THE
DICTIONARY
OF
NATIONAL BIOGRAPHY

Note on the Dictionary

THE *Dictionary of National Biography* comprises the following distinct works:

1. *The D.N.B. from the earliest times to 1900.*

   In two alphabetical series:

   Vols. I–XXI.

   Vol. XXII (Supplementary).

   > At the end of each of the 21 volumes is an alphabetical index of the lives in that volume and of those in vol. 22 which belong to the same part of the alphabet.

2. *The Twentieth-Century D.N.B.*

   (a) *1901–1911*, three volumes in one.

   (b) *1912–1921*, with an index covering 1901–1921.

   (c) *1922–1930*, with an index covering 1901–1930.

3. *The Concise D.N.B.* One volume.

   > An epitome of the main work and its supplement to 1900 in one alphabet, followed by an epitome of the Twentieth-Century D.N.B. in one alphabet.

NOTE

In reprinting the twenty-two volumes of the main Dictionary in 1921–2 and again in 1937–8 it seemed best to leave the text unaltered. The bulk of the corrections hitherto received or collected by the present Publishers is insignificant when compared with the magnitude of the work, and would not justify the issue of a 'new edition' purporting to supersede the editions now in the libraries and in private hands. The collection and classification of such corrections for future use is, however, being steadily carried on; and students of biography are invited to communicate their discoveries to the Publishers.

Two changes have been made in reprinting:—

1. The lists of Contributors originally prefixed to each of the sixty-six volumes, and later combined in twenty-two lists, have been combined in one list which is now printed in Volume 1 only.

2. In using the main Dictionary (to 1900) it is necessary to remember that it is in *two* alphabetical series: Vols. 1–21, and the supplementary Vol. 22, in which were added lives of persons who had died too late for inclusion in their places (as well as lives of some who had been accidentally omitted). It has been sought to mitigate the inconvenience arising from this by adding to the index at the end of each volume those names, occurring in Vol. 22, which belong to the same part of the alphabet. These 'supplementary' names are added at the bottom of each page. It is thus possible to ascertain, by reference to a single volume, whether any person (who died before 1901) is or is not in the 22-volume Dictionary.

The opportunity has been taken, in accordance with the wishes of the donors, to commemorate upon each title-page the name of the munificent Founder.

CONTENTS OF VOLS. 1–22

Note.—*Vols.* 1–21, *as originally issued* 1885–1890, *were edited by Sir Leslie Stephen; Vols.* 22–26, 1890–1891, *by Sir Leslie Stephen and Sir Sidney Lee; Vols.* 27–66, 1891–1901, *by Sir Sidney Lee.*

DICTIONARY

OF

NATIONAL BIOGRAPHY

FINCH, ANNE (*d.* 1679), metaphysician. [See CONWAY, ANNE, VISCOUNTESS.]

FINCH, ANNE, COUNTESS OF WINCHILSEA (*d.* 1720), poetess, was the daughter of Sir William Kingsmill of Sidmonton, near Southampton, and the wife of Heneage Finch, second son of Heneage, second earl of Winchilsea [q. v.] Her husband succeeded to the title as fourth earl on the death of his nephew Charles in 1712. Finch was gentleman of the bedchamber to James II when Duke of York, and his wife maid of honour to the second duchess. Anne Finch was a friend of Pope, of Rowe, and other men of letters. Her most considerable work, a poem on 'Spleen,' written in stanzas after Cowley's manner, and published in Gildon's 'Miscellany,' 1701, inspired Rowe to compose some verses in her honour, entitled 'An Epistle to Flavia.' Pope addressed 'an impromptu to Lady Winchilsea' (*Miscellanies,* 1727), in which he declared that 'Fate doomed the fall of every female wit' before 'Ardelia's' talent. She replied by comparing 'Alexander' to Orpheus, who she said would have written like him had he lived in London. The only collected edition of her poems was printed in 1713, containing a tragedy never acted, called 'Aristomenes, or the Royal Shepherd,' and dedicated to the Countess of Hertford, with 'an Epilogue to [Rowe's] Jane Shore, to be spoken by Mrs. Oldfield the night before the poet's day' (printed in the *General Dictionary,* x. 178, from a manuscript in the countess's possession). Another poem, entitled 'The Prodigy,' written at Tunbridge Wells, called forth Cibber's regret that the countess's rank made her only write occasionally as a pastime. Wordsworth sent a selection of her poems with a commendatory sonnet of his own to Lady Mary Lowther, and remarked in a prefatory essay to his volume of 1815 that Lady Winchilsea's 'nocturnal reverie' was almost unique in its own day, because it employed new images 'of external nature.' On her death, 5 Aug. 1720, she left a number of unpublished manuscripts to her friends, the Countess of Hertford and a clergyman named Creake, and by their permission some of these poems were printed by Birch in the 'General Dictionary.' She left no children. Her husband died 30 Sept. 1726. Her published works were: 1. The poem on 'Spleen,' in 'A New Miscellany of Original Poems,' published by Charles Gildon, London, 1701, 8vo; republished under the title of 'The Spleen, a Pindarique Ode; with a Prospect of Death, a Pindarique Essay,' London, 1709, 8vo. 2. 'Miscellany Poems, written by a Lady,' 1713, 8vo.

[General Dict. x. 178; Biog. Brit. vii. Suppl. p. 204; Cibber's Lives of the Poets, iii. 321; Walpole's Royal and Noble Authors, ed. Park, iv. 87; Collins's Peerage, ed. 1779, iii. 282; Cat. of Printed Books, Brit. Mus.]   E. T. B.

FINCH, DANIEL, second EARL OF NOTTINGHAM and sixth EARL OF WINCHILSEA (1647–1730), born in 1647, was the eldest son of Heneage Finch, first earl of Nottingham [q. v.], by Elizabeth, daughter of Daniel Harvey, a London merchant. Like his father he was educated at Westminster School, and proceeded to Christ Church, Oxford, as a gentleman-commoner in 1662. He left without a degree, entered the Inner Temple, and was chosen F.R.S. 26 Nov. 1668. He seems to have been first elected to parliament for Great Bedwin, Wiltshire, 10 Feb. 1672-3, but does not appear to have sat till he was returned by the borough of Lichfield 7 Aug. 1679. He had been made lord of the admiralty 22 April 1679. He adhered to the tory politics of his family, became a privy councillor 4 Feb. 1679–80, and was first lord of the admiralty from 19 Feb. following to 22 May 1684. He was elected M.P. by both Lichfield and Newtown in March 1681, but was called to the House of Lords by his father's death, 18 Dec. 1682. As a privy councillor he signed the order for the proclamation of James II, and up to the time of Monmouth's insurrection was one of that king's steadiest supporters. But the ecclesiastical policy afterwards adopted by the government damped the loyalty of the cavaliers and laid the foundation of that new tory party which held itself aloof from the Jacobites. Nottingham came in time to be recognised as their head. Their distinguishing tenet was devotion to the established church in preference even to hereditary right. In the reign of Anne they were called the Hanoverian tories, and sometimes known by the nickname of the 'Whimsicals.' Nottingham's career was consistent throughout. He was one of the last men in England to accept the revolution settlement; but having once accepted it, he was one of the very few eminent statesmen of his time who never seem to have intrigued against it. Though Swift accuses him of having corresponded with the Stuarts, the charge, made in a moment of great exasperation, is not countenanced by any of his contemporaries. His private character is universally represented as stainless. Rowe tells us that he had an intrigue with an opera singer, Signora Margaretta, afterwards Mrs. Tofts. But this was empty gossip. Both his principles and his virtues marked him out to be a leader of the clergy, with whom his influence was unbounded. This influence was the secret of Nottingham's importance for nearly a generation after the death of Charles II.

In the spring of 1688 the whigs resolved to take Nottingham into their confidence, and invite his co-operation in the intended revolution. He was for a time inclined to join in the appeal to the Prince of Orange; but on second thoughts he declared that he could take no active part against his rightful sovereign. He admitted that his share in their confidence had given the whigs the right to assassinate him on breaking with them, and some of them were rather inclined to take him at his word. But they ended by relying on his honour, and had no reason to regret it.

Nottingham was a prominent figure in the parliamentary debates which followed James's flight from England. The tories were in favour of Sancroft's plan—a regency, that is, during the minority of the Prince of Wales; and this was the policy proposed by Lord Nottingham in the House of Lords. The motion was only lost by 51 votes to 49; and then the lords proceeded to consider the resolution which had been adopted by the commons declaring the throne vacant. This was opposed by Nottingham, and the resolution was rejected by 55 votes to 41. But the House of Commons refused to give way, and the House of Lords found it necessary to yield. Nottingham proposed a modification of the oaths of allegiance and supremacy for the sake of tender consciences, which was accepted by both houses, and he then fairly threw in his lot with the new régime, though he still maintained in theory his allegiance to the Stuarts. Nottingham, according to Bishop Burnet, was the author of the distinction between the king *de jure* and the king *de facto*, in which the old cavalier party found so welcome a refuge.

In December 1688 he was made one of the secretaries of state with charge of the war department, an office which he retained till December 1693. One of his first duties was the introduction of the Toleration Act. He seems to have sincerely believed it to be conducive to the stability of the church. It left the Act of Uniformity, the Test and Corporation Acts, the Conventicle Act, the Five Mile Act, and the act making attendance at church compulsory, in full force, only enacting that on certain conditions dissenters might be exempted from the penalties attaching to the violation of the law. These conditions were intended to serve as a test by which dangerous dissenters could be distinguished from harmless ones. Those, it was thought, who would subscribe five of the Thirty-nine Articles, take the oath of allegiance, and sign the declaration against popery might be safely trusted. Ten years before, Nottingham, as a member of the House of Commons, had framed a bill on much the same lines, which only failed to become law by an artifice. At the same time he now brought in a less popular measure, a comprehension bill, for enabling dissenters to conform to the church of England. The Bishop of London supported the bill in the House of Lords, where, oddly enough, it was violently opposed by Bishop Burnet. But Nottingham would probably have succeeded in his efforts had it not been for the dissenters themselves. Those who were unwilling to accept the compromise were naturally interested in preventing others from accepting it, and between the active hostility of its enemies and the lukewarm support of its friends, the measure fell to the ground. An attempt made at the same time by some members of the whig party to repeal the Test Act was dropped with it.

When William III set out for Ireland in the summer of 1690 he left behind him a council of nine, of whom Nottingham was one, to act as the advisers of Mary, and it fell to his lot to bring her the tidings of the battle of the Boyne. Nottingham, who was admitted to a greater share of the queen's confidence than any other English statesman, always said that if she survived her husband William she would bring about the restoration of her father James. He had, however, bitter enemies in parliament. He was hated by the extreme men of both sides, and was perhaps not much loved even by those who respected him. Much discontent was caused by the failure to follow up the victory of La Hogue in May 1692. The public threw the blame on Admiral Russell, the commander of the allied fleet, and Russell in turn threw the blame on Nottingham, from whom he received his orders. A parliamentary inquiry ended in nothing; but Russell was acquitted of all blame by the House of Commons, though Nottingham was defended by the lords. The king found it necessary to do something; he was very unwilling to part with Nottingham, and accordingly persuaded Russell to accept a post in the household, Admirals Killigrew and Delaval, both tories, being entrusted with the command of the Channel fleet. They thus became responsible for the disaster which happened to the convoy under the command of Sir George Rooke [q. v.] in the Bay of Lagos in June 1693, and when parliament met in November they were forced to retire. Russell was appointed first lord of the admiralty and commander of the Channel fleet, and Nottingham's resignation was inevitable. The king parted from him with great reluctance. He thanked him for his past services, and declared that he had no fault to find with him.

Nottingham remained out of office till the accession of Anne. Six weeks after William's death (8 March 1702) he was appointed secretary of state, with Sir Charles Hedges for his colleague. Though a consistent anti-Jacobite, Nottingham was a staunch tory. He upheld during the war of the Spanish succession the doctrine, thenceforward identified with the tory policy, that in a continental war we should act rather as auxiliaries than as principals, and that our operations should be exclusively maritime. This opinion, whenever the opportunity offered, Nottingham upheld in his place in parliament. But his heart was in the church question, to which he was ready to sacrifice even his party allegiance.

As soon as the new parliament assembled a bill for the prevention of occasional conformity was introduced in the House of Commons by St. John, no doubt after due consultation with the leader of the church party. Both the Corporation Act and the Test Act were designed to keep all places of public trust or authority in the hands of members of the church of England. And the question that arose during the last years of the seventeenth century was simply this, whether the evasion of the law by dissenters should be connived at or prevented. It was supposed that no honest dissenters would communicate according to the rites of the church of England merely to obtain a qualification for office, but it was found in practice that the large majority of them did so, and indeed had been in the habit of so communicating before the passing of the Test Act. Nottingham had shown both in 1679 and 1689 that he was no bigot, and it is possible that circumstances of which we know nothing may have contributed to make him prefer an attempt to enforce the test to the alternative policy of connivance at conduct which could hardly raise the reputation of the occasional conformists themselves. Three sessions running, 1702, 1703, and 1704, the bill was passed through the commons, and Nottingham exerted himself to the utmost to get it carried through the upper house. But it was all in vain, and the question was allowed to rest again for seven years.

Nottingham resigned in 1704, when he found it impossible to agree with his whig colleagues. He told the queen that she must either get rid of the whig members of the cabinet or accept his own resignation. Greatly to the minister's mortification she decided on the latter, and from this time Nottingham's zeal as a political tory began to cool, and the very next year he took his revenge on the court by persuading some of his tory friends to join with him in an address to the crown, begging that the Electress Sophia might be invited to reside in England. Anne, who was exceedingly sensitive on this point, never forgave Nottingham, and he in his turn continued to drift further and further away from his old associates. Against Harley he was supposed to nurture a special grudge. He had committed the grave offence of accepting the seals which Nottingham had thrown up, and the ex-secretary was quite willing to retaliate whenever an opportunity should occur.

In 1710 the trial of Sacheverell took place. Nottingham throughout took Sacheverell's side, and signed all the protests recorded by the opposition peers against the proceedings of his accusers.

His rupture with the court may be said to have been complete when, on the death of Lord Rochester, lord president of the council, in April 1711, the post was conferred on the Duke of Buckingham. The privy seal, which became vacant about the same time, was given to Bishop Robinson, and from that moment it is no want of charity to conclude that Nottingham felt his cup was full. When it was known that the new government were bent on putting an end to the war, the whig opposition became furious. But in the House of Commons the tories had a large majority, and in the House of Lords the whigs required some help from the other side. Nottingham was in a similar predicament with regard to the Occasional Conformity Bill. He was sure of the commons, but in the upper house he had hitherto been unsuccessful, and was likely to be so unless the opposition could be disarmed. The bargain was soon struck. The whigs agreed to withdraw their resistance to the Church Bill on condition that Nottingham in turn would support them in an attack upon the government. He readily accepted an offer which enabled him to gratify his love of the church and his hatred of the ministry at the same moment. On 7 Dec. 1711 he moved an amendment to the address, declaring that no peace would be acceptable to this country which left Spain and the Indies in the possession of the house of Bourbon. It was carried by a majority of twelve, and Harley and St. John replied by the creation of twelve new peers.

Nottingham, however, claimed his reward. A week after the division the Occasional Conformity Bill was reintroduced into the House of Lords, and on 22 Dec. received the royal assent. It provided that 'if any officer, civil or military, or any magistrate of a corporation obliged by the acts of Charles the Second to receive the sacrament, should during his continuance in office attend any conventicle or religious meeting of dissenters such person should forfeit 40*l.*, be disabled from holding his office, and incapable of being appointed to another till he could prove that he had not been to chapel for twelve months.' In this unprincipled transaction Nottingham, though sincere enough in his zeal for the church, was actuated quite as much by jealousy of the Earl of Oxford as by disapproval of the policy of Bolingbroke. Nottingham can have had no concern in a tract published in 1713 bearing his name. The tract, entitled 'Observations on the State of the Nation,' maintains the ultra low-church view of church government and doctrine. It was reissued in the 'Somers Tracts' in 1751 as 'The Memorial of the State of England in Vindication of the Church, the Queen, and the Administration.'

Nottingham, who probably expected that the vote of the House of Lords would bring the ministry to the ground and pave the way for his own return to office, was mistaken.

It is to his credit that having gained all that he thought necessary for the church in 1711 he opposed the Schism Bill, which was carried in June 1714 to please the still more ultra section of the high church tories. Yet by so doing he again served his own interests, for it helped to cement his good understanding with the whigs and to insure his being recommended for high office on the accession of George I. The new king landed at Greenwich on 18 Sept. 1714, and in the first Hanoverian ministry Nottingham was made president of the council, with a seat in the cabinet, then consisting of nine peers. But he only held office for about a year and a half. In February 1716 it was moved in the House of Lords that an address should be presented to the king in favour of showing mercy to the Jacobite peers, then lying under sentence of death for their share in the rebellion of 1715. The government opposed the motion, but Nottingham supported the address, which was carried by a majority of five. It produced no effect, except on the unlucky intercessor, who was immediately deprived of his appointment, and never again employed in the service of the crown. His only parliamentary appearances of any importance after this date were in opposition to the Septennial Bill in 1716, and the repeal of the Occasional Conformity Bill in 1719. His name appears in the protest against the first; but the second passed with less difficulty, and no protest appears on the minutes.

After his retirement from office Nottingham lived principally at Burley-on-the-Hill, near Oakham, Rutlandshire, a very fine country seat which had been purchased by his father from the second Duke of Buckingham, and which is still in possession of a branch of the Finch family. It was here that he wrote 'The Answer of the Earl of Nottingham to Mr. Whiston's Letter to him concerning the eternity of the Son of God,' 1721, which restored all his popularity with the clergy, rather damaged by his acceptance of office with the whigs. The pamphlet rapidly reached an eighth edition. Nottingham died 1 Jan. 1729–30, shortly after he had succeeded to the earldom of Winchilsea on the decease of John, fifth earl, 9 Sept. 1729, the last heir in the elder branch of Sir Moyle Finch, whose heir Thomas was first earl of Winchilsea [see under FINCH, SIR THOMAS]. Nottingham married, first Lady Essex Rich, second daughter and coheiress of Robert, earl of Warwick, and secondly Anne, daughter of Christopher, viscount Hatton. By his first wife he had a daughter, Mary; by his second five sons and seven daughters. Edward Finch-Hatton, the youngest son, is separately noticed.

In person Nottingham was tall, thin, and dark-complexioned. His manner was so solemn and the expression of his countenance was, generally speaking, so lugubrious, that he acquired the nicknames of Don Diego and Don Dismal, he and his brother, Heneage, first earl of Aylesford [q. v.], being known as the Dismals. He figures as Don Diego in the 'History of John Bull' and in the 'Tatler' (1709), and Swift in his correspondence is always making fun of him. He is the subject of a famous ballad, 'An Orator Dismal of Nottinghamshire,' by the same eminent hand. When he joined the whigs in 1711 the 'Post Boy' (6 Dec.) offered a reward of ten shillings to any one who should restore him to his friends, promising that all should be forgiven. Reference is there made to his 'long pockets.'

[Macaulay's Hist. of England; Stanhope's Hist. of England and Queen Anne; Burnet's Hist. of his own Time; Somerville's Hist. of Queen Anne and Political Transactions; Somers Tracts; Swift's Diary and Correspondence; Coxe's Life of Marlborough; Walpole's Letters; Cunningham's Hist. of the Revolution; Wyon's Reign of Queen Anne; Stoughton's Religion in England; Doyle's Baronage; Welch's Alumni Westmonast. p. 570; Wood's Athenæ Oxon (Bliss), iv. 651.] T. E. K.

FINCH, EDWARD (*fl.* 1630–1641), royalist divine, is said by Walker and others to have been brother of John, lord Finch of Fordwich [q. v.], and thus younger son of Sir Henry Finch [q. v.], by Ursula, daughter of John Thwaites of Kent. The genealogists state that John was Sir Henry's only son, but there is little doubt that they are wrong. On 9 Dec. 1630 Edward was admitted to the vicarage of Christ Church, Newgate. Walker celebrates him as the first of the parochial clergy actually dispossessed by the committee for scandalous ministers. A resolution of parliament, 8 May 1641, declared him unfit to hold any benefice. The articles against him allege that he had set up the communion-table altarwise, and preached in a surplice; they also detail a list of charges more or less affecting his character. Walker, who had not seen the pamphlet containing the articles and evidence in the case, makes the best of Finch's printed defence, but on Finch's own showing there was ground for scandal. Finch died soon after his sequestration; his successor, William Jenkyn, was admitted on 1 Feb. 1642, 'per mort. Finch.' There is a doubt as to whether he was married. It was said that he had lived seven years apart from his wife, but he denied that he had a wife. Finch published 'An Answer to the Articles,' London, 1641, 4to. This was in reply to 'The Petition and Articles . . . exhibited in Parliament against Edward Finch,

Vicar of Christ's Church, London, and brother to Sir J. Finch, late Lord Keeper,' &c., 1641, 4to. This pamphlet has a woodcut of Finch, and a cut representing his journey to Hammersmith with a party of alleged loose characters. The main point of Finch's defence on this charge was that one of the party was his sister.

[Walker's Sufferings, 1714, i. 69 sq., ii. 170; Calamy's Continuation, 1727, i. 17, 18; pamphlets above cited.] A. G.

FINCH, EDWARD (1664–1738), composer, born in 1664, was the fifth son of Heneage, first earl of Nottingham [q. v.] He proceeded M.A. in 1679, and became fellow of Christ's College, Cambridge. He represented the university of Cambridge in the parliament of 1689–90. He was ordained deacon at York in 1700, became rector of Wigan, was appointed prebendary of York 26 April 1704, and resided in the north end of the treasurer's house in the Close, taking an active interest in musical matters, as appears from the family correspondence. Finch was installed prebendary of Canterbury 8 Feb. 1710. He died 14 Feb. 1737–8, aged 75, at York, where a monument erected by him in the minster to his wife and brother (Henry, dean of York) bears a bust and inscription to his memory.

Finch's 'Te Deum' and anthem, 'Grant, we beseech Thee,' both written in five parts, are to be found in Dr. Tudway's 'Collection of Services' (Harleian MSS. 7337–42); 'A Grammar of Thorough Bass,' with examples, a manuscript of sixty-six pages, is in the Euing Library at Glasgow. Of Finch's manuscript letters, that addressed to his brother Daniel, second Earl of Nottingham [q. v.], and dated Winwick, 12 July 1702, is of interest; he there enunciates his views of a sinecure and discusses other questions of preferment.

[Collins's Peerage, iii. 290; Graduati Cantabrigienses, 1823, p. 168; Le Neve's Fasti, iii. 650; Dict. of Musicians, 1827, i. 247; Willis's Survey of Cathedrals, 1742, i. 176; Drake's Eboracum, 1736, pp. 513, 559, 570; Addit. MSS. 28569 f. 130, 29588 f. 88, 32496 f. 48 *b*; Hasted's Hist. of Canterbury, 1801, ii. 63; Harleian MSS. 2264 f. 267, 7342 p. 306; Gent. Mag. viii. 109; Brown's Biog. Dict. of Musicians, p. 246.] L. M. M.

FINCH, EDWARD (1756–1843), general, fourth son of Heneage, third earl of Aylesford, by Lady Charlotte Seymour, daughter of Charles, sixth duke of Somerset, was born on 26 April 1756. He went to Westminster School as a queen's scholar in 1768, and was elected to Trinity College, Cambridge, in 1773, proceeding B.A. in 1777. He entered the army as a cornet in the 11th dragoons on 27 Dec. 1778, exchanged into the 20th light dragoons, and on 7 Oct. 1779 was promoted lieutenant into the 87th regiment. He accompanied this regiment to the West Indies in January 1780, and served there and in America until he was promoted lieutenant and captain into the 2nd or Coldstream guards on 5 Feb. 1783. On 11 May 1789 he was elected M.P. for Cambridge, a seat which he held for thirty years, and on 3 Oct. 1792 he was promoted captain and lieutenant-colonel. He accompanied the brigade of guards to Flanders under General Lake in 1793, and served throughout the campaigns under the Duke of York with great credit. He was present at the actions of Cæsar's Camp and Famars, in the famous engagement of Lincelles, and at the battles of Hondschoten, Lannoy, Turcoing, and round Tournay. He remained with his corps until the withdrawal of the British troops from the continent in April 1795. He was promoted colonel on 3 May 1796, and nominated to command the light companies of the guards in Coote's expedition to cut the sluices at Ostend [see COOTE, SIR EYRE, 1762–1823], but was prevented from going by an accidental injury he received the day before the expedition sailed. He was present with the guards in the suppression of the Irish rebellion of 1798, and in 1799 commanded the 1st battalion of the Coldstreams in the expedition to the Helder and at the battles of Bergen. In the following year Finch was appointed to the command of the brigade of cavalry, consisting of the 12th and 26th light dragoons, which accompanied Sir Ralph Abercromby's army to Egypt. His regiments hardly came into action at all in the famous battles of March 1801, for the ground was not well adapted for cavalry, and he only covered the siege operations against Alexandria. He received the thanks of parliament with the other generals, and on 1 Jan. 1801 he was promoted major-general. In 1803 he took command of the 1st brigade of guards, then stationed at Chelmsford, consisting of the 1st battalion of the Coldstreams and the 1st battalion 3rd guards, and commanded that brigade in the expedition to Denmark in 1809, and at the siege of Copenhagen. In 1802 he was appointed a groom of the bedchamber to the king, on 25 April 1808 he was promoted lieutenant-general, and on 3 Aug. 1808 appointed colonel of the 54th regiment. On 18 Sept. 1809 he was transferred to the colonelcy of the 22nd foot, and on 12 Aug. 1819 he was promoted general. His seniority to Lord Wellington prevented him from being employed in the Peninsula, and he never saw service after 1809. He continued to sit in the House of Commons for Cambridge, through the influence of the Duke of Rutland, until December 1819, when he accepted the Chiltern Hundreds, and throughout the thirty years of his parliamentary career his seat was only once contested, in 1818. Finch, after 1819, entirely retired from public life, and he died on 27 Oct. 1843, at the age of eighty-seven, being at the time of his death the sixth general in order of seniority in the English army.

[Royal Military Calendar; Hart's Army List; Mackinnon's History of the Coldstream Guards; Welch's Alumni Westmonast. p. 397; Gent. Mag. December 1843.] H. M. S.

FINCH, FRANCIS OLIVER (1802–1862), water-colour painter, son of Francis Finch, a merchant in Friday Street, Cheapside, London, was born 22 Nov. 1802, and spent his boyhood at Stone, near Aylesbury. When twelve years of age, at that time fatherless, he was placed under John Varley, with whom he worked altogether five years, a friend having paid a premium of 200l. Among his earliest patrons was Lord Northwick, a patron of the fine arts, who employed the youth in making views of his mansion and grounds. Some time after leaving his master's studio the same friend who had assisted in placing him there afforded him the benefit of a tour through Scotland. After his return he doubted for some time whether he should continue the practice of landscape or enter as a student at the Royal Academy. He joined Sass's life academy and produced several portraits, but circumstances drawing him back to landscape-painting he became a candidate for admission into the then newly formed Society of Painters in Water Colours. On 11 Feb. 1822 he was elected an associate, and on 4 June 1827 a member of that society. He first exhibited at the Royal Academy in 1817, at that period living at 44 Conduit Street, Bond Street. He married in the spring of 1837, and resided for some time in Charlotte Street and afterwards in Argyle Square, Euston Road. On 10 Oct. 1861 Finch lost the use of his limbs, and died 27 Aug. 1862. He possessed a fine voice, and was a thorough musician, as well as a poet. He printed a collection of sonnets entitled 'An Artist's Dream.' Among his best works may be mentioned 'Garmallon's Tomb,' oil (1820); 'View of Loch Lomond' (1822); 'View on the River Tay' (1827); 'View of Windsor Castle' (1829); 'View of the College of Aberdeen' (1832); scene from Milton's 'Comus' (1835); 'Alpine Scene, Evening' (1838); 'A Watch Tower' (1840); 'The

Thames near Cookham, Berkshire' (1845); 'Ruined Temple, Evening' (1852); 'Rocky Glen, Evening' (1855); 'The Curfew—Gray's Elegy' (1860); 'Pastoral Retreat' (1861); and 'Moonlight over the Sea' (1862). His portrait has been engraved by A. Roffe.

[Memoir and Remains of F. O. Finch, by Mrs. E. Finch, London, 1865, 8vo.]   L. F.

FINCH, SIR HENEAGE (d. 1631), speaker of the House of Commons, was the fourth son of Sir Moyle Finch of Eastwell, Kent, and grandson of Sir Thomas Finch [q. v.] His mother was Elizabeth, daughter of Sir Thomas Heneage of Copt Hall, Essex, and granddaughter on the mother's side of Thomas, lord Berkeley of Berkeley Castle. Admitted a member of the Inner Temple in November 1597, he was called to the bar in 1606. At a by-election in 1607 he was returned to parliament for Rye. He spoke in July 1610 in the debate on 'impositions,' maintaining the following positions: (1) 'that the king, though upon a restraint for a time, may impose for a time, much more for ever;' (2) 'that he may dispense with a law for ever, because the law is for ever;' (3) 'that he may make a bulwark in any land, but not take money not to do it;' (4) 'that the king hath power only to make war. If all the subjects will make war without the king, it is no war' (Parl. Debates, 1610, Camden Soc., p. 116). He was one of the lawyers who argued before the king and council on 6 April 1612 the moot point 'whether baronets and bannerets were the same promiscuously;' and desiring to give dignity to the argument, opened 'with a philosophical preamble, omne principium motus est intrinsecum,' at which the king, being much displeased, said: 'Though I am a king of men, yet I am no king of time, for I grow old with this;' and therefore, if he had anything to speak to the matter, bade him utter it. Whereupon Finch, with great boldness, undertook to prove much, but did nothing (Hist. MSS. Comm. 10th Rep. App. pt. iv. 9). In 1616 he was employed in conjunction with Bacon in an attempt to reduce the statute law to some sort of consistency with itself (SPEDDING, Letters and Life of Bacon, vi. 71). In 1620–1 he was returned to parliament for West Looe, otherwise Portpighan, Cornwall. He took part in the debate of 3 Dec. 1621 on the Spanish match, supporting the proposal to petition the king against it (Parl. Hist. i. 1320). In the preceding February he had been appointed recorder of London (Index to Remembrancia, p. 295), and he represented the city in parliament between 1623 and 1626. On 22 June 1623 he was knighted at Wanstead, and three days later he was called to the degree of serjeant-at-law. On 8 July

following he was further honoured by the elevation of his mother, then a widow, to the peerage as Viscountess Maidstone, with remainder to her heirs male. This honour was procured through the interest of Sir Arthur Ingram at the price of a capital sum of 13,000l. and an annuity of 500l., to secure which Copt Hall manor and park were mortgaged. She was afterwards, viz. on 12 July 1628, created Countess of Winchilsea, also with remainder to her heirs male. She died in 1633, and was buried at Eastwell under a splendid monument. Sir Heneage's eldest brother, Thomas, succeeded her as first earl of Winchilsea (cf. art. FINCH, SIR THOMAS; NICHOLS, Progr. James I, iii. 768, 875, 878; DUGDALE, Chron. Ser. 105; COLLINS, Peerage, ed. Brydges, iii. 387; Cal. State Papers, Dom. 1619–23, pp. 223, 623; Hist. MSS. Comm. 4th Rep. App. 283 b, 290 a). On 7 July 1625 Finch read the report of a committee of the House of Commons to which had been referred the consideration of two works recently published by Richard Montagu, afterwards bishop of Chichester, viz. 'A New Gag for an Old Goose' and 'Appello Cæsarem,' which were thought to savour somewhat rankly of Arminianism and popery. The result of the report was that the publication of the books was treated as a breach of privilege and Montagu arrested. The plague then raging severely, the debtors in the Fleet petitioned the House of Commons for a habeas corpus. Finch on 9 July spoke in favour of granting a release, but so as to save the rights of the creditors. On 9 Aug. he was present at a conference with the lords touching certain pardons illegally granted by the king to some jesuits, but is not recorded to have done more than read the lord keeper's speech. On 10 Aug. he spoke in favour of granting the subsidies in reversion demanded by the king, but advised that the grant should be accompanied with a protestation never to do the like upon any necessity hereafter (Commons' Debates, 1625, Camden Soc., pp. 47, 51, 65, 94, 113; Commons' Journ. i. 805; Parl. Hist. ii. 18–19, 35). On 6 Feb. 1625–6 he was elected to the speaker's chair (Commons' Journ. i. 816). His speech at the opening of parliament was divided between the conventional self-abasement, praise of the 'temperate' character of the laws, 'yielding a due observance to the prerogative royal, and yet preserving the right and liberty of the subject,' fulsome flattery of the king, and denunciation of popery and Spain. In 1628 he was elected to the bench of his inn. On 10 April 1631 he was nominated one of the commissioners for the repair of St. Paul's Cathedral. He died on 5 Dec. following and was buried at Ravenstone in Buckinghamshire (*Cal. State Papers*, Dom. 1625–6 p. 248, 1631–3 pp. 6, 207; NICHOLS, *Progr. James I*, iii. 768; *Parl. Hist.* ii. 41). Finch married twice. His first wife was Frances, daughter of Sir Edmund Bell of Beaupré Hall, Norfolk, and granddaughter of Sir Robert Bell [q. v.], chief baron of the exchequer and speaker of the House of Commons in the reign of Elizabeth. She died on 11 April 1627, and on 16 April 1629 Finch married, at St. Dunstan's in the West, Elizabeth, daughter of William Cradock of Staffordshire, relict of Richard Bennett, mercer and alderman of London, an ancestor of the Earls of Arlington. By his first wife Finch had issue seven sons and four daughters. His eldest son, Heneage [q. v.], was lord keeper and first earl of Nottingham. Another son, Sir John [q. v.], was a physician. For the hand of Mrs. Bennett, who brought Finch a fortune, he had several rivals, among them Sir Sackville Crow and Dr. Raven, a conjunction which afforded much amusement to the town. Another suitor was Sir Edward Dering (*Coll. Top. et Gen.* v. 218; *Proceedings in Kent*, 1640, Camden Soc.) By this lady Finch had issue two daughters only, viz. (1) Elizabeth, who married Edward Madison, and (2) Anne, who married Edward, viscount and earl of Conway.

Finch compiled 'A Brief Collection touching the Power and Jurisdiction of Bishops,' which remains in manuscript (*Hist. MSS. Comm.* 4th Rep. App. 353).

[Morant's Essex, i. 47; Berry's County Genealogies (Kent), p. 207; Hasted's Kent, iii. 199, 387; Official Return of Lists of Members of Parliament; Inner Temple Books; Collins's Peerage, ed. Brydges, iii. 387; Manning's Lives of the Speakers.] J. M. R.

FINCH, HENEAGE, first EARL OF NOTTINGHAM (1621–1682), successively solicitor-general, lord keeper, and lord chancellor, was born 23 Dec. 1621, probably at Eastwell in Kent (WOOD, *Athenæ Oxon.*), and was the eldest son of Sir Heneage Finch [q. v.], knight, recorder of London, and speaker in Charles I's first parliament, and of Frances, daughter of Sir Edmund Bell of Beaupré Hall in Norfolk. He was grandson of Elizabeth, created Countess of Winchilsea by Charles I [see under FINCH, SIR THOMAS], and nephew of Sir John, lord Finch [q. v.], keeper of the seals to Charles I. He was educated at Westminster School, whence he went to Christ Church, entering in the Lent term of 1635. He then joined the Inner Temple, where he soon became a distinguished student, with special proficiency in municipal law. He took no part in the troubles of the civil war, and during the usurpation conducted an extensive private practice (COLLINS, *Peerage*). Of

this, however, there does not seem to be any direct evidence. By the time of the Restoration he was evidently well known, for he was returned for the Convention parliament both for Canterbury and St. Michael's in Cornwall, electing to sit for the former. In honour of the occasion he was entertained by the city at a banquet (*Hist. MSS. Comm.* 9th Rep. 165 *b*). On 6 June 1660 he was made solicitor-general, and on the next day was created a baronet of Ravenstone in Buckinghamshire (COLLINS, *Peerage*). He at once became the official representative of the court and of the church in the House of Commons. In the great debate of 9 July 1660 on the future form of the church, Finch in an uncompromising speech treated the matter as not open to argument, since there was 'no law for altering government by bishops;' he jeered at 'tender consciences,' and hoped the house would not 'cant after Cromwell.' On 30 July he urged the expulsion from their livings of all ministers who had been presented without the consent of the patrons, and opposed any abatement in the articles or oaths. In the matter of the Indemnity Bill he was deputed by the commons to manage the conference between the two houses on 16 Aug., and strongly supported the exclusion from pardon of the late king's judges, a compromise which he felt to be necessary to secure the passing of the measure so warmly desired by the king and Clarendon. On 12 Sept. he spoke against the motion that the king should be desired to marry a protestant, and on 21 Nov. proposed the important constitutional change whereby the courts of wards and purveyance were abolished, and the revenue hitherto raised by them was for the future levied on the excise. It is significant of the real objects of the court that as law officer of the crown he opposed (28 Nov.) the bill brought in by Sir Matthew Hale for giving effect to the king's declaration regarding ecclesiastical affairs by embodying it in an act. And in the debate regarding the ill-conduct of the troops, on 14 Dec., he spoke against the proposal to accompany the bill of supply with a complaint of grievances (*Parl. Hist.* vol. iv.) He was of course one of the prosecuting counsel in the trial of the regicides in October 1660, where he is described in one account as effectually answering Cooke, the framer of the impeachment of Charles I (*Hist. MSS. Comm.* 5th Rep. 181 *b*), though by the report in the state trials he appears only to have formally opened the case against the prisoner. In April 1661 Finch was elected to Charles's second parliament, both for the university of Oxford and for Beaumaris in

Anglesey, electing to sit for the former (*Journals of the House of Commons*, 13 May 1661). He was carried by the influence of Clarendon, whose son Laurence Hyde stood with him, of the Bishop of Oxford, and of the heads of houses, against strong opposition aroused apparently by the conduct of their former representative, Selden (*Cal. State Papers*, 1660–1). He appears to have disappointed his constituents by not assisting to get rid of the hearth-tax (WOOD, *Athenæ Oxon.*) In this year also he was made treasurer and autumn reader of the Inner Temple. He chose as the subject of his lectures, which excited much attention, lasting from 4 to 17 Aug., the statute of the 39th of Elizabeth, concerning the recovery of debts of the crown, which had never previously been discussed. The favour in which he stood was shown by the presence of the king and all the great officers of state at a banquet in his honour on the 15th in the Inner Temple (*ib.*; PEPYS, *Diary*; DUGDALE, *Origines Juridiciales*). It is noticeable that in one matter upon which Charles seemed really bent, toleration of dissent, he certainly opposed the court. In February 1663 he was made chairman of the committee of the commons which drew up in the most uncompromising terms an address to the king praying for the withdrawal of his declaration of indulgence (*Parl. Hist.* vol. iv.), and in March was the representative of the house in the conference with the lords about a bill against the priests and jesuits (*Cal. State Papers*, Dom. Ser. 1663–4). In October 1664 he was leading counsel for the Canary merchants in their endeavour to acquire a new charter (EVELYN, *Diary*, 27 Oct.) When the house met at Oxford in 1665 he again vehemently espoused the intolerant policy of the Anglican church by pressing forward the Five Mile Act; and at the prorogation he, with Hyde, Colonel Strangways, and Sir John Birkenhead, received the honorary degree of D.C.L. (7 Nov.), having with the two latter (*Commons' Journals*, 31 Oct. 1665), by order of the commons, communicated to the university on 31 Oct. 1665 the thanks of the house for its 'loyalty in the late rebellion, especially in refusing to submit to the visitation of the usurped powers, and to take the solemn league and covenant' (*Cal. State Papers*, Dom. Ser. 1664–5). In the debate on the Five Mile Act, when Vaughan wished to add the word 'legally,' to 'commissioned by him,' Finch pointed out that the addition was unnecessary, and his argument was adopted by Anglesey in the lords, where Southampton moved the same addition (BURNET, *Own Time*, i. 225). In the session of 1666 he spoke against the Irish Cattle Bill

(*Cal. State Papers*, Dom. Ser. 1666–7), and in October 1667 on Clarendon's impeachment. The account is obscure, but apparently he did what he could to check the violence of the commons, insisting on sworn evidence, though willing that it should be kept secret. On 18 Feb. 1668 he did the court good service by shelving the bill for holding frequent parliaments on the ground of informal introduction (*Parl. Hist.*); and in the same month, in the celebrated Skinner controversy, he pleaded against Skinner before the lords on behalf of the East India Company (PEPYS, 22 Feb. 1668). In December 1668, on the motion for impeaching the Earl of Orrery, he warned the house against acting upon 'out-of-door accusation' (*Parl. Hist.*) On 10 May 1670 he became attorney-general, and soon afterwards councillor to Queen Catherine. He was chamberlain of Chester from 1673 to 1676. He exercised a moderating influence in the debates on the bill for 'preventing malicious maiming,' which followed the outrage on Sir John Coventry [q. v.], and he successfully opposed the proposal for a double assessment of defaulting members of the house by the argument that by tacking it to the subsidy bill a matter affecting the commons only would come before the lords. In April 1671 he conducted with great skill the conferences between the lords and commons on the subject of the interference of the former in money bills, from which dates practically the cessation of the practice. His ability in the conduct of this matter was recognised by the formal thanks of the house. On 6 Feb. 1673 he argued in favour of the 'chancellor's writs,' the writs issued for parliamentary elections during the recess by Shaftesbury, on the ground that parliamentary privilege was then dormant, but could not make head against the determination of the house to suffer no court interference. In the great debate of 10 Feb. on the king's declaration of indulgence, while repudiating the doctrine advanced by Shaftesbury of a distinction between the exercise of the royal power in ecclesiastical and temporal affairs, he defended the legality and expediency of the declaration. 'A mathematical security,' he said, 'we cannot have; a moral one we have from the king.' Seeing the temper of the house, however, he concluded by the illogical motion that the king be petitioned 'that it might be so no more.' In March 1673 he passionately opposed the Naturalisation of Foreigners Bill, and in October did his best in vain to combat the determination of the commons to refuse further supplies for the Dutch war (*Parl. Hist.*)

On the dismissal of Shaftesbury, Finch became lord keeper of the seals, 9 Nov. 1673, and as such was made on 4 Jan. 1674 the unconscious mouthpiece of the first direct lie which Charles had ventured openly to tell his parliament (*ib.*) On 10 Jan. he was raised to the peerage as Baron Finch of Daventry, from the manor in Northamptonshire of which he was owner (COLLINS, *Peerage*). On 19 Dec. he surrendered the seals, to receive them again immediately with the higher title of lord chancellor, the office carrying with it apparently the very large salary of 4,000*l.* a year (*Autobiography of Roger North*, p. 165).

In 1675 Finch was, according to the evidence of Burnet, one of the chief arguers for the non-resisting test (*Own Time*, i. 383). As lord chancellor he had at the beginning of each session to supply an elaboration of the king's speech, and this he did, 'spoiling what the king had said so well by overstraining to do it better' (RALPH). In this year he conducted the case of the lords in the great Fagg controversy. In 1677 he presided as lord high steward of England on the trial of the Earl of Pembroke for manslaughter (WOOD, *Athenæ Oxon.*) A signal instance of the adroitness, joined, it should be said, with unimpeached probity, by which, almost alone among his contemporaries, he managed to secure at once permanence in office and freedom from parliamentary attack, occurred in the matter of Danby's impeachment. Charles, to the great anger of the commons, had given Danby a pardon in bar of the impeachment. The house appointed a committee, who demanded from Finch an explanation of the fact that the pardon bore the great seal. Finch's statement was that he neither advised, drew, nor altered it; that the king commanded him to bring the seal from Whitehall, and being there he laid it upon the table; thereupon his majesty commanded the seal to be taken out of the bag, which it was not in his power to hinder; and the king wrote his name on the top of the parchment, and then directed to have it sealed, whereupon the person who usually carried the purse affixed the seal to it. He added that at the time he did not regard himself as having the custody of the seal (*Parl. Hist.* iv. 1114). When the case of Danby was before the lords he argued for the right of bishops to vote in trials for treason, and carried his view as to preliminaries, though not as to final judgment (BURNET, *Own Time*, i. 460; COLLINS, *Peerage*). There is among Sir Charles Bunbury's manuscripts at Bury, Suffolk, a treatise on the king's power of granting pardons, ascribed with

most probability to Finch (*Hist. MSS. Comm.* 3rd Rep. 241 *a*). Some autograph notes, certainly his, on the Habeas Corpus Act of 1679 belong to Alfred Morrison, esq. (*ib.* 9th Rep. 457 *a*). He conducted the examination before the privy council of the 'party' lords who came from Scotland in 1678 to complain of Lauderdale, and, though evidently holding a brief for the duke, was unable to shake their position (BURNET, *Own Time*, i. 420). That Finch was not above using the ordinary jargon of court flattery appears in his exclamation, when Charles tried the experiment of a newly modelled privy council, 'It looked like a thing from heaven fallen into his master's breast.' During the popish terror Finch appears to have given no offence to either side. He presided, however, as lord high steward at the trial of Lord Stafford, and his conduct formed a pleasing contrast to that which so often disgraced the courts in the latter years of Charles's reign. He showed personal courtesy to the prisoner, provided him with all proper means of defence, and pronounced sentence in a speech greatly admired at the time, 'one of the best he had ever made' (BURNET, *Own Time*, i. 492). He, however, gave his own vote against Stafford, and complied so far with the prevailing fashion as to assume the whole truth of the 'plot,' and even to father the absurd cry that London had been burned by the papists (*ib.* i. 492; *State Trials*). Burnet accounts for his patronage of the plot as the result of fear of parliamentary attack in consequence of his conduct in the matter of Danby's pardon (*ib.* ii. 261). Only one slip does Finch appear to have made in his discreet avoidance of giving offence. In 1679, on receiving Gregory, the new speaker of the house, he allowed himself to declare that the king 'always supports the creatures of his power.' Shaftesbury at once fastened on the expression; Finch was compelled to apologise, and a resolution was carried not to enter it upon the minutes of the house (RANKE, *Hist. England*, iv. 77). In the great question of the succession, Finch was of course against exclusion. But by Charles's command he proposed the middle and entirely impracticable scheme of 'limitations' (*ib.* iv. 80). On 12 May 1681 he was created Earl of Nottingham, and died 18 Dec. 1682, in the sixty-first year of his age, after a life spent in unremitting official and professional toil. He was buried at Ravenstone, near Newport Pagnell in Buckinghamshire, of which place he was the owner and benefactor (COLLINS, *Peerage*). He married Elizabeth Harvey, sister of Daniel Harvey, merchant of London (probably one of the members for Surrey in the Convention parliament), by whom he had a numerous family. The eldest son, Daniel [q. v.], became second earl. Heneage, the second son [q. v.], was solicitor-general, and was created earl of Aylesford. The fifth son, Edward [q. v.], was a musical composer. Nottingham's favourite residence, Kensington House, he bought of his younger brother John [q. v.] His son Daniel [q. v.] sold it to William III.

The fact that throughout an unceasing official career of more than twenty years, in a time of passion and intrigue, Finch was never once the subject of parliamentary attack, nor ever lost the royal confidence, is a remarkable testimony both to his probity and discretion. His success in the early part of the reign arose from the fact that he was in the first place a constitutional lawyer of the highest repute, 'well versed in the laws' (BURNET, *Own Time*, i. 365). Dryden bears the same testimony in 'Absalom and Achitophel,' where he is described as Amri. These qualifications made him a man of extreme usefulness at a time when the constitution had to be restored after many years of dislocation. Until he finally left the house scarcely a committee of importance was formed on which he was not placed, usually as chairman. He was appointed to draw up the letter of congratulation from the commons to Charles on his arrival in England; and he had the management of almost all the important controversies which were so frequently held with the lords. His forensic eloquence is testified to on all hands; though Burnet says he was too eloquent on the bench, in the lords, and in the commons, and calls his speaking laboured and affected. Roger North in his autobiography (p. 198) confirms this view, saying that his love of 'a handsome turn of expression gave him a character of a trifler which he did not so much deserve.' In the high-flown language of the time he was named the English Roscius and the English Cicero.

Burnet states to his credit that, though he used all the vehemence of a special pleader to justify the court before the lords, yet, as a judge, Finch carried on the high tradition of his predecessor, Shaftesbury. In his own court he could resist the strongest applications even from the king himself, though he did it nowhere else. The same historian calls him 'ill-bred; and both vain and haughty; he had no knowledge of foreign affairs, and yet he loved to talk of them perpetually.' Burnet's last words about him are, however, a recognition of the purity and fitness of his presentations of clergymen to livings in the chancellor's gift. His portrait was painted by Lely. There is a print by Houbraken.

[The chief authorities are the Journals of the House of Commons; Wood's Athenæ Oxon. (Bliss), iv. 66; Parliamentary History; Burnet's Own Time; Collins's Peerage.]   O. A.

FINCH, HENEAGE, second EARL OF WINCHILSEA (*d.* 1689), was the son of Thomas, the first earl, whose mother Elizabeth had been created Countess of Winchilsea in her widowhood by Charles I (1628). Heneage, educated at Emmanuel College, Cambridge, succeeded to the title of Viscount Maidstone in 1633, and of Earl of Winchilsea in 1639. He distinguished himself on the royalist side during the great rebellion, providing auxiliary troops (horse and foot) at his own expense, and supplying 'with great hazard' Charles II's 'necessities in foreign parts.' He was a friend of Monck and was made governor of Dover Castle in 1660. Upon the Restoration he was created a baron, by the title of Lord Fitzherbert of Eastwell (from which family the Finches claimed descent), 26 June 1660, and on 10 July was appointed lord-lieutenant of Kent. Early in 1661 he went on an important embassy to Sultan Mahomet Chan IV, and published an account of it the same year. He remained as English ambassador at Constantinople eight years, and on his return journey wrote from Naples to the king a description, afterwards printed, of the eruption of Mount Etna. At home he was reinstated lord-lieutenant of Kent and governor of Dover Castle, and was lord-lieutenant of Somerset from 1675 to 1683. He was, with a long list of other lieutenants, dismissed from Kent in 1687. When James II was stopped at Feversham by the Kentish fishermen, he sent for Winchilsea, who was at Canterbury. The earl arrived before night (12 Dec.), and interposed on behalf of the king besides moving him to a more suitable lodging in a private house (*Add. MS.* 32095, f. 298; RALPH, *History*, i. 1068). When James fled for the second time, Winchilsea was one of those who voted for offering the vacant throne to William and Mary, and in March 1689 was again made lord-lieutenant of Kent. He died in August the same year. He married four times: (1) Diana, daughter of Francis, fifth lord Willoughby of Parham; (2) Mary, daughter of William Seymour, marquis of Hertford; (3) Catherine, daughter of Sir Thomas Norcliff; (4) Elizabeth, daughter of John Ayres, esq. Out of twenty-seven children sixteen lived to 'some maturity.'

His published works were: 1. 'Narrative of the Success of his Embassy to Turkey

The Voyage of the Right Honourable Heneage Finch from Smyrna to Constantinople. His Arrival there, and the manner of his Entertainment and Audience with the Grand Vizier and Grand Seignieur,' London, 1661. 2. 'A true and exact Relation of the late prodigious Earthquake and Eruption of Mount Etna, or Mount Gibello, as it came in a Letter written to his Majesty from Naples. By the Right Honourable the Earl of Winchelsea, his Majesty's late Ambassador at Constantinople, who on his return from thence, visiting Catania, in the Island of Sicily, was an eye-witness of that dreadful spectacle. Together with a more particular Narrative of the same, as it is collected out of several relations sent from Catania. With a View of the Mountain and Conflagration,' London, 1669, fol.

[Collins's Peerage, ed. 1779, iii. 280 ; Walpole's Royal and Noble Authors, ed. Park, iii. 316; Rycaut's Hist. of the Turks, ii. 97, &c.; Luttrell's Relation of State Affairs, i. 422, 575 ; Brit. Mus. Cat. ; Doyle's Baronage.]   E. T. B.

FINCH, HENEAGE, first EARL OF AYLESFORD (1647 ?–1719), second son of Heneage Finch, first earl of Nottingham [q.v.], was educated at Westminster School and Christ Church, Oxford. He left the university without a degree, and entering the legal profession was admitted a barrister of the Inner Temple. His name soon became known as the author of various reports of celebrated trials and other legal tracts; he was appointed king's counsel 10 July 1677, and solicitor-general in 1679, entering parliament as member for the university of Oxford in the same year. In 1686 he was deprived of the solicitor-generalship by James II, and two years later pleaded as leading counsel on the side of the seven bishops. He sat for Guildford in the parliament of 1685, again representing the university of Oxford in the Convention parliament of 1689–90, and all subsequent ones (except that elected in 1698), till his promotion to the peerage in 1703 (*Members of Parliament Blue Book*, pt. i. see Index). Burnet relates that in the debate on the Act of Settlement of 1701 Finch attempted to alter the clause for abjuring the Prince of Wales into an obligation not to assist him, and pressed his point 'with unusual vehemence in a debate that he resumed seventeen times in one session against all rules' (BURNET, *History of my own Time*, ed. 1823, iv. 537–8 and note). In August 1702 he was chosen by the university to present a complimentary address to Queen Anne on her visit to Oxford, and in 1703 was created, 'in consideration of his great merit and abilities,' Baron Guernsey, and sworn of the privy council. Burnet remarks that there

were great reflections on the promotion of Finch and others, to make, it was said, a majority for the Stuarts in the House of Lords. On the accession of George I he was advanced in the peerage, taking the title of Earl of Aylesford, an estate having been left to him there, with a large fortune, by his wife's father. Besides this new dignity he was again sworn of the privy council, and created chancellor of the duchy of Lancaster, which office he resigned in 1716. He died 22 July 1719, and was buried at Aylesford, Kent. He married Elizabeth, daughter and coheir of Sir John Banks of Aylesford, by whom he had nine children. His son Heneage, M.P. for Surrey, was made in 1711 master of the jewel house.

His portrait appears in the print engraved by White in 1689 of the counsel of the seven bishops.

[Collins's Peerage, ed. 1779, iv. 316; Sharpe's Peerage, i. 20; Welch's Alumni Westmon. p. 571; Poynter's Chron. 1703, 1711; Luttrell's Relation of State Affairs; Burnet's History of my own Time, ed. 1823, ii. 106, 397; Macaulay's Hist.] E. T. B.

FINCH, SIR HENRY (1558–1625), serjeant-at-law, was second son of Sir Thomas Finch [q. v.] of Eastwell, Kent, by Catherine, daughter and heir of Sir Thomas Moyle. His elder brother, Sir Moyle Finch, was the father of Sir Heneage Finch [q. v.], speaker of the House of Commons in the reign of Charles I, whose son Heneage [q. v.], first earl of Nottingham, was lord chancellor to Charles II. Wood's statement that Finch was 'for a time' at Oriel College, Oxford, seems doubtful. He was probably the pensioner of his name who matriculated in May 1572 from Christ's College, Cambridge, and graduated B.A. 1575–6 (cf. ANDREW WILLET, *Harmony of I Samuel*, pref.) Finch was admitted of Gray's Inn in 1577, and called to the bar there in 1585 (DOUTHWAITE, *Gray's Inn*, p. 62). He seems to be identical with a certain Henry Finch of Canterbury, who held from the archbishop a lease of Salmstone rectory, except the timber and the advowson, between 1583 and 1600. In Feb. 1592–3 he was returned to parliament for Canterbury, and he retained the seat at the election of 1597. He became an 'ancient' of his inn in 1593, and the same year counsel to the Cinque ports. He was reader at his inn in the autumn of 1604. In 1613 he was appointed recorder of Sandwich, on 11 June 1616 he was called to the degree of serjeant-at-law, and nine days later was knighted at Whitehall (*Cal. State Papers*, Dom. 1598–1601 p. 533, 1611–1618 p. 373; *Lists of Members of Parliament*; Boys, *Collections for History of Sandwich*, pp. 423, 779). At this time he was engaged, in conjunction with Bacon, Noy, and others, upon an abortive attempt at codifying the statute law, described by Bacon as ' the reducing of concurrent statutes heaped one upon another to one clear and uniform law.' About the same time his opinion was taken by the king on the ' conveniency' of monopoly patents, and to him, jointly with Bacon and Montague, was entrusted the conduct of the business connected with the patent intended to be granted to inns and alehouses (SPEDDING, *Letters and Life of Bacon*, vi. 71, 84, 99). He took part in the argument on the question whether baronets ranked as bannerets before the king and council on 6 April 1612. In 1614 he was elected M.P. for St. Albans. In 1621 he published a work entitled ' The World's Great Restauration, or Calling of the Jews, and with them of all Nations and Kingdoms of the Earth to the Faith of Christ,' in which he seems to have predicted as in the near future the restoration of temporal dominion to the Jews and the establishment by them of a world-wide empire. This caused King James to treat the work as a libel, and accordingly Finch was arrested in April 1621. He obtained his liberty by disavowing all such portions of the work as might be construed as derogatory to the sovereign and apologising for having written unadvisedly. Laud, in a sermon preached in July 1621, took occasion to animadvert on the book. It was suppressed and is now extremely rare (*Notes and Queries*, 2nd ser. xi. 127; *Cal. State Papers, Dom.* 1619–23, pp. 247, 248). He must have been in embarrassed circumstances in 1623, as his son John [q. v.] having become surety for him was only protected from arrest for debt by an order under the sign-manual (*Cal. State Papers, Dom.* 1619–23, p. 515). He died in October 1625, and was buried in the parish church of Boxley, Kent (HASTED, *Kent*, iv. 624). By his wife Ursula, daughter of John Thwaites of Kent, he was father of John, lord Finch of Fordwich [q. v.] (BERRY, *County Genealogies* (Kent), p. 206), and of Edward (*fl.* 1630–1641) [q. v.], royalist divine, whom the genealogists overlook. Besides the 'Great Restauration,' Finch published a legal treatise of considerable merit entitled ' Νομοτεχνία, cestascavoir un Description del Common Leys d'Angleterre solonque les Rules del Art Parallelees ove les Prerogative le Roy, &c., &c., Per Henrie Finch de Graye's Inne, Apprentice del Ley,' Lond. 1613, fol. It is dedicated in remarkably good Latin, ' Augustissimo Principi omnique virtutum genere splendidissimo Jacobo Magno Dei gratia Britanniæ Regi.' It consists of four books. The first treats of what is now called jurisprudence, and is mainly devoted to expounding the distinction between natural and ' positive' law. It is learnedly written, Plato and Cicero being frequently cited. The second book deals with the common law, customs, prerogative, and statute law; the third with procedure, and the fourth with special jurisdictions, e.g. those of the admiral and the bishop. The treatise is written in law French. An English version, entitled ' Law, or a Discourse thereof in Four Books, written in French by Sir Henry Finch, Knight, His Majesty's Serjeant-at-law, done into English by the same author,' appeared in London in 1627, 8vo; 1636, 12mo; 1678, 8vo; and was edited with notes by Danby Pickering of Gray's Inn, in 1789, 8vo. It differs in some important particulars from the original work. Another and much closer translation was published in the last century under the title, ' A Description of the Common Laws of England according to the Rules of Art compared with the Prerogatives of the King,' &c., London, 1759, 8vo. As an exposition of the common law, Finch's Law, as it was called, was only superseded by Blackstone's ' Commentaries,' so far as it dealt with jurisprudence only by the great work of Austin. A little abstract of the work, entitled ' A Summary of the Common Law of England,' appeared in London in 1673, 8vo.

[Wood's Athenæ Oxon. (Bliss), ii. 387; Woolrych's Lives of Eminent Serjeants-at-law, i. 391–3; Berry's County Genealogies (Kent).] J. M. R.

FINCH, HENRY (1633–1704), ejected minister, was born at Standish, Lancashire, and baptised on 8 Sept. 1633. He was educated at the grammar schools of Standish and Wigan. Calamy does not say at what university he graduated. After preaching in the Fylde country (between the Lune and the Ribble) he was presented in 1656 to the vicarage of Walton-on-the-Hill, Lancashire, a parish which then included the town of Liverpool. He was a member of the fifth presbyterian classis of Lancashire. In July 1659 he took a rather active part in the plans for the rising of the ' new royalists' under Sir George Booth (1622–1684) [q. v.] His property was seized by the parliamentary sequestrators, and not restored; but for the restoration of the monarchy in the following year he would probably have lost his benefice. Unable to accept the terms of the Uniformity Act, he was ejected in 1662. He retired to Warrington, where he lived for some years in dependence on his wife's relatives. The Five Mile Act (1665) compelled him to leave, and he settled in Manchester (not then a corporate town), where he supported himself by keeping a school. Both at

Warrington and Manchester he attended the ordinary services in the established church, preaching only occasionally on Sunday evenings in his own dwelling to such restricted gatherings as the law allowed. On the indulgence of 1672 he took out a license as a 'general presbyterian minister,' and officiated in the licensed 'private oratory' (Birch Chapel), which was in the hands of Thomas Birch of Birch Hall, Lancashire, though the legal owners were the warden and fellows of the collegiate church of Manchester. On 29 Oct. 1672 he took part in the first ordination conducted by the ejected nonconformists, in the house of Robert Eaton at Deansgate, Manchester. On the outbreak of the Monmouth rebellion (1685) Finch was imprisoned at Chester; this was probably the occasion when, as Calamy relates, 'they thrust a conformist into his place' at Birch Chapel, but 'that project dropt,' and Finch was allowed to resume his ministry.

The Toleration Act (1689) was the means of calling attention to the insecurity of his position. Birch Chapel, being a consecrated place, could not be licensed as a dissenting meeting-house. Finch, however, stayed on until the death of Thomas Birch the younger in 1697, when the chapel was ceded by his son, George Birch, to the legal owners. Finch then preached at licensed houses in Platt and Birch, till his friends built a meeting-house at Platt (1700), Finch himself contributing 20l. towards the erection, which cost 95l. in all. The opening discourse was preached by Finch's son-in-law, James Grimshaw of Lancaster, author of 'Rest from Rebels,' 1716.

Finch was a member of the provincial meeting of united ministers (presbyterian and congregational) formed in Lancashire in 1693 on the basis of the London 'agreement' of 1691, involving a doctrinal subscription. He preached before this meeting on two occasions, 4 Aug. 1696, and 13 Aug. 1700, both at Manchester. Calamy acknowledges the value of Finch's corrections to his account of the silenced ministers. It is interesting to note that, though a strong supporter of the revolution of 1688, Finch was 'a charitable contributor while he liv'd' to the distressed nonjurors. Finch died on 13 Nov. 1704, and was succeeded by Robert Hesketh, early in whose ministry the chapel was conveyed (25–6 Oct. 1706) in trust for the maintenance of an 'orthodox' ministry.

PETER FINCH (1661–1754), presbyterian minister, son of the above, was born on 6 Oct. 1661. On 3 May 1678 he entered the nonconformist academy of Richard Frankland [q. v.] at Natland, Westmoreland. He soon removed to the university of Edinburgh, where

he graduated M.A. on 16 July 1680. His first employment was as chaplain in the family of William Ashurst, afterwards knighted [see ASHURST, HENRY]. In 1691 he was invited to become colleague at Norwich to Josiah Chorley [q. v.]; his first entry in the presbyterian register of baptisms is dated 1 June 1692. He remained at his post for over sixty-two years, and survived Edward Crane [q. v.] and Thomas Dixon the younger [see under DIXON, THOMAS], both of whom had been designated as his successor. Himself a strict Calvinist, he contributed much, by his love of peace, to preserve concord when doctrinal differences threatened to divide his flock. From 1733 John Taylor, the Hebraist, was his colleague. He died on his ninety-third birthday, 6 Oct. 1754, and was buried in the church of St. Peter Mancroft, Norwich. A small portrait of him hangs in the vestry of the Octagon Chapel. His great-grandson, Peter, was mayor of Norwich in 1827.

[Calamy's Account, 1713, p. 404 sq.; Continuation, 1727, i. 564; Monthly Repository, 1811, p. 261; Taylor's Hist. Octagon Chapel, Norwich, 1848, p. 15 sq.; Booker's Hist. Ancient Chapel of Birch (Chetham Soc.), 1858; Cat. of Edinb. Graduates (Bannatyne Club), 1858; Halley's Lancashire Nonconformity, 1869, p. 94, &c.; Manuscript Minutes of Provincial Meeting of Lancashire Ministers (1693–1700), in possession of trustees of Cross Street Chapel, Manchester; papers relating to Platt Chapel, in possession of G. W. Rayner Wood.]   A. G.

FINCH, SIR JOHN, BARON FINCH OF FORDWICH (1584–1660), speaker of the House of Commons and lord keeper, son of Sir Henry Finch [q. v.], by Ursula, daughter of John Thwaites, was born on 17 Sept. 1584, admitted a member of Gray's Inn in February 1600, and called to the bar on 8 Nov. 1611. Clarendon states that he 'led a free life on a restrained fortune,' and that he 'set up upon the stock of a good wit and natural parts, without the superstructure of much knowledge in the profession by which he was to grow' (Rebellion, Oxford ed. i. 130), and Finch himself, on the occasion of his instalment as lord chief justice, publicly confessed that the first six years of his pupilage were mainly devoted to other pursuits than the study of the law (RUSHWORTH, Hist. Coll. ii. 256). In 1620 he was returned to parliament for Canterbury. In 1617 he was elected a bencher of his inn, where, in the autumn of the following year, he discharged the duties of reader (DOUTHWAITE, Gray's Inn, p. 66). Foss says, without giving his authority, that in 1617 he was elected recorder of Canterbury. He was certainly recorder of the city in March 1618–19 (Egerton *MS.* 2584, f. 177), and was dismissed by the corporation shortly afterwards. The cause of his removal does not appear. Finch himself, in a letter dated 4 Jan. 1619, soliciting the interest of Lord Zouch, warden of the Cinque ports, with the privy council, from which he had obtained a mandamus against the corporation for his reinstatement, speaks vaguely of the 'factious carriage' of one Sabin (*ib.* f. 100). The corporation had refused to obey the order of the privy council, and it remained as yet unenforced. On 19 May 1620 the corporation wrote to the Archbishop of Canterbury and Lord Zouch praying that they might not be compelled to re-elect Finch, as it would be 'against their consciences and their charter, and greatly to the disquiet of the city.' On 28 May, however, they changed their tone, humbly informing the council that they were willing to re-elect Mr. Finch as their recorder,' and craving 'pardon for discontenting their lordships' (*Cal. State Papers*, Dom. 1619–1623, pp. 108, 144, 146, 148). Finch was returned to parliament for Winchelsea in February 1623–4, but was unseated on petition on the ground that certain voters had been excluded by the mayor. A new writ issued on 19 March, and Finch was re-elected (*Comm. Journ.* i. 739). He exchanged Winchelsea for Canterbury at the election of 1625. On 31 May the king, and on 13 June 1625 the king and queen paid a visit to Canterbury, and were received with an address by Finch as recorder. The addresses, notes of which are preserved in Sloane MS. 1455, ff. 1–6, must have been remarkable only for the style of fulsome adulation in which they were conceived. In 1626 he was knighted and appointed king's counsel and attorney-general to the queen (*Cal. State Papers*, Dom. 1625–6, p. 456; RYMER, *Fœdera*, Sanderson, xiii. 633, 866). On 17 March 1627–8 he was elected speaker of the House of Commons, being still member for Canterbury (*Comm. Journ.* i. 872). His speech to the throne, couched though it was in language of the most extravagant loyalty, nevertheless concluded with three petitions: (1) that the house might be assured of the immunity of its members from arrest, (2) that freedom of debate might be respected, (3) that access to the royal person might be granted on suitable occasions (*Parl. Hist.* ii. 225). On 14 April 1628 he presented a petition against the practice of billeting soldiers on private citizens. On 5 May he conveyed to the king the answers of the commons to various royal messages, in particular to the demand of the king to know whether the commons would rest content with his 'royal word and pro-

mise' for the redress of their grievances. Finch expressed on behalf of the commons at once their entire confidence in the royal word, and their settled conviction that 'no less than a public remedy will raise the dejected hearts' of the people at large (*ib.* pp. 281, 346). In the debate on the royal message of 5 June, enjoining the commons not to meddle with affairs of state or asperse ministers, Sir John Eliot having risen ostensibly to rebut the implied charge of aspersing ministers, Finch, 'apprehending Sir John intended to fall upon the duke' (Buckingham), said, with tears in his eyes: 'There is a command laid upon me to interrupt any that should go about to lay aspersion on the ministers of state;' upon which Eliot sat down, the house, after some desultory conversation, resolved itself into a committee of public safety, and Finch repaired to the king, from whom next day he brought a conciliatory message. On this occasion he seems to have acted as a mediator between the king and the commons. Sir Robert Philips, who replied to the royal message on behalf of the house, while expressing himself very cautiously on the general question, lauded Finch as one who had 'not only at all times discharged the duty of a good speaker, but of a good man' (*ib.* pp. 402–7; *Cal. State Papers*, Dom. 1628–9, p. 153). In September and October 1628 Finch was associated with the attorney-general, Sir Robert Heath, in investigating the circumstances attending the assassination of the Duke of Buckingham (*ib.* pp. 332, 343). On 25 Feb. 1628–9 Finch delivered a message from the king commanding the adjournment of the house. Several members objected that adjournment was a matter for the house to determine, and Sir John Eliot proceeded to present a remonstrance on the subject of tonnage and poundage, which Finch refused to read. Eliot then read it himself. Finch, however, refused to put the question, and, rising to adjourn the debate, was forced back into the chair, and held there by Denzil Holles, Valentine, and others, Holles swearing 'God's wounds he should sit still till it pleased them to rise.' Finch burst into tears, exclaiming, 'I will not say I will not, but I dare not,' reminding the house that he had been their 'faithful servant,' and protesting 'he would sacrifice his life for the good of his country, but durst not sin against the express command of his sovereign.' Meanwhile with locked doors the substance of Eliot's remonstrance was adopted by the house and declared carried. Shortly afterwards parliament was dissolved, not to meet again for eleven years (*Parl. Hist.* ii. 487–91). In 1631 Finch was much employed in Star-chamber and high commission cases (*Reports of Cases in the Courts of Star-chamber and High Commission*, Camd. Soc.) In the autumn of 1633, the Inns of Court having decided to provide a grand masque for the entertainment of the king and queen, by way at once of testifying their loyalty and protesting against the austere views lately published by Prynne in his 'Histrio-Mastix,' Finch was elected one of the committee of management. The performance, which took place on Candlemas day (2 Feb. 1633–4), is described at some length by Whitelocke, and seems to have been a very splendid pageant. The masquers went in procession from Ely House, Holborn, by way of Chancery Lane and the Strand to Whitehall. The dancing took place in the palace, the queen herself dancing with some of the masquers. The revels were prolonged far into the night, and terminated with a stately banquet. Finch was subsequently deputed to convey the thanks of the members of the four inns to the king and queen for their gracious reception of the masquers. The entertainment was afterwards repeated by royal command in the Merchant Taylors' Hall (WHITELOCKE, *Memoirs*, pp. 19, 22). About the same time Finch was busily engaged in the proceedings taken against Prynne in the Star-chamber. His speech, in which he charges Prynne with veiling under the name of Herodias a libel on the queen, is reported in 'Documents relating to William Prynne' (Camd. Soc. pp. 10, 11). Attorney-general Noy dying in the following August was succeeded by Sir John Banks, and Sir Robert Heath having been removed from the chief-justiceship of the court of common pleas on 14 Sept., Finch was appointed to succeed him on 16 Oct., having taken the degree of serjeant-at-law on 9 Oct. Notes of his speeches on being sworn in as serjeant, taking leave of Gray's Inn on 12 Oct., and being sworn in as chief justice, are preserved in Sloane MS. 1455, ff. 7–15. These changes inspired some legal wit with the following couplet :—

Noy's floods are gone, the Banks appear,
The Heath is cropt, the Finch sings there.

(DUGDALE, *Chron. Ser.* 106–7; CROKE, *Rep.* Car. p. 375; *Cal. State Papers*, Dom. 1634–5, p. 221). On the bench Finch distinguished himself by the height to which he carried the royal prerogative, and the severity of his sentences. Thus a certain James Maxwell and his wife Alice having been found guilty in the Star-chamber (17 April 1635) of libelling the king and the lord keeper, and Lord Cottington proposing a fine of 3,000*l.* for the offence against the king and the same sum to the lord keeper, the lord chief baron moved to add in the case of the woman a whipping, in which he was supported by Finch. The motion, however, was lost. In another Star-chamber case (27 Jan. 1636–7) one Elmstone having been sentenced to imprisonment and also to stand in the pillory at Westminster, Finch moved to add that he lose his ears. The motion was lost. On Prynne's second trial (1637) Finch surpassed himself in brutality. He drew the attention of the court to the fact that some remnants of Prynne's ears still remained, and moved that they be cut close, and that he be stigmatised with the letters S. L. (seditious libeller) on his cheeks, which proposals were adopted into the sentence. In the case of John Langton (1638), one of the subordinate officials of the exchequer, charged with abuse of the royal prerogative, Finch doubled the fine of 1,000*l.* proposed by Lord Cottington, and added the pillory, imprisonment, and disability to hold office, in which the rest of the court concurred, Archbishop Laud, however, being for raising the fine to 5,000*l.* Finch also added a whipping to the sentence of fine, pillory, and mutilation proposed by Lord Cottington for one Pickering, a Roman catholic, found guilty in 1638 of libelling the king and queen by calling them Romanists, and sacrilegiously converting part of a churchyard into a pigsty (*Cal. State Papers*, Dom. 1635 p. 31, 1636–7 p. 398, 1637 p. 214, 1637–8 pp. 384, 474; COBBETT, *State Trials*, iii. 717, 725).

On 12 Feb. 1636–7 the king laid before the judges a case for their opinion on the legality of ship-money. The opinion which they all subscribed, but for which, according to Clarendon, Finch was mainly responsible, was to the effect that the king had an uncontrolled discretion in the matter. To this opinion Finch and the majority of his colleagues adhered on the occasion of the trial of Hampden in the exchequer chamber. He delivered a long and somewhat rambling judgment, concluding with the statement that 'upon common law and the fundamental policy of the kingdom the king may charge his subjects for the defence of the kingdom when it is in danger,' and 'that the king is sole judge of the danger, and ought to direct the means of defence' (COBBETT, *State Trials*, iii. 843, 1243). Of this judgment Clarendon says that it made ship-money 'more abhorred and formidable than all the commitments by the council table, and all the distresses taken by the sheriffs in England ; the major part of men looking upon these proceedings with a kind of applause to themselves, to see other men punished for not doing as they had done; which delight was quickly determined when they found their own interest, by the unnecessary logic of that argument, no less concluded than Mr. Hampden's' (*Rebellion*, i. 127, 130). In March 1638-9 Finch was sworn of the privy council, and on 17 Jan. 1639-40 he obtained through the influence of the queen the place of lord keeper, then vacant by the death of Lord Coventry. His appointment was far from giving universal satisfaction. Thus, Sir Richard Cave writes to Sir Thomas Roe, under date 7 Feb. 1639-40: 'The lord keeper keeps such a clatter in his new place that they are more weary of him in the chancery than they were before in the common pleas.' On 7 April 1640 he was created Baron Finch of Fordwich in Kent (*Letters of Lady Brilliana Harley* (Camd. Soc.), p. 32; *Cal. State Papers*, Dom. 1639-40 pp. 341, 344, 436, 1640 p. 12). The Short parliament of 1640 was opened by the king on 13 April with a few words indicative of the gravity of the situation, the task of more fully setting forth the royal wishes and intentions being devolved upon the lord keeper. After dwelling upon the magnanimity shown by the king in 'sequestering the memory of all former discouragements,' and once more summoning a parliament, Finch proceeded to expatiate upon the threatening aspect of Scottish affairs, and the consequent necessity of obtaining immediate supplies. On this theme he again enlarged on 20 April, but with no effect, the commons resolving that grievances must take precedence of supply. On 5 May parliament was dissolved. One of the first acts of the Long parliament was the exhibition of articles of impeachment against Finch. The principal counts in the indictment were three: (1) his arbitrary conduct when speaker on the occasion of Eliot's motion on tonnage and poundage; (2) malpractices on the bench in 1635 for the purpose of extending the royal forest in Essex beyond its legal boundaries; (3) his conduct in Hampden's case (*Harleian Miscellany*, v. 566-9; *Somers Tracts*, iv. 129-32; *Trevelyan Papers*, Camd. Soc. iii. 199-200). Finch appeared at the bar of the House of Commons during the preliminary stage (21 Dec.), and made an elaborate speech in his own defence, but took refuge in Holland before the form of the articles was finally determined, arriving at the Hague on 31 Dec. 1640. According to Clarendon (*Rebellion*, i. 311, 526) the house was 'wonderfully indisposed to hear anything against' him, though Falkland denounced him as the 'chief transgressor' in the matter of ship-money. His estates in Kent and Middlesex were sequestrated in 1644, being estimated as of the annual value of 338*l.*;

but his wife, Lady Mabel, was permitted to occupy them at the annual rent of 100*l.* so long as they should continue in sequestration (*Lords' Journals*, vi. 568 *a*, vii. 272; *Add. MS.* 5494, f. 206). They seem to have been subsequently redeemed for 7,000*l.*, though Finch's name does not appear in Dring's 'Catalogue' (1733) (*Parl. Hist.* ii. 528-34, 552-60, 685-98; COBBETT, *State Trials*, iv. 18; *Cal. State Papers*, Dom. 1661-2, p. 328). During his exile Finch seems to have resided principally at the Hague. Here in 1641 Evelyn met him, and lodged for a time in the same house with him, the house, oddly enough, of a Brownist, where, says Evelyn, 'we had an extraordinary good table' (*Diary*, 26 July and 19 Aug. 1641). Two letters to Finch, one from Henrietta Maria, the other from Elizabeth, queen of Bohemia, belonging to this period, may be read in 'Archæologia,' xxi. 474 et seq. They are of slight historical importance, but by the familiarity of their style serve to show the intimate terms on which he stood with the writers. A letter to Sir Christopher Hatton, dated 3 Jan. 1640-1, announcing his arrival at the Hague (*Add. MSS.* 28218 f. 9, 29550 f. 49), was printed in 1641 (*Brit. Mus. Cat.* 'Finch'). Another to Dr. Cosin, dean of Peterborough, written in a very inflated style, but not without touches of humour, is undated, but must have been written in 1641 or 1642, as it contains a reference to the 'danger that hangs over the head' of Cosin, viz. the prosecution in the high commission court for innovating in religion, which terminated 22 Jan. 1642 in sequestration. It was printed in 1642 (*ib.*), and reprinted in 1844 (*Newcastle Reprints of Rare Tracts, Historical*, i.) On 14 July 1647 Finch petitioned the House of Lords for leave to return home to die in his native country. The petition was ordered to be considered, and was entered in the journal of the house, but no leave appears to have been granted (*Lords' Journals*, vii. 331). In October 1660 Finch was one of the commissioners for the trial of the regicides, but took little part in the proceedings. He died on the 27th of the following month, and was buried in St. Martin's Church, near Canterbury. As he left no male issue the peerage became extinct. Finch married first Eleanor, daughter of George Wyat; and secondly, Mabel, daughter of the Rev. Charles Fotherby, dean of Canterbury. Smith (*Obituary*, Camd. Soc., p. 52) calls him a 'proud and impious man, but loyal to his prince.' His character has been painted in black colours by Campbell; but though a bigoted supporter of despotic power, there is no reason to suppose that he was other than a conscientious man. His view of the duty of a judge was certainly very humble, if we may credit the statement of Clarendon (*Rebellion*, i. 130) that while lord keeper he announced his intention of giving effect on all occasions to the mandates of the privy council. It has, however, never been suggested that he was open to pecuniary corruption. Wood says that he was the author of a 'Manuale Mathematicum,' curiously written on vellum with his own hand, formerly preserved in the Ashmolean Museum, but now missing from the Ashmolean collection at the Bodleian. He was also one of the first donors to Gray's Inn library (DOUTHWAITE, *Gray's Inn*, p. 176).

[Berry's County Genealogies (Kent); Campbell's Lives of the Chancellors; Foss's Lives of the Judges.] J. M. R.

FINCH, SIR JOHN (1626–1682), physician, younger son of Sir Heneage Finch, speaker of the House of Commons [q. v.], was born in 1626, and, after education at Mr. Sylvester's school in All Saints parish, Oxford, was admitted pensioner of Christ's College, Cambridge, 11 April 1645. Subsequently he entered Balliol College as a gentleman commoner and graduated B.A. 22 May 1647, being incorporated at Cambridge the same year. In 1648 he left Oxford, and in 1649 graduated M.A. at Christ's College, Cambridge; then went to Padua and took the degree of M.D. in that university. He became English consul at Padua, and was made syndic of the university. The Grand Duke of Tuscany afterwards appointed him to a professorship at Pisa. He returned to England at the Restoration, and on 26 Feb. 1661 was elected an extraordinary fellow of the College of Physicians of London. 'Ob præclara doctoris Harvei merita,' say the college annals, probably in reference to the fact that Harvey had been a doctor of physic of the university of Padua. Lord Clarendon presented Finch to the king, who knighted him on 10 June 1661, and on 26 June in the same year he was created M.D. at Cambridge, Dr. Carr appearing as his proxy. He was one of the fellows admitted by the council of the Royal Society, in virtue of the power given them for two months, on 20 May 1663. The house now called Kensington Palace belonged to Finch, and in 1661 he sold it to his elder brother, Sir Heneage Finch, afterwards Lord Nottingham. In 1665 he was sent as minister to the Grand Duke of Tuscany, and in 1672 was promoted to be ambassador at Constantinople. On his voyage thither he stopped at Leghorn and at Malta to arrange the restitution of some goods belonging to the basha of Tunis, which had been seized by English privateers. On 2 May 1675 he left his house in Pera, with a retinue of one hundred and twenty horses and fifty-

five carts of baggage, and after a nine days' journey reached Adrianople. The object of the visit was to obtain the sultan's confirmation of privileges granted to English residents in his dominions, and after tedious delays this was accomplished on 8 Sept. The town was crowded, and the ambassador, who had at first wretched lodgings, was later obliged to live in tents in the fields owing to an epidemic of plague, of which some of his household died. He returned to Constantinople, and in 1682 to England. He died of pleurisy on 18 Nov. 1682 in London, whence his body was conveyed by his kinsmen to Cambridge and there buried, as he had desired, near that of his friend Sir Thomas Baines [q.v.], in the chapel of Christ's College. Their friendship is the most interesting circumstance of the life of Finch. It began at Cambridge, where Henry More the Platonist introduced Finch, on his migration from Oxford, to Baines, already a member of Christ's College. They pursued the same studies and lived in the same places, both graduated in medicine at Padua, were admitted fellows of the College of Physicians of London on the same day, and were together created doctors of physic at Cambridge. When Finch had been knighted he sought the same honour for Baines, and when he went abroad as an ambassador he took Sir Thomas Baines with him as physician to the embassy. They consulted together on every difficulty, and at Constantinople were known as the ambassador and the chevalier, and it was considered as important to secure the influence of the one as of the other. Thus constant throughout life they are buried side by side, under the same marble canopy, and are every year commemorated as benefactors of their college, where they jointly founded two fellowships and two scholarships, anxious to encourage in future generations the formation of friendships at the university as true and as lasting as their own.

[Munk's Coll. of Phys. i. 298; Pepys's Diary, 6th ed. iii. 446; Cambridge University Calendar, 1868; North's Life of the Hon. Sir Dudley North, Knt., London, 1744; tomb in the chapel of Christ's College, Cambridge; Dodd's Church History, iii. 257; Wood's Fasti, ed. Bliss, ii. 101.] N. M.

FINCH, ROBERT (1783–1830), antiquary, born in London on 27 Dec. 1783, was the only son of Thomas Finch, F.R.S. He was educated for a short time at St. Paul's School, and at eighteen was admitted at Balliol College, Oxford. He graduated B.A. 1806, M.A. 1809. He was ordained in 1807, and officiated at Maidstone and elsewhere. In 1814 he went abroad, visiting Portugal,

France, Switzerland, Italy, Greece, and the Holy Land. For several years before his death he lived in Rome. He died at his residence, the Palazzo del Re di Prussia, in Rome, on 16 Sept. 1830, from malarial fever. Finch had a great love of the fine arts, and studied antiquities and topography. He left his library, pictures, coins, and medals to the Ashmolean Museum, Oxford, and his plate to Balliol College. He was a fellow of the Society of Antiquaries, and a contributor to the 'Gentleman's Magazine' and other periodicals. He married in 1820, when in Italy, Maria, eldest daughter of Frederick Thomson of Kensington, but left no issue.

[Gent. Mag. 1830, vol. c. pt. ii. pp. 567–8.]
W. W.

FINCH, ROBERT POOLE (1724–1803), divine, son of the Rev. Richard Finch, was born at Greenwich 3 March 1723–4, entered Merchant Taylors' School in 1736, and was admitted a member of Peterhouse, Cambridge, whence he graduated B.A. 1743, M.A. 1747, D.D. 1772. He became a preacher of some eminence, published numerous sermons, and was also an author of a treatise upon oaths and perjury, which passed through many editions. In 1771 he was appointed rector of St. Michael's, Cornhill, but resigned in 1784, on becoming rector of St. John the Evangelist, Westminster. In 1781 he was made prebendary of Westminster, and retaining this appointment until his death, 18 May 1803, was buried in the abbey.

He published in 1788 'Considerations upon the Use and Abuse of Oaths judicially taken,' which became a standard work among the publications of the Society for Promoting Christian Knowledge.

[Robinson's Reg. of Merchant Taylors' School; Chester's Westminster Abbey Reg. p. 469.]
C. J. R.

FINCH, Sir THOMAS (d. 1563), military commander, was second son of Sir William Finch, who was knighted for his services at the siege of Terouenne in 1513, and attended Henry VIII with a great retinue in 1520. His mother, his father's first wife, was Elizabeth, daughter of Sir James Cromer of Tunstall, Kent, and widow of Sir Richard Lovelace. An elder brother, Lawrence, died without issue, and Thomas succeeded to his father's property. He was trained as a soldier, and in 1553 was engaged in suppressing Wyatt's rebellion in Kent. On the day after Mary's coronation (2 Oct. 1553) he was knighted. Soon after Elizabeth's accession (1559), Nicholas Harpsfeld [q. v.], archdeacon of Canterbury, threatened violent resistance to the new ecclesiastical legislation, and Finch was despatched to Canterbury to disarm his household. Early in 1563 he was appointed, in succession to Sir Adrian Poynings, knight-marshal of the army then engaged in war about Havre. He at once sent his half-brother, Sir Erasmus Finch, to take temporary charge, and his kinsman Thomas Finch to act as provost-marshal. He himself embarked in the Greyhound in March with two hundred followers, among them James and John Wentworth, brothers of Lord Wentworth, another brother of his own, a brother of Lord Cobham, and a nephew of Ambrose Dudley, earl of Warwick. When nearing Havre the ship was driven back by contrary winds towards Rye. Finch and his friends induced the captain—' a very good seaman,' says Stow—' to thrust into the haven before the tide,' and ' so they all perished' with the exception of ' seven of the meaner sort' (19 March). The news reached the court two days later, and produced great consternation (Cecil to Sir Thomas Smith in WRIGHT, Queen Elizabeth, i. 133). A ballad commemorating the misfortune was licensed to Richard Griffith at the time (COLLIER, Stationers' Registers, 1557–70, Shakespeare Soc. 73). Finch was buried at Eastwell, Kent.

Finch married Catherine, daughter and coheiress of Sir Thomas Moyle, chancellor of the court of augmentations, and thus came into possession of Moyle's property of Eastwell, at his death 2 Oct. 1560. He owned other land in Kent, and on 9 Dec. 1558 Aloisi Pruili, Cardinal Pole's secretary, requested Cecil to direct Finch to allow the officers of the cardinal, then just dead, to dispose of oxen, hay, wood, and deer belonging to their late master in St. Augustine's Park, Canterbury (Cal. State Papers, Dom. 1547–80, p. 116). His widow remarried Nicholas St. Leger, and died 9 Feb. 1586–7. Of his children, three sons and a daughter survived him. The second son, Sir Henry Finch, serjeant-at-law, is separately noticed. The third, Thomas, died without issue in the expedition to Portugal in 1589. The daughter, Jane, married George Wyatt of Bexley, son of Sir Thomas Wyatt of Allington, Kent. Finch's heir, Moyle, created a baronet 27 May 1611, married in 1574 Elizabeth, daughter of Sir Thomas Heneage of Copt Hall, Essex; inherited Eastwell on his mother's death in 1587; obtained a license to enclose one thousand acres of land there, and to embattle his house, 18 Jan. 1589, and died 14 Dec. 1614. His widow was created, in consideration of her father's services, Viscountess Maidstone, 8 July 1623, and Countess of Winchilsea, 12 July 1628, both titles being granted with limitation to heirs male. She died and was buried at Eastwell in 1633. Her eldest son, Thomas, succeeded her as Earl of Winchilsea. Her fourth son, Sir Heneage [q. v.], was speaker of the House of Commons, 1626–31.

[Collins's Peerage, ed. Brydges, iii. 378–9; Hasted's Kent, iii. 198–9; Stow's Chronicle, 1614, pp. 654–5; Wright's Queen Elizabeth, i. 127, 133; Froude's Hist. vi. 201; Machyn's Diary, pp. 302, 308.]　　　　　S. L.

FINCH, WILLIAM (d. 1613), merchant, was a native of London. He was agent to an expedition sent by the East India Company, under Captains Hawkins and Keeling, in 1607 to treat with the Great Mogul. Hawkins and Finch landed at Surat on 24 Aug. 1608. They were violently opposed by the Portuguese. Finch, however, obtained permission from the governor of Cambay to dispose of the goods in their vessels. Incited by the Portuguese, who seized two of the English ships, the natives refused to have dealings with the company's representatives. During these squabbles Finch fell ill, and Hawkins, proceeding to Agra alone, obtained favourable notice from the Emperor Jehanghire. Finch recovered, and joined Hawkins at Agra on 14 April 1610. The two remained at the mogul's court for about a year and a half, Finch refusing tempting offers to attach himself permanently to the service of Jehanghire. Hawkins returned to England, but Finch delayed his departure in order to make further explorations, visiting Byana and Lahore among other places. Finch made careful observations on the commerce and natural products of the districts visited. In 1612 the mogul emperor confirmed and extended the privileges he had promised to Finch and Hawkins, and the East India Company in that year set up their first little factory at Surat. Finch died at Babylon on his way to Aleppo from drinking poisoned water in August 1613.

[Purchas; Prévost's Histoire de Voyages; Dow's Hist. of Hindostan; Cal. State Papers, East Indies, 1513–1617, Nos. 449, 649, 650.]　　　　　J. B–y.

FINCH, WILLIAM (1747–1810), divine, son of William Finch of Watford, Hertfordshire, was born 22 July 1747, entered Merchant Taylors' School in 1754, and was elected thence in 1764 to St. John's College, Oxford. He graduated B.C.L. in 1770 and D.C.L. in 1775. In 1797 he accepted the college living of Tackley, Oxfordshire, and in the same year was appointed Bampton lecturer. He took as his subject 'The Objections of Infidel Historians and other writers against Christianity.' The lectures were published in 1797, together with a sermon preached before the

university on 18 Oct. 1795. Finch, who also published a sermon preached before the Oxford Loyal Volunteers (Oxford, 1798), died 8 June 1810, and was buried at Tackley.

[Robinson's Reg. of Merchant Taylors' School, ii. 114; Oxf. Matr. Reg.]　　　　　C. J. R.

FINCH-HATTON, EDWARD (d. 1771), diplomatist, was fifth son of Daniel Finch [q. v.], sixth earl of Winchilsea and second earl of Nottingham. He proceeded M.A. of Trinity College, Cambridge, in 1718, was elected M.P. for his university to every parliament that met between 1727 and 1768, and instituted with his fellow-member, Thomas Townshend, the Members' Prizes in the university for essays in Latin prose. A brother William, who was secretary to Lord Carteret 1719–20, was envoy to Sweden 1720–4 and afterwards to Holland. Edward held a longer succession of diplomatic posts. He was envoy extraordinary at the diet of Ratisbon, 1723. On 8 Feb. 1724–5 he was appointed to the court of Poland, where he remained two years. He was appointed in 1729 to the court of Sweden, and on 11 Jan. 1739 to that of Russia. On returning home he became groom of the royal bedchamber (1742), master of the robes (June 1757), and surveyor of the king's private woods in November 1760. He assumed in 1764 the additional name of Hatton, under the will of his aunt, Elizabeth (5 Oct. 1764), daughter of Christopher, viscount Hatton. He died 16 May 1771. In 1746 he married Elizabeth, daughter of Sir Thomas Palmer of Wingham, Kent, by whom he had two sons, George (1747–1823), the father of George William Finch-Hatton[q.v.], and John Emilius Daniel Edward (b. 19 May 1755), besides three daughters.

[Collins's Peerage, iii. 296–7.]

FINCH-HATTON, GEORGE WILLIAM, ninth EARL OF WINCHILSEA AND fifth EARL OF NOTTINGHAM (1791–1858), politician, born at Kirby, Northamptonshire, on 19 May 1791, was grandson of Edward Finch-Hatton [q. v.], and son of George Finch-Hatton (1747–1823) of Eastwell Park, near Ashford, Kent, M.P. for Rochester 1772–84, by his wife whom he married in 1785, Elizabeth Mary, eldest daughter of David Murray, second earl of Mansfield. She died 1 June 1825. George William, the elder son, was educated at Christ's College, Cambridge, where he proceeded B.A. in 1812. On 13 Oct. 1809 he became a captain in the Ashford regiment of Kentish local militia, on 14 Dec. 1819 commenced acting as a lieutenant of the Northamptonshire regiment of yeomanry, and on 7 Sept. 1820 was named a deputy-lieutenant for the county of Kent. His cousin, George Finch, eighth earl of Winchilsea and fourth earl of Nottingham, having died on 2 Aug. 1826, he succeeded to these peerages. He presided at a very large and influential meeting held on Pennenden Heath, Kent, on 10 Oct. 1828, when strongly worded resolutions in favour of protestant principles were carried. In his place in the House of Lords he violently opposed almost every liberal measure which was brought forward. He was particularly noted as being almost the only English nobleman who was willing to identify himself with the Orange party in Ireland, and he was accustomed to denounce in frantic terms Daniel O'Connell, Maynooth, and the system of education carried out in that college. Occasionally he took the chair at May meetings at Exeter Hall, but his intemperate language prevented him from becoming a leader in evangelical politics. The Catholic Relief Bill of 1829 encountered his most vehement hostility, and ultimately led to a duel with the Duke of Wellington. Lord Winchilsea, in a letter to the secretary of King's College, London, wrote that the duke, ' under the cloak of some coloured show of zeal for the protestant religion, carried on an insidious design for the infringement of our liberties and the introduction of popery into every department of the state.' The duke replied with a challenge. The meeting took place in Battersea Fields on 21 March 1829, the duke being attended by Sir Henry Hardinge, and his opponent by Edward Boscawen, viscount Falmouth. The duke fired and missed, whereupon Winchilsea fired in the air and then apologised for the language of his letter (*Annual Register*, 1829, pp. 58–63; STOCQUELER, *Life of Wellington*, ii. 147–8, with portrait of Winchilsea; STEINMETZ, *Romance of Duelling*, ii. 336–43). He was a very frequent speaker in the lords, and strenuously opposed the Reform Bill and other whig measures. He was gazetted lieutenant-colonel commandant of the East Kent regiment of yeomanry 20 Dec. 1830, named a deputy-lieutenant for the county of Lincoln 26 Sept. 1831, and created a D.C.L. of Oxford 10 June 1834. He died at Haverholme Priory, near Sleaford, Lincolnshire, 8 Jan. 1858.

He was the writer of a pamphlet entitled ' Earl of Winchilsea's Letter to the "Times," calling upon the Protestants of Great Britain to unite heart and soul in addressing the Throne for a Dissolution of Parliament,' 1851.

Winchilsea was married three times : first, on 26 July 1814, to Georgiana Charlotte, eldest daughter of James Graham, third duke of Montrose, she died at Haverholme Priory 13 Feb. 1835 ; secondly, on 15 Feb. 1837, to Emily Georgiana, second daughter of Sir Charles Bagot, G.C.B., she died at Haverholme Priory 10 July 1848 ; thirdly, on 17 Oct. 1849, to Fanny Margaretta, eldest daughter of Edward Royd Rice of Dane Court, Kent.

[Portraits of Eminent Conservatives and Statesmen, 1st ser. 1836, with portrait ; Doyle's Baronage (1886), iii. 690, with portrait after T. Phillipps ; Carpenter's Peerage for the People (1841), pp. 772–3 ; Gent. Mag. February 1858 pp. 211–12.] G. C. B.

FINDEN, EDWARD FRANCIS (1791–1857), engraver, was younger brother, fellow-pupil, and coadjutor of William Finden [q. v.], and shared his successes and fortunes. He executed some separate works, among early ones being a set of etchings for Duppa's 'Miscellaneous Opinions and Observations on the Continent,' 1825, and 'Illustrations of the Vaudois in a Series of Views,' 1831. He was also a large contributor of illustrations to the annuals, books of beauty, poetry, and other sentimental works then in vogue. The separate engravings executed by him included 'The Harvest Waggon,' after Gainsborough ; 'As Happy as a King,' after W. Collins ; 'Captain Macheath in Prison,' after G. S. Newton ; 'The Little Gleaner,' after Sir W. Beechey ; 'The Princess Victoria,' after Westall ; 'Othello telling his Exploits to Brabantio and Desdemona,' after Douglas Cowper, &c. He died at St. John's Wood, aged 65, on 9 Feb. 1857.

[Art Journal, 1852 ; Bryan's Dict. of Painters and Engravers, ed. Graves ; Redgrave's Dict. of Artists ; Athenæum, September 1852 ; Encycl. Brit. 9th ed. ; Brit. Mus. Cat.] L. C.

FINDEN, WILLIAM (1787–1852), engraver, was apprenticed to James Mitan, an engraver, one of the articles of his apprenticeship being that he was never to be a candidate for academy honours ; it is probable, however, that he derived much instruction from his careful study of the works of James Heath (1766–1834) [q. v.] He worked chiefly in conjunction with his younger brother and fellow-pupil, Edward Finden [q. v.], and was at first employed in his master's line of engraving, illustrating the books published by Sharpe, Sutton, and others, engraving Smirke's drawings for 'Don Quixote.' This rather cramped style of book illustration the Findens developed to a very great extent. They established a large school of pupils, who worked under their direction, and executed most of the works which bear the Findens' name, the Findens confining themselves principally to supervision, and to giving the few touches necessary to produce the elaborate finish and precision in which their productions excelled. This mechanical elaboration perhaps renders their works cold, and prevents their great excellency from being duly appreciated. Among the earlier works produced by William Finden were the illustrations to Sir Henry Ellis's edition of Dugdale's 'History of St. Paul's,' 1818, Dibdin's 'Ædes Althorpianæ,' 1822, &c. The brothers were both employed in engraving the Elgin marbles for the British Museum, and also on the illustrations for 'The Arctic Voyages' published by Murray; Brockedon's 'Passes of the Alps,' 1829; Campbell's 'Poetical Works,' 1828; and Lodge's 'Portraits,' 1821–34. They published on their own account and at their own cost in 1833 the illustrations to Moore's 'Life and Works of Lord Byron.' This last-named work created a great sensation. It was followed by other works of a popular nature, 'The Gallery of the Graces,' from pictures by Chalon, Landseer, and others, 1832–4; 'Landscape Illustrations of the Bible,' after Turner, Callcott, Stanfield, and others, 1834–6; 'Byron Beauties,' 1834; 'Landscape Illustrations to the Life and Poetical Works of George Crabbe,' 1834; 'Portraits of the Female Aristocracy of the Court of Queen Victoria,' after Chalon, Hayter, and others, 1838–9; 'Tableaux of National Character, Beauty, and Costume,' first edited by Mrs. S. C. Hall, then by Mary Russell Mitford (among the contributors of poetry was Elizabeth Barrett, afterwards Mrs. Browning [q. v.]), &c. The large profits which the brothers Finden gained from these works were risked and finally dissipated in an ambitious production, 'The Royal Gallery of British Art,' 1838, &c.; this publication, though admirably planned and beautifully executed, was unsuited to a public whose taste for annuals and illustrations of poetry had been surfeited to excess. It was the deathblow to the fortunes of the two Findens. William Finden died a widower after a short illness on 20 Sept. 1852, in his sixty-fifth year, and was buried in Highgate cemetery; one of his last acts was to sign a petition to the queen for the recognition of the claims of engravers to the full honours of the Royal Academy. Besides the publications above mentioned and numerous other illustrative works he produced some important single works, notably the full-length portrait of George IV, painted by Sir Thomas Lawrence for the Marchioness of Conyngham (a collection of progressive proofs of this engraving is in the print room at the British Museum); 'Sheep Washing' and 'The Village Festival,' by Sir David Wilkie (in the National Gallery); 'The Highlander's Return,' 'The Highlander's Home,' and 'The

Naughty Boy,' after Sir Edwin Landseer; and 'The Crucifixion,' after W. Hilton, Finden's last work, which was purchased by the Art Union for 1,470l.

[For authorities see under FINDEN EDWARD FRANCIS.] L. C.

FINDLATER, EARLS OF. [See OGILVY, JAMES, fourth EARL, 1664–1730; OGILVY, JAMES, sixth EARL, 1714 ?–1770.]

FINDLATER, ANDREW (1810–1885), compiler, born at Aberdour, Aberdeenshire, in 1810, was educated at the university of Aberdeen, where he graduated and for some time attended the divinity classes. On leaving college he became schoolmaster at Tillydesk, and subsequently head-master of Gordon's Hospital, Aberdeen. In 1853 he began a life-long connection with the publishing firm of Messrs. Chambers, Edinburgh. In the same year was published his essay on 'Epicurus' in the 'Encyclopædia Metropolitana.' His first work for Messrs. Chambers was an edition of their 'Information for the People,' which appeared in 1857. Shortly afterwards he was entrusted with the editorship of their 'Encyclopædia,' in which he wrote several articles. He also prepared for the 'Educational Course' of the same firm manuals on language, astronomy, physical geography, and physiography, and put forth new editions of their 'Etymological Dictionary' and the 'Miscellanies.' In addition to these literary productions, he contributed a series of essays entitled 'Notes of Travel' and various other articles to the 'Scotsman.' In 1864 he received the degree of LL.D. from the university of Aberdeen. His work is characterised by singular clearness of exposition. He died on 1 Jan. 1885. He married a daughter of Thomas Barclay, sheriff-clerk of Fifeshire, who died in 1879.

[Scotsman, 2 Jan. 1885.] W. B-E.

FINDLATER, CHARLES (1754–1838), agricultural writer and essayist, was born 10 Jan. 1754 in the manse of West Linton, Peeblesshire. His grandfather, Alexander Findlater, was a native of Moray, and married into the famous Scotch family, Kirkaldy of Grange. Thomas (1697–1778), his son, was minister of West Linton, but his settlement there in 1729 was resolutely opposed by certain of the parishioners, and led to the rise of a secessionist congregation, which still survives. Charles was Thomas Findlater's son by his second wife, Jean, daughter of William Brown, an Edinburgh bookseller. He graduated at Edinburgh University 14 Nov. 1770. In 1777 he was ordained assistant to his father, and in 1790 was presented by the Duke of Queensberry to the neighbouring parish, Newlands, where he lived until 1835, and then retiring from duty, died at Glasgow 28 May 1838, aged 84. His appointment at Newlands, like his father's at West Linton, was opposed, and led to the establishment of a seceding congregation, which yet exists. He married (26 July 1791) Janet Hay Russell (who was accidentally burnt to death in 1828). He was father of the synod of Lothian and Tweeddale, and was buried at Newlands. A marble bust of him, executed at the cost of many admirers, is in the Peebles Art Gallery.

Himself of the moderate theological school, Findlater's liberal opinions and neglect of conventionalities, united with much kindness of heart and intellectual power, marked him among his brother clergy. The cordiality of his friendship and correctness of his life were universally acknowledged. He established one of the first local savings banks, and used to carry his account-book for it regularly with him on his pastoral visitations. He would sing a song at a cottar's wedding, and on many wintry Sundays gather his congregation round him in his kitchen and give them dinner afterwards.

Findlater's books show him to have been well read in moral and political economy. He published: 1. 'Liberty and Equality; a Sermon or Essay, with an Appendix on Godwin's system of society in his "Political Justice,"' 1800. This sermon, preached at Newlands, was directed against the 'new doctrine of French philosophy, the monstrous doctrine of equality.' Few of his parishioners could have understood a word of it. Yet some sympathisers with the obnoxious doctrine attacked Findlater, and he was obliged to hide himself until the lord advocate, Sir James Montgomery, was able to appease the outcry. The sermon was dedicated to Montgomery when printed. 2. 'General View of the Agriculture of the County of Peebles,' Edinburgh, 1802. This is descriptive rather than didactic. He states that pigeons and bees are rather disadvantageous than otherwise to the Peebles farmers from their impoverishing the ground, and, curiously enough, never mentions in his survey either the game or the fish of the county. The industry and sobriety of the inhabitants are commended, 'with the exception of a few instances of perversion of principle, occasioned by the introduction of the French philosophy, and these chiefly confined to the county town.' 3. 'Sermons or Essays, as the Reader shall chuse to design them, upon Christian Duties,' 1830. In these are contained 'a plain statement of some of the most obvious principles of political economy.' 4. Accounts of West Linton and of Newlands in Sinclair's 'Statistical Account' and in the new 'Statistical Account.'

[Findlater's Works in Brit. Mus.; Dr. Hew Scott's Fasti Ecclesiæ Scoticanæ, pt. i. 247, 253; Presbytery and Synod Records at Newlands, Peeblesshire; private information from the Rev. J. Milne, minister of Newlands.]   M. G. W.

FINDLAY, ALEXANDER GEORGE (1812–1875), geographer and hydrographer, born in London, 6 Jan. 1812, was a descendant of the Findlays of Arbroath, Forfarshire. His grandfather was a shipowner of that port, who transferred his business to the river Thames about the middle of the eighteenth century. Findlay's father, Alexander Findlay, also a geographer, was born in London in 1790, and became one of the original fellows of the Royal Geographical Society on its foundation in 1830. Among his numerous undertakings successfully completed was an atlas sheet of the environs of London (1829) to a distance of thirty-two miles from St. Paul's (upon a half-inch scale), every line of which was his own handiwork. He died in London in the year 1870.

The son, Alexander George Findlay, under the father's encouragement, early devoted himself to the compilation of geographical and hydrographical works, and his atlases of 'Ancient and Comparative Geography' are known all over the world. In 1851 he completed the revision of Brookes's 'Gazetteer,' and the same year published his earliest important work, on the 'Coasts and Islands of the Pacific Ocean,' in 2 vols. of 1,400 pages. By the death of John Purdy, the hydrographer, in 1843, he succeeded to the foremost position in this branch of nautical research and authorship. His researches in the kindred science of meteorology further attracted the attention of Admiral Fitzroy, who in the earlier days of meteorological investigation invited him to join an official department then about to be established, but Findlay preferred an independent career. In the course of years of immense labour he prepared and issued six large nautical directories, which have proved invaluable to the maritime world. These directories are accompanied by illustrations, charts, &c., and include 'The North Atlantic Ocean,' 'The South Atlantic Ocean,' 'The Indian Ocean,' 'Indian Archipelago, China, and Japan,' 'The South Pacific Ocean,' and 'The North Pacific Ocean.' 'These works,' observes Sir Henry Rawlinson, 'constitute a monument of industry and perseverance, and are accepted as standard authorities in every quarter of the globe.' As a cartographer Findlay exhibited a wide practical knowledge of the sailor's requirements which even the hydrographic department of the admiralty was not able to surpass, and he executed a series of charts universally known and appreciated by the mercantile marine. The Society of Arts awarded Findlay its medal for his dissertation on 'The English Lighthouse System.' Subsequently he published 'Lighthouses and Coast Fog Signals of the World.' At the time of Sir John Franklin's catastrophe he carefully sifted all the probable and possible routes, and as a member of the Arctic committee of the Royal Geographical Society materially assisted in preparing the arguments which induced the government to send out the Alert and Discovery expedition of 1875. On the death of Laurie, the London geographical and print publisher, in 1858, Findlay took up his business, which soon sprang into renewed activity under his guidance, and in 1885, on the dispersal of the navigation business of Van Keulen of Amsterdam, founded in 1678, it became the oldest active firm in Europe for the publication of charts and nautical works. Findlay devoted much time to the labours of his friend, Dr. Livingstone, in central Africa, and he also carefully investigated the question of the sources of the Nile. For the record of the Burton and Speke explorations in the lake regions of central equatorial Africa during 1858-9 he constructed a map of the routes traversed. He also wrote a paper on the connection of Lake Tanganyika with the Nile, accompanying it by a comparative series of maps relating to the northern end of the lake. Findlay served on various committees appointed by the British Association for the Advancement of Science, and contributed the following papers to section E : at Liverpool in 1853, 'On the Currents of the Atlantic and Pacific Oceans;' Exeter, 1869, 'On the Gulf Stream, and its supposed influence upon the Climate of N.-W. Europe.'

In 1844 Findlay was elected a fellow of the Royal Geographical Society, and soon became an active member of its council and committees. To the 'Journal' of the society he contributed several papers, as well as to the 'Transactions of the Royal United Service Institution,' and to the 'Transactions of the Society of Arts.' Findlay's services were pronounced equally worthy of remembrance with those of Arrowsmith and Petermann. In 1870 the Società Geografica Italiana elected him one of its foreign honorary members. Findlay's various publications embrace a total of no less than ten thousand pages, all of which are in active use. He died at Dover on 3 May 1875.

[Royal Geographical Society's Journal, vol. xlv. 1875; Athenæum, May 1875; Bookseller, June 1875 ; private memoranda.] G. B. S.

FINDLAY, ROBERT, D.D.(1721-1814), Scotch divine, son of William Findlay of Waxford, Ayrshire, born 23 Nov. 1721, was educated at Glasgow, Leyden, and Edinburgh, and was ordained a minister of the kirk of Scotland in 1744. He had charges successively at Stevenston (1743), Galston (1745), Paisley (1754), and St. David's Church, Glasgow (1756), was appointed professor of divinity in the university of Glasgow in 1782, and died 15 June 1814. He published in the 'Library' for July 1761 'A Letter to the Rev. Dr. Kennicott vindicating the Jews from the Charge of Corrupting Deut. xxvii. 4,' which, on Kennicott's replying in the 'Library,' he followed up with 'A Second Letter to Dr. Kennicott upon the same subject, being an Answer to the Remarks in the "Library" for August 1761, and a further illustration of the argument.' This letter he sent to the 'Library;' but the editor of that magazine having had enough of the controversy, it appeared separately in January 1762. Both letters were signed 'Philalethes.' A more ambitious task next engaged Findlay's attention, viz. an examination of the views on the credibility of Josephus and the Jewish and Christian Scriptures propounded by Voltaire in his 'Philosophie de l'Histoire.' This work appeared under the title of 'A Vindication of the Sacred Books and of Josephus, especially the former, from various misrepresentations and cavils of the celebrated M. de Voltaire,' Glasgow, 1770, 8vo. Findlay also published a pamphlet on 'The Divine Inspiration of the Jewish Scriptures and Old Testament,' London, 1803, 8vo.

[Irving's Book of Eminent Scotsmen; Brit. Mus. Cat.; Cleland's Annals of Glasgow, ii. 114; Hew Scott's Fasti Eccl. Scot. ii. 26, 116, 187, 203.] J. M. R.

FINET or **FINETT**, SIR JOHN (1571-1641), master of the ceremonies, was son of Robert Finet of Soulton, near Dover, Kent, who died early in 1582. His mother was Alice, daughter and coheiress of John Wenlock, a captain of Calais. His great-grandfather, John Finet, an Italian of Siena, came to England as a servant in the train of Cardinal Campeggio in 1519, settled here and married a lady named Mantell, maid of honour to Catherine of Arragon. John was brought up at court and commended himself to James I by composing and singing witty songs in the royal presence after supper. Sir Anthony Weldon (*Court of King James*, 1812, i. 399) credits Finet's songs with much coarseness. On 17 Jan. 1617-18 he is said to have offended his master by the impropriety of some verses that he introduced into a play produced at court (*Cal. State Papers*, Dom. 17 Jan. 1618). Finet was in Paris early in 1610, and sent home an account of the treatment accorded to duellists in France, dated 19 Feb. 1609–10 (see *Cott. MS.* Titus, C. iv.) He seems to have been at the time in the service of Lord-treasurer Salisbury (*Cal. State Papers*, Dom. 29 April 1612). Wood states that he was in France on diplomatic business in 1614, but on 15 Dec. 1614 he was reported in a contemporary news-letter to have just returned from Spain, whither he had been despatched to present gifts of armour and animals to members of the royal family (*ib.* 15 Dec. 1614). Next year he was with the king at Cambridge. On 23 March 1615–16 he was knighted, and on 13 Sept. 1619 he was granted the reversion of the place of Sir Lewis Lewknor, master of the ceremonies, whom he had already begun to assist in the performance of his duties. On 19 Feb. 1624–5 he was granted a pension of 120*l.*, vacant by the death of Sir William Button, assistant-master of the ceremonies, and on 18 March 1624–5 he was formally admitted into Button's office on the understanding that on Finet's promotion to Lewknor's place the office should be abolished. On Lewknor's death Finet succeeded to the mastership of ceremonies (12 March 1625–6). Thenceforward Finet was busily employed in entertaining foreign envoys at the English court, and determining the numerous difficulties regarding precedence which arose among the resident ambassadors. He was intimate with all the courtiers. Lord Herbert of Cherbury (*Autobiography*, ed. S. L. Lee, p. 164) had made his acquaintance before 1616. In 1636 it was proposed at Oxford to confer on him the degree of D.C.L., but it is doubtful if the proposal was carried out. Finet died 12 July 1641, aged 70, and was buried on the north side of the church of St. Martin's-in-the-Fields. Sir Charles Cotterell [q. v.] was his successor at court.

In 1618 Finet married Jane, the 'lame' daughter of Henry, lord Wentworth, of Nettlestead, Suffolk, whose brother Thomas was created Earl of Cleveland 7 Feb. 1624–5. By her he had a son, John, and two daughters, Lucy and Finetta.

Finet was the author of the following: 1. 'The Beginning, Continvance, and Decay of Estates. Written in French by R. de Lusing, L. of Alymes, and translated into English by I. F.' (London, 1606); dedication, signed Iohn Finet, to Richard Bancroft, archbishop of Canterbury: an essay on the history of the Turks in Europe. 2. 'Finetti Philoxenis: some choice observations of Sᵣ John Finett, knight, and master of the cere-

monies to the two last kings, Touching the Reception and Precedence, the Treatment and Audience, the Puntillios and Contests of Forren Ambassadors in England,' London, 1656. The dedication to Philip, viscount Lisle, is signed by the editor, James Howell [q. v.] The incidents described by Finet chiefly concern the reign of James I. A manuscript copy of the book belongs to C. Cottrell Dormer, esq., of Rousham, near Oxford (*Hist. MSS. Comm.* 2nd Rep. 83). An interesting letter from Finet to Lord Clifford is among the Duke of Devonshire's MSS. at Bolton Abbey (*ib.* 3rd Rep. 39). Others are at Hatfield and the Record Office. Some recipes by Finet appear in a manuscript volume belonging to the late E. P. Shirley of Ettington Hall, Oxford (*ib.* 5th Rep. 365).

[Wood's Fasti, ed. Bliss, ii. 492–3; Cal. State Papers, Dom. 1611–41; Berry's County Genealogies, Kent, p. 449; authorities cited in the text.] S. L.

FINEUX, Sɪʀ JOHN (1441 ?–1527), judge. [See Fʏɴᴇᴜx.]

FINGALL, second Eᴀʀʟ ᴏꜰ. [See Pʟᴜɴᴋᴇᴛ, Cʜʀɪsᴛᴏᴘʜᴇʀ, *d.* 1649.]

FINGER, GODFREY ᴏʀ GOTTFRIED (*fl.* 1685–1717), composer, a native of Olmütz in Moravia, came to England probably about 1685. This date is fixed by the preface to his first composition, 'Sonatæ XII,' in which he says that it was the fame of James II which led him to bid farewell to his native land. The work was published in 1688, but from his calling the king 'tutissimum contra æmulos et invidos zoilos patrocinium' it may be inferred that he had at that time been long enough in England to make enemies, who no doubt resented the intrusion of a foreigner. The title of his opus primum is 'Sonatæ XII, pro diversis instrumentis . . . authore Godefrido Finger Olmutio-Moravo Capellæ Serenissimi Regis Magnæ Britaniæ Musico' (no publisher's name is given). A beautifully engraved frontispiece shows the composer protected by Minerva, offering before a bust of the king his musical production, on which is inscribed the motto, 'Puras non plenas aspice manus.' A false interpretation of this title seems to have given rise to the impression that Finger was appointed chapel-master to the king (Rᴏɢᴇʀ Nᴏʀᴛʜ, *Memoirs of Musick*, ed. Rimbault; Gʀᴏᴠᴇ, *Dictionary*), but it is plain that no such office was claimed in the title, and it is also almost a matter of certainty that Nicholas Staggins held the post during the whole period of Finger's residence in England. For some time Finger was no doubt a member of the king's band. His Op. 2 (published by Walsh) consisted of six sonatas for two flutes, and in 1690 he published (privately, according to Rimbault) 'VI Sonatas or Solos,' three for violin and three for flute, dedicated to the Earl of Manchester. On 5 Nov. 1691 a set of 'Ayres, Chacones, Divisions, and Sonatas for violins and flutes,' composed by Finger and John Banister, was advertised in the 'London Gazette' (No. 2712) as being on sale at Banister's house. Shortly afterwards, says the authority above quoted, he joined Godfrey Keller in a set of sonatas in five parts for flutes and hautboys (PLAYFORD, *General Catalogue*, 1701). Other instrumental works are stated by Hawkins to be in Estienne Roger's catalogue. On 5 Feb. 1693 Finger's setting of Theophilus Parsons's ode on St. Cecilia's day was performed 'at the consort in York-buildings' (advertised in the 'London Gazette,' No. 2945). He had already begun writing music for the theatre, having made a first attempt in this capacity in the previous year, on the production of Southerne's 'Wives' Excuse' at Drury Lane. The list of plays for which he wrote music is, as far as can be ascertained, as follows : Congreve's 'Love for Love,' 1695, and 'The Mourning Bride,' 1697 ; Ravenscroft's 'Anatomist,' in which was inserted the masque by Motteux, entitled 'The Loves of Mars and Venus,' 1697 (the music, written in conjunction with J. Eccles, was published by Heptinstall and dedicated to Sir Robert Howard) ; N. Lee's 'The Rival Queens' (with Daniel Purcell) ; Elkanah Settle's 'Virgin Prophetess,' Baker's 'Humours of the Age,' Mrs. Trotter's 'Love at a Loss,' Cibber's 'Love makes a Man,' and Farquhar's 'Sir Harry Wildair,' all in 1701. These were most probably written, though not performed, before the 'Prize Music,' as it was called, was publicly heard. On 18 March 1699 the 'London Gazette' contained an advertisement to the effect that 'several persons of quality' had offered a sum of two hundred guineas for the best musical settings of a certain work not named in the advertisement. This was Congreve's masque 'The Judgment of Paris,' and the four prizes were to be in this proportion : one hundred, fifty, thirty, and twenty guineas. As to how long a time was allowed for the work information is not forthcoming ; the successful compositions were, however, performed early in the new century. The prizes were awarded in this order : John Weldon, John Eccles, Daniel Purcell, and Godfrey Finger. The early authorities seem to agree in considering Finger to have been the best of the competitors, and the award is generally explained as the result

of animosity against a foreigner. At this point of musical history English music enjoyed for a brief space exceptional popularity. The foreign element which had made its appearance with the Elizabethan madrigalists had died out, and the advent of the Italian opera and Handel did not take place until a few years later. The judges of the compositions were not masters of the art, but members of the fashionable world. The Hon. Roger North says, in recounting the history of the affair in his 'Memoirs of Musick' (ed. Rimbault, p. 117) : 'I will not suppose, as some did, that making interest as for favour and partiality influenced these determinations, but it is certain that the comunity of the masters were not of the same opinion with them. Mr. G. Finger, a german, and a good musitian, one of the competitors who had resided in England many years, went away upon it, declaring that he thought he was to compose music for men and not for boys.' Some authorities allege as the reason of his departure the inadequate performance of his work, which Fétis states, but without giving his source of information, to have taken place on 11 March 1701. In 1702 he was appointed chamber-musician to Sophia Charlotte, queen of Prussia, and for some years he lived at Breslau. After the queen's death an opera, 'Der Sieg der Schönheit über die Helden,' was performed in Berlin in December 1706. It was composed by Finger and A. R. Stricker, and the ballets were by Volumier. He is said to have produced another opera, 'Roxane' (Telemann's account, quoted by MATTHESON), but the fact that Stricker wrote an opera, 'Alexanders und Roxanens Heirath,' produced at Berlin in 1708, makes it uncertain whether Telemann was not in error, especially as he does not express his meaning very lucidly. In 1717 he was appointed chapel-master at the court of Gotha. He is said to have held the title of 'Churpfalzischer Kammerrath' at the time of his death, but the date is not forthcoming.

[Sonatæ XII, &c., title quoted above ; Hon. Roger North's Memoirs of Musick, ed. Rimbault, 1846, p. 117 et seq. and notes ; Grove's Dict. i. 524, &c. ; Burney's Hist. iii. 579, iv. 632 ; Hawkins's Hist. (ed. 1853), 701, 764, 824 ; London Gazette, references given above ; Fétis's Dictionnaire, sub voce ; Mattheson's Grundlage einer Ehrenpforte, Hamburg, 1740, p. 362 ; Schneider's Geschichte der Oper, &c., 1852, pp. 23, 24 ; Addit. MS. in Brit. Mus. 31466, consisting of sixty-six sonatas for violin, thirteen of which are by Finger. Manuscript scores of the music in the 'Rival Queens' and the 'Virgin Prophetess' are in the Fitzwilliam Museum at Cambridge.]

J. A. F. M.

FINGLAS, PATRICK (*fl.* 1535), Irish judge, was appointed baron of the exchequer in Ireland by Henry VIII in or before 1520, and afterwards, by patent dated at Westminster 8 May 1534, he was constituted chief justice of the king's bench in that kingdom in the place of Sir Bartholomew Dillon. He resigned the latter office in or before 1535.

He wrote 'A Breviat of the getting of Ireland, and of the Decaie of the same.' Printed in Harris's 'Hibernica,' edit. 1770, i. 79–103. It appears that the original manuscript of this work is in the Public Record Office (*State Papers, Henry VIII,* Ireland, vol. xii. art. 7). It is described in the calendar as 'An Historical Dissertation on the Conquest of Ireland, the decay of that land, and measures proposed to remedy the grievances thereof arising from the oppressions of the Irish nobility.'

[Ware's Writers of Ireland (Harris), p. 93; Liber Hiberniæ, ii. 30, 49; Cal. of State Papers relating to Ireland, 1509–73 (Hamilton), pp. 3, 9, 14, 161.] T. C.

FINGLOW, JOHN (*d.* 1586), catholic divine, born at Barnby, near Howden, Yorkshire, was educated at the English College of Douay, during its temporary removal to Rheims, where he was ordained priest on 25 March 1581. Being sent on the mission he laboured zealously in the north of England until he was apprehended and committed to the Ousebridge Kidcote at York. He was tried and convicted of high treason, for being a priest made by Roman authority, and for having reconciled some of the queen's subjects to the catholic church. He was executed at York on 8 Aug. 1586.

[Douay Diaries, pp. 10, 28, 160, 176, 178, 261, 293; Challoner's Missionary Priests (1741), i. 183; Dodd's Church Hist. ii. 106; Morris's Troubles of our Catholic Forefathers, 3rd series; Stanton's Menology, p. 387.] T. C.

FININGHAM, ROBERT DE (*d.* 1460), a brother in the Franciscan or Greyfriars' monastery at Norwich, where he was also educated, was born at Finingham in Suffolk, and flourished in the reign of Henry VI. He was a very learned man, skilled, as Pits expresses it, in all liberal arts, excelling especially in canon law, and was the author of numerous Latin works. The chief purpose of his writings was in defence of the Franciscans against the common accusation that their profession of poverty was hypocritical. The titles given of his works are as follows: 1. 'Pro Ordine Minorum.' 2. 'Pro dignitate Status eorum.' 3. 'Casus Conciliorum Angliæ.' 4. 'De Casibus Decretorum.' 5. 'De Casibus Decretalium.' 6. 'De Extra-

vagantibus.' 7. 'De Excommunicationibus.' Tanner describes a manuscript of the last in Bishop Moore's library, now in the Cambridge University Library (E. e. v. 11).

[Pits, De Angliæ Scriptt. p. 652; Bale's Scriptt. Brit. cent. viii. § 23; Tanner's Bibl. Brit. p. 280; Blomefield's Hist. of Norfolk, iv. 113; Wadding's Scriptt. Min. Ord. (1650), p. 308.] E. T. B.

FINLAISON, JOHN (1783–1860), statistician and government actuary, son of Donald Finlayson (who spelt the name thus), was born at Thurso in Caithness-shire, 27 Aug. 1783, and at the age of seven was by the death of his father left an orphan. In 1802 he became factor to Sir Benjamin Dunbar (afterwards Lord Duffus), whose whole estates, together with those of Lord Caithness, were entrusted to his management when he was only nineteen years of age. He soon after went to Edinburgh to study for the bar, but having visited London in 1804 on business, he became attached to Elizabeth, daughter of the Rev. James Glen, and receiving the offer of an appointment under the board of naval revision, which enabled him to marry at once, he entered the government service in July 1805. He was shortly after promoted to be first clerk to the commission, and filled that office till the board closed its labours in August 1808. For some time previously he had also acted as secretary to a committee of the board, and in that capacity, although but twenty-three, he framed the eleventh and twelfth reports of the commission (*Eleventh and Twelfth Reports of the Commissioners for Revising the Civil Affairs of His Majesty's Navy,* 1809; *Parl. Papers,* 1809, vol. vi.), and was the sole author of the system for the reform of the victualling departments. The accounts had seldom been less than eighteen months in arrear, but by Finlaison's system they were produced, checked, and audited in three weeks, when the saving made in Deptford yard only in the first year, 1809, was 60,000*l.* In 1809 he was employed to devise some plan for arranging the records and despatches at the admiralty, and after nine months of incessant application produced a system of digesting and indexing the records by which any document could be immediately found. This plan met with such universal approval that it was adopted by France, Austria, and Russia, and its inventor received as a reward the order of the Fleur-de-lys from Louis XVIII in 1815 (BARON CHARLES DUPIN, *Voyages dans la Grande-Bretagne,* 1821, pt. ii. vol. i. pp. 65–67). In the same year he was appointed keeper of the records and librarian of the admiralty, and became reporter and précis writer on all difficult and complicated inquiries arising from day to day. During the twelve years while he held this post he was also engaged in many other confidential duties. He was desired by Lord Mulgrave to prepare the materials for a defence of the naval administration before parliament in 1810, and with three months' labour collected a mass of information which enabled Mulgrave to make a successful defence. In 1811 Finlaison compiled an exact account of all the enemy's naval forces. Such information had never before been obtained with even tolerable accuracy. Experience proved it to be correct, and it was quoted in parliament as an authority. In the same year he was employed to investigate the abuses of the sixpenny revenue at Greenwich Hospital, a fund for the support of the out-pensioners, and in his report showed that by other arrangements, as well as by the reform of abuses and the abolition of sinecure places, the pensions might be much increased. The subject of the increase of the salaries of the government clerks having twice been forced on the notice of parliament, John Wilson Croker in 1813 directed Finlaison to fully inquire into the case of the admiralty department, when, after six months of close attention, he completed a report, upon which was founded a new system of salaries in the admiralty. In 1814 he compiled the first official 'Navy List,' a work of great labour, accuracy, and usefulness. It was issued monthly, and he continued the duty of correcting and editing it until the end of 1821. From 1817 to 1818 he was occupied in framing a biographical register of every commissioned officer in the navy, in number about six thousand, describing their services, merits, and demerits; this work he engrafted on to his system of the digest and index, where it formed a valuable work of reference for the use of the lords of the admiralty. He introduced into the naval record office a hitherto unknown degree of civility towards the public and of readiness to impart information. Having as librarian found many valuable state papers relating to the American war, he was in 1813 induced to attempt the completion of Redhead Yorke's 'Naval History,' which was intended to form a part of Campbell's 'Lives of the Admirals.' He carried out his design in part by continuing the history down to 1780. This portion of the work was printed for private circulation, but its further progress was abandoned. In 1815 Dr. Barry O'Meara, physician to Napoleon at St. Helena, commenced a correspondence with Finlaison, his private friend, on the subject of the emperor's daily life. In 1824, by the desire of the writer,

the letters were burnt. Some copies of them, however, had fallen into other hands and were published in 1853 in a book entitled 'Napoleon at St. Helena and Sir Hudson Lowe.' Finlaison now completed a work on which he had been employed since 1812, the fund for the maintenance of the widows and orphans of all who were employed in the civil departments of the royal navy. Through Lord Melville's intervention his efforts terminated successfully in the establishment of the fund by order in council 17 Sept. 1819. The naval medical supplemental fund for the widows of medical officers also owed to him its existence and subsequent prosperity. Until 1829 he remained the secretary, when the directors treated him so ungenerously that he resigned, and by mismanagement this fund was ruined in 1860. The success of these charities, together with his subsequent investigation into the condition of friendly societies, upon which he was employed by a select committee of the House of Commons in 1824, introduced him to a private practice among benefit societies; he constructed tables for many of these, furnished the scheme of some, and entirely constituted others. Among other societies with which he became connected were: the London Life, the Amicable Society, the Royal Naval and Military Life Assurance Company, and the New York Life Assurance and Trust Company. The government in 1808 instituted a new system of finance based upon the granting of life annuities, the tables used being the Northampton tables of mortality. On 1 Sept. 1819 Finlaison made a first report to Nicholas Vansittart [q. v.], in which he demonstrated the great loss that was sustained by the government in granting life annuities at prices much below their value, the loss in eleven years having been two millions sterling (WALFORD, *Insurance Cyclopædia*, v. 496–514). His report was not printed till 1824, when he was directed to make further investigations into the true laws of mortality prevailing in England. The result of his studies was the discovery that the average duration of human life had increased during the century. His tables were also the first which showed the difference between male and female lives ('Life Annuities. Report of J. Finlaison, Actuary of the National Debt, on the Evidence and Elementary Facts on which the Tables of Life Annuities are founded,' 1829).

Before the close of 1819 he furnished the chancellor of the exchequer with a statement of the age of each individual in the receipt of naval half-pay or pensions, fourteen thousand persons, thence deducing the decrement of life among them. In 1821 Mr. Harrison employed him for several months in computations relative to the Superannuation Act, and in 1822 he was occupied in considerations relative to the commutation of the naval and military half-pay and pensions. The measure consequently suggested by him was finally established by negotiations with the Bank of England in 1823 for its acceptance of the charge for public pensions in consideration of the 'dead weight' annuity. All the calculations were made by him, and it was plainly stated in the House of Commons that in the whole establishment of the Bank of England there was not one person capable of computing the new annuity at the fractional rate of interest agreed upon. On 1 Jan. 1822 he was removed from the admiralty to the treasury, and appointed actuary and principal accountant of the check department of the national debt office, the duties of which position he performed for twenty-nine years. For many years after he had sought to impress on the government the loss which the country was sustaining by the use of erroneous tables, he was treated with neglect and contempt, and it was only by the accidental production of one of his letters before Lord Althorpe's committee of finance in March 1828 that the matter was brought forward. This letter proved that the revenue was losing 8,000*l.* a week, and that this loss was concealed by the method of preparing the yearly accounts. The immediate suspension of the life annuity system took place, and, remodelled upon the basis of Finlaison's tables, it was resumed in November 1829 with a saving in five years of 390,000*l.* In 1831 he made computations on the duration of slave and creole life, preliminary to the compensation made to the slaveowners 1 Aug. 1834. He was consulted by the ecclesiastical commissioners on the means of improving church property, on the question of church leases, and finally on the subject of church rates; he made various reports on these matters, and on one occasion was summoned to attend the cabinet to explain his views to the ministers. On the passing of the General Registration Act in 1837, his opinion was taken on the details of the working of the scheme, and he was the first witness called before the parliamentary committee on church leases in the following year. The Institution of Actuaries being formed in 1847, he was elected the first president, and retained that position until his death. In 1848 he wrote two reports on the act for lending money to Irish landlords. He retired from the public service in August 1851, and employed his remaining days in his favourite study of scripture chronology,

and the universal relationship of ancient and modern weights and measures. He died at 15 Lansdowne Crescent, Notting Hill, London, 13 April 1860. He married in London, first, in 1805, Elizabeth, daughter of the Rev. James Glen, she died at Brighton in 1831; secondly, in 1836, Eliza, daughter of Thomas Davis of Waltham Abbey. His son Alexander Glen Finlaison, who was born at Whitehall on 25 March 1806, was also an author and an authority on insurance statistics.

Finlaison was the author of: 1. 'Report of the Secretary to the Supplemental Fund for the Relief of the Widows and Orphans of the Medical Officers of the Royal Navy,' 1817. 2. 'Tables showing the Amount of Contributions for Providing Relief in Sickness,' 1833. 3. 'Rules of the Equitable Friendly Institution, Northampton, with Tables,' 1837. 4. 'Account of some Applications of the Electric Fluid to the Useful Arts by A. Bain, with a Vindication of his Claim to be the First Inventor of the Electro-Magnetic Printing Telegraph, and also of the Electro-Magnetic Clock,' 1843. 5. 'Tables for the use of Friendly Societies, for the Certificate of the Actuary to the Commissioners for the Reduction of the National Debt. Constructed from the original computations of J. Finlaison, by A. G. Finlaison,' 1847. He also produced some lyrical poems of considerable merit.

[Times, 17 April 1860, p. 9, and 23 April, p. 9; Gent. Mag. August 1860, pp. 194–5; Assurance Mag. April 1862, pp. 147–69; Walford's Insurance Cyclopædia (1874), iii. 300–3; Macaulay's England (1858), i. 284; Southwood Smith's Philosophy of Health (1835), i. 115–47.]

G. C. B.

FINLAY, FRANCIS DALZELL (1793–1857), Irish journalist, son of John Finlay, tenant farmer, of Newtownards, co. Down, by his wife, Jane Dalzell, was born 12 July 1793 at Newtownards, and began life as a printer's apprentice in Belfast, where he started as a master printer in 1820. The letterpress which issued from his works was distinguished by both accuracy and elegance, being far superior to any that had previously been produced in Ireland. In 1824 he founded the 'Northern Whig.' Liberalism being then a very unpopular creed in Ulster, Finlay was frequently prosecuted for press offences. On 21 July 1826 he was indicted for publishing in the 'Northern Whig' a libel tending to bring into disrepute the character of a certain 'improving' landlord. The libel consisted in a letter purporting to be by a small farmer in which the improvements alleged to have been effected by the landlord in question were denied to be improvements at all, and in which a character for litigiousness was imputed to the landlord. Finlay was sentenced to three months' imprisonment, without the option of a fine, and the publication of the 'Northern Whig' was suspended from August 1826 until May 1827. From the first Finlay advocated the emancipation of the Roman catholics, and it was in the columns of the 'Northern Whig' that William Sharman Crawford [q. v.] propounded his celebrated views on tenant-right. Some comments in the 'Northern Whig' on the conduct of Lord Hertford's agent led to another prosecution for libel in 1830, which, however, was abandoned when it transpired that Daniel O'Connell had volunteered for the defence. On a similar charge he was found guilty on 23 July 1832 and sentenced to three months' imprisonment and fined 50l. In spite, however, of these proceedings, the 'Northern Whig' continued from time to time to give expression to similar views which were adjudged libellous and occasioned its proprietor very heavy legal expenditure. To the extension of the suffrage, the disestablishment of the Irish church, and the reform of the land laws Finlay through his paper gave a steady and zealous support; but, though a personal friend of O'Connell, he opposed the movement for the repeal of the union and the later developments of Irish disaffection, such as the Young Irelandism of Mitchel and the agitation which resulted in the abortive insurrection of Smith O'Brien. He died on 10 Sept. 1857, bequeathing his paper to his son, Francis Dalzell Finlay, by whom it was conducted until 1874, when it was transferred to a limited company. Finlay married in 1830 Marianne, daughter of the Rev. William Porter, presbyterian minister, of Newtonlimavady, co. Derry.

[Northern Whig, 12 Sept. 1857 ; information from F. D. Finlay, esq.]   J. M. R.

FINLAY, GEORGE (1799–1875), historian, was son of Captain John Finlay, R.E., F.R.S., and brother of Kirkman Finlay (d. 1828) [q. v.] His grandfather, James Finlay, was a Glasgow merchant. He was born 21 Dec. 1799, at Faversham, Kent, where his father was inspector of the government powder mills. The latter died in 1802, and George was for some time instructed by his mother, to whose training he attributed his love of history. His education was continued at an English boarding-school, and in the family of his uncle, Kirkman Finlay of Glasgow [q. v.], under private tutors. He subsequently studied law in Glasgow, and proceeded about 1821 to the university of Göttingen to acquaint himself with Roman jurisprudence. While there he began to doubt his vocation for law, and, partly influenced

by his acquaintance with a Greek fellow-student, 'resolved to visit Greece and judge for myself concerning the condition of the people and the chances of the war.' In November 1823 he met Byron at Cephalonia. 'You are young and enthusiastic,' said Byron, 'and therefore sure to be disappointed when you know the Greeks as well as I do.' The number of Hellenes and Philhellenes about Byron gave umbrage to the Ionian government, which was bound to remain neutral. Finlay quitted the island on a hint from Sir Charles Napier, and, after narrowly escaping shipwreck, made his way successively to Athens and Missolonghi, where for two months he spent nearly every evening with Byron, who, Parry says, 'wasted much of his time' in conversation with the future historian and other such frivolous persons. Quitting Missolonghi before Byron's death, Finlay joined Odysseus on an expedition into the Morea, but, disgusted with the general venality and rapacity, returned to the headquarters of the government, where things were no better. A malarious fever compelled him to return to Scotland, where he passed his examination in civil law, but was soon again in Greece at the invitation of his intimate friend Frank Abney Hastings [q. v.], who had built a steamer in which Finlay took his passage. He continued fighting for Greece, or engaged in missions on her behalf, until the termination of the war, when he purchased an estate in Attica, 'hoping to aid in putting Greece into the road that leads to a rapid increase of production, population, and material improvement.' 'I lost my money and my labour, but I learned how the system of tenths has produced a state of society, and habits of cultivation, against which one man can do nothing. When I had wasted as much money as I possessed, I turned my attention to study.' His unfortunate investment had at least the good results of compelling his continual residence in the country, with which he became most thoroughly acquainted, and of stimulating his perception of the evils which, in the past as in the present, have deteriorated the Greek character and injured the credit and prosperity of the nation. The publication of his great series of histories commenced in 1844, and was completed in 1861, when he wrote the autobiographical fragment which is almost the sole authority for his life. His correspondence is lost or inaccessible, and, notwithstanding his courteous hospitality, acknowledged by many travellers, little more seems to be known of his life in Greece than his constant endeavours to benefit the country by good advice, sometimes expressed in language of excessive

if excusable acerbity, but which, if little followed, was never resented by the objects of
it. His most important effort was the series
of letters he addressed to the 'Times' from
1864 to 1870, which, being translated by the
Greek newspapers, produced more effect than
his earlier admonitions. He also contributed
to 'Blackwood's Magazine,' the 'Athenæum,'
and the 'Saturday Review,' and occasionally
visited England, not later, however, than
1854. He wrote in Greek on the stone age
in 1869, and in the following year published
the French narrative of Benjamin Brue, the
interpreter who accompanied the Vizier Ali
on his expedition into the Morea in 1715.
Among his other writings are an essay on the
site of the holy sepulchre (1847), and pamphlets on Greek politics (1836) and finance
(1844). His essays on classical topography,
never collected by himself, were published
in 1842 in a German translation by S. F. W.
Hoffmann. He died at Athens 26 Jan. 1875;
the date 1876 given in the Oxford edition of
his history is an unaccountable mistake.

Finlay's great work appeared in sections,
as follows: 'Greece under the Romans,' 1844;
'Greece to its Conquest by the Turks,' 1851;
'Greece under Ottoman and Venetian Domination,' 1856; 'Greek Revolution,' 1861. After
the author's death the copyright of these several works was offered to the delegates of the
Clarendon Press by his representatives, and
in 1877 all were brought together under the
title of 'A History of Greece from its Conquest by the Romans to the present time,
B.C. 146 to A.D. 1864,' and published in seven
volumes under the able editorship of the
Rev. H. F. Tozer. The whole had been
thoroughly revised by Finlay himself, who,
besides aiming throughout at a greater con-
densation of style, had added several new
chapters, chiefly on economical subjects, entirely recast the section on Mediæval Greece
and Trebizond, and appended a continuation
from 1843 to the enactment of the constitution of 1864. The period covered by the
history, therefore, is no less than two thousand and ten years.

Finlay is a great historian of the type of
Polybius, Procopius, and Machiavelli, a man
of affairs, who has qualified himself for treating of public transactions by sharing in them,
a soldier, a statesman, and an economist.
He is not picturesque or eloquent, or a master of the delineation of character, but a singular charm attaches to his pages from the
perpetual consciousness of contact with a
vigorous intelligence. In the latter portion
of his work he speaks with the authority of
an acute, though not entirely dispassionate,
eye-witness; in the earlier and more exten-

sive portion it is his great glory to have shown
how interesting the history of an age of slavery
may be made, and how much Gibbon had
left undone. Gibbon, as his plan requires,
exhibits the superficial aspects of the period
in a grand panorama; Finlay plunges beneath
the surface, and brings to light a wealth of
social particulars of which the mere reader
of Gibbon could have no notion. This being
Finlay's special department, it is the more to
his praise that he has not smothered his story
beneath his erudition. He may, indeed, even
appear at a disadvantage beside the Germans
as regards extent and profundity of research,
but this inferiority is more than compensated
by the advantages incidental to his prolonged
residence in the country. His personal disappointments had indeed caused a censorious-
ness which somewhat defaces the latter part
of his history, and is the more to be regretted
as it affected his estimate of the value of his
own work, and of its reception by the world.
In character he was a frank, high-minded,
public-spirited gentleman.

[Autobiography prefixed to vol. i. of the Oxford edition of Finlay's History; Memoir in
Athenæum, 1875; Sir Charles Newton in Academy, and Professor Freeman in Saturday Review,
1875.] R. G.

FINLAY, JOHN (1782–1810), Scottish
poet, was born of humble parents at Glasgow
in December 1782. He was educated in one
of the academies at Glasgow, and at the age
of fourteen entered the university, where he
had as a classmate John Wilson ('Christopher North'), who states that he was distinguished 'above most of his contemporaries.'
While only nineteen, and still at the university, he published 'Wallace, or the Vale
of Ellerslie, and other Poems' in 1802, dedicated to Mrs. Dunlop of Dunlop, the friend
of Burns, a second edition with some additions appearing in 1804, and a third in 1817.
Professor Wilson describes it as displaying 'a
wonderful power of versification,' and possessing 'both the merits and defects which we look
for in the early compositions of true genius.'
The prospect of obtaining a situation in one
of the public offices led him to visit London
in 1807, and while there he contributed to
the magazines some articles on antiquarian
subjects. Not finding suitable employment
he returned to Glasgow in 1808, and in that
year he published 'Scottish Historical and
Romantic Ballads, chiefly ancient, with Explanatory Notes and a Glossary.' As the
title indicates, the majority of the ballads
were not his own composition, but Sir Walter
Scott nevertheless wrote of the book: 'The
beauty of some imitations of the old Scottish

ballads, with the good sense, learning, and modesty of the preliminary dissertations, must make all admirers of ancient lore regret the early loss of this accomplished young man.' He also published an edition of Blair's 'Grave,' wrote a life of Cervantes, and superintended an edition of Adam Smith's 'Wealth of Nations.' In 1810 he left Glasgow to visit Professor Wilson at Ellerlay, Westmoreland, but on the way thither was seized with illness at Moffat, and died there on 8 Dec. He had begun to collect materials for a continuation of Warton's ' History of Poetry.'

[Memoir with specimens of his poetry in Blackwood's Mag. ii. 186–92 ; J. Grant Wilson's Poets and Poetry of Scotland, ii. 46–8; C. Rogers's Scottish Minstrel, iii. 57–62.] T. F. H.

FINLAY, KIRKMAN (*d.* 1828), philhellene, was son of Captain-lieutenant John Finlay, R.E., F.R.S., who died at Glasgow in 1802 (*Scots Mag.* lxiv. 616), and brother of George Finlay [q. v.] His education was cared for by his uncle, Kirkman Finlay [q. v.], lord provost of Glasgow. When about twenty years of age, being in possession of a handsome fortune, he proceeded to Greece for the purpose of engaging in the war of independence. In February 1824 he became acquainted with Lord Byron and Prince Mavrocordatos, both then at Missolonghi, who entrusted him with conciliatory messages for Odysseus and other refractory chiefs. At Byron's request, Finlay with two comrades set out in March in charge of powder and other military stores, forwarded from Missolonghi to Odysseus for his war in Negropont. On crossing the stream of the Phidari, which had been much swollen by the rains, he missed the ford, lost the most valuable part of his baggage and papers, and very nearly his life. Finlay continued one of the few philhellenes, undaunted by disappointment and disgust, constant and persistent to the cause he had adopted. On that cause he spent his fortune, energies, and life. During a sortie of the Turks from the fortress of Scio on 29 Jan. 1828 he was shot through the head at the first attack, as he was attempting to rally a body of men under his command. He fell dead on the spot.

[Moore's Life of Lord Byron ; Count Gamba's Narrative of Lord Byron's Last Journey to Greece, pp. 223–4 ; Gent. Mag. vol. xcviii. pt. i. p. 372.] G. G.

FINLAY, KIRKMAN (1773–1842), lord provost of Glasgow, the son of James Finlay, merchant, was born in Glasgow in 1773. He was educated at the grammar school and at the university, and at an early age entered on business on his own account. In 1793 he took a prominent part in opposing the monopoly of the East India Company in the cotton trade. He became a magistrate of Glasgow in 1804, and in 1812 lord provost of the city. He was M.P. for Glasgow from 1812 to 1818, and for Malmesbury 1818–20. He was a political economist of an advanced type. In 1819 he was appointed rector of the university of Glasgow, and contested the city unsuccessfully in 1830. He was a founder of the commerce of Glasgow, on the wider basis which it took after the failure of the tobacco trade with America. He married Janet, daughter of John Struthers. He died 4 March 1842, at Castle Toward, a residence which he built on the Firth of Clyde. George, the Greek historian, and Kirkman Finlay, both separately noticed, were his nephews.

[MacGeorge's History of Glasgow ; Glasgow Past and Present.] W. B-E.

FINLAYSON, GEORGE (1790–1823), naturalist and traveller, born of humble parents at Thurso in 1790, was clerk to Dr. Somerville, chief of the army medical staff in Scotland, and afterwards to Dr. Farrel, chief of the army medical staff in Ceylon, whence he was removed to Bengal, and attached to the 8th light dragoons as assistant-surgeon in 1819. In 1821–2 he accompanied the mission to Siam and Cochin China in the character of naturalist, returning with it to Calcutta in 1823. By this time his health was thoroughly broken, and he soon afterwards died. The journal which he had kept during the mission was edited, with a prefatory notice of the author, by Sir Stamford Raffles, F.R.S., under the title of ' The Mission to Siam and Hue, the capital of Cochin China, in the years 1821–2, from the Journal of the late George Finlayson, Esq.,' London, 1826, 8vo.

[Raffles's memoir, noticed above; Quarterly Review, 1826.] J. M. R.

FINLAYSON, JAMES, D.D. (1758–1808), divine, was born on 15 Feb. 1758, at Nether Cambushenie, in the parish of Dunblane, Perthshire, where his ancestors had been settled for several centuries. He made rapid progress at school, and began his studies in the university of Glasgow at the age of fourteen. He held two tutorships, and subsequently became amanuensis to Professor Anderson, who had discovered his abilities. In 1782 he became domestic tutor to two sons of Sir William Murray of Ochtertyre. As the family spent the winter in Edinburgh, Finlayson continued his studies at the university. He was licensed to preach in 1785.

In this year the Duke of Atholl offered Finlayson the living of Dunkeld, which he was induced to decline, as Sir William Murray informed him that an arrangement was proposed to procure for him the chair of logic in the university of Edinburgh. He was offered the living of Borthwick, near Edinburgh, of which parish he was ordained minister on 6 April 1787. He had assumed the duties of the logic professor in the winter session of 1786–7. He was now rising into reputation with a rapidity the more remarkable from his modest disposition. The most experienced sages of the church respected his judgment in questions of ecclesiastical policy. He therefore dedicated much of his leisure to study the laws, constitution, and history of the Scottish church, and began to take an active part in the details of its political government. This made him gradually lean more to the ecclesiastical than to the literary side of his functions. He soon became a leader on the moderate side in the church courts. In 1790 he was presented by the magistrates of Edinburgh to Lady Yester's church; in 1793 he was appointed to succeed Robertson, the historian, in the collegiate church of the old Grey Friars; in 1799, on a vacancy occurring in the high church, he was chosen by the town council to fill that collegiate charge. This last is considered the most honourable appointment in the church of Scotland, and it was, at the time, rendered more desirable from the circumstance that he had for his colleague Hugh Blair [q. v.], whose funeral sermon he was called upon to preach in little more than a year. The university of Edinburgh conferred on Finlayson the degree of D.D. (28 March 1799), and in 1802 he was elected moderator of the general assembly. He was elected king's almoner in the same year, but resigned the post almost immediately. These honours indicate the general estimate of Finlayson's merits. Finlayson established his ascendency on the wisdom of his councils and his knowledge of the laws and constitution of the church, and among his own party his sway was unlimited. Those who differed from him in church politics freely acknowledged his honourable character and the purity of his motives: his political opponents, in points of business unconnected with party, were occasionally guided by his judgment. His manner was simple and unpresuming; he was below the average height. He wrote the life of Dr. Hugh Blair, and a volume of his sermons was published after his death. In 1805 his constitution began to decline. In 1807 he was constrained to accept the assistance of one of his earliest friends, Principal G. H. Baird [q. v.], who

taught the class during the remainder of that session. On 25 Jan. 1808, while conversing with Baird, he was seized with a paralytic affection. Among the few words he was able to articulate was the following sentence: 'I am about to pass to a better habitation, where all who believe in Jesus shall enter.' On his deathbed the senatus academicus of the university and the magistrates of Edinburgh waited on him and asked him to name the successor to his chair. In deference to his advice, an offer of the chair was made to Principal Baird, the gentleman he had named. He died on 28 Jan. 1808, and was honoured with a public funeral in the cathedral church of Dunblane. His students and others erected a monument to his memory at Dunblane, and a memorial window of stained glass was placed in Grey Friars by his old pupil Principal Lee of Edinburgh University. He published: 1. 'Heads of an Argument in support of the Overture respecting Chapels of Ease,' 1798. 2. 'A Sermon on Preaching,' Edinburgh, 1801. 3. 'Sermons,' Edinburgh, 1809.

[Life by Baird; Encyclopædia Perthensis; Chambers's Biog. Dict. of Eminent Scotsmen; Anderson's Scottish Nation; Hew Scott's Fasti Eccl. Scot.; Proceedings of the General Assembly of the Church of Scotland; private information.] A. R. M. F.

FINLAYSON or **FINLEYSON**, JOHN (1770–1854), disciple of Richard Brothers [q. v.], was born in Scotland in 1770. His descendants make him the second son of Colonel John Hamilton M'Finlay, who married, about 1765, Lady Elizabeth Mary Alexander, eldest sister of the last Earl of Stirling. He was originally a writer at Cupar-Fife, and removed thence to Edinburgh. His relations with Brothers, which began in 1797, are detailed in the article on that enthusiast. He printed at Edinburgh a couple of pamphlets before repairing to London. In London he was 'in considerable practice as a house-agent.' Brothers led him to change the spelling of his name, by telling him his ancestors had some 'fine leys' of land granted them for deeds of valour. Brothers, who died (1824) in Finlayson's house at Marylebone, made it his dying charge to his friend that he should write against a rival genius, Bartholomew Prescot of Liverpool. This Finlayson did, describing Prescot's 'System of the Universe,' very correctly, as a 'misapprehended mistaken elaborate performance, or book.'

He printed a variety of pamphlets, reiterating Brothers's views, and developing his own peculiar notions of astronomy, for which he claimed a divine origin. The heavenly bodies were created, he thinks, partly 'to amuse us in observing them.' The earth he decides to be a perfect sphere, 'not shaped like a garden turnip, as the Newtonians make it;' the sun is a created body 'very different from anything we can make here below;' the stars are 'oval-shaped immense masses of frozen water, with their largest ends foremost.'

Finlayson was reduced in extreme and widowed age to a parish allowance of 3s. 6d. weekly, supplemented by 5s. from Busby, in whose house Brothers had lived from 1806 to 1815. Prescot and John Mason (a brushmaker), though a disciple of Brothers, refused to assist him. He died on 19 Sept. 1854, and was buried in the same grave as Brothers at St. John's Wood. He married, in 1808, Elizabeth Anne (d. 1848), daughter of Colonel Basil Bruce (d. 1800), and had ten children. His eldest son, Richard Brothers Finlayson, who took the name of Richard Beauford, was a photographer at Galway, where he died on 17 Dec. 1886, aged 75.

Finlayson printed: 1. 'An Admonition to the People of all Countries in support of Richard Brothers,' 8vo (dated Edinburgh, 7 Sept. 1797). 2. The same, 'Book Second,' containing 'The Restoration of the Hebrews to their own Land,' 8vo (dated Edinburgh, 27 Jan. 1798). 3. 'An Essay,'&c. 8vo (on Dan. xii. 7, 11, 12; dated London, 2 March 1798). 4. 'An Essay on the First Resurrection, and on the Commencement of the Blessed Thousand Years,' 8vo (dated London, 14 April 1798). 5. 'The Universe as it is. Discovery of the Ten Tribes of Israel and their Restoration to their own Land,' 1832, 8vo. 6. 'God's Creation of the Universe,' 1848, 8vo (contains some of his letters to the authorities respecting his claims on Brothers's estate; Mason and Prescot were angry at this publication, but Finlayson had 'a dream and vision' of Brothers, approving all he had done). 7. 'The Seven Seals of the Revelations.' 8. 'The Last Trumpet,' &c., 1849, 8vo (incorporates No. 7; there are several supplements, the latest dated 21 Feb. 1850). Also nine large sheets of the ground plan of the New Jerusalem (with its 56 squares, 320 streets, 4 temples, 20 colleges, 47 private palaces, 16 markets, &c.); and twelve sheets of views of its public buildings; all these executed by Finlayson for Brothers (the original copperplates were in the hands of Beauford, whose price for a set of the prints was 38l.) Finlayson's pamphlets are scarce; he deposited his stock with Mason, after whose death it was destroyed.

[Finlayson's Works; information from his eldest son, and from H. Hodson Rugg, M.D.; tombstone at St. John's Wood.]   A. G.

FINLAYSON, THOMAS (1809–1872), united presbyterian minister, second son of Thomas Finlayson, a farmer, was born at Coldoch, Blair Drummond, Perthshire, 22 Dec. 1809. He received his elementary education at the parish school of Kincardine in Menteith, and preparatory to entering college engaged in a special study of the classics at a school in the village of Doune in Kilmadock parish. At the university of Glasgow and at the theological hall of the united secession church he went through the usual course of training, and was licensed as a preacher of the gospel in April 1835 by the presbytery of Stirling and Falkirk. Part of his period of study was spent in teaching a school at Dumbarton, where he formed a friendship with the Rev. Dr. Andrew Somerville, who afterwards became the secretary of the foreign mission of the united presbyterian church. In November 1835 Finlayson was ordained minister of the Union Street congregation, Greenock, where he founded a missionary society, and in two years persuaded his people to pay off the large debt existing on the church. After twelve years of admirable ministerial work in Greenock he was called to be colleague and successor to the Rev. John M'Gilchrist of Rose Street Church, Edinburgh, and, having accepted the call, was inducted to the ministry there in September 1847. The congregation to which he now became minister was one of very few churches which at that time set an example and gave a tone to the whole church. They at once attached themselves to their new minister. He was elected moderator of the supreme court of his church in 1867, and shortly afterwards received the degree of D.D. from the university of Edinburgh. As one of the most ardent promoters of the manse fund, he was the chief agent in raising 45,000l., which led to the spending of 120,000l. in building and improving manses in two hundred localities. In the management of the augmentation fund he also took a deep interest. As a preacher he excelled in distinct and powerful exhibition of the truth; whatever he had to say came fresh from his own independent thought, went straight to the heart of the subject, and made an immediate impression on his hearers. The untimely death in 1868 of his eldest son Thomas, a promising advocate at the Scottish bar, caused him intense grief, from which he never fully recovered. On 7 Oct. 1872 his congregation celebrated the semi-jubilee of his ministry in Edinburgh. Having gone to Campbeltown to take part in an induction service there, he was suddenly attacked with failure of the heart's action, and was found dead in his bed on 17 Oct. 1872. He was buried in the Grange cemetery, Edinburgh, on 22 Oct. He married, in 1836, Miss Chrystal, by whom he had six children.

[Memorials of the Rev. Thomas Finlayson, D.D., 1873, with portrait; John Smith's Our Scottish Clergy, 1849, 2nd ser. pp. 295–301.]

G. C. B.

FINN BARR, SAINT and BISHOP (*d.* 623), of Cork, was son of Amergin, of the tribe of Ui Briuin Ratha of Connaught, who were descended from Eochaidh Muidmheadhon, brother of Olioll Olum, king of Munster. Amergin left Connaught for Munster and settled in the territory of Muscraidhe (Muskerry), in the county of Cork, where he obtained an inheritance and land at a place called Achaidh Durbchon; he was also chief smith to Tigernach, king of the Ui Eachach of Munster, who lived at Rathlin in the neighbourhood of Bandon. Amergin married in defiance of the king's prohibition, and the couple were ordered to be burnt alive. A thunderstorm which prevented the sentence from being carried out was regarded as a divine interposition, and they were set free. A child having been born from this union, they returned to Achaidh Durbchon, where he was baptised by a bishop named MacCorb, who gave him the name of Luan (or Lochan according to another account). When he was seven years old three clerics of Munster—Brendan, Lochan, and Fiodhach—who had been on a pilgrimage to Leinster, came to revisit their native territories, and stopping at the house of Amergin admired the child. Eventually they were allowed to take him away to be educated. On their return with him they arrived at a place called Sliabh Muinchill, where it was thought suitable that he should read his alphabet (or elements), be tonsured, and have his name changed. The cleric who cut his hair is said to have observed : 'Fair [finn] is this hair [barra] of Luan.' Let this be his name, said another, 'Barr-finn or Finn-barr.' His name, however, in popular usage, as well as in many authorities, has always been Barra or Bairre. On this occasion Brendan was observed to weep and then soon after to smile, and when asked the reason replied, 'I have prayed to Almighty God to grant me three territories in South Munster for my use and that of my successors, viz. from the Blackwater to the Lee, from the Lee to the Bandon, and from the Bandon to Bere Island, but they have been granted to Barra for ever. I wept because I fear I am blameworthy in God's sight, and I smiled again for joy because of the love which God manifested for Barra.' The three clerics, with

Barra, proceeding on their journey, arrived at Belach Gabhran, now Gowran, in the county of Kilkenny. Here he read his psalms and began his studies, and his diligence was shown by his prayer that a heavy fall of snow might continue to block his hut until he could read his 'saltair.' It is said to have continued accordingly. He next went to Cuil Caisin (now Coolcashin), in the barony of Galmoy, county of Kilkenny, where he marked out and founded that church, and thence to Aghaboe, where he blessed a church and stayed for a while. He departed at the request of his predecessor, St. Canice, after some negotiation, and went to MacCorb, by whom he had been baptised. The latter had been a fellow-pupil of St. David, and both were reputed to have been pupils of Pope Gregory, which probably means that they studied his writings, which were held in high esteem by the Irish. About this time Fachtna, an aged chieftain of Muscraidhe Breogain, now the barony of Clanwilliam, in county of Tipperary, whose son and daughter Finn Barr had cured, and whose wife he was said to have brought to life, made a grant to him of Rath Mhartir in perpetuity. Here there is an important difference between the Irish and Latin lives, the latter giving Fiachna as the name of the chieftain, whom Ussher, appearing to have known only the Latin life, identifies with the king of West Munster. But the Irish life evidently gives the correct account. With MacCorb Finn Barr read the gospels of St. Matthew and the ecclesiastical rules, to which another authority adds the Epistles of St. Paul. It was while in this neighbourhood that he stayed at Lough Eirce, in a place called Eadargabhail (Addergoole), where, according to the Irish life, he had a school in which many famous saints are said to have been educated. There has been much discussion as to the situation of Lough Eirce, chiefly owing to an error of Colgan, who placed it in the neighbourhood of Cork. There is a townland of Addergoole in the parish of Aghmacart in the south of Queen's County, and adjoining it in co. Kilkenny is the parish of Eirke, in a low-lying district. Here the site of the school must be looked for. At Lough Eirce there was also a female school, presided over by a sister of Finn Barr's. Coming now to his own country, he founded a church at Achaidh Durbchon. 'Near this,' says the Irish life, 'is the grotto [*cuas*] of Barra, and there is a lake or tarn there, from which a salmon is brought to him every evening.' This appears to be the lake of Gougane Barra, at the source of the river Lee, which probably derives its name from the cuadhan, pronounced cuagán (the little cavity) of Barra. Warned, as we are informed, by an angel not to stay at the hermitage, as his resurrection was not to be there, he set out, and crossing the Avonmore (Blackwater) proceeded in a north-easterly direction until he arrived at Cluain, where he built a church. This place, which has been strangely confounded with Cloyne, near Cork, is stated by Colgan to have been situated between Sliabh g-Crot (the Galtees) and Sliabh-Mairge, and appears to be Cluain-ednech, now Clonenagh, a townland near Mountrath, in the Queen's County. Here, when he had stayed some time, he was visited by two pupils of St. Ruadan, whose church of Lothra was some thirty miles distant. These clerics, Cormac and Baithin, had asked Ruadan for a place to settle in. 'Go,' he said, 'and settle wherever the tongues of your bells strike.' They went on until they arrived at the church of Cluain, where their bells sounded. They were much disappointed at finding the place already occupied, not thinking they would be allowed to stay there, but Barra gave them the church and all the property in it, and leaving the place returned to co. Cork, and came to Corcach Mor, or 'The Great Marsh,' now the city of Cork. Here he and his companions were engaged in fasting and prayer, when Aodh, son of Conall, the king of the territory, going in search of one of his cows which had strayed from the herd, met with them and granted them the site of the present cathedral. Before settling there finally, Barra was admonished by an angel, we are told, to go to the place to the westward, 'where,' he said, 'you have many waters, and where there will be many wise men with you.'

A long time after this, Barra, with Eolang, David, and ten monks, is said to have gone to Rome to be consecrated a bishop, but the pope refused to consecrate him, saying the rite would be performed by Jesus Christ himself. The Latin lives, instead of Barra's journey to Rome, tell of a message brought by MacCorb from the pope informing him how he was to be consecrated. At this time, MacCorb having died, Barra desired to have Eolang of Aghabulloge as a soul-friend or confessor in his place. According to the 'Calendar' of Oengus, Eolang was originally at Aghaboe, and probably accompanied Barra, whose pupil he had been. Eolang declined, saying, 'Christ will take your hand from mine and hear your confession.' It was reported that Barra afterwards wore a glove on one of his hands which Christ had touched, to hide its supernatural brightness. Seventeen years after the foundation of Cork, feeling that his death was near, he went to Clonenagh, and there died suddenly. His remains were brought to Cork and honourably interred,

and in after times his bones were taken up and enshrined in a silver casket. His pastoral character is thus described: 'The man of God abode there [at Cork], building up not so much a house of earthly stones as a spiritual house of true stones, wrought by the word and toil through the Holy Spirit.' His generosity is often referred to. Cumin of Condeire, in his poem, says: 'He never saw any one in want whom he did not relieve;' and the 'Calendar' of Oengus at 25 Sept. notices 'the festival of the loving man, the feast of Barre of Cork,' and in his 'Life' he is the 'amiable champion' (athleta). In after times, when Fursa was at the city of Cork, 'he saw [in vision] a golden ladder near the tomb of the man of God, to conduct souls to the kingdom of Heaven, and he beheld the top of it reach to the sky.'

Barra's travels are scarcely referred to in his 'Life.' He is said to have gone to Britain with St. Maidoc. In Reeves's edition of Adamnan's 'St. Columba' reference is made to 'his repeated and perhaps protracted visits to St. Columba at Hy,' though no notice of them is found in his 'Life.' There is an extraordinary story in the Rawlinson manuscript of his having borrowed a horse from St. David in Wales and ridden over to Ireland, in memory of which a brazen horse was made and kept at Cork, but there is nothing of this in the other lives. He is the patron saint of Dornoch, the episcopal seat of Caithness, where his festival is performed riding on horseback, a usage which seems to have some connection with the legend just mentioned. The island of Barra also claims him as patron and derives its name from him. According to Gerald de Barré, or Giraldus Cambrensis, his family name was derived from this island, and thus ultimately from the saint. Mr. Skene thinks the name Dunbarre is connected with him, as Dunblane with St. Blane. The name undergoes many modifications. He is termed Finn Barr, Barr-fhinn, or Barr-fhind, which by the silence of fh becomes Barrind, and then Barrindus. He is also Barr-og, or Barrocus, Bairre, Barra, and Barre, the last being his name in popular usage. In the parallel lists of Irish and foreign saints in the 'Book of Leinster' he is said to have been 'like Augustine, bishop of the Saxons, in his manner of life.' He died on 25 Sept. most probably in 623.

[Beatha Barra MS. 23 a, 44, Royal Irish Academy; Codex Kilkenniensis, fol. 132 b, 134; Codex Bodl. Rawlinson B. 485, both published by Dr. Caulfield in his Life of St. Finn Barr; Lanigan's Eccl. Hist. ii. 314–18; Calendar of Oengus at 25 Sept.; Reeves's Adamnan, lxxiv.]
T. O.

FINNCHU, SAINT (*fl.* 7th cent.), of Brigobann, now Brigown, in the county of Cork, was son of Finnlug, a descendant of Eochaidh Muidhmeadhon, and an inhabitant of Cremorne, county of Monaghan. Finnlug's first wife, Coemell, was of the Ciannachta of Glen Geimhin. After a married life of thirty years Coemell died, and Finnlug married Idnait, daughter of Flann, also of the Ciannachta. Soon after he was expelled from Ulster with his followers, and making his way to Munster the king, Aengus Mac Nadfraoich, granted him land in the province of Mog-Ruth (Fermoy). Here Idnait gave birth to the child Finnchu, who was baptised by Ailbe of Imlach Ibair (Emly), and 'a screpall, that is seven pennies of gold, paid as a baptismal fee.' The form of his name given in the ' Calendar ' of Oengus is Chua, to which Finn (fair) being added makes Chua-finn, and by transposition Finnchua. The Irish life and the ' Martyrology of Donegal ' make him son of Finnlug, son of Setna, but in other authorities he is son of Setna. He was placed with Cumusgach, king of Teffia (in Westmeath and Longford), with whom he remained seven years. At the end of that time Comgall [q. v.] of Bangor (county of Down) obtained leave to educate the child as an ecclesiastic at Bangor. Here he distinguished himself by his courage in bearding the king of Ulaidh, who had insisted on grazing his horses on the lands of the monastery. Nine years later Comgall died, and Finnchu succeeded him as abbot, though he does not appear in the regular lists. Seven years afterwards he was expelled from Bangor and the whole of Ulaidh, ' because of the scarcity of land.' He then returned to Munster, where the king of Cashel allowed him to choose a place of residence. Finnchu said : ' I must not settle in any place save where my bell will answer me without the help of man.' From Cashel he proceeded to the territory of Fermoy, and on the morrow his bell answered him at Fán Muilt (the wether's slope). As this was the queen's home farm, he would have been evicted had he not consented to pay rent. After this Finnchu ' marked out the place and arranged his enclosure, and covered his houses, and allotted lands to his households.' Hither came to him Conang, king of the Déisi, who prostrated himself to him, and Finnchu gave him, ' as a soul-friend's jewel, his own place in heaven.' Then, in order to obtain a place in heaven instead of that which he had given away, he suspended himself by the armpits from hooks in the roof of his cell, so that ' his head did not touch the roof, nor his feet the floor.' Thenceforth the place was called Bri gobann (Smith's Hill), now Mit-

chelstown, from the skill shown by the smiths who manufactured the hooks. During seven years he continued to practise this self-mortification until he was visited by St. Ronan Finn with an urgent request for help from the king of Meath, who was distressed by the inroads of British pirates. After much persuasion he saw St. Ronan, ' though sorely ashamed of his perforated body holed by chafers and beasts.' Accompanying St. Ronan to Tara, on the night of his arrival an inroad took place, and by Finnchu's advice, ' all, both laymen and clerics, turned right-handwise and marched against the intruders,' with the result that they slew them, burnt their ships, and made a mound of their garments.

At this time, dissensions having arisen between the two wives of Nuadu, king of Leinster, he sent off his favourite wife to Munster ' on the safeguard of Finnchua of Sliabh Cua.' Arrived near Brigown the saint desired she should not come any further until her child was born, for at that time ' neither wives nor women used to come to his church.' On the birth of the child he was baptised by Finnchu, and named Fintan. In a war which ensued between the king of Leinster and the kinsmen of his neglected wife, Finnchu was successful in obtaining the victory for the king. Fintan was with him, and when the king begged that the boy might be left with him, Finnchu consenting gave him ' his choice between the life of a layman and that of a cleric.' Having chosen the latter the land was bestowed on him, from which he was afterwards known as St. Fintan of Cluain-ednech. The St. Fintan (*d.* 634) [q. v.] generally known by this title was the son of Tulchan, but it appears from his ' Life ' that there were four of the name at Cluain-ednech. Returning to Munster, Finnchu was next called to repel an attack from the north, the queen of Ulaidh having instigated her husband to invade Munster to provide territory for her sons. The king of Munster was then living at Dun Ochair Maige (the fort on the brink of the Maige), now Bruree, in the county of Limerick, and when he and his consort beheld ' the splendid banners floating in the air, and the tents of royal speckled satin pitched on the hill,' they sent for Finnchu, who had promised, if occasion required, to come, ' with the Cenn Cathach [head battler], even his own crozier.' After vainly trying to make peace, he ' marched in the van of the army with the Cenn Cathach in his hand, and then passed right-handwise round the host.' For the complete victory which followed the king awarded ' a cow from every enclosure from Cnoc Brenain to Dairinis of Emly, and a milch cow to the cleric carrying his crozier in battle.' Ciar Cuircech, nephew of the king of Kerry, having been sent adrift on account of suspected treason, had been taken by pirates, and was retained by them as guide, and for three autumns they harried Kerry, and carried off the corn. The king sent for his relative, Finnchu (the Ciarraige and Finnchu's mother being both of the seed of Ebir). The saint came to the rescue, and 'his wrath arose against the maurauders, and the howling and rending of a hound possessed him on that day, wherefore the name of Finnchu [fair hound] clave to him.' Ciar was spared by Finnchu, who took him away, and placed him in the territory since called from him Kerrycurrihy, in the county of Cork.

The last warlike adventure in whichFinnchu was engaged was the repelling an invasion of the Clanna Neill. The people of Munster, who were then without an overking, elected Cairbre Cromm, a man of royal descent, who was at this time 'in waste places hunting wild swine and deer.' He consented to lead them on condition that Finnchu accompanied him. On coming in sight of the enemies' camp the Munster men 'flinch from the fight in horror of the Clanna Neill,' but stirred by the warning of Finnchu that not a homestead would be left to them if they did not fight, they gained the victory. Cairbre Cromm was then made king of Munster, but being dissatisfied with his appearance, as 'his skin was scabrous,' he besought Finnchu to bestow a goodly form on him, and the saint 'obtained from God his choice of form for him.' His shape and colour were then changed, so that he was afterwards Cairbre the Fair.

After this he made a vow that he would not henceforth be the cause of any battles. He gave his blessing to the rulers of Munster, and they promised to pay the firstlings of cows, sheep, and swine to him and his successors, together with an alms 'from every nose in Fermoy.' Then he went to his own place, and thence it is said to Rome, for he was penitent for the battles and deeds he had done for love of brotherhood. He is associated in Oengus with two foreign saints, Mammes and Cassian. Little of a religious character appears in the present life, but in Oengus he is said to have been 'a flame against guilty men,' and that 'he proclaimed Jesus.' His religion appears to have chiefly consisted in ascetic practices of an extreme character. He was supposed to lie the first night in the same grave with every corpse buried in his church. In an Irish stanza current in the north of the county of Cork he is associated with Molagga, Colman of Cloyne, and Declan, all very early saints, and he is termed 'Finnchu the ascetic.' The anachronisms in this life are more formidable than usual, but may possibly be explained by the habit of using the name of a well-known king for the reigning sovereign, as in the case of Pharaoh and Cæsar. The year of his death is not on record, but it must have been a long time after he left Bangor, which was in 608. His day is 25 Nov.

[The Irish life in the Book of Lismore, translated by Whitley Stokes, D.C.L.; Martyrology of Donegal, p. 317; Reeves's Eccles. Antiq. of Down, &c., p. 381; Calendar of Oengus, cxix, clxxii.] T. O.

FINNERTY, PETER (1766 ?–1822), journalist, born in or about 1766, was the son of a trader at Loughrea in Galway. He was brought up as a printer in Dublin, and became the publisher of 'The Press,' a nationalist newspaper started by Arthur O'Connor in September 1797. The violence of that journal caused it to be prosecuted by the government. On 22 Dec. 1797 Finnerty was tried before the Hon. William Downes, one of the justices of the court of king's bench in Ireland, upon an indictment for a seditious libel. The prosecution was instituted in consequence of the publication of a letter signed 'Marcus,' on the subject of the conviction and execution of William Orr, a presbyterian farmer, on a charge of administering the United Irish oath to a private in the Fifeshire Fencibles. Finnerty refused to divulge the writer's name, and, although John Philpot Curran made a most eloquent speech in his defence, he was found guilty. The sentence was that he should stand in and upon the pillory for the space of one hour; that he should be imprisoned for two years from 31 Oct. 1797 (the day he was arrested); that he should pay a fine of 20l. to the king; and that he should give security for his future good behaviour for seven years from the end of his imprisonment, himself in 500l., and two sureties in 250l. each. The whole of this sentence was eventually carried into effect. Finnerty, on 30 Dec., stood for one hour in the pillory opposite the sessions house in Green Street, in the presence of an immense concourse of sympathising spectators. He was accompanied by some of the leading men in the country. On being released from the pillory he said to the people: 'My friends, you see how cheerfully I can suffer—I can suffer anything, provided it promotes the liberty of my country.' The crowd cheered this brief address enthusiastically, but they were quickly dispersed by the military (HOWELL, *State Trials*, xxvi. 902–1018; CURRAN, *Speeches*, 2nd edit. by Davis, p. 276).

On regaining his liberty Finnerty came to

London and obtained an engagement as a parliamentary reporter on the staff of the 'Morning Chronicle.' In 1809 he accompanied the Walcheren expedition as special correspondent, in order to supply the 'Chronicle' with intelligence, but his bulletins soon induced the government to ship him home in a man-of-war. This he attributed to Lord Castlereagh, whom he libelled accordingly. On 7 Feb. 1811 he was sentenced by the court of queen's bench to eighteen months' imprisonment in Lincoln gaol for a libel charging his lordship with cruelty in Ireland. The talent and courage which he displayed at the trial obtained for him a public subscription of 2,000*l.* He memorialised the House of Commons on 21 June against the treatment he had experienced in prison, accusing the gaolers of cruelty in placing him with felons, and refusing him air and exercise. The memorial gave rise to several discussions, in which he was highly spoken of by Whitbread, Burdett, Romilly, and Brougham (HANSARD, *Parl. Debates*, 1811, xx. 723–43). He died in Westminster on 11 May 1822, aged 56.

Finnerty was an eccentric Irishman, extremely quick, ready, and hot-headed. Much of his time was spent with Paul Hiffernan [q. v.], Mark Supple, and other boon companions at the Cider Cellars, 20 Maiden Lane, Covent Garden. He published: 1. 'Report of the Speeches of Sir Francis Burdett at the late Election,' 1804, 8vo. 2. 'Case of Peter Finnerty, including a Full Report of all the Proceedings which took place in the Court of King's Bench upon the subject . . . with Notes, and a Preface comprehending an Essay upon the Law of Libel,' 4th edit. London, 1811, 8vo.

[Phillips's Curran and his Contemporaries, p. 184; Gent. Mag. vol. xcii. pt. i. p. 644; Biog. Dict. of Living Authors, p. 116; Andrews's British Journalism, ii. 31, 66; Notes and Queries, 2nd ser. ix. 306; Grant's Newspaper Press, ii. 224; Hunt's Fourth Estate, ii. 275.] T. C.

FINNEY, SAMUEL (1719–1798), miniature-painter, born at Wilmslow, Cheshire, 13 Feb. 1718–19, was eldest son of Samuel Finney of Fulshaw, Cheshire, and Esther, daughter of Ralph Davenport of Chorley. His family being in pecuniary difficulties, Finney came up to London to study law, but quitted that profession for painting. He established himself as a miniature-painter, working both in enamel and on ivory, and was very successful. He exhibited miniatures at the Exhibition of the Society of Artists in 1761, and in 1765 exhibited a miniature of Queen Charlotte, having been appointed 'enamel and miniature painter to her majesty.' He was a member of the Incorporated Society of Artists, and in 1766 subscribed the declaration roll of that society. Having amassed a fortune sufficient to pay off the encumbrances on the old family estate, Finney in 1769 retired to Fulshaw, became a justice of the peace, and devoted the remainder of his life to quelling the riots, then so prevalent in that part of Cheshire, and in local improvements. He also compiled a manuscript history of his family, part of which was printed in the 'Cheshire and Lancashire Historical Collector,' vol. i. A small portrait of Finney is in the possession of his descendant, Mr. Jenkins of Fulshaw; it was engraved by William Ford of Manchester, and the plate was destroyed after twelve copies had been struck off. He died in 1798, and was buried at Wilmslow. He was twice married, but left no children.

[Redgrave's Dict. of Artists; Graves's Dict. of Artists, 1760–1880; Earwaker's East Cheshire, i. 154.] L. C.

FINNIAN, SAINT (*d.* 550), of Cluainiraird, now Clonard, in the county of Meath, son of Finlugh, son of Fintan, a descendant of Conall Cearnach, one of the heroes of the Red Branch, was born in Leinster. He was baptised by a Saint Abban, and afterwards placed when of suitable age under the charge of Fortchern. With him he read 'the Psalms and the Ecclesiastical Order.' On reaching the age of thirty he crossed the sea, and according to the Irish life went to Tours, called by the Irish Torinis, where he became a friend of St. Caeman. But the Latin life, the author of which, according to Dr. Todd, had the Irish before him, substitutes Dairinis, an island in the bay of Wexford, in which there was a well-known monastery. The resemblance in sound may have suggested the correction, as Caeman was connected with Dairinis. But as the 'Office of St. Finnian' also mentions a visit to Tours, and two of St. Finnian's pupils, Columcille and Columb Mac Criomthainn, are said to have visited Tours, the Irish life may be correct. Finnian, probably on his way back, was at Cell Muine, or St. David's in Wales, where he met David, Gildas, and Cathmael or Docus. Here he is said to have stayed thirty years, and to have spoken the British language 'as if it was his own native tongue.' Finnian was employed to negotiate with the Saxon invaders, and failing in this is said to have overthrown them by supernatural means. An angel warned him to return to Ireland, which was in need of his teaching, instead of visiting Rome as he wished to do. He obeyed the divine call, and landed, according to Dr. Lanigan, first at the island of Dairinis, where he paid a second visit to St. Caeman. Leaving the island he coasted along, and finally landed at one of the harbours of Wexford, where he was well received by Muiredach, son of the king of Leinster, who honoured him, not as Dr. Lanigan says, by prostrating himself before him, but by taking him on his back across the fields. The king having offered him any site he pleased for a church, he selected Achad Aball, now Aghowle, in the barony of Shillelagh, in the county of Wicklow. Here he is said to have dwelt sixteen years. Moving about and founding churches in several places, he arrived at Kildare, where he 'stayed for a while, reading and teaching,' and on leaving was presented by Brigit with a ring of gold, which she told him he would require. Afterwards a slave at Fotharta Airbrech, in the north-east of the King's County, complained that the king demanded an ounce of gold for his freedom. Finnian having weighed the ring (ring money?) given him by Brigit, found it to be exactly one ounce, and he purchased the man's freedom. This slave was St. Caisin of Dal m Buain. Crossing the Boyne, he next founded a church at Ross Findchuill, also called Esgar Brannain, now Rosnarea. One of a raiding party from Fertullagh in Westmeath passing by his church became his disciple, and afterwards his successor at Clonard. This was Bishop Senach of Cluain Foda Fine, now Clonfad, in the county of Westmeath. It was probably at this time that he established his school at Clonard, in A.D. 530, according to Dr. Lanigan. Disciples came to him from all parts of Ireland till the number is said to have reached three thousand, and he acquired the title of 'the Tutor of the Saints of Ireland.' Many celebrated men were educated under him, among them Columcille, Columb of Tir da Glas, the two Ciarans, and others. To each of his pupils on their departure he gave a crozier or a gospel (i.e. a book of the gospels), or some well-known sign. These gifts became the sacred treasures of their respective churches. From his disciples he selected twelve who were known as 'the twelve Apostles of Ireland.' These, according to Dr. Todd, formed themselves into a kind of corporation, and exercised a sort of jurisdiction over the other ecclesiastics of their times. They were especially jealous of the right of sanctuary which they claimed for their churches.

A bard named Gemman, also termed 'the master,' and mentioned in Adamnan's 'Columba' as a tutor, brought him a poem celebrating his praises, and asked in return that 'the little land he had should be made fer-

tile.' Finnian replied, 'Put the hymn which thou hast made into water, and scatter the water over the land.' This is in accordance with Bede's description of the virtues of Irish manuscripts when immersed in water (*Eccl. Hist.* bk. i. chap. i.) In the Latin life he orders Gemman 'to sing the hymn over the field.' Some of the pupils of Finnian having been attracted to St. Ruadan of Lothra, formerly one of his disciples, he visited that saint at the request of his school, and an amicable contest took place between them, with the result that Ruadan consented 'to live like other people.' The special reason for the flocking of students to Lothra is said to have been 'a lime tree from which there used to drop a sweet fluid in which every one found the flavour he wished.' His next journey was into Luigne, now the barony of Leyney, co. Sligo, whither he was accompanied by Cruimther (or presbyter) Nathi. Here he founded a church in a place called Achad caoin conaire, now Achonry, where his well and his flagstone were shown.

When he had thus 'founded many churches and monasteries, and had preached God's word to the men of Ireland,' he returned to Clonard. Here his pupil, Bishop Senach, observing 'his meagreness and great wretchedness,' and 'seeing the worm coming out of his side in consequence of the girdle of iron which he wore,' could not restrain his tears. Finnian comforted him by reminding him that he was to be his successor. His food was a little barley bread, and his drink water, except on Sundays.

In the 'Martyrology of Donegal' he is compared to St. Paul, the parallel being carried out in detail. Finnian was the chief of the second order of Irish saints; he is sometimes said to have been a bishop, but it is not so stated in his life, and it is improbable, as the second order were nearly all presbyters. He died at Clonard, and, according to the 'Chronicon Scotorum,' of the pestilence known as the Buidhe Conaill, or yellow plague, which ravaged Ireland in A.D. 550. The language of his life is ambiguous, but seems to agree with this: 'As Paul died in Rome for the sake of the Christian people, even so Finnian died in Clonard that the people of the Gael might not all die of the yellow plague.' The 'Annals of the Four Masters' place his death at 548 (549), which is too early. Colgan's opinion that he lived as late as 563 is founded on a statement referring not to him but to St. Finnian of Maghbile. He is said in the Irish life to have reached the age of 140, and if his stay in different places was so long as mentioned, this would seem to be necessary, but the numbers can scarcely be intended to be taken literally. 'Thirty' seems to be used indefinitely in the lives of Irish saints. St. Finnian's day in the 'Martyrology of Donegal' is 12 Dec., though 11 Feb., 3 Jan., and 26 March have also been mentioned.

[Lives from the Book of Lismore, translated by Whitley Stokes, D.C.L., pp. 222-30; Lanigan's Eccl. Hist. i. 468, &c., ii. 21, 22; Dr. Todd's St. Patrick, pp. 98-101; Martyrology of Donegal, p. 333; Annals of the Four Masters, A.D. 548; Reeves's Adamnan, p. 136.]   T. O.

FINTAN, SAINT (*d.* 595), of Cluain-ednech, according to his pedigree in the 'Book of Leinster,' and his life as quoted by Colgan, was the son of Gabren and Findath, and a descendant of Feidlimid Rectmar. In the 'Codex Kilkenniensis' his father is called Crymthann, but Gabren is added in the margin, apparently as a correction. Again, in the 'Life of Finnchu' he is said to have been the son of Nuadu, king of Leinster, by his wife, Anmet. But as, according to some accounts, there were four Fintans at Cluain-ednech, the son of Nuadu was evidently a different person from the subject of the present notice. On the eighth day after his birth our Fintan was baptised at Cluain mic Trein, which may be presumed to have been in or near Ross, anciently called Ros mic Trein. He studied with two companions, Coemhan and Mocumin, under Colum, son of Crimthann, afterwards of Tirdaglas, now Terryglas, barony of Lower Ormond, county of Tipperary. Coemhan became eventually abbot of Enach Truim, now Annatrim, in Upper Ossory, and Mocumin, otherwise Natcaoim, was also subsequently of Tirdaglas.

The party of students and their master moved about, and on one occasion stayed at Cluain-ednech, where there was then no monastery. Here such numbers flocked to them that they had to move to Sliabh Bladma, now Slieve Bloom. Looking back from the mountain-side it was said that angels were hovering over the place they had left, and Fintan was at once advised to build his monastery there, which he did about A.D. 548. This place is now Clonenagh, a townland near Mountrath in the Queen's County. Here he led a life of the severest asceticism, but notwithstanding the strictness of his rule many sought admission to his community. 'The monks laboured with their hands after the manner of hermits, tilling the earth with hoes, and, rejecting all animals, had not even a single cow. If any one offered them milk or butter it was not accepted; no one dared to bring any flesh meat.'

This mode of life being felt as a reproach by the neighbouring clergy, a council assembled, at which St. Cainnech of Kilkenny and others were present, who visited St. Fintan and requested him for the love of God to relax the extreme rigour of his rule. Fintan after much persuasion conceded the changes proposed as regarded his community, but refused to alter his own mode of living. His discernment of character is shown in the case of two relatives of one of his monks. After the young man had failed to convert them, Fintan visited them and pronounced that one would be converted, but that the case of the other was hopeless. He seems to have been kind to his community, for when some of them, eager, like all the Irish of the period, for foreign travel, went away without his leave, and proceeded to Bangor in Ulster, and thence to Britain, he said to those who spoke of them, 'They are gone for God's work.'

A warlike party once left the heads of their enemies at the gate of Clonenagh. They were buried by the monks in their own cemetery, Fintan saying that all the saints who lay in that burial-ground would pray for them, as the most important part of their bodies was buried there. At this time the king of North Leinster held the son of the king of South Leinster (or Hy Censelach) prisoner, intending to kill him as a rival, but Fintan and twelve disciples went to the king at a town named Rathmore, in the north-east of the county of Kildare, to remonstrate with him. The king ordered the fortress to be firmly closed against him, but Fintan overcame all resistance, and rescued the youth, who afterwards became a monk at Bangor.

Walking on one occasion in the plain of the Liffey, he met Fergna, son of Cobhthach, and kneeled before him. The man was much surprised, but Fintan told him he was to become a monk. He said: 'I have twelve sons and seven daughters, a dear wife, and peaceful subjects,' but he eventually gave up all. Bishop Brandubh, 'a humble man of Hy Censelach,' went to Fintan to become one of his monks. Fintan met him in the monastery of Achad Finglas, near Slatey, and desired him to remain in this monastery, 'where,' he added, 'the mode of life is more tolerable than in mine.'

His most famous pupil was Comgall [q. v.] of Bangor, who came to him at Cluain-ednech. Here he joined the community, but so hard was the life that he grew weary of it, and the devil tempted him to return to his native place. He told Fintan of this, but shortly after, when praying at a cross to the west of Cluain-ednech, a supernatural light broke in on him, and he became quite happy. Fintan then sent him back to his native place to build churches and rear up servants to Christ.

He subsequently founded the famous monastery of Benchor (Bangor) in Ulster.

Fintan when on his deathbed appointed as his successor Fintan Maeldubh. In the 'Lebar Brecc' notes on the 'Calendar' of Oengus there are said to have been four Fintans there. His life was a continual round of fasts, night watches, and genuflexions. He is termed by Oengus 'Fintan the Prayerful,' and on the same authority we read, 'he never ate during his time, save woody bread of barley, and clayey water of clay.' In the parallel list of Irish and foreign saints, he, as 'chief head of the monks of Ireland,' is compared with Benedict, 'head of the monks of Europe.' His day is 17 Feb.

[Colgan's Acta Sanct. Hiberniæ, p. 349, &c.; Codex Kilkenniensis; Marsh's Library, Dublin, p. 74 aa; Calendar of Oengus, lii. liii.; Martyrology of Donegal, p. 51; Lanigan's Eccl. Hist. ii. 227–30.]　　　　　　　　　　　T. O.

FINTAN or **MUNNU**, Saint (d. 634), of Tech Munnu, now Taghmon, co. Wexford, was son of Tulchan, a descendant of Conall Gulban, son of Niall of the Nine Hostages, his mother, Fedelm, being of the race of Maine, son of Niall. He used to leave his father's sheep to go for instruction to a holy man named Cruimther (or presbyter) Grellan, who lived at Achad Breoan. The sheep did not suffer, and it was even rumoured that two wolves were seen guarding them. St. Comgall of Bangor on his way from Connaught met with him at Uisnech (now Usny), in the parish of Killare, barony of Rathconrath, co. Westmeath. Comgall allowed the boy to join him, and on the first day initiated him into his discipline by refusing to allow him a draught of water until vespers in spite of the heat.

Fintan is said to have gone next to the school of St. Columba at Cill mor Ditraibh; but this seems inconsistent with the dates of his life. His regular studies were carried on under Sinell of Cluaininis, an island in Lough Erne, who is described as 'the most learned man in Ireland or in Britain.' With him he continued nineteen years, studying the Scriptures in company with nine others. In making their bread they were not permitted to separate the chaff from the wheat; but all being ground together, the flour was mixed with water and baked by means of stones heated in the fire.

On the completion of his studies he went to Hy to enter the monastery, but found that St. Columba was dead, and Baithin, his successor, refused to accept him, alleging that St. Columba had anticipated his coming, and directed him not to receive him. 'He will not like this,' he added, 'for he is a rough man; therefore assure him that he will be an abbot and the head of a congregation.' This story, which is not only found in his lives, but in Adamnan's 'Life of Columba,' is stated in the latter to have been communicated to the author by Oissene, who had it from the lips of Fintan himself. Fintan is described as fair, with curly hair and a high complexion. On his return to Ireland he took up his abode in an island named Cuimrige or Cuinrigi, where he founded a church at a place called Athcaoin; but having ascended a mountain to pray he was so disturbed by the cries and tumult at the battle of Slenne (perhaps of Sleamhain, near Mullingar, A.D. 602) that he left the island. He next passed on to his own neighbourhood in the territory of Ely, but did not visit or salute any one. Here he built Tech Telle (now Tehelly), in the north of the King's County, where he remained five years. He permitted his mother to visit him with his two sisters, but said that if she came again he would depart to Britain. Probably in allusion to this a poem attributed to Colum Cillé, says: 'The mother that bore thee, O Fintan, O Munnu, bore a son hard to her family.' Soon afterwards a virgin with five companions presented herself at Tech Telle, and said to the steward: 'Tell the strong man who owns this place to give it to me, for he and his fifty youths are stronger than I and my five, and let him build another for himself.' Fintan complied, ordering his pupils to bring only their axes, books, and chrismals with their ordinary clothing, and the two oxen which drew the wagon with the books. But he refused to bless her, and told her that the church would not be associated with her name, but with that of Telle, son of Segein. He and his party then proceeded to the Ui Bairrche (now the barony of Slieve Margy in the Queen's County), where there was a monastery of Comgall of Bangor, over which one of his pupils named Aed Gophan (or Guthbinn?) presided. He was obliged to go away into exile for twelve years, and left Fintan to take charge during his absence. Meanwhile, Comgall having died, 'the family' of the monastery came to Fintan, but he refused their several requests either to accept the abbacy of Bangor, or to become one of the monks there, but said that he would leave the place if he could surrender it to Aed Gophan, who entrusted it to him. Then they said: 'You had better go and seek for him, even if you have to go to Rome, and we will wait your return.' He therefore set out with five companions, but after crossing one field he met with Aedh returning after twelve years of exile. Leaving Ui Bairrche, Fintan came to Achad Liacc, in the barony of Forth, co. Wexford. Here one day when in the woods he met three men clothed in white garments, who told him, 'Here will be your city,' and they marked out in his presence seven places in which afterwards the chief buildings of his city should be erected, and Fintan placed crosses there. The chieftain of the country of Forth, named Dimma, who had offended him by unseemly rejoicing over a homicide, repenting, 'offered him the land where his city Taghmon now is.' He asked for a reward, and when Fintan promised him the kingdom of heaven, said : 'That is not enough, unless you also give me long life and all my wishes, and allow me to be buried with your monks in holy ground.' All these requests Fintan granted to him. The community of Fintan consisted of fifty monks, and their daily food was bread with water and a little milk. Dimma, chieftain of the territory, had placed his two sons in fosterage—one, Cellach, at Airbre in Ui Cennselaigh with St. Cuan; the other, Cillin, with Fintan at Taghmon. The father going to visit them found Cellach dressed in a blue cloak, with a sheaf of purple arrows on his shoulder, his writing tablet bound with brass, and wearing shoes ornamented with brass. Cillin, in a cloak of black undyed sheep's wool, a short white tunic, with a black border and common shoes, chanting psalms with other boys behind the wagon. The king was displeased, but Fintan told him that Cellach would be slain by the Leinster people, while Cillin would be 'the head of a church, a wise man, a scribe, bishop, and anchorite,' and would go to heaven.

Fintan's rugged character is illustrated in an imaginary dialogue between him and the angel who used to visit him. Fintan asked why another, whom he mentioned, was higher in favour than himself. Because, was the reply, 'he never caused any one to blush, whereas you scold your monks shamefully.' 'Then,' Fintan indignantly replied, 'I will go into exile and never take any more pains with my monks.' 'No,' said the angel, 'but the Lord will visit you.' That night Fintan became a leper, and continued so for twenty-three years. This is referred to in the 'Calendar' of Oengus, where he is called 'crochda,' crucified or bearing a cross.

Fintan's most remarkable appearance was at the council of Magh Ailbe or Whitefield, where the propriety of adopting changes made on the continent in the Rule of Easter was discussed. Laisrean or Molaisse of Leighlin, with his friends, defended the new system and the new order. Fintan and all others maintained the old. The king of Ui Bairrche, impatient at Fintan's delay in coming, spoke tauntingly of his leprosy. When he arrived the king asked him to speak. 'Why,' said Fintan, turning fiercely to him, 'do you ask me, a leprous man, for a speech? When you were abusing me Christ blushed at the right hand of the Father, for I am a member of Christ.' Fintan proposed the ordeal by fire and then by water, or a contest in miraculous power; but Laisrean would not risk the danger of defeat. Dr. Lanigan is not accurate in saying that 'Fintan soon after withdrew his opposition, and agreed with his brethren of the south,' for the 'Codex Salmanticensis' states that the council broke up, assenting to his conclusion : 'Let every one do as he believes, and as seems to him right,' words which fairly express the tolerant spirit of the Irish church. It is added by the writer of his 'Life' that whenever he addressed a guest in rough or hasty language he would not eat until he had apologised, saying: 'At that moment I was the son of Tulchan according to the flesh, but now I am spiritually the son of God.' Lanigan does not allow that he was at Clonenagh; but Bishop Reeves, following Colgan, holds that he was 'fourth in a succession of Fintans there.' He has given his name to a Taghmon, also in Westmeath, and is commemorated at Kilmun in Cowall (Scotland), where he is buried according to the 'Breviary of Aberdeen.' There was also a church in Loch Leven called after him. In the 'Litany' of Oengus 'one hundred and fifty true martyrs' who lived under his rule are invoked, and two hundred and thirty-three are referred to in the 'Martyrology' of Tamlaght; but this does not imply that they were all living at one time. The name Mundu or Munnu is interpreted in the 'Lebar Brecc' as a contraction of mo-Fhindu, the F in the compound becoming silent; Fintan is also a contraction of Findu-án. His day is celebrated 21 Oct.

[Acta Sanct. Hiberniæ ex codice Salmanticensi, London, 1888; Calendar of Oengus, clix.; Lanigan's Eccl. Hist. ii. 404–8; Ussher's Works, vi. 503; Reeves's Adamnan, pp. 18, 27; the Rev. James Gammack, in Dict. of Christian Biography, ii. 520.] T. O.

FIRBANK, JOSEPH (1819–1886), railway contractor, son of a Durham miner, was born at Bishop Auckland in 1819. At the age of seven he was sent to work in a colliery, and attended a night-school. In 1841 he secured a sub-contract in connection with the Woodhead tunnel on the Stockton and Darlington railway, and in 1845 and 1846 took contracts on the Midland railway. The opposition to railway construction was so great at this time that on one occasion Firbank was captured and kept a prisoner for twenty-four hours. Noblemen would not permit the contractors or their workmen to approach their demesnes. In 1848 Firbank was engaged on the Rugby and Stamford branch of the North-Western railway, and lost most of his savings by the bankruptcy of the former contractor of the line. When the Monmouthshire Railway and Canal Company transformed their mineral tramways and canals into passenger railways in 1854, Firbank took the contract for dealing with the canals in the town of Newport, Monmouthshire. He also took the contract for the maintenance of the lines for seven years, and this contract was several times renewed.

Firbank established himself at Newport, where he formed an intimate friendship with Mr. Crawshaw Bailey, the ironmaster, who supported him in his early undertakings. He was employed in South Wales for thirty years, until the absorption of the Monmouthshire company by the Great Western. In 1856 Firbank took a contract for the widening of the London and North-Western railway near London, and afterwards (1859–66) various contracts on the Brighton line. He was also engaged upon the Midland Company's Bedford and London extension (1864–1868), which involved great difficulties and ultimately cost the company upwards of 3,000,000*l.* He was contractor in 1870 on the Settle and Carlisle extension of the Midland railway. He was afterwards contractor for many lines, the most difficult undertaking being the Birmingham west suburban section of the Midland railway.

In 1884 Firbank built the St. Pancras goods depôt of the Midland railway. The last contract taken by him was for the Bournemouth direct line from Brokenhurst to Christchurch. It proved to be the most troublesome of all his undertakings, and was finally completed by his son, Joseph T. Firbank. The lines constructed by Firbank from 1846 to 1886 amounted to forty-nine. All through his career he was a generous employer, doing his best to promote the welfare of those whom he employed.

Firbank died at his residence, near Newport, on 29 June 1886. He was twice married, and was survived by his second wife and seven children. Firbank has been described as 'an excellent specimen of the class of Englishmen who rise up not so much by any transcendent talents, as by intelligence and energy,' and above all by a scrupulous 'honesty, inspiring confidence' (SAMUEL LAING). He was indefatigable in work, retiring to rest by nine o'clock and rarely rising later than five. His business faculties were very great. He was a justice of the peace

and deputy-lieutenant for the county of Monmouth.

[F. M'Dermott's Life and Work of Joseph Firbank, 1887.] G. B. S.

FIREBRACE, HENRY (1619–1691), royalist, sixth son of Robert Firebrace of Derby, who died in 1645, by Susanna, daughter of John Hierome, merchant, of London, held the offices of page of the bedchamber, yeoman of the robes, and clerk of the kitchen to Charles I, which he obtained through the interest of the Earl of Denbigh. He became much attached to the king, and was able to be of service to him on more than one occasion—at Uxbridge, in connection with the negotiations there in 1644, Oxford, and elsewhere. After the king's surrender to the Scots at Newark, in 1646, Firebrace joined him at Newcastle, and attended him to Holmby House and Hampton Court, and again after his flight to the Isle of Wight he obtained permission to attend him as page of the bedchamber during his confinement in Carisbrooke Castle. Here he determined, if possible, to effect the king's escape, and accordingly contrived one evening, as Charles was retiring to rest, to slip into his hand a note informing him of a place in the bedchamber where he had secreted letters from friends outside. A regular means of communication was thus established between the king and his most trusted supporters. They thus concerted a plan of escape. At a signal given by Firebrace Charles was to force his body through the aperture between the bars of his bedchamber window, and let himself down by a rope; Firebrace was then to conduct him across the court to the main wall of the castle, whence they were to descend by another rope and climb over the counterscarp, on the other side of which men and horses were to be in waiting to carry them to a vessel. On a night, the precise date of which cannot be fixed, but which was probably early in April 1648, Firebrace gave the signal by throwing something against the bedchamber window. The king thrust his head into the aperture, and succeeded in squeezing some portion of his body through it, but then stuck fast, and could with difficulty get back into the room. Firebrace was not slow in devising a new plan, which he communicated to the king by a letter. A bar was to be cut in one of the windows, from which the king would be able to step upon a wall and escape over the outworks. The king, who had already begun filing one of the bars of his bedchamber window, expressed approval of the new plan as an alternative scheme. In the end, however, he abandoned an attempt at secret flight as impracticable. In a letter (26 April) he commanded Firebrace 'heartily and particularly to thank, in my name, A. C. F. Z., and him who stayed for me beyond the works, for their hearty and industrious endeavours in this my service.' The cipher letters are supposed to stand for Francis Cresset, Colonel William Legg, groom of the bedchamber, Abraham Doucett, and Edward Worsely. The person 'who stayed beyond the works' appears to have been one John Newland of Newport, who had provided the vessel for the king's use. On the day before his execution Charles charged Dr. William Juxon to recommend Firebrace to Prince Charles as one who had been 'very faithful and serviceable to him in his greatest extremities.' After this we lose sight of Firebrace until the Restoration, when he petitioned to be appointed to one or other of the posts which he had held under the late king. The petition, which was supported by a certificate from Juxon, then archbishop of Canterbury, of Charles's recommendation, was granted, and Firebrace was appointed to the several offices of chief clerk of the kitchen, clerk-comptroller-supernumerary of the household, and assistant to the officers of the green cloth. He died on 27 Jan. 1690-1.

Firebrace married, first, Elizabeth, daughter of Daniel Dowell of Stoke-Golding, Leicestershire; secondly, Alice, daughter of Richard Bagnall of Reading, relict of John Bucknall of Creek, Northamptonshire; and thirdly, Mary, of whom nothing seems to be known except that she was buried in the north cloister of Westminster Abbey on 1 Feb. 1687-8. By his first wife he had issue four sons and one daughter. His eldest son, Henry, became a fellow of Trinity College, Cambridge, and entered the church; his second son, Basil (d. 1724), went into business, was sheriff of London in 1687, and was created a baronet on 28 July 1698. In December 1685 a royal bounty of 1,694l. was paid him (*Secret Services of Charles II and James II*, Camd. Soc. p. 114). Reference is made to him in Luttrell's 'Relation.' The dignity became extinct in 1759. The original form of the name Firebrace, sometimes spelt Ferebras, is said to have been Fier à bras; the family was probably of Norman lineage.

[Nichols's Leicestershire, iv. pt. ii. 726; Hist. MSS. Comm. 4th Rep. App. 274 b, 7th Rep. App. 224 a; Sir Thomas Herbert's Memoirs, 1702, pp. 185-200; Dr. Peter Barwick's Life of Dr. John Barwick (translation by Hilkiah Bedford, pp. 87-9, 380-7; Wotton's Baronetage, iv. 65-77; Cal. State Papers, Dom. 1660-1, p. 20; Coll. Top. et Gen. vii. 163, viii. 20.] J. M. R.

FIRMIN, GILES (1614-1697), ejected minister, son of Giles Firmin, was born at Ipswich in 1614. As a schoolboy he received religious impressions from the preaching of John Rogers at Dedham, Essex. He matriculated at Emmanuel College, Cambridge, in December 1629, his tutor being Thomas Hill, D.D. [q. v.] At Cambridge he studied medicine. In 1632 he went with his father to New England. While at Boston, Massachusetts, he was ordained deacon of the first church, of which John Cotton was minister. At Ipswich, Massachusetts, he received in 1638 a grant of 120 acres of land. He practised medicine in New England, and had the repute of a good anatomist. About 1647 he returned to England, leaving a wife and family in America. He was shipwrecked on the coast of Spain ; Calamy relates, as a 'well-attested' fact, that at the very time when he was in danger of being drowned his little daughter of four years old roused the family in New England by continually crying out 'My father!'

In 1648 Firmin was appointed to the vicarage of Shalford, Essex, which had been vacant a year since the removal of Ralph Hilles to Pattiswick. At Shalford he was ordained a presbyter by Stephen Marshall [q. v.] and others. He is returned in 1650 as 'an able, godly preacher.' He appears to have been a royalist in principle, for he affirms that he was one of those who 'in the time of the usurpation' prayed for 'the afflicted royal family.' Very soon he got into controversy on points of discipline. He was a strong advocate for the parochial system, insisted on imposition of hands as requisite for the validity of ordination, and denied the right of parents who would not submit to discipline to claim baptism for their children. With Baxter he opened a correspondence in 1654, complaining to him that 'these separatists have almost undone us.' The quakers also troubled his parish. In ecclesiastical politics he followed Baxter, preferring a reformed episcopacy to either the presbyterial or the congregational model, but laying most stress on the need of a well-ordered parish. He actively promoted in 1657 the 'agreement of the associated ministers of Essex' on Baxter's Worcestershire model.

After the king's return he writes to Baxter (14 Nov. 1660) that he is most troubled about forms of prayer; these, he says, 'will not downe in our parts.' He is ready to submit to bishops, 'so they will not force me to owne their power as being of divine authoritie,' and adds, 'some episcopacies I owne.' In spite of the persuasion of his seven children he refused to conform. As the result of his ejection (1662), Shalford Church was closed for some months.

Firmin retired to Ridgewell, Essex, perhaps on the passing of the Five Mile Act (1665). He supported himself by medical practice, and was much in request. The neighbouring justices, who valued his professional services, took care that he should not be molested, though he regularly held conventicles, except once a month, when there was a sermon at Ridgewell Church which he attended. On 22 July 1672 Daniel Ray, who had been ejected from Ridgewell, took out licenses qualifying him to use his house as a 'presbyterian meeting-place.' Firmin on 1 Dec. took out similar licenses. Ray removed in 1673, and Firmin remained till his death in sole charge of the congregation. It still exists, and now ranks with the independents.

Firmin retained robust health as an octogenarian, and was always ready to take his part in polemics. He had broken a lance with his old friend Baxter in 1670, and in 1693 he entered the lists of the Crispian controversy, which was then breaking up the newly formed 'happy union' of the London presbyterians and independents. He was a well-read divine, if somewhat captious. Calamy reckons him at his best in an experimental treatise. He was taken ill on a Sunday night after preaching, and died on the following Saturday, in April 1697. He married, in New England, Susanna, daughter of Nathaniel Ward, pastor of the church at Ipswich, Massachusetts.

Davids gives an imperfect list of seventeen of Firmin's publications. His chief pieces are: 1. 'A Serious Question Stated,' &c., 1651, 4to (on infant baptism). 2. 'Separation Examined,' &c., 1651 [i.e. 15 March 1652], 4to. 3. 'Stablishing against Shaking,' &c., 1656, 4to (against the quakers; the running title is 'Stablishing against Quaking;' answered by Edward Burrough [q. v.] 4.'Tythes Vindicated,'&c.,1659,4to. 5.'Presbyterial Ordination Vindicated,' &c., 1660, 4to. 6. 'The Liturgical Considerator Considered,' &c., 1661, 4to (anon., in answer to Gauden). 7. 'The Real Christian,' &c., 1670, 4to; reprinted, Glasgow, 1744, 8vo (in this he criticises Baxter; it is his best piece according to Calamy). 8.'The Question between the Conformist and the Nonconformist,' &c., 1681, 4to. 9. 'Πανουργία,' &c., 1693 (against Davis and Crisp). 10. 'Some Remarks upon the Anabaptist's Answer to the Athenian Mercuries,' &c. (1694), 4to (apparently his last piece). He wrote also in defence of some of the above, and in opposition to John Owen, Daniel Cawdry [q. v.], Thomas Grantham (d. 1692) [q. v.], and others.

[Benjamin Calamy's Account of his Life and Times, 1713, p. 295; Continuation, 1727, p. 458; Davids's Annals of Evang. Nonconf. in Essex, 1863, pp. 440, 449, 457; Dexter's Congregationalism of the last Three Hundred Years, 1880, p. 574 n.; Firmin's letters to Baxter, in the collection of Baxter MSS. at Dr. Williams's Library (extracts, occasionally needing correction, are given by Davids); Hunter's manuscripts, Addit. MSS. 24478, p. 114 b.] A. G.

FIRMIN, THOMAS (1632–1697), philanthropist, son of Henry and Prudence Firmin, was born at Ipswich in June 1632. Henry Firmin was a parishioner of Samuel Ward, the puritan incumbent of St. Mary-le-Tower, by whom in 1635 he was accused of erroneous tenets; the matter was brought before the high commission court, but on Firmin's making satisfactory submission the charge (particulars of which are not disclosed) was dismissed. Thomas was apprenticed in London to a mercer, who attended the services of John Goodwin [q. v.] the Arminian, then vicar of St. Stephen's, Coleman Street. He learned shorthand, and took down Goodwin's sermons. As an apprentice his alacrity gained him the nickname of 'Spirit.' An elder apprentice accused him of purloining 5l., but afterwards confessed that the theft was his own. The late story (KENNETT) according to which Firmin, during his apprenticeship, presented a petition in favour of John Biddle [see BIDDLE, JOHN], and was dismissed by Cromwell as a 'curl-pate boy,' does not tally with earlier accounts. Kennett, however, gives as his authority John Mapletoft, M.D. [q. v.], who was a relative of Firmin.

With a capital of 100l. Firmin began business as a girdler and mercer. His shop was at Three Kings Court, in Lombard Street; he had a garden at Hoxton, in which he took great delight. Slender as were his means he contrived to keep a table for his friends, especially ministers. His frank hospitality brought him (after 1655) into relations with such men as Whitchcote, Worthington, Wilkins, Fowler, and Tillotson. In this way, somewhat earlier, he became acquainted with Biddle, whose influence on Firmin's philanthropic spirit was important. It was from Biddle that he learned to distrust mere almsgiving, but rather to make it his business to fathom the condition of the poor by personal investigation, and to reduce the causes of social distress by economic effort. Biddle also deepened Firmin's convictions on the subject of religious toleration, and without converting him to his own specific opinions made him heterodox in the article of the Trinity. Biddle was Firmin's guest in 1655, prior to his banishment, and it was largely through Firmin's exertions that a pension of one hundred crowns was granted by Cromwell to the banished man.

Sympathy with the oppressed had something to do with Firmin's religious leanings. He expressed himself as hating popery ' more for its persecuting than for its priestcraft.' In 1662 he raised money partly by ' collections in churches ' for the exiled anti-trinitarians of Poland ; but when (1681) the Polish Calvinists met the same fate Firmin was foremost in efforts for their relief, collecting about 680*l.* His acquaintance with religious controversies was gained in conversation, for he was never a student. There was scarcely a divine of note whom he did not know. He helped young clergymen to preferment, and it is said that Tillotson, after becoming dean of Canterbury (1672), when obliged to leave town, ' generally left it to Mr. Firmin to provide preachers ' for his Tuesday lecture at St. Lawrence, Jewry. Tillotson was aware that Firmin's freedom of opinion did not bias his judgment of men.

Firmin's first philanthropic experiment was occasioned by the trade disorganisation of the plague year (1665). He provided employment at making up clothing for hands thrown out of work. It was the only one of his enterprises by which he suffered no pecuniary loss. During the great fire (1666) his Lombard Street premises were burned. He secured temporary accommodation in Leadenhall Street, and in a few years was able to rebuild in Lombard Street, and to carry on his business with increased success. In 1676 he left the management of the concern in the hands of his nephew and partner, Jonathan James (son of his sister Prudence), who had been his apprentice ; he was then worth about 9,000*l.* Henceforth he devoted his time and great part of his means to works of public benefit. He had been elected about 1673 a governor of Christ's Hospital, the first public recognition of his worth.

He had two schemes already in operation. About 1670 he had erected a building by the river for the storage of corn and coals, to be retailed to the poor in hard times at cost price ; how this plan worked is not stated. Early in 1676 he had started a ' workhouse in Little Britain, for the employment of the poor in the linen manufacture ; ' he built new premises expressly for it. Tillotson suggests that the hint of this ' larger design ' was taken from the example of Thomas Gouge [q. v.], who was one of the frequenters of Firmin's table. Firmin employed as many as seventeen hundred spinners, besides flax-dressers, weavers, &c. He paid them for their work at the current rate, but, finding that they must work sixteen hours a day to earn sixpence, he added to their earnings in various ways, giving a sort of bonus in coal to good workers. His arrangements for the comfort and cleanliness of his hands, and for the industrial training of children rescued from the streets, were admirable. Nothing is said of his directly fostering the education of the children, but he printed large editions of a ' Scripture Catechism' (probably by Bishop Edward Fowler [q.v.]), and gave rewards to such as learned it.

The scheme never paid its way. Firmin sold his linens at cost price, but the sale flagged ; for the first five years the annual loss was 200*l.* He invoked the aid of the press, in the hope of getting the corporation of London to take the matter up as a public enterprise, but in vain. The scale of production was diminished, yet the loss increased. Two or three friends helped to make it good, but the main burden rested on Firmin. In 1690 the patentees of the linen manufacture took over the scheme, retaining Firmin as its manager at a salary of 100*l.* a year, and reducing the rate of wages. The new arrangement was unsuccessful, Firmin's honorarium was not paid, and the enterprise was once more thrown on his hands. He kept it up to the day of his death, and nominally contrived to make it pay, only however by keeping the wages low, and supplementing them by private doles to his workers. His last wish was for two months more of life, in order that he might remodel his ' workhouse.' This was done after his death by James, his partner, a prudent man, who had saved Firmin from ruining himself by drawing too largely on the ready money of the firm. He had put down his coach rather than drop some of his spinners. The higher rate of wages obtainable at the woollen manufacture led Firmin to attempt its introduction as a London industry. He took for this purpose a house in Artillery Lane ; but wool was too dear ; his hands were too slow ; after losing money for two years and a quarter he abandoned the trial.

Firmin deserves notice as a prison philanthropist. From about 1676 he interested himself in the condition of prisoners for debt, freeing several hundreds who were detained for small sums, and successfully promoting acts of grace for the liberation of others. He visited prisons, inquired into the treatment pursued, and prosecuted harsh and extortionate gaolers. His biographer relates that one of these incriminated officials hanged himself rather than face a trial.

Firmin was a strong patriot as regards English manufactures, strenuously opposing the importation of French silks. But when the protestant refugees came over from France in 1680 and following years he was the first to assist them to set up their own trades. Most of the moneys devoted to their relief passed through his hands, he himself collecting some 4,000*l.* His pet project of a linen manufacture he started for them at Ipswich in 1682.

In politics Firmin does not seem to have taken any part till 1685. His opposition to James II's unconstitutional proceedings cost him for a time his governorship at Christ's Hospital. Not won by James's declaration for liberty of conscience he largely aided the circulation of pamphlets which sounded the alarm against it. His principles seem to have been republican, but he was a devoted adherent to William of Orange. To Robert Frampton [q. v.], the nonjuring bishop of Gloucester, Firmin remarked, 'I hope you will not be a nonconformist in your old age.' Frampton retorted that Firmin himself was 'a nonconformist to all Christendom besides a few lowsy sectarys in Poland.' On the protestant exodus from Ireland in 1688–9 Firmin was the principal commissioner for the relief of the refugees; more than 56,000*l.* went through his hands, and eight of the protestant hierarchy of Ireland addressed to him a joint letter of thanks. He was rendering a similar service for the nonjurors in 1695, when he was stopped by the interference of the government.

In conjunction with his friend, Sir Robert Clayton [q. v.], Firmin was an indefatigable governor of Christ's Hospital, carrying out many improvements, both of structure and arrangement. On Sunday evenings it was his custom to attend the scholars' service, and see that their 'pudding-pies' for supper were of proper 'bigness.' In April 1693 he was elected a governor of St. Thomas's Hospital, of which Clayton had been made president in the previous year. Firmin carried through the work of rebuilding the hospital and church. Among his admirable qualities was the faculty for interesting others in benevolent designs and calling forth their liberality. He was a kind of almoner-general to the metropolis, keeping a register of the poor he visited, recommending their cases, and apprenticing their children.

Luke Milbourn [q. v.] in 1692 speaks of Firmin as a 'hawker' for the Socinians, 'to disperse their new-fangled divinity.' Only four books of this class are known with certainty to have been promoted by him. In 1687 was printed at his expense 'A Brief History of the Unitarians, called also Socinians.' It is in the shape of four letters, written for his information, probably by Stephen Nye, and is noteworthy as marking the first appearance in English literature of the term 'unitarian,' a name unknown to Biddle. In 1689 he printed 'Brief Notes on the Creed of St. Athanasius,' a sheet by an unknown author. Tillotson, who had lectured on the Socinian controversy at St. Lawrence, Jewry, in 1679–80, felt himself compelled by 'calumnies' to publish the lectures in 1693. He sent a copy to Firmin, who printed a letter (29 Sept. 1694) in reply, probably by Nye, under the title 'Considerations on the Explications of the Doctrine of the Trinity' (sometimes confounded with a tract of 1693 with similar title, and by the same hand). This he laid before Tillotson, who remarked that Burnet's forthcoming exposition of the articles 'shall humble your writers.' In 1697, at Firmin's instance, appeared 'The Agreement of the Unitarians with the Catholick Church,' a work which more closely expresses his own views than any of the foregoing. He never departed from the communion of the church of England, but put a Sabellian sense on the public forms. At the time of his death he was meditating a plan of 'unitarian congregations' to meet for devotional purposes as fraternities within the church.

Firmin was an original member of the 'Society for the Reformation of Manners' (1691), and was very active in the enforcement of fines for the repression of profane swearing. Kettlewell's biographer speaks of his disinterested charity, and Wesley, who abridged his life for the 'Arminian Magazine,' calls him 'truly pious.'

Firmin had injured his health by over-exertion and neglecting his meals, and had become consumptive. He was carried off in a couple of days by a typhoid fever, dying on 20 Dec. 1697. Bishop Fowler [q. v.] attended him on his deathbed. He was buried in the cloisters at Christ's Hospital, where a marble slab is placed to his memory. A memorial pillar stands in the grounds of Marden Park, Surrey, the seat of his friend Clayton, where 'Firmin's Walk' perpetuates his name. There is no portrait of Firmin; he is described as a little, active man, of frank address and engaging manner. His autograph will (dated 7 Feb. 1694) shows illiteracy.

Firmin died worth about 3,000*l.* He was twice married: first, in 1660, to a citizen's daughter with a portion of 500*l.*; she died while Firmin was at Cambridge on business, leaving a son (*d.* about 1690) and a daughter (*d.* in infancy); secondly, in 1664, to Margaret (*d.* 14 Jan. 1719, aged 77), daughter of Giles Dentt, J.P., of Newport, Essex, alderman of London; by her he had several children, who all died in infancy, except the eldest, GILES, born 22 May 1665 (Tillotson was his godfather). Giles received his mother's portion and became a promising merchant ; he married Rachel (*d.* 11 April 1724), daughter of Perient Trott and sister of Lady Clayton ; died at Oporto on 22 Jan. 1694, and was buried at Newport on 13 April ; his widow afterwards married Owen Griffith, rector of Blechingley, Surrey.

Firmin's only known publication was 'Some Proposals for the Imploying of the Poor, especially in and about London, and for the Prevention of Begging. In a Letter to a Friend. By T. F.,' 1678, 4to. An enlarged issue appeared in 1681, 4to ; two editions same year. It was reprinted in a collection of 'Tracts relating to the Poor,' 1787, 4to.

[The Charitable Samaritan, or a Short and Impartial Account of . . . Mr. T. F. . . . by a gentleman of his acquaintance, 1698, 4to; Life of Mr. Thomas Firmin, 1698, 8vo, 2nd edition, 1791, 12mo (the writer had known him since 1653 ; appended is a funeral sermon, probably by the same writer, ' preached in the country') ; Vindication of the memory of Thomas Firmin from the Injurious Reflections of . . . Milbourn, 1698, 4to (apparently by the writer of the Life); Account of Mr. Firmin's Religion, &c., 1698, 8vo ; Tillotson's Funeral Sermon for Gouge, 1681 ; Penn's Key Opening the Way, 1692 ; Milbourn's Mysteries in Religion, 1692 ; Grounds and Occasions of the Controversy concerning the Unity of God, 1698 ; Life of Kettlewell, 1718, p. 420 ; Kennett's Register, 1728, p. 761 ; Burnet's Hist. of his own Time, 1734, ii. 211 sq.; Birch's Life of Tillotson, 1753, p. 292 sq.; Life by Cornish, 1780 ; Arminian Magazine, 1786, p. 253 ; Wallace's Antitrin. Biog., 1850, i. (historical introduction), iii. 353 sq.; Life of Bishop Frampton (Evans), 1876, p. 187 ; State Papers, Dom. Chas. I, cclxi. 105 ; Cole's manuscripts, v. 27 sq.; Hunter's manuscript (Addit. MS. 24478, p. 114 *b*); Firmin's will at Somerset House.]

A. G.

FIRTH, MARK (1819–1880), founder of Firth College, Sheffield, was born at Sheffield 25 April 1819 and left school in 1833. His father, Thomas Firth, was for several years the chief melter of steel to the firm of Sanderson Brothers & Co., Sheffield, receiving 70*s.* a week; here his two sons, Mark and Thomas, on leaving school, joined him, and each had 20*s.* a week. Their demand for an increase of wages being refused, they commenced a business of their own with a six-hole furnace in Charlotte Street (1843). At first they manufactured steel exclusively for home consumption, and then gradually extended their business to Birmingham. By perseverance and energy they at last acquired an immense American connection, and in 1849 erected the Norfolk Works at Sheffield, which cover thirteen acres of ground. In 1848

Thomas Firth, senior, died, and Mark became the head of the firm, which soon acquired other works at Whittington in Derbyshire, which occupy twenty-two acres, and several forges at Clay Wheels, near Wadsley. A speciality of the business was casting steel blocks for ordnance, and shot both spherical and elongated, in addition to all kinds of heavy forgings for engineering purposes. From gun-blocks of seven inches diameter they went up to sixteen inches for the 81-ton gun, the heaviest single casting made. The whole of the steel employed in the manufacture of guns for the British government was Firth's steel. When the government found it necessary to have a steel core for their great guns, the Firths laid down machinery which cost them 100,000*l.*, it being understood that they should be compensated for their outlay by receiving the government work. The principal feature of their business was the refining and manufacture of steel, in which they were unrivalled. They supplied foreign iron, which they imported in immense quantities from Swedish mines, of which they had concessions. After supplying the Italians with a 100-ton gun, they cast a dozen similar ingots for massive ordnance. The British government obtained four of these, but they were never used in the armament of any war ship. The Firths furnished nearly all the steel gun tubes afloat in the British navy, and a large proportion of those used by the French. Three younger brothers, John, Edward, and Henry, became members of the firm of T. Firth & Sons. Mark Firth was one of the original members of the Iron and Steel Institute on its establishment in 1869, and remained connected with it to his decease. Having gained a large fortune, he made many donations to his native place. His first gift of any magnitude was 1,000*l.*, which he added to a legacy of 5,000*l.* left by his brother Thomas (*d.* 1858) for the erection of a Methodist New Connexion training college and the education of young men about to enter the ministry. In 1869 he erected and endowed Mark Firth's Almshouses at Ranmoor, near his own residence, at a cost of 30,000*l.*; in this building are thirty-six houses, which are left to the poor of Sheffield for ever. For three successive years he held the office of master cutler, and in his third year entertained Henry, duke of Norfolk, 2 Sept. 1869, on the occasion of his taking possession of his estates as lord of Hallamshire. His next gift was a freehold park of thirty-six acres for a recreation ground. The Prince and Princess of Wales opened this park on 16 Aug. 1875, and were for two days Firth's guests at Sheffield.

Perhaps the most useful act of his life was the erection and fitting up of Firth College at a cost of 20,000*l.*, its endowment with 5,000*l.*, and the foundation of a chair of chemistry with 150*l.* a year. This building was opened by Prince Leopold 20 Oct. 1879, and a great educational work has since been carried on in the institution. Firth, who was mayor of Sheffield in 1875, died of apoplexy and paralysis at his seat, Oakbrook, 28 Nov. 1880, and was buried in Sheffield general cemetery on 2 Dec., when a public procession nearly two miles in length followed his remains to the grave. His personalty was sworn under 600,000*l.* in January 1881. He married first, 15 Sept. 1841, Sarah Bingham, who died in 1855, and secondly Caroline Bradley, in September 1857, and left nine children.

[Practical Magazine (1876), vi. 289–91, with portrait; Gatty's Sheffield Past and Present (1873), pp. 305, 312, 332–4, with view of Firth's Almshouses; Hunter's Hallamshire (Gatty's ed. 1869), p. 215; Times, 29 Nov. 1880, p. 9, and 3 Dec., p. 3; Illustrated London News, 21 Aug. 1875, pp. 185–90, and 28 Aug., pp. 193, 196, 208, with portrait; Engineer, 3 Dec. 1880, p. 417; Journal of Iron and Steel Institute, 1880, No. 2, pp. 687–8.] G. C. B.

FISCHER, JOHANN CHRISTIAN (1733–1800), oboist and composer, lived many years in London, was chamber musician to the queen (Charlotte), and took a prominent part in the Bach-Abel and other concerts of modern classical music which were to bring about a great change in musical taste. Born at Freiburg (Breisgau) in 1733, Fischer was in 1760 a member of the Dresden court band, and later entered the service of Frederick the Great for a short time. In the course of his travels he came to London, took lodgings, according to an advertisement of the time, at Stidman's, peruke-maker, Frith Street, Soho, and announced his concert for 2 June 1768. As early as 1774 he joined the quartet parties at court, but his appointment as queen's musician dates from 1780, with a salary of 180*l.* 'The original stipend of the court musicians,' says Mrs. Papendiek in her journals, 'had been 100*l.*; but on giving up their house 30*l.* had been added, and 25*l.* for the Ancient Music concerts. They had four suits of clothes, fine instruments, and able masters to instruct them when required.' The same lady gives a lively account (p. 143) of the practical jokes played on the popular oboist by the Prince of Wales and his friends (see also KELLY, Reminiscences, i. 9, and PARKE, p. 48, for anecdotes). Fischer established his reputation in England by his brilliant playing at the Professional, Nobility, and New Musical Fund concerts, and espe-

cially at the Handel commemoration performances at Westminster Abbey. In 1780 he married Mary, the beautiful younger daughter of Gainsborough; it is said that a separation soon followed. Perhaps it was because he was refused the post of master of the king's band and composer of minuets that Fischer left England in 1786, but in spite of disappointments of various kinds he returned in 1790 to London. On the night of 29 April 1800, while performing a solo part in his concerto at the Queen's House, and 'after having executed his first movement in a style equal to his best performance during any part of his life,' he was seized with an apoplectic fit. Prince William of Gloucester supported him out of the room, and the king, who was much affected, had the best medical assistance called; but Fischer died within an hour at his lodgings in Soho, desiring in his last moments that all his manuscript music might be presented to his majesty.

George III has recorded his appreciation of his faithful musician's performance in a critical note appended in his own handwriting to the proof-sheets of Dr. Burney's 'Account of the Handel Commemoration.' The testimony of the younger Parke, himself an oboist of repute, is of even greater value. After remarking that Fischer arrived in this country in very favourable circumstances, the two principal oboe players, Vincent and Simpson, using an instrument which in shape and tone bore some resemblance to a post-horn, he continues : 'The tone of Fischer was soft and sweet, his style expressive, and his execution at once neat and brilliant.' A. B. C. Dario compared the tone of his oboe to that of a clarionet, Giardini commented on its power, and Burney and Mrs. Papendiek agree in praising him. Mozart, on the other hand, writing from Vienna 4 April 1787, observes that whereas Fischer's performance had pleased him upwards of twenty years ago in Holland, it now appeared to him undeserving of its reputation. Mozart was even more severe upon Fischer's compositions, yet he paid a substantial compliment to the celebrated minuet (composed by Fischer for a court ball on the occasion of the king of Denmark's visit to England) by writing and often playing a set of variations upon it (Köchel, No. 179); and Burney bears witness to the merit of his style.

There were published at Berlin : Oboe concerto ; pianoforte concerto ; popular rondo ; concerto for violin, flute, or oboe ; six duos for two flutes, Op. 2 ; ten solos for flute and oboe. In London appeared : Three concertos for principal oboe, Nos. 8, 9, 10 ; the same for pianoforte ; seven divertimentos for two flutes; ten sonatas for flute; three quartets and two trios for German flutes, violin, viola, and cello, from eminent masters, revised by J. C. Fischer (GERBER). Pohl mentions 'God save great George our King,' for four solo voices, chorus and harp accompaniment, newly harmonised; and 'The Invocation of Neptune,' solo quartet and chorus.

Gainsborough's portrait of Fischer, now at Hampton Court, is full of expression; another by the same artist is mentioned by Thicknesse, 'painted at full length . . . . in scarlet and gold, like a Colonel of the Foot Guards.' It is said to have been exposed for sale at a picture dealer's in Catherine Street.

[Burney's History of Music, iv. 673; Mendel, iii. 540; Grove's Dict. i. 528; Pohl's Mozart und Haydn in London, ii. 53; The Gazetteer, No. 12, p. 246; Mrs. Papendiek's Journals, i. 65, ii. 125; Parke's Musical Memoirs, pp. 48, 334; Fulcher's Life of Gainsborough, pp. 74, 118, 200; Thicknesse's Gainsborough, 1788, p. 24; Times, 1 May 1800; Gent. Mag. vol. lxx. pt. i. p. 488; D'Arblay's Memoir of Burney, 1832, ii. 385; Jahn's Mozart, 1882, ii. 343; Gerber's Tonkünstler-Lexikon, 1812, i. 137.] L. M. M.

FISCHER, JOHN GEORGE PAUL (1786–1875), painter, born at Hanover on 16 Sept. 1786, was the youngest of three sons of a line-engraver, who died very soon after the birth of the youngest child, leaving his family in poverty. Fischer at the age of fourteen was placed as pupil with J. H. Ramberg, the fashionable court painter, by whom he was employed in painting portraits, theatrical scenery, and generally assisting his master. He became capable of earning enough money to support his mother. In 1810 he betook himself to England, and his Hanoverian connection rendered it easy for him to obtain the patronage of royalty. He painted miniature portraits of Queen Charlotte and the junior members of the royal family, and was employed by the prince regent to paint a series of military costumes. He painted the present queen twice, once in 1819 as an infant in her cradle, and again in 1820. In 1817 he began to exhibit at the Royal Academy, and continued to do so up to 1852, occasionally contributing also to the Suffolk Street Exhibition. His works were chiefly portraits in miniature, but he occasionally exhibited landscapes in water-colours. He continued to paint up to his eighty-first year, and died 12 Sept. 1875. Fischer was an industrious but inferior artist. Some sketches by him in the print room at the British Museum show spirit and intelligence, especially two pencil portraits of William Hunt and his wife. He published a few etchings and lithographs.

[Redgrave's Dict. of Artists; Graves's Dict. of Artists, 1760–1880; Royal Academy Catalogues.] L. C.

FISH, SIMON (d. 1531), theologian and pamphleteer, was a member of the university of Oxford, and entered Gray's Inn about 1525, which is the first date that can be approximately fixed in his life. In London he formed one of a circle of young men who gave expression to the popular dislike of Wolsey and denounced the riches of the church. One of their boldest undertakings was the production of an interlude, written by one Mater Roo (a member of Queens' College, Cambridge), the object of which was to hold up Wolsey to ridicule. Fish acted a part in this interlude, and, fearing the wrath of Wolsey, fled into the Low Countries, where he consorted with other English exiles, chief of whom were Tyndale and Roy. From them it would seem that he learned the principles of protestantism, and he turned his energies to the promotion of the Reformation in England. Wolsey's wrath against him soon passed away, and he returned to London, where he acted as an agent for the sale of Tyndale's New Testament. He lived in a house by the White Friars, and one Necton confessed that he bought from him copies of Tyndale's prohibited book, 'now five, now ten, to the number of twenty or thirty' (Necton's confession in STRYPE, Memorials, i. App. No. 22). Such conduct drew on him suspicion, and he again fled to the Low Countries, probably about the end of 1527. There he wrote his famous 'Supplication of the Beggars.'

So far it is possible to adapt Foxe's narrative (Acts and Monuments, ed. 1837, iv. 656, &c.) to other known facts about Fish's life. About the date of the 'Supplication' and its influence in England, Foxe gives two contradictory accounts without seeing that they are contradictory: (1) He tells us that Fish found means to send a copy of the 'Supplication' to Anne Boleyn early in 1528; Anne was advised by her brother to show it to Henry VIII, who was much amused by it and kept the copy. On hearing this Mrs. Fish made suit to the king for her husband's return, but apparently received no answer. However, on Wolsey's fall, in October 1529, Fish ventured to return, and had a private interview with Henry VIII, who 'embraced him with a loving countenance,' and gave him his signet ring as a protection against Sir Thomas More, in case the new chancellor should continue the grudge of his predecessor. (2) He tells us that the book was brought to the king by two London merchants, who read it aloud. When they had done the king said, 'If a man should pull down an old stone wall, and begin at the lower part, the upper part thereof might chance to fall upon his head,' meaning that Fish's exhortation to deal with the monks and friars was hazardous advice until the royal supremacy had been established. After saying this the king took the book and put it away, commanding the merchants to keep their interview a secret. Of these accounts the first is very improbable in itself, and makes Fish a much more important personage than he was. Moreover, Foxe evidently thought that Wolsey was Fish's personal enemy, and he did not know of Fish's return to London and of his second flight. The second account of Henry VIII's interview with the London merchants is quite credible in itself, and the king's remark is so characteristic both of the man and of the times as to make the story extremely probable. If this be accepted, Fish's 'Supplication' was written in 1528, was brought secretly to London at the end of that year, and was presented to Henry VIII early in 1529. Henry VIII, who was feeling his way towards an ecclesiastical revolution, appreciated the advantage of winning popular support. Fish's pamphlet was admirably fitted to impress men's minds, and just before the assembling of parliament in November London was flooded with copies of it, in a way which suggests the connivance of some one in authority. 'The Supplication of the Beggars' was exactly suited to express in a humorous form the prevalent discontent. It purported to be a petition from the class of beggars, complaining that they were robbed of their alms by the extortions of the begging friars; then the monks and the clergy generally were confounded with the friars, and were denounced as impoverishing the nation and living in idleness. Statistics were given in an exaggerated form; England was said to contain fifty thousand parish churches (the writer was counting every hamlet as a parish), and on that basis clerical revenues were computed, with the result that a third of the national revenue was shown to be in the hands of the church. The pamphlet was judged by Sir Thomas More to be of sufficient importance to need an answer, 'The Supplication of Poor Soules in Purgatory,' which is fairly open to the criticism that it makes the penitents in purgatory express themselves in very unchastened language about events on earth.

At the end of 1529 Fish returned to England; but, though Henry VIII was ready to use Fish's spirited attack upon the church, he was not prepared to avow the fact, or to stand between him and the enemies whom he had raised up. It is not surprising that he was suspected of heresy, that his book was condemned by Archbishop Warham (WILKINS, *Concilia*, iii. 737), and that he was in great difficulties. Whether the pressure of his difficulties overcame him, or he underwent a change of opinion we cannot tell; but Sir Thomas More wrote: 'This good zele had, ye wote well, Symon Fysh when he made the Supplication of Beggars; but God gave him such grace afterwards that he was sorry for that good zele, and repented himself, and came into the church again, and forswore and forsook all the whole hill of those heresies out of which the fountain of that same good zele sprang' (*Works*, ed. 1557, p. 881). Perhaps More overestimated the result of his answer to Fish. At all events, Fish's perplexities were ended by his death of the plague early in 1531. Very soon after his death his wife married James Bainham [q. v.], who was burned as a heretic in April 1532.

Fish's 'Supplication' was not only remarkable for its vigorous style and for its immediate influence, but was the model for a series of pamphlets couched in the same form. It was first printed in England in 1546, and was embodied in Foxe's 'Acts and Monuments' (iv. 660, &c., ed. 1837). It has also been edited, with three of its successors in the same style, in 'Four Supplications,' by Furnivall and Cooper, for the Early English Text Society, 1871. Besides this work Foxe also ascribes to Fish a 'Summe of Scripture done out of Dutch,' of which a unique copy exists in a volume of pamphlets in the British Museum (C. 37, *a*), where it was first identified by Mr. Arber in his introduction to a 'Proper Dialogue in Rede me and be not Wroth' (*English Reprints*, 1871). There are also assigned to Fish 'The Boke of Merchants, rightly necessary to all Folks, newly made by the Lord Pantopole' (London, 1547), and 'The Spiritual Nosegay' (1548).

[Foxe's Acts and Monuments, iv. 656, &c.; Wood's Athenæ Oxon. ed. Bliss, i. 59; Tanner's Bibliotheca, p. 280; Furnivall's Introduction to the Supplication (Early English Text Soc.), 1871.] M. C.

FISH, WILLIAM (1775–1866), a musician of Norwich, was born in that city in 1775. He commenced his musical career as violinist (GROVE) in the orchestra of the theatre, and, after studying under Sharp, the oboist, and Bond, the pianist and organist, was fitted to take part in various capacities in the important local concerts and cathedral festivals. He was organist of St. Andrew's, Norwich, opened a music warehouse, and became well known in the neighbourhood as a teacher. He died 15 March 1866, a later date than that suggested by the musical dictionaries. Fish's Opus I., a sonata in the Mozartean manner, was followed by a number of less interesting pianoforte pieces, some ballads (words and music by the composer), among which 'The Morning Star' may be singled out, an oboe concerto, and some fantasias for the harp. His unpublished works are said to have included a manuscript cantata to words by Mrs. Opie, and some pieces (presumably for band) played at the Norwich Theatre.

[Grove's Dict. i. 530; Dict. of Musicians, 1827, i. 249; History of Norfolk, 1829, ii. 1283; Notes from Register Office, Norwich; Norfolk News, 17 March 1866; Fish's music in Brit. Mus. Library.]   L. M. M.

FISHACRE, FISSAKRE, FISHAKLE, or FIZACRE, RICHARD DE (d. 1248), Dominican divine, is said to have been a native of Devonshire (FULLER, i. 442, iii. 20). Trivet styles him 'natus Oxonia,' where, however, other manuscripts read Exonia (p. 230). Bale makes him study 'the scurrilities of the Sophists' at Oxford and Paris; but the whole story of the latter visit is probably nothing more than the expansion of a very dubious suggestion in Leland's 'Commentaries' (BALE, p. 294; LELAND, ii. 275). Like Robert Bacon [q. v.], Fishacre in his old age became a Dominican; but as the two friends continued to read divinity lectures for several years after entering the order in the schools of St. Edward, his entry can hardly be dated later than 1240, and perhaps like Robert Bacon's should be placed ten or more years earlier (TRIVET, pp. 229-30). The two comrades died in the same year, 1248 (MATT. PARIS, v. 16). In their own days they were considered to be without superior, or even equal, in theology or other branches of science; nor was their eloquence in popular preaching less remarkable (ib.) Leland calls Fishacre, Robert Bacon's 'comes individuus,' and adds that the two were as fast linked together in friendship as ever Theseus was to Pirithous. He even hints that the former died of grief on hearing of his friend's decease (LELAND, ii. 275; FULLER, ubi supra). Fishacre was buried among the Friars Preachers at Oxford. He was the first of his order in England who wrote on the 'Sentences' (Oriel MS. No. 43, quoted in Coxe). Wood makes him a friend and auditor of Edmund Rich (Hist. II. ii. 740).

Fishacre's works are: 1. Commentaries on Peter Lombard's 'Book of Sentences,' four books (manuscripts at Oriel College, Nos. 31, 43, and Balliol, No. 57, Oxford, and, according to Echard, at the Sorbonne in Paris, &c.) 2. Treatises on the Psalter (to the seventieth Psalm only according to Trivet). 3. 'Super Parabolas Salamonis.' To these Bale adds other dissertations: 'De Pœnitate,' 'Postillæ Morales,' 'Commentarii Bibliæ,' 'Quæstiones Variæ,' 'Quodlibeta quoque et alia plura.' Pits says he was the first Englishman to become a doctor in divinity. The same writer states that Thomas Walden, the great anti-Wycliffite theologian of the early part of the fifteenth century, often appeals to Fishacre's authority; while Bale adds that William Woodford (d. 1397), the Franciscan, and William Byntre relied on him for the same purpose. Echard assigns him another work, 'De Indulgentiis.'

[Matt. Paris, ed. Luard (Rolls Ser.), vol. v.; Trivet, ed. Hog (Engl. Hist. Soc.); Leland's Commentaries, ed. 1709; Bale's Scriptores, ed. 1559, p. 294; Pits's Commentaries, ed. 1619, p. 317; Fuller's Worthies, ed. 1840, i. 422, iii. 419-20; Anthony à Wood's Hist. and Antiquities of Oxford, ed. Gutch, ii. 740; Echard's Scriptores Ordinis Prædicatorum, i. 118-19; Coxe's Cat. of Oxford MSS.; Tanner's Scriptores.]   T. A. A.

FISHER, CATHERINE MARIA (d. 1767), afterwards NORRIS, generally known as KITTY FISHER, courtesan, seems to have been of German origin, since her name is frequently spelt Fischer, and once by Sir Joshua Reynolds Fisscher. She became the second wife of John Norris of Hempsted Manor, Benenden, Kent, sometime M.P. for Rye. Her later life, in which she devoted herself to building up her husband's dilapidated fortunes, was in striking contrast with her previous career, which was sufficiently notorious. Ensign (afterwards Lieutenant-general) Anthony George Martin (d. 1800) is said to have introduced her into public life. In London she was known as a daring horsewoman, and also credited with the possession of beauty and wit. A satire in verse, 'Kitty's Stream, or the Noblemen turned Fishermen. A comic Satire addressed to the Gentlemen in the interest of the celebrated Miss K——y F——r. By Rigdum Funnidos,' 1759, 4to, of which a copy, with manuscript notes by the Rev. John Mitford, is in the British Museum, says that her parentage was 'low and mean,' that she was a milliner, and had neither sense nor wit, but only impudence. Other tracts concerning her, mentioned in the 'Gentleman's Magazine,' 1760, are 'An odd Letter on a most interesting subject to Miss K. F—h—r,' 6d., Williams; 'Miss K. F—'s Miscellany,' 1s., Ranger (in verse); and 'Elegy to K. F—h—r.' A further satire on her among the satirical tracts in the king's library at the British Museum is 'Horse and Away to St. James's Park on a Trip for the Noontide Air. Who rides fastest, Miss Kitty Fisher or her gay gallant?' It is a single page, and claims to have been written and printed at Strawberry Hill. Mme. d'Arblay states (*Memoirs*, i. 66) that Bet Flint once took Kitty Fisher to see Dr. Johnson, but he was not at home, to her great regret. She died at Bath, and at her own request was placed in the coffin in her best dress. This gave rise to 'An Elegy on Kitty Fisher lying in state at Bath' (query same as the elegy previously mentioned?), an undated broadside with music assigned to Mr. Harrington. She was buried at Benenden. The Benenden registers give the date of her burial as 23 March 1767. It has been attempted to associate her with folklore in the expressions, ' My eye, Kitty Fisher,' and in a rhyme beginning ' Lucy Locket lost her pocket, Kitty Fisher found it.' Her chief claim to recognition is that Sir Joshua Reynolds more than once painted her portrait. Several paintings of her by him seem to be in existence. One was in the possession of John, first baron Tollemache, of Peckforton, Cheshire. Others were in 1867 lent to the National Portrait Gallery by the Earl of Morley and by Lord Crewe. The last is doubtless that concerning which in Sir Joshua's diary, under the date April 1774, is the entry, ' Mr. Crewe for Kitty Fisher's portrait, 52*l*. 10*s*.' This is curious, however, in being seven years after Mrs. Norris's death. Mitford says in his manuscript notes before mentioned that a portrait by Sir Joshua is ' at Field-marshal Grosvenor's, Ararat House, Richmond,' and one is gone to America. Two portraits, one representing her as Cleopatra dissolving the pearls, are engraved. In the 'Public Advertiser' of 30 March 1759 is an appeal to the public, signed C. Fisher, against ' the baseness of little scribblers and scurvy malevolence.' After complaining that she has been ' abused in public papers, exposed in printshops,' &c., she cautions the public against some threatened memoirs, which will have no foundation in truth. The character of Kitty Willis in Mrs. Cowley's 'The Belle's Stratagem' is taken from Kitty Fisher. Hone's ' Every-day Book' says in error that ' she became Duchess of Bolton,' and Cunningham's ' Handbook to London' states that she lived in Carrington Street, Mayfair.

[Notes and Queries, 3rd ser. viii. 81, 155, 4th ser. v. 319, 410; Bromley's Cat. of Engraved Portraits; Ann. Reg. ii. 168; Boswell's Johnson, ed. Birkbeck Hill; works cited.]   J. K.

FISHER, DANIEL (1731–1807), dissenting minister, born at Cockermouth in 1731, was appointed in 1771 tutor in classics and mathematics at Homerton College, where he was afterwards divinity tutor. He was a rigid Calvinist and staunch dissenter. He died at Hackney in 1807 after a lingering illness, in which he lost the use of all his faculties. Two funeral sermons were preached on the occasion, one of which, by the Rev. Samuel Palmer, was published under the title of 'The General Union of Believers,' London, 1807, 8vo.

[Brit. Mus. Cat.; Evans's Cat. of Engraved British Portraits, ii. 152.]   J. M. R.

FISHER, DAVID, the elder (1788?– 1858), actor, one of the managers of Fisher's company, which had a monopoly of the Suffolk theatres, was the son of David Fisher (*d*. 6 Aug. 1832), manager of the same circuit. Fisher made his first appearance in London at Drury Lane, as Macbeth, 3 Dec. 1817. This was followed on the 5th by Richard III, and on the 10th by Hamlet. The recovery from illness of Kean arrested his career. On 24 Sept. 1818, at Drury Lane, then under Stephen Kemble, he played Jaffier in ' Venice Preserved.' Subsequently he appeared as Lord Townly in the ' Provoked Husband,' and Pyrrhus in ' Orestes.' He was the original Titus in Howard Payne's ' Brutus, or the Fall of Tarquin,' 3 Dec. 1818, and Angelo in Buck's ' Italians, or the Fatal Accusation,' 3 April 1819. He failed to establish any strong position, and discovered at the close of the second season that his presence was necessary on the Suffolk circuit. On 7 Nov. 1823 he appeared at Bath in ' Hamlet,' and subsequently as Shylock, Leon, and Jaffier. He was pronounced a sound actor, but with no claim to genius, and failed to please. Returning again to the eastern counties, he built theatres at Bungay, Beccles, Halesworth, Eye, Lowestoft, Dereham, North Walsham, and other places. About 1838 he retired to Woodbridge, where he died 20 Aug. 1858. He was a musician and a scene-painter, and in the former capacity was leader for some time of the Norwich choral concerts.

[Genest's Account of the English Stage; Gent. Mag. 1858, ii. 422; Theatrical Inquisitor, vol. xi.]   J. K.

FISHER, DAVID, the younger (1816?– 1887), actor, the son of David Fisher the elder [q. v.], was born at East Dereham, Norfolk, a town on a circuit established by his grandfather, and managed by his father and his uncle. An accident to his leg disqualified him for the stage, and he appeared as principal violinist at local concerts. A recovery, never perfect, enabled him to join the company at the Prince's Theatre, Glasgow. After a stay of four years he appeared 2 Nov. 1853 at the Princess's Theatre, under Charles Kean's management, as Victor in the 'Lancers, or the Gentleman's Son,' an adaptation of 'Le Fils de Famille' of Bayard. During six years he played at this house in various novelties and revivals, including a trifling production from his own pen entitled 'Music hath Charms' (June 1858). In 1859 he joined the Adelphi under B. Webster's management, where he was the original Abbé Latour in the 'Dead Heart' of Watts Phillips. In 1863 he gave, at the Hanover Square Rooms and at St. James's Hall, an entertainment called 'Facts and Fancies,' and in the autumn of the same year rejoined the Princess's, then under Vining's management. In 1865 he played, at the Haymarket, Orpheus in Planché's 'Orpheus in the Haymarket.' In 1866–8 he was at Liverpool as stage-manager for Mr. H. J. Byron, playing at the Amphitheatre and Alexandra Theatre. When the Globe Theatre, London, opened, 28 Nov. 1868, he was the first Major Treherne in Byron's 'Cyril's Success.' He appeared in succession at Drury Lane, the Olympic, the Globe, the Opera Comique, the Criterion, the Mirror (Holborn) Theatre, now destroyed, and the Princess's, playing in pieces by H. J. Byron, Mr. Boucicault, and other writers. His last appearance in London was at the Lyceum in 1884, as Sir Toby Belch. After that period he played in the country. He died in St. Augustine's Road, Camden Town, on 4 Oct. 1887, and was buried at Highgate cemetery. The 'Era' says that not a single actor attended his funeral. Fisher was below the middle height, a stiff-built man, who tried to conceal his lameness by a dancing-master elegance. Concerning his Abbé Latour, John Oxenford said in the 'Times' that 'he came to the Adelphi a second-rate eccentric comedian, and showed himself an able supporter of the serious drama.' He left a son on the stage, who perpetuated the name of David Fisher borne by at least four generations of actors.

[Pascoe's Dramatic List, 1879; The Players, 1860; Cole's Life and Times of Charles Kean; Era newspaper, 8 and 15 Oct.; personal recollections.]   J. K.

FISHER, EDWARD (*fl.* 1627–1656), theological writer, was the eldest son of Sir Edward Fisher, knight, of Mickleton, Gloucestershire. In 1627 he entered as a gentleman commoner at Brasenose College, Oxford, and graduated B.A. on 10 April 1630. He was noted for his knowledge of ecclesiastical history and his skill in ancient languages. He was a royalist, and a strong upholder of the festivals of the church against the puritans. He based the obligation of the Lord's day purely on ecclesiastical authority, declining to consider it a sabbath. He succeeded to his father's estate in 1654, but finding it much encumbered he sold it in 1656 to Richard Graves. Getting into debt he retired to Carmarthen and taught a school, but his creditors found him out, and he fled to Ireland. Here he died, at what date is not known. His body was brought to London for burial. He was married, but his wife died before him. The only publications which can be safely identified as his are: 1. 'The Scriptures Harmony . . . by E. F., Esq.,' &c., 1643, 4to (a tract somewhat on the lines of Hugh Broughton's 'Concent of Scripture,' 1588). 2. 'An Appeale to thy Conscience,' &c., without place, 'printed in the 19th yeare of our gracious lord King Charles,' &c. (British Museum copy dated 20 April 1643; it is quite anonymous, but easily identified as Fisher's). 3. 'The Feast of Feasts, or the Celebration of the Sacred Nativity,' &c., Oxf. 1644, 4to (quite anonymous, but identified as Fisher's by the Bodleian Catalogue, and in his style). 4. 'A Christian Caveat to the old and new Sabbatarians, or a Vindication of our Gospel Festivals . . . By a Lover of Truth; a Defender of Christian Liberty; and an hearty Desirer of Peace, internall, externall, eternall to all men,' &c., 1649 (i.e. 1650), 4to; 4th edit. 1652, 4to, 'By Edward Fisher, Esq.,' has appended 'An Answer to Sixteen Queries touching the . . . observation of Christmass, propounded by Joseph Hemming of Uttoxeter' (reprinted 'Somers Tracts,' 1748, vol. iv.); 5th edit. 1653, 4to; another edit. 1655, 4to, has appended 'Questions preparatory to the more Christian Administration of the Lord's Supper . . . by E. F., Esq.' The 'Caveat,' which reckons Christmas day and Good Friday as of equal authority with the Lord's day, was attacked by John Collinges, D.D. [q. v.], and by Giles Collier [q. v.] Parts of the 'Caveat' were reprinted by the Seventh Day Baptists of America, in 'Tracts on the Sabbath,' New York, 1853, 18mo.

In Tanner's edition of Wood's 'Athenæ,' 1721, Fisher is identified with E. F., the author of the 'Marrow of Modern Divinity' [see BOSTON, THOMAS, the elder]; and the identification has been accepted by Bliss, Hill Burton, and others. It is doubted by Grub, and internal evidence completely disproves it. The author of the 'Marrow' has been described as 'an illiterate barber,' but nothing seems known of him except that in his dedication to John Warner, the lord mayor, he speaks of himself as a 'poore inhabitant' of London. The following publications, all cast into the form of dialogue, and bearing the imprimatur of puritan licensers, may be safely ascribed to the same hand: 1. 'The Marrow of Modern Divinity ... by E. F.,' &c., 1645, 8vo; 4th edit. 1646, 8vo, has recommendatory letters by Burroughes, Strong, Sprigge, and Prittie. 2. 'A Touchstone for a Communicant ... by E. F.,' &c., 1647, 12mo (Caryl's imprimatur). 3. 'The Marrow of Modern Divinity: the Second Part ... by E. F.,' &c., 1649, 8vo. The 19th edit. of the 'Marrow' was published at Montrose, 1803, 12mo. It was translated into Welsh by John Edwards, a sequestered clergyman; his dedication is dated 20 July 1650; later editions are Trefecca, 1782, 12mo; Carmarthen, 1810, 12mo. 4. 'London's Gate to the Lord's Table,' &c., 1647, 12mo; the title-page is anonymous, but the signature 'E. F.' appears at the end of the dedication to Judge Henry Rolle of the pleas, and Margaret his wife. 5. 'Faith in Five Fundamentall Principles ... by E. F., a Seeker of the Truth,' &c., 1650, 12mo.

[Wood's Athenæ Oxon. 1691 i. 866, 1692 ii. 132; Wood's Athenæ Oxon. (Bliss), iii. 407 sq.; Burton's History of Scotland, 1853, ii. 317; Grub's Ecclesiastical History of Scotland, 1861, iv. 54; Cox's Literature of the Sabbath Question, 1865, i. 237, &c. ii. 418; Rees's History of Protestant Nonconformity in Wales, 1883, p. 77 (compare Walker's Sufferings, 1714, ii. 237); publications of Fisher and E. F.] A. G.

FISHER, EDWARD (1730–1785?), mezzotint engraver, born in Ireland in 1730, was at first a hatter, but took to engraving, went to London, and became a member of the Incorporated Society of Artists in 1766, where he exhibited fourteen times between 1761 and 1776. His earliest dated print is 1758, and his latest 1781. He resided in 1761 in Leicester Square, and moved to Ludgate Street in 1778. It is said that Reynolds called him 'injudiciously exact' for finishing too highly the unimportant parts of the plate. After his death, about 1785, most of his coppers were dispersed among several printsellers, and in some cases tampered with. He engraved over sixty plates of portraits, including George, earl of Albemarle, after Reynolds; Robert Brown, after Chamberlin; William Pitt, earl of Chatham, after Brompton; Colley Cibber, after Vanloo; Christian VII of Denmark, after Dance; David Garrick, after Reynolds; Simon, earl Harcourt, after Hunter; Roger Long, after B. Wilson; Hugh, earl of Northumberland, and Elizabeth, countess of Northumberland, after Reynolds; Paul Sandby, after F. Cotes; Laurence Sterne, after Reynolds; and the following fancy subjects: 'Lady in Flowered Dress,' after Hoare; 'Hope Nursing Love,' or, according to Bromley, Theophila Palmer,

afterwards Mrs. Gwatkin, after Reynolds; and 'Heads from "Vicar of Wakefield,"' ten plates engraved from his own designs and published in 1776.

[Redgrave's Dict. of Artists; J. Chaloner Smith's Descriptive Catalogue of British Mezzotints, pt. ii. p. 485.] L. F.

FISHER, GEORGE (1794–1873), astronomer, was born at Sunbury in Middlesex on 31 July 1794. One of a large family left to the care of a widowed mother, he received little early education, and entered the office of the Westminster Insurance Company at the age of fourteen. Here his devotion to uncongenial duties won the respect and rewards of his employers. His scientific aspirations had, however, been fostered by Sir Humphry Davy, Sir Joseph Banks, Sir Everard Home, and other eminent men, and he entered St. Catharine's College, Cambridge, in 1817, whence he graduated B.A. in 1821, M.A. in 1825. His university career was interrupted by his appointment, on the recommendation of the Royal Society, as astronomer to the polar expedition fitted out in H.M. ships Dorothea and Trent in 1818. The highest latitude attained was 80° 34', and both vessels returned to England disabled before the close of the year; but Fisher had made a series of pendulum experiments at Spitzbergen, from which he deduced the value $\frac{1}{303}$ for the ellipticity of the earth. The results of his observations on the ships' chronometers were embodied in a paper read before the Royal Society on 8 June 1820, entitled 'On the Errors in Longitude as determined by Chronometers at Sea, arising from the Action of the Iron in the Ships upon the Chronometers' (Phil. Trans. cx. 196).

Fisher soon afterwards took orders, and qualified himself by formally entering the navy to act as chaplain as well as astronomer to Parry's expedition for exploring the northwest passage in 1821–3. A 'portable' observatory, embarked on board the Fury, was set up first at Winter Island, later at Igloolik, and Captain Parry testified to the 'unabated zeal and perseverance' with which Fisher pursued his scientific inquiries. He devoted much care to the preparation of the results for the press, and they formed part of a volume, published at government expense in 1825, as an appendix to Parry's 'Journal of a Second Voyage for the Discovery of a North-West Passage.' Astronomical, chronometrical, and magnetic observations were accompanied by details of experiments on the velocity of sound, and on the liquefaction of chlorine and other gases at very low temperatures, as well as by an important discussion of nearly four thousand observations on astronomical refraction in an arctic climate.

Fisher was elected a fellow of the Royal Society in 1825, and of the Astronomical Society in 1827, acted several times as vice-president of the latter body, and was a member of the council from 1835 until 1863. Appointed in 1828 chaplain to H.M. ships Spartiate and Asia he carried on magnetic observations in various parts of the Mediterranean, and on 24 Jan. 1833 laid a paper on the subject before the Royal Society, entitled 'Magnetical Experiments made principally in the South part of Europe and in Asia Minor during the years 1827 to 1832' (ib. cxxiii. 237; Proc. R. Soc. iii. 163). His theory of 'The Nature and Origin of the Aurora Borealis' was communicated to the Royal Society on 19 June 1834 (ib. p. 295), and to the British Association at Cambridge in 1845 (Report, pt. ii. p. 22). Founded on a close study of the phenomenon in arctic regions, it included the ideas, since confirmed, of its being the polar equivalent of lightning, and of its origin in a zone surrounding at some distance each pole. Auroræ were thus regarded as a means of restoring electrical equilibrium between the upper and lower strata of the atmosphere, disturbed by the development of positive electricity through rapid congelation.

Fisher accepted in 1834 the post of headmaster of Greenwich Hospital School, and greatly improved the efficiency of the institution. He erected an astronomical observatory in connection with it, which he superintended during thirteen years, observing there the solar eclipse of 18 July 1860 (Monthly Notices, xxi. 19). At the request of Lord Herbert in 1845, he wrote text-books of algebra and geometry for use in the school, of which he became principal in 1860. His retirement followed in 1863, and after ten years of well-earned repose he died without suffering on 14 May 1873.

Besides the papers already mentioned Fisher presented to the Royal Society accounts of magnetic experiments made in the West Indies and North America by Mr. James Napier (Proc. R. Soc. iii. 253), and on the west coast of Africa by Commander Edward Belcher (Phil. Trans. cxxii. 493), and reduced those made on the coasts of Brazil and North America from 1834 to 1837 by Sir Everard Home (ib. cxxviii. 343). He contributed to the 'Quarterly Journal of Science' essays 'On the Figure of the Earth, as deduced from the Measurements of Arcs of the Meridian, and Observations on Pendulums' (vii. 299, 1819); 'On the Variation of the Compass, observed in the late Voyage of Discovery to the North Pole' (ix. 81); and

'On Refractions observed in High Latitudes' (xxi. 348, 1826).

[Monthly Notices, xxxiv. 140; Weld's Hist. of Royal Society, ii. 280; Royal Society's Catalogue of Scientific Papers.]   A. M. C.

FISHER, JAMES (1697–1775), one of the founders of the Scottish secession church, was born on 23 Jan. 1697 at Barr in Ayrshire, where his father, Thomas, was minister, studied at Glasgow University, and was ordained minister of Kinclaven, Perthshire, in 1725. In 1727 he married the daughter of the Rev. Ebenezer Erskine [q. v.] of Portmoak, Kinross-shire, with whom he was afterwards associated as a founder of the secession body. Fisher concurred with Erskine and other likeminded ministers in their views both as to patronage and doctrine, and in opposition to the majority of the general assembly, by whom their representations were wholly disregarded. In 1732 Erskine preached a sermon at the opening of the synod of Perth, in which he boldly denounced the policy of the church as unfaithful to its Lord and Master. For this he was rebuked by the general assembly; but against the sentence he protested, and was joined by three ministers, of whom Fisher was one. The protest was declared to be insulting, and the ministers who signed it were thrust out of the church, and ultimately formed the associate presbytery. The people of Kinclaven adhered almost without exception to their minister, and the congregation increased by accessions from neighbouring parishes. Fisher was subsequently translated to Glasgow (8 Oct. 1741), but was deposed by the associate antiburgher synod 4 Aug. 1748. In 1749 the associate burgher synod gave him the office of professor of divinity. His name is associated with a catechism designed to explain the 'Shorter Catechism of the Westminster Assembly.' What is known as Fisher's 'Catechism' (2 parts, Glasgow, 1753, 1760) was in reality the result of contributions by many ministers of the body, which were made use of by three of the leading men, Ebenezer and Ralph Erskine and Fisher. Fisher survived the other two; and as the duty of giving a final form to the work, as well as executing his own share, devolved on him, it is usually spoken of as his. It is a work of great care, learning, and ability; it has passed through many editions; it was long the manual for catechetical instruction in the secession church; and it was a favourite with evangelical men outside the secession like Dr. Colquhoun of Leith and Robert Haldane [q. v.] Fisher was the author of various other works, chiefly bearing on matters of controversy at the time, and illustrative of

Erskine's work. Though not so attractive a preacher as the Erskines, nor so able an apologist as Wilson, yet by the weight of his character and his public position he exerted a very powerful influence on the secession, and contributed very materially to its progress and stability. He died 28 Sept. 1775, in the seventy-eighth year of his age.

[Scott's Fasti, pt. iv. 802; Memorials of the Rev. James Fisher, by John Brown, D.D. (United Presbyterian Fathers), 1849; M'Kerrow's Hist. of the Secession; Life and Diary of the Rev. E. Erskine, A.M., by Donald Fraser; Walker's Theology and Theologians of Scotland; McCrie's Story of the Scottish Church.]　W. G. B.

FISHER, JASPER (*fl.* 1639), divine and dramatist, born in 1591, was the son of William Fisher of Carleton, Bedfordshire, deputy-auditor for the county of York (descended from a Warwickshire family), by Alice Roane of Wellingborough (*Visitation of Bedfordshire*, Harl. Soc. 1884, xix. 107). Fisher matriculated at Magdalen Hall, Oxford, 13 Nov. 1607; he was admitted B.A. 28 Jan. 1610–11, M.A. 27 Jan. 1613–14, B.D. and D.D. 1639 (CLARK, *Register*, ii. 300). About 1631 (according to Wood) he became rector of Wilsden, Bedfordshire, and in 1633 published his one considerable work, a play, entitled 'Fuimus Troes, the True Trojans, being a story of the Britaines valour at the Romanes first invasion. Publickly presented by the gentlemen students of Magdalen College in Oxford,' London, 1633, 4to. The drama is written in blank verse, interspersed with lyrics; Druids, poets, and a harper are introduced, and it ends with a masque and chorus. Fisher held at Magdalen College the post of divinity or philosophy reader (WOOD). He also published some sermons, one on Malachi ii. 7, 1636, 8vo, and 'The Priest's Duty and Dignity, preached at the Triennial Visitation in Ampthill 18 Aug. 1635, by J. F., presbyter and rector of Wilsden in Bedfordshire, and published by command,' London, 1636, 12mo. The exact date of Fisher's death is uncertain; it is only known that he was alive in 1639, when he proceeded D.D. According to Oldys's manuscript notes to Langbaine he became blind, whether from old age or an accident is not known. Wood calls him 'an ingenious man, as those that knew him have divers times informed me' (*Athenæ*, ii. 636, ed. Bliss). He married Elizabeth, daughter of the Rev. William Sams of Burstead, Essex. Gideon Fisher, who went to Oxford in 1634 and succeeded to the estate at Carleton, was the son, not of Jasper, but of Jasper's elder brother Gideon (*Visitation of Bedfordshire*, 1634, Harl. Soc. 107).

[Brit. Mus. Cat. of Printed Books; Langbaine's English Dramatic Poets, 1691, p. 533; Baker's Biographia Dramatica, 1812.]　E. T. B.

FISHER, JOHN (1459–1535), bishop of Rochester, eldest son of Robert Fisher, mercer, and Agnes, his wife, was born at Beverley in Yorkshire in 1459 (*Sloane MS.* 1898, f. 9), and was probably first educated in the school attached to Rochester Cathedral. There is no serious difficulty in accepting so early a date for Fisher's birth (see *Life* by Lewis, i. 1–2). His portrait by Holbein bears the words, 'Aº Aetatis 74.' As this could scarcely have been painted after his imprisonment in the Tower, it is obvious that Fisher must have been at least seventy-six years of age at the time of his execution. Fisher was clearly well over twenty-six at the time of his admission to the B.A. degree, an unusual age, especially in those days, but not an impossible one. When only thirteen years old he lost his father; the latter would seem to have been a man of considerable substance, and, judging from his numerous bequests to different monastic and other foundations, religious after the fashion of his age. Fisher was subsequently entered at Michaelhouse, Cambridge, under William de Melton, fellow, and afterwards master of the college. In 1487 he proceeded to his degree of bachelor of arts; was soon after elected fellow of Michaelhouse, proceeded to his degree of M.A. in 1491, filled the office of senior proctor in the university in 1494, and became master of his college in 1497. The duties of the proctorial office necessitated, at that time, occasional attendance at court; and Fisher on his appearance in this capacity at Greenwich attracted the notice of the king's mother, Margaret, countess of Richmond, who in 1497 appointed him her confessor.

In 1501 he was elected vice-chancellor of the university. We learn from his own statements, as well as from other sources, that the whole academic community was at that time in a singularly lifeless and impoverished state. To rescue it from this condition, by infusing new life into its studies and gaining for it the help of the wealthy, was one of the chief services which Fisher rendered to his age. In 1503 he was appointed by the Countess of Richmond to fill the newly founded chair of divinity, which she had instituted for the purpose of providing gratuitous theological instruction in the university; and it appears to have been mainly by his advice that about the same time the countess also founded the Lady Margaret preachership, designed for supplying evangelical instruction of the laity in the surrounding county and elsewhere. The preaching was to be in the vernacular, which had at that period almost fallen into disuse in the pulpit.

A succession of appointments now indicated the growing and widespread sense of his services. In 1504 he was elected to the chancellorship of the university, an office to which he was re-elected annually for ten years, and eventually for life. A papal bull (14 Oct. 1504) ratified his election to the see of Rochester, but for this preferment he was indebted solely to King Henry's favour and sense of his 'grete and singular virtue' (*Funeral Sermon*, ed. Hymers, p. 163). On 12 April 1505 Fisher was elected to the presidency of Queens' College, but held the office only for three years. His appointment to the post, it has been conjectured, was mainly with the design of providing him with a suitable residence during the time that he was superintending the erection of Christ's College, which was founded by the Lady Margaret under his auspices in 1505. On the death of Henry VII, Fisher preached the funeral sermon at St. Paul's, and his discourse was subsequently printed at the request of the king's mother. Three months later it devolved upon him to pay a like tribute to the memory of his august benefactress, a discourse which forms a memorable record of her virtues and good works. By a scheme drawn up during her lifetime it was proposed to dissolve an ancient hospital at Cambridge, that of the Brethren of St. John, and to found a college in its place. Fisher was shortly after nominated to attend the Lateran council in Rome (19 April 1512), and a sum of 500*l.* had been assigned for his expenses during 160 days ; but at the last moment it was decided that he should not be sent. This happened fortunately for the carrying out of the Lady Margaret's designs, for Fisher, by remaining in England, was enabled to defeat in some measure the efforts that were made to set aside her bequest ; and it was mainly through his strenuous exertions that St. John's College was eventually founded, its charter being given 9 April 1511. In connection with the college he himself subsequently founded four fellowships and two scholarships, besides lectureships in Greek and Hebrew. In 1513, on Wolsey's promotion to the see of Lincoln, Fisher, in the belief that one who stood so high in the royal favour would be better able to further the interests of the university, proposed to retire from the office of chancellor, advising that Wolsey should be elected in his place. The university acted upon his advice ; but Wolsey having declined the proffered honour,

under the plea of being already overburdened with affairs of state, Fisher was once more appointed. Notwithstanding the deference which he showed to Wolsey on this occasion, there existed between him and the all-powerful minister a strongly antagonistic feeling, of which the true solution is probably indicated by Burnet when he says that Fisher being 'a man of strict life' 'hated him [Wolsey] for his vices' (*Hist. of the Reformation*, ed. Pocock, i. 52). At a council of the clergy held at Westminster in 1517, Fisher gave satisfactory proof that he was actuated by no spirit of adulation ; and in a remarkable speech, wherein he severely censured the greed for gain and the love of display and of court life which characterised many of the higher ecclesiastics of the realm, he was generally supposed to have glanced at the cardinal himself. In 1523 he opposed with no less courage, by a speech in convocation, Wolsey's great scheme for a subsidy in aid of the war with Flanders (HALL, p. 72).

Fisher's genuine attachment to learning is shown by the sympathy which he evinced with the new spirit of biblical criticism which had accompanied the Renaissance. It was mainly through his influence that Erasmus was induced to visit Cambridge, and the latter expressly attributes it to his powerful protection that the study of Greek was allowed to go on in the university without active molestation of the kind which it had to encounter at Oxford (*Epist.* vi. 2). Notwithstanding his advanced years, Fisher himself aspired to become a Greek scholar, and appears to have made some attainments in the language. On the other hand, his attachment to the papal cause remained unshaken, while his hostility to Luther and the Reformation was beyond question. He preached in the vernacular, before Wolsey and Warham, at Paul's Cross, on the occasion of the burning of the reformer's writings in the churchyard (12 May 1521), a discourse which was severely handled by William Tyndale (LEWIS, *Life*, i. 181-3). He replied to Luther's book against the papal bull in a treatise entitled 'A Confutation of the Lutheran Assertion' (1523), and was supposed, although without foundation, to have been the real writer of the royal treatise against Luther, entitled 'Assertio septem Sacramentorum,' published in 1521. He again replied to Luther in his 'Defence of the Christian Priesthood' (1524), and again, for the third time, in his 'Defence' of Henry's treatise, in reply to the reformer's attack (1525). He also wrote against Œcolampadius and Velenus.

With advancing years his conservative

instincts would appear, indeed, sometimes to have prevailed over his better judgment. To the notable scheme of church reform brought forward in the House of Commons in 1529 he offered strenuous resistance, and his language was such that it was construed into a disrespectful reflection on that assembly, and the speaker was directed to make it a matter of formal complaint to the king. Fisher was summoned into the royal presence, and was fain to have recourse to a somewhat evasive explanation, which seems scarcely in harmony with his habitual moral courage and conscientiousness. The statutes which he drew up about this time, to be the codes of Christ's College and St. John's College, are also characterised by a kind of timorous mistrust, and, while embodying a wise innovation on the existing scheme of study, exhibit a pusillanimous anxiety to guard against all subsequent innovations whatever. In the revised statutes which he gave to St. John's College in 1524 and 1530 this tendency is especially apparent; but it is to be observed that some of the new provisions in the latter code were taken from that given by Wolsey to Cardinal College (afterwards Christ Church), Oxford. In 1528 the high estimation in which his services were held by St. John's College was shown by the enactment of a statute for the annual celebration of his exequies.

The unflinching firmness with which he opposed the doctrine of the royal supremacy did honour to his consistency. When convocation was called upon to give its assent, he asserted that the acceptance of such a principle would cause the clergy of England 'to be hissed out of the society of God's holy catholic church' (BAILY, p. 110); and his opposition so far prevailed that the form in which the assent of convocation was ultimately recorded was modified by the memorable saving clause, 'quantum per legem Dei licet' (11 Feb. 1531).

His opposition to the royal divorce was not less honourable and consistent, and he stood alone among the bishops of the realm in his refusal to recognise the validity of the measure. As Queen Catherine's confessor he naturally became her chief confidant. Brewer goes so far as to say that he was 'the only adviser on whose sincerity and honesty she could rely.' From the evidence of the State Papers it would seem, however, that Wolsey, in his desire to further Henry's wishes, did succeed for a time in alienating Fisher from the queen, by skilfully instilling into the bishop's mind a complete misapprehension as to the king's real design in inquiring into the validity of his marriage. But he could not succeed in inducing Fisher

to regard the papal dispensation for Catherine's marriage as invalid, and in 1528 the latter was appointed one of her counsellors. On 28 June 1529 he appeared in the legate's court and made his memorable declaration that 'to avoid the damnation of his soul,' and 'to show himself not unfaithful to the king,' he had come before their lordships 'to assert and demonstrate with cogent reasons that this marriage of the king and queen could not be dissolved by any power, divine or human' (BREWER, *Reign of Henry VIII*, ii. 346). Henry betrayed how deeply he was offended by drawing up a reply (in the form of a speech) in which he attacked both Fisher's character and motives with great acrimony and violence. The copy sent to Fisher is preserved in the Record Office, and contains brief comments in his own handwriting on the royal assertions and misrepresentations. In the following year, one Richard Rouse having poisoned a vessel of yeast which was placed in the bishop's kitchen 'in Lambith Marsh,' several members of the episcopal household died in consequence. By Sanders (*De Schismate*, p. 72) this event was represented as an attempt on the bishop's life by Anne Boleyn, dictated by resentment at his opposition to the divorce.

The weaker side of Fisher's character was shown in the credence and countenance which he gave to the impostures of the Nun of Kent [see BARTON, ELIZABETH]; while the manner in which the professedly inspired maid denounced the projected marriage of Henry and Anne Boleyn brought the bishop himself under the suspicion of collusion. This suspicion was deepened by the fact that the nun, when interrogated before the Starchamber, named him as one of her confederates. He was summoned to appear before parliament to answer the charges preferred against him. On 28 Jan. 1533–4 he wrote to Cromwell describing himself as in a pitiable state of health, and begging to be excused from appearing as commanded. In another letter, written three days later, he speaks as though wearied out by Cromwell's importunity and frequent missives. Cromwell in replying broadly denounces his excuses as 'mere craft and cunning,' and advises him to throw himself on the royal mercy. Chapuys, the imperial ambassador, writing 25 March to Charles V, says that Fisher, whom he characterises as 'the paragon of Christian prelates both for learning and holiness,' has been condemned to 'confiscation of body and goods,' and attributes it to the support which he had given to the cause of Catherine. Fisher was sentenced, along with Adyson, his chaplain, to be attainted of misprision, to be imprisoned at the king's will, and to forfeit all his goods (*Letters and Papers Henry VIII*, vol. ii. No. 70). He was, however, ultimately permitted to compound for his offence by a payment of 300*l*.

On 13 April he was summoned to Lambeth to take the oath of compliance with the Act of Succession. He expressed his willingness, as did Sir Thomas More, to take that portion of the oath which fixed the succession in the offspring of the king and Anne Boleyn, but, like More, he declined the oath in its entirety. Their objection is sufficiently intelligible when we consider that while one clause declared the offspring of Catherine illegitimate, another forbade 'faith, truth, and obedience' to any 'foreign authority or potentate.' The commissioners were evidently unwilling to proceed to extremities, and Cranmer advised that both Fisher and More should be held to have yielded sufficiently for the requirements of the case. Both, however, were ultimately committed to the Tower (Fisher on 16 April), and their fate now began to be regarded as sealed. On the 27th an inventory of the bishop's goods at Rochester was taken, which has recently been printed in 'Letters and Papers' (u. s. pp. 221–2). His library, which he had destined for St. John's College, and, according to Baily, the finest in Christendom, was seized at the same time. In his confinement, Fisher's advanced age and feeble health procured for him no relaxation of the rigorous treatment ordinarily extended to political offenders, and Lee, the bishop of Coventry and Lichfield, who visited him, described him as 'nigh gone,' and his body as unable 'to bear the clothes on the back.' He was deprived of his books, and allowed only insufficient food, for which he was dependent on his brother Robert. It is to the credit of the society of St. John's College that they ventured under the circumstances to address to him a letter of condolence.

With the passing of the Act of Supremacy (November 1534) Fisher's experiences as a political offender entered upon a third phase. Under the penalties attaching to two special clauses both Fisher and More were again attainted of misprision of treason, and the see of Rochester was declared vacant from 2 Jan. 1534–5. The bishop was thus deprived of all privileges attaching to his ecclesiastical dignity. On 7 May 1535 he was visited by Mr. Secretary Cromwell and others of the king's council. Cromwell read aloud to him the act, and Fisher intimated his inability to recognise the king as 'supreme head' of the church. A second act, whereby it was made high treason to deny the king's right to that title, was then read to him; and Fisher's previous denial, extracted from him when uninformed as to the exact penalties attaching thereto, would appear to have constituted the sole evidence on which he was found guilty at his trial. It is probable, however, that Henry would still have hesitated to put Fisher to death had it not been for the step taken by the new Roman pontiff, Paul III, who on 20 May convened a consistory and created Fisher presbyter cardinal of St. Vitalis. Paul was at that time aiming at bringing about a reformation of the Roman church, and with this view was raising various ecclesiastics of admitted merit and character to the cardinalate. According to his own express statement, volunteered after Fisher's execution, he was ignorant of the extremely strained relations existing between the latter and the English monarch. His act, however, roused Henry to almost ungovernable fury. A messenger was forthwith despatched to Calais to forbid the bearer of the cardinal's hat from Rome from proceeding further, and Fisher's death was now resolved upon. With the design, apparently, of entrapping him into admissions which might afford a further justification of such a measure, two clerks of the council, Thomas Bedyl and Leighton, were sent to the Tower for the purpose of putting to Fisher thirty distinct questions in the presence of Walsingham, the lieutenant, and other witnesses. Fisher's replies, subscribed with his own hand, are still extant. He had already, in an informal manner, been apprised of the honour designed for him by Paul, and among other interrogatories he was now asked simply to repeat what he had said when he first received the intelligence. He replied that he had said, in the presence of two witnesses (whom he named), that 'yf the cardinal's hat were layed at his feete he wolde not stoupe to take it up, he did set so little by it' (LEWIS, *Life*, ii. 412). According to the account preserved in Baily, however, Cromwell was the interrogator on this occasion, and the question was put hypothetically; whereupon Fisher replied: 'It any such thing should happen, assure yourself I should improve that favour to the best advantage that I could, in assisting the holy catholic church of Christ, and in that respect I would receive it upon my knees' (p. 171). A third account is given by Sanders (see LEWIS, *Life*, i. xv, ii. 178); but amid such conflicting statements it seems reasonable to attach the greatest weight to Fisher's own account upon oath. It is certain that his replies, if they did not further inculpate him, in no way served to soften Henry's resentment, and he was forthwith brought to trial on the charge that he did, '7 May 27 Hen. VIII, openly declare in English, "The king our sovereign lord is not supreme head in earth of the church of England"' (*Letters and Papers Henry VIII*, vol. viii. No. 886). The jury found one bill against Fisher, and presented another, and were then discharged. On 17 June he was brought to the bar at Westminster, pronounced guilty, and sentenced to die a traitor's death at Tyburn. But on the 21st Walsingham received a writ in which the sentence was changed to one of beheading (instead of the ordinary hanging, disembowelling, and quartering), and Tower Hill was assigned as the place of execution, instead of Tyburn. The accounts of Fisher's execution, which took place 22 June 1535, and of the incidents which immediately preceded and succeeded that tragical event, are conflicting, and it seems that on certain points there was a confusion in the traditions preserved of the details with those which belonged to More's execution, which took place just a fortnight later. (The incidents recorded by Baily are partly taken from the account by Maurice Chauncy ; see authorities at end of art.) All the narratives, however, agree in representing Fisher as meeting death with a calmness, dignity, and pious resignation which greatly impressed the beholders. His head was exposed on London Bridge; his body left on the scaffold until the evening, and then conveyed to the churchyard of Allhallows Barking, where it was interred without ceremony. A fortnight later it was removed to the church of St. Peter ad Vincula in the Tower, and there laid by the side of the body of his friend Sir Thomas More, who, but a short time before his own career was similarly terminated, had left it on record as his deliberate conviction that there was 'in this realm no one man in wisdom, learning, and long approved vertue together, mete to be matched and compared with him' (MORE, *English Works*, p. 1437).

The intelligence of Fisher's fate was received with feelings approaching to consternation not only by the nation but by Europe at large. Paul III declared that he would sooner have had his two grandsons slain, and in a letter (26 July) to Francis I says that he 'is compelled, at the unanimous sollicitation of the cardinals, to declare Henry deprived of his kingdom and of the royal dignity' (*Letters and Papers Henry VIII*, vol. viii. No. 1117).

As a theologian Fisher was to some extent an eclectic; and, according to Volusenus

(*De Tranquillitate Animi*, ed. 1751, p. 280), inclined, on the already agitated question of election and free will, to something like a Calvinistic theory. The same writer tells us (*ib.* p. 250) that he also frequently expressed his high admiration of the expositions of some of the Lutheran divines, and only wondered how they could proceed from heretics. Professor John E. B. Mayor observes : 'If *bonus textuarius* is indeed *bonus theologus*, Bishop Fisher may rank high among divines. He is at home in every part of scripture, no less than among the fathers. If the matter of his teaching is now for the most part trite, the form is always individual and life-like. Much of it is in the best sense catholic, and might be illustrated by parallel passages from Luther and our own reformers' (pref. to *English Works*, p. xxii).

The best portrait of Fisher is the drawing by Hans Holbein in the possession of the queen. Another, by the same artist, also of considerable merit, is in the hall of the master's lodge at St. John's College. A third (supposed to have been taken shortly before his execution) is in the college hall. There are others at Queens', Christ's, and Trinity Colleges. In the combination room of St. John's there are also three different engravings.

A collected edition of Fisher's Latin works, one volume folio, was printed at Würzburg in 1597 by Fleischmann. This contains : 1. 'The Assertio septem Sacramentorum' of Henry VIII against Luther, which finds a place in the collection as being 'Roffensis tamen hortatu et studio edita.' 2. Fisher's 'Defence' of the 'Assertio,' 1523. 3. His treatise in reply to Luther, 'De Babylonica Captivitate,' 1523. 4. His 'Confutatio Assertionis Lutheranæ,' first printed at Antwerp, 1523. 5. 'De Eucharistia contra Joan. Œcolampadium libri quinque,' first printed 1527. 6. 'Sacri Sacerdotii Defensio contra Lutherum.' 7. 'Convulsio calumniarum Vlrichi Veleni Minhoniensis, quibus Petrum nunquam Romæ fuisse cauillatus est,' 1525. 8. 'Concio Londini habita vernaculè, quando Lutheri scripta publicè igni tradebantur,' translated by Richard Pace into Latin, 1521. 9. 'De unica Magdalena libri tres,' 1519. Also the following, which the editor states are printed for the first time : 10. 'Commentarii in vii. Psalmos pœnitentiales, interprete Joanne Fen à monte acuto.' 11. Two sermons : (*a*) 'De Passione Domini,' (*b*) 'De Justitia Pharisæorum.' 12. 'Methodus perveniendi ad summam Christianæ religionis perfectionem.' 13. 'Epistola ad Hermannum Lætmatium Goudanum de Charitate Christiana.' At the end (whether printed before or not does not appear) are 14. 'De

Necessitate Orandi.' 15. ' Psalmi vel precationes.'

An edition of his English works has been undertaken for the Early English Text Society by Professor John E. B. Mayor, of which the first volume (1876) only has as yet appeared. This contains the originals of 8, 10, 11 *a*, and 12; the two sermons of the funerals of Henry VII and his mother; and ' A Spiritual Consolation,' addressed to Fisher's sister, Elizabeth, during her confinement in the Tower. Of these, the two funeral discourses and the originals of 8 and 10 are reprinted from early editions by Wynkyn de Worde. An ' Advertisement' to this edition gives a valuable criticism by the editor on Fisher's theology, English style, vocabulary, &c. The second volume, containing the ' Letters ' and the ' Life ' by Hall, is announced, under the editorship of the Rev. Ronald Bayne.

A volume in the Rolls Office (27 Hen. VIII, No. 887) contains the following in Fisher's hand : 1, prayers in English; 2, fragment of a ' Commentary on the Salutation of the Virgin Mary;' 3, theological commonplace book, in Latin; 4, draft treatises on divinity ; 5 and 6, treatises on the rights and dignity of the clergy; 7, observations on the history of the Septuagint Version (this annotated and corrected only by Fisher). He also wrote a ' History of the Divorce,' which, if printed, was rigidly suppressed; the manuscript, however, is preserved in the University Library, Cambridge.

[Fisher's Life, professedly written by Thomas Baily, a royalist divine, was first published in 1665, and was really written by Richard Hall, of Christ's College, Cambridge, who died in 1604 [see art. BAYLY, THOMAS]; a manuscript in University Library, Cambridge, No. 1266, contains Maurice Chauncy's account of the martyrdoms of More and Fisher; a considerable amount of original matter is also given in the appendices to the Life by the Rev. John Lewis (a posthumous publication), ed. T. Hudson Turner, 2 vols. 1855. The following may also be consulted: The Funeral Sermon of Margaret, Countess of Richmond, with Baker's Preface, ed. Hymers, 1840 ; Baker's Hist. of St. John's College, ed. Mayor, 2 vols. 1869 ; Cooper's Memoir of Margaret, Countess of Richmond and Derby, 1874 ; Early Statutes of the College of St. John the Evangelist, ed. Mayor, 1859; Mullinger's Hist. of the University of Cambridge, vol. i. 1873; a paper by Mr. Bruce in Archæologia, vol. xxv. ; Letters and Papers of the Reign of Henry VIII, vols. iv. to viii., with Brewer's and Gairdner's Prefaces; Brewer's Reign of Henry VIII, 2 vols., 1884 ; T. E. Bridgett's Life of Blessed John Fisher, Bishop of Rochester, Cardinal of the Holy Roman Church, and Martyr under Henry VIII, London and New York, 1888.]   J. B. M.

FISHER, JOHN (1569–1641), jesuit, whose real name was PERCY, son of John Percy, yeoman, and his wife, Cecilia Lawson, was born at Holmside, co. Durham, on 27 Sept. 1569. At fourteen years of age he was received into the family of a catholic lady, and soon afterwards joined the Roman church. He then proceeded to the English College at Rheims, where he studied classics and rhetoric for three years. On 22 Sept. 1589 he entered the English College at Rome for his higher studies. He was ordained priest on 13 March 1592–3, by papal dispensation, before the full canonical age, in consequence of the want of priests for the mission. After publicly defending universal theology at the Roman college, he was admitted into the Society of Jesus by Father Aquaviva, and began his noviceship at Tournay on 14 May 1594. In the second year of his noviceship he was ordered to England for the sake of his health, which had been impaired by over-application to study. On his way through Holland he was seized at Flushing by some English soldiers on suspicion of being a priest, and cruelly treated. Immediately after his arrival in London he was arrested and committed to Bridewell, from which prison, after about seven months' confinement, he succeeded in making his escape through the roof, together with two other priests and seven laymen. In 1596 he was sent by Father Henry Garnett to the north of England, where he laboured till 1598, when he was appointed companion to Father John Gerard in Northamptonshire. In that locality he exercised his priestly functions, and he occasionally visited Oxford, where he became acquainted with William Chillingworth [q. v.], whom he persuaded to renounce the protestant faith (WOOD, Athenæ Oxon. ed. Bliss, iii. 87). He was professed of the four vows in 1603. For some time he and Gerard resided first at Stoke Poges, and subsequently at Harrowden, in the house of Mrs. Elizabeth Vaux, widow of William, second son of Lord Vaux of Harrowden. Fisher was afterwards chaplain to Sir Everard Digby [q. v.] In August 1605 he went on a pilgrimage to St. Winifred's well with Sir Everard Digby's wife, Mrs. Vaux, and others. He was arrested in November 1610, with Father Nicholas Hart, at Harrowden, was conveyed to London, and committed to the Gatehouse prison, and after upwards of a year's confinement was released at the instance of the Spanish ambassador, and with Father Hart sent into banishment. Both of them had been tried and condemned to death, and had received several notices to prepare for execution.

After landing in Belgium, Fisher discharged the duties at Brussels of vice-prefect of the English jesuit mission, in the absence of Father Anthony Hoskins. He was next professor of holy scripture at St. John's, Louvain. At length he returned to England, but was at once seized and confined in the new prison on the banks of the Thames. He appears, however, to have been allowed considerable freedom of action, and it is said that during his three years' confinement there he reconciled 150 protestants to the Roman church. He was famous for his dialectic skill, and held several controversial conferences with eminent protestant theologians. When James I desired a series of disputations to be held before the Countess of Buckingham (who was leaning to catholicism), Fisher defended the catholic side against Francis White, afterwards bishop of Ely. The king and his favourite (Buckingham, the countess's son) attended the conferences, the third and last of which was held on 24 May 1622, when Laud, bishop of St. David's and afterwards archbishop of Canterbury, replaced White. The countess was converted by the jesuit, whose arguments, however, failed to convince her son and the king. James himself proposed to Fisher nine points in writing upon the most prominent topics of the controversy, in a document headed ' Certain Leading Points which hinder my Union with the Church of Rome until she reforms herself, or is able to satisfy me.' Fisher's replies to these questions were revised by Father John Floyd [q.v.] The relation of the conference between Laud and Fisher forms the second volume of Laud's works (Oxford 1849). On 27 June 1623 another religious disputation was held in the house of Sir Humphry Lynde, between Dr. White, then dean of Carlisle, Dr. Daniel Featley, and the jesuits Fisher and John Sweet.

When the king of France gave his daughter in marriage to Prince Charles (afterwards Charles I) in 1625, the French ambassador obtained a free pardon for twenty priests, including Fisher, who apparently enjoyed some ten years of liberty under the royal letters of pardon. In December 1634, however, he was arrested, brought before the privy council at Whitehall, and ordered to depart from the realm, after giving bail never to return. As he refused to find sureties, he was imprisoned in the Gatehouse till August 1635, when he was released at the urgent intercession of the queen. During the last two years of life he suffered severely from cancer. He died in London on 3 Dec. 1641.

His works are : 1. 'A Treatise of Faith ; wherein is briefly and plainly shown a Direct Way by which every Man may resolve and settle his Mind in all Doubts, Questions, and Controversies concerning Matters of Faith,' London, 1600, St. Omer, 1614, 8vo. 2. ' A Reply made unto Mr. Anthony Wotton and Mr. John White, Ministers, wherein it is showed that they have not sufficiently answered the Treatise of Faith, and wherein also the Chief Points of the said Treatise are more clearly declared and more strongly confirmed,' St. Omer, 1612, 4to. 3. ' A Challenge to Protestants, requiring a Catalogue to be made of some Professors of their Faith in all Ages since Christ.' At the end of the preceding work. 4. An account of the conference in 1622, under the initials A. C. Laud answered this in a reply to the ' Exceptions of A. C.,' which is printed with his own account of the conference. 5. ' An Answer to a Pamphlet, intitvled : " The Fisher catched in his owne Net. . . . By A. C.,"' s. l. 1623, 4to. The pamphlet by Daniel Featley, to which this is a reply, appeared in 1623, and contains ' The Occasion and Issue of the late Conference had between Dr. White, Deane of Carleil, and Dr. Featley, with Mr. Fisher and Mr. Sweet, Jesuites.' 6. ' An Answere vnto the Nine Points of Controuersy proposed by our late Soveraygne (of Famous Memory) vnto M. Fisher. . . . And the Rejoinder vnto the Reply of D. Francis White, Minister. With the Picture of the sayd Minister, or Censure of his Writings prefixed ' [St. Omer], 1625–1626, 8vo.

Among the protestant writers who entered into controversy with Fisher were G. Walker, G. Webb, and Henry Rogers.

[De Backer's Bibl. des Écrivains de la Compagnie de Jésus (1869), i. 1870 ; Dodd's Church Hist. ii. 394 ; Foley's Records, i. 521, vi. 180, 212, 526, vii. 585, 1028, 1032, 1098 ; Gardiner's History of England, iv. 279, 281 ; Heylyn's Cyprianus Anglicus, p. 95 ; Lawson's Life of Laud, i. 217–19, ii. 533 ; Le Bas' Life of Laud, p. 55 ; More's Hist. Missionis Anglic. Soc. Jesu, p. 378 ; Morris's Condition of Catholics under James I ; Oliver's Jesuit Collections, p. 91 ; Southwell's Bibl. Scriptorum Soc. Jesu, p. 487 ; Calendar of State Papers ; Tanner's Societas Jesu Apostolorum Imitatrix, p. 707 ; Wood's Athenæ Oxon. (Bliss), iv. 971.]   T. C.

FISHER, JOHN, D.D. (1748–1825), bishop of Salisbury, the eldest of the nine sons of the Rev. John Fisher, successively vicar of Hampton, Middlesex, vicar of Peterborough, rector of Calbourne, Isle of Wight, and prebendary of Preston in the cathedral of Salisbury, was born at Hampton in 1748. His father became chaplain to Bishop Thomas, the preceptor of George III, on his appointment to the see of Peterborough in 1747, and was by him presented to the incumbency of St. John the Baptist in that city. The son received his early education at the free school at Peterborough, whence at the age of fourteen he was removed to St. Paul's School, of which Dr. Thicknesse was then head-master. In 1766 he passed to Peterhouse, Cambridge, on a Pauline exhibition. Dr. Edmund Law, afterwards bishop of Carlisle, was then head of the college, and Fisher became the intimate friend of his two distinguished sons, afterwards respectively Lord-chief-justice Ellenborough and Bishop of Elphin. He took his degree of B.A. in 1770, appearing as tenth wrangler, and being also eminent for his classical attainments. In 1773 he became M.A., and in the same year was appointed to a Northamptonshire fellowship at St. John's, of which college he was chosen tutor, the duties of which office, we are told, 'he fulfilled to the great advantage of his pupils, being distinguished not only for his various talents, but for the suavity of his manners and the peculiarly felicitous manner in which he conveyed instruction.' Fisher then became private tutor to Prince Zartorinski Poniatowski, and to the son of Archbishop George of Dublin, and spent some time with Sir J. Cradock, governor of the Cape, but 'deriving no great benefit from these connections,' he undertook parochial work, as curate of his native parish of Hampton. In 1780 he became B.D., and on the recommendation of Bishop Hurd he was appointed preceptor to Prince Edward, afterwards Duke of Kent, father of Queen Victoria, and became royal chaplain and deputy clerk of the closet. This appointment he held five years, until in 1785 his royal pupil went to the university of Göttingen. On this Fisher visited Italy, where he became known to Mrs. Piozzi, who describes him in one of her letters as 'a charming creature, generally known in society as "the King's Fisher"' (WHALLEY, *Correspondence*, ii. 367). The following year, 14 July, he was recalled from Naples by his nomination by the king to a canonry at Windsor, where he took up his residence, and in September of the next year he married Dorothea, the only daughter of J. F. Scrivenor, esq., of Sibton Park, Suffolk, by whom he had one son and two daughters. The refined simplicity and courteousness of his manners and the amenity of his temper rendered Fisher a favourite with George III, whose esteem he also gained by his unaffected piety and his unswerving fidelity to him. The king, we are told, treated him rather as a friend than as a subject, and reposed in him almost unlimited confidence. In 1789 he took the degree of D.D. From 1793 to 1797 he held the vicarage of Stowey, in the gift of the chapter of Windsor. When the

bishopric of Exeter became vacant by the death of Bishop Courtenay, Fisher was chosen by the king to be his successor, and was consecrated in Lambeth Chapel, 16 July 1803. In 1805 George III appointed him to superintend the education of the Princess Charlotte of Wales. He fulfilled the duty, we are told, 'with exemplary propriety and credit.' The autobiography of Miss C. Knight and other contemporary memoirs give some glimpse of the difficulties of this post, which he would have thrown up but for his respect for his sovereign. His union of gentleness, firmness, and patience carried him through. His chief concern, we are told, was to train the princess in the self-command naturally foreign to her. At the outset of his charge a correspondence sprang up between him and Hannah More, who had published anonymously 'Hints towards Forming the Character of a Princess.' An interview took place, and Hannah More records that 'the bishop appeared to have a very proper notion of managing his royal pupil, and of casting down all high imaginations' (H. MORE, *Correspondence*, ed. Roberts, iii. 230). Fisher was no favourite with Miss C. Knight, who narrates that he used to come three or four times a week to 'do the important;' his great point being to arm the princess against popery and whiggism, 'two evils which he seemed to think equally great;' she adds, what is contradicted by all other estimates of his character, that 'his temper was hasty, and his vanity easily alarmed.' His 'best accomplishment,' in this lady's opinion, was 'a taste for drawing, and a love of the fine arts' (MISS C. KNIGHT, *Autobiography*, i. 232 sq.) Dr. Parr gives the following estimate of his character:—

Unsoiled by courts and unseduced by zeal,
Fisher endangers not the common weal.

In 1804 he accepted the office of vice-president of the British and Foreign Bible Society. In 1807, on the death of Bishop Douglas, Fisher was translated from Exeter to Salisbury, where he won general respect and affection by his faithful and unobtrusive performance of his episcopal duties. His mode of life was dignified, but unostentatious. He was very liberal in works of charity, devoting a large portion of his episcopal revenues to pious and beneficent uses, leaving his bishopric no richer than he came to it, his personal estate amounting at his death to no more than 20,000*l*. In 1818 Fisher, under a commission from Bishop North, visited the Channel Islands for the purpose of holding confirmations and consecrating a church, being the first time, since the islands were placed under the jurisdiction of the see of Winchester, that they had enjoyed episcopal visitation (*Ann. Reg.* lx. 92, 104). He died in Seymour Street, London, after long protracted sufferings borne with exemplary patience, 8 May 1825, aged 76, and was buried at Windsor. He published nothing beyond his primary charge as bishop of Exeter, and two or three occasional sermons, which were given to the world under pressure. In his charge he declared himself against intolerant treatment of Roman catholics, but expressed his opinion that bare toleration was all that peaceable and conscientious dissenters from the established church had any claim to. In the same charge he repudiated the alleged Calvinism of the church of England, which he said was flatly contradicted by the articles of the church. Fisher was a generous patron both of authors and of artists, whom he is recorded to have treated with liberality and unaffected kindness. A portrait of him hangs in the dining-room of the palace at Salisbury. Fisher's only published works are: 1. 'Charge at the Primary Visitation of the Diocese of Exeter,' Exeter, 1805, 4to. 2. 'Sermon at the Meeting of the Charity Children in St. Paul's, 3 June 1806,' London, 1806, 4to. 3. 'Sermon preached before the House of Lords, 25 Feb. 1807, on the occasion of a General Fast, on Is. xl. 31,' London, 1807, 4to. 4. 'Sermon in behalf of the S. P. G. on Is. lx. 5,' London, 1809, 4to. 5. 'Sermon preached at the Consecration of St. James's Church, Guernsey, on Col. i. 24,' Guernsey, 1818.

[Baker's St. John's College, ed. Mayor, p. 731; Annual Register, 1825, also lvi. 218, lx. 92-104; Imperial Mag. August 1825; Gent. Mag. 1825, ii. 82; Sandford's Thomas Poole, pp. 65, 170, 241.]   E. V.

FISHER, JOHN ABRAHAM (1744–1806), violinist, son of Richard Fisher, was born at Dunstable in 1744. He was brought up in Lord Tyrawley's house, learning the violin from Pinto, and his appearance at the King's Theatre (1763), where he played a concerto, was 'by permission' of his patron. The following year Fisher was enrolled in the Royal Society of Musicians. He matriculated at Magdalen College, Oxford, 26 June 1777 (FOSTER, *Alumni Oxon.* ii. 465). His indefatigable industry obtained him the degrees of Bac. and Doc. Mus. on 5 July 1777, his oratorio 'Providence' being performed at the Sheldonian Theatre two days previously. The work was afterwards heard several times in London; but Fisher's name as a composer is more closely connected with theatrical than with sacred music. He became entitled to a sixteenth share of Covent Garden Theatre by his marriage about 1770 with Mrs. Powell

[see under POWELL, WILLIAM]. He devoted his musical talent and business energy to the theatre. When his wife died Fisher sold his share in the theatre, and made a professional tour on the continent, visiting France, Germany, and Russia, and reaching Vienna in 1784. The Tonkünstler-Societät employed three languages in a memorandum—'Monsieur Fischer, ein Engelländer und virtuoso di Violino'—which probably refers to the stranger's performance at a concert of the society. Fisher won favour also at court, and became as widely known for his eccentricities as for his ingenious performances. It was not long before he drew odium upon himself through his marriage with, and subsequent ill-treatment of, Anna Storace, the prima donna. The wedding had taken place with a certain amount of éclat, but when the virtuoso bullied and even struck his bride, the scandal soon became public, and a separation followed. The emperor (Joseph) ordered Fisher to quit his dominion. Leaving his young wife he sought refuge in Ireland. The cordiality with which his old friend Owenson welcomed him to Dublin, his personal appearance, and introduction into the family circle, have been amusingly described by Lady Morgan, one of Owenson's daughters. Fisher gave concerts at the Rotunda, and occupied himself as a teacher. He died in May or June 1806. As an executant Fisher pleased by his skill and fiery energy. In his youth he appears to have revelled in his command of the instrument, and in his maturer years he offended the critics by a showiness that bordered on charlatanism. Among Fisher's compositions, his 'Six Easy Solos for a Violin' and 'Six Duettos' were useful to amateurs of the time; while his 'Vauxhall and Marybone Songs,' in three books, were made popular by the singing of Mrs. Weichsel, Vernon, and Bellamy. Another favourite book was a collection of airs forming 'A comparative View of the English, French, and Italian Schools,' which, however, contains no critical remarks. The songs 'In vain I seek to calm to rest' and 'See with rosy beam' deserve mention. The 'Six Symphonies' were played at Vauxhall and the theatres; the pantomime, with music, 'Master of the Woods,' was produced at Sadler's Wells; the 'Harlequin Jubilee' at Covent Garden, and, with the 'Sylphs' and the 'Sirens,' gave evidence of the professor's facility in manufacturing musicianly serio-comic measures. The 'Norwood Gipsies,' 'Prometheus,' 'Macbeth,' and lastly 'Zobeide,' point to a more serious vein, though belonging equally to Fisher's theatrical period, about 1770–80; but the well-written anthem, 'Seek ye the Lord,' sung at Bedford Chapel and Lincoln Cathedral, is of later date. Three violin concertos were published at Berlin, 1782.

[Grove's Dict. i. 530; Brown's Biog. Dict. p. 247; A. B. C. Dario, p. 20; Pohl's Mozart and Haydn in London, i. 42, &c.; Royal Society of Musicians, entry 2 Sept. 1764; Oxford Graduates, p. 231; Kelly's Reminiscences, i. 231; Musical World, 1840, p. 276; Hanslick's Geschichte des Concertwesens in Wien, p. 108; Mount-Edg-cumbe's Reminiscences, 1834, p. 59; Clayton's Queens of Song, i. 215; Lady Morgan's Memoirs, 1863, p. 80; Gent. Mag. vol. lxxvi. pt. i. p. 587; Gerber's Tonkünstler-Lexikon, 1770, i.418; Fisher's music in Brit. Mus. Library.] L. M. M.

FISHER, SIR JOHN WILLIAM (1788-1876), surgeon, son of Peter Fisher of Perth, by Mary, daughter of James Kennay of York, was born in London 30 Jan. 1788, and apprenticed to John Andrews, a surgeon enjoying a large practice. After studying at St. George's and Westminster Hospitals, he was admitted member of the Royal College of Surgeons in 1809, became a fellow in 1836, and was a member of the council in 1843. The university of Erlangen, Bavaria, conferred on him the degree of M.D. in 1841. He was appointed surgeon to the Bow Street patrol in 1821 by Lord Sidmouth, and promoted to the post of surgeon-in-chief to the metropolitan police force at the time of its formation in 1829, which position he held until his retirement on a pension in 1865. He was knighted by the queen at Osborne on 2 Sept. 1858. He was a good practitioner, honourable, hospitable, and steadfast in duty. He died at 33 Park Lane, London, 22 March 1876, and was buried in Kensal Green cemetery on 29 March, when six of his oldest medical friends were the pallbearers. His will was proved on 22 April, the personalty being sworn under 50,000*l.* He married, first, 18 April 1829, Louisa Catherine, eldest daughter of William Haymes of Kibworth Harcourt, Leicestershire, she died in London, 5 Oct. 1860; and secondly, 18 June 1862, Lilias Stuart, second daughter of Colonel Alexander Mackenzie of Grinnard, Ross-shire.

[Proceedings of Royal Medical and Chirurgical Soc. (1880), viii. 173-4; Illustrated London News, 1 April 1876, p. 335, and 27 May, p. 527; Lancet, 1 April 1876, p. 515.] G. C. B.

FISHER, JONATHAN (*d.* 1812), landscape-painter, was a native of Dublin, and originally a draper in that city. Having a taste for art, he studied it by himself, and eventually succeeded in obtaining the patronage of the nobility. He produced some landscapes which were clever attempts to reproduce nature, but were too mechanical and cold in colour to be popular. They were, however, very well suited for engraving, and a set of views of Carlingford Harbour and its neighbourhood were finely engraved by Thomas Vivares, James Mason, and other eminent landscape engravers of the day. In 1792 Fisher published a folio volume called 'A Picturesque Tour of Killarney, consisting of 20 views engraved in aquatinta, with a map, some general observations, &c.' He also published other illustrations of scenery in Ireland. Fisher did not find art profitable, but was fortunate enough to obtain a situation in the Stamp Office, Dublin, which he continued to hold up to his death in 1812. There is a landscape by Fisher in the South Kensington Museum, 'A View of Lymington River, with the Isle of Wight in the distance.' A painting by him of 'The Schomberg Obelisk in the Boyne' was in the Irish Exhibition at London in 1888.

[Redgrave's Dict. of Artists; Catalogues of the South Kensington Museum and the Irish Exhibition, 1888; Lowndes's Bibl. Man.; engravings in Print Room, Brit. Mus.] L. C.

FISHER, JOSEPH (*d.*1705), archdeacon of Carlisle, was born at Whitbridge, Cumberland, and matriculated at Queen's College, Oxford, in Michaelmas term 1674; took his B.A. degree 8 May 1679, his M.A. 6 July 1682, was fellow of that college, and on the death of Christopher Harrison, 1695, was presented to the rectory of Brough or Burgh-under-Stanmore, Westmoreland. Before that time he had filled the office of lecturer or curate, living in a merchant's house in Broad Street, London, to be near his work. At this place he wrote, 1695, the dedicatory epistle to his former pupil Thomas Lambard, prefacing his printed sermon, preached 27 Jan. 1694 at Sevenoaks, Kent, on 'The Honour of Marriage,' from Heb. xiii. 4. This is his only literary production, although we are told that he was well skilled in Hebrew and the oriental languages. On the promotion of William Nicolson [q. v.] to the see of Carlisle, the archdeaconry was accepted by Fisher 9 July 1702, and his installation took place 14 July. To the archdeaconry was attached the living of St. Cuthbert, Great Salkeld, which he held in conjunction with Brough till his death, which took place early in 1705. He was succeeded in office by George Fleming [q. v.], afterwards Sir George Fleming, bishop of Carlisle, 28 March 1705. He was buried at Brough.

[Wood's Athenæ Oxon. ed. Bliss, iv. 539; Nicolson's and Burn's Hist. of Westmoreland and Cumberland, i. 569; Le Neve's Fasti Eccles.

Angl.; Watt's Bibl. Brit. 1824; Willis's Survey of Cathedrals, i. 307; Jefferson's Antiquities of Cumberland, i. 266.] E. C. S.

FISHER, MARY (*fl.* 1652–1697), quakeress, was born in a village near York about 1623. She joined the Friends before 1652, in which year she was admitted a quaker minister. Shortly afterwards she was imprisoned in York Castle for having addressed a congregation at Selby at the close of public worship. This imprisonment lasted for sixteen months, during which she wrote with four fellow-prisoners a tract called 'False Prophets and Teachers Described.' Immediately after her release she proceeded on a missionary journey to the south and east of England, in company with Elizabeth Williams, a quaker minister. At the close of 1653 they visited Cambridge, and, preaching in front of Sidney Sussex College, were stoned by the 'scholars,' whom Mary Fisher irritated by terming the college a cage of unclean birds. The Friends were apprehended as disorderly persons by the mayor of Cambridge, who ordered them to be whipped at the market cross 'until the blood ran down their bodies.' The sentence was executed with much barbarity. This is the first instance of quakers being publicly flogged. Shortly afterwards Mary Fisher 'felt called to declare the truth in the steeple-house at Pontefract,' and for so doing was imprisoned for six months in York Castle, at the completion of which term she was imprisoned for another period of three months, at the request of the mayor of Pontefract, for being unrepentant and refusing to give securities for good behaviour. In 1655, while travelling in the ministry in Buckinghamshire, she was also imprisoned for several months for 'giving Christian exhortation' to a congregation. Later in this year she 'felt moved' to visit the West Indies and New England. On her arrival, accompanied by Ann Austin, at Boston the authorities refused to allow them to land, and searched their baggage for books and papers, confiscating more than a hundred volumes, which were destroyed. The quakeresses then disembarked and were kept in close confinement in the common gaol, the master of the ship which brought them being compelled to pay for their support and to give a bond that he would remove them. During their imprisonment they were deprived of writing materials, and their beds and Bibles were confiscated by the gaoler for his fees. They were stripped naked to see if they had witch-marks on their persons, and would have been starved if some inhabitants had not bribed the gaoler to be allowed to feed them. Mary Fisher returned to England in 1657, visiting the

West Indies again at the end of that year. In 1660 she deemed it her duty to attempt to convert Mahomet IV, and for that purpose made a long and hazardous journey, largely on foot, to Smyrna, where she was ordered to return home by the English representative. She retraced her steps to Venice, and at length succeeded in reaching Adrianople, where the sultan lay encamped with his army. The grand vizier, hearing that an Englishwoman had arrived with a message from the 'Great God to the sultan,' kindly offered to procure her an interview with the sultan, which he did. Mary spoke through an interpreter, whom the sultan heard with much patience and gravity, and when she had concluded acknowledged the truth of what she said and offered her an escort of soldiers to Constantinople, which she declined. He then asked her what she thought of Mahomet, 'a pitfall she avoided by declaring that she knew him not.' She afterwards journeyed on foot to Constantinople, where she obtained passage in a ship to England. In 1662 she married William Bayley of Poole, a quaker minister and master mariner, who was drowned at sea in 1675, and by whom she is believed to have had issue. During his lifetime she appears to have chiefly exercised her ministry in Dorsetshire and the adjacent counties. Her 'testimony concerning her deceased husband' appears at the end of Bayley's collected writings in 1676. In 1678 she married John Cross, a quaker of London, in which town she resided until—when uncertain—they emigrated to America. In 1697 she was living at Charlestown, South Carolina, where she entertained Richard Barrow, a quaker, after he had been shipwrecked, and from a letter of Barrow's it appears she was for a second time a widow. No later particulars of her life are known. Mary Fisher was a devoted, untiring, and successful minister, and Croese describes her as having considerable intellectual faculties, which were greatly adorned by the gravity of her deportment.

[Croese's Hist. of the Quakers, ii. 124; Besse's Sufferings, &c. i. 85, ii. 85, &c.; Manuscript Sufferings of the Friends; Manuscript Testimony of the Yearly Meeting (London); Neal's Hist. of New England, i. 292; Minutes of the Two Weeks' Meeting (London); Bowden's Hist. of the Friends in America, i. 35; Smith's Friends' Books, i. 220, 612; Sewel's Hist. of the Society of Friends, ed. 1853, i. 440, ii. 225; Bishop's New England Judged.] A. C. B.

FISHER, PAYNE (1616–1693), poet, son of Payne Fisher, one of the captains in the royal life guard while Charles I was in Oxfordshire, and grandson of Sir William Fisher, knight, was born at Warnford, Dorsetshire, in the house of his maternal grand-father, Sir Thomas Neale. He matriculated at Hart Hall, Oxford, in Michaelmas term, 1634; three years after he removed to Magdalene College, Cambridge. While at Cambridge he first developed 'a rambling head' and a turn for verse-making (WOOD, *Athenæ*, Bliss, iv. 377). He quitted the university very speedily, about 1638, and entered the army in the Netherlands. There he fought in the defence of Boduc, but, returning to England before long, enlisted as an ensign in the army raised (1639) by Charles I against the Scots, and during this campaign made acquaintance with the cavalier poet, Lovelace. Subsequently Fisher took service in Ireland, where he rose to the rank of captain, and, returning about 1644, was made, by Lord Chichester's influence, sergeant-major of a foot regiment in the royalist army. By Rupert's command he marched at the head of three hundred men to relieve York, but was present at Marston Moor, but, finding himself on the losing side, he deserted the royalist cause after the battle, and retired to London, where he lived as best he could by his pen.

Fisher's first poem, published in 1650, celebrating the parliamentary victory of Marston Moor, was entitled ' Marston Moor, Eboracense carmen; cum quibusdam miscellaneis opera studioque Pagani Piscatoris, . . .' London, 1650, 4to. He always wrote under the above sobriquet, or that of Fitzpaganus Fisher. By his turn for Latin verse and his adulatory arts, or, as Wood termed it, by his ability 'to shark money from those who delighted to see their names in print,' Fisher soon became the fashionable poet of his day. He was made poet-laureate, or in his own words after the Restoration, 'scribbler' to Oliver Cromwell, and his pen was busily employed in the service of his new master. He wrote not only Latin panegyrics and congratulatory odes on the Protector, dedicating his works to Bradshaw and the most important of the parliamentary magnates, but also composed a constant succession of elegies and epitaphs on the deaths of their generals. Thus the 'Irenodia Gratulatoria, sive illus. amplissimique Oliveri Cromwellii . . . Epinicion,' London, 1652, was dedicated to the president (Bradshaw) and the council of state, and concluded with odes on the funerals of Ludlow and Popham (London, 1652). To another, 'Veni vidi, vici, the Triumphs of the most Excellent and Illustrious Oliver Cromwell . . . set forth in a panegyric, written in Latin, and faithfully done into English verse by T. Manly' (London, 1652, 8vo), was added an elegy upon the death of Ireton, lord deputy of

Ireland. The 'Inauguratio Oliveriana, with other poems' (Lond. 1654, 4to), was followed the next year by 'Oratio Anniversaria in die Inaugurationis . . . Olivari . . .' (London, 1655, fol.), and again other panegyrics on the second anniversary of ' his highness's' inauguration (the 'Oratio . . .' and 'Pæan Triumphalis,' both London, 1657). To the 'Pæan' was added an epitaph on Admiral Blake, which, like most of Fisher's odes and elegies, was also published separately as a ' broadsheet' (see list in WOOD, ed. Bliss, *Athenæ Oxon.* iv. 377, &c.) He celebrated the victory of Dunkirk in an ' Epinicion vel elogium . . . Ludovici XIIII . . . pro nuperis victoriis in Flandria, præcipue pro desideratissima reductione Dunkirkæ captæ . . . sub confœderatis auspiciis Franco-Britannorum' (London ? 1655 ?). The book has a portrait of the French king in the beginning, and French verses in praise of the author at the end. Fisher afterwards presented Pepys with a copy of this work ' with his arms, and dedicated to me very handsome' (PEPYS, *Diary*, ed. 1849, i. 118, 121, 122). It was a usual habit of the poet's to put different dedications to such of his works as might court the favour of the rich and powerful. His 'vain, conceited humour' was so notorious that when he once attempted to recite a Latin elegy on Archbishop Ussher in Christ Church Hall, Oxford (17 April 1656), the undergraduates made such a tumult that he never attempted another recitation at the university. He printed 'what he had done' in the 'Mercurius Politicus' (1658), which called forth some satire doggerel from Samuel Woodford in 'Naps upon Parnassus' (1658) (see WOOD). It was not till 1681 that the elegy on Ussher was separately issued, and then an epitaph on the Earl of Ossory was printed with it. With the return of the Stuarts the time-server turned his coat, and his verses were now as extravagant in praise of the king as they had been of the Protector. His most despicable performance was a pamphlet entitled ' The Speeches of Oliver Cromwell, Henry Ireton, and John Bradshaw, intended to have been spoken at their execution at Tyburne 30 June 1660, but for many weightie reasons omitted, published by Marchiament Needham and Pagan Fisher, servants, poets, and pamphleteers to his Infernal Highness,' 1660, 4to (Bodl.) Fisher's character was too notorious for him to gain favour by his palpable flatteries, and he lived poor and out of favour after the Restoration. He spent several years in the Fleet prison, whence he published two works on the monuments in the city churches, written before or just after the great fire, and therefore of some value. The first of these compilations is 'A Catalogue of most of the Memorable Tombs, &c., in the Demolisht or yet extant Churches of London from St. Katherine's beyond the Tower to Temple Barre,' written 1666, published 1668, 'two years after the great fire,' London, 4to. The second is 'The Tombs, Monuments, and Sepulchral Inscriptions lately visible in St. Paul's Cathedral . . . by Major P. F., student in antiquity, grandchild to the late Sir William Fisher and that most memorable knight, Sir Thomas Neale, by his wife, Elizabeth, sister to that so publick-spirited patriot, the late Sir Thomas Freke' of Shroton, Dorsetshire; from the Fleet, with dedication to Charles II, after the fire, London, 1684, 4to. Several editions were published of both these catalogues; the latest is that revised and edited by G. B. Morgan, entitled 'Catalogue of the Tombs in the Churches of the City of London,' 1885. Fisher died in great poverty in a coffee-house in the Old Bailey 2 April 1693, and was buried 6 April in a yard belonging to the church of St. Sepulchre's.

Besides the works above enumerated, and a quantity of other odes and epitaphs (see list in WOOD and *Brit. Mus. Cat.*), Fisher edited poems on several choice and various subjects, occasionally imparted by an eminent author [i. e. James Howell, q. v.]; collected and published by Sergeant-major P. F., London, 1663; the second edition, giving the author's name, is entitled 'Mr. Howel's Poems upon divers emergent occasions,' and dedicated to Dr. Henry King, bishop of Chichester, with a preface by Fisher about Howell, whom he describes as having 'asserted the royal rights in divers learned tracts,' London, 1664, 8vo. Fisher also published: 1. 'Deus et Rex, Rex et Episcopus,' London, 1675, 4to. 2. 'Elogia Sepulchralia,' London, 1675, a collection of some of Fisher's many elegies. 3. 'A Book of Heraldry,' London, 1682, 8vo. 4. 'The Anniversary of his Sacred Majesty's Inauguration, in Latin and English; from the Fleet, under the generous jurisdiction of R. Manlove, warden thereof,' London, 1685.

Winstanley sums up Fisher's character in the following words: 'A notable undertaker in Latin verse, and had well deserved of his country, had not lucre of gain and private ambition overswayed his pen to favour successful rebellion.' Winstanley adds that he had intended to 'commit to memory the monuments in the churches in London and Westminster, but death hindered him' (*Lives of the Poets*, pp. 192, 193).

[Chalmers's Biog. Dict. p. 433; Cat. of Printed Books in Brit. Mus.; Bodleian Cat.] E. T. B.

FISHER, SAMUEL (1605–1665), quaker, son of John Fisher, a hatter in Northampton, was born in Northampton in 1605. After attending a local school he matriculated at Trinity College, Oxford, in 1623, and graduated B.A. in 1627. Being puritanically inclined he removed to New Inn Hall, whence he proceeded M.A. in 1630. Croese (*Gen. Hist. of Quakers*, p. 63, ed. 1696) says he was chaplain to a nobleman for a short time, and became a confirmed puritan. In 1632 he was presented to the lectureship of Lydd, Kent, a position variously estimated as being worth from two to five hundred pounds a year. Wood (*Athenæ Oxon.* iii. 700, ed. 1813) says he was presented to the vicarage of Lydd, but the register shows this to be incorrect. He rapidly obtained the character of a powerful preacher, and was a leader among the puritans of the district. In his 'Baby-Baptism' (p. 12) Fisher states that he was made a priest (? presbyter) by certain presbyterian divines after episcopacy was laid aside. While at Lydd Fisher took a warm part in favour of some anabaptists, attending their meetings and offering them the use of his pulpit, in which he was stopped by the churchwardens. About 1643 he returned his license to the bishop and joined the baptists, with whom he had for some time consorted, supporting himself by farming. He was rebaptised, and after taking an active part in the baptist community became minister to a congregation at Ashford, Kent, some time previous to 1649, in which year he was engaged in a controversy on infant baptism with several ministers in the presence of over two thousand people. He also disputed with Dr. Channel at Petworth, Sussex, in 1651, and was engaged in at least eight other disputes within three years, and is said to have been considered a 'great honour to the baptist cause' (CROSBY, *Hist. of the Baptists*, i. 363). He wrote several tractates in defence of his principles, and 'Baby-Baptism meer Babism.' In 1654 William Caton and John Stubbs, while on a visit to Lydd, stayed at Fisher's house, and convinced him of the truth of quakerism. Shortly afterwards he joined the Friends, among whom he subsequently became a minister, probably before his meeting with George Fox at Romney in 1655. On 17 Sept. 1656 Fisher attended the meeting of parliament, and when the Protector stated that to his knowledge no man in England had suffered imprisonment unjustly attempted a reply. He was prevented completing his speech, which he afterwards published. He subsequently attempted to address the members of parliament at a fast-day service in St. Margaret's Church, Westmin-

Oxfordshire, being made collector of the king's revenue within that borough and hundred, as also governor of the castle, with a fee of 66s. 7d. a year for exercising the office of steward and keeping the king's court within that manor. It was generally believed that the Duke of Northumberland, anticipating want of money to pay the forces which would be required in the event of his daughter-in-law Lady Jane Grey being proclaimed queen, 'privately conveyed a vast summe' to Fisher's keeping, which was hidden by him in Bishop's Itchington pool. After the attainder and execution of the duke in 1553, Fisher was questioned about the money by orders from the queen, but he sturdily refused to deliver it up, and even suffered his fingers to be pulled out of joint by the rack rather than discover it. Fisher represented Warwick in the second parliament of Mary, 1554, and in the first (1554), second (1555), and third (1557–8) of Philip and Mary (*Lists of Members of Parliament, Official Return*, pt. i. pp. 387, 391, 395, 398). In 1571, when Robert Dudley, earl of Leicester, celebrated the order of St. Michael in the collegiate church of Warwick, the bailiff and burgesses of the borough were invited to attend the earl from the Priory, where he was Fisher's guest for six or seven days, and thence went in grand procession to the church. Immediately on the conclusion of the ceremony, at which he had been present, William Parr, marquis of Northampton, brother of Queen Catherine Parr, died suddenly at the Priory. The following year Elizabeth paid a sudden visit to the Priory, when returning to Warwick from Kenilworth, on Saturday night, 17 Aug., having dined with Fisher's son, Edward, at his house at Itchington on the Monday previously. After supping with Mrs. Fisher and her company, her majesty withdrew for the kind purpose of visiting 'the good man of the house . . . who at that time was grevously vexid with the gowt,' but with most gracious words she so 'comfortid him that forgetting, or rather counterfeyting, his payne,' he resolved 'in more haste than good spede to be on horseback the next tyme of her going abrode.' Though his resolution was put to the proof as soon as the following Monday, he actually accomplished it, attending the queen on her return to Kenilworth and riding in company with the Lord-treasurer Burghley, to whom, it would seem, he talked with more freedom than discretion (NICHOLS, *Progresses of Queen Elizabeth*, i. 310, 318–19). Fisher died 12 Jan. 1576–7, and was buried at the upper end of the north aisle in St. Mary's Church, Warwick. His

tomb, which bore the recumbent effigies of himself and his first wife Winifred, daughter of William Holt, probably perished in the great fire of 1694; it has been engraved by Hollar (DUGDALE, p. 350). His son and heir, EDWARD FISHER, was thirty years old at the time of his father's death. His inheritance, Dugdale informs us, was then worth 3,000l. a year, but he soon squandered it, and hastened his ruin by making a fraudulent conveyance to deceive Serjeant Puckering, to whom in 23 Elizabeth he sold the Priory and lands adjoining. The serjeant commenced a prosecution against him in the Star-chamber, and had not Leicester interposed, his fine would have been very severe. He ultimately consented that an act of parliament should be made to confirm the estate to Puckering, but being encumbered with debts he was committed prisoner to the Fleet, where he spent the rest of his life. He married Katherine, daughter of Sir Richard Longe, by whom he had issue, Thomas, John, Dorothy, and Katherine.

Fisher is sometimes mistaken for the John Fisher who compiled the 'Black Book of Warwick.' The latter was in all probability John Fisher, bailiff of Warwick, in 1565.

[Dugdale's Warwickshire (1656), pp. 364–5, and passim; Colvile's Worthies of Warwickshire, pp. 287–91; Cal. State Papers, Dom. 1547–80, Addenda, 1547–65; Visitation of Warwickshire, 1619, Harl. Soc. 20.]   G. G.

FISHER, THOMAS (1781?–1836), antiquary, born at Rochester in or about 1781, was the younger of the two sons of Thomas Fisher, printer, bookseller, and alderman of that city. His father, who died on 29 Aug. 1786, was author of the 'Kentish Traveller's Companion,' 12mo, 1776, and, with Samuel Denne, F.S.A. [q. v.], and W. Shrubsole, of a useful little 'History of Rochester' published in 1772 (*Gent. Mag.* vol. lvi. pt. ii. pp. 908, 995, vol. lvii. pt. ii. p. 696). In 1786 Fisher entered the India House as an extra clerk, but in April 1816 was appointed searcher of records, a post for which his knowledge and literary attainments well fitted him. From this situation he retired on a pension in June 1834, after having spent in different offices under the company altogether forty-six years. He died unmarried on 20 July 1836, in his sixty-fifth year, at his lodgings in Church Street, Stoke Newington, and was buried on the 26th in Bunhill Fields. From the time of his coming to London he had resided at Gloucester Terrace, Hoxton, in the parish of Shoreditch.

Before he left Rochester Fisher's talents as a draughtsman attracted the attention of

Isaac Taylor, the engraver. He was besides eminent as an antiquary. Some plates in the 'Custumale Roffense,' published by John Thorpe in 1788, are from drawings by Fisher; while it appears from the same work (pp. 155, 234, 262) that he had helped Samuel Denne, one of the promoters of the undertaking, in examining the architecture and monuments of Rochester Cathedral. His first literary effort, a description of the Crown inn at Rochester and its curious cellars, was printed with a view and plan in the 'Gentleman's Magazine' for 1789, under the pseudonym of 'Antiquitatis Conservator' (vol. lix. pt. ii. p. 1185). He had previously contributed drawings for one or two plates. In 1795 Denne communicated to the Society of Antiquaries a letter on the subject of watermarks in paper, enclosing drawings by Fisher of sixty-four specimens, together with copies of several autographs and some curious documents discovered by him in a room over the town hall at Rochester. The letter, accompanied by the drawings, is printed in 'Archæologia,' xii. 114–31. By Fisher's care the records were afterwards placed in proper custody. His next publications were 'An Engraving of a fragment of Jasper found near Hillah, bearing part of an inscription in the cuneiform character,' s. sh. 4to, London, 1802, and 'An Inscription [in cuneiform characters] of the size of the original, copied from a stone lately found among the ruins of ancient Babylon,' s. sh. fol., London, 1803. In 1806 and 1807 Fisher was the means of preserving two beautiful specimens of Roman mosaic discovered in the city of London; the one before the East India House in Leadenhall Street, and the other, which was presented to the British Museum, in digging foundations for the enlargement of the Bank of England. These he caused to be engraved from drawings made by himself, and he published a description of them in the 'Gentleman's Magazine,' vol. lxxvii. pt. i. p. 415.

In the summer of 1804 Fisher discovered some legendary paintings on the roof and walls of the chapel belonging to the ancient Guild of Holy Cross in Stratford-on-Avon. A work founded upon this and muniments lent to him by the corporation appeared in 1807 as 'A Series of antient Allegorical, Historical, and Legendary Paintings . . . discovered . . . on the walls of the Chapel of the Trinity at Stratford-upon-Avon . . . also Views and Sections illustrative of the Architecture of the Chapel,' parts i–iv. (Appendix, No. 1, pp. 1–4), fol. (London), 1807. His account of the guild, with copious extracts from the ledger-book, appeared in the 'Gentleman's Magazine,' new ser. iii. 162, 375.

Between 1812 and 1816 Fisher published ninety-five plates from his drawings of monumental and other remains in Bedfordshire, under the title of 'Collections Historical, Genealogical, and Topographical for Bedfordshire,' 4to, London, 1812–16. A second part, consisting of 114 folio plates, appeared only a few weeks before his death in 1836. He gave up his intention of adding letterpress descriptions on account of the tax of eleven copies imposed by the Copyright Act. He published numerous remonstrances in petitions to parliament, in pamphlets, and in essays in periodicals. See his essay in the 'Gentleman's Magazine' for 1813, vol. lxxxiii. pt. ii. pp. 513–28, and his petition in 1814, printed in the 'Gentleman's Magazine,' vol. lxxxvii. pt. i. p. 490. In 1838 John Gough Nichols added descriptions to a new edition.

Meanwhile Fisher had printed at the lithographic press of D. J. Redman thirty-seven drawings of 'Monumental Remains and Antiquities in the county of Bedford,' of which fifty copies were issued in 1828. Fisher was one of the first to welcome lithography in this country. As early as 1808 he published an account of it, under the title of 'Polyantography,' with a portrait of Philip H. André, its first introducer into England, in the 'Gentleman's Magazine,' vol. lxxviii. pt. i. p. 193. In 1807 he published in four lithographic plates: 1. 'A Collection of all the Characters . . . which appear in the Inscription on a Stone found among the Ruins of ancient Babylon . . . now deposited in the East Indian Company's Library at Leadenhall Street.' 2. 'A Pedestal, and Fragment of a Statue of Hercules . . . dug out of the Foundations of the Wall of the City of London.' 3. 'Ichnography, with Architectural Illustrations of the old Church of St. Peter le Poor in Broad Street, London.' 4. 'Sir W. Pickering, from his Tomb in St. Helen's Church, London.' Shortly afterwards he issued several plates of monumental brasses to illustrate Hasted's 'Kent' and Lysons's 'Environs of London.' In order to encourage a deserving artist, Hilkiah Burgess, Fisher had ten plates etched of 'Sepulchral Monuments in Oxford.' These were issued in 1836.

Fisher was in 1821 elected F.S.A. of Perth, and on 5 May 1836 F.S.A. of London, an honour from which he had been hitherto debarred, as being both artist and dissenter. Many of the more valuable biographies of distinguished Anglo-Indians in the 'Gentleman's Magazine' were contributed by Fisher. That of Charles Grant, father of Lord Glenelg (Gent. Mag. vol. xciii. pt. ii. p. 561), was afterwards enlarged and printed for private circulation, 8vo, London, 1833. He was likewise a contributor to the 'European Magazine,' the 'Asiatic Journal,' and to several religious periodicals. He was one of the projectors of the 'Congregational Magazine,' and from 1818 to 1823 conducted the statistical department of that serial. When elected a guardian of Shoreditch, in which parish he resided, he assisted John Ware, the vestry clerk, in the compilation of a volume entitled 'An Account of the several Charities and Estates held in trust for the use of the Poor of the Parish of St. Leonard, Shoreditch, Middlesex, and of Benefactors to the same,' 8vo, London, 1836. He was also zealous in the cause of anti-slavery. In 1825 he published 'The Negro's Memorial, or Abolitionist's Catechism. By an Abolitionist,' 8vo, London. He was a member, too, of various bible and missionary societies. A few of his letters to Thomas Orlebar Marsh, vicar of Steventon, Bedfordshire, are in the British Museum, Addit. MS. 23205. His collections of topographical drawings and prints, portraits and miscellaneous prints, books, and manuscripts, were sold by Evans on 30 May 1837 and two following days.

[Gent. Mag. new ser. vi. 220, 434–8; Notes and Queries, 5th ser. xi. 228, 339; Cat. of Library of London Institution, iii. 350.]   G. G.

FISHER, WILLIAM (1780–1852), rear-admiral, second son of John Fisher of Yarmouth, Norfolk, was born on 18 Nov. 1780, and entered the navy in 1795. After serving in the North Sea, at the Cape of Good Hope, and in the Mediterranean, and as acting lieutenant of the Foudroyant on the coast of Egypt, he was confirmed in the rank on 3 Sept. 1801. In 1805 he was lieutenant of the Superb during the chase of Villeneuve to the West Indies; and in 1806 was promoted to be commander. In 1808 he commanded the Racehorse of 18 guns in the Channel, and in the same ship, in 1809–10, was employed in surveying in the Mozambique. In March 1811 he was promoted to post-rank, and in 1816–17 commanded in succession the Bann and Cherub, each of 20 guns, on the coast of Guinea, in both of which he captured several slavers and pirates, some of them after a desperate resistance. From March 1836 to May 1841 he commanded the Asia in the Mediterranean, and in 1840, during the operations on the coast of Syria [see STOPFORD, SIR ROBERT], was employed as senior officer of the detached squadron off Alexandria, with the task of keeping open the mail communication through Egypt. For this service he received the Turkish gold medal and diamond decoration. He had no further

service afloat, but became, in due course, a rear-admiral in 1847. During his retirement he wrote two novels: 'The Petrel, or Love on the Ocean' (1850), which passed through three editions, and 'Ralph Rutherford, a Nautical Romance' (1851). He died in London, on 30 Sept. 1852. A man who had been so long in the navy during a very stirring period, who had surveyed the Mozambique, and captured slavers and pirates, had necessarily plenty of adventures at command, which scarcely needed the complications of improbable love stories to make them interesting; but the author had neither the constructive skill nor the literary talent necessary for writing a good novel, and his language throughout is exaggerated and stilted to the point of absurdity.

Fisher married, in 1810, Elizabeth, sister of Sir James Rivett Carnac, bart., governor of Bombay, by whom he had two children, a daughter and a son.

[O'Byrne's Nav. Biog. Dict.; Gent. Mag. 1852, new ser. xxxviii. 634.]   J. K. L.

FISHER, WILLIAM WEBSTER, M.D. (1798?–1874), Downing professor of medicine at Cambridge, a native of Westmoreland, was born in or about 1798. He studied in the first instance at Montpellier, where he took the degree of M.D. in 1825 (D. M. I. 'De l'inflammation considérée sous le rapport de ses indications,' 4to, Montpellier, 1825). Two years later he was entered at Trinity College, Cambridge, of which his brother, the Rev. John Hutton Fisher, was then fellow and assistant-tutor. Subsequently he removed to Downing College, where he graduated as M.B. in 1834. Shortly afterwards he succeeded to a fellowship, but the Downing professorship of medicine falling vacant in 1841, Fisher was elected and resigned his fellowship. He, however, held some of the college offices. In 1841 he proceeded M.D. His lectures were well attended. He acted for many years as one of the university examiners of students in medicine, and was an *ex officio* member of the university board of medical studies. In addition to fulfilling the duties of his professorship, Fisher had a large practice as a physician at Cambridge. He was formerly one of the physicians to Addenbrooke's Hospital, and on his resignation was appointed consulting physician to that institution. Although for some time he had relinquished the practice of his profession, he regularly delivered courses of lectures until 1868, since which time they were read by a deputy, P. W. Latham, M.D., late fellow of Downing. Fisher was a fellow of the Cambridge

Philosophical Society, and a contributor to its 'Transactions.' He was highly esteemed in the university for his professional attainments and his conversational powers. He died at his lodge in Downing College, 4 Oct. 1874, in his seventy-sixth year.

[Brit. Med. Journ. 10 Oct. 1874, p. 481; Med. Times and Gaz. 10 Oct. 1874, p. 434, 17 Oct. 1874, p. 461; Lancet, 10 Oct. 1874, p. 533.]

G. G.

FISK, WILLIAM (1796–1872), painter, born in 1796 at Thorpe-le-Soken, Essex, was the son of a yeoman farmer at Can Hall in that county, of a family which boasted of some antiquity, dating back to the days of Henry IV. Drawing very early became Fisk's favourite occupation, but his inclination to art was discouraged by his father, who sent him to school at Colchester, and at nineteen years of age placed him in a mercantile house in London. In this uncongenial profession Fisk remained for ten years, though he never neglected his artistic powers, and in 1818 sent to the Royal Academy a portrait of Mr. G. Fisk, and in 1819 a portrait of a 'Child and Favourite Dog.' He married about 1826, and after the birth of his eldest son he devoted himself seriously to art as a profession. In 1829 he sent to the Royal Academy a portrait of William Redmore Bigg, R.A., and continued to exhibit portraits there for a few years. At the British Institution he exhibited in 1830 'The Widow,' and in 1832 'Puck.' About 1834 he took to painting large historical compositions, by which he is best known. These compositions, though a failure from an artistic point of view, possessed value from the care Fisk took to obtain contemporary portraits and authorities for costume, which he faithfully reproduced on his canvas. Some of them were engraved, and the popularity of the engravings led to his painting more. They comprised 'Lady Jane Grey, when in confinement in the Tower, visited by Feckenham' (British Institution, 1834); 'The Coronation of Robert Bruce' (Royal Academy, 1836); 'La Journée des Dupes' (Royal Academy, 1837); 'Leonardo da Vinci expiring in the arms of Francis I' (Royal Academy, 1838); 'The Chancellor Wriothesley approaching to apprehend Katherine Parr on a charge of heresy,' and 'Mary, widow of Louis XII of France, receiving Charles Brandon, Duke of Suffolk, ambassador from Henry VIII' (British Institution, 1838); 'The Queen Mother, Marie de Medici, demanding the dismissal of Cardinal Richelieu' (British Institution, 1839); 'The Conspiracy of the Pazzi, or the attempt to assassinate Lorenzo de Medici' (Royal Academy, 1839); the last-named picture was in 1840 awarded the gold medal of the Manchester Institution for the best historical picture exhibited in their gallery. About 1840 Fisk commenced a series of pictures connected with the reign of Charles I, namely, 'Cromwell's Family interceding for the life of Charles I' (Royal Academy, 1840); 'The Trial of the Earl of Strafford' (never exhibited, engraved by James Scott in 1841, and now in the Walker Art Gallery, Liverpool); 'The Trial of Charles I in Westminster Hall' (Royal Academy, 1842); 'Charles I passing through the banqueting-house, Whitehall, to the Scaffold' (Royal Academy, 1843); 'The last interview of Charles I with his Children' (British Institution, 1844). After these his productions were of a less ambitious nature, and he eventually retired from active life to some property at Danbury in Essex, where he died on 8 Nov. 1872. He was also a frequent contributor to the Suffolk Street exhibition.

[Art Journal, 1873, p. 6; Redgrave's Dict. of Artists; Graves's Dict. of Artists, 1760–1880; Catalogues of the Royal Academy and British Institution.]

L. C.

FISK, WILLIAM HENRY (1827–1884), painter and drawing-master, son of William Fisk [q. v.], was a pupil of his father, and also a student of the Royal Academy. He was a skilled draughtsman, and as such was appointed anatomical draughtsman to the Royal College of Surgeons. In painting he was a landscape-painter, and exhibited for the first time in 1846. In 1850 he exhibited at the Royal Academy, subsequently being an occasional exhibitor at the other London exhibitions and also in Paris. He was teacher of drawing and painting to University College School, London, and in that capacity was very successful and of high repute. A series of drawings of trees which he produced for the queen were much esteemed. He was a clear and logical lecturer on the practical aspect of art, and succeeded in attracting large audiences in London and the provinces. He also occasionally contributed articles on painting to the public press. He died on 13 Nov. 1884, in his fifty-eighth year.

[Athenæum, 22 Nov. 1884; Graves's Dict. of Artists, 1760–1880; Catalogues of the Royal Academy, &c.]

L. C.

FISKEN, WILLIAM (d. 1883), presbyterian minister, the son of a farmer, was born on Gelleyburn farm, near Crieff, Perthshire. After attending school at the neighbouring village of Muthill, he was sent to St. Andrews College to study for the ministry under Professor Duncan. Subsequently he removed to the university of Glasgow, and thence to the Divinity Hall of the Secession church. While there he taught a school at Alyth, near his birthplace. Upon receiving license in the presbytery of Dundee, he commenced his career as a preacher in the Secession church. He visited various places throughout the country, including the Orkney Islands, where he would have received a call had he cared to accept it. He was next sent to the presbytery at Newcastle-upon-Tyne, and preached as a probationer at the adjoining village of Stamfordham, where in 1847 he received a call, and was duly ordained. He there laboured zealously until his death. In the double capacity of governor and secretary he did much towards promoting the success of the scheme of the endowed schools at Stamfordham. Fisken and his brothers Thomas (a schoolmaster at Stockton-upon-Tees) and David studied mechanics. Thomas and he invented the steam plough. A suit took place between the Fiskens and the Messrs. Fowler, the well-known implement makers at Leeds, and the finding of the jury was that the former were the original discoverers. The appliance which perfected the plan of the brothers occurred to them both independently and almost simultaneously. William Chartres of Newcastle-upon-Tyne, the solicitor employed by the Fiskens, used to tell how the two brothers wrote to him on the same day about the final discovery, but that he received William's letter first. Fisken also invented a potato-sowing machine, a safety steam boiler, a propeller, an apparatus for heating churches, which worked excellently, and the 'steam tackle' which, patented in July 1855, helped to render the steam plough of practical use. This system of haulage, which obtained second prize at the royal show at Wolverhampton, has undergone great modifications since its early appearance in Scotland in 1852, its exhibition at Carlisle in 1855, and at the show of the Royal Agricultural Society of England in 1863 (*Journal of Royal Agricultural Society*, xx. 193, xxiv. 368). Fisken worked on the fly-rope system. An endless rope set into motion direct by the fly-wheel of the engine drove windlasses of an extremely ingenious type, by which the plough or other implement was put in motion. A great deal of excellent work was done on this system, especially with tackle made by Messrs. Barford & Perkins of Peterborough, but for some reason the system never quite took with farmers, and very few sets of Fisken's tackle are now in use (*Engineer*, 11 Jan. 1884, p. 37). Fisken was the author of a pamphlet on 'The Cheapest System of Steam Cultivation and Steam Cartage,' and of another 'On the Comparative Methods of Steam Tackle,'

which gained the prize of the Bath and West of England Society. A man of liberal views, great generosity of character, and wide reading, he made friends wherever he went. He died at his manse, Stamfordham, on 28 Dec. 1883, aged upwards of seventy.

[Times, 4 and 8 Jan. 1884; Newcastle Courant, 4 Jan. 1884.]   G. G.

FITCH, RALPH (1550?-1611), traveller in India, was among the first Englishmen known to have made the overland route down the Euphrates Valley towards India. He left London on 12 Feb. 1583 with other merchants of the Levant Company, among whom were J. Newberry, J. Eldred, W. Leedes, jeweller, and J. Story, a painter. He writes: 'I did ship myself in a ship of London, called the Tiger, wherein we went for Tripolis in Syria, and from thence we took the way for Aleppo' (HAKLUYT, ii. 250). Fitch and his companions arrived at Tripolis on 1 May, thence they made their way to Aleppo in seven days with the caravan. Setting out again on 31 May for a three days' journey on camels to Bir (Biredjik) on the Euphrates, there they bought a large boat, and agreed with a master and crew to descend the river, noticing on their way the primitive boat-building near the bituminous fountains at Hit (cf. CHESNEY, ii. 636). On 29 June Fitch and his company reached Felújah, where they landed. After a week's delay, for want of camels, they crossed the great plain during the night, on account of the heat, to Babylon (i.e. Bagdad) on the Tigris. On 22 July they departed hence in flat-bottomed boats down this river to Bussorah at the head of the Persian Gulf, where they left Eldred for trade.

On 4 Sept. Fitch and his three companions arrived at Ormuz, where within a week they were all imprisoned by the Portuguese governor at the instance of the Venetians, who dreaded them as their rivals in trade. On 11 Oct. the Englishmen were shipped for Goa in the East Indies unto the viceroy, where, upon their arrival at the end of November, as Fitch puts it, 'for our better entertainment, we were presently put into a fair strong prison, where we continued until 22 Dec.' (HAKLUYT, vol. ii. pt. i. 250). Story having turned monk, Fitch, Newberry, and Leedes were soon afterwards set at liberty by two sureties procured for them by two jesuit fathers, one of whom was Thomas Stevens, sometime of New College, Oxford, who was the first Englishman known to have reached India by the Cape of Good Hope, four years before, i.e. 1579 (cf. HAKLUYT, vol. ii. pt. i. 249). After 'employing the remains of their money in precious stones,' on Whitsunday, 5 April 1584, Fitch and his two companions, Newberry and Leedes, escaped across the river from Goa, and made the best of their way across the Deccan to Bijapur and Golconda, near Haiderabad, thence northwards to the court of Akbar, the Great Mogore (i.e. Mogul, Persian corruption for Mongol), whom they found either at Agra or his newly built town of Fatepore (Fatehpur Sikri), twelve miles south from it. They stayed here until 28 Sept. 1585, when Newberry proceeded north to Lahore, with a view to returning through Persia to Aleppo or Constantinople ; as Newberry was never heard of afterwards it is supposed he was murdered in the Punjab. Story remained at Goa, where he soon threw off the monk's habit and married a native woman, and Leedes, the jeweller, accepted service under the Emperor Akbar. From Agra Fitch took boat with a fleet of 180 others down the Jumna to Prage (Allahabad), thence he proceeded down the Ganges, calling at Benares and Patna, to 'Tanda in Gouren,' formerly one of the old capitals of Bengal, the very site of which is now unknown. From this point Fitch journeyed northward twenty days to Couch (Kuch Behar), afterwards returning south to Húgli, the Porto Piqueno of the Portuguese, one league from Satigam. His next journey was eastward to the country of Tippara, and thence south to Chatigam, the Porto Grande of the Portuguese, now known as Chittagong. Here he embarked for a short voyage up one of the many mouths of the Ganges to Baçola (Barisol) and Serampore, thence to Sinnergan, identified by Cunningham (xv. 127) as Sunargaon, an ancient city formerly the centre of a cloth-making district, the best to be found in India at this period. On 28 Nov. 1586 he re-embarked at Serampore in a small Portuguese vessel for Burma. As far as can be learned from this obscure part of his narrative, Fitch, after sailing southwards to Negrais Point, ascended the western arm of the Irawadi to Cosmin (Kau-smin, the old Talaing name for Bassein), thence by the inland navigation of the Delta, across to Cirion (Syriam, now known as Than-lyeng, near Rangoon), calling at Macao (Meh-Kay of Williams's map), and so on to Pegu. Fitch's sketches of Burmese life and manners as seen in and near Pegu deserve perusal upon their own merits, apart from the fact of their having been drawn by the first Englishman to enter Burma. With a keen eye to the prospects of trade, he also proved himself to be a persistent questioner upon state affairs. In describing the king of Pegu's dress and splendour of his court retinue, he adds : 'He [the

king] hath also houses full of gold and silver, and bringen in often, but spendeth very little' (HAKLUYT, ii. 260). From Pegu Fitch went a twenty-five days' journey north-east to Tamahey (Zimmé) in the Shan States of Siam ; this must have been towards the end of 1587, for on 10 Jan. 1588 he sailed from Pegu for Malacca, where he arrived 8 Feb., soon after its relief by P. de Lima Pereira for the Portuguese (cf. LINSCHOTEN, p. 153). On 29 March Fitch set out on his homeward journey from Malacca to Martaban, and on to Pegu, where he remained a second time. On 17 Sept. he went once more to Cosmin (Bassein), and there took shipping for Bengal, where he arrived in November. On 3 Feb. 1589 he shipped for Cochin on the Malabar coast, where he was detained for want of a passage nearly eight months. On 2 Nov. he sailed for Goa, where he remained for three days, probably in disguise. Hence he went up the coast to Chaul, where after another delay of twenty-three days in making provision for the shipping of his goods, he left India for Ormus, where he stayed for fifty days for a passage to Bussorah. On his return journey Fitch ascended the Tigris as far as Mosul, journeying hence to Mirdui and Urfah, he went to Bir, and so passed the Euphrates. He concludes the account of his travels thus : 'From Bir I went to Aleppo, where I stayed certain months for company, and then I went to Tripolis, where, finding English shipping, I came with a prosperous voyage to London, where, by God's assistance, I safely arrived the 29th April 1591, having been eight years out of my native country' (HAKLUYT, vol. ii. pt. i. 265).

Fitch's narrative, which was printed by Hakluyt in 1598, largely copies its description of places from Thomas Hickock's translation (from the Italian) of the travels of Cæsar Frederick (Cesare Federici), which was published independently in 1588, and was also incorporated in Hakluyt's collections (1598). Fitch was often consulted when the first charter to the East India Company of 31 Dec. 1601 was under consideration. On 2 Oct. 1600 it was 'Orderid that Captein Lancaster (and others), together with Mr. Eldred and Mr. ffitch, shall in the meetinge to-morrow morning conferre of the merchaundize fitt to be provided for the (first) voyage' (STEVENS, p. 26). Again, 29 Jan. 1600-1 : 'Order is given to . . . Mr. Hacklett . . . [who] was required to sette downe in wryting a note of the principal places in the East Indies where trade was to be had, to th' end the same may be used for the better instruction of oᵣ factors in the said voyage' (ib. p. 123). Again court minutes,

31 Dec. 1606: 'Letters to be obtained from K. James to the king of Cambaya, gouernors of Aden, etc. . . . their titles to be inquired of Ralph Fitch' (SAINSBURY, *State Papers*, No. 36). Fitch, who was mentioned in the second charter of the Levant Company (7 Jan. 1592–3), was long a member of the board. His signature appears thirteen times in the Company's records between 2 Feb. 1607–8 and 26 Oct. 1610. He was also for many years associated with the Leather-sellers' Company, and was on the court of assistants until 7 June 1611. He died, according to his will in Somerset House, between 3 and 5 Oct. of the last year.

In 1606 was produced Shakespeare's 'Macbeth;' the line (I. iii. 8) 'Her husband's to Aleppo gone, master of the Tiger,' plainly echoes the opening passage of Fitch's narrative.

[Chesney's Survey of the Euphrates and Tigris, 1850; Cunningham's India; Archæological Survey Reports, vol. xv., Calcutta, 1882; Hakluyt's Navigations, 1599, vol. ii.; Linschoten's Voyages 1598; Stevens and Birdwood's Records of the East India Company, 1599–1603; Sainsbury's State Papers, East Indies, 1513–1616.]   C. H. C.

FITCH, THOMAS (*d.* 1517), ecclesiastic and compiler. [See FICH.]

FITCH, WILLIAM (1563–1611). Capuchin friar. [See CANFIELD, BENEDICT.]

FITCH, WILLIAM STEVENSON (1793–1859), antiquary, born in 1793, was for more than twenty-one years postmaster of Ipswich, but devoted his leisure to studying the antiquities of Suffolk. His collections were dispersed on his death, but the West Suffolk Archæological Association, of which he was a founder, purchased the drawings and engravings, arranged in more than thirty quarto volumes, and they were deposited in the museum of the society at Bury St. Edmunds. Fitch published: 1. 'A Catalogue of Suffolk Memorial Registers, Royal Grants,' &c. (in his possession), Great Yarmouth, 1843, 8vo. 2. 'Ipswich and its Early Mints' (Ipswich), 1848, 4to. He contributed notices of coins and antiquities found in Suffolk to the 'Journal of the British Archæological Association' (vols. i. ii. iii. xxi.), and the 'Proceedings of the East Suffolk Archæological Society.' Fitch died 17 July 1859, leaving a widow, a daughter, and two sons.

[C. R. Smith's Collect. Antiqua, vi. 323–4; C. R. Smith's Retrospections, i. 245–8; Gent. Mag. 1859, 3rd ser. vii. 202; Index to Journ. Brit. Arch. Assoc. vols. i–xxx.]   W. W.

FITCHETT, JOHN (1776–1838), poet, the son of a wine merchant at Liverpool, was born on 21 Sept. 1776, and having lost his parents before he attained the age of ten, was removed to Warrington by his testamentary guardian, Mr. Kerfoot, and placed at the Warrington grammar school under the Rev. Edward Owen. In 1793 he was articled to his guardian, and in due time, having been admitted an attorney, was taken into partnership with him, subsequently attaining a high place in his profession. His first published work, 'Bewsey, a Poem' (Warrington, 1796, 4to), written at the age of eighteen, had considerable success. He afterwards wrote many fugitive pieces, which were collected and printed at Warrington in 1836, under the title of 'Minor Poems, composed at various Times' (8vo, pp. ii, 416). The great work of his life was one which occupied his leisure hours for forty years, and in the composition of which he bestowed unwearied industry and acute research. It was printed at Warrington for private circulation at intervals between 1808 and 1834, in five quarto volumes. It was cast in the form of a romantic epic poem, the subject being the life and times of King Alfred, including, in addition to a biography of Alfred, an epitome of the antiquities, topography, religion, and civil and religious condition of the country. He rewrote part of the work, but did not live to finish it. He left money for printing a new edition, and the work of supervising it was undertaken by his pupil, clerk, and friend, Robert Roscoe [q. v.] (son of William Roscoe of Liverpool), who completed the task by adding 2,585 lines, the entire work containing more than 131,000 lines, and forming probably the longest poem in any language. This prodigious monument of misapplied learning and mental energy was published by Pickering in 1841–2, in six volumes, 8vo, with the title of 'King Alfred, a Poem.'

Fitchett died unmarried at Warrington on 20 Oct. 1838, and was buried at Winwick Church. His large and choice library was left to his nephew, John Fitchett Marsh, and was sold, with that gentleman's augmentations, at Sotheby's rooms in May 1882.

[Marsh's Lit. Hist. of Warrington in Warrington Mechanics' Inst. Lectures (1859), p. 85; Palatine Note-book, ii. 168, 175; Kendrick's Profiles of Warrington Worthies; Notes and Queries, 1st ser. x. 215, 334; Manchester City News Notes and Queries, iii. 89, 98; Lanc. and Cheshire Hist. and Geneal. Notes, iii. 35, 55.]   C. W. S.

FITTLER, JAMES (1758–1835), engraver, was born in London in 1758, and became a student at the Royal Academy in 1778. Besides book illustrations, he distinguished himself by numerous works after English and foreign masters, chiefly portraits. He engraved also landscapes, marine subjects, and topographical views, and was appointed marine engraver to George III. He was elected an associate of the Royal Academy in 1800; died at Turnham Green 2 Dec. 1835, and was buried in Chiswick churchyard. Fittler exhibited at the Royal Academy between 1776 and 1824. In 1788 he resided at No. 62 Upper Charlotte Street, Rathbone Place. Among his most important works are : two views of Windsor Castle, after George Robertson ; a view of Christ Church Great Gate, Oxford, after William Delamotte ; 'The Cutting of the Corvette la Chevrette from the Bay of Camaret, on the night of 21 July 1801,' 'Lord Howe's Victory,' and 'The Battle of the Nile,' after P. J. de Loutherbourg ; several naval fights, after Captain Mark Oates, Thomas Luny, and D. Serres ; a classical landscape, with a temple on the left, after Claude Lorraine ; the celebrated portrait known by the name of 'Titian's Schoolmaster,' after Moroni ; portrait of Lord Grenville, after T. Phillips ; portrait of Dr. Hodson, after T. Phillips ; Pope Innocent X, after Velasquez ; he also executed the plates for Forster's 'British Gallery,' many of those for Bell's ' British Theatre,' and all the illustrations in Dibdin's ' Ædes Althorpianæ,' published in 1822, after which time he undertook no important work. His prints, books, and copper-plates were sold at Sotheby's 14 July 1825, and two following days.

[Redgrave's Dictionary of Artists.] L. F.

FITTON, Sir ALEXANDER (d. 1699), lord chancellor of Ireland, was the younger son of William Fitton of Awrice, co. Limerick, by Eva, daughter of Sir Edward Trevor, knt., of Brynkinallt, Denbighshire (*Harl. MS.* 2153, f. 36). This William Fitton was next male kinsman to Sir Edward Fitton, bart., the possessor of Gawsworth, Cheshire, who resolved in 1641 to restore the old entail of his estates, and settled them by indenture, which he was said to have confirmed by deed-poll, on the above William Fitton, with remainder to his two sons. Sir Edward died in August 1643, shortly after the taking of Bristol, and 'his heart, his brain, and soft entrails' were buried in a fragile urn in the church of St. Peter in that city (*Gloucestershire Notes and Queries*, iii. 353). On the death of Felicia, lady Fitton, in January 1654–5, William Fitton became possessed of Gawsworth. His son Alexander was admitted a law student of the Inner Temple in 1655, and was called to the bar on 12 May 1662. He married, about 1655, Anne, elder daughter of Thomas Jolliffe (or Jollie) of Cofton, Worcestershire, with whom he probably received a fortune, for shortly after

the mortgages on the family estates were paid off; and his elder brother, Edward, having died without issue, he became, on his father's death, the possessor of the whole. His wife died 7 Oct. 1687, and was buried in St. Patrick's Cathedral, Dublin, under the monument of her husband's ancestor, Sir Edward Fitton [q. v.] Their issue was Anne, an only child.

In 1661 Charles, lord Gerard of Brandon, laid claim to Fitton's estates in right of his mother, who was sister to Sir Edward, and a will was produced, nineteen years after Sir Edward's death, giving the estates to Lord Gerard. A litigation took place, in the course of which it was alleged by Lord Gerard's solicitor that the deed-poll executed by Sir Edward Fitton, upon which Fitton relied, was forged by one Abraham Granger. An issue was then directed by the court of chancery to try the genuineness of the document, and the jury finally found against it. Then Granger withdrew a previous confession, and stated that the deed was duly signed (ORMEROD, *Cheshire*, iii. 259). The House of Lords on hearing of this ordered that Fitton should be fined 500*l.* and committed to the king's bench prison until he should produce Granger, and find sureties for good behaviour during life. Having lost his money in the fruitless prosecution of his case, Fitton remained in gaol until taken out by James II to be made chancellor of Ireland, when he was knighted.

On 12 Feb. 1686–7 he received the appointment of lord chancellor of Ireland, and on 1 April 1689 was raised to the peerage as Baron Fitton of Gawsworth, but this title, granted by James after his abdication, was not allowed. Little is known of Fitton's qualifications for his office beyond his long experience of litigation. The absence of any complaints from the bar or bench is so far in his favour. Archbishop King has asserted that Fitton ' could not understand the merit of a cause of any difficulty, and therefore never failed to give sentence according to his inclination, having no other rule to lead him' (*State of the Protestants of Ireland under King James,* 1691, p. 59). A recent biographer says : ' I have looked carefully through those [decrees] made while Lord [Fitton of] Gawsworth held the seals, but could observe nothing to mark ignorance of his duty, or incapacity to perform it. He confirms reports, dismisses bills, decrees in favour of awards, grants injunctions, with the confidence of an experienced equity judge' (O'FLANAGAN, *Lives of the Lord Chancellors of Ireland,* 1870, i. 487).

After the flight of James II from Ireland, Fitton, Chief Baron Rice, and Plowden assumed the office of lords justices of Ireland. In 1690 Sir Charles Porter was appointed lord chancellor in succession to Fitton, who was attainted; fled to France; and died at St. Germains in November 1699 (LUTTRELL, *Relation*, iv. 586). The husbands of the two coheiresses of the Fitton estates, Lord Mohun and the Duke of Hamilton, killed each other (1712) in the famous duel arising from a dispute as to the partition, 'and Gawsworth itself passed into an unlineal hand by a series of alienations complicated beyond example' (*Cheshire*, iii. 295).

[Authorities cited above; Burke's Extinct Baronetcies (1844), p. 199; Earwaker's East Cheshire, ii. 555, 560–3, 591; Nash's Worcestershire, i. 250; Smyth's Law Officers of Ireland, p. 36.]

B. H. B.

FITTON, SIR EDWARD, the elder (1527–1579), lord president of Connaught and vice-treasurer of Ireland, was the eldest son of Sir Edward Fitton of Gawsworth, Cheshire, and Mary, daughter and coheiress of Guicciard Harbottle, esq., of Northumberland (ORMEROD, *Cheshire*, iii. 292). He was knighted by Sir Henry Sidney in 1566 (*Cal. Carew MSS.* ii. 149), and on the establishment of provincial governments in Connaught and Munster he was in 1569 appointed first lord president of Connaught and Thomond (patent, 1 June 1569; *Liber Hiberniæ*, ii. 189). Arrived in Ireland on Ascension day he was established in his office by Sir H. Sidney in July. On 15 April 1570 he wrote to Cecil : ' We began our government in this province at Michaelmas, from thence till Christmas we passed smoothly . . . but after Christmas, taking a journey into Thomond, all fell upside down ' (*State Papers*, Eliz. xxx. 43). Ere long he found himself so closely besieged in Galway by the Earl of Thomond and the sons of the Earl of Clanricarde that Sidney was obliged to send a detachment to extricate him from his position. With their assistance and that of the Earl of Clanricarde, 'and such others as made profession of their loyalty,' he made a dash at Shrule Castle, a place of strategical importance, which he captured. An attack on his camp by the Burkes was successfully averted; but during the conflict he was unhorsed and severely wounded in the face. His conduct was approved by the deputy, who wrote that ' he in all his doings, both formerly since these troubles began, and otherwise in following the same, hath shewed great worthiness, as well in device as in attempt, and of good counsel according to the success and state of things ' (*ib.* xxx. 56). The short period of calm that followed served only as the prelude to a fresh storm. O'Conor Don. whom he held in Athlone Castle as se-

curity for the good conduct of his sept, having escaped one night he next morning marched against his castle of Ballintober, which he speedily captured. But the Burkes were up in arms and were vigorously supported by a large body of Scots. Notwithstanding all his exertions he gradually lost ground during 1571–2, and believing that the Earl of Clanricarde was secretly instigating his rebellious sons he arrested him and clapped him in Dublin Castle. His conduct in the matter led to a quarrel with Sir William Fitzwilliam [q. v.], who had succeeded Sidney as deputy. Fitzwilliam complained that Fitton had imprisoned Clanricarde, and refused to reveal the nature of his offence, either to the council or to himself as in duty bound, which, he declared, ' implieth an accusation of me.' When called upon to explain, Fitton could only say that the proofs of the earl's guilt, though satisfactory to himself, were not likely to weigh much with the council. After six months' imprisonment Clanricarde was allowed to return home, when he endeavoured to signalise his loyalty by hanging his own son, his brother's son, his cousin-german's son, and one of the captains of his own galloglasses, besides fifty of his followers that bore armour and weapons ; but he never forgave Fitton the injury he had done him. Meanwhile the lord president, cooped up within Athlone, prayed earnestly that fresh reinforcements might be sent him, or that he might be relieved of his government. In midsummer 1572 the rebels burnt Athlone to the ground, and his position becoming one of extreme peril he was shortly afterwards recalled, and the office of president allowed to sink for the nonce into abeyance.

In October he retired to England, and seems to have spent his time chiefly at Gawsworth. In December he was appointed vice-treasurer and treasurer at wars (queen to Fitzwilliam, HAMILTON, *Cal.* i. 491). On 25 March 1573 he returned to Dublin in charge of Gerald, fifteenth earl of Desmond, and on 1 April entered upon his duties as treasurer. Shortly afterwards a fresh quarrel broke out between him and Fitzwilliam. It arose out of a brawl between his servant Roden and one Burnell, a friend of Captain Harrington, the lord deputy's nephew. It appears that Roden, having broken Burnell's head with a dagger, was himself a day or two after run through the body by Harrington's servant, Meade. Meade was acquitted by the coroner's jury, but found guilty of manslaughter by the queen's bench. Thereupon the deputy stepped in with a general pardon, which coming into the possession of Fitton he refused to surrender it, and was forthwith committed to gaol for contempt. Next day, regretting his hasty action, the deputy summoned him to take his place at the council board; but he, declining to be thus thrust out of gaol privily, complained to the queen, who, evidently without due consideration of the merits of the case, sharply reprimanded the deputy, praised Fitton for his loyalty, and then bade them become friends again. No doubt Fitzwilliam lost his temper, but the treasurer's conduct was exasperating to the last degree (BAGWELL, *Ireland*, ii. 256). On 18 June he was commissioned, along with the Earl of Clanricarde, the archbishop of Tuam, and others, to hold assizes in Connaught. On his return he accompanied the deputy to Kilkenny; but when it was proposed that he should proceed into Munster and endeavour to prevent the disturbances likely to arise there owing to the escape of the Earl of Desmond, he flatly refused to play the part of 'a harrow without pynnes,' protesting to Burghley that 'if I must neuely be thrown upon all desperate reckes (I meane not for life but for honesty and credit) I may say my hap is hard' (*State Papers*, Eliz. xlvi. 46).

In May 1575 he escorted the Earl of Kildare and his two sons, suspected of treason, into England, but returned in September with Sir H. Sidney, Fitzwilliam's successor, whom he attended on his northern journey. In April 1578 he was the cause of another 'scene' at the council board owing to his refusal, apparently on good grounds, to affirm with the rest of the council that there had been an increase in the revenue. The only governor with whom he seems to have cordially co-operated was Sir William Drury. With him he was indefatigable in his preparations to meet the threatened invasion of James Fitzmaurice. He died on 3 July 1579 'from the disease of the country,' caught during an expedition into Longford. 'I know,' wrote Drury, 'he was, in many men's opinions, over careful of his posterity, and was not without enemies that sought to interpret that to his discredit; but I wish in his successor that temperance, judgment, and ability to speak in her majesty's causes that was found in him. And for my own part, if I should (as of right I ought) measure my liking of him by his good affection to me, truly my particular loss is also very great' (*ib.* lxvii. 25).

He was buried on 21 Sept. in St. Patrick's Cathedral beside the 'wyef of his youth, Anne, the second daughter of Sʳ Peter Warburton, of Areley in the county of Chester, knight, who were borne both in one yere, viz. he yᵉ last of Marche 1527, and she the first of Maye in the same yeare, and were maried on Sonday next after Hillaries daye 1539, being

yᵉ 19 daye of Januarie, in the 12 yere of their age, and lyved together in true and lawfull matrymonie iuste 34 yeres, for yᵉ same Sonday of the yeare wherein they were maried yᵉ same Sondaie 34 yeres following was she buried, though she faithfully depted this lyef 9 daies before, viz. on Saturdaie yᵉ 9 daie of Januarie 1573, in wᶜʰ tyme God gave theim 15 children, viz. 9 sonnes and 6 daughters' (from a brass in St. Patrick's, of which there is a rubbing in Brit. Mus. Add. MS. 32485, Q. 1).

SIR EDWARD FITTON the younger (1548?–1606), son and heir of the above, being disappointed in his expectation of succeeding his father as vice-treasurer, retired to England shortly after having been knighted by Sir William Pelham (HAMILTON, *Cal.* ii. 175; cf. *Domestic Cal. Add.* p. 25). His interest in Ireland revived when it was proposed to colonise Munster with Englishmen, and he was one of the first to solicit a slice of the forfeited estates of the Earl of Desmond. On 3 Sept. 1587 he passed his patent for 11,515 acres in the counties of Limerick, Tipperary, and Waterford; but the speculation proved to be not so profitable as he had anticipated, and on 19 Dec. 1588 he wrote to Burghley that he was 1,500*l.* out of pocket through it, and begged that his rent might be remitted on account of his father's twenty years' service and his own (HAMILTON, *Cal.* iv. 87). He was most energetic in his proposals for the extirpation of the Irish, but failed to fulfil the conditions of the grant, and was noted as an absentee. He was M. P. for Boroughbridge in 1588. He married Alice, daughter and sole heiress of Sir John Holcroft of Holcroft, Lancashire, who survived him till 5 Feb. 1626, and who, after his death in 1606, erected a monument to his memory in Gawsworth Church (ORMEROD, *Cheshire*, iii. 295). His daughter Mary is noticed below.

[Authorities as in the text; Newdegate's Gossip from a Muniment Room, 1897; J. P. Earwaker's East Cheshire.] R. D.

FITTON, MARY (*fl.* 1600), maid of honour to Queen Elizabeth, and fantastically alleged to be 'the dark lady' of Shakespeare's sonnets, was fourth child and second daughter of Sir Edward Fitton the younger [see above], by his wife, Alice, daughter of Sir John Holcroft. She was baptised at Gawsworth Church, Cheshire, 24 June 1578. In 1595 Mary was one of the maids of honour to the queen. In 1600 Queen Elizabeth attended the festivities which celebrated the marriage of Anne Russell, another of her maids of honour, and Lord Herbert, son of the Earl of Worcester. Mary Fitton took a prominent part in the masque performed then by ladies of the court, and she led the dances (*Sidney Papers*, ii. 201, 203). Her vivacity made her popular with the young men at court, and she became the mistress of William Herbert (1580–1630) [q. v.], the young earl of Pembroke. 'During the time that the Earl of Pembroke favoured her she would put off her head-tire, and tuck up her clothes, and take a large white cloak and march as though she had been a man to meet the said earl out of the court' (*State Papers*, Dom. Add. vol. xxxiv.) Early in 1601 she was 'proved with child' (*Cal. Carew MSS.* 1601–3, p. 20). Pembroke admitted his responsibility, and both were threatened with imprisonment. The earl 'utterly renounced all marriage' and was sent to the Fleet in March, but his mistress, who was delivered of a son, seems to have escaped punishment. The child died soon after birth. According to Sir Peter Leycester (1614–1678) Mary Fitton also bore two illegitimate daughters to Sir Richard Leveson, knight (SHAKESPEARE, *Sonnets*, ed. Tyler, xxii.; *Academy* for 15 Dec. 1888, p. 388). There seems no doubt that she married Captain William Polwhele in 1607. But there is some likelihood of his having been her second husband, for as early as 1599 her father corresponded with Sir Robert Cecil about her marriage portion. In Sir Peter Leycester's manuscripts the name of Captain Lougher appears beside that of Captain Polwhele as one of her husbands. But it would appear that Mary Fitton married Polwhele before Lougher. Hence it would seem either that the marriage conjecturally assigned to 1599 did not take place, and that when mistress of Pembroke and Leveson, Mary Fitton was unmarried; or that her first husband's name is lost, and that Lougher was a third husband.

On the elaborate tomb erected by Mary Fitton's mother over her father's grave in 1606 in Gawsworth Church, kneeling figures of herself, her brothers, her sister, and her mother still remain.

An attempt has been made to identify Mary Fitton with the 'mistress' of 'raven black' eyes to whom Shakespeare appears to make suit in his sonnets (cxxvii–cliv). The theory rests on the questionable assumptions that the earlier sonnets celebrate Shakespeare's friendship with William Herbert, earl of Pembroke, and that the later sonnets describe how Shakespeare supplanted this friend in the affections of a dark-complexioned beauty of the court. This beauty, it is suggested, was Mary Fitton. But the association of Pembroke with the sonnets rests on no safe ground, and it is only Herbert's relations with Mary Fitton which have brought her name into the discussion. It is very possible that all the sonnets deal with a fictitious situation.

The objection raised to the circumstance that a lady moving in high society should have entered into a *liaison* with a man of Shakespeare's low social rank of actor and playwright has been met by the discovery of the fact that William Kemp, the actor, dedicated to Mistress *Anne* Fitton, whom he calls maid of honour to the queen, his 'Nine Daies Wonder,' 1600, in terms approaching familiarity. Mistress *Anne* Fitton was Mary Fitton's elder sister, and there is no good reason for supposing (as has been suggested) that Kemp intended Mary when he wrote Anne. Anne Fitton, baptised 6 Oct. 1574, married about 1595 Sir John Newdegate of Erbury, Warwickshire. Kemp's employment of her maiden name alone in his dedication is in accordance with a common contemporary practice of addressing married women.

Mary Fitton's alleged identity with Shakespeare's 'dark lady' is a fanciful theory, which does not admit of serious consideration.

[Lady Newdegate's Gossip from a Muniment Room: passages in the lives of Anne and Mary Fytton, 1897, is the chief authority. The introduction to Shakespeare's Sonnets, edited by Thomas Tyler, London, 1890, propounds the theory of Mary Fitton's identification with the 'dark lady' of the sonnets. The theory is contested in Sidney Lee's Life of Shakespeare (1898, 6th ed. 1908); cf. Tyler's Herbert-Fitton theory, 1899. See also J. P. Earwaker's East Cheshire, ii. 566; Ormerod's Cheshire; Nichols's Progresses of Queen Elizabeth; Gerald Massey's Secret Drama of Shakespeare's Sonnets (1888), adverse to the Fitton theory.]　　　S. L.

FITTON, MICHAEL (1766–1852), lieutenant in the navy, was born in 1766 at Gawsworth in Cheshire, the ancient seat of his family. He entered the navy in June 1780, on board the Vestal, with Captain George Keppel. On 10 Sept. the Vestal gave chase to and captured the Mercury packet, having on board Mr. Laurens, late president of congress, on his way to Holland as ambassador of the revolted colonies. During the chase young Fitton, being on the foretop-gallant yard, hailed the deck to say that there was a man overboard from the enemy. The Vestal sent a boat to pick him up, when the object was found to be a bag of papers, which, being insufficiently weighted, was recovered. On examination these papers were found to compromise the Dutch government, and led to a declaration of war against Holland a few months afterwards. Fitton continued with Captain Keppel during the war in different ships, and as midshipman of the Fortitude was present at the relief of Gibraltar in 1782,

In 1793 he was again with Captain Keppel in the Defiance of 74 guns, as master's mate. In 1796 he was appointed purser of the Stork in the West Indies, and in 1799 was acting lieutenant of the Abergavenny of 54 guns, from which he was almost immediately detached in command of one of her tenders. One of his first services was, in the Ferret schooner, to cruise in the Mona Passage, in company with the Sparrow cutter, commanded by Mr. Whylie. The two accidentally separated for a few days. On rejoining, Fitton invited Whylie by signal to come to breakfast, and while waiting caught a large shark that was under the stern. In its stomach was found a packet of papers relating to an American brig Nancy. When Whylie came on board, he mentioned that he had detained an American brig called the Nancy. Fitton told him that he had her papers. Whylie said that he had 'sealed up her papers and sent them in with her.' Fitton replied: ' Those were her false papers; here are her real ones.' And so it proved. The papers, which are now in the Institute of Jamaica, were lodged in the admiralty court at Port Royal, and by them the brig was condemned. The shark's jaws were set up on shore, with the inscription, ' Lieut. Fitton recommends these jaws for a collar for neutrals to swear through.' Other papers, taken from the Nancy, are in the museum of the Royal United Service Institution.

Fitton's whole service during the three years in which he commanded the Abergavenny's tenders was marked by daring and good fortune. Several privateers of superior force he captured or beat off. One, which he drove ashore, he boarded by swimming, himself and the greater part of his men plunging into the sea with their swords in their mouths (O'BYRNE: a friend of the present writer often heard Fitton tell the story). When the war was renewed in 1803, Fitton was again sent out to the West Indian flagship, and appointed to command her tender, the Gipsy schooner. At the attack on Curaçao in 1804, being the only officer in the squadron who was acquainted with the island, he piloted the ships in, and had virtually the direction of the landing. On the failure of the expedition the Gipsy was sent to the admiral with despatches, and Fitton, in accordance with the senior officer's recommendation, was at last promoted to be lieutenant, thus receiving, as ' the bearer of despatches announcing a defeat, what years of active employment and of hard and responsible service, what more than one successful case of acknowledged skill and gallantry as a commanding officer had failed to procure him' (JAMES, iii. 296).

His promotion, however, made no difference in his employment. In the Gipsy and afterwards in the Pitt, a similar schooner, he continued to wage a dashing and successful war on the enemy's privateers, and on 26 Oct. 1806, after a weary chase of sixty-seven hours, drove on shore and captured the Superbe, a French ship of superior force, which had long been the scourge of English trade, and on board of which a list of captures made showed a value of 147,000l. The captain of the Superbe afterwards equipped a brig which he named La Revanche de la Superbe, and sent an invitation to Fitton to meet him at a place named; but before the message arrived Fitton had been superseded by a friend of the admiral, Sir Alexander Cochrane, ' not to be promoted to the rank of commander, but to be turned adrift as an unemployed lieutenant' (ib. iv. 184). All that he seems to have got for capturing or destroying near forty of the enemy's ships, many of them privateers, was the thanks of the admiralty, a sword valued at 50l. from the Patriotic Society, and his share of the prize-money, which, from his being in command of a tender, was only counted to him as one of the officers of the flagship. He was left unemployed till 1811, when he was appointed to the command of a brig for service in the North Sea and Baltic, and which was paid out of commission in 1815. In 1831 he was appointed a lieutenant of the ordinary at Plymouth, and in 1835 was admitted into Greenwich Hospital, where he continued till his death, which took place at Peckham on 31 Dec. 1852.

It is now impossible to say what was the cause of Fitton's being so grievously neglected. The record of his services is brilliant beyond that of any officer of his standing; and the story of his career is in marked and painful contrast with that of Sir Thomas Cochrane, whose rapid promotion by the admiral who superseded Fitton has been already related.

[O'Byrne's Nav. Biog. Dict.; Gent. Mag. 1853, new ser. xl. 312; United Service Journal, 1835, pt. i. p. 276; Allen's Battles of the British Navy (see index). Allen was an intimate friend of Fitton in the days of his retirement at Greenwich, and his notices of Fitton's achievements may be considered as practically related by Fitton himself.]   J. K. L.

FITTON, WILLIAM HENRY, M.D. (1780–1861), geologist, born in Dublin in January 1780, was a descendant of an ancient family, originally of Gawsworth in Cheshire, but long settled in Ireland. Fitton went to school in Dublin with Moore (the poet) and Robert Emmet. He carried off the senior classical scholarship at Trinity College, Dublin, in 1798, and took his B.A. degree there in 1799. He was destined for the church, but his bent towards natural science induced him to adopt the medical profession.

Before 1807 he had determined barometrically the heights of the principal mountains of Ireland, had made excursions to Wales and to Cornwall to study their minerals and rocks, and had been arrested on suspicion as a rebel while engaged in collecting fossils in the neighbourhood of Dublin. In 1808 Fitton went to the university of Edinburgh, where he attended the lectures of Professor Jameson, through whose influence many able men were led to the study of geology. In 1809 Fitton removed to London, where he continued to study medicine and chemistry, and in 1812 he established himself in Northampton, assured of a good reception there as a physician by the introduction of Lord and Lady Spencer, and with the anticipation also of succeeding to the practice of Dr. Kerr, the father of Lady Davy.

At Northampton Fitton's mother and three sisters kept house for him, till in 1820 he married Miss James, a lady of ample fortune, by whom he had five sons and three daughters. In 1816 Fitton was made M.D. of Cambridge University, but after his marriage he gave up the active practice of his profession, removed to London, and devoted himself entirely to scientific researches, mainly geological. After acting for several years as secretary of the Geological Society, Fitton was made president in 1828. He established the 'Proceedings' of the society.

Fitton was a man of very independent spirit. He strongly supported Herschel in opposition to the Duke of Sussex for the chair of the Royal Society. His house was a hospitable meeting-place for scientific persons, and while president of the Geological Society he held a regular conversazione on Sundays. Fitton was elected a fellow of the Royal Society in 1815; he also belonged to the Linnean, Astronomical, and Geographical Societies. He was awarded the Wollaston medal by the Geological Society in 1852. He died at his house in London on 13 May 1861.

Fitton's scientific work began in 1811 with his paper, 'Notice respecting the Geological structure of the vicinity of Dublin ('Trans. Geological Society,' 1811). Between 1817 and 1841 he contributed a series of papers to the 'Edinburgh Review' upon contemporaneous geological topics, such as 'William Smith's Geological Map of England,' 'Lyell's Geology,' the 'Silurian System,' &c. But Fitton's best work was done between 1824 and 1836, when he laid down the proper suc-

cession of the strata between the oolite and the chalk; dividing the 'greensand' into an upper and a lower division, separated by a bed of clay, the gault. This work forms a distinct landmark in the history of geology. His principal papers descriptive of the greensand are contained in the 'Proceedings' and in the 'Transactions' of the Geological Society for 1834–5, and in the 'Journal' of the same society, 1845–6. It was Fitton's delight to instruct others in practical geology, and many travellers, including Sir John Franklin, Sir George Back, and Sir John Richardson, received valuable assistance from him.

Fitton's last paper (he published twenty-one altogether) was 'On the Structure of North-West Australia' in the 'Proceedings of the Geographical Society' for 1857.

[Quart. Journ. Geological Society, president's address, 1862, p. xxx; Royal Society's Catalogue of Scientific Papers.]   W. J. H.

FITZAILWIN, HENRY (*d.* 1212), first mayor of London, is of doubtful origin. Dr. Stubbs holds that he 'may have been an hereditary baron of London' (*Const. Hist.* i. 631). Mr. Loftie confidently asserts that he was a grandson of Leofstan, portreeve of London before the Conquest (*London*, pp. 22, 36, 129). The present writer has shown (*Antiquary*, xv. 107–8) that this is a fallacy, partly based on the confusion of three or four Leofstans, who are similarly confused by Mr. Freeman (*Norman Conquest*, v. 469). It is just possible that the clue may be found in an entry in the 'Pipe Roll' of 1165 (*Rot. Pip.* 11 Hen. II, p. 18), where a Henry Fitzailwin Fitzleofstan, with Alan his brother, pay for succeeding apparently to lands in Essex or Hertfordshire, since we learn that our Henry Fitzailwin held lands at Watton and Stone in Hertfordshire by tenure of serjeanty (*Testa de Nevill*, p. 270 *a*), which descended to his heirs (*ib.* pp. 276 *b*, 266 *b*). In that case his grandfather was a Leofstan, but as yet unidentified. It has been urged by the writer (*Academy*, 12 Nov. 1887) that Henry's career should be divided into two periods: the first, in which he is styled Henry Fitzailwin (i.e. Æthelwine), and the second, in which he figures as mayor of London. He appears as a witness under the former style in a document printed by Palgrave (*Rot. Cur. Reg.* cvii), in a duchy of Lancaster charter (Box A. No. 163), and in two of the St. Paul's muniments (9th Rep. i. 25, 26). A grant of his also is printed by Palgrave (*Rot. Cur. Reg.* cv). As mayor he occurs far more frequently, namely five times, in the St. Paul's muniments (9th Rep. i. 8, 10, 20, 22, 27), twice in the 'Rot. Cur. Reg.' (pp. 171, 432), viz. in 1198 and 1199, and once in an Essex charter of 1197 (*Harl. Cart.* 83 A, 18). His last dated appearance in the first capacity is 30 Nov. 1191, and he first appears as mayor in April 1193 (HOVEDEN, iii. 212). He probably therefore became mayor between these dates. This is fatal to the well-known assertion in the 'Cronica Maiorum et Vice-comitum Londoniæ' (*Liber de Ant. Leg.*) that 'Henricus filius Eylwini de London-stane' was made mayor in '1188' or 1189, and is even at variance with Mr. Coote's hypothesis that the mayoralty originated in the grant of a communa 10 Oct. 1191 (vide infra). Dr. Stubbs, however, leans to this date as the commencement of Henry's mayoralty (*Sel. Chart.* p. 300; *Const. Hist.* i. 630). Though he continued mayor, as far as can be ascertained, uninterruptedly till his death, the only recorded event of his mayoralty is his famous 'assize' (*Liber de Ant. Leg.* p. 206; *Liber Albus*, p. 319). And even this is only traditionally associated with his name. In 1203 he is found holding two knight's fees of the honour of 'Peverel of London' (*Rot. Canc.* 3 John). He derived his description as 'de London-stane' from his house, which stood on the north side of St. Swithin's Church in Candlewick (now Cannon) Street, over against London Stone. He also held property at Hoo in Kent, Warlingham and Burnham in Surrey, and Edmonton in Middlesex. He is found presiding over a meeting of the citizens, 24 July 1212, consequent on the great fire of the previous week (*Liber Custumarum*, p. 88). The earliest notice of his death is a writ of 5 Oct. 1212, ordering his lands to be taken into the king's hands (*Rot. Pat.* 14 John). It is often erroneously placed in 1213. His wife, Margaret, survived him (*Rot. Claus.* 14 John), as did his three younger sons, Alan, Thomas, and Richard (*ib.* 15 John), but his eldest son, Peter, who had married Isabel, daughter and heir of Bartholomew de Cheyne, had died before him, leaving two daughters, of whom the survivor was in 1212 Henry Fitzailwin's heir.

[Patent Rolls (Record Commission); Close Rolls (ib.); Testa de Nevill (ib.); Palgrave's Rotuli Curiæ Regis (ib.); Rot. Canc. (ib.); Pipe Roll Society's works; Duchy Charters (Public Record Office); Roger Hoveden (Rolls Series); Riley's Munimenta Gildhalle Londoniensis (ib.); Reports on Historical MSS.; Stapleton's Liber de Antiquis Legibus (Camd. Soc.); Stubbs's Select Charters and Constitutional Hist.; Freeman's Norman Conquest; Antiquary, 1887; Academy, 1887; Coote's A Lost Chapter (London and Middlesex Arch. Trans. vol. v.); Loftie's London (Historic Towns).] J. H. R.

FITZALAN, BERTRAM (*d.* 1424), Carmelite, said to have been a member of the great family of the Fitzalans, entered the Carmelite fraternity at Lincoln, and studied at Oxford, presumably in the house of his order, where William Quaplod, also a Carmelite, who became bishop of Derry (not of Kildare, as Bale has it) in 1419, was his friend and patron. Fitzalan, after proceeding to the degree of master, seems to have returned to Lincoln, and to have there founded a library, in which Bale saw the following works of his: 'Super quarto Sententiarum liber i.,' 'Quæstiones Theologiæ,' and 'Ad plebem Conciones.' Pits also assigns to him a volume of 'Excerpta quædam ex aliis auctoribus,' which he mentions as existing in the library of Balliol College, Oxford. The book has, however, either been lost, or else Pits was misled by a codex there (clxv. B) of miscellaneous contents, some of which are by Cardinal Peter Bertrand. Fitzalan died on 17 May 1424.

[Leland, Comm. de Scriptt. Brit. dxxviii. p. 436 (ed. A. Hall, 1709); Bale, Scriptt. Brit. Cat. vii. 64, p. 558; Pits, De Angl. Scriptt. p. 610 et seq.; Tanner's Bibl. Brit. 282.] R. L. P.

FITZALAN, BRIAN, LORD OF BEDALE (*d.* 1306), was descended from a younger branch of the Counts of Brittany and Earls of Richmond. His father, Brian Fitzalan, an itinerant justice (Foss, *Judges*, ii. 326), and sheriff of Northumberland between 1227 and 1235 and of Yorkshire between 1236 and 1239 (*Thirty-first Report of Deputy-Keeper of Records*, pp. 321, 364), was grandson of Brian, a younger son of Alan of Brittany, and brother, therefore, of Count Conan, the father of Constance, wife of Geoffrey of Anjou (DUGDALE, *Baronage*, i. 53; cf. *Harl. MS.* 1052, f. 9). He was summoned to the Welsh war of 1282, and in 1287 to the armed council at Gloucester. In 1290 he was appointed by Edward warden of the castles of Forfar, Dundee, Roxburgh, and Jedburgh. They remained in his custody till 1292 (STEVENSON, *Doc. illustrative of Scott. Hist.* i. 207–8, 350). In 1292 he was made by Edward one of the guardians of Scotland during the vacancy of the throne (*Fœdera*, i. 761; cf. RISHANGER, p. 250, Rolls Ser.) He took a leading share in the judicial proceedings which resulted in John Baliol being declared by Edward king of Scotland, and after witnessing the new king's homage to Edward surrendered his rolls and official documents to the new king (*Fœdera*, i. 782, 785). In 1294 he was summoned to repress the Welsh revolt. In 1295 he received a summons to the famous parliament of that year. Henceforth he was regularly summoned, but always as 'Brian Fitzalan,' though in 1301 he subscribed the letter of the magnates sent from the Lincoln parliament to the pope as 'Lord of Bedale.' In 1296 and the succeeding years he was almost constantly occupied in Scotland. On 10 July 1296 he was present at Brechin when John Baliol submitted to Edward (STEVENSON, ii. 61). Though summoned on 7 July 1297 to serve in person beyond sea, he was on 12 July appointed captain of all garrisons and fortresses in Northumberland. On 14 Aug. 1297 he was appointed guardian of Scotland in succession to Earl Warenne (*Fœdera*, i. 874). An interesting letter is preserved, in which he remonstrates with the king for appointing one of so small ability and power as himself to so great a post. He was only worth 1,000*l.*, and feared that the salary of his office, inadequate for so great a noble as his predecessor, would be still more insufficient for himself (STEVENSON, ii. 222–4). But on 24 Sept. he was ordered to go at once to Scotland and act with Warenne (*ib.* ii. 232). On 28 Sept. the musters from Nottinghamshire and Derbyshire were ordered to assemble under his command, and in October he was made captain of the marches adjoining Northumberland. In 1298 Earl Warenne was again the royal representative (HEMINGBURGH, ii. 155). In 1299, 1300, and lastly in 1303, Fitzalan was again summoned against the Scots. His last parliamentary summonses were for 1305 to Westminster, and for May 1306, for the occasion of making Edward, the king's son, a knight. He died, however, before June 1306 (see note in *Parl. Writs*, i. 598; cf. *Calendarium Genealogicum*, p. 619). He was buried in Bedale Church, 'where he hath a noble monument, with his effigies in armour cross-leg'd thereon' (DUGDALE). He left by his wife Matilda two daughters, Matilda, aged 8, and Catharine, aged 6, who were his coheiresses (*Cal. Geneal.* p. 619). His possessions were partly in Yorkshire and partly in Lincolnshire.

[Parl. Writs, i. 598–9; Rymer's Fœdera, vol. i.; Stevenson's Documents illustr. of Hist. of Scotland; Calendarium Genealogicum; Dugdale's Baronage, i. 53.] T. F. T.

FITZALAN, EDMUND, EARL OF ARUNDEL (1285–1326), son of Richard I Fitzalan, earl of Arundel [q. v.], and his Italian wife Alisona, was born on 1 May 1285 (*Cal. Genealogicum*, ii. 622). In 1302 he succeeded to his father's titles and estates. On Whitsunday (22 May) 1306 he was knighted by Edward I, on the occasion of the knighting of Edward the king's son and many others, and was at the same time married to Alice, sister and ultimately heiress of John, earl Warenne (*Ann. Worcester* in *Ann. Mon.*

iv. 558; LANGTOFT, ii. 368). He then served in the campaign against the Scots, and was still in the north when Edward I died. At Edward II's coronation he was a bearer of the royal robes (*Fœdera*, ii. 36). On 2 Dec. 1307 he was beaten at the Wallingford tournament by Gaveston, and straightway became a mortal enemy of the favourite (MALMESBURY, in STUBBS's *Chron. Ed. I and Ed. II*, Rolls Series, ii. 156). In 1309 he joined Lancaster in refusing to attend a council at York on 18 Oct. (HEMINGBURGH, ii. 275), and in 1310 was appointed one of the lords ordainers (*Rot. Parl.* i. 443 *b*). In 1312 he was one of the five earls who formed a league against Gaveston (MALMESBURY, p. 175), and he warmly approved of the capture of the favourite at Scarborough. Even after Gaveston's murder Arundel adhered to the confederate barons and was with Lancaster one of the last to be reconciled to the king. In 1314 he was one of the earls who refused to accompany Edward to the relief of Stirling, and thus caused the disaster of Bannockburn (*ib.* p. 201). In 1316 he was appointed captain-general of the country north of the Trent, and in 1318, after being one of the mediators of a fresh pacification, was made a member of the permanent council then established to watch the king. In 1319 he served against the Scots.

The Despensers now ruled Edward, and the marriage of Arundel's eldest son to the daughter of the younger Hugh was either the cause or the result of an entire change in his political attitude. He consented indeed to their banishment in 1321, but afterwards pleaded the coercion of the magnates. When Edward's subsequent attempt to restore them began, Arundel still seemed to waver in his allegiance. Finally in October 1321 he joined Edward at the siege of Leeds Castle, and henceforth supported consistently the royal cause (*ib.* p. 263, 'propter affinitatem Hugonis Despenser,' a phrase suggesting that the marriage had already been arranged). In 1322 he persuaded the Mortimers to surrender to the king at Shrewsbury (*Ann. Paul.* in STUBBS's *Chron. Ed. I and Ed. II*, i. 301), acted as one of the judges of Thomas of Lancaster at Pontefract (*ib.* p. 302), and received large grants from the forfeited estates of Badlesmere and the Mortimers. The great office of justice of Wales was transferred from Mortimer to him (*Abbrev. Rot. Orig.* i. 262), and in that capacity he received the writs directing the attendance of Welsh members to the parliament at York (*Rot. Parl.* i. 456). His importance in Wales had been also largely increased by his acquisitions of Kerry, Chirk, and Cydewain. In 1325 he also became warden of the Welsh marches (*Parl. Writs*, II. iii. 854), and in 1326 he still was justice of Wales (*Fœdera*, ii. 641). In 1326 he and his brother-in-law Earl Warenne were the only earls who adhered to the king after the invasion of Mortimer and Isabella. He was appointed in May chief captain of the army to be raised in Wales and the west; but he does not seem to have been able to make effectual head against the enemy even in his own district. He was captured in Shropshire by John Charlton, first lord Charlton of Powys [q. v.], and led to the queen at Hereford, where on 17 Nov. he was executed without more than the form of a trial, to gratify the rancorous hostility of Mortimer to a rival border chieftain (*Ann. Paul.* p. 321, says beheaded, but KNIGHTON, c. 2546, says 'distractus et suspensus '). His estates were forfeited, and the London mob plundered his treasures.

By his wife Alice, sister of John, earl Warenne, Arundel had a fairly numerous family. His eldest son, Richard II Fitzalan [q. v.], ultimately succeeded to his title and estates. He had one other son, Edmund, who seems to have embraced the ecclesiastical profession, and to have afterwards abandoned it. Of his daughters, Aleyne married Roger L'Estrange, and was still alive in 1375 (NICOLAS, *Testamenta Vetusta*, p. 94), and Alice became the wife of John Bohun, earl of Hereford. A third daughter, Jane, is said to have been married to Lord Lisle (compare the genealogies in EYTON, *Shropshire*, vii. 229, and in YEATMAN, *House of Arundel*, p. 324).

[Rymer's Fœdera, vol. i.; Rolls of Parliament, vol. ii.; Parl. Writs, vol. ii.; Stubbs's Chronicles of Edward I and Edward II (Rolls Series); Knighton in Twysden, Decem Scriptores; Walter of Hemingburgh (Engl. Hist. Soc.); Dugdale's Baronage, i. 316–17; Doyle's Official Baronage, i. 70; Tierney's Hist. of Arundel, 212–24; Vincent's Discoverie of Errours in Brooke's Catalogue of Nobility, p. 26.] T. F. T.

FITZALAN, HENRY, twelfth EARL OF ARUNDEL (1511?–1580), born about 1511, was the only son of William Fitzalan, eleventh earl of Arundel, K.G., by his second wife, Lady Anne Percy, daughter of Henry Percy, fourth earl of Northumberland. He was named after Henry VIII, who personally stood godfather at his baptism (*Life*, King's MS. xvii. A. ix. f. 5). Upon entering his fifteenth year his father proposed to place him in the household of Cardinal Wolsey, but he preferred the service of the king, who received him with affection (*ib.* ff. 3–7). He was in the train of Henry at the Calais interview of September 1532 (GAIRDNER, *Let-*

ters and Papers of Reign of Henry VIII, vol. v. App. No. 33). In February 1533 he was summoned to parliament by the title of Lord Maltravers (*ib.* vol. vi. No. 123). In July 1534 he was one of the peers summoned to attend the trial of William, lord Dacre of Gillesland (*ib.* vol. vii. No. 962). In May 1536 he was present at the trial of Anne Boleyn and Lord Rochford (*ib.* vol. x. No. 876). In 1540 he succeeded Arthur Plantagenet, viscount Lisle, in the office of deputy of Calais. During a successful administration of three years he devoted himself to the improvement of military discipline and to the strengthening of the town. At his own expense the fortifications were extended or repaired, and large bodies of serviceable recruits were raised. The death of his father in January 1543–4 recalled him home. On 24 April of that year he was elected K.G. (*Harl. MS.* 4840, f. 729; BELTZ, *Memorials*, p. clxxv), and during the two following months appears to have lived at Arundel Place. On war being declared with France Arundel and the Duke of Suffolk embarked in July 1544 with a numerous body of troops for the French coast; Henry himself followed in a few days, and on 26 July the whole force of the English, amounting to thirty thousand men, encamped before the walls of Boulogne. Arundel on being created 'marshal of the field ' began elaborate preparations for investing the town. The besieged made a most determined resistance. In the night, however, of 11 Sept. a mine was successfully sprung. He immediately ordered a sharp cannonade, and at the head of a chosen body of troops marched to the intrenchments, and when the artillery had effected a breach by firing over his head, successfully stormed the town. On his return to England Arundel was rewarded with the office of lord chamberlain, which he continued to fill during the remainder of Henry's reign. 'The boke of Henrie, Earle of Arundel, Lorde Chamberleyn to Kyng Henrie th' Eighte,' containing thirty-two folio leaves and consisting of instructions to the king's servants in the duties of their several places, is preserved in Harl. MS. 4107, and printed from another copy in Jeffery's edition of the 'Antiquarian Repertory,' 4to, 1807, ii. 184–209. In his will the king bequeathed him 200*l*. At Henry's funeral Arundel was present as one of the twelve assistant mourners, and at the offering brought up, together with the Earl of Oxford, 'the king's broidered coat of armes' (STRYPE, *Memorials*, 8vo ed. vol. ii. App. pp. 4, 15).

On the accession of Edward VI, in 1547, Arundel was retained in the post of lord chamberlain and chosen to act as high constable at the coronation. He had also been named, in the will of Henry VIII, as a member of the council of twelve, intended to assist the executors in cases of difficulty; but his influence was destroyed when Somerset became protector. Somerset soon disgusted the other members of the cabinet, and Arundel was among the first to urge his dismissal in favour of the Earl of Warwick. At length, in 1549, Somerset was sent to the Tower, while Arundel, Warwick, and four other lords were appointed to take charge of the king. Warwick quickly grew jealous of Arundel's influence. When the bill for the infliction of penalties on Somerset was brought before parliament in 1550 Arundel was still in office; but a series of ridiculous charges had been collected against him from the last twelve years of his life, and when the late protector obtained his release the earl had been dismissed from his employments. It was asserted that he had abused his privileges as lord chamberlain to enrich himself and his friends, that he had removed the locks and bolts from the royal stores at Westminster, had distributed 'the king's stuff' among his acquaintance, and had been guilty of various other acts of embezzlement. The proof of these charges was never exhibited, and Edward himself in his 'Diary' terms the offences only 'crimes of suspicion against him;' but the 'suspicion' was sufficient for the purposes of Warwick. Arundel was removed from the council, was ordered to confine himself to his house, and was mulcted in the sum of 12,000l., to be paid in equal annual instalments of 1,000l. each. His confinement, however, was of short duration, and the injustice of the accusations having been ascertained, 8,000l. of the fine was remitted. Arundel had been sent into Sussex to allay the insurrection of 1549. By his influence tranquillity was perfectly restored throughout Sussex (*Cal. State Papers*, Dom. 1547–80, p. 19). When renewed symptoms of uneasiness appeared shortly after his release, the council made a second request for his assistance in repressing the disturbance. Arundel returned a severely dignified refusal. His late punishment, he said, for offences which he had never committed had injured him both in his fortune and his health, and he did not understand why his services, which had formerly been so ill requited, were again demanded. The council, after attempting to frighten him into submission, were glad to despatch the Duke of Somerset in his stead.

His opposition to Warwick and the ruling party at court subjected him to much persecution. Finding the necessity of offering a united resistance to the aggressions of Warwick, he formed a friendship with his old enemy the Duke of Somerset. On 16 Oct. 1551 Somerset was a second time committed to the Tower on charges of felony and treason. In the original depositions no mention was made of Arundel as an accomplice, but in a few days the evidence of one of the accused, named Crane, began to implicate him; by degrees Crane's recollections became more vivid, and on 8 Nov. Arundel was arrested and conveyed to the Tower ('King Edward's Diary' in *Cotton MS.* Titus, B. ii.) It was said that he had listened to overtures from Somerset, and that he was privy to the intended massacre of Northumberland, Northampton, and Pembroke, at the house of Lord Paget. These accusations rest entirely on the doubtful testimony of Crane (*Cal. State Papers*, Dom. 1547–80, p. 36). During more than twelve months that Arundel was confined to the Tower, Northumberland, although he plotted unceasingly against the life of his prisoner, never ventured to bring him to his trial; Arundel's subsequent confession was exacted as the condition of his pardon, and on a subsequent occasion he publicly asserted his innocence in the presence, and with the assent, of Pembroke himself. On 3 Dec. 1552 he was called before the privy council, required to sign a submission and confession, and fined in the sum of six thousand marks, to be paid in equal portions of one thousand marks annually; he was bound in a recognisance of ten thousand marks to be punctual in his payment of the fine, and was at length dismissed with an admonition (STRYPE, *Memorials*, ii. 383, from the Council Book). The declining health of the king suggested to Northumberland the expediency of conciliating the nobility. Arundel was first restored to his place at the council board, and four days before Edward's death was discharged entirely of his fine. In June 1553 he strongly protested against Edward's 'device' for the succession, by which the king's sisters were declared illegitimate. He ultimately signed the letters patent, but not the bond appended, with a deliberate intention of deserting Northumberland whenever a chance should present itself. On the death of the king, 6 July 1553, Arundel entered with apparent ardour into the designs of the duke. But on the very same evening, while the council were still discussing the measures necessary to be adopted before they proclaimed the Lady Jane, he contrived to forward a letter to Mary, in which he informed her of her brother's death; assured her that Northumberland's motive in conceding it was 'to entrap her before she knew of it;' and concluded by urging her to retire to a position of safety. Mary followed his advice; while Arundel continued during more than ten days to concur in Northumberland's schemes with a view to his betrayal. He attended the meetings of the council, he signed the letter to Mary denouncing her as illegitimate, and asserted the title of her rival; he accompanied Northumberland and others when they informed Jane of her accession to the crown, and attended her on the progress from Sion House to the Tower preparatory to her coronation. Arundel and the other secret partisans of Mary persuaded Northumberland to take the command in person of the force raised to attack Mary, and assured him of their sympathy when he started. His speeches strongly betrayed his distrust of Arundel (STOW, *Annales*, ed. Howes, 1615, pp. 610, 611; HOLINSHED, *Chronicles*, ed. Hooker, 1587, iii. 1086).

Arundel lost no time in endeavouring to sound the dispositions of the councillors. They were still under the eyes of the Tower garrison. Their first meeting to form their plans was within the Tower walls, and Arundel said 'he liked not the air.' On 19 July 1553 they managed to pass the gates under pretence, says Bishop Godwin, of conference with the French ambassador, Lavall (*Annals of Queen Mary*, pp. 107, 108), and made their way to Pembroke's house at Baynard's Castle, above London Bridge, when they sent for the mayor, the aldermen, and other city magnates. Arundel opened the proceedings in a vehement speech. He denounced the ambition and violence of Northumberland, asserted the right of the two daughters of Henry VIII to the throne, and concluded by calling on the assembly to unite with him in vindicating the claim of the Lady Mary. Pembroke pledged himself to die in the cause, amid general applause. The same evening Mary was proclaimed queen at the cross at Cheapside, and at St. Paul's. Pembroke took possession of the Tower, and Arundel, with Lord Paget, galloped off with the great seal and a letter from the council, which he delivered to Mary at Framlingham Castle in Suffolk (the draft of this letter is printed in Sir Henry Ellis's 2nd series of 'Original Letters,' ii. 243, from Lansdowne MS. 3). He then hastened to Cambridge to secure Northumberland. Their meeting is described by Stow (p. 612) and by Holinshed (iii. 1088). In Harl. MS. 787, f. 61, is a copy of the piteous letter which Northumberland addressed to Arundel the night before his execution (cf. *Hist. MSS. Comm.* 5th Rep. p. 213).

In reward of his exertions Mary bestowed on Arundel the office of lord steward of the household; to this were added a seat at the council board, a license for two hundred retainers beyond his ordinary attendants (STRYPE, *Memorials*, iii. 480), and a variety of local privileges connected with his possessions in Sussex. He was also appointed to act as lord high constable at the coronation, and was deputed to confer on any number of persons not exceeding sixty the dignity of knighthood (HARDY, *Syllabus of Rymer's Fœdera*, ii. 792). Though favoured by the queen he deemed it politic to make some show of resenting her derogatory treatment of Elizabeth. In September 1553 he was a commissioner for Bishop Bonner's restitution (STRYPE, *Memorials*, iii. 23). On 1 Jan. 1553-4 he was nominated a commissioner to treat of the queen's marriage, and on 17 Feb. 1554 he was lord high steward on the trial of the Duke of Suffolk. He bore, too, a part in checking the progress of Wyatt's shortlived rebellion. On Philip's landing at Southampton, 20 July 1554, Arundel received him and immediately presented him with the George and Garter (SPEED, *Historie of Great Britaine*, ed. 1632, p. 1121). Along with William, marquis of Winchester and others, he received from Philip and Mary, 6 Feb. 1555, a grant of a charter of incorporation by the name of Merchant Adventurers of England for the discovery of unknown lands (*Cal. State Papers*, Dom. Addenda, 1547-65, p. 437; the grant is printed in HAKLUYT, i. 298-304). In May 1555 he was selected with Cardinal Pole, Gardiner, and Lord Paget to urge the mediatorial offices of the queen at the congress of Marque, and to effect, if possible, a renewal of amity between the imperial and French crowns. He accompanied Philip to Brussels in the following September. In the same year (1555) he was elected high steward of the university of Oxford. When the troubles with France commenced, the queen appointed Arundel, 26 July 1557, lieutenant-general and captain of the forces for defence of the kingdom (*Cal. State Papers*, Dom. 1547-80, p. 93). The following year he was deputed with Thirlby, bishop of Ely, and Dr. Nicholas Wotton to the conferences held by England, France, and Spain, in the abbey of Cercamp, and was actually engaged in arranging the preliminaries of a general peace, when the death of Mary, in November 1558, caused him to abruptly return home in December (cf. *MS. Life*, f. 53; also the letter addressed by Arundel and Wotton to their colleague, the Bishop of Ely, which is printed, from the original preserved at Norfolk House, in Tierney's 'Hist. of Arundel,' pp. 335-7.

It is dated 'Ffrom Arras, the xvth of Novembre, 1558,' and relates to a proposed meeting at that town. Other letters and despatches will be found in *Cal. State Papers*, For. 1558).

By Elizabeth, Arundel was retained in all the employments which he had held in the preceding reign, although he was trusted by no one (FROUDE, ch. xxxvi.), chiefly because she could not afford to alienate so powerful a subject. A commission, dated 21 Nov. 1558, empowers Arundel, William, lord Howard of Effingham, Thirlby, and Wotton to treat with Scotland; it was made out on 27 Sept. in the last year of Mary, and the alterations are in the handwriting of Sir William Cecil (*Cal. State Papers*, Scottish Ser. i. 107). Disgusted by the 'sinister workinge of some meane persons of her counsaile,' Arundel had surrendered the staff of lord steward shortly before the death of Mary (*MS. Life*, ff. 49–51). Elizabeth on her accession replaced it in his hands; she called him to a seat in the council, and added to his other honours the appointments of high constable for the day before, and high steward for the day of her coronation, on which occasion he received a commission to create thirty knights (HARDY, *Syllabus of Rymer's Fœdera*, ii. 798, 799). In January 1559 he was elected chancellor of the university of Oxford, but resigned the office, probably from religious motives, in little more than four months (WOOD, *Fasti Oxon.* ed. Bliss, i. 86, 87). In August 1559 Elizabeth visited him at Nonsuch in Cheam, Surrey, where for five days she was sumptuously entertained with banquets, masques, and music (*Cal. State Papers*, Dom. 1547–80, p. 136). At her departure she accepted 'a cupboard of plate' (NICHOLS, *Progresses of Queen Elizabeth*, i. 74), as she had before received the perquisites obtained by the earl at her coronation. The queen paid several subsequent visits to Nonsuch (LYSONS, *Environs*, i. 154–5). In August 1560 he was one of the commissioners appointed to arrange a commercial treaty with the Hanse Towns. During the same year Arundel, in the queen's presence, sharply rebuked Edward, lord Clinton, who advocated the prosecution of the war with Scotland [see CLINTON, EDWARD FIENNES DE, ninth BARON CLINTON AND SAYE, EARL OF LINCOLN], and Elizabeth herself could scarcely prevent them from coming to blows. 'Those,' Arundel exclaimed, 'who had advised the war with Scotland were traitors to their country' (FROUDE, ch. xxxviii.) Being a widower Arundel was named among those who might aspire to the queen's hand, a fact which led to a violent quarrel with Leicester in 1561 (*ib.* ch. xl.)

Upon the queen's dangerous illness in October 1562 a meeting was held at the house of Arundel in November to reconsider the succession. The Duke of Norfolk, Arundel's son-in-law, was present. The object was to further the claims of Lady Catherine Grey, to whose son Norfolk's infant daughter was to be betrothed. The discussion ended at two in the morning without result. When the queen heard of it she sent for Arundel to reproach him, and Arundel, it is said, replied that if she intended to govern England with her caprices and fancies the nobility would be forced to interfere (*ib.* ch. xl.) In 1564 he resigned the staff of lord steward 'with sundry speeches of offence' (STRYPE, *Annals*, i. 413), and Elizabeth, to resent the affront, restrained him to his house.

Though released within a month from his confinement, Arundel felt deeply the humiliation of his suit. Early in 1566 a smart attack of gout afforded him a pretext for visiting the baths at Padua. He returned in March 1567. On his arrival at Canterbury he was met by a body of more than six hundred gentlemen from Kent, Sussex, and Surrey; at Blackheath the cavalcade was joined by the recorder, the aldermen, and many of the chief merchants of London, and as it drew near to the metropolis the lord chancellor, the earls of Pembroke, Huntingdon, Sussex, Warwick, and Leicester, with others, to the number of two thousand horsemen, came out to meet him. He passed in procession through the city, and having paid his respects to the queen at Westminster went by water to his house in the Strand.

It has often been asserted, but quite erroneously, that on this occasion Arundel appeared in the first coach, and presented to Elizabeth the first pair of silk stockings ever seen in England. The subject has been fully discussed by J. G. Nichols in the 'Gentleman's Magazine' for 1833 (vol. ciii. pt. ii. p. 212, *n.* 12). That he sent the queen some valuable presents appears from her letter to him, dated at Westminster, 16 March 1567 (*Cal. State Papers*, Dom. 1547–80, p. 289).

Arundel was now partially restored to favour, so that when the conferences relative to the accusations brought by the Earl of Murray against the Queen of Scots were removed in November 1568 from York to Westminster, he was joined in the commission (*ib.* Scottish Ser. ii. 864). His hopes of gaining Elizabeth in marriage had long been buried. As the leader of the old nobility and the catholic party he now resolved that the Queen of Scots should marry Norfolk; Cecil and

Bacon were to be overthrown, Elizabeth deposed, and the catholic religion restored. He became intimate with Leslie, bishop of Ross, and with Don Gueran, the Spanish ambassador. In 1569 he undertook to carry Leslie's letter to Elizabeth, wherein it was falsely asserted that the king of Spain had directed the Duke of Alva and Don Gueran 'to treat and conclude with the Queen of Scots for her marriage in three several ways,' and thus alarm the queen by the prospect of a possible league between France and Spain and the papacy. He followed up the blow by laying in writing before her his own objections to extreme measures against Mary Stuart (FROUDE, ch. li.) When at length the discovery of the proposed marriage determined Elizabeth to commit the Duke of Norfolk to the Tower, Arundel was also placed under arrest, and restrained to his house in the Strand in September 1569 (*Cal. State Papers,* Scottish Ser. ii. 880). The northern insurrection which broke out a few weeks later added to the length and rigour of his confinement. From Arundel House he was removed to Eton College, and thence to Nonsuch (*ib.* Dom. Addenda, 1566–79, pp. 269, 279, 284, 286), where a close imprisonment brought on a return of the gout, and by withdrawing him from his concerns contributed to involve him in many pecuniary difficulties, which, however, his son-in-law, Lord Lumley, did much to alleviate. Though his name appeared conspicuously in the depositions of the prisoners examined after the northern rebellion, he had been too prudent to commit himself to open treason. ' He was able to represent his share of the conspiracy as part of an honest policy conceived in Elizabeth's interests, and Elizabeth dared not openly break with the still powerful party among the nobles to which Arundel belonged.' Leicester, desiring to injure Cecil, had little difficulty in inducing the queen to recall Arundel to the council board during the following year. With Arundel was recalled also Lord Lumley, and both of them renewed their treasonable communications with Don Gueran and La Mothe Fénelon. He violently opposed himself to Elizabeth's matrimonial treaty with the Duke of Alençon. He strongly remonstrated against the Earl of Lennox being sent with Sir William Drury's army to Scotland as the representative of James. At length the discovery of the Ridolfi conspiracy, to which he was privy, in September 1571, afforded indubitable evidence that he had been for years conspiring for a religious revolution and Elizabeth's overthrow (FROUDE, ch. lvi.) He was again placed under a guard at his own house, and did not regain his liberty

until December 1572 (*Cal. State Papers,* Dom. Addenda, 1566–79, p. 454).

Arundel passed the remainder of his days in seclusion. He died 24 Feb. 1579–80 at Arundel House in the Strand, and on 22 March was buried, in accordance with his desire, in the collegiate chapel at Arundel, where his monument, with a long biographical inscription from the pen of Lord Lumley, may still be seen (TIERNEY, *Hist. of Arundel,* pp. 628–9, and ' College Chapel at Arundel,' *Sussex Archæol. Coll.* iii. 84–7). The programme of his funeral is printed in the ' Sussex Archæological Collections,' xii. 261–262. In his will, dated 30 Dec. 1579, and proved 27 Feb. 1579–80, he appointed Lumley his sole executor and residuary legatee (registered in P. C. C. 1, Arundell). In person Arundel appears to have been of the middle size, well proportioned in limb, ' stronge of bone, furnished with cleane and firme fleshe, voide of fogines and fatnes.' His countenance was regular and expressive, his voice powerful and pleasing; but the rapidity of his utterance often made his meaning ' somewhat harde to the unskilfull' (*MS. Life,* ff. 63, 68). His dislike of ' new-fangled and curious tearmes ' was not more remarkable than his aversion to the use of foreign languages, although he could speak French (PUTTENHAM, *Arte of English Poesie,* 1589, p. 227). According to his anonymous biographer he was ' not unlearned,' and with the counsel of Humphrey Lhuyd [q. v.], who lived with him, he formed a library, described by the same authority as ' righte worthye of remembrance.' His collection merged in that of Lord Lumley [q. v.] With Lumley and Lhuyd he became a member of the Elizabethan Society of Antiquaries enumerated in the introduction to vol. i. of the ' Archæologia,' p. xix.

Arundel was twice married. His first wife, whom he had married before November 1532 (GAIRDNER, vol. v. No. 1557), was Katherine, second daughter of Thomas Grey, marquis of Dorset, K.G., by whom he had one son, Henry, lord Maltravers, born in 1538, who died at Brussels, 30 June 1556, and two daughters, Jane and Mary. Jane was married before March 1552 to John, lord Lumley, but had no issue, and nursed her father after the death of his second wife, and died in 1576–7. Mary, born about 1541, became the wife (between 1552 and 1554) of Thomas Howard, duke of Norfolk, and the mother of Philip Howard, who inherited the earldom of Arundel. She died 25 Aug. 1557, and was buried at St. Clement Danes. Both these ladies were eminent for their classical attainments. Their learned exercises are preserved in the

British Museum among the Royal MSS., having been handed down with Lord Lumley's library (*Gent. Mag.* vol. ciii. pt. ii. pp. 494–500). Arundel married secondly Mary, daughter of Sir John Arundell of Lanherne, Cornwall, and widow of Robert Ratcliffe, first earl of Sussex of that family, and K.G. She had no children by Arundel, and dying 21 Oct. 1557 at Arundel House, was buried 1 Sept. in the neighbouring church of St. Clement Danes, but was afterwards reinterred at Arundel (*Sussex Archæol. Coll.* iii. 81–2). A curious account of her funeral is contained in a contemporary diary, Cotton MS. Vitellius, F. v. Arundel thus died the last earl of his family.

His portrait was painted by Sir Anthony More; another by Hans Holbein, now in the collection of the Marquis of Bath, has supplied one of the best illustrations of Lodge's 'Portraits.' A third portrait, dated 1556, is at Parham House, Sussex. There is also an engraved likeness of him in armour, half-length, with a round cap and ruff, the work of an unknown artist.

[The chief authority is The Life of Henrye Fitzallen, last Earle of Arundell of that name, supposed to have been written by his chaplain in the interval between the earl's death in February 1580 and the following April, and now preserved among the King's MSS. xvii. A. ix. in the British Museum. It has been largely drawn on by Tierney (Hist. of Arundel, pp. 319–50), and printed by J. G. Nichols in Gent. Mag. for 1833 (vol. ciii. pt. ii. pp. 11, 118, 210, 490), accompanied by notes and extracts from other writers, and is also cursorily noticed in Dallaway's History of the Rape of Arundel. The Life in Lodge's Portraits is both inadequate and inaccurate. Other authorities are Dugdale's Baronage, i. 324; Chronicle of Queen Jane (Camd. Soc.); Froude's Hist. of England; Tytler's England under Edward VI and Mary; Sussex Archæol. Coll.; Cal. State Papers, For. 1547–69, Venetian, 1554–8; Nicolas's Historic Peerage (Courthope), p. 30; Nichols's Literary Remains of Edward VI (Roxb. Club), 1857.]   G. G.

FITZALAN, JOHN II, LORD OF OSWESTRY, CLUN, AND ARUNDEL (1223–1267), was the son of John I Fitzalan, one of the barons confederated against King John, and of his first wife Isabella, sister and finally one of the four coheiresses of Hugh of Albini, last earl of Arundel of that house. In his father's lifetime he was married to Matilda, daughter of Theobald le Butiler and Rohese de Verdun. In 1240 his father's death put him in possession of the great Shropshire estates of his house, of which the lordship of Oswestry had been in its possession since the days of Henry I, and that of Clun since the reign of Henry II. Until 1244, when he attained

his majority, the estates remained in the custody of John L'Estrange, sheriff of Shropshire, while in 1242 his father's executors were quarrelling with Rohese de Verdun, apparently about his wife's portion (*Rot. Finium*, i. 387). In 1243 he received his mother's share of one-fourth of the inheritance of the Albinis, including the town and castle of Arundel. In 1244 he entered into actual possession of all his estates.

In general politics Fitzalan's attitude was rather inconsistent. He was no friend of foreigners. In 1258 he quarrelled with Archbishop Boniface about the right of hunting in Arundel Forest, and in 1263 carried on a sharp feud with Peter of Aquablanca, the Poitevin bishop of Hereford. In the course of this he seized and plundered the bishop's stronghold of Bishop's Castle (WEBB, *Introduction to Expenses Roll of Bishop Swinfield*, I. xxi–xxii. Camd. Soc.) In 1258 he seems to have adhered to the baronial party against Henry III, and so late as December 1261 was among those still unreconciled to the king. Yet in 1258 and 1260 he had acted as chief captain of the English troops against Llewelyn of Wales, who was on the baronial side. Finally he seems to have adopted the middle policy of his patron Edward, the king's son, whom in 1263 he attended in Wales, acting in the same year as conservator of the peace in Shropshire and Staffordshire. He joined Edward and other magnates in the agreement to refer all disputes to the arbitration of St. Louis (*Fœdera*, i. 433). In April 1264 he was actively on the king's side, and besieged with Earl Warenne in Rochester Castle (LELAND, *Collectanea*, i. 321). After the king had relieved the siege, Fitzalan joined the royal army and was taken prisoner at the battle of Lewes (14 May). Next year Montfort's government required him to surrender either his son or Arundel Castle as a pledge of his faithfulness (*Fœdera*, i. 454). He died in November 1267, having in October made his will, in which he ordered that his body should be buried in the family foundation of Haughmond, Shropshire. He was succeeded (*Calend. Geneal.* i. 132) by his son John III Fitzalan (1246–1272), who in his turn was succeeded by his son Richard I Fitzalan [q. v.]

John Fitzalan is loosely described by Rishanger (p. 28, Rolls Ser.; cf. p. 25 *Chron. de Bello*, Camd. Soc.) as Earl of Arundel, but in all writs and official documents he is simply spoken of as John Fitzalan, and he never described himself in higher terms than lord of Arundel. His history does not, then, bear out the notion that the possession of the castle of Arundel conferred an earl's dignity on its holders (but cf. TIERNEY, *Hist. Arundel*, who holds the contrary view). His son John also is never spoken of by contemporaries as Earl of Arundel.

[Rymer's Fœdera, i. 399, 412, 420, 434, 454; Rot. Finium, i. 387, 411, 417; Eyton's Shropshire, vii. 253–6; Dugdale's Baronage, i. 314–15; Doyle's Official Baronage, i. 68–9; Lords' Report on the Dignity of a Peer, pp. 411–15 (1819); Yeatman's Genealogical Hist. of the House of Arundel, pp. 334–5; Tierney's Hist. of Arundel, 193–200.]   T. F. T.

FITZALAN, JOHN VI, EARL OF ARUNDEL (1408–1435), born in 1408, was the son of John Fitzalan, lord Maltravers, and of his wife, Eleanor, daughter of Sir John Berkeley of Beverston. His father, the grandson of Sir John Arundel, marshal of England, and of Eleanor, heiress of the house of Maltravers, inherited, in accordance with an entail made by Earl Richard II [see FITZALAN, RICHARD II], the castle and earldom of Arundel after the decease, without heirs male, of Earl Thomas [see FITZALAN, THOMAS], and was in 1416 summoned to parliament as Earl of Arundel. But Thomas Mowbray, duke of Norfolk, the husband of Earl Thomas's eldest sister, contested his claim both to the estate and title, and he received no further summons as earl. On his death, in 1421, the question was still unsettled, and the long minority both of his son and of John, duke of Norfolk, his rival, still further put off the suit.

The younger John, called Lord Maltravers, was knighted in 1426, at the same time as Henry VI at Leicester (*Fœdera*, x. 357). On attaining his majority he was summoned to parliament as a baron (12 July 1429). But he still claimed the earldom, and official documents describe him as 'John, calling himself Earl of Arundel' (NICOLAS, *Proceedings and Ord. of Privy Council*, iv. 28). At last, in November 1433, on his renewed petition, it was decided in parliament that his claims were good, and 'John, now Earl of Arundel, was admitted to the place and seat anciently belonging to the earls of Arundel in parliament and council' (*Rot. Parl.* iv. 441–3; cf. *Lords' Report on the Dignity of a Peer*, p. 405 sq.; and TIERNEY, *Hist. of Arundel*, pp. 107–39, for very different comments on the whole case).

Arundel's petition had been sent from the field in France, where his distinguished services had warmly enlisted the regent Bedford in his favour, and possibly hastened the favourable decision. In February 1430 he had entered into indentures to serve Henry in the French wars, and on 23 April was among the magnates that disembarked with the young king at Calais (WAURIN, *Chroniques*, 1422–31, p. 360). In June he joined Bedford at Compiègne, and brilliantly distinguished himself in the siege of that place (SAINT-REMY, ii. 181–4). He was thence sent by Bedford to co-operate with a Burgundian force in saving Champagne from the victorious course of the French governor, Barbasan. He compelled Barbasan to raise the siege of Anglure, a place situated between Troyes and Chalons, but he could not force an engagement, and was constrained to retreat, leaving Anglure a ruin to save it from falling into the enemies' hands (WAURIN, pp. 395, 396; cf. MARTIN, *Hist. de France*, vi. 245). In the summer of 1431 he was called with Talbot from the siege of Louviers to defend the Beauvaisis from invasion, and took part in the action in which Saintrailles was captured (SAINT-REMY, ii. 263). On 17 Dec. he was at Henry VI's coronation at Paris, and next day shared with the bastard of St. Pol 'the applause of the ladies for being the best tilters' at a tournament (MONSTRELET, liv. ii. ch. 110).

In February 1432 Arundel was made captain of the castle of Rouen, and on the night of 3 March was surprised in his bed by Ricarville and 120 picked soldiers, admitted by the treachery of a Béarnais soldier. Arundel had only time to escape from capture; but the gallant attack was unsupported by a larger force, and Arundel managed to confine the assailants to the castle, where twelve days later they were forced to surrender (CHÉRUEL, *Rouen sur les Anglais*, p. 113; cf. *Pièces Justificatives*, p. 94; MONSTRELET, liv. ii. ch. 113). Soon after he was despatched by Bedford with twelve hundred men to reconquer some French fortresses in the Isle de France. He captured several, but was checked at Lagny-sur-Marne, where, after partial successes, the greater part of his troops deserted. Not even the arrival of Bedford could secure the capture of Lagny. In November Arundel returned to Rouen as captain of the town, castle, and bridge (LUCE, *Chronique de Mont Saint-Michel*, ii. 14). In 1433 he was at the head of a separate army, which operated mostly upon the southern Norman frontier, where his troops held Vernon on the Seine and Verneuil in Perche (STEVENSON, *Wars of English in France*, ii. 256, 542, 543); while he was engaged on countless skirmishes, forays, and sieges (POLYDORE VERGIL, p. 482, ed. 1570). With such success were his dashing attacks attended that he was able to carry his arms beyond Normandy into Anjou and Maine (*ib.*) He is described as 'lieutenant of the king and regent in the lower marches of Normandy' (LUCE, ii. 20). His cruelty, no less than his success, made him exceptionally odious to French patriots (BLONDEL, *Reductio Normanniæ*, pp. 190–6, is very eloquent on this subject; cf. MONSTRELET, liv. ii. ch. 158). In the summer of 1534 he was despatched with Lord Willoughby to put down a popular revolt among the peasants of Lower Normandy. This gave them little difficulty, though in January 1435 Arundel was still engaged on the task (LUCE, ii. 53). The clemency with which he sought to spare the peasants and punish the leaders only was so little seconded by his troops that it might well have seemed to the French a new act of cruelty (POL. VERG. p. 483). In February 1435 his approach led Alençon to abandon with precipitation the siege of Avranches (LUCE, ii. 54).

In May 1435 Arundel was despatched by Bedford to stay the progress of the French arms on the Lower Somme; but on his arrival at Gournay he found that the enemy had repaired the old fortress of Gerberoy in the Beauvaisis, whence they were devastating all the Vexin. He accordingly marched by night from Gournay to Gerberoy, and arrived at eight in the morning before the latter place. But La Hire and Saintrailles had secretly collected a large force outside the walls, and simultaneous attacks on the English van from the castle and from the outside soon put it in confusion, while the main body was driven back in panic retreat to Gournay. Arundel and the small remainder of the van took up a strong position in the corner of a field, protected in the rear by a hedge, and in front by pointed stakes; but cannon were brought from the castle, and the second shot from a culverin shattered Arundel's ankle. On the return of La Hire from the pursuit the whole body was slain or captured (MONSTRELET, liv. ii. ch. 172). Arundel was taken to Beauvais, where the injured limb was amputated. He was so disgusted at his defeat that he rejected the aid of medicine (BASIN, i. 111), and on 12 June he died. His body was first deposited in the church of the Cordeliers of that town. A faithful Shropshire squire, Fulk Eyton, bought the remains from the French, and his executors sold them to his brother William, the next earl but one, who deposited them in the noble tomb in the collegiate chapel at Arundel, which Earl John had himself designed for his interment (TIERNEY in *Sussex Arch. Collections*, xii. 232–9). His remains show that he was over six feet in height. The French regarded the death of the 'English Achilles' with great satisfaction. 'He was a valiant knight,' says Berry king-at-arms, 'and if he had lived he would have wrought

great mischief to France' (GODEFROY, p. 389). 'He was,' says Polydore Vergil, 'a man of singular valour, constancy, and gravity.' But his exploits were those of a knight and partisan rather than those of a real general. He had just before his death been created Duke of Touraine, and in 1432 had been made a knight of the Garter.

Arundel had been twice married. His first wife was Constance, daughter of Lord Fanhope; his second Maud, daughter of Robert Lovell, and widow of Sir R. Stafford. By the latter he left a son, Humphrey (1429–1438), who succeeded him in the earldom. On Humphrey's early death, his uncle, William IV Fitzalan (1417–1487), the younger son of John V, became Earl of Arundel. He was succeeded by his son, Thomas II Fitzalan (1450–1524), whose successor was William V Fitzalan (1483–1544), the father of Henry Fitzalan [q. v.]

[Monstrelet's Chronique, ed. Douet d'Arcq (Soc. de l'Histoire de France); Waurin's Chroniques, 1422–31 (Rolls Series); Jean le Fèvre, Seigneur de Saint-Remy, Chroniques (Soc. de l'Histoire de France); Thomas Basin's Histoire de Charles VII, vol. i. (Soc. de l'Histoire de France); Godefroy's Histoire de Charles VII, par Jean Chartier, Jacques le Bonvier, &c. (Paris, 1661); Stevenson's Wars of English in France (Rolls Series); Blondel's De Reductione Normanniæ (Rolls Series); Hall's Chronicle, ed. 1809; Polydore Vergil's Hist. Angl. ed. 1570; Rolls of Parl., vol. iv.; Luce's Chron. de Mont Saint-Michel, vol. ii. (Soc. des Anciens Textes Français); Doyle's Official Baronage, i. 76; Tierney's Hist. of Arundel, pp. 106–27, 292–303, and 625, corrected in Sussex Arch. Coll. xii. 232–9; Lords' Rep. on Dignity of a Peer; Martin's Hist. de France, vol. vi.] T. F. T.

FITZALAN, RICHARD I, EARL OF ARUNDEL (1267–1302), was the son of John III Fitzalan, lord of Arundel, by his wife Isabella, daughter of Roger Mortimer of Wigmore, and was therefore the grandson of John II Fitzalan [q. v.] He was probably born on 3 Feb. 1267 (EYTON, vii. 258, but cf. *Calendarium Genealogicum*, i. 347, which makes him a little older). His father died when he was five years old, and his estates were scandalously wasted by his grandmother Matilda, and her second husband, Richard de Amundeville (EYTON, iv. 122). He was himself, however, under the wardship of his grandfather, Mortimer, though several custodians, among whom was his mother (1280), successively held his castle of Arundel. In 1287 he received his first writ of summons against the rebel Rhys ap Maredudd, and was enjoined to reside on his Shropshire estates until the revolt was put down (*Parl. Writs.* i. 599). He is there described as Richard Fitzalan, but in 1292 he is called Earl of Arundel in his pleas, in answer to writs of quo warranto (*Placita de quo warranto*, pp. 681, 687). It is said, without much evidence, that he had been created earl in 1289 (VINCENT, *Discovery*, p. 25), when he was knighted by Edward I. But the title was loosely and occasionally assigned to his father and grandfather also, though certainly without any formal warranty, for the doctrine of the act of 11 Henry VI, that all who possessed the castle of Arundel became earls without other title, was certainly not law in the thirteenth century (*Lords' Report on the Dignity of a Peer*, but cf. DUGDALE, *Baronage*, i. 315). In 1292 his zeal to join the army was the excuse for a humiliating submission to Bishop Gilbert of Chichester, after a quarrel about his right of hunting in Houghton forest (TIERNEY, pp. 203–7, from Bishop Rede's *Register*). In 1294 he was again spoken of as earl in his appointment to command the forces sent to relieve Bere Castle, threatened by the Welsh insurgent Madoc (*Parl. Writs*, i. 599). In all subsequent writs he equally enjoys that title, though his absence in Gascony prevented his being summoned to the model parliament of 1295. In 1297 he again served in Gascony. In 1298, 1299, and 1300 he held command in Scotland, and in the latter year appeared, a 'beau chevalier et bien amé' and 'richement armé,' at the siege of Carlaverock (NICOLAS, *Siege of Carlaverock*, p. 50). His last attendance in parliament was in 1301 at Lincoln, where he was one of the signatories of the famous letter to the pope. His last military summons was to Carlisle for 24 June 1301. He died on 9 March 1302 (DOYLE, i. 70).

Fitzalan married Alice or Alisona, daughter of Thomas I, marquis of Saluzzo (MULETTI, *Memorie Storico-diplomatiche di Saluzzo*, ii. 508), an alliance which is thought to point to a lengthened sojourn in Italy in his youth. By her he left two sons, of whom the elder, Edmund Fitzalan [q. v.], succeeded him, while the younger, John, was still alive in 1375 (NICOLAS, *Testamenta Vetusta*, p. 94). Of their two daughters, one, Maud, married Philip, lord Burnell, and the other, Margaret, married William Botiler of Wem (DUGDALE, i. 315).

[Parliamentary Writs, i. 599–600; Calendarium Genealogicum, ii. 622; Nicolas's Le Siège de Carlaverock, pp. 50, 283–5; Doyle's Official Baronage, i. 69–70; Dugdale's Baronage, i. 315; Eyton's Shropshire, iv. 122, 123, vii. 260–1; Lords' Report on the Dignity of a Peer, pp. 420, 421; Tierney's Hist. of Arundel, pp. 201–12.]

T. F. T.

FITZALAN, RICHARD II, EARL OF ARUNDEL AND WARENNE (1307?–1376), son of Edmund Fitzalan, earl of Arundel [q. v.], and his wife, Alice Warenne, was born not before 1307. About 1321 his marriage to Isabella, daughter of the younger Hugh le Despenser, cemented the alliance between his father and the favourites of Edward II. In 1326, however, his father's execution deprived him of the succession both to title and estates. In 1330, after the fall of Mortimer, he petitioned to be reinstated, and, after some delay, was restored in blood and to the greater part of Earl Edmund's possessions (*Rot. Parl.* ii. 50). He was, however, forbidden to continue his efforts to avenge his father by private war against John Charlton, first lord Charlton of Powys [q. v.] (*ib.* ii. 60). In 1331 he obtained the castle of Arundel from the heirs of Edmund, earl of Kent. These grants were subsequently more than once confirmed (*ib.* ii. 226, 256). In 1334 Arundel received Mortimer's castle of Chirk, and was made justice of North Wales, his large estates in that region giving him considerable local influence. The justiceship was afterwards confirmed for life. He was also made life-sheriff of Carnarvonshire and governor of Carnarvon Castle. Arundel took a conspicuous part in nearly every important war of Edward III's long reign. After surrendering in 1336 his 'hereditary right' to the stewardship of Scotland to Edward for a thousand marks (*Fœdera*, ii. 952), he was made in 1337 joint commander of the English army in the north. Early in 1338 he and his colleague Salisbury incurred no small opprobrium by their signal failure to capture Dunbar (KNIGHTON, c. 2570; cf. *Liber Plus-cardensis*, i. 284, ed. Skene). On 25 April he was elevated to the sole command, with full powers to treat with the Scots for truce or peace (*Fœdera*, ii. 1029, 1031), of which he availed himself to conclude a truce, as his duty now compelled him to follow the king to Brabant (*Chron. de Melsa*, ii. 385), where he landed at Antwerp on 13 Dec. (FROISSART, i. 417, ed. Luce). In the January parliament of 1340 he was nominated admiral of the ships at Portsmouth and the west that were to assemble at Mid Lent (*Rot. Parl.* ii. 108). On 24 June he comported himself 'loyally and nobly' at the battle of Sluys, and was one of the commissioners sent by Edward from Bruges in July to acquaint parliament with the news and to explain to it the king's financial necessities (*ib.* ii. 118 *b*). Later in the same year he took part in the great siege of Tournay (LUCE, *Chronique des Quatre Premiers Valois*, p. 4, ed. Soc. de l'Histoire de France). In 1342 he was at the great feast given by Edward III in honour of the Countess of Salisbury (Froissart, iii. 3). His next active employment was in the same year as warden of the Scottish marches in conjunction with the Earl of Huntingdon. In October of the same year he accompanied Edward on his expedition to Brittany (*ib.* iii. 225), and was left by the king to besiege Vannes (*ib.* iii. 227) while the bulk of the army advanced to Rennes. In January 1343 the truce put an end to the siege, and in July Arundel was sent on a mission to Avignon. In 1344 he was appointed, with Henry, earl of Derby, lieutenant of Aquitaine, where the French war had again broken out; and at the same time was commissioned to treat with Castile, Portugal, and Aragon (*Fœdera*, iii. 8, 9). In 1345 he repudiated his wife, Isabella, on the ground that he had never consented to the marriage, and, having obtained papal recognition of the nullity of the union, married Eleanor, widow of Lord Beaumont, and daughter of Henry, third earl of Lancaster. This business may have prevented him sharing in the warlike exploits of his new brother-in-law, Derby, in Aquitaine. He was, however, reappointed admiral of the west in February 1345, and retained that post until 1347 (Nicolas, *Hist. of Royal Navy*, ii. 95). In 1346 he accompanied Edward on his great expedition to northern France (Froissart, iii. 130), and commanded the second of the three divisions into which the English host was divided at Crecy (*ib.* iii. 169, makes him joint commander with Northampton, but Murimuth, p. 166, includes the latter among the leaders of the first line). He was afterwards with Edward at the siege of Calais (*Rot. Parl.* ii. 163 *b*). In 1348 and 1350 Arundel was on commissions to treat with the pope at Avignon (*Fœdera*, iii. 165, 201). In 1350, however, he took part in the famous naval battle with the Spaniards off Winchelsea (Froissart, iv. 89). In 1351 he was employed in Scotland to arrange for a final peace and the ransom of King David (*Fœdera*, iii. 225). In 1354 he was one of the negotiators of a proposed truce with France, at a conference held under papal mediation at Guines (*ib.* iii. 253), but on the envoys proceeding to Avignon (*ib.* iii. 283), to obtain the papal ratification, it was found that no real settlement had been arrived at, and Innocent VI was loudly accused of treachery (*Cont.* Murimuth, p. 184). In 1355 Arundel was one of the regents during the king's absence from England (*Fœdera*, iii. 305). In 1357 he was again negotiating in Scotland, and in 1358 was at the head of an embassy to Wenzel,

duke of Luxemburg (*ib.* iii. 392). In August 1360 he was joint commissioner in completing the ratifications of the treaty of Bretigny. In 1362 he was one of the commissioners to prolong the truce with Charles of Blois (*ib.* iii. 662). In 1364 he was again engaged in diplomacy (*ib.* iii. 747).

The declining years of Arundel's life were spent in comparative seclusion from public affairs. In 1365 he was maliciously cited to the papal court by William de Lenne, the foreign bishop of Chichester, with whom he was on bad terms. He was supported by Edward in his resistance to the bishop, whose temporalities were ultimately seized by the crown. He now perhaps enlarged the castle of Arundel (Tierney, *Hist. of Arundel*, p. 239). His last military exploit was perhaps his share in the expedition for the relief of Thouars in 1372.

Arundel was possessed of vast wealth, especially after 1353, when he succeeded, by right of his mother, to the earldom of Warenne or Surrey. He frequently aided Edward III in his financial difficulties by large advances, so that in 1370 Edward was more than twenty thousand pounds in his debt. Yet at his death Arundel left behind over ninety thousand marks in ready money, nearly half of which was stored up in bags in the high tower of Arundel (*Harl. MS.* 4840, f. 393, where is a curious inventory of all his personal property at his death).

One of Arundel's last acts was to become, with Bishop William of Wykeham, a general attorney for John of Gaunt during his journey to Spain (*Fœdera*, iii. 1026). He died on 24 Jan. 1376. By his will, dated 5 Dec. 1375, he directed that his body should be buried without pomp in the chapter-house of Lewes priory, by the side of his second wife, and founded a perpetual chantry in the chapel of St. George's within Arundel Castle (Nicolas, *Testamenta Vetusta*, pp. 94–6). By his first marriage his only issue was one daughter. By his second he had three sons, of whom Richard, the eldest [see Fitzalan, Richard III], was his successor to the earldom. John, the next, became marshal of England, and perished at sea in 1379. According to the settlement made by Earl Richard in 1347 (*Rot. Parl.* iv. 442), the title ultimately reverted to the marshal's grandson, John VI Fitzalan. The youngest, Thomas [see Arundel, Thomas], became archbishop of Canterbury. Of his four daughters by Eleanor, two are mentioned in his will, namely Joan, married to Humphrey Bohun, earl of Hereford, and Alice, the wife of Thomas Holland, earl of Kent. His other daughters, Mary and Eleanor, died before him

E

[Rymer's Fœdera, vol. iii. Record edit. ; Rolls of Parl. vol. ii. ; Dugdale's Baronage, i. 316–18 ; Doyle's Official Baronage, i. 71–2 ; Froissart's Chroniques, vols. i–iv. ed. Luce (Société de l'Histoire de France); Murimuth and his Cont. (Engl. Hist. Soc.); Knighton in Twysden, Decem Scriptores; Tierney's Hist. of Arundel, pp. 225–240.]   T. F. T.

FITZALAN, RICHARD III, EARL OF ARUNDEL AND SURREY (1346–1397), born in 1346, was the son of Richard II Fitzalan, earl of Arundel [q. v.], and his second wife, Eleanor, daughter of Henry, third earl of Lancaster. He served on the expedition to the Pays de Caux under Lancaster (NICOLAS, *Scrope and Grosvenor Roll*, i. 220). In January 1376 he succeeded to his father's estates and titles. Though the petitions of the Good parliament contain complaints of the men of Surrey and Sussex against the illegal jurisdiction exercised by his novel ' shire-court' at Arundel over the rapes of Chichester and Arundel (*Rot. Parl.* ii. 348), he was appointed one of the standing council established in that parliament to restrain the dotage of Edward III (*Chron. Angliæ*, 1328–1388, p. lxviii, Rolls Ser.) At Richard II's coronation he acted as chief butler (*Rot. Parl.* iii. 131). He was placed on the council of regency (*ib.* iii. 386), and in 1380 put on a commission to regulate the royal household. In 1377 he was appointed admiral of the west. His earlier naval exploits were but little glorious, yet French authorities credit him with the merit of having saved Southampton from their assault (LUCE, *Chronique des Quatre Premiers Valois*, p. 263, ed. Soc. de l'Histoire de France). About Whitsuntide 1378 he attacked Harfleur, but was subsequently driven to sea (*ib.* p. 273). In the same year he and the Earl of Salisbury were defeated by a Spanish fleet, though they afterwards compelled Cherbourg to surrender (WALSINGHAM, i. 371). He next accompanied John of Gaunt on his expedition to St. Malo, where his negligence on the watch gave the French an opportunity to destroy a mine and so compel the raising of the siege (FROISSART, liv. ii. ch. xxxvi. ed. Buchon). Arundel barely escaped with his life (*Chronique des Quatre Premiers Valois*, p. 275). The earl showed an equal sluggishness in defending even his own tenants when the French ravaged the coasts of Sussex (WALS. i. 439 ; cf. *Chron. Angliæ*, p. 168). In 1381 he and Michael de la Pole were approved in parliament as councillors in constant attendance upon the young king and as governors of his person (WALS. ii. 156; *Rot. Parl.* iii. 104 *b*). In 1383 he was proposed as lieutenant of Bishop Spencer of Norwich's crusading army,

but the bishop refused to accept him (*ib.* iii. 155 *a*). In 1385 he took part in the expedition to Scotland.

Arundel definitely joined the baronial opposition that had now reformed under Gloucester, the king's uncle. He took a prominent part in the attack on the royal favourites in 1386, acted as one of the judges of M. de la Pole (WALS. ii. 152), and was put on the commission appointed in parliament to reform and govern the realm and the royal household (*Rot. Parl.* iii. 221). His appointment as admiral was now renewed with a wider commission, rendered necessary by the projected great invasion of England, which brought Charles VI to Sluys (FROISSART, iii. 47; cf. WALLON, *Rich. II*, liv. v. ch. iii.) In the spring of 1387 he and Nottingham prepared an expedition against the French, which, on 24 March, defeated a great fleet of Flemish, French, and Spanish ships off Margate, and captured nearly a hundred vessels laden with wine (WALS. ii. 154–6; *Monk of Evesham*, p. 78; FROISSART, iii. 53. The different accounts vary hopelessly; see NICOLAS, *Hist. of Royal Navy*, ii. 317–24). This brilliant victory won Arundel an extraordinary popularity, which was largely increased by the liberality with which he refused to turn the rich booty to his own advantage. For the whole year wine was cheap in England and dear in Netherlands (FROISSART, iii. 54). Immediately after he sailed to Brest and relieved and revictualled the town, which was still held for the English, and destroyed two forts erected by the French besiegers over against it (KNIGHTON, c. 2692). He then returned in triumph to England, plundering the country round Sluys and capturing ships there on his way. All danger of French invasion was at an end.

In 1387 Richard II obtained from the judges a declaration of the illegality of the commission of which Arundel was a member. His rash attempt to arrest the earl produced the final conflict. Northumberland was sent to seize Arundel at Reigate, but, fearing the number of his retainers, retired without accomplishing his mission (*Monk of Evesham*, p. 90). Warned of this treachery, Arundel escaped by night and joined Gloucester and Warwick at Harringhay, where they took arms (November 1387). At Waltham Cross on 15 Nov. they first appealed of treason the evil councillors of the king, and on 17 Nov. forced Richard to accept their charges at Westminster Hall. When the favourites attempted resistance, another meeting of the confederates was held on 12 Dec. at Huntingdon, where Arundel strongly urged the capture and deposition of the king. But the reluctance of the new associates, Derby and Nottingham, caused this violent plan to be rejected (*Rot. Parl.* iii. 376). But Arundel continued the fiercest of the king's enemies. In the parliament of February 1388 he was one of the five lords who solemnly renewed the appeal (*ib.* iii. 229; KNIGHTON, cc. 2713–2726). He specially pressed for the execution of Burley, though Derby wished to save him, and for three hours the queen interceded on her knees for his life (*Chronique de la Traison*, p. 133).

In May 1388 Arundel again went to sea, still acting as admiral, and now also as captain of Brest and lieutenant of the king in Brittany. Failing to do anything great in that country, he sailed southward, conquered Oléron and other small islands off the coast, and finally landed off La Rochelle, and took thence great pillage (FROISSART, iii. 112, 113, 129). Next year, however, he was superseded as admiral by Huntingdon (KNIGHTON, c. 2735), and in May was, with the other lords appellant, removed from the council. He was, however, restored in December, when Richard and his old masters finally came to terms (NICOLAS, *Proceedings of Privy Council,* i. 17).

For the next few years peace prevailed at home and abroad. The party of the appellants began to show signs of breaking up, though Arundel still remained faithful to his old policy. In 1392 he was fined four hundred marks for marrying Philippa, daughter of the Earl of March and widow of John Hastings, earl of Pembroke (*Rot. Pat.* 15 Rich. II, in DALLAWAY'S *Western Sussex,* II. i. 134, new edit.) A personal quarrel of Arundel with John of Gaunt marks the beginning of the catastrophe of Richard II's reign. The new Countess of Arundel was rude to Catharine Swynford (FROISSART, iv. 50). Henry Beaufort [see BEAUFORT, HENRY, bishop of Winchester], if report were true, seduced Alice, Arundel's daughter (POWEL, *Hist. of Cambria,* p. 138, from a pedigree of the Stradlings, whose then representative married the daughter born of the connection; cf. CLARK, *Limbus Patrum Morganiæ et Glanmorganiæ,* p. 435). In 1393, when Arundel was residing at his castle of Holt, a revolt against John of Gaunt broke out in Cheshire, and Arundel showed such inactivity in assisting in the restoration of peace that the duke publicly accused him in parliament of conniving at the rising (WALS. ii. 214; *Ann. Ric. II,* ed. Riley, p. 161). Arundel answered by a long series of complaints against Lancaster (*Rot. Parl.* iii. 313). Some of these so nearly touched the king as to make him very angry, and Arundel was compelled to apologise for

what he had said. The actual English words that he uttered in his recantation are preserved in the Rolls of Parliament. A short retirement from court now seems to have ensued (*Ann. Ric. II,* p. 166), but Arundel soon returned, only to give Richard fresh offence by coming late to the queen's funeral and yet asking leave to retire at once from the ceremony (*ib.* p. 169; WALS. ii. 215). The king struck Arundel with a cane with such force as to shed blood and therefore to pollute the precincts of Westminster Abbey. On 3 Aug. Arundel was sent to the Tower (*Fœdera,* vii. 784), but was released on 10 Aug. (*ib.* vii. 785), when he re-entered the council. The appointment of his brother Thomas as archbishop of Canterbury may mark the final reconciliation.

After the stormy parliament of February 1397, Arundel and Gloucester withdrew from court, after reproaching the king with the loss of Brest and Cherbourg. It was probably after this, if ever, that Arundel entertained Gloucester, Warwick, and his brother the archbishop at Arundel Castle, when they entered into a solemn conspiracy against Richard (*Chronique de la Traison,* pp. 5–6, though the date there given, 23 July 1396, must be wrong, and 28 July 1397, the editor's conjecture, is too late, one manuscript says 8 Feb.; *Chronique du Religieux de Saint-Denys,* ii. 476–8, in *Collection de Documents Inédits,* cf. FROISSART, iv. 56. The statement is in no English authority, and has been much questioned, cf. WALLON, ii. 161, 452). Nottingham, who, though Arundel's son-in-law and one of the appellants, had now deserted his old party, informed Richard of the plot. The king invited the three chief conspirators to a banquet on 10 July (*Ann. Ric. II,* p. 201). From this Arundel absented himself without so much as an excuse, but the arrest of Warwick, who ventured to attend, was his justification. He was, however, in a hopeless position. His brother pressed him to surrender, and persuaded him that the king had given satisfactory promises of his safety (*ib.* 202–3; WALS. ii. 223). He left accordingly his stronghold at Reigate, and accompanied the archbishop to the palace. Richard at once handed him over into custody, while Thomas returned sorrowfully to Lambeth (*Eulog. Hist.* iii. 371). This was on 15 July. Arundel was hurried off to Carisbrooke and thence after an interval removed to the Tower. On 17 Sept. a royalist parliament assembled. The pardons of the appellants were revoked (*Rot. Parl.* iii. 350, 351). On 20 Sept. Archbishop Arundel was impeached. Next day the new appellants laid their charges against the Earl of Arundel before the lords. He was brought before them, arrayed in scarlet. With much passion he protested that he was no traitor, and that the charges against him were barred by the pardons he had received. A long and angry altercation broke out between him and John of Gaunt and Henry of Derby, his old associate. He refused to answer the charges, denounced his accusers as liars, and when the speaker declared that the pardon on which he relied had been revoked by the faithful commons, exclaimed, 'The faithful commons are not here' (*Monk of Evesham*, pp. 136–8; *Rot. Parl.* iii. 377; *Ann. Ric.* pp. 214–19). He was, of course, condemned, though Richard commuted the barbarous penalty of treason into simple decapitation. The execution immediately followed. He was hurried through the streets of London to Tower Hill, amidst the lamentations of a sympathising multitude. Brutally illtreated by the bands of Cheshiremen who had been collected to overawe the Londoners, he displayed extraordinary firmness and resolution, ' no more shrinking or changing colour than if he were going to a banquet' (WALS. ii. 225–6; cf. *Religieux de Saint-Denys*, ii. 552). He rebuked with much dignity his treacherous kinsfolk (Nottingham was not present, though Walsingham and Froissart, iv. 61, say that he was), and exhorted the hangman to sharpen well his axe. Slain by a single stroke, he was buried in the church of the Augustinian friars. The people reverenced him as a martyr, and went on pilgrimage to his tomb. At last Richard, conscience-stricken though he was at his death, avoided a great political danger by ordering all traces of the place of his burial to be removed. But after the fall of Richard the pilgrimages were renewed, and the next generation did not doubt that his merits had won for him a place in the company of the saints (ADAM OF USK, p. 14, ed. Thompson). Arundel was very religious and a bountiful patron of the church. So early as 1380 he was admitted into the brotherhood of the abbey of Tichfield. In the same year he founded the hospital of the Holy Trinity at Arundel for a warden and twenty poor men (DUGDALE, *Monasticon*, ed. Caley, &c. vi. 736–7). Between 1380 and 1387 he enlarged the chantry projected by his father into the college of the Holy Trinity, also at Arundel. This establishment now included a master and twelve secular canons, and superseded the confiscated alien priory of St. Nicholas (*ib.* vi. 1377–1379; TIERNEY, *Arundel*, pp. 594–613). In his will he left liberal legacies to several churches.

By his first wife, Elizabeth (*d.* 1385), daughter of William de Bohun, earl of North-

ampton, Arundel had three sons and four daughters. The second son, Thomas [see FITZALAN, THOMAS], ultimately became earl of Arundel. Of his daughter Elizabeth's four husbands, the second was Thomas Mowbray, earl of Nottingham [q. v.] Another daughter, Joan, married William, lord Bergavenny. A third, Alice, married John, lord Charlton of Powys. By Philippa Mortimer Arundel had no children.

[Walsingham's Chronicle of Richard II, ed. Riley; Eulogium Historiarum; Wright's Political Poems and Songs; Chronicon Angliæ, 1328–1388 (all in Rolls Series); Chronique de la Traison et Mort de Richard (Engl. Hist. Soc.); French Metrical History of the Deposition of Richard II, in Archæologia, vol. xx.; Monk of Evesham's Hist. Rich. II, ed. Hearne, 1729; Knighton in Twysden, Decem Scriptores; Chronique du Religieux de Saint-Denys, vol. i. (Documents Inédits sur l'Histoire de France); Froissart, vols. iii. and iv. ed. Buchon, is often wrong in details; Rolls of Parliament, vols. ii. and iii.; Rymer's Fœdera, vol. vii.; Dugdale's Baronage, i. 318–320; Doyle's Official Baronage, i. 73–4; Sir N. H. Nicolas's History of the Royal Navy, vol. ii.; Wallon's Richard II. with good notes on the authorities, is, with Stubbs's Constitutional History of England, vol. ii., the fullest modern account; Dallaway's Western Sussex, II. i. 130–7, new edit.; Tierney's History of Arundel, pp. 240–276; Nichols's Collection of Royal Wills, pp. 120–143, contains in full Arundel's long and curious testament, written in French and dated 1392; it is taken from the Register of Archbishop Arundel.]   T. F. T.

FITZALAN, *alias* ARUNDEL, THOMAS (1353–1414), archbishop of Canterbury. [See ARUNDEL.]

FITZALAN, THOMAS, EARL OF ARUNDEL AND SURREY (1381–1415), the second and only surviving son of Richard III Fitzalan, earl of Arundel [q. v.], and his first wife, Elizabeth Bohun, was born on 13 Oct. 1381. He was only sixteen when his father was executed. Deprived by his father's sentence of the succession to the family titles and estates, he was handed over by King Richard II to the custody of his half-brother, John Holland, duke of Exeter, who also received a large portion of the Arundel estates. In after years Fitzalan retained a bitter remembrance of the indignities he and his sister had experienced at Exeter's hands; how he drudged for him like a slave, and how many a time he had taken off and blacked his boots for him (*Chronique de la Traison* p. 97). He was no better off when confined in his father's old castle of Reigate, under the custody of Sir John Shelley, the steward of the Duke of Exeter, who also compelled him to submit to great humiliations (*Ann. Ric. II*, ed. Riley, p. 241; LELAND, *Collectanea*, i. 483). At last Fitzalan managed to effect his escape, and with the assistance of a mercer named William Scot arrived safely on the continent, either at Calais or at Sluys. He joined his uncle, the deposed Archbishop Arundel, at Utrecht, but was so poor that he would have starved but for the assistance of his powerful kinsfolk abroad. The conjecture, based on a slight correction of Froissart's story of Archbishop Arundel's commission from the Londoners to Henry of Derby, that Fitzalan bore a special message from the London citizens to Henry, that he should overthrow Richard and obtain the English crown, seems neither necessary nor probable. Froissart's whole account of the movements of the exiled Henry is too inaccurate to make it necessary to explain away his gross blunders. However, Archbishop Arundel left his German exile and joined Henry at Paris, and his nephew doubtless accompanied him, both on this journey and on the further travels of Henry and the archbishop to Boulogne. Fitzalan embarked with Henry on his voyage to England, and landed with him at Ravenspur early in July 1399. There is no foundation for the story of the French anti-Lancastrian writers that when Richard II fell into Henry's hands the latter entrusted Fitzalan and the son of Thomas of Woodstock (who was already dead) with the custody of the captive prince, with an injunction to guard closely the king who had put both their fathers to death unjustly, and that they conveyed Richard to London 'as strictly guarded as a thief or a murderer' (*Chronique de la Traison*, p. 210; *Religieux de Saint-Denys*, ii. 717; cf. *Archæologia*, xx. 173). On 11 Oct. Fitzalan was one of those knighted by Henry in the great hall of the Tower of London on the occasion when the order of the Bath is generally considered to have been instituted. Next day he marched, with the other newly-made knights, in Henry's train to Westminster, all dressed alike and 'looking like priests.' At Henry's coronation, on Monday 13 Oct., he officiated as butler (ADAM OF USK, p. 33, ed. Thompson). The new king even anticipated the commons' petition in his favour by restoring him to his father's titles and estates (*Rot. Parl.* iii. 435–6; *Cal. Rot. Pat.* p. 238 *b*; *Cont. Eulog. Hist.* iii. 385). Though still under age he at once took his seat as Earl of Arundel, and on 23 Oct. was one of the magnates who advised the king to put Richard II under 'safe and secret guard' (*Rot. Parl.* iii. 426–7). Early in 1400 Arundel took the field against the Hollands and the other insurgent nobles.

On the capture of John Holland, now again only Earl of Huntingdon, by the followers of the Countess of Hereford, in Essex, Arundel, if we can believe the French authorities, hastened to join his aunt in wreaking an unworthy revenge on his former captor (*Chronique de la Traison*, p. 97 sq.) After taunting Huntingdon with his former ill-treatment of him, Arundel procured his immediate execution, despite the sympathies of the bystanders and the royal order that he should be committed to the Tower (*Fœdera*, viii. 121). He then marched through London streets in triumph with Huntingdon's head on a pole, and ultimately bore it to the king (*Religieux de Saint-Denys*, ii. 742).

Arundel's great possessions in North Wales were now endangered by the revolt of Owain of Glyndyfrdwy [see GLENDOWER, OWEN], who had begun life as an esquire of Earl Richard. Earl Thomas was much employed against the Welsh chieftain during the next few years. In 1401 he fought with Hotspur against the rebels near Cader Idris. In August 1402 he commanded that division of the threefold expedition against the Welsh which assembled at Hereford. Within a month all three armies were compelled by unseasonable storms to retreat to England. In 1403 he was again ordered to assemble an army at Shrewsbury. After attending, in October 1404, the parliament at Coventry, where he was one of the triers of petitions for Gascony, he entered into an agreement with the king, in accordance with the ordinance of that parliament, to remain for eight weeks with a small force at his castle of Oswestry; but in February 1405 he confessed that he was able to do nothing against the insurgents (*Rot. Parl.* iii. 545–7; NICOLAS, *Proceedings of Privy Council*, i. 246–7).

In the early summer of 1405 the revolt of Archbishop Scrope and the earl marshal brought Arundel to the north. After the capture of the two leaders Arundel joined Thomas Beaufort in persuading Henry to disregard his uncle, Archbishop Arundel's, advice to respect the person of the captive archbishop. On 8 June, while Archbishop Arundel was delayed at breakfast with King Henry, his nephew was placed at the head of a commission which hastily condemned both Scrope and Mowbray, and ordered their immediate execution (*Ann. Hen. IV*, p. 409; RAYNALDI, *Ann. Eccl.* viii. 143; but cf. Maidstone, in RAINE, *Historians of the Church of York*, ii. 306 sq., Rolls Ser., for a different account). This violence seems to have caused a breach between Arundel and his uncle. Henceforth the earl inclined to the policy of the Beauforts and the Prince of Wales against the policy of the archbishop. Arundel next accompanied Henry in August into Wales, where he is said to have successfully defended Haverfordwest against Owain and his French allies under Montmorency (HALL, p. 25, ed. 1809). But in the autumn he was engaged in negotiating a marriage with Beatrix, bastard daughter of John I, king of Portugal, by Agnes Perez, and sister therefore of the Duke of Braganza. John's wife was sister of King Henry IV, and English assistance had enabled him to secure his country's freedom against Castile. The projected marriage was but part of the close alliance between the two countries, and Henry IV actively interested himself in its success. As Arundel's means were much straitened by the devastation of his Welsh estates, the king advanced the large sums necessary to bring the bride ' with magnificence and glory' to England. On 26 Nov. the marriage was celebrated at London in the presence of the king and queen (*Ann. Hen. IV*, p. 417; WALSINGHAM, ii. 272; *Collectanea Topog. et Geneal.* i. 80–90).

In 1406 Arundel was present at the famous parliament of that year, and supported the act of succession then passed (*Rot. Parl.* iii. 576, 582). In May 1409 he was again ordered to remain on his North Welsh estates to encounter Owen (*Fœdera*, viii. 588), and in November was ordered to continue the war, notwithstanding the truce made by his officers, which the Welsh persisted in not observing (*ib.* viii. 611).

In 1410 Arundel's ally, Thomas Beaufort, became chancellor, and the frequency of the appearance of his name in the proceedings of the council shows that he took, in consequence, a more active part in affairs of state. The old differences with his uncle, now driven from power, continued, and in one letter Arundel complained to the archbishop that he had been misrepresented (*Proceedings of Privy Council*, ii. 117–18). The triumph of the Beauforts involved England in a Burgundian foreign policy, and when in 1411 an English expedition was sent to help Philip of Burgundy against the Armagnacs, Arundel, the Earl of Kyme, and Sir J. Oldcastle were appointed its commanders. He was also one of the commissioners appointed to negotiate the marriage of the Prince of Wales with a sister of the Duke of Burgundy (*ib.* ii. 20). He was well received by Burgundy, whom he accompanied on his march to Paris, arriving there on 23 Oct. On 9 Nov. he fought a sharp and successful engagement with the Orleanists, which resulted in the capture of St. Cloud (WALSINGHAM, ii. 286; JEAN LE FÈVRE, *Chronique*, i.

36–43; PIERRE DE FENIN, *Mémoires*, pp. 22–23, both in Soc. de l'Histoire de France; cf. MARTIN, *Histoire de France*, v. 521). The result was the retirement of the Armagnacs beyond the Loire. The English, having been bought out of their scruples against selling their prisoners to be tortured to death by their allies, returned home with large rewards soon afterwards. The fall of the Beauforts and the return of Archbishop Arundel to power kept Earl Thomas in retirement until Henry IV's death. Before this date he had become a knight of the Garter (ASHMOLE, *Order of the Garter*, p. 710).

The day after his accession Henry V turned Archbishop Arundel out of the chancery and made the Earl of Arundel treasurer in place of Lord le Scrope. Arundel was also appointed on the same day constable of Dover Castle and warden of the Cinque ports. In 1415 the commons petitioned against his aggressions and violence in Sussex (*Rot. Parl.* iv. 78), and an Italian merchant complained of his unjust imprisonment and the seizure of his effects by him (*ib.* iv. 90). He was also engaged in a quarrel with Lord Furnival about some rights of common in Shropshire, which ultimately necessitated the king's intervention (*Gesta Hen. V*, pref. p. xxviii, Engl. Hist. Soc.) From such petty difficulties he was removed by his summons to accompany Henry on his great invasion of France. He took a leading part in the siege of Harfleur, but was one of the many who were compelled to return home sick of the dysentery and fever that devastated the victorious army. On 10 Oct. he made his will; on 13 Oct. he died. He was buried in a magnificent tomb in the midst of the choir of the collegiate chapel that his father had founded at Arundel. There is a vignette of the tomb in Tierney, p. 622.

Earl Thomas was in character hot, impulsive, and brave. He was a good soldier, and faithful to his friends; but he showed a vindictive thirst for revenge on the enemies of his house, and a recklessness which subordinated personal to political aims. He left no children, so that the bulk of his estates was divided among his three surviving sisters, while the castle and lordship of Arundel passed to his second cousin, John V Fitzalan (1387–1421), grandson of Sir John Arundel, marshal of England, and of his wife, Eleanor Maltravers [see JOHN VI FITZALAN, EARL OF ARUNDEL]. The earldom of Surrey fell into abeyance on Thomas's death.

[Annales Ric. II et Hen. IV, ed. Riley (Rolls Ser.); Eulogium Historiarum (Rolls Ser.); Walsingham's Hist. Angl. and Ypodigma Neustriæ (Rolls Ser.); Otterbourne's Chronicle, ed. Hearne;

Monk of Evesham, Hist. Ric. II, ed. Hearne; Chronique de la Traison et Mort de Richart II (Engl. Hist. Soc.); French Metrical History of the Deposition of Richard II in Archæologia, vol. xx.; Henrici V Gesta (Engl. Hist. Soc.); Froissart's Chronique, ed. Buchon; Chroniques du Religieux de Saint-Denys (Documents Inédits sur l'Histoire de France); Waurin's Chroniques (Rolls Ser.); Hall's Chronicle, ed. 1809; Nicolas's Proceedings and Ordinances of the Privy Council, vols. i. ii.; Rymer's Fœdera, vols. viii. ix., original edition; Rolls of Parliament, vols. iii. iv.; Calendarium Rotulorum Patentium, Record Commission; Stubbs's Constitutional History of England, iii.; Doyle's Official Baronage, i. 74; Wylie's History of Henry IV, 1399-1404; Biography in Tierney's History of Arundel, pp. 277-87.]   T. F. T.

FITZALAN, WILLIAM (d. 1160), rebel, was the son and heir of Alan Fitzflaald, by Aveline or Adeline, sister of Ernulf de Hesding (EYTON, Shropshire, vii. 222-3). His younger brother, Walter Fitzalan (d. 1177), was 'the undoubted ancestor of the royal house of Stuart' (ib.) His father had received from Henry I, about the beginning of his reign, extensive fiefs in Shropshire and Norfolk. William was born about 1105 and succeeded his father about 1114 (ib. pp. 222, 232). His first appearance is as a witness to Stephen's charter to Shrewsbury Abbey (Monasticon, iii. 519) in 1136. He is found acting as castellan of Shrewsbury and sheriff of Shropshire in 1138, when he joined in the revolt against Stephen, being married to a niece of the Earl of Gloucester (ORD. VIT. v. 112-13). After resisting the king's attack for a month, he fled with his family (August 1138), leaving the castle to be defended by his uncle Ernulf, who, on his surrender, was hanged by the king (ib.; Cont. FLOR. WIG. ii. 110). He is next found with the empress at Oxford in the summer of 1141 (EYTON, vii. 287), and shortly after at the siege of Winchester (Gesta, p. 80). He again appears in attendance on her at Devizes, witnessing the charter addressed to himself by which she grants Aston to Shrewsbury Abbey (EYTON, ix. 58). It was probably between 1130 and 1138 that he founded Haughmond Abbey (ib. 286-7). In June 1153 he is found with Henry, then duke of Normandy, at Leicester (ib. p. 288). With the accession of Henry as king he regained his paternal fief on the fall of Hugh de Mortimer in July 1155. He is found at Bridgnorth with the king at that time, and on 25 July received from his feudal tenants a renewal of their homage (ib. i. 250-1, vii. 236-7, 288). His first wife, Christiana, being now dead, he received from Henry the hand of Isabel de Say, heiress of the barony of Clun (ib. vii. 237), together

with the shrievalty of Shropshire, which he retained till his death (Pipe Rolls, 2-6 Hen. II), which took place in 1160, about Easter (ib. 6 Hen. II, p. 27). Among his benefactions he granted Wroxeter Church to Haughmond in 1155 (EYTON, vii. 311-12), and, though not the founder of Wombridge Priory, sanctioned its foundation (ib. p. 363). He was succeeded by William Fitzalan the second, his son and heir by his second wife. By his first he left a daughter, Christiana, wife of Hugh Pantulf.

[Ordericus Vitalis (Société de l'Histoire de France); Gesta Stephani (Rolls Ser.); Florence of Worcester (Engl. Hist. Soc.); Monasticon Anglicanum, new ed.; Pipe Rolls (Record Commission and Pipe Roll Soc.); Eyton's Hist. of Shropshire.]   J. H. R.

FITZALDHELM, WILLIAM (fl. 1157-1198), steward of Henry II and governor of Ireland, is described as the son of Aldhelm, the son of William of Mortain (DUGDALE, Baronage, i. 693; 'if our best genealogists are not mistaken,' as he cautiously adds), whose father, Robert of Mortain, earl of Cornwall, was half-brother of the conqueror, but after Tenchebrai was deprived of his earldom, imprisoned for over thirty years, and only exchanged his dungeon for the habit of a Cluniac monk at Bermondsey. A brother of Aldhelm is said to have been the father of Hubert de Burgh [q. v.] But there seems no early authority for this rather improbable genealogy, and the absence of contemporary references to his family makes it probable that his descent was obscure. Fitzaldhelm first appears as king's steward (dapifer) as witnessing two charters of Henry II to the merchants of Cologne and their London house, which apparently belong to July 1157 (LAPPENBERG, Urkundliche Geschichte des hansischen Stahlhofes zu London, Urkunden, pp. 4-5, 'aus dem Cölner Copialbuche von 1326'). He appears as an officer of the crown in the Pipe Roll of 1159-60, 1160-1, and 1161-2 (Pipe Roll Society's publications, passim). In 1163 he attested a charter which fixed the services of certain vassals of the Count of Flanders to Henry II (Fœdera, i. 23). He again appears in the Pipe Rolls of 1163, 1165, and 1170, and about 1165 is described as one of the king's marshals and acted as a royal justice (HEARNE, Liber Niger, i. 73, 74; EYTON, pp. 80, 85, 139). In October 1170 he was one of the two justices consulted by Becket's agents prior to their appearance before the younger king at Westminster (Memorials of Becket, vii. 389). In July 1171 he was with Henry in Normandy and witnessed at Bur-le-Roy a charter in favour of Newstead Priory (DUGDALE, Monas-

ticon, vi. 966 ; EYTON, p. 159). Almost immediately afterwards Henry was at Valognes, whence he despatched Fitzaldhelm to Ireland to act as the royal representative until Henry obtained leisure to settle the affairs of the island in person (*Fœdera*, i. 36, dated by the Record commissioners' editors in 1181, but assigned to this date with more probability by EYTON, *Itinerary*, p. 159 ; GILBERT, *Viceroys*, p. 41, gives the date 1176–7). In the letter of appointment he is described as the king's steward. It cost 27*s*. 6*d*. to convey him and his associates, with their armour, to Ireland (*Calendar of Documents*, Ireland, 1171–1251, No. 40). On 18 Oct. he, with his followers, was at Waterford to meet the king, who had landed close by on the previous day (BENEDICTUS ABBAS, i. 25 ; REGAN's statement that he accompanied Henry, p. 124, is of less authority). He remained in Ireland with Henry, witnessing among other acts the charter which gave Dublin to the men of Bristol (GILBERT, *Historical and Municipal Documents of Ireland*, p. 1). He was sent by Henry with Hugh de Lacy on a mission to Roderick O'Conor, king of Connaught, to receive his homage (GIRALDUS CAMBRENSIS in *Opera*, v. 279, Rolls Ser.) He also made a recognition of the lands given to the monks of St. Mary's Abbey, Dublin, before his arrival in Ireland (*Chartulary of St. Mary's*, i. 138, Rolls Ser.) Giraldus also says that when Henry went home he left Fitzaldhelm behind as joint-governor of Wexford (*ib.* p. 286), but this may be a confusion with a later appointment (REGAN, p. 39, says that Strongbow was governor of Wexford in 1174). Fitzaldhelm was also sent in 1174 or 1175 with the prior of Wallingford to produce the bull of Pope Adrian, granting Ireland to Henry, and a confirmatory bull of Alexander III to a synod of bishops at Waterford (*Exp. Hib.* p. 315). He soon left Ireland, for he appears as a witness of the treaty of Falaise in October 1174 (*Fœdera*, i. 30 ; BENED. ABBAS, i. 99), and in 1175 and 1176 he was constantly in attendance at court in discharge of his duties as steward or seneschal (EYTON, pp. 191, 194, 195, 198, from Pipe Rolls ; LAPPENBERG, *Stahlhof*, p. 5).

On 5 April 1176 Strongbow, conqueror and justiciar of Ireland, died (DICETO, i. 407), and Henry sent Fitzaldhelm to Ireland to take his place (BENED. ABBAS, i. 125 ; HOVEDEN, ii. 100) and to seize all the fortresses which his predecessor had held. With him were associated several other rulers, very different lists of which are given by Giraldus (*Exp. Hib.* p. 334) and 'Benedict of Peterborough' (BENED. ABBAS, i. 161). It was at this time that Wexford and its elaborately

defined dependencies were assigned to Fitzaldhelm (*ib.* i. 163). It is remarkable that he is never called 'justice' of Ireland, like most viceroys of the period, but generally ' dapifer regis' (e.g. *Hist. MSS. Comm.* 10th Rep. pt. v. p. 211). Giraldus calls him 'procurator' (*Exp. Hib.* p. 334). Fitzaldhelm had no easy task before him. John de Courci [q. v.], one of his colleagues, almost at once defied his prohibition, and, under the pretext of disgust at his inactivity, set forth on his famous expedition to Ulster (BENED. ABBAS, i. 137). He also had a difference with Cardinal Vivian, the papal legate, which led to Vivian's withdrawal to Scotland (WILL. NEWBURGH, i. 239, Rolls Ser.) But his most formidable opponents were the ring of Welsh adventurers who resented the intrusion of a royal emissary to reap the fruits of their private exploits. Their literary representative, Giraldus, draws the blackest picture of Fitzaldhelm, which, though suspicious, cannot be checked from other contemporary sources. Fitzaldhelm was fat, greedy, profligate, and gluttonous. Plausible and insinuating, he was thoroughly deceitful. He was only brave against the weak, and shirked the duties of his office. His inactivity drove De Courci and the choicer spirits into Ulster. From the day on which Raymond, the acting governor, came to meet him at Waterford he envied the bravery, the devotion, and the success of the Geraldines, and vowed to humble their pride. When Maurice Fitzgerald died he cheated his sons of their stronghold of Wicklow, though compelled ultimately to give them Ferns as an inadequate compensation. He refused to restore Offaly to Fitzstephen, and deprived Raymond of his lands in the valley of the Liffey. His nephew, Walter the German, was suborned by Irish chieftains to procure the destruction of Ferns. He went on progress through the secure coast towns, but feared to penetrate into the mountainous haunts of the natives. He had little share in Miles de Cogan's dashing raid into Connaught. The only good thing that he did was to transfer the wonder-working staff of Jesus from Armagh to Dublin. Giraldus forgets that Fitzaldhelm was also the founder of the monastery of St. Thomas of Canterbury at Donore in the western suburbs of Dublin (charter of foundation printed in LELAND, *Hist. of Ireland*, i. 127 ; cf. *Monasticon*, vi. 1140). It was also during his tenure of office that John became lord of Ireland. At last Henry listened to the complaints which a deputation from Ireland laid before him at Windsor just after Christmas 1178 (BENED. ABBAS, i. 221), and removed Fitzaldhelm and his colleagues from office, and for a long time withheld all marks of favour from him (*ib.*; *Exp. Hib.* ccxv–xx, 334–47, for the whole history of Fitzaldhelm's government, but it should be checked by the less rhetorical and more impartial account of BENED. ABBAS, with which it is often in direct conflict). This makes it probable that Fitzaldhelm was not quite equal to the difficulties of his position. Substantially his fall was a great triumph for the Geraldines.

Fitzaldhelm now resumed his duties as 'dapifer' at the English court. From 1181 onwards he was sufficiently in favour for his name to appear again in the records (e.g. EYTON, pp. 245, 267). In 1188 he became sheriff of Cumberland, and in 1189 acted also as justice in Yorkshire, Northumberland, and his own county (*ib.* pp. 298, 336). He remained sheriff of Cumberland until 1198 (*Thirty-first Report of Deputy-Keeper of Records*, p. 276). In 1189 he witnessed a charter of Christ Church, Canterbury (GERVASE, *Op. Hist.* i. 503). In 1194 he attested a grant of lands to the cook of Queen Eleanor (*Fœdera*, i. 63). These are the last appearances of his name in the records. He is said to have married Juliana, daughter of Robert Doisnell (HEARNE, *Liber Niger Scaccarii*, i. 73).

Fitzaldhelm has been generally identified with a WILLIAM DE BURGH (*d.* 1204), who occupies a very prominent position in the first years of John's reign in Ireland. A William de Burgh appears with his wife Eleanor in the 'Pipe Roll' of 1 Richard I (p. 176), but he is undoubtedly different from Fitzaldhelm, as the latter appears by his regular name in the same roll. In 1199 William de Burgh received from John large grants of land and castles in Ireland (*Rot. Chart.* pp. 19 *b*, 71 *b*, 84 *b*, 107 *b* ; the earliest grants of John to him were before the latter became king, *Hist. MSS. Comm.* 3rd Rep. p. 231). Of these Limerick was the most important. In 1200 he became the terror of the Irish of Connaught. He supported the pretender, Cathal Carrach, in his attempts to dispossess Cathal Crobhderg, the head of the O'Conors, from the throne of Connaught. 'There was no church from the Shannon westwards to the sea that they did not pillage or destroy, and they used to strip the priests in the churches and carry off the women without regard to saint or sanctuary or to any power upon earth' (*Annals of Loch Cé*, i. 213). Cathal Crobhderg was expelled and took refuge with John de Courci. But in 1202 he made terms with William de Burgh, and a fresh expedition from Munster again devastated Connaught (the *Four Masters*, iii. 129, put this expedition in 1201). Cathal Carrach

was slain, but the treacherous Cathal Crobhderg contrived a plot to assassinate in detail the followers of De Burgh. Nine hundred or more were murdered, but the remainder rallied and the erection of the strong castle of Meelick secured some sort of conquest of Connaught for the invaders. A quarrel between De Burgh and the king's justice, Meiler Fitzhenry [q. v.], for a time favoured the Irish. In 1203, while De Burgh was in Connaught, Meiler invaded his Munster estates (*Ann. Loch Cé*, i. 229–31). This brought William back to Limerick, but Meiler had already seized his castles. The result was an appeal to King John. William appeared before John in Normandy (*Rot. de Liberate*, 5 John, p. 67, summarised in *Cal. Doc. Ireland*, 1171–1251, No. 187), leaving his sons as hostages in the justiciar's hands. In March 1204 a commission, at the head of which was Walter de Lacy, was appointed to hear the complaints against De Burgh (*Pat.* 5 John, m. 2 ; *Cal. Doc. Ireland*, No. 209). The result was the restoration of his Munster estates, though Connaught, 'whereof he was disseised by reason of certain appeals and the dissension between the justiciary and himself,' was retained in the king's hands 'until the king knows how he shall have discharged himself' (*Pat.* 6 John, m. 8 ; *Cal. Doc. Ireland*, No. 230). Connaught, however, had not been restored when soon after William de Burgh died, 'the destroyer of all Erinn, of nobility and chieftainship' (*Ann. Loch Cé*, i. 235). The Irish believed that 'God and the saints took vengeance on him, for he died of a singular disease too shameful to be described' (*Four Masters*, iii. 143). He was the uncle of Hubert de Burgh [q. v.] He was the father of Richard de Burgh [q. v.] (*Rot. Claus.* p. 551), who in 1222–3 received a fresh grant of Connaught and became the founder of the great house of the De Burghs. He founded the abbey of Athassell for Austin canons (ARCHDALL, *Monast. Hiber.* p. 640), and is said to have been buried there.

[For Fitzaldhelm: Giraldus Cambrensis, Expugnatio Hibernica, in Opera, vol. v. ed. Dimock (Rolls Ser.); Benedictus Abbas, ed. Stubbs (Rolls Ser.); Rymer's Fœdera, vol. i. (Record ed.); Eyton's Itinerary, &c. of Henry II; Pipe Roll, 1 Richard I (Record ed.), and the French poem on the conquest of Ireland, ed. Michel. For De Burgh: Annals of Loch Cé, i. 211–35 (Rolls Ser.); Annals of the Four Masters; Rotuli Chartarum, Rotuli Literarum Patentium, Rotuli de Oblatis, Rotuli de Liberate. For both: Sweetman's Calendar of Documents relating to Ireland, 1171–1251; Book of Howth; Gilbert's Viceroys of Ireland; Dugdale's Baronage; Lodge's Peerage of Ireland (Archdall).] T. F. T.

FITZALWYN, HENRY (*d.* 1212), first mayor of London. [See FITZAILWIN.]

FITZCHARLES, CHARLES, EARL OF PLYMOUTH (1657 ?–1680), born in or about 1657, was the illegitimate son of Charles II, by Catherine, daughter of Thomas Pegge of Yeldersley, Derbyshire. 'In the time of his youth,' writes the courtly Dugdale, 'giving much testimony of his singular accomplishments,' he was elevated to the peerage, 28 July 1675, as Baron of Dartmouth, Viscount Totness, and Earl of Plymouth, ' to the end he might be the more encouraged to persist in the paths of virtue, and thereby be the better fitted for the managery of great affairs when he should attain to riper years' (*Baronage*, iii. 487). He was colonel of the 2nd Tangier regiment. He married on 19 Sept. 1678 at Wimbledon, Surrey, Lady Bridget Osborne, third daughter of Thomas, first duke of Leeds, but died without issue at Tangier on 17 Oct. 1680, aged 23, and was buried on 18 Jan. 1680–1 in Westminster Abbey (CHESTER, *Registers of Westminster Abbey*, p. 201). His wife remarried, about August 1706, Philip Bisse, bishop of Hereford, and died on 9 May 1718 (*Hist. Reg.* 1718, Chron. Diary, p. 21). According to Wood (*Fasti Oxon.* ed. Bliss, ii. 270) he was commonly called ' Don Carlos.'

[Authorities as above.]   G. G.

FITZCLARENCE, LORD ADOLPHUS (1802–1856), rear-admiral, an illegitimate son of William IV, by Mrs. Jordan, entered the navy in 1814, on board the Impregnable, bearing the flag of his father, then Duke of Clarence. Afterwards he served in the Mediterranean, on the North American station, or the coast of Portugal, and was promoted to be lieutenant in April 1821. In May 1823 he was made commander, and captain in December 1824. In 1826 he commanded the Ariadne in the Mediterranean, in 1827 the Challenger, in 1828 the Pallas, and in July 1830 was appointed to the command of the royal yacht, which he retained till promoted to flag rank, 17 Sept. 1853. He was groom of the robes 1830–3, and naval aide-de-camp to Queen Victoria 1846–53. He died 17 May 1856. On his father's accession he was granted, 24 May 1831, the title and precedency of younger son of a marquis, and on 24 Feb. 1832 became G.C.H.

[O'Byrne's Naval Biog. Dict.; Foster's Peerage, s n. 'Munster.']   J. K. L.

FITZCLARENCE, GEORGE AUGUSTUS FREDERICK, first EARL OF MUNSTER (1794–1842), major-general, president of the Royal Asiatic Society of London, the eldest of the numerous children of the Duke of Clarence, afterwards William IV, by Mrs. Jordan (1762 ?–1816) [q. v.], was born in 1794. He was sent to a private school at Sunbury, and afterwards to the Royal Military College at Marlow, and on 5 Feb. 1807, before he was fourteen, was appointed cornet in the 10th hussars. He went with his regiment to Spain next year, and was aide-de-camp to General Slade at Corunna. He returned to the Peninsula the year after as galloper to Sir Charles Stewart, afterwards second marquis of Londonderry, then Lord Wellington's adjutant-general, and made the campaigns of 1809–11. He was wounded and taken prisoner at Fuentes d'Onoro, but effected his escape in the mêlée. He was promoted to a troop in the 10th hussars at home soon after. He accompanied his regiment to Spain in 1813, and made the campaigns of 1813–14 in Spain and the south of France, first as a deputy assistant adjutant-general (GURWOOD, *Wellington Despatches*, vi. 452), and afterwards with his regiment, while leading a squadron of which he was severely wounded at Toulouse. On the return of the regiment to England he was one of the chief witnesses against the commanding officer, Colonel Quentin, who was tried by a general court-martial at Whitehall, in October 1814, on charges of incapacity and misconduct in the field. The charges were partly proved ; but as the officers were believed to have combined against their colonel, the whole of them were removed to other regiments, ' as a warning in support of subordination,' a proceeding which acquired for them the name of the 'elegant extracts.' Fitzclarence and his younger brother Henry, who died in India, were thus transferred to the since disbanded 24th light dragoons, then in India, where George became aide-de-camp to the Marquis of Hastings, governor-general and commander-in-chief, in which capacity he made the campaigns of 1816–17 against the Mahrattas. When peace was arranged with the Maharajah Scindiah the event was considered of sufficient importance to send the despatches in duplicate, and Fitzclarence was entrusted with the duplicates sent by overland route. He started from the western frontier of Bundelkund, the furthest point reached by the grand army, 7 Dec. 1817, and travelling through districts infested by the Pindarrees, witnessed the defeat of the latter by General Doveton at Jubbulpore, reached Bombay, and quitted it in the H.E.I.C. cruiser Mercury for Kosseir 7 Feb. 1818, crossed the desert, explored the pyramids with Salt and Belzoni, descended the Nile, and reached London, *via* Alexandria and Malta, 16 June 1818. He subsequently published an account of his travels, entitled 'Journal of a Route across India and through Egypt to England in 1817–18,' London, 1819, 4to, a work exhibiting much observation, and containing some curious plates of Indian military costumes of the day from sketches by the author.

Fitzclarence became a brevet lieutenant-colonel in 1819, and the same year married a natural daughter of the Earl of Egremont and sister of his old brother officer, Colonel Wyndham, M.P., by whom he had a numerous family. He subsequently obtained a troop in the 14th light dragoons, commanded the 6th carabiniers for a short time as regimental major in Ireland, and served as captain and lieutenant-colonel Coldstream guards from July 1825 to December 1828, afterwards retiring as lieutenant-colonel on half-pay unattached. In June 1831 he was raised to the peerage, under the titles of the Earl of Munster (one of the titles of the Duke of Clarence) and Baron Tewkesbury in the United Kingdom, his younger brothers and sisters at the same time being given the precedence of the younger children of a marquis. For a short time he was adjutant-general at the Horse Guards, a post which he resigned. The Duke of Wellington appointed him lieutenant of the Tower (1831–3) and colonel 1st Tower Hamlets militia, but refers to him (*Wellington Corresp.* vii. 195, 498) as having done a good deal of mischief by meddling with Mrs. Fitzherbert's affairs. He appears to have busied himself a good deal with politics before the passing of the Reform Bill (*ib.* viii. 260, 274, 306, 326), and after the resignation of the whig cabinet in 1832 became very unpopular, on the supposition that he had attempted to influence the king against reform, a charge he emphatically denied (*Parl. Debates*, 3rd ser. xiii. 179–80). At the brevet on the birth of the Prince of Wales he became a major-general, and was soon after appointed to command the Plymouth district. His health had been for some time impaired by suppressed gout, which appears to have unhinged his mind. He committed suicide by shooting himself, at his residence in Upper Belgrave Street, 20 March 1842. He was buried in the parish church at Hampton.

Munster was a privy councillor, governor and captain of Windsor Castle, a fellow of the Royal Society, and of the Royal Geographical, Antiquarian, Astronomical, and Geological societies of London. He became a member of the Royal Asiatic Society on its first formation in 1824, was elected a member of the council in March 1825, in 1826 was one of the committee commissioned to draw up a plan for a committee of correspondence, was many years vice-president, and was chosen president the year before his death. On 4 Oct. 1827 he was nominated by the society member of a committee to prepare a plan for publishing translations of oriental works, and was subsequently appointed deputy-chairman and vice-president of the Oriental Translation Fund, which was largely indebted to his activity in obtaining subscriptions and making the necessary arrangements, and particularly in securing the co-operation of the Propaganda Fide and other learned bodies in Rome (*Oriental Transl. Fund*, 3rd Rep., 1830). He was also president of the Society for the Publication of Oriental Texts. He communicated to the Société Asiatique of Paris a paper on the employment of Mohammedan mercenaries in Christian armies, which appeared in the 'Journal Asiatique,' 56 cahier (February 1827), and was translated in the 'Naval and Military Magazine' (ii. 33, iii. 113–520), a magazine of which four volumes only appeared. With the aid of his secretary and amanuensis, Dr. Aloys Sprenger (the German orientalist, afterwards principal of Delhi College), Munster had collected an immense mass of information from the great continental libraries and other sources for a 'History of the Art of War among Eastern Nations' (see Ann. Rep. p. v, *Journal Royal Asiatic Society*, vol. vii.) With this object he sent out, two years before his death, an Arabic circular, 'Kitab-i-fibrist al Kutub,' &c. (or 'A List of Desiderata in Books in Arabic, Persian, Turkish, and Hindustani on the Art of War among Mohammedans'), compiled, under the order of Munster, by Aloys Sprenger, London, 1840. Munster was likewise the author of 'An Account of the British Campaign in Spain and Portugal in 1809,' London, 1831, which originally appeared in Colburn's 'United Service Magazine.'

Munster is described as having been a most amiable man in private life, and much beloved by his old comrades of the 10th hussars.

[Burke's Peerage, under 'Munster;' Jerdan's Nat. Portraits, vol. iii., with portrait after Atkinson; Proceedings of Court-martial on Colonel Quentin, printed from the shorthand writer's notes (1814); Fitzclarence's Account of a Journey across India, &c. (1819); Wellington Correspondence, vols. vii. and viii.; Greville Correspondence, 1st ser. ii. 10, 43, 168; Royal Asiatic Society, London, Comm. of Correspondence (London, 1829); Annual Report in Journal Royal Asiatic Society, London, vol. vii. (1843); Gent. Mag. new ser. xvii. 358, xviii. 677 (will); a letter from Lord Munster to the Duke of Montrose in 1830 is in Egerton MS. 29300, f. 119.]

H. M. C.

FITZCOUNT, BRIAN (*fl.* 1125–1142), warrior and author, was the son of Count Alan 'Fergan' (*Anglo-Saxon Chron.* 1127) of Brittany (*d.* 1119), but apparently illegitimate. From a most interesting letter addressed to him by Gilbert Foliot (vide infra), we learn that Henry I reared him from his youth up, knighted him, and provided for him in life. A chief means by which he was provided for was his marriage with 'Matilda de Wallingford,' as she was styled, who brought him the lands of Miles Crispin (*Testa de Nevill*, p. 115), whose widow (*ib.*) or daughter she was. He was further made *firmarius* of Wallingford (but not, as asserted, given it for himself), then an important town with a strong fortress. This post he held at least as early as 1127 (*Pipe Roll*, 31 Hen. I, p. 139). He was despatched in that year (1127) with the Earl of Gloucester to escort the Empress Maud to Normandy (*Anglo-Saxon Chronicle*), and was engaged with him shortly afterwards in auditing the national accounts at the treasury at Winchester (*Pipe Roll*, 31 Hen. I, pp. 130–1). He also purchased for himself the office and part of the land of Nigel de Oilli (*ib.* p. 139), and held land by 1130 in at least twelve counties (*ib.* passim). From the evidence of charters it is clear that he was constantly at court for the last ten years of the reign. Though a devoted adherent of the Empress Maud, he witnessed as a 'constable' Stephen's charter of liberties (1136), as did the Earl of Gloucester. On her landing (1139), however, he at once declared for her (*Gesta*, p. 57), met the Earl of Gloucester as he marched from Arundel to Bristol, and concerted with him their plans (WILL. MALM. ii. 725). Stephen promptly besieged Wallingford, but failing to take it, retired, leaving a blockading force (*Gesta*, pp. 57–8). But the blockade was raised, and Brian relieved by a dashing attack from Gloucester (*ib.* p. 59). Thenceforth Wallingford, throughout the war, was a thorn in Stephen's side, and Brian was one of the three chief supporters of the empress, the other two being her brother Robert and Miles of Gloucester [q. v.] These three attended her on her first visit to Winchester (March 1141), and were sureties for her to the legate (WILL. MALM. ii. 743). Charters prove that Brian accompanied her to London (June 1141), and that at Oxford he was with her again (25 July 1141). Thence he marched with her to Winchester (*Gesta*, p. 80), and on her defeat fled with her to Devizes, 'showing that as before they had loved one another, so now neither adversity nor danger could sever them' (*ib.* p. 83).

A Brien de Walingofort
Commanda a mener la dame
E dist, sor la peril de s'alme,
Qu'en nul lieu ne s'aresteiisent. (MEYER)

He is again found with her at Bristol towards the close of the year (*Monasticon*, vi. 137), and at Oxford in the spring of 1142. And when escaping from Oxford in December following, it was to Brian's castle that the empress fled (HEN. HUNT. p. 276).

It was at some time after the landing of the empress (1139) that Gilbert Foliot wrote to Brian that long and instructive letter, from which we learn that this fighting baron had apparently composed an eloquent treatise in defence of the rights of the empress (ed. Giles, ep. lxxix.) Another ecclesiastic, the Bishop of Winchester, endeavoured in vain to shake his allegiance on behalf of the king, his brother. Their correspondence is still extant in the 'Liber Epistolaris' of Richard de Bury (*Hist. MSS. Comm.* 4th Rep. p. 390 *b*). Brian must therefore have received, for these days, an unusually good education, probably at the court of Henry 'Beauclerc.'

His later history is very obscure. On the capture of William Martel at Wilton in 1143 he was sent prisoner to Brian, who placed him in a special dungeon, which he named 'cloere Brien' (MATT. PARIS, ii. 174). In 1146 he was again besieged by Stephen, who was joined by the Earl of Chester (HEN. HUNT. p. 279), but he surprised and captured shortly after a castle of the Bishop of Winchester (*Gesta*, p. 133). In 1152 Stephen besieged him a third time, and he found himself hard pressed; but in 1153 he was brilliantly relieved by Henry (HEN. HUNT. pp. 284, 287). Thus the 'clever Breton,' as Gervase (i. 153) terms him, held his fortress to the end. At this point he disappears from view.

The story that he went on crusade comes from the utterly untrustworthy account of him in the 'Abergavenny Chronicle' (*Mon. Angl.* iv. 615). An authentic charter of 1141–2 (Pipe Roll Soc.) proves that he held Abergavenny, but, like everything else, in right of his wife. She, who died without issue (*Note-book*, iii. 536), founded Oakburn Priory, Wiltshire, circa 1151 (*Mon. Angl.* vi. 1016).

[Anglo-Saxon Chronicle (Rolls Series); Gesta Stephani (ib.); Henry of Huntingdon (ib.); Matt. Paris's Chronica Major (ib.); Gervase of Canterbury (ib.); Pipe Roll of 31 Hen. I (Record Commission); Testa de Nevill (ib.); William of Malmesbury (Engl. Hist. Soc.); Monasticon Anglicanum (new edit.); Round's Charters (Pipe Roll Soc.); Maitland's Bracton's Note-book; Meyer's L'histoire de Guillaume le Maréchal (Romania, vol. xi); Hist. MSS. Comm. 4th Rep.;

Giles's Letters of Foliot (Patres Ecclesiæ Anglicanæ); Athenæum, 22 Oct. 1887; the Rev. A. D. Crake's Brian Fitzcount (1888) is an historical romance, founded on Brian's legendary career.]

J. H. R.

FITZGEFFREY, CHARLES (1575?–1638), poet and divine, son of Alexander Fitzgeffrey, a clergyman who had migrated from Bedfordshire, was born at Fowey in Cornwall about 1575. He was entered in 1590 at Broadgates Hall, Oxford, proceeded B.A. 31 Jan. 1596–7, and M.A. 4 July 1600. In 1596 he published at Oxford a spirited poem entitled 'Sir Francis Drake, his Honorable Lifes Commendation and his Tragical Deathes Lamentation,' 8vo. It was dedicated to Queen Elizabeth, and commendatory verses were prefixed by Richard Rous, Francis Rous, 'D.W.,' and Thomas Mychelbourne. A second edition, with a revised text and additional commendatory verses, was published in the same year. Meres, in 'Palladis Tamia,' 1598, has a complimentary notice of 'yong Charles Fitz-Ieffrey, that high touring Falcon;' and several quotations from the poem occur in 'England's Parnassus,' 1600. In 1601 Fitzgeffrey published an interesting volume of Latin epigrams and epitaphs: 'Caroli Fitzgeofridi Affaniæ; sive Epigrammatum libri tres; Ejusdem Cenotaphia,' 8vo. Epigrams are addressed to Drayton, Daniel, Sir John Harington, William Percy, and Thomas Campion; and there are epitaphs on Spenser, Tarlton, and Nashe. Fitzgeffrey's most intimate friends were the brothers Edward, Laurence, and Thomas Mychelbourne, who are so frequently mentioned in Campion's Latin epigrams. There is an epigram 'To my deare freind Mr. Charles Fitz-Ieffrey' among the poems 'To Worthy Persons' appended to John Davies of Hereford's 'Scourge of Folly,' n. d., 1610–11. It appears from the epigram ('To thee that now dost mind but Holy Writ,' &c.) that Fitzgeffrey was then in orders. By his friend Sir Anthony Rous he was presented to the living of St. Dominic, Eastwellshire. In 1620 he published 'Death's Sermon unto the Living,' 4to, 2nd ed. 1622, a funeral sermon on the wife of Sir Anthony Rous; in 1622 'Elisha, his Lamentation for his Owne,' 4to, a funeral sermon on Sir Anthony; in 1631 'The Curse of Corne-horders: with the Blessing of seasonable Selling. In three sermons,' 4to, dedicated to Sir Reginald Mohune, reprinted in 1648 under the title 'God's Blessing upon the Providers of Corne,' &c.; in 1634 a devotional poem, 'The Blessed Birth-Day celebrated in some Pious Meditations on the Angels Anthem,' 4to, reprinted in 1636 and 1651; and in 1637, 'Compassion towards Captives, chiefly

towards our Brethren and Country-men who are in miserable bondage in Barbariē: urged and pressed in three sermons . . . preached in Plymouth in October 1636,' 4to, with a dedication to John Cause, mayor of Plymouth. Fitzgeffrey died 24 Feb. 1637–8, and was buried under the communion-table of his church. Robert Chamberlain has some verses to his memory in 'Nocturnall Lucubrations,' 1638.

Fitzgeffrey prefixed commendatory verses to Storer's 'Life and Death of Thomas, Earl of Cromwell,' 1599 (two copies of Latin verse and two English sonnets), Davies of Hereford's 'Microcosmus,' 1603, Sylvester's 'Bartas, his Devine Weekes and Workes,' 1605, and William Vaughan's 'Golden Grove,' 1608. He was among the contributors to 'Oxoniensis Academiæ funebre officium in Memoriam Elizabethæ,' 1603, 4to, and 'Academiæ Oxoniensis Pietas erga Jacobum,' 1603, 4to. There is an epigram to him in John Dunbar's 'Epigrammaton Centuriæ Sex,' 1616; Campion addressed two epigrams to him, and Robert Hayman in 'Quodlibets,' 1620, has an epigram to him, from which it appears that he was blind of one eye. A letter of Fitzgeffrey, dated from Fowey, March 1633, giving an account of a thunderstorm, is preserved at Kimbolton Castle. 'Sir Francis Drake' and 'The Blessed Birth-Day' have been reprinted in Dr. Grosart's 'Occasional Issues.'

[Wood's Athenæ, ed. Bliss, ii. 607–9; Dr. Grosart's Memorial Introduction to Fitzgeffrey's Poems; Boase and Courtney's Bibliotheca Cornubiensis; Hunter's Chorus Vatum.] A. H. B.

FITZGEFFREY, HENRY (*fl.* 1617), writer of satires and epigrams, is commonly assumed to have been a son of Charles Fitzgeffrey [q. v.], but no evidence in support of the conjecture has been adduced. A Henry Fitz-Jeffrey, who is on the list of Westminster scholars elected to Cambridge in 1611 (WELCH, *Alumni Westmonast.* p. 81), may, or may not, be the satirist. In 1617 appeared 'Certain Elegies, done by Sundrie excellent Wits. With Satyres and Epigrames,' 8vo; 2nd edition, 1618; 3rd edition, 1620; 4th edition, undated. The elegies are by F[rancis] B[eaumont], N[athaniel?] H[ooke?], and M[ichael] D[rayton]. They are followed by 'The Author in Praise of his own Booke,' four lines; and 'Of his deare Friend the Author H. F.,' eight lines, signed 'Nath. Gvrlyn,' to which is appended 'The Author's Answer.' In the first satire there are some curious notices of popular fugitive tracts. After the second satire is a copy of commendatory verses by J. Stephens. Then follows 'The Second Booke: of Satyricall

Epigram's,' with a dedication ' To his True Friend Tho: Fletcher of Lincoln's Inn, Gent.;' and at the end of the epigrams is another copy of commendatory verses by Stephens. 'The Third Booke of Humours: Intituled Notes from Black-Fryers,' opens with an epigram 'To his Lou: Chamber-Fellow and nearest Friend Nat. Gvrlin of Lincolnes-Inn, Gent.' The notes are followed by some more verses of Stephens, the epilogue ' The Author for Himselfe,' and finally a verse ' Post-script to his Book-binder.' Twelve copies of the little volume were reprinted, from the edition of 1620, for E. V. Utterson at the Beldornie Press in 1843.

[Corser's Collectanea Anglo-Poetica, pt. vi. pp. 356–60; Wood's Athenæ Oxon. ed. Bliss, ii. 608.] A. H. B.

FITZGERALD, DAVID (*d.*1176), bishop of St. David's. [See DAVID the Second.]

FITZGERALD, LORD EDWARD (1763–1798), Irish rebel, was one of the seventeen children of James Fitzgerald, viscount and first duke of Leinster [q. v.], by Emilia Mary, daughter of Charles, duke of Richmond. His father died in 1773, and his mother married William Ogilvie. The Duke of Richmond lent his house at Aubigny in France to the family, who resided there till 1779 ; Ogilvie undertook Edward's education, which had been commenced by a tutor named Lynch. The boy had a marked military bent, and on returning to England joined the Sussex militia, of which his uncle, the Duke of Richmond, was colonel. He next entered the 96th infantry as lieutenant, served with it in Ireland, exchanged into the 19th in order to get foreign service, and in 1781 went out to Charleston. His skill in covering a retreat got him the post of aide-de-camp to Lord Rawdon, on whose retirement he rejoined his regiment. At the engagement of Eutaw Springs, August 1781, he was wounded in the thigh, was left senseless on the field, and might have succumbed had not a negro, Tony, carried him to his hut and nursed him. Tony was thenceforth, to the end of Fitzgerald's life, his devoted servant or slave. After his recovery Fitzgerald was on O'Hara's staff at St. Lucia, but soon returned to Ireland, where his eldest brother had him elected M.P. for Athy. He voted in the Dublin parliament in the small minority with Grattan and Curran. After a course of professional study at Woolwich a disappointment in love drove him to New Brunswick to join his regiment, the 54th, of which he was now major. Cobbett was the sergeant-major, and was grateful to Fitzgerald for procuring him his discharge,

describing him to Pitt in 1800 as the only really honest officer he had ever known. Infected by the fashionable Rousseau admiration for savage life, Fitzgerald made his way by compass through the woods from Frederickton to Quebec, was formally admitted at Detroit into the Bear tribe, and went down the Mississippi to New Orleans, but was refused the expected permission to visit the Mexican mines. On returning home he found himself M.P. for Kildare, became intimate with the whig leaders in London, joined in April 1792 their Society of the Friends of the People, shared their enthusiasm for the French revolution, and in October 1792 visited Paris. He stayed at the same hotel as Paine, took his meals with him, and at a British dinner to celebrate French victories joined in Sir Robert Smith's toast to the abolition of all hereditary titles. Cashiered from the army for attendance at this revolutionary banquet, he was not, however, so immersed in politics as to neglect the theatres. Hence his brief courtship and his marriage, 27 Dec. 1792 [see FITZGERALD, PAMELA]. He took his bride over to Ireland, and six days after his arrival at Dublin caused a scene in parliament by describing the lord-lieutenant and the majority as ' the worst subjects the king has.' He was ordered into custody, but refused to make any serious apology. When not attending parliament he enjoyed the society of his wife and child and of his flowers at Kildare. His dismissal from the army and the political reaction consequent on the atrocities in France converted the light-hearted young nobleman into a stern conspirator. Early in 1796 he joined the United Irishmen, who now avowedly aimed at an independent Irish republic, and in May he went with Arthur O'Connor to Bâle to confer with Hoche on a French invasion ; but the Directory, apprehensive of accusations of Orleanism, on account of Pamela's supposed kinship with the Orleans family, declined to negotiate with Fitzgerald, who rejoined his wife at Hamburg, leaving O'Connor to treat with Hoche. Returning to Ireland he visited Belfast with O'Connor, then a candidate for Antrim, but in July 1797 he declined to solicit re-election, telling the Kildare voters that under martial law free elections were impossible, but that he hoped hereafter to represent them in a free parliament. In the following autumn the United Irishmen became a military organisation, 280,000 men, according to a list given by Fitzgerald to Thomas Reynolds, being prepared with arms, and a military committee, headed by Fitzgerald, was deputed to prepare a scheme of co-operation with the French, or of a rising if their arrival could not be awaited. Fitzgerald was himself colonel of the so-called Kildare regiment, but induced Reynolds to take his place. The latter alleges that three months after his appointment he learned the intention of the conspirators to begin the rising by murdering eighty leading noblemen and dignitaries, and that to save their lives he gave the authorities information which led to the arrest, on 12 March 1798, at Oliver Bond's house, of the Leinster provincial committee. He does not state whether Fitzgerald was cognisant of the intended murders, but anxious for his escape he had on the 11th given him a vague warning and urged flight, whereupon Fitzgerald expressed a desire to go to France that he might induce Talleyrand to hasten the invasion. Owing perhaps to Reynolds's warning, Fitzgerald was not at Bond's meeting; but being told there was no warrant against himself was about to enter his own house, then being searched by the police, when Tony, on the look-out, gave him timely notice. So far from distrusting Reynolds, Fitzgerald, while in concealment, sent for him on the 14th and 15th, the first time to propose taking refuge in Kilkee Castle, the property of the Duke of Leinster, then occupied by Reynolds. Reynolds objected to the plan as unsafe, and next day took him fifty guineas and a case of pocket pistols. Reynolds clearly gave no information of these interviews, and Lord-chancellor Clare, if not other members of the Irish government, was also desirous of an escape. Fitzgerald, however, remained in or near Dublin, paid two secret visits, once in female attire, to his wife, who had prudently removed from Leinster House, walked along the canal at night, and actively continued preparations for a rising fixed for 23 May. The authorities were therefore obliged in self-defence to take more serious steps for his apprehension, and on 11 May they offered a reward of 1,000*l.* Madden gives reasons for thinking that the F. H. or J. H. (the first initial was indistinctly written in the original document from which he copied the entry) to whom on 20 June the sum was paid, was John Hughes, a Belfast bookseller, one of Fitzgerald's so-called body-guard. However this may be, the authorities knew that on the 19th he would be at Murphy's, a feather dealer. Fitzgerald, having dined, was lying with his coat off on a bed upstairs, and Murphy was asking him to come down to tea, when Major Swan and Ryan mounted the stairs and entered the room. After a desperate struggle, in which Ryan was mortally wounded, Fitzgerald was captured. Shot in the right arm by Major Sirr, who had also entered the room, his wound was pronounced free from danger, whereupon he said, 'I am sorry for it.' He

was taken first to the castle and then to Newgate. Inflammation set in; his brother Henry and his aunt (Lady Louisa Conolly) were allowed to see him in his last moments, and on 4 June he expired. His remains were interred in St. Werburgh Church, Dublin, and Sirr, forty-three years later, was buried a few paces off in the churchyard. A bill of attainder was passed against Fitzgerald, but the government allowed his Kilrush estate, worth about 700*l.* a year, to be bought by Ogilvie at the price of the mortgage, 10,400*l.*, and in 1819 the attainder was repealed. Fitzgerald was of small stature (Reynolds says 5 feet 5 inches, Murphy 5 feet 7 inches), and Moore, who once saw him in 1797, speaks of his peculiar dress, elastic gait, healthy complexion, and the soft expression given to his eyes by long dark eyelashes. He left three children: Edward Fox (1794–1863), an officer in the army; Pamela, wife of General Sir Guy Campbell; and Lucy Louisa, wife of Captain G. F. Lyon, R.N.

[Moore's Life of Lord E. Fitzgerald; Life of Thomas Reynolds; Madden's United Irishmen; Teeling's Personal Narrative of the Irish Rebellion.]   J. G. A.

FITZGERALD, EDWARD (1770?–1807), Irish insurgent leader, born at Newpark, co. Wexford, about 1770, was a country gentleman of considerable means. At the breaking out of the insurrection in 1798 he was confined in Wexford gaol on suspicion, but on being released by the populace, commanded in some of the engagements that took place in different parts of the county during the occupation of the town, exhibiting, it is said, far better generalship than the commander-in-chief, Bagenal Beauchamp Harvey [q. v.] Madden commends his humanity to the prisoners that fell into his hands at Gorey. At the battle of Arklow he commanded the Shemalier gunsmen. He afterwards joined in the expedition against Hacketstown, and surrendered upon terms to General Wilford in the middle of July. With Garrett, Byrne, and others he was detained in custody in Dublin until the ensuing year, when he was permitted to reside in England. He was, however, re-arrested on 25 March 1800, imprisoned for a while, and then allowed to retire to Hamburg, where he died in 1807. In person Fitzgerald is described as a 'handsome, finely formed man;' he was besides a speaker of great eloquence.

[Madden's United Irishmen; Webb's Compendium of Irish Biog. pp. 194–5.]   G. G.

FITZGERALD, EDWARD (1809–1883), poet and translator, born at Bredfield House, near Woodbridge, Suffolk, on 31 March

1809, was the third son of John Purcell, who, on the death of his wife's father in 1818, took the name and arms of Fitzgerald. In 1821 Fitzgerald was sent to King Edward the Sixth's Grammar School at Bury St. Edmunds, under the charge of Dr. Malkin. In 1826 he entered at Trinity College, Cambridge, and took his degree in 1830. He made lifelong friendships with his schoolfellows, James Spedding and W. B. Donne [q. v.], and with his college contemporaries, W. M. Thackeray, W. H. Thompson, afterwards master of Trinity, and John Allen, afterwards archdeacon of Salop. The three brothers Tennyson were also at Cambridge at the same time, but he did not know them till a later period. With Frederic, the eldest, he kept up a correspondence for several years, and the laureate dedicated to him his poem 'Tiresias,' but, as Fitzgerald died just before it was published, their long friendship is further commemorated in the touching epilogue. Carlyle was a friend of a later date, but firm and true to the last. Fitzgerald spent the greater part of his life in Suffolk. His youth was passed at Bredfield, where he was born, and where he lived, with the exception of a short sojourn in France, till about 1825. His home was then for some time at Wherstead Lodge, near Ipswich, till 1835, when the family removed to Boulge Hall in the adjoining parish to Bredfield, and for several years Fitzgerald occupied a small cottage close by the park gates. Here his chief friends were George Crabbe, the son of the poet and vicar of Bredfield, and Bernard Barton, the quaker poet of Woodbridge, whose daughter he afterwards married. He had no liking for the conventional usages of society, and was therefore somewhat of a recluse. But he was by no means unsocial, and to those whom he admitted to his intimacy he was the most delightful of companions. His habits were extremely simple; his charity large and generous, but always discriminating; his nature tender and affectionate. He lived at Boulge till about the end of 1853, and then settled for a time at Farlingay Hall, an old farmhouse just outside Woodbridge, where Carlyle visited him in 1855. About the end of 1860 he went to live in Woodbridge itself, taking lodgings on the Market Hill, and there he remained till, at the beginning of 1874, he removed to his own house, Little Grange, which he had enlarged some years before, and where he continued till his death. His chief outdoor amusement was boating, and the great part of each summer was spent in his yacht, in which he cruised about the neighbouring coast. But he gradually withdrew from the sea, and after the death of his old boatman in 1877, the river had no longer any pleasure for him, and he was driven to console himself with his garden. On 14 June 1883 he died suddenly while on a visit at Merton Rectory, Norfolk, and was buried at Boulge.

Beyond occasional contributions to periodical literature Fitzgerald does not appear to have published anything till he wrote a short memoir of Bernard Barton, prefixed to a collection of his letters and poems, which was made after the poet's death in 1849. In 1851 was issued 'Euphranor, a Dialogue on Youth,' which contains some beautiful English prose. In 1852 appeared 'Polonius: a Collection of Wise Saws and Modern Instances,' with a preface on proverbs and aphorisms. Both these were anonymous. In 1853 he brought out the only book to which he ever attached his name, 'Six Dramas of Calderon, freely translated by Edward Fitz-Gerald,' but the reception it met with at the hands of reviewers, who did not take the trouble to understand his object, did not encourage him to repeat the experiment. He consequently never issued, except to his personal friends, the translations or adaptations of 'La Vida es Sueño' and 'El Mágico Prodigioso.' These translations never professed to be close renderings of their originals. They were rather intended to produce, in one who could not read the language from which they were rendered, something of the same effect as is conveyed by the original to those familiar with it. On this principle he translated the 'Agamemnon' of Æschylus, which was first issued privately without date, and was afterwards published anonymously in 1876. A year or two before his death he completed on the same lines a translation of the 'Œdipus Tyrannus' and the 'Œdipus Coloneus' of Sophocles. But the work on which his fame will mainly rest is his marvellous rendering of the 'Quatrains' of Omar Khayyám, the astronomer poet of Persia, which he has made to live in a way that no translation ever lived before. In his hands the 'Quatrains' became a new poem, and their popularity is attested by the four editions which appeared in his lifetime. But when they were first published in 1859 they fell upon an unregarding public, as heedless of their merits as the editor of a magazine in whose hands they had been for two years previously. His Persian studies, which were begun at the suggestion of his friend, Professor Cowell, first led him in 1856 to translate the 'Salámán and Absál' of Jámí. After this he was attracted to Attar's 'Mantik-ut-tair,' and by 1859 he had made a kind of abridged translation of it, which he called the 'Bird Parliament;' but it remained in manuscript till his death.

Fitzgerald was a great admirer of Crabbe's poetry, and, in order to rescue it from the disregard into which it had fallen, he published in 1882, with an introduction, 'Readings in Crabbe,' a condensed version of the 'Tales of the Hall.'

His collected writings were edited, with selections from his correspondence, in 1889 (3 vols.) by the writer of this article. Fitzgerald's 'Letters to Fanny Kemble, 1871–83,' followed in 1895, and 'More Letters of Fitzgerald' in 1901. A complete edition of his 'Letters and Literary Remains,' edited by the present writer, appeared in 1902 (7 vols.)

[Fitzgerald's Collected Works, ed. W. Aldis Wright, LL.D.; F. H. Groome, Two Suffolk Friends, 1895; W. F. Prideaux, Notes for a Bibliography of Fitzgerald, 1901; Thomas Wright's Life, 1904; A. C. Benson's monograph in Men of Letters Series, 1905.] W. A. W.

FITZGERALD, LADY ELIZABETH, called the FAIR GERALDINE (1528?–1589), was youngest daughter of Gerald Fitzgerald, ninth earl of Kildare [q. v.], by his second wife, Lady Elizabeth, fourth daughter of Thomas Grey, marquis of Dorset. Born apparently about 1528 at her father's castle at Maynooth, she was brought to England by her mother in 1533, when her father was involved in his son's treasonable practices. Her father died in 1534, and she lived with her mother at Beaumanoir, Leicestershire, the house of her uncle, Lord Leonard Grey. In 1538 she entered the household of the Princess Mary at Hunsdon, and when that establishment was broken up in 1540, she transferred her services to Queen Catherine Howard at Hampton Court. At Hunsdon Henry Howard, earl of Surrey [q. v.], first saw her. He renewed his acquaintance with her at Hampton, and began about 1540 the series of songs and sonnets, first printed in Tottel's 'Miscellany' (1557), in which he extolled her beauty and declared his love for her. One sonnet, in which he refers to the Florentine origin ascribed to the Geraldine family and to the Lady Elizabeth's education, is entitled 'Description and Praise of his love Geraldine.' The lady is only mentioned by name in this one poem. Surrey at the time was husband of Lady Frances, daughter of John Vere, fifteenth earl of Oxford, whom he married in 1534; a first child was born in 1536. Surrey's relationship with Lady Elizabeth would seem to have imitated Petrarch's Platonic association with Laura. According to Nashe's romance, called 'The Unfortunate Traveller, or the Life of Jack Wilton' (1594), Surrey while in Venice consulted Cornelius Agrippa

as to the welfare of his ladylove, and saw her image in a magic mirror. When he arrived in Florence he challenged to combat all who disputed his mistress's loveliness. Drayton utilised these stories in his beautiful poetical epistle of 'The Lady Geraldine to the Earl of Surrey,' first published in his 'Heroicall Epistle,' 1597. Sir Walter Scott has also introduced the first episode into his 'Lay of the Last Minstrel' (canto vi. stanzas xvi–xx.) Although these reports were widely disseminated in the seventeenth century, there seems no foundation for them. They are to all appearance the outcome of Nashe's imagination.

In 1543 Lady Elizabeth, who was then no more than fifteen, married Sir Anthony Browne (d. 1548) [q. v.], a widower aged sixty. The poverty-stricken condition of her family perhaps explains this union, which Surrey has been assumed to deplore in his later verse. The wedding was attended by Henry VIII and his daughter Mary, and a sermon was preached by Ridley. Surrey was executed in 1547, and Lady Elizabeth's husband died in 1548. About 1552 she became the third wife of Edward Fiennes de Clinton, earl of Lincoln (1512–1585) [q. v.] She would seem to have been greatly in her second husband's confidence, and the facsimile of a letter (dated 14 Sept. 1558), written partly by her, acting as her husband's secretary, and partly by himself, is printed by the Rev. James Graves in the 'Journal of the Archæological and Historical Association of Ireland' (1873). Clinton died in 1585, and made his wife executrix of his will, but she appears to have been on bad terms with the children of her husband's second marriage. She died in March 1589, without issue, and was buried beside her second husband in St. George's Chapel, Windsor, where she had already erected an elaborate monument to his memory. Her sister Margaret was chief mourner, and sixty-one old women, numbering the years of her life, followed her to the grave. A fine portrait by C. Ketel, showing a lady with auburn hair, of very attractive appearance, is at Woburn Abbey. A copy belonging to the Duke of Leinster is at Carton, Maynooth. An engraving by Scriven was published in 1809, and Mr. Graves gives a photograph from the original painting in the journal noticed above.

[Rev. James Graves in Archæological and Historical Association of Ireland, 1873, pp. 560 et seq. publ. Kilkenny Archæolog. Soc.; Tottel's Miscellany, 1557, reprinted by Arber; Poems of Surrey and Wyatt, ed. Dr. Nott, 1815; Nashe's works, ed. Grosart, vol. v.; Duke of Leinster's Earls of Kildare, 1858, pp. 126–9.] S. L.

FITZGERALD, GEORGE, sixteenth EARL OF KILDARE (1611–1660), was son of Thomas, second son of William Fitzgerald, thirteenth earl of Kildare, by Frances, daughter of Thomas Randolph, postmaster-general in England under Queen Elizabeth. George Fitzgerald was in his ninth year when, in 1620, he inherited the Kildare peerage, on the death of Gerald, the fifteenth earl, at the age of eight years and ten months. Earl George was given in wardship by the king to the Duke of Lennox. On the decease of the latter his widow transferred the wardship of the minor and his estates to Richard Boyle, earl of Cork, for 6,600*l.* Kildare studied for a time at Christ Church, Oxford, and in his eighteenth year married Joan, fourth daughter of Lord Cork. He appears to have been much under the influence of that astute adventurer; but occasional differences occurred between them, for the settlement of which the intervention of the lord deputy, Wentworth, was obtained. A portrait of Kildare, painted in 1632, in which he is represented as of diminutive stature, is extant at Carton, the residence of the Duke of Leinster. There is also preserved at Carton a transcript, made in 1633 for Kildare, of an ancient volume known as the 'Red Book of the Earls of Kildare.' Kildare sat for the first time in the House of Peers, Ireland, in 1634, and was appointed colonel of a foot regiment in the English army in Ireland. With pecuniary advances from Lord Cork Kildare rebuilt the decayed castle of his ancestors at Maynooth in the county of Kildare. James Shirley, the dramatist, during his visit to Dublin in 1637–8, was befriended by Kildare, and dedicated to him his tragi-comedy entitled 'The Royal Master,' acted at the castle and the theatre, Dublin, in 1638. Kildare was about that time committed to prison for having disobeyed an order made by the lord deputy for the delivery of documents connected with a suit at law with Lord Digby. In 1641 Kildare was appointed governor of the county of Kildare, and subsequently took part with the leaders of the protestant party in Ireland in opposing the movements of the Irish catholics to obtain from Charles I redress of their grievances. Correspondence between Kildare and the viceroy, Ormonde, in 1644 appears in the third and fourth volumes of the 'History of the Irish Confederation and War.' In January 1645–6 Kildare and the Marquis of Clanricarde became sureties to the extent of 10,000*l.* each for the Earl of Glamorgan, on the occasion of his liberation from prison at Dublin. Kildare acted as governor of Dublin under the parliamentarian colonel, Michael Jones, in 1647,

and in 1649 he received a pension of 46*s.* weekly from the government. In a subsequent petition to the chief justice of Munster Kildare stated that during eleven years he and his family had been driven to great extremities and endured much hardship in England and Ireland through his constant adherence and faithful affection to the parliament of England; that he was then, for debt, under restraint in London, and had despatched his wife and some of his servants to Ireland in hopes to raise a considerable sum out of his estate for his enlargement and subsistence. By his wife, who died in 1656, he had three sons and six daughters. Kildare died early in 1660. He was buried at Kildare. His second son, Wentworth Fitzgerald, succeeded him as seventeenth earl of Kildare.

[Archives of the Duke of Leinster; Ormonde Archives (Kilkenny Castle); Diaries of the Earl of Cork; Carte Papers (Bodleian Library), vol. xvi.; History of the Irish Confederation and War, 1643–6 (Dublin, 1885–9); Works of James Shirley, 1833; History of the City of Dublin, 1854; Hist. MSS. Comm. 9th Rep. 1884; The Earls of Kildare, by the Marquis of Kildare, 1858–62.] J. T. G.

FITZGERALD, GEORGE ROBERT (1748 ?–1786), known as 'Fighting Fitzgerald,' was a descendant of the Desmond branch of the great Geraldine family, anciently settled in Waterford, but removed in the time of Cromwell to county Mayo. He was the eldest son of George Fitzgerald, who was for some time an officer in the Austrian service, by Lady Mary Hervey, formerly maid of honour to the Princess Amelia, and sister to the Earl of Bristol, bishop of Derry. He was educated at Eton, which he left to join the army, his first quarters being at Galway. He soon became noted for his gallantry, his recklessness, and his duels. Having at Dublin made the acquaintance of the sister of the Right Hon. Thomas Conolly of Castletown, cousin of the Duke of Leinster, he married her against the wishes of her parents, receiving with her a fortune of 10,000*l.* Soon afterwards he went to the continent, where his wife died, leaving an only daughter. In 1773 he gained celebrity in connection with a fracas at Vauxhall relating to an actress, Mrs. Hartley. A clergyman, the Rev. Henry Bate [see DUDLEY, SIR HENRY BATE], who protected the actress against the familiarities of Fitzgerald and his friends, had, however, much the best of the quarrel (see *The Vauxhall Dispute, or the Macaronies Defeated: being a compilation of all the Letters, Squibs, &c., on both sides of the Dispute,* 1773). Fitzgerald married a second time the only daughter and heiress of Mr. Vaughan of Carrowmore, Mayo. He now began to take an active interest in politics. He was a strong supporter of the legislative independence of Ireland, and assisted in the formation of the volunteer companies. On his estate in county Mayo he boasted with truth that he had introduced numerous improvements, much attention being devoted by him to the growth of wheat. His serious occupations were relieved by wild adventures, including a habit introduced by him of hunting at night. For a sum of 8,000l. per annum paid down his father granted him a rent-charge of 1,000l. per annum, and agreed to settle his whole estates on him and his issue male. As, however, it now seemed unlikely that young Fitzgerald would ever have any issue male, he became jealous of his younger brother, whose issue would ultimately inherit the property. The father having fallen in arrears in the payment of the rent-charge to the amount of 12,000l., young Fitzgerald, by an order of the court of exchequer, got possession of the property, his father being allowed a comparatively small annuity. This annuity the son neglected to pay, and carried off his younger brother to his house at Turlough. Thereupon his brother brought an action against him for forcible abduction, and being found guilty he was sentenced to three years' imprisonment and a fine of 1,000l. The sentence proved for a time a dead-letter. He retreated to Sligo with his father, and, being closely followed, embarked with him in a boat for a small island in Sligo Bay. Here his father proposed to him that if he would pay him 3,000l. to clear his debts, and give him a small yearly stipend, he would convey to him the reversion in the estate and exonerate him of all blame in the forcible abduction. To this he agreed, and, proceeding by unfrequented roads, the two together reached Dublin. No sooner had they reached it than the father set him at defiance. A reward of 3,000l. having previously been offered for his capture, it was not long before he was arrested. He endeavoured to move for a new trial, but without effect, and he was sent to prison, where he remained till a serious illness induced the authorities to liberate him. Soon afterwards one Patrick Randal M'Donnell, who had been in league against him, was shot at and wounded in the leg. One Murphy, a retainer of Fitzgerald, was arrested on suspicion, but would reveal nothing. Fitzgerald now procured a warrant for the arrest of M'Donnell and others for false imprisonment of Murphy, but it could not be immediately executed on account of M'Donnell's illness

from the wound in his leg. Knowing, however, that M'Donnell would on a certain day proceed from Castlebar to Chancery Hall, they beset him on his return and took him prisoner. In the scuffle one of the escort was shot. The volunteers coming up, the tables were, however, turned against Fitzgerald, who was captured and lodged in gaol. While there he was in some inexplicable way attacked by a mob of men, who left him in a very weak condition on the supposition that he was dead; but he survived to stand his trial for murder, and being found guilty was executed at Castlebar in the evening of Monday, 12 June 1786. He was interred at midnight in the family tomb in a chapel which, now in ruins, adjoins a round tower.

[Memoirs of G. R. Fitzgerald, 1786; Life, in Dublin University Magazine, xvi. 1–21, 179–197, 304–24, reprinted in 1852; Appeal to the Jockey Club, &c., 1775; Case of G. R. Fitzgerald 1786; Gent. Mag. vol. lvi. pt. i. 346–7, 434, 518–20; Sir Jonah Barrington's Memoirs.]

T. F. H.

FITZGERALD, GERALD, Lord of OFFALY (d. 1204), was the son of Maurice Fitzgerald (d. 1176) [q. v.], the invader of Ireland. Though the Geraldines had already become a well-known family, Gerald is more often called Fitzmaurice than Fitzgerald. Accompanying his father from Wales to Ireland, he and his brother Alexander showed great valour in the battle against Roderick O'Conor, outside the walls of Dublin in 1171 (*Exp. Hib.* in GIRALDUS, *Opera*, v. 268, Rolls Ser.) After his father's death, William Fitzaldhelm [q. v.] deprived him and his brothers of their stronghold of Wicklow, though after a time compelled to give them Ferns in exchange (*ib.* p. 337). He had already received from Strongbow, Naas and other districts in Kildare, and had erected Maynooth Castle (GILBERT, *Viceroys of Ireland*, p. 93). In 1199, though receiving King John's letters of protection, he was ordered to do right to Maurice Fitzphilip for the lands of 'Gessil and Lega' (? Leix), whereof he had already deforced Maurice (*Chart.* 1 John, m. 6, p. i.; *Oblate* 1 John, m. 12; *Cal. Doc. Ireland*, Nos. 101, 102). But on his death, Gerald was still in possession of those estates (*Cal. Doc. Ireland*, No. 195). He is often described as 'Baron Offaly,' the middle cantred of which had been among his father's possessions. He died before 15 Jan. 1204 (*ib.* No. 195), though generally said to have died in 1205 (*Book of Howth*, p. 118, which describes him erroneously as justice of Ireland). He married Catherine, daughter of Hamon of Valognes, justiciar of Ireland between 1197 and 1199 (GILBERT, *Viceroys*, pp. 57, 93). He left by her two sons (LODGE, *Peerage of Ireland*, i. 59), one of whom, his successor, was Maurice Fitzgerald, lord of Offaly (1194?–1257) [q. v.] Gerald is described by his cousin, Giraldus Cambrensis, as small in stature, but distinguished for prudence and honesty (*Exp. Hib.* p. 354). He was the ancestor of the earls of Kildare.

[Authorities referred to in text.]   T. F. T.

FITZGERALD, GERALD, fourth EARL OF DESMOND (*d.* 1398), justiciar of Ireland, was the son of Maurice Fitzthomas, the first earl of Desmond [q. v.], by his second wife, Evelina or Eleanor Fitzmaurice, and was generally styled Gerald Fitzmaurice. He was in 1356 taken prisoner by the Irish, but released on a truce being made (*Cal. Rot. Pat. et Claus. Hib.* p. 59). His father's death in the same year was soon followed by that of his elder brother, Maurice, the second earl. This produced great disturbances in Munster. To appease them Edward III granted to Gerald the lands of his brother Maurice, together with the custody of his idiot brother, Nicholas, who seems to have been regarded as incompetent to succeed (*ib.* p. 72). This was on 3 July 1359. On 20 July the king renewed the grant on condition of Gerald's marrying Eleanor, the daughter of James Butler, earl of Ormonde, then justiciar of Ireland (*Fœdera*, iii. 433). The peerage writers describe Gerald as the fourth earl, on the assumption that either Nicholas or another brother, John, previously bore the title (LODGE, *Peerage of Ireland*, i. 65; cf. 'Pedigree of the Desmonds,' in GRAVES, *Unpublished Geraldine Documents*, pt. ii.) But the authorities only know of Maurice and his father as his predecessors in the title. The 'Book of Howth' (p. 118) describes him rightly as third earl.

In 1367 Desmond succeeded Lionel, duke of Clarence, as justiciar of Ireland (GRACE, *Annals*, p. 154). The appointment was a confession of weakness of the home government, for Gerald carried on even further than his father that policy of amalgamation with the native Irish which it had been Lionel's main object to prevent. The period of his rule was almost exceptionally turbulent. A great meeting was held at Kilkenny to induce the Birminghams to live in peace with the government, and the king's officials petitioned for the removal of the exchequer from Carlow, where it was exposed to the Irish attacks. In 1368 the Irish parliament petitioned that all who held land in Ireland should be compelled to defend their estates in person or by sufficient deputies. In 1369 Desmond was superseded by Sir William de Windsor. In the same year Desmond was

defeated near Nenagh and taken prisoner by Brien O'Brien, king of Thomond, whose victorious army now plundered and destroyed Limerick (*Annals of Loch Cé*, ii. 43; *Annals of the Four Masters*, iii. 649). It was one of the greatest victories ever won by the Irish of Munster. In 1370 Windsor led an expedition to effect Desmond's release, but in 1372 O'Brien was again in arms and threatening Limerick (*Cal. Rot. Pat. et Claus. Hib.* p. 84 *b*).

In 1377 Desmond was at war with Richard de Burgh (*ib.* p. 103 *b*). In 1381 he was appointed to 'repress the malice of the rebels' in Munster, where no justiciar ventured to show his face after the death of the Earl of March (*ib.* pp. 114, 115). In 1386 he again acted as deputy of the justiciar in Munster (*ib.* p. 127 *b*). In 1393 he obtained from the council an order compelling the town of Cork to pay him a rent already granted 'considering the great expenses which he continually sustains in the king's wars in Munster' (*King's Council in Ireland*, 16 *Richard II*, p. 126, Rolls Ser.) During the latter part of his life he was constantly at war with his hereditary foes, the Butlers (*ib.* p. 261; cf. *Cal. Rot. Pat. et Claus. Hib.* pp. 121, 122 *b*).

Desmond is generally described in the records as the chief upholder of the king's cause in Munster. Yet his policy was to set the law at defiance and adopt Irish customs and sympathies. He obtained in 1388 a royal license to allow his son James to be fostered among his old enemies, the O'Briens, notwithstanding the statute of Kilkenny (*Cal. Rot. Pat. et Claus. Hib.* p. 139). The Irish annalists are enthusiastic in his praises. The 'Four Masters' describe him as 'a cheerful and courteous man, who excelled all the English and many of the Irish in the knowledge of the Irish language, poetry, and history' (iv. 761, cf. note on p. 760). He was a man of some culture and refinement. He was called 'Gerald the poet,' and some short French verses attributed to him still survive in the 'Book of Ross or Waterford,' in Harl. MS. 913, f. 15 *b*, with the title 'Proverbia Comitis Desmond.' 'The point of these is not very evident beyond an ingenious play on words' (CROKER, *Popular Songs of Ireland*, p. 287). He is also described as a mathematician and magician. He died in 1398, but the Munster peasantry long believed that he had only disappeared beneath the waters of Lough Air, near Limerick, and that every seven years he revisited its castle.

By his wife, Eleanor Butler, who died in 1392, and is described as a 'charitable and bountiful woman' (*Annals of Loch Cé*, ii. 75), Desmond left several children. The eldest son, John, the fifth earl, according to the ordinary reckoning, was drowned in the river Suir, within a few months of his father's death (*Four Masters*, iv. 761). The next son, Maurice, died without male issue in 1410. The third son, James, the O'Brien's foster-son, usurped the earldom from his nephew Thomas, the sixth earl, son of John. James was the father of Thomas Fitzgerald, eighth earl of Desmond [q. v.] Two daughters of Gerald and Eleanor are also mentioned ('Pedigree of the Desmonds,' in GRAVES, *Unpublished Geraldine Documents*, pt. ii.)

[Chartularies, &c., of St. Mary's Abbey, Dublin; Annals of Loch Cé, both in Rolls Series; Calendar of the Patent and Close Rolls of Ireland, Record Comm.; Annals of the Four Masters; Clyn's Annals and Grace's Annals (Irish Archæological Soc.); Lodge's Peerage of Ireland, vol. i. (Archdall); Graves's Unpublished Geraldine Documents, first printed in Journal of Kilkenny Archæological Society, and then separately; Gilbert's Viceroys of Ireland; and the other authorities referred to in the text.] T. F. T.

FITZGERALD, GERALD, eighth EARL OF KILDARE (*d.* 1513), was son of Thomas Fitzgerald, seventh earl of Kildare [q. v.], by his wife Joan, daughter of James, earl of Desmond. Gerald became Earl of Kildare on the death of his father in 1477, and was elected by the council at Dublin to succeed him as deputy-governor in Ireland. Edward IV, however, nominated Henry, lord Grey, to that office. In connection with the appointment serious complications arose. Kildare and Grey respectively asserted rights as governors, and presided over rival parliaments of the English settlement in Ireland. After the termination of the contest Kildare was, in 1481, appointed as deputy in Ireland for the viceroy, Richard, duke of York, and during the closing years of Edward IV advanced much in wealth and influence. He married Alison, daughter of Sir Rowland Fitzeustace, baron of Portlester, and formed alliances with the most important Irish and Anglo-Irish families. Richard III, on his accession, laboured to secure the interest of Kildare, and appointed him deputy-governor in Ireland for his son, Prince Edward. Kildare identified himself prominently with the Yorkist movement in Ireland, which led to the battle at Stoke. In 1488, through the medium of Sir Richard Edgecombe, Kildare was taken into favour by Henry VII, and received pardon under the great seal. As lord deputy he acted energetically against some of the hostile Irish, but was subsequently suspected of favouring the claims of Perkin Warbeck. Kildare deferred compliance with a royal mandate for his appearance in England. His messengers, sent with despatches to the king, were imprisoned at London, for which no explanation was accorded to him. In a letter to the Earl of Ormonde Kildare complained of this treatment, and mentioned that he understood that he had been falsely accused of having favoured Perkin Warbeck. He declared that he had never aided or supported him, and that his loyalty had been certified to the king by the principal lords of Ireland. At the same time the Earl of Desmond, and other chief personages in Ireland, by letter entreated the king not to require Kildare to attend on him in England, as they alleged that the English interest in Ireland would be severely prejudiced by his absence, and they assured the king that he was a true and faithful subject. Kildare was attainted in a parliament convened by Sir Edward Poynings at Drogheda in November 1494, and sent as prisoner to the Tower of London. After a detention there for two years the earl was pardoned, and appointed lord deputy in 1496. In that year he married, as his second wife, Elizabeth St. John, first cousin to Henry VII. In 1498 Kildare presided at the first parliament held in Ireland under Poynings' law. The statutes enacted on that occasion were afterwards officially declared to have been lost, but they have been brought to light and published by the writer of the present notice. Of Kildare's military operations the most important was that in 1504 at Cnoctuagh, near Galway, in which he obtained a victory over forces commanded by some of the chief nobles of Connacht and Munster. He was installed as a knight of the Garter in May 1505, and continued as deputy in Ireland in the early years of the reign of Henry VIII. Kildare died in September 1513 of a wound which he received in an engagement with a sept of Leinster. He was interred in a chapel which he had erected in the convent of the Holy Trinity, now known as Christ Church, Dublin. Contemporary chroniclers styled him 'the great earl,' and described him as 'a mighty made man, full of honour and courage, soon hot and soon cold, somewhat headlong and unruly towards the nobles whom he fancied not.' His son Gerald succeeded as ninth earl [q. v.] A covenant in the Irish language, executed about 1510, between Kildare and the sept of MacGeoghegan, extant in the British Museum, has been reproduced in the third part of 'Facsimiles of National MSS. of Ireland,' London, 1879.

[Archives of the Duke of Leinster; Unpublished Statute Rolls of Ireland; Patent Rolls, Henry VII; State Papers, Public Record Office, London; Harleian MS. 433; Holinshed's Chronicles, 1586; Obits of Christ Church, Dublin, 1844; Papers of Richard III, 1861; Earls of Kildare, 1862; Hist. of Viceroys of Ireland, 1865; Report of Hist. MSS. Commission, 1883.]

J. T. G.

FITZGERALD, GERALD, ninth EARL OF KILDARE (1487–1534), son of Gerald Fitzgerald, eighth earl [q. v.], by his first wife, Alison Eustace, daughter and coheiress of Rowland, baron of Portlester, was born in 1487. Sent into England in 1493 as a pledge of his father's loyalty, his youth was spent at court, where he was treated as befitted his rank. In 1503 he married Elizabeth, daughter of Sir John Zouche of Codnor in Derbyshire, ' a woman of rare probity of mind and every way commendable.' Shortly after his marriage he was allowed to return to Ireland, and on 28 Feb. 1504 was appointed lord high treasurer. In the same year he accompanied his father, the lord deputy, on an expedition against MacWilliam of Clanricarde and O'Brien of Thomond. In the battle of Knockdoe on 19 Aug. he commanded the reserve, but 'seeing the battle joining, could not stand still to wait his time as was appointed,' and by his indiscreet valour allowed the Irish horse to capture the baggage train, together with a number of English gentlemen (*Annals of the Four Masters*, ed. O'Donovan, v. 1277; *Book of Howth*, p. 185; HARDIMAN, *Galway*, p. 76). The account in the 'Book of Howth' must be received with caution; Ware prudently remarks regarding MacWilliam and O'Brien: ' De particulari eorum machinatione non possum aliquid pro certo affirmare' (*Annales*, p. 71). In May 1508 he was again in England, but for what purpose is not clear (BERNARDI ANDREÆ *Annales*, p. 115). On 9 Nov. 1510 he obtained from Henry VIII a grant during pleasure, afterwards confirmed in tail male, of the manor of Ardmolghan, co. Meath. His father dying on 30 Sept. 1513, he was elected lord justice by the council pending his appointment as lord deputy. In the following year he undertook an expedition against the O'Moores and O'Reillies, and having slain Hugh O'Reilly he returned to Dublin laden with plunder. For this and other services done against the ' wild Irish' he was rewarded with the customs and dues of the ports of Strangford and Ardglass. As yet nothing had happened to mar the friendly relations between him and his brother-in-law, Piers Butler. In 1514 he presented Sir Piers with a chief horse, a grey hackney, and a haubergeon, and about the same time united with him to frame regulations for the government of the counties of Kilkenny and Tipperary. In June 1515 he crossed over into England to confer with the king about the affairs of the kingdom, and in October he was authorised to summon a parliament, which met in January 1516. At the same time (October 1515) he was, by license of the king, permitted to carry into execution a scheme, originated by his father, for the foundation and endowment of a college in honour of the Virgin at Maynooth, co. Kildare, which, however, was shortly afterwards suppressed with other religious houses in 1538. In 1516 he conducted an expedition against the O'Tooles, who by their constant depredations considerably annoyed the citizens of Dublin. Marching west he next invaded Ely O'Carroll, where he was joined by several noblemen of Munster and Leinster, including Piers, earl of Ormonde, and James, eldest son of the Earl of Desmond. Having captured and razed the castle of Lemyvannan (Leim-Ui-Bhanain, i.e. O'Banan's leap) he marched rapidly on Clonmel, which having surrendered on conditions he returned to Dublin in December ' laden with booty, hostages, and honour.' In March 1517 he held a parliament at Dublin, after which he invaded Lecale, where he stormed and recaptured the castle of Dundrum. Thence he marched against Phelim Magennis, whom he defeated and took prisoner, and having captured the castle of Dungannon and laid waste Tyrone, ' he reduced Ireland to a quiet condition.' Shortly after his return, in October, his wife, whom he dearly loved, died at Lucan, and was by him buried with great pomp near his mother in the monastery of the Friars Observant at Kilcullen, co. Kildare. Hitherto there had been no question made of his loyalty. In 1515, however, Sir Piers Butler [q. v.] succeeded to the earldom of Ormonde, and shortly afterwards the old hereditary feud between the two houses broke out with redoubled violence. (There is a judicious account of this quarrel in the 'History of St. Canice's Cathedral.' Mr. Froude's narrative is distorted by his extreme partiality for Ormonde. On the other hand, the story in Stanihurst, manifestly derived from Geraldine sources, must be received with caution. One noticeable feature is the vehement animosity of the Countess of Ormonde towards her brother.) At the instigation of Ormonde a charge of maladministration was preferred against him in 1518, and early in the following year he sailed for England. The investigation of the charges against him was committed to Wolsey, but Wolsey, either from policy or pressure of other business, continually postponed the inquiry. In 1520 Kildare married the Lady Elizabeth Grey, fourth daughter of Thomas, marquis of Dorset, granddaughter of Elizabeth Woodville, queen of Edward IV and first cousin of Henry VIII. The same year he was removed from office and the Earl of Surrey appointed lord-lieutenant. Polydore Vergil was perhaps not an unprejudiced observer, but he undoubtedly expressed the general feeling when he remarked that in making this change Wolsey was actuated rather by hatred of Kildare than by any love for Surrey (*Historia Anglica*, lib. xxvii.) In June Kildare accompanied Henry to the Field of the Cloth of Gold, where he was distinguished for his gallant bearing. Fretting, however, under his detention, he seems to have entered into treasonable negotiations with the wild Irish to invade the Pale, but the charge was never brought home to him, and it ought to be noted that the chief witness against him, O'Carroll, was a kinsman of Ormonde's. He was placed under restraint, and though shortly afterwards released, it was not till July 1523 that he was allowed to return to Ireland. In 1521 Ormonde had been appointed deputy to the Earl of Surrey. For a brief period peace prevailed between the two rivals, but in October the feud broke out afresh. In November they consented to a treaty of peace 'for one year only.' But the murder of Robert Talbot, a retainer of Ormonde's, suspected of spying upon Kildare, by James Fitzgerald, in December, at once led to further acts of hostility on both sides. A new charge of treason was preferred against him, but by the influence of the Marquis of Dorset the commission of investigation was appointed to sit in Ireland, with the result that in August 1524 Ormonde was removed from office and Kildare established in his stead. Immediately afterwards he was ordered to arrest the Earl of Desmond, believed to be engaged in treasonable negotiations with Francis I, 'but whether willingly or wittingly he omitted the opportunity, as being loath to be the minister of his cousin Desmond's ruin, or that it lay not in his power and hands to do him hurt or harm, he missed the mark at which he aimed' (RUSSEL, *Narrative*). On his return he advanced into Ulster to afford assistance to his cousin, Con O'Neill, assailed on one side by O'Donnell and on the other by his rival, Hugh O'Neill. In May 1525 he held a parliament at Dublin, and shortly afterwards 'crucified' Maurice Kavanagh, archdeacon of Leighlin, for the murder of his kinsman, Maurice Doran, bishop of Leighlin (DOWLING, *Annals*). The same year the charge of treasonable practices was renewed against him by the Earl of Ossory (he had recently resigned the earldom of Ormonde to Sir Thomas Boleyn [q. v.]) on the ground that he had wilfully neglected to arrest the Earl of Desmond and that he had

connected himself by marriage with the 'Irish enemy.' Accordingly, in compliance with a summons from Henry he passed over next year into England, and was immediately clapped in the Tower. As to the story told by Stanihurst of his trial before the council and of Wolsey's abortive attempt to have him secretly executed, it can only be said that there is perhaps a grain of truth in it. But that Wolsey's hatred should have led him to commit such an egregious piece of folly is incredible, if indeed it is not absolutely disproved by state documents (*State Papers*, Hen. VIII, ii. 138). However this may have been, he was shortly liberated on bail and went to reside at Newington in Middlesex, a seat of the Duke of Norfolk's. His detention proving irksome, he, in July 1528, sent his daughter Alice, lady Slane, to instigate his Irish allies to invade the Pale; but his intrigues being suspected he was again confined to the Tower, and the office of deputy transferred to Ossory. In 1530, on the appointment of Sir W. Skeffington, he was allowed to return to Ireland, and in 1531 accompanied him on an expedition against O'Donnell. But he regarded the appointment with unconcealed dislike, and Ossory, ever ready to strike a blow at him, combined with the deputy. Once again was he compelled to appear in England, but this time he acquitted himself so successfully as to obtain Skeffington's removal and his own appointment. On his return in August 1532 he received an ovation from the populace of Dublin and forthwith proceeded with little ceremony to remove his enemies from office. In May 1533 he held a parliament at Dublin, and afterwards went to the assistance of his son-in-law, O'Carroll (son of Mulrony), whose position was challenged by the sons of John O'Carroll; but during the siege of Birr Castle he received a bullet wound in his side, which partially deprived him of the use of his limbs and speech (Cox's assertion that he was wounded in the head is without foundation in fact). Meanwhile Ossory, Archbishop Allen, and Robert Cowley were busily complaining of his conduct to the king, and in consequence of their representations he was again summoned to England. Suffering acutely from his wound he, on 3 Oct., sent his wife to make his excuses, but the king was resolved on his coming, and gave him permission to appoint a vice-deputy. Accordingly, having held a council at Drogheda in February 1534, at which he delivered up the sword of state to his son and heir, Thomas, lord Offaly [q. v.], he shortly afterwards set sail on his last and fatal voyage (his speech before the council recorded by Stanihurst, has every appearance of being apocryphal). On his arrival in April he was examined before the council, and his reply being deemed unsatisfactory, he was committed to the Tower, though so ill both in brain and body, according to Chapuys, that he could do nothing either good or evil. He would have been put there immediately on his arrival, says the imperial ambassador, 'had it not been that the king always hoped to bring over and entrap his son.' On being informed of Lord Thomas's rebellion he did not care to blame him, but showed himself very glad of it, 'only wishing his son a little more age and experience.' About the beginning of September he was allowed somewhat greater liberty, his wife being permitted to visit him freely, there being some proposal when he got a little better to send him into Ireland to influence his son; but he died before the month expired, and was buried in St. Peter's Church in the Tower. Valiant even to rashness, beloved by his friends and dependents, a faithful husband, a lover of hospitality, he was by no means a match for his rival in diplomacy, and whatever of treason there may have been in his actions it was due rather to imprudence than to premeditated disloyalty. The office of deputy he regarded as the prerogative of his house. By the admission of his enemies he was 'the greatest improver of his lands' in Ireland. Methodical in his habits he in 1518 commenced an important book called 'Kildare's Rental' (edited by H. Hore in 'Kilkenny Arch. Soc. Journal,' 1859, 62, 66), which affords us a curious glimpse of the peculiar relations existing between landlords and their tenantry at this period. His picture, painted in 1530 by Holbein, is preserved in the library at Carton, Maynooth, co. Kildare.

[There is a serviceable but rather uncritical life in The Earls of Kildare, by C. W. Fitzgerald, late Duke of Leinster. The chief authorities are the State Papers (printed), Henry VIII, vol. ii., supplemented by Mr. Gairdner's admirable calendars; Sir James Ware's Annals; Annals of the Four Masters; Annals of Loch Cé; Lodge's Peerage (Archdall).]   R. D.

FITZGERALD, GERALD, fifteenth EARL OF DESMOND (d. 1583), was the son of James, fourteenth earl [q. v.], whom he succeeded in 1558, doing homage before the lord deputy, Sussex, at Waterford (28 Nov.) Shortly afterwards, attended by 'one hundred prime gentlemen,' he crossed over into England, where he was graciously received by Elizabeth, and confirmed by her (22 June 1559) in all the lands, jurisdictions, seignories, and privileges that were held in times past by his predecessors. Already, during the lifetime of his father, he had become notorious for his turbulent disposition, and for his proneness to private war. In 1560 a dispute arose between him and Thomas Butler, tenth earl of Ormonde [q. v.], about the prize wines of Youghal and Kinsale, which the latter claimed, and certain debatable lands on the river Suir, into which Desmond swore Ormonde had entered by force. The dispute, conducted in the usual Irish fashion, obliged the government to intervene, and the two earls were accordingly summoned to submit their claims in person to Elizabeth. Ormonde alone showed any willingness to obey; but at last, after alleging many frivolous pretexts for his non-compliance, Desmond appeared at court about the beginning of May 1562, attended by a numerous retinue. Being charged before the council with openly defying the law in Ireland, he answered contumaciously, and refusing to apologise was forthwith committed into the custody of the lord treasurer, a slight confinement, as the queen wrote to his countess, which would do him no harm, and which Sir William Fitzwilliam hoped would have the effect of bringing him to such senses as he had. Though soon released, he was not allowed to return to Ireland till the beginning of 1564, after he had consented to such stipulations as were deemed essential to the public peace (MORRIN, Patent Rolls, i. 485). Almost immediately after his return he involved himself in a quarrel between the Earl of Thomond and his rival Sir Donnell O'Brien. In October he and Ormonde were again on evil terms with one another, and in November the latter complained to Cecil that he was continually invading his territories, killing the queen's subjects, and carrying off his cattle, and that in self-defence he must retaliate. The death of the Countess Joan, the wife of Desmond, and the mother of Ormonde, early in 1565, removed the last restraint on his conduct, and on 1 Feb. he entered the territories of Sir Maurice Fitzgerald, viscount Decies, and baron of Dromana, with a considerable body of men in order to enforce his claim to certain disputed arrears of rents and services. The Baron of Dromana, however, being anxious to liberate himself from his feudal superior, had meanwhile enlisted the support of the Earl of Ormonde, who, nothing loth, under this plausible pretext of maintaining the peace to revenge himself on his rival, immediately assembled his men and marched southwards. The two armies met at the ford of Affane on the Blackwater; a bloody skirmish followed, in which Desmond was wounded in the thigh with a bullet and taken prisoner. The queen, enraged at this fresh outbreak, summoned both earls to appear before her. On Easter Tuesday Desmond arrived at Liverpool in custody of Captain Nicholas Heron, having suffered much from sea-sickness. Ormonde was already at court. Charges and counter-charges of high treason followed. Eventually then two earls submitted, and consented to enter into recognisances of 20,000*l*. each to stand to such order for their controversies as her majesty should think good. On 7 Jan. 1566 the lord deputy was informed that the earls were reconciled and licensed to depart into Ireland, but Desmond was not to leave Dublin until he had paid what debts he had incurred. The original controversy between them, however, remained, and seemed likely to remain, undecided. 'I will never,' wrote Sir H. Sidney to Cecil on 27 April, 'unpressed, upon my allegiance, deal in the great matters of my lord of Ormonde, until another chancellor come, or some other commissioner out of England, to be joined with me for hearing and determining of that cause; for how indifferently soever I shall deal, I know it will not be thought favourably enough on my lord of Ormonde's side.' He protested that he was not prejudiced against Ormonde, only the case had been 'forejudged.' On 12 Dec. he renewed his request, and soon afterwards (27 Jan. 1567) began a tour of inspection through Munster, in consequence of which he was most unfavourably impressed with Desmond's character. At Youghal he entered into an examination of the controversy between the earls, and having found that the disputed lands were in the possession of Ormonde 'at the time of the fray-making,' he gave judgment accordingly, 'whereat the Earl of Desmond did not a little stir, and fell into some disallowable heats and passions.' 'From this time forward, nor never since,' he wrote to Elizabeth, 'found I any willingness in him to come to any conformity or good order,' but, on the contrary, found him to be 'a man void of judgment to govern and will to be ruled,' the cause in short of the turbulent state of Munster. He therefore arrested him at Kilmallock, and, carrying him to Dublin, locked him up in the Castle, leaving his brother, Sir John of Desmond, of whose capabilities he seems to have had a higher opinion, seneschal or captain of the country. In August 1567 Sidney left Ireland, and during his absence, as he himself said, Sir John was by the lord justices inveigled up to Dublin, taken prisoner, sent over to England with the earl, and both of them committed to the Tower. 'And truly, Mr. Secretary,' said he, 'this kind of dealing with Sir John of Desmond was the origin of James Fitzmaurice's rebellion.' The earl and Sir John landed at Graycoite, near Beaumaris, on 14 Dec., and on their arrival in London they were confined to the Tower, where they remained until midwinter 1570, when the state of Sir John's health necessitated his removal. They were then placed under the supervision of Sir Warham St. Leger, at his house at Southwark. In August 1571 St. Leger complained to the council that the earl had refused to accompany him into Kent, and that during his absence he had rashly ranged abroad into sundry parts of London. Next summer he tried to bribe Martin Frobisher, who revealed the plot to Burghley, to assist him to escape by sea. Meanwhile, on 30 June 1569, the question of the prize wines had been settled in Ormonde's favour. In the following year Eleanor, countess of Desmond (the earl's second wife), came to England, where she remained with her husband till his release. The government was undecided what to do with him. Sir John Perrot, then president of Munster, strenuously urged that he should be detained for another year or two, but that Sir John should be allowed to return. However, in March 1573, after signing articles for his future good conduct (*Cal. Carew MSS.* i. 430), he was permitted to return to Ireland, to Perrot's disgust, who marvelled much that her majesty should so act in regard to 'a man rather meet to keep Bedlam than to come to a new reformed country.' The Irish government thought with Perrot, and on his arrival in Dublin on Lady-day they rearrested him; but on 16 Nov. he managed to escape, and within a month afterwards he had destroyed almost every trace of Perrot's government in the province. Elizabeth was now anxious to recapture him, and a certain Edward Fitzgerald, brother of the Earl of Kildare, and presumably *persona grata*, was in December commissioned to remonstrate with him. The attempt failed, as did also the intervention of the Earl of Essex in June 1574. Desmond was profuse in his protestations of loyalty, but refused to surrender unconditionally. Required to consent to the abolition of coyne and livery, the surrender of certain castles and other things embodied in the articles of 8 July, he declined, and his conduct was approved by his kinsmen, who bound themselves by oath (18 July) 'to maintain and defend this our advice against the lord deputy or any others that will covet the earl's inheritance' (this combination, printed in MORRIN's *Patent Rolls*, ii. 109, and the deed of feoffment that followed, have an interesting history. See Wallop to Burghley, *Ham. Cal.* iii. 63). Thereupon he was proclaimed, a price set on his head, and in August Fitzwilliam and Ormonde advanced into Munster, attacked Derrinlaur Castle, captured it, and put the garrison to the sword. Convinced of the necessity of temporising, Desmond appeared at Cork and humbly submitted himself (2 Sept.); but on 10 Sept. he made over all his lands to Lord Dunboyne, Lord Power, and Sir John Fitzedmund Fitzgerald of Cloyne [q. v.], in trust for himself and his wife during their joint lives, with provision for his daughters and remainder to his son James (*Carew MSS.* i. 481). This feoffment, though suspicious, does not necessarily imply that he had, when he made it, any premeditated intention of rebelling. In March 1575 James Fitzmaurice [q. v.] left Ireland for the express purpose of soliciting foreign aid, but whether he did so, as MacGeoghegan asserts, with the connivance of the earl is extremely doubtful. Certain it is that during the government of Sir H. Sidney (1575–8) he manifested no rebellious intentions, though occasionally resenting President Drury's arbitrary conduct, and he even revealed to the deputy the nature of Fitzmaurice's negotiations on the continent. 'This and other good shows in the Earl of Desmond,' wrote Sidney to the queen, 'maketh demonstration that his light and loose dealings (whereunto he runneth many times rashly) proceedeth rather of imperfection of judgement, than of malicious intendment against your majesty.' 'I hold him,' he added, 'the least dangerous man of four or five of those that are next him in right and succession . . . being such an impotent and weak body, as neither can he get up on horseback, but that he is holpen and lift up, neither when he is on horseback can of himself alight down without help, and therefore, in mine opinion, the less to be feared or doubted, if he would forget himself, as I hope now he will not.' Sidney's is probably the most correct, as it is the most charitable, explanation of his subsequent foolhardy conduct. On the arrival of Fitzmaurice (17 July 1579) Desmond rejected his overtures to join with him in re-establishing the old religion, notified the fact to Drury, protested his own loyalty, declared his intention of marching against the invader, and did what he could in that direction. The death of Fitzmaurice, of whom he seems to have been extremely jealous, and the representations of Sanders exercised a prejudicial effect upon him. His conduct aroused the suspicion of Drury, who on 7 Sept. 'restrained him from liberty' for two days, until he promised to send his son as hostage for his conduct to Limerick. Fascinated by the rhetoric of Sanders and yet unwilling to risk everything by openly rebelling, he endeavoured to temporise. Warned by Malby

that he was suspected, he refused to take the only safe course open to him, and on 1 Nov. he was proclaimed a traitor. Compelled to act, he marched against Youghal, which he sacked, while the Earl of Clancar did the same for Kinsale. This did little to add to his strength. In March 1580 Pelham captured the castle of Carrigafoyl, and in April Askeaton and Ballyloughan, his last fortresses, shared the same fate. On 14 June he and Sanders narrowly escaped being surprised by Pelham, and in August he was reduced to such extremities that he sent his countess to the lord justice to intercede for him. About the same time he applied to Admiral Winter, who was cruising in Kinsale waters, to transport him to England to beg his pardon personally from the queen. After the destruction of the Spaniards in Fort-del-Ore the government of Munster was entrusted to the Earl of Ormonde, while Captain Zouche with 450 men was deputed to hunt him down. On 15 June 1581 he was surprised in the neighbourhood of Castlemange and obliged to fly in his shirt into the woods of Aharlow. During the winter he was compelled to keep his Christmas in Kilquegg wood, near Kilmallock, where he was nearly captured by the garrison stationed there. In September 1582 he was reported to have two hundred horse and two thousand foot under his command. In January 1583 he had two remarkable escapes. All attempts to capture him seemed useless. The Munster officials were at their wits' end. Fenton suggested that he should be assassinated, while St. Leger advised the queen to adopt a policy similar to that which her father had found useful in the case of 'Silken Thomas.' Meanwhile Ormonde, by more legitimate means, was bringing him to the end of his resources. On 5 June his countess left him, and a proclamation of pardon deprived him of most of his followers. Deserted by all except a priest, two horsemen, one kerne, and a boy, he wandered about helplessly from one place to another. On 19 Sept. he was nearly captured on the borders of Slievloghra. On Monday, 11 Nov., just as day was breaking, he was surprised in a cabin in the wood of Glanaginty by five soldiers of the garrison of Castlemange, led on by Owen MacDonnell O'Moriarty, whose brother-in-law had just been plundered by the earl. Fearing a rescue, his head was cut off by Daniel O'Kelly and sent into England. His body was conveyed, according to tradition, through the byways of the hills to the little mountain churchyard of Kill-na-n-onaim, or the 'Church of no Name.' In 1586 an act of parliament declared his estates forfeited to the crown.

He married (1) Joan, daughter and heiress of James, eleventh earl of Desmond, widow of James, ninth earl of Ormonde, and mother of his rival, Thomas, tenth earl; (2) Eleanor, daughter of Edmund Butler, lord Dunboyne, by whom he had James, called 'the Queen's Earl' [q. v.], Thomas, and five daughters.

SIR JOHN OF DESMOND, who had immediately on his landing joined Fitzmaurice, signalising his adhesion by the murder of Captain Henry Davells at Tralee, became, on the death of Fitzmaurice and till the accession of the earl, head of the rebel army. Sharing with his brother in the vicissitudes of the war, he was in December 1581, after having been wounded on several occasions, entrapped by Captain Zouche in the neighbourhood of Castlelyons. His body was sent to Cork and 'was hanged in chaynes ouer the citty gates, where it hanged up for 3 or foure yeares togeather as a spectacle to all the beholders to looke on, vntill at length a greate storme of wynd blew it off, but the head was sent to Dublin, and there fastened to a pole and set over the castle wall.'

[The chief authorities are Hamilton's Calendar of State Papers, vols. i. and ii.; Collins's Sydney State Papers, vol. i.; Calendar of Carew MSS. vols. i. and ii.; O'Daly's Initium, incrementa, et exitus familiæ Geraldinorum; O'Sullevan's Historiæ Catholicæ Iberniæ Compendium; Annals of the Four Masters; Annals of Loch Cé; Morrin's Calendar of Patent Rolls, vols. i. and ii.; Unpublished Geraldine Documents, ed. Hayman and Graves; Thomas Churchyard's A Scourge for Rebels; Bishop Carleton's A Thankful Remembrance of God's Mercy; Kerry Mag. vol. i., where, under the title 'Antiquities of Tralee,' will be found a most excellent discussion on that part of Desmond's life which relates to his rebellion, said to be by the late Archdeacon Rowan; Cox's Hibernica Anglicana, vol. i.; Bagwell's Ireland under the Tudors, vol. ii.]   R. D.

FITZGERALD, GERALD, eleventh EARL OF KILDARE (1525–1585), was son of Gerald Fitzgerald, ninth earl of Kildare [q. v.], by his second wife, Elizabeth, daughter of Thomas Grey, marquis of Dorset. In 1537 Gerald's father was executed for high treason and attainted, with forfeiture of title and estates. Mainly through the exertions of his tutor, Thomas Leverous, subsequently bishop of Kildare, Gerald was conveyed to France, whence he went to Rome, where he was received by his relative, Cardinal Pole. He subsequently took part with knights of Rhodes in expeditions against the Moors, and entered the service of Cosmo de' Medici at Florence. After the death of Henry VIII Gerald came to England, and married Mabel, daughter of Sir Anthony Browne, knight of the Garter.

Edward VI, in 1552, restored to him some of his paternal estates. In 1554 he served against Sir Thomas Wyatt. Queen Mary conferred upon Gerald the earldom of Kildare, with possessions of his father, which, under the attainder, had been confiscated. The original grant for the re-establishment of the earldom is in the possession of the Duke of Leinster, now the chief representative of the earls of Kildare. The document has, with autographs of the eleventh earl, been reproduced in the fourth part of 'Facsimiles of National MSS. of Ireland.' Gerald conformed to the protestant religion early in the reign of Elizabeth. He sat in parliament in Ireland in 1559. The attainder of his family was annulled by statute in 1568. In 1577 he attended before the privy council in England in relation to complaints made concerning the assessment imposed upon landholders in Ireland. He took an active part in the warfare against hostile Irish and the Spaniards who had landed in Munster. In 1582, on suspicion of treason, the earl's estates were placed under sequestration, and he, his son Henry, and his son-in-law Lord Delvin, were imprisoned in the Tower of London. After examinations before the lord chancellor of England and other judges, the earl was released from the Tower on giving a bond for 2,000l., in June 1583, to remain within twenty miles of London and not to come within three miles of her majesty's court. In the following year the queen granted him permission to wait upon her, and to return to Ireland, where he sat in the parliament at Dublin in April 1585. He died in London on 16 Nov. following, and was interred at Kildare. He is stated by contemporaries to have been an expert horseman, valiant, small of stature, slender of person, very courteous, but hard and angry at times, a great gatherer of money, and addicted to gambling.

[Archives of the Duke of Leinster; Patent and Statute Rolls; State Papers, Public Record Office, London; Carew MSS., Lambeth; Carte Papers, Bodleian Library; The Earls of Kildare, 1862; Report of Hist. MSS. Commission, 1883.]   J. T. G.

FITZGERALD, JAMES FITZJOHN, fourteenth EARL OF DESMOND (d. 1558), second son of Sir John Desmond [see FITZGERALD, JAMES Fitzmaurice, thirteenth earl], de facto thirteenth earl of Desmond, and More, daughter of Donogh O'Brien of Carrigogunnell, co. Limerick, lord of Pobble O'Brien, immediately on the death of his grandfather in June 1536 assumed the position and title of Earl of Desmond, and in order to support it united himself with the head of the discontented party in Ireland, O'Brien of Thomond. Naturally the government, which had just suppressed the rebellion of Thomas, earl of Kildare, could not brook such insolence, and accordingly on 25 July the lord deputy, Grey, marched against him, and having come to the border of Cashel encamped in the field three days expecting his coming, as he had promised the chief justice, with the intention of separating him from O'Brien, 'so as we might have entangled but with one of them at once.' Not keeping his appointment, the deputy marched forward and took possession of his castle in Lough Gur, the doors and windows of which had been carried away and the roof burnt by the rebels themselves, which was then entrusted to Lord James Butler, who made it defensible. But Fitzgerald had no intention of imitating his unfortunate kinsman Thomas, earl of Kildare, and, although he refused to place his person within the power of the deputy, 'he showed himself in gesture and communication very reasonable,' offering to deliver up his two sons as hostages for his loyalty, and to submit his claims to the earldom to the decision of Lord Grey. Though renewed in December nothing for the nonce came of the proposal. 'And as far as ever I could perceive,' wrote Grey to Cromwell in February 1537, 'the stay that keepeth him from inclining to the king's grace's pleasure is the fear and doubt which he and all the Geraldines in Munster have in the Lord James Butler, both for the old malice that hath been betwixt their bloods, and principally for that he claimeth title by his wife to the earldom of Desmond' (*State Papers*, Hen. VIII, ii. 404). Grey argued in favour of the acknowledgment of his claims, and in August Anthony St. Leger, who was at the time serving on the commission 'for the order and establishment to be taken and made touching the whole state of Ireland,' was advised by Cromwell 'to handle the said James in a gentle sort.' Accordingly on 15 Sept. he was invited to submit his claims to the commissioners at Dublin; but suspecting their intention he declined to place himself in their power, though signing articles of submission and promising to deliver up his eldest son as hostage for his good faith. The negotiations continued to hang fire. In March 1538 the commissioners wrote that 'he hath not only delivered his son, according to his first promise, to the hands of Mr. William Wyse of Waterford to be delivered unto us, but also hath affirmed by his secretary and writing all that he afore promised' (*ib.* p. 550). Nor was he without good reason for his cautious conduct. The

Ormonde faction in the council, violently opposed to Grey and St. Leger, were assiduously striving to effect his ruin by entangling him in rebellious projects. In July 1539 John Allen related to Cromwell how the 'pretended Earl of Desmond' had confederated with O'Donnell and O'Neill 'to make insurrection against the king's majesty and his subjects, not only for the utter exile and destruction of them, but also for the bringing in, setting up, and restoring young Gerald (the sole surviving scion of the house of Kildare) to all the possessions and pre-eminences which his father had; and so finally among them to exclude the king from all his regalities within this land' (*ib.* iii. 136). In April 1540 the council informed the king that 'your grace's servant James Fitzmaurice, who claimed to be Earl of Desmond, was cruelly slain the Friday before Palm Sunday, of unfortunate chance, by Maurice Fitzjohn, brother to James Fitzjohn, then usurper of the earldom of Desmond. After which murder done, the said James Fitzjohn immediately resorted to your town of Youghal, where he was well received and entertained, and ere he departed entered into all such piles and garrisons in the county of Cork as your majesty's deputy, with the assistance of your army and me, the Earl of Ormonde, obtained before Christmas last' (*ib.* p. 195). Ormonde was sent to parley with him, but he refused to trust him. On the arrival of St. Leger, as deputy, however, he again renewed his offer of submission, and promised, upon pledges being given for his safety, to meet him at Cashel. This he did, and on bended knees renounced the supremacy of the pope. 'And then,' writes St. Leger, 'considering the great variance between the Earl of Ormonde and him, concerning the title of the earldom of Desmond . . . I and my fellows thought it not good to leave that cancer remain, but so laboured the matter on both sides, that we have brought them to a final end of the said title.' St. Leger assured the king 'that sith my repair into this your land I have not heard better counsel of no man for the reformation of the same than of the said Earl of Desmond, who undoubted is a very wise and discreet gentleman,' for which reason, he said, he had sworn him of the council and given him 'gown, jacket, doublet, hose, shirts, caps, and a riding coat of velvet, which he took very thankfully, and ware the same in Limerick and in all places where he went with me' (*ib.* p. 285). By such conciliatory conduct did St. Leger, in the opinion of Justice Cusack, win over to obedience the whole province of Munster (*Cal. Carew MSS.* i. 245) In July 1541 he was appointed chief executor of the ' ordinances for the reformation of Ireland ' in Munster, and in token of the renunciation of the privilege claimed by his ancestors of not being obliged to attend the great councils of the realm, he took his seat in a parliament held at Dublin. In June 1542 he visited England, where, being admitted to the presence of the king, he was by him graciously received, his title acknowledged, and the king himself wrote to the Irish council ' that the Earl of Desmond hath here submitted himself in so honest, lowly, and humble a sort towards us, as we have conceived a very great hope that he will prove a man of great honour, truth, and good service.' Nor did he, during the rest of his life, fail to justify this opinion. On 9 July 1543 he obtained a grant of the crown lease of St. Mary's Abbey, Dublin, ' for his better supporting at his repair' to parliament. By Edward VI he was created lord treasurer on the death of the Earl of Ormonde (patent 29 March 1547), and on 15 Oct., when thanking him for his services in repressing disorders in Munster, the king offered to make a companion of his son. During the government of Bellingham he was suspected of treasonable designs, and having refused a peremptory order to appear in Dublin, the deputy swooped down upon him unexpectedly in the dead of winter, 1548, and carried him off prisoner. He was soon released and continued in office by Mary. In the summer of 1558 he was attacked by a serious illness, and died at Askeaton on Thursday 27 Oct. He was buried in the abbey of the White Friars, Tralee. ' The loss of this good man was woful to his country ; for there was no need to watch cattle, or close doors from Dun-caoin, in Kerry, to the green bordered meeting of the three waters, on the confines of the province of Eochaidh, the son of Lachta and Leinster' (*Annals of the Four Masters*). He married four times : first, Joan Roche, daughter of Maurice, lord Fermoy, and his own grandniece, for which reason she was put away, and her son, Thomas Roe (father of James Fitzthomas Fitzgerald, the Sugan Earl [q. v.]), known as Sir Thomas of Desmond, disinherited ; secondly, More, daughter of Sir Maolrony McShane O'Carroll, lord of Ely O'Carroll, by whom he had Gerald, his heir, also John and four daughters—she died in 1548 ; thirdly, Catherine, second daughter of Piers, earl of Ormonde, and widow of Richard, lord Power—she died at Askeaton, 17 March 1553 ; and fourthly, Ellen, daughter of Donald MacCormac, MacCarthy Mór, by whom he had a son, Sir James-Sussex Fitzgerald, and a daughter, Elinor.

[State Papers, Hen. VIII, vols. ii. and iii. ; Lodge's Peerage (Archdall) ; Ware's Annales ; Stanihurst's Chronicle ; Cal. Carew MSS. vol. i. ; Hamilton's Cal. vol. i. ; Liber Hiberniæ, ii. 41 ; O'Clery's Book of Pedigrees, Kilkenny Arch. Soc. Journal, 1881, p. 413.] R. D.

FITZGERALD, JAMES Fitzmaurice, thirteenth EARL OF DESMOND (*d.* 1540), was the son of Maurice Fitzthomas, only son and heir-apparent of Thomas, twelfth earl of Desmond, and Joan, daughter of John Fitzgibbon, the White Knight. Immediately on the death of his grandfather, Thomas, twelfth earl, in 1534, the succession was disputed by John Fitzthomas, brother of the twelfth earl, and fourth son of Thomas, eighth earl [q. v.], on the ground of the invalidity of the marriage of Maurice Fitzthomas with the daughter of the White Knight. Whether it was so or not was never determined, but John Fitzthomas having taken forcible possession remained earl *de facto* during his life, and after his death in 1536 the earldom was seized by his son James, fourteenth earl [q. v.], the title being cleared by the ' accidental' death of James Fitzmaurice, thirteenth earl *de jure*, at the hand of Maurice à *totane*, brother of the fourteenth earl. Lodge, who correctly describes James Fitzmaurice as thirteenth earl, incorrectly states that he was succeeded by his uncle, John Fitzthomas, which was impossible, John having died in 1536. This alteration makes Lodge's fifteenth and sixteenth earls, fourteenth and fifteenth respectively (cp. *Unpublished Geraldine Documents*, edited by Hayman and Graves, pt. ii. pp. 103–17).

James Fitzmaurice, thirteenth earl, being in England at the time of his grandfather's death was, at the suggestion of the Irish council, who had their own purposes to serve (*State Papers*, Hen. VIII, iii. 106), allowed to return home, being ' sufficiently furnished with all things fitting and necessary for such a journey and enterprise' by the bounty of the king. Landing at Cork, he was proceeding through the territory of Lord Roche, when he was waylaid and slain by Sir Maurice of Desmond on 19 March 1540 (*ib.* p. 195). He married Mary, daughter of his great-uncle, Cormoc Og MacCarthy, but had no male issue (LODGE, *Peerage*, Archdall). She remarried Daniel O'Sullivan Mor, and died in 1548.

[Authorities cited above.] R. D.

FITZGERALD, JAMES Fitzmaurice (*d.* 1579), ' arch traitor,' was the second son of Maurice Fitzjohn à *totane*, i. e. of the burnings, and Julia, second daughter of Dermot O'Mulryan of Sulloghade, co. Tipperary, nephew of James, fourteenth, and cousin of

Gerald, fifteenth earl of Desmond Earl James had shown his appreciation of the 'accident' that had removed his competitor, James Fitzmaurice, the so-called thirteenth earl [q. v.], from his path, by rewarding his brother, Maurice *à totane*, with the barony of Kerrykurrihy. But the cordial relations thus established between the two families came to an end with the accession of Gerald, fifteenth earl [q. v.], who appears to have regarded his uncle with jealousy, and to have treated him in a way that was resented by Maurice and his sons, who were soon at 'hot wars' with him. During the detention of the earl and his brother Sir John in England (1565-73), Fitzmaurice assumed the position of captain of Desmond, in which he was confirmed by the warrant of the earl himself, though not without protest on the part of Thomas Roe Fitzgerald. His conduct gave as little satisfaction to the government as had that of the earl. In July 1568 he entered Clanmaurice, the country of Thomas Fitzmaurice, lord of Lixnaw, nominally to distrain for rent, and, having captured two hundred head of cattle and wasted the country, was returning homewards when he was met by Lord Lixnaw himself (29 July), and utterly defeated by him. Hitherto he had lived on fairly good terms with the earl his cousin; but about the end of 1568 the earl granted to Sir Warham St. Leger, in return probably for services rendered or to be rendered to him during his confinement, a lease of the barony of Kerrykurrihy. This he naturally regarded as an act of base ingratitude, and from that moment he seems to have entered on a line of conduct which could only have for its ultimate object the usurpation of the earldom of Desmond. 'James Fitzmaurice,' wrote Sir H. Sidney, 'understanding that I was arrived, and had not brought with me neither the earl nor Sir John his brother, which he thought I might and would have done, assembling as many of the Earl of Desmond's people as he could, declared unto them that I could not obtain the enlargement either of the earl or of his brother John, and that there was no hope or expectation of either of them but to be put to death or condemned to perpetual prison. And therefore (saying that that country could not be without an earl or a captain) willed them to make choice of one to be their earl or captain, as their ancestors had done. . . And according to this his speech, he wrote unto me, they forthwith, and as it had been with one voice, cried him to be their captain' (*Cal. Carew MSS.* ii. 342). Eleanor, countess of Desmond, was a shrewd woman, and she wrote to her husband (26 Nov. 1569) that Fitzmaurice had rebelled in order to

bring him into further displeasure, and to usurp all his inheritance 'by the example of his father.' In June 1569 he and the Earl of Clancarty invaded Kerrykurrihy, spoiled all the inhabitants, took the castle-abbey of Tracton, hanged the garrison, and vowed never to depart from Cork unless Lady St. Leger and Lady Grenville were delivered up to him. His policy, even now, seems to have been to create a strong Roman catholic and anti-English sentiment, and to make an alliance with him as the head of the Irish catholic party an object of importance to the catholic powers of Europe. And here perhaps we may trace the finger of Father Wolf, the jesuit. To this end he seduced the brothers of the Earl of Ormonde, and entered into a bond with the Earl of Thomond and John Burke, son of the Earl of Clanricarde. On 12 July he wrote to the mayor and corporation of Cork, ordering them to 'abolish out of that city that old heresy newly raised and invented.' When Sidney took the field about the end of July the rebellion had extended as far as Kilkenny, while at Cork Lady St. Leger and the English inhabitants were in instant danger of being surrendered to the enemy. By the end of September the deputy had practically broken the back of the rebellion, and, leaving Captain (afterwards Sir) Humphrey Gilbert to suppress Fitzmaurice, he returned to Dublin. Gilbert soon brought him 'to a very base estate,' compelling him to seek safety in the woods of Aharlow. No sooner, however, had Gilbert departed than he succeeded in collecting a new force, with which he spoiled Kilmallock (9 Feb. 1570). On 1 March a commission was given to Ormonde 'to parley, protect, or prosecute' the Earl of Thomond, James Fitzmaurice, and others, but without leading to any result. On 27 Feb. 1571 Sir John Perrot landed at Waterford as lord president, and prepared to put him down with a strong hand. But he, we are told, 'knowing that the lord president did desire nothing more than the finishing of those wars,' proposed to terminate them by a duel, 'believing that the president's longing for a speedy issue, and his expectation thereof, would keep him for a time from further action.' He had, indeed, no intention of fighting, 'not so much,' he said, 'for fear of his life, but because on his life did depend the safety of all such as were of his party.' When Perrot at last discovered the artifice he was so enraged that he vowed 'to hunt the fox out of his hole' without delay. This he eventually did, but not without undergoing enormous fatigue, for his foe was a past master in the art of Irish strategy. After holding out for more than a year he was forced to sue for pardon, 'which at length the lord president did consent to, and James Fitzmaurice came to Kilmallock, where in the church the lord president caused him to lie prostrate, taking the point of the lord president's sword next his heart, in token that he had received his life at the queen's hands, by submitting himself unto her mercy. And so he took a solemn oath to be and continue a true subject unto the queen and crown of England' (23 Feb. 1573). He gave up one of his sons as hostage, and Perrot wrote to Burghley that from his conduct he almost expected him to prove 'a second St. Paul.' On the return of the Earl of Desmond he exerted himself to induce that nobleman to assume a position of irreconcilable enmity to England, but, finding him more inclined to submit to 'reasonable terms,' he determined to retire to the continent. His object in so doing, he said to some, was to obtain pardon from Elizabeth through the mediation of the French court; to others he declared that he was compelled to leave Ireland by the unkindness of his cousin. One excuse was probably as good as another. In March 1575, accompanied by the White Knight and the seneschal of Imokilly, he and his family sailed on board La Arganys for France, and a few days afterwards landed at St. Malo, where they were all cordially received by the governor. From St. Malo he proceeded to Paris, where he had several interviews with Catherine de' Medici. He promised largely, we are told, offering in return for assistance to make Henry III king of Ireland. During 1575-6 he remained in the neighbourhood of Paris, and received a pension of five thousand crowns, which, considering the scarcity of money, Dr. Dale shrewdly conjectured was not 'pour ses beaux yeux.' But finding that he was merely a pawn in the delicate game that Elizabeth and Catherine were playing, he, early in 1577, left France to try his fortunes at the Spanish court. Here the crown of Ireland was offered to Don John; but Philip, with the Netherlands and Portugal on his hands, had no inclination to break openly with England; so, leaving his two sons Maurice and Gerald under the protection of Cardinal Granvelle, who had taken a fancy to them, he went on to Italy, where he met with a much more satisfactory reception from Gregory XIII. At the papal court he fell in with Stukely, and a plan was soon on foot for the invasion of Ireland, the crown this time being promised to the pope's nephew. Leaving Stukely to follow with the main body of the invading force, Fitzmaurice, accompanied by Dr. Sanders, papal nuncio, and Matthew de Oviedo, sailed from Ferrol in

Galicia on 17 June 1579 with a few troops which he had gathered together, having with him his own vessel and three Spanish shallops. In the Channel two English vessels were captured, and on 16 July they arrived in the port of Dingle in Kerry, where they took possession of the Fort del Ore. On the 18th they cast anchor in Smerwick harbour, where on the 25th they were joined by two galleys with a hundred soldiers. Four days later, however, their ships were captured by the English fleet. Fitzmaurice's first concern was to despatch an urgent but ineffectual exhortation to the Earls of Desmond and Kildare, as heads of the Geraldines, to join with him in throwing off the yoke of the heretic, and then, leaving his soldiers in the Fort del Ore to await the arrival of Stukely, he went to pay a vow at the monastery of the Holy Cross in Tipperary. On his way thither he was slain in a skirmish (the merits of which are somewhat uncertain) by his cousin, Theobald Burke. He married Katherine, daughter of W. Burke of Muskerry, by whom he had two sons, Maurice and Gerald, and a daughter.

[The chief authorities for his life are Hamilton's Irish Calendar; Crosby's Foreign Calendar; Geraldine Documents, ed. Hayman and Graves; Rawlinson's Life of Sir John Perrot; Hogan's Ibernia Ignatiana; Moran's Catholic Archbishops of Dublin; Calendar of Carew MSS. i. 397; Kerry Magazine, No. 31; O'Daly's Initium, incrementa, et exitus familiæ Geraldinorum; O'Sullevan's Historiæ Catholicæ Iberniæ Compendium; Annals of the Four Masters; Annals of Loch Cé; Cox's Hibernia Anglicana; Bagwell's Ireland under the Tudors, vol. ii. In the Kilkenny Archæological Society's Journal, July 1859, will be found a collection of Irish letters by Fitzgerald, translated and edited by Dr. O'Donovan.] R. D.

FITZGERALD, JAMES, commonly called the TOWER EARL, or the QUEEN'S EARL OF DESMOND (1570?-1601), was elder son of Gerald Fitzgerald, fifteenth earl of Desmond (d. 1583) [q. v.], by his second marriage with Eleanor, daughter of Edmund Butler, lord Dunboyne. He was born in England about 1570, and the queen was his godmother. When his father renounced his allegiance to the English crown in 1579, the child seems to have been resident in Ireland. His mother, to dissociate him from his father's ill fortune, delivered him up to Sir William Drury, an acting lord justice, who sent him to Dublin Castle. On 28 Aug. 1582 the countess bitterly complained to Lord Burghley that his education was utterly neglected, and petitioned for better treatment (HAYMAN and GRAVES, 91). On 17 Nov. 1583, and on 9 July

1584 his gaolers applied to the English authorities for his removal to the Tower of London. Their second petition was successful, and before the close of 1584 the lad was carried to the Tower, to remain a prisoner there for sixteen years. On 17 June 1593 he wrote pathetically to Cecil that 'only by being born the unfortunate son of a faulty father, [he] had never since his infancy breathed out of prison.' Between 1588 and 1598 innumerable accounts are extant detailing payment in behalf of 'James Garolde,' as the prisoner was called, for medicines, ointments, pills, syrups, and the like, particulars which suggest a very feeble state of health. The 'wages' of the youth's schoolmaster appear in the accounts, and many letters are extant to testify to the thoroughness of the teaching as far as it went.

Fitzgerald's condition underwent a great change in the autumn of 1600. Tyrone's rebellion was still unchecked. In Munster the Geraldine faction was united by Tyrone's influence against the English government, in the support of James Fitzthomas Fitzgerald, the Sugan Earl [q. v.], who, being the heir of the disinherited elder son of James, fourteenth earl of Desmond, had been put forward by the rebel leaders as the only rightful earl of Desmond. To break the union between the Geraldine faction and the other rebels, Sir George Carew, president of Munster, suggested that the imprisoned James Fitzgerald should be sent to the province, and paraded as the genuine earl of Desmond. It was confidently expected that the Geraldine faction would at once transfer their allegiance to the youthful prisoner. Elizabeth disliked the scheme. Cecil doubted its wisdom, but finally gave way. Fitzgerald was to assume the title of Earl of Desmond, and a patent passed the great seal, with the proviso that if the earl had an heir, the heir should bear the title of Baron Inchiquin. The new earl was to have none of his father's lands restored to him, and was to be in the custody of a governor, Captain Price, together with a gentleman named Crosbie, and the protestant archbishop of Cashel, Miler Magrath. Captain Price was ordered to indoctrinate his charge with the necessity of supporting the queen, of adhering to the protestant religion, and of maintaining a very frugal household. Cecil directed Carew to leave Fitzgerald all the appearances of liberty, but he was to be closely watched and placed under restraint if he showed the slightest sign of sympathy with the government's enemies. The party left Bristol for Cork on 13 Oct. 1600. The earl suffered terribly from sea-sickness, and was landed at Youghal. The Geraldines welcomed him with enthusiasm, although the mayor of Cork was not very courteous. The earl travelled quickly to Carew's headquarters at Mallow, and thence to the centre of the Geraldine district at Kilmallock (18 Oct.), where Sir George Thornton, the English commander, provided him with lodging. The people still treated him with favour, and although he found his position irksome, he faithfully preached to them Elizabeth's clemency and the desirability of making peace with her. But on Sunday, the 19th, while his followers were expecting him to join them at worship in the catholic chapel, he ostentatiously made his way to the protestant church. This act broke the spell, and the people's acclamations changed to hooting. On 14 Nov., however, Thomas Oge, an officer in the service of the Sugan Earl, who held a fortress called Castlemang, surrendered it to the new earl, and the latter dwelt with pride on the victory in a letter to Cecil (18 Dec.) But this was Desmond's only success. Cecil saw that his presence in Ireland had no effect on the rebellious population, and his guardians found him difficult to content with the narrow means at their command. He resented living on 500l. a year, the allowance made him by the government, and desired to marry a certain widow Norreys, to which Cecil objected. Cecil held out hopes that a more suitable marriage could be arranged in England. At the end of March 1601 he came to London with a letter from Carew highly recommending him for a grant of land and a settled income in consideration of his loyalty. On 31 Aug. 1601 he appealed to Cecil for aid, and for some of the lands lately held by the Sugan Earl. He described himself as penniless, despised, and without the means to present himself at court. Chamberlain, writing to Carleton, 14 Nov. 1601, says that 'the young earl of Desmond died here [i.e. London] the last week' (*Letters temp. Eliz.*, Camd. Soc., 122); but it was not until 14 Jan. 1601–2 that the privy council formally announced his death, and released the persons who had accompanied him to Ireland from the charge of attendance upon him. On 17 Jan. 1601–2 one of these persons, named William Power, appealed for pecuniary assistance in behalf of the earl's four sisters, who were suffering greatly from poverty. Irish writers suggest that the earl was poisoned, but there is nothing to support the suggestion.

[Hayman and Graves's Unpublished Geraldine Documents, pt. ii. pp. 80 et seq.; Pacata Hibernia, 1633, i. cap. 14, p. 800; Gent. Mag. 1863 pt. ii. 414–25, 1864 pt. ii. 28–39; Cal. State Papers (Domestic), 1601–3, pp. 13, 134; Cal. Carew MSS. 1600–1.] S. L.

FITZGERALD, JAMES Fitzthomas, the Sugan Earl of Desmond (*d.* 1608), was the eldest son of Sir Thomas Fitzgerald, commonly called Thomas Roe or Red Thomas. Thomas Roe had been bastardised and disinherited by his father, James Fitzjohn Fitzgerald, fourteenth earl of Desmond [q. v.], and though inclined to dispute the claim of his younger brother Gerald, fifteenth earl [q. v.], to the earldom of Desmond, circumstances had proved too strong for him, and he had sunk into obscure privacy. By his wife Ellice, daughter of Richard, lord Poer, he had two sons, James and John, and a daughter, who married Donald Pipi MacCarthy Reagh. When of an age to understand his position James Fitzthomas repaired to court to petition Elizabeth for a restoration of his rights. His petition was regarded with favour, some slight encouragement held out to him, and a small yearly allowance promised him. Consequently, during the rebellion of his uncle Gerald, both he and his father remained staunch in their allegiance to the crown, and after the death of the earl and the suppression of the rebellion in 1583 they naturally looked for their restoration to the earldom. But their petitions no longer found favour at court, for Munster was to be 'planted' with Englishmen, and for ever to be made loyal to England. So matters remained until 1598, when Munster, in the words of the Irish annalists, again became 'a trembling sod.' Instigated by his brother John and by Hugh O'Neill, earl of Tyrone, James Fitzthomas assumed the title of Earl of Desmond, and before long found himself at the head of eight thousand clansmen. To the expostulations of the Earl of Ormonde he replied, on 12 Oct. 1598, by a statement of his grievances, and by an avowal of his intention, seeing he could obtain no justice, 'to maintain his right, trusting in the Almighty to further the same.' The struggle lasted for three years. But in October 1600, while withdrawing his forces from the open into the woods of Aharlow, he was surprised by Captain Greame and the garrison of Kilmallock. From that day the Geraldines never rallied again to any purpose. Dismissing his followers the earl took to the woods for safety, where, in May 1601, Sir George Carew was informed that he was living 'in the habit of a priest,' but determined 'to die rather than to depart the province, retaining still his traitorly hopes to be relieved out of Ulster or out of Spain' (*Cal. Carew MSS.* iv. 55). Carew made several attempts to procure his capture or death, but without success, for 'such is the superstitious folly of these people, as for no price he may be had, holding the same to be so heinous as no

priest will give them absolution' (*ib.* iii. 471). Eventually, on 29 May 1601, he was captured by Edmund Fitzgibbon, the White Knight [q. v.], while hiding in 'an obscure cave many fathoms underground' in the neighbourhood of Mitchelstown. He was placed in irons to prevent a rescue, 'so exceedingly beloved of all sorts' was he, and conveyed to Shandon Castle, where he was immediately arraigned and adjudged guilty of treason. For a time Carew hoped to make use of him against a still greater rebel, Hugh O'Neill; but finding him to be after all but a 'dull-spirited traitor,' he on 13 Aug. handed him over to Sir Anthony Cooke, who conveyed him to England, where, on his arrival, he was placed in the Tower. Of his life in prison there remains only the following pathetic notice: 'The demands of Sir John Peyton, Lieutenant of Her Majesty's Tower of London, for one quarter of a year, from St. Michael's day 1602 till the feast of our Lord God next. For James M'Thomas. Sayd tyme at 3*l.* per week, physicke, sourgeon, and watcher with him in his Lunacy.' He is said to have died in 1608, and to have been buried in the chapel of the Tower. He married Ellen, widow of Maurice, elder brother of Edmund, the White Knight, but had no issue.

John Fitzthomas, his brother, who had shared with him in the vicissitudes of the rebellion, and who indeed seems to have been the prime instigator of it, after his brother's capture, escaped with his wife, the daughter of Richard Comerford of Dangenmore, Kilkenny, into Spain, where he died a few years afterwards at Barcelona. His son Gerald, known as the Conde de Desmond, entered the service of the Emperor Ferdinand II, and was killed in 1632. As he left no issue, in him ended the heirs male of the four eldest sons of Thomas, eighth earl of Desmond [q. v.]

[The principal references to the life of the Sugan Earl will be found collected together in the Unpublished Geraldine Documents, edited by Hayman and Graves, pt. ii.]   R. D.

FITZGERALD, JAMES, first Duke of Leinster (1722–1773), was the second but eldest surviving son of Robert, nineteenth earl of Kildare, and head of the great family of the Geraldines, by Lady Mary O'Brien, eldest daughter of William, third earl of Inchiquin. He was born on 29 May 1722, and, after receiving his preliminary education at home, travelled on the continent from February 1737 to September 1739. In the following year he became heir-apparent to the earldom of Kildare, on the death of his elder brother, and on 17 Oct. 1741 he entered the Irish House of Commons as member for Athy, with the courtesy title of Lord Offaly. On 20 Feb. 1744 he succeeded his father as twentieth earl of Kildare, and in the rebellion of the following year he offered to raise a regiment at his own expense to serve against the Pretender. He was sworn of the Irish privy council in 1746, and on 1 Feb. 1747 he received a seat in the English House of Lords as Viscount Leinster of Taplow, Buckingham- shire, an estate belonging to his uncle, the Earl of Inchiquin. This peerage was conferred on Kildare on the occasion of his marriage with Lady Emily Lennox, second daughter of Charles, second duke of Richmond, and sister of Lady Holland, Lady Louisa Conolly, and Lady Sarah Napier, which took place on 7 Feb. 1747. Kildare after his marriage took an active part in Irish politics; he built Leinster House in Dublin, and exercised a princely hos- pitality; and from his wealth, high birth, and influential family connections, soon formed a powerful party. This party followed im- plicitly all the directions of Kildare, who pursued an intermediate policy between the radical ideas of Speaker Boyle (afterwards Earl of Shannon) [see BOYLE, HENRY, 1682– 1764] and his friends, and the ministerialists, headed by the primate, George Stone, arch- bishop of Dublin. Stone was an especial ob- ject of hatred to Kildare, who in 1754 sent a most violent protest to the king, attacking the primate's nomination to be a lord deputy during the absence of the lord-lieutenant, and declaring the inalienable right of the Irish par- liament to dispose of unappropriated sums of money when voted in excess of the ministerial demands. Stone's chief supporter, the Duke of Dorset, was at once recalled; the primate was struck out of the Irish privy council; and the Marquis of Hartington, a personal friend of Kildare's, was appointed lord-lieutenant. The Irish people, or perhaps it is more correct to say the population of Dublin, were delighted at the earl's behaviour; a medal was struck in his honour, and he remained until the day of his death one of the most popular noblemen in Ireland. He justified the confidence of the English ministry by bringing round the speaker and Richard Malone, the chancellor of the Irish exchequer, to the support of the Irish administration, and in 1756 he accepted the post of lord deputy. In 1758 he was made master-general of the ordnance in Ireland, in March 1760 he raised the Royal Irish regi- ment of artillery, of which he was appointed colonel, and on 3 March 1761 he was created Earl of Offaly and Marquis of Kildare in the peerage of Ireland. Five years later he re- ceived the final step in the peerage. There were at that time no Irish dukes, and the marquis was eager to maintain his precedence

over all Irish noblemen. The king promised that he should be created a duke whenever an English duke was made, and in compliance with this promise, when Sir Hugh Smithson- Percy, Earl Percy, was promoted to be Duke of Northumberland, Kildare was created Duke of Leinster in the peerage of Ireland on 16 March 1766. After this last promotion he began to take less part in politics, but in 1771 he drew up and signed a protest in the Irish House of Lords against the petition of the majority of the Irish parliament for the continuance of Lord Townshend in the office of lord-lieu- tenant. The duke died at Leinster House, Dublin, on 19 Nov. 1773, and was buried at Christ Church in that city. He left a large family, among whom the most notable were William Robert [q. v.], who succeeded as second duke of Leinster; Charles James, a distinguished naval officer, who was created Lord Lecale in the peerage of Ireland; Lord Henry Fitzgerald, who married Charlotte, baroness De Ros in her own right; Lord Ed- ward Fitzgerald, the rebel [q. v.]; and Lord Robert Stephen Fitzgerald, a diplomatist of some note, who was minister *ad interim* in Paris during the early years of the French revolution, and afterwards British representa- tive at Berne.

[The Marquis of Kildare's Earls of Kildare and their Ancestors from 1057 to 1773, Dublin, 1858.] H. M. S.

FITZGERALD, JAMES (1742–1835), Irish politician, descended from the family of the White Knight [see FITZGIBBON, EDMUND Fitzjohn], was younger son of William Fitz- gerald, an attorney of Ennis, and younger brother of Maurice Fitzgerald, clerk of the crown for Connaught. He was born in 1742, and educated at Trinity College, Dublin, where he greatly distinguished himself. In 1769 he was called to the Irish bar, and he soon obtained a large practice, and won a great reputation both as a sound lawyer and an eloquent pleader. From 1776 to 1783 he was member for Fore, co. Westmeath, in the Irish House of Commons; in 1783 he was elected both for Killybegs and Tulsk in Ros- common, and sat for the latter; in 1790 he was re-elected for Tulsk; and in 1797 he was chosen to represent the borough of Kil- dare in the last Irish parliament. His elo- quence soon made him as great a reputa- tion in the Irish parliament as at the Irish bar, and he was recognised as one of the leading orators in the days of Gratton and Flood. Though an eloquent speaker, Fitz- gerald was not much of a statesman; he, however, supported all the motions of the radical party, and in 1782 he made his most famous speech in proposing a certain measure of catholic relief. In that year he married Catherine, younger daughter of the Rev. Henry Vesey, who was grandson of John Vesey, archbishop of Tuam, and cousin of Lord Glentworth, ancestor of the Viscounts de Vesci. Fitzgerald never sought political office, but he eagerly accepted professional appointments, which helped him at the bar. He thus became in rapid succession third serjeant in 1779, second serjeant in 1784, and prime serjeant in 1787. In all the debates which preceded the final abolition of the independent Irish parliament Fitzgerald distinguished himself. He opposed the project of the union with all his might, and he was certainly disinterested in his cause, for in 1799 he was dismissed from his post of prime serjeant to make way for St. George Daly, who had been converted to the unionist policy. The Irish bar insisted on showing their respect for him, and continued to give him the precedence in court over the attorney-general and solicitor-general which he had held as prime serjeant. When the union was carried Fitzgerald accepted it, and he sat in the imperial parliament for Ennis from 1802 to February 1808, when he resigned the seat to his son, William Vesey Fitzgerald. He, however, was re-elected in 1812, but again resigned in January 1813, when he finally retired from politics. His name, like his son's [see FITZGERALD, WILLIAM VESEY, 1783-1843], was unfortunately mixed up in the Mary Anne Clarke scandal with the Duke of York. This son, who was thoroughly reconciled to the union, held many important political offices, and in recognition of his services his mother was created Baroness Fitzgerald and Vesey on 31 July 1826, when James Fitzgerald himself refused a peerage. James Fitzgerald died at Booterstown, near Dublin, on 20 Jan. 1835, aged 93; the baroness had predeceased him 3 Jan. 1832. His youngest son, HENRY VESEY FITZGERALD, was dean of Emly (1818–26), and dean of Kilmore from 1826 till his death, on 30 March 1860. He succeeded his eldest brother as third Lord Fitzgerald and Vesey in 1843.

[Gent. Mag. March 1835; Blue Book of the Members of the House of Commons; Blacker's Booterstown, pp. 241–3; Sir John Barrington's Memoirs of the Union; Grattan's Life of Henry Grattan; Hardy's Life of the Earl of Charlemont.]   H. M. S.

FITZGERALD, JOHN, first EARL OF KILDARE. [See FITZTHOMAS, JOHN, *d.* 1316.]

FITZGERALD, JOHN FITZEDMUND (*d.* 1589), seneschal of Imokilly, was the son of Edmund Fitzmaurice Riskard, seneschal of Imokilly and Shylie, daughter of Maolrony O'Carroll. He was a prominent actor in the two great rebellions that convulsed Munster during 1563 to 1583. In 1569, being 'a principal communicator with James Fitzmaurice,' 'arch traitor' [q. v.], he was besieged in his castle of Ballymartyr by Sir Henry Sidney; but after a stout defence, in which several of the besiegers were wounded, finding the place untenable, he 'and his company in the dead of night fled out of the house by a bog, which joins hard to the wall where no watch could have prevented their escape.' He continued to hold out with Fitzmaurice in the woods of Aharlow till February 1573, when he humbly submitted himself before Sir John Perrot in the church of Kilmallock, and was pardoned. In 1575 he accompanied Fitzmaurice to France, but returned to Ireland a few weeks afterwards. From that time till the date of Fitzmaurice's landing we hear nothing of him with the exception that on 16 Nov. 1576 he complained to the president of Munster, Sir William Drury, that the Earl of Desmond was coshering sixty horses and a hundred horse-boys on Imokilly, an incident quite sufficient to show how the wind was blowing meanwhile. Instantly on the arrival of Fitzmaurice in July 1579 he went into rebellion. An adept in all the stratagems of Irish warfare, and personally brave in carrying his schemes into execution, he became, after the death of the 'arch traitor,' the unquestionable, though not nominal, head of the rebellion. It was against him, and not the Earl of Desmond, that Ormonde mainly directed his efforts. More than once during that terrible struggle he was reported to have been slain. He was, indeed, once severely wounded and his brother killed, but he manifested no intention of submitting. In February 1581 he narrowly missed capturing Sir Walter Raleigh. In May 1583 his aged mother was taken and executed by Thomas Butler, tenth earl of Ormonde [q. v.] But it was not till 14 June, when he was reported to have not more than twenty-four swords and four horse, that he consented to recognise the hopelessness of his cause. His submission was accepted conditionally; but Ormonde, who greatly respected him for his bravery, pleaded earnestly with Burghley for his pardon. He was, he declared, a man 'valiant, wise, and true of his word.' Ever since his submission 'he and his people had been employed in order and husbandry.' Ormonde's intervention was successful so far as his life was concerned; but as for his lands, that was to be left an open question. Thirty-six thousand acres of good land, which the undertakers had come to regard as their property, were not to be surrendered by them without a struggle. He was represented as the most dangerous man in the province, as ' having more intelligence from Spain than any one else.' Their representations were not without their calculated effect on Elizabeth, who had at first been inclined to treat him leniently. Not suspecting any attack, he was in March 1587 arrested by Sir Thomas Norreys and confined to Dublin Castle, where he died in February 1589 (*Ham. Cal.* iv. 126, but cf. p. 253), a few days after it had been finally decided that he should enjoy the profit of his lands. He married Honora, daughter of James Fitzmaurice, by whom he had Edmund and Richard, seven weeks old in 1589, and two daughters, Catherine and Eleanor. His son and heir, Edmund, at the time of his father's death being a year and a half old, was found by inquisition to be heir to Ballymartyr and other lands in co. Cork, and was granted in wardship to Captain Moyle. He obtained livery of his lands on coming of age, and in 1647 defended Ballymartyr against his nephew, Lord Inchiquin, when the castle was burnt and himself outlawed.

[The principal references to Fitzgerald's life contained in the State Papers will be found in the Unpublished Geraldine Documents, edited by Hayman and Graves, pt. ii. pp. 118-36.] R. D.

FITZGERALD, Sir JOHN Fitzedmund (1528–1612), dean of Cloyne, son of Edmund Fitzjames, born in 1528, was a devoted loyalist, being almost the only gentleman of note who refused to join in the rebellion of James Fitzmaurice Fitzgerald [q. v.] in 1569, whereupon he was appointed sheriff of the county of Cork, and for his good services in that office was ' so maliced and hated of the rebels, as they not only burned all his towns and villages to the utter banishing of th' inhabitants of the same, but also robbed and spoiled and consumed all his goods and cattle, and thereby brought him from a gentleman of good ability to live to extreme poverty, not able to maintain himself and his people about him in the service of her majesty as his heart desired.' His petition for compensation was supported by Sir Henry Sidney, who declared that he well deserved the same both for the losses he had sustained as also for his honesty and civility. On the outbreak of Desmond's rebellion he again threw in his lot with the government, and was again exposed to the attacks of the rebels, insomuch that he was obliged to take refuge in Cork. In January 1581 his condition was described to Burghley as truly pitiful, and in May 1582 the queen gave order that he should receive an annuity of one hundred marks and a grant of one

hundred marks land of the escheats in Munster. In 1586 he strenuously opposed the bill for the attainder of the Earl of Desmond, and by trying to maintain the legality of the earl's feoffment almost made shipwreck in one moment of the reputation gained by a long life of loyalty. Being charged with conniving at the marriage of Florence MacCarthy (whose godfather he was) and Ellen, daughter of the Earl of Clancar, he denied it, declaring to Burghley that on the contrary he had done his best to prevent it; while, as for his action in regard to Desmond's deed of feoffment, it was with him a thing of conscience and honesty before God and the world, and not a thing desired by him. His loyalty was confirmed by Justice Smythes, who wrote that he was a gentleman ' wise and considerate in all his doings, of great learning in good arts, and approved loyalty in all times of trial, just in his dealings, and may serve for a pattern to the most of this country' (*Ham. Cal.* iv. 46).

During the rebellion of the Sugan Earl [see FITZGERALD, JAMES Fitzthomas] he more than once proved himself 'the best subject the queen had in Munster,' and in order ' to requite his perpetual loyalty to the crown of England, as also to encourage others,' Lord Mountjoy, while visiting him at Cloyne (7 March 1601), on his way from the siege of Kinsale to Dublin, knighted him. The castle of Cloyne had originally been the palace of the bishops of Cloyne. The way in which it came into the possession of Fitzgerald very well illustrates the general laxity in ecclesiastical matters prevailing during Elizabeth's reign. In order to make leases of bishops' lands valid it was necessary to have them confirmed by the dean and chapter, the church thus having, as it were, double security that its estates should not be recklessly given away. In order to obviate this difficulty Fitzgerald, though a layman, got himself appointed to the deanery of Cloyne, after which he filled the chapter with his dependents. Thereupon Matthew Shehan, bishop of Cloyne, in consideration of a fine of 40*l.*, leased out on 14 July 1575, at an annual rent of five marks for ever, the whole demesne of Cloyne to a certain Richard Fitzmaurice, one of Fitzgerald's dependents. The dean and chapter confirmed the grant, and Fitzmaurice handed over his right and title to his master. The castle, which stood at the south-east angle of the four crossways in the centre of the town of Cloyne, was repaired by Fitzgerald, and only disappeared in 1797, having been recovered for the church in 1700. He married Honor O'Brien, niece of the Earl of Thomond, by whom he had three sons: Edmund, who married the widow of John Fitzedmund Fitzgerald [q. v.], seneschal of Imokilly; Thomas (*d.* 1628), who married Honor, daughter of O'Sullivan Beare; James (o.s.p.), and two daughters, Joan and Eleanor. He died on 15 July 1612, and was buried with his ancestors in the cathedral of Cloyne. Two months later he was followed by his eldest son. 'In the N.-E. angle of the north transept of the cathedral,' says the late Rev. James Graves, 'was erected, doubtless during his lifetime, a very fine monument in the renaissance style, originally consisting of an altar-tomb, above which was reared a pillared superstructure crowned by an ornamented entablature; whilst, from the fragments still remaining, it would appear that two kneeling armed figures surmounted the first-named part of the monument.' According to the epitaph he was 'hospitio celebris, doctrina clarus et armis.'

[The principal references to Fitzgerald's life contained in the State Papers have been collected together in the Unpublished Geraldine Documents, ed. Hayman and Graves, pt. ii. He must be carefully distinguished from his relative the seneschal of Imokilly. See also the Life and Letters of Florence MacCarthy Reagh, by Daniel MacCarthy, and Dr. Brady's Clerical and Parochial Records of Cork, Cloyne, and Ross, vol. iii.]

R. D.

FITZGERALD, Sir JOHN FORSTER (1784?–1877), field marshal, colonel 18th royal Irish foot, was a younger son of Edward Fitzgerald of Carrigoran, co. Clare, who sat for that county in the Irish parliament, was a colonel of Irish volunteers in 1782, and died in 1815, by his second wife, the daughter and coheiress of Major Thomas Burton, 5th dragoon guards, and granddaughter of Right Hon. John Forster, lord chief justice of Ireland [q. v.], and consequently was younger brother of the first two baronets of Carrigoran. The date of his birth is variously given as 1784 and 1786. On 29 Oct. 1793 he was appointed ensign in Captain Shee's independent company of foot in Ireland, and became lieutenant in January 1794. In May 1794 he was given a half-pay company in the old 79th (royal Liverpool volunteers) regiment of foot, which had been disbanded before he was born. After seven years as a titular captain on the Irish half-pay list, on 31 Oct. 1800 he was brought into the 46th foot, and joined that corps, then consisting of two strong battalions of short-service soldiers, in Ireland. The regiment was much reduced by the discharge of the latter at the peace of Amiens, and young Fitzgerald was again placed on half-pay, but the year after was brought on full pay again in the newly raised New Brunswick fencibles,

in which he was senior captain and brevet major. In 1809 he was promoted major in the 60th royal Americans, afterwards known as the 60th rifles, and in 1810 became brevet lieutenant-colonel. He joined the 5th or Jäger battalion, 60th, in the Peninsula, and was present at the storming of Badajoz, where he was among the regimental commanding officers specially commended by Sir Thomas Picton (GURWOOD, *Well. Desp.* v. 379), at Salamanca, Vittoria, the Pyrenees, and many minor affairs. Part of the time he was in command of a provisional battalion of light companies, and in the Pyrenees commanded a brigade and was taken prisoner by the French, but exchanged (*ib.* vii. 237). At the end of the war he was made C.B. and received the gold cross given to commanding officers of regiments and others of higher rank who had been present in four or more general actions entitling them to a gold medal for each, which medals were replaced by the cross. He accompanied the 5th battalion, 60th, from the south of France to Ireland in 1814, and thence in 1816 to the Mediterranean. In 1818 it was brought home from Gibraltar and disbanded, Fitzgerald, then senior major, with most of the other officers and men, being transferred to the 2nd battalion, 60th, at Quebec, which then became the 1st battalion and was made rifles. Fitzgerald, who became brevet colonel in 1819, remained some years in Canada, most of the time as commandant of Quebec, and afterwards of Montreal. On 5 Feb. 1824 he exchanged with Lieutenant-colonel Bunbury to the command of the 20th foot in Bombay, which he held until promoted to major-general in 1830. He was made K.C.B. the year after. In 1838 he was appointed to a divisional command at Madras, but was afterwards transferred to Bombay, and commanded a division of the Bombay army until his promotion to lieutenant-general in November 1841. He was colonel of 85th foot (1840–3), colonel of 62nd foot in 1843, transferred to colonelcy 18th royal Irish 1850, general 1854, G.C.B. 1862, and field marshal 29 May 1875. He was liberal M.P. for Clare county from 1852 to 1857, when he was defeated.

Fitzgerald married first, in New Brunswick, in 1805, Charlotte, daughter of the Hon. Robert Hazen of St. John's, New Brunswick, by whom he had a son, John Forster Fitzgerald—killed as a captain 14th light dragoons in the second Sikh war—and two daughters. He married secondly, in 1839, Jean, daughter of Hon. Donald Ogilvy of Clova, formerly of the Madras army, and afterwards colonel Forfarshire militia (see

DEBRETT, *Peerage*, under ' Earl of Airlie '), and by her had a family.

Fitzgerald, who some short time before had been received into the Roman catholic communion, died at Tours on 24 March 1877, being at the time the oldest officer in the British army. By order of the French minister of war, the garrison of Tours paid him the funeral honours prescribed for a marshal of France.

[Foster's Baronetage, under 'Fitzgerald of Carrigoran;' Debrett's Peerage, under 'Cunningham' and 'Airlie;' Wallace's Chronicle King's Royal Rifles (London, 1879); Times, 4 April 1877. The records of the old 5th or Jäger battalion, 60th, with which Fitzgerald served in the Peninsula, were arranged by the late Major-general Gibbes Rigaud, and have been published in the 'Maltese Cross,' the regimental newspaper of the 1st battalion king's royal rifles, in 1886–7.]

H. M. C.

FITZGERALD, KATHERINE (*d.* 1604), the 'old' COUNTESS OF DESMOND, was daughter of Sir John Fitzgerald, lord of Decies, and became the second wife of Thomas Fitzgerald, twelfth earl of Desmond, some time after 1505. The first wife of the earl was Sheela, daughter of Cormac Mac-Carthy. To her (under the equivalent name of Gilis ny Cormyk), as 'wife to Sir Thomas of Desmond,' on 9 June 20 Henry VII, i.e. 1505, Gerald (son of Thomas) Fitzgerald, eighth earl of Kildare, granted a lease of lands for five years, a copy of which is preserved in the rental-book of the ninth earl, now in the possession of the Duke of Leinster. On its first discovery it was supposed by some to be dated 20 Henry VIII, i.e. 1528; but the earlier date is shown to be correct not only by a facsimile given in the 'Journal of the Kilkenny Archæological Society,' but also by the fact (unnoticed by those who have commented on the document) that the Earl of Kildare who granted it died in 1513. The Earl of Desmond who was the husband of Sheela and Katherine died in 1534, at the age of eighty. As he left a daughter by his second wife, it may safely be assumed that 1524 is the latest date at which his marriage to her could have taken place, while, as we have seen, 1506 is the earliest. The tradition, therefore, preserved by Sir Walter Raleigh, to which Horace Walpole gave its popular currency, that this second wife was married in the time of Edward IV, is at once disposed of; but it may very probably be true of her predecessor. In the same way the further tradition of her having danced with Richard III may be accounted for. Mr. Sainthill, in his 'Inquiry,' referred to at the end of this article, endea-

voured to support these traditions by the theory that Thomas of Desmond might have divorced his first wife and married his second long before 1505, but this was a mere suggestion, opposed to such evidence as exists. That the 'old countess' was living in 1589, 'and many years since,' is asserted by Sir W. Raleigh in his ' History of the World' (bk. i. ch. 5, § 5); and he had good reason for knowing the truth of this, inasmuch as in that year and in the year preceding he granted leases of lands in Cork at a reduced rent pending the life of 'the ladie Cattelyn, old countess dowager of Desmond,' who had some life-interest in them. It appears from the terms of these leases that her life was not supposed to be likely to last more than five years from their date. That her death occurred in 1604 is stated in a manuscript of Sir George Carew's, preserved in Lambeth Library (No. 626). From these data it follows that, at the lowest computation, she can hardly have been less than 104 years old at the time of her decease; and it has been thought by some that the traditional 140 may possibly have had its rise in an accidental transposition of these figures. It is in Fynes Morison's 'Itinerary,' published in 1617, that the number 140 is first given. He visited Youghal, near which the Castle of Inchiquin, in which the countess resided, is situated, in 1613, and states that 'in our time' she had lived to the age of 'about' 140 years, and was able in her last years to go on foot three or four miles weekly to the market town, and that only a few years before her death all her teeth were renewed. From him Bacon appears to have derived the notices which he gives in his 'Hist. Vitæ et Mortis' and his 'Sylva;' and from Bacon and Raleigh, and a Desmond pedigree, Archbishop Ussher makes mention of the countess in his 'Chronologia Sacra,' where he says that 'meo tempore' she was both living and lively. A diary kept by the Earl of Leicester some thirty years later also records the stories which he had heard. One additional and original witness has, however, been recently found, not known to previous writers on the subject, whose evidence corroborates the general account. Sir John Harington, who was twice for some time in Ireland, for the first time soon after 1584, and for the second time in 1599, speaking in 1605 of the wholesomeness of the country, says: 'Where a man hath lived above 140 year, a woman, and she a countess, above 120, the country is like to be helthy.' Of the case of the man whom he mentions nothing is known, but his allusion to the case of the countess evidently implies that her story, as well as that of the former, was then a familiar one. On the whole, it may be concluded that the countess reached at least the age of 104, and that, until some further evidence, such as the date of her marriage, be forthcoming, it may further reasonably be conjectured that the addition of ten years would very probably be a nearer approximation to the truth. The stories of her death being caused by a fall from an apple, a walnut, or a cherry tree, may be dismissed as fictions; while that of her journey to London to beg relief from Queen Elizabeth or James I has been shown by Mr. Sainthill to belong to the Countess Elinor, widow of Gerald, the fifteenth and attainted earl of Desmond. Nine or ten portraits of the old countess are said to be in existence; but only two of these, respectively at Muckross Abbey and Dupplin Castle, with possibly a third at Chatsworth, are supposed to represent her, the others being pictures of other persons by Rembrandt and Gerard Douw.

[Article in the Quarterly Review for March 1853, pp. 329–54; Archd. A. B. Rowan's Olde Countesse of Desmonde, 1860; Richard Sainthill's Old Countess of Desmond, an Inquiry, 2 vols. (privately printed), 1861–3; article (by J. Gough Nichols) in the Dublin Review, 1862, li. 51–91; Journal of the Kilkenny Archæol. Soc., new ser. iv. 111, 1864; W. J. Thoms's Longevity of Man, 1879; Sir J. Harington's Short View of the State of Ireland, 1879, p. 10; see also Notes and Queries, 2nd ser. vii. 313, 365, 431, 3rd ser. i. 301, 377, 5th ser. xi. 192, 332.] W. D. M.

FITZGERALD, MAURICE (*d.* 1176), an English conqueror of Ireland, was the son of Nesta, daughter of Rhys the Great, king of South Wales (*Exp. Hib.* p. 229), and thus half-brother to Robert Fitzstephen [q. v.], uncle of Meiler Fitzhenry [q. v.], and brother of David II [q. v.], bishop of St. David's (*ib.*; GIRALD. *Itin. Cambr.* p. 130; *Earls of Kildare*, p. 3). His father Gerald, according to later genealogists, was grandson of Walter Fitzother, who figures in 'Domesday' as a tenant at Windsor and elsewhere, and lord of manors in Surrey, Hampshire, Berkshire, Middlesex, and Buckinghamshire. In the early years of the twelfth century his father was steward of Pembroke Castle. He was probably dead by 1136, in which year the Welsh annals show that Nesta's second husband, Stephen, and the 'sons of Gerald' were fighting against the Welsh prince, Owen (*Domesday*, 30 *a* 1, 36 *a* 1, 61 *b* 1, 130 *a* 1, 151 *a* 1; *Ann. Cambr.* pp. 30, 34, 40). In 1168, when Dermot, king of Leinster, was in South Wales seeking for aid to reestablish himself in his kingdom, Rhys ap Griffith had just released his three-year prisoner, Robert Fitzstephen, on condition

that he should help him against Henry II. Robert's half-brother, Maurice Fitzgerald, now petitioned that he might carry his kinsman to Ireland instead; for Dermot had promised to give the two knights Wexford and the two adjoining 'cantreds' in return for their services (*Exp. Hib.* p. 229; *Ann. Cambr.* p. 50). Robert crossed at once (May 1169), but Maurice did not land till some months later, when he reached Wexford with 140 followers. Here Dermot came to meet him, and led him to his royal city of Ferns. In the expedition against Dublin, Maurice commanded the English contingent, while Robert Fitzstephen stayed behind to fortify the rock of Carrick, near Wexford (*Exp. Hib.* pp. 229, 233, 245; REGAN, p. 56; cf. *Ann. Cambr.* p. 52; *Annals of the Four Masters*, sub 1169, 1170; *Annals of Boyle*, p. 28). Dermot had already fulfilled his promise as regards Wexford, and when the Earl of Clare did not come according to his engagement, he offered his daughter, with the succession to the kingdom, to Robert or Maurice, an offer which both declined on the plea that they were already married (*Exp. Hib.* p. 246). Earl Richard at last landed at Waterford, 24 Aug. 1170. The town was taken next day, Maurice and Robert arriving with Dermot in time to save the lives of the nobler captives (*ib.* p. 255).

Next year Maurice was present at the great siege of Dublin. His anxiety for the safety of his half-brother Robert, whom the Irish of Wexford were besieging in the turf fort of Carrick, led him to propose the famous sally from the city, when some ninety Norman knights routed King Roderic's army of thirty thousand men. Though the English started southwards on the day after the victory, they were too late to relieve Robert Fitzstephen, who had surrendered on receiving false news as to the fall of Dublin (*ib.* p. 266, &c.)

Henry II's arrival seems to have brought the temporary downfall of the Geraldines. The men of Wexford attempted to curry favour with the king by giving him their prisoner; and, though Robert was soon set free, he and Maurice were seemingly deprived of Wexford and the neighbouring cantreds (*ib.* p. 278). Henry kept Wexford in his own hands, entrusting it to William Fitzaldhelm before he left the country, but now, or a little later, Earl Richard gave Maurice 'the middle cantred of Ophelan,' i.e. the district about Naas in Kildare (*ib.* pp. 286, 314; REGAN, pp. 146–7). On leaving Dublin, Henry charged the two brothers, at the head of twenty knights, to support the new governor of this city, Hugh de Lacy; and it must have been shortly after this that Maurice, forewarned by his nephew's dream, saved his leader's life from the ambush set for his destruction at his interview with O'Rourke, the 'rex monoculus' of Meath (*Exp. Hib.* pp. 286, 292-4).

The remainder of Maurice's life is obscure. During the great rebellion of the young princes (1173-4) Henry had to withdraw the greater part of his own retainers from Ireland; but there seems to be no evidence that Maurice accompanied his half-brother Robert to the king's assistance in England and Normandy. When Earl Richard was restored to power, an attempt was made to consolidate the English interests by a system of intermarriage. It was now that Maurice's daughter Nesta wedded Hervey of Mountmaurice, the great enemy of the Irish Geraldines; while Maurice's son took Earl Richard's daughter, Alina, to wife. This alliance procured a grant of Wicklow Castle and the restoration of Naas, which had seemingly been confiscated, but which was henceforward held as a fief of the earl. The rest of Ophelan in North Kildare was divided between Maurice's kinsmen, Robert Fitzstephen and Meiler Fitzhenry (*ib.* p. 314; REGAN, pp. 146-7).

Some three years later, Maurice Fitzgerald died at Wexford (*c.* 1 Sept. 1176), 'not leaving a better man in Ireland.' The death of Earl Richard and the appointment of William Fitzaldhelm as governor caused the momentary downfall of the Geraldines, who soon forced Maurice's sons to give up Wicklow Castle in exchange for Ferns (*Exp. Hib.* pp. 336-7).

Giraldus Cambrensis has described Maurice's personal appearance and his character. His face was somewhat highly coloured but comely, his height moderate, 'neither too short nor too tall,' and his body well proportioned. In bravery no one surpassed him, and as a soldier he struck the happy mean between rashness and over-caution. He was sober, modest, and chaste, trustworthy, staunch, and faithful; 'a man not, it is true, free from every fault, but not guilty of any rank offence.' He was little given to talk, but when he did speak it was to the point. It would seem that when he crossed over to Ireland he was fairly advanced in life, since the same author applies to him the epithets 'venerabilis et venerandus' (*ib.* p. 297). He was buried in the Grey Friars monastery outside Wexford, where, in Hooker's days (1586), his ruined monument was still to be seen 'wanting some good and worthy man to restore so worthy a monument of so worthy a knight' (HOLINSHED, vi. 198).

Maurice Fitzgerald left several sons and a daughter, Nesta. His wife is said to have been Alice, granddaughter of Roger de Mont-gomery, who led the centre of the Norman army at Hastings (*Earls of Kildare*, p. 10). She was living in 1171, as Giraldus tells us that she and some of Maurice's children were with Fitzstephen when the Irish were laying siege to Carrick (*Exp. Hib.* p. 266). Of his sons two, Gerald (*d.* 1204) [q. v.] and Alexander, greatly distinguished themselves in the sally from Dublin (*ib.* pp. 268-9). Alexander seems to have left no issue (*Nat. MSS. of Ireland*, pp. 125-6), and Gerald, 'a man small of stature, but of no mean valour and integrity,' succeeded to his father's estates, and became, through his heir, Maurice Fitzgerald II [q. v.], the ancestor of the Fitzgeralds of Offaly and Kildare (*Exp. Hib.* p. 354). Nesta married Hervey of Mountmaurice; William, another son, must have died before, or not long after his father, as he can hardly be the William Fitzmaurice who died about 1247 A.D. (SWEETMAN, i. No. 2903, cf. Nos. 89, 94). The Irish genealogists, however, make him succeed his father in Naas, but die without a son. They also assign Maurice another son, Thomas the Great, who, marrying Eleanor, daughter of Sir William Morrie, acquired extensive property in Munster, and became the ancestor of the earls of Desmond, the White Knight, the Knight of Kerry, &c. (*Earls of Kildare*, p. 10). A Thomas Fitzmaurice (*d.* 1210-1215) appears not unfrequently in the Irish rolls (SWEETMAN, i. Nos. 406, 529; cf. *Earls of Kildare*, p. 10, where his death is assigned to 1213) [see FITZTHOMAS, MAURICE, first EARL OF DESMOND].

[Giraldus Cambrensis, Expugnatio Hibernica, ed. Dimock (Rolls Series, vol. v.); Anglo-Norman poem on the Conquest of Ireland, ed. Thomas Wright, London, 1841, cited as Regan; Annales Cambriæ, ed. Williams ab Ithel (Rolls Series); Annals of the Four Masters, ed. O'Donovan; The Earls of Kildare and their Ancestors, by the Marquis of Kildare (Dublin, 1858), represents the popular genealogy, &c., of the Geraldine family at the time the book was written. See also Sir William Bethel's Pedigree of the Fitzgeralds, printed in the Journal of the Hist. and Archæolog. Society of Ireland for 1868-9 (3rd ser. vol. i.); Holinshed, ed. 1808; Calendar of Documents relating to Ireland, ed. Sweetman, vol. i.; Sweetman's Cal. of Documents, vol. i.; Annals of Boyle, ap O'Conor, vol. ii.; Nat. MSS. of Ireland, ed. Gilbert.] T. A. A.

FITZGERALD, MAURICE II, BARON OF OFFALY (1194?-1257), justiciar of Ireland, was born about 1194 (SWEETMAN, i. 91, 118). His father, Gerald (*d.* 1204) [q. v.], through whom he was grandson of the great Irish 'conquistador,' Maurice Fitzgerald [q. v.], died towards the end of 1203 (*ib.* No. 195). His mother is said to have been 'Catherine, daughter of Hamo de Valois, lord justice of Ireland in 1197' (*Earls of Kildare*, p. 11; LODGE, i. 59). Though ordered seisin of his father's lands on 5 July 1215, he had not entered into full possession on 19 July 1215, by which time he was already a knight. In December 1226 he was engaged in a lawsuit with the Irish justiciar, Geoffry de Mariscis. In 1232 he was himself appointed to this office (2 Sept.), in succession to Richard Burke, the head of the great house, which for over a century was to be the most powerful rival of the Fitzgeralds (SWEETMAN, Nos. 793, 1458, 1977).

These were the days of popular discontent against Peter des Roches and the foreign favourites. Maurice, though a vassal of the great constitutional leader, Richard the Earl Marshal, laid waste the earl's Irish lands at the instigation of the king or his councillors. The earl crossed the Channel, induced, so ran the scandal of the day, by forged letters to which Maurice had attached the royal seal. The justiciar, at a conference held on the Curragh of Kildare, offered such terms that the earl preferred battle, though he had but fifteen knights against a hundred and fifty. A desperate attempt on the justiciar's life failed. Earl Richard was defeated, and carried to his own castle at Kildare, then in Maurice's hands (1 April 1234). He died a fortnight later of his wounds, aggravated, says Roger of Wendover, by a physician hired for this purpose by Maurice the justiciar, who was summoned to England to defend his honour. The Archbishop of Canterbury became surety for his safety (24 July), but a reconciliation at Marlborough (21 Sept. 1234) with the new Earl Gilbert was only apparent. Next year the feud was further embittered by the murder, attributed to Earl Gilbert, of Henry Clement, who represented the accused Irish nobles in London. The two barons were not reconciled till the summer of 1240, when Maurice Fitzgerald, hearing that the earl had made his peace with the king, came to London offering to prove his innocence by the judgment of his peers. At Henry's intercession, Gilbert Marshal reluctantly accepted this declaration. Maurice engaged to found a monastery for the soul of the dead man, and in acquittance of his vow is said to have founded the Dominican abbey at Sligo. Matthew Paris's words, when chronicling his death, show that his innocence was never believed (MATT. PARIS, iii. 265-6, 273-6, 327, iv. 56-7, v. 62; *Annals of the Four Masters*, ii. 272-3; *Loch Cé*, p. 319; SWEETMAN, i. 313, 317, 374; *Earls of Kildare*, p. 12; *Oseney Annals*, p. 78; WYKES, p. 78; *Royal Letters*, i. 448, 470, 480; cf. art. BURGH, RICHARD DE, *d.* 1243).

Roderic O'Conor (*d.* 1198), king of Connaught, had been succeeded by his brother, Cathal Crobdherg (*d.* 28 May 1224). On Cathal's death the succession was disputed between the sons of Roderic O'Conor, Turlough and Ædh, and those of Cathal, Ædh, and Felim. After various changes of fortune, in which Richard de Burgh, made justiciar of Ireland 13 Feb. 1228, played a great part, Ædh O'Conor was placed on the throne in 1232. Before the end of 1233 he was displaced by Felim, who destroyed the castles built by Richard de Burgh. In 1235 Maurice and Richard led an army to ravage Connaught, but turned aside to attack Donnchadh O'Briain, prince of Munster. Felim was driven off to O'Domhnaill, while Maurice the justiciar was mustering the spoil at Ardcarna, launching his fleet on the eastern Atlantic, and storming the rock of Loch Cé. The expedition closed when Felim made peace with the justiciar, and was granted the five 'king's cantreds.' Next year Maurice banished Felim again, and supplanted him by his cousin, Brian O'Conor. A great victory at Druimraithe restored Felim to the throne; he once more received the 'king's cantreds' (1237) (*Loch Cé*, pp. 203-347; *Annals of Boyle*, p. 44; *Ann. Four Masters*, sub an.)

In 1238 Maurice was warring in Ulster. With Hugh de Lacy he deposed Domhnall MacLochlainn (*d.* 1241) from his lordship over the Cenel Eoghain, and Cenel-Conaill in favour of Brian, son of Ædh O'Neill. Domhnall recovered his office next year and maintained it, despite the justiciar's efforts, till his death in 1241. Meanwhile Felim, who had long been suffering from the depredations of the De Burghs, appealed to Henry III for protection. At London (1240) his request was granted, and he returned with orders that Maurice should see that he had justice. Next year Maurice and Felim forced Maelsechlainn O'Domhnaill and the Cenel-Conaill to give hostages. In 1246 he was again in Tir-Conaill, half of which he now gave to Cormac O'Conor. Maelsechlainn renewed his hostages for the other half, but on All Saints' day took his revenge by burning the town near Maurice's castle of Sligo. In 1247 he led an army as far as Sligo and Assaroe (on the Erne), and his retreat was cut off by Maelsechlainn with the Cenel-Conaill and Cenel-Eoghain (3 July). Maurice, by a skilful manœuvre, won a great victory, in which Maelsechlainn was slain (*Loch Cé*; *Ann. Four Masters*).

During the years of his office Maurice had been largely occupied in the attempt to supply Henry III with funds. His salary as justiciar was 500*l.* a year; but he seems to have left office in debt. In 1233 he was ordered to seize Miloc Castle from Richard de Burgh, and distrain for this noble's debts to the king (February 1234), and was afterwards empowered to take further measures (*Royal Letters*, i. 410–14). In May 1237 he was bidden to let the earl's friends buy their pardon. The marriage of Henry's sister, Isabella, to the emperor Frederic II brought with it fresh demands, and Maurice was expected to wring a scutage of two marks and a thirtieth from his Irish subjects. He was granted safe-conducts to England in May and July 1234, as well as in 1237 and 1242. He seems to have actually been in England late in 1234 or early in 1235, and perhaps in 1244. He was ordered to provide men, money, provisions, and galleys for the Gascon expedition of 1242. In January 1245 he was bidden to build four wooden towers for the expedition against Wales (SWEETMAN, i. 302, 304, 313, &c.; GRACE, p. 31). Accompanied by Felim he took a part in this war, in which he seems to have incurred the king's displeasure by putting some of his Irish followers to death in Anglesey. In 1237 the king sent over a commissioner to audit his accounts, and on 4 Nov. 1245 he resigned his office to John Fitzgeoffrey, the son of a previous justiciar (SWEETMAN, i. 408, 440, &c.; GRACE, p. 31; CAMPION, pp. 76–7; HANMER, p. 191, &c.) Matters were finally compromised by the infliction of a fine of four hundred marks (2 July 1248). This fine Maurice was at first permitted to pay off by instalments; later the payments were respited (29 April 1250), and finally (10 June 1251) in a great measure remitted (September 1252). In August 1248 Maurice had gone to Gascony on the king's service. In December 1253 he was again summoned to Gascony to take part in the meditated war with the king of Castile. A later brief seems, however, to show that the new justiciar crossed the sea (*Loch Cé*, p. 405), leaving Maurice as his deputy in Ireland (SWEETMAN, vol. i. Nos. 305–7, 356–7).

Meanwhile, though no longer justiciar, he had been equally active in Ireland. In 1248 he expelled Roderic O'Canannan from Tir-Conaill. Next year he invaded Connaught to avenge the death of Gerald Mac Feorais, and a little later led an expedition from Munster and Connaught to meet another under the justiciar at Elphin. The united armies deposed Felim O'Conor, setting up his nephew Turlough in his place. Felim was restored by Brian O'Neill and the Cenel-Eoghain in 1250. In the same year, probably in return for Brian's interference in Connaught, Maurice invaded the land of the Cenel-Eoghain, but failed to reduce its lord. In 1253 he made

another futile attack upon Brian O'Neill and the Cenel-Eoghain, and two years later he crossed over 'to meet the king of the Saxons' at about the same time as Felim's envoys. The 'Four Masters' represent him as in 1257 accompanying the new lord justice against Godfrey O'Domhnaill, and distinguished himself in a single combat with Godfrey. Matthew Paris, however, seems to put Maurice's death in the beginning of 1257, whereas the 'Irish Annals' date Godfrey's death, which was due to wounds received in this expedition, in 1258. The State Papers show conclusively that he was alive on 8 Nov. 1256, but dead by Christmas 1257 (*Loch Cé*; *Ann. Four Masters*; MATT. PARIS, v. 642; SWEETMAN, ii. 524, 563; cf. DOWLING, p. 15).

Fitzgerald had served the king long and faithfully. In 1255 Henry wrote to thank him for his strenuous defence of the country. As justiciar he was vigorously engaged in fortifying castles against the Irish; by 2 Nov. 1236 he had already fortified three, and was bidden to build two more in the coming summer. For their construction he was allowed to draft workmen from Kent (*Royal Letters*, i. 400; SWEETMAN, p. 352, &c.) On Richard de Burgh's resignation he was empowered to take over all the royal castles, even including the great stronghold of Miloc. When the same noble died his castles were put in Maurice's charge (23 Aug. 1243), and ten years later (3 Aug. 1253) Richard's son, Walter, brought an assize 'mort d'ancestor' against the warden. His deposition from the justiciarship was due to his remissness on the Welsh expedition of 1245; but, adds the chronicler, he bore the disgrace patiently, as since his son's death he had learned to despise the honours of earth (SWEETMAN; MATT. PARIS, iv. 488). In character Maurice was 'miles strenuus et facetus nulli secundus.' 'He lived nobly all his life.' His piety may be seen from his religious foundations: Sligo (Dominican), Ardfert (Franciscan, 1253), and Youghal (Franciscan, 1224) (MATT. PARIS, v. 642; *Loch Cé*; *Ann. Four Masters*, sub an.; *Earls of Kildare*). In 1235, when his soldiers were laying Connaught waste, Maurice protected the canons of Trinity on the island of Loch Cé. Later he presented (1242) the hospital of Sligo to the same foundation (*Loch Cé*, pp. 329, 359), and, according to Clyn (p. 8), he died in the habit of a Franciscan.

Fitzgerald is reckoned the second or third baron of Offaly. This barony he held of the Earl of Pembroke (to whom on 30 May 1240 he was ordered to do homage) or of his heirs. He appears as Lord of Maynooth and Gallos in Decies. According to the later genealogists

(*Earls of Kildare*, p. 15) Fitzgerald's wife was Juliana, daughter of John de Cogan. His eldest son seems to have been Gerald, who predeceased him probably in 1243, and had a son Maurice, who is noticed below. The justiciar's eldest surviving son was Maurice Fitzmaurice [q. v.] (Sweetman, vol. ii. No. 563). Another was probably Thomas MacMaurice (*d.* 1271, cf. *Loch Cé*, p. 469), father of John Fitzthomas, the first earl of Kildare [q. v.]. Robert Fitzmaurice, who figures so frequently in the Irish documents of the latter half of the thirteenth century, may possibly have been another son.

Maurice Fitzgerald (*d.* 1268), son of Gerald, the eldest son, inherited the barony of Offaly (Sweetman, vol. ii.) He married Agnes, daughter of William de Valence, uncle of Edward I, and appears to have been drowned in crossing between England and Ireland, 28 July 1268 (Clyn, p. 9; *Annals of Ireland*, ii. 290, 316; *Loch Cé*, p. 459; *Ann. Four Masters*, ii. 404). He must be distinguished from his uncle Maurice Fitzmaurice Fitzgerald (*d.* 1277) [q. v.] He left an infant heir, Gerald Fitzmaurice, aged three and a half years (Sweetman, Nos. 1106, 2163, p. 467, &c.; *Book of Howth*, p. 324; Dugdale, i. 776). This child was the ward of Thomas de Clare, brother to the Earl of Gloucester, and, by purchase, of William de Valence. In 1285 he, as baron of Offaly in succession to his father, was attacked by the native Irish of the barony. We find this Gerald Fitzmaurice coming of age about 1286 (Sweetman, vol. ii. Nos. 866-7, 957, 970, 1039, &c.; vol. iii. Nos. 29, 238, 456, p. 75, &c.; *Abbrev. Plac.* pp. 263, 283), and it is probably he to whom Clyn refers (p. 10) in his crucial passage on the Geraldine succession where he says that 'Gerald, filius Mauricii, capitaneus Geraldinorum' died in 1287 and left his inheritance to his grand-uncle's son John Fitzthomas [q. v.] Some genealogists contend that Gerald Fitzmaurice was son of Maurice Fitzmaurice Fitzgerald (*d.* 1277) [q. v.], the justiciar. But he was clearly that justiciar's grand-nephew.

[The principal authorities for the life of Maurice Fitzgerald are the English State Documents and the contemporary English chroniclers. The Irish documents may be found in Sweetman's Calendar of Irish Documents, vols. i. and ii. (Rolls Series); Rymer's Fœdera, ed. 1720, vol. i. The chief contemporary English chroniclers are Roger of Wendover, ed. Coxe (Engl. Hist. Soc.); Matthew Paris, ed. Luard, vols. iii. iv. v. (Rolls Series); Thomas Wykes, the Oseney Annals, the Dunstable Annals, ap. Riley's Annales Monastici (Rolls Series), vols. iii. iv. Other important contemporary documents are to be found in the Royal Letters, ed. Shirley, vol. i. (Rolls Series); Documents of the Anglo-Normans in Ireland, ed. Gilbert, vol. i. (Rolls Series). The chief Irish Annals are the Annals of Loch Cé (Rolls Series), vol. i. ed. Hennessy; Annals of Boyle ap. O'Conor's Scriptores Rerum Hibernicarum, vol. ii.; and the collection known as the Annals of the Four Masters, ed. O'Donovan, vol. ii. Then come the Latin-writing Irish chroniclers: Clyn (*fl.* 1348) (Irish Archæol. Soc.), ed. R. Butler; a fourteenth-century Annales Hiberniæ, with its fifteenth-century continuation and expansion, both cited above as Annals of Ireland, ap. Chartulary of St. Mary's, Dublin, ed. Gilbert, vol. ii. (Rolls Series); the Annals of Jas. Grace (*fl.* 1537) (Irish Arch. Soc.), ed. Butler. Hanmer's Chronicle of Ireland (*c.* 1571) and Campion's History of Ireland (1633) may be found reprinted in the Ancient Irish Histories (Dublin, 1809), but are very untrustworthy, as also are Ware's Annals (English edition, 1705); and Cox's Hibernia Anglicana (ed. 1689). The Earls of Kildare, by the Marquis of Kildare (Dublin, 1857), represents the current genealogy of the Fitzgeralds, and is a careful compilation of facts. See, too, Lodge's Peerage of Ireland, ed. Archdall, 1789, vol. i.; Gilbert's Viceroys of Ireland (Dublin, 1865); and Archdall's Monasticon Hibernicum (editions 1786 and 1873). See also the Book of Howth, ed. Brewer and Bullen, and Hist. and Municipal Documents of Ireland, ed. Gilbert (Rolls Series).] T. A. A.

FITZGERALD, MAURICE Fitzmaurice (1238?–1277?), justiciar of Ireland, was the son and heir of Maurice Fitzgerald (*d.* 1257) [q. v.], the justiciar (Sweetman, vol. ii. No. 563). His mother is said to have been Juliana de Cogan (*Earls of Kildare*, p. 15). Being still a minor at his father's death he was claimed as the ward of Margaret de Quinci, countess of Lincoln, the widow of Walter Marshall, of whom the elder Maurice had held the barony of Offaly (Sweetman, vol. ii. No. 563; Doyle, ii. 376, iii. 7; Dugdale, i. 102, 607). He had perhaps come of age two years later (7 Nov. 1259), when he was granted Athlone Castle and the shrievalty of Connaught (Sweetman, vol. ii. No. 631). Next year he was defeated in an expedition against Conor O'Brian at Coill-Berrain in Munster, but succeeded in plundering the O'Donnells, who retaliated on Cairpre (Carbery, co. Sligo) in North Ireland (*Loch Cé*, pp. 435-7; *Ann. Four Masters*, sub an.) He led another expedition against Brian Ruadh O'Brien in 1272 or 1273. For the expenses of this campaign he received a hundred marks; and it was perhaps on this occasion that he borrowed from the Dublin citizens the 86*l.* 19*s.* which they asked the king to repay in June 1275. This expedition of 1273 was a success, and, according to the Irish annals, Maurice 'took hostages and obtained sway over the O'Briens' (Sweetman,

ii. 170, No. 1139; *Loch Cé*, p. 473). He is said on this occasion to have been aided by Theobald Butler (WARE, from *Earls of Kildare*, p. 16; but cf. WARE, ed. 1705, pp. 57–8).

Fitzgerald was summoned to England in 1262, and in 1264 was ordered to secure for the young Earl of Gloucester seisin of his Irish lands. The new justiciar, Richard de Rochelle (1261–*c.* May 1265), was at feud with the Geraldines, and within a short time the island was in arms (DOWLING, p. 16; CAMPION, p. 77; GRACE, p. 37; HANMER, ii. 401–402; CLYN, p. 8; *Earls of Kildare*, p. 16). The quarrel extended to the De Burghs, and in 1264 Maurice took the justiciar Theobald Butler and John Cogan prisoners, and incarcerated the former at his castle of Leigh (*Annals of Ireland*, ii. 290; GRACE, p. 37; *Book of Howth*, p. 323). With the justiciar it is said that Walter de Burgh, earl of Ulster, was also taken (*Earls of Kildare*, p. 16). But this statement seems due to a confusion with the reported action in 1294 of Fitzgerald's nephew, John Fitzthomas, first earl of Kildare [q. v.]. Next year he and his nephew, Maurice Fitzgerald [see FITZGERALD, MAURICE, *d.* 1257, *ad fin.*], on whose behalf the feud with the De Burghs may have originated, received royal letters exhorting them to peace; in April 1266 he was twice granted letters of protection to England (SWEETMAN, Nos. 727, 795, 798). About August 1272 he was appointed justiciar of Ireland in the place of James Audeley. On Henry III's death he was renewed in the office and received the oaths of succession from the Irish nobles to the new king. About August 1273 he was supplanted by Geoffrey de Geneville (*ib.* vol. ii. Nos. 924, 927, &c.; RYMER, ii. 2). According to the Earl of Kildare, quoting from Ware, in 1273 'he invaded Offaly, but was betrayed by his own people into the hands of the O'Conors' (*Earls of Kildare*, p. 16, but cf. WARE, p. 57). With this may be connected a later statement that about 23 Aug. 1273 he was deprived of part of the barony of Offaly. But this story seems altogether erroneous. Fitzmaurice, although often reckoned one of the Barons Offaly, never held the barony, which passed on his father's death in 1257 to his nephew (son of his elder brother Gerald) Maurice (*d.* 1268), and thence to Maurice's son Gerald Fitzmaurice. The latter Gerald was attacked by the native Irish in 1285, and it is probably this incident which has found its way disguisedly into our Fitzmaurice's biography [see FITZGERALD, MAURICE, *d.* 1257? *ad fin.*] An entry in the Irish treasury accounts of 1276–7 shows that he led an expedition to Glendory (Glenmalure, co.

Wicklow). On 24 July 1276 he was ordered to England to do fealty for his wife's inheritance (SWEETMAN, ii. 258, Nos. 1249, 1321–2; cf. CLYN, p. 9; Cox, p. 73). Later in the same year (1277) he accompanied his son-in-law against Brian Ruadh O'Brien, king of Thomond. Brian was taken prisoner and beheaded; but a little later the two kinsmen were besieged in Slow-Banny, and reduced to such straits that they had to give hostages for their lives and yield up the castle of Roscommon (HANMER, ii. 406; WARE, p. 58; Cox, p. 73; *Earls of Kildare*, pp. 16, 17; cf. *Loch Cé*, i. 481; *Annals of Ireland*, p. 318). Maurice is said to have died shortly after (1277) at Ross (*Earls of Kildare*, p. 17; cf. SWEETMAN, vol. ii. No. 1527).

Maurice Fitzmaurice married Emelina, daughter and heiress of Emelina de Riddlesford, the wife of Hugh de Lacy (*d.* 1242), and Stephen Longsword (*Abbrev. Plac.* p. 227; SWEETMAN, vol. ii. No. 1028; DUGDALE, *Monast.* vi. 443; MATT. PARIS, iv. 232). This Emelina was probably born *c.* 1252 A.D. (*Cal. Gen.* i. 236). He is wrongly said to have been succeeded by a son Gerald Fitzmaurice, an assertion due to a confusion noted under MAURICE FITZGERALD (*d.* 1257?) (*Earls of Kildare*, p. 18; SAINTHILL, ii. 47; cf. CLYN, p. 10). He left two daughters: (1) Juliana, who married Thomas de Clare (*d.* 1286), brother of Gilbert de Clare, earl of Gloucester, and, secondly, Adam de Cretinge (*Cal. Gen.* i. 448, ii. 431; SWEETMAN, vol. ii. No. 2210, vol. iii. Nos. 940, 1142; CLYN, p. 40); (2) Amabilia, who seems to have died unmarried, and to have enfeoffed her cousin, John Fitzthomas [q. v.], of part of her estates (SWEETMAN, vol. iii. No. 940; *Earls of Kildare*, p. 17).

In the complicated genealogy of the Geraldines, some of the entries ascribed to this Maurice Fitzmaurice properly belong to his nephew MAURICE FITZGERALD (*d.* 1268), who is noticed under MAURICE FITZGERALD II (1194?–1257).

[See authorities cited in text. For editions and value of the various chroniclers see MAURICE FITZGERALD II.] T. A. A.

FITZGERALD, MAURICE, first EARL OF DESMOND. [See FITZTHOMAS, MAURICE, *d.* 1356.]

FITZGERALD, MAURICE, fourth EARL OF KILDARE (1318–1390), justiciar of Ireland, born in 1318, was the youngest son of Thomas Fitzgerald, the second earl [q. v.], and his wife, Joan de Burgh, and was generally called Maurice Fitzthomas. He lost his father in 1328, and became earl on his brother Earl Richard's death in 1331. His lands remained in the custody of Sir John D'Arcy, his mother's second husband. Kildare was involved in the opposition led by Maurice Fitzthomas, earl of Desmond [q. v.], to the new policy which the justiciar, Ralph D'Ufford, endeavoured to enforce, of superseding the ' English born in Ireland' by ' English born in England.' In 1345 Ufford sent a knight named William Burton to Kildare with two writs, one summoning him to an expedition to Munster, the other a secret warrant for his arrest. Burton was afraid to carry out the latter in the earl's own estates, but enticed him to Dublin, where he was suddenly arrested while sitting in council at the exchequer (*Ann. Hib.* Laud MS. p. 386). Next year Kildare was released, on 23 May, on the surety of twenty-four manucaptors (*ib.* p. 389). He at once invaded the O'More's country, and compelled that chieftain to submit. In 1347 he was present with Edward III at the siege and capture of Calais (CLYN, *Annals*, p. 34). He was then knighted by the king, and married to a daughter of Sir Bartholomew Burghersh (GRACE, *Annals*, p. 143). There are preserved in the archives of the Duke of Leinster some interesting indentures of fealty of various Irish chieftains to Kildare (*Hist. MSS. Comm.* 9th Rep. ii. 270–1).

On 30 March 1356 Kildare was appointed justiciar of Ireland (*Fœdera*, iii. 326), but he was almost at once succeeded by Thomas de Rokeby. On 30 Aug. 1357, however, Kildare was made *locum tenens* for Almaric de St. Amand, who had been appointed justiciar on 14 July, until the arrival of the latter in Ireland (*ib.* iii. 361, 368). In 1358 his Leinster estates were invaded by the De Burghs, and in the same year he and his county made a liberal grant for the war against the 'O'Morthes' (*Cal. Rot. Pat. et Claus. Hib.* pp. 69, 75). In 1359 his mother, the Countess Joan, died (*Ann. Hib.* Laud. MS. p. 393).

In 1359 Kildare was made *locum tenens* for James Butler, earl of Ormonde, justiciar of Ireland, and continued in office in 1360, being on 30 March 1361 definitely appointed as justiciar (*Ann. Hib.* Laud. MS. p. 394). He resigned, however, on Ormonde's return from England. In 1371 Kildare was made justiciar, and again in 1376, in succession to Sir William de Windsor; but on neither occasion did he hold the post for any time. On the latter occasion he was specially instructed to remain in Leinster, while the custody of Munster was more particularly entrusted to Stephen, bishop of Meath. He refused, however (GILBERT, *Viceroys*, p. 243), to take office again in 1378. In 1386 he was one of the council of De Vere, the marquis of Dublin (*ib.* p. 551). He died on 25 Aug.

1390, and was buried in the church of the Holy Trinity, now called Christ Church, in Dublin.

By his wife, Elizabeth Burghersh, he left four sons, of whom the eldest, Gerald, became the fifth earl, and died in 1410. He was succeeded by his son John, the sixth earl (*d.* 1427), the father of Thomas Fitzgerald, the seventh earl [q. v.]

[Chartularies, &c., of St. Mary's Abbey, Dublin (Rolls Ser.); Rymer's Fœdera; Clyn's Annals and Grace's Annals (Irish Archæol. Soc.); Calendar of the Patent and Close Rolls of Ireland; Gilbert's Viceroys of Ireland; Kildare's Earls of Kildare, pp. 31–5.] T. F. T.

FITZGERALD, MAURICE (1774–1849), hereditary Knight of Kerry and Irish statesman, was the elder son of Robert Fitzgerald, knight of Kerry, by his third wife, Catherine, daughter of Launcelot Sandes of Kilcavan, Queen's County. The dignity of Knight of Kerry was first borne in the fourteenth century by Maurice, son of Maurice Fitzgerald of Ennismore and Rahinnane. The latter was third son by a second marriage of John Fitzthomas Fitzgerald (*d.* 1261) [cf. FITZTHOMAS, MAURICE, first EARL OF DESMOND], stated to be grandson of Maurice Fitzgerald (*d.* 1176) [q. v.], the founder of the Geraldine family in Ireland. Maurice Fitzgerald was born 29 Dec. 1774, and entered public life almost before he was legally competent to do so. On the representation of his native county suddenly becoming vacant in 1794, Fitzgerald was elected to fill it. He then wanted some months of coming of age, and could not take his seat in parliament, but when he eventually made his appearance in the parliament house at Dublin he gave high promise. For thirty-seven years uninterruptedly he continued to represent Kerry in the Irish and imperial parliaments. The Knight of Kerry entered public life at the same period as two of his personal friends, the Duke of Wellington and Lord Castlereagh. Up to the time of the union Fitzgerald sat in the Irish parliament, and he voted in favour of that measure throughout its stages.

From July 1799 until January 1801—one and a half years—Fitzgerald acted as a commissioner of customs in Ireland. In 1801 he was returned for the county of Kerry to the imperial parliament. Soon after he entered the House of Commons he was called to a seat in the privy council, and at the board of the Irish treasury. The latter office he resigned at the dissolution of the whig ministry in 1807. While he had not much general sympathy with the whigs, he agreed with them on the catholic question. The partial fusion of parties in the Canning ministry called him to office as lord of the English treasury (July 1827). The passing of the Catholic Emancipation Act, which had always been warmly supported by Fitzgerald, removed the only barrier between him and the tories. Feeling himself bound, as an emancipationist, to support the Duke of Wellington, he again took office in 1830 as vice-treasurer of Ireland. Shortly afterwards his active political career terminated, for although he once more held office as a lord of the admiralty in Sir Robert Peel's short-lived administration of December 1834, he never again recovered his seat in parliament, which he lost in the struggle attendant on the Reform Bill. He was defeated at the Kerry election of 1831, and again in 1835. He was frequently invited to seek the suffrages of an English constituency, but declined. In 1845 Fitzgerald addressed a 'Letter to Sir Robert Peel on the Endowment of the Roman Catholic Church of Ireland.' The Duke of Wellington and the writer were the only survivors of those who professed Pitt's politics in the Irish parliament, and Fitzgerald's letter, while partly explanatory of Pitt's views and pledges, also established the fact that this great statesman was the originator of the 'treasonable and sacrilegious scheme' of Peel. When Pitt left office he drew up a paper explaining the causes of his resignation, which was delivered by Lord Cornwallis to the Knight of Kerry for circulation among the leading Roman catholics. Pitt's views were subsequently more fully revealed in the 'Castlereagh Correspondence.' Fitzgerald approved the means by which the union was carried, declaring it to be a very popular measure among the Munster and Connaught population; and with respect to the parliament on College Green, with whose inner workings he was intimately acquainted, he stated that he was 'thoroughly disgusted with its political corruption, its narrow bigotry, and the exclusive spirit of monopoly with which it misgoverned Ireland.' On the passing of the Act of Union, Lord Castlereagh addressed a confidential letter to Fitzgerald, acknowledging the pledges given to the Irish catholics, and announcing his intention to support the endowment of their church.

In private Fitzgerald was an excellent friend and landlord. He died at Glanleam, Valentia, 7 March 1849, having married (1), 5 Nov. 1801, Maria (d. 1827), daughter of the Right Hon. David Digges la Touche of Marlay, Dublin; and (2) Cecilia Maria Knight, a widow, who died 15 Oct. 1859. By his first wife he had six sons and four daughters. His four eldest

sons predeceased him, and he was succeeded in his 'feudal' honours by his fifth son, Peter George Fitzgerald [q. v.]

[Gent. Mag. 1849; Cork Southern Reporter and Kerry Post, March 1849.]   G. B. S.

FITZGERALD, PAMELA (1776?–1831), wife of Lord Edward Fitzgerald [q. v.], was described in her marriage contract of 1792 as Anne Stéphanie Caroline Sims, daughter of Guillaume de Brixey and Mary Sims, as a native of Fogo Island, Newfoundland, and as about nineteen years of age. Though she has generally been regarded as the daughter of Madame de Genlis by the Duke of Orleans (Égalité), this statement of her Newfoundland birth is confirmed by information now obtained from Fogo. Henry Sims, a respectable planter who died there in 1886, at the age of eighty-two, believed Pamela to have been his cousin. Mr. James Fitzgerald, the present magistrate of Fogo, on arriving in the island in 1834, made the acquaintance of Sims, who informed him that his grandfather, an Englishman living at Fogo in the latter part of last century, had a daughter Mary, that she was delivered of a child at Gander Bay, and in the following summer sailed with her infant for Bristol, in a vessel commanded by a Frenchman named Brixey, and that the Simses heard nothing more of mother or child until they learned from Moore's book that Lord E. Fitzgerald married a Nancy Sims from Fogo. Newfoundland had no parish registers at that date, but Henry Sims's story may be true, though there is the bare possibility of the death of the child in infancy, and of the transfer of her pedigree to a second child placed under Mary's charge. It may be conjectured that when in 1782 she was sent over by Forth, ex-secretary to the British embassy at Paris, to be brought up with the Orleans children, and familiarise them with English, the object was to divert attention from the arrival a little later of a child known as Fortunée Elizabeth Hermine de Compton (afterwards Madame Collard), who died in 1822 at Villers Hélon. Hermine, who, unlike Pamela, was recognised by the Orleans family in after life as a quasi-relative, was in all probability Madame de Genlis's daughter by Égalité, and was perhaps born at Spa in 1776. In a scene between Madame de Genlis and Pamela, witnessed by the latter's daughter, there was moreover a positive disclaimer of maternity (Journal of Mary Frampton, letter of Lady Louisa Howard to Mrs. Mundy, 1876). Unveracious, therefore, though the lady was, her story may be credited that Forth casually saw the child at Christchurch, that he sent

Orleans 'the handsomest filly and the prettiest little girl in England,' that, enraptured by the girl's beauty and talents, she had unconditionally baptised, conferring on her her own name, Stéphanie, and the pet name, Pamela, and that to guard against extortion by the mother, she paid the latter in 1786 twenty-four guineas for a legal renunciation of all claims. The belief of the Fitzgerald family, in deference to which Moore retracted his original acceptance of the Orleans-Genlis parentage, and Louis-Philippe's opposite conduct to his two old playmates, strengthen this conclusion. Against it must be set Pamela's alleged likeness to the Orleans family; the rumour of 1785 (see GRIMM, *Correspondence*), that Monsieur de Genlis had acknowledged both Pamela and Hermine as his own children, sent away in infancy to test the difference between children brought up with and without knowledge of their status; Égalité's settlement on Pamela about 1791 of fifteen hundred francs, increased on her marriage to six thousand francs; and Madame de Genlis's statement in her memoirs (1825), assigning the paternity to a legendary Seymour of good family, who married a woman of low birth named Sims, took her to Newfoundland, and there died, whereupon widow and child returned to England. Of winning manners, though devoid of application or reflection, Pamela was applauded by the mob on their way to Versailles (Madame de Genlis had sent her out, with grooms in Orleans livery, to ride through the crowd), was the ornament of her adoptive mother's political receptions, and went with her to England in 1791, when Sheridan is said to have offered her marriage, and been accepted, he being struck by her resemblance to his late wife. To that resemblance is also attributed her conquest of Lord Edward Fitzgerald, who, objecting to 'blue stockings,' had refused to meet the Genlis party in England, but saw Pamela at a Paris theatre, was immediately introduced to her, was invited to dinner next day, joined the party on the road, on their expulsion from Paris as *émigrées*, accompanied them to Tournai, and there married her, 27 Dec. 1792. The Tournai register, which, like the marriage contract, overstates her age by at least three years, gives her father's name as Guillaume Berkley, and London as her birthplace, but this may be imputed to the carelessness of the officiating priest. The future Louis-Philippe was present at the ceremony. Arrived at Dublin, Pamela indulged her passion for dancing, but failed to win popularity. Meanwhile the Paris revolutionists, misled by a report of her travelling in Switzerland with her adoptive mother, issued a warrant against

her. She gave birth to a son in Ireland, and in 1796 her second child, Pamela, was born at Hamburg. Madame de Genlis, then staying there, represents herself as remonstrating against Lord Edward's political vehemence, and Pamela as replying that she avoided discussing politics with him for obvious reasons. Their domestic happiness seems to have been unalloyed. Her third child was born while her husband was in concealment and paying her secret visits. On his arrest she was ordered to quit Ireland, and after his death repaired to Hamburg, whence she had had an invitation from her old companion, Henriette de Sercey, Madame de Genlis' niece. Henriette had married a Hamburg merchant, Mathiesson, and Pamela hoped there to be able to recover the Orleans annuity. Her children seem to have stayed behind. She shortly afterwards married Pitcairn, the American consul at Hamburg, by whom she had a daughter (who was married and living at New York in 1835), but a separation soon ensued. She is next heard of as encountering, about 1812, in a Dover hotel, Casimir, another of Madame de Genlis's adopted children, and as giving her English creditors the slip by accompanying him to Paris. Resuming the name of Fitzgerald, she first lived at the Abbaye-aux-Bois, next lodged with Auber, the composer's father, and then went to Montauban to lodge with the Duc de la Force, commandant of Tarn-et-Garonne. There she is said to have had the freak of acting as a shepherdess in the costume of Fontenelle's pastoral heroines. She appears to have paid at least one visit to Paris about 1820, when Madame de Genlis forgave her abrupt departure from Paris and cessation of correspondence. At this period her home was at Toulouse. After the revolution of 1830 she revisited Paris, apparently in the hope of royal favour, but received little notice, and died eleven months after her adoptive mother, in November 1831, in a small hotel in the rue Richepance. Though enjoying a pension of at least ten thousand francs, she is said to have left nothing, so that Louis-Philippe had to be applied to—probably by Talleyrand, who attended it—to provide a proper funeral at Montmartre. In 1880, a legal informality necessitating the removal of her remains, they were interred by her grandchildren at Thames Ditton.

[Information through Sir G. W. Des Vœux from Mr. James Fitzgerald, J.P., Fogo; Mémoires de Madame de Genlis; Tournai register; Moore's Life of Lord E. Fitzgerald; Madden's United Irishmen; Mémoires d'Alexandre Dumas; Parisot's article in Biographie Universelle; Times, 25 Aug. 1880.]   J. G. A.

FITZGERALD, Sir PETER GEORGE (1808–1880), nineteenth Knight of Kerry, eldest surviving son of the Right Hon. Maurice Fitzgerald [q. v.] of Glanleam, by Maria, daughter of the Right Hon. David la Touche of Marlay, co. Dublin, was born 15 Sept. 1808. He began life in the banking-house of his maternal grandfather at Dublin. He subsequently entered the public service, and was appointed vice-treasurer of Ireland in the 1841-6 ministry of Sir Robert Peel. Succeeding his father in 1849, from that period he resided almost constantly on the island of Valentia, devoting himself indefatigably to the duties of an Irish landlord, the improvement of his estates, and the welfare of his tenantry. He especially earned the thanks of the people by the erection of substantial homesteads in place of the wretched cabins with which the middleman system had covered the west of Ireland. Fitzgerald manifested a keen interest in all questions which had a practical bearing on the progress or prosperity of Ireland; and in able contributions to the 'Times' he deprecated the censure which at that time and since was cast indiscriminately upon all Irish landlords. His own admirable personal qualities, his hatred of abuses, his engaging manners, and his generous nature, made him a great favourite with the Irish peasantry. His hospitality at Glanleam was enjoyed by the Prince of Wales and other distinguished guests. The Atlantic cable had its British termination on his estates, and he evinced much public spirit and energy in connection with the successful laying of the cable. He married in 1838 Julia Hussey, daughter of Peter Bodkin Hussey of Farranikilla House, co. Kerry, a lineal descendant of the Norman family of Hoses, which settled on the promontory of Dingle in the thirteenth century. By this lady he had four sons and seven daughters. Fitzgerald was a magistrate and deputy-lieutenant for co. Kerry, and was high sheriff of Kerry in 1849, and of co. Carlow in 1875. On 8 July 1880 the queen conferred upon him a baronetcy. Fitzgerald was then, however, suffering from a dangerous malady, and he died on 6 Aug. following. He was succeeded in the title and estates by his eldest son, Captain Maurice Fitzgerald, who served with distinction in the Ashantee war, being present at the battles of Amoaful, Becquah, and Ordahau, and at the capture of Coomassie.

[Times, 9 Aug. 1880; Guardian, vol. xxxv.; Kerry Evening Post, 11 Aug. 1880.] G. B. S.

FITZGERALD, RAYMOND, surnamed LE GROS (d. 1182), was the son of William, the elder brother of Maurice Fitzgerald, d. 1176

[q. v.], and Robert Fitzstephen [q. v.] (Expugnatio Hibernica, pp. 248, 310), who preceded him in the invasion of Ireland, whither he was sent as Strongbow's representative in April 1170 [see CLARE, RICHARD DE, d. 1176]. He landed at Dundunnolf, near Waterford (c. 1 May), at the head of ten knights and seventy archers, and at once entrenched himself behind a turf fortification. Here he was besieged by the Ostmen of Waterford in alliance with the Irish of Decies and Idrone. A sudden sally repelled the assailants with a loss of seventy prisoners. Raymond spared their lives against the advice of Hervey de Mountmaurice, who had represented Strongbow in Ireland before he himself arrived, and a long feud arose from this (Exp. Hib. pp. 250-3; REGAN, pp. 70-2; Ann. Four Masters, i. 1177; Annals of Inisf. p. 114).

Four months later Earl Strongbow reached Ireland, and the fall of Waterford was due to Raymond, who, in the words of Giraldus, was 'totius exercitus dux et tribunus militiæque princeps' (25 Aug. 1170). After the earl's marriage to Dermot's daughter, Raymond accompanied his lord to Ferns. In the Dublin expedition he led the centre of the army, having eight hundred 'companions' under his orders. There Raymond and Miles de Cogan, tired of negotiations, broke into the place and drove its ruler Asculf to his ships, 21 Sept. 1170 (Exp. Hib. pp. 256-8; REGAN, pp. 73-82; Ann. Four Masters, p. 1177; Annals of Boyle, p. 28).

Raymond was soon afterwards sent by the earl to place all his conquests at the disposal of Henry II. Raymond seems to have met Henry in Aquitaine (c. December 1170 to January 1171). He led the first or second squadron in the famous sally from Dublin about July 1171. He probably returned to England with Henry II in April 1172, as he was not one of those to whom the king gave grants of Irish land on leaving the country. A year later, when Strongbow's services in Normandy were rewarded by permission to return to Ireland, he insisted upon taking Raymond with him (Exp. Hib. pp. 256-98; REGAN, pp. 73-8).

During the earl's absence Henry de Mountmaurice had apparently occupied his post. The Irish had revolted, the earl's soldiers were unpaid, and threatened to return to England or join the Irish unless Raymond became their constable. The earl yielded, and Raymond led his old troops on a plundering expedition against Offaly; Dermot MacCarthy was routed near Lismore, and four thousand head of cattle were driven into Waterford. Three or four years before the earl had given the constableship of Leinster to Robert de Quenci, along with his sister's hand. Robert was soon slain, leaving an infant daughter; and Raymond now wished to marry the widow, and thus become the guardian of the baby heiress. When his petition was refused Raymond made the death of his father an excuse for crossing over into Wales, and Hervey once more became the acting constable. An unfortunate expedition into Munster was the signal for a general Irish rising. Strongbow was besieged in Waterford (1174); Roderic of Connaught had burst into Meath, and was laying everything waste as far as Dublin (*Exp. Hib.* pp. 308–11; REGAN, pp. 130–7; *Ann. Four Masters*, ii. 15–18; *Annals of Boyle*, p. 29; *Annals of Inisf.* p. 116).

The earl now offered his sister's hand to Raymond in reward for help. Raymond and his cousin Meiler hurried over to Wexford just in time to save the town, marched to Waterford, and brought back the earl to Wexford. The marriage took place a few days later, and on the morrow Raymond started for Meath. Roderic retreated before him and peace was restored, though the new constable did not leave this province until he had repaired the ruined castles of Trim and Duleek (*Exp. Hib.* pp. 310–14; REGAN, pp. 142–3; cf. *Ann. Four Masters*; *Boyle*; *Inisfallen*). A short calm followed. Raymond took part in promoting the alliances by which the Normans solidified their interests. His cousin Nesta married Hervey de Mountmaurice, and his influence brought about the union of William Fitzgerald and Alina, the earl's daughter (*Exp. Hib.* p. 314).

In the summer of 1175 Donald O'Brien, king of Munster, threw off his allegiance to King Henry, and Raymond was despatched with some eight hundred men against Limerick. There he found the Irish drawn up on the opposite bank of the river (Shannon *sic*) in such strength that his soldiers feared to cross until Meiler Fitzhenry passed over alone, and Raymond, going to his rescue, was at last followed by the army. The town was taken, provisioned and garrisoned, and the constable turned back towards Leinster (*ib.* pp. 320–3; REGAN, pp. 160–4; cf. *Ann. Four Masters, Boyle,* and *Inisf.*)

Meanwhile Hervey de Mountmaurice had accused Raymond before the king of endeavouring to supplant the royal authority in Leinster and all Ireland. Henry recalled Raymond, who was about to obey, when Donald O'Brien again revolted. The earl's household refused to march without Raymond to command them. The king's envoys consented, and the constable started for Limerick once more at the head of a mixed army of English and Irish. On Easter eve (3 April 1176) he forced his way through the pass of Cashel, and three days later entered Limerick, upon which Donald and Roderic of Connaught renewed their fealty to the king of England (*Exp. Hib.* pp. 327–31). From Limerick he set out for Cork to aid Dermot Macarthy, prince of Desmond, who had been expelled by his son Cormac. News of the earl's death (*c.* 1 June 1176) called him back to Limerick, which he now determined to evacuate in order that he might have larger forces for the defence of Connaught in the event of a general rebellion among the Irish. Donald O'Brien undertook to hold the town for the king of England, but fired it as soon as it was evacuated (*ib.* pp. 327–34; *Ann. Four Masters,* p. 25; *Inisfallen,* p. 117).

Raymond now ruled Ireland till the coming of William Fitzaldhelm, the new governor, to whom he at once handed over the castles in his possession. If we may trust Giraldus, Fitzaldhelm, unmollified by this conduct, set himself to destroy the whole power of the Geraldines, who were soon despoiled of their lands. Raymond now lost his estates near Dublin and Wexford. Next year Hugh de Lacy succeeded Fitzaldhelm, and a general redistribution of Ireland among the English adventurers took place in May 1177. It was now that Robert Fitzstephen and Miles de Cogan received the kingdom of South Munster (i.e. of Desmond or Cork) from Lismore west (HOVEDEN, ii. 134; cf. *Inisfallen,* p. 117). A few years later, when Fitzstephen's sons had perished (1182 according to the *Irish Annals*) and the Irish seemed on the point of winning back their land, Raymond hurried from Waterford to the help of his uncle, who was closely besieged in Cork. According to Giraldus, who himself came to Ireland about this time, Raymond succeeded to his uncle's estates, became master of Cork, and reduced the country to quiet (*Exp. Hib.* pp. 349–50, &c.) The date of his death is not given by the contemporary English chroniclers, but the 'Irish Annals' seem to assign it to 1182. This is almost certainly a mistake, as the latter writers associate his decease with that of Fitzstephen's son (Ralph), while the words of Giraldus are hardly compatible with such a synchronism (*Annals of Loch Cé,* sub an. 1182, and the note, with quotations, from the *Annals of Ulster* and *Clonmacnoise;* cf. *Ann. of Boyle,* p. 31). Raymond Fitzgerald left no legitimate issue (*Exp. Hib.* pp. 345, 409).

Raymond Fitzgerald was a man 'big-bodied and broad-set,' somewhat above the middle height, and inclining to corpulence. His eyes were large, full, and grey, his nose rather prominent, and his features well-coloured and pleasant. He would spend sleepless nights in his anxiety for the safety of his troops. Careless in the matters of food and drink, raiment, or personal comfort, he had the art to appear the servant rather than the lord of his followers, to whom he showed himself liberal and gentle. Though a man of undoubted spirit, he always tempered his valour with prudence, and, 'though he had much of the knight about him, he had still more of the captain. He was specially happy in this, that he rarely or never failed in any enterprise he took in hand through rashness or imprudence' (*ib.* pp. 323–4; cf. the quaint englishing of this passage in HOLINSHED, p. 190; and the *Book of Howth*, pp. 297–8).

[It is hardly possible to make Giraldus's account of Raymond's movements harmonise completely with that of Regan, and the Irish Annals give little or no help in settling the details of the chronology from 1172 to 1176. Giraldus Cambrensis, Expugnatio Hibernica, ed. Dimock (Rolls Series), vol. v.; the Anglo-Norman poet cited as Regan, ed. Michel and Wright (London, 1837); Annals of Loch Cé, ed. Hennessy (Rolls Series); Annals of the Four Masters, ed. O'Donovan; Annals of Inisfallen and Boyle, ap. O'Conor's Scriptores Rerum Hibernicarum, vol. ii.; Hoveden, ed. Stubbs (Rolls Series), vol. ii.]

T. A. A.

FITZGERALD, THOMAS, second EARL OF KILDARE (*d.* 1328), twice justiciar of Ireland, was the son of John Fitzthomas, the first earl, and of his wife Blanche 'de Rupe' [see FITZTHOMAS, JOHN, first EARL OF KILDARE], and was therefore generally called Thomas Fitzjohn. On 16 Aug. 1312 his marriage at Greencastle, on Carlingford Bay, with Joan, daughter of Richard de Burgh, the 'red earl' of Ulster, was the symbol of the union of the two greatest Norman families in Ireland (*Ann. Hib.* MS. Laud in *Chart. St. Mary's*, ii. 341). On 8 Sept. 1316 he succeeded to the new earldom of Kildare on his father's death (*ib.* p. 352). He at once gathered a great army to fight against Edward Bruce and the Scots, and served against them. His free use of the system of 'bonaght,' or 'coigne and livery,' to support these troops afterwards became a very bad precedent. In 1317 he was thanked by Edward II for his services against Bruce (*Fœdera*, ii. 327), and in the same year he received from the king the office of hereditary sheriff for his county of Kildare, which involved full jurisdiction and liberties within the earldom (*ib.* ii. 354). In 1319 and again in 1320 he served on a commission to inquire into the treasons committed during the Bruce invasion (*ib.* ii. 396, 417). In 1320 he was made justiciar of Ireland, though he only acted as viceroy for a year (*Ann. Hib.* MS. Laud, p. 361). During his tenure of office Archbishop Bicknor [q. v.] attempted to found a university in Dublin. Kildare received a patent empowering him to subject to English law such of his Irish tenants as chose to be governed by it. In 1322 he was summoned to serve against the Scots, but the truce prevented his services being required (*Fœdera*, ii. 501, 523). In 1324 he was at the Dublin parliament, where the magnates of Ireland pledged themselves to support the crown (*Rot. Claus. Hib.* 18 Edw. II, p. 30 *b*, Record Comm.) In 1324 he was accused of being an adherent of Roger Mortimer and of corresponding with him after his escape from the Tower of London (*Parl. Writs*, vol. ii. pt. iii. p. 1052). This seems probably true, for one of the first acts of Mortimer's party after the accession of Edward III was to reappoint Kildare justiciar of Ireland. This was before 13 Feb. 1327 (*Fœdera*, ii. 688). He experienced some difficulty before the partisans of Edward II would accept him. In July several great barons, including John de Bermingham [q. v.], were still refractory (*ib.* ii. 710). But a local feud which involved the Berminghams, the Butlers, the Poers, and De Burghs in a private war with the Geraldines of Desmond, because Arnold le Poer had called Maurice Fitzthomas, first earl of Desmond [q. v.], a rhymer, was probably at the bottom of this disobedience (*Ann. Hib.* MS. Laud, p. 365; cf. GILBERT, *Viceroys*, pp. 163–4). However, Kildare compelled the chief offenders to sue for pardon at the parliament of Kilkenny. During his viceroyalty a native 'king' of Leinster ventured to set up his standard within two miles of Dublin, but was soon subdued. The burning of one of the O'Tooles for heresy was another example of Kildare's vigour (GRACE, pp. 107–8). In 1327 he granted the advowson of Kilcullen to the priory of Holy Trinity, Dublin (*Hist. MSS. Comm.* 9th Rep. pt. ii. p. 269). He died, still in office, on 9 April 1328 at Maynooth, and was buried in the chapel of St. Mary which he had built in the Franciscan convent at Kildare (ARCHDALL, *Monast. Hib.* p. 312). He is described as wise and prudent (GRACE, p. 76). His wife, Joan de Burgh, remarried, on 3 July 1329, his successor as justiciar, John D'Arcy (*Ann. Hib.* MS. Laud, p. 371). He had by her three sons, of whom John, the eldest, died in 1323 or 1324 at the age of nine (*ib.* p. 362), being then in the hands of the king as a hostage for his father (CLYN, p. 16). The second Richard succeeded his father as third earl, but died in July 1331 (*Hist. MSS. Comm.* 9th Rep. pt. ii. p. 268), aged 12. The youngest son, Maurice Fitzgerald (1318–1390) [q. v.], then became the fourth earl.

[Chartularies, &c. of St. Mary's Abbey, Dublin (Rolls Ser.), especially Annales Hiberniæ, MS. Laud, in vol. ii.; Grace's Annales Hib. (Irish Archæol. Soc.); Calendar of Patent and Close Rolls, Ireland (Record Comm.); Book of Howth; Rymer's Fœdera, vol. ii., Record edit.; Gilbert's Viceroys of Ireland; Lodge's Peerage of Ireland (Archdall), vol. i.; Marquis of Kildare's Earls of Kildare; Hist. MSS. Comm. 9th Rep. pt. ii. p. 263 sq.]   T. F. T.

FITZGERALD, THOMAS, eighth EARL OF DESMOND (1426?–1468), deputy of Ireland, was the son of James, seventh earl, and of his wife Mary, daughter of Ulick Burke of Connaught (LODGE, *Peerage of Ireland*, i. 67). In 1462 Thomas succeeded his father to the earldom (*Annals of Loch Cé*, ii. 165, says 1463, and speaks of him as 'the chief of the foreigners of the south'). In 1463 he was made deputy to George, duke of Clarence, the lord-lieutenant of Ireland. He showed great activity. He built border castles to protect the Pale, especially in the passes of Offaly, the ordinary passage of the O'Conors in their invasions; but the break-up of the English power in Ireland was now so complete that he had to sanction the parliamentary recognition of the tax exacted by that sept on the English of Meath, and to relax the prohibition of traffic with the 'Irish enemies.' He carried on the hereditary feud with the Butlers, whose lands he devastated in 1463. He was less successful in an expedition against Offaly. In 1464 he quarrelled with Sherwood, bishop of Meath, and both went to England to lay their grievances before the king (*Ann. Ireland, 1443–68, in Irish Archæol. Miscellany*, p. 253). The Irish parliament certified that he had 'rendered great services at intolerable charges and risks,' had 'always governed himself by English laws,' and had 'brought Ireland to a reasonable state of peace.' But a Drogheda merchant accused him of extorting 'coigne and livery,' and of treasonable relations with the natives. In the end Edward restored Desmond to office and granted him six manors in Meath as a mark of his favour.

The period of Desmond's government of Ireland was one of considerable legislative activity. But laws had little effect in repressing the Irish. Two expeditions of Desmond against the O'Briens did not prevent the border septs' attacks on Leinster. The Irish of Meath called in a son of the lord of Thomond to act as their 'king,' but his death of a fever averted this danger. Yet Desmond's rule was so far successful, or his hold over Munster so strong, that for the first time for many years representatives of the county of Cork appeared in the Irish parliament.

In 1467 Desmond was superseded as deputy by John Tiptoft, earl of Worcester [q.v.] It was believed that he was a strong supporter of Warwick in his hostility to Edward IV's marriage, and had incurred the hostility of Queen Elizabeth in consequence. Tiptoft convoked a parliament at Drogheda, in which, on the petition of the commons, Desmond was attainted, along with the Earl of Kildare [see FITZGERALD, THOMAS, seventh EARL OF KILDARE] and Edward Plunket. The charges brought against them were 'fosterage and alliance with the Irish, giving the Irish horses, harness, and arms, and supporting them against the faithful subjects of the king' ('Carew MSS.,' *Book of Howth*, &c. p. 483). On these charges Desmond was executed at Drogheda on 14 Feb. 1468, at the age of forty-two (CLYN, *Annals*, p. 46, Irish Archæol. Soc.) William Wyrcester (*Annals in Wars of English in France*, II. ii. 789) says that Edward was at first displeased with his execution. This suggests that the actual charges rather than secret relations with English parties were the causes of his fall. Desmond was soon looked on as a martyr (GRACE, p. 165). It was soon believed that Tiptoft, with his usual cruelty, had also put to death two infant sons of Desmond (HALL, p. 286, ed. 1809; cf. *Mirrour for Magistrates*, ii. 203, ed. 1815, and note in GILBERT's *Viceroys*, pp. 589–91), but there is no native or contemporary evidence for this. Richard III described Desmond as 'atrociously slain and murdered by colour of the law against all manhood, reason, and sound conscience' (GAIRDNER, *Letters, &c. of Richard III and Henry VII*, i. 68). The Munster Geraldines avenged his death by a bloody inroad into the Pale. The Irish writers celebrate Desmond for 'his excellent good qualities, comely fair person, affability, eloquence, hospitality, martial feats, almsdeeds, humanity, bountifulness in bestowing good gifts to both clergy and laity, and to all the learned in Irish, as antiquaries, poets' (*Annals of Ireland, 1443–68*, p. 263; cf. *Four Masters*, iv. 1053). He founded a college at Youghal for a warden, eight fellows, and eight choristers (HAYMAN, *Notes of the Religious Foundations of Youghal*, p. xxxiii), and procured an act of parliament allowing the corporation to buy and sell of the Irishry (HAYMAN, *Annals of Youghal*, p. 13). He was buried at Drogheda, but Sir Henry Sidney removed his tomb to Dublin (LODGE, i. 70). The 'Four Masters' (iv. 1053) say that his body was afterwards conveyed to the burial-place of his predecessors at Tralee. He married Elizabeth or Ellice Barry, daughter of Lord Buttevant, by whom he had a large family. Four of his sons, James, Maurice, Thomas, and John, became in succession earls of Desmond.

[Gilbert's Viceroys of Ireland; Annals of Loch Cé; Annals of Ireland in Irish Archæological Miscellany; Annals of the Four Masters (O'Donovan), with the note on iv. 1050–2; Carew MSS., Book of Howth, &c.; Hayman's unpublished Geraldine Documents, i. 11–13; Lodge's Peerage of Ireland (Archdall), vol. i.]   T. F. T.

FITZGERALD, THOMAS, seventh EARL OF KILDARE (d. 1477), deputy of Ireland, was son of John, sixth earl, and his wife, Margaret de la Herne (LODGE, i. 82). He succeeded to his father in 1427, when he must have been quite young. Between 1455 and 1459 he was deputy for Richard, duke of York, the lord-lieutenant. In 1459 he warmly welcomed York on his taking refuge in Ireland. The Lancastrian government in vain sought to weaken his position by intriguing with the native Irish against him. On 30 April 1461 Kildare was appointed deputy to George, duke of Clarence (Cal. Rot. Pat. Hib. 1 Edward IV, p. 268); and on 5 July the confirmation of a grant of Duke Richard's was Edward IV's further reward for his fidelity to the Yorkist cause (ib. p. 268 b). Next year he was superseded by Sir Roland Fitzeustace, but in January 1463 he was made lord chancellor of Ireland. In 1464 he and his wife Joan founded the Franciscan convent at Adare in county Limerick (Annals of the Four Masters, iv. 1035). In 1467 he incurred, with his brother-in-law Desmond [see FITZGERALD, THOMAS, eighth EARL OF DESMOND], the hostility of the new deputy, John Tiptoft, earl of Worcester. Both were attainted at the parliament of Drogheda, but the reprisals which followed the execution of Desmond brought out so clearly the weakness of a government deprived of the support of the Fitzgeralds, that Kildare was respited. The Archbishop of Dublin and other grandees became his sureties, and on his promise of faithful service the parliament of 1468 repealed the attainder and restored him to his estates. In the same year he was reappointed deputy, but on the fall of Clarence, Tiptoft himself became lord-lieutenant, and Edmund Dudley his deputy. But on Clarence's reappointment Kildare became deputy again, and remained in office until 1475. By building a dyke to protect the Pale, and by excluding 'disloyal Irish' from garrisons, he sought to uphold the English rule. In 1472 eighty archers were provided for him as the nucleus of a permanent force, but he was expected to de-

fray half the cost. In 1474 the archers were increased to 160, with 63 spearmen; and in 1475 a 'Brotherhood of St. George' was established for the defence of the Pale, of which Kildare was president, while his son Gerald was its first captain. This put a further force of 120 mounted archers, 40 men-at-arms, and 40 pages in his hands ('Carew MSS.,' Book of Howth, &c., p. 403). His government is an epoch of some importance in the history of the Irish coinage. In 1475 he was superseded by William Sherwood, bishop of Meath. He died on 25 March 1477 and was buried in the monastery of All Hallows in Dublin. By his wife, Joan, daughter of James, seventh earl of Desmond, and sister of Thomas, the eighth earl [q. v.], he is said to have left four sons and two daughters (LODGE, i. 83). He was succeeded by his eldest son, Gerald Fitzgerald, the eighth earl [q. v.]

[Gilbert's Viceroys of Ireland; Lodge's Peerage of Ireland, vol. i.; Annals of the Four Masters; Carew MSS., Book of Howth, &c.; Marquis of Kildare's Earls of Kildare, pp. 38–42.]
                                                      T. F. T.

FITZGERALD, THOMAS, LORD OFFALY, tenth EARL OF KILDARE (1513–1537), son of Gerald Fitzgerald, ninth earl [q. v.], by his first wife, Elizabeth, daughter of Sir John Zouche of Codnor, Derbyshire, was born in 1513. Like his father he spent a considerable portion of his life in England, but it was not till 1534 that he began to play an important part in history. In February of that year he was appointed deputy-governor of Ireland on the occasion of his father's last and ill-fated journey to England. About the beginning of June a report obtained currency in Ireland, through the machinations of the Ormonde faction, that his father had been summarily executed in the Tower, and that his own death and that of his uncles had been determined upon by his government. Full of indignation at what he considered an act of gross perfidy, he summoned the council to St. Mary's Abbey, whither on 11 June he rode through the city, accompanied by 140 horsemen with silken fringes on their helmets (whence his sobriquet 'Silken Thomas'), and there, despite the remonstrances of his advisers and the chancellor Cromer, he publicly renounced his allegiance, and formally declared war on the government. After which he returned to Oxmantown, where he placed himself at the head of his army. His enemies, terrified by his decisive action, took refuge in Dublin Castle, whence several of them made their way to England. Archbishop Allen was not so fortunate. By the aid of his servant Bartholomew Fitzgerald, he obtained a small vessel in which he hoped to effect his escape; but owing either to the unskilfulness of the sailors, or the contrariness of the winds, he was driven ashore near Clontarf, whence he hastened to the neighbouring village of Tartaine (Artane) to the house of a Mr. Hothe. On the following day, 28 July, a little before dawn, Offaly, accompanied by his uncles, John and Oliver Fitzgerald, and James Delahide, arrived on the spot, when, it is said, he ordered the trembling wretch to be brought before him, and then commanded him to be led away. But his servants, either misunderstanding or disobeying him, slew him on the spot. Whether Thomas was privy to the murder it is impossible to say; but it is certain that he shortly afterwards despatched his chaplain to Rome to obtain absolution for the crime (v. R. Reyley's Examination, *State Papers*, Hen. VIII, ii. 100, and GAIRDNER, *Cal.* viii. 278, Dr. Ortez to Charles V). Meanwhile he had been endeavouring by every means within his power to strengthen his position. On 27 July, Dublin Castle, his chief object, was besieged, and those of the nobility who declined to take an oath to support him clapped in the castle of Maynooth. His overtures to the Earl of Ossory were rejected with scorn by that astute and prudent nobleman, who, shortly after his return from England in August, created a diversion by invading and devastating Carlow and Kildare. But an attempt made by his son, Lord James Butler, to surprise Offaly recoiled on his own head, and he was only rescued from his dilemma by the news that the citizens of Dublin had turned on the besiegers of the castle and made prisoners of them. Having concluded a short truce with him, Offaly marched rapidly on Dublin. An assault made by him on the castle was repulsed with loss, and in a gallant sortie the citizens succeeded in completely routing his army. He himself narrowly escaped capture, being obliged to conceal himself in the Abbey of Grey Friars in Francis Street. On the same day Sir William Skeffington and an English army set sail from Beaumaris; but encountering a storm in the Channel were driven to take shelter under Lambay Island. Intending himself to sail to Waterford, he allowed Sir W. Brereton, with a portion of the fleet, to make for Dublin, and shortly afterwards landed a small contingent near Howth to support him by land. It was, however, intercepted by Offaly, who thereupon retired to his principal fortress of Maynooth. During the winter Skeffington remained idle, but about the middle of March

1535 he concentrated his forces about Maynooth, which he carried on the 23rd—an important event from a military point of view (FROUDE, *Hist. of England*, ii. 317). The garrison, including the commandant Parese, who was charged by the Irish, but on insufficient evidence, with having betrayed the place, were with one or two exceptions put to the sword. The 'Pardon of Maynooth' practically determined the fate of a rebellion which at one time threatened to prove fatal to the English authority in Ireland. Offaly, or as he was now, since the death of his father (though Stanihurst roundly asserts that he never obtained recognition of his title), Earl of Kildare, who was advancing to the relief of the place with seven thousand men, saw his army 'melt away from him like a snow-drift.' Still he ventured to risk a battle with Brereton near the Naas, but was utterly defeated, and obliged to seek shelter in Thomond, whence he meditated a flight into Spain. From this he was dissuaded by O'Brien, with whose assistance and that of O'Conor Faly he managed for several months to keep up a sporadic sort of warfare. He had married Frances, youngest daughter of Sir Adrian Fortescue, but he now sent her into England, declaring that he would have nothing to do with English blood. Seeing his fate to be certain, his allies submitted one by one to the government. On 28 July Lord Leonard Grey arrived in Ireland, and to him he wrote from O'Conor's Castle, apologising for what he had done, desiring pardon 'for his life and lands,' and begging his kinsman to interest himself in his behalf. If he could obtain his forgiveness he promised to deserve it; if not he 'must shift for himself the best he could.' He was still formidable, and to reject his overtures might prolong the war indefinitely. Acting on his own responsibility, Grey guaranteed his personal safety, persuaded him to submit unconditionally to the king's mercy, and a few weeks after his arrival had the satisfaction of carrying him over into England. For a few days he was allowed to remain at liberty, but about the beginning of October was sent prisoner to the Tower. 'Many,' wrote Chapuys, 'doubt of his life, although Lord Leonard, who promised him pardon on his surrender, says that he will not die. The said Lord Leonard, as I hear, has pleaded hard for his promise to the said Kildare, but they have stopped his mouth, the king giving him a great rent and the concubine a fine chain with plenty of money. It is quite certain, as I wrote last, that the said Kildare, without being besieged or in danger from his enemies, stole away from his men to yield himself to Lord Leonard, I know not from what motive, inclination or despair' (GAIRD-NER, *Cal.* Hen. VIII, ix. 197). The government, though hampered by Grey's promise, had no intention of pardoning him. ' Quod defertur non aufertur,' said the Duke of Norfolk, when asked his opinion. After suffering much from neglect, Earl Thomas and his five uncles, whose capture and death reflected the utmost discredit on the government, three of them being wholly free from participation in the rebellion, were on 3 Feb. 1537 executed at Tyburn, being drawn, hanged, and quartered. One member only of the family, his half-brother, Gerald Fitzgerald, afterwards eleventh Earl of Kildare [q. v.], managed to escape. On 1 May 1537, at a parliament held at Dublin, Gerald Fitzgerald, earl of Kildare, Thomas Fitzgerald, his son and heir, Sir John and Oliver Fitzgerald, with other their accomplices, were attainted for high treason. It is curious that this act should have been directed against Earl Gerald, who had not been concerned in the rebellion. In the same year an English act was passed for the attainder of Thomas ' earl of Kildare,' his five uncles and their accessories. Thomas is described as a man of great natural beauty, ' of stature tall and personable; in countenance amiable; a white face, and withal somewhat ruddy, delicately in each limb featured, a rolling tongue and a rich utterance, of nature flexible and kind, very soon carried where he fancied, easily with submission appeased, hardly with stubbornness weighed; in matters of importance an headlong hotspur, yet nathless taken for a young man not devoid of wit, were it not as it fell out in the end that a fool had the keeping thereof.' Among the inscriptions in the Beauchamp Tower is that of THOMAS FITZGERA.

[Lodge's Peerage(Archdall),vol.i.; StatePapers Hen. VIII, vol. ii., supplemented by Mr. Gairdner's Calendar, vols. viii. and ix.; Ware's Annales; Stanihurst's Chron.; Froude's Hist. of England, chap. viii.; The Earls of Kildare.] R. D.

FITZGERALD, SIR THOMAS JUDKIN-(*d.* 1810). [See JUDKIN-FITZGERALD.]

FITZGERALD, WILLIAM (1814–1883), bishop of Killaloe, son of Maurice Fitzgerald, M.D., by his second wife, Mary, daughter of Edward William Burton of Clifden, county Galway, and younger brother of Francis Alexander Fitzgerald, third baron of the exchequer, was born at Lifford, Limerick, 3 Dec. 1814. He was first educated at Middleton, co. Cork, and then entering Trinity College, Dublin, in November 1830, obtained a scholarship in 1833, the primate's Hebrew prize in 1834, and the Downes's premium for composition in 1835 and 1837. He took his

degree of B.A. 1835, his M.A. 1848, and his B.D. and D.D. 1853. He was ordained deacon 25 April 1838, and priest 23 Aug. 1847, and while serving as curate of Lackagh, Kildare, made his first essay as an author. Philip Bury Duncan of New College, Oxford, having offered a sum of 50*l.* for an essay on ' Logomachy, or the Abuse of Words,' Fitzgerald bore off the prize with the special commendation of the donor and an additional grant of 25*l.* for the expense of printing the essay. After serving the curacy of Clontarf, Dublin, from 1846–8 he was collated to the vicarage and prebend of Donoghmore, in the diocese of Dublin, on 16 Feb. in the latter year. From 1847 to 1852 he was professor of moral philosophy in Trinity College, Dublin, and from 1852 to 1857 was professor of ecclesiastical history in the same university. His next promotion was to the vicarage of St. Anne's, Dublin, 18 July 1851, whence he removed to the perpetual curacy of Monkstown, Dublin, on 13 May 1855, being in the same year also appointed prebendary of Timothan, Dublin, and archdeacon of Kildare. On 8 March 1857 he was consecrated bishop of Cork, Cloyne, and Ross, and in 1862 was translated to Killaloe by letters patent dated 3 Feb. He was a voluminous author both under his own name and as an anonymous writer, and was the chief contributor to the series of papers called ' The Cautions for the Times,' which was edited by Archbishop Whately in 1853. His edition of Bishop Butler's ' Analogy' displays such judgment and ' learning without pedantry' that it superseded all the previous editions. He died at Clarisford House, Killaloe, 24 Nov. 1883, and was buried at St. Nicholas Church, Cork, on 28 Nov. He married, in 1840, Anne, elder daughter of George Stoney of Oakley Park, Queen's County, and by her, who died 20 Oct. 1859, he had six children.

He was the author of the following works, some of which were the cause of controversy and published replies: 1. ' Episcopacy, Tradition, and the Sacraments considered in reference to the Oxford Tracts,' 1839. 2. 'Holy Scripture the Ultimate Rule of Faith to a Christian Man,' 1842. 3. 'Practical Sermons,' 1847. 4. ' A Disputation on Holy Scripture against the Papists, by W. Whitaker,' translated, Parker Soc., 1849. 5. ' The Analogy of Religion, by G. Butler, with a Life of the Author,' 1849; another ed. 1860. 6. 'A Selection from the Nicomachean Ethics of Aristotle with Notes,' 1850. 7. 'The Connection of Morality with Religion,' a sermon, 1851. 8. 'The Irish Church Journal,' vol. ii., ed. by W. Fitzgerald and J. G. Abeltshauser, 1854. 9. 'National Humiliation, a step towards Amendment,' a sermon, 1855. 10. 'Duties of the Parochial Clergy,' a charge, 1857. 11. 'The Duty of Catechising the Young,' a charge, 1858. 12. 'A Letter to the Laity of Cork in Communion with the United Church of England and Ireland,' 1860. 13. 'Speech in the House of Lords on Lord Wodehouse's Bill for Legalising Marriage with a Deceased Wife's Sister,' 1860. 14. 'Thoughts on Present Circumstances of the Church in Ireland,' a charge, 1860. 15. 'The Revival of Synods in the United Church of England and Ireland,' a charge, 1861. 16. 'Some late Decisions of the Privy Council considered,' a charge, 1864. 17. 'A Charge to the Clergy of Killaloe,' 1867. 18. 'The Significance of Christian Baptism,' three sermons, 1871. 19. 'Remarks on the New Proposed Baptismal Rubric,' 1873. 20. 'The Order of Baptism, Speeches by Bishop of Meath and Bishop of Killaloe,' 1873. 21. 'Considerations upon the Proposed Change in the Form of Ordaining Priests,' 1874. 22. 'The Athanasian Creed, a Letter to the Dioceses of Killaloe and Kilfenora, Clonfert, and Kilmacduagh,' 1875. 23. 'Lectures on Ecclesiastical History, including the Origin and Progress of the English Reformation,' ed. by W. Fitzgerald and J. Quarry, 2 vols. 1882.

[W. M. Brady's Records of Cork, Cloyne, and Ross (1864), iii. 87–8; Dublin University Mag. April 1857, pp. 416–26.] G. C. B.

FITZGERALD, WILLIAM ROBERT, second DUKE OF LEINSTER (1749–1804), second son of James, first duke of Leinster [q. v.], by Lady Emily Lennox, was born on 2 March 1749. He succeeded his elder brother as heir-apparent to his father, and in the courtesy title of Baron Offaly in 1765, and in the following year took the title of Marquis of Kildare when his father was created Duke of Leinster. He then travelled on the continent, and in his absence he was elected M.P. for Dublin by his father's interest, after an expensive contest with La Touche, head of the principal Dublin bank. He was elected both for the county of Kildare and the city of Dublin to the Irish House of Commons at the general election of 1769, and preferred to sit for Dublin. In 1772 he served the office of high sheriff of Kildare. On 19 Nov. 1773 he succeeded his father as second Duke of Leinster, and soon after he married Olivia, only daughter and heiress of St. George Ussher, Lord St. George in the peerage of Ireland. In the Irish House of Commons he had made no mark, and when he succeeded to the dukedom he rather eschewed politics, though his high rank and influential connections caused his support to be sought by all parties. When the movement of the volunteers was started Leinster showed himself a moderate supporter of the scheme, and he was elected a general of the volunteers, and colonel of the Dublin regiment. In 1783, when the order of St. Patrick was founded for the Irish nobility in imitation of the Scotch order of the Thistle, Leinster was nominated first knight, and in 1788 he was appointed to the lucrative office of master of the rolls. In the movement of 1798 the behaviour of the duke was greatly discussed, but though Lord Edward Fitzgerald [q. v.] was his brother he himself was never even suspected of complicity in the rebellion. He made every effort to save his brother's life, alleging his own loyalty, and it was no secret that the determination of the government to proceed to extremities was highly displeasing to him. At the time of the proposal for the abolition of the independent Irish parliament in 1799, he was therefore on bad terms with the government, yet as the leading Irish nobleman Leinster was one of the first persons consulted by Lord Cornwallis. His cordial adhesion to the idea of union was not in any way actuated by personal motives, for by the abolition of the Irish parliament his own position as premier peer and most influential person in Ireland was entirely destroyed, and his support of the scheme influenced many other peers. When the Act of Union was passed the duke received 28,800l. as compensation for the loss of his borough influence, 15,000l. for the borough of Kildare, and 13,800l. for the borough of Athy. He died at Cartons, his seat in Kildare, on 20 Oct. 1804, and was buried in Kildare Abbey. He appointed by will his cousin Charles James Fox and another guardians of his only son, Augustus Frederick Fitzgerald, who succeeded him as third duke of Leinster (1791–1874). In a notice of his death it is said of him that 'he was not shining but good-tempered; good-natured and affable; a fond father, an indulgent landlord, and a kind master.'

[The Marquis of Kildare's Earls of Kildare and their Ancestors; Hardy's Life of Lord Charlemont; Moore's Life of Lord Edward Fitzgerald; Cornwallis Correspondence; Gent. Mag. November 1804.] H. M. S.

FITZGERALD, SIR WILLIAM ROBERT SEYMOUR VESEY (1818–1885), governor of Bombay, son of William, second baron Fitzgerald and Vesey, who died in 1843, was born in 1818. He matriculated from Christ Church, Oxford, 21 Feb. 1833, and migrated to Oriel, where he was New-digate prizeman in 1835, and graduated B.A., being placed second class in classics in 1837, and M.A. in 1844. He was called to the bar by the Honourable Society of Lincoln's Inn at Hilary term 1839, and went the northern circuit. In 1848 he was returned for Horsham, Sussex, in the conservative interest, but was unseated on petition. He was returned again for the same borough in 1852, and retained his seat until 1865. He was under-secretary of state for foreign affairs under the Derby administration, in which Lord Malmesbury was foreign secretary, from February 1858 to June 1859. He was appointed governor of Bombay in Nov. 1866, and was sworn in a member of the privy council, and made knight commander of the order of the Star of India in the same year, and grand cross of the same order in 1868. He was relieved in March 1872. In February 1874 Fitzgerald was returned to parliament for the fifth time for the borough of Horsham, and sat until November 1875, when he was appointed chief commissioner of charities in England. Fitzgerald, who was an honorary D.C.L. Oxon. (1863), and a magistrate and deputy-lieutenant of Sussex, died at his residence in Warwick Square, London, 28 June 1885. He married in 1846 Maria Triphena, eldest daughter of the late Edward Seymour, M.D., and by her, who died in 1865, left issue.

[Foster's Knightage, 1882; Law Times, 4 July 1885; Times, 30 June 1885.] H. M. C.

FITZGERALD, WILLIAM THOMAS (1759?–1829), versifier, was born in England of an Irish father (see preface to his 'Tears of Hibernia dispelled by the Union'), and claimed connection with the Duke of Leinster's family. He was educated partly at a school in Greenwich and partly in Paris, and entered the navy pay office as a clerk in 1782. 'On all public occasions,' as the 'Annual Register' for 1829 remarks, his 'pen was ever ready.' His more notable productions are either prologues for plays or appeals to England's loyalty and valour. These latter he was in the habit of reciting, year after year, at the public dinners of the Literary Fund, of which he was one of the vice-presidents. It is to this that Byron refers in the first couplet of 'English Bards and Scotch Reviewers':—

Still must I hear?—shall hoarse Fitzgerald bawl
His creaking couplets in a tavern hall?

The 'Annual Register' for 1803 speaks of the company at the dinner for that year as being 'roused almost to rapture' by Fitzgerald's 'Tyrtæan compositions,' and says that 'words cannot convey an idea of the

force and animation' with which he recited, 'or of the enthusiasm with which he was encored.' A collection of Fitzgerald's poems appeared in 1801 as 'Miscellaneous Poems,' dedicated to the Right Honourable the Earl of Moira, by William Thomas Fitzgerald, esq.,' and they are very bad. Perhaps the one which most nearly approaches the famous parody in the 'Rejected Addresses' is the 'Address to every Loyal Briton on the Threatened Invasion of his Country;' but the 'Britons to Arms!' of a later date is almost of equal merit. Fitzgerald's 'Nelson's Triumph' appeared in 1798, his 'Tears of Hibernia dispelled by the Union' in 1802, and his 'Nelson's Tomb' in 1806. In 1814 Fitzgerald issued a collected edition of his verses in denunciation of Napoleon Bonaparte. It is, however, unquestionably in the 'Loyal Effusion' of the 'Rejected Addresses,' and the opening couplet of 'English Bards and Scotch Reviewers' that Fitzgerald will live. It is only just to record that this 'small beer poet,' as Cobbett called him, bore no malice against James and Horace Smith for their parody. Meeting one of them, probably the latter, at a Literary Fund dinner, he came to him with great good humour, and said, 'I mean to recite. . . . You'll have some more of "God bless the regent and the Duke of York."' Fitzgerald died at Paddington on 9 July 1829. A portrait appears in the 'European Magazine' for 1804.

[Gent. Mag. 1829, ii. 471–3; Annual Register, 1829; notes to the later editions of Rejected Addresses.] F. T. M.

FITZGERALD, WILLIAM VESEY, BARON FITZGERALD AND VESEY (1783–1843), statesman, was the elder son of the Right Hon. James Fitzgerald [q. v.], by his wife Catherine Vesey, who was in 1826 created Baroness Fitzgerald and Vesey in the peerage of Ireland. He was born in 1783, and spent three years at Christ Church, Oxford, where he made some reputation as a young man of ability, and he entered the united House of Commons as member for Ennis, in his father's room, in 1808. He was greatly involved in the famous scandal resulting from the connection of the Duke of York with Mrs. Mary Ann Clarke [q. v.], but rendered services to the government and the court in bringing facts to light, and secured his appointment as a lord of the Irish treasury and a privy councillor in Ireland in February 1810. His motives at this time were impugned by Mrs. Clarke in a 'Letter' which she published in 1813, but though there probably was a grain of truth in her assertions, there was not enough to damage Fitzgerald's reputation, and the lady was condemned to nine months' imprisonment for libel. In 1812 he was sworn of the English privy council, and appointed a lord of the treasury in England, chancellor of the Irish exchequer, and first lord of the Irish treasury, and in January 1813 he again succeeded his father as M.P. for Ennis. He held the above offices until their abolition in 1816, when the English and Irish treasuries were amalgamated. A year earlier he had assumed his mother's name of Vesey in addition to his own, on succeeding to some of the Vesey estates. In 1818 he was elected M.P. for the county of Clare. In 1820 he was appointed minister plenipotentiary and envoy extraordinary to the court of Sweden, where he spent three years in fruitless attempts to persuade Bernadotte, who had succeeded to the throne of that kingdom, to repay the large sums of money advanced to him during the war with Napoleon. His efforts were of no avail, and in 1823 he was recalled in something like disgrace. Lord Liverpool, however, knew his value as a speaker and man of business, and in 1826 made him paymaster-general to the forces. After the retirement of Huskisson and others from the Duke of Wellington's administration in June 1828, the duke selected Vesey-Fitzgerald for a seat in his cabinet as president of the board of trade, and this nomination made it necessary for him to seek re-election for the county of Clare. He was opposed by Daniel O'Connell, and was beaten at the poll, a defeat involving important political consequences. A seat was, however, found for Vesey-Fitzgerald at Newport in Cornwall in 1829, and in August 1830 he was elected for Lostwithiel. In February 1830 he resigned office, being succeeded by John Charles Herries [q. v.], and gave up his seat in parliament, but next year was again elected for Ennis, and sat for that borough until his accession to his mother's Irish peerage in February 1832. When Sir Robert Peel came into office with his tory cabinet in 1835, he did not forget the services of Vesey-Fitzgerald, who was created an English peer, Lord Fitzgerald of Desmond and Clan Gibbon in the county of Cork, 10 Jan. 1835. He did not form part of Sir Robert Peel's original cabinet when he next came into office in 1841, but he succeeded Lord Ellenborough as president of the board of control on 28 Oct. 1841, and held that office until his death in Belgrave Square, London, on 11 May 1843. Vesey-Fitzgerald was not a great statesman, but he was a finished speaker, a good debater, a competent official, and had refined literary tastes. At the time of his death he was a trustee of the British Museum, president of the Institute of Irish Architects, and a fellow of the Society of Antiquaries. At his death his United Kingdom peerage became extinct, but he was succeeded in his Irish peerage by his brother Henry, dean of Kilmore, at whose death in 1860 that also became extinct.

[Gent. Mag. July 1843; Mary Anne Clarke's Letter to the Right Hon. W. Fitzgerald, 1813.]
H. M. S.

FITZGIBBON, EDMUND FITZJOHN (1552?–1608), the White Knight, second son of John Oge Fitzgerald, *alias* Fitzgibbon (*d.* 1569), and Ellen, daughter of Patrick Condon, lord of Condons, accompanied James Fitzmaurice to France in March 1575, returning in July. Being by the attainder of his father (13 Eliz. c. 3) deprived of his ancestral possessions, he in 1576 obtained a lease of a large portion of them (*Cal. of Fiants*, Eliz. 2873), which he surrendered in 1579, receiving in return a new one comprising the lands contained in the former and others which had in the meantime reverted to the crown through the death of his mother (*ib.* 3583). Charged by his hereditary enemy, Lord Roche, viscount Fermoy, with aiding and abetting the rebellion of Gerald, earl of Desmond, he appears to have trimmed his way through the difficulties that beset him with considerable skill, but without much regard for his honour. The English officials, Sir H. Wallop in particular, were greatly provoked that the lands forfeited by his father's rebellion were not to be allotted among the planters, and did their best to blacken his character. In 1584 he accompanied Sir John Perrot on his expedition against Sorley Boy MacDonnell, and being wounded on that occasion was much commended for his valour by the deputy. In April 1587 the government thought it advisable to arrest him, though it declined to follow St. Leger's advice to make him shorter by his head. In 1589, when all immediate danger had passed away, he was released on heavy recognisances. In the following year he paid a visit to England and obtained a grant in tail male of all the lands he held on lease (MORRIN, *Cal. of Patent Rolls*, ii. 198). He was appointed sheriff of the county of Cork in 1596, and appears to have fulfilled his duties satisfactorily. But he still continued to be regarded with suspicion, and not without reason, for it is almost certain that he was implicated in the rebellion of Hugh O'Neill. He, however, on 22 May 1600, submitted unconditionally to Sir George Thornton, and was ready enough when called upon to blame the folly of his son John, who had joined the rebels (*Pac. Hib.* i. 74, 133). Still Cecil was not quite satisfied, and advised Sir George Carew to take good pledges for him, 'for, it is said, you will be cozened by him at last' (*Cal. Carew MSS.* iii. 462). In May 1601 he again fell under suspicion for not attempting to capture the Sugan Earl [see FITZGERALD, JAMES Fitzthomas, *d.* 1608], while passing through his territories; but, 'being earnestly spurred on to repair his former errors' by Sir George Carew, 'did his best endeavours which had the success desired.' His capture of the Sugan Earl in the caves near Mitchelstown purchased him the general malice of the province. Such service could not pass unrewarded, and on 12 Dec. 1601 the queen declared her intention that an act should pass in the next parliament in Ireland for restoring him to his ancient blood and lineage. This intention was confirmed by James I on 7 July 1604, and the title of Baron of Clangibbon conferred on him. But as no parliament assembled before 1613, and as by that time he and his eldest son were both dead, it took no effect. In 1606 he again fell under suspicion, and was committed to gaol, but shortly afterwards liberated on promising to do service against the rebels. He died at Castletown on Sunday, 23 April 1608, a day after the death of his eldest son, Maurice. They were buried together in the church of Kilbeny, where they lay a week, and were then removed to Kilmallock, and there lie in their own tomb. He married, first, Joan Tobyn, daughter of the Lord of Cumshionagh, co. Tipperary, by whom he had two sons, Maurice (who married Joan Butler, daughter of Lord Dunboyne, by whom he had issue Maurice and Margaret), and John, and four daughters; secondly, Joan, daughter of Lord Muskerry, having issue Edmund and David, who died young. Maurice and John dying, Maurice, the grandson, succeeded, but dying without issue the property passed to Sir William Fenton through his wife, Margaret Fitzgibbon.

[All the references to Fitzgibbon's life contained in the State Papers, the Carew MSS., and Pacata Hibernia have been collected together in the Unpublished Geraldine Documents, pt. iv., ed. Hayman and Graves.]   R. D.

FITZGIBBON, EDWARD (1803–1857), who wrote under the pseudonym 'Ephemera,' son of a land agent, was born at Limerick in 1803. He was devotedly attached to fishing from boyhood. When he was fourteen years old his father died, and he came to London. At sixteen he was articled to a surgeon in the city, but quitted the profession in disgust two years later, and became a classical tutor in various parts of England for three years, finding time everywhere to practise his favourite sport. He then visited Marseilles, where he remained six years, devoting himself to politics and the French language and literature, and becoming a welcome guest in all literary and polite circles. Having taken some part in the revolution of 1830, he returned to England and recommended himself to the notice of Black, the editor of the 'Morning Chronicle.' Being admitted to the staff, he worked with success in the gallery of the House of Commons. For a long series of years he wrote on angling for 'Bell's Life in London,' his knowledge of the subject and the attractive style in which his articles were written giving them great celebrity. For twenty-eight years he was a diligent worker for the daily press. His 'Lucid Intervals of a Lunatic' was a paper which at the time obtained much attention. He wrote often for the 'Observer,' and was a theatrical critic of considerable acumen.

With his fine genius, excellent classical attainments, and perfect knowledge of French, Fitzgibbon would have been more famous but for an unfortunate weakness. He had periodical fits of drinking. Physicians viewed his case with much interest, as his weakness seemed almost to amount to a kind of monomania, in the intervals of which his life was marked by abstemiousness and refined tastes. Fitzgibbon often promised that he would write his experiences of intoxication, which his friends persuaded themselves would have won him fame. But he became a wreck some years before his death, on 19 Nov. 1857, after a month's illness. He died in the communion of the Roman catholic church. He left no family, and was buried in Highgate cemetery.

Fitzgibbon made a great impression upon all who knew him by the brilliancy of his gifts. He possessed unblemished integrity, a kind and liberal disposition, much fire and eloquence, and the power of attaching to him many friends. From 1830 to the time of his death his writings had given a marvellous impulse to the art of fishing, had caused a great improvement in the manufacture and sale of fishing tackle, and largely increased the rents received by the owners of rivers and proprietors of fishing rights. He once killed fifty-two salmon and grilse on the Shin river in fifty-five hours of fishing. His 'Handbook of Angling' (1847), which reached a third edition in 1853, is perhaps the very best of the enormous number of manuals on fishing which are extant. Besides it Fitzgibbon wrote, in conjunction with Shipley of Ashbourne, 'A True Treatise on the Art of Fly-fishing as practised on the Dove and the Principal Streams of the Midland Counties,' 1838; and 'The Book of the Salmon,' together with A. Young, who added to it many notes on the life-history of this fish, 1850. 'Ephemera' regarded this as the acme of his teachings on fishing. He also edited and partly re-wrote the section on 'Angling' in Blaine's 'Encyclopædia of Rural Sports' (1852), and published the best of all the practical editions of 'The Compleat Angler' of Walton and Cotton in 1853.

[Bell's Life in London, 22 and 29 Nov. 1857; Francis's By Lake and River, p. 221; Annual Register, 1857, p. 347; Quarterly Review, No. 278, p. 365.]   M. G. W.

FITZGIBBON, GERALD (1793–1882), lawyer and author, the fourth son of an Irish tenant farmer, was born at Glin, co. Limerick, on 1 Jan. 1793, and, after receiving such education as was to be had at home and in the vicinity of his father's farm, obtained employment as a clerk in a mercantile house in Dublin in 1814. His leisure hours he devoted to the study of the classics, and in 1817 entered Trinity College, where he graduated B.A. in 1825, and proceeded M.A. in 1832, having in 1830 been called to the Irish bar. During his college course and preparation for the bar he had maintained himself by teaching. In the choice of a profession he was guided by the advice of his tutor, Dr. (afterwards Bishop) Sandes. His rise at the bar was rapid, his mercantile experience standing him in good stead, and in 1841 he took silk. In 1844 he unsuccessfully defended Dr. (afterwards Sir John) Gray, one of the traversers in the celebrated state prosecution of that year, by which O'Connell's influence with the Irish masses was destroyed. In the course of the trial Fitzgibbon used language concerning Cusack Smith, the Irish attorney-general, which was construed by the latter into an imputation of dishonourable motives, and so keenly resented by him that he sent Fitzgibbon a challenge. Fitzgibbon returned the cartel, and on the attorney-general declining to take it back, drew the attention of the court to the occurrence. Thereupon the chief justice suspended the proceedings, in order to afford the parties time for reflection, observing that 'the attorney-general is the last man in his profession who ought to have allowed himself to be betrayed into such an expression of feeling as has been stated to have taken place.' The attorney-general thereupon expressed his willingness to withdraw the note, in the hope that Fitzgibbon would withdraw the words which had elicited it, and Fitzgibbon disclaiming any intention to impute conduct unworthy of a gentleman to the attorney-general, the matter dropped, and the trial proceeded (*Annual Register*, 1844, Chron. 323). Fitzgibbon continued in large

practice until 1860, when he accepted the post of receiver-master in chancery. He published in 1868 a work entitled 'Ireland in 1868, the Battle Field for English Party Strife; its Grievances real and fictitious; Remedies abortive or mischievous,' 8vo. The book, which displays considerable literary ability, dealt with the educational, agrarian, religious, and other questions of the hour. The last and longest chapter, which was entitled 'The Former and Present Condition of the Irish People,' was published separately the same year. Its design is to show, by the evidence of history and tradition, that such measure of prosperity as Ireland has enjoyed has been due to the English connection. A second edition of the original work also appeared in the course of the year, with an additional chapter on the land question, in which stress is laid on the duties of landowners. This Fitzgibbon followed up with a pamphlet entitled 'The Land Difficulty of Ireland, with an Effort to Solve it,' 1869, 8vo. The principal feature of his plan of reform was that fixity of tenure should be granted to the farmer conditionally upon his executing improvements to the satisfaction of a public official appointed for the purpose. In 1871 he published 'Roman Catholic Priests and National Schools,' a pamphlet in which the kind of religious instruction given by Romanist priests, particularly with regard to the dogma of eternal punishment, is illustrated from authorised works. A second edition with an appendix appeared in 1872. Having in 1871 been charged in the House of Commons with acting with inhumanity in the administration of certain landed property belonging to wards of the Irish court of chancery, he published in pamphlet form a vindication of his conduct, entitled 'Refutation of a Libel on Gerald Fitzgibbon, Esq., Master in Chancery in Ireland,' 1871, 8vo. Fitzgibbon also published 'A Banded Ministry and the Upas Tree,' 1873, 8vo. He resigned his post in 1878, and died in September 1882. As an advocate he enjoyed a high reputation for patient and methodical industry, indefatigable energy, and great determination, combined with a very delicate sense of honour, and only a conscientious aversion to engage in the struggles of party politics precluded him from aspiring to judicial office. Fitzgibbon married in 1835 Ellen, daughter of John Patterson, merchant, of Belfast, by whom he had two sons, (1) Gerald, now Lord Justice Fitzgibbon, (2) Henry, now M.D. and vice-president of the Royal College of Surgeons in Ireland.

[Catalogue of Dublin Graduates; British Museum Catalogue; information from members of the family.]   J. M. R.

FITZGIBBON, JOHN, EARL OF CLARE (1749–1802), lord chancellor of Ireland, the second son of John Fitzgibbon of Mount Shannon, co. Limerick, a successful Irish barrister, was born near Donnybrook in 1749. At school and at the university of Dublin he gained great distinction. Grattan was his great rival at Dublin, and had the superiority in the early, while Fitzgibbon succeeded best in the later years of the course. In 1765 Fitzgibbon obtained an optime for a translation of the 'Georgics,' 'the very rarest honour in our academic course' (*Dublin University Mag.* xxx. 672). He graduated B.A. of Trinity College, Dublin, in 1767, and afterwards entered Christ Church, Oxford, where he graduated M.A. in 1770. In 1772 he was called to the Irish bar, and stepped at once into a large and growing practice. He received in his first year 343*l*. 7*s*., between 1772 and 1783 (when he became attorney-general) 8,973*l*. 6*s*. 3*d*., and between 1783 and 1789 (when he became lord chancellor) 36,939*l*. 3*s*. 11*d*. (*ib.* xxx. 675). His father is said to have allowed him 600*l*. a year in addition. He conducted a successful election petition in 1778 against the return of Hely Hutchinson for the university, succeeded to the seat, and, along with Hussey Burgh, represented the university till 1783. In his early parliamentary days he gave a moderate support to the national claims. In 1780 he opposed Grattan's declaration of the legislative rights of Ireland; but, in consequence of an appeal from his constituents, promised to support it on the next occasion. 'I have always been of opinion,' he said, 'that the claim of the British parliament to make laws for the country is a daring usurpation of the rights of a free people, and have uniformly asserted the opinion in public and in private.' The total repeal of Poynings's law, however, seemed to him undesirable. On the necessity of repealing the Perpetual Mutiny Bill and of making the judges independent, he entirely agreed with his constituents (see his letter in O'FLANAGAN, *Lord Chancellors of Ireland*, ii. 160).

He succeeded in keeping on good terms both with the government and with the nationalists. On several important questions he supported the latter, and had his reward in 1783, when Grattan, to his own subsequent regret, pressed for his appointment as attorney-general (GRATTAN, *Memoirs*, iii. 202). Fitzgibbon was never fortunate enough to find a suitable occasion for expressing the national feelings with which Grattan credited him. Until the union he remained practically the directing head of the Irish government, and consistently used his great influence to resist every proposal of reform and concession. His first conflict was over the question of parliamentary reform in the House of Commons, where he now represented Kilmallock. He opposed Flood's bill of 1784 as the mandate of a turbulent military congress; and, when the sheriffs of Dublin convened a meeting for the purpose of electing delegates to a national congress to consider the question, he wrote a letter threatening them with prosecution if they proceeded. He had the courage to appear at the meeting and repeat his threat. Reilly, the sheriff who was present, yielded, but was nevertheless fined for contempt of the court of king's bench in calling an illegal meeting. In the House of Commons Fitzgibbon defended both the legality and the expediency of this proceeding, and stated that it had been taken by his advice. In 1785 he supported the government's commercial policy with such power as to produce a special message of thanks from the king. In a speech on the treaty (15 Aug.) he referred to Curran as 'the politically insane gentleman,' whose declamation was better calculated for Sadler's Wells than the House of Commons. Curran retorted by saying that if he acted like Fitzgibbon he should be glad of the excuse of insanity. A duel followed, 'but,' says Lord Plunket in narrating the incident, 'unluckily they missed each other.' Curran is reported to have accused Fitzgibbon of determined malignity, shown by taking aim for nearly half a minute after his antagonist had fired (PHILLIPS, *Curran and his Contemporaries*, p. 145). Mr. Froude ingeniously suggests that Fitzgibbon's deliberate aim was 'perhaps to make sure of doing him no serious harm' (*English in Ireland*, ii. 484). The enmity lasted through life; and Curran freely accused Fitzgibbon of purposely seeking opportunities to injure him.

In the Whiteboy Act of 1787 Fitzgibbon may be said to have begun his consistent policy of repression. He was presumably responsible for a clause, which had to be abandoned, giving power to destroy any popish chapel in or near which an illegal oath had been tendered. In later years he recurred repeatedly to the evil influence of the priests. At the same time he saw clearly the causes of outrage which repressive measures could not remove. In an often-quoted passage he gave his experience of Munster: 'If landlords would take the trouble to know their tenants,' he said, 'and not leave them in the hands of rapacious agents and middlemen, we should hear no more of discontents. The great source of all these miseries arises from the neglect of those whose duty and interest it is to protect them.' On the other hand, he steadily opposed a reform of the tithe system such as Pitt advised in 1785 and as Grattan urged in the Irish parliament in 1787, 1788, and 1789 (LECKY, *Hist. of England*, vi. 401).

In the debates on the regency in 1789 the duty of advocating the case of the government rested mainly on Fitzgibbon. In his speeches, which Mr. Lecky has justly described as 'of admirable subtlety and power,' may be found probably the best defence which was made of Pitt's proposal. They show, however, that the idea of a union with England was already in his mind, though he spoke of it as only the least of two evils. Since the 'only security of your liberty,' he said, 'is your connection with Great Britain, he would prefer a union, however much to be deprecated, to separation.' During the debate on the lord-lieutenant's refusal to transmit to the Prince of Wales the address of the Irish parliament Fitzgibbon unguardedly said he recollected how a vote of censure on Lord Townshend had been followed by a vote of thanks which cost the nation half a million, and that therefore he would oppose the present censure, which might lead to an address which would cost half a million more (PLOWDEN, *Hist. of Ireland*, ii. 286; GRATTAN, *Memoirs*, iii. 377. See Fitzgibbon's subsequent explanation in a speech of 19 Feb. 1798, reprinted after his reply to Lord Moira on the same day).

In 1789 Fitzgibbon succeeded Lord Lifford as lord chancellor of Ireland, with the title of Baron Fitzgibbon of Lower Connello. Thurlow for a long time opposed his appointment, partly on the ground that the office should not be held by an Irishman, and partly owing to reports of Fitzgibbon's unpopularity, but yielded at last to the pressure of Fitzgibbon himself, the Marquis of Buckingham, and others (BUCKINGHAM, *Courts and Cabinets of George III*, ii. 157; O'FLANAGAN, *Lord Chancellors of Ireland*, ii. 200). In 1793 he received the title of Viscount Fitzgibbon and in 1795 that of Earl of Clare, and in 1799 he was made a peer of Great Britain as Lord Fitzgibbon of Sidbury, Devonshire.

In his judicial capacity he displayed great rapidity of decision, which, though called precipitancy and attributed to his despotic habits, was rather the simple result of his extraordinary power of work and of concentration. An anonymous biographer says that he had heard Peter Burrowes [q. v.], an eminent counsel and strong political opponent, testify to the extraordinary correctness of Clare's judgments (*Dublin University Mag.* xxx. 682). With equal energy he devoted

himself to the task of law reform, and down to the day of his death he sought every opportunity to remove legal abuses.

In politics he maintained an uncompromising resistance to all popular movements, and especially to all attempts to improve the position of the Roman catholics. A detailed record of his chancellorship would be a history of Ireland during the same period. His position and opinions can be most conveniently indicated by a reference to four speeches in the Irish House of Lords, published by himself or his friends, which are of great historical importance : 1. A speech on the prorogation of parliament in 1790, in which he angrily attacked the Whig Club for interfering in a question which had been raised concerning the election of the lord mayor (see pamphlet entitled *Observations on the Vindication of the Whig Club: to which are subjoined the speech of the Lord Chancellor as it appeared in the newspapers, the Vindication of the Whig Club*, &c., and see also GRATTAN, *Miscellaneous Works*, pp. 266, 270). 2. A speech on the second reading of a bill for the relief of his majesty's Roman catholic subjects in Ireland, 13 March 1793 (1798; reprinted in 1813). Reviewing at great length the history of the Roman catholic church in Ireland, and the claims of the catholic church in general, he urged vehemently the impolicy and danger of entrusting catholics with power in the state, but agreed that after the promises which had been made it might be essential to the momentary peace of the country that the bill should pass. His peculiar bitterness on this occasion was partly due to the fact that only a few months before he had vainly sought to dissuade the viceroy and the English government from any conciliatory language towards the catholics (LECKY, *Hist. of England*, vi. 528), and that as a member of the government he was speaking against a government measure. Comparing the speech with that of the Bishop of Killala, who preceded him, Grattan wrote to Richard Burke : 'The bishop who had no law was the statesman; the lawyer who had no religion was the bigot' (*Memoirs*, v. 557). The attempt at conciliation which Lord Fitzwilliam was allowed to make for a few months in 1794 and 1795 must have been intensely repugnant to him. Fitzwilliam had marked out the lord chancellor as one of the men who had to be got rid of (BUCKINGHAM, *Courts and Cabinets*, p. 312), and the influence of the chancellor had doubtless a good deal to do with the viceroy's recall. On the day of Lord Camden's arrival the Dublin mob attacked Clare's house, and he was saved only by the skill with which his sister led off the crowd to seek him elsewhere. 3. Speech in the House of Lords, 19 Feb. 1798, on Lord Moira's motion (printed 1798). Lord Moira attacked the government for its coercive policy. Clare justified that policy in a long reply, containing an elaborate account of the progress of disaffection, and of the failure of conciliation during a period, as he considered it, of rapid advance. He excused a case of picketing, on the ground that it led to the discovery of two hundred pikes within two days, and has been therefore denounced as the defender of torture. Clare himself, however, was inclined to temper a rigorous policy by moderation to individuals. Both he and Castlereagh supported Cornwallis's proposal of a general amnesty after Vinegar Hill, and in the case of Lord Edward Fitzgerald he went so far as to warn his friends that his doings were fully known to the government, and to promise that if he would leave the country every port should be open to him. This did not affect his determination to crush out disaffection at any cost. (The share of Clare in the government policy cannot be profitably separated from the general history, as to which see the *Cornwallis* and *Castlereagh Correspondence*, the *Lords' Report of the Committee of Secrecy*, which is understood to have been carefully edited by Clare, and Macneven's *Pieces of Irish History*.) 4. Speech in the House of Lords, 10 Feb. 1800, on a motion made by him in favour of a union (printed 1800). Clare narrated the history of the English connection, of the religious divisions, and of the land confiscations, recalled the circumstances in which the 'final adjustment of 1782' was made, the designs of the revolutionists, and the disorganised state of Irish finances, and insisted that union was the only alternative to separation and bankruptcy. Grattan replied in an indignant pamphlet, vindicating the action of himself and his friends, and rebuking Clare for the insulting language in which he spoke of his country. The speech is certainly that of an advocate, not of an historian; but it is impossible not to admire its skilful marshalling of facts and the vigour of its language. There is little doubt that the passing of the Act of Union was due to Clare more than to any other man. For the last seven years, he said, he had urged its necessity on the king's ministers, and this statement is borne out by an unpublished letter which he wrote to Lord Auckland in 1798. 'As to the subject of the union with the British parliament,' he said, 'I have long been of opinion that nothing short of it can save this country. I stated this opinion very strongly to Mr. Pitt in the year 1793, immediately after that fatal mistake into which he was betrayed by Mr.

Burke and Mr. Dundas, in receiving an appeal from the Irish parliament by a popish democracy.' He states his continued adherence to this view, and concludes: 'It makes me almost mad when I look back at the madness, folly, and corruption in both countries which has brought us to the verge of destruction' (British Museum *Additional MS.* 29475, f. 43). Yet in 1793 he told the House of Lords that a separation and a union were 'each to be equally dreaded.' On 16 Oct. 1798 he wrote to Castlereagh: 'I have seen Mr. Pitt, the chancellor, and the Duke of Portland, who seem to feel very sensibly the critical situation of our damnable country (highly complimentary, but it was between themselves), and that the union alone can save it' (*Castlereagh Correspondence*, i. 393).

Clare was equally eager that no attempt should be made to change, as a part of the union, the existing catholic laws. 'Even the chancellor,' wrote Cornwallis to Pitt, 25 Sept. 1798, 'who is the most right-minded politician in this country, will not hear of the Roman catholics sitting in the united parliament' (*Cornwallis Correspondence*, ii. 416; and see letter of Lord Grenville, 5 Nov. 1798, in BUCKINGHAM, *Courts and Cabinets*, ii. 411; and CORNEWALL LEWIS, *Administrations of Great Britain*, p. 185).

Clare even ventured to try humour in his anxious desire for a union. In 1799 appeared a tract entitled 'No Union! But Unite and Fall! By Paddy Whack, in a loving letter to his dear mother, Sheelah, of Dame Street, Dublin,' of which he is said to have been the author, and in which Paddy Whack advises Sheelah to marry 'the rich, and generous, and industrious, and kind, and liberal, and powerful, and free, honest John Bull.' Its humour is somewhat coarse and clumsy.

After the union Clare appeared several times in the House of Lords, but he did not increase his reputation. His sharp temper brought him into frequent conflict, while the studied disrespect with which he referred to his countrymen, and his passionate insistence on the madness of conceding anything to the Roman catholics, excited a feeling of repugnance. 'Good God!' Pitt is reported to have said when listening to him on one occasion, 'did you ever hear in all your life such a rascal as that?' (GRATTAN, *Memoirs*, iii. 403). He died on 28 Jan. 1802. His funeral was followed by a Dublin mob, whose curses violently expressed the hate with which a great part of his fellow-countrymen regarded him (account by an eye-witness in *Dublin Univ. Mag.* xxvii. 559; CLONCURRY, *Personal Recollections*, p. 146).

On his deathbed he is said to have sent for

his wife, and requested her to burn all his papers—'should they remain after me, hundreds may be compromised '—and his wishes were observed (*Curran and his Contemporaries*, p. 154). A report that he repented of his action with regard to the union (PLOWDEN, *Hist. of Ireland*, ii. 558) is based on a sentence in an abusive statement of his nephew Jeffreys, who had quarrelled with his uncle over private matters: 'I afterwards saw Lord Clare die, repenting of his conduct on that very question' (GRATTAN, *Memoirs*, iii. 403).

Clare married in 1786 Anne, eldest daughter of R. C. Whaley of Whaley Abbey, co. Wicklow, who died in 1844. He left two sons, both of whom succeeded to the earldom. John, the elder (1792–1851), second earl, educated at Christ Church, Oxford, was governor of Bombay, 1830–4. Richard Hobart, the younger son (1793–1864), third and last earl, had an only son, John Charles Henry, viscount Fitzgibbon (1829–1854), who fell in the charge of the light brigade at Balaklava.

Clare has been described as the basest of men, without one redeeming virtue (see the account of him by Grattan's son in GRATTAN's *Memoirs*, iii. 393), and he has been represented as an unsullied patriot, thinking only of his country's good (FROUDE, *English in Ireland*, ii. 526). The one picture is as false as the other. In Clare's cold and unemotional manner there was a good deal of affectation, and his friends claimed for him that in private life he was kindly and true. There is evidence that he was an indulgent landlord—'the very best of landlords,' Plowden calls him. It is unreasonable, moreover, to question the general sincerity of his political opinions. He had a fixed purpose clearly before his mind, and he held firmly to it, undeterred by the abuse and the hate which he excited. He was ambitious, not very scrupulous, vain, and intolerably insolent; but whether he used his power for good or evil he acted with uniform courage, and in point of ability stood head and shoulders above all the other Irishmen of his time who sided with the government (*Curran and his Contemporaries*, p. 139; Magee's funeral sermon in *Annual Register*, 1802, p. 705; BARRINGTON, *Rise and Fall of the Irish Nation*).

[O'Flanagan's Lives of the Lord Chancellors of Ireland; Grattan's Memoirs; Phillips's Curran and his Contemporaries; Dublin Univ. Mag. xxx. 671; Metropolitan Mag. xxiv. 337, xxv. 113; Gent. Mag. lxxii. 185; Irish Parliamentary Debates; Cornwallis and Castlereagh Correspondence.] G. P. M.

FITZGILBERT, RICHARD (*d.* 1090?), founder of the house of Clare. [See CLARE, RICHARD DE, *d.* 1090?]

FITZGILBERT, RICHARD (*d.* 1136?), warrior. [See CLARE, RICHARD DE.]

FITZHAMON, ROBERT (*d.* 1107), conqueror of Glamorgan, belonged to a great family whose ancestor, Richard, was either the son or nephew of Rollo, and which since the tenth century had possessed the lordships of Thorigny, Creully, Mézy, and Evrecy in Lower Normandy (*Roman de Rou*, ed. Andresen, l. 4037 sq.) Richard's son, 'Haim as Denz' (Haimo Dentatus), was one of the rebels slain at Val ès Dunes in 1047 (*ib.* l. 4057 sq.), and Robert is generally described as his son (PEZET, *Les Barons de Creully*, p. 50). But William of Malmesbury expressly states that Robert was the grandson of this Haimo (*Gesta Regum*, bk. iii. p. 393, Engl. Hist. Soc.) If so, Robert's father must have been some other Haimo, probably the 'Haimo vicecomes' mentioned in the 'Domesday Book' as holding lands in chief in Kent and Surrey, and who presided as sheriff over the great suit between Odo and Lanfranc in the Kentish shire moot (ANDRESEN, *Roman de Rou*, Anmerkungen, ii. 768; cf. LE PRÉVOST's note to his edition of ORDERICUS VITALIS, iii. 14, 'grace aux renseignements de M. Stapleton;' cf. also ANSELM, *Epistolæ*, iv. 57, complaining of the outrages of Hamon's followers). Those who regard Haimo Dentatus as the grandfather of Robert, the conqueror of Glamorgan, suppose that the former had, besides 'Haimo vicecomes,' another son called Robert Fitzhamon, to whom the earlier notices of the name really refer. In that case, Haimo the sheriff was probably the father of Haimo Dapifer, a tenant-in-chief in Essex, though Mr. Ellis (Introduction to *Domesday Book*, i. 432) identifies the two Haimos. There is, however, no direct evidence for this, and it is quite certain that 'Hamon the steward' was brother, though hardly, as Professor Freeman (*William Rufus*, ii. 82–3) says, elder brother, of Robert Fitzhamon (WILLIAM OF JUMIÈGES in DUCHESNE, *Hist. Norm. Scriptt. Ant.* 306 c.) Robert held all the family estates, and Haimo was still alive in 1112 (CLARK in *Arch. Journal*, xxxv. 3). It is therefore not quite certain whether the earlier notices of Robert Fitzhamon refer to the nephew or the uncle; but in any case a Robert Fitzhamon is mentioned in Bayeux charters of 1064 and 1074 (*ib.* xxxv. 2). Between 1049 and 1066 the same person assented as lord to the foundation of the priory of St. Gabriel (DE LA RUE, *Essais Historiques sur la Ville de Caen*, ii. 409; cf. *Nouveaux Essais*, ii. 39; PEZET, p. 23). In 1074 he attested a charter of William I (*Mémoires de la Société des Antiquaires de la Normandie*, xxx. 702). There is no certain mention of him in 'Domesday Book,' despite the appearance of the two Hamons, his kinsmen.

When the feudal party under Odo of Bayeux revolted in 1088, Robert is mentioned among the select band of 'legitimi et maturi barones' who supported the royal cause (ORD. VIT. ed. Le Prévost, iii. 273). His Kentish connections may have given him special grievances against Odo as earl of Kent. In reward for his services William assigned him great estates, particularly the lands mostly in Gloucestershire, but partly in Buckinghamshire and Cornwall, which had passed from Brictric to Queen Matilda (Cont. WACE in ELLIS, ii. 55, and *Chron. Angl. Norm.* i. 73, which is manifestly wrong in making William I grantor of Brictric's lands to Fitzhamon; see FREEMAN, *Norman Conquest*, iv. 762–3). These Rufus had for a time allowed his brother Henry to possess, but about 1090 he transferred them to Fitzhamon (ORD. VIT. iii. 350). It is possible that the Gloucestershire estates were now erected into an honour (DUGDALE, *Monasticon*, ii. 60). Robert's marriage with Sibyl (ORD. VIT. iii. 118), daughter of Roger of Montgomery and sister of Robert of Bellême [q. v.], must have still further improved his position on the Welsh marches.

The next few years were marked by the definitive Norman conquest of South Wales. But while authentic history records the settlements of Bernard of Neufmarché in Brecheiniog, and of Arnulf of Montgomery in Dyfed and Ceredigion, the history of Fitzhamon's conquest of Glamorgan has to be constructed out of its results, and the untrustworthy, though circumstantial, legend that cannot be traced further back than to fifteenth or sixteenth century pedigree-mongers. In 1080 the building of Cardiff, subsequently the chief castle of Fitzhamon's lordship, was begun (*Brut y Tywysogion*, sub anno, Rolls Ser.), and this event may mark the beginning of Fitzhamon's conquests. If we can rely on the authenticity of the charter of 1086 (*Hist. Glouc.* i. 334), by which William I confirmed to Abbot Serlo Fitzhamon's grant of Llancarvan to the abbey of Gloucester, there can be no doubt but that the end of William's reign saw the beginning of the conquest. But probability suggests that it was not until after he had obtained the honour of Gloucester that he was able to win so large a territory as Glamorgan. The legend fits in with this, for it tells us how about 1088 Eineon [q. v.], son of Collwyn, went to London and 'agreed with Robert Fitzhamon, lord of Corbeil in France and cousin of the Red King, to come to the assistance of Iestin, prince

of Morganwg.' 'Twelve other honourable knights' were persuaded by Robert to accompany him. Uniting his forces with Iestin, Robert defeated and slew Rhys ab Tewdwr at Hirwaun Wrgan, received from Iestin his recompense in sterling gold, and returned towards London. But Eineon, disappointed by Iestin's treachery of Iestin's daughter, besought them to return. At Mynydd Bychan, near Cardiff, Iestin was put to flight and despoiled of his country. 'Robert Fitzhamon and his men took for themselves the best of the vale and the rich lands, and allotted to Eineon the uplands.' Robert himself, 'their prince,' took the government of all the country and the castles of Cardiff, Trevuvered, and Kenfig, with the lands belonging to them. The rest of the valley between the Taff and the Neath he divided among his twelve companions. Such is the story as told in the so-called Gwentian 'Brut y Tywysogion,' the manuscript of which is no older than the middle of the sixteenth century. The same story is repeated, with more detail and with long genealogical accounts of the descendants of Fitzhamon's twelve followers, in Powel's 'History of Cambria,' first published in 1584, on the authority of Sir Edward Stradling, described as 'a skilful and studious gentleman of that country,' but whose more than doubtful pedigree it was a main purpose of the story to exalt. There is in some ways a still fuller account in Rhys Meyrick's 'Book of Glamorganshire Antiquities' (1578). The 'Gwentian Brut's' authority is singularly small, and the details of the pedigrees in the later versions are of no authority at all. Rhys ab Tewdwr was really slain by Bernard of Neufmarché and the French of Brecheiniog (*Brut y Tywysogion*, sub anno 1091; but the date of FLORENCE OF WORCESTER (ii. 31), 1093, is better; cf. FREEMAN, *William Rufus*, ii. 91). But his death was followed by the French conquests of Dyved and Ceredigion, which must surely have succeeded the occupation of Glamorgan. Fitzhamon's grants to English churches and the inheritance which his daughter brought to her husband equally prove Fitzhamon to have been the conqueror of Glamorgan. There is almost contemporary proof of the existence of some at least of his twelve followers, and for their possession of the lordships assigned to them in the legend (e.g. *Liber Landavensis*, p. 27, for Pagan of Turberville, Maurice of London, and Robert of St. Quentin; cf. *Hist. Glouc.* passim). We can gather from the records of the next generation that Glamorgan was organised into what was afterwards called a lordship marcher, with institutions and government based on those of an English county ('Vicecomes Glamorganscirae,' *Hist. Glouc.*

i. 347; 'Comitatus de Cardiff,' *ib.*; *Liber Landavensis*, pp. 27–8, speaks of 'Vicecomes de Cardiff' when Robert of Gloucester was still alive). Except perhaps in name, Fitzhamon founded in Wales a county palatine as completely organised as the earldom of Pembroke.

Fitzhamon was a liberal benefactor to the church. He so increased the wealth and importance of Tewkesbury Abbey that he was regarded as its second founder. Hitherto Tewkesbury had been a cell of Cranborne in Dorsetshire, but in the reign of William Rufus (ORD. VIT. iii. 15), or in 1102 (*Ann. Theok.* in *Ann. Mon.* i. 44), the abbot Giraldus transferred himself, with the greater part of the fraternity, to the grand new minster that was now rising under Robert's fostering care on the banks of the Severn. William of Malmesbury can hardly find words to express the splendour of the buildings and the charity of the monks (*Gesta Regum*, bk. v. p. 625; cf. *Gesta Pont.* p. 295). The major part of the endowments was taken from Robert's Welsh conquest. Among the churches Fitzhamon handed over to Tewkesbury were the parish church of St. Mary's, Cardiff, the chapel of Cardiff Castle, and the famous British monastery at Llantwit. He also granted the monks of Tewkesbury tithes of all his domain revenues in Cardiff, and of all the territories of himself and his barons throughout Wales (DUGDALE, *Monasticon*, ii. 66, 81). He was only less liberal to the great abbey of St. Peter's, Gloucester, to which he granted the church of Llancarvan with some adjoining lands, and for which he witnessed a grant of Henry I of the tithe of venison in the Forest of Dean and the lands beyond the Severn (*Hist. Glouc.* i. 93, 122, 223, 334, ii. 50, 51, 177, 301). Traces of Fitzhamon's concessions still remain in the patronage of many Glamorganshire churches belonging to the chapter of Gloucester.

Little reference is made to Fitzhamon by chroniclers of the time of William Rufus, but he was in the close confidence of the king until his death. Before William's fatal hunting expedition on 2 Aug. 1100, Fitzhamon, then in attendance at Winchester, had reported to him the ominous dream of the foreign monk, and his representations at least postponed William's hunting until after dinner (WILL. MALM. bk. iv. p. 507). When William's corpse was discovered Fitzhamon was one of the barons who stood around it in tears. Fitzhamon's new mantle covered the corpse on its last journey to the cathedral at Winchester (GEOFFRY GAIMAR, ed. Wright, ll. 6357–96, Caxton Soc. The details are perhaps mythical, some others

are certainly false; the whole account shows the impossibility of Pezet's notion that Fitzhamon was away on crusade with Robert). But no former differences about the lands of Queen Matilda prevented Fitzhamon and his brother Hamon the steward from immediately attaching themselves with an equal zeal to Henry I. Both are among the witnesses of the letter despatched by Henry imploring Anselm to return from exile (STUBBS, *Select Charters*, p. 103). Fitzhamon was among the few magnates who strenuously adhered to Henry when the mass of the baronage openly or secretly favoured the cause of Robert of Normandy (WILL. MALM. bk. v. p. 620). When in 1101 Robert landed in Hampshire and approached Henry's army at Alton, Fitzhamon and other barons who held estates both of the king and the duke procured by their mediation peace between the brothers (WACE, l. 10432 sq. ed. Andresen; cf. ORD. VIT. iv. 199). In March 1103 he was one of Henry's representatives in negotiating an alliance with Robert, count of Flanders (*Fœdera*, i. 7, Record ed.) He also witnessed the Christmas charter of Henry, which assigned punishment to the false managers (*ib.* i. 12). When war again broke out, Fitzhamon still adhered to Henry, and busied himself in Normandy in a partisan warfare against the friends of Robert. Early in 1105 he was surprised by Robert's troops from Bayeux and Caen, and forced to take refuge in the tower of the church of Secqueville-en-Bessin. The church was set on fire, and he was compelled to descend a prisoner. For some time he was imprisoned at Bayeux, where the governor, Gontier d'Aulnay, protected him from the fury of the mob, which regarded him as a traitor to the duke (WACE, ll. 11125–60, ed. Andresen; cf. *Chronique de Normandie* in BOUQUET, xiii. 250–1). This news at once brought Henry to Normandy, where he landed at Barfleur just before Easter (ORD. VIT. iv. 204), and at once besieged Bayeux to rescue his faithful follower. Gontier sought to win the king's favour by surrendering Fitzhamon (*ib.* iv. 219), but valiantly defended the town, which Henry finally reduced to ashes, not sparing even the cathedral. The guilt of this sacrilege was, it was believed, shared by Henry and Fitzhamon (WILL. MALM. bk. v. p. 625; WACE, l. 11161 sq.; cf. DE TOUSTAIN, *Essai historique sur la prise et l'incendie de Bayeux*, Caen, 1861, who satisfactorily establishes the date as May 1105; cf. LE PRÉVOST's note to ORD. VIT. iv. 219). So detested did the house of Fitzhamon become in Bayeux, that a generation later a long resistance was made to the appointment of his son-in-law's bastard to the bishopric (HERMANT, *Hist. du Diocèse de Bayeux*, pp. 167–9; CHIGOUESNEL, *Nouvelle Histoire de Bayeux*, p. 131). Yet Fitzhamon held large estates under Bayeux, and was hereditary standard-bearer to the church of St. Mary there (*Mémoires de la Soc. des Ant. de la Normandie*, viii. 426).

Soon after Fitzhamon bought from Robert of Saint Remi the prisoners taken at Bayeux, and intrigued so successfully with those of them that came from Caen that they treacherously procured the surrender of Caen to Henry (WACE, l. 11259; BOUQUET, xiii. 251). Fitzhamon next served in the siege of Falaise, where he was struck by a lance on the forehead with such severity that his faculties became deranged (WILL. MALM. bk. v. p. 625; cf. *Gwentian Brut*, p. 93). He survived, however, until March 1107. He was buried in the chapter-house of Tewkesbury Abbey, whence his body was in 1241 transferred to the church and placed on the left side of the high altar (*Ann. Theok. in Ann. Mon.* i. 120). In 1397 the surviving rich chapel of stone was erected over the founder's tomb. The 'vast pillars and mysterious front of the still surviving minster' (FREEMAN, *Will. Rufus*, ii. 84) still testify to Fitzhamon's munificence. He may have built the older parts of the castle of Creully (PEZET).

By his wife, Sibyl of Montgomery, a benefactress of Ramsey (*Cart. Ramsey*, ii. 274, Rolls Ser.), Fitzhamon left no son, and his possessions passed, with the hand of his daughter Mabel, to Henry I's favourite bastard, Robert, under whom Gloucester first became an earldom (WILL. MALM. *Hist. Nov.* bk. i.; ROBERT OF THORIGNY in DUCHESNE, 306 c, who erroneously calls her Sibyl and her mother Mabel; ORD. VIT., iii. 318, calls her Matilda). Mabel was probably Fitzhamon's only daughter (WYKES in *Ann. Mon.* iv. 22), and certainly inherited all her father's estates, as well as those of Hamon the steward, her uncle (ROBERT OF THORIGNY, 306 c). The Tewkesbury tradition was, however, that she had three younger sisters, of whom Cecily became abbess of Shaftesbury, Hawyse abbess of the nuns' minster at Winchester, and Amice the wife of the 'Count of Brittany' (DUGDALE, *Monasticon*, ii. 60, 452, 473).

[Ordericus Vitalis, ed. Le Prévost (Société de l'Histoire de France); William of Malmesbury's Gesta Regum and Hist. Novella (Engl. Hist. Soc.); Wace's Roman de Rou, ed. Andresen; G. Gaimar's Estorie des Engles (Caxton Soc.); History and Chartulary of St. Peter's, Gloucester (Rolls Ser.); Dugdale's Monasticon, vol. ii. ed. Caley, Bandinel, and Ellis; Gwentian Brut, pp. 69–77 (Cambrian Archæological Association); Powel's Hist. of Cambria, ed. 1584, pp. 118–41; Merrick's Book of Glamorganshire Antiquities, privately printed by Sir T. Phillips (1825); Freeman's Norman Conquest, ii. 244, iv. 762–4, v. 820; Freeman's William Rufus, i. 62, 197, ii. 79–89, 613–15; G. T. Clark's Land of Morgan, reprinted from Archæological Journal, xxxiv. 11–39, xxxv. 1–4; Pezet's Les Barons de Creully, pp. 21–52 (Bayeux, 1854); De Toustain's Essai historique sur la prise et l'incendie de Bayeux, 1105.]

T. F. T.

FITZHARDING, ROBERT (*d.* 1170), founder of the second house of Berkeley, appears to have been the second son of Harding, son of Eadnoth [q. v.], the staller (*Gesta Regum*, i. 429; ELLIS, *Landholders of Gloucestershire*, p. 59; EYTON, *Somerset Domesday*, i. 58; FREEMAN, *Norman Conquest*, iv. 760). Local antiquaries have endeavoured to make out that he was the grandson of a Danish king or sea-rover (SEYER, i. 315; *Bristol, Past and Present*, i. 56), a futile imagination which has been traced to John Trevisa (MACLEAN), and is probably older than his date. Robert's eldest brother, Nicolas, inherited his father's fief, Meriet in Somerset (ELLIS). Robert was provost or reeve of Bristol, and was possessed of great wealth; he upheld the cause of Robert, earl of Gloucester, who fought for the empress, and purchased several estates from the earl, among them the manor of Billeswick on the right bank of the Frome, which included the present College Green of Bristol, and the manor of Bedminster-with-Redcliff. He had other lands, chiefly in Gloucestershire, and held of Humphrey de Bohun in Wiltshire, and William, earl of Warwick, in Warwickshire (*Liber Niger*, pp. 109, 206). Before Henry II came to the throne he is said to have been assisted by Robert, probably by loans of money; when he became king he granted him the lordship of Berkeley Hernesse, and Robert is held to have been the first of the second or present line of the lords of Berkeley [NICOLAS; see BERKELEY, FAMILY OF]. He granted a charter to the tenants of his fee near the 'bridge of Bristou.' By his wife Eva he had Maurice, who succeeded him, and four other sons and three daughters. On his estate in Billeswick he founded in 1142 the priory or abbey of St. Augustine's for black canons, the present cathedral, and is said to have assumed the monastic habit before his death, which occurred on 5 Feb. 1170 (ELLIS). He also founded a school in a building, afterwards called Chequer Hall, in Wine Street, Bristol, for the instruction of Jews and other strangers in the Christian faith. His wife Eva was the founder of a nunnery on St. Michael's Hill, Bristol. Both Robert and Eva were buried in St. Augustine's Church.

[Smyth's Lives of the Berkeleys, i. 19–62, ed. Maclean; Ellis's Landholders of Gloucestershire named in Domesday, pp. 59, 111, from Bristol and Glouc. Archæol. Soc.'s Trans. iv.; Eyton's Domesday Studies, Somerset, i. 59, 70, 101; Notes and Queries, 6th ser. i. 20; Freeman's Norman Conquest, iv. 757–60; Liber Niger de Scaccario, pp. 95, 109, 171, 206 (Hearne); Will. Malm. Gesta Regum, i. 429 (Engl. Hist. Soc.); Robert of Gloucester, p. 479 (Hearne); Ricart's Kalendar, p. 20 (Camden Soc.); Dugdale's Monasticon, vi. 365; Baronage, i. 350; Tanner's Notitia, p. 480; English Gilds, p. 288 (Early Eng. Text Soc.); Seyer's Hist. of Bristol, i. 313; Nicholls and Taylor's Bristol, Past and Present, i. 56–8, 91, ii. 46, 125; Britton's Bristol Cathedral, pp. 3–7, 57.]

W. H.

FITZHARDINGE, Baron. [See Berkeley, Maurice Frederick Fitzhardinge, 1788–1867.]

FITZHARRIS, EDWARD (1648?–1681), conspirator, son of Sir Edward Fitzharris, was born in Ireland about 1648, and brought up in the Roman catholic faith. According to his own relation he left Ireland for France in 1662 to learn the language, returning home through England in 1665. Three years later he went to Prague with the intention of entering the service of the emperor Leopold I in his operations against Hungary, when, finding that the expedition had been abandoned, he wandered through Flanders to England again. He next obtained a captain's commission in one of the companies raised by Sir George Hamilton in Ireland for Louis XIV, but on being discharged from his command soon after landing in France, he went to Paris, 'and, having but little money, he lived there difficulty about a year.' Returning to England in October 1672 he received, in the following February, the lieutenancy of Captain Sydenham's company in the Duke of Albemarle's regiment, which he was forced to resign on the passing of the Test Act in 1673. For the next eight years he was busily intriguing with influential Roman catholics, among others with the Duchess of Portsmouth. At length in February 1681 he wrote a libel, 'The True Englishman speaking plain English in a Letter from a Friend to a Friend' (Cobbett, Parl. Hist. vol. iv., Appendix, No. xiii.), in which he advocated the deposition of the king and the exclusion of the Duke of York. He possibly intended to place this in the house of some whig, and then, by discovering it himself, earn the wages of an informer. He was betrayed by an accomplice, Edmond Everard, and sent first to Newgate and afterwards to the Tower, where he pretended he could discover the secret of Sir Edmondbury Godfrey's murder. Eventually he succeeded in implicating Danby. Fitz-

harris was impeached by the commons of high treason, not to destroy but to serve him in opposition to the court. His impeachment brought into discussion an important question of constitutional law. The lords having voted for a trial at common law, the commons declared this to be a denial of justice. Parliament, however, was suddenly dissolved after eight days' session on 28 March, probably to avoid a threatened collision between the two houses; others, according to Luttrell, thought that the court feared that Fitzharris might be driven by the impeachment to awkward disclosures (Relation of State Affairs, 1857, i. 72). He had had, in fact, more than one interview with the king through the Duchess of Portsmouth (Burnet, Own Time, Oxford edition, ii. 280–1). The dissolution decided his fate. He was tried before the king's bench in Easter term, and entered a plea against the jurisdiction of the court on the ground that proceedings were pending against him before the lords. This plea was ruled to be insufficient, and Fitzharris was proceeded against at common law, 9 June 1681, and convicted. His wife, daughter of William Finch, commander in the navy, exhibited wonderful courage and resource on his behalf. At his request Burnet afterwards visited him, and soon satisfied himself that no reliance whatever could be placed on his testimony. Francis Hawkins, chaplain of the Tower, then took him in hand in the interests of the court, and, by insinuating that his life might yet be spared, persuaded him to draw up a pretended confession, in which Lord Howard of Escrick, who had befriended Fitzharris, was made the author of the libel, while Sir Robert Clayton [q. v.] and Sir George Treby, before whom his preliminary examination had been conducted, together with the sheriffs, Slingsby Bethel [q. v.] and Henry Cornish [q. v.], were severally charged with subornation. 'Yet at the same time he writ letters to his wife, who was not then admitted to him, which I saw and read,' says Burnet, 'in which he told her how he was practised upon with the hopes of life' (ib. ii. 282). Fitzharris was executed on 1 July 1681, the concocted confession appeared the very next day, and Hawkins was rewarded for his pains with the deanery of Chichester. The justices and sheriffs in their reply, 'Truth Vindicated,' had little difficulty in proving the so-called 'confession' to be a tissue of falsehoods. The indictment against Lord Howard of Escrick was withdrawn, as the grand jury refused to believe the evidence of the two witnesses, Mrs. Fitzharris and her maidservant. The court, fearful of further exposures, persuaded

Mrs. Fitzharris to give up her husband's letters under promise of a pension; 'but so many had seen them before that, that this base practice turned much to the reproach of all their proceedings' (BURNET, ut supra). In 1689 Sir John Hawles, solicitor-general to William III, published some 'Remarks' on Fitzharris's trial, which he condemns as being as illegal as it was odious. During the same year the commons recommended Mrs. Fitzharris and her three children to the bountiful consideration of the king (*Commons' Journals*, 15 June 1689).

[Cobbett's State Trials, viii. 223–446; Cobbett's Parl. Hist. vol. iv. col. 1314, Appendix No. xiii.; Burnet's Own Time, Oxford edit. ii. 271, 278, 280; Luttrell's Relation of State Affairs, 1857, vol. i.; Reresby's Diary; North's Examen; Eachard's Hist. of England, pp. 1010, 1011; Hallam's Const. Hist. 8th edit. ii. 446; Macpherson's Hist. of Great Britain, vol. i. ch. v. pp. 341–3; Notes and Queries, 3rd ser. i. 303.]   G. G.

FITZHENRY, MEILER (d. 1220), justiciar of Ireland, was the son of Henry, the bastard son of King Henry I, by Nesta, the wife of Gerald of Windsor, and the daughter of Rhys ab Tewdwr, king of South Wales (GIRALDUS CAMBRENSIS, *Itinerarium Kambriæ*, in *Opera*, vi. 130, Rolls Ser.; cf. *Annales Cambriæ*, p. 47, and *Brut y Tywysogion*, p. 189). He was thus the first cousin of Henry II, and related to the noblest Norman and native families of South Wales. Robert Fitzstephen [q. v.], Maurice Fitzgerald (d. 1176) [q. v.], and David II [q. v.], bishop of St. David's, were his half-brothers. Raymond le Gros [see FITZGERALD, RAYMOND] and Giraldus Cambrensis were among his cousins. In 1157 his father Henry was slain during Henry II's campaign in Wales, when Robert Fitzstephen so narrowly escaped (GIRALDUS, *Opera*, vi. 130). Meiler, then quite young, now succeeded to his father's possessions of Narberth and Pebidiog, the central and northeastern (*ib.* i. 59) parts of the modern Pembrokeshire. In 1169 he accompanied his uncle Fitzstephen on his first expedition to Ireland. He first distinguished himself in the invasion of Ossory along with his cousin Robert de Barry, brother of Giraldus (GIRALDUS, *Expugnatio Hibernica*, in *Opera*, v. 234–5). The French poet (REGAN, p. 37) fully corroborates as regards Meiler. If the partial testimony of their kinsman is to be credited, Robert and Meiler were always first in every daring exploit. In 1173 the return of Strongbow to England threw all Ireland into revolt. Meiler was then in garrison at Waterford, and made a rash sortie against the Irish. He pursued them into their impenetrable woods and was surrounded. But he cut a way through

them with his sword, and arrived safely at Waterford with three Irish axes in his horse and two on his shield (*ib.* pp. 309–10). In 1174 he returned with Raymond to Wales, but when Strongbow brought Raymond back Meiler came with him and received as a reward the 'more distant cantred of Offaly' (Carbury barony, co. Kildare) (*ib.* p. 314, and Mr. Dimock's note). In October 1175 he accompanied Raymond in his expedition against Limerick, was the second to swim over the Shannon, and with his cousin David stood the attack of the whole Irish host until the rest of the army had crossed over (cf. *Exp. Hib.* and REGAN, p. 162 sq.) He was one of the brilliant band of Geraldines who under Raymond met the new governor, William Fitzaldhelm [q. v.], at Waterford, and at once incurred his jealous hatred (*Exp. Hib.* p. 335). Hugh de Lacy, the next justiciar, took away Meiler's Kildare estate, but gave him Leix in exchange. This was in a still wilder, and therefore, as Giraldus thought, a more appropriate district than even the march of Offaly for so thorough a border chieftain (*ib.* pp. 355–6). In 1182 Lacy again became justice and built a castle on Meiler's Leix estate at 'Tahmeho,' and gave him his niece as a wife. It seems probable that Meiler had already been married, but he hitherto had no legitimate children (*ib.* p. 345). This childlessness was in Giraldus's opinion God's punishment to him for the want of respect to the church. Giraldus gives us a vivid picture of his cousin in his youth. He was a dark man, with black stern eyes and keen face. In stature he was somewhat short, but he was very strong, with a square chest, thin flanks, bony arms and legs, and a sinewy rather than fleshy body. He was high-spirited, proud, and brave to rashness. He was always anxious to excel, but more anxious to seem brave than really to be so. His only serious defect was his want of reverence to the church (*ib.* pp. 235, 324–5).

In June 1200 Meiler was in attendance on King John in Normandy (*Chart.* 2 John, m. 29, summarised in SWEETMAN, *Cal. Doc. Ireland*, 1171–1251, No. 122), and on 28 Oct. of that year received a grant of two cantreds in Kerry, and one in Cork (*Chart.* 2 John, m. 22, *Cal.* No. 124). About the same time he was appointed to 'the care and custody of all Ireland' as chief justiciar, the king reserving to himself pleas touching the crown, the mint, and the exchange (*Chart.* 2 John, m. 28 *dors.*, *Cal.* No. 133). During his six years' government Meiler had to contend against very great difficulties, including the factiousness of the Norman nobles. John de Courci [q. v.], the conqueror of Ulster, was a constant source of trouble to him (*Pat.* 6 John, m. 9, *Cal.* No. 224). The establishment of Hugh de Lacy as Earl of Ulster (29 May 1205) was a great triumph for Fitzhenry. Before long, however, war broke out between Lacy and Fitzhenry (*Four Masters*, iii. 155). Another lawless Norman noble was William de Burgh [see under Fitzaldhelm, William], who was now engaged in the conquest of Connaught. But while De Burgh was devastating that region, Fitzhenry and his assessor, Walter de Lacy, led a host into De Burgh's Munster estates (1203, *Annals of Loch Cé*, i. 229, 231). De Burgh lost his estates, though on appeal to King John he ultimately recovered them all, except those in Connaught (*Pat.* 6 John, m. 8, *Cal.* No. 230). Fitzhenry had similar troubles with Richard Tirel (*Pat.* 5 John, m. 4, *Cal.* No. 196) and other nobles. Walter de Lacy, at one time his chief colleague, quarrelled with him in 1206 about the baronies of Limerick (*Pat.* 8 John, m. 2, *Cal.* No. 315). In 1204 he was directed by the king to build a castle in Dublin to serve as a court of justice as well as a means of defence. He was also to compel the citizens of Dublin to fortify the city itself (*Close*, 6 John, m. 18, *Cal.* No. 226). Fitzhenry continued to hold the justiciarship until 1208. The last writ addressed to him in that capacity is dated 19 June 1208 (*Pat.* 10 John, m. 5). Mr. Gilbert (*Viceroys*, p. 59) says that he was superseded between 1203 and 1205 by Hugh de Lacy, but many writs are addressed to him as justiciary during these years (*Cal. Doc. Ireland*, pp. 31–44 passim). On several occasions assessors or counsellors were associated with him in his work, and he was directed to do nothing of exceptional importance without their advice (e.g. Hugh de Lacy in 1205, *Close*, 5 John, m. 22, *Cal.* No. 268).

Fitzhenry remained one of the most powerful of Irish barons, even after he ceased to be justiciar. About 1212 his name appears immediately after that of William Marshall in the spirited protest of the Irish barons against the threatened deposition of John by the pope, and the declaration of their willingness to live and die for the king (*Cal. Doc. Ireland*, No. 448). Several gifts from the king marked John's appreciation of his administration of Ireland (*ib.* No. 398). But it was not till August 1219 that all the expenses incurred during his viceroyalty were defrayed from the exchequer (*ib.* No. 887). He must by that date have been a very old man. Already in 1216 it was thought likely that he would die, or at least retire from the world into a monastery (*ib.* No. 691). There is no reference to his acts after 1219, and he died in 1220 (Clyn, *Ann. Hib.* p. 8). He had long ago atoned for his early want of piety by the foundation in 1202 ('Annals of Ireland' in *Chart. St. Mary's*, ii. 308 ; Dugdale, *Monasticon*, vi. 1138) of the abbey of Connall in county Kildare, which he handed over to the Austin canons of Llanthony, near Gloucester. This he endowed with large estates, with all the churches and benefices in his Irish lands, with a tenth of his household expenses, rents, and produce (*Chart.* 7 John, m. 7, *Cal.* No. 273). He was buried in the chapter-house at Connall (*Ann. Ireland*, ii. 314). He had by the niece of Hugh de Lacy a son named Meiler, who in 1206 was old enough to dispossess William de Braose of Limerick (*Close*, 8 John, m. 3, *Cal.* No. 310), and whose forays into Tyrconnell had already spread devastation among the Irish (*Annals of Loch Cé*, i. 231). The brother of the elder Meiler, Robert Fitzhenry, died about 1180 (*Exp. Hib.* p. 354).

[Giraldus Cambrensis, Expugnatio Hibernica, in Opera, vol. v. (Rolls Ser.) ; The Anglo-Norman Poem on the Conquest of Ireland, wrongly attributed to Regan, ed. Michel; the Patent, Close, Charter, Liberate, and other Rolls for the reign of John, printed by the Record Commissioners, and summarised, not always with quite the necessary precision, in Sweetman's Calendar of Documents relating to Ireland, 1171–1251 ; Chartularies, &c., of St. Mary's Abbey, Dublin (Rolls Ser.) ; Gilbert's Viceroys of Ireland is not in this part always quite accurate ; Annals of Loch Cé, vol. i. (Rolls Ser.)]   T. F. T.

FITZHENRY, Mrs. (*d.* 1790 ?), actress, was the daughter of an Irishman named Flannigan, who kept the old Ferry Boat tavern, Abbey Street, Dublin. She contributed by her needle to the support of her father, and married a lodger in his house, a Captain Gregory, commander of a vessel engaged in the trade between Dublin and Bordeaux. After the death, by drowning, of her husband, followed by that of her father, she proceeded to London in 1753 and appeared at Covent Garden 10 Jan. 1754 as Mrs. Gregory, 'her first appearance upon any stage,' playing Hermione in the 'Distressed Mother.' Alicia in 'Jane Shore' followed, 23 March 1754. Her Irish accent impeded her success, and at the end of the season she went, at a salary of 300*l.*, soon raised to 400*l.*, to Smock Alley Theatre, Dublin, under Sowdon and Victor, where she appeared (? 3 Jan. 1755) as Hermione, and played (14 March 1755) Zara in the 'Mourning Bride,' Zaphira in 'Barbarossa' (2 Feb. 1756), and Volumnia in 'Coriolanus.' These representations gained her high reputation. On 5 Jan. 1757 she reappeared at Covent Garden as Hermione, and added to her repertory Calista in the 'Fair Penitent,' and for her benefit Lady Macbeth.

About this time she married Fitzhenry, a lawyer, by whom she had a son and a daughter. He also predeceased her. She reappeared at Smock Alley in October 1757 as Mrs. Fitzhenry in Calista. At one or other of the Dublin theatres, between 1759 and 1764, she played Isabella in 'Measure for Measure,' Emilia in 'Othello,' Cleopatra in 'All for Love,' the Queen in 'Hamlet' (then held to be a character of primary importance), Mandane in the 'Orphan of China,' Queen Katharine, and other parts. On 15 Oct. 1765, as Calista, she made her first appearance at Drury Lane, and added to her characters, 9 April 1766, Roxana in the 'Rival Queens.' Returning to Dublin she played at Smock Alley or Crow Street theatres, both for a time under the management of Mossop, the Countess of Salisbury and Aspasia in 'Tamerlane.' Her last recorded appearance was at Smock Alley 1773–4 as Mrs. Belleville in the 'School for Wives.' Not long after this she retired with a competency and lived with her two children. She returned to the stage, Genest supposes, on no very strong evidence, about 1782–3, and acted successfully many of her old parts. She then finally retired, and is said to have died at Bath in 1790. The date and place are doubted by Genest, a resident in Bath, who thinks there is a confusion between her and Mrs. Fitzmaurice, who died in Bath about this epoch. The monthly obituary of the 'European Magazine' for November and December 1790 says: '11 Dec. Lately in Ireland, Mrs. Fitzhenry, a celebrated actress.' Mrs. Fitzhenry was an excellent actress. She lacked, however, the personal beauty of Mrs. Yates, to whom she was opposed by the Dublin managers, and was in consequence treated with much discourtesy and cruelty in Dublin. Her acting was original, and her character blameless. She was prudent, and it may almost be said sharp, in pecuniary affairs.

[The chief authority for the life of Mrs. Fitzhenry is the Thespian Dictionary, a not very trustworthy production. Other works from which information has been derived are Genest's Account of the English Stage; Hitchcock's View of the Irish Stage; Tate Wilkinson's Memoirs; Notes and Queries, 7th ser. v. 372. A notice in Gilliland's Dramatic Mirror is copied from the Thespian Dictionary.] J. K.

FITZHERBERT, ALLEYNE, BARON ST. HELENS (1753–1839), was fifth and youngest son of William Fitzherbert of Tissington in Derbyshire, who married Mary, eldest daughter of Littleton Poyntz Meynell of Bradley, near Ashbourne, in the same county. His father, who was member for the borough of Derby and a commissioner of the board of trade, committed suicide on 2 Jan. 1772 through pecuniary trouble. He was numbered among the friends of Dr. Johnson, who bore witness to his felicity of manner and his general popularity, but depreciated the extent of his learning. Of his mother the same authority is reported to have said 'that she had the best understanding he ever met with in any human being.' Alleyne, who inherited his baptismal name from his maternal grandmother, Judith, daughter of Thomas Alleyne of Barbadoes, was born in 1753, and received his school education at Derby and Eton. In July 1770 he matriculated as pensioner at St. John's College, Cambridge, his private tutor being the Rev. William Arnald, and in the following October Gray wrote to Mason that 'the little Fitzherbert is come as pensioner to St. John's, and seems to have all his wits about him.' Gray, attended by several of his friends, paid a visit to the young undergraduate in his college rooms, and as the poet rarely went outside his own college, his presence attracted great attention, and the details of the interview were afterwards communicated to Samuel Rogers, and printed by Mitford. Fitzherbert took his degree of B.A. in 1774, being second of the senior optimes in the mathematical tripos, and he was also the senior chancellor's medallist. Soon afterwards he went on a tour through France and Italy, and when abroad was presented to one of the university's travelling scholarships. In February 1777 he began a long course of foreign life with the appointment of minister at Brussels, and this necessitated his taking the degree of M.A. in that year by proxy. He remained at Brussels until August 1782, when he was despatched to Paris by Lord Shelburne as plenipotentiary to negotiate a peace with the crowns of France and Spain, and with the States-General of the United Provinces; and on 20 Jan. 1783 the preliminaries of peace with the first two powers were duly signed. The peace with the American colonies, which was agreed to at about the same date, was not brought to a conclusion under Fitzherbert's charge, but he claimed to have taken a leading share in the previous negotiations which rendered it possible. This successful diplomacy led to his promotion in the summer of 1783 to the post of envoy extraordinary to the Empress Catherine of Russia, and he accompanied her in her tour round the Crimea in 1787. His conversation was always attractive, and among his best stories were his anecdotes of the empress and her court, some of which are preserved in Dyce's 'Recollections of Samuel Rogers' (pp. 104–5). At the close of 1787 he returned to England to accompany the Marquis of Buckingham, the newly appointed lord-lieutenant of Ireland, as his chief secretary, and he was in consequence sworn a member of the privy council (30 Nov.) His health was bad, and the first Lord Minto wrote to his wife (9 Dec. 1787) that Fitzherbert was going to Ireland 'with the greatest danger to his life, his health being very bad in itself, and such as the business and vexation he is going to must make much worse.' In spite of these gloomy prognostications he continued to hold the post until March 1789, being M.P. for Carysfort in the Irish parliament 1788–90. When he resigned the chief secretaryship in 1789, he was sent to the Hague as envoy extraordinary, 'with the pay of ambassador in ordinary, in all about 4,000l.' a year. His reputation had reached its highest point, and Fox described him as 'a man of parts and of infinite zeal and industry.' As years went on his attention to minutiæ flagged. One hostile critic complained in 1793 that his letters were left unanswered by Fitzherbert, and in 1794 he was described by the first Lord Malmesbury as 'very friendly, but *insouciant* as to business and not attentive enough for his post.' Yet in important matters he acted with promptness and energy. When differences broke out between Great Britain and Spain respecting the right of British subjects to trade at Nootka Sound and to carry on the southern whale fishery, he was despatched to Madrid (May 1790) as ambassador extraordinary (gazetted Nov. 1789) and under his care all disputes were settled in October 1790, for which services he was raised to the Irish peerage as Baron St. Helens. A treaty of alliance between Great Britain and Spain was concluded by him in 1793, but as the climate of that country did not agree with his health he returned home early in 1794. Very shortly after his landing in England St. Helens was appointed to the ambassadorship at the Hague (25 March 1794), where he remained until the French conquered the country, when the danger of his situation caused much anxiety to his friends. A year or two later a great misfortune happened to him. On 16 July 1797 his house, containing everything he possessed, was burnt to the ground, and he himself narrowly escaped a premature death. 'He has lost,' wrote Lord Minto, 'every scrap of paper he ever had. Conceive how inconsolable that loss must be to one who has lived his life. All his books, many fine pictures, prints and drawings in great abundance, are all gone.' His last foreign mission was to St. Petersburg in April 1801 to congratulate the Emperor Alexander on his accession to the throne,

and to arrange a treaty between England and Russia. The terms of the agreement were quickly settled, and on its completion he was promoted to the peerage of the United Kingdom. In the next September he attended the coronation of Alexander in Moscow, and arranged a convention with the Danish plenipotentiary, which was followed in March 1802 by a similar settlement with Sweden. This completed his services abroad, and on 5 April 1803 he retired from diplomatic life with a pension of 2,300l. a year. When Addington was forced to resign the premiership, St. Helens, who was much attached to George III, and was admitted to more intimate friendship with that king and his wife than any other of the courtiers, was created a lord of the bedchamber (May 1804), and the appointment is said to have been made against Pitt's wishes. He declared that he could not live out of London, and he therefore dwelt in Grafton Street all the year round. His consummate prudence and his quiet, polished manners are the theme of Wraxall's praise. Rogers and Jeremy Bentham were included in the list of his friends. To Rogers he presented in his last illness Pope's own copy of Garth's 'Dispensary,' with Pope's manuscript annotations. Bentham had been presented to St. Helens by his elder brother, sometime member for Derbyshire, and many letters to and from him on subjects of political interest are in Bentham's works. Two letters from him to Croker on Wraxall's anecdotes are in the 'Croker Papers' (ii. 294–7), and a letter to him from the first Lord Malmesbury is printed in the latter's diaries. St. Helens died in Grafton Street, London, on 19 Feb. 1839, and was buried in the Harrow Road cemetery on 26 Feb. As he was never married, the title became extinct, and his property passed to his nephew, Sir Henry Fitzherbert. From 1805 to 1837 he had been a trustee of the British Museum, and at the time of his death he was the senior member of the privy council.

Sir William Fitzherbert (1748–1791), gentleman-usher to George III, born 27 May 1748, was Lord St. Helens's eldest brother, and was educated at St. John's College, Cambridge, receiving the degree of M.A. *per literas regias* in 1770. He was called to the bar and became recorder of Derby. After serving as gentleman-usher to the king, he was promoted to be gentleman-usher in extraordinary, and was created a baronet in recognition of his services 22 Jan. 1784. He resigned his post at court soon afterwards in consequence of a personal quarrel with the Marquis of Salisbury (lord chamberlain). He died 30 July 1791 at his house at Tissington, which he had inherited from his father in 1772. He was author of 'A Dialogue on the Revenue Laws,' and of a collection of moral 'Maxims.' He is also credited with an anonymous pamphlet 'On the Knights made in 1778.' By his wife Sarah, daughter of William Perrin, esq., of Jamaica, whom he married 14 Oct. 1777, he was father of two sons, Anthony (1779–1798) and Henry (1783–1858), who were respectively second and third baronets.

[Gray's Works (ed. 1884), iii. 384–5; Hill's Boswell, i. 82–3; Hutton's Bland-Burges Papers, pp. 141–5, 189–90, 243, 250–1; Collins's Peerage (Brydges's ed.), ix. 156–7; Lord Minto's Life and Letters, i. 175, 295, ii. 413–14, iii. 341; Wraxall's Posthumous Memoirs (ed. 1884), v. 35; Lord Malmesbury's Diaries, i. 504–5, ii. 38–9, iii. 98, 199, 223–5; Bentham's Works, x. 261–2, 305–6, 319–20, 362, 429–31, xi. 118–120; Mary Frampton's Journal, p. 83; Gent. Mag. 1791 pt. ii. 777–8, April 1839 pp. 429–30, December 1839 p. 669; Burke's and Foster's Baronetages.]   W. P. C.

FITZHERBERT, SIR ANTHONY (1470–1538), judge, sixth son of Ralph Fitzherbert of Norbury, Derbyshire, by Elizabeth, daughter of John Marshall of Upton, Leicestershire, was a member of Gray's Inn. Wood states that he 'laid a foundation of learning' in Oxford. He was called to the bar from Gray's Inn. His shield was emblazoned on the bay window of the hall not later than 1580, where it was to be seen in 1671, but from which it has since disappeared; and he is included in an authentic list of Gray's Inn readers compiled in the seventeenth century by Sir William Segar, Garter king of arms, and keeper of Gray's Inn library (DOUTHWAITE, Gray's Inn, p. 46). On 20 March 1508–9 he was appointed recorder of Coventry (Extracts from Leet Book, fol. 304 b), an office which he also held in 1510 and 1511 (ib. ff. 309, 311). On 18 Nov. 1510 he was called to the degree of serjeant-at-law, and on 24 Nov. 1516 he was appointed king's serjeant. About 1521–2 he was raised to the bench as a justice of the court of common pleas and knighted (DUGDALE, Chron. Ser. pp. 79, 80, 81; Letters and Papers. For. and Dom. Henry VIII, vol. iii. pt. ii. p. 889). In April 1524 he was commissioned to go to Ireland with Sir Ralph Egerton, and Dr. James Denton, dean of Lichfield, to attempt the pacification of the country. The commissioners arrived about midsummer, and arranged a treaty between the deputy, the Earl of Ormonde, and the Earl of Kildare (concluded 28 July 1524), whereby, after making many professions of amity, they agreed to refer all future differences to arbitration, the final decision, in the event of the arbitrators disagreeing, to rest with the lord chancellor of England and the privy council, Kildare in the meantime making various substantial concessions. The commissioners left Ireland in September. On their return they received the hearty thanks of the king. During the next few years Fitzherbert's history is all but a blank. There is, however, extant a letter from him to Wolsey dated at Carlisle, 30 March 1525, describing the state of the country as very disturbed, and hinting that it was the 'sinister policy' of Lord Dacre to make and keep it so (State Papers, ii. 104–8; Letters and Papers, For. and Dom. of the reign of Henry VIII, vol. iv. pt. i. pp. 244, 352, 534; HALL, Chron. 1809, p. 685).

On 11 June 1529 Fitzherbert was one of the commissioners appointed to hear causes in chancery in place of the chancellor, Wolsey (RYMER, Fœdera, xiv. 299). On 1 Dec. following he signed the articles of impeachment exhibited against Wolsey, one of them being to the effect that 'certain bills for extortion of ordinaries' having been found before Fitzherbert, Wolsey had the indictments removed into the chancery by certiorari, 'and rebuked the same Fitzherbert for the same cause.' On 1 June 1533 he was present at the coronation of Anne Boleyn. In 1534 he was with the council at Ludlow (COBBETT, State Trials, i. 377; Letters and Papers, For. and Dom. of the reign of Henry VIII, vol. iv. pt. iii. p. 272, vi. 263, vii. 545, 581). He was one of the commission that (29 April 1535) tried the Carthusians, Robert Feron, John Hale, and others, for high treason under the statute 25 Hen. VIII, c. 22, the offence consisting in having met and conversed too freely about the king's marriage. He was also a member of the tribunals that tried Fisher and More in the following June and July. He appears as one of the witnesses to the deed dated 5 April 1537, by which the abbot of Furness surrendered his monastery to the king (Letters relating to the Suppression of Monasteries, Camd. Soc. p. 154). He died on 27 May 1538, and was buried in the parish church of Norbury.

Fitzherbert married twice: first, Dorothy, daughter of Sir Henry Willoughby of Wollaton, Nottinghamshire; second, Matilda, daughter and heir of Richard Cotton of Hamstall Ridware, Staffordshire. He had no children by his first wife, but several by his second [cf. FITZHERBERT, NICHOLAS and THOMAS]. The manor of Norbury is still in the possession of his posterity. The family has been settled at Norbury since 1125, when William, prior of Tutbury, granted the manor to William Fitzherbert. Though he never attained the position of chief justice, Fitzherbert possessed a profound knowledge of English law combined with a strong logical faculty and remarkable power of lucid exposition His earliest and greatest work, 'La Graunde Abridgement,' first printed in 1514, is a digest of the year-books arranged under appropriate titles in alphabetical order; it is also more than this, as some cases are there mentioned which are not to be found in the year-books, but which have nevertheless been accepted as authorities in the courts. Coke (*Rep. Pl.* pref.) describes it as 'painfully and elaborately collected,' and it has always borne a very high character for accuracy. It was the principal source from which Sir William Staunforde [q. v.] derived the material for his 'Exposition of the King's Prerogative,' London, 1557, 4to, and is frequently cited by Richard Bellew [q. v.] in 'Les Ans du Roy Richard le Second.' Besides the first edition, which seems to have been printed by Pinson, an edition appeared in 1516, of which fine specimens are preserved in the British Museum and Lincoln's Inn. The work is without printer's name or any indication of the place of publication, but is usually ascribed to Wynkyn de Worde, whose frontispiece is found in the second and third volumes. A summary by John Rastell, entitled 'Tabula libri magni abbreviamenti librorum legum Anglorum,' was published in London in 1517, fol.; reprinted under a French title in 1567, 4to. The original work was reprinted by Tottel in 1565, and again in 1573, 1577, and 1786, fol. Though not absolutely the earliest work of the kind, for Statham's abridgment seems to have had slightly the start of it, Fitzherbert's was emphatically the 'grand abridgment,' the first serious attempt to reduce the entire law to systematic shape. As such it served as a model to later writers, such as Sir Robert Broke or Brooke [q. v.], whose 'Graunde Abridgement' is indeed merely a revision of Fitzherbert's with additional cases, and Henry Rolle [q. v.], chief justice of the king's bench in 1648, whose 'Abridgement des Plusieurs Cases et Resolutions del commun Ley,' published 1668, was designed to supplement Fitzherbert and Brooke. Two works addressed to the landed interest are also attributed to Fitzherbert, viz.: (1) 'The Boke of Husbandrie,' London (Berthelet), 1523, 1532, 1534, 1548, 8vo; (Walle) 1555, 8vo; (Marshe) 1560, 8vo; (Awdeley) 1562, 16mo; (White) 1598, 4to; edited by Prof. Skeat for English Dialect Society 1882. (2) 'The Boke of Surveyinge and Improvements,' London (Berthelet), 1523, 1539, 1546, 1567, 8vo; (Marshe) 1587, 16mo. 'The Boke of Husbandrie' is a manual for the farmer of the most practical kind. 'The Boke of Surveyinge and Improvements' is an exposition of the law relating to manors as regards the relation of landlord and tenant, with observations on their respective moral rights and duties and the best ways of developing an estate. It purports to be based on the statute 'Extenta Manerii,' now classed as of uncertain date, but formerly referred to the fourth year of Edward I. This is important, because we know that Fitzherbert selected that statute as the subject of his reading at Gray's Inn. This book is therefore in all probability an expansion of the reading. The authenticity of the 'Boke of Husbandrie' has been called in question, and Sir Anthony's brother John has been suggested as its probable author on two grounds: (1) That Fitzherbert's professional engagements would not permit of his acquiring the forty years' experience of agriculture which the author claims to possess; (2) that the author is described in the printer's note, not as Sir Anthony, but as Master Fitzherbarde. The latter argument applies equally to the 'Boke of Surveyinge,' which is also stated to be the work of Master Fitzherbarde. In the prologue to the latter treatise, however, the author distinctly claims the 'Boke of Husbandrie' as his own work. He says that he has 'of late by experience' 'contrived, compiled, and made a treatise' for the benefit of the 'poor farmers and tenants and called it the book of husbandry.' There seems no reason to doubt that this claim was honestly made. The argument from the designation 'Master' is of no real weight. A clause in Archbishop Warham's will (1530) provides that all disputes as to the meaning of any of its provisions shall be referred to the decision of 'Magistri Fitzherbert unius justiciarii, &c.' (*Wills from Doctors' Commons*, Camd. Soc. p. 25), and Cromwell, writing to Norfolk on 15 July 1535, refers to Fitzherbert as 'Mr. FitzHerberd.' Even less substantial, if possible, is the argument from the claim of forty years' experience put forward by the author. Considering how much of the legal year consists of vacation, and how comparatively light the pressure of legal business was until recent times, there is nothing startling, much less incredible, in the supposition that Fitzherbert during forty years found leisure to exercise such general supervision over his farm-bailiffs as would entitle him to say that he had had practical experience of agriculture during that period.

Other works by Fitzherbert are the following: 1. 'La Novelle Natura Brevium,' a manual of procedure described by Coke (*Reports*, pt. x. pref.) as an 'exact work exquisitely penned,' London, 1534, 1537; (Tottell), 1553 8vo, 1557 16mo, 1567 8vo, 1576 fol., 1567, 1581, 1588, 1598, 1609, 1660, 8vo; another edition in 4to appeared in 1635, an English translation in 1652 (reprinted 1666), 8vo. The translation (with marginalia by Sir Wadham Wyndham, justice, and a commentary by Sir Matthew Hale, chief justice of the king's bench, 1660) was republished in 1635, 1652, 1718, 1730, 1755, 4to, and 1794, 8vo. 2. 'L'Office et Auctoritie de Justices de Peace,' apparently first published by Tottell in the original French in 1583, 8vo, with additions, by R. Crompton, republished in 1593, 1606, and 1617, 4to. An English translation had, however, appeared in 1538, 8vo, which was frequently reprinted under the title of 'The Newe Booke of Justices of Peas made by A. F., judge, lately translated out of Frenche into English.' The last edition of the translation seems to have appeared in 1594. 3. 'L'Office de Viconts Bailiffes, Escheators, Constables, Coroners,' London, 1538. This treatise was translated and published in the same volume with the translation of the work on justices of the peace, in 1547, 12mo. The original was also republished along with the original of the latter work, by R. Crompton, in 1583. 4 'A Treatise on the Diversity of Courts,' a translation of which was annexed by W. Hughes to his translation of Andrew Horne's 'Mirrour of Justices,' London, 1646, 12mo. 5. 'The Reading on the Stat. Extenta Manerii,' printed by Berthelet in 1539.

[Bale's Script. Illustr. Maj. Brit. (Basel, 1557), p. 710 ; Pits, De Rebus Anglicis (Paris, 1619), p. 707 ; Fuller's Worthies (Derbyshire) ; Wood's Athenæ Oxon. (Bliss), i. 110 ; Biog. Brit. ; Foss's Lives of the Judges ; Bridgman's Legal Bibliography ; Ames's Typogr. Antiq. (Dibdin), ii. 210, 455, 506–8, iii. 287 n., 305 n., 328, 332, iv. 424, 431, 437, 446, 451, 534, 566 ; Marvin's Legal Bibliogr. ; Brit. Mus. Cat. ; Nichols's Leicestershire, iv. pt. ii. 853 ; Notes and Queries, 6th ser. ii. 392, iii. 196, iv. 467.]   J. M. R.

FITZHERBERT, MARIA ANNE (1756–1837), wife of George IV, born in July 1756, was the youngest daughter of Walter Smythe, esq., of Brambridge, Hampshire, second son of Mr. John Smythe of Acton Burnell, Shropshire. Little is known of her childhood beyond the fact that she visited Paris, and was taken to see Louis XV at dinner. When the king pulled a chicken to pieces with his fingers she burst out laughing, upon which his majesty presented her with a box of sugar-plums. She married in 1775 Edward Weld, esq., of Lulworth Castle, Dorsetshire, who died in the same year. In 1778 his widow married Thomas Fitzherbert of Swynnerton in Staffordshire, by whom she was left a widow a second time in 1781.

Mrs. Fitzherbert, with a jointure of 2,000l. a year, now took up her abode at Richmond, where she soon became the centre of an admiring circle. In 1785 she first saw the Prince of Wales (born 1762). He fell, or thought he fell, desperately in love with her at first sight, and on one occasion pretended to stab himself in despair. On this occasion she was induced to visit him at Carlton House in company with the Duchess of Devonshire, but soon after went abroad to escape further solicitations. After remaining some time in Holland and Germany, she received an offer of marriage from the prince, which she is said to have accepted with reluctance. They were married on 21 Dec. 1785 in her own drawing-room, by a clergyman of the church of England, and in the presence of her brother, Mr. John Smythe, and her uncle, Mr. Errington. By the Marriage Act of 1772 every marriage contracted by a member of the royal family under twenty-five years of age without the king's consent was invalid ; and by the Act of Settlement if the heir-apparent married a Roman catholic he forfeited his right to the crown. It was argued, however, that a man could not be said to marry when he merely went through a ceremony which he knew to be invalid. According to one account, repeated by Lord Holland in his 'Memoirs of the Whig Party,' Mrs. Fitzherbert took the same view, said the marriage was all nonsense, and knew well enough that she was about to become the prince's mistress. The story is discredited by her well-known character, by the footing on which she was always received by other members of the royal family, and by the fact that, even after the marriage of the prince regent with Caroline of Brunswick, she was advised by her own church (Roman catholic) that she might lawfully live with him. Nobody seems to have thought the worse of her ; she was received in the best society, and was treated by the prince at all events as if she was his wife.

In April 1787, on the occasion of the prince applying to parliament for the payment of his debts, Fox, in his place in the House of Commons, formally denied that any marriage had taken place. It is unknown to this day what authority he had for this statement. Common report asserted that 'a slip of paper' had passed between the prince and his friend ; and Lord Stanhope, in his 'History of England,' declares his unhesitating belief that Fox had the best reasons for supposing the statement to be true. The prince himself, however, affected to be highly indignant. The next time he saw Mrs. Fitzherbert he went up to her with the words, 'What do you think, Maria? Charles declared in the House of Commons last night that you and I were not man and wife.' As the prince was now approaching the age at which he could make a legal marriage, the curiosity of parliament on the subject is perfectly intelligible. But after a lame kind of explanation from Sheridan, who tried to explain away Fox's statement, without contradicting it, the subject dropped, and the prince and the lady seem to have lived happily together till the appearance of the Princess Caroline [see CAROLINE, AMELIA ELIZABETH, 1768–1821]. At the trial of Warren Hastings in 1788 Mrs. Fitzherbert, then in the full bloom of womanly beauty, attracted more attention than the queen or the princesses. On the prince's marriage (8 April 1795) to Caroline she ceased for a time to live with him. But being advised by her confessor, who had received his instructions from Rome, that she might do so without blame, she returned to him; and oddly enough gave a public breakfast to all the fashionable world to celebrate the event. She and the prince were in constant pecuniary difficulties, and once on their return from Brighton to London they had not money enough to pay for the post-horses, and were obliged to borrow of an old servant, yet these, she used to say, were the happiest years of her life. As years passed on, however, the prince appears to have fallen under other influences; and at last at a dinner given to Louis XVIII at Carlton House, in or about 1803, she received an affront which she could not overlook, and parted from the prince for ever. She was told that she had no fixed place at the dinner-table, and must sit ' according to her rank,' that is as plain Mrs. Fitzherbert. She was not perhaps sorry for the excuse to break off a connection which the prince's new ties had already made irksome to her; and resisting all further importunities she retired from court on an annuity of 6,000l. a year, which, as she had no children, was perhaps a sufficient maintenance. She was probably the only woman to whom George IV was ever sincerely attached. He inquired for her in his last illness, and he died with her portrait round his neck.

Mrs. Fitzherbert survived him seven years, dying at Brighton on 29 March 1837. From George III and Queen Charlotte, the Duke of York, William IV, and Queen Adelaide she had always experienced the greatest kindness and attention, and seems never to have been made to feel sensible of her equivocal position. The true facts of the case were long unknown to the public.

[In 1833 a box of papers was deposited with Messrs. Coutts, under the seals of the Duke of Wellington, Lord Albemarle, and a near connection of Mrs. Fitzherbert, Lord Stourton. Among other documents the box contained the marriage certificate, and a memorandum written by Mrs. Fitzherbert, attached to a letter written by the clergyman by whom the ceremony was performed, from which, however, she herself had torn off the signature, for fear it should compromise him. At her death she left full powers with her executors to use these papers as they pleased for the vindication of her own character. And on Lord Stourton's death in 1846 he assigned all his interest in and authority over them to his brother, the Hon. Charles Langdale, with a narrative drawn up by himself, from which all that we know of her is derived. On the appearance of Lord Holland's Memoirs of the Whig Party in 1854, containing statements very injurious to Mrs. Fitzherbert's reputation, Mr. Langdale was anxious to avail himself of the contents of the sealed box. But the surviving trustees being unwilling to have the seals broken, and thinking it better to let the whole story be forgotten, Mr. Langdale made use of the narrative entrusted to him to compose a Life of Mrs. Fitzherbert, which was published in London early in 1856, and is so far our only authority for the facts above stated. In an article in the Quarterly Review in 1854 a hope was expressed that the contents of the box will soon be given to the public; but it has not at present been fulfilled.]

T. E. K.

FITZHERBERT, NICHOLAS (1550–1612), secretary to Cardinal Allen, second son of John Fitzherbert of Padley, Derbyshire, by the daughter of Edward Fleetwood of Vache, was grandson of Sir Anthony Fitzherbert [q. v.], and first cousin to Thomas Fitzherbert [q. v.], the jesuit. He became a student in Exeter College, Oxford, and was 'exhibited to by Sir Will. Petre, about 1568, but what continuance he made there,' says Wood, 'I know not.' His name appears in the matriculation register as a member of Exeter College in 1571 and 1572, he being then the senior undergraduate of that college. About that time he went abroad in order that he might freely profess the catholic religion. He matriculated in the university of Douay during the rectorship of George Prielius (Douay Diaries, p. 275). He studied the civil law at Bologna, where he was residing in 1580. During his absence from England he was attainted of treason, 1 Jan. 1580, on account of his zeal for the catholic cause, and especially for his activity in raising funds for the English College at Rheims. Afterwards he settled in Rome, and received from Pope Gregory XIII an allowance of ten golden scudi a month. When Dr. Allen was raised to the purple in 1587, Fitzherbert became his secretary, and continued to reside in his household till the cardinal's death in 1594. He strenuously opposed the policy adopted by Father Parsons in reference to English catholic affairs. An instance of this is recorded in the diary of Roger Baynes, a former secretary to Cardinal Allen : 'Father Parsons returned from Naples to Rome, 8 Oct. 1598. All the English in Rome came to the College to hear his reasons against Mr. Nicholas Fitzherbert.'

He never could be induced to take orders. When a proposal was made to the see of Rome in 1607 to send a bishop to England, Fitzherbert was mentioned by Father Augustine, prior of the English monks at Douay, as a person worthy of a mitre. Fitzherbert, however, deemed himself unworthy even of the lowest ecclesiastical orders (DODD, *Church Hist.* ii. 159). While on a journey to Rome he was accidentally drowned in an attempt to ford a brook called La Pesa, a few miles south of Florence, on 6 Nov. 1612. He was buried in the Benedictine abbey at Florence.

His works are: 1. 'Ioannis Casæ Galathævs, sive de Moribus, Liber Italicvs. A Nicolao Fierberto Anglo-Latine expressvs,' Rome, 1595, 8vo. Dedicated to Didacus de Campo, chamberlain to Clement VIII. Reprinted, together with the original Tuscan 'Trattato . . . cognominato Galateo ovvero de' Costumi, colla Traduzione Latina a fronte di Niccolò Fierberto,' Padua, 1728, 8vo. 2. 'Oxoniensis in Anglia Academiæ Descriptio,' Rome, 1602, 8vo, dedicated to Bernardinus Paulinus, datary to Clement VIII. Reprinted by Thomas Hearne in vol. ix. of Leland's 'Itinerary,' 1712. 3. 'De Antiquitate & Continuatione Catholicæ Religionis in Anglia, & de Alani cardinalis vita libellus,' Rome, 1608 and 1638, 8vo, dedicated to Pope Paul V. The biography was reprinted at Antwerp, 1621, 8vo, and in Knox's 'Letters and Memorials of Cardinal Allen,' 1882, pp. 3–20.

[Biog. Brit. iii. 1941; Boase's Register of Exeter Coll. pp. 185, 208, 223; Dodd's Church Hist. ii. 158; Foley's Records, ii. 229, 230; Knox's Letters and Memorials of Card. Allen, pp. 3, 190, 201, 375, 465; Oliver's Jesuit Collections, p. 93; Pits, De Scriptoribus Angliæ, p. 814; Wood's Athenæ Oxon. (Bliss), vol. ii.]   T. C.

FITZHERBERT, THOMAS (1552–1640), jesuit, was the eldest son and heir of William Fitzherbert, esq., of Swynnerton, Staffordshire, by Isabella, second daughter and coheiress of Humphrey Swynnerton, esq., of Swynnerton. He was a grandson of Sir Anthony Fitzherbert [q. v.], justice of the common pleas. Born at Swynnerton in 1552, he was sent either to Exeter or to Lincoln College, Oxford, in 1568. Having openly defended the catholic faith, he was obliged to live in concealment for two years, and being at last seized in 1572 he was imprisoned for recusancy. After his release he found it prudent to remove to London, where he was an active member of the association of young men founded by George Gilbert in 1580 for the assistance of the jesuits Parsons and Campion. In that year he married Dorothy, the only daughter of Edward East, esq., of Bledlow, Buckinghamshire. He retired with his wife to France in 1582. There he was 'a zealous solicitor' in the cause of Mary Queen of Scots. After the death of his wife, in 1588, he went to Spain, where, on the recommendation of the Duke of Feria, he received a pension from the king. His name is repeatedly mentioned in the letters and reports preserved among our State Papers. When on a visit to Brussels in 1595 he was charged before the state of Flanders with holding a correspondence with the English secretary of state, and with a design to set fire to the magazine at Mechlin, but was extricated by the Duke of Feria. In 1598 Fitzherbert and Father Richard Walpole were charged with conspiring to poison Queen Elizabeth (see SQUIRE, EDWARD; JESSOPP, *One Generation of Norfolk House,* p. 294).

After a brief stay at Milan in the service of the Duke of Feria, Fitzherbert proceeded to Rome, where he was ordained priest 24 March 1601–2. For twelve years he acted as agent at Rome for the English clergy. In 1606 he made a private vow to enter the Society of Jesus. In 1607, when the court of Rome had some thoughts of sending a bishop to England, Fitzherbert was on the list, with three other candidates. He resigned the office of agent for the clergy in consequence of the remonstrance of the archpriest George Birkhead [q. v.] and the rest of the body, who appointed Dr. Richard Smith, bishop of Chalcedon, to take his place. Dodd says 'they were induced to it by a jealousy of some long standing. They had discovered that Fitzherbert had constantly consulted Father Parsons and the jesuits in all matters relating to the clergy, and that, too, contrary to the express order lately directed to the archpriest from Rome.'

In 1613 he carried into effect his vow to enter the order of jesuits, and in 1616 was appointed superior of the English mission at Brussels, an office which he filled for two years. In 1618 he succeeded Father Thomas Owen as rector of the English College at Rome, and governed that establishment till March 1639, when he was succeeded by Father Thomas Leeds, *alias* Courtney. He died in the college on 7 Aug. (O.S.) 1640, and was buried in the chapel.

Wood says : ' He was a person of excellent parts, had a great command of his tongue and pen, was a noted politician, a singular lover of his countrymen, especially those who were catholics, and of so graceful behaviour and generous spirit that great endeavours were used to have him created a cardinal some years after Allen's death, and it might have been easily effected, had he not stood in his own way.'

His portrait was formerly in the English College at Rome, and a copy of it by Münch was in the sacristy at Wardour Castle.

His works are: 1. 'A Defence of the Catholycke Cause, contayning a Treatise of sundry Untruthes and Slanders published by the heretics, ... by T. F. With an Apology of his innocence in a fayned Conspiracy against her Majesty's person, for the which one Edward Squyre was wrongfully condemned and executed in November 1598,' St. Omer, 1602, 8vo. 2. 'A Treatise concerning Policy and Religion, wherein the infirmitie of humane wit is amply declared, . . . finally proving that the Catholique Roman Religion only doth make a happy Commonwealth,' 2 vols. or parts, Douay, 1606–10, 4to, and 1615, 4to ; 3rd edit. London, 1696, 8vo. The work is dedicated to the author's son, Edward Fitzherbert, who died on 25 Nov. 1612. Wood says that a third part was published at London in 1652, 4to. 3. 'An sit Utilitas in Scelere : vel de Infelicitate Principis Macchiavelliani, contra Macchiavellum et politicos ejus sectatores,' Rome, 1610 and 1630, 8vo. This and the preceding work were most favourably received both by catholics and protestants. 4. A long preface to Father Parson's 'Discussion of the Answer of M. William Barlow, D.D., to the book entitled "The Judgment of a Catholick Englishman concerning the Oath of Allegiance,"' 1612. 5. 'A Supplement to the Discussion of M. D. Barlow's Answer to the Judgment of a Catholike Englishman,' &c., St. Omer, 1613, 4to, published under the initials F. T. 6. 'A Confutation of certaine Absurdities, Falsities, and Follies, uttered by M. D. Andrews in his Answer to Cardinall Bellarmine's Apology,' St. Omer, 1613, 4to, also published under the initials F.T. Samuel Collins, D.D., replied to it in ' Epphata, to F. T., or a Defence of the Bishop of Ely [Lancelot Andrewes] concerning his Answer to Cardinal Bellarmine's Apology against the calumnies of a scandalous pamphlet,' Cambridge, 1617, 4to. 7. ' Of the Oath of Fidelity or Allegiance against the Theological Disputations of Roger Widdrington,' St. Omer, 1614, 4to. Widdrington (vere Thomas Preston) published two replies to this work. 8. ' The Obmutesce

of F. T. to the Epphata of D. Collins ; or, the Reply of F. T. to Dr. Collins his Defence of my Lord of Winchester's [Lancelot Andrewes] Answere to Cardinal Bellarmine's Apology,' St. Omer, 1621, 8vo. 9. 'Life of St. Francis Xavier,' Paris, 1632, 4to, translated from the Latin of Horatius Tursellinus.

[Addit. MS. 5815, ff. 212, 213 b; Dr. John Campbell, in Biog. Brit. ; Catholic Spectator (1824), i. 171 ; Constable's Specimens of Amendments to Dodd's Church Hist. pp. 202–12 ; De Backer's Bibl. des Écrivains de la Compagnie de Jésus ; Dodd's Church Hist. ii. 410, 491–6, iii. 77 ; Erdeswick's Survey of Staffordshire, p. 110 ; Foley's Records, ii. 198–233, vi. 762, vii. 258 ; Gage's English-American, p. 208 ; Gillow's Bibl. Dict. ; Intrigues of Romish Exiles, pp. 31, 35 ; Morus, Hist. Missionis Anglic. Soc. Jesu, p. 235 ; Morris's Condition of Catholics under James I, p. ccxlii ; Oliver's Jesuit Collections, p. 92 ; Panzani's Memoirs, pp. 82, 83 ; Pits, De Angliæ Scriptoribus, p. 813 ; Southwell's Bibl. Scriptorum Soc. Jesu, p. 762 ; Calendars of State Papers ; Wadsworth's English-Spanish Pilgrim, p. 65 ; Wood's Athenæ Oxon. (Bliss), ii. 662.]

T. C.

FITZHERBERT, WILLIAM (d. 1154), archbishop of York and Saint, is also called sometimes William of Thwayt (*Chron. de Melsa*, i. 114, Rolls Ser.) and most commonly SAINT WILLIAM OF YORK. He was of noble birth (WILLIAM OF NEWBURGH, i. 55, Rolls Ser.), and brought up in luxury (JOHN OF HEXHAM, c. 274, in TWYSDEN), but of his father Herbert very little is certainly known. John of Hexham calls him Herbert of Winchester, and says that he had been treasurer of Henry I. Hugh the Chanter (in RAINE, *Historians of the Church of York*, ii. 223) says Herbert was also chamberlain. Thomas Stubbs (*ib.* p. 390) calls him the ' very strenuous Count Herbert,' and says that his wife was Emma, the sister of King Stephen. But of her nothing else is known (FREEMAN, *Norman Conquest*, v. 315), and her very existence depends on the trustworthiness of a late authority. John of Hexham mentions that William was a kinsman of Roger, king of Sicily, but it is suspicious that no contemporary writer, even when speaking in some detail of William's dealings with Stephen and his brother Henry of Winchester, says a word of his relationship to the king. One nephew of Stephen was almost elected archbishop before him. Another nephew of Stephen succeeded him as treasurer of York. It is hardly probable that William was a nephew of Stephen also.

Many of William's kinsfolk lived in Yorkshire, and his elder brother Herbert held lands there, to which he apparently succeeded about 1140. William himself probably became treasurer and canon of York before 1130, at latest before 1138 (DUGDALE, *Monasticon*, iv. 323–4, ed. Caley, &c.) In that capacity he accompanied Archbishop Thurstan on his visitation of St. Mary's Abbey, and witnessed his charter of foundation of Fountains Abbey (WALBRAN, *Memorials of Fountains*, i. 157). He also joined his brother Herbert in conferring benefactions on the Austin Priory of Nostell (*Rot. Chart.* p. 215). Stephen made him one of his chaplains, and granted him certain churches in the north which he had hitherto held of his brother in fee (*Monasticon*, vi. 1196).

On the death of Archbishop Thurstan (February 1140) there were great disputes in the chapter as to the choice of his successor. When the election of Henry de Coilli, King Stephen's nephew, had been determined upon, it was rendered ineffective by his refusal to comply with the papal request to resign the abbey of Fécamp on accepting the archbishopric. At last, in January 1142, the majority agreed to elect as their archbishop William the treasurer. Their choice was, however, hardly unfettered; for King Stephen strongly pressed for his election, and the presence of William, earl of Albemarle, in the chapter-house to promote it doubtless stimulated their zeal (JOHN OF HEXHAM, c. 268; cf. GERVASE, *Op. Histor.* i. 123, Rolls Ser.) A minority persisted in voting for the strict Cistercian, Henry Murdac of Fountains (HOVEDEN, i. 198, Rolls Ser.), and the whole of that famous order believed that bribes of the treasurer had supplemented the commands of the king. The archdeacon of York, Osbert, called Walter of London in John of Hexham and in the 'Additions to Hugh the Chanter' (RAINE, *Historians of York*, ii. 221), and other archdeacons hurried to the king to complain of the election. They were seized by Albemarle on their way and confined in his castle of Bytham, Lincolnshire. William meanwhile was well received by Stephen at Lincoln, and there received the restitution of his temporalities. But he was unable to obtain consecration from Archbishop Theobald, and Henry, bishop of Winchester, the legate, Stephen's brother, who was his friend, could only direct him to go to Rome, where Richard, abbot of Fountains, William, abbot of Rievaulx, and his other enemies had already appealed against his election as tainted by simony and royal influence. A strong letter of St. Bernard to Innocent II (S. BERNARDI, *Omnia Opera*, i. 316, ed. Mabillon; also printed in WALBRAN, pp. 80–1), to the pope that he had made, showed that the whole influence of the Cistercian order was to be directed against William. For a time Inno-

cent hesitated, but at last, in Lent 1143, he decided that William might be consecrated if William, dean of York, would swear that the chapter received no royal commands from Albemarle, and if the archbishop elect would clear himself on oath from the charge of bribery. These points were to be ascertained in England, whither William arrived in September. The Dean of York, who had in the meanwhile been made bishop of Durham, was unable to attend in person the council at Winchester, where the case was to be settled; but his agents gave the necessary assurances, and William's innocence was so clearly established that all clamoured for his consecration. On 26 Sept. the legate Henry himself consecrated William in his own cathedral at Winchester (*Additions to Hugh the Chanter*, p. 222).

William now ruled at York in peace, and St. Bernard could only exhort the abbot of Rievaulx to bear with equanimity the triumph of his foe (*Epistolæ*, ccclii. and ccclx. in *Opera*, i. 556, 561, ed. Migne). Meanwhile William busied himself in drawing up constitutions that prohibited the profane use of the trees and grass in churchyards, and prevented clerks turning the money received for dilapidations from the heirs of their predecessors to their own personal uses (WILKINS, *Concilia*, i. 425–6). On a visit to Durham William succeeded in reconciling the turbulent William Comyn with Bishop William his old friend. On the same day he enthroned the former dean of York as bishop in Durham Cathedral, and absolved Comyn from his sins against the church (SYMEON, *Hist. Eccl. Dunelm.* pp. 283–4, 292; also *Anglia Sacra*, i. 717).

Though popular from his extraordinary kindness and gentleness, William was of a sluggish temperament. When in 1146 the cardinal bishop Hincmar arrived in England on a mission from the new pope, Lucius II, he brought with him the pallium for the new archbishop. Occupied, as was his wont, on other matters of less necessity (JOHN OF HEXHAM, c. 274), William neglected to obtain it from Hincmar at an early opportunity. Before long Lucius died. The new pope, Eugenius III, was a violent Cistercian and the slave of St. Bernard. The enemies of William took advantage of his accession to renew their complaints against William. Hincmar took his pall back again to Rome. Bernard plied Eugenius with new letters. Henry Murdac, who was now, through Bernard's influence, abbot of Fountains, led the attack. In 1147 William was compelled to undertake a fresh journey to Rome to seek for the pallium. To pay his expenses he was

Berwick was made governor of the Limousin by the king of France, and the king of Spain arranged a marriage between Berwick's only son by his first marriage and Donna Catherina de Veraguas, the richest heiress in Spain, and created the boy Duke of Liria and a grandee of the first class. In 1709 the marshal was recalled from Spain to defend the south-eastern frontier of France against the Austrians and Sardinians under Prince Eugène. This he did in a series of defensive campaigns, unmarked by a single important battle, which have always been considered as models in the art of war.

After the peace of Utrecht Berwick was long unemployed. He refused to co-operate in the attempt of his legitimate brother, the 'Old Pretender,' to regain the throne of England in 1715, and preferred French politics to English. He kept clear of party intrigues, and his advice on military questions was received with the highest respect. He cordially supported the English alliance maintained by the Regent Orleans and Fleury, in spite of his family relationship to the exiled Stuart family.

In 1733 the war of the Polish succession broke out, and Berwick was placed in command of the most important French army, which was destined to invade Germany from Strasbourg, and act against Berwick's old adversary, Prince Eugène. He took command of his army, and in October 1733 occupied Kehl, and then went into winter quarters. In March 1734 he again joined his army at Strasbourg; on 1 May he crossed the Rhine, and carried the lines at Ettlingen, and on 13 May he invested Philipsbourg. The siege was carried on in the most scientific manner, and the third parallel had just been opened, when on 12 June the marshal started on his rounds with his eldest son by his second marriage, the Duc de Fitzjames. He had not proceeded far when his head was carried off by a cannon-ball. The news of this catastrophe aroused the greatest sorrow in France, and the marshal's body was brought to France to be interred in the church of the Hôpital des Invalides at Paris.

Berwick was a cautious general of the type of Turenne and Moreau, whose genius shone in sieges and defensive operations. He served in twenty-nine campaigns, in fifteen of which he commanded in chief, and in six battles, of which he only commanded in one, the famous victory of Almanza. Montesquieu, in the éloge prefixed to the marshal's memoirs, says of him: 'He was brought up to uphold a sinking cause, and to utilise in adversity every latent resource. Indeed, I have often heard him say that all his life he had earnestly desired the duty of defending a first-class fortress.' Berwick left descendants both in France and Spain, who held the highest ranks in both those countries, in Spain as Dukes of Liria and in France as Ducs de Fitzjames.

[The Duke's Mémoires were first published by his grandson in 1777; they only go down to 1705, and are generally published with the prefatory éloge by Montesquieu, into whose hands they were placed to be prepared for the press, and with a continuation to 1734 by the Abbé Hook, who published an English translation in 1779. They have been many times reprinted, notably in Michaud and Poujoulat's great collection of French memoirs. All French histories of the period and all French biographical dictionaries contain information about Berwick and his campaigns, and in English reference may be made to James II and the Duke of Berwick, published 1876, and The Duke of Berwick, published 1883, by C. Townshend Wilson.] H. M. S.

FITZJAMES, Sir JOHN (1470?–1542?), judge, son of John Fitzjames of Redlynch, Somersetshire, and nephew of Richard, bishop of London [q.v.], was a member of the Middle Temple, where he was reader in the autumn of 1504 and treasurer in 1509 (DUGDALE, *Orig.* pp. 215, 221). He also held the office of recorder of Bristol in 1510, a place worth 19*l*. 6*s*. 8*d*. per annum, which he does not seem to have resigned until 1533, when he was succeeded by Thomas Cromwell. In 1511 he was one of the commissioners of sewers for Middlesex (*Letters and Papers of the Reign of Henry VIII*, Foreign and Domestic, i. 157, 301, iii. pt. ii. 1458, vi. 263, vii. 557). On or about 26 Jan. 1518–19 he was appointed attorney-general, and in this capacity seems to have been sworn of the council, as his signature is appended to a letter dated 13 June 1520 from the council to the king, then at Calais, congratulating him on his 'prosperous and fortunate late passage.' About the same time he was appointed, with Sir Edward Belknap and William Roper, to assist the master of the wards in making out his quarterly reports. He was also attorney-general for the duchy of Lancaster between 1521 and 1523, and probably from a much earlier date; and he seems to be identical with a certain John Fitzjames who acted as collector of subsidies for Somersetshire between 1523 and 1534. As attorney-general he conducted, in May 1521, the prosecution of the Duke of Buckingham. The same summer he was called to the degree of serjeant-at-law. On 6 Feb. 1521–2 he was advanced to a puisne judgeship of the king's bench, and two days later he was created chief baron of the exchequer. About the same time he was knighted. In the autumn of 1523 he was entrusted by the king with the delicate task of negotiating a marriage between Lord Henry Percy, who was supposed to be engaged to Anne Boleyn, and Lady Mary Talbot, daughter of the Earl of Shrewsbury. Fitzjames's diplomacy was crowned with success. On 23 Jan. 1525–6 he succeeded Sir John Fyneux [q. v.] as chief justice of the king's bench. He was a trier of petitions in parliament in November 1529, and signed the articles of impeachment exhibited against Wolsey on 1 Dec. of the same year. He seems to have exerted himself at Wolsey's request to save Christchurch from sequestration (*ib*. iii. pt. i. 12, 197, pt. ii. 873, 1383, iv. pt. iii. 2690, 2714, 2928; COBBETT, *State Trials*, i. 296; BREWER, *Reign of Henry VIII*, ed. Gairdner, ii. 177; *Proceedings and Ordinances of the Privy Council*, vii. 338; DUGDALE, *Chron. Ser.* 80, 81). Two letters are extant from Fitzjames to Cromwell, one dated 29 Oct. 1532, describing the state of legal business and the ravages of the plague, the other, dated 8 March, and apparently written at Redlynch in 1533, in which he complains much of illness, and begs to be excused attendance in London. He was present, however, at the coronation of Anne Boleyn on 1 June 1533. His name is appended to a proclamation of 7 Nov. 1534, fixing the maximum price of French and Gascon wines at 4*l*. per tun, pursuant to statute 23 Hen. VIII, c. 7. He was a member of the special tribunals that tried in April 1535 the Carthusians, Robert Feron, John Hale, and others, for high treason under statute 25 Hen. VIII, c. 22, the offence consisting in having conversed too freely about the king's marriage. He also helped to try Fisher and More in the ensuing June and July. It is probable that he secretly sympathised with the prisoners, as he preserved a discreet silence throughout the proceedings, broken only when the lord chancellor directly appealed to him to say whether the indictment against More was or was not sufficient by the curiously cautious utterance, ' By St. Gillian, I must needs confess that if the act of parliament be not unlawful, then the indictment is not in my conscience invalid.' On 2 Sept. 1535 he wrote to Cromwell, interceding on behalf of the abbot of Glastonbury, who he thought was being somewhat harshly dealt with by the visitors of the monasteries. In October 1538 he made his will, being then ' weak and feeble in body.' He retired from the bench in the same year, or early in the following year, his successor, Sir Edward Montagu, being appointed on 21 Jan. 1538–9. The exact date of his death is uncertain. His will was proved on 12 May 1542. He was buried in the parish church of Bruton, Somersetshire (*State Papers*, i. 384, 387; *Trevelyan Papers*, Camden Soc. ii. 55–7; *Letters and Papers of the Reign of Henry VIII*, Foreign and Domestic, viii. 229, 350, 384, ix. 85; COBBETT, *State Trials*, i. 393). The reputation of Fitzjames suffered much at the hands of Lord Campbell, whose errors and fabrications were ably exposed by Foss. It is impossible, with the meagre materials at our command, to say how far Fitzjames may have allowed subserviency to the king to pervert justice. His complicity in the judicial murders of 1535 leaves a stain on his memory. On the other hand he seems to have been superior to bribes.

[Fuller's Worthies, Somersetshire; Lloyd's State Worthies, i. 125–9; Collinson's Somersetshire, i. 226 ; Hutchins's Dorset, ii. 222 ; Foss's Lives of the Judges.]   J. M. R.

FITZJAMES, RICHARD (*d.* 1522), bishop of London, son of John and grandson of James Fitzjames, who married Eleanor, daughter of Simon Draycot, was born at Redlynch, in the parish of Bruton, Somersetshire. Nothing is known of him till he became a student at Oxford, which Wood says was about 1459. He was elected fellow of Merton College in 1465, and had taken his degree of M.A. before he was ordained acolyte (XIV Kal. Maii, 1471). Fuller speaks of him as being of right ancient and worthy parentage; but Campbell, in his life of his nephew, Sir John Fitzjames [q. v.], speaks of him as of low origin, though he gives no authority for the statement. He served the office of proctor in the university of Oxford in 1473, and in 1477 became prebendary of Taunton in the cathedral church of Wells, in succession to John Wansford, subdean of Wells, resigned. He was afterwards chaplain to Edward IV, and took degrees in divinity. He was principal of St. Alban Hall from Michaelmas day 1477 to the same day 1481, and treasurer of St. Paul's 1483–97 and prebendary from 1485 to 1497. In 1485 he became rector of Aller and vicar of Minehead, both in Somerset, and in 1495 was incorporated M.A. at Cambridge. He held Aller till 1497, when he was succeeded by Christopher Bainbridge, afterwards cardinal and archbishop of York. He was, says Wood, a frequent preacher, but read, not preached, his sermons. On 12 March 1483 he succeeded John Gygur in the wardenship of his college. This post he held till 1507, and won golden opinions for his liberality and excellent government of the college. He considerably enlarged the warden's lodge, and was otherwise so great a benefactor to the college as almost to be considered its second founder. Among other reforms he procured an enactment that no one admitted into the society should be ordained till he had completed his regency in arts, the object being to remedy the ignorance of candidates for holy orders. In 1511, being at that time bishop of London, he was appointed by the university to inquire into its privileges, and the relation in which it stood to the town of Oxford. He also contributed to the completion of St. Mary's Church. In 1495 he became almoner to Henry VII, and was consecrated bishop of Rochester, 2 Jan. 1497, at Lambeth by Cardinal Morton, assisted by the bishops of Llandaff and Bangor. He appears to have been employed at Calais in March 1499 in negotiations for a commercial treaty with the Low Countries, in conjunction with Warham and Sir Richard Hatton, and was one of the bishops appointed to be in the procession for receiving the Princess Catherine of Arragon on her arrival in this country in 1501, and to attend on the Archbishop of Canterbury on his celebration of the marriage with Prince Arthur. In January 1504 he was translated to Chichester, and to London on 14 March 1506, soon after which he resigned the wardenship of his college. During his tenure of this see he did much for the restoration and beautifying of St. Paul's Cathedral. Bernard André commemorates his preaching on Sunday 31 Oct. 1507 at Paul's Cross. He lived till 15 Jan. 1521-2, and was buried in the nave of his cathedral, a small chapel being erected over his tomb, which was destroyed by fire in 1561. In conjunction with his brother John, father of the lord chief justice of England [see FITZ-JAMES, SIR JOHN], he founded the school of Bruton, near the village where he was born. The palace at Fulham was also built by him.

He seems to have been a man of high character and greatly respected, in this respect very unlike his brother the chief justice. While at Oxford he acted as commissary (an office which corresponds to that of the vice-chancellor of this day) in 1481, under the chancellorship of Lionel Woodville, bishop of Salisbury, and again served the same office in 1491 and 1492, under John Russell, bishop of Lincoln; and in 1502, upon the resignation of William Smith, bishop of Lincoln, being then warden of Merton and bishop of Rochester, became, as Wood says, 'cancellarius natus.'

Fitzjames belonged to the strongly conservative type of bishop. In a letter from Fitzjames to Cardinal Wolsey (printed by Foxe) the bishop defended his chancellor, Horsey, who had been imprisoned on the charge of murdering Hunne, a merchant tailor of London charged with heresy. Fitzjames asked that the cause might be tried before the council, because he felt assured that a jury in London would condemn any clerk, be he as innocent as Abel, as they were so maliciously set 'in favorem hæreticæ pravitatis.' Horsey was condemned and afterwards pardoned. Foxe prints a document the authenticity of which Mr. Brewer doubts, to the effect that the king orders Horsey to recompense Roger Whapplot and Margaret his wife, daughter of Richard Hunne, for the wasting of his goods, which were of no little value. It appears from Fitzjames's 'Register' that there were a few other cases of prosecution for heresy during his episcopate, all of which ended in a recantation and abjuration. Fitzjames deprecated Dean Colet's efforts at church reform, and from 1511 onwards the dean complained of the persecution he suffered at his bishop's hands [see COLET, JOHN].

[Wood's Athenæ, ed. Bliss, ii. 720; Wood's History and Antiquities, ed. Gutch; Burnet's Reformation; Fuller's Worthies; Lupton's Life of Colet, 1887; Cooper's Athenæ Cantabr. i. 25, 26, 526; Stubbs's Registrum Sacrum Anglicanum; Foxe's Acts and Monuments; Le Neve's Fasti; Godwin, De Præsulibus; Brewer's Calendar of State Papers; Bernard André's Hist. of Henry VII, ed. Gairdner; Gairdner's Letters of Richard III and Henry VII; Fitzjames's Register.] N. P.

FITZJOCELIN, REGINALD (1140?–1191), archbishop-elect of Canterbury, son of Jocelin de Bohun, bishop of Salisbury, and nephew of Richard de Bohun, bishop of Coutances (1151–79), of the house of Bohun of St. George de Bohun, near Carentan, was born about 1140, for he is said to have been thirty-three in 1174 (*Anglia Sacra*, i. 561), and was brought up in Italy, whence he was called the Lombard (BOSHAM, *Materials for Life of Becket*, iii. 524). He was made archdeacon of Salisbury by his father, and was reckoned a young man of prudence, industry, high spirit, and ability. Like most of the young archdeacons of his time he loved pleasure, and was much given to hawking (PETER OF BLOIS, *Ep.* 61). In early life he was one of the friends of Thomas, possibly while Thomas was chancellor, and in 1164 received from Lewis VII the abbey of St. Exuperius in Corbeil (*Archæologia*, l. 348). During the progress of the quarrel between Henry II and Archbishop Thomas the archbishop excommunicated Reginald's father, the Bishop of Salisbury. Reginald, who had a strong affection for his father, wholly withdrew from the archbishop, and became one of his most dangerous and outspoken opponents. He was constantly employed by the king, who sent him on embassies to Pope Alexander III in 1167 and 1169, and the archbishop complained of his boasting of his success at the papal court (*Ep. Becket*, vi. 643). On 15 Aug. 1169 Henry sent him to meet the pope's commissioners at Damfront, and shortly afterwards Thomas wrote of him in violent terms, declaring that he had betrayed him, had spoken disrespectfully of the pope and the curia, and had advised Henry to apply to the pope to allow some bishop to discharge duties that pertained to his see (*ib.* vii. 181). Peter of Blois, who was much attached to Reginald, sent a letter to the archbishop's friends, defending his conduct, chiefly on the ground that he was acting in support of his father (*ib.* p. 195). After the murder of the archbishop he was sent in 1171 to plead the king's innocence before the pope (*ib.* pp. 471–5; HOVEDEN, ii. 25). The see of Bath having been vacant for more than eight years, the king, in 1173, procured the election of Reginald, who, in company with Richard, archbishop elect of Canterbury, went to procure the pope's confirmation. On 5 May 1174 he wrote to the king, saying that though the pope had consecrated Richard his own matter was still undecided. Before long he obtained his desire by, it is said, offering the pope a purse of money (*De Nugis Curialium*, p. 35). He was consecrated at S. Jean de Maurienne by the archbishops of Canterbury and Tarentaise on 23 June, after having cleared himself by oath of all complicity in Thomas's death, and brought forward witnesses to swear that he had been begotten before his father became a priest (DICETO, i. 391). His election scandalised Thomas's party, and while it was yet unconfirmed Peter of Blois wrote a letter, declaring that it was unfair to speak of him as one of the archbishop's persecutors and murderers, that he had loved the archbishop, and only turned against him for his father's sake (*Epistolæ, Becket*, vii. 554).

Immediately after his consecration Reginald went to the Great Chartreuse, and persuaded Hugh of Avalon to come over to England and take charge of the house which the king had built at Witham in Somerset (*Magna Vita S. Hugonis*, p. 55); he then rejoined the archbishop, early in August consecrated the church of St. Thomas the Martyr at St. Lo (*Somerset Archæol. Proc.* xix. 11, 94), and on the 8th met the king at Barfleur (BENEDICT, i. 74). On 24 Nov. he was enthroned by the archbishop (DICETO, i. 398). He enriched the church of Wells, added to the canons' common fund, founded

several new prebends, and, as there is reason to believe, built a portion of the nave of the church. He appears to have desired to strengthen the cathedral organisation by bringing the rich abbey of Glastonbury into close connection with it, for he made the abbot a member of the chapter, set apart a prebend for him, and erected the liberty of the abbey into an archdeaconry. He granted two charters to the town of Wells, creating it a free borough. At Bath he founded the hospital of St. John in 1180 for the succour of the sick poor who came to use the baths there. He obtained from Richard I a charter granting to him and his successors in the see the right of keeping sporting dogs throughout all Somerset. He continued to take an active share in public affairs. In 1175 he was at the council which the archbishop held at Westminster in May (BENEDICT, i. 84); in March 1177 he attended the council called by the king which met at London to arbitrate between the kings of Castile and Navarre (*ib.* pp. 144, 154), and two months later attended the councils which Henry held at Geddington and Windsor. He was appointed one of the commissioners sent in 1178 by the kings of England and France to put down the heretics of Toulouse, and in company with the Viscount of Turenne and Raymond of Châteauneuf tried and excommunicated the heretical preachers there. Then, in company with the abbot of Clairvaux, he visited the diocese of Albi, and thence proceeded to the Lateran council which was held in the March of the following year (*ib.* pp. 199–206, 219; HOVEDEN, ii. 171). He was on terms of friendship with the king's natural son Geoffrey, and in 1181 persuaded him to resign his claim to the see of Lincoln. In 1186 he promoted the election of Hugh of Avalon to the bishopric of Lincoln, was present at the council of Eynsham, near Oxford, and attended the marriage of William the Lion, the Scottish king, at Woodstock (BENEDICT, i. 351). At the coronation of Richard I on 3 Sept. 1189 he walked on the left hand of the king when he advanced to the throne, the Bishop of Durham being on his right (*ib.* ii. 83). He attended the council of Pipewell held on the 15th (HOVEDEN, iii. 15), and was probably the 'Italus' who unsuccessfully offered the king 4,000*l.* for the chancellorship (RICHARD OF DEVIZES, p. 9). The next year he obtained the legatine office for the chancellor, Bishop William Longchamp (*ib.* p. 14); he seems to have been requested to make the application when he and others of the king's counsellors crossed over in February to meet Richard in Normandy. He took the side of Geoffrey against the chancellor, and in October 1191 assisted in overthrowing Longchamp (BENEDICT, ii. 218). The monks of Christ Church found in him a steady and powerful friend during their quarrel with Archbishop Baldwin. In this matter he largely employed the help of his kinsman, Savaric, archdeacon of Northampton, the cousin, as he asserted, of the emperor. When the death of Baldwin was known in England the monks, on 27 Nov., elected Reginald to the archbishopric, acting somewhat hastily, for they were afraid that the suffragan bishops would interfere in the election (GERVASE, i. 511). The justiciar, Walter of Coutances, is said to have desired the office, and the ministers called in question the validity of the election. Reginald went down to his old diocese to secure the election of Savaric as his successor, and as he was returning was, on 24 Dec., seized with paralysis or apoplexy at Dogmersfield in Hampshire, a manor belonging to the see of Bath. On the 25th he sent to the prior of Christ Church, bidding him hasten to him and bring him the monastic habit. He died on the 26th, and was buried near the high altar of the abbey church of Bath on the 29th (*Epp. Cantuar.* pp. 354, 355; RICHARD OF DEVIZES, pp. 45, 46, where an epitaph is given). Peter of Blois notices that he who had no small hand in causing the demolition of the archbishop's church at Hackington, dedicated to St. Stephen and St. Thomas the Martyr, died on St. Stephen's day, and was buried on the day of St. Thomas (*Epp. Cantuar.* p. 554).

[Materials for the history of Thomas Becket, archbishop, iii, vi, vii (Rolls Ser.); Walter Map's De Nugis Curialium (Camden Soc.); Benedictus Abbas, i. and ii. passim (Rolls Ser.); Ralph de Diceto, i. and ii. (Rolls Ser.); Roger de Hoveden, ii. and iii. (Rolls Ser.); Magna Vita S. Hugonis (Rolls Ser.); Memorials of Rich. I, ii, Epp. Cantuar. (Rolls Ser.); Gervase, i. (Rolls Ser.); Peter of Blois, Epistolæ, ed. Giles; Richard of Devizes (Engl. Hist. Soc.); Wharton's Anglia Sacra, i. 561; Reginald, bishop of Bath, Archæologia, l. 295–360; Reynolds's Wells Cathedral, pref. lxxxi; Freeman's Cathedral Church of Wells, pp. 70, 170; Somerset Archæol. Soc.'s Journal, xix. ii. 9–11; Dugdale's Monasticon, vi. 773; Cassan's Bishops of Bath and Wells, p. 105.] W. H.

FITZJOHN, EUSTACE (*d.* 1157), judge and constable of Chester, was the son of John de Burgh, and the nephew and heir of Serlo de Burgh, lord of Knaresborough, and the founder of its castle (DUGDALE, *Monasticon*, vi. 957–72; cf., however, *Notes and Queries*, 5th ser. xii. 83–4). Like his brother, Pain Fitzjohn [q. v.], he became attached to the court of Henry I. He witnessed some charters of 1133. In the only extant Pipe Roll of Henry's reign he appears as acting as justice itinerant in the north in conjunction with Walter Espec. He won Henry's special favour (*Gesta Stephani*, p. 35, Engl. Hist. Soc.), received grants that made him very powerful in Yorkshire, and was reputed to be a man of great wisdom (AILRED OF RIEVAULX in TWYSDEN, *Decem Scriptores*, c. 343; cf. WILLIAM OF NEWBURGH, i. 108, Rolls Ser.) Dugdale gives from manuscript sources a list of Henry's donations to Eustace (*Baronage*, i. 91). He was also governor of Bamburgh Castle (JOHN OF HEXHAM in TWYSDEN, *Decem Scriptores*, c. 261). He witnessed the charter of Archbishop Thurstan to Beverley (*Fœdera*, i. 10). On the death of Henry, Fitzjohn remained faithful to the cause of Matilda, and was in consequence taken into custody and deprived of his governorship of Bamburgh (JOHN OF HEXHAM). He joined David, king of Scots, when that king invaded the north in 1138 (*Gesta Stephani*, p. 35). He surrendered Alnwick Castle to David (RICHARD OF HEXHAM in TWYSDEN, c. 319), and held out against Stephen in his own castle of Malton (HENRY OF HUNTINGDON, *Hist. Anglorum*, p. 261, Rolls Ser.) He was present at the Battle of the Standard (AILRED, c. 343), where he and his followers fought alongside the men of 'Cumberland' and Teviotdale in the second line of King David's host. In the latter part of Stephen's reign he lived quietly in the north under the government of the Scottish king, by whose grants his possessions were confirmed.

Fitzjohn was a lavish patron of the church and the special friend of new orders of regulars. In 1131 he witnessed the charter by which his colleague, Walter Espec [q. v.], founded Rievaulx, the first Cistercian house established in Yorkshire (*Monasticon*, v. 281). When the first monks of Fountains were in the direst distress and had given away their last loaves in charity, Eustace's timely present of a load of bread from Knaresborough was looked on as little less than a miracle (WALBRAN, i. 50). He also made two gifts of lands to Fountains (*ib.* i. 55, 57). In 1147 he founded the abbey of Alnwick for Premonstratensian canons. This was the first house of that order in England, and was erected only two years after the order was founded (*Monasticon*, vi. 867–8). Fitzjohn was a friend of St. Gilbert of Sempringham [q. v.], and established two of the earliest houses for the mixed convents of canons and nuns called, after their founder, the Gilbertines. Between 1147 and 1154 Fitzjohn, in conjunction with his second wife, Agnes, founded a Gilbertine house at Watton in Yorkshire (*ib.* vi. 954–7), and another at Old Malton in the same county (*ib.* vi. 970–4).

A few years later his grants to Malton were confirmed (*Thirty-first Report of Deputy-Keeper of Records*, p. 3). He also made grants to the monks of St. Peter's, Gloucester, the church of Flamborough, and to the Austin canons of Bridlington (*Monasticon*, vi. 286).

Fitzjohn made two rich marriages. His first wife was Beatrice, daughter and heiress of Ivo de Vesci. She brought him Alnwick and Malton (*ib.* vi. 868). She died at the birth of his son by her, William (*ib.* vi. 956), who adopted the name of Vescy, and was active in the public service during the reign of Henry II (EYTON, *Court and Itinerary of Henry II*, passim), and was sheriff of Northumberland between the fourth and sixteenth years of Henry II (*Thirty-first Report of Deputy-Keeper of Records*, p. 320). He was the ancestor of the Barons de Vescy. His son Eustace was prominent among the northern barons, whose revolt from John led to the signing of Magna Charta. Fitzjohn's second wife was Agnes, daughter and heiress of William, baron of Halton and constable of Chester (*Monast.* vi. 955), one of the leading lords of that palatinate. He obtained from Earl Ranulph II of Chester a grant of his father-in-law's estates and titles. He was recognised in the grant as leading counsellor to the earl, 'above all the nobles of that country.' In his new capacity he took part in Henry II's first disastrous expedition into Wales, and was slain (July 1157) in the unequal fight when the king's army fell into an ambush at Basingwerk. He was then an old man (WILL. NEWBURGH, i. 108). By his second wife he left a son, Richard Fitzeustace, the ancestor of the Claverings and the Lacies.

[Besides the chronicles quoted in the article, Dugdale's Baronage, i. 90–1, largely 'ex vet. Cartulario penes Car. Fairfax de Menstan in Com. Ebor.,' which gives a pedigree of the Vescies; Dugdale's Monasticon, vol. vi.; Walbran's Memorials of Fountains (Surtees Soc.); Foss's Judges of England, i. 115–17; Eyton's Itinerary of Henry II; Thirty-first Report of Deputy-Keeper of Public Records.]   T. F. T.

FITZJOHN, PAIN (*d.* 1137), judge, was a brother of Eustace Fitzjohn [q. v.] The evidence for this is a charter of Henry I (1133) to Cirencester Priory, in which Eustace and William are styled his brothers. He belonged to that official class which was fostered by Henry I. Mr. Eyton (*Shropshire*, i. 246–7, ii. 200) holds (on the authority of the 'Shrewsbury Cartulary') that he was given the government of Salop about 1127. In the 'Pipe Roll' of 1130 he is found acting as a justice itinerant in Staffordshire, Gloucestershire, and Northamptonshire, in conjunction with Miles of Gloucester, whose son eventually married his daughter. He is frequently, during the latter part of the reign, found as a witness to royal charters. In 1134 his castle of Caus on the Welsh border was stormed and burnt in his absence by the Welsh (ORD. VIT. v. 37). At the succession of Stephen he was sheriff of Shropshire and Herefordshire. At first he held aloof, but was eventually, with Miles of Gloucester, persuaded by Stephen to join him (*Gesta*, pp. 15, 16). His name is found among the witnesses to Stephen's Charter of Liberties early in 1136 (*Sel. Charters*, p. 114). In the following year, when attacking some Welsh rebels, he was slain (10 July 1137), and his body being brought to Gloucester, was there buried (*Gesta*, p. 16; *Cont.* FLOR. WIG. ii. 98). By a charter granted shortly afterwards (*Duchy of Lancaster; Royal Charters*, No. 20) Stephen confirmed his whole possessions to his daughter Cicily, wife of Roger, son of Miles of Gloucester. Dugdale erroneously assigns him Robert Fitzpain as a son.

[Pipe Roll, 31 Hen. I (Record Comm.); Florence of Worcester (Engl. Hist. Soc.); Gesta Stephani (Rolls Series); Ordericus Vitalis (Soc. de l'Histoire de France); Stubbs's Select Charters; Duchy Charter (Publ. Rec. Office); Cott. MS. Calig. A. vi.; Eyton's Hist. of Shropshire.]
                                                    J. H. R.

FITZJOHN, THOMAS, second EARL OF KILDARE. [See FITZGERALD, THOMAS, *d.* 1328.]

FITZMAURICE, HENRY PETTY, third MARQUIS OF LANSDOWNE (1780–1863). [See PETTY-FITZMAURICE.]

FITZMAURICE, JAMES (*d.* 1579), 'arch traitor.' [See FITZGERALD, JAMES FITZMAURICE.]

FITZMAURICE, PATRICK, seventeenth LORD KERRY and BARON LIXNAW (1551?–1600), son and heir of Thomas Fitzmaurice, sixteenth lord Kerry [q. v.], was sent at an early age into England as a pledge of his father's loyalty. When he had attained the age of twenty he was allowed by Elizabeth to return to Ireland (LODGE, *Peerage* (Archdall), ii.) In 1580 he joined in the rebellion of the Earl of Desmond, but shortly afterwards with his brother Edmund was surprised and confined to the castle of Limerick. In August 1581 he managed to escape with the connivance, it was suspected, of his gaoler, John Sheriff, clerk of the ordnance (*State Papers*, Eliz. lxxxv. 9, 14). In September 1582 he was reported to have gone to Spain with the catholic bishop of Killaloe (*Ham. Cal.* ii. 399); but he was in January 1583 wounded at the Dingle, and in April 1587 captured and committed to Dublin Castle (*ib.* iii. 278 ; *Cal. Carew MSS.* ii. 442). In 1588 Sir William Herbert made a laudable effort to procure his release, offering to pawn his bond to the uttermost value of his land and substance for his loyal and dutiful demeanour, 'knowing him to be of no turbulent disposition' (*Ham. Cal.* iii. 502). He was, however, opposed by St. Leger and Fitzwilliam, and despite a loving attempt on the part of his wife to obtain his freedom (*ib.* iv. 208) he remained in prison till 1591-2. During the last great rebellion that convulsed Ireland in Elizabeth's reign he, perhaps more from compulsion than free choice, threw in his lot with the rebels (*Carew Cal.* iii. 203, 300) ; but the evident ruin that confronted him and the loss of his castle of Lixnaw so affected him that he died shortly afterwards, August 1600 (*Pacata Hib.* ch. xi.) He was buried with his uncle Donald, earl of Clancar, in the Grey Friary of Irrelaugh in Desmond. He married Joan or Jane, daughter of David, lord Fermoy, and by her had Thomas, his heir [q. v.], Gerald, and Maurice, and two daughters, Joan and Eleanor (LODGE (Archdall), vol. ii.)

[Authorities as in the text.] R. D.

FITZMAURICE, THOMAS, sixteenth LORD KERRY and BARON LIXNAW (1502–1590), was the youngest son of Edmund Fitzmaurice, tenth lord Kerry, and Una, daughter of Teige MacMahon. Made heir to the ancestral estates in Clanmaurice by the death of his elder brothers and their heirs, he owed his knowledge of that event to the fidelity of his old nurse, Joan Harman, who, together with her daughter, made her way from Dingle to Milan, where he was serving in the imperial army. On his return he found his inheritance contested by a certain John Fitzrichard, who, however, surrendered it in 1552. He was confirmed in his estate by Mary, and on 20 Dec. 1589 executed a deed settling it on his son Patrick and heirs male, remainder to his own right heirs (LODGE, *Peerage* (Archdall), vol. ii.) He is said to have sat in the parliament of 1556, and in March 1567 he was knighted by Sir H. Sidney (*Cal. Carew MSS.* ii. 149). His conduct during the rebellion of James Fitzmaurice (1569–73) was suspicious, but he appears to have regained the confidence of the government, being commended by Sidney on the occasion of his visit to Munster in 1576 (*Ham. Cal.* ii. 90). Like most of the would-be independent chiefs in that province, he complained bitterly of the aggressions of the Earl of Desmond. Charged by Sir W. Pelham with conniving at that earl's rebellion, he grounded his denial on the ancient

and perpetual feud that had existed between his house and the head of the Geraldines (*Cal. Carew MSS.* ii. 296, 303). His sons Patrick and Edmund, who had openly joined the rebels, were surprised and incarcerated in Limerick Castle. On 3 Sept. 1581 he and the Earl of Clancar presented themselves before the deputy at Dublin 'in all their bravery. And the best robe or garment they wore was a russet Irish mantle worth about a crown apiece, and they had each of them a hat, a leather jerkin, a pair of hosen which they called trews, and a pair of brogues, but not all worth a noble that either of them had' (BRADY, *State Papers*). Two months previously (23 July) he had given pledges of his loyalty to Captain Zouche, but in May 1582 we read that after killing Captain Acham and some soldiers he went into rebellion, whereupon his pledges were hanged by Zouche (*Ham. Cal.* ii. 365, 369, 376). His position indeed was intolerable, what with the 'oppressions' of the rebels and the 'heavy cesses' of the government. The Earl of Ormonde mediated for him, and in May 1583 he was pardoned (*ib.* pp. 430, 431, 439, 468). He sat in the parliament of 1585-6, but he seems to have been regarded with suspicion till his death on 16 Dec. 1590 (*ib.* iv. 346, 383). He was buried in the tomb of Bishop Philip Stack, in the cathedral of Ardfert, Zouche refusing to allow his burial in the tomb of his ancestors in the abbey, which then served as a military station. He married, first, Margaret, 'the fair,' second daughter of James Fitzjohn, fourteenth earl of Desmond (*d.* 1563), by whom he had Patrick, his heir [q. v.], Edmund, killed at Kinsale, Robert, slain in the isles of Arran, and one daughter; secondly, Catherine, only daughter and heir of Teige MacCarthy Mór (o. s. p.); thirdly, Penelope, daughter of Sir Donald O'Brien, brother of Conor, third earl of Thomond.

He is said to have been the handsomest man of his age, and of such strength that within a few months of his death not more than three men in Kerry could bend his bow. 'He was,' says the 'Four Masters,' 'the best purchaser of wine, horses, and literary works of any of his wealth and patrimony in the greater part of Leath-Mogha at that time' (LODGE (Archdall); *Annals of Four Masters,* s. a. 1590).

[Authorities as in text.] R. D.

FITZMAURICE, THOMAS, eighteenth LORD KERRY and BARON LIXNAW (1574–1630), was son of Patrick, seventeenth lord Kerry [q. v.], whom he followed into rebellion in 1598. After the death of his father and the capture of Listowel Castle by Sir Charles Wilmot in November 1600, finding himself excluded by name from all pardons offered to the rebels (*Cal. Carew MSS.* iii. 488, 499), he repaired into the north, where he was soon busily negotiating for aid with Tyrone and O'Donnell (*ib.* iv. 10). Finding that he was 'like to save his head a great while,' the queen expressed her willingness that he should be dealt with for pardon of his life only (*ib.* p. 15). But by that time he had managed to raise twelve galleys, and felt no inclination to submit (*ib.* p. 60). After the repulse of the northern army from Thomond in November 1601, he was driven 'to seek safety in every bush' (*ib.* p. 405). In February 1603 an attempt was made to entrap him by Captain Boys, but without success (RUSSELL and PRENDERGAST, *Cal.* i. 5–6). On 26 Oct. 1603 Sir Robert Boyle, afterwards Earl of Cork, wrote that 'none in Munster are in action saving MacMorris, whose force is but seven horse and twelve foot, and they have fed on garrans' flesh these eight days. He is creeping out of his den to implore mercy from the lord deputy in that he saith he never offended the king' (*ib.* p. 22). His application was more than successful, for he obtained a regrant of all the lands possessed by his father (king's letter, 26 Oct. 1603; *ib.* p. 98; cf. *Erck's Cal.* p. 101). His son and heir, however, was taken away from him and brought up with the Earl of Thomond as a protestant. He sat in the parliament of 1615, when a quarrel arose between him and Lords Slane and Courcy over a question of precedence (*ib.* v. 25), which was ultimately decided in his favour (*Cal. Carew MSS.* v. 313, 320). Between the father, a catholic and an ex-rebel, and the son, a protestant and 'a gentleman of very good hope,' there was little sympathy. The former had promised to assure to the latter a competent jointure at his marriage, but either from inability or unwillingness refused to fulfil his promise. The son complained, and the father was arrested and clapped in the Fleet (RUSSELL and PRENDERGAST, *Cal.* v. 289, 361, 392). After a short period of restraint he appears to have agreed to fulfil his contract, and was allowed to return home. Again disdaining to acknowledge the bond, and falling under suspicion of treason, he was rearrested and conveyed to London (*ib.* pp. 530, 535, 547). This time, we may presume, surety for his good faith was taken, for he was allowed to return to Ireland, dying at Drogheda on 3 June 1630. He was buried at Cashel, in the chapel and tomb of St. Cormac. He married, first, Honora, daughter of Conor, third earl of Thomond, by whom he had Patrick, his heir, Gerald, and Joan;

secondly, Gyles, daughter of Richard, lord Power of Curraghmore, by whom he had five sons and three daughters (LODGE (Archdall), vol. ii.)

[Authorities as given in text.] R. D.

FITZNEALE or **FITZNIGEL**, RICHARD, otherwise RICHARD OF ELY (*d.* 1198), bishop of London, was the son—legitimate, if he were born before his father was in holy orders—of Nigel, bishop of Ely, treasurer of the kingdom, the nephew of the mighty Roger, bishop of Salisbury, chancellor and justiciar of Henry I. He received his education in the monastery of Ely, where he acquired the reputation of 'a very quick-witted and wise youth' (*Hist. Eliens.*; WHARTON, *Anglia Sacra*, i. 627), and laid the foundations of wide and accurate learning and literary power. He belonged to a family which for nearly a century and a half held a leading place in the royal household and in the legal and financial administration of the kingdom. The year of his birth is not recorded, but he must have been still young when in 1169 his father, the bishop of Ely, purchased for him for a hundred marks the treasurership which he had long filled himself. The flourishing condition of the treasury on Henry's death proved the excellence of his administration, more than a hundred thousand marks being found in the royal coffers, in spite of Henry's continued and costly wars. He had been appointed archdeacon of Ely by his father before 1169, became justice itinerant in 1179, and held the prebendal stall of Cantlers in St. Paul's Cathedral. In 1184 we find him dean of Lincoln, and in 1186 the chapter elected him bishop of that see, the election, however, being annulled by Henry II, who had resolved that one of the holiest and wisest men of his day, Hugh, prior of Witham, should fill the office, and compelled Fitzneale and his canons to elect the royal nominee (BENEDICT. ABBAS, i. 345). On the death of Gilbert Foliot [q. v.], he was appointed to the see of London shortly before the king's death in 1189. The canons of St. Paul's were summoned to Normandy to elect the king's nominee, but political troubles and domestic sorrows allowed Henry no time or thought for ecclesiastical affairs. The election was postponed from day to day, and was still pending on the king's death. Immediately after his accession Richard I held a great council at Pipewell on 5 Sept. 1189, the first act of which was to fill the five sees then vacant, confirming his father's nomination of Fitzneale to the see of London (MATT. PARIS, ii. 351), to which he was consecrated in the chapel at Lambeth by Archbishop Baldwin on

31 Dec., at the same time with Richard's chancellor, William Longchamp, to the see of Ely. His episcopate was nearly commensurate with the reign of Richard, and his career was on the whole as peaceful as that of his sovereign was warlike. The new king showed his value for Fitzneale's services as treasurer by continuing him in his office, which he held undisturbed till his death. Baldwin, archbishop of Canterbury, accompanying Richard to the Holy Land the same year, the newly consecrated bishop of London was appointed to act as his commissary during the primate's absence (*Annals of Dunstaple*, iii. 25). In this capacity a correspondence took place between Baldwin and Fitzneale in 1190 relative to the suspension of Hugh, bishop of Lichfield, who had illegally assumed the shrievalty, and his absolution on submission (MATT. PARIS, ii. 358 ; DICETO, ii. 77, 78). In the bitter conflict between Longchamp and Prince John Fitzneale took an influential part, chiefly as a peacemaker, an office for which he was specially qualified, not only by his benignity and the sweetness of his address, but by his practical common sense and large experience. At the personal meeting between John and the chancellor, demanded by the latter to settle the points in dispute, held at Winchester on 25 April 1191, Fitzneale was one of the three episcopal arbitrators, and was put in charge of the castle of Bristol, one of the strongholds nominally surrendered by John. He was present also at the second assembly held at Winchester, and took part in the new settlement then attempted (HOVEDEN, iii. 135, 136 ; RIC. DEVIZES, pp. 26, 32, 33). When Geoffrey Plantagenet, the natural son of Henry II, recently appointed by Richard to the see of York, on his landing at Dover on 14 Sept., had been violently dragged from the altar of St. Martin's priory by the men-at-arms of Richenda, the wife of the constable of Dover Castle, Longchamp's sister, and committed to prison, the protests of Fitzneale against so impious an act were only second in influence to those of the sainted Hugh of Lincoln in obtaining the release of the archbishop-elect, for which Fitzneale pledged his bishopric to the chancellor. On his arriving in London he afforded him a reception suitable to his dignity at St. Paul's, and entertained him magnificently at his palace (DICETO, ii. 97 ; MATT. PARIS, *Chron. Maj.* ii. 372 ; *Hist. Angl.* ii. 22).

When Longchamp was summoned by John to give an account of his conduct before him and the justiciars at Loddon Bridge, between Reading and Windsor, on 5 Oct., Fitzneale gave the chancellor security for his safety, and on his non-appearance took a leading part in the discussion of the complaints against his administration, and joined in the solemn excommunication in Reading parish church of all concerned in Archbishop Geoffrey's seizure and imprisonment (MATT. PARIS, *Chron. Maj.* p. 380 ; DICETO, ii. 98). On 8 Oct. he took the oath of fealty to King Richard in St. Paul's, together with the bishops and barons, 'salvo ordine suo.' He was present at the deposition of Longchamp from his secular authority on 10 Oct. (HOVEDEN, iii. 145, 193). Perhaps as a gracious act of courtesy, perhaps as a measure of policy, we find him at this period making a present to Prince John of a wonderful hawk which had caught a pike swimming in the water, and the fish itself (MATT. PARIS, *Chron. Maj.* ii. 383 ; DICETO, ii. 102). We find him also at the same time giving the benediction to the Abbot of Westminster at the high altar of St. Paul's (DICETO, ii. 101), and in 1195 to John de Cella, on his appointment as abbot of St. Albans (MATT. PARIS, ii. 411), and, not forgetful of the privileges of his order, posting down to Canterbury in company with one of the justiciars to protect the rights of himself and his brother bishops in the matter of the election to the vacant primatial see. He summoned the whole episcopal body to meet him in London to decide the matter, and on the monks of Canterbury anticipating their action by the election of Fitzjocelin of Bath, he, in the name of the bishops, despatched an appeal to the pope (DICETO, ii. 103). In December 1192 he appears in controversy with his former friend, Archbishop Geoffrey, who had ventured to carry his cross erect in his portion of the province of Canterbury. The archbishop was visited with excommunication, and the New Temple, in which he was lodged and where the offence took place, was suspended from divine service (HOVEDEN, iii. 187). In 1193 he was one of the treasurers of Richard's ransom (*ib.* p. 212), and the following year joined in the sentence of excommunication passed on John for open rebellion against his royal brother in the infirmary chapel at Westminster Abbey (*ib.* p. 237). He was also present at Richard's coronation at Winchester on 17 April 1194, which succeeded his return from his Austrian captivity (*ib.* p. 247), and in 1197, when Richard endeavoured to enforce the rendering of military service for his continental wars on the English bishops, a demand thwarted by the bold independence of Hugh of Lincoln, Fitzneale followed Archbishop Hubert, by whom the illegal measure was proposed, in declaring his readiness as a loyal subject to take his share of the burden (GERV. CANT. i. 549 ; *Mag. Vit. S. Hugonis*, pp. 249, 250). Fitzneale died six months before, on 10 Sept. 1198. Few prelates of his day are spoken of in more eulogistic terms by the contemporary chroniclers, and a review of the events of his life shows that the eulogy was not undeserved. The Winchester annalist describes him as 'vir venerandæ et piissimæ recordationis et plurimæ scientiæ,' most benign and most merciful, whose words distilled sweetness; 'vir exactissimæ liberalitatis et munificentiæ,' whose bounty was so profuse that all others in comparison with him appeared covetous, admitting all without distinction to his table, except those who were repelled by their own evil deeds (*Annal. Winton.* i. 70). It is, however, on his literary ability that Fitzneale's fame most deservedly rests. To him, 'the first man of letters who occupied the episcopal throne of London' (MILMAN, *Annals of St. Paul's*), we are almost certainly indebted for the two most valuable authorities for the financial and political history of the kingdom. In his preface to the work Madox has proved by unanswerable arguments that the 'Dialogus de Scaccario,' termed by Bishop Stubbs 'that famous and inestimable treatise,' on the principles and administration of the English exchequer, begun in 1176, but describing the system of the year 1178, was written by Fitzneale. Bishop Stubbs advanced but afterwards withdrew a theory that in the 'Acts of King Henry and King Richard,' which have long passed under the name of Benedict (*d.* 1193 [q. v.], abbot of Peterborough, we have really, though altered from its inconvenient tripartite form, the chronicle of the events of Fitzneale's own lifetime, begun in the days of his youth, of which the writer of the 'Dialogue' declares himself the author, which was designated 'Tricolumnus,' from its original division into three columns, containing the affairs respectively of church and state, and miscellaneous matters and judgments of the courts of law (STUBBS, Introduction to BENEDICTUS ABBAS, i. lvii–lx, and to DICETO, ii. xxxi). Fitzneale, distinguished among his contemporaries in the pursuits of literature, employed his high position for its advancement in others, exhibiting a large and liberal patronage towards students and men of letters. The celebrated Peter of Blois [see PETER] was appointed by him to the archdeaconry of London, and he assigned to the support of the school of his cathedral of St. Paul's the tithes of the episcopal manors of Fulham and Hornsey. Ralph de Diceto [q. v.], the distinguished chronicler, was dean of St. Paul's during the whole of the episcopate, and there can hardly fail to have been much sympathy between two men of such congenial tastes brought into such close official relations.

[Matt. Paris, Chron. Majora, vol. ii.; Hist. Angl. vol. ii. ll. cc.; Hoveden, vol. iii. ll. cc.; Diceto, vol. ii. ll. cc.; Richard of Devizes, ll. cc.; Annales Monastici, ll. cc.; Stubbs's Introd. to Benedictus Abbas; Wright's Historia Literaria, ii. 286–90; Miss Norgate's England under the Angevin Kings, ii. 279, 296–301, 305–10, 349, 439; Dugdale's St. Paul's, pp. 217, 258; Milman's Annals of St. Paul's.]   E. V.

FITZOSBERN, WILLIAM, EARL OF HEREFORD (*d.* 1071), was the son and heir of Osbern the seneschal, who was connected with the ducal house of Normandy, and was murdered while guardian to the future Conqueror. His son became an intimate friend of the duke, and was, after him, in Mr. Freeman's words, 'the prime agent in the conquest of England.' On the accession of Harold he was the first to urge the duke to action, and at the council of Lillebonne (1066) he took the lead in pressing the scheme upon the Norman barons. He himself offered the duke a contribution of sixty ships. At the battle of Hastings he is mentioned by Wace as fighting in the right wing of the invading host. He received vast estates in the conquered land, chiefly in the west, and became Earl of Hereford. Florence of Worcester (ii. 1) states that he had already received the earldom when the Conqueror left England in March 1067. His English career may be dealt with under two heads: first in his capacity as Earl of Hereford (1067–71); secondly in his special character as joint viceroy during William's absence in 1067. In the first of these, his function as earl was to defend the English border against the South Welsh. For this purpose his earldom was invested with a quasi-palatine character, and was essentially of the nature of a military settlement. William of Malmesbury (*Gesta Regum*, iii. 256) asserts that he attracted a large number of warriors to his standard by liberal rewards, and made a special ordinance reducing the penalties to which they would be liable by crime. During his brief tenure of the earldom he was almost always engaged in border warfare with the Welsh, and Meredith, son of Owen, was among the princes of South Wales whom he fought and overthrew. In Heming's 'Cartulary of Worcester' are several references to his doings, in which he usually figures as a despoiler of the church. Several of the knights who followed him to the west, or joined him when established there, are mentioned afterwards (1086) in 'Domesday.'

As viceroy in William's absence he played an important part. To Bishop Odo was entrusted the guard of Kent and of the south coast, while Earl William was left to guard the northern and western borders, with Hereford and Norwich as his bases of operation. He is accused by Ordericus and by the English chronicler of great severity, and especially of building castles by forced labour, but in the then precarious state of the Norman rule a stern policy was doubtless necessary. There were, however, outbursts of revolt, especially in his own Herefordshire, where Eadric 'the Wild' successfully defied him. We do not find that he lost favour in consequence of this with the Conqueror, for in January 1069 he was entrusted with the new castle which William built at York on the suppression of the local revolt, and shortly after he successfully crushed an attempt to renew the insurrection. From a somewhat obscure passage in Ordericus it would seem that he was despatched the following September to retake Shrewsbury, which had been captured by Eadric 'the Wild,' who retired before his advance. The last deed assigned to him in England is the searching of the monasteries by William, at his advice, early in 1070, and the confiscation of all the treasures of the English found therein (FLOR. WIG.)

It was about Christmas 1070 that the earl was sent by William to Normandy to assist his queen in administering the duchy. But at the same time Baldwin, count of Flanders, died, leaving him one of the guardians to his son Arnulf. The count's widow, Richildis, attacked by her brother-in-law, offered her hand to the earl if he would come to her assistance. He did so, and was slain at the battle of Cassel, where her forces were defeated early in 1071. He was buried at Cormeilles, one of the two monasteries which he had founded in Normandy.

His estates, according to the practice of the time, were divided between his two sons; William, the elder, succeeding to the Norman fief, and Roger, the younger [see FITZWILLIAM, ROGER], to the English one. Some seventy years after his death Herefordshire was granted to the Earl of Leicester as the husband of his heir, to be held as fully and freely as it had been by himself (*Duchy of Lancaster, Royal Charters*).

[Freeman's Hist. of the Norman Conquest gives all that is known of William Fitzosbern's life, together with the authorities, of which Ordericus Vitalis is the chief.]   J. H. R.

FITZOSBERT, WILLIAM (*d.* 1196), demagogue, is first mentioned as one of the leaders of the London crusaders in 1190, who fought the Moors in Portugal (HOVEDEN, iii. 42 ; BENED. ii. 116). He was a member of an eminent civic family, which was said to have been conspicuous for wearing the beard 'as a mark of their hatred for the Normans' (MATT. PARIS, ii. 418). William himself was known as 'Longbeard,' from the excess to which he carried this distinction. Of commanding stature and of great strength, an effective popular speaker, and with some knowledge of law (HOVEDEN, iv. 5), he threw himself into the social struggles of his day with an energy and a success of which the measure is preserved in that spirit of bitter partisanship in which the chroniclers narrate his career. William of Newburgh, who, according to Dr. Stubbs, 'treats him judicially,' but who clearly takes the very worst view of him, has devoted to him a long chapter (lib. v. cap. 20), in which he traces William's conduct to his extravagance and lack of means, which led him, when his elder brother, Richard, refused to supply him with money, first to threaten him, and then to go to the king, whom he knew personally, and accuse him of treason. That he did bring this charge (cf. R. DE DICETO, vol. ii.) is certain from the 'Rotuli Curiæ Regis' (p. 69), which record that (21 Nov. 1194) he accused his brother, before the justices, of speaking treason against the king and primate and denouncing their exactions. Meanwhile he appears, on the one hand, to have posed as zealous for the interest of the king, who was defrauded, he urged, by financial corruption, of the treasure that should be his ; while, on the other, he accused the city magnates, who had to apportion the heavy 'aids' laid upon London for the king's ransom (1194), of saving their own pockets at the expense of the poorer payers. He made himself, on both these grounds, hateful to the ruling class, but succeeded in obtaining a seat on the civic council and pursued his advantage. He had clearly found a genuine grievance in the system of assessment, and 'fired,' says Hoveden, 'with zeal for justice and equity, he made himself the champion of the poor' (iv. 5). Addressing the people on every occasion, especially at their folkmoot in St. Paul's churchyard, he roused them by stinging invective against the mayor and aldermen. An abstract of one of his speeches, or rather sermons, is given by William of Newburgh (ii. 469), who tells us that 'he conceived sorrow and brought forth iniquity.' The craftsmen and the populace flocked to hear him, and he was said to have had a following of more than fifty thousand men. The primate, alarmed at the prospect, sided with the magnates against him, but William, crossing to France, appealed successfully to the king (HOVEDEN, iv. 5 ; WILL. NEWBURGH, ii. 468). The primate now determined to crush him, took hostages from his supporters for their good behaviour, and then ordered his arrest. Guarded by his followers, William defied him, and the panic-stricken magnates were in hourly expectation of a general rising and of the sacking of the city. Soon, however, surprised by a party of armed men, the demagogue slew one of his assailants and fled for refuge to Bow Church, together with a few friends, and, his enemies said, with his mistress. He trusted that the sanctuary would shelter him till his followers assembled; but the primate, dreading the delay, ordered him to be dragged out by force. On his taking refuge in the church tower, his assailants set fire to the fabric and smoked him out. Badly wounded by a citizen as he emerged, he was seized and fastened to a horse's tail, and so dragged to the Tower. Being there sentenced to death, he was dragged in like manner through the city to the Elms (at Smithfield) and there hanged in chains (6 April 1196), 'dying,' says Matthew Paris, 'a shameful death for upholding the cause of truth and of the poor.' William of Newburgh writes that he 'perished, according to justice, as the instigator and contriver of troubles.' His nine faithful friends were hanged with him (R. DE DICETO, ii. 143; GERVASE, i. 533, 534). It is admitted by William of Newburgh that his followers bewailed him bitterly as a martyr. Miracles were wrought with the chain that hanged him. The gibbet was carried off as a relic, and the very earth where it stood scooped away. Crowds were attracted to the scene of his death, and the primate had to station on the spot an armed guard to disperse them. Dr. Stubbs pronounces him 'a disreputable man, who, having failed to obtain the king's consent to a piece of private spite, made political capital out of a real grievance of the people' (Const. Hist. i. 508). This is probably the right view.

[William of Newburgh (Rolls Ser.); Benedictus Abbas (ib.); Matthew Paris, Chronica Major (ib.); Ralph de Diceto (ib.); Gervase of Canterbury (ib.); Palgrave's Rotuli Curiæ (Record Commission); Stubbs's Roger de Hoveden (Rolls Ser.), and Const. Hist. vol. i.] J. H. R.

FITZPATRICK, SIR BARNABY, LORD OF UPPER OSSORY (1535?–1581), son and heir of Brian Fitzpatrick or MacGillapatrick, first lord of Upper Ossory, was born probably about 1535. Sent at an early age into England as a pledge of his father's loyalty, he was educated at court, where he became a favourite schoolfellow and companion of Prince Edward, whose 'proxy for correction' we are informed he was (FULLER, Church Hist. bk. vii. par. 47). On 15 Aug. 1551 he and Sir Robert Dudley were sworn two of the six

gentlemen of the king's privy chamber (Edward VI's Diary). Edward VI, who continued to take a kindly interest in him, sent him the same year into France in order to perfect his education, sagely advising him to 'behave himself honestly, more following the company of gentlemen, than pressing into the company of the ladies there.' Introduced by the lord admiral, Lord Clinton, to Henry II, he was by him appointed a gentleman of his chamber, in which position he had favourable opportunities for observing the course of French politics. On his departure on 9 Dec. 1552 he was warmly commended for his conduct by Henry himself and the constable Montmorency (Cal. State Papers, For. vol. i.) During his residence in France Edward VI continued to correspond regularly with him, and so much of the correspondence as has survived has been printed in the 'Literary Remains of Edward VI,' published by the Roxburghe Club, i. 63–92. (Some of these letters had previously been printed by Fuller in his 'Worthies,' Middlesex, and his 'Church History of Britain;' by Horace Walpole in 1772, reprinted in the 'Dublin University Magazine,' xliv. 535, and by Halliwell in his 'Letters of the Kings of England,' vol. ii., and in 'Gent. Mag.' lxii. 704.) On his return he took an active part in the suppression of Sir Thomas Wyatt's rebellion (1553). The same year it appears from the 'Chronicle of Queen Jane' that 'the Erle of Ormonde, Sir [blank] Courteney Knight, and Mr. Barnaby fell out in the night with a certayn priest in the streate, whose parte a gentyllman comyng by by chance took, and so they fell by the eares; so that Barnabye was hurte. The morrowe they were ledd by the ii sheryves to the counter in the Pultry, where they remained [blank] daies' (ed. Camd. Soc. p. 33). Shortly afterwards he went into Ireland with the Earl of Kildare and Brian O'Conor Faly (Annals of Four Masters; Ham. Cal. i. 133). It is stated both by Collins and Lodge that he was in 1558 present at the siege of Leith, and that he was there knighted by the Duke of Norfolk; but for this there appears to be no authority. He sat in the parliament of 1559. In 1566 he was knighted by Sir H. Sidney, who seems to have held him in high estimation (Cal. Carew MSS. ii. 148). His proceedings against Edmund Butler for complicity with James Fitzmaurice were deeply resented by the Earl of Ormonde, and led to a lifelong feud between them (Ham. Cal. i. 457, 466). In 1573 he was the victim of a cruel outrage, owing to the abduction of his wife and daughter by the Graces (ib. i. 502, 510, 525; Carew, i. 438; BAGWELL, Ireland, ii. 254). In 1574 the Earl of Ormonde made fresh allegations against his loyalty, and he was summoned to Dublin to answer before the council, where he successfully acquitted himself (*Ham. Cal.* ii. 23, 24, 31, 33; *Carew*, i. 472). In 1576 he succeeded his father, who had long been impotent, as Baron of Upper Ossory, and two years afterwards had the satisfaction of killing the great rebel Rory Oge O'More (COLLINS, *Sydney Letters*, i. 264; *Somers Tracts*, i. 603). Owing to a series of charges preferred against him by Ormonde, who declared that there was 'not a naughtier or more dangerous man in Ireland than the baron of Upper Ossory' (*Ham. Cal.* ii. 237; cf. *ib.* pp. 224, 246, 250), he and Lady Fitzpatrick were on 14 Jan. 1581 committed to Dublin Castle (*ib.* p. 280). There was, however, 'nothing to touch him,' he being in Sir H. Wallop's opinion 'as sound a man to her majesty as any of his nation' (*ib.* p. 300). He, however, seems to have been suddenly taken ill, and on 11 Sept. 1581 he died in the house of William Kelly, surgeon, Dublin, at two o'clock in the afternoon (LODGE (Archdall), vol. ii.; *A.F.M.* v. 1753). He was, said Sir H. Sidney, 'the most sufficient man in counsel and action for the war that ever I found of that country birth; great pity it was of his death' (*Carew*, ii. 344). He married in 1560 Joan, daughter of Sir Rowland Eustace, viscount Baltinglas, by whom he had an only daughter, Margaret, first wife of James, lord Dunboyne. His estates passed to his brother Florence Fitzpatrick (LODGE, Archdall).

[Authorities as in the text.] R. D.

FITZPATRICK, RICHARD, first BARON GOWRAN (d. 1727), second son of John Fitzpatrick of Castletown, Queen's County, by Elizabeth, fourth daughter of Thomas, viscount Thurles, and relict of James Purcell, baron of Loughmore, entered the royal navy and was appointed on 14 May 1687 commander of the Richmond. On 24 May 1688 he was made captain of the Assurance, from which in 1689 he was transferred to the Lark, in which he cruised against the French in the German Ocean. Having distinguished himself on that station, he was advanced on 11 Jan. 1690 to the command of the St. Alban's, a fourth-rate, with which on 18 July he captured off Rame Head a French frigate of 36 guns, after a fight of four hours, in which the enemy lost forty men killed and wounded, the casualties on board the St. Alban's being only four; and the French ship was so shattered that she had to be towed into Plymouth. In February 1690-1 he drove on shore two French frigates and helped to cut out fourteen merchantmen from a convoy of twenty-two. In command of the

Burford (70 guns) he served under Lord Berkeley in 1696, and in July was detached to make a descent on the Groix, an island near Belle Isle, off the west coast of Brittany, from which he brought off thirteen hundred head of cattle, with horses, boats, and small vessels. He was promoted to the command of the Ranelagh (80 guns) on the outbreak of the war of the Spanish succession, and took part in Ormonde's mismanaged expedition against Cadiz (1702), and in the successful attack on Vigo which followed; but soon after retired from the service. In 1696 he had received a grant of the town and lands of Grantstown and other lands in Queen's County. He was M.P. for Harristown in the Irish House of Commons from 1703 to 1713, and for Queen's County from 1713 to 1715. On 27 April 1715 he was raised to the Irish peerage as Baron Gowran of Gowran, Kilkenny. He took his seat on 12 Nov., and on 14 Nov. helped to prepare an address to the king congratulating him upon his accession. He died on 9 June 1727. Fitzpatrick married in 1718 Anne, younger daughter of Sir John Robinson of Farmingwood, Northamptonshire, by whom he had two sons, John and Richard. The former, promoted to the Irish earldom of Upper Ossory on 5 Oct. 1751, was father of Richard Fitzpatrick [q. v.]

[Charnock's *Biog. Navalis*, ii. 134–8; Burchell's Naval History, pp. 545, 547; Luttrell's Relation of State Affairs, ii. 80, 435; Hist. Reg. Chron. Diary (1727), p. 23; Lodge's Peerage of Ireland (Archdall), ii. 347.] J. M. R.

FITZPATRICK, RICHARD (1747–1813), general, politician, and wit, was second son of John, first earl of Upper Ossory in the peerage of Ireland and M.P. for Bedfordshire, by Lady Evelyn Leveson Gower, daughter of the second Earl Gower, and was grandson of Richard Fitzpatrick, lord Gowran [q. v.] He was born in January 1747, and was educated at Westminster School, where he formed an intimacy with Charles James Fox, which lasted until the death of Fox in 1806. Stephen Fox, the elder brother of Charles James, married Lady Mary Fitzpatrick, the sister of his friend. On 10 July 1765 Fitzpatrick entered the army as an ensign in the 1st, afterwards the Grenadier, guards, and on 13 Sept. 1772 he was gazetted lieutenant and captain, but he had no opportunity of going on service, and devoted himself to the pleasures of London life. He lived in the same lodgings with Fox in Piccadilly, and shared his love for gambling and betting, classical scholarship and brilliant conversation. The two friends were recognised as the leaders of the young men of fashion about town, and both were devoted to amateur theatricals, in which Fitzpatrick was voted to be superior to Fox in genteel comedy, though his inferior in tragedy. Both indulged in *vers de société*, and Fitzpatrick published 'The Bath Picture, or a Slight Sketch of its Beauties,' in 1772, and 'Dorinda, a Town Eclogue,' which was printed at Horace Walpole's press at Strawberry Hill in 1775. When Fox entered the House of Commons he expressed the keenest desire that his friend should join him there. From 1770 to 1774 Fitzpatrick was M.P. for Okehampton, and from 1774 to 1807 for Tavistock, a seat which he owed to the Duke of Bedford. Fitzpatrick had none of Fox's debating power, but his political influence was very great on account of his confidential relations with Fox, who generally followed his advice. Fitzpatrick was strongly opposed to the American war, but when he was ordered with a relief belonging to his battalion to the scene of action, he at once obeyed and refused to throw up his commission. He arrived in America in March 1777, and served with credit in the guards in the action at Westfield, the battle of Brandywine, the capture of Philadelphia, and the battle of Germantown, and he returned to England in May 1778 on receiving the news that he had been promoted captain and lieutenant-colonel on 23 Jan. in that year. In 1782 he first took office, when Lord Rockingham formed his second administration, and in that year he accompanied the Duke of Portland, lord-lieutenant of Ireland, as chief secretary. He was promoted colonel 20 Nov. 1782, was M.P. for Maryborough in the Irish House of Commons 1782–3, and in April 1783 he entered the coalition ministry of Fox and Lord North as secretary at war. Fitzpatrick shared the subsequent exclusion of the whigs from power, and he warmly supported the policy of Fox and Sheridan regarding the French revolution. During this period Fitzpatrick was best known as a man of fashion and gallantry, and as a wit; he was one of the principal authors of the 'Rolliad;' he was a constant attendant in the green-rooms of the theatres and at Newmarket, and he was so noted for his fine manners and polite address that the Duke of Queensberry left him a considerable legacy on this account alone. On 12 Oct. 1793 he was promoted major-general, and in 1796 he made his most famous speech in the House of Commons, protesting against the imprisonment of Lafayette and his companions by the Austrians. In answer to this speech Henry Dundas remarked that 'the honourable general's two friends [Fox and Sheridan] had only impaired the impres-

sion made by his speech.' On 1 Jan. 1798 Fitzpatrick was promoted lieutenant-general, and on 25 Sept. 1803 general. When the ministry of All the Talents came into power in 1806, Fox appointed Fitzpatrick once more secretary at war, and he was concurrently lieutenant-general of the ordnance. On 20 April 1806 he was made colonel of the 11th regiment, from which he was transferred to the colonelcy of the 47th on 25 Feb. 1807. The death of Fox profoundly affected Fitzpatrick, and the great orator left him in his will a small personal memento 'as one of his earliest friends, whom he loved excessively.' In 1807 Fitzpatrick was elected M.P. for Bedfordshire, and in 1812 once more for Tavistock, but his health was seriously undermined, and he was little better than a wreck during the latter years of his life. He died in South Street, Mayfair, on 25 April 1813, leaving behind him one of the best known names in the history of the social life of the last half of the eighteenth century, and the proud title of being the most intimate friend of Charles James Fox.

[Army Lists; Military Panorama, Life, with portrait, September 1813; Gent. Mag. May 1813, and supplement; Hamilton's History of the Grenadier Guards; Sir G. O. Trevelyan's Early Life of Fox; Lord John Russell's Memorials of Fox; Horace Walpole's Letters.] H. M. S.

FITZPETER, GEOFFREY, EARL OF ESSEX (*d.* 1213), younger brother of Simon Fitzpeter, sheriff of Northamptonshire, Buckinghamshire, and Bedfordshire in the reign of Henry II, marshal in 1165, and justice-itinerant in Bedfordshire in 1163 (NORGATE, *Angevin Kings*, ii. 355, *n.* 2), married Beatrice, daughter and coheiress of William de Say, eldest son of William de Say, third baron, who married Beatrice, sister of Geoffrey de Mandeville, earl of Essex. In 1184 Geoffrey shared the inheritance of his father-in-law with William de Bocland, the husband of his wife's sister (DUGDALE). During the last five years of Henry's reign he was sheriff of Northamptonshire, and acted occasionally as a justice of assize and judge of the forest-court (EYTON, *Itinerary of Henry II*; NORGATE). He took the cross, but in 1189 paid a fine to Richard I for not going on the crusade (RICHARD OF DEVIZES, p. 8). On the departure of the king he was left one of the five judges of the king's court, and baron of the exchequer, and was therefore one of the counsellors of Hugh, bishop of Durham, the chief justiciar (HOVEDEN, iii. 16, 28). On the death of William de Mandeville, earl of Essex, in this year, his inheritance was claimed by Geoffrey in right of his wife as daughter of the elder son of Beatrice de Say, aunt and heiress of the earl; her claim was disputed by her uncle Geoffrey, who was declared heir by his mother. William Longchamp, the chancellor, adjudged the inheritance to Geoffrey de Say, on condition that he paid seven thousand marks, and gave him seisin. As he made default, the chancellor transferred the inheritance to Geoffrey Fitzpeter for three thousand marks (*ib.* Preface, xlviii, *n.* 6; *Monasticon*, iv. 145; *Pipe Roll*, 2 Ric. 1). The patronage of the priory of Walden in Essex formed part of the Mandeville inheritance; but, while the succession was disputed, the monks on 1 Aug. 1190 prevailed on Richard, bishop of London, to change their house into an abbey. When Geoffrey went to Walden he declared that the abbot and monks had defrauded him of his rights by thus renouncing his patronage; he seized their lands, and otherwise aggrieved them. They appealed to the Bishop of London, who excommunicated those who disturbed them, and William Longchamp also took their part, and caused some of their rights to be restored. This greatly angered Geoffrey, who set at naught Longchamp's authority, and continued to aggrieve the monks. Nor did he pay any attention to a papal mandate which they procured on their behalf. About this time his wife Beatrice died in childbed, and was buried in the priory of Chicksand in Bedfordshire, which also formed part of the Mandeville inheritance. Towards the end of his reign Richard exhorted Geoffrey to satisfy the monks, but he delayed to do so, and the dispute went on until in the reign of John he restored part of the lands which he had taken away, and the matter was arranged (*Monasticon*, iv. 145–8). Meanwhile, in February 1191, Richard, who had heard many complaints against Longchamp, wrote from Messina to Geoffrey and the other justices bidding them control him if they found it necessary, and informing them that he was sending over Walter, archbishop of Rouen, to guide their actions (DICETO, ii. 90, 91). Geoffrey took part in the league against the chancellor, served as one of the coadjutors of Archbishop Walter, the new chief justiciar (GIRALDUS CAMBRENSIS, iv. 400; BENEDICTUS, ii. 213), and was one of the persons excommunicated for the injuries done to Longchamp. When Hubert Walter resigned the chief justiciarship, Richard, on 11 July 1198, appointed Geoffrey as his successor (*Fœdera*, i. 71). The new justiciar gathered a large force, marched to the relief of the men of William of Braose, who were besieged by Gwenwynwyn, son of the prince of Powys, in Maud's Castle, and inflicted a severe defeat on the Welsh (HOVEDEN, iv. 53). Richard was in constant need of money, and Geoffrey,

as his minister, carried out the oppressive measures by which his wants were supplied. The religious houses refused to pay the carucage, and their compliance was enforced by the outlawry of the whole body of the clergy. A decree was issued that all grants were to be confirmed by the new seal, and the people were oppressed by the over-sharp administration of justice, and by a visitation of the forests (*ib.* pp. 62–6). When Richard died, Geoffrey took a prominent part in securing the succession of John at the council of Northampton. At the king's coronation feast he was girded with the sword of the earldom of Essex, though he had been called earl before, and had exercised certain administrative rights which Roger of Hoveden speaks of as pertaining to the earldom (*ib.* p. 90); the chronicler seems to confuse the office of sheriff and the title of earl. He was sheriff of several counties, and among other marks of the king's favour received grants of Berkhamsted and Queenhythe. He was confirmed in his office, and evidently lived on terms of some familiarity with the king (Foss). John is said to have made him the agent of his extortion, and he was reckoned among the king's evil counsellors; he served his master faithfully, and the work he did for him earned him the hatred of the oppressed people. At the same time John disliked him, for the earl was a lawyer, brought up in the school of Glanville, and though no doubt ready enough to gain wealth for himself or his master by any means within the law, can scarcely have been willing to act in defiance of it. He was one of the witnesses of John's charter of submission to the pope on 15 May 1213, and when the king set sail on his intended expedition to Poitou, was left as his vicegerent in conjunction with the Bishop of Winchester. He was present at the assembly held at St. Albans on 4 Aug., and promised on the king's behalf that the laws of Henry I should be observed. He died on 2 Oct. When the king heard of his death he rejoiced, and said with a laugh, 'When he enters hell let him salute Hubert, archbishop of Canterbury, whom no doubt he will find there;' adding that now for the first time he was king and lord of England. Nevertheless the death of his minister left him without any hold on the baronage, and was an important step towards his ruin (STUBBS). By his first wife Geoffrey left three sons, Geoffrey and William, who both succeeded to his earldom, and died without issue, and Henry, a churchman, and a daughter, Maud, who married Henry Bohun, earl of Hereford; and by a second wife, Aveline, a son named John, who inherited his father's manor of Berkhamsted. Geoffrey founded

Shouldham Priory in Norfolk (*Monasticon*, vi. 974), and a hospital at Sutton de la Hone in Kent (*ib.* p. 669), and was a benefactor to the hospital of St. Thomas of Acre in London (*ib.* p. 647).

[Roger of Hoveden, pref. to vol. iii., and 16, 28, 153, iv. 48, 53, 62–6; Benedictus, ii. 158, 213, 223; Ralph of Diceto, ii. 90; Matt. Paris, ii. 453, 483, 553, 559; Walter of Coventry, ii. pref. (all Rolls Ser.); Roger of Wendover, ii. 137, 262 (Engl. Hist. Soc.); Dugdale's Baronage, i. 702, and Monasticon, iv. 145–8; Foss's Judges of England, ii. 62; Norgate's Angevin Kings, ii. 355, 393; Stubbs's Const. Hist. ii. 527.]   W. H.

FITZRALPH, RICHARD, in Latin Ricardus filius Radulphi, often referred to simply as 'Armachanus' or 'Ardmachanus' (*d.* 1360), archbishop of Armagh, was born probably in the last years of the thirteenth century at Dundalk in the county of Louth. The place is expressly stated by the author of the St. Albans 'Chronicon Angliæ' (p. 48, ed. E. M. Thompson) and in the 'Annales Hiberniæ' (an. 1337, 1360, in *Chartularies of St. Mary's Abbey, Dublin*, ii. 381, 393, ed. J. T. Gilbert, 1884). Fitzralph has been claimed by Prince (*Worthies of Devon*, p. 294 et seq., Exeter, 1701) for a Devon man, solely on the grounds of his consecration at Exeter, and of the existence of a family of Fitzralphs in the county.

Fitzralph was educated at Oxford, where he is said to have been a disciple of John Baconthorpe [q. v.], and where he devoted himself with zeal and success to the scholastic studies of the day, which he afterwards came to regard as the cause of much profitless waste of time (*Summa in Quæstionibus Armenorum*, xix. 35, f. 161 *a*. col. 1). He became a fellow of Balliol College, and it was as an ex-fellow that he subscribed in 1325 his assent to a settlement of a dispute in the college as to whether members of the foundation were at liberty to follow studies in divinity. The decision was that they were not permitted to proceed beyond the study of the liberal arts (*Hist. MSS. Comm. 4th Rep.* p. 443).

It has been commonly stated that Fitzralph was at one time a fellow or scholar of University College; but the assertion is part of the well-known legend about that college fabricated in 1379, when the society, desirous of ending a wearisome lawsuit, endeavoured to remove it to the hearing of the king's council. For this purpose they addressed a petition to the king, setting forth that the college was founded by his progenitor, King Alfred, and thus lay under the king's special protection. They further added, to show the services which the college had

performed in the interest of religious education, 'que les nobles Seintz Joan de Beverle, Bede, Richard Armecan, et autres pluseurs famouses doctours et clercs estoient jadys escolars en meisme votre college' (printed by James Parker, *Early History of Oxford*, App. A. 22, p. 316, Oxford, 1885; cf. WILLIAM SMITH, *Annals of University College*, pp. 124–8, Newcastle-on-Tyne, 1728). This audacious fiction with its wonderful inversion of chronology can scarcely be said to establish any fact about Fitzralph, except the high, if not saintly, reputation which he had acquired within twenty years of his death.

Fitzralph seems to have continued residence at Oxford for some time after the lapse of his fellowship, and about 1333 he is said to have been commissary (or vice-chancellor) of the university. It is more likely, however, that he was chancellor, although Anthony à Wood expressly states (*Fasti Oxon.* p. 21) that this is an error; for when he goes on to say that the chancellor at that time was necessarily resident, and that Fitzralph could not be so since he was dean of Lichfield, it is clear that he has mistaken the date of the latter's preferment; and one can hardly doubt his identity with 'Richard Radyn,' who appears in Wood's list as chancellor in the very year 1333, but whose name is written in another copy 'Richardus Radi' (SMITH, p. 125, Radi being evidently Radi, the usual contraction for Radulphi). Fitzralph was now a doctor of divinity. On 10 July 1334 he was collated to the chancellorship of Lincoln Cathedral (LE NEVE, *Fasti Eccl. Anglic.* ii. 92, ed. Hardy), and probably soon afterwards was made archdeacon of Chester. The last preferment must have been some time after 1330 (*ib.* i. 561). Bale, by an error, calls him archdeacon of Lichfield (*Scriptt. Brit. Cat.* v. 93, p. 444); it was to the deanery of Lichfield that he was advanced by the provision of Pope Benedict XII in 1337, and installed 20 April (T. CHESTERFIELD, *De Episc. Coventr. et Lichf.* in WHARTON, *Anglia Sacra*, i. 443). An express notice of William de Chambre (*Cont. Hist. Dunelm.* in *Hist. Dunelm. Script. tres*, p. 128, Surtees Soc., 1839) mentions Fitzralph, in company with Thomas Bradwardine, the future primate, Walter Burley, Robert Holcot, and others, among those scholars who were entertained in the noble household of Richard of Bury, bishop of Durham, a reference which probably belongs to a date subsequent to Bury's elevation to the see in 1333. From his deanery at Lichfield Fitzralph was advanced by provision of Clement VI to the archbishopric of Armagh, and was consecrated at Exeter by Bishop John of Grandison and three other prelates on 8 July 1347 (STUBBS,

Reg. Sacr. Angl. p. 55; CHESTERFIELD, l. c.; SIR J. WARE, *De Præsul. Hibern.* p. 20, Dublin, 1665).

The fact that Fitzralph owed both his highest preferments to papal influence renders it probable that he was held in favour at the court of Avignon, though it is certain that he was never made, as has been stated, a cardinal. It has not, however, been noticed that he was frequently in Avignon previously to his well-known visit in 1357. Among his collected sermons (of which, either in full or in reports, the Bodleian MS. 144 contains no less than eighty-eight) there are some which were delivered before the pope on 7 July 1335, in November 1338, in December 1341, in September and December 1342, and in December 1344, dates which may possibly even point to a continuous residence at Avignon, taken in connection with the circumstance that his sermons preached in England begin in 1345. He was once more in Avignon in August 1349, having been sent thither by the king of England on business connected with the jubilee announced for 1350. A memorial of this remains in the manuscript already referred to (f. 246 *b*), and in other copies, containing under this date Fitzralph's 'Propositio ex parte illustris principis domini regis Edwardi III in consistorio pro gratia jubilea eiusdem domini regis populo obtinenda.' It is highly probable that it was this opportunity which brought Fitzralph into connection with the negotiations then going on between the Armenian church and the pope. The Armenians had sought help from Boniface XII against the advance of the Mussulman, and the pope had required them as an antecedent condition to abjure their heresies, which were set out in 117 articles (enumerated at length in RAYNALD. *Ann.* an. 1341, xlix et seq.; summarised by GIESELER, *Eccl. Hist.* iii. 157 n. 2, Engl. trans., Philadelphia, 1843). The Armenians held a council in 1342 (see the text in MARTÈNE and DURAND, *Vet. Scriptt. Ampliss. Coll.* vii. 312 et seq.); the pope sent them legates, and a correspondence followed, which led to the visit of two of their body—Nerses, archbishop of Melasgerd (Manasgardensis), and John, elect of Khilát (Clatensis)—to Avignon for further consultation. Fitzralph took part in the interviews which were arranged with them, and at their request wrote an elaborate treatise in nineteen books, examining and refuting the doctrines in which the Armenians differed from catholic Christians. The book is called on the title-page 'Richardi Radulphi Summa in Quæstionibus Armenorum,' but the first book is headed 'Summa de Erroribus Armenorum.' It was edited by Johannes Sudoris, and printed by Jean Petit at Paris in 1511. The facts

that Fitzralph dwells upon his personal intercourse with Nerses and John, and that he mentions Clement VI as living, seem to expose an error in Raynaldus, who says (an. 1353, xxv. vol. vi. 588) that it was Innocent VI who invited them in 1353. If this correction is accepted, there is no reason to doubt that the meetings with the Armenians, described at the opening of Fitzralph's treatise, took place during his visit to Avignon in 1349. On the other hand, the concluding chapter of the last book, which alludes to the troubles he had suffered from opponents, looks as though it were added at a later date, if, indeed (which is questionable on internal grounds), it is the work of Fitzralph at all.

If his efforts to promote a reconciliation with the Armenian church redounded to Fitzralph's fame abroad as a champion of catholic orthodoxy, in England he had already won a position of high eminence as a divine, both by solid performances as a teacher and writer on school theology, and by sermons, many of which are extant, preached at various places in England and Ireland. These, though preserved or reported in Latin, are generally stated to have been delivered in English ('in vulgari'). One of them was preached 'in processione Londoniæ facta pro rege,' after the French campaign of 1346. He appears to have been popular on all hands, and in great request as a preacher. His visit to Avignon, however, in 1349, brought him, so far as is known, for the first time into that conflict with the mendicant orders which lasted until the end of his life, and left his posthumous reputation to be agitated between the opposed parties in the church. Previously he had often preached in the friars' convents at Avignon. Thus we possess his sermon at the general chapter of the Dominicans there, 8 Sept. 1342 (*Bodl. MS.* 144, f. 141), and another in the Franciscan church on St. Francis's day in this very year 1349. He was charged, however, on this visit, with a petition from the English clergy reciting certain well-known complaints against the friars. This memorial, 'Propositio ex parte prælatorum et omnium curatorum totius Ecclesiæ coram papa in pleno consistorio ... adversus ordines mendicantes' (*Bodl. MS.* 144, f. 251 *b*), he presented on 5 July 1350. Before this, not later than the beginning of May, Pope Clement had appointed a commission, consisting of Fitzralph and two other doctors, to inquire into the main points at issue; but after long deliberation they seem to have come to no positive decision, and Fitzralph was urged by certain of the cardinals to write an independent treatise on the subject. This work, as he completed it some years later, is the treatise 'De Pauperie

Salvatoris' mentioned below (see the dedication to that work). In the meantime some complaints appear to have been laid against him before the king in respect of his behaviour in Ireland, where he was said to have presumed upon the favour he enjoyed at the pope's hands. The king's decision went against him. First, 20 Nov. 1349, the archbishop's license to have his cross borne before him in Ireland was revoked (RYMER, *Fœdera*, iii. pt. i. 190 seq., ed. 1825), and next, 18 Feb. 1349–50, the king wrote to the Cardinal of St. Anastasia to procure the disallowal of Fitzralph's claim of supremacy over the see of Dublin, and to the archbishop commanding his return to his diocese (*ib.* 192; the two letters of 18 Feb. appear, in this edition of the *Fœdera* only, also under date 1347–8, at pp. 154 seq.) But down to the end of the year at least we find Fitzralph's claims supported by riots which called for active measures on the part of the government (*ib.* pp. 211 seq.)

At Avignon, as has been seen, Fitzralph had thus appeared as the official spokesman of the secular clergy, and this attitude he maintained after his return to Ireland. How matters reached a crisis six years later is not quite certain. Wadding, speaking for the Franciscans, asserts that he had attempted to possess himself of an ornament from one of their churches, and, being foiled in this, proceeded to a general attack upon the order, for which he was summoned, at the instance of the warden of Armagh, to make his defence at the papal court (*Ann. Min.* vii. 127, ed. 1733). He does not, however, name his authority. Fitzralph's own account, in the 'Defensio Curatorum,' is that in 1356 he visited London on business connected with his diocese, and there found a controversy raging about the question of 'evangelical poverty.' On this subject he at once preached a number of sermons, laying down nine propositions, which centred in the assertion that poverty was neither of apostolic observance nor of present obligation, and that mendicancy was without warrant in scripture or primitive tradition. Out of these 'seven or eight' sermons four were printed by Johannes Sudoris at the end of his edition of the 'Summa in Quæstionibus Armenorum.' They were all preached in English at St. Paul's Cross, and range in date from the fourth Sunday in Advent to the third Sunday in Lent 1356–7. The dean of St. Paul's, Richard Kilmington (or Kilwington), his old friend from the time when they were together in Bishop Bury's household, stood by him (W. REDE, *Vitæ Pontif.* ap. TANNER, *Bibl. Brit.* p. 197); but the anger of the English friars was hotly excited, and the Franciscan, Roger Conway [q. v.], wrote a set reply to the archbishop's positions. It was then, and in consequence of this discussion, Fitzralph asserts (*Defensio Curatorum*, ad init.), that his opponents succeeded in procuring his citation to defend his opinions before the pope, Innocent VI, at Avignon. The king forbade him, 1 April 1357, to quit the country without special leave (RYMER, iii. pt. i. 352); but the prohibition seems to have been withdrawn, since he was at the papal court before 8 Nov., on which day he preached a sermon in support of his position, which has been frequently published, and exists in numerous manuscripts, under the title of 'Defensio Curatorum contra eos qui privilegiatos se dicunt' (printed by John Trechsel, Lyons, 1496; also in Goldast's 'Monarchia,' ii. 1392 et seq., Frankfurt, 1614; Brown's 'Fasciculus Rerum expetendarum et fugiendarum,' ii. 466 et seq., and elsewhere).

It was probably in connection with this sermon that Fitzralph completed and put forth his treatise 'De Pauperie Salvatoris,' in seven books, of which the first four will shortly be published for the first time as an appendix to Wycliffe's book 'De Dominio Divino' (edited by R. L. Poole for the Wyclif Society). The interest of this work is partly that it resumes the catholic contention against the mendicant orders which had been accepted by the council of Vienne and by Pope John XXII, and links this to a general view of human relations towards God which was taken up in its entirety by Wycliffe, and made by him the basis of a doctrinal theory which was soon discovered to be, if not heretical, at least dangerous. Fitzralph, however, suffered no actual condemnation; it is hard to see how he could have been made to suffer for maintaining a position which had been upheld in recent years, though in different circumstances, by the highest ecclesiastical authority; and it is likely that he died at Avignon before judgment was pronounced, or perhaps even contemplated. A notarial instrument of the case, of which there is a copy in the Bodleian MS. 158, f. 174, contains the information that Fitzralph's case was entrusted by the pope to four cardinals for examination, 14 Nov., and gives the particulars on which this should proceed. But unfortunately we have no record of the conclusion arrived at. Wadding (*Ann. Min.* viii. 127 et seqq., ed. 1733) states that while the inquiry was going on the pope wrote letters, 1 Oct. 1358, to the English bishops restraining them for the time from any interference with the practices of the friars to which Fitzralph had made objections; and that in the end silence was imposed upon the archbishop, and the friars were confirmed in their privileges. This last fact is not disputed; the friars gained their point (cf. WALSINGHAM, *Hist. Anglic.* i. 285, ed. H. T. Riley): but whether they succeeded in obtaining Fitzralph's condemnation is more than doubtful. Hermann Corner (in ECCARD, *Corp. Hist. Med. Ævi,* iii. 1097) goes so far as to say that he was arrested at Avignon and there perished miserably. But Wadding himself admits in his margin that he died 're infecta,' and the common account is that he died in peace at an advanced age before any formal decision upon his propositions had been reached (F. BOSQUET, *Pontif. Rom. Gall. Hist.* p. 131, Paris, 1632). It is significant that some time before this a subsidy had been levied upon the clergy of the diocese of Lincoln, where he had formerly been chancellor, to contribute towards his expenses during his stay at the papal court (*Reg. Gynewell.* ap. TANNER, 284 note *c*), and Wycliffe implies that a collection of a more general kind was made for his support (*Fascic. Zizan.* p. 284; *Trialogus,* iv. 36, p. 375, ed. G. V. Lechler) ; while a Benedictine chronicler asserts roundly, under the year 1368, that it was in consequence of the default of the English clergy and the abundant resources of the friars that the latter received a confirmation of their privileges, 'adhuc pendente lite' (*Chron. Angl.* p. 38; WALSINGHAM, *Hist. Anglic.* i. 285).

The date of Fitzralph's death was probably 16 Nov. 1360 (WARE, *De Præsul. Hib.* p. 21; COTTON, *Fast. Eccl. Hib.* iii. 15) ; but the 'Chronicon Angliæ,' p. 48, and, among modern writers, Bale (l. c.) give the day as that of St. Edmund the king or 20 Nov. The former date, '16 Kal. Dec.,' has been sometimes misread as 16 Dec. (*Ann. Hib.* an. 1360, p. 393 ; WADDING, viii. 129), and Wadding hesitates whether the year was 1360 or 1359, the latter year being given by Leland (*Comm. de Scriptt. Brit.* p. 373). That Fitzralph's death took place at Avignon may be accepted as certain. The discordant account is in fact obviously derived from the statement in Camden's edition of the 'Annales Hiberniæ' (*Britannia,* p. 830, ed. 1607) that he died 'in Hannonia,' which was pointed out by Ware (l. c.) two hundred and fifty years ago as a mistake for 'Avinione' (see J. T. GILBERT, introduction to the *Chart. of St. Mary's Abbey, Dublin,* ii. pp. cxviii, cxix, where he prints 'Aviniona'). Hannonia then becomes localised in 'Montes Hannoniæ' or Mons in Hainault, and Wadding (l. c. p. 129) conjectures that his death took place in the course of his homeward journey. In this identification of the place he is followed by Mansi (note to RAYNALD. *Ann.* vii. 33).

About ten years after Fitzralph's death his bones are said to have been taken by Stephen de Valle, bishop of Meath (1369–1379), and removed to the church of St. Nicholas at Dundalk; but some doubted whether the bones were his or another's (*Ann. Hib.* l. c.; WARE, p. 21). The monument was still shown in the beginning of the seventeenth century, when Ussher wrote to Camden (30 Oct. 1606) that it 'was not long ago by the rude soldiers defaced' (CAMDEN, *Epist.* p. 86, 1691). However this may be, the statement that miracles were wrought at the tomb in which his remains were laid rests upon early testimony. The first continuator of Higden, whose manuscript is of the first part of the fifteenth century, asserts of the year 1377 that 'about this time God, declaring the righteousness wrought by master Richard whiles that he lived on the earth, that that might be fulfilled in him which is said in the psalm, "The righteous shall be in everlasting remembrance," through the merits of the same Richard worketh daily at his tomb at Dundalk in Ireland many and great miracles, whereat it is said that the friars are ill-pleased ' (*Polychron.* viii. 392, ed. J. R. Lumby; *Chron. Angl.* p. 400). A like statement occurs in the 'Chronicon Angliæ' (an. 1360, p. 48). In consequence of these miracles Ware says that Boniface IX caused a commission, consisting of John Colton, archbishop of Armagh, and Richard Yong, abbot of Osney, and elect of Bangor (therefore between 1400 and 1404), to inquire into his claims to canonisation ; but the inquiry led to no positive action in the matter. Still, popular usage seems to have placed its own interpretation upon the miracles, and as late as the seventeenth century a Roman catholic priest, Paul Harris, speaks of Fitzralph as 'called . . . by the inhabitants of this countrey S. Richard of Dundalke' (*Admonition to the Fryars of Ireland,* pp. 15, 34, 1634). Ussher had used almost the same words in his letter already quoted. Wood states that there was an effigy of Fitzralph in Lichfield Cathedral, but it had been destroyed before the time at which he wrote (*Fasti Oxon.* p. 21).

Besides his chief works already enumerated Fitzralph was the author of a number of minor tracts in the mendicant controversy (among them a reply to Conway), sermons (one collection entitled 'De Laudibus Mariæ Avenioni'), 'Lectura Sententiarum,' 'Quæstiones Sententiarum,' 'Lectura Theologiæ,' 'De Statu universalis Ecclesiæ,' 'De Peccato Ignorantiæ,' 'De Vafritiis Judæorum,' 'Dialogus de Rebus ad S. Scripturam pertinentibus,' 'Vita S. Manchini Abbatis,' and 'Epistolæ ad Diversos,' most of which are still extant in manuscript. For fuller particulars see Tanner's ' Bibl. Brit.,' p. 284 et seq. The statement that Fitzralph translated the Bible or parts of the Bible into Irish, though often repeated, rests simply upon a guess—given merely as a guess—of Foxe (*Acts and Monuments*, ii. 766, ed. 1854).

[Authorities cited above.]   R. L. P.

FITZRICHARD, GILBERT (*d.* 1115?). [See CLARE, GILBERT DE.]

FITZROBERT, SIMON, bishop of Chichester (*d.* 1207). [See SIMON DE WELLS.]

FITZROY, AUGUSTUS HENRY, third DUKE OF GRAFTON (1735–1811), grandson of Charles (1683–1757), second duke and eldest surviving son of Lord Augustus Fitzroy (*d.* 28 May 1741), by Elizabeth, daughter of Colonel William Cosby of Strodbell in Ireland, governor of New York, was born 1 Oct. 1735, and educated at Westminster School and at Peterhouse, Cambridge, taking the degree of M.A. in 1753, as Earl of Euston. Stonehewer, the friend of Gray, was his tutor at Cambridge, and afterwards his private secretary and intimate friend. Grafton subsequently declined the degree of LL.D. usually conferred on its chancellor, from a dislike to subscribing the articles of the church of England. He was returned in December 1756 as member by the boroughs of Boroughbridge in Yorkshire and Bury St. Edmunds in Suffolk, when he chose the latter constituency. On 6 May 1757 he succeeded as third Duke of Grafton, and was at once created lord-lieutenant of Suffolk, a position which he held until 1763, when he was dismissed by Lord Bute, and again from 1769 to 1790. He was appointed in November 1756 as lord of the bedchamber to the Prince of Wales, afterwards George III, but resigned the post early in June 1758. His first active appearance in politics was on the accession to power of Lord Bute, when he flung himself into opposition. At this time he was intimately allied with Lord Temple, and followed his lead by visiting Wilkes in the Tower in May 1763 ' to hear from himself his own story and his defence, and to show that no influence ought to stop the means of every man's justifying himself from an accusation, though it should be of the most heinous nature,' but he offended Temple by refusing in that month to become bail for Wilkes. His rise in parliament was so rapid that when Pitt was summoned by the king to form a ministry in August 1763 he had it in contemplation to enlist Grafton as a member of his cabinet. In December of that year Horace Walpole records in his letters that the Duke of Grafton is much commended, and, although he had never been in office, he was now in the front rank of politics. Pitt was again called upon to form a ministry, when he named Grafton and himself as the principal secretaries of state; but the projected administration fell through in consequence of Lord Temple's refusal to take office. The Marquis of Rockingham thereupon took the treasury, and Grafton became his secretary of state for the northern department (July 1765). Then, as ever, he was anxious to obtain Pitt's assistance, but the great commoner was not enamoured of the new cabinet, and especially objected to the Duke of Newcastle's inclusion in it. Weak as it was, without the support of the king or of Pitt, and without cohesion among themselves, the Rockingham ministry dragged on for some months. Grafton threw up the seals in May 1766, when he stated in the House of Lords that he had not gone out of office 'from a love of ease and indulgence to his private amusements, as had been falsely reported, but because they wanted strength, which one man only could supply;' and that ' though he had carried a general's staff, he was ready to take up a mattock or spade under that able and great minister.' At the end of July all Grafton's colleagues followed his example, and Pitt was forced to take upon himself the cares of office. Grafton very reluctantly accepted the headship of the treasury, and Pitt, to the disgust of his friends, took a peerage and the privy seal (July 1766). With a view to strengthening the cabinet by the inclusion of the Duke of Bedford's party, the first lord endeavoured to obtain Lord Gower in lieu of Lord Egmont as first lord of the admiralty, but in this he was unsuccessful. The new ministry was soon involved in difficulty. Wilkes came to London, and on 1 Nov. 1766 addressed to Grafton a letter in which he professed loyalty and implored pardon, but on the advice of Chatham no notice was taken of the communication, and Wilkes thereupon repaired to Paris and sent a second communication on 12 Dec. The state of the East India Company presented even greater dangers to the new administration. The views of Conway and Charles Townshend were antagonistic to those of Chatham, and but for the latter's illness, Townshend would have been dismissed from office. Their defeat over the amount of the land tax was ' a most disheartening circumstance,' and when Townshend was taunted with the necessity of providing some means to recoup the reduction, he, ' without the concurrence of the rest of the cabinet, intimated that he had thought of a method of taxing America without giving offence, and the ministry found themselves under the necessity of bringing forward the port duties upon glass, colours, paper, and tea.' Grafton became more anxious than ever for Chatham's advice in the cabinet's deliberations, and for his presence in parliament. An interview between them was at last arranged on 31 May 1767, but the only effect of their consultation was for the ministry to continue in its course, with Conway taking the lead in the commons. As Chatham's malady became worse, it was necessary for Grafton either to retire, which he often threatened, or to assume greater responsibility in business. He adopted the latter alternative, and from September 1767 the ministry was known by his name. Townshend died in that month and Lord North succeeded as chancellor of the exchequer, and Lord Gower with the members of the Bedford party was included in the government in the following December. The effect of these changes was to render the ministry more united in council but to weaken its liberal character. Wilkes was returned for Middlesex, and Grafton, though personally adverse to arbitrary acts of power, was at the head of affairs when an elected representative to parliament was first expelled the House of Commons, and then declared incapable of election. The cabinet decided that the port duties levied in the American colonies should be repealed, but were divided upon the question whether the duty upon tea should not be retained as an assertion of the right. Grafton was for the repeal of all, but, ' to his great surprise and mortification, it was carried against him by the casting vote of his friend Lord Rochford, whom he had himself lately introduced into the cabinet.' To make matters worse, he began to neglect business, and to outrage the lax morality of his day, thinking, to use the strong language of Horace Walpole, 'the world should be postponed to a whore and a horse race.' Junius thundered against him, accusing him, as hereditary ranger of Whittlebury and Salcey forests, of malversation in claiming and cutting some of the timber— an accusation which would appear from the official minutes in 'Notes and Queries,' 3rd ser. viii. 231–3, to have been unfounded— and denouncing him, both in his letters and in a poem called 'Harry and Nan,' an elegy in the manner of Tibullus, which was printed in 'Almon's Political Register,' ii. 431 (1768), for what could not be gainsaid, his connection with Nancy Parsons. This woman was the daughter of a tailor in Bond Street, and she first lived with Hoghton or Horton, a West India captive merchant, with whom she went to Jamaica, but from whom she fled to England. She is de-

scribed as ' the Duke of Grafton's Mrs. Horton, the Duke of Dorset's Mrs. Horton, everybody's Mrs. Horton.' Her features are well known from Gainsborough's portrait, and she was endowed with rare powers of attraction, for which Grafton threw away ' his beautiful and most accomplished wife,' and Charles, second viscount Maynard, raised her to the peerage by marrying her 12 June 1776. It was in April 1768 that the prime minister appeared with her at the opera and thus afforded Junius an opportunity for some of his keenest invectives. Under the influence of these private distractions and public troubles over Wilkes and America, resignation of the premiership was often threatened by Grafton. In October 1768 Chatham resigned his place as lord privy seal, although several of his friends still adhered to their places. At the close of 1769 Chatham recovered the full possession of his faculties, and the effect upon the ministry of his reappearance in the political world was instantaneous. Lord Granby voted against them, and then resigned. Lord Camden was dismissed from his post of lord chancellor, and the seals were given to Charles Yorke. The death of the new chancellor followed immediately on his appointment, and Grafton, naturally timid and indolent, and with a set of discontented friends around him, seized the opportunity of resigning on 28 Jan. 1770. His temporary difference with Chatham was intensified by some words which passed between them in the following March, when Grafton was pronounced unequal 'to the government of a great nation.' After much persuasion from the king's friends he took office as privy seal in Lord North's administration (June 1771), but, 'with a kind of proud humility,' refused a seat in the cabinet. This step exposed him to varying comment. The king wrote, 'Nothing can be more handsome than his manner of accepting the privy seal,' but Horace Walpole sneeringly wrote, that it came ' of not being proud.' Grafton himself gave out in after years that he accepted this office in the hope of preventing the quarrel with America from being pushed to extremities, and his views probably always leant to the side of the colonists. In August 1775 he wrote to Lord North, warmly urging the desirability of a reconciliation, but the prime minister did not reply for seven weeks, when the substance of his answer was a draft of the king's speech. His resignation was daily expected, and on 3 Nov. the king thought that the seal of office should be sent for, but on 9 Nov. Grafton resigned, and at once took public action against his late colleagues. An attempt was made in February

1779 to attach him and some of Chatham's followers to the North ministry, but it failed, and he remained out of office until the foundation of the Rockingham ministry in March 1782, when he joined the cabinet as lord privy seal. Though he acquiesced in the accession of Lord Shelburne on Rockingham's death in the following July, he did not cordially act with his new chief, and the downfall of the administration in April 1783 was probably a relief to him. From that time he remained out of office, and to his credit be it said that although he had a numerous family he obtained 'no place, pension, or reversion whatever.' He had been declining in health for more than two years, but his fatal illness lasted for some weeks. He died at Euston Hall, Suffolk, on 14 March 1811, and was buried at Euston on 21 March. He was invested K.G. at St. James's Palace 20 Sept. 1769, was recorder of Thetford and Coventry, high steward of Dartmouth, hereditary ranger of Whittlebury and Salcey forests, and the holder of several sinecures, including places in the king's bench, common pleas, and court of exchequer. His first wife, whom he married 29 Jan. 1756, was Anne, daughter and heiress of Henry Liddell, baron Ravensworth. After a married life of twelve years she eloped with John Fitzpatrick, second earl of Upper Ossory, whom she married on 26 March 1769, the act dissolving her first marriage having come into law three days previously. By her the duke had two sons, George Henry, fourth duke [q. v.], and Lord Charles [q. v.], and a daughter, Georgiana. He married in May 1769 Elizabeth, third daughter of the Rev. Sir Richard Wrottesley, dean of Windsor. She is described as 'not handsome, but quiet and reasonable, and having a very amiable character.' She bore him twelve children.

Grafton's tastes first leant entirely to pleasure. His pack of hounds at Wakefield Lodge, his official residence in Whittlebury forest, and the races of Newmarket absorbed his thoughts and his spare time. Latterly he became of a more serious disposition, and he was for many years a regular worshipper at the unitarian chapel in Essex Street, Strand, London. He was the author of: 1. 'Hints submitted to the serious attention of the Clergy, Nobility, and Gentry, by a Layman,' 1789, two editions, the first edition having been called in in consequence of the king's illness. It urged the propriety of amendment of life by the upper classes, and greater attention to public worship, to insure which a revision of the liturgy was necessary. 2. 'The Serious Reflections of a Rational Christian from 1788 to 1797' [anon.], 1797. In favour of unitarianism and against the in-

fallibility of the writers of the Old and New Testaments. It was through some of Bishop Watson's little tracts that Grafton first turned his attention to religious inquiry, and when his views were condemned by several writers they found a defender in the bishop. A volume of 'Considerations on the expediency of Revising the Liturgy and Articles of the Church of England' (1790, two edits.), written by Watson, was printed under the duke's auspices, and seven hundred copies of an edition of Griesbach's Greek New Testament, with the various readings in manuscript, printed at his sole expense in 1796, were gratuitously circulated according to his direction. Late in life he wrote a 'Memoir' of his public career, and several extracts from it have been published in Lord Stanhope's 'History,' Walpole's 'Memoirs of George III,' vol. iv., Appendix, and in Campbell's 'Lives of the Chancellors;' but the whole work has not yet been printed, although it has for some time been included among the publications of the Camden Society. On 29 Nov. 1768 Grafton was unanimously elected chancellor of Cambridge University, and on 1 July 1769 he was installed in the senate house. Through Stonehewer's interest Gray had been appointed by Grafton to the professorship of modern history at Cambridge, and he thought himself bound in gratitude to write on the installation. The ode was begun in 1768, finished in April 1769, and printed after July in that year. Much to Dr. Burney's chagrin it was set to music by Dr. John Randall, the then music professor. Particulars of the proceedings on this occasion may be found in Nichols's 'Illustrations of Literature,' v. 315-317; Cradock's 'Memoirs,' i. 105-17, iv. 156-9; and in the 'Gentleman's Magazine,' xxxix. 361-2. His expenses on this occasion were estimated at 2,000l., and to celebrate his appointment he offered 500l. towards lighting and paving the town. The duke's career disappointed the expectations of his friends. His disinterestedness of motive and the sincerity of his friendship have received high praise, nor was he wanting in judgment or good sense, but these qualities were allied with many drawbacks, and notably with timidity of conduct, which led him in times of danger to threaten resignation of office, and disregard of public opinion in social life. It is perhaps his highest praise that Fox in 1775 wrote that he could act with him 'with more pleasure in any possible situation than with any one I have been acquainted with,' and Chatham in 1777 sent him 'unfeigned respect.'

[Grenville Papers, passim; Stanhope's History, 1713-83, vols. v-vii.; Chatham Corresp. passim; Walpole's Memoirs of Reign of George III;

Walpole's Letters, iii. 138, iv. 139, 500, v. 106, 163, 225, 305, 347, vii. 89; Corresp. of George III and North, i. 75-6, 281-3, ii. 225; Almon's Anecdotes, i. 1-34; Gent. Mag. 1811, p. 302; Taylor's Sir Joshua Reynolds, i. 176; Dyer's Cambridge, ii. 29-31; C. H. Cooper's Annals of Cambridge, iv. 353-61; Gray's works (1884 ed.), i. 92-7, ii. 242, 277, iii. 318, 342-6; Baker's Northamptonshire, ii. 170-1; Nichols's Illustr. of Lit. vi. 768; Nichols's Lit. Anecdotes, i. 582, ii. 67, viii. 145, ix. 87, 457, 461, 487; Notes and Queries, 2nd ser. ii. 456, 462, iii. 57; Belsham's Lindsey, pp. 320-36; John Williams's Belsham, pp. 611-12; Uncorrupted Christianity, &c., a sermon on the duke's death by Belsham, 1811.]
W. P. C.

FITZROY, CHARLES, first DUKE OF SOUTHAMPTON and CLEVELAND (1662-1730), natural son of Charles II, by Barbara, countess of Castlemaine [see VILLIERS, BARBARA], was born in 1662 and baptised on 18 June in that year in St. Margaret's Church, Westminster, the king, the Earl of Oxford, and Lady Suffolk (sister of the Countess of Castlemaine) being sponsors. The entry in the register was 'Charles Palmer, lord Limerick, son to the Right Honourable Roger, earl of Castlemaine, by Barbara,' and he bore the title of Lord Limerick until 1670, when the patent which created his mother Countess of Southampton and Duchess of Cleveland, with remainder in tail male, conferred upon him the right to use the title of Earl of Southampton during his mother's life, and from that date he is commonly referred to as Lord Southampton. He was installed knight of the Garter on 1 April 1673, and on 10 Sept. 1675 was created Baron of Newbury in the county of Berkshire, Earl of Chichester in the county of Sussex, and Duke of the county of Southampton. On the death of his mother in 1709 he succeeded to the barony of Nonsuch in the county of Surrey, the earldom of Southampton, and the dukedom of Cleveland. He took his seat in the House of Lords as Duke of Cleveland on 14 Jan. 1710. His life was uneventful. He was suspected of intriguing for the restoration of James II in 1691, received a pension of 1,000l. per annum, charged on the proceeds of the lotteries in 1697, took little or no part in the debates of the House of Lords, but joined in the protest against the abandonment of the amendments to the Irish Forfeitures and Land Tax Bill in 1700. He died in 1730. Fitzroy married, first, Mary, daughter of Sir Henry Wood, one of the clerks of the green cloth, through whom, as next of kin to her father, he acquired after much litigation in 1692 a life interest of the annual value of 4,000l.; secondly, in November 1694, Ann, daughter of Sir William Pulteney of

Misterton, Leicestershire. By his first wife he had no issue; by his second, three sons and three daughters. His eldest son and successor, William, died without issue in 1774. Two other sons died in his lifetime. Of his daughters, Grace married Henry Vane [q. v.], third baron Barnard, and their grandson, William Harry Vane, created Duke of Cleveland in 1833, was father of the second, third, and fourth dukes of this creation.

[Gent. Mag. new ser. 1850, p. 368; Pepys's Diary, 26 July 1662; Hist. MSS. Comm. 6th Rep. App. 367, 7th Rep. App. 210 b, 465 b; Nicolas's Knighthood, ii. lxviii; Lords' Journals, xix. 37; Luttrell's Relation, ii. 606, 630, iii. 397, iv. 636; Cal. Treas. Papers, 1697-1701-2, p. 76; Hist. Reg. Chron. Diary, 1730, p. 58; Nicolas's Peerage (Courthope).]
J. M. R.

FITZROY, CHARLES (1737-1797), first BARON SOUTHAMPTON, third son of Lord Augustus Fitzroy (second son of Charles, second duke of Grafton), by Elizabeth, daughter of Colonel William Cosby, was born on 25 June 1737. He was gazetted to a lieutenancy in the 1st regiment of foot in 1756, was rapidly advanced to the rank of lieutenant-colonel, and served as aide-de-camp to Prince Ferdinand of Brunswick at the battle of Minden (1 Aug. 1759), when he carried the famous order for the advance of the cavalry, which Lord George Sackville (afterwards Sackville-Germain) neglected. He gave evidence before the court-martial on Sackville [see GERMAIN, GEORGE SACKVILLE]. He was M.P. for Oxford 1759-61, for Bury St. Edmunds 1761-74, and for Thetford 1774-80. In 1760 he was appointed groom of the bedchamber to the king, an office which he resigned in 1762. He was present at the battle of Kirchdenkern on 15 July 1761. On 11 Sept. 1765 he succeeded the Marquis of Lorne in the command of the 14th regiment of dragoons. On 20 Oct. 1772 he was appointed colonel of the 3rd or king's own dragoons. On 17 Oct. 1780 he was raised to the peerage as Baron Southampton, and on 27 Dec. following he became groom of the stole to the Prince of Wales. He moved the address to the throne at the opening of parliament in 1781, and spoke (18 Feb. 1782) on Lord Carmarthen's motion protesting against the elevation to the peerage of 'any person labouring under a heavy censure of a court-martial,' a motion aimed at Lord George Sackville-Germain, who had just been created Viscount Sackville of Drayton, denying that, as had been alleged or insinuated, the court-martial in question had been animated by a factious spirit. He also spoke, without definitely committing himself to either side, on the Regency Bill on 16 Feb.

1789. He was advanced to the rank of general on 25 Oct. 1793. He died on 21 March 1797. He married, on 27 July 1758, Anne, daughter of Sir Peter Warren, K.B., vice-admiral of the red, by whom he had issue nine sons and seven daughters. He was succeeded by his eldest son, George Ferdinand. He was lord of the manor of Tottenham Court, Middlesex, and had his principal seat at Fitzroy Farm, near Highgate, the grounds of which he laid out in the artificial style then in vogue.

[Brydges's Peerage (Collins), vii. 451 ; Gent. Mag. 1756 p. 362, 1759 p. 144, 1760 pp. 47, 136, 1761 p. 331, 1762 p. 391, 1765 p. 444, 1797 i. 355 ; Beatson's Polit. Index, i. 429, 455 ; Lords' Journ. xxxvi. 180 b ; Parl. Hist. xxii. 637, 1013, xxvii. 1274 ; Walpole's Journ. of the Reign of Geo. III. ii. 475 ; Lysons's Environs, 1795, iii. 272 n.]　　　　　J. M. R.

FITZROY, Lord CHARLES (1764–1829), general, the second son of Augustus Henry, third duke of Grafton [q. v.], by his first wife, Anne, daughter of Henry Liddell, baron Ravensworth, was born on 17 July 1764. He took the degree of M.A. at Trinity College, Cambridge, in 1784. Having entered the army as an ensign in 1782 he was appointed captain of the 3rd foot guards in 1787, and in 1788 equerry to the Duke of York, under whom he served in the campaign in Flanders in 1793–4, being present at the siege of Valenciennes. In 1795 he became aide-de-camp to the king with the rank of colonel, was advanced to major-general in 1798, served on the Irish staff from February 1798 to April 1799, and then on the English staff until 1809, with the exception of the 'year of peace,' 1802. He also commanded the garrison of Ipswich. He was colonel-commandant of a battalion of 60th foot 1804–5 and colonel of 48th foot 1805 until death. He was gazetted lieutenant-general in January 1805, and on 4 Jan. 1814 general. From 1787 to 1796 and 1802 to 1818 he was M.P. for Bury St. Edmunds. He never spoke in the house. During the last twenty years of his life he resided principally at his seat at Wicken, near Stony Stratford, where he endeared himself to the poor by many acts of charity. He died at his house in Berkeley Square on 20 Dec. 1829, and was buried on the 30th at Wicken. Fitzroy married, first, on 20 June 1795, Frances, daughter of Edward Miller Mundy, sometime M.P. for Derbyshire, by whom he had one son, Charles Augustus [q. v.]; and secondly, on 10 March 1799, Lady Frances Anne Stewart, eldest daughter of Robert, first marquis of Londonderry, by whom he had two sons, George and Robert [q. v.], and one daughter.

[Collins's Peerage (Brydges), i. 219 ; Grad. Cant. ; Gent. Mag. 1788 pt. i. 278, 1795 pt. i. 243, 1798 pt. i. 90, 1805 pt. i. 577, 1818 pt. ii. 499, 1830 pt. i. 78 ; List of Members of Parl. (Official Return of) ; Cornwallis Corresp. (Ross), ii. 422.]　　　　　J. M. R.

FITZROY, Sir CHARLES AUGUSTUS (1796–1858), colonial governor, eldest son of Lord Charles Fitzroy [q. v.], the second son of Augustus Henry, third duke of Grafton [q. v.], was born 10 May 1796. He obtained a commission in the Horse Guards, and was present at the battle of Waterloo, where he was attached to the staff of Sir Hussey Vivian. After his retirement from active service he was elected in 1831 as member for Bury St. Edmunds, and voted for the Reform Bill. He did not sit in the reformed parliament. In 1837 he was appointed lieutenant-governor of Prince Edward Island, being knighted on his departure to the colony. In 1841 he was appointed governor and commander-in-chief of the Leeward Islands, where he won great favour by his conciliatory demeanour. Before his term of office was completed he was recalled (1845), in order that he might be sent to the colony of New South Wales, then in a state of considerable excitement and in peculiar need of a governor of proved moderation and courtesy. He succeeded Sir George Gipps [q. v.] in August 1846. The colonists had insisted on constitutional changes, and had been irritated by Gipps's unsympathetic behaviour. The immediate question was the claim of the council, then partly composed of nominee members, to specific appropriation of the public funds. The appointment of Fitzroy enabled the colonists to agree to what was really a postponement of the full acknowledgment of their claim. Their confidence was shown in the universal sympathy on the occasion of the fatal accident to Lady Mary Fitzroy, 7 Dec. 1847. Mr. Gladstone had suggested to the Legislative Council of New South Wales a revival of the system of transportation, a proposal to which a select committee had assented on the condition that an equal number of free emigrants should be sent out by the home government. Lord Grey, however, had determined to send convicts alone. The whole colony was roused to excitement by the arrival (11 June 1849) of the Hashemy with convicts on board. The convicts were landed and sent to the up-country districts. Fitzroy reported their objections, but declared that he would firmly resist coercion. Fortunately, Lord Grey yielded the point. In 1850 Fitzroy was appointed governor-general of Australia, and soon afterwards the Port Phillip district was separated into the independent colony of Victoria. Upon the discovery of gold Fitzroy steadily pressed on the home authorities the advisability of establishing a mint at Sydney. His influence was also used on behalf of a favourable consideration for the Constitutional Act which Wentworth had passed through the colonial legislature in 1853. He was made K.C.B. in June 1854. His departure, 17 Jan. 1855, was greatly regretted, and when news of his death reached the colony the legislature adjourned. Fitzroy was present at the opening of Sydney University, and under his auspices the first railway was commenced, the first stone of the Fitzroy Dock laid, and the Exchange begun.

He died in London on 16 Feb. 1858. He was twice married: first, on 11 March 1820, to Lady Mary Lennox, eldest daughter of the fourth Duke of Richmond, who died 7 Dec. 1847; secondly, on 11 Dec. 1855, to Margaret Gordon.

[Records of the British Army, Royal Horse Guards; Antigua and the Antiguans; Rusden's Hist. of Australia; Sydney Morning Herald; European Mail (for Australia), February 1858.]

E. C. K. G.

FITZROY, GEORGE, DUKE OF NORTHUMBERLAND (1665–1716), third and youngest son of Charles II, by Barbara, countess of Castlemaine [See VILLIERS, BARBARA, DUCHESS OF CLEVELAND], born at Oxford in December 1665, was created Baron of Pontefract in the county of York, Viscount Falmouth in the county of Cornwall, and Earl of Northumberland on 1 Oct. 1674. He was employed on secret service at Venice in 1682, and on his return to England was created Duke of Northumberland (6 April 1683), and elected and installed knight of the Garter (10 Jan. and 8 April 1684). He served as a volunteer on the side of the French at the siege of Luxembourg in the summer of the same year, returning to England in the autumn. Evelyn, who met him soon after his return, describes him as 'of all his majesty's children the most accomplished and worth the owning,' 'extremely handsome and well shaped,' and skilled in horsemanship (*Diary*, 24 Oct. and 18 Dec. 1684). He was made colonel 2nd troop of horse guards in 1686, which he commanded in 1687, was appointed a lord of his majesty's bedchamber in December 1688, constable of Windsor Castle in 1701, and succeeded the Earl of Oxford as colonel of the royal regiment of horse March 1702–3, from which he was transferred to the 2nd troop of horse guards Jan. 1711–2. On 10 Jan. 1709–10 he obtained the rank of lieutenant-general, became lord-lieutenant of Berks in 1712, was sworn of the privy council on 7 April 1713, and was appointed lord-lieutenant of Surrey on 9 Oct. 1714. He was also chief butler of England. Frogmore House, Berkshire, was one of his seats. He was deprived of his lord-lieutenancies and his colonelcy after George I's accession. He died without issue at Epsom on 28 June 1716. He married in 1686 Catherine, daughter of Robert Wheatley, a poulterer, of Bracknell, Berkshire, and relict of Robert Lucy of Charlecote.

[Lodge's Peerage of Ireland (Archdall), iv. 89; Courthope's Hist. Peer.; Burke's Extinct Peerage; Secret Services of Charles II and James II (Camd. Soc.), p. 66; Luttrell's Relation of State Affairs, i. 295, 304, 307, 322, 373, 434, 544, 615, v. 46, 268, 277, 278, vi. 711, 723; Magn. Brit. Notit. 1702, p. 549; Angl. Notit. 1687 pt. i. p. 179, 1714 pt. ii. p. 336; Lysons's Magn. Brit. i. 433; Haydn's Book of Dignities; Hist. Reg. i. 352.]

J. M. R.

FITZROY, GEORGE HENRY, fourth DUKE OF GRAFTON (1760–1844), son of Augustus Henry Fitzroy [q. v.], third duke, by his first wife, was born 14 Jan. 1760. As Earl of Euston he was sent at eighteen years of age to Trinity College, Cambridge, where he contracted an intimate friendship with the younger Pitt. He proceeded M.A. in 1799. He was afterwards for a time Pitt's warm partisan in the House of Commons, and for many years his colleague in the representation of the university. In 1784 he married the Lady Maria Charlotte Waldegrave, second daughter of James, second earl of Waldegrave. He was M.P. for Thetford 1782–4. In 1784 the tories attacked many whig seats, including those of Cambridge University. The sitting members were Lord John Townshend and James (afterwards Chief Justice) Mansfield. The election excited great interest throughout the country, and the return of Pitt and Euston was hailed with enthusiasm by the tory party. The numbers were: Pitt, 351; Euston, 299; Townshend, 278; and Mansfield, 181. Euston's career in the House of Commons was useful, but not brilliant. At the outset he supported the government of Pitt, but he rarely addressed the house. He was appointed lord-lieutenant of Suffolk in 1790, receiver-general in the courts of king's bench and common pleas, and king's gamekeeper at Newmarket. From 1784 to 1807 he was ranger of Hyde Park and of St. James's Park. In addition to these offices, conferred upon him by the prime minister, he was hereditary ranger of Whittlebury Forest, recorder of Thetford, a trustee of the Hunterian Museum, president of the Eclectic Society of London, &c. Twice, in 1790 and 1807, his seat at Cambridge was stoutly contested, on the latter occasion by Lord Palmerston, but in both instances unsuccessfully. Euston sat for his university from 1784 to 1811, when he succeeded to the peerage on the death of his father, 14 March 1811. A considerable time before this event Euston had changed his political views. He was unable to support all the measures of the government in relation to the war against France, and seceded from Pitt when embarrassments began to surround that minister. In fact, long before the death of Pitt, Euston had become a whig. From the time of his accession to the dukedom Euston steadfastly cast his votes and exercised all his influence in favour of civil and religious liberty. He did not, however, show bitterness towards his former friends, being considerate and urbane in speech and action. When the bill of pains and penalties against the queen of George IV was presented to the House of Lords, he spoke vehemently against the measure, and this was almost the last occasion on which he took a prominent part in the business of parliament. For nearly twenty years he lived in retirement, surrounded by his numerous descendants; but he had become a widower in 1808. He received the Garter in 1834. He died at his seat, Euston Hall, Suffolk, 28 Sept. 1844. He was succeeded in the title and estates by his eldest son Henry, who, as Earl of Euston, had sat in the House of Commons for eleven years, first as member for Bury St. Edmunds, and then as member for Thetford. The fifth Duke of Grafton married a daughter of Admiral Sir George Cranfield Berkeley, by whom he had issue.

[Times, 30 Sept. 1844; Ipswich Express, 1 Oct. 1844; Annual Register, 1844.]   G. B. S.

FITZROY, HENRY, Duke of Richmond (1519–1536), was the son of Henry VIII and Elizabeth Blount, a lady in waiting on Queen Catherine of Arragon, daughter of John Blount, esq., who, according to Wood, came from Knevet in Shropshire, perhaps Kinlet, an old seat of the Blount family. His mother afterwards married Gilbert, son of Sir George Talboys of Goltho, Lincolnshire, and certain manors in that county and Yorkshire were assigned to her for life by act of parliament.

At the age of six, on 7 June 1525, he was made knight of the Garter, in which order he was subsequently promoted to the lieutenancy (17 May 1533). A few days after his installation he was created Earl of Nottingham and Duke of Richmond and Somerset, with precedence over all dukes except the king's lawful issue. The ceremony, which took place at Bridewell on 18 June 1525, is minutely described in an heraldic manuscript quoted in the 'Calendar of State Papers

of Henry VIII.' On the same day he was appointed the king's lieutenant-general north of Trent, and keeper of the city and castle of Carlisle. The following month (16 July) he received a patent as lord high admiral of England, Wales, Ireland, Normandy, Gascony, and Aquitaine, and on the 22nd a further commission as warden-general of the marches of Scotland. He was also receiver of Middleham and Sheriff Hutton, Yorkshire. Lands and income were at the same time granted to him amounting to over 4,000l. in yearly value. Other offices bestowed on him were the lord-lieutenantship of Ireland in June 1529, and the constableship of Dover Castle, with the wardenry of the Cinque ports, about two months before his death. It was commonly reported that the king intended to make him king of Ireland, and perhaps his successor, for which these high offices were meant to be a preparation. Shortly after his creation he travelled north, and resided for some time at Sheriff Hutton and Pontefract, where his council transacted all the business of the borders. His education was entrusted to Richard Croke [q. v.], one of the most famous of the pioneers of Greek scholarship in England, and to John Palsgrave, author of 'Lesclarcissement de la langue Francoyse,' the earliest English grammar of the French language. Both his tutors took great pains with his education, in spite of the hindrance of those of his household who preferred to see him more proficient in horsemanship and hunting than in literature. When ten years old he had already read some Cæsar, Virgil, and Terence, and knew a little Greek. Croke appears to have been much attached to him, and when in Italy, after leaving his service, writes offering to send him models of a Roman military bridge and of a galley. Singing and playing on the virginals were included in his education. Various matrimonial alliances were proposed for him, some perhaps merely as a move in the game of politics. Within the short space of a year there was some talk of his marrying a niece of Pope Clement VII, a Danish princess, a French princess, and a daughter of Eleanor, queen dowager of Portugal, sister of Charles V, who afterwards became queen of France; but he eventually married (25 Nov. 1533) Mary [see Fitzroy, Mary], daughter of Thomas Howard, third duke of Norfolk, by his second wife, and sister of his friend Henry, earl of Surrey, who commemorated their friendship in his poems.

In the spring of 1532 he came south, residing for a time at Hatfield, and in the autumn accompanied his father to Calais, to be present at his interview with Francis I. Thence he went on to Paris with his friend the Earl of Surrey, and remained there till September 1533. On his return he was married, and it was intended he should go to Ireland shortly after; but this intention was not carried out, perhaps owing to the state of his health, and he remained with the court. He is mentioned as being present at the execution of the Carthusians in May 1535, and at that of Anne Boleyn in May 1536. On 22 July the same year he died in 'the kinges place in St. James,' not without suspicion of being poisoned by the late queen and her brother, Lord Rochford. He was buried in the Cluniac priory of Thetford, but at the dissolution his body and tomb, together with that of his father-in-law, the Duke of Norfolk, were removed to St. Michael's Church, Framlingham, Suffolk. The tomb now stands on the north of the altar. 'It is of freestone, garnished round with divers histories of the Bible, and on the top were twelve figures, each supporting a trophy of the Passion, but all of them are miserably defaced. His arms in the Garter, with a ducal coronet over them, are still perfect.' A miniature portrait of the young duke was formerly in the Strawberry Hill collection, and was engraved by Harding. There is a sketch of it in Doyle's 'Baronage,' and also a facsimile of his signature from one of his letters, preserved among the public records.

[Cal. State Papers Hen. VIII, vols. iv–viii. ; Grafton's Chronicle, pp. 382, 443 ; Wriothesley's Chronicle, i. 41, 45, 53, 54 ; Chronicle of Calais, pp. 41, 44, 164 ; Friedmann's Anne Boleyn, ii. 176, 286–7, 294 ; Doyle's Official Baronage, iii. 120 ; Blomefield's Norfolk, ii. 125 ; Statute 14 Hen. VIII c. 34, 22 Hen. VIII c. 17, 23 Hen. VIII c. 28, 25 Hen. VIII c. 30, 26 Hen. VIII c. 21, 27 Hen. VIII c. 51, 28 Hen. VIII c. 34 ; Nott's Life of Surrey, p. xxviii ; Green's Guide to Framlingham, 1878, p. 16 ; Dodd's Church Hist. i. 167.]
C. T. M.

FITZROY, HENRY, first DUKE OF GRAFTON (1663–1690), second son of Charles II by Barbara Villiers, countess of Castlemaine, afterwards Duchess of Cleveland [see VILLIERS, BARBARA], was born on 20 Sept. 1663, and was, after, it is said, some hesitation, acknowledged by Charles as his son. A rich wife was early provided for him in Isabella, daughter and heiress of Henry Bennet, earl of Arlington. She was only five years old when, on 1 Aug. 1672, she was married by Archbishop Sheldon to her young husband in the presence of the king and court (EVELYN, Diary, 1 Aug. 1672). On 16 Aug. he was made Earl of Euston, the title being derived from Arlington's house in Suffolk, of which he was now the probable heir. In September 1675 he was made Duke of Grafton. Arlington and his family were

very unwilling to sanction the alliance, and so late as 1678 there were rumours that it was broken off (Hist. MSS. Comm. 6th Rep. p. 386) ; but in 1679 the couple were remarried, though Evelyn looked with the greatest anxiety to the union of the 'sweetest and most beautiful child' to a 'boy that had been rudely bred' (Diary, 6 Sept. 1679). Grafton was, however, 'exceeding handsome, by far surpassing any of the king's other natural issue,' and his father's resolution to bring him up for the sea soon made him, as Evelyn had hoped, 'a plain, useful, and robust officer, and, were he polished, a tolerable man.' He was sent as a volunteer to learn his profession under Sir John Berry [q. v.], and in his absence on 30 Sept. 1680 was installed by proxy as knight of the Garter. In 1682–3 he was master of the Trinity House, was colonel of the 1st foot guards 1681–8 and 1688–9, and, on the death of Prince Rupert, vice-admiral of England. In 1683 he became captain of the Grafton, a ship of 70 guns. In 1684 he visited Louis XIV at Condé, and, at some personal danger, won experience of military service at the siege of Luxemburg (Hist. MSS. Comm. App. to 7th Rep. pp. 84, 263, 302). At the coronation of James II he acted as lord high constable. He shared in suppressing the rebellion of Monmouth ; showed great gallantry at the skirmish at Philip's Norton, near Bath, on 27 June, where he fell into an ambuscade, and it was only with great risk that he succeeded in effecting his retreat (London Gazette, 2 July 1685 ; Hist. MSS. Comm. 9th Rep. pp. 3, 4). He was also present at Sedgmoor. He first took his seat in parliament on 9 Nov. 1685 (ib. 11th Rep. pt. ii. p. 321). Early in 1686 he fought two fatal duels ; in one case, however, Evelyn acknowledges 'after almost insufferable provocation from Mr. Stanley, brother of Lord Derby' (Diary, 19 Feb. 1686). A few days afterwards he helped his brother Northumberland in an attempt to 'spirit away' his wife (ib. 29 Feb. 1686). On 3 July 1687 he carried his complaisance to his uncle so far as to act as conductor for the papal nuncio D'Adda on his public entry into London. But soon after he started with a fleet on an expedition which first conveyed the betrothed queen of Pedro II of Portugal from Rotterdam to Lisbon, where Grafton was magnificently entertained. Thence he sailed on a cruise among the Barbary states, where at Algiers, Tunis, and Tripoli he renewed treaties, and procured the release of English captives. He returned in March 1688, and, though not much of a politician, and less of a churchman (BURNET, iii. 317), was disgusted at his uncle's proceedings, and hurt at Dartmouth being preferred to him in the command of the fleet (CLARKE, *Life of James II*, ii. 208). Falling under the influence of Churchill, he excited discontent not only among the ships at Portsmouth, where he now joined the fleet as a volunteer (*Hist. MSS. Comm.* 10th Rep. pt. iv. p. 397), but also through his own regiment of guards. He signed the petition to James II for a ' free and regular parliament.' Yet he accompanied James on his march against William, and joined with Churchill in protesting that he would serve him with the last drop of his blood. He was suspected, however, of having joined the conspiracy, and on 24 Nov. ran away with Churchill to join William at Axminster (CLARKE, *Life of James II*, ii. 219; MACPHERSON, *Original Papers*, i. 280–3). The success of William restored him to his regiment, at the head of which he was sent to siege Tilbury fort. He was one of the forty-nine lords who voted for a regency; but he took the oaths to William and Mary on the very first day, and carried the orb at their coronation. Disappointed of any great command, he served in his ship the Grafton at the battle of Beachy Head, 30 June 1690, and showed great gallantry in assisting distressed Dutch vessels in that unlucky action (*Hist. MSS. Comm.* 7th Rep. p. 482). Finally he took service as a volunteer under Churchill, now Lord Marlborough, on his expedition to the south of Ireland. On 28 Sept. Grafton went with four regiments, who ' waded through water up to their armpits,' to effect a landing under the walls of Cork, and storm the town through the breach. They had almost succeeded when a musket-ball from the walls broke two of his ribs, and he was conveyed dangerously wounded into the captured city. He lingered some time, but died 9 Oct. 1690 (*London Gazette*, September and October 1690; cf. *Life of Joseph Pike*, in Friends' Library, ii. 368). His body was conveyed to England and buried at Euston. The most popular and ablest of the sons of Charles II, his strong and decided character, his reckless daring, and rough but honest temperament, caused him to be widely lamented. It was generally believed that he had the prospect of a brilliant career as a sailor (BURNET, iii. 317, iv. 105; cf. *An Elegy on the Death of the Duke of Grafton*, a broadside, licensed 27 Oct. 1690; and the ballad on *The Noble Funeral of that renowned Champion the Duke of Grafton*).

He was succeeded by his only son, Charles, born on 25 Nov. 1683, who died 6 May 1757. His widow, whose sweetness and beauty were universally commended, subsequently married Sir Thomas Hanmer.

[Evelyn's Diary; London Gazette; Burnet's Hist. of his own Time; Kennett's Hist. of England, vol. iii.; Clarke's Life of James II; Doyle's Official Baronage, ii. 48–9; Charnock's Biographia Navalis, ii. 98–105; Ranke's Engl. Hist. vol. iv.; Granger's Biog. Hist. iii. 199–200; Macaulay's Hist. of Engl.; Hist. MSS. Comm. Appendices, 6th, 7th, and 9th Reps.] T. F. T.

FITZROY, HENRY (1807–1859), statesman, second son of George Ferdinand, second Baron Southampton, by his second wife, Frances Isabella, second daughter of Lord Robert Seymour, was born 2 May 1807 in Great Stanhope Street, Mayfair, London. He matriculated at Magdalen College, Oxford, on 27 April 1826, but afterwards left Oxford and graduated M.A. at Trinity College, Cambridge, in 1828, and was returned to parliament for Great Grimsby in 1831 as a conservative. He was elected for Lewes on 21 April 1837, and represented it till death. He spoke frequently upon practical and administrative topics, and in 1845 became a lord of the admiralty in Sir Robert Peel's government. He joined the Peelites and ultimately became a liberal. In Dec. 1852 he returned to office under Lord Aberdeen as under-secretary of the home department, and was largely instrumental in passing the Hackney Carriages (Metropolis) Act and Aggravated Assaults Act of 1853, 16 and 17 Vict. c. 30 and 33, and the County Courts Extension Act Explanation Act of 1854, having been equally active in passing the County Courts Extension Act in 1850, 17 and 18 Vict. c. 94, and 13 and 14 Vict. c. 61. Quitting this office in February 1855, he was elected chairman of committees in March, and in Lord Palmerston's administration of 1859 became chief commissioner of the board of works, without a seat in the cabinet. After a long and painful illness he died at Sussex Square, Kemptown, Brighton, 22 Dec. 1859. He married, 29 April 1839, Hannah Meyer, second daughter of Baron Nathan Meyer Rothschild, who survived him five years, and had issue Arthur Frederic, who died in 1858, and Caroline Blanche, who married Sir Coutts Lindsay, bart.

[Hansard's Parliamentary Debates; Annual Register, 1859; Foster's Alumni Oxonienses; Gent. Mag. 1859.] J. A. H.

FITZROY, JAMES, otherwise CROFTS, afterwards SCOTT, DUKE OF MONMOUTH and BUCCLEUCH (1649–1685). [See SCOTT.]

FITZROY, MARY, DUCHESS OF RICHMOND (d. 1557), was the only surviving daughter of Thomas Howard, third duke of Norfolk [q. v.], by his second wife, Lady Elizabeth Stafford, eldest daughter of Edward Stafford, duke of Buckingham. Her childhood was passed in the summer at Tendring Hall, Suffolk, and in the winter at Hunsdon, Hertfordshire. In 1533 a dispensation, bearing date 28 Nov. of that year, was obtained for her marriage to Henry Fitzroy, duke of Richmond [q. v.], the natural son of Henry VIII. Owing to the tender age of both, the duchess continued to live with her own friends, and Richmond probably went to reside at Windsor Castle. The duke died on 22 July 1536, and the duchess afterwards remained a widow. She had some trouble before she could obtain a settlement of her dowry, as appears from a letter to her father preserved in Cotton MS. Vespasian, F. xiii. f. 75. A bill was signed in the duchess's favour, 2 March, 30 Hen. VIII (1539–40), by which she received for life the manor of Swaffham in Norfolk, and perhaps others. In 1546 her father offered her in marriage to Sir Thomas Seymour, proposing other alliances between the two families (expostulation addressed to the privy council, Cotton MS. Titus, B. ii.)

When the Duke of Norfolk and his son, the Earl of Surrey, were arrested in December 1546, three commissioners were sent to her father's mansion, Kenninghall, near Thetford, Norfolk, to examine her and a certain Elizabeth Holland, 'an ambiguous favourite' of the duke. The commissioners reached Kenninghall by daybreak, 14 Dec. The duchess, on learning the object of their visit, at first almost fainted. She promised to conceal nothing. The two ladies were forthwith brought to London (report of commissioners to the king, State Papers, Hen. VIII, i. 888–90; FROUDE, Hist. of England, cabinet edit. 1870, ch. xxiii.) From the evidence of Sir Wymound Carew it appeared that her brother, the Earl of Surrey, had advised her to become the mistress of Henry. Carew's evidence was supported by another witness, who spoke of her strong abhorrence of the proposal. The duchess effectually screened her father; but against her brother her evidence told fatally. She confirmed the story of his abominable advice, and 'revealed his deep hate of the "new men"' (FROUDE, loc. cit.)

Surrey had recently set up a new altar at Boulogne, while his sister was a patroness of John Foxe, the martyrologist. When Surrey's children were taken from their mother, and committed to the care of their aunt, she immediately engaged Foxe as their preceptor. The duchess's household was usually kept at the castle of Reigate, which was one of the Duke of Norfolk's manors.

Her father appears to have always retained a kindly feeling towards her. In his will, dated 18 July 1554, he bequeathed her 500l.

as an acknowledgment of her exertions to obtain his release from confinement, and of her care in the education of his grandchildren. About two years before she had been granted by the crown an annuity of 100l. towards the support of the children.

The Duchess of Richmond died on 9 Dec. 1557. A portrait, drawn by Holbein, of 'The Lady of Richmond' remains in the royal collection, and is engraved by Bartolozzi in the volume of 'Holbein Heads' published in 1795 by John Chamberlain, with a biographical notice by Edmund Lodge. A manuscript volume of poetry, chiefly by Sir Thomas Wyatt, in the library of the Duke of Devonshire, is supposed by Dr. Nott to have belonged to the Duchess of Richmond. At p. 143 is written 'Madame Margaret et Madame de Richemont.' Nott imagined that several pieces in the volume were written by her hand (preface to Works of Wyatt, p. ix).

[Life by J. G. Nichols in Gent. Mag. new ser. xxiii. 480–7; Lord Herbert's Reign of King Henry VIII; Letters and Papers of Reign of Henry VIII (Gairdner), vols. vi. vii.] G. G.

FITZROY, ROBERT (1805–1865), vice-admiral, hydrographer, and meteorologist, second son by a second marriage of Lord Charles Fitzroy [q. v.], was grandson of Augustus Henry, third duke of Grafton [q. v.], and on the mother's side of the first Marquis of Londonderry. He was born at Ampton Hall, Suffolk, on 5 July 1805; entered the navy from the Royal Naval College in 1819, and was promoted to the rank of lieutenant on 7 Sept. 1824. After serving in the Mediterranean and on the coast of South America, he was appointed in August 1828 to be flag-lieutenant to Rear-admiral Sir Robert Otway, commander-in-chief on the South American station, and on 13 Nov. 1828 was promoted to the command of the Beagle brig, vacant by the melancholy death of Commander Stokes. The Beagle was at that time, and continued to be, employed on the survey of the coasts of Patagonia, Tierra del Fuego, and more especially of the Straits of Magellan, under the orders of Commander King in the Adventure [see KING, PHILIP PARKER]. The two vessels returned to England in the autumn of 1830, and in the following summer Fitzroy was again appointed to the Beagle, to continue the survey of the same coasts. The Beagle sailed from Portsmouth on 27 Dec. 1831, having Charles Robert Darwin [q. v.] on board as naturalist of the expedition. After an absence of nearly five years, and having, in addition to the survey of the Straits of Magellan and a great part of the coast of South America, run a chronometric line round the world, thus approximately fixing the longitude of many secondary meridians, the Beagle returned to England in October 1836. In July 1835 Fitzroy had been advanced to post rank, and his work for the next few years was the reduction and discussion of his numerous observations. In 1837 he was awarded the gold medal of the Royal Geographical Society, and in 1839 he published the 'Narrative of the Surveying Voyages of H.M. ships Adventure and Beagle between the years 1826 and 1836, describing their Examination of the Southern Shores of South America, and the Beagle's Circumnavigation of the Globe,' 8vo, 3 vols.; but the third volume is by Charles Darwin. Of Fitzroy's work as a surveyor it is unnecessary now to speak in any detail. Though the means at his disposal were small, the results were both great and satisfactory, and even twelve years later Sir Francis Beaufort, in a report to the House of Commons (10 Feb. 1848), was able to say: 'From the Equator to Cape Horn, and from thence round to the river Plata on the eastern side of America, all that is immediately wanted has been already achieved by the splendid survey of Captain Robert Fitzroy.' At the general election in June 1841 Fitzroy was returned to parliament as member for Durham, virtually as a nominee of his uncle, the Marquis of Londonderry. The preceding canvass led to a violent quarrel with a Mr. Sheppard, who agreed to contest the city in the conservative interest in concert with Fitzroy, but afterwards withdrew, without, as Fitzroy thought, giving him proper notice. The quarrel led to a challenge; a meeting was arranged, but Sheppard failed to appear, alleging that his affairs compelled him to go to London. He afterwards assaulted Fitzroy in front of the United Service Club, and was summarily knocked down. The matter was referred to a few naval and military officers of high rank, who decided that, under the circumstances, Fitzroy could not give his opponent a meeting. And so it ended, both Fitzroy and Sheppard publishing pamphlets giving the angry correspondence in full detail ('Captain Fitzroy's Statement,' August 1841, 8vo, 82 pp.; 'The Conduct of Captain Robert Fitzroy . . . , by William Sheppard, esq.,' 1842, 8vo, 80 pp.) In September 1842 Fitzroy accepted the post of conservator of the river Mersey, but resigned it early in 1843, on being appointed governor and commander-in-chief of New Zealand. He arrived in his government in December, at a time of great excitement. Questions relating to the purchase of land were then, as for a long time afterwards, the source of much trouble. The settlers conceived their interests to be of paramount importance.

Fitzroy held that the aborigines had an equal claim on his care, and said so with more candour than prudence. His sentiments roused the fiercest indignation among men whose near relations had been massacred by the Maoris. His manner, in face of this opposition, was not conciliatory. It was spoken of as arrogant and dictatorial, as savouring more of the quarter-deck than of the council chamber. His financial policy, too, proved unfortunate, and incurred the bitter enmity of the New Zealand Company, which was strongly represented in parliament. The government yielded to the storm, and superseded him in November 1845.

In September 1848 he was appointed superintendent of the dockyard at Woolwich, and in March 1849 to the command of the Arrogant, a screw frigate, which had been fitted out under his own supervision, and in which he was desired to carry out a series of trials. In 1850 he retired from active service, though in course of seniority he became rear-admiral in 1857 and vice-admiral in 1863. In 1851 he was elected a fellow of the Royal Society, and in 1854, after serving for a few months as private secretary to his uncle, Lord Hardinge—then commander-in-chief of the army —he was, at the suggestion of the president of the Royal Society, appointed to be chief of the meteorological department of the board of trade. His reputation as a practical meteorologist already stood high, and it is by his more popular work in this office that his name is now best known. A cheap and serviceable barometer, constructed on a plan suggested by him, is still commonly called 'the Fitzroy barometer,' and his 'Weather Book,' published in 1863, inaugurated a distinct advance in the study of the science. He instituted, for the first time, a system of storm warnings, which have been gradually developed into the present daily forecasts; and by his constant labours in connection with the work of the office, and as secretary of the Lifeboat Association, built up a strong claim to the gratitude of all seafaring men. The toil proved too much for a temperament naturally excitable, and a constitution already tried by the severe and anxious service in the Straits of Magellan. He refused to take the prescribed rest, and under the continued strain his mind gave way, and he committed suicide 30 April 1865. He married, in December 1836, Mary Henrietta, daughter of Major-general Edward James O'Brien, by whom he had several children. His eldest son, Robert O'Brien Fitzroy, is at the present time (1888) a captain in the navy and a C.B.

Besides the works already named, he published: 1. 'Remarks on New Zealand,' 1846.

2. 'Sailing Directions for South America,' 1848. 3. 'Barometer and Weather Guide,' 1858. 4. 'Passage Table and General Sailing Directions,' 1859. 5. 'Barometer Manual,' 1861. He was also the author of official reports to the board of trade (1857–65), of occasional papers in the 'Journal of the Royal Geographical Society'—of which society he was for several years a member of council—and in the 'Journal of the Royal United Service Institution.'

[O'Byrne's Nav. Biog. Dict.; Journal of the Royal Geogr. Soc. vol. xxxv. p. cxxviii; A. S. Thomson's Story of New Zealand, ii. 82; E. J. Wakefield's Adventure in New Zealand, ii. 504; Report from the Select Committee on New Zealand, 29 July 1844 (Parliamentary Papers, 1844, xiii.); Parliamentary Debates, 3rd ser. (11 March 1845), lxxviii. col. 644, and (5 May 1845) lxxx. cols. 172, 183.]   J. K. L.

FITZSIMON, HENRY (1566–1643), jesuit, born at Dublin on 31 May 1566, was son of Nicholas Fitzsimon, an alderman or 'senator' of that city, by his wife Anne, sister of Christopher Sidgreaves of Inglewight, Lancashire. At the age of ten he was 'inveigled into heresy,' and afterwards he studied grammar, humanities, and rhetoric for four years at Manchester. He matriculated at Oxford, as a member of Hart Hall, on 26 April 1583. 'In December following,' says Wood, 'I find one Henry Fitz-Simons, to be elected student of Christ Church, but whether he be the same with the former, I dare not say.' It does not appear how long he continued at Oxford, nor whether he took a degree. In 1587 he became a student in the university of Paris. At this period he imagined that he was 'able to convert to Protestancie any encounterer whatsoever;' but at length he was overcome in argument by Father Thomas Darbyshire [q. v.], nephew of Bishop Bonner, and was reconciled to the catholic church. After his conversion he appears to have visited Rome. He went to the university of Pont-à-Mousson before the close of 1587, and studied rhetoric for one year, philosophy for three years, from 1588 to 1591, and took the degree of M.A., after which he read theology for three months at Pont-à-Mousson, and for seven weeks at Douay, privately studying casuistry at the same time. He took minor orders, was admitted into the Society of Jesus by Father Manæreus, the provincial of Flanders, and began his noviceship at Tournay on 15 or 26 April 1592. On 2 June 1593 he was sent to pursue his theological studies at Louvain under Father Leonard Lessius, and while there he also formed an intimate acquaintance with Father Rosweyde and

Dr. Peter Lombard. He so distinguished himself that he was appointed to the chair of philosophy in the university of Douay.

Being sent, at his own earnest petition, to the Irish mission, he reached Dublin late in 1597. Wood states that 'he endeavoured to reconcile as many persons as he could to his religion, either by private conference or public disputes with protestant ministers. In which work he persisted for two years without disturbance, being esteem'd the chief disputant among those of his party, and so ready and quick that few or none would undertake to deal with him.' The hall of a nobleman's house in Dublin having been placed at his disposal, he caused it to be lined with tapestry and covered with carpets, and had an altar made and magnificently decorated. Here high mass was celebrated with a full orchestra, composed of harps, lutes, and all kinds of instruments except the organ. The catholics used to go armed to mass in order to protect the priests and themselves. Father Field, superior of the Irish jesuit mission, reported in September 1599 that Fitzsimon was working hard, that crowds flocked to hear him and were converted, that he led rather an open, demonstrative life, never dining without six or eight guests, and that when he went through the country, he rode with three or four gentlemen, who served as companions. His zeal led to his arrest in 1599, and he was committed to Dublin Castle, where he remained in confinement for about five years. While in prison he held disputations with Dr. Challenor, Meredith Hanmer, Dean Rider, and James Ussher, afterwards primate of Ireland. On 12 March 1603–4 James I ordered Fitzsimon's release, but he was not actually liberated until three months later. About 1 June 1604 he was taken from Dublin Castle and placed on board a ship which landed him at Bilboa in Spain.

After some time he left Spain for Flanders, and in 1608 he was summoned on the business of the Irish mission to Rome, where he made his solemn profession of the four vows, and where he appears to have remained till after April 1611, when he returned to Flanders. On 1 July 1620 he reached the imperial camp in Bohemia, and, in the capacity of army chaplain, went through the campaign, of which he wrote a history. He was again in Belgium in 1626. At length, after an exile of twenty-six years, he returned in 1630 to his native country. Having been condemned to be hanged for complicity in the rebellion he was forced to leave the Dublin residence of the jesuits and to fly by night to distant mountains, in company with many catholics who were expelled from the city in the winter of 1641. He died, probably at Kilkenny, on 29 Nov. 1643, though other accounts give 1 Feb. 1643–4 and 29 Nov. 1645 as the date of his decease.

Wood remarks that 'by his death the Roman Catholics lost a pillar of their church, [he] being esteem'd in the better part of his life a great ornament among them, and the greatest defender of their religion in his time' (*Athenæ Oxon.* ed. Bliss, iii. 96).

His works are: 1. 'Brief Collections from the Scriptures, the Fathers, and principal Protestants, in proof of six Catholic Articles,' which John Rider, dean of St. Patrick's, and afterwards bishop of Killaloe, had challenged him to prove. Manuscript sent on 2 Jan. 1600–1 to Rider, who published an answer entitled 'A Caveat to Irish Catholics' on 28 Sept. 1602. 2. Manuscript reply to the 'Caveat,' sent to Rider on 4 Feb. 1602–3. Rider's 'Rescript' was published on 30 March 1604. 3. 'A Catholick Confutation of Mr. John Rider's Claim to Antiquitie, and a calming Comfort against his Caveat. In which is demonstrated . . . that all Antiquitie . . . is repugnant to Protestancie . . . And a Reply to Mr. Rider's Rescript, and a Discoverie of Puritan Partialitie in his behalfe,' Rouen, 1608, 4to. 4. 'An Answer to sundrie Complaintive Letters of Afflicted Catholics, declaring the Severitie of divers late Proclamations,' 1608. Printed at the end of the preceding work. It was reprinted by the Rev. Edward Hogan, S.J., under the title of 'Words of Comfort to Persecuted Catholics,' Dublin, 1881, 8vo. 5. 'Narratio Rerum Ibernicarum,' or an 'Ecclesiastical History of our Country.' He was engaged on this work in 1611. It was never printed. The Bollandists often quote Fitzsimon's manuscript collections. 6. 'The Justification and Exposition of the Divine Sacrifice of the Masse, and of al Rites and Ceremonies thereto belonging' [Douay], 1611, 4to. 7. 'Catalogus præcipuorum Sanctorum Hiberniæ.' Manuscript finished 9 April 1611. The Bollandists cite the editions of 1611 and 1619; there were also those of Douay, 1615 and 1619; Liège, 1619; Lisbon, 1620; Antwerp, 1627. The catalogue was also appended to 'Hiberniæ sive Antiquæ Scotiæ Vindiciæ adversus Thomam Dempsterum. Auctore G. F.,' Antwerp, 1621, 8vo, and it was printed at Rome in Porter's 'Annales.' 8. 'Britannomachia Ministrorum in plerisque fidei fundamentis et articulis dissidentium,' Douay, 1614, 4to. A reply to this was published by Francis Mason, B.D., archdeacon of Norfolk, in his 'Vindiciæ Ecclesiæ Anglicanæ,' 2nd edit. London, 1638, fol. 9. 'Pugna

Pragensis. A Candido Eblanio,' Brünn, 1620. It went through three editions at least. 10. 'Buquoy Quadrimestre Iter, Progressusque, quo, favente numine, ac auspice Ferdinando II Rom. Imp., Austria est conservata, Bohemia subjugata, Moravia acquisita, eademque opera Silesia solicitata, Hungariaque terrefacta. Accedit Appendix Progressus ejusdem Generalis, in initio Anni 1621. Authore Constantio Peregrino,' Vienna, 1621, 4to. It was printed twice at Brünn and twice at Vienna, and translated into Italian in 1625 by Aureli of Perugia. The work was attacked by Berchtold von Rauchenstein in 'Constantius Peregrinus Castigatus,' Bruges, 1621, 4to. Portions of Fitz-Simon's work are printed by Hogan, together with the 'Words of Comfort,' under the title of 'Diary of the Bohemian War of 1620.' It is erroneously stated in the British Museum Catalogue that 'Constantius Peregrinus' was Boudewyn de Jonge. 11. Treatise to prove that Ireland was originally called Scotia. Manuscript quoted in Fleming's 'Life of St. Columba.' 12. Many of his letters, some written from his cell in Dublin Castle, are printed by Hogan with the 'Words of Comfort to Persecuted Catholics.'

[Life by the Rev. Edmund Hogan, 1881; Dodd's Church Hist. iii. 112; Ware's Writers of Ireland (Harris), p. 118; Foley's Records, vii. 260; Hogan's Cat. of the Irish Province, S. J., p. 8; Oliver's Jesuit Collections, p. 245; Catholic Miscellany (1828), ix. 33; Bernard's Life of Ussher (1656), p. 32; Duthilloeul's Bibliographie Douaisienne (1842), p. 99; De Backer's Bibl. de la Compagnie de Jésus (1869), i. 1875; Shirley's Library at Lough Fea, p. 113; Lowndes's Bibl. Man. (Bohn), p. 805; Gillow's Bibl. Dict.; Dwyer's Diocese of Killaloe, p. 86; Hogan's Ibernia Ignatiana, i. 33, 43, 51, 52, 72–6, 81, 102, 104, 111, 124, 131, 222; Southwell's Bibl. Scriptorum Soc. Jesu, p. 224; Irish Ecclesiastical Record, viii. 214, 268, 313, 347, 504, 553, ix. 15, 78, 187, 272, 430; Patrignani's Menologio (1730), vol. i. pt. ii. p. 8.] T. C.

FITZSIMONS or **FITZSYMOND, WALTER** (*d.* 1511), archbishop of Dublin, was precentor of St. Patrick's Cathedral in 1476; he was the chapter's proxy in a parliament held in 1478 (*King's Collections* and *Cod. Clar.* p. 46); and was also official, or vicar-general, of the diocese. He has been described in old records as a learned divine and philosopher, a man of great gravity of character and of a commanding aspect. Having first sued out a charter of pardon from Henry VII, for accepting promotion by a papal provision, he was appointed by Pope Sixtus IV to the archbishopric of Dublin on 14 June 1484, and was the first archbishop consecrated in St. Patrick's (MONCK MASON, *History of St. Patrick's Cathedral*, p. 139). Along with the Earl of Kildare, lord deputy of Ireland, he espoused, in 1487, the cause of Lambert Simnel, to whose coronation in Christ Church Cathedral he was accessory. The pope directed an inquiry to be held, and a full report of the matter having been made, the archbishop, with the bishops of Meath and Kildare, was found guilty. In the following year, however, he was permitted with others to renew his allegiance to the king, and received pardon through Sir Richard Edgecombe. The archbishop, 'when the mass was ended in the choir of the said church [St. Mary's Abbey], began Te Deum, and the choir with the organs sung it up solemnly, and at that time all the bells in the church rang' (HARRIS, *Hibernica*, pt. i. p. 33). He was subsequently taken into great favour by the king, who made him lord deputy of Ireland in 1492, lord chancellor in 1496 and 1501, and again, in 1503, lord deputy.

Fitzsimons strenuously exerted himself, while holding the office of lord deputy in 1492, to lessen the number of useless idlers in Ireland. He represented to the king the idleness of the younger brothers of the nobility, and the indolence of the common people 'on account of the great plenty of all kinds of provisions.' At his suggestion vagrancy was strictly forbidden, and workhouses were everywhere erected for the employment of able-bodied vagabonds, beadles being appointed by him 'to look after the several cities, towns, and parishes, to keep beggars out, and to take up strangers' (*Council Books*, temp. Henry VII).

In 1496, the king, having made his son Henry, duke of York, lord-lieutenant of Ireland, appointed Fitzsimons lord chancellor of Ireland (RYMER, *Fœdera*, ed. 1727, vol. xii.) In the same year Fitzsimons held a provincial synod, on which occasion an annual contribution for seven years was settled by the clergy of the province, to provide salaries for lecturers of the university in St. Patrick's Cathedral (ALLEN, *Registry*, f. 105). In 1509 he was again lord chancellor, by appointment of Henry VIII, and held that office until his death, at Finglas, near Dublin, on 14 May 1511. He was buried in the nave of St. Patrick's, but no memorial of him remains.

[Sir James Ware's Works, ed. Harris, i. 343; Cotton's Fasti Ecclesiæ Hibernicæ, ii. 17, 110, v. 79; D'Alton's Memoirs of the Archbishops of Dublin, p. 171; Monck Mason's Hist. of St. Patrick's Cathedral; Leeper's Hist. Handbook to St. Patrick's (2nd ed.), p. 89; Smyth's Law Officers of Ireland, pp. 15, 16.]   B. H. B.

FITZSTEPHEN, ROBERT (*d.* 1183?), one of the original Norman conquerors of Ireland, was the son of Stephen, constable of Aberteivi (Cardigan), and of Nesta, daughter of Rhys ab Tewdwr, king of South Wales. Whether Stephen was, as is sometimes stated, a second husband of Nesta is at least very doubtful (DIMOCK, Preface to *Expugn. Hib.* in GIRALDUS CAMBRENSIS, *Opera*, v. ci; cf. *Cal. Carew MSS., Book of Howth*, &c., p. 435). If the list of Nesta's children given by her grandson (GIRALDUS, *De Rebus a se Gestis* in *Opera*, i. 59) is arranged in order of their birth, her amour with Stephen must have been after her marriage with Gerald of Windsor and the birth of her eldest son, William Fitzgerald, and before the birth of her son, Meiler Fitzhenry [q. v.], by Henry I. As Aberteivi did not fall into English hands before 1110 or 1111 (*Annales Cambriæ*, p. 34), Robert could hardly have been born before that date. The birth of Nesta's son by King Henry must have followed his expedition to Dyved in the summer of 1114. Robert was therefore born between these two dates. In 1157 Robert followed Henry II's expedition into North Wales, and narrowly escaped the ambush in which his half-brother, the king's son, was slain. His inheritance included Cardigan and Cemmes, and he became constable of Cardigan town in succession apparently to his father. In November 1166 he was betrayed by his own men ('dolo Rigewarc clerici,' *Ann. Cambr.* p. 50) into the hands of his cousin, Rhys ab Gruffydd, with whom he was then at war. He was released after three years' captivity on the mediation of his half-brother, David II, bishop of St. David's [q. v.], and at the instance of Dermot, the exiled king of Leinster, whom he agreed to help in restoring to his kingdom as an easy release from his promise to join the 'Lord Rhys' in his war against the English. In the spring of 1169 Fitzstephen, with his half-brother, Maurice Fitzgerald (*d.* 1176) [q. v.], landed in Ireland at Baganbon or Bannow, near Wexford (*Exp. Hib.* p. 230; cf. REGAN, p. 23, and Introduction, p. xvi). They were accompanied by thirty knights, sixty men-at-arms, and three hundred Welsh foot soldiers. In conjunction with Dermot's forces they took Wexford, which was assigned, with the two adjacent cantreds, to Fitzstephen. The successful invasion of Ossory followed, but the approach of Roderick O'Conor, king of Connaught, now caused Dermot's Irish followers to desert. But Fitzstephen contemptuously rejected Dermot's bribes, and built so strong a camp at Ferns that Roderick accepted terms that left Dermot king of Leinster. Maurice Fitzgerald now joined Fitzstephen with additional troops from Wales. Fitzstephen was busy in fortifying Carrig, two miles from Wexford, while Dermot and Fitzgerald were attacking Dublin; but he marched westwards to aid Donnell, king of Limerick, against Roderick. Dermot now, if Giraldus could be believed, offered the brothers the hand of his daughter and the succession to his throne, and on their refusal to give up their present wives he at their advice called in Strongbow [see CLARE, RICHARD DE, d. 1176], who was now encouraged by Fitzstephen's successes to undertake what he had formally feared to venture. But Giraldus is so extravagantly partial to his uncle that the constant attempt to exalt him over Strongbow fails by reason of its obvious exaggeration. Fitzstephen's exploits are reduced to more modest, though still solid, proportions by the French poet, who derived his information from Maurice Regan.

In 1171 Fitzstephen was shut up in Carrig with five knights and a few archers by his own Wexford subjects, while the mass of the invaders were besieged by Roderick in Dublin. The false intelligence, vouched for by the oath of two Irish bishops, that Dublin had surrendered to the Irish induced him to surrender. They retreated with him, murdering the inferior prisoners, to the island of Begerin ('Little Erin,' REGAN, p. 85), when the news came of the defeat of Roderick at Dublin. There the fears or jealousy of Strongbow (Exp. Hib. p. 271) prevented his deliverance; but on the arrival of Henry II in October at Waterford the men of Wexford brought their lord bound and in chains before the king. Henry ordered him still to be kept in prison 'in Reginald's Tower,' 'because he had invaded Ireland before getting his assent.' But he released Fitzstephen before his own departure, though he took away from him Wexford and the two cantreds. Immediately afterwards Henry left him at Dublin under Hugh de Lacy. By fighting with distinction on Henry's side in the civil war in 1173 and 1174, both in France and England, Fitzstephen completely recovered the king's favour. In May 1177, at a council at Oxford, he and Miles Cogan received a grant of the kingdom of Cork on condition of the service of sixty knights. Cork city, however, the king kept in his own hands (BENEDICTUS ABBAS, i. 163; the charter is printed in LYTTLETON, Henry II, app. iii. to bk. v.) If Giraldus can be trusted, Fitzstephen was actually associated with William Fitzaldhelm [q. v.] in the government of Ireland (Exp. Hib. p. 334; but cf. BEN. ABB. i. 161). On their arrival in Ireland they decided by lot that the three eastern cantreds should be the portion of Fitzstephen, while the tribute of the twenty-four cantreds farmed out and

the custody of the city was common to both. Soon after he accompanied Philip de Braose on an expedition against Limerick with thirty knights, but nothing was done. Soon after Maredudd, a bastard son of Robert, a youth of great promise, died at Cork.

For the next five years Fitzstephen and Cogan reigned in peace at Cork, the modest ambition of the elderly leaders restraining the impetuosity of their youthful followers (Exp. Hib. p. 350). But in 1182 the treacherous murder of Miles Cogan and Ralph, another bastard of Fitzstephen, and Miles's son-in-law, by a chieftain called Mac Tire, was followed by a general revolt against Fitzstephen throughout all Desmond. The old warrior was now closely besieged in Cork, but was relieved by his nephew, Raymond Fitzgerald [q. v.] In 1183 he was joined by his nephews Philip and Gerald de Barri. The latter boasts of the help he gave to his uncle (ib. p. 351). Fitzstephen granted Philip three cantreds of his Desmond territory (Cal. Doc. Ireland, 1171–1251, No. 340). He probably died very soon after. Giraldus describes Fitzstephen as by turns the luckiest and most wretched of men. He was rather short in stature, stout, and full of body, liberal and pleasant in his manners. His great faults were his immoderate devotion to wine and women. He left no legitimate offspring.

[The main authority is Giraldus, Expugnatio Hibernica, in Opera, vol. v. (Rolls Ser.) See also the anonymous French poem on Irish history, said to be translated from the original of Maurice Regan.]   T. F. T.

FITZSTEPHEN, WILLIAM (d. 1190?), the biographer of Becket, styles himself the archbishop's 'concivis.' He was in the closest connection with Becket for ten years or more, as his 'clericus et convictor.' When Becket became chancellor, he appointed Fitzstephen to be 'dictator in cancelleria ejus.' Later William became subdeacon in his chapel, and was entrusted with the duty of perusing letters and petitions. Sometimes at Becket's bidding, he either decided these cases on his own authority, or was appointed advocate to one of the parties—'patronus causarum.' He was present at the great council of Northampton (13 Oct. 1164), and was sitting at the archbishop's feet, when Herbert of Bosham gave his master the rash advice to excommunicate his enemies if they laid hands upon him. William induced the archbishop to refuse this counsel, as the archbishop afterwards confessed when during his exile he met William at St. Benedict's on the Loire (Vit. S. Thomæ, pp. 1, 2, 59).

Fitzstephen appears to have escaped most of the disadvantages of intimacy with Becket. He has himself preserved a rhyming Latin poem, some ninety lines long, which he composed and presented to Henry II in the chapel of 'Bruhull.' In return for this petition the king pardoned him. It would appear, however, that when Becket was reconciled to the king, his old clerk once more entered his service, for he was an eye-witness of his murder: 'passionem ejus Cantuariæ inspexi.' Of the rest of his life we have no certain knowledge; but Mr. Foss is inclined to identify this author with William Fitzstephen, who along with his brother, Ralph Fitzstephen, was sheriff of Gloucester from 18 Henry II to 1 Richard I, i.e. 1171-90 (Foss, i. 370; FULLER, i. 569). This William Fitzstephen is probably the same William Fitzstephen whom Henry II in 1176 placed at the head of one of the six circuits into which he divided the country. The circuit in question included the county of Gloucester, and his pleas are recorded in that and the four following years, not only in fourteen counties, but 'ad scaccarium' also. His name appears as a justice itinerant in 1 Richard I (Foss, *ib.*; cf. MADOX, i. 83, 127, &c.; HOVEDEN, ii. 88), about which time he perhaps died.

William Fitzstephen's most important work is the 'Vita Sancti Thomæ.' This is the main authority for the archbishop's early life. The curious preface, entitled 'Descriptio nobilissimæ civitatis Londoniæ,' is by far the most graphic and elaborate account of London during the twelfth century yet remaining. It has been printed separately in Stow's 'Survey of London,' and Hearne's ed. of Leland's 'Itinerary.' The 'Vita Thomæ' was first printed in Sparke's 'Historiæ Anglicanæ Scriptores' (1723). The chief later editions are those of Dr. Giles (1845), and that by the Rev. J. C. Robertson (Rolls Ser. 1877). To the same author are also attributed, though, as it seems, on doubtful grounds, 'Libri quinque de Miraculis B. Thomæ' (cf. also HARDY, ii. 382).

[Materials for the Hist. of Thomas Becket, ed. Robertson (Rolls Ser.), vol. iii. contains Fitzstephen's Vita Sti Thomæ; Roger of Hoveden, ed. Stubbs (Rolls Ser.), vol. ii.; Madox's Hist. of the Exchequer (ed. 1769), vols. i. and ii.; Foss's Judges, vol. i; Wright's Biographia Literaria, vol. ii.; Hardy's Cat. of Manuscript Materials for Hist. of Great Britain and Ireland, ii.] T. A. A.

FITZTHEDMAR, ARNOLD (1201-1274?), alderman of London, was descended on both sides from German settlers in London, where he was born on 9 Aug. 1201. His father, Thedmar, a man of wealth and position, was a native of Bremen. His mother,

Juliana, was the daughter of Arnold, a citizen of Cologne, and of his wife Ode. This couple had made a pilgrimage to St. Thomas's shrine at Canterbury to pray for children. Their prayers being heard, they were induced to settle in London, where two children were born to them. The elder, Thomas, destined to become a monk, died during the fourth crusade. The younger, Juliana, became the wife of Thedmar and the mother of a numerous family, of which only one son, Arnold, and four daughters grew up to maturity. Wonderful dreams preceded Arnold's birth. On his father's death he succeeded to all his property. His career illustrates very remarkably the position of the foreign merchants settled in London. English by birth, and taking a prominent part in London political life, he was still a member of the 'domus quæ Guildhalla Teutonicorum nuncupatur,' the later Steelyard, and kept up close relations with the merchants of the country of his origin. On 1 Aug. 1251 he appears as a witness to a treaty with Lübeck (LAPPENBERG, *Geschichte des Stahlhofes*, pp. 11-12, 'aus dem Lübecker Urkundenbuche'). He is described as 'alderman of the Germans.' He held the office for at least ten years.

Fitzthedmar was conspicuous among the few leading citizens who, in opposition to the general current of feeling in the city, were stout supporters of Henry III and his son Edward throughout all the barons' wars. In February 1258, before the meeting of the Mad parliament, the Londoners accused the mayor and other rulers of the city of levying the city tallages in an unjust way. Henry appointed John Mansel to investigate the charges. Then, on 11 Feb., Fitzthedmar, who had hitherto not been involved, was included in the attack. His special offence was that he had altered the method of weighing used in the city without the king's permission. Before long the aldermen were deposed, and new ones appointed, except for Fitzthedmar's ward, which remained in the mayor's hands. But next year the proceedings were reversed. On 6 Nov. 1259 a full folk-moot was held in the king's presence at Paul's Cross, and it was declared on John Mansel's attestation that Fitzthedmar had been unjustly degraded. He was therefore restored to royal favour and to his aldermanship. Between this date and Michaelmas 1260 Arnold bought, on behalf of the German merchants, of William, son of William Reyner, the yearly rent of 2s. for a piece of land situated to the east of the Germans' Guildhall, in the parish of All Hallows in Thames Street (the site of the Steelyard). For this he paid two marks sterling. He is described in the charter as 'aldermanus mercatorum Alemaniæ in Angliam venientium' (*ib.* Urkunden, p. 13). This then seems to have been the office recently restored to him by the king. It is often thought he was also the regular alderman of a ward, though which ward is unknown. Immediately afterwards the grant of fresh privileges to the Germans in London, on the petition of Richard, king of the Romans, seems to have followed (17 June 1260).

Arnold next distinguished himself by his strong hostility to the democratic mayor, Thomas Fitzthomas. He and his friends only escaped a plot for their destruction by the arrival of the news of the battle of Evesham (4 Aug.), in the middle of the folk-moot at which the attack was to have been made. This was on Thursday, 6 Aug. 1265. Arnold's loyalty did not, however, save him from paying a heavy share in the fines imposed by the victorious king on the rebellious city. At last he got royal letters which protected him from further exactions. Many years later the city of Bremen complained that even one of Arnold's servants, Hermann, a Bremen citizen, had been severely fined on the same account, and that his resistance had caused a feud between London and Bremen (*Fœdera,* i. 534). In 1270 the chest containing the city archives (*scrinium civium*) was under Arnold's care, while three other citizens held the keys of it. In 1274 Arnold was among those who resisted the validity of the charters granted by the mayor, Walter Hervey, without the consent of the aldermen and 'discretiores' of the city. They gained their point, and got Hervey removed from his aldermanship.

Nearly all our knowledge of Arnold's acts comes from the 'Chronica Majorum et Vicecomitum Londoniarum,' contained in the so-called 'Liber de Antiquis Legibus' in the Guildhall, and edited by Mr. Stapleton for the Camden Society in 1846. The special particularity with which his birth, family, and adventures are recorded, the scrupulous absence of comment on him, yet the apologetic tone of the references to his acts, have given rise to the conjecture that he is himself its author. The full references to his patron, Richard, king of the Romans, increase the probability. The entrusting of the city archives to him just before the time that the chronicle, which contains a large number of official documents, closes, makes this as near a certainty as can be gathered from merely indirect internal evidence. The chronicle breaks off in August 1274 with the preparations for Edward I's coronation. He must have died before 10 Feb. 1275, on which date his will was read and enrolled in the Hustings court (RILEY, Introduction to *Chronicle of the Mayors,* &c., p. ix). He left part of his property in the city to the monks of Bermondsey, and to his kinsman, Stephen Eswy, for his own use and for that of Arnold's wife. The latter's name was probably Dionysia, who married Adam the Taylor after Arnold's death, and was alive in 1292. Another 'alderman of the Germans' appears as holding office in 1282. Dr. Lappenberg's conjecture (p. 16) that he was alive in 1292, and even (p. 156) in 1302, is sufficiently disproved by the date of his birth. There is no reference in the chronicle to Arnold's wife or children, but a John Thedmar appears as a witness in 1286 (*Placita de quo warranto* 14 Ed. I), and again acts as an executor in 1309.

[Liber de Antiquis Legibus (Camden Soc.), pp. 34, 37, 43, 115, 165, 238–42, 253; Riley's Chronicles of the Mayors and Sheriffs of London, the above translated, with notes and illustrations; Lappenberg's Urkundliche Geschichte des Hansischen Stahlhofes zu London, pp. 11, 14–16, 156, and Urkunden, p. 13; Hardy's Descriptive Cat. of Manuscript Materials for Hist. of Great Britain and Ireland, iii. 205.] T. F. T.

FITZTHOMAS, JOHN, first EARL OF KILDARE and sixth BARON OF OFFALY (*d.* 1316), belonged to the great Anglo-Irish family of the Fitzgeralds, though the genealogies are contradictory. The Earl of Kildare (*Earls of Kildare,* pp. 15–22) makes him grandson of Maurice Fitzgerald II [q. v.], the justiciar, who died in 1257, and so far the descent is undoubted. In all probability his father was the justiciar's younger son, Thomas Macmaurice, whose death the Irish 'Annals' enter as taking place at Lough Mask Castle, co. Mayo, in 1271 (*Loch Cé,* p. 469). In 1287 died Gerald Fitzmaurice (CLYN, p. 10), who was this Thomas's grandnephew, and being descended from Thomas's eldest brother Gerald, had come to own Offaly and Maynooth [see FITZGERALD, MAURICE, 1194 ?–1257 *ad fin.*] On Gerald Fitzmaurice's death (1287) he bequeathed this inheritance to John Fitzthomas, his granduncle's son and his own first cousin once removed.

Besides the inheritance of this cousin, John Fitzthomas seems about the same time to have come in for that of his first cousin, Amabilia, one of the two coheirs of his uncle Maurice Fitzmaurice Fitzgerald [q. v.], the justiciar, who died in 1277 (SWEETMAN, *ib.*; *Cal. Gen. ib.*) He makes his first appearance in the receipt rolls of the Irish exchequer in connection with a payment of 50*l.* from co. Limerick through his more distant kinsman, Thomas Fitzmaurice, the father of Maurice

Fitzthomas [q. v.], first earl of Desmond (SWEETMAN, iii. 54). In the summer of 1288 the new justiciar of Ireland proclaimed a muster against the Irish of Offaly and Leix, who were in a state of open rebellion. They had in 1285 taken Gerald Fitzmaurice, Fitzthomas's predecessor in the barony, prisoner on his own lands (*ib.* iii. 265; CLYN, pp. 10, 11). John Fitzthomas was one of the three chief leaders of the host, and was appointed to guard the marchers from Rathemegan (Rathangan? in co. Kildare) to Baly-madan. The expedition was on the whole successful, but there is an entry of 11*l.* 13*s.* 4*d.* for the 'rescue of John Fitzthomas' (SWEETMAN, pp. 267, 273); and Clyn, under 1289, tells us that 'lord John Fitzthomas lost many horses and followers (garciones) in Offaly.' Four years later the castle of Sligo was granted to him (*Annals of the Four Masters*).

In 1291 Fitzthomas seems to have been in England, and a little earlier had been on an expedition against the king's enemies in Ireland (SWEETMAN, No. 915, p. 428). In May 1292 he was empowered to treat with the king's adversaries. In 1294 'Mac Maurice' (i.e. in all probability John Fitzthomas) leagued with the great Anglo-Norman family of the Berminghams in a disastrous expedition against Calbach Mor O'Conor, one of the most dangerous of the rebellious Irish princes of Leinster (*Loch Cé*, p. 501). When Magnus O'Conor, king of Connaught, died in 1293, William de Vescy, the new justiciar (12 Sept. 1290–18 Oct. 1294), put Ædh O'Conor, a scion of the rival race of Cathal Crobdherg, on the throne, but so great was Fitzgerald's power in Connaught, that within ten days the new king was a prisoner. Before the year was out Fitzgerald had set Ædh free, and the justiciar had made his own candidate king (*Loch Cé*, p. 509; *Annals of the Four Masters*, p. 459). This opposition on the part of a mere noble seems to have roused the anger of William de Vescy (*Abbrev. Plac.* p. 231; SWEETMAN, vol. ii. sub 13 Nov. 1278, Nos. 2025, &c.) The feud was at its height by April 1294, and William de Vescy accused John Fitzthomas of felony. John accused the justiciar of saying that the great lords of Ireland need care very little for a king like Edward, who was 'the most perverse and dastard knight in his realm.' William denied the charge, and offered wager of battle. From Ireland the case was transferred to Westminster, and a day appointed for the combat. At the fixed time (24 July) William de Vescy appeared in full armour, and, as his opponent had not arrived, claimed judgment by default (*ib.* Nos. 135, 137, 147; *Abbrev. Plac.* pp. 231–4; RYMER, ii. 631).

Other accounts represent that William de Vescy, to avoid fighting, fled to France, and the king gave to John all that was his, including Kildare and Rathangan. But it would seem, from a note to Butler's 'Grace,' that Kildare remained in the king's hands till 16 May 1316, whereas William de Vescy was still receiving summons to parliament in 24 Edward I, and did not surrender Kildare and his Irish estates till 1297 (*Annals of Ireland*, p. 323; *Parl. Rolls*, i. 127–34; GRACE, p. 43; and note in Irish Close Rolls, i. 36, Nos. 45–6). The famous Fitzgerald legend of this quarrel may be read in Campion, p. 115, Holinshed, p. 241, and Burke's 'Peerage.' The justiciarship was transferred in the same year (18 Oct. 1294) to William de Oddyngeseles (SWEETMAN, vol. iv. Nos. 165–6).

By this time the rivalry of the De Burghs and the Geraldines had become violent, and in December 1294 John Fitzthomas took Richard de Burgh, the earl of Ulster, prisoner, and kept him in his castle of Ley till 12 March 1295. For this the lord of Offaly was once more impleaded at Westminster; he had to find twenty-four sureties by 11 Nov., and was finally mulcted in Sligo and all his Connaught estates (CLYN, p. 10; *Annals of Ireland*, p. 323; SWEETMAN, p. 104; cf. CAMPION, p. 79; *Parl. Rolls*, i. 135–6). The same year John Wogan, the new justiciar, made a peace between the two earls for two years, and it was made permanent about 28 Oct. 1298 (*Annals of Ireland*, pp. 325, 328).

From 1295 John Fitzthomas's name figures frequently on the writs for military service. In 1296 he accompanied the justiciar and Richard de Burgh on the Scotch expedition, and was sumptuously entertained by the king of England on Whitsunday (13 May). When summoned to London for a campaign against the king of the French, he and the Earl of Ulster were allowed a grace of three weeks (till 1 Aug.) beyond the English barons, 'pour la longe mer qu'il ount a passer' (*ib.* p. 326; *Annals of the Four Masters*, p. 467; *Parl. Writs*, pp. 280, 284, &c.; *Dignity of a Peer*, ii. 278, 322). In 1301 he was again serving in Scotland with Edward I from August to November, and probably again in 1303, unless he was excused on this occasion because of his son's death (*ib.*; *Parl. Writs*, i. 367; RYMER, ii. 897). He received similar summons to attend the Earl of Ulster against the Scotch for the nativity of St. John, 1310, and for the Bannockburn campaign of 1314 (*Parl. Writs*, ii. 392, 424).

During all these years there seems to have

been great confusion in Offaly and Kildare. Ley, the chief stronghold of John Fitzthomas in Offaly, had been taken and burned on 25 Aug. 1284; the castle of Kildare was captured in 1294, and the country round laid waste by bands of predatory Irish and English; and though the great Irish chief of Offaly, Calbhach O'Conor, was slain in 1305, yet two years later 'the robbers of Offaly burned the town of Ley, and laid siege to the castle till they were driven back by the combined forces of John Fitzthomas and Edmund Butler.' In 1309 he crossed over to England with the Earl of Ulster and Roger Mortimer. Three years later (1312) his friendship with the De Burghs was ratified by a double marriage. At Green Castle in co. Down his ward, Maurice Fitzthomas [q. v.], the head of the Desmond branch of the family, married (5 Aug.) Richard de Burgh's daughter Catherine; and on 16 Aug. his son Thomas Fitzjohn married Joan, another daughter of the same earl. At Christmas he held a great court at Adare in co. Limerick, and knighted Nicholas Fitzmaurice, the knight of Kerry (*Annals of Ireland*, pp. 319, 323, &c.; *Loch Cé*, p. 531, &c.; *Annals of the Four Masters*, pp. 481, &c.; CLYN, p. 11). On 26 May 1315 Edward Bruce landed at Carrickfergus (*Annals of Ireland*, p. 348, &c.; *Loch Cé*, p. 563; *Annals of the Four Masters*), and Barbour seems to make John Fitzthomas take part in the Earl of Ulster's expedition which, in the ensuing summer (July–September 1315), forced the Scotch back from Dundalk to the Bann (BARBOUR, xiv. 140–6). After a few months spent in Ulster Edward Bruce made a definite advance south, and by the beginning of 1316 was laying waste John Fitzthomas's own county. At Arscoll in co. Kildare he was met by three hosts, each of which outnumbered his own. But the leaders, Edmund Butler, John Fitzthomas, and Arnold Poer, were at variance, and the Scotch gained an easy victory (26 Jan. 1316). Bruce, however, almost at once began to retreat north, burning John Fitzthomas's great castle of Ley on his way (*Annals of Ireland*, pp. 296–7, 244–8; CLYN, p. 12). John Fitzthomas and the other Irish magnates gathered at Dublin (c. 2 Feb.) and took an oath of fealty to the king of England's new agent, John de Hotham (*Annals of Ireland*, p. 350; *Lib. Hib.* pt. iv. p. 6). In mid-February the Scotch were still lying at Greashill in Offaly, while the English army lay at Kildare (*Annals of Ireland*, p. 349). A little later John Fitzthomas crossed over to England, and it was probably soon after this that he was created Earl of Kildare. The patent is dated 16 May 1316 (see patent

in extenso, LODGE, i. 78–9). Immediately after this the Earls of Kildare and Ulster seem to have taken a second oath (c. 3 July), and two months later, just as the news of Robert Bruce's landing reached Dublin, John Fitzthomas died at Laraghbryan, co. Kildare, on Sunday, 12 Sept. (*Annals of Ireland*, pp. 247, 352). He was buried at the Franciscan monastery in Kildare (*ib.* p. 297).

John Fitzthomas is said to have married Blanche Roche, daughter of John Baron of Fermoy (*Earls of Kildare*, p. 28; LODGE, p. 79). His children were (1) Gerald, 'his son and heir' (d. 1303) (CLYN, p. 10; GRACE, p. 47; *Annals of Ireland*, p. 331); and his successor, (2) Thomas Fitzjohn, second earl of Kildare [see FITZGERALD, THOMAS, d. 1328]. To these the Earl of Kildare adds Joan, who in 1302 married Sir Edmund Butler (cf. *Annals of Ireland*, p. 331), and thus became ancestress to the later marquises of Ormonde; and Elizabeth, who married Sir Nicholas Netterville, ancestor of the viscounts Netterville (*Earls of Kildare*, p. 28).

John Fitzthomas seems to have been one of the most unruly even of the Irish barons. Besides the feuds already noticed, he appears to have had another with the De Lacies in 1310 (*Pat. Rolls of Ireland*, No. 58, p. 13, cf. No. 240, and p. 16, No. 50). He is said to have built and endowed the Augustinian abbey at Adare (*Earls of Kildare*, p. 27; ARCHDALL, *Monasticon*, p. 414), 'for the redemption of Christian captives.' His fame was of long continuance in his own country, where an Irish poet, in 1601, wrote of him: 'The first Leinster Earl without reproach ... John the redoubtable, than whom no poet was more learned' (*Earls of Kildare*, p. 28). At one time or another he must have had under his control no inconsiderable part of Ireland. The fact that he was never justiciar seems to point to some distrust as to his perfect trustworthiness, and his power is shown by his equality in the quarrel with the great house of Ulster, which latterly seems to have been willing to secure peace by mutual marriages. His elder son, Gerald, is said to have been betrothed to a daughter of Richard de Burgh; but if this was so, the agreement seems to have been broken short by the young noble's death.

[Sweetman's Calendar of Documents relating to Ireland, vols. i.–v.; Rymer's Fœdera, ed. 1720; Calendarium Genealogicum, ed. Roberts; Irish Close and Patent Rolls, ed. Ball and Tresham, 1828; Parliamentary Writs (Palgrave, 1827); Liber Munerum Hiberniæ (Thomas, 1824); Report on the Dignity of a Peer; Book of Howth, ed. Bond and Brewer; Annals of the Four Masters, vol. ii., ed. O'Donovan; Annals of Loch Cé, ed. Henessy (Rolls Series); Clyn's Annals, ed. Butler (Irish Archæol. Soc. Publications); Grace's Annals, ed. Butler (Irish Archæol. Soc.); Campion's Annals in Irish Chroniclers (Dublin, 1809); Holinshed, vol. vi., ed. 1808; Annals of Ireland ap. Cart. and Doc. of St. Mary's, Dublin, ed. Gilbert (Rolls Series); Archdall's Monasticon, ed. 1789; Burke's Extinct Peerages; Marquis of Kildare's Earls of Kildare; Lynch's Feudal Dignities of Ireland; Barbour's Bruce, ed. Herrtage (Early Engl. Text Soc.); J. T. Gilbert's Hist. of the Irish Viceroys; Rolls of Parliament, Edward I.]   **T. A. A.**

FITZTHOMAS or **FITZGERALD, MAURICE**, first EARL OF DESMOND (d. 1356), justiciar of Ireland, was the son of Thomas Fitzmaurice 'of the ape,' justice of Ireland in 1295, and of his wife Margaret 'the king's cousin' (*Cal. Doc. Ireland*, 1293–1301, No. 533). His grandfather, Maurice Fitzjohn, was slain along with his father, John Fitzthomas, at the battle of Callan (1261). John Fitzthomas was the son of Thomas Fitzmaurice, who seems to have been a younger son of Maurice Fitzgerald (d. 1176) [q. v.], the invader and the founder of the Geraldine family. The genealogy is, however, not quite clear.

Maurice's father died in 1298 (*Ann. Hib.* in *Chart. St. Mary's*, ii. 328; *Annals of Loch Cé*, i. 521), when Maurice was still a child. He left his vast estates in Munster, second only to those of the De Burghs among the Anglo-Irish nobility, to be protected by royal nominees, whose services could thus be cheaply rewarded (e.g. *Cal. Doc. Ireland*, 1302–7, Nos. 38, 43). In 1299 Maurice's mother married Reginald Russel without the royal license (*Rot. Orig. Abbrev.* i. 109). The right of his marriage was assigned to Thomas of Berkeley (*Cal. Doc. Ireland*, 1293–1301, No. 773). John Fitzthomas, afterwards first earl of Kildare, ultimately became guardian of his lands. On 5 Aug. 1312 his marriage to Catherine, daughter of Richard de Burgh, second earl of Ulster [q. v.], at Greencastle, reconciled for a time a long-standing family feud (*Ann. Hib.* p. 341; CLYN, p. 11, says on 25 Dec. 1413). Barbour says he played a conspicuous part in 1315 in resisting Edward Bruce (*Bruce*, xiv. 140–6, Early Engl. Text Soc.), but his authority is hardly conclusive. About this time, however, his active career begins. In 1326 the death of the great Earl of Ulster, his father-in-law, was the beginning of new feuds in which Maurice vigorously played his part. In 1327 a private war broke out between him and Arnold le Poer (Power), who had called him a 'rhymer.' Supported by the Butlers and William Bermingham, Maurice ravaged his enemies' lands in Ofath, and drove his allies, the Burkes, into

Connaught. But the intervention of the viceroy [see FITZGERALD, THOMAS, second EARL OF KILDARE] led to Arnold's leaving the country and Maurice's craving pardon at a parliament at Kilkenny. Yet in 1328 he again collected a strong army against the Poers. He also quarrelled with the Earl of Ulster, but in March 1329 the justiciar, Roger Outlaw, effected their reconciliation.

In 1329 Maurice was created Earl of Desmond, and received a grant of the county palatine of Kerry, with royal liberties therein to be held of the English crown. This was part of the policy which about the same time gave earldoms to the other leaders of the English colony. At the same time he received the grant of the advowson of Dungarvan, and a remission of his rents to the crown for that term (*Fœdera*, ii. 770). In 1330 he helped the viceroy, D'Arcy, against the clans of Leinster. Ten thousand men, including the chief of the O'Briens, followed his standards. He defeated the O'Nolans and the O'Mores and took Ley Castle. But Desmond and Ulster soon renewed their quarrels (*ib.* ii. 793) until the justiciar shut both up in prison. Desmond, who had been captured at Limerick (CLYN, p. 23), soon escaped, and resisted the next viceroy, Anthony de Lucy. He refused to attend the Dublin parliament of June 1331, though he appeared after it had been transferred to Kilkenny, where he swore oaths of faithfulness, and was pardoned. But in August Lucy seized him at Limerick, and shut him up in October in Dublin Castle. After eighteen months' imprisonment, Desmond was liberated on the petition of the three estates. The greatest lords of Ireland bound themselves under heavy penalties to be his sureties, and he swore before the high altar of Christ Church that he would attend the next parliament and be faithful to the king. In the same year, 1333, he broke his leg by a fall from a horse. In 1335 he served under the viceroy, D'Arcy, in the expedition of Edward III against Scotland (*Cal. Rot. Claus. Hib.* 9 Edw. III, p. 41; CLYN, p. 26). In 1339 he inflicted a crushing defeat on the MacCarthies and Irish of Kerry, of whom twelve hundred were slain.

A plan of Edward III to supersede the Anglo-Norman settlers by English ministers produced a terrible dissension between the 'English born in Ireland' and the 'English born in England' (GRACE, p. 133). Desmond took the lead in the struggle. He refused to attend the parliament of October 1341 at Dublin, and collected a great gathering of the nobles and townsfolk of English blood at Kilkenny in November. This assembly sent a long complaint to Edward III against the policy of his viceroy, and denounced the greed and incompetence of the 'needy men sent from England without knowledge of Ireland.' But the new justiciar, Ralph D'Ufford, persevered in the new policy. Desmond absented himself therefore from the parliament of June 1345 at Dublin. Ufford treated this as a declaration of war (CLYN, p. 31). He invaded his territories, and captured his castles of Iniskilty and Castleisland, where he hanged the leaders of the garrison. Many of the other nobles abandoned Desmond in alarm. The Earl of Kildare was imprisoned. Desmond's estates were declared forfeited. The grandees who had been his sureties in 1333 were ruined by Ufford's insisting on their forfeiture. Ufford died on Palm Sunday 1346, but all that Desmond got by his death was a respite and a safe-conduct. In August John Maurice was made seneschal of Clonmel, Decies, Dungarvan, and other lands formerly belonging to Desmond (*Cal. Rot. Pat. Hib.* 20 Edw. III, p. 51). In September 1346 he sailed from Youghal with his wife and two sons to answer his accusers or to prosecute his complaints in England. He surrendered himself to the king, and was retained for some time in prison. In 1347 he was present at the siege of Calais (CLYN, p. 34). In 1349 he was finally released from his difficulties (*Cal. Rot. Pat.* 23 Edw. III, p. 158), received back his lands, and was restored to the king's favour. In 1348 Ralph, lord Stafford, and others had bound themselves by heavy penalties as his sureties (*Fœdera*, iii. 154). He never ventured again on his old course of contumacy.

In 1355 Desmond was taken under the king's special protection (*ib.* iii. 300), the forfeits of his manucaptors of 1333 were restored (*ib.* iii. 306), and he himself was appointed viceroy of Ireland on 8 July, in succession to Thomas Rokesby. He remained in office until his death on 25 Jan. 1356 (*Ann. Hib.* MS. Laud, p. 392; *Obits and Martyrology of Christ Church*, p. 61, Irish Arch. Soc.; GILBERT, *Viceroys*, p. 21, places his death in July), 'not without great sorrow of his followers and all lovers of peace.' He was buried in the choir of the church of the Dominicans at Dublin, but his body was afterwards transferred to the general burying-place of his race, the church of the same order at Tralee. He is described as 'a good man and just, who hanged even his own kinsfolk for theft,' and 'well castigated the Irish.' He was the foremost Irish noble of his time, and the spokesman of the Anglo-Irish party which aspired to practical independence.

Desmond is said to have been married thrice. His first wife, Catherine de Burgh

(*d.* 1331), was the mother of Maurice and John, who became in succession earls of Desmond. An elder son, named Nicholas, was deprived of his inheritance as an idiot (*Fœdera*, iii. 433). His second wife is described as Eleanor, daughter of Nicholas Fitzmaurice, lord of Kerry. Her real name was Evelina (*Cal. Rot. Claus.* 32 Edw. III, p. 67). She was the mother of Gerald Fitzgerald [q. v.], the fourth earl, called 'Gerald the poet' (LODGE, *Peerage of Ireland*, i. 64, ed. Archdall). His third wife is said to have been Margaret, daughter of O'Brien, prince of Thomond.

[A valuable communication from Mr. T. A. Archer has been utilised for this article. The Annals of Ireland from the 15th Century, Laudian MS., published in Gilbert's Cartularies, &c., of St. Mary's Abbey, Dublin, vol. ii., forms the 'chief authority for the history of the English settlement,' and copious in their accounts of Desmond. See also Grace's Annales Hiberniæ (Irish Archæol. Soc.); Clyn's Annals of Ireland (Irish Archæol. Soc.); Sweetman's Calendar and Documents relating to Ireland; Rymer's Fœdera; Liber Munerum Hiberniæ; Lynch's Feudal Dignities of Ireland; Gilbert's Viceroys of Ireland; Graves's Unpublished Geraldine Documents; Book of Howth; Lodge's Peerage of Ireland, vol. i.]
T. F. T.

FITZURSE, REGINALD (*fl.* 1170), one of the murderers of St. Thomas of Canterbury, was the eldest son of Richard Fitzurse, on whose death about 1168 he inherited the manor of Williton, Somersetshire (COLLINSON, iii. 487); he also held the manor of Barham, Kent (HASTED, iii. 536), and lands in Northamptonshire (*Liber Niger*, p. 216). He is sometimes called a baron, for he held of the king in chief. He was one of the four knights who were stirred up by the hasty words of Henry II to plot the archbishop's death. They left Bures, near Bayeux, where the king then was, and proceeded, it is said, by different routes to England, all meeting at Saltwood, then held by Ranulf de Broc, on 28 Dec. 1170. The next day they set out with a few men, and having gathered reinforcements, especially from the abbot of St. Augustine's, at whose house they halted, they entered the archbishop's hall after dinner, probably about 3 P.M., and demanded to see him. Reginald told him that he bore a message from the king, and took the most prominent and offensive part in the interview which ensued (FITZSTEPHEN, *Becket*, iii. 123, *Vita anon., ib.* iv. 71). He had been one of Thomas's tenants or men while he was chancellor; the archbishop reminded him of this; the reminder increased his anger, and he called on all who were on the king's side to hinder the archbishop from escaping. When the knights went out to arm and post their guards, Reginald compelled one of the archbishop's men to fasten his armour, and snatched an axe from a carpenter who was engaged on some repairs. While Thomas was being forced by his monks to enter the church, the knights entered the cloister, and Reginald was foremost in bursting into the church, shouting 'King's men !' He met the archbishop, and after some words tried to drag him out of the church. Thomas called him 'pander,' and said that he ought not to touch him, for he owed him fealty [for the whole story of the murder see THOMAS, SAINT]. After the murder had been done the knights rode to Saltwood, glorying, it is said, in their deed (*Becket*, iv. 158), though William de Tracy afterwards declared that they were overwhelmed with a sense of their guilt. On the 31st they proceeded to South Malling, near Lewes, one of the archiepiscopal manors, and there it is said a table cast their armour from off it (*ib.* ii. 285). They were excommunicated by the pope, and the king advised them to flee into Scotland. There, however, the king and people were for hanging them, so they were forced to return into England (*ib.* iv. 162). They took shelter in Knaresborough, which belonged to Hugh Morville, and remained there a year (BENEDICT, i. 13). All shunned them and even dogs refused to eat morsels of their meat (*ib.* p. 14). At last they were forced by hunger and misery to give themselves up to the king. He did not know what to do with them, for as murderers of a priest they were not amenable to lay jurisdiction (NEWBURGH, ii. 157 ; JOHN OF SALISBURY, *Epp.* ii. 273); so he sent them to the pope, who could inflict no heavier penalty than fasting and banishment to the Holy Land. Before he left Reginald Fitzurse gave half his manor of Williton to his brother and half to the knights of St. John. He and his companions are said to have performed their penance in the 'Black Mountain' (various explanations of this name have been given; none are satisfactory; it was evidently intended to indicate some place, probably a religious house, near Jerusalem), to have died there, and to have been buried at Jerusalem before the door of the Templars' church (HOVEDEN, ii. 17). It was believed that all died within three years of the date of their crime. There are some legends about their fate (STANLEY). Reginald Fitzurse is said to have gone to Ireland and to have there founded the family of McMahon (*Fate of Sacrilege*, p. 183).

[Materials for the History of Becket, vols. i-iv. (Rolls Ser.); Benedict, i. 13 (Rolls Ser.); Ralph de Diceto, i. 346 (Rolls Ser.); William of Newburgh, lib. ii. c. 25 (Engl. Hist. Soc.) ; John of Salisbury, Epp. ii. 273, ed. Giles ; Garnier, pp. 139–51, ed. Hippeau; Stanley's Memorials of Canterbury, pp. 71–107, 4th edit.; Robertson's Becket, pp. 266–80 ; Collinson's Hist. of Somerset, iii. 487; Hasted's Kent, iii. 536; Liber Niger de Scaccario, p. 216, ed. Hearne ; Spelman's Sacrilege, p. 183, ed. 1853; Norgate's Angevin Kings, ii. 432 n.] W. H.]

FITZWALTER, ninth BARON (1452?–1496). [See RATCLIFFE, JOHN.]

FITZWALTER, JOHN (*d.* 1412?), astrologer. [See WALTER.]

FITZWALTER, ROBERT (*d.* 1235), baronial leader, lord of Dunmow and Baynard's Castle, was the son of Walter Fitzrobert, by his wife Matilda, daughter of Richard de Lucy, the faithful justiciar of Henry II. Walter was the son of Robert, steward of Henry I, to whom the king had granted the lordship of Dunmow and of the honour or soke of Baynard's Castle in the south-west angle of the city of London, both of which had become forfeited to the crown by William Baynard. Robert is generally described as the younger son of Richard Fitzgilbert, founder of the great house of Clare [see CLARE, RICHARD DE, *d.* 1090?], who certainly had a son of that name (ORDERICUS VITALIS, ii. 344, ed. Le Prévost, Soc. de l'Histoire de France). This genealogy was accepted by Dugdale (*Baronage*, i. 218), but some doubt has been thrown upon it on chronological grounds by Mr. Eyton (*Addit. MS.* 31938, f. 98). If it be true, it connects Robert Fitzwalter with the Norman counts of Brionne, descendants of Richard the Fearless, and therefore with the higher ranks of the nobility of the Conquest [see CLARE, FAMILY OF]. But in any case the house of Fitzwalter belongs properly to the administrative families, who in the latter part of the twelfth century had stepped into the place of the old feudal houses. Its possession of the soke of Baynard's Castle, to which the hereditary office of standard-bearer of the city was annexed, and which grew into an ordinary ward (LOFTIE, *London*, pp. 74–80, Historic Towns Series), brought it into intimate relations with the Londoners. Robert Fitzwalter was himself engaged in trade, and owned wine ships which received special privileges from King John (*Rot. Lit. Pat.* i. 73 *b*).

Baron Walter died in 1198, and was buried at Little Dunmow, in the choir of the priory of Austin canons (DUGDALE, *Monasticon*, vi. 147, ed. Caley). Robert Fitzwalter now succeeded to his estates, being already more than of full age. His mother and father are said to have been married in 1148, though this hardly seems likely (*ib.* vi. 147). He was already married to Gunnor, daughter and heiress of Robert of Valognes (*Rot. Curiæ Regis*, i. 157), from whom he inherited 30½ knight's fees, mainly situated in the north, so that his interests now became largely identical with the 'Aquilonares,' whom he afterwards led in the struggle against King John. He also acquired two knight's fees through her uncle Geoffry of Valognes, and about 1204 obtained livery of seisin of the lands of his own uncle, Geoffry de Lucy, bishop of Winchester (DUGDALE, *Baronage*, i. 218).

In 1200 Robert Fitzwalter was surety for half the fine incurred by his brother, Simon Fitzwalter, for marrying without the royal license (*Rotuli de Oblatis*, p. 111). In 1201 he made an agreement in the curia regis with St. Albans Abbey with respect to the wood of Northawe ('Ann. Dunst.' in *Ann. Mon.* iii. 28). He was now engaged in several other lawsuits. One of these sprang from his claim to the custody of the castle of Hertford as of ancient right (*Rot. Curiæ Regis*, ii. 185). But he withdrew this suit for a time, though in August 1202 he procured his appointment as warden of Hertford Castle by royal letters patent (*Rot. Lit. Pat.* i. 17 *b*).

Early in 1203 Fitzwalter was in attendance on King John in Normandy. In February and March he was with John at Rouen (*Rot. Norm.* pp. 74, 78, 80, 82; *Hist. MSS. Comm.* 9th Rep. i. 353). But he was now made joint-governor of Vaudreuil Castle (near the mouth of the Eure) with Saer de Quincy [q. v.], afterwards Earl of Winchester. After Easter King Philip of France took the field. The governors of Vaudreuil were so disgusted with John that they surrendered at the first summons. They thus incurred the derision of the whole French army, and Philip, disgusted at their cowardice, shut them up in close confinement at Compiègne (COGGESHALL, pp. 143–4; MATT. PARIS, *Hist. Major*, ii. 482). There they remained until redeemed by the heavy ransom of five thousand marks. On 5 July John issued letters patent from Rouen to certify that they had surrendered the castle by his precept (*Rot. Lit. Pat.* i. 31). But at the end of November his cousin William of Albini was still engaged in selling some of Fitzwalter's lands to raise his ransom (*ib.* i. 37 *b*).

In October 1206 Fitzwalter witnessed the truce made between John and Philip Augustus at Thouars (*Fœdera*, i. 95, Record edit.) The misgovernment of John provoked his profound resentment, and in 1212 he entered into intrigues with Eustace de Vescy [q.v.] and Llewelyn ab Iorwerth [q. v.] against the king. John's suspicions were aroused by private intelligence as he was preparing at Nottingham to march against his rebellious son-in-law, the Welsh prince. Most of the barons cleared themselves, but Fitzwalter and De Vescy, who were afraid to appear, were condemned to perpetual exile (COGGESHALL, p. 171). But John was so much alarmed that he shut himself up from his subjects, and abandoned his projected Welsh campaign. Eustace escaped to Scotland, and Robert took refuge in France (WALT. COV. ii. 207; 'Ann. Wav.' in *Ann. Mon.* ii. 268; 'Ann. Wig.' in *Ann. Mon.* iv. 400). John now seized upon Fitzwalter's estates, and on 14 Jan. 1213 destroyed Castle Baynard. He also demolished Robert's castle of Benington and his woods in Essex ('Ann. Dunst.' in *Ann. Mon.* iii. 35).

Fitzwalter remained in exile until John's submission to Innocent III. On 13 May 1213 John promised peace and security to him as part of the conditions of his reconciliation with Rome (MATT. PARIS, ii. 542), and on 27 May issued letters patent informing him that he might safely come to England (*Rot. Lit. Pat.* i. 99). On 19 July his estates were restored (*ib.* i. 101). John also granted a hundred marks to his steward as compensation (*Rot. Lit. Claus.* i. 146), and directed a general inquest into his losses like those made in the case of the clerks who had suffered by the interdict. Fitzwalter, however, was a vigorous opponent of John's later measures. It was said that John specially hated him, Archbishop Langton, and Saer de Quincy (MATT. PARIS, ii. 482). In 1215 Fitzwalter was the first mentioned in the list of barons who assembled in Easter week (April 19–26) at Stamford (*ib.* ii. 585; WALT. COV. ii. 219). He accompanied the revolted lords on the march to Brackley in Northamptonshire (27 April). But John now formally refused to accept the long list of demands which they forwarded to him at Oxford. Thereupon the barons elected Fitzwalter their general, with the title of 'Marshal of the army of God and Holy Church.' They solemnly renounced their homage to John and proceeded to besiege Northampton. They failed there and at Bedford, where Fitzwalter's standard-bearer was slain. But the adhesion of London secured their success. On 17 May the lord of Baynard's Castle entered the city at the head of the 'army of God,' though the partisans of John still held out in the Tower. Fitzwalter and the Earl of Essex specially busied themselves with repairing the walls of London, using for the purpose the stones taken from the demolished houses of the Jews

(COGGESHALL, p. 171). On 15 June John gave way and signed the Great Charter. Fitzwalter was one of the twenty-five executors appointed to see that its provisions were really carried out (MATT. PARIS, ii. 605).

For a short time nominal peace prevailed. Fitzwalter now got back the custody of Hertford Castle (*Rot. Lit. Pat.* i. 144 *b*). But the barons remained under arms, and Fitzwalter was still acting as 'Marshal of the army of God and Holy Church.' He now made a convention with John, by which London remained in the barons' hands till 15 Aug. (*Fœdera*, i. 133). But he was so fearful of treachery that within a fortnight of the Runnymede meeting he thought it wise to postpone a tournament fixed to be held at Stamford on the Monday after the feast of SS. Peter and Paul (29 June) for another week, and chose as the place of its meeting Hounslow Heath, that the barons might be near enough to protect London (*ib.* i. 134). After the failure to arrange terms at a meeting at Staines on 26 Aug. open war broke out. The twenty-five executors assigned to themselves various counties to secure them for their side. Fitzwalter, who with Eustace de Vescy was still the leading spirit of the movement, became responsible for Northamptonshire (WALT. COV. ii. 224). On 17 Sept. John granted Fitzwalter's Cornish estates to his young son Henry (*Rot. Lit. Claus.* i. 228; cf., however, i. 115 *b*, 200). But the pope's annulling the charter had paralysed the clerical supporters of the popular side, and the thoroughgoing policy of the twenty-five under Fitzwalter's guidance had alienated some of the more moderate men. Fearing lest Archbishop Langton might be forced to surrender his castle of Rochester, Fitzwalter, with the assent of the warden of the castle, Reginald of Cornhill, secretly occupied it with a large force. John's troops soon approached, and strove, by burning Rochester bridge and occupying the left bank of the Medway, to cut off Fitzwalter from his London confederates. But Fitzwalter succeeded in keeping his position, though before long he was forced (11 Oct.) to retreat to London, and allow the royalists to occupy the town and besiege the castle (COGGESHALL, pp. 174–5). John now tried to deceive him by forged letters (*ib.* p. 176). Fitzwalter, conscious of the weakness of his position, sought to negotiate. On 9 Nov. he received with the Earl of Hertford and the citizens of London a safe-conduct for a conference; but nothing came of it. In vain the beleaguered garrison of Rochester bitterly reproached him for deserting them (MATT. PARIS, ii. 624). On 16 Nov. they were forced

to surrender. On 16 Dec. the barons, including Fitzwalter, were excommunicated by name (*Fœdera*, i. 139). French help was now their only refuge. Fitzwalter went over to France with the Earl of Winchester and offered the throne to Louis, the son of King Philip, putting into his hands twenty-four hostages and assuring him of the support of their party. Fitzwalter was back in England early in 1216. Louis landed in May, and, as John made great progress in the east, Fitzwalter busied himself in compelling Essex and Suffolk, his own counties, to accept the foreign king (MATT. PARIS, ii. 655–6). The tide of fortune now turned, but after John's death on 19 Oct. Fitzwalter's difficulties increased. Gradually the English went over to the side of Henry III. Those who remained in arms were not respected by the French. On 6 Dec. Louis captured Hertford Castle from the followers of the new king Henry. Fitzwalter naturally asked for the custody of a stronghold that had already been so long under his care. The French urged that a traitor to his own lord was not to be trusted, and Louis told him he must wait until the end of the war (*ib.* iii. 5). Fitzwalter was too deeply pledged to Louis to join the deserters. He was sent from London on 30 April 1217 at the head of a strong French force to raise the siege of Mountsorrel in Leicestershire, now closely pressed by the Earl of Chester (WALT. COV. ii. 237). On his way he rested at St. Albans, where his hungry troops ate up all the supplies of the abbey (MATT. PARIS, iii. 16). He raised the siege of Mountsorrel and advanced to Lincoln. He was met by the regent, William Marshall, whose forces were now joined by the Earl of Chester with the army that had besieged Mountsorrel. Fitzwalter was anxious for an immediate battle. On 20 May the battle of Lincoln was fought, and the baronial forces thoroughly defeated. Fitzwalter himself was taken prisoner along with his son (GERVASE CANT. ii. 111) and most of the leaders of his party. The Londoners still held out until Hubert de Burgh's great naval victory on 24 Aug. On 11 Sept. the treaty of Lambeth ended the struggle. But the reissue of the charter as the result of the treaty showed that Fitzwalter's cause had triumphed in spite of his personal failure.

On 8 Oct. 1217 Fitzwalter's release from prison was ordered (*Rot. Lit. Claus.* i. 328 *b*). On 24 Jan. 1218 the king granted him his scutage (*ib.* i. 349 *b*). In July he received the custody of his nephew, Walter Fitzsimon Fitzwalter, whose father was now dead (*ib.* i. 379 *b*; *Excerpta e Rot. Finium*, i. 15). In the same year he witnessed the understanding that the great seal was to be affixed to no letters patent or charters until the king came of age (*Fœdera*, i. 152). But the fifth crusade must have offered a convenient opportunity to him and others. In 1219 he sailed for the Holy Land along with Earl Saer of Winchester and Earl William of Arundel. Before he arrived the crusading host had been diverted to the siege of Damietta. There he seems to have arrived along with Saer de Quincy and other English, at the same time as the cardinal legate Pelagius (*Flores Hist.* iv. 44 ; MATT. PARIS, iii. 41). This was in the autumn of 1219 (KUGLER, *Geschichte der Kreuzzüge*, p. 319). Saer de Quincy died on 3 Nov. ('Ann. Wav.' in *Ann. Mon.* ii. 292). This date makes impossible the statement of Walter of Coventry that they only arrived after Damietta had been captured (ii. 246). The town fell into the crusaders' hands on 5 Nov. Fitzwalter, therefore, though he is not mentioned, must have taken part in the latter part of the siege (see for all points connected with the crusade RÖHRICHT, 'Die Belagerung von Damiette' in VON RAUMER'S *Hist. Taschenbuch* for 1876, and his other article in *Forschungen zur deutschen Geschichte*, 1876). Eracles, in 'Recueil des Histor. des Croisades,' ii. 343, says that Fitzwalter arrived in the seventh month of 1219 (cf. also *Publications de la Société de l'Orient Latin*, Série Historique, iii. 55, 62, 65, 69).

The crusaders remained in Egypt until August 1221. But Fitzwalter had gone home sick ('Ann. Dunst.' in *Ann. Mon.* iii. 56), probably at some earlier period. He spent the rest of his life peaceably in England, thoroughly reconciled now to the government of Henry III. He must have by this time become well advanced in years. He was called 'Robert Fitzwalter, senior,' in the list of executors of the charter, and his son, presumably Robert Fitzwalter, junior, was taken prisoner along with him at Lincoln. On 11 Feb. 1225 Fitzwalter was one of the witnesses of Henry III's third confirmation of the great charter ('Ann. Burton.' in *Ann. Mon.* i. 232). In June 1230 he was one of those assigned to hold the assize of arms in Essex and Hertfordshire (SHIRLEY, *Royal Letters*, i. 375). He died on 9 Dec. 1235 ('Ann. Theok.' in *Ann. Mon.* i. 99 ; MATT. PARIS, iii. 334), and was buried before the high altar at Dunmow priory, the chief foundation of his house. He is described by Matthew Paris (iii. 334) as a 'noble baron, illustrious by his birth, and renowned for his martial deeds.' Administration of his goods and chattels was granted to his executors on 16 Dec. (*Excerpta e Rot. Finium*, i. 294). His heir, Walter, was at the time under age, so that the son who fought with him at Lincoln must have been dead (*ib.* i. 301). This Walter (*d.* 1257) must have been either a younger son or a grandson. After the death of Gunnor (she was alive in 1207) it is said that Fitzwalter married a second wife, Rohese, who survived him. He had also a daughter, Christina, who married William Mandeville, earl of Essex (DOYLE, *Official Baronage*, i. 685).

A large legendary and romantic history gradually gathered round the memory of the first champion of English liberty. A picturesque tale, first found in the manuscript chronicle of Dunmow (*MS. Cotton.* Cleop. C. 3, f. 29), and reproduced in substance in the 'Monasticon' (ed. Caley, Ellis, and Bandinel, vi. 147), tells how Fitzwalter had a very beautiful daughter named Matilda, who indignantly rejected the immoral advances of King John. At last, as the maiden proved obdurate, John caused her to be poisoned, so that the bitterest sense of personal wrong drove Fitzwalter to take up the part of a constitutional leader. So generally was the story believed that an alabaster figure on a grey altar-tomb in Little Dunmow Church is still sometimes pointed out as the effigy of the unfortunate Matilda. Several poems and plays have been based upon this picturesque romance. In them the chaste Matilda is curiously mixed up with Maid Marian, the mistress of Robin Hood. Such are the plays called 'The Downfall of Robert, Earl of Huntingdon, afterwards called Robin Hood, with his Love to Chaste Matilda, the Lord Fitzwater's daughter, afterwards his faire Maid Marian,' and 'The Death of Robin Hood with the lamentable Tragedy of Chaste Matilda, his faire Maid Marian, poisoned at Dunmowe by King John.' Both were printed in 1601, and were written by Henry Chettle [q. v.] and Anthony Munday [q. v.] They are reprinted in the eighth volume of Hazlitt's 'Dodsley.' Michael Drayton [q. v.] also published in 1594 a poetical account of 'Matilda, the faire and chaste Daughter of the Lord Robert Fitzwalter,' as well as two letters in verse, purporting to be written between her and King John. Before 1639 Robert Davenport [q. v.] wrote another play, 'The Tragedy of King John and Matilda.' It was also believed in the seventeenth century that Robert Fitzwalter, 'or one of his successors,' was the founder of the famous Dunmow custom of giving a flitch of bacon to the couple that had never repented of their union for a year and a day.

[Matthew Paris's Hist. Major, vols. ii. and iii., ed. Luard ; Flores Historiarum, vols. iii. and iv. (Engl. Hist. Soc.) ; R. de Coggeshall's Chronicon Anglicanum (Rolls Ser.) ; Walter of Coventry's Memoriale (Rolls Ser.); Annales Monastici (Rolls Ser.); Rymer's Fœdera, vol. i., Record ed.; Rotuli Literarum Patentium, Rotuli Literarum Clausarum, Record Commission; Dugdale's Baronage, i. 209, 218–20; Dugdale's Monasticon, vi. 147–9, ed. Caley, Ellis, and Bandinel; Thomson's Essay on Magna Carta, especially pp. 504–11.]   T. F. T.

FITZWARINE, FULK, was the name of several persons living in Shropshire in the twelfth and thirteenth centuries, some of whose actions are attributed to one individual in the romance of 'Foulques Fitz-Warin.' FULK FITZWARINE I was the second son of Warin de Metz, and of a daughter of the Peverels, then very powerful in Shropshire and the marches. He was the head of his family in 1156, when Henry II had given him the Gloucestershire manor of Alveston (R. W. EYTON, *Antiquities of Shropshire*, vii. 67), and died 1170–1. He had four sons, of whom the eldest, FULK II, married Hawise, daughter and coheiress of Joceas of Dinan, and is traditionally stated to have made a claim upon Ludlow, which was never allowed (*ib.* vii. 69). The Shropshire Pipe Roll of 1177 shows that he had been amerced forty merks by Henry II for forest trespass. About 1180 he successfully disputed the right of Shrewsbury Abbey to the advowson of Alberbury. Ten years later he was fined 100*l.* for his wife's share of an inheritance (*Rot. Pipe*, 2 Ric. I, 'Wilts'), and through her probably acquired an interest in several Wiltshire manors (*Testa de Nevill*, 1807, p. 150). On 6 Nov. 1194 he was named as attorney for his wife in a suit of *mort d'ancestre* on account of lands in the same county (*Rot. Curiæ Regis*, 1835, i. 35, 37); and was fined ten merks to be excused transfretation to Normandy (*Rot. Canc. de 3° Joannis*, 1833, p. 122). In 1195 he is entered as owing forty merks for the castle of Whittington adjudged to him in the curia regis. The fine remained unliquidated in 1202 (*ib.* p. 225). He died in 1197. Next year his widow paid thirty merks that she might not be obliged to remarry (*Rot. Pipe*, 10 Ric. I, 'Wilts'). Her name constantly appears as a litigant down to 1226 (*Testa de Nevill*, 1807, p. 128). Fulk had six sons, of whom the eldest, FULK III, in the year ending Michaelmas 1200, was 'fined 100*l.* with King John to have judgment concerning Witinton Castle and its appurtenances as his right, which had been adjudged to him by consideration of the curia regis' (EYTON, *Antiquities*, vii. 72). The king was bribed by Meuric de Powis to confirm the latter in the possession of Whittington, whereupon in 1201 Fulk, his brothers, and friends rebelled. The traditional story of the rebellion may be seen in the romance mentioned later. The outlawry was revoked by patent dated from Rouen, 11 Nov. 1203 (*Rot. Patent*, 1835, i. 36). In the next year John restored Whittington (*ib.* i. 46). Probably before 1 Oct. 1207 Fulk married Matilda, daughter of Robert le Vavasour, and widow of Theobald Walter. He received several marks of favour from the king (*Rot. Litt. Claus.* an. 9° et an. 14° Joannis, 1833, i. 92, 126, 129), and was with him in 1212 at Allerton and Durham (*Rot. Chart.in turri Lond. asserv.* 1837, i. pt. i. 187, 188), and at Bere Regis in 1213 (*ib.* pp. 193, 199). In 1215 he was making war upon his neighbours, had lost the royal favour, and had been despoiled of fiefs (*Rot. Litt. Claus.* i. 270). He was one of the malcontent barons who met at Stamford and Brackley in 1215 (MATT. PARIS, *Chronica*, 1874, ii. 585), and was among those specially excommunicated in the bull of Innocent III of 16 Dec. (RYMER, *Fœdera*, 1816, i. 139). Henry III bestowed some of the lands of the rebellious baron upon his own adherents (*Testa de Nevill*, pp. 45, 48, 49, 55, 56). The king styles him 'manifestus inimicus noster' in 1217 (*Rot. Litt. Claus.* i. 321). Fulk made his peace in the following year (*ib.* pp. 352, 376). Some time between 1220 and 1230 he founded Alberbury Priory. In 1221 and 1222 sufficient confidence was not placed in him to be permitted to strengthen Whittington without giving security for loyal behaviour (*ib.* i. 460, 520). Full seisin was granted to him by writs of 11 July and 9 Oct. 1223 (*ib.* pp. 554, 565). On 30 June 1245 an assembly of the barons sent him as their representative to order the papal nuncio to quit the country (MATT. PARIS, *Chronica*, iv. 420). His first wife having died he married Clarice de Auberville (*Excerpta e Rot. Fin.* 1836, ii. 89). He probably died about 1256–1257. The romance states that he was blind during the last seven years of his life. He died before August 1260, and his affairs were managed for some time before his death by his son, FULK IV, who was drowned at the battle of Lewes in 1264. By the death of an infant in 1420 the elder male line of this family became extinct. Eleven Fulk Fitzwarines in succession bore the same christian name.

In the traditional history Fulk I is omitted, and the career of his two successors combined as that of 'Fouke le Brun,' the outlaw and popular hero. We are told how he roamed through the country with his four brothers (recalling the 'Quatre Fils Aimon'), cousins, and friends, and the nimble-witted jongleur, John de Rampayne, seeking forest adventures of the Robin Hood type, spoiling the king, and succouring the poor, and how he was twice compelled to quit England and encounter sea perils from the Orkneys to Barbary. The story is preserved in a single manuscript in French in the British Museum (*Reg.* 12, c. xii.), first printed privately by Sir T. Duffus Hardy, and then published as 'Histoire de Foulques Fitz-Warin, par Francisque Michel,' Paris, 1840, large 8vo, and with an English translation and notes by Thomas Wright for the Warton Club in 1855. It is included by L. Moland and C. d'Héricault in 'Nouvelles Françoises en prose du xive siècle,' Paris, 1858, 12mo. The text and a new translation are given in J. Stevenson's edition of 'Radulphi de Coggeshall Chronicon' (Rolls Series, 1875). The manuscript was transcribed before 1320, and is evidently paraphrased from an earlier record written before the end of the thirteenth century in octosyllabic verses, some of which remain unaltered. An English version in alliterative verse was seen by Leland, who reproduces 'Thinges excerptid owte of an old Englisch boke yn Ryme of the Gestes of Guarine' (*Collectanea*, 1774, i. 230–7). Pierre de Langtoft of Bridlington (*Cottonian MS.* Julius A. v.), writing probably before 1320, refers to the romance, and Robert de Brunne, writing about the same period, says :

Thus of dan Waryn in his boke men rede.

It is a compilation from family records and traditions first put into shape by 'an Anglo-Norman trouvère in the service of that great and powerful family, and displays an extraordinarily minute knowledge of the topography of the borders of Wales, and more especially of Ludlow and its immediate neighbourhood' (T. Wright's ed. 1855, p. xv). There are historical anachronisms and other inaccuracies. As a story it is full of interest.

[Eyton's Antiquities of Shropshire, ii. 2–12, vii. 66–99, xi. 29–42 ; T. Wright's Sketch of Ludlow Castle, 2nd ed. 1856, and Essays on the Middle Ages, 1846, ii. 147–63 ; Frère's Bibliographe Normand, 1860, ii. 616, 619 ; Histoire Littéraire de la France, 1877, xxvii. 164–86 ; Revue Contemporaine, 1858, iii. 308–17 ; Ward's Cat. of Romances in the British Museum, 1883, i. 501–8. The account of the Fitzwarines by Dugdale (Baronage, 1675, pp. 443, &c.) is full of errors.] H. R. T.

FITZWILLIAM, CHARLES WILLIAM WENTWORTH, third EARL FITZWILLIAM in the peerage of the United Kingdom (1786–1857), only son of William Wentworth Fitzwilliam [q. v.], second earl, by his first wife, Lady Charlotte Ponsonby, youngest daughter of the second Earl of Bessborough, born in London 4 May 1786, was educated at

Trinity College, Cambridge. In 1806 he married Mary, fourth daughter of Thomas, first lord Dundas, by whom he had ten children. The countess died in 1830.

In 1806 the earl, as Viscount Milton, was returned to the House of Commons for Malton, and in 1807 for Yorkshire. Through five successive parliaments he represented the latter constituency. In 1830 he was elected for Peterborough, in 1831 (with Lord Althorp) for Northamptonshire, and in 1832 for the northern division of the same county. This seat he retained until his elevation to the peerage by the death of his father, 8 Feb. 1833. Fitzwilliam was a man of chivalrous honour, high moral courage, and perfect independence and disinterestedness. In the outset of his political career he was opposed to parliamentary reform, but afterwards became an ardent advocate of that measure, although his family possessed several pocket boroughs and had been known for its aristocratic exclusiveness. He was also an early advocate of the repeal of the corn laws, when his own fortune depended mainly upon the land. He took a similar view of the then interesting question of the export of wool. A powerful deputation of Yorkshire manufacturers waited upon the earl (then Lord Milton) soliciting him to oppose a projected measure permitting the export. Fitzwilliam replied that he had embraced the principles of free trade without qualification. He concurred with his father in openly condemning the conduct of the Manchester magistrates at the Peterloo riots of 1819, when for petitioning that the event might be inquired into the earl was deprived of the lordlieutenancy of the West Riding. In 1851 Fitzwilliam was created a knight of the Garter. In 1853 he was appointed a deputy-lieutenant for Northamptonshire, and in 1856 received the royal authorisation to adopt the surname of Wentworth before that of Fitzwilliam, as it had been previously used by his father to mark his descent from Thomas, first marquis of Rockingham. The earl gave a general support in the House of Lords to the liberal government, but in the debate of 1857 relative to the conduct of Sir John Bowring in the matter of the Arrow he spoke and voted with the opposition. Fitzwilliam published in 1839 his 'First, Second, and Third Addresses to the Landowners of England on the Corn Laws,' in which he supported the free trade policy. By the will of the widow of Edmund Burke, who died in 1812, power was given to Fitzwilliam's father, Walker King, bishop of Rochester, and William Elliot to print and publish such parts of the works of Burke as were not published before her decease, and all the statesman's papers were bequeathed to them for this purpose. One considerable portion of the task was successfully executed, but after the death of all the three literary executors a number of Burke's papers came into the possession of Fitzwilliam. Accordingly in 1844 there appeared, in four vols., the 'Correspondence of the Right Hon. Edmund Burke between the year 1744 and the period of his decease in 1797. Edited by Charles William, Earl Fitzwilliam, and Lieut.-General Sir Richard Bourke, K.C.B.' In 1847 Fitzwilliam published a 'Letter,' addressed to a Northamptonshire rector, in which he recommended that Ireland should be extricated out of her difficulties by the application of imperial resources. Fitzwilliam died at Wentworth House, Yorkshire, 4 Oct. 1857. His eldest son having predeceased him, he was succeeded as fourth earl in the peerage of the United Kingdom by his second son, William Thomas Spencer, viscount Milton, born in 1815, who sat in the lower house with only one intermission from 1837 to 1857. The fourth earl married, in 1838, Lady Frances Douglas, eldest daughter of the eighteenth Earl of Morton.

[Times, 5 Oct. 1857; Gent. Mag. 1857; Ann. Reg. 1857; Leeds Mercury, 7 Oct. 1857.]

G. B. S.

FITZWILLIAM, EDWARD (1788–1852), actor, was born of Irish parents near Holborn in London on 8 Aug. 1788. In 1806 he was actor and property man with Trotter, manager of the theatres at Southend and Hythe. At Gosport in 1808 he was seen by Elliston, who engaged him for his theatre at Birmingham. As Hodge in 'Love in a Village' he made, at the West London Theatre, his first appearance in London. In 1813 he was a leading actor at the Olympic, under Elliston, with whom he migrated to the Royal Circus, subsequently known as the Surrey, his first part at this house being Humphrey Grizzle in 'Three and the Deuce.' Under the management of Thomas Dibdin [q. v.] he rose at this house to the height of his popularity, his best parts being Leporello, Dumbiedykes in the 'Heart of Midlothian,' Patch, Partridge in 'Tom Jones,' and Humphry Clinker. At the Surrey he met Miss Copeland [see FITZWILLIAM, FANNY ELIZABETH], whom on 2 Dec. 1822 he married. Fitzwilliam—who had once appeared at Drury Lane for the benefit of T. P. Cooke, playing Sancho in 'Lovers' Quarrels' and singing a song, 'Paddy Carey,' in which he was very popular—joined the regular company at that house 10 Nov. 1821 as O'Rourke O'Daisy in 'Hit or Miss.' From this time his reputation dwindled. Padreen Gar in 'Giovanni in Ire-

land,' Loney Mactwolter in the 'Review,' and other Irish parts were assigned him. After a time he practically forsook the stage and became a comic vocalist at city entertainments. About 1845 he retired on an annuity from the Drury Lane Theatrical Fund, and died at his house in Regent Street 30 March 1852. In society, in which he was popular, he was known as 'Little Fitz.' He was about 5 ft. 3 in. in height, robustly built, and had a good-humoured characteristically Irish physiognomy. His son is noticed below.

[Genest's Account of the English Stage; Oxberry's Dramatic Biography, vol. ii.; Biography of the British Stage; Era newspaper, 4 April 1852; Era Almanack various years; Oxberry's Dramatic Chronology.] J. K.

FITZWILLIAM, EDWARD FRANCIS (1824–1857), song-writer, born at Deal in Kent on 2 Aug. 1824, was the son of Edward Fitzwilliam, an actor [q. v.], by his wife, Fanny Elizabeth Fitzwilliam, actress [q. v.] He was educated at the Pimlico grammar school, at St. Edmund's College, Old Hall, Hertfordshire, and at the institution of L'Abbé Haffrénique at Boulogne. Sir Henry Bishop was his instructor in an elementary course of harmony, and for a few months he resided with John Barnett at Cheltenham studying instrumentation. When in his twenty-first year he composed a 'Stabat Mater,' which was performed at the Hanover Square Rooms on 15 March 1845, with much success. In October 1847 he was appointed by Madame Vestris musical director of the Lyceum Theatre, and remained there for two years. About this time he wrote a cantata entitled 'O Incomprehensible Creator,' which was performed at Hullah's concert, 21 May 1851. At Easter 1853 he became musical director of the Haymarket Theatre, and held that position until his death. His principal compositions were 'The Queen of a Day,' a comic opera, and 'A Summer Night's Love,' an operetta, both produced at the Haymarket. He also wrote the overture, act, and vocal music of the 'Green Bushes' for the Adelphi Theatre, the overtures and music of all the Haymarket pantomimes, and of many that were brought out at the Theatre Royal, Liverpool. The music of Perea Nena's Spanish ballets, 'El Gambusino' and 'Los Cautivos,' were entirely his composition. His works were distinguished by an intelligence which gave promise of great excellence had he lived to fully master the technicalities of his art. After suffering for two years from consumption, he died at 9 Grove Place, Brompton, London, 19 Jan. 1857, aged 33, and was buried (27 Jan.) in Kensal Green cemetery.

Fitzwilliam's chief published compositions were : 1. 'O Incomprehensible Creator,' a cantata, 1850. 2. A 'Te Deum' for solo voices and chorus, 1852. 3. 'A Set of Songs; the Poetry chiefly Selected,' 1853. 4. 'Songs for a Winter's Night; the Poetry chiefly Selected,' 1855. 5. 'Seaside Musings; Six Morceaux for the Pianoforte,' 1855. 6. 'Four-Part Song for Four Voices,' 1855. 7. 'Dramatic Songs for Soprano, Contralto, Tenor, and Bass Voices; Four Books and an Appendix,' 1856. 8. 'Three Sacred Songs for a Child,' 1857. 9. 'Songs of a Student.' 10. 'Miniature Lyrics.' 11. 'Christmas Eve, a Lyric Ode.' His music to J. B. Buckstone's libretto for the opera 'Love's Alarms' was very popular, and ten songs from that piece were separately published in 1854. He was also the composer of songs, ballads, romances, cavatinas, serenades, and glees, and of quadrilles, polkas, schottisches, minuets, and marches. Of the music that he wrote for songs probably the best known is that composed for Barham's 'As I laye a thynkynge,' and for two songs from the 'Green Bushes'—'The Maid with the Milking Pail,' and 'The Jug of Punch.' Some of his compositions appeared in Hullah's 'Sacred Music for Family Use,' and in Davison's 'Musical Bouquet.'

ELLEN FITZWILLIAM (1822–1880), actress, his wife, whom he married on 31 Dec. 1853, was eldest daughter of Thomas Acton Chaplin (d. November 1859). She made her first appearance in London at the Adelphi Theatre on 7 Oct. 1841, when she played Wilhelm in the aquatic spectacle 'Die Hexen am Rhein.' She was for twenty-two years a prominent member of the Haymarket company under the management of J. B. Buckstone. Leaving England for Australia in 1877 she soon became a great favourite in the colonies. After a twelve months' engagement with Mr. Lewis of the Academy of Music, Melbourne, she joined the Lingard company. She was taken ill in Murrundi, New South Wales, but was able to proceed to New Zealand, and acted at Auckland, where she died from acute inflammation, 19 Oct. 1880, aged 58 (Era, 26 Dec. 1880, p. 4; Theatrical Times, 18 Nov. 1848, p. 439, with portrait).

[Era, 25 Jan. 1857, p. 9; Grove's Dictionary of Music (1879), i. 530; Planché's Extravaganzas (1879), iv. 261.] G. C. B.

FITZWILLIAM, FANNY ELIZABETH (1801–1854), actress, daughter of Robert Copeland, manager of the Dover theatrical circuit, was born in 1801 at the dwelling-house attached to the Dover theatre. When an infant of two or three years she was brought on the stage as one of the children in the 'Stranger.' After one or two similar experiments she played, when twelve years of age, the piano at a concert in Margate. Three years later, as Norah in the 'Poor Soldier,' she began a career as leading actress at the Dover theatre. Her first appearance in London took place at the Haymarket, at which house she played in 1817 Lucy in the 'Review,' Cicely in the 'Beehive,' and the page (Chérubin) in 'Follies of a Day' ('Le Mariage de Figaro'). Thence she proceeded to the Olympic, where she played the Countess of Lovelace in 'Rochester.' Engaged by Thomas Dibdin [q. v.] she went to the Surrey, where she replaced Mrs. Egerton [q. v.] as Madge Wildfire in the 'Heart of Midlothian.' In June 1819, in Dibdin's 'Florence Macarthy,' she is said to have displayed 'distinguished merit' (Theatrical Inquisitor, xiv. 468). As Fanny in 'Maid or Wife,' by Barham Livius, she made, 5 Dec. 1821, her first appearance at Drury Lane, where, 9 Feb. 1822, she was the original Adeline in Howard Payne's 'Adeline or the Victim of Seduction.' On 2 Dec. 1822 she married Edward Fitzwilliam [q. v.] After playing in Dublin and in the country, at the Coburg, the (old) Royalty, and other theatres she was engaged at the Adelphi, appearing 10 Oct. 1825, in a drama called 'Killigrew.' On 31 Oct. 1825 she was the original Kate Plowden in the 'Pilot,' Fitzball's adaptation of the novel by Fenimore Cooper. She was also the original Louisa Lovetrick in the 'Dead Shot,' and 21 Oct. 1830 Bella in Buckstone's 'Wreck Ashore.' She played in other dramas of Buckstone and attained high popularity. In 1832 she undertook the management of Sadler's Wells, to which house she transferred the Adelphi success, the 'Pet of the Petticoats,' a ballad burletta. At the Adelphi in 1835 she gave, on the Wednesdays and Fridays in Lent, a monologue entitled 'The Widow Wiggins.' She went in 1837 with Webster to the Haymarket, and shortly afterwards started for America, opening at New York as Peggy in the 'Country Girl.' On 4 Nov. she played twelve nights in Boston, and Wemyss, ex-manager of the Chestnut Street Theatre, who saw her, predicted that she would make more money in the United States than any actress, with the exception of Fanny Kemble, who had visited them (see his Theatrical Biog. p. 263, ed. 1848). The prediction appears to have been fulfilled, since America was revisited. She played with Buckstone in New Orleans and went with him to Havannah. After visiting many country towns in England she returned to the Adelphi and played, September 1844, in the 'Belle of the Hotel' and what is called a monopologue. Her Nelly O'Neil in Buckstone's 'Green Bushes,' 27 Jan. 1845, and her Starlight Bess in his 'Flowers of the Forest,' 11 March 1847, raised her reputation to its height. A few years later she returned to the Haymarket, where she played Nan in 'Good for Nothing,' Margery in the 'Rough Diamond,' and Dorinne in a version of 'Tartuffe.' At this house she continued to act until the Saturday before her death. On Monday, 11 Sept. 1854, she was seized with cholera, and died at six that evening. She was buried on the Thursday following at Kensal Green. She was a good actress of the Mrs. Jordan school. Elliston said her Lady Teazle was, on account of the rusticity she displayed, the best he had seen. She was unequalled in country girls, Irish peasants, &c. Her acting had much sweetness and womanliness. She had studied singing under Mrs. Bland [q. v.], and her rendering of ballads and of bravura songs, which she sang with John Reeve, was excellent. A French chanson, 'Portrait Charmant,' which she sang in Dibdin's 'Harlequin Hoax,' enjoyed extreme popularity. She had also great imitative faculty. She was light-complexioned, with blue eyes, and was below the middle height. She left two children—a son, a musical composer, Edward Francis [q. v.], and a daughter, Kathleen, who attained some reputation as an actress. Her brother was also on the stage. Had she lived she would within a month have married Buckstone.

[Genest's Account of the English Stage; Biography of the British Stage, 1824; Oxberry's Dramatic Biography, vol. i.; Cole's Life and Times of Charles Kean; Tallis's Drawing-Room Table-Book; Era Almanack; Era newspaper, 17 Nov. 1854; Dramatical and Musical Review; Theatrical Times; works cited.] J. K.

FITZWILLIAM, JOHN, D.D. (d. 1699), nonjuring divine, was educated at Magdalen College, Oxford, where he entered as a servitor in 1651, and was elected to a demyship in the same year. At the Restoration, according to Anthony à Wood, 'he turned about and became a great complier to the restored liturgy.' But Fitzwilliam himself appeals to 'the zeal I had for the present government even while it was merely to be enjoyed in hopes, and we could only wish it might be restored' (sermon preached in 1683). In 1661 he was elected fellow of Magdalen, and held his fellowship until 1670. He was made librarian of the college in 1662, being at the same time university lecturer on music. His first patron was Dr. George Morley, afterwards bishop of Winchester, who recommended him to the lord treasurer, Thomas Wriothesley, the virtuous earl of Southampton, in 1664, in whose family

he resided as chaplain, and instructed Lady Rachel Wriothesley and her sisters. On the death of the Earl of Southampton Bishop Morley 'took him into his own household,' and on 'his dismission from his service with a fair reward' recommended him in 1666 as chaplain to the Duke of York, afterwards James II, to whose daughter, the Princess Anne, he became tutor. In 1669 he was appointed by Bishop Morley to the living of Brightstone in the Isle of Wight, on the resignation of Dr. Thomas Ken, who was collated to the living of Woodhay. He was afterwards presented by his friend, Bishop Turner of Ely, to the living of Cottenham, near Cambridge, and promoted by the crown to a canonry at Windsor in 1688. He was a friend both of Thomas Ken and of his brother-in-law, Izaak Walton, who sent him presentation copies of all his works. He was also on terms of intimacy with John Kettlewell. He attended, with Ken, Bishop Morley's deathbed in 1684. At the revolution he resigned his preferments, because his conscience forbad him to take the oaths of allegiance to the new dynasty. In January 1690-1691 he appeared as a witness at the trial of John Ashton [q. v.], executed for a Jacobite conspiracy. It was reported that Ashton was a Roman catholic, and Fitzwilliam testified that 'he had received the sacrament of the Lord's supper only six months before in Ely Chapel'—that is, in the chapel at Ely House, Hatton Garden, the Bishop of Ely's London residence, which was a great resort of the nonjurors until Bishop Turner was deprived. Fitzwilliam appears to have been a regular attendant at these services, for he admits that 'he had been a hundred times at prayers in their altered state,' that is, when the names of King William and Queen Mary were omitted. He professed his willingness to submit peaceably, though he would not take the oaths. His correspondence with Lady Russell consists of fifty-seven letters which she wrote to him, and four or five which he wrote to her. Thomas Selwood, who edited the first edition of Lady Russell's letters in 1773, says: 'All the letters to Dr. Fitzwilliam were by him returned in one packet to her ladyship, with his desire they might be printed for the benefit of the public.' The correspondence indicates the greatest veneration on the part of Lady Russell for her old instructor, and a pastoral, almost a parental, solicitude on his part for his old pupil. Lady Russell consults him on the appointment of a chaplain, the education of her children, the marriage of her daughter, and, above all, her own griefs upon the execution of Lord William Russell, whom

Fitzwilliam had attended before his execution, and at whose trial he was one of the witnesses for the defence. She expresses the deepest reverence for his character, and the utmost value for his counsel. After the revolution she strove in vain to convince him that he 'might honestly submit to the present government.' Fitzwilliam's replies to her arguments show the conscientious and unselfish character of the man, and also give some insight into his life. He begs her to use her influence, not for himself, but for his parishioners, 'to get some person presented to my living, upon my resignation, in whom I may confide without any, the least capitulation, direct or indirect, beforehand. He whom I design is one Mr. Jekyl, minister of the new chapel, Westminster, and a favourite of the present government.' Anticipating that he would not be able to comply, he adds: 'I beg of your honour three things: first, that you would have the same good opinion of my integrity, and of my zealous addiction to your service, as ever you had; secondly, that you would permit me, in entire trust and confidence, to make over all my worldly goods to you; for I fear some men's heats may drive affairs so far as to bring all remnants of it into a premunire; thirdly, that I may have some room in your house, if any can be spared, to set up my books in, and have recourse to them if, on refusal, we may be permitted to stay in town.' If Lady Russell cannot grant these last requests, he intimates that he will apply to one of her sisters, Lady Gainsborough or Lady Alington. He died 26 March 1699, appointing 'my ever dear friend, and now my truly honoured father,' Dr. Ken, his sole executor under his will, with a life interest in 500l., which he bequeathed to the library of Magdalen College. He also left books and manuscripts to the Bodleian Library.

The only publication of Fitzwilliam extant is 'A Sermon preached at Cotenham, near Cambridge, on 9 Sept. 1683, being the day set apart for Public Thanksgiving for deliverance of His Sacred Majesty and Government from the late Treasonable Conspiracy,' that is, the Rye House plot, for his supposed complicity in which Lord William Russell lost his life. Fitzwilliam, however, thoroughly believed in his innocence, and testified to that effect at the trial. On the anniversaries of the arrest, the trial, and the execution of her husband, Fitzwilliam always sent letters of comfort and advice to Lady Russell.

Fitzwilliam was one of the few nonjurors who are mentioned with unqualified praise by Lord Macaulay. He groups him with the saintly John Kettlewell, and thinks they are deserving of 'special mention, less on account of their abilities and learning than on account of their rare integrity, and of their not less rare candour.'

[Letters of Rachel, Lady Russell, 3rd edition, 1792, and a new edition by 'J. R.,' 1853; Some Account of the Life of Rachel Wriothesley, Lady Russell, by the editor of Madame du Deffand's Letters, 3rd edition, 1820; Lathbury's Hist. of the Nonjurors; Life of Thomas Ken, Bishop of Bath and Wells, by a Layman, 1851; State Trials, xii. 792; Bloxam's Register of Magdalen College, Oxford; private information from the Dean of Wells (Dr. Plumptre).] J. H. O.

FITZWILLIAM, RALPH (1256?-1316), baron, was the son of William Fitzralph of Grimthorpe in Yorkshire, and of his wife Joan, daughter of Thomas de Greystock (DUGDALE, *Baronage*, i. 740). He was probably born in 1256, as he is described in 24 Edward I as forty years old and more (*Calendarium Genealogicum*, p. 515). In 1277 he served on behalf of his uncle, William de Greystock, in the Welsh war, and again on his own account in 1282, and in 1287 against the same enemy (*Parl. Writs*, i. 615). In 1291 he was first summoned to serve against the Scots, and in 1295 was first summoned to parliament. In July 1297 he was appointed captain of the royal garrisons in Northumberland (STEVENSON, *Doc. Scotland*, ii. 195), and for his services against the Scots thanked in November, in which month he was also appointed one of the captains of the Scottish marches. In 1298 he was put at the head of the troops levied in Yorkshire. He was constantly serving against Scotland and in parliament. In 1300 he was at the siege of Carlaverock. In 1301 he signed as 'lord of Grimthorpe' the letter of the barons at the Lincoln parliament to the pope. He was also employed as a representative of the East Riding before the exchequer in 1300, and as the king's agent empowered to 'use all friendly ways' to exact a purveyance of grain from the Yorkshire monasteries in 1302. In 1304 he was commissioned with John de Barton to act as a justice to execute the statute of 'trailbaston' in Yorkshire (HEMINGBURGH, ii. 235); but in the commissions of 'trailbaston' in 1305 his name does not appear (*Fœdera*, i. 970). In the reign of Edward II he attached himself to the baronial opposition. In 1309 he was appointed a justice to receive in Northumberland complaints of prises taken contrary to the statute of Stamford. In 1313 he was among the adherents of Thomas of Lancaster who received a pardon for their complicity in the death of Gaveston (*ib.* ii. 231). In the same year he was made 'custos' of Cumberland, and in 1314 one of the justices of oyer and terminer in Cumberland and Westmoreland for the trial of offenders indicted before the conservators of the peace. In January 1315 the magnates of the north appointed him one of the wardens of the marches. The king ratified their choice, and nominated him captain and warden of Newcastle-upon-Tyne and of all Northumberland. In March 1315 he was also made captain and warden of Carlisle and of the adjoining marches. In June 1316 he was appointed one of the wardens to defend Yorkshire against the Scots. The last writ addressed to him as a commissioner of array was on 15 Sept. 1316. He died soon after, apparently about November, certainly before February 1317, and is said to have been buried in Nesham Priory, Durham (DUGDALE).

Fitzwilliam inherited and acquired very considerable estates in Northumberland, Yorkshire, and Cumberland (*Cal. Inq. Post Mortem*, i. 282). In 1296 he was declared nearest heir to Gilbert Fitzwilliam (*Cal. Geneal.* p. 515). In 1303 he got one-fourth of the manors in Northumberland belonging to John Yeland (*ib.* p. 646). In 1306 he succeeded to the estates of his cousin John de Greystock (*ib.* p. 713), for the repose of whose soul he founded a chantry at Tynemouth.

Fitzwilliam married, about 1282, Marjory, daughter and coheiress of Hugh of Bolebec and widow of Nicholas Corbet. She died before 1303. His eldest son William died before him. He was succeeded by his second son Robert, who died before the end of 1317 (*Cal. Inq. Post Mortem*, i. 282). The estates then went to Ralph, the son of Robert, who assumed the name of Greystock. The barony remained in the family until 1487, when it passed through females to the Dacres of the north (DUGDALE, ii. 24).

[Parl. Writs, i. 615–16, vol. ii. pt. iii. pp. 880–1; Rymer's Fœdera, vols. i. and ii. Record ed.; Calendarium Genealogicum; Stevenson's Documents illustrative of the History of Scotland, vol. ii.; Calendarium Inquisitionum Post Mortem, vol. i.; Dugdale's Baronage, i. 740; Foss's Judges of England, iii. 89–91; Biographica Juridica, p. 272.]   T. F. T.

FITZWILLIAM, RICHARD, seventh VISCOUNT FITZWILLIAM of Meryon (1745–1816), founder of the Fitzwilliam Museum at Cambridge, eldest son of Richard, sixth viscount, and Catharine, eldest daughter and coheiress of Sir Matthew Decker, bart., of Richmond, Surrey, was descended from a member of the English family of Fitzwilliam, who, attending Prince John to Ireland on his appointment to the office of chief governor, founded the branch which flourished in that kingdom

till the early part of the present century. He was born in August 1745, and having entered Trinity Hall, Cambridge, graduated M.A. in 1764. On 25 May 1776 he succeeded his father in his Irish titles of viscount and baron and to his large estates. He was a fellow of the Royal Society, vice-admiral of the province of Leinster, and M.P. for Wilton from 1790 till he died on 4 Feb. 1816, in Bond Street, London. Most of his property passed, in accordance with his will (dated 18 Aug. 1815, and printed in Acts 3 & 4 Wm. IV, c. xxvi. s. 1, and 5 & 6 Vict. c. xxiii. s. 1), to George Augustus, eleventh earl of Pembroke, while the titles devolved upon the viscount's brother, John, by whose death without issue in 1833 they became extinct.

Playfair, in his 'British Family Antiquity,' gives a high character of Fitzwilliam. Though a member of the church of England and Ireland, he was the author of a rather remarkable publication, entitled 'The Letters of Atticus' (or, 'Protestantism and Catholicism considered in their comparative Influence on Society'). These letters, composed in French, and issued from the press at different dates, were collected and reprinted anonymously in London in 1811. Another edition appeared in Paris in 1825; and in the following year, in London, an English version with the author's name on the title-page. He is best known by his bequest to the university of Cambridge, of his splendid collection of printed books, illuminated manuscripts, pictures, drawings, engravings, &c., together with the dividends of 100,000*l*. South Sea annuities for the erection of a museum. The dividends having accumulated to more than 40,000*l*., the existing building was commenced on 2 Nov. 1837, from the designs of George Basevi [q. v.], and the work was carried on under his superintendence until his death in 1845, when C. R. Cockerell [q. v.], the architect of the public library, was selected as his successor.

[Lodge's Peerage of Ireland, ed. Archdall, iv. 306; Graduati Cantabrigienses; Cambridge University Calendar (1887), p. 451; Playfair's British Family Antiquity, v. 38; Blacker's Brief Sketches of the Parishes of Booterstown and Donnybrook, pp. 89, 108, 314; Gent. Mag. (1816), vol. lxxxvi. pt. i. pp. 189, 367, 627; Annual Register (1816), lviii. Chron. 213.]   B. H. B.

FITZWILLIAM, ROGER, *alias* ROGER DE BRETEUIL, EARL OF HEREFORD (*fl.* 1071–1075), was the younger son of William Fitzosbern [q. v.], to whose earldom and English estates he succeeded at his death (1071). He is described by William of Malmesbury as 'a youth of hateful perfidy,' and the letters of Lanfranc complain of his violence and rebellious tendencies, for which the writer eventually excommunicated him. In 1075 he gave his sister Emma in marriage to Ralf, earl of Norfolk, against the will of the Conqueror, according to Florence of Worcester. At the 'bride-ale' there was hatched a conspiracy between the two earls and their friends against William's rule. Roger returning to his earldom rose in revolt, but was prevented by the royal forces from crossing the line of the Severn. For this revolt he was fined in the king's court at the following Christmas (1075), and sentenced to forfeiture of his lands and perpetual imprisonment. His rage against the king, according to Ordericus, made William resolve to keep him in prison so long as he lived, but on his deathbed he sanctioned his release. He was, however, never released, and when Ordericus wrote in the time of Henry I, his two sons, Reginald and Roger, were gallantly striving to regain by their services that royal favour which their house had lost.

[Freeman's Norman Conquest. The history of Roger's revolt is told by Ordericus Vitalis in chap. xiii. of his 4th book.]   J. H. R.

FITZWILLIAM, Sir WILLIAM (1460 ?–1534), sheriff of London, was son of John Fitzwilliam. His mother was Ellen, daughter of William Villiers of Brokesby in Leicestershire. It has been claimed that the family was descended from one William Fitzwilliam of Green's Norton, who is stated to have been a natural son of William the Conqueror. But the existence of this natural son receives no confirmation from contemporary documents, and he is probably a figment of the genealogists. Fitzwilliam lived and traded in Bread Street, London, afterwards in St. Thomas Apostle, having a country house at Gaynes Park, Chigwell, Essex. He was admitted to the livery of the Merchant Taylors' Company of London in 1490, of which he was warden in 1494 and 1498, and master in 1499, obtaining a new charter for the company on 6 Jan. 1502. In 1505 he was an unsuccessful candidate for the shrievalty of London, but was appointed to the office on the king's nomination in 1506, and was elected alderman of Broad Street ward in the same year. Elected sheriff of London in 1510 he refused to serve, and was in consequence disfranchised and fined one thousand marks by the lord mayor. The franchise was restored and the fine remitted by order of the Star-chamber, 10 July 1511. He became treasurer and high chamberlain to Cardinal Wolsey, who appointed him one of the king's council. In 1515 he was nominated sheriff of Essex, was knighted in 1522, and was sheriff of Northampton in

1524. He entertained Wolsey during his disgrace, 1–5 April 1530, at Milton Manor, Northampton (the seat of the present Earl Fitzwilliam), which he purchased in 1506 from Richard Wittelbury. Fitzwilliam rebuilt the church of St. Andrew's Undershaft, London, and the chancel of Marholm, Northamptonshire. By deed (26 May 1533) he settled twelve hundred marks on the Merchant Taylors' Company for certain religious uses since applied (under scheme of 1887) to divinity scholars at St. John's College, Oxford. Fitzwilliam married, first, Ann, daughter of Sir John Hawes; secondly, Mildred, daughter of Sir R. Sackville of Buckhurst; thirdly, Jane, daughter of John Ormond. He had by his first wife issue Sir William, his heir (father of Sir William Fitzwilliam, 1526–1599 [q. v.]), Richard, Elizabeth, and Ann; by his second wife, Christopher, Francis, and Thomas. He died 9 Aug. 1534. His will is dated 21 May 1534. He was buried at Marholm.

[Bibl. Top. Brit. vol. x.; Gibson's Castor, p. 187; Manuscript Records of Merchant Taylors' Company; Corporation of London Repertory Book; Collins's Peerage, iv. 387 sq.; Testamenta Vetusta, ii. 665; Greyfriars Chronicle (Camd. Soc.); Cavendish's Life of Wolsey.]   W. C–E.

FITZWILLIAM, WILLIAM, Earl of Southampton (d. 1542), lord high admiral of England, was the younger son of Sir Thomas Fitzwilliam of Aldwarke, West Riding of Yorkshire, by Lucy, daughter and coheiress of John Neville, marquis of Montacute. From the time when he was not more than ten years of age he had been brought up with the king, and was perfectly familiar with his personal habits, his likings and dislikings. He shared in the king's love of sportsmanship, but was ignorant of Latin, and though he spoke French fluently was a poor French scholar (BREWER, Reign of Henry VIII). In 1509, as one of the king's cupbearers, he was awarded many grants and privileges; two years later he obtained the place of esquire of the body in reversion. In 1513, being one of the chief commanders in the fleet sent out against the French, he was 'sore hurt with a quarell' in a fight near Brest in Brittany (HOLINSHED, Chronicles, ed. Hooker, 1587, iii. 816). Before the end of that year, on 25 Sept., he was knighted for his good services at the siege of Tournay (ib. p. 824), and shortly afterwards created vice-admiral of England. In 1518 he was treasurer of Wolsey's household. In February 1521 Wolsey sent him as ambassador to the French court, seeing that he would be a useful instrument. He was keen, bold, sagacious, able to resist flattery and cajolery, and never lost his presence of mind. The French king received him cordially, talked of sport, and presumed upon his want of experience. Fitzwilliam meanwhile kept his eyes open to all that went on, and gave the highest satisfaction to Wolsey. After many difficulties and much tedious negotiations both powers consented to accept Henry's mediation. When war was declared against France in the following year, Fitzwilliam was appointed vice-admiral of the navy, under the command of the Earl of Surrey, his special duty being to protect the English merchantmen from the attacks of the enemy (HERBERT, *Reign of Henry VIII*, p. 123). He commanded in 1523 the fleet stationed in the Channel to bar Albany's passage to Scotland. On 10 May 1524 he left England to take up his appointment as captain of the garrison of Guisnes in Picardy, where he remained until the spring of 1525. By April 1525 he was again in France, and with Sir Robert Wingfield attended a council at Mechlin, which he quitted for Guisnes on 21 May. In October 1525 he was deputed with John Taylor, LL.D., to take the oath of the lady regent, Louise of Savoy, then at Lyons (Francis I being a prisoner in Spain), for ratifying the articles of a treaty just concluded between the crowns of England and France (HOLINSHED, iii. 892 ; HERBERT, p. 181). Ill-health obliged him to return home in January 1526. On 24 April of that year, being then comptroller of the king's household, he was elected K.G. (BELTZ, *Memorials of the Garter*, p. clxxiii). At the end of the year he was sent, along with Clerk, bishop of Bath and Wells, to offer Francis I the hand of the Princess Mary, and thus promote an alliance with France.

In June 1528 he narrowly escaped falling a victim to the sweating sickness, then epidemic (*Letters and Papers of Reign of Henry VIII*, ed Brewer, iv. 1932). In May 1529 he accompanied the Duke of Suffolk on an embassy to France. During the same year he was elected M.P. for Surrey and subscribed the articles exhibited against Wolsey. He was present when the great seal was taken from Wolsey, 17 Oct. 1529, and with Gardiner was appointed to see that no part of the cardinal's goods were embezzled. About this time Fitzwilliam, 'on the part of the king, mediated' a quarrel which had arisen between the two houses of parliament in consequence of Fisher's hasty declaration 'that nothing now would serve with the commons but the ruin of the church' (*ib.* p. 293). In October 1529 Fitzwilliam succeeded More as chancellor of the duchy of Lancaster. For a short time in 1533 he acted as lord privy seal. On 26 May

1535 he took passage for Calais to be present at the diet of French and English commissioners, returning in June. In the same capacity of commissioner he arrived at Calais on the following 17 Aug. to redress 'such things as were out of order in the town and marches,' and remained thus employed until October. Soon afterwards he was joined in another embassy to France, with the Duke of Norfolk and Dr. Cox, regarding the marriage of the Duke of Angoulême, the French king's third son, with the Princess Elizabeth (*ib.* p. 383). He was on the council in 1536, when Sir Henry Norris confessed to adultery with Anne Boleyn. He also formed one of the tribunal appointed to try Norris and the three other commoners of a similar crime. Norris at his trial declared that he was deceived into making his confession by Fitzwilliam's trickery (FROUDE, *History of England*, cabinet edit., 1870, ch. xi.) He succeeded the Duke of Richmond as lord high admiral 16 Aug. 1536, and held the office until 18 July 1540. In the same year he took part in the suppression of the insurrection in Lincolnshire. On 18 Oct. 1537, having in the meantime been made treasurer of the king's household, Fitzwilliam was raised to the peerage as Earl of Southampton. He remained treasurer for about a year. In November 1538 he was sent down to Warblington in Hampshire to examine the Countess of Salisbury, who was implicated in the nun of Kent's conspiracy (see his letter to Cromwell in SIR H. ELLIS's *Original Letters*, 2nd ser. ii. 110–14). She denied all knowledge of the plot, and was removed to Cowdray, near Midhurst in Sussex, a place belonging to Fitzwilliam himself, where she was detained (FROUDE, ch. xv.) Cowdray had been sold to Fitzwilliam by Sir David Owen in 1528 (*Sussex Archæol. Coll.* v. 178, vii. 40). In 1539, when an invasion of England was threatened, he took command of the fleet at Portsmouth. At the parliamentary election of 1539 he put out his utmost strength to secure for the king a manageable House of Commons, going in person round Surrey, Sussex, and Hampshire, where his own property was situated (Letter of Fitzwilliam to Cromwell, Cotton MS. Cleopatra, E. 4, cited in FROUDE, ch. xvi.) On 11 Dec. 1539 he met Anne of Cleves at Calais to conduct her to her future country. Detained by the bad weather for fifteen days, Fitzwilliam, to beguile the time, taught the princess to play at cards. Meanwhile he wrote to advertise the king of her arrival, and, thinking that he must make the best of a matter which was past remedy, repeated the praises of the lady's appearance. Cromwell afterwards accused Fitzwilliam of having encouraged false hopes in his letters from Calais (FROUDE, ch. xvii.; deposition of the Earl of Southampton in STRYPE, *Memorials*, 8vo ed. vol. ii.) He witnessed the arrest of Cromwell, 10 June 1540, when, according to Marillac, 'to show that he was as much his enemy in adversity as in prosperity he had pretended to be his friend, he stripped the Garter off the fallen minister' (FROUDE, ch. xvii.) Shortly afterwards, 'upon some discontent between Henry and the king of France, whereupon the French raised forces in Picardy, Fitzwilliam, with John, lord Russel, then newly made high admiral, carried over two troopes of northern horse into those parts' (HERBERT, p. 484). He died at Newcastle-upon-Tyne in October 1542, while on his march into Scotland, leading the van of the English army commanded by the Duke of Norfolk. In honour of his memory 'his standard was borne in the foreward throughout that whole expedition' (*ib.* p. 483). In his will, dated 10 Sept. 1542, he desired to be buried in the parish church of Midhurst, where a new chapel was to be built for a tomb for himself and his wife Mabel, at an expense of five hundred marks, 'if he should die within one hundred miles of it' (abstract of will registered in P. C. C. 16, Spert, in NICOLAS, *Testamenta Vetusta*, ii. 707–9). The chapel remains, but there are no signs of a tomb; he was therefore probably buried at Newcastle. To the king he gave 'his great ship with all her tackle, and his collar of the Garter, with his best George beset with diamonds.' He married in 1513 Mabel, daughter of Henry, lord Clifford, and sister of Henry, first earl of Cumberland, but by this lady, who died in 1535, he had no issue. Consequently the earldom of Southampton at his decease became extinct, while his entailed estates would rightly devolve upon his two nieces, daughters of his elder brother, Thomas Fitzwilliam, who was slain at Flodden Field in 1515: Alice, married to Sir James Foljambe, and Margaret, the wife of Godfrey Foljambe. The Cowdray estate fell to his half-brother, Sir Anthony Browne [q. v.]

There is a portrait of Fitzwilliam in the Fitzwilliam Museum, Cambridge, which is considered to be a copy of the one by Holbein, destroyed at Cowdray by the fire in September 1793 (*Sussex Archæol. Coll.* vii. 29 *n.*)

[Dugdale's Baronage, ii. 105–6; Letters and Papers of Reign of Henry VIII, ed. Brewer and Gairdner; Cal. State Papers, Venetian, vols. iii. iv. vi. (Appendix); Collectanea Topographica et Genealogica, i. 360, ii. 69; Sussex Archæol. Coll.]   G. G.

FITZWILLIAM, SIR WILLIAM (1526–1599), lord deputy of Ireland, eldest son of Sir William Fitzwilliam of Milton in the

hundred of Nassaburgh, Northamptonshire, and Anne, daughter of Sir Richard Sapcote of Elton, Huntingdonshire, was born at Milton in 1526. He was grandson of Sir William Fitzwilliam, sheriff of London [q. v.] Related through his mother to Sir John Russell, first earl of Bedford, he was on his entrance into court placed under the protection of that nobleman, who presented him to Edward VI, by whom he was created marshal of the king's bench. From a lease granted to William Fitzwilliam, esq., 'one of the gentlemen of the king's chamber,' of certain lands in Ireland on 10 July 1547, it would appear that he had already at that time formed a connection with Ireland, which throughout a long life was the chief sphere of his labours (COLLINS, *Peerage*; LODGE, *Peerage* (Archdall); BRIDGES, *Northamptonshire*, vol. ii.; WIFFIN, *House of Russell*; *Cal. of Fiants*, Ed. VI, 70).

When the succession to the throne was threatened through Lady Jane Grey, he loyally (though a protestant) stood by Mary, and in 1555 was created temporary keeper of the great seal of Ireland (*Lib. Hib.* ii. 14). Coming under the influence of the Earl of Sussex, who spoke of him as a friend, he took that nobleman's side against Sir A. St. Leger (*Hamilton Cal.* i. 133, 231; *Cal. Carew MSS.* i. 257, 260). On 24 July 1559 he was made vice-treasurer and treasurer at wars in Ireland, a post he held till 1 April 1573, when he was relieved by Sir Edward Fitton (*Lib. Hib.* ii. 43; *Ham. Cal.* i. 157). In 1559, too, he was elected M.P. for Carlow county in the Irish House of Commons. In 1560, during the temporary absence of the Earl of Sussex, he was appointed lord justice, taking the oath and receiving the sword at Christ Church on Thursday 15 Feb. (patent, 18 Jan. 1560). His conduct was approved by the queen (*Ham. Cal.* i. 160), who again entrusted the government to him during the absence of Sussex in 1561 (patent, 10 Jan. 1561). Meanwhile Shane O'Neill had entered upon a course of conduct which for the next eight years was destined to perplex and madden the government. On the return of Sussex in June a campaign was undertaken against him which, though ending in failure, reflected great credit on Fitzwilliam, by whose 'worthiness,' and that of Captain Warne, the English army was, according to Sussex, saved from annihilation (*ib.* i. 177). In August he was sent into England to explain the state of affairs to the council; but immediately afterwards returned to Ireland. On Thursday, 22 Jan. 1562 he was again sworn chief governor during the absence of Sussex from 16 Jan. to 24 July (patent, 20 Dec. 1561). On 3 Dec. he and Justice Plunket were despatched into England to acquaint the council with the situation of affairs in Ireland. He returned about the end of January 1563; but appears to have spent the greater part of that year and the beginning of the next in England. In May 1564 Sir Nicholas Arnold, late commissioner for reforming and introducing economy into the Irish government, was appointed lord justice, and having insinuated many things against him as vice-treasurer, which he wholly failed to substantiate, the latter retorted by saying that he could have governed Ireland as well as Arnold and saved the queen twenty thousand marks (*State Papers*, Eliz., xiii. 57, xviii. 1, 2, 3). Arnold was succeeded by Sir Henry Sidney, and he being summoned home, Fitzwilliam and Dr. R. Weston were on 14 Oct. 1567 sworn lords justices, much against the will of the former, who declared that his last justiceship had cost him 2,000*l.* This was bad enough, but to be charged by the queen with not preventing the landing of the Scots in Antrim was intolerable, and he complained bitterly against it, protesting that he had for eight years and more truly and faithfully served her majesty without bribery, robbery, or friendly gifts (*ib.* xxiii. 13). Though 'not bred up to arms,' he, in the spring of the following year (1568), undertook an expedition into the north; but it was badly managed, and ended in disgraceful failure (BAGWELL, *Ireland*, ii. 133). Fortunately Sidney returned in October and relieved him from his more onerous duties. In 1570 he appears to have resided chiefly in England; but on 29 Jan. 1571 he returned to Ireland. In March Sidney departed, and on 1 April he was appointed lord justice. He was suffering severely at the time from ague, and protested his unfitness for the government, and his impoverishment after thirteen years' service, tending to his utter ruin (*Ham. Cal.* i. 454, 457). His petition, supported by the entreaties of Lady Fitzwilliam, who implored the queen to allow her husband to return to England before the winter came on, was unsuccessful, and instead he was appointed lord deputy, and sworn into office on 13 Jan. 1572 (patent, 11 Dec. 1571).

Forced into the gap against his will, and miserably supplied with money, Fitzwilliam's government (1572–5) was not remarkably successful, though he declared that Ireland in 1575 was in a much better state than it was in 1571 (*ib.* ii. 49). With Sir Edward Fitton in Connaught and Sir John Perrot in Munster, his attention was chiefly directed to Ulster. Here the grants of land made by Elizabeth to Malby, Chatterton, Sir Thomas Smith, and the Earl of Essex (1572–3), lead-

ing as they did to serious complications with the Irish, and with Turlough Luineach O'Neill in particular, greatly added to his difficulties; but his conduct in the matter appears to have been much misrepresented. He was not, he declared, opposed to the plantation scheme; on the contrary, he warmly approved of it, only he objected to the way in which it was carried into execution. There was too much talk about it. The thing ought to have been done quietly and with celerity. Instead of that the Irish obtained wind of what was intended, and had time to band together, thereby not only obstructing the plantation, but considerably embarrassing him in the government. His views on the subject were undoubtedly sound, and were indeed recognised to be so by Essex himself, who, however much he might feel inclined to resent his unwillingness to co-operate and the alacrity with which he obeyed the order to disband, was obliged to admit that he had no other choice in the matter (*Ham. Cal.* 1572–5, passim; BAGWELL, *Ireland*, ch. xxix–xxxii.; DEVEREUX, *Lives of the Earls of Essex*, vol. i.; SHIRLEY, *Monaghan*).

The post of treasurer, which he resigned in 1573 to Sir Edward Fitton, far from being a lucrative appointment, had involved him in debts amounting to nearly 4,000*l.* The deputyship profited him nothing, and unless shortly relieved he declared he would be obliged to sell Milton; as it was, his wife had already been instructed to sell part of the stock on the property. At the last moment Elizabeth remitted 1,000*l.* and 'stalled' the rest, thus saving him from absolute beggary. These private difficulties, superadded to his bodily infirmities, rendered him extremely irritable, and led to one quarrel after another with Sir E. Fitton [q. v.] Despite his advice and that of Sir J. Perrot, the Earl of Desmond had in 1573 been allowed to return to Ireland, and though promptly rearrested in Dublin, he had a few months later managed to escape into Munster. Mischief was of course anticipated; but nothing was done—nothing indeed could be done so long as Fitton proved insubordinate. The queen was enraged, declaring that her honour was wounded so long as the traitor was allowed to continue abroad (*Ham. Cal.* ii. 15; *Cal. Carew MSS.* i. 464, 466, 473). Fitzwilliam replied that he had neither men nor credit to enable him to take the field. Compelled at length to act, he in August 1574 marched into Munster, captured in rapid succession Derinlaur Castle, Castlemagne, and Ballymartyr, and obliged the earl to submit himself at Cork on 2 Sept. For this service he had Elizabeth's thanks (*Cal. Carew*, i. 483), but he still continued to be hampered by the reports of his detractors at court (just retribution for his own attacks on Sir Anthony St. Leger), and especially of his brother-in-law Sir H. Sidney. He was seriously ill, so ill in fact that in March 1575 he thought he could not live a year longer, and that he was likely to be buried in Ireland and slandered in England. Lady Fitzwilliam, who his enemies asserted was the real lord deputy, was despatched to solicit his recall. His prayer was at last listened to, and the arrival of Sir H. Sidney on 12 Sept. restored him to private life (*Lib. Hib.* ii. 4).

During the next twelve years he remained in England quietly engaged, we may presume, in attending to his own affairs. In 1582 there was some talk of appointing him successor to Lord Grey (*Ham. Cal.* ii. 364, 374, 499), but nothing came of it. He, however, obtained a crown lease of Fotheringay Castle (LEMON, *Cal.* ii. 395), and it was during his governorship that Mary of Scotland met her doom there. His conduct on that occasion reflected great credit on him. The only one who showed any respect for her feelings, Mary gratefully acknowledged his kindness to her, and in token of her esteem presented him with the picture of her infant son, James, which is still carefully preserved by his successors (*Topog. Brit.* vol. iv.)

On 17 Feb. 1588 he was reappointed lord deputy of Ireland in the room of Sir John Perrot, and on 23 June, being Sunday, he landed at the Ring's End, about six o'clock in the morning, and on Sunday following received the sword of state in Christ's Church. The country was at peace, but the period was one of critical importance. The timely storm that dissipated the Armada relieved the government of its chief danger, but there were still a number of ships in the narrow seas to cause considerable anxiety. Fitzwilliam's vigilance was worthy the high trust reposed in him. A number of Spaniards, it was reported, who had escaped the clutches of the sea, were roaming about the country, and likely, if they were allowed to band together, to prove dangerous. On 22 Sept. 1588, therefore, he issued orders to the provincial governors to take all hulls of ships, stores, treasure, &c., and to apprehend and execute all Spaniards they might find in their districts (*Cal. Carew MSS.* ii. 490). For himself he proposed to make a journey into Connaught and O'Donnell's country, 'as well for the riddance of such Spaniards thence who were reported to be dispersed in great numbers throughout that province, as also for that the Irishry of that province towards

the Pale and Feagh MacHugh O'Byrne, with the rest upon the mountain's side, grew into such pride upon hope of those Spaniards and their assistants.' His design was approved by the council, and on 4 Nov. he set out from Dublin. Proceeding directly to Athlone and thence to Sligo, he held on towards Ballyshannon, 'where, as I heard, lay not long before twelve hundred or thirteen hundred of the dead bodies.' A little before coming to Donegal, 'I being then accompanied with Sir Owen O'Tool, whom by courteous entreaty I had drawn thither to help the compounding of some good course for the well-ordering of his country,' he was met by O'Donnell and courteously entertained by him. At Strabane Sir John O'Dogherty came to him, 'whereof I was not a little glad, for then I made account before his and Sir Owen O'Tool's departures to settle her majesty in some good surety for the 2,100 beeves and 1,000 more for a fine, which at Dungannon, the Earl of Tyrone's house, upon handling of the matter, was accomplished, and by them both and O'Donnell agreed that they should be cut upon the country and paid, and in the meantime that Sir Owen and Sir John should go and remain with me till such pledges as I then named were put in.' (A very different account of this transaction will be found in Fynes Moryson's history.) On 23 Dec. he returned to Dublin without the loss of a single man (*Ham. Cal.* iv. 53, 73, 92).

In January 1589 Sir Ross MacMahon, captain of Monaghan, exasperated by the exactions of the sheriff, Captain Willis, and his soldiers, a collection of arrant rascals according to Fizwilliam, took the law into his own hand and expelled them from his country. Thereupon in March Fitzwilliam invaded and spoiled his country so thoroughly that he left not a house standing or a grain of corn unburnt. Shortly afterwards Sir Ross died, and his brother, Hugh, being entitled to succeed him, was by the deputy established in possession in August (*ib.* iv. 224). The Irish (see FYNES MORYSON) asserted that he was bribed; but this he denied. According to Fitzwilliam the new MacMahon immediately entered upon treasonable courses, and was by him arrested. Process, however, was for a time delayed owing to the unwillingness of the privy council to proceed to extremities in what might be construed into a mere border raid (*ib.* iv. 263). Convinced at last by the deputy's representations, order was on 10 Aug. 1590 given to proceed with his trial.' Wherein, for the avoiding the scandal of justice with severity, he had the favour to be tried in his own country, and by a jury of the best gentlemen of his own name and blood' (*Add. MSS.*

12503, f. 389–90. What the Irish said about this transaction may be read in FYNES MORYSON's *History*, bk. i. ch. i.; cf. also SHIRLEY, *Monaghan*, ch. iv.)

In 1589 a quarrel arose between him and the president of Connaught, Sir Richard Bingham, which created considerable excitement at the time. Bingham had been charged by the natives with extreme harshness in his government and as being the sole cause for their rebellious attitude. The deputy, therefore, on 2 June 1589, undertook a journey into that province for the purpose of pacifying it and inquiring into the charges against Bingham. These proceedings Bingham resented and poured out the vials of his wrath upon Fitzwilliam. The charges preferred against him he categorically denied, with the result that the deputy was severely reprimanded by Elizabeth. In reply, he could only say that 'Sir Richard hath unjustly dealt with me, as in his answers in several parts appeareth, to which upon the margin I have set down some notes of truth. God make him his, but I fear if there be an atheist upon earth, he is one, for he careth not what he doeth, nor to say anything (how untrue soever), so it may serve his turn' (*Ham. Cal.* iv. 194–281 passim). Never of a strong constitution, his health had of recent years been very bad. During the journey into Connaught 'he swooned twice on one day, and after had three fits of a tertian.' His enemies caricatured him as being 'blind, lame, burst and full of dropsy;' nevertheless he contrived manfully to attend to his business, and his conduct in suppressing the mutiny of Sir Thomas Norreys's soldiers (May 1590) won him the high praise of Sir George Carew (*Cal. Carew MSS.* iii. 33). Hugh MacMahon out of the way, he in October 1591 partitioned Monaghan (with the exception of Donnamyne, which belonged to the Earl of Essex) among the principal gentlemen of the MacMahons, the termon or ecclesiastical lands being reserved for English officials. In July 1592 he proceeded to Dundalk in order to determine certain border disputes between Tyrone and Turlough Lunieach, and in June in the following year he, at the same place, concluded a treaty between them (*Ham. Cal.* iv. 568, v. 99; *Cal. Carew MSS.* iii. 73). Hardly had he done this when he was called upon to suppress the rebellion of Maguire, setting out from Dublin on 4 Dec. 'into the Cavan, whither by easy journeys, yet through very foul ways and deep fords by reason of continual rain, he arrived within five days after his departure' (*Ham. Cal.* v. 190). His expedition was successful so far as the capture of Enniskillen Castle and the proclaiming Maguire traitor went; but the rebellion was only the first act of a tragedy, the end of which he was not to see. His health had been fairly good while in the field, but on his return he was confined closely to his chamber. On 30 Jan. 1594 he wrote: 'It is God's good blessing that this state is reduced to that staidness of quiet that the infirmities of the governor, old, weak in body, sick in stomach, racked with the stone, bedrid with the gout, and disgraced with restraints, do not make it stagger' (*ib.* p. 201). In the spring death seemed so near that he deemed it necessary to provide for the government by nominating lords justices. On 31 July his successor, Sir W. Russell, arrived, and on 12 Aug. he and his family sailed for England. His infirmities increased, and eventually he lost his sight entirely. He lived to hear of Tyrone's rebellion, and to hear it laid to his charge. One of his last acts was to dictate a vindication of his conduct during his last deputyship (*Addit. MS.* 12503, Brit. Mus.)

He married Anne, daughter of Sir William Sidney, and sister of Sir Henry Sidney, by whom he had two sons (William, who succeeded him, and John, a captain in the wars in Scotland) and three daughters. He died in 1599 at his house at Milton, and was buried in the church of Marham, where, on the north side, is a noble monument erected to him by his widow. One of the ablest of Elizabeth's viceroys, it was his misfortune to be vilified by his contemporaries and to be misrepresented in history as the most avaricious and wantonly cruel of English governors.

[Authorities as in the text. In addition to the State Papers calendared by Mr. Hamilton and Mr. Brewer there are in the great Carte collection in the Bodleian at Oxford four volumes of State Papers (lv–viii.) specifically known as the 'Fitzwilliam Papers,' relating to Ireland during the period of his government there.] R. D.

FITZWILLIAM, WILLIAM WENTWORTH, second EARL FITZWILLIAM in the peerage of the United Kingdom (1748–1833), statesman, eldest son of William, first earl Fitzwilliam, was born 30 May 1748, and succeeded to the earldom on the death of his father (9 Aug. 1756). He was educated at Eton, where he began a lifelong friendship with his schoolfellows Charles James Fox and Lord Carlisle. From Eton he proceeded to Cambridge, and took his seat in the House of Lords in 1769. On 11 July 1770 he married Lady Charlotte Ponsonby, youngest daughter of William, second earl of Bessborough, by Lady Caroline Cavendish, daughter of the Duke of Devonshire. He adhered to the whig politics of his family, and steadily opposed the North administration. On the death of his uncle, Lord Rockingham, in 1782, he succeeded to estates valued at 40,000*l.* a year. He kept up a princely establishment at Wentworth House in Yorkshire, and had probably the finest stables and kennels in England. In 1783 Fox had intended him for the head of his new India board; and in their regency arrangements of 1788 the whigs designed him for the lord-lieutenancy of Ireland. The Prince of Wales in September 1789 honoured him by a visit at Wentworth, when nearly forty thousand persons were entertained in the park. After the outbreak of the French revolution Fitzwilliam acted with the 'old whigs,' and in July 1794, in company with the Duke of Portland and others, joined the government, and was appointed president of the council.

In December 1794 Pitt sent Fitzwilliam to Ireland as lord-lieutenant, where he became the centre of a political misunderstanding which it is very difficult to unravel. Fitzwilliam was known to be a friend to the Roman catholic claims, and his appointment in the place of Lord Westmorland, a favourer of the protestants, was regarded as an indication of approaching concessions. Before Fitzwilliam left England Grattan saw Pitt, and received what he took to be assurances that the catholic claims would be granted, though Pitt disavowed this interpretation of his words, and even told Fitzwilliam that he was to give the Roman catholics no encouragement, but to postpone the question until the fullest inquiries had been made. Fitzwilliam, when he reached Dublin, seems to have thought that delay was impossible, after Grattan had so raised the hopes of the party, and upon writing to the government was surprised to receive a repetition of his former instructions from the Duke of Portland, who declared that no steps would be taken at the present time in the interests of the catholics. It is impossible to say how far Pitt, Fitzwilliam, or the Duke of Portland was responsible for the misunderstanding. Fitzwilliam was not aware that Pitt was contemplating the union as a condition antecedent to emancipation, and therefore could hardly understand the premier's policy. He supposed himself to have received instructions subsequently disavowed by their author; nor was this the only point of disagreement between himself and the cabinet. Pitt, who had appointed Fitzwilliam chiefly to please his new allies, had stipulated, among other things, that the 'supporters of government should not be displaced on the change.' Portland explained this to Fitzwilliam, or, as Lord Stanhope thinks, tried ineffectually to ex-

plain it. In any case Fitzwilliam disregarded it (*Life of Pitt*, ii. 293). Fitzwilliam landed at Dublin on Sunday evening, 4 Jan. 1795, was in bed all Monday, and on Wednesday Beresford, commissioner of the customs, Cooke, secretary in the military department, Wolfe and Toler, attorney- and solicitor-general, were dismissed. Beresford appealed to the government and was at once reinstated; and Fitzwilliam was informed that the resignations of Wolfe and Toler would not be accepted. But in spite of this rebuff he did not send in his own resignation for nearly three weeks, and remained at the castle till 25 March, when he was succeeded by Lord Camden. 'The day of his departure was one of general gloom; the shops were shut; no business of any kind was transacted; and the greater part of the citizens put on mourning, while some of the most respectable among them drew his coach down to the water-side' (STANHOPE, *Life of Pitt*, ii. 365).

Fitzwilliam now drew up his own version of the whole story in two letters addressed to the Earl of Carlisle. He maintained, without the least justification, that his dismissal was caused by Pitt's deliberate wish to humiliate his new allies. On his return to England motions for inquiry were made in both houses of parliament, and rejected by large majorities; and Beresford sent him a challenge which led to a meeting between them at old Tyburn turnpike on 26 June. The duel was stopped by the constables.

Fitzwilliam soon made his peace with the government, and in 1798, when the Duke of Norfolk was dismissed from the lord-lieutenancy of the West Riding for a seditious toast, Fitzwilliam was appointed to succeed him. On the formation of the Addington ministry in February 1801 Fitzwilliam, with the other whig conservatives, went into opposition. On Addington's resignation in April 1804 it was intended by Pitt to make Fitzwilliam one of the secretaries of state, but the allies standing out for the admission of Fox, the negotiation came to nothing, and Pitt went on without him. Under the short-lived ministry of Lord Grenville in 1806 he was president of the council; and during the political uncertainty occasioned by the king's illness in 1811 he was sometimes spoken of as a possible whig prime minister. All his official hopes, however, vanished with the determination of the prince regent to keep the tory government in power. He was afterwards one of the little knot of whig magnates in the House of Lords who protested against the government policy, and especially the maintenance of the Roman catholic disabilities. On 31 Jan. 1812 he brought on a resolution in the House of Lords charging the crown solicitor in Ireland with tampering with the panel of the jury selected to try one of the catholic delegates, but was defeated by a majority of 162 to 79. In the following March he was offered the vacant Garter, which he declined. In 1819 he attended a public meeting at York convened for the purpose of censuring the Manchester magistrates for their conduct at the Peterloo massacre, and was dismissed from the lord-lieutenancy for violent language.

The first Lady Fitzwilliam died on 13 May 1822, leaving one son, Charles William Wentworth, third earl [q. v.] On 21 July 1823 Fitzwilliam married Louisa, widow of the first Lord Ponsonby, and daughter of the third Viscount Molesworth. She died without issue, on 1 Sept. 1824. Fitzwilliam died on 8 Feb. 1833.

[Diary of Lord Colchester; Cornwallis Correspondence; Rockingham Papers; Froude's English in Ireland; Plowden's Hist. of Ireland; Lord Stanhope's Life of Pitt; Massey's Hist. of England; Rose's Diary; Lord Malmesbury's Diary.]   T. E. K.

FLAHAULT, COMTESSE DE (1788–1867). [See ELPHINSTONE, MARGARET MERCER.]

FLAKEFIELD, WILLIAM (*fl.* 1700), first weaver of checked linen in Great Britain, was, it is said, son of a native (named Wilson) of Flakefield, in the parish of East Kilbride, Lanarkshire, who became a merchant in Glasgow about 1650, and was called Flakefield in order to distinguish him from another merchant named Wilson. However this may be, Richard Fleckfield was deacon of the incorporation of weavers of Glasgow in 1640, John Fleckfield in 1670, and Robert Fleckfield in 1673, 1675, and 1676 (CLELAND, *Annals of Glasgow*, p. 425). William Flakefield may probably have been the son of John or Robert Fleckfield. After having learnt the art of weaving, he enlisted about 1670 in the Cameronian regiment; from this he was afterwards transferred to the Scots guards. While on service abroad he came across a blue and white check handkerchief of German make. He resolved immediately to imitate it when he returned to Glasgow, and when he obtained his discharge in 1700 he carried out his intention. With some difficulty he got together the means for making a web of two dozen handkerchiefs. The novelty of the blue and white check and the unusual fineness of the texture made the article so popular that it was soon very largely manufactured in Glasgow and its neighbourhood. As late as 1771 striped and checkered linen cloth and handkerchiefs were among the most important textile manufactures of Glasgow (GIBSON, *History of Glasgow*, pp. 239, 248). Probably in consequence of being outstripped by imitators with larger means of carrying on the new manufacture, Flakefield himself seems to have obtained no benefit from the success of his scheme, for in his old age he was made town-drummer of Glasgow, and died in that office.

[Ure's Hist. of Rutherglen and East Kilbride, pp. 169–72.]   E. C–N.

FLAMBARD, RANNULF (*d.* 1128), bishop of Durham and chief minister of William Rufus, was of obscure origin (ORD. VIT. iii. 310, iv. 107; WILLIAM OF MALMESBURY, ii. 497), a phrase perhaps not to be taken too strictly in those days (cf. ORD. VIT. iv. 144). Domesday shows that Rannulf Flambard (Flamard, Flanbard, or Flanbart) was a landowner in Godalming hundred, Surrey, at Middleton-Stoney, Oxfordshire, and at 'Bile' and 'Becleslei' in Hampshire. He was also tenant of a house in Oxford, and appears to have been dispossessed of part of his Hampshire property on the making of the New Forest (*Domesday*, 1 fol. 30b2, 157a1, 51a2, 154a1). He may also, as Mr. Freeman has remarked, be the Rannulf Flamme who holds land, in the Survey, at 'Funtelei' in Titchfield hundred, Hampshire (*ib.* fol. 49a2). Orderic says that he was the son of Turstin of Bayeux. His mother was still living in 1101, and his brother possibly in 1130–1, so that he could hardly have been settled in this country under Edward the Confessor (ORD. VIT. iii. 310, iv. 109–10), as has been sometimes held.

Rannulf seems to have attached himself in boyhood to the court of William I, where his comely person, intelligence, eloquence, and generosity soon cleared the road to success (*ib.* iii. 310; but cf. *Cont. Hist. Dun. Eccles.* i. 135). He pushed his way by flattery, treachery, and coarse indulgences (ORD. VIT. *ib.*) Though no scholar, he had a pliant wit and argumentative quickness. Even before the Conqueror's death he was feared by many nobles, whose failings he revealed to the king. Mr. Freeman suggests with probability that he is the Rannulf whom William I sent (*c.* 1072) to force his 'new customs' on the bishopric of Durham, and who was driven from the diocese by the saint's vengeance (SIMEON OF DURHAM, i. 105–7; cf. FREEMAN, iv. 521). According, however, to Simeon's continuator, who appears to have possessed special knowledge as to Rannulf's early career, Rannulf was originally in the service of Maurice, bishop of London (1085–1107), whom he only left 'propter decaniam sibi ablatam,' and in the hope of doing better in the service of the king (apparently William II) (*Cont. Hist.*

Dun. Eccles. i. 135). If so it was probably late in William I's days or early in those of William II that he acquired his surname or nickname, Flambard. The exact meaning of the epithet is very obscure, but appears to have some reference to Rannulf's 'consuming' greed and ambition (ORD. VIT. iii. 310–11; cf. ANSELM, *Epp.* l. iv. ep. ii. col. 201; see, too, FREEMAN, *William Rufus*, ii. 555).

All the direct contemporary evidence tends to show that it was in the early years of William II's reign that Rannulf came into prominence. He was plainly the prime mover of the shameless ecclesiastical policy which reached its climax when the see of Canterbury was left vacant for over four years, from 28 May 1089 to 20 Sept. 1093 (FLORENCE OF WORCESTER, ii. 45–6; WILLIAM OF MALMESBURY, ii. 407–8; SIMEON OF DURHAM, ii. 231–2; cf. HENRY OF HUNTINGDON, pp. 232–3; and *Anglo-Saxon Chronicle*, ii. 203–4). Hence it is almost certain that he is the 'Rannulfus' who was sent down by the king to open a plea against Anselm at Canterbury on the day Of that archbishop's enthronement, 25 Sept. 93 (EADMER, *Hist. Nov.* pp. 41–2).

Rannulf does not seem to have borne as yet any distinct legal office or title. He may have been the king's chancellor, but in contemporary documents and chronicles he is generally styled 'Rannulf the chaplain' or 'the king's clerk' (Rannulfus Cappellanus) (DUGDALE, i. 164, 174; cf. *Cont. Hist. Dun. Eccles.* i. 135; and the 'Rannulfe his capellane' of the *Anglo-Saxon Chronicle*, i. 364). Later he appears to have held all the authority of the twelfth-century justiciar, even if he did not enjoy this specific title, which is given him by Orderic Vitalis (iv. 107). But his position may very well have been somewhat abnormal, as the chroniclers give him various titles and run off into rhetorical phrases. In 1094 he sent back from Hastings twenty thousand English soldiers, whom William had summoned to Normandy, and confiscated the 10s. with which the shire had supplied each man for his expenses abroad (FLORENCE OF WORCESTER, ii. 35; SIMEON OF DURHAM, ii. 224; cf. *Anglo-Saxon Chronicle*, ii. 197).

Rannulf seems to have been mainly occupied in supplying the king with the money he required for his court, his new buildings, the wages of his stipendiary soldiers, and, in the latter half of his reign, for the purchase of Normandy and Aquitaine from their crusading dukes (ORD. VIT. iii. 476, iv. 80). According to Orderic he urged William Rufus 'to revise the description of all England,' a phrase which has generally been interpreted as

referring to the compilation of a new Domesday Book. Both Dr. Stubbs and Mr. Freeman consider this to be a misdated reference to the Great Survey of the previous reign, in which they admit that Rannulf took a more or less prominent part. Though this is not improbable, Orderic's words refer more naturally to a revision of a previous survey. Orderic seems to imply that the main offence of this survey lay in superseding the old and vague measures of land by new ones made after a fixed standard (ORD. VIT. iii. 311; WILLIAM OF MALMESBURY, ii. 497; cf. also STUBBS, i. 298–9; FREEMAN, *Norm. Conq.* v. 377–8, *Will. Rufus*, i. 331, &c.) Mr. Round seems to have shown that there was a special levy of 4s. the hide imposed for the purchase of Normandy in 1096. This might imply such stringent application of the Domesday records as would justify Orderic's words with reference to its revision (cf. ROUND, ap. *Domesday Studies*, pp. 83–4).

Florence of Worcester probably gives the true chronology of Rannulf's rise when he tells us that he began by buying the custody of vacant bishoprics, abbeys, and other benefices. For these he paid not only a sum of ready money, but an annual rent, and this system continued till the end of the reign, when the king 'had in his own hand the archbishopric of Canterbury, the bishoprics of Winchester and Salisbury, and eleven abbeys all set out to gafol' (FLORENCE OF WORCESTER, ii. 46; *Anglo-Saxon Chron.* i. 364). With these sources of wealth Rannulf's 'craft and guile' raised him higher and higher, till the king made him the head of his realm, both in matters of finance and justice. Once in this position Rannulf turned his hands against laymen as well as clergy, the rich and the poor (FLORENCE OF WORCESTER, ii. 46).

All the chroniclers recognise Rannulf as the mainspring of the king's iniquity (WILLIAM OF MALMESBURY, ii. 497, 619; cf. ORD. VIT. iii. 311). His rule was one of violence and legal chicanery; in those days 'almost all justice slept, and money was lord' in the great man's courts (FLORENCE OF WORCESTER, p. 46). When William Rufus laid a tax upon the land, Rannulf levied it at twofold or a threefold rate, thus winning from the king the dubious compliment of being the only man who would rack his brains without caring about other men's hatred so long as he pleased his lord (WILLIAM OF MALMESBURY, *Gesta Reg.* ii. 497; cf. *Gesta Pont.* p. 274). So great was the terror of these days that there went abroad a rumour that the devil had shown himself in the woods to many Normans, and commented on the doings of Rannulf and the king (FLORENCE OF WORCESTER, ii. 46).

It was perhaps towards the end of his ministerial career that Rannulf was entrapped by a pretended message from his old patron, Maurice, the bishop of London, on board a boat belonging to a certain Gerold, one of Rannulf's own vassals. He was carried off to sea in a larger ship, full of armed men; but, after three days, during which the manner of his death was disputed, he obtained his liberty by an appeal to Gerold's fealty and the promise of a large reward to the pirates. Gerold fled, distrusting his lord's word, while Rannulf, attended by a great train of knights, made an imposing entry into London, became a greater favourite with the king than ever, and was not entrapped again (*Cont. Hist. Dun. Eccles.* i. 135–8).

On the Whitsuntide festival of 1099 (29 May) William Rufus gave him the bishopric of Durham, which had been vacant since about New-year's day 1096 (*Anglo-Saxon Chronicle*, ii. 203; SIMEON OF DURHAM, *Hist. Dun. Eccl.* i. 133–5; HENRY OF HUNTINGDON, p. 232; FLORENCE OF WORCESTER, ii. 44). A week later (5 June) Rannulf was consecrated in St. Paul's Cathedral by Thomas, archbishop of York, to whom, however, he would make no profession of obedience (*Cont. Hist. Dun. Eccles.* i. 138; SIMEON OF DURHAM, *Hist. Reg.* ii. 230; FLORENCE OF WORCESTER, ii. 44). A year later William Rufus was slain (2 Aug. 1100), and, immediately after his accession, Henry I flung Rannulf into the Tower (15 Aug.) (*Cont. Hist. Dun. Eccles.* i. 138; *Anglo-Saxon Chron.* ii. 204; &c.), partly, as it seems, to gratify a private grudge (ORD. VIT. iv. 107).

Anselm, when he returned to England (23 Sept. 1100), found the people rejoicing over Rannulf's captivity, 'as if over that of a ravaging lion.' When brought up before the king's curia 'pro pecunia . . . male retenta,' Rannulf appealed to his 'brother bishop,' and Anselm offered to help him, though at his own risk, if he could clear himself of simony. Rannulf failed to do this, and was imprisoned in the Tower. He was not severely treated, and managed to escape by a rope conveyed to him in a wine-stoup, after having intoxicated his warders at a banquet. He reached the sea-coast, where he and his mother—according to Orderic, a witch who had lost one eye in communications with devils—embarked with all their treasure in two different ships. The mother, while trying to subdue a storm with her incantations, was taken by pirates and put ashore in Normandy 'moaning and naked' (ORD. VIT. iv. 108–10; cf. WILLIAM OF MALMESBURY, ii. 620; *Anglo-Saxon Chron.*

ii. 205; HENRY OF HUNTINGDON, p. 234; FLORENCE OF WORCESTER, ii. 48). Anselm, writing to Paschal II early in 1101, says that the bishop has escaped into Normandy, 'and, joining himself with the king's enemies, has made himself "Lord of the Pirates," whom, as is said for a certainty, he has sent out to sea' (ANSELM, *Epp.* l. iv. ep. 1; cf. HERMANN OF LAON, ii. c. 6).

Robert of Normandy received Rannulf eagerly, and made him ruler of Normandy (ORD. VIT. iv. 110, 116). Rannulf in return urged the duke to invade England (FLORENCE OF WORCESTER, ii. 48; WILLIAM OF MALMESBURY, ii. 620; ORD. VIT. iv. 107, 110; *Anglo-Saxon Chron.* ii. 205). When the fleets of Robert and Henry were mustered, Rannulf counselled the bribery of the English sailors (FLORENCE OF WORCESTER, ii. 48). After the treaty of Winchester, August–September 1101 (*Cont. Hist. Dun. Eccles.*), or more probably after Robert's defeat at Tenchebrai (28 Sept. 1106), Rannulf obtained the king's favour. He sent envoys to the king, who came on to Lisieux, where the bishop received him with splendour. There Henry pardoned Rannulf's offences, and restored him the see of Durham (*Anglo-Saxon Chron.* ii. 205, 208–9; *Cont. Hist. Dun. Eccles.* i. 138; ORD. VIT. iv. 273–4; FLORENCE OF WORCESTER, ii. 49; WILLIAM OF MALMESBURY, p. 625).

Rannulf seems to have been a fully ordained priest by the time Anselm left the kingdom (c. 30 Oct. 1097) (ANSELM, *Epp.* l. iv. ep. 2); cf. FLOR. OF WORC. ii. 46), for the primate speaks of him as being 'professione sacerdos.' A somewhat apocryphal account shows us Rannulf, probably about the same date, as pulling down and rebuilding the primitive church at Twyneham (Christchurch, Hampshire), with its surrounding canon's houses (*Reg. de Twinham*, ap. DUGDALE, vi. 303). After the peace of Winchester Rannulf seems to have returned to Normandy. Gilbert Maminot, the aged bishop of Lisieux, died in August 1101 (ORD. VIT. iv. 116), and in the following June Rannulf procured the appointment of his brother Fulcher, who, though almost an illiterate person, held the post till his death in January 1102 or 1103 (*ib.*) Rannulf then persuaded the duke to make his son Thomas, a boy of some twelve years of age, his successor, on the condition that should Thomas die the succession was to pass to Rannulf's second son (*ib.*) During the boyhood of these two children Rannulf, seemingly with Henry's consent, ruled the bishopric for three years 'non ut præsul sed ut præses' (*ib.*; cf. IVO OF CHARTRES, *Epp.* 153, 154, 157, and 159). At last, apparently on his final restoration to Durham, he gave up all claim on Lisieux (ORD. VIT. iv. 274; cf. pp. 116–17).

Rannulf was at times in England during this period, and was at Durham when the relics of St. Cuthbert and Bede were translated (August 1104). He was sceptical as to the discovery till the great day of the ceremony —perhaps till the arrival of Alexander of Scotland—when he preached a sermon to the people (SIM. OF DURH. *Auct.* i. 252, 258, 260; cf. SIM. OF DURH. *Hist. Reg.* ii. 236; FLORENCE OF WORCESTER, ii. 53). He took part in Anselm's great consecration of Roger of Salisbury, and the four other bishops at Canterbury (11 Aug. 1107) (EADMER, *Hist. Nov.* p. 187). Next year he fruitlessly proposed to consecrate Thurgod to St. Andrews in Scotland, on the plea that Thomas, the new archbishop of York, could not legally perform the ceremony (*ib.* pp. 198–9). At the council of Northampton (1109) Henry confirmed Rannulf's claims against the men of Northumberland (*Script. Tres*, App. p. xxxii). Ten years later Henry sent him to the council of Rheims with orders to forbid the consecration of Thurstan to the archbishopric of York (19 Oct. 1119); but he arrived too late (ROGER OF HOVEDEN, i. 173–4). In 1127 he set out to attend the great ecclesiastical council at Westminster (13–16 May), but was forced to turn back through sickness, and in the same or the next year assisted his suffragan bishop of the Orkneys, Radulph, and Archbishop Thurstan in consecrating King Alexander's nominee to St. Andrews (*Cont.* of FLOR. OF WORC. ii. 86, 89; with which cf. HENRY OF HUNTINGDON, p. 247).

The concluding years of Rannulf's life were spent in architectural works. He completed to the very roof the nave of the cathedral, begun by his predecessor, William of St. Carilef [q. v.] He was a strenuous defender of the liberties of his see, and according to Surtees the charter is still extant in which Henry confers on him the privileges of his county palatine (SURTEES, i. xx). He was never, however, able to recover Carlisle and Teviotdale, which had been severed from his see in the days of his exile; and we are told that King Henry's hatred caused William II's charter to be destroyed (*Cont. Hist. Dun. Eccles.* i. 139–40). He renewed the walls of Durham, and guarded against a fire by removing all the mean dwellings that were huddled between the cathedral and the castle. He threw a stone bridge across the Wear, and founded a great castle (Norham) on the Tweed to guard against the incursions of the Scotch. His restless activity, says his biographer, was impatient of ease, and he 'passed from one work to another, reckoning nothing

finished unless he had some new project ready.' Two years before his death his health began to fail. As the dog-days drew on he took to his bed (1128). The fear of death made him distribute his money to the poor, and even induced him to pay his debts. The king, however, reclaimed all this wasted money after the bishop's decease. A month before his death he had himself borne into the church, bemoaned his evil doings, placed his ring upon the altar as a sign of restitution, and even attached his golden ring to the charter of his penitence (*ib.* pp. 139–41; cf. SURTEES, p. xx, note 9). He died on 5 Sept. 1128 (SIMEON OF DURHAM, *Hist. Reg.* ii. 283; cf. FLORENCE OF WORCESTER, ii. 91; *Anglo-Saxon Chron.* ii. 225).

In earlier life Rannulf was of a comely figure (ORD. VIT. iii. 310); but in later years he became full-bodied, and Orderic gives a curious account of the difficulties he had in escaping from the Tower (iv. 109). He was generous to the poor (*Cont. Hist. Dun. Eccles.* i. 140), and munificent to his own friends (ORD. VIT. iii. 310; cf. *Cont. Hist. Dun. Eccles.* i. 135–40). Besides the Thomas mentioned above Rannulf had at least two other children: Elias, a prebendary of Lincoln Cathedral, and Radnulf, the patron of St. Godric (DUGDALE, vi. 1273; *Vita Sti Godrici*, c. xx.), in whom Rannulf himself took an interest. Foss adds a brother, Geoffrey, 'whose daughter is mentioned in the Great Roll of Henry I' (Foss, i. 66; but cf. *Pipe Roll*, p. 79, where the entry is merely 'Fratris episcopi'). Rannulf's charters are sometimes signed by his nephews, Osbern (to whom he gave Bishop Middleton manors) and 'Raulf,' or Rannulf. For his other nephews, &c., see Surtees, p. xx and App. pp. cxxv–vi.

Both Dr. Stubbs and Mr. Freeman consider Rannulf to have introduced into England the most oppressive forms of military tenure; and he is 'distinctly charged with being the author of certain new and evil customs with regard to spiritual holdings' (FREEMAN, v. 377–8). Under William I, on a prelate's death, his immediate ecclesiastical superior, whether bishop or archbishop, became guardian of the ecclesiastical estates. But under Rannulf's rule the king claimed the wardship, and kept office vacant until he had sold it for money (ORD. VIT. iii. 313). Thus under Rannulf's influence the theory arose that all land on its owner's death lapsed back to the supreme landowner, the king, and had to be 'redeemed' by the next heir; the old English heriot was transformed into the 'relief;' and there came into prominence those almost equally annoying feudal incidents as to marriage, wardship, and right of testament which Henry I had to promise to reform in his charter. These had existed in embryo under William the Conqueror, or even earlier; but during Rannulf's rule they stiffened into abuses, and in this respect his influence was permanent; for Henry I did not abolish the new customs, he only amended them (FREEMAN, *Norman Conquest*, v. 374, &c., and *William Rufus*, p. 4). Constitutionally speaking, the days of Rannulf's power mark the time when the definite office (of the justiciarship) seems first to stand out distinctly (*Norman Conquest*, v. 203).

[Orderic Vitalis, ed. Le Prévost (Soc. de l'Hist. de France), 5 vols. The chief passages relating to Flambard are l. viii. c. 8, x. c. 18, xi. c. 31 ; Florence of Worcester, ed. Thorpe (Engl. Hist. Soc.); William of Malmesbury, Gesta Regum Angl. ed. Hardy (Engl. Hist. Soc.), paragraphs 314, 394, and Gesta Pontificum, ed. Stubbs (Rolls Ser.); Simeon of Durham and his continuators (ed. Arnold); Historia Dunelmensis Ecclesiæ, &c., vol. i.; Historia Regum, &c., vol. ii. (Rolls Ser.); Eadmer, Historia Novorum, ed. Rule (Rolls Ser.); Letters of Anselm, ap. Migne's Cursus Theologiæ, vol. clix. coll. 201–2; Letters of Ivo, bishop of Chartres, ap. Migne, vol. clxii. coll. 162, &c.; Henry of Huntingdon, ed. Arnold (Rolls Ser.); Roger of Hoveden, ed. Stubbs (Rolls Ser.); Anglo-Saxon Chronicle, ed. Thorpe, vol. i. text, vol. ii. translation (Rolls Ser.); Historiæ Dunelmensis Scriptores Tres, ed. Raine (Surtees Soc. 839); Domesday Book, vol. i. (ed. 1783); Dugdale's Monasticon, ed. 1817–30; Foss's Judges ; Campbell's Lives of the Chancellors (1848); Hardy's List of Chancellors, &c.; Domesday Studies, vol. i. (1888); Stubbs's Constitutional History, vol. i.; Freeman's Norman Conquest, vols. iv. v.; William Rufus, vols. i. ii.; Surtees's Durham, vol. i.; Vita Godrici, ed. Raine.]

T. A. A.

FLAMMOCK, THOMAS (*d.* 1497), rebel, usually described as a lawyer and attorney of Bodmin, was eldest son of Richard Flamank or Flammock of Boscarne, by Johanna or Jane, daughter of Thomas Lucombe of Bodmin (cf. *Visitation of Cornwall*, 1620, Harl. Soc. 71). The family is of great antiquity at Bodmin, having held the manor of Nanstallan in uninterrupted succession from the fourteenth to the nineteenth century (1817). In early times the name appeared as Flandrensis, Flemang, Flammank, and in other forms (MACLEAN). Thomas Flammock was the chief instigator of the Cornish rebellion of 1487. At the time Henry VII was attempting to collect a subsidy in Cornwall for the despatch of an army to Scotland to punish James IV for supporting Perkin Warbeck. Flammock argued that it was the business of the barons of the north, and of no other of the king's subjects, to defend the Scottish border, and that the tax was

illegal. Working with another popular agitator and fellow-townsman, Michael Joseph, a blacksmith, he suggested that the Cornishmen should march on London and present a petition to the king setting forth their grievances, and urging the punishment of Archbishop Morton and Sir Reginald Bray, and other advisers of the king who were held responsible for his action. Flammock and Joseph modestly consented to lead the throng until more eminent men took their place. Rudely armed with bills and bows and arrows, a vast mob followed Flammock to Taunton, where they made their first display of violence and slew ' the provost of Perin,' i.e. Penryn. At Wells, James, lord Audley [see TUCHET, JAMES], joined them and undertook the leadership. They marched thence by way of Salisbury and Winchester to Blackheath. London was panic-stricken; but the rebels had grown disheartened by the want of sympathy shown them in their long march. Giles, lord Daubeney, was directed to take the field with the forces which had been summoned for service in Scotland. On Saturday, 22 June 1497, Daubeney opened battle at Deptford Strand. At the first onset he was taken prisoner, but he was soon released, and the enemy, who had expected to be attacked on the Monday, and were thus taken by surprise, were soon thoroughly routed. Each side is said to have lost three hundred men, and fifteen hundred Cornishmen were taken prisoners. Audley, Flammock, and Joseph were among the latter. Audley was beheaded at Tower Hill. Flammock and Joseph were drawn, hanged, and quartered at Tyburn (24 June), and their limbs exhibited in various parts of the city. Most of their followers were pardoned. Flammock married Elizabeth, daughter of John Trelawny of Menwynick, and had a daughter Joanna, wife of Peter Fauntleroy.

[Bacon's Hist. of Henry VII; Thomas Gainsford's Hist. of Perkin Warbeck, 1618, in Harl. Miscellany, 1810, xi. 422–7 ; Stow's Annals, s. a. 1497; Boase and Courtney's Bibl. Cornub. p. 1181; Maclean's Trigg Minor, i. 44, 279–84, ii. 518 ; Polwhele's Hist. of Cornwall, iv. 53–4; Hals's Hist. of Cornwall, p. 24.]   S. L.

FLAMSTEED, JOHN (1646–1719), the first astronomer royal, born at Denby, five miles from Derby, 19 Aug. 1646, was the only son of Stephen Flamsteed, a maltster ; his mother, Mary, daughter of John Spateman, an ironmonger in Derby, died when he was three years old. He was educated at the free school of Derby, where his father resided. A cold caught in the summer of 1660 while bathing produced a rheumatic affection of the joints, accompanied by other ailments. He became unable to walk to school, and finally left it in May 1662. His self-training now began, and it was directed towards astronomy by the opportune loan of Sacrobosco's ' De Sphærâ.' In the intervals of prostrating illness he also read Fale's ' Art of Dialling,' Stirrup's ' Complete Diallist,' Gunter's 'Sector' and 'Canon,' and Oughtred's ' Canones Sinuum.' He observed the partial solar eclipse of 12 Sept. 1662, constructed a rude quadrant, and calculated a table of the sun's altitudes, pursuing his studies, as he said himself, ' under the discouragement of friends, the want of health, and all other instructors except his better genius.' Medical treatment, meantime, as varied as it was fruitless, was procured for him by his father. In the spring of 1664 he was sent to one Cromwell, ' cried up for cures by the nonconformist party; ' in 1665 he travelled to Ireland to be 'stroked' by Valentine Greatrakes [q. v.] A detailed account of the journey was found among his papers. He left Derby 16 Aug., borrowed a horse in Dublin, which carried him by easy stages to Cappoquin, and was operated upon 11 Sept., ' but found not his disease to stir.' His faith in the supernatural gifts of the ' stroker,' however, survived the disappointment, and he tried again at Worcester in the February following, with the same negative result, ' though several there were cured.'

His talents gradually brought him into notice. Among his patrons was Imanuel Halton of Wingfield Manor, who lent him the ' Rudolphine Tables,' Riccioli's ' Almagest,' and other mathematical books. For his friend, William Litchford, Flamsteed wrote, in August 1666, a paper on the construction and use of the quadrant, and in 1667 explained the causes of, and gave the first rules for, the equation of time in a tract, the publication of which in 1673, with Horrocks's 'Posthumous Works,' closed controversy on the subject. His first printed observation was of the solar eclipse of 25 Oct. 1668, which afforded him the discovery ' that the tables differed very much from the heavens.' Their rectification formed thenceforth the chief object of his labours.

Some calculations of appulses of the moon to fixed stars, which he forwarded to the Royal Society late in 1669 under the signature ' In Mathesi a sole fundes ' (an anagram of 'Johannes Flamsteedius '), were inserted in the 'Philosophical Transactions' (iv. 1099), and procured him a letter of thanks from Oldenburg and a correspondence during five years with John Collins (1625–1683) [q. v.]

About Easter 1670 he ' made a voyage to see London ; visited Mr. Oldenburg and Mr. Collins, and was by the last carried to see the Tower and Sir Jonas Moore ' (master of the ordnance), ' who presented me with Mr. Townley's micrometer and undertook to procure me glasses for a telescope to fit it.'

On his return from London he made acquaintance with Newton and Barrow at Cambridge, and entered his name at Jesus College. His systematic observations commenced in October 1671, and ' by the assistance of Mr. Townley's curious mensurator' they 'attained to the preciseness of 5″.' ' I had no pendulum movement,' he adds, 'to measure time with, they being not common in the country at that time. But I took the heights of the stars for finding the true time of my observations by a wood quadrant about eighteen inches radius fixed to the side of my seven-foot telescope, which I found performed well enough for my purpose.' This was by necessity limited to such determinations as needed no great accuracy in time, such as of the lunar and planetary diameters, and of the elongations of Jupiter's satellites. He soon discovered that the varying dimensions of the moon contradicted all theories of her motion save that of Horrocks, lately communicated to him by Townley, and its superiority was confirmed by an occultation of the Pleiades on 6 Nov. 1671. He accordingly undertook to render it practically available, fitting it for publication in 1673, at the joint request of Newton and Oldenburg, by the addition of numerical elements and a more detailed explanation (HORROCCII Op. Posth. p. 467). An improved edition of these tables was appended to Flamsteed's 'Doctrine of the Sphere,' included in Sir Jonas Moore's ' New System of the Mathematicks' (vol. i. 1680).

A ' monitum' of a favourable opposition of Mars in September 1672 was presented by him both to the Paris Academy of Sciences and to the Royal Society, and he deduced from his own observations of it at Townley in Lancashire a solar parallax ' not above 10″, corresponding to a distance of, at most, 21,000 terrestrial radii' (Phil. Trans. viii. 6100). His tract on the real and apparent diameters of the planets, written in 1673, furnished Newton with the data on the subject, employed in the third book of the ' Principia;' yet the oblateness of Jupiter's figure was, strange to say, first pointed out to Flamsteed by Cassini.

At Cambridge on 5 June 1674, he took a degree of M.A. per literas regias, designing to take orders and settle in a small living near Derby, which was in the gift of a friend of his father's. He was in London as a guest of Sir Jonas Moore's at the Tower 13 July to 17 Aug., and by his advice compiled a table of the tides for the king's use ; and the king and the Duke of York were each supplied with a barometer and thermometer made from his models, besides a copy of his rules for forecasting the weather by their means. Early in 1675 Moore again summoned him from Derby for the purpose of consulting him about the establishment of a private observatory at Chelsea to be placed under his direction.

A certain 'bold and indigent Frenchman,' calling himself the Sieur de St. Pierre, proposed at this juncture a scheme for finding the longitude at sea, and through the patronage of the Duchess of Portsmouth obtained a royal commission for its examination. Flamsteed was, by Sir Jonas Moore's interest, nominated a member, and easily showed the Frenchman's plan to be futile without a far more accurate knowledge of the places of the fixed stars, and of the moon's course among them, than was then possessed. Charles II thereupon exclaimed with vehemence that 'he must have them anew observed, examined, and corrected for the use of his seamen.' Flamsteed was accordingly appointed 'astronomical observator' by a royal warrant dated 4 March 1675, directing him 'forthwith to apply himself with the most exact care an 1 diligence to the rectifying the tables of the motions of the heavens, and the places of the fixed stars, so as to find out the so much desired longitude of places for the perfecting the art of navigation.' A site in Greenwich Park was chosen for the new observatory by Sir Christopher Wren, and the building was hastily run up from his design at a cost of 520l., realised by the sale of spoilt gunpowder.

Flamsteed was ordained by Bishop Gunning at Ely House at Easter 1675, and continued to observe at the Tower and afterwards at the queen's house in Greenwich Park, until 10 July 1676, when he removed to the Royal Observatory. He found it destitute of any instrument provided by the government; but Sir Jonas Moore gave him an iron sextant of seven feet radius, with two clocks by Tompion, and he brought from Derby a three-foot quadrant and two telescopes. His salary was 100l. a year, cut down by taxation to 90l., and for this pittance he was expected, not only to reform astronomy, but to instruct two boys from Christ's Hospital. His official assistant was a 'surly, silly labourer,' available for moving the sextant; and his large outlay in procuring skilled aid and improved instruments obliged him to take private pupils, numbering, between 1676 and 1709, about 140, many of them of the highest rank. Under these multiplied disadvantages, and in spite of continued ill-health, he achieved amazing results. The whole of the theories

and tables of the heavenly bodies then in use were visibly and widely erroneous. Flamsteed undertook the herculean task of revising them single-handed. 'My chief design,' he wrote to Dr. Seth Ward on 31 Jan. 1680, 'is to rectify the places of the fixed stars, and, of them, chiefly those near the ecliptic and in the moon's way' (BAILY, *Flamsteed*, p. 119). His first observation for the purpose was made on 19 Sept. 1676, and he had executed some twenty thousand by 1689. But they were made in the old way, by measuring intermutual distances, and gave only the relative places of the stars. He had as yet no instrument fit to determine the position of the equinox, but was compelled to take it on trust from Tycho Brahe. A small quadrant, lent to him by the Royal Society, was withdrawn after Sir Jonas Moore's death on 27 Aug. 1679, with which event, he remarks, 'fell all my hopes of having any allowance of expenses for making such instruments as I still wanted.' After some fruitless applications to government, he resolved to construct at his own cost a mural quadrant of fifty inches radius, which he himself set up and divided in 1683. With its aid he took the meridional altitudes of a number of stars with an estimated error of half a minute, and formed a rough working catalogue of some of the principal. But the quadrant proved too slight for stability, and the old sextant was after a time again resorted to.

In 1684 Flamsteed was presented by Lord North to the living of Burstow in Surrey, and his circumstances were further improved by his father's death in 1688. With the aid of Abraham Sharp [q. v.] he was thus enabled to undertake the construction of the mural arc with which all his most valuable work was executed. Its completion marked a great advance in the art of mathematical instrument making. The limb, firmly fixed in the meridian, was of 140°, and was divided with hitherto unapproached accuracy; the radius was of seven feet. Observations with it were begun on 12 Sept. 1689. 'From this moment,' Baily writes (*Flamsteed*, p. xxix), 'everything which Flamsteed did . . . was available to some useful purpose, his preceding observations being only subsidiary, and dependent on results to be afterwards deduced from some fixed instrument of this kind.' His first concern was to determine the latitude of the observatory, the obliquity of the ecliptic, and the position of the equinox; and the method employed for this last object, by which he ascertained absolute right ascensions through simultaneous observations of the sun and a star near both equinoxes, was original, and may be called the basis of modern astronomy. He determined in this way in 1690 the right ascensions of forty stars to serve as points of reference for the rest. The construction of a catalogue, more accurate and extensive than any yet existing, was his primary purpose; but he continued, as he advanced with it, to compute the errors and correct the tables of the sun, moon, and planets.

Flamsteed was elected into the Royal Society on 8 Feb. 1677; he sat on the council 1681–4, and again 1698–1700. But some years later he allowed his subscription to drop, and his name was, on 9 Nov. 1709, erased from the list of fellows. In December 1677 Dr. Bernard offered to resign the Savilian professorship of astronomy in his favour; but the project was soon found to be hopeless, owing to Flamsteed's not being a graduate of Oxford.

His observations on the great comet, extending from 22 Dec. 1680 to 15 Feb. 1681, were transmitted to Newton, and turned to account in the 'Principia.' He firmly held that they referred to the body already seen in November, which reappeared after passing the sun; while Newton believed that there were two comets, and only acknowledged his error in September 1685. His letter on the subject, however, shows no trace of the 'magisterial ridicule' which Flamsteed, in his subsequent ill-humour, declared had been thrown upon his opinion.

In a letter dated 10 Aug. 1691 Newton advised Flamsteed to print at once a preliminary catalogue of a few leading stars. But Flamsteed had large schemes in view which he could not bear to anticipate by partial publication, and importunities irritated without persuading him. Hence he drifted into a position of antagonism to his scientific contemporaries, which his infirmities of temper deplorably aggravated.

He attributed Newton's suggestion to the inimical influence of Halley [q. v.], of whom, in his reply, he spoke in rancorous terms. He never, it would seem, forgave him for indicating, in 1686, a mistake in his tide-tables (*Phil. Trans.* xvi. 192), and certainly did what he could to frustrate his hopes of the Savilian professorship in 1691. He disliked him besides for his 'bantering' manner, and rejected all efforts towards reconciliation.

Newton's resumption of his toil upon the lunar theory brought him into constant intercourse with the astronomer royal. 'Sir Isaac,' Flamsteed said afterwards, 'worked with the ore he had dug.' 'If he dug the ore,' Sir Isaac replied, 'I made the gold ring' (BREWSTER, *Memoirs of Newton*, ii. 178).

On 1 Sept. 1694 Newton visited the Royal Observatory, and Flamsteed, 'esteeming him to be an obliged friend,' explained the progress of his work, and gave him a hundred and fifty observed places of the moon with their tabular errors, for his private use in correcting the theory of her motions. He stipulated, however, that they should be imparted to no one else without his consent. Similar communications were repeated at intervals during sixteen months, not without chafings of spirit on both sides. Flamsteed was often ill, and always overworked; Newton was in consequence frequently kept waiting. There is evidence that he was occasionally kept waiting of set purpose; and his petulant letter of 9 July 1695 is largely excused by Flamsteed's admission that 'I did not think myself obliged to employ my pains to serve a person that was so inconsiderate as to presume he had a right to that which was only a courtesy. And I therefore went on with my business of the fixed stars, leaving Mr. Newton to examine the lunar observations over again' (BAILY, *Flamsteed*, p. 63). An offer of a pecuniary recompense for his communications was rejected with justifiable warmth; yet the consequence of their grudging bestowal probably was that Newton desisted in disgust from his efforts to complete the lunar theory (EDLESTON, *Correspondence of Newton and Cotes*, p. lxiv).

Flamsteed occasionally visited Newton in Jermyn Street after his appointment as warden of the mint, and found him civil, though less friendly than formerly. He, however, came to Greenwich on 4 Dec. 1698, and took away twelve lunar places.

In January 1694, on tabulating his observations of the pole-star, Flamsteed was surprised to find its polar distance always greater in July than in December. 'This is the first time, I am apt to think,' he wrote, 'that any real parallax hath been observed in the fixed stars.' The apparent displacements noted by him were, in fact, caused by the aberration of light, the value of which his observations, discussed by Peters, gave, with a close approach to accuracy, as $=20''.676$ (GRANT, *Hist. of Astron.* p. 477). He might easily have perceived that they were of a different character from any attributable to annual parallax, as J. J. Cassini at once pointed out (*Mém. de l'Ac. des Sciences*, 1699, p. 177). Flamsteed's 'Letter to Dr. Wallis on the Parallax of the Earth's Annual Orb' was published, turned into Latin, in Wallis's 'Opera Mathematica' (iii. 701, 1699). It contained a paragraph, inserted for the purpose of refuting the charge of uncommunicativeness current against him, referring to the lunar data imparted to Newton. Newton obtained the suppression of the statement; but Flamsteed's feelings towards him were thenceforth of unmitigated bitterness.

Newton nevertheless dined at the Royal Observatory on 11 April 1704. The real object of the visit was to ascertain the state of the catalogue, which Flamsteed, 'to obviate clamour,' had announced to be sufficiently forward for printing. It was about half finished, and Newton offered to recommend its publication to Prince George of Denmark. The astronomer royal 'civilly refused' the proposal. 'Plainly,' he added, 'his design was to get the honour of all my pains to himself.'

Yet the suggested plan was carried out. A committee of the Royal Society, including Newton, Wren, Arbuthnot, and Gregory, was appointed by the prince, and on 23 Jan. 1705 reported in favour of publication. The prince undertook the expense; arrangements were made for printing the catalogue and observations, and articles between Flamsteed, the 'referees' (as the members of the committee were called), and the printers were signed on 10 Nov. 1705.

A prolonged wrangle ensued. Each party accused the other of wilfully delaying the press, and a deadlock of many months was no unfrequent result of the contentions. Flamsteed gave free vent to his exasperation. His observations were made with his own instruments, and computed by his paid servants. He understood better than any man living how such a series ought to be presented, and naturally thought it a gross hardship to be placed at the mercy of a committee adverse to all his views.

There were discreditable suspicions on both sides. 'I fear,' Flamsteed wrote to Sharp on 28 Nov. 1705, 'Sir Isaac will still find ways to obstruct the publication of a work which perhaps he thinks may make him appear less. I have some reason to think he thrust himself into my affairs purposely to obstruct them.' On the other hand, it was resolved at a meeting of the referees on 13 July 1708 'that the press shall go on without further delay,' and 'that if Mr. Flamsteed do not take care that the proofs be well corrected and go on with dispatch, another corrector be employed.'

By Christmas 1707 the first volume, containing only the observations made with the sextant, 1676–89, was at last printed off, but as to the arrangement of the second there was total disagreement. While it was at its height the prince died, on 28 Oct. 1708, and the publication was suspended. Not illpleased, Flamsteed resumed his work with the catalogue. A board of visitors to the observatory, consisting of the president (Newton) and other members of the Royal Society, appointed by a royal order, dated 12 Dec. 1710, was, however, empowered both to superintend the publication and to take cognisance of official misconduct on the part of the astronomer-royal. Flamsteed's indignant protest elicited from Mr. Secretary St. John only the haughty reply that 'the queen would be obeyed.'

The visitors resumed without Flamsteed's knowledge the suspended printing of his catalogue. Two imperfect copies, comprising about three-fourths of the whole, had been deposited with the referees on 15 March 1706, and 20 March 1708, respectively. The first only was sealed, and Flamsteed raised a needless clamour about Newton's 'treachery' in opening it. The truth seems to be that the act complained of under the influence of subsequent wrath was accomplished, with Flamsteed's concurrence, as early as 1708. On 2 March 1711 he was applied to by Arbuthnot to complete the catalogue from his later observations, and at first appeared disposed to temporise; but on learning that Halley was the editor he kept no further terms, writing to Arbuthnot on 29 March 'that the neglect of me, and the ill-usage I had met with, was a dishonour to the queen and the nation, and would cause just reflections on the authors of it in future times' (BAILY, *Flamsteed*, p. 227).

In this temper he was summoned, on 26 Oct. 1711, to meet the president and other members of the board at the Royal Society's rooms in Crane Court. Requested to state the condition of his instruments, he declared they were his own, and he would suffer no one to concern himself with them. Whereupon Newton exclaimed, 'As good have no observatory as no instruments!' 'I proceeded from this,' Flamsteed relates, 'to tell Sir Isaac (who was fired) that I thought it the business of their society to encourage my labours, and not to make me uneasy for them, and that by their clandestine proceedings I was robbed of the fruits of my labours; that I had expended above 2,000*l.* in instruments and assistance. At this the impetuous man grew outrageous, and said, "We are, then, robbers of your labours." I answered, I was sorry they acknowledged themselves to be so. After this, all he said was in a rage. He called me many hard names—*puppy* was the most innocent of them. I only told him to keep his temper, restrain his passion, and thanked him as often as he gave me ill names (*ib* p. 228).

We have only Flamsteed's account of this unseemly altercation. It at any rate put the finishing touch to the hostility between him and Newton, and inspired Flamsteed's resolution of printing his observations according to his own plan and at his own expense. His petition to the queen for the suppression of what he termed a 'surreptitious' edition of his works was without effect. The 'Historia Cœlestis' appeared in 1712, in one folio volume, made up of two books, the first containing the catalogue and sextant observations; the second, observations made with Sharp's mural arc, 1689–1705. But the catalogue was the avowedly imperfect one deposited with the referees in 1708, and completed, without Flamsteed's concurrence, from such of his observations as could be made available. Halley was said to have boasted, in Child's coffee-house, of his pains in correcting its faults. Flamsteed called him a 'lazy and malicious thief,' and declared he had by his meddling 'very effectually spoiled' the work. The observations were incompletely and inaccurately given, and Halley's preface was undoubtedly an offensive document.

The energy displayed by Flamsteed during the last seven years of his life, in the midst of growing infirmities, was extraordinary. He was afflicted with a painful disease, prostrated by periodical headaches, and crippled with gout. 'Though I grow daily feebler,' he wrote in 1713, 'yet I have strength enough to carry on my business strenuously.' He observed diligently till within a few days of his death, while prosecuting his purpose of independent publication in spite of numerous difficulties. Newton's refusal to restore 175 sheets of his quadrant observations put him to an expense of 200l. in having them recopied; and he was compelled in 1716 to resort to legal proceedings for the recovery from him of four quarto volumes of 'Night Notes' (original entries of observations), entrusted to him for purposes of comparison in 1705. In the second edition of the 'Principia' Newton omitted several passages in which he had in 1687 acknowledged his obligations to his former friend.

The enlarged catalogue was hastily printed before the close of 1712, but only a few copies were allowed to be seen in strict confidence. The death of Queen Anne on 1 Aug. 1714, quickly followed by that of Halifax, Newton's patron, brought a turn in Flamsteed's favour. The new lord chamberlain was his friend, and a memorial to the lords of the treasury procured him possession of the three hundred remaining copies (out of four hundred) of the spurious 'Historia Cœlestis,' delivered to him by order of Sir Robert Walpole. Sparing only from each ninety-seven sheets of observations with the sextant, he immediately

committed them to the flames, 'as a sacrifice to heavenly truth,' and 'that none might remain to show the ingratitude of two of his countrymen who had used him worse than ever the noble Tycho was used in Denmark.' The extreme scarcity of the edition thus devastated is attested by the following inscription in a copy presented to the Bodleian Library by Sir Robert Walpole in 1725: 'Exemplar hoc "Historiæ Cœlestis," quod in thesauraria regia adservabatur, et cum paucis aliis vitaverat ignem et iram Flamsteedianum, Bibliotheca Bodleiana debet honorabili admodum viro Roberto Walpole, Scaccarii Cancellario,' &c. Its value is enhanced by a letter from Mrs. Flamsteed pasted into it, requesting its removal as an 'erroneous abridgment of Mr. Flamsteed's works.'

Taken ill on Sunday, 27 Dec. 1719, Flamsteed expired about 9.30 P.M. on the 31st. He remained sensible to the last, but speech failed, and his last wishes remained unuttered. He was buried in the chancel of the parish church of Burstow, but though funds were, by Mrs. Flamsteed's will, appropriated to the purpose, no monument has ever marked his grave (E. Dunkin, *Observatory*, iv. 234). He married, on 23 Oct. 1692, Margaret, daughter of Mr. Ralph Cooke of London, but had no children. He left about 350l. in ready money, and settled upon his widow 120l. a year in Exchequer and South Sea stock. He made no arrangements for the completion of his great work, of which the first and most of the second volume were printed at his decease. The devotion of his assistant, Joseph Crosthwait, supplied the omission. 'He has not left me in a capacity to serve him,' he wrote, 'notwithstanding he has often told me he would; but this I impute to his not being sensible of his near approach till it was too late; but the love, honour, and esteem I have, and shall always, for his memory and everything that belongs to him, will not permit me to leave Greenwich or London before, I hope, the three volumes are finished' (Baily, *Flamsteed*, p. 333). This was accomplished, with Sharp's assistance, in 1725.

Of the three folio volumes constituting the 'Historia Cœlestis Britannica,' the first comprised the observations of Gascoigne and Crabtree, 1638–43; those made by Flamsteed at Derby and the Tower, 1668–74, with the sextant observations at Greenwich 1676–89, spared from destruction with the edition of 1712. The second volume contained his observations with the mural arc, 1689–1720. The third opened with a disquisition entitled 'Prolegomena to the Catalogue,' on the progress of astronomy from the earliest ages, chiefly valuable for the description, with which it terminated, of the Greenwich instruments and methods; the catalogues of Ptolemy, Ulugh Beigh, Tycho Brahe, the Landgrave of Hesse, and Hevelius followed; finally came the 'British Catalogue' of 2,935 stars observed at Greenwich, to which Halley's southern stars were appended. A dedication to George I, by Margaret Flamsteed and James Hodgson (the husband of Flamsteed's niece), was prefixed to the first volume; but Flamsteed's vindication of his conduct was cancelled from the preface, doubtless out of regard to the reputation of Newton and Halley.

The appearance of the 'Atlas Cœlestis,' corresponding to the 'British Catalogue,' was delayed, owing to difficulties with engravers and lack of funds, until 1729. The figures of the constellations were drawn by Sir James Thornhill. Crosthwait's labours in editing his master's works thus extended over ten years, and involved the sacrifice of his own prospects in life. Yet he never received one farthing. For this signal act of injustice Mrs. Flamsteed was responsible. She showed, nevertheless, an active zeal for her husband's honour, and resisted with spirit and success the outrageous claim made by the government after his death to the possession of his instruments. She died on 29 July 1730, and was buried with him at Burstow.

Flamsteed was in many respects an excellent man—pious and conscientious, patient in suffering, of unimpeachable morality, and rigidly abstemious habits. His wife and servants were devoted to him, living and dead; but his naturally irritable temper, aggravated by disease, could not brook rivalry. He was keenly jealous of his professional reputation. His early reverence for Newton was recorded in the stray note among his observations: 'I study not for present applause; Mr. Newton's approbation is more to me than the cry of all the ignorant in the world.' Later he was not ashamed to call him 'our great pretender,' and to affect scorn for his 'speculations about gravity,' 'crotchets,' and 'conceptions.' The theory of gravitation he described in 1710 as 'Kepler's doctrine of magnetical fibres, improved by Sir C. Wren, and prosecuted by Sir I. Newton,' adding, 'I think I can lay some claim to a part of it.' He had certainly, in 1681, spoken of the attraction of the sun as determining the fall towards him of the great comet, but attributed the curve of its path to the resistance of the planetary vortex.

'Flamsteed,' Professor De Morgan wrote, 'was in fact Tycho Brahe with a telescope; there was the same capability of adapting instrumental means, the same sense of the in-

adequacy of existing tables, the same long-continued perseverance in actual observation' (*Penny Cyclopædia*). Nor was he a mere observer piling up data for others to employ, but diligently turned them to account for improving the power of prediction. His solar tables were constructed at the age of twenty-one, published in 1673 with Horrocks's 'Opera Posthuma,' and constantly, in subsequent years, amended. The discovery of the importance of the Horroxian lunar theory was due to him; he extended it to include the equations given by Newton in 1702, and he formed thence improved tables published in Lemonnier's 'Institutions Astronomiques' in 1746. He remarked the alternately and inversely accelerated and retarded movements of Jupiter and Saturn; determined the elements of the solar rotation, fixing its period at 25¼ days, and formed from diligent observations of sun-spots a theory of the solar constitution similar to that introduced later by Sir William Herschel, viz. 'that the substance of the sun is terrestrial matter, his light but the liquid menstruum encompassing him' (BREWSTER, *Newton*, ii. 103). He observed Uranus six times as a fixed star, the observation of 13 Dec. 1690 affording the earliest datum for the calculation of its orbit.

Flamsteed's 'British Catalogue' is styled by Baily 'one of the proudest productions of the Royal Observatory at Greenwich.' Its importance is due to its being the first collection of the kind made with the telescope and clock. Its value was necessarily impaired by defective reduction, and Flamsteed's neglect of Newton's advice to note the state of the barometer and thermometer at the time of his observations rendered it hopeless to attempt to educe from them improved results by modern processes of correction. The catalogue showed besides defects attributable to the absence of the author's final revision. Sir William Herschel detected errors so numerous as to suggest the need of an index to the original observations printed in the second volume of the 'Historia Cœlestis.' Miss Herschel undertook the task, and showed, by recomputing the place of each star, that Flamsteed had catalogued 111 stars which he had never observed, and observed 560 which he had not catalogued (*Phil. Trans.* lxxxvii. 293). Her catalogue of these inedited stars was published by order of the Royal Society in 1798; they were by Baily in 1829 arranged in order of right ascension, and identified (all but seventy) by comparison with later catalogues (*Memoirs R. Astr. Soc.* iv. 129).

Flamsteed's portrait was painted by Gibson in 1712. An engraving by Vertue was prefixed to the 'Historia Cœlestis,' and the original was bequeathed by Mrs. Flamsteed to the Royal Society. A replica is preserved in the Bodleian Library. The features are strongly marked, and bear little trace of age or infirmity ; the expression is intelligent and sensitive. Flamsteed was described by an old writer as a 'humorist and of warm passions.' That he occasionally relished a joke is shown in an anecdote related by him to his friend, Dr. Whiston, concerning the unexpected success with which he once assumed the character of a prophet (COLE, *Athenæ Cantabr.*; *Add. MS.* 5869, f. 77 ; *Notes and Queries*, 2nd ser. iii. 285). Peter the Great visited the Royal Observatory, and saw Flamsteed observe several times in February 1698.

Flamsteed's communications to the Royal Society extended from 1670 to 1686 (*Phil. Trans.* iv-xvi.), and his observations during 1713, 'abridged and spoiled,' as he affirmed, were sent to the same collection by Newton (*ib.* xxix. 285). 'A Correct Table of the Sun's Declination,' compiled by him, was inserted in Jones's 'Compendium of the Art of Navigation' (p. 103, 1702), and 'A Letter concerning Earthquakes,' in which he had attempted in 1693 to generalise the attendant circumstances of those phenomena, was published at London in 1750.

[The chief source of information regarding Flamsteed is Francis Baily's Account of the Rev. John Flamsteed, the first Astronomer Royal (London, 1835, 4to). The materials for this valuable work were derived largely from a mass of Flamsteed's manuscript books and papers, purchased by the Board of Longitude for 100*l.* in 1771, which lay in disorder at the Royal Observatory until Baily explored them. The incentive to the search was, however, derived from a collection of Flamsteed's original letters to Sharp, discovered after long years of neglect in a garret in Sharp's house at Little Horton in Yorkshire, and submitted to Baily in 1832. They were exhibited before the British Association in 1833 (Report, p. 462), and are now in the possession of the Rev. R. Harley, F.R.S., who has kindly permitted the present writer to inspect them. The collection includes 124 letters from Flamsteed, 60 from Crosthwait, and 1 from Mrs. Flamsteed, dated 15 Aug. 1720, all addressed to Sharp, whose replies are written in shorthand on the back of each. The first part of Baily's Account contains Flamsteed's History of his own Life and Labours, compiled from original manuscripts in his own handwriting. The narrative is in seven divisions. The first, designated 'The Self-Inspections of J. F.,' being an account of himself in the Actions and Studies of his twenty-one first years,' was partially made known in the life of the author published in the General Dictionary (v. 1737), the materials for which were supplied by James Hodgson. The second division, entitled 'Historica Narratio Vitæ Meæ,

ab anno 1646 ad 1675,' was composed in November 1707. Of the succeeding four, derived from scattered notices, No. 5 had been published in Hone's Every-day Book (i. 1091) ; while the seventh division, written February 1717, is the suppressed portion of the Original Preface to the Historia Cœlestis, and brings down the account of his life to 1716. An Appendix contains a variety of illustrative documents, besides Flamsteed's voluminous correspondence with Sharp, Newton, Wren, Halley, Wallis, Arbuthnot, Sir Jonas Moore, and others. The second part comprises the British Catalogue, corrected and enlarged to include 3,310 stars by Baily. An elaborate Introduction is prefixed, and a Supplement, added in 1837, gives Baily's reply to criticisms on the foregoing publication. See also Biog. Brit. arts. 'Flamsteed,' iii. 1943 (1750), 'Halley,' iv. 2509 (1757), 'Wallis,' vi. 4133 (1763); Rigaud's Correspondence of Scientific Men; Whewell's Flamsteed and Newton; Brewster's Memoirs of Sir Isaac Newton, vol. ii. ; Weld's Hist. R. Society, i. 377 ; Roger North's Life of Lord Keeper North, p. 286 ; Edinburgh Review, lxii. 359 (Galloway) ; Gent. Mag. 1866, i. 239 (Carpenter) ; Annuaire de l'Observatoire de Bruxelles, 1864, p. 288 (Mailly) ; Grant's Hist. of Astronomy, p. 467 ; Whewell's Hist. of the Inductive Sciences, ii. 162; Cunningham's Lives of Eminent Englishmen, iv. 366 ; Noble's Continuation of Granger, ii. 132 ; Montucla's Hist. des Mathématiques, iv. 41 ; Bailly's Hist. de l'Astr. Moderne, ii. 423, 589, 650; Delambre's Hist. de l'Astr. au xviii° Siècle, p. 93 ; Mädler's Gesch. der Himmelskunde, i. 397, 453 ; André et Rayet's Astr. Pratique, i. 3; Watt's Bibl. Brit.; Acta Eruditorum, 1721, p. 463 ; Journal R. Society, xvii. 129 ; Rigaud MSS. in Bodleian, Letter L; MSS. Collegii Corporis Christi, Oxon. Codex ccclxi. (correspondence of Flamsteed with Newton and Wallis in forty original letters, mostly printed in General Dict.) ; C. H. F. Peters on Flamsteed's Lost Stars, Memoirs American Academy, 1887, pt. iii. Flamsteed's horoscope of the Royal Observatory, 10 Aug. 1675, inscribed 'Risum teneatis, amici ? ' is reproduced in Hone's Everyday Book, i. 1090.] A. M. C.

FLANAGAN, RODERICK (1828–1861), journalist, son of an Irish farmer, was born near Elphin, co. Roscommon, in April 1828. His parents, with a numerous family, emigrated to New South Wales in 1840, and settled in Sydney, where Flanagan received his education. At the age of fourteen he was apprenticed to a printer, and on the completion of his indentures became attached to the 'People's Advocate.' After contributing to the 'Advocate,' the 'Empire,' the 'Freeman's Journal,' and other newspapers for several years, he founded, in conjunction with his brother, E. F. Flanagan, a weekly journal called 'The Chronicle.' It had only a brief existence, and upon its cessation

Flanagan became a member of the staff of the 'Empire.' He was subsequently chief editor of that journal, and during his connection with it published a series of essays on the aboriginals which attracted much attention. The writer dealt with the manners and customs of the natives, and severely criticised the treatment they had received at the hands of the colonists. In 1854 Flanagan joined the literary corps of the 'Sydney Morning Herald,' and in the columns of that newspaper he shortly began to grapple with the numerous events which tended to the making of New South Wales. For nearly four years he laboured arduously at his task of writing the history of the colony, and by November 1860 had made such progress in his undertaking that he left Sydney for London, bearing his manuscript with him. He succeeded in making arrangements for the publication of the work, but while engaged in revising the proof-sheets of the first volume was seized with illness, the result of over-exertion. He died towards the close of 1861, and was buried at a cemetery near London, where a public monument has been erected to his memory. Flanagan's work was posthumously issued in 1862, in 2 vols., under the title of the 'History of New South Wales; with an Account of Van Diemen's Land (Tasmania), New Zealand, Port Phillip (Victoria), Moreton Bay, and other Australasian Settlements.' While narrating the events which have marked the progress of New South Wales from the earliest times till beyond the middle of the nineteenth century, Flanagan also succeeded in bringing into one view the whole of the British Australasian territories. The work was pronounced to be the most comprehensive, moderate, and most generally accurate of any which had hitherto appeared dealing with the Australasian colonies.

[Heaton's Australian Dictionary of Dates and Men of the Time, 1879; Athenæum, 25 Oct. 1862.]   G. B. S.

FLANAGAN, THOMAS (1814–1865), historical compiler, born in 1814, was educated at Sedgley Park School, Staffordshire, and at St. Mary's College, Oscott, where he remained as a professor, and was prefect of studies for many years. In 1851 he was appointed vice-president of Sedgley Park, and in August the same year he became the ninth president of that institution, in succession to Dr. James Brown, who, on the restoration of the catholic hierarchy by Pope Pius IX, had been advanced to the see of Shrewsbury. Flanagan was also nominated one of the original canons of the newly erected chapter of Birmingham. In July 1853 he resigned the presidentship of Sedgley Park, and returned to Oscott as prefect of studies. In 1854 he was appointed resident priest at Blackmore Park, and in 1860 he removed to St. Chad's Cathedral, Birmingham. He died on 21 July 1865 at Kidderminster, whither he had gone for the benefit of his health.

In addition to some controversial tracts, he wrote: 1. 'A Manual of British and Irish History; illustrated with maps, engravings, and statistical, chronological, and genealogical tables,' London, 1847, 12mo, 1851, 8vo. 2. 'A Short Catechism of English History, ecclesiastical and civil, for children,' London, 1851, 16mo. 3. 'A History of the Church in England, from the earliest period, to the re-establishment of the Hierarchy in 1850,' 2 vols., London, 1857, 8vo, the only work hitherto published which gives a continuous history of the Roman catholic church in England since the revolution of 1688. 4. 'A History of the Middle Ages,' manuscript, commenced at Sedgley Park, but never completed.

[Husenbeth's Hist. of Sedgley Park School, pp. 243, 244; Tablet, 29 July 1865, p. 468; Weekly Register, 5 Aug. 1865, p. 85; Gillow's Bibl. Dict.]   T. C.

FLANN (d. 1056), Irish historian, commonly called Mainistrech (of the monastery), son of Eochaidh Erann, was twenty-second in descent from Ailill Oluim, king of Munster, according to some Irish historians (McFIRBIS in CURRY, Cath Muighe Leana, p. 175); but this genealogy may justly be suspected to be an attempt to connect Flann after he became famous with St. Buite [q. v.], founder of Mainister Buite, now Monasterboice, co. Louth, the monastery in which this historian spent most of his life. He attained a great reputation for historical learning in his own time, and has since been constantly quoted by all writers of history in the Irish language. He is called 'airdferleighinn ocus sui senchusa Erenn,' archreader and sage of historical knowledge of Ireland (Annals of Ulster, i. 599, ed. Hennessy), and 'ferléighind Mainistreach Buithe,' reader of Monasterboice (Annala R. Eireann, ii. 870). O'Curry (Manners and Customs of the Ancient Irish, vol. ii.) has tried to prove that he was not an ecclesiastic; but the verses on his death quoted in the annals (A. R. I. ii. 870) prove the contrary, 'Fland a primchill Buithi bind' (Flann of the chief church of melodious Buithe), while the ages of his sons, with the date of his compositions, favour the conclusion that he began life as a poetical historian, wandering through the northern half of Ireland,

and that he retired for his later years into the monastic clan of St. Buite. He had two sons, of whom Echtighern, the elder, became airchennach of Monasterboice, died 1067 (*ib.* ii. 890), and left two sons, Eoghan, who died in 1117, and Feargna, who became a priest, and died in 1122. His second son, Feidhlimidh, died in 1104, and was also famous as an historian. The third son mentioned in some accounts is due to a clerical error. The local writings of Flann refer mainly to the northern half of Ireland. He calls Brian Boroimhe [see BRIAN] 'sun of the hills of West Munster,' but chiefly celebrates the achievements of the descendants of Nial Naighiallach, and nowhere extols the Dal Cais, so that he is to be regarded as a northern writer. His writings are interesting as the genuine productions of an Irish historian of the eleventh century. They have never been critically examined, and the lists given by O'Reilly, who enumerates fourteen (*Transactions of the Iberno-Celtic Society* for 1820, p. 75), and by O'Curry (*Manners and Customs of the Ancient Irish*, ii. 149), who mentions nineteen, require revision. His poem on the kings of Tara (*Book of Leinster*, facs. 132 *b*, line 6) ends with Maelsechlainn, who died in 1021; that on the Cinel Eoghain ends with an O'Neill who died in 1036. Flann himself died on 17 Nov. 1056 (*A. R. I.* ii. 870). The beautiful stone cross of Muiredach, still standing in the enclosure of Monasterboice, was there in the time of Flann, and it is probable that he was also familiar with the loftier carved cross and with the curious leaning round tower. The earliest extant manuscript text of any of his writings comes within fifty years of his death, and is a poem on King Aedh Sláine in 'Lebar na h-Uidhre' (fol. 53 *a*, line 3), beginning 'Muguin ingen choncruid mac Duach don desmumhain' (Muguin, daughter of Conchruid, son of Duach, of South Munster), and relating how, through the prayers of a saint, the queen, till then childless, first gave birth to a salmon, then to a lamb, and last of all to the famous king, Aedh Sláine. 'The Book of Leinster,' a manuscript of the latter part of the twelfth century, contains eleven poems of his, viz. (1) f. 27 *b*, 54, on a famous assembly of poets; (2) f. 131 *b*, 34, on the kings of Tara to the death of Dathi; (3) 132 *b*, 6, on the kings of Tara from Loeghaire to Moelsechlainn; (4) 145 *b*, 19, a later text of the poem on Aedh Sláine; (5) 181 *a*, 1, on the fortress of Ailech (co. Donegal); (6) 181 *b*, 11, on Ailech; (7) 182 *a*, 24, on the deeds of the seed of Eoghain; (8) 182 *b*, 12, on sixty victories of the clan Eoghain; (9) 183 *b*, 17, on clan Eoghain; (10) 184 *b*, 20, on kings

of Meath; (11) 185 *b*, 1, the names of the kings of the race of Aedh Sláine. 'The Book of Ballymote,' a manuscript of the beginning of the fifteenth century, contains (f. 11) a copy of 'Leabhar comaimsirech du Flainn' (i.e. Flann's Book of Synchronisms), a tale of the kings of the outer world and of Ireland in prose and verse. 'The Book of Lecan,' written in 1416, contains (PETRIE, *Ecclesiastical Architecture of Ireland*, p. 142) a poem on the household of St. Patrick. Part of the same poem is quoted in the 'Annals' (*A. R. I.* i. 130).

[O'Reilly, Transactions of Iberno-Celtic Society for 1820, Dublin; Curry's Cath Muighe Leana (Celtic Society), Dublin, 1855; Manuscript Materials of Ancient Irish History, Dublin, 1873; Petrie's Ecclesiastical Architecture of Ireland, Dublin, 1845; Dunraven's Notes on Irish Architecture, London, 1877; Royal Irish Academy, Facsimiles of Lebar na h-Uidhre, Book of Leinster; Book of Ballymote.] N. M.

FLANNAN, SAINT and BISHOP of Cill-da-Lua, now Killaloe (*fl.* 7th cent.), was son of Torrdelbach (called also Theodoric), son of Cathal, king of Munster. Torrdelbach ruled the territory of Ui Torrdelbaigh, nearly co-extensive with the present diocese of Killaloe. He was a very pious and charitable king. Flannan was sent at an early age to St. Blathmac, 'who surpassed all the saints.' Blathmac trained him in sacred literature and taught him 'to plough, sow, reap, grind, sift, and bake with his own hands for the monks.' He was next sent to Molua, who was reckoned among the greatest saints in Ireland, and is mentioned by St. Bernard as the 'founder of a hundred monasteries.' Molua is said to have resigned his bishopric in consequence of his engagements in England and Scotland, and to have appointed Flannan as his successor. But Molua or Lua, the founder of Killaloe, died, according to the 'Annals of the Four Masters,' in 588, or 592 in Bishop Reeves's 'Adamnan.' The date of his death proves that the alleged transaction with Flannan is impossible. It was probably meant to account for Flannan's being the patron saint of Killaloe, though not the founder.

Flannan, now appointed to a bishopric, wished to visit Rome and receive holy orders from Pope John; and, according to Ware, he was consecrated at Rome by Pope John IV in 639, who, however, was not pope until 640. His parents and friends had strenuously objected to the journey; St. Bracan, probably St. Berchan of Cluain Sosta or Clonsast in the King's County, who flourished, according to O'Curry, in 690, had vainly endeavoured to dissuade Flannan from his purpose, but finding his resolution fixed, they had earnestly prayed for a ship, and Flannan had been granted a miraculous voyage on a smooth stone. This legend, which has probably no foundation in fact at all, was known 'all over the south of Ireland when the Emperor Frederick took Milan.' Returning home through Tuscany, Burgundy, and France. Torrdelbach with his chieftains conducted him to Killaloe, and some Romans who attended him received permission to settle on an island near. Then all the saints and chiefs of the kingdom, far and near, came to hear what 'new rules and instructions and sacraments of holy church he had brought from the church and court of Rome.' Flannan's discourse in answer so affected Torrdelbach that the king sought the monastery of St. Colman at Lismore, where he became a monk, and with his companions laboured in clearing the ground. On Torrdelbach's return to Killaloe by direction of St. Colman he refused Flannan's entreaties to resume his kingdom, and died on his way back to Lismore.

Flannan, disappointed by the lukewarmness of his hearers, set sail for the Isle of Man. There nine men of horrid aspect demanded of him nine black rams. When he hesitated about complying, they threatened to 'defame him as long as they lived.' Flannan used to 'sing his psalter in cold rivers,' and fearing that he might be called on to desert his religious life and become king, he besought his Creator to send him some disfiguring blemish. In answer to his prayer he was visited by the 'disease called morphea, which is the sixth species of elephantiasis, and forthwith rashes and erysipelas and boils began to appear on his face, so that it became dreadful and repulsive.' Thus by native law he was ineligible for the throne. There is no record of the time or place either of his birth or death, but Dr. Lanigan conjectures that he was born in 640 or 650. In after times his bones were placed in a shrine wrought with wondrous art, and covered with gold and silver, which was placed on the altar of Cill-da-Lua. His memorials, that is his gospels, bells, and staff, were also ornamented with artistic skill and covered with the purest gold. There are still to be seen at Killaloe the church of Molua, on an island in the Shannon, and the oratory of St. Flannan, also called his 'house.' They are coeval with these saints according to Dr. Petrie, and the oratory served the twofold purpose of a church and a house like that at St. Doulough's. Ware, referring to St. Flannan's occupancy, says : 'While he sat there his father Theodoric endowed the church of Killaloe with many estates, and dying full of years

was magnificently interred in this church by his son Flannan.'

The life from which most of the foregoing particulars are taken was evidently written by one who desired to flatter the O'Briens, who were descended from Torrdelbach. This family was mainly instrumental in bringing in the customs of the Roman church to the south of Ireland, and hence the account of St. Flannan's visit to Rome, which would be highly improbable in the seventh or eighth century, though not in the twelfth or thirteenth, when in all probability this life was written. Flannan's day is 18 Dec.

[Vita Flannani Episcopi et Confessoris Codex Salmanticensis, pp. 643–80, London, 1888; Lanigan's Eccl. Hist. ii. 205, 211, iii. 147–9 ; Petrie's Round Towers, pp. 274–8 ; Martyrology of Donegal, pp. 179, 341; O'Curry's MS. Materials, p. 412; Reeves's Adamnan, pp. 34, 371 ; Ussher's Works, vi. 476.]
T. O.

FLATMAN, THOMAS (1637–1688), poet and miniature-painter, was admitted a scholar of Winchester College 22 Sept. 1649, being eleven years of age at the previous Michaelmas, and from Winchester he was admitted 11 Sept. 1654 to a scholarship at New College, Oxford. In the register of his admission to Winchester he is stated to have been born in Red Cross Street, London ; in the New College register he is said to have come from Aldersgate Street. He was a fellow of New College in 1656, and in that year contributed to the collection of Oxford verses on the death of Charles Capel. In 1657 he left Oxford, without a degree, for the Inner Temple. He was created M.A. of Cambridge by the king's letters, dated 11 Dec. 1666, 'being then A.B. of Oxford, as is there described' (BAKER, ap. WOOD, *Athenæ*, ed. Bliss).

Having settled in London he devoted his talents to painting and poetry. As a miniature-painter he was, and is, greatly esteemed; but his poetry, which was received with applause by his contemporaries, has been unduly depreciated by later critics. Granger declares that 'one of his heads is worth a ream of his Pindarics.' His Pindarics deserve the derision of Rochester :—

Flatman, who Cowley imitates with pains,
And rides a jaded muse whipt with loose reins.

But his other poems are better. 'A Thought of Death' (which Pope imitated in 'The Dying Christian to his Soul') and 'Death. A Song,' are singularly impressive; the 'Hymn for the Morning' and 'Another for the Evening' are choice examples of devotional verse ; and some of the lighter poems, notably the paraphrases of select odes of Horace, are elegant.

Flatman's 'Poems and Songs' were first collected in 1674, 8vo, and reached a fourth edition in 1686. Prefixed are commendatory verses by Walter Pope (only in first edition), Charles Cotton, Richard Newcourt, and others. In the third and fourth editions are a portrait of the author, engraved by R. White, and a dedicatory epistle to the Duke of Ormonde, who is said to have been so pleased with the ode on the death of his son, the Earl of Ossory (published in 1680), that he sent the poet a diamond ring. The edition of 1686 is the most complete. Some of the poems were in the first instance published separately, or had appeared in other collections. 'A Panegyrick . . . to Charles the Second,' s. sh. fol. 1660, and two copies of verses prefixed to Sanderson's 'Graphice,' 1658, were not reprinted; but Flatman was careful to collect most of his scattered poems. Among his 'Poems and Songs' he included his commendatory verses before Faithorne's 'Art of Graveing,' 1662, 'Poems by Mrs. Katherine Philips, the Matchless Orinda,' 1667, Creech's translation of 'Lucretius,' 2nd edit. 1683, and Izaak Walton's edition of Chalkhill's 'Thealma and Clearchus,' 1683; also some satirical verses contributed to 'Naps upon Parnassus,' 1658 [see AUSTIN, SAMUEL, the younger].

He died in Three-leg Alley, St. Bride's, London, 8 Dec. 1688, and was buried in the parish church. On 26 Nov. 1672 he had married a 'fair virgin' of some fortune, and in Hacket's epitaphs there is an epitaph upon one of his sons. Flatman is said to have possessed a small estate at Tishton, near Diss. Two miniature portraits of him, painted by himself, are preserved; one in the collection of the Duke of Buccleuch, and another in the Dyce collection at South Kensington. There are also portraits of him by Sir Peter Lely and by Faithorne.

Wood ascribes to him 'Montelion's Almanac' for 1661 and 1662; also a mock romance, 'Don Juan Lamberto: or, a Comical History of the Late Times. By Montelion, Knight of the Oracle,' &c., b. l., two parts, 1661, 4to (reprinted in vol. vii. of 'Somers Tracts,' 1812), 'to both which parts (very witty and satyrical), tho' the disguis'd name of Montelion, Knight of the Oracle, &c., is set, yet the acquaintance and contemporaries of Th. Flatman always confidently aver'd that the said Flatman was the author of them.' A satirical tract, 'Heraclitus Ridens,' 1681, has been attributed to Flatman. Wood (*Fasti*, ed. Bliss, ii. 37) states that in May 1672 'there had like to have been a poetical war' between Flatman and Dr. Robert Wild; but 'how it was ended I cannot tell.'

[Wood's Athenæ, ed. Bliss, iv. 244–6; Granger's Biog. Hist. 2nd ed. iv. 54–6, 117–18; Walpole's Anecdotes of Painting. 1849, pp. 460–1; Gent. Mag. March 1834; Notes and Queries, 4th ser. iv. 251; Godwin's Lives of Edward and John Phillips, p. 113, &c.; Hunter's Chorus Vatum, Addit. MS. 24490, fol. 206; Corser's Collectanea; Redgrave's Dictionary of Artists; information kindly supplied by the Warden of New College, Oxford.]   A. H. B.

FLATTISBURY, PHILIP (*fl.* 1500), compiler, was of a family members of which, from the thirteenth century, held important positions as landowners in the county of Kildare, Ireland, and occasionally filled legal offices under the English government there. Flattisbury appears to have been a retainer of Gerald Fitzgerald, eighth earl of Kildare [q. v.], deputy-governor of Ireland under Henry VII and Henry VIII. In 1503 Flattisbury made for that nobleman a compilation styled the 'Red Book of the Earls of Kildare.' This volume consists mainly of documents connected with or bearing upon the lands and possessions of the Geraldine house of Kildare. This volume was sought for eagerly, but in vain, by the governmental agents at the time of the attainder of the heads of the house of Kildare in 1537. It is now in the possession of the Duke of Leinster. A reproduction from it was given on plate lx. of the third part of 'Facsimiles of National MSS. of Ireland,' published in 1879.

Flattisbury also transcribed for Gerald, ninth earl of Kildare [q. v.], in 1517, a collection of Anglo-Irish annals in Latin, terminating in 1370 [see PEMBRIDGE, CHRISTOPHER]. To them he appended at the end a few lines of additional matter, with a brief panegyric on the Earl of Kildare. The manuscript bears the following title: 'Hic inferius sequuntur diversæ Cronicæ ad requisitionem nobilis et præpotentis domini, Geraldi filii Geraldi, deputati domini regis Hiberniæ, scriptæ per Philippum Flattisbury de Johnston juxta le Naas, anno Domini mdxvii. et anno regni Henrici Octavi ix.' Edmund Campion, in his 'History of Ireland,' written in 1571, and Richard Stanihurst, somewhat later, referred erroneously to Flattisbury as the author of the annals of which he was the transcriber. Stanihurst did not record the date of Flattisbury's death, but mentioned that it took place 'at his town styled Johnstown,' near Naas, in Kildare, and observes that he was a 'worthy gentleman and a diligent antiquary.' The original annals, from which Flattisbury transcribed, were printed for the first time in 1607 by Camden, in his 'Britannia,' from a manuscript lent to him by Lord Howard of Naworth, and subsequently presented by Archbishop Laud to the Bodleian Library, where it is now preserved. A new edition from the manuscript used by Camden, and collated with fragments of an older one unknown to him, was published by the writer of the present notice in the appendix to the 'Chartularies of St. Mary's Abbey, Dublin,' Rolls Series, 1885.

[State Papers, Ireland, Public Record Office, London; Patent Rolls and Chancery Inquisitions, Ireland; MSS., Trinity College, Dublin; Holinshed's Chronicles, 1586; Hist. of Ireland, Dublin, 1633; Ware, De Scriptoribus Hiberniæ, 1639; William Nicholson's Historical Library, 1724; Hist. MSS. Comm., 8th Rep. 1881.]

J. T. G.

FLAVEL, JOHN (1596–1617), logician, was born in 1596 at Bishop's Lydeard, Somersetshire, where his father was a clergyman. He matriculated, 25 Jan. 1610–11, at Trinity College, Oxford, and developed a turn for logical disputation. In 1613 he was made one of the first scholars of Wadham College. He graduated B.A. on 28 June 1614, and lectured on logic. Proceeding M.A. on 23 June 1617, he was in the same year chosen professor of grammar. He had skill in Greek and Latin verse. He died on 10 Nov. 1617, and was buried in Wadham College chapel.

After Flavel's death, Alexander Huish, of Wadham College, edited from his manuscript a logical treatise, with the title, 'Tractatus de Demonstratione Methodicus et Polemicus,' &c., Oxford, 1619, 16mo. The treatise, which is in four books, was not intended for publication. Huish dedicates it (1 March 1618–19) to Arthur Lake, bishop of Bath and Wells.

Wood mentions 'Grammat. Græc. Enchyridion,' 8vo (not seen), by Joh. Flavell, possibly the subject of this article.

[Wood's Athenæ Oxon. (Bliss), ii. 207, 355, 371; Flavel's Tractatus; Oxf. Univ. Reg. (Oxf. Hist. Soc.), ii. ii. 321, iii. 328.]

A. G.

FLAVEL, JOHN (1630?–1691), presbyterian divine, eldest son of the Rev. Richard Flavel, described as 'a painful and eminent minister,' who was incumbent successively of Bromsgrove, Worcestershire, Hasler and Willersey, Gloucestershire (from which last living he was ejected in 1662), was born in or about 1630 at Bromsgrove. Having received his early education at the schools of the neighbourhood, he entered University College, Oxford, at an early age, and gained a good reputation for talent and diligence. On 27 April 1650 he was sent by 'the standing committee of Devon' to Diptford, a parish on the Avon, five miles from Totnes, where the minister, Mr. Walplate, had become infirm. On 17 Oct. 1650, after examination and the preaching of a 'trial

sermon,' he was ordained Mr. Walplate's assistant by the classis at Salisbury. He continued to minister at Diptford for about six years, succeeding the senior minister when he died, and endearing himself greatly to the people, not only by his earnestness, but by his easy dealings with them in the matter of tithes. In 1656 he removed to Dartmouth, though the Diptford emoluments were much greater. On the passing of the Act of Uniformity (1662) he was ejected, but continued to preach in private until the Five Mile Act drove him from Dartmouth. He kept as near it, however, as possible, removing to Slapton, five miles off, and there preached twice each Sunday to all who came, among whom were many of his old parishioners. On the granting of the indulgence of 1671 he returned to Dartmouth, and continued to officiate there even after the liberty to do so was withdrawn. In the end he found himself obliged to remove to London, travelling by sea and narrowly escaping shipwreck in a storm, which is said to have ceased in answer to his prayers. Finding that he would be safer at Dartmouth he returned there, and met with his people nightly in his own house, until in 1687, on the relaxation of the penal laws, they built a meeting-house for him. Just before his death he acted as moderator at a meeting of dissenting ministers held at Topsham. He died suddenly of paralysis at Exeter on 26 June 1691, and was buried in Dartmouth churchyard. Wood bitterly comments on the violence of his dissent.

Flavel was four times married: first to Jane Randal; secondly, to Elizabeth Morries; thirdly, to Ann Downe; and, lastly, to a daughter of the Rev. George Jeffries. There is a portrait of him in Dr. Williams's library, London.

He was a voluminous and popular author. There is a play of fine fancy in some of them, such as the 'Husbandry Spiritualised.' All display vigorous diction and strong evangelical sentiments. They comprise: 1. 'Husbandry Spiritualised,' Lond. 1669. 2. 'Navigation Spiritualised,' Lond. 1671. 3. 'The Fountain of Life Opened, or a Display of Christ in his Essential and Mediatorial Glory, containing forty-two sermons,' Lond. 1672. 4. 'A Saint indeed,' Lond. 1671. 5. 'A Token for Mourners,' Lond. 1674. 6. 'The Seaman's Companion,' Lond. 1676. 7. 'Divine Conduct, or the Mystery of Providence Opened, Lond. 1678, 1814, 1822. 8. 'The Touchstone of Sincerity,' Lond. 1678. 9. 'The Method of Grace in the Gospel Redemption,' Lond. 1680. 10. 'A Practical Treatise of Fear, wherein the various Kinds, Uses, Causes, Effects, and Remedies thereof are distinctly opened and prescribed,' Lond. 1682. 11. 'The Righteous Man's Refuge,' Lond. 1681. 12. 'Preparations for Sufferings, or the Best Work in the Worst Times,' Lond. 1682. 13. 'England's Duty under the present Gospel Liberty,' Lond. 1689. 14. 'Mount Pisgah, or a Thanksgiving Sermon for England's Delivery from Popery,' Lond. 1689. 15. 'Sacramental Meditations upon divers select places of Scripture,' Lond. 1689. 16. 'The Reasonableness of Personal Reformation and the Necessity of Conversion,' Lond. 1691. 17. 'An Exposition of the Assembly's Catechism,' Lond. 1693. 18. 'Pneumatologia, a Treatise of the Soul of Man,' Lond. 1698. 19. 'Planelogia, a succinct and seasonable Discourse of the Occasions, Causes, Nature, Rise, Growth, and Remedies of Mental Errors.' 20. 'Vindiciarum Vindex, or a Refutation of the weak and impertinent Rejoinder of Mr. Philip Carey' (a leading anabaptist in Dartmouth). 21. 'Gospel Unity recommended to the Churches of Christ.' 22. 'A Faithful and Succinct Account of some late and wonderful Sea Deliverances.' 23. 'Antipharmacum Saluberrimum, or a serious and seasonable Caveat to all the Saints in this Hour of Temptation.' 24. 'Tydings from Rome, or England's Alarm.' 25. 'A pathetic and serious Dissuasive from the horrid and detestable Sins of Drunkenness, Swearing, Uncleanness, Forgetfulness of Mercies, Violation of Promises, and Atheistical Contempt of Death.' 26. 'The Balm of the Covenant applied to the Bleeding Wounds of afflicted Saints.' 27. 'Vindiciæ Legis et Fœderis.' 28. 'A Familiar Conference between a Minister and a doubting Christian concerning the Sacrament of the Lord's Supper.' 29. 'A Table or Scheme of the Sins and Duties of Believers.' Many editions of several of these treatises have appeared. Collected editions were issued in 1673, 1701, 1716, 1754, 1770 (Paisley), and 1797 (6 vols. Newcastle). Charles Bradley [q. v.] edited a selection in 1823.

[Life prefixed to collected edition of his Works, Glasgow, 1754; Palmer's Nonconf. Mem. ii. 18–22; Wood's Athenæ Oxon. (Bliss), iv. 323–6.]

T. H.

FLAXMAN, JOHN (1755–1826), sculptor and draughtsman, was born at York on 6 July 1755. According to a family tradition four brothers Flaxman, coming from Norfolk, had fought against the king at Naseby, and the youngest of the four, named John, had settled as a farmer and carrier in Buckinghamshire. From him was descended another John, who towards the middle of the eighteenth century carried on, partly in London and partly in the provinces, the trade of a maker and seller of plaster casts. He had a good connection among artists, and was employed as a modeller by some of the chief sculptors of the day, including Roubilliac and Scheemakers. He and his wife (whose maiden name was Lee) were on business at York at the time when their second son, the subject of the present article, was born. Six months afterwards the family returned to London, and the childhood of the sculptor was spent almost entirely in his father's shop at the sign of the Golden Head, New Street, Covent Garden. As an infant he was rickety and ill-shapen, could only move with crutches, and was not expected to live; but an alert and stubborn spirit animated the puny frame, and from about his tenth year his health began to mend. His mother, a woman of little thrift, dying about the same time, his father took a second wife, of whom we know nothing except that her maiden name was Gordon, and that she proved a kind and careful stepmother. Except for a brief interval of schooling, under a master whose cruelty he never forgot, the young John Flaxman was kept at home. Unfitted for the play or the exercises of his age, he found in his father's stock-in-trade all the occupation and all the pastime for which he cared. Customers, among whom were men of note in arts and literature, soon began to take an interest in the sickly lad whom they found always busy drawing or modelling behind the counter, or trying to teach himself the classic fables and Latin. Among the earliest of those who noticed and encouraged his talents were the painter Romney and a lettered and amiable clergyman named Mathew; whose wife, herself a woman of culture, used to invite the boy to her house, and read out translations of the ancient poets while he made sketches to such passages as struck his fancy. His earliest commission was from a friend of the Mathews, Mr. Crutchley of Sunninghill Park, for a set of six classical drawings of this kind. He became a precocious exhibitor and prize-winner, gaining at twelve the first prize of the Society of Arts for a medal, and another similar prize at fifteen. In 1767, and for two years following, he was a contributor to the exhibitions of the Free Society of Artists in Pall Mall; and to those of the Royal Academy from the second year of their foundation, 1770. In this year he became a student at the Academy schools, and presently carried off the silver medal. But when it came to the competition for the gold medal in 1772, the successful youth received a check, the president and council awarding the prize to a rival, Thomas Engleheart [q. v.], who did nothing afterwards to justify the choice. This reverse is said to have had a salutary effect on the character of the young Flaxman, in whose composition a certain degree of dogmatism and self-sufficiency went together with many amiable qualities of kindness, simplicity, enthusiasm, generosity, and piety. Some experience of the former qualities, naturally most conspicuous in early youth, caused Thomas Wedgwood to write of him in 1775, 'It is but a few years since he was a most supreme coxcomb.' By the time these words were written Wedgwood's partner, Thomas Bentley [q. v.], who had already had some business relations with the elder Flaxman, had secured the services of his second son as a designer for the cameo wares of their firm, then freshly in fashion. Wedgwood himself quickly learnt to rate the talents of the young coxcomb at their true value, and to call him 'the genius of sculpture.' It was by designing and preparing wax models for classical friezes and portrait medallions in Wedgwood ware that Flaxman chiefly maintained himself during the first part of his career.

That career falls into three main divisions: first, his early life in London, brought to a close in 1787 by his departure for Rome; next, the period of his residence in Italy, from his thirty-second to his thirty-ninth year (1787–94); and, lastly, his second residence in London, as an artist of acknowledged fame and standing, from 1794 until his death in 1826.

In 1775, the year in which young Flaxman began to be regularly employed by the Wedgwoods, his family, and he with it, moved from New Street, Covent Garden, to a larger shop, No. 420 Strand. He had been for four years a frequent exhibitor at the Royal Academy (1770, a wax model of Neptune; 1771, four portrait models in wax; 1772, figure of a child in wax, portrait bust in terra-cotta, figure of History; 1773, a figure of the Grecian Comedy, a Vestal in bas-relief); and continued to contribute somewhat more irregularly during the next twelve years. In 1780 he showed his first design for a monument to be erected in a church, that, namely, in honour of Chatterton for St. Mary Redcliffe at Bristol; this was followed in 1784 by one in memory of Mrs. Morley for Gloucester Cathedral, and in 1785 by another, for Chichester, in memory of the Rev. Thomas and Mrs. Margaret Ball. It was by works of this class that Flaxman came in due time to earn the best part both of his livelihood and his fame. Meantime his incessant industry (for he is described as continually reading or drawing when not actually at work for his employers) did not prevent him from increasing the circle of his acquaintance. His chosen companions of his own age and calling were Thomas Stothard and William Blake. For a time these three young artists used to frequent together the drawing-room of Mrs. Mathew in Rathbone Place, which was the resort of a lettered society, including such models of female accomplishment and decorum as Mrs. Montague, Mrs. Barbauld, and Mrs. Chapone. There was that about Flaxman already, and still more as time went on, which secured him personal liking and respect wherever he went. His appearance was singular, for though his frame had acquired a wiry tenacity which enabled him to bear much fatigue, yet he looked feeble, and was high-shouldered almost to deformity, with a head somewhat too large for his body, and a sidelong gait in walking. His mouth and set of jaw had something of plebeian stubbornness, corresponding to his inflexible rigidity of opinion on certain subjects; but the eyes were fine and full of enthusiasm, the forehead noble, the smile quaint and winning, and in youth long brown hair curled to his shoulders. Such as he was, Flaxman won the affections of a girl about his own age, Ann (1760?–1820), daughter of William Denman, a gunstock-maker of Mansell Street, Whitechapel; she proved the best of wives. She shared his studies and interests, was enthusiastic, sensible, somewhat sententious, according to the Johnsonian fashion of the age, in speech, the pleasantest and most frugal of housekeepers, his inseparable companion, helpmate, and 'dictionary' (to use his own expression). The pair were married in 1782, and went to live in a very small house, No. 27 Wardour Street; where Flaxman was elected to the parochial office of collector of the watchrate. Shortly afterwards the sculptor was made known by Romney to his friend William Hayley [q. v.], the Sussex squire and poet. This maudlin writer, but genial and generous man, conceived a warm attachment both for Flaxman and his wife. The young couple spent the summer holidays of several years following their marriage at Hayley's country house at Eartham in the South Downs; and his patronage, equally assiduous and delicate, was of great use to Flaxman, particularly in procuring him commissions for monumental works in the neighbouring cathedral of Chichester.

After five years of married life Flaxman determined to start on a journey to Rome, on which his heart had long been set. Wedgwood helped him both with recommendations and with a money advance for services to be rendered in superintending the work of the designers and modellers employed for the firm in Italy. The young couple set out in August

1787, and took up their quarters at Rome in the Via Felice. They meant to stay abroad only two years, but stayed seven. Their residence at Rome was varied with summer trips to other parts of Italy, the records of some of which are preserved in the artist's extant sketch-books and journals. These prove him to have been a zealous and intelligent student, not only of the remains of classic art, to which by sympathy and vocation he was more especially attracted, but also of the works, then generally despised, of the Gothic and early Renaissance ages in Italy. At Rome he soon attracted the notice of the resident and travelling English dilettanti. A Mr. Knight, of Portland Place, for whom he had already executed a figure of Alexander, and just before leaving England a Venus and Cupid, ordered from him a reduced copy of the Borghese vase (these works are now at Wolverley Hall, Worcestershire); ' Anastasius ' Hope of Deepdene, a group of ' Cephalus and Aurora ; ' the notorious Frederick Hervey, earl of Bristol and bishop of Derry, one on a great scale of the ' Fury of Athamas.' Flaxman's relations with the last-named patron and his agent were a source of great annoyance to him ; the price fixed was 600*l.* ; the instalments were unpunctually doled out ; the work remained long on hand, and when completed left the sculptor heavily out of pocket (the group is now at Ickworth, Bury St. Edmunds). Flaxman also spent much time on his own account on an attempt, not very successful, to restore and complete as a group the famous ancient fragment at the Vatican known as the Belvedere torso ; the cast of this group he in later life destroyed. He was further engaged while at Rome in preparing designs for a monument in relief to the poet Collins for Chichester Cathedral, and for one in the round to Lord Mansfield for Westminster Abbey. On behalf of the Wedgwoods he found much to employ him at first, less afterwards. The occupation which brought him most repute, though at first slender enough profit, during his stay at Rome was not that of a sculptor or modeller, but that of a designer of illustrations to the poets. Mrs. Hare Naylor (born Georgiana Shipley, and mother of the distinguished brothers, Francis, Augustus, and Julius Hare [q. v.]) gave him the commission for the designs to the ' Iliad ' and ' Odyssey,' seventy-three drawings in all at fifteen shillings each. These drawings no sooner began to be shown about among artistic circles at Rome than they aroused the greatest enthusiasm. Mr. Hope followed suit with a commission for similar designs for Dante ; Lady Spencer with one for a set of

Æschylus subjects (at a guinea each). All four series were successively handed over to Piroli to be engraved, and the first copies of each were printed at Rome in 1793 ; the plates were then shipped to England, for home publication, and those for the ' Odyssey ' getting lost on the voyage, the designs were re-engraved for Flaxman by his friend Blake. The engraved versions of the designs fall far short of the originals, neither Piroli nor Blake (in this his first attempt) having at all succeeded in rendering with the burin the delicacy and expressiveness of Flaxman's pen work.

In an age much given to the cultivation of classic art and *virtù*, Flaxman, even as a lad, with no models before him except the plaster casts of his father's shop, had shown in his drawings and models an instinct beyond that of any of his contemporaries for the true qualities of Greek design. He had the secret, almost lost to modern art, of combining ideal grace of form and rhythmical composition of lines with spontaneousness and truth of pose and gesture, and the unaffected look of life. Sketching constantly, as was his habit, with pen and pencil the leading lines and masses of every scene and every action of daily humanity that caught his attention within doors or without, and at the same time studying ardently, since his arrival in Italy, the works of Greek design in ancient vases and bas-reliefs, he had greatly strengthened his natural gifts both for linear design and the expression of life and action. The best of the outlines to the Greek poets and Dante —and they are those which represent subjects of grace and gentleness, rather than subjects of violence or terror—are worthy of all the praise they have won. Their success was immediate and universal. Fuseli, whose foible was certainly not diffidence, at once declared himself outdone as a designer. Canova, the prince of Italian sculptors, was generous in recognising those qualities in Flaxman which he lacked himself, and praised his work without stint. Schlegel, the chief of German critics, extolled it a few years later more vehemently still. French taste, then running towards ancient ideals, was equally favourable, and from within a few years of the publication of these designs until our own time the name of Flaxman has been perhaps more known and honoured abroad than that of any other English artist.

Flaxman's last occupation in Italy was that of getting packed and despatched the collection of casts from the antique which Romney had commissioned him to form, intending to place it for the use of students in his great painting room at Hampstead. The sculptor and his wife left Italy in the summer of 1794,

and travelled to England without any such
molestation as they apprehended from the
disturbed state of the continent. They established themselves in a house in Buckingham Street, Fitzroy Square, where Flaxman
continued to live until his death. A son
of Hayley's, who showed some talent for
art, was placed with him as a pupil, but
within a few years died of a decline, and is
commemorated by a small memorial relief, in
Flaxman's best manner, in Eartham Church.
From the date of his return, commissions for
memorial sculptures, both public and private,
brought Flaxman employment and reward
more than sufficient for his modest desires and
frugal way of living. In the most lucrative
branch of his profession, the production of
ordinary busts and portrait statues, he found
comparatively little employment, the strength
of his art not lying in individuality of likeness and character. Among the best of his
emblematic groups in memory of private persons, executed during the years following his
return from Rome, were those to Miss Emily
Mawley, for Chertsey Church (model exhibited 1797); to Miss Lushington, for Lewisham; to Miss Cromwell, for Chichester, 1800;
and to Mrs. Knight, for Milton Church, Cambridge, 1802. Among public monuments he
exhibited in 1796 the model of that to Lord
Mansfield for Westminster Abbey, and in
1798 of that to Corsican Paoli for the same
place. Through Mrs. Hare Naylor he obtained the commission for a monument to
Sir William Jones (her brother-in-law) for
St. Mary's, Oxford (the model exhibited
1797; the finished portrait statue, 1801), and
afterwards executed another for University
College, Oxford. These commissions led the
way to an Indian connection, and Flaxman
afterwards carried out several monumental
works for the East India Company and one
for the rajah of Tanjore. In 1800 he showed
a design for a monument to a Captain Dundas, and in 1802 that for the monument of
Captain Montagu in Westminster Abbey. In
the meantime he had in 1797 been elected an
associate of the Royal Academy, and a full
member in 1800, in which year was exhibited his diploma work, a marble relief of
'Apollo and Marpessa.'

There remain evidences of Flaxman's industry in other forms during these years. It
was his yearly habit to give his wife on her
birthday a drawing of their friend Stothard.
In 1796 he gave her instead, with a charming
dedication, a set of forty outline drawings
of his own in illustration of a little allegorical
poem he had written in blank verse, called
'The Knight of the Blazing Cross' (this volume is now in the Fitzwilliam Museum,

Cambridge). In 1797 he published in the
'Gentleman's Magazine' a letter to the president and council of the Royal Academy, deprecating, with more point and vigour of style
than are shown in any other of his writings,
the scheme of the French government for
ransacking Italy of its art treasures and bringing them to Paris. The progress of the war
with France fired his patriotism, and in 1800
he addressed a pamphlet to the committee
then considering the proposal to erect a great
naval pillar in honour of British arms. Flaxman urged in opposition the erection of a
colossal statue of Britannia triumphant, two
hundred feet high, on Greenwich Hill. The
next year he exhibited his sketch model
for such a monument, and was somewhat
wounded at the indifference with which his
project was received. About the same time
he published another letter to the president
and council of the Royal Academy on the
encouragement of the arts in England. In
1802 the act of rapine against which he
pleaded five years before had been accomplished, and the peace of Amiens brought all
Europe to Paris to gaze on the spoils of Italy
there assembled. Flaxman, notwithstanding
his disapproval, went too, but stiffly declined
all interchange of courtesies with the French
artists and others who had been instrumental
in the spoliation.

After 1802 the tenor of Flaxman's life continued with little change until 1810, when he
was appointed to the newly created post of
professor of sculpture in the academy. Not
only his fame as an artist, but particularly
his assiduity and popularity as a teacher in
the academy schools, recommended him to
this post. Simplicity and earnestness of
manner are said to have been his chief
characteristics as a lecturer. 'The Rev. John
Flaxman' he was once styled by the obstre-
perous Fuseli in the act of leaving a jovial
party to go and hear him. His lectures
in their published form show no power of
style, and not much of order or arrangement,
and on points of scholarship and archæology
are now quite without authority; they are at
the same time distinguished for sound sense
and native insight into the principles and
virtues alike of Greek and Gothic art. Among
the chief works of sculpture which occupied
Flaxman in the years preceding and following his appointment as academy professor
were the beautiful and elaborate monument
in relief for the Baring family in Micheldever
Church, Hampshire, of which the various parts
were exhibited at intervals between 1805 and
1811; the monument, only less rich, for the
Yarborough family at Campsall Church, Yorkshire; a model for a monument to Sir Joshua

Reynolds in St. Paul's (1807); one for a monument to Josiah Webbe for India (1810); monuments to Captains Walker and Beckett in Leeds Church (1811); a monument to Lord Cornwallis for Prince of Wales' Island (1812); one in honour of Sir J. Moore for Glasgow (1813); one to General Simcoe, and one to a Mr. Bosanquet for Leyton Church (1814). Since 1793 he had published no drawings in illustration of the poets except three for an edition, undertaken by Hayley, of Cowper's translations into English of the Latin poems of Milton (published 1810). Other sets of drawings made but not published about this time were one for the 'Pilgrim's Progress' and one to illustrate a Chinese tale in verse, called 'The Casket,' which he wrote (1812) to amuse his womankind. In 1817 he brought out the outlines to Hesiod, which are both the best in themselves of his designs to the Greek poets, and much the best rendered by the engraver, in this instance again Blake. For the next few years classical and decorative subjects in various forms began to occupy a larger share than usual of his time, side by side with monumental sculpture for churches. In the same year (1817) he designed a tripod to be executed by the goldsmiths Rundell and Bridge, and presented to John Kemble on his taking leave of the stage; and in 1818, on a commission from the same goldsmiths, set to work on the drawings and models for a shield of Achilles, to be executed in relief according to the description in the 18th book of the 'Iliad.' This task gave him much labour and much pleasure, and in the result added considerably to his fame; though nothing, as we now know, could be more unlike the art of the Homeric age than Flaxman's suave and flowing work, which resembles a number of his happiest outline designs worked into a single ring-shaped composition. In 1820 Flaxman was engaged on a pedimental group in marble of 'Peace, Liberty, and Plenty' for the Duke of Bedford's new sculpture gallery at Woburn. A group of 'Maternal Love' for the monument to Mrs. Fitzharris (1817); two reliefs of 'Faith' and 'Charity' for the monument of Lady Spencer, exhibited in 1819; and one of 'Religious Instruction' in 1820, for a monument to the Rev. John Clowes at St. John's Church, Manchester, show that the artist had at the same time not broken off his usual labour on pious memorials for the dead, and symbols of Christian hope and consolation. His literary industry at the same time is shown by several articles on art and archæology contributed to Rees's 'Cyclopædia' (published 1819–20).

Flaxman's home life in Buckingham Street during these years was one of great contentment. He was childless, but his half-sister, Mary Ann Flaxman, who was thirteen years younger than himself, and his wife's half-sister, Maria Denman (b. 1779), joined his household. He went little into society, but kept up an unpretending hospitality at home. Crabb Robinson, who was first acquainted with Flaxman in 1810, has borne witness to the spirit of pleasantness which reigned there; to the dignity and simplicity of Flaxman's character, the charm and playfulness of his ordinary conversation, and the goodness of heart which made him beloved alike by pupils, servants, models, and the poor folk and children of the neighbourhood, among whom he went habitually armed with a sketch-book to note down their actions and groupings, and a pocketful of coppers to relieve their distress. Similar testimonies of affectionate and admiring regard have been left by others, especially by E. H. Baily the sculptor, who was his pupil from 1807 to 1814; by Watson the sculptor; and by Allan Cunningham, who only knew him in the last years of his life. In conduct Flaxman seems to have been faultlessly kind, upright, and generous, and in conversation sweetness itself; except on the subject of religion, in which he held stiffly to certain private opinions, compounded partly of puritan orthodoxy and partly of Swedenborgian mysticism. The mystical 'Book of Enoch' supplied many subjects to his pencil, and he had a sympathy with religious seers and enthusiasts. But he was not haunted, like Blake, by visions more real to him than reality; and when Sharp, the engraver, came to him with a message from the prophet Brothers, declaring that he must accompany them in leading back the Jews to Jerusalem, and undertake the office of architect to the Temple, he was able to put by the offer with a smile and speak of it humorously afterwards.

In 1820 Mrs. Flaxman, who had made a good recovery from a stroke of paralysis six years before, died on 7 Feb. The blow to Flaxman was very great. His health and spirits were never the same again, though he did not suffer the shock to diminish or interrupt his industry. The next year he finished and exhibited the group of 'Michael and Satan,' for Lord Egremont, in marble, and in 1824 a 'Pastoral Apollo' for the same patron. Both are now at Petworth. In 1822 he gave an address at the Royal Academy on the occasion of the death of Canova, and in 1823 received a visit from his old admirer, Schlegel. He was at work about the same time on statuettes of Raphael and Michael Angelo, on small figures of Cupid and Psyche, on designs for a statue of Burns, and for one of John Kemble for Westminster Abbey, and on sketches for friezes for the external decoration of Buckingham Palace, then uncompleted. In his seventy-second year he lived still surrounded by honour and affection, and as busy almost as ever, though visibly failing in strength; when, on 3 Dec. 1826, he caught a cold in church, which turned quickly to inflammation. On the morning of the 7th he died. He was buried, with no public mourning, in the burial-ground of St. Giles-in-the-Fields.

The most important and complete monumental works of Flaxman, including those above mentioned and others, are to be found in Westminster Abbey, in St. Paul's, at Glasgow, and in Calcutta; his most ambitious classical and decorative groups and figures at Petworth, Ickworth, Woburn, Deepdene, and Wolverley Hall. But neither of these classes of work represent him at his best. His occupation on wax models for Wedgwood had accustomed him in youth to work chiefly on a minute scale; and on a large scale he never learnt to design or execute with complete mastery. Many of the shortcomings of his heroic monuments are due to the fact of his having used half-sized, or even smaller, instead of full-sized models in their preparation. They are, moreover, often marred by inexpressiveness and lack of thoroughness in the treatment of the marble; Flaxman not having been himself very skilful with the chisel, and having been content, except in a few instances (as the 'Fury of Athamas' and the Academy relief of 'Apollo and Marpessa,' which he is said to have finished in great part with his own hand), with the empty mechanical polish which the Italian workmen of the time imitated from the Roman imitations of Greek originals. His real genius appears far better in the memorial reliefs in honour of the private dead, which are to be found in so many churches throughout England—in Chichester Cathedral no less than eight, in the cathedrals of Winchester and Gloucester, in the churches of Leeds, Manchester, Campsall, Tewkesbury, Ledbury, Micheldever, Heston, Chertsey, Cookham, Lewisham, Beckenham, Leyton, Milton, and many more. For this class of work his favourite form of design was one of symbolic figures or groups in relief, embodying some simple theme of sorrow or consolation, a beatitude, or a text from the Lord's Prayer. Such motives lose all triteness in his hands, and are distinguished by a unique combination of typical classic grace with heartfelt humanity and domestic pathos. But of these, too, the execution in marble is often not equal to the beauty of the motive, and in many cases

they can be studied almost better in the collection of casts from the clay models preserved in the Flaxman Hall at University College than in the marbles themselves. Perhaps the most entirely satisfactory class of Flaxman's works is to be found, not among his sculptures, but his drawings and sketches and pen outline, pen and wash, or pencil. These are very numerous, and include ideas and essays for almost all his extant or projected works, whether in sculpture or outline illustrations, as well as many hundred studies and motives from life or fancy not afterwards used. Slight as they commonly are, abstract and generalised as is their treatment of anatomical forms, they stand alone by the peculiar quality of their beauty; expressing, in lines of a charm equal to, and partly caught from, that of antique vase-paintings and bas-reliefs, the inventions and observations of a singularly gifted, pure, lofty, and tender spirit. The best public collections are in the British Museum, the South Kensington Museum, in the Flaxman Hall at University College (founded by Maria Denman), and the Fitzwilliam Museum, Cambridge; many remain in private hands.

John Flaxman's elder brother, WILLIAM FLAXMAN (1753?–1795?), was also a modeller and exhibitor. He contributed to the exhibition of the Free Society of Artists in 1768, and to those of the Academy at intervals between 1781 (when he sent a portrait of John Flaxman in wax) and 1793. He is said to have been distinguished as a carver in wood. No details of his life have been preserved in any published memoir or correspondence of his brother.

Of more note as an artist, and more closely associated with the sculptor's career, was his half-sister, MARY ANN FLAXMAN (1768–1833). She lived as governess in the family of the Hare Naylors for several years, first in Italy and afterwards at Weimar; and from 1810 was an inmate of John Flaxman's house at Buckingham Street until his death. Her work in art was strongly influenced by his example, and shows both talent and feeling. She is best known by the six designs for Hayley's 'Triumphs of Temper,' engraved by Blake, and published in 1803. Her contributions to the Royal Academy occur at intervals between 1786 and 1819, and consist chiefly of designs in illustration of poetry and romance.

[Anonymous 'Brief Memoir' prefixed to Flaxman's Lectures, ed. 1829; Allan Cunningham's Lives of the most Eminent British Painters, Sculptors, and Architects; J. T. Smith's Nollekens and his Times; Dr. Lonsdale's Life of Watson; Mrs. Bray's Life of Stothard; Gilchrist's and Rossetti's Life of Blake; Miss Meteyard's

Life of Josiah Wedgwood; Crabb Robinson's Diaries and Reminiscences; Redgrave's Dict. of Artists; articles by G. F. Teniswood in the Art Journal for 1867, 1868, and 1872; Sidney Colvin's Drawings of Flaxman (atlas fol. 1876); unpublished correspondence.]
                            S. C.

FLECCIUS, GERBARUS (*fl.* 1546–1554), painter. [See FLICCIUS.]

FLECKNOE, RICHARD (*d.* 1678?), poet, is said to have been an Irishman and a Roman catholic priest. From his own account of his travels it appears that he went abroad in 1640, and spent three or four years in the Low Countries. He travelled to Rome in 1645, where, as he says, he was chiefly occupied with pictures and statues. From Rome he made a voyage to Constantinople about 1647, and he afterwards went to Portugal, and visited Brazil in 1648. Thence he returned to Flanders and to England. At Rome he was visited by Andrew Marvell, who described him in 'Fleckno, an English priest at Rome.' Marvell, with his hyperbolic humour, gives a quaint description of Flecknoe's extreme leanness, his narrow lodging up three pairs of stairs, and his appetite for reciting his own poetry. Flecknoe, as appears from his dedications, was known to many distinguished people on the continent and in England. Langbaine says that he was more acquainted with the nobility than with the muses. He speaks as a moderate catholic, though one of his books (see below) contains a panegyric upon Cromwell at the Protector's death. He says that nobody prints more or publishes less than he. He amused himself by writing plays, only one of which ('Love's Kingdom') was acted, and giving lists of the actors whom he would have wished to represent the parts. He disapproved of the license of the stage, and was regarded with special contempt and dislike by the popular writers. Dryden refers to him in his dedication of 'Limberham' (1678), and a rather obscure phrase, that there is a worse poet in the world than 'he of scandalous memory who left it last,' is supposed to intimate that Flecknoe was then recently dead. Dryden in his later satire, 'MacFlecknoe,' 1682, says that Flecknoe

In prose and verse was owned, without dispute,
Through all the realms of nonsense, absolute.

The causes of Dryden's antipathy, if they were anything more than a general dislike to bad poetry, are not discoverable. In one of his epigrams Flecknoe praises Dryden,

the Muses' darling and delight,
Than whom none ever flew so high a flight.

Southey has pointed out some good lines in Flecknoe, and Lamb prefixed some pleasing verses on silence to his essay 'On a Quaker's Meeting.' He is also praised in the 'Retrospective Review.' It must, however, be admitted that Flecknoe's verses, excepting a few happy passages, are of the kind which chiefly pleases the author. They were printed for private circulation, and are often rare.

His works are: 1. 'Hierothalamium, or the Heavenly Nuptials of our Blessed Saviour with a Pious Soule,' 1626. 2. 'The Affections of a Pious Soule unto our Saviour Christ, expressed in a mixed Treatise of Verse and Prose,' 1640. 3. 'Miscellania, or Poems of all Sorts, with divers other Pieces,' 1653. 4. 'Love's Dominion, a dramatick piece full of excellent Moralities, written as a pattern for the reformed stage,' 1654 (anon.) 5. 'A Relation of Ten Years' Travels in Europe, Asia, Affrique, and America,' 1656. 6. 'The Diarium or Journal, divided into twelve Jornadas in burlesque Rhime or Drolling Verse,' 1656. 7. 'Enigmaticall Characters, all taken to the Life from several Persons, Humours, and Dispositions,' 1658. (A second edition, called 'Sixty-nine Characters,' &c., in 1665; and also in 1665 'Enigmatical Characters, &c. . . . being rather a new work than a new impression of the old,' differing greatly from the other two.) 8. 'The Marriage of Oceanus and Britannia,' 1659. 9. 'The Idea of his Highness Oliver, late Lord Protector, with certain brief Reflections on his Life,' 1659. 10. 'Heroick Portraits, with other Miscellany Pieces,' 1660. 11. 'Love's Kingdom, a Pastoral Trage-Comedy' ('Love's Dominion' altered); appended is a short treatise of the English stage, 1664 (reprinted in Hazlitt's 'English Drama and Stage,' Roxburghe Library, 1869). 12. 'Erminia, or the Fair and Virtuous Lady, a Trage-Comedy,' 1661 and 1665. 13. 'A Farrago of Several Pieces,' 1666. 14. 'The Damoiselles à la Mode,' 1667 (taken, according to the preface, 'out of several excellent pieces of Molière'). 15. 'Sir William Davenant's Voyage to the other World, with his Adventures in the Poets' Elyzium: a Poetical Fiction,' 1668 (with a postscript to the actors at the theatre in Lincoln's Inn Fields). 16. 'Epigrams of all Sorts,' 1 bk. 1669. 17. 'Epigrams of all Sorts, made at divers times on several occasions,' 1670, with 'Epigrams Divine and Moral.' Another book with same title ('rather a new work than a new impression'), 1671. 18. 'A Collection of the choicest Epigrams and Characters of R. F.' (rather a 'new work than a new impression'), 1673 (from previous 'Epigrams' and 'Enigmatical Characters'). 19. 'Euterpe Revived, or Epigrams made at several times . . . on persons . . . most of them now living,' 1675. 20. 'A Treatise of the Sports of Wit,' 1675 (only two copies known, one in the Huth Library).

[Langbaine's Dramatic Poëts, 1691, pp. 199–202; Ware's Writers of Ireland; Southey's Omniana, i. 105–10; Scott's Dryden, 1808, vi. 7, x. 441; Marvell's Works (Grosart), pp. xxxiv, 229; Retrospective Review, v. 266–75.] L. S.

FLEET, SIR JOHN (d. 1712), governor of the East India Company, was, according to Luttrell, by trade a sugar baker, but according to Le Neve a wine cooper. He was elected alderman of Langbourn ward on 9 Oct. 1688, and sheriff of London two days later, being knighted soon afterwards. He was also chosen captain of the city horse volunteers in July 1689, and lord mayor on 1 Oct. 1692. His accession to the latter office was celebrated by a pageant called 'The Triumphs of London,' written by Elkanah Settle and performed in the Grocers' Hall on 29 Oct. He represented the city of London in parliament between March 1692–3 and 1705, with the exception of the short parliament which sat from 30 Dec. 1701 to 2 July 1702. On 25 April 1694 he was elected governor of the East India Company, and served two years. He was re-elected for 1698–1700, 1702–4, and 1706–8. It was a critical epoch in the history of the company, the charter having become legally forfeit in consequence of the interest due to the government having fallen into arrear. The government was itself in financial straits. A rival company had also been projected which offered the government a loan of 2,000,000*l.* at 8 per cent., while the best offer which Fleet was authorised to make on behalf of the old company was an advance of 700,000*l.* at 6 per cent. The new company was accordingly incorporated on 5 Sept. 1698, and the old company found it necessary to effect an amalgamation. This was carried out on 22 July 1702. Fleet was appointed, on 11 July 1702, one of the commissioners to execute the office of lieutenant of London, and on 14 March 1704–5 he was elected president of St. Bartholomew's Hospital. He married twice, his second wife being the relict of Newcomb, the king's printer. He died in 1712 and was buried at Battersea.

[Luttrell's Relation of State Affairs, passim; Le Neve's Pedigrees of Knights (Harl. Soc.), p. 417; Anderson's Hist. of Commerce, ii. 222, 233; Lysons's Environs, 1792, i. 35.]   J. M. R.

FLEETWOOD, CHARLES (d. 1692), soldier, was the third son of Sir Miles Fleetwood of Aldwinkle, Northamptonshire, and of Anne, daughter of Nicholas Luke of Woodend, Bedfordshire (pedigree communicated by W. S. Churchill, esq.) Sir Miles Fleetwood was receiver of the court of wards, and died in 1641. His eldest son, Sir William (b. 1603), who succeeded to his father's estates and office, took the side of the king, and died in 1674. George, the second son, sought his fortune in the service of Sweden, and is noticed below. Charles, who appears to have been much younger than his brothers, was left by his father an annuity of 60*l.*, chargeable on the estate of Sir William Fleetwood (*Royalist Composition Papers*, 2nd ser. xxiii. 165). He was admitted a member of Gray's Inn 30 Nov. 1638 (*Harleian MS.* 1912). In 1642 he and other young gentlemen of the Inns of Court entered the life-guard of the Earl of Essex (LUDLOW, ed. 1751, p. 17). Though a simple trooper Fleetwood was in September 1642 employed by Essex to bear a letter to the Earl of Dorset, containing overtures of peace to the king, but was dismissed without an answer (CLARENDON, ed. Macray, ii. 340). He was wounded at the first battle of Newbury, by which time he had risen to the rank of captain (*Bibliotheca Gloucestrensis*, p. 244). In May 1644 parliament rewarded him with the receivership of the court of wards, forfeited by his brother (WHITELOCKE, i. 256, ed. 1853). In the same year he was in command of a regiment in the Earl of Manchester's army, and already notorious as a favourer of sectaries. 'Look at Colonel Fleetwood's regiment,' writes a presbyterian; 'what a cluster of preaching officers and troopers there is !' (*Manchester's Quarrel with Cromwell*, p. 72). His support of preaching officers involved him in a quarrel with Sir Samuel Luke (ELLIS, *Original Letters*, 3rd ser. iv. 260–6). Fleetwood commanded a regiment of horse in the new model, fought at Naseby, and assisted in the defeat of Sir Jacob Astley at Stow-on-the-Wold (SPRIGGE, *Anglia Rediviva*, pp. 67, 107, 174; RUSHWORTH, vi. 140). In May 1646 Fleetwood entered the House of Commons as member for Marlborough (*Return of Members of Parliament*, i. 496). In the quarrel between the army and the parliament in the summer of 1647 he played an important part. His regiment was one of those which unanimously refused to take service in Ireland; he himself was one of the four military commissioners sent to explain the votes of parliament to the army (30 April 1647), and also one of the officers appointed by the army to treat with the commissioners of parliament (1 July 1647) (RUSHWORTH, vi. 468, 475, 603). According to the statements of Lilburn and Holles he was deeply engaged in the plot for seizing the king at Holmby (LILBURN, *An Impeachment of High Treason against Oliver Cromwell*, 1649, p. 55;

MASERES, *Tracts*, i. 246). Fleetwood does not appear to have been actively employed in the second civil war, and took no part in the king's trial. He was appointed on 14 Aug. 1649 governor of the Isle of Wight, in conjunction with Colonel Sydenham (*Cal. State Papers, Dom.* 1649–50, p. 277). In the summer of 1650 he accompanied Cromwell to Scotland, and, as lieutenant-general of the horse, helped to gain the battle of Dunbar. During his absence Fleetwood was elected a member of the third council of state (17 Feb. 1651), and was recalled from Scotland and charged with the command of the forces retained in England (*ib.* 1651, pp. 44, 103). This position gave him the command of the forces collected to oppose Charles II's march into England. He met Cromwell on 24 Aug. at Warwick to concert measures with him, gathered at Banbury the militia of about twenty counties, and crossing the Severn established himself at Upton, on the south-west of Worcester (29 Aug.) From this point Fleetwood commenced the battle of 3 Sept., forcing his way across the Teme, and driving the royalists into Worcester (*Old Parliamentary History*, xx. 25, 33, 41, 60). His services were acknowledged by the thanks of the House of Commons, and his re-election to the council of state. In the following year Fleetwood's importance was further increased by his appointment as commander-in-chief in Ireland and his marriage with Cromwell's daughter. A few weeks after the battle of Worcester Fleetwood had lost his wife, Frances, daughter of Thomas Smith of Winston, Norfolk, who was buried at St. Anne's, Blackfriars, 24 Nov. 1651 (*Notes and Queries*, iv. 3, 156). Two days later died Henry Ireton, the husband of Cromwell's eldest daughter, Bridget, and before the end of 1652 the widow became Fleetwood's second wife (CARLYLE, *Cromwell*, Letter clxxxix.) The marriage was attributed at the time to Mrs. Ireton's desire to regain the position she had lost; but this is hardly consistent with the account of her character given by the writer who tells the story (*Memoirs of Colonel Hutchinson*, ii. 189, 202, ed. 1885). Fleetwood's appointment to the command of the Irish army was due to Lambert's refusal to hold the post except with the rank of lord deputy, which office parliament had resolved to abolish. Accordingly the council of state nominated Fleetwood (8 July 1652), parliament approved, and Cromwell, as captain-general of the forces of the Commonwealth, granted him a commission as commander-in-chief in Ireland, 10 July 1652 (THURLOE, i. 212). He was also made one of the commissioners for the civil government of that country (*Instructions*

24 Aug. 1652, *Old Parliamentary History*, xx. 92).

Fleetwood remained in Ireland from September 1652 to September 1655. On 27 Aug. 1654, or earlier, he was given the higher rank of lord deputy, and continued to hold that title until superseded by Henry Cromwell in November 1657 (*14th Report of the Deputy-Keeper of Irish Records*, p. 28; *Mercurius Politicus*, 3780). The chief work of Fleetwood's government was the transplantation of the condemned Irish landholders to Connaught, and he was also able to begin the settlement of the disbanded soldiers on the confiscated estates (PRENDERGAST, *Cromwellian Settlement of Ireland*, ed. 1875, pp. 228, 267). Fleetwood was personally a warm supporter of the policy of transplantation, and eager to punish Vincent Gookin [q. v.] for his book against it (THURLOE, iii. 139). A bitter persecutor of catholic priests, he showed himself ever ready to protect and favour the anabaptists and extreme sectaries among the soldiers, and was accordingly disliked by the presbyterians. This was probably one of the causes of his recall to England (*Reliquiæ Baxterianæ*, i. 74). The sectarian party and the army in general petitioned for his return (THURLOE, iv. 276, 421). Fleetwood approved and furthered the foundation of the protectorate. According to Ludlow he procured the proclamation of the Protector by a trick, and took care that all the Irish members in the parliament of 1654 should be staunch friends of the government (*Memoirs*, pp. 184, 189, ed. 1751). But according to Colonel Hewson it was Fleetwood's 'sweet healing peaceable spirit' which drew over the hearts of the scrupulous, and convinced them that 'the interest of God's people' could only be secure by Cromwell's rule (THURLOE, iv. 276). But he was always ready to intervene on behalf of old companions in arms who were dissatisfied with the new government. He interceded for Colonel Alured, Colonel Rich, and Adjutant-general Allen, proceeded against Ludlow with great reluctance, and strove hard to win him over (*ib.* ii. 728, iii. 246, vi. 251; LUDLOW, pp. 205, 210). Fleetwood was also in complete agreement with Cromwell in the various breaches which took place between him and his parliaments. On the dissolution of the first (January 1655) he wrote to Thurloe, declaring that freedom for tender consciences, and the limitation of the powers and duration of parliament were the two essentials of any settlement (THURLOE, iii. 23, 112, 136). In December 1654 Fleetwood had been appointed one of Cromwell's council, and on his return to England (September 1655) he at once assumed a leading place in the Protector's court (*ib.* iv. 406). He was appointed also one of the major-generals, having under his charge the counties of Norfolk,.Suffolk, Essex, Oxford, Cambridge, Huntingdon, and Buckingham, but seems usually to have exercised his functions through a deputy. Fleetwood approved of the exclusion of those who refused to sign a recognition of the protectorate from the parliament of 1656, and though he opposed the proposal to make Cromwell king accepted willingly the rest of the articles of the petition and advice (LUDLOW, pp. 222, 225; THURLOE, vi. 219, 244, 281, 310). He took his seat in the new House of Lords, believing that the revised constitution would secure the desired settlement, and was deeply disappointed at the breach which followed (THURLOE, vi. 752, 840). He advocated the speedy summons of.another parliament, and was one of the committee of nine appointed to consider the necessary measures (*ib.* vii. 192). In foreign as well as domestic policy Fleetwood, moved by his strong religious sympathies, was in complete accord with Cromwell. He was inclined to believe that the latter was 'particularly raised up' to be a shelter to poor persecuted protestants in foreign parts, and held 'the cause of the protestant interest against the common enemy' to be the supreme interest of England (*ib.* iii. 468, vii. 190). So for public, as well as for personal, reasons Fleetwood watched with anxiety Cromwell's last illness, and lamented his death. 'There is none,' he wrote, 'but are deeply concerned in this that have a true love to this blessed cause.' 'His heart was full of love to the interest of the Lord's people, and made everything else bow down unto it' (*ib.* vii. 355, 375). Fleetwood's position as head of the army and this thorough agreement with Cromwell's views lend some plausibility to the story that Cromwell once designed Fleetwood to succeed him. It is stated that the Protector some time before his death nominated Fleetwood in writing as his successor; but that the document was lost or destroyed (BAKER, *Chronicle*, ed. Phillips, 1670, p. 653; BATES, *Elenchus*, ed. 1685, pt. ii. pp. 236, 242). If a protector were to be chosen other than one of Cromwell's sons, no one had stronger claims than Fleetwood. He was the officer highest in rank in the armies of the three kingdoms. The military services of Lambert and Harrison might have made them dangerous rivals, but both had been distinguished by their opposition to the existing government, and neither was at present a member of the army. Fleetwood's connection with the Cromwell family furnished a guarantee to the adherents of Cromwell, and he was

at the same time trusted by the extreme sectaries. These reasons induced the discontented officers to put him forward as their leader in the attempt to render the army independent of the civil power. Fleetwood took part in the elevation of Richard Cromwell, presented the address in which the army declared their resolution to support him, and wrote to Henry Cromwell expressing his joy at his brother's peaceable accession (THURLOE, vii. 405). The first movement came from the superior officers of the army, who early in October 1659 met and drew up an address demanding that a general should be appointed, and that in future no officer should be cashiered without a council of war. The Protector refused these demands, pointing out that he had already made Fleetwood lieutenant-general of all the army, and so by consequence commander-in-chief under himself (*ib.* vii. 436, 449, 452). Fleetwood was suspected of instigating these petitions, and the responsibility which he incurred by permitting them was clearly pointed out to him by Henry Cromwell. He endeavoured to vindicate himself, and based his defence on the necessity of preserving 'the honest interest' in the army (*ib.* pp. 454, 500).

In February 1659 the officers assembled again, and entered into communication with the republican party in the House of Commons. They intended to present a petition, but their own dissensions and Fleetwood's reluctance to press matters to extremity prevented the plan from being carried out (GUIZOT, *Richard Cromwell*, i. 304–6; *Clarendon Papers*, iii. 430, 432; THURLOE, vii. 612–18). The attacks of parliament upon the soldiers who had been Cromwell's instruments led to a fresh meeting in April, ending in the presentation of 'the Humble Representation of 6 April, which insisted in strong terms on the danger of the good old cause' from the intrigues of the cavaliers. The Protector, backed by parliament, ordered these meetings of officers to be brought to an end, but Fleetwood now placed himself at the head of the movement, refused to obey the Protector's orders, and by a military demonstration forced him to dissolve parliament (22 April 1659).

In thus acting Fleetwood's conduct was dictated, not by hostility to the Protector, but by hostility to his parliament. Immediately after the dissolution he had a long interview with Richard Cromwell, and made him large promises of support (GUIZOT, i. 372; BAKER, *Chronicle*, p. 660). Fleetwood, Desborough, and most of the Wallingford House party were anxious to patch up an agreement with the Protector, while the subordinate officers were eager for a commonwealth, and for the revival of the Long parliament. They lost their influence with the officers, 'being looked upon as self-seekers in that they are for a protector now they have got a protector of wax whom they can mould as they please, and lay aside when they can agree upon a successor' (THURLOE, vii. 666; BAKER, p. 660). They were therefore obliged to yield, and to recall the expelled members of the Long parliament (6 May 1659). At the same time Lambert's [see LAMBERT, JOHN] re-admission to the army still further diminished Fleetwood's influence. Nominally his authority was much increased by this revolution. He was appointed a member of the committee of safety (7 May), one of the council of state (13 May), and one of the seven commissioners for the reorganisation of the army (LUDLOW, pp. 248–51). The twelfth article of the army address of 13 May demanded that Fleetwood should be made commander-in-chief, and an act was passed for that purpose. He received his commission on 9 June 1659 (THURLOE, vii. 679). But his powers were to last 'only during the continuance of parliament, or till parliament should take further order,' and all commissions were to be signed by the speaker (BAKER, p. 669; LUDLOW, pp. 251–3). On the suppression of Sir George Booth's rising [see BOOTH, GEORGE, 1622–1684], Lambert's brigade petitioned that these restrictions should be removed, Fleetwood's commission be made permanent, and other general officers be appointed (BAKER, p. 677). These demands were backed by a second petition signed by most of the officers of the English army (*Old Parliamentary History*, xxi. 460). Parliament answered by cashiering nine leading officers, and by voting Fleetwood's commission to be void, and vesting the chief command in seven commissioners, of whom he was to be one (11 Oct.) Fleetwood seems at first to have attempted to mediate. His wife told Ludlow 'that her husband had been always unwilling to do anything in opposition to the parliament, that he was utterly ignorant of the contrivance of the officers at Derby to petition the parliament in so insolent a manner, and had not any part in their proceedings upon it afterwards' (*Memoirs*, p. 295). Ludlow also says that Fleetwood was in the House of Commons when the vote of 11 Oct. was passed, and promised to submit to it (*ib.* p. 275). In the violent expulsion of parliament on 12 Oct. Lambert played the principal part. Fleetwood assisted but kept in the background. As before, when events came to a crisis he sided with the army. He was now again declared commander-in-chief (18 Oct.), but he was in reality little more

than president of the council of officers. While Lambert went north to meet Monck, he stayed in London to maintain order in the city and union in the army. He made every effort, publicly and privately, to come to an agreement with Monck, and signed a treaty with his commissioners on 15 Nov. 1659, which Monck refused to ratify (BAKER, pp. 685–95). In a speech to the common council, Fleetwood endeavoured to vindicate the conduct of the army. 'I dare say our design is God's glory. We have gone in untrodden paths, but God hath led us into ways which, if we know our own hearts, we have no base or unworthy designs in. We have no design to rule over others' (*Three Speeches made to the Lord Mayor, &c., by the Lord Whitelocke, the Lord Fleetwood, and the Lord Desborough,* 8 *Nov.* 1659). With the same object and with equally little success Fleetwood engaged in epistolary controversy with Haslerig (*The True Copy of Several Letters from Portsmouth,* 1659). There is also printed a reply to Colonel Morley's remonstrance (THURLOE, vii. 771), entitled 'The Lord-General Fleetwood's Answer to Colonel Morley, and some other late Officers of the Army,' 8 Nov. 1659, but this is denounced as 'a mere fiction' (*Mercurius Politicus,* 10–17 Nov. 1659). Defections increased rapidly, and in December it was simply a question with whom to make terms. Fleetwood was generally suspected of a desire to restore Richard Cromwell, and his acts were jealously watched by Vane's party (LUDLOW, p. 288). Ludlow urged him to recall the Rump (*ib.* p. 295). Royalist agents had for some time been soliciting him on behalf of the king, and he was now vigorously pressed by his brother, Sir William Fleetwood, and by Bulstrode Whitelocke to enter into negotiations with Charles, and to declare for a free parliament (WHITELOCKE, iv. 381, ed. 1853). If he did not seize the opportunity and make terms with the king, Monck would bring him back without terms. Fleetwood was on the point of agreeing with the city for this object, but he was held back by a promise to take no step of the kind without consulting Lambert, and by the opposition of the inferior officers (*Clarendon State Papers,* iii. 633). 'He replied to the assistance and conjunction offered by the city, that God had spit in his face, and he was to submit to the late dissolved body of members of parliament' (*ib.* pp. 633, 647; BAKER, p. 698). The soldiers declared for the restoration of the Rump (24 Dec.), which immediately deprived Fleetwood of his post of commander-in-chief (26 Dec.) His regiment of horse was given to Sir A. Cooper. Fleetwood was included in the vote of indemnity which was immediately passed (2 Jan.), but was summoned (24 Jan.) to appear before parliament on 31 Jan. 1660 to answer for his conduct. Pepys was told on 31 Jan. that Fleetwood had written a letter 'and desired a little more time, he being a great way out of town. And how that he is quite ashamed of himself, and confesses how he had deserved this for his baseness to his brother. And that he is like to pay part of the money paid out of the exchequer during the committee of safety out of his own purse again' (*Diary*, 31 Jan. 1660). The day fixed for his appearance was several times adjourned, and he does not appear to have been actually punished.

Fleetwood's escape at the Restoration was due to the fact that he had taken no part in the king's trial, and was not regarded as politically dangerous. The commons excepted twenty persons not regicides from the act of indemnity for penalties not extending to life, and among these was Fleetwood (18 June 1660) (*Old Parliamentary History*, xxii. 351). When the act came before the lords the Earl of Lichfield exerted himself on behalf of Fleetwood, and, thanks to his influence and that of other friends, Fleetwood was ultimately included in the list of eighteen persons whose sole punishment was perpetual incapacitation from all offices of trust (LUDLOW, *Memoirs*, p. 354; *Act of Indemnity*, 29 Aug. 1660). The rest of his life was therefore passed in obscurity. Shortly after the Restoration occurred the death of Bridget Fleetwood, who was buried at St. Anne's, Blackfriars, 1 July 1662 (*Notes and Queries*, 4th ser. iii. 156). Eighteen months later, 14 Jan. 1663-4, Fleetwood married Dame Mary Hartopp, daughter of Sir John Coke of Melbourne, Derbyshire, and widow of Sir Edward Hartopp, bart. (*ib.* 4th ser. ii. 600). From the date of his third marriage he resided at Stoke Newington, in a house belonging to his wife, which was afterwards known as Fleetwood House. This house was demolished in 1872 (*ib.* 4th ser. ix. 296, 364, 435, 496). During this period he was a member of the congregation of Dr. John Owen, two of whose letters to him are printed by Orme (*Life of Owen*, pp. 368, 516). Fleetwood's third wife died on 17 Dec. 1684, Fleetwood himself on 4 Oct. 1692; both were buried in Bunhill Fields cemetery. His will, dated 10 Jan. 1689-90, is printed in 'Notes and Queries' (4th ser. ix. 362), and also by Waylen (*House of Cromwell*, p. 69). In 1869, when the cemetery was reopened as a public garden, Fleetwood's monument, which had been discovered seven feet below the surface of the ground, was restored at the expense of the corporation

of London. An engraving of it was given in the 'Illustrated London News' of 23 Oct. 1869.

Fleetwood left issue by two of his wives, but his descendants in the male line became extinct about the middle of the eighteenth century. By his first wife, Frances Smith, he had (1) Smith Fleetwood (1644-1709), who married Mary, daughter of Sir Edward Hartopp, their descendants became extinct in 1764 (NOBLE, ii. 367); (2) Elizabeth, married Sir John Hartopp, third baronet, from whom the existing Cradock-Hartopp family is descended (*ib.* ii. 367; FOSTER, *Baronetage*, ed. 1883). By Bridget Cromwell, Fleetwood was the father of (1) Cromwell Fleetwood, born about 1653, married in 1679 Elizabeth Nevill of Little Berkhampstead, Hertfordshire (CHESTER, *Marriage Licenses*, ed. Foster, p. 491); administration of his goods was granted in September 1688; he seems to have died without issue. (2) Anne Fleetwood, buried in Westminster Abbey, and exhumed at the Restoration (CHESTER, *Westminster Abbey Registers*, p. 522); (3) Mary, who married Nathaniel Carter (21 Feb. 1678), and other children, most of whom died young, and none of whom left issue (WAYLEN, p. 88; *Notes and Queries*, 5th ser. vi. 390).

[Pedigree of the Fleetwood family, drawn up by J. P. Earwaker, esq., and communicated by W. S. Churchill, esq.; articles by Colonel Chester in Notes and Queries; Noble's House of Cromwell, 1787; Waylen's House of Cromwell, 1880; Cal. State Papers, Dom.; Thurloe Papers; Carlyle's Cromwell's Letters and Speeches.] C. H. F.

FLEETWOOD, GEORGE (*fl.* 1650?), regicide, was probably son of Charles Fleetwood and grandson of Sir George Fleetwood, knt., of the Vache, near Chalfont St. Giles, Buckinghamshire, who married Catherine, daughter of Henry Denny of Waltham, Essex. Sir George Fleetwood died 21 Dec. 1620, and his son Charles, whose wife Anne was daughter of Nicholas and Margery Watkins, died in 1628. The future regicide was baptised at Chalfont St. Giles 15 Feb. 1621-2 (*Notes and Queries*, 9th ser. ix. 261, 10th ser. i. 422-424). According to 'Mercurius Aulicus,' 7 Dec. 1643, 'Young Fleetwood of the Vache' had raised a troop of dragoons for the parliament, to defend the Chiltern parts of Buckinghamshire; and in an ordinance of 27 June 1644 the name of Fleetwood appears in the list of the Buckinghamshire committee (HUSBAND, *Ordinances*, 1646, p. 54). He entered the Long parliament in July 1647 as member for Buckinghamshire. In 1648 he was appointed one of the commissioners for the trial of the king, attended two sittings of the court, and was present also when sentence was pronounced, and signed the death-warrant (NALSON, *Trial of Charles I*). In 1649 and 1650 he was colonel of the Buckinghamshire militia, and was chosen a member of the eighth and last council of state of the Commonwealth (1 Nov.–10 Dec. 1653, *Cal. State Papers*, Dom. 1653–4, p. xxxvi). He represented the county of Buckingham in the assembly of 1653, and again in the parliament of 1654 (*Old Parliamentary History*, xx. 176, 297). Cromwell knighted him in the autumn of 1656, and summoned him to his House of Lords in December 1657 (*Perfect Politician*, ed. 1680, p. 293; *Old Parliamentary History*, xxi. 168). On the occasion of Sir George Booth's rising parliament authorised Fleetwood to raise a 'troop of well-affected volunteers' (*Cal. State Papers*, Dom. 1659–60, pp. 125, 565). He refused to assist Lambert against Monck, opposed the oath of abjuration in parliament, was entrusted with the command of a regiment by Monck in the spring of 1660, and proclaimed Charles II at York (11 May 1660) (*Hist. MSS. Comm.* 7th Rep. p. 159). When the regicides were summoned to surrender he gave himself up (16 June), but was excepted from the Act of Indemnity (KENNETT, *Register*, pp. 181, 240). At his trial (October 1660) Fleetwood pleaded guilty, was sentenced to death, and said, weeping, that he had confessed the fact, and wished he could express his sorrow (*Trial of the Regicides*, pp. 28, 276). A saving clause in the Act of Indemnity suspended the execution of those who claimed the benefit of the king's proclamation, unless their conviction was followed by a special act of parliament for their execution. Fleetwood accordingly petitioned parliament, stating that his name was inserted in the list of commissioners without his knowledge and against his will, and that his signature to the warrant was extorted by Cromwell, 'whose power, commands, and threats (he being then young) frighted him into court.' He produced certificates from Monck and Ashley of his services in forwarding the Restoration, and begged 'to be represented to his majesty as a fit object of his royal clemency and mercy to hold his life merely by his princely grace' (*Hist. MSS. Comm.* 7th Rep. p. 159). His life was spared, but his estate of the Vache confiscated and given to the Duke of York. In 1664 a warrant was issued for Fleetwood's transportation to Tangier, but it seems to have been suspended at the solicitation of his wife. According to Noble he was finally released and went to America. He was twice married and had issue. A miniature of Fleetwood by S. Cooper, dated 1647, belongs to G. Milner Gibson Cullum, Esq., F.S.A.

[Pedigree and wills kindly communicated by W. S. Churchill, esq.; Dom. State Papers; Noble's Lives of the Regicides, 1798.] C. H. F.

FLEETWOOD, GEORGE (1605–1667), Swedish general and baron, was second son of Sir Miles Fleetwood of Cranford and Aldwinkle, Northamptonshire, receiver of the court of wards, and was grandson of the first Sir William of Aldwinkle. Sir Miles had two other sons, William (afterwards Sir William of Aldwinkle) and Charles, the parliamentary general [q. v.] George was baptised at Cople, Bedfordshire, 30 June 1605, and in 1629 raised a troop of horse with which he went to Germany and joined the Swedish army under Gustavus Adolphus, who gave him the rank of lieutenant-colonel. He returned to England, and having collected a regiment of foot conducted it to the scene of war in 1630. He became a Swedish knight 3 June 1632, and in 1636 was sent on a mission to England. He was commandant of Greifswald and Colberg in 1641, and having returned to Sweden in 1653 was raised to the rank of baron by Queen Christina, 1 June 1654. In the following year he was sent by Charles X as envoy extraordinary to Cromwell, in response to Whitelocke's embassy. He was accompanied by his eldest son, Gustavus Miles Fleetwood, who was enrolled among the life-guard of Charles II, and pursued in England his education in the civil and military accomplishments of the day. Fleetwood became a Swedish lieutenant-general in 1656, and, having left England in 1660, member of the council of war in 1665. In 1640 he married Brita Gyllenstjerna, of the family of that Christina Gyllenstjerna who, in 1520, defended Stockholm against the Danes. By that lady he had four sons and two daughters. He died 11 June 1667, and was buried at Nyköping. He was a man of great energy and prudence, much trusted by his superiors. Whitelocke mentions him frequently in his 'Journal of the Swedish Embassy in the years 1653 and 1654,' and a letter from Fleetwood to his father in 1632, describing the battle of Lützen, at which he was present, is published in the 'Camden Miscellany,' vol. i. 1847. There are several branches of his descendants now in Sweden. Nathaniel Whiting, minister of Aldwinkle, dedicated his 'Old Jacob's Altar newly repaired,' 1659, 4to, to the three brothers, William, George, and Charles.

[Information kindly supplied by W. S. Churchill, esq., of Manchester; Whitelocke's Swedish Embassy; Camden Miscellany, vol. i. Attartaflor, or Swedish Tables of Nobility, Stockholm (1859), gives the correct genealogy. Burke in his Extinct and Dormant Baronetcies repeats genealogical errors of Mark Noble.] C. H. D.

FLEETWOOD, JAMES, D.D. (1603–1683), bishop of Worcester, the seventh son of Sir George Fleetwood of the Vache, Chalfont St. Giles, Buckinghamshire, by Catherine, daughter of Henry Denny of Waltham, Essex, was baptised at Chalfont St. Giles 25 April 1603. He was educated first at Eton and then at King's College, Cambridge, of which he was elected scholar in 1623. Having taken holy orders, he was appointed in 1632 chaplain to the Bishop of Lichfield (Dr. Robert Wright), by whom he was presented to the vicarage of Prees, Shropshire, and subsequently, 12 July 1636, collated to the prebend of Eccleshall in the church of Lichfield, in which he was installed on 9 Sept. following. On the outbreak of the rebellion he attached himself as chaplain to the regiment of John, earl of Rivers, and was of so much service at the battle of Edgehill—whether he limited himself strictly to prayers and exhortations or took a more active part in the fighting is not clear—that at Charles's special command the university of Oxford conferred upon him the degree of D.D. on 1 Nov. 1642. He was afterwards preferred to the rectory of Sutton Coldfield, Warwickshire, from which, however, he was ejected by the parliament. He was tutor to several noblemen and chaplain to Prince Charles, who made him his chaplain in ordinary on the Restoration. In accordance with a royal mandate the fellows of King's College, Cambridge, elected him provost in June 1660. Dr. Whichcote, the existing provost, supported by a minority of the fellows, held out in his rooms, and Fleetwood was compelled to apply to Charles for a 'letter mandatory' before he would quit. He was restored to the living of Prees and presented to the rectory of Anstey in Hertfordshire and that of Denham in Buckinghamshire. He was vice-chancellor of Cambridge University in 1663 and 1667. On 29 Aug. 1675 he was consecrated bishop of Worcester in the church of St. Peter le Poer, Broad Street, London. He died 17 July 1683, being buried in Worcester Cathedral. A mural tablet inscribed with his name was placed in Jesus Chapel the same year. Wood states he was buried in the lady chapel, and that 'a marble monument with an epitaph of his own making' was placed over his grave in 1687. No trace of this is now to be seen. By his wife, Martha Mercer of Reading, he had two sons, Arthur and John (the latter became archdeacon of Worcester), and four daughters.

[Wood's Fasti Oxon. ii. 51; Alumni Etonenses; Le Neve's Fasti Eccl. Angl.; Hist. MSS. Comm. 1st Rep. App. 67, 7th Rep. App. 106; Britton's Worcester Cathedral, App. 2; information from J. P. Earwaker, esq.] J. M. R.

FLEETWOOD, SIR PETER HESKETH (1801–1866), founder of the town of Fleetwood, descended from the ancient Lancashire families of Hesketh and Fleetwood, son of Robert Hesketh, esq., of Rossall, Lancashire, was born at Wennington Hall, near Lancaster, on 9 May 1801. He was educated at Trinity College, Oxford, and graduated B.A. in 1823 and M.A. in 1826. He was high sheriff of Lancashire in 1830, and sat as M.P. for Preston from 1832 to 1847, at first as a conservative, and subsequently as a member of the opposite party. He assumed the surname of Fleetwood by royal license 5 March 1831, and was created a baronet in June 1838. He projected, and in 1836 commenced to build the present flourishing town and port of Fleetwood, situated on his estate of Rossall, at the mouth of the river Wyre, in the Fylde, Lancashire. He was a strong advocate for the abolition of the death penalty, and in 1840 published a translation of Victor Hugo's 'Last Days of a Condemned,' to which he prefixed 'Observations on Capital Punishment.'

He was twice married: first in 1826 to Eliza Debonnaire, daughter of Sir T. J. Metcalfe; and secondly, in 1837, to Virginia Marie, daughter of Señor Pedro Garcia, who still (1889) survives. Sir Peter died at his residence, 127 Piccadilly, London, on 12 April 1866. His son, the Rev. Sir Peter Louis Hesketh Fleetwood, died in 1880, when the baronetcy became extinct.

[Gent. Mag. June 1866, p. 906; Illustrated London News, April 1886, p. 426; Hardwick's History of Preston (1857), p. 555; Baines's History of Lancashire (1870), ii. 517–18; Lancashire and Cheshire Historical and Genealogical Notes, ii. 113, 118.] C. W. S.

FLEETWOOD, THOMAS (1661–1717), drainer of Marton or Martin Meer, eldest son of Sir Richard Fleetwood, bart., of Calwick, Staffordshire, who survived him, was born in 1661, and having married the daughter and heiress of Christopher Bannister, esq., of Bank Hall, Lancashire, he purchased from the Mainwarings, about 1690, the manor of Marton Grange, or Marton Sands, in the same county. His land adjoined a large lake called Marton (or Martin) Meer, occupying an area of 3,132 acres, with a circumference of about eighteen miles, and this he boldly resolved to drain. Having first obtained from the neighbouring proprietors a lease of their rights in the meer for the duration of three lives and thirty-one years, he procured in 1692 an act of parliament allowing him to proceed, and commenced operations in the following year. On these extensive works as many as two thousand labourers were sometimes engaged at the same time. The result was fairly successful for about sixty years, but in 1755, five years after the lease had expired, the sea broke in, almost destroying all that had been done. In 1781 draining operations were resumed by Thomas Eccleston of Scarisbrick, Lancashire; but it was not until after the middle of the nineteenth century that Sir Peter Hesketh succeeded in triumphing over every difficulty, converting this large tract of fertile land, traversed by good roads, to profitable use. Fleetwood died 22 April 1717, and was buried in the church of North Meols, Lancashire, where there is a monument to his memory eulogising his enterprise and spirit. His only daughter and heiress, Henrietta Maria, married Thomas Legh, younger brother of Peter Legh, esq., of Lyme in Cheshire (EARWAKER, *East Cheshire*, ii. 301).

[Burke's Extinct and Dormant Baronetcies, 1844; Baines's History of the County Palatine and Duchy of Lancaster, 1836; Leigh's Natural History of Lancashire, Cheshire, and the Peak, 1700.] C. H. D.

FLEETWOOD, WILLIAM (1535 ?-1594), recorder of London, son of Robert Fleetwood, third son of William Fleetwood of Hesketh in Lancashire, was born about 1535, and after being educated at Brasenose College, Oxford, which he left without a degree, was called to the bar of the Middle Temple. He became freeman by patrimony of the Merchant Taylors' Company of London on 21 June 1557; autumn reader of his inn on 21 May 1563; steward of the company's manor of Rushbrook in 1564, and counsel in their suit against the Clothworkers in 1565. In 1559 he was one of the commissioners to visit the diocese of Oxford, Lincoln, Peterborough, Coventry, and Lichfield, and was elected M.P. for Lancaster to the first two parliaments of Elizabeth's reign, having previously sat for Marlborough in the last of Mary's parliaments. In 1568 he became 'double reader in Lent' to his inn. By the Earl of Leicester's influence he was elected (26 April 1571) recorder of London, and the same year was made a commissioner to inquire into the customs, besides being returned to parliament for the city of London (8 May 1572). As recorder he was famous for rigorously and successfully enforcing the laws against vagrants, mass-priests, and papists. In 1576 he was committed to the Fleet prison for a short time for breaking into the Portuguese ambassador's chapel under colour of the law against popish recusants. His own account of his action, dated 9 Nov., is printed in Strype's 'Annals.' In 1580 he was made serjeant-at-law, and in 1583 a commissioner

for the reformation of abuses in printing. In the same year he drafted a scheme for housing the poor and preventing the plague in London by maintaining open spaces. On 27 April 1586 he was promised, but did not receive, the post of baron of the exchequer. He was re-elected M.P. for London in 1584, 1586, and 1588. In 1588 he reported, with the solicitor-general, as to proceedings to be taken against the jesuits, and in 1589 on the right of sanctuary for criminals attaching to St. Paul's churchyard. In 1591 the common council voted him a pension of 100*l.*, whereupon he resigned his office. He was made queen's serjeant in 1592, and died at his house in Noble Street, Aldersgate, on 28 Feb. 1593–4. He had formerly lived at Bacon House, Foster Lane, and at his death owned an estate at Great Missenden, Buckinghamshire, where he was buried. Fleetwood was a hard-working judge, and was disappointed at not receiving higher preferment. His connection with Leicester was insisted on by Leicester's enemies, and he is called 'Leicester's mad Recorder' in 'Leicester's Commonwealth,' but he was at the same time assiduous in cultivating Lord Burghley's favour. He was noted for his witty speeches, and his eloquence is eulogised by Thomas Newton in his 'Encomia,' 1589. He married Mariana, daughter of John Barley of Kingsey, Buckinghamshire, by whom he left a family. His elder son, Sir William, succeeded to Missenden, and the younger son, Sir Thomas, of the Middle Temple, was attorney to Henry, prince of Wales. One daughter (Cordelia) married Sir David Foulis [q. v.], and another (Elizabeth) Sir Thomas Chaloner (1561–1615) [q. v.] Fleetwood's works are: 1. 'An Oration made at Guildhall before the Mayor, concerning the late attempts of the Queen's Maiesties evil seditious subjects,' 15 Oct. 1571, 12mo. 2. 'Annalium tam Regum Edwardi V, Ric. III, et Hen. VII quam Hen. VIII, titulorum ordine alphabetico digestorum Elenchus,' 1579, 1597. 3. 'A Table to the Reports of Edmund Plowden' (in French), 1578, 1579, 1599. 4. 'The Office of a Justice of the Peace,' 1658, 8vo (posthumous). 5. Verses before Sir Thomas Chaloner's 'De Republica Anglorum instauranda,' 1579, and Lambarde's 'Perambulation of Kent,' 1576. Many of Fleetwood's works remain in manuscript. Among them are 'Observacons sur Littleton' (*Harl. MS.* 5225), besides four volumes of reports and law commonplaces (*Harl. MS.* 5153–6), and an imperfect but interesting 'Itinerarium ad Windsor' (*Gent. Mag.* 1857, i. 602). Wood saw in manuscript 'Observations upon the Eyre of Pickering,' and on Lambarde's 'Archeion.' In the preface to the 'Office of a Justice' Fleetwood mentions a work by himself 'De Pace Ecclesiæ,' not otherwise known.

[Baines's Lancashire, iv. 440; Middle Temple MS. Records; Merchant Taylors' MS. Records; Parl. Hist. i. 734 sq.; Stow's London; Strype's Annals; Wood's Athenæ, ed. Bliss, i. 598; Wright's Elizabeth and her Times; Biog. Brit. (1750); Official Lists of M.P.'s.]   W. C–E.

FLEETWOOD, WILLIAM (1656–1723), bishop of Ely, a descendant of the ancient family of Fleetwood of Hesketh, Lancashire, fifth of six children of Captain Geoffrey Fleetwood by Anne, daughter of Mr. Richard Smith, prothonotary to the Poultry Compter, and nephew of James Fleetwood [q. v.], bishop of Worcester, was born on 1 Jan. 1656, in the Tower of London, where his father resided till his death in April 1665. William was on the foundation at Eton, and was elected scholar of King's College, Cambridge, on 27 Nov. 1675, and in due course became a fellow. He graduated B.A. 1679, M.A. 1683, D.D. 1705. On the death of Provost Copleston in 1689, the appointment of his successor being claimed by the crown, Fleetwood and another fellow were deputed to assert the right of the college to elect their own provost, which they succeeded in maintaining (Cole MSS. xvi. 35). In the same year, not long after his admission to holy orders, he gained his earliest celebrity as a preacher by a sermon delivered in King's College Chapel, at the commemoration of the founder, Henry VI, on 25 March, deservedly admired by his contemporaries as ' a perfect model and pattern of that kind of performance.' Fleetwood speedily became one of the most celebrated preachers of the day. He was often appointed to preach before the royal family, the houses of parliament, and other public bodies on great occasions. A sweet voice and graceful delivery commended, we are told, the sound sense and fervent piety of his sermons. His sermons were rendered more useful by 'the fine vein of casuistry which ran through most of them, wherein he displayed a peculiar talent, and gave ease to many weak and honest minds' (Memoir, p. viii). Fleetwood's reading was wide and his learning accurate. Browne Willis terms him a 'general scholar,' and one specially 'versed in antiquities.' His first work besides occasional sermons was a collection of pagan and Christian inscriptions, illustrated with notes, chiefly original, entitled 'Inscriptionum Antiquarum Sylloge' (1691). In 1707 he published anonymously his 'Chronicon Pretiosum,' a book very valuable for its research and general accuracy on the value of money and the price of corn and other commodities for the previous six centuries. The question had occurred whether the statutes of a college making the possession of an estate of 5l. per annum a bar to the retention of a fellowship were to be interpreted literally, or with regard to the altered value of money. Fleetwood clearly makes good the more liberal interpretation (AUBREY, Lives, i. 150). Fleetwood was a generous patron of letters. He encouraged Hickes in the publication of his 'Thesaurus Septentrionalis.' Hearne in the preface to his ' Liber Scaccarii,' and Browne Willis in the 'History of the Cathedral of St. Asaph,' acknowledge his 'communicativeness' (Cathedrals, iii. 367). The Boyle lectureship was offered to him, but ill-health prevented him from lecturing. The materials he had prepared were subsequently published by him in 1701, as 'An Essay on Miracles,' those, namely, of Moses and of Jesus Christ. Hoadly wrote a reply to this essay, to which Fleetwood, from his extreme aversion to controversy, made no rejoinder.

Fleetwood was a zealous whig, an ardent friend of the revolution and of the Hanoverian succession. Soon after the accession of William and Mary he was appointed chaplain to the king, but no other mark of royal favour followed till just before William's death, when he was nominated to a canonry at Windsor. The letters of nomination had not received the royal seal when the king died, and the House of Commons endeavoured to set them aside in favour of one of their own chaplains. Queen Anne, however, replied to their petition that ' if the king had given the canonry to Dr. Fleetwood, Dr. Fleetwood should have it.' He was installed on 2 June 1702. By the interest of Dr. Henry Godolphin [q. v.], provost of Eton and canon of St. Paul's, he was appointed to a fellowship at Eton and to the chapter rectory of St. Augustine and St. Faith's on 26 Nov. 1689, to which was speedily added the lectureship of St. Dunstan's-in-the-West, Fleet Street, where he usually preached three times a week to admiring crowds. But his love of retirement and his attachment to Eton and Windsor induced him in 1705 to exchange his London preferments for the living of Wexham, Buckinghamshire, worth only 60l. per annum, where he devoted much of his time to his favourite historical and antiquarian studies. In 1708 Queen Anne, of her own personal act and without his knowledge, appointed him to the see of St. Asaph, vacant by the death of Beveridge, to which he was consecrated on 8 June of that year. Anne called Fleetwood ' my bishop,' attended his sermons, and favoured him till her death, in spite of the outspoken whiggism which made him specially offensive to her favourite party. His fulfilment of the duties of the episcopate rose much above the standard of the age, and overcame the prejudice with which he was at first regarded by his clergy. His conciliatory manners, unblemished life, and high reputation secured respect in a diocese where party animosities were unusually strong (*Biograph. Brit.*) His first charge, issued in 1710, which covers nineteen closely printed folio pages of small type, will still repay reading. It is in the form of a series of remarks on the 'Articles of Enquiry' issued to his diocese, and throws much light on the condition of the church at the time. It closes with an impassioned defence of his own party against the charge of disloyalty to the church. He gives some sensible advice to his clergy upon the use of Welsh ('British,' he calls it) in their sermons. This charge exhibits Fleetwood as one who aimed sensibly and sincerely at promoting the good of his diocese. He paved the greater part of the cathedral at his own cost, and laid out above 100*l.* in the decoration of the choir (*Cole MSS.* xvi. 35). On the fall of the whigs Fleetwood absented himself from court, and openly expressed his indignation at the peace of Utrecht. Being selected to preach before the House of Lords on the general fast day, 16 Jan. 1711–1712, he chose for his subject 'the people that delight in war' (Ps. lxviii. 30), and defended the necessity of the war, of which the advantages were to be thrown away. The tory ministry adjourned the house beyond the day fixed for the sermon, so that it was not delivered; but it was at once printed, and though his name was concealed the authorship was no secret. His courageous attack upon the Jacobite tendencies of the government was quickly punished. Fleetwood at this time published four sermons preached by him on the deaths of Queen Mary, the Duke of Gloucester, William III, and the accession of Anne to the throne, and in an outspoken preface assailed the principle of non-resistance, and eloquently repudiated the doctrine that Christianity was favourable to political slavery. The tory ministry at first proposed to impeach Fleetwood for the publication. Eventually the House of Commons resolved, by a vote of 119 to 54, that the preface was malicious and factious, and sentenced it to be burnt by the common hangman. It was at once issued as No. 384 (21 May) of the 'Spectator,' and thus, as Fleetwood says to Burnet in answer to a sympathetic letter, conveyed 'above fourteen thousand copies into people's hands who would otherwise never have seen or heard of it.' Swift attacked it bitterly in a couple of papers (*Works*, 1814, iv. 276–93). Fleetwood took little part in public affairs during the brief remainder of Anne's reign, and could 'hardly endure to think of them,' and was especially indignant at the Schism Act of 1714. Soon after the accession of George I several bishoprics became vacant. Of these Ely was the first filled up, and Fleetwood was chosen for it. He was elected on 19 Nov. 1714, three months after the king's accession. Though advanced in years he was still assiduous in discharging his duties, and as the cathedral of Ely was too spacious for his voice, his sermons were commonly delivered in the chapel of Ely House in London, usually every Sunday.

As bishop of Ely he delivered two charges to his clergy in 1716 and 1722. Both enforce the solemnity of the ministerial office, and warmly eulogise George I. The case between Bentley and his fellows had been heard out before Fleetwood's predecessor, Dr. Moore [q. v.], whose death had put a stop to a definitive sentence of deprivation against Bentley. Application was at once made to the new bishop to carry on the case. Fleetwood declared that if he visited the college at all he would hold a general visitation, and take cognisance of all delinquencies reported to him of the fellows as well as of the master. Such a prospect frightened several of Bentley's opponents, whose moral character was not of the highest, into a mutual compact of forbearance. When the quarrel again broke out Fleetwood adhered to his refusal (MONK, *Life of Bentley*, i. 367–70, ii. 88, 247). He died at Tottenham, near London, to which place he had removed for the amendment of his health, from Ely House, Holborn, where he had chiefly resided, on 4 Aug. 1723, aged 67, and was buried in the north choir aisle of Ely Cathedral, 10 Aug. A monument bears an epitaph, laudatory, but not beyond his deserts. He left a widow and one son, James, on whom his father had conferred the archdeaconry of Ely.

In both his dioceses Fleetwood secured the love and esteem of his clergy, in spite of opinions generally unpalatable to them. Few bishops have left a more unspotted reputation behind them. He endeavoured to dispense his patronage to the most deserving without regard to personal influence. He always refused to enter into personal controversy. When attacked he would say: 'I write my own sense as well as I can. If it be right it will support itself; if it be not it is fit it should sink.' He liberally assisted his clergy with money, books, and in the remission of their fees. As a preacher his style is dignified, but simple, with much calmness of expression and clearness of thought. Archbishop Herring, who when at Lincoln's Inn was one of the most celebrated preachers of the day, was Fleetwood's domestic chaplain, and is said to have derived his excellent style of pulpit oratory from him as a model.

Many of Fleetwood's sermons were published anonymously to avoid prejudice and allow greater freedom of speech. Besides separate sermons on various occasions his works include: 1. 'Sermon on 2 Cor. ix. 12, preached before the University of Cambridge in King's College Chapel, 25 March 1689, at the Commemoration of Henry VI,' 1689, 4to. 2. 'Inscriptionum Antiquarum Sylloge,' 1691, 8vo. 3. 'A Method of Christian Devotion, translated from the French of M. Jurieu,' 1692, 8vo. 4. 'An Essay on Miracles, in two Discourses,' dedicated to Dr. Godolphin, provost of Eton, 1701. 5. 'The Reasonable Communicant,' London, 1704, 8vo (anonymous, erroneously ascribed to Mr. Theophilus Dorrington). 6. 'Sixteen Practical Discourses on Relative Duties, with Three Sermons upon the Case of Self-murther, addressed to the parishioners of St. Austins and St. Faith,' London, 1705, 2 vols. 1736. 7. 'Chronicon Pretiosum, or an Account of English Gold and Silver Money' (anonymous), London, 1707, 8vo. 8. 'Charge to the Clergy of the Diocese of St. Asaph,' London, 1710, 4to. 9. 'Romans xiii. vindicated from the Abusive Senses put upon it. Written by a Curate of Salop,' London, 1710, 8vo (anonymous). 10. 'Sermon in Refutation of Dr. Sacheverell's Doctrine of Passive Obedience and Non-resistance.' 11. 'Sermon preached before the Society for the Propagation of the Gospel in Foreign Parts at Bow Church, 16 Feb. 1710–11' (this sermon produced a powerful effect on behalf of the society, and was widely circulated). 12. 'Sermon on Ps. lxviii. 30, on the Fast Day, Jan. 16, 1711–12, against such as delight in war. By a Divine of the Church of England,' London, 1712 (see above). 13. 'The Judgment of the Church of England of Lay Baptism and of Dissenters' Baptism, in two parts' (in reply to Dr. Hickes, who denied its validity), London, 1712, 8vo (anonymous). 14. 'Four Sermons,' with preface, 1712 (see above). 15. 'The Life and Miracles of St. Wenefred, together with her Litanies, with some Historical Observations made thereon,' London, 1713, 8vo (anonymous) (directed against the superstitious pilgrimages made to St. Winifred's well in his diocese of St. Asaph). 16. 'Funeral Sermon on 2 Sam. xii. 5, on Mr. Noble, who was executed at Kingston for the murder of a gentleman with whose wife he had criminal conversation' (without name or date). 17. 'The

Counsellor's Plea for the Divorce of Sir G. D[owning] and Mrs. F[orrester]' (without name or date) [see DOWNING, SIR GEORGE, 1684?–1749]. 18. 'Charge to the Clergy of the Diocese of Ely, 1716,' London, 1716, 4to. 19. 'Papists not excluded from the Throne upon the account of Religion, being a vindication of Bishop Hoadly's "Preservative"' (without his name). The title is ironical. 20. Letter from Mr. J. Burdett, executed at Tyburn for the murder of Captain Falkland (without name or date). 21. Letter to an inhabitant of St. Andrew's, Holborn, about new ceremonies in the church, of which Dr. Sacheverell was the rector (without name or date). 22. 'A Defence of Praying before Sermon as directed by the IVth Canon' (without name or date). 23. 'Charge to the Clergy of the Diocese of Ely in August 1722.' A complete collection of his works was published in one volume folio in 1737, with a prefatory memoir by his nephew, Dr. W. Powell, dean of St. Asaph and prebendary of Ely.

[Biographical preface to Fleetwood's collected works; Bentham's Ely, pp. 208–9; Monk's Bentley, i. 367, 370, ii. 88, 247; Biog. Brit. 1750; Abbey's English Church, i. 120–7.]   E. V.

FLEMING, MISS, afterwards MRS. STANLEY (1796?–1861), actress, was born, according to Oxberry's 'Dramatic Chronology,' 31 Oct. 1796, but more probably four years earlier. She is said to have been a granddaughter of John West Dudley Digges [q. v.] In Liverpool and Manchester she played Lady Macbeth, Helen McGregor, and other characters. She married George Stanley, a low comedian, who appeared 9 Oct. 1834 at the Lyceum as Nicholas Trefoil in 'Before Breakfast,' went to America, and there died. Mrs. Stanley's first appearance in London took place at the Lyceum, assumably near the same date. She is chiefly remembered in connection with the Haymarket, where she played old women both in comedy and tragedy. She was a tall, well-built woman, and seems to have been a fine actress. Her daughter, Emma Stanley, born 13 Nov. 1823, made her first appearance at the Lyceum, in May 1843, as Catherine in 'The Exile.' Mrs. Stanley died suddenly of bronchitis in Jermyn Street, 17 Jan. 1861, at the reputed age of sixty-nine years.

[Such meagre particulars as are obtainable concerning Miss Fleming are derived from Oxberry's Dramatic Chronology, an untrustworthy source; and Gent. Mag. 1861, pt. i. p. 234.]   J. K.

FLEMING, ABRAHAM (1552?–1607), antiquary and poet, born in London in or about 1552, was matriculated at Cambridge as a sizar of Peterhouse in November 1570, but did not go out B.A. until 1581–2. He took holy orders, and became chaplain to the Countess of Nottingham. Between 1589 and 1606 he preached eight times at St. Paul's Cross. On 19 Oct. 1593 he was collated by Archbishop Whitgift to the rectory of St. Pancras, Soper Lane, London. He died at Bottesford, Leicestershire, on 18 Sept. 1607, while on a visit to his brother Samuel, the rector of that parish, and was buried in the chancel of the church there.

Though a poor poet, Fleming was an excellent antiquary. Most, if not all, of his manuscript collections were in 1732 in the possession of Francis Peck [q. v.], who designed to print them in the second volume of his 'Desiderata Curiosa.' They cannot now be traced.

A list of fifty-nine of his works will be found in Cooper's 'Athenæ Cantabrigienses.' Among these are: 1. 'Virgil's Eclogues, translated into English Verse,' London, 1575, and with the 'Georgics,' 1589. 2. 'The Bukolikes of P. Virgilius Maro . . . Drawne into plaine and familiar English Verse,' London, 1575, 4to. 3. 'A Panoplie of Epistles, or, a Looking-Glasse for the Vnlearned. Conteyning a perfecte plattforme of inditing letters of all sorts,' London, 1576, 4to; a translation from the Latin. 4. 'A Register of Hystories,' from the Greek of Ælianus, London, 1576, 4to. 5. 'Of English Dogges,' from the Latin of John Caius, London, 1576, 4to. 6. 'A Straunge and Terrible Wunder wrought very late in the Parish Church of Bongay . . . . the fourth of this August 1577, in a great tempest of violent raine, lightning, and thunder . . . With the appearance of a horrible-shaped Thing, sensibly perceived of the people then and there assembled,' London, 1577, 12mo; reprinted, London, 1826, 8vo. 7. 'Of all Blasing Starrs in Generall,' from the Latin of Frederick Nause, bishop of Vienna, London, 1577, 4to. 8. 'Historie of Leander and Hero,' written by Musæus. Translation, published about 1577. This is mentioned in a marginal note to Fleming's translation of Virgil's 'Georgics,' 1589. 9. 'Jerom of Ferrara his meditations, on the 51 & 31 Psalms; translated and augmented,' London, n. d., and 1588, 16mo. Licensed in 1578. 10. 'A Paradoxe, proving by reason and example that baldnesse is much better than bushie haire, &c. Written by that excellent philosopher Synesius, or (as some say) Cyren. A prettie pamphlet to pervse, and replenished with recreation. Englished by Abraham Fleming. Herevnto is annexed the pleasant tale of Hemetes the Heremite, pronounced be-

fore the Queens Maiestie. Newly recognised both in Latine and Englishe, by the said A.F.,' London, 1579, 8vo. The tale of Hermetes is, with a few verbal changes, that which George Gascoigne presented to Queen Elizabeth (COOPER, *Athenæ Cantabr.* i. 377). 11. 'Fred. Nawse, his generall Doctrine of Earthquakes,' translated, London, 1580, 8vo. The translator has added a history of earthquakes in England from the time of William the Conqueror to the last earthquake on 6 April 1580. 12. 'A Memoriall of the Famous Monumentes and Charitable Almes Deedes of the Right Worshipfull Mr. Willm. Lambe . . . who deceased the xxi. of Aprill 1580,' London, 1580, 8vo. 13. 'The Footpath to Felicitie,' London, 1581, 24mo, reprinted in 'The Diamond of Deuotion,' 1586. 14. 'A Monomachie of Motives in the mind of man: Or a battell between Vertues & Vices of contrarie qualitie,' newly Englished, London, 1582, 24mo. 15. 'Verborvm Latinorvm cvm Græcis Anglicisqve conivnctorvm locupletissimi Commentarij,' London, 1583, fol. 16. Poetical translations for Reginald Scot's 'Discoverie of Witchcraft,' 1584. 17. 'A Shorte Dictionarie in Latine and English,' London, 1586 and 1594, 4to. 18. 'The Diamond of Deuotion; cut and squared into six severall pointes: namelie (1) The Footpath of Felicitie; (2) A Guide to Godlines; (3) The Schoole of Skill; (4) A Swarme of Bees; (5) A Plant of Pleasure; (6) A Grove of Graces. Full of manie fruitfull lessons auailable vnto the leading of a godlie and reformed life,' London, 1586, 24mo. 19. 'The Historie of England, . . . &c. By Raphael Holinshed. Now newlie digested, &c. by Abr. Fleming.' In the first volume of Holinshed's 'Chronicles,' 1587. The third volume of the same edition was enlarged by Fleming with interpolations from the collections of Francis Thynne, the abridgment of R. Grafton, and the summary of John Stow. 20. 'The Bucoliks of Publius Virgilius Maro, Prince of all Latine Poets . . . Together with his Georgiks or Ruralls, otherwise called his husbandrie, conteyning foure books. All newly translated into English verse,' London, 1589, 4to, dedicated to Archbishop Whitgift. This version of the 'Bucolics' is not the same as that published by Fleming in 1575. 21. Historical and miscellaneous articles in manuscript enumerated in Peck's 'Desiderata Curiosa.'

[Addit. MS. 5869, f. 20; Ames's Typogr. Antiq. (Herbert); Bibl. Anglo-Poetica, p. 105; Bodleian Cat.; Brydges's Brit. Bibl. ii. 313, 583; Brydges's Censura Literaria, 2nd edit. vi. 11, x. 4; Brydges's Restituta, ii. 203, iii. 47; Collier's Poetical Decameron, i. 105, 109, 114, 116, 117,

194; Collier's Register of Stationers' Company, ii. 87, 97, 114–16, 118, 197; Cooper's Athenæ Cantabr. ii. 459; Eller's Belvoir, p. 386; Haslewood's Ancient Critical Essays, ii. 35, 54; Hone's Every-day Book, i. 1066; Lowndes's Bibl. Man. (Bohn), p. 808; Newcourt's Repertorium, i. 519; Nichols's Leicestershire, ii. 98, 99; Notes and Queries, 1st ser. i. 85; Oldys's British Librarian, pp. 89, 91; Peck's Desiderata Curiosa, folio edit. lib. vi. 49–56; Peck's Historical Pieces, p. 28; Ritson's Bibl. Poetica, p. 207; Strype's Annals, ii. 548 fol.; Suckling's Suffolk, i. 124; Tanner's Bibl. Brit. p. 287; Warton's Hist. of English Poetry; Watt's Bibl. Brit.; Wood's Athenæ Oxon. (Bliss), i. 412, 485, 752.] T. C.

FLEMING, ALEXANDER, M.D. (1824–1875), was born in 1824 at Edinburgh, where he studied medicine and graduated M.D. in 1844. His chief work was his college essay on the 'Physiological and Medicinal Properties of Aconitum Napellus,' Lond. 1845, which led to the introduction of a tincture of aconite of uniform strength known as Fleming's tincture. Having spent some years at Cork as professor of materia medica in the Queen's College, he went in 1858 to Birmingham, where he held the honorary office of physician to the Queen's Hospital until his retirement through ill-health in 1873. He died at Brixton, London, on 21 Aug. 1875. Besides the works above mentioned, he published two introductory addresses and two papers in the 'Dublin Quarterly Journal of Medical Science' (on measles of the pig, and on the classification of medicines).

[Brit. Med. Journ. ii. 1875.] C. C.

FLEMING, CALEB, D.D. (1698–1779), dissenting polemic, was born at Nottingham on 4 Nov. 1698. His father was a hosier; his mother, whose maiden name was Buxton, was a daughter of the lord of the manor of Chelmerton, Derbyshire. Brought up in Calvinism, Fleming's early bent was for the independent ministry. As a boy he learned shorthand, in order to take down sermons. In 1714 John Hardy [q. v.] became one of the ministers of the presbyterian congregation at the High Pavement, Nottingham, and opened a nonconformist academy. Fleming was one of his first pupils. He was admitted as a communicant in 1715. Hardy (who conformed in 1727) taught him to discard his ancestral theology. He gave up the idea of the ministry and took to business, retaining, however, his theological tastes.

In 1727 he left Nottingham for London. By this time he had married and had a family. How he maintained himself is not clear. He probably relied upon his pen; but though he began at once to publish pamphlets which attracted some attention, he 'was often in sight of real want.' In 1727 'a popish seducer' tried to make a convert of him, but desisted on discovering that he had to deal with an anti-trinitarian (Survey of the Search, p. 101). Some help in further classical and biblical study was given to him by John Holt, then a presbyterian minister in London, afterwards mathematical tutor at Warrington Academy, and he learned Hebrew from a rabbi. Through William Harris, D.D., presbyterian minister at Crutched Friars, an offer was made for his services as a government pamphleteer. He replied that he 'would sooner cut off his right hand.' In 1736 he published a pamphlet, 'The Fourth Commandment abrogated by the Gospel,' dedicating it to his namesake, Sir George Fleming [q. v.], bishop of Carlisle. It would appear that he had been advised to do this by John Thomas, afterwards bishop of Winchester. Bishop Fleming offered him the living of Lazonby, Cumberland, worth some 600l. a year. Dr. Thomas was ready to advance what was needed for his removal, but Fleming could not conform. In his refusal he was warmly supported by his wife.

His friends now began to urge him to enter the dissenting ministry. In his fortieth year he preached his first sermon to the presbyterian congregation at Wokingham, Berkshire, Catcot, the minister, publicly thanking him for his services. After this he officiated at a few places in the neighbourhood of London. At length, on the death of John Munckley (August 1738), he was strongly recommended by Benjamin Avery [q. v.] as a suitable candidate for the charge of the presbyterian congregation at Bartholomew Close. Here Fleming and William May were ordained as joint pastors in 1740. Fleming had scruples about presbyterian forms, and classed himself as an independent. At his ordination, conducted by Samuel Chandler, D.D. [q. v.], Jeremiah Hunt, D.D., a learned independent, and others, he refused to submit to the imposition of hands. His confession of faith was unique. He would only say that he believed the New Testament contained 'a revelation worthy of God to give and of man to receive;' and this he promised to teach in the sense in which he should 'from time to time' understand it. It was soon rumoured that Fleming was a Socinian. His congregation was never large, and the scantiness of his stipend reduced him to straits. His friends fell off, with the exception of Jeremiah Hunt. After Hunt's death (1744) Fleming contracted a close intimacy with Nathaniel Lardner, D.D., his neighbour in Hoxton Square, and co-operated with him in literary work.

In January 1752 James Foster, D.D. [q.v.],

became disabled from preaching. John Weatherley (*d.* May 1752), a general baptist minister, who supplied Foster's place, met Fleming at Hamlin's Coffee-house, and engaged him for a Sunday at Pinners' Hall (independent). He attracted the notice of Timothy Hollis, was soon afterwards elected as Foster's assistant, and on Foster's death (5 Nov. 1753) as pastor. The Bartholomew Close congregation then came to an end, its few remaining members joining Pinners' Hall. For nearly a quarter of a century Fleming remained at his post; his ministry, though painstaking, was not popular, and when he ceased to preach, in December 1777, his congregation became extinct, the lease of their meeting-house expiring in 1778. He had admirers, who left him considerable legacies, among them being a bequest by a Suffolk gentleman (Reynolds), who had once heard him preach but did not know his name. A wealthy widow placed her whole fortune at his disposal. Fleming, however, declined to be enriched at the expense of her needy relatives.

Fleming's chief work is 'A Survey of the Search after Souls,' 1758, 8vo, dedicated to Nicolas Munckley, M.D. The title and topic were suggested by the writings of William Coward (1657?–1725) [q.v.] To prove, against Coward, the existence of a separate soul, Fleming employs the arguments of Clarke, and especially of Andrew Baxter [q. v.] He does not contend that the soul is inherently immortal, but simply that it possesses a 'capacity of immortality.' His view of the resurrection was adopted by John Cameron (1724–1799) [q. v.]

Fleming was an unwearied writer of argumentative and combative pamphlets, the greater part of them being anonymous. His political brochures, in defence of civil liberty and against the Jacobites, church establishments, and the toleration of popery, are tart enough. Against the theological writers of his time, high and low, he entered the field with confident vigour. He attacked Sherlock, Soame Jenyns, Wesley, the Sabbatarians as represented by Robert Cornthwaite, and the Muggletonians. His most severe, and perhaps his best remembered, publication is his 'character' of Thomas Bradbury [q.v.], 'taken from his own pen.' The topics to which he most frequently recurred were the defence of infant baptism and of the authority of the New Testament against the deists, especially Chubb, whom he is said to have impressed. His own theology, as may be seen in his 'True Deism, the Basis of Christianity,' 1749, 8vo, was little more than a specially authenticated deism. He retains the 'supernatural conception,' minimised after a fashion of his own, and the miracles of our Lord, which 'did not introduce a single unnatural phenomenon,' but 'removed defects in nature' (*True Deism*, p. 14). In a manuscript sermon (10 Oct. 1773) he ranks Confucius, Socrates, Plato, Cicero, and Seneca among organs of divine revelation. Many of his pamphlets and sermons attempt to deal with the problem of a general depravity of morals. Under the title of 'A Modern Plan,' 1748, 8vo, he drew up 'a compendium of moral institutes,' in the shape of a catechism in which the learner asks the questions.

In his old age his 'dear friend,' William Dalrymple, D.D., of Ayr (Burns's 'D'rymple mild'), procured for him the degree of D.D. from St. Andrews. Fleming was inclined to reject this 'compliment;' but his friend Thomas Hollis 'put it into the public papers,' so Fleming accepted it in a very characteristic letter (6 April 1769).

After completing his seventy-ninth year Fleming retired from public duty. He died on 21 July 1779, and was buried in Bunhill Fields. He married a daughter of John Harris of Hardstoft, Derbyshire, and had ten children, of whom one survived him. He left an epitaph for his gravestone, in which he describes himself as 'dissenting teacher,' and expresses a conditional hope of immortality. For this, however, was substituted a eulogistic inscription by Joseph Towers, LL.D. His funeral sermon was preached by John Palmer at New Broad Street. A fine portrait of Fleming, by William Chamberlain, was bequeathed by him to Dr. Williams's Library. An engraving by Hopwood is given in Wilson.

Wilson enumerates sixty of Fleming's publications. It may suffice to add such as are not included in Wilson's list. Most of them will be found in Dr. Williams's Library, Grafton Street, W.C.; others are from a collection formed by Fleming's nephew: 1. 'The Parent Disinherited by his Offspring,' &c., 1728, 8vo. 2. 'Observations on Some Articles of the Muggletonians' Creed,' &c., 1735, 8vo (answered in 'The Principles of the Muggletonians,' &c., 1735, 8vo, by A. B., i.e. Arden Bonell). 3. 'An Appeal to the People of England,' &c. [1739], 8vo. 4. 'The Challenge . . . on . . . Baptism,' &c., 1743, 8vo. 5. 'A Fine Picture of Enthusiasm,' &c., 1744, 8vo. 6. 'A Letter to the Rev. Charles Willats upon his Assize Sermon,' &c., 1744, 8vo. 7. 'Remarks upon the Life of John Duke of Argyle,' &c., 1745, 8vo. 8. 'Tracts on Baptism,' &c., 1745, 8vo (a collection of six previous pieces, with an introduction). 9. 'A Fund raising for the Italian Gentleman,' &c.,

1750, 8vo (the reference is to the 'Young Pretender'). 10. 'The Devout Laugh,' &c., 1750, 8vo. 11. 'Natural and Revealed Religion at Variance,' &c., 1758, 8vo (against Thomas Sherlock). 12. 'A Letter to the Rev. John Stevens,' &c., 1760, 8vo. 13. 'The Pædo-Baptist's sense of Positive Institutions,' &c., n.d. 8vo. 14. 'Grammatical Observations on the English Language,' &c., 1765, 8vo. 15. 'A few Strictures relative to the Author,' prefixed to 'An Enquiry,' &c., 1776, 8vo, by Paul Cardale [q. v.] 16. 'Two Discourses,' &c., 1778, 8vo. Some of Cardale's anonymous pieces have sometimes been ascribed to Fleming. He edited many works by divines and others, including the first volume (1756) of Amory's 'Life of John Buncle.'

[Fleming left memoirs, which were to have been published by Joseph Lomas Towers (son of Dr. Towers), who died insane in 1832. A memoir was drawn up by Fleming's nephew, J. Slipper, corrected by Laurence Holden, and published in the Monthly Repository, 1818, p. 409 sq.; Kippis's Life of Lardner, 1769, p. 96; Palmer's Funeral Sermon, 1779; Aikin's Gen. Biog. art. 'Fleming;' Wilson's Dissenting Churches, 1808, i. 103, ii. 91, 255, 283 sq., iii. 384; Turner's Lives of Eminent Unitarians, 1840, i. 275 sq.; Jeremy's Presbyterian Fund, 1885, pp. 2, 165 sq.; Fleming's tracts; and a collection of his manuscript sermons in the possession of the present writer.] A. G.

FLEMING, CHRISTOPHER (1800–1880), surgeon, was born at Boardstown in co. Westmeath on 14 July 1800, and in 1821 graduated B.A. in the university of Dublin. He became a licentiate of the Irish College of Surgeons in 1824, and a member in 1826. In 1838 he took an M.D. degree in the university of Dublin, but did not obtain a hospital appointment till 1851, when he became surgeon to the House of Industry Hospitals. In 1856 he was elected president of the College of Surgeons of Ireland, and in 1877 collected some papers which he had previously published in medical journals into a volume entitled 'Clinical Records of Injuries and Diseases of the Genito-Urinary Organs.' His only other work is 'Remarks on the Application of Chloroform to Surgical purposes,' Dublin, 1851, and both are without permanent value. He married a Miss Radcliff, and had seven children, of whom a son and a daughter survived him. He retired from practice a few years before his death, and went to live at Donnybrook, near Dublin, where he died 30 Dec. 1880.

[Sir A. Cameron's Hist. of the Royal College of Surgeons in Ireland; British Medical Journal, 8 Jan. 1881; index Cat. of Library of the Surgeon-General's Office, U.S. Army.] N. M.

FLEMING, Sir DANIEL (1633–1701), antiquary, eldest son of William Fleming of Coniston, North Lancashire, and Rydal, Westmoreland, by Alice, eldest daughter of Roger Kirkby of Kirkby, Lancashire, was born on 25 July 1633, and educated at Queen's College, Oxford, which he entered in 1650, and Gray's Inn. By the death of his father in 1653 he inherited considerable estates in the neighbourhood of Rydal, for which he paid heavy fines to the parliament. At the Restoration he was appointed sheriff of Cumberland. He was a constant correspondent of Secretary Williamson, and his letters in the Record Office, some of which have been calendared, afford a lively picture of the state of affairs in Cumberland and Westmoreland during the latter half of the seventeenth century, and exhibit him as a staunch supporter of the church of England, and enemy alike of the protestant dissenter and the Roman catholic. He regretted the release of George Fox in 1666 as likely to discourage the justices from acting against the quakers, and credited to the full the reports of their burning 'steeple houses.' He was knighted on 15 May 1681 at Windsor, and in the parliament of 1685–1687 sat as member for Cockermouth, in which character he opposed the declaration of indulgence. He occupied his leisure in antiquarian researches, chiefly in connection with his native county, and left some manuscript collections, which have recently been edited for the Cumberland and Westmoreland Antiquarian Society under the title 'Description of the County of Westmoreland,' by Sir G. F. Duckett, bart., London, 1882, 8vo. He died in 1701. He is said by Wotton (Baronetage, iv. 120) to have been, 'not without grateful acknowledgment, a considerable assistant to the learned annotator of Camden's "Britannia."' No such acknowledgment, however, is to be found in the preface to Gibson's edition of Camden, which must be the one referred to. It was at Fleming's suggestion that Thomas Brathwaite left his collection of upwards of three hundred coins of the Roman era to the university of Oxford. Fleming married in 1655 Barbara, eldest daughter of Sir Henry Fletcher of Hutton, Cumberland, who was slain at Rowton Heath on the side of the king in 1645. His eldest son, William, created a baronet 4 Oct. 1705, died in 1736, and was succeeded by his brother George, bishop of Carlisle, who is separately noticed.

[Nicolson and Burn's Westmoreland, i. 164–71; Cal. State Papers, Dom. 1660–7; Luttrell's Relation of State Affairs, i. 93; Hist. MSS. Comm. 10th Rep. App. pt. iv.; Lists of Members of Parliament (Official Return of).] J. M. R.

FLEMING, Sir GEORGE (1667-1747), bishop of Carlisle, fifth son of Sir Daniel Fleming [q. v.] of Rydal, Westmoreland, and of Barbara, his wife, eldest daughter of Sir Henry Fletcher, bart., of Hutton, Cumberland, was born at Rydal Hall, 10 June 1667, the ninth of fifteen children. He succeeded his elder brother, Sir William, who died without heir-male, as second baronet of Rydal in 1736. He entered St. Edmund Hall, Oxford, June 1688. In 1690 he contributed to some congratulatory verses upon the king's safe return from Ireland. He proceeded B.A. 13 April 1692, and M.A. 7 March 1694. Leaving Oxford in 1699, he became domestic chaplain to Dr. Thomas Smith [q. v.], bishop of Carlisle, by whom he had been ordained, and who, 1695, presented him to the living of Aspatria, Cumberland. He resigned Aspatria on his collation by Bishop Nicolson [q. v.] in 1703 to the church of St. Michael, Stanwix, which he held as vicar till 1705 (HUTCHINSON, *Hist. of Cumberland*, ii. 285, 583). He was instituted to the second prebend in Carlisle Cathedral 7 March 1700-1. He was nominated by Bishop Nicolson to the archdeaconry of Carlisle 28 March 1705. Attached to the archdeaconry was the rectory of St. Cuthbert, Great Salkeld, which he held in conjunction with future preferment till his accession to the episcopate (JEFFERSON, *Antiquities of Cumberland*, i. 262, 266), a portion of this preferment being the living of Ousby, to which he was presented by Bishop Bradford, 1719, and to which a prebend was attached. According to the edition of Willis's 'Survey of Cathedrals,' containing the manuscript notes by W. Cole (i. 307), he succeeded Joseph Fisher [q. v.] as vicar of Brough or Burgh-under-Stanmore, Westmoreland. He was created LL.D. by diploma at Lambeth 10 March 1726-7 (Wotton MSS.) He was installed dean of Carlisle 7 April 1727; and 30 Oct. 1734 was nominated bishop. He was consecrated bishop at Lambeth 19 Jan. 1734-1735. On 1 May 1736 he lost his wife Catherine, daughter of Robert Jefferson, to whom he had been married 28 Oct. 1708. He had by her one son, William, a prebendary, and his successor in the archdeaconry, who died in 1743, during his father's lifetime, and four daughters (*Gent. Mag.*), the youngest of whom, Mildred, was married in 1737 to Edward Stanley, esq., of Ponsonby Hall, where there was a portrait of Fleming by Vanderbank.

When the Pretender entered Carlisle in November 1745, he installed Thomas Coppock [q. v.] as bishop. It seems (*Gent. Mag.* 1745, p. 575) that the bishop had accompanied the sheriff to oppose the rebels at Penrith, when the force ran away at the sight of a few highlanders. Fleming contributed his share (HUTCHINSON, *Hist. of Cumberland*, ii. 437) towards repairing and beautifying the episcopal palace, for he ' laid new floors and wainscotted the drawing-room, dressing-room, and kitchen chambers.' He died in his palace at Rose Castle 2 July 1747, and was buried at the east end of the south aisle of the cathedral, where there is a marble monument with a panegyrical inscription. Two letters of Fleming are in the Wotton MSS. in the British Museum (*Add. MSS.* 24120, ff. 331-2), in answer to a request for information from Thomas Wotton, author of the 'Baronetage.' The second letter gives full details about the Fleming family and his own life. His title and estates passed to his nephew William, son of his next brother, Michael, likewise deceased, the sixth son of Sir Daniel. This Sir William was father to Michael, the fourth baronet—the ' brilliant baronet,' incidentally noticed for his social and literary gifts by Sir W. Scott, in whose person the prefix 'le,' which had dropped out of the family name since the time of Edward IV, was revived at baptism (BURKE, *Landed Gentry*).

[Wotton MSS. Brit. Mus. (Add. MSS. 24120, ff. 331-2, &c.); Gent. Mag. anno 1747; Le Neve's Fasti Eccles. Angl. (Hardy); Cat. of Graduates Oxon. 1851; Stubbs's Reg. Sacr. Angl.; Willis's Survey of Cathedrals, with manuscript notes by W. Cole; Jefferson's Hist. of Carlisle, and Hist. Antiquities of Cumberland; Willing's Carlisle Cathedral; Nicolson's and Burn's Hist. of Cumberland; Hutchinson's Hist. of Cumberland; Walcott's Memorials of Carlisle; British Chronologist; old newspapers, 1745-7.]

E. C. S.

FLEMING, JAMES, fourth BARON FLEMING (1534?-1558), lord high chamberlain of Scotland, was the eldest son of Malcolm, third lord high chamberlain, by his wife Johanna or Jonet Stewart, natural daughter of James IV. The father, who had been taken prisoner at the rout of Solway in 1542, and had been tried and acquitted of treason in 1545 for his connection with the English party, was slain at the battle of Pinkie 10 Sept. 1547. In August 1548 young Fleming, along with Lord Erskine, accompanied the young Queen Mary to France, Lady Fleming, his mother, being governess to the queen. He also accompanied the queen dowager into France in 1549 (KEITH, *Hist.* i. 135). On 21 Dec. 1553 he was continued great chamberlain of Scotland for life (*Reg. Mag. Sig.* 1546-80, entry 877). About the same time he was appointed guardian of the east and middle marches, and invested with a power of justiciary within the limits of his jurisdiction. He was one of the eight commissioners elected by parliament 8 Dec. 1557 to represent the Scottish nation at the nuptials of Queen Mary with Francis, dauphin of France, 24 April 1558. Though the commissioners agreed to swear fealty to the king-dauphin as the husband of the queen, they affirmed that their instructions did not permit them to agree that he should receive the ensigns of royalty. They were thereupon requested to support this proposal in the Scottish parliament, but when they left for Scotland, the French court appears to have been doubtful of the intentions of certain members of the commission. In such circumstances the death of four of their number on the way home awakened grave suspicions that they had been designedly poisoned. The Earls of Rothes and Cassilis and Bishop Reid succumbed sooner to the attack than Fleming, who, in the hope of recovery, returned to Paris, but died there on 18 Dec. By his marriage to Lady Barbara Hamilton, eldest daughter of James, duke of Chatelherault, he had one daughter, Jane, married first to John lord Thirlestane, who died 3 Oct. 1595 ; and secondly, to John, fifth earl of Cassilis, by neither of whom had she any issue.

[Douglas's Scotch Peerage (Wood), ii. 634 ; Crawfurd's Officers of State, pp. 327–8; Keith's History of Scotland ; Hunter's Biggar and the House of Fleming, pp. 525–8.]   T. F. H.

FLEMING or FLEMMING, JAMES (1682–1751), major-general, colonel 36th foot, was wounded at Blenheim when serving as a captain in the Earl of Derby's regiment (16th foot, now 1st Bedford), and afterwards for many years commanded the royal fusiliers, until promoted on 9 Jan. 1741 colonel of the 36th foot (now 2nd Worcester). He became a brigadier-general in 1745, was present at Falkirk and Culloden, and became major-general in 1747. He died at Bath 31 March 1751. A tablet with medallion portrait was erected to his memory in Westminster Abbey.

[Cannon's Hist. Records 16th Foot and 36th Foot ; Evans's Cat. of Engraved Portraits (London, 1836–53), vol. ii. ; Scots Mag. xiii. 165.]
H. M. C.

FLEMING, JOHN, fifth BARON FLEMING (d. 1572), was the younger brother of James, fourth lord Fleming [q. v.], and the second son of Malcolm, third lord Fleming, by his wife Johanna or Jonet Stewart, natural daughter of James IV. He succeeded to the title on the death of his brother, 18 Dec. 1558. He is mentioned in a letter of Randolph to Cecil, 3 June 1565, as one of those who 'shamefully left Moray when he endea-

voured to prevent the marriage between Mary and Darnley' (KEITH, ii. 292). By commission dated 30 June 1565 he was appointed great chamberlain of Scotland, and he took the oaths on 1 Aug. following (Reg. Privy Council Scot. i. 347). In the 'round-about raid' against Moray he accompanied the king, who led the battle (ib. 379). He was one of those in waiting on Mary when Rizzio was murdered (Letter of Queen Mary to the Archbishop of Glasgow, 9 May 1566, printed in KEITH, ii. 418), but succeeded in making his escape from the palace of Holyrood. In 1567 he was made justiciary within the bounds of the overward of Clydesdale, appointed to the sheriffdom of Peebles, and received the important office of governor of Dumbarton Castle. Though he was in Edinburgh at the time of the murder of Darnley, he had no connection with the tragedy. He, however, signed the bond in favour of the marriage of Mary and Bothwell. After the flight of Bothwell from Carberry Hill, Fleming, along with Lord Seton, accompanied him to the north of Scotland, but both ultimately abandoned him (Illustrations of the Reign of Mary, p. 223). He joined the party of the queen's lords, who resolved to take measures to effect her escape from Lochleven (KEITH, ii. 656). Refusing the invitation to attend a parliament to be held at Edinburgh on 15 Dec. (CALDERWOOD, ii. 388), he withdrew with other lords to Dumbarton Castle, of which he was keeper, where a bond was entered into for the queen's liberty (KEITH, ii. 718). In the hope of obtaining assistance from France he refused to deliver up the castle (CALDERWOOD, ii. 402). After Queen Mary's escape from Lochleven, he assembled with other lords at Hamilton to take measures for securing the triumph of her cause. Rather than trust herself to the Hamiltons, Mary would have preferred meanwhile to shut herself up in the stronghold of Dumbarton under the protection of Fleming, but the Hamiltons, who had determined that she should marry Lord Arbroath, would not permit her out of their hands, and resolved against her wishes to stake the cause of the queen on a battle against the forces of Moray. The result was the disaster at Langside. Fleming was one of the three noblemen who with the queen watched the battle from an adjoining eminence. He, along with Lords Herries and Livingstone, conducted her from the field (HERRIES, Memoirs, p. 103), and accompanied her in her gallop for life through the Ayrshire and Galloway moors. The small party crossed the Solway in a fishing-boat, and on 15 May arrived at Workington. A day or two afterwards they lodged her in the castle of Carlisle (State Papers, For. Ser.

1566–8, entry 2199). Shortly afterwards Fleming was sent along with Lord Herries to ask Elizabeth's assistance to restore her to her throne (LABANOFF, *Lettres de Marie Stuart*, ii. 87). Mary also asked for Elizabeth's permission for Fleming to go on a mission to France (for the exact nature of the mission see 'Instructions données par Marie Stuart à Lord Fleming, envoyé vers le roi de France,' in LABANOFF, ii. 86–90; and 'Instructions données &c., vers le Cardinal de Lorrain,' *ib.* 90–3), but Elizabeth declined her permission, asserting that the only object of a mission of the chatelain of Dumbarton to France must be to take measures for bringing the French into the country. Fleming sounded the Spanish ambassador as to whether it might not be possible to bribe Cecil, Pembroke, and Bedford, but de Silva gave no countenance to the proposal, and advised that for the present it would be best for the interests of Mary that she should submit to Elizabeth's wishes (FROUDE, *Hist. England*, cab. ed. viii. 362). Mary made more than one effort to obtain Elizabeth's consent to Fleming's embassy to France, but at last, finding it hopeless to break her resolution, Fleming left for the north. Reaching Mary at Carlisle on 5 July, he went thence to Scotland and joined the forces under Huntly and Argyll. Fleming was one of the commissioners appointed by Mary to represent her cause at the conference at York (SIR JAMES MELVILLE, *Memoirs*, p. 265). On his return he shut himself up in Dumbarton Castle, which he held in Queen Mary's name, thus keeping open a door of communication with France. At a parliament held at Edinburgh he and his relative, John Fleming of Boghall, were denounced, on 17 Nov. 1569, as traitors, and their arms were 'riven' at the cross, in presence of the regent and the lords (CALDERWOOD, ii. 506). In his stronghold he bade defiance for a time to all proclamations and threats. It became the centre of intrigues on Mary's behalf. De Virac, the French ambassador, took up his residence in it to superintend the arrival of supplies of arms and money. According to Buchanan, Fleming had persuaded the king of France that he 'held the fetters of Scotland in his own hands; and that, whenever the French had leisure from other wars, if they would but send him a little assistance he would easily clap them on and bring all Scotland to their assistance.' In January 1569–70 the regent Moray went to Dumbarton in the hope that the favourable terms he proposed, and his own personal interposition, would induce Fleming to deliver it up, but returned disappointed. In fact his visit suggested to the Hamiltons and others who

were in the castle the scheme for his assassination, and it was within its walls that the plot was completed and the assassin chosen (*ib.* iii. 570). After the assassination Hamilton, uncle of the assassin, and an indirect agent in the murder, took refuge in the castle, which was supposed to be almost impregnable to assault. In May 1570 Drury was sent to Scotland to treat with those in arms in the cause of Mary (*Cal. State Papers*, Scot. Ser. i. 287), and when attempting a parley with Fleming he was stated to have been treacherously shot upon (ballad of 'The Tressoun of Dumbartune,' printed at Edinburgh by Lekprevick, 1570). For more than a year after the death of the regent Moray, the flag of Mary waved above the battlements of Wallace's Tower. Suddenly, on the morning of 2 May, its precipices were scaled by Captain Thomas Crawford [q. v.], and the garrison overpowered with scarcely an attempt at resistance (see narrative in RICHARD BANNATYNE's *Memorials*, pp. 106–7). Fleming made his way out alone by a postern gate; and, the tide being full, obtained a boat and escaped to Argyll (HERRIES, *Memoirs*, p. 132; CALDERWOOD, *History*, iii. 57). He left Lady Fleming in the castle, but she was very courteously treated by the regent Lennox, and permitted to pass out freely with all her plate and baggage (HERRIES, p. 133). She also subsequently obtained a part of the forfeited rents of Lord Fleming for her support. Fleming proceeded to France, where he endeavoured to concert measures for foreign assistance to the friends of Mary. An expedition under his direction was wrecked on the coast of England, but although his papers were seized he himself escaped (*Correspondance de Fénelon*, iv. 401). Ultimately he succeeded in returning to Scotland, and obtained entrance to Edinburgh Castle, still held by the supporters of Mary. On 5 July 1572 he was mortally wounded by French soldiers discharging their pieces on their entrance into Edinburgh, some of the bullets rebounding from the pavement and striking him in the knee. After lying for some time in the castle he was removed in a litter to Biggar, where he died of his wounds on 6 Sept. By his marriage to Elizabeth, only child of Robert Master of Ross, killed at the battle of Pinkie in 1547, he had, besides three daughters, one son,

JOHN FLEMING, first EARL OF WIGTOWN or WIGTON (*d.* 1619). He held the office of chief 'janitor et custos domus et cubiculi regis' from 30 July 1587, and was granted large estates united into the lordship of Cumbernauld (18 Jan. 1588–9 and 31 Jan. 1595–6). He was created Earl of Wigtown or Wigton 19 March 1606–7, and died in April 1619.

By his first wife, Lillias, daughter of John, earl of Montrose, he had four sons and six daughters.

His heir, JOHN FLEMING, second EARL OF WIGTOWN or WIGTON (d. 1650), was one of the committee of estates in 1640; became a privy councillor in 1641; entered into an association framed at his house at Cumbernauld in support of Charles I, and died at Cumbernauld 7 May 1650. He married Margaret, second daughter of Alexander Livingston, second earl of Linlithgow, by whom he left issue. The earldom became extinct on the death of Charles Fleming, seventh earl, in 1747.

[Illustrations of the Reign of Mary (Maitland Club); Lord Herries's Memoirs (Abbotsford Club); Sir James Melville's Memoirs (Bannatyne Club); Diurnal of Occurrents (Bannatyne Club); History of James Sext (Bannatyne Club); Richard Bannatyne's Memorials; Labanoff's Lettres de Marie Stuart; Fénelon's Correspondance; Register of the Privy Council of Scotland; State Papers, Reign of Elizabeth; Histories of Keith, Calderwood, Buchanan, Tytler, Burton, and Froude; Douglas's Scottish Peerage (Wood), ii. 634–5; Crawfurd's Officers of State, pp. 330–1; Hunter's Biggar and the House of Fleming, pp. 525–44.] T. F. H.

FLEMING, JOHN (d. 1815), botanist, was educated at Douai, took his degree of M.D. at Edinburgh, and became president of the Bengal medical service. He is stated to have been a good classic, and contributed to several journals, but the only memoir of his which can be cited is his 'Catalogue of Indian Medicinal Plants and Drugs' in the eleventh volume of 'Asiatick Researches,' which was reprinted with additions, Calcutta, 1810, 8vo, and translated into Dutch and German. He died of a paralytic stroke in London, 10 May 1815. Dr. Roxburgh dedicated the genus *Flemingia* to him, and his name is further commemorated by the genus of fossil plants, *Flemingites*.

[Gent. Mag. vol. lxxxv. pt. i. p. 568; Roxburgh's Corom. Pl. iii. 44.] B. D. J.

FLEMING, JOHN, D.D. (1785–1857), naturalist, son of Alexander Fleming, was born near Bathgate in Linlithgowshire 10 Jan. 1785. Moved by the strong wishes of his mother, he studied for the ministry, but he discovered at an early age an intense love of nature and natural science, which he took all opportunities, in harmony with other duties, to cultivate. Being asked by Sir John Sinclair to make a mineralogical survey of the northern isles, he became acquainted with the ministers of Shetland, and on the occurrence of a vacancy in the parish of Bressay, the right of presentation to which fell, *jure devo-*

luto, to the presbytery, he was nominated by them, with consent of the people, to the charge (licensed 22 April 1806, called 6 Aug. and ordained 22 Sept. 1808). His 'Economical Mineralogy of the Orkney and Zetland Islands' was published in 1807. A paper 'On the Narwal or Sea-Unicorn' was communicated at the same time to the Wernerian Society. In 1810 he was translated to Flisk in Fifeshire, a neighbouring parish to Kilmeny, where Dr. Chalmers was minister. Many papers on local natural history and cognate topics were written for the learned societies, and Fleming soon became known as the first zoologist in Scotland. On 16 May 1814 the degree of D.D. was conferred on him by the university of St. Andrews. In 1822 he published the 'Philosophy of Zoology.' To remedy certain difficulties of classification in Cuvier's method, Fleming advocated the dichotomous or binary method, a proposal which Cuvier did not approve, and for which Fleming had to fight stoutly against other antagonists. The book attracted much interest from many quarters in consequence of the attention devoted by the writer to the characters of animals. It was translated into Italian by Signor Zandrini, and was for many years a standard work among Italian savants. In 1828 the publication of 'British Animals' added yet more to his fame as a naturalist. The number of genera and species described was much in advance of previous catalogues. Buckland's 'Reliquiæ Diluvianæ' (1823) led to the publication of a pamphlet 'On the Geological Deluge as interpreted by Baron Cuvier and Professor Buckland,' which is said to have caused the suppression of a new edition of Buckland's work. Fleming's connection and correspondence with scientific men widened as the years went on, and he was in request for articles in the 'Quarterly' and a series of volumes, which, however, did not appear, for Murray's 'Family Library.' His total contributions to science in books, journals, &c., amounted to 129.

While zealous for science, Fleming was active and earnest in parochial duties; a proof of this was that on the occurrence of a vacancy in the neighbouring church of Auchtermuchty, a petition signed by four hundred parishioners (virtually all) was presented to the patron in his favour; but he did not receive the appointment. In 1832 he was presented by Lord Dundas to the parish of Clackmannan. In 1834 he was appointed to the chair of natural philosophy in the University and King's College, Aberdeen. A petition from 418 inhabitants of Clackmannan was presented to him asking him to remain, but he elected to go to Aberdeen.

Although his chair was connected with a different branch of science, he continued to prosecute his old pursuits. The old red sandstone engaged a large share of his attention, and its fossils were the subject of several papers contributed to the scientific journals. But many other departments of natural science likewise engaged his attention and his pen.

From the nature of his pursuits Fleming had been little implicated in the discussions going on in the church and the country with reference to patronage. But he had always been in favour of the popular side. When the disruption occurred in 1843 he joined the free church. Sir David Brewster [q. v.] had done the same at St. Andrews, where the presbytery of the established church took steps with the intention of compelling him to conform to the church or to resign his office in the university. Fleming had every reason to believe that a similar course would be taken with reference to himself. Ultimately he agreed to accept a chair of natural science which Dr. Chalmers and others had deemed it desirable to establish in connection with the Free Church College at Edinburgh. His appointment to this chair in 1845 enabled him to devote his whole heart and time to the subjects with which he was most conversant. In undertaking to conduct such a class, mainly for divinity students, he acted on the conviction that a right knowledge of nature was fitted to be of great use to all engaged in pastoral duty; and that there was need at the present time of special steps to defend the Christian faith from what he regarded as theories 'resting on foundations that it would take a powerful lens to discover.' During his tenure of this chair, besides writing as usual for the scientific journals, he sent several important contributions to the 'North British Review,' started by his friend and colleague, Dr. Welsh; he published a popular work, 'The Temperature of the Seasons' (1851), forming the second volume of a series called 'The Christian Athenæum,' and he prepared for publication his latest work, published after his death, 'The Lithology of Edinburgh' (Edinburgh, 1859).

Fleming had a vein of sarcasm which he allowed to operate somewhat freely, and a way of hitting opponents which could not be very agreeable. But the genuine kindness and honesty of the man came to be appreciated even by those whom, like Buckland, he had once somewhat alienated. He died, after a short illness, on 18 Nov. 1857.

[Scott's Fasti, iv. 494, 697, v. 424; Fleming's Lithology of Edinburgh, with a Memoir by the Rev. John Duns; personal knowledge.] W. G. B.

FLEMING, Sir MALCOLM, Earl of WIGTOWN (d. 1360 ?), the son of Sir Malcolm Fleming of Cumbernauld, was, like his father, a staunch adherent of King Robert Bruce. He was appointed steward of the household to David, earl of Carrick, and continued to hold the office after the young prince [see BRUCE, DAVID, 1324–1371] succeeded to the throne. He was also bailie of Carrick, sheriff of Dumbarton, and keeper of the castle of Dumbarton, for which last-named office he had an annual salary of a hundred merks. He was engaged in the battle of Halidon in 1333, the loss of which by the Scots left their country at the mercy of Edward III, who quickly reduced it all to subjection, save four castles and an island peel, the principal of which was the castle of Dumbarton. Fleming had escaped from the battle-field, and hastening home, placed this castle in a position to hold out for any length of time. Hither, says Wyntoun, resorted all who yearned to live freely. Here too he kept safely David II and his queen, until the king of France sent means to convey them thence to France, whither Fleming accompanied them. On his return he received in the following year Robert, the steward of Scotland, afterwards Robert III, who had effected his escape from Rothesay. David II and his consort returned from France to Scotland on 4 May 1341, and the loyalty of Fleming was rewarded on 9 Nov. following by a royal charter, dated at Ayr, granting him and his heirs male the sheriffdom of Wigtown and other lands, and creating him Earl of Wigtown, with right of regality and special judicial powers. Fleming followed David II into England in 1346, and with him was taken prisoner at the battle of Durham, 17 Oct., conveyed to London and incarcerated in the Tower. After a lengthened captivity he was liberated, and took a prominent part in the negotiations for the ransom of David II. At the meeting of the Scottish parliament at Edinburgh on 26 Sept. 1357 he was appointed one of the commissioners to conclude the treaty at Berwick on 3 Oct. following, and his seal was appended to that document. He died about 1360, and was succeeded by his grandson Thomas, earl of Wigtown, who sold the earldom to Archibald, third earl of Douglas, 8 Feb. 1371–2. Fleming married a foster sister of King Robert Bruce, who was called Lady Marjory, countess of Wigtown. The royal connection is shown in the fact that in 1329 Fleming received a royal gift of money on the occasion of his son's marriage. He had one son, Thomas or John, who predeceased him, and two daughters: (1) Lady Marjory, who married William of

Fawside, and received during her lifetime a grant of part of the crown lands of Clackmannan; (2) Lady Eva, who married John of Ramsay, and with her husband received from the king the thanage of Tannadice.

[Wyntoun's Chronicle, bk. viii. chaps. xxvii. xxviii. xl.; Fordun à Goodall; Rymer's Foedera; Hailes's Annals, ii. 185, 186, 239, 267, iii. 110; Robertson's Index of Missing Charters; Registrum Magni Sigilli; Exchequer Rolls of Scotland, v. 43.]   H. P.

FLEMING, MARGARET (1803–1811), called PET MARGARIE or MARJORIE, born 15 Jan. 1803, was daughter of James Fleming of Kirkcaldy, by Elizabeth, daughter of James Rae, and sister of Mrs. Keith of Ravelston, the friend of Sir Walter Scott. Scott frequently saw Margaret Fleming at the house of her aunt, Mrs. Keith, became attached to the child, and delighted in playing with her. She showed extraordinary precocity; she read history when six years old, and wrote diaries and poems, which were preserved by her family. They show singular quickness, vivacity, and humour, while there is no trace of the morbid tendencies too often associated with infant prodigies. She composed an historical poem upon Mary Queen of Scots,

Who fled to England for protection
(Elizabeth was her connection);

an excellent epitaph upon three young turkeys,

A direful death indeed they had,
That would put any parent mad;
But she [their mother] was more than usual calm,
She did not give a single dam;

and made many quaint remarks upon various lovers, including a gentleman who offered to marry her with his wife's permission, but failed to carry out his promise, and sundry religious reflections, especially upon the devil. That her talents were limited is proved by her statement: 'I am now going to tell you the horrible and wretched plaege that my multiplication table givis me; you can't conceive it. The most devilish thing is 8 times 8 and 7 times 7; it is what nature itself can't endure.' No more fascinating infantile author has ever appeared, and we may certainly accept the moderate anticipation of her first biographer, that if she had lived she might have written books. Unfortunately she had an attack of measles, and when apparently recovering was taken ill and died after three days of 'water on the brain,' 19 Dec. 1811. Her father could never afterwards mention her name. Her life is probably the shortest to be recorded in these volumes, and certainly she is one of the most charming characters.

[Pet Margarie; a Story of Child Life Fifty Years Ago, Edinburgh, 1858. This was reviewed in the North British Review for November 1863 by Dr. John Brown, who had the original diaries, &c., before him, and gives details not recorded in the previous account. His very pleasing article has been republished with Rab and his Friends; Scotsman, 6 July 1881 (notice of death of her elder sister, Elizabeth Fleming).]   L. S.

FLEMING, PATRICK (1599–1631), a Franciscan friar of the Strict Observance, was born on 17 April 1599 at Bel-atha-Lagain, now the townland of Lagan, in the parish of Clonkeen and county of Louth, Ireland. His father, Gerald Fleming, was great-grandson of Christopher Fleming, baron of Slane and treasurer of Ireland. His mother was Elizabeth, daughter of Robert Cusack of Cushinstown, a baron of the exchequer, by Catharine Nugent, daughter of Christopher, heir to the barony of Delvin. He was baptised by Father William Jacson, and received the family christian name of Christopher. At the age of thirteen he was sent by his parents to Flanders, and placed under the care of his uncle, the Rev. Christopher Cusack, who was administrator of the Irish colleges for the secular clergy in that country. Having studied humanities at Douay he removed to the college of St. Anthony of Padua at Louvain, where, on 17 March 1616–17, he took the probationary habit of St. Francis from the hands of Anthony Hickey, the superior; and on the same day in the following year he made his solemn profession, assuming in religion the name of Patrick. In 1623 he journeyed to Rome in company with Hugh Mac Caghwell, then definitor-general of the Franciscan order, and afterwards archbishop of Armagh. In passing through Paris, Fleming contracted a close friendship with Father Hugh Ward, to whom he promised a zealous co-operation in searching out and illustrating the lives of the early saints of Ireland. He completed his philosophical and theological studies in the Irish college of St. Isidore at Rome (WADDING, Scriptores Ordinis Minorum, ed. 1806, p. 185), and afterwards he was sent to teach philosophy at Louvain, where he continued to lecture for some years. He removed to Prague in Bohemia on being appointed the first superior of, and divinity lecturer in, the college of the Immaculate Conception, recently founded in that city for Irish Franciscans of the Strict Observance. When the elector Palatine invaded Bohemia, Fleming fled from the city, in company with Matthew Hoar, a deacon. On 7 Nov. 1631 they were suddenly attacked near the small town of Beneschau, by a party of armed peasants, who killed them on the spot. Fleming's body was conveyed to the monastery of Voticium, about four miles from the scene of the murder, and solemnly interred in the presence of forty brethren.

His works are: 1. 'Vita S. Columbani, Abbatis Bobiensis, cum annotationibus.' This work, and the lives of some other Irish saints, with their 'Opuscula,' Fleming, before his departure for Prague, gave to Moretus, the famous printer of Antwerp, with a view to publication, but the design was not then carried into effect. The manuscripts afterwards were edited by Thomas Sirinus, or O'Sherrin, jubilate lector of divinity in the college of St. Anthony of Padua at Louvain, who published them under the title of 'Collectanea Sacra, seu S. Columbani Hiberni Abbatis, magni Monachorum Patriarchæ, Monasteriorum Luxoviensis in Gallia, et Bobiensis in Italia, aliorumque, Fundatoris et Patroni, Necnon aliorum aliquot è Veteri itidem Scotiâ seu Hiberniâ antiquorum Sanctorum Acta & Opuscula, nusquam antehàc edita, partem ab ipso brevibus Notis, partem fusioribus Commentariis, ac speciali de Monastica S. Columbani institutione Tractatu, ilustrata,' Louvain, 1667, fol. pp. 455. This work is of even greater rarity than the scarce volumes of Colgan. A detailed account of its contents, by William Reeves, D.D., will be found in the 'Ulster Journal of Archæology,' vol. ii. 2. 'Vita Reverendi Patris Hugonis Cavelli [MacCaghwell],' 1626. This biography was incorporated by Vernulæus in the panegyric of the deceased primate which he delivered at Louvain; and its chief facts are preserved by Lynch in his manuscript 'History of the Bishops of Ireland.' 3 'Chronicon Consecrati Petri Ratisbonæ,' manuscript, being a compendium of the chronicle of the monastery of St. Peter at Regensberg. 4. Letters on Irish hagiology addressed to Hugh Ward, and printed in the 'Irish Ecclesiastical Record.'

[Life by O'Sherrin, prefixed to Fleming's Collectanea; Ware's Writers of Ireland (Harris), p. 112; Preface to Colgan's Acta Sanctorum; Ulster Journal of Archæology, ii. 253; Sbaralea's Suppl. et Castigatio ad Scriptores Trium Ordinum S. Francisci a Waddingo aliisve descriptos, p. 573; Irish Ecclesiastical Record, vii. 59, 193; Brenan's Eccl. Hist. of Ireland, p. 512; Lowndes's Bibl. Man. (Bohn), p. 809.] T. C.

FLEMING, RICHARD (d. 1431), bishop of Lincoln and founder of Lincoln College, Oxford, was born of a good family in Yorkshire—Tanner says at Croston, but the name suggests a doubt as to the identification—probably about 1360. He entered the university of Oxford, and became a member of University College. He was junior proctor in 1407 (WOOD, Fasti Oxon. p. 37 et seq.), his year of office being still remembered in consequence of the fact that he caused one of the books of statutes and privileges of the university, still preserved in the archives and known as the 'Junior Proctor's Book' (or Registrum C), to be transcribed for him (Munimenta Academica Oxon. i. intr. xiv, 237, ed. H. Anstey, 1868). In 1408 there is a record of his payment of 6s. 8d. for the use of one of the schools belonging to Exeter College (C. W. BOASE, Register of Exeter College, p. 14, 1879), probably with a view to proceeding to a degree in divinity. He had already held, since 22 Aug. 1406, the prebend of South Newbald in the church of York (LE NEVE, Fasti Ecclesiæ Anglicanæ, iii. 205, ed. Sir T. D. Hardy).

At present Fleming was, in some points at least, a warm adherent of the Wycliffite party, which still maintained its strength among the scholars of Oxford. In 1407 Archbishop Arundel had held a provincial council there, at which stringent decrees were passed against the reading of Wycliffe's books and an attempt made to regulate the studies of the university (WILKINS, Conc. Magn. Brit. iii. 305). Two years later the archbishop persuaded convocation at its session in London to appoint a committee of twelve persons to examine the writings of Wycliffe, and to condemn them if any heresy should be found therein. Among these judges was Fleming, described as a student of theology (ib. p. 172, where the date is erroneously given as 1382; cf. H. C. MAXWELL LYTE, History of the University of Oxford, p. 283, n. 2, 1886). After long debate and a delay which called forth a complaint from the archbishop, the majority drew up a report condemning 267 propositions attributed to Wycliffe as erroneous or heretical (WILKINS, iii. 339). But the discussion appears to have excited the smouldering elements of heterodox opinion. The university was disturbed by disorderly manifestations of lollard feeling, and Fleming with another member of the committee itself declared openly for some of the obnoxious tenets. In December 1409 the archbishop addressed a mandate to the chancellor of the university, bidding him to warn the malcontents to abstain from defending Wycliffe's doctrines under heavy penalties. The language employed is remarkable for its contemptuous severity as applied to a man who had already been chosen by the masters of arts some years before to be their official representative as proctor: 'Certæ personæ,' wrote the archbishop, 'dictæ universitatis, quibus digna non esset cathedra, attamen graduatæ, quæ et puerilia rudimenta non transcendunt, vix adhuc ab adolescentiæ cunabulis exeuntes, quarum una, ut asseritur, est Richardus cognomento Flemmyng, quæ etiam velut elingues pueri, quorum nondum barbas cæsaries decoravit, prius legentes quam syllabicent, ponentes os in cœlum, tanta ambitione tumescunt quod certas dictarum conclusionum damnatarum publice asserere et velut conclusionabiliter in scholis tenere et defendere damnabiliter non verentur' (*ib.* p. 322). The passage has needed quotation at length since doubts have been cast upon Fleming's attachment to Wycliffism; at the same time his theological obliquity cannot be proved to have extended to Wycliffe's more radical heresies, and it would be hasty to conclude with Wood (*Hist. and Antiq. of Oxford, Colleges and Halls,* p. 234, ed. Gutch) that he was so active in the cause 'that had not his mouth been stopped with preferment the business would then have proved pernicious' (cf. LYTE, pp. 280–5). Whether or not frightened by the primate's energetic measures, Fleming seems to have soon tempered his judgment and to have won recognition as an authority on the method of theological disputation. Thomas Gascoigne, the most correct of divines, who was chancellor in 1434, says that about 1420 (the date is evidently some years too late) he introduced the procedure in such exercises which continued in force in his own day (*Loci e Libro Veritatum,* p. 183, ed. J. E. T. Rogers).

In 1413 Fleming appears signing a petition, as B.D., promising to receive the visitation of Repyngdon, bishop of Lincoln, himself formerly, like Fleming, conspicuous on the lollard side. On 21 Aug. 1415 he received the prebend of Langtoft in the church of York (LE NEVE, iii. 199); afterwards he became rector of Boston; and on 20 Nov. 1419 he succeeded Repyngdon as bishop of Lincoln. He was consecrated at Florence 28 April 1420 (STUBBS, *Reg. Sacr. Anglic.* 65), and the temporalities were restored to him 23 May (RYMER, *Fœdera,* ix. 909). On 18 Dec. 1421 he received instructions to head an embassy to Germany to seek armed support from the king of the Romans (*ib.* x. 161–3). But it was in ecclesiastical affairs that his interest directly lay. So little now was there any taint of lollardy about him that on 22 June 1423 he appeared as president of the English nation at the general council of Pavia (JOHN OF RAGUSA, *Initium et prosecutio Basiliensis concilii,* in the *Monum. Concil. Gen. sec. xv.,* i. 11, Vienna, 1857; MANSI, *Conc. Collect. Ampliss.* xviii. 1059 D). The council was transferred to Siena, and on 21 July Fleming was the preacher before it (JOHN OF RAGUSA,

p. 12). At the beginning of the following year he was appointed to hear evidence on behalf of the council (*ib.* p. 46); then on 23 Jan. he preached a sermon in which he made himself conspicuous as a champion of the rights of the papacy as against the council, an advocacy which produced a good deal of dissatisfaction among the fathers. It was said that he was scheming for higher preferment from the pope (*ib.* p. 64). The council ended in no positive decisions of moment; but it is singular that Fleming's name is not mentioned in connection with its anti-Wycliffite decree of 8 Nov. 1423. If, as his epitaph asserts, Fleming was chamberlain to Pope Martin V, he was probably appointed to the office in the course of this visit to Italy.

On his return to England he was given a more signal mark of the pope's favour. The archbishopric of York became vacant in the autumn of 1423, and Fleming received the see by his 'provision,' 20 July 1424. The Bishop of Worcester, however, had already in January been elected by the chapter, and the royal consent had been obtained. Moreover, Fleming displeased the king's ministers (GODWIN strangely says, Henry V, *De Præsulibus,* i. 297, ed. Cambr. 1743) by his acceptance of the archbishopric without asking permission, and it was seized into the king's hands. In the end he had to submit, under humiliating conditions, to re-translation to Lincoln, and neither of the candidates obtained their desire, the archbishopric being given by the king's nomination, after a long interval, to the chancellor, John Kemp (LE NEVE, iii. 110).

Not long after his return to Lincoln, Fleming began to prepare a plan for the foundation of a college at Oxford. The royal license was given by letters patent on 13 Oct. 1427, and although the bishop did not live to carry out more than the elements of his design, his preface to the body of statutes of Lincoln College (which were actually drawn up, nearly half a century later, by Bishop Rotherham) shows clearly enough the objects which he had in view. It was expressly with the desire of counteracting the spread of heresy and error and encouraging the sound study of divinity, that he proposed to found a little college ('collegiolum') of theologians in connection with the three parish churches of St. Mildred, St. Michael, and Allhallows. The college which he founded had little endowment from him beyond the churches and the site, and some books of which an inventory is preserved (*Hist. MSS. Comm.* 2nd Rep. 131, 1871), and it was not established upon a firm footing until the last quarter of the century, when Rotherham drew up a code of statutes on the principle (he said) and in the spirit of Fleming's design. The ninth chapter of these statutes appointed an annual mass for the 'first founder' on the feast of the Conversion of St. Paul, the day of his death.

So far as can be judged from his earlier Memorandum Register (that for his later years is unfortunately lost), Fleming appears to have been an active administrator of his immense diocese, and particularly diligent in the visitation of monasteries within its limits. The muniments of Lincoln Cathedral include a number of injunctions which he addressed to them. The best known act of his episcopate belongs almost exactly to the time when he was planning his foundation for the overthrow of heresy. The old man believed that the movement which he had seen strong at Oxford in his youth was still vigorous. It was in 1428, after an urgent reminder from the pope, 9 Dec. 1427 (RAYNALD. *Ann.* ix. 55 seq.), that he gave effect to the vindictive sentence of the council of Constance of 4 May 1415, by exhuming the bones of John Wycliffe from Lutterworth churchyard; he burned them and cast them into the river Swift (W. LYNDWODE, *Provinciale*, v., f. cliv. b, ed. 1501). As a writer he is credited only with sermons preached at the council of Siena and with a work, apparently lost, 'Super Angliæ Etymologia' (BALE, *Scriptt. Brit. Catal.* vii. 90, p. 575).

Fleming died at his palace at Sleaford on 25 Jan. 1430-1, and was buried in Lincoln Cathedral. His altar-tomb, with effigy, still exists. The epitaph, which has been attributed to his own authorship (cf. WOOD, *Colleges and Halls*, p. 236), may be found also in manuscript, with panegyric verses attached by one Stoon, a Cistercian monk of Shene (*Bodleian MS.* 496, f. 225). He bore, barry of six ar. and az., three lozenges in chief gules; on the fess point a mullet for difference sable (WOOD, p. 244).

Fleming's name is spelt variously with one or two m's and with i or y in the second syllable.

[Letters patent for the foundation of Lincoln College and Fleming's preface to the Statutes, in Statutes of Lincoln College, Oxford, 1853; Tanner's Bibl. Brit. p. 286; Wood's Hist. and Antiq. of the Univ. of Oxford, i. 551, ed. Gutch; Lincoln Cathedral registers.] R. L. P.

FLEMING, ROBERT (d. 1483), dean of Lincoln. [See FLEMMING.]

FLEMING, ROBERT, the elder (1630–1694), Scottish ejected divine, was born in December 1630 at Yester, Haddingtonshire, of which parish, anciently known as St. Bathan's, his father, James Fleming (d.

8 April 1653), was minister. James Fleming's first wife was Martha, eldest daughter of John Knox, the Scottish reformer; Robert was the issue of a second marriage with Jean Livingston. His childhood was sickly, and he nearly lost his sight and life owing to a blow with a club. He speaks of an 'extraordinary impression' made upon him as a boy by a voice which he heard when he had climbed up into his father's pulpit at night; but he dates the beginning of his religious life from a communion day at Greyfriars Church, Edinburgh, at the opening of 1648. At this time he was a student of Edinburgh University, where he graduated M.A. on 26 July 1649, distinguishing himself in philosophy. He pursued his theological studies at St. Andrews under Samuel Rutherford. At the battle of Dunbar (3 Sept. 1650) he was probably in the ranks of the Scottish army, for he speaks of his 'signal preservation.' After license he received a call to Cambuslang, Lanarkshire, and was ordained there in 1653. His health was then so bad that 'it seemed hopeless,' and on the day of his ordination there was an 'extraordinary storm,' which he deemed an assault of Satan.

Fleming's ministry was popular and successful. On the restoration of episcopacy the Scottish parliament passed an act (11 June 1662) vacating benefices that had been filled without respect to the rights of patrons, unless by 20 Sept. the incumbent should obtain presentation (this patrons were enjoined to grant) and episcopal collation, and renounce the covenant. Failing to comply with these conditions, Fleming was deprived by the privy council on 1 Oct. During the next ten years he remained in Scotland, preaching wherever he found opportunity. Indulgences were offered to the ejected ministers in 1669 by the king, and on 3 Sept. 1672 by the privy council. By the terms of this latter indulgence Fleming was assigned to the parish of Kilwinning, Ayrshire, as a preacher. He disobeyed the order; when cited to the privy council on 4 Sept. he did not attend, and a warrant was issued for his apprehension. He fled to London, where his broad Scotch 'idiotisms and accents' somewhat 'clouded' his usefulness. In 1674 he was again in Scotland, at West Nisbet, Roxburghshire, where he had left his wife. She died in that year, and Fleming returned to London.

In 1677 he removed to Rotterdam, having been called to a collegiate charge in the Scots Church there. Next year he visited Scotland for the purpose of bringing over his children. While there he held conventicles in Edinburgh, and was thrown into the Tolbooth. Brought before the privy council in June 1679, he agreed to give bail, but declined to promise a passive obedience. He was sent back to prison, but soon obtained his liberty and returned to Rotterdam. On 2 April 1683 proceedings were taken against him in the high court of judiciary at Edinburgh, on suspicion of harbouring some of the assassins of Archbishop Sharpe; his innocence appearing, the accusation was dropped on 17 April 1684. He did not formally demit the charge of Cambuslang till March 1688, on the death of David Cunningham, who had been appointed in his place. The act of April 1689 restored him to his benefice, but he preferred to remain in Holland. During a visit to London he was seized with fever on 17 July, and died on 25 July 1694. His funeral sermon was preached by Daniel Burgess (1645–1713) [q. v.] He married Christian, daughter of Sir George Hamilton of Binny, Linlithgowshire, and had seven children. His son Robert [q. v.] succeeded him at Rotterdam. In 1672 Fleming had the infeftment of the lands of Marbreck and Formontstoun.

Fleming's 'Fulfilling of the Scripture,' his best-known work, is a treatise on particular providences; it is rich in illustrative anecdote, and contains valuable material mixed with legend relating to the puritan biography of Scotland and the north of Ireland.

He published: 1. 'The Fulfilling of the Scripture,' &c., Rotterdam, 1669, fol. Second part, 'The Faithfulness of God,' &c. Third part, 'The Great Appearances of God,' &c. [1677?] All three parts, Lond., 1681, 12mo, two vols.; third edit., 1681, 8vo; fourth edit., 1693, 8vo; fifth edit., 1726, fol.; last edit., Edinb., 1845, 8vo, two vols.; an abridgment is published by the Religious Tract Society. 2. 'An Account of the Roman Church and Doctrine,' 1675, 8vo (not seen). 3. 'A Survey of Quakerism,' &c., 1677, 8vo (anon.) 4. 'Scripture Truth confirmed and cleared,' 1678, 8vo (not seen). 5. 'The Truth and Certainty of the Protestant Faith,' 1678, 8vo (not seen). 6. 'The Church wounded and rent,' &c., 1681, 4to (not seen). 7. 'The One Thing Necessary,' 1681 (not seen). 8. 'Joshua's Choice,' 1684 (previously printed in Dutch, not seen). 9. 'The Confirming Worke of Religion,' Rotterdam, 1685, 12mo. 10. 'True Statement of Christian Faith,' 1692, 8vo (not seen). 11. 'The Present Aspect of our Times,' &c., 1694 (not seen). Also two separate sermons, 1692. Hew Scott adds, 'A Discourse on Earthquakes,' 1693, by his son; also, without dates, 'The Healing Work,' &c., and 'Epistolary Discourse,' two parts (this is by his son).

[Fleming left a diary, which was not published; his rather confused list of thirty-eight memorable occurrences of his life, entitled A Short Index, &c., is printed at the end of Memoirs by Daniel Burgess, prefixed to the 1726 edition of the Fulfilling; a fuller memoir is prefixed to the 1845 edition; Hew Scott's Fasti Eccles. Scot.; Wilson's Dissenting Churches, 1808, ii. 469; Grub's Ecclesiastical History of Scotland, 1861, iii. 200; Anderson's Scottish Nation, 1870, ii. 221 sq.]   A. G.

FLEMING, ROBERT, the younger (1660?–1716), presbyterian minister, son of Robert Fleming the elder [q. v.], was born at Cambuslang, Lanarkshire, about 1660. His early education was at the school of his uncle by marriage, John Sinclair, minister of Ormiston, Haddingtonshire. He entered into a religious 'covenant' at the age of thirteen, and set his heart on the ministry. In 1679 his father took him to Holland, where he studied at Leyden and Utrecht. He pursued his own course of reading, gaining a wide familiarity with classics and the fathers, and with theological writers of the most opposite schools. On 9 Feb. 1688 he was privately ordained by Scottish divines in Holland, without special charge. He removed to England, and was domestic chaplain in a private family for about four years. In 1692 he accepted a call to the pastorate of the English presbyterian congregation at Leyden. On his father's death he was invited to succeed him in the Scots Church at Rotterdam, to which he was inducted in 1695.

In 1698 Fleming received a call to the Scots Church, Founders' Hall, Lothbury. His acceptance was urged by William Carstares [q. v.], and William III, who had known him in Holland, 'signified his desire to have him near his person.' Fleming began his ministry at Founders' Hall on 19 June 1698. The meeting-house was rebuilt for him about 1700. His position was one of great influence, though he never became a public man. William III consulted him on the ecclesiastical affairs of Scotland, and he was in friendly relations with Archbishop Tenison. Through the influence of his kinsman, John, lord Carmichael, secretary of state for Scotland, he had the offer of the principalship of Glasgow University, but this he declined. On 15 May 1701 he succeeded Vincent Alsop as one of the Tuesday lecturers at Salters' Hall, a lectureship which represented the liberal side in the Calvinistic controversy. On 7 May 1707 he was the spokesman of the London ministers of the three denominations in presenting an address of congratulation to Queen Anne on the union with Scotland. These appointments were unusual in the case of one who, like Fleming, was distinctively a Scottish presbyterian. But Fleming's views were broad, and indeed he was the pioneer of a principle which afterwards became the symbol of the most liberal section of English dissent. His 'Christology' (1705–8) shows that while himself orthodox on the person of Christ, he was resolutely opposed to any form of subscription. He held the tenet of the pre-existence of our Lord's human soul.

Fleming inherited from his father a strong taste for studies directed by the aim of tracing the divine hand in history. To the speculations advanced in his 'Apocalyptical Key' (1701) he chiefly owes his posthumous fame. In 1793, and again in 1848, attention was directed to the apparent historical verification of some of his conjectures. He predicted the fall of the French monarchy by 1794 at latest, and fixed on a period 'about the year 1848' as the date at which the papacy would receive a fatal, though not immediately destructive blow. Fleming makes no pretensions to the character of a prophet; his speculations are put forward with the modesty of a devout student of history and scripture.

A serious illness laid Fleming aside for a time. On his recovery he paid a visit to Holland, where he took some part in political negotiations in the protestant interest. He returned, shortly before the accession of King George, in improved but still uncertain health. His weakness increased, and he died on 21 May 1716. Joshua Oldfield, D.D., preached his funeral sermon. He left a widow and several children.

He published: 1. 'The Mirror of Divine Love . . . a poetical Paraphrase on the . . , Song of Solomon . . . other Poems,' &c., 1691, 8vo. 2. 'An Epistolary Discourse . . . with a Second Part,' 1692, 8vo. 3. 'A Discourse on Earthquakes,' &c., 1693, 8vo; reprinted 1793. 4. 'The Rod and the Sword,' &c., 1694, 8vo; reprinted 1701 and 1793. 5. 'Apocalyptical Key. An extraordinary Discourse on the Rise and Fall of Papacy,' &c., 1701, 8vo (dedicated to Lord Carmichael); reprinted 1793, and Edinb. 1849, with memoir by Thomas Thomson. 6. 'Discourses on Several Subjects,' 1701, 8vo (includes No. 5). 7. 'A Brief Account of Religion,' &c., 1701, 8vo. 8. 'Christology,' &c., vol. i. 1705, 8vo (dedicated to Queen Anne); vols. ii. and iii., 1708, 8vo; an abridgment was published in one vol., Edinb. 1795, 8vo. 9. 'The History of Hereditary Right,' &c., 8vo (anon.; not seen; mentioned by Wilson). Also eight separate sermons at funerals and special occasions between 1688 and 1716.

[General Preface to Fleming's Christology, 1701 (many biographical details); Oldfield's Funeral Sermon, 1716; Protestant Dissenter's Magazine, 1799, p. 431; Wilson's Dissenting Churches, 1808, ii. 468 sq.; Calamy's Hist. Acc. of My Own Life, 1830, i. 441, ii. 63, 363; Thomson's Memoir, 1849; Anderson's Scottish Nation, 1870, ii. 222 sq.] A. G.

FLEMING, Sir THOMAS (1544–1613), judge, son of John Fleming of Newport, Isle of Wight, by his wife, Dorothy Harris, was born at Newport in April 1544. He entered Lincoln's Inn on 12 May 1567, and was called to the bar there on 24 June 1574. In 1579 he was sent to Guernsey as commissioner to inquire into certain alleged abuses connected with the administration of the island. He entered parliament in 1584 as member for Winchester, of which place he was then recorder. He was re-elected for the same borough in 1586 and 1588. In 1587 he was made a bencher of his inn, and in Lent 1590 discharged the duties of reader there. He retained his seat for Winchester at the election of 1592. On 29 Nov. 1593 he was called to the degree of serjeant-at-law. On 27 March 1594 he succeeded Serjeant Drew as recorder of London (*Index to Remembrancia*, 93). A speech delivered by him in that capacity on presenting the lord mayor, Sir John Spencer, to the court of exchequer will be found in Nichols's 'Progresses of Elizabeth,' iii. 254. It is eminently judicious in tone, as may be judged by the following extract: 'He that taketh upon him the office of a magistrate is like to a good man to whose custody a precious jewel is committed; he taketh it not to retain and challenge it for his own, nor to abuse it while he hath it, but safely to keep, and faithfully to render it to him that deposed it when he shall be required. He must do all things not for his private lucre, but for the public's good preservation and safe custody of those committed to his charge, that he may restore them to him that credited in a better and more happy state, it may be, than he received them.' On 5 Nov. 1595 he was appointed to the solicitor-generalship over the head of Bacon, who acknowledged that he was an 'able man' (SPEDDING, *Letters and Life of Bacon*, i. 365, 369). In this capacity, in 1596, he assisted Sir Edward Coke, attorney-general, in taking the confession of Sir John Smith [q. v.], sometime ambassador to the king of Spain in the Netherlands, who had been committed to the Tower for having, as by his confession he admitted, on 12 June 1596, in company with his kinsman, Seymour, the second son of the Earl of Hertford, incited the militia in the neighbourhood of Colchester to mutiny. He also assisted in the examination of John Gerard, a jesuit charged with blasphemy, on 13 May 1597 (STRYPE, *Annals* (fol.), iv. 297–300). On 26 Sept. following he was returned to parliament for the county of Southampton. In January 1600-1 he received a commission from the queen to inquire into the abuses connected with patents, a work which was soon interrupted by the more urgent duty of investigating the Essex plot (*Cal. State Papers*, Dom. 1598–1601, pp. 560, 563). His speech on the prosecution of Sir Christopher Blunt, Sir Charles Davers, and others of the conspirators, is reported at length in Cobbett's 'State Trials,' i. 1435. In the parliament of 1601 he represented the borough of Southampton. On the accession of James I he was retained in office as solicitor-general, and placed on the commission for perusing and suppressing unlicensed books ; and he received the honour of knighthood at Whitehall on 23 July 1603. At the general election of March 1603-4 he retained his seat for the borough of Southampton. On 27 Oct. 1604 he was created chief baron of the exchequer (NICHOLS, *Progresses of James I*, i. 208 ; STRYPE, *Whitgift* (fol.), ii. 577 ; DUGDALE, *Chron. Ser.* 99, 100). His elevation to the bench disqualified him for sitting in the House of Commons, but he was permitted to attend the debates in the upper house. A new writ was issued for Southampton in his place 9 Nov. 1605, little more than a year after his promotion to the chief justiceship. He helped to try the conspirators concerned in the gunpowder treason on 27 Jan. 1606 (COBBETT, *State Trials*, ii. 159) ; and the same year delivered an elaborate judgment on the important case of Bates, a Levant merchant, who had refused to pay the duty on certain currants imported by him, on the ground that it had been imposed without the consent of parliament. The duty had in the first instance been imposed by the Levant Company under a patent by Elizabeth ; but James I, soon after his accession, by letters patent, directed the revenue officers to levy the duty upon all currants imported, thus subjecting the Levant Company to the impost (*ib.* ii. 382, 391). Fleming's judgment, which proceeded wholly 'upon reasons politic and precedents,' was for the crown. He argued that it was part of the royal prerogative to impose customs, and that the amount was in the absolute discretion of the king, and moreover that in the particular case, currants being a luxury, no real hardship was suffered. The judgment, which is reported at length in Cobbett's 'State Trials,' ii. 388, was subjected to much severe criticism by Hakewill and Whitelocke, in the course of the great debate on impositions in June and July 1610 (*ib.* p. 477 ; *Debates* in 1610, Camden Soc. 79, 103, 157). Coke roundly says that it was 'against law and

divers express acts of parliament' (*Inst.* pt. ii. cap. 30, *ad fin.*) On 25 June 1607 Fleming was advanced to the chief-justiceship of the king's bench. In that capacity he delivered a judgment in the case of the postnati tried in the exchequer chamber in 1608 (COBBETT, *State Trials*, ii. 609), the question being whether the accession of James I had the effect of naturalising in England persons born in Scotland, and in Scotland persons born in England after the event. It was decided in the affirmative, two judges only dissenting. Fleming's judgment has not been preserved. On 13 Feb. 1610 he was commissioned to supply the place of the lord chancellor during his sickness (*Cal. State Papers*, Dom. 1603–10, p. 58). In 1612 he was a member of the committee of the privy council that sat at York House to determine whether the Countess of Shrewsbury had been guilty of an offence in refusing to give information to the privy council concerning the escape of her niece, Arabella Stuart, to which she had been privy. Fleming took occasion to enlarge upon the several privileges incident to nobility by the law of England, arguing that being derived from the king, they entailed on persons of quality a correlative obligation 'to answer, being required thereto by the king, to such points as concern the safety of the king and quiet of the realm,' the breach of which was a high contempt and ingratitude. The committee were unanimous that the matter was cognisable in the Star-chamber, and resolved that if sentence should there be given the countess should be fined 20,000*l.* and imprisoned during the king's pleasure (COBBETT, *State Trials*, ii. 774–6). Anthony à Wood (*Fasti Oxon.* (Bliss), ii. 355) states that on 7 Aug. 1613 it was 'granted by the venerable convocation that Sir Thomas Fleming, chief justice of England, might be created M.A., but whether it was effected appears not.' Fleming died the same night in his bed, after entertaining his tenantry at his seat, Stoneham Park, Hampshire. He was buried in the parish church of North Stoneham. It has been said that Bacon regarded Fleming as an 'able man.' Coke is more explicit, giving him credit for 'great judgment, integrity, and discretion,' and 'a sociable and placable disposition' (*Rep.* x. 34). Fleming and his eldest son, Sir Thomas, were both members of a club founded in 1609 for the practice of the gentle game of bowls, at East Standen, Isle of Wight, where the members usually dined with the governor twice a week during the season (WORSLEY, *Isle of Wight*, p. 223). Fleming married in 1570. By his wife, of whom we know nothing beyond the fact that her christian name was Mary, he had issue eight sons and seven daughters. His eldest son, Thomas, who was knighted by James I at Newmarket on 26 Feb. 1604–5, married Dorothy, youngest daughter of Sir Henry Cromwell of Hinchinbroke, Huntingdonshire, known as 'the golden knight.' This lady, who was an aunt of the Protector, has been erroneously identified by Foss with Fleming's own wife. Fleming's posterity failed in the male line in the last century, but Browne Willis, the antiquary, having married one of the judge's descendants in the female line, his grandson succeeded to Stoneham Park and assumed the name of Fleming. The present owner, John Edward Browne Willis Fleming, is thus a lineal descendant of the judge in the female line.

[Spedding's Letters and Life of Bacon, iv. 378; Woodward's General History of Hampshire, ii. 110–12; Noble's Cromwell Memoirs, ii. 167; Nichols's Progr. of James I, i. 496; Foss's Lives of the Judges.]   J. M. R.

FLEMING, THOMAS (1593–1666), Roman catholic archbishop of Dublin, third son of William Fleming, sixteenth baron of Slane in the peerage of Ireland, by his cousin Ellinor, younger daughter of Thomas, fifteenth baron, was born in 1593. He became a Franciscan friar, and was for six or seven years a professor of theology at Louvain. While there, on 23 Oct. 1623, he was promoted to the archbishopric of Dublin, which was vacant by the death of Eugene Matthews, by Pope Urban VIII, from whom he thereupon obtained letters apostolic, assuring protection and patronage to the colleges founded on the continent for the Irish priesthood, and also sanctioning the mission in Ireland (DE BURGO, *Hibernia Dominicana*, p. 874). Paul Harris, a secular priest of the diocese, inveighed bitterly against this and other selections of prelates from the order of the regulars, and attacked the archbishop in his 'Olfactorium' and similar publications. In July 1640 Fleming presided over a provincial synod in the county of Kildare. When the parliamentary declaration of March 1641 excluded the smallest tendency of royal clemency to the members of his community, the archbishop selected Joseph Everard to attend as his proxy at the synod of the clergy which met at Kilkenny in May 1642. In October of the same year he felt constrained to appear in person at the general convention of the Roman catholic confederates at Kilkenny, and he rather strangely selected Dr. Edmund Reilly, whose acts at this period of his life were of a violent political tendency, to act as vicar-general during his absence from the diocese. On 20 June 1643 Fleming and the Archbishop of

Tuam were the only prelates who signed the commission authorising Lord Gormanston, Sir Lucas Dillon, Sir Robert Talbot, and others, to treat with the Marquis of Ormonde for the cessation of hostilities. In the following month Scarampa arrived in Ireland as minister of the pope, with supplies of money and ammunition; but Fleming rejected both, and with two other bishops signed a letter to the lords justices ratifying the articles of cessation. He was present in July 1644 at the general assembly held at Kilkenny when an oath was agreed upon by which each confederate swore to bear true faith and allegiance to the king and his heirs. Scarampa remained in the discharge of his office until November 1645, when Rinuccini, archbishop of Fermo, arrived as apostolic nuncio extraordinary. During the greater part of 1649 Fleming resided quietly in his diocese; but he was not long allowed to enjoy repose from political labours. His better judgment and prudence were no longer overruled by the nuncio's presence, and therefore, when the meeting of Irish prelates was held at Clonmacnoise on 4 Dec. 1649, Fleming was one who signed the declaration of oblivion of all past differences. But Charles, on his restoration, declared the peace with the confederates to be null and void. This step Ormonde had advised, and the archbishop consequently pronounced his excommunication. As a leading member of the Roman catholic party in Ireland, Fleming was involved in most of the political and religious controversies of his time, and in common with many of his co-religionists suffered considerable annoyance and persecution. In the midst of his troubles he died in 1666, and was succeeded in 1669 by Peter Talbot, the administration of the diocese being entrusted in the meantime to James Dempsey, vicar apostolic and capitulary of Kildare.

[Burke's Dormant and Extinct Peerages, 1883, p. 217; D'Alton's Memoirs of the Archbishops of Dublin, pp. 390–429; Moran's History of the Catholic Archbishops of Dublin since the Reformation, i. (all published) 294–411.]   B. H. B.

FLEMMING, JAMES (1682–1751), colonel. [See FLEMING.]

FLEMMING, RICHARD (d. 1431), bishop of Lincoln. [See FLEMING.]

FLEMMING, ROBERT (d. 1483), dean of Lincoln, nephew of Bishop Richard Fleming [q. v.], the founder of Lincoln College, Oxford, was probably connected with the earlier days of the college, the foundation of which was left by his uncle in an incomplete and unfinished state. At any rate, he displayed afterwards his care for this society by some valuable presents. Probably also he had an early connection with the church at Lincoln, inasmuch as twenty years after his uncle's death, under the episcopate of Bishop Lumley, he was chosen to be dean (1451). Lincoln Cathedral was then in a most disturbed state from the long and bitter struggle which had been carried on between the late dean, Mackworth, and the bishop, Alnwick. Doubtless the disputes between the episcopal and decanal powers still continued, and this may have induced Flemming to leave his cathedral and become a resident in Italy. Here also he had far greater facilities for cultivating his literary tastes. Flemming is said by Leland and Pits to have distinguished himself at Oxford, and to have gained a reputation for his elegant Latin scholarship. His journey to Italy is attributed to his eager desire for instruction. He visited, according to the same writers, all the more celebrated universities, and formed friendships with their most learned scholars. At Ferrara he became the pupil of Baptista Guarino, professor of Greek and Latin, and attended his lectures for a considerable period. He then went to Rome, where he remained several years intent upon study. Here he formed a friendship with Platina, the author of the 'Lives of the Popes,' and librarian of the Vatican, and other learned men, and became known to the reigning pontiff, Sixtus IV, a pope whose sole recommendation was his love of letters. Pope Sixtus appointed Flemming to the office of prothonotary, and he thus became employed in the complicated affairs of the Roman see. In summer, during the hot season, it was his custom to retreat to Tivoli, and here he composed his poems, written in heroic metre and dedicated to the pope. These poems were entitled: 1. 'Lucubrationes Tiburtinæ.' 2. 'Epistolæ ad diversos.' 3. 'Carmina diversi generis.' In addition to these Flemming is said to have compiled a dictionary of the Greek and Latin tongues, but whether this was written during his sojourn in Italy or after his return to England does not appear. Other works (unspecified) are attributed to him. Flemming, on his return from Italy, bestowed some valuable manuscripts, curiously illuminated, and, according to Wood, 'limned on their margins with gold,' on Lincoln College, which are probably still to be found among the manuscript collections of that college. He also gave the college copies of his own works, and a table for the high altar in the college chapel. He had probably returned to England before 1467, in which year he was installed into the prebend of Leighton Manor

in Lincoln Cathedral. This he exchanged in 1478 for that of Leighton Buzzard. There does not appear to be any special record of his work as dean of Lincoln. Both his predecessor and his successor were remarkable for their turbulence. But the great number of dispensations from Pope Sixtus found to be existing in Lincoln Cathedral at the visitation in 1501 may have been due to Flemming's influence with that pope. He died in 1483.

[Wood's Athenæ, vol. ii.; Pits, De Script. Illustr. s. v.; Bishop Smyth's Memorandum Register, MS. Lincoln.]   G. G. P.

FLEMYNG, MALCOLM, M.D. (*d.* 1764), physiologist, was born in Scotland early in the eighteenth century. He was a pupil of Monro at Edinburgh and of Boerhaave at Leyden. In the first of his five printed letters to Haller (*Epist. ad Hallerum*, vol. iii.) he speaks of Boerhaave as their common preceptor, and as having been 'mihi supra fidem amicus et beneficus,' but to Haller himself he would be 'prorsus ignotus,' although they may have been at Leyden at the same time. He began practice in Scotland about 1725, and removed after a time to Hull. In 1751, finding his health unequal to a country practice, he came to London, and made an attempt to support a wife and three children by teaching physiology. His lessons were intended for medical pupils who had not been at the universities, and were unable to read the standard books in learned or foreign languages. He seems to have read only one course of lectures, in the winter of 1751–2; in 1752 he issued a syllabus of the lectures, but probably he got no more pupils, the attempt being premature for London. About the end of 1752 he left London and settled at Brigg in Lincolnshire, on account of his wife's health, and to obtain practice. In a letter to Haller (February 1753), shortly after his arrival at Brigg, he hints at a possibility of teaching physiology at Oxford and Cambridge. The last letter to Haller (Brigg, June 1753) contains a Latin ode on the peace of Aix, 'to fill up the page.' In 1763 he was living at Lincoln, and still in practice. He died there 7 March 1764 (*Gent. Mag.* 146).

Flemyng's writings show him to have been well abreast of the best physiological teaching of his time, and an original experimenter and reasoner as well. One of the Haller letters (iii. 369) contains a statement of the fact that motor and sensory nerves are anatomically distinct, although they might coexist in the same bundle; the experimental proof came many years after. The ossicles of the ear serve the same purpose, he says, as the wooden rod inside a violin, 'ad continuandos tremores.' His 'Introduction to Physiology,' 369 pages, 8vo, Lond. 1759, being the substance of his London lectures increased to twenty-eight, is full of the latest information well digested. He employed a person in the Norway trade to get for him a manuscript copy of a paper on the resuscitation of the drowned by a Copenhagen authority. His first work, dated from Hull in June 1738 and published at York in 1740, was 'Neuropathia,' a Latin poem in three books on hypochondriasis and hysteria, with a prose summary and additions prefixed, dedicated to Peter Shaw ('Doctissime Shavi!'); it was republished at Rome, with an Italian translation by Moretti, in 1755. His next venture was 'A Proposal for the Improvement of Medicine, &c.,' being a collection of therapeutic essays on the use of bark in small-pox, on limes and other fruits and vegetables in scurvy, &c.; it was dedicated to Mead, who had been pleased with the 'Neuropathia.' In 1748 he published a new edition, much enlarged, and with remarks on Berkeley's tar-water doctrine and on the bishop's use of the term 'panacea.' In 1751 he published in London 'The Nature of the Nervous Fluid, or Animal Spirits,' an attempt to adapt the latter doctrine to current nervous physiology. In the same year he published anonymously 'A new Critical Examination of an Important Passage in Mr. Locke's Essay on Human Understanding [on the possibility of thought being superadded to matter], in a familiar letter to a friend.' In 1753 he issued a physiological comment on Solano's prognostics from the pulse (dicrotism, intermittence, &c.), an account of which had been brought to England by Dr. Nihell, physician to the English factory at Madrid. In 1755 Flemyng published a paper in the 'Philosophical Transactions' on the imbibition of the liquor amnii by the fœtus. Another paper, on corpulency, was read at the Royal Society in 1757, but not issued until the author printed it in 1760; it was translated into German by J. J. Plenk at Vienna in 1769, and reprinted in London as late as 1810. In 1754 he published at York 'A Proposal to diminish the Progress of the Distemper among the Horned Cattle' (2nd edition, Lond. 1755). His other writings are a 'Dissertation on James's Fever Powder' (Lond. 1760), and 'Adhesions or Accretions of the Lungs to the Pleura' (Lond. 1762), discussing the divergent views of Boerhaave and Haller as to the effects on the breathing. A disparaging criticism of this unimportant piece by a London reviewer caused him to issue the remainder

of the impression with a 'Vindication' in 1763.

[Epistolæ ad Hallerum, vol. iii. ; Flemyng's writings.]   C. C.

FLETA, though sometimes loosely used as if it were the name of a person, is really the name of a Latin text-book of English law, which, from internal evidence, seems to have been written in 1290 or thereabouts. It was printed with a dissertation by Selden in 1647, and again in 1685. The one old manuscript in which it is found (*Cotton MS.* Julius, B. viii., fourteenth century) bears on its frontispiece the title 'Fleta,' and in the preface there is a statement to the effect that 'this book may well be called Fleta, for it was composed in Fleta.' This seems to mean that it was written in the Fleet prison, and the conjecture has been made that it was the work of one of the corrupt judges whom Edward I imprisoned.

[The manuscript; Selden's Dissertation; Nichols's Introduction to edition of Britton (1865).]
F. W. M.

FLETCHER, ABRAHAM (1714–1793), mathematician, born in 1714 at Little Broughton, Bridekirk, Cumberland, was the son of a tobacco-pipe maker, who taught him his own trade, but gave him no higher instruction. The boy learnt to read, write, and cipher as he best could, applying himself particularly to the study of arithmetic, from which he proceeded to the investigation of mathematical theorems. After the day's toil in the workshop he would hoist himself by a rope into the loft over his father's cottage, in order to pursue his studies uninterruptedly. Having worked through Euclid he set up as a schoolmaster at the age of thirty, and acquired considerable reputation as a teacher of mathematics. He married early. His wife, like his parents, discouraged the pursuit of learning as an unprofitable thing. Turning his attention to botany, Fletcher studied the properties rather than the classification of plants; increased his income by the sale of herbal decoctions, and was known to his neighbours as 'Doctor Fletcher.' He also studied judicial astrology, and cast his own nativity, which Hutchinson found in one of his books. 'This gives,' says another astrologer, 'seventy-eight years and fifty-five days' duration of life. Fletcher lived seventy-eight years seventy-one days, dying on 1 Jan. 1793.

Fletcher published: 1. 'The Universal Measurer; the Theory of Measuring in all its various uses, whether artificers' works, gauging, surveying, or mining,' Whitehaven, 1753, 2 vols. 8vo. 2. 'The Universal Measurer and Mechanic, a work equally useful to the Gentleman, Tradesman, and Mechanic, with copperplates,' London, 1762, 8vo.

[Hutchinson's Hist. of Cumberland, ii. 324; Watt's Bibl. Brit.] R. H.

FLETCHER, ALEXANDER (1787–1860), presbyterian divine, son of William Fletcher, minister at the Bridge of Teith, near Doune, Perthshire, by Jean Gilfillan, sister of the Rev. Michael Gilfillan, was born at the Bridge of Teith 8 April 1787, and educated in the village of Doune and at Stirling grammar school. At the age of eleven he was sent to Glasgow College, whence he passed to the divinity hall in 1802, and ultimately became M.A. of the university of Glasgow. Having been received into the associated synod of Scotland 23 Dec. 1806, his first labours in the ministerial office were as co-pastor with his father at the Bridge of Teith, 16 Sept. 1807. In November 1811 he came to London as minister of Miles Lane Chapel, Meeting-house Yard, London Bridge. Here he very soon obtained popularity as a preacher. The church accommodation became too limited, and the congregation erected a new place of worship in London Wall, under the name of Albion Chapel, which was opened 7 Nov. 1816. This building cost upwards of 10,000l., and was soon crowded in every part. Here he began his annual Christmas sermon to the young, a practice he kept up with unabating success to the last. He was now in the height of his power and fame, especially popular as a preacher to the young. In April 1824 he was prosecuted in the civil and ecclesiastical courts in a breach of promise case with Miss Eliza Dick. In the king's bench no verdict was given, but in the meeting of the united associate synod at Edinburgh he was suspended from the exercise of his office and from church fellowship (Trial of the Rev. Alexander Fletcher before the United Associate Synod, London, 1824, pp. xvi, 120; Trial of the Rev. A. Fletcher before the Lord Chief Justice of the Court of Common Sense, 1825; An Appeal to the Public against the Associate Synod of Scotland, by A. Fletcher, 1824; The Injustice of the United Associate Synod Exposed, presented by A. Fletcher, 1825; The Loves of the Saints, or the Diverting History of Sandy and Bobby, 1825). The result was his separation from the secession church. He removed with the greater part of his congregation to Grub Street, and afterwards to their new and spacious temple in Finsbury Circus, an edifice which cost about 13,000l., and was at the time the largest chapel in London. Here for thirty-five years he continued to minister with

acceptance and success. He was honoured with the degree of D.D. from America, and after a long separation was again welcomed as a minister of the united presbyterian church. His last sermon was preached to nearly three thousand children, in Surrey Chapel, in February 1860, and from that time he gradually declined in health. His fame mainly rests upon his talent in preaching to children, and upon his 'Family Devotions,' of which fifty thousand copies were sold in England, besides numerous editions in the United States. He died of bronchitis and dropsy at 4 Portland Place, Lower Clapton, Middlesex, 30 Sept. 1860, and was buried in Abney Park cemetery 8 Oct., in the presence of six thousand persons. He married, 13 Jan. 1846, Lydia, daughter of Richard Baynes of Rayne Lodge, Essex.

He was the author of very numerous works, and his name is also found attached to the prefatory introductions to many books on theological subjects. The following are his chief publications: 1. 'The Tendency of Infidelity and Christianity contrasted,' two sermons, 1815. 2. A sermon on the death of Queen Caroline, 1821. 3. 'A Spiritual Guardian for Youth,' a sermon, 1822. 4. 'A Collection of Hymns for Albion Chapel,' 1822. 5. 'The Christian Ambassador,' a sermon, 1827. 6. 'The History of Miles Lane Chapel,' 1832. 7. 'A Guide to Family Devotion, containing a Hymn, a portion of Scripture, with Reflections and a Prayer for the Morning and Evening of every Day in the Year,' 1834. 8. 'Finsbury Chapel Collection of Hymns,' 1835. 9. 'The Juvenile Preacher, including twelve sermons by A. Fletcher,' 1836. 10. 'Scripture History designed for the Improvement of Youth,' 1839. 11. 'The Illustrated Watts's Hymns, edited by A. Fletcher,' 1840. 12. 'The Master's Joy, the Servant's Reward,' the funeral sermon of E. Temple, 1841. 13. The funeral sermon of Augustus Frederick, duke of Sussex, 1843. 14. 'The Sabbath School Preacher and Juvenile Miscellany,' 1848–50, 2 vols., continued as 'Dr. Fletcher's Juvenile Magazine,' 1850–1, 1 vol. 15. 'Address to the Young,' 1851. 16. 'The Bible the Great Exhibition for all Nations,' 1851. 17. Sermon on the funeral and death of the Duke of Wellington, 1852. 18. The annual Christmas-day sermon to children, 1855. 19. Address at the grave of H. Althans, 1855. 20. 'Closet Devotional Exercises for the Young,' 1859. 21. 'Scripture Teaching for the Young,' 1859.

[Macfarlane's Altar-Light, a tribute to the memory of the Rev. A. Fletcher, 1860; Blair's The Prince of Preachers, Rev. A. Fletcher, 1860;

The Christian Cabinet Illustrated Almanack, 1860, p. 31, with portrait; Gent. Mag., November 1860, p. 563; Times, 10 Oct. 1860, p. 10; Fletcher's History of Miles Lane Chapel, 1832, pp. 45–9.]   G. C. B.

FLETCHER, ANDREW, LORD INNER-PEFFER (d. 1650), judge, was the eldest son of Robert Fletcher of Innerpeffer and Beucleo, Forfarshire, a burgess of Dundee. He succeeded Sir John Wemyss of Craigtoun as an ordinary lord of session, 18 Dec. 1623, and retained his seat in 1626, when many of the lords were displaced. In 1630 he was placed upon a commission upon Scotch law, and in 1633 was a member of commissions to revise the acts and laws of Scotland with a view to constructing a code, a project which was not proceeded with, and to report upon the jurisdiction of the admiral and chamberlain. He was also ordered to examine Sir Thomas Craig's work ' Jus Feudale,' with a view to its publication. In 1638 he was a commissioner to take subscriptions to the confession of faith of 1580. He was employed in 1639 in regulating the fees of writers to the signet and others, and parliament adopted the scales which he laid down. On 13 Nov. 1641 he, with others, was appointed to his judgeship afresh by the king and parliament, and his appointment was objected to by the laird of Moncrieff, upon the ground that he was incapacitated by having purchased lands the subject of litigation before him. The matter was referred to the privy council, and as Fletcher retained his seat the charge was presumably disproved. In the same year he was a commissioner for the plantation of kirks, and about this time was elected member for Forfarshire, but his election was avoided for illegality. He represented that county, however, in parliament in 1646, 1647, and 1648. On 1 Feb. 1645 he was appointed a commissioner of the exchequer, was on the committee of war for Haddingtonshire in 1647, and on the committee of estates for Haddingtonshire and Forfarshire in 1647 and 1648. He was fined 5,000l. by the Protector in 1648. Upon the question whether conditions should be obtained from the English army on behalf of Charles I, he was one of the four who voted against abandoning the king, and was removed in 1649 from his offices of judge and commissioner of the exchequer, on account of his accession to ' the engagement,' for the carrying on of which he had subscribed in the previous year 8,500l. (Scots), repaid by order of parliament in 1662 after his death to his son Robert. He was also ' ordained to lend money to the public.' In March 1650 he died at his house in East Lothian. He married a daughter of Peter Hay of Kirkland of Megginch, brother to George, first earl of Kinnoull, by whom he had a son Robert, afterwards knighted, who was father of Andrew Fletcher of Saltoun.

[Acts Scots Parl.; Books of Sederunt; Brunton and Haig's Senators; Guthrie's Memoirs; Lamont's Diary, p. 14; Gordon's Hist. Scots Affairs (Spalding Club), i. 109.]   J. A. H.

FLETCHER, ANDREW (1655–1716), Scotch patriot, born in 1655 at Salton (formerly Saltoun), East Lothian, was the son and heir of Sir Robert Fletcher (1625–1664), a country gentleman of good estate, at whose pressing instance Gilbert Burnet [q. v.], afterwards bishop of Salisbury, became parish minister of Salton in 1665. In his epicedial 'discourse' on his patron Burnet describes him as a man of singular devoutness, very charitable, and somewhat a cultivator of philosophy and science. Sir Robert is said (BUCHAN, p. 6) to have expressed a desire on his deathbed that Burnet should superintend the education of his son, then a boy of ten, and this Burnet seems to have done during the remaining five years of his stay at Salton. Their acquaintance long survived this connection, and Burnet, in the 'History of his own Time' (iii. 24), speaks of Fletcher as 'a Scotch gentleman of great parts and many virtues, but a most violent republican, and extremely passionate.' Fletcher became one of the most accomplished Scotchmen of his time. While young, he made a tour on the continent, and after his return to Salton soon became a marked man through his local opposition to Lauderdale. In July 1680 he was rebuked by the Scotch privy council for obstructing the drafting of a number of men from the militia into the standing force maintained to overawe presbyterian malcontents (FOUNTAINHALL, Hist. Notices, i. 270). In the Scotch convention of estates which met in June 1678 Fletcher sat as a commissioner for his county (FOUNTAINHALL, Hist. Observes, 'Accompt of the Convention of Estates,' &c., pp. 270–1), the statement in the official lists of that assembly (Acts of the Parliaments of Scotland, viii. 214; Members of Parliament: Return to the House of Commons, 1878, pt. iii. p. 583) that ' a James Fletcher' was one of the commissioners for East Lothian being undoubtedly incorrect. He voted in it with the Duke of Hamilton in opposition to Lauderdale's policy. He was punished as a malcontent by having soldiers quartered on him, and a petition which he and others presented, complaining of this proceeding as 'contrare to law,' was ' much resented' by the council (FOUNTAINHALL, Hist. Notices, i. 281). He was again a commissioner for East Lothian in the Scotch parliament which met in July 1681, and he industriously opposed the measures of Lauderdale's successor, the Duke of York. Sir John Dalrymple, in a statement seemingly unsupported (pt. i. bk. i. p. 39), asserts that Fletcher broached the successful proposal to make a profession of presbyterianism part of the test which was imposed by that parliament (cf. WODROW, iii. 298, and BURNET, ii. 301-2, who differ materially as to the early history of the test). Certainly he had the courage with only one other member to record a protest against the provision of the act which made subscription to the test imperative on county electors, as well as on their representatives (*Acts of the Parliaments of Scotland*, viii. 245). He is said to have addressed to members of the parliament anonymous letters beseeching them to oppose the Duke of York's succession (FOUNTAINHALL, *Hist. Observes*, p. 209). In April 1682, as a commissioner of cess and excise, he, with some colleagues, was again brought before the privy council on a charge of not having levied a local tax to be applied in supplying the soldiery with corn (FOUNTAINHALL, *Hist. Notices*, i. 352). Fletcher took part in the exodus of Scotch malcontents which followed the condemnation of Archibald, ninth earl of Argyll [q. v.], for refusing more than a qualified acceptance of the test. It is said (FOUNTAINHALL, *Hist. Observes*, p. 214) that when he was about this time an exile at Brussels the Duke of York asked the Spanish governor there to have him arrested. Hearing of this Fletcher came secretly to London and was taken into the confidence of Monmouth, Russell, and Sydney, who were planning their movement for a change in the system of government. With its collapse and Monmouth's flight to Holland, Fletcher left England and was for a time in Paris, where Lord Preston, Charles II's envoy extraordinary to Louis XIV, wrote to Halifax, 5 Oct. 1683 : 'Here is one Fletcher, laird of Salton, lately come from Scotland. He is an ingenious but a violent fanatic, and doubtless hath some commission, for I hear he is very busy and very virulent' (Appendix to *Hist. MSS. Comm.* 7th Rep. 343 *b*). Fletcher is next heard of as in Holland, and as one of the most intimate associates and advisers there of Monmouth, from whom he hoped for at the very least the convocation of a 'free parliament' in England. In spite of his impetuosity Fletcher was earnest in dissuading Monmouth from imprudent enterprises. He was strongly opposed to Argyll's disastrous expedition to Scotland, and to Monmouth's own expedition to England (BURNET, iii. 25, from Fletcher's own information; FERGUSON, p. 210). To Lord Grey of Wark's argument in its favour,

founded on the success of Henry VII's expedition, Fletcher replied that Henry reckoned, as Monmouth could not, on the support of a strong party of powerful English nobles (BURNET, *ib.*)

Fletcher nevertheless sailed with Monmouth and landed at Lyme 11 June 1685. On the 13th he was to have been joined with Lord Grey in the command of a troop of horse in an expedition to Bridport. He rode, or insisted on riding, a fine charger brought in that day by one Dare, who also accompanied the duke to England. Dare, formerly a disaffected goldsmith and alderman of Taunton, joined the refugees in Holland, and made himself useful to them and to Monmouth by aiding them to communicate with their friends in England. After having been Monmouth's secretary he was appointed paymaster of the expeditionary force, and much benefit to the enterprise was expected from his knowledge of the district and his old connection with Taunton. Dare angrily disputed Fletcher's claim to the use of his horse, and after having reviled him for some time shook a switch at him, on which Fletcher drew a pistol and shot him dead. Monmouth was forced to part with Fletcher, who embarked on board the vessel which had been hired to bring the expedition to England, and the papers of which were made out for Bilbao. According to Lord Buchan (p. 18) Fletcher told his friend Keith, the earl marischal, that he quitted Monmouth, not on account of the Dare incident, but out of disgust at Monmouth's proclamation of himself at Taunton as king. But the Dare catastrophe occurred on 13 June, and Monmouth was not proclaimed king at Taunton until the 20th. The contemporary authorities, while differing more or less as to details, agree that the death of Dare alone produced Fletcher's separation from Monmouth. Fletcher was incapable of falsehood. Keith must have misunderstood or misreported him (cf. BUCHAN, *ib.*; BURNET, iii. 44-5; ROBERTS, i. 272-4; FERGUSON, 221-2; *State Trials*, xi. 1055).

According to the earl marischal's further reports of conversations with him (see BUCHAN, pp. 19-23) Fletcher was thrown into prison soon after he landed at Bilbao, and his extradition was demanded by the English minister at Madrid. He is represented to have made a romantic escape from prison, and then to have wandered through Spain in disguise, viewing the country and the people, studying in the conventual libraries, and purchasing rare and curious books, some of which found their way to his library at Salton. When his Spanish wanderings were over, he went to Hungary and fought as a volunteer against the Turks (*ib.* p. 22, with a reference to family manuscripts), whom in one of his writings Fletcher calls 'the common enemy of mankind.' In his absence he was tried at Edinburgh, 4 Jan. 1686, for treasonable complicity in Monmouth's rebellion, when he was sentenced to death and his estate forfeited. One of the two witnesses on whose evidence he was condemned described him as 'a little man,' wearing 'a brown periwig, of a lean face, pock-marked' (*State Trials,* xi. 1054). Of the amnesty proclaimed by James II in his letter to the parliament of Scotland, 29 April 1686 (*Acts,* &c., viii. 879–80), Fletcher, unlike some other Scotchmen in his predicament, did not avail himself, because it was given in virtue of 'the dispensing power,' and not by an act of the legislature (see BUCHAN, p. 30, &c.)

Fletcher joined William of Orange at the Hague in 1688, and with the revolution returned to Scotland. He was not a member of the Scottish convention which met 14 March 1689, and which became a parliament in June 1690, when his estates were restored to him by a special act. He became, however, one of the busiest members of 'the club' (*Leven and Melville Papers,* p. 159), an association consisting mainly of the leaders and members of the majority of the parliamentary opposition formed soon after William's accession, ostensibly to diminish the power of the crown in Scotland. Fletcher, as a republican and a hater of English domination, naturally approved this object. He now began to attempt to create a Young Scotland and Scotch home rule party. When William Paterson proposed to form the association which became in 1695, by an act of the Scotch parliament, 'The Company of Scotland trading with Africa and the Indies,' the principal operation of which was the disastrous attempt to colonise the isthmus of Darien, Fletcher is said to have brought Paterson down from London to Salton, to have introduced him to his neighbour, the Marquis of Tweeddale, then minister for Scotland, and to have aided in persuading that nobleman to support the scheme (DALRYMPLE, vol. iii. pt. iii. p. 129; BUCHAN, p. 46). These statements are not supported by any contemporary authority. In the original list of shareholders (1696) Fletcher figures as the subscriber of 1,000*l.* to the stock of the company (*Darien Papers,* p. 373).

In 1698 appeared, without author's name, Fletcher's earliest published writings, three in number: 1. 'A Discourse of Government relating to Militias,' an able and vigorous contribution to a controversy which was at that time being fiercely waged in England. Fletcher argued that in warfare a militia

was more effective than a standing army. He sketched a plan for the establishment of a national militia by the formation of camps of military instruction, in which all the adult youth of the country were to be trained and disciplined with Spartan rigour, and from which ecclesiastics were to be excluded. 2. 'Two Discourses concerning the Affairs of Scotland, written in the year 1698.' In the first of these Fletcher urged that the 84,000*l.* annually spent on maintaining a force of regulars in Scotland might be much more usefully employed in promoting industry. In the second 'Discourse' Fletcher proposed a sweeping measure of social reform. He estimated at two hundred thousand at that time of scarcity, and at one hundred thousand in ordinary times, the number of beggars and vagrants who infested and preyed upon Scotland. He proposed that every man of a certain estate should be obliged to take a proportional number of them into his service. They were to be servants not slaves, to call them so was to be punishable, and they were to be protected by law like ordinary servants, with the important exceptions that their servitude was to be compulsory and hereditary, and that they and their children might be 'alienated,' i.e. sold by their masters. Fletcher found precedents for his scheme in Scotch acts of parliament passed in 1579 and 1597, the first of which, Fletcher said, allowed the compulsory servitude of the children of beggars for a term of years, which the second extended to their lifetime. The act of 1579, as Fletcher failed to observe, permitted the compulsory servitude of even an adult beggar for a year, and this term also was extended to his lifetime by the act of 1597. In the same 'Discourse' Fletcher made suggestions for the improvement of the condition of the Scotch farmer. He denounced rack-renting, to which he ascribed the general poverty of Scotland. 3. 'Discorso delle cose di Spagna scritto nel mese di Luglio, 1698,' with the imprint 'Napoli,' but in all probability printed at Edinburgh. This curious Italian tractate, written at the time of the negotiation of the first partition treaty, shows how measures might be taken, unsuspected by any one except Fletcher himself, for the attainment of universal monarchy by Spain. There seems to have been a second edition of the 'Discorso,' to which Fletcher prefixed an 'Aviso' which was not in the first (see his *Political Works,* ed. 1737, p. 179). Fletcher returned to the subject of Spain in what professes to be 'A Speech upon the State of the Nation in April 1701,' but it probably never was spoken, and does not seem to have been published in Fletcher's lifetime. It attributes to William III a project for making himself an absolute monarch, in connivance with Louis XIV.

Fletcher entered, as a commissioner for East Lothian once more, the new Scotch parliament of 1703. The Scotch were irritated by the failure of the Darien scheme, and by the unsatisfactory character of the English proposals for a treaty of union. Fletcher and the national party saw an opportunity for wresting from Queen Anne a large measure of political independence for Scotland by making her acceptance of their terms a preliminary to their entering on the question of the succession. Fletcher took a very prominent part in the parliamentary controversy between the national and the court parties. On 27 May 1703 he carried a resolution to defer a grant of supply until guarantees were obtained for the security of the religion and liberties of Scotland. On 22 June he produced a draft act of security, which, if accepted by the parliament of Scotland and by Queen Anne, would have given after her death home rule to Scotland. Fletcher's scheme of security was only to take effect if Queen Anne's successor on the throne of England should also be sovereign of Scotland. He proposed that in this contingency the Scotch executive should be chosen not by the sovereign of both countries, but by a committee of the parliament of Scotland. The Scotch parliament was to meet annually, and the votes in it were to be taken by ballot. For every nobleman added to the parliament a 'lesser baron,' or county member, was to be added. A national militia was to be established as soon as the Act of Security became law. For these 'limitations' Fletcher pleaded throughout the stormy session of 1703. Among Fletcher's proposals, which were embodied in the Act of Security passed by the Scotch parliament, and in 1704 assented to by Queen Anne, was that for the immediate formation and arming of a Scotch national militia, a measure which was regarded by the English government and parliament as a menace of civil war. Another of his proposals, to deprive the sovereign of the power of declaring war and making peace, was embodied in a special act, which also was touched with the sceptre. When the queen's commissioner announced in the session of 1703 that all the acts passed by the parliament during it would be thus touched, except the Act of Security, Fletcher rose and moved a resolution declaring that ' after the decease of her majesty we will separate our crown from that of England.' Fletcher's defiant speeches, along with the adoption of some of the measures advocated in them, con-

tributed powerfully to induce Queen Anne's advisers to revive, this time successfully, the project of a legislative union of England and Scotland.

Fletcher issued, without his name, in the year of their delivery, 'Speeches by a Member of the Parliament which began at Edinburgh the 6th of May, 1703.' In 1704 appeared, also anonymously, the most attractive, to modern readers, of his political writings, 'An Account of a Conversation concerning a Right Regulation of Governments for the common good of Mankind. In a Letter to the Marquis of Montrose, the Earls of Rothes, Roxburg, and Haddington, from London the 1st of December, 1703'—a dialogue described in the text as between Fletcher himself, the Earl of Cr[o]m[a]rty, Sir Ed[ward] S[ey]-m[ou]r, and Sir Chr[istopher] M[u]sgr[a]ve. Fletcher supports his theories with much dramatic force against his interlocutors. In the 'imaginary conversation' occurs an often quoted and misquoted remark of Fletcher's. 'I knew,' he says, 'a very wise man so much of Sir Christopher's sentiment that he believed if a man were permitted to make all the ballads he need not care who should make the laws of a nation.' In the remaining sessions, 1704 to 1707, of the Scotch parliament Fletcher continued very active, but with diminished influence, the majority deciding on assenting to the union. In all its sessions he displayed great irritability, the assembly having on several occasions to interfere to prevent him fighting duels with the Duke of Hamilton and Lord Stair, among others (see SIR DAVID HUME, pp. 147, 160, &c., and a detailed narrative of a duel just on the point of being fought by him in BURTON's *Queen Anne*, i. 164–5). Once, July 1705 (SIR DAVID HUME, p. 167), he seems to have gone the length of proposing that the (first) king of Prussia should be named successor to Queen Anne in the sovereignty of Scotland. He and the Jacobites voted together against the chief clauses of the Act of Union. It had been touched by the sceptre when, 27 Jan. 1707, he made his last noticeable appearance in the last parliament of Scotland, with a motion, apparently successful, incapacitating noblemen's eldest sons for election by the expiring Scotch legislature to the first union parliament of Great Britain.

Fletcher was one of the members of the motley party opposed to the union who, in April 1708, were brought in custody to London on a suspicion of having been privy to the attempted French invasion of Scotland in the previous month in the interest of the Pretender (BOYER, *History of Queen Anne*, ed. 1722, p. 338); but he was soon discharged, and with this incident he disappeared from public life. What is known of his subsequent career entitles him to a place among the early improvers of Scotch agriculture. In Holland he had been struck by the efficacy of the mill-machinery used there for removing the husk of barley and converting it into 'pot' barley, and of the fanners for winnowing corn. In 1710 he engaged James Meikle, an ingenious millwright in the neighbourhood of Salton, father of the better known Andrew Meikle, to go to Amsterdam and, under his direction, to see to the construction of such portions of the ironwork of the barley-mills as could not easily be made in Scotland. Meikle took them to Salton and there erected a barley-mill, which found constant employment (cf. ALLARDYCE, ii. 70, where the Salton mill is said to have been erected upon a plan made from memory by 'William Adam, the architect,' doubtless the father of the three brothers Adam). 'Salton barley' became conspicuous on the signboard of almost every Scotch retailer of such articles, yet for more than forty years that barley-mill remained the only one in Great Britain, Ireland, or America. Fanners also were erected at Salton, but apparently not until a few years after Fletcher's death (HEPBURN, pp. 145–6; SMILES, p. 198). Fletcher died in London in September 1716, and his remains were taken to Salton, where they were deposited, and rest in the family burial-vault.

Fletcher's ardent, courageous, and disinterested patriotism raise him far above the Scotch politicians of his time. Historians from Wodrow to Macaulay unite in bearing testimony to his worth. Hume calls him 'a man of signal probity and fine genius' (*History of England*, ed. 1854, vi. 396). The Jacobite Lockhart of Carnwath, who sat with him in the Scotch parliament of 1703–7, declared him (p. 75) to be 'so steadfast to what he thought right that no hazard nor advantage, no, not the universal empire, nor the gold of America, could tempt him to yield or desert it.' The strict Wodrow (iv. 227), after speaking of him as 'one of the brightest of our gentry, remarkable for his fine taste in all manner of polite learning, his curious library, his indefatigable diligence in every thing he thought might benefit and improve his country,' praises the 'sobriety, temperance, and good management' which he exhibited in private life. As a writer he is superior to any Scotchman of his age, and his oratory, nervous and incisive, is made eloquent by his sincerity and earnestness. His chief fault was his irritability of temper. The story retailed to Mrs. Calderwood during her journey in Holland (*Coltness Papers*, pp. 166–7, and reproduced in CHAMBERS, iii. 319 *n*.) of a Dutch skipper deliberately sent out of the world by 'old Fletcher of Salton' from a dislike of his tobacco-smoking, may have been meant to refer to the patriot, though this is by no means certain, since the date of her narrative is 1756, forty years after his death. If told of him it is probably apocryphal. Macky (p. 223) describes him as 'a low,' i.e. short, 'thin man, brown complexion, full of fire, with a stern, sour look.' He died unmarried.

All the writings of Fletcher previously mentioned are contained in the first collection of his 'Political Works,' London, 1737; the 'Character of the Author, from a MS. in the Library of the late Thomas Rawlinson,' prefixed to it, and often reprinted subsequently with the same account of its source, being simply that given by Macky in the volume already quoted from. In the next edition of the 'Political Works,' Glasgow, 1747, the 'Discorso delle cose di Spagna' appears in an English translation solely. The volume, London, 1798, professing to contain the 'Political Works,' gives only Fletcher's 'Discourse on Militias' and the 'Account of a Conversation,' with notes, &c., to which is prefixed a sketch of his life, with observations, moral, philosophical, and political, by R. Watson, M.D.' The life is valueless. To Lord Buchan's 'Memoir' are appended Fletcher's parliamentary speeches of 1703. 'An Historical Account of the Ancient Rights and Power of the Parliament of Scotland,' &c., published anonymously at Edinburgh in 1703, and reprinted at Aberdeen in 1823 as 'undoubtedly' written by Fletcher, may be pronounced to have been undoubtedly not written by him were it only because a very complimentary reference is made in it to the author of the 'Discourse of Government with relation to Militias.' The catalogue of the Edinburgh Advocates' Library attributes to Fletcher two pamphlets, nowhere else referred to, in connection with him: 1. 'Scotland's Interest, or the great Benefit and Necessity of a Communication of Trade with England,' &c., 1704. 2. 'State of the Controversy betwixt United and Separate Parliaments,' &c. Neither of these pamphlets is in the Library of the British Museum. Fletcher left behind him a manuscript 'Treatise on Education,' of which nothing seems now to be known. The library which he formed is still preserved at Salton Hall, in a room built expressly for it in 1775 by his grand-nephew, also an Andrew Fletcher.

[Fletcher's writings; Earl of Buchan's Essays on the Lives and Writings of Fletcher of Saltoun and the Poet Thomson (1792): Biographical,

Critical, and Political, 1792; Bishop Burnet's History of his own Time, ed. 1823; Wodrow's History of the Sufferings of the Church of Scotland, 1829-30; Fountainhall's Historical Observes of Memorable Occurrences in Church and State, 1840, and Historical Notices of Scottish Affairs, 1847-8 (Bannatyne Club); Sir David Hume of Crossrigs' Diary of the Proceedings in the Parliament . . . of Scotland, 1700-7 (Bannatyne Club); Lockhart Papers, 1817; Macky's Memoirs, 1733; Sir John Dalrymple's Memoirs of Great Britain and Ireland, ed. 1790; G. Roberts's Life, &c., of James, Duke of Monmouth, 1844; J. Ferguson's Robert Ferguson the Plotter, 1887; Howell's State Trials; J. Hill Burton's History of Scotland, 2nd edit. 1873, and History of the Reign of Queen Anne, 1880; R. Chambers's Domestic Annals of Scotland, 1858-61; Allardyce's Scotland and Scotsmen in the Eighteenth Century (from the manuscripts of John Ramsay of Ochtertyre), 1888; G. Buchan Hepburn's General View of the Agriculture and Rural Economy of East Lothian, 1794; Smiles's Lives of the Engineers, 'Andrew Meikle;' other authorities cited; family information; communications from Sir W. Fraser, deputy-keeper of the Records of Scotland. The chief authority for a life of Fletcher is the quasi-biographical rhapsody of David Steuart Erskine [q. v.], the eccentric (eleventh) earl of Buchan (1742-1829), who did not turn to much account the papers relating to Fletcher which were lent to him from the family archives, and which were afterwards, unfortunately, lost. When Lord Buchan's statements can be tested, he is too often found untrustworthy. Before the papers were lost they were also consulted by the writer of the memoir of Fletcher in the third edition of the Encyclopædia Britannica, 1797. He extracted from them the interesting statement that while the Jacobite George Keith, the well-known (tenth) earl marischal, who had been with Fletcher a member of the Scotch parliament of 1703-7, was governor of Neufchatel, he asked Rousseau to write a life of Fletcher, for which he promised the needful material. There are brief reports of several of Fletcher's parliamentary speeches, sometimes given as those of a nameless 'member,' in Boyer's Annals of Queen Anne, 1703-7, but the most instructive indications of his parliamentary career are in Sir David Hume's Diary. Some depreciatory remarks on Fletcher's parliamentary influence and tactics in the manuscript memoirs of Sir John Clerk are quoted in Somerville's History of Great Britain during the Reign of Queen Anne, p. 204 n., and in Howell's State Trials, xi. 1050 n. The Retrospective Review (first series), vol. iv. part i., contains an article on 'Fletcher's Political Writings.' There are interesting references to Fletcher and his schemes, political and social, in Lord Macaulay's History of England, and still more of the kind in Dr. Hill Burton's History of Scotland. A brief notice appears in Anderson's Scottish Nation.]

F. E.

FLETCHER, ANDREW, Lord Milton (1692-1766), lord justice clerk, was the eldest son of Henry Fletcher of Salton, Haddingtonshire, by his wife Margaret, daughter of Sir David Carnegie of Pittarrow, bart., and nephew of Andrew Fletcher of Salton [q. v.] He was born in 1692, and having been educated for the bar was admitted an advocate on 26 Feb. 1717. In the following year he was nominated a cashier of the excise. In 1724, when only thirty-two years of age, he was appointed an ordinary lord of session in the place of Sir John Lauder of Fountainhall, and took his seat on the bench on 4 June in that year. On 22 June 1726 he became a lord justiciary on the resignation of James Hamilton of Pencaitland, and by patent dated 7 July 1727 was nominated one of the commissioners for improving the fisheries and manufactures of Scotland. On 21 June 1735 he succeeded James Erskine of Grange as lord justice clerk, and on 10 Nov. 1746 was appointed principal keeper of the signet. In 1748 he resigned the office of justice clerk, 'but retained the charge of superintending elections, which he considered as his masterpiece' (*Scotland and Scotsmen in the Eighteenth Century*, 1888, i. 89). The acuteness of his judgment, and his accurate knowledge of the laws and customs of Scotland, early recommended him to the notice and confidence of Lord Islay, afterwards Archibald, third duke of Argyll, to whose hands the chief management of Scottish affairs was then entrusted, and for a number of years Milton acted as his confidential agent in Scotland. As lord justice clerk he presided at the trial of Captain Porteous in 1736, and in May of the following year was examined at the bar of the House of Lords with regard to matters arising out of those proceedings. During the rebellion of 1745 he acted with great leniency and discretion, and after its suppression strenuously exerted himself in the promotion of the trade and agriculture of the country. He took an active part in the abolition of the exceptional heritable jurisdictions, and under his advice the greater part of the government patronage in Scotland was dispensed. Milton died at Brunstane, near Edinburgh, on 15 Dec. 1766, in the seventy-fifth year of his age, after a long illness. He married Elizabeth, daughter of Sir Francis Kinloch of Gilmerton, bart. His mother appears to have been a woman of great energy and enterprise. Taking with her a millwright and a weaver she went to Holland, where 'by their means she secretly obtained the art of weaving and dressing what was then, as it is now, commonly called holland (fine linen), and introduced the manufacture into the village and neigh-bourhood of Salton' (*The Bee*, xi. 2). A number of Milton's letters relating to affairs in Scotland in 1745 will be found in the appendix to John Home's 'History of the Rebellion in the year 1745' (1802). Two portraits of Milton by Allan Ramsay were exhibited in the Scotch Loan Collection at Edinburgh in 1884 (*Catalogue*, Nos. 121 and 187). A small engraving by R. Scott, after one of Ramsay's portraits, forms the fronti-spiece to the eleventh volume of 'The Bee.'

[The Bee, or Literary Weekly Intelligencer, xi. 1–5; Brunton and Haig's Senators of the College of Justice (1832), pp. 498–9; Anderson's Scottish Nation (1863), ii. 226; Chalmers's Biog. Dict. of Eminent Scotsmen (1869), ii. 36; Scots Mag. 1746 viii. 550, 1748 x. 509, 1766 xxviii. 671; Burke's Landed Gentry (1879), i. 574.]

G. F. R. B.

FLETCHER, ARCHIBALD (1746–1828), reformer, was descended from the highland clan of Fletcher, his ancestors, ac-cording to tradition, being the first who 'had raised smoke or boiled water on the braes of Glenorchy.' He was the eldest son of Angus Fletcher, a younger brother of Archibald Fletcher of Bennice and Dunans, Argyle-shire, by his second wife, Grace M'Naghton, and was born at Pooble in Glenlyon, Perth-shire, in 1746. After attending the gram-mar school of Kenmore in Breadalbane he entered the high school of Perth in his thir-teenth year. He served an apprenticeship to a writer to the signet in Edinburgh, and became confidential clerk to Lord-advocate Sir James Montgomery, who introduced him to Mr. Wilson of Howglen, with whom he became partner. In his earlier years he de-voted much of his spare time to study, rising at four in the morning to read Greek, attend-ing a debating society, and enrolling himself in some of the university classes, including that of moral philosophy, where he had as one of his fellow-students Dugald Stewart, with whom he became intimately acquainted. In 1778 he was chosen, on account of his knowledge of Gaelic, to negotiate with the M'Cra highlanders, who refused to embark at Leith for service in America. When about this time the Faculty of Advocates brought forward a resolution that no one above the age of twenty-seven should be admitted a member of their body, Fletcher wrote a pamphlet against the proposal, which was so successful that the resolution was withdrawn. The pamphlet gained him the friendship of Henry Erskine. He also distinguished him-self by an 'Essay on Church Patronage,' in which he supported the popular side. In 1784, when burgh reform was first agitated

in Scotland, he became secretary of the so-ciety then formed in Edinburgh, and drew up the principal heads of a reform bill to be submitted to parliament. He was deservedly called 'father of burgh reform,' both on ac-count of his initiation of the agitation and the skill and energy with which he directed it. In 1787 he was sent as delegate to London by the Scottish burghs to promote this object, when he gained the friendship of Fox and other leaders. It was not till 1790 that he was called to the Scottish bar. The following year he married Miss Eliza Dawson, a lady of literary tastes [see FLETCHER, ELIZA]. At first his success at the bar was hindered by his advanced political opinions, but he gradually acquired a considerable practice. He was a supporter of the American war of independence, a prominent abolitionist, and so strong a sympathiser with the French revolution that he attended every anniver-sary of the fall of the Bastille from 14 July 1789. He acted without fee as counsel for Joseph Gerrald and 'other friends of the people' charged with sedition in 1793, and in 1796 was one of the minority of thirty-eight who opposed the deposition of Henry Erskine, dean of the faculty. In 1816 he retired from the bar on account of declining health, and took up his residence at Park-hill, Stirlingshire. Still taking a special in-terest in questions affecting the burghs of Scotland, he published in 1825 'An Exami-nation of the Grounds on which the Conven-tion of Royal Burghs claimed the right of altering and amending the Setts or Consti-tution of the Individual Burghs.' He died at Auchindinny House, near Edinburgh, 20 Dec. 1828. He is described by Lord Brougham as 'one of the most upright men that ever adorned the profession, and a man of such stern and resolute firmness in public prin-ciple as is very rarely found united with the amiable character which endeared him to pri-vate society.'

[Account by Mrs. Fletcher in Appendix to her Autobiography; Kay's Edinb. Portraits, ii. 445–447; Cockburn's Life of Lord Jeffrey; Ferguson's Henry Erskine and his Times.]   T. F. H.

FLETCHER, ELIZA (1770–1858), auto-biographer, was born on 15 Jan. 1770, at Ox-ton, near Tadcaster in Yorkshire, where her father, named Dawson, descendant of a race of yeomen, was a land surveyor, and lived on a little family estate. Eliza was the only child of his marriage with the eldest daughter of William Hill. The mother died ten days after the birth. At eleven years old Eliza, a beautiful, intelligent girl, was sent to the Manor School at York. The mistress (Mrs.

Forster) was 'a very well-disposed, conscientious old gentlewoman,' but incapable of proper superintendence. 'Four volumes of the "Spectator" constituted the whole school library.' Miss Dawson had a profound admiration for William Mason the poet, then a York notability, especially on account of his 'Monody' upon his wife's death, and was shocked at seeing him 'a little fat old man of hard-favoured countenance,' devoted to whist. When she was seventeen accident brought to her father's house a Scotch advocate, Archibald Fletcher [q. v.], 'of about forty-three, and of a grave, gentlemanlike, prepossessing appearance.' They carried on a literary correspondence for a year, and after another meeting became engaged, though the father opposed the union, preferring a higher suitor, Lord Grantley. Miss Dawson got a friend, Dr. Kilvington, to tell Lord Grantley of her engagement. On 16 July 1791 the lovers were married in Tadcaster Church. Her father did not sanction the ceremony by his presence, but he could not withhold his blessing. For seven-and-thirty years, at the end of which time her husband died, 'there was not a happier couple in the three kingdoms.' Fletcher's steady adherence to his whig principles prevented his getting into practice, and they were often reduced to their last guinea. Her sympathy prevented her from ever regretting the sacrifice to principle. Afterwards success in life set steadily in with little interruption. Mrs. Fletcher died at Edinburgh 5 Feb. 1858. Her 'Autobiography,' of which a few copies had been printed for private circulation, 8vo, Carlisle, 1874, was published at Edinburgh the following year under the editorship of her surviving child, the widow of Sir John Richardson, the Arctic explorer. The 'Life' also contains a memoir by Mrs. Fletcher of her daughter Grace, and another of her son Archibald, by his widow. It is an attractive book about a most lovable woman, who seems, according to her portraits, at fifteen and eighty, to prove 'that there is a beauty for every age.'

[Autobiography of Mrs. Fletcher of Edinburgh; Gent. Mag. 3rd ser. iv. 340; Athenæum, 1 May 1875.] G. G.

FLETCHER, GEORGE (1764–1855), a reputed centenarian, son of Joseph Fletcher, was baptised at Clarborough, Nottinghamshire, 15 Oct. 1764, but according to his own account on 2 Feb. 1747, and worked as a labourer. On 2 Nov. 1785 he enlisted in the 23rd foot, the royal Welsh fusiliers, from which regiment he deserted on 16 March 1792. Under a royal proclamation dated 1793 all deserters were pardoned, and their services restored on certain conditions. Fletcher, taking advantage of this amnesty, re-enlisted into the 3rd foot guards on 14 March 1793, stating that he had originally entered the army in October 1773. This addition of twelve years to his army services he continued to claim throughout the remainder of his life. He remained in his regiment for ten years, and was then pensioned from Chelsea Hospital on 18 April 1803 on 1s. 2½d. a day. By some oversight he was credited with twenty-four and a half years' service, and his age at the time of his discharge was entered as forty-nine instead of thirty-nine. After this period he was in the service of the West India Dock Company for thirty-six years, at the end of which time he retired on a pension. He was a local preacher in the Wesleyan methodist connexion, and in his sermons gave sketches of his own career, when he took credit for his great age, and related details of his services at the battle of Bunker's Hill in July 1775, although he was then only eleven years of age. The fame of his age caused large congregations to attend his preaching, and his portrait as a man of a hundred and six, who had lived in four reigns, was extensively sold in 1853. One of his later announcements says : 'Finsbury Chapel, Moorfields. Two sermons will be delivered Wednesday, June 21, 1854, by the Venerable George Fletcher, in his 108th year. For the benefit of an aged minister.' He died at 41 Wade Street, Poplar, London, 2 Feb. 1855, aged 91.

[Thoms's Human Longevity, 1873, pp. 64, 164–70 ; Registrar-general's Weekly Return, 17 Feb. 1855, p. 49 ; Gent. Mag. April 1855, p. 440, and June, p. 657 ; Illustrated London News, 10 March 1855, p. 221, with portrait ; Times, 13 Feb. 1855, p. 7, col. 6.] G. C. B.

FLETCHER, GILES, LL.D. (1549?–1611), civilian, ambassador, and poet, was certainly born in or about 1549 at Watford, Hertfordshire, as appears from his own statement on being admitted to the university of Cambridge. It has hitherto been supposed that he was a native of Kent. His father, Richard Fletcher, was vicar of Bishops Stortford, Hertfordshire, from 1551 to 1555, and was subsequently rector of Cranbrook and vicar of Smarden, Kent. Giles was educated at Eton, whence he was elected to King's College, Cambridge, being admitted a scholar on 27 Aug. 1565, and a fellow on 28 Aug. 1568. He proceeded B.A. in 1569, and commenced M.A. in 1573. In 1576 he took an active part in opposition to the provost, Dr. Goad, and signed articles accusing the provost of maladministration and infringement of the college statutes. These articles were laid before Lord Burghley as chancellor of the university.

His decision was unfavourable to the provost's opponents, and Fletcher had to sign a formal submission and apology.

He was deputy orator of the university in 1577. On 28 Oct. 1579 the provost of his college enjoined him to divert to the study of the civil law. On 3 July 1580 he was constituted commissary to Dr. Bridgwater, the chancellor of the diocese of Ely. On 16 Jan. 1580–1 he married Joan Sheafe of Cranbrook. In 1581 he was created LL.D., and on 5 July in that year was in a commission for visiting the church of Chichester, of which diocese he occurs as chancellor in 1582. Subsequently he appears to have been living at Cranbrook. In the parliament which began 23 Nov. 1585 he served for Winchelsea. He was remembrancer of the city of London from January 1586–7 to 1605.

He was sent to Scotland with Thomas Randolph, the English ambassador in that country. There is a letter from Fletcher to Sir Francis Walsingham, dated Edinburgh, 17 May 1586, giving an account of the proceedings of the general assembly, and in conclusion begging to be employed in some honest service in England. At a subsequent period he was employed in negotiations in Germany, Hamburg, and Stade. In 1588 he was despatched on a special embassy to Russia, being probably recommended to this post by Randolph, who had formerly been ambassador to that country. Before he set out Fletcher was made a master extraordinary of the court of requests. In Russia he was treated with the greatest indignity, but he nevertheless contrived to secure for the English merchants very considerable concessions. The queen sent a formal complaint to the emperor, remonstrating on the manner in which Fletcher had been treated. He returned to England in 1589, and it is believed that he was soon afterwards made a master of requests in ordinary. He was certainly about the same time constituted secretary or remembrancer to the city of London.

In 1590 he formed the design of writing an extensive history of the reign of Queen Elizabeth in Latin. He applied to Lord Burghley for assistance and the communication of state papers, and consulted him on his plan, especially as to whether he should undertake to justify at length the marriage of Henry VIII with Anne Boleyn, and at what point he should commence his work. He forwarded a scheme in Latin of his first book, to comprise the first year of Elizabeth's reign, with a paper of articles in which he desired information.

His account of Russia, which appeared in 1591, excited no little alarm on the part of the Eastland merchants of England. Point-

ing out the passages which they believed were calculated to give offence to the emperor, they memorialised Lord Burghley. The book was quickly suppressed, and it is only within the last few years that this very curious and interesting work has reappeared in its integrity.

Fletcher was one of the commissioners empowered by the privy council on 25 Oct. 1591 to examine Eustace White, a seminary priest, and Brian Lacey, a disperser of letters to papists, being empowered to cause them to be put to the manacles and such other tortures as were used in Bridewell. His brother, the bishop of London, a few months before his death made strenuous efforts to obtain for Fletcher the situation of master extraordinary in chancery. It does not appear that he was successful. Fletcher was one of the bishop's executors. This trust involved him in great difficulties, and he was only saved from arrest by the interposition of the Earl of Essex. On 20 June 1597 he was presented by the queen to the office of treasurer of the church of St. Paul, vacant by the elevation of Dr. Bancroft to the see of London. In 1600 he obtained from King's College, Cambridge, a lease of the rectory of Ringwood, Hampshire, for ten years. It had been previously leased by the college in 1596 for a similar term to Richard Sheafe of Cranbrook, clothier. An expression of sympathy for his unfortunate patron, the Earl of Essex, led to his being committed in February 1600–1 to the private custody of Mr. Lowe, one of the aldermen of London. On 14 March following he appealed for release to Sir Robert Cecil in a letter stating that he was infirm through grief of mind for this restraint, and the affliction of his wife and children.

In the reign of Elizabeth he was plaintiff in a suit in chancery against Nathaniel Pownall on personal matters. There was also a bill filed by him, Joan, his wife, and Phineas, his eldest son, against John Hall, respecting the site of the manor of Hynwick, Worcestershire, and a pasture lying on the banks of the Severn below the park of Hallow, under a lease granted by the Bishop of Worcester. In November 1610 he was employed by the Eastland merchants to treat with Dr. Jonas Charisius, the king of Denmark's ambassador, touching the removal of the trade from the town of Krempe. He died in the parish of St. Catherine Colman, Fenchurch Street, London, where he was buried on 11 March 1610–1611. His daughter Judith was baptised at St. Thomas the Apostle, London, 1 Aug. 1591. His son Nehemias was buried at Chelsea 12 June 1596. His sons Phineas and Giles are noticed in separate articles.

Fletcher's lease of Ringwood had been renewed by King's College in 1605. On 5 Aug. 1611 James I sent a letter to the provost and fellows to grant his widow the term of ten years in that parsonage.

The following is a list of the works written by or ascribed to Fletcher : 1. Latin verses (*a*) in the collection presented by the Eton scholars to Queen Elizabeth at Windsor Castle, 1563; (*b*) prefixed to Foxe's 'Acts and Monuments,' 2nd edit. 1570; (*c*) subjoined to Carr's 'Demosthenes,' 1571; (*d*) with Walter Haddon's poems, 1576; (*e*) before Peter Baro's 'Prelections on Jonah,' 1579; (*f*) on the motto and crest of Maximilian Brooke in Holinshed's 'Chronicles,' p. 1512; (*g*) in the Cambridge University collection, on the death of Sir Philip Sidney, 1587. 2. A Latin letter in the name of the university of Cambridge. In 'Epistolæ Academiæ,' MS. ii. 455. 3. A brief of his 'Negotiation in Moscovia.' In Lansd. MS. 60, art. 59; Ellis's 'Letters of Eminent Literary Men,' 76–85; and Bond's 'Russia at the Close of the Sixteenth Century,' p. 342. 4. 'Of the Russe Common Wealth; or, Manner of Government by the Russe Emperour (commonly called the Emperour of Moskouia), with the Manners and Fashions of the People of that Country,' London, 1591, 8vo. Dedicated to Queen Elizabeth. Abridged, with the suppression of material passages, in Hakluyt's 'Voyages,' i. 474. Reprinted also, with the suppression of some passages and many verbal differences, in 'Purchas, his Pilgrimes,' iii. 413. Epitomised by Harris, in his 'Collection of Voyages,' i. 542. Reprinted as 'The History of Russia, or the Government of the Emperour of Muscovia, with the Manners and Fashions of the People of that Countrey,' London, 1643, 1657, 12mo; also with the proper title, from the original edition, in Edward A. Bond's 'Russia at the Close of the Sixteenth Century,' published for the Hakluyt Society, London, 1856, 8vo. There is a manuscript copy of the 'Russe Common Wealth' at University College, Oxford (MS. No. 144). Another manuscript copy is preserved at Queens' College, Cambridge. 5. 'Answers to matters objected against Mr. Horsey by the Emperour's Counsel of Rusland.' In Bond's 'Russia at the Close of the Sixteenth Century,' p. 373, from a manuscript in the state paper office. 6. 'Licia, or Poemes of Love: in Honour of the admirable and singular Vertues of his Lady, to the imitation of the best Latin Poets, and others. Whereunto is added the Rising the Crowne of Richard the Third,' 4to, n. d. Dedication to Lady Molineux, wife of Sir Richard Molineux, dated from the author's chamber 4 Sept. 1593. An edition of this work, prepared by the Rev. Alexander B.

Grosart, who has prefixed a 'Memorial-Introduction,' was printed for private circulation in the 'Miscellanies of the Fuller Worthies' Library,' 1871. Cf. Hunter's 'New Illustrations of Shakespeare,' ii. 77,78; Dyce's 'Account of the Lives and Writings of Beaumont and Fletcher,' pp. xv, xvi. 7. 'Reasons to moue her Majesty in some Commisseration towards the Orphanes of the late Bisshopp of London,' Lambeth MS. 658, f. 193; Dyce's 'Account of the Lives and Writings of Beaumont and Fletcher,' p. xiv, and less correctly in Birch's 'Elizabeth,' ii. 113. 8. 'De literis antiquæ Britanniæ, Regibus præsertim qui doctrina claruerunt, quique Collegia Cantabrigiæ fundarunt,' in Latin verse, Cambridge, 1633, 12mo. Edited by his son Phineas. 9. 'An Essay upon some probable grounds that the present Tartars, near the Cyprian Sea, are the Posterity of the Ten Tribes of Israel.' Printed in Samuel Lee's 'Israel Redux,' 1677, from the author's manuscript, furnished by his grandson, Phineas Fletcher, citizen of London; and again by Whiston in his 'Memoirs,' 1749, p. 576, from a manuscript formerly in Sir Francis Nethersole's library, under the following title: 'A Discourse concerning the Tartars, proving, in all probability, that they are the Israelites, or Ten Tribes, which, being captivated by Salmanaser, were transplanted into Media.' 10. Three Eclogues in 'Poemata varii argumenti,' 1678. They are entitled respectively 'Contra Prædicatorum Contemptum,' 'Querela Collegii Regalis,' and 'De morte Boneri.'

[Addit. MS. 6177, p. 151; Ames's Typogr. Antiq. (Herbert), p. 1128; Baker MS. iv. 14 seq.; Beloe's Anecdotes, v. 222; Biog. Brit.; Birch's Elizabeth, ii. 77, 78, 100, 101, 113, 114, 150, 171, 223, 224; Memoir by E. A. Bond; Chamberlain's Letters, temp. Eliz. p. 106; Cooper's Athenæ Cantabr. iii. 34 (unpublished); Cotton. MS. Nero B. v. 333; Dixon's Personal Hist. of Lord Bacon, p. 317; Dyce's Lives of Beaumont and Fletcher; Ellis's Letters of Eminent Lit. Men, p. 76; Faulkner's Chelsea, ii. 128, 196; Fuller's Worthies, 'Kent;' Green's Cal. State Papers, Dom. James I, ii. 66; Grosart's Memorial-Introduction to Licia; Heywood and Wright's King's and Eton Colleges, pp. 239–41, 245, 248, 252; Horne's Cat. of Queen's Coll. Library, p. 1002; Hunter's Illustr. of Shakespeare, ii. 77, 78; Jardine on Torture, p. 92; Lansd. MSS. xxiii. art. 18–20, 24, 26, 36, lx. art. 59, lxv. f. 154, lxxii. art. 28, cxii. art. 39; Ledger Coll. Regal. ii. 537, iii. 19, 132; Lemon's Cal. State Papers, Dom. ii. 100, 646; Le Neve's Fasti (Hardy), ii. 357; Lloyd's State Worthies, p. 662; Lowndes's Bibl. Man. (Bohn), pp. 810, 1358; Lodge's Illustr. ii. 547; Newcourt's Repertorium, i. 107; Lib. Protocoll. Coll. Regal. i. 227, 238, ii. 19; Stephenson's Suppl. to Bentham's Ely, p. 32; Strype's Annals, ii. 420, 422, iv. 268

fol.; Strype's Grindal, 267 fol.; Thorpe's Cal.
State Papers, Scottish Ser. p. 521; Willis's Not.
Parl. iii. (2) 107; Wood's Fasti Oxon. (Bliss),
i. 191.] T. C.

FLETCHER, GILES, the younger (1588?–
1623), poet, younger son of Giles Fletcher,
LL.D., the elder [q. v.], and younger brother
of Phineas Fletcher [q. v.], was (according to
the account given to Fuller by John Ramsey,
who married the poet's widow) born in London, and educated at Westminster School.
Neither statement has been corroborated.
Before 1603 Fletcher matriculated at Cambridge. He was elected scholar of Trinity
College on 12 April 1605; proceeded B.A. in
1606; became a minor fellow of his college
on 17 Sept. 1608, reader in Greek grammar
in 1615, and in Greek language in 1618.
To Thomas Nevile, D.D., master of Trinity,
Fletcher acknowledged special indebtedness.
About 1618 he left Cambridge to hold a college living, which he soon exchanged for the
rectory of Alderton, Suffolk. It has been suggested that the great Francis Bacon presented
him to the latter living. In Fletcher's latest
work, 'The Reward of the Faithfull,' which
he dedicated to Sir Roger Townshend, he
expresses his gratitude for favours rendered
him to Sir Nathaniel Bacon of Stiffkey, the
father of Sir Roger's wife, and to Francis
Bacon, Sir Nathaniel's half-brother. He refers
to the latter as his 'honourable benefactor,'
although he admits that he had no personal
acquaintance with him. Fuller writes that
Fletcher's 'clownish, low-parted parishioners,
having nothing but their shoes high about
them, valued not their pastor, according to
his worth, which disposed him to melancholy
and hastened his dissolution.' He died in
1623; the registers of Alderton are not extant at that date. Letters of administration were granted to his widow Anne on
12 Nov. 1623. She afterwards married John
Ramsey.

Fletcher wrote his poems at a very early
age. In 1603 he contributed a somewhat
frigid 'Canto upon the death of Eliza' to a
volume of academic verse issued at Cambridge
to celebrate Elizabeth's death and James I's
accession. His chief work followed in 1610,
while he was still at Trinity. It is entitled
'Christ's Victorie and Triumph in Heaven
and Earth over and after Death' (Cambridge,
by C. Legge, small 4to), in two parts, with
separate title-pages ('Christ's Triumph over
Death,' and 'Christ's Triumph after Death'),
dedicated to Dr. Nevile, master of Trinity,
with prefatory verses by Francis (afterwards
Sir Francis) Nethersole, and by the author's
brother Phineas. The poet in a prose preface
defends the application of verse to sacred

subjects, and acknowledges his obligations to
'thrice-honoured Bartas, and our (I know no
name more glorious than) Edmund Spencer,
two blessed soules.' Fletcher tells the story
of Christ's life with many digressions, and
concludes with an affectionate reference to
the poetic work of his brother Phineas, whom
he calls 'Young Thyrsilis.' His admiration
of Spenser is very apparent. Allegorical descriptions of vices and virtues abound in his
poem. There is a wealth of effective imagery,
with which the occasional simplicity of some
passages descriptive of natural scenery contrasts attractively. But exaggerated Spen-
serian characteristics mar the success of the
work as a whole. The versification, although
based on Spenser's, is original. Each stanza
has eight lines, the last an Alexandrine,
rhyming thus: ababbccc. Milton borrowed
something from 'Christ's Triumph' for his
'Paradise Regained.' Fletcher's poem was
reissued at Cambridge in 1632, and (in four
parts) in 1640; it was again issued in 1783
(with Phineas Fletcher's 'Purple Island'), in
1824, in 1834 (as vol. xx. of Cattermole and
Stebbing's 'Sacred Classics'), and in 1888
in the 'Library of Theological Literature.'

Fletcher also published a prose tract (dedicated to Sir Roger Townshend, bart.), 'The
Reward of the Faithfull: the Labour of the
Faithfull: the Ground of our Faith,' London,
1623. A few verse translations from Boethius
and Greek epigrams are scattered through
the book. Among the Tanner MSS. (465 f. 2)
at the Bodleian are some verses by Fletcher,
'after Petronius,' and in the library of King's
College, Cambridge, is a manuscript entitled
'Ægidii Fletcheri Versio Poetica Lamenta-
tionum Ieremiæ,' which was presented to
the college on 2 Feb. 1654–5 by 'S[amuel]
Th[oms] soc.'

Fletcher's poetical works appear in Chalmers's and Sandford's collections; in Dr.
Grosart's 'Fuller's Worthies Library' (1868),
and his 'Early English Poets' (1876); and
in 'Giles and Phineas Fletcher—Poetical
Works,' ed. F. S. Boas (Cambridge Univ.
Press) 1908.

[Hunter's MS. Chorus Vatum in Addit. MS.
24487, f. 122; Cole's MS. Athenæ Cantabr.; Grosart's introduction; Fuller's Worthies.] S. L.

FLETCHER, HENRY (*fl.* 1710–1750),
engraver, worked in London, and produced
engravings possessing some merit. He most
excelled as an engraver of flowers, notably
'The Twelve Months of Flowers' and 'The
Twelve Months of Fruits,' engraved from
drawings by Peter Casteels [q. v.], made in
1730 for a publication by Robert Furber,
the well-known gardener. He also engraved

some fine plates of birds from drawings by Casteels and Charles Collins. He engraved some of the vignettes and tail-pieces to the first edition of Voltaire's 'Henriade,' published in London in 1728. Among his other works were 'Bathsheba,' after Sebastiano Conca; a set of views of Venice, engraved with L. P. Boitard after Canaletto; 'A View of Stocks Market in 1738,' and 'A View of the Fountain in Temple Gardens,' after Joseph Nichols; 'A View of Bethlehem Hospital, Moorfields,' and portraits of Robert Nelson (1715), after Kneller, Ebenezer Pemberton (1727), and the Rev. Robert Warren.

[Dodd's manuscript History of English Engravers; Le Blanc's Manuel de l'Amateur d'Estampes; Cohen's Guide de l'Amateur des Livres à Figures du xviiime Siècle; Redgrave's Dict. of Artists.]   L. C.

FLETCHER, SIR HENRY (1727–1807), politician, a native of Cumberland, was born in 1727. Brought up in the service of the East India Company, he successively commanded two of its vessels, the Stormont and the Middlesex. When he retired from his command, after rendering conspicuous services to the company, he was chosen a director of the East India board, and filled that office for eighteen years (1769–87), being always re-elected when he retired by rotation. He was chairman in 1782–3. Fletcher entered parliament in 1768 for Cumberland, where he had fought successfully against a very powerful influence. He joined the whig opposition in the House of Commons, and on the accession of that party to power was rewarded with a baronetcy, 20 May 1782. In 1783 he gave a general approval to the treaty of peace with France, so far as related to the settlements of the East India Company. When Fox introduced his India Bill, Fletcher, then chairman of the company, was nominated one of the seven commissioners for the affairs of Asia. Fletcher declared in the House of Commons in 1783 that it would have been much better for England, and Europe in general, if the navigation to the East Indies had never been discovered. But having once acquired these Indian possessions, the British must never give them up. Fletcher considered the retention and proper government of India of supreme moment, and sacrificed private interests so as to advocate his views in parliament. Fox's measure, however, was lost, and administrative reform in India was postponed. In 1796 Fletcher voted with the great whig leader for a direct censure upon ministers, on the ground of having advanced money to the Emperor of Germany and the Prince of Condé without the knowledge or consent of parliament. He also supported Grey in the following session in his motion on parliamentary reform. Fletcher continued to represent the county of Cumberland until the general election of 1806. He died on 25 March 1807, and was succeeded in the title by his only son of the same name. The character of Fletcher stood high among his contemporaries for generosity and integrity.

[Gent. Mag. 1807; Hansard's Parliamentary Debates.]   G. B. S.

FLETCHER, JOHN (1579–1625), dramatist, a younger son of Dr. Richard Fletcher [q.v.], afterwards bishop of London, by his first wife Elizabeth, was born in December 1579 at Rye in Sussex, where his father was then officiating as minister. A 'John Fletcher of London' was admitted 15 Oct. 1591 a pensioner of Bene't (Corpus) College, Cambridge, of which college Dr. Fletcher had been president. Dyce assumes that this John Fletcher, who became one of the bible-clerks in 1593, was the dramatist. Bishop Fletcher died, in needy circumstances, 15 June 1596, and by his will, dated 26 Oct. 1593, left his books to be divided between his sons Nathaniel and John.

Fletcher's intimacy with Francis Beaumont (1584–1616) appears to date from about 1607. Aubrey states that there was a 'wonderful consimility of phansy' between the two poets; that they lived together on the Bankside in Southwark, near the Globe; and that they shared everything in common. Beaumont probably began his literary career before Fletcher; although the attribution to him of 'Salmacis and Hermaphroditus' (anonymously published in 1602, and printed in 1640 among 'Poems by Francis Beaumont, Gent.') is doubtful. The earliest of the plays attributed to 'Beaumont and Fletcher' is the 'Woman Hater,' which was entered in the 'Stationers' Register' 20 May 1607 and published anonymously in the same year. It is largely written in a mock-heroic style. Dyce assumed that it was wholly by Fletcher, but later critics more reasonably claim it for Beaumont, who had undeniably a rich vein of burlesque. The versification has none of Fletcher's peculiarities. Beaumont in 1607 prefixed some commendatory verses to the 'Fox,' and a similar compliment was paid to Jonson by Fletcher, who also commended 'Catiline,' 1611.

'The Faithful Shepherdess,' n. d., 4to, the unassisted work of Fletcher, was published not later than 1610 (probably in 1609), for one of the three persons to whom it was dedicated, Sir William Skipwith, died 3 May

1610. John Davies of Hereford, in the 'Scourge of Folly,' n. d. [1611], has an allusion to Fletcher's pastoral. On the stage it was not successful, but the printed copy was ushered into notice with commendatory verses by Field, Beaumont, Jonson, and Chapman. The 'Faithful Shepherdess,' which was under some obligations to Tasso's 'Aminta' and Guarini's 'Pastor Fido,' is the most famous and the best of English pastoral plays. The lyrical portions supplied Milton with hints for 'Comus.' In January 1633–4 it was successfully revived at court. The 'Scornful Lady,' published in 1616, has a mention of the Cleve wars, which began in 1609. It was performed, as Mr. Fleay remarks, by the children of Her Majesty's Revels at Blackfriars, which theatre was in possession of the king's company after 1609. The 'Scornful Lady' is an excellent comedy of English domestic life, and was very popular both before and after the Restoration. The character of Vellum in Addison's 'Drummer' was sketched (as Addison himself informed Theobald) from that of the steward Savil. To Beaumont may be assigned the first two acts; they are chiefly written in prose, which Fletcher very rarely employed. In the later acts Fletcher seems to have had the larger share.

The 'Maid's Tragedy,' 1619, 4to, and 'Philaster,' 1620, 4to, were produced not later than 1611. Dryden asserts without authority that the 'first play that brought Fletcher and Beaumont in esteem was their "Philaster."' Some modern critics have denied that Fletcher had any hand in 'Philaster,' but John Davies of Hereford, in the 'Scourge of Folly' [1611], mentions this play, with the 'Faithful Shepherdess' and the 'Maid's Tragedy,' in his epigram to Fletcher. Detached passages in the fourth act and two scenes in the fifth (scenes three and four), with the rhetorical harangues in act i. scene 1, are in Fletcher's manner. But Beaumont's genius dominates the play; and the poetry at its highest is of a subtler quality than can be found in any play that Fletcher wrote singlehanded. 'Philaster' held the stage for many years. Elkanah Settle in 1695 produced a new version without success. Another alteration, the 'Restauration, or Right will take place,' was printed in the first volume of the 'Works,' 1714, of George Villiers, duke of Buckingham, and a third, by the elder Colman, was performed at Drury Lane in 1764. The 'Maid's Tragedy' was composed before 31 Oct. 1611, for on that day Sir George Buc licensed a play to which he gave the title of 'The Second Maiden's Tragedy.' In the first three acts Fletcher's hand cannot be traced

to any noticeable extent; but he was mainly responsible for the fourth and fifth acts. Until the closing of the theatres the 'Maid's Tragedy' was frequently performed, and it again became popular at the Restoration. Waller absurdly turned it into a comedy by rewriting (in rhyme) the last act.

'A King and No King,' which in some respects is a more solid piece of work than the 'Maid's Tragedy,' was licensed for the stage in 1611 and printed in 1619, 4to. Arbaces, in his insolence and magnanimity, is certainly one of the most striking figures in the English drama. Garrick prepared an alteration of 'A King and No King,' in which he had intended to personate Arbaces; but at the last moment the play was withdrawn. Beaumont unquestionably had the chief share in the authorship; Fletcher's contributions were confined to the fourth and fifth acts.

'Four Plays or Moral Representations in One,' first printed in the 1647 folio, is an early work. Mr. Fleay adduces some arguments (*Englische Studien*, ix. 14) to show that it was brought out as early as 1608. The Induction and the first two pieces, the 'Triumph of Honour' and the 'Triumph of Love,' are usually and with probability ascribed to Beaumont, and the last two, the 'Triumph of Death' and the 'Triumph of Time,' to Fletcher.

The 'Knight of the Burning Pestle,' written in ridicule of such extravagant plays as Heywood's 'Four Prentices of London,' was published anonymously in 1613, 4to. W. B[urre] the publisher, in a dedicatory epistle to Robert Keysar, states that he 'had fostered it privately in his bosom these two years,' and that it was the elder of Don Quixote (i. e. Shelton's translation, which appeared in 1612) 'above a year.' Hence the date of composition cannot be later than 1611. From the same epistle we learn that the play was written in eight days and that it was not successful on the stage. It is probable that Beaumont had but slight help from Fletcher in this drollest and most delightful of burlesques, for Fletcher nowhere shows any inclinations towards the mock-heroic. At its revival in 1635 the 'Knight of the Burning Pestle' was received with great applause, as Brome testifies in the 'Sparagus Garden;' and it was occasionally acted after the Restoration.

'Cupid's Revenge' was published in 1615 as the work of Fletcher, but from internal evidence it is clear that Beaumont was concerned in the authorship. The colloquy between Bacha and Leucippus in act iii. scene 2 is in Beaumont's most strenuous manner; and in the second act his hand can be clearly traced. Mr. Robert Boyle (*Englische Studien*, viii. 39) detects the presence of a third author, and Mr. Fleay supposes that this third author was Nathaniel Field [q. v.] The play was acted by the children of Her Majesty's Revels at Whitefriars in January 1611–12. For the groundwork of the plot the playwrights were indebted to Sidney's 'Arcadia.'

The 'Coxcomb,' first printed in the 1647 folio, was acted in 1612–13, and may have been produced earlier. The underplot, relating to Viola, may be attributed to Beaumont; but in other parts of the play we are more frequently reminded of William Rowley than of Beaumont or Fletcher. It is a somewhat unpleasing play. The 'Captain,' 1647, was composed some time before 20 May 1613, when Hemings and his company were paid for representing it at court. No portion can be definitely assigned to Beaumont; but Fletcher certainly had assistance from some quarter. Mr. Fleay suggests that 'Jonson worked with Fletcher on the original play.' There are occasional traces of Middleton's hand. The most powerful and most repulsive scene, act iv. sc. 5, cannot be ascribed to Fletcher, although he probably supplied the song 'Come hither you that love.'

In honour of the marriage of the Count Palatine with the Princess Elizabeth, February 1612–13, Beaumont composed the 'Masque of the Inner Temple and Grayes Inne,' n. d., 4to, which was dedicated to Sir Francis Bacon. The songs are of rare beauty. The 'Honest Man's Fortune,' 1647, was performed in 1613. In the Dyce Library is preserved the manuscript copy which was licensed in 1624 by Sir Henry Herbert for the king's company. It is entitled 'The Honest Mans Fortune, plaide in the yeare 1613.' The fifth act is plainly by Fletcher, and Mr Boyle has given excellent reasons for ascribing the third act, or part of it, to Massinger. Mr. Fleay's suggestion that the fourth act (with perhaps part of the third) belongs to Field is very plausible. Acts i. and ii. are by some other playwright. Appended to the play is a curious copy of verses ' Upon an Honest Man's Fortune. By Master John Fletcher.' Not a trace of Beaumont's hand can be found in this comedy. Nor can any part of the 'Knight of Malta,' 1647, produced before Burbage's death (March 1618–1619), be safely assigned to Beaumont. Mr. Macaulay (*A Study of Francis Beaumont*, p. 196) gives the fifth act to him; but the poverty of the lyrical passages affords sufficient evidence that he was not the author. Three scenes (iii. 2, 3, iv. 1) are shown by Mr. Boyle to belong to Massinger, and to

these may be added part of another (v. 2). The second act, which contains the strongest writing in the play, is wholly by Fletcher, who also contributed iii. 1. Some other dramatist wrote the first act and part of the fifth. No portions of 'Thierry and Theodoret,' published in 1621 and written probably about 1616, can be confidently given to Beaumont. The most impressive scene (iv. 1), in which Ordella declares her readiness to lay down her life for her husband, is unmistakably Fletcher's. In depicting womanly heroism Fletcher always overshoots the mark; when he essays to be profoundly pathetic he becomes sentimental. Massinger largely assisted him in this play, but the third act appears to be by some unknown author. 'Wit at Several Weapons,' 1647, produced about 1614, is a merry comedy of intrigue, and the scene is laid in London. In reading it we are strongly reminded of Middleton's town-comedies, or of the mixed work of Middleton and Rowley.

Beaumont died 6 March 1615–16, and appears to have given up dramatic work as early as 1614. Dyce printed from Harleian MS. 6057, fol. 34, some lines, 'Come, sorrow, come,' signed 'I. F.,' that may have been written by Fletcher on the occasion of Beaumont's death. Aubrey states, on the authority of Earle, that Beaumont's ' main businesse was to correct the overflowings of Mr. Fletcher's witte,' and Dryden declares that Beaumont was 'so accurate a judge of plays' that Ben Jonson ' submitted all his writings to his censure.' Little weight can be attached to these statements; but the stage tradition, that Beaumont was superior in judgment to Fletcher, is supported by sound criticism. In the most important plays that they wrote together Beaumont's share outweighs Fletcher's, both in quantity and quality. Beaumont had the firmer hand and statelier manner; his diction was more solid; there was a richer music in his verse. Fletcher excelled as a master of brilliant dialogue and sprightly repartee. In the management of his plots and in the development of his characters he was careless and inconsistent. But in his comedies the unceasing liveliness and bustle atone for structural defects; and in tragedy his copious command of splendid declamation reconciles us to the absence of rarer qualities. Fletcher's metrical characteristics are strongly marked. He sought by various devices to give greater freedom to the movement of blank verse. Thus he introduces redundant syllables in all parts of the line, and he is particularly fond of ending the line with an emphatic extra monosyllable, a practice in which he stands alone. Having introduced so much freedom into his blank verse, he was able to dispense almost entirely with the use of prose. Fletcher's verse, however, becomes monotonous, owing to his habit of pausing at the end of the line; and for tragic purposes it is wanting in solidity. His metrical peculiarities are of importance in helping us to distinguish his work from the work of his coadjutors.

The following fifteen plays may be confidently regarded as Fletcher's unaided compositions. 'Wit without Money,' 1639, 4to, was produced (as appears from a reference to the 'dragons in Sussex,' ii. 4) not earlier than August 1614. Langbaine says that he had often seen this comedy acted 'at the Old House in little Lincoln's-Inn-Fields with very great applause.' In the eighteenth century it was frequently performed at Covent Garden. 'Bonduca,' 1647, produced some time before Burbage's death (March 1618–19), presents in the person of Caratach a worthy portrait of a magnanimous soldier; and the frank, fearless boy Hengo, nephew of Caratach, is sketched with loving tenderness. An alteration of 'Bonduca' was produced and published in 1696; another, by the elder Colman, was acted at the Haymarket and published in 1778; a third, by J. R. Planché (entitled 'Caractacus'), was performed at Drury Lane in 1837. 'Valentinian,' 1647, also produced before March 1618–19, displays to good effect Fletcher's command of dramatic rhetoric. It would be hard to overrate the delightful songs. A wretched alteration by the Earl of Rochester was printed in 1685. The 'Loyal Subject,' 1647, was licensed for the stage 16 Nov. 1618. Archas, the 'loyal subject,' in his submission (under the most severe provocations) to kingly authority, surpasses even Aecius in 'Valentinian.' The play was performed at Whitehall 10 Dec. 1633, and Sir Henry Herbert records that it was 'very well likt by the king.' The 'Mad Lover,' 1647, produced before March 1618–19, is a strangely grotesque piece of work, but it held the stage both before and after the Restoration. The 'Humorous Lieutenant,' 1647, is of uncertain date; but as Burbage's name is not found in the list of 'principal actors,' we may infer that the date of production is later than March 1618–19. In the Dyce Library is preserved a manuscript copy, dated 1625, with the title 'Demetrius and Enanthe, a pleasant comedie, written by John Fletcher, Gent.,' differing somewhat from the printed comedy; it was edited by Dyce in 1830. 'Women Pleased,' 1647, was probably produced about 1620. The most entertaining

personage in this well-ordered play is the hungry serving-man, Penurio. Fletcher was indebted for his plot to three stories of Boccaccio's 'Decameron,' and to Chaucer's 'Wif of Bathes Tale.' From Sir Henry Herbert's 'Office-Book' it appears that three of Fletcher's plays were presented at court in 1621—the 'Island Princess,' 1647, the 'Pilgrim,' 1647, and the 'Wildgoose-Chase,' 1652. The first, which is of slender merit, was revived with alterations in 1669; again in 1687, with alterations by Nahum Tate; and in 1699 the play was turned into an opera by Motteux, the music being composed by Daniel Purcell, Clarke, and Leveridge. The 'Pilgrim' is of far more interest. Coleridge declared that 'this play holds the first place in Beaumont and Fletcher's romantic entertainments' (Remains, ii. 315). An alteration by Sir John Vanbrugh was published in 1700. When Humphrey Moseley brought out the folio of 1647 he was unable to obtain a copy of the 'Wildgoose-Chase.' This brilliant comedy was first published in 1652, 4to, 'Retriv'd for the publick delight of all the Ingenious; and private Benefit of John Lowin and Joseph Taylor, servants to His Late Majestie. By a Person of Honour.' In a dedicatory epistle Lowin and Taylor observe: 'The play was of so general a received acceptance that, he himself a spectator, we have known him unconcerned, and to have wished it had been none of his; he, as well as the thronged theatre (in despite of his innate modesty), applauding this rare issue of his brain.' Commendatory verses by Richard Lovelace and others follow the epistle. The first four acts of Farquhar's 'Inconstant,' 1702, are taken from the 'Wildgoose-Chase.' 'Monsieur Thomas,' probably one of the later works, was first published in 1639, with a dedicatory epistle by Richard Brome to Charles Cotton the elder, and with a copy of verses by Brome in Fletcher's praise. D'Urfey's 'Trick for Trick,' 1678, is little more than a revival of 'Monsieur Thomas.' The 'Woman's Prize,' 1647, was described by Sir Henry Herbert as 'an ould play' in 1633. 'Upon complaints of foule and offensive matters conteyned therein' he suppressed the performance on 19 Oct. 1633. The players brought the manuscript to him the next day for revision, and he returned it to them, 'purgd of oathes, prophaness, and ribaldrye,' on 21 Oct. It was acted before the king and queen 28 Nov., and was 'very well likt.' Fletcher wrote the 'Woman's Prize' to serve as a sequel to the 'Taming of the Shrew;' he lays the scene in England, and represents Petruchio in complete subjection to his second wife, Maria. 'A Wife for a Month,' 1647, was licensed by

Herbert 27 May 1624. As Nicholas Tooley, who personated one of the principal characters, died in June 1623, this play must have been produced some time before it was licensed. It is a singular and powerful play, but its performance had been discontinued in the time of Langbaine, who mentions it as 'well worth reviving.' 'Rule a Wife and have a Wife,' 1640, was licensed by Herbert 19 Oct. 1624, and performed at court twice in that year. It is among the very best of Fletcher's comedies, and met with great success. In 1759, having undergone some alteration, it was revived by Garrick, and it has been occasionally played in the nineteenth century. The underplot is founded on the eleventh of Cervantes's 'Novelas Exemplares.' Davies mentions a somewhat absurd tradition that the character of Cacafogo 'was intended as a rival to Falstaff' (*Dram. Miscell.* ii. 406). The 'Chances,' 1647, probably a late work, was deservedly popular. The plot is taken from 'La Señora Cornelia,' one of Cervantes's 'Novelas Exemplares.' In 1682 an alteration by Villiers, duke of Buckingham, who completely rewrote acts iv. and v., was produced at the theatre in Dorset Gardens; in 1773 Garrick brought out another alteration at Drury Lane; and in 1821 'Don John, or the Two Violettas, a musical drama in three acts,' was played at Covent Garden.

Massinger's hand has been already traced in three plays—the 'Honest Man's Fortune,' the 'Knight of Malta,' and 'Thierry and Theodoret,' but there are many others to which he contributed. Sir Aston Cokaine, in his 'Epitaph on Mr. John Fletcher and Mr. Philip Massinger' (*Poems*, 1662, p. 186), expressly states: 'Playes they did write together, were great friends.' In an address 'To my Cousin Mr. Charles Cotton' (the elder Cotton) he mentions that Massinger was associated with Fletcher in the authorship of several of the plays published in the 1647 folio. Cokaine also addressed some lines of remonstrance to the publishers of the folio of Beaumont and Fletcher's plays, Humphrey Moseley and Humphrey Robinson, saying that

. . . Beaumont of those many writ in few,
And Massinger in other few.

Although he claims to have been a friend of Massinger, Cokaine's information was derived from the elder Cotton, 'Fletcher's chief bosome-friend informed me so.' Shirley, who edited the 1647 folio (or advised the publishers), makes no mention of Massinger in his address to the reader. Humphrey Moseley in a prefatory note states that he had once had the intention of printing Fletcher's works by themselves, 'because single and alone he would make a just volume;' but he also is silent on the subject of Massinger. Internal evidence shows clearly that Cokaine was abundantly justified in claiming for Massinger a share in some of the plays printed in the 1647 folio. But Fletcher collaborated with others besides Massinger. Among the 'Henslowe Papers' is preserved a letter addressed to Henslowe by Field, Daborne, and Massinger, in which the three playwrights beg for an advance of 5*l*. to supply their urgent necessities; and to this letter, which was written some time before January 1615–1616, Daborne appends a postscript: 'The mony shall be abated out of the mony remaynes for the play of Mr. Fletcher and ours' (the play to which Daborne refers may perhaps be the 'Honest Man's Fortune'). External and internal evidence agree in attributing to William Rowley a share in some of the dramas that pass as the work of 'Beaumont and Fletcher;' and it is certain that others were either altered or completed by James Shirley.

The 'Queen of Corinth,' 1647, was produced some time before March 1618–19, as one of the principal characters was personated by Burbage. Fletcher's hand can only be detected in the second act; the first and fifth acts are by Massinger, and the rest of the play appears to be by Middleton and Rowley. The fine tragedy of 'Sir John Van Olden Barnavelt,' first printed from manuscript by the present writer (*A Collection of Old English Plays*, vol. ii.), is unquestionably the joint work of Massinger and Fletcher. It was produced in August 1619, shortly after Barneveldt's execution. Mr. S. L. Lee (*Athenæum*, 19 Jan. 1884) discovered among the State Papers two letters of Thomas Locke to Carleton, the English ambassador at the Hague. On 14 Aug. 1619 Locke wrote that when the players 'were bringing of Barnevelt upon the stage' the Bishop of London at the last moment forbade the performance. On 27 Aug. he announced: 'Our players have fownd the meanes to go through wth the play of Barnevelt, and it hath had many spectators and received applause.' Mr. Boyle (BULLEN, *Old Plays*, vol. ii., Appendix) has drawn up an elaborate analysis of the play, assigning to each their respective shares in the composition. To 1619 probably belongs the lost play of the 'Jeweller of Amsterdam,' which was entered in the 'Stationers' Books,' 8 April 1654, as the work of Fletcher, Field, and Massinger. Mr. Fleay's suggestion that the subject of this play was the murder of John Van Wely is highly probable. The

'Little French Lawyer,' 1647, written about 1620, is mainly by Fletcher; but Massinger's hand is seen in the first act, and occasionally in acts iii. and v. The character of La-Writ, which Coleridge declared to be 'conceived and executed from first to last in genuine comic humour,' is Fletcher's creation. 'A Very Woman,' printed in 1655 as the work of Massinger, was written by Fletcher and revised by Massinger. It is to be identified with a comedy called 'The Woman's Plot,' which was acted at court in 1621. On 9 Sept. 1653 it was entered in the 'Stationers' Register' by Humphrey Moseley under the title of 'A Very Woman, or the Woman's Plot,' as a play of Massinger. It was again entered by Moseley 29 June 1660 under the title of 'A Right Woman;' and in the second entry it is ascribed to Beaumont and Fletcher. In its present state it is probably (as Mr. Fleay observes) the version revised by Massinger for representation in 1634. The amusing scene in the slave market (iii. 1), and the still more amusing scene (iii. 5) in which Borachia is overcome by Candy wine, are in Fletcher's raciest manner, and the beautiful colloquy (iv. 1) between Almira and Antonio is in his sweetest vein of romantic tenderness. The 'Custom of the Country,' 1647, is mentioned in Sir Henry Herbert's 'Office-Book,' 22 Nov. 1628, as an 'old play.' Part of the story is taken from the 'Travels of Persiles and Sigismunda,' 1619, translated (through the French version) from Cervantes, and part from a novel in Cinthio's 'Hecatommithi.' Mr. Boyle adduces good reasons for assigning several scenes of this skilfully conducted play to Massinger; for the grosser portions Fletcher must be held responsible. Colley Cibber's 'Love makes a Man,' 1700, and Charles Johnson's 'Country Lasses,' 1715, were partly borrowed from this play. The opening scene, modelled on 'Julius Cæsar' (ii. 1), of the 'Double Marriage,' 1647, composed about 1620, is unquestionably by Massinger; and probably he contributed some scenes in the fourth and fifth acts. The 'False One,' 1647, composed about 1620, deals with the fortunes of Julius Cæsar in Egypt. The rhetorical passages are of very high merit, and the Masque of Nilus in the third act is a graceful lyrical interlude. Massinger's contributions are confined to the first and fifth acts. 'Beggar's Bush,' 1647, was performed at court at Christmas 1622. Coleridge is reported to have said, 'I could read it from morning to night; how sylvan and sunshiny it is!' The scenes in which the woodland life of the beggars is depicted are much in the manner of William Rowley (or Rowley and Middleton, as in the 'Spanish Gipsy'). Mr. Boyle assigns to Massinger the first act and 'act ii. sc. 3, act v. sc. 1 and 2 down to line 110;' but Massinger's share is not clearly marked in this play. 'Beggar's Bush' continued to be popular after the Restoration, and three alterations have appeared, the last in 1815 under the title of 'The Merchant of Bruges,' when Kean took the part of Flores with success at Drury Lane. The 'Prophetess,' 1647, licensed by Sir Henry Herbert 14 May 1622, is an odd jumble of history and supernaturalism. Massinger's share was very considerable. An alteration by Betterton 'after the manner of an opera,' with a prologue by Dryden, was produced in 1690. The 'Sea Voyage,' 1647, an interesting romantic comedy licensed by Herbert 22 June 1622, is partly modelled, as Dryden observed, on the 'Tempest.' A poor alteration by D'Urfey, entitled 'A Common-Wealth of Women,' was produced in 1686 and published in the same year. The 'Elder Brother,' published in 1637 as a work of Fletcher, was probably revised and completed by Massinger after Fletcher's death. A contemporary manuscript copy (unknown to Dyce) is preserved in Egerton MS. 1994. Colley Cibber formed from the 'Elder Brother' and the 'Custom of the Country' his 'Love makes a Man.' Both the date and the authorship of the powerful tragedy the 'Bloody Brother' are uncertain. On the title-page of the first quarto, 1639, it is ascribed to 'B. J. F.' (Ben Jonson and Fletcher?); in the second quarto, 1640, 'John Fletcher, Genf.,' is given as the author's name. It had been entered in the 'Stationers' Register,' 4 Oct. 1639, as the work of 'J. B.' Mr. Fleay contends that the date is 1616-17, and that the authors were Fletcher, Massinger, and Field, with the assistance of Jonson in one scene, iv. 2. Mr. Boyle tentatively assigns iv. 1 to Daborne, who was not only incapable of writing it, but had probably retired from the stage and taken holy orders before 1617, its earliest possible date. A plausible view is that the 'Bloody Brother' was written in the first instance by Fletcher and Jonson, and that it was revised by Massinger on the occasion of its revival at Hampton Court in January 1636-7. It was one of the plays surreptitiously acted at the Cockpit in 1648; during the performance a party of foot-soldiers beset the house and carried off the actors in their stage habiliments to prison. After the Restoration it was very popular. The 'Lovers' Progress,' 1647, is a play of Fletcher's with large alterations by Massinger; the plot is taken from D'Audiguier's 'Histoire Tragi-comique de notre temps,' 1615. In the prologue the reviser, with the modesty for which Massinger was distinguished, declares himself to be

ambitious that it should be known
What's good was Fletcher's and what ill his own.

This play is unquestionably a revised version of the 'Wandering Lovers,' a play licensed 6 Dec. 1623, and may be identified with the 'Tragedy of Cleander' (ascribed to Massinger), which was performed at Blackfriars 7 May 1634. A play called 'The Wandering Lovers, or the Picture,' was entered in the 'Stationers' Register,' 9 Sept. 1653, as a work of Massinger. In spite of the puzzling after-title the entry probably refers to the 'Lovers' Progress.' The 'Spanish Curate,' 1647, was licensed 24 Oct. 1622. Both plot and under-plot are taken from a Spanish romance (of Gonçalo de Cespides), which had been translated into English by Leonard Digges under the title of 'Gerardo the Unfortunate Spaniard,' 1622. The excellent comic scenes are Fletcher's, but the more serious portions of the play belong to Massinger. In the preface to his alteration of 'Philaster,' 1763, the elder Colman states that the 'Spanish Curate' had been recently revived without success. An alteration was acted at Covent Garden in 1840. 'Love's Pilgrimage,' 1647, a romantic comedy of high merit, appears to be almost entirely by Fletcher. In the first act are found some passages that occur, with slight alterations, in Ben Jonson's 'New Inn,' published in 1629. Weber's explanation, which Dyce accepted, is that Shirley introduced these passages when he revised Fletcher's play. Mr. Fleay is of opinion that 'Love's Pilgrimage' was written as early as 1612, and that Ben Jonson was the borrower. He urges that the disputed passages are 'distinctly Fletcher's in style and metre;' but this is a very bold assertion, for nothing could be more Jonsonian than Colonel Tipto's elaborate enumeration of his various articles of finery (*New Inn*, ii. 2; *Love's Pilgrimage*, i. 1). Nor is it possible to accept Mr. Fleay's identification of 'Love's Pilgrimage' with the lost play 'Cardema' or 'Cardano,' acted in 1613. The story of 'Love's Pilgrimage' is taken from 'Las dos Doncellas,' one of the 'Novelas Exemplares' of Cervantes. 'Love's Cure,' 1647, has an allusion to the Russian ambassador who was in England in 1622; and there are references to the renewal of the war between Spain and Holland, and to 'the miraculous maid in Flanders' who 'lived three year without any other sustenance than the smell of a rose.' The date would seem to be about 1623, and the play is probably by Massinger and Middleton. Mr.

Fleay fixes 1608 as the date of the original production, and contends that 'Love's Cure' is an alteration by Massinger of a play by Beaumont and Fletcher. The 'Nice Valour, or the Passionate Madman,' 1647, is an amusingly eccentric comedy. In v. 3 mention is made of a prose-tract that was not published until 1624, but the original play may have been written earlier. Mr. Fleay suggests that much of the play was rewritten by Middleton. The verbal quibbles are strongly suggestive of Middleton, and the poetry is frequently in his manner. To this play belongs the beautiful song 'Hence all you vain delights,' which gave Milton hints for 'Il Penseroso.' In a contemporary commonplace-book preserved among the Malone MSS. the song is ascribed to William Strode; but Fletcher's claim to this and the other songs in the 'Nice Valour' cannot be seriously disputed. Fletcher's hand can hardly be traced in the 'Laws of Candy,' 1647, which is largely by Massinger. The principal plot is taken from the ninth novel of the tenth decade of Cinthio's 'Hecatommithi.' The 'Fair Maid of the Inn,' 1647, licensed for the stage 22 Jan. 1625-6, was brought out after Fletcher's death. Only a small portion can be assigned to Fletcher; the chief contributors seem to have been Rowley and Massinger. Part of the story is drawn from 'La Ilustre Fregona,' one of Cervantes's 'Novelas Exemplares.' From Sir Henry Herbert's 'Office-Book' it appears that the 'Maid in the Mill,' licensed 29 Aug. 1623, and acted three times at court in that year, was a joint work of Rowley and Fletcher. The plot is taken partly from Gonçalo de Cespides's 'Gerardo,' and partly from a novel of Bandello. To Fletcher may be safely assigned the whole of the first act, part of the third, and the early part of v. 2 (scene between Otrante and Florimel). The 'Night-Walker, or the Litte Thief,' was published in 1640 as the work of John Fletcher. Herbert's 'Office-Book' shows that this comedy was 'corrected' by Shirley in 1633. We learn from the same source that it was acted at court before the king and queen in January 1633-4, and was 'likt as a merry play.' Langbaine says that he had seen it acted by the king's servants with great applause both in town and country. Weber plausibly conjectured that the 'Night-Walker is an alteration by Shirley of Fletcher's 'Devil of Dowgate, or Usury put to Use,' mentioned by Sir Henry Herbert as 'a new play' in October 1623. The 'Coronation,' printed in 1640 as a work of Fletcher, was licensed in February 1634-5 as written by Shirley, who in 1652 claimed it in a list of his plays appended to the 'Cardinal.' There is no reason for supposing that Fletcher had any hand in it. The 'Noble Gentleman,' 1647, was licensed on 3 Feb. 1625-6. It is impossible to assign to Fletcher any portions of this poor play. Still worse is the 'Faithful Friends,' which was entered in the 'Stationers' Register,' 29 June 1660, as a work of Beaumont and Fletcher. Weber printed it in 1812 from a manuscript which is now preserved in the Dyce Library.

The 'Two Noble Kinsmen' is stated on the title-page of the first edition, 1634, to have been written by Fletcher and Shakespeare. It is difficult to ascribe to Shakespeare any share in the conduct of the plot, but it is infinitely more difficult to conceive that any other hand wrote the first scene (with the opening song), Arcite's invocation to Mars (v. 1), and the description of the accident that resulted in Arcite's death (v. 4). Outside Shakespeare's later plays there is nothing that can be compared with these passages. To Fletcher belong acts ii., iii. (with the exception of the first scene), iv., and v. 2. Mr. Boyle has shown that Massinger had a hand in the 'Two Noble Kinsmen,' and some of the Shakespearean portions have suffered from Massinger's interpolations. There is no reason for supposing that Shakespeare and Fletcher worked together on this play. Shakespeare's contributions may have been written (towards the close of his career) for a revival of the old play of 'Palamon and Arsett,' mentioned by Henslowe in 1594, and these 'additions' may have come into the hands of Fletcher and Massinger after Shakespeare's death.

It is generally agreed that Fletcher was largely concerned in the authorship of 'Henry VIII.' That play in its present state appears to be in the main a joint production of Fletcher and Massinger, composed about 1617, some Shakespearean passages (notably the trial-scene of Catherine) having been incorporated. Wolsey's famous soliloquy, 'So farewell to the little good you bear me' (iii. 2), and his parting words to Cromwell, may be safely attributed to Fletcher, who must also be held responsible for Cranmer's somewhat fulsome prophecy at the close of the play. The 'History of Cardenio,' entered by Humphrey Moseley in the 'Stationers' Register,' 9 Sept. 1653, as a joint work of Fletcher and Shakespeare, is to be identified with the lost play 'Cardano' or 'Cardema,' acted at court in 1613. Late seventeenth-century entries in the 'Stationers' Register' carry no authority so far as Shakespeare is concerned.

A comedy, the 'Widow,' composed about 1616, was printed in 1652 as the work of Jonson, Fletcher, and Middleton. It was attributed to the three dramatists on the authority of the actor Alexander Gough, but appears to belong wholly to Middleton.

Fletcher was buried on 29 Aug. 1625 at St. Saviour's, Southwark. 'In the great plague, 1625,' says Aubrey (*Letters written by Eminent Persons*, vol. ii. pt. i. p. 352), 'a knight of Norfolk or Suffolk invited him into the countrey. He stayed but to make himselfe a suite of cloathes, and while it was makeing fell sick of the plague and died. This I had from his tayler, who is now a very old man, and clarke of St. Mary Overy's.' Sir Aston Cokaine, in his 'Epitaph on Mr. John Fletcher and Mr. Philip Massinger,' wrote that Fletcher and Massinger were buried in the same grave. Dyce supposed that 'the same grave' means nothing more than 'the same place of interment,' but there is no reason why the words should not be accepted in their literal sense.

Fletcher is seen at his best in his comedies. Few poets have been endowed with a larger share of wit and fancy, freshness and variety. Such plays as the 'Wildgoose-Chase' and 'Monsieur Thomas' are a feast of mirth from beginning to end. The 'Faithful Shepherdess' is (not excepting Ben Jonson's 'Sad Shepherd') the sweetest of English pastoral plays; and some of the songs scattered in profusion through Fletcher's works are hardly surpassed by Shakespeare. In tragedy he does not rank with the highest. 'Bonduca' and 'Valentinian' are impressive works, but inferior to the tragedies that he wrote with Beaumont, the 'Maid's Tragedy' and 'A King and No King.'

Beaumont and Fletcher's plays were collected in 1647, fol., prefaced by various copies of commendatory verses; and a fuller collection appeared in 1679, fol. An edition in 10 vols., commenced by Theobald and completed by Seward and Sympson, was published in 1750; another, under the general editorship of the elder Colman, appeared in 1778, 12 vols.; an edition by Weber in 14 vols. followed in 1812; and in 1840 George Darley wrote an introduction to the 2-vol. edition. The edition long reckoned the best is that of Alexander Dyce, 11 vols. 1843-6. In 1904 a new variorum edition directed by A. H. Bullen (in 12 vols.) began publication, and in 1905 a reprint (in 10 vols.), edited by A. R. Waller (in 'Cambridge English Classics').

[Dyce prefixed a memoir to vol. i. of his edition of Beaumont and Fletcher; and his prefatory remarks before the various plays supply full bibliographical and other details. Mr. Fleay in his Shakspere Manual, and in papers contributed to the New Shakspere Society's Transactions, has rendered valuable aid towards distinguishing Fletcher's work from the work of Beaumont and others.

His paper on the chronology of Beaumont and Fletcher's plays in the ninth volume of Englische Studien deserves attention. Mr. Robert Boyle's investigations in Englische Studien, and in the Transactions of the New Shakspere Society, are particularly important for the light they throw on Fletcher's connection with Massinger. Mr. Macaulay's Study of Francis Beaumont, 1883, is brightly written.]

A. H. B.

FLETCHER, JOHN, M.D. (1792–1836), medical writer, born in 1792, was the son of Thomas Fletcher, merchant, of London. Finding his father's counting-house irksome, he began the study of medicine at Edinburgh, having already been an occasional hearer of Abernethy and C. Bell in London. He graduated M.D. in 1816. After making a start in practice at Henley-on-Thames, whither his family had retired suddenly in reduced circumstances, he returned to Edinburgh and took private pupils in medicine. His Latin scholarship and systematic methods brought him many pupils. In 1828–9 he joined the Argyll Square school of medicine, having McIntosh, Argyle Robertson, and, for a time, James Syme, as his colleagues. He lectured on physiology, and afterwards on medical jurisprudence. His repute as a lecturer stood very high; in 1836 he gave a course of popular lectures on physiology to large audiences of the educated laity of both sexes, illustrated by preparations and diagrams of his own making. He died of a sudden illness the same year. His earliest publication was 'Rubi Epistolæ Edinburgenses,' being a collection of good-humoured satirical pieces on students and professors. In 1822 he published 'Horæ Subsecivæ,' a dialogue in Latin, and said to be a very useful little book. His principal work was 'Rudiments of Physiology,' in three parts, Edinb. 1835–7, the last part (on sensation, &c.) having been brought out by R. Lewins, M.D. It is distinguished by originality and erudition. His 'Elements of Pathology,' published several years after his death (1842) by two of his pupils, John J. Drysdale, M.D., and J. R. Russell, M.D., shows a certain leaning to the teaching of Hahnemann. A paper entitled 'Vieles Sprechen ist gesund,' in Behrend's 'Wöchentl. Repert.' iv. 175 (1837), is attributed to him. Besides one or two introductory lectures, his only other publication is a tract on the trial of Robert Reid for the murder of his wife, 29 June 1835; Reid was thought to have got off unfairly, on a medico-legal plea urged by Fletcher.

[Brit. and For. Med. Rev. 1836, ii. 302; biographical preface, by Lewins, to pt. iii. of Rudiments of Physiology.]

C. C.

FLETCHER, JOHN, D.D (*d.* 1848?), catholic divine, a native of Ormskirk, Lancashire, was educated at Douay College, and at the English seminary of St. Gregory in Paris. When the seminary was dissolved he proceeded to the college of St. Omer, of which his great-uncle, the Rev. William Wilkinson, was for some time president. Fletcher was one of the professors at St. Omer throughout the imprisonment of the members of the college at Arras and Dourlens. Upon their release in 1795 Fletcher accompanied them to England, and was successively missioner at Hexham, Blackburn, and Weston Underwood. He was created D.D. by Pope Pius VII on 24 Aug. 1821, in recognition of his missionary merit and excellent sermons. Fletcher became chaplain to the Dowager Lady Throckmorton, and served the mission at Leamington. In 1844 he removed to the mission at Northampton, which he resigned in 1848, owing to his advanced age. He died shortly afterwards.

His works are: 1. 'Sermons on various Religious and Moral Subjects, for all the Sundays after Pentecost,' 2 vols., London, 1812, 8vo; 2nd edit. 1821. Prefixed is 'An Essay on the Spirit of Controversy,' which was also published separately. 2. 'The Catholic's Manual,' translated from the French of Bossuet, with preliminary reflections and notes, London, 1817, 12mo, 1829, 8vo. 3. 'Thoughts on the Rights and Prerogatives of the Church and State; with some observations upon the question of Catholic Securities,' London, 1823, 8vo. 4. 'Comparative View of the Grounds of the Catholic and Protestant Churches,' London, 1826, 8vo. 5. 'The Difficulties of Protestantism,' London, 1829, and again 1832, 8vo. 6. 'The Catholic's Prayer-Book,' London, 1830, 12mo. For some time this manual was extensively used. It was chiefly compiled from the manuscript of 'A Prayer-Book for the Use of the London District,' 1813, by the Rev. Joseph Berington [q. v.] 7. 'The Prudent Christian,' London, 1834, 12mo. 8. 'Guide to the True Religion,' a series of sermons, 2nd edit., London, 1836, 8vo. 9. 'Transubstantiation, &c. A Letter,' London, 1836, 8vo. 10. 'Short Historical View of the Rise, Progress, and Establishment of the Anglican Church,' London, 1843, 8vo.

He also published translations of several works, including Father Edmund Campion's 'Ten Reasons' (1827), Antonio de Dominis's 'Motives for Renouncing the Protestant Religion' (1827), and De Maistre's 'Letters on the Spanish Inquisition' (1838).

[Gillow's Bibl. Dict. of the English Catholics; Catholic Magazine and Review (1833), iii. 112; Butler's Hist. Memoirs (1822), iv. 441.]

T. C.

FLETCHER or DE LA FLECHERE, JOHN WILLIAM (1729–1785), vicar of Madeley, was born in 1729 at Nyon in Switzerland. His father was an officer in the army. His schooldays were spent at Nyon, whence he proceeded to the university of Geneva. Both at school and at college he was distinguished for his attainments, especially in classical literature. He was intended by his friends for the sacred ministry, but he himself determined to be a soldier. With this intention he went, without his parents' consent, to Lisbon, accepted a captain's commission, and engaged to serve the king of Portugal on board a man-of-war which was about to sail to Brazil. Being prevented by an accident from carrying out his resolution, he returned to Switzerland. His uncle, who was a colonel in the Dutch service, procured a commission for him, and he set out for Flanders; but his uncle having died before the arrangement was completed, he gave up all thoughts of being a soldier, and went on a visit to England. During this visit he was recommended as a tutor to the two sons of Thomas Hill, esq., of Tern Hall in Shropshire, and in 1752 entered Mr. Hill's family in that capacity. He was soon afterwards deeply impressed with the preaching of the methodists, and determined to seek holy orders. In 1757 he was ordained deacon and priest on two successive Sundays by the Bishop of Bangor (John Egerton), at the Chapel Royal, St. James's. His first ministerial work was to help Wesley at the West Street Chapel, and to preach in various places to the French refugees in their native tongue. He was urged to return to Switzerland, but preferred to remain in the land of his adoption, and again made Tern Hall his home. He was accustomed to help the vicar of Madeley, a large parish ten miles distant, and he 'contracted such an affection for the people of Madeley as nothing could hinder from increasing more and more until the day of his death' (BENSON). His intimacy with the brothers Wesley, especially Charles, with whom he kept up a constant correspondence, increased, but, unlike them, he preferred parochial to itinerant work, and in 1760 he accepted the living of Madeley, of which Mr. Hill was the patron, in preference to one which was double its value. Madeley is said to have been a rough parish, 'remarkable for little else than the ignorance and profaneness of its inhabitants, among whom respect to men was as rarely to be observed as piety towards God' (ib.) It therefore offered abundant scope for the untiring and self-denying efforts of its new vicar, who continued, amid much opposition, to labour there

for a quarter of a century. Mr. Gilpin, a gentleman who lived in the neighbourhood, and was well acquainted with Madeley, writes in the most rapturous terms of his ministerial work, and Wesley says that 'from the beginning of his settling there he was a laborious workman in the Lord's vineyard, endeavouring to spread the truth of the gospel, and to suppress vice in every possible way. Those sinners who endeavoured to hide themselves from him he pursued to every corner of his parish, by all sorts of means, public and private, early and late, in season and out of season, entreating and warning them to flee from the wrath to come. Some made it an excuse for not attending the church service on a Sunday morning that they could not awake early enough to get their families ready. He provided for this also. Taking a bell in his hand, he set out every Sunday for some months at five in the morning, and went round the most distant parts of the parish, inviting all the inhabitants to the house of God.' He established 'societies,' after the Wesley pattern, at Madeley Wood and Coalbrook Dale, two outlying hamlets, and was so lavish in his liberality that he injured his own health by his abstinence in order that he might give his money to the poor. Mr. Ireland, a rich and pious gentleman of Bristol, whose name frequently appears in connection with the evangelical revival, helped him with his purse, and persuaded him to make a tour with him in Italy and Switzerland. 'As they approached the Appian Way, Fletcher directed the driver to stop before he entered upon it. He then ordered the chaise door to be opened, assuring his fellow-traveller that his heart would not suffer him to ride over that ground upon which the apostle Paul had formerly walked, chained to a soldier, on account of preaching the everlasting gospel. As soon as he had set his foot upon this old Roman road, he took off his hat, and walking on, with his eyes lifted up to heaven, returned thanks to God, in a most fervent manner, for that light, those truths, and that influence of the Holy Spirit which were continued to the present day.' In 1768 Selina, countess of Huntingdon, invited him to take the superintendence of her college at Trevecca in Wales, founded for the education of 'pious young men of whatever denomination for the ministry.' He was not to reside at Trevecca, but was to visit the college as frequently as he could. He made there, as he did everywhere, an extraordinary impression. Benson his principal biographer, was head-master at the time, and thus writes of him : ' Mr. Fletcher visited them [the students] frequently, and was received as an angel of God. It is not possible for me to describe the veneration in which we all held him. Like Elijah, in the schools of the prophets, he was revered, he was loved, he was almost adored, and that not only by every student, but by every member of the family. And indeed he was worthy.' When the Calvinistic controversy broke out in 1771 he resigned his office, because he sympathised with Wesley and not with Lady Huntingdon on the points in dispute ; but he maintained, in relation to the college, the same truly Christian spirit which he had shown throughout the whole of that unhappy controversy. 'Take care, my dear sir,' he wrote to Mr. Benson, who was dismissed from the head-mastership because, like Fletcher, he took the Arminian side, 'not to make matters worse than they are ; and cast the mantle of forgiving love over the circumstances that might injure the cause of God, so far as it is put into the hands of that eminent lady [Lady Huntingdon] who hath so well deserved of the church of Christ. Rather suffer in silence, than make a noise to cause the Philistines to triumph.'

By his incessant work in his parish, his frequent journeys in all weathers to Trevecca, his self-denying abstinence, and his literary labours, he injured his health, which was not naturally strong, and to recruit it he paid a long visit at the house of Charles Greenwood, who lived at Stoke Newington. But he could not find there the rest and retirement which he needed ; for 'he was continually visited by high and low, and by persons of various denominations, one of whom being asked when he went away what he thought of Mr. Fletcher, said: "I went to see a man that had one foot in the grave ; but I found a man that had one foot in heaven !"' During his enforced absences from Madeley he frequently wrote pastoral letters to his parishioners, which breathe the spirit of the most ardent piety; and always took care to provide a 'locum tenens' who would carry on his work on his own lines. Partly to see his relations, and partly in the hope of recovering his health, he made another journey to Switzerland, and stayed for some time at Nyon, his birthplace, where he lodged in the same house with William Perronet, son of that vicar of Shoreham whom Charles Wesley called the archbishop of methodism. He returned to England with his health greatly improved in 1781, and in the same year married Mary Bosanquet, a lady of a kindred spirit with his own. With her he settled quietly down at Madeley, and spent the remainder of his life in active parochial work. He showed a particular interest in the children of the parish, teaching them himself every day, and warmly took up the new scheme of Sunday schools, establishing a large one at Madeley. In all his labours he was cordially helped by Mrs. Fletcher. The laying the foundation of the Sunday schools at Madeley was his last public work. After about a week's illness he died at Madeley on 14 Aug. 1785, leaving behind a reputation of saintliness such as few have ever attained. John Wesley, in a funeral sermon on the suggestive text, 'Mark the perfect man, and behold the upright, for the end of that man is peace,' said that he had never met so holy a man, and never expected to do so on this side of eternity ; and the testimony of others is equally explicit.

Fletcher was a voluminous and very much admired writer. His best-known work is his 'Checks to Antinomianism,' which was called forth by the disputes between the Arminians (so called) and Calvinists in 1771. It was written in defence of the minutes of the Wesleyan conference of 1770, which aroused the hostility of Lady Huntingdon and her friends, and had special reference to a 'circular printed letter,' under the name of the Hon. and Rev. Walter Shirley, inviting all 'real protestants' to meet and protest against the obnoxious minutes. John Wesley 'knows not which to admire most [in the 'Checks'], the purity of the language (such as scarce any foreigner wrote before), the strength and clearness of the argument, or the mildness and sweetness of the spirit that breathes throughout the whole.' Much of this praise is thoroughly deserved ; and there is another feature in the work which Mr. Wesley has not noticed. The 'Checks' show that the writer had a great sense of humour, and a vein of delicate satire, which, if he had not been restrained by that spirit of Christian charity to which Mr. Wesley refers, would have made him a most dangerous antagonist to meddle with. But, unfortunately, the 'Checks to Antinomianism' are so inextricably mixed up with the most feeble, bitter, and unprofitable controversy of the eighteenth century, that justice has scarcely been done to their intellectual merits. His other works are: 1. 'An Appeal to Matter of Fact and Common Sense ; or a Rational Demonstration of Man's Corrupt and Lost Estate,' which was addressed 'to the principal inhabitants [that is, the gentry] of the parish of Madeley,' and was published in 1772, though written a year earlier. 2. 'An Essay on Truth ; or a Rational Vindication of the Doctrine of Salvation by Faith,' which he dedicated to Lady Huntingdon and published in 1773. 3. 'Scripture Scales

to weigh the Gold of Gospel Truth,' 1774.
4. 'Zelotus [? Zelotes] and Honestus Reconciled; or an Equal Check to Pharisaism and Antinomianism'(which includes the first and second parts of the 'Scripture Scales'), 1775. 5. 'The Fictitious and Genuine Creed,' 1775. 6. 'A Polemical Essay on the Twin Doctrines of Christian Imperfection and a Death Purgatory,' popularly called his 'Treatise on Christian Perfection,' 1775. 7. 'A Vindication of Mr. Wesley's Calm Address to our American Colonies, in Three Letters to Mr. Caleb Evans.' 8. 'American Patriotism further confronted with Reason, Scripture, and the Constitution; being Observations on the Dangerous Politics taught by the Rev. Mr. Evans and the Rev. Dr. Price,' 1776 ('I carried one of them' (these tracts), wrote Vaughan to Wesley, 'to the Earl of D. His lordship carried it to the lord chancellor, and the lord chancellor handed it to the king. One was immediately commissioned to ask Mr. Fletcher whether any preferment in the church would be acceptable? Or whether he [the chancellor] could do him any service? He answered, "I want nothing but more grace"'). 9. 'The Reconciliation; or an Easy Method to Unite the Professing People of God, by placing the Doctrines of Grace and Justice in such a Light as to make the candid Arminians Bible-Calvinists, and the candid Calvinists Bible-Arminians,' 1776. This was preceded by a tract entitled 'The Doctrines of Grace and Justice equally essential to the Pure Gospel; with some Remarks on the mischievous Divisions caused among Christians by parting those Doctrines;' but this was intended as an introduction to the 'Reconciliation,' and the two were subsequently printed and sold in one volume. During the last nine years of his life his health was too delicate to allow him to write anything except letters to his friends and the pastoral addresses already referred to.

[Life of the Rev. John W. de la Flechere, compiled from the narrative of the Rev. J. Wesley (1786); the Biographical Notes of the Rev. Mr. Gilpin, his own Letters, &c., by the Rev. Joseph Benson; Fletcher's Checks to Antinomianism, and Works, passim.]   J. H. O.

FLETCHER, JOSEPH (1582?–1637), religious poet, son of Thomas Fletcher, merchant tailor of London, was, according to his epitaph, sixty years old at the time of his death in 1637. There can be little doubt that he was four or five years younger. He was entered at Merchant Taylors' School on 11 March 1593–4, and was elected to St. John's College, Oxford, in 1600, matriculating on 23 Jan. 1600–1, at the age of eighteen.

He proceeded B.A. in 1604–5 and M.A. in 1608. He took part in a burlesque pageant called 'The Christmas Prince,' played at Oxford in 1607, together with his fellow-collegiate, Laud (TRIPHOOK, *Miscellanea Antiqua Anglicana*, 1816). In the autumn of 1609 he was presented to the rectory of Wilby, Suffolk, by Sir Anthony Wingfield, and he died there on 28 May 1637, being buried in the church. A mural brass above his grave with verses inscribed upon it is still extant. He married, first, in May 1610, Grace, daughter of Hugh Ashley, vicar of St. Margaret's, Ilkettshall, a parish in the neighbourhood of Wilby. By her he had six children: Joseph (baptised 7 April 1611), William (baptised 13 April 1612), Grace (baptised 28 Dec. 1613), Marie (baptised 27 Aug. 1605), John (baptised 18 May 1617), and a sixth child, born in December 1618. Fletcher's first wife died in giving birth to the sixth child, and she was buried in Wilby Church on 4 Dec. 1618. Her husband, when entering her death in the burial register, added two elegiac poems, one in Latin and the other in English. Fletcher's second wife (Anne) survived him, and to her he left all his property by a will dated 1 May 1630.

Fletcher was the author of a volume of poetry—now very rare—entitled 'The Historie of the Perfect, Cursed, Blessed Man: setting forth man's excellencie, miserie, felicitie by his generation, degeneration, regeneration, by I. F., Master of Arts, Preacher of God's Word, and Rector of Wilbie in Suffolk,' London, 1628, 1629. This is dedicated to the author's patron, Sir Anthony Wingfield. A long prose address to the reader precedes the poem, which is written throughout in heroic verse, and rarely rises above mediocrity. Emblematical designs by Thomas Cecil are scattered through the volume. No copy is in the British Museum. A poem of far higher literary quality called 'Christes Bloodie Sweat, or The Source of God in his Agonie, by I. F.' (London, 1613), has also been attributed to Fletcher by Dr. Grosart and Mr. W. C. Hazlitt. The British Museum Catalogue accepts the identification of 'I. F.' with Fletcher's initials. But the authorship is very uncertain, and little of the fervour of the earlier work is discernible in the later. Dr. Grosart reprinted the two volumes in his 'Fuller's Worthies Library' as Joseph Fletcher's poetical works (1869).

[Robinson's Merchant Taylors' School Reg. i. 34; Clark's Oxf. Univ. Reg. (Oxf. Hist. Soc.), II. ii. 245, iii. 250; Dr. Grosart's preface to Fletcher's Poetical Works; Notes and Queries, 3rd ser. viii. 268.]   S. L.

FLETCHER, JOSEPH, D.D. (1784–1843), theological writer, was born 3 Dec. 1784 at Chester, where his father was a goldsmith. In his boyhood he was deeply impressed by the gospel, and after attending the grammar school of his native city, prepared for the ministry in the independent church by studying, first at Hoxton and then at the university of Glasgow, where he took the degree of M.A. in 1807. Receiving a call from the congregational church of Blackburn, Lancashire, he began his ministry the same year, and continued there till 1823, when he became minister of Stepney meeting, in the metropolis. In 1816 he added to his duties that of theological tutor in the Blackburn college for training ministers. While discharging the duties both of the congregation and the chair, with marked ability and success, Fletcher was also a voluminous writer. The 'Eclectic Review' had just begun its career, and Fletcher was one of its regular contributors. His papers gave proof of ample stores of information, and of a scholarly and powerful pen. On particular subjects Fletcher published tracts and treatises that won considerable fame. His lectures on the 'Principles and Institutions of the Roman Catholic Religion' (1817) won great appreciation, Dr. Pye Smith, Robert Hall, and others expressing a very high opinion of them. A discourse on 'Personal Election and Divine Sovereignty' (1825) was also much commended. A volume of poems (1846) was the joint production of himself and his sister, Mary Fletcher. In 1830 the senatus of the university of Glasgow conferred on him the degree of D.D. He was chairman of the Congregational Union in 1837. Without reaching the first rank, he showed a combination of reasoning power and emotional fervour which made him an instructive preacher. As a writer who gave birth to all his literary offspring amid the whirl of constant practical work and endless engagements he did little more than show what he might have done with leisure and other facilities for literary work. He died 8 June 1843.

JOSEPH FLETCHER the younger (1816–1876), congregational minister, Dr. Fletcher's fourth son by his wife Mary France, was born at Blackburn 7 Jan. 1816; was educated at Ham grammar school, near Richmond, Surrey; went from a Manchester counting-house in 1833 to study at Coward College; was called to the congregational church of Hanley in 1839; was transferred to Christchurch, Hampshire, in 1849, in succession to Daniel Gunn [q. v.]; resigned his charge owing to paralysis at the close of 1873, and died at Christchurch 2 June 1876. He kept a school for a time at Christchurch, but the death by drowning of seven of his pupils in May 1868 caused him to close his establishment. He published, besides the memoirs of his father in 1846, 'Six Views of Infidelity,' a series of lectures given at Hanley in 1843; 'History of Independency,' an important work in 4 vols. 1847–9, reissued 1853; and 'Life of Constantine the Great,' 1852 (Congregational Year-Book, 1877). He is also credited with the libretto of an oratorio entitled 'Paradise,' by John Fawcett the younger [q. v.]

[Memoirs of the Rev. Joseph Fletcher, D.D., by his son, 1846; Waddington's Congregational Hist.] W. G. B.

FLETCHER, JOSEPH (1813–1852), statistician, born in 1813, was educated as a barrister. From the age of nineteen he was engaged upon works and reports in connection with the health, occupations, and well-being of the people. He acted as secretary to the handloom inquiry commission, and afterwards to the children's employment commission. His valuable reports of these commissions formed the basis of useful legislation. The disclosures of the children's employment commission in particular established the necessity of parliamentary control. In 1844 Fletcher was appointed one of her majesty's inspectors of schools; and his voluminous reports were among the most serviceable contributions to British educational statistics. For many years Fletcher was one of the honorary secretaries of the Statistical Society of London, and in this post he earned wide recognition among statists at home and abroad. He was also during the same period editor of the 'Statistical Journal,' and responsible for the collation and arrangement of the vast collection of documents published in that journal. Fletcher was a member of the council of the British Association, and on several occasions acted as secretary to the statistical section, contributing also a series of memoirs to the association reports. In 1850 Fletcher published a 'Summary of the Moral Statistics of England and Wales;' and in the following year a work on 'Education: National, Voluntary, and Free.' He paid great attention to foreign educational systems, and issued (1851–2) two treatises on 'The Farm School of the Continent, and its Applicability to the Preventive and Reformatory Education of Pauper and Criminal Children in England and Wales.' Fletcher died at Chirk, Denbighshire, 11 Aug. 1852. He was an ideal statistician, having in a singular degree the power of grasping facts and realising their relative significance. He was buried in the graveyard of Tottenham Church.

[Gent. Mag. 1852; Journal of the Statistical Society, 1852; Athenæum, 1852.]   G. B. S.

FLETCHER, Mrs. MARIA JANE (1800–1833), authoress. [See Jewsbury.]

FLETCHER, PHINEAS (1582–1650), poet, was elder son of Giles Fletcher, LL.D. [q. v.], by his wife, Joan Sheafe, and was baptised at his birthplace, Cranbrook, Kent, of which his grandfather, Richard Fletcher, was rector, on 8 April 1582. Like his father, he was educated at Eton, and was thence elected on 24 Aug. 1600 a scholar of King's College, Cambridge, where he graduated B.A. in 1604, M.A. in 1607–8, and afterwards B.D. He obtained a fellowship before midsummer 1611; contributed English verse to the university collections in 1603, and acquired the reputation of a poet among his Cambridge friends. In 1614 he wrote a pastoral play, 'Sicelides,' to be acted before James I on his visit to Cambridge, but the royal party left the university before it was ready, and the piece was performed later at King's College. Fletcher remained at King's College till midsummer 1616. In his 'Piscatory Eclogues,' where he writes of himself under the name of Thyrsil, he asserts that he left the university—'ungrateful Chame,' he calls it—in resentment for some slight cast upon him by the authorities:

Not I my Chame, but me proud Chame refuses,
His froward spites my strong affections sever;
Else from his banks could I have parted never.

For the next five years Sir Henry Willoughby seems to have entertained Fletcher as his chaplain at Risley, Derbyshire. In 1621 Willoughby presented the poet to the rectory of Hilgay, Norfolk, where he lived for the rest of his life. Soon after settling at Hilgay he married Elizabeth Vincent. In 1627 the publication of his 'Locustæ,' an attack on Roman catholicism, seems to have involved him in a quarrel with some neighbours. His intimate friends included Edward Benlowes [q. v.], his junior by more than twenty years, and Benlowes introduced him to Francis Quarles. In Quarles's 'Emblems' (1635), bk. v. No. vi., a globe representing the world is inscribed with the name of four places, one of them being Hilgay. Fletcher died at the close of 1650. His will, dated 21 June 1649, was proved by his widow, the sole executrix, 13 Dec. 1650. Mention is made there of two sons, Phineas and William, and four daughters, Ann, Elizabeth, Frances, and Sarah.

Fletcher's chief volume, 'The Purple Island or the Isle of Man, together with Piscatorie Eclogs and other Poeticall Miscellanies by P. F.,' was printed by the printers to the university of Cambridge in 1633. The dedication to Benlowes is dated 'Hilgay, 1 May 1633.' There Fletcher describes the poems that follow as 'these raw essayes of my very unripe yeares, and almost childehood,' and says that Benlowes insisted on their publication. A commendatory preface by Daniel Featley, D.D., is succeeded by eulogistic verses by E. Benlowes, his brother William, Francis Quarles (two poems), Lodowick Roberts, and A. C., who has been identified with Cowley. 'The Piscatory Eclogs and other Poeticall Miscellanies' has a separate title-page. The seven 'Eclogs' contain much autobiographical matter, but the names of the author's friends are disguised. Thelgon is the poet's father, Thyrsil himself, and Thomalin is John Tomkins. The 'Miscellanies' include epithalamia in honour of the author's cousins, 'Mr. W.' and 'M. R.' (perhaps Walter and Margaret Robarts) of Brenchley, and poems addressed to Cambridge friends, the initials of whose names alone are given, together with metrical versions of the psalms. Members of the Courthope family are believed to be intended by 'W. C.' and 'E. C.' Cole suggested that 'E. C., my son by the university,' was one Ezekiel Charke. A third title-page introduces another poem, 'Elisa: an Elegie upon the unripe demise of Sr Antonie Irby.' The lady had died in 1625, and at the time that the elegy was published the husband was on the point of marrying again. A poem by Quarles closes the volume. In the British Museum is the presentation copy given by Fletcher to Benlowes. 'The Piscatory Eclogs' was edited separately by Lord Woodhouselee in 1771. 'The Purple Island' was reissued separately in 1784 and 1816; the latter edited by Headley.

'The Purple Island,' in twelve cantos of seven-line stanzas, is an elaborate allegorical description of the human body and of the vices and virtues to which man is subject. There are many anatomical notes in prose. The body is represented as an island, of which the bones stand for the foundations, the veins for brooks, and so forth in minute detail. Fletcher imitates the 'Faery Queene.' Quarles calls him 'the Spencer of this age,' and Fletcher eulogises his master in canto vi. stanzas 51–2. But Fletcher's allegory is overloaded with detail, and as a whole is clumsy and intricate. His diction is, however, singularly rich, and his versification melodious. Incidental descriptions of rural scenes with which he was well acquainted are charmingly simple, and there is a majesty in his personifications of some vices and virtues which suggest Milton, who knew Fletcher's works well.

Fletcher's other works are: 1. 'Locustæ vel Pietas Jesuitica. The Locusts or Apollyonists,' Cambridge, Thomas & John Bucke, 1627. The first part in Latin verse is dedicated to Sir Roger Townshend, the patron of Phineas's brother Giles, and has commendatory verse by S. Collins. The second part in English verse, in five cantos of nine-line stanzas, is dedicated to Lady Townshend, and has prefatory verse by H. M., perhaps Henry More. Two manuscript copies of the Latin part are in the British Museum. One Harl. MS., 3196, is dedicated in Latin prose to Thomas Murray, provost of Eton (d. 1625), and in Latin verse to Prince Charles. The second manuscript (Sloane MS. 444) is dedicated to Montague, bishop of Bath and Wells. The poem is a sustained attack on Roman catholicism, and the English version suggested many phrases to Milton. 2. 'Sicelides, or Piscatory, as it hath been acted in King's College in Cambridge,' London, 1631. The piece is in five acts, partly in blank, and partly in rhymed verse. Songs are interspersed, and there are comic scenes in prose. 3. 'The Way to Blessedness; a treatise . . . on the First Psalm,' with the text, London, 1632 (prose). 4. 'Joy in Tribulation; a Consolation for afflicted Spirits,' London, 1632 (prose). 5. 'Sylva Poetica Auctore P. F.,' Cambridge, 1633; a collection of Latin poems and eclogues; dedicated to Edward Benlowes. 6. 'A Father's Testament, written long since for the benefit of a particular relation of the Author,' London, 1670 (prose, with some verse, chiefly translations from Boethius). Fletcher also edited a previously unpublished Latin poem by his father, entitled 'De Literis Antiquæ Britanniæ,' Cambridge, 1633. He contributed verses to 'Sorrowe's Joy,' Cambridge, 1603 (a collection of Cambridge poems in English on the death of Elizabeth and accession of James I) ; to 'Threno-Thriambeuticon,' Cambridge, 1603 (a similar collection in Latin); to his brother Giles's 'Christ's Victory,' 1610; and to his friend Benlowes's 'Theophila,' 1632. Dr. Grosart has credited Fletcher with the authorship of a love-poem of considerable beauty, and somewhat lascivious tone, entitled 'Brittain's Ida,' an account of the loves of Venus and Anchises. This poem was first issued in 1627, and was described as by Edmund Spenser. It is clear that Spenser was not the author. There is much internal resemblance between Fletcher's other works and 'Brittain's Ida,' and no other name has been put forward to claim the latter poem. But no more positive statement is possible.

Fletcher's poetical works were edited by Grosart in 'Fuller's Worthies Library' (4 vols.) and by Mr. F. S. Boas in ' Giles and Phineas Fletcher—Poetical Works' (Cambridge Univ. Press) 2 vols., 1908–9.

[Grosart's Memoir, in his edition; Grosart's Fuller's Worthies Misc., iii. 70, where Fletcher's will is printed; Hunter's MS. Chorus Vatum in Addit. MS. 24487, f. 125; Cole's MS. Hist. of King's College, Cambridge (Cole's MSS. xv. 35); Howell's Letters, ii. 64; Retrospective Rev., ii. 341; Phillips's Theatr. Poet.]　S. L.

FLETCHER, RICHARD, D.D. (d. 1596), bishop of London, was son of a Richard Fletcher, ordained by Ridley in 1550, and vicar of Bishops Stortford till his deprivation by Mary in 1555. In July of the same year he and his son witnessed the martyrdom of Christopher Wade at Dartford in Kent, of which an account signed by both was furnished to Foxe (Acts and Mon. iii. 317, ed. 1684). On the accession of Elizabeth the elder Fletcher became vicar of Cranbrook, Kent. Young Fletcher was appointed by Archbishop Parker to the first of the four Norfolk fellowships founded by him in Corpus Christi College, Cambridge; on the college books he is styled 'Norfolciensis.' He was admitted a pensioner of Trinity College, Cambridge, 16 Nov. 1562, and a scholar in 1563. He became B.A. in 1565–6, M.A. in 1569, B.D. in 1576, and D.D. in 1581. He was made fellow of Corpus Christi in 1569. In 1572 he was incorporated M.A. of Oxford, and in the same year was appointed to the prebendal stall of Islington in St. Paul's Cathedral. According to Masters (Hist. of Corpus Christi College, pp. 285–8) he received this stall from Matthew Parker, son of the archbishop, who appears to have had the patronage made over to him (for this turn) to carry out his father's design of getting prebendal stalls annexed by act of parliament to his Norfolk fellowships. He vacated his fellowship on his marriage with Elizabeth Holland, which took place in Cranbrook Church in 1573. In 1574 he was minister of Rye in Sussex, where his son John [q. v.] the dramatist and three of his elder children were born. He was introduced by Archbishop Parker to Queen Elizabeth, who was attracted by his handsome person, courtly manners, and ability as a preacher.

Sir John Harington says of him 'he could preach well and speak boldly, and yet keep decorum. He knew what would please the queen, and would adventure on that though that offended others.' Elizabeth's favour insured rapid preferment. On 19 June 1575 he was presented by the queen to the living of Bradenham, Buckinghamshire. In 1581 he became one of her chaplains in ordinary. Whitgift recommended him unsuccessfully for the deanery of Windsor. On 15 Nov. 1583 he was appointed to the deanery of Peterborough, and on 23 Jan. 1585-6 he was installed prebendary of Stow Longa in Lincoln Cathedral, and in the same year became rector of Barnack, Northamptonshire, on the presentation of Sir Thomas Cecil. He also held the rich living of Algarkirk in South Lincolnshire, which, together with his stall, on his becoming bishop of Bristol, he was allowed to retain *in commendam* (*Calendar of State Papers*, Dom. p. 663). He was also chaplain to Archbishop Whitgift, and in that capacity is stated to have helped to draw up the original of the present 55th canon, ordaining the form of bidding prayer to be used by preachers before sermons. He is said, however, the canon notwithstanding, to have used a form of his own composing. He held the deanery of Peterborough for six years. He preached before the commissioners for the trial of Mary Queen of Scots, in the chapel of Fotheringay Castle, 12 Oct. 1586, drew up a detailed report of the examination of the queen, and officiated as chaplain at her execution, 8 Feb. 1586-7. He obtruded his 'unwelcome ministrations' upon Mary with the insolence of unfeeling bigotry, and the 'stern Amen' with which his solitary voice echoed the Earl of Kent's imprecation, 'So perish all the queen's enemies,' was an evident bidding for high preferment, followed up without delay by a sermon (preserved in manuscript in the library of St. John's College, Cambridge) delivered before Elizabeth immediately after the execution of her rival. Two years later Elizabeth resolved to confer upon her 'well-spoken' chaplain the see of Bristol, which her father founded in 1542 and she had kept vacant thirty years. He was consecrated by Whitgift in Lambeth Chapel 14 Dec. 1589 (STRYPE, *Whitgift*, i. 616). According to Sir John Harington, his elevation was helped forward by some of the queen's court, who were on the look-out for compliant candidates, and obtained the bishopric for him on terms by which he almost secularised the see (COLLIER, *Church Hist.* vii. 222; STRYPE, *Whitgift*, ii. 112). He took part in the consecration of Bishop Coldwell of Salisbury, 16 Dec. 1591. Fletcher had a house of his own at Chelsea, where he chiefly resided, spending much more of his time at court than in his diocese. Here his first wife, Elizabeth, died, December 1592, shortly after the birth of her daughter Mary (baptised 14 Oct.), and was buried in Chelsea Church beneath the altar. After three years' stay at Bristol he

was translated to the much richer see of Worcester, his election taking place 24 Jan. 1592-3.

In June 1594 the see of London became vacant by the death of John Aylmer [q. v.] Fletcher wrote (29 June) to Lord Burghley, giving reasons for his translation thither. He 'delighted in' London, had been educated there, was beloved by many of the citizens to whom he could be useful, and would be near the court, 'where his presence had become habitual and looked for' (STRYPE, *Whitgift*, ii. 214-15). The queen signified her assent to his translation, and as bishop-elect of London he took part with Whitgift and others in drawing up the so-called 'Lambeth Articles,' happily never accepted by the church, in which some of the most offensive of the peculiar doctrines of Calvinism were dogmatically laid down. The queen condemned both the articles and their authors very severely. Fletcher soon offended her still more by an ill-advised second marriage. She objected to the marriage of all bishops, and thought it specially indecorous in one two years a widower to contract a second marriage, and that with a widow. The new wife was the widow of Sir Richard Baker of Sissinghurst in Kent, and sister of Sir George Gifford, one of the gentlemen pensioners attached to the court. She was a very handsome woman, probably wealthy, 'a fine lady,' but with a tarnished reputation. A very coarse satirical ballad preserved by Cole (*MS.* xxxi. 205) says of the bishop, 'He of a Lais doth a Lucrece make.' Fletcher was forbidden the court, and the queen demanded from the primate his suspension from the exercise of all episcopal functions. The inhibition was issued on 23 Feb. 1594-5, hardly more than a month after his confirmation as bishop of London. The next day he entreated Burghley's good offices for his restitution to the royal favour in a letter of the most degrading adulation and self-abasement (STRYPE, *Whitgift*, ii. 216). Through Burghley's mediation the suspension was relaxed at the end of six months, and the queen became partially reconciled to him. He continued piteous appeals to Burghley for readmission to the court. 'His greatest comfort seculor' (*sic*, Fletcher's spelling in his autograph letters is not only irregular but ignorant) 'for twenty years past had been to live in her Highness' gratious aspect and favour. Now it was a year all but a week or two since he had seen her' (*ib.* p. 218). This letter was written on 7 Jan. 1595-6. Elizabeth is said to have visited him at Chelsea, but he appears to have been still excluded from court. He had so far resumed his official position as to assist at the consecration of Bishop Day of Winchester and Bishop Vaughan of Bangor, 25 Jan. 1596; in March he issued orders regulating the exercise of their authority by ecclesiastical officers within his diocese (COLLIER, *Eccl. Hist.* ix. 352–6), and in the following May he ventured to ask for the appointment of his brother, Dr. Giles Fletcher the elder [q. v.], as an extraordinary master of requests (*Lansd. MSS.* lxxxii. 28). But his spirit was broken. On 13 June 1596 he assisted at the consecration of Bilson as bishop of Worcester. He sat in commission on 15 June till 6 P.M., and was smoking a pipe of tobacco (of which he was immoderately fond, and to which Camden, prejudiced against a novel habit, groundlessly attributes his end) when he suddenly exclaimed to his servant, 'Boy, I die,' and breathed his last. He was buried in St. Paul's Cathedral without any memorial, leaving eight children, several of whom were still very young. He died insolvent, with large debts due to the queen and others, his whole estate consisting of his house at Chelsea, plate worth 400*l.*, and other property amounting to 500*l.* A memorial on behalf of his family was at once presented to the queen. It was urged that his debts were caused partly by his rapid promotions, involving heavy payments of first-fruits, partly by 'allowances or gratifications' made to members of her court, by her desire, while he had spent the whole revenue of his see on hospitality and other duties incumbent on his office. His death, chiefly due to the queen's anger at his marriage, had atoned for the offence so given. His children had no resources, and their uncle with nine children of his own had barely enough for his family (GREEN, *Calendar of State Papers*, Dom. June 1596). What was the result of this appeal to Elizabeth's generosity we are not informed. His widow took for her third husband Sir Stephen Thornhurst, knight, and dying in 1609 was buried in Canterbury Cathedral. Five of his eight children were: Nathanael (*b.* 1575), Theophilus (*b.* 1577), Elizabeth (*b.* 1578), John, the famous dramatist [q. v.], and Maria (*b.* in London 1592). His will is dated 26 Oct. 1593, and was proved 23 June 1596.

Camden styles Fletcher 'præsul splendidus.' Fuller describes him as 'one of a comely person and goodly presence. . . . He loved to ride the great horse, and had much skill in managing thereof; condemned for being proud (such was his natural stately gait) by such as knew him not, and commended for humility by those acquainted with him. He lost the queen's favour by reason of his second marriage, and died suddenly more of grief than

any other disease' (FULLER, *Church Hist.* v. 231).

From the leading part he took in the composition of the 'Lambeth Articles,' and his patronage of Robert Abbot [q. v.], afterwards bishop of Salisbury, his theology was evidently Calvinistic. Fletcher published nothing. The manuscripts of the two sermons (see above) preached at Fotheringay and before Elizabeth after Mary's execution are in the library of St. John's College, Cambridge (i. 30), together with (1) a relation of the proceedings against the queen of Scots at Fotheringay on 12, 14, and 20 Oct., (2) a relation of divers matters that passed at Fotheringay on 8 Feb. 1586–7, and of the execution of Mary, and (3) the manner of the solemnity of the funeral of Mary on 1 Aug. Strype has printed his exhortation to Mary upon her execution (*Annals*, III. i. 560), and Gunton his prayer at the execution (*Hist. of Peterborough*, p. 75). His articles of visitation are to be found in Strype (*Annals*, iv. 350), and some of his letters to Burghley (STRYPE, *Whitgift*, ii. 204–57).

[Strype's Annals; Cooper's Athenæ Cantabr. ii. 205, 548; Dyce's Beaumont and Fletcher, i. 7, 38; Faulkner's Chelsea, ii. 127, 197; Fuller's Ch. Hist. v. 231; Collier's Ch. Hist. vii. 222, 396, ix. 352; Milman's St. Paul's, p. 301; Camden's Annals, sub an. 1596; Cole MSS. xxvii. 22, xxxi. 305; Masters's Hist. of C.C.C. (ed. Lamb), p. 323.]   E. V.

FLETCHER, SIR RICHARD (1768–1813), lieutenant-colonel royal engineers, son of the Rev. R. Fletcher, who died at Ipswich 17 May 1813, was born in 1768. He passed through the Royal Military Academy, Woolwich, was gazetted a second lieutenant in the royal artillery 9 July 1788, and transferred to the royal engineers on 29 June 1790. In 1791 he was sent to the West Indies, and took part in the capture of Martinique, Guadaloupe, and St. Lucia. At the storming of the Morne Fortuné in the latter island, he was wounded in the head by a musket-ball. He for a time commanded the royal engineers at Dominica, and, returning to England at the end of 1796, was appointed adjutant of the royal military artificers at Portsmouth. On 27 Nov. of this year he married a daughter of Dr. Mudge of Plymouth, and continued to serve at Portsmouth until December 1798, when he was ordered to Constantinople, and appointed a major while employed in Turkey. On his way out he was shipwrecked off the Elbe, and had to cross two miles of ice to reach the shore. He reached Constantinople in March 1799, and in June of that year accompanied the grand vizier in his march to Syria. On his return from this expedition he was employed on the defences of the Dardanelles. In January 1800, 'equipped as a Tartar,' he left Constantinople on a special mission to Syria and Cyprus, returning in April, when he received a 'beniche' of honour from the sultan. In June he embarked with the division for Syria, landed at Jaffa, and was employed in constructing works of defence there and at El Arish.

In December he was sent off in the Camelion to Marmorice with despatches for Sir Ralph Abercromby, who, with the army, was on his way to Egypt. He was then sent with Major McKerras in the Penelope frigate to survey the coast of Egypt, with a view to the disembarkation of the troops. On arriving off Alexandria they shifted into the Peterel sloop of war, and proceeded in one of her boats to reconnoitre Aboukir Bay, and with great enterprise landed at the spot which appeared the most favourable for, and which was subsequently chosen as the place of, disembarkation. At dawn of day, as they were returning to the Peterel, they were surprised by a French gunboat. McKerras was killed by a musket-ball, and Fletcher was taken prisoner.

After the capture of Cairo and Alexandria and the capitulation of the French, Fletcher was released, and received for his services a gold medal from the sultan. He returned to England in 1802, and was stationed at Portsmouth, where he was employed in the extension of the Gosport lines of fortification. He was afterwards appointed brigade major to Brigadier-general Everleigh, and held the appointment until July 1807, when he joined the expedition, under Lord Cathcart and Admiral Gambier, to Copenhagen. In 1808 he was ordered to the Peninsula, where Sir H. Dalrymple was then commander-in-chief; he took over the command of the royal engineers from Major Landmann on 27 Aug., just after the battle of Vimeiro. The convention of Cintra followed, and Fletcher accompanied the army to Lisbon. On 21 June 1809 he was promoted lieutenant-colonel, having held local rank as such, with extra command pay of twenty shillings a day since the March previous.

On the appointment of Wellington as commander-in-chief, Fletcher joined his staff as commanding royal engineer, and accompanied him in the campaigns of 1809 and 1810 in Spain and Portugal. He took part in the battle of Talavera on 27 and 28 July 1809, and was complimented by Wellington in his despatch of 29 July. In October 1809 Wellington retired into Portugal. Fletcher, as chief engineer, superintended the designing and execution of the lines of Torres Vedras,

under the immediate orders of Wellington, from October 1809 to July 1810, when the works were nearly complete. Fletcher then handed over the works to Captain (afterwards Sir John) Jones, and hastened to the scene of active operations on the Coa. He was present at the battle of Busaco, and Wellington in his despatch of 30 Sept. 1810 mentioned his particular indebtedness to Fletcher. The army retired behind the lines upon which Fletcher had bestowed so much labour, and he had the satisfaction of seeing the French effectually checked by them. In November 1810, in a despatch to Lord Liverpool, Wellington again specially noticed Fletcher's services.

Fletcher was present at the battles of Sabugal (2 April), Fuentes d'Onoro (5 May), and at the evacuation of Almeida by the French on 10 May 1811. At the first English siege of Badajoz in May, and at the second in June 1811, Fletcher had the direction of the siege operations, and was mentioned in despatches. In January 1812 he had the direction of the siege of Ciudad Rodrigo, and on its capture, Wellington, in his despatch of 20 Jan. 1812, stated that Fletcher's 'ability exceeded all praise.' The third siege of Badajoz took place in March and April 1812, and Fletcher again directed the attack. On 19 March the garrison made a sortie, and Fletcher was struck in the groin by a musket-ball. A silver dollar piece received the blow and saved his life, but inflicted a wound which disabled him. Wellington, however, insisted that Fletcher should retain the direction of the attack, and consulted him in his bed every morning until near the end of the siege. After the assault and capture of Badajoz, Fletcher remained there to place it again in a state of defence. and then proceeded on leave of absence to England.

In May 1811 the master-general of ordnance had represented his important services to the prince regent, and a pension had consequently been granted him of twenty shillings a day from 7 May 1811. He was now made a knight commander of Hanover, created a baronet, decorated with the gold cross for Talavera, Busaco, Ciudad Rodrigo, and Badajoz, and permitted to accept and wear the insignia of the Portuguese order of the Tower and Sword.

On his return to the Peninsula, Fletcher took part in the battle of Vittoria (21 June 1813), and was again mentioned in despatches. He then made all the arrangements for the blockade of Pampeluna, under Sir Rowland Hill, and arriving at St. Sebastian shortly after the commencement of the siege he directed the operations under Sir T. Graham, until in the final and successful assault on 31 Aug. 1813 he was killed by a musket-ball in the forty-fifth year of his age. Sir Augustus Fraser says, in a letter written at the time: 'We cannot get Sir Richard's loss from our minds; our trenches, our batteries, all remind us of one of the most amiable of men I ever knew, and one of the most solid worth. No loss will be more deeply felt, no place more difficult to be filled up.'

Fletcher was buried with three other engineer officers on the height of St. Bartholomew, opposite St. Sebastian, where a tombstone recorded the fact. A monument to his memory, designed by E. H. Baily, R.A., was erected in Westminster Abbey by his brother-officers of the corps of royal engineers. It stands at the west end of the north aisle.

Fletcher left a son and five daughters, his wife having died before him; his only son died in 1876 without issue, and the baronetcy became extinct.

[Jones's Sieges in Spain; Jones's War in Spain; Wellington Despatches; Napier's History of the War in the Peninsula; Alison's History of Europe; Landmann's Recollections; Sabine's Letters of Colonel Sir A. S. Fraser; Conolly's Notitia Historica of the Corps of Royal Engineers; Corps Records.]   R. H. V.

FLETCHER, ROBERT (*fl.* 1586), verse writer, seems to be identical with a student of Merton College, Oxford, who came from Warwickshire, proceeded B.A. in 1564, and M.A. in 1567. He was admitted a fellow in 1563, but in 1569 quarrelled with Bickley, the new warden. 'For several misdemeanors he was turned out from his fellowship of that house (i.e. Merton) in June 1569,' whereupon he became schoolmaster at Taunton, and afterwards 'preacher of the word of God' (WOOD). He wrote two works, both very rare, viz.: 1. 'An Introduction to the Looue of God. Accoumpted among the workes of St. Augustine, and translated into English by Edmund [Freake], bishop of Norwich that nowe is . . . and newlie turned into Englishe Meter by Rob. Fletcher,' London (by Thomas Purfoot), 1581, dedicated to Sir Francis Knollys. 2. 'The Song of Solomon,' in English verse, with annotations, London, by Thomas Chard, 1586. A third very rare volume—a copy is in the Grenville Library at the British Museum—by a Robert Fletcher, who may be identical with the author of the two former volumes, is entitled 'The Nine English Worthies . . . beginning with King Henrie the first, and concluding with Prince Henry, eldest sonne to our soueraigne Lord the King,' London, 1606, dedicated to Prince Henry, and to the Earls of Oxford and Essex,

'and other young lords attending the princes highnesse.' Fletcher commends Ascham's advice as to the need of learning in men of high rank. Prefatory verse is contributed by R. Fenne, Thomas, lord Windsor, Sir Will. Whorewood, John Wideup, Jo. Guilliams, Paul Peart, and others. A brief life of each monarch in prose is followed by an epitaph in verse, except in the last case, where the life is wholly in verse.

[Wood's Fasti Oxon. ed. Bliss, i. 179; Oxford Univ. Reg. (Oxf. Hist. Soc.), i. 253; Ames's Typ. Antiq. ed. Herbert, pp. 998, 1195; Brodrick's Memorials of Merton Coll., pp. 54, 267.] S. L.

FLETCHER, THOMAS (1666–1713), poet, eldest son of John Fletcher of Winchester, was born at Avington, Hampshire, on 21 March 1666, and was educated at Winchester School. He matriculated at Balliol College, Oxford, 9 April 1685, and on 12 Sept. 1685 entered at New College, Oxford, where he graduated B.A. on 10 April 1689, M.A. on 14 Jan. 1692–3, B.D. and D.D. on 25 June 1707. He became fellow of New College, but resigned on his marriage in 1702. He held the living of Fairfield, Somerset in 1694, was prebendary of Barton David in the cathedral of Wells from 1696 until his death, and became an undermaster of Winchester School in 1701, and fellow of Winchester 12 Sept. 1711, resigning in 1712. Fletcher was an admirer of Bishop Ken, and wrote in youth some fulsome verses to him on his promotion to the see of Bath and Wells in 1685. It is probable that Ken, who was deprived of the see in 1691, still retained and exerted sufficient influence with the dean and chapter of Wells to secure in 1696 Fletcher's appointment to the prebend of Barton David in Wells Cathedral. Fletcher died in 1713, and was buried in Winchester Cathedral. By his wife, a daughter of William Master, fellow of New College, he had three sons, Thomas, Philip, and William.

Fletcher is the author of a small volume of verse entitled 'Poems on Several Occasions and Translations, wherein the first and second books of Virgil's Æneis are attempted in English,' London, 1692, 8vo. A dedication to the Rev. William Harris, D.D., 'schoolmaster of the college near Winton,' explains that the poems are chiefly juvenile exercises. The first book of the Æneid is translated in heroic couplets, part of the second and also part of the fourth in blank verse. The volume also contains a translation of the second epode of Horace, and of part of the first book of Boethius's 'De Consolatione Philosophiæ,' the verses to Ken referred to in the text, a 'pastoral' on the birth of Christ, and some other pieces of a conventional stamp.

[Notes and Queries, 8th ser. i. 510; Wood's Athenæ Oxon. (Bliss), iv. 559; Hearne's Collections (Oxford Hist. Soc.), i. 291; Le Neve's Fasti; Cat. Oxford Graduates; Burke's Landed Gentry; Brit. Mus. Cat.]   J. M. R.

FLETE, JOHN (*fl.* 1421–1465), a Benedictine monk, prior of Westminster Abbey in the reign of Henry VI, and the author of a Latin chronicle of the early history of that foundation, entered the monastery of St. Peter's, Westminster, about 1421, ascending step by step the different posts available to the brethren, till in 1448 he was unanimously elected prior. During the suspension of Abbot Norwych, who succeeded Kirton as abbot in 1462, Flete, assisted by two monks, administered the spiritual and temporal affairs of the monastery, and had he lived would probably have been made abbot on the death of Norwych (1469). But in 1465 he resigned the post of prior and seems to have died soon afterwards. He was a pious and learned man, 'addicted to reading of history, and zealous for the gaining of souls' (STEVENS). His homilies, which are mentioned as 'notable' by several writers, are no longer extant, and the only remaining record of him is his manuscript history of the abbey. He began to write it in 1443, and intended to carry it on to that year, but it ends with Abbot Littington's death in 1386, and in all probability Flete's duties as prior and acting-abbot prevented his carrying out his original plan. The first chapters of the 'Chronicle' are devoted to the legends of the foundation and dedication of the abbey; these are followed by an account of the benefactors and the relics, and it concludes with the lives of the abbots up till 1386. The book has been much used by later historians of the abbey, but is inexact in many particulars. The original manuscript is in the Chapter Library, Westminster, and there is a later and abridged manuscript copy in Lambeth Library.

[Widmore's Hist. of St. Peter's, Westminster; Tanner's Bibliotheca; Pits, De Illustr. Brit. Script.]   E. T. B.

FLEXMAN, ROGER, D.D. (1708–1795), presbyterian minister, was born on 22 Feb. 1708 at Great Torrington, Devonshire, where his father was a manufacturer. He showed early promise, and at the age of fifteen (1723) was admitted to the academy of John Moore, presbyterian minister at Tiverton, Devonshire, to study for the ministry. He declined an offer from Moore of the post of tutor in the academy, and applied to the Exeter assembly on 7 May 1728 to admit him to examination for license. His application was granted, in spite of his youth, in consideration of his long study, and the 'great want of ministers.' On examination he gave full satisfaction to that staunch Calvinist, John Ball (1665?–1745) [q. v.] He was licensed at Tiverton in the course of the summer. According to the records of the Exeter assembly he began his ministry at Great Torrington. He was ordained at Modbury, Devonshire, on 15 July 1730. In 1731 he became minister at Bow, near Crediton, Devonshire, and appears to have assisted Josiah Eveleigh, the presbyterian minister at Crediton. In 1735 he removed to Chard, Somersetshire, and in 1739 to Bradford, Wiltshire. He came to London in 1747, having accepted a call to the presbyterian congregation in Jamaica Row, Rotherhithe. In 1754 he was chosen one of the preachers of the Friday morning lecture, founded in 1726 at Little St. Helen's, Bishopsgate, by William Coward (*d.* 1738) [q. v.]

Flexman was an assiduous, and for some time a successful, minister at Rotherhithe. In 1770 he received the degree of D.D. from the Marischal College, Aberdeen. Preferment was offered him in the established church. Owing partly to the failure of his health, partly, perhaps, to his adoption of Arian views, his congregation declined, and on his resignation in 1783 became extinct. He retained his lectureship to extreme old age. Heterodox on a main point of theology, Flexman was conservative in his religious philosophy, and in later life exhibited 'uncommon ardour' in opposition to materialists and necessarians.

Flexman was remarkable for historical attainments, and especially for his minute and accurate knowledge of the constitutional history of England. His extraordinary memory was invaluable in historical research. His reputation in this respect introduced him to some of the leading politicians of his day, and, having already shown skill as an index-maker, he was appointed (1770) one of the compilers of the general index to the journals of the House of Commons. His plan was adopted by a committee of the house, and the period 1660–97 was assigned to him. He completed his work in four folio volumes (viii–xi.) in 1780; it was his best paid piece of literary work. George Steevens, in conversation with Johnson, happened to mention Flexman's 'exact memory in chronological matters;' Johnson impatiently characterised him as 'the fellow who made the index to my "Ramblers," and set down the name of Milton thus: Milton, *Mr.* John.' Flexman compiled a bibliography appended to his edition of Burnet's 'Own Time,'

1753–4, 8vo, 4 vols.; a memoir and bibliography prefixed to the 'Twenty Sermons,'
1755, 8vo, of Samuel Bourn the younger
[q. v.]; and bibliographies annexed to the
funeral sermons for Samuel Chandler, D.D.
[q.v.], 1766, and Thomas Amory, D.D. [q.v.],
1774. He was a trustee of Dr. Williams's
foundations from 1778 to 1786, and librarian
from 1786 to 1792.

In 'Psalms and Hymns for Divine Worship,' 1760, 12mo, edited by Michael Pope,
presbyterian minister of Leather Lane, are
four compositions, signed ' *F.*,' which were
contributed by Flexman. One of them appears, with improvements, in Kippis's 'Collection,' 1795, 12mo, and has found a place
in similar collections of more recent date.

During his last years Flexman was subject
to a painful disorder, which seems to have
weakened his mind. He died on 14 June
1795, at the house of his daughter in Prescot
Street, Goodman's Fields. His funeral sermon was preached by Abraham Rees, D.D.,
of the 'Cyclopædia.' He married (1747) a
daughter of a member of his congregation at
Bradford, named Yerbury.

Flexman's contributions to periodical literature have not been identified. Besides the
above he published: 1. 'The Connexion and
Harmony of Religion and Virtue,' &c., 1752,
8vo (charity sermon). 2. 'Critical, Historical, and Political Miscellanies,' &c., 1752,
8vo; 1762, 8vo. 3. 'The Plan of Divine
Worship in the Churches of Protestant Dissenters,' &c., 1754, 8vo (against forms of
prayer). 4. 'The Nature and Advantage of
a Religious Education,' &c., 1770, 8vo (sermon). Also funeral sermon for Amory, 1774,
8vo.

[Rees's Funeral Sermon, 1795; Protestant
Dissenters' Magazine, 1795, pp. 264, 399 sq.;
Wilson's Dissenting Churches, 1808, iv. 361 sq.;
Murch's Hist. Presb. and Gen. Bapt. Churches in
West of Engl. 1835, pp. 64, 67, 456; Boswell's
Johnson (Wright), 1859, viii. 327; Jeremy's
Presbyterian Fund, 1885, p. 170; manuscript
minutes of Exeter assembly (May 1723 to Sep-
tember 1728) in Dr. Williams's Library; manu-
script list of ordinations, preserved in the records
of the Exeter assembly.]   A. G.

FLEXMORE, RICHARD (1824–1860),
pantomimist, whose real name was Richard
Flexmore Geatter, son of Richard Flexmore
Geatter, a well-known dancer, who died at
an early age, was born at Kennington, London, 15 Sept. 1824. At the age of eight he
commenced his theatrical career at the Victoria Theatre, where his juvenile drollery
soon attracted attention. In 1835 he appeared at a small theatre which then existed
in Chelsea in a fantastic piece called 'The

Man in the Moon,' and danced very effectively
a burlesque shadow dance. He subsequently
became a pupil of Mr. Frampton, and showed
great aptitude for stage business in his own
peculiar line. As a grotesque dancer his
services soon became in request at various
theatres, and in 1844 he appeared as clown
at the Grecian Saloon. The winter following
he made his first great hit when taking the
part of clown at the Olympic Theatre, which
was then under the management of T. D.
Davenport. His wonderful activity and
abundant flow of animal spirits became
quickly recognised, and he was then engaged
for the Princess's Theatre, where he remained
for several seasons. On 28 July 1849 he
married, at St. Mary's parish church, Lambeth, Francisca Christophosa, daughter of
Jean Baptiste Auriol, the famous French
clown, and with her acted with great success
in the chief cities of the continent. He afterwards appeared at the Strand, the Adelphi,
and Covent Garden theatres, and more recently at Drury Lane, where he performed in
the pantomime 'Jack-in-the-Box' at Christmas 1859. He was especially noted for his
close and natural imitation of the leading
dancers of the day, such as Perrot, Carlotta
Grisi, Taglioni, Cerito, and others; but although chiefly known as a dancing clown, he
could when required also take the part of
clown *à la* Grimaldi in a very efficient manner, and was one of the most diverting
pantomimists who ever delighted a holiday
audience. His physical strength and activity
were remarkable; but he overtaxed his powers
to obtain the applause of the public, and
brought on a consumption, of which he died
at 66 Hercules Buildings, Lambeth, London,
20 Aug. 1860, and was buried at Kensal
Green on 27 Aug. His widow, who married
her cousin, Monsieur Auriol, died in Paris
3 Sept. 1862. His mother, Ann Flexmore
Geatter, whom he had supported for many
years, died 26 Dec. 1869, aged 88.

[Gent. Mag., October 1860, p. 440; Times,
23 Aug. 1860, p. 8; Era, 26 Aug. 1860, p. 10,
2 Sept. p. 10; Illustrated Sporting and Dramatic
News, 19 Dec. 1874, p. 268 (portrait), 18 Dec.
1875, p. 294; Mrs. Evans Bell's A First Appearance, 1872, i. 129–33, iii. 195–7.]   G. C. B.

FLICCIUS or FLICCUS, GERBARUS,
GERLACHUS or GERBICUS (*fl.* 1546–
1554), a native of Germany, was the painter
of the interesting portrait of Archbishop
Cranmer which was presented to the British
Museum in 1776 by John Michell, M.P., of
Bayfield Hall, Norfolk, and in June 1879
was transferred to the National Portrait
Gallery. This portrait was painted in 1546,

when the archbishop was fifty-seven years of age, and shows Cranmer without the long white beard which he suffered to grow after Henry VIII's death in the following year. The picture is signed 'Gerbarus Fliccus Germanicus faciebat.' It has been frequently engraved, viz. in Thoroton's 'History of Nottinghamshire' (1677), Strype's 'Memorials of Cranmer,' Lodge's 'Illustrious Portraits,' and other works. Other portraits from the hand of the same painter have been noted, viz. 'Thomas, first Lord Darcy of Chiche' (painted in 1551), at Irnham in Lincolnshire; 'James, second Earl of Douglas and Mar' (painted in 1547), at Newbattle Abbey, East Lothian; and others. The last-named portrait, which is probably a copy of an older one, as the earl was killed at Otterbourne in 1388, is stated to be signed 'Gerbicus Flicciis Germanicus faciebat ætatis 40.' A curious double portrait was offered for sale at Christie's auction-rooms on 25 July 1881; it contained two small portraits of the painter and a friend named Strangways, who were fellow-prisoners in London at the time (1554) when it was painted, and the painting was executed in prison, according to the inscriptions. This picture was then in the possession of Robert de Ruffiero, Belsize Park Road, and had formerly belonged to Dr. Edward Monkhouse, F.S.A. All these portraits are painted in the style of Lucas Cranach, the great Lutheran painter of Saxony, and this, taken with the date of imprisonment and the painter's connection with Cranmer, would point to his being one of the victims of the religious persecutions of Queen Mary's reign and himself an ardent protestant.

[J. G. Nichols, in Archæologia, xxxix. 25; Cat. of the National Portrait Gallery, 1888; information from G. Scharf, C.B., F.S.A.]   L. C.

FLIGHT, BENJAMIN (1767?–1847), organ-builder, was son of Benjamin Flight, of the firm of Flight & Kelly, organ-builders. In conjunction with his son J. Flight and Joseph Robson he constructed the apollonicon, an instrument with five manuals, forty-five stops, and three barrels. This ingenious contrivance was exhibited in 1817 and the following years until 1840. The partnership with Robson was afterwards dissolved, but Flight continued to interest himself in certain inventions and improvements in the mechanism of organs. He died, aged 80, in 1847, leaving the business in the hands of his son, J. Flight, who carried it on until 1885.

[Grove's Dict. i. 74, 532; Rees's Cyclopædia, vol. xxv. under 'Organs;' private information.]
L. M. M.

FLIGHT, WALTER (1841–1885), mineralogist, son of William P. Flight of Winchester, was born in Winchester 21 Jan. 1841. He was educated at Queenwood College, Hampshire, where Debus then taught chemistry and Professor Tyndall physics, and in after life Debus was his constant friend. After coming of age Flight proceeded to Germany and spent the winter session of 1863–1864 studying chemistry under Professor Heintz at the university of Halle. He passed the next two years at Heidelberg, and acquired a thorough knowledge of chemistry. His studies in Germany were completed at Berlin, where he acted for some time as secretary and chemical assistant to Professor Hofmann. In 1867 Flight returned to England, and took the degree of doctor of science at London University. In 1868 he was appointed assistant examiner there in chemistry under Professor Debus. On 5 Sept. 1867 he became an assistant in the mineralogical department of the British Museum under Professor N. Story-Maskelyne. In the laboratory, which was now specially fitted up, he commenced a series of researches upon the mineral constituents of meteorites and their occluded gases, which rapidly brought him into notice. He was appointed examiner in chemistry and physics at the Royal Military Academy, Woolwich, in 1868, and in 1876 examiner to the Royal Military Academy, Cheltenham. He also acted for several years as a member of the committee on luminous meteors appointed by the British Association. In 1880 he married Kate, daughter of Dr. Fell of Ambleside.

Flight wrote twenty-one papers on scientific subjects, of which the first three, all on chemical subjects, appeared in German periodicals in 1864–5–70. The later papers were chiefly upon meteorites, dealing in detail with the recorded circumstances of their fall, and with their mineralogical and chemical constituents; several, written in conjunction with Professor Story-Maskelyne, give accounts, published in the 'Philosophical Transactions,' of the meteorites which fell at Rowton in Shropshire, at Middlesborough, and at Cranbourne in Australia. A paper, thus jointly written, on 'Francolite, Vivianite, and Cronstedtite from Cornwall,' appeared in the 'Journal of the Chemical Society' for 1871. The last paper Flight wrote was on the meteorite of Alfianello in Italy. Between 1875 and 1883 Flight contributed a series of twenty-three papers to the 'Geological Magazine,' entitled 'A Chapter in the History of Meteorites' (published in book form in 1887). Flight was elected a fellow of the Royal Society on 7 June 1883. In 1884 he was taken so seriously ill that he was compelled to resign his post in the British Museum, and died on 4 Nov. 1885, leaving a widow and three young children.

[Geol. Mag., December 1885 ; A Chapter in the History of Meteorites, by W. Flight (with obituary notice), 8vo, 224 pp., seven plates and six woodcuts, 1887.]   W. J. H.

FLINDELL, THOMAS (1767–1824), newspaper editor and printer, was born in 1767 at Helford, in the parish of Manaccan, Cornwall, and was, to use his own words, 'bred an illiterate half-seaman.' He was apprenticed to a printer, and in 1790, when twenty-three years old, was sent to Yorkshire to conduct the 'Doncaster Gazette,' the circulation of which he largely increased through his happy audacity in anticipating the decision of the jury in the trials of Hardy and Horne Tooke by publishing the verdict of 'not guilty.' About 1798 he returned to Helston in his native county, where he opened business as a printer, starting the 'Stannary Press,' and publishing several works by the Rev. Richard Polwhele and Dr. Hawker, as well as an edition of Pope's 'Essay on Man.' In 1800 he removed to Falmouth, and in that year was published the first volume of his impression of the Bible, which he issued in numbers. The introduction and notes to three of the books of the Old Testament were contributed by the Rev. John Whitaker, and Polwhele wrote the notes on the other books; but the work was left incomplete, and copies are now very scarce. The first number of the 'Cornwall Gazette and Falmouth Packet,' a weekly paper, was started at Falmouth under his editorship on 7 March 1801, and it lasted until 16 Oct. 1802, when it ceased through the bankruptcy of his partners. Flindell possessed abundant energy and a vigorous style of composition, and when backed by the support of the leading Cornish gentry he was emboldened into establishing at Truro in the following year a larger newspaper called the 'Royal Cornwall Gazette.' Its first number appeared on 2 July 1803, and it still survives. A rival newspaper in the opposite political interest was started in a few years, when the two editors (Flindell and Edward Budd) opened a fierce controversy in their own journals and in separate publications. To damage his political antagonist Flindell would have published the details of a private conversation, and a letter of remonstrance with him on this point is in the 'Life of Samuel Drew,' pp. 369–72. He parted with his interest in this paper in 1811, but he continued the printing business at Truro during the next year. His next venture was the 'Western Luminary,' a weekly newspaper of tory principles, which he set on foot at Exeter early in 1813. It prospered for some years, until the fierceness of his political zeal led him to stigmatise Queen Caroline as 'notoriously devoted to Bacchus and Venus,' when Wetherell brought the matter before the House of Commons (24 and 25 July 1820), and moved that it was a breach of the house's privileges. This was not unreasonably resisted by Lord Castlereagh, and as it appeared in the subsequent discussion that a prosecution would be instituted the motion was withdrawn. For this indiscretion Flindell was prosecuted, and on 19 March 1821 was sentenced to an imprisonment of eight months in Exeter gaol. During his confinement he composed a volume entitled 'Prison Recreations: the philosophy of reason and revelation attempted, with a view to the restoration of the theory of the Bible on the ruins of infidelity.' The discussion of religious topics was one of his chief pleasures, and the pages of his Exeter paper contained a lengthened controversy from three divines, named Cleeve, Dennis, and Carpenter, on the Trinitarian question, which Flindell 'closed at last in a somewhat perplexed manner,' and provoked from Colton the epigram printed in Archdeacon Wrangham's catalogue of his English library, p. 564, to the effect that the three parsons had proved 'not one incomprehensible but three,' and Flindell had shown 'not three incomprehensible but one.' His prison restraint impaired his health ; he wrote in January 1824 that he was breaking up fast, and his illness was aggravated by his indignation at the severe treatment which he had received, while others who had used equally strong language had escaped scot-free. After a protracted illness he died at Exeter on 11 July 1824, aged 57. His wife and a numerous family survived him ; he had eight children in 1806, some of whom are mentioned in Boase's 'Collectanea Cornub.,' p. 251. Several letters by Flindell are in J. E. Ryland's 'Kitto,' pp. 124–9, 155; Polwhele's 'Traditions and Recollections,' ii. 778–81; 'Reminiscences,' i. 125–6; and 'Biographical Sketches in Cornwall,' ii. 57. 'A man of strong understanding, though by no means polished or refined,' was Polwhele's accurate estimate of Flindell's character.

[Boase and Courtney's Bibl. Cornub. ; Andrews's British Journalism, ii. 128–33; Timperley's Typographical Anecdotes, pp. 853, 879, 893; Gent. Mag. 1824, ii. 93 ; Hansard, new ser. ii. 586–609.]   W. P. C.

FLINDERS, MATTHEW (1774–1814), captain in the navy, hydrographer and discoverer, was born on 16 March 1774 at Donington, near Boston in Lincolnshire, where his father, grandfather, and great-grandfather had practised as surgeons. He was intended for the same profession, but being, in his own phrase, 'induced to go to sea, against the wish of friends, from reading "Robinson Crusoe,"' he applied himself to the study of geometry and navigation with such assiduity that he obtained a competent knowledge of them without a master or other assistance. In May 1790, acting, it would seem, on the advice of a cousin who was governess in the family of Captain (afterwards Sir Thomas) Pasley, he offered himself on board Captain Pasley's ship, the Scipio, at Chatham. Pasley received him kindly, placed him on the quarter-deck, took him with him to the Bellerophon during the Spanish armament, and in the end of the year, when the Bellerophon was paid off, sent him to the Providence with Captain William Bligh [q. v.], on the point of sailing to the South Sea on his second and successful attempt to transplant the bread-fruit tree to the West Indies. His preliminary study of navigation now proved serviceable, and he was entrusted by Bligh with a greater share of the navigation and chart-drawing than was due to his few months' service at sea. On his return to England in 1793 Commodore Pasley was again commissioning the Bellerophon, and again took Flinders with him. On returning to Portsmouth after the battle of 1 June, Flinders was taken by Captain Waterhouse, formerly a lieutenant of the Bellerophon, on board the Reliance, which he was then fitting out for a voyage to New South Wales, in order to carry out Captain John Hunter [q. v.], the newly appointed governor of the colony. The Reliance arrived at Port Jackson in September 1795, and for the next five years Flinders devoted the whole of the time that he could be spared from the duties of the ship to exploring or surveying the adjacent parts of Australia. In this work he was associated with the surgeon of the Reliance, George Bass [q. v.], who, while Flinders was detained on board, made an extended coasting voyage by himself in a whaleboat. Bass's observations were, however, so imperfect that it was not till they were plotted, after his return, that the meaning of what he had done became apparent. It was then seen that he must have passed between New South Wales and Van Diemen's Land, till then believed to be connected with it, a discovery which the governor considered so important that, in September 1798, he appointed Flinders to command the Norfolk, a sloop of twenty-five tons, and despatched him to examine behind the Furneaux Islands, with instructions, if he found a strait, to pass through it, sail round Van

Diemen's Land, and return by the south and east sides. This was happily done in a voyage extending from 7 Oct. to 11 Jan. 1799, and the existence of the strait being thus demonstrated the governor, acting on Flinders's suggestion, gave it the name of Bass's Strait. It is unnecessary to speak in detail of the many other coasting voyages which Flinders made at this period, in boats varying in size from an 8-foot dingey to the sloop of twenty-five tons. During the commission of the Reliance he had, by his own exertions, allowed indeed and sanctioned by the governor, explored and in a rough way surveyed the coast from Hervey Bay in the north to the circuit of Van Diemen's Land in the south.

When the Reliance arrived in England in the latter part of 1800, and some account of the new discoveries was made public, a desire was at once expressed for a more systematic examination of these coasts. Sir Joseph Banks was earnest in the cause, and, mainly at his instigation, an expedition for that purpose was resolved on. Flinders had already been promoted to the rank of lieutenant on 31 Jan. 1798, and was now, on Banks's recommendation, appointed to command the Xenophon, receiving the rank of commander a few weeks later, 16 Feb. 1801. The Xenophon, a north-country ship of 334 tons which had been bought into the navy some years before, was now rechristened the Investigator, and was fitted out in a very liberal manner, the East India Company also allowing the officers 600l. for their outfit. The instructions, dated 22 June 1801, prescribed the survey of New Holland, beginning with King George's Sound and the south coast. Provided with these, with all existing charts and books of voyages, and with a passport from the French government, the Investigator sailed from Spithead on 18 July 1801. Touching in Simon's Bay, from which she sailed on 9 Nov., on 6 Dec. she was off Cape Leeuwin, and on the 8th arrived in King George's Sound. This had already been examined by Vancouver in 1791, and was now more carefully surveyed by Flinders, after which he examined, in more or less detail, the whole coastline to the eastward as far as Port Phillip. The greater part of this was new ground, seen for the first time, and the names given by Flinders to the different bays, gulfs, headlands, and islands still call attention to the names of the officers of the Investigator, to some of the incidents of the voyage, and to the fact that the captain, his brother, the second lieutenant, and a midshipman named John Franklin [q. v.] were natives of Lincolnshire. Cape Catastrophe commemorates the loss of the cutter with her crew and two officers, whose names, Thistle and Taylor, live in two neighbouring islands. Hard by is Memory Cove, and a few miles further are Port Lincoln, Cape Donington, Boston Island, Spalding Cove, Grantham Island, and Spilsby Island, one of the Sir Joseph Banks group. On Kangaroo Island they found a countless number of kangaroos, of which they killed thirty-one, knocking them down with sticks. On 8 April, off Encounter Bay, they met the French exploring ship Géographe, under the command of Captain Nicolas Baudin, of his conversation with whom Flinders has left an amusing account. Whether from the excitement of meeting the French ship or from the state of the weather, which prevented the ship's entering the bay, the embouchure of the Darling escaped his notice, but with this exception he seems to have obtained a chart of the coast which, under the circumstances of a running survey —and, for the most part, it was nothing more—was wonderfully accurate, and is still the basis of our admiralty charts. From Port Phillip eastward the coast which had been first explored by Bass had been examined more closely by Lieutenant Grant of the Lady Nelson in 1800 (JAMES GRANT, *A Voyage in the Lady Nelson to New South Wales*, London, 4to, 1803)—a priority of discovery and survey which was contested by the French, who, in ignorance of Grant's work, also surveyed the coast in 1802, renaming the several noticeable points, not only in that part, but also in that further west, which had been examined by Flinders (MM. PERON et FREYCINET, *Voyage aux Terres Australes*, 1800-4, Paris, 1807-16). On 9 May 1802 the Investigator arrived at Port Jackson, where she found the Lady Nelson, ordered to act as her tender during the further progress of the survey. While the ship was refitting, an observatory was established on shore under the charge of Lieutenant Flinders and Franklin. The ship's company was badly in want of fresh provisions, but the price was prohibitive; none could be purchased on the public account, and all that could be done was to pay the men what savings' allowance was due, so that they might buy some for themselves, when fortunately the Géographe came in in a very distressed state, owing to the ravages of scurvy, so that out of a complement of 170 not more than twelve were capable of doing their duty. All the resources of the colony were at once put at their disposal, and some few cattle which the governor had as breeding stock were slaughtered for the stranger. One quarter of beef—only one—Flinders managed to secure for his own men.

On 22 July the Investigator sailed from Port Jackson, with the Lady Nelson, as a tender, in company. The tender proved, however, of but little use; she was so bad a sailer that she retarded the work, and, after being aground and having lost part of her false keel, was worse than ever. She was accordingly sent back, and the Investigator, rounding Cape York on 31 Oct., proceeded with the survey of the Gulf of Carpentaria. The ship, however, was leaking badly; on examination it was found that many of her timbers were rotten, and the examining officers reported that if she had fine weather she might last six months without much risk. Flinders was naturally much disappointed. He had hoped 'to make so accurate an investigation of the shores of Terra Australis that no future voyage to the country should be necessary.' This was now impossible. He finished the survey of the Gulf of Carpentaria, and to the westward as far as Arnhem Bay; then finding his men sickly went to Timor for refreshments, and returned to Port Jackson on 9 June 1803. The ship was then officially surveyed and pronounced incapable of being repaired. Flinders therefore, in consultation with the governor, determined to go home as a passenger in the Porpoise, an old Spanish prize attached to the colony. Fowler, the first lieutenant, of the Investigator, was appointed to command her, with twenty-two officers and men; the rest of the ship's company staying at Port Jackson to await Flinders's return with another vessel. She put to sea on 10 Aug. in company with the East India Company's ship Bridgewater and the Cato of London; and standing to the north on the 17th, the Porpoise and Cato both struck on Wreck Reef. The Porpoise stuck fast, but the Cato rolled over and sank in deep water, her men having barely time to scramble on shore. The Bridgewater sailed away, leaving them to their fate; and after earnest deliberation, it was determined that Flinders should attempt to fetch Port Jackson in one of the boats. This he succeeded in doing, and the governor at once engaged the Rolla, bound to China, to relieve the party and to carry them on to Canton; two schooners accompanying her; one to bring back to Port Jackson those who preferred it, and one, the Cumberland of twenty-nine tons, to go with Flinders to England. At the wreck the master, the boatswain, and eight men agreed to accompany him on this risky voyage; and the little craft parted from the Rolla on 11 Oct., passing through Torres Straits. In crossing the Indian Ocean the Cumberland proved to be very leaky; her pumps were worn out and the labour was excessive; so much so that Flinders determined to fetch Mauritius in hopes of finding some more convenient way of getting home. According to his last news from home France and England were at peace; and even if not, he believed that the passport given him by the French government before he left England would meet the case. Unfortunately, as the instructions given him by Governor King, on leaving Port Jackson, did not clearly warrant his touching at Mauritius, he considered it prudent to state his reasons in the log; in doing which he laid little stress on the necessities of his case, but dwelt, with the ardour of a surveyor, on the opportunities that would be afforded him of obtaining information on many points of interest. He anchored on 15 Dec. in Baie du Cap, from which he was directed to go round to Port Louis and see the governor, M. Decaen. Decaen at once objected that the passport was for the Investigator, and had no mention of the Cumberland. Flinders was therefore detained, his men were made prisoners, and his books and papers taken for examination. The last entry in his log was sufficient to excite suspicion; and Flinders, burning with anxiety to get to England and renew his survey, appears, even from his own account, to have acted with want of temper and tact. The governor was omnipotent; his personal ill-will put the worst construction on Flinders's unlucky explanations; he declared that the man was there as a spy, attempting to take a base advantage of the passport which had been granted to aid a scientific voyage. Flinders was accordingly kept in close confinement; and though, after nearly two years, he was allowed to reside in the country with leave to go about within two leagues of the house, his imprisonment was continued for nearly seven years. All exchanges were refused; instructions for his release were sent out from France, but Decaen chose to consider them optional, or not sufficiently explicit, and still detained him; nor did he release him till 7 June 1810, when he gave him permission to return to England, by Bombay, on parole not to serve against France during the course of the war. Accordingly, on 9 June, Flinders left Mauritius in a cartel for Bombay, but meeting with a man-of-war sloop bound to the Cape, he took passage in her to that place, where he found a ship going to England. He arrived at Portsmouth on 24 Oct. 1810. As soon as his release was known in England, he had been promoted to post rank, with seniority dated back as far as the patent of the existing board of admiralty would allow, 7 May 1810. It was admitted that had he

come home in the Cumberland or at that time, he would have been then, in 1804, promoted; but it was impossible to date the commission back without an order from the king in council, which would involve more trouble than the admiralty were willing to undertake.

A few months after his return he was desired to prepare a narrative of his voyage, to which task he steadily devoted himself for the next three years. The sedentary employment aggravated the symptoms of a disease due probably, in its origin, to the hardships to which he had been exposed, and which had become more developed during the term of his long imprisonment. He lived to complete his work, and died, 19 July 1814, shortly before it was published. He had married in April 1801, while fitting out the Investigator, and at his death left one daughter, a child two years old.

Flinders appears to have had an extraordinary natural gift as a surveyor, so that with little or no instruction he became one of the best of the hydrographers who have graced our naval service. His survey of a large proportion of the Australian coast, though carried out under great disadvantages, has stood the test of time, and forms the basis of our modern charts. He was also one of the first, if not actually the first, to investigate the error of the compass due to the attraction of the iron in the ship, and contributed a paper on the subject to the Royal Society, written while detained in Mauritius (*Phil. Trans.* 1805, p. 187).

[The principal authority for Flinders's professional life and for the history of his work is his own narrative: A Voyage to Terra Australis undertaken for the purpose of completing the discovery of that vast country, and prosecuted in the years 1801–2–3, in his Majesty's ship the Investigator, and subsequently in the armed vessel Porpoise and Cumberland schooner, with an account of the shipwreck of the Porpoise, arrival of the Cumberland at Mauritius, and imprisonment of the commander during six years and a half in that island (2 vols. 4to, with atlas fo. 1814); see also Observations on the Coasts of Van Diemen's Land, on Bass's Straits, its Islands, and on parts of the Coasts of New South Wales (4to, 1801). The memoir in the Naval Chronicle, xxxii. 177 (with a portrait), is based on information supplied by Flinders himself; it is in this (p. 182 *n*.) that the suggestion was first made to give the name of Australia or Australasia to 'the tract of land hitherto most unscientifically called "New Holland,"' and which Flinders wrote of as Terra Australis. His correspondence with Sir Joseph Banks and many letters from Robert Brown (1773–1858) [q. v.], the botanist of the Investigator, are in Addit.

MSS. 32439 passim, and 32441, ff. 424–33. His correspondence with Sir Edward Pellew in 1805 is in the Public Record Office, Admirals' Despatches (East Indies), vol. 18.]   J. K. L.

FLINTER, GEORGE DAWSON (*d.* 1838), soldier of fortune, by birth an Irishman, entered the British army in 1811 as an ensign in the 7th West India regiment of foot, and was advanced to the rank of lieutenant on 22 July 1813. He was sent with his regiment to Curaçao in the West Indies in 1812, and in 1815 visited Caracas, then in the throes of an unusually bloody and exasperated civil war, in which many horrible atrocities were committed. Here he acted as interpreter to the British embassy. In the following year he was placed on the half-pay list, and seeing no prospect of promotion in the British service, he fixed his residence at Caracas, where he was treated with great distinction by the governor-general Gagigal, and obtained employment as interpreter between the Spaniards and the English and Americans. He afterwards travelled through most of the European colonies in the West Indies and on the continent of America, married a Spanish American lady, through whom he acquired a large property in land and slaves, obtained a commission in the Spanish army, and though remaining on the British half-pay list until 1832, had for some years before that date held the position of a staff officer in the Spanish service. On the outbreak of the Carlist war in 1833 he declared for Isabella, and in 1834–5 he served under Mina and Valdez in their unsuccessful operations against Zumalacarregui in the Basque provinces. In 1836, while engaged in organising the militia in Estremadura, he was surprised by some of the troops of Gomez and Cabrera, taken prisoner, and thrown into a loathsome dungeon, from which by the connivance of his gaoler he contrived to escape, and made his way to Madrid. He was then placed in command of Toledo, whence on 18 Feb. 1838 he made a sortie, inflicting a severe defeat on the Carlists under Jara and Peco, who were in great force in the neighbourhood. In this action he placed nearly eighteen hundred of the enemy *hors de combat* without the loss of a single man killed or wounded. On his return to Toledo on the 20th, he was saluted by the municipal authorities as the liberator of the province, and on the 22nd the Cortes recognised his services by a vote of thanks. On 16 March, though outnumbered by two to one, he drove Basileo Garcia out of Val de Penas, but was prevented by lack of reinforcements from improving his advantage. His conduct on this occasion was severely censured by the Spanish govern-

ment, and he was removed from his command. Maddened by disappointment and disgust, he committed suicide at Madrid by cutting his throat on 9 Sept. 1838. Flinter was a knight of the royal order of Isabella the Catholic, and the author of the following works: 1. 'The History of the Revolution of Caracas, comprising an impartial Narrative of the Atrocities committed by the contending parties, illustrating the real state of the contest both in a commercial and political point of view. Together with a Description of the Llaneros, or People of the Plains of South America,' London, 1819, 8vo. 2. 'An Account of the present State of the Island of Puerto Rico,' London, 1834, 8vo. 3. 'Consideraciones sobre la España y sus Colonias,' Madrid, 1834.

[Army Lists 1812, 1813, 1816, 1832; Gent. Mag. 1838, ii. 553; Ann. Reg. 1838, pp. 422–3; App. to Chron. p. 224; Borrow's Bible in Spain (Murray's Home and Colonial Library), cap. xxxiv.]   J. M. R.

FLINTOFT, LUKE (*d.* 1727), composer, took the degree of B.A. at Queens' College, Cambridge, in 1700, and was appointed priest-vicar at Lincoln Cathedral in 1704. He remained there until 1714. On 4 Dec. 1715 he was sworn as a gentleman of the Chapel Royal, and is described in the 'Cheque Book' as 'from Worcester,' which therefore was probably his birthplace. On 9 July 1719 he was appointed reader in Whitehall Chapel, and was subsequently made a minor canon of Westminster. He died on 3 Nov. 1727, and was buried in the cloisters of Westminster Abbey. His claim to a place in musical history depends upon the question whether a certain 'double chant' in G minor, attributed to him, is or is not the first specimen of the kind in existence. The arguments for and against this will be found in 'Notes and Queries,' 3rd ser. x. 206, xi. 267, 391, and 445.

[Grove's Dict. i. 533; Bemrose's Chant Book; Cheque Book of the Chapel Royal, ed. Rimbault; Graduati Cantabr. (1823), p. 172; Notes and Queries, as above.]   J. A. F. M.

FLITCROFT, HENRY (1697–1769), architect, son of Jeffery Flitcroft, gardener to William III at Hampton Court, and grandson of Jeffery Flitcroft of Twiss Green, Winwick, Lancashire, was born on 29 Aug. 1697, and on 6 Nov. 1711 was apprenticed to Thomas Morris, citizen and joiner of London, for seven years, being admitted to the freedom of that company on 3 Nov. 1719. It is said that Flitcroft was employed as a carpenter in the house of Richard Boyle, third earl of Burlington [q. v.], and broke his leg by falling from a scaffold; hence he attracted the notice of the earl, who employed him as draughtsman on the edition of Inigo Jones's designs, published by Kent in 1727 at the Earl of Burlington's expense; some of these drawings are in the library of the Royal Institute of British Architects. Burlington's patronage insured Flitcroft's success, and even gained the architect the nickname of 'Burlington Harry.' In 1726 Flitcroft was employed in the office of the board of works; he continued to be engaged as clerk of the works at Whitehall, St. James's, and Westminster, as well as at Richmond and Kew, until 20 Nov. 1746, when he was appointed master-carpenter; on 10 May 1748 he succeeded Kent as master-mason; and on 10 March 1758 he succeeded Ripley as comptroller of the works in England, which post he held until his death. In 1729 Flitcroft designed a mansion for John Baynes near Havering in Essex; in 1733 he was commissioned to make the necessary alterations in Carlton House, then recently purchased, for Frederick, prince of Wales. In 1731 he entered into a contract to pull down the old church of St. Giles-in-the-Fields and to erect a new church and steeple in its place; the new church was opened in 1734, having been erected at a cost of over 10,000l., exceeding the original estimate by about 3,000l. It is perhaps too closely copied from Gibbs's church of St. Martin-in-the-Fields. In 1737-9 Flitcroft was employed in erecting the church of St. Olave, Tooley Street, Southwark, which was completed at a cost of 5,000l. About 1745 he designed the church of St. John at Hampstead. Flitcroft made considerable alterations in Wentworth House, Yorkshire, for the Marquis of Rockingham, and in Woburn Abbey, Bedfordshire, for the Duke of Bedford; in 1747 he designed for Mary Lepel, lady Hervey, a house in St. James's Place, looking on the Green Park, afterwards occupied by the Earl of Moira; and in 1749 he rebuilt the church at Wimpole in Cambridgeshire. Flitcroft's general repute led to his being elected sheriff of London and Middlesex in June 1745, but he paid the fine to be excused serving the office; in 1747 he paid a similar fine on being elected renter warden of the Joiners' Company. He built for himself a house at Frognal, Hampstead, called Montagu Grove, where he resided for some time. He died on 25 Feb. 1769, in his seventy-second year, and was buried at Teddington in Middlesex. In the Royal Library at the British Museum there is a volume of architectural drawings and designs by Flitcroft, executed about 1750, and dedicated to William, duke of Cumberland.

[The Dictionary of Architecture; Redgrave's Dict. of Artists; Cunningham's Handbook to London.]   L. C.

FLOOD, Sir FREDERICK (1741-1824), Irish politician, was the younger son of John Flood of Farmley, county Kilkenny, and nephew of Warden Flood, chief justice of the court of king's bench in Ireland, the father of the Right Hon. Henry Flood [q. v.] He was born in 1741, and was educated at Trinity College, Dublin, where he proceeded B.A. in 1761, M.A. in 1764, LL.B. in 1766, and LL.D. in 1772. He was called to the Irish bar in 1763, soon attained considerable legal practice, and in the social circles of Dublin was immensely popular from his wit and oddity. He succeeded to handsome estates from both his parents, and in 1776 was elected to the Irish House of Commons as member for Enniscorthy. He sat for that constituency till 1783. From 1783 to 1790 he was M.P. for Ardfert, and in 1796-7 for Carlow borough. His relationship to Henry Flood did more for his reputation than his own abilities, and he consistently followed in his cousin's footsteps. In 1778 he was made a K.C. and elected a bencher of the King's Inns, and on 3 June 1780 he was created a baronet of Ireland 'of Newton Ormonde, co. Kilkenny, and Banna Lodge, co. Wexford.' Two years later he married Lady Juliana Annesley, daughter of the fifth Earl of Anglesey, and he took a prominent part in the volunteer movement, being elected colonel of the Wexford regiment. In many debates which preceded the abolition of the Irish parliament Flood was a frequent speaker. Sir Jonah Barrington calls him an ostentatious blunderer, whose 'bulls' did not contain the pith of sound sense which underlay the mistakes of Sir Boyle Roche. He adds that Flood would rashly accept any suggestions made to him while speaking, and one day, just after he had declared 'that the magistrates of Wexford deserved the thanks of the lord-lieutenant,' he added, on some wit's suggestion, 'and should be whipped at the cart's tail' (Barrington, Personal Sketches, i. 111). He steadily opposed the Act of Union, but when that measure was carried he did not retire from politics, but sat in the united House of Commons for the county of Wexford from 1812 to 1818. He made no particular impression there. His only son died unmarried in 1800, and it was proposed to perpetuate Flood's title by creating him a baronet of the United Kingdom, with remainder to his only daughter Frances, who was married to Richard Solly, esq. He died before the patent for this new honour had passed the great seal on 1 Feb. 1824, and left his estates to his grandson, Richard Solly, who took the name of Flood in addition to his own.

[Burke's Extinct Baronetage; Sir Jonah Barrington's Memoirs and Personal Sketches; Grattan's Life and Times of Henry Grattan; Hardy's Life of Lord Charlemont.] H. M. S.

FLOOD, HENRY (1732–1791), statesman and orator, illegitimate son of the Right Hon. Warden Flood, chief justice of the king's bench in Ireland, was born in 1732, and when sixteen entered Trinity College, Dublin, as a fellow commoner. After three years' residence he matriculated at Christ Church, Oxford, where he graduated M.A. 1752. He was admitted a member of the Inner Temple on 19 Jan. 1750, and for some time pursued the study of the law in England. He returned to Ireland in his twenty-seventh year, and having been elected a member for the county of Kilkenny in the Irish House of Commons, he took his seat on the opposition benches in 1759. Parliament was dissolved upon the death of George II in the following year, and Flood was returned for the borough of Callan in the place of James Agar, who was declared 'not duly elected.' It is generally asserted that Flood's maiden speech was an attack upon Primate Stone, who at that time was the recognised leader of the English party, and it is related that 'during the first part of Mr. Flood's speech, his grace, who was in the House of Commons, and did not know precisely what part the new member would take, declared that he had great hopes of him; when Flood sat down his grace asserted, with some vehemence, that a duller gentleman he had never heard' (*Memoirs of the Earl of Charlemont*, i. 157). His first speech, however, of which there is any authentic record was delivered on 12 Oct. 1763 (CALDWELL, *Irish Debates*, 1766, i. 31–7). Owing to his eloquence and social position, Flood quickly became the most prominent leader of the popular party, and it was through his untiring exertions that a powerful opposition was at length organised within the Irish House of Commons. The principal objects which Flood kept steadily in view were the shortening of the duration of parliaments, the reduction of pensions, the creation of a constitutional militia, and the independence of the Irish legislature. But though these measures of reform were frequently brought forward, they were for many years rejected either by parliament or the privy council as a matter of course. For the first seven years of the new reign the political history of Ireland was uneventful, and in 1767 Flood contemplated entering the English House of Commons, but his over-

tures for a seat appear to have been unsuccessful (*Letters to Flood*, p. 42). In October 1767 Lord Townshend went over as the new lord-lieutenant. A different line of policy was adopted by the government, and in the following year the Octennial Bill was passed. With the aid of the undertakers, Flood was able successfully to oppose the ministerial scheme for the augmentation of the Irish army, and parliament was dissolved in May 1768. At the general election Flood was returned for the borough of Longford as well as for Callan, and elected to sit for the latter. About this time he became involved in a quarrel, arising out of the election contest for Callan, with James Agar of Ringwood, with whom he fought two duels. Agar challenged Flood on the second occasion in September 1769. They met in Dunmore Park, near Kilkenny, and the former was mortally wounded. Flood was formally tried at the Kilkenny assizes in April 1770, and a verdict of manslaughter in his own defence was duly returned. In order to break down the power of the undertakers, who were now in alliance with Flood and the popular party, Townshend strongly urged the government to call Flood to office. The advice was not taken, and when the new parliament met in 1769 the money bill was rejected, and a resolution declaring that it had been thrown out 'because it did not take its rise in the House of Commons' was carried by the opposition. On 26 Dec. parliament was suddenly prorogued, and was not summoned again for fourteen months. Flood now systematically opposed the government on every occasion, and devoted all his energies to obtain Townshend's recall. A series of papers relating to recent Irish politics, written by Langrishe, Flood, Grattan, and others, appeared from time to time in the 'Freeman's Journal.' These papers, which created a great sensation, were afterwards published in a collected form under the title of 'Baratariana,' with a dedication to Lord Townshend, written by Grattan. The contributions signed 'Sindercombe,' which have been attributed on insufficient grounds to Hugh Boyd, were written by Flood. Though powerful and well reasoned, they are laboured in style, and 'certainly give no countenance to the notion started at one time that he was the author of the "Letters of Junius"' (LECKY, *Leaders of Public Opinion in Ireland*, p. 75). Townshend was at length recalled in September 1772, and upon the appointment of the Earl of Harcourt as lord-lieutenant the government was conducted for a time on more liberal principles. Flood now ceased from opposition and vigorously supported the introduction of the absentee tax. Harcourt writing to North, 27 Nov. 1773, says: 'Mr. Flood was violent and able in behalf of the bill in a degree almost surpassing everything he had ever uttered before' (*The Harcourt Papers*, ix. 117). But in spite of his eloquence, and without any open hostility on the part of the government, the measure was defeated. After a long period of negotiation Flood in October 1775 accepted the post of vice-treasurer of Ireland, a sinecure worth 3,500*l.* a year. Flood contended that after Townshend's recall 'the only way anything could be effected for the country was by going along with government and making their measures diverge towards public utility' (GRATTAN, *Life*, i. 206); and he seems to have thought that by obtaining a seat in the Irish privy council he would be better able to influence the government for the good of the country. The history of his negotiations for office, as related in the letters of Harcourt and Blaquiere, is by no means creditable to him, and Harcourt, writing to North on 9 Oct. 1775, says: 'Since I was born I never had to deal with so difficult a man, owing principally to his high-strained ideas of his own great importance and popularity. But the acquisition of such a man, however desirable at other times, may prove more than ordinarily valuable in the difficult times we may live to see, and which may afford him a very ample field for the display of his great abilities' (*The Harcourt Papers*, ix. 361). After the general election in 1776 Flood was unseated for Callan, but was subsequently returned at a by-election for the borough of Enniskillen. During Harcourt's administration, and while Flood was in office, an embargo was placed on Irish exports for two years, and four thousand Irish troops, termed by Flood 'armed negotiators,' were sent to America. Both these measures were very unpopular, and to the latter Grattan afterwards referred when describing Flood as standing 'with a metaphor in his mouth and a bribe in his pocket,' and giving 'a base suffrage against the liberty of America, the eventual liberty of Ireland, and the cause of mankind' (GRATTAN, *Life*, iii. 94). When Buckingham became lord-lieutenant, Flood frequently absented himself from the meetings of the privy council. and rarely voted for the government in the House of Commons. He identified himself with the volunteer movement and became colonel of one of the regiments. In 1779, though still a minister, Flood spoke in support of the amendment to the address in favour of free trade. At length his attitude became so hostile to the government that at the

request of the Earl of Carlisle, Buckingham's successor in office, he was in the autumn of 1781 removed from the post of vice-treasurer as well as from his seat in the privy council. When Flood once more took his seat on the opposition benches he found his popularity gone, and his place as leader of the popular party filled by Grattan. On 11 Dec. 1781, in a speech lasting three hours and a half, Flood maintained that the power of the Irish privy council to alter heads of bills before sending them to England rested solely on an erroneous decision of the judges in 1692, but the committee for inquiry for which he asked was refused by a considerable majority (*Parl. Reg.* i. 153–74). A few days afterwards he spoke in the debate on Yelverton's bill for the repeal of Poynings's law, and grievously complained that 'after a service of twenty years in the study of a peculiar question it was taken out of his hands and entirely wrested from him.' 'The hon. gentleman (he added) was erecting a temple of liberty; he hoped therefore at least he should be allowed a niche in the fane.' Whereupon Yelverton cleverly retorted that, as Flood seemed to think he had *espoused* this question, he would remind him that according to the law, 'if any man married a wife and lives with her in constancy it was a crime to take her away from him; but if a man shall separate from his wife, desert and abandon her for seven years, another then might take her up and give her his protection' (*ib.* p. 189). On 22 Feb. 1782 Flood supported Grattan's motion for an address to the king in favour of the independence of the Irish parliament, and in the same year an attempt was made by Montgomery in the House of Commons to obtain Flood's restoration to his old office of vice-treasurer. The Duke of Portland, who succeeded Carlisle as viceroy in April 1782, being anxious to enter into negotiations with Flood, asked for authority to offer him a seat in the Irish privy council, if he should deem it expedient. The nomination, which was intended to be at the option of the viceroy, was by some extraordinary mistake sent directly to the 'Gazette,' and Flood straightway refused to accept the nomination. Legislative independence having been obtained, Flood took up the subject of 'simple repeal,' and contended that the mere repeal of the Declaratory Act (6 Geo. I, c. 5) was not sufficient, but that an act of parliament expressly disclaiming the right to legislate for Ireland should be obtained without delay. In this view he was supported by the greater portion of the volunteers, and by this means Flood in some measure regained his old popularity. Grattan differed with him on the question as well as on the advisability of continuing the volunteer convention, and on 28 Oct. 1783, in the debate on Sir Henry Cavendish's motion for retrenchment in the expenses of the country, the famous collision between the two great Irish orators took place. The speeches of both were full of the bitterest personal invective. Flood, alluding to the grant which parliament had bestowed upon Grattan, referred to him as 'the mendicant patriot who was bought by my country for a sum of money, and then sold my country for prompt payment,' and concluded by saying that 'if the gentleman enters often into this kind of controversy with me, he will not have much to boast of at the end of the session.' While Grattan, after comparing Flood to an 'ill-omen'd bird of night with sepulchral notes, a cadaverous aspect and broken beak,' and asserting that neither minister nor people could trust him, concluded his speech with the following words: 'I therefore tell you in the face of your country, before all the world, and to your beard, you are not an honest man' (ib. ii. 35–43). The quarrel nearly ended in a duel. On their way to a hostile meeting at Blackrock they were arrested and bound over to keep the peace. On 1 Nov. Flood was allowed to make a further speech in vindication of his character, in which he gave an explanation of his political conduct during the whole of his parliamentary career (ib. pp. 61–70). With this incident their friendship of twenty years terminated, but though they never became reconciled, they successfully co-operated in opposing Orde's Commercial Propositions in 1785. At the general election a few months previously Flood had been returned with Curran for the borough of Kilbeggan. In November 1783 the volunteer convention met in Dublin, and Flood was appointed assessor to the committee appointed to draw up a scheme of parliamentary reform. The Bishop of Derry brought forward the question of extending the franchise to the Roman catholics, but was successfully opposed by Flood and Charlemont. At length a comprehensive plan of reform which had been drawn up by Flood, and gave no political rights to the Roman catholics, was agreed to on 28 Nov. 1783. On the following day Flood brought forward the measure in the Irish House of Commons. The house, however, refused to receive the bill by 157 to 77 (*Journals of the Irish House of Commons*, xi. 144), and, resenting the interference of the volunteers, passed a resolution that it had 'now become indispensably necessary to declare that this house will maintain its just rights and privileges against encroachments whatsoever' (ib.) The volunteer convention was dis-

solved, but in March of the following year Flood again brought forward the Reform Bill. Though supported by petitions from twenty-six counties, it was rejected on the question of committal by a majority of 74 (*Parl. Reg.* iii. 13–23, 43–85). Meanwhile, in October 1783, Flood was returned to the English House of Commons as one of the members for Winchester, having purchased his election from the Duke of Chandos for 4,000l. His English career was a failure. As Grattan remarked, 'he misjudged when he transferred himself to the English parliament; he forgot that he was a tree of the forest too old and too great to be transplanted at fifty' (GRATTAN, *Miscellaneous Works*, 1822, p. 118). On 3 Dec. he took part in the debates for the first time, and made a lengthy speech against Fox's East India Bill (*Parl. Hist.* xxiv. 56–9). The subject was one of which he had little knowledge, and by want of tact he managed to prejudice both sides of the house against him. In a curious passage Wraxall thus refers to Flood's speech: 'The slow, measured, and sententious style of enunciation which characterised his eloquence, however calculated to excite admiration in the sister kingdom, appeared to English ears cold, stiff, and deficient in some of the best recommendations to attention. Unfortunately, too, for Flood, one of his own countrymen, Courtenay, instantly opened upon him such a battery of ridicule and wit, seasoned with allusions or reflections of the most personal and painful kind, as seemed to overwhelm the new member' (*Memoirs*, 1884, iii. 185–6). Having had a misunderstanding with the Duke of Chandos, Flood was not returned again for Winchester at the general election in 1784. After two unsuccessful contests for the borough of Seaford he obtained the seat upon petition. On 15 Feb. 1787 he spoke at great length against the treaty of commerce with France (*Parl. Hist.* xxvi. 425–38, 465), and on 4 March 1790 asked for leave to introduce a bill for the reform of parliament, providing for the addition of one hundred new members, to be elected by the resident householders in every county. Fox 'owned that he thought that the outlines of the present proposition the best of all which he had yet heard suggested,' but Pitt's motion for an adjournment was carried, and Flood's bill was consequently lost (ib. xxviii. 452–79). At the general election in 1790 Flood was not returned to either parliament. He retired to his seat at Farmley in the county of Kilkenny, where he died on 2 Dec. 1791, in the fifty-ninth year of his age, and was buried in the family vault at Burnchurch near Farmley. Flood married, on 13 April 1762, Lady Frances Maria Beresford, the sixth daughter of Marcus, first earl of Tyrone. There was no issue of the marriage. His widow survived him many years, and died at Clifton on 18 April 1815. By his will he left a considerable amount of property to Trinity College, Dublin, after his wife's death, for the establishment of a professorship of Irish, the maintenance of a prize fund for the best compositions in English, Irish, Greek, and Latin, and for the purchase of Irish books and manuscripts. The validity of the will was contested, and the gift to Trinity College having been declared void, as being contrary to the law of mortmain, John Flood of Flood Hall, a nephew of Chief-justice Flood, was successful in establishing his claim to the property in question.

Flood was a man of ample fortune and many social qualities. Possessing brilliant conversational powers, delighting in field sports and private theatricals, genial and frank in manner, he was popular in all classes of society. In his youth Flood had a fine figure and a handsome countenance; but in later life he was somewhat gaunt in appearance, and was described by Wraxall as 'a man of the most forbidding physiognomy.' With the exception, perhaps, of Malone, Flood was the first great orator which Ireland produced. His speeches, though too laboured and sententious, were remarkable for the closeness of their reasoning. As a master of grave sarcasm and fierce invective he had no equal, while his readiness of reply, his extensive knowledge of constitutional questions, and his consummate mastery of parliamentary tactics, made him a most formidable opponent to the government in the Irish House of Commons. Curran declared that 'Flood was unmeasurably the greatest man of his time in Ireland.' In Grattan's opinion Flood 'had faults; but he had great powers, great public effect. He persuaded the old, he inspired the young; the Castle vanished before him. On a small subject he was miserable. Put into his hand a distaff, and like Hercules he made sad work of it; but give him the thunderbolt, and he had the arm of Jupiter' (GRATTAN, *Miscellaneous Works*, 1822, p. 118). Flood was identified with all the great measures of Irish reform in his time; but though he was prepared to give complete religious toleration to the Roman catholics in Ireland, he consistently refused to give them any political power. Though he cannot be charged with corruption in accepting office, Flood committed a grave error in judgment in doing so, which proved fatal to his reputation. Moreover, instead of resigning when he found

that he had over-estimated his influence with the government, he clung to office as long as he was able. His long silence during the debates on the many constitutional questions which he had vigorously supported when in opposition is an indelible stain upon his political character. The loss of his popularity had a perceptible influence on his nature, and his career from the time of taking office was that of a soured and disappointed man. A portrait of Flood 'speaking in the Irish House of Commons' was exhibited in the Loan Collection of National Portraits of 1867 (*Catalogue*, No. 796). An engraving from a drawing by Comerford will be found in Barrington's 'Historic Memoirs' (1833), ii. opp. 106, and a lithograph of the portrait, in the possession of the university of Dublin, forms the frontispiece to Flood's 'Memoirs.'

While at Oxford Flood wrote some English verses on the death of Frederick, prince of Wales, which were published in 'Epicedia Oxoniensia,' &c. (1751), pp. 127–8. While preparing for his parliamentary career he translated several speeches of Demosthenes, and other portions of the classics; but his manuscripts were all destroyed shortly after his death. The authorship of 'A Letter to the People of Ireland on the Expediency and Necessity of the Present Associations in Ireland in favour of our own Manufactures, with some Cursory Observations on the effects of a Union,' Dublin, 1799, 8vo, has been attributed to him. His 'sepulchral verses' on Dr. Johnson are to be found in Boswell's 'Life of Johnson' (G. B. Hill's edition), iv. 424–5. He was the author of the following works: 1. 'An Ode on Fame and the First Pythian Ode of Pindar' (anon.), London, 1775, 4to. 2. 'Speech of the Right Hon. Henry Flood in the House of Commons of Great Britain, Feb. 15, 1787, on the Commercial Treaty with France,' Dublin, 1787, 8vo. 3. 'Speech and Proposition of the Right Hon. Henry Flood in the House of Commons of Great Britain, March 4, 1790, for a Reform in the Representation of Parliament,' London, 1790, 8vo.

[Warden Flood's Memoirs of Henry Flood (1838); Original Letters, principally from Lord Charlemont . . . to the Right Hon. Henry Flood (1820); Lecky's Hist. of England, vol. iv. chap. xvi. xvii., vol. vi. chap. xxiv.; Lecky's Leaders of Public Opinion in Ireland (1871), pp. 63–103; Froude's English in Ireland (1881), vols. ii. iii.; Memoirs of the Life and Times of Henry Grattan, vols. i. ii. iii.; Hardy's Memoirs of the Earl of Charlemont (1812); Charles Phillips's Curran and his Contemporaries (1857); Wills's Irish Nation (1875), iii. 171–90; Webb's Compendium of Irish Biography (1878), pp. 207–

210; Dublin University Mag. vii. 652–72, viii. 80–112; Dublin Review, xiii. 100–55; Monthly Review, xcvii. 187–99; Burke's Landed Gentry (1879), i. 574–5; Gent. Mag. 1791, vol. lxi. pt. ii. pp. 1163–4, 1224–32, 1792 vol. lxii. pt. i. pp. 44–8, 1793 vol. lxiii. pt. i. p. 477, 1813 vol. lxxxv. pt. i. p. 473; Notes and Queries, 2nd ser. viii. 101–3, 189–90, 259, x. 305, xi. 171; Official Return of Lists of Members of Parliament, pt. ii. pp. 168, 184. 659, 665, 670, 674, 675, 681; Watt's Bibl. Brit.]   G. F. R. B.

FLOOD, ROBERT (1574–1637), rosicrucian. [See FLUDD.]

FLOOD, VALENTINE, M.D. (d. 1847), anatomist, was born in Dublin, where his father practised as a barrister, and was educated at Trinity College, Dublin, as a member of which he took the degrees of B.A. in 1820, M.B. and M.A. in 1823, and M.D. in 1830 (Cat. of Graduates in University of Dublin, 1591–1868, p. 199). After serving the apprenticeship, at that time necessary for becoming licensed by the Irish College of Surgeons, to Richard Carmichael [q. v.], he took out the letters testimonial of the college, of which he ultimately became a fellow, and in 1828 or 1829 was appointed demonstrator of anatomy in the school of medicine connected with the Richmond Hospital. His increasing reputation as an anatomist led to his being chosen a lecturer on anatomy in the Richmond school about 1831–2. For a few seasons he gave his undivided attention to this branch of the profession, and became a favourite among the pupils. As a private teacher he eventually commanded one of the best classes in Dublin. Had Flood continued these pursuits, for which he was so admirably adapted, it is certain that he would have enjoyed a highly prosperous career. But becoming ambitious of succeeding as a general practitioner, he connected himself with one of the Dublin dispensaries about 1835, and laboured incessantly among the poor of the district in which he lived. To follow out his intention of becoming by this means introduced into general practice, his classes were neglected; students first complained, then rebelled, and finally deserted him. Having lost position both as a lecturer and a private teacher, Flood was at length obliged to leave Dublin. He went to London, and became associated with a medical school in Charlotte Street, Fitzroy Square; but he did not succeed. His health became impaired, and in 1846 he returned to Ireland. He then obtained one of the appointments afforded by the board of health to some fever sheds at Tubrid, in the county of Tipperary, and there contracted the epidemic typhus, of which he died 18 Oct. 1847. A stone was erected to his memory by the clergy of both denominations, and the principal members of the relief committee at Tubrid.

As early as 1828 Flood published at Dublin the first volume of a work never completed, entitled 'The Anatomy and Physiology of the Nervous System,' 12mo, which, though not without merit, lacked lucidity of style, and attracted little attention. In 1839 he issued the treatise upon which his fame will chiefly rest, 'The Surgical Anatomy of the Arteries, and Descriptive Anatomy of the Heart: together with the Physiology of the Circulation in Man and inferior Animals,' 12mo, London, 1839 (new edition by John Hatch Power, M.D., 16mo, Dublin, 1850). During his connection with the Richmond school he brought out a work on 'The Anatomy and Surgery of Femoral and Inguinal Hernia. Illustrated with eight folio plates, drawn on stone by Mr. William Lover, from dissections and designs by Dr. Flood,' fol., London, 1843, an excellent compilation. Flood was a member of the Royal Irish Academy.

[Dublin Quarterly Journ. of Med. Science, v. 282–5; Webb's Compendium of Irish Biogr. p. 210; Med. Directory of Great Britain and Ireland for 1845, p. 565.]   G. G.

FLORENCE OF WORCESTER (d. 1118), chronicler, a monk of Worcester, is said by one of his continuators, who praises his skill and industry, to have died on 7 July 1118 (FLOR. WIG. ii. 72). This is all that is known of his personal history. He wrote the 'Chronicon ex Chronicis,' which is based on the work of Marianus, an Irish monk. Marianus, who died in 1082 or 1083, composed a general chronicle from the creation to his own time, containing a few notices of events relating to Britain and Ireland. The additions of Florence nearly all refer to English affairs. From 455 to 597 he uses the 'Anglo-Saxon Chronicle,' then chiefly Bæda to 732, and then again the 'Chronicle' and lives of saints, and later Asser's 'Life of Alfred,' together with some short extracts from Abbo. From 946 to 971 he relies on the 'Lives' of Dunstan, Oswald, and Æthelwold, and then again returns to the 'Chronicle,' which he amplifies from other sources. Some events specially connected with Worcester receive notice, though passed over by the English chronicle-writers. After the conclusion of the work of Marianus, Florence still goes on recording some pieces of continental history. His own work ends at 1117; he has several continuators. One of the earliest of them was a monk of Worcester named John. Orderic (p. 504) says that John, a monk of Worcester, added to the work of Marianus matters belonging to the reigns of the Conqueror and his sons, William Rufus and Henry, down to his own day, and that his chronicle, which covered nearly a hundred years, was undertaken at the command of Bishop Wulfstan. He no doubt found John employed on the works of Marianus and Florence when he visited Worcester about 1136, and probably confused the continuator, and possibly transcriber, of Florence with the original author. One continuator went down to 1031, another probably to 1037, another to 1141, and one manuscript has a continuation to 1295. Florence used a version of the 'Chronicle' which has since been lost; it was no doubt a version written at Worcester, which is to some extent represented by the Peterborough 'Chronicle.' This fact invests his work with peculiar importance, indeed it is one of the most valuable of the authorities for early English history; but it is impossible to say how much of the passages which are not to be traced to extant versions of the 'Chronicle' or other early sources is to be set down as translation from this lost Worcester chronicle, or is to be regarded as merely the amplifications of the twelfth-century compiler. Florence is an industrious and careful writer, but either he or the work which he copied adopted views on certain subjects, such, for example, as the causes of the English defeats in the reign of Æthelred the Unready, which seem exaggerated (GREEN, Conquest of England, p. 381). He wrote a list of the English bishops and genealogies of the kings, and, according to Bale, a book 'De Rebus sui Cœnobii.' Nine manuscripts of Florence's 'Chronicle' are extant. The first in the list of Sir T. D. Hardy, MS. C. C. C. Oxford, 12th cent. fol., ends abruptly at 1140; it belonged to the church of Worcester, contains the lists and genealogies, and insertions and a continuation by a contemporary monk of Worcester. MS. Lambeth, 12th cent. fol., ends at 1131, contains some lists, formerly belonged to Abingdon, and has some special Abingdon notices. MS. Bodl. 297, fol., also 12th cent., ends at 1131 and has notices of charters of Bury St. Edmunds. MS. C. C. C. Cambr. xcii., 13th cent. fol., ends at 1131 and has a continuation to 1295; it formerly belonged to Peterborough. Florence's 'Chronicle' was first printed in 1592 at London, 4to, under the editorship of William Howard of Naworth, third son of Thomas, duke of Norfolk, who dedicated his work to Lord Burghley; it was reprinted faultily at Frankfort, along with the 'Flores Historiarum,' 1601, fol. The two manuscripts used by Howard belong to Trinity College, Dublin; his edition ends with 1141. The portion from 450 to 1066 is edited by Petrie in the 'Monumenta Historica Britannica,' pp. 616–44, 1848, fol., where the portions taken from Marianus are omitted in the text, and the whole work from 450 with the C. C. C. Cambr. continuation to 1295 was edited by B. Thorpe for the English Historical Society, 1849, 2 vols. 8vo. Florence's 'Chronicle' has been translated by T. Forester for Bohn's 'Historical Library,' 1847, 8vo, and by J. Stevenson in his 'Church Historians,' vol. ii. pt. i. 1853, 8vo.

[Florence of Worcester, ii. 72 (Engl. Hist. Soc.); Orderic, p. 504, ed. Duchesne; Hardy's Descriptive Cat. ii. 130 (Rolls Ser.); Mon. Hist. Brit., Preface, pp. 83–7; Wright's Biog. Lit. ii. 73; Green's Conquest of England, pp. 341, 381.] W. H.

FLORIO, JOHN (1553?–1625), author, was born about 1553, according to the inscription on his portrait issued in 1611, where he was described as fifty-eight years old. His father, MICHAEL ANGELO FLORIO, a Florentine protestant, whose family was originally settled at Sienna, fled to England shortly before Edward VI's reign from persecution in the Valteline, and was in 1550 preacher to a congregation of Italian protestants in London. Sir William Cecil and Archbishop Cranmer both patronised him, but charges of gross immorality were brought against him; he was ultimately banished from Cecil's house, where he had resided, and he temporarily severed his connection with the Italian church in London (cp. STRYPE, Memorials, II. i. 377–378; STRYPE, Cranmer, pp. 343, 881, 883). A manuscript by him in the Cambridge University Library, 'Regole de la Lingua Thoscana,' shows that he was for some time a teacher of Italian in London, perhaps in the service of William Herbert, first earl of Pembroke, to whose son Henry, 'Signore Arrigo Herbert,' this work is dedicated (London, 21 Aug. 1553). The elder Florio also wrote, 'Catechismo, cioè forma breve per amaestrare i fanciuli: Laquale di tutta la Christiana disciplina cõtiene la somma . . . Tradotta di Latino in lingua Thoscana,' without date or place, and 'Historia de la vita e de la morte de l'illustrissima Signora G. Graia, già Regina eletta e publicata d'Inghilterra: e de le cose accadute in quel regno dopo la morte del re Edoardo VI,' with Italian translations of several works attributed to Lady Jane Grey, 1607. The former work was probably published in London; the latter has been conjecturally assigned to a Dutch publishing house: on its title-page the author is described as 'Fiorentino già predicatore famoso del Sant' Euangelo in più città d'Italia et in Londra.' ' Apologia . . . scritta contro un heretico,' 1557, is also attributed to him. After the accession of Queen Mary, the elder Florio, according to Wood, took his family to the continent again, and there John received his early education.

We know that John Florio resided in his youth at Oxford, and about 1576 became tutor in foreign languages to Emanuel, son of Robert Barnes, bishop of Durham, who was a commoner of Magdalen College. Florio matriculated at Magdalen in 1581 (WOOD), ' and was a teacher and instructor of certain scholars in the university.' He dedicated his ' First Fruites ' to Leicester in 1578, from ' his lodgings in Worcester Place,' Oxford. He similarly dated from Oxford a translation from the Italian of Ramuzio, dedicated to Edmund Bray, high sheriff of Oxfordshire, 25 June 1580; and inscribed to Sir Edward Dyer a manuscript collection of Italian proverbs, also from Oxford, 12 Nov. 1582. In his ' Second Frutes,' 1591, he writes that his first patron, Leicester, whom ' every miscreant does strike, being dead,' had been succeeded by one Nicholas Saunders of Ewell. In the same place he makes highly appreciative reference to Spenser, ' the sweetest singer of all our western shepherds,' who, he says, had heralded Leicester's virtues. A few years later Florio was, according to his own account, taken into ' the pay and patronage' of the Earl of Southampton, in which he ' lived some years' (*The Worlde of Wordes*, 1598 dedication), and to the Earl of Pembroke he was soon under heavy obligations.

At the close of the sixteenth century Florio was living in London on intimate terms with all the chief literary men and their patrons. In 1598 he dedicated his great Italian-English dictionary to Roger, earl of Rutland, Henry, earl of Southampton, and Lucy, countess of Rutland. He there calls himself ' Resolute John Florio,' and venomously attacks one ' H. S.' who had insulted the sonnets of one of his friends. Hunter suggests that ' H. S.' may be Henry Salisbury, author of a Welsh dictionary, and a protégé of the Earl of Pembroke. Florio's admirable translation of Montaigne's ' Essays ' was licensed to Edward Blount in 1599, but was not published till 1603. Each of the three books is separately dedicated—the first to Lucy, countess of Bedford, and Anne, lady Harington; the second to Elizabeth, countess of Bedford, and Penelope, lady Rich; the third to Elizabeth, lady Grey, and Mary, lady Nevill. To the countess of Bedford's exhortations and to Sir Edward Wotton's advice Florio attributes his preparation of the work and acknow-

ledges assistance from Theodore Diodati [see DIODATI, CHARLES] and his ' sympathising friend, Maister Doctor Gwinne' [see GWINNE, MATTHEW, M.D.] The latter is doubtless author of the many pieces of commendatory verse contributed to this and other of Florio's works under the title of ' Il Candido.' Sir William Cornwallis [q. v.], writing of a recent translation of Montaigne in his ' Essayes,' (1600), says : ' Montaigne speaks now good English. It is done by a fellow less beholding to nature for his fortunes than wit, yet lesser for his face than his fortune. The truth is he looks more like a good fellow than a wise man, and yet he is wise beyond either his fortune or education.' This is undoubtedly a reference to Florio. Cornwallis obviously saw in manuscript Florio's translation, which was entered at Stationers' Hall four years before its publication.

Farmer and Warburton have argued that Shakespeare ridiculed Florio in Holofernes in ' Love's Labour's Lost.' They chiefly rely on the bombastic prefaces to the ' Worlde of Wordes' and to Montaigne. But there is really nothing there to justify the suggestion. Florio writes more in the vein of Armado than of Holofernes, and beyond the fact that he was a teacher of languages in London he bears no resemblance whatever to the latter, a village schoolmaster. Florio as the protégé of Lords Southampton and Pembroke doubtless met Shakespeare, but this is pure conjecture. We are on safer ground in tracing the original of Gonzago's description of an ideal state in the ' Tempest ' to Florio's translation of Montaigne's essay. One copy of the 1603 edition of the Montaigne at the British Museum contains an autograph signature said to be by Shakespeare himself. It was purchased as a genuine autograph for 140*l.* in 1838, having been in the possession of the Rev. Edward Patteson of East Sheen, Surrey, whose father, Edward Patteson, minister of Smethwick, Staffordshire, had had it in his possession at least as early as 1780. Sir Frederick Madden, in a letter originally addressed to the Society of Antiquaries (26 Jan. 1837), and afterwards republished from the ' Archæologia' as a separate pamphlet, vouched for the authenticity of the autograph. But later investigation has left little doubt that it is an eighteenth-century forgery. Another copy of the same date in the same collection bears a signature alleged to be that of Ben Jonson. This is doubtless genuine.

In 1603 Florio became reader in Italian to Queen Anne at a salary of 100*l.* a year, and on 5 Aug. 1604 was appointed by the king gentleman-extraordinary and groom of the privy chamber. In 1610 John Healey dedicated to him his translation of 'Epictetus.' After 1620 Florio resided at Fulham, and he died there in August or September 1625. Wood says that he retired to Fulham shortly before his death on account of the plague; but although he owned the lease of a house in Shoe Lane, Fleet Street, Fulham was his ordinary place of residence for at least five years before he died. By his will, dated 20 July 1625, and proved 1 May 1626, he left most of his small property to his wife Rose. A daughter, Aurelia, married to John Molins, a surgeon of Shoe Lane, is mentioned. To the Earl of Pembroke he bequeathed 'all my Italian, French, and Spanish books, as well printed as unprinted, being in number about 340, viz. my new and perfect Dictionary, as also my ten dialogues in Italian and English and my unbound volume of divers written collections and rhapsodies.' Florio desired these books and manuscripts to be placed in Pembroke's library, either at Wilton or Baynard's Castle in London, and begged the earl to protect his wife from the molestation of his enemies, and to hand over to her any profit arising from the publication of his manuscripts. His executors were Theophilus Field [q. v.], bishop of Llandaff and afterwards of Hereford, and Richard Cluett, vicar of Fulham. Nothing is certainly known of the fate of Florio's manuscripts. Oldys possessed an autograph of 'Giardino di Ricreatione,' which is now in the British Museum (see No. 3 below), and Wood says that Pembroke handed over much manuscript material to Torriano, who edited Florio's Italian-English Dictionary in 1659, adding an English-Italian part. A suit of arms impaling Florio's was granted to his son-in-law Molins on 23 Aug. 1644. The poet Samuel Daniel [q. v.] has been claimed as Florio's brother-in-law, on the ground that in the commendatory verse prefixed by Daniel to the 1613 edition of the Montaigne the translator is addressed as 'brother,' whereas in the earlier edition of 1603 Daniel had merely called Florio his friend. But the difference in the designation is amply accounted for by the fact that Florio and Daniel were in 1613 brother-officers in the queen's household. There is no other evidence of a family relationship, and the theory may safely be rejected.

Florio's works are: 1. 'His First Fruits, which yield familiar speech, merry proverbs, witty sentences, and golden sayings,' London, 1578, with which is bound up 'Perfect Induction to the Italian and English Tongues,' both dedicated to Robert, earl of Leicester. The 'First Fruits' consist mainly of simple dialogues in English and Italian. The British Museum has only an imperfect copy. 2. 'A Short and Briefe Narration of the Two Navigations and Discoueries to the North-weast Partes called New Fraunce. First translated out of French into Italian by that famous learned Man, Geo. Bapt. Ramutius [Ramuzio], and now turned into English by John Florio,' London, 1580; dedicated to Edmund Bray. 3. 'Giardino di Ricreatione.' London (Woodcock), 1591; dedicated to Master Nicholas Saunders of Ewell, esq.—a collection of 6,150 proverbs, all in Italian. A manuscript is in the British Museum with a dedication to Sir Edward Dyer (Addit. MS. 15214). It has been in the possession successively of Oldys, Isaac Heard, and B. H. Bright. 4. 'Florio's Second Frutes to be gathered of twelve Trees of diuers but delightsome tastes to the tongues of Italian and English men. To which is annexed his Garden of Recreation, yielding 6,000 Italian proverbs,' London (Thomas Woodcock), 1591; dedicated to Nicholas Saunders. This work consists mainly of Italian and English dialogues, with a reprint of No. 3. 5. 'A Worlde of Wordes: a most copious and exact Dictionarie in Italian and English, collected by John Florio,' London (for E. Blount), 1598 [see dedication noticed above]; sonnets by Il Candido, i.e. Gwynne, and verses by B. B. are affixed. A list of seventy-six books consulted by the compiler is given. In 1611 the dictionary was reissued as 'Queen Anna's New World of Words, or Dictionarie of the Italian and English Tongues, collected and newly much augmented by Iohn Florio,' London (for E. Blount and W. Barret). An Italian dedication to the queen is followed by an English address by the author, an Italian poem by Alberico Gentili, an Italian and English sonnet by Il Candido, and English verses by Samuel Daniel, James Mabbe, and John Thorys. 'Necessary Rules and Short Observations for the True Pronouncing and Speedie Learning of the Italian, collected for Queen Anne,' forms an appendix of 73 pages. A third edition, 'Vocabolario Italiano et Inglese,' revised by Gio. Torriano, appeared in 1659, together with an English-Italian part, apparently prepared from Florio's manuscripts. A fourth edition in 1688, further revised by J. Davis, M.D., was dedicated to Maria d'Este, queen of England. 6. 'The Essayes on Morall, Politike, and Millitarie Discourses of Lo. Michaell de Montaigne. First written by him in French, and now done into English,' London (for E. Blount), 1603 [for dedication see above]. There are prefatory verses by Il Candido and Daniel. The second edition, dated 1613, is dedicated to Queen Anne, and is declared to be translated from the last French edition. A reprint with introduction by Prof. George Saintsbury appeared in 1892–3 (in 'Tudor Translations,' 3 vols.)

A fine portrait of Florio, aged 58, engraved by W. Hole, is prefixed to the 1611 edition of the Italian Dictionary. A painting by Mytens is said to have belonged to the Earl of Dorset, and to be now at Knole Park, Sevenoaks.

[Hunter's New Illustrations of Shakespeare, i. 23, 145, 146, 261, 273, 281 ; Wood's Athenæ Oxon. ed. Bliss, ii. 380 ; Notes and Queries, 3rd ser. viii. 4 ; Florio's Works in Brit. Mus. Libr.]

S. L.

FLOWER, BENJAMIN (1755–1829), political writer, born in London in 1755, was the son of a prosperous tradesman, to a share of whose business he succeeded. Edward Fordham Flower [q. v.] was his nephew. Through unfortunate speculations, however, described with much candour by himself in a 'Statement of Facts,' he soon found himself greatly embarrassed, and ultimately, in 1785, accepted an engagement to travel in business on the continent for half the year, spending the other half in the service of a firm at Tiverton. He thus had opportunities of visiting Holland, Germany, and Switzerland, and spent six months in France in 1791, 'the most innocent part of the revolution.' The impressions thus imbibed inspired his work on the French constitution (1792), which is, however, much less an account of the French constitution than an attack on the alleged defects of the English, and is too discursive and irrelevant to be of much value for either purpose. It contributed to his being about this time selected to edit the 'Cambridge Intelligencer,' which his brother Richard, a farmer and staunch liberal, had a considerable share in establishing. It was almost the only provincial newspaper in the kingdom which denounced the war with France as 'absurd and wicked,' and advocated the removal of the grievances of the dissenters on the broad grounds of religious liberty. It thus attracted attention out of all proportion to its ability. Flower's hostility to the war was vigorously expressed in his 'National Sins Considered,' 1796; but here again he is exceedingly digressive. In 1799 he was summoned before the House of Lords for an alleged libel upon Bishop Watson, whose political conduct he had censured, and after a very short hearing was adjudged guilty of a breach of privilege, and sentenced to six months' imprisonment in Newgate, and a fine of 100l. The proceedings seem to have been of a very arbitrary nature; but Flower's attempts to obtain their revision by application to the court of king's bench were unsuccessful. His captivity was alleviated by the visits of Miss Eliza Gould,

a young lady who had herself suffered for her liberal opinions. Shortly after his release he married her, and, relinquishing his newspaper, established himself in business as a printer at Harlow in Essex, where he printed the works of his favourite divine, Robert Robinson, and carried on a monthly magazine, entitled 'The Political Register,' from 1807 to 1811. His other publications were the 'Life of Robinson' accompanying the latter's works, a preface to his brother Richard's 'Letters from Illinois,' and some pamphlets on family affairs. His wife died in 1810, leaving him two highly gifted daughters [see ADAMS, SARAH FLOWER ; FLOWER, ELIZA]. In his latter years he retired to Dalston, where he died on 17 Feb. 1829. Circumstances have given him a more important place in the history of English journalism than his literary or political abilities could have procured him. His style has the warmth imparted by conscientious conviction, but he has no great argumentative power. As a man he is entitled to honour for his disinterested consistency, and his independence of thought preserved him from some of the extremes to which the vehemence of his temper might have inclined him. Though an advocate of the French republic, he was not a republican at home, and in religion he belonged to the most conservative school of English unitarianism.

[The principal authority for Flower's life up to 1808 is the Statement of Facts published by him in that year on occasion of a lawsuit for defamation, in which he recovered damages. See also an obituary notice, probably by W. J. Fox, in the Monthly Repository, new ser. vol. iii.]

R. G.

FLOWER, EDWARD FORDHAM (1805–1883), author, younger son of Richard Flower, a brewer, banker, agriculturist, and breeder of sheep, was born at Marden Hall, Hertfordshire, on 31 Jan. 1805. Benjamin Flower [q. v.] was his uncle. At the age of twelve he went with his father to Illinois, United States, but returning in 1824 he in 1827 married Celina, eldest daughter of John Greaves of Radford House, near Leamington, and, settling at Stratford-on-Avon, opened a brewery in 1832, which was so successful that in thirty years he was able to retire and leave the business to his sons. He four times held the office of mayor of Stratford, the last occasion being in 1864, the year of the Shakespeare tercentenary. In this celebration he took a leading part, and was well known to all visitors to Shakespeare's birthplace, more especially to Americans, many of whom he hospitably entertained at his residence, The Hill, built in 1855. As a liberal he contested Coventry in 1865, and

North Warwickshire in 1868, but was not elected. In 1873 he removed his residence to London, and being a great lover of horses he spent the remainder of his life in an endeavour to mitigate the sufferings caused by the use of improper harness, tight bearing-reins, and gag-bits. In these efforts he was to a certain extent successful. He died at 35 Hyde Park Gardens, London, 26 March 1883, and his widow Celina died 2 March 1884, aged 79. He left three sons, Charles Edward Flower, founder of the Shakespeare Memorial Theatre at Stratford-on-Avon (*d.* 3 May 1892), (Sir) William Henry Flower, K.C.B. [see SUPPLEMENT], and Edgar Flower, chairman of the Shakespeare Birthplace Trustees (*d.* 29 July 1903). The books he published were: 1. 'A Few Words about Bearing Reins,' 1875. 2. 'Bits and Bearing Reins,' 1875; seventh edition, 1886. 3. 'Horses and Harness,' 1876. 4. 'The Stones of London, or Macadam *v.* Vestries,' 1880.

[Bits and Bearing Reins, 1886, pp. 3–15, with portrait and memoir; Victoria Mag. May 1878, pp. 67–8, with portrait; Live Stock Journal, 30 March 1883, p. 282; Times, 27 March 1883, p. 7.]

G. C. B.

FLOWER, ELIZA (1803–1846), musical composer, elder daughter of Benjamin Flower [q. v.], was born at Harlow, Essex, 19 April 1803. Her first published compositions, a series of 'Fourteen Musical Illustrations of the Waverley Novels' (1831), followed by 'Songs of the Seasons' and a number of other pieces, indicated the musician's power of sympathetic expression. Among a few political songs, 'The Gathering of the Unions,' a juvenile composition, has been republished as having been performed at the great Birmingham meeting in May 1832, where, in fact, the words had been sung, but to another musical setting. Of a higher character, though equally simple, is the widely known chorus, 'Now pray we for our country' (1842). The chief work of Miss Flower's musical life was the composition of 'Hymns and Anthems, the words chiefly from Holy Scripture and the writings of the poets,' arranged in five parts, 'Adoration' (1841), 'Aspiration,' 'Belief,' 'Heaven upon Earth' (1846), and 'Life in Death' (as yet unprinted). Eighteen of these pieces were republished in 1888, and a further selection is contemplated. The object of the composer was to supply a musical service for the congregation of South Place Chapel, Finsbury, which had no liturgy, and was accustomed to simple psalmody led by a precentor. A choir was, however, formed, and many of these compositions, full of melody and musical feeling, and at the same time truly devotional in character, were performed.

Among the anthems deserving special mention are several to poetry written by her sister, Mrs. Sarah Flower Adams [q. v.], including 'Darkness shrouded Calvary,' and the well-known 'Nearer, my God, to Thee,' to the music of which many admirers of this hymn are strangers. Among the more simple hymns are Sir John Bowring's 'Ancient of Ages' and Milton's 'Defend the Poor and Desolate.' For the South Place Chapel choir a hymn-book was specially compiled by Mr. W. J. Fox, to which music from the best composers was adapted by Miss Flower. This highly gifted and enthusiastic musician died of consumption 12 Dec. 1846, and was buried in her father's grave near Harlow. Her portrait, drawn from memory by Mrs. Bridell Fox, lithographed by Vinter, has been published by Charles Fox.

[Private information ; Brown's Dict. of Musicians, p. 249 ; The Reasoner, December 1846.]

L. M. M.

FLOWER, JOHN (*fl.* 1658), puritan divine and preacher, born about 1624, was the son of William Flower of Cubley, Derbyshire. He became a commoner of New Inn Hall, Oxford, in Act term 1640, proceeded B.A. 2 April 1647, and was created M.A. by the parliamentary visitors, 14 April 1648. According to Wood 'he was soon after preacher of God's word at Ilmington in Warwickshire, and afterwards at Staunton in the county of Nottingham, where I find him in 1658' (*Fasti Oxon.* ed. Bliss, ii. 101, 112). He wrote: 1. 'The Free and Honourable Servant, set forth in his Privileges and Prerogatives,' 8vo, London, 1652. 2. 'Several Quæries concerning the Church of Jesus Christ upon Earth, briefly explained and resolved,' 8vo, London, 1658.

[Wood's Fasti Oxon. (Bliss), ii. 101, 112 ; Notes and Queries, 2nd ser. xii. 46.]

G. G.

FLOWER, ROGER (*d.* 1428?), speaker of the House of Commons, son of William Flower, sheriff of Rutland in 1386–7, by Elena his wife, was returned to parliament for the county of Rutland in 1396–7, again in 1399, 1402, 1404, 1413–14. He was one of the feoffees of the Brigitine nunnery founded by Henry V in 1414. Still representing Rutland county he was chosen speaker four times—in 1416, 1417, 1419, and 1422—a distinction hitherto unprecedented except in the case of Thomas Chaucer [q. v.] From his holograph will (dated 15 April 1424, proved 20 June 1428) it is clear that he was a lawyer. Not only is it plainly the composition of one well versed in legal technicalities, but it contains a bequest of chattels 'in mine inn' in London, where the inn referred to can only be one of the Inns of Court. From this document it appears that besides his ancestral manor of Okeham or Oakham in Rutlandshire, he held estates in Leicestershire; that he had four sons, Robert, Roger, John, and William, and two daughters, Anneys and Joan, the latter being married to Sir Henry Plesyngton of Burley in Rutland, grandson of Sir Robert Plesyngton [q. v.], chief baron of the exchequer in the reign of Richard II, and that his wife, Cecile, daughter of Anneys Sainon, was then living. The latter was his second wife, his first wife being Catherine, daughter and heiress of William Dalby of Exeter, founder of certain almshouses mentioned in the will, and of which Flower seems to have been the patron. The probate of the will being dated 20 June 1428, Flower presumably died in that year. The manor of Okeham was in the possession of Sir Richard Flower, a descendant, who died in 1523. Sir William Flower, Sir Richard's great-great-grandson, distinguished himself during the Irish rebellion of 1641, and was grandfather of William, created Baron of Castle Durrow (Irish peerage) in 1733, whose son Henry was created, in 1751, Viscount Ashbrook (Irish peerage), a title still extant.

[Wright's Rutland, i. 29, 136; Official Return of Lists of Members of Parliament; Rot. Parl. iv. 95 a, 107 a, 117 a, 170 a; The Fifty Earliest English Wills (Early English Text Soc.), 55–64; Manning's Speakers, 62.]   J. M. R.

FLOWER, WILLIAM (1498?–1588), Norroy king of arms, born at York about 1498, was probably the elder son of John Flower, tailor and corn merchant, of the parish of All Saints upon the Pavement, York, whose goods were administered on 2 Nov. 1523 by Margaret, his widow. He married Helen Davyes, and had two sons and three daughters, of whom Elizabeth married first, about 1570, Robert Glover [q. v.], Somerset herald, and secondly, in April 1588, a Mr. Woolward. Noble rightly says 'few have been more assiduous in the duties of their profession than this Norroy, as the visitations of his province evince' (Hist. of Coll. of Arms, p. 172). He became Guisnes pursuivant extraordinary upon the removal of Fulke ap Howell at Westminster, 10 July 28 Henry VIII. When Calais pursuivant extraordinary he was sent, 1 April 1543, to Rouen to visit the merchants and marines who had been captured by the French, and were confined there (NOBLE, loc. cit.) On 30 May 1544 he was appointed Rouge Croix, and promoted to the office of Chester herald about 37 Henry VIII. With Sir Gilbert Dethick [q. v.], Garter, he attended the Marquis of Northampton into France, when he

had an allowance of 10s. per diem for his 'dyett.' The deputation from Thomas Hawley, Clarenceux, to Flower, constituting him his marshal and deputy, is dated at the house of the said Clarenceux in Barbican, London, 1555, 1 and 2 Philip and Mary. His patent as Norroy is dated 29 Jan. 1561–2 (RYMER, Fœdera, xvi. 620; MACHYN, Diary, Camden Soc., p. 276). A commission of visitation was addressed to him on 10 July, 6 Elizabeth. On 9 March 1580 he obtained a patent joining Robert Glover, Somerset, his son-in-law, with himself for the office of Norroy, in which patent he is stated to be then eighty-two years of age. Flower died at Windsor in the autumn of 1588. His will, bearing date 14 Oct., 30 Elizabeth, 1588, was proved in London 22 Nov. following. The effects were small, and the legacies consisted chiefly of articles of furniture and wearing apparel (will registered in P. C. C. 9, Leicester).

Flower's 'Visitation of Yorkshire' in 1563 and 1564 was edited for the Harleian Society in 1881 by Charles Best Norcliffe of Langton, Yorkshire, from the original manuscript, which has been in the possession of the family since 1738. Two copies of this visitation, one with additions, are in the College of Arms; a portion only is to be found in the British Museum, Harleian MS. 1171. In 1567 Flower undertook a 'Visitation of the County Palatine of Lancaster,' on which occasion he appointed Robert Glover his marshal or deputy; the visitation has for that reason been sometimes described as 'Glover's Visitation.' The original manuscript is preserved in the College of Arms, but a carefully written transcript of it by Glover is in the British Museum, Harleian MS. 2086. A second copy in the same collection, Harleian MS. 6159, with additional and enlarged pedigrees, was made by William Smith [q. v.], Rouge Dragon pursuivant, in 1598. Transcripts of this visitation, all in the libraries of Humphrey Chetham of Manchester, and of Queen's College, Oxford, and other copies, more or less inaccurate, are in several public and private collections. It was printed by the Chetham Society in 1870 under the editorship of Canon F. R. Raines. Flower's last undertaking was a 'Visitation of the County Palatine of Durham' in 1575, in which he was again greatly assisted by Glover. One hundred and forty copies of this visitation were printed at Newcastle-upon-Tyne in 1820 from a copy in the possession of Nicholas John Philipson, F.S.A., of that town. Manuscript copies exist in the libraries of the British Museum (Harl. MSS. 1171 and 1540), of the College of Arms, of Queen's College, Oxford, and of Durham Cathedral.

[Raines's Introduction to Lancashire Visitation (Chetham Soc.); Norcliffe's Preface to Yorkshire Visitation (Harl. Soc.); Calendar of State Papers, Domestic, 1547-80, Foreign, 1553-8, p 312; Noble's History of the College of Arms; Sims's Manual for the Genealogist, 2nd ed., pp. 165, 168, 176.]

G. G.

FLOWERDEW, EDWARD (d. 1586), judge, fourth son of John Flowerdew of Hethersett, Norfolk, a large landed proprietor, was educated at Cambridge, but took no degree. He became a member of the Inner Temple 11 Oct. 1552, and in the autumn of 1569 and Lent of 1577 was reader, and in 1579 treasurer. He obtained considerable celebrity as a lawyer in his own county. In 1571 he became counsel to the dean and chapter of Norwich, and in 1573 to the town of Great Yarmouth. He was counsel also to Sir Thomas Gresham. The town of Norwich gave him a silver cup in 1571, presumably for professional services, and various grateful clients settled annuities on him, Thomas Grimesdiche settling 40s. and John Thornton 26s. 8d. in 1573, and Simon Harcourt of Stanton Harcourt, Oxfordshire, one third of five marks in 1575. On 12 Feb. 1584 he received a grant from the clerk of the royal kitchen of a buck in summer and a doe in winter yearly from any royal forest in Norfolk or elsewhere. He was M.P. for Castle Rising 1572-84. He became serjeant and recorder of Great Yarmouth, 16 Oct. 1580, and on 23 Oct. 1584 third baron of the exchequer, when he resigned his recordership. On 20 Feb. 1585 he was a member of the special commission for the county of Middlesex, before which Dr. Parry was tried and convicted for high treason. In the winter of 1585 and 1586 he went circuit in South Wales, and in March held the assizes at Exeter. Here gaol fever broke out, and, seizing upon him, carried him off between 14 March and 4 April. He was buried at Hethersett Church. He was a man of grasping temper, but apparently not of fine feelings. In 1564 he purchased Stanfield Hall and its furniture of John Appleyard, in order to live there, and also married Elizabeth, daughter of William Foster of Wymondham, who had long been Appleyard's mistress. In 1575 he acquired the site of the dissolved abbey of Wymondham. The parishioners, wishing to preserve the church, petitioned the crown to be allowed to buy it at a valuation, and paid the money. Flowerdew, however, stripped it of its lead and carried off a quantity of freestone, whereupon the exasperated parishioners dismantled it. His lands were dispersed on his death, and he left no issue. According, however, to another account, he had a daughter, who married Thomas Skelton.

[Foss's Judges of England; Blomefield's Norfolk, i. 721, 724; Dugdale's Origines Jurid.; Holinshed's Chron. iv. 868; Leicester Correspondence, p. 224; Burgon's Gresham, ii. 493, 499; Cooper's Athenæ Cantabr. ii. 5; Manship's Yarmouth, i. 295; Palmer's continuation of Manship's Yarmouth, ii. 337 et seq. and Vincent's Norfolk Collections there cited; Monro's Acta Cancellariæ; Strype's Annals, iv. 310, and Parker, 453; Weever's Fun. Mon. p. 864; Lemon's Domestic Papers, 1581-90; App. 4, Rep. Publ. Records, p. 273; Gawdy MSS., Hist. MSS. Comm. Rep., 1885.]

J. A. H.

FLOWERS, FREDERICK (1810-1886), police magistrate, third son of the Rev. Field Flowers, rector of Partney, Lincolnshire, 1815-18, was born at Boston in 1810, and educated at Louth grammar school, Lincolnshire. He was admitted a student of Lincoln's Inn 10 Nov. 1828, called to the bar 18 Nov. 1839, joined the midland circuit, and for many years practised as a special pleader. In 1862 he was appointed recorder of Stamford, and was for some time revising barrister for the northern division of Nottinghamshire. He was named by Sir George Grey police magistrate at Bow Street, London, 6 July 1864, and sat at that court until his death. He also acted as a magistrate for Middlesex, Kent, Surrey, Hertfordshire, and Essex. As a police magistrate he was extremely well known and greatly respected. His common sense, combined with a sound knowledge of the law, prevented him from making many mistakes in his decisions. He possessed kindness, tact, and discrimination, and a strong sense of justice, especially towards those who were poor and weak. He died at his residence, Holmesdale, Tottenham Lane, Hornsey, Middlesex, 26 Jan. 1886, and was buried at Partney on 30 Jan., where on his grave is a monumental cross, and in the church there is a memorial brass. He married in 1841 Ann, only daughter of R. Kirby, by whom he left one son.

[Law Times, 13 Feb. 1886, p. 275; Solicitors' Journal, 30 Jan. 1886, p. 225; Law Journal, 30 Jan. 1886, p. 79; Graphic, 8 Jan. 1881, p. 32, with portrait; Saturday Review, 30 Jan. 1886, pp. 145-6.]

G. C. B.

FLOWERS, GEORGE FRENCH (1811-1872), composer and musical theorist, fourth son of the Rev. Field Flowers, was born in 1811 at Boston, Lincolnshire; he studied music under Rink and Von Wartensee in Germany, graduated Mus. Bac. from Lincoln College, Oxford, in 1839, and proceeded doctor of music in 1865. In the meantime he was organist at the Chapel of the British Embassy, Paris,

St. Mark's, Myddelton Square, and St. John's, Paddington, successively. Flowers founded the Contrapuntists' Society in 1843, was responsible for some contrapuntal and musical reviews in the 'Literary Gazette' about that time, and was author of an analysis of Goss's 'Harmony' in the 'Fine Arts Journal' (1847, p. 445 et seq.) His 'Essay on the Construction of Fugue with . . . new Rules for Harmony' appeared in London in 1846; the 'Pictorial Representation of the Science of Harmony,' a translation of Basler's 'Reisekarte,' in 1850; and a poem on 'Muscular Vocalisation,' Barrow-on-Humber, in 1861. Flowers introduced and developed Vogler's system of progressive cadences (cf. his papers in *Musical World* of 1848, pp. 501 and 554). He contributed opinions on musical matters for many years to the 'Musical Examiner' and 'Musical World.' In 1850 (*Mus. World,* p. 650) he announced his determination to cultivate and bring forward English vocal talent by means of a British school of vocalisation. His attempt was justified a year or two later by some measure of success, strikingly illustrated by the excellent singing of his young pupils in St. James's Hall, yet no trace remains of the institution which promised so well. The late Mrs. Howard Paul may be cited as having been its most distinguished member. Flowers displayed in the composition of his 'Organ Fugues,' 'Pastoral Chorus,' and 'Choral Fugue' all the erudition expected from so earnest a follower of Bach and Vogler. His elaborate first mass, about 1860, probably marks the date of his reception in the church of Rome. Flowers died of cholera, 14 June 1872.

[Grove's Dict. of Music, i. 535 ; Brown's Dict. of Musicians, p. 249 ; Musical World, 1844–52 ; other periodicals mentioned above; Gorman's Converts to Rome, p. 39; Foster's Alumni Oxon.]

L. M. M.

FLOYD, FLOUD, or **LLOYD, EDWARD** (*d.* 1648?), was a catholic barrister who became steward in Shropshire to Lordchancellor Ellesmere and the Earl of Suffolk. In 1621, when he was a prisoner in the Fleet at the instance of the privy council, he was impeached in the House of Commons for having said : 'I have heard that Prague is taken ; and Goodman Palsgrave and Goodwife Palsgrave have taken their heels ; and as I have heard, Goodwife Palsgrave is taken prisoner.' These words, it was alleged, were spoken by him in a most despiteful and scornful manner, to insult the prince palatine and his wife. The case led to an important constitutional decision. The commons condemned him on 1 May to pay a fine of 1,000*l.*, to stand in the pillory in three different places

for two hours each time, and to be carried from place to place upon a horse without a saddle, with his face towards the horse's tail, and holding the tail in his hand. Floyd immediately appealed to the king, who the next morning sent to inquire upon what precedents the commons grounded their claim to act as a judicial body in regard to offences which did not concern their privileges. A debate of several days led to a conference of the two houses, when it was agreed that the accused should be arraigned before the lords, and that a declaration should be entered on the journals that his trial before the commons should not prejudice the just rights of either house. The lords added to the severity of the first judgment. On 26 May Floyd was condemned to be degraded from the estate of a gentleman ; his testimony not to be received ; he was to be branded, whipped at the cart's tail, to pay 5,000*l.*, and to be imprisoned in Newgate for life. When he was branded in Cheapside he declared that he would have given 1,000*l.* to be hanged in order that he might be a martyr in so good a cause. Some days afterwards, on the motion of Prince Charles, it was agreed by the lords that the whipping should not be inflicted, and an order was made that in future judgment should not be pronounced, when the sentence was more than imprisonment, on the same day on which it was voted. The remainder of the monstrous sentence on Floyd seems to have been carried into effect. But he was liberated on 16 July 1621, after the new lord keeper Williams had prevailed with Buckingham to recommend to James I a liberal exercise of his prerogative of mercy in the case of political prisoners (GARDINER, *Hist.* iv. 137). On the petition of Joane, his wife, the lords on 6 Dec. 1621 ordered his trunk and writings to be delivered up to her; the clerk first taking out 'such popish beads and popish books' as were therein (*Lords' Journals,* iii. 183). Perhaps he is the person whose death is thus recorded by Smyth: 'July 1648, Mr. Fludd (an honest recusant), my old acquaintance, about this time died' (*Obituary,* p. 26).

Hallam speaks with great severity of the cruelty of these proceedings. 'The cold-blooded, deliberate policy of the lords is still more disgusting than the wild fury of the lower house' (*Constitutional Hist.,* 7th edit. i. 361). A collection, made by Sir Harbottle Grimstone, bart., of the proceedings in Floyd's case in the House of Commons is preserved in the Harleian MS. 6274, art. 2.

[Gardiner's History of England, iv. 119–22; Birch's James I, ii. 252–8; Camden's James I; Campbell's Lord Chief Justices, i. 366, 389, 390;

Commons' Journals, i. 596–624; Howell's State Trials, ii. 1153 seq. viii. 92; Lingard's Hist. of England (1849), vii. 223; Lords' Journals, iii. 110–83; Parliamentary Hist. v. 427–47.] T. C.

FLOYD, Sir GODFREY (*fl.* 1667), military engineer. [See LLOYD.]

FLOYD, HENRY (1563–1641), jesuit, elder brother of Father John Floyd [q. v.], born in Cambridgeshire in 1563, received his education in the English College of Douay during its temporary removal to Rheims. On 8 May 1589, being then a deacon, he was sent with other students by Dr. Richard Barret, president of the college, to assist in commencing the new English College founded by Father Parsons at Valladolid (*Records of the English Catholics*, i. 220, 224). For a time he was stationed at the 'residence' or seminary established by Parsons at Lisbon. He was probably ordained priest in 1592, and he defended universal theology with great applause at Seville on 20 Feb. 1592–3. From Lisbon he crossed over to England about 1597, and for nineteen years he was chaplain to Sir John Southcote. In 1599 he entered the Society of Jesus, and in 1618 was professed of the four vows. He underwent many vicissitudes owing to his great zeal, and at various times was incarcerated in Newgate, the Clink, and the Fleet prisons in London, and in Framlingham and Winchester gaols. On James I's accession, being sent into banishment with many other priests, he returned to Lisbon, but soon revisited England, and again fell into the hands of the pursuivants. After serving the mission in the London district for many years, he died in London on 7 March 1640–1.

[More's Hist. Missionis Angl. Soc. Jesu, p. 286; Oliver's Jesuit Collections, p. 93; Foley's Records, i. 503–13, vii. 267.]   T. C.

FLOYD, JOHN (*d.* 1523), composer. [See LLOYD.]

FLOYD, JOHN (1572–1649), jesuit, called also DANIEL À JESU, younger brother of Father Henry Floyd [q. v.], was born in Cambridgeshire in 1572. After studying in the school of the English jesuits at Eu in Normandy, he was admitted on 17 March 1587–8 into the English College at Rheims, where he made his course of humanities and philosophy. Next he proceeded to Rome, was admitted into the English College there 9 Oct. 1590, and joined the Society of Jesus 1 Nov. 1592 (FOLEY, *Records*, vi. 185). On 18 Aug. 1593 he received minor orders at Rheims or Douay, and on the 22nd of the same month he was sent back to the English College at Rome with nine companions (*Douay Diaries*, pp. 232, 233). He taught philosophy and theology with great success, and acquired fame as a

preacher. In 1609 he became a professed father of the jesuit order. He laboured long and zealously on the English mission. Having ventured to visit Father Edward Oldcorne in Worcester gaol in 1606, he was detained, and he was unable either by entreaties or bribes to escape the clutches of Popham (MORUS, *Hist. Missionis Anglic. Soc. Jesu*, p. 287). After a year's imprisonment he was sent into exile with forty-six other priests, and he spent four years in preaching at St. Omer and composing controversial works. Then he returned to England, where he was often captured, and as often contrived by payments of money to escape from the pursuivants. Finally he settled at Louvain, where he was professor of theology. He died suddenly at St. Omer on 15 Sept. 1649 (*Florus Anglo-Bavaricus*, p. 51).

Wood describes him as 'a person excellently learned, as well in philosophy as theology' (*Athenæ Oxon.* ed. Bliss, iii. 483). He wrote the following works, some of which appeared under the pseudonyms of Daniel à Jesu, Hermannus Lœmelius, George White, and Annosus Fidelis Verimentanus, and the name Flud, and the initials J. R.: 1. 'The Overthrow of the Protestants Pulpit-Babels, convincing their Preachers of Lying and Rayling, to make the Church of Rome seeme mysticall Babell' [St. Omer], 1612, 4to. This contains an answer to 'The Jesuites Gospell,' by William Crashaw [q. v.], published in 1610. Floyd's work, which purports to be by 'J. R., Student in Divinity,' has been erroneously ascribed to Father Robert Jenison (GILLOW, *Bibliographical Dict.* iii. 611). In reply to this or some other work by Floyd, Sir Edward Hoby wrote 'A Counter-Snarle for Ishmael Rabshakeh, a Cecropedian Lycaonite, being an Answer to a Roman Catholic, who writes himself J. R.,' London, 1613. 2. 'Purgatories Triumph over Hell, maugre the barking of Cerberus in Syr Edward Hobyes Counter-Snarle. Described in a Letter to the said Knight, from J. R., authour of the Answere unto the Protestants Pulpit-Babels,' 1613, 4to, to which Hoby rejoined in a book entitled 'Curry-comb for a Coxcombe,' 1615. 3. 'Synopsis Apostasiæ Marci Antonii de Dominis, olim Archiepiscopi Spalatensis, nunc apostatæ, ex ipsiusmet libro delineata,' Antwerp, 1617, 8vo, translated into English by Father Henry Hawkins, St. Omer, 1617, 8vo, and again edited by John Fletcher, D.D. [q. v.]. Lond. 1828, 8vo. 4. 'Hypocrisis M. A. de Dominis detecta, seu censura in ejus libros de Republica Ecclesiastica,' Antwerp, 1620, 8vo. 5. 'Censura X Librorum de Republica Ecclesiastica M. A. de Dominis,' Antwerp, 1620, 12mo; Cologne, 1621, 8vo.

6. 'God and the King ; or a Dialogue wherein is treated of Allegiance due to ... K. James within his Dominions, which (by removing all Controversies and Causes of Dissentions and Suspitions) bindeth Subjects by an inviolable band of Love and Duty to their Soveraigne,' translated from the Latin, Cologne, 1620, 12mo. 7. 'St. Augustine's Meditations,' translated, St. Omer, 1621, 16mo, Paris, 1655, 16mo. 8. ' Monarchiæ Ecclesiasticæ ex scriptis M. Antonii de Dominis ... Demonstratio, duobus libris comprehensa, seu Respublica Ecclesiastica M. Ant. de Dominis, per ipsum a fundamentis eversa,' Cologne, 1622, 8vo. 9. ' A Word of Comfort ; or a Discourse concerning the late lamentable Accident of the Fall of a Roome at a Catholike Sermon in the Black-Friars at London, wherewith about fore-score persons were oppressed ... By J. R. P.,' St. Omer, 1623, 4to. This relates to the ' Fatal Vespers' [see DRURY, ROBERT, 1587–1623]. 10. 'Of the Sacrifice of the Mass,' translated from the Spanish of Antonio Molina, St. Omer, 1623, 4to. 11. 'On the Real Presence,' St. Omer, 1624, 12mo. 12. 'An Answer to Francis White's [successively bishop of Norwich and Ely] Reply to Mr. Fisher's Answer to the Nine Articles offered by King James to Father John Fisher, S. J.,' St. Omer, 1625, 4to. Francis Mason replied to Floyd in the second edit. of his ' Vindiciæ Ecclesiæ Anglicanæ,' 1625. 13. ' An Apology of the Holy Sea Apostolicks Proceedings for the Government of the Catholicks of England during the tyme of persecution. With a Defence of a Religious State, written by Daniel of Jesus,' Rouen, 1630, 4to. The first part is translated from the French. An enlarged Latin edition was published at Cologne and St. Omer in 1631. This work relates to the disputes between the jesuits and the secular priests in the matter of the episcopacy. It drew down the censure of the theological faculty of the Sorbonne upon its author, who replied with No. 15 below. 14. ' A Paire of Spectacles for Sir Humphrey Linde to see his way withall ; or, an Answeare to his booke called Via Tuta, a Safe Way,' s.l. 1631, 8vo. This has been sometimes attributed to Father Robert Jenison, but with no apparent foundation. Lynde's ' Via Tuta,' 1628, was answered more fully by John Heigham. 15. 'Hermanni Loemelii ... Spongia quâ diluuntur Calumniæ nomine Facultatis Parisiensis impositæ libro qui inscribitur Apologia Sanctæ Sedis Apostolicæ circa Regimen Catholicorum Angliæ,' &c., St. Omer, 1631, 8vo. A rejoinder was published on the part of the Sorbonne. Gillow gives a list of the principal books occasioned by Floyd's works

against Dr. Richard Smith, bishop of Chalcedon, and the French clergy who supported him (*Bibl. Dict.* ii. 304, 305). 16. 'Answer to a Book intituled "Instructions for the Catholicks of England."' 17. ' The Church Conquerant over Human Wit,' St. Omer, 1638, 4to, being a reply to Chillingworth's ' Religion of Protestants.' 18. ' The Total Summ,' St. Omer, 1638, 4to, reprinted in 1639 with ' The Judgment of an University Man on Mr. Chillingworth's Book, by Father William Lacy.' 19. 'The Imposture of Puritan Piety,' St. Omer, 1639. 20. 'A Treatise on Holy Pictures.' 21. ' Vita Brunehildis, Francorum Reginæ, liber primus,' manuscript folio, at St. Omer. It is cited by Bollandus in his notes to the life of St. Nicet, bishop of Besançon, under 8 Feb.

[Gillow's Bibl. Dict. of the English Catholics; Foley's Records, iv. 237, vii. 268; Oliver's Jesuit Collections, p. 94; Notes and Queries, 3rd ser. ix. 38; Panzani's Memoirs, pp. 124, 125; Southwell's Bibl. Scriptorum Soc. Jesu, p. 449; De Backer's Bibl. des Écrivains de la Compagnie de Jésus (1869), i. 1888; Dodd's Church Hist. iii. 105; Wood's Athenæ Oxon. (Bliss), ii. 195, iii. 92, 386, 995, iv. 309.]   T. C.

FLOYD, SIR JOHN (1748–1818), general, was elder son of Captain John Floyd of the 1st or king's dragoon guards (killed in Germany during the seven years' war), by Mary, daughter of the Rev. James Bate, rector of Chilham, Kent. He was born on 22 Feb. 1748, and entered the army on 5 April 1760, at the age of twelve, as a cornet in Eliott's light horse, afterwards the 15th or king's royal hussars. He is said to have received his commission without purchase, as some recognition of his father's gallantry, and he at once joined the regiment, and distinguished himself at the battle of Emsdorf. He was promoted lieutenant on 20 April 1763, and made riding-master to his regiment. His skill in this capacity brought him under the notice of the authorities. General Eliott, afterwards Lord Heathfield, spoke most favourably of his abilities, and he was 'lent' to the 1st dragoons, the royals, in order to improve their riding. Under the patronage of Eliott, Floyd was promoted, without purchase, captain-lieutenant on 20 May 1770, and captain on 25 May 1772 in the 15th hussars, and on 5 May 1779 major in the newly raised 21st light dragoons. In 1781 it was determined to raise a cavalry regiment expressly for service in India, and on 24 Sept. in that year Floyd was gazetted lieutenant-colonel of this new regiment, which was styled first the 23rd, and then the 19th light dragoons. He reached Madras in 1782, in which year he was gazetted a local colonel in the East Indies, and remained in that presidency for eighteen years, during which he showed himself the most accomplished English cavalry commander who ever served in the south of India. On 18 Nov. 1790 he was promoted colonel, and was in the same year appointed by Lord Cornwallis to command all the cavalry upon the Coromandel coast. In the three campaigns of Lord Cornwallis against Tippoo Sultan Floyd greatly distinguished himself. Before Lord Cornwallis had assumed the command in person, Floyd performed his greatest feat of arms. He had occupied Coimbatore on 21 July 1790 with the van of the army, and, after leaving headquarters there, he established himself on 26 Aug. at Satyamangalam with a detachment of the 36th regiment, and some of his own troopers of the 19th light dragoons. He was attacked by the enemy's cavalry in greatly superior force, but succeeded in retreating in good order. Cornwallis hereupon gave Floyd the command of the van-guard. He was wounded during the siege of Bangalore in March 1791, distinguished himself on the left wing in the battle of Arikera in May 1791, and served in the general action in May 1792 near Seringapatam, which induced Tippoo to sue for terms. After the conclusion of this war Floyd took his regiment into cantonments at Bangalore; he served as second in command to Colonel Braithwaite in the capture of Bangalore in 1793, and was promoted major-general on 5 Oct. 1794. When the second war with Tippoo Sahib broke out, Floyd again commanded the cavalry, and acted as second in command to General Harris. He led the advance of the army into Mysore, and the charges of his cavalry did much to win the battle of Malavalli. When the siege of Seringapatam was formed, Floyd commanded the covering army, and brought the Bombay column, under Major-general James Stuart, safely into camp. In the year after the capture of Seringapatam, Floyd, who had acquired great wealth from the lucrative appointments he had held in India, and from the booty of Seringapatam, returned to England. He was received with great distinction, was appointed colonel of the 23rd light dragoons on 11 Sept. 1800, and was promoted lieutenant-general on 1 Jan. 1801. He never again saw service, but spent some years on the staff in Ireland, commanding the Limerick division from 1803 to 1806, and the Cork division from 1809 to 1812. He was transferred to the colonelcy of the 8th light dragoons on 13 Sept. 1804, promoted general on 1 Jan. 1812, and in 1813 he received the honourable but sinecure office of governor of Gravesend and Tilbury. On 30 March 1816 he was

created a baronet, and a special crest of a lion rampant, bearing the standard of Tippoo Sultan in its paws, was granted to him. Floyd was twice married: first, in 1771, to Rebecca Juliana, daughter of Charles Darke of Madras; and secondly, in 1803, to Anna, daughter of Crosbie Morgell, and widow of Sir Barry Denney, bart., of Tralee Castle. By his first wife he left one son (an officer who served in the Peninsula and at Waterloo, and who succeeded him as second baronet) and two daughters, one married to General Sir Joseph Fuller, G.C.H., and the other to the Right Hon. Sir Robert Peel, the second baronet. Floyd died suddenly of gout in the stomach, on 10 Jan. 1818, shortly before completing his seventieth year.

[Royal Military Calendar, 1st edit.; Foster's Baronetage; Military Record of the 8th Hussars; Cornwallis Correspondence; Mackenzie's Sketch of the War with Tippoo Sultan from 1789 to 1792; Dirom's Narrative of the Campaign in India in 1792; Beatson's War with Tippoo Sultan in 1799; Lushington's Life and Services of General Lord Harris; Wellesley Despatches.]
H. M. S.

FLOYD, THOMAS (*fl.* 1603), author, a Welshman, entered New Inn, Oxford, as a commoner in 1589, graduated B.A. on 9 Feb. 1592–3, afterwards transferred himself to Jesus College, and took the degree of M.A. on 5 Feb. 1595-6. He was the author of 'The Picture of a Perfect Commonwealth, describing as well the Offices of Princes and inferior Magistrates over their Subjects, as also the Duties of Subjects towards their Governors,' &c., London, 1600, 12mo. He also wrote some Latin verses in 'Academiæ Oxoniensis Pietas erga Jacobum Regem,' 1603.

[Wood's Athenæ Oxon. (Bliss), i. 744; Fasti, i. 257, 270.]
J. M. R.

FLOYER, SIR JOHN (1649–1734), physician, born in 1649, was the son of Richard Floyer of Hintes, Staffordshire. He entered as commoner of Queen's College, Oxford, at the beginning of 1664, being then fifteen years of age. He was B.A. 16 April 1668, M.A. 1671, B.M. 27 June 1674, D.M. 8 July 1680 (WOOD). After twelve years' residence in Oxford, he settled at Lichfield as a physician. He was knighted in or before 1686, whether merely for professional eminence or for political services does not appear; but he would seem to have been in some way mixed up with the intrigues of James II in 1686 to obtain control over the corporation of Lichfield. There is no record of any other notable events in his life, except the publication of his several books. Floyer's name is known in connection with that of Samuel Johnson, who was, by his advice, sent up to be touched by Queen Anne for the 'evil.' It is also noteworthy that some of Floyer's books were printed for Michael Johnson, bookseller, of Lichfield, father of the lexicographer. Floyer attained considerable eminence in his profession, and died on 1 Feb. 1734.

Floyer was one of the most original physicians of the great scientific period in which he lived. His works show independence of thought and the spirit of research; while some have been important as being the starting-points of new methods in medical practice.

His first book, 'The Touchstone of Medicines,' contains a number of operations on the taste and smell of plants and other drugs, considered as a guide to their medicinal virtues, a subject treated of by Galen and other ancient writers, and by some of the moderns, though not now held to be worth consideration. This work, as well as that on animal humours, which is of the same class, contains many chemical and microscopical observations, but it appears to have been treated with some ridicule.

His work on the pulse watch is much more important. Floyer was the first to make regular observations upon the rate of the pulse, counting the number of beats in a minute by the watch. Before his time, though other points connected with the pulse had been carefully studied, this had been neglected. The pulse watch was merely a watch constructed to go for exactly one minute. Though Floyer's observations were not perfectly accurate, still, in Haller's words, he 'broke the ice,' and introduced a practice now universal. Floyer did good service also by his advocacy of cold bathing in a work published under different titles in several editions. He showed that the Roman customs of bathing had been prevalent in Britain in former times, and attributed to their disuse the occurrence of many diseases. He even went so far as to ascribe salutary physical consequences to infant baptism by immersion, and advocated the restoration of this ancient method of performing the rite. Indeed he succeeded more than once in getting children thus baptised according to the rubric ; and his authority has been quoted by theological advocates of baptism by immersion. He also built or got built a cold bath in the neighbourhood of Lichfield.

The work on asthma is also very noteworthy, not only as containing excellent clinical observations, but as giving the first account, derived from dissection, of the change in the lungs now called emphysema, which is found in one of the forms of asthma as then

understood. This observation, which has been often quoted in modern text-books, was made not on the human subject, but on a broken-winded mare. Floyer clearly distinguishes spasmodic asthma (from which he himself suffered), and assigns for it the same cause as do most modern authorities, viz. : ' contraction of the muscular fibres of the bronchia.' His other medical writings are less important. Haller remarks that Floyer's works were less known abroad than they deserved to be, and even in this country he has hardly received full justice. He was evidently a man of miscellaneous as well as medical learning, and greatly interested himself in the study of prophecy.

He wrote: 1. 'Φαρμακο-Βάσανος, or the Touchstone of Medicines,' London, printed for Michael Johnson at Lichfield, vol. i. 1687, vol. ii. 1690, 8vo. 2. 'Preternatural State of the Animal Humours, described by their Sensible Qualities,'London, 1696, 8vo. 3. 'An Enquiry into the Right Use of Baths,' London, 1697, 8vo; afterwards under other titles, viz.: 'The Ancient Psychrolusia Revived,' London, 1702, 1706; 'History of Hot and Cold Bathing,' with appendix by Dr. Baynard, London, 1709, 1715, 1722; Manchester, 1844, 12mo; in German, Breslau, 1749; in Latin, Leyden, 1699, Amsterdam, 1718. 4. 'Treatise on the Asthma,' London, 1698 ; 3rd ed. 1745, 8vo ; in French, Paris, 1761 (WATT, *Bibl. Brit.*) 5. 'The Physician's Pulse Watch,' vol. i. 1707, vol. ii. 1710, 8vo. 6. A letter on bathing in Dr. Joseph Browne's account of cures performed by cold baths, London, 1707. 7. ' A Letter concerning the Rupture of the Lungs,' London, 1710, 8vo (WATT). 8. 'The Sibylline Oracles, translated from the Greek,' London, 1713, 8vo. 9. 'A Vindication of the Sibylline Oracles,' London, 1715, 8vo. 10. 'Two Essays, on the Creation and on the Mosaic System,' Nottingham, 1717, sm. 8vo. 11. 'An Exposition of the Revelations,' London and Lichfield, 1719. 12. ' Exposition and Vindication of Esdras' (announced as on sale 1722; not seen). 13. 'An Essay to restore the Dipping of Infants in their Baptism,' London, 1722, 8vo. 14. 'Medicina Geronocomica, or the Galenic Art of Preserving Old Men's Healths,' London, 1724, 1725, 8vo. 15. 'A Comment on Forty-two Histories described by Hippocrates in his "Epidemics,"' &c., London, 1726, 8vo. 16. Two memoirs in ' Philos. Transactions,' vols. xxi. and xxiii., of no great importance.

Floyer states that the following manuscripts were left in the library of Queen's College, Oxford, but they are not named in Coxe's Catalogue of Oxford MSS.: (1) ' Advice to a Young Physician ; ' (2) ' Medicines distributed into Classes by their Tastes;' (3) 'The Third and Fourth Parts of the Pulse Watch;' (4) 'Essay on Air, Exercise,' &c. Two letters of Floyer's, without importance, are among the Brit. Mus. MSS.

[Wood's Athenæ Oxon. ii. 979 (1721); Harwood's Lichfield, 1806; Haller, Bibl. Med. Pract. iv. 10; Gent. Mag. March 1734.]   J. F. P.

FLUD, JOHN (d. 1523), composer. [See LLOYD.]

FLUDD or FLUD, ROBERT, M.D. (1574–1637), rosicrucian, second, or, according to Waite, fifth son of Sir Thomas Fludd, knight, by Elizabeth, daughter of Philip Andros of Taunton, Somerset, was born in 1574 at Milgate House, in the parish of Bearsted, Kent. The family was of Welsh origin; Robert's grandfather, David Fludd, was of Morton, Shropshire. Sir Thomas Fludd was 'sometime treasurer of war to Q. Elizabeth in France and the Low Countries.' In 1591 Fludd became commoner of St. John's College, Oxford, and graduated B.A. on 3 Feb. 1596; M.A. on 8 July 1598. As a student of medical science he travelled for nearly six years on the continent, visiting France, Spain, Italy, and Germany, and teaching in noble families. Returning with considerable repute as a proficient in chemistry, he became a member of Christ Church, Oxford, and on 16 May 1605 received the degrees of M.B. and M.D. Early in 1606 he was twice examined by the College of Physicians; on the second occasion (7 Feb.) the censors reported that although he had not fully satisfied the examiners, he was qualified to practise medicine. In consequence of alleged expressions of contempt for the Galenic system, he was cited before the censors on 2 May 1606. He denied the charges; his accusers not appearing, he was dismissed with an admonition. Thrice in the same year he was examined for the fellowship, and on 22 Dec. was pronounced 'dignus.' But he got into further trouble with the authorities, and 'tam insolenter se gessit' that on 21 March 1608 he was again admonished. On 20 Sept. 1609 he was elected a fellow of the College of Physicians; he was censor in 1618, 1627, 1633, and 1634.

Fludd practised in London as a physician, and kept a handsome establishment. His success in the healing art is ascribed by Fuller to his influence on the minds of his patients, producing a 'faith-natural' which aided the 'well working' of his drugs. He had his own apothecary under his roof, which was unusual; and he was always provided with an amanuensis, to whom he dictated at untimely hours his numerous and elaborate treatises on things divine and human. He claims notice as a mechanician; by his own account he had constructed a wooden bull that bellowed, an automatic dragon, and a self-performing lyre.

As a writer, Fludd is the chief English representative of that school of medical mystics which laid claim to the possession of the key to universal science. With less of original genius than Paracelsus, he has more method, and takes greater pains to frame a consistent system. The common idea of this school, that the biblical text contains a storehouse of hints for modern science, has lost interest, its potency expiring with the Hutchinsonians. And since Fludd did not make, like Paracelsus, any permanent addition to the pharmacopœia, or foreshadow, like Servetus, any later discoveries in chemistry or physiology, his lucubrations have passed into oblivion. His writings obtained more attention abroad than at home, though Selden highly valued them, and an admiring writer (John Webster) esteems their author 'one of the most Christian philosophers that ever writ.' Kepler and Gassendi entered the lists against him. De Quincey, following Buhle, makes him oddly enough the 'immediate father' of freemasonry.

Fludd is best remembered for his connection with the fraternity of the rosy cross, a society so obscure that its very existence has been denied. It was introduced to the public in 1614 by an anonymous work in German, best known as the 'Fama Fraternitatis,' which promised a 'universal and general reformation of the whole world' through the 'Orden des Rosenkreuzes.' This publication, which Gottfried Arnold regards as an elaborate skit on the part of Johann Valentin Andreas (1586–1654), ascribed the foundation of the fraternity to one Christian Rosenkreuz, in the fifteenth century. In addition to the attainment of the usual prizes of the alchemist, one of its practical objects was reported to be the gratuitous healing of the sick. The movement was commended to Fludd's notice by the German alchemist, Michael Maier, who visited him in London. Fludd came forward in vindication of the fraternity, especially from the suspicions of theologians. To a manuscript 'Declaratio breuis,' which he addressed to James I, are appended the confirmatory letters of French and German associates. On behalf of German writers of the fraternity, Justus Helt testifies (20 April 1617) that they are neither popish nor Lutheran, in short that 'Fratrum theosophiam esse Calvinistarum theologiam.'

Flood takes the position that all true natural science is rooted in revelation. He opposes the 'ethnic philosophy' of Aristotle, and is equally opposed to all modern astronomy, for he denies the diurnal revolution of the earth. Holding with the neoplatonists that all things were 'complicitly and ideally in God' before they were made, he advances to a doctrine of the divine immanence which betrays a strong pantheistic tendency. In the dedication of one of his works (1617) he addresses the deity, 'O natura naturans, infinita et gloriosa.' St. Luke he calls his 'physicall and theosophicall patron' (*Mosaicall Philos.*)

Fludd died unmarried on 8 Sept. 1637 at his house in the parish of St. Catherine, Coleman Street; he had previously lived in Fenchurch Street. He was buried with some ceremony in the chancel of Bearsted Church, under a stone which he had laid for the purpose; it bears an English inscription. He left directions for a monument in the style of that of Camden at Westminster; this, with bust and long Latin epitaph, was erected 10 Aug. 1638 within the chancel rails at Bearsted, by his nephew, Thomas Fludd or Floyd of Gore Court, Otham, Kent. His portrait was engraved by Mathias Merran of Basle, and again by Cooper. It represents a man with bald head, high forehead, and good features. Granger mentions five different prints of him. A sister of Fludd married Sir Nicholas Gilbourne of Charing, Kent (*Answer to Foster*, p. 108).

In his printed works his name is given indifferently as Flud or Fludd; the former seems to represent his earlier usage, and it is that of the manuscript 'Declaratio breuis' (1617). The punning translation, 'De Fluctibus,' used by Fludd in his second publication, and adopted by Kepler and others, argues an ignorance of Welsh, as the rendering bears no relation either to 'llwyd' (grey), or 'llwydd' (luck). Once he employs (1617) the name Rudolf Otreb, an anagram for Robert Floud. He published also under the name of Joachim Frizius; and a posthumous work, which has been assigned to him, appeared under the name of Alitophilus.

His principal works are: 1. 'Apologia Compendiaria, Fraternitatem de Rosea Cruce suspicionis ... maculis aspersam, veritatis quasi Fluctibus abluens,' &c., Leyden, 1616, 8vo. (the assailant of the rosicrucians was Andreas Libavius). 2. 'Tractatus Apologeticus integritatem Societatis de Rosea Cruce defendens,' &c., Leyden, 1617, 8vo (a revision of No. 1). 3. 'Tractatus Theologo-philosophicus,' &c., Oppenheim, 1617 [the date is given in a chronogram], 4to (this treatise 'a Rudolfo Otreb Britanno' is dedicated to the rosicrucian fraternity, and

consists of three books, 'De Vita,' 'De Morte,' and 'De Resurrectione;' in the third book he contends that those filled with the spirit of Christ may rise before his second advent). 4. 'Utriusque Cosmi ... metaphysica, physica atque technica Historia,' &c., Oppenheim and Frankfort, 1617–24, fol. (has two dedications, first to the Deity, secondly to James I; very curious copperplates; it was to have been in two volumes, the first containing two treatises, the second three; it was completed as far as the first section of the second treatise of the second volume). 5. 'Veritatis Proscenium,' &c., Frankfort, 1621, fol. (reply to Kepler, who had criticised him in appendix to 'Harmonice Mundi,' 1619, fol.) 6. 'Monochordon Mundi Symphoniacum,' &c., Frankfort, 1622, 4to (reply to Kepler's 'Mathematice,' 1622, fol.) 7. 'Anatomiæ Amphitheatrum,' &c., Frankfort, 1623, fol. (includes reprint of No. 6). 8. 'Philosophia Sacra et vere Christiana,'&c., Frankfort, 1626, fol. (portrait; dedicated to John Williams, bishop of Lincoln). 9. 'Medicina Catholica,' &c., Frankfort, 1629–31, fol. (in five parts; the plan included a second volume, not published). 10. 'Sophiæ cum Moria Certamen,' &c., Frankfort, 1629, fol. (reply to the 'Quæstiones Celebres in Genesim,' by Marin Mersenne). 11. 'Summum Bonorum,' &c. [Frankfort], 1629, fol. ('per Joachim Frizium;' further reply to Mersenne, who had accused Fludd of magic; Gassendi took up the controversy in an 'Examen Philosophiæ Fluddanæ,' 1630). 12. 'Doctor Fludds Answer vnto M. Foster, or, The Sqvesing of Parson Fosters Sponge,' &c., London, 1631, 4to (defence of weapon-salve, against the 'Hoplocrisma-Spongus,' 1631, 4to, of William Foster [q. v.], of Hedgerley, Buckinghamshire); an edition in Latin, 'Responsum ad Hoplocrisma-Spongum,' &c., Gouda, 1638, fol. Posthumous were: 13. 'Philosophia Moysaica,' &c., Gouda, 1638, fol.; an edition in English, 'Mosaicall Philosophy,' &c., London, 1659, 4to. 14. 'Religio Exculpata,' &c. [Ratisbon], 1684, 4to ('Autore Alitophilo Religionis fluctibus dudum immerso, tandem ... emerso;' preface signed J. N. J.; though assigned to Fludd, this work wholly differs in character from his genuine productions). 15. 'Tractatus de Geomantia,' &c. (four books), included in 'Fasciculus Geomanticus,' &c., Verona, 1687, 8vo. 16. An unpublished manuscript, copied by an amanuensis, and headed 'Declaratio breuis, &c.,' is in the British Museum, Royal MSS., 12 C. ii.; the manuscript 12 B. viii., which seems to have been another copy of this, with a slightly different title, has perished by fire. Fludd's 'Opera' consist of his folios, not reprinted, but collected and arranged in six volumes in 1638; appended is a 'Clavis Philosophiæ et Alchimiæ Fluddanæ,' Frankfort, 1633, fol.

[Fuller's Worthies, 1672, p. 78 sq. (second pagination), gives the name as Floid; Wood's Athenæ Oxon. 1691, i. 504, 509 (i.e. 519), 773, 778, 793; additions in Bliss, ii. 618; Ebert's Lexicon, 1821–30, No. 7701; Webster's Displaying of Supposed Witchcraft, 1677; Granger's Biog. Hist. of Engl. 1824, ii. 119; De Quincey's Historico-Crit. Inquiry into the Origin of the Rosicrucians and the Freemasons (1824), Works, xvi. 406 sq.; Hunt's Relig. Thought in Engl. 1870, i. 240 sq.; Munk's Coll. of Phys. 1878, i. 150 sq.; Waite's Real Hist. of the Rosicrucians, 1887, p. 284 sq.; Fludd's Works.]   A. G.

FLUDYER, SIR SAMUEL (1705–1768), lord mayor of London, born in 1705, was the son of Samuel Fludyer, a clothier in the city of London. His mother was Elizabeth Monsallier, and her sister Judith was grandmother of the eminent legist, Sir Samuel Romilly. 'The Fludyers (i.e. Samuel and his brother Thomas) began their career in very narrow circumstances, but by extraordinary industry, activity, enterprise, and good fortune they acquired inordinate wealth' (ROMILLY, *Memoirs*). Romilly would have become a clerk in their counting-house had not their deaths put an end to the scheme. In due course the brothers became common councillors in the city of London, Samuel for Bassishaw ward, Thomas for Aldgate. In 1751 Samuel was elected alderman of Cheap ward. Three years later he served the office of sheriff, was elected M.P. for Chippenham in 1754, was knighted in 1755 by George II, made a baronet in 1759, and became lord mayor in 1761. On this occasion George III attended the inauguration dinner, while the queen and royal family witnessed the lord mayor's show from David Barclay's house opposite Bow Church in Cheapside. This 9 Nov. was also distinguished by the last known exhibition of a play written expressly for the day by the 'city poet' (NICHOLS, *Anecd.* i. 44). Fludyer failed in an attempt to represent the city of London at the election of 1761, but was then re-elected for Chippenham. He was deputy-governor of the Bank of England at the time of his death, which took place, of apoplexy, on 18 Jan. 1768. His fortune was estimated at 900,000*l*. (*Gent. Mag.*) Sir Thomas, who succeeded his brother in the representation of Chippenham, died in March 1769.

[Orridge's Citizens of London, 153–7; Memoirs of Sir S. Romilly; Taubman's Pageants; Nichols's Lit. Anecd. i. 44; Gent. Mag. 1768.]   R. H.

FOGG, LAURENCE (1623–1718), dean of Chester, son of Robert Fogg (who was an active worker for the parliament, rector of Bangor-is-y-Coed, Flintshire, ejected 1662, died 1676), was born at Darcy Lever, in the parish of Bolton, in 1623, and educated at Bolton grammar school and at Cambridge. He was admitted pensioner of Emmanuel College on 28 Sept. 1644, and was afterwards of St. John's College. He held the office of taxor of the university in 1657. The degree of S.T.P. was granted to him in 1679. He was appointed rector of Hawarden, Flintshire, in 1655 or 1656, and was among the first who restored the public use of the liturgy. In 1662 he resigned his living, owing to an apparent ambiguity in an act of parliament relating to subscription, but he afterwards conformed. He preached at Oldham on 20 May 1666, being then curate of Prestwich, and described as theol. baccal. In 1672 he was appointed vicar of St. Oswald's, Chester, and on 4 Oct. 1673 was inducted prebendary of Chester Cathedral. In the latter year he became vicar of Plemonstall, Cheshire, on the presentation of the lord keeper Bridgeman, and on 14 Nov. 1691 was installed dean of Chester. He was a candid, sober-minded churchman, and much esteemed by the more moderate and pious dissenters, with whom he was on intimate terms. Philip and Matthew Henry both refer to him with appreciation. The latter in 1698 listened to one of Fogg's sermons with 'singular delight.' 'I have from my heart forgiven,' he writes, 'so I will endeavour to forget all that the dean has at any time said against dissenters, and against me in particular.' He wrote: 1. 'Two Treatises; i. A General View of the Christian Religion; ii. An Entrance into the Doctrine of Christianity by Catechistical Instruction,' Chester, 1712, 8vo. 2. 'Theologiæ Speculativæ Schema,' Lond. 1712, 8vo. 3. 'God's Infinite Grace in Election, and Impartial Equity in Preterition Vindicated,' Chester, 1713, 8vo. He died on 27 Feb. 1717–18, and was buried in Chester Cathedral, where a monument to his memory was erected by his son Arthur (1668–1738), prebendary of Chester, but, although it was extant in Ormerod's time, it is no longer to be found there.

[Cf. Calamy's Abridgment, 1713, ii. 708; Continuation, 1727, ii. 826; Ormerod's Cheshire, 1819, i. 427; Booker's Prestwich Church, 1852, p. 118; Sir J. B. Williams's Mem. of M. Henry, 1828; Philip Henry's Diaries and Letters (Lee), 1882; Worthington's Diary (Chetham Soc.), i. 20, 90, 104; Palatine Note-book, iv. 55, 79; Gastrell's Notitia Cestriensis (Raines), i. 135-6, 138; Le Neve's Fasti (Hardy), iii. 265, 271;

Graduati Cantabr. 1823; Watt's Bibl. Brit.; communications from Mr. W. H. Gladstone of Hawarden, Mr. Thomas Hughes, F.S.A., of Chester, and Mr. J. C. Scholes, Bolton.]   C. W. S.

FOGGO, GEORGE (1793–1869), historical painter, younger brother of James Foggo [q. v.], born in London 14 April 1793, received his early education with his brother at Paris, and joined him in London in 1819, after which date he was inseparably associated with him in his works and life. With his brother he founded the society for obtaining free access to our museums, public edifices, and works of art, of which the Duke of Sussex was president, Joseph Hume chairman of committees, and George Foggo honorary secretary. He worked as a lithographer also with his brother, and they lithographed their large picture of ' Parga ' and other original works; in 1828 he published by himself a set of large lithographs from the cartoons by Raphael. Foggo published in 1844 a catalogue of the pictures of the National Gallery, with critical remarks, the first attempt to make the collection intelligible to the public. Together with his brother, he was an unsparing critic of the Royal Academy and its system of education, and published some pamphlets on the subject. He was associated with other plans for the advancement of art, and was a man of great energy. He also published in 1853 the ' Adventures of Sir J. Brooke, Rajah of Sarawak.' He died in London 26 Sept. 1869, aged 76.

[Redgrave's Dict. of Artists; Ottley's Dict. of Recent and Living Painters; Graves's Dict. of Artists, 1760–1880; Art Journal, 1860 p. 372, 1869 p. 360; Catalogues of Royal Academy, British Institution, &c.; manuscript and other notes in Anderdon's Illustrated Academy Catalogues, print room, British Museum.]   L. C.

FOGGO, JAMES (1789–1860), historical painter, was born in London 11 June 1789. His father was a native of Fifeshire, and a watchmaker of good repute, but an advanced republican. He strenuously advocated negro emancipation in repeated visits to North and South America. Towards the end of 1799 the free assertion of these principles led him to fear persecution, and he took refuge in France with his wife and children. Unfortunately the Foggos arrived just at the commencement of Napoleon's military despotism, and were unable to quit Paris and return to their native land as they desired. James and his younger brother George [q. v.], wishing to become painters, were placed in the academy at Paris under the instruction of Jean Baptiste Regnault. They became desirous of emulating the work done, under the encourage-

ment of their country, by the French historical painters. In 1815, on Napoleon's return from Elba, Foggo quitted France for England, where he found all the friends of his family dead or dispersed. He set up a studio in Frith Street, Soho. In 1816 he exhibited ' Jane Shore ' at the Royal Academy, and in 1818 ' Hagar and Ishmael ' at the British Institution, contributing also to the latter a study of ' An Assassin's Head.' The picture of ' Hagar ' was well hung, and attracted attention, but did not find a purchaser. Foggo was obliged to support himself by teaching, and occasionally painting portraits. In 1819 his father had to go on a journey to Brazil, and his mother, with his brother George, joined him in London. From this time for forty years the two brothers lived and worked together, painting on the same canvas, and devoting themselves to historical compositions. They spent about three years in painting a very large picture, representing ' The Christian Inhabitants of Parga preparing to emigrate.' This, when completed, was too large for exhibition in the ordinary galleries, and the Foggos were compelled to exhibit it separately at their own expense. They were forced to eke out their means by all kinds of artistic drudgery. By sketching in accessories to architectural and sculptural designs they became acquainted with Francis Goodwin, the architect, who advised them to paint pictures suitable for altar-pieces in churches. They subsequently produced ' The Pool of Bethesda ' for the Bordesley Chapel at Birmingham; ' Christ blessing little Children ' for St. Leonard's Church, Bilston; ' Christ confounding the Rulers of the Synagogue,' exhibited at the Royal Academy, and much admired, but mysteriously lost on its way to Manchester, for which town it was destined; ' Nathan reproving David ' for Macclesfield town hall, and ' The Entombment of Christ,' presented by Mr. Edward Moxhay to the French protestant church, St. Martin's-le-Grand. The brothers lost patronage by their open advocacy of a more liberal system of education in art than that provided by the Academy. They were unsuccessful competitors at the Westminster Hall exhibitions in 1843–7, but exhibited their works with Haydon and others at the Pantheon. Among other historical pictures painted by them were : ' The Martyrdom of Anne Askew,' ' Wat Tyler killing the Tax Collector, ' The Barons taking the Oath at Bury St. Edmunds,' ' Napoleon signing the Death-warrant of the Duc d'Enghien,' ' General Williams among the Inhabitants of Kars,' &c.

In 1852 they undertook the arrangement and care of the exhibition at the Pantheon in Oxford Street, and continued it for three years. Mr. Hart, a well-known picture dealer, offered to purchase all the unsold works which the Foggos had by them. The offer, gladly accepted, came to nothing, owing to the premature death of the purchaser. The brothers were much esteemed in private life for many excellent qualities, and their friends were numerous and sincere. Foggo died in London 14 Sept. 1860, and was buried in the Highgate cemetery.

[Authorities under GEORGE FOGGO.]   L. C.

FOILLAN, SAINT and BISHOP (d. 655), brother of Fursa [q. v.], left Ireland with his brother, and passing through Wales settled in East Anglia, where he was received by King Sigebert. When Fursa, having completed his monastery of Cnoberesburgh, was about to retire to the hermitage of his brother Ultan, he placed the monastery in charge of Foillan and two others. Fursa, some time after, was driven abroad by the disturbed state of the country, and settled in the territory of Neustria. Foillan some time later left Cnoberesburgh, and with Ultan followed Fursa to the continent. Here they were invited to settle in Brabant, to the north of Peronne, by Gertrude, daughter of Pepin, abbess of Nivelles. She wished them to instruct her community, especially in music, for which the Irish were famous. With the aid of Gertrude they erected a monastery at Fosse, not far from Nivelles, over which Ultan was placed, Foillan remaining in charge of the establishment at Nivelles. Foillan, when travelling through the forest of Soignies in Hainault with three of his disciples, was set upon by robbers and slain on 31 Oct., and probably in 655. The bodies were not discovered until 16 Jan. following. This day was afterwards observed as that of the Invention of St. Foillan. He was buried at Fosse, and in the calendar of Œngus and other authorities is accounted a martyr, doubtless because he was killed in the discharge of his duty. He appears to have been a bishop, but the story of his having been consecrated by Pope Martin I seems to have no better foundation than the idea which possessed many mediæval writers that every one ought to have gone to Rome. The monasteries of Fosse and Peronne, with that of St. Quinton, formed one of those groups of Irish monasteries which were so frequent on the continent in that age, and performed an important part in sowing the seeds of religion and civilisation among barbarian tribes.

[Colgan, Acta Sanct. 99–103 ; Lanigan's Eccl. Hist. ii. 464–6 ; Ussher's Works; Calendar of Œngus, clxi.]   T. O.

FOLBURY, GEORGE (d. 1540), master of Pembroke Hall, Cambridge, graduated B.A. at Cambridge in 1514, was preacher to the university in 1519, took the degree of B.D. in 1524, was presented to a canonry and to the prebend of North Newbald in the church of York in March 1531, to the rectory of Maidwell, Northamptonshire, on 20 Feb. 1533–4, elected master of Pembroke Hall in 1537, and died between 10 July and 10 Nov. 1540. He is said to have been for a time tutor to Henry Fitzroy, duke of Richmond, natural son of Henry VIII, but this is not confirmed by the memoir of the duke published in 'Camden Miscellany,' vol. iii. Bale states that he took the degree of D.D. at Montpelier, and that he was a poet, orator, and epigrammatist. His works seem to have perished.

[Cooper's Athenæ Cantabr. ; Le Neve's Fasti Eccl. Angl. iii. 674 ; Letters and Papers, For. and Dom. Henry VIII, vol. v. g. 166, 31 ; Bale's Scriptt. Illustr. Maj. Brit. (Basel, 1557), cent. ix. 27.]   J. M. R.

FOLCARD or FOULCARD (fl. 1066), hagiographer, a Fleming by race and birth, was a monk of St. Bertin's in Flanders, who is supposed to have come over to England in the reign of Edward the Confessor. He entered the monastery of the Holy Trinity or Christ Church, Canterbury, and was renowned for his learning, and especially for his knowledge of grammar and music; his manners were affable and his temper cheerful. Soon after the Conquest the king set him over the abbey of Thorney, Cambridgeshire; but he was never strictly abbot, for he did not receive the benediction. After holding the abbey about sixteen years he retired, owing to a dispute with the Bishop of Lincoln, evidently Remigius, and returned, as may be fairly inferred from Orderic, to his own land. The statement in the 'Monasticon' that he was deposed by Lanfranc at the council of Gloucester in 1084 seems to lack foundation. Either while he was a monk at Canterbury, or during his residence at Thorney, which seems more probable, he and his monastery were in some trouble, and were helped by Aldred [q. v.], archbishop of York, who persuaded the queen either of the Confessor or of the Conqueror to interest herself in their cause. In return Folcard wrote the 'Life of Archbishop John of Beverley' for Aldred. His works are: 1. 'Vita S. Bertini,' dedicated to Bovo, abbot of St. Bertin's from 1043 to 1065, and printed in Mabillon's 'Acta SS. O. S. B.' III. ii. 104, and in Migne's 'Patrologia,' cxlvii. 1082. 2. 'Vita Audomari,' in Mabillon, ii. 557, and Migne. 3. A poem 'in honorem

S. Vigoris Episcopi,' written between 1045 and 1074, in Achery's 'Spicilegium,' iv. 576, and Migne. 4. 'Vita S. Oswaldi' in Mabillon, i. 727, the Bollandists' 'Acta SS.,' Capgrave, and Migne. 5. 'Responsoria for the Festival of St. John of Beverley,' composed before 'Vita S. Johannis Episcopi Eboracensis,' which was written before 1070, and is printed in the Bollandists' 'Acta SS.' May, ii. 165, Migne, and 'Historians of York' (Rolls Ser.), i. 238. 6. 'Vita S. Botulfi,' suggested by the fact that the relics of the saint were at Thorney, dedicated to Walkelin, bishop of Winchester, and therefore written in or after 1070, in Mabillon, III. 1, the Bollandists' 'Acta SS.' June iv. 324, and Migne.

[Ordericus Vitalis, Eccles. Hist. lib. xi. 835, Duchesne; Histoire Littéraire de la France, ed. 1868, viii. 132; Cave's Scriptt. Eccles. Historia. p. 531; Bale's Scriptt. cent. ii. 164; Dugdale's Monasticon, ii. 594; Wright's Biog. Lit. i. 512; Hardy's Cat. I. i. 373, 423, ii. 790; Raine's Historians of York, i., Pref. lii. (Rolls Ser.)]   W. H.

FOLDSONE, JOHN (*d.* 1784?), painter, obtained some note as a painter of small portraits, which he executed with great rapidity. He used to attend his sitters at their dwellings in the morning, dine with them if they lived at a distance, and finish his work before evening. His portraits, though naturally of no great merit, had sufficient likeness to gain him employment. Two portraits by him of Miss Elizabeth Haffey, a child, and her brother, John Burges Haffey, were engraved in mezzotint by Robert Laurie, and a picture by him, entitled 'Female Lucubration,' was similarly engraved by P. Dawe. Foldsone exhibited first at the Society of Artists in 1769 and 1770, and afterwards at the Royal Academy from 1771 to 1783, shortly after which date he died. He painted madonnas, mythology, history, and portraits, but his artistic productions seem to have been indifferent and on a par with his general character. He left a wife and family; his eldest daughter, Sarah, attained some note as a miniature-painter [see MEE, ANNE].

[Edwards's Anecdotes of Painters; Redgrave's Dict. of Artists; Graves's Dict. of Artists, 1760–1880; Chaloner Smith's British Mezzotinto Portraits; Royal Academy Catalogues.]   L. C.

FOLEY, DANIEL (1815–1874), professor of Irish, was born at Tralee, co. Kerry, in 1815. His parents were poor people, and he had never worn shoes, when he obtained employment in the shop of Patrick Grey in Tralee. Under the influence of a clergyman in the neighbourhood he left the church of Rome, and was sent to study for ordination in the then established church of Ireland at

Trinity College, Dublin. He was in time ordained, and took the degree of B.D., and obtained the prebend of Kilbragh, in the cathedral of Cashel, and the rectory of Templetuohy. Irish was his native tongue, and in 1849 he was appointed professor of that language in the university of Dublin, and held the office till 1861. While holding this office he wrote a preface to a small Irish grammar by Mr. C. H. H. Wright, and 'An English-Irish Dictionary, intended for the use of Students of the Irish Language,' Dublin, 1855. This work is based upon a dictionary prepared early in this century by Thaddeus Connellan [q. v.], but published without date, long kept in sheets, and issued in Dublin from time to time with a variety of false title-pages. Foley altered some of the Irish interpretations, and added a good many words. Many of the Irish words are inventions of his own, as *fuam-ainm* (sound-name) for onomato-poeia; or paraphrases, as *duine* (person) for microcosm, *eudaigh* (clothes) for caparison; or errors due to defective education, as *ainis* (anise) for caraway. The university of Dublin made a grant towards the publication, but as a dictionary it is of no authority. Foley took an active part in opposition to disestablishment of the church in Ireland, and lectured on the subject in England. He died at Blackrock, near Dublin, 7 July 1874, and was buried in the cemetery of Kill o' the Grange.

[A. Webb's Compendium of Irish Biog.; information from Joseph Manning of Tralee; Foley's Works.]   N. M.

FOLEY, JOHN HENRY (1818–1874), sculptor, was born in Dublin on 24 May 1818. At the age of thirteen he entered the schools of the Royal Dublin Society, and gained the first prizes for human form, ornamental design, animals, and architecture. In 1834 he came to London, and was admitted a student of the Royal Academy in the following year. In 1839 he exhibited 'The Death of Abel' and 'Innocence,' which at once attracted attention, and in the following year a group of 'Ino and Bacchus,' which was purchased by the Earl of Ellesmere. In 1841 came 'Lear and Cordelia,' followed in 1842 by 'Venus rescuing Æneas from Diomed,' and by 'Prospero and Miranda' in 1843. In 1844 he sent a figure, 'Youth at the Stream,' to the competition at Westminster Hall for the decoration of the houses of parliament, and in 1847 he received a commission to execute the statue of Hampden, which now stands in the entrance corridor, together with that of Selden, afterwards commissioned. In 1849 he was elected an associate of the Royal Academy,

N

and in 1858 a royal academician. He continued to contribute to the exhibitions of the Academy till 1861, but in consequence of a dispute about the arrangement of the sculpture at the following exhibition he refused to exhibit again. Among the finest of his exhibited works not already mentioned were 'The Mother,' 1851; 'Egeria,' 1856; 'The Elder Brother in Comus,' his diploma work, 1860; and 'Oliver Goldsmith,' 1861. More important, however, than these were some of his subsequent works, the three equestrian statues of Lord Canning, Lord Hardinge, and Sir James Outram for Calcutta; and the group of Asia and the figure of the prince for the Albert Memorial, the latter of which was not erected till after his death. Among his other works in public places are: 'Caractacus' and 'Egeria' at the Mansion House, 'John Stuart Mill' on the Thames Embankment, 'Sir Charles Barry' in the House of Commons, and 'Lord Herbert' in Pall Mall. His statues of O'Connell, Lord Gough, Goldsmith, and Burke are at Dublin, Lord Clyde at Glasgow, Father Mathew at Cork, Clive at Shrewsbury, the Hon. J. Stuart at Ceylon, and General Stonewall Jackson in America. Of Foley's sepulchral monuments the most remarkable are those erected to Admiral Sir William Cornwallis and others in Melfield Church, Hampshire, to General the Hon. Robert Bruce in Dunfermline Abbey, and to Brigadier-general John Nicholson in Lisburn Cathedral. If we add his statues of Grattan, Faraday, and Reynolds, his monument to James Ward, R.A., and his relief of Miss Helen Faucit (Lady Martin), the list of his more celebrated works will be nearly complete; but he also designed the seal of the Confederate States of America, and we must take account of a large number of busts and other commissions of minor importance before we can fully appreciate the fulness of his employment and the industry of his life. He was a very conscientious and fastidious workman, consulting his friends as to his designs, and altering them continually in course of execution. After a life of devotion to his art he died at Hampstead of pleuritic effusion of the heart, 27 Aug. 1874. He left his models to the Dublin Society, and the bulk of his property to the Artists Benevolent Fund.

Foley fully deserved the favour which he enjoyed almost from the beginning to the end of his career. His earlier and more ideal works, like 'Ino and Bacchus,' 'Innocence,' and 'The Mother,' were marked by a natural grace and freshness of conception which were at that time rare in modern sculpture. His later figure of 'Egeria' is touched with finer poetry, and in his conception of 'Caractacus' he displayed that vigour of imagination and grasp of character which distinguished his statues of public men from the work of most of his contemporaries. His three noble equestrian statues of Indian worthies are perhaps his greatest works. They are all very different from one another; but that of Sir James Outram, reining up his horse and turning round as it were suddenly in his saddle, is the most vivacious and original.

[Redgrave's Dict. of Artists, 1878; Art Journal, 1865, 1875, 1877; Works of John Henry Foley, R.A.; English Encyclopædia; Encyclopædia Britannica; Clement and Hutton's Artists of the Nineteenth Century.]   C. M.

FOLEY, PAUL (1645?–1699), speaker of the House of Commons, second son of Thomas Foley [q. v.] of Witley Court, Worcestershire, founder of the Old Swinford Hospital, was born in or about 1645 (*Mon. Inscript.*) In 1670 he purchased the estate of Stoke Edith, Herefordshire, from Alice Lingen, and between 1697 and 1699 pulled down the old house and built the present one. In 1679 he was chosen by the city of Hereford as one of its representatives, and served in the same capacity in seven parliaments in three successive reigns. He bore a high reputation for integrity and personal piety, due, perhaps, in part to the good influence of Richard Baxter, his father's bosom friend. In politics he was a strong tory, but was among those who insisted most strenuously upon the vacancy of the throne caused by the flight of James II. He was a member of the Convention parliament, and was one of the managers of the free conference between the two houses of parliament which took place in 1689 and led to the settlement of the succession. In 1690 (26 Dec.) Foley was elected by the House of Commons one of the commissioners for stating the public accounts, and showed himself a good financier, though his opinions on certain points were singular. If we may credit Roger North, he held that 'all foreign trade was loss and ruinous to the nation' (*Life of Lord Guilford*, i. 293)—a statement which may have meant only that by means of foreign trade the crown was rendered too independent of parliamentary supplies. But his honesty and industry were conspicuous and commended him to the House of Commons when it had to choose a speaker in place of the venal Sir John Trevor. An attempt was made by Wharton to impose on the house a nominee of the king, but, a division taking place, Foley was elected on 14 March 1694–5, and in the next parliament (November 1695) was again unanimously chosen. His conduct in the chair, which he occupied until December 1698, was upright and impartial. His independence showed itself conspicuously in his remarks on the king's rejection of the Place Bill. Foley took part in the debates from time to time. He spoke openly against the employment of Dutch and French officers in the English army and navy, and steadily opposed the attainder of Sir John Fenwick in 1696. Earlier in the same year Foley joined with Harley in proposing to parliament the establishment of a national land bank. A bill was passed authorising the government to borrow 2,564,000*l.* at seven per cent. It received the royal assent on 27 April. If before 1 Aug. half the sum had been subscribed, the subscribers were to be incorporated into a land bank, which was to lend annually on mortgages of land alone a sum of not less than 500,000*l.* Foley was one of the commissioners for raising the loan, but his efforts failed, and, in spite of various modifications of the original scheme, he and his colleagues were unable to borrow more than 2,100*l.* The land bank thus proved a disastrous failure. The library at Stoke Edith contains a valuable collection of books and pamphlets, which bear out Roger North's observation (*ib.* i. 292) that Foley was a busy student of records and had compiled a treatise which went further into the subject of precedents than either Cotton or Prynne had gone. Bishop Burnet, who naturally disparages a political opponent, yet gives him credit for being 'a learned lawyer and a man of virtue and good principles'. (*Hist.* iv. 191), and Macaulay considers him to have been 'superior to his partisan, Harley, both in parts and elevation of character' (*ib.* iv. 67). Foley died from gangrene in the foot on 13 Nov. 1699 (*MS. Family Notes*), and was buried at Stoke Edith, where the inscription on his monument antedates his death by two days. He was not a man of extraordinary ability, but his political career was wholly free from those vices which most of the public men of his day displayed. He married Mary, daughter of Alderman Lane of London, and by her had two sons, Thomas (*d.* 1737), who was an active member of parliament, and Paul, a barrister-at-law. The grandson of the elder son, also Thomas, was raised to the peerage as Baron Foley of Kidderminster 20 May 1776. A similar peerage, held by a cousin, had become extinct ten years earlier [see FOLEY, THOMAS]. The peerage of the second creation is still extant.

[Manning's Lives of the Speakers; Nash's Materials for Hist. of Worcestershire, ii. 460–2, App. 82–4; Parl. Hist. v. 64–108; Kennett, pp. 510–512; Luttrell's Brief Relation, iv. 583; Robinson's Manor Houses of Herefordshire, pp. 257–8; Macaulay's History.]   C. J. R.

FOLEY, SAMUEL (1655–1695), bishop of Down and Connor, was eldest son of Samuel Foley of Clonmel and Dublin (*d.* 1695), younger brother of Thomas Foley [q. v.], founder of the Old Swinford Hospital. His mother, Elizabeth, was sister of Colonel Solomon Richards of Polsboro, Wexford. He was born at Clonmel 25 Nov. 1655, was admitted fellow-commoner of Trinity College, Dublin, 8 June 1672, was elected fellow 11 June 1697, and was ordained in the church of Ireland in 1678. On 14 Feb. 1688–9 he was installed chancellor of St. Patrick's Cathedral, Dublin, and was attainted by James II's parliament in the same year. On 4 April 1691 he became dean of Achonry and precentor of Killala. He proceeded D.D. of Trinity College in the same year. On 4 Oct. 1694 he was enthroned bishop of Down and Connor in succession to Thomas Hacket, who had been deprived for gross neglect of duty. He died of fever at Lisburn 22 May 1695, and was buried there. The bishop was married, and left issue. He wrote: 1. Two sermons, one preached 19 Feb. 1681–2, and the other 24 April 1682. 2. 'An Account of the Giant's Causeway,' published in the 'Philosophical Transactions' for 1694. 3. 'An Exhortation to the Inhabitants of Down and Connor concerning the Religious Education of their Children,' Dublin, 1695. Foley left some manuscripts on the controversy between protestantism and Roman catholicism to the library of Trinity College, Dublin.

[Burke's Peerage, s.v. 'Foley;' Cotton's Fasti Eccles. Hibern. i. 270, ii. 118, iii. 208, iv. 84, 105; Ware's Bishops of Ireland, ed. Harris, i. 214; Ware's Writers of Ireland, ed. Harris, 253.]   S. L.

FOLEY, THOMAS (1617–1677), founder of the hospital at Old Swinford, Worcestershire, was eldest son of Richard Foley of Stourbridge, by a second marriage with Alice, daughter of William Brindley of Hide, Staffordshire. His father was engaged in the iron manufactory near Stourbridge (four miles from the town), died 6 July 1657, aged 77, and was buried in the chancel of Old Swinford Church. His mother died 26 May 1663, aged 75. There is a legend (cf. SMILES, *Self-Help*, ed. 1877, pp. 205–7) that Richard Foley the father was originally a fiddler. On perceiving that the supremacy of the Stourbridge ironworks was threatened by the competition of ironworkers in Sweden, who had discovered the process of 'splitting,' he is said to have worked his way to a Swedish iron port and obtained access to the factories, where he learned the secret of the successful process. On his return home he induced some friends to join him in erecting machinery for the purpose of working the process. The first experiments failed, and Foley paid a second secret visit to Sweden to perfect his knowledge. His second attempt at Stourbridge succeeded, and he thus laid the foundations of his family's fortune. The splitting machine introduced by Foley is still in use in the neighbourhood of Stourbridge. Coleridge tells the story as 'the best attested instance of enthusiasm existing,' but unfortunately confuses Richard with his son Thomas (*Table-talk*, ed. Ashe, pp. 332–3).

Born 3 Dec. 1617, Thomas actively pursued the iron industry of his native place, and amassed a large fortune, which was increased by a wealthy marriage. He acquired much landed property in the neighbourhood of Stourbridge and Old Swinford, and secured valuable church patronage at Kidderminster and elsewhere. His association with Kidderminster brought him the acquaintance of Richard Baxter [q. v.], with many of whose opinions he strongly sympathised. Baxter describes Foley as 'a truly honest man . . . who from almost nothing did get about 5,000*l.* per ann. or more by ironworks, and that with so just and blameless dealing that ever he had to do with that ever I heard of magnified his great integrity and honesty, which was questioned by none.' As a church patron he always chose, according to Baxter, 'the most conformable ministers that could be got.' Foley was also on good terms with Baxter's friend, James Berry [q. v.], a well-known major-general under Cromwell's régime. When Cromwell urged that Foley should become high sheriff of Worcestershire—an office which few country gentlemen were ready to undertake— Berry wrote to Thurloe (17 Nov. 1655): 'Mr. Foley I know to be an honest man, but I fear it would be much to his prejudice to have the place, he having no conveniency in the country, and being a friend, I hope my lord will favour him a little' (*Thurloe State Papers*, iv. 211). A day or two later Berry wrote more emphatically in the same sense (*ib.* iv. 215). Although no avowed enemy to Cromwell's government, Foley, like Baxter, had royalist leanings, and desired apparently to have as little as possible to do with the Commonwealth. He none the less seems to have been high sheriff in 1656, when Baxter preached a sermon before him, and in the same year was one of the commissioners for levying the property-tax in Worcestershire. In 1659, while the Rump was sitting at Westminster, Foley and John Bridges presented a petition, drawn up by Baxter, 'in favour of tithes and the ministry.' He sat in the Convention parliament of 1660 as mem-

ber for Bewdley. In later life he settled at Witley, where he had a fine estate, now the property of the Earl of Dudley, whose trustees purchased it for 900,000*l.* In 1667 he founded a hospital at Old Swinford, endowing it with land producing 600*l.* a year. Sixty poor boys between the ages of seven and eleven, selected in fixed numbers from different parishes in Worcestershire and Staffordshire, were to be fed, clothed, and educated there free of charge, and were to be afterwards apprenticed by the trustees. The hospital is still standing, and the endowment now produces 5,500*l.* a year. There are 160 boys in the school. Foley died at Witley 1 Oct. 1677, and was buried in the church there, under a monument with a long Latin inscription.

Foley was married to Anne, daughter of George Brown of Spelmonden, Kent, by whom he had four sons: Thomas, Nathaniel (1647–1663), Paul [q. v.], afterwards speaker of the House of Commons, and Philip. Foley had also two daughters: Martha, wife of William Jolliffe, a London merchant, and Sarah, the wife of (1) Essex Knightly of Fawsley, Northamptonshire, and (2) of John Hampden, grandson of the patriot. A portrait of Foley is in the Old Swinford Hospital. It was painted by William Trabute, and is engraved in Nash's 'Materials.'

A grandson, THOMAS FOLEY (heir of Foley's eldest son), was M.P. for Stafford for eighteen years, from 1694 until he was raised to the peerage on 1 Jan. 1711–12, being one of the twelve peers made by the tory administration of Harley and St. John to secure a majority for their peace negotiations in the House of Lords. He died 22 Jan. 1732–3. This peerage became extinct 8 Jan. 1766. It was revived in the person of a kinsman [see FOLEY, PAUL, ad fin.] in 1776, and is still extant.

[Nash's Materials for Hist. of Worcestershire, ii. 210–12, 464–6, App. 82–4; Baxter's Reliquiæ; Chambers's Biog. Illustrations of Worcestershire, p. 187; Noake's Worcestershire Notes and Queries, p. 264; Noake's Guide to Worcestershire, p. 331; Official Lists of Members of Parl. i. 517; Collins's Peerage, viii. 364 et seq.; information kindly communicated by P. H. Foley, esq., Prestwood, Stourbridge.]   S. L.

FOLEY, SIR THOMAS (1757–1833), admiral, second son of John Foley of Ridgeway in Pembrokeshire, where the family had been settled for several centuries, a nephew of Thomas Foley, a captain in the navy (*d.* 1758), who had been round the world with Anson in the Centurion, was born in 1757, and entered the navy on board the Otter in 1770. After serving in her on the Newfoundland station for three years he was in 1774 appointed to the Antelope, going out to Jamaica as flagship of Rear-admiral Clark Gayton [q. v.] While in her he was repeatedly lent to the small craft on the station, and saw a good deal of active cruising against the colonial privateers. He returned to England in the Antelope in May 1778; on the 25th was promoted to the rank of lieutenant, and on the 28th was appointed to the America, with Lord Longford. In her, he took part in the operations of the fleet under Keppel [see KEPPEL, AUGUSTUS, VISCOUNT] in 1778, and Sir Charles Hardy [q. v.] in 1779. In October 1779 he was appointed to the Prince George with Rear-admiral Robert Digby [q. v.], in which he was present at the capture of the Spanish convoy off Cape Finisterre on 8 Jan. 1780, the defeat of Langara off Cape St. Vincent on 16 Jan. and the subsequent relief of Gibraltar [see RODNEY, GEORGE BRYDGES, LORD]. Continuing in the Prince George when she went to North America in 1781, and afterwards to the West Indies with Sir Samuel Hood [see HOOD, SAMUEL, VISCOUNT], Foley was present as a lieutenant in the attempted relief of St. Kitts, and in the engagements to leeward of Dominica on 9 and 12 April 1782. In the following October, on the invaliding of Captain Elphinstone [see ELPHINSTONE, GEORGE KEITH, LORD KEITH], he was for a few weeks acting captain of the Warwick at New York, and on 1 Dec. was confirmed in the rank of commander, and appointed to the Britannia, armed ship. In her he continued after the peace and till the beginning of 1785, when he brought her to England and paid her off. From December 1787 to September 1790 he commanded the Racehorse sloop on the home station, and from her was advanced to post rank on 21 Sept. In April 1793 he was appointed to the St. George of 98 guns as flag-captain to Rear-admiral John Gell [q. v.], with whom he went to the Mediterranean, took part in the operations at Toulon (August–December 1793), and, when Gell invalided, continuing as flag-captain to Rear-admiral Sir Hyde Parker (1739–1807) [q. v.], assisted in driving the French squadron into Golfe Jouan (11 June 1794), and in defeating the French fleet in the two engagements off Toulon (13 March, 13 July 1795). In March 1796 he accompanied Parker to the Britannia, in which he remained with Vice-admiral Thompson, who relieved Sir Hyde towards the close of the year. As flag-captain to the commander in the second post, Foley thus held an important position in the battle off Cape St. Vincent on St. Valentine's day, 1797. He was shortly afterwards appointed to com-

mand the Goliath of 74 guns, one of the ships sent into the Mediterranean under Captain Troubridge in May 1798 to reinforce Rear-admiral Sir Horatio Nelson [see NELSON, HORATIO, VISCOUNT; TROUBRIDGE, SIR THOMAS]. He thus shared in the operations of the squadron previous to the battle of the Nile, in which he had the distinguished good fortune to lead the English line into action. In doing so he passed round the van of the French line as it lay at anchor, and engaged it on the inside; the ships immediately following did the same, and a part at least of the brilliant and decisive result of the battle has been commonly attributed to this manœuvre. It has also been frequently and persistently asserted that in doing this Foley acted solely on his own judgment, and that Nelson, had time permitted, would have prevented him. But this assertion is distinctly contradicted by the positive statements of Sir Edward Berry [q. v.] in his 'Narrative,' that Nelson's projected mode of attack was 'minutely and precisely executed,' and also by the fact that Captain Miller of the Theseus, writing a very detailed account of the commencement of the battle, gives no hint that the Goliath's manœuvre was at all unexpected by him or the other captains who followed Foley (LAUGHTON, Letters and Despatches of Viscount Nelson, pp. 151, 156). The probable explanation of the apparent contradiction would seem to be that the advisability of passing inside had been fully discussed between the admiral and the captains of the fleet, and that the doing or not doing it was left to the discretion not only of the captain of the leading ship but of all the others. If this was the case, Foley merely exercised the right of judgment which Nelson had entrusted, not to him alone, but to whoever happened to lead (HERBERT, pp. 40–3; Journal of the Royal United Service Institution, 1885, xxix. p. 916). The Goliath continued on the Mediterranean station, attached to the command of Lord Nelson, till towards the close of 1799, when she was sent home. In the following January Foley was appointed to the Elephant of 74 guns for service in the Channel fleet. In 1801 she was sent into the Baltic, in the fleet under Sir Hyde Parker; and when it was decided to attack the Danish position at Copenhagen, Nelson, on whom the duty devolved, hoisted his flag on board her, his own flagship, the St. George, drawing too much water for the contemplated operations. It was thus that Foley, as flag-captain, assisted in drawing out the detailed instructions for the several ships to be employed on this service, and, in Nelson's own words, with 'his advice on many and important occasions during the battle' (NICOLAS, *Nelson Despatches*, iv. 304, 315). Immediately after the battle Nelson went back to the St. George, and the Elephant, continuing attached to the fleet, returned to England in the autumn, when she was paid off. In September 1805, when Nelson was going out to resume the command of the fleet off Cadiz, he called on Foley and offered him the post of captain of the fleet. Foley's health, however, would not at that time permit him to serve afloat, and he was obliged to refuse (HERBERT, p. 41). On 28 April 1808 he was promoted to the rank of rear-admiral, and in 1811 was appointed commander-in-chief in the Downs, in which post he continued till the peace. On 12 Aug. 1812 he became a vice-admiral; was nominated a K.C.B. in January 1815, a G.C.B. on 6 May 1820, and attained the rank of admiral on 27 May 1825. In May 1830 he was appointed commander-in-chief at Portsmouth, where he died 9 Jan. 1833. He was buried in the Garrison Chapel, in a coffin made of some fragments of oak kept from his old ship Elephant when she was broken up.

Foley married, in July 1802, Lady Lucy Fitzgerald, youngest daughter of the Duke of Leinster, and cousin, on the mother's side, of Sir Charles and Sir William Napier. During his married life he had lived for the most part at Abermarlais, an estate in Carmarthenshire, which he purchased about 1795, apparently with his share of a rich Spanish prize which had been the subject of a very singular law case (*ib.* p. 16). He left no issue, and after his death Lady Lucy resided principally at Arundel till 1841, when she moved to the south of France, where, in the neighbourhood of Marseilles, she died in her eightieth year in 1851. Foley is described as 'above six feet in height, of a fine presence and figure, with light brown hair, blue eyes of a gentle expression, and a mouth combining firmness with good humour' (*ib.* p. 40). His portrait by Sir William Beechey is now in the possession of Mr. H. Foley Vernon of Hanbury Hall, Worcestershire; an engraved copy is prefixed to Herbert's 'Memoir.'

[Life and Services of Admiral Sir Thomas Foley, by J. B. Herbert (Cardiff, 1884, reprinted with additions from the Red Dragon, vol. v.); Marshall's Royal Naval Biography, i. 363; Nicolas's Nelson Despatches.]   J. K. L.

FOLIOT, GILBERT (*d.* 1188), bishop successively of Hereford and London, was born early in the twelfth century, as in 1170 he is described by a chronicler as *grandævus*.

He was of a Norman family which had been settled in England from the Conquest, and was related to the Earls of Hereford. It appears that some of his connections were among the Normans who had acquired estates in Scotland. Hence Dean Milman conjectures he may have been a Scotchman, but incorrectly (*Latin Christ.* vol. iii.) The earliest fact known about him is his profession as a monk in the famous monastery of Clugny, where he must have been under Peter the Venerable, the great antagonist of St. Bernard. Foliot rose to the rank of prior of this house of three hundred monks, from which post he was promoted to the headship of the affiliated house of Abbeville, and from this to the abbacy of Gloucester. A letter from Hugh of Clugny to him lauds his religion, wisdom, and eloquence as the honour of the church of God, and felicitates the church of Clugny, which was thought worthy to have such a son (*Materials for Life of Becket,* v. 30). In 1148 Foliot was promoted to the bishopric of Hereford, which he held for about sixteen years. In the vast mass of materials now collected for the illustration of the life of Becket there are abundant notices of the character of Foliot, his great antagonist. The testimony of all these is that he was the most remarkable among all the bishops of England for his learning, eloquence, and great austerities, and that he was very high in favour with Henry II, who used him as his most trusted counsellor. They are also unanimous in declaring that he aspired to the primacy, which is probably true, in spite of the disclaimer which Foliot afterwards made of this ambition. There is a letter to him from Pope Alexander III, written in a very laudatory strain, and earnestly cautioning him against too great austerities, lest by the failure of his health the church of God should suffer grievous loss (*ib.* v. 44). When in 1161 the Bishop of London became imbecile, the king proposed to Foliot to administer the diocese, finding what was necessary for the support of the bishop, and paying over the balance to him. This Foliot declined, as being 'perilous to his soul,' and begged the king to excuse him from the charge (*ib.* v. 15). The turning-point in Foliot's career was his opposition to the election of Becket at Westminster, May 1162. This is recorded by all Becket's biographers, but with varying circumstances. There is no doubt that Becket was held, at the time of his election, by the English churchmen generally as altogether a king's man, and as one likely to oppress the church. Foliot, it appears, was the only one who had the courage of his opinions. There may have been jealousy at the bottom, but this ascetic and high-born churchman would naturally object to Becket, both as having lived a very secular life, and as being of low extraction. He afterwards withdrew his objection, but he himself declares that he merely did this on the threat of banishment of himself and his kindred. The saying attributed to him by William Fitzstephen, that the king had wrought a miracle by turning a secular man and a soldier into an archbishop, is probably true (*ib.* iii. 36). Soon after this the Bishop of London died, and Henry, with the consent of the pope, translated Foliot to the see (28 April 1163). Upon this occasion Becket wrote him a very kind letter. Canon Robertson (*Life of Becket*) thinks that he was insincere in doing this; but though the archbishop afterwards had the bitterest feelings against Foliot, it is not clear that they existed at this time. Becket speaks as though the promotion were due to his influence. ' We have called you to the care of this greater church, being confident that, by God's mercy, we have done well. Your character, your well-known religion, the wisdom given to you from above, the good work done by you in the diocese of Hereford, have merited that it should be said to you, "Friend, go up higher"' (*Materials*, v. 29). Becket mentions in this letter that the pope had specially appointed Foliot to be the director of the king's conscience, and there is a letter from the pope to Foliot suggesting certain matters which were to be urged upon the king. But very soon after the translation the feelings of the archbishop towards Foliot underwent a change. The new bishop of London refused to make the usual profession of obedience to the metropolitan see of Canterbury. A vast deal has been written on this subject. Among the materials published by the Rolls Commission there is a long treatise upon it. The contention of the Bishop of London was that he had already promised canonical obedience as bishop of Hereford, and that the promise ought not to be renewed. For the archbishop it was contended that Foliot had entered on a new office, which required a new oath of obedience. The most remarkable thing about the matter was that the pope refused to interfere. He had already begun to look coldly on Becket, fearing to offend the king. Foliot's refusal was the commencement of the open hostility between the two bishops, which continued ever increasingly till Becket's death. With regard to the question of the clerical immunities it is probable that Foliot's views coincided with those of Becket, as all the bishops appear to have been of one mind on this point at the council of Westminster

(1163). But Foliot saw that it was necessary or politic to yield to the king, and he secretly agreed with him to concede the point. Now also, by way of opposing Becket, he began to claim metropolitical dignity for the see of London, and to assert that it owed no subjection to Canterbury (*ib.* vi. 590). At Clarendon (1164) Foliot witnessed with satisfaction the humiliation of Becket, and at Northampton, in the same year, when the archbishop was so hardly dealt with in money matters, he counselled him to resign his see, and otherwise acted an unfriendly part towards him. At the famous scene, when the archbishop went to the king, carrying his cross in his own hand, Foliot actually tried to wrest it from him by force, declaring that it was his right to carry it as dean of the province. Being unable to obtain it, he exclaimed, ' You have always been a fool, and always will be one' (WILL. CANT. GERVASE). On Becket's escape, Foliot was one of the envoys sent by Henry to the French king, to ask him not to receive the fugitive—an embassy which was altogether unsuccessful. Nor was he more successful with Pope Alexander at Sens, though, as has been seen, he was highly esteemed by that pope. In declaiming against Becket, he said, 'The wicked flee when no man pursueth.' 'Spare, brother,' said the pope. 'I will spare him,' returned the bishop. 'I said not spare him,' said Alexander,' but rather spare yourself' (ALANUS). Throughout Becket's exile Foliot was the chief ecclesiastical adviser of the king, and the leader of the opposition against Becket. He administered the affairs of the see of Canterbury, and when all Becket's friends and adherents were banished, he is charged by the archbishop with having denied them any help, and carefully cut off their means of support. On these grounds Becket was specially infuriated against Foliot. He brings some serious charges against his episcopal acts, asserting that he had taken bribes to allow clerical matrimony, and had ordained the sons of priests to their father's benefices. These charges the bishop denied. At Argentan (1167) Foliot appeared before the pope's legates and the king of England and inveighed against Becket, deriding him as thinking that his debts were quashed by his consecration, as sins are done away in baptism. He declared that if the pope would not help the church of England against him the king and nobles would recede from the Roman church. Upon this, Becket excommunicated him, but the pope, being appealed to, restrained the archbishop from issuing such sentence till a reconciliation could be effected. This prohibition, he afterwards informed Becket, only held good to the beginning of Lent 1169. Foliot therefore knew what he had to expect when that time came, and, in anticipation of the sentence, he appealed to Rome against it when it should be issued. This precaution was soon shown to be needed, for on Palm Sunday, 1169, at Clairvaux, the sentence of excommunication was again pronounced against him by Becket. This sentence was brought to England and published with great adroitness and courage by a young Frenchman named Berengar, who, in St. Paul's Cathedral, on Ascension day, 1169, when the priest, Vitalis, was saying mass, presented himself at the altar during the offertory and handed the priest a paper, which was accepted on the supposition that it was intended for an offering. Then, holding the paper in the priest's hand, he demanded that it should be read before mass was proceeded with. The priest opened the paper and found the sentence of excommunication against the bishop, and as he did so Berengar proclaimed loudly to the people that the Bishop of London was excommunicated. Then, by the aid of one of the archbishop's friends, he succeeded in making his escape through the people, who were inclined to use him roughly. The bishop, being informed of what had been done, came from his manor of Stepney, and, calling all the clergy of his church together, explained to them that he had previously appealed against this sentence, which was therefore null and void. He, however, submitted to it for the time, but immediately despatched a messenger to the king abroad, requesting his intervention with the pope, and his license for himself to go abroad. Henry wrote strongly to the pope, and sent his license to Foliot, who at Michaelmas crossed the sea on his way to the papal court. Foliot found or suspected all sorts of dangers blocking his way; but he succeeded in reaching Milan in safety, where he found letters from the pope informing him that he had empowered the bishops of Rouen and Exeter to absolve him. He returned to Rouen, where he was formally absolved on Easter day, 1170 (RADULPH DE DICETO). But he was not to remain long free from Becket's curse. On 14 June he joined with the Archbishop of York in crowning the king's son. This was a matter of the direst offence to Becket, and when, by a nominal reconciliation between the archbishop and the king, the former was able to return to England (December 1170), he had secretly sent letters before him excommunicating all the bishops who had taken part in the ceremony. These prelates hastened to the king with their complaints, and the anger felt by Henry on hearing them led to the murder of Becket by the four knights. There is no reason to suppose that Foliot in any way suggested this crime, but so great was the horror caused by it that the Bishop of London did not obtain absolution from the sentence of excommunication till May 1172, after taking an oath that he had not received any letter from the pope prohibiting the coronation, and that he had not contributed to Becket's death. Foliot remained at the height of favour with King Henry. In 1173 he was summoned to Normandy, and carried back to England letters from the pope's legates, written at the request of the king, promising that the vacancies in the various sees should be filled up by free election. In 1174, on the occasion of Henry's famous pilgrimage to Canterbury, the Bishop of London preached the sermon, and maintained with earnestness that the king had no complicity whatever in causing the death of St. Thomas. Foliot took a leading part in the elections of Archbishop Richard and Archbishop Baldwin (ROGER DE HOVEDEN), and continued to hold a prominent position among the English bishops until his death in the spring of 1187-8 (LE NEVE). His character has been judged harshly, or favourably, by the numerous writers who have employed themselves on the career of Becket, according as they favoured the archbishop or the contrary. All, however, including the monkish chroniclers, allow Foliot the praise of great ability and of a strict ascetic life. As to the former, his numerous letters, printed in the Becket collection, abundantly testify; especially the famous letter or pamphlet (printed in 'Materials for Becket's Life,' vol. v.) which reviews and denounces with great force the career of Becket. The authorship of this letter has been questioned, but the balance of authorities is in favour of its being Foliot's (ROBERTSON, *Life of Becket*, appendix v.) The only work attributed to Foliot by the bibliographers is 'A Treatise on Solomon's Song.'

[Materials for the Life of Becket, ed. Robertson, published in Rolls Series, 1877, 6 vols., superseding Dr. Giles's publications; Historia Radulphi de Diceto, ed. Stubbs, Rolls Series, 1876, 2 vols.; Chronica Rogeri de Hoveden, ed. Stubbs, Rolls Series, 1869, 4 vols.; Matthew Paris's Chronica Majora, ed. Luard, Rolls Series, 1876, 7 vols.; Robertson's Life of Becket, 1859; Milman's Latin Christianity, vol. iii. 1854.]

G. G. P.

FOLIOT, ROBERT (*d.* 1186), bishop of Hereford, a near kinsman of Gilbert Foliot [q. v], bishop of London, has been confusedly credited by Bale and others with early experiences which really belong to his predecessor in the see of Hereford, Robert of Melun [see ROBERT]. Bale quite erroneously states that he was called 'Melundinensis,' from the place of his studies. This must mean Melun, but the epithet applies alone to Robert of Melun

By Becket's influence Robert Foliot was made archdeacon of Oxford towards the close of 1151. While holding this office he wrote a letter of consolation and advice to Gilbert Foliot [q. v.], Robert of Melun's predecessor in the see of Hereford, who, having been excommunicated by Becket, had written to Robert Foliot in affectionate terms (BECKET, *Materials*, vi. 606-9). In 1155 he was the first occupant of the newly founded stall of Wellington in Hereford Cathedral. In 1174 the see of Hereford had been vacant seven years, since the death of Robert of Melun in 1167, in consequence of Henry II's refusal to issue a license of election. Foliot was then appointed, and after some further delay was consecrated with three other bishops at Canterbury by the recently appointed Archbishop Richard, 6 Oct. 1174. In 1179 he was one of the four English bishops deputed to attend the Lateran council (HOLINSHED, *Chronicle*, ii. 178; D'ACHERY, *Spicileg.* xii. 650). He consecrated the abbey church of Wigmore, to which, on the same day, he is said to have presented various jewels (LELAND, *Itin.* viii. 78). He died 9 May 1186. His liberality was shown by his large gifts of lands, books, vases, and ornaments to his cathedral at Hereford, where a yearly commemoration was celebrated on the anniversary of his death. Bale attributes to him 'a most lucid work,' 'De Sacramentis Antiquæ Legis,' 'Conciones Aliquot,' and certain other unnamed works.

[Godwin, De Præsulibus, ii. 6; Bale's Scriptores Illustres, p. 216, ed. Basil, 1557; Leland's Itin. viii. 78 ; Britton's Hereford Cathedral.]
E. V.

FOLKES, MARTIN (1690-1754), antiquary and man of science, born in Queen Street, Lincoln's Inn Fields, London, on 29 Oct. 1690, was the eldest son of Martin Folkes, bencher of Gray's Inn, by his wife Dorothy, second daughter of Sir William Hovell, knt., of Hillington Hall, near Lynn, Norfolk. When a boy he was sent to the university of Saumur, and his tutor Cappel, son of Lewis Cappel, described him as 'a choice youth of a penetrating genius and master of the beauties of the best Roman and Greek writers.' Soon after February 1706-7 Folkes was sent to Clare Hall, Cambridge, and there made great progress in mathematics and other studies. He held the degrees of M.A., Cambridge (6 Oct. 1717), and D.C.L., Oxford (July 1746). On 29 July 1714, when

only twenty-three, he was elected a fellow of the Royal Society. In 1722-3 he was appointed vice-president of the society, and often presided in the absence of Sir Isaac Newton. On Newton's death he was a candidate with Sir Hans Sloane for the presidentship. Sloane was chosen, but Folkes became president (30 Nov. 1741) on Sloane's retirement. Under Folkes the meetings were literary rather than scientific. Stukeley describes them at that time as 'a most elegant and agreeable entertainment for a contemplative person.' Folkes contributed ten papers to the 'Transactions' of the society, his communications being chiefly on astronomy and metrology. He resigned the presidentship from ill-health on 30 Nov. 1752. As president he was a principal object of attack in Sir John Hill's 'Review of the Works of the Royal Society' (1751), and the book is 'dedicated' to him (DISRAELI, *Calamities and Quarrels of Authors*, 1860, pp. 364-6).

In 1733 Folkes went with his family to Italy and remained abroad about two years and a half. He went to Paris in May 1739. On 5 Sept. 1742 he was elected a member of the French Academy, in succession to Edmund Halley. Folkes was elected a fellow of the Society of Antiquaries on 17 Feb. 1719-20. He was afterwards vice-president, and from 1749-50 till his death president of the society. His communications were on Roman antiquities and coins (NICHOLS, *Lit. Anecd.* ii. 581). He published at his own expense: 1. 'A Table of English Gold Coins from the 18th year of King Edward III,' with weights and values, London, 1736, 4to. 2. 'A Table of English Silver Coins from the Norman Conquest to the Present Time,' with weights, values, and remarks, 1745, 4to. The 'Tables' were much consulted by antiquaries. Folkes had more than forty plates engraved to illustrate his 'Tables,' and these, purchased after his death by the Society of Antiquaries, were utilised in the society's reprint of the 'Tables' published in 1763, 4to, 3 parts, and edited by J. Ward and Dr. A. Gifford. Folkes was an associate of the Egyptian Club and a member of the Spalding Society (instituted 1710, *ib.* vi. 13). He was a friend of Sir I. Newton and a patron of George Edwards, the naturalist. He gave some help to Theobald for his notes on Shakespeare. He was a man of extensive knowledge and is described as upright, modest, and affable. He contested Lynn as a whig in 1747. He died from a paralytic attack on 28 June 1754, and was buried in the chancel of Hillington Church, Norfolk. In 1792 a monument by Ashton, after Tyler, was erected to him in Westminster Abbey in the south aisle of the choir. He bequeathed to the Royal Society 200*l.*, a cornelian ring for the use of the president, a portrait of Bacon, and his portrait by Hogarth. The sale of his library, prints, drawings, gems, pictures, coins, &c., in 1756 lasted fifty-six days and brought 3,090*l.* 5*s.* He destroyed much autograph writing before his death.

Folkes married at St. Helen's, Bishopsgate, on 18 Oct. 1714 LUCRETIA BRADSHAW, an actress who appeared as 'Mrs. Bradshaw' at the Haymarket Theatre in 1707 and at Drury Lane from 1710 to 1714 (*ib.* ii. 588, 589; GENEST, *English Stage*, vol. i. ; Regist. of St. Helen's, Bishopsgate). She acted Sylvia in the 'Double Dealer,' Corinna in the 'Confederacy,' and other parts. She spoke an epilogue (about 1712) to the 'Generous Husband,' 'in boy's cloaths.' The author of the 'History of the English Stage,' 1741 (cited by NICHOLS, loc. cit.) calls her 'one of the greatest and most promising genii of her time,' and says that Folkes took her off the stage for her 'exemplary and prudent conduct.' Nichols gathers that she was a handsome woman, probably only of second-rate abilities. At the time of her husband's death she was living in confinement at Chelsea, her mind having been for some time deranged.

The issue of this marriage was : 1. A son Martin, who entered Clare Hall, and was killed, during his father's lifetime, by a fall from his horse at Caen in Normandy, whither he had gone to finish his studies. He inherited his father's taste for coins. 2. Dorothy Rishton, who married and had a son and two daughters. 3. Lucretia, married in 1756 to (Sir) Richard Betenson.

Portraits of Folkes were produced by J. Richardson (1718), Vanderbank, Hogarth (1741), Hudson, and Gibson. There is a portrait-medal of him (specimens in British Museum) by J. A. Dassier (1740), described by G. Vertue (manuscript notes in Brit. Mus.) as 'done very like him.' A curious portrait-medal (specimens in British Museum) with the reverse type of a sphinx, the sun, and the tomb of Caius Sestius, was executed at Rome. It bears a date of the era of masonry corresponding either to A.D. 1738 or 1742, and there is a story (referred to in HAWKINS, *Medallic Illustrations*, ii. 571) that it was made by command of the pope as a surprise to Folkes on his visit ; but Folkes is not known to have been in Rome either in 1738 or 1742.

[Memoir in Nichols's Lit. Anecd. ii. 578–98, and numerous references in indexes in vii. 137, 566 of ib. ; and in index in viii. 39 of Nichols's Lit. Illustr. ; Memoir in Weld's Hist. of the Royal Society, i. 479 ff., and other references in vols. i. and ii. ; Gent. Mag. 1754, xxiv. 292 ; Brit. Mus. Cat. ; Hawkins's Medallic Illustr.

(ed. Franks and Grueber), ii. 558, 571 ; Stukeley's Memoirs (Surtees Soc.), where Folkes's wife is called 'Mrs. Bracegirdle.']   W. W.

FOLLETT, SIR WILLIAM WEBB (1798–1845), attorney-general, second and eldest surviving son of Benjamin Follett, a timber merchant, of Topsham, near Exeter, and formerly a captain in the 13th regiment of foot, by his wife, a daughter of John Webb of Kinsale, was born 2 Dec. 1798. At first his health was very feeble, but in 1809 he was put to school under Dr. Lemprière at Exeter grammar school, and in 1810 to Mr. Hutchinson's school at Heavitree, near Exeter, whence he proceeded to Trinity College, Cambridge, and took a B.A. ægrotat degree in 1818 and an M.A. in 1830. In 1836 he was appointed counsel to the university. In Michaelmas term 1814 he joined the Inner Temple, and read in the chambers of Robert Bayly and Godfrey Sykes. He became a special pleader in 1821, but early in 1824 was obliged from illness, the rupture of a blood-vessel in the lungs, to give up work for some months. In Trinity term, however, of the same year he was called to the bar, and joined the western circuit in the following summer. His first reported case is Moore *v.* Stockwell, 6 Barnwell and Cresswell, p. 76, in Michaelmas term 1826. From the time he came to London he was a tory, and lived very much with John Wilson Croker [q. v.], though at Cambridge his opinions are said to have been whig. He was a cousin of Mrs. Croker, and eventually married Croker's ward, Jane Mary, eldest daughter of Sir Ambrose Hardinge Giffard, chief justice of Ceylon, in October 1830, by whom he had five sons and two daughters. From the first, except for a few early appearances at sessions, his professional career was one unbroken success, and yet it provoked neither envy nor detraction. The years 1831–3 brought him an election petition practice of unprecedented magnitude. In 1832 he contested Exeter unsuccessfully against Buller and Divett, but in 1835 was returned for it, heading the poll with 1,425 votes. He succeeded well in the House of Commons, but for the most part contented himself with speaking on legal and not on general topics. He became a king's counsel in Michaelmas term 1834, and was solicitor-general in Sir Robert Peel's administration from November 1834 to April 1835, and was also knighted. His first speech was on 31 March 1835 upon Lord John Russell's Irish church motion. On 23 June of the same year he moved an amendment to clause 9 of the Government Corporation Bill for the purpose of preserving the rights of freemen to the parliamentary franchise, and was only defeated by 278 to 232.

When, later in the year, the House of Lords, on Lyndhurst's advice and against Peel's, recast the bill, and so produced a conflict between the two houses, the high tories formed plans for dispensing with Peel and coming in with Lyndhurst as prime minister, and Follett and Praed to lead the commons. In 1837 he was re-elected at Exeter without a contest, and in 1841 headed the poll with 1,302 votes. In Peel's second administration in the same year he became again solicitor-general, and in April 1844, when Pollock became chief baron, Follett succeeded him as attorney-general, and, his re-election being opposed, again won with 1,293 votes. His health, however, failed, and symptoms of paralysis appeared in his lower limbs. When he addressed the House of Lords for the crown on O'Connell's appeal, he was obliged to do so sitting on a high chair. He spent some months on the continent, but returning home in March 1845, soon fell ill again, and for some months before his death had given up all hope of recovery. He died 28 June 1845 at Cumberland Terrace, Regent's Park, and was buried in the south-eastern vault of the Temple Church on 4 July. He was universally popular and universally regretted. 'In every qualification of intellect and grace of manner,' writes Lord Hatherley (*Life*, i. 270), 'he was as nearly perfect as man can be.' His best-known cases at the bar were his defence of Lord Cardigan for his duel with Captain Tuckett, in which he obtained an acquittal on technical grounds, and the action of Norton against Lord Melbourne, in which he appeared for the plaintiff. With little knowledge of classical and modern languages and literatures, with much general information, there was a complete absence of rhetoric or fire, but he was unrivalled for lucidity, dexterity, promptitude, and persuasiveness. He was unfortunately parsimonious and too eager to accumulate a fortune, and fell a victim to his application to professional work. In person he was tall and slim, with a fine brow, large mouth, and grey eyes. His voice was mellow and full, and his gestures, though limited, were very graceful. He has left behind him the reputation of having been the greatest advocate of the century. His personal property was sworn at 160,000*l.* There is a statue of him in Westminster Abbey, and a portrait by F. R. Say, which has been engraved by G. R. Ward. One speech of his on the second reading of the Dissenters' Chapels Bill, 6 June 1844, has been published.

[Times, 30 June 1845; Hansard's Parliamentary Debates; Croker Papers, ii. 367; Duke of Buckingham's Courts and Cabinets, ii. 199; McCullagh Torrens's Melbourne, ii. 191; Raikes's Journal, ii. 77; Ballantyne's Experiences, i. 125; Blackwood's Mag. lix. 1; Dublin Univ. Mag. xx. 117; Fraser's Mag. xxxii. 165; Gent. Mag. 1845.] J. A. H.

FOLLOWS, RUTH (1718–1809), quakeress, born in 1718 at Weston in Nottinghamshire, was the daughter of Richard and Ruth Alcock, who were poor quakers. When twenty-three years old she married George Follows, quaker, of Castle Donington in Leicestershire, with whom she lived sixty years, and by whom she had two children. When about thirty years of age she received a certificate enabling her to travel as a minister, and visited and preached at the majority of the quaker meetings in the United Kingdom. Her first sermon was preached in 1748 at Castle Donington, whence she proceeded to London, attending over eighty meetings on her way. She remained in London until the middle of 1749, from which time till 1758 she appears to have done little more than attend to meetings in the neighbourhood of her own residence, and those at Atherstone and Matlock. In 1758 she visited Yorkshire and Lancashire, and in 1760 made an extended tour, which embraced most of the meetings in the western and midland counties, as well as London and Norfolk. During the following year she visited Ireland, where she remained several months, working so arduously as to seriously injure her health. Quakerism was at this time at a low ebb in Ireland, and her letters show that she was greatly dispirited. In 1764 she laboured in Wales, and between that time and 1788 she visited nearly every part of England and Wales, and made several excursions into Scotland. In 1782–3 she spent several months in ministerial work in Ireland. From 1788 till her death she was almost incapacitated by the infirmities of age; but she was able to make occasional journeys, the last she undertook being in 1795, when seventy-seven years old. She died on 3 April 1809, and was buried seven days later in the quaker burial-ground at Castle Donington. She is not known to have been the author of any works. Her life was very self-denying and her piety intense, her ministry being highly valued for its simplicity and earnestness.

[Stansfield's Memoirs of Ruth Follows, 1829; Smith's Cat. of Friends' Books.] A. C. B.

FONBLANQUE, ALBANY (1793–1872), journalist, was born in London in 1793, and was the third son of John de Grenier Fonblanque [q. v.], jurist. He was intended for service in the royal engineers, but his education at Woolwich having been interrupted for two years by a dangerous illness, he studied law under Chitty. Before he was twenty, however, he had gained such success as a contributor to newspapers as to determine him to devote himself entirely to journalism. His career was again interrupted by a serious attack of illness, but upon his recovery he resumed his journalistic labours, chiefly upon the 'Morning Chronicle' and the 'Times.' In 1820 he married, and, after a short engagement on the 'Atlas,' became in 1826 principal leader writer upon the 'Examiner,' which found in his brilliant pen a substitute for Leigh Hunt, whose connection with the paper had ceased upon his departure for Italy. He was intimate with Bentham, the Mills, Grote, and the chiefs of the utilitarian school in general, and was a leading contributor to the 'Westminster Review' from its establishment in 1823. The publishers of the 'Examiner' were deeply embarrassed, and about 1828 the paper was purchased by the Rev. Dr. Robert Fellowes [q. v.], author of 'The Religion of the Universe.' Dr. Fellowes, in September 1830, placed the entire management in Fonblanque's hands, and sold the paper to him a few years afterwards. Its reputation as the chief organ of high-class intellectual radicalism was recognised by a subscription to defray the cost of improved machinery to allow of its being issued at a lower price. The contribution took the form of a prepayment of subscriptions for ten years, and the measure produced a large increase of circulation. Fonblanque, in an unpublished letter, gives W. J. Fox and Stuart Mill the chief credit for their exertions in accomplishing the end in view. Mill had already regularly contributed letters which aroused the attention of Carlyle; and Disraeli, then coquetting with radicalism, was among the subscribers. In 1837 Fonblanque republished his most remarkable articles of the preceding ten years, under the title of 'England under Seven Administrations.' Macaulay disputed the wisdom of the step. 'Fonblanque's leading articles in the "Examiner,"' he tells Macvey Napier, 'were extolled to the skies while they were considered merely as leading articles. . . . Fonblanque had not considered that in that form they would be compared, not with the rant and twaddle of the daily and weekly press, but with Burke's pamphlets, with Pascal's letters, with Addison's Spectators and Freeholders.' This is evidently true, and yet the publication has preserved Fonblanque from becoming a mere *nominis umbra*. The book counts among the authorities for the history of the period, and brings together the choicest examples of the indomitable spirit and caustic wit which constituted his chief distinction as a journalist.

The publication of the 'Seven Administrations' indicated the high water-mark of Fonblanque's public influence. It was the time when, as a eulogist in the 'Scotsman' said, 'an epigram in the "Examiner" went off like a great gun, echoing all over the country.' This position could not but be affected by the decline of the liberal party in reputation from 1836 onward, and its ultimate rehabilitation through the acceptance of new ideas, chiefly of financial and commercial reform, which Fonblanque, though approving, could not make his own. In the divisions among his own section of the party he inclined rather to the support of the whig cabinet than to the combative radicalism of Mill. The two schools of old-fashioned London radicalism and of Benthamite utilitarianism, with both of which Fonblanque had intimate affinities, waned more and more, and when at length in 1847 the liberals were returned to office, Fonblanque consented to relinquish the editorship of the 'Examiner,' and accepted an appointment, apparently most uncongenial to a wit and satirist, in the statistical department of the board of trade. He had been offered the government of Nova Scotia, but he could not tear himself away from London. The editorship of the 'Examiner' passed into the hands of John Forster (1812–1876) [q. v.] Fonblanque, however, remained proprietor until 1865, and continued until about 1860 to contribute articles distinguished by all his old pungency, though less and less abreast with the spirit of the new time. He felt himself entirely out of place as the board of trade's statistician. Traditions linger in the office of his late arrivals, his early departures, his panics when called upon for official information, his general inaccessibility, but gentle and almost mournful courtesy to those with whom he deigned to communicate. He was understood to suffer from domestic troubles, and his health was never good. He dropped almost entirely out of society for the last ten years of his life, and was rarely to be seen except in the library of the Athenæum, or absorbed in a game of chess at the St. James's Club. He died 13 Oct. 1872. A second collection of his leading articles, with a memoir by his nephew, Edward Barrington de Fonblanque, was published in 1874.

Fonblanque is one of the few English journalists who, merely as such, have gained a permanent place in literature. This is due partly to his gifts of humour and sarcasm, partly to the republication of his best work, but chiefly to his instinct for literary form. The finish and polish of his articles give them a literary value independent of the subject. Fonblanque wrote slowly and rewrote much. He did not consider his early articles in daily newspapers worth reprinting, and when at a later period he was tempted by great offers to write in the 'Morning Chronicle,' he felt himself unequal to the task and soon abandoned it. No editor, perhaps, has ever more strongly impressed his personality upon his journal, or habitually written in a more individual and recognisable style, even to the risk of monotony. His slowness of composition makes the great extent and overwhelming proportion of his contributions to the 'Examiner' the more remarkable. His negative bent made him before all things a censor and a critic, and disabled him from taking broad surveys of measures and men. His strong positive views on legislation, derived from Bentham, made his journalistic work in that department more fruitful if less brilliant. In politics he was no revolutionist, but a staunch radical reformer, whose hostility to abuses did not involve hostility to institutions, some few excepted, which he thought decisively condemned by his utilitarian standard. He may be taxed with occasional injustice to individuals, but not with deliberate unfairness; he was in purpose thoroughly impartial, and never employed his powers of satire for the mere sake of giving pain. Being sarcastic he naturally passed for a cynic, but the character did him great injustice. He seems to have been shy and sensitive, patient in a never-ending contest with ill-health and domestic unhappiness, scrupulously honourable and delicate in all personal relations, and subdued in manner, except when he held the pen or became animated in discussion. All his friends who have left notices of him celebrate his social charm and his disinterested kindness. He was a brilliant talker, a finished scholar, and a theoretical student of music and art.

[Life and Labours of Albany Fonblanque, ed. E. B. de Fonblanque, 1874; H. R. Fox Bourne's English Newspapers, vol. ii.; Horne's Spirit of the Age, vol. ii.; obituary notices in Examiner, Daily News, and Scotsman.] R. G.

FONBLANQUE, JOHN DE GRENIER (1760-1837), jurist, son of Jean de Grenier Fonblanque, a naturalised Englishman and banker in London, who was descended from an ancient and noble Huguenot family of Languedoc, was born in 1760. He was educated at Harrow and Oxford; became a student of the Middle Temple, and was called to the bar by that society 24 Jan. 1783. He soon obtained a good practice as an equity lawyer. He is said to have caused quite a sensation by disputing the then established, but now exploded, doctrine of *scintilla juris*. He was leading counsel on behalf of the merchants of London in their opposition to the Quebec Bill of 1791, and pleaded their cause at the bar of the House of Commons. By the influence of the Duke of Bedford he sat for Camelford, 1802-6. In 1804 he was made king's counsel. Fonblanque was a steady whig and a personal friend of the Prince of Wales, for whom he is supposed to have written the letters addressed to George III on his exclusion from the army. He died 4 Jan. 1837, and was interred in the Temple Church, in the vault belonging to the Middle Temple, of which society he was senior bencher. At the time of his death Fonblanque was called 'Father of the English Bar.' Writing to one of his sons Lord Lyndhurst says of him: 'I have known jurists as profound as your father, but I have known no one who was so perfect a master of the philosophy of law.' In 1786 Fonblanque married the daughter of Colonel John Fitzgerald, by whom he left three sons and a daughter. He assumed the old family prefix de Grenier in addition to the name of Fonblanque by royal license in May 1828. Fonblanque edited the 'Treatise on Equity' ascribed to Henry Ballow [q. v.], with such additions and improvements that it became almost a new work. It enjoyed considerable reputation as an authority on the subject, and went through several editions (5th ed. 1820). He also wrote two tracts, ' A Serious Exhortation to the Electors of Great Britain' (1791 ?), and 'Doubts as to the Expediency of adopting the Recommendation of the Bullion Committee,' 1810.

[Gent. Mag. March 1837, p. 325; Fonblanque's Life of Albany Fonblanque, pp. 1-4 (1874); County Courts Chron. and Bankruptcy Gaz. 1 Feb. 1866, p. 44; Brit. Mus. Cat.] F. W-T.

FONBLANQUE, JOHN SAMUEL MARTIN DE GRENIER (1787-1865), legal writer, eldest son of John de Grenier Fonblanque [q. v.], was born in Brook Street, Grosvenor Square, London, in March 1787. He was educated at the Charterhouse and at Caius College, Cambridge, where he was one of the founders of the Union Debating Society. He also kept his terms at Lincoln's Inn. At college he burst a blood-vessel and was advised change for his health, whereupon, having obtained a commission in the 21st fusiliers, he served with the regiment in Cadiz and Gibraltar, and in Italy under Lord W. Bentinck, by whom he was appointed deputy judge advocate-general. He took an active part in the war between Great Britain and the United States, was present at the taking of Washington, the battle of Baltimore, and the disastrous attempt on New Orleans, where he was captured by the enemy. After the battle of Waterloo he served in France with the army of occupation, and returning to England in 1816 he was called to the bar, and appointed by Lord Eldon in the following year a commissioner of bankruptcy. On the institution of the bankruptcy court by 1 & 2 William IV, c. 56, he was appointed one of the original commissioners. Fonblanque died at Brighton 3 Nov. 1865. He wrote (jointly with Dr. J. A. Paris) 'Medical Jurisprudence,' 3 vols. 1823—for this work the first award of the Swiney prize was made to the authors—and 'Observations on the Bill now before Parliament for the Consolidation and Amendment of the Laws relating to Bankrupts,' &c. 1824. He also was one of the founders of 'The Jurist, or Quarterly Journal of Jurisprudence and Legislation,' vols. i-iv. 1827-33.

[Gent. Mag. December 1865, p. 801; County Courts Chronicle and Bankruptcy Gazette, 1 Feb. 1866, p. 44; Brit. Mus. Cat.] F. W-T.

FONNEREAU, THOMAS GEORGE (1789-1850), author and artist, was the second and posthumous son of Thomas Fonnereau (son of Z. P. Fonnereau, the descendant of an ancient family from the neighbourhood of Rochelle, which settled in England at the edict of Nantes and realised a fortune in the linen trade), who married on 19 Oct. 1786 Harriet, daughter of John Hanson of Reading. His father died at Topsham, Devonshire, on 26 Dec. 1788; his mother survived until 2 Feb. 1832. He himself was born at Reading on 25 Aug. 1789, and his elder brother, John Zachary, who married Caroline Sewell, died without issue at Douai in 1822. After practising as an attorney in partnership with John Gregson at 8 Angel Court, Throgmorton Street, from 1816 to 1834, he succeeded, by the death of a relation, to a good property, and devoted himself for the rest of his life to his books and his friends. His political opinions leaned to conservatism, and he published in 1831 a 'Practical View of the Question of Parliamentary Reform,' which, unlike most of the swarm of pamphlets issued at that crisis, passed through two editions. It was written mainly to prove that a purely democratic government is inapplicable to the circumstances of England, and that the existing system was 'founded on a concentration of the various interests of the country in the House of Commons.' While still a lawyer he occupied chambers in the Albany, and as a 'great lover and liberal patron of art' enter-

tained a distinguished set of artists and wits at 'choice little dinners,' which are commemorated in the pages of Planché's 'Recollections.' With one of these friends he travelled in Italy about 1840, and on his return there were printed for private distribution, at the expense of D. Colnaghi, a few copies of 'Mems. of a Tour in Italy, from Sketches by T. G. F., inspired by his friend and fellow-traveller, C. S., esq., R.A.' (probably Clarkson Stanfield), containing thirteen sketches of scenery. On inheriting his fortune he gratified an inclination which had long possessed him by building, with the assistance of his friend, Decimus Burton, 'a bachelor's kennel,' his own depreciatory designation of 'an Italian villa with colonnade and campanile,' which arose at Haydon Hill, near Bushey in Hertfordshire. There he died on 13 Nov. 1850, and was buried in a vault in Aldenham churchyard, with many members of the family of Hibbert, his nearest relatives.

Fonnereau printed for private circulation in 1849 a few copies of 'The Diary of a Dutiful Son, by H. E. O.,' the second letters of his three names. A copy fell accidentally into the hands of Lockhart, who inserted numerous extracts from its pages into the 'Quarterly Review,' lxxxvi. 449-63 (1850). The introduction to the volume sets out that his father urged him to keep a diary of the remarks which he heard in the house of a distant relation, 'a literary man in affluent circumstances,' and that some little time afterwards he showed the diary as a proof that he had adopted the suggestion. A concluding paragraph reveals that this was an imposition, as the conversations were the product of his own inventive powers. They contained many original and acute observations, from a thinker not dissatisfied with the world, and not anxious for much change, on poetry, philosophy, and political economy, and they present in style and substance an accurate representation of his talk. Lockhart suggested its publication to the world, and a copy, evidently prepared for the press, was found among Fonnereau's papers after his death. This was published by John Murray in 1864.

[Gent. Mag. 1786 pt. ii. 907, 1788 pt. ii. 1183, 1851 p. 107; Cussans's Hertfordshire, iii. pt. i. 268, pt. ii. 179; Planché's Recollections, i. 233; Preface to 1864 ed. of Diary of a Dutiful Son; Agnew's Protestant Exiles, iii. 234.] W. P. C.

FONTIBUS (FOUNTAINS), **JOHN** DE (d. 1225), ninth abbat of Fountains, sixth bishop of Ely, who is erroneously called PHERD by Burton, was elected abbat of Fountains in 1211, and blessed on 13 Dec. at Melrose Abbey by Ralph, bishop of Down. All that is known of his rule at Fountains is that he prosecuted the work of his predecessor vigorously, continuing the erection of the choir and lady chapel. He made himself useful to King John, from whom there are several letters extant to him, one showing that the king had entrusted many of his valuables to the care of the abbey. On 24 Dec. 1219 he was elected bishop of Ely, after the two elections of Geoffrey de Burgh and Robert of York had been quashed by the pope. This was chiefly through Pandulf's influence (*Annal. Monast.* iv. 412), whose letter to the king in his favour is given by Prynne (WALBRAN, *Memorials of Fountains Abbey*, i. 171). He was consecrated at Westminster by Archbishop Langton on 8 March 1219-20, and enthroned on 25 March. In 1221, in conjunction with the Bishop of Salisbury, Richard le Poore, he was appointed by Honorius III to investigate the complaints of the monks of Durham against their bishop, Richard de Marisco. He went to Durham, summoned the bishop to appear before him, and seems to have found the accusations true (*Dunstable Annals*, iii. 62, 67). The bishop appealed to the pope, but the pope referred the matter back to the two bishops (R. WENDOVER in MATT. PARIS, iii. 62, 63). While still abbat of Fountains he had been appointed by the pope one of a commission to inquire into the merits of Hugh, bishop of Lincoln, before his canonisation. In 1223, in conjunction with his successor at Fountains and the abbat of Rievaulx, he received a similar injunction with respect to William, archbishop of York. In 1225 he witnessed Magna Charta (*Burton Annals*, i. 231). He died at his palace at Downham on 6 May 1225, and was buried in Ely Cathedral. He gave the tithes of Hadham to the Ely monks to provide for his anniversary, and endowed them with the churches of Witchford and Meldreth, with a view to their hospitality. His skeleton was found entire in 1770, when the choir was repaired and altered (Stevenson's supplement to BENTHAM's *Ely*, *Notes*, p. 76).

[Annales Monastici, i. 231, iii. 62, 67, iv. 412; Roger of Wendover and Matt. Paris, iii. 58, 62, 63, 93; Chron. de Mailros (Fulman), p. 184; Historia Eliensis, in Wharton's Anglia Sacra, i. 634–5; Hardy's Le Neve, i. 328; Walbran's Memorials of Fountains Abbey, i. pp. lxiv, lxv, 134–6, 164–5, 171.] H. R. L.

FOOT, JESSE (1744–1826), surgeon, was born at Charlton in Wiltshire in 1744. He received a medical education in London, becoming a member of the Surgeons' Company, and about 1766 went to the West Indies, where he practised for three years in the island of Nevis, returning in 1769. After this he went to St. Petersburg, where he became 'a privileged practitioner of the College of St. Petersburg,' as he afterwards described himself, and practised there some time profitably. Returning to England, he was appointed house-surgeon to the Middlesex Hospital, and on the conclusion of his term of office began practice in Salisbury Street, Strand, afterwards removing to Dean Street, Soho, where he had a large practice for many years. He died at Ilfracombe on 27 Oct. 1826.

Foot's principal branch of practice may be gathered from the titles of his numerous professional books and pamphlets. His belief in his own merits was great, and he aspired to surpass John Hunter in fame; but finding himself unable to succeed, he endeavoured to defame his rival, to prove that his discoveries were plagiarisms or of little merit, to denounce him as an embittered, ill-tempered man, and to represent that his works were written by Smollett. His 'Life of Hunter' shows in almost every page the intense jealousy by which he was actuated. Foot's inclination to biography is also seen in his lives of the seducer and duellist Bowes and his wife, Mary Eleanor, countess of Strathmore [q. v.], whom he attended professionally for thirty-three years, and of his friend Arthur Murphy [q. v.], whose executor he was. He was also strongly prejudiced in favour of the West Indian planters and their treatment of their slaves, and his vigorous 'Defence' ran through three large editions in three weeks. He attacked Wilberforce and the abolition party on several occasions.

Foot wrote: 1. 'A Critical Inquiry into the Ancient and Modern Manner of Treating Diseases of the Urethra, and an Improved Method of Cure,' London, 1774; 6th edit. 1811. 2. 'Observations on the New Opinions of John Hunter in his Treatise on the Venereal Disease,' in three parts, 1786–7. 3. 'An Essay on the Bite of a Mad Dog, with Observations on John Hunter's Treatment of the Case of Master R—— [Rowley], and also a Recital of the Successful Treatment of Two Cases,' 1788; 2nd edit. 1791. 4. 'A New Discovered Fact of a relative nature in the Venereal Poison,' 1790. 5. 'A Defence of the Planters in the West Indies, comprised in Four Arguments,' &c., 1792. 6. 'A Complete Treatise on the Origin, Theory, and Cure of the Lues Venerea and Obstruction in the Urethra, illustrated by a great variety of Cases, being a course of twenty-three lectures read in Dean Street, Soho, 1790 and 1791;' 4to, 1792; new edit., 8vo, 1820, amended and corrected; German translation, Leipzig, 1793–4. 7. 'A Plan for Preventing the Fatal Effects of the Bite of a Mad Dog, with Cases,' 1792. 8. 'Life of John Hunter,' 1794; 2nd edit. 1797. 9. 'Dialogues between a Pupil of the late John Hunter and Jesse Foot, including passages in Darwin's "Zoonomia,"' 1795. 10. 'Cases of the Successful Practice of the Vesicæ Lotura in the Cure of Diseased Bladders,' pt. i. 1798, pt. ii. 1803. 11. 'Observations principally upon the Speech of Mr. Wilberforce on his Motion in the House of Commons, 30 May 1804, for the Abolition of the Slave Trade,' 1805. 12. 'Important Researches upon the Existence, Nature, and Consummation of Venereal Infection in Pregnant Women, New-born Infants, and Nurses, by the late P. S. O. Mahon, contrasted with the Opinions of the late John Hunter upon the subject,' 1808. 13. 'The Lives of Andrew Robinson Bowes, Esq., and the Countess of Strathmore, written from thirty-three years' professional attendance, from Letters and other well-authenticated Documents,' 1810. 14. 'Life of Arthur Murphy, Esq.,' 1811. 15. 'Review of Everard Home's Observations on the Diseases of the Prostate Gland,' 1812. 16. 'Facts relative to the Prevention of Hydrophobia,' in 'Medical Facts and Observations,' iii. 33. 17. 'Two Letters on the Necessity of a Public Inquiry into Cause of the Death of the Princess Charlotte and her Infant,' 1817. See also for several minor contributions 'Index to the London Medical and Physical Journal,' vols. i–xl., 1820.

FOOT, JESSE, the younger (1780–1850), surgeon, was not the son but the nephew of the preceding. He practised for many years as a surgeon at Clarendon, Jamaica, returned home about 1819, and lived with his uncle in Dean Street, Soho, for two years, marrying Miss Foot (presumably his cousin) on 4 Sept. 1819. He succeeded to his uncle's practice, and in 1826 brought out a new edition of his work on the urethra, which is described as the eighth edition. He became surgeon to the Royal Westminster Ophthalmic Hospital. He published 'Ophthalmic Memoranda,' 1838, and wrote several papers in the 'Lancet' and the 'London Medical and Surgical Journal,' enumerated in Déchambre. In 1834 he published 'The Medical Pocket-book for 1835.' Foot died at Ilfracombe, aged 70, on 5 Jan. 1850 (*Gent. Mag.* 1850, i. 225).

[Georgian Era, ii. 574; Déchambre's Dictionnaire Encyclopédique des Sciences Médicales, 4th ser. vol. iii. 1879; Foot's Works.] G. T. B.

FOOTE, SIR EDWARD JAMES (1767–1833), vice-admiral, youngest son of the Rev. Francis Hender Foote, rector of Bishopsbourne, near Canterbury, and, on the mother's side, nephew of Sir Horace Mann [q. v.], was born at Bishopsbourne on 20 April 1767. In 1779 he was entered at the naval academy at Portsmouth, and in 1780 joined the Dublin of 74 guns, under Captain Samuel Wallis. In November he was moved into the Belle Poule frigate, and in her was present in the action on the Dogger Bank, 5 Aug. 1781. He shortly afterwards joined the Endymion frigate, in which he was present in the battle of Dominica, 12 April 1782. After the peace he was appointed to the Europa, bearing the flag of Vice-admiral Gambier, on the Jamaica station; served as acting lieutenant of the Swan, the Antelope, and the Janus, and was confirmed in the rank on 12 Aug. 1785. In 1787 he was for a few months in the Royal Sovereign, and in September 1788 was appointed to the Crown, going out to the East Indies with the broad pennant of Commodore Cornwallis, by whom, in the summer of 1791, he was made commander of the Atalanta sloop. He was afterwards transferred to the Ariel, which he brought home and paid off in October 1792. In 1793 he commanded the Thorn sloop, and on 7 June 1794 was advanced to post rank, and appointed to the Niger frigate, in which for the next two years he was employed in the Channel and on the coast of France. He then joined the Mediterranean fleet under Sir John Jervis, and had the good fortune, on the early morning of 14 Feb. 1797, to bring the first positive intelligence of the immediate proximity of the Spanish fleet, and, a few hours later, to assist in its defeat. The Niger shortly afterwards returned to England, and attended the king at Weymouth during the autumn; on going back to Spithead, Foote was, at the king's especial desire, appointed to the Seahorse of 38 guns, and ordered out to the Mediterranean. He was on his way to join the detached squadron under Sir Horatio Nelson, when, off the coast of Sicily, on 26 June 1798 he fell in with and captured the French frigate Sensible of 36 guns, carrying General Baraguay d'Hilliers and his staff. From his prisoners Foote learned the destination of the expedition; he at once made sail for the coast of Egypt, and in company with the Terpsichore arrived off Alexandria on 20 July. After seeing the French ships there and in Aboukir Bay, the frigates went in search of Nelson, but, not meeting with him, returned to Egypt on 17 Aug., when they found that the French fleet had been meantime destroyed. On the departure of Nelson for Naples, Foote remained attached to the blockading squadron; but the following spring he rejoined Nelson at Palermo, and in March was sent with Captain Troubridge into the Bay of Naples, where, on Troubridge being called away in May, he was left as senior officer [see TROUBRIDGE, SIR THOMAS ; NELSON, HORATIO, VISCOUNT]. In this capacity, on 22 June, he, in conjunction with Cardinal Ruffo and the Russian and Turkish admirals, signed the capitulation of the forts Uovo and Nuovo; a capitulation which Nelson, on arriving in the bay two days later, pronounced invalid, and refused to carry into effect. Nelson does not seem to have seriously blamed Foote for his share in the transaction, considering that he had yielded to the false representations of Ruffo, who had received express orders not to admit the rebels to terms; nor, on the other hand, did Foote present any remonstrance against the capitulation being annulled. On the contrary, throughout July, August, and September—in which month he was ordered home—he repeatedly addressed Nelson in terms of gratitude and devotion, which went far beyond the submission required from a junior officer (NICOLAS, *Nelson Despatches*, iii. 517 *n.*, 518). It was not till 1807, after Nelson's death, that he, publicly at least, found out what wicked things had been done in the Bay of Naples in 1799, and published a 'Vindication' of his conduct, which had never been attacked, and a virulent criticism of Lord Nelson's, which he had till then inferentially approved of. The fact was that he had learned from Harrison's 'Life of Nelson' that the great admiral had described the capitulation as 'infamous,' a term correct enough when applied, as Nelson had applied it, to the conduct of Ruffo, but which Nelson's personal bearing towards Foote had clearly shown was not applied to him. That Foote had exceeded his powers was perfectly certain; he had been guilty of an error of judgment and a weakness which Nelson had pointed out and had condoned; Ruffo's treating with armed rebels, contrary to the orders of his sovereign, was on a totally different footing.

On his return to England in the early part of 1800, Foote, still in the Seahorse, was again sent out to the Mediterranean, with Sir Ralph Abercromby [q. v.] and staff as passengers, and in charge of a convoy of store-ships and transports. He was appointed to attend on the king at Weymouth during the summer of 1801, and was then sent to India in charge of convoy. In October 1802 the Seahorse was paid off, and the following year, at the particular desire of the

king, who had conceived a strong partiality for him, Foote was appointed to the royal yacht Princess Augusta, in which he remained till promoted to flag rank in August 1812. It is said that he would have much preferred active service, but that, as his attendance seemed grateful to the king in his derangement, he felt that the yacht was his proper sphere of duty. In 1814 he hoisted his flag as second in command at Portsmouth, but struck it at the peace, and had no further service, becoming in due course a vice-admiral in 1821. He was nominated a K.C.B. in 1831, and died at his house in the neighbourhood of Southampton on 23 May 1833. He was twice married: first, to Nina, daughter of Sir Robert Herries, banker; secondly, to Mary, daughter of Vice-admiral Patton; and had issue by both wives.

[Ralfe's Naval Biography, iii. 130 ; Marshall's Roy. Nav. Biog. i. 559 ; United Service Journal (1833), pt. ii. p. 379 ; Gent. Mag. (1833), vol. ciii. pt. ii. p. 180 ; Foote's Vindication of his Conduct (1807) ; Nicolas's Despatches and Letters of Lord Nelson, iii. 477.] J. K. L.

FOOTE, MARIA, COUNTESS OF HARRINGTON (1797 ?–1867), actress, was born 24 July 1797 (?) at Plymouth. Her father, Samuel T. Foote (1761–1840), who claimed to be a kinsman of Samuel Foote [q. v.], sold out of the army, became manager of the Plymouth theatre, and married a Miss Hart. In July 1810 Miss Foote appeared as Juliet at her father's theatre, in which also she played as Susan Ashfield in 'Speed the Plough,' and Emily Worthington in the 'Poor Gentleman.' Foote afterwards took an hotel in Exeter. The experiment not succeeding, his daughter appeared at Covent Garden, 26 May 1814, as Amanthis in the 'Child of Nature' of Mrs. Inchbald. In this part, which specially suited her, she made a great success. Her second appearance was at the same theatre in the same character in the following season, 14 Sept. 1814. On 6 Dec. she was the original Ulrica in 'The King and the Duke, or Which is Which ?' attributed to Jameson. On 2 Jan. 1815 she played Miranda in the 'Tempest,' and 17 April 1815 was the original Adela in the 'Fortune of War,' attributed to Kenney. For her benefit, 6 June 1815, she appeared as Statira in 'Alexander the Great,' Betty acting, for that occasion only, Alexander. This was her first appearance in tragedy. Fanny in the 'Clandestine Marriage,' Hippolita in an alteration of the 'Tempest,' Lady Percy in 'King Henry IV,' Helena in the 'Midsummer Night's Dream,' and many other parts, chiefly secondary, in old pieces and new, followed. Her abilities proved to be limited. She had, however, a reputation for beauty sufficient to secure her constant engagements at the patent theatres and in the country. She played with success in both Ireland and Scotland, and accompanied Liston, Tyrone Power, and other actors to Paris, where they all acted with very unsatisfactory results. In 1815 she formed at Cheltenham an intrigue with Colonel Berkeley, by whom she had two children. An alleged promise of marriage made by him was not kept. ' Pea Green ' Haynes then proposed to her and was accepted. He retracted, however, his offer, and as the result of an action for breach of promise of marriage had to pay 3,000*l.* damages. These proceedings gave rise to a keen pamphlet warfare, through which and through some opposition on the stage Miss Foote retained a large measure of public sympathy. At Covent Garden she played every season up to 1824-5 inclusive, frequently in subordinate parts, but taking occasionally characters such as Miss Letitia Hardy in the 'Belle's Stratagem,' Miss Hardcastle, and, for her benefit, Lady Teazle. She was the original Isidora in Barry Cornwall's ' Mirandola.' On 9 March 1826 she made as Letitia Hardy her first appearance at Drury Lane, where also she played Violante in the ' Wonder,' Rosalind, Virginia, Maria in ' A Roland for an Oliver,' Imogen, and Maggy in the ' Highland Reel.' Other parts of importance in which she was seen at one or other house were Maria Darlington, Beatrice, Roxalana, Violante, Imogen, Ophelia, Desdemona, Juliana in the ' Honeymoon,' and Clara in ' Matrimony.' At Bath on 13 and 14 Jan. 1826 she was the object of ill-natured demonstrations on the part of a portion of the audience. Chronicling these and condensing them, Genest says that ' she was a very pretty woman and a very pleasing actress, but she never would have travelled about as a star if it had not been for circumstances totally unconnected with the stage ' (*Account of the Stage,* ix. 358-9). A writer in the ' New Monthly Magazine 'for March 1821, variously stated to be Talfourd, Campbell, and Horace Smith, writes warmly concerning ' the pure and innocent beauty with which she has enriched our imaginations,' and, referring to her then anticipated departure, asks rhapsodically, ' Is comedy entirely to lose the most delicate and graceful of its handmaidens and tragedy the loveliest of its sufferers?' Talfourd speaks highly of the grace of her movements, and specially commends her singing of the song ' Where are you going, my pretty maid?' Her singing and dancing and her power of accompanying herself upon the harp, guitar,

and pianoforte added to her popularity. She was indefatigable in the pursuit of her profession, and is said to have traversed England, Ireland, and Scotland every year for five years, in course of which she posted twenty-five thousand miles. Her theatrical career closed at Birmingham on 11 March 1831, and on 7 April of the same year she married Charles Stanhope, fourth earl of Harrington. She died 27 Dec. 1867. She was of medium height, her face oval, and her features expressive. She had an abundance of light brown hair. By those most under her influence the character of her acting was described as fascinating. A whole-length portrait by Clint of Miss Foote as Maria Darlington was sold in June 1847, with the effects of Thomas Harris, lessee of Covent Garden.

[The Stage, 1815 ; Burke's Peerage ; Dramatic Magazine ; Genest's Account of the English Stage ; Facts illustrative of the Evidence in the trial of Foote v. Haynes, 1835 ; Notes and Queries, 7th ser. vi. 6.]   J. K.

FOOTE, SAMUEL (1720-1777), actor and dramatist, second son of Samuel and Eleanor Foote, was born at a house in Truro long known as Johnson Vivian's, and was baptised at St. Mary's in that city 27 Jan. 1720. His father (1679-1754) was a commissioner of the prize office and fine contract, and at one time filled the office of mayor of Truro. His mother, Eleanor Goodere, through the death of her brother, Sir John Dinely Goodere, bt., murdered by another brother, Captain Samuel Goodere [q. v.], inherited a considerable fortune. Foote was educated at Worcester under Dr. Miles, and matriculated at Worcester College, Oxford, 1 July 1737. His college life, like his subsequent career, was marked by extravagance. Without taking a degree he proceeded to the Temple. A turn for mimicry had already displayed itself, and after wasting his entire fortune as a man of fashion at the Grecian, the Bedford, and other coffee-houses, he appeared at the Haymarket, 6 Feb. 1744, as ' a gentleman ' in ' Othello,' playing with a company of novices collected and trained by Macklin, at that period excluded from Drury Lane. He repeated this impersonation three or four times, and gave it for a benefit at Drury Lane on 10 March. On 2 March, at the Haymarket, he played Lord Foppington in the ' Relapse,' and recited an epilogue, apparently of his own composition. He is also said to have played Pierre in ' Venice Preserved.' These ill-judged experiments were complete failures. Foote then proceeded to Dublin, where, according to Hitchcock (*Irish Plays,* i. 147), ' he brought a few crowded houses and was well received.'

On 1 Nov. 1745 he appeared at Drury Lane as Sir Harry Wildair in the 'Constant Couple.' He afterwards appeared as Lord Foppington, Bayes, Sir Courtly Nice, and other parts played by Colley Cibber. He had meanwhile conceived the idea of turning to advantage his talent for mimicry, and on 22 April 1747 he opened the Haymarket with a concert, a farce extracted from the 'Old Bachelor,' called 'The Credulous Husband,' in which Foote was Fondlewife, and an entertainment by himself called 'The Diversions of the Morning.' In this, with the assistance of Shuter and other actors, he met with much success. His career was, however, stopped by the Westminster magistrates, and Foote then hit upon the device of summoning his friends, for 25 April at noon, to take with him a 'dish of chocolate,' for which was subsequently substituted a 'dish of tea.' Tickets for this were obtained at George's Coffee-house, Temple Bar. On the invitation appeared 'N.B.—Sir Dilbury Diddle will be there, and Lady Betty Frisk has absolutely promised.' According to a statement of Tate Wilkinson (*Memoirs*, i. 24 et seq.), which Genest says 'is not to be reconciled with the bills,' the entertainment was principally made up of satirical mimicry of actors, such as Quin, Delane, Ryan, Woodward, Mrs. Woffington, and of Garrick, upon whom he was especially severe. In November 1747 Foote, still at the Haymarket, gave 'Tea at 6.30;' in March 1748 he substituted for this 'Chocolate in Ireland,' and soon afterwards produced an entertainment similar in kind called 'An Auction of Pictures.' In 1748-9 this class of entertainment was continued until March or April, when Foote produced the two-act comedy, the 'Knights,' printed 1754, 8vo, in which he played Hartop. This piece ended with a feigned concert between two cats, in which Italian opera was ridiculed. Various persons of more or less importance had been libelled in these productions; but the complaints and retorts of those injured only added to the piquancy of the production. A second fortune having been left him, Foote disappeared to Paris, whence, after some years' absence, he returned with 'Taste,' a two-act comedy produced unsuccessfully at Drury Lane 11 Jan. 1752, 8vo, 1753, with a prologue written and spoken by Garrick. The 'Englishman in Paris,' Covent Garden, 24 March 1753, 8vo, 1756, was more fortunate. Foote let Macklin have the piece for his benefit. Macklin played Buck, a character which Foote took when he transferred the play, 20 Oct. 1753, to Drury Lane stage. In the course of this season Foote played Fondlewife, Ben in 'Love for Love.' Brazen

in the 'Recruiting Officer,' and gave his lastingly popular 'Tea.' The following two seasons he appeared at Covent Garden, where he played, 3 Feb. 1756, Buck in the 'Englishman Returned from Paris,' a piece in three acts, 8vo, 1756, the idea and incidents of which Foote took from Murphy, the dramatist, who indiscreetly confided them to him. On 1 March 1756 he played Sir Paul Plyant in the 'Double Dealer,' and 30 March Lady Pentweazel in 'Taste.' In 1756-7 he returned to Drury Lane, where, 5 Feb. 1757, he produced the 'Author,' 8vo, 1757, a two-act piece, in which, as Cadwallader, he mimicked a Mr. Aprice, a friend of his own, who had interest enough to obtain the suppression of the play. An additional scene, which he intended to introduce into it for his benefit, is given in the 'Monthly Mirror,' vii. 39–41. He also played Gomez in Dryden's 'Spanish Friar.' In December 1757, in company with Tate Wilkinson, Foote visited Dublin, where he had a favourable reception, socially and artistically, but played no new part. Wilkinson and Foote were engaged by Garrick, and appeared at Drury Lane 17 Oct. 1758. For his benefit Foote appeared, 18 Dec. 1758, as Shylock, and was a failure. With 100*l.*, which he borrowed from Garrick, he visited Scotland. According to the 'Courant' he reached Edinburgh 15 March 1759, and appeared on the 20th at the Canongate Concert Hall. He played many parts, and was made much of. He is said to have given the first afternoon entertainment in Edinburgh. He returned in May, and in the autumn went once more to Dublin, where, at the Crow Street Theatre, he produced, 28 Jan. 1760, his comedy the 'Minor,' originally in two acts, 8vo, 1760. In this he played Shift, a character designed to satirise his associate, Tate Wilkinson. Piece and excursion alike failed, and Foote, in want of funds, opened in the summer of 1760 the Haymarket, where, with a company hastily assembled, he produced the 'Minor,' now enlarged to three acts. In this, Foote's best comedy, his title to a portion of which has been disputed, he satirised Whitefield and the methodists. In its new shape it was a great success. Foote, who played at the Haymarket the characters of Shift, Smirke, and Mrs. Cole, is said to have sent the manuscript to the Archbishop of Canterbury, with a request that he would excise or alter whatever was objectionable. It was returned untouched, the archbishop shrewdly surmising that Foote wished to advertise it as 'corrected and prepared for the press by his Grace the Archbishop of Canterbury.' Once more at Drury Lane he was the original Scotchman in the 'Register

Office' of Joseph Reed, a piece from which he was accused by Reed of having stolen the character of Mrs. Cole in the ' Minor.' In partnership with Murphy, Foote leased Drury Lane for a summer season. On 15 June 1761 the management produced Murphy's ' All in the Wrong,' a version of Molière's ' Cocu Imaginaire.' Foote wrote and spoke the prologue. The ' Citizen,' also by Murphy, was played 2 July 1769, Foote appearing as Young Philpot. The ' Old Maid ' of Murphy was given for the first time the same night. ' Wishes, or Harlequin's Mouth Opened,' a comedy by Thomas Bentley, with a speaking harlequin, closed the season with a failure. Foote, who played in this Distress a poet, took over 300*l.* for his share of the entire venture, though he had broken his contract and supplied no novelty. In 1762, at the Haymarket, Foote produced the ' Orators,' 8vo, 1762, ridiculing, in Peter Paragraph, George Faulkner, the Dublin printer, who had lost a leg, and who brought an action against him. At Covent Garden, 12 Jan. 1762, he played Young Wilding in the ' Lyar,' 8vo, 1764, his adaptation of ' Le Menteur' of Corneille. From this period the original characters of Foote, with the exception of Ailwould in Bickerstaffe's ' Dr. Last in his Chariot,' Haymarket, 31 Aug. 1769, and Francisco in the ' Tailors,' Haymarket, 2 July 1767, were confined to the Haymarket and to his own comedies. Many of these were played in the afternoon. Their order is as follows: Major Sturgeon and Matthew Mug in the ' Mayor of Garratt,' two acts, 1763, 8vo, 1764 ; Sir Thomas Lofty and Sir Peter Pepperpot in the ' Patron,' three acts, 1764, 8vo, 1764 ; Zachary Fungus in the ' Commissary,' three acts, 1765, 8vo, 1765 ; Foote in ' An Occasional Prelude,' one act, printed in the ' Monthly Mirror,' vol. xvii.; the Devil in the ' Devil upon Two Sticks,' three acts, 30 May 1768, 8vo, 1778 (by this piece Foote reaped between 3,000*l.* and 4,000*l.*; on his way to Ireland he lost 1,700*l.* at Bath to cardsharpers, and had to borrow 100*l.* to proceed on his journey); Sir Luke Limp in the ' Lame Lover,' 8vo, 1770, three acts, 27 Aug. 1770; Flint in the ' Maid of Bath,' three acts, 26 June 1771, 8vo, 1778 ; Sir Matthew Mite in the ' Nabob,' three acts, 29 June 1772, 8vo, 1778 ; Sir Robert Riscounter in the ' Bankrupt,' three acts, 21 July 1773, 8vo, 1776 (this season Foote gave an entertainment with puppets known as ' The Primitive Puppet Show,' and produced an unprinted entertainment entitled ' The Handsome Housemaid, or Piety in Pattens '); Aircastle in the ' Cozeners,' 1774, 8vo, 1778, and O'Donnovan in the ' Capuchin,' three acts,

17 Aug. 1776, 8vo, 1778. This piece was an alteration of the famous ' Trip to Calais,' the performance of which was stopped by the censor. In 1766 Foote was visiting at Lord Mexborough's, where he met an aristocratic party, including the Duke of York. Playing on his vanity they mounted him on a high-mettled horse, which threw him and fractured his leg in two places. He accepted the accident with philosophy, and asked for the removal of the leg, which was accomplished. As a compensation for this loss the Duke of York obtained for Foote a patent to erect a theatre in the city and liberties of Westminster, with the privilege of exhibiting dramatic pieces there from 14 May to 14 Sept. during his natural life. This was a fortune. Foote purchased his old premises in the Haymarket, and erected a new theatre on the site, which he opened in May 1767 with the ' Prelude,' in which he referred to the loss of limb and to the gift of his patron, &c. In 1767 he engaged Spranger Barry [q. v.] and Mrs. Ann Dancer, subsequently Mrs. Spranger Barry [q. v.], and produced tragedy, announcing as the cause of such a proceeding that they were dangerous neighbours. Upon his visit to Dublin in 1768 Foote found his ' Devil upon Two Sticks ' once more a source of fortune. In 1770 he rented the Edinburgh Theatre for the winter season, and took over his company. The result was unsatisfactory, and he resigned his lease to West Digges [q. v.] The year previously Foote, whose treatment of Garrick consisted in alternately sponging upon him and ridiculing him, intended to caricature the famous procession in the jubilee, but by influence from without was induced to abandon the idea. A notion previously entertained of caricaturing Dr. Johnson was given up in consequence of Johnson sending word to Foote that, in case the threat was carried out, ' he would go from the boxes on the stage and correct him before the audience ' (*Monthly Review*, lxxvi. 374). Few of Foote's plays had been produced without an acknowledged purpose of caricaturing some known individual. For a long time this practice succeeded. Foote was wise enough to withdraw when, as in the case of Johnson, he found his man too strong for him. When, after the production of the ' Nabob,' two members of the East India Company called upon him with the intention of castigating him, he had tact enough to keep them talking until he had disarmed their resentment and induced them to stay to dinner. The most he ordinarily had to fear was an interference of the censor, and a consequent diminution of profits. Those who winced most under his attacks held it prudent to

hold their tongues. Garrick, who smarted more frequently than most, said that nobody in London thought it worth while to quarrel with him. So accustomed was Foote to this process that, when he heard his leg was to be cut off, he said, 'Now I shall take off old Faulkner to the life,' Faulkner having lost one of his legs. The privilege of the buffoon was at length to be denied him. In preparing the 'Trip to Calais' he hit upon the celebrated Duchess of Kingston, and told his acquaintance, with customary garrulity and indiscretion, that she was to be shown in the character of Lady Crocodile. The influence of the duchess sufficed to secure the prohibition of the play. A correspondence undignified on both sides, though marvellously clever on that of Foote, took place between the author and the duchess, and resulted in Foote abandoning some hastily formed schemes of vengeance, and in the production of the 'Capuchin,' in which the satire was transferred from the duchess to Jackson, an Irish clergyman who was in her pay, and who ultimately committed suicide to avoid the penalty of death, to which he had been condemned for treason. This man, under the disguise, transparent to a large number of people, of Dr. Viper, Foote lashed in the 'Capuchin.' Jackson's answer was by insinuations conveyed in the paper of which he was editor, and copied into other periodicals, charging Foote with the most odious form of crime. For a time Foote, on the advice of his friends, kept silence. He opened the Haymarket on 20 May 1776 with his comedy, the 'Bankrupt.' An organised opposition upon the part of a portion of the audience drew Foote before the curtain to appeal for justice, and to say that he had taken steps in the court of king's bench to bring the charges to an issue. A further mine was, however, sprung beneath Foote, a discharged servant appearing (8 July 1776) to prefer a bill of indictment against the author for a criminal assault. Under these circumstances Foote received the full support of friends convinced of his innocence. Those whom he had libelled thronged to defend him. Evidence that the charge was due to Jackson was forthcoming, and on the trial in the court of king's bench the jury returned an unhesitating verdict of acquittal. Foote was, however, much shaken. On 16 Jan. 1777 he disposed of his patent to George Colman for 1,600l. a year and a specific sum for the right of acting Foote's unpublished pieces. Foote, who had undertaken to play at another house, appeared at the Haymarket in the 'Devil upon Two Sticks,' the 'Nabob,' the 'Minor,' and other pieces.

A great falling off in power was, however, apparent. On 30 July, in the 'Maid of Bath,' his name appeared in the bills for the last time. Acting on medical advice he started for the South of France, and arrived at Dover 20 Oct. 1777 on his way to Calais. He was in good spirits, joking with the servants at the Ship Inn. At breakfast next morning he was seized with a shivering fit, a second followed, and on the same day, 21 Oct. 1777, he died. The body was removed to his house, Suffolk Street, Pall Mall East, by William Jewell, the treasurer to the Haymarket, who had been sent for, and on the Monday night following (3 Nov.) he was buried by torchlight in the west cloister in Westminster Abbey. The register of the abbey calls him Samuel Foote, esq., and gives his age as fifty-five (CHESTER, *Registers of Westminster*, p. 424). No monument is erected to him, though a tablet was put up by Jewell in St. Martin's Church, Dover. His will, dated 13 Aug. 1768, was proved the day after his death. It bequeathed his possessions in trust to his illegitimate sons, Francis Foote and George Foote, with remainder in case they should die in their minority to Jewell, to Foote's mother, who, however, was dead, and to his brother, Edward Goodere Foote. In addition to the plays mentioned Foote wrote 'A Treatise on the Passions so far as they regard the Stage; with a Critical Enquiry into the Theatrical merit of Mr. G—k, Mr. Q—n, and Mr. Barry . . .' London, 8vo (no date), 1747; 'The Roman and English Comedy consider'd and compar'd. With remarks on the "Suspicious Husband." And an Examen into the merits of the Present Comic Actors,' London, 1747, 8vo; 'A Letter from Mr. Foote to the Reverend Author of the Remarks, critical and christian, on the Minor,' London, 1760, 8vo; 'Apology for the "Minor," with a Letter to the Rev. Mr. Bain,' Edinburgh, 1771, 8vo and 12mo (same date). He is credited with the authorship of an account of the murder of his uncle, which is said to have been his first production. There is, however, reason for sparing him this ignominy. 'Wit for the Ton! the Convivial Jester, or Sam Foote's Last Budget opened,' &c., London (no date), 1777, contains some of his jokes, but is, of course, not by him. A long list of polemical works to which his pieces gave rise, many of them claiming to be by him, but ordinarily virulent attacks upon him, is given in Mr. Lowe's useful 'Bibliographical Account of English Theatrical Literature,' 1888. Mr. Lowe believes that 'A Letter to the Licenser' (regarding the prohibition of the 'Trip to Calais') was published, but has never seen it catalogued.

Its only appearance seems to have been in a daily newspaper for 3 Aug. 1775, whence it was copied into the 'Westminster Magazine,' August 1775. The 'Methodist, a comedy; being a Continuation and Completion of the plan of the "Minor," written by Mr. Foote,' &c., 3rd edit. London (no date), 1761, 8vo, is, according to the 'Biographia Dramatica,' 'a most impudent catchpenny job of Israel Pottinger.' Foote's prose tracts, like his letters, are forcibly, wittily, and logically written. It is, however, as a dramatist, a wit, and an actor that he has to be judged. all these qualities he is noteworthy. No complete collection of his plays has been made, more than one of his pieces, chiefly his early entertainments, having never been printed. From the dates given it will be seen that the plays were in many cases not printed until long after their appearance on the stage. What are called his dramatic works were issued in 4 vols. 8vo, 1778, and with life by John Bee, i.e. Badcock, in 3 vols. 12mo, 1830. Three dramatic trifles are given in 'The Memoirs of Samuel Foote, with a Collection of his Genuine Bon Mots, &c. By William Cooke,' London, 1805, 12mo, 3 vols. In the series edited by Cumberland, Mrs. Inchbald, Lacy, and in innumerable similar collections, various plays are to be found, and collections of the 8vo editions are in the British Museum and other libraries. In the 'Comic Theatre,' being a free translation of all the best French comedies by S. Foote and others, London, 1762, 5 vols. 12mo, one play only, the 'Young Hypocrite,' is said in the 'Biographia Dramatica' to be by Foote. A play of Foote's occasionally appears on the present stage. To the list already given may be added the 'Tryal of Samuel Foote, esq., for a Libel on Peter Paragraph,' acted in 1761 at the Haymarket, and the 'Diversions of the Morning,' compiled from his 'Taste' and other sources, and played at Drury Lane in 1758. These pieces, previously unprinted, Tate Wilkinson gives at the close of vol. iv. of his 'Wandering Patentee,' 12mo, 1795. 'Lindamira, or Tragedy à-la-mode,' a burlesque tragic bagatelle, by Foote, is included in 'Thespian Gleanings,' by T. Meadows, comedian, Ulverstone, 8vo, 1805. It is taken from 'Diversions of the Morning.' The 'Slanderer,' a comedy, is said to have been left in manuscript, and appears to be lost. As a rule the plays are invertebrate, and the manners they sketch are not to be recognised in the present day. Foote had, however, a keen eye to character, and on the strength of the brilliant sketches of contemporary manners which he afforded, and of the wit of the dialogue, they may be read with pleasure to this

day. Foote's satire is direct and scathing. Much of it is directed against individuals, not seldom with no conceivable vindication, since Foote singled out those, such as Garrick, to whom he was under deepest obligations. During his lifetime and for some years subsequently Foote was known as the English Aristophanes. Without being deserved, the phrase is less of a misnomer than such terms ordinarily are. As an actor Foote seems to have attracted attention only in his own pieces. Tom Davies, who speaks with something not far from contempt of his general performances, praises his Bayes in the 'Rehearsal.' In this, however, Foote, like Garrick, used to introduce allusions to contemporary events. This, of course, was quite in Foote's line. The words of Davies are: 'Public transactions, the flying follies of the day, debates of grave assemblies, absurdities of play-writers, politicians, and players, all came under his cognisance, and all felt the force of his wit; in short, he laid hold of everything and everybody that would furnish merriment for the evening. Foote could have written a new "Rehearsal" equal to the old' (*Dram. Misc.* iii. 304–5). What is this but an account of Foote's own entertainments? Such success as he obtained as an actor in early life was due to an imitation, conscientious at first, but subsequently degenerating into buffoonery, of Colley Cibber. Even as a mimic Johnson disputed his capacity, saying, 'His imitations are not like. . . . He goes out of himself without going into any other people.' As a conversationalist and wit he stood alone. Many of the jokes fathered upon him by his biographer Cooke are to be found in early collections, such as Taylor the Water Poet's 'Wit and Mirth.' More anecdotes concerning Foote are to be found among theatrical ana than are told of any half-dozen of his contemporaries or successors. The opinions expressed with regard to him by those who lived in his society or under his influence show a curious mixture of fear and admiration. Garrick was distinctly afraid of him, and, in spite of being his equal in wit and his superior in scholarship, sought at almost any cost to cajole him. His favourable utterances are accordingly to be taken with allowances. Johnson, who despised without fearing him, says: 'The first time I was in company with Foote was at Fitzherbert's. Having no good opinion of the fellow I was resolved not to be pleased, and it is very difficult to please a man against his will. I went on eating my dinner pretty sullenly, affecting not to mind him. But the dog was so very comical that I was obliged to lay down my knife and fork, throw myself back upon my chair, and fairly laugh it out. No, sir, he was irresistible' (BOSWELL, *Johnson*, ed. Hill, iii. 69, 70). Fox told Rogers that, meeting Foote at Lord William Bentinck's, he anticipated that the actor would prove a bore, and continued: 'We were mistaken; whatever we talked about, whether fox-hunting, the turf, or any other subject, Foote instantly took the lead and delighted us all' (ROGERS, *Table Talk*, ed. Dyce, pp. 101–2). Sir Joshua Reynolds is credited with having said that 'by Foote's buffoonery and broad-faced merriment, private friendship, public decency, and everything estimable among men were trod under foot' (CLARK RUSSELL, *Representative Actors*, p. 137). Tate Wilkinson declared that 'if any man possessed the gift of pleasing more than another Mr. Foote was the man,' and Colman the younger says Foote always made him laugh. Testimony of the kind may be indefinitely extended. He was short, fat, and flabby in appearance, his face intelligent, and his eye bright. He was a gourmand, an egotist, and a thoroughly selfish man, with a few redeeming traits, which the contrast with his general character gave almost the appearance of virtues. A portrait of Foote by Sir Joshua Reynolds is in the Mathews collection in the Garrick Club. Another portrait by Zoffany in a scene from 'The Commissary' was given by the actor to Fitzherbert, and is now in the collection of the Earl of Carlisle. Zoffany also painted Foote as Sturgeon in the 'Mayor of Garratt,' and in other characters.

[The chief authorities for the life of Foote are the Memoirs of Samuel Foote, esq., with a Collection of his Genuine Bon Mots, Anecdotes, Opinions, &c., by William Cooke, 3 vols. 1805, and the Memoir prefixed to the Works of Samuel Foote, esq., by John Bee (Badcock), esq., 3 vols. 1830; Memoirs of the Life and Writings of Samuel Foote, esq., the English Aristophanes, &c., London (no date), 1777, is an anonymous and untrustworthy work; the Garrick Correspondence; Walpole's Letters; Forster's Historical and Biographical Essays; Boswell's Life of Johnson, ed. Dr. Birkbeck Hill; Genest's Account of the Stage; Tate Wilkinson's Memoirs and Wandering Patentee and Davies's Life of Garrick overflow with information; George Colman's Random Recollections; Peake's Memoirs of the Colman Family; O'Keeffe's Recollections; Boaden's Life of Siddons and Life of Bannister. The Life and Times of Frederic Reynolds, by himself, Notes and Queries, 2nd and 4th ser., and Dibdin's History of the Edinburgh Stage, 1888, may also be consulted, as may the Town and Country Magazine, and other periodicals of the last century. Lives of Foote appear in the Biographical Dictionaries of Chalmers and of Rose. Lowe's Bibliography of the Stage and Boase and Courtney's Bibliotheca Cornubiensis, i. 152–7, 1181–3, supply useful bibliographies. There are few books dealing with the stage from which particulars, frequently untrustworthy and contradictory, may not be gleaned.] J. K.

FORANNAN, SAINT and BISHOP (*d.* 982), was, according to the 'Book of Leinster,' eighteenth in descent from Fiacha Suidhe, brother of Conn the Hundred Battler [q. v.] His clan held the plain of Magh Feimhin, near Clonmel. Forannan was chosen bishop by popular election, and consecrated, according to his 'Life,' in 'the city called in the barbarous dialect of the Irish Domhnach mor,' i.e. Donoughmore, which, it is added, is the metropolis of Ireland. From this Lanigan erroneously inferred it to have been in Armagh. But the 'Book of Leinster,' the 'Lebar Brecc,' and the 'Martyrology of Donegal' all term him of 'Donoughmore in Magh Feimhin,' the territory of his family. In obedience to a vision directing him to go to the Meuse, Forannan, with twelve companions, left Ireland about 969, and, as usual with Irish saints, was miraculously conveyed across the sea. While in search of the appointed place they met Count Eilbert, who had built many churches, and among them one dedicated to St. Patrick. He then led them to Rome, that they might obtain the instruction in monastic learning which they sought for. There Forannan received the episcopal dignity and the title of abbot; he was ordered to turn aside for further instruction in the Benedictine rule to a monastery named Gorzia. Thence he went to Walciodorus, now Wassor, between Dinant and Givet. The pious emperor Otto heard of his fame, and, after some hesitation in acknowledging Forannan's rank, took the abbey under his protection. Walciodorus had been founded in 945 by Eilbert, and Macallen, an Irishman, was the first abbot. Macallen, on leaving Ireland, had first gone to Peronne, the Irish monastery founded by St. Fursa [q. v.], and there won the patronage of Hersendis, the wife of Count Eilbert. Walciodorus was one of a group of such monasteries supplied with inmates from Ireland. By Forannan's influence a place called Hasteria (now Hastières) was added to his monastery. He also obtained a village called Gruthen, which he made over to the monastery, in order that its vineyards might supply the monks with wine. Several interpretations of the name Walciodorus have been proposed; some taking it to be from 'vallis decora,' the beautiful valley, others from 'waltz-dor,' the torrent of the wood. Seven years after his arrival Count Eilbert died. He was attended during his illness by Forannan, and was buried in the Basilica of Walciodorus. Forannan died in 982. His day is 30 April.

[Bollandists' Acta Sanct. 30 April, tom. iii. p. 807; Lanigan's Eccl. Hist. iii. 401; Book of Leinster, p. 348 *d*; Lebar Brecc, p. 15 *b*; Martyrology of Donegal, 30 April.] T. O.

FORBES, ALEXANDER, first BARON FORBES (*d.* 1448), was the eldest son of Sir John de Forbes of that ilk. The lands of Forbes in Aberdeenshire gave name to the family, who trace back their ancestors in it to the time of King William the Lion (1165–1214). Sir John de Forbes was justiciar and coroner for Aberdeenshire in the time of Robert III, and leaving four sons was the common ancestor of the families of the Lords Forbes, Forbes Lord Pitsligo, and the Forbeses of Tolquhoun, Foveran, Watertoun, Culloden, Brux, &c. The eldest son, Sir Alexander de Forbes, succeeded to the estates in 1405, on his father's death, and during his time both added considerably to their extent and obtained their consolidation into a barony, with his own elevation to the peerage as a baron of parliament. In 1407 he was one of four knights who went to England to hold a friendly tournament with an equal number of English knights. Wyntoun calls him a knight of Mar, and praises the worthy manner in which he and his comrades upheld the honour of their country on the field of chivalry. In 1419 he formed one of the contingent of Scottish knights who with their followers responded to the appeal of Charles, dauphin of France, to Scotland for help against the English. He took part in the war then going on, and was present at the battle of Beaugé, 22 March 1421. During the same year he visited James I in his captivity in London, and afterwards returned to Scotland, but came again into England as far as Durham in 1423, to convoy James I into his kingdom. Between 1436 and 1442 he was created by James II a lord of parliament, under the title of Baron Forbes. He died in 1448. He married about 1423 Lady Elizabeth Douglas, only daughter of George, first earl of Angus [q. v.], and granddaughter of Robert II. By her, who afterwards became the wife of David Hay of Yester, he left issue two sons and three daughters: (1) James, second lord Forbes, (2) John, provost of the church of St. Giles, Edinburgh, (3) Annabella, who married Patrick, master of Gray, (4) Margaret, who married the laird of Fyvie, and (5) Elizabeth, who married Irvine of Drum. Through his marriage to Elizabeth Douglas his children were heirs of entail to the earldom of Angus.

[Registrum Magni Sigilli, ii. Nos. 54–9, 127, 134, 279, 1239, 1298, &c.; Rymer's Fœdera, x.

308; Rotuli Scotiæ; Wyntoun's Fordun à Goodall, ii. 460; Exchequer Rolls; Sir William Fraser's Douglas Book, ii. 23.] H. P.

FORBES, ALEXANDER, fourth BARON FORBES (*d.* 1491), was the eldest son of William, third lord Forbes, and succeeded his father in or before 1483. The gift of the fine payable to the crown on his marriage was acquired by Margaret, lady Dirleton, who wished him to marry her own daughter, Margaret Ker. But he declined her proposals, and without her consent married Lady Margaret Boyd, daughter of Thomas, earl of Arran. For this he was condemned by the lords auditors on 5 July 1483 to pay Lady Dirleton double the value of his marriage or two thousand merks. He espoused the cause of James III when the son of that monarch rose in rebellion in 1488 against him. After the king's death at Sauchieburn he was summoned to answer before parliament to a charge of treason and conspiracy, but instead of obeying the summons he exposed the blood-stained shirt of the slain king on his spear at Aberdeen, and raised a considerable force there with the object of avenging his death. But his hopes of success were suddenly extinguished by the defeat of the Earl of Lennox (with whom he had been acting in concert) at Tillymoor, near Stirling, and on submitting to James IV, he was pardoned and received into favour. He died about 1491, survived by his widow, who was a granddaughter of James II, and who in 1509 married David, lord Kennedy, afterwards first earl of Cassilis, but leaving no issue. He was succeeded by his two brothers, Arthur, fifth lord, and John, sixth lord, Forbes.

[Acta Auditorum Dominorum, pp. 113*, 121*; Acts of the Parliaments of Scotland, ii. 169–215; Treasurer's Accounts, i. xlii; Registrum Magni Sigilli, ii. Nos. 1678, 2529, 2530, 3371, 3696, &c.; Pinkerton's Hist. of Scotland, ii. 8.] H. P.

FORBES, ALEXANDER (1564–1617), bishop of Aberdeen, belonged to the Brux branch of the Forbes family. He was the son of John Forbes of Ardmurdo in Aberdeenshire, by his second wife, a daughter of Graham of Morphie. Educated at St. Andrews, where he took his degree of A.M. in 1585, he was appointed in 1588 minister of Fettercairn in Kincardineshire, and soon began to take a position of some prominence in the church. So early as 1594 we find him associated by the general assembly in a committee of the most eminent ministers appointed 'to treate upon the offence conceaved by the king against John Ross,' a too freespoken preacher. Between 1593 and 1602 he was a member of eight out of ten general assemblies, and seems consistently to have supported the king's efforts to restore episcopacy in the church of Scotland. On 12 Nov. 1604 he was advanced to the bishopric of Caithness, retaining, however, his benefice of Fettercairn, a circumstance which explains the charge specially brought against him in the libellous verses in which (1609) the Scottish bishops were assailed—

Rarus adis parochos, O Catanæe, tuos.

He was one of the bishops who, 'clothed in silk and velvet,' rode in procession between the earls and the lords at the opening of the parliament at Perth in 1606. The general assembly at Linlithgow in December of the same year appointed him, as bishop, perpetual moderator of the presbytery of Caithness, which was charged by the privy council (17 Jan. 1607) to receive him as such within twenty-four hours on pain of rebellion. He was a member of the assembly of 1608, of the conference at Falkland in the following year, and of the important assembly at Glasgow in 1610, which completed the restoration of episcopal government in the church of Scotland. In the same year the episcopal succession was reintroduced from England, and Forbes was consecrated in 1611 in the cathedral of Brechin by the Archbishop of St. Andrews and the Bishops of Dunkeld and Brechin. In 1610, and again in 1615, the king appointed him a member of the court of high commission (Scotland). In the latter year he was in London, and incurred much blame by assenting, on the part of the Scottish prelates but without their authority, to an act which all parties in Scotland looked on as an encroachment on the rights of the Scottish church—the absolution by the Archbishop of Canterbury of the Marquis of Huntly, who lay under excommunication in Scotland. His compliance was not desired by the king, but it pleased Huntly, and may have paved Forbes's way for translation (1616) to the see of Aberdeen, where Huntly's influence was paramount. The general assembly which met at Aberdeen the same year called his conduct in question, and expressed a wish that Patrick Forbes [q. v.] should be appointed to the vacant see. But the promotion of the Bishop of Caithness seems to have been already decided on at court, and he was formally elected by the chapter of the diocese. He was instituted at St. Andrews 23 Feb. 1617, and died at Leith 14 Dec. in the same year. Calderwood tells an ill-natured story, that on his deathbed 'fain would he have spoken with the Bishop of St. Andrews [Spotiswood], but he being loathe to leave his play at cards,

howbeit it was the Lord's day, the other departed before he came to him.' He adds that Bishop Forbes 'was impudent and shameless. He was not ashamed, when the lords of session and advocates came out of the Tolbooth at twelve hours, to follow them into their houses uncalled, and sit down at their tables; therefore he was nicknamed Collie.' On the other hand, he is described by Spotiswood as 'a man well-born and of good inclination.' Forbes is said to have written against Gordon the jesuit. He married Christian, daughter of Straton of Crigie, and had seven sons and three daughters. One of his sons, John Forbes, minister of Auchterless, Aberdeenshire, suffered for his loyalty in the civil war, and was recommended for compensation by the parliament of the Restoration; another, Colonel William Forbes, is probably the same as an officer of that name and rank in the army of Montrose.

[Calderwood's History of the Kirk of Scotland; Grub's Eccl. History of Scotland; Scott's Fasti; Lumsden's Family of Forbes; Row's Historie of the Kirk of Scotland; Bishop Patrick Forbes's Funerals; Keith's Catalogue of Scottish Bishops, &c.]   J. C.

FORBES, ALEXANDER, fourth and last BARON FORBES OF PITSLIGO (1678–1762), Jacobite, only son of the third lord, by Lady Sophia Erskine, third daughter of John, ninth earl of Mar, was born 22 May 1678. He succeeded to the estates and title on the death of his father in 1691. In early manhood he travelled in France, and having made the acquaintance of Fénelon, was introduced by him to Madame Guyon and other 'quietists.' Their influence left a deep impression on his mind, and led him to devote much of his attention to the study of the mystical writers. He was an adherent of the protestant episcopal church of Scotland, and a warm supporter of the exiled Stuart family. He was strongly opposed to the Act of Union, and on the oath of abjuration being extended to Scotland, ceased to attend parliament. Having taken part in the rebellion of 1715 he was compelled, after the retreat of Mar, to take refuge on the continent, but was never attainted, as has sometimes been erroneously stated, and in 1720 returned to Scotland, taking up his residence chiefly at Pitsligo, where he continued a correspondence with the quietists, and engaged in a kind of transcendental devotion. In 1734 he published 'Essays Moral and Philosophical.' On the outbreak of the rebellion of 1745, though sixty-seven years of age and asthmatic, he again took up arms in behalf of the Stuarts. His decision, from his sober and staid character, had great influence in the surrounding district, but it was taken after much hesitation. 'I thought,' he says, 'I weighed, and I weighed again. If there was any enthusiasm in it, it was of the coldest kind; and there was as little remorse when the affair miscarried as there was eagerness at the beginning.' He raised a regiment of well-appointed cavalry, numbering about a hundred, and composed chiefly of Aberdeenshire gentlemen and their tenants. When they were drawn up ready to set out, he moved to the front, lifted his hat, and said, 'O Lord, Thou knowest that our cause is just;' then added the signal, 'March, gentlemen.' He arrived at Edinburgh 8 Oct. 1745, a few days after the victory at Prestonpans. After the disaster at Culloden he remained in hiding near Pitsligo, protected by the general regard in which he was held in the district. His principal place of concealment was a cave constructed in the arch of a bridge at a remote spot in the moors of Pitsligo. He adopted the disguise of a mendicant, and on one occasion actually received a small coin from one of the soldiers sent in search of him. Occasionally he took refuge in the neighbouring bogs. His estates were seized in 1748, but in the act of attainder he was named Lord Pitsligo, a misnomer for Lord Forbes of Pitsligo. On this account he endeavoured to obtain a reversal of the attainder, but though the court of session gave judgment in his favour 10 Nov. 1749, this decision was reversed on appeal to the House of Lords 1 Feb. 1750. After this the search for him relaxed, and he resided for the most part with his son at Auchiries, under the name of Mr. Brown. In March 1756 a party was sent to search for him, but he was hid in a small recess behind a wainscot, which was concealed by a bed in which a lady slept. He died 21 Dec. 1762. He was twice married: first, to Rebecca, daughter of John Norton, merchant, London, by whom he had one son, John, master of Pitsligo; and secondly, to Elizabeth Allen, who had been companion to his first wife, but by this marriage there was no issue. He wrote 'Thoughts concerning Man's Condition' in 1732, and it was published in 1763, and again in 1835, with memoir by his kinsman Lord Medwyn.

[Memoir prefixed to Thoughts concerning Man's Condition; Walpole's Royal and Noble Authors (Park), ii. 158; Chambers's Eminent Scotsmen, ii. 36-8.]   T. F. H.

FORBES, ALEXANDER PENROSE (1817–1875), bishop of Brechin, second son of John Hay Forbes, lord Medwyn [q. v.], by his wife Louisa, daughter of Sir Alexander Cum-

ming Gordon, bart., of Altyre, Elgin, was born at Edinburgh 6 June 1817. He was sent to the Edinburgh Academy, and to a school kept by Canon Dale at Beckenham, Kent. In 1833 he matriculated at Glasgow University. After studying for one session there he obtained a nomination to Haileybury, where he took prizes and medals for classics, mathematics, political economy, law, history, Arabic, and Sanskrit, showing special aptitude for oriental languages. In September 1836 Forbes sailed for Madras, and a year after his arrival was appointed assistant to the collector and magistrate of Rajahmundry. In 1839 he was acting head assistant to the Sudder and Foujdarry Adawlut, when his health broke down. After nine months' leave of absence at the Cape of Good Hope, he returned to India and resumed his post at Rajahmundry, but was again attacked by fever, and sent back to England for two years. He never returned to India, though he had no idea of throwing up his appointment when he matriculated at Brasenose College, Oxford, 23 May 1840. During his residence, however, he came strongly under the influence of the prevailing 'Oxford movement,' and determined to take orders. As an undergraduate he won the Boden Sanskrit scholarship. He took the B.A. degree 29 Feb. 1844, and resigned his Indian appointment 5 June following. He proceeded M.A. 19 Nov. 1846, and received the honorary D.C.L. on his appointment as bishop of Brechin in May 1848. He was ordained at Trinity 1844, and was curate at Aston Rowant, a village near Oxford, till the following January, when he transferred his services to St. Thomas's, Oxford. A year later Forbes became incumbent of Stonehaven, Kincardine, having expressed to Moir, bishop of Brechin, his wish to serve the Scotch episcopal church. He remained there till May 1847, when, on the nomination of Dr. Pusey, who had become his intimate friend at Oxford, he was appointed to the vicarage of St. Saviour's, Leeds, a church built for the purpose of giving practical illustration to 'Tractarian' doctrine. In the following August Moir, bishop of Brechin, died. Mr. Gladstone, in conversation with Bishop Wilberforce, suggested that Forbes might fit the post. His name was presented to the electors at the diocesan synod, and he was elected by a large majority over the Rev. W. Henderson. The headquarters of the bishopric he changed from Brechin to Dundee, becoming vicar of St. Paul's, Dundee, and prosecuting parochial together with episcopal duties. On 5 Aug. 1857, at a meeting of the diocesan synod at Brechin, Forbes delivered his primary charge, which took the form of a manifesto on the Eucharist.

inculcating the doctrine of the real presence, and vindicating the Scotch communion office. Great stir was made by the charge, which was published, and in the following December it was proposed at an episcopal synod that a declaration on the doctrine of the Eucharist should be issued on the authority of the college of bishops. The motion was lost, but a declaration of similar purport was issued by Terrot, Ewing, and Trower, bishops respectively of Edinburgh, Argyll, and Glasgow, and clearly directed against Forbes. Keble wrote a lengthy answer to the bishops, and published pamphlets on various aspects of the case. In May 1858 the college of bishops issued a pastoral letter, in spite of an elaborate protest by Forbes, announcing that they felt bound to resist the teaching of the Bishop of Brechin on the matter in dispute. A year and a half later Forbes was presented to the college for erroneous teaching in this primary charge by Mr. Henderson, his rival for the bishopric, and two vestrymen. He was formally tried, and the final finding of the court in March 1860 was a declaration of admonition and censure to the bishop to be more careful in future. Throughout the long period of suspense, as both before and after, Forbes continued his incessant labours in the service of the church. When he took up his residence in Dundee, the churchmen there were so few that their only place of worship was a room over a bank. He left behind him the pro-cathedral of St. Paul, and the churches of St. Salvador and St. Mary Magdalene. He founded schools in connection with the churches, was a visitor of the Royal Infirmary, on the committee of a Model Lodging-house Association and the Dundee Free Library, a member of the Dundee school board, and a director of the Prisoners' Aid Society. He took great interest in sisterhoods and their work, and founded that of St. Mary and Modwenna. His work was interfered with by frequent attacks of ill-health, and consequent journeys abroad. On the continent he became the intimate friend of Dr. von Döllinger, and sympathised with the Old Catholic movement. He constantly corresponded with Mr. Gladstone, who was a warm friend and adviser. On 8 Oct. 1875 Forbes died from a sharp gastric attack. He was buried beneath the chancel of St. Paul's, Dundee. His many admirers erected in his memory Forbes Court, Dundee, the existing episcopal see-house. As a theologian Forbes takes high rank. He was deeply versed in the whole range—patristic, mediæval, and modern—of his subject, and in his own treatment of it gave it an exact systematic and dogmatic form. This appears in his two chief works: (1) 'A Short Ex-

planation of the Nicene Creed,' 1852 (2nd ed. considerably enlarged, 1866), which is a brief handbook of dogmatic theology, founded largely on the fathers and schoolmen, and more technical than is usual with English text-books; (2) 'An Explanation of the Thirty-nine Articles,' 2 vols. 1867 and 1868, which aims at elucidating the positive doctrine of the articles and defends the catholic as distinguished from the ultra-protestant or puritan interpretation; this book was written at the suggestion of Dr. E. B. Pusey, whose help 'in each step of its progress to maturity' is acknowledged by Forbes in the dedication. Many of Forbes's numerous publications are sermons (including a collected edition in four volumes), pastoral charges, and manuals of devotion. Of the others the more important are: 'Commentary on the Seven Penitential Psalms,' 1847; 'The Prisoners of Craigmacaire; a Story of the '46,' 1852; 'Commentary on the Canticles,' 1853; 'The Pious Life and Death of Helen Inglis,' 1854. Forbes also translated the first part of 'Memoriale Vitæ Sacerdotalis,' from the Latin of Arvisenet, 1853; edited with his brother, G. H. Forbes, the 'Arbuthnot Missal,' 1864; translated the Scotch communion office into Greek, 1865; edited 'Meditations on the Passion by the Abbot of Monte Cassino,' 1866; published with elaborate preface 'Kalendars of Scottish Saints, with Personal Notices of those of Alba, Laudonia, and Strathclyde,' 1872; wrote an introduction to Miss Kinloch's 'History of Scotland,' 1873; and edited Lady Eleanor Law's 'Translation from Pinart,' and from manuscript 'Lives of St. Ninian, St. Kentigern, and St. Columba,' 1875. At the time of his death he was engaged on a translation of the works of St. Columban. He contributed at various times to the 'Ecclesiastic,' the 'Christian Remembrancer,' the 'North British,' the 'Edinburgh,' and the 'Quarterly Review.' By Forbes's express wish the greater portion of his correspondence and journals has not been made public.

[Mackey's Bishop Forbes, a Memoir (with photogravure portrait); Memoir of Alexander, Bishop of Brechin, anon.; Prinsep's Madras Civil Servants, 1885, p. 54.]   A. V.

FORBES, SIR ARTHUR, first EARL OF GRANARD (1623–1696), eldest son of Sir Arthur Forbes of Corse in Aberdeenshire (who went to Ireland in 1620 with the Master of Forbes's regiment, of which he was lieutenant-colonel, and was granted large estates in Leitrim and Longford by James I), by Jane, daughter of Sir Robert Lauder of the Isle of Bass, and widow of Sir Alexander

Hamilton of Killeshandra, co. Cavan, a lady of singular ability and courage, was born in 1623, and at an early age exhibited conspicuous spirit and ability. His father was killed in a duel in 1632, and he was trained entirely under his mother's care. During the rebellion of 1641 she was besieged in Castle Forbes, the family seat, for nine months, and Forbes raised men for her relief, though only eighteen years old. He is next heard of in Scotland, serving under Montrose in the cause of Charles I. On the defeat of Montrose in 1645 he was taken prisoner, and for two years confined in Edinburgh Castle. On his release he still embraced every opportunity to aid the fallen fortunes of the Stuarts, but, all efforts to restore them failing, he returned to Ireland in 1655. In 1660 he was sent to Charles at Breda to assure him that if he would only go over to Ireland the whole kingdom would declare for him. At the Restoration he was appointed a commissioner of the court of claims in Ireland, and received additional grants of land in Westmeath. In 1661 he entered parliament as member for the family borough of Mullingar. In 1663 he did good service in the north of Ireland by nipping in the bud efforts there in support of Blood's plot. Honours now flowed rapidly in on him. In 1670 he was sworn of the Irish privy council, and appointed marshal and commander-in-chief of the army. In 1671 he was one of the lords justices. On several subsequent occasions he held the same post. In 1672 he was the means of rendering to the presbyterian church of Ireland, of which he was an attached member, an important service, by procuring for it the first grant of *regium donum*, which that body continued to enjoy until the passing of the Irish Church Act in 1869, with the exception of a short interval. Kirkpatrick, in his 'Presbyterian Loyalty,' gives an account of his action in this matter, which, he says, came 'from Sir Arthur Forbes's own mouth,' to the effect that he (Forbes) being in London, the king inquired of him as to the welfare of the Irish presbyterian ministers, of whose loyalty and sufferings in his cause he had often heard. Forbes having told him that 'they lived in no great plenty,' the king said 'that there was 1,200*l.* a year in the settlement of the revenue of Ireland which he had not yet disposed of, but designed it for a charitable use, and he knew not how to dispose of it better than by giving it to these ministers.' It subsequently appeared that only 600*l.* was available for the purpose, and at this figure the grant was made to Forbes (*Presbyterian Loyalty*, p. 384).

In 1675 he was created Baron Clanehugh

and Viscount Granard. In 1684 he raised the 18th regiment of foot, and was made colonel thereof, and in the same year was advanced to the dignity of Earl of Granard. James II, when he came to the throne, endeavoured to make use of his services for the promotion of the interests of Romanism, but Granard could not be induced to betray his fellow-protestants. He was accordingly removed from the command of the army, Tyrconnel being put in his place. When James's Dublin parliament passed the acts of repeal and attainder, he boldly remonstrated with the king. Finding his arguments vain, he went to the House of Lords, entered his solemn protest against these measures, and retired to Castle Forbes. Here he was besieged by the Irish, but in vain. When William went over to Ireland, no one welcomed him more heartily than Granard. He was placed by the king in command of a force of five thousand men for the reduction of Sligo, the surrender of which he secured. This was his last public service. His closing years were spent quietly at Castle Forbes, where he died in 1696.

He married Catherine, daughter of Sir Robert Newcomen of Mosstown, co. Longford, and widow of Sir Alexander Stewart, ancestor of the Mountjoy family, by whom he had five sons and one daughter.

[Forbes's Memoirs of the Earls of Granard; Kirkpatrick's Historical Essay upon the Loyalty of Presbyterians; Adair's True Narrative; Reid's History of the Presbyterian Church in Ireland.]

T. H.

FORBES, Sir CHARLES (1774–1849), politician, of Newe and Edinglassie, Aberdeenshire, son of the Rev. George Forbes of Lochell, was born in 1774. He was a descendant of Alexander Forbes of Kinaldie and Pitsligo, and was in 1833 served heir male in general to Alexander, third lord Forbes of Pitsligo, father of Alexander, fourth lord Forbes [q. v.], attainted in 1745. Forbes was educated at Aberdeen University, of which, late in life, he was elected lord rector. Shortly after leaving the university he went out to India, and became the head of the first mercantile house in our eastern dependency, Forbes & Co. of Bombay. His name ranked high in the commercial world for ability, foresight, and rectitude of character. On returning to England, he was elected to parliament for the borough of Beverley, and represented that place from 1812 to 1818. In the latter year he was returned for Malmesbury, and continued to represent that town until the passing of the Reform Bill of 1832. As a member of the House of Commons he enjoyed the respect of all parties, for his love of justice, kindly feeling, and plain, straightforward honesty. Though a tory of the tories, he 'never allowed his political creed to cloud his fine judgment and keen sense of right and wrong, and his manly spirit was readily engaged in favour of the poor, the weak, and the persecuted.' He warmly supported catholic emancipation; and when the Duke of Wellington incurred great unpopularity in 1830, Forbes pronounced in the House of Commons a warm panegyric on the duke's conduct. Forbes was one of the earliest to advocate the claims of women to the franchise. In the session of 1831 he asked upon what reasonable grounds they could be excluded from political rights, pointing out that ladies had the power of voting for directors of the East India Company, and maintaining that if the right of voting was grounded on the possession of property, there ought to be no distinction of sex. Forbes was a strong opponent of the Reform Bill of 1831-2. During the debates in the former session he spoke of the measure as 'the vile Reform Bill, that hideous monster, the most frightful that ever showed its face in that house.' He promised to pursue it to the last with uncompromising hostility, and if it were carried to abandon parliament. He put forward an urgent plea for Malmesbury. The borough, after much angry discussion, was left with one member only. Forbes vainly contested Middlesex against Joseph Hume at the general election of 1832. He was most distinguished in connection with India. From his long residence in the East, he knew the people intimately, and he spent a large portion of his fortune in their midst. In parliament and in the proprietors' court of the East India Company his advocacy of justice for India was ardent and untiring. One of his last acts was the appropriation of a very large sum of money to procure for the inhabitants of Bengal a plentiful supply of pure water in all seasons. His fame spread from one end of Hindostan to the other. When he left India he was presented by the natives with a magnificent service of plate, and twenty-seven years after his departure from Bombay the sum of 9,000l. was subscribed for the erection of a statue to his honour. The work was entrusted to Sir Francis Chantrey, and the statue now stands in the town hall of Bombay, between those of Mountstuart Elphinstone and Sir John Malcolm. It was the first instance on record of the people of India raising a statue to any one unconnected with the civil or military service of the country. An address, signed by 1,042

of the principal native and other inhabitants of Bombay, expatiated upon his services to the commercial development of the country and the improvement in the position of the natives. In his private charities Forbes was most liberal; he was also a munificent contributor to the leading public charities of Scotland. Forbes was of a bluff but kindly nature, diffident as to his own merits, of a straightforward and manly character. On the death of his uncle in 1821 Forbes succeeded to the entailed estates of the Forbeses of Newe, and was created a baronet by patent in 1823. He married in 1800 Elizabeth, daughter of Major John Cotgrave, of the Madras army, and by that lady he left four sons and two daughters. He died in London 20 Nov. 1849.

[Ann. Reg. 1849; Gent. Mag. 1850; Hansard's Parliamentary Debates; Aberdeen Journal, 28 Nov. 1849.]   G. B. S.

FORBES, Sir CHARLES FERGUSSON, M.D. (1779–1852), army surgeon, was born in 1779 and educated to the medical profession in London. He joined the army medical staff in Portugal in 1798, was gazetted next year assistant-surgeon to the royals, served in Holland, at Ferrol, in Egypt, the Mediterranean, the West Indies, and through the Peninsular war, having been appointed to the staff in 1808 and made deputy inspector-general of hospitals in 1813. He retired in 1814 with that rank and the war medal with five clasps, and commenced practice as a physician in Argyll Street, London. He had graduated M.D. at Edinburgh in 1808, and joined the College of Physicians of London in 1814, becoming a fellow in 1841. In 1816 he was appointed physician to the newly founded Royal Westminster Infirmary for Diseases of the Eye in Warwick Street, Golden Square, having George James Guthrie [q. v.] as his surgical colleague. In 1827 some difference of opinion arose between Forbes and Guthrie as to the treatment of inflammatory affections of the eye; the subject was noticed in the 'Lancet' adversely to Guthrie, who commenced an action for libel against the journal, but abandoned it on learning that Forbes had been subpœnaed as a witness. Having been insulted at the hospital by one Hale Thomson, a young surgeon in Guthrie's party, Forbes challenged the former to a duel. It was fought with pistols on Clapham Common at half-past three in the afternoon of 29 Dec. 1827; when each had fired twice without effect, the seconds interposed, but another encounter was demanded by the principals, which was also harmless. The seconds then declared the duel at an end, against the wishes of the parties. Forbes resigned his appointment at the hospital, carrying a number of its subscribers with him. He declined an offer by Guthrie to give him the satisfaction of a gentleman and an officer of the same service, on the ground that the offer was not made until after events at the hospital had been allowed to take their course. He had a considerable practice among a number of families of the nobility, and was much esteemed. His only writings are two small pamphlets of correspondence, &c., on the Guthrie affair (1828), and a brief record of a case of fatal thrombosis of the thigh veins in the 'Medico-Chirurgical Transactions,' xiii. (1827). He was a knight of the Crescent, in 1837 was made a Guelphic knight of Hanover, and in 1844 an English knight. He died at Argyll Street on 22 March 1852.

[Gent. Mag. April 1852; Med. Times and Gaz. 1852, i. 355; Munk's Coll. of Phys. vol. iii.; pamphlets on the Guthrie incident.]   C. C.

FORBES, DAVID (1777?–1849), major-general, was the son of a Scotch minister in the county of Elgin, and entered the army when a mere boy as an ensign in the 78th highlanders, or Ross-shire buffs, when Francis Humberstone Mackenzie, afterwards Lord Seaforth, raised that regiment in March 1793. He was promoted lieutenant on 3 May 1794, and in the following September his regiment joined the army in the Netherlands, under the command of Lieutenant-colonel Alexander Mackenzie Fraser [q. v.] He served with distinction in all the affairs of the disastrous retreat before Pichegru, and was especially noticed for his behaviour at Geldermalsen on 5 Jan. 1795. He was present at the affair of Quiberon and the attack on Belle Isle in that year, and in 1796 he proceeded with his regiment first to the Cape and then to India. He remained in India more than twenty years, seeing much service. In 1798 his regiment formed the escort of Sir John Shore when he advanced into Oude to dethrone the nawab, and it was engaged throughout the Maráthá campaign of 1803, and especially at the storm of Ahmednagar. For his services in this campaign Forbes was promoted captain on 25 June 1803, and he remained in garrison until 1811, when his regiment was selected to form part of the expedition sent against Java in 1811, under Sir Samuel Auchmuty. He was placed in command of the flank companies of the various British regiments, and at their head led the assaults on the lines of Waltevreede and the lines of Cornelis, and was to the front in every engagement with

the Dutch troops. For these services he was five times thanked in general orders, received the gold medal for Java, and was promoted major on 29 Aug. 1811. In May 1812 he commanded the grenadiers of the 59th regiment and the light companies of the 78th in an expedition for the reduction of the sultan of Djocjocarta, and in May 1813 he suppressed the serious insurrection which broke out among the Malays at Probolingo in the east of the island of Java. In this insurrection Lieutenant-colonel Fraser of the 78th was killed, and Forbes, as major, received the step in promotion on 28 July 1814. In 1817 he returned to Scotland, being the only officer who returned out of forty-two, and bringing with him only thirty-six out of twelve hundred rank and file. He went on half-pay and settled at Aberdeen, where he lived without further employment for the rest of his life. On 10 Jan. 1837 he was promoted colonel, in 1838 made a C.B., and in 1846 promoted major-general. He died at Aberdeen on 29 March 1849.

[Hart's Army List; Gent. Mag. May 1849; and for the affair at Probolingo the Military Panorama for February 1814.]   H. M. S.

FORBES, DAVID (1828–1876), geologist and philologist, born at Douglas, Isle of Man, on 6 Sept. 1828, was one of the nine children of Edward Forbes of Oakhill and Croukbane, near Douglas, and Jane, eldest daughter and heiress of William Teare of the same island. He was younger brother of Edward Forbes [q. v.] David Forbes showed an early taste for chemistry; he was sent to school at Brentwood in Essex, whence he passed to Edinburgh University. Leaving Edinburgh about the age of nineteen, Forbes spent some months in the metallurgical laboratory of Dr. Percy in Birmingham, but he was still under twenty when he accompanied Mr. Brooke Evans to Norway, where he received the appointment of superintendent of the mining and metallurgical works at Espedal, a post which he held for ten years. Forbes showed courage in arming four hundred of his miners to aid the government against a threatened revolution in 1848, and received the personal thanks of the king. He was elected fellow of the Royal Society in June 1856. Entering into partnership with the firm of Evans & Askin, nickel-smelters of Birmingham, Forbes went to South America in 1857 in search of the ores of nickel and cobalt. From 1857 to 1860 he traversed the greater part of Bolivia and Peru, and embodied his observations on the minerals and rock-structure of those countries in a classical paper, which is printed in the 'Quarterly Journal' of the Geological

Society for 1860. He visited England in 1860, when it was proposed to appoint him as a representative of the English government in South America. Sir Roderick Murchison and Lord John Russell were memorialised, but the appointment was not considered necessary. Returning to South America he traversed the mining districts of the Cordilleras, and increased the large collection of minerals already formed in Norway. From South America Forbes made an expedition to the South Sea Islands, studying more especially their volcanic phenomena. In 1866 he travelled in Europe and in Africa. He had a talent for learning languages, and a remarkable power of securing the confidence of the half-savage miners of America. Forbes settled in England, and became foreign secretary to the Iron and Steel Institute. In that capacity he wrote the half-yearly reports on the progress of metal-working abroad which appeared in the journal of the institute from 1871 to 1876. During his later years Forbes was so entirely absorbed in his literary and scientific pursuits that he neglected to take sufficient exercise; the death of his wife, to whom he was profoundly attached, caused him to suffer severe mental trouble; his constitution, already enfeebled by a recurrent fever caught in South America, gave way, and he died on 5 Dec. 1876. Many representative men of science attended his funeral at Kensal Green cemetery, London, on 12 Dec. 1876. Forbes joined the Geological Society in 1853, and had been one of the secretaries since 1871. He was also a member of the Ethnological Society, to which he contributed a paper on the 'Aymara Indians of Bolivia and Peru.'

He wrote fifty-eight papers on scientific subjects, including three in conjunction with other investigators. Sixteen of his papers appeared in the 'Geological Magazine' from 1866 to 1872. His first paper, 'On a Simple Method of Determining the Free and Combined Ammonia and Water in Guano and other Manures,' appeared while he was a lad of seventeen in the 'Chemical Gazette' for 1845. Among his last papers were those 'On Aerolites from the Coast of Greenland,' published in the 'Quarterly Journal of the Geological Society' for 1872, and 'The Application of the Blow-pipe to the Quantitative Determination or Assay of Certain Minerals' in the 'Journal of the Chemical Society' for 1877. He was one of the first to apply the microscope to the study of rocks, and his paper in the 'Popular Science Review' on 'The Microscope in Geology' was translated, and appeared in the leading foreign scientific periodicals.

Igneous and metamorphic phenomena occupied much of Forbes's attention, and at Espedal he experimented on a large scale on the action of heat on minerals and rocks. He wrote some important papers on this subject, including 'The Causes producing Foliation in Rocks' (Geological Society, 1855), 'The Igneous Rocks of Staffordshire' ('Geol. Mag.' iii. 23), and 'On the Contraction of Igneous Rocks in Cooling' ('Geol. Mag.' vii. 1). Forbes tried hard to direct the attention of British geologists to chemical geology. His views are expressed in his articles on 'Chemical Geology' ('Chemical News,' 1867 and 1868) and 'On the Chemistry of the Primeval Earth' ('Geol. Mag.' 1867, p. 433, and 1868, p. 105). During his travels he had amassed a large fund of geological information, of which only a part was used in his published papers. He postponed an intended publication until too late.

[Geol. Mag., 1877, p. 45, obituary notice by Professor John Morris; Nature, xv. 139 ; Quart. Journ. Geol. Soc., president's address, 1877, pp. 41–8 ; Journal of the Iron and Steel Institute, 1876, pp. 519–24 ; Times, 12 Dec. 1876, p. 6.]

W. J. H.

FORBES, DUNCAN (1644 ?–1704), genealogist, was the eldest son of John Forbes of Culloden, Inverness-shire, M.P. and provost of Inverness, by Anna, eldest daughter of Alexander Dunbar of Grange (marriage contract dated 1643). He received an excellent education at Bourges and elsewhere on the continent, and on the death of his father about 1688 succeeded to the family estates. He represented Nairnshire in the convention of 1678 and 1681–2, Inverness-shire in the convention of 1689 and in the parliament of 1689–1702, and Nairnshire in the parliament of 1702, remaining undisturbed in his seat until his death (FOSTER, *Members of Parliament of Scotland*, 2nd edit. pp. 138–9). He was among the most active of those patriots who in Scotland contributed to bring about the expulsion of James II. The year after the revolution his estates at Culloden and Ferintosh were ravaged by the Jacobite hordes of Buchan and Cannon, and damage done to the amount of 54,000*l.* Scots, or 4,500*l.* sterling. The Scotch parliament met his claim for compensation by voting him a perpetual grant of a liberty to distil into spirits the grain of the barony of Ferintosh upon his paying a small specific composition in lieu of excise (Introduction to *Culloden Papers*, pp. v–vii). Forbes married Mary, second daughter of the second Sir Robert Innes, bart., of Innes, Morayshire (contract dated 1668), and felt a warm interest in his wife's family. For this reason, and also for the specific purpose of warranting a grant or confirmation of arms by the Lord Lyon, he compiled in 1698 'Ane Account of the Familie of Innes,' a very honest, painstaking work. Long after it had served its first purpose the work had become known from Pennant having extracted from it the account of the family tragedy of 1580 (*Tour in Scotland*, 5th edit. i. 331–7). A formal copy being found in the Innes charter-chest along with the Lord Lyon's patent, they were privately printed at Edinburgh in 1820 at the expense of the then Duke of Roxburghe, who wanted, as he afterwards observed to a friend, 'to show those proud Kerrs that he was of as good blood on his father's side as on his great-grandmother's.' Another edition was edited for the Spalding Club in 1864 by Cosmo Innes, who had discovered the author's original manuscript at Culloden. Appended are valuable charters and notes, chiefly from the Innes charter-chest at Floors, and from those of Leuchars and Dunkintie. Following a suggestion of Forbes, a member of the family, Robert Innes of Blairtoun in Balhelvie, writer to the signet and Lyon clerk, copied the early part of Forbes's manuscript and added his own genealogy down to 1729; it is now preserved at Edingicht, Banffshire. Forbes died 20 June 1704. He had, with seven daughters, two sons: John, who succeeded him in the representation of Nairnshire, and died without issue in 1734; and Duncan [q. v.], lord president of the court of session. Forbes is represented as a person of great worth; he certainly possessed some share of the ability which shone in the next generation of his house. He had turned his attention, as his son Duncan did afterwards, to the dangerous state of the clans, and is known as the author of 'A Plan for Preserving the Peace of the Highlands.' His 'MS. Diary,' to judge from the extract given in the Introduction to the 'Culloden Papers,' would be well worth printing.

[Memoirs of the Life of Lord President Forbes (8vo. London, 1748), pp. 9–10; Hill Burton's Life of Lord President Forbes (1847), pp. 273–4; The Familie of Innes (Spalding Club), preface, pp. 191, 255.] G. G.

FORBES, DUNCAN (1685–1747), president of the court of session, born 10 Nov. 1685, was the second son of Duncan Forbes (1644?–1704) [q. v.], of Culloden and Bunchrew, near Inverness, by his wife, Mary Innes. Duncan and his elder brother, John, were sent to the grammar school of Inverness. Here, according to his first biographer, who preserves some details omitted from more decorous records, the brothers became known as 'the greatest boozers in the north' from their convivial prowess. Duncan drank freely until, about 1725, delicate health compelled greater temperance, for a period at least. The same writer states that on the occasion of his mother's funeral (in 1716, see BURTON, 303), Forbes and the rest of the party drank so hard that when they went to the burial-place they left the body behind. On his father's death in 1704 Forbes's elder brother took the estate and Forbes inherited a small sum of money which he lost in mercantile speculations. He then went to study law at Edinburgh, under John Spottiswood, but, finding the teaching inadequate, proceeded in 1705 to Leyden. He had been present in March 1705 at the remarkable trial of Captain Thomas Green for piracy (HOWELL, *State Trials*, xiv. 1311). The execution of a man afterwards proved to be innocent made a deep impression upon him, as appears from a remarkable passage in his speech in the House of Commons on the Porteous case. At Leyden he studied both the civil law and oriental languages. He returned to Scotland in 1707. Soon after his return he married Mary, daughter of Hugh Rose, twelfth baron of Kilravock, near Culloden. She died early, though the exact date is not known, certainly before 1717. He was admitted an advocate 26 July 1709, and was soon afterwards appointed sheriff of Midlothian (BRUNTON and HAIG). This appointment was due to the favour of John, second duke of Argyll. The duke's brother, Lord Islay (afterwards third duke of Argyll), was also a warm friend. Forbes, it is said, managed the duke's estates gratuitously, though he might have had 500*l.* or 600*l.* a year for his services. He took an active part in politics on the whig side. On a canvass for his brother on one occasion his liberality in distributing claret and his vigour in consuming his own share carried the election. In 1715 he distinguished himself by loyal exertions against the rebels. His brother John joined the famous Simon Fraser, twelfth lord Lovat [q. v.], at Stirling, and accompanied him to Inverness. The brothers had raised forces to support the government. Culloden and Kilravock (the house of Duncan's father-in-law) were garrisoned; and, in combination with Lovat, they threatened Inverness, which surrendered just before the battle of Sheriffmuir. Duncan Forbes was rewarded by the office of depute-advocate, upon which he entered 12 March 1716. He accepted the office with great reluctance. He was expected, as he thought, to take part in the trial of some of the rebels in Carlisle. The law which provided that trials should take place in the counties in which the treasonable actions were alleged to have taken place was suspended. Forbes regarded this as unjust. He was not called upon to prosecute. He even collected money to support the Scottish prisoners at Carlisle. He wrote an anonymous letter to Sir Robert Walpole, protesting against severity to the rebels (*Culloden Papers*, pp. 61–5). His sentiments exposed him to suspicion of Jacobite leanings.

In 1721–2 Forbes was M.P. for Ayr burgh. In 1722 he stood against Alexander Gordon of Ardoch for the Inverness burghs. Gordon was returned, but upon a petition Forbes was declared to be duly elected. He had already been frequently employed as counsel in appeals to the House of Lords, and he made acquaintance with many eminent statesmen, and, it is said, with Pope, Arbuthnot, and their circle (*Scots Mag.* lxiv. 539). He knew Thomson the poet, who apostrophises him in 'Autumn,' and patronised Ruddiman and other men of letters. On 29 May 1725 he was appointed lord advocate in succession to Robert Dundas of Arniston [q. v.], and is said to have distinguished himself by his humanity. His salary was only 500*l.* or 600*l.* a year, and he had to discharge many of the duties previously attached to the office of secretary of state for Scotland, which was suspended during the years 1725–1731, and finally abolished in 1746.

Forbes had to take active measures during the troubles which arose from the extension of the English system of taxation to Scotland. A riot took place at Glasgow in 1725, when Shawfield, the house of Daniel Campbell, M.P. for Glasgow, who had supported the malt tax, was sacked by the mob. Forbes at once accompanied a force, commanded by General Wade, which marched upon Glasgow. Forbes, as lord advocate, ordered the arrest of the Glasgow magistrates for their negligence, and brought them, with some of the rioters, to Edinburgh (WODROW, *Analecta*, Maitland Club, iv. 215–17). They were liberated after a short time. The same act provoked a strike of the Edinburgh brewers, who had been ordered by the court of session to sell their ale at a fixed price. The court, at Forbes's request, ordered them to continue their trade, and threatened to commit them to prison. After a sharp dispute the brewers yielded, and Forbes received warm thanks from Walpole. He afterwards proposed very stringent regulations for the protection of the revenue. Forbes was a tenant of the infamous Francis Charteris [q. v.], at the old manor house of Stoneyhill, near Edinburgh. The anonymous biographer says that he defended Charteris, who died in 1732. In gratitude for this and for some other reasons

Charteris left him 1,000*l.* and the life-rent of Stoneyhill (BURTON, pp. 309, 310).

In 1735 Forbes succeeded to the family estates on the death of his brother, and undertook agricultural improvements at Bunchrew, a small property near Culloden. In 1737 he took a conspicuous part in opposing the bill inflicting penalties upon the city of Edinburgh for the Porteous affair. He made two firm, though temperate, speeches, reported in the 'Parliamentary History' (x. 248, 282), on 16 May and 9 June. The Duke of Argyll and all the Scottish members took the same side, and the bill was reduced to a measure 'for making the fortune of an old cook-maid' (Mrs. Porteous), and even then carried by a casting vote. Though Forbes had thus opposed government while holding an official position, he was immediately appointed lord president of the court of session, and took his seat 21 June 1737. He soon gained a very high character as a judge (*Culloden Papers*; *Edinb. Rev.* xxvi. 108; LORD COCKBURN). Many of the cases which he decided are given in Kilkerran's reports. He immediately made regulations for improving the despatch of business, and reported in February 1740 that all arrears had been cleared off (BURTON, p. 361). He enforced respect for his office upon all classes, and at the same time laboured at other incidental tasks. He made an elaborate investigation, at the request of the House of Lords, into the origin and history of Scottish peerages. He tried hard to convert various friends to a favourite crotchet. He held that the commercial prosperity of the country, otherwise in a satisfactory state, was threatened by the 'excessive use of tea.' He proposed to limit the use of tea by all persons with an income under 50*l.* a year. But memorials to the solicitor-general, Murray (afterwards Lord Mansfield), and other eminent persons met no response.

The approach of the rebellion of 1745 brought more serious difficulties. Forbes strongly, but vainly, urged preventive measures, and especially the plan, afterwards adopted by Chatham, of the formation of highland regiments (BURTON, p. 368). In August 1745 he went to Inverness and corresponded with many of the highland leaders, especially Lovat, who had been known to his father, intimate with his brother John, and had kept up a friendly correspondence with Duncan Forbes since 1715 (*ib.* p. 119). Forbes had assisted Lovat in some of his complex lawsuits (*ib.* pp. 127, 128). Forbes now endeavoured to detach Lovat from the Pretender's cause. Lovat's clan made a sudden raid upon Culloden, which was fortified and garrisoned; but Lovat disavowed his complicity, and for a time kept to his mask (*ib.* pp. 227–42). Forbes was meanwhile left, by Cope's departure to the south in September, the sole representative of government in the north of Scotland. Blank commissions were sent to him for distribution among the loyal clans. After Prestonpans his position became very difficult. He was joined by the Earl of Loudon, and they raised a force of two thousand men. When the highlanders moved northwards in the beginning of 1746 Forbes and Loudon retreated into Ross-shire, and ultimately to Skye, where they heard of the battle of Culloden. Forbes then returned to Inverness. He protested against the cruelties of the Duke of Cumberland, who showed his spirit by calling Forbes 'that old woman who talked to me about humanity' (*ib.* p. 382). Forbes had been obliged to raise sums upon his own credit. 'Small sums' amounted to 1,500*l.*, and he advanced besides three times his annual rents. The consequent anxiety and the labours which he had gone through seem to have broken his health. He died 10 Dec. 1747. A statue by Roubiliac was raised to him in the parliament house at Edinburgh.

He left an only son, John, who was a friend of Thomson's, and is said to be described as the 'joyous youth' who kept the Castle of Indolence in a 'gay uproar.' He entered the army, served at Fontenoy, and after his father's death lived in retirement at Stradishall, Suffolk, slowly paying off the encumbrances upon his paternal estates.

Forbes is also known as the author of some theological works. As lord advocate he had been engaged in 1728 in the prosecution of James Carnegie of Finhaven, who had been grossly insulted during one of the usual convivial parties at a funeral by a Mr. Bridgeton, and, trying to stab Bridgeton, had killed Lord Strathmore (Howell, *State Trials*, xvii. 73–154). Carnegie was acquitted after long arguments, in which frequent reference was made to the Mosaic law and Jewish cities of refuge. Forbes, according to his anonymous biographer, was so much impressed by these arguments that he set to work to learn Hebrew. The result of his studies appeared in three treatises, which were published soon after his death as his 'Works, now first collected' (undated). They contain: 1. 'A Letter to a Bishop, concerning some important Discoveries in Religion and Theology,' 1732 (an exposition of Hutchinson's 'Moses's Principia'). 2. 'Some Thoughts concerning Religion, natural and revealed . . . tending to show that Christianity is, indeed, *very near* as old as the Creation,' 1735 (an answer to Tindal's 'Christianity as Old as the Creation,'

chiefly from prophecy). 3. 'Reflections on the Sources of Incredulity with respect to Religion' (posthumous). The two first were translated into French by Charles François Houbigant in 1769; but, it is said, 'the solidity of a Scottish lawyer could not be expected to suit with the vivacity of French reasoners.' Another peculiarity perhaps had more importance. Forbes was a follower of the fanciful school founded by John Hutchinson (1674–1737) [q. v.], and afterwards represented by Bishop Horne, Jones of Nayland, Parkhurst, and others, with which his translator seems to have been in sympathy. His piety was superior to his scholarship, but his books show an attractive enthusiasm and seriousness. Warburton in 1750 (*Letters*, 2nd edition, p. 40) recommends the posthumous work on incredulity as 'a little jewel. I knew and venerated the man,' he adds; 'one of the greatest that ever Scotland bred, both as a judge, a patriot, and a Christian.' Though Warburton is not a safe critic, he seems to have expressed a general opinion.

[Memoirs of the Life, &c., of the late Right Hon. Duncan Forbes, 1748; Culloden Papers, with memoir by Duff, 1815; Tytler's Life of Kames, 1814, i. 45–8; Elchies's Notes on Jurisdiction, No. 14; Brunton and Haig, pp. 508–12; Lives of Simon, Lord Lovat, and Duncan Forbes of Culloden, by John Hill Burton, 1847. The last is founded upon an examination of original papers preserved at Culloden, many extracts from which are given.] L. S.

FORBES, DUNCAN (1798–1868), orientalist, was born of humble parentage at Kinnaird in Perthshire on 28 April 1798. His parents emigrated to America in the spring of 1801, taking only their youngest child with them, while Duncan was consigned to the care of his paternal grandfather in Glenfernate. His early schooling was of the scantiest, and he knew no English till he was about thirteen years old, but he soon showed intellectual independence and plain commonsense. When barely seventeen years old he was chosen village schoolmaster of Straloch, and soon after began to attend Kirkmichael school as a student. In October 1818 he entered Perth grammar school, and qualified himself to matriculate two years after at the university of St. Andrews, where he took the degree of M.A. in 1823. In the summer of the same year he accepted an appointment in the Calcutta Academy, then newly established, and arrived at Calcutta in the following November. Ill-health, however, obliged him to return to England early in 1826, when he became, soon after his arrival in London, assistant to Dr. John Borthwick

Gilchrist [q. v.], teacher of Hindustani, and afterwards to Dr. Sandford Arnot. In 1837 he was appointed professor of oriental languages in King's College, London, a post which he occupied until 1861, when he was elected to an honorary fellowship of the college. From 1849 to 1855 Forbes was employed by the trustees of the British Museum to make a catalogue of the collection of Persian MSS., previously uncatalogued, and numbering at that time just over a thousand. This work is contained in four large volumes of manuscript in the department of Oriental MSS. The plan of arrangement, the absence of bibliographical apparatus, probably due to want of revision from the cataloguer, and, lastly, the addition of new collections equal in bulk to the old, rendered it necessary to entirely recast Forbes's work in the new printed 'Catalogue of Persian MSS.' The preface to the latter (vol. iii. p. xxviii) states that 'the use of Dr. Forbes's catalogue was practically confined to the help it afforded in the preliminary classing of the MSS.' He was a successful teacher, and writer of useful publications. His habits were singularly self-denying, and his chief relaxation was chess-playing, on the history of which in the Orient he wrote 'Observations on the Origin and Progress of Chess, containing a brief account of the theory and practice of the Chaturanga, the primæval game of the Hindūs, also of the Shatranj, the mediæval game of the Persians and Arabs,' &c., 8vo, London, 1855. This was followed by a work of great research, entitled 'The History of Chess, from the time of the early Invention of the Game in India till the period of its Establishment in Western and Central Europe,' 8vo, London, 1860. Some portions of it have, however, been handled with great severity by Dr. van der Linde in his 'Geschichte des Schachspiels.' Forbes, who was a member of the Royal Asiatic Society, was created honorary LL.D. of St. Andrews University in 1847. He died on 17 Aug. 1868. With Sandford Arnot, Forbes was joint author of 'A New Persian Grammar, containing . . . the elementary principles of that . . . language,' 8vo, London, 1828, and 'An Essay on the Origin and Structure of the Hindostanee Tongue, . . . with an account of the principal elementary works on the subject,' 8vo, London, 1828; second edition, 8vo, London, 1844; 3rd edit., enlarged (appendix), 3 pts. 8vo, 1861. He also added to the new edition of Arnot's 'Grammar of the Hindūstāni Tongue,' 8vo, London, 1844, 'a selection of easy extracts for reading in the Persi-Arabic and Devanagari character, with a copious vocabulary and explanatory notes.'

He also published: 1. 'The Hindustani Manual; a pocket companion for those who visit India. Part 1. A compendious grammar. Part 2. A vocabulary of useful words,' 18mo, London, 1845; new edit., 24mo, 1850; new edit., revised by J. T. Platts, 24mo, 1874. 2. 'A Grammar of the Hindūstāni Language in the Oriental and Roman Character. To which is added a copious selection of easy extracts for reading in the Persi-Arabic and Devanagari characters,' 8vo, London, 1846. 3. 'A Dictionary, Hindustani and English. To which is added a reversed Part, English and Hindustani,' 2 vols. 8vo, London, 1848; 2nd edit., greatly enlarged, 2 pts. 8vo, 1857; new edit., printed entirely in the Roman character, 2 pts. 8vo, 1859. 4. 'Oriental Penmanship; an essay for facilitating the reading and writing of the Tàlik character . . .,' 4to, London, 1849. 5. 'Two Letters addressed to E. B. Eastwick,' attacking Eastwick's 'Lucubrations on the Bāgh o Bahār,' 8vo, London, 1852. 6. 'A smaller Hindustani and English Dictionary,' sq. 8vo, London, 1861. 7. 'A Grammar of the Bengālī Language,' 8vo, London, 1861. 8. 'The Bengālī Reader . . . A new edition . . . revised,' 8vo, London, 1862. 9. 'A Grammar of the Arabic Language,' 8vo, London, 1863. 10. 'Arabic Reading Lessons,' 8vo, London, 1864. 11. 'Catalogue of Oriental Manuscripts, chiefly Persian, collected within the last five-and-thirty years,' 8vo, London, 1866. For the Oriental Translation Fund he translated the Persian romance 'The Adventures of Hatim Taï,' 4to, London, 1830. He edited, with a vocabulary, the 'Bāgh o Bahār' in 1846, 1849, and (with the Hindustani text 'printed in the Roman character'), 1859; revised and corrected L. F. Smith's translation of the same work in 1851, and published his own version in 1862. In 1852 appeared his edition of the 'Totā-Kahānī' in Hindustani, and in 1857 his edition of the 'Baitāl-Pachīsi' in Hindi. Writing as 'Fior Ghael' Forbes discussed Celtic dialects, denying that Welsh was one, in the 'Gentleman's Magazine' for May 1836, and led the warm controversy which followed (cf. *Gent. Mag.* 1838-9). Forbes was also author of a privately printed autobiography.

Forbes's books, though clear and convenient to use, show little original research. It is indeed to be regretted that he endeavoured to cover, without due equipment of scholarship, an area of oriental study extending into fields so widely separated as Arabic and Bengali, in neither of which was he really at home. Still his elementary manuals are often of greater use to beginners than more learned works.

[Annual Report of the Royal Asiatic Society, May 1869, pp. vii-viii; St. Andrews Univ. Calendar, 1800-53, pp. 24, 70 ; King's College Calendar ; Brit. Mus. Catalogues of Printed Books and of Persian MSS. ; Cat. of Printed Books in Library of Faculty of Advocates, iii. 206-7 ; information kindly supplied by Professor Cecil Bendall.]

FORBES, EDWARD (1815-1854), naturalist, son of Edward Forbes, banker, and brother of David Forbes (1828-1876) [q. v.], was born at Douglas, Isle of Man, on 12 Feb. 1815, and was educated at home and at a day-school at Douglas. He very early displayed marked and widespread tastes for natural history, literature, and drawing. When at school he is described as tall and thin, with limbs loosely hung, and wearing his hair very long. His school-books were covered with caricatures and grotesque figures, and his parents were so impressed by his artistic talent that at the age of sixteen they sent him to London to study art. Being, however, refused entrance to the Royal Academy School, and found not sufficiently promising by his teacher, Mr. Sass, Forbes entered at Edinburgh University in November 1831 as a medical student. While in London he had made his first contribution to the 'Mirror' (August 1831), 'On some Manx Traditions.' In his first year at Edinburgh he attended Knox's lectures on anatomy, Hope's on chemistry, and Graham's on botany, and became a devoted student of natural history in Jameson's museum and in the country round Edinburgh. At this early period his powers of generalisation and abstraction were as noticeable as his perfect familiarity with natural objects and his varied experimental studies. His peculiar vein of humour showed itself in sketches of the most grotesque kind, and equally broad comic verses. During the vacation of 1832 he investigated the natural history of the Isle of Man. He returned to Edinburgh with a bias against medicine, which turned his note-books into portfolios of caricatures, and he was far more congenially employed in 1834-5 in writing and drawing for the 'University Maga,' which he and a few other students brought out weekly from 8 Jan. to 26 March 1835. In this the professors and other prominent persons were severely satirised, and the complete volume was dedicated to 'Christopher North.' The death, early in 1836, of his mother, who had particularly wished him to become a physician, left him free to resign medical study. Meanwhile the Maga Club had developed into a 'Universal Brotherhood of the Friends of Truth,' whose membership demanded good work already done as well as good fellowship, and the maintenance of a character free from stain. In this society Forbes always continued to take an interest.

Meanwhile Forbes's vacations had been utilised for much natural history work. In the summer of 1833, with his friend Campbell, afterwards principal of Aberdeen University, he went to Norway, sailing from the Isle of Man to Arendal in a brig. Both the voyage and the land trip were occupied with the keenest observation of natural history, and an account of it was given by Forbes in the 'Magazine of Natural History,' vols. viii. and ix. The return journey was through Christiania and Copenhagen, and at these places Forbes made several botanical friends. In the summer of 1834 Forbes dredged in the Irish Sea and continued to explore the natural history of the Isle of Man. The results of the dredging appeared in the 'Magazine of Natural History,' vols. viii. and ix. In the summer of 1835 he visited France, Switzerland, and Germany, and was so much attracted by the Jardin des Plantes that he resolved to spend the winter of 1836-7 in Paris, studying at the Jardin and attending the lectures of De Blainville and Geoffroy Saint-Hilaire. From their lectures he was much impressed with the necessity of studying the geographical distribution of animals. After this winter he travelled in the south of France and in Algeria, collecting many natural history specimens, on which he based a paper in the 'Annals of Natural History,' vol. ii.

In 1837-8 Forbes was back in Edinburgh, working at natural history, bringing out his little volume on 'Manx Mollusca,' and taking an active part on behalf of the students in the notable snowball riots of 1838, which were the subject of much of the contents of the revived 'University Maga' of 1837-8. He also published, under the title of 'The University Snowdrop,' a collection of his songs and squibs on the riots, being especially severe on the town council, who, as patrons of the university, had made themselves obnoxious to the students by calling out the military. Owing largely to Forbes's exertions, the thirty-five students who were arrested were fully acquitted. In the summer of 1838, after a fruitful tour through Austria, during which he collected about three thousand plant specimens, Forbes attended the British Association meeting at Newcastle, read before it a paper 'On the Distribution of Terrestrial Pulmonifera in Europe,' and was asked to prepare another on the distribution of pulmoniferous mollusca in the British Isles, which he presented at the succeeding meeting after much original study. After studying the star-fishes of the Irish Sea

After the Restoration he invented a mode of coining farthings. Each piece was to differ minutely from another to prevent forgery. He failed in procuring a patent for these in England, but obtained one for Ireland. He died in Ireland before he could carry his design into execution, on 3 Sept. 1670. His body was brought to England, and interred in the family burial-place at Harting. Wood says: 'He was a great virtuoso of his time, yet none of the Royal Society, and might have done greater matters if that he had not been disincouraged for those things he had done before' (*Athenæ Oxon.* ed. Bliss, iii. 906).

By the marriage of his only daughter, Catharine, to Ralph lord Grey of Werke, Up Park became the property of the earls of Tankerville until it was sold in 1745.

He wrote: 1. 'A Design for bringing a Navigable River from Rickmansworth in Hartfordshire to St. Giles's in the Fields,' &c., London, 1641, 4to, with an answer by Sir Walter Roberts, printed the same year, and both reprinted in 1720. Ford's pamphlet is also reprinted in the 'Harleian Miscellany.' 2. 'Experimented Proposals how the King may have money to pay and maintain his Fleets with ease to his people. London may be rebuilt, and all proprietors satisfied. Money be lent at six per cent. on pawns. And the Fishing-Trade set up, which alone is able and sure to enrich us all. And all this without altering, straining, or thwarting any of our Laws or Customes now in use,' London, 1666, 4to. To this was added a 'Defence of Bill Credit.' 3. 'Proposals for maintaining the Fleet and rebuilding London, by bills to be made payable on the taxes to be given to the King by Parliament,' manuscript in Public Record Office, 'State Papers,' Dom. Charles II, vol. clxxi. 4. Important letters of intelligence preserved among the 'Clarendon State Papers' in the Bodleian Library at Oxford.

[Clarendon's Hist. of the Rebellion (1843), pp. 477, 478, 626; Calendar of the Clarendon State Papers, i. 545; Dallaway's Sussex; Notes and Queries, 3rd ser. ix. 80; Calendars of State Papers, Dom. 1649-50 p. 46, 1659-60 p. 97, 1661-2 p. 146, 1663-4 pp. 396, 655, 1664-5 pp. 72, 214, 230, 1665-6 p. 170, 1666-7 pp. 127, 439; Hist. MSS. Comm. 6th Rep. 330, 331, 7th Rep. 686, 9th Rep. 393; Sussex Archæological Collections, v. 36-63, ix. 50-3, xix. 94, 118; Tierney's Arundel, pp. 58-68.]   T. C.

FORD, EDWARD (1746-1809), surgeon, is stated to have been 'the son of Dr. Ford, a prebendary of Wells,' and to have been born in that city 'in 1750' (*Gent. Mag.* vol. lxxix. pt. ii. p. 1168). As, however, his

age at the time of his death is given as '62' (*ib.* p. 984), he would have been born in 1746, the son of Thomas Ford, prebendary of St. Decuman, Wells, and vicar of Banwell and of Wookey, Somersetshire, who died 29 Aug. of the same year (*ib.* xvi. 496; LE NEVE, *Fasti*, ed. Hardy, i. 185, 197). He received his medical training under Dr. John Ford, then in practice at Bristol. At an early age he settled as a surgeon in London, was admitted a member of the court of assistants of the Royal College of Surgeons, acquired an excellent practice, and was greatly liked. In 1780 he was appointed surgeon to the Westminster General Dispensary, which office he resigned, after more than twenty years' service, on 16 July 1801. At this time, the finances of the charity being very low, Ford generously presented it with the arrears of his salary, amounting altogether to four hundred guineas, and his example was followed by the physicians to the institution, Drs. Foart Simmons and Robert Bland (*Gent. Mag.* vol. lxxi. pt. ii. p. 661). He died 15 Sept. 1809 at Sherborne, Dorsetshire, when on his way from Weymouth to Bath, 'a very humane and benevolent gentleman, well known in the abodes of poverty, wretchedness, and disease.' Besides papers in various medical serials (REUSS, *Alphabetical Register of Authors*, p. 138, supplement, pt. i. pp. 360-1), Ford was author of a valuable treatise entitled 'Observations on the Disease of the Hip Joint; to which are added some Remarks on White Swellings of the Knee . . . illustrated by cases and engravings,' 8vo, London, 1794 (WATT, *Bibl. Brit.* i. 257 *d*, 377 *e*), of which revised editions were published in 1810 and 1818 by his nephew and successor Thomas Copeland [q. v.], to whom he bequeathed his house in Golden Square, London, and a considerable legacy. He was elected a fellow of the Society of Antiquaries, 3 May 1792 (GOUGH, *Chronological List of Soc. Antiq.* 1798, p. 51). He was twice married. His first wife, Sarah Frances, daughter of Hugh Josiah Hansard, died in 1783, and was buried at Hillingdon, Middlesex (LYSONS, *Parishes in Middlesex*, p. 161).

[David Rivers's Literary Memoirs of Living Authors, 1798, i. 191; Noble's Continuation of Granger, iii. 115.]   G. G.

FORD, EMANUEL (*fl.* 1607), romance writer, was the author of 'Parismus, the renovmed prince of Bohemia. His most famous, delectable, and pleasant historie, conteining his noble battailes fought against the Persians, his love to Laurana, the king's daughter of Thessaly, and his strange adventures in the desolate Island.' London, by Thomas Creede, 1598. This work was licensed to Creede on 22 Nov. 1597 (ARBER, iii. 98), and was dedicated to Sir Robert Radcliffe, the Earl of Sussex, Viscount Fitzwaters, Lord Egremond and Burnell. At the close is a recommendatory epistle from the author's friend L[azarus] P[lot], the pseudonym of Anthony Munday. The book imitated the Spanish romances. Its style was euphuistic, but its story was for the most part original. It was extraordinarily well received, and on 25 Oct. 1598 Creede obtained a license for a second part. It is called in the 'Stationers' Registers' (ib. iii. 129) 'Parismenos. The triall of true friendship,' but when published it was entitled 'Parismenos. The second part of the most famous, delectable, and pleasant Historie of Parismenos, the renowned prince of Bohemia,' London, 1599, and was dedicated to the Countess of Essex. Innumerable reprints of the whole work followed. In 1608 a volume was issued containing 'The First Part of Parismus' with a second title-page introducing 'Parismenos, the second part.' The latter bears the date 1609 and the words 'The third time imprinted and amended.' A fourth edition of the whole is dated 1615: others are dated 1630, 1636, 1649 (13th edit.), 1657, 1663, 1664, 1665, 1668-9, 1671, 1677, 1684, 1690, 1696, and 1704. The romance was also frequently issued in an abridged form as a chapbook without date. A reference to the work in Thomas May's 'Old Couple' (not published till 1658, although acted earlier) illustrates the book's popularity (DODSLEY, Old Plays, ed. Hazlitt, xii. 12; cp. Notes and Queries, 2nd ser. vi. 310).

Another of Ford's romances is entitled 'The most pleasant history of Ornatus and Artesia, wherein is contained the unjust reign of Thaeon, king of Phrygia.' The Douce collection in the Bodleian Library has a copy dated 1607, dedicated to Bryan Stapleton, esq., of Carleton, Yorkshire. Heber had an imperfect copy, which he believed to have been published before 1598. Editions of 1634, 1650, 1669, and 1683 are known. The British Museum Library has none earlier than 1650. A third romance by Ford is called 'The Famous History of Montelion, knight of the oracle, son of the true mirrour of Princes, the most renowned king Persicles of Assyria.' In a jovial preface the author states that the success of 'Parismos' encouraged him to produce this work. The earliest edition now known is dated 1633. J. O. Halliwell-Phillipps had in his possession at one time a copy of earlier date. Other editions are dated 1663, 1668,

1671, 1683, 1687, 1695. It also appeared frequently as an undated chapbook. Ford's title of 'Montelion, knight of the oracle,' was the pseudonym adopted by John Phillipps [q. v.], one of Milton's nephews, who issued almanacks under that name in 1660 and 1661. Flatman [q. v.] also employed the same nom-de-guerre in his mock romance of 'Don Juan Lamberto.' Both 'Ornatus and Artesia' and 'Montelion' are written on the same models as 'Parismos.'

[Dunlop's Hist. of Fiction, ed. Wilson, 1888, ii. 547; Hazlitt's Handbooks; Brit. Mus. and Bodl. Libr. Catalogues.] S. L.

FORD, SIR HENRY (1619?–1684), secretary of state, born in or about 1619, was the eldest son of Henry Ford of Bagtor in Ilsington, Devonshire, by Katharine, daughter and heiress of George Drake of Spratshays in Littleham, in the same county. He was absurdly supposed to have been grandson of John Ford the dramatist [q. v.] (LYSONS, Magna Britannia, vol. vi. Devonshire, pt. ii. pp. 291-2); his grandfather was Thomas Ford, son and heir of George Ford of Ilsington (Visitation of Devonshire in 1620, Harl. Soc., p. 108). He was for a time fellow-commoner of Exeter College, Oxford (BOASE, Reg. of Exeter Coll. p. lxi), but his father dying, and his mother marrying again, he went home to look after his patrimony. With his stepfather, John Cloberry of Bradstone, Devonshire, he had many hot disputes over the property, which had to be settled in the law courts. In the reign of Charles II he purchased Nutwell Court, in the parish of Woodbury, near Exeter, which he made the place of his future abode. He was put in the commission of the peace for the county, and was lieutenant-colonel, under Sir John Drake of Ash, his kinsman, in the militia for the eastern division of the shire, of which he was likewise a deputy-lieutenant. On the death of Sir Thomas Stucley he was elected member for Tiverton, 6 April 1664, and kept his seat until the dissolution of Charles's last parliament, 28 March 1681 (Lists of Members of Parliament, Official Return, pt. i. pp. 522, 535, 541, 547). Prince, who knew him well, describes Ford as 'an excellent orator,' and witty, but the single specimen he gives of his wit is by no means brilliant (Worthies of Devon, ed. 1701, p. 315). In 1669 he accompanied John, lord Robartes, the lord-lieutenant, to Ireland as secretary of state, but 'to his no little damage and disappointment' was recalled along with his chief the very next year. In 1672 Ford, having been knighted at Whitehall on 20 July in that year (LE NEVE, Knights, Harl. Soc., p. 279), acted in the same capacity to Arthur Capel, earl of Essex. He did not, however, continue in office long, 'for being sent into England on some important affair, contrived by those who were willing to put him out of the way, he returned no more unto Ireland' (PRINCE, p. 316). The fact was that his brusque, overbearing manner made him everywhere disliked. He died in 1684, aged 65, at Nutwell Court, and was buried in Woodbury Church (LYSONS, *Magna Britannia*, vol. vi, Devonshire, pt. i. pp. cxcv–vi, pt. ii. pp. 291–292). He left a son Charles, supposed to have died in his minority, and three daughters, married to Drake, Holwell, and Egerton (*ib.* vol. vi. pt. ii. p. 571). On 22 July 1663 he was elected F.R.S. (THOMSON, *Hist. of Roy. Soc.*, appendix iv.), and remained in the society until 1682 (*Lists of Roy. Soc.* in Brit. Mus.)

[Prince's Worthies of Devon, 1701, pp. 314–16.]
G. G.

FORD, JAMES (1779–1850), antiquary, born at Canterbury on 31 Oct. 1779, was the eldest son of the Rev. James Ford, B.A., minor canon of Durham, and afterwards minor canon of Canterbury. He entered the King's School, Canterbury, in 1788, matriculated at Trinity College, Oxford, 8 July 1797, and became fellow of his college 2 June 1807. He graduated B.A. 1801, M.A. 1804, B.D. 1812, and in 1811 was junior proctor of the university. He held the perpetual curacies of St. Laurence, Ipswich, and of Hill Farrance, Somersetshire. He was subsequently presented (28 Oct. 1830) to the vicarage of Navestock in Essex, and died 31 Jan. 1850. His quaint directions (see SIDEBOTHAM, *Memorials*, p. 96) for a funeral of great simplicity were carried out when he was buried in Navestock churchyard. There is a monument to him in Navestock Church, and a portrait of him in the common room of Trinity College, Oxford. He married, on 19 Nov. 1830, Lætitia, youngest daughter of Edward Jermyn, bookseller, of Ipswich, but left no children. To the university of Oxford Ford bequeathed 2,000*l.* for the endowment of 'Ford's Professorship of English History,' and to Trinity College, Oxford, 4,000*l.* for the purchase of advowsons, as well as 4,000*l.* for the endowment of four 'Ford's Studentships,' two of which were to be confined to youths educated at the King's School, Canterbury. Ford was a collector and compiler on antiquarian subjects. His large collection for a new edition of Morant's 'History of Essex' is in the library of Trinity College, Oxford, and his manuscript collections for a history of bishops from the Re-

volution onwards were purchased by the British Museum. He was also a contributor to the 'Gentleman's Magazine' and to Nichols's 'Literary Illustrations,' vols. vi. and viii., and was the author of 'The Devout Communicant,' 1815, 12mo, and 'A Century of Christian Prayers,' 2nd ed. Ipswich, 1824, 8vo.

[Sidebotham's Memorials of the King's School, Canterbury (1865), pp. 95–8 ; Brit. Mus. Cat.; Nichols's Lit. Illustr. viii. 659, 668 ; Gent. Mag. 1848, new ser. xxx. 330.]
W. W.

FORD, JOHN (*fl.* 1639), dramatist, second son of Thomas Ford of Ilsington, Devonshire, was baptised at Ilsington 17 April 1586. His mother was a sister of Lord-chief-justice Popham. He is probably the John Ford, 'Devon, gen. f.,' who matriculated at Exeter College, Oxford, 26 March 1601, aged sixteen years (*Oxford Univ. Reg.* vol. ii. pt. ii. p. 246). On 16 Nov. 1602 Ford was admitted a member of the Middle Temple. In 1606 he published an elegy on the Earl of Devonshire, 'Fames Memoriall ; or the Earle of Devonshire Deceased. With his honourable life, peacefull end, and solemne Funerall,' 4to, with a dedicatory sonnet to the Lady Penelope, countess of Devonshire, and commendatory verses by Barnabe Barnes and 'T. P.' Ford seems to have had no personal acquaintance with the earl or with Lady Penelope, and he is careful to state that his elegy was not written from any mercenary motive. In the course of the poem he makes mysterious allusions to a lady, 'bright Lycia the cruel, the cruel-subtle,' whose affections he had vainly sought to engage. To 1606 also belongs 'Honor Trivmphant; or the Peeres Challenge, by Armes defensible, at Tilt, Turney, and Barriers. . . . Also the Monarches Meeting ; or the King of Denmarkes welcome into England,' 4to. His earliest dramatic work was an unpublished comedy entitled 'An Ill Beginning has [or may have] a Good End,' acted at the Cockpit in 1613. On 25 Nov. 1615 'A booke called Sir Thomas Overburyes Ghost, contayneing the history of his life and vntimely death, by John Fford, gent.,' was entered in the Stationers' Register. This must have been a prose-tract or a poem, as a play on the subject would certainly have been forbidden. In 1620 Ford published a moral treatise, 'A Line of Life. Pointing out the Immortalitie of a Vertuous Name,' 12mo.

First on the list of Ford's plays in order of publication is 'The Lovers Melancholy. Acted at the Private House in the Blacke Friers, and publikely at the Globe by the Kings Maiesties seruants,' 1629, 4to, which had been brought out 24 Nov. 1628. Four copies of commendatory verses are prefixed, and the play is dedicated 'To my worthily respected friends, Nathaniel Finch, John Ford, Esquires; Master Henry Blunt, Master Robert Ellice, and all the rest of the Noble Society of Gray's Inn.' In the dedicatory epistle Ford states that this was his first appearance in print as a dramatic writer, and hints that it may be his last. Gifford rightly pronounces the comic portions of 'The Lovers Melancholy' to be despicable; but it contains some choice poetry, notably the description (after Strada) of the contention between the nightingale and the musician.

In 1633 was published 'Tis Pity Shee's a Whore. Acted by the Queenes Maiesties Seruants at the Phœnix in Drury Lane,' 4to, with a dedicatory epistle to John, first earl of Peterborough, to whom the dramatist acknowledges his indebtedness for certain favours. In this tragedy, of which the subject is singularly repulsive, Ford displays the subtlest qualities of his genius. The final colloquy between Annabella and Giovanni is one of the most memorable scenes in the English drama. In the same year (1633) was published 'The Broken Heart. A Tragedy. Acted by the Kings Maiesties Seruants at the private House in the Black-Friers. Fide Honor,' 4to, dedicated to William, lord Craven. 'Fide Honor' is an anagram of 'John Forde.' 'I do not know,' says Lamb, 'where to find in any play a catastrophe so grand, so solemn, and so surprising as this;' but Hazlitt and others have remarked on the fantastic unreality, the violent unnaturalness, of the closing scenes. A third play was printed in 1633, 'Loues Sacrifice. A tragedie receiued generally well. Acted by the Queenes Majesties Seruants at the Phœnix in Drury Lane,' 4to, with a dedicatory epistle to the author's cousin, John Ford of Gray's Inn, and commendatory verses by James Shirley. Detached passages and scenes are excellently written, but the plot is unsatisfactory, and the characters badly drawn. 'The Chronicle Historie of Perkin Warbeck. A Strange Truth. Acted (some-times) by the Queenes Maiesties Servants at the Phœnix in Drurie Lane. Fide Honor,' 1634, 4to, with a dedicatory epistle to William Cavendish, earl of Newcastle, and five copies of commendatory verses, is the most faultless, but not the greatest, of Ford's plays—well planned and equably written, a meritorious and dignified composition. It was reprinted in 1714, 12mo, when the movements of the Pretender's adherents in Scotland were attracting attention, and it was revived at Goodman's Fields in 1745. 'The Fancies Chast and Noble,' 1638, 4to, a comedy acted at the Phœnix, dedicated to Randal Macdonnel, earl of Antrim, is ingeniously conceived but awkwardly executed. From a passage in the prologue it has been hastily supposed that Ford was abroad when the play was produced. 'The Ladies Triall. Acted by both their Majesties Servants at the private house in Drvry Lane. Fide Honor,' 4to, was brought out 3 May 1638, and was published in the following year with a dedicatory epistle to John Wyrley, esq., and his wife, Mistress Mary Wyrley. The prologue was written by Theophilus Bird, the actor. There is much to admire in the first four acts, but the conclusion is strangely huddled. Pepys notices its revival at the Duke of York's theatre in March 1688.

'The Sun's Darling: A Moral Masque: As it hath been often presented at Whitehall by their Majesties Servants, and after at the Cock-pit in Drury Lane with great applause. Written by John Foard and Tho. Decker, Gent.,' 4to, was posthumously published in 1656, some copies being dated 1657. This play, which may have been an alteration of Dekker's unpublished 'Phaeton,' was licensed for the Cockpit 3 March 1623–4. The lyrical portions, which doubtless belong to Dekker, are the most attractive. From Sir Henry Herbert's 'Diary' it appears that two other plays by Ford and Dekker, 'The Fairy Knight' and 'The Bristowe Merchant,' were produced in 1624, but they were not published. 'The Witch of Edmonton; A known True Story. Composed into a Tragi-comedy by divers well-esteemed Poets, William Rowley, Thomas Dekker, John Ford, &c.,' 4to, first published in 1658, was probably written in 1621, soon after the execution of the reputed witch, Elizabeth Sawyer. Ford seems to have contributed little or nothing to the powerful scenes in which Mother Sawyer figures, but he must be credited with no small share of the scenes that deal with Frank Thorney. In September 1624 was licensed for the stage 'A new Tragedy, called A late Murther of the Sonn upon the Mother, written by Forde and Webster,' which was not published. A copy of commendatory verses by Ford was prefixed to Webster's 'Duchess of Malfi,' 1623.

A tragedy by Ford, 'Beauty in a Trance,' was entered in the Stationers' Register 9 Sept. 1653, and three comedies, 'The London Merchant,' 'The Royal Combat,' and 'An Ill Beginning has a Good End,' were entered 29 June 1660. These four unpublished pieces were among the plays destroyed by Warburton's cook. Ford prefixed commendatory verses to Barnabe Barnes's 'Foure Bookes of Offices,' 1606, Sir Thomas Overbury's 'Wife,' 1616, Shirley's 'Wedding,' 1629, Richard Brome's 'Northern Lass,' 1632; and he was one of the contributors to 'Jonsonus Virbius,' 1638. Dyce was of opinion that the verses to Barnabe Barnes were by the dramatist's cousin.

Ford drops from sight after the publication of the 'Ladies Trial' in 1639; but in Gifford's time 'faint traditions in the neighbourhood of his birth-place' led to the supposition that, having obtained a competency from his professional practice, he retired to Devonshire to end his days. In the 'Time-Poets' ('Choice Drollery,' 1656) occurs the couplet—

Deep in a dump John Forde was alone got,
With folded arms and melancholy hat.

It is certain that he had very little comic talent. That he was a favourite with playgoers is shown by his familiar appellation, 'Jack Ford,' mentioned by Heywood in the 'Hierarchie of Blessed Angels,' 1635—

And hee's now but Jacke Foord that once was John.

He was not dependent on the stage for his livelihood, and his plays bear few marks of haste. In the prologue to the 'Broken Heart' he declared that his 'best of art hath drawn this piece,' and in all his work the diction is studiously elaborated.

Ford's works were first collected by Weber in 1811, 2 vols. 8vo. A more accurate edition was published by Gifford in 1827, 2 vols. 8vo. An edition of Ford and Massinger, by Hartley Coleridge, appeared in 1848; and in 1869 Dyce issued a revised edition of Gifford's 'Ford,' 3 vols. 8vo.

[Memoir by Gifford, revised by Dyce, prefixed to Ford's Works, 1869; Lamb's Specimens of Dramatic Poets; Swinburne's Essays and Studies.]
A. H. B.

FORD, MICHAEL (d. 1758?), mezzotint engraver, was a native of Dublin, and a pupil of John Brooks, the mezzotint engraver [q. v.] When Brooks quitted Ireland about 1747, Ford set up as his successor at a shop on Cork Hill. He engraved a number of portraits in mezzotint, which on account of their scarcity are highly valued by collectors. Among them were James, earl of Barrymore, after Ottway; Maria Gunning, countess of Coventry, after F. Cotes; George II, after Hudson; William, earl of Harrington, after Du Pan; Richard St. George, after Slaughter; and William III, after Kneller. He also painted portraits, and engraved some himself, viz. Henry Boyle, speaker of the House of Commons in Ireland, Henry Singleton, lord chief justice of Ireland, and a double portrait of William III and Field-marshal Schomberg, the heads being copied from Kneller. Ford's address as publisher appears on some of the mezzotint engravings by Andrew Miller [q. v.] and James MacArdell [q. v.] With the former he seems to have been in rivalry, as they engraved the same subjects, notably Hogarth's full-length portrait of Gustavus Hamilton, viscount Boyne, in which Ford's print seems to be the earlier of the two. It is probable that Ford visited London, but this is not certain. On 28 Oct. 1758 the ship Dublin Trader, Captain White, left Parkgate for Dublin, and was never heard of again; she carried 70,000l. in money and 80,000l. in goods, and numerous passengers, among whom were Edward, fifth earl of Drogheda, and his son, Theophilus Cibber [q. v.], and others. There are grounds for supposing that Ford was also among the passengers.

[Chaloner Smith's Brit. Mezzotinto Portraits J. T. Gilbert's Hist. of Dublin, vol. ii.] L. C.

FORD, RICHARD (1796–1858), critic and author of 'The Handbook for Travellers in Spain,' was the son of Sir Richard Ford, a descendant of an old Sussex family, who was M.P. for East Grinstead in 1789, and eventually chief police magistrate of London. He died, at the age of forty-seven, on 3 May 1806, leaving a family of three children, of whom Richard was the eldest. Richard, born in 1796, was educated at Winchester School, from which he joined Trinity College, Oxford, where he graduated (B.A. 1817, M.A. 1822). He afterwards entered at Lincoln's Inn, and read in the chambers of Pemberton Leigh and Nassau Senior, but though called to the bar he never practised. In 1824 he married, and six years later he took up his quarters with his family in the south of Spain, where he spent the next four years, and acquired his extraordinary knowledge of the country by a series of long riding tours made between 1830 and 1834 from his headquarters in the Alhambra or at Seville. Shortly after his return from Spain he bought a small property at Heavitree, near Exeter, where his brother, the Rev. James Ford, a prebendary of the cathedral, was living. He there built himself a house and laid out grounds with an artistic taste which made his residence one of the local lions of East Devon. His employment suggested an essay on cob walls, in which he traced the analogy between the earthen walls of the Devonshire peasantry and the tapia or concrete structures of the Moors and Phœnicians, and this, written in 1837, was the first of a series of articles that continued to appear in the 'Quarterly Review' until the year before his death, when it ended with his genial review of 'Tom Brown's School Days.' He was an occasional contributor also to the 'Edinburgh,' 'British and Foreign Quarterly,' and 'Westminster' reviews, and for the 'Penny Cyclopædia' he wrote the admirable article on Velazquez. In 1840 he undertook to write a 'Handbook for Travellers in Spain,' and finished it in 1845. Of this an article in the 'Times' on his death, commonly attributed to Sir W. Stirling Maxwell, truly said that ' so great a literary achievement had never before been performed under so humble a title; ' and a sale of two thousand copies within a few months proved the public estimate of its merits. Its only fault was that it gave too much for the convenience of the traveller, for the two stout volumes of over a thousand closely-printed pages contained in the guise of a manual the matter of an encyclopædia. In the next edition (1847) it was cut down to the ordinary dimensions of Murray's 'Handbooks for Travellers,' and the parings, with the addition of some new matter, made the delightful little volume published in 1846 under the title of 'Gatherings from Spain.' In 1855 it was restored to its first shape, but in the interval alterations had been found necessary, and the use of a somewhat larger type made the exclusion of much of the preliminary matter unavoidable; and thus the 'Handbook for Spain' in its original form has now come to be included among those treasures that book lovers covet. The revision was nearly his last work; his health had latterly shown signs of failing, and he died at Heavitree on 1 Sept. 1858. The year before his death he had been nominated as one of the committee to decide upon a site for the National Gallery, but resigned on account of his health. He was three times married: first, in 1824, to a daughter of the Earl of Essex; secondly, in 1838, to the Hon. Eliza Cranstoun, eldest daughter of Lord Cranstoun; and in 1851 to Mary, only daughter of Sir A. Molesworth. Ford's love of art was hereditary. His maternal grandfather, Mr. Booth, was an eminent connoisseur and collector of pictures, and his mother, Lady Ford, an amateur artist of exceptional ability; and in the opinion of competent judges he himself might have been no less distinguished as a painter than as a man of letters. His sketches, brought home from Spain, often served as the originals of his friend David Roberts's illustrations of Spanish architecture and scenery. He was an indefatigable collector of pictures, etchings, drawings, and prints; his collection of majolica ware was reckoned one of the choicest in existence, and in all matters of connoisseurship there was no higher authority. Spain at the time of his visit was an unworked mine of artistic treasure. He may be said to have been the first to make Velazquez known to English readers, for in Madrid alone Velazquez is to be seen, as he says, ' in all his protean variety of power.' His article upon Velazquez in the 'Penny Cyclopædia' was followed by one in the 'Quarterly Review' (No. clxv.) upon the predecessors of Velazquez and Murillo, and the history of the various schools of painting in Spain; and these, with the masterly article in No. cliv. upon the history of Spanish architecture, make up a treatise on Spanish art no less remarkable for its learning than for its lucidity and brilliancy. In the handbook the infectious spirit of enjoyment is perhaps the quality that most of all commends it to the ordinary reader, but there too the critical faculty and the artist's eye are always felt. He was a kindly critic, although severe to pretended erudition.

Besides the writings already mentioned he wrote in 1837 a pamphlet called ' Historical Enquiry into the Unchangeable Character of a War in Spain,' a trenchant reply to 'The Policy of England in Spain,' a pamphlet in support of Lord Palmerston. He also wrote the explanatory letterpress for 'Apsley House and Walmer Castle, illustrated by plates,' 1853; for the 'Guide to the Diorama of the Campaigns of the Duke of Wellington,' 1852; and for ' Tauromachia, or the Bull Fights of Spain, illustrated,' 1852.

[Times, 4 Sept. 1858 ; Fraser's Mag. October 1858.]   J. O.

FORD, ROGER OF (*fl.* 1170), hagiographer. [See ROGER.]

FORD, SIMON (1619 ?–1699), divine, son of Richard Ford, was born at East Ogwell, near Newton Bushel, Devonshire, about 1619, was educated at the grammar schools of Exeter and Dorchester, and entered Magdalen Hall, Oxford, in 1636. He was lineally related to Nicholas Wadham, founder of Wadham College, but failed to obtain a scholarship there. In 1641 he proceeded B.A., and was expelled from Oxford soon afterwards on account of his strong puritan leanings (WOOD, *Fasti*, ii. 147). When the parliamentary visitors were sent to Oxford in 1647, Ford returned and was received with much honour. He took the degree of M.A. 12 Dec. 1648, was made a delegate of the visitors in 1649, and was created B.D. 'by dispensation of the delegates,' 16 Feb. 1649–50. His friend Dr. Edward Reynolds, who had become dean of Christ Church, admitted him as a senior student there, and he frequently preached at St. Mary's. A sermon delivered against the Engagement of 1651 led to his removal from his studentship. He became lecturer of Newington Green, London, and later vicar of St. Lawrence, Reading. There he engaged in much local controversy. In an assize sermon preached in 1654 he denounced the people of Reading for their support of extravagant religious views, and was called before the grand jury to explain his conduct (cf. *The Case of the Town of Reading stated*, 1654, p. 17). Two years later a quaker named Thomas Speed excited his wrath. Ford and Christopher Fowler [q. v.], another Reading clergyman, published jointly 'A Sober Answer to an Angry Epistle . . . written in haste by T. Speed,' London, 1656, to which Speed replied in 'The Guilty-covered Clergyman unvailed,' 1656. In July 1659 Ford left Reading to become vicar of All Saints, Northampton. On 30 Jan. 1660–1 he preached at Northampton against 'the horrid actual murtherers of Charles I.' In 1665 he proceeded D.D. at Oxford. On 30 March 1670 he was chosen minister of Bridewell, London, but resigned the post on becoming vicar of St. Mary, Aldermanbury, 29 Dec. following. Failing health compelled him to remove to the rectory of Old Swinford, Worcestershire, which was conferred on him by Thomas Foley [q. v.] on 22 May 1676. He died at Old Swinford 7 April 1699, and was buried in his church. His wife, Martha Stampe of Reading, died 13 Nov. 1684.

Ford's chief works are : 1. ' Ambitio Sacra. Conciones duæ Latine habitæ ad Academicos Oxon.,' Oxford, 1650. 2. 'Two Dialogues concerning Infant Baptism,' the first published in 1654 and the two together in 1656, with a commendatory preface by the Rev. Thomas Blake of Tamworth. 3. 'The Spirit of Bondage and Adoption largely and practically handled, together with a Discourse on the Duty of Prayer in an Afflicted Condition,' London, 1655. 4. 'A Sober Answer' [see above], London, 1656. 5. 'A Short Catechism declaring the practical use of the Covenant interest of Baptism of the Infant Seed of Believers,' London, 1657, an epitome of No. 2. 6. 'Three Poems relating to the late dreadful Destruction of the City of London by Fire . . . entituled: I. Conflagratio Londinensis [in Latin hexameters with English translation in heroic verse]; II. Londini quod reliquum [in Latin elegiacs with English translation]; III. Actio in Londini Incendarios' [in Latin hexameters only], London, 1667. The first two parts have separate title-pages. A copy in the Bodleian of the first poem is entitled 'The Conflagration of London, poetically deleniated,' and has commendatory manuscript verses by John Mill addressed to Thomas Barlow (afterwards bishop). A fourth part, 'Londini renascentis Imago poetica,' published in Latin only in 1668,

was issued in an English translation in 1669. In its Latin form it is sometimes bound up with the three earlier poems. 7. 'Carmen Funebre ex occasione Conflagrationis Northamptonæ, 20 Sept. an. 1675 conflagratæ, concinnatum,' London, 1676 ; republished in an English translation by F. A., M.A., as 'The Fall and Funeral of Northampton in 1677.' 8. 'A Plain and Profitable Exposition of, and Enlargement upon, the Church Catechism,' London, 1684, 1686. 9. 'A new version of the Psalms of David,' in metre, London, 1688. Ford also translated two discourses for the first volume of the English version of 'Plutarch's Morals,' London, 1684. His published sermons are also very numerous. They include sermons on the king's return, 1660 ; on the burial of Elizabeth, wife of Sir James Langham, 1665 ; on the Duke of York's victory over the Dutch, 1665. 'A Discourse concerning God's Judgments,' London, 1678, was prepared as a preface to James Illingworth's account of ' a man [John Duncalf] whose hands and legs rotted off in the parish of King's Swynford in Staffordshire, where he died 21 June 1677.' Both tracts were reissued in 1751 with a notice of the circumstances by William Whiston, 'with his reasons for the republication thereof, taken from the Memoirs.' Edward Stillingfleet, bishop of Worcester, wrote a preface for ' the substance of two sermons preached ' by Ford 'at the performance of publick penance by certain criminals on the Lord's Day, usually called Midlent Sunday, 1696, in the parish church of Old Swinford,' London, 1697. A graceful piece of Latin verse by Ford, entitled 'Piscatro,' and dedicated by him to Archbishop Sheldon, was first published in ' Musarum Anglicanarum Analecta,' vol. i. 1721, and was issued in an English verse translation (by Tipping Silvester) at Oxford in 1733.

[Wood's Athenæ Oxon., ed. Bliss, iv. 756–60; Burrows's Visitation of Oxford University, Camden Soc.; Brit. Mus. Cat.; art. infra, FOWLER, CHRISTOPHER.] S. L.

FORD, STEPHEN (*d.* 1694), nonconformist divine, is said to have been a servant to the head of a college at Oxford. He certainly studied at Oxford, though at what college does not appear. During the Commonwealth he was presented to the vicarage of Chipping Norton, Oxfordshire, where, after his ejectment in 1662, he still continued to preach privately as he had opportunity. But he was sadly harassed by reason of his nonconformity, and at length, on some of his enemies threatening his life, he removed to London. There he settled with a congregation in Miles Lane, Cannon Street, and continued to officiate as their pastor nearly thirty years. He often preached in the time of the plague, when other ministers had fled into the country. In May 1692 Matthew Clarke (1664–1726) [q. v.] was ordained joint-pastor with him. Ford is said to have died 'some time in the year 1694' (WALTER WILSON, *Dissenting Churches*, i. 473). He published : 1. 'The Evil Tongue condemned ; or, the Heinousness of Defaming and Backbiting,' 8vo, London, 1672. 2. 'A Gospel-Church : or, God's Holy Temple opened,' 8vo, London, 1675, and other tracts vaguely mentioned by Calamy. Ford was one of the twenty-one divines who subscribed John Faldo's 'Quakerism No Christianity,' 8vo, 1675.

[Calamy and Palmer's Nonconf. Memorial (1802–3), iii. 121–2 ; Walter Wilson's Dissenting Churches, i. 472–3, 476–7 ; Joseph Smith's Bibliotheca Anti-Quakeriana, p. 188.] G. G.

FORD, THOMAS (*d.* 1648), composer, was one of the musicians of Henry, Prince of Wales. The appendix to Dr. Birch's 'Life' of the prince shows that in 1611 Ford received a salary of 30*l.* per annum, which was soon afterwards increased to 40*l.* He with the rest of the musicians may possibly have been appointed before the prince was created Prince of Wales (see BIRCH, p. 427 *n.*) It is probable that after the prince's death the salaries were continued, for in 1626 he received a grant of 80*l.* per annum, ' 40*l.* for the place he formerly held, and 40*l.* for that which John Ballard deceased held' (RYMER, *Fœdera*, ed. 1715, xviii. 728). In 1607 he published 'Musicke of Sundrie Kindes. Set forth in two Bookes. The first whereof are Aries (*sic*) for four Voices to the Lute, Orphorion, or Basse-Viol, with a Dialogue for two Voices, and two Basse-Viols in parts tunde the Lute way. The second are Pavens, Galiards, Almaines, Toies, Iigges, Thumpes, and such like, for two Basse-Viols, the Liera way, so made as the greatest number may serve to play alone, very easy to be performde. Composed by Thomas Ford. Imprinted at London by Iohn Windet at the Assignes of William Barley, and are to be sold by Iohn Browne in Saint Dunstons churchyard in Fleetstreet, 1607.' The first book, containing eleven songs, among which are the celebrated 'Since first I saw your face,' and 'There is a Lady sweet and kind,' is dedicated to Sir Richard Weston, and the second, containing eighteen pieces, to Sir Richard Tichborne. An anthem, in five parts, 'Let God arise,' is printed in the Musical Antiquarian Society's publication for 1845 (p. 61), from a set of manuscript part-books in the possession of the

editor, Mr. Rimbault, and formerly in that of John Evelyn. Ford contributed to Sir William Leighton's 'Tears and Lamentacions of a Sorrowfull Soule' (1614) two anthems, ' Almighty God, which hast me brought,' for four voices with lute and treble-viol, and 'Not unto us' for five voices. In Hilton's 'Catch that catch can' (1652) three sacred canons by Ford are contained : ' I am so weary' (reprinted in BURNEY's *Hist.* iii. 415), ' O Lord, I lift my heart to Thee,' and 'Look down, O Lord' (*ib.* p. 416). Another canon, 'Haste thee, O Lord,' contained in Tudway's collection (*Harl. MS.* 7337), ascribed to Ramsey, is considered by Mr. T. Oliphant to be by Ford (pencil note in MS.) Ford died in November 1648, and was buried on the 17th in St. Margaret's, Westminster.

[Hawkins's Hist. ed. 1853, pp. 566, 570 ; Birch's Life of Henry, Prince of Wales, 1760, pp. 427, 455, 467 ; Grove's Dict. i. 540 ; Registers of St. Margaret's, Westminster ; authorities quoted above.] J. A. F. M.

FORD, THOMAS (1598–1674), nonconformist divine, was born at Brixton, Devonshire, in 1598. According to Wood he was entered, in Easter term 1619, a batler in Magdalen Hall, Oxford, as a member of which he proceeded B.A. 22 Feb. 1624, and M.A. 1 June 1627 (*Fasti Oxon.* ed. Bliss, i. 414, 431). When taking orders he became 'a very faithful' tutor in his house for several years. His puritanical opinions, which he took no pains to conceal, subjected him to considerable persecution at the hands of Laud. Accepted Frewen [q. v.], then president of Magdalen College, ' changed the communion-table in the chapel into an altar,' as the puritans considered. Several of the preachers at St. Mary's inveighed against this innovation. Ford in his turn preached on 2 Thess. ii. 10, 12 June 1631, and offered some ' smart reflections 'on making the eucharist a sacrifice, setting up altars instead of tables, and bowing to them. This plain speaking having excited the wrath of the Laudian party, the next Saturday the vice-chancellor (William Smith) called Ford before him and demanded a copy of his sermon. Ford offered to give him one if he demanded it 'statutably.' The vice-chancellor then ordered him to surrender himself prisoner at the castle. He refused to go unless accompanied by a beadle or a servant. The following Saturday the vice-chancellor sealed up his study, and afterwards searched his books and papers, but found nothing that could be urged against him, as Ford had taken care to secrete his private memoranda. In the meantime an information was sent to Laud, then chancellor of the university, who returned orders to punish the preachers. Thereupon a citation in his name was fixed on St. Mary's, 2 July, commanding Ford's appearance before the vice-chancellor on the 5th. Appearing on the day appointed he was pressed to take an oath, *ex officio*, to answer any questions about his sermon; but he refused it, because there were no interrogatories in writing. He again offered a copy of his sermon if demanded according to the statutes, and the next day delivered one, which was accepted. But on pretence of former contumacy the vice-chancellor commanded him again to surrender himself prisoner. Ford appealed from him to the congregation, and delivered his appeal in writing to the proctors (Atherton Bruch and John Doughty). They carried it to convocation, who referred the cause to delegates, a majority of whom, upon a full hearing, acquitted him of all breach of the peace. From them the vice-chancellor himself appealed to convocation, who again appointed delegates; but the time limited by statute expired before they could arrive at a decision. Laud then brought the cause before the king and council, who heard it at Woodstock 23 Aug. Ford, when questioned by the king, stuck manfully to his statement. In the end he was sentenced to quit the university within four days (RUSHWORTH, *Hist. Coll.* pt. ii. vol. i. pp. 110–11). His popularity was such that many of the scholars, arrayed in their gowns, assembled at Magdalen to conduct him out of the city with all honour. The affair has been minutely set forth by Wood (*Antiquities of Oxford*, ed. Gutch, vol. ii. pt. i. pp. 374–9), who is very severe on Ford for his 'insolencies.' Soon afterwards Ford was invited by the magistrates of Plymouth to become their lecturer. Laud was no sooner informed of this than he procured letters from the king forbidding the townsmen to elect Ford on pain of his majesty's displeasure, and another to the Bishop of Exeter, commanding him not to admit him in case he should be elected (PRYNNE, *Canterburies Doome*, pp. 175–6). Ford, finding the bishop bent upon excluding him from all preferment in England, embraced an opportunity of going abroad as chaplain to an English regiment under the command of Colonel George Fleetwood [q. v.], in the service of Gustavus Adolphus. He travelled with the colonel into Germany, and was for some time in garrison at Stode and Elbing. The English merchants at Hamburg invited him to be their minister, with the promise of a stipend of 200*l.* a year. But growing weary of life abroad he returned home. Laud having probably forgotten his existence, no opposition was offered to his institution to the rectory of Aldwinkle All Saints, Northamptonshire, 18 Oct. 1637, a preferment which he owed to Sir Myles Fleetwood (BRIDGES, *Northamptonshire*, ii. 210, where his name is misprinted 'Forth'). In 1640 he was elected proctor for the clergy of the diocese of Peterborough in the convocation which framed the so-called 'et cætera oath.' He held his rectory for ten years; but on the outbreak of the civil war, after a short stay at Exeter, he retired to London, and was chosen minister of St. Faith's, and in 1644, on the death of Mr. Bolls, a member of the Westminster Assembly. Ford afterwards settled at Exeter, where he exercised his ministry with such success that 'the whole city was mightily reformed, and a good relish of the best things appeared in the generality.' He preached in the choir of the cathedral (as his brother pastors, Lewis Stucley and Thomas Mall, did in the nave), 'but,' relates Calamy, 'he was once put out of it, in 1649, by Major-general Desborough, who quartered there, for refusing the "Engagement."' He was appointed minister of St. Lawrence, Exeter, and also acted as an assistant-commissioner for Devonshire. The enforcement of the Bartholomew Act in 1662 obliged him to desist from preaching publicly. A year later he was compelled by the Oxford Act to remove to Exmouth, about nine miles from Exeter, where he lived very privately. When the 'Indulgence' came out he returned to Exeter, but in feeble health. He died in December 1674, in his seventy-sixth year, and was buried on the 28th in St. Lawrence's Church, Exeter, near his wife, Bridget Fleetwood, and several of his children. His writings are as follows: 1. 'Singing of Psalmes the duty of Christians under the New Testament, or a vindication of that Gospel-Ordinance in V sermons upon Ephesians v. 19,' 12mo, London, 1659; 2nd edit., 'with many additions,' the same year. 2. 'The Sinner condemned of himself: being a Plea for God against all the Ungodly, proving them alone guilty of their own destruction,' 8vo, London, 1668. 3. 'Scripture's Self-Evidence, proving it to be the only Rule of Faith' (cited by Calamy). He preached once before the commons, 30 July 1645, and once before the lords, at a fast held 29 April 1646, and his sermons were undoubtedly published. Wood, who otherwise is grossly unfair to Ford, states that 'a certain doctor of divinity of his time and persuasion, that knew him well, hath several times told me that this our author was a man of very great parts and of unbyassed principles, one and the same in all times and changes.' Calamy's account of Ford is probably more correct than that given by Wood. According to the latter Ford was born about 1603, went to college at sixteen, and died in 1676.

[Wood's Athenæ Oxon. (Bliss), iii. 1096–8; Calamy and Palmer's Nonconf. Memorial (1802–1803), ii. 26–31; Brook's Puritans, ii. 395–6.]

G. G.

FORD or FOORD, WILLIAM (*fl.* 1616), divine, was educated at Trinity College, Cambridge, where he graduated B.A. in 1578. He was elected fellow of his college in 1581, proceeded M.A. in 1582, and commenced B.D. in 1591. He afterwards became chaplain to the Levant Company at Constantinople. On 31 July 1611 he petitioned the court for an augmentation of his salary of two hundred sequins; on the following 1 Oct. the court allowed him an advance from 30*l.* to 50*l.* on the ground of his being 'well spoken of for paines and merits in his charge.' On 1 Sept. 1613 he intimated a wish to resign his post, but was requested to remain a year longer. He received permission to return home, 6 July 1614. His only known publication is 'A Sermon [on Gen. xxiii. 2–4] preached at Constantinople, in the Vines of Perah, at the Funerall of the vertuous and admired Lady Anne Glover, sometime Wife to the Honourable Knight Sir Thomas Glover, and then Ambassadour ordinary for his Maiesty of Great Britaine, in the Port of the Great Turke,' 4to, London, 1616. In dedicating this discourse to Lady Wentworth the author would perhaps be encouraged, should it prove acceptable to her, 'to second it with some more pleasing and delightfull subiect, which mine owne experience hath gathered from no lesse painefull then farre forraigne obseruations.'

[John B. Pearson's Biographical Sketch of the Chaplains to the Levant Company, pp. 12, 13, 46.]

G. G.

FORD, WILLIAM (1771–1832), bookseller and bibliographer, son of John Ford, tinman, was born at Manchester in 1771, and educated at the grammar school of that town. Though intended originally for the medical profession, he went into the Manchester trade, and subsequently became a book and print seller. While in business as a manufacturer, he formed a curious and valuable library, which when he commenced as a bookseller served as the basis of the stock described in his first catalogue, dated 1805. In this catalogue were many rarities, one of which was a volume containing 'Licia, or Poems of Love,' and the original edition of Shakespeare's 'Venus and Adonis,' 1593, now in the

Malone collection, Bodleian Library. The catalogue attracted the attention of bibliophiles all over the country, and brought him into correspondence with Dibdin, Malone, Heber, Bindley, and other collectors. The collection produced upwards of 6,000*l.* In a letter to Dibdin, Ford wrote: 'It was my love of books, not of lucre, which first induced me to become a bookseller.' His second catalogue came out in 1807, and his third, containing more than fifteen thousand articles, in 1800–11. Other catalogues followed, and all were esteemed for their accurate descriptions and curious bibliographical notes. He was a chief contributor to a series of papers in 'Aston's Exchange Herald,' of which twenty-four copies were reprinted in octavo, with the title, 'Bibliographiana, or Bibliographical Essays, by a Society of Gentlemen,' Manchester, 1817. Of a continuation of these papers, printed in the 'Stockport Advertiser,' only ten reprints were made up. In the same paper he wrote a useful chronology of Manchester. He was also one of the early contributors to the 'Retrospective Review.' In 1816 he met with a reverse of fortune, and his large stock was sold by auction. He resumed business soon after, but was not rewarded with the success which, in the opinion of Dibdin, his efforts and merit deserved. His last catalogue was printed at Liverpool in 1832, where he had carried on business for a few years. Books from his stock, frequently containing annotations in his handwriting, are still to be met with. He published a series of local views and portraits, some of which were etched by himself. His portrait was painted and etched by Wyatt in 1824. He died at Liverpool on 3 Oct. 1832, and was buried in St. James's cemetery.

His son John carried on the same business, and that of an auctioneer. A second son, William Henry, survived until 1882.

[Notice by J. Crossley in Manchester School Register (Chetham Soc.), ii. 79; Earwaker's Local Gleanings, 1875, i. 38, 52, 79; Palatine Notebook, i. 190 (a memoir by Ford of the Stringers, Cheshire artists), ii. 124, 269, iii. 88 (list of his portraits, &c.); Dibdin's Bibliomania, 1811, pp. 164, 629; Dibdin's Library Companion, p. 696; Dibdin's Remin. of a Literary Life, 1836, i. 317; Procter's Byegone Manchester, 1880.] C. W. S.

FORDE, FRANCIS (*d.* 1770), conqueror of Masulipatam and friend of Clive, was the second son of Mathew Forde of Seaforde, co. Down, and M.P. for Downpatrick in the Irish House of Commons, by Anne, daughter of William Brownlow of Lurgan. He is said to have married in 1728 Mrs. Martha George (Burke, *Landed Gentry*, ed. 1882); but this is improbable, for he is first mentioned in the 'Army List' as having been appointed a captain in Adlercron's (the 39th) regiment on 30 April 1746. This regiment was the first ever sent to India of the king's army, and it is worthy of remark that Eyre Coote (1726–1783) [q. v.], afterwards Sir Eyre, was only the junior captain when Forde was promoted major in it on 13 Nov. 1755. He first appears in Anglo-Indian history as the commander of a small party which was defeated at Nellore (MALCOLM, *Life of Clive*, ii. 26); but Clive early perceived his great military abilities, and it was upon Clive's express invitation that Forde resigned his commission in the royal army in June 1758, and proceeded to Bengal in order to act as second in command to Clive in that presidency, and to be ready to succeed him in case of need.

The victory of Plassey had secured the possession of Bengal to the East India Company, but Clive felt that the British authority could not be considered as safely established until the French were driven out of the Deccan. The great danger lay in the powerful dominion erected by M. Bussy, the ablest French officer who ever served in India in the Northern Circars between the company's two eastern presidencies. Bussy had secured the grant of the coast districts known as the Northern Circars from the nizam, where he had established an efficient system of administration and organised a powerful army. At the beginning of 1759 the Comte de Lally, the governor-general at Pondicherry, suddenly recalled Bussy from Masulipatam, and appointed M. Conflans, an incompetent officer, to succeed him. At this juncture Colonel Forde, as he was called in anticipation of the colonel's commission which Clive had promised him from the East India Company, landed at Vizagapatam with a small force of five hundred Europeans, two thousand sepoys, and twelve guns. He at once advanced against Conflans, and, after defeating him at Condore, took Rájámahendri and all the baggage of the French army. He was then hindered by want of money; the ally of the English, Bassalat Jang, refused to pay; the European soldiers mutinied; and Forde was obliged to remain inactive for fifty days. At last he determined that any action was better than no action; he feared that the French fleet might throw reinforcements into Masulipatam, or that Bussy might return; and he quieted his soldiers by promising them the whole booty of the city. He thereupon determined to assault Masulipatam, though he had barely nine hundred men with him after deducting his losses by sickness and the garrisons he had left at Rájámahendri and Vizagapatam. At midnight on 25 April the assault took place; 284, or nearly one-third of Forde's little army, were killed or wounded, but the city was taken, and five hundred French soldiers and 2,100 sepoys surrendered themselves prisoners. The result of this gallant action was that the French lost their foothold in the Deccan, and the Northern Circars were ceded to the East India Company. Forde was both publicly and privately thanked by Clive, but his disappointment was bitter when he found, on returning to Calcutta, that after having resigned his commission in the king's army the directors of the East India Company had refused to confirm his commission in their service. His disappointment was aggravated by the return to India of his junior, Eyre Coote, with the rank of lieutenant-colonel in the king's service, and the command of a fine regiment. Nevertheless he was ready to assist Clive in his operations against the Dutch at Chinsurah, and it was to Forde that Clive pencilled his famous note when Forde reported that the Dutch were in a favourable position to be attacked, and that he only wanted an order in council to attack. 'Attack at once; will send order in council,' was Clive's response on the back of a playing-card, and he then resumed his game. Forde did attack, and completely defeated the Dutch, and in the following year he returned to England with Clive. Clive obtained a company's commission for Forde, and his great quarrel with Sulivan and his party in the India House was largely due to Clive's advocacy of Forde for high military command in India, in opposition to the Sulivan candidate, Eyre Coote. Forde remained for some time in England. In 1769 he was appointed, on Clive's recommendation, to be one of the three supervisors who were to examine in India every department of administration. The three supervisors, Henry Vansittart, M.P., Luke Scrafton, and Forde, set sail from Portsmouth in Sept. 1769 on board the Aurora frigate; they touched at the Cape of Good Hope on 27 Dec. 1769, and were never heard of again.

[Burke's Landed Gentry, ed. 1882; Army Lists, 1754–8; Elphinstone's Rise of British Power in India, p. 492; Orme's Narrative of Affairs in Hindostan; Malcolm's Life of Clive; Mill's History of India; Stubbs's History of the Bengal Artillery, which contains good plans.]

H. M. S.

FORDE, SAMUEL (1805–1828), painter, born at Cork on 5 April 1805, was son of Samuel Forde, a tradesman, who became involved in difficulties, and went to America, deserting his family. The elder brother was a talented musician, and was able to earn sufficient to send young Samuel to school, where he learnt Latin and French. A friend, Mr. Aungier, taught him Latin, and he learnt Greek by his own perseverance. Forde very soon displayed a talent for art, and though Cork did not offer much to inspire a youthful artist, his taste for literature helped to nourish and foster the high aspirations which distinguished, even in his schoolboy days, the numberless sketches on which he employed himself. He became a student in the Cork Academy, drawing from the collection of casts which Lord Listowel had obtained for that institution. The master, Chalmers, was also a scene painter, and taught Forde distemper painting, so that he was able to be employed at the theatre. He had an intention of becoming a mezzotint engraver, and taught himself the art with materials roughly made by his own hands, but soon relinquished any further practice, and became a teacher of drawing, and subsequently master in the Cork Mechanics' Institute. Among his fellow-students and intimate friends was Daniel Maclise [q. v.] Up to about twenty years of age Forde was principally engaged on works of a decorative character painted in distemper; in 1826 he was able to execute works of his own invention, and give expression to the grand projects which his poetical mind conceived. His first picture was the 'Vision of Tragedy,' the idea taken from Milton, which was painted in distemper, in grey and white. A cartoon for this subject was in the possession of Mr. Justice Willes, and was presented by his nephew to the South Kensington Museum. Forde was continually occupied in projecting pictures of an ambitious nature. In November 1827 he painted in two days a 'Crucifixion' for the chapel of Skibbereen. In October 1827 his lungs first became affected. Early in 1828 he commenced a large picture of the 'Fall of the Rebel Angels,' but although he was able to dispose of the picture, he was not destined to complete it. He slowly sank under the increase of his consumptive symptoms, and died on 29 July 1828, at the early age of twenty-three. He was buried in St. Finn Barr's churchyard at Cork.

[Dublin Univ. Mag. (March 1845), xxv. 338; O'Driscoll's Life of Daniel Maclise; Redgrave's Dict. of Artists.] L. C.

FORDE, THOMAS (*d.* 1582), catholic divine, was born in Devonshire and educated at Trinity College, Oxford, where he obtained a fellowship. He proceeded B.A. 13 May 1563, and commenced M.A. 14 July 1567 (BOASE, *Register of the Univ. of Oxford*, p. 251). On being converted to the Roman catholic faith he went in 1570 to the Eng-

lish College at Douay. In March 1572–3 he was ordained priest at Brussels, with Richard Bristow [q. v.] and Gregory Martin, these being the first three alumni who were presented for holy orders from Douay College. He took the degree of B.D. in the university of Douay in 1576, and soon afterwards returned to England upon the mission. On 17 July 1581 he was apprehended with Edmund Campion [q. v.] and John Colleton [q. v.], in the house of Mr. Yates at Lyford, Berkshire. He was conveyed to London with the other priests and committed to the Tower. On the testimony of two perjured witnesses he was convicted of complicity in the pretended conspiracy of Rheims and Rome, although he had never been in either of those cities. Sentence of death was pronounced 21 Nov. 1581. On 28 May 1582 he was executed with two other priests, John Shert and Robert Johnson. Between the time of their condemnation and execution they were examined in the Tower by the attorney- and solicitor-general, Popham and Egerton, and two civilians, Dr. Hammond and Dr. Lewis, in order to elicit from them opinions which might be considered treasonable in reference to the bull of Pope Pius V and the deposing power of the holy see. Forde was beatified by the decree of Pope Leo XIII, dated 29 Dec. 1886.

[Bridgewater's Concertatio Ecclesiæ Catholicæ, ff. 85 *b*, 86 *b*; Challoner's Missionary Priests (1741), i. 77; Dodd's Church Hist. ii. 107; Douay Diaries, p. 423; Hist. del Glorioso Martirio di diciotto Sacerdoti (Macerata, 1585), p. 127; Raissius, Catalogus Christi Sacerdotum, p. 28; Simpson's Life of Campion, p. 220 seq.; Stanton's Menology, p. 238; Stow's Annales (1615), p. 694; Tablet, 15 Jan. 1887, pp. 81, 82.] T. C.

FORDE, THOMAS (*fl.* 1660), author, describes himself as belonging to the neighbourhood of Maldon, Essex, being of the same kindred as John Udall, the puritan (FORDE, *Fœnestra*, p. 135). He was a staunch and pious royalist. His books indicate some classical attainments. James Howell was apparently intimate with him. His earliest work was 'The Times Anatomized in several characters, by T. F.,' London, 1647. This series of pointed essays on such topics as 'A Good Subject,' 'A Soldier of Fortune,' 'Religion,' and the like, has sometimes been wrongly assigned to the famous Fuller. Oldys first showed that Forde was the author. An early manuscript note in the copy in the British Museum gives the writer's name as 'T. Ford, servant to Mr. Sam. Man.' 'Lusus Fortunæ, the play of Fortune; continually acted by the severall creatures on the Stage of the World,' London, 1649, consists of a number of moral essays, illustrated by quotations from ancient and modern literatures. Among modern writers, Spenser, Cowley, Donne, Cornwallis, Bacon, Fuller, Hall, Heylyn, and Sylvester are represented. A Latin poem prefixed is signed I. H. (James Howell?). In 1660 appeared five tracts which are sometimes met with as separate publications and sometimes bound together in a single volume, bearing the general title 'Virtus Rediviva, with several other pieces from the same pen.' Each piece has a separate title-page and is separately paged. (1) 'Virtus Rediviva, or a Panegyrick on the late king, Charles I,' consists of a prose tract and two elegies in verse, written on the anniversaries of Charles I's execution in 1657 and 1658 respectively. (2) 'Love's Labyrinth, or the Royal Shepherdess, a Tragi-Comedie, by Tho. Forde Philothal,' is partly imitated from Robert Greene's 'Menaphon,' and partly borrowed from Gomersal's 'Sforza, Duke of Milan.' One of its songs is taken bodily from Greene; another is a version of Anacreon's 'Love's Duel.' The play is in blank verse. It was never acted. Verses by 'N. C.' and Edward Barwick are prefixed. (3) 'A Theatre of Wits, Ancient and Modern,' a collection of apophthegms. (4) 'Fænestra in Pectore, or Familiar Letters,' apparently a selection from Forde's actual correspondence with his father, a friend at Barbadoes, E. B. (Edward Barwick?), and others. In a letter addressed to 'Mr. T. F.,' i.e. the famous Thomas Fuller, he praises unstintedly Fuller's 'Church History' (p. 135). On p. 166 he translates Martial's 'Non amo te Sabidi,' &c., as 'I do not like thee, Nell,' &c., the prototype of the better-known 'I do not like thee, Dr. Fell' [cf. FELL, JOHN, and BROWN, THOMAS or TOM]. (5) 'Fragmenta Poetica, or Poetical Diversions with a panegyrick upon his sacred Majestie's most happy return on the 29 May 1660.' Besides sacred poems, there are some verses here in praise of George Herbert and Thomas Bastard. The description 'Philothal,' which commonly follows Forde's name on his title-pages, is apparently an abbreviation of 'Philo-thalassios,' a lover of the sea.

[Hunter's manuscript Chorus Vatum in Addit. MS. 24489, f. 400; Forde's works; Brit. Mus. Cat.; Bailey's Life of Thomas Fuller, pp. 585–6, 759.]   S. L.

FORDHAM, GEORGE (1837–1887), jockey, son of James Fordham, was born at Cambridge on 24 Sept. 1837. He was trained for the turf by Richard Drewitt and Edward Smith, and at the age of thirteen had his earliest mount at Brighton. In October 1851 he gained his first victory in the Trial Stakes at the Brighton autumn meeting. He carried off the Cambridgeshire in 1853 on Little David, and in the following year he unexpectedly won the Chester Cup on Epaminondas. From this time Fordham became a very popular rider. In 1855 he was at the head of the list of winning jockeys, and during eight succeeding years he occupied the same position, his best record being 165 wins in 1862. In 1859 he won his first important race, the One Thousand Guineas. The same year he won the Oaks on Summerside. Fordham won the Ascot Cup five times, the Alexandra Plate once, the Gold Vase six times, the Ascot Stakes twice, and the Prince of Wales's Stakes four times. He rode several favourites for the Derby, but only won it in 1879 upon Sir Bevys. Fordham had in all twenty-two mounts for the Derby, his last appearance in the race being in 1883, when he was unplaced on Ladislas. He never won the St. Leger, though he rode twenty-two races. He won the Oaks five times. For the Two Thousand Guineas Fordham had also twenty-two mounts, but only won twice. He secured the One Thousand Guineas seven times out of twenty-one mounts for that race. Many of Fordham's best efforts were in small races, when he frequently succeeded against expectation by his singular skill and resolution. His greatest achievement is said to have been in 1871, when he won the Cambridgeshire on Sabinus. His only Cesarewitch victory was in 1857, when the famous dead heat occurred between three.

Fordham was a great favourite on the continent, and especially in France, where he frequently rode. He won the Grand Prix de Paris in 1867, 1868, and 1881, the French Derby in 1861 and 1868, and the French Oaks in 1880. He had no superior as a rider of two-year-olds. His weight was only 3st. 12lb. when he won his first Cambridgeshire. His services were much in request from a very early period; and one owner presented him with a Bible, a testimonial pin, and a gold-mounted whip, all of which he preserved through life, religiously following the motto engraved upon the whip of 'Honesty is the best policy.' He also received souvenirs from the Rothschilds, the Prince of Wales, and other patrons of the turf. He was frequently offered 1,500l. a year to ride in England and France, but he would never agree to receive a fixed salary.

During the latter part of his career failing health frequently kept Fordham out of the saddle. Between 1875 and 1878 he was not seen in public. His last win was in

Leopold de Rothschild's colours on Brag in the Brighton Cup of 1883, and his last race the Park Stakes at Windsor in August 1884. He carried the most implicit confidence of all his employers, and was kind to young jockeys. It was said that he never attempted to take advantage of a youngster at the start.

Fordham was twice married : first to Miss Hyde of Lewes, who died in 1879; and secondly to her cousin, Miss Leith. After the loss of his first wife he went to reside at West Brighton, where an accident in riding produced a concussion of the brain. He was for weeks in a serious condition. At the close of 1884 Fordham left Brighton and returned to Slough, where he had previously lived, and he died there 12 Oct. 1887.

Fordham was devoted to his family. He was never known to give a vote for a parliamentary candidate in his life. He was extremely reticent on horse-racing, had a deep aversion to gambling of all kinds, and ever showed the greatest anxiety to keep his son from being in any way associated with the turf. His own career was scrupulously honourable.

[Times, Sportsman, and Morning Post, 13 Oct. 1887.]

FORDUN, JOHN (*d.* 1384 ?), is the writer upon whom Walter Bower [q. v.] based the earlier part of his great work, the 'Scotichronicon.' At the end of his chronicle Walter Bower claims for himself books vi–xvi., while to his predecessor he allows books i–v. (*Scotichron.* i. 1, ii. 513). Fordun wrote fifteen of the first twenty-three chapters of book vi. also (*ib.* i. 338), and the rest of Bower's work down to 1383 is very largely based upon Fordun's notes (Prolog. *Scotichron.* i. 1). Even in the first five books of the 'Scotichronicon' there are, however, many passages [see BOWER, WALTER] interpolated by Bower.

The prefaces to the later redactions of the 'Scotichronicon' are our only authority for Fordun's life. He only once intimates his name by an acrostic (FORDUN, p. 3; *Scotichron.* i. 3). The important manuscript of the 'Scotichronicon' in the British Museum (Royal Library, 13 EX), commonly known as the 'Black Book of Paisley' (a fifteenth-century manuscript), calls John de Fordun 'capellanus ecclesiæ Aberdonensis,' while the 'prologue' to the 'Scotichronicon' styles him 'dominus Joannes Fordoun, presbyter' (SKENE, pref. p. xvii ; MURRAY, pp. 2, 15). From these indications Mr. Skene has inferred that he was a 'chantrey priest' in the cathedral at Aberdeen (p. xiv). From the preface to another manuscript we learn that

Edward 'Langschankes,' the tyrant, had carried off to England or burnt all the truly national records of the Scotch history. After their loss, 'a certain venerable' priest, Lord John Fordon, desired to repair the loss, and, after collecting in his own country, wandered like a 'curious bee' with his manuscript ('Codex Sinualis') in his breast, 'in prato Britanniæ et in oraculis Hiberniæ, per civitates et oppida, per universitates et collegia, per ecclesias et cœnobia, inter historicos conversans et inter chronographos perendinans' (Pref. to *Book of Cupar*; the Dublin MS. of *Scotichron.* ap. SKENE, pp. 49, 50). This journey in quest of materials is calculated, from internal evidence, to have taken place between 1363 and 1384. In the prologue to the 'Scotichronicon' Bower tells us of a conversation in which a certain venerable doctor remarked that he could very well recollect this writer of whom the company made so much : 'He was an unlearned man (homo simplex), and not a graduate of any school' (*Scotichron.* i. 1). Mr. Murray suggests that the John Fordun whose name appears in the 'Exchequer Rolls of Scotland' as making certain payments on behalf of the burgesses of Perth in 1393–5 was the historian (MURRAY, pp. 2, 3 ; cf. *Exchequer Rolls of Scotland*, iii. 366). He also remarks that Fordun must have been the friend of Walter Wardlaw, the bishop of Glasgow and *legatus a latere* in Scotland, and, if a chantry-priest of Aberdeen, must likewise have known John Barbour [q. v.] (MURRAY, pp. 2, 3 ; cf. FORDUN, bk. v. c. 50). Fordun probably died soon after 1384, the year in which his annals end.

Fordun's writings, as now preserved, consist of : 1. 'Chronica Gentis Scotorum.' 2. 'Gesta Annalia.' Some manuscripts also include certain 'materials.' Of these materials a great part has been worked up into the later books of his 'Chronica ;' the rest consist of documents relating to the 'controversy with England as to the independence of Scotland.' These 'Independence' documents appear in book vi. of the 'Chronica' as contained in the Wolfenbüttel MS., and before the 'Gesta Annalia.' In the Trinity Coll. Cambridge MS. they are found in the middle of the 'Gesta Annalia' at the year 1284. Of the 'Chronica Gentis Scotorum,' book i. is almost entirely mythical ; book ii. continues the story of the Scots from their first king in Great Britain, Fergus, to the days of Maximus and Theodosius (*c.* 395 A.D.); book iii. extends to the days of Charles the Great (*c.* 814 A.D.) ; book iv. down to the reign of Macbeth (1057 A.D.); book v. from Malcolm Canmore's accession to the death of King David (1153 A.D.) The last eighteen chapters of this book are made up of extracts from Abbot Baldred or Ailred of Rievaulx, 'Lamentatio pro morte regis David.' At this point the 'Gesta Annalia' take up the narrative, and continue it from the accession of Malcolm IV (1153 A.D.) down to 1383 A.D. The historical chapters of book vi. (i.e. cc. 9–23) are a sketch of English history from Cerdic, or rather Woden, down to the death of Edward the Confessor.

From Mr. Skene's careful analyses of the extant manuscripts of these works it appears that Fordun compiled the materials for book v. and the still extant part of book vi. before his journey into England; for the additions which these books in their later form contain ' are frequently taken from William of Malmesbury, while in the materials there is no allusion to that writer.' Of the 'Gesta Annalia' there also seem to be two texts, the earlier one of which (represented by Cotton Vitellius MS. E. xi., a sixteenth-century manuscript, and Trinity Coll. Dublin MS. E. 2, 28, a sixteenth- or seventeenth-century manuscript) was plainly drawn up in 1363, for the list of English kings in chapter 80 ends with ' Edwardus tertius qui nunc est,' and the history of events breaks off with the year 1363. On the other hand, the Wolfenbüttel MS. (fourteenth century) carries on the narrative to 1383, and, after recording the Black Prince's death, winds up the list o English kings with ' Edwardus princeps genuit Ricardum qui nunc est' (SKENE, pref. pp. xxxii–iii; cf. FORDUN, pp. 319, 382, 383). It was apparently after his journey into England that Fordun compiled the first four books, and brought the 'Gesta Annalia' down to 1384 or 1385.

Fordun's authorities are collected by Mr. Skene at the end of the second volume of his edition. He was an historian of no great discernment when dealing with early times, but becomes more valuable the nearer he gets to his own days. There can be little doubt that he made use of Irish materials in his work.

[Johannis de Fordun, Chronica Gentis Scotorum, vols. i. and ii. ed. Skene, for the Historians of Scotland (Edinburgh, 1871-2); Johannis de Fordun, Scotichronicon, ed. Hearne, 5 vols. (Oxford, 1722); Gale's Scriptores, vol. iii.; Bower's Scotichronicon, ed. Goodall (Edinburgh, 1759). All the references to Fordun are to Skene's edition; those to the Scotichronicon to Goodall's Notes on the Black Book of Paisley (New Club Series) by David Murray (Paisley, 1885); Die Handschriften der herzoglichen Bibliothek zu Wolfenbüttel (Otto von Heinemann, Wolfenbüttel, 1886), vol. i. pt. ii. p. 26. Mr. Skene's preface to the first volume of his Fordun contains a precise account of the various manuscripts of Fordun and Bower; he has here collected everything that can be said about his author's life and work.]   T. A. A.

FORDYCE, ALEXANDER (d. 1789), banker, youngest son of Provost Fordyce of Aberdeen, and brother to David, James, and William Fordyce, each of whom is separately noticed, was educated under his uncle, Thomas Blackwell the younger [q. v.], and was afterwards for some time in the hosiery trade at Aberdeen. Abandoning this occupation, he went to London, and obtained a situation as outdoor clerk to a banker named Boldero. Eventually he became the most active partner in the firm of Neale, James, Fordyce, & Down. Under his guidance this firm speculated freely, and gained a large sum by obtaining early intelligence of the signature of the preliminaries of the peace of Paris in 1763, and a still larger one when East India stock rose greatly in 1764–5. With the proceeds of these and other speculations Fordyce purchased an estate and built a fine house at Roehampton, where he lived in great magnificence. He stood as a candidate for the borough of Colchester at the general election of 1768, and spent nearly 14,000l., but was defeated by twenty-four votes. On this he proceeded to build a hospital and otherwise ' nurse' the borough. In 1770 he married Lady Margaret Lindsay, second daughter of the Earl of Balcarres. The tide of fortune then turned; he lost heavily at the beginning of 1771 in the fluctuations of the market caused by the dispute with Spain about the Falkland Islands. His partners became alarmed, but it is said he succeeded in quieting their fears by the simple expedient of showing them a pile of bank notes which he had borrowed for the purpose for a few hours. His losses continuing, he absconded, and the bank stopped payment on 10 June 1772. The stoppage precipitated a crisis which was impending in consequence of the collapse of a speculative mania in Scotland; no bankruptcies of importance happened for a few days, but then a great panic arose in the city. Sir Richard Glyn and Hallifax stopped payment temporarily, and the stoppage of Sir George Colebrooke was only prevented with difficulty. Fordyce returned and went through his examination at the Guildhall, although his life was threatened by the mob. His deficiency was about 100,000l. He was again the defeated candidate at Colchester in 1780. He died 8 Sept. 1789, at Mr. Mead's in George Street, Portman Square. A sermon by Thomas Toller, published in London in 1775, describes Fordyce's fall. His widow married in 1812 Sir James Bland Burges [q. v.]

[Gent. Mag. xlii. 310, 311, and 292, 293, 296, 392, 434-6, xxxviii. 274, xl. 344, vol. lix. pt. ii. p. 866; Grenville Papers, iv. 539-43; Walpole's Letters, v. 393-6; Anderson's Scottish Nation.]
E. C-N.

FORDYCE, DAVID (1711-1751), professor at Aberdeen, born at Broadford, near Aberdeen, and baptised 1 April 1711, was the second son of George Fordyce of Broadford, provost of Aberdeen. After attending Aberdeen grammar school he was entered of Marischal College in 1724, where he went through a course of philosophy under Professor Daniel Garden, and of mathematics under Mr. John Stewart. He took his M.A. degree in 1728. Being intended for the church he next studied divinity under Professor James Chalmers, and obtained in due time license as a preacher, though he never received a call. In 1742 he was appointed professor of moral philosophy in Marischal College. By Dodsley he was employed to write the article 'Moral Philosophy' for the 'Modern Preceptor,' which was afterwards published separately as 'The Elements of Moral Philosophy,' 12mo, London, 1754. It reached a fourth edition in 1769, and was translated into German, 8vo, Zurich, 1757. Previously to this Fordyce had attracted some notice by his anonymous 'Dialogues concerning Education,' 2 vols. 8vo, London, 1745-8. In 1750 he made a tour through France, Italy, and other countries, and was returning home in September 1751 when he lost his life in a storm off the coast of Holland. His premature end is noticed by his brother, Dr. James Fordyce [q. v.], in one of his 'Addresses to the Deity,' and a bombastic epitaph from the same pen will be found in the 'Gentleman's Magazine' for 1796 (vol. lxvi. pt. ii. pp. 1052-1053). Fordyce's posthumous works are: 1. 'Theodorus: a Dialogue concerning the art of Preaching,' 12mo, London, 1752, which was often reprinted, along with James Fordyce's 'Sermon on the Eloquence, and an Essay on the Action of the Pulpit.' 2. 'The Temple of Virtue. A Dream [by D. Fordyce]. Published [with some additions] by James Fordyce,' 16mo, London, 1757 (other editions in 1759 and 1775).

[Chalmers's Biog. Dict. 1814, xiv. 468-70; Chambers's Eminent Scotsmen, ii. 54-5; Irving's Book of Scotsmen, p. 149; Watt's Bibl. Brit.]
G. G.

FORDYCE, GEORGE (1736-1802), physician, born at Aberdeen on 18 Nov. 1736, was the only and posthumous son of George Fordyce of Broadford, a small property near that city. His father was one of a family of twenty children, several of whom became well known, e.g. David, the professor of philosophy [q. v.]; James, the divine [q. v.]; Sir William, the physician [q. v.]; and John, also a physician. George Fordyce was sent to school at Fouran, and afterwards to the university of Aberdeen, where he became M.A. at the age, it is said, of fourteen. A year later he was sent to his uncle, Dr. John Fordyce of Uppingham, to prepare for the medical profession, and, after spending four years with him, entered as a medical student in the university of Edinburgh. Here he became a favourite pupil of Cullen, from whom he imbibed a fondness for chemistry and materia medica, as well as an insight into practical medicine. He graduated M.D. in October 1758 with a dissertation 'De Catarrho,' which shows considerable knowledge of chemistry and contains results which the author thought worth quoting in his public lectures thirty years later. Immediately afterwards he came to London, but in 1759 passed over to Leyden, where he studied anatomy under Albinus. Returning to London in the same year he resolved to settle there as a lecturer on medical science, a career which was at that time, owing to the absence of regular medical schools, a comparatively open one. Before the end of the year he had commenced a course of lectures on chemistry, and in 1764 added courses on materia medica and the practice of physic. These subjects he continued to teach for nearly thirty years, lecturing on the three in succession from seven to ten on six mornings in the week the whole year through. Such arduous labour probably soon began to bear fruit, as we find that Fordyce married in 1762, and in after years his lectures were extremely popular, being attended successively by thousands of students, among them many who subsequently became distinguished. Several full copies of notes by his pupils still exist in manuscript.

Fordyce was admitted licentiate of the College of Physicians on 25 June 1765. Five years afterwards, a vacancy having occurred for a physician at St. Thomas's Hospital through the death of Akenside, Fordyce became a candidate, and, after a close contest with Dr. (afterwards Sir William) Watson, was elected on 11 July 1770 to that office, which he held till his death. In 1776 he was made F.R.S., and wrote several papers in the 'Philosophical Transactions.' In 1787 he was elected 'speciali gratia' fellow of the College of Physicians, the greater honour because at that time only graduates of English universities were generally eligible to the fellowship, and because Fordyce had been an active partisan of the licentiates in their quarrel with the college. Fordyce took an important part in the compilation of the new 'Pharmacopeia Londinensis,' which was issued in 1788. In 1793 he assisted in forming a Society for the Improvement of Medical and Chirurgical Knowledge, to the 'Transactions' of which he also contributed.

Fordyce was not at first successful in practice, owing, it is said, partly to disregard of appearances in manner and dress; but in later life he was fully occupied till his health began to give way. His habits had always been such as to try his constitution; and in early life, it is said, he often reconciled the claims of pleasure and business by lecturing for three hours in the morning without having gone to bed the night before. He had conceived the idea that man ought to eat only once in the day, and consequently took no meal but a dinner, though this, if anecdotes are trustworthy, was a very liberal one (MUNK, Coll. of Phys. 1878, ii. 375). He died of disorders connected with gout on 25 May 1802, at his house in Essex Street, Strand. He was the father of two sons, who died young, and two daughters, who survived him. His portrait, by T. Phillips, is preserved at St. Thomas's Hospital, and was engraved by S. Phillips in 1796.

Fordyce was a man of much intellectual force and of great attainments in medicine. His friend Dr. Wells, no mean judge, thought him more generally skilled in the medical sciences than any other person of his time. He was also a good chemist and mineralogist. One of his chemical papers in the 'Philosophical Transactions' (No. 7 in list below) is important as confirming by an indirect method the views of Priestley and Lavoisier in opposition to the doctrine of Phlogiston. His medical lectures, judging from the manuscript notes, seem to have been lucidly arranged and remarkable for rather elaborate logical analysis. They are said by Dr. Wells to have been composed and delivered entirely without notes, and with a slow, hesitating manner. The 'Elements of Physic' was the text-book for these lectures; but it is on the 'Treatise on Digestion' and the 'Dissertations on Fever' that Fordyce's reputation rests. The former, which was first delivered as the Gulstonian lecture before the College of Physicians, is a work of great ability and conceived in a scientific spirit. Rejecting all purely mechanical and chemical theories, he treats digestion as a physiological process. A similar reaction against the scholastic medical systems of the last century is shown in the 'Dissertations on Fever,' in which the leading principle is that 'observation of the disease is entirely to be adhered to, without

any reasoning why or how anything in it takes place.' Fordyce's observations on the temperature of the human body were numerous and historically important. He devised experiments, the results of which were communicated to the Royal Society by Sir C. Blagden, which showed that the body preserves a constant temperature even in heated rooms.

He wrote: 1. 'Elements of Agriculture and Vegetation,' Edinburgh, 1765, 8vo; 2nd edition, London; 3rd edition, ib., 1779 (lectures given to a class of gentlemen interested in agriculture). 2. 'Elements of the Practice of Physic,' 2 vols., London; 2nd edition, 1768–70; 6th edition, ib., 1791. 3. 'Treatise on the Digestion of Food,' London, 1791; 2nd edition, 1791. 4. 'Dissertation on Simple Fever,' London, 1794; 2nd edition, ib., 1800; 'Second Dissertation on Tertian Intermittent Fever,' ib., 1795; 'Third Dissertation on Continued Fever,' 2 pts., 1798–9; 'Fourth Dissertation,' ib., 1802; 'Fifth Dissertation' (edited after the author's death by Dr. Wells), ib., 1803. 5. 'Syllabus of Lectures on Chemistry,' 12mo, s. d. The first four were translated into German. In 'Philosophical Transactions:' (1) 'Of the Light produced by Inflammation,' vol. lxvi.; (2) 'Examination of Ores in Museum of Dr. W. Hunter,' vol. lxix.; (3) 'New Method of Assaying Copper Ores;' (4) 'On Loss of Weight in Bodies on being Melted or Heated,' vol. lxxv.; (5) 'Account of an Experiment on Heat,' vol. lxxvii.; (6) 'The Croonian Lecture on Muscular Motion;' (7) 'On the Cause of the Additional Weight which Bodies acquire on being Calcined,' vol. lxxxii.; (8) 'Account of a New Pendulum, being the Bakerian Lecture,' vol. lxxxiv. In 'Transactions' of a society above mentioned: (1) 'Observations on the Small-pox and Causes of Fever;' (2) 'An Attempt to Improve the Evidence of Medicine;' (3) 'Some Observations upon the Composition of Medicines.'

[Gent. Mag. June 1802 (memoir by Dr. Wells, the original authority); Monthly Mag. July 1802; Archives of St. Thomas's Hospital.]

J. F. P.

FORDYCE, JAMES, D.D. (1720–1796), presbyterian divine and poet, third son of George Fordyce of Broadford, merchant and provost of Aberdeen (who had twenty children), was born at Aberdeen in the last quarter of 1720. David Fordyce [q. v.] was his elder brother, Alexander Fordyce [q. v.] and Sir William Fordyce [q. v.] were his younger brothers; George Fordyce, M.D. [q. v.], was his nephew. From the Aberdeen High School Fordyce proceeded to Marischal

College, where he was educated for the ministry. On 23 Feb. 1743 he was licensed by the Aberdeen presbytery. In September 1744 he was presented by the crown to the second charge at Brechin, Forfarshire. His admission was delayed, as the parishioners stood out for their right of election ; he was ordained at Brechin on 28 Aug. 1745. His position was not comfortable, and he did not get on with his colleague. In 1753 he took his degree of M.A. at Marischal College, and in the same year he received a presentation to Alloa, Clackmannanshire. The parishioners wanted another man ; however, Fordyce got a call on 5 June, demitted his charge at Brechin on 29 Aug., and was admitted at Alloa on 12 Oct. 1753. Here he won the affections of his flock, and rapidly acquired reputation as a preacher. He published several sermons; in 1760 his sermon before the general assembly on the 'folly, infamy, and misery of unlawful pleasures' created a profound impression, and stamped him as a pulpit orator of the first rank. The university of Glasgow made him a D.D.

Already Fordyce had turned his thoughts to London, where several members of his family had established themselves. During a visit to his brother Alexander in 1759 an unsuccessful effort had been made by his friends to procure for him a call to a vacant pastorate in Carter Lane. In 1760 he was chosen as colleague to Samuel Lawrence, D.D., minister of the presbyterian congregation in Monkwell Street. He demitted his charge at Alloa on 30 May, and was released from it on 18 June 1760. Lawrence died on 1 Oct., and Fordyce became sole pastor. He preached only on Sunday afternoons, the morning lecturer being Thomas Toller, Lawrence's son-in-law.

Fordyce's eloquence soon drew crowds to Monkwell Street. He had the natural advantages of a dignified presence and a piercing eye; his delivery and gestures were studied with great care. His topics were didactic, but he freed them from dryness by his powers of imagination and a polish and pomp of his style which satisfied cultured tastes. He forsook generalities, and dealt with the ethics of actual life. Garrick is said to have heard him more than once, and to have spoken highly of his oratory. Boswell speaks of his 'long and uninterrupted social connection' with Johnson ; he introduced Johnson to Blair. His sympathetic account (in 'Addresses to the Deity,' 1785) of Johnson's religious character has often been quoted. From this and other passages of his writing it is evident that, while he avoided the position of a party preacher and steered clear of

controversy, his moderation had not destroyed his evangelical faith.

Fordyce's popularity lasted for about twelve years. Several causes contributed to its decline. In 1772 the failure of his brother Alexander involved the ruin of some of Fordyce's warmest adherents, and the alienation of many friends. In 1775 the congregation was rent by a quarrel between Fordyce and Toller ; the ground of the ill-feeling is not stated, but may perhaps be gathered from the tone of Toller's funeral sermon on Alexander Fordyce. Fordyce's part in the dispute is not excused by his friends ; he procured the dismissal of Toller on 28 Feb. 1775 ; a large part of the congregation withdrew with Toller to an independent meeting-house in Silver Street. Fordyce now undertook the whole of the duties at Monkwell Street; his audience thinned, and disappointment preyed upon his health. Under medical advice he resigned his office at Christmas 1782. His charge at the ordination of his successor, James Lindsay, D.D., on 21 May 1783, is regarded as his finest effort of pulpit eloquence.

He retired to a country residence near Christchurch, Hampshire, where he was a neighbour of Lord Bute, who gave him the range of his library. Several publications, including a poor volume of poems, were the fruits of his leisure. On the death (1792) of his brother, Sir William Fordyce, he removed to Bath. He was troubled with asthma, and, after much suffering from this cause, died suddenly of syncope on 1 Oct. 1796 in his seventy-sixth year, and was buried in one of the parish churches of Bath. A funeral sermon was preached by Lindsay at Monkwell Street on 16 Oct. He married (1771) Henrietta Cummyng, who died at Bath on 10 Jan. 1823, aged 89. There was no issue of the marriage.

He published: 1. 'The Eloquence of the Pulpit,' &c., 1752, 8vo (ordination sermon ; often reprinted with David Fordyce's 'Theodorus'). 2. 'The Temple of Virtue,' &c., 1757, 12mo (by David Fordyce; but this edition has additional matter by James Fordyce). 3. 'The Folly . . . of Unlawful Pleasures,' &c., 1760, 8vo ; 2nd edit. Edinb. 1768, 8vo. 4. 'Sermons to Young Women,' 1765, 2 vols. 12mo, often reprinted. 5. 'The Character and Conduct of the Female Sex,' 1776, 8vo. 6. 'Addresses to Young Men,' 1777, 2 vols. 8vo. 7. 'Addresses to the Deity,' 1785, 8vo. 8. 'Poems,' 1786, 8vo. 9. 'A Discourse on Pain,' 1791, 8vo (Chalmers refers to a certain 'cure for the cramp' here given, and connects it with a passage from Beaumont and Fletcher). Also sermon on popery (1754), reprinted 1779; ordination sermon and charge

(1755); sermon on Eccles. xi. 1 (1757); funeral sermon for Lawrence (1760); sermon on Prov. viii. 6, 7 (1775); charge at ordination of Lindsay (1783).

[Hew Scott's Fasti Eccles. Scot.; Lindsay's Funeral Sermon, 1797; Protestant Dissenting Magazine, 1796 p. 399 sq., 1797 p. 81 sq.; Wilson's Dissenting Churches, 1808, iii. 114, 209 sq.; Chalmers's Gen. Biog. Dict. 1814, xiv. 470 sq.; Mitchell's Scotsman's Library, 1825, p. 30 sq.; Bogue and Bennett's Hist. of Dissenters, 1833, ii. 606 sq.; Boswell's Johnson (Wright), 1859, ii. 168, viii. 413, x. 155; Anderson's Scottish Nation, 1870, ii. 244 sq. (gives the family pedigree).] A. G.

FORDYCE, Sir WILLIAM (1724–1792), physician, son of Provost Fordyce of Aberdeen, and brother of David Fordyce [q. v.], was born at Aberdeen in 1724, and educated at Marischal College, also serving a medical pupilage with a local practitioner and with his brother John at Uppingham in 1743. It has been inferred that he qualified at Edinburgh, from the fact that he was admitted a member of the Royal Medical Society there, 22 Dec. 1744; but it is more probable that he left Edinburgh without qualifying, volunteering for the army during the war with France which ended in 1748, and obtaining an appointment as surgeon to the guards, with whom he served in three campaigns, enduring many hardships. Probably after the peace he travelled and studied in France. He was at Turin in 1750 (*Fragmenta Chirurgica*, p. 21), but returned to London in the same year. While retaining for many years his connection with the army, he entered upon general practice in London, and this and the growing note of his brothers introduced him to the best circles. In 1770 he was created M.D. at Cambridge by royal mandate, and was admitted licentiate of the Royal College of Physicians on 10 April 1786. He was knighted on 20 Dec. 1782. It is stated (*Gent. Mag.* lxii. 1218) that he was sent for to greater distances and received greater sums than almost any physician of his time, and accumulated much money. He aided his brother Alexander [q. v.] to his dazzling rise of fortune, and suffered great loss when he failed, generously taking upon himself the burden of his brother James's loss also. His generosity and hospitality were very great. His medical skill and knowledge were considerable for his time, as testified by his works, some of which went through numerous editions. The Society of Arts voted him a gold medal for his work on rhubarb. He died at Brook Street, Grosvenor Square, after a long illness, on 4 Dec. 1792, aged 68. At the time of his death he was lord rector of Marischal College, Aberdeen, to which he left 1,000*l.*

Fordyce's works (all published in London) are: 1. 'A Review of the Venereal Disease and its Remedies,' 1767, fifth edition 1785; German translation, Altenburg, 1769. 2. 'A New Inquiry into the Causes, Symptoms, and Cure of Putrid and Inflammatory Fevers, with an Appendix on the Hectic Fever and on the Ulcerated Sore Throat,' 1773, fourth edition 1777; German translation, Leipzig, 1774. 3. 'The Great Importance and Proper Method of Cultivating and Curing Rhubarb in Britain for Medical Uses,' 1784. 4. 'Fragmenta Chirurgica et Medica,' 1784. 5. 'Letter to Sir John Sinclair on the Virtues of Muriatic Acid in curing Putrid Diseases,' 1790.

[Gent. Mag. lxii. 1217; Fordyce's Works; Chalmers's Biog. Dict.; Munk's Coll. of Phys. ii. 359–60.] G. T. B.

FOREST, JOHN (1474?–1538), martyr, entered the convent of Franciscans of the Observance at Greenwich when about seventeen years of age. Some nine years later he was sent by the convent to study theology in the Franciscan house without Watergate at Oxford. In due time he supplicated the regents for admission to oppose in divinity for the degree of bachelor, but there is no evidence of his having taken any degree, though Pits calls him doctor of theology. After returning to Greenwich he was appointed minister of the English province, but the date is doubtful. In January 1525 Cardinal Wolsey attempted to hold a visitation of the Observants by virtue of his legatine power. This was strongly opposed by most of the friars, but Forest supported his authority, and went so far as to curse nineteen of his recalcitrant brethren at Paul's Cross. This, according to Francis à S. Clara, proves him to have been provincial minister. On the other hand, certain letters from the convent at Greenwich seem to show that he was elected minister to succeed Friar William Peto, who had displeased Henry VIII by his expression of opinion about the divorce. A list of names in Cromwell's hand apparently implies that Forest might be reckoned on as an opponent of Peto on the king's behalf, and he was probably appointed for that reason. The king knew him personally from the fact of his being confessor to the queen (Catherine of Arragon), and at a later time he said that Forest had promised to preach in his support. But after his appointment as minister he became an ardent advocate of the queen's cause, preaching himself on her behalf and preventing other members of his convent from preaching on the other side. Meanwhile discontented friars of his convent frequently complained to Cromwell of his conduct. In the spring of 1533 the king succeeded in procuring his deposition and the appointment of Fr. Jean de la Hey, a Frenchman, as commissary. Forest was sent to some convent in the north, but in the following year was back in London imprisoned at Newgate on a charge of heresy, the basis of which was denial of the king's supremacy. He at first submitted to the court. His confinement, therefore, was not strict, and he was allowed to celebrate divine service and hear confessions. It was found that he used this opportunity of confirming his visitors in the old faith, and employed his leisure in writing a book, 'De auctoritate Ecclesiæ et Pontificis Maximi,' inveighing with great vehemence against the pride and impiety of the king in assuming the title of head of the church. Sentence of death had been passed upon him at the commencement of his imprisonment, and when his relapse was discovered it was immediately carried out. He was burnt on 22 May 1538 in Smithfield with unusual barbarity, being slung alive over a fire instead of being surrounded by faggots. An image called Dderfel Gadern, which had been long venerated in North Wales, was used as fuel to fulfil a Welsh prophecy, which said that it would set a forest on fire. Bishop Hugh Latimer preached a sermon on the occasion, urging him in vain to recant, and the lord mayor, Cromwell, and other great people were present. The book mentioned above is the only literary work which he is said to have composed, and that is not known to be extant. There are, however, some letters of his to Queen Catherine and others printed by Wadding and Parkinson.

[Cal. Hen. VIII, vols. v. vi. vii.; Hall's Chron. pp. 135, 232 b; Bourchier's Hist. Eccl. de Martyrio Fratrum Angl. Ingoldstadt, 1583, p. 28; Francis à S. Clara, Supplem. Hist. Prov. Angl., Douay, 1671, p. 8; Athenæ Oxon. i. 107; Foxe, iv. 590, v. 179; Pits, i. 726; Tanner's Bibl. Brit.-Hib. p. 292; Wadding's Annales Minorum, xvi. 365, 390, 419; Parkinson's Collect. Anglo-Minoritica, pp. 234, 241; Gasquet's Hen. VIII and English Monasteries, i. 193–201; Froude, iii. 295; Parker Soc.: 1 Lat. xi. 266, 2 Lat. pp. 391–2, 2 Tyn. p. 302, 2 Cran. pp. 365–6, Bale pp. 139, 509; Rawlinson MS. B. 488, f. 41 b.] C. T. M.

FORESTER, JAMES (fl. 1611), theological and medical writer, matriculated in the university of Cambridge as a sizar of Clare Hall, 26 May 1576. He proceeded B.A. in 1579–80, M.A. in 1583, and practised physic (COOPER, Athenæ Cantabr. iii. 58). By procurement of Henry Barrow, the puritan, he wrote out part of the book entitled 'A brief

Description of the False Church,' but he says that he found fault with ' the sharpe maner of wrytyng,' and caused it to be reformed, but never saw the book in print. He was indicted with Barrow, Greenwood, and others, on 21 March 1592–3, for writing and publishing books against the church of England and the queen's ecclesiastical prerogative. As he expressed penitence, his life was spared.

He was the author of: 1. 'The Pearle of Practise, or Practisers Pearle for Phisicke and Chirurgerie found out by J[ohn] H[ester] a Spageriche or Distiller, amongst the Learned Observations and Proved Practises of many expert Men in both Faculties. Published and drawn into methode,' London, 1594, 4to. 2. 'The Marrow and Juice of 260 Scriptures,' London, 1611, 4to.

[Ames's Typogr. Antiq. (Herbert), p. 1256; Egerton Papers, pp. 166, 178; Strype's Annals, iv. 93; Watt's Bibl. Brit.] T. C.

FORFAR, EARLS OF. [See DOUGLAS, ARCHIBALD, first EARL, 1653–1712; DOUGLAS, ARCHIBALD, second EARL, 1693–1715.]

FORGAILL, DALLAN (fl. 600), Irish saint. [See DALLAN.]

FORGLEN, LORD (d. 1727), Scottish judge. [See OGILVY, SIR ALEXANDER.]

FORMAN, ANDREW (d. 1522), archbishop of St. Andrews, is said to have been of the Formans of Hatton, near Berwick-on-Tweed (Scotichron. p. 242). The 'Lord Treasurer's Accounts' record a small payment to him on 22 Oct. 1489 (p. 123; cf. p. 128). According to Mr. Dickson, he was protonotary by September 1491, and his name appears in that capacity several times in the treasury accounts. In May 1492 he distributed the royal alms in St. Giles's, and in April 1498 won money from James IV at cards (ib. pp. 187, 386; cf. pp. 172, 187, &c.) When Perkin Warbeck landed in Scotland (November 1495) the protonotary appears to have been told off to attend him. He received 74l. 8s. in connection with this service (21 Sept. 1496) at the time of the futile expedition across the Tweed. He probably remained with Warbeck till the impostor sailed from Ayr for Ireland in July 1497 (ib. pp. 299, 344–5, Pref. pp. cxxvii–cliii). Next September 'Andrew Forman, protonotary apostolic and prior of May,' was despatched with the Bishop of Aberdeen and Sir Patrick Hume to make terms with Henry VII. A truce was signed for seven years at Aytoun in Berwickshire (30 Sept. 1497). He was employed in other embassies in 1499 and 1501, and on 8 Oct. 1501 was empowered to treat for the marriage of James IV to Henry VII's daughter

Margaret (RYMER, pp. 673, 721, 772, 778–780; PAUL, No. 2602).

Forman was rewarded by permission to hold benefice in England (24 May 1498), and with a pension of a thousand merks 'till he be *promovit* to a bishoprik or abbasy' (13 Oct.) (DICKSON, Pref. p. clviii); and by the grant of the wardship of the Rutherford heiress (12 Nov. 1502), who ultimately married his brother, Sir John Forman (*Reg. of Great Seal*, Nos. 2677, 3612). By 8 Oct. 1501 he was postulate of Moray, and by 12 Nov. 1502 full bishop of this see (*ib.* No. 2677; RYMER, p. 778). In 1502 he was also commendator of Pittenweem in Fife and of Cottinghame in England (*Reg. of Great Seal*, No. 2677). On 30 July 1509 Forman was appointed ambassador to Henry VIII. Early in 1511 (January?) James IV commissioned him to bring about a general peace among Christian princes with a view to a great crusade. For the next few years he was occupied in this work. The pope, Julius II, determined to make him a cardinal (BREWER, i. 1459, 1461, 1643, &c.) Forman succeeded in making a truce between Julius and Louis XII (*ib.* ii. 776), but not in securing universal peace. James IV made an alliance with Louis for an attack on England, and Louis made the ambassador archbishop of Bourges, for which see, after a contested election, he did homage on 12 Sept. 1513 (MICHEL, i. 318–21; *Gallia Christiana*, ii. 93–4). Henry, suspecting the king of France's intentions, refused the bishop a safe-conduct through his country (12 Nov. 1512); but Forman was abroad by April 1513, and sent news of Julius II's death to Scotland. In these days he was reckoned omnipotent with James (BREWER, No. 3651). Leo X, who succeeded Julius II in the papacy, had promoted the Bishop of Moray to St. Andrews (by 27 Jan. 1514), then vacant by the death of Alexander Stewart, James IV's son, who was slain at Flodden (No. 4682, LESLIE, p. 95). His election to this see was contested by Gavin Douglas [q. v.] and John Hepburn. It was generally believed that Forman was supported by the new regent, the Duke of Albany, whom, however, the bishop did not accompany to Scotland. In March 1515 the bishop was at Lyons, and about 3 June he left Bruges for Scotland. Leo had already appointed the new archbishop his legate in Scotland, but promised to revoke the commission on hearing of Henry VIII's disapproval (2 March 1515) (BREWER, ii. Nos. 210, 291, 365, 576, 593).

The archbishop was so unpopular in Scotland that in January 1515 it was reported that the lords would league against him, and that 'the duke will be the *werr ressavit* if he tak his part.' His great offence seems to have been the accumulation of ecclesiastical benefices which the lords thought would be better in the hands of members of their own family. Besides the offices already noticed he had held the monasteries of Dryburgh, Dunfermline, Kilwinning, and Arbroath, and was accused of aiming at the see of Glasgow also (*ib.* ii. Nos. 27, 50, 776; LESLIE, p. 101). He appears, however, to have very soon resigned everything, except St. Andrews and Dunfermline (No. 776); and in February 1516 the three competitors for St. Andrews consented to abide by Albany's decision. Albany gave St. Andrews to Forman, and promoted James Hepburn to the see of Moray (LESLIE, p. 106). In May 1516 Albany was still urging his claims to the cardinalate (No. 1869); and it appears that, notwithstanding Henry VIII's opposition, he was 'legatus natus cum potestate legati a latere' (regni Scotiæ) (*Great Seal*, ii. No. 389). As bishop of Moray he had procured for this see an exemption from the authority of St. Andrews, much to the displeasure of James IV and his son. As archbishop of St. Andrews he sought to limit, though he could not at once annul, the exemption and authority of Glasgow (ROBERTSON, pp. ccxxvi–ccxxviii). As primate of Scotland he issued an important series of constitutions in 1515–16, which are printed in the 'Scotiæ Concilia' (pp. cclxx, &c.) He died in 1522, and was buried at Dunfermline (*Scotichron.* p. 245).

Forman is praised for his generosity, his political capacity, and his scholarship. Demster makes Forman the author of three works: 1. 'Contra Lutherum.' 2. 'De Stoica Philosophia.' 3. 'Collectanea Decretalium' (*ib.* p. 243). Robertson, in the notes to his 'Scotiæ Concilia,' prints some interesting documents showing the debts Forman incurred in his candidature for the cardinalate, and how the bishop laid his ill-success to the charge of Henry VIII, who would not suffer him to pass through England (i. p. cxxvi).

[Accounts of the Lord High Treasurer of Scotland, ed. T. Dickson; Reg. of the Great Seal of Scotland, ed. J. B. Paul, vols. i. and ii.; Cal. of Doc. Henry VIII, vols. i. and ii., ed. Brewer; Rymer's Fœdera, vol. xii., ed. 1792; Michel, Les Ecossais en France, vol. i., ed. 1862; Exchequer Rolls of Scotland, ed. Burnet; Burton's The Scot Abroad, i. 138–40; Registrum Moraviense (Maitland Soc.); Concilia Scotiæ, ed. Jos. Robertson; Gordon's Scotichronicon, ed. 1867; Keith's List of Scotch Bishops, ed. 1824; Leslie's Hist. of Scotland (sixteenth cent. translation).]

T. A. A.

FORMAN, SIMON (1552–1611), astrologer and quack-doctor, was fifth son of the eight children of William Forman and his wife Mary, daughter of John Foster, by Marianna Hallam. Simon's grandfather, Richard Forman, was governor of Wilton Abbey before the suppression of the monasteries, and when the abbey was made over to William Herbert, earl of Pembroke, held some office about the park. Dying in 1556 Richard was buried at Foulson, Devonshire. Simon's father, William, born at Quidhampton, Wiltshire, in 1524, served as page to Lady Willoughby; married in 1544 Mary Foster, who came from the neighbourhood of Andover; was deprived of property which he should have inherited from his father, and died 1 Jan. 1564, being buried at Foulson. Simon's mother lived to the age of ninety-seven, dying in 1602, and being buried with her husband. She was vigorous to the last, walking two miles within a fortnight of her death. Simon, who paid much attention to the genealogy of his family, claimed descent from some apocryphal Richard Forman, earl of Devonshire in the time of William I, who is said to have built the church of St. James at Exeter. A Sir George Forman was created K.B. in 1485, and Sir William Forman, haberdasher, was lord mayor of London in 1538–9. With both of these Simon declared that he was connected.

Simon was born at Quidhampton, 30 Dec. 1552. Lilly's statement that he was son of a chandler, and was born in Westminster, is untrue. He suffered as a child from bad dreams, presaging 'the troubles of his riper years.' A clergyman of Salisbury, named Riddout, who had formerly been a cobbler, and who removed to Quidhampton, when the plague raged in Salisbury, first taught Simon his accidence. Afterwards he went for two years to a free school in the Close at Salisbury, under a master named Boole or Bowle, 'a severe and furious man,' and was thence removed to the care of one Minterne, prebendary of the cathedral, a person of unpleasantly frugal habits. The death of Simon's father in January 1563–4 left him destitute. His mother neglected him, and made him do menial work. On 8 Feb. 1567 he apprenticed himself to Matthew Comin, a general dealer, of Salisbury. His master treated him kindly, but his mistress had a violent temper, and he left after a serious quarrel with her (29 June 1572). He had kept up his studies by getting a schoolboy who lodged with his master to teach him at night all he learned by day. He went through the Isle of Wight on his way home to Quidhampton. His mother still declined to maintain him; he became a schoolmaster near his native place, and received 40s. for half a year's work. On 20 May 1573 Simon made his way to Oxford with a friend, Thomas Ridear. He entered Magdalen College as a poor scholar, and studied at the school attached to the college. John Thornborough, a demy of the college (afterwards bishop of Limerick), and his friend Robert Pinkney of St. Mary's Hall, two pleasure-loving young gentlemen, took him into their service. He had to attend them on hunting expeditions to Shotover, and to walk to Cowley almost every day to assist them in the courtship of a young lady for whose hand they were both suitors. Forman left Oxford 12 Sept. 1574, and until midsummer 1578 found employment as an usher in several small schools at Wilton, Ashmore, and Salisbury. Early in 1579 he was lodging in the parsonage of Fisherton, and it was about that date that he discovered what he claimed to be his miraculous powers. 'I did prophesy,' he records in his diary, 'the truth of many things which afterwards came to pass, and the very spirits were subject to me.' In June he was robbed of his goods and books, and, on the information of one William Estcourt, was sent to gaol for sixty weeks, apparently on the ground of practising magic. This proved the first of a long series of similar experiences. He was set free 14 July 1580, begged his way to London, and obtained work as a carpenter at Greenwich. On 14 Aug. he first practised his healing arts, which cured one Henry Jonson of London of a pulmonary complaint. In September he accompanied his patient to Holland; stayed for a fortnight at the Hague, and largely increased his knowledge of astrology and medicine. He was home again in October, and went to Quidhampton for a year, 'curing sick and lame folk,' but the justices at the Lent assizes bound him over to abstain from his quackery, and he had often to 'thresh and dig and hedge' for his living. In the autumn of 1581 he hired a house at Salisbury, and renewed his practice of physic and surgery. In August 1582 he went to sea, and landed in Studland. On his return he travelled much, but finally set up in the next year (1583) in London as a doctor and astrologer. There he remained till the end of his life. He lived at different times in New Street, St. Thomas's Churchyard, Philpot Street, and elsewhere. The authorities invariably condemned his methods of gaining a livelihood, and he repeatedly suffered imprisonment, but gradually he acquired a lucrative practice, although for the most part a disreputable one. The Bishop of London summoned him in 1583; he was imprisoned for nearly the whole of July 1584, and in the summer of 1585 he was robbed, assaulted, and sent to prison. The assault was perhaps due to his personal immoralities, of which he left an elaborate record in his diaries. Women figured largely among his patients, and his treatment of them was very unprofessional. In 1588 he began to publicly practise necromancy, and to 'call angels and spirits.' In 1589 he was impressed for the Portugal voyage, but he seems to have been released from service within a month. On 26 July 1590 he was threatened with process in the Star-chamber. His fortunes suffered eclipse, and he was near starvation. With a view to improving his position he began writing a treatise on mathematics and medicine. In 1592 the tide turned in his favour. He worked assiduously and with great success among the poor in plague-stricken districts of London, where few doctors ventured. He himself caught the infection. The College of Physicians summoned him in May 1593 for practising without a license. He confessed that he had practised in England for sixteen years, but in London for two only; claimed to have effected many cures; acknowledged that the only medical authors he studied were 'Cockes and Wainefleet' (the first is probably a reference to Francis Coxe [q. v.]), and boasted that he used no other help to know diseases than the 'Ephemerides.' He declared that celestial signs and aspects gave him all the information about diseases that he required. The physicians reported that he was laughably ignorant of medicine and astronomy. He was interdicted from the practice of medicine, and was fined 5l., which he promised to pay.

Forman had no intention of relinquishing his work. In 1594 he began experiments with the philosopher's stone and wrote a book on magic. Persons moving in high society, especially ladies, began to employ him. In 1595 he went aboard ' my Earl of Cumberland's ship' to attend Lady Hawkins, and in September 1601 he wrote that he had made the acquaintance of Lord Hertford. To his poor patients he always remained accessible. But the physicians still refused to tolerate him. On 7 Nov. 1595 he was re-examined by them and was sent to prison and fined 10l. On 22 Dec. the lord keeper Egerton ordered his release and demanded from the physicians an explanation of their conduct. In September 1596 he was charged by the college with administering a water of his own manufacture, in the success of which he thoroughly believed, to a patient who died after drinking it. The physicians again sent him to prison, but he was set free in November.

In September 1597 he was charged before the lord mayor with assaulting a woman, and was in the Counter for a fortnight. In 1597 he took a house at Lambeth so as to be within the jurisdiction of the Archbishop of Canterbury and free from the attacks of the physicians. But he seems to have suffered again at their hands in 1598, and on 25 June 1601 the College of Physicians petitioned Archbishop Whitgift to allow them to proceed against him once more.

Forman had now acquired many powerful friends. On 26 June 1603 the university of Cambridge gave him a license to practise medicine (*Ashmole MS.* 1301, now 1763, f. 44), and on 27 June he proceeded M.D. from Jesus College. On 30 March 1607 a number of patients complained to the College of Physicians of Forman's prophetic methods of cure, and of the high charges which he demanded for his drugs. But until the end of his life Forman's connection among ladies of the court increased. At the trial of those charged with the murder of Sir Thomas Overbury in 1615, four years after Forman's death, it was shown that one of the defendants, Mrs. Turner, had constantly consulted Forman in order not only to forward an intrigue of her own with Sir Arthur Mainwaring, but also to assist her friend the Countess of Essex, who was seeking a divorce from the Earl of Essex (D'EWES, *Autob.* i. 87). A very familiar letter was produced in court, written by the countess to Forman, in which she asked him to alienate by his magical philtres the love of her husband Essex, and to draw towards her the love of the Earl of Somerset. Indecent images in wax of the persons concerned in these scandals were brought into court by Forman's widow. A book in his handwriting was also produced containing the names of his female clients and accounts of their intrigues with gentlemen about the court of which they had given the doctor secret knowledge. It is stated that Lord-chief-justice Coke was about to read out these notes when his attention was attracted to the name of his own wife (*State Trials*, ii. 931–2; WELDON, *Court of James I*, ed. Sir W. Scott, i. 418; cf. *Ashmole MS.* 411, f. 179). Forman was likewise reported to be especially skilful in tracking thieves and stolen treasure by 'horary' speculations. Ben Jonson refers to the fame of his philtres in 'Epicene' (iv. 1). In Richard Niccols's poem entitled 'Overbury's Vision' (1616), Overbury is made to say that he often crossed the river to Lambeth, where

Forman was, that fiend in human shape,
That by his art did act the devil's ape.

Forman died 12 Sept. 1611, and was buried

the same day in the church of St. Mary, Lambeth. His friend Lilly reports that on the previous Sunday Forman's wife had asked him whether he or she should die first. He answered that she would bury him on the following Thursday. On the Monday, Tuesday, and Wednesday Forman was in his usual health, and his wife twitted him with the falseness of his prophecy. But on Thursday after dinner he took a boat at Southwark to cross the Thames to Puddle Dock, and having rowed into mid stream fell down dead. A storm arose immediately after his death. With this curious story may be compared the account of the death of Sir John Davies [q. v.], which his wife Eleanor foretold.

Forman seems to have married twice. Weldon describes one of his wives as 'a very pretty wench' who was noted for her infidelity. At Lambeth on 29 July 1599, when he was forty-seven, he married his first wife, Anne Baker, a niece on her mother's side of Sir Edward Moninges, and a member of a Canterbury family. This lady was only seventeen at the date of the marriage, and the union does not seem to have been a happy one. The name of Forman's second wife, who survived him, was Jane, and she had a sister, Susan Browne of London. She was her husband's executrix, and a letter from her to a friend referring to her troubles since her husband's death, and dated from Lambeth Marsh 26 Feb. 1611-1612, is in Ashmole MS. 240, f. 107. By his first wife Forman had a son Clement. He left 1,200*l.* in money and a large illegitimate family.

The sole work which Forman is known to have printed in his lifetime is 'The Grounds of the Longitude, with an admonition to all those that are incredulous and believe not the trueth of the same. Written by Simon Forman, student in astronomie and philosophy,' London, 1591, by Thomas Dawson. No copy is in the British Museum. One is in the Ashmolean collection at the Bodleian. Forman left a mass of manuscripts to Richard Napier, 'who had formerly been his scholar.' Napier bequeathed them to Sir Richard Napier his nephew, whose son Thomas gave them to Elias Ashmole [q. v.] They are now among the Ashmolean MSS. at the Bodleian. The manuscripts, which Wood remarks Forman did not live to methodise, include much autobiographical material. One of the most interesting features is a folio manuscript pamphlet entitled 'The Bocke of Plaies and notes thereof per Formans for common pollicie.' The earliest extant accounts are here supplied of the performances of Shakespeare's 'Macbeth' (at the Globe Theatre on Saturday, 20 April 1610), of the 'Winter's Tale' (at the Globe on Wednesday, 15 May 1611), and of 'Cymbeline.' A representation of a play, acted 30 April 1611, by another dramatist on the subject of Richard II is also described. The passages relating to Shakespeare were first printed in J. P. Collier's 'New Particulars,' 1836, pp. 6-26; facsimiles are given in Mr. J. O. Halliwell-Phillipps's 'Folio Shakespeare' (1853-65). A diary from 1564 to 1602, with an account of Forman's early life (from Ashmole MS. 208), was printed by Mr. J. O. Halliwell-Phillipps in 1843 for the Camden Society, but the astrologer's frank confessions of his immoral habits led the committee to cancel the publication after a few sheets had passed through the press. Sixteen copies were alone struck off. Mr. Halliwell-Phillipps added to this collection some genealogical notes by Forman, and issued it privately in an edition of 105 copies in 1849. The transcript is not always intelligible, but the difficulty of transcribing Forman's crabbed handwriting is very great. A diary for 1607 (*Ashmole MS.* 802, f. 152) was examined by Mr. Halliwell-Phillipps and deemed unfit for publication. Bliss has printed in his notes to Wood's 'Athenæ Oxon.' ii. 101-2, an 'Argumente between Forman and Deathe in his Sicknes 1585, Sept. the 4th,' in verse from Ashmole MS. 208, f. 13 *b.* Six books of medical practice, dated between March 1596 and December 1600, give the names of Forman's patients and their diseases. Chemical and medical collections, astrological papers, alchemical notes, verses on miscellaneous topics, and Forman's letters to Napier, fill a large number of the remaining manuscript volumes. There are also separate treatises on the plague, on the art of geomancy, on prayer, on the astrological judgments of diseases, on the creation of the world, the restoration of the Jews, and the life of Merlin, besides a poem on antichrist, prayers in Latin and English verse, and the astrologer's accounts of his dreams. In the printed diary Forman mentions that in 1600 he wrote out the two books of 'De Arte Memoratus' by Appolonius Niger, and copied also the four books of Stegonnographia and divers other books (p. 30). There are, moreover, manuscript verses on his troubles with the doctors in the Plymouth Library, and these were printed by Mr. J. O. Halliwell-Phillipps in his privately printed account of that library in 1853. Sir S. E. Brydges printed in 'Censuria Literaria,' iv. 410, a short account by Forman 'of Lucifer's creation and of the world's creation,' from a manuscript in St. John's College, Oxford.

Forman states that his portrait was painted in 1600, when he was arrayed in elaborate raiment. In the 'Antiquarian Repertory' (1780), i. 275, is an engraved portrait 'from the original drawing in the collection of the Right Hon. Lord Mountstuart,' now the property of the Marquis of Bute.

[Wood's Athenæ Oxon. ed. Bliss, ii. 98; William Lilly's History of his Life and Times (1715), pp, 12–16 (Lilly obtained his information from Forman's widow); the publications of Forman's manuscripts described above, edited by Mr. J. O. Halliwell-Phillipps; Hist. MSS. Comm. 8th Rep. 226–8 (archives of the College of Physicians); Black's Catalogue of the Ashmolean MSS.; Weldon's Court of King James, ed. Scott, 1812, i. 417–18; D'Ewes's Autobiography, i. 87–89; Halliwell-Phillipps's Outlines of the Life of Shakespeare, ed. 1887, i. 230–1, ii. 85–7 (with specimen of Forman's handwriting in facsimile), 258–259; Sidney Lee's Life of Shakespeare, 5th edit. 1905, pp. 248, 259; Lysons's Environs, i. 303, where Forman figures among notable inhabitants of Lambeth; Halliwell's Archæologist, p. 34; Loseley MSS. ed. Kempe, p. 387; Strype's Whitgift, ii. 457. A manuscript completed in 1615 and dealing with astrology and medicine, said to be the work of a pupil of Forman's, perhaps Richard Napier, was sold at the auction rooms in Wellington Street, Strand, of Messrs. Sotheby, Wilkinson and Hodge, 21 May 1857, and is said to throw light on Forman's life; cf. Notes and Queries, 6th ser. ix. 230–1, and articles infra on WILLIAM LILLY and RICHARD NAPIER.]   S. L.

FORREST, ARTHUR (d. 1770), commodore, served as lieutenant in the expedition against Carthagena in 1741, and is said to have specially distinguished himself under Edward Boscawen [q.v.], afterwards admiral, who was attached to the expedition in command of the Shoreham in the attack on the Baradera battery on shore on 17–18 March 1740–1. On 25 May 1741 Forrest was promoted by Vernon to the command of the Alderney bomb. In November 1742 he was appointed to the Hawk sloop, in which, and afterwards in the Success, he was employed on the home station and in convoy service to America. In 1745 he was posted to the command of the Wager, in which he took out a large convoy to Newfoundland. In November he was at Boston, where, by pressing some seamen contrary to colonial custom, he got into a troublesome dispute, ending in a serious fray, in which two men were killed. The boatswain of the Wager was arrested on a charge of murder, was convicted, and sentenced to death; the sentence, however, does not appear to have been carried out. Forrest afterwards went to the West Indies, where, in the following year, he captured a Spanish privateer of much superior

force. In 1755 he commanded the Rye, in which he was again sent to the West Indies, and in 1757 was moved into the Augusta of 60 guns. In October he was detached, with two other ships—Dreadnought and Edinburgh—under his command, to cruise off Cape François; and on the 21st fell in with a powerful French squadron of four ships of the line and three heavy frigates accompanying the large convoy for which he was on the look-out. After a short conference with his colleagues—said to have lasted just half a minute—Forrest determined on attempting to carry out his orders, and bore down on the enemy. It was gallantly done, but the odds against him were too great to permit him to achieve any success; and after a sharp combat for upwards of two hours, the two squadrons parted, each disabled. The French returned to the Cape, where they refitted and then proceeded on their voyage, while Forrest went back to Jamaica. On 24 Dec., being detached singly off Petit Guave, he cleverly bagged the whole of a fleet of eight merchant ships, capturing in the night the sloop of war which was escorting them, and using her as a tender against her own convoy. In August 1759 he took the Augusta to England, and on paying her off, in April 1760, commissioned the Centaur, one of the ships taken by Boscawen off Lagos in the preceding year. After a few months with the grand fleet in the Bay of Biscay, he went out to Jamaica, where, by the death of Rear-admiral Holmes in November 1761, he was left senior officer. On this he moved into the Cambridge, hoisted a broad pennant, and took on himself both the duties and privileges of commander-in-chief, till Sir James Douglas [q. v.], coming from the Leeward Islands in April 1762, summarily dispossessed him. He returned to England, passenger in a merchant ship, when, on reporting himself to the admiralty, he was told that his conduct in constituting himself commodore was 'most irregular and unjustifiable;' and that the officers whom he had promoted would not be confirmed. This led to a long correspondence, in which the admiralty so far yielded as to order him to be reimbursed for the expenses he had incurred, though without sanctioning the higher rate of pay. In 1769, however, he was sent out to the same station as commander-in-chief, with his broad pennant in the Dunkirk. He enjoyed the appointment but a short time, dying at Jamaica within the twelvemonth, on 26 May 1770. He married a daughter of Colonel Lynch of Jamaica, by whom he had a family. Mrs. Forrest survived her husband many years, and died in 1804 at the age of eighty-two.

[Naval Chronicle, xxv. 441 (with a portrait); Charnock's Biog. Navalis, v. 380 ; Beatson's Nav. and Mil. Memoirs ; official letters and other documents in the Public Record Office.] J. K. L.

FORREST, EBENEZER (*fl.* 1774), attorney, resided at George Street, York Buildings, London, and was intimate with Hogarth and John Rich, proprietor of the Lincoln's Inn Theatre. He was the father of Theodosius Forrest [q. v.] His opera entitled ' Momus turn'd Fabulist, or Vulcan's Wedding,' was performed at the Lincoln's Inn Theatre on 3 Dec. 1729 and some subsequent nights. He also wrote ' An Account of what seemed most remarkable in the five days' peregrination of the five following persons, viz. Messrs. Tothall, Scott, Hogarth, Thornhill, and F. Begun on Saturday, 27 May 1732, and finished on the 31st of the same month,' London, 1782 (illustrated with plates by Hogarth): reprinted with W. Gostling's Hudibrastic version, London, 1872, 4to.

[Gent. Mag. 1824, i. 410, 581–2; Brit. Mus. Cat.] J. M. R.

FORREST or FORRES, HENRY (*d.* 1533?), Scottish martyr, is referred to by Knox as ' of Linlithgow,' and Foxe describes him as a ' young man born in Linlithgow.' David Laing, in his edition of Knox's 'Works,' conjectures that he may have been the son of ' Thomas Forrest of Linlithgow' mentioned in the treasurer's accounts as receiving various sums for the ' bigging of the dyke about the paliss of Linlithgow.' He also states that the name ' Henricus Forrus' occurs in the list of students who became bachelors of arts at the university of Glasgow in 1518, but supposes with more likelihood that he was identical with the ' Henriccus Forrest' who was a determinant in St. Leonards College, St. Andrews, in 1526, which would account for his special interest in the fate of Patrick Hamilton. Forrest was a friar of the order of Benedictines. Knox states that Forrest suffered martyrdom for no other crime than having in his possession a New Testament in English ; but Foxe gives as the chief reason that he had ' affirmed and said that Mr. Patrick Hamilton died a martyr, and that his articles were true.' Before being brought to trial Forrest, according to Knox, underwent ' a long imprisonment in the sea tower of St. Andrews.' Foxe and Spotiswood both state that the evidence against him was insufficient until a friar, Walter Laing, was sent on purpose to confess him, when he unsuspiciously revealed his sentiments in regard to Patrick Hamilton. According to Foxe he was first degraded before the ' clergy in a green place,' described, with apparently a

somewhat mistaken knowledge of localities, as ' being between the castle of St. Andrews and another place called Monimail.' He was then condemned as a heretic and burned at the north church stile of the abbey church of St. Andrews, 'to the intent that all the people of Anguishe' (Angus or Forfar, on the north side of the Firth of Tay) ' might see the fire, and so might be the more feared from falling into the like doctrine.' When brought to the place of execution he is said to have exclaimed, ' Fie on falsehood ! fie on false friars, revealers of confession !' Calderwood supposes the martyrdom to have occurred in 1529 or the year following, but as Foxe places it within five years after Hamilton's martyrdom, and Knox refers to Forrest's ' long imprisonment,' it in all probability took place in 1532 or 1533.

[Foxe's Acts and Monuments ; Calderwood's History of the Church of Scotland, i. 96–7 ; Knox's Works, ed. Laing, i. 52–3, 516–18 ; Spotiswood's History of the Church of Scotland i. 129–30.] T. F. H.

FORREST, JOHN (1474?–1538), martyr. [See FOREST.]

FORREST, ROBERT (1789?–1852), sculptor, was born in 1788 or 1789 at Carluke, Lanarkshire. He was an entirely self-taught artist, and was brought up as a stonemason in the quarries of Clydesdale. His first public work was the statue of the ' Wallace wight ' which occupies a niche in the steeple of Lanark parish church, and was erected in 1817. He was subsequently employed to cut the colossal figure of the first Viscount Melville which surmounts the pillar in the centre of St. Andrew Square, Edinburgh, and he was also the sculptor of the statue of John Knox in the necropolis of Glasgow. One of his best works is the statue of Mr. Ferguson of Raith at Haddington ; it was erected in 1843. In 1832 Forrest opened his public exhibition of statuary on the Calton Hill with four equestrian statues, under the patronage of the Royal Association of Contributors to the National Monuments. In progress of time the gallery was extended to about thirty groups, all executed by Forrest. He died at Edinburgh, after an illness of about six weeks' duration, 29 Dec. 1852.

[Redgrave's Dict. of Artists ; Builder, 1853, p. 32.] L. F.

FORREST, THEODOSIUS (1728–1784), author and lawyer, son of Ebenezer Forrest [q. v.], a solicitor, author of ' Momus turn'd Fabulist,' and a friend of Rich and Hogarth, was born in London in 1728. He studied drawing under Lambert, one of the first landscape-painters of his time, and until a year or two before his death annually (1762–81) exhibited at the Royal Academy. He then entered his father's business; and became a steady solicitor, retaining, however, his artistic tastes. He had a passion for music, and could catch and reproduce an air with surprising quickness. He was a member of the Beefsteak Club, and his society was prized by Garrick and Colman. As solicitor to Covent Garden Theatre, Forrest was thrown into close relations with the dramatic profession, and he composed a musical entertainment, 'The Weathercock,' produced at Covent Garden 17 Oct. 1775, said by Genest to be 'poor stuff.' As a writer of songs, however, Forrest was more successful. He is said to have been exceedingly generous, a man of strict integrity, a good judge in matters of art, and an agreeable and entertaining companion. He earned considerable reputation for the rendering of his own ballads. Towards the close of his life Forrest was afflicted with a painful nervous disorder, attended with a black jaundice. He was thrown into a condition of deep melancholy, and on 5 Nov. 1784 killed himself at his chambers in George Street, York Buildings, London. Forrest had a plentiful income, and was very charitable.

A portrait of Forrest, with Francis Grose the antiquary [q. v.] and Hone, was painted by Dance and engraved by Bartolozzi.

[Baker's Biographia Dramatica, 1812; Gent. Mag. 1784, p. 877 (article by Thomas Tyers), and 1824, i. 582; Nichols's Lit. Anecd. iii. 659; Genest's Hist. of the Stage, v. 512; Graves's Dict. of Artists.] G. B. S.

FORREST, THOMAS (d. 1540), Scottish martyr. [See FORRET.]

FORREST, THOMAS (fl. 1580), was author of 'A Perfite Looking Glasse for all Estates: most excellently and eloquently set forth by the famous and learned Oratour Isocrates, as contained in three Orations of Morall Instructions, written in the Greeke tongue, of late yeeres: Translated into Latine by ... Hieronimus Wolfius. And nowe Englished ... with sundrie examples of pithy sentences, both of Princes and Philosophers, gathered and collected out of divers writers, Coted in the margent, approbating the Author's intent. ... Imprinted in Newgate Market, within the new Rents, at the Signe of the Lucrece, 1580.' The volume is a quarto of forty-six leaves, and is dedicated by the translator, Tho. Forrest, to Sir Thomas Bromley. There are also prefixed 'An Epistle to the Reader;' 'The Author's Enchomion upon Sir Thomas Bromley;' 'J. D. in Commendation of the Author;' 'In Praise

of the Author, S. Norreis;' 'The Booke to the Reader.' The volume is probably 'certen orations of Isocrates' found in the Stationers' Register under date 4 Jan. 1580. Ritson puts Forrest among the English poets because of the 'Enchomion' above mentioned.

[Ames's Typogr. Antiq. (Herbert), p. 997; Ritson's Bibl. Poet. p. 209; Arber's Stationers' Registers, ii. 165; Hunter's Chorus Vatum, iii. 296 (Addit. MS. Brit. Mus. 24489).] R. B.

FORREST, THOMAS (1729?–1802?), navigator, appears to have served for some time in the royal navy, and to have been a midshipman in 1745. It was probably after the peace in 1748 that he entered the service of the East India Company, and different passages in his own writings show that he was employed in Indian seas from 1753 almost continuously, though he implies that during part of the seven years' war he was on board the Elizabeth, a 64-gun ship, in the squadron under Admiral Steevens. His name, however, does not appear in the Elizabeth's pay-book. In 1762 he had command of a company's ship, from which he seems to date his experience when, writing in 1782, he spoke of himself as having above twenty years' practice in 'the country trade;' as having made fifteen voyages from Hindostan to the East, and four voyages from England to India, and thus being permitted to claim some knowledge of the winds, weather, and sailing routes of the station, adding, however, that of the Persian and Red Sea Gulfs he knew little, never having been there. With this accumulation of practical learning he published at Calcutta 'A Treatise on the Monsoons in East India' (sm. 4to, 1782), a 2nd edition of which was published in London (12mo, 1783), a little book of interesting experiences and exploded theories. In 1770 he was engaged in forming the new settlement at Balambangan, which had been recommended by Alexander Dalrymple [q. v.], and in 1774, when the council, in accordance with their instructions, and with a view to developing new sources of trade, were desirous of sending an exploring party in the direction of New Guinea, Forrest offered his services, which were readily accepted. He sailed on 9 Dec. in the Tartar, a native boat of about ten tons burden, with two English officers and a crew of eighteen Malays. In this, accompanied during part of the time by two small boats, he pushed his explorations as far as Geelvink Bay in New Guinea, examining the Sulu Archipelago, the south coast of Mindanao, Mandiolo, Batchian, and more especially Waygiou, which he first laid down on the chart with some approach to accuracy, and returned to Achin in March 1776. The voyage was one of examination and inquiry rather than of discovery, and the additions made to geographical knowledge were corrections of detail rather than startling novelties; but the tact with which Forrest had conducted his intercourse with the natives, and the amount of work done in a crazy boat of ten tons, deservedly won him credit as a navigator. He published a detailed account of the voyage, under the title, 'A Voyage to New Guinea and the Moluccas from Balambangan . . . during the years 1774-5-6' (4to, 1779), with a portrait. In December 1782 Forrest was employed by the governor-general, Warren Hastings, to gain intelligence of the French fleet, which had left the coast of India, and evaded the observation of Sir Edward Hughes [q. v.], the English commander-in-chief. It was believed that it had gone to Mauritius. Forrest found it at Achin, and bringing back the information to Vizagapatam, just before the return of the French, saved many country vessels from falling into their hands. In the following June he sailed again to survey the Andaman Islands, but falling to leeward of them, passed through the Preparis Channel to the Tenasserim coast, which he examined southwards as far as Quedah; the account of the voyage, under the title, 'A Journal of the Esther Brig, Capt. Thomas Forrest, from Bengal to Quedah, in 1783,' was afterwards edited by Dalrymple, and published at the charge of the East India Company (4to, 1789). In 1790 he made a fuller examination of the same coast and of the islands lying off it, in, as he discovered, a long row, leaving a sheltered passage 125 miles long between them and the main land, to which he gave the name of Forrest Strait, by which it is still known. The results of this voyage were published as 'A Voyage from Calcutta to the Mergui Archipelago' (4to, 1792), with which were included some minor essays and descriptive accounts, as well as a reprint of the 'Treatise on the Monsoons.' This volume is dedicated to William Aldersey, president of the board of trade in Bengal, by his 'most affectionate cousin,' with which solitary exception we have no information as to his family. Forrest is said to have died in India about 1802.

[Forrest's own writings, as enumerated above, seem the only foundation of the several memoirs that have been written, the best of which is that in the Biographie Universelle (Supplément). Some letters to Warren Hastings in 1784–5, in Addit. MSS. 29164 f. 171, 29166 f. 135, 29169 f. 118, show that before 1790 he had already examined the Mergui Islands.] J. K. L.

FORREST, WILLIAM (*fl.* 1581), catholic priest and poet, is stated by Wood to have been a relative of John Forest [q.v.], the Franciscan friar. He received his education at Christ Church, Oxford, and he was present at the discussions held at Oxford in 1530, when Henry VIII desired to procure the judgment of the university in the matter of the divorce. He appears to have attended the funeral of Queen Catherine of Arragon at Peterborough in 1536. He was an eyewitness of the erection of Wolsey's college upon the site of the priory of St. Frideswide, and there can be no doubt that he was appointed to some post in the college as refounded by the king, as his name occurs among the pensioned members after its dissolution as the recipient of an annual allowance of 6*l.* in 1553 and 1556. In 1548 he had dedicated his version of the treatise 'De regimine Principum' to the Duke of Somerset, as also in 1551 his paraphrase of some of the psalms. This continued choice of patron, coupled with the character of the latter work, affords some ground for Warton's suspicion that Forrest 'could accommodate his faith to the reigning powers.' In 1553, however, he came forward with warm congratulations on the accession of Mary, and, being in priest's orders, he was soon afterwards nominated one of the queen's chaplains. Among Browne Willis's manuscript collections for Buckinghamshire, preserved in the Bodleian Library, double entries are found of the presentation of William Forest by Anthony Lamson on 1 July 1556 to the vicarage of Bledlow in that county; but in Lipscomb's 'Buckinghamshire' the name of the presentee is given as William Fortescue, and the discrepancy has not yet been cleared up. In 1558 Forrest presented to Queen Mary his poem of 'The Second Gresyld.' Of his career after the death of his royal mistress nothing certain is known. He was probably protected by Thomas Howard, duke of Norfolk, to whom he dedicated his 'History of Joseph' shortly before the duke's execution in 1572. Forrest remained in the same faith to the last. This is shown by the fact that the two dates '27 Oct. 1572, per me Guil. Forrestum,' and '1581' occur in a volume (Harl. MS. 1703) containing a poem which in a devout tone treats of the life of the Blessed Virgin and of the Immaculate Conception. But, although a Roman catholic, he was not papal, and in one of his poems he speaks strongly of the right of each national branch of the church to enjoy self-government. He was well skilled in music, and had a collection of the choicest compositions then in vogue. These manuscripts came into the hands of Dr. Heather, founder of the musical praxis and professorship at Oxford, and are preserved in the archives belonging to that institution. Forrest was on terms of friendship with Alexander Barclay [q. v.], the translator of Brant's 'Ship of Fools,' of whom he gives some interesting particulars. There is a portrait of him in the Royal MS. 17 D. iii. He is represented as a young man in a priest's gown, and with long flowing hair not tonsured (NICHOLS, *Literary Remains of Edward VI*, i. p. cccxxxv).

His poetical works are: 1. 'The History of Joseph the Chaiste composed in balladde royall crudely; largely derived from the Testaments of the Twelve Patriarchs. In two parts.' Dedicated to Thomas Howard, duke of Norfolk, and dated as having been finished 11 April 1569, but said by the author to have been originally written twenty-four years before. The first part, written on vellum, is in the library of University College, Oxford, and the second part is in the Royal Library, British Museum, 18 C. xiii. A copy of both parts in one folio volume of 286 pages, written on paper, is in the possession of the Rev. J. E. A. Fenwick, at Thirlestane House, Cheltenham, being in the collection of Sir Thomas Phillipps, which that gentleman inherited. 2. 'A Notable Warke called the pleasant Poesie of princelie Practise, composed of late by the simple and unlearned sir William Forrest, priest, much part collected out of a booke entitled the "Governance of Noblemen," which booke the wyse philosopher Aristotle wrote to his disciple Alexander the Great,' Royal MS. in British Museum, 17 D. iii. This work, written in 1548, and dedicated to the Duke of Somerset, was intended, when sanctioned by him, for the use of Edward VI. A long extract from it is printed in 'England in the Reign of Henry VIII. Starkey's Life and Letters' (Early English Text Society), 1878, pt. i. p. lxxix seq. The treatise referred to in the title, 'De regimine Principum,' was written, not by Aristotle, but by Ægidius Romanus. 3. A metrical version of some of the Psalms, written in 1551, and also dedicated to the Duke of Somerset. In the Royal Library, British Museum, 17 A. xxi. 4. 'A New Ballade of the Marigolde. Imprinted at London in Aldersgate Street by Richard Lant' [1553]. Verses on the accession of Queen Mary. A copy of the original broadside is in the library of the Society of Antiquaries (LEMON, *Catalogue of Broadsides*, p. 12). The ballad was reprinted by Park in the second edition of the 'Harleian Miscellany' (1813), x. 253. 5. Pater Noster and Te Deum, versified as a prayer and a thanksgiving for Queen Mary. In the first edition of Foxe's 'Acts and Monu-

ments' (1563), pp. 1139–40. 6. 'A true and most notable History of a right noble and famous Lady, produced in Spain, entitled The Second Gresyld, practised not long out of this time, in much part Tragedious, as delectable both to Hearers and Readers,' folio. In the manuscripts of Anthony à Wood in the Bodleian Library No. 2, being the copy presented by the author to Queen Mary. It was given to Wood by Ralph Sheldon of Weston Park, Warwickshire. The work, which was finished 25 June 1558, is a narrative in verse of the divorce of Queen Catherine of Arragon. Wood extracted some passages for his English 'Annals of the University of Oxford.' These are printed in Gutch's edition of the 'Annals' (1796), ii. 47, 115. The whole of the ninth chapter was contributed by Dr. Bliss in 1814 to Sir S. E. Brydges's 'British Bibliographer,' iv. 200. The entire poem has since been printed by the Roxburghe Club, with the title of 'The History of Grisild the Second,' London, 1875, 4to, under the editorial supervision of the Rev. W. D. Macray, rector of Ducklington, Oxfordshire, who remarks that Forrest's poems, 'however prosaic under the form of verse, are all of them full of interest, alike as illustrations of the history and manners of his times, and as illustrations of language.' 7. 'An Oration consolatorye to Queen Marye.' At the end of the preceding work. 8. Life of the Blessed Virgin Mary, being a poem in praise of her and in honour of the Immaculate Conception, followed by miscellaneous, moral, and religious verses, dated from 1572 to 1581. In Harl. MS. 1703. This appears to be the volume described by Wood as having been in the possession of the Earl of Aylesbury.

[Memoir by Macray; Wood's Athenæ Oxon. (Bliss), i. 297; Warton's English Poetry (1840), iii. 257; Dodd's Church Hist. i. 515; Tanner's Bibl. Brit. p. 292; Addit. MS. 24490, f. 192 *b*; Foxe's Acts and Monuments, ed. Townsend, vii. 124; Ritson's Bibl. Poetica, p. 209; Cal. State Papers, Dom. Eliz. 1591–4, p. 297.]   T. C.

FORRESTER, ALFRED HENRY, artist, best known under the name of ALFRED CROWQUILL (1804–1872), younger brother of Charles Robert Forrester [q. v.], was born in London on 10 Sept. 1804, and educated at a private school in Islington. Although connected with his brother in business for many years, he was never a sworn notary, and in 1839 took the earliest opportunity of retiring from his connection with the city. In 1822 he wrote for the 'Hive' and in 1823 for the 'Mirror,' which was then under the editorship of John Timbs. He next applied himself to the study of drawing and model-ling, as well as to wood and steel engraving. The two brothers were always on the most intimate and friendly terms, and the elder's novel, 'Castle Baynard,' published in 1824, bore the following inscription, 'To Alfred, this little volume is dedicated by his affec-tionate brother, the author.' A. H. Forrester furnished the illustrations to his brother's 'Absurdities' in 1827, and to his contribu-tions to Bentley's 'Miscellany' in 1840-1, when the pseudonym of Alfred Crowquill was conjointly used by the writer and the artist. The best of A. H. Forrester's illustra-tive work, mostly designs on wood, were exe-cuted for Bentley, and afterwards reappeared in the 'Phantasmagoria of Fun.' He was also the writer of burlesques, drew panto-mimic extravaganzas for the pictorial papers, and exhibited pen-and-ink sketches in the miniature room of the Royal Academy in 1845 and 1846. About 1843 C. R. Forrester retired from literary life, and from that time onward the other brother used the name Al-fred Crowquill as sole representative of the previous partnership, and owing to his more numerous works and to his much longer life came at last to be considered as the only Alfred Crowquill, his elder brother being almost completely forgotten. For a time he contributed sketches to 'Punch,' where his work will be found in vols. ii. iii. and iv., and then went over to the 'Illustrated Lon-don News' as a member of the literary and pictorial staff. As a writer and as an illus-trator of his own writings he was very popu-lar; upwards of twenty works came from his pen, many of them being children's books. For some years the London pantomimes were indebted to him for designs, devices, and effects. He supplied some of the woodcuts to Chambers's 'Book of Days,' he was one of the illustrators of Miss Louisa H. Sheridan's 'Comic Offering,' 1831, &c., and he was the designer in 1839 of the cover for 'Hood's Own.' In 1851 he modelled a statuette of the Duke of Wellington, which he produced a fortnight before the duke's death and pre-sented to Queen Victoria and the allied so-vereigns. At the time when he originally started as an artist there was not much com-petition, and he consequently found constant work. He was inferior in many respects to Kenny Meadows, although a useful and in-genious man, and many of his works have enjoyed a considerable amount of popularity.

He died at 3 Portland Place North, Clap-ham Road, London, 26 May 1872, and was buried in Norwood cemetery on 31 May. The works mentioned below were written by Forrester and contain illustrations by him-self: 1. A. Crowquill's 'Guide to Watering Places,' 1839. 2. 'Sketches of Pumps, handled by R. Cruikshank, with some Tem-perate Spouting by A. Crowquill,' 1846. 3. 'A good Natural Hint about California,' 1849. 4. 'A Missile for Papists, a few Remarks on the Papacy, by the Ghost of Harry the Eighth's Fool,' 1850. 5. 'Gold, a Legendary Rhyme,' 1850. 6. 'A Bundle of Crowquills, dropped by A. Crowquill in his Eccentric Flights over the Fields of Literature,' 1854. 7. 'Fun,' 1854. 8. 'Picture Fables,' 1854. 9. 'Gruf-fel Swillendrinken, or the Reproof of the Brutes,' 1856. 10. 'The Little Pilgrim,' 1856. 11. 'Tales of Magic and Meaning,' 1856. 12. 'Fairy Tales,' 1857. 13. 'A New Story Book, comprising the Good Boy and Simon and his Great Acquaintance,' 1858. 14. 'Honesty and Cunning,' 1859. 15. 'Kind-ness and Cruelty, or the Grateful Ogre,' 1859. 16. 'The Red Cap,' 1859. 17. 'The Two Sparrows,' 1859. 18. 'What Uncle told us,' 1861. 19. 'Fairy Footsteps, or Lessons from Legends,' 1861 (with Kenny Meadows). 20. 'Tales for Children,' 1863. 21. 'Sey-mour's Humorous Sketches, illustrated in Prose and Verse,' 1866. 22. 'The Two Pup-pies,' 1870. 23. 'The Boys and the Giants,' 1870. 24. 'The Cunning Fox,' 1870. 25. 'Dick Do-little, the Idle Sparrow,' 1870. 26. 'The Pictorial Grammar,' 1875.

In the following list the works were illus-trated by A. Crowquill, sometimes in con-junction with other artists: 27. 'Ups and Downs,' 1823. 28. 'Der Freischütz Tra-vestied,' 1824. 29. 'Paternal Pride,' 1825. 30. 'Despondency and Jealousy,' 1825 (with G. Cruikshank and others). 31. 'Eccentric Tales, by W. F. von Kosewitz' (i.e. C. R. Forrester), 1827. 32. 'Absurdities, in Prose and Verse,' by C. R. Forrester, 1827. 33. 'Faust, a Serio-comic Poem,' 1834. 34. 'Leaves from my Memorandum Book,' 1834. 35. 'The Tour of Dr. Syntax,' 1838. 36. 'Comic Latin Grammar,' 1840 (with J. Leech). 37. 'The Vauxhall Papers,' edited by Alfred Bunn, a periodical, 1841, 1 vol. 38. 'The Sea Pie,' a periodical, 1842, 1 vol. 39. 'Phantasmagoria of Fun,' by C. R. For-rester; edited and illustrated by A. Crow-quill, 1843, 2 vols. 40. 'Beauty and the Beast,' by Albert R. Smith, 1843. 41. A Comic Arithmetic,' 1844. 42. 'Woman's Love,' by G. H. Rodwell, 1846. 43. 'The Wanderings of a Pen and Pencil,' by F. P. Palmer, 1846, eight numbers. 44. 'The Ex-citement, a Tale of our Time,' 1849. 45. 'The Book of Ballads,' by Bon Gaultier, 1849 (with Doyle and Leech). 46. 'The Sisters,' by H. Cockton, 1851. 47. 'Little Plays for Little Actors,' by Miss J. Corner, 1856.

by the crown of Portugal, made him commander of the orders of Christ and Isabella la Catolica, and received the cross of chevalier of various orders of his adopted country. He was member of the Royal Academies of Lisbon and Oporto, of the Royal Academy of Sciences of Turin, of the English Society of Antiquaries, of the Royal Geographical Societies of London, Paris, and Berlin, and received the highest gold medals reserved for learned foreigners by the pope and by the emperors of Russia, Austria, and France. Charles Albert, king of Piedmont, during his residence in Oporto, not long before his death, detached from his own breast the cross of SS. Maurice and Lazarus, worn by him throughout his campaigns, in order to affix it to the coat of Baron de Forrester.

[Annual Register, 1861, ciii. 438; Gent. Mag. 3rd ser. July 1861, ii. 88; private information from W. Offley Forrester, esq.]   E. M. C.

FORRESTER, THOMAS (1588?–1642), satirist and divine, graduated A.M. at St. Andrews University 22 July 1608. On 10 March 1623 the Archbishop of Glasgow recommended him for the ministry of Ayr, but the session reported 'that he was not a meet man.' Thereupon James I presented him to the post (10 April). About 1632 he gave 20l. to the fund for building the library at Glasgow University. He succeeded John Knox, a nephew of the reformer, as minister of Melrose in 1627. As an enthusiastic episcopalian, he took delight in uttering words and performing acts fitted to shock the feelings of presbyterians. At the assembly of 1638 he was accused of popery, Arminianism, &c., and was deposed 11 Dec. 1638. He took his revenge in satire. A mock litany threw ridicule on the leading covenanters and the most solemn of their doings. This was published as 'A Satire in two parts, relating to public affairs, 1638–9,' in Maidment's 'Book of Scottish Pasquils,' 1828. An epitaph on Strafford, attributed to Forrester, is printed in Cleveland's poems. Forrester died in 1642, aged 54. He married Margaret Kennitie, who died 19 Jan. 1665–6, and had a daughter, Marjory, who married a tailor of Canon-

in 1664. The perusal of John Brown's (1610?–1679) [q. v.] 'Apologetical Relation' led him to renounce episcopacy, and he became a field preacher. He was imprisoned in Edinburgh, but liberated by the indemnity of March 1674, and was deposed on the 29th of the same month. He was proclaimed a fugitive 5 May 1684, and settled at Killearn. After the revolution he became in succession minister of Killearn (1688) and of St. Andrews (May 1692). He refused calls to Glasgow and other places, and was appointed principal of the new college at St. Andrews on 26 Jan. 1698 (St. Mary's), in which office he died in November 1706. He is well known as one of the ablest advocates of presbyterianism of his day. His principal work is 'The Hierarchical Bishop's Claim to a Divine Right tried at the Scripture Bar,' 1699. Here he controverts Dr. Scott, in the second part of his 'Christian Life,' Principal Monro's 'Inquiry,' and Mr. Honeyman's 'Survey of Naphtali.' Other works bore the titles of 'Rectius Instruendum,' 1684; 'A Vindication and Assertion of Calvin and Beza's Presbyterian Judgment and Principles,' 1692; 'Causa Episcopatus Hierarchici Lucifuga,' 1706.

[Scott's Fasti, ii. 356, 391, 691; Wodrow's Hist.; Wodrow's Analecta.]   W. G. B.

FORRET, THOMAS (d. 1540), vicar of Dollar, Clackmannanshire, and Scottish martyr, was descended from an old family which possessed the estate of Forret in the parish of Logie, Fifeshire, from the reign of William the Lion till the seventeenth century. The name is sometimes erroneously given as Forrest. His father had been master stabler to James IV. The catholic priest, Sir John Forret, for permitting whom to administer the sacrament of baptism at Swinton in 1573 the Bishop of St. Andrews was complained against (CALDERWOOD, *History*, iii. 272), was probably a near relative. After obtaining a good preliminary education, Forret was, through the 'help of a rich lady,' sent to study at Cologne. On his return he became a canon regular in the monastery of 'Sanct

Q

the parishioners when any one died, of 'the cow and the uppermost cloth,' remarking that the people would expect others to do as he did. He advised Forret, therefore, if he was determined to preach, to preach only on ' one good Epistle or one good Gospell that setteth forth the libertie of the holie church.' On Forret explaining that he had never found any evil epistle or gospel in the New or Old Testament, then 'spake my lord stoutlie and said, "I thank God that I never knew what the Old and the New Testament was."' This innocent instance of devout gratitude on the part of the bishop gave rise to a proverb in Scotland : ' Ye are like the Bishop of Dunkeld that knew neither the new law nor the old law.' Forret systematically warned his parishioners against the sellers of indulgences. He also took care specially to teach them the ten commandments, and composed a short catechism for their instruction on points of prime importance in Christian belief. He was in the habit of carrying bread and cheese in his gown sleeve to any poor person who was ill. He studied from six in the morning till twelve, and again from dinner till supper ; and, in order the better to hold his own against disputants, committed three chapters in Latin of the New Testament to memory every day, making his servant, An-

gate, Edinburgh, named James Alison. She obtained a pension of 20l. from Charles II 14 March 1678-9.

[Scott's Fasti, pt. ii. p. 559; Chambers's Eminent Scotsmen; A Book of Scottish Pasquils, 1828.] W. G. B.

FORRESTER, THOMAS (1635?-1706), Scotch theologian, brother of David Forrester, a merchant and burgess of Stirling, was born at Stirling about 1635, and admitted minister of Alva in Stirling under the bishop

dlesex, at the annual rent of 16l. 11s. 8d. As a justice of peace he showed himself very active in the examination of those concerned in the Gunpowder plot, and he occasionally took charge of the Tower during the absence of the lieutenant, Sir William Waad. He was chosen M.P. for Wells in 1606. He also held a surveyor's place in the office of works, and in May 1609 was commissioned to repair Oatlands Park (Cal. State Papers, Dom. Ser. Addenda, 1580–1625, p. 516). On 8 June 1611 James I granted him the manor of Tyburn, with all its appurtenances, excepting the park, for the sum of 829l. 3s. 4d. (ib. 1611-1618, p. 40). It passed to his great-grandson, John Austen, who sold it in 1710. Forsett died in 1629 or 1630, probably at his chamber in Charing Cross House. He married about 1585 Elizabeth, daughter of Robert Carr, of Hillingdon, Middlesex; she predeceased him. His will (P. C. C. 46, Scroope), dated 13 Oct. 1629, was proved 25 May 1630 by his son, Robert Forsett, and his daughter Frances (d. 1668), wife of Mr. (afterwards Sir) Matthew Howland of Holborn and Streatham, Surrey, one of the king's gentlemen pensioners. Therein he describes himself as ' of Maribone in the countie of Middlesex esquier,' and desires to be buried in Marylebone Church, in a vault of his own in the chancel. He is the author of two ably written pamphlets: 1. 'A

the wine country he is still remembered as the ' protector of the Douro.' An interesting sketch of his home in Oporto is contained in 'Les Arts en Portugal,' by Count Raczynski, who records a visit paid to him in August 1844. He left six children, but had been a widower for many years before his death. There is an excellent portrait of him, a large print in lithography, by Banquiet of London, 1848. He was created Baron de Forrester for life

Comparative Discovrse of the Bodies Natvral and Politiqve. Wherein . . . is set forth the true forme of a Commonweale, with the dutie of Subiects, and the right of the Soueraigne,' 4to, London, 1606. At page 51 he makes interesting allusion to the Gunpowder plot; he also argues strongly for union with Scotland (p. 58). 2. 'A Defence of the Right of Kings; wherein the power of the papacie ouer princes is refuted, and the oath of allegeance iustified. (An examination of a position published by P. R. [i.e. Robert Parsons] in the preface of his treatise . . . concerning the lawfullnesse of the Popes power ouer princes),' 4to, London, 1624, dedicated to James I. It had been written ten or twelve years previously, and was at length published by a friend who signs himself 'F. B.' Wood confounds the above Edward Forsett with another of the same names, whom he describes as ' a gentleman's son of Lincolnshire, and of the same family with the Forsets of Billesby in that county' (*Athenæ Oxon.* ed. Bliss, ii. 5). In 1590, ' or thereabouts, he became a commoner of Lincoln College, Oxford, aged eighteen; but leaving that house without the honour of a degree, retired at length to his patrimony.' An Edward Forsett ' of Billesby, co. Lincoln, gent.,' was examined before Popham and Coke in April and May 1600, when he was charged with being a papist and with denying the queen's title to the crown (*Cal. State Papers*, Dom. 1598–1601, pp. 423–5, 430, 434).

[Prof. Moore Smith's Introduction to the Latin comedy Pedantius, Louvain, 1905, pp. xii–xvii; Lysons's Environs, iii. 249, 254; Lysons's Middlesex Parishes, p. 2; Newcourt's Repertorium, i. 695; Cal. State Papers, Dom. Ser.; Overall's Remembrancia, pp. 555–6; Chester's London Marriage Licenses (Foster), col. 501; Administration Act re Ann Forsett, granted May 1645 (P. C. C.); Will of Robert Forsett, proved by decree, January 1688 (P. C. C. 125, Exton); Administration Act re Edward Forsett, April 1674 and Oct. 1693 (P. C. C.); Will of Anne Forsett, proved May 1690 (P. C. C. 69, Dyke).] G. G.

FORSHALL, JOSIAH (1795–1863), librarian, born at Witney in Oxfordshire on 29 March 1795, was the eldest son of Samuel Forshall. He received some of his education at the grammar schools of Exeter and Chester, and in 1814 entered Exeter College, Oxford. He graduated B.A. in 1818, taking a first class in mathematics and a second in litt. hum. He became M.A. in 1821, and was elected fellow and tutor of his college. He was appointed an assistant librarian in the manuscript department of the British Museum in 1824, and became keeper of that department in 1827. In 1828

he was elected a fellow of the Royal Society. He edited the catalogue of the manuscripts in the British Museum (new series): pt. i. the Arundel MSS.; pt. ii. the Burney MSS.; pt. iii. index, 1834, &c. fol., and also the ' Catalogus Codicum Manuscriptorum Orientalium [in the Brit. Mus.]: Pars Prima Codices Syriacos et Carshunicos amplectens,' 1838, &c. fol. He also edited the ' Description of the Greek Papyri ' in the Brit. Mus., pt. i. 1839, 8vo. In 1828 he had been appointed secretary to the museum, and in 1837 resigned his keepership in order to devote himself exclusively to his secretarial duties. He was examined before the select committee appointed to inquire into the museum in 1835–6, and made some curious revelations on the subject of patronage. As secretary he had much influence with the trustees. He was greatly opposed to any attempts to ' popularise ' the museum. In 1850 he published a pamphlet entitled ' Misrepresentations of H.M. Commissioners [who inquired into the British Museum in 1848–9] exposed,' and about that time retired from the museum on account of ill-health. After his resignation Forshall lived in retirement, spending much of his time, till his death, at the Foundling Hospital, of which he had been appointed chaplain in 1829. He died at his house in Woburn Place, London, on 18 Dec. 1863, after undergoing a surgical operation. Forshall was a man of ability, and of a kindly disposition. Besides the catalogues already mentioned he published, in conjunction with Sir F. Madden, the wellknown edition of ' The Holy Bible . . . in the earliest English Versions made by John Wycliffe and his followers,' 1850, 4 vols. 4to. To this work he had given up much time during twenty-two years. He also published editions of the Gospels of St. Mark (1862, 8vo), St. Luke (1860, 8vo), and St. John (1859, 8vo), arranged in parts and sections, and some sermons. His works ' The Lord's Prayer with various readings and critical notes' (1864), 8vo, and ' The First Twelve Chapters of . . . St. Matthew ' in the received Greek text, with various readings and notes, 1864, 8vo, were published posthumously.

[Gent. Mag. 1864, 3rd ser. xvi. 128; Statutes and Rules of the Brit. Mus. (1871); Cowtan's Memories of the Brit. Mus. 6, 66, 69, 365–76; Brit. Mus. Cat.] W. W.

FORSTER, BENJAMIN (1736–1805), antiquary, was born in Walbrook, London, 7 Aug. 1736, being the third son of Thomas Forster, a descendant of the Forsters of Etherston and Bamborough, and his wife

Dorothy, granddaughter of Benjamin Furly [q. v.], the friend and correspondent of Locke. He was educated at Hertford school and at Corpus Christi College, Cambridge, where he had as friends and fellow-students the antiquarians Richard Gough and Michael Tyson. He graduated as B.A. in 1757, becoming M.A. and fellow of his college in 1760, and B.D. 1768. Having taken orders, 'though he was never very orthodox,' he became in succession curate of Wanstead and of Broomfield and Chignal Smeely in Essex (1760), Lady Camden lecturer at Wakefield (1766), and rector of Boconnoc, Broadoak, and Cherichayes in Cornwall (1770). He died at Boconnoc parsonage on 2 Dec. 1805, his tomb being, by his orders, merely inscribed 'Fui.' He was somewhat eccentric, surrounding himself with multifarious pet animals, to whom he was much attached; but his letters show him to have been a man of taste and learning, and a skilful antiquary. These letters are preserved in Nichols's 'Literary Anecdotes,' ix. 648–50, and 'Literary Illustrations,' v. 280–90, while many of Gough's letters to him are in a volume privately printed at Bruges (1845–50) by his great-nephew, Thomas Ignatius Maria Forster [q. v.], entitled 'Epistolarium Forsterianum.' Among his other friends were the poets Mason and Gray.

[Gent. Mag. 1849, xxxii. 431; Nichols's Illustrations, viii. 554; Boase and Courtney's Bibl. Cornub.] G. S. B.

FORSTER, BENJAMIN MEGGOT (1764–1829), man of science, second son of Edward Forster the elder [q. v.] and his wife Susanna, was born in Walbrook, London, 16 Jan. 1764. He was educated with his brothers at Walthamstow, and became a member of the firm of Edward Forster & Sons, Russia merchants, but attended very little to business. During his whole life he was attached to the study of science, especially botany and electricity. He executed many fine drawings of fungi, communicated various species to Sowerby, and in 1820 published, with initials only, 'An Introduction to the Knowledge of Fungusses,' 12mo, pp. 20, with two plates. He contributed numerous articles to the 'Gentleman's Magazine' under various signatures and on various subjects, and is credited with eight scientific contributions to the 'Philosophical Magazine' in the Royal Society's Catalogue. They deal with fungi, the electric column, and atmospheric phenomena. He invented the sliding portfolio, the atmospherical electroscope, and an orrery of perpetual motion, the last being a failure. Ceaseless in his exertions in the cause of humanity, he was one of the earliest advocates of emancipation, and one of the first members of the committee of 1788 against the slave trade. He also joined the societies for the suppression of climbing chimney-sweepers, for diffusing knowledge respecting capital punishments, for affording refuge to the destitute, and for repressing cruelty to animals, he being conscientiously opposed to field sports. He also framed the child-stealing act. He never married, living with his father and mother till their death, when he took a cottage called Scotts, at Hale End, Walthamstow, where he died 8 March 1829.

[Gent. Mag. (1829), xcix. 279; Nichols's Illustrations, viii. 553; Epistolarium Forsterianum, vol. ii. pp. xiii–xv.] G. S. B.

FORSTER, EDWARD, the elder (1730–1812), banker and antiquary, the son of Thomas and brother of Benjamin Forster [q. v.], was born 11 Feb. 1730, and was educated at Felstead school. He then went to Holland to his relative Benjamin Furly, from whom he received the original letters of Locke, afterwards published by his grandson. He married Susanna Furney, a member of an old Somerset family, by whom he left three sons, Thomas Furly [q. v.], Benjamin Meggot [q. v.], and Edward (1765–1849) [q. v.], and a daughter Susanna Dorothy (1757–1822), who married the Rev. J. Dixon, rector of Bincombe, Dorsetshire. In 1764 he settled at Walthamstow, where his leisure was employed in riding in search of scenery and antiquities, in sketching, etching, and writing of occasional verses. In 1774 he published the speeches made by him at the bar of the House of Commons on the linen and Russia trades, his only other publication being 'Occasional Amusements,' 12mo, 1809, pp. 87, a volume of verse. He was a member of the Mercers' Company, a director of the London Docks, governor of the Royal Exchange, and, for nearly thirty years, of the Russia Company, in which capacity he gave an annual ministerial dinner. When consulted by Pitt as to a forced paper currency he was offered a baronetcy. He died at Hoe Street, Walthamstow, 20 April 1812. Though neither a sportsman nor a practical naturalist, he was very fond of horses and dogs, and was an ardent lover of nature. Addison, Swift, and Rousseau were his favourite authors, and Gray, Gough, and Tyson were among his personal friends. One of his letters (Epistolarium Forsterianum, i. 205–26) contains a reference to Gray's 'Elegy' as early as 1751. Edward Forster is stated (NICHOLS, Anecdotes, viii. 596) to have been the introducer of bearded wheat from Smyrna. His portrait was painted by Shee for the Mercers' Company in 1812, and by Hoppner for the Royal Exchange, the latter having been privately engraved in mezzotint.

[Nichols's Anecdotes, vi. 331–3, 616, viii. 1, 596, ix. 720; Gent. Mag. 1849, xxxii. 431; Epistolarium Forsterianum, 1845, i. 205–26, Bruges, privately printed.] G. S. B.

FORSTER, EDWARD (1769–1828), miscellaneous writer, born at Colchester, Essex, on 11 June 1769, was the only son of Nathaniel Forster, D.D. (1726?–1790) [q. v.], rector of All Saints in that town. After receiving some instruction at home, he was placed at Norwich grammar school, then presided over by his father's intimate friend, Samuel Parr. On 5 May 1788 he matriculated at Balliol College, Oxford, where he divided his time in desultory study of medicine and law. Towards the end of 1790 he married Elizabeth, widow of Captain Addison, and youngest daughter of Philip Bedingfeld of Ditchingham Hall, Norfolk (BURKE, Landed Gentry, 4th edit. p. 80). In order to renew his acquaintanceship with Parr, Forster took a house at Hatton, Warwickshire, where he resided for some time; but his wife, by whom he had no children, lived only four years after their union. He ultimately became a member of St. Mary Hall, Oxford, where he graduated B.A. on 21 Feb. 1792, and entered himself at Lincoln's Inn on 15 June of the same year (FOSTER, Alumni Oxon. p. 478). Deciding, however, to become a clergyman, he was ordained priest by Porteus, bishop of London, in 1796. He proceeded M.A. on 16 Feb. 1797 (Oxford Graduates, 1851, p. 237). On 3 Aug. 1799, being then resident at Weston, Oxfordshire, he married as his second wife Lavinia, only daughter of Thomas Banks, R.A. [q. v.], the sculptor (Gent. Mag. lxix. pt. ii. 716). He now entered into an engagement with a bookseller, William Miller of Old Bond Street, subsequently of Albemarle Street, to issue tastefully printed editions of the works of standard authors, illustrated by the best artists of the day. His first venture was an edition of Jarvis's translation of 'Don Quixote,' 4 vols. 8vo, 1801, 'with a new translation of the Spanish poetry, a new life of Cervantes, and new engravings.' Having been successful in this, he published some works of less importance, while he was preparing for the press a new translation, from the French of Antoine Galland, of the 'Arabian Nights,' 5 vols. 4to, London, 1802, with twenty-four engravings from pictures by R. Smirke, R.A. During the same year he brought out in quarto an edition of 'Anacreon,' for which Bulmer furnished a peculiarly fine Greek type; the

title-plates and vignettes were from the pencil of Mrs. Forster. Various editions of dramatic authors, under the titles of 'British Drama,' 'New British Theatre,' 'English Drama,' some of them illustrated with engravings from designs by the first artists, successively employed his time.

In 1803 he was presented to the rectory of Aston Somerville, Gloucestershire, by an old friend, Lord Somerville, who had procured for him the appointment of chaplain to the Duke of Newcastle in 1796; but there being no parsonage-house on the living residence was dispensed with, and he settled in London, where his pulpit oratory was in demand. He was from 1800 to 1814 successively morning preacher at Berkeley and Grosvenor chapels; and at Park Street and King Street chapels, in which he divided the duty alternately with Sydney Smith, Stanier Clarke, T. F. Dibdin, and other admired preachers. In 1805 Forster entered into a correspondence with Scott on the subject of a projected edition of Dryden, subsequently abandoned. Forster had at a later period intended publishing an 'Essay on Punctuation,' which he had made his especial study, and on which his views were approved by Scott. An elegant quarto edition of 'Rasselas,' with engravings by A. Raimbach, from pictures painted for the purpose by Smirke, was issued by Forster in 1805; it was followed in 1809 by a small privately printed volume of verse, entitled 'Occasional Amusements,' which appeared without his name. But his chief publication was the splendid work in folio entitled 'The British Gallery of Engravings,' consisting of highly finished prints in the line manner from paintings by the old masters 'in the possession of the king and several noblemen and gentlemen of the United Kingdom.' Descriptions in English and French accompany each engraving. The first number of this work appeared in 1807, and in 1813 the first volume only was completed, when, the expenses considerably exceeding the profits, it was found necessary to abandon its further publication altogether. After the peace of 1815 Forster removed with his family to Paris, his finances having suffered by his publications. He was then engaged in publishing a 'Plautus,' and three volumes were already completed, when it was stopped by the sudden death of the printer. About a year after he had settled in Paris Forster began to preach in the French protestant church of the Oratoire, and eventually obtained a grant from the consistory for the use of the church when it was not required for French service. Here he officiated until the autumn of 1827, when ill-health compelled him to resign. In 1818 he was appointed to the post, founded at his suggestion, of chaplain to the British embassy, which he continued to hold until his death. In 1824 the Earl of Bridgewater made him his chaplain. Forster died at Paris on 18 Feb. 1828, after a lingering illness, and was buried in the cemetery of Père la Chaise in that city. He left a widow and three daughters, for whose benefit were published 'Sermons preached at the Chapel of the British Embassy, and at the Protestant Church of the Oratoire, in Paris, by Edward Forster, with a short Account of his Life' [edited by Lavinia Forster], 2 vols. 8vo, Paris, 1828. Forster had been elected F.R.S. on 10 Dec. 1801, and F.S.A. previously. He was also an active supporter of the Royal Institution from its commencement, was appointed honorary librarian by the directors, and was engaged to deliver lectures there during three following seasons.

[Gent. Mag. xcviii. pt. i. 566.]   G. G.

FORSTER, EDWARD, the younger (1765–1849), botanist, was born at Wood Street, Walthamstow, 12 Oct. 1765, being the third and youngest son of Edward the elder [q. v.] and Susanna Forster. He received his commercial education in Holland, and entered the banking-house of Forster, Lubbocks, Forster, & Clarke. He began the study of botany in Epping Forest at fifteen, and in conjunction with his two brothers he afterwards cultivated in his father's garden almost all the herbaceous plants then grown, and contributed the county lists of plants to Gough's edition of Camden (1789). In 1796 he married Mary Jane, only daughter of Abraham Greenwood, who died in 1846 without surviving issue. Forster was one of the early fellows of the Linnean Society, founded in 1788, was elected treasurer in 1816, and vice-president in 1828. With his brothers he was one of the chief founders of the Refuge for the Destitute in Hackney Road. He died of cholera, 23 Feb. 1849, two days after inspecting the refuge on the occasion of an outbreak of that disease. He was buried in the family vault at Walthamstow. He was exceedingly temperate and methodical, shy, taciturn, and exclusive, rising early to work among his extensive collections of obscure British plants before banking hours, and devoting his evenings to reading and to his large herbarium, collected in many parts of England. He resided chiefly at Hale End, ·Walthamstow, but at the time of his death at the Ivy House, Woodford, Essex. In 1817 he had printed a catalogue of British birds (*Catalogus avium in insulis Britannicis habitantium cura et studio Eduardi Forsteri jun.*, London, 1817, 8vo, pp. 48), but seems

subsequently to have devoted his attention to plants exclusively. He printed various papers on critical species of British plants in the 'Transactions' of the Linnean Society, the 'Annals and Magazine of Natural History,' and the 'Phytologist,' and collected material towards a flora of Essex. His knowledge of British plants was critically exact, several species being described by him in the 'Supplement to English Botany' (1834). At his death his library and herbarium were sold, the latter being purchased by Robert Brown and presented to the British Museum. There is an oil painting of Forster by Eddis at the Linnean Society, and a lithograph by T. H. Maguire, published in the year of his death.

[Gent. Mag. 1849, xxxii. 432; Nichols's Illustrations, viii. 554; Proc. Linn. Soc. ii. 39; Epistolarium Forsterianum, 1850, vol. ii. p. xv, Bruges, privately printed; Gibson's Flora of Essex, 1862, p. 448.]   G. S. B.

FORSTER, GEORGE (d. 1792), traveller, a civil servant of the East India Company on the Madras establishment, undertook and safely accomplished in 1782 the then remarkable feat of travelling from Calcutta overland into Russia. His journey took him through Cashmere, Afghanistan, Herat, Khorassan, and Mazanderan to the Caspian Sea, which he crossed. While in England he prepared for the press 'Sketches of the Mythology and Customs of the Hindoos' (8vo, 84 pp., 1785), and on his return to India he wrote an account of his journey, the first volume of which was published at Calcutta in 1790. In 1792 he was sent on an embassy to the Mahrattas, and died at Nagpore. The narrative of his journey was completed from his papers, and published in London by an unknown editor as 'A Journey from Bengal to England through the Northern part of India, Kashmire, Afghanistan, and Persia, and into Russia by the Caspian Sea' (2 vols. 4to, 1798). He is often confused with Johann Georg Adam Forster [q. v.], as, for example, in 'Monthly Review,' December 1798 (xxvii.361n.), where, in a review of the journey, he is described as the son of Johann Reinhold Forster.

[Authorities in text.]   J. K. L.

FORSTER, HENRY PITTS (1766?– 1815), orientalist, entered the Bengal service of the East India Company 7 Aug. 1783 (we may thus place his birth in or about 1766), became collector of Tipperah in 1793, and registrar of Diwani Adalat of the twenty-four Pargannas in 1794. To Forster belongs the credit of publishing the first English work of lexicography for the Bengali language. The first part of this book, the 'English and

Bengalee Vocabulary,' appeared at Calcutta in 1799. It is evident, from the lengthy preface to this work, that it was undertaken on political and practical, as well as on literary, grounds. Bengali at this time was, officially at least, an unrecognised vernacular, and Forster rightly insists on the absurdity and inconvenience of continuing to use Persian in courts of law. It was thus due to the efforts of Forster, seconded among Europeans by Carey, Marshman, and the other Serampur missionaries, and among the natives by Rāmamohan Ray and his friends, that Bengali not only has become the official language of the presidency, but now ranks as the most prolific literary language of India. The second volume appeared in 1802. Meanwhile Forster was also directing his attention to Sanskrit. We find from the advertisement of the 'Bengali Vocabulary,' appearing in the 'Calcutta Gazette' 26 Aug. 1802, that he had then finished, and proposed to publish by subscription, an 'Essay on the Principles of Sanskrit Grammar,' and as a sequel the text and translation of a native grammar, the 'Mugdhabodha' of Vopadeva. The latter work seems not to have been published; no trace of it, at all events, is to be found in the ordinary bibliographical works on the subject. The essay finally appeared in 1810, and from its preface we learn that it was submitted in manuscript to the 'College Council' in 1804, at which time 'none of the elaborate works on Sanskrit by Mr. Colebrooke, Mr. Carey, or Mr. Wilkins had made their appearance.' It is a laborious work, not, indeed, calculated to attract students to the pursuit of oriental learning, but abounding in tabular and statistical information, founded on the intricate and often merely theoretical lucubrations of the ancient native schools of grammar. In 1803–4 Forster was employed at the Calcutta Mint, of which he rose to be master. In 1815 he was 'nominated to sign stamp paper.' He died in India 10 Sept. of the same year.

[Dodwell and Miles's Bengal Civil Servants; Calcutta Gazette, as above.] C. B.

FORSTER, JOHANN GEORG ADAM (1754–1794), commonly known as GEORGE, naturalist, descended from a Yorkshire family which left England on the death of Charles I and settled in Polish Prussia, eldest son of Johann Reinhold Forster, also known as a traveller, naturalist, and writer, and a minister of the reformed church, was born in his father's parish of Nasserhuben, near Danzig, on 27 Nov. 1754. Reinhold Forster, who had become a minister at the desire of his father, was by inclination a student and a naturalist, and under his teaching George's talents were early developed in the same direction. In 1765 Reinhold accepted an invitation to Russia, and from that time, throwing off his clerical capacity, devoted himself entirely to scientific and literary pursuits. George was placed at a school in St. Petersburg, where he acquired a knowledge of Russian, and again accompanied his father when he went to England towards the end of 1766. Here Reinhold was from 1768 tutor of French, German, and natural history in the Warrington academy, and George, pursuing his general studies, was also acquiring a remarkable mastery of English. In 1770 the family removed to London, on a proposal from Alexander Dalrymple [q. v.] to employ Reinhold in the service of the East India Company. The plan fell through, and for the next two years the father supported his family by translating, in which work he was assisted by George, and especially, it is said, in the translation into English of Bougainville's voyage, published under the father's name in 1772. Reinhold Forster accompanied Cook in his second voyage as naturalist [see COOK, JAMES], taking George with him as his assistant. On their return in 1775 the two in concert published 'Characteres Generum Plantarum quas in Itinere ad Insulas Maris Australis collegerunt, descripserunt, delinearunt, annis MDCCLXXII–MDCCLXXV, Johannes Reinhold Forster et Georgius Forster' (fol. 1775). A second edition, really the same with a new title-page, was issued in 1776. The publication obtained for George his election as fellow of the Royal Society, an honour which had been conferred on the father before the voyage. The Forsters, however, were in want of money; Reinhold was always in difficulties, and of the 4,000l. which had been paid him for the services of himself and son during the three years' voyage, much had been swallowed up in necessary expenses. He had expected to have to write the narrative of the voyage, and to reap a large profit; but Cook determined to write it himself, and as Reinhold would not submit to any compromise he was ordered by the admiralty not to write at all. He complied with the letter of the order, but set George to do it instead, and a few weeks before the publication of Cook's narrative George Forster's was published under the title, 'A Voyage round the World in his Britannic Majesty's sloop Resolution, commanded by Captain James Cook, during the years 1772–5' (2 vols. 4to, 1777). A translation into German was published in 1779. The circumstances of this publication naturally drew down on the Forsters the ill-will of the admiralty on the one hand and of Cook's friends on the other;

and Wales, the astronomer of the expedition, published as a pamphlet, 'Remarks on Mr. Forster's Account of Captain Cook's last Voyage . . .' (8vo, 1778), in which Forster and his father and his book were criticised with more ill-nature than good judgment. Forster answered in much better taste with a 'Reply to Mr. Wales's Remarks' (4to, 1778), and a few months later published 'A Letter to the Right Honourable the Earl of Sandwich, First Lord Commissioner of the Admiralty' (4to, 1778), in which he accused his lordship of going back from his agreement, of forfeiting his plighted word, and of persecuting his father in order to gratify the spite and malice of Miss Ray [see MONTAGU, EDWARD, fifth EARL OF SANDWICH]. The statement, however, was unsupported by proof, and Sandwich was too well accustomed to such charges to take them to heart. Reinhold Forster had meantime been imprisoned for debt, and George, who in October 1777 had gone to Paris for a short time, apparently in the hope of getting some assistance, now, in October 1778, crossed over to Germany, where he found influential friends. This was the end of his connection with England. He obtained a post as teacher in the gymnasium of Cassel, and was afterwards professor of natural history in the university of Wilna, an appointment which he relinquished on the invitation of the empress of Russia to take part in a Russian voyage of discovery. The outbreak of the war with Turkey put an end to the plan, and Forster became librarian at Mainz, where he continued from 1788 to 1792. During this time, in 1790, he accompanied Alexander von Humboldt on a three months' tour down the Rhine, and through Belgium and Holland, the account of which he afterwards published as 'Ansichten vom Niederrhein u. s. w.,' perhaps the most popular of his many writings. Forster had married in 1783 Therese, the daughter of Heyne, the celebrated critic and philologist. The marriage seems to have been one of mutual attachment; but in the course of years love grew cold, and Therese, who is described as having imbibed the communistic views of the marriage tie, did not feel herself bound to a husband for whom she no longer felt a passion. Forster, though he still loved her ardently, seems to have been willing to take measures for a divorce. He entered with enthusiasm into the schemes for a democracy and a republic, and early in March 1793 was sent by the citizens of Mainz as their representative and deputy to the national convention of Paris. He was still there when, on 10 Jan. 1794, he died of a scorbutic fever. He left one child, a daughter, who in 1843

published a collected edition of his works in nine volumes. These, however, are but a small part of what he wrote, for his translations, on which he laboured almost incessantly, have no place among them, except, indeed, the German version of the 'Voyage round the World.' The style of his English writings, which have been already named, is uncommonly pure and good, and Germans speak most highly of the charm and polish of his writings in his mother-tongue (KNIGGE, *Briefe auf einer Reise . . . geschrieben*, 1793, p. 58). He is spoken of as a man capable of inspiring feelings of warm affection, and loved by all who knew him (*Monthly Review*, 1794, xiii. 544). But his life was a continual hard struggle with penury, and the breakdown of his domestic happiness seems to have unhinged his mind during the last two years of his life.

His English works bear on the title-page the name of George Forster, as, indeed, do most of his German publications. In consequence of this he is frequently confused with his namesake, George Forster [q. v.], who died in 1792, the confusion being sometimes most insidious and puzzling; as, for instance, in Chalmers's 'Biographical Dictionary,' where he is said to have been, about 1790, studying the oriental languages with a view to travelling in Thibet and India. His linguistic attainments were remarkable, but it does not appear that they included any of the languages of Asia.

[Allgemeine deutsche Biographie, art. by Alfred Dove.]   J. K. L.

FORSTER, JOHN (1812–1876), historian and biographer, was born at Newcastle on 2 April 1812. He was the eldest of the four children of Robert Forster and Mary his wife, daughter of the keeper of a dairy-farm in Gallowgate. Robert Forster and his elder brother, John, were grandsons by a younger son of John Forster, landowner, of Corsenside in Northumberland. Having nothing to inherit from the family property, the brothers became cattle-dealers in Newcastle; and Robert's children were chiefly indebted for their education to their uncle John, whose especial favourite from the first was his nephew and namesake. John Forster was placed by him at an early age in the grammar school of Newcastle. There he became the favourite pupil of the headmaster, the Rev. Edward Moises. Eventually he became captain of the school, as Lord Eldon and Lord Collingwood had been before him. A tale written by him when he was fresh from the nursery appeared in print. While yet a mere child he took delight in going to the theatre. In answer to remonstrances he wrote a singularly clever and elaborate paper, in June 1827, entitled 'A Few Thoughts in Vindication of the Stage.' On 2 May 1828 a play of his in two acts, called 'Charles at Tunbridge, or the Cavalier of Wildinghurst,' was performed at the Newcastle Theatre, written 'expressly,' as 'by a gentleman of Newcastle,' for the benefit of Mr. Thomas Stuart. Forster's success at school induced his uncle John to send him to Cambridge in October 1828, but within a month he decided to move on to London. By his uncle's help he was at once sent to the newly founded University College, and entered as a law student at the Inner Temple on 10 Nov. 1828. His instructor in English law at University College was Professor Andrew Amos [q. v.] Among his fellow-students and fast friends for life were James Emerson Tennent [q. v.] and James Whiteside [q. v.] In the January number of the 'Newcastle Magazine' for 1829 a paper of Forster's appeared (his earliest contribution to the periodicals) entitled 'Remarks on two of the Annuals.' In that year he first made the acquaintance of Leigh Hunt, of whom he afterwards wrote: 'He influenced all my modes of thought at the outset of my life.' As early as March 1830 he projected a life of Cromwell. He was already studying in the chambers of Thomas Chitty [q. v.] In 1832 Forster became the dramatic critic on the 'True Sun.' He became a valued acquaintance of Charles Lamb; in 1831 Lamb had written to him: 'If you have lost a little portion of my good will, it is that you do not come and see me oftener.' In December 1832 both Lamb and Leigh Hunt were contributing to a series of weekly essays which Moxon had just then commenced under Forster's direction, called 'The Reflector,' of which a few numbers only were published. In 1833 Forster was writing busily on the 'True Sun,' the 'Courier,' the 'Athenæum,' and the 'Examiner.' Albany Fonblanque [q. v.], who had just become editor, appointed Forster the chief critic on the 'Examiner,' both of literature and the drama. In 1834, being then twenty-two years of age, he moved into his thenceforth well-known chambers at 58 Lincoln's Inn Fields. In 1836 he published in 'Lardner's Cyclopædia' the first of the five volumes of his 'Lives of the Statesmen of the Commonwealth,' including those of Sir John Eliot and Thomas Wentworth, earl of Strafford. Vol. ii., containing those of Pym and Hampden, appeared in 1837; vol. iii., giving those of Vane and Marten, in 1838; vols. iv. and v., completing the work in 1839, being devoted to the life of Oliver Cromwell. While engaged in the composition of this work he

was betrothed to the then popular poetess, L. E. L[andon]. An estrangement, however, took place between them, and in 1838 Miss Landon married George Maclean. Forster for two years, 1842 and 1843, edited the 'Foreign Quarterly Review,' where his papers on the Greek philosophers bore evidence of scholarship. On 27 Jan. 1843 he was called to the bar at the Inner Temple. Besides writing in Douglas Jerrold's 'Shilling Magazine' 'A History for Young England,' Forster in 1845 contributed to the 'Edinburgh Review' two masterly articles on 'Charles Churchill' and 'Daniel Defoe.' His intimate personal friends by that time included some of the most intellectually distinguished of his contemporaries, and on 20 Sept. 1845 Forster, in association with several of these, began to take part in a series of amateur theatricals, which for ten years enjoyed a certain celebrity. As Ford in the 'Merry Wives of Windsor,' as Kitely in 'Every Man in his Humour,' as Ernani in Victor Hugo's drama so entitled, he took part in the 'splendid strolling' which, under the lead of Dickens and Lytton, was intended to promote, among other objects, the establishment of the Guild of Literature and Art. On 9 Feb. 1846 Forster was installed editor of the 'Daily News,' in succession to Dickens, but resigned the post in October. In 1847 he assumed the editorship of the 'Examiner,' succeeding Albany Fonblanque, and held the post for nine years. He was now rewriting, for the twelfth time, his unpublished life of Goldsmith. In 1848 it appeared in one volume, as 'The Life and Adventures of Oliver Goldsmith.' Daintily illustrated by his friends Maclise, Stanfield, Leech, Doyle, and Hamerton, it won instant popularity. Six years afterwards Forster expanded the work into two volumes, with the enlarged title of the 'Life and Times' of Goldsmith. In this, as in more than one later instance, he marred the original outline by his greater elaboration, overcrowding his canvas with Goldsmith's contemporaries. When the first draft of the work was in preparation, Dickens humorously said of him that 'nobody could bribe Forster' unless it was with a 'new fact' for his life of Goldsmith. He contributed to the 'Quarterly Review,' in September 1854, a brilliant paper on Samuel Foote, and in March 1855 a sympathetic monograph on Sir Richard Steele. At the end of 1855 he was appointed secretary to the commissioners of lunacy, with an income of 800l. a year. He withdrew at once from the editorial chair of the 'Examiner,' for which he never afterwards wrote a line, devoting his leisure from that time forward exclusively to literature. On the appearance of Guizot's 'History of the

English Commonwealth,' Forster, in January 1856, wrote a criticism of it in the 'Edinburgh Review,' entitled 'The Civil Wars and Oliver Cromwell.' On 24 Sept. 1856 he married Eliza Ann, daughter of Captain Robert Crosbie, R.N., and widow of Henry Colburn, the well-known publisher. He began his happy home life at 46 Montagu Square, where he remained until his removal to Palace Gate House, which in 1862 he built for himself at Kensington. In 1858 he collected his 'Historical and Biographical Essays' in two volumes, among which there appeared for the first time his two important papers headed respectively 'The Debates on the Grand Remonstrance' and 'The Plantagenets and Tudors, a Sketch of Constitutional History.' In 1860 he published his next work, 'The Arrest of the Five Members by Charles I, a chapter of History Rewritten,' and in the same year he brought out, in a greatly enlarged form, 'The Debates on the Grand Remonstrance, November and December 1641, with an Introductory Essay on English Freedom under Plantagenet and Tudor Sovereigns.' In November 1861 Forster resigned his secretaryship to the lunacy commission on his appointment as a commissioner of lunacy, with a salary of 1,500l. a year. In 1864 he expanded his 'Life of Sir John Eliot' into two large volumes, and apparently intended to elaborate in the same way his other memoirs of the statesmen of the Commonwealth. The deaths, within six years of each other, of three of his intimate friends gave him, however, other occupation. Landor dying on 17 Sept. 1864, Forster saw through the press a complete edition of his 'Imaginary Conversations,' and in 1869 published his 'Life of Landor' in 2 vols. Upon the death of Alexander Dyce in 1869, Forster corrected and published his friend's third edition of Shakespeare, and prefixed a memoir to the official catalogue of the library bequeathed by Dyce to the nation. Dickens's death, on 9 June 1870, led to his last finished biography. His 'Life of Dickens' was published, the first volume in 1872, the second in 1873, and the third in 1874. His failing health had induced him, in 1872, to resign his office of lunacy commissioner. He survived all his relations, and felt deeply each successive death. His father died in 1836; his younger brother, Christopher, in 1844; his mother, who is described as 'a gem of a woman,' in 1852; his sister Jane in 1853; and his sister Elizabeth in 1868. Forster had long meditated another work, for which he had collected abundant materials. This was the 'Life of Jonathan Swift.' The preface to it was dated June 1875, but the first

and only finished volume was not published until the beginning of 1876. The hand of death was already upon him while he was correcting the last sheets of vol. i. for the press. He died on 1 Feb. 1876, almost upon the morrow of the book's publication. He was followed to his grave at Kensal Green, on 6 Feb., by a group of attached friends, his remains being buried there beside those of his favourite sister Elizabeth.

Those who knew Forster intimately were alone qualified to appreciate at their true worth his many noble and generous peculiarities. Regarded by strangers, his loud voice, his decisive manner, his features, which in any serious mood were rather stern and authoritative, would probably have appeared anything but prepossessing. Beneath his unflinching firmness and honesty of purpose were, however, the truest gentleness and sympathy. Outsiders might think him obstinate and overbearing, but in reality he was one of the tenderest and most generous of men. A staunch and faithful friend, he was always actively zealous as the peacemaker. While he had the heartiest enjoyment of society he had a curious impatience of little troubles, and yet the largest indulgence for the weakness of others. It was regarded as significant that Dickens allotted to him, in Lord Lytton's comedy of 'Not so bad as we seem,' the character of Mr. Hardman, who, with a severe and peremptory manner, is the readiest to say a kindly word for the small poet and hack pamphleteer. By his will, dated 26 Feb. 1874, he bequeathed to the nation 'The Forster Collection,' now at South Kensington. The library of eighteen thousand books includes the first folio of Shakespeare, the first edition of 'Gulliver's Travels,' 1726, with Swift's corrections in his own handwriting, and other interesting books. The manuscripts in the collection embrace nearly the whole of the original manuscripts of the world-famous novels of Charles Dickens. These, with forty-eight oil-paintings and an immense number of the choicest drawings, engravings, and curiosities, were left by Forster to his widow during her life, and afterwards, for the use of the public, to the Department of Science and Art at South Kensington. Mrs. Forster at once, however, surrendered her own right, to secure without delay the complete fulfilment of her husband's intention.

[The two principal sources of information in regard to the subject of this memoir, apart from the writer's own personal knowledge, are Professor Henry Morley's Sketch of John Forster, prefixed to the Handbook of the Forster and Dyce Collections, pp. 1–21, 1877, and the Rev. Whitwell Elwin's Monograph on John Forster, prefixed to the Catalogue of the Forster Library, pp. i–xxii, 1888. Reference may also be made to the Times of 2 and 7 Feb. 1876; Athenæum, 5 Feb. 1876; Alderman Harle's sketch of John Forster in Newcastle Daily Chronicle of 15 Feb. 1876, reprinted, in February 1888, in Monthly Chronicle of North-Country Lore and Legend, ii. 49–54; Men of the Time, 9th edit. p. 413; Annual Register for 1876, p. 134.]　　　C. K.

FORSTER, JOHN COOPER (1823–1886), surgeon, was born on 13 Nov. 1823 in Mount Street, Lambeth, his father and grandfather having been medical practitioners there. After being at King's College School Forster entered at Guy's Hospital in 1841, became M.R.C.S. in 1844, M.B. London in 1847, gaining a gold medal in surgery, and F.R.C.S. in 1849. In 1850 he was appointed demonstrator of anatomy at Guy's, in 1855 assistant surgeon, and in 1870 full surgeon. In 1880, when senior surgeon, he resigned his appointment, at the same time that Dr. Habershon resigned the senior physiciancy, as a mark of disapproval of the conduct of the governors and treasurer of the hospital in disregarding the opinions of the medical staff on questions relating to the nursing staff. After their resignation over four hundred Guy's men subscribed to a testimonial and presentation of silver plate to both. After being long a member of the council of the College of Surgeons and examiner in surgery he was in 1884–5 president of the college, and did much to facilitate the starting of the combined examination scheme of the colleges of physicians and surgeons. On the termination of his year of office he retired from practice, having long ceased to extend it owing to his large private means. After a stay at Cannes and Nice in January and February following he returned home prostrated by the cold of travelling, and died of an obscure disease on 2 March 1886 (see Mr. Jonathan Hutchinson's remarks on the case, *British Medical Journal*, 13 March 1886).

Forster was a good practical surgeon, prompt and decisive in the wards, and by no means lacking in boldness as an operator. He was the first to perform gastrostomy in England in 1858, and went to Aberdeen to study Pirrie's procedure of acupressure in 1867, and in various papers in the Pathological and Clinical Society's 'Transactions,' and by his reports of surgical cases in 'Guy's Hospital Reports,' showed enlarged views and keen observation. His clinical lectures were terse, emphatic, and full of common sense. His only published volume was on 'The Surgical Diseases of Children,' 1860. There is no doubt that Forster would have done more as a surgeon but for his easy circumstances. He

was a good practical horticulturist, a very skilful oarsman, having a very wide and complete knowledge of English waterways, and a devoted fly-fisher; he was also noted for his cheery and well-planned hospitality.

[Guy's Hospital Reports, vol. xliv. 1887, Memorial Notice by W. H. A. Jacobson.] G. T. B.

FORSTER, NATHANIEL, D.D. (1718–1757), classical and biblical scholar, was born on 3 Feb. 1717–18 at Stadscombe, in the parish of Plymstock, Devonshire, of which his father, Robert Forster, was then minister. His mother was Elizabeth, daughter of the Rev. John Tindal, vicar of Cornwood in the same county. She was sister of the Rev. Nicholas Tindal, translator of Rapin's 'History of England,' and niece of Dr. Matthew Tindal, author of 'Christianity as Old as the Creation' (see Tindal pedigree in NICHOLS, *Lit. Anecd.* ix. 303). He received the rudiments of education at Plymouth, where his father had removed on being appointed lecturer of St. Andrew's Church. After a course of instruction in the grammar school of that town under the Rev. John Bedford, he was removed in 1731–2 to Eton, being at the same time entered at Pembroke College, Oxford, in order to entitle him to the benefit of an exhibition of 40l. a year. He spent about sixteen months at Eton, and then repaired to his college at Oxford, where he became a pupil of Dr. Radcliff. On 13 June 1733 he was admitted scholar of Corpus Christi College, Oxford. He proceeded B.A. in 1735, and M.A. 10 Feb. 1738–9, was elected a fellow of Corpus in 1739, and graduated B.D. in 1746 and D.D. in 1750 (FOSTER, *Alumni Oxon.* ii. 479).

In 1749 he was presented by the Lord-chancellor Hardwicke, on the recommendation of Bishop Secker, to the small rectory of Hethe, Oxfordshire. In 1750 he became domestic chaplain to Dr. Butler, on that prelate being translated from Bristol to Durham. The bishop bequeathed to him a legacy of 200l., appointed him executor of his will, and died in his arms at Bath [see BUTLER, JOSEPH]. Forster, overwhelmed with grief at the loss of his friend, returned to his college for a short time, and in July 1752 was appointed one of the chaplains to Dr. Herring, archbishop of Canterbury. In the autumn of 1754 the archbishop gave him the valuable vicarage of Rochdale, Lancashire. Although a scholar and a preacher of the highest order, he was little understood and not very popular at Rochdale, where he did not long reside. The many letters addressed to him by Dr. Herring show that the primate's regard for him was most cordial and sincere. The lord chancellor promoted him on 1 Feb. 1754–5 to a prebendal stall in the church of Bristol (LE NEVE, *Fasti*, ed. Hardy, i. 231).

On 1 May 1755 he was elected a fellow of the Royal Society (THOMSON, *List of the Fellows*, p. xlviii), and on 12 May 1756 he was sworn one of the chaplains to George II. In the summer of 1757 he was, through the interest of Lord Royston, appointed by Sir Thomas Clarke to succeed Dr. Terrick as preacher at the Rolls Chapel. In August the same year he married Susan, widow of John Balls of Norwich, a lady possessed of considerable fortune. Forster took a house in Craig's Court, Charing Cross, about two months before his death, which took place on 20 Oct. 1757, in consequence of excessive study. He was buried in St. Martin's Church, Westminster. His widow (who afterwards married Philip Bedingfeld, esq., of Ditchingham, Norfolk) erected a monument to his memory in Bristol Cathedral. It is inscribed with an elegant Latin epitaph, composed by Dr. Hayter, then bishop of Norwich.

Forster, who was an accomplished scholar, and thoroughly conversant with the Greek, Latin, and Hebrew languages, published: 1. 'Reflections on the Natural Foundation of the high Antiquity of Government, Arts, and Sciences in Egypt,' Oxford, 1743, 8vo. 2. 'Platonis Dialogi quinque. Recensuit, notisque illustravit Nathan. Forster,' Oxford, 1745, 8vo, reprinted 1765. 3. 'Appendix Liviana; continens, (I.) Selectas codicum MSS. et editionum antiquarum lectiones, præcipuas variorum Emendationes, et supplementa lacunarum in iis T. Livii, qui supersunt libris. (II.) I. Freinshemii supplementorum libros X in locum decadis secundæ Livianæ deperditæ,' Oxford, 1746. 4. 'Popery destructive of the Evidence of Christianity,' a sermon on Mark vii. 13, preached before the university of Oxford on 5 Nov. 1746, Oxford, 8vo; reprinted in 'The Churchman Armed,' vol. ii. (1814). 5. 'A Dissertation upon the Account supposed to have been given of Jesus Christ by Josephus. Being an attempt to show that this celebrated passage, some slight corruptions only excepted, may be esteemed genuine,' 1749, 8vo. 6. 'Biblia Hebraica sine punctis,' Oxford, 1750, 4to. 7. 'Remarks on the Rev. Dr. Stebbing's "Dissertation on the Power of States to deny Civil Protection to the Marriages of Minors," &c.,' London, 1755.

[Nichols's Lit. Anecd. ix. 289; Gent. Mag. lxxxvi. (i.) 537; Darling's Cyclopædia Bibliographica, p. 1166; Cat. of Oxford Graduates, 1851, p. 238; Watt's Bibl. Brit.; Lowndes's Bibliographer's Manual (Bohn), p. 821; Bodleian Cat.] T. C.

FORSTER, NATHANIEL, D.D. (1726?–1790), writer on political economy, son of the Rev. Nathaniel Forster of Crewkerne, Somerset, and cousin of Nathaniel Forster, D.D., the editor of Plato [q. v.], was born in 1726 or 1727. He matriculated at Oxford, as a member of Balliol College, 12 Feb. 1741–2, but migrated to Magdalen College (where he was elected a demy in 1744), and graduated B.A. in 1745, and M.A. in 1748. He resigned his demyship in 1754 (BLOXAM, *Magdalen College Register*, vi. 264). Returning to Balliol College on being elected a fellow of that society, he took the degrees of B.D. and D.D. by cumulation in 1778. He became rector of All Saints Church, Colchester, and chaplain to the Countess Dowager of Northington. When Dr. Samuel Parr left Stanmore in 1777 to become master of the school at Colchester, he was received by Forster with open arms, and was offered by him the curacies of Trinity Church and St. Leonard's in addition to the school. The conversation of Forster was peculiarly interesting to Parr, who never mentions him in his correspondence without some term of admiration. Forster was instituted to the rectory of Tolleshunt Knights, Essex, in 1764. He died on 12 April 1790, aged 63. He left an only son, Edward (1769–1828) [q. v.]

Besides four single sermons, which are characterised by Parr as very excellent, he published the following political treatises: 1. 'An Answer to a pamphlet entitled "The Question Stated, whether the Freeholders of Middlesex forfeited their right by voting for Mr. Wilkes at the last Election."' London, 1749, 4to (anon.) 2. 'An Enquiry into the Causes of the present High Price of Provisions,' London, 1767, 8vo (anon.) M'Culloch remarks that 'this is perhaps the ablest of the many treatises published about this period on the rise of prices. It contains, indeed, not a few principles and conclusions that are quite untenable; but the comprehensiveness of the author's views and the liberal and philosophical spirit by which the work is pervaded make it both valuable and interesting' (*Literature of Political Economy*, p. 193). 3. 'A Letter to Junius, by the author of the Answer to "The Question Stated,"' London, 1769, 4to. 4. 'An Answer to Sir John Dalrymple's pamphlet on the Exportation of Wool,' Colchester, 1782, 8vo. He also compiled the 'General Index to the twelfth–seventeenth volumes of the Journals of the House of Commons,' printed by order of the house, London, 1778, fol.

[Foster's Alumni Oxon. ii. 479; Darling's Cyclop. Bibl. i. 1167; Gent. Mag. lx. 376, 473, 1145; Cat. of Oxford Graduates, 1851, p. 238; Parr's Works, ed. Johnstone, i. 94.] T. C.

FORSTER, RICHARD, M.D. (1546?–1616), physician, son of Laurence Forster, was born at Coventry about 1546, and was educated at All Souls' College, Oxford. He graduated at Oxford, M.B. and M.D., both in 1573. He became a fellow of the College of Physicians of London about 1575, but his admission is not mentioned in the 'Annals.' In 1583 he was elected one of the censors, in 1600 treasurer, and Lumleian lecturer in 1602. He was president of the college from 1601 to 1604, and was again elected in 1615 and held office till his death on 27 March 1616. He had considerable medical practice, and was also esteemed as a mathematician. Camden, when recording his death, describes him as 'Medicinæ doctor et nobilis Mathematicus.' Clowes, the surgeon, praises him, and in 1591 (*Prooved Practice*, p. 46) speaks of him as 'a worthie reader of the surgerie lector in the Phisition's college,' showing that he gave lectures before the Lumleian lectures were formally instituted in 1602. Forster had been introduced to Robert, earl of Leicester, by Sir Henry Sidney, and dedicated to the earl in 1575 his only published work, a thin oblong quarto, entitled 'Ephemerides Meteorologicæ Richardi Fosteri artium ac medicinæ doctoris ad annum 1575 et positum finitoris Londini emporii totius Angliæ nobilissimi diligenter examinatæ.' Besides the prose dedication, in which astronomy is said to be the handmaid of medicine, twenty lines of Latin verse on Leicester's cognisance, the bear, precede the tables of which the book is made up.

[Munk's Coll. of Phys. i. 74; Wood's Fasti Oxon. vol. i.; Preface to Forster's Ephemerides; Clowes's Surgical Works.] N. M.

FORSTER, SIR ROBERT (1589–1663), lord chief justice. [See FOSTER.]

FORSTER, THOMAS (*fl.* 1695–1712), limner, is known from a number of small portraits, drawn with exquisite care and feeling, in pencil on vellum. The majority of these were no doubt intended for engraving as frontispieces to books, and the following were so engraved by Michael Vander Gucht and others: J. Savage, Sir Thomas Littleton, the speaker, William Lloyd, bishop of St. Asaph, Dr. Humphry Hody, Rev. John Newte, and others. Unlike David Loggan [q. v.], Robert White [q. v.], and John Faber, sen. [q. v.], who drew portraits 'ad vivum' in the same style, Forster does not appear to have been an engraver himself. A number of his drawings were exhibited at the special Exhibition of Portrait Miniatures at the South Kensington Museum in 1865; they included Robert, lord Lucas, Archbishop Ussher, Sir Thomas Pope Blount, bart., Lady Blount, John, lord Somers, and Admiral Sir George Rooke. A drawing of Margaret Harcourt is in the print room at the British Museum. His portraits are highly valued.

[Redgrave's Dict. of Artists; Cat. of Special Exhibition of Miniatures, South Kensington Museum, 1865; Bromley's Cat. of Engraved British Portraits.] L. C.

FORSTER, THOMAS (1675?–1738), the Pretender's general, was a high-church tory squire of Ederstone or Etherston, Northumberland, who at the outbreak of the rebellion in Scotland in 1715 represented his county in parliament (first elected 27 May 1708, expelled 10 Jan. 1715–16). He was a man of influence, and was mentioned as one of the disaffected to parliament in 1715, when an order for his arrest was issued with the consent of the house. Timely notice was given him, and at the head of a body of servants and a few friends he at once joined some of the north-country gentry. They failed in an attempt to seize Newcastle, and after proclaiming James III at various places in Northumberland and Durham, and avoiding an encounter with General Carpenter, they succeeded in joining the south-country Scots on 19 Oct. at Rothbury, and the following day a body of highlanders under Mackintosh at Kelso. On account of his social position, and to propitiate the protestants, the Pretender appointed Forster to the command of this little army. He had no experience or capacity. When once face to face with the king's forces at Preston he seems to have lost heart. He at once surrendered at discretion, in spite of the entreaties of his officers. He was among the prisoners of the better class who were sent to be tried in London, and was led with a halter on his horse's head. At Barnet he and others were pinioned, to add to their abject appearance rather than for security, and from Highgate they were escorted into the city by a strong detachment of the guards, horse and foot, amidst the enthusiastic cheers of a vast concourse of people. He was lying in Newgate 10 April 1716, three days before his intended trial. His servant had, by a cunning device, got the head-keeper's servant locked in the cellar, and Forster, who had induced Pitts the governor and another friend to have wine with him, left the room. A few minutes later Pitts tried to follow, and found that he was locked in. Forster and his servant had been provided with keys, by which they not only secured their liberty, but delayed pursuit; and notwithstanding the offer of 1,000*l.* reward, they made good their escape by a small vessel from Rochford in Essex, and landed in France. He is said to have spent some time in Rome. He died, however, at Boulogne, France, 'of an asthma,' on 3 Nov. 1738 (*Gent. Mag.* 1738, p. 604). There is a small engraved portrait of Forster by Wedgwood after a miniature by Rosalba.

[R. Patten's Hist. Rebellion in 1715, 3rd ed. 1745; A Full and Authentick Narrative of the Intended and Horrid Conspiracy, &c., 1715; Penrice's Account of Charles Ratcliffe, 1747; Hibbert-Ware's Lancashire during Rebellion of 1715 (Chetham Soc.), 1845; Commons' Journals, xviii. 325, 336, 449; Hist. MSS. Comm. 11th Rep. App. pt. iv. pp. 168–71; Evans's Cat. of Portraits, i. 127.]

A. N.

FORSTER, THOMAS FURLY (1761–1825), botanist, was born in Bond Street, Walbrook, 5 Sept. 1761, being the eldest son of Edward Forster the elder [q. v.] and Susanna his wife. His father retired to Walthamstow in 1764, and, being a great admirer of Rousseau, brought up his son on his principles. From his uncle Benjamin [q. v.] Forster early acquired a taste for antiquities, coins, prints, and plants. He was introduced to the Linnean system of classification, to which he always remained a firm adherent, by the Rev. John Dixon, and was further encouraged in his studies by Joseph Cockfield of Upton, Michael Tyson, Sir John Cullum, and Richard Warner, author of the 'Plantæ Woodfordienses'(1771). Between 1775 and 1782 he made many drawings of plants, studying exotic species in the garden of Mr. Thomas Sikes at Tryon's Place, Hackney. In 1784 was printed a list of additions to Warner's 'Plantæ Woodfordienses,' attributed by Dryander to Thomas Forster. In 1788 Forster married Susanna, daughter of Thomas Williams of West Ham, and niece of Mr. Sikes. He was one of the first fellows of the Linnean Society, founded in that year, and he visited Tunbridge Wells in that and almost every succeeding year of his life. In conjunction with his brothers he drew up the county lists of plants in Gough's 'Camden' (1789), and communicated various plants to the 'Botanical Magazine' and to 'English Botany.' From 1796 to 1823 he mainly resided at Clapton, and, as he had grown hardy plants in his home at Walthamstow, then devoted himself to greenhouse exotics, giving much assistance to the Messrs. Loddiges in establishing their nursery at Hackney. A list of the rare plants of Tunbridge Wells, pp. 14, 12mo, belonging probably to 1800, is attributed to him by Dryander; and in 1816 he published a 'Flora Tonbrigensis,' pp. 216, 8vo, dedicated to Sir J. E. Smith, which was reissued by his son in 1842. His fondness for animals made him refuse to prepare

an account of the fauna. In 1823 he moved to Walthamstow on the death of his mother, and died there 28 Oct. 1825, leaving two sons and three daughters. He contributed two papers to the Linnean Society's 'Transactions,' and left an extensive hortus siccus of algæ, as well as of flowering plants, together with collections of fossils, music, &c., and more than a thousand drawings of churches and other ancient buildings, executed by himself. His natural history journals of weather prognostics, &c., were published by his son in 1827 as 'The Pocket Encyclopædia of Natural Phenomena,' pp. xlviii and 440, 12mo. He was a member of many scientific and philanthropic societies, and among his friends were Porson and Gough, as well as the botanists, Sir J. E. Smith, Sir Joseph Banks, Dryander, Dickson, Robert Brown, and Afzelius of Upsala.

[Gent. Mag. 1849, xxxii. 431; Nichols's Illustrations of Literary History, viii. 553; Flora Tonbrigensis, 2nd ed. 1842; Epistolarium Forsterianum, i. 33–41.]

G. S. B.

FORSTER, THOMAS IGNATIUS MARIA, M.D. (1789–1860), naturalist and astronomer, eldest son of Thomas Furly Forster [q.v.], was born in London on 9 Nov. 1789. He was brought up mainly at Walthamstow, and, both his father and grandfather being followers of Rousseau, his literary education was neglected. During his life, however, he acquired familiarity with the Latin, Greek, French, German, Italian, Spanish, and Welsh languages, while from his uncle Benjamin Meggot [q. v.] he obtained his first notions of astronomy, mechanics, and aërostatics. In 1805 he compiled a 'Journal of the Weather' and a 'Liber Rerum Naturalium,' and in the following year, being attracted by the writings of Gall, he began to study that branch of psychology to which he afterwards gave the name of 'phrenology.' In 1808, under the signature 'Philochelidon,' he published 'Observations on the Brumal Retreat of the Swallow,' of which the sixth edition appeared, with a catalogue of British birds annexed, in 1817. In 1809 he took up for a time the study of the violin, to which he returned forty years later; and in 1810, having been ill, his attention was first directed to the influence of air upon health, upon which subject he wrote in the 'Philosophical Magazine.' The great comet of 1811 directed his attention to astronomy; and in 1812, having been, from his study of Pythagorean and Hindu philosophy and an inherited dislike of cruelty to animals, for some years a vegetarian, he published 'Reflections on Spirituous Liquors,' denying man to be by birth a carnivor. This work made him acquainted with Abernethy. In the same year appeared his 'Researches about Atmospheric Phenomena,' of which a third edition was published in 1823; and, having been already elected a fellow of the Linnean Society, his father permitted him to enter Corpus Christi College, Cambridge, to study law. This study, however, he soon abandoned, graduating as M.B. in 1819. In 1815 he issued an annotated edition of the 'Diosemeia' of Aratus, which he partially suppressed, and a volume of songs in German, 'Lieder der Deutschen.' Making the personal acquaintance of Spurzheim, he studied with him the anatomy and physiology of the brain, and accompanied him to Edinburgh, where he communicated a paper on the comparative anatomy of the brain to the Wernerian Society. On his return to London he published a sketch of Gall and Spurzheim's system, which, like many of his writings, appeared in the 'Pamphleteer,' together with an essay on the application of the organology of the brain to education. He became a frequenter of Sir Joseph Banks's Sunday gatherings in Soho Square. He declined the fellowship of the Royal Society from dislike of some of its rules. In 1817 he married Julia, daughter of Colonel Beaufoy, F.R.S., and settled at Spa Lodge, Tunbridge Wells, where in the same year he wrote his 'Observations on the . . . Influence of . . . the Atmosphere on . . . Diseases, particularly Insanity.' In the following year his only daughter, Selena, was born, and he moved to Hartwell in Sussex. This year he published an edition of Catullus, and on 3 July 1819 he discovered a comet. The next three years he spent mainly abroad, and in 1824 issued his 'Perennial Calendar,' containing numerous essays by himself, though variously signed, during the preparation of which work he seems to have been converted to Roman catholicism. Having become a fellow of the Royal Astronomical Society, he, in conjunction with Sir Richard Phillips, founded a short-lived Meteorological Society. After his father's death he took (1827) a house at Boreham, near Chelmsford, so as to be near New Hall Convent, where his daughter was at school, and while there published various essays on the atmospheric origin of diseases and especially of cholera, in connection with which subject he made a balloon ascent in April 1831, with Green, ascending six thousand feet. In 1830 he published the original letters of Locke, Shaftesbury, and Algernon Sydney, which he had inherited from his ancestor Benjamin Furly, with a metaphysical preface, partly inspired by his recent acquaintance with Lady Mary Shepherd. After 1833 he appears to have lived mainly abroad, finally

settling at Bruges; but he reissued his father's 'Flora Tonbrigensis,' with a memoir of the author, at Tunbridge Wells in 1842, and his works were issued at Frankfort, Aix, or Brussels as often as at Bruges. Many of his later writings are poetical, and he composed various pieces for the violin, having formed a valuable collection of specimens of that instrument. In 1836 he was engaged in a controversy with Arago as to the influence of comets, and he also had some difficulty in demonstrating the orthodoxy of his Pythagorean doctrine of 'Sati,' or universal immortality, including that of animals. In conjunction with his friend Gompertz he founded the Animals' Friend Society. The autobiographical 'Recueil de ma Vie' (Frankfort-on-Main, 1835), and still more the two volumes, 'Epistolarium Forsterianum,' which he printed privately at Bruges in 1845 and 1850, contain much information about himself and other members of his family. Besides the works already mentioned and those enumerated below, he contributed largely to the 'Gentleman's Magazine,' and is credited with thirty-five scientific papers in the Royal Society's 'Catalogue,' several dealing with colours, their names, and classification. He died at Brussels on 2 Feb. 1860, though Hoefer had killed him (*Biographie Universelle*, vol. xviii.) ten years previously. Among his personal friends this remarkable man numbered, besides those already mentioned, Gray, Porson, Shelley, Peacock, Herschel, and Whewell.

He published: 1. 'Observations sur la variété dans le pouvoir dispersif de l'Atmosphère,' in 'Phil. Mag.,' 1824. 2. 'On the Colours of the Stars' (*ib.*) 3. 'Pocket Encyclopædia of Natural Phenomena,' 1826. 4. 'Memoir of George Canning,' 1827. 5. 'The Circle of the Seasons,' 1828. 6. 'Medicina Simplex,' 1829. 7. 'Beobachtungen über den Einfluss des Luftdruckes auf das Gehör,' 1835. 8. 'Onthophilos,' 1836. 9. 'Florilegium, Poeticæ Aspirationes, or Cambridge Nugæ,' 1836. 10. 'Observations sur l'influence des Comètes,' 1836. 11. 'Philozoia,' 1839. 12. 'Elogio e Vita di Boecce,' 1839. 13. 'Pan, a Pastoral,' 1840. 14. 'Essay on Abnormal Affections of the Organs of Sense,' 1842. 15. 'Philosophia Musarum,' 1842. 16. 'Discours préliminaire à l'étude de l'Histoire Naturelle,' 1843. 17. 'Harmonia Musarum,' 1843. 18. 'Sati,' 1843. 19. ''Η τῶν παιδῶν ἀγωγή,' 1844. 20. 'Piper's Wallet,' 1845. 21. 'Annales d'un Physicien Voyageur,' 1848. 22. 'L'Age d'Or,' 1848.

[Hoefer, xviii. cols. 206–8; Annual Reg. cii. 440; Roy. Soc. Cat. ii. 670–1; Gillow's Bibl. Dict. of Engl. Catholics; Recueil de ma Vie, 1835; Epistolarium Forsterianum, 1845–50.] G. S. B.

FORSTER, WILLIAM (*fl.* 1632), mathematician, was a pupil of William Oughtred [q. v.], and afterwards taught mathematics 'at the Red bull over against St. Clements churchyard with out Temple bar.' While staying with Oughtred at Albury, Surrey, during the long vacation of 1630, the latter showed him a horizontal instrument for delineating dials upon any kind of plane, and for working most questions which could be performed by the globe. This invention Oughtred had contrived for his private use thirty years before. Forster persuaded him to make it public, and was ultimately allowed to translate and publish his master's treatise on the subject as 'The Circles of Proportion and the Horizontall Instrvment. Both invented, and the vses of both written in Latine by Mr. W[illiam] O[ughtred]. Translated into English and set forth for the publique benefit by William Forster,' 4to, London, 1632 (another edition, 1639), which he dedicated to Sir Kenelm Digby. A revised edition of this book was published by Arthur Haughton, another disciple of Oughtred, 8vo, Oxford, 1660. Forster had his name affixed to an 'Arithmetick, explaining the grounds and principles of that Art, both in whole numbers and fractions,' 12mo, London, 1673 (new edition, by Henry Coley, 12mo, London, 1686). The former edition is adorned by a supposed portrait of Forster, which is really that of John Weever, the antiquary.

[Ward's Lives of the Gresham Professors, i. 88; Chalmers's Biographical Dictionary, xxiii. 428; Granger's Biographical History of England (2nd edit.), ii. 328.] G. G.

FORSTER, WILLIAM (1739–1808), the founder of a family of eminent musical instrument makers and publishers, known in the trade as 'Old Forster,' was the son of a maker of spinning-wheels and repairer and maker of violins in Cumberland. William made his way southwards as a cattle-drover, and reached London in 1759. At home he had been carefully taught music and the making of instruments, and the violins with which he supplied the shops were accepted and sold without difficulty. His talent obtained him permanent employment from Beck, a music-seller of Tower Hill, until Forster started a business of his own in Duke's Court, St. Martin's Lane, whence he removed about 1785 to No. 348 Strand. The tone of his violins is penetrating; great attention was paid to their varnish and finish, and even now the earlier 'Forsters,' especially the violoncellos and double basses, are considered of some value. As a publisher Forster became honourably known through his connection with Haydn. Orchestral and chamber music was not at that time popular in England, and the enterprise which introduced more than one hundred of Haydn's important works to this country deserved the success it ultimately gained. Among letters published in 'The History of the Violin' are several of interest from Haydn, referring to the purchase of his compositions by the Forsters between 1781 and 1788. WILLIAM FORSTER (1764–1824), son of the above William Forster, made instruments of a fair quality. Music-seller to the Prince of Wales and the Duke of Cumberland, he was distinguished as 'Royal' Forster, although his father had enjoyed similar court favours. WILLIAM FORSTER (1788–1824), eldest son of the second William Forster, made no more than twelve or fifteen violins, &c., but occupied himself as violoncellist in theatre orchestras. SIMON ANDREW FORSTER (1801–1870), the fourth son of the second William Forster, carried out the instructions of his father and his brother in Frith Street, and later in Macclesfield Street, Soho. He was part author of the 'History of the Violin' (1864), from which some of the details in this article have been taken.

[Grove's Dict. of Music, i. 555; Brown's Biog. Dict. p. 252; Sandys and Forster's Hist. of the Violin, 1864, p. 290, &c.] L. M. M.

FORSTER, WILLIAM (1784–1854), minister of the Society of Friends, was born at Tottenham, near London, 23 March 1784. His father, who was a land agent and surveyor, and his mother were pious members of the Society of Friends, and they took much pains in bringing up their children. From his earliest years William, their second son, manifested a profoundly spiritual disposition, and in after years would say that 'in looking back on his earliest religious experience he could not remember a time when he was not sensible of the work of the Holy Spirit in his heart.' After his education was completed he declined to follow his father's profession, and, having taken part in quaker meetings for two years, was recognised as a minister in 1805, in his twenty-second year. For several years he was an itinerant minister, and visited many parts of England and Scotland. For a time he settled at Tottenham. In October 1816 he married, at Shaftesbury, Anna Buxton, a daughter of Thomas Fowell Buxton of Earl's Colne, Essex, and sister of Sir Thomas Fowell Buxton [q. v.] Anna Buxton, whose family were residing at Weymouth, was a handsome girl of fascinating manners. She had attracted the interest of George III, to whom Weymouth was a favourite resort, and

made governor of Meaux, the eldest being Sir Henry Fortescue [q. v.], sometime chief justice of the common pleas in Ireland, and the third Sir Richard Fortescue, who was killed at the battle of St. Albans in 1455 (see the family pedigree in CLERMONT'S supplement to *Family History*). The date of his birth cannot be precisely stated, but it was certainly before the beginning of the fifteenth century. He is said to have been educated at Exeter College, Oxford; he was a 'gubernator' of Lincoln's Inn in 1425, 1426, and 1429 (DUGDALE, *Orig. Jud.* p. 257: in the first two years he is called 'Fortescue junior'), and in 1429 or 1430 he received the degree of serjeant-at-law. No one, he says in the 'De Laudibus,' chap. l., had received this degree who had not spent at least sixteen years in the general study of the law, which enables one to form a guess as to the date of his birth (but cf. *De Natura Legis Naturæ*, ii. 10, and PLUMMER, p. 40). Thenceforth his name appears with increasing frequency in the year-books. About 1436 he married the daughter of John Jamyss of Philips Norton in Somersetshire. In an exchequer record of 20 Hen. VI he is mentioned as a justice of assize (*Kal. Exch.* iii. 381). In 1442 he was made chief justice of the king's bench, and was soon afterwards knighted. Frequent references to him occur in the privy council records for the following years. In 1443 he sat on a commission of inquiry into certain disturbances in Norwich caused by ecclesiastical exactions, and received the thanks of the council for 'his grete laboures' in the matter ; and later in the year he was member of another commission to inquire into similar disturbances in Yorkshire. From 1445 to 1455 he was appointed by each parliament one of the triers of petitions. In a grant of 1447 admitting Fortescue and his wife to the fraternity of the convent of Christchurch, Canterbury, we find him thus described in the reasons for his admission : 'Vir equidem justus, quem omnes diserti justum discernunt, obsequuntur, venerantur, et diligunt, cum et omnibus velit prodesse sed obesse nulli, nemini nocens sed nocentes prohibens' (PLUMMER, p. 48), and this agrees with the character which tradition has given to him. A few years afterwards, however, he appears as an object of popular displeasure. In Cade's proclamation (1450), in which an inquiry by some true justice is demanded, it is said : 'Item, to syt upon this enqwerye we refuse no juge except iij chefe juges, the which ben fals to beleve' (*Three Fifteenth Century Chronicles*, Camd. Soc. p. 98, see also p. 102 ; and WRIGHT, *Political Poems and Songs*, ii. lvii n.) ; and Sir John Fastolf's

servant writing in 1451 says : 'The Chief Yistice hath waited to ben assauted all this sevenyght nyghtly in hes hous, but nothing come as yett, the more pite' (GAIRDNER, *Paston Letters*, i. 185). Probably the only reason for his unpopularity was that he was known to belong to the court party ; for as judge there is every reason to believe that he was distinguished for his impartiality. Among the cases with which he had to deal as chief justice may be mentioned that of Thomas Kerver, a prisoner in Wallingford Castle, whom he refused to release on the simple command of the king (CLERMONT, *Life*, p. 10) ; and Thorpe's case (31 Hen. VI), in which he and Prisot, chief judge of the common pleas, expressed the opinion of all the judges that they ought not to answer the question put to them by the lords whether the speaker, who had been arrested during the recess, should be set at liberty, 'for it hath not been used aforetime, that the judges should in any wise determine the privilege of this high court of parliament' (13 Rep. p. 64 ; HATSELL, i. 29 ; STUBBS, *Const. Hist.* iii. 491). The cases in the year-books (21 Hen. VI–38 Hen. VI) in which Fortescue took part as chief justice are reprinted, with a translation, in the appendix to Lord Clermont's edition of his works. After the battle of Northampton in 1460 the fortunes of Fortescue followed those of the house of Lancaster, to which he remained faithful as long as any hope remained. Whether he was among the judges who declined to advise on the Duke of York's claim to the crown or had accompanied the queen to Wales does not appear. But he was present at the battle of Towton in 1461 (*Collections of a London Citizen*, Camd. Soc. p. 217, where he is called 'the Lord Foschewe'), and was included in the act of attainder passed against those who had taken part against the new king, Edward IV. At the time of his attainder he was a man of considerable landed property, acquired through his wife and by his own purchases (see PLUMMER, pp. 42–4). He spent the next two years in Scotland with the deposed family, and wrote several treatises in favour of the title of the house of Lancaster, including the 'De Natura Legis Naturæ.' The question has been discussed whether Fortescue was ever Henry VI's chancellor, as he describes himself in the 'De Laudibus ; the better opinion is that he was only chancellor 'in partibus' (CAMPBELL, *Lord Chancellors*, i. 367 ; FOSS, iv. 312 ; PLUMMER, p. 57 ; CLERMONT, pp. 15–17). In 1463 he followed Queen Margaret to Flanders, and remained abroad, living in poverty, with her and the Prince of Wales till 1471, first at

Bruges and afterwards at St. Mighel in Barrois. The 'De Laudibus,' written towards the end of her exile, suggests that he devoted himself to the education of the prince; while he seems to have spared no effort to procure assistance from Louis XI and others in order to bring about a restoration. After the Earl of Warwick's defection from Edward IV, Fortescue was particularly active. He took great pains in forwarding the marriage between Prince Edward and Warwick's daughter, and would seem to have been in frequent communication with the French king (his papers to Louis XI are not preserved: Lord Clermont prints a memorandum of them, dated 1470, which is in the *Bibliothèque Nationale* : p. 34 of *Life*). By Warwick's aid the Lancastrian restoration was accomplished in the autumn of 1470; but it was not until April 1471 that the queen, Prince Edward, and Fortescue landed in England, and then only to find that on the day of their landing King Henry had been defeated at Barnet. Fortescue joined the Lancastrian army, and was taken prisoner at the battle of Tewkesbury, at which Prince Edward was killed. Frankly acknowledging that nothing remained for which to struggle, he recognised King Edward, received his pardon (1471), and was admitted to the council (*Works*, p. 533). It was evidently made a condition of his restoration to his estates that he should formally retract and refute his own arguments in favour of the Lancastrian, which he did in his 'Declaracion upon certayn wrytinges sent oute of Scotteland.' Thereupon he petitioned for a reversal of his attainder, alleging among other things that he had so clearly disproved all the arguments that had been made against King Edward's right and title 'that nowe there remayneth no colour or matere of argument to the hurt or infamye of the same right or title, by reason of any such writyng;' and his prayer was granted by parliament (1473: CLERMONT, *Life*, pp. 41–3). He himself feared that his change of front would lay him open to the charge of doubleness. But whether it was a purely conscientious change of opinion or not (see Coke's vindication, pref. to 10th Rep.), it must be remembered that Fortescue had given the best proof of his honesty by the extraordinary sacrifices which he had made for the lost cause. On the reversal of his attainder, he went to live at Ebrington, where he died, and in the parish church of which he was buried. The date of his death is unknown, the last mention of him being in 1476 (*Kal. Exch.* iii. 8). 'According to local tradition,' says Lord Clermont, 'which the present oc-

cupant of the manorhouse repeated to me, he lived to be ninety years old' (*Life*, p. 44). He left one son, Martin, who died in 1471, and two daughters. The present Earl Fortescue is descended from Martin's elder son, Lord Clermont from the younger.

Fortescue's fame has rested almost entirely on the dialogue 'De Laudibus.' Coke, speaking with the exaggeration which he used in referring to Fortescue's contemporary, Littleton, described it as worthy, 'si vel gravitatem vel excellentiam spectemus,' of being written in letters of gold (Pref. to 8th Rep.), and Sir W. Jones, following him, called it 'aureolum hunc dialogum' (AMOS, p. x). In the history of law it is still a work of importance. The editor of his less known treatise, 'On the Governance of England,' however, has good reason for his opinion that the historical interest of the latter is far higher. It is less loaded with barren speculations, and it shows a real insight into the failure of the Lancastrian experiment of government; while it is invaluable as the earliest of English constitutional treatises (on Fortescue's constitutional theories, see STUBBS, iii. 240). Except for the minute student his other writings have no interest.

The following are Fortescue's works: 1. Tracts on the title to the crown. For Henry VI, (1) 'De Titulo Edwardi Comitis Marchiæ' (in Clermont, with translation by Stubbs, pp. 63*–90*); (2) 'Of the Title of the House of York' (a fragment, Clermont, pp. 499–502; Plummer prints what was probably the beginning of the tract 'Governance,' p. 355); (3) 'Defensio juris Domus Lancastriæ' (Clermont, with translation, pp. 505–16); (4) a short argument on the illegitimacy of Philippa, daughter of Lionel, duke of Clarence (Clermont, pp. 517–18; more fully in Plummer, p. 353). For Edward IV, 'The Declaracion made by John Fortescu, knyght, upon certayn wrytinges sent oute of Scotteland agenst the Kinges Title to the Roialme of England' (Clermont, pp. 523–41; in the form of a dialogue between Fortescue and 'a lernid man in the lawe of this lande,' written 1471–1473). 2. 'De Natura Legis Naturæ, et de ejus censura in successione regnorum suprema.' The treatise written in support of the claim of the house of Lancaster consists of an argument on this abstract case : 'A king, acknowledging no superior in things temporal, has a daughter and a brother. The daughter bears a son ; the king dies without sons. The question is, whether the kingdom of the king so deceased descends to the daughter, the daughter's son, or the brother of the king.' The first part is devoted to a consideration of the law of nature, by which the question is to be decided; in the second part, Justice, sitting as judge, hears the arguments of the rival claimants, the daughter, the grandson, and the brother, and decides in favour of the last. The treatise was one of Fortescue's 'writings sent out of Scotland,' and therefore written between 1461 and 1463. First printed by Lord Clermont, with translation and notes by Mr. Chichester Fortescue (Lord Carlingford). 3. 'De Laudibus Legum Angliæ.' Written for the instruction of Edward, prince of Wales, while he was in exile in Berry, with his mother, Queen Margaret: date about 1470. It is in the form of a conversation between Fortescue and the prince, who is encouraged to acquaint himself with the laws of England. First printed in 1537. Subsequent editions: (*a*) containing translation by Robert Mulcaster, 1573, 1575, 1578, 1599, 1609, 1616 (with preface and notes by Selden, but without his name, and containing also the 'Summæ' of Hengham), 1660 (reprint of 1616), 1672 (with Selden's name, said to be a faulty edition); (*b*) translation by Francis Gregor, 1737, 1741, 1775, 1825 (with notes by A. Amos), 1869 (Lord Clermont). Also 'Fortescutus illustratus; or a commentary on that nervous treatise, "De Laudibus Legum Angliæ,"' &c., by Edward Waterhouse, 1663. The work still waits a competent and careful editor. It is said to have suffered from interpolations; in particular, chapter xlix., on the inns of court, &c., has been questioned (see PULLING, *Order of the Coif*, pp. 153–4). 4. A treatise on the monarchy of England, variously entitled 'The Difference between an Absolute and Limited Monarchy,' 'On the Governance of the Kingdom of England,' 'De Dominio Regali et Politico,' probably written after Fortescue's return to England in 1471 (see PLUMMER, pp. 94–6). Having repeated the distinction which he draws in the 'De Natura' and the 'De Laudibus' between 'dominum regale,' or absolute monarchy, and 'dominum politicum et regale,' or constitutional monarchy, he discusses the means of strengthening the monarchy in England, taking many illustrations, by way of contrast, from his experience in France; the increase of the king's revenues, for 'ther may no realme prospere, or be worshipful and noble, under a poer kyng;' the perils that arise when subjects grow over-mighty; that the safeguard against rebellion is the wellbeing of the commons; a scheme for the reconstitution of the king's council; and the bestowal by the king of offices and rewards. The treatise is referred to in Selden's preface to the 'De Laudibus;'

it was first published in 1714 by Lord Fortescue of Credan (another edition in 1719), and the same text was printed in Lord Clermont's collection. In 1885 a revised text was published by Mr. Charles Plummer with an historical and biographical introduction and elaborate notes. Mr. Plummer's work is a mine of information concerning not only Fortescue himself, but also the history of his time, and every historical and constitutional question suggested by his treatise. 5. 'A Dialogue between Understanding and Faith,' wherein Faith seeks to resolve the doubts raised by Understanding as to the Divine justice which permits the affliction of righteous men (first printed in Lord Clermont's collection, date unknown).

Lord Clermont prints several other short pieces, including one on 'The Comodytes of England' and a rhymed 'legal advice to purchasers of land,' but the evidence of Fortescue's authorship is not strong (see PLUMMER, pp. 80–1).

[Plummer's Introduction to The Governance of England; Life of Fortescue in Lord Clermont's edition of Fortescue's works; Foss's Judges, vol. iv.; Biog. Brit.; Gairdner's Paston Letters.]   G. P. M.

FORTESCUE, SIR JOHN (1531?–1607), chancellor of the exchequer, was the eldest of the three sons of Sir Adrian [q. v.], by his second wife, Anne, daughter of Sir W. Rede. He was eight years old at the date of his father's execution, and was brought up under his mother's care. He is said by Lodge (*Peerage of Ireland*, 1789, iii. 346) to have been educated at Oxford, and afterwards entered at one of the inns of court, but there is no further evidence of his having been at either. In 1551 an act of parliament was passed for his 'restitution in blood' (*Statutes at Large*, v. p. xiv), which removed the effect of his father's attainder and gave him possession of his property at Shirburn in Oxfordshire. On the accession of Mary, his mother, who had married Sir Thomas Parry, comptroller of the royal household, was taken into the queen's service, and received various grants of lands in Gloucestershire, which were, after her death, inherited by her eldest son. About the same time Fortescue was appointed to superintend the studies of Queen Elizabeth (CAMDEN, *Annales*, 1625, ii. 27), while his youngest brother, Anthony, received the appointment of comptroller of the household of Cardinal Pole, whose niece, Katherine Pole, he had recently married. Fortescue owed his place no doubt in part to the reputation which he enjoyed throughout his life as a Greek and Latin scholar, but perhaps still more to the fact that he was second cousin once removed to Elizabeth, through the marriage of his grandfather, Sir John Fortescue of Punsborne, to Alice, daughter of Sir Geoffrey Boleyn and great-aunt of Anne Boleyn. The same marriage brought Fortescue into kinship one degree more distant with Robert Devereux, earl of Essex, who in his letters invariably addresses him as his 'loving cosen.' In one of these letters (*Add. MSS.* Brit. Mus. 4119), undated, but no doubt written in 1596, the Earl of Essex asks Fortescue's interest on behalf of the appointment of Francis Bacon to the mastership of the rolls.

On the accession of Queen Elizabeth, Fortescue was appointed keeper of the great wardrobe (*Patent Rolls*, 1 Eliz. pt. vii. m. 10). The great or standing wardrobe was situated in Blackfriars, near Carter Lane. It contained, in addition to a collection of armour and royal costumes, a large number of state documents and papers, as well as a house in which Fortescue, when in London, resided during the whole reign of Elizabeth (STOW, *Survey*, vol. i. bk. iii. p. 224). Here, in addition to his ordinary guests, he had, like other statesmen of the period, to act on occasion as host or gaoler to state prisoners, a duty which he seems to have found peculiarly burdensome, as he complains several times in his letters to Burghley of the unfitness of his house for such a purpose. Fortescue entered parliament for the first time in 1572, when he was returned for the borough of Wallingford. He sat in every subsequent parliament during the reign of Elizabeth as member first for the borough and afterwards for the county of Buckingham, until the parliament of 1601, when he was returned for Middlesex (*Return of Members of Parliament*, pt. i.) His name hardly occurs as a speaker in D'Ewes's 'Journal' until 1589, after which date he seems to have spoken frequently in the House of Commons, chiefly, however, in his capacity of chancellor of the exchequer, in proposing subsidies, suggesting means of taxation, or expressing the wishes or commands of the queen. In the midst of graver matters he appears once as an advocate of parliamentary propriety, when, on 27 Oct. 1597, three days after the meeting of parliament, he 'moved and admonished that hereafter no member of the house should come into the house with their spurs on, for offending of others' (D'EWES, *Journal*, ed. 1693, p. 550). On the death of Sir Walter Mildmay in 1589, Fortescue succeeded him in the office of chancellor of the exchequer and under-treasurer, and was sworn a member of the privy council (CAMDEN, *Annales*, ii. 27). The office of chancellor of the exchequer was an exceedingly lucrative one. A curious account of his sources of official income exists in a paper drawn up after his death, endorsed 'Sir John Fortescue's meanes of gaine, by Sir Richard Thekstin, told me, 26 Nov. 1608' (*Add. MS.* Brit. Mus. 12497, f. 143). It appears from this paper that Fortescue received from the queen a number of grants of land in several counties, leases in reversion of great value, and sinecure places, and from Burghley 'many advantageous imployments in the custom-house,' and other means of enriching himself. After a few years of office he grew to be a remarkably wealthy man, bought large estates in Buckinghamshire and Oxfordshire, maintained a retinue of sixty or seventy servants, and lived in much state. He built on his estate of Salden a house of great size and beauty at an expense of some 33,000*l.*, equal to not less than 120,000*l.* at the present day. He also bought or hired the manorhouse of Hendon, where he principally resided during the sitting of parliament, and he possessed a house in Westminster in addition to his official residence in Blackfriars. In November 1601 he was appointed chancellor of the duchy of Lancaster, so that he held during the remainder of the queen's lifetime three offices of importance at the same time. He also served upon a number of commissions, notably upon all those which concerned jesuits or seminary priests, and sat as a member of the Star-chamber, and as an ecclesiastical commissioner (RYMER, vol. vii.) After the death of Elizabeth, Osborne (*Works*, ed. 1701, p. 379) relates that Fortescue, with Lord Cobham, Sir Walter Raleigh, and other members of the privy council, made some efforts to impose conditions upon James VI, apparently with a view to prevent his appointing an unlimited number of Scotchmen to office in England. The story is to a certain extent confirmed by Bishop Goodman, who says: 'I have heard it by credible persons that Sir John Fortescue did then very moderately and mildly ask whether any conditions should be proposed to the king' (*Court of King James*, 1839, p. 14). According to Osborne, Lord Cobham and the others were 'all frowned upon after by the king,' but in Fortescue's case no very serious results followed. He was, it is true, deprived of the most important of his offices, the chancellorship of the exchequer, which was bestowed upon Sir George Home, created Earl of Dunbar; but he received on 20 May 1603 a new patent for life of the chancellorship of the duchy of Lancaster, and was continued in his office of master of the great wardrobe by patent of 24 May 1603 (RYMER, vol. vii.

pt. ii. p. 65; NAPIER, *Swyncombe*, p. 401). In the same year he twice entertained King James; in May at Hendon, and in June, with Queen Anne and Prince Henry, at Salden (NICHOLS, *Progresses of James I*, i. 165; NAPIER, p. 402).

The election for Buckinghamshire in January 1604 gave rise to a serious constitutional struggle between the crown and the House of Commons. Fortescue was defeated in his candidature by Sir Francis Goodwin. When the writs were returned, the court of chancery at once declared that the election was void, on the ground that a judgment of outlawry had been passed against Goodwin, and on a second election Fortescue was returned, and took his seat in the parliament which met 19 March 1604. The question of this election was raised immediately after the meeting of the House of Commons, and after hearing Sir F. Goodwin the house decided in his favour. The lords then demanded a conference with the commons on the subject, declaring that they did so by the king's orders. The commons thereupon sent a deputation to wait upon the king, who asserted the right of the court of chancery to decide upon disputed returns; the commons, on the other hand, maintained their exclusive right to judge of the election of their own members, and after several interviews with the king, and a conference with the judges, James suggested a compromise, which was accepted by the House of Commons, that both Goodwin and Fortescue should be set aside and a new writ issued (*Commons' Journal*, i. 149–69). In February of the next year, 1605–6, Fortescue was returned for the county of Middlesex, for which he sat for the brief remainder of his life. He died in his seventy-fifth year, on 23 Dec. 1607, and was buried in Mursley Church, Buckinghamshire.

Few men have more narrowly missed such fame as history can bestow than Fortescue. He held a considerable place in the government during one of the most eventful periods of English history. Although the greater part of his correspondence, preserved in the Record Office and at Hatfield, deals with official matters, there are a sufficient number of private letters to show that he counted among his friends such men as Burghley, Francis and Anthony Bacon, Raleigh and Essex, and that his assistance and good offices with the queen were constantly asked by persons of note and importance in the state. That he enjoyed in a high degree the confidence of Elizabeth is clearly evident from these letters, which serve to confirm the words which Lloyd attributes to her: 'Two men, Queen Elizabeth would say, outdid her

expectation, Fortescue for integrity, and Walsingham for subtlety and officious services' (*State Worthies*, ed. 1670, p. 556). He had a considerable reputation for scholarship; Camden calls him 'an excellent man and a good Grecian' (*Annales*, ii. 27); while Lloyd speaks of him as 'a great master of Greek and Latin.' Among his friends was Sir Thomas Bodley, to whose newly founded library at Oxford he presented a number of books and several manuscripts.

Fortescue was twice married: first, to Cecily, daughter of Sir Edmund Ashfield; and secondly, to Alice, daughter of Christopher Smyth.

By his first wife Fortescue had two sons, Sir Francis, K.B., and Sir William, and one daughter. The eldest son of Sir Francis was created a baronet of Nova Scotia in 1636. The direct male line of the house ceased with the death of Sir John, the third baronet, in 1717. The only portrait of Fortescue known to exist was, after long search, discovered by Thomas Fortescue, Lord Clermont (1815–1887). A copy of this picture was presented by him to the Bodleian Library, and two engravings of it are given in his family history.

[Lord Clermont's Hist. of the Family of Fortescue; Napier's Hist. Notices of the parishes of Swyncombe and Ewelme.] G. K. F.

FORTESCUE, SIR NICHOLAS, the elder (1575?–1633), chamberlain of the exchequer, was the eldest son of William Fortescue of Cookhill, and grandson of Sir Nicholas Fortescue, groom porter to Henry VIII, to whom the Cistercian nunnery of Cookhill, on the borders of Worcestershire and Warwickshire, was granted in 1542. Fortescue, who was throughout his life a zealous Roman catholic, for several years harboured at Cookhill the Benedictine monk, David Baker [q. v.] In 1605, after the Gunpowder plot and the rising of the Roman catholics of Warwickshire, Fortescue underwent several examinations, and fell under some suspicion on account of a large quantity of armour found in his house. His name appears twice in the 'Calendar of State Papers' in connection with the plot. A letter from Chief-justice Anderson and Sheriff Warburton to the privy council states that Fortescue of Warwickshire, though summoned to appear before them, had not come forward to be examined. A declaration by himself says that the armour in question has been in his house for five years, and adds that he has not seen Winter, the conspirator, for eight years, and was not summoned to join the rising in Warwickshire (*Cal. State Papers*, 1603–10, pp. 253, 304). He succeeded in clearing himself from these suspicions and lived at Cookhill unmolested until about 1610, when he was appointed a commissioner of James's household and of the navy; he was knighted in 1618, and in the same year, on the death of Sir John Points, he obtained the lucrative and honourable post of chamberlain of the exchequer, which he held until May 1625, when he resigned it (*Ashmole MS.* 1144, ix.; *Cal. State Papers*, 1625–6, p. 109). During 1622 and 1623 his name appears as serving on royal commissions, to inquire into the state of the plantations of Virginia and of Ireland, into the depredations committed by pirates on the high seas, and on royal grants of lands (RYMER, *Fœdera*, vol. vii. pt. iii. p. 247, pt. iv. pp. 46, 63).

Fortescue died at his house in Fetter Lane on 2 Nov. 1633, and was buried in the private chapel of Cookhill, where his tomb may still be seen. He married Prudence, daughter of William Wheteley of Holkham, Norfolk, by whom he had five sons, William, Francis, Edmund, Nicholas, John, and two daughters.

[Lord Clermont's Hist. of the Family of Fortescue.] G. K. F.

FORTESCUE, SIR NICHOLAS, the younger (1605?–1644), knight of St. John, was the fourth son of Sir Nicholas Fortescue, chamberlain of the exchequer [q. v.] His father was throughout his life a member of the Roman catholic church, and his sons were brought up in that religion. It is probable that the memory of Sir Adrian Fortescue [q. v.], who had late in his life become a member of the order of St. John, was cherished among his kinsmen, who adhered to the faith for the sake of which they believed him to have died a martyr, and it may be assumed that this feeling inspired Nicholas with the ambition to resuscitate the order, which had completely died out in England. In 1637 he went to Malta, furnished, if we are to believe Pozzo, the historian of the order, with a direct commission from Queen Henrietta Maria, who, 'in her zeal for the restoration of the true religion' in her adopted country, desired to revive the English langue of the order. Fortescue was received as a knight of Malta in 1638, and his project was favourably reported upon to the grand master, the pope, and Cardinal Barbarino, protector of the order, by a commission appointed to investigate the matter. The chief difficulty, which proved insuperable, was to procure the sum of twelve thousand scudi, to be expended in buildings, fees, and other expenses necessary to the refoundation of the order in England. The negotiations extended over some years, during

which time Fortescue travelled to and from England several times. During one of his journeys he was a guest at the English College at Rome, where, as the strangers' book of the college shows, he dined with John Milton, like himself travelling abroad. In 1642 the scheme was finally abandoned, owing, says Pozzo, to the 'impious turbulence of the English people, which overthrew alike the cause of holy religion and of its royal patroness.' Sir Nicholas, with his brothers William and Edmund, joined the royal army. According to the 'Loyal Martyrology' (sect. 38, p. 68) he was slain in a skirmish in Lancashire while advancing with Prince Rupert's army to the relief of York; but it is more probable that he was killed at the battle of Marston Moor, since he was buried at Skipton on 5 July 1644.

The following character of Sir Nicholas is given in Lloyd's 'Memoirs:' 'Sir Nicholas Fortescue, a knight of Malta, slain in Lancashire, whose worth is the more to be regarded by others, the less he took notice of himself; a person of so dextrous an address that when he came into notice he came into favour; when he entered the court he had the chamber, yea the closet of a prince; a gentleman that did much in his person, and, as he would say, let reputation do the rest; he and Sir Edmund Fortescue were always observed so wary as to have all their enemies before them and leave none behind them' (LLOYD, *Memoirs*, p. 669). The allusion to Sir Edmund may refer to Sir Edmund Fortescue of Fallapit [q. v.]; but it seems more probable that it relates to Edmund, brother of Sir Nicholas, who held a post at court as sewer to the queen.

[Lord Clermont's Hist. of the Family of Fortescue; Pozzo's Hist. della Rel. Milit. di S. Giovanni Geros. tom. ii.] G. K. F.

FORTESCUE, THOMAS (1784–1872), Anglo-Indian civilian, son of Gerald Fortescue, by Elizabeth, daughter of John Tew, was born in 1784, acted as secretary to his cousin, Henry Wellesley (afterwards Lord Cowley), lieutenant-governor of the recently ceded province of Oude, 1801–3, and on the capture of Delhi, October 1803, was appointed civil commissioner there. He married on 19 March 1859 Louisa Margaret, second daughter of Thomas Russell, esq., and died on 7 Sept. 1872. Part of his official correspondence is preserved at the British Museum in Addit. MSS. 13560, 13562, 13563, 13565, 13568, 13570, 13572, 13574.

[Lord Clermont's Hist. of the Family of Fortescue, p. 206.] J. M. R.

'Two Visits to the Tea Countries of China and the British Plantations in the Himalayas,' London, 1853, 2 vols. 8vo. In 1853 he visited Formosa and described the manufacture of rice-paper carried on there, and about the same time paid several visits to Japan, whence he introduced the variegated China-rose (*Kerria japonica*), *Aucuba japonica*, *Lilium auratum*, and the golden larch (*Larix Kæmpferi*), with many other species now widely known in our gardens. In 1857 he published 'A Residence among the Chinese,' describing the culture of the silkworm, and in the same year was commissioned to collect tea-shrubs and other plants in China and Japan on behalf of the United States government. The story of this journey was told in his last work, 'Yeddo and Peking,' London, 1863, 8vo, written after his retirement, when he engaged for a time in farming in Scotland. He died at Gilston Road, South Kensington, 13 April 1880.

[Gardener's Chronicle, 1880, i. 487; Garden, 1880, xvii. 356; Cottage Gardener, xix. 192.]

G. S. B.

FOSBROKE, THOMAS DUDLEY (1770–1842), antiquary, born 27 May 1770, was the only son of William Fosbroke by his second wife, Hesther, daughter of Thomas Lashbroke of Southwark, and was a descendant of a family first settled at Forsbrook in Staffordshire (for the family history see FOSBROKE, *Brit. Monachism*, 3rd ed. pp. 14–23). When nine years old he was sent to St. Paul's School, London, and in 1785 was elected to a Teasdale scholarship at Pembroke College, Oxford. He graduated B.A. 1789, M.A. 1792 (*Catal. Oxf. Graduates*). He was ordained in 1792, and was curate of Horsley in Gloucestershire from 1792 to 1810. From 1810 to 1830 he was curate of Walford, near Ross, Herefordshire, and from 1830 till his death was vicar of the parish. He died at Walford vicarage on 1 Jan. 1842. He married, in 1796, Miss Howell of Horsley, and had four sons and six daughters. His wife and seven of his children (see *Gent. Mag.* 1842, new ser. xvii. 216) survived him. There is a portrait of him prefixed to his 'British Monachism' (3rd edit.)

Fosbroke was elected a fellow of the Society of Antiquaries in 1799, and from about that time devoted himself to archæology and Anglo-Saxon literature, studying eight or nine hours a day. His 'British Monachism' was published in 1802 (London, 2 vols. 8vo), and was well received (also 1817, 4to; 1843, 8vo). His other chief work, the 'Encyclopædia of Antiquities,' a treatise on the elements of classical and mediæval archæology,

was published in 1825 (London, 2 vols. 4to; also London, 1840, 1 vol. 8vo). He contributed many reviews to the 'Gentleman's Magazine,' and among his other publications are: 1. 'Abstracts of Records and MSS. respecting the County of Gloucester,' Gloucester, 1807, 2 vols. 4to. 2. 'Key to the Testament; or Whitby's Commentary abridged,' 1815, 8vo. 3. 'History of the City of Gloucester,' London, 1819, fol. 4. 'Berkeley Manuscripts' (pedigrees of the Berkeleys; history of parish of Berkeley, &c.), London, 1821, 4to. 5. 'Companion to the Wye Tour: Ariconensia' (on Ross and Archenfield), Ross, 1821, 12mo. He also made additions to Gilpin's 'Wye Tour' (see *Brit. Mus. Cat.*) 6. 'The Tourist's Grammar' (on scenery, antiquities, &c.), London, 1826, 12mo. 7. 'Account of Cheltenham,' Cheltenham, 1826, 12mo. 8. 'Foreign Topography' (an account of ancient remains in Africa, Asia, and Europe), London, 1828, 4to. 9. 'A Treatise on the Arts, Manufactures, Manners, and Institutions of the Greeks and Romans' (in Lardner's 'Cabinet Cyclopædia'), 1833, 8vo.

[Gent. Mag. 1842, new ser. xvii. 214–16; Fosbroke's Works; Brit. Mus. Cat.] W. W.

FOSS, EDWARD (1787–1870), biographer, eldest son of Edward Smith Foss, solicitor, of 36 Essex Street, Strand, London, by Anne, his wife, daughter of Dr. William Rose of Chiswick, was born in Gough Square, Fleet Street, 16 Oct. 1787. He was educated under Dr. Charles Burney [q. v.], his mother's brother-in-law, at Greenwich, and remained there until he was articled in 1804 to his father, whose partner he became in 1811. In 1822 he became a member of the Inner Temple, but never proceeded further towards a call to the bar. Upon his father's death, in 1830, he removed to Essex Street, and carried on the practice alone until 1840, when he retired. During his professional career he had, owing to his literary tastes and connections, been specially concerned with questions relating to publishers and literary men. In 1827–8 he served the office of undersheriff of London. He was connected with the Law Life Assurance Society from its foundation in 1823, first as auditor and afterwards as director, and was active in founding the Incorporated Law Society, of which he was president in 1842 and 1843. In 1844 he removed from Streatham to Canterbury, where he proved himself a useful chairman of the magistrates' bench, in 1859 to Dover, and in 1865 to Addiscombe. From an early age he had made various essays in writing. He contributed, while still a very young man, to the 'Monthly Review,' 'Aikin's

'Athenæum,' the 'London Magazine,' the 'Gentleman's Magazine,' and the 'Morning Chronicle.' In 1817 he published 'The Beauties of Massinger,' and in 1820 an abridgment of Blackstone's 'Commentaries,' begun by John Giffard and published under his name, which has since been translated into German. On retiring from professional practice he devoted himself to collecting materials for the history of the legal profession, which he lent to Lord Campbell for his 'Lives of the Chancellors.' He published in 1843 'The Grandeur of the Law,' and in 1848 the first two volumes of the 'Judges of England' appeared. The work was at first unsuccessful, owing to the obscurity and unpopularity of the subject—judges of the Norman period; but as it progressed it rose in favour, until it is now established as the standard authority in its particular field. In recognition of his labours Lord Langdale, to whom the first two volumes were dedicated, procured for him a grant of the entire series of publications of the Record Commission. The third and fourth volumes appeared in 1851, fifth and sixth in 1857, and seventh, eighth, and ninth in 1864. In 1865 he published 'Tabulæ Curiales,' and the printing of his 'Biographia Juridica'—an abbreviation of his 'Judges of England '—was far advanced when he died of an apoplexy, 27 July 1870. He also contributed to the 'Standard.' He was an original member of the Archæological Institute, and contributed a paper on Westminster Hall to its publication, 'Old London,' 1867. He contributed to 'Archæologia' papers ' On the Lord Chancellors under King John,' ' On the Relationship of Bishop Fitz-James and Lord Chief Justice Fitzjames,' 'On the Lineage of Sir Thomas More,' and ' On the Office and Title of Cursitor Baron of the Exchequer.' For the Kent Archæological Association, which he helped to found, he wrote a paper ' On the Collar of S.S.' (*Archæol. Cantiana*, vol. i. 1858), and a privately printed volume of poems, ' A Century of Inventions,' appeared in 1863. He was elected a fellow of the Society of Antiquaries in 1822, was a member of the council of the Camden Society from 1850 to 1853, and from 1865 to 1870, a member of the Royal Society of Literature from 1837, and on the council of the Royal Literary Fund, and until 1839 secretary to the Society of Guardians of Trade. He was a magistrate and deputy-lieutenant for Kent. He married in 1814 Catherine, eldest daughter of Peter Martineau, by whom he had one son, who died in infancy, and in 1844 Maria Elizabeth, eldest daughter of William Hutchins, by whom he had six sons (of whom the eldest, Edward, a barrister,

assisted in the preparation of the 'Biographia Juridica ') and three daughters.

[Memoir by J. C. Robertson, prefixed to Biographia Juridica; Law Times, 24 Sept. 1870; Notes and Queries, 4th ser. vi. 126.] J. A. H.

FOSTER, Sir AUGUSTUS JOHN (1780–1848), diplomatist, second son of John Thomas Foster, M.P. for Ennis in the Irish House of Commons (nephew of Anthony Foster, lord chief baron of Ireland, and first cousin of John Foster, lord Oriel [q. v.]), by Lady Elizabeth Hervey, daughter of Frederick Augustus, earl of Bristol and bishop of Derry, was born on 1 Dec. 1780, and through the influence of his mother, who had remarried William, fifth duke of Devonshire, he was appointed secretary to the legation of the Right Hon. Hugh Elliot [q. v.] at Naples. In August 1811 he was nominated minister plenipotentiary to the United States of America. His manners were not conciliatory, and he did nothing to stave off the war which broke out in 1812. In that year he returned to England, and was elected M.P. for Cockermouth, and in May 1814 he was nominated minister plenipotentiary at Copenhagen. He remained in Denmark for ten years, during which nothing of importance happened, and in 1815 he married Albinia Jane, daughter of the Hon. George Vere Hobart, who received a patent of precedency as an earl's daughter when her brother succeeded to the earldom of Buckinghamshire in 1832. In 1822 Foster was sworn of the privy council, and in 1824 he was transferred to the court of Turin, and was knighted and made a G.C.H. in the following year. He was further created a baronet ' of Glyde Court, county Louth,' on 30 Sept. 1831, and he remained at Turin for no less than sixteen years, until 1840, during which period no event happened to bring his name into notice. In that year he retired from the diplomatic service. On 1 Aug. 1848 he committed suicide by cutting his throat, in a fit of temporary insanity, at Branksea Castle, near Poole, Dorsetshire.

[Foster's Baronetage; Gent. Mag. September 1848.] H. M. S.

FOSTER, HENRY (1796–1831), navigator, born in August 1796, was the eldest son of Henry Foster, incumbent of Wood Plumpton, near Preston, Lancashire, and was educated under Mr. Saul at Green Row, Cumberland. It was his father's wish that he should take orders, but in 1812 he entered the navy as a volunteer under Captain Morton in the York, and was appointed sub-lieutenant 13 June 1815. In 1815 he served in the Vengeur with Captain Alexander, and in

1817 in the Eridanus with Captain King in the North Sea and Channel fleets. In 1817 he joined Captain Hickey in the Blossom, with whom he served until 1819. When the Blossom visited the Columbia River with the commissioners to establish the boundary line between Great Britain and the United States, he surveyed the river's mouth. When in the Creole with Commodore Bowles in 1819 he made a useful survey of the north shore of the river La Plata. In 1820 he accompanied Captain Basil Hall in the Conway in his voyage to South America, and assisted him greatly in his pendulum and other observations. His next appointment, in 1823, was to the Griper, Captain Clavering, on her voyage with Captain Sabine to the coasts of Greenland and Norway, and on the return of this ship in 1824 he received full lieutenant's rank, being also elected F.R.S. on 6 May. As astronomer to the expedition Foster sailed with Sir Edward Parry on his third voyage of north-western discovery, May 1824 to October 1825, and again accompanied him, April–September 1827, in his attempt to reach the north pole. At Port Bowen and other stations within the Arctic circle he made, with the assistance of Parry and others, an extensive series of observations upon the diurnal variation, diurnal intensity of the magnetic needle, and upon other subjects connected with terrestrial magnetism and astronomical refractions, which formed an entire fourth part of the 'Philosophical Transactions' for 1826, and was printed at the expense of the board of longitude. For these papers he received the Copley medal of the Royal Society, 30 Nov. 1827, and in half an hour afterwards the rank of commander. Another valuable paper contributed by him to the same serial was ' A Comparison of the Changes of Magnetic Intensity throughout the Day in the Dipping and Horizontal Needles at Treurenburgh Bay in Spitzbergen' (*Phil. Trans.* cxviii. 303–11). On 12 Dec. 1827 he was appointed to the command of the Chanticleer, a sloop sent out by the government to the South Seas at the suggestion of the Royal Society, in order to determine the specific ellipticity of the earth by a series of pendulum experiments at various places, and to make observations on magnetism, meteorology, and the direction of the principal ocean currents. Foster sailed from Spithead 27 April 1828. He commenced the pendulum experiments on Rat Island, Montevideo. He rounded Cape Horn on 27 Dec., and on 5 Jan. 1829 observed Smith's Island, one of the New South Shetland group. Two days later he touched at Trinity Island, which he christened ' Clarence Land,' and of which he

took possession in the name of Great Britain, not being aware of its previous discovery in 1599 by Dirck Gherritz, and of its position in most of the old charts by the name of 'Gherritz Land.' From 9 Jan. to 4 March he remained at an island on these coasts, to which he gave the name of ' Deception Island,' busied with astronomical and geodesic observations, then returned to Cape Horn 25 March, and anchored in St. Martin's Cove. Here he was joined on 17 April by Captain King in the Adventure, employed on a survey of the islands adjacent. Leaving Cape Horn on 24 May Foster bore away for the Cape of Good Hope, which he reached by 16 July, and where he stayed until 13 Dec. He then visited St. Helena, and afterwards various South American ports, arriving at Porto Bello on 22 Dec. 1830. Here he wished to measure the difference of longitude across the isthmus of Panama by means of rockets. After various preparations and one failure, he left for Panama on 28 Jan. 1831, to make the final experiment. It proved successful, and the meridian distance between Panama and Chagres having been thus measured, Foster, in high spirits, embarked in a canoe at Cruces on 5 Feb. to return down the river Chagres. In the evening he was sitting upon the awning when it gave way, and he fell into the river and was drowned. His remains were recovered on 8 Feb. and buried on the river bank, nearly halfway between Palamatio Viejo and Palamatio Nueva. A monument marks the spot. A simple tablet was also raised to his memory by the officers of the Chanticleer in the port of San Lorenzo at Chagres; another monument to him is in the north aisle of Wood Plumpton Church. 'There were few officers in the service whose minds could have been more highly cultivated than Foster's,' writes one of his comrades in the Arctic expedition (*United Service Journal,* 1835, pt. ii. pp. 83–4). Foster's notebook, containing all his observations since leaving Porto Bello, was stolen from his body by the canoe-men, but he left an immense mass of observations of various kinds, which the admiralty confided partly to the Royal Society and partly to the Astronomical Society. A report on the pendulum experiments of Foster was drawn up by Francis Baily, the president of the Astronomical Society, and inserted in vol. vii. of their ' Memoirs ;' it was also printed by the admiralty. The preparation of the report on his chronometrical observations was entrusted to Dr. J. L. Tiarks, F.R.S. These, with other valuable papers, form the appendix to the ' Narrative of a Voyage to the Southern Atlantic Ocean, in the years 1828, 29, 30, performed in H.M.

Sloop Chanticleer, under the command of the late Captain Henry Foster, F.R.S., &c. By order of the Lords Commissioners of the Admiralty. From the Private Journal of W. H. B. Webster, surgeon of the Sloop,' 2 vols. 8vo, London, 1834. A French translation by A. de Lacaze appeared in 1849.

[Webster's Narrative, i. preface, ii. 190–208 ; United Service Journal, 1831, pt. ii. pp. 286, 489–96; Gent. Mag. vol. ci. pt. i. p. 643, pt. ii. pp. 64–5, vol. cii. pt. i. pp. 87–8 ; Navy Lists.]
G. G.

FOSTER, JAMES (1697–1753), divine, was born at Exeter on 16 Sept. 1697. His father, a fuller at Exeter, had become a dissenter, although he was the son of a clergyman of Kettering, Northamptonshire. Foster was educated at the free school of Exeter, and afterwards at an academy in that town kept by Joseph Hallet (*d.* 1722). He began to preach in 1718. At this time the dissenters in the west were inclining to Arianism. The proposal that they should make a declaration of orthodoxy led to the Salters' Hall conference, and to the expulsion of James Peirce and Joseph Hallet (*d.* 1722), both friends of Foster, from their congregation at Exeter. Foster took the side of the non-subscribers. His opinions gave offence to the majority of the dissenters in Exeter, and he accepted an invitation from a congregation at Milborne Port in Somersetshire. Milborne Port was also too orthodox for him, and he left it to live in the house of Nicholas Billingsley (son of Nicholas Billingsley [q. v.]) at Ashwick, under the Mendip Hills. An inscription, afterwards placed in a summer-house where he wrote and studied, is given in Collinson's 'History of Somersetshire' (ii. 449). He preached to two small congregations at Colesford and Wokey, near Wells, his salary from both amounting to only 15*l.* a year. He next moved to Trowbridge, Wiltshire, where he boarded with a glover, and had a congregation of from fifteen to twenty persons. In 1720 he published a sermon, 'The Resurrection of Christ proved,' preached at Trowbridge ; and afterwards in the same year an 'Essay on Fundamentals,' arguing that the doctrine of the Trinity should not be regarded as essential. An appendix seems to imply that his own views were Arian. He was converted by the writings of John Gale [q. v.] against infant baptism. He was baptised by Gale in London. Although his congregation did not object, they were only able to give him so small a salary that he thought of entering his landlord's trade as a glover. A Mr. Robert Houlton, however, took him as a domestic chaplain. In 1724 he was chosen

as the colleague of Joseph Burroughs [q. v.] at the chapel in the Barbican, a position previously occupied by Gale. In 1728 he was also appointed to give the Sunday evening lecture at the Old Jewry. Foster became known as an eloquent preacher, and took part in many controversies. In 1731 he wrote one of the best-known replies to Tindal's 'Christianity as Old as the Creation' (the 'Usefulness, Truth, and Excellency of the Christian Religion defended against . . .'), and Tindal is said to have spoken with great regard (CALEB FLEMING) of an answer which, in fact, implies a very close approximation of opinion. In 1735 he had a controversy with Henry Stebbing [q. v.] upon heresy, in which his main point was the innocency of intellectual error. Foster made replies to two 'Letters' by Stebbing, and to a 'True State of the Controversy,' in which Stebbing answered the second letter; and Stebbing again answered the last reply (1735-6-7). In 1744 he became pastor of the independent church at Pinners' Hall. In 1746 he visited Lord Kilmarnock in the Tower, administered the sacrament to him, and was present at his execution (18 Aug.) He published an account of Kilmarnock's behaviour (partly printed in HOWELL, *State Trials*, xviii. 503–14), which was attacked in various pamphlets. It was insinuated that the dissenters were willing to accept the Pretender in order to get rid of the Test Act, as some had been willing to submit to James II. The attack was apparently very unfair. Foster seems to have shown good feeling, and it is said that his health declined from this time on account of the shock to his nerves (FLEMING and HAWKINS, *Anecdotes*, p. 164).

Foster published four volumes of sermons (1744, &c.), besides separate sermons. The first volume produced 'A Vindication of some Truths of Natural and Revealed Religion, in answer to the false teaching of James Foster,' by J. Brine (1746). His great reputation is indicated by Pope's familiar lines (Epilogue to the *Satires*, i. 132–3) :

Let modest Foster, if he will, excel
Ten Metropolitans in preaching well;

though Johnson explained the remark to Beauclerk by saying, 'Sir, he [Pope] hoped that it would vex somebody' (Langton's 'Collectanea,' in BOSWELL). Hawkins, in his 'History of Music,' said that it had become a proverbial phrase that 'those who had not heard Farinelli sing and Foster preach were not qualified to appear in genteel company.' A contemporary eulogist gives the less conclusive proof that the sermons were attended by numbers of the fair sex. His published

others belonged, was founded in Glasgow College 10 Jan. 1752, and Foulis was admitted the next year. It was the duty of each member in turn to read a paper, and he delivered fifteen discourses, chiefly on philosophical subjects (see list in DUNCAN, op. cit. pp. 134–135). He is said to have anticipated some of Beccaria's views.

In 1755 the Select Society of Edinburgh offered a silver medal for the best printed and most correct book of at least ten sheets (*Scots Mag.* 1755, pp. 126–30), which was awarded the following year to the Foulises for their sm. folio Callimachus, 1755 (*ib.* 1756, p. 195). This is one of their masterpieces, and is much sought after; it contains some rather commonplace plates, designed by pupils of the academy. The Horace (3rd edition, 1756) also received a medal. An edition of the 'Nubes' of Aristophanes in Greek (1755) and a translation of Hierocles (1756) are prized by collectors. The 'Anacreon,' 8vo (1757), and Virgil, 8vo (1758), are commended by Harwood for their beauty and correctness. Medals were bestowed by the Select Society for the 'Iliad' (1756) and for the 'Odyssey' (1758), the famous Greek Homer in four stately folio volumes, which for accuracy and splendour is the finest monument of the Foulis press. Flaxman's designs were executed for this book. 'As the eye is the organ of fancy,' says Gibbon, 'I read Homer with more pleasure in the Glasgow folio; through that fine medium the poet's sense appears more beautiful and transparent' (*Miscellaneous Works*, 1814, v. 583). In Harwood's opinion a Thucydides of 1759 is 'by far the most correct of all the Greek classics published at Glasgow' (*View*, p. 29).

During this time Foulis had struggled with great difficulty in his academy. Proper teachers were scarce, and the public seemed unwilling to patronise native artists. Some promising students were sent abroad to study at the expense of the academy. One of these was William Cochrane, another was Archibald Maclauchlane, who married a daughter of Foulis. It should not be forgotten that David Allan and James Tassie were also pupils. Foulis advertised proposals (*Scots Mag.* 1759, p. 47) for gentlemen to subscribe to the academy with the right of choosing prints, designs, paintings, models, or casts to the value of their subscriptions. The objects were shown at Edinburgh in the shop of Robert Fleming, as well as at the gallery in Glasgow. An Herodotus (1761, 9 vols. sm. 8vo) 'is beautifully printed and reflects distinguished honour on the university of Glasgow,' says Harwood (*View*, p. 23). On the occasion of the coronation of George III the inner

court of the college was decorated with paintings from the academy, shown in a print after a picture by D. Allan (reproduced in MACGEORGE's 'Old Glasgow,' 1880, pp. 134–5). The academy pictures were exhibited on the king's birthday in subsequent years down to about 1775. In January 1763 Foulis states that 'the academy is now coming into a state of tolerable maturity.... Modelling, engraving, original history-painting, and portrait-painting' were 'all in a reputable degree of perfection' (Letter ap. DUNCAN, p. 86). About this time there was printed 'for the use of subscribers' a folio priced list showing the great variety of the productions, 'Catalogue of Pictures, Drawings, Prints, Statues, and Busts in Plaister of Paris, done at the Academy,' including 'a Collection of Prints, the plates of which are the property of R. and A. Foulis.' It is reprinted by Duncan (op. cit. pp. 91–115).

Towards the end of 1767 Foulis obtained permission from Gray, through Dr. Beattie, to publish an edition of his poems, which were then being issued in London by James Dodsley. In a letter to Beattie (1 Feb. 1768) Gray says: 'I rejoice to be in the hands of Mr. Foulis, who has the laudable ambition of surpassing his predecessors, the Etiennes and the Elzevirs, as well in literature as in the proper art of his profession' (*Works*, 1836, iv. 102). The book accordingly appeared in the middle of 1768, a handsome quarto, whose special features are explained by Beattie in a letter to Arbuthnot (*Letters*, 1820, i. 47–49). Beattie also had a share in the literary direction of the folio 'Paradise Lost' (1770), which he calls 'wonderfully fine' (Letter to Foulis, 20 June 1770, ap. DUNCAN, pp. 35–36).

Archibald Ingram, one of the partners in the academy, died 23 July 1770. The academy was dissolved. Never pecuniarily successful, it was now eclipsed by the new Royal Academy in London. The printing office was continued, but with lessened activity. A series of plates after the cartoons of Raphael, issued in 1773, may be considered to belong rather to the work of the academy than to the press. They printed down to the death of Andrew in 1775. This blow quite crushed Robert, for the two brothers were deeply attached. The increased commercial responsibility was too much for him, and he decided to send the pictures, which had been used as models in the academy, to London, where he arrived in April 1776 with Robert Dewar from the printing office, who married his daughter. The season was late, and the sale proceeded against the advice of Christie, the auctioneer. The collection is described in 'A Catalogue of Pictures, composed and painted chiefly by the most admired masters, in which many of the most capital are illustrated by descriptions and critical remarks by Robert Foulis,' London, 1776, 3 vols. 12mo. The net result of the three nights' sale was very disappointing, for which some cause may be discovered in the absence of any evidence of genuineness in the printed descriptions. Foulis was deeply mortified, and on his way home died suddenly at Edinburgh 2 June 1776, aged 69.

'A Catalogue of Books, being the entire stock in quires of the late Messrs. R. and A. Foulis,' announces the sale by auction at Glasgow 1 Oct. 1777. Their affairs were finally wound up in 1781 by Robert Chapman, printer, and James Duncan, bookseller. The debts amounted to over 6,500l.; nearly the whole of the stock was purchased by James Spottiswood of Edinburgh. The printing house in Shuttle Street was advertised for sale 31 Oct. 1782.

In the course of thirty-six years Robert and Andrew Foulis produced over 554 works, the number (known to be incomplete) in the list given by Duncan (*Notices and Documents*, pp. 49-78, 147-9); 461, being one of the most extensive collections extant, are in the Mitchell Library, Glasgow. Most of the books are reprints of standard authors; few are original. When published their chief merits were careful editing, convenient size, good paper, artistic appearance, and cheapness. They are now much sought after as admirable specimens of typography, and are noticeable for their severely plain elegance. 'Nothing has ever been done [in Glasgow] to rival the results attained by the Foulis press,' says Professor Ferguson. 'The works produced by it are quite entitled to rank with the Aldines, Elzevirs, Bodonis, Baskervilles, which are all justly renowned for the varied excellencies they possess, but no provincial, and certainly no metropolitan, press in this country has ever surpassed that of the two brothers' (*The Library*, March 1889, p. 95).

There is a medallion portrait of Foulis by Tassie, of which an engraving is given by Duncan (op. cit.) and by Dibdin (*Bibl. Tour*, ii. 765). A print of an engraving of the academy in the fore-hall, Glasgow College, after a drawing by D. Allan, is in MacGeorge's 'Old Glasgow' (p. 302).

Robert was of short stature, robust, well-proportioned, amiable, and sociable. During the winter the brothers sold books by auction. Andrew usually acted as auctioneer, for Robert was not a businesslike salesman. On one occasion he refused to sell 'Tom Jones,' as 'improper for the perusal of young persons.' He was twice married: first, in September 1742, to Elizabeth, daughter of James Moor; she died in 1750, having had five daughters. His second wife was a daughter of William Boutcher, seedsman, of Edinburgh; she also died before her husband, who survived several of his daughters. His son, ANDREW the younger, carried on the printing in the same style, and many of his books are not inferior to those of the older firm, whose name he used. A Virgil, 2 vols. folio (1778), a 'Cicero de Officiis,' 12mo (1784), and a Virgil, 12mo (1784), deserve mention. He died in 1829 in great poverty. Alexander Tilloch entered into partnership with Foulis in 1782, in order to carry on his reinvention of stereotyping.

ANDREW FOULIS the elder (1712-1775), born at Glasgow 23 Nov. 1712, was originally intended for the church, and received a more regular education than his elder brother Robert. For some time he taught Greek, Latin, French, and philosophy in Glasgow. From 1738 to his last moments the life of Andrew cannot be dissociated from that of his partner Robert. Of the two brothers Andrew was more strictly the man of business; after the foundation of the academy the responsibility of the printing, bookselling, and binding departments fell mainly on him. Between 1764 and 1770 he read eleven papers (see list in DUNCAN, p. 135) before the Literary Society of Glasgow, to which he was elected in 1756. He died suddenly of apoplexy 18 Sept. 1775, at the age of sixty-three (*Scots Mag*. 1775, p. 526).

[Information obligingly contributed by Dr. David Murray from his forthcoming work, An Account of the Foulis Academy and of the Progress of Literature, Art, and Science in Glasgow. Many facts are given in Notices and Documents illustrative of the Literary History of Glasgow (by William James Duncan), Maitland Club, 1831, 4to, reprinted with additions, Glasgow, 1886; see also an interesting article by Professor John Ferguson on the Brothers Foulis and early Glasgow Printers in The Library, March 1889; T. Mason's Public and Private Libraries of Glasgow, 1885; T. B. Reed's Old English Letter Foundries, 1887; J. Strang's Glasgow and its Clubs, 2nd ed. 1857; Dibdin's Bibl. Tour in Northern Counties and Scotland, 1838, vol. ii.; Nichols's Lit. Anecd. iii. 217, 691, viii. 475, 569, and Illustrations, ii. 167.] H. R. T.

FOULKES, PETER, D.D. (1676-1747), scholar and divine, was the third son of Robert Foulkes of Llechryd, Denbighshire, deputy baron of the court of exchequer of Chester, by Jane Ameredith of Landulph, Cornwall. He was admitted king's scholar at Westminster in 1690, and was elected thence to a Westminster studentship at Christ

Church in 1694. While an undergraduate he published, in conjunction with John Freind and under Aldrich's auspices, an edition of ' Æschines against Ctesiphon and Demosthenes on the Crown,' with a Latin translation (Oxford, 1696). He took the degrees of B.A. in 1698, M.A. in 1701. He was chosen censor at Christ Church in 1703, in preference to Edmund Smith, the poet, and was junior proctor for 1705. His cousin, Dr. William Jane, regius professor of divinity, who died in 1707, left him residuary legatee and devisee of his property, which included land in Liskeard and Bodmin, and was supposed to be worth ten or twelve thousand pounds; consequently he was a grand compounder for the degrees of B.D. and D.D. in 1710. He was appointed canon of Exeter in 1704, and became sub-dean in 1723, chancellor in May 1724, and precentor in 1731. Of Christ Church he was made canon in November 1724, and was sub-dean from 1725 to 1733. He was instituted rector of Cheriton Bishop, Devonshire, in 1714, and vicar of Thorverton in 1716. Andrew Davy of Medland, Cheriton Bishop, who died in 1722, left him the manor of Medland and other lands in trust for his second son, William Foulkes. He married first in 1707 Elizabeth Bidgood of Rockbeare, Devonshire, who died in 1737; and secondly, on 26 Dec. 1738, Anne, widow of William Holwell, and daughter of Offspring Blackall, bishop of Exeter. He died 30 April 1747, and was buried in Exeter Cathedral.

Besides the work already mentioned he published a Latin poem in ' Pietas Universitatis Oxoniensis in obitum augustissimæ et desideratissimæ Reginæ Mariæ,' Oxford, 1695; another on the east window in Christ Church in ' Musarum Anglicanarum Analecta,' Oxford, 1699, ii. 180; another (No. 15) in ' Pietas Universitatis Oxoniensis in obitum serenissimi Regis Georgii I et gratulatio in augustissimi Regis Georgii II inaugurationem,' Oxford, 1727; ' A Sermon preached in the Cathedral Church of Exeter, Jan. 30, 1723, being the day of the martyrdom of King Charles I,' Exeter, 1723.

[Manuscript records and genealogical table in the possession of Mrs. Peter Davy Foulkes; Chester Recog. Roll, 16 Car. ii. No. 326; Register of St. Mary's, Chester; List of Queen's Scholars of Westminster; Polwhele's Devonshire, vol. ii. Dioc. of Exeter, p. 41 and p. 62; Hearne's Collections, ed. Doble, i. 68, 334, 338, 339; Wood's Hist. and Antiq. iii. 515; Gent. Mag. ix. 46; Dr. Jane's will; Johnson's Lives of the Poets, ' Edmund Smith;' Cat. of Oxford Grad.; Oxford Honours Register; Le Neve's Fasti Eccl. Angl. (Hardy); Christ Church MS. Registers; Diocesan Reg. Exon. ; Provincial Register of Canterbury; Bodl. Libr. Cat. of Printed Books.]   E. C–N.

FOULKES, ROBERT (*d.* 1679), murderer, ' became,' says Wood, ' a servitor of Christ Church College, Oxford, in Michaelmas term 1651, where he continued more than four years, under the tuition and government of presbyterians and independents. Afterwards entering into the sacred function he became a preacher, and at length vicar of Stanton Lacy in his own county of Shropshire, and took to him a wife ' (*Athenæ Oxon.* ed. Bliss, iii. 1195). He seduced a young lady who resided with him, took a lodging for her in York Buildings in the Strand, and there made away with the child that was born. The next morning he went down into Shropshire. His companion eventually made a full confession. Foulkes was tried and convicted at the Old Bailey sessions, 16 Jan. 1678-9. After receiving sentence he manifested great penitence, and was visited by several eminent divines, among whom was Burnet. William Lloyd, dean of Bangor, who came to him the very evening after his condemnation, managed to obtain for him, through Compton, bishop of London, a few days' reprieve, which he employed in writing forty pages of cant, entitled ' An Alarme for Sinners: containing the Confession, Prayers, Letters, and Last Words of Robert Foulkes, . . . with an Account of his Life. Published from the Original, Written with his own hand, . . . and sent by him at his Death to Doctor Lloyd,' 4to, London, 1679. He speaks of his unfortunate companion with ill-concealed malignity. On the morning of 31 Jan. 1678-9 he was executed at Tyburn, 'not with other common felons, but by himself,' and was buried by night at St. Giles-in-the-Fields.

[A True and Perfect Relation of the Tryal, &c. of Mr. Robert Foulks, 1679.]   G. G.

FOUNTAINE, Sir ANDREW (1676-1753), virtuoso, born in 1676, was the eldest son of Andrew Fountaine, M.P., of Narford, Norfolk, by his wife Sarah, daughter of Sir Thomas Chicheley, master of the ordnance, and belonged to an old Norfolk family (see BURKE, *Landed Gentry*, 1886, i. 673; BLOMEFIELD, *Norfolk*, vi. 233 f.) He was educated at Christ Church, Oxford, under Dr. Aldrich, proceeding B.A. 1696 and M.A. 1700, and studied Anglo-Saxon under Dr. Hickes, in whose 'Thesaurus' he published 'Numismata Anglo-Saxonica et Anglo-Danica illustrata,' Oxford, 1705, folio. Fountaine was knighted by William III at Hampton Court on 30 Dec. 1699, and succeeded to the estate at Narford on his father's death, 7 Feb. 1706. In 1701 he went with Lord Macclesfield on a mission to the elector of Hanover. He then passed through Munich, and travelled in Italy, buying antiquities and curiosities. In 1714 he stayed for a long time in Paris, and again visited Italy, staying nearly three years at Rome and Florence. In 1725 he was made vice-chamberlain to Princess Caroline, and he held the same office when she became queen. He was also tutor to Prince William, and was installed for him (as proxy) knight of the Bath, and had on that occasion a patent granted him (14 Jan. 1725) for adding supporters to his arms. On 14 July 1727 he succeeded Sir Isaac Newton as warden of the mint (RUDING, *Annals*, i. 29), and held the office until his death, which took place on 4 Sept. 1753 at Narford, where from 1732 he had chiefly lived surrounded by his collections. He was buried at Narford.

Fountaine was not married. His sister, Elizabeth, became the wife of Colonel Edward Clent. Their grandson, Mr. Brigg Price of Narford, assumed the name of Fountaine and has descendants. There are two busts of Fountaine, by Roubiliac and Hoare of Bath, in Wilton House (MICHAELIS, *Ancient Marbles*, p. 46), and at least three portraits (one a miniature) are, or were, preserved at Narford. A well-known portrait at Holland House, assumed to represent Addison, has been identified as a portrait of Fountaine [see under ADDISON, JOSEPH]. There is a portrait-medal of Fountaine, made in 1744 by J. A. Dassier, in the British Museum (HAWKINS, *Medallic Illustrations*, ii. 590), and a rarer portrait-medal (specimen in Brit. Mus.) made at Florence in 1715 by Antonio Selvi. On the reverse is Pallas standing amidst ruins, works of art, coins, &c. (*ib.* ii. 433; cf. p. 434).

Fountaine was distinguished as a connoisseur, and his advice was much sought by English collectors of classical antiquities. He formed collections of china, pictures, coins, books, and other objects. When laying out money on his seat at Narford he sold his coins to the Earl of Pembroke, the Duke of Devonshire, and the Venetian ambassador, Cornaro. He lost many of his miniatures, &c., in a fire at White's Chocolate-house, in St. James's Street, London, where he had hired two rooms for his collections before removing them to Narford. The remarkably fine Fountaine collection of Palissy ware, Limoges enamels, Henri Deux ware, and majolica—sold at Christie's for a large sum 16–19 June 1884—owed its origin to Fountaine. His descendant, Mr. Andrew Fountaine (*d.* 1873), had, however, added many choice specimens, especially of majolica (see the *Fountaine Sale Catalogue*; and the *Academy*, 1884, pp. 446, 464). Fountaine incurred the displeasure of

Pope, who unfairly attacks him as the antiquary Annius (according to the seemingly correct identification of Warton) in the 'Dunciad' (iv. l. 347 ff.; see ELWIN and COURTHOPE, *Pope*, iv. 361; A. W. WARD, *Pope*, Globe ed. 1876, p. 415):—

But Annius, crafty Seer, with ebon wand,
And well-dissembled em'rald on his hand,
False as his Gems, and cancer'd as his Coins,
Came, cramm'd with capon, from where Pollio
    dines.

The 'ebon wand' is his vice-chamberlain's black rod. The 'emerald'—a genuine stone —was said some time ago to be in existence at Narford (for other references in Pope and Young to Fountaine as a virtuoso, see ELWIN and COURTHOPE, *Pope*, iii. 171–2).

Fountaine was a friend and correspondent of Leibnitz, who says in a letter that his wit and good looks made much noise at court when he was abroad. He became intimate at Florence with Cosmo III, grand duke of Tuscany, and their correspondence has been preserved. When in Ireland in 1707 with Pembroke, the lord-lieutenant, Fountaine became acquainted with Swift (cf. H. CRAIK, *Life of Swift*, pp. 136, 143). Swift and Fountaine were very intimate when in London from 1710 to 1712. Swift speaks, in his 'Journal to Stella,' of 'sauntering at chinashops and booksellers' with Fountaine, of playing ombre and 'punning scurvily' with him. They often visited the Vanhomrighs' house together at this time. When Fountaine was seriously ill in December 1710, Swift visited him and foretold his recovery, though the doctors had given him up. Fountaine seems to have corrected the original designs for Swift's 'Tale of a Tub.'

[Nichols's Lit. Anecd. i. 18, ii. 4, 250, 258, 581, v. 253–4 (memoir), 330, 697, viii. 511, ix. 415, 416, 419, 603; Nichols's Lit. Illustr. i. 804, 819, iv. 441, vi. 612; Sale Catalogue of the Fountaine Collection (with memoir), 1884; Joseph Addison and Sir Andrew Fountaine, London, 1858; Notes and Queries, 2nd ser. v. 389; Burke's Hist. of the Commoners, 1837, i. 225, and his Landed Gentry, editions of 1868 and 1886, s. v. 'Fountaine;' Swift's Journal to Stella for the years 1710–12; Gent. Mag. 1753, xxiii. 445; Michaelis's Ancient Marbles in Great Britain pp. 46, 57, 522; Burke's Visitations of Seats and Arms, 2nd ser. i. 194; Hawkins's Medallic Illustrations, ed. Franks and Grueber; authorities cited above.] W. W.

FOUNTAINE, JOHN (1600–1671), judge, son of Arthur Fountaine of Dalling, Norfolk, by Anne, daughter of John Stanhow, was admitted a member of Lincoln's Inn on 30 Oct. 1622, and called to the bar on 21 June

1629. Wood is certainly wrong in identifying him with the John Fountaine who graduated B.A. at Oxford in 1634, and proceeded M.A. in 1637, who is much more likely to be the John Fountaine, M.A., who was rector of Woolston in Buckinghamshire in 1649 (BLOMEFIELD, *Norfolk*, iii. 522; WOOD, *Fasti Oxon.* i. 473; LIPSCOMB, *Buckinghamshire*, iv. 425). Fountaine distinguished himself in 1642 by refusing to pay the war tax levied by the parliament, and accordingly, pursuant to a resolution of the House of Commons, he was 'secured and disarmed,' and on 12 Oct. lodged in the Gatehouse. The death of his wife, which occurred about the same time, procured him four days' liberty. He was also on his own petition granted liberty (2 Nov.) to attend service in St. Margaret's Church, from which it is probable that he was a member of parliament. His name, however, is given neither by Browne Willis nor in the official list. He was still at the Gatehouse on 20 Dec. 1642, when his petition to be allowed bail was refused. He emerges into history again at Oxford in 1645. Here he was associated with Sir John Stawel in a scheme for uniting the freeholders of the western counties on the side of the king. The Prince of Wales was appointed general of the association, and went to Bristol to take command of the forces which the association were to raise. The scheme, however, came to nothing. Fountaine seems shortly afterwards to have perceived that the royalist cause was lost. On 11 April 1646 Colonel Rainsford, in command at Woodstock, reported to the parliament that 'Mr. Fountaine, the lawyer, was come in to him,' and was then at Aylesbury. The letter was read to the house on 25 April, and the house then resolved that Fountaine should be sent prisoner to Bristol. While at Aylesbury Fountaine had written to Dr. Samuel Turner a letter on the situation. It is a document of considerable interest, being marked by much sagacity. He begins by pointing out that the moderates were then in the ascendant while the king's cause was desperate, and advises the acceptance of 'such conditions of peace as may be had;' he then proceeds to argue at some length that episcopacy is not *jure divino*, and that the alienation of church lands by parliament is legally within the powers of parliament. The letter elicited a reply by Dr. Richard Stewart, entitled 'An Answer to a Letter written at Oxford [*sic*], and superscribed to Dr. Samuel Turner concerning the church and the revenue thereof' (for both letter and answer see *Brit. Mus. Cat.*, 'Turner, Samuel'). On 17 Jan. 1651–2 he was elected, though not without opposition, into the parliamentary committee for 'con-

sidering of the inconveniencies' of the law and how to remove them. On 17 March following he was formally pardoned his delinquency and restored to full status as a citizen (WHITELOCKE, *Mem.* 63, 202, 520; *Commons' Journal*, ii. 804, 832, 896, iv. 523, vii. 74, 268; CLARENDON, *Rebellion*, v. 85–7, 141). He paid a composition of 480*l.* for his estates (DRING, *Catalogue*). He was placed on a commission appointed by the council of state on 29 April 1653 to investigate the condition of the prison of the upper bench, and suggest regulations for its better management, and on a similar commission of 13 June following to 'consider about the inspecting and improving of the public offices.' On 27 Nov. 1658 he was called to the degree of serjeant-at-law, and on 3 June 1659 he was made joint commissioner with Bradshaw and Tyrell of the 'broad seal' for the term of five months. On 1 Nov. following the lord president, Bradshaw, delivered the seal to Whitelocke by order of the committee of public safety. It was, however, again put in commission, Fountaine being one of the commissioners on 17 Jan. 1659–60, and so continued until the Restoration. On that event Fountaine was confirmed in his status of serjeant-at-law (27 June 1660), but he never again held judicial office (*Cal. State Papers*, Dom. 1652–3, pp. 300, 405; *ib.* 1653–4, p. 61; NOBLE, *Cromwell*, i. 438; WHITELOCKE, *Mem.* pp. 680, 686, 693; LUDLOW, *Mem.* p. 282; SIDERFIN, *Rep.* i. 3). Fountaine survived until 1671, when he died on 14 June, after a year's illness. His chambers are said to have been at Boswell Court, Carey Street. He was buried in the parish church of Salle, Norfolk, the original seat of his family. Fountaine is called a turncoat by Anthony à Wood, and Foss follows suit; perhaps, however, it would be nearer the truth to describe him as a moderate and practical royalist. Burnet states that he was in favour of Cromwell's assuming the royal dignity on the ground that 'no government could be settled legally but by a king' (*Own Time*, fol. i. 68). After the death of his first wife Fountaine married Theodosia, daughter of Sir Edward Harrington of Ridlington, Norfolk, by whom he had issue John Fountayne of Lincoln's Inn, and Melton, Yorkshire (*d.* 1680), and Thomas Fountayne, who succeeded his brother at Melton, and died in 1709. John Fountayne, the elder son, had two daughters, of whom the second, Theodosia, married Robert Monckton, and was the mother of the first Viscount Galway. The grandson of the younger son, Thomas, was the Rev. John Fountayne, D.D. [q. v.], dean of York. The family is now represented in the direct line by Andrew Montagu of Melton Park,

Yorkshire, and Papplewick, Nottinghamshire.

[Foss's Lives of the Judges; Hunter's South Yorkshire, i. 367.] J. M. R.

FOUNTAINHALL, LORD (1646–1722), Scottish judge. [See LAUDER, SIR JOHN.]

FOUNTAINS, JOHN (*d.* 1225), bishop of Ely. [See FONTIBUS, JOHN DE.]

FOUNTAYNE, JOHN, D.D. (1714–1802), dean of York, born in 1714, second son of John Fountayne of Melton in South Yorkshire, by Elizabeth, daughter of Francis Carew of Beddington, Surrey, was great-grandson of John Fountaine, the judge [q. v.] He graduated B.A. at St. Catharine's Hall, Cambridge, in 1735, proceeded M.A. in 1739, being installed prebendary of Salisbury on 16 April of the same year. He was appointed by patent of 3 Jan. 1740–1 to a canonry of Windsor, which he resigned in 1748, having the previous year been appointed dean of York. He took the degree of D.D. in 1751. On the death of his elder brother in 1739 he succeeded to the manor of Melton. He closed a long and uneventful life at the deanery on 14 Feb. 1802. Fountayne married first, in 1744, Ann, daughter of William Bromley, speaker of the House of Commons; secondly, Frances Maria, daughter of Thomas Whichcote of Harpswell, Lincolnshire; and thirdly, in 1754, Ann, only daughter of Charles Montagu of Papplewick, Nottinghamshire. By his first wife he had no issue; by his second, who died on 22 Aug. 1750, he had one daughter only, viz. Frances Maria, who married, on 27 Feb. 1773, William Tatton of Withenshaw, Cheshire, who took the name of Egerton; by his third wife he had two sons, both of whom died unmarried, and three daughters, of whom the eldest and youngest died unmarried, and the second married Richard, second son of Dr. Christopher Wilson, bishop of Bristol. Fountayne published: 1. A sermon on the Lisbon earthquake, 1755. 2. A fast sermon, 1756.

[Hunter's South Yorkshire, i. 367; Le Neve's Fasti Eccl. Angl. ii. 670, iii. 408; Grad. Cant.; Gent. Mag. 1802, pt. i. p. 190; Britton's York Cathedral, p. 86; Ormerod's Cheshire, ed. Helsby, iii. 610.] J. M. R.

FOURDRINIER, HENRY (1766–1854), inventor, was born on 11 Feb. 1766, in Lombard Street, London. His father was a papermaker and wholesale stationer, and was in all probability grandson of Paul Fourdrinier [see under FOURDRINIER, PETER]. Henry Fourdrinier succeeded his father as a paper manufacturer. In conjunction with his brother Sealy he devoted himself for many years to the invention and improvement of paper-making machinery. Their first patent was taken out in 1801. In 1807 they perfected their machine for making continuous paper. This machine imitated with some improvements the processes used in paper by hand. Its chief advantages were that it produced paper of any size, and with greatly increased rapidity. The experiments were very costly, and much litigation was required to protect the patent. When the invention was completed they had expended 60,000*l.*, and became bankrupt. Parliament extended the Fourdriniers' letters patent for fourteen years, and the new system of paper-making was widely adopted, but the brothers were greatly hampered by the defective state of the law of patents. In 1814 the Emperor Alexander, while visiting England, was interested in Fourdriniers' machine. An agreement was made that the Fourdriniers should receive 700*l.* annually for the use of two machines for ten years. The machines were erected at Peterhoff under the superintendence of Henry Fourdrinier's son, but no portion of the stipulated yearly sum was ever paid. Henry Fourdrinier repeatedly asserted his claim, and at the age of seventy-two, attended by his daughter, made a journey to St. Petersburg, and placed his petition personally in the hands of the Emperor Nicholas. No result followed. Meanwhile the Fourdriniers had petitioned parliament for compensation for the losses sustained by them. On 25 April 1839 a motion was brought forward in the House of Commons, when the chancellor of the exchequer promised to go into the merits of the case. On 8 May 1840 7,000*l.* was voted to the Fourdriniers. Many persons thought this inadequate, and a few years later a subscription, raised by firms in the paper trade, enabled annuities to be purchased for Henry Fourdrinier, the then surviving patentee, and his two daughters, insuring a comfortable income during their respective lives. Henry Fourdrinier died on 3 Sept. 1854, in his eighty-ninth year, at Mavesyn Ridware, near Rugeley, where he spent the last years of his life in humble but cheerful retirement.

His brother, SEALY FOURDRINIER, participated in the parliamentary compensation, but died in 1847 before the subscription had been applied.

[Hansard, vols. xlvii. liii., 3rd ser.; Illustrated London News, 9 Sept. 1854; British and Colonial Printer and Stationer, September 1888.] J. B-y.

FOURDRINIER, PETER (*fl.* 1720–1750), engraver, a member of a French refugee family which fled from Caen to Holland, was a pupil of Bernard Picart at Amsterdam for six years, and came to England in 1720. He was employed in engraving portraits and book illustrations; among the former were the portraits of Cardinal Wolsey and Bishop Tonstall in Fiddes's 'Life of Wolsey,' John Radcliffe, M.D., after Kneller, William Pattison, poet, after J. Saunders, William Conolly, speaker of the House of Commons in Ireland, after Jervas, Jonathan Swift, after Jervas, Dr. John Freind, after M. Dahl, and Thomas Wright, after G. Allen. He was more frequently employed on architectural works, to which his mechanical style of engraving was well suited. He engraved plates for Cashel's 'Villas of the Ancients,' Ware's 'Views and Elevations of Houghton House, Norfolk,' Sir W. Chambers's 'Civil Architecture,' Wood's 'Ruins of Palmyra,' and others from the designs of Inigo Jones, W. Kent, and other architects. He also engraved 'The Four Ages of Man,' after Lancret, one of Lemprière's views of Belem, near Lisbon, before the earthquake, and the illustrations to Spenser's 'Calendarium Pastorale' (London, 1732, 8vo). He is perhaps identical with Pierre Fourdrinier, who married at Amsterdam in 1689 Marthe Theroude, and came to England. Other authorities mention a PAUL FOURDRINIER as engraver of some of the works mentioned, and he has been identified with Paul Fourdrinier who was of the parish of St. Martin's-in-the-Fields, and died in January or February 1758, leaving by his wife Susanna Grolleau a son Henry, whose daughter Jemima was the mother of Cardinal John Henry Newman. The engravings are in all cases signed 'P. Fourdrinier,' but the title-page of Chambers's 'Civil Architecture' says that the plates were engraved by 'Old Rooker, Old Fourdrinier, and others,' which points to there having probably been two engravers of the name.

[Redgrave's Dict. of Artists; Vertue's MSS. (Addit. MS. Brit. Mus. 23079); Dodd's manuscript History of English Engravers; Bromley's Engraved British Portraits; Lowndes's Bibl. Man.; information from H. Wagner, F.S.A.]

L. C.

FOURNIER, DANIEL (d. 1766?), engraver and draughtsman, was probably a member of a French refugee family, and originally educated as a chaser. He also practised the varying professions of 'à-la-mode beef-seller, shoemaker, and engraver,' according to the inscription on a small portrait of him etched by himself. He likewise dealt in butter and eggs, modelled in wax, and taught drawing. In 1761, at about the age of fifty, he wrote and published 'A Treatise of the Theory and Practice of Perspective,

wherein the Principles of that most Useful Art are Laid Down by Dr. Brook Taylor, are fully and clearly Explained by Means of Moveable Schemes properly Adapted for the Purpose,' &c. It is said that at the time he was writing it he used to draw the diagrams on the alehouse tables with chalk, and was known by the name of the 'Mad Geometer.' He was a good etcher, and etched a survey of the Leeward Islands. He also engraved in mezzotint a portrait of Cuthbert Mayne, a priest executed for heresy in 1579. In addition to these accomplishments he is said to have made a fiddle, and taught himself to play upon it. He died in Wild Court, Wild Street, about 1766.

[Redgrave's Dict. of Artists; Dodd's manuscript History of English Engravers; Grose's Olio; Chaloner Smith's British Mezzotinto Portraits.]

L. C.

FOWKE, FRANCIS (1823–1865), captain royal engineers, architect and engineer of the Science and Art Department, South Kensington, born at Ballysillan 7 July 1823, was educated at Dungannon College, and at a military tutor's at Woolwich; entered the Royal Military Academy, Woolwich, in 1839, and passed out sixth in a batch of sixteen in 1841. His proficiency in drawing secured his appointment to the royal engineers, in which he was commissioned as second lieutenant 18 June 1842. He married, 22 May 1845, Louisa Charlotte, daughter of the Rev. R. Rede Rede of Ashmans, Suffolk (*Gent. Mag.* new ser. xxiii. 538). He became first lieutenant 1 April 1846, and second captain 17 Feb. 1854. After serving some years at Bermuda, Fowke was employed at Devonport, where he prepared the working drawings for the new Raglan barracks, and is credited with originating the many sanitary improvements introduced there. About the period of the Russian war he brought under notice of the government numerous suggestions regarding the use of elongated projectiles for rifled ordnance, and later, a design for a collapsing canvas pontoon described in 'Professional Papers, Corps of Royal Engineers,' new ser. vii. 81, and 'Journal United Service Institution,' iv. (1860), none of which led to any results. In 1854 he was sent to Paris in charge of the machinery for the Paris Exhibition, and when the late Colonel H. Cunliffe Owen, royal engineers, was ordered to the Crimea, he was appointed secretary to the British commission in that officer's place. He carried out a series of valuable experiments on the strength of colonial woods, the results of which were published in the 'Parliamentary Reports of the Paris Exhibition,' and afterwards as a separate pamphlet, and are said, in Jamaica alone, to have raised the annual exports of lancewood spars fourfold, and of mahogany over eightfold (*Proc. Inst. Civil Engineers*, xxx. 469). He prepared the reports on 'Construction' and 'Naval Construction' in the exhibition reports. He was made a chevalier of the Legion of Honour, but was debarred by the rules of the British service from wearing the decoration, it not having been given for service in the field. A paper by him on 'Coast Defence Batteries' appeared in the 'Papers, Corps of Royal Engineers,' vol. v. (1856).

Fowke remained in Paris until 1857, and was there again in 1858. The international technical commission on improved navigation of the Danube which was sitting there had come to a deadlock. The British members had submitted all the papers to Sir John Fox Burgoyne [q. v.], inspector of fortifications, and Fowke was sent to present Burgoyne's conclusions. An independent report which Fowke made confidentially to Lord Cowley, the British ambassador, was printed privately. Meanwhile (1 April 1857) Fowke became an inspector for science and art in the Science and Art Department in London. In 1860 there was conferred on him in addition the office of architect and engineer, to which was added in 1862 (when he ceased to be inspector) that of superintendent of the construction of South Kensington Museum. In 1863 he was also made science referee of the Museum. On the removal of the department from Marlborough House to South Kensington, Fowke at once adapted (in the summer of 1857) the iron buildings originally erected by Sir William Cubitt, and popularly known as the 'Brompton Boilers,' and a nest of old residences adjoining, work which he executed with economy and despatch. In the midst of it he was called upon to build a picture-gallery for the Sheepshanks gift of pictures, one of the conditions of the bequest being that a suitable apartment should be provided by the nation within twelve months. In this work Fowke was associated with Mr. Redgrave, R.A., who had discovered a formula for a top-light gallery. The object sought—that the pictures should be seen without glare or reflection—was in most respects satisfactorily accomplished, and Fowke further devised arrangements for lighting them by gas, together with an ingenious contrivance, now in use, for lighting many hundred gas-burners at once. Before the work was finished the Vernon and Turner galleries were required, which Fowke erected with fireproof floors at very small cost.

As architect and engineer of the Science and Art Department, Fowke designed the new Museum of Science and Art, Edinburgh, and the improvements and enlargement of the Dublin National Gallery. He designed and erected the Officers' Library, Aldershot, which was executed at the private cost of the prince consort, and erected a drill shed for the 1st Middlesex volunteer engineers (the first engineer volunteer corps formed), which Sir Joseph Paxton pronounced to be the cheapest structure he had ever seen. He planned the buildings for the International Exhibition of 1862, in which the main feature was originally a noble hall, which was omitted altogether owing to want of funds. The lighting, ventilation, and general arrangement of the buildings were allowed to be a success; for their artistic shortcomings Fowke was not responsible. Subsequently Fowke prepared designs, which were not executed, for adapting the Exhibition buildings to permanent uses. In 1864 his design for the Natural History Museum at South Kensington won the first prize in a public competition, but he died before it could be executed, and finally Alfred Waterhouse's design was substituted. Plans which he left for the completion of the South Kensington (now Victoria and Albert) Museum were ultimately superseded by those of Sir Aston Webb. Fowke designed the main buildings at South Kensington of the Royal Horticultural Society (1861), which in 1887 were added to the Imperial Institute. Shortly before his death he designed the Royal Albert Hall, which was in its main features erected after his plans (1867–71). Fowke died at his official residence, South Kensington, 4 Dec. 1865, and was buried at Brompton cemetery. A bust of him, by Woolner, is in the South Kensington Museum.

Fowke was author of 'A Description of the Buildings at South Kensington for the Reception of the Sheepshanks Pictures,' London, 1858, 8vo, and 'Some Account of the Buildings designed for the International Exhibition of 1862,' London, 1861, 8vo. He wrote for the 'Cornhill Magazine' on 'National Gallery Difficulty Solved' (March 1860), and 'London, the Stronghold of England' (July 1860). Fowke was the inventor of a military fire-engine, made to limber up like a field gun, which is now in use in the service. On 31 May 1856 he patented a folding photographic camera; in carrying out instructions (11 June 1857) of the Science and Art Department to design a camera of larger size, he adapted to his purpose a principle of the concertina, on which he was a player, and thus invented the 'bellows' camera, which came into general use.

[Memoir by Sir H. Cole in Papers on Professional Subjects, Corps of Royal Engineers,

xv. 9; Proceedings Inst. Civil Engineers (London), xxx. 468–70; Athenæum, 1865, ii. 808.]

H. M. C.

FOWKE, JOHN (d. 1662), lord mayor, third son of William Fowke of Tewkesbury, Gloucestershire, by his wife, Alice Carr of Newcastle-under-Lyme, Staffordshire (*Visitation of London*, 1633–5, Harl. Soc. i. 288; STOW, *Survey*, ed. Strype, bk. v. p. 145), came to London, and eventually rose to be one of its leading merchants. He was a member of the Haberdashers' Company, and an alderman (ORRIDGE, *Citizens of London and their Rulers*, p. 236). In 1627 Fowke, in obedience to the vote and declaration of the commons against paying tonnage and poundage, persistently refused to pay, although 'a man of great trading at that time.' Accordingly he had 'currans, muscadels, grograms, mohairs, raw-silk, and other goods, seized to his prejudice of 5,827*l*.' In August 1627 and January 1628, for attempting to obtain legal redress, he was imprisoned and lost more merchandise. In the following February he was prosecuted by the Star-chamber for 'pretended riot and seditious words' used by him to the officers sent to execute the replevin. About the same time Charles openly expressed his displeasure against him at the council table, and shortly afterwards named him in a declaration printed and published in March 1628. In October 1629, on Fowke again refusing to pay the impost, an information was laid against him at the council, and 'great endeavours used to take away his life and estate upon false pretences of clipping of money and piracies.' After witnesses had been examined he was committed to the Fleet, 'without any cause expressed,' and his ship and cargo, with a prize of sugar, seized. All his endeavours to regain his liberty proved ineffectual, and, after spending a large sum on law costs, he was forced 'to give 40,000*l*. bail in the admiralty about the said prize.' In June 1641 he petitioned the commons for relief, as he had previously done in 1628, setting forth that he had then lost 20,000*l*. The house, by an order of 30 June 1645, nominated a committee to consider how he might have reparation out of delinquent's estates (*Commons' Journals*, vols. iv. vi. vii.) Fowke served the office of sheriff in 1643. He had naturally become a bitter opponent of the court party. Charles, in his answer to the city petition of 4 Jan. 1642–3, speaks of Fowke as one of the leaders of the parliamentary party in the city, and a person 'notoriously guilty of schism and high treason' (cf. also the King's Letter and Declaration to the City, 17 Jan. 1642–3, and the Speech of Pym, 13 Jan. 1642–3, in reply to Charles's Answer to the City Petition). In the ordinance of 29 March 1642–3 for assessing such as had not contributed according to the propositions of the parliament for raising money, Fowke was one of the persons empowered to nominate collectors in each ward. Having afterwards been appointed a commissioner of the customs, and refusing to deliver up an account upon oath of what money he had received, he was fined for this contempt 100*l*. by the committee of accompts, 18 April 1645, and in the end sent to the Fleet. Thereupon a deputation from the common council, headed by his friend William Gibbs, goldsmith, then sheriff, petitioned the commons on 23 July for his release on bail, praying besides that the house would appoint a committee to hear his cause; 'he being committed not upon the matter of his accompt, but upon the manner of his accompting.' After a 'serious and long' debate on 4 Aug. it was resolved that Fowke ought to 'accompt jointly with the rest of the late commissioners and collectors of the customs;' it was further ordered that he 'do accompt for the three hundred pounds and such other monies and goods for which he is accomptable' (*Commons' Journals*, vol. iv.) Despite these irregularities he appears to have retained his commissionership, for so late as July 1658 he was reported to have in his keeping 1,500*l*. of public money, which he refused to deliver up (cf. *Cal. State Papers, Dom.* 1658–9, pp. 58, 102). He was in fact treated by all factions, until the Restoration, with the greatest deference. By virtue of two decrees made by Lord-keeper Coventry, on 21 Nov. 1631 and 9 June 1635, the East India Company had detained Fowke's 'adventures in their hands, by him alleged to be sixteen hundred pounds in their second joint stock, and twenty-one hundred pounds more in three of their voyages.' Fowke therefore petitioned the lords, 8 July 1646, to have these decrees reversed. On 6 May 1647 judgment was given in his favour. He obtained full restitution, with interest, and 100*l*. costs (*Lords' Journals*, vols. viii. ix.) At a meeting of the common council for nominating a new committee for the militia of London, 27 April 1647, Fowke's name was ordered to be omitted from the list to be presented to parliament. However, on the following 12 June, upon a rumour of the army's near approach to London, he was asked to head a deputation to parliament to desire its approbation of the city's answer to Fairfax, and early next morning he set out along with his fellow-commissioners to carry it to the general at St. Albans. He was restored to the militia committee by an ordinance of both houses dated 23 July and 2 Sept. 1647. On 12 July 1648 Fowke presented to both houses a 'petition for peace in the name of divers well-affected magistrates, ministers, and other inhabitants in the city of London, and parts adjacent,' and delivered himself of a short speech. The petition, which with the speech was published, expressed a hope that the parliament might take a course to secure peace. When, a few weeks later, the army returned to London, ' some false brothers in the city,' says Lord Holles, ' as Alderman Foulks and Alderman Gibbs, bewitcht the city and lull'd it into a security' (*Memoirs*, 1699, pp. 110, 160). At the sale of bishops' lands Fowke acquired, 28 Sept. 1648, the Gloucestershire manors of Maysmore, Preston, Longford, and Ashleworth, the property of the sees of Gloucester and Bristol, for 3,819*l*. 14*s*. (*Collectanea Topographica et Genealogica*, i. 124). He was named one of the king's judges, but refused to attend. On 27 Feb. 1651 a parliamentary committee reported that compensation to the extent of 27,615*l*. ought to be awarded him (*Commons' Journals*, vii. 99–100). The matter was referred to a committee of the council of state, 9 Sept. 1652 (*ib*. vii. 177), who suggested, 25 Oct., that state lands in Waltham Forest, Essex, worth 500*l*. a year should be settled on him and his heirs for ever, ' according to his own propositions given into council' (*Cal. State Papers*, Dom. 1651–2, p. 455). This proposal, although backed up by innumerable petitions from Fowke, did not receive the assent of the council until 9 May 1654 (*ib*. 1654, p. 162). Elated by his success, Fowke now besought them to take his ' sufferings' into consideration. Finally, it was enacted, 4 Aug. 1654, that 5,000*l*. be assigned him from the fines set by the Act of Grace for Scotland, ' and if any part remained unpaid, it should be provided for some other way' (*ib*. 1654, p. 287). During 1652–3 Fowke served the office of lord mayor. In January 1653 he was acting as a commissioner for the sale of the king's goods (*Cal. of Clarendon State Papers*, ii. 171). Along with four other commissioners he was appointed, 10 March 1653–4, to consider ' how the business of the forests might be best improved for the benefit of the state,' and to draw up a report thereon (*Cal. State Papers*, Dom. 1654, pp. 19, 97). He was one of the committee chosen by the city to confer with Fleetwood, 9 Dec. 1659 (*Mercurius Politicus*, 8–15 Dec. 1659, p. 945). Three weeks later he laid before the court of common council a report which was printed on the ' imminent and extraordinary danger of the City.' When the city corporation agreed to send their thanks to Monck for his services, Fowke was one of the three commissioners appointed for that purpose, 19 Jan. 1659–60 (*ib*. 19–26 Jan. 1660, p. 1043). On 30 Jan. he reported to the lord mayor, in the name of the other commissioners, the effect of their journey (*ib*. 26 Jan. to 2 Feb. 1650, p. 1068). In March he appears as a commissioner for the City of London militia (*ib*. 8–15 March 1660, p. 1170). When the Restoration seemed inevitable, Fowke hastened to clear himself of all complicity in the king's death by issuing an advertisement (*ib*. 22–9 March 1660, p. 1199), denying that he was 'one of those persons that did actually sit as judges upon the tryal,' to which he appended a certificate to the like effect from Henry Scobell, clerk of the parliament, dated 28 March 1660. For a while he appears to have lived in retirement at his country seat at Clayberry, situated in the north-east side of Barking, near Woodford Bridge, Essex. He was, however, elected M.P. for the city of London on 19 March 1660–1, when he headed the poll (*Lists of Members of Parliament, Official Return*, pt. i. p. 525), and was chosen in the same year president of Christ's Hospital (TROLLOPE, *Hist. of Christ's Hospital*, p. 310), to which and to Bethlehem Hospital he proved a liberal benefactor. He bequeathed to the former institution certain estates in Essex for the maintenance of eight boys, of whom two were to be of the parish of Barking and two of Woodford (LYSONS, *Environs*, iv. 104, 286; TROLLOPE, p. 117, note). Under this bequest Clayberry was sold by his trustees in 1693 (LYSONS, iv. 85). Fowke's portrait, dated 1691, is at Christ's Hospital (TROLLOPE, p. 344). He died of apoplexy on 22 April 1662 (SMYTH, *Obituary*, Camden Soc., p. 55). By his wife Catherine, daughter of Richard Briggs of London, he had two sons, John and Bartholomew, and a daughter, Elizabeth.

[Wood's Athenæ Oxon. (Bliss), iii. 683; Noble's Lives of the English Regicides, i. 237–242; Rushworth's Historical Collections, pt. iv. vol. i. pp. 472, 558, 634, pt. iv. vol. ii. p. 797.]

G. G.

FOWKE, PHINEAS, M.D. (1638–1710), physician, son of Walter Fowke, M.D., was born at Bishop Burton, Yorkshire, and there baptised on 7 Jan. 1639. His mother was sister of Sir John Micklethwaite [q. v.], physician to Charles II and to St. Bartholomew's Hospital. He was admitted at Queens' College, Cambridge, 21 April 1654, and graduated B.A. 1658, and on 26 March in the same year was admitted a fellow of the college. His family connections directed him to the profession of medicine, and he graduated M.D. at Cambridge 1668. He practised in London, residing in Little Britain, and was admitted a fellow of the College of Physicians 12 Nov. 1680. In 1684 he married Sarah, daughter of Sir Vincent Corbet, bart., at Shrewsbury. She died 6 Dec. 1686. He retired to his paternal estate in Shropshire, and there died at Little Worley Hall 21 Jan. 1710. He was buried in the neighbouring church of Brewood, and his death is recorded on his wife's monument in St. Chad's Church, Shrewsbury. He was learned in theology as well as in medicine, and was an admirer of Dr. Seth Ward, bishop of Sarum, whose views on passive obedience he warmly supported. In some manuscript notes on a sermon of Ward's, on the text 'And they that resist shall receive to themselves damnation,' Fowke expresses his contempt of the conduct of the university of Oxford in 1688, saying, 'These great pretenders to loyalty invited ye Prince of Orange. They had no patience when King James bore upon their priviledges in Oxford, but exclamed bitterly against ye king and joyned with the wiggs and dissenters to bring in ye Prince of Orange.' Among the Sloane manuscripts in the British Museum there is a private letter of Fowkes.

[Munk's Coll. of Phys. i. 417; Original Lists Coll. of Phys. of London; Seven Sermons, by Seth Ward, Bishop of Sarum, 1674, annotated in manuscript by Ph. Fowke, M.D., C.R.C.S.]

N. M.

FOWLER, ABRAHAM (*fl.* 1577), poet, was a queen's scholar at Westminster, whence he was elected to Christ Church, Oxford, in 1568. His name does not appear on the university register. He contributed a poem in alternate rhymes to 'A Philosophicall discussion entituled The Anatomie of the Minde newlie made and set forth by T[homas] R[ogers],' London, 1576. Rogers [q. v.] was a student of Christ Church. Fowler's verse is followed by a poem by Camden.

[Welch's Alumni Westmonast. p. 47; Wood's Athenæ Oxon. (Bliss), ii. 163; Brydges's Censura Literaria, vi. 33.] S. L.

FOWLER, CHRISTOPHER (1610 ?–1678), ejected minister, son of John Fowler, was born at Marlborough, Wiltshire, about 1610. He entered Magdalen College, Oxford, as a servitor in 1627, and graduated B.A. on 9 Feb. 1632. Removing to St. Edmund Hall, he graduated M.A. on 29 Oct. 1634. To John Prideaux, regius professor of divinity, he owed his strong attachment to the Calvinistic theology. He took holy orders, and was a puritan preacher in and about Oxford till he obtained a settlement at West Woodhay, Berkshire, before 1641. On the

surrender of Reading (26 April 1643), Thomas Bunbury, vicar of St. Mary's, joined the king at Oxford; his living was sequestered and given to Fowler. He took the covenant (1643), and distinguished himself by his zeal for the presbyterian cause. Thinking himself unsafe in the neighbourhood of the royalist troops at the manor-house of Donnington, Berkshire, garrisoned for the king at the time of the second battle of Newbury (27 Oct. 1644), Fowler went up to London. Here his fanatical preaching attracted a crowd of hearers. Wood suggests that he was at this time preacher at St. Margaret's, Lothbury; it seems, however, that he obtained an appointment at Albourn, Sussex (*Funeral Sermon*); the engagement at St. Margaret's belongs to a later date; his name first occurs in the registers in 1652. In 1649 Fowler refused to take the 'engagement' to be faithful to the Commonwealth without king or House of Lords. Notwithstanding this disqualification, he was subsequently made fellow of Eton College.

Fowler was an assistant to the commissioners for Berkshire, appointed under the ordinance of 28 Aug. 1654, for ejecting scandalous ministers. In this capacity he was mixed up with the proceedings against a noted mystic and astrologer, John Pordage [q. v.], formerly of St. Lawrence's, Reading, whom the commissioners ejected (by order 8 Dec. 1654, to take effect 2 Feb. 1655) from the rectory of Bradfield, Berkshire. Fowler wrote an account and defence of this business, in which he and John Tickel, presbyterian minister at Abingdon, Berkshire, had taken a leading part. Somewhat later he entered the lists against the quakers. In conjunction with Simon Ford [q. v.], vicar of St. Lawrence's, Reading, he published (1656) an answer to the 'quaking doctrines' of Thomas Speed of Bristol, and he engaged in a controversy (1659) with Edward Burrough [q. v.]

On the restoration of the monarchy Fowler lost his fellowship at Eton, but retained the Reading vicarage till he was ejected by the Uniformity Act of 1662. He then moved to London, had his abode successively at Kennington and Southwark, and exercised his ministry in private. He had a turn for the explication of prophecy, wherein he displayed 'a singular gift in chronology.' According to Wood, he was 'esteemed a little better than crazed or distracted for some time before his death.' It is possible that his powers failed, but of his general ability a high estimate is given by William Cooper [q. v.], no mean judge. A warrant was out for his apprehension as a conventicle preacher at the time of his death. He died in Southwark on [15 ?] January 1678, and was buried within the precincts of St. John the Baptist, Dowgate Hill. Cooper preached his funeral sermon.

He published: 1. 'Dæmonium Meridianum,' &c., 1655, 4to (an account of the proceedings against Pordage, who had already published his own account, 1654, 4to; with appendix in reply to Pordage's 'Innocency Appearing,' 1655, fol.) 2. 'Dæmonium Meridianum. The Second Part,' &c., 1656, 4to (in reply to Pordage's 'Truth Appearing,' 1655, 4to, and a tract entitled 'The Case of Reading,' 1656, 4to; appendices on infant baptism in answer to John Pendarves, and on the Reading case addressed to the municipal authorities). 3. 'A Sober Answer to an angry Epistle . . . by Thomas Speed,' &c., 1656, 4to (by Fowler and Ford; Speed replied to these and another adversary in 'The Guilty-Covered Clergyman,' &c., 1657, 4to). 4. 'A True Charge in Ten Particulars against the people called Quakers' [1659] (does not seem to have been separately printed; it is handled in 'A Discovery,' &c., 1659, 4to, by Edward Burrough, and is reprinted in Burrough's 'Works,' 1672, fol. 5. 'Sermon on John xix. 42,' 1666, 4to (this is mentioned by Wood, but not seen by him; the date seems to show that Fowler was one of those nonconformists who resumed their ministry after the great fire in defiance of the law, and it may give some colour to the conjecture that he founded the presbyterian congregation which met in a wooden structure at Unicorn Yard, Tooley Street). Also a sermon in the 'Morning Exercise at Cripplegate,' 1674–6, 4to, and another in the 'Morning Exercise against Popery preached in Southwark,' 1675, 4to.

[Funeral Sermon by Cooper, 1677 (i.e. 1678); Wood's Athenæ Oxon. 1691 i. 870, 1692 ii. 449 sq., 728; Calamy's Account, 1713, p. 97 sq.; Palmer's Nonconf. Memorial, 1802, i. 294 sq. (misprints the date of death, 1676, an error which has been followed by later writers); Chalmers's Gen. Biog. Dict. 1814, xv. 14 sq.; Wilson's Diss. Churches, 1814, iv. 228; Smith's Biblioth. Anti-Quak., 1873, p. 189 sq.; Fowler's Dæmonium]
A. G.

FOWLER, EDWARD, D.D. (1632–1714), bishop of Gloucester, was born in 1632 at Westerleigh, Gloucestershire. His father, Richard Fowler, whom Calamy describes as a man of great ability, was ejected as a nonconformist in 1662 from the perpetual curacy of Westerleigh. At the same time the bishop's elder brother, Stephen Fowler, B.A., was ejected from a fellowship at St. John's, Cambridge, and from the rectory of Crick, Northamptonshire. He became presbyterian minister at Newbury, Berkshire, in 1684, and died soon after. Edward Fowler was educated at the college school in Gloucester

under William Russell, who had married his sister. At the beginning of 1650 he was admitted a clerk of Corpus Christi College, Oxford, and became a chaplain on 14 Dec. 1653, having a gift of extemporary prayer. He graduated B.A. on 23 Dec. 1653. After this he became a member of Trinity College, Cambridge, and graduated M.A. about 1655. Returning to Oxford, he was incorporated M.A. on 5 July 1656.

Fowler's first post on leaving the university was that of presbyterian chaplain to Amabella, dowager countess of Kent. Through the influence of his patroness he obtained in 1656 the rectory of Norhill, Bedfordshire, a donative in the gift of the Grocers' Company. On the passing of the Uniformity Act (1662), he was inclined to cast in his lot with his father and brother; he appears to have been nonresident till after 1664, though this was contrary to the terms of the donative; subsequently he conformed, and retained his rectory. He did not forfeit the respect of nonconformists; Calamy speaks of him as 'a very worthy man.' His theology was of the Baxterian type, a mean between Calvinism and Arminianism. He accepted the articles in Ussher's sense, as 'instruments of peace,' and deplored the combative zeal alike of the high churchman and the puritan. In 1670 he presented his views, without giving his name, in a 'Free Discourse,' an animated, if somewhat rambling dialogue between Philalethes and Theophilus. This piece is avowedly a defence of the latitudinarian divines, though Fowler never belonged to the inner circle of the Cambridge men of that school. It was followed next year by his 'Design of Christianity,' dedicated to Sheldon, in which the authorship of the 'Free Discourse' is admitted, and stress is laid on the moral purpose of revelation. Baxter criticised the argument ('How far Holiness is the Design of Christianity,' 1671, 4to); while Bunyan vehemently assailed the author from Bedford gaol ('Defence of the Doctrine of Justification by Faith,' 1672, 4to). An undignified retort ('Dirt Wip'd Off') is with too much reason connected with Fowler, nor is the matter mended by the suggestion that for some of his vocabulary of abuse he may have been indebted to his curate. Bunyan described the 'Design' as a mixture of 'popery, socinianism, and quakerism;' on the other hand Joseph Smith includes the book in his 'Bibliotheca Anti-Quakeriana,' though he admits that the reference to Friends is 'very slight.'

Fowler's 'Discourse' and 'Design' commended him to Sheldon, who brought him to London as rector of Allhallows, Bread Street.

He was collated to the living on 25 Aug. 1673; whether he then resigned Norhill is not certain. As a London preacher he became intimate with Thomas Firmin [q.v.], who subsequently circulated among his workers large editions of a 'Scripture Catechism,' which is believed to have been drawn up by Fowler. He was installed in the fourth prebend in Gloucester Cathedral on 29 Feb. 1676. In 1680 he published his ' Libertas Evangelica,' a sequel to his 'Design.' Next year, resigning other cure of souls, he was instituted (31 March) to the vicarage of St. Giles, Cripplegate. On 10 June 1681 he accumulated the degrees of B.D. and D.D. at Oxford. Two years later he began to write against popery (already attacked with some vigour in his 'Design'), pursuing the topic with so much eagerness as to give offence in high quarters under James II. At the instance of some parishioners, who considered him 'guilty of whigism,' he was prosecuted in the court of arches for uncanonical practices, such as admitting excommunicated persons without absolution, and was suspended on 9 Dec. 1685. When the London clergy met to consider whether they should read James's declaration for liberty of conscience (11 April 1687), Fowler delivered a manly speech, described by Macaulay, which converted the whole meeting to the views of a small but resolute minority. Patrick was the first and Fowler the second to subscribe a general pledge against reading the declaration. Upon the revolution of 1688–9, Fowler thought the time come for the consolidation of the protestant interest by a comprehension of the dissenters. As a member of the royal commission of thirty divines (appointed 13 Sept. 1689) for revising the prayer-book, Fowler proposed that the use of the Athanasian Creed be left optional. The whole scheme was dropped lest any change should strengthen the cause of the nonjuring schism. After the execution (28 Jan. 1691) of John Ashton [q. v.], the Jacobite conspirator, a 'Paper' which he had produced at the gallows was published, and made a great impression. Fowler immediately prepared and printed (though without his name) an 'Answer' to its political argument. His reward was his elevation to the bishopric of Gloucester. On 1 Feb. 1691 Robert Frampton [q. v.] was deprived as a nonjuror; Fowler was nominated on 23 April, elected 2 July, and consecrated 5 July 1691. He still held *in commendam* his London vicarage, and continued to preach at St. Giles's till age incapacitated him. It seems that for twenty-five years, from 1683, he provided a lecturer at his own cost, and in consideration of this the vestry

in 1701 repaired the chancel. In 1708, when he 'could no longer preach in a morning,' the vestry at his request, he 'having a large family and but small profits from the vicarage,' undertook to provide a lecturer. His episcopate was a quiet one ; the non-jurors in his diocese were few, and Frampton did nothing to encourage a schism. Fowler took little part as a bishop in public affairs. After the attack on nonconformist academies as political seminaries (made in the dedications to the second and third volumes of Clarendon's ' History,' 1703–4), he and Williams, bishop of Chichester, endeavoured to get the dissenters to put forth a declaration disclaiming antimonarchical principles. On the advice of Lord Somers the suggestion was not entertained.

Fowler's speculations on the Trinity belong to the later period of his life, and may be traced to his desire to satisfy the objections of Firmin. In his 'Twenty-eight Propositions' he to some extent anticipated Clarke, attempting, with the aid of patristic authority, to strike a line between the errors of Arianism and the later developments of dogmatic orthodoxy. His patristic learning was not deep ; and the Socinians, who felt themselves challenged, admitted his reasonableness, but thought his argument halted. He attended Firmin on his deathbed, receiving from him a confession of faith which he accepted as adequate. Fowler had little tincture of the platonism characteristic of the Cambridge men whom he admired. He kept up a correspondence with Henry More, supplying him between 1678 and 1681 with ghost stories, as the empirical basis of a spiritual philosophy. From More he borrowed a doctrine of the pre-existence of our Lord's human soul, urging it with some vehemence in a special 'Discourse' (1706). The opinion was 'examined' by William Sherlock, 'vindicated' by Thomas Emlyn [q. v.], and espoused at a later date by Watts and Doddridge.

Fowler survived Frampton over six years, dying at Chelsea on 26 Aug. 1714. He was buried in the churchyard of Hendon, Middlesex; in 1717 his remains were removed to a vault in the same churchyard ; a monument to his memory is erected in the chancel of the church. He married, first, Ann (*d.* 19 Dec. 1696), daughter of Arthur Barnardiston, master in chancery; and secondly, Elizabeth (*d.* 2 April 1732), daughter of Ralph Trevor, a London merchant, and widow of Hezekiah Burton, D.D. [q. v.] By his first wife he had three sons and five daughters, of whom Edward and Richard and three daughters survived him.

He published : 1. 'The Principles and

Practices of certain Moderate Divines . . . called Latitudinarians . . . in a Free Discourse,' &c., 1670, 8vo (anon.) ; 1671, 8vo ; 1679, 8vo. 2. 'The Design of Christianity,' &c., 1671, 8vo ; 1676, 8vo ; 1699, 8vo ; 1760, 8vo (reprinted in vol. vi. of Bishop Watson's 'Collection of Theological Tracts,' Cambr. 1785, 8vo). 3. 'Dirt Wip'd Off: or, a Manifest Discovery of the . . . Wicked Spirit of one John Bunyan,' &c., 1672, 4to. 4. 'Libertas Evangelica . . . a further pursuance of The Design of Christianity,' &c., 1680, 8vo. 5. 'The Resolution of this Case of Conscience, whether the Church of England, symbolising . . . with . . . Rome, makes it lawful to hold Communion with the Church of England,' &c., 1683, 4to. 6. 'A Defence of the Resolution . . . in answer to A Modest Examination,' &c., 1684, 4to. 7. 'The Great Wickedness . . . of Slandering,' &c., 1685, 4to (sermon at St. Giles's, 15 Nov., with vindicatory preface and appendix). 8. 'An Examination of Cardinal Bellarmine's Fourth Note of the Church,' &c., 1687, 4to. 9. 'The Texts which Papists cite . . . for the proof of . . . the obscurity of the Holy Scriptures,' &c., 1687, 4to ; 1688, 4to (Nos. 8 and 9 are reprinted in Bishop Gibson's 'Preservative against Popery,' 1689, 3 vols. fol., several times reprinted, the latest edition being 1848–1849, 18 vols. 8vo). 10. 'An Answer to the Paper delivered by Mr. Ashton at his Execution,' 1690 [i.e. 1691], 4to (anon.) 11. 'Twenty-eight Propositions, by which the Doctrine of the Trinity is endeavoured to be explained,' 1693, 4to (anon.) (WALLACE). 12. 'Certain Propositions, by which the Doctrin of the H. Trinity is so explain'd,' &c., 1694, 4to (anon. ; a reissue of No. 11, with a 'Defence' against 'Considerations,' 1694, 4to, probably by Stephen Nye); 1719, 8vo. 13. 'A Second Defence of the Propositions . . . with a Third Defence,' &c., 1695, 4to (the 'Second Defence' is in reply to 'a Socinian MS.,' which seems to have been submitted to Fowler by Firmin; the 'Third Defence' is in reply to 'A Letter to the Reverend the Clergy,' 1694, 4to; [see FRANKLAND, RICHARD]). 14. 'A Discourse of the Descent of the Man, Christ Jesus, from Heaven,' &c., 1706, 8vo. 15. 'Reflections upon the late Examination of the Discourse of the Descent,' &c., 1706, 8vo. Also fourteen separate sermons (1681–1707) and a charge (1710).

[Calamy's Account, 1713, pp. 90, 95, 330, 494; Continuation, 1727, pp. 128, 506, 639; Own Life, 1830, i. 63, ii. 305; Wood's Athenæ Oxon. 1692, ii. 780, 790, 888; Wood's Athenæ Oxon. (Tanner), 1721, ii. 1029; Biog. Brit. 1750, iii. 2012 (article by C., i.e. Philip Morant); Glanvill's Sadducismus Triumphatus, 1681, ii. 230 sq.;

Barrington's Letter of Advice to Protestant Dissenters, 1720, p. 18; Emlyn's Works, 1746, i. 361 sq.; Birch's Life of Tillotson, 1753, p. 294; Watt's Bibliotheca Britannica, 1824; Chalmers's Gen. Biog. Dict. 1814, xv. 16 sq.; Cardwell's Hist. of Conferences, 1841, p. 411 sq.; Lathbury's Hist. of Nonjurors, 1845, p. 78 sq.; Macaulay's Hist. of Engl. 1848, ii. 349; Wallace's Antitrinitarian Biog. 1850, i. 280 sq., 323 sq.; Hunt's Rel. Thought in Engl. 1871, ii. 38, &c.; Tulloch's Rational Theol. 1872, ii. 35 sq., 437 sq.; Smith's Bibliotheca Anti-Quakeriana, 1873, p. 190; Evans's Life of Bishop Frampton, 1876, p. 219; information from the Rev. F. Pott, rector of Norhill.]
A. G.

FOWLER, HENRY (1779–1838), hymnwriter, was born at Yealmpton, Devonshire, 11 Dec. 1779. In early life he followed some trade, but occasionally preached in independent meeting-houses in Devonshire and at Bristol. At length, in October 1813, he 'received a call' to Birmingham, where he continued until the end of 1819. Ultimately he settled in London, becoming in July 1820 minister of Gower Street Chapel. He died 16 Dec. 1838, and was buried on Christmas-day morning at the New Bunhill Fields burying-ground at Islington. As 'a close, searching preacher,' Fowler had for some years an excellent congregation, and a tolerable one to the close of his life. 'His discourses were delivered chiefly in short, pithy sentences.' It has been said that his own frame of mind seemed, in general, rather gloomy; certainly his autobiography, which he called 'Travels in the Wilderness,' 8vo, London, 1839, is not cheerful reading. In addition to this and numerous religious tracts and biographies, he wrote 'Original Hymns, Doctrinal, Practical, and Experimental, with prose reflections,' 2 vols. 18mo, Birmingham, London, 1818–1824, and edited 'A Selection of Hymns, by various authors,' 18mo, London, 1836. His portrait has been engraved by R. Cooper.

[Fowler's Autobiography; John Dixon's Autobiography, pp. 9–10.]
G. G.

FOWLER, JOHN (1537–1579), catholic printer and scholar, born at Bristol in 1537, was admitted in 1551 to Winchester School, whence he proceeded to Oxford, and was a fellow of New College in that university from 4 Oct. 1553 to 1559. He was admitted B.A. 23 Feb. 1556–7, and took the degree of M.A. in 1560, though he did not complete it by standing in the comitia. Dr. George Acworth [q. v.], in his reply to Sanders, asserts that Fowler, in the first year of Elizabeth's reign, took the oath renouncing the pope's supremacy, in order that he might retain the valuable living of Wonston, Hampshire, **to**

which he had been instituted (*De visibili Romanarchiâ*, pp. 33, 34). However this may be, he left England in consequence of the changes of religion soon after the queen's accession and retired to Louvain, where he set up a printing press, which he afterwards removed to Antwerp, and finally to Douay. He printed and published several important works written by the exiled clergy, in support of the catholic cause. Henry Simpson, in his examination at York on 11 Oct. 1571, stated that Fowler printed all the English books at Louvain, written by Harding or others, and that the Duke of Alva's printer in Brussels produced all the Latin works which were written against the doings in England. He added that William Smith, a Welshman, servant to Dr. Harding, commonly brought the books to the press (*Cal. of State Papers*, Dom. Eliz. 1566–79, p. 365). Wood says 'he was well skill'd in the Greek and Latin tongues, a tolerable poet and orator, and a theologian not to be contemn'd. So learned he was also in criticisms, and other polite learning, that he might have passed for another Robert or Henry Stephens' (*Athenæ Oxon.* ed. Bliss, i. 441). Dr. (afterwards Cardinal) Allen calls him 'catholicissimus et doctissimus librorum impressor,' in a letter addressed from Rheims in 1583 to Father Alphonsus Agazzari, rector of the English seminary at Rome, asking his interest in favour of Fowler's brother Henry, then in necessitous circumstances in that city (*Records of the English Catholics*, ii. 216). Fowler married Alice, daughter of John Harris, formerly secretary to Sir Thomas More, and died at Namur on 13 Feb. 1578–9, being buried near the body of his father-in-law, in the church of St. John the Evangelist (PITS, *De Angliæ Scriptoribus*, p. 772). His widow lived afterwards at Douay, where she entertained several of the English exiles as boarders (DODD, *Church Hist.* i. 532).

His works are: 1. 'An Oration against the unlawful Insurrections of the Protestantes of our Time under pretence to reforme Religion,' translated from the Latin of Peter Frarinus, Antwerp, 1566, 8vo. A reply by Dr. William Fulke appeared under the title of 'An apologie of the professors of the Gospel in Fraunce against the railing declamation of Peter Frarine, a Louvanian, turned into English by John Fowler,' was afterwards printed with William Clarke's 'Treatise against the Defense of the Censure,' Cambridge, 1586, 8vo. 2. 'Ex Universa Summa . . . S. Thomæ Aquinatis desumptæ Conclusiones,' Louvain, 1570, 8vo; Venice, 1572, 8vo, dedicated to Goldwell, the exiled bishop of St. Asaph. 3. 'M. Maruli Dictorum factorumque memo-

rabilium libri sex,' edited with numerous corrections by Fowler, Antwerp, 1577, 8vo; Paris, 1586, 8vo. 4. Additiones in Chronica Genebrandi, 1578. 5. 'A Psalter for Catholics,' a controversial work, which elicited from Thomas Sampson, dean of Christ Church, 'A Warning to take heed of Fowler's Psalter,' Lond. 1578, 8vo (STRYPE, *Annals*, i. 476, Append. p. 159, fol.) 6. Epigrams and other verses.

He also edited Sir Thomas More's 'Dialogue of Comfort against Tribulation,' Antwerp, 1573, 8vo. Wood ascribes to him the English version of the 'Epistle of Orosius' (Antwerp, 1565), but the title-page shows that the translation was really made by Richard Shacklock.

[Ames's Typogr. Antiq. (Herbert), iii. 1617, 1618, 1619, 1620, 1622, 1626, 1635, 1836; Tanner's Bibl. Brit. p. 294; Gillow's Bibl. Dict.; Boase's Register of the Univ. of Oxford, i. 354; Kirby's Winchester Scholars, p. 130; Lansd. MS. 96, art. 51; Fulke's Defence of the Translations of the Scriptures (Hartshorne), p. x; Fulke's Stapleton's Fortress Overthrown (Gibbings), pp. 3, 215.] T. C.

FOWLER, JOHN (1826–1864), inventor of the steam plough, was born at Melksham, Wiltshire, 11 July 1826. He was at first engaged in the corn trade, but in 1847 entered the works of Gilke, Wilson, & Co. at Middlesborough. While in Ireland in 1849 he became impressed by the necessity of draining waste lands, and conceived the idea of a mechanical system. In 1850 he conducted experiments with Albert Fry at Bristol, which resulted in the completion of the drain plough, which was first worked by horses. He then undertook a contract for the drainage of Hainault Forest, Essex, and there introduced his patent drainage plough. Finding, however, that the application of steam to the cultivation of the soil was yet a desideratum, he henceforth applied all his energies to supply that want. Some of his experimental appliances were made by Ransome & Sims at Ipswich in 1856, others by George and Robert Stephenson at Newcastle. He was afterwards introduced by his father-in-law to Jeremiah Head, and working with that gentleman, they succeeded in producing at Stephenson's works a plough which fulfilled all the conditions laid down by the Royal Agricultural Society, and received at the Chester show in 1858 the prize of 500*l*. offered 'for a steam cultivator that shall, in the most efficient manner, turn over the soil and be an economic substitute for the plough or the spade.' In this invention, discarding the idea of using a locomotive digger, a stationary engine was employed, which moved the plough up and down the field by means of ropes attached to a drum. By its use a great saving was effected in the cost of labour, and the soil was left in a better state for all purposes of husbandry. In 1860 Fowler made further improvements by bringing out his double engine tackle, the invention of which has given a great impetus to steam cultivation not only in Great Britain but also on the continent, and in the cotton districts of Egypt. The cost of one of these machines being upwards of 2,000*l.*, their use could not become general, but by a system of lending the ploughs and charging so much a week for the loan, they at last came into greater demand. In 1860, in conjunction with Mr. Kitson and Mr. Hewitson, he established extensive manufacturing works at Hunslet, Leeds, where in 1864 nine hundred hands were employed. Between 1850 and 1864 he took out himself, and in partnership with other persons, thirty-two patents for ploughs and ploughing apparatus, reaping machines, seed drills, horseshoes, traction engines, slide valves, laying electric telegraph cables, and making bricks and tiles. The mental strain to which Fowler had been subject had wrought his brain into a state of undue activity, and he now retired to Ackworth, Yorkshire, for repose. Being recommended active exercise, he began to hunt, and in November 1864 fractured his arm by falling from his horse; tetanus ensued, from the effect of which he died at Ackworth 4 Dec. 1864. He married, 30 July 1857, Elizabeth Lucy, ninth child of Joseph Pease, M.P. for South Durham, by whom he left five children.

[Leeds Mercury, 6, 9, and 16 July, and 7 Dec. 1864 ; Taylor's Biographia Leodiensis, 1865, pp. 525–8, 672 ; Practical Mag. 1875, v. 257–62, with portrait ; Gent. Mag. January 1865, p. 123 ; Proceedings of the Institution of Mechanical Engineers, 1865. p. 14 ; Journal of Royal Agricultural Soc. 1854–63, vols. xv–xxiv. ; Transactions of the Soc. of Engineers for 1868, pp. 299–318.]

G. C. B.

FOWLER, RICHARD (1765–1863), physician, was born in London 28 Nov. 1765, and, though he lived to a greater age than any other member of the College of Physicians, was of feeble health when a child. He was educated at Edinburgh and studied medicine there, but while a student visited Paris in the times before the revolution. Returning to Edinburgh in 1790 he continued his medical studies, and graduated M.D. 12 Sept. 1793 with a dissertation 'De Inflammatione.' He was also a member of the celebrated 'Speculative Society,' to which he contributed essays. He was admitted licentiate of the College of Physicians of London

21 March 1796, and settled in practice at Salisbury, where he passed the remainder of his life. He was at once elected physician to the Salisbury Infirmary, and held the office till 1847. He was elected F.R.S. in 1802, and often took part in the meetings of the British Association, to attend which and to read a paper there he made the journey from Salisbury to Aberdeen in 1859, when close upon ninety-four years of age. He was successful in practice, and occupied a leading position in Salisbury for many years. He died 13 April 1863 at Milford, near Salisbury, in his ninety-eighth year, an age reached by very few persons in the annals of medicine.

Fowler always kept up an interest in science, without producing any notable original work. When a student in Edinburgh, after his return from Paris, he was interested in the recent discoveries of Galvani on the form of electricity called by his name, and made numerous experiments on the subject, which were published in a small volume entitled 'Experiments and Observations on the Influence lately discovered by M. Galvani, and commonly called Animal Electricity,' 8vo, Edinburgh, 1793. It contains, also, observations on the action of opium on nerves and muscles. Many years after Fowler published two small books on the psychology of persons in whom the senses are defective, viz. 'Observations on the Mental State of the Blind and Deaf and Dumb,' 12mo, Salisbury, 1843 ; 2nd edit. 1860 ; and 'The Physiological Processes of Thinking, especially in Persons whose Organs of Sense are Defective,' 12mo, Salisbury, 1849 ; 2nd edit. 1852. These works show some reading, and contain interesting observations, but are wanting in lucidity and in philosophical method. He also wrote 'On Literary and Scientific Pursuits as conducive to Longevity,' Salisbury, 1855, 12mo. Fowler appears to have written nothing on purely medical subjects, but contributed memoirs to the 'Proceedings of the British Association,' some of which were published separately.

[Salisbury and Winchester Journal, 18 April 1863 (original memoir) ; Lancet, 25 April 1863 ; Munk's Coll. of Phys. 1878, ii. 447.]   J. F. P.

FOWLER, ROBERT (1726?–1801), archbishop of Dublin and chancellor of the order of St. Patrick, third son of George Fowler of Skendleby Thorpe, Lincolnshire, by Mary, daughter and coheiress of Robert Hurst, was a king's scholar at Westminster School in 1744. Thence he went to Trinity College, Cambridge, and graduated B.A. 1747, M.A. 1751, and D.D. 1764. In 1756 he was appointed chaplain to George II, and in January 1765 became prebendary of Westminster. He was promoted from his prebend to the bishopric of Killaloe and Kilfenora by patent dated 29 June 1771, and on 8 Jan. 1779 was translated to the archbishopric of Dublin, with a seat in the Irish privy council. While he held the bishopric of Killaloe he caused the present see-house to be erected. Philip Skelton [q. v.] has spoken of him in terms of high respect for his great regard for religion, as well as for his kindness and affability, not, however, unattended by warmth of temper—an ordinary 'concomitant of good nature;' and he has noticed as unrivalled his solemnity of manner in reading the services of the church (BURDY, *Life of Skelton*, 1792, p. 183). John Wesley makes a similar remark (*Journal*, xx. 14). In 1782, as a member of the Irish House of Lords, Fowler was one of twelve spiritual peers who protested against the bill for the relief of dissenters, as likely to promote clandestine and improvident marriages. In 1789 he concurred with fourteen other peers in protesting against the memorable address to the Prince of Wales (*Lords' Journals*, vi. 243). He also joined in protesting against the resolution condemning the answer of the lord-lieutenant refusing to transmit the address. He married, in 1766, Mildred, eldest daughter of William Dealtry of Gainsborough, Lincolnshire, and coheiress of her brother, William Dealtry of Ashby in the same county, and had an only son, Robert, who was promoted to the bishopric of Ossory in 1813, and two daughters, Mary, countess of Kilkenny, and Frances, who married the Hon. and Rev. Richard Bourke (subsequently bishop of Waterford and Lismore), and was mother of Robert, fifth earl of Mayo. Fowler died suddenly at Bassingbourne Hall, near Dunmow, Essex, where he had resided two years for his health, on 10 Oct. 1801.

[Graduati Cantabr.; Cotton's Fasti Ecclesiæ Hibernicæ, i. 471, ii. 27; Mant's Hist. of Church of Ireland, ii. 648, 660; Cooke's Diocesan Hist. of Killaloe, &c. p. 62; D'Alton's Memoirs of Archbishops of Dublin, p. 347; Gent. Mag. 1801, lxxi. pt. ii. 965, 1049; Ann. Reg. 1801, xliii. Chron.74; Burke's Landed Gentry, 3rd ed. p. 409.] B. H. B.

FOWLER, **WILLIAM** (*fl.* 1603), Scottish poet, son of Thomas Fowler (*d.* 1590), executor to the Countess of Lennox, Arabella Stuart's grandmother, is described as at one time pastor of Hawick, a living formerly held by Gavin Douglas. Before 1581 he was driven from France by the jesuits. In 1581 he published, with Robert Lekprewick, at Edinburgh, 'An Answer to the Calumnious Letter and erroneous propositiouns of an apostat named M. Jo.

Hammiltoun.' The dedication, dated from Edinburgh 2 June 1581, is addressed to Francis, earl Bothwell. Fowler sets forth what he alleges to be the errors of Roman catholicism, and claims acquaintance incidentally with the Earl of Crawford, Sir James Balfour, and other distinguished Scottish statesmen. He was subsequently prominent as a burgess of Edinburgh, and about 1590 became secretary to James VI's wife, Queen Anne. He was engaged in political negotiations with England, and in 1597 wrote an epitaph on his friend, Robert Bowes [q. v.], the English agent at Berwick. In 1603 he accompanied his royal mistress to England, and was reappointed not only her secretary but her master of requests. His leisure was always devoted to poetry, and soon after his arrival in London he enclosed two sonnets addressed to Arabella Stuart in a letter to the Earl and Countess of Shrewsbury; they are printed in Nichols's 'Progresses of James I,' i. 250, 260–1. In September 1609 a grant was made him of two thousand acres in Ulster.

Fowler's sister married John Drummond, first laird of Hawthornden, and was mother of William Drummond, the poet [q. v.] Fowler seems to have left the chief part of his poetry, none of which has been published, to his nephew William. This consists of two volumes, entitled 'The Tarantula of Love' and 'The Triumphs of Petrarch.' The former is composed of seventy-two sonnets in the manner of the Italian sonneteers, and the latter is a somewhat diffuse translation from Petrarch. These manuscripts were presented by Drummond of Hawthornden to the university of Edinburgh in 1627. The esteem in which Fowler was held by his contemporaries is illustrated by the commendatory sonnets, including one by the king himself, prefixed to his poems. His style is marked by the verbal and sentimental affectation of the period, but it is not seldom scholarly and graceful.

[Masson's Life of William Drummond of Hawthornden, pp. 7–8; E. T. Bradley's Arabella Stuart, 1889; Register of Privy Council of Scotland, iv. 383, v. 423, vii. lxxix, 330; Nichols's Progresses of James I, i. passim; Manuscripts of Fowler's poems in Edinburgh University Library; Scottish Descriptive Poems, edited by J. Leyden; Irving's Hist. of Scottish Poetry.]

FOWLER, **WILLIAM** (1761–1832), artist, was born at Winterton, Lincolnshire, 12 March 1761, not, as is wrongly stated in the parish register, 13 March 1760. He became an architect and builder at Winterton, and about 1796 made drawings of Roman pavements discovered there. These were so much admired that he took them to London to be engraved. He there studied the process of copper-plate engraving, and in April 1799 brought out a fine coloured engraving of a Roman pavement at Roxby. From that time to 30 Jan. 1829, the date of his latest engraving, he published three volumes, containing coloured engravings of twenty-five pavements, thirty-nine subjects from painted glass, five brasses and incised slabs, four fonts, and eight miscellaneous subjects. He also executed at least twenty-nine engravings, mostly of objects of antiquity, which were never published. Many of the published plates are accompanied by printed broadsides. Most of the lettering on the plates was done by professed engravers. Those which he did himself are much more characteristic and interesting. He became acquainted with Sir Joseph Banks, Sir Walter Scott, and other celebrities, and was once at least presented to the royal family at Windsor.

Fowler, though an earnest member of the church of England, was at the same time a 'class-leader' among the methodists. Some of his neighbours used to say that they 'did not know whether he was more of a methodist or a catholic.' He died 22 Sept. 1832, and was buried at Winterton under a cruciform slab, in accordance with his own desire. Sir Joseph Banks once said: 'Others have shown us what they thought these remains ought to have been, but Fowler has shown us what they are, and that is what we want.' His works are distinguished by a strict fidelity especially remarkable at the time. Whenever it was possible he worked from tracings, rubbings, &c., reducing the scale by means of the pantograph. It is said that he was the first to introduce the lead-lines in representations of painted glass. There is a characteristic portrait of him by W. Bond, from a painting by G. F. Joseph, A.R.A., dated 4 June 1810.

[Notes on William Fowler and his Works, by H. W. Ball of Barton-on-Humber, reprinted from the North Lincolnshire Monthly Illustrated Journal, April 1869; Bibliotheca Lindesiana; Collections and Notes, No. 2; Fowler's Mosaic Pavements, &c., by Ludovic, earl of Crawford and Balcarres, London, 1883; information from the Rev. J. T. Fowler.] H. W. B.

FOWNES, GEORGE (1815–1849), chemist, born on 14 May 1815, was educated first at Enfield in Middlesex, and afterwards at Bourbourg, near Gravelines, in France. He was intended for commerce, but at an early age he resolved to adopt chemistry as a profession. When seventeen years old he attended a philosophical class at the Western Literary Institution, a London society. In January 1837 he became a pupil of Professor Thomas Everitt at Middlesex Hospital, and afterwards studied at Giessen in Germany, where he became Ph.D.

Fownes was assistant to Professor Graham in the laboratory of University College, a post which he resigned about 1840 to become lecturer on chemistry at Charing Cross Hospital. In 1842 he became professor of chemistry to the Pharmaceutical Society, and in the same year he resigned his post at Charing Cross to succeed Professor Everitt as chemical lecturer at Middlesex Hospital. In 1844 Fownes delivered an able course of lectures at the London Institution. Symptoms of pulmonary disease compelled him to resign his post at Middlesex Hospital in 1845, and at the Pharmaceutical Society in 1846. But in 1846 he accepted the professorship of practical chemistry in the Birkbeck laboratory at University College, a post which he held till his death. He visited Barbadoes in search of health in the spring of 1847, but caught cold on his return in 1848, and died at his father's house in Brompton on 31 Jan. 1849.

Fownes was an excellent public lecturer, and at the time of his death was secretary of the Chemical Society, in whose journal many of his papers appeared. He also wrote a capital general text-book of chemistry, which was published in 1844, and which, under the careful editorship of Mr. Henry Watts, has since passed through twelve editions. He won the prize offered by the Royal Agricultural Society in 1842 for an essay on the 'Food of Plants,' and the Actonian prize of one hundred guineas for an 'Essay on Chemistry, as exemplifying the Wisdom and Beneficence of God.' He published eighteen papers in various scientific periodicals. The first of these, 'On the Equivalent of Carbon,' appeared in the 'Philosophical Magazine' for 1839; and the last, 'On the Equivalent or Combining Volumes of Solid Bodies,' in the 'Pharmaceutical Journal' for 1849. Of the others we may name those on the 'Direct Formation of Cyanogen from its Elements' ('British Association Report,' 1841); 'Artificial Yeast,' 'Action of Oil of Vitriol on Ferrocyanide of Potassium,' 'Hippuric Acid,' 'Phosphoric Acid in Felspar of Jersey' (all in the 'Proceedings of the Chemical Society'). Organic chemistry was his special study. He succeeded 'for the first time in the artificial production of a vegeto-alkali or organic salt-base (furfurine), and was also the discoverer of benzoline.' For his researches on these substances (see *Philosophical Transactions*, 1845) Fownes was awarded a royal medal by the Royal Society.

[Journal of the Chemical Society for 1850, ii. 184; Royal Society's Catalogue of Scientific Papers, 1868.] W. J. H.

FOWNS, RICHARD (1560?–1625), divine, 'a minister's son and Worcestershire man born,' was elected student of Christ Church, Oxford, in 1577, at the age of seventeen, and graduated B.A. 30 Jan. 1581, M.A. 3 April 1585 (WOOD, *Fasti Oxon.* ed. Bliss, i. 217, 230). He took the degrees of B.D. and D.D. by accumulation, 16 May 1605 (*ib.* i. 306, 307). He became chaplain to Prince Henry, and in 1602 was rector of Severn Stoke, Worcestershire, in the church of which he was buried 25 Nov. 1625. His monument was 'miserably defaced' during the civil war. He was the author of: 1. 'Concio [on 2 Thess. ii. 3, 4] ad Clerum celeberrimæ florentissimæq; Academiæ Oxoñ. habita Iulij decimo, Anno Domini 1606,' 4to, London, 1606, dedicated to Henry, prince of Wales. 2. 'Trisagion, or the three Holy Offices of Iesvs Christ, the Sonne of God, priestly, prophetical, and regall; how they ought of all his Church to be receiued. With a Declaration of the violence and iniuries offered vnto the same by the Spirituall and Romish Babylon,' London, 1619, a stout quarto of 782 pages, inscribed to Prince Charles.

[Wood's Athenæ Oxon. (Biiss), ii. 388–9; Nash's Worcestershire, ii. 347.]   G. G.

FOX, CAROLINE (1819–1871), diarist, born at Falmouth on 24 May 1819, was second daughter of Robert Were Fox of Penjerrick. From her earliest years she displayed great intelligence and refinement of mind. In 1835 she began to keep the journal which has rendered her celebrated, not so much from its considerable literary merits, as from its association with distinguished persons. Most of these were men of science, attracted by Robert Were Fox's scientific reputation, and his especial knowledge of Cornish mineralogy; but the most remarkable were thinkers and men of letters brought to her remote nook of Cornwall by their own delicacy of constitution or that of their friends. At the beginning of 1840 John Sterling was staying at Falmouth, partly on account of his own health, partly in attendance on his sick friend, Dr. Calvert; Stuart Mill's mother, with her daughters Clara and Harriet, was nursing her youngest son Henry in a hopeless illness, and was soon joined by Mill himself. Sterling and Mill soon became exceedingly intimate with the Fox family, especially with Caroline and her brother Barclay, to whom Mill wrote several letters published in the second edition of Caroline's journal. Caroline's account of their conversations is exceedingly interesting, and adds considerably to our knowledge of both, especially of Mill, who has not elsewhere found a Boswell. The intimacy was the means of introducing her to Carlyle and other remarkable persons, few of whom are mentioned without some bright touch of appreciative portraiture. Her tendency was always to admiration and sympathy, recognising what seemed to her excellent, ignoring or minimising points of difference; it would not be possible to point out a cavil or an ill-natured expression from one end of the record to the other. The intimacy with Mill gradually diminished, while that with Sterling increased in warmth, and his death in 1844 may not have been unconnected with the depression into which Caroline fell in that year, and which left its traces on all her subsequent life. From this time her diary becomes less copious and interesting, partly from the comparative infrequency of remarkable acquaintances, partly from the interruptions occasioned by ill-health, but partly also from a loss of buoyancy and a comparative limitation and timidity of thought. Every line nevertheless indicates the gentle, spiritual, and at the same time intellectual and accomplished woman, and it will always be valued as a highly important illustration of the most characteristic thought of the Victorian era. Caroline died on 12 Jan. 1871, having never married, or quitted her home except for occasional visits to the continent. With her sister, Anna Maria Fox (*d.* Dec. 1897), she translated into Italian several English religious works, of which the latest, 'Il Mozzo Bertino,' was published in Florence in 1867.

[Memories of Old Friends, being extracts from the Journals and Letters of Caroline Fox, edited by Horace N. Pym (London, 1882); Boase and Courtney's Bibliotheca Cornubiensis, pp. 160, 1189.]   R. G.

FOX, CHARLES (1749–1809), Persian scholar, was, according to one account, son of Joseph Fox, quaker and grocer at Falmouth, and was born there in 1749; but he may possibly be identified with Charles Fox, who was the eldest son of John Fox by his wife, Rebecca Steevens of High Wycombe (FOSTER, *Fox Family*, p. 15). He kept a bookseller's shop in his native town, and is the person mentioned in Southey's 'Espriella' (i. 6), who, when his house was on fire and he realised that nothing could be saved, 'went upon the nearest hill and made a drawing of the conflagration—an admirable instance of English phlegm.' Polwhele, who refers to this incident, adds that 'his friend Wolcot saved the horses in the stable by muffling up their heads in blankets.' After this loss, which does not seem to have involved him in pecuniary difficulties, Fox followed the bent of his inclination in landscape and portrait painting. He accompanied his brother, the master of a merchant vessel, on a voyage to the Baltic, and then made a tour, on foot and alone, through Sweden, Norway, and part of Russia, drawing hundreds of views on the way. On his return he stopped for a short time in London, but soon fixed his abode permanently in Bristol. He was facile in acquiring languages, and made a special study of oriental literature, collecting numerous Persian manuscripts. In 1797 Joseph Cottle published for him a volume of 'Poems, containing the Plaints, Consolations, and Delights of Achmed Ardebeili, a Persian Exile, with notes historical and explanatory.' The verses are said to have evinced much vigour of thought and beauty of expression, and the notes have been lauded for their illustration of Eastern subjects; but their value in a monetary sense may be judged from the fact that Cottle, after selling his copyrights to Longmans, found that Fox's 'Achmed'and Wordsworth's 'Lyrical Ballads' had been 'reckoned as nothing.' As both authors were his personal friends, Cottle begged them back again, and, the request being readily granted, returned to the former his receipt for twenty guineas, and to Coleridge, for Wordsworth, his receipt for thirty guineas. Fox's nominal profession made slight demand upon his time, and for many years before his death it was abandoned altogether for poetry. About 1803 he had prepared for the press two volumes of poems from the Persian, but growing weakness of health hindered their publication, though he still continued versifying. He died at Villa Place, Bathwick, Bath, on 1 March 1809. From the description in Hone's 'Table Book' (i. 762), he was 'a great natural genius, which employed itself upon trivial and not generally interesting matters. He was self-taught, and had patience and perseverance for anything.' His eccentricity is acknowledged, but he is credited with 'the quickest reasoning power, and consequently the greatest coolness, of any man of his day who was able to reason.' He married, in 1792, Miss Feniers, the daughter of a Dutch merchant, who survived him. They were hospitable people, and to young persons with literary tastes their house and conversation were ever open. Southey says: 'I knew him well, and met Adam Clarke at his house. I have profiles of him, his wife, and the parrot, &c.' Claudius James Rich, author of a memoir on the ruins of Babylon and other works, was attracted to the study of the oriental languages when a boy by accidentally seeing some Arabic manuscripts in Fox's library, and by constant access to these books, and the loan of

an Arabic grammar and lexicon, he soon made himself master of the language. From him William Isaac Roberts, a young Bristol poet whose poems and letters were issued in 1811, 'experienced continual kindness and encouragement in his literary pursuits.' It was during Dr. Adam Clarke's second residence in Bristol, beginning in 1798, that he obtained much aid from Fox in his study of Persian; and he is said to have repaid these services by turning his friend into a 'devout believer.' Many of Fox's manuscripts, including the illustrated narrative of his travels, passed into the doctor's hands. They are described in J. B. B. Clarke's catalogue of the 'European and Asiatic Manuscripts of the late Dr. Adam Clarke' (1835), and the particulars are copied into the 'Bibliotheca Cornubiensis,' iii. 1186. Proofs of Fox's 'humour and accurate observation of character' are found in his Cornish dialogues printed by Polwhele and other authors.

[Gent. Mag. 1809, pt. i. 385; Corresp. of Southey and Caroline Bowles, p. 281; Polwhele's Reminiscences, ii. 182; Polwhele's Biog. Sketches in Cornwall, ii. 62–9; Annual Register, 1809, pp. 658–9; Monthly Mag. April 1809, pp. 311–312; Cottle's Early Recollections, ii. 26–7; Etheridge's Adam Clarke, pp. 265, 384; Memoir of Rich in Residence in Koordistan; Boase and Courtney's Bibl. Cornub.]   W. P. C.

FOX, CHARLES (1794–1849), line-engraver, born on 17 March 1794, was the son of the steward to Lord Stafford at Cossey Hall, Norfolk, where he was brought up in the gardens, spending his early years in agricultural and horticultural occupations. An accidental visit from William Camden Edwards [q. v.], the engraver, led to young Fox being placed by his father as a pupil with Edwards at Bungay in Suffolk. He had already received some instruction in drawing from Charles Hodgson at Norwich. On the completion of his engagement with Edwards, Fox came to London, and became an inmate of the studio of John Burnet [q. v.], the engraver, who was then engaged on his large plates after Sir David Wilkie's pictures, in which Fox assisted him. Fox's most important plates, of his own execution, were from pictures by Wilkie, viz. 'Village Politicians' and 'Queen Victoria's First Council.' He also engraved some illustrations by Wilkie for Cadell's edition of Sir Walter Scott's novels. He was employed on the annuals, then so much in vogue, Stark's 'Rivers of Norfolk,' and other works. Among other engravings by him were the full-length portrait of Sir George Murray, after Pickersgill, in which his best work was shown, 'A Cauchaise Girl,' after G. S. Newton, &c. He also painted in water-colours, mostly portraits of his friends. During his whole life Fox never ceased to take interest in floriculture, and was considered one of the best judges of flowers. When Dr. John Lindley [q. v.] was appointed superintendent of the Horticultural Society, Fox was chosen as judge and arbitrator, in which capacity he gained universal esteem. He superintended the illustrations of the 'Florist.' While on a visit to a friend at Leyton in Essex, Fox died from an affection of the heart on 28 Feb. 1849. He was engaged on an engraving of Mulready's 'The Fight Interrupted,' which remained unfinished at his death. A portrait of Fox was etched from a drawing by W. Carpenter, jun. for publication in the 'Florist.'

[Redgrave's Dict. of Artists; Ottley's Dict. of Recent and Living Painters; Cunningham's Life of Sir David Wilkie; Gent. Mag. (1849), new ser. xxxi. 434; Florist, 1849; other obituary notices.]

L. C.

FOX, Sir CHARLES (1810–1874), engineer, youngest of four sons of Francis Fox, M.D., was born at Derby 11 March 1810. He was originally destined for his father's profession, but abandoned this intention as his taste for mechanics developed. He was deeply interested in the projected scheme for the Liverpool and Manchester railway, and at the age of nineteen he was articled to Captain Ericsson. With Ericsson he was engaged in designing and constructing the 'Novelty' engine, one of the three which competed at Rainhill in October 1829. He was also employed with Ericsson in experimenting with rotary engines. His mechanical talents having attracted the attention of Robert Stephenson, he was appointed by him one of the constructing engineers of the London and Birmingham railway. He designed the tunnel at Watford, and afterwards carried out the extension of the line from Camden Town to Euston Square. These works were wholly constructed within a covered way and retaining walls, thus realising for the first time the idea of a metropolitan railway. While engaged on this line Fox read a paper before the Royal Institution upon the correct principles of skew arches, which he had carried out in the works. The new mechanical departure was the development of these arches, not from the intrados or the extrados, but from a line midway between the two. Fox now entered into partnership with the contractor Bramah, and upon the retirement of the senior partner the firm assumed the title of Fox, Henderson, & Co. of London, Smethwick, and Renfrew. This firm was the first to carry out the manufacture of railway plant and stock upon a

complete and systematic plan. Great improvements were effected in bridges, roofs, cranes, tanks, and railway wheels. Fox was the inventor of the system of four feet plates for tanks, combined with a very simple formula for calculating weight and contents. He also introduced the switch into railway practice, thus superseding the old sliding rail. Many improvements in iron structures were due to him, and in connection with his experiments upon links he read a paper before the Royal Society (March 1865) 'On the Size of Pins for connecting Flat Links in the Chains of Suspension Bridges.' From 1857 Fox practised in London as a civil and consulting engineer, with his two eldest sons, the firm still being known under the style of Sir Charles Fox & Sons.

During the forty-five years of his professional life Fox was engaged in works of magnitude in all parts of the world. His chief undertaking was the building in Hyde Park for the Great Exhibition of 1851, designed by Paxton. This work was begun towards the end of September 1850, and finished before the close of April 1851, Fox having been engaged exclusively upon it for eighteen hours a day during a period of seven weeks. Together with Cubitt and Paxton he received the honour of knighthood (22 Oct. 1851) in connection with the exhibition. Fox's firm afterwards removed the building from Hyde Park and re-erected it, with many alterations and improvements, at Sydenham for the Crystal Palace Company. Fox was a consistent advocate for economy in railway construction, and it was through his exertions that the 'light railway' clauses were inserted in the Railway Facilities Act. In conjunction with G. Berkley he constructed the first narrow-gauge line in India. He made a special study of the narrow-gauge system, and eventually constructed lines upon this principle in various parts of the world. While strenuously advocating the narrow-gauge system, however, Fox was strongly opposed to break of gauge, except under special circumstances. His main principle was 'to retain the gauge of the country, and to reduce the weight on the engine wheels to the same as that on the wheels of the stock, to limit the speed, and then to reduce the weight of the permanent way and other works.' He was also in favour of vertical rails and cylindrical tyres.

The works executed by Fox as a manufacturer and contractor include the bridge over the Medway at Rochester; three bridges over the Thames, at Barnes, Richmond, and Staines; the swing bridge over the Shannon; a bridge over the Saône at Lyons; and the

Great Western railway bridges. In roofs he executed those at the Paddington station, at the Waterloo station, and at the New Street station, Birmingham, and slip roofs for several of the royal dockyards. The railways upon which he was engaged included the Cork and Bandon, the Thames and Medway, the Portadown and Dungannon, the East Kent, the Lyons and Geneva (eastern section), the Mâcon and Geneva (eastern section), and the Wiesbaden and the Zealand (Denmark). He was also one of the constructors of the Berlin waterworks. Fox was engineer to the Queensland railways, the Cape Town railways, the Wynberg railway (Cape of Good Hope), the Toronto narrow-gauge railway, and (with Berkley) the Indian Tramway Company. Fox & Sons were engineers to the comprehensive scheme of high-level lines at Battersea for the London and Brighton, Chatham and Dover, and London and South-Western companies, with the approach to the Victoria station, Pimlico, including the widening of the Victoria railway bridge over the Thames. Fox was a member of the Institute of Civil Engineers, and for many years a member of the council of the Institution of Mechanical Engineers. He was an original life member of the British Association, a member of the Society of Arts, and a fellow of the Royal Asiatic and Royal Geographical Societies. Early in his career he took an active part in the affairs of the Society of Arts, and, in conjunction with his elder brother Douglas, who was well known as a medical practitioner at Derby, he elaborated the process of casting in elastic moulds, for which the society's silver medal was awarded.

Fox married in 1830 Mary, second daughter of Joseph Brookhouse, by whom he had three sons and one daughter. The two elder sons, Charles and Francis Fox, constitute the firm of Sir Charles Fox & Sons, civil and consulting engineers. Fox was of a most urbane and generous disposition. He died at Blackheath 14 June 1874.

[Engineering, 17 July 1874; Ann. Reg. 1874.]
G. B. S.

FOX, CHARLES (1797–1878), scientific writer, seventh son of Robert Were Fox, by Elizabeth, daughter of Joseph Tregelles of Falmouth, and younger brother of Robert Were Fox, F.R.S. [q. v.], was born at Falmouth 22 Dec. 1797, and educated at home. He became a partner in the firm of G. C. and R. W. Fox & Co., merchants and shipping agents at Falmouth, and was also a partner in the Perran Foundry Company at Perranarworthal, Cornwall, where from 1824 to 1847 he was the manager of the foundry and the engine manufactory.

He was one of the projectors and founders of the Royal Cornwall Polytechnic Society at Falmouth in 1833, and, in conjunction with Sir Charles Lemon, led the way to a movement which resulted in the offer of a premium of 600l. for the introduction of a man-engine into Cornish mines, the result of which was the erection of the first man-engine at Tresavean mine in 1842. This machine was a great success, and its invention has been the means of saving much unnecessary labour to the tin and copper miners in ascending and descending the mine shafts. He was president of the Polytechnic Society for 1871 and 1872, in connection with which institution he founded in 1841 the Lander prizes for maps and essays on geographical districts. He was president of the Royal Geological Society of Cornwall from 1864 to 1867, and president of the Miners' Association of Cornwall and Devon from 1861 to 1863. He interested himself particularly in such discoveries, philological and antiquarian, as tended to throw light on Bible history, and with this object in view he visited Palestine, Egypt, and Algiers. In all branches of natural history he was deeply read, making collections and examining with the microscope the specimens illustrative of each department.

On the introduction of boring machines into mines he was one of the first to recognise their use, and as early as 1867 he wrote papers on this subject. He made many communications to the three Cornish societies, as well as to the 'Mining Journal' and 'Hardwicke's Science Gossip.' 'Extracts from the Spiritual Diary of John Rutty, M.D.,' was edited by Fox in 1840, and in 1870 he wrote a small work, 'On the Ministry of Women.' He was largely interested in Cornish mines throughout his life, and latterly was much impoverished by the failure of the greater number of these undertakings. For the last twenty-five years of his life he resided at Trebah, near Falmouth, and died there 18 April 1878, and was buried in the Friends' cemetery at Budock 23 April. He married, 20 Dec. 1825, Sarah, only daughter of William Hustler. She was born at Apple Hall, Bradford, Yorkshire, 8 Aug. 1800, and died at Trebah 19 Feb. 1882. Her writings were: 'A Metrical Version of the Book of Job,' 1852–4; 'Poems, Original and Translated,' 1863; 'Catch who can, or Hide and Seek, Original Double Acrostics,' 1869; and 'The Matterhorn Sacrifice, a Poem,' in 'Macmillan's Magazine,' 1865.

[Records from Papers and Letters respecting C. Fox, Falmouth, 1878; Journal of the Royal

Institution of Cornwall, November 1878, pp. 2–3;
Boase and Courtney's Bibliotheca Cornubiensis,
pp. 160, 165, 1186, 1189; Joseph Foster's De-
scendants of Francis Fox, 1872, p. 11; Weekly
Welcome, April 1879, pp. 215–16, with portrait.]
G. C. B.

FOX, CHARLES JAMES (1749–1806),
statesman, third son of Henry Fox [q. v.],
afterwards Baron Holland of Foxley, and
Lady Caroline Georgina, daughter of Charles
Lennox, second duke of Richmond, grandson
of Charles II, was born in Conduit Street on
24 Jan. 1749; Holland House, which was
then rented by his father, being under repair.
He was a clever, lively child, and a great
favourite with his father. When his mother
grieved over his passionate temper, Henry
Fox said that he was a 'sensible little fellow,'
and would soon cure himself; nothing was
to be done 'to break his spirit' (WRAXALL,
Memoirs, ii. 2). At his own request he was
in 1756 sent to a school at Wandsworth, kept
by a M. Pampellone, where there were many
boys of high rank, and in the autumn of 1758
he went to Eton, where Dr. Philip Francis
[q. v.] was his private tutor. At Eton he
was studious and popular. Unfortunately
in 1763 his father, then Lord Holland, who
'brought up his children without the least
regard to morality,' interrupted his school life
by taking him with him to Paris and to Spa.
During this excursion, which lasted for four
months, Lord Holland encouraged the boy
to indulge in vice, and at Spa sent him to
the gaming-table well supplied with money
(Life and Times, i. 4). Fox returned to Eton,
and the tone of the school is said to have
suffered from the 'extravagant, vulgar indulgence' with which his father treated him and
his brother (Early Life, p. 52); he learnt to
write creditable Latin verses, had a good acquaintance with French, took a prominent
part in the school debates and recitations, and
was looked upon by his schoolfellows as certain to become famous as an orator. In October 1764 he entered at Hertford College,
Oxford, then much frequented by young men
of family. Unlike his companions, Fox studied diligently, giving much time to mathematics, which he liked 'vastly,' and professed
to consider 'entertaining' (Memorials, i. 19).
He visited Paris in the spring of the next
year, returned to Oxford in July, and spent
the greater part of the long vacation in study.
He left the university in the spring of 1766,
having spent his time there to good purpose;
for he read much of the early English dramatists, and acquired the power of enjoying
Latin and Greek literature, which proved an
unfailing source of pleasure to him in later
life. In the autumn he joined his father and

mother at Lyons, and spent the winter with
them at Naples. When they returned to
England in the spring, he remained in Italy
with two friends of his own age. He joined
Lord and Lady Holland in the autumn at
Paris, and spent the winter with them at
Nice, for he was a good and affectionate son.
In the spring of 1768 he returned to Italy
with his cousin, Lord Carlisle, and visited
Bologna, Florence, and Rome. On his homeward journey he called on Voltaire at Ferney,
and was received graciously. His birth and
connections secured him a welcome at foreign
courts, and his father's great wealth enabled
him to travel magnificently, and indulge every
whim, however extravagant. At the same
time he did not give himself up to frivolity.
He visited picture galleries with appreciation,
perfected himself in French, learnt Italian,
and studied Italian literature. He returned
to England on 2 Aug., and soon afterwards
made a short tour with his elder brother
Stephen and his wife in the Austrian Netherlands and Holland.

As a young man Fox was strongly built;
his frame was large, and he had a handsome
face, bright eyes, high colour, and black hair.
He soon became very stout, and his enemies
considered that in manhood his swarthy countenance had a 'saturnine' aspect, but his smile
was always pleasant (WRAXALL, Memoirs,
ii. 3). From childhood he was courted for
his gaiety, originality, and genius. He was
perfectly good-natured, eager, warm-hearted,
and unselfish. With great natural abilities,
a singular quickness of apprehension, and
a retentive memory, he combined the habit
of doing all things with his might. He
was, as he said, a 'very painstaking man,'
and even when secretary of state wrote copies
for a writing-master to improve his handwriting (ROGERS, Table-talk, p. 85). He
delighted in literature and art, his critical
faculty was acute, and his taste cultivated.
Poetry was to him 'the best thing after all,'
and he declared that he loved 'all the poets.'
He had already acquired a considerable store
of learning, and the works of his favourite
authors, Greek, Latin, English, French, Italian, and in his later years Spanish, never
failed to afford him refreshment and, when
he needed it, consolation. He was fond of
exercise, and even after he had become very
fat retained his activity; he played cricket
and tennis well, loved hunting, racing, and
shooting, and was a good walker and swim-
mer. During his long tour he constantly
referred in his letters to acting plays; he
took pains to excel as an amateur actor, and
retained his love for this amusement for
some few years. Unfortunately his father's

teaching was not thrown away, and he early acquired extravagant and dissolute habits. In his younger days he was an outrageous fop, and led the fashion among the 'macaronis.' After his visit to Italy he and his cousin posted from Paris to Lyons simply in order to choose patterns for their waistcoats (*ib.* p. 74); he appeared in London in red-heeled shoes and blue hair-powder, and up to the age of twenty-five, sometimes at least, wore a hat and feather in the House of Commons. In later life he became careless both as to dress and cleanliness. He drank, though perhaps not so hard as many men in his position, and was much addicted to gambling. When a mere boy he became a member of Almack's [see ALMACK, WILLIAM] gaming club, which was the scene of the most reckless play, and night after night lost sums that soon reached a ruinous amount.

In March 1768, when Fox was in his twentieth year, he was returned for the borough of Midhurst in Sussex, which his father and uncle, Lord Ilchester, had bought for their sons. He took his seat in the following November, and, influenced by the wishes and resentments of his father, joined the supporters of the Duke of Grafton's administration. His first speech was probably made on 9 March 1769, on a point of order. He took an active part in promoting the candidature of Colonel Luttrell for Middlesex, in opposition to Wilkes. On 14 April he spoke with some insolence in support of the motion that Luttrell ought to have been returned, and in the debate on the Middlesex petition on 8 May answered Wedderburn and Burke in a speech which, in spite of some boyishness, delighted his friends, and was praised even by the opposition (*ib.* p.53; CAVENDISH, *Debates,* i. 406). This speech won him a place among the foremost members of the house. On 9 Oct. he went to Paris with his father and mother, and while there lost heavily at play (*Lettres de la Marquise du Deffand,* i. 355, 356). He returned to England early in January 1770, and won great applause by two speeches on the Middlesex election. On 24 Feb., when just past twenty-one, he entered Lord North's administration as one of the lords of the admiralty. Fox delivered his speeches without previous preparation, and their power lay not in rhetorical adornments, but in the vigour of the speaker's thoughts, the extent of his knowledge, the quickness with which he grasped the significance of each point in debate, the clearness of his conceptions, and the remarkable plainness with which he laid them before his audience. Even in his longest speeches he never strayed from the matter in hand; he never rose above the level of his

hearers' understanding, was never obscure, and never bored the house. Every position that he took up he defended with a large number of shrewd arguments, plainly stated and well ordered. The training in elocution that he had received at Eton and his practice as an amateur actor gave him confidence and ease, while the accuracy and readiness of his memory supplied him with a store of quotations, and rendered him never at a loss for a word. At the same time he does not appear to have been particularly fluent until he became warmed with his subject; then he spoke with a stormy eloquence which carried his hearers with him. His voice was naturally poor, and though he generally modulated it skilfully, he was apt when excited to speak with shrillness. His action was ungraceful. His attempts at pathos generally failed; he was prone to invective, and is said to have been the wittiest speaker of his time. Although some of his speeches introducing subjects to the house are magnificent, he especially excelled in reply; for great as he was as an orator, he was certainly greater in debate. During the first period of his political career, when he was generally contemptuous of popular rights, he spoke with too much flippancy; but 'in his best days,' when he was attacking North's administration during the American war, he was in Grattan's opinion the best speaker he had ever heard (*Last Journals,* i. 85, with a comparison between Fox, Burke, and Townshend; ERSKINE, *Preface to Speeches;* BROUGHAM, *Statesmen,* i. 236; *Quarterly Review,* art. by Frere, October 1810; *Early Life,* p. 331).

In June Fox was in Paris with his father; in November he was supping with Lauzun at the Clob à l'Anglaise, and he returned to England about the middle of January 1771. Much as he loved Paris, he was no favourite with Mme. du Deffand, who described him as 'hard, bold, and ready;' he did not, she complained, put his mind to hers, and cared only for play and politics (*Lettre,* 13 Jan. 1771, ii. 139. See also a somewhat similar character of him by Mme. Neckar, who in 1777 spoke of him as knowing everything, and as cold and cynical, GIBBON, *Miscell. Works,* ii. 194). Of the two she preferred Richard Fitzpatrick [q. v.], Fox's connection by marriage, and his constant companion, who at this time shared the lodgings in Piccadilly where Fox lived when his father was absent from Holland House. After joining the administration Fox took a prominent part in several unpopular measures, and especially in the attempt to restrain the press. When on 6 Dec. a committee on the press laws was moved for, he opposed the motion, and jeered the opposition for their declaration that they wished to 'satisfy the people.' Where, he asked, was he to look for the complaints of the people? he refused to recognise the people apart from the majority of the house, their legal representatives (*Speeches,* i. 5). He took the same line on 25 March 1771, when urging the committal of Alderman Oliver for discharging the printers apprehended by the officers of the house. His action in this affair rendered him exceedingly unpopular, and on the 27th he and his brother were attacked by a mob as they drove down to the house, and he was rolled in the mud. Zealous for privilege of every kind, he gave much satisfaction to his party ' by the great talents he exerted' in opposing the *Nullum Tempus* Bill. Junius had hitherto virtually left him alone, but his opposition to the popular cause of the Duke of Portland called forth a sharp rebuke in the 'Public Advertiser' of 4 March, signed ' Ulysses.' Fox wished to challenge the writer, but was unable to identify him (*Life of Sir P. Francis,* i. 255). A letter of Junius in October provoked an answer signed 'An Old Correspondent,' which was attributed to Fox. A reply appeared signed 'Anti-Fox,' in which the writer warns ' my pretty black boy' that if provoked Junius might cease to spare Lord Holland and his family (*Letters of Junius,* ii. 384). His contempt for the wishes of the people provoked a caricature entitled ' The Death of the Foxes' in the ' Oxford Magazine' of February 1770. In this he appears with his father and brother, and his corpulence is ridiculed. Another caricature in the same magazine in December 1773 represents him as picking his father's pocket, in reference to his gambling debts (WRIGHT).

On 6 Feb. 1772 Fox spoke against the clerical petition for relief from subscription to the articles, though he condemned the custom of requiring subscription from lads at the universities. He prepared himself for his defence of the church ' by passing twenty-two hours in the pious exercise of hazard,' losing during that time 11,000*l.* (GIBBON, *Miscellaneous Works,* ii. 74). A twelvemonth later he supported a motion for a committee on the subject of subscription, and further showed that, in spite of his zeal for privilege, he was not to be reckoned among those who were content to forward the king's wishes on all points, for he acted as teller for a bill for the relief of protestant dissenters; the king declared that ' his conduct could not be attributed to conscience, but to his aversion to all restraints' (*Speeches,* i. 17; *George III, Letters to Lord North,* i. 89; this letter, dated 1772, seems to belong to 1773; comp. *Parl. Hist.* xvii. 758). On 20 Feb. 1772 he resigned office. Although he had some private grounds of dissatisfaction

with North (*Memorials,* i. 73; *Last Journals,* i. 23), the chief cause of his resignation was that he intended to oppose the Royal Marriage Bill. The circumstances of his parents' marriage rendered him jealous of all needless restrictions on marriage; he had already obtained leave to bring in a bill to amend the marriage act, and he chose to sacrifice office rather than assent to the restrictions that the king was bent on placing on the marriages of his house. North was terrified by the report of his intended resignation, and withdrew one of the most objectionable clauses of the bill. Fox joined Conway and Burke in opposing the bill, and was 'universally allowed to have seized the just point of argument throughout with amazing rapidity and clearness' (*ib.* p. 59). At least as early as 1766 he had become acquainted with Burke, and had learnt to respect his opinion (*Memorials,* i. 26), and this temporary co-operation with him can scarcely have been without some effect on his later career. Fox introduced his own marriage bill on 7 April, having that morning, after a night spent in drinking, returned from Newmarket, where he had lost heavily; he spoke with effect, but took no more trouble about the bill, which was thrown out at a later stage. In December he re-entered the administration as a junior lord of the treasury. Although Clive had been absolved by parliament, Fox took the opportunity of a debate on the affairs of India in June 1773 to attack him with unsparing vehemence. He recommended his assaults on the press. In a debate he had raised on this subject on 16 Feb. 1774 he rebuked T. Townshend for coupling the name of Johnson with that of Shebbeare (*Speeches,* i. 25). Johnson never forgot his warm defence (BOSWELL, *Life,* iv. 315). Fox had lately been elected a member of the club; he was generally silent when Johnson was present (*ib.* 179). He was naturally shy, but when in the society of those with whom he felt at ease would ' talk on for ever with all the openness and simplicity of a child' (ROGERS, *Table-talk,* p. 75); his conversation was always easy and full of anecdote. Office exercised no restraint upon him. He forced North against his will to persist in a proposal that the printer Woodfall should be committed to the Gatehouse for printing a letter containing charges against the speaker. The minister was defeated, and the king, who already disliked Fox for the part he had taken against the Royal Marriage Bill, and in support of the relief bill of the year before, was furious at his presumption. ' That young man,' he wrote, ' has so thoroughly cast off every principle of common honour and honesty that he must soon become as contemptible as he is odious' (*George III, Letters to North*, i. 170). North was reluctantly compelled to inform him on the 24th that the king had dismissed him from office. Meanwhile his money difficulties had come to a crisis. For four years he had played constantly and for high stakes, and his losses were very heavy. Although his horses were generally beaten on the turf, his bets were judicious, and in 1772 he won 16,000*l.* on a single race. Nor was he a loser in games that required skill, such as whist and picquet. He was ruined by his losses at hazard, and it seems tolerably certain that the 'immoderate, constant, and unparalleled advantages' gained over him at the gaming-table were the result of unfair play (*Memorials*, i. 91). In order to pay his gambling debts he had recourse to Jewish money-lenders, and, always light-hearted, used to call the room where these men waited for him his 'Jerusalem chamber.' Friends, and especially Lord Carlisle, paid large annuities on his behalf. In the summer of 1773 his difficulties induced him to put faith in an adventuress who promised to procure him a wife with 80,000*l.* In that year the wife of his elder brother bore a son, and the money-lenders refused to give him further credit. 'My brother Ste's son,' he said, 'is a second Messiah, born for the destruction of the Jews' (GIBBON, *Miscell. Works*, ii. 132). He thought of reading for the bar, in the hope of retrieving his fortune by professional industry. Lord Holland paid his debts in the winter of 1773–4, at a cost of 140,000*l.* He did not give up the habit of gambling (*Last Journals*, i. 7, 283; WRAXALL, *Memoirs*, ii. 9; *Early Life*, pp. 478–92). In the course of 1774 Fox lost his father, mother, and elder brother. He received King's Gate, near Margate, from his father, and on his brother's death succeeded to the Irish clerkship of the pells, which was worth 2,000*l.* a year for life; he shortly afterwards sold both the house and the clerkship (WRAXALL, *Memoirs*, ii. 8).

At the time of Fox's dismissal the dispute with the American colonies had reached a critical stage; the tea riot in Boston took place in December 1773, and Gage landed in May 1774 to put in force the Boston Port Bill. Fox now began to act with the Rockingham party; he carried on a constant opposition to the war, and his speeches, hitherto occasional and for the most part misdirected, were during this period the most effective expositions of the policy of the Rockingham whigs. His jealousy for the rights of parliament, hitherto exhibited in unworthy measures against the liberty of the press, now took a nobler turn, and on 24 March he declared

that the quarrel with Massachusetts was with the parliament not with the crown, and that it therefore belonged to parliament to decide on the restoration of the port of Boston (*Speeches*, i. 27). On 19 April he voted for the repeal of the tea duty, declaring that the tax was a mere assertion of a right which would force the colonists 'into open rebellion' (*ib.* p. 28). It is said that in December an attempt was made to negotiate between Fox and North, but that Fox's demands were too high (*Last Journals*, i. 437). Fox upheld Burke, on 23 Jan. 1775, in complaining of the disregard shown to the merchants' petition, and pointed out that Gage's troops were in a ridiculous position. He made a violent attack on North on the 27th, and when the minister complained that Fox and Burke were threatening him, declared that he would join Burke in bringing him to answer for his conduct. In moving an amendment to a ministerial address on 2 Feb. 'he entered into the whole history and argument of the dispute, and made the greatest figure he had yet done in a speech of an hour and twenty minutes' (*ib.* p. 455); 'taking the vast compass of the question' he 'discovered power for regular debate which neither his friends hoped, nor his enemies dreaded' (GIBBON, *Miscell. Works*, ii. 132). On the 20th he exposed the hollowness of North's plan of conciliation, as, according to his ideas, 'carrying two faces on its very first appearance' (*Speeches*, i. 37). The affair at Lexington took place in April. When parliament met on 26 Oct. Fox supported the amendment to the address, censuring the ministers for increasing the discontent in America. The ministers, he said, 'have reason to triumph. Lord Chatham, the king of Prussia, nay, Alexander the Great, never gained more in one campaign than the noble lord has lost—he has lost a whole continent.' The colonists, he admitted, had gone too far, though he denied that they were aiming at independence, they were aiming at freedom, and he urged that they should be placed in the same position as in 1763 (*ib.* i. 49). On 20 Feb. 1776 he moved for a committee on the war, contending that the ministers lacked wisdom and integrity, parliament public spirit, and the commanders either military skill or liberty to carry out what they were sent to do. The motion was lost by 240 to 104. Speaking in support of the amendment to the address on 31 Oct. he denied that it was 'not for the interest of Spain and France to have America independent;' injury to the trade of this free country must be advantageous to old corrupted governments. If, however, the question lay between conquering and abandoning

America, he was for abandoning it; for our advantages from America arose from trade and from relationships with a people of the same ideas and sentiments. They would be cut off by war; while the army in America would oppress the people there, and would be dangerous to liberty at home (*ib.* p. 61). Fox was at this time the animating spirit of the Rockingham party, though he had not as yet avowedly joined it; he brought recruits to it, declared himself 'far from being dismayed by the terrible news from Long Island,' urged perseverance, and tried to dissuade the marquis from secession (*Memoirs of Rockingham*, ii. 297). The king recognised his power; for he wrote to North, saying that he heard that Fox was about to leave for Paris on 16 Nov., and that the minister would do well to press on business in his absence (*Letters to North*, ii. 40). While, however, Fox, according to Gibbon, 'in the conduct of a party' thus 'approved himself equal to the conduct of an empire' (*Miscell. Works*, i. 222), he did not abandon his gaming or rakish life, and was seldom in bed before 5 A.M., or up before 2 P.M. (*Last Journals*, ii. 4). He went to Paris with Fitzpatrick, played high there, and returned to England about the middle of January 1777 (MME. DU DEFFAND, iii. 207, 218).

When the Rockingham party seceded from parliament, Fox still continued to attend, and on 10 Feb. opposed the suspension of the Habeas Corpus Act. In the summer he made a tour in Ireland with Lord John Townshend, met Grattan at Lord Charlemont's, and formed a friendship with him, and was much fêted at Dublin (*Memorials*, i. 156). While in Ireland he received a letter from Burke, exhorting him to lay his 'foundations deep in public opinion,' and expressing the writer's wish that he would avowedly join the Rockingham party (BURKE, *Works*, ix. 148). On the meeting of parliament in November he delivered a 'bitter philippic on Lord George Germaine,' describing him as 'that inauspicious and ill-omened character, whose arrogance and presumption, whose ignorance and inability,' had damaged the country. 'Charles,' Lord North said, for in spite of political differences they were on friendly terms, 'I am glad you did not fall on me to-day, for you was in full feather' (*Memorials*, i. 159). When Germaine confirmed the news of the disaster at Saratoga, Fox renewed his attack with great vehemence, and expressed his hope of seeing Germaine 'brought to a second trial' (*Last Journals*, ii. 170). In moving for papers with reference to the surrender at Saratoga, Fox, in January 1778, compared the reign to that of James II. Luttrell said that he was

talking treason, which he denied. The 'Morning Post,' the paper of the court party, taunted him with not challenging Luttrell. Its tone gave rise to a suspicion that there was a scheme to get rid of Fox by provoking a duel. Luttrell complained of the tone of the paper, said he had been misrepresented, and threatened to have the gallery cleared. Fox, so greatly had he changed his ground as regards press matters, asserted that the 'public had a right to know what passed in parliament' (*Speeches*, i. 101). On 2 Feb. he made a motion on the state of the nation, and reviewed the whole conduct of the ministers in a speech of two hours and forty minutes. His speech was not answered, and the motion was rejected by 259 to 165, which was considered a very good division for the opposition (*ib.* pp. 102–11). The treaty between France and the revolted colonies was signed 6 Feb., and on the 17th Fox, while in the main approving North's new scheme for conciliation, asked 'what punishment would be sufficient for those who adjourned parliament in order to make a proposition of concession, and then had neglected to do it until France had concluded a treaty with the independent states of America' (*ib.* p. 117). Negotiations were opened in March to induce Fox to join the administration. Fox is reported to have said 'that except with Lord G. Germaine he could act with the present ministers: but he disavowed every possibility of accepting singly and alone.' This report has been discredited (*Memorials*, i. 181, *note* by Lord Russell). He had not yet made 'engagements to any set of men,' but felt bound in honour to the Rockingham party (*ib.* p. 170). As, however, he seems on 31 May to have thought that a 'compromise ought to be made' (*Memoirs of Rockingham*, ii. 354), the report does not seem incredible. Fox evidently thought it possible that the king would sanction a change of policy, and a considerable change in the administration; while the king only contemplated reinforcing the existing administration by the admission of two or three men of ability (LEWIS, *Administrations*, p. 14; STANHOPE, *History*, vi. 222–6). Soon after this Fox definitely attached himself to the Rockingham party. He still thought a coalition possible, and on 24 Jan. 1779 urged it on Rockingham as an opportunity of restoring the whig party to power. His uncle, the Duke of Richmond, pointed out his mistake, insisted that the negotiations then afoot meant simply 'an offer of places without power,' and exhorted him to be patient and steadfast (*Memoirs of Rockingham*, ii. 371; *Memorials*, i. 213). He followed this advice. Meanwhile he had not abated the vehemence of his opposition. In the debate on the address in November 1778 he criticised the naval arrangements, and advocated the withdrawal of troops from America and the prosecution of the war against France. 'America,' he said, 'must be conquered in France; France can never be conquered in America,' and he declared that the war of the Americans was a 'war of passion,' the war of France a 'war of interest' (*Speeches*, i. 131–8). After Christmas he attacked the admiralty, which was wretchedly mismanaged by Lord Sandwich, and on 3 March moved a vote of censure on the ground that when Keppel had been sent to prevent a junction of two French squadrons the previous June he had only twenty ships, though there were twenty-seven ships of the line in the Brest waters, and five more nearly ready for sea. The motion was lost by 204 to 170, an unusually large minority (*ib.* pp. 140–60). He warmly espoused the cause of Keppel against Palliser and Sandwich with reference to the engagement off Ushant. When the news of Keppel's acquittal reached London at 3 A.M. on 11 Feb., he and some of his friends were drinking at Almack's; they sallied out into the streets, and one of the party is said to have incited the mob to break Lord G. Germaine's windows (*Last Journals*, ii. 343).

By this time it had become abundantly evident that the king's determination to carry on the war was at the bottom of the resistance offered by North and the majority of the commons to the policy of the opposition. Accordingly, on 25 Nov., at the opening of the session, Fox referred to the unconstitutional character of the doctrine that the king might be his own minister, spoke of the punishments that befell Charles I and James II, and compared the king and his reign to Henry VI and the period of his losses in France. He also made a violent attack on Adam. This led to a duel on the 29th, in which Fox was slightly wounded [see under ADAM, WILLIAM]. He was now the 'idol of the people.' On 2 Feb. 1780 he took the chair at a great meeting in Westminster Hall, where a petition was adopted praying the commons to reform abuses in the public expenditure. At this meeting he was received as candidate for the city of Westminster at the approaching election. At another meeting of the same sort on 5 April he declared for yearly parliaments and an additional hundred knights of the shire, and when a motion was brought forward on 8 May for triennial parliaments upheld it on the ground that it would lessen the influence of the crown, to which he traced all the misfortunes of the country (*Speeches*, i. 276). He took a prominent part in the debates on economical

reform [see under BURKE, EDMUND]; on 8 March combated Rigby's theory that the house was not competent to disturb the existing arrangement with the crown, declaring that if this was so there 'was an end of the constitution,' and he would never enter the house again, and insisting that the only way to narrow influence was by the reduction of the civil list (*ib.* p. 224). During the Gordon riots in the first week of June Fox joined a party of young men who kept guard over the Marquis of Rockingham's house in Grosvenor Square, and on the 20th made a fine speech of three hours in favour of relief of the Roman catholics, declaring himself a 'friend to universal toleration.' In July fresh negotiations were set on foot between North and the leaders of the opposition. Rockingham proposed that Fox should be 'considered.' The king objected to Fox on the ground that he advocated shortening the duration of parliaments, but added, 'As to Mr. Fox, if any lucrative, not ministerial, office can be pointed out for him, provided he will support the ministry, I shall have no objection. He never had any principle, and can therefore act as his interest may guide him' (*Memorials*, i. 252). The negotiations failed. While the king's opinion of Fox was harsh, some of the circumstances of his early career, his insubordination in office, and his rapid change from toryism to 'virulent and unqualified opposition to his former chief,' even though he had never defended the quarrel with the American colonies, and though American questions had not become urgent until the time of his secession, certainly gave his enemies some excuse for speaking ill of him, while his dissipated life deprived him of the weight that attaches to character (LECKY, *History*, iii. 528). This was the period of his greatest pecuniary embarrassments. In January 1779 he is said to have jestingly asked for a place on the council for India as a means of gaining a livelihood (*Life of Sir P. Francis*, ii. 172). Two years later he won 70,000*l.*, at least so it is said, in partnership with others at hazard, lost it all at Newmarket, and was 30,000*l.* 'worse than nothing' (*Auckland Correspondence*, i. 320). Although he was then lodging in St. James's Street, near the gambling club, where he spent nearly all his spare time, he was often in need of the smallest sums, and on 20 June 1781 his books were sold under a writ of execution (*Memorials*, i. 265). He bore his losses with great equanimity. Immediately after a run of ill-luck that left him penniless he was found quietly reading Herodotus; at other times he would at once fall sound asleep. By 1781 his dissipation is said to have brought on internal pains, but he used each year to lay in a fresh store of health by spending some weeks in shooting in Norfolk (WRAXALL, *Memoirs*, ii. 15, 23; WALPOLE, *Letters*, viii. 41; but as regards Fox's health compare *Memorials*, i. 264 *n.*) His embarrassments rendered his faithfulness to his party especially praiseworthy; his opposition to the American war was sincere, and the emoluments of office could not tempt him to be false to his principles.

In October 1780 Rodney and Fox were returned for Westminster, the ministerial candidate being defeated by a large majority. During the canvass the whig electors adopted a resolution to defend Fox's safety, as he would probably be made the ' object of such attacks as he had already experienced, and to which every unprincipled partisan of power is invited by the certainty of a reward.' Fox at this time adopted the blue frock-coat and buff waistcoat which are said to have given the whigs their party colours, still commemorated on the cover of the ' Edinburgh Review' (WRAXALL, *Memoirs*, ii. 27; the connection is doubtful, and rests on Wraxall's assertion, which, however, is perhaps corroborated by the phrase ' our buff and blue chief,' *Auckland Correspondence*, ii. 369). The appointment of Palliser as governor of Greenwich Hospital provoked Fox to renew his attacks upon him, and on 1 Feb. he spoke severely of the exercise of the royal influence in driving Keppel from the borough of Windsor. This greatly annoyed the king (*Speeches*, i. 295; *Letters to North*, ii. 357). On 7 March he attacked North on finance, pointing out that the minister's proposal to raise twelve millions by annuities and 480,000*l.* by lottery showed utter disregard of the public interest, and that the profit on the loan would be 900,000*l.*, which North would have the power of distributing among his supporters, and which would thus become a means of maintaining a majority; the lottery scheme he considered as injurious to the morals of the people. When pursuing this subject on 30 May he made a violent attack on North, personating the minister at his levee as inducing members to vote for the continuance of the war by representing that he had 900,000*l.* to distribute (*Speeches*, i. 316, 364; WRAXALL, *Memoirs*, i. 98). On 15 June he carried the commitment of a bill to amend the marriage act, making a speech of remarkable power, in which he compared the results of lawful and unlawful union (*Speeches*, i. 413). When parliament met on 27 Nov. news had been received of the surrender of Yorktown. Fox moved an amendment to the address, and, angered by a remark that the house had heard

with impatience the narratives of the American disasters, declared that the ministers ' must by the aroused indignation and vengeance of an injured and undone people hear of them at the tribunal of justice and expiate them on the public scaffold;' he exposed the wretched condition of the navy, and appealed to the house not to go on with the war. His amendment was lost by 218 to 129 (*ib.* pp. 427, 436). During January and February 1782 he continued his attacks on the maladministration of the navy, and the majority rapidly decreased. On 8 March Adam taunted him with looking outside the house for the wishes of the people, especially as regards the duration of parliaments. In reply Fox made a sort of confession of the principles he would follow if the ministry was overthrown; he spoke of the corrupt state of the house, and declared that it ought to be made to represent the people, but that it would be of little use to shorten parliaments unless the influence of the crown was abated; he desired an administration formed on the broadest basis (*ib.* ii. 40; *Parl. Hist.* xxii. 1136; WRAXALL, *Memoirs*, ii. 222). North resigned on the 20th.

On the 25th Fox took office as foreign secretary in Lord Rockingham's administration. His appointment was immensely popular (he appears in the caricature ' The Captive Prince' as the ruler of the mob). As minister he was ' indefatigable,' and for the time wholly gave up play (WALPOLE, *Letters*, viii. 217; *Memorials*, i. 320 *n.*) He was not satisfied with the composition of the ministry; it consisted, he said, ' of two parts, one belonging to the king, the other to the public;' the king's part was led by Shelburne, the other secretary, and it soon became evident that he and Fox regarded each other with the distrust and jealousy natural to men who are forced by circumstances to act together while they are rivals and enemies at heart, as well as with an intense personal dislike' (*ib.* pp. 314, 316; LECKY, *History*, iv. 216). On 17 May Fox brought in the bill for the repeal of the declaratory act of George I and for other concessions to Ireland. He had already, on 6 Dec. 1779, expressed in parliament his approval of the Irish association, and of ' the determination that in the *dernier ressort* flew to arms to obtain deliverance' (*Speeches*, i. 221). He now said that he ' would rather see Ireland totally separated from the crown of England than kept in obedience by mere force.' In acceding to the four demands of the Irish he was anxious ' to meet Ireland on her own terms,' and contemplated a formal treaty which should regulate the relationship between the two kingdoms. Finally, he praised the moderation of the volunteers (*ib.* ii. 64). He supported Pitt's motion for parliamentary reform on the ground that it gave power to those who had a stake in the country (*ib.* p. 67). In his special department he desired to counterbalance the power of France by alliances with Russia and Prussia, and in order to satisfy Russia made offers to Holland on the basis of the 'armed neutrality' (MALMESBURY, *Diaries*, i. 497–517; *Memorials*, iii. 300; *Life*, i. 299). The discord between the two secretaries increased (*Grafton MSS.*, quoted LECKY, *History*, iv. 224), and came to a crisis about the negotiations for peace. Fox desired that the independence of America should be acknowledged unconditionally, and not as part of the joint treaty with America and France. Shelburne preferred to receive the acknowledgment for the joint treaty, and use it as a set-off to claims for territory. The treaty with France belonged to Fox's department, negotiations with the American colonies to Shelburne's. A merchant named Oswald was employed, first informally by Shelburne, and then by the cabinet, to negotiate with Franklin at Paris. Oswald was unfit for his work, and encouraged Franklin to expect large concessions, embodied in a paper which Shelburne concealed from Fox. On 23 May the cabinet came round to Fox's ideas, and authorised Grenville, Fox's envoy to Vergennes, 'to propose the independency of America in the first instance' (*Memorials*, i. 357). Fox contended that, as America was thus recognised as independent, negotiations belonged for the future to him as foreign minister, while Shelburne claimed them as secretary for the colonies (*ib.* p. 439). The king agreed with Shelburne, for he desired that Oswald might be a 'check' on Fox (*Life of Shelburne*, iii. 184). Fox was outvoted in the cabinet, and Oswald was sent back to Paris. When Oswald returned, Grenville, who had been negotiating with Franklin, found that Franklin became reserved; he complained to Fox and told him of the private paper, for Oswald informed him of it. Fox was indignant at Shelburne's duplicity, and demanded Oswald's recall. The majority of the cabinet, however, decided to grant him full powers. On 30 June Fox desired that the independence of America should be unconditionally acknowledged, which would have put the whole negotiations into his hands. Shelburne declared that the instructions of 23 May only indicated a recognition that might be withdrawn in case other negotiations failed; he was supported by the majority of the cabinet, and Fox announced his intention of resigning (*ib.* p. 218;

Memorials, i. 434–9; FRANKLIN, *Works*, ix. 335; LEWIS, *Administrations*, pp. 31–50; LECKY, *History*, iv. 223–35, where this intricate subject is admirably elucidated).

Fox's resignation was delayed, for Rockingham was on his deathbed, and died the next day. Fox advised the king to send for one of the Rockingham party, and wished for the appointment of the Duke of Portland. The king preferred Shelburne, and Fox, Lord John Cavendish, 'with Burke, Sheridan, and some others not in the cabinet, resigned.' Fox's resignation broke up the Rockingham party. He has been much blamed for it (*Memorials*, i. 472); but the king knew that it would be impossible for him to work with Shelburne (*Life of Shelburne*, iii. 220), Burke advised him not to try it (*Memorials*, i. 457), and Elliot thought resignation necessary to his credit (*Life of Sir G. Elliot*, i. 80). He defended his resignation on the grounds that he felt general want of confidence, that Rockingham's 'system' had been abandoned, and that, while he maintained that the acknowledgment of American independence should be unconditional, Shelburne wished to make it the price of peace (*Speeches*, ii. 73, 97). Considering the differences between him and Shelburne on this subject, and, indeed, on other matters, and the fact that if he had remained in office he would always have been in a minority in the cabinet, his resignation appears justified. His loss of office was made the subject of three famous caricatures, one by James Sayer entitled 'Paradise Lost,' the other two by J. Gillray, who represents him in one as in the envious mood of Milton's Satan, and in the other, 'Guy Vaux and Judas Iscariot,' as wrangling with Shelburne (WRIGHT). His party could now count on ninety votes, and he held the balance between the supporters of the minority and the party of North. A design was at once formed to bring about a coalition between Fox and North (*Auckland Correspondence*, i. 9, 28). Political sympathy dictated a union between the Foxites and the ministerial party; personal dislike prevented it. In February an attempt was made to induce Fox to come to terms with the Shelburne whigs. He refused to enter any administration of which Shelburne was the head. On the 17th his coalition with North became patent, and on the 21st the two combined parties defeated the ministry on a motion concerning the peace. The coalition with North forcibly illustrates Fox's levity and indiscretion; he defended it on the plea that quarrels should be short, friendships abiding; but his differences with North were not personal, they were matters of political principle. He declared that the cause of quarrel, the American war, had passed, and that there was therefore no reason why he should not act with North. But his late censures on North had not been confined to the minister's persistence in the war, he had attacked North's character as a statesman, had maintained that he was a bad and corrupt minister, and had threatened him with impeachment. Besides, North was, and remained, a tory, while Fox had embraced the principles of the Rockingham whigs. Fox himself declared that nothing could justify the junction but success; he hoped that it would lead to the establishment of a strong administration which would be able to resist the intrigues of the crown; the king was to be treated with respect, but was to have only the semblance of power, and there was to be no government by departments (*Memorials*, ii. 38, iv. 40, 102). The coalition ruined the whigs, disgusted the nation, and was overthrown by the king. George struggled hard against it; he hated Fox not merely for political reasons, but because he believed that he encouraged the Prince of Wales in evil courses, and in unfilial conduct (*ib.* i. 269). The prince was intimate with Fox, and upheld him as a politician, greatly to his father's annoyance. Although the king used every effort to exclude Fox from the administration (*Courts and Cabinets*, i. 169, 172, 213), he was beaten by the coalition, and on 2 April Fox took office as foreign secretary with North and under the headship of the Duke of Portland. He was re-elected for Westminster on the 7th without opposition, though amid some hissing.

The coalition was violently disapproved by the nation; it offended the democratic party equally with the court, and was held up to public ridicule both in print and in caricatures (e.g. by Sayer in the 'Medal' and the 'Mask,' in the 'Drivers of the State-coach' and 'Razor's Levee,' and by Gillray in his double picture, 'The Astonishing Coalition'). As minister Fox was respectful to the king, but he could get no more in return than bare civility, for George smarted under his defeat, and was determined to get rid of his new ministers. In foreign politics Fox tried to follow the line which has already been noticed in the account of his official work during the Rockingham administration; he describes the formation of 'a continental alliance as a balance to the house of Bourbon' as his guiding principle. He was thwarted by the indifference of the king and the unwillingness of Frederic of Prussia. In May he supported Pitt's resolutions for reform of parliament (*Speeches*, ii. 172), while

North opposed them. By his persuasion the ministers pledged themselves to obtain a grant of 100,000*l.* a year for the prince. The king proposed 50,000*l.* a year to be taken from his own civil list. On 17 June it seemed likely that the matter would end in the dismissal of the ministers, but it was arranged by the prince himself. Fox acted in this affair rather as a friend to the prince than as a minister of the crown (WRAXALL, *Memoirs*, iii. 111). With respect to Ireland he exhorted the lord-lieutenant, Lord Northington, 'not to be swayed in the slightest degree by the armed volunteers' associations;' he considered that the concessions of 1782 'closed the account,' and would have nothing yielded to threats (*Memorials*, ii. 163). The condition of Indian finance, the abuses of the administration, and the conduct of the court of proprietors in retaining Warren Hastings as governor-general of Bengal rendered it necessary to reform the government of India, and on 18 Nov. Fox brought in a bill for that purpose; the conception and the particulars of the bill must be ascribed to Burke, but Fox made the measure his own and recommended it with uncommon power (NICHOLLS, *Recollections*, i. 55). Although he was conscious that by bringing in this India bill before the ministry was firmly established he was risking his power, he did not hesitate to incur that danger 'when the happiness of so many millions was at stake' (*ib.* p. 219). He exposed the deplorable condition of the company, defended the recall of Hastings, and, as illustrations of the bad government of which he was the principal agent, dwelt on the iniquities of the transactions with Cheyt Sing and the begums of Oude and the Rohilla war. In order to remedy abuses he proposed to constitute a supreme council in England, consisting of seven commissioners, to be named by the legislature, who should hold office for four years and have complete control over government, patronage, and commerce. At the end of their period of office the right of nomination was to vest in the crown. A board of assistant-directors chosen from the largest proprietors was to manage commercial details; these assistants were to be appointed in the first instance for four years by parliament, and vacancies were to be filled up by the proprietors. Provision was made in a second bill for giving security to landowners and for certain other matters (*Speeches*, ii. 194). The first bill was carried in the commons, but the opposition raised a strong feeling against it by representing that it struck at chartered rights and at royal prerogative. All public companies were said to be endangered; the bill was declared to provide opportunities for corruption, and, above all, the tories represented that it gave the whig majority in the commons the virtual sovereignty of India. Fox was said to be attempting to make himself 'king of Bengal,' and Sayer's fine caricature, 'Carlo Khan's Triumphal Entry into Leadenhall Street,' gave, so he declared, the severest blow to his bill in the public estimation (WRIGHT). The king was easily induced to believe that his prerogative was attacked. As the right of nomination only belonged to the parliament for four years, and the nominees were liable to be removed by the king on address by either house of parliament, the declaration that the bill was an attempt to deprive the sovereign of his rights was certainly exaggerated and was due to party considerations. The king used his personal influence through Lord Temple to secure the rejection of the bill and the defeat of his ministers in the House of Lords on 17 Dec., and the next day Fox and his colleagues were dismissed.

Fox's large majority in the commons made it probable that the king would dissolve the house in order to gain a majority in favour of the new ministry which was formed by Pitt. Fox determined to prevent a dissolution and an appeal to the nation, and was confident that he should be able to force the king to recall the late ministry. The king could not dissolve until the Land Tax Bill had been passed, and the house deferred the third reading and presented an address against dissolution. On 12 Jan. 1784 Fox moved for a committee on the state of the nation, endeavouring to make a dissolution impossible, and declaring that 'it would render gentlemen in some degree accomplices in the guilt of a dissolution without cause, if they suffered the land bill to go out of their hands without taking measures to guard against the evils which might be expected from a dissolution' (Speeches, ii. 305). The motion was carried by a majority of thirty-nine. On the 23rd he spoke against, and procured the rejection of, Pitt's East India Bill. He endeavoured to force Pitt to resign by a series of votes of censure and addresses to the crown, and took his stand on the principle that a minister who persisted in retaining office against the wishes of a majority in the commons was guilty of contempt of the opinion of the house. In this long attack on the ministry he committed some grave mistakes; he attempted to restrain the crown from exercising its undoubted right, and he showed that he was unwilling to submit his cause to the judgment of the country. As a matter of tactics he foolishly gave Pitt time to gain a hold upon the constituencies, and he showed

a want of political knowledge in staking his success on the stability of his majority in the house. On the 20th the section styled the 'country gentlemen' called for a coalition, and the attempt was renewed on 2 Feb. Fox, while professing that he was not averse to the idea, declared that a junction was impossible, as it could not be founded on principle (ib. p. 353). The king and Pitt remained firm, but Fox's majority gradually dwindled. On 20 Feb. an address to the crown was carried by twenty-one; on 1 March Fox moved another address and had a majority of twelve, this sank to nine on a motion to delay the Mutiny Bill on the 5th, and on the 8th a representation on public affairs was only carried by 191 to 190. On the 10th the Mutiny Bill was passed without a division, and on the 25th parliament was dissolved. Thus ended the struggle in which Dr. Johnson said 'Fox divided the kingdom with Cæsar; so that it was a doubt whether the nation should be ruled by the sceptre of George III or the tongue of Fox' (BOSWELL, Life of Johnson, iv. 315). Fox's defeat was caricatured by Sayer in the 'Fall of Phaeton' (WRIGHT).

His popularity had been ruined by the coalition, the India bill, and his attempt to prevent an appeal to the country, and in the general election upwards of 160 members lost their seats, almost all of whom were 'friends of the late administration' (Annual Register, 1784-5, xxv. 147). Fox was opposed at Westminster by Sir Cecil Wray. The poll was opened on 1 April and closed on 17 May, when the numbers were—Lord Hood, 6,694; Fox, 6,234; Wray, 5,998. During the whole period the city was a scene of riot. By far the most efficient canvasser for Fox was Georgina, duchess of Devonshire, who was aided by other whig ladies, and was shamefully libelled in the 'Morning Post' and 'Advertiser.' He also received much help from the songs of Captain Morris. No other occasion probably has called forth such a profusion of lampoons and caricatures (WRIGHT, Caricature History, p. 387; for squibs and history of the election see under authorities. The most noteworthy caricatures are on Fox's side those attributed to Rowlandson to be found in the 'History of the Election' and elsewhere, the 'Champion of the People,' the 'State Auction,' and the 'Hanoverian Horse and the British Lion,' and against him Gillray's 'Returning from Brooks's'). At the close of the poll the high bailiff granted Wray a scrutiny, and on the meeting of parliament the next day simply reported the numbers, making no return to the writ on pretence of not having finished the scrutiny (Annual Re-

gister, xxv. 279). Fox, however, was enabled to take his seat, as he was returned for Kirkwall. On 8 June he spoke on the subject of the scrutiny, arguing that by Grenville's act such questions should not be decided by votes of the house, and that the bailiff had acted on insufficient evidence and had no right to grant a scrutiny to be continued after the writ became returnable (*Speeches*, ii. 451). A struggle on this matter was kept up during two sessions. At last it became evident that there was no chance of unseating Fox, and on 3 March 1785 the high bailiff was ordered to make his return, and Hood and Fox were declared duly elected. All the expenses of the election were paid by Fox's political friends. He was in great difficulties ; all his effects were seized, and he was forced to leave his lodgings in St. James's. Shortly before this time he had formed a connection with Elizabeth Bridget Cane, otherwise Armistead or Armstead, a woman of good manners and some education, who is said to have begun life as waiting-woman to Mrs. Abington [q. v.] (*Early Life of Samuel Rogers*, p. 264). She took him to St. Anne's Hill, a house beautifully situated, with about thirty acres of land, near Chertsey in Surrey. Mrs. Armistead, to give her the title invariably used by Fox, appears to have bought this property about 1778 (BRAYLEY, *History of Surrey*, ii. 238). There Fox indulged his tastes for gardening and literature, and thoroughly enjoyed a country life in company with a woman to whom he was sincerely attached, and who devoted herself to promoting his happiness. For some years he stayed in London during the sessions of parliament, and actively though vainly led the opposition. When Pitt brought forward his resolutions regulating the conditions of commerce between Great Britain and Ireland, he condemned them on the grounds that they would injure the mercantile interests of England, and would place Ireland in a position of dependence by imposing uncertain restraints 'at the arbitrary demand of another state' (*Speeches*, iii. 57 sq.) As one of the champions of English commercial interests he received a warm welcome at Manchester in September; this greatly pleased him, for he loved popularity (*Memorials*, ii. 270). In the previous April he expressed his approval of the principle of Pitt's motion for parliamentary reform, but objected to the proposal for buying up the borough seats, contending that the franchise was not a property but a trust. The attack on Hastings was begun the next year, and in May appeared Gillray's caricature, 'Political banditti assaulting the Saviour of India,'

in which Fox appears attacking Hastings with a dagger. On 2 June Fox made an effective reply to Grenville's defence of Hastings against the charges brought against him by Burke with reference to the Rohilla war, and on the 13th laid before the committee the Benares charge, accusing Hastings of plundering Cheyt Sing, of causing the women taken at Bidgigur to be ill-treated, and of acting tyrannically at Benares; he concluded with a motion of impeachment. Pitt unexpectedly declared that he would vote for the motion, which was carried. Early in 1787 he took part in the debate on the Oude charge. He served on the committee appointed to draw up articles of impeachment, was one of the managers, and urged that Francis should be added to the number. During the progress of the trial, in 1788, he argued on the course of proceedings, opened the first part of the Benares charge in a speech which lasted five hours, and on 23 Dec. 1789 spoke with much force against the abatement of the impeachment by reason of the dissolution of parliament (*Speeches*, iv. 126).

In February 1787 Fox assailed the commercial treaty with France, though it certainly promised to be of great advantage to England. His opposition was based on political grounds. France, he said, was 'the natural political enemy of Great Britain;' she was endeavouring to draw England into 'her scale of the balance of power,' and to prevent it from forming alliances with other states. He advocated the claims of the dissenters to be exempt from disabilities on the score of religion, as he had advocated the cause of the Roman catholics seven years before. On 28 March he supported a motion for the repeal of the Test and Corporation Acts, and when the motion was renewed, on 1 May 1789, expressed his conviction that every country ought to have an established church, and that that church ought to be the church of the majority. He did not think it probable that the church of England would lose that position, but if the majority of the people should ever be for its abolition 'in such a case the abolition ought immediately to follow.' On 2 March following he moved the repeal himself. But the French revolution, and the writings of Priestley and Price, had convinced the house that it was possible that the church might be overthrown in England as it had been overthrown in France; Burke opposed his motion, and it was lost by nearly three to one (*ib*. iii. 315, iv. 1, 55). During 1785 the Prince of Wales often visited St. Anne's Hill in order to rave to Fox and his mistress about his passion for

T

Mrs. Fitzherbert. In the December of that year Fox, believing that he contemplated marrying that lady, wrote him an able letter pointing out the serious dangers that would arise from such a step. The prince replied that the world would soon see that there never existed any grounds for the reports to which Fox referred, and ten days later, without Fox's knowledge, married Mrs. Fitzherbert privately. On 20 April 1787 a reference was made in a debate to the alleged marriage, and Fox took an early opportunity of denying the report in the strongest terms, adding that he did so 'from direct authority.' His truthfulness is beyond question. A few days later he found out the deceit that had been practised upon him, and for about a year avoided meeting the prince (*Parl. Hist.* xxvi. 1064, 1070; *Memoirs of the Whig Party,* ii. 120–42; *Life of Mrs. Fitzherbert,* i. 28 sq.; *Life,* ii. 177 sq.; *Memorials,* ii. 289 *n.*) In August Fox had some hope of being enabled, by his friends' help, to extricate himself from his money difficulties, and wrote to Fitzpatrick that Coutts was willing to lend him 6,000*l.* (*Memorials,* ii. 290). He was deeply impressed with the evils of the slave trade, and when Pitt brought forward a resolution on the subject in May 1788, declared that the trade should not be regulated but destroyed (*Speeches,* iii. 388). He often urged the abolition of the trade in later years.

In the summer Fox and Mrs. Armistead went abroad. Gibbon, with whom he spent two days at Lausanne in September, writes that 'his powers were blended with the softness and simplicity of a child' (*Miscell.* i. 252, 253, 282). It was rumoured in England at this time that he was about to marry Miss Pulteney, afterwards created Baroness Bath, who married Sir James Murray, and who was in Italy while Fox was there (*Auckland Correspondence,* ii. 212). Fox stayed in Italy longer than he intended, for Mrs. Armistead sprained her ankle (*Life of Sir G. Elliot,* i. 225). During his whole tour he never opened a newspaper except once to see how his bets had been decided at Newmarket, and as he had left no address had no news from England (*ib.* p. 236). In November a messenger from the Duke of Portland found him at Bologna. His party were anxious for his presence, for the king had become insane. After travelling incessantly night and day for nine days he arrived in London on the 24th, suffering in health from his hurried journey (*ib.* p. 240). It at once became evident that the prince, if constituted regent, would dismiss his father's ministers and 'form a Foxite administration' (LEWIS). Whatever anger Fox may have

felt at the deceit the prince had practised on him, he put it aside and entered into close relations with him, but found to his annoyance that during his absence Sheridan had become prime favourite (*Auckland Correspondence,* ii. 267, 279). Although the prince was distrusted and disliked, and the change of ministers would have been extremely unpopular, Fox, in spite of his whig theories, determined to assert his right to the regency as independent of the will of parliament, and when on 10 Dec. Pitt proposed a committee to search for precedents, on the principle that the appointment of a regent was within the right of parliament, he opposed the motion, declaring that 'the Prince of Wales had as clear, as express a right to assume the reins of government' as in the case of the king's 'natural and perfect demise' (*Speeches,* iii. 401). As Pitt listened to this speech he slapped his thigh and said to a friend: 'I'll unwhig the gentleman for the rest of his life' (*Life of Sheridan,* ii. 38). He made the most of the difference between them. Fox explained that he did not intend to annul the authority of parliament, but held that the royal authority belonged to the prince from the moment of the king's incapacity. Constitutionally, his contention was that as a limited hereditary monarchy had been established as the form of government best suited to the wants of the nation, it would be dangerous to disturb that settlement by vesting the executive in a regent elected by the two houses; and that as parliament had no legislative power apart from the sanction of the crown, it was not competent to elect a regent or impose restrictions on the exercise of the royal power (LECKY, *History,* v. 103–20), for the question really at issue was not a matter of abstract right, but concerned the imposition of restrictions (LEWIS). Whatever may be thought of his reasoning, there can be no doubt as to his indiscretion. The ministerial party rejoiced greatly over his errors (*Courts and Cabinets,* ii. 49–54). On the 15th he believed that he and his party would be in power 'in about a fortnight' (*Memorials,* ii. 299). But after much debating Pitt's resolutions were agreed to. During the latter part of the discussions Fox was seriously unwell, and was forced to be at Bath to recruit his health (*Auckland Correspondence,* ii. 261, 267). On 21 Jan. 1789 he made out a list of the intended administration, placing the Duke of Portland at the head, and taking for himself the foreign department and the chairmanship of the India board (*Memorials,* iv. 284), and on 17 Feb. wrote of the regency as about to commence at once, for the bill had been carried in the commons four days before. Two days later the king was pronounced convalescent.

After hearing of the taking of the Bastille, Fox wrote to Fitzpatrick on 30 July 1789: 'How much the greatest event it is that ever happened in the world! and how much the best!' and bade him tell the Duke of Orleans that, if the revolution had the consequences he expected, his dislike of French connections for this country would be at an end (ib. ii. 361). During the succeeding period he advocated the revolutionary cause in the same spirit of vehement partisanship that he had exhibited during the American war; indeed 'there was no end to his indiscretions' (Auckland Correspondence, ii. 387). When opposing the army estimates on 5 Feb. following, he praised the French army for taking part against the crown, and for showing that 'in becoming soldiers they did not cease to be citizens.' In replying to Burke on the 9th he protested that he was no friend to democracy; he upheld a mixed form of government, but he applauded the French soldiers for disobeying their leaders and joining the people in a struggle for liberty, and, while he deplored bloodshed, considered that the severe tyranny of the old régime should cause the excesses of the revolutionists to be regarded with compassion [see under BURKE, EDMUND]. He opposed the foreign policy of Pitt during the war between Russia and the Porte, arguing in March 1791 that the Turks were in fault, and were, he suspected, set on by Great Britain, that Catherine's terms were moderate, and that it was mistaken to strive to compel her to restore Oczakoff and accept conditions of the status quo ante; for the advance of Russia in the south could never be prejudicial to English interests. The czarina affected a romantic attachment for Fox, and sent to England for his bust, in order to place it between the busts of Demosthenes and Cicero (Malmesbury Correspondence, i. 325 n.; COLCHESTER, Diary, i. 18). His conduct as regards the visit of Sir Robert Adair [q. v.] to Russia was declared by Burke to have 'frustrated the king's minister' (BURKE, Works, vii. 227). While Burke's accusation was untrue, Fox certainly appears to have treated foreign politics at this period mainly as an instrument of party. When Oczakoff was yielded to Russia by the treaty of Jassy (January 1792), he taunted Pitt in a sarcastic and witty speech for having lowered his tone. He opposed the Quebec Government Bill, objecting to the provisions for the duration of the Canadian parliaments, the reserves for the clergy, and the institution of an hereditary nobility to sit in the council.

The references he made to French politics in the course of the debates on this subject widened the breach between him and Burke, and on 6 May their old friendship and their political alliance was finally broken by public declaration in the commons [see under BURKE]. On the 20th Fox brought forward his Libel Bill, which was carried in the commons without opposition, and became law the next year. This act, which is declaratory, maintained the rights of juries, and secured to the subject a fair trial by his peers (MAY, Const. Hist. ii. 263). During the summer of 1792 some of the followers of Fox who disapproved of his sympathy with the revolution, and feared the total break-up of their party, engaged in a scheme with the Duke of Portland for a coalition with Pitt. Fox declared himself 'a friend to coalition,' and Pitt professed to be favourable to the idea. As, however, Fox objected to serve under Pitt, though it is possible that he might have been brought to do so, and as Pitt held that after Fox's declarations relative to the revolution it would be impossible for him to go 'at once' into the foreign department, the negotiations, which lasted about seven weeks, virtually ended by 30 July (MALMESBURY, ii. 453–72; Life of Sir G. Elliot, ii. 43, 53). Fox found some excuse for the revolutionary outbreak of 10 Aug., but not a shadow for the massacre of September (Memorials, ii. 368, 371); he was indignant at the Duke of Brunswick's proclamation and the invasion of France, and declared that no 'public event, not excepting Saratoga and Yorktown,' had so pleased him as the retreat of the Germans (ib. p. 372). He was now rapidly losing the confidence of a large section of his party, who took the Duke of Portland as their head. In the course of the winter Portland, Lord Fitzwilliam, Windham, Sir G. Elliot, T. Grenville, and many others separated themselves from him and gave their support to Pitt. He felt their secession deeply. Nor was he in full sympathy with Grey and others who joined the Association of the Friends of the People, for he considered it an inopportune time for pressing parliamentary reform, and was indeed never especially eager in the cause (MALMESBURY, ii. 482 sq.; Life of Elliot, ii. 82; Memorials, iii. 20, iv. 292). On 13 Dec. he moved an amendment to the address, mocking at the reason given in the king's speech for embodying the militia, which was declared to be rendered necessary by the spirit of disorder shown in acts of insurrection; instead of trying to suppress opinion it would, he said, be better to redress grievances. He was in a minority of 50 against 290; the larger number of his party had left him, and he was a 'head forsaken and alone' (*Auckland Correspondence*, ii. 498).

On 1 Feb. 1793 Fox opposed Pitt's address to the crown, pledging the house to resist the aggrandisement of France. The position that he took with regard to the war then imminent was that it was an unjustifiable attempt to interfere with the internal affairs of another nation, that the ministers were taking advantage of the opening of the Scheldt to press on the war, that they should have asked for reparation for the decree of 19 Nov., and that their demand that the French troops should be withdrawn from the Austrian Netherlands was insolent; in short that they were seizing on excesses to begin what would be a 'war of opinion' (*Speeches*, v. 16). After war was declared, he moved on the 18th a series of resolutions condemning the policy of the ministers, and was defeated by 44 to 270. His conduct brought him much unpopularity, and he was attacked by Gillray in some bitter caricatures; in 1791 he was represented in the 'Hopes of the Party' as beheading the king; he is learning to fire in 'Patriots amusing themselves,' 1792, and is in sans-culotte dress in a drawing of 1793. To Grey's motion for reform he gave on 7 May a general support, and in the course of his speech said some things that, considering the special needs of the time, were violent and unstatesmanlike (*ib.* p. 115). Some trials and sentences for sedition deeply moved his indignation. He was in a small minority in moving an amendment to the address recommending peace in January 1794. Before the opening of parliament the more important of his former allies formally signified their intention of supporting the ministers. He wrote to his nephew, Lord Holland, on 9 March that if he could have done it with honour he should best have liked to retire from politics altogether (*Memorials*, iii. 65). Pitt's plan of subsidising Prussia to prevent its threatened defection drew forth an able and sarcastic speech from him on 30 April (*Speeches*, v. 261), and a month later he made another attack on the policy of the ministers, both as regards the grounds of the war and the mode in which it was prosecuted (*ib.* p. 307). Although separated from his former allies, unpopular with a large part of the nation, and in a hopeless minority in parliament, Fox was cheerful and unsoured. There was nothing small in his nature, and he felt no envy; he understood the delight of literary leisure, and enjoyed it thoroughly as far he could get it. During this period his letters to his nephew, whom he loved as a son, and who was then abroad, are full of the pleasure he derived from the society of

Mrs. Armistead, the fine weather, and the beauties of St. Anne's Hill, of the pictures that pleased him most in Italy, and of his reading. He would have Lord Holland take note in the Pitti of Titian's 'Paul III, the finest portrait in the world.' Titian's masterpiece he holds to be his 'Peter Martyr' at Venice, and he speaks of his delight in the pictures of Guercino at Cento, and so on. Besides reading the 'Iliad' and the 'Odyssey,' as he did constantly, he was studying Spanish literature. He was at last fairly at ease about money, for in 1793 his friends subscribed 70,000*l.* to pay his debts and buy him an annuity (*Memorials*, iii. 40; *Life of P. Francis*, ii. 443). On 28 Sept. 1795 he married his mistress at Wytton, Huntingdonshire, but kept the fact of his marriage secret until 1802 (*Life*, iii. 78; BRAYLEY, *History of Surrey*, ii. 240). He continued his opposition to the war in 1795, and, regarding the Treason and Sedition Bills brought forward in November as a deathblow to the constitution, declared in the house that if such bills were vigorously enforced, he should advise the people 'that their obedience was no longer a question of moral obligation and duty, but of precedence' (*Speeches*, vi. 31). This remark was severely reprobated. In moving an address on the conduct of the war on 10 May 1796, he maintained that Austria and Prussia would not have moved in 1792 against the will of England, and that after the treaty of Pilnitz England should have taken a neutral position and become the moderator of peace; that the war had been conducted without any fixed aim, it was neither wholly for the restoration of the French monarchy nor wholly for English interests, and that it had caused the country to leave Poland to its fate. He was in a minority of 42 to 206. In May 1797 he censured the measures adopted to put an end to the mutiny at Spithead; his censure has been pronounced just (RUSSELL), but it is impossible to agree with this opinion; indeed the line he took on this occasion, and his attack on the government the next month with reference to the mutiny at the Nore, seem to prove that he regarded the difficulties of the country mainly as opportunities for attempting to win a party triumph. To this year belongs Isaac Cruikshank's [q. v.] caricature of Fox as the 'Watchman of the State.' On 26 May he supported Grey's motion for reform, declaring himself in favour of household suffrage in boroughs (*Speeches*, vi. 339). On the close of the session he and several of his friends, without pledging themselves to a systematic secession, ceased to attend parliament.

For more than five years Fox seldom appeared in parliament. During this period he led a quiet and regular life, spending much of his time in reading. He carried on a correspondence (1796–1801) with the famous Greek scholar, Gilbert Wakefield, and his letters show that he not only loved classical literature, but took a deep interest in the niceties of scholarship. The masterpieces of the greatest Latin, Greek, French, Italian, and Spanish authors were his constant companions. The four finest compositions of the century were, he said, the 'Isacco' of Metastasio, Pope's 'Eloisa,' Voltaire's 'Zaire,' and Gray's 'Elegy.' Burnet he held to be a master of historical style; he delighted in Dryden's works, and thought of editing them; Milton's prose he could not endure, and he did not admire Wordsworth. He read Homer through every year, enjoying the 'Odyssey' more than the 'Iliad,' though admitting that it was not so fine a work. Euripides he preferred to Sophocles. 'I should never finish,' he wrote, 'if I let myself go upon Euripides.' The 'Æneid' he read over and over again, dwelling with special pleasure on the pathetic passages (Memorials, iii. passim; Table-talk of S. Rogers, pp. 89–93). He began his 'History of the Revolution of 1688' in 1797 ; he made very slow progress with it, writing, Sydney Smith said, 'drop by drop.' A dinner of the Whig Club was held at the Crown and Anchor tavern on 24 Jan. 1798 to celebrate his birthday. At this dinner the Duke of Norfolk gave as a toast 'Our sovereign, the people,' and was in consequence dismissed from his lord-lieutenancy. Fox repeated the toast at a dinner held early in May, and on the 9th his name was erased from the privy council (Life of Pitt, iii. 128; MALMESBURY, iv. 303). He disliked the proposed Irish union, and thought that a scheme of federation would be preferable (19 Jan. 1799, Memorials, iii. 150, 295; COLCHESTER, Diary, ii. 39); the ministerial proposal was, he declared, 'an attempt to establish the principles as well as the practice of despotism' (Life of Grattan, iv. 435), but 'nothing would induce him to attend the union debates.' In September 1799 he was severely injured in the hand by the bursting of a gun while he was out shooting. He was indignant at Lord Grenville's reply to the overtures in the First Consul's letter of 25 Dec., and in deference to the wishes of his friends attended the debate on it on 3 Feb. 1800. His speech, except at the end, is rather an indictment of the ministers for entering on the war than a condemnation of Grenville's letter (Speeches, vi. 420). He was indignant at the sentences passed on Lord Thanet and Wakefield ; wrote bitterly of the ministers, declaring that, with them in office, invasion would

mean slavery ; condemned their Irish policy, disapproved of their proposal to compensate Irish borough-holders, and held that they were wrong in their pretensions as regards the right of searching neutral ships (Memorials, iii. 284, 292, 306, 326).

When Addington succeeded Pitt, in February 1801, Fox determined to test the feeling of the house by joining in the debate on Grey's motion on the state of the nation on 25 March. He spoke with much ability on the dispute with the northern powers, the ill-success of the war, and the rights of catholics, warmly vindicated the character of the Irish people, and made a sarcastic reference to the new chancellor of the exchequer (Speeches, vi. 423). The motion was rejected, and he declared that he should not attend again that session except to uphold Tooke's claim. The House of Commons, he thought, 'had ceased, and would cease, to be a place of much importance.' He approved of the peace of Amiens, and on 10 Oct., at a dinner at the Shakespeare tavern, exulted in the thought that the peace was glorious to France. 'Ought not glory,' he said, 'to be the reward of such a glorious struggle ? ' (Life of Pitt, iii. 357). On 3 Nov. he criticised the terms of the peace in parliament. He was re-elected for Westminster after a contest in July 1802, and on the 29th set out for a tour in the Netherlands, Holland, and France. While at Paris he had several interviews with Bonaparte. They did not raise his opinion of the First Consul, whom he pronounced to be a 'young man considerably intoxicated with success' (TROTTER, Memoirs, p. 36; LAS CASES, Journal de l'Empereur, iv. 171). Much of his time was spent in working at the archives, getting materials for his history. He paid a short visit to Lafayette, and returned to England on 17 Nov. On his return he expressed his conviction that Bonaparte wished for peace, and would do everything in his power to maintain it (Memorials, iii. 381, 384). Nevertheless, on 8 March 1803, he found himself forced to support a warlike address. On 24 May, after the declaration of war, he made a speech of three hours' duration in favour of an attempt to restore peace. This speech is universally praised. 'It was calm, subtle, argumentative pleasantry' (Memoirs of Horner, i. 221; MALMESBURY, iv. 257 ; Life of Sidmouth, ii. 182). He condemned the retention of Malta, but blamed the conduct of France with respect to Switzerland and Holland. Piedmont, he declared, was a part of France ; we had no right to complain of France there. In the matter of insults, as distinguished from injuries, he scorned the idea of checking the freedom of the press, or expelling refugees to please a foreign power. While he allowed that a check should be put on the designs of Bonaparte, he condemned the war as undertaken for British interests, for the retention of Malta (*Speeches*, vi. 485). For Addington he had an unmitigated contempt. Grenville, the leader of the 'new opposition,' wished a union between himself, Fox, and Pitt to turn Addington out, and, as Pitt held aloof, proposed in January 1804 that Fox, the leader of the old opposition, should join with him 'for the purpose of removing the ministry, and forming one on the broadest possible basis' (*Memorials*, iii. 449). Fox agreed, and resumed regular attendance in parliament. After the Easter recess Pitt, without pledging himself to Fox, let him know that in case of a change of ministers he would use earnest endeavours to induce the king to receive him and Grenville (*Courts and Cabinets*, iii. 349); Pitt entered into opposition, and on 30 April Addington was forced to resign.

Pitt submitted a plan of an administration to the king which included the principal men of both the oppositions, and in which Fox was proposed as foreign secretary. The king 'positively proscribed Fox and no one else' (MALMESBURY, iv. 300), and wished it to be known that Fox was 'excluded by his express command' (*Life of Sidmouth*, ii. 288). Meanwhile Fox, who thought it not improbable that the king would take this course, informed both his own friends and the Grenvilles that he hoped that his exclusion would not prevent them from taking office. Both sections declined entering an administration from which he was shut out (MALMESBURY, iv. 321). In the summer he went to Cheltenham for the benefit of his health. He had announced his marriage before going abroad in 1802, and his wife was now received at the houses at which he visited. Mrs. Fox had grown plain and fat, but her 'manners were pleasing and gentlewomanlike.' Fox read much to her, and never wearied of her society. He was extremely anxious that every one should do her honour, and it was said that considerations of this sort weighed too much with him. He enjoyed shopping with her; and Sir Gilbert Elliot marvelled to see them setting off together to buy cheap china, and notes that they were both very economical (*Life of Elliot*, 1805, iii. 361-2; *Life of Sir P. Francis*, ii. 352). On 13 May 1805 Fox made a remarkable speech in introducing a motion founded on the Roman catholic petition, but was defeated by 336 to 124 (*Speeches*, vi. 587). In July, and again in September, Pitt endeavoured to persuade the king to allow him to offer Fox office, but was

unsuccessful [see under GEORGE III]. Fox's accession would have secured the adhesion of Lord Grenville. According to his own account he hoped that the scheme would be defeated, for he declared that he would not enter a cabinet of which Pitt was the head. If he was to take office the administration must be changed (*Memorials*, iv. 90–114). When Pitt lay dying, on 21 Jan. 1806, a political meeting was held at Fox's house, but Fox refused to proceed to business. He could not do so, he said, at such a time, adding 'mentem mortalia tangunt' (*Life of Horner*, i. 328). He opposed the motion for public honours to Pitt on the ground that he had not been an 'excellent statesman,' but agreed cheerfully to the payment of his debts.

On Pitt's death the king sent for Lord Grenville, who at once said that the first person he should consult on the formation of an administration would be Fox; the king readily assented (*ib.* p. 331). By the end of the month Fox took office as foreign secretary in Grenville's administration, called 'All the Talents' or the 'Broad-bottomed,' and was caricatured by Gillray in 'Making Decent,' and as a led bear, for he was supposed to be under Grenville's influence. His union with Grenville was not like his coalition with North; there was no difference of principle, for he now recognised the necessity of checking Bonaparte's aggressions, and he had no cause to think ill of his colleague. At the same time he gave way to his old partiality for coalition by bringing into the cabinet Sidmouth, whom he despised, and who was wholly opposed to his principles (*Life of Sidmouth*, ii. 412). Nor was he justified in the part he took in involving the chief criminal judge in party politics by giving cabinet office to Lord Ellenborough, the chief justice, a course which he defended by laying down the maxim that the cabinet is not a body recognised by the constitution (*Parl. Debates*, vi. 308; this maxim was ridiculed by Canning). He agreed to submit any plan for withdrawing the army from the control of the crown, through the commander-in-chief, to the king's approval (*Life of Sidmouth*, ii. 415), and, in deference to the king's known desire, abstained from attempting to forward the claims of the catholics, for which the state of the king's health is some excuse (*ib.* p. 435). George received him graciously, and was turned from his old dislike of him by his minister's respectful and conciliatory manners. On 20 Feb. Fox informed Talleyrand of the offer of a Frenchman to assassinate Napoleon. This led to a correspondence which gave some hope of a treaty between Great Britain and France. Negotiations were begun but failed. Fox was convinced that the French were 'playing a false game;' he 'insisted that Russia should be made a party to the treaty,' and was stedfastly resolved to do nothing that could alienate our allies (*Life*, iii. 371–7; *Memorials*, iv. 136). Towards the end of May Fox's health became much impaired, but, in spite of increasing weakness, he moved for the abolition of the slave trade on 10 June, declaring that after forty years of political life he should feel that he could retire with contentment if he carried his motion (*Speeches*, vi. 658). A few days later he was forced to give up attendance in parliament. At the end of June his friends suggested that he should accept a peerage. 'I will not,' he said, 'close my politics in that foolish way, as so many have done before me' (*Memoirs of the Whig Party*, i. 249). His disease was found to be dropsy. He was moved from London to the Duke of Devonshire's house at Chiswick, and hoped to go on to St. Anne's, but was unable to do so. During his illness he listened with pleasure to Virgil, Dryden, Johnson's 'Lives of the Poets,' and Crabbe's 'Parish Register.' He was 'no believer in religion;' to content Mrs. Fox he consented to have prayers read, but 'paid little attention to the ceremony' (Lord Holland's account of his death in *Greville Memoirs*, iv. 159, ed. 1888). He died peacefully in the evening of 13 Sept., in his fifty-eighth year, and was buried in Westminster Abbey, close by the grave of Pitt.

Although Fox's private character was deformed by indulgence in vicious pleasures, it was in the eyes of his contemporaries largely redeemed by the sweetness of his disposition, the buoyancy of his spirits, and the unselfishness of his conduct. As a politician he had liberal sentiments, and hated oppression and religious intolerance. He constantly opposed the influence of the crown, and, although he committed many mistakes, and had in George III an opponent of considerable knowledge of kingcraft and immense resources, the struggle between him and the king, as far as the two men were concerned, was after all a drawn game. While his change of politics in 1772–4, though coincident with private pique, must not, considering his age, be held as a proof of irritability, the coalition of 1783 shows that he failed to appreciate the importance of political principles and was ignorant of political science. An immediate access of numerical strength always seemed to him a sure means of attaining a strong and stable government. Although his speeches are full of common sense, he made serious mistakes on some critical occasions, such as were the

struggle of 1783–4, and the dispute about the regency in 1788. The line that he took with reference to the war with France, his idea that the Treason and Sedition bills were destructive of the constitution, and his opinion in 1801 that the House of Commons would soon cease to be of any weight, are instances of his want of political insight. The violence of his language constantly stood in his way; in the earlier period of his career it gave him a character for levity; later on it made his coalition with North appear especially reprehensible, and in his latter years afforded fair cause for the bitterness of his opponents. The circumstances of his private life helped to weaken his position in public estimation. He twice brought his followers to the brink of ruin and utterly broke up the whig party. He constantly shocked the feelings of his countrymen, and 'failed signally during a long public life in winning the confidence of the nation' (Lecky, *Hist.* iii. 465 sq.) With the exception of the Libel Bill of 1792, the credit of which must be shared with others, he left comparatively little mark on the history of national progress. Great as his talents were in debate, he was deficient in statesmanship and in some of the qualities most essential to a good party leader. He occasionally wrote verses, and some lines of his are preserved in his memoirs (*Life*, iii. 191). His 'History of the Early Part of the Reign of James II, with an Introductory Chapter,' 4to, was published by Lord Holland in 1808. It ends with the death of the Duke of Monmouth. It is written in a cold, uninteresting style, and represents the chief aim of James to be the establishment of civil despotism rather than the overthrow of the church of England. The appendix contains the transcripts of Barillon's correspondence made during Fox's visit to Paris in 1802. Mrs. Fox continued to reside at St. Anne's Hill after her husband's death, and died there at the age of ninety-two on 8 July 1842 (*Annual Register*, pp. 84, 276). Fox had an illegitimate son, who was deaf and dumb, and died at the age of fifteen; he treated him with much affection (*Table-talk of S. Rogers*, p. 81).

[Earl Russell's Memorials and Correspondence of C. J. Fox, 1853–7, full of information, but awkwardly arranged, and the same writer's Life and Times of C. J. Fox, 1859–66, valuable but dull and with strong whig leanings, cited as Life; Sir G. O. Trevelyan's Early History of C. J. Fox, 1880, interesting though discursive, with some new facts about Fox's gaming, ends at 1774; Fell's Memoirs of Public Life, 1808, poor and now useless; Trotter's Memoirs of the Later Years of C. J. Fox, 1811, by Fox's private secretary, the first-hand authority for many details of private life from 1802 to 1806, according to S. Rogers 'inaccurate though pleasing,' both epithets seem disputable; a spiteful criticism of Fox's character by Francis in Parkes and Merivale's Life of Sir P. Francis, 1867; Brougham's estimate in his Historical Sketches of Statesmen, I., Knight's Weekly, 1845, is worthy of attention; Lecky's Hist. of England in Eighteenth Cent. vols. iii-vi., 1882–7; Lewis's Administrations, 1864; May's Constitutional History, 1875; Speeches of C. J. Fox, 1815; Walpole's Memoirs of the Reign of Geo. III, 1859, Last Journals, 1859, and Letters, ed. Cunningham, 1880; Wraxall's Historical and Posthumous Memoirs, 1884; Lettres de la Marquise du Deffand, 1810; Letters of Junius, ed. Woodfall, 1878; Donne's Correspondence of Geo. III with Lord North, 1867; Boswell's Life of Johnson, 1807; Gibbon's Miscellaneous Works, ed. Lord Sheffield, 1814; Lord Albemarle's Memoirs of the Marquis of Rockingham, 1852; Duke of Buckingham's Courts and Cabinets of Geo. III, 1853; Fitzmaurice's Life of Shelburne, 1875; Franklin's Works, ed. Sparks, vol. ix. 1840; Nicholls's Recollections of the Reign of Geo. III, 1820. For the Westminster election of 1784: History of the Westminster Election, 1784; Book of the Wars of Westminster, 1784; Oriental Chronicles, 1785; Collection of Squibs in the British Museum, 1784. For caricatures of Fox: Wright's History of Caricature, 1865; and Caricature History of the Georges, 1868. Lord Holland's Memoirs of the Whig Party, 1852; Moore's Life of Sheridan, 1825; Lord Malmesbury's Diaries, 1844; Prior's Life of Burke, 1853; Grattan's Life of Grattan, 1836; Stanhope's Life of Pitt, 1862; Lord Auckland's Journal and Correspondence, 1862; Horner's Memoirs of F. Horner, 1853; Rose's Diaries, 1865; Pellew's Life of Lord Sidmouth, 1847; Lord Colchester's Diary and Correspondence, 1861; Lady Minto's Life of Sir G. Elliot, 1874; Maltby's Samuel Rogers's Table-talk, ed. Dyce, 1887; Clayden's Early Life of S. Rogers, 1887; Princess Liechtenstein's Holland House, 1874, contains, among other matters, notices of the portraits and statues of Fox.]   W. H.

FOX, CHARLES RICHARD (1796–1873), numismatist, was the son of Henry Richard Vassall Fox [q. v.], third lord Holland, by Elizabeth, daughter of Richard Vassall, formerly wife of Sir Godfrey Webster, born (in 1796) before their marriage. He served in the navy from 1809 to 1813, and was present at the sieges of Cadiz (1810) and Tarragona (1813). He left the navy and entered the grenadier guards in June 1815. He became colonel in 1837 and general in 1863. He represented Calne and Tavistock in parliament, and was elected for Stroud in 1835. In November 1832 he was appointed surveyor-general of the ordnance, and was afterwards secretary to the master-general of the ordnance. He became equerry to Queen

Adelaide in July 1830, and aide-de-camp to William IV in May 1832. He was elected a member of the Dilettanti Society in 1837. At the time of his death he was receiver-general of the duchy of Lancaster, having held the appointment some time.

Fox began coin-collecting early in life, and a journey to Greece and Asia Minor in 1820 stimulated his taste. He obtained many coins from the peasants, and at Priene found several specimens in dry watercourses. In 1851 he acquired one of the collections of Whittall of Smyrna. He also bought at the Pembroke, Thomas, Devonshire, and other sales. In 1840 Burnes gave him the whole of his Bactrian coins. In 1862 his collection consisted of more than ten thousand Greek coins. He published a description of part of it entitled 'Engravings of Unedited or Rare Greek Coins,' with descriptions and plates. Part I. ('Europe') London, 1856, 4to. Part II. ('Asia and Africa'), London, 1862, 4to. The collection was purchased (after his death) in 1873 by the Royal Museum at Berlin. Dr. J. Friedlaender, who published a notice of it in the 'Archäologische Zeitung' for 1873 (pp. 99–103; 'Die Fox'sche Münzsammlung'), declares that this acquisition for the first time enabled the Berlin coin-cabinet to aspire to the rank of the national collections of England and France. The Fox collection consisted of 11,500 Greek coins, among which were 330 in gold, and more than 4,000 in silver. It was remarkable for the rarity of the specimens (not a few being unique), and for the admirable state of preservation throughout (cp. FRIEDLAENDER and VON SALLET, Das königliche Münzkabinet, 1877, pp. 43–5). Fox died at his house in Addison Road on 13 April 1873, after a long illness. He married, first, on 19 June 1824, Lady Mary Fitzclarence, second daughter of the Duke of Clarence and Mrs. Jordan, a woman of great social ability, who was raised to the rank of a marquis's daughter in May 1831, was for many years state housekeeper of Windsor Castle, and died in 1864; and secondly, in August 1865, Katherine, second daughter of John Maberly, M.P., who survives him. There was no issue of the marriages. Fox's portrait when a midshipman was painted by Sir Martin Archer Shee, and a portrait of him in his sixty-sixth year is prefixed to part i. of his 'Engravings of Unedited Coins.' Fox had a remarkable memory and, though not a savant, much facility in acquiring knowledge. He was a man of great amiability, and a wit without cynicism. He endeavoured to make his house a literary centre, especially of some of the younger archæologists. In politics he called himself 'a movement whig.'

[Times, 16 April 1873, p. 7, col. 6; Michaelis's Ancient Marbles in Great Britain, pp. 64, 165; Fox's Engravings, &c.; information from Reginald Stuart Poole, LL.D.]   W. W.

FOX, EBENEZER (d. 1886), journalist, was born in England, and practised his profession in the north until he had nearly attained middle age. For several years he was chief reporter on the 'Manchester Guardian.' His account of the great floods at Holmfirth in 1852 was widely quoted. Delicate health induced Fox to emigrate to Australia. In 1862 he went to Dunedin and joined the staff of the 'Otago Daily Times,' being associated with Sir Julius Vogel and B. L. Farjeon, the novelist. When Vogel established the 'Sun,' Fox assisted him. The two friends moved to Auckland, and soon after Vogel joined William Fox's ministry in 1869 as colonial treasurer, Fox became his private secretary. In 1870 he was appointed confidential clerk and secretary to the treasury, which position he held up to his death. For sixteen years he was implicitly trusted by successive ministries. In the columns of the 'New Zealand Times' Fox wrote a series of articles on the denudation of the forests, which attracted much attention. Fox, who was kindly but eccentric in character, died of muscular atrophy at Wellington in January 1886.

[New Zealand Times, 9 Jan. 1886; Phonetic Journal, 20 March 1886.]   G. B. S.

FOX, EDWARD (1496?–1538), bishop of Hereford, was born at Dursley in Gloucestershire. He was educated at Eton, whence he proceeded to King's College, Cambridge, the date of his admission being 27 March 1512. According to Lloyd, he was 'wild' in his youth, but his brilliant talents afterwards made him the 'wonder of the university.' The same writer implies that Fox was partly indebted for his advancement as a scholar to his relationship to Richard Foxe [q. v.], bishop of Winchester; but these are statements with respect to which we have no confirmatory evidence. His whole career gives us the impression that he possessed not only great abilities, but also a readiness, tact, and indomitable energy which rendered him especially adapted for difficult negotiations. His early success must, however, be to a great extent attributed to the fact that he obtained the appointment of secretary to Wolsey. At what time this occurred does not appear, but his admission as prebendary of Osbaldwicke in the county of York, which took place 8 Nov. 1527, was probably one of the earliest proofs of the archbishop's favour. In the early part of 1528 he was sent with Gardiner by Wolsey to Rome, for the purpose of overcoming Clement VII's scruples as to granting a commission and a dispensation with respect to King Henry's marriage with Catherine. They were enjoined especially to represent the dangers that would ensue from a disputed succession, and the likelihood in that event of England declining from obedience to the holy see (*Letters and Papers*, Hen. VIII, ed. Brewer, IV. ii. passim). In a letter (12 May) written to Gardiner on his return, Fox gives a detailed account of his reception at court, together with the report of their mission, which he gave to the king and council, and of the manner in which it was received (POCOCK, *Records of the Reformation*, pp. 141–55). On 22 Sept. 1528, being D.D., he was elected provost of King's College, on the recommendation of the king and Wolsey. On the arrival of Campeggio in England in the same year, and his first audience with the king (22 Oct.), Fox made an 'elegant reply' to the address of Florian, the legate's spokesman. It was in the following August (1529) that, being at Waltham in attendance on the king, he held with Cranmer [see CRANMER, THOMAS] their historic conversation respecting the legality of the royal marriage. It was Fox who reported Cranmer's observation to Henry, and thus became the means of introducing him to the king, and of bringing about his rapid rise in the royal favour. In October Fox was sent on an embassy to Paris, and in December he was presented to the mastership of the hospital of Sherburn, Durham. In the following January (1529–30) he appears as intervening at Cambridge for the purpose of putting an end to a controversy which had there arisen between Latimer and the Romanist party, his influence evidently inclining in favour of the former, mainly, it would seem, because Latimer was known to have pronounced in favour of the royal divorce. Fox, however, admits in his letter that Latimer is perhaps 'more vehement than becomes the very evangelist of Christ, and purposely speaks paradoxes to offend and slander people.' In the ensuing month he visited the university along with Stephen Gardiner, in order to wring from the academic body a formal expression of opinion in favour of the divorce. Their object was not accomplished without difficulty, and the means by which it was ultimately brought about cast a slur on the chief agents in the matter. In the following April Fox was sent on a similar errand to Oxford, along with John Longland, bishop of Lincoln, and John Bell, afterwards bishop of Worcester [q. v.] His account of their proceedings, transmitted to the king, is still extant in his own handwriting (Pocock, *Records*, pp. 291–3). He next went with the same object to Paris ; and Reginald Pole, writing to Henry (7 July) and giving some account of the circumstances under which the conclusion of the university there was arrived at, states that the adverse party had used every effort to prevent its being carried, but that Fox (who appears to have been the bearer of his letter) had ' used great prudence and diligence in withstanding them.' In May 1531 he again proceeded to France on the same business. Chapuys, in a letter to the emperor, describes him as an ' habile galant, and one of the boutefeus in this matter of the divorce.' On 26 Sept. the same writer states that Fox has again been sent to Paris, and adds that, in order ' to enable him to do it better, the lady' (Anne Boleyn) ' has given him benefices and the office of almoner.' In December Fox returned to England ; and on New Year's day we find the queen presenting him with a piece of arras.

The tact and ability which he showed in these difficult and delicate negotiations led to his frequent employment in other political business. In 1532 he appears as one of the signatories to the treaty with France ; and when, at the celebration of high mass, the treaty received the signature of Henry and the French ambassador, Fox, according to Chapuys, made a speech in praise of the alliance, describing it as ' inviolable and eternal' and ' the best means of resisting the Turk.' In April 1533 he was appointed on the commission to conclude a yet stricter ' league and amity' with Francis I, and in 1534 discharged a like function in arranging terms of peace with Scotland. The whole conduct of the divorce transactions appears to have now been mainly in his hands, and Sir George Casale refers to him as the best informed among English statesmen with respect to the negotiations on the subject which had been going on in Italy. In April 1533, when the lawfulness of Henry's first marriage was under discussion by convocation, he presided in the place of the prolocutor. In the following May, on the occasion of an official conference with Chapuys at Westminster, he was appointed to reply to Chapuys, to whom he represented that ' the king, by his great learning, moved by the Divine Spirit, had found that he could not keep the queen as his wife, and, like a catholic prince, he had separated from her, and that there was no occasion to discuss the matter further' (Rolls Series, 25 Hen. VIII, No. 465). He took a leading part in the attempts made to induce Catherine to give her assent to the statute respecting the succession, and in 1534 he published his treatise ' De vera Differentia

Regiæ Potestatis et Ecclesiæ.' It was printed by Berthelet, and a second edition was published in 1538. Fox, by this time, had definitely taken his stand as a reformer, and Chapuys describes him as, along with Cranmer and Cromwell, ' among the most perfect Lutherans in the world.'

In the meantime honours and preferments had been showered liberally upon him. On 3 Jan. 1528 he was presented to the rectory of Combemartin in the diocese of Exeter. In 1531 he was appointed archdeacon of Leicester, and continued to hold that office until his election as bishop of Hereford. In January 1532 he received a grant, in augmentation of the royal alms, of all goods and chattels of deodands and suicides in England. In 1533 he was promoted to the deanery of Salisbury and the archdeaconry of Dorset. In May 1535 he was presented to a canonry and prebend in the collegiate church of SS. Mary and George in Windsor Castle. In the following August he was elected to the bishopric of Hereford, the royal assent being given on 2 Sept. During the former month he appears to have been much with Cranmer at Lambeth, occupied probably in discussing with the primate the various points on which he would have to confer with the Lutheran divines in Germany, to whom it was proposed he should go as a delegate for the purpose of winning them over to Henry's side. On the 31st he received his credentials from the king at Bromham in Wiltshire, and in October he set out with Dr. Nicolas Heath, archdeacon of Stafford, for Germany. They were instructed to proceed first to the elector of Saxony, and afterwards to the other German princes. On their arrival at Wittenberg they had an interview with Luther, who, although he could not conceal his amazement at their apparent confidence in the justice of their cause, expressed himself willing to listen to their arguments. He, however, became wearied by their pertinacity and prolonged stay, which was protracted to April, Fox, in that month, even going so far as to follow the doctors of the university to the diet at Frankfort. At length he and his colleagues were dismissed, taking back to England as the reply of the protestant divines of Germany, that, although the king had doubtless been moved by very weighty reasons, and it was impossible to deny that his marriage was against natural and moral law, they could not persuade themselves that he had acted rightly in the matter of the divorce.

In 1536 Fox was sent on a similar errand to France. In the same year his growing sympathy with Lutheran doctrine was shown by the support which he gave to Alexander Alane [see ALESIUS], on the occasion when the young reformer pleaded his own cause before convocation. The whole of Fox's remarkable speech is printed in the 8th book of Foxe's 'Acts and Monuments;' it contains, among other noteworthy utterances, an explicit declaration, that 'the lay people do now know the Holy Scriptures better than most of us.' In the same year Martin Bucer dedicated to him the edition of his 'Commentaries on the Gospels' printed at Basle.

Fox died in London 8 May 1538, and was buried in the church of St. Mary Mounthaw there. His will, dated on the day of his death, was proved 20 March 1538-9. Some of his sayings have become proverbial. 'The surest way to peace is a constant preparedness for war.' 'Oft was this saying in our bishop's mouth,' says Lloyd, 'before ever it was in Philip the Second's—" Time and I will challenge any two in the world " ' (*State Worthies*, ed. 1670, pp. 88–9).

Fox's chief work was the 'De vera Differentia' above mentioned, which his warm friend and admirer, Henry Stafford, only son of Edward, duke of Buckingham, translated into English (8vo, 1548). He appears to have been the joint author, along with Stokesley, bishop of London, and Dr. Nicolas, of a volume 'afterwards translated into English, with additions and changes, by my lord of Canterbury,' entitled 'The Determinations of the most famous and mooste excellent universities of Italy and Fraunce, that it is so unleful for a man to marie his brothers wyfe, that the pope hath no power to dispence therewith,' London, 8vo, 1531.

[Letters and Papers of the Reign of Hen. VIII, ed. Brewer and Gairdner; Cooper's Athenæ Cantabrigienses, vol. i.; manuscript notes to Baker's copy of the De vera Differentia in St. John's College Library, A. 3, 36; Pocock's Records of the Reformation; Lloyd's State Worthies; Lelandi Encomia.]   J. B. M.

FOX, ELIZABETH VASSALL, LADY HOLLAND (1770–1845), daughter of Richard Vassall of Jamaica, was born in 1770, and was married on 27 June 1786 to Sir Godfrey Webster, bart., of Battle Abbey, Sussex. The marriage was dissolved on 3 July 1797 on the ground of adultery committed by her with Henry Richard [q. v.], third baron Holland, to whom she was married at Rickmansworth three days afterwards. Lord Holland had just restored Holland House, and there he gathered round him that brilliant circle of statesmen, wits, men of letters, and other people of distinction, which gave the house a European celebrity. Lady Holland possessed a remarkable power of making her guests

display themselves to the best advantage. Traits in her character that were by no means attractive rendered her power of fascination the more extraordinary. Cyrus Redding says of her: 'Polite, cold, haughty to those she met first in social intercourse, she was offensive to those to whom she took a dislike,' adding, as an instance, that Campbell having jestingly taken her to task for using the expression 'take a drive,' she treated him 'with an hauteur to which he would not again expose himself' (*Fifty Years' Recollections*. iii. 176–8). 'Elle est toute assertion,' said Talleyrand, 'mais quand on demande la preuve, c'est là son secret' (RAIKES, *Journal*, i. 300). Moore tells how on one occasion she asked him how he could write those 'vulgar verses' about Hunt, and on another occasion attacked his 'Life of Sheridan' as 'quite a romance' showing a 'want of taste and judgment.' To 'Lalla Rookh' she objected, 'in the first place because it was eastern, and in the second place because it was in quarto.' 'Poets,' says Moore, 'inclined to a plethora of vanity would find a dose of Lady Holland now and then very good for their complaint.' To Lord Porchester she once said: 'I am sorry to hear you are going to publish a poem. Can't you suppress it?' 'Your poetry,' she said to Rogers, 'is bad enough, so pray be sparing of your prose.' To Matthew Gregory (better known as Monk) Lewis, complaining that in 'Rejected Addresses' he was made to write burlesque, which he never did, she replied, 'You don't know your own talent' (MOORE, *Diary*, Russell, ii. 328, v. 262, vi. 41; *Quarterly Review*, cxxv. 427). Byron, supposing that she had prompted the article on 'Hours of Idleness' in the 'Edinburgh Review,' satirised her in 'English Bards and Scotch Reviewers,' but afterwards made reparation by dedicating the 'Bride of Abydos' to her husband. In Ticknor, the historian of Spanish literature, she met her match. Referring to New England she told him that she understood the colony had originally been a convict settlement, to which Ticknor answered that he was not aware of the fact, but that in the King's Chapel, Boston, was a monument to one of the Vassalls, some of whom had been among the early settlers of Massachusetts (*Life of Ticknor*, i. 264 n.) She kept a tight rein on her guests when they seemed inclined to monopolise the conversation. Macaulay once descanting at large on Sir Thomas Munro, she told him brusquely she had had enough of the subject and would have no more. The conversation then turned on the Christian Fathers, and Macaulay was copious on Chrysostom and Athanasius till Lady Holland abruptly turned to him with, 'Pray, Macaulay, what was the origin of a doll? when were dolls first mentioned in history?' This elicited a disquisition on the Roman doll, which in its turn was cut short by Lady Holland (GRE-VILLE, *Memoirs*, 1837–52, i. 367–8). On another occasion she sent a page to ask him to cease talking, as she wished to listen to Lord Aberdeen. She would also issue her orders to her more intimate friends with very little ceremony. 'Ring the bell, Sydney,' she said once to Sydney Smith, to which he re-plied, 'Oh yes! and shall I sweep the room?' She dined at the unfashionably early hour of six or half-past six, merely, according to Talleyrand, 'pour gêner tout le monde,' and often overcrowded her table. 'Make room,' she said to Henry Luttrell [q. v.] on one of these occasions. 'It must certainly be *made*,' he observed, 'for it does not exist.' Lord Dudley declined her invitations, because 'he did not choose to be tyrannised over while he was eating his dinner.' Lord Melbourne, being required to change his place, got up with 'I'll be d——d if I dine with you at all,' and walked out of the house. Neverthe-less her beauty, vivacity, and the unrivalled skill with which she managed the conversa-tion so that there should never be either too much or too little of any one topic, atoned for everything. Her house was neutral ground on which men of the most opposite schools of thought met and conversed freely and with mutual forbearance and respect. Though herself a sceptic she never encouraged an irreverent treatment of religion; and though, like her husband, a staunch whig, she im-pressed a temperate tone on the discussion of all political questions.

In 1800 she became entitled, under the will of her grandfather, Florentius Vassall, to some estates in Jamaica, on condition that she as-sumed the name of Vassall only after her christian name. She did this by royal license 18 June 1800 (in Heralds' College, I. 36, 20). She aspired to exert an influence on politics. 'Lady Holland,' writes Lord Hobart, under date 16 Sept. 1802, 'is deep in political in-trigue, and means for the preservation of peace to make it necessary that Fox should be in power' (*Journal of William, first lord Auckland*, iv. 163). By degrees Holland House came to be the headquarters of the opposition, where the leaders of the party were accustomed to hold council every Sun-day (BUCKINGHAM, *Memoirs of the Court of the Regency*, i. 169–70). On the collapse of Lord Goderich's coalition ministry (1828) Lady Holland was ambitious of high office for her husband. 'Why should not Lord Holland be secretary for foreign affairs,' she asked, 'why not, as well as Lord Lansdowne

for the home department?' Lord John Rus-sell is said to have quietly replied, 'Why, they say, ma'am, that you open all Lord Holland's letters, and the foreign ministers might not like that' (CROKER, *Corresp.* i. 400). During the progress of the Reform Bill, some of the cabinet ministers often dined with her, and freely discussed the political situation. Brougham accuses her of pursuing him with bitter spite on account of an affront put on her by his mother (*Memoirs*, ii. 102), but much importance cannot be attached to such a charge emanating from Brougham. He and Lady Holland were, however, at feud for a great many years; she made an advance in the direction of a reconciliation by sending him an invitation to dinner in 1839, which he declined (GREVILLE, *Memoirs*, 1837–52, i. 245–6). She was an ardent admirer of Napoleon, to whom she was introduced at Malmaison in 1802, and sent him a message of respect and sympathy at Elba in 1814, and parcels of books and Neapolitan sweet-meats at St. Helena. He bequeathed to her a gold snuff-box ornamented with a fine cameo, the gift of Pius VI after the signature of the treaty of Tolentino, 1797, and she procured and preserved as relics a ring and cross of the Legion of Honour which had belonged to him, a sock which he had worn at his death, and a copy of the 'Edinburgh Review' (October-December, 1816) containing pencil marks in his handwriting. Dr. John Allen lived in her house, and Macaulay says she treated him like a negro slave [see ALLEN, JOHN, 1771–1843]. By the death of Lord Holland in 1840 the gaiety of her house suffered a brief eclipse. But three months afterwards Greville was pre-sent at one of her most brilliant dinner parties (*ib.* 1837–52, i. 367). These, however, were now for the most part given at her house in South Street, Grosvenor Square, and to a some-what smaller company. Thiers and Palmerston were both present at the last she ever gave (October 1845). Her own death, the approach of which seemed to cause her neither fear nor concern, took place at her house in South Street, Grosvenor Square, at two o'clock on the morning of 16 Nov. 1845. She was buried at Ampthill Park, Bedfordshire. Her will was unnatural, her children being almost entirely excluded. She was a kind mistress to her servants, and a warm, sympathetic, and faithful friend. Greville says that 'she dreaded solitude above everything.' A portrait of her, painted by Gauffier at Florence in 1795, and another by Fagan are at Holland House. Lady Holland had issue by her first husband two sons (Godfrey Vassall, who succeeded his father in title and estates, represented Sussex in parliament, and died in 1836; and Henry, who entered the army, and rose to the rank of colonel) and one daughter, Harriet, who married in 1816 the Hon. Sir Fleetwood Pellew, captain R.N. and C.B. She also had a son by Lord Holland before her marriage with that nobleman, viz. Charles Richard Fox [q. v.], who entered the army, and married in 1824 Lady Mary Fitzclarence, second daughter of William IV by Mrs. Jordan.

[Lords' Journals, xli. 333, 348, 379; Gent. Mag. 1797 pt. ii. 614, 1846 pt. i. 89; Burke's Extinct Peerage; Lord Holland's Foreign Reminiscences, pp. 188–205; Trevelyan's Life of Macaulay, i. 207, 211, 230, 234, 266, 339, 352; Quarterly Review, cliii. 116, cliv. 110; Princess Liechtenstein's Holland House; Addit. MSS. 20117 f. 17, 20125 f. 259, 20140 f. 54, 20158 ff. 12 b, 13; Greville's Mem. (Geo. IV–Wm. IV), ii. 130, 245, iii. 316; Sir Henry Holland's Recollections of Past Life (2nd ed.), 228 et seq.; Hayward's Biographical and Critical Essays, new ser. ii. 262–3.] J. M. R.

FOX, FRANCIS (1675–1738), divine, son of Francis Fox, was born at Brentford in 1675. He entered St. Edmund Hall, Oxford, as a commoner in April 1698, after having, according to Hearne, served six and a half years of his time as apprentice to a glover in London. He took the degree of B.A. in 1701, and that of M.A. in 1704. In 1705 he was chaplain to the lord mayor, Sir Owen Buckingham, and apparently about this time was 'commonly known as Father Fox.' Bishop Burnet appointed him rector of Boscombe, Wiltshire, in 1708, and promoted him thence to the vicarage of Potterne, a better living, in 1711. He was chaplain to Lord Cadogan, and, from 1713 till his death, prebendary of Salisbury. In 1726 the lord chancellor presented him to the vicarage of St. Mary's in Reading, a living worth 300l. a year. There he died in July 1738.

He was, at any rate for most of his life, a strong whig, and in 1727 he preached at what was called the Reading lecture a sermon which gave great offence to a number of the clergy who formed the audience. After being repeated as an assize sermon at Abingdon, it was published under the title of 'Judgment, Mercy, and Fidelity, the Weightier Matters or Duties of the Law' (Matt. xxiii. 23). It was considered to undervalue the efficacy of the sacraments, and to depreciate unduly the usefulness of preaching against dissenters. Angry letters about it were exchanged between Fox and the Rev. Joseph Slade of St. Laurence's, Reading, who eventually published a sermon in reply to it, with the letters prefixed. This in its turn was attacked by the Rev. Lancelot Carleton in 'A Letter to the Rev. Jos. Slade.'

Besides the sermon, 'Judgment, Mercy, and Fidelity,' Fox published: 1. 'The Superintendency of Divine Providence over Human Affairs,' a sermon preached in St. Paul's before the lord mayor on Restoration-day, 1705. 2. An anonymously printed folio sheet entitled 'The Obligations Christians are under to shun Vice and Immorality and to practise Piety and Virtue shown from the express words of Holy Scripture,' about 1707. 3. 'The Lawfulness of Oaths and the Sin of Perjury and Profane Swearing,' an assize sermon at Salisbury, 1710. 4. 'The Duty of Public Worship proved, with directions for a devout behaviour therein,' 1713 (19th ed. S.P.C.K., 1818). 5. 'A Sermon on the Sunday next after 5 Nov.' (Num. xxiii. 23), 1715. 6. 'The New Testament, with references and notes,' 1722. 7. 'An Introduction to Spelling and Reading, containing lessons for children,' 7th ed. 1754 (17th ed. S.P.C.K., 1805).

[Coates's Hist. of Reading, pp. 116, 117, and extract from Rawlinson MS. J., 4to, iii. 286, in the supplement; Hearne's Collections, ed. Doble, i. 34, ii. 6, 75, 107; Hearne's MS. Diary, lxxxvi. 11, cxi. 115; Hoare's Modern Wiltshire, Underditch, p. 164, Ambresbury, p. 116; Hutchins's Hist. of Dorset (3rd ed.), ii. 572; Political State, July 1738, lvi. 93; Oxford Cat. of Grad.; Brit. Mus. and Bodleian Catalogues of Printed Books.] E. C–N.

FOX, GEORGE (1624–1691), founder of the Society of Friends, son of Christopher Fox ('righteous Christer'), a puritan weaver in good circumstances, was born at Fenny Drayton (otherwise Drayton-in-the-Clay), Leicestershire, in July 1624. Fox mentions that his mother, Mary Lago, was 'of the stock of the martyrs,' in allusion probably to the family of Glover of Mancetter (see RICHINGS, *The Mancetter Martyrs*, 1860). Penn describes her as 'a woman accomplished above most of her degree.' Whether Fox had any schooling (CROESE) is doubtful; his spelling was always uncouth, but his illiteracy has been somewhat exaggerated. The accounts of his early seriousness are chiefly remarkable for bringing to the front the ethical element in the puritan character and training. His parents intended George for the ministry of the church of England; he speaks of no objection on his own part, 'but others persuaded to the contrary.' Accordingly he was apprenticed to a shoemaker (at Nottingham, according to Croese). His master did business as a grazier and wool dealer, and employed George as a trusted agent, whose 'verily' was accepted as a final word in a bargain.

Early in the summer of 1643 (before July) an incident at a fair determined Fox's future.

His cousin Bradford, with another puritan youth, would have initiated him into the practice of drinking healths. He paid his shot, but left the company; spent a night in religious exercises, and felt a divine call to forsake all his existing associations. This call he obeyed on 9 Sept. 1643. Turning his face southward, he disappeared for nine months, dividing his time between Lutterworth, Northampton, and Newport Pagnel, shunning society and declining religious fellowship. In June 1644 he moved on to Barnet; here he doubted whether he had done right in leaving home, and his religious melancholy deepened towards despair. After a stay at Barnet, he took a lodging in London, and visited his uncle Pickering, a baptist. Hearing that his relatives were troubled at his absence, he at length returned to Drayton.

From that return he dates (*Epistles*, p. 2) the beginning of his religious community (1644). This, however, is a retrospective judgment. His course was still far from clear. His relatives wished him to marry. Others proposed his joining the 'auxiliary band' among the parliamentary forces; this he refused, being 'tender,' a word which in his phraseology means religiously affected. He was attracted to Coventry, a puritan stronghold, and found sympathisers there. Returning to Drayton in 1645, he spent something like a year in fruitless resorts to neighbouring clergy. The curate of Drayton, Nathaniel Stephens (rector from 1659), a studious and kindly man, paid much attention to him, but Fox disliked his bringing the subjects of their conversations into the pulpit. He describes Stephens as subsequently his 'great persecutor,' an unwarranted expression. The old vicar of Mancetter, Richard Abell, advised him to 'take tobacco, and sing psalms.' John Machin, afterwards lecturer at Atherstone, prescribed physic and bleeding; the bleeding was tried without success. He got more satisfaction from his visits of charity among the poor; he had some independent means, whence derived he does not say; he reports without comment the remark of his relatives, 'When hee went from us hee had a greate deale of gould and sillver about him' (original manuscript of *Journal*, p. 17).

During a Sunday morning's walk, early in 1646, the new idea presented itself to him that a minister must be more than a scholar. Henceforward he gave up attendance at church; going rather to the orchard or the fields, with his Bible. For more than a year he wandered about in the midland counties, mixing with separatists of all sorts, but 'never joined in profession of religion with any.' The rumour of a 'fasting woman' drew him to Lancashire, but his curiosity was soon satisfied. On his way back he visited Dukinfield, a Cheshire village, where, according to Edwards (*Gangræna*, iii. 164), the earliest independent church in England was organised. Among its members, who had lately (1646) been troubled by a supernatural drum, Fox in 1647 'declared truth.' Sewel marks this as 'the first beginning of George Fox's preaching.' It was continued at Manchester, and consisted of 'few, but powerful and piercing words.' A conference of baptists and others at Broughton, Leicestershire (probably Broughton-Astley), gave him an opportunity of addressing a large concourse of people. From this time he was much sought after; 'one Brown' prophesied great things of him; and when Brown died, Fox lay in a trance, which was a fourteen days' wonder. He attended the religious meetings and discussions which then abounded, usually taking some part. The first mention of his speaking in a 'steeple-house' is at a great disputation in Leicester (1648), when 'presbyterians, independents, baptists, and common-prayer-men' all took part; the debate came to an abrupt conclusion, but was resumed at an inn. In the same year he first mentions 'a meeting of Friends,' at Little Eaton, near Derby.

At this period the mysticism of Fox was not confined to matters of spiritual insight. He claimed to have received direct knowledge of the occult qualities of nature, so that he was 'at a stand' in his mind, whether he should 'practise physick for the good of mankind.' In this respect, as in some others, he reminds us of Jacob Boehme, whose writings, a contemporary affirms, were 'the chief books' bought by Fox's followers (MUGGLETON, *Looking Glass for G. Fox*, 2nd ed. 1756, p. 10). But this phase passed away, and he devoted himself to a spiritual reform. Fox's idealism was not that of the visionary; his mind was strongly set on realities. It was a sore trial to him to reach by degrees the conclusion that the religious disputes of his day, even that between protestant and papist, turned upon trivial matters. With much modesty of conviction, but a daring thoroughness of sincerity, he strove to get at the core of things. Unconventional ways, which he now adopted, his retention of the hat, and disuse of complimentary phrases, were dictated by a manly simplicity. Too much has been made of his peculiarities of dress. He rejected ornaments. His 'leathern breeches' are first mentioned by him in his journal under date 1651. Croese makes his whole dress of leather, and Sewel appears to corroborate this, denying, however, that it had any connection with 'his former leather-work.' For Carlyle's rhapsody (*Sartor Resartus*, iii. 1) on the leathern suit stitched by Fox's own hands there is no foundation.

His first incarceration was at Nottingham in 1649, for the offence of brawling in church. He was described in the charge-sheet as 'a youth,' though now in his twenty-fifth year. Though he complains of the foulness of his cell, the action of the authorities was gentle as compared with the fury of the villagers of Mansfield Woodhouse on a similar occasion shortly after. By this time Fox had fairly entered upon a course of aggressive action as an itinerant preacher. He sought an interview (1649) with Samuel Oates and other general baptist preachers, at Barrow-upon-Soar, Leicestershire. Barclay is probably right in inferring (*Inner Life*, p. 256) that there was enough in common between his objects and their free methods and Arminian views to make him think an approximation possible; but 'their baptism in water' stopped the way. It does not appear that Fox's society was recruited from the baptists more largely than from other sects, though it exhibits the influence of baptist ideas. The earliest documentary name for the new society is 'Children of Light,' which Barclay traces to a baptist source (*ib.* p. 262). It was soon, however, superseded by the happy designation of 'Truth's Friends,' or 'Friends of Truth,' abbreviated into 'Friends.' Their popular nickname was given to them at Derby on 30 Oct. 1650 by the wit of Gervase Bennet, a hard-headed oracle of the local bench (MUGGLETON, *Acts of the Witnesses*, 1699, p. 94 sq.) Fox had bidden the magistrates 'tremble at the word of the Lord,' whereupon Bennet retorted upon Fox and Fretwell the name of 'quakers.' The term got into the House of Commons' journals as early as 1654.

The rise of this body synchronises with the parliamentary attempt to regulate the affairs of the church of England on the Scottish model; the new society was a collective protest against the presbyterian system, as inefficient for purposes of evangelisation. Fox's earliest recorded convert was a middle-aged widow at Nottingham, Elizabeth Hooton [q. v.] (mentioned 1647), who became the first woman preacher in the society. His adherents were soon numbered by thousands. They came for the most part from the lower middle class, drawn not merely from the puritan folds, but from the fringes of all the sects, from ranters, shakers, seekers, and visionaries of all sorts, who brought with them an exuberant emotional piety tending to pantheism, and a marvellous unrestraint of speech. The commu-

nity exhibited all the signs, mental and physical, of strong religious enthusiasm. Their symbolic acts, grotesque and sometimes gross, were regarded as fanaticism gone mad. With the early characteristics of his society Fox has been often reproached. It is more to the point to observe how by degrees his calmer spirit prevailed over those whom his fervour had attracted, while his genius for organisation reduced to order an otherwise unmanageable mass. His discipline of religious silence had a sobering influence, and the growth of a systematic network of meetings, dependent on each other, induced a sense of corporate responsibility. Barclay notices (*Inner Life*, p. 11) that, with all its freedom, the society from the first was not 'independent' but 'connexional' in its character. There is shrewdness in Baxter's remark that the quakers were 'the ranters revers'd,' turned from wild extravagances to 'extream austerity' (CALAMY, *Abridgement*, 1713, p. 102). Baxter ascribes the change to Penn. But the ranter spirit reached its climax and its fall in the Bristol ride (1656) of James Nayler [q. v.], who died in 1660, many years before the adhesion of either Robert Barclay (1667) or William Penn (1668). By this time the Perrot schism (1661–3) had removed the remaining elements of insubordination, and Fox had given final shape to his rules for the management of 'meetings for discipline' (printed as 'Friends Fellowship,' &c., 1668; reprinted, but not by a quaker, as 'Canons and Institutions,' &c., 1669; given in Beck and Ball). The system was completed by the institution of the yearly meeting, first held on 6 Jan. 1669.

In the organisation of his mission Fox had the valuable help of a remarkable woman, whom he afterwards married, Margaret Fell [q. v.], named by Barclay 'the Lady Huntingdon of the new society' (*Inner Life*, p. 259). She had been carried away by the teaching of William Lampett, who then held the perpetual curacy of Ulverston; he is explicitly described by Fox as 'a ranter' (original manuscript of *Journal*, p. 61). It was by degrees that Fox's teaching exerted a regulative influence over her mind. Her first letter to him in 1652 (facsimile in WILKINSON, *Quakerism Examined*, 1836) has the ranter swell which inflates the well-known letter of John Audland, printed by Leslie (*Snake in the Grass*, 1698, p. 369). Her husband's residence, Swarthmoor Hall, Lancashire, became the headquarters of the movement, the travelling preachers, of whom Fox had thirty in 1653, sixty in the following year (they usually went out in pairs), sending in their reports to her. At his own expense Fox built and endowed the meeting-house at Swarthmoor, which bears the inscription 'Ex Dono : G : F. 1688;' his 'tryacle' bible (1541) is here preserved.

The quaker organisation was thus gaining in cohesion and stability during a period of repressive legislation which was fatal to the continuity of corporate life in the other non-conformist sects. Fox waited for no indulgence, and regarded no conventicle act. 'Now is the time,' said Fox, ' for you to stand . . . go into your meeting-houses as at other times.' Throughout the interval between the restoration of 1660 and the toleration of 1689 the Friends kept up regular meetings, and their numbers increased. When the preachers were carried to prison, the people met in silence ; the lawyers were puzzled to prove such meetings illegal. The meeting-places were nailed up or demolished ; they assembled outside or amid the ruins. At Reading (1664) and Bristol (1682) nearly all the adult members were thrown into gaol ; the meetings were punctually kept by the children. Equal firmness was shown in the matter of oaths and marriages. Fox's admirable system for the registration of births, marriages, and burials began in 1652, and was probably suggested by the practice of the baptist churches. There was no indiscriminate almsgiving, but a constant effort to improve the condition of the poorer members.

The persistent fidelity of Fox's personal labours can hardly be exaggerated. On his missionary journeys, continued from year to year until his death, he visited nearly every corner in England and Wales. He travelled to Scotland in 1657, to Ireland in 1669, to the West Indies and North America in 1671–1672, to Holland in 1677, and again in 1684. Eight times he suffered imprisonment, the longest period of his incarceration being at Lancaster and Scarborough (1663–6), and the latest at Worcester for nearly fourteen months (1673–4). Among the many public services rendered by the early Friends, that of compelling attention to the hideous condition of the common gaols must not be forgotten. In addition to his work as a preacher Fox found time for a constant stream of publications, sometimes all his own, sometimes produced in conjunction with others. He early perceived (or, as seems probable, Margaret Fell perceived for him) the power of the press as a missionary agency. On 18 Feb. 1653 Margaret writes to her husband begging him to see after the printing of tracts by Fox, Nayler, and John Lawson, which she encloses (WEBB, *Fells*, 2nd edit., 1867, p. 41). In an age of pamphlet-writers the quakers were the most prolific, and in some respects the most virulent, in others the most impressive

of pamphleteers. Admitting no weapon but the tongue, they used it unsparingly. In Fox's own pamphlets, though his emotion sometimes renders him inarticulate, there is often a surprising elevation of thought, and an unstudied dignity of expression.

Fox died at the house of Henry Gouldney, in White Hart Court, Gracechurch Street, on Tuesday, 13 Jan. 1691. He was interred on 16 Jan. in Whitecross Street (or Chequer Alley) burying-ground (present entrance in Roscoe Street), near Bunhill Row (BECK and BALL, *London Friends' Meetings*, 1869, p. 329). Eleven Friends took part in the funeral service at the meeting-house ; four delivered testimonies at the graveside, amid a concourse of four thousand people. A headstone was placed over the grave, but this was removed about 1757, when the body was reinterred in order to facilitate the enlargement of the burial-ground. A stone about six inches square, bearing the initials 'G. F.,' was then built into the wall. This also became displaced, and was knocked to pieces as 'nehushtan' by Robert Howard (*d.* January 1812) (*ib.* p. 331 ; WEBB, *Fells,* p. 322). When the old graveyard was laid out as a garden (1881) an inscribed headstone, about two feet high, was placed on the supposed site of Fox's grave. In 1872 a small obelisk, with an incorrect inscription, was erected at Drayton, by C. H. Bracebridge of Atherstone Hall.

Fox had no issue of his marriage on 18 Oct. 1669 to Margaret Fell ; she was ten years his senior, and had been eleven years a widow. Her ' testimony ' to him draws a vivid picture of his character. Fox's will (dated October 1688, proved 30 Dec. 1697) disposes of little more than papers and keepsakes. This ' will ' consists of three distinct autograph papers of direction ; in the Spence collection are other signed papers, giving orders for the disposal not only of a thousand acres in Pennsylvania, assigned to Fox by William Penn, but of 'land and sheep' (to his brother John Fox of Polesworth), and of money laid out ' in ships and trade.' In 1767 his heirs-at-law were the descendants, in Pennsylvania, of his brother John (WEBB, *Fells,* p. 321). Of his ' bulky person,' his abstemious ways and little need of sleep, his manners, ' civil beyond all forms of breeding,' his ' awful, living, reverent frame ' in prayer, we have glimpses in Penn's preface to the ' Journal.' Leslie speaks of his ' long, straight hair, like rats' tails' (*Theol. Works,* 1721, ii. 357). A painting ascribed to William Honthorst, 1654 (engraved by Holmes), is said to represent Fox at the age of thirty ; the face is too young for that age (yet compare the

Nottingham description in 1649), the hair curls, and it seems a fancy picture. When lent to the National Portraits Exhibition in 1866, it was in the possession of Mrs. Watkins. A small and rude woodcut without date (reissued by Joseph Smith) is probably an authentic contemporary likeness of Fox in middle age; the visage is homely, massive and dignified. It is evidently the source of later portraits, such as the neat engraving published by W. Darton (1822), of which there is an enlarged reproduction in lithography by Thomas Fairland [q. v.] about 1835. An engraving by Samuel Allen, from a painting by S. Chinn, was published in 1838 (*Notes and Queries*, 1st ser. vi. 156).

The bibliography of Fox's writings fills fifty-three pages of Smith's 'Catalogue.' Most modern readers will be contented with 1. 'A Journal, or Historical Account of the Life . . . of . . . George Fox,' &c., 1694, fol., a work of the highest interest. A shorter journal, preserved among the manuscripts at Devonshire Square, is described by Barclay (*Inner Life*, p. 277 sq.) The published journal was revised by a committee, under the superintendence of Penn, and transcribed for the press by Thomas Ellwood [q. v.] Fox had himself (in a paper dated 24 June 1685) named a committee for this purpose, including Ellwood; he says, 'And ye great jornall of my Life, Sufferings, Travills, and Imprisonments, they may bee put together, they Lye in papers; and ye Little Jornall Books, they may bee printed together in a Book' (autograph in *Spence Collection*). The original manuscript (wanting sixteen folios at the beginning) is in the possession of Robert Spence, esq., North Shields; it is not in autograph, but has been dictated to successive amanuenses. After publication, a further revision (24 Sept. 1694) substituted a new leaf for pp. 309-10 (story of Justice Clark); copies with the uncancelled leaf are very scarce. Wilson Armistead's edition, 1852, 2 vols. 8vo, with notes, and divided into chapters, is handy for reference; but it has 'improvements' (some of them from Phipps's 'third edition,' 1765, fol.) which sometimes miss the sense. An abridgment, by Henry Stanley Newman, 'Autobiography of George Fox,' &c. (n.d., preface dated Buckfield, Leominster, 1886), is rather a partisan selection. 2. 'A Collection of . . . Epistles,' &c., 1698, fol. (called 'the second volume,' the 'Journal' being considered the first). 3. 'Gospel-Truth . . . a Collection of Doctrinal Books,' &c., 1706, fol. This forms a third volume, though it is not so designated. In this and the preceding Fox's principal works will be found, the most important omission being 4. 'The Great Mis-

tery,' &c., 1659, fol. There is no complete collection of Fox's writings, the fullest being the Philadelphia edition of the 'Works,' 1831, 8 vols. 8vo.

Macaulay's epigram on Fox, as 'too much disordered for liberty, and not sufficiently disordered for Bedlam,' is well known. De Morgan admits (*Budget of Paradoxes*) that, though not a 'rational,' Fox was certainly a 'national' man. Marsden has done more justice to the intellectual merit of Fox's doctrine of the inner light, which 'rested upon one idea, the greatest that can penetrate the mind of man: God is a spirit, and they that worship him must worship him in spirit and truth' (*Hist. of the Later Puritans*, 1872, p. 240). There can be no question of the healthiness and strength of his moral fibre. It is remarkable that Wesley, who was acquainted with Barclay's 'Apology,' never mentions Fox. Yet the early quakerism anticipated methodism in many important points, as well as in the curious detail of conducting the business of meetings by means of answers to queries. The literary skill of the 'Apology' has drawn readers to it rather than to Fox's amorphous writings; but for pure quakerism, not yet fixed (1676) in scholastic forms, it is necessary to go to Fox; and the student will be rewarded, as Professor Huxley observed (*Nineteenth Century*, April 1889), by passages of great beauty and power.

GEORGE FOX, called for distinction 'the younger,' not in years, but 'the younger in the truth,' was of Charsfield, Suffolk. He reached independently (about 1651) similar views to those of his namesake, and joined his society, in which he was a preacher. He began to write in 1656. He died at Hurst, Sussex, on 7 July 1661, and was buried at Twineham. His works were collected in a small volume, 1662, 8vo; 2nd edition, enlarged, 1665, 8vo.

[For the facts of Fox's life the great authority is the Journal. Gerard Croese's Historia Quakeriana, 1695; 2nd edit. 1696; English translation, 1696, is based on materials supplied by William Sewel. Sewel's own History, 1722, embodies some few fresh particulars from a paper by Fox, 'in his lifetime drawn up by his order, at my request, and sent to me.' Besse's Collection of the Sufferings, 1753; Gough's History, 1789. Among the numerous biographies may be mentioned those of Henry Tuke (1813), William and Thomas Evans (1837), Josiah Marsh (1847) from an Anglican point of view, Samuel M. Janney (1853) a Hicksite friend, John Selby Watson (1860), and A. C. Bickley (1884), with a facsimile letter (2 Oct. 1680) from Fox to Barclay. The Swarthmoor MSS. were first employed by Maria Webb in The Fells of Swarthmoor

Hall, 1865, with plates and facsimiles. An able essay on George Fox: his Character, Doctrine, and Work, 1873, by a member of the Society of Friends [Edward Ash, M.D.], deals with the limitations of Fox's mind; a reply, Immediate Revelation True, 1873, was published by George Pitt. In the Inner Life of the Religious Societies of the Commonwealth, 1876, by Robert Barclay (1833–1876) [q. v.], much new light was thrown on Fox's aims and methods, and the genesis of his movement; the writer somewhat over-estimates the direct influence of the ideas of the Mennonite baptists. Joseph Smith's Descriptive Catalogue of Friends' Books, 1867, 2 vols.; Biographical Catalogue, 1888, by Beck, Wells, and Chalkley. Articles by the present writer : Theological Review, January 1874, July 1877. The exact date of Fox's birth is not recoverable: the early registers of Fenny Drayton are lost, and there is no transcript for 1624 in the records of the archdeaconry; the first entry relating to the family is the baptism of Fox's sister Dorothy on 9 April 1626. Use has been made of the Swarthmoor MSS., of the original manuscript of the printed Journal, and of a large number of manuscripts from Swarthmoor in the Spence collection; also of Southey's manuscript Life of Fox (unfinished) in the same collection; and of a contemporary manuscript account of Fox's funeral per C. Elcock ; works cited above.] A. G.

FOX, GEORGE (1802?–1871), topographer, a native of Pontefract, Yorkshire, carried on the business of a bookseller and stationer, in partnership with his father, John Fox, in Market Place in that town, and was for some years a member of the corporation. He died at his residence, Friar Wood House, on 23 Aug. 1871, aged 69. He compiled an excellent and now scarce 'History of Pontefract,' 8vo, Pontefract, 1827, illustrated with plates from his own drawings.

[Pontefract Advertiser, 26 Aug. 1871 ; Pontefract Telegraph, 26 Aug. 1871 ; Boyne's Yorkshire Library, pp. 147-8 ; Pigot's Directories.] G. G.

FOX, HENRY, first BARON HOLLAND (1705–1774), younger son of Sir Stephen Fox [q. v.], by his second wife, Christian, daughter of the Rev. Francis Hopes, rector of Haceby, and afterwards of Aswarby, Lincolnshire, was born at Chiswick on 28 Sept. 1705, and was educated at Eton, where he was the contemporary of Pitt, Fielding, and Sir Charles Hanbury Williams. It has been generally asserted that Fox went up to Oxford University, but there is no record of his matriculation in 'Alumni Oxonienses 1715–1886.' Indulging recklessly in gambling and other extravagances, he soon squandered the greater part of his private fortune, and went abroad to extricate himself from his pecuniary embarrassments. Upon his return to England

Fox was elected to parliament for the borough of Hindon in Wiltshire in February 1735. Being by profession a whig he attached himself to Sir Robert Walpole, whom he served with unswerving fidelity, and was quickly rewarded for his services with the post of surveyor-general of works, to which he was appointed on 17 June 1737. At the general election in 1741 Fox was returned for the borough of Windsor, for which he continued to sit until the dissolution in March 1761. Upon the fall of Walpole in 1742 Fox resigned office, but was appointed a lord of the treasury in the Pelham administration on 25 Aug. 1743. After holding this post nearly three years he was appointed secretary at war in May 1746, and was admitted a member of the privy council on 23 July following. During the debate on the Regency Bill in 1751, Fox repelled with great warmth an attack made on his patron, the Duke of Cumberland, by Pitt. So incensed was Fox with his colleague's speech that he left the house without voting. When Pelham, remonstrating with him afterwards, told him that he had not spoken like himself, Fox spiritedly replied, ' Had I indeed spoken like myself I should have said ten times more against the bill.' In 1753 he attacked Lord Hardwicke, whom he had never forgiven for deserting Sir Robert Walpole. When the lord chancellor's Marriage Bill appeared in the commons, Fox vehemently opposed it, and neither spared the bill nor the author of it (Parl. Hist. xv. 67–74). Upon the death of Pelham in March 1754, the Duke of Newcastle opened negotiations with Fox, through the Marquis of Hartington. It was proposed that Fox should be secretary of state with the lead of the House of Commons, but that the disposal of the secret service money should be left in the hands of the first lord of the treasury, who should keep Fox informed of the way in which the fund was employed. In his interview with Fox, however, the duke declared that he should not disclose to any one how he employed the secret service money. Fox refused to accept these altered terms, but promised to remain in the administration as secretary at war. But though Fox continued in office it can hardly be said that he continued to support the ministry. Reconciled by a common enmity, Fox and Pitt combined in seizing every opportunity which arose during the debate for the purpose of making Sir Thomas Robinson, the newly appointed secretary of state, ridiculous. The covert sarcasms of Fox and the open denunciations of Pitt quickly rendered Newcastle's position intolerable, and in

January 1755 fresh negotiations were opened with Fox, which this time proved successful, though the terms offered him were not so favourable as on the last occasion. Fox, having consented in future to act under Robinson, and to give the king's measures his active support in the House of Commons, was admitted to the cabinet, and his temporary alliance with Pitt was thereupon dissolved. Though Fox suffered in reputation by his desertion of Pitt and his subservience to Newcastle, he speedily gained his object, and before the year was out was leader of the House of Commons. Robinson, receiving a pension, was reappointed master of the great wardrobe, and Fox was appointed in his place secretary of state on 25 Nov. 1755. Thinking himself ill-used both by the king and Newcastle, and suspecting that the latter was intriguing to cast the loss of Minorca upon his shoulders, Fox obtained the king's permission to resign in October 1756. Newcastle's resignation soon followed. The king then sent for Fox and directed him to form an administration with Pitt, but the latter refused to act with him; and the Duke of Devonshire thereupon formed an administration with Pitt's help and without Fox. During the ministerial interregnum in 1757 Fox, at the request of the king, who was incensed at Newcastle's refusal to act with Pitt, consented to become chancellor of the exchequer, with Lord Waldegrave as first lord of the treasury. At the last moment, however, the king yielded to Newcastle, and Fox accepted the subordinate post of paymaster-general without a seat in the cabinet. In this office, which during the continuance of the war was probably the most lucrative one in the government, Fox contented himself with amassing a large fortune, and took but little part in the debates. Upon Grenville's resignation of the seals of secretary of state in October 1762, Fox, with considerable reluctance, once more accepted the leadership of the House of Commons. Refusing to become secretary of state on the ground of bad health, he was admitted to Bute's cabinet, and while retaining the post of paymaster-general accepted the sinecure office of writer of the tallies and clerk of the pells in Ireland. Fox had assured the king that parliament should approve of the peace by large majorities, and by the employment of the grossest bribery and intimidation he kept his word. Having broken with all his old political friends, he turned upon them with relentless fury. 'Strip the Duke of Newcastle of his three lieutenancies immediately,' wrote Fox to Bute, in November 1762; 'I'll answer for the good effect of it, and then go on to the general rout, but let this beginning be made immediately.' In the following month he wrote again to Bute in the same strain : 'The impertinence of our conquered enemies last night was great, but will not continue so if his majesty shows no lenity. But, my lord, with regard to their numerous dependents in crown employments, it behoves your lordship in particular to leave none of them. . . . And I don't care how much I am hated if I can say to myself, I did his majesty such honest and essential service' (*Life of the Earl of Shelburne*, i. 179–80). The peace of Paris was signed in 1763, and Fox having accomplished his task took but little further trouble about the business of the ministry in the House of Commons. Ill supported by his colleagues and hated on all sides, Fox became anxious to retire from the house, and, claiming his reward for his apostasy, was created Baron Holland of Foxley, Wiltshire, on 16 April 1763. After a long altercation with Bute and Shelburne, which is fully recorded in the 'Life' of the latter (i. 199–229), Fox managed to retain the post of paymaster. Shelburne, who had acted as Bute's agent in the negotiations with Fox in the previous year, was denounced by him as 'a perfidious and infamous liar.' But the familiar tradition that Bute attempted to justify Shelburne's conduct by telling Fox that the whole affair was a 'pious fraud,' and that Fox replied, 'I can see the fraud plainly enough, but where is the piety ?' is stated by Lord Edmond Fitzmaurice to be 'valueless for the purposes of history' (*ib.* p. 228). On leaving the House of Commons Fox practically retired from public life, and it does not appear that he took any part in the debates of the upper house. In May 1765 he was forced to resign the post of paymaster-general, which was conferred upon Charles Townshend (*Cal. of Home Office Papers*, 1760–5, p. 553). On Grenville's fall he made some advances towards a reconciliation with his old friends, which were scornfully rejected by Rockingham. In 1769 the lord mayor presented the king with a petition from the livery of the city of London against his ministers, in which Fox was referred to as 'the public defaulter of unaccounted millions' (*Annual Reg.* 1769, p. 202). Proceedings against Fox had been actually commenced in the court of exchequer, but had been stayed by a warrant from the crown. After some correspondence with Beckford, Fox published a statement clearly proving that the delay which had occurred in making up the accounts of his office was neither illegal nor unusual in those days. It has, however, been asserted that the interest on the balances which were outstanding when he left the office brought him no less than a quarter of a million pounds. He tried several times to obtain an earldom, but isolated from all parties in the state, and out of favour at court, he asked for it in vain. Disappointed in ambition and broken down in health, he divided most of his time in travelling on the continent, and in constructing at Kingsgate, near the North Foreland, a fantastic habitation purporting 'to represent Tully's Formian Villa.' He died at Holland House, near Kensington, on 1 July 1774, in the sixty-ninth year of his age, and was buried at Farley in Wiltshire. During Fox's last illness George Selwyn called at Holland House and left his card. Glancing at it, and remembering his old friend's peculiar taste, Fox humorously said: 'If Mr. Selwyn calls again show him up: if I am alive I shall be delighted to see him; and if I am dead he would like to see me.' Fox married, on 2 May 1744, Lady Georgiana Caroline Lennox, eldest daughter of Charles, second duke of Richmond. The marriage was secretly solemnised at the house of Sir Charles Hanbury Williams, the lady's parents having refused their consent. The stir which this wedding made in the town is amusingly recorded in 'Walpole's Letters' (i. 303), and it was not until after some years that the duke and duchess became reconciled to their daughter. The match was a peculiarly happy one, and the correspondence between Fox and his wife is a remarkable record of conjugal felicity. Lady Caroline was created Baroness Holland of Holland, Lincolnshire, in the peerage of Great Britain, on 6 May 1762. She survived her husband only a few weeks, and died on 24 July 1774. They had four sons, viz. Stephen, Henry, Charles James [q. v.], and Henry Edward [q. v.] Stephen succeeded to the two baronies of Holland, and died 16 Dec. 1774. Henry died an infant. The last Lady Holland was the widow of Henry Fox's great grandson, Henry Edward, fourth baron Holland, upon whose death in 1859 the titles became extinct. Fox was a man of many talents, of indomitable courage and extraordinary activity. Gifted with great sagacity and shrewdness, he was confident in manner and decisive in action. Though not a great orator, he was a formidable debater. 'His best speeches,' says Lord Waldegrave, 'are neither long nor premeditated; quick and concise replication is his peculiar excellence' (*Memoirs*, p. 25). Devoid of principle, and regardless of the good opinion of his fellow-men, he cared more for money than for power. Chesterfield declares

that 'he had not the least notion of, or regard for, the public good or the constitution, but despised those cares as the objects of narrow minds, or the pretences of interested ones' (*Letters*, ii. 467). Though at one time the rival of Pitt, Fox never rose above the rank of a political adventurer. His jovial manners and many social qualities gave him much influence in society, but his unscrupulous conduct during the five months which he spent in Bute's cabinet made him the best hated minister in the country. Churchill in his 'Epistle to William Hogarth,' Gray in his 'Stanzas suggested by a View of the Seat and Ruins at Kingsgate in Kent, 1766,' Mason in his 'Heroic Epistle,' as well as the political writers of the day, all bear witness to his great unpopularity. In appearance he was unprepossessing, his figure was heavy, and his countenance dark and lowering. Portraits of him by Hogarth and Reynolds are preserved at Holland House, where there are also several portraits of his wife, and a small collection of his poems. The authorship of a short-lived periodical entitled 'The Spendthrift,' which commenced on 29 March 1766, and lasted through twenty weekly numbers, has been attributed to him. On the first page of the copy of 'The Spendthrift' in the British Museum is the following manuscript note: 'These papers are supposed to have been written by Lord Holland. Mr. Nichols, who printed them, informs me that the copy always came from that nobleman's house.—Ic. Reed.' Holland House was bought by Fox in 1767, having previously rented it since 1749.

[Coxe's Memoirs of Horatio, Lord Walpole (1802); Coxe's Memoirs of the Pelham Administration (1829); The Grenville Papers (1852); Diary of the late George Bubb Dodington (1784); Chatham's Correspondence (1838–40); Correspondence of John, fourth Duke of Bedford (1842–6); Memoirs from 1754 to 1758, by James, Earl Waldegrave (1821); Walpole's Memoirs of the Reign of George II (1847); Walpole's Memoirs of the Reign of George III (1845); Walpole's Letters (ed. Cunningham); Fitzmaurice's Life of the Earl of Shelburne (1875), vol. i.; Lecky's Hist. of England, vols. i. ii. iii.; Lord Mahon's Hist. of England (1858), vols. iii. iv. v.; Trevelyan's Early Life of Charles James Fox (1881); Macaulay's Essays (1885), pp. 301–6, 309, 762–4, 767; Jesse's George Selwyn and his Contemporaries (1844); Sir Edward Creasy's Memoirs of Eminent Etonians (1876), 308–11; The Fox Unkennelled, or the Paymaster's Accounts Laid Open (1769); Princess Mary Liechtenstein's Holland House (1874); Chester's Westminster Abbey Registers (1876), pp. 262, 473; Collins's Peerage (1812), iv. 538, vii. 308–10; Foster's Peerage (1883), p.

383; Gent. Mag. 1774, xliv. 333–4, 335, 543; Annual Register 1777, pp. 16–18; Haydn's Book of Dignities (1851); Official Return of Lists of Members of Parliament, pt. ii. pp. 80, 85, 98, 109, 131; Brit. Mus. Cat.]   G. F. R. B.

FOX, HENRY EDWARD (1755–1811), general, was the third son who reached manhood of Henry Fox, first lord Holland [q. v.], by Lady Georgiana Caroline Lennox, eldest daughter of the second Duke of Richmond, and younger brother of the celebrated orator and statesman, Charles James Fox [q. v.] He was born on 4 March 1755, and a curious quotation from one of his father's letters in 1764, when the boy was but nine years old, shows what his disposition then was. 'Harry,' he writes, 'has a little horse to ride, and the whole stable full to look after. He lives with the horse, stinks, talks, and thinks of nothing but the stable, and is not a very good companion' (TREVELYAN, Early Life of Charles James Fox, p. 276). After a short time at Westminster School, Fox was gazetted to a cornetcy in the 1st or king's dragoon guards in 1770, from which he was promoted lieutenant into the 38th regiment in 1773. This regiment was then quartered at Boston in America, and Henry Fox served all through the war of American independence. On 14 Feb. 1774 he was promoted captain; in 1775 he served at Concord and at the battle of Bunker's Hill; in 1776 he was present at the battles on Long Island and of White Plains; in 1777 he was at the battle of Brandywine and in the advance on Philadelphia, and on 12 July 1777 he was promoted major into the 49th regiment. This regiment was placed under orders for the West Indies, but before it started Fox was promoted lieutenant-colonel of the 38th regiment on 12 Oct. 1778. He continued to serve until the end of the American war of independence, and it is curious to notice that while Charles James Fox was inveighing against the war with the Americans, his brother Henry was constantly employed in it. On his return to England he was received, perhaps for this reason, with the greatest favour by the king, who made him one of his aides-de-camp with the rank of colonel on 12 March 1783. In 1786 he married Marianne, daughter of William Clayton, and sister of the Baroness Howard de Walden. On 20 Dec. 1793 he was promoted major-general, and soon after offered a command in the army under the Duke of York in Flanders. He joined this army during the retreat through Belgium, and was posted to the command of the brigade formerly commanded by Major-general Ralph Abercromby, consisting of the 14th, 37th, and 53rd regiments. With this brigade he served at the

battles of Roubaix and Mouveaux, and on 23 May 1794 he performed his greatest feat of arms, the repulse of the whole French army at Pont-à-Chin. He was upon the extreme right of the retreating army, when he was isolated and attacked in force, and his gallant stand and the successful extrication of his brigade is the brightest feature in the history of the whole war in Flanders from 1793 to 1795. On 28 June 1795 Fox was appointed colonel of the 10th regiment, and on 26 June 1799 he was promoted lieutenant-general. On 25 July 1801 he was appointed a local general in the Mediterranean, with his headquarters at Minorca, where he remained until the signature of the peace of Amiens, and in 1803 he was appointed commander-in-chief of the forces in Ireland. His tenure of office there was signalised by the outbreak and the suppression of the rebellion of Robert Emmet, when Fox was seized with the panic which assailed all the Castle authorities, and made elaborate preparations for dispersing the wretched pikemen, who were easily defeated by the ordinary night guard before the troops had begun to concentrate. In 1804 Fox was appointed lieutenant-governor of Gibraltar, which, as the titular governor, the Duke of Kent, did not reside there, practically meant governor of that important fortress. From this office he was removed, after his brother's accession to office in 1806, to the command of the army in Sicily, and he was also appointed ambassador to the court of Naples, then residing at Palermo. Sir John Moore was his second in command, and as Fox was in very bad health, Moore really undertook the entire management of both military and diplomatic matters. When Fox assumed the command, Major-general John Stuart had just won the victory of Maida, and the queen of Naples pressed his successor to undertake a similar expedition on a larger scale, and thus drive the French from Naples. But Fox knew that Stuart's success was very much due to chance, and that it would be ridiculous for the English to leave the island of Sicily for the mainland, where Murat could soon outnumber them. He was the more determined to refuse, since by the directions of his government he had materially weakened his army by sending five thousand men, under Major-general Mackenzie Fraser, to Egypt. This conflict with the Neapolitan court continued until 10 July 1807, when the new English ministry recalled Fox, and after a time replaced him in the supreme military and civil command by Lord William Bentinck. Soon after his return to England Fox was promoted general on 25 July 1808, and made governor of Portsmouth, where he died on 18 July 1811. He left one son, Henry Stephen Fox [q. v.], diplomatist, and two daughters, the elder married to General Sir Henry Bunbury, bart., and the younger to General Sir William Napier, K.C.B.

[Army Lists; Historical Record of the 10th Foot; Hamilton's History of the Grenadier Guards; Jones's Historical Journal of the campaign on the continent in 1794; and for his command in Sicily Bunbury's Narrative of some Passages in the Great War with France.]

H. M. S.

FOX, HENRY RICHARD VASSALL, third BARON HOLLAND, BARON HOLLAND of Holland in the county of Lincoln, and BARON HOLLAND of Foxley in the county of Wilts (1773–1840), only son of Stephen, second lord Holland, by Lady Mary Fitzpatrick, daughter of John, earl of Upper Ossory, was born at Winterslow House, Wiltshire, on 21 Nov. 1773. He was saved by his mother at the risk of her own life in a fire which destroyed the house on 9 Jan. 1774. His father died on 16 Dec. 1774, his mother in 1778, and he was brought up by his maternal grandfather and his uncle, Charles James Fox [q. v.] He was educated at Eton, whence he proceeded, 19 Oct. 1790, to Christ Church, Oxford, where he was created M.A. on 20 June 1792. Among his friends at school and college were Lord Carlisle, Canning, Hookham Frere, and Robert ('Bobus') Smith. During the long vacation of 1791 he visited Paris, was introduced to Lafayette and Talleyrand, and returned to England in 1792 after visiting Denmark and Prussia. His guardians, to quench a premature interest in politics, sent him abroad in March 1793. He travelled in Spain and in Italy, where he met Nelson (at Leghorn), and settled at Florence in the autumn of 1794. Early in 1796 he returned to England, through Germany, with the wife of Sir Godfrey Webster [see Fox, ELIZABETH VASSALL]. She continued to reside with him in England, and then gave birth to a son, whom he acknowledged for his own. Sir Godfrey Webster obtained a decree for a separation in February 1797 (Ann. Reg. 1797, Chron. p. 12) Lord Holland took his seat in the house of peers on 5 Oct. 1796, where, on 9 Jan. 1798, he made his maiden speech in the debate on the Assessed Taxes Bill. In spite of an ungraceful action and hesitating delivery he showed himself a useful recruit to the whig party. A clear and terse protest against the bill, which he entered on the journals of the house, was the first of a long series of similar documents afterwards collected and published under the title of 'Opinions of Lord Holland.' He at once became the recognised exponent in the

House of Lords of his uncle's policy, resisting in the most determined manner suspensions of the Habeas Corpus Act, openly countenancing the United Irishmen, denouncing the union with Ireland as both unjust and impolitic, and afterwards endeavouring to insert a clause for the admission of Roman catholics to seats in parliament. In 1800 a royal license was granted to Lord and Lady Holland jointly (18 June) to take 'the name of Vassall only after their own respective christian names' (Heralds' Coll. I. 36, 20) [see Fox, ELIZABETH VASSALL]. In 1807 they adopted the signature Vassall Holland, although Vassall was no part of the title. In the summer of 1800 Lord Holland paid a short visit to North Germany, returning to England, under a passport obtained through Talleyrand, by way of the Netherlands and France in the autumn. On the conclusion of the peace of Amiens in 1802 the Hollands went to Paris, and were presented to the first consul. From Paris they travelled to Spain, where they remained, chiefly at Madrid, until the spring of 1805. They returned to England in time to permit of Lord Holland's speaking in support of Lord Grenville's motion for a committee to consider the petition of the Irish Roman catholics for the removal of their disabilities (10 May 1805). The United States having sent commissioners to England to complain of various alleged infringements of their rights as a neutral power committed by English naval commanders, Lord Holland was appointed (20 Aug. 1806) with Lord Auckland to negotiate with Messrs. Monroe and Pinckney, the American plenipotentiaries, an adjustment of the dispute. A treaty was concluded on 31 Dec., making some concessions, but as the question of impressment was left unsettled, President Jefferson refused to submit it to the senate for ratification, and it accordingly lapsed (LORD HOLLAND, Memoirs of the Whig Party in my Time, ii. 98–103; TUCKER, Life of Jefferson, ii. 247). Though in right of his wife the owner of extensive plantations in Jamaica, Lord Holland was a consistent advocate of the emancipation of the slaves in the West Indies, and throughout life supported all measures against the slave trade. On 27 Aug. 1806 he was sworn of the privy council, and on 15 Oct. he entered the cabinet of All the Talents as lord privy seal, and was dismissed with his colleagues in March 1807. Lord Holland accompanied Sir David Baird to Corunna in September 1808, thence he passed into Spain, where he made a prolonged tour, returning in the autumn of 1809. On his return he moved (30 May) the second reading of the bill for the abolition of capital punishment in cases of stealing, took part in the debate on the state of the nation and the king's illness (27 Dec.), and led the opposition to the proposal to establish the regency by legislation (4 Jan. 1811). He moved for a return of all informations issued *ex officio* by the attorney-general between 1 Jan. 1801 and 31 Dec. 1810. The motion was negatived after a prolonged debate. On 21 May he energetically opposed Sidmouth's measure for licensing dissenting ministers. In the debate on the orders in council (28 Feb. 1812) he urged the expediency of an immediate rescission of the order of November 1807 prohibiting the trade with France to all the world; later on he supported the catholic claims, proposed to regulate the law of *ex-officio* information, and was in favour of treating with Napoleon as emperor. He vehemently attacked the treaty with Sweden (2 April 1813), by which England agreed, in consideration of some commercial concessions, to abet the Swedish designs on Norway. He visited Murat at Naples in 1814. On 8 April 1816 he vigorously opposed the bill for the detention of Napoleon as a prisoner of war, arguing that the detention must be justified by the law of nations or not at all. In 1817 he moved for papers relating to Napoleon's treatment at St. Helena. After the insurrection in Barbadoes, he moved (28 June 1816) for an inquiry into the condition of the negroes. He energetically opposed the various repressive measures which were carried out by Lord Sidmouth in 1817 and 1818. He also opposed the Foreign Enlistment Bill, introduced in order to prevent persons being enlisted on British soil for the service of the insurgent Spanish colonies. Lord Holland took comparatively little public action in the case of Queen Caroline beyond expressing emphatically (7 June 1820) his disapproval of the ministerial plan of investigation by a secret committee, and supporting a regular legal procedure. During the following period he consistently supported the whig policy in regard to domestic and foreign affairs. He supported the cause of the Greeks, proposed forcible intervention in favour of Donña Maria on the usurpation of the Portuguese throne by Dom Miguel in 1828, and strongly condemned ministers in 1830 for preventing her adherents who had sailed from Plymouth from landing at Terceira. When at last the whigs were restored to power by the reform agitation, Lord Holland became chancellor of the duchy of Lancaster (25 Nov.) in Lord Grey's administration. He held the place, with the exception of the brief interregnum in 1832 between Lord Grey's resignation

(10 May) and his recall (18 May), until the dismissal of Lord Melbourne's administration (14 Nov. 1834). He accepted the same place on Lord Melbourne's second administration (23 April 1835), and held it until he died, after a short illness at Holland House, on 22 Oct. 1840. He was buried on 28 Oct. in Millbrook Church, near Ampthill, Bedfordshire (the family seat). The following lines were found in his handwriting on his dressing-table after his death :—

> Nephew of Fox, and friend of Grey,
> Enough my meed of fame
> If those who deigned to observe me say
> I injured neither name.

A portrait of him (half-length) by Leslie is at Holland House, and another, by the same artist (full-length, with Lady Holland and John Allen), is in the possession of Earl Grey. At Holland House also are his portrait by Fabre and his bust by Nollekens; his statue by Watts is in the grounds. Greville, who knew him well, speaks of his 'imperturbable temper, unflagging vivacity and spirit, his inexhaustible fund of anecdote, extensive information, sprightly wit,' and 'universal toleration and urbanity' (*Mem.* 1837–52, i. 341). Brougham is equally complimentary to his engaging social qualities as well as to his high statesmanship and political magnanimity (*Statesmen of the Time of George III*, 1843, iii. 329, 340; *Memoirs*, iii. 446). Sydney Smith declares that 'there never existed in any human being a better heart, or one more purified from all the bad passions, more abounding in charity and compassion, and which seemed to be so created as a refuge to the helpless and the oppressed.' In his premeditated speeches, though closely reasoned and occasionally witty, he never escaped from his early defects; he was, however, more effective in his replies (BROUGHAM, *Statesmen of the Time of George III*, 1843, iii. 329, 332, 340; *Memoirs*, iii. 446; MACAULAY, *Essays*, 7th ed., iii. 213; LADY HOLLAND, *Memoir of the Rev. Sydney Smith*, i. 282). Lord Holland had lawful issue by Lady Holland, two sons, viz. Stephen, who died in 1800, and Henry Edward, who succeeded to the title and estate; and two daughters, viz. Mary Elizabeth, who married in 1830 Thomas Atherton, third baron Lilford, and Georgiana Anne, who died in her tenth year. Lord Holland appears to have had rather more than the ordinary dilettante's appreciation of art, but no ear whatever for music. He was an accomplished scholar not only in the classical but in the modern languages, and made some trifling contributions to literature. These are: 1. 'Observations on the Tendency of a Pamphlet entitled "Sound Argument Dictated by Common Sense,'" London, 1795, 8vo, anon., showing that Horne's arguments against the pseudo-prophet Brothers were much of a kind with those of freethinkers against the Hebrew prophets. 2. 'Secession' and 'The Yeoman,' 1798–9. Two satires in imitation of Juvenal, suggested by the course of events in Ireland, apparently printed for private circulation only. Lord Holland says that he infused into them, if little of the poetry and force, at least much of the bitterness of the original (*Memoirs of the Whig Party in my Time,* i. 134). 3. Chapter ix. of the 'Annual Register' for 1806, dealing with the abortive negotiations with France. 4. 'Some Account of the Lives and Writings of Lope Felix de Vega Carpio,' London, 1806, 8vo, anon. (republished with Lord Holland's name, together with the 'Life of Guillen de Castro,' London, 1817, 8vo). 5. 'Three Comedies from the Spanish,' London, 1807, 8vo (two from Calderon, one from Antonio de Solis). 6. 'A Dream,' London, 1818 (printed for private circulation, a dialogue between George III, Sir Thomas More, Bacon, Locke, Berkeley, and other eminent personages on education and the encouragement of letters by the state). 7. 'Sketch of a Constitution for the Kingdom of Naples, suggested in 1815 to the Duca di Gallo,' London, 1818, 8vo, reprinted in 1848, 8vo. 8. 'Letter to the Rev. Dr. Shuttleworth, warden of New College, Oxford,' London, 1827, 8vo (on the Roman catholic question). 9. 'Parliamentary Talk, or the Objections to the late Irish Church Bill, considered in a Letter to a Friend abroad, by a Disciple of Selden,' 3rd ed., with additions, London, 1836, 8vo (this elicited a reply entitled 'Irish Church, by a Pupil of Canning,' London, 1836, 8vo). 10. Two translations from Ariosto, printed in vol. v. of W. S. Rose's translation of the 'Orlando Furioso.' He wrote introductions and prefaces to Fox's 'James II,' Townshend's 'Dissertation on the Poor Laws,' 'Doblado's Letters on Spain' (Blanco White), and edited Waldegrave's 'Memoirs' and Horace Walpole's 'George II.' A brief epistle in verse, ascribed to Lord Holland, is printed in the article on him in Jerdan's 'National Portrait Gallery,' 1833, and a sonnet by him on the Greek question, written in 1827, will be found in 'Notes and Queries,' 4th ser. viii. 414.

After his death the protests entered by Lord Holland in the journals of the House of Lords were collected and edited by Dr. Moylan of Lincoln's Inn, barrister-at-law, under the title of 'The Opinions of Lord Holland as recorded in the Journals of the House of Lords from 1797 to 1841,' Lond. 1841,

8vo (see MACAULAY's review of this work, *Essays,* iii. 205). 'Foreign Reminiscences,' a miscellaneous collection of anecdote and gossip, often piquant, sometimes scandalous, concerning various persons of distinction whom Lord Holland had met in his travels abroad, accepted apparently without any very careful scrutiny, and thrown together in a loose and desultory way, was edited by his son Henry Edward, lord Holland, London, 1850, 8vo, and translated into French. It was highly praised in the 'Edinburgh Review' (January 1851), and savagely denounced by Croker in the 'Quarterly Review' in the following March as little less than a scandalous libel. The bulk of the anecdotes seem to be fairly authentic, but Lord Holland was misled, by his lively sympathy with the revolutionary movement of his time, to give undue credit to stories disparaging some of the prominent actors on the other side. It was followed by a more serious contribution to the history of that eventful period, viz. Lord Holland's 'Memoirs of the Whig Party during my Time' (also edited by his son), London, 1852, 2 vols. 8vo. This work covers the period from Lord Holland's first entrance into public life to 1809. It is written with commendable precision, lucidity, and conciseness, and, its author having been during that period rather the whig party itself in the House of Lords than its leader, constitutes a first-hand historical authority of great value. Lord Holland also spent much of his leisure time in collecting materials for a life of Fox, which were subsequently edited by Lord John Russell, and published under the title of 'Memorials and Correspondence of Charles James Fox,' Lond. 1853, 3 vols. 8vo.

[The principal authorities are the Memoirs and the Reminiscences referred to above, with the Parliamentary History and Debates; Jerdan's National Portrait Gallery, 1833; Gent. Mag. (1840), pt. ii. p. 653. The English Cyclopædia Biog. vol. iii., and the Encyclopædia Britannica also contain more or less elaborate articles. See supra, art. Fox, ELIZABETH VASSALL.] J. M. R.

FOX, HENRY STEPHEN (1791–1846), diplomatist, only son of General Henry Edward Fox [q. v.], by Marianne Clayton, sister of Lady Howard de Walden, was born on 22 Sept. 1791. He was educated at Eton and matriculated at Christ Church, Oxford, 26 Jan. 1809, but soon sought a diplomatic and political career. Deprived by the tory supremacy of any chance of preferment, and inheriting little from his father, Fox spent his time in the fashionable world, where he made himself popular by his wit and charming manners. He was a friend of all the whigs and well known in the clubs. After the peace of 1815 he travelled on the continent with Lord Alvanley and Thomas Raikes, and at Rome had a bad attack of fever. When Grey's reform ministry was formed in 1830, Lord Holland pressed the claims of his cousin, who was appointed the first minister plenipotentiary and envoy extraordinary at Buenos Ayres. He was moved to Rio de Janeiro in 1832 and thence to Washington in 1835. The relations between England and the United States were then disturbed by much ill-feeling, and Fox's tact and courteous manners did much to improve them. When Sir Robert Peel came into office in 1841, he sent Lord Ashburton to settle outstanding difficulties, and the success of the Ashburton treaty was in great measure due to Fox, whose services were cordially acknowledged by Ashburton. In December 1843 Fox was superseded, but he continued to reside in Washington, where he died in October 1846.

[Gent. Mag. 1847, i. 82; Raikes's Journal, iii. iv.; Foster's Alumni Oxon.]   H. M. S.

FOX, HENRY WATSON (1817–1848), Indian missionary, son of George Townshend Fox of Durham, was born at Westoe in 1817. He was sent to Durham grammar school, and thence to Rugby, where he was in the house of Bonamy Price. A lecture delivered by Price in 1833 and the weekly sermons of Arnold strengthened his early religious impressions. In 1836 he gained one of the university exhibitions, and commenced residence at Wadham College, Oxford, in October of that year. Proceeding B.A. in December 1839, he was ordained deacon in December 1840, and shortly afterwards married Elizabeth, daughter of G. H. James, esq., of Wolverhampton. Early in 1841 the Church Missionary Society appointed him a missionary to the Telugu people, inhabiting the northeastern districts of the Madras presidency. He reached Madras in July 1841 with his colleague, the Rev. R. T. Noble [q. v.] Noble managed a school at Masulipatam for natives of the higher classes, while Fox, as soon as he had mastered the language, preached to the people in Masulipatam and the adjoining district. Ill-health compelled him to reside on the Nilgiri hills from 1843 to October 1844, with the exception of some time spent on a tour among the mission stations of Travancore and Tinnivelly. The illness of his wife, who died a few hours after embarking at Madras, compelled him to visit England in the latter part of 1845. In 1848 he was obliged by his own health finally to return to England. He was able a few months later to accept the appointment of assistant-secretary to the Church Missionary Society,

but on 14 Oct. 1848, after a severe attack of the malady which had driven him from India, he died in his mother's house at Durham.

Fox's short and interrupted career was made remarkable by his single-minded and intelligent devotion. His last illness was brought on by his exertions in working and preaching for the society when his strength was unequal to the task. His letters and journals show that his work and the spread of missions were with him all-engrossing topics. In 1846 he wrote a little book entitled 'Chapters on Missions in South India,' published a few months before his death, giving a popular account of mission life in India, and of his observations of Hindu religion and manners. Shortly after Fox's death subscriptions were raised by his friends at Rugby and elsewhere, which resulted in the endowment of a Rugby Fox mastership in the Church Mission School, now called the Noble College, at Masulipatam. It was at the same time arranged that an annual sermon should be preached in the school chapel at Rugby in aid of the funds of the endowment. In 1872 the preacher was Fox's son, the Rev. H. E. Fox.

[Memoir of the Rev. Henry Watson Fox, by the Rev. George Townshend Fox of Durham, with a preface by the Rev. H. V. Elliott, 1850; Chapters on Missions in South India, by the Rev. H. W. Fox, 1848; A Sermon preached at Hampstead, 7 Aug., on the death of the Rev. H. W. Fox, by the Rev. J. Tucker, B.D., 1849; Posthumous Fragment by the Rev. H. W. Fox, with a notice of the extent of his influence, 1852.]   A. J. A.

FOX, JOHN (1516–1587), martyrologist. [See FOXE.]

FOX, JOHN (*fl.* 1676), nonconformist divine, took the degree of B.A. at Cambridge, as a member of Clare Hall, in 1624 (*Notes and Queries*, 2nd ser. v. 438). During the Commonwealth he held the vicarage of Pucklechurch, Gloucestershire. After his ejectment in 1662 he became pastor of a congregation at Nailsworth in the same county. He is the author of two treatises of considerable merit, entitled: 1. 'Time, and the End of Time. Or Two Discourses: The first about Redemption of Time, the second about Consideration of our latter End,' 12mo, London, 1670 (many subsequent editions). It was translated into Welsh by S. Williams, 8vo, yng Ngwrecsam, 1784. 2. 'The Door of Heaven opened and shut. . . . Or, A Discourse [on Matt. xxv. 10] concerning the Absolute Necessity of a timely Preparation for a Happy Eternity,' 12mo, London, 1676 (and again in 1701). He has been frequently confounded with John Foxe [q. v.] the 'martyr-maker.'

[Palmer's Nonconf. Memorial (London, 1802), ii. 253 ; Wood's Athenæ Oxon. (Bliss), i. 533.]
G. G.

FOX, JOHN (1693–1763), biographer, was born at Plymouth on 10 May 1693. His father, a zealous presbyterian, 'devoted' him 'to the ministry, from an infant.' His mother was the daughter of a Plymouth tradesman named Brett. After an education at Tavistock grammar school, and under 'old Mr. Bedford' at Plymouth, he read the Greek Testament and Virgil for a few months with Nicodemus Harding, son of Nathaniel Harding, independent minister at Plymouth. The two young men were preparing for entrance at the Exeter academy, under Joseph Hallet (d. 1722) [q. v.] In May 1708 he entered the academy, where he soon quarrelled with Harding, and formed an intimacy with his tutor's son, Joseph Hallet (d. 1744) [q. v.], who put doubts into his mind respecting the Trinity.

When he left the academy in 1711 he had 'no great disposition of being a minister.' His reluctance to comply with the Toleration Act, by subscribing the doctrinal articles, produced a coolness with his father. After some months, Isaac Gilling, minister at Newton Abbot, Devonshire, came to Plymouth in disguise ; a process was out against him for illegally keeping a Latin school. He was a first cousin of the elder Fox, who allowed his son to accompany Gilling on his flight from Devonshire, on a promise that Gilling would do all in his power to remove young Fox's aversion to the ministry. At Salisbury Fox was introduced to Sir Peter King, then recorder of London, an old friend of Gilling. Arrived in London, he slipped out of Gilling's hands, and stayed with another relative. He was not favourably impressed with John Shower, the only London minister he met, and spent his time in getting glimpses of great people and visiting the theatres. At the end of a fortnight in town, Gilling was able to return to Newton Abbot, and took Fox with him. The accidental sight of a letter from his father to Gilling 'determined [him] to be a minister at all events.' With this view he remained with Gilling three-quarters of a year (1712–13), the pleasantest part of his life. Gilling directed his studies, and he fell in love with Gilling's daughter. In May 1713 Edmund Calamy, D.D. [q. v.], visited the west of England, and, hearing of Fox's scruples, made him easy by telling him confidentially that he himself had never subscribed, and that if Fox 'kept himself to himself' the omission would never be suspected.

In October 1714 Fox went to London, where he remained till April 1716. He lodged with four young ministers in Austin Friars ; it is probable that he attended the classes of John Eames [q. v.] He became intimate with Secker and Samuel Chandler [q. v.] (who lived in Calamy's house); to both of whom, and especially to Secker (who kept up a correspondence with him till 1718), he ascribes his progress in freedom of opinion. His father wished him to be licensed as a preacher before he returned to Plymouth. This implied an examination, from which he shrank. After interviews with Williams and Calamy, he abandoned the idea of passing his trials in London. His friend Jeremy Burroughs (a young minister who afterwards became collector of the customs at Bristol) came to his relief, by advising him simply to take the oath of allegiance, as if he had been licensed. He chose a time when, in consequence of the rebellion of 1745, all ministers were ordered to take the oath afresh. As he was signing his name in the court of exchequer with the rest, Calamy 'looked very hard at' his rather advanced pupil.

Returning to Plymouth it occurred to Fox that he was not yet a communicant. Harding admitted him without question, but at once guessed that he had not been licensed. He preached his first sermon at Chumleigh, Devonshire, whereupon there was 'a whispering and grumbling among the ministers,' who suspected him of being an intruder.' He preached elsewhere, but soon found that without a license the Exeter assembly would not recognise him. Accordingly he applied for leave to choose his own examiners. After some manœuvring between parties in the assembly, he got what he wanted, dealt cleverly with the test questions, and was licensed on 17 Oct. 1717. In the assembly of May 1719 he threw in his lot with Peirce, the leader of the heterodox party, and the result was that he got no preaching engagements except to 'the poor remains of a few broken congregations.' It does not appear that he was ever ordained.

On 12 May 1723 his father died, and Fox at once abandoned the ministry. He was now master of 'a humble competence,' which enabled him to marry (23 Dec. 1723) Miss Gilling (b. 11 Dec. 1695); and henceforth he lived in obscure comfort, 'between the sunshine of life and the clouds and darkness of it.' His health was good, and he took pleasure in his books and the society of a few friends. In 1736 he writes to Secker that for some years past he had conformed 'out of regard to public peace and . . . respect to the public.' The ailments of his wife, to whom he was strongly attached, were his only trouble. On her death, 19 Dec. 1762, he lost heart. He died on 25 Oct. (according to Hazlitt 22 Oct.) 1763, aged 70. A daughter, Mary (b. 26 Dec. 1725), married John Cleather, 3 Sept. 1747.

It was some time after 1744 that Fox penned his own very entertaining 'Memoirs' and the 'Characters' of some of his contemporaries. They throw much light on dissenting history. Fox writes with great freedom and pungency, and his estimates of men are valuable, though sometimes hasty, and always coloured by his dislikes, and by his contempt for the surroundings of his early life. In 1814 some use was made of the 'Characters' by Toulmin, to whom the manuscript had been lent by Fox's grandson, George Cleather of Stonehouse, near Plymouth; Toulmin had evidently not seen the 'Memoirs.' In 1821 the 'Memoirs' and nine 'Characters' were published in the 'Monthly Repository,' with nine letters from Secker to Fox, one from Fox to Secker, and two from Chandler to Fox. Notes were added by John Towill Rutt. The editor, Robert Aspland [q. v.], speaks of the manuscripts as having come into his possession through a descendant of Fox. Aspland thought of reprinting the papers, and promised to deposit the originals in Dr. Williams's Library; unfortunately neither intention was carried out. In 1822 an additional letter from Fox to Secker was supplied by Clifford, of the Theatre Royal, Norwich, who reported that he possessed other memoirs by Fox. Northcote's transcript of Fox's papers (containing some addition to the 'Memoirs') is now in the public library at Plymouth.

[Monthly Repository, 1821, p. 128 sq., 1822, p. 219 sq.; Toulmin's Hist. View, 1814, p. 568 sq.; Worth's Hist. Nonconf. in Plymouth, 1876, p. 16; Northcote's Conversations (Hazlitt), 1881, p. 287 sq.; MS. Minutes of Exeter Assembly, 1691–1717, in Dr. Williams's Library; Northcote's MS. Worthies of Devon in Plymouth Libr.]
A. G.

FOX, LUKE (1586–1635), navigator, son of Richard Fox, seaman and assistant of the Trinity House at Kingston-upon-Hull, was born at Hull 20 Oct. 1586. 'Having been sea-bred from his boystime,' he acquired his knowledge of seamanship in voyages southward to France, Spain, and the Mediterranean, and northward to the Baltic, Denmark, and Norway, varied by 'imployments along the coasts' of England and crossing the North Sea. In 1606 he offered his services as mate to John Knight in that able seaman's last and fatal voyage to Greenland, but was rejected by the promoters on account of his youth. Henceforth the whole of his thoughts

were devoted to Arctic exploration, but more particularly to the north-west passage. He writes: 'At the returnes home of all ships from thence I enquired of the masters, mates, and others that were that way imployed, whereby I gathered from reports and discourse and manuscripts how farre they had proceeded.' If we except Captain Hawkridge's abortive voyage of 1619, Fox was the true successor of Bylot and Baffin (1615) in Arctic exploration. Earlier voyages had been made by Sir Thomas Button [q. v.] in 1612, by Henry Hudson [q. v.] in 1606, by Captain Weymouth in 1601, and by John Davis [q. v.] in 1585–7.

Fox's earliest patron was the famous mathematician, Henry Briggs [q. v.], also a Yorkshireman, and professor of geometry at Oxford. He, with the assistance of his friend, Sir J. Brooke, was the first to direct the royal attention to Fox's voyage. The project first took shape in 1629, in a 'Petition of Luke Fox to the king for a small supply of money towards the discovery of a passage by the north-west to the South Sea, Hudson and Sir Thomas Button having discovered a great way, and given great hopes of opening the rest' (State Papers, p. 105). In reply to this a pinnace of the royal navy of seventy tons was placed at the disposal of the adventurers, but the setting forth was deferred until the following year. In the interval Briggs died; half the adventurers having fallen away, the voyage would have been abandoned but for the news that the Bristol merchants had projected a similar voyage from their port. Their rival scheme was the well-known voyage of Captain Thomas James [q. v.], which left Bristol 3 May 1631. This news caused a spirit of emulation among the London merchants, which, with the assistance of Sir T. Roe and Sir J. Wolstenholme, resulted in the setting forth of Fox in the Charles pinnace with a crew of twenty men and two boys victualled for eighteen months. Fox sailed from the Pool below London Bridge 30 April 1631 (MS. Journal, f. 23). He anchored off Whitby, where he landed, and reached Kirkwall in the Orkneys 19 May. Sailing thence due west on the sixty parallel he made land 20 June on the north side of Frobisher Bay; two days later he sighted Cape Chidley, off the south shore of Hudson's Strait, six leagues distant. Passing Resolution Island two leagues south on 23 June, his crew saw in the harbour on the west side the smoke of the camp-fire of Captain James, who had put in there for repairs. From this date until 11 July Fox worked his way along the north shore of Hudson's Strait until he reached a position between Mill and Salisbury Islands. Thence he proceeded to the south of Coates Island until 19 July, when he commenced his search for the undiscovered passage by the north-west. On 27 July he reached the furthest point of Button, on 'Sir T. Roe's Welcome' Island, where he found traces of native sepulture, which he carefully examined. Being prohibited by his instructions from proceeding to a higher latitude than 63° N. in this direction, he turned southward along the west shore of Hudson's Bay until 27 Aug., when he entered the mouth of the Nelson River, where he found the remaining half of an inscribed board erected by Button, which he replaced by a new one of his own. Hence he sailed E.S.E. sixty-one leagues until 30 Aug., when he met his rival, Captain James, in the Maria of Bristol, with whom, after some trouble in getting on board, he dined and spent seventeen hours. Fox bluntly tells us that he found his host 'no seaman.' After adieux, Fox proceeded on his course down to 55° 14', or Wolstenholme's *ultima vale*, now known as Cape Henrietta Maria, at the head of James Bay. On 3 Sept. he turned the head of his ship northward until he reached Cape Pembroke on Coates Island five days later. From 15 to 20 Sept. Fox was employed in making the remarkable series of observations on the channel that bears his name on the west shore of what is now known as Baffin Land. On 22 Sept., after reaching 'Fox his farthest,' Fox turned the head of his ship homeward, continuing his observations among the numerous islands and sounds off the north shore of Hudson's Strait, which have never been marked in our admiralty charts. On 28 Sept. Fox found himself, with nearly half his crew worn out with cold and fatigue, once more off Resolution Island, at the entrance to the strait. On 5 Oct. he made Cape Chidley; two days later he writes that they were 'revived by warmth in open sea, most of us ready to fall down with the rest who were down already.' On account of the absence of the moon he directed his course homeward south-east to the English Channel instead of the shorter, but more dangerous one by way of the North Sea. On 31 Oct. he concludes: 'Came into the Downs with all my men recovered and sound, not having lost one man or boy, nor any manner of tackling, having been forth neere six months.' Fox is best known by the following work, which contains the results of his voyage: 'North-west Fox, or Fox from the North-west Passage . . . with briefe Abstracts of the Voyages of Cabot, Frobisher, Davis, Weymouth, Knight, Hudson, Button, Gibbons, Bylot, Baffin, Hawkridge . . . Mr. James

Hall's three Voyages to Groynland . . . with the Author his owne Voyage, being the xvi[th] . . . T. Fawcett and B. Alsop, imp. London,' 1635, 4to. This curious book was entered for the Stationers' Company 15 Dec. 1634 (ARBER, iv. 331). It was accompanied by a large folded map of the Arctic regions, now rarely found in the book, but which is one of the most interesting and important documents in the history of Arctic exploration. References to two other journals of the voyage will be found below. It would appear that Fox was allowed to pass the closing years of his life in neglect. Towards the end of his book he says that he had 'wash't the Blackmore these five yeares, having yet received neither sallery, wages, or reward, except what some few gentlemen hath, I know not whether in curtesse or charity, bestowed upon me, having before had my meanes taken from me in the time of warres, betwixt France, Spain, and us' (p. 268). Fox, who was a younger brother of the Trinity House, died at Whitby in July 1635.

[Arber's Reg. Stat. Company, iv. 305-6; Charlton's Hist. of Whitby, 1779, p. 315; Corlass's Hull Authors, 1879 (Captain Luke Fox (N. W. Fox), London, 1635, &c.); Rundell's Voyages toward the North-West, 1849 (Hakluyt Soc.); Sheahan's Hist. of Hull, 1864; Sainsbury's State Papers, Col. Ser., America and West Indies, 1574–1660, 8vo, p. 105; Brit. Mus. Addit. MS. 19302 (two Journals, one by Captain Luke Fox, the other by the master of the Charles, eighteenth-century copies, more or less perfect).] C. H. C.

FOX, RICHARD (1448?–1528), bishop of Winchester. [See FOXE.]

FOX, ROBERT (1798?–1843), antiquary, was admitted a member of the Royal College of Surgeons, 5 March 1819, and practised in Huntingdon and the neighbourhood. He was the founder of the Literary and Scientific Institution of Huntingdon in 1841, and was himself an able lecturer on subjects connected with antiquities, geology, natural history, and philosophy. His only publication, 'The History of Godmanchester, in the county of Huntingdon,' 8vo, London, 1831, one of the best of its class, gained him admission to the Society of Antiquaries. He was also a member of the Numismatic Society. In 1826 and 1831 he served as a bailiff of Godmanchester, and died there on 8 June 1843, aged forty-five, greatly esteemed for his benevolence. He left a small but choice collection of coins and antiquities, mostly local 'finds.' This, together with his philosophical apparatus, was purchased by subscription after his death, and placed in the Huntingdon Literary and Scientific Institution as a testimonial to his memory.

[Gent. Mag. new ser. xx. 99 ; Lists of Members of Royal Coll. of Surgeons; Lists of Soc. of Antiq.; Kelly's Directory of Bedfordshire, Huntingdonshire, &c. (1885), pp. 207–8.]   G. G.

FOX, ROBERT WERE (1789–1877), scientific writer, born at Falmouth in Cornwall on 26 April 1789, belonged to a quaker family. His father, a shipping agent, was also named Robert Were Fox; his mother was Elizabeth, daughter of Joseph Tregelles of Falmouth. He was privately educated, and showed a special taste for mathematics. His mother taught him to study natural phenomena. He married in 1814 Maria, fourth daughter of Robert Barclay of Bury Hill, Surrey, and during his wedding trip, taken that year on the continent, he formed lasting friendships with Humboldt and other foreign savants. In 1848 Fox was elected a fellow of the Royal Society. He was one of the founders of the Royal Cornwall Polytechnic Society in 1833, and was several times vice-president. Fox died at his house, Penjerrick, near Falmouth, on 25 July 1877, in the eighty-ninth year of his age. He was buried in the Friends' burial-ground at Budock. His wife, who was born in 1786, died 4 June 1858.

Fox's original scientific researches were commenced in 1812, when he made, in conjunction with Joel Lean, a series of costly experiments on the elasticity of high-pressure steam, hoping to improve Watt's engines employed in pumping the Cornish mines. Fox aided Trevithick in several of his mechanical inventions. In 1815 Fox commenced an important series of researches upon the internal temperature of the earth, which he continued to prosecute more or less throughout his life. His lifelong connection with the Cornish mines gave him great facilities for this work ; and, commencing in the ' Crenver' mine, the temperature was tested regularly at intervals of a few feet, by means of thermometers embedded in the rocks, down to the greatest depths attainable in the Dolcoath and other deep mines in Cornwall. Fox was the first to prove definitively that the heat increased with the depth; he also showed that this increase was in a diminishing ratio as the depth increased. The results are contained in a series of papers, of which we may mention those ' On the Temperature of Mines,' in Thomson's 'Annals of Philosophy' for 1822; ' Some Facts which appear to be at Variance with the Igneous Hypothesis of Geologists,' ' Philosophical Magazine' for 1832 ; ' Report on some Observations on Subterranean Temperature,' ' British Association Report,' 1840; and ' Some Remarks on the High Temperature in the United Mines,' ' Edinburgh New Philosophical Journal' for 1847. Fox con-

tributed fifty-two papers to various scientific periodicals. The first of these is on the ' Alloys of Platinum,' and was published in Thomson's ' Annals of Philosophy ' for 1819. A very important discovery made by Fox was the 'Electro-Magnetic Properties of Metalliferous Veins in the Mines of Cornwall' ('Philosophical Transactions' for 1830). Continuing this work Fox published in the 'Edinburgh New Philosophical Journal' for 1838 a paper on the ' Lamination of Clay by Electricity,' showing that miniature mineral veins could be formed in clay by the long-continued passage of an electric current.

Fox devoted much time to the study of magnetic phenomena, especially those belonging to the earth's magnetism. In 1831 and 1832 he read papers before the Royal Society on the ' Variable Magnetic Intensity of the Earth,' and on the ' Influence of the Aurora on the Compass Needle.' To aid in the study of these subjects Fox constructed a new dipping-needle of great delicacy and accuracy. This instrument was afterwards employed by Sir James Clarke Ross in his voyage to the Antarctic Ocean in 1837, and by Captain Nares in the last expedition to the North Pole in 1875–7.

[Athenæum, 4 Aug. 1877 ; Royal Society's Catalogue of Scientific Papers, 1868 ; Royal Cornwall Polytechnic Society's Report for 1877 ; J. H. Collins's Catalogue of the Works of R. W. Fox, F.R.S., 1878 ; Boase and Courtney's Bibliotheca Cornubiensis, i. 162–5, iii. 1188–9, where a full list of Fox's scientific papers is given.]
          W. J. H.

FOX, SAMUEL (1560–1630), diarist. [See FOXE.]

FOX, SIMEON (1568–1642), president of the College of Physicians. [See FOXE.]

FOX, SIR STEPHEN (1627–1716), statesman, born on 27 March 1627, was the youngest son of William Fox of Farley, Wiltshire, by his wife Elizabeth, daughter of Thomas Pavey of Plaitford, in the same county. As a boy he is said to have been in the choir of Salisbury Cathedral. He also received a thorough and early drilling in the art of bookkeeping. At the age of fifteen his ' beauty of person and towardliness of disposition,' aided, it is probable, by a letter from an early patron, Brian Duppa [q. v.], recommended him to the notice of the Earl of Northumberland, high admiral of England. Some five years later he passed into the household of the earl's brother, Lord Percy, under whom he had the supervision of the ordnance board during the campaign which ended with the battle of Worcester, 3 Sept. 1651. He then took an active part in assisting the escape of Charles to Normandy. When the prince was obliged to leave France in 1654, Clarendon persuaded him to entrust the management of his household affairs unreservedly to Fox, 'a young man bred under the severe discipline of the Lord Peircy, . . . very well qualified with languages, and all other parts of clerkship, honesty, and discretion, that were necessary for the discharge of such a trust' (*Hist. of the Rebellion*, Oxf. edit. bk. xiv. par. 89). Under Fox's discreet stewardship the prince, wherever he might choose to fix his court, was never without the means of living in comfort. 'Mr. Fox,' writes Ormonde to Charles from Breda, 9 Aug. 1658, 'knows to a stiver what money you can depend upon' (*Cal. State Papers*, Dom. 1658–9, p. 104). At Spa he won the favour of the king's sister, the widowed Princess of Orange, and was employed subsequently in several important missions to her, as well as to other great persons in Holland. He was able to procure frequent and regular supplies of money for the royal household. Charles intended rewarding him by a grant of the place of cofferer of the household, but finding William Ashburnham held already the reversion, he granted Fox, by a special instrument dated at Brussels 23 Nov. 1658, an honourable augmentation to his arms out of the royal ensigns and devices, to wit, 'in a canton Azure, a Fleur de Lis, Or' (*Addit. MS.* 15856, f. 89 *b*). Fox was the first to bring his master the news of Cromwell's death, and to salute him as the real king of Great Britain. The king afterwards employed Fox on various secret missions to England, as one the royalists could thoroughly rely on. With Sir Edward Walker, Garter king at arms, he was sent to the Hague in May 1660 to adjust the ceremonies for the king's public reception there. After the Restoration Fox's fortunes rose rapidly. Ormonde, then lord high steward, nominated him first clerk of the board of green cloth. In October 1660 he received a grant of the remainder of the lease of part of the manor of East Meon, Hampshire, to the value of 400*l*. a year, which had been forfeited by the treason of Francis Allen, goldsmith and alderman of London (*ib*. 1660–1661, p. 337, 1661–2, p. 131). In March 1661 he became receiver and paymaster of two regiments of guards appointed for the king's safety upon the outbreak of Venner's plot in the preceding January (*ib*. 1660–1, p. 556). During the same year he was constituted paymaster-general, an enormously lucrative office. He deigned, however, to accept the receivership of the garrison at Portsmouth, 20 Feb. 1662, with the nominal fee of 100*l*.

a year (*ib*. 1661–2, p. 279). The people of Salisbury, 'for the love they bore to a gentleman who did them the honour of owing his birth to their neighbourhood,' chose him as their member, 30 Nov. 1661, in succession to Francis Swanton, deceased. He was knighted 1 July 1665. Despite his position at court he contrived to maintain his independence. He strenuously asserted the integrity of Clarendon, and voted against his impeachment, 12 Nov. 1667, 'although he was in a manner commanded by the king to act in a contrary part.' On 27 Feb. 1678–9 he was elected for Westminster. In November 1679 he became one of the lords commissioners of the treasury, and his name appeared in every subsequent commission except that of July 1684, when Laurence, earl of Rochester, was lord treasurer. He was, however, reinstated in the following September. In December 1680, having been gazetted first commissioner of horse, he resigned his office of paymaster-general, but contrived that his eldest son, Charles Fox, should share it along with Nicholas Johnson. On Johnson's death in April 1682 Fox made interest to have it solely conferred on his son, who three years afterwards was independent enough to vote with the opposition against granting money to James II until grievances had been redressed. On 18 Feb. 1684 Fox was made sole commissioner of horse.

Fox's places brought him enormous profits. In 1680 his friend Evelyn computed him to be worth at least 200,000*l*., 'honestly got and unenvied, which is next to a miracle.' Evelyn himself tells how Fox contrived to escape the jealousy of his colleagues. At the height of his prosperity he continued 'as humble and ready to do a courtesy as ever he was' (*Diary*, ed. 1850–2, ii. 147–8). He made an intelligible use of his riches. He showed his regard to his birthplace, Farley, by building a church, and in 1678 a set of almshouses and a charity school, there. 'In the North Part of Wilts he built a Chancel intirely new.' He built almshouses at Broome, Suffolk, and at Ashby, Northamptonshire. He also erected the church of Culford in Suffolk. At Redlinch in Somersetshire he founded a charity school, in addition to repairing the church. Canon Richard Eyre, who preached his funeral sermon, tells us that 'he pew'd the body of the cathedral church of Sarum in a very neat manner, suitable to the neatness of that church, to which he was many other ways a great benefactor' (p. 18 *n*.) After twenty years at the pay office he thought of a magnificent device for restoring to the army some part of the fortune which he had got by it. He inspired Charles in 1681 with that idea of founding an asylum at Chelsea for disabled soldiers, the credit of which is generally ascribed to Nell Gwyn. In furthering the enterprise through all its stages he derived assistance from Evelyn (*Diary*, ii. 159, 163). His contribution to the building and maintenance fund was above 13,000*l*. (EYRE, *Funeral Sermon*, p. 8 *n*.)

On James coming to the throne a peerage was offered to Fox on the condition of his turning Roman catholic. He adhered, however, manfully to his religion. The priests then intrigued to have him removed from the commission of the treasury, but the king had sense enough to insist on keeping Fox and Godolphin as members of an otherwise inexperienced board. He was also suffered to retain his clerkship of the green cloth. On 26 March 1685 he was returned once more for Salisbury. Greatly to James's anger he opposed the bill for a standing army, though he otherwise endeavoured to serve him faithfully. When the Prince of Orange landed, Compton, bishop of London, attempted to tamper with the fidelity of Fox. Fox refused to take an active part against his old master. His anonymous biographer, however, can only say that 'he never appeared at his highness's court to make his compliments there till the king had left the country.' William, who had dined with him when on a visit to England, 23 July 1681, soon won him over to his side. In February 1689–1690 Luttrell heard that Fox 'hath lately kist his majesties hand, and is received into favour' (*Historical Relation of State Affairs*, 1857, ii. 16). The next month he took his seat once more at his accustomed boards. Thenceforward whatever changes might occur at the treasury Fox's name was always on the new commission. On 9 Nov. 1691 he succeeded, on the death of Sir William Pulteney, in being returned a second time for Westminster, and he was re-elected by the same constituency on 29 Oct. 1695. In May 1692, James, having arrived at La Hogue, excepted Fox by name in his declaration promising pardon to all who returned to their allegiance. In 1696–7 Fox was a rival with Montague for the place of first commissioner, but at length withdrew from the competition, though not with a very good grace. He wished it to be notified in the 'London Gazette' that the place had been offered to him and declined by him. This would have been an affront to Montague. But from tenderness to Fox the promotion of his rival was not announced in the 'London Gazette' (MACAULAY, *Hist. of Engl.* ch. xxi.) By a commission, which bears the date 1 Feb. 1696-7, Fox succeeded Henry Frederick Thynne in

the office of treasurer and receiver-general to the queen dowager, 'Sir Christopher Musgrave haveing refused it;' it is certain that Charles Fox was acting as such by 1700 (CHAMBERLAYNE, *Angliæ Notitia*, ed. 1700, pt. iii. p. 515). On 26 Jan. 1698–9 Fox was chosen member for Cricklade, Wiltshire, in place of Charles Fox, who elected to serve for Salisbury, and was returned again 7 Jan. 1700-1. Upon Anne's accession he wished to retire into private life, but by the queen's express desire he led the commons in procession at her coronation, 23 April 1702, and also acted for a time as first commissioner of horse. He consented to be chosen for Salisbury, 15 March 1713-14, in succession to his son, who had died in the preceding September. In 1685 he had purchased a copyhold estate at Chiswick, Middlesex, on which he built a villa, which excited the admiration of William III, but not that of Evelyn (LYSONS, *Environs*, ii. 209; EVELYN, ii. 169, 175). There he died, 28 Oct. 1716, and was buried at Farley (the date, '23 Sept.,' is wrongly given on his monument). Ninety years later his grandson, Charles James Fox [q. v.], died in the same place. About 1654 he married Elizabeth, daughter of William Whittle of Lancashire, and sister of Sackvill Whittle, chief surgeon to Charles II, by whom he had seven sons and three daughters. Charles, the eldest son, who was named after his godfather, Charles II, died childless in September 1713, and was buried at Farley (RICHARD EYRE, *Funeral Sermon on C. Fox, Esq.*) Five other sons, who died young, were buried in Westminster Abbey (CHESTER, *Westminster Abbey Registers*). Of the two surviving daughters, Elizabeth, the elder, married, 27 Dec. 1673, Charles, third lord Cornwallis, a disreputable gambler. Evelyn (ii. 156–7) gives an amusing sketch of the 'grave and dexterous courtesy' with which Fox foiled Lady Sunderland's attempt to secure his younger daughter Jane for her son, Lord Spencer. Jane Fox was married in 1686 to George, fourth earl of Northampton. Lady Fox died 11 Aug. 1696, 'much lamented by the poor for her charity' (LUTTRELL, iv. 96), and was buried at Farley. In his seventy-seventh year, Fox, 'unwilling that so plentiful an estate should go out of the name, and being of a vegete and hale constitution,' married as his second wife, 11 July 1703, Christian, daughter and coheiress of Francis Hopes, rector, first of Haceby and afterwards of Aswarby, both in Lincolnshire (CHESTER, p. 262, *n*. 3). By this lady, who was then in her twenty-sixth year, Fox became the father of four more children: Stephen (*b*. 1704), afterwards Earl of Ilchester; Henry (*b*. 1705), first Lord

Holland [q. v.]; a daughter, Christian, twin with Henry (*d.* 1708); and another daughter, Charlotte, married in July 1729 to Edward, third son of William, fifth lord Digby. The second Lady Fox dying at Bath, 17 Feb. 1718-1719, was buried at Farley. In the picture at Holland House Sir Godfrey Kneller endows her 'with small and pretty features, and hair and complexion as dark as her grandson's.'

Fox's reputation for courtesy, kindliness of disposition, and generosity has been amply confirmed by Evelyn. Pepys, too, has much to say in commendation of the paymaster, who confided to him the secrets whereby he was enabled to make such large profits (*Diary,* ed. Bright, iv. 206). He does not forget to celebrate the 'very genteel' dinners of his host, while Lady Fox and her seven children noted for their comeliness received unstinted praise, 'a family governed so nobly and neatly as do me good to see it' (*ib.* v. 335). Fox's portrait by Lely has been engraved by Scriven; of that by J. Baker there are engravings by Simon, Earlom, and Harding (EVANS, *Cat. of Engraved Portraits,* ii. 158). A large mass of his official papers and correspondence is preserved in the Additional Manuscripts in the British Museum.

[Memoirs of the Life of Sir Stephen Fox, kt. 8vo, London, 1717 (reprinted fol. London, 1807, and 8vo, London, 1811); Richard Eyre's Sermon preach'd at the Funeral of Sir Stephen Fox, kt. 8vo, London, 1716; Richard Eyre's Sermon preach'd at the Funeral of Charles Fox, esq., 4to, Oxford, 1713; Historical Register, 1716, i. 546-7; Trevelyan's Early Hist. of C. J. Fox, ch. i.; Collins's Peerage (Brydges), iii. 260, iv. 529, v. 382; Le Neve's Pedigrees of the Knights (Harl. Soc.), p. 197; Cal. State Papers (Dom. Ser.); Evelyn's Diary (1850-2); Pepys's Diary (Bright); Luttrell's Relation of State Affairs (1857); Noble's Continuation of Granger's Biog. Hist. i. 150-1; Chester's London Marriage Licences (Foster), col. 508; Chester's Westminster Abbey Registers; Lysons's Environs, ii. 155, 208-10; Hoare's Wiltshire, Hundred of Alderbury, sub 'Farley;' Notes and Queries, 1st ser. ix. 271, xi. 325, 395, 2nd ser. i. 301, 410, ix. 419, 5th ser. iii. 416, iv. 114; Memorials and Correspondence of C. J. Fox (Russell), vol. i. bk. i.; Earl Russell's Life and Times of C. J. Fox, vol. i. ch. i.; Will of Sir Stephen Fox (P. C. C. 133, Fox); Will of Sackvill Whittle (P. C. C. 52, North); Cal. Clarendon State Papers; Cal. State Papers, Treas., 1692-1719.]   G. G.

FOX, TIMOTHY (1628-1710), nonconformist divine, was born in 1628, and educated at Birmingham, whence he proceeded to Christ's College, Cambridge. He was admitted by the commissioners of the great seal to the rectory of Drayton, Staffordshire, but on being ejected by the Bartholomew act of 1662 he settled for a while in a neighbouring town, where he made a shift to live by his pen and the help of relations, till the Oxford act forced him to remove, and rent a farm in Derbyshire. Afterwards, in May 1684, he was committed to Derby gaol upon that act, not for any exercise of religion, but merely for coming to see his son, then an apprentice in that town, and remained a prisoner until the following November. He again suffered imprisonment when Monmouth was in the west, on this occasion in Chester gaol. No cause whatever was assigned for his detention. After enduring a month's confinement he was released on finding ample security for his good behaviour. From the time of his ejectment he preached in private as he had opportunity, and after public liberty was granted, he opened a meeting in his own house at Caldwell, Derbyshire, where he preached twice a day and catechised. He died in May 1710.

[Calamy's Nonconf. Memorial, ed. Palmer, 1802, iii. 232-3.]   G. G.

FOX, WILLIAM (1736-1826), founder of the Sunday School Society, son of J. Fox, renter of the Clapton Manor estate, Gloucestershire, was born at Clapton 14 Feb. 1736. The youngest of a large family he was left fatherless in early childhood. He had extraordinary resolution, and at the age of ten formed business plans which were afterwards completely realised. He ultimately became lord of the manor of Clapton. Fox was apprenticed to a draper and mercer at Oxford in 1752, and before the expiration of his indentures his master gave up to him his house and shop and stock of goods, valued at about 4,000*l.* Fox married in 1761 the eldest daughter of Jonathan Tabor, a Colchester merchant. Three years later he removed to London, and entered upon a large business in Leadenhall Street. Impressed with the degradation of the poorer classes of the population, he endeavoured unsuccessfully, by the aid of members of both houses of parliament, to move the government in their behalf. About 1784, when he became the proprietor of Clapton, he began his humanitarian work unaided, not only clothing all the poor of the parish—men, women, and children—but founding a free day school. Writing to Robert Raikes in 1785 he stated that long before the establishment of Sunday schools he had designed a system of universal education, but had met with little support from the clergy and laity, who were alarmed by the magnitude of the undertaking. A meeting was held at Fox's instance in the Poultry, London, on 16 Aug. 1785, when it was resolved to issue a circular recommending the formation of a society for the establishment and support of Sunday schools throughout the kingdom of Great Britain. Fox was cordially supported by Raikes, Jonas Hanway, and other friends of education, and the result was the foundation of the Sunday School Society, with a body of officers and governors, and a committee of twenty-four persons, chosen equally from the church of England and the various bodies of protestant dissenters. The Earl of Salisbury was elected president. Before eight months had elapsed from the first meeting in the Poultry, thirty schools had been established, containing 1,110 scholars, and by the following January (1787) these had been increased to 147 schools with 7,242 children. In 1797 the Baptist Home Missionary Society was formed, with Fox as treasurer. Five years later Fox left London and went to reside at Lechlade House, Gloucestershire. He remained here till 1823, when he moved to Cirencester, where he lost his wife, a lineal descendant of Sir Harbottle Grimstone [q. v.] Fox died at Cirencester on 1 April 1826, and was buried at Lechlade beside his wife and daughter. Among the friends and supporters of Fox were Granville Sharp and William Wilberforce.

[Ivimey's Memoir of Fox, 1831.] G. B. S.

FOX, WILLIAM JOHNSON (1786–1864), preacher, politician, and man of letters, was born at Uggeshall Farm, Wrentham, in the north of Suffolk, 1 March 1786. From his father, a sturdy peasant-farmer, who had once got into trouble as a poacher, he inherited, he says in a fragmentary autobiography, 'sluggish tenacity of brain;' from his mother, a woman of sweet and liberal nature, 'nervous irritability.' Both parents were strict Calvinistic independents. When Fox was only three years of age his father gave up farming, and barely supported himself in several callings at Norwich. Fox was sent to a chapel school, became a weaver's boy, an errand-boy, and in 1799 clerk in a bank. Here he found leisure for self-improvement, worked hard at mathematics, and, like Leigh Hunt, Peacock, and De Quincey, won prizes offered by the 'Monthly Preceptor,' and planned a course of study which would have occupied him for seven years. He first studied Latin and Greek with a view to progress in mathematics, and improved his knowledge of them with a view to divinity. He appreciated, however, the melody of Greek versification, and the shrewd philosophy of Horace, 'though much of it used to elbow and jostle my morality.' He took to authorship, competed for essay prizes, and

wrote occasionally for a local newspaper; until at length it was suggested that the pulpit was his proper destination. In September 1806 he entered the Independent College at Homerton under Dr. Pye Smith. He found there a considerable tendency to free inquiry, 'which gradually subsided as the time came for the student to exchange his sure and safe retreat for the fiery ordeal of the deacon and the pew.' Early in 1810 he took charge of a congregation at Fareham. He studied the unitarian controversy, reading books treating upon it for hours in bed. By March 1812 he had entirely broken with orthodoxy, and had become minister of the unitarian chapel at Chichester, after a brief and unsuccessful experience as pastor of a small seceding congregation at Fareham. At Chichester he studied hard, and formed an ill-advised engagement to his future wife, Eliza, daughter of James Florance, barrister. In 1817 he became minister of Parliament Court Chapel, London. He had now, by dint of assiduous practice, made himself a consummate rhetorician. His celebrity was enhanced by several published sermons, one of which, 'On the Duties of Christians towards Deists,' occasioned by the trial of Carlile, excited warm controversy. In 1820 he married, and the next few years of his life were marked by a severe illness, a visit to Scotland, his first regular contributions to a newspaper, the 'Norwich Mercury,' the removal of his congregation from Parliament Court to a chapel built especially for him in South Place, Finsbury (1824), a controversy with Dr. Blomfield on the gospel of St. John, and increasing connection with literature and politics. He began to be celebrated for his taste as a dramatic critic; he wrote on Nathaniel Lee, 'Sethos,' and other subjects for the 'Retrospective Review;' and, on the establishment of the 'Westminster Review,' he wrote the first article, entitled 'Men and Things in 1824.' He had already become editor, with Robert Aspland (1782–1845) [q. v.], of the 'Monthly Repository,' the leading organ of the unitarian denomination, which he conducted as a theological periodical until 1831, when he purchased the copyright from the Unitarian Association, and made it an organ of political and social reform, combined with literary criticism. Fox's quick recognition of youthful genius was especially shown in his welcome of Browning's 'Pauline,' which occasioned a lifelong friendship with the poet. Mill contributed philosophical papers under the signature 'Antiquus;' and in Fox's periodical appeared Crabb Robinson's remarkable series of papers on 'Goethe;' Harriet Martineau's poems and essays; Eliza Flower's musical contributions; Browning's poems; and W. Bridges Adams's essays on social subjects, signed 'Junius Redivivus,' whose freedom of tone gave offence in unitarian circles. Hazlitt pronounced Fox superior to Irving as a preacher, and his celebrity was extended beyond metropolitan limits by the publication of two collections of sermons, 'Christ and Christianity' and 'Christian Morality.' He was, however, drifting further and further away from theology; and during the agitation for reform he took a prominent part as a popular leader, daily addressing open-air meetings in Lincoln's Inn Fields. 'He was,' says Francis Place, 'the bravest of us all.' In 1834 his domestic difficulties came to the knowledge of leading members of his congregation. He resented their consequent interference; the majority of his congregation stood by him; and the controversy was closed by the secession of the minority in September 1834. No tangible imputation rested upon his personal conduct, but the confidence of many of his most influential supporters had been undermined by the advocacy in the 'Repository' of the dissolubility of marriage, and his evident alienation from theology. A separation on account of incompatibility of temper was arranged between him and Mrs. Fox.

Fox was disowned by his brother unitarian ministers, and resigned his office as a trustee of the Williams Library. His freedom from restraint, already irksome, gave him a more independent position in the pulpit. The service, under Eliza Flower's direction, became musical, Fox himself contributing some highly poetical hymns; his addresses ranged widely over the fields of morals and politics, and attracted a very intellectual auditory, including many members of parliament. Twenty-six of these discourses, published between 1835 and 1840 under the title of 'Finsbury Lectures,' represent the general topics and tone of his teaching. Discourses on such themes as 'Morality illustrated by the various Classes into which Society is divided' alternate with secular subjects, as the coronation, the corn laws, and national education. The tone, however, is invariably lofty. They were usually delivered after a few days' meditation, with slight assistance from a shorthand abstract, but published entirely from the reporter's notes. They gained greatly in delivery from the impressive intonation of the speaker. Rapturous descriptions of Fox's oratory will be found in John Saunders's sketch in the 'People's Journal' and in Evans's 'Authors and Orators of Lancashire.' Their testimony is confirmed by James Grant (1802–1879) [q. v.], writing in 1840,

who infers, however, from his statue-like absence of gesture, that he would fail with a popular audience. In 1843 Fox was thrilling enthusiastic popular assemblages. To meet heavy expenses he wrote more than ever, especially upon politics. Bulwer, Talfourd, Macready, and Forster were now among his most intimate friends, and his relations with Mill led Carlyle to believe that he was to be offered the editorship of the 'London and Westminster Review.' He transferred the proprietorship and editorship of the unprofitable 'Repository' to R. H. Horne in 1836, and for a time chiefly devoted himself to journalism. Daniel Whittle Harvey [q. v.] enlisted him in the 'Sunday Times,' and when Harvey became proprietor of the 'True Sun' (1835) Fox's contributions raised the circulation from two thousand to fifteen thousand copies. He laboured at the office regularly for five days a week until the end of 1837, when Harvey's sudden relinquishment of his journal terminated the engagement. Fox joined the 'Morning Chronicle,' where his politics were much more under restraint. He devoted especial attention to the performances of Macready, of whom he was an intense admirer.

When, in 1840, an address from the Anti-Cornlaw League to the nation was required, Cobden drew up a paper of memoranda, and entrusted the composition to Fox as the person most competent to administer ' a blister to the aristocracy and the House of Commons.' The address was followed by a long series of most effective letters to leading public characters published in the 'League' newspaper, under the signature of 'A Norwich Weaver Boy.' Fox became a leading orator of the league, speaking especially at Drury Lane and Covent Garden. 'The speech read well,' says Prentice, 'but the reader could have no conception of the effect as delivered with a beauty of elocution which Macready on the same boards might have envied.' His connection with the 'Morning Chronicle' ceased about this time, and was followed by an engagement with the 'Daily News,' to which, as to the 'Chronicle,' he contributed four leaders weekly. When Forster retired in September 1846, Fox followed his example. He further undertook a course of Sunday evening lectures to the working classes at the National Hall in Holborn, commenced in 1844, and continued until 1846; which, after being published first in 'The Apprentice,' and afterwards in the 'People's Journal,' were collected into four volumes in 1849. They showed the author to be one of the wisest as well as the warmest friends of the working classes. This character, even more than the eloquence of his Anti-Cornlaw League orations, gained Fox an invitation to stand for the working-class constituency of Oldham, for which he was returned after a keen contest in July 1847. His congregation had already found it necessary to provide an assistant minister. He was relieved from embarrassment by the munificence of Samuel Courtauld of Braintree, who settled upon him an annuity of 400*l*. His last address to his congregation was given in February 1852. He had previously summed up his conclusions in his lectures of the 'Religious Ideas' (published in 1849), in which these ideas are treated as the natural production of the human mind in the course of its development, corresponding to external realities, as yet but dimly surmised.

Fox's later exertions were mainly confined to parliament and the composition of the 'Publicola' letters for the 'Weekly Dispatch,' which he continued until 1861. His success in parliament was limited by his age and the didacticism acquired in the pulpit. Regarded at first as 'a sort of heterodox methodist parson,' he soon gained general respect by his tact, discretion, and moderation. His most remarkable speeches were that delivered on seconding Mr. Hume's motion for an extension of the franchise in 1849, and that on the introduction of his own bill for establishing compulsory secular education in 1850. He made the subject of education in large measure his own, and always regretted that Lord John Russell had taken it out of his hands. He usually acted with the politicians of the Manchester school, but differed from them on the Crimean war, and declared his dissent in a great speech to his constituents in the winter of 1855. His success at Oldham had involved the rejection of John Fielden [q. v.], who had thrown in his lot with Mr. J. M. Cobbett. Fox thus excited the fiercest antagonism in a section of the liberal party. He was defeated in 1852, regained his seat in the autumn of the same year, after tumults described as 'sacrificial games dedicated to the manes of the late Mr. John Fielden,' was again ejected in 1857, and re-elected in the same year upon another unexpected vacancy. He then held the seat without opposition until his retirement in 1863, though taking little part in public business. He died after a short illness on 3 June 1864, and was buried in Brompton cemetery. His memory was celebrated in the most fitting manner by a memorial edition of his complete writings.

Fox's master passion was philanthropy, and he had adopted the philosophy of Bentham as that apparently most conducive to human welfare. But his temperament was that of a poet, his tastes were literary, dramatic, musical. His utilitarianism was pervaded with imagination, and he was far more effective as a man of letters than as a thinker, and a speaker than as a reasoner. The orator in him was rather made than born, his seeming gift of improvisation was the acquisition of long and careful practice. The construction of his speeches was in the highest degree rhetorical, and they owed much of their effect to his marvellous elocution. They are, however, admirable for powerful diction, manly sense, and abound in fancy, humour, and sarcasm; nor were his innumerable contributions to the press less excellent in their way. No one could better popularise a truth or embody an abstraction. The great aim of his life was to benefit the classes from which he had sprung. No one has counselled those classes more freely, or on the whole more wisely. His nature, though not exempt from angularities, was genial and affectionate; he said of himself that he could never learn to say 'No' till he had attained middle life, and then but imperfectly. He craved for sympathy, and when disappointed of obtaining it, took refuge in a reserve which, combined with the phlegm of his physical constitution, sometimes made him appear inert and inanimate, when in reality his mind was actively at work.

[About 1835 Fox began to dictate an autobiography, which he only brought down to his settlement at Fareham, with many gaps and omissions. He began another in 1858, but made still less progress. These documents, with many other unpublished papers, have been placed at the writer's disposal by Fox's daughter, Mrs. Bridell Fox. See also the memoir in vol. xii. of his collected writings; Memoirs of Eliza Fox; James Grant's Public Characters; Evans's Lancashire Authors and Orators; Prentice's History of the Anti-Cornlaw League; Sir John Bowring in the Theological Review for 1864; John Saunders in the People's Journal for 1848.] R. G.

FOX, WILLIAM TILBURY (1836–1879), physician, son of Luther Owen Fox, M.D., of Broughton, Winchester, was born in 1836, and entered the medical school of University College, London, in 1853. In 1857 he obtained the scholarship and gold medal in medicine at the M.B. examination of the university of London, and graduated M.D. in 1858. After a short period of general practice at Bayswater, he selected midwifery as a specialty, and was appointed physician-accoucheur to the Farringdon General Dispensary. At this period he wrote some good papers on obstetrical subjects, published in the 'Transactions' of the Obstetrical Society. Becoming interested in the study of microscopic fungi attacking the skin and hair, he wrote a book on the subject, and gradually became a specialist on dermatology. In 1864 he travelled in the East with the Earl of Hopetoun, but returned much enfeebled in health. The experience gained abroad was utilised in several works mentioned below. Settling in Sackville Street, Piccadilly, Fox soon acquired a large practice in dermatology. In 1866 he became physician to the skin department of Charing Cross Hospital, and not long after succeeded Dr. Hillier as physician to the same department of University College Hospital, where he established an excellent system of baths. He proved a good teacher and attracted many foreigners to his clinique. His book on 'Skin Diseases,' enlarged and more copiously illustrated in successive editions, made his name widely known, and his 'Atlas' finally established his reputation. He did not seek to revolutionise the treatment of his subject, but based his classification on Willan and Bateman's, while insisting on the value of general medical knowledge and insight to the dermatologist. Thus he had worthily gained a position second to few if any specialists, when his life was threatened by aortic disease, with frequent angina. He was taking a brief holiday in Paris, and preparing for the presidency of the Dermatological subsection of the British Medical Association at Cork, when an attack of angina carried him off on 7 June 1879. He was buried at Willesden cemetery, 14 June 1879.

For many years and up to the time of his death Fox was a prominent member of the editorial staff of the 'Lancet.' His intense energy was always at work promoting the interests of dermatology as a branch of medical practice. His genial manners and conscientiousness made him very popular with patients.

Fox's principal writings are the following: 1. 'Skin Diseases of Parasitic Origin,' 1863. 2. 'Skin Diseases, their Description, Pathology, Diagnosis, and Treatment,' 1864; 3rd edit., rewritten and enlarged, 1873. 3. 'The Classification of Skin Diseases,' 1864. 4. 'Cholera Prospects,' 1865. 5. 'The Action of Fungi in the Production of Disease,' 1866. 6. 'Leprosy, Ancient and Modern; with notes taken during recent travel in the East,' 1866. 7. 'Eczema, its Nature and Treatment,' 'Lettsomian Lectures,' 1870. 8. 'Prurigo and Pediculosis,' 1870. 9. 'Scheme for obtaining a better knowledge of Endemic Skin Diseases of India' (with Dr. T. Farquhar); prepared for the India Office, 1872. 10. 'Key to Skin Diseases,' 1875. 11. 'Atlas of Skin Diseases' (based on Willan's); 4to, with plates, 1875-7. 12. 'On certain Endemic Skin and other Diseases of India and Hot Climates generally' (with Dr. T. Farquhar), 1876. 13. 'Epitome of Skin Diseases' (with T. Colcott Fox), 1877, 2nd edit. 14. 'On Ringworm and its Management,' 1878. Fox edited and revised editions of Tanner's 'Manual of Clinical Medicine,' published in 1869 and 1876. He also contributed numerous papers on skin diseases to the medical societies and journals.

[Lancet, Medical Times, and British Medical Journal, 14 June 1879.]　　　　　G. T. B.

FOX, WILSON (1831-1887), physician, son of a manufacturer belonging to a well-known quaker family in the west of England, was born at Wellington, Somersetshire, on 2 Nov. 1831. He was educated at Bruce Castle, Tottenham, and University College, London, graduating B.A. in 1850, M.B. in 1854, and M.D. in 1855, at London University. After a year spent as house physician at the Edinburgh Royal Infirmary, he passed several years in Paris, Vienna, and Berlin, being for two years in the last city a pupil of the great pathologist Virchow. Here he made important observations on the degeneration of the gastric glands (see Fox's 'Contributions to the Pathology of the Glandular Structures of the Stomach,' *Med.-Chir. Transactions*, xli. 1858). In 1859 he married Miss Emily Doyle, and settled at Newcastle-under-Lyme, where he became physician to the North Staffordshire Infirmary. In 1861, supported by Virchow's strong recommendation, he was appointed professor of pathological anatomy at University College, London, and soon afterwards assistant physician to University College Hospital. In 1866 he became fellow of the Royal College of Physicians, and in 1867 full physician to his hospital and Holme professor of clinical medicine. In 1870 he was appointed physician extraordinary to the queen, and was elected F.R.S. He afterwards became physician in ordinary, and frequently attended the queen while in Scotland. He acquired a large practice, and was an active member of the leading medical societies and of the College of Physicians. In April 1887 he was suddenly summoned to the deathbed of his eldest brother at Wellington. Thence he went northwards towards his seat at Rydal Mount for a rest, but was seized with pneumonia on the way and died on 3 May at Preston in Lancashire. He was buried at Taunton on 6 May 1887. A bust in the Shire Hall, Taunton, was unveiled 25 Oct. 1888 (*Times*, 26 Oct. 1888, p. 8). His first wife died in 1870; by her he left three sons and three daughters. In 1874 he married Evelyn, daughter of Sir Baldwin W. Walker, bart., and widow of Captain Burgoyne, lost in his ship the Captain [see BURGOYNE, HUGH TALBOT].

In personal appearance Fox was tall, spare, and erect, with a refined expression. Although he was somewhat reserved in manner, his sincerity and earnestness gave him a strong hold on those with whom he came in contact. He was a man of great benevolence, and was in the habit of placing his house at Rydal at the disposal of the Bishop of Bedford during the summer months for the use of invalided East-end clergymen and their families.

Equally as a teacher and as an investigator and writer Fox ranked high. His cases were thoroughly studied, with special attention to the mental and emotional state of his patients, in whom he inspired great confidence. He was the first physician to save life in cases of rheumatic fever where the temperature was excessively high, by placing the patient in baths of iced water. His lectures were highly valued by the students, and the characteristic of his teaching was the ability with which the facts of pathology were made the basis of practical diagnosis and treatment. All his writings manifested great research and labour, and are encyclopædic on their subjects. Besides the works enumerated below, he had been for many years preparing a treatise on diseases of the lungs and an atlas of their pathological anatomy, works that were nearly complete at his death.

Fox's principal writings were : 1. 'On the Origin, Structure, and Mode of Development of Cystic Tumours of the Ovary,' 'Med.-Chir. Trans.,' 1864, xlvii. 227–86. 2. 'On the Artificial Production of Tubercle in the Lower Animals,' a lecture before the Royal College of Physicians, 1864. 3. 'On the Development of Striated Muscular Fibre,' 'Phil. Trans.' clvi. 1866. 4. 'On the Diagnosis and Treatment of the Varieties of Dyspepsia,' 1867 ; 3rd edition, enlarged, 1872, under the title 'The Diseases of the Stomach,' substantially a reproduction of his articles in Reynolds's 'System of Medicine,' vol. ii. 1868. 5. Articles on 'Pneumonia,' &c., in Reynolds's 'System,' iii. 1871. 6. 'On the Treatment of Hyperpyrexia by means of the External Application of Cold,' 1871.

[Lancet, 7 and 14 May 1887 ; British Medical Journal, 7 May 1887.]   G. T. B.

FOXE, JOHN (1516–1587), martyrologist, was born at Boston, Lincolnshire, in 1516. The date is supplied by a grant of arms made to his family on 21 Dec. 1598 (MAITLAND, Notes, pt. i. 8–10). He is there said to be lineally connected with Richard Foxe [q. v.], bishop of Winchester, but this relationship is improbable. The father, of

whom nothing is known, died while his sons were very young. Foxe had at least one brother. The mother married a second husband, Richard Melton, to whom Foxe dedicated an early work, 'An Instruccyon of Christen Fayth,' with every mark of affection. He was a studious youth, and attracted the notice of one Randall, a citizen of Coventry, and of John Harding or Hawarden, fellow of Brasenose College, Oxford. His stepfather's means were small, and these friends sent him to Oxford about 1532, when he was sixteen years old. According to the untrustworthy biography of 1641, attributed to Foxe's son Samuel, Foxe entered at Brasenose College, where his patron Hawarden was tutor. He is not mentioned in the college books. It must, however, be admitted that Foxe, when dedicating his 'Syllogisticon' (1563) to Hawarden, writes of him as if he had been his tutor ; and that Alexander Nowell, afterwards dean of St. Paul's (stated in the biography of 1641 to have been Foxe's chamber-fellow at Oxford), was a member of Brasenose, and was one of Foxe's lifelong friends. Foxe also refers to Brasenose thrice in his 'Actes and Monuments,' but the absence of any comment indicating personal association with the place does not give this circumstance any weight. If he resided at Brasenose at all, it was probably for a brief period as Hawarden's private pupil. He must undoubtedly have attended Magdalen College School at the same time. A close connection with both Magdalen School and College is beyond question. The matriculation register for the years during which Foxe would have been ' in statu pupillari ' is unfortunately lost. But he became probationer fellow of Magdalen in July 1538, and full fellow 25 July 1539, being joint lecturer in logic with Baldwin Norton in 1539–1540, and proceeding B.A. 17 July 1537 and M.A. in July 1543 (Oxf. Univ. Reg., Oxf. Hist. Soc., i. 188). Foxe repeatedly identifies himself with Magdalen in his works and private letters. 'For which foundation,' he writes in the 'Actes,' iii. 716, ' as there have been and be yet many students bound to yield grateful thanks unto God, so I must needs confess to be one, except I will be unkind.' About 1564, when one West (formerly of Magdalen) was charged in the court of high commission with making rebellious speeches, Foxe used his influence to procure the offender's pardon, on the sole ground that he had belonged to the same school and college at Oxford as himself. As fellow of Magdalen Foxe had his difficulties. His intimate friends and correspondents at Oxford included, besides Nowell, Richard Bertie [q. v.], John Cheke of Cambridge [q. v.], Hugh Latimer, and

William Tindal, and like them he strongly favoured extreme forms of protestantism. His colleagues at Magdalen were divided on doctrinal questions, and the majority inclined to the old forms of religious belief. He was bound by the statutes to attend the college chapel with regularity, and to proceed to holy orders within seven years of his election to his fellowship. He declined to conform to either rule. Complaint was made to the president, Dr. Owen Oglethorp, and Foxe defended himself in a long letter (*Lansd. MS.* 388). He expressly objected to the enforcement of celibacy on the fellows. Finally, in July 1545, he and five of his colleagues resigned their fellowships. There was no expulsion, as Foxe's biographer of 1641 and most of his successors have asserted. The college register records that 'ex honesta causa recesserunt sponte a collegio,' and Foxe's future references to his college prove that he bore it no ill-will.

Before leaving Oxford, Foxe mentioned in a letter to Tindal that he had derived much satisfaction from a visit to the Lucy family at Charlecote, Warwickshire. Thither he now directed his steps. William Lucy seems to have given him temporary employment as tutor to his son Thomas. On 3 Feb. 1546-7 Foxe married, at Charlecote Church, Agnes Randall, daughter of his old friend of Coventry—a lady who seems to have been in the service of the Lucys. He thereupon came up to London to seek a livelihood. The biographer of 1641 draws a dreary picture of his disappointments and destitution, and relates how an unknown and anonymous benefactor put a purse of gold into his hand, while in a half-dying condition in St. Paul's Cathedral, and how he received soon afterwards an invitation to visit Mary Fitzroy [q. v.], duchess of Richmond, at her residence, Mountjoy House, Knightrider Street. The latter statement is well founded. It is undoubted that Foxe and his friend Bale, whose acquaintance he first made at Oxford, were both, early in 1548, entertained by the duchess, who was at one with them on religious questions (*Actes*, iii. 705). Through the joint recommendation of his hostess and of Bale, Foxe was moreover appointed before the end of the year tutor to the orphan children of Henry Howard, earl of Surrey, who had been executed 19 Jan. 1546-7. The duchess was the earl's sister, and Bale was intimate with Lord Wentworth, who had been the children's guardian since their father's death. There were two boys, Thomas, afterwards duke of Norfolk (*b.* 1536), and Henry Howard, afterwards earl of Northampton (*b.* 1539), together with three girls. Foxe joined his pupils at the

castle of Reigate, a manor belonging to their grandfather, the Duke of Norfolk. He remained there for five years.

In that interval Foxe published his earliest theological tracts. All advocated advanced reforming views. Their titles are: 'De non plectendis morte adulteris consultatio Ioannis Foxi,' London, per Hugonem Syngletonum, 1548, dedicated to Thomas Picton; 'A Sarmon of Jhon Oecolampadius to Yong Men and Maydens,' dedicated to 'Master Segrave,' London? 1550?; 'An Instruccyon of Christen Fayth,' London, Hugh Syngleton, 1550? dedicated to Melton, his stepfather, a translation from Urbanus Regius; and 'De Censura, sive Excommunicatione Ecclesiastica, Interpellatio ad archiepiscopum Cantabr.,' London, Stephen Mierdmannus, 1551. The first work was reissued in 1549 under the new title 'De lapsis in Ecclesiam recipiendis consultatio,' with a 'Præfaciuncula ad lectorem' substituted for the dedication to Picton (MAITLAND, *Early Books in Lambeth Library*, pp. 223-4). Furthermore, he prepared a school book, 'Tables of Grammar,' London, 1552. According to Wood, eight lords of the privy council subscribed to print this work, but its brevity disappointed its patrons. Meanwhile Foxe was reading much in church history with a view to an elaborate defence of the protestant position. On 24 June 1550 he was ordained deacon by Ridley, bishop of London, in St. Paul's Cathedral. He stayed for the purpose in Barbican, at the house of the Duchess-dowager of Suffolk, who became the wife of his friend, Richard Bertie [see BERTIE, CATHARINE]. Subsequently he preached as a volunteer at Reigate, being the first to preach protestantism there.

The accession of Mary in July 1553 proved of serious import to Foxe. One of the queen's earliest acts was to release from prison the old Duke of Norfolk (*d.* 1554), the grandfather of Foxe's pupils. The duke was a catholic, and promptly dismissed Foxe from his tutorship. It is probable that Foxe thereupon took up his residence at Stepney, whence he dates the dedication of 'A Fruitfull Sermon of the moost Euangelicall wryter, M. Luther, made of the Angelles' (London, by Hugh Syngleton, 1554?). The elder lad, Thomas, had formed a strong affection for his teacher, and when he was sent from Reigate to be under the care of Bishop Gardiner at Winchester House, he contrived that Foxe should pay him secret visits. Foxe was soon alarmed by the obvious signs of a catholic revival. A rumour that parliament was about to re-enact the six articles of 1539 drew from him a well-written Latin petition denouncing any change in the religious esta-

with Parkhurst, and as having preached in his diocese. The bishop invited him to Norwich (29 Jan. 1563–4), but there is no evidence of an earlier visit. From the autumn of 1561 Foxe was chiefly engaged in translating his latest volume into English and in elaborating its information. The papers of Ralph Morice, Cranmer's secretary, had fallen into his hands, together with much new and, as Foxe believed, authentic material. Most of his time was clearly spent in London at the Duke of Norfolk's house in Aldgate, but every Monday he worked at the printing-office of John Day in Aldersgate Street, who had undertaken the publication.

In 1564, after the death of the Duchess of Norfolk, Foxe removed from the duke's house to Day's house in Aldersgate Street, and took a prominent part in Day's business. He petitioned Cecil (6 July 1568) to relax in Day's behalf the law prohibiting a printer from employing more than four foreign workmen. Day's close connection with Foxe's great undertaking is commemorated in the lines on Day's tombstone in the church of Little Bradley, Suffolk :—

He set a Fox to wright how martyrs runne
By death to lyfe: Fox ventured paynes and health
To give them light : Daye spent in print his
                        wealth.
      (*Notes and Queries*, 6th ser. viii. 246.)

But Foxe's stay in Day's house was probably only temporary. In 1565 he spent some time at Waltham. The register states that two of his children, Rafe and Mary, were baptised there on 29 Jan. 1565–6. Fuller in 'The Infant's Advocate,' 1653, not only credits Waltham with being Foxe's home when he was preparing 'his large and learned works,' but says that he left his posterity a considerable estate in the parish. The biographer of 1641 writes that Foxe was on very good terms with Anne, the wife of Sir Thomas Heneage [q. v.], who was a large landowner in the neighbourhood of Waltham. On 24 July 1749 the antiquary Dr. Stukeley made a pilgrimage to the house associated with Foxe at Waltham, and it then seems to have been a popular show-place (*Memoirs*, ii. 211). About 1570 Foxe removed to Grub Street, where he probably lived till his death.

On 20 March 1562–3 Foxe's 'Actes and Monuments' issued from Day's press, on the very same day as Oporinus published at Basle the second part of the Latin original containing Pantaleone's account of the persecutions on the continent. The title of the 'Actes and Monuments' seems to have been borrowed from a book called 'Actiones et Monimenta Martyrum,' printed by Jean Crespin at Geneva in 1560. Grindal had written of Foxe's pro-

jected work as 'Historia Martyrum,' 19 Dec. 1558. From the date of its publication it was popularly known as the 'Book of Martyrs,' and even in official documents as 'Monumenta Martyrum.' The first edition has four dedicatory epistles : to Jesus Christ, the queen, ad doctum lectorem (alone in Latin), and to the persecutors of God's truth. A preface 'on the utility of the story' is a translation from the Basle volume of 1559. Foxe forwarded a copy to Magdalen College, with a letter explaining that the work was written in English 'for the good of the country and the information of the multitude,' and received in payment 6*l.* 13*s.* 4*d.* The success of the undertaking was immediate, and at the suggestion of Jewell, bishop of Salisbury, the author received his first reward in the shape of a prebend in Salisbury Cathedral, together with the lease of the vicarage of Shipton (11 May 1563). Before the year was out he had brought out an elaborate treatise on the Eucharist, entitled 'Syllogisticon,' with a dedication to his old friend Hawarden, now principal of Brasenose, and in 1564 he published a Latin translation of Grindal's funeral sermon in memory of the Emperor Ferdinand I. But he also spent much time in helping the plague-stricken, and made a powerful appeal to the citizens for help for the afflicted (1564). His poverty did not cease. His clothes were still shabby; the pension which the Duke of Norfolk gave him was very small, and when he bestowed the vicarage of Shipton on William Master he appealed to the queen (August 1564) to remit the payment of first-fruits, on the ground that neither of them had a farthing. He also informed her, in very complimentary terms, that he contemplated writing her life. At Salisbury he declined to conform or to attend to his duties regularly. He had conscientious objections to the surplice. He was absent from Jewell's visitation in June 1568, and in the following December was declared contumacious on refusing to devote a tithe of his income to the repair of the cathedral.

On the Good Friday after the publication of the papal bull excommunicating the queen (1570), Foxe, at Grindal's bidding, preached a powerful sermon at St. Paul's Cross, and renewed his attacks on the catholics. The sermon, entitled 'A Sermon of Christ Crucified,' was published by Day immediately, with a prayer and 'a postscript to the papists,' and was reissued, 'newly recognised by the authour,' in 1575, 1577, and 1585. A very rare edition was printed for the Stationers' Company in 1609. On 1 Oct. 1571 Foxe translated it into Latin, and Day issued it under the title 'De Christo Crucifixo Concio.' In this shape it was published at Frankfort in 1575.

Foxe's correspondence was rapidly increasing, and his position in ecclesiastical circles grew influential. Parkhurst (29 Jan. 1563–4) solicited his aid in behalf of Conrad Gesner, who was writing on the early Christian writers. Lawrence Humphrey, president of Magdalen, appealed to him to procure for him an exemption from the regulations affecting clerical dress, but Humphrey afterwards conformed. On 20 Nov. 1573 one Torporley begged him to obtain for him a studentship at Christ Church. Strangers consulted him repeatedly about their religious difficulties. Francis Baxter (4 Jan. 1572) inquired his opinion respecting the lawfulness of sponsors, and another correspondent asked how he was to cure himself of the habit of blaspheming. About the same time Foxe corresponded with Lord-chief-justice Monson respecting the appointment of a schoolmaster at Ipswich, and recommended a lady to marry one of his intimate friends.

Much of his correspondence also dealt with the credibility of his monumental work. The catholics had been greatly angered by its publication. They nicknamed it 'Foxe's Golden Legend,' and expressed special disgust at the calendar prefixed to the book, in which the protestant martyrs took the place of the old saints (STRYPE, *Annals*, i. 375–80). Foxe's accuracy was first seriously impugned in the 'Dialogi Sex,' published in 1566 under the name of Alan Cope [q. v.], although the author was without doubt Nicholas Harpsfield. Foxe showed some sensitiveness to such attacks. He instituted inquiries with a view to corrections or corroborations for a second edition, which the puritan party deemed it desirable to issue before the meeting of parliament in April 1571. This edition (1570) was in two volumes, the first of 934 pages, and the second of 1378. New engravings were added; there was a new dedication to the queen, in which Foxe declared that he only republished the book to confute the attacks of evil-disposed persons, who had made it appear that his work was as 'full of lies as lines.' The address to the persecutors of God's truth was omitted; a protestation to the true and faithful congregation of Christ's universal church, and four questions addressed to the church of Rome were added. Magdalen College paid 6l. 8s. for a copy of this new edition, and another copy belonging to Nowell was bequeathed by him to Brasenose, where it still is. Convocation meeting at Canterbury on 3 April resolved that copies of this edition, which was called in the canon 'Monumenta Martyrum,' should be placed in cathedral churches and in the houses of archbishops, bishops, deacons, and archdeacons. Although this canon was never confirmed by parliament, it was very widely adopted in the country.

About the same time Foxe prepared, from manuscripts chiefly supplied by Archbishop Parker, a collection of the regulations adopted by the reformed English church, which was entitled 'Reformatio Legum.' A proposal in parliament to accept this collection as the official code of ecclesiastical law met with no success, owing to the queen's intervention and her promise—never fulfilled—that her ministers should undertake a like task. But it was printed by Day in 1571, and held by the puritans in high esteem. It was reissued in 1640, and again by Edward Cardwell in 1850. In the same year (1571) Foxe performed for Parker a more important task. He produced, with a dedication to the queen, an edition of the Anglo-Saxon text of the Gospels. This was similarly printed by Day, and is now a rare book. Two years later he collected the works of Tindal, Frith, and Barnes, giving extracts from his own account of the writers in his 'Actes.'

On 2 June 1572 Foxe's pupil and patron, the Duke of Norfolk, was executed, at the age of thirty-six, for conspiring with Mary Queen of Scots and the catholic nobility against Elizabeth. Foxe attended him to the scaffold. Some time before he had heard the rumours of Norfolk's contemplated marriage with the Queen of Scots, and had written a strong protest against it. Foxe's biographers have exaggerated the influence which his early training exerted on the duke and on his brother, Henry Howard, afterwards earl of Northampton. It is obvious that they assimilated few of their tutor's religious principles. On the scaffold the duke denied that he was a catholic; but he, like his brother in after years, had shown unmistakable leanings to catholicism. It is to the credit of both Foxe and the duke that their affection for each other never waned. The duke directed his heirs to allow Foxe an annuity of 20l. On 14 Oct. of the same year Bishop Pilkington installed Foxe in a prebendal stall at Durham Cathedral; but Foxe was still obstinately opposed to the surplice, and within the year he resigned the office. Tanner asserts that he was at one time vicar of St. Giles's, Cripplegate. Foxe's friend, Robert Crowley [q. v.], held this benefice for a long period; but he was suspended between 1569 and 1578, when Foxe may have assisted in the work of the parish. In 1575 Foxe energetically sought to obtain the remission of the capital sentence in the case of two Dutch anabaptists condemned to the stake for their opinions. He wrote to the queen, Lord Burghley, and Lord-chief-justice Monson, pointing out the disproportion between the offence and the punishment, and deprecating the penalty of death in cases of heresy. He also appealed to one of the prisoners to acknowledge the errors of his opinion, with which he had no sympathy. A respite of a month was allowed, but both prisoners were burnt at the stake 22 July. In 1576 and 1583 the third and fourth editions of the 'Actes' were issued. On 1 April 1577 Foxe preached a Latin sermon at the baptism of a Jew, Nathaniel, in Allhallows Church, Lombard Street (cf. 'Elizabethan England and the Jews,' by the present writer, in *New Shakspere Soc. Trans.* 1888). The title of the original ran : 'De Oliva Evangelica. Concio in baptismo Iudæi habita. Londini, primo mens. April.' London, by Christopher Barker, 1577, dedicated to Sir Francis Walsingham. At the close is a prose 'Appendicula de Christo Triumphante,' dedicated to Sir Thomas Heneage. A translation by James Bell appeared in 1578, with the Jew's confession of faith. In 1580 the same translator issued a tract entitled 'The Pope Confuted,' which professed to be another translation from Foxe, although the original is not identified. Tanner assigns 'A New Years Gift touching the deliverance of certain Christians from the Turkish gallies' to 1579, and says it was published in London. Foxe completed Haddon's second reply to Osorius in his 'Contra Hieron. Osorium . . . Responsio Apologetica,' dedicated to Sebastian, king of Portugal (Latin version 1577, English translation 1581). In 1583 he contested Osorius's view of 'Justification by Faith' in a new treatise on the subject, 'De Christo gratis iustificante. Contra Osorianam iustitiam, Lond., by Thomas Purfoot, impensis Geor. Byshop,' 1583. Tanner mentions an English translation dated 1598. 'Disputatio Ioannis Foxij Angli contra Iesuitas' appeared in 1585 at Rochelle, in the third volume of 'Doctrinæ Iesuiticæ Præcipua Capita.' According to Tanner, Foxe also edited in the same year Bishop Pilkington's 'Latin Commentary on Nehemiah.'

Foxe's health in 1586 was rapidly breaking. An attempt in June of that year on the part of Bishop Piers of Salisbury to deprive him of the lease of Shipton much annoyed him ; but the bishop did not press his point when he learned that he might by forbearance 'pleasure that good man Mr. Foxe.' Foxe died after much suffering in April 1587, and was buried in St. Giles's Church, Cripplegate, where a monument, with an inscription by his son Samuel, is still extant. His final work, 'Eicasmi seu Meditationes in Sacram Apocalypsin,' was printed posthumously in 1587 by George Bishop, and dedicated by Foxe's son Samuel to Archbishop Whitgift. Foxe was charitable to the poor, although he never was well-to-do, and would seem to have been of a cheerful temperament, despite his fervent piety. A letter to him from Bishop Parkhurst shows that he was a lover and a judge of dogs. His wife, who possessed all the womanly virtues, died 22 April 1605. Two sons, Samuel and Simeon, are separately noticed. A daughter, born in Flanders in 1555, and the two children Rafe and Mary, baptised at Waltham Abbey early in 1566, seem to have completed his family.

Of Foxe's great work, the 'Actes and Monuments,' four editions were published in his lifetime, viz. in 1563, 1570, 1576, and 1583. Five later editions are dated respectively 1596, 1610, 1632, 1641, and 1684. All are in folio. The first edition was in one volume, the next four in two volumes, and the last four named in three. The fifth edition (1596) consisted of twelve hundred copies. The edition of 1641 includes for the first time the memoir of the author, the authenticity of which is much contested. All have woodcuts, probably by German artists, inserted in the printed page. The first eight editions are all rare ; the first two excessively rare. No quite perfect copy of the 1563 edition is extant. Slightly imperfect copies are at the British Museum, the Bodleian, the Cambridge University Library, Magdalen and Christ Church, Oxford. In the Huth Library a good copy has been constructed out of two imperfect ones. Early in the seventeenth century the first edition had become scarce, and Archbishop Spotiswood, writing before 1639, denied its existence. The corrected edition of 1570, which convocation directed to be placed in all cathedral churches, is more frequently met with. Many Oxford colleges possess perfect copies, but as early as 1725 Hearne wrote that this edition also was excessively rare. The British Museum possesses a complete set of the nine early editions.

Foxe's 'Actes' is often met with in libraries attached to parish churches. This was not strictly in obedience to the order of convocation of 1571, which only mentioned cathedral churches ; but many clergymen deemed it desirable to give the order a liberal interpretation, and to recommend the purchase of the book for their churches. According to the vestry minutes of St. Michael, Cornhill, it was agreed, 11 Jan. 1571–2, 'that the booke of Martyrs of Mr. Foxe and the paraphrases of Erasmus shalbe bowght for the church and tyed with a chayne to the Egle bras.' Foxe's volumes cost the parish 2*l.* 2*s.* 6*d.* At the church of St. John the Baptist, Glastonbury, the 1570 edition is also known to have been bought at the same time. Various editions—mostly mutilated but still chained—are known to exist or have very recently existed in the parish churches of Apethorpe (Northamptonshire), Arreton (Isle of Wight), Chelsea, Enstone (Oxfordshire), Kinver (Staffordshire), Lessingham (Norfolk), St. Nicholas (Newcastle-on-Tyne), Northwold (Norfolk), Stratford-on-Avon, Waltham, St. Cuthbert (Wells).

Of modern editions that edited by S. R. Cattley, with introduction by Canon Townsend, in eight volumes (1837–41), is the best known. It professed to be based on the 1583 edition, with careful collation of other early editions. But Dr. Maitland proved these pretensions to be false, and showed that the editing was perfunctorily and ignorantly performed. Slight improvements were made in a reissue (1844–9). In 1877 Dr. Stoughton professed to edit the book again in eight volumes, but his text and notes are not very scholarly. The earliest abridgment was prepared by Timothy Bright and issued, with a dedication to Sir Francis Walsingham, in 1589. Another, by the Rev. Thomas Mason of Odiham, appeared, under the title of 'Christ's Victorie over Sathans Tyrannie,' in 1615. Slighter epitomes are Leigh's 'Memorable Collections,' 1651 ; 'A brief Historical Relation of the most material passages and persecutions of the Church of Christ . . . collected by Jacob Bauthumley,' London, 1676 ; and 'ΜΑΡΤΥΡΟΛΟΓΙΑ ΑΛΦΑΒΕΤΙΚΗ,' by N. T., M.A., T.C.C., London, 1677. A modern abridgment, by John Milner (1837), was reissued in 1848 and 1863, with an introduction by Ingram Cobbin [q. v.] Numerous extracts have been published separately, mainly as religious tracts. John Stockwood appended to his 'Treasure of Trueth,' 1576, 'Notes appertayning to the matter of Election gathered by the Godly and learned father, I. Foxe.' Hakluyt appropriated Foxe's account of Richard I's voyage to Palestine (*Voyages*, 1598, vol. ii.) Foxe's accounts of the martyrs of Sussex, Suffolk, and other counties have been collected and issued in separate volumes.

With the puritan clergy, and in almost all English households where puritanism prevailed, Foxe's 'Actes' was long the sole authority for church history, and an armoury of arguments in defence of protestantism against catholicism. Even Nicholas Ferrar, in his community of Little Gidding, Huntingdonshire, directed that a chapter of it should be read every Sunday evening along with the Bible, and clergymen repeatedly made its stories of martyrdom the subject of their sermons. But as early as 1566, when Nicholas

Harpsfield wrote his 'Sex Dialogi,' which his friend, Alan Cope, published under his own name, Foxe's veracity has been powerfully attacked. Robert Parsons the jesuit condemned the work as a carefully concocted series of lies in his 'Treatise of the Three Conversions of England,' 1603. Archbishop Laud in 1638 refused to license a new edition for the press (RUSHWORTH, ii. 450), and was charged at his trial with having ordered the book to be withdrawn from some parish churches (LAUD, *Works*, iv. 405). Peter Heylyn denied that Foxe was an authority on matters of doctrine affecting the church of England. Jeremy Collier contested his accuracy in his 'Ecclesiastical History,' 1702–14. Dr. John Milner, the Roman catholic bishop of Castabala (*d.* 1826), and George Leo Haydock, in 'A Key to the Roman Catholic Office,' 1823, are the best modern representatives of catholic critics. William Eusebius Andrews's 'Examination of Foxe's Calendar,' 3 vols. 1826, is an intemperate attack from the same point of view. But the most learned impugner of Foxe's honesty and accuracy was Dr. S. R. Maitland [q. v.], who in a series of pamphlets and letters issued between 1837 and 1842 subjected portions of his great work to a rigorous scrutiny.

The enormous size of Foxe's work has prevented a critical examination of the whole. But it is plain from such examination as the work has undergone that Foxe was too zealous a partisan to write with historical precision. He is a passionate advocate, ready to accept any *primâ facie* evidence. His style has the vigour that comes of deep conviction, and there is a pathetic picturesqueness in the forcible simplicity with which he presents his readers with the details of his heroes' sufferings. His popularity is thus amply accounted for. But the coarse ribaldry with which he belabours his opponents exceeds all literary license. His account of the protestant martyrs of the sixteenth century is mainly based on statements made by the martyrs themselves or by their friends, and they thus form a unique collection of documents usually inaccessible elsewhere and always illustrative of the social habits and tone of thought of the English protestants of his day. 'A Compendious Register' (Lond. 1559) of the Marian martyrs by Thomas Brice [q. v.] doubtless supplied some hints. Foxe's mistakes sometimes arise from faulty and hasty copying of original documents, but are more often the result of wilful exaggeration. A very friendly critic, John Deighton, showed that Foxe's account of the martyrdom of 'Jhon Horne and a woman' at Newent on 25 Sept. 1556 is an amplification of the suffering at the stake of *Edward* Horne on 25 Sept. 1558 (NICHOLS, p. 69). No woman suffered at all. The errors in date and christian name in the case of the man are very typical. Foxe moreover undoubtedly included among his martyrs persons executed for ordinary secular offences. He acknowledged his error in the case of John Marbeck, a Windsor 'martyr' of 1543 whom he represented, in his text of 1563 to have been burnt, whereas the man was condemned, but pardoned. But Foxe was often less ingenuous. He wrote that one Greenwood or Grimwood of Hitcham, near Ipswich, Suffolk, having obtained the conviction of a 'martyr' John Cooper, on concocted evidence, died miserably soon afterwards. Foxe was informed that Greenwood was alive and that the story of his death was a fiction. He went to Ipswich to examine witnesses, but never made any alteration in his account of the matter. At a later date (according to an *obiter dictum* of Coke) a clergyman named Prick recited Foxe's story about Greenwood from the pulpit of Hitcham church. Greenwood was present and proceeded against Prick for libel, but the courts held that no malicious defamation was intended (see CROKE, *Reports*, ed. Leach, ii. 91). Foxe confessed that his story of Bishop Gardiner's death is derived from hearsay, but it is full of preposterous errors, some of which Foxe's personal knowledge must have enabled him to correct. With regard to the sketch of early church history which precedes his story of the martyrs, he undoubtedly had recourse to some early documents, especially to bishops' registers, but he depends largely on printed works like Crespin's 'Actiones et Monimenta Martyrum,' Geneva, 1560, or Illyricus's 'Catalogus Testium Veritatis,' Basle, 1556. It has been conclusively shown that his chapter on the Waldenses is directly translated from the 'Catalogus' of Illyricus, although Illyricus is not mentioned by Foxe among the authorities whom he acknowledges to have consulted. Foxe claims to have consulted 'parchment documents' on the subject, whereas he only knew them in the text of Illyricus's book. This indicates a loose notion of literary morality which justifies some of the harshest judgments passed on Foxe. In answering Alan Cope's 'Sex Dialogi' in the edition of 1570 he acknowledges small errors, but confesses characteristically, 'I heare what you will saie; I should have taken more leisure and done it better. I graunt and confesse my fault; such is my vice. I cannot sit all the daie (M. Cope) fining and minsing my letters and combing my head and smoothing myself all the daie at the glasse of Cicero. Yet notwithstanding, doing what I can and doing my good will, me thinkes I should not

be reprehended.' He was a compiler on a gigantic scale, neither scrupulous nor scholarly, but appallingly industrious, and a useful witness to the temper of his age.

Dr. Maitland insisted that Foxe's name should be spelt without the final *e*. He himself spelt it indifferently Fox and Foxe, and latinised it sometimes as Foxus, sometimes as Foxius. His contemporaries usually write of him as Foxe.

Foxe's papers, which include many statements sent to him by correspondents in corroboration or in contradiction of his history, but never used by him, descended through his eldest son Samuel to his grandson, Thomas Foxe, and through Thomas to Thomas's daughter and sole heiress, Alice. Alice married Sir Richard Willys, created a baronet in 1646, and their son, Sir Thomas Fox Willys, died a lunatic in 1701. Strype obtained the papers shortly before that date, and when Strype died in 1737, they were purchased by Edward Harley, earl of Oxford. The majority of them now form volumes 416 to 426 and volume 590 in the Harleian collection of manuscripts at the British Museum. A few other papers are now among the Lansdowne MSS. 335, 388, 389, 819, and 1045. Strype has worked up many of these papers in his 'Ecclesiastical Memorials,' 'Life of Cranmer,' and elsewhere. An interesting selection is printed by J. G. Nichols in 'Narratives of the Reformation' (Camden Society, 1859).

A portrait by Glover has been often engraved. A painting by an unknown artist is in the National Portrait Gallery, and is inscribed 'An. Dom. 1587. Ætatis suæ 70.' There is also an engraving in Holland's 'Herωologia,' p. 200.

[The earliest life of Foxe, which forms the basis of the many popular lives that have been issued for religious purposes by Foxe's admirers, is that prefixed in both English and Latin to the second volume of the 1641 edition of the Actes and Monuments, and has been generally attributed to his son Samuel, who died in 1630. The authorship is very doubtful. Samuel died eleven years before it was issued. The writer says in a brief introductory address that his memoir was written thirty years before publication, and there is no sign that it was regarded as a posthumous production. The handwriting of the original in Lansd. MS. 388 is not like that of Samuel Foxe's known manuscripts, and the manuscript has been elaborately corrected by a second pen. Samuel's claim is practically overthrown, and the suggestion that Simeon, Foxe's second son, who died in 1642, was the author, is not of greater value, when the writer's ignorance of Foxe's real history is properly appreciated. The dates are very few and self-contradictory. The writer, who refers to Foxe as 'Foxius noster' or 'sæpe audivi Foxium narrantem,' gives no hint outside the prefatory address to the reader that the subject of the biography was his father, and confesses ignorance on points about which a son could not have been without direct knowledge. Its value as an original authority is very small, and its attribution to Foxe of the power of prophecy and other miraculous gifts shows that it was chiefly written for purposes of religious edification. In 1579 Richard Day, John Day's son, edited and translated Foxe's Christus Triumphans, and his preface supplies some good biographical notes. Strype, who intended writing a full life, is the best authority, although his references to Foxe are widely scattered through his works. The Annals, I. i. 375 et seq., give a good account of the publication of the Actes. The careless memoir by Canon Townsend prefixed to the 1841 edition of the Actes and Monuments has been deservedly censured by Dr. Maitland. In 1870 it was rewritten by the Rev. Josiah Pratt, who took some advantage of the adverse criticism lavished on Townsend's work, and produced an improved memoir, forming the first volume of the Reformation series of Church Historians of England. Wood's Athenæ Oxon.; Fuller's Worthies and Church History; Tanner's Bibl. Brit.; the Troubles at Frankfort; Nichols's Narratives of the Reformation; Dr. Maitland's pamphlets; Notes and Queries, 2nd ser.; and W. Winter's Biographical Notes on John Foxe, 1876, are all useful.]   S. L.

FOXE or FOX, RICHARD (1448?– 1528), bishop of Winchester, lord privy seal to Henry VII and Henry VIII, and founder of Corpus Christi College, Oxford, was born at Ropesley, near Grantham, Lincolnshire, about 1447 or 1448. In his examination touching the marriage of Henry VIII and Queen Catherine before Dr. Wolman on 5 and 6 April 1527 he speaks of himself as seventy-nine years old. The house in which he was born, part of which is still standing, seems to have been known as Pullock's Manor. His parents, Thomas and Helena Foxe, probably belonged to the class of respectable yeomen, for, though it became afterwards common to speak of his mean extraction, his earliest biographer, Thomas Greneway (president of Corpus Christi College 1562–8), describes him as 'honesto apud suos loco natus.' According to Wood, he was 'trained up in grammar at Boston, till such time that he might prove capable of the university.' According to another account, he received his school education at Winchester, but there is no early or documentary evidence of either statement. From Greneway onwards, his biographers agree that he was a student of Magdalen College, Oxford, though the careful antiquary, Fulman (1632–1688), adds ' most probably;' but the explicit statement of Greneway, writing in 1566, appears to derive striking confir-

mation from the large number of Magdalen men who were imported by Foxe into his new college of Corpus Christi. From Oxford he is said to have been driven by the plague to Cambridge, with which university he was subsequently connected as chancellor, and, at a still later period, as master of Pembroke. He did not linger in either seat of learning. 'Long continuance in those places,' says William Harrison in his 'Description of England' (2nd ed., 1586), ' is either a sign of lack of friends or of learning, or of good and upright life, as Bishop Fox sometime noted, who thought it sacrilege for a man to tarry any longer at Oxford than he had a desire to profit.' In 1477 one Richard Fox, B.A., was master of the grammar-school at Stratford-on-Avon. Impelled by love of learning or desire of adventure and advancement, the future bishop soon after repaired to Paris.

'During his abode there,' according to Fulman, Henry, earl of Richmond, was in Paris soliciting help from the French king, Charles VIII, ' in his enterprise upon the English crown.' He took Foxe, then a priest and doctor of the canon law, ' into special favour and familiarity,' and, upon his departure for Rouen, ' made choice of Doctor Foxe to stay behind and pursue his negotiations in the French court, which he performed with such dexterity and success as gave great satisfaction to the earl.'

The first definite notice we have of Foxe is in a letter of Richard III, dated 22 Jan. 1484–5 (preserved in STOW, London and Westminster, sub. 'Stepney,' a reference due to Mr. Chisholm Batten), in which the king intervenes to prevent his institution to the vicarage of Stepney, on the ground that he is with the 'great rebel, Henry ap Tuddor.' The king's nominee, however, was never instituted, and Foxe (who is described in the register as L.B.) obtained possession of the living, 30 Oct. 1485.

After the victory of Bosworth Field (22 Aug. 1485) the Earl of Richmond, now Henry VII, constituted a council in which were included the two friends and fellow-fugitives, Morton, bishop of Ely, and Richard Foxe, ' vigilant men and secret,' says Bacon, ' and such as kept watch with him almost upon all men else.' On Foxe were conferred in rapid succession, besides various minor posts, the offices of principal secretary of state, lord privy seal, and bishop of Exeter. The temporalities of the see of Exeter were restored on 2 April 1487, and he at once appointed a suffragan bishop, evidently reserving himself for affairs of state. 'In conferring orders,' says Fulman, ' and such like episcopal administrations, he made use of Thomas [Cornish, afterwards provost of Oriel and precentor of Wells], titular bishop of Tine, as his suffragan; himself, for the most part, as it seems, being detained by his public employments about the court.' On 28 Nov. of this same year was signed at Edinburgh a treaty between Henry VII and James III, which had been negotiated, on the part of England, by Foxe and Sir Richard Edgcombe, controller of the king's household. This treaty provided for a truce and also for certain intermarriages, including that of the king of Scots to Queen Elizabeth, widow of Edward IV, but the negotiations were afterwards broken off, in consequence, it is said, of Henry's unwillingness to cede Berwick. In the summer of 1491 Foxe was honoured by being asked to baptise the king's second son, Prince Henry, afterwards Henry VIII. [In Foxe's examination before Wolman he is reported as having distinctly stated that he baptised (baptizavit) Prince Henry. This statement is fully confirmed by a document in the College of Arms, of which a copy may be found in the Ashmolean MSS. vol. mcxv. fol. 92. The statement of Harpsfield (*Hist. Angl. Eccl.*) and others that Foxe was godfather is founded, probably, on a perverted tradition of the baptism.] Shortly afterwards (by papal bull dated 8 Feb. 1491-2) he was translated to the see of Bath and Wells, the episcopal work being, as at Exeter, delegated to the titular bishop of Tine, who already combined the duties of suffragan of this diocese with those of the diocese of Exeter. In the treaty of Estaples (3 Nov. 1492), which terminated the siege of Boulogne and the war recently commenced with Charles VIII of France, Foxe is mentioned first of the English ambassadors, Giles, lord Daubeney, being second, and others following. In 1494 (the temporalities were restored on 8 Dec.) Foxe was translated to Durham, probably not merely for the sake of advancement, but because his diplomatic talents were likely to be useful to the king on the Scottish border. In this diocese he seems to have been resident, and he left a permanent memorial of himself in the alterations which he made in the banqueting hall of the castle. It may be noticed that the woodwork in these alterations, which bears the date of 1499, already exhibits Foxe's device of the pelican in her piety, with his usual motto, 'Est Deo gracia.' In April 1496 Foxe acted as first commissioner in settling the important treaty called 'Intercursus Magnus' (see BACON, *Henry VII*) with Philip, archduke of Austria, regulating divers matters concerning commerce, fishing, and the treatment of rebels, as between England and Flanders. In the summer of 1497, during the troubles connected with

Perkin Warbeck, James IV of Scotland invaded England, and besieged the castle of Norham. 'But,' says Bacon, 'Foxe, bishop of Duresme, a wise man, and one that could see through the present to the future, doubting as much before, had caused his castle of Norham to be strongly fortified, and furnished with all kind of munition, and had manned it likewise with a very great number of tall soldiers more than for the proportion of the castle, reckoning rather upon a sharp assault than a long siege. And for the country, likewise, he had caused the people to withdraw their cattle and goods into fast places, that were not of easy approach; and sent in post to the Earl of Surrey (who was not far off in Yorkshire) to come in diligence to the succour. So as the Scottish king both failed of doing good upon the castle, and his men had but a catching harvest of their spoils. And when he understood that the Earl of Surrey was coming on with great forces, he returned back into Scotland.' This fruitless siege was followed by certain negotiations with the king of Scots carried on by Foxe with the assistance of D'Ayala, the Spanish envoy of Ferdinand and Isabella, who had been interested by Henry in his affairs. The result was that, though James refused to surrender Perkin Warbeck to the king of England, he contrived to facilitate his withdrawal to Ireland, and in December 1497 a long truce was concluded between the two kingdoms. In the following year (probably in November 1498) the peace thus established was in great danger of being again broken through the rough treatment which some Scottish stragglers had received at the hands of the English soldiery quartered in Norham Castle. James was highly indignant at this outrage, but Foxe being appointed by Henry to mediate, and obtaining an interview with the Scottish king at Melrose Abbey, skilfully brought about a reconciliation. The Scottish king appears to have taken advantage of the occasion to propose, or rather revive (for as early as 1496 a commission to treat in this matter had been issued to Foxe and others), a project for a closer connexion between the two kingdoms by means of his own marriage with the Princess Margaret, eldest daughter of Henry VII. The offer was readily, if not greedily, accepted by Henry, though, on Foxe's advice, he determined to move in the matter slowly. It was not till 11 Sept. 1499 that the second, and more effective, commission was issued to Foxe, empowering him to arrange the preliminaries of this marriage with the Scottish court. The marriage itself, which resulted in the permanent union of the English and Scottish crowns under James VI, did not take place till August 1503. Another marriage, almost equally important in its consequences, that between Prince Arthur, the king's eldest son, and Catherine of Arragon, subsequently the divorced wife of Henry VIII, had been solemnised on 14 Nov. 1501. The ceremonial was regulated by Foxe, who, says Bacon, 'was not only a grave counsellor for war or peace, but also a good surveyor of works, and a good master of ceremonies, and any thing else that was fit for the active part belonging to the service of court or state of a great king.' Shortly before this event Foxe had been translated from Durham to Winchester, the temporalities of which see were restored to him on 17 Oct. 1501. It is probable that, besides his desire to reward Foxe still further (for Winchester is said to have been then the richest see in England), the king was anxious to have him nearer the court, especially as the differences with Scotland might now seem to have been permanently settled. In 1500 Foxe also held the dignity of chancellor of the university of Cambridge.

It is probably to 1504 that we may refer the story told of Foxe by Erasmus (*Ecclesiastes*, bk. ii. ed. Klein, ch. 150; cp. HOLINSHED, *Chronicles*), and communicated to him, as he says, by Sir Thomas More. Foxe had been appointed chief commissioner for the purpose of raising a loan from the clergy. Some came in splendid apparel and pleaded that their expenses left them nothing to spare; others came meanly clad, as evidence of their poverty. The bishop retorted on the first class that their dress showed their ability to pay; on the second that, if they dressed so meanly, they must be hoarding money, and therefore have something to spare for the king's service. A similar story is told of Morton, as having occurred at an earlier date, by Bacon (*Hist. Henry VII*), and the dilemma is usually known as Morton's fork or Morton's crutch. It is possible that it may be true of both prelates, but the authority ascribing it to Foxe appears to be the earlier of the two. It is curious that Bacon speaks only of 'a tradition' of Morton's dilemma, whereas Erasmus professes to have heard the story of Foxe directly from Sir Thomas More, while still a young man, and, therefore, a junior contemporary of Foxe.

The imputation cast on Morton and Foxe by Tyndale (*The Practice of Prelates*, Parker Soc. ed. p. 305), that they revealed to Henry VII 'the confessions of as many lords as his grace lusted,' is one which it is now impossible to examine, but it may be due merely to the ill-natured gossip of the enemies

of these prelates, or of the catholic clergy generally. It is equally impossible, with the materials at our disposal, to estimate the justice of the aspersion put in the mouth of Whitford, Foxe's chaplain, while attempting to dissuade Sir Thomas More from following the bishop's counsel (ROPER, *Life of More*, ad init.), that 'my lord, to serve the king's turn, will not stick to agree to his own father's death.'

The year before the king's death (1508) Foxe with other commissioners succeeded in completing at Calais a treaty of marriage between the king's younger daughter, the Princess Mary, and Charles, prince of Castile and archduke of Austria, subsequently the emperor Charles V. Though the marriage itself never took place, the child-prince was betrothed, by proxy, to the child-princess at Richmond on 17 Dec. of this year (see RYMER, *Fœdera*, xiii. 236–9), and the immediate objects of the alliance were thus secured.

On 22 April 1509 Henry VII died. Foxe was one of his executors, Fisher, bishop of Rochester, whose preferment had been given to him solely on Foxe's recommendation, being another. It is said by Harpsfield that Henry had specially commended his son to Foxe's care, and it is certain that he was continued in all the places of trust which he had occupied in the previous reign. According to Archbishop Parker (*De Antiquitate Britannicæ Ecclesiæ*), Warham and Foxe, the two first named on the new king's council, took different sides on the first question of importance which was discussed within it. Warham was averse to, while Foxe advised the marriage with Catherine, who had remained in England ever since the death of her first husband, Prince Arthur. The marriage was solemnised almost immediately afterwards by the archbishop himself, and the new king and queen were crowned together at Westminster within a few weeks of the marriage. It is insinuated by Parker that Foxe's advice was dictated solely by reasons of state, Warham's by religious scruples. Foxe had been present, on 27 June 1505, when Henry, instigated, or at least not opposed, by his father (see RANKE, *History of England*, bk. ii. ch. 2), had solemnly protested, on the ground of his youth, against the validity of the engagement with Catherine; but this conduct does not necessarily prove inconsistency, as the object of Henry and his father may have been merely to keep the question open, and subsequent events may have persuaded Foxe of the desirability of the marriage, while he probably never doubted its legitimacy.

The king's coronation was speedily followed by the death of his grandmother, the

'Lady Margaret,' as she is usually called, countess of Richmond and Derby [see BEAUFORT, MARGARET]. This pious lady named Foxe, in whom she appears to have reposed great confidence, together with Fisher and others, as one of her executors. He was thus concerned in what was probably the congenial employment of settling the incomplete foundation of St. John's College, Cambridge (that of Christ's had been completed before the Lady Margaret's death), though the principal merit of this work must be assigned to Fisher. In 1507 Foxe had been elected master of Pembroke College or Hall, in the same university, and continued to hold the office till 1519. Richard Parker (LELAND, *Collectanea*, vol. v.), writing in 1622, describes him as a former fellow of Pembroke, and Doctor of Law of Paris.

According to Polydore Vergil, the chief authority in Henry's council soon fell into the hands of Foxe and Thomas Howard, earl of Surrey. And according to the same writer (in whom, however, as Lord Herbert of Cherbury remarks, 'I have observed not a little malignity'), mutual jealousies and differences soon sprang up between these two powerful counsellors. One cause at least assigned for these differences seems highly probable, namely, the propensity of Surrey to squander the wealth which, under the previous reign, Foxe and his master had so diligently collected and so carefully husbanded.

The altercation between Warham and Foxe (1510-13) as to the prerogatives of the Archbishop of Canterbury with regard to the probate of wills and the administration of the estates of intestates, is narrated at length by Archbishop Parker in the work above cited, and is confirmed by documentary evidence. Foxe, supported by Bishops Fitzjames, Smith, and Oldham, appealed to Rome, but, as the cause was unduly spun out in the papal court, they finally procured its reference to the king, who decided the points mainly in their favour. In 1510 Foxe was employed, in common with Ruthall, bishop of Durham, and the Earl of Surrey, to conclude a treaty of peace with Louis XII of France. But this peace was not destined to last long, and the war with France, which broke out in 1513, brought another and a younger counsellor to the front. 'Wolsey's vast influence with the king,' says J. S. Brewer (*Reign of Henry VIII*), 'dates from this event. Though holding no higher rank than that of almoner, it is clear that the management of the war, in all its multifarious details, has fallen into his hands. . . . Well may Fox say, "I pray God send us with speed, and soon deliver you out of your outrageous charge and labour, else ye shall have

a cold stomach, little sleep, pale visage, and a thin belly, *cum pari egestione.*"' Wolsey, Foxe, and Ruthall all attended the army which invaded France, the former with two hundred, the two latter with one hundred men each; but it does not follow that these ecclesiastics were present at any engagement. On 7 Aug. 1514 a treaty of peace and also a treaty of marriage between Louis XII and the Princess Mary were concluded at London, Foxe being one of the commissioners. At this time J. S. Brewer regards him as still powerful in the council, though his influence was inferior to that of Wolsey, of Surrey (now Duke of Norfolk), and of Charles Brandon, duke of Suffolk. 'Foxe was,' says Giustinian, the Venetian ambassador, 'a lord of extreme authority and goodness.' But advancing years, combined probably with weariness of political life, with a certain disinclination to the foreign policy, favourable to the empire and antagonistic to France, which now prevailed, and, there can be no doubt from his extant letters, with genuine compunction for the prolonged neglect of his spiritual duties, made him anxious to retire from affairs of state. At the beginning of 1516 he resigned the custody of the privy seal, which was committed to Ruthall, and henceforth he seldom appeared at the council.

The traditional story of Wolsey's ingratitude to Foxe, of the growing alienation between them, and of Foxe being ultimately driven from the council board through the intrigues of Wolsey, 'owes its parentage,' as Brewer says, 'to the spite of Polydore Vergil, whom Wolsey had committed to prison. The historian would have us believe that Wolsey paved the way for his own advancement by supplanting Fox, and driving him from the council. . . . The insinuation is at variance with the correspondence of the two ministers. We see in their letters not only the cordial friendship which existed between them, but also the rooted disinclination of Fox to a life of diplomacy. It is only with the strongest arguments that Wolsey can prevail on him to give his attendance at the court and occupy his seat at the council table. He was always anxious to get away. He felt it inconsistent with his duties as a bishop to be immersed in politics, and he laments it to Wolsey in terms the sincerity of which cannot be mistaken. . . . So far from driving Fox from the court, it is the utmost that Wolsey can do to bring him there, and when he succeeds it is evidently more out of compassion for Wolsey's incredible labours than his own inclination.' In a letter to Wolsey, dated 23 April 1516 (*Letters and Papers of the Reign of Henry VIII*, ii. pt. i. 515), Foxe protests that he never had greater will to serve the king's father than the king himself, especially since Wolsey's great charge, 'perceiving better, straighter, and speedier ways of justice, and more diligence and labour for the king's right, duties, and profits to be in you than ever I see in times past in any other, and that I myself had more ease in attendance upon you in the said matters than ever I had before.' Had he not good impediment and the king's license to be occupied in his cure, to make satisfaction for twenty-eight years' negligence, he would be very blameable and unkind not to accept the invitation to court, considering Wolsey's goodness to him in times past. In a letter to Wolsey, written at a later date, 30 April 1522, Foxe speaks with still greater compunction of his former neglect of his spiritual duties, and with a still more fixed determination to take no further part in the affairs of state, to which Wolsey was endeavouring to recall his attention: 'Truly, my singular good lord, since the king's grace licensed me to remain in my church and thereabouts upon my cure, wherein I have been almost by the space of thirty years so negligent, that of four several cathedral churches that I have successively had, there be two, scilicet, "Excestre and Wellys," that I never see; and "innumerable sawles whereof I never see the bodyes;" and specially since by his licence I left the keeping of his privy seal, and most specially since my last departing from your good lordship and the council, I have determined, and, betwixt God and me, utterly renounced the meddling with worldly matters; specially concerning the war [with France] or anything to it appertaining (whereof for the many intolerable enormities that I have seen ensue by the said war in time past, I have no little remorse in my conscience), thinking that if I did continual penance for it all the days of my life, though I shall live twenty years longer than I may do, I could not yet make sufficient recompence therefor.' The tone of this letter, though the bishop's determination is firm, is throughout most friendly to Wolsey. Foxe's aversion to the French war had, it is plain from the passage quoted, as well as from subsequent parts of the letter, something to do with his disinclination to quit his pastoral charge, even for ever so brief a period, for the secular business of the court. In fact, of the two parties into which the council and the country were divided, the French and the German party, Foxe, as comes out plainly in the despatches of Giustinian, favoured the former.

The closing years of Foxe's life were spent in the quiet discharge of his episcopal duties, in devotional exercises, and the acts of liberality and munificence through which his memory now mainly survives. He was not, however, without trouble in his diocese. Writing to Wolsey, 2 Jan. 1520–1, he expresses satisfaction at Wolsey's proposed reformation of the clergy, the day of which he had desired to see, as Simeon desired to see the Messiah. As for himself, though, within his own small jurisdiction, he had given nearly all his study to this work for nearly three years, yet, whenever he had to correct and punish, he found the clergy, and particularly (what he did not at first suspect) the monks, so depraved, so licentious and corrupt, that he despaired of any proper reformation till the work was undertaken on a more general scale, and with a stronger arm. Once more we hear of him in a public capacity in 1523. The enormous subsidy of that year was energetically opposed in convocation, according to Polydore Vergil, by Foxe and Fisher, though of course without success. The charge on Foxe himself amounted to 2,000*l*., on the Archbishop of Canterbury to 1,000*l*., on Wolsey to 4,000*l*. The largeness of the revenues of the great sees at this time is strikingly illustrated by the fact that Foxe's newly founded college of Corpus was rated only at 133*l*. 6*s*. 8*d*., and the two richest colleges in Oxford, Magdalen and New Colleges, only at 333*l*. 6*s*. 8*d*. each.

The story that shortly before his death Wolsey proposed to Foxe that he should retire from his bishopric on a pension, and that Foxe tartly replied that though he could no longer distinguish white from black, yet he could well discern the malice of an ungrateful man, and bade him attend closer to the king's business, leaving Winchester to the care of her bishop, rests solely on the authority of Archbishop Parker. It is inconsistent with what we know otherwise of Foxe's relations with Wolsey, and has an apocryphal flavour.

Foxe, who appears to have been totally blind for ten years before his death, died, probably at his castle of Wolvesey in Winchester, on 5 Oct. 1528. According to a document found in his coffin, from which this date is taken, he was buried on the very same day, the place of sepulture being the splendid Gothic chapel in Winchester Cathedral, which he had previously constructed. The ecclesiastical historian, Harpsfield, says that, being then a boy at Winchester School, he was present at the funeral. This devout and gentle prelate passed away at an opportune moment, when the troubles connected with the divorce were only in their initial stage. He was succeeded by Wolsey, who held the see of Winchester as perpetual Administrator.

The most permanent memorial of Foxe is

his college of Corpus Christi at Oxford, the foundation and settlement of which attracted great attention at the time (1515–16). Its most distinctive characteristic was the recognition of the new learning, a public lecturer in Greek being one of its principal officers. The foundation of this lectureship appears to have been the first official recognition of the Greek language in either university. Innovations almost equally startling were his bringing over the distinguished humanist, Ludovicus Vives, from the south of Italy to be reader of Latin, and his provision that the reader in theology should, in his interpretations of scripture, follow the Greek and Latin fathers rather than the scholastic commentators. The reader in Latin was carefully to extirpate all 'barbarism' from ' our bee-hive,' the name by which Foxe was accustomed fondly to designate his college. Indeed, Corpus and the subsequent foundations of Christ Church at Oxford and Trinity at Cambridge were emphatically the colleges of the Renaissance. Among the early fellows was Reginald Pole (afterwards cardinal), who with several others was transferred from Magdalen to his new college by the founder himself. Erasmus, writing in 1519 to John Claymond [q.v.], the first president, who had previously been president of Magdalen (*Ep.* lib. iv.), speaks of the great interest which had been taken in Foxe's foundation by Wolsey, Campeggio, and Henry VIII himself, and predicts that the college will be ranked 'inter præcipua decora Britanniæ,' and that its 'trilinguis bibliotheca' will attract more scholars to Oxford than were formerly attracted to Rome. It had been Foxe's original intention to establish a house in Oxford, after the fashion of Durham and Canterbury Colleges, for the reception of young monks of St. Swithin's monastery at Winchester while pursuing academical studies; but he was persuaded by Bishop Oldham of Exeter (himself a great benefactor to the college) to change his foundation into the more common form of one for the secular clergy. ' What, my lord,' Oldham is represented as saying by John Hooker, *alias* Vowell, in Holinshed, ' shall we build houses and provide livelihoods for a company of bussing monks, whose end and fall we ourselves may live to see; no, no, it is more meet a great deal that we should have care to provide for the increase of learning, and for such as who by their learning shall do good in the church and commonwealth.' The college (which it may be noted was founded out of the private revenues of Foxe and his friends, and not, as was the case with some other foundations, out of ecclesiastical spoils) still possesses the crosier, the gold chalice and patin, with many other relics of its founder. In addition to this notable foundation Foxe also built and endowed schools at Taunton and Grantham (the school of Sir Isaac Newton), besides making extensive additions and alterations in Winchester Cathedral, Farnham Castle, and the hospital of St. Cross. His alterations in Durham Castle and his fortifications at Norham have been already noticed. He was a benefactor also to the abbeys of Glastonbury and Netley, to Magdalen College, Oxford, and Pembroke College, Cambridge, and seems to have contributed largely to what we should now call the 'restoration' of St. Mary's Church, Oxford, as well as to the reduction of the floods in Oxford in the year of pestilence, 1517 (WOOD, *Annals*, sub ann.) He is also said to have been concerned in the building of Henry VII's Chapel at Westminster, the architecture of which, though on a much larger scale, resembles that of his own chapel in Winchester Cathedral. Notwithstanding these numerous benefactions, his household appointments seem to have been on a magnificent scale. Harpsfield tells us that he had no less than 220 serving-men.

In 1499 a little book, entitled ' Contemplacyon of Synners,' was printed by Wynken de Worde, ' compyled and fynyshed at the devoute and dylygent request of the ryght reverende fader in God the lorde Rycharde bysshop of Dureham,' &c. It is possible that Foxe himself may have had a hand in this work. He also edited the 'Processional,' according to the use of Sarum, which was printed at Rouen, in 1508. At a later period he translated the Rule of St. Benedict for the benefit of the ' devout, religious women' of his diocese. The book was beautifully printed by Pynson on 22 Jan. 1516–17. From a letter to Wolsey, written on 18 Jan. 1527–28, it would appear that Foxe had at a subsequent time much trouble with some of his nuns.

There are several portraits of Foxe at Corpus Christi College, the principal of which is the one in the hall by ' Joannes Corvus, Flandrus' [see CORVUS], which represents him as blind. Some of these portraits are independent, and apparently independent of them all are one at Lambeth Palace, and one, taken in 1522, at Sudeley Castle, Gloucestershire. Among the engraved portraits are one by Vertue, 1723, and one by Faber, *circa* 1713; the former of the picture by Corvus, the latter of a picture, also in the possession of the college, representing the bishop while still having his sight.

[Greneway's MS. Life of Foxe, and Fulman MSS. vol. ix. in C. C. C. Library; Wood's Colleges and Halls of Oxford; Fowler's Hist. C.C. Coll.,

Oxford (Oxf. Hist. Soc.), 1893 ; Cooper's Athenæ Cantab. ; Holinshed's Chronicles ; Polydore Vergil ; Parker's Antiquitates Britannicæ ; Harpsfield's Hist. Anglicana Ecclesiastica ; Harrison's Description of England ; Godwin, De Praesulibus Angliæ ; Rymer's Fœdera ; Bacon's Henry VII ; Brewer's Henry VIII ; Letters and Papers of the Reigns of Henry VII and Henry VIII ; Giustinian's Despatches ; Ellis's Original Letters, 2nd ser. ; Surtees's Hist. of Durham ; William de Chambre in the Historiæ Dunelmensis Scriptores tres, published by the Surtees Soc. ; Cassan's Lives of the Bishops of Winchester and of the Bishops of Bath and Wells; information from Mr. Chisholm Batten and the Rev. F. A. Gasquet, O.S.B.]   T. F.

FOXE, SAMUEL (1560–1630), diarist, eldest son of John Foxe, the martyrologist [q. v.], was born at Norwich on 31 Dec. 1560 (*Diary*), and admitted into Merchant Taylors' School, London, on 20 Oct. 1572 (*School Register*). In 1574 he went to Oxford, where he was elected demy of Magdalen College. In 1576 he left for France without permission of his tutors or knowledge of his father. He was, however, readmitted to the college, although he is said to have acquired a fondness for dress, which displeased his father. In 1579 he was elected probationer, and in 1580 fellow of his college. In 1581 he was expelled on religious grounds. He seems to have quarrelled with some of his colleagues who adopted the extremer forms of puritanism. His father temperately pleaded for his restoration, and wrote to a bishop, probably Horn of Winchester, soliciting his help in the matter. Meanwhile Samuel spent more than three years in foreign travel, visiting the universities of Leipzig, Padua, and Basle. He returned to England in 1585, and was restored to his fellowship. His father gave him a lease of Shipton, Wiltshire, attached to the prebend which the elder Foxe held in Salisbury Cathedral. In 1587 he was admitted into the service of Sir Thomas Heneage of Copt Hall, Essex, and became custodian of Havering-atte-Bower and clerk of Epping. On 15 April 1589 he married Anne Leveson, a kinswoman of Sir Thomas Heneage. He was chosen burgess for the university of Oxford in 1590. The parliament in which he sat was of very brief duration, but it passed—probably with Foxe's aid—a valuable and much needed act directed against abuses in the election to fellowships, scholarships, and similar positions. About 1594 he settled at Warlies, near Waltham Abbey, and died there in January 1629–30. He was buried at Waltham Abbey 16 Jan. His will was dated 22 June 1629 (see *MS. Lansd.* 819, f. 32). The Latin treatise on the Apocalypse, dedicated by him to Arch-

bishop Whitgift, was written by his father. The 'Life' of his father, prefixed to the second volume of the 'Actes and Monuments' in the edition of 1641, has been repeatedly ascribed to him. But internal evidence is much opposed to this theory of authorship [see FOXE, JOHN, *ad fin.*] His 'Diary,' very brief and extending over only a portion of his life, will be found in the appendix to Strype's 'Annals.' The original is in 'MS. Lansd.' 679. A letter to his brother Simeon is in 'MS. Harl.' 416, f. 222, and a continuation of his travels in 'MS. Lansd.' 679. The latter pieces are printed in W. Winter's 'Biographical Notes on Foxe the Martyrologist,' 1876.

By his wife Anne, who was buried by her husband 18 May 1630, Foxe had three sons, Thomas, John, and Robert. THOMAS FOXE, M.D. (1591–1652), born at Havering Palace 14 Feb. 1591; matriculated from Magdalen Hall, Oxford, 19 June 1607; was demy of Magdalen College 1608–13, and fellow 1613–30 (BLOXAM, v. 30), proceeding B.A. 1611 and M.A. 1614. He was bursar of his college in 1622, and junior proctor of the university 1620–1. He afterwards studied medicine, proceeding M.D. at Oxford, and was a candidate of the London College of Physicians 25 June 1623. A letter describing Ben Jonson's reception at Oxford, written by Thomas Foxe to his father, is preserved in 'MS. Harl.' 416, f. 226, and has been printed by Mr. Winters. On 8 May 1634 James Hay, earl of Carlisle, applied to him for a loan of 500*l.* He seems to have acquired much property, and to have been friendly with men eminent in literature and society. He died at Warlies 20 Nov. 1662, and was buried in Waltham Abbey 26 Nov. He married Anne, daughter of Richard Honeywood of Charing, Kent, and Marleshall, Essex, and grand-daughter of Mrs. Mary Honeywood, the pious friend of his grandfather, the martyrologist. By her he left a daughter Alice, who married Sir Richard Willys, bart. Robert, Samuel's youngest son, was a captain in the navy, and died in 1646. He wrote to his elder brother an interesting letter descriptive of the trial of the Earl and Countess of Somerset.

[Wood's Athenæ Oxon. ed. Bliss, i. 533 ; Bloxam's Reg. of Magd. Coll. iv. 190–9; Strype's Annals, bk. ii. No. xlviii.; Winters's Biographical Notes, 1876.]   C. J. R.

FOXE, SIMEON, M.D. (1568–1642), president of the College of Physicians, born in 1568 'in the house of the Duke of Norfolk,' was the youngest son of John Foxe, the martyrologist [q. v.]. He was educated at Eton, and on 24 Aug. 1583 was elected a scholar of King's College, Cambridge, where he proceeded B.A. in 1587, having become a fellow 24 Aug. 1586. He graduated M.A. in 1591. Bishop Piers promised him a prebend, but he preferred to study medicine. After leaving college he resided for some time with Archbishop Whitgift, then visited Italy, and took the degree of M.D. at Padua. On his return home he engaged in military service, and was with Sir John Norris and the Earl of Southampton in Ireland and the Netherlands. In the Low Countries he is said to have been taken prisoner and detained for a time at Dunkirk. He reached London in 1603, and shortly afterwards commenced to practise, attaining to the highest eminence in his profession. He was admitted a candidate of the College of Physicians on 30 Sept. 1605, and a fellow on 25 June 1608. He was censor in 1614, 1620, 1621, 1623, 1624, 1625, 1631, and 1632; registrar on 20 Nov. 1627, on the death of Dr. Matthew Gwinne; treasurer on 3 Dec. 1629, on Harvey's resignation of that office; anatomy reader, 1630; elect, 22 Dec. 1630, in place of Dr. Thomas Moundeford, deceased; president from 1634 to 1640; consiliarius in 1641. He died at the college house at Amen Corner, Paternoster Row, on 20 April 1642. In his will, dated 21 Oct. 1641, proved by his nephew, Thomas Fox, he describes himself as of the parish of St. Martin's, Ludgate, London, and desires 'to be buried in Christian buriall within the Cathedrall Church of St. Paule in London, as neere to the monument of Doctor Lynacer as conveniently may be,' bequeathing the sum of 20l. 'towards the repayring of the same Cathedrall' (registered in P.C.C. 51, Cambell). He was buried according to his directions on 24 April. He also bequeathed to the college 40l., to which his nephew added another 60l. 'On 22 Dec. 1656 the college, on the proposition of Dr. Baldwin Hamey, unanimously voted the erection of a marble bust to his memory in the Harveian Museum;' the statue was destroyed in the great fire of 1666, as was his monument in St. Paul's erected by his nephew. His portrait in the college was one of two pictures rescued from the fire, but has disappeared. He attended John Donne, dean of St. Paul's, and contributed liberally towards the erection of a monument to his memory. In Harleian MS. 416 (ff. 203b, 210, 214) are three Latin letters of Fox, two of which are addressed to his father and brother Samuel respectively. The life of his father prefixed to the second volume of the 1641 edition of the 'Actes and Monuments,' long attributed to his brother Samuel, has lately been assigned, on very feeble grounds, to Simeon himself. He was certainly alive at the date of its publication, when Samuel had been dead twelve years. But internal evidence does not justify Simeon's claim to the memoir [see FOXE, JOHN, ad fin.]

[Munk's Coll. of Phys. (1878), i. 147–8; Harwood's Alumni Eton. p. 193; Winters's Biographical Notes on John Foxe, pp. 33, 36–38.]

G. G.

FOY, NATHANIEL, D.D. (d. 1707), bishop of Waterford and Lismore, son of John Foy, M.D., was born at York, and educated at Trinity College, Dublin, of which he became a senior fellow (M.A. 1671, B.D. and D.D. 1684). He was ordained priest in 1670, and in the same year was installed as a canon of Kildare. On 20 Dec. 1678 he was appointed minister of the parish of St. Bride, Dublin. In the reign of James II he stood up boldly in defence of the established church. Crowds assembled at St. Bride's every alternate Sunday to hear his replies to the sermons delivered at Christ Church on the preceding Sundays by a doctor of the Sorbonne in the presence of the king. This task he accomplished by means of abstracts of his antagonist's arguments supplied to him by gentlemen who wrote shorthand. He was prevented from preaching on several occasions by the menaces of some of the king's guard, and his firmness in supporting the protestant faith led to his being imprisoned, together with Dr. King and other clergymen.

After the battle of the Boyne his constancy was rewarded by William III, who promoted him to the united sees of Waterford and Lismore by letters patent 13 July 1691. In September 1695 he was imprisoned in Dublin Castle for three days by order of the House of Lords, because he had spoken disrespectfully of that assembly in a protest against the rejection of a bill for union and division of parishes. He died in Dublin on 31 Dec. 1707, and was buried at the west end of Waterford Cathedral, in St. Saviour's Chapel.

During his lifetime he expended 800l. on the improvement of the palace at Waterford, and by his will he established and endowed the free school at Grantstown. His only publication is 'A Sermon preached in Christ's Church, Dublin, on 23 Oct. 1698, being the anniversary thanksgiving for putting an end to the Irish Rebellion, which broke out on that day 1641. Before the House of Lords,' Dublin 1698, 4to.

[Ware's Bishops (Harris), p. 543; Cotton's Fasti, i. 130, ii. 250, v. 29, 273; Taylor's Univ. of Dublin, p. 416; Todd's Cat. of Dublin Graduates, p. 207; Killen's Eccl. Hist. of Ireland, ii. 184; Luttrell's Hist. Relation of State Affairs, ii. 213,

vi. 265; Smith's Waterford (1774), p. 188; Mant's Hist. of the Church of Ireland, ii. 12, 23, 63, 92, 195, 196.]　　　　　　　　　　　T. C.

FRADELLE, HENRY JOSEPH (1778–1865), historical painter, was born at Lille in 1778, studied in Paris, and afterwards in Italy. He settled in London in 1816, and sent to the Royal Academy in the following year 'Milton dictating Paradise Lost to his Daughter.' He then resided at No. 4 Nassau Street, Middlesex Hospital. He also contributed thirty-six pictures to the British Institution, and two in Suffolk Street, between 1817 and 1854. In this latter year his address was 5 Brecknock Crescent, Camden New Town, where he painted the portrait of the son of W. T. Barnes of Rowley Lodge, Shenley, Hertfordshire. This was exhibited at the Royal Academy. The following rank among his best works: 'The Escape of Mary Queen of Scots from Lochleven Castle,' engraved by H. Dawe; 'The Earl of Leicester's Visit to Amy Robsart at Canmore Place,' engraved by Charles Turner in 1826; 'Queen Elizabeth and Lady Paget,' engraved by William Say in 1828; 'Mary Queen of Scots and her Secretary, Chastelard,' 'Rebecca and Ivanhoe,' 'Belinda at her Toilet,' and 'Lady Jane Grey,' most of which are in the collections at Petworth, Munich, Holland House, &c. The original drawing, dated 1824, in black chalk, of the picture representing the Earl of Leicester's visit to Amy Robsart is in the department of prints and drawings, British Museum. He died 14 March 1865.

[Redgrave's Dict. of Artists.]　　　L. F.

FRAIGNEAU, WILLIAM (1717–1788), Greek professor at Cambridge, was the son of John Fraigneau, of Huguenot extraction. He was born in London in 1717, and became a queen's scholar at Westminster School in 1731. He proceeded to Trinity College, Cambridge, in 1736. Graduating B.A. 1739 and M.A. 1743, he took holy orders, and was elected a fellow. In 1743 he was appointed professor of Greek to the university, and held that position till 1750, when he resigned it. He then accepted the post of tutor to the family of Frederick, lord Bolingbroke, and in March 1758 was by him presented to the living of Battersea. Three years later the same patron gave him the living of Beckenham, Kent, and in 1765 a dispensation passed to enable Fraigneau to hold the two livings conjointly. He retained both appointments till his death, which took place at Brighton 12 Sept. 1788. He is described by Cole (*Athenæ Cantab.* F. p. 109) as 'a little man of great life and vivacity.'

[Le Neve's Fasti Eccl. Angl.; Hasted's Kent, i. 88; Manning and Bray's Surrey, iii. 341; Gen. Even. Post, 15 Sept. 1788; Nichols's Lit. Anecd. iv. 278; Welch's Alumni Westmonast. 303, 313, 314.]　　　　　　　A. V.

FRAIZER, SIR ALEXANDER (1610?–1681), physician, was born in Scotland about 1610, and graduated M.D. at Montpelier on 1 Oct. 1635. He was incorporated at Cambridge 9 March 1637, and was elected a fellow of the College of Physicians of London on 23 Nov. 1641. He was a faithful royalist, followed Charles II abroad, and became his physician. The king placed confidence in him, and he was in turn courted and abused by the violent rival factions which grew up among the English exiles on the continent. He was once friendly with Hyde, and at another time avoided communication with him. He was declared by the king to be excellent as a physician, and was employed in court affairs. There was probably some resemblance of character which sustained the confidential relation; but the conclusion stated by some contemporary writers, that the physician was as unprincipled as his royal patient, is unsupported by evidence, and no weight attaches to the abuse of Sir John Denham and of Pepys. Denham's attacks are founded on personal enmity, of which the cause is not now known. Pepys's informant was Pierce, a groom of the privy chamber, who repeated backstairs' gossip. The respect with which Fraizer is mentioned by Dr. Edward Browne (*Travels*, ed. 1685, p. 115), and the fact that on 26 July 1666 he was chosen an elect at the College of Physicians, a distinction which his being king's physician would not have obtained for him had his professional character been low, are evidences of his general uprightness. Sir Edmundbury Godfrey, who dealt in wood, arrested Fraizer for a wood bill of about 30*l.* The bailiffs were beaten by the king's order, but this was not due to any misconduct on the physician's part, but to royal indignation at a supposed breach of a prerogative. Few records of Fraizer's practice remain; he attended the princess royal in the attack of small-pox which ended fatally on Christmas eve, 1660, and the young Dukes of Cambridge and Kendal in the illness which killed both in 1667, and he superintended the successful trepanning of Prince Rupert's skull on Sunday, 3 Feb. 1666. At Cologne Mr. Elburg was his apothecary. Soon after the Restoration he was knighted, and his wife made a dresser to the queen. He died 3 May 1681. He had a son, Charles, who became a fellow of Trinity College, Cambridge, was physician in ordinary to Charles II, and was elected a fellow of the College of Physicians in 1684.

[Munk's Coll. of Phys. i. 233; Pepys's Diary, 6th ed. i. 134, ii. 168, iii. 55, 118, iv. 179.]

N. M.

FRAMPTON, JOHN (*fl.* 1577–1596), merchant, was resident for many years in Spain, and on his retirement about 1576 to his native country employed his leisure in translating from Spanish into English the following: Escalante's 'A Discourse of the Navigation which the Portugales doe Make,' dedicated to Edward Dyer, 1579, 4to; Monardes's 'Joyfull Newes ovt of the Newe Founde Worlde,' dedicated to Edward Dyer, 1577, 1580 (with three other tracts by Monardes), 1596, 4to; Marco Polo's 'Travels,' 1579, 4to; 'An Account of the Empire of China in 1579' (in 'Harleian Collection of Voyages,' 1745, vol. ii.)

[Joyfull Newes, 1st ed. pref.; Tanner's Bibl. Brit. p. 297; Brit. Mus. Cat. of Books before 1640.]

B. D. J.

FRAMPTON, MARY (1773–1846), writer of a journal, was the daughter of James Frampton of Moreton, Dorsetshire, by his second wife Phillis, who had been previously married to Dr. Charlton Wollaston. Frampton died in 1784, but his widow survived until 1829, when she had reached her ninety-second year. She was evidently an accomplished person, with a wide circle of well-connected relations and friends. Mary Frampton during the earlier part of her life went with her parents to London once every two years, and was present at the Gordon riots, the Warren Hastings trial, and the thanksgiving service for the recovery of George III in 1789. About two years after her father's death she and her mother settled at Dorchester, and formed a centre for the society of the county. Miss Frampton is said by all who have any recollection of her to have been a most agreeable person. Her views were evidently those of a strong tory. She died, unmarried, on 12 Nov. 1846.

Miss Frampton's 'Journal from the year 1779 until the year 1846, edited with notes by her niece, Harriot Georgina Mundy,' was published in 1885. It begins in 1803, prefaced by reminiscences from 1779, and incorporating a large correspondence from friends and acquaintances, together with much additional information supplied by the editor, Mrs. Mundy, who died in January 1886. The whole forms an interesting picture of the times, and gives, in particular, a good deal of information about the court. The Framptons became acquainted with the family of George III during his frequent visits to Weymouth, and their correspondents supplied them with many stories about the prince regent and his relations with Mrs. Fitzherbert, Lady Jersey, and Caroline of Brunswick; also about the Princess Charlotte, whose governess, Mrs. Campbell, was a great friend of the Framptons. The book deals with public affairs and society talk, giving anecdotes about Mrs. Montagu, 'Mary of Buttermere,' Archbishop Sumner, Miss Edgeworth, Napoleon and his widow, the Empress Maria Louisa, Charles X of France, and Baron Stockmar, and touching upon events like the outbreak of the French revolution, the French invasion of Wales in 1797, the visit of the allied sovereigns to London in 1814, and the riots and Swing fires of 1830.

[Mary Frampton's Journal mentioned above; information from the Mundy family. For reviews of the Journal see the Athenæum, Academy, and Saturday Review, 7 Nov. 1885, and the Spectator, 10 April 1886.]

L. C. S.

FRAMPTON, ROBERT (1622–1708), bishop of Gloucester, was born at Pimperne, near Blandford in Dorsetshire, 26 Feb. 1622. He was the youngest of eight children, his father being a respectable farmer. He was educated at the Blandford grammar school, whence he went to Oxford as an exhibitioner at Corpus Christi College. Here he was much neglected by his tutor, and by the aid of some influential friends was transferred to Christ Church, where he was placed under the tuition of Mr. Zouch. He took his degree with credit, and soon afterwards set up a private school at Farnham, Dorsetshire. He then obtained the appointment of head-master of the school of Gillingham in the same county, where he had a hundred boys under him. During the period of the war between the king and parliament, Frampton, professing high loyal principles, was involved in a quarrel with one Gage, a parliamentary officer in the neighbourhood. It appears that on more than one occasion they came to blows. Frampton and his brothers were on the king's side in the battle of Hambledon Hill (3 Aug. 1645). He now determined, despite the difficulties of the time, to take orders, and was privately ordained by Skinner, bishop of Oxford. He then became domestic chaplain to the Earl of Elgin, but was also a frequent preacher in London and elsewhere, and was much admired for his oratorical powers. By the influence of Mr. Harvey, a well-known Levant merchant, Frampton obtained the appointment of chaplain to the English factory at Aleppo (30 Aug. 1655).

Here he spent, with some short intervals of absence, twelve years, and by his abilities as a linguist and his straightforward character obtained great influence. He became a proficient in Arabic and in Italian, and lived on friendly terms with the chief men among the Mussulmans at Aleppo. He enjoyed the fullest confidence of the Europeans at Aleppo, who entrusted him with an important mission to the Porte, in which he succeeded, against all the influence of the pasha of Aleppo, in obtaining the redress of certain grievances under which foreigners were made to suffer in Syria. After many years spent at Aleppo, Frampton returned to England, where in 1667 he married Miss Mary Canning. Hearing, however, that the plague had broken out at Aleppo, he gallantly determined to return thither almost immediately after his marriage. He remained at Aleppo actively ministering to the sufferers till 1670, having himself escaped the disease. In this year he finally returned to England, where his reputation stood high. In two months' time he was appointed preacher at the Rolls, living in the house of Sir Harbottle Grimston. He was also made chaplain to the lord keeper, Sir Orlando Bridgeman [q. v.] Any amount of preferment was now within his reach, and he was confessedly one of the first preachers of the day. Pepys, writing in 1667, says : 'All the church crammed, and, to my great joy, find Mr. Frampton in the pulpit, and I think the best sermon for goodness and oratory, without affectation or study, that I ever heard in my life. The truth is he preaches the most like an apostle that ever I heard man, and it was much the best time that I ever spent in my life at church.' In 1671 Frampton was made prebendary of Gloucester, and shortly afterwards of Salisbury. In 1673, on the death of Dr. Vines, he was made dean of Gloucester. At this time he preached a sermon at court against the encouragement of infidelity, to which the king objected as personal, and the dean apologised. Frampton obtained the livings of Fontmell, Dorsetshire, and Oakford Fitzpaine, Devonshire, which he held with his deanery. In 1680 he was appointed bishop of Gloucester, in succession to Dr. John Pritchard. He was consecrated by Archbishop Sancroft in the chapel of All Souls' College, Oxford, 27 March 1681. At first he held his livings *in commendam*, but at Sancroft's desire he resigned them, being afterwards appointed to the living of Standish, Gloucestershire, the emoluments of which were very small, while his parsonage house was in ruins. Frampton proved himself a great builder and restorer. He did much both at the deanery and the episcopal palace of Gloucester, and rebuilt the house at Standish.

He was a frequent preacher at Whitehall, and in the administration of his diocese was tolerant towards dissenters, and universally popular. After the accession of James II the king complained to the archbishop that Frampton was in the habit of denouncing popery. When the famous declaration of indulgence was published, and ordered to be read in churches, the bishop went strongly with those of his brethren who opposed it. When the petition of the bishops was drawn up, he authorised the appending of his signature, but he was not present with the seven at its presentation. He sent a direction to his clergy bidding them not to read the declaration, and when the seven were committed to the Tower he spent most of his time there with his brethren. But, though thus strongly opposed to the illegal proceedings of James, he would not transfer his allegiance to the new dynasty. On his refusal to take the oath his diocese was greatly moved. The gentry of the county offered to have the sessions deferred that he might have more time for deliberation. The grand jury petitioned for him. But neither side would yield, and the bishop was deprived of his see as a nonjuror on 1 Feb. 1690–1. He was allowed, however, by connivance, to hold the small benefice of Standish, where he resided. Here his life was not altogether tranquil. Frequent accusations were made against him of favouring popery, and he was actually arrested and imprisoned on suspicion of being concerned in a plot for murdering the king. The only definite act which could be proved against Frampton was his having sent round circular letters to the nonjuring clergy. But he was able to show that this was only done by way of raising some funds for the relief of those of them who were greatly in need. At the archbishop's request Frampton was accordingly liberated. In the Tower the deprived bishop had the opportunity of visiting Judge Jeffreys, whom he found in a very sad and melancholy state, and to whom he ministered christian consolation. At Standish it was Frampton's habit to attend the church services, and to take part in them, omitting the names of the royal family, and preaching from his pew. So greatly was he respected in the diocese that those who were instituted to livings by the legal bishop did not consider their institution complete until they had obtained the ratification, secretly given, of the deprived nonjuror. Frampton had no wish to continue the nonjuring schism, and consequently incurred the ill-will of the more violent members of the party. His views about the schism corresponded with those of Henry Dodwell in the

'Case in View' (1705). He regarded it altogether as a personal matter, and, though he could not himself feel justified in taking the oaths, he did not condemn others who might do so. He agreed in this to a great degree with Bishop Ken [q. v.] At the accession of Queen Anne the position of the nonjurors appeared to alter, and many of them returned to allegiance. The queen took particular notice of Frampton, and went so far as to offer him the see of Hereford, which was to be regarded as a 'translation,' thus recognising the position he still claimed as bishop of Gloucester. But Frampton, who was now a very aged man, declined this delicate offer. He died at Standish 25 May 1708, at the age of eighty-six, and was buried in the church there, his grave being marked by a black marble slab with the inscription, 'Robertus Frampton, Episcopus Glocestrensis—Cetera quis nescit?'

A portrait of Frampton hangs in the episcopal palace at Gloucester, and has been reproduced in the anonymous contemporary memoir first published in 1876, which corrects some of the mistakes made by Wood and others, and was unknown to Lathbury, author of the 'History of the Non-jurors.'

[Memoir of Robert Frampton, Bishop of Gloucester, edited by Rev. T. S. Evans, London, 1876; Lathbury's Hist. of the Nonjurors, London, 1845; Wood's Athenæ, ed. Bliss, vol. iv.; Diary and Correspondence of Samuel Pepys, vol. iii. London, 1858; Dodwell's A Case in View Considered, London, 1705; J. B. Pearson's Chaplains of the Levant Company, 1883, pp. 21, 56, 57.]

G. G. P.

FRAMPTON, TREGONWELL (1641–1727), 'the father of the turf,' born in 1641 at Moreton in Dorsetshire, was the fifth son of William Frampton, lord of the manor of Moreton, by his wife, Katharine Tregonwell of Milton Abbas. He probably passed his youth at home in the country, and there acquired a taste for field sports. He is described by Chafin (Anecdotes of Cranbourne Chase, p. 47) as being in 1670 the most active pursuer of hawking in the west of England. He was at the same period a regular attendant at race meetings, kept horses in training, and owned a house at Newmarket, though he passed the greater part of the year in Dorsetshire. At the former place he speedily acquired a reputation for bold and successful gambling. Coventry, in a despatch dated March 1675, mentions a horse-racing match 'wherein Mr. Frampton, a gentleman of some 120l. rent, is engaged 900l. deep.' He adds: 'I hope the world will see we have men who dare venture as well as M. de Turenne.' Frampton won his money, and in the racing records of the time his name

appears far more frequently as a winner than a loser, the amounts at stake being considerably greater than was usual. In April 1676, for example, he had two matches in the same week, the one at Newmarket and the other at Salisbury, each for 1,000l. A well-known incident belongs to this period. The commonly accepted tradition is that embodied by Hawkesworth in an essay on instances of cruelty to animals (Adventurer, No. 37). This story is that Frampton's horse Dragon beat a certain mare, winning a stake of 10,000l. On the conclusion of the match the owner of the mare instantly offered to run her on the following day for double the sum against any gelding in the world, and Frampton accepted the challenge. He then castrated Dragon, who was brought out the next day, and again beat the mare, but fell down at the post and died almost immediately. Hawkesworth declares that he remembers the facts as thus stated to be true, but he could have had no personal knowledge of them. Lord Conway, in a letter dated 7 Oct. 1682, says: 'His majesty's horse Dragon, which carried seven stone, was beaten yesterday by a little horse called Post Boy, carrying four stone, and the masters of that art conclude this top horse of England is spoiled for ever.' This last sentence would seem to imply that some such operation as Hawkesworth alleges had been performed on a horse called Dragon; but it also contradicts his statement that the horse died at the post, and there is not the remotest evidence for supposing that Frampton had any connection with the racing establishment of Charles II. On the other hand Lawrence (Philosophical and Practical Treatise on Horses) quotes a letter from a Mr. Sandern of Newmarket: 'The abominable story which is told of Mr. Frampton . . . is entirely without foundation, for I had an uncle who was well acquainted with Mr. F., and who frequently assured me that no such circumstance ever happened. . . . Cruelty was no part of the old gentleman's character.' A letter written by the Duke of York to the Prince of Orange eighteen months after the date of Frampton's alleged cruelty mentions a forthcoming match between the 'famous horses Dragon and Why Not.' Frampton, though probably not guilty of this atrocity, was by no means always scrupulous. On one occasion he had made a match with Sir William Strickland, a Yorkshire baronet. Frampton managed to arrange a private trial, and secretly put 7lbs. overweight upon his horse, which was just beaten. The greatest interest was excited by the match, which was looked upon as a struggle between the north and south, and it has been said that the bets arising from it were far in excess of anything that had been previously known. Several estates changed hands after the event, and so many gentlemen were completely ruined that, if Whyte (*Hist. of British Turf*, i. 397) may be believed, it was in consequence of the vast sums lost that the act (9 Anne c. 14, s. 3) was passed, forbidding the recovery of any sum due through bets above 10*l*. Frampton's horse was again beaten, and his losses must have been considerable. He had before known what it was to be in want of money, for in a letter dated September 1690 he says he 'shall be for a fortnight tumbling up and down in Dorset and Wiltshire till I have got up some money to make up part of my engagements; but I doubt shan't all,' and it may have been at this defeat of his horse by Merlin that he made over the family estate, to which he had succeeded on the death of his brother William in 1689, to his cousin Giles Frampton, the next heir, in consideration of 5,000*l*. down. But the dates of both the match and the transfer of property are unknown, though the latter took place some time prior to 1702.

It was probably in 1695 that Frampton first assumed the duties of the position ascribed to him on his tombstone of 'keeper of the running horses to their sacred majesties William III, Queen Anne, George I and George II.' In October of that year he won with the king's horse the town plate at Newmarket, and in the accounts of the master of the horse for the same year there is mention of a payment to him 'for settling the establishment of racehorses at the Green Cloth and Avery, and for a plate at Newmarket.' In 1700 he first appears in Chamberlayne's 'Angliæ Notitia' (pt. iv. p. 506), as receiving 1,000*l*. per annum as supervisor of the racehorses at Newmarket, for the maintenance of ten boys, their lodgings, &c., and for provisions of hay, oats, bread, and all other necessaries for ten racehorses. From that date till his death he regularly received a salary, which sometimes, however, dropped as low as 600*l*., the amount apparently being reckoned at 100*l*. for every horse in training. It is not now possible to ascertain the precise nature of Frampton's duties. He certainly trained the royal horses, and made matches for them, and they generally ran in his name. He continued to breed horses on his own account, some of which he used to dispose of at high prices to the master of the horse, and he remained a steady and persistent gambler. That part of his time which was not given up to horses was devoted to hawking, coursing, and cock-fighting. He was particularly successful with his cocks,

and his taste was largely shared by his royal master, William III, who, during his visits to Newmarket, spent many of his afternoons in watching his trainer's cocks do battle. Frampton kept his post till his last day, which was 12 March 1727. He was buried in the church of All Saints, Newmarket, where on the south side of the altar is a mural monument of black and white marble inscribed to his memory.

Notwithstanding the comparative humility of Frampton's position there were few men of his time who enjoyed more widespread notoriety through the country. The author of 'Newmarket, or an Essay on the Turf,' London, 1771 (attributed by Cole to Mr. Anstey of Trumpington), thus describes him (p. 171 *n*.): 'I cannot here omit to instance the famous song which begins—

Four and twenty Yorkshire knights
Came out of the north countree,
And they came down to Newmarket
Mr. Frampton's horses to see.

At the same time I take this opportunity of paying my respects to the memory of old Frampton. This gentleman (whose picture may be seen in many a house in Newmarket) was as great an oddity as perhaps ever was heard of. He was a known woman hater, passionately fond of horse-racing, cocking, and coursing; remarkable for a peculiar uniformity in his dress, the fashion of which he never changed, and in which, regardless of its uncouth appearance, he would not unfrequently go to court and enquire in the most familiar manner for his master or mistress, the king or queen. Queen Anne used to call him Governor Frampton.' Another writer quoted by Whyte (*British Turf*, i. 398), in an account of Newmarket in the reign of Anne, remarks: 'There was Mr. Frampton, the oldest, and, as they say, the cunningest jockey in England; one day he lost 1,000 guineas, the next he won 2,000, and so alternately. He made as light of throwing away 500*l*. or 1,000*l*. at a time as other men do of their pocket-money, and was perfectly calm, cheerful, and unconcerned when he had lost a thousand pounds as when he won it.' Noble (additions to GRANGER, ii. 387) gives further testimony to his qualities. It has been said of this man that he was 'a thorough good groom only, yet would have made a good minister of state if he had been trained for it . . . Frampton was supposed to be better acquainted with the genealogy of the most celebrated horses than any man of his time. . . . Not a splint or sprain, or bad eye, or old broken knee, or pinched foot, or low heel, escaped in the choice of a horse.' On the other hand he is tersely dismissed as a mere tout by Sir George Etherege in the couplet:—

I call a spade a spade, Eaton a bully,
Frampton a pimp, and brother John a cully.

The time when Frampton was first given the
title 'father of the turf' is uncertain. It may
have been towards the close of his long life;
but he does not appear to have been so described in print till the publication of an engraving of his portrait by Wooton in 1791,
which bears his name and the descriptive
title. On another portrait, also by Wooton
and engraved by Faber, he is called 'royal
stud-keeper at Newmarket,' which is not accurate, the keeper of the stud holding a distinct office. Frampton's portrait has since
frequently served as a frontispiece to books
on racing, and occupies that position in Taunton's 'Portraits of Celebrated Racehorses'
(London, 1886 and 1887).

[Hutchins's Dorsetshire, 3rd ed. 1861, i. 398
and 400; Addit. MS. 5807, fol. 132; Hore's
History of Newmarket, 1886, vols. ii. and iii.
passim; Chafin's Anecdotes of Cranbourne Chase,
p. 47 et seq.; Chamberlayne's Angliæ Notitia,
1700–27; J. C. Whyte's History of the British
Turf, i. 389–99; State Papers, Dom. unpublished; Luttrell's Diary, iii. 540; Smith's
Currant Intelligence; the Postman and Post
Boy, &c. passim.]   A. V.

FRAMYNGHAM, WILLIAM (1512–
1537), author, was born in February 1512 at
Norwich, and educated at the grammar school,
where he was contemporary with Dr. John
Caius. From Norwich he went to Cambridge,
and was at first at Pembroke Hall and afterwards at Queen's College, 'in aula Pembro-
kiana per adolescentiam educatus, per juven-
tutem in Collegium reginale ascitus.' He
proceeded B.A. 1530, M.A. 1533, and was
scholar of Queen's College from 1530 till his
death, and bursar for three years from 1534.
He died 25 Sept. 1537. He left all his books
to his friend and schoolfellow Dr. John Caius,
who tells us that along with Framyngham
he wrote 'Scholia' and notes upon them, but
could never recover them from those in whose
care he left them when he went to Italy.
Long afterwards, in 1570, Edmund, bishop
of Rochester, professed to know of them, but
Caius apparently did not follow up the clue.
Dr. Caius describes his friend as 'homo tena-
cissimæ memoriæ, fœcundi ingenii, infinitæ
lectionis, indefatigati laboris atque diligen-
tiæ,' and gives the following list of his works:
1. 'De Continentia lib. ii.' (prose). 2. 'De
Consolatione ad Æmilianum cæcum lib. i.'
(verse; suggested by the author's blindness,
brought on by immoderate study). 3. 'D.
Laurentii Martyrium' (verse). 4. 'Ἐκπύ-
ρωσις, sive Incendium Sodomorum' (verse).
5. 'Idololatria' (verse). 6. ''Ἀρέτη, sive in

laudem virtutis' (verse). 7. 'Epigrammatum lib. ii.'

[J. Caius de libris propriis, 1570, p. 2; N.
Carlisle's Endowed Grammar Schools, ii. 186;
Tanner's Bibliotheca, p. 297; Cooper's Athenæ
Cantab. i. 63, 531.]   R. B.

FRANCATELLI, CHARLES ELMÉ
(1805–1876), cook, born in London in 1805,
was of Italian extraction, and was educated
in France. He studied the culinary art under
Carême, and advanced it to unprecedented
perfection in this country. He became successively chef de cuisine to the Earl of
Chesterfield, the Earl of Dudley, Lord Kinnaird, &c. Afterwards he managed the well-
known Crockford's, or the St. James's Club,
whence he removed to the royal household,
becoming maître d'hôtel and chief cook in
ordinary to the queen. He next farmed the
once flourishing Coventry House Club, and
for seven years was chef de cuisine to the
Reform Club. He afterwards managed the
St. James's Hotel, Berkeley Street, Piccadilly,
and finally the Freemasons' Tavern, which post
he held until within a short period of his death.
Francatelli was very successful as an author.
In 1845 he published the 'Modern Cook,'
which ran through twelve editions. This
was succeeded in 1861 by 'The Cook's Guide
and Butler's Assistant.' The same year he
issued his 'Plain Cookery Book for the Working Classes,' and in 1862 the 'Royal English
and Foreign Confectionery Book.' In the
latter work he discussed the art of confectionery in all its branches as practised in
England and in all the leading European
countries. While able to dress the costliest
banquets, Francatelli was likewise a culinary
economist. On one occasion he characteristically remarked that he could feed every
day a thousand families on the food that was
wasted in London. His cookery book for the
working classes contained information of
practical value to the poor. Francatelli died
at Eastbourne on 10 Aug. 1876.

[Men of the Time, 8th edit.; Ann. Reg. 1876;
Illustr. Lond. News, 19 Aug. 1876.]   G. B. S.

FRANCE, ABRAHAM (*fl.* 1587–1633),
poet. [See FRAUNCE.]

FRANCIA, FRANÇOIS LOUIS THO-
MAS (1772–1839), water-colour painter, was
born at Calais 21 Dec. 1772, and was brought
early in life to London by his father, a refugee. He was for some time employed as an
assistant of a drawing-master named Barrow,
who was the master of John Varley [q. v.]
He commenced to exhibit at the Royal Aca-

demy in 1795, and contributed from that year to 1821 (inclusive) eighty-five works in all to its exhibitions. He was one of the sketching society formed by Thomas Girtin [q. v.] about 1799, and there is a moonlight composition in the South Kensington Museum dated in that year. He was a member of the (now Royal) Society of Painters in Water-Colours, and for some time its secretary, but he resigned his membership, and became in 1816 an unsuccessful candidate for the associateship of the Royal Academy. The next year he retired to Calais, where he resided till his death on 6 Feb. 1839. Here he gave instruction to R. P. Bonington [q. v.], whose coast scenes bear much resemblance to the later works of Francia. Francia's earlier drawings are broad and simple in execution, rich, but sombre in colour, like those of Girtin; but his later work, while still retaining its breadth and harmony, is brighter and lighter in tone, and more subtle in handling. Though he painted landscape of different kinds, his favourite subjects were shore scenes, which he executed with great truth and beauty of aerial effect. He was an excellent draughtsman of boats and shipping, and some of his drawings were engraved to illustrate a book of sketches of shipping by E. W. Cooke [q. v.] He was one of the earliest and most accomplished of English water-colourists, and his works are distinguished by their fine colour and poetical feeling. There are several of his drawings at the South Kensington Museum, and a few at the British Museum. In 1810 he published 'Studies of Landscapes by T. Gainsborough, J. Hoppner, R.A., T. Girtin, &c., imitated from the originals by L. F.'

[Redgrave's Dict. of Artists; Graves's Dict. of Artists; Bryan's Dict. (Graves); English Encyclopædia; private information.]   C. M.

FRANCILLON, JAMES (1802–1866), legal writer, sixth son of Francis Francillon of Harwich, Essex, descended from a Huguenot family settled in this country since 1685, was born 21 Nov. 1802, educated at the king's school, Rochester, 'served his articles' and was admitted an attorney, thereafter entered a student at Gray's Inn, and was called to the bar by that society in 1833. He went the Oxford circuit, enjoyed a fair practice, but was chiefly employed in chamber work. In 1847, when the modern county courts were constituted, he was appointed judge for the Gloucestershire district. He was also a magistrate for Gloucestershire and Wiltshire, and deputy-chairman of the Gloucestershire quarter sessions. Francillon, who was married and had issue, died at Lausanne of cholera 3 Sept. 1866. He wrote

'Lectures, Elementary and Familiar, on English Law,' first and second series, 1860-1. This work, written in a popular style, had some reputation.

[County Court Chronicle and Bankruptcy Gazette, 1 Oct. 1866, p. 227; Gent. Mag. October 1866, p. 559.]   F. W–T.

FRANCIS, ALBAN (d. 1715), Benedictine monk, a native of Middlesex, became a professed monk on 9 May 1670, in the abbey of St. Adrian and St. Denis at Lansperg or Lambspring in the kingdom of Hanover (WELDON, Chronicle, App. p. 24). He assumed in religion the name of Placid. He was sent to the mission in Cambridgeshire. On 7 Feb. 1686-7 James II addressed a mandatory letter under his signet manual to Dr. John Peachell, master of Magdalene College, and vice-chancellor of Cambridge, commanding him to admit Francis to the degree as master of arts 'without administering unto him any oath or oaths whatsoever, or tendering any subscription to be made by him.' This letter was laid before a congregation of the university on 21 Feb., and the senate advised that the king should be petitioned to revoke his mandate. The esquire-bedels and the registrars were sent to inform Francis that the senate were ready to admit him to the degree provided that he would swear as the law appointed, but he refused to do so, insisting upon the royal dispensation. On the same afternoon the heads met in the consistory, and agreed to send a letter to the Duke of Albemarle and another to the Earl of Sunderland, secretary of state, through whose hands the mandate had passed. A second letter from the king dated 24 Feb. was read in the senate on 11 March. The senate, confirmed by the approval of several eminent lawyers, persisted in its refusal to comply with the royal letters. Consequently the vice-chancellor and the senate (by its deputies) were cited to appear before the ecclesiastical commissioners at Whitehall. The lord chancellor (Jeffreys) pronounced the decision of the commissioners on 7 May 1687. Peachell was deprived of the office of vice-chancellor and was suspended, ab officio et beneficio, of his mastership during his majesty's pleasure. At a subsequent sitting (12 May) the lord chancellor reprimanded the deputies of the senate. Another vice-chancellor was elected, Dr. Balderston, master of Emmanuel College, but Francis never got his degree.

At the revolution Francis withdrew to Lambspring, whence he removed in 1699 to the English Benedictine college of St. Gregory at Douay. He was again sent to the mission in the south province of England, where he died on 27 July 1715 (SNOW, *Necrology*, p. 87).

[Howell's State Trials, **xi.** 1319–37; Cooper's Annals of Cambridge, iii. 614; Dodd's Church Hist. iii. 424, 489; Macaulay's Hist. of England; Addit. MSS. 5869, f. 71, 32095, f. 238; Corrie's Notices of the Interference of the Crown with the Affairs of the English Universities, p. 62; Burnet's Hist. of his own Time (1838), p. 443; Echard's Hist. of England; Pepys's Memoirs, **v.** 117.] T. C.

FRANCIS, ANNE (1738–1800), authoress, daughter of the Rev. Daniel Gittins, rector of South Stoke, near Arundel, Sussex, was educated by her father in the classics and Hebrew, and became a competent scholar. She married the Rev. Robert Bransby Francis, rector of Edgefield, near Holt, Norfolk. She died on 7 Nov. 1800. She published: 1. 'A Poetical Translation of the Song of Solomon from the original Hebrew, with a preliminary Discourse and Notes, historical and explanatory,' 1781, 4to. 2. 'The Obsequies of Demetrius Poliorcetes: a Poem,' 1785, 4to. 3. 'A Poetical Epistle from Charlotte to Werther,' 1788, 4to. 4. 'Miscellaneous Poems,' 1790, 12mo.

[Dallaway's Western Sussex, ii. 193.]
J. M. R.

FRANCIS, ENOCH (1688–1740), Welsh baptist, was born in 1688 at Pantyllaethdy, on the banks of the Tivy, and began to preach in 1707. He was settled first at Capel Iago, Llanbyther, but removed in 1730 to Newcastle Emlyn, Carmarthenshire. He became one of the most popular and successful ministers of his denomination. He was moderator of the baptist association at Hengoed, Glamorganshire, in 1730, 'but the meeting,' says Thomas, 'was uncomfortable. There were very warm debates upon general redemption and other articles connected with it. Mr. E. Francis had work enough to moderate some tempers.' The disturbing element at Hengoed was Charles Winter. Francis's publications were: 1. 'The Work and Reward of the Faithful Minister of the Gospel,' 1729. 2. 'A Word in Season,' 1733. He was also the author of some of the association letters; that of 1734 is specially mentioned. He died 4 Feb. 1739–40. Mary, his wife, died 23 Aug. 1739, aged 49, and the inscription on the tomb tells us 'Enoch walked with God;' 'Mary has chosen the better part.' The historian of the baptists concludes his memoir with an elegy by Jenkin Thomas, Drewen.

[Thomas's Hist. Baptist Association; Thomas's Hanes y Bedyddwyr; Rees's Hist. of Nonconformity in Wales.] R. J. J.

FRANCIS, FRANCIS (1822–1886), writer on angling, born in 1822 at Seaton, Devonshire, was son of Captain Morgan, R.N., his mother being the only daughter of Mr. Hartley, who founded the Hartley Institution at Southampton. He changed his name on coming of age and inheriting property. After being educated at various private schools, and with several tutors, he adopted the profession of a civil engineer, but on completing his articles abandoned it for sport and sporting literature. In 1851 he married Mary Cole of Oxford, and henceforth, happy in his domestic life, enthusiastically devoted himself to angling and all connected with it. No kind of fishing, from gudgeon to salmon, came amiss to him, and he speedily made himself familiar with every mode of catching fish. His ardour never flagged; a lifetime of fishing found him, when he reeled up his last line at Houghton, Hampshire, as enthusiastic as when in his boyhood he caught his first fish. He was angling editor of the 'Field' for more than a quarter of a century, and frequently wrote his experiences as an angler, together with reminiscences of angling literature, and papers on cognate subjects in the columns of that newspaper. He found time also to make himself a fair classical scholar, and to obtain a knowledge of the masterpieces of the English language. The collection of a good angling library formed a congenial entertainment to him. Francis established the Thames Rights Defence Association, throughout life advocated the cause of fish culture, and suggested the plan of 'The National Fish-Culture Association,' which has since been carried out. He had a large share, too, in introducing the ova of English trout to the New Zealand and Tasmanian streams. Thus he occupied himself with his rod and pen during many happy years until he was seized with a severe stroke of paralysis in 1883. Though he eventually recovered from this, he grew thinner month by month, and an old cancerous affection, for which he had previously undergone two operations, recurring, he died in his chair on 24 Dec. 1886. He had long lived at Twickenham and was buried there.

Francis was a member of the commission on oyster culture from 1868 to 1870, and was always enthusiastic about the improvement of English streams. As naturalist director for some years of the Brighton Aquarium he had special opportunities of observing fish and making experiments on their culture. He was of fine stature, active in mind and body, quick with his pen, and never unemployed; cheerful, bright, sympathetic, and independent, his courage was extraordinary, and was well exhibited in the indomitable fortitude with which he bore the pains and necessary operations of the attempts to cure the cancer in his tongue. Scrupulously fair in word and thought, his nervous temperament made him no respecter of persons, and at times caused him to be hasty both in temper and judgment, but he was always ready to own himself mistaken, and was quick to forgive as well as to forget. On the Test and Itchen, and among the Scotch lochs and rivers, which he loved to frequent, his name will long be remembered. 'His memory is the memory of a man who spent his life not merely in selfish amusement, but in contributing largely to the amusement of others' (Memoir in *Book of Angling*). More perhaps than any other he instructed and delighted the enormous number of anglers who have sprung into existence during the last thirty years by his writings, his geniality, and his prowess as a fisherman.

Besides 'The Diplomatic History of the Greek War' (1878) which he wrote in early life, Francis was the author of: 1. 'Pickacki-fax,' a novel in rhyme, 1854. 2. 'The Real Salt,' a yachting story, 1854. 3. 'The Angler's Register,' 1858, 1860, 1861, from which sprang the 'Angler's Diary.' 4. 'Newton Dogvane,' a novel, 3 vols., illustrated by Leech, 1859. 5. 'Fish Culture,' 1863. 6. 'A Book on Angling,' 1867, his best work, which has often been enlarged and reissued in subsequent years. 7. 'Sidney Bellew,' a sporting novel, 2 vols., 1870. 8. 'Reports on Salmon Ladders,' 1870. 9. 'By Lake and River,' rambles in the north of England and in Scotland. 10. 'Angling' (often reissued), 1877. 11. 'Sporting Sketches with Pen and Pencil,' 1878 (in conjunction with Mr. A. W. Cooper). 12. 'Miscellaneous Papers from the "Field,"' 1880. 13. 'The Practical Management of Fisheries,'1883. 14. 'Angling Reminiscences,' a posthumous work, 1887, containing almost his last contributions to the 'Field' paper. Besides these he wrote the articles on angling in 'Chambers's Encyclopædia,' and contributed a number of scattered papers to other magazines and journals.

[Fishing Gazette; Field and Academy for 1 Jan. 1887; Westwood and Satchell's Bibliotheca Piscatoria; Memoir prefixed to the sixth edition of his Book on Angling; private information.] M. G. W.

FRANCIS, GEORGE GRANT (1814–1882), Welsh antiquary, eldest son of John Francis of Swansea, Glamorganshire, by his wife, Mary Grant, was born in that town in January 1814, and educated at the high school there. Until within a few years of his death Francis took a very prominent part in every question affecting the interest of his native town. 'It mattered little,' writes one who knew him well, 'whether the subject was one of antiquarian research, . . . or a question of modern improvement and progress, such as railways, docks, or tramways. Whatever his hand found to do he did it with a might which certainly deserved success, though it by no means uniformly commanded it. . . . As with many other men of a similar temperament, his enthusiasm ran away with him.' His numerous schemes for local improvements were, in fact, somewhat in advance of his time, and being always financially weak, met with an imperfect appreciation. In 1835 he helped to found the Royal Institution of South Wales, and presented it with his large collections of local fossils, antiquities, coins, and seals, together with one of the best libraries of works relating to Wales extant, of which he compiled and printed a catalogue, afterwards adding a supplementary volume. He also shared in the formation of the Cambrian Archæological Association in 1846, and frequently contributed to its journal, the 'Archæologia Cambrensis.' To the volume for 1848 he sent for insertion the original contract of affiance between Edward of Carnarvon, prince of Wales, and Isabella, daughter of Philip the Fair, king of France, dated at Paris 20 May 1303, which he had discovered in Swansea Castle. It was printed separately the same year. He was active in restoring to public use the ancient grammar school of Bishop Gore, of which he was many years chairman and one of the trustees. His connection with it enabled him to collect materials for his book, 'The Free Grammar School, Swansea; with brief Memoirs of its Founders and Masters, and copies of original deeds,' 8vo, Swansea, 1849. By the town council he was entrusted with the restoration and arrangement of their neglected and scattered muniments, which task he performed so admirably as to call forth a warm eulogium from Lord Campbell in the court of queen's bench. He afterwards privately printed one hundred copies of 'Charters granted to Swansea. . . . Translated, illustrated, and edited by G. G. Francis,'Latin and English, fol., London, 1867. The preservation and restoration of Oystermouth Castle, near Swansea—one of the many ancient ruins pertaining to the house of Beaufort, lords of Gower and Kilvey—were also owing to his exertions, for which he was presented with a piece of plate. In 1851 Francis was selected to represent the Swansea district as local commissioner at the Great Exhibition. During the same year the British Association appointed him secretary to its department of ethnology when holding its meeting at Swansea. He was mayor of the borough in 1853-4, and was also colonel of the 1st Glamorgan artillery volunteers, a corps raised by his exertions in 1859. In 1867 Francis communicated to the Swansea newspaper, 'The Cambrian,' 'as the earliest organ of the copper trade,' some curious papers which he had discovered in the Record Office on the metallurgy of the district. These papers excited considerable attention, and the author consented to gather them together and print fifty copies for presents as 'The Smelting of Copper in the Swansea District, from the Time of Elizabeth to the Present Day,' 8vo, Swansea, 1867. So numerous, however, were the inquiries for this book that he published it in 1881 as a quarto volume, illustrated with autotype portraits of men connected with the copper trade, and sketches of places historically interesting from their connection with copper smelting. From a large mass of original documents extant among the Gnoll papers at Neath, Francis was able to add to this second edition many new and important facts; while he personally examined each of the copper-smelting works described in the book.

Francis died at his town house, 9 Upper Phillimore Place, Kensington, 21 April 1882, and was buried on the 26th in Swansea cemetery. By his marriage in 1840 to Sarah, eldest daughter of John Richardson of Swansea, and of Whitby Lodge, Northumberland, he left issue three sons. He was elected F.S.A. 16 Jan. 1845, was its honorary secretary for South Wales, and was also a corresponding member of the Society of Antiquaries of Scotland and of the Welsh Manuscripts Society. In addition to those already named Francis wrote many other monographs on Welsh history and topography, of which we may mention: 1. 'Original Charters and Materials for a History of Neath and its Abbey,' with illustrations, now first collected,' 8vo, Swansea, 1845 (fifty copies privately printed). 2. 'The Value of Holdings in Glamorgan and Swansea in 1545 and 1717, shown by rentals of the Herbert Family. Edited from the originals,' fol., Swansea, 1869 (twenty-five copies printed). 3. 'Notes on a Gold Chain of Office presented to the Corporation of Swansea in . . . 1875, . . . together with a list of [mayors] from 1835 to 1875,' 4to, Swansea, London (printed), 1876. He also assisted L. W. Dillwyn in the latter's 'Contributions towards a History of Swansea,' 8vo, Swansea, 1840, joined the Rev. Thomas Bliss in writing 'Some Account of Sir Hugh Johnys, Deputy Knight Marshal of England, temp. Henry VI and Edward IV, and of his

Monumental Brass in St. Mary's Church, Swansea,' 8vo, Swansea, 1845, and readily gave Dr. Thomas Nicholas the benefit of his varied knowledge in the compilation of the 'Annals of Counties and County Families of Wales,' 1872, 1875.

[Swansea and Glamorgan Herald, 26 April and 3 May 1882; Nicholas's Annals, ii. 628; Thomas's Handbook to the Public Records, Introd. p. xviii; Lists of Soc. Antiq.; Brit. Mus. Cat.; Athenæum, 22 April 1882, pp. 510-11.] G. G.

FRANCIS, GEORGE WILLIAM (1800-1865), botanical writer, was born in London in 1800. Besides the works enumerated below, he edited the first five volumes of the 'Magazine of Science and School of Arts,' 1840-5. His family increasing he emigrated to Australia, arriving in the colony by the Louisa Baillie 2 Sept. 1849. Shortly after his arrival he took the old botanical garden, north of the Torrens river, as a yearly tenant, and was subsequently appointed director of the Adelaide botanic garden. This position he held until his death, after a long illness, of dropsy on 9 Aug. 1865; he was buried the next day. He left a widow and ten children.

He published: 1. 'Catalogue of British Plants and Ferns,' 1835; 5th edition, 1840. 2. 'Analysis of British Ferns,' 1837; 5th edition, 1855. 3. 'Little English Flora,'1839. 4. 'Grammar of Botany,' 1840. 5. 'Chemical Experiments,'1842, abridged by W. White, 1851, and republished as 'Chemistry for Students.' 6. 'Favourites of the Flower Garden,' 1844. 7. 'Manual of Practical Levelling for Railways and Canals,' 1846. 8. 'Art of Modelling Wax Flowers,' 1849. 9. 'Electrical Experiments,' 8th edition, 1855. 10. 'Dict. Practical Receipts,'new edition, 1857. 11.'Acclimatisation of Animals and Plants,' Royal Society, South Australia, 1862.

[South Australian Register, 10 Aug. 1865.] B. D. J.

FRANCIS, JAMES GOODALL (1819-1884), Australian statesman, was born in London in 1819. In 1834 he arrived in Tasmania. He obtained employment in the firm of Boys & Pointer at Hobart. In 1847 the business was transferred to himself together with a partner named Macpherson. In 1853 the firm, Francis & Macpherson, opened a branch establishment in Victoria. Francis became managing partner there and took up his permanent residence in Melbourne. His position rapidly grew in influence. He became director of the bank of New South Wales in 1855, vice-president of the chamber of commerce in 1856, and president in 1857. In

October 1859 he was elected to the Victorian Legislative Assembly (the Lower House) for Richmond, and he sat in the house for the same constituency till his retirement fifteen years later. He entered the cabinet of William Nicholson on 25 Nov. 1859 as vice-president of the Board of Lands and Works and commissioner of public works. He held the office till 3 Sept. 1860. When James M'Culloch formed a ministry on 27 June 1863, Francis became commissioner of trade and customs, and retired with his chief 6 May 1868. M'Culloch held office for a third time, 9 April 1870–19 June 1871, when Francis joined him as treasurer. Francis supported the protectionist revision of the tariff, 1865–6, and was always a protectionist, although he deemed five and ten per cent. duties adequate to protect native industries. After the fall of Charles Gavan Duffy's administration in June 1872, Francis was entrusted by Viscount Canterbury, the governor, with the formation of a ministry. He retired on 3 July 1874, having passed a free education act and other important measures, including railway bills involving an expenditure of 2,250,000l. A dangerous attack of pleurisy was the chief cause of his resignation. On recovery he paid a long visit to England. In 1878 he reentered political life, and was returned to the Victoria Assembly as member for Warrnambool. On the retirement of Sir James M'Culloch he took office once again under James Service, but a painful illness compelled him to retire into private life in 1882. Francis frequently declined the honour of knighthood, and business reasons prevented his acceptance of the post of agent-general for the colony in London, when offered him by Sir Bryan O'Loghlan. Francis was not a polished speaker, but his integrity gave him enormous influence in the assembly. As premier he avoided constitutional strife or sensational appeals to the people. His practical good sense was widely appreciated. He died at Queenscliff, Victoria, on 25 Jan. 1884, and was buried privately, according to the wishes of his family, on 28 Jan.

[Private information; Heaton's Australian Dict. pp. 72–3, 160–2; Times, 29 Jan. 1884.]

FRANCIS, JOHN (1780–1861), sculptor, was born in Lincolnshire 3 Sept. 1780, and brought up to farming, but showing some talent for the arts, he was advised by a few friends to settle in London, where he became a pupil of Chantrey. He first exhibited at the Royal Academy in 1820 a bust of T. W. Coke, esq., and another of Captain Sir W. Bolton, R.N. At this period his residence was at Thornham, Norfolk. In 1822, when he sent

to the same institution a bust of Miss Horatia Nelson, he was living at 2 New Norfolk Street, Park Lane. In 1844 he executed by command of her majesty in marble a bust of his Royal Highness Prince Albert, and a few years earlier a bust of Queen Victoria, now in the hall of the Reform Club. About this period Francis removed to 56 Albany Street, Regent's Park. Among his other works may be mentioned the following: Busts of the Duke and Duchess of Norfolk (1844); bust in bronze of the Duke of Sussex (1847); marble bust of Lord John Russell, now in the National Portrait Gallery (1848); a bronze medal of Eos, a favourite greyhound of Prince Albert (1848); marble bust of the Hon. Edward Petre (1848); four busts, in marble, of various members of the Eaton family (1851); posthumous bust of the Earl of Carlisle (1852); bust of the Duke of Wellington, now in the National Portrait Gallery (1852); posthumous bust of the Hon. and Rev. James Norton (1854); bust of Vice-admiral Sir Charles Napier (1855); cabinet bust of the Right Hon. Earl of Aberdeen (1856). Francis died in Albany Street, 30 Aug. 1861.

[Redgrave's Dict. of Artists.] L. F.

FRANCIS, JOHN (1811–1882), publisher of the 'Athenæum,' was born in Bermondsey on 18 July 1811. His father, James Parker Francis of Saffron Walden, Essex, married Elizabeth, daughter of Thomas Perkins of Ware, and came to London to carry on the business of a leather-dresser. For twenty-five years he was honorary secretary of the Leather-dressers' Trades Union, and died 24 Aug. 1850, aged 73. John received his earliest education from F. Painter, in Long Lane, Bermondsey. He afterwards attended a nonconformist school in Unicorn Yard, Tooley Street, Southwark, the master of which helped him in 1823 to apprentice himself to E. Marlborough, the well-known newspaper agent, 4 Ave Maria Lane. Having served his full time, in September 1831 he entered the office of the 'Athenæum' as a junior clerk, but he showed such ability that he became business manager and publisher of the journal on 4 Oct. At fourteen years of age he taught in the Sunday school of Dr. John Rippon's chapel, Carter Lane, Southwark, and was superintendent when Dr. Rippon removed to New Park Street in 1833. In 1849 Francis joined the new Bloomsbury Chapel under the pastorate of Dr. William Brock, and did good service as a district visitor in St. Giles's. At an early period of his business career his attention was drawn to the heavy fiscal restrictions on the newspaper press, and he took an active and prominent part in trying to remove them. While Milner Gibson fought the battle in parliament, Francis did more than any man out of doors towards bringing about the repeal of the advertisement duty of 1s. 6d. on each advertisement, of the stamp duty of 1d. on each newspaper, and lastly of the paper duty of 1½d. per pound, which charges were successively repealed in 1853, 1855, and 1861. During the long agitation on this question he was constantly engaged in deputations to the leading ministers of the day, and was really the founder of the Association for the Repeal of the Paper Duty, on behalf of which he visited Edinburgh and Dublin in company with John Cassell [q. v.] and Henry Vizetelly. In 1863 his services were rewarded by the presentation, at 47 Paternoster Row, of a testimonial from gentlemen representing the press and the Association for the Repeal of the Taxes on Knowledge. 'The Bookseller' of 26 April 1861 (pp. 215–216) contains a paper by him on 'The Progress of Periodical Literature from 1830 to 1860,' and on 7 Jan. 1870 he contributed to the 'Athenæum' an essay on 'The Literature of the People.' He undertook the charge of the commercial affairs of 'Notes and Queries' in 1872, in addition to his other work, and in October 1881 he celebrated the fiftieth anniversary of his becoming publisher of the 'Athenæum.' For many years he resided at 2 Catherine Street and then at 20 Wellington Street, in connection with his publishing offices. Later on he lived at 11 Burghley Road, Highgate Road; but he returned in 1881 to 20 Wellington Street, Strand, London, where he died on 6 April 1882, and was buried in Highgate cemetery on 18 April, near the grave of Faraday, in the presence of many literary men. In his memory two John Francis pensions were founded in connection with the Newsvendors' Benevolent Institution. His wife, Charlotte Collins, died 7 Dec. 1879, aged 71.

Francis's elder son, John Collins Francis, succeeded him as publisher of the 'Athenæum,' and his younger son, Edward James Francis, was manager of the 'Weekly Dispatch' from 1875 till his death, 14 June 1881.

[J. C. Francis's John Francis, publisher of the Athenæum, 1888, i. 1–19, 45–7, 226, ii. 173 et seq., 545–50, with portrait; Times, 11 April 1882, p. 5, 12 April, p. 1, 19 April, p. 12; Athenæum, 15 April 1882, p. 476, and 27 Dec. 1884, p. 826; Sunday School Chronicle, 21 April 1882, p. 205; Grant's Newspaper Press (1871), ii. 299, 313, 320; Henry J. Nicoll's Great Movements, 1881, 269–339; Bookseller, 3 May 1882, and 5 March 1883 and 1885.]   G. C. B.

FRANCIS, PHILIP (1708?–1773), miscellaneous writer, son of Dr. John Francis, rector of St. Mary's, Dublin (from which living he was for a time ejected for political reasons), and dean of Lismore, was born about 1708. He was sent to Trinity College, Dublin, taking the degree of B.A. in 1728, and was ordained, according to his father's wish, in the Irish branch of the English church. He held for some time the curacy of St. Peter's parish, Dublin, and while resident in that city published his translation of Horace, besides writing in the interests of 'the Castle.' Soon after the death of his wife, Elizabeth Rowe, whom he married in 1739, he crossed to England, and in 1744 obtained the rectory of Skeyton in Norfolk. If he ever took up his abode on this living he soon abandoned it for literature and society in London. In January 1752, when Gibbon became an inmate of his house, Francis was keeping or supposed to be keeping a school at Esher; but the boy's friends quickly found that the nominal instructor 'preferred the pleasures of London to the instruction of his pupils,' and in a month or two Gibbon was removed. To maintain himself in the social life of London, Francis tried many expedients, but most of them were failures. Twice was a play of his composition produced on the stage, and each time without success. He tried translation, but, except in his rendering of the works of Horace, he was beaten out of the field by abler writers. His fortune was made when he secured, through the kindness of Miss Bellamy, who pitied him for his ill-success in play-writing and recommended him to Fox, the post of private chaplain to Lady Caroline Fox, and became domesticated in her family, where he taught Lady Sarah Lennox to declaim and Charles James Fox to read. At the end of 1757 Fox was sent to Eton, and Francis accompanied him to assist the boy in his studies. The father, Henry Fox, best known as Lord Holland, found the Irish tutor a useful ally. It has sometimes been said that he was the chief writer in the paper called 'The Con-test,' which lived from November 1756 to August 1757, but the accuracy of this statement is more than doubtful. He is also said to have contributed to the 'Gazette' daily newspaper on behalf of the court interest. When Pitt resigned, in 1761, Francis wrote a libel against him under the title of 'Mr. Pitt's Letter Versified,' the notes to which, according to Horace Walpole, were supplied by Lord Holland, and he followed this with 'A Letter from the Anonymous Author of "Mr. Pitt's Letter Versified,"' in which he reflected on Pitt's indifference to the truculent language of Colonel Barré. Even so late as 1764 he attacked Pitt and Wilkes with great bitterness in the 'Political Theatre.' On 22 June 1761 he was inducted to the vicarage of Chilham in Kent, but resigned in the summer of 1762, and through Lord Holland's influence he held from May 1764 to 1768 the chaplaincy at Chelsea Hospital, and the rectory of Barrow in Suffolk, to which he was instituted on 26 Feb. 1762, and which he retained until his death. These preferments did not exhaust the whole of the wages which he received for political services. He was recommended in January 1764 by George Grenville for a crown pension of 300*l.* a year, and his letters of thanks for these and other favours are printed in the 'Grenville Papers,' ii. 250–5, when he announced, as is common with the recipients of pensions, that he used to 'love and revere the constitution.' The editor quotes from a list of pensioners on the Irish establishment for 1770 the entry, 'John Stear, esq., assignee of Philip Francis, esq., 600*l.* for 31 years from Sept. 16, 1762.' Francis was still unsatisfied. He quarrelled with Lord Holland because he had not been made an Irish bishop, and threatened to expose his patron's villainy. Walpole relates that on Churchill's death a collection of letters from Holland to Francis, which had been supplied by him, were found among the poet's papers, and that, to stop any future exposure, the peer paid 500*l.* and obtained Francis's nomination to the chaplaincy at Chelsea. It should be noticed, however, that the appointment of Francis to that position preceded the date of Churchill's death, and that Churchill attacked him in the poem of the 'Author' as 'the atheist chaplain of an atheist lord,' and in the 'Candidate' sneered at his endeavours to translate. He was 'very feeble and languid in October 1766,' and next year he was 'struck with palsy from head to foot.' In June 1771 he was seized by a paralytic stroke, and after lingering for some years died at Bath 5 March 1773. He was fond of his son Sir Philip Francis [q. v.], and numerous letters to and from him are in the son's memoir; but he resented his son's marriage, and they were consequently at variance, but were afterwards reconciled. His first start in life was obtained through his rendering of Horace, of which Dr. Johnson said : 'The lyrical part of Horace never can be perfectly translated. Francis has done it the best. I'll take his five out of six against them all.' The first part, consisting of the 'Odes, Epodes, and Carmen Seculare of Horace in Latin and English,' in which he was assisted by Dr. Dunkin, is said to have been issued at Dublin in two volumes in 1742. It was republished in London in the next year, and in 1746 two more volumes, containing the 'Satires,

Epistles, and Art of Poetry,' appeared with a dedication in prose to Lord Newport, lord chancellor of Ireland, who had encouraged the translation. The whole version was reissued in 1747, on this occasion with a poetical dedication to Lord Newport, and it ran into many subsequent editions, that edited by Edward Dubois being the best. It was also included in the set of poets edited by Chalmers, the 'British Poets,' vols. xcvii–viii., and in Whittingham's 'Greek and Roman Poets,' vol. xii. Francis was at work, as appears from a letter of Lord Chesterfield to Madame du Boccage, in 1751 on his play of 'Eugenia,' an adaptation of the French tragedy of 'Cenie,' and it was acted at Drury Lane Theatre on 17 Feb. 1752, but 'verged towards dullness,' and was naturally unsuccessful, when Chesterfield attributed its failure to the fact that pit and gallery did not like a tragedy without bloodshed. A similar failure attended his play of 'Constantine,' which was produced at Covent Garden on 23 Feb. 1754, and expired on the fourth night. Genest styles it 'a cold and uninteresting play, the plot avowedly taken in part from a French piece.' Both pieces were printed, the former being dedicated to the Countess of Lincoln, and the latter to Lord Chesterfield. For eight years he was employed in studying the 'Orations' of Demosthenes, and his translation appeared in two volumes in 1757–8, but it was deemed inferior to that by Leland, and Francis was much depressed by his disappointment.

An anonymous volume, which was written by John Taylor, and was that writer's first publication on the subject, was printed in 1813 with the title of 'A Discovery of the Author of the "Letters of Junius," founded on Evidence and Illustrations.' It attributed the authorship to Francis and his son, Sir Philip Francis, and claimed that all the peculiarities of language in the writings of the elder Francis are discernible in some parts of Junius. The doctor's connection with the 'Letters of Junius' may at once be dismissed from consideration. It is wholly without foundation.

[Gent. Mag. 1773, p. 155, 1785, pt. i. 245 ; Hill's Boswell, iii. 356 ; Notes and Queries, 2nd ser. ii. 156, 5th ser. ix. 355, x. 97 ; Gage's Suffolk, p. 18 ; Blomefield's Norfolk (1807 ed.), vi. 364 ; Chesterfield's Works (Stanhope's ed.), iii. 445, iv. 8 ; Faulkner's Chelsea, p. 198 ; Walpole's Memoirs of George III, i. 123, ii. 36 ; Webb's Irish Biography ; Trevelyan's Fox, p. 48 ; Gibbon's Miscell. Works (1814), i. 40 ; Churchill's Works (1804), i. 314, 329, ii. 281 ; Genest's Hist. of English Stage, iv. 345–7, 397–8 ; Hasted's Kent, iii. 144 ; Merivale's Sir P. Francis, vol. i.]
W. P. C.

FRANCIS, Sir PHILIP (1740–1818), reputed author of 'Junius's Letters,' only child of the Rev. Philip Francis [q. v.], by his wife, Elizabeth Rowe, was born in Dublin, 22 Oct. 1740. His mother died about 1744–5, and his father soon after removed to England, leaving the son at a school kept by a Mr. Roe in Dublin. About 1751–2 Francis came to England to be educated by his father. Among his fellow-pupils was the historian Gibbon. On 17 March 1753 Francis was entered at St. Paul's School, then flourishing under an able head-master, George Thicknesse. He became a good classical scholar. Henry Sampson Woodfall [q. v.], afterwards the publisher of 'Junius,' was a schoolfellow. Francis was captain of the school in 1756, and left it in the same year to take a junior clerkship in the secretary of state's office. The appointment came from his father's patron, Henry Fox, afterwards the first Lord Holland. John Calcraft (1726–1772) [q. v.] was intimate both with Fox and the elder Francis, and Francis had many opportunities of seeing the leading statesmen of the day. He continued to educate himself, spent his savings on books, and became favourably known to Robert Wood, secretary of the treasury, a man of classical parts and a trusted subordinate of Pitt in the seven years' war. Through Wood's influence Francis was appointed secretary to General Edward Bligh [q. v.], whom he accompanied in the expedition to Cherbourg and St. Cas in 1758. In January 1760 he was appointed, again on Wood's recommendation, secretary of Lord Kinnoul's embassy to Portugal. He found time to learn French, Portuguese, and Spanish, and to compile elaborate note-books containing many diplomatic documents, besides discharging his official duties. Upon the conclusion of Kinnoul's mission in November 1760, Francis returned to his clerkship and his studies. His note-books show careful study both of classical and modern authors. He compiled careful financial and statistical tables, and made elaborate notes upon English constitutional questions. Wood recommended him to Pitt, to whom he acted as amanuensis between January 1761 and May 1762, writing despatches occasionally in French and Latin. Pitt, according to Lady Francis, was struck by the youth's talents, but no preferment resulted. In October 1761 Lord Egremont succeeded Pitt as secretary of state. Francis, who was in his department, tried, without success, to obtain the secretaryship to Hans Stanley's mission to Paris in 1761. He was acquainted with the course of later negotiations, and copied part of the correspondence between Egremont and the Duke of Bedford during the final negotiations for peace in the autumn of 1762. A remarkable reference is made to the relations between Egremont and Bedford at this time in the Junius letter of 29 Sept. 1769. Francis referred to his own employment on this occasion in a speech of 29 Feb. 1792. In 1761 he fell in love with Elizabeth Macrabie, then living with her parents at Fulham. She was an accomplished musician, and an attractive and sensible girl. She had no fortune, and the connection was disapproved by both families. They were both of age, however, and married at St. Martin's-in-the-Fields, 27 Feb. 1762. A coolness resulted between Francis and his father, till in 1766 the father's illness brought about a reconciliation.

At the end of 1762 Welbore Ellis succeeded Charles Townshend as secretary-at-war. He appointed Francis, upon Wood's recommendation, first clerk at the war office, and directly afterwards appointed as his deputy Christopher d'Oyly, who became Francis's most intimate friend. From 1765 the secretary-at-war was Lord Barrington. Both Barrington and D'Oyly left the greatest part of the official correspondence to be drafted by Francis. From this point Francis's career involves disputed questions. His biographer, Joseph Parkes, attributes to him many anonymous writings upon evidence of varying cogency. Francis told his second wife that he 'scarcely remembered when he did not write.' He was only treading in his father's steps, although his official position made a public acknowledgment of his writings inexpedient. A letter signed 'One of the People' in the 'Public Ledger' of 2 March 1763, dealing with a theatrical 'O. P.' riot, is claimed in his papers (PARKES, i. 69). In May 1766 Francis sent a long letter to the Duke of Richmond, then secretary of state, upon English trade with Portugal. The duke did not return it till 2 Aug., when he was leaving office. A strong hint had been given in a letter signed 'Tantum' in the 'Public Advertiser' of 1 Aug., which may therefore be plausibly attributed to Francis. His interest in Portuguese questions may also justify Parkes's opinion that he wrote letters signed 'Lusitanicus' and one signed 'Ulisippo' in the same paper for 2 and 13 Jan. and 3 March 1767 (ib. i. 132, 136). The statement is relevant only as showing that Francis was writing in the papers. Parkes also attributes to Francis two pamphlets in 1764. The first was published by John Almon [q. v.] in September as 'A Letter to the "Public Advertiser."' Part of it had appeared in that paper on 2 Aug. under the signature 'Candor,' but Woodfall declined to publish the rest without having the author's name. On 29 Nov.

Almon published a longer 'Enquiry into the doctrine . . . concerning Libels, Warrants, and the Seizure of Papers . . . in a Letter . . . from the Father of Candor.' These pamphlets, dealing with the Wilkes controversy, made some impression, went through several editions, and have been attributed to Dunning, Lord Temple, and others. Parkes attributes them to Francis upon internal evidence of little cogency, and also upon the evidence of a letter from 'Candor' to Woodfall, with a list of corrections, which is said to be 'unquestionably' in the handwriting of Francis (not the feigned hand of 'Junius'). The original, of which a facsimile is given by Parkes and Merivale, is in Addit. MS. 27777. It may be added that 'Candor' (2nd edit. p. 27) and the 'Father of Candor' (2nd edit. p. 37) speak pointedly of the practice in the secretary of state's office (see PARKES, i. 75–81, 85–96, 99–101). Woodfall addresses his correspondent as 'C.,' the signature afterwards used by Junius. Parkes also attributes to Francis a pamphlet called 'Irenarch' (1774), which he considers to be a continuation of the 'Candor' pamphlets. It was really written by R. Heathcote, in whose name it was afterwards published (Notes and Queries, 3rd series, xii. 456). Besides this Parkes identifies Francis with 'Anti-Sejanus,' the writer of letters to the 'Public Advertiser' in January 1765 and later, who is probably the 'Anti-Sejanus Junior' identified with Junius as author of one of the 'Miscellaneous Letters' in Woodfall's (1812) edition. 'Anti-Sejanus' was certainly James Scott, a clergyman patronised by Lord Sandwich, as was stated by a correspondent of the 'Public Advertiser' of 16 April 1770 (see also NICHOLS, Lit. Anecd. ix. 125; Chatham Corr. iv. 66). Parkes again attributes to Francis a letter signed 'A Friend to Public Credit' in the 'Public Advertiser' of 28 June 1768, of which he found a copy among Francis's papers. He failed to observe that this is one of a series by the same writer, and that a later letter of 11 Oct. 1768 is sharply attacked by 'Brutus,' and (19 Oct.) 'Atticus' (two of the letters assigned both by Parkes and Woodfall to Junius). If Francis wrote it, he was not Junius. But it is as inconsistent with Francis's views at the time as with the views of Junius. The 'Atticus' letter in which it is assailed was specially praised by Calcraft, with whom Francis was then acting, in a letter to the elder Francis (PARKES, i. 216). A copy of the letter of 28 June was no doubt kept by Francis, because it professes to give details of an operation upon the funds contemplated by the government. These palpable blunders go far to destroy the authority of Parkes's identifications. The following

period of Francis's career is remarkably illustrated by the autobiographical fragment, written not later than 1776, and published by Parkes and Merivale (i. 355–70). His great patron was Calcraft. Francis says that he 'concurred heartily' in Calcraft's schemes, which offered his only 'hope of advancement.' Calcraft had been in close connection both with Chatham and with Chatham's brothers-in-law, Lord Temple and George Grenville, and kept upon terms with all these after the quarrel which separated them upon Chatham's acceptance of office in 1766. From the spring of 1767 Chatham's illness had caused his retirement from active participation in the government, and he finally resigned in October 1768. Calcraft's plan was to discredit the rump of Chatham's administration, to reconcile Chatham to the Grenville party, and to attack ministers by a combination, including the Rockinghams as well as the Grenvilles. This political combination succeeded so well that in the beginning of 1770, as Francis observes, victory seemed assured. The great support of the opposition was the agitation on behalf of Wilkes, who returned to England at the beginning of 1768. His election for Middlesex, his expulsions and re-election, final exclusion, and other disputes arising out of these questions were the main topics of controversy from 1768 till 1772. Junius was undoubtedly the close (even if unknown) ally of the clique to which Calcraft and Francis belonged throughout the whole movement. The very questionable authenticity of the 'Miscellaneous Letters' makes it impossible to speak confidently of the earlier attitude of Junius. We know, however, that on 2 Jan. 1768 he wrote privately to Chatham (Chatham Corr. iii. 302), warning him, with expressions of 'respect and veneration,' of treachery on the part of his colleagues. Chatham soon discovered, says Francis (PARKES, i. 361), 'that he had been cajoled and deceived.' During 1768 Junius also wrote three remarkable private letters to George Grenville (Grenville Corr. iv. 254, 355, 379). They claim the authorship of a letter called 'the Grand Council,' of the 'Atticus' of 19 Oct. 1768, of letters signed 'Lucius,' of others in defence of Grenville and criticising the commission of trade, and of 'almost everything that for two years past has attracted the attention of the public.' The author, who signs himself 'C.,' expects to make himself known to Grenville when Grenville becomes a minister, and will then not be 'a needy and troublesome dependent.' During 1768 Junius (assuming him to have written the 'Miscellaneous Letters,' some of which are thus claimed) bitterly attacked the government, and especially the Duke of Grafton. If 'C.' be always his signature, he also attacked Wilkes at his first appearance, apparently because he first thought that ministers could be best assailed for want of energy, though he afterwards assails them for their arbitrary measures. He alludes disrespectfully to Chatham ('Lucius' 29 Aug. and 'Atticus' 19 Oct.), for Chatham's fame was still of use to ministers. He especially insists at length upon the dismissal of Amherst, which was regarded as a personal slight to Chatham, and therefore served to detach him from office.

The signature 'Junius' first appeared on 21 Nov. 1768, when Grafton and Camden were attacked for their behaviour to Wilkes. The first Junius of the collected edition appeared 21 Jan. 1769. It led to the sharp controversy with Sir William Draper [q. v.], which made the letters famous. The signature was afterwards used by Junius for his most careful writings, though he used many others. Junius now appeared as the advocate of Wilkes during the contest produced by his expulsions, and assailed the Duke of Bedford, whose influence was now on the government side, with singular ferocity. He culminated with the famous letter to the king on 19 Dec. 1769, which produced more sensation than any other letter.

At the beginning of 1770 Chatham came to the front with restored health. His friends Camden and Granby retired; Yorke committed suicide from remorse after taking Camden's place; Grafton himself resigned in January, and was succeeded by North. While Junius carried on the attack in his letters, Francis endeavoured to get Chatham's speeches diffused through the press. He claimed long afterwards, in a private note in Belsham's 'History' (ed. 1805), to have reported the speeches of Mansfield and Chatham on 9 Jan. 1770, and 'all Chatham's speeches on the Middlesex election,' &c., in this year (*Chatham Corr.* iv. 194). On the publication in the 'Parliamentary History' in 1813 he claimed to have reported Chatham's speeches of 9 and 22 Jan. and of 22 Nov., the only fully reported speeches of this period (*Parl. Hist.* xvi. 647, 741, 1091, and preface to vol. xxxiv.) He stated in pamphlets of 1811 that he had heard Chatham's speeches of January (see *Junius Identified*, 1816, pp. 289, 325). The speeches of January had appeared, as given for the first time by a 'gentleman of strong memory,' in Almon's 'Anecdotes of Chatham,' 1792, to which Francis made other contributions (PARKES, i. 160; TAYLOR's Appendix, p. 28). Notes taken from a speech of Chatham's on 2 Feb. 1770 are given from Francis's papers in Parkes and Merivale (i. 390-

393). Francis's claim has at least a *prima facie* justification. Taylor in his 'Junius Identified' pointed out a number of coincidences, some of them very remarkable, between the reports of the January speeches, the writings of Junius both before and after, and some of Francis's own writings. Dilke (*Papers of a Critic*, vol. ii.) endeavoured to meet this by stating that extracts from the speech of 9 Jan. had appeared at the time in the papers. The document to which Dilke apparently refers contains only a few brief fragments, in different language and without the specific phrases. He could find no report of the speech of 22 Jan. which contains, besides other coincidences, a sentence, quoted verbatim by Junius, in a private letter to Wilkes (7 Sept. 1771). This proves that Junius had seen the report, which, so far as we know, was still in Francis's desk. The nature of the brief and disguised reports of the time makes it highly improbable that any other report than that mentioned was published, and Almon's statement that he was the first publisher seems to be justified.

When parliament met in November 1770, the opposition dwelt chiefly upon the Falkland Islands difficulty, and upon the conduct of Mansfield in the trials of Woodfall and others for publishing Junius's letter to the king. On 22 Nov. Chatham delivered a great speech upon the Falkland Islands difficulty. Francis says in his autobiography (PARKES, i. 363) that he took it down from memory and had it published 'in a few days.' It appeared accordingly (*Papers of a Critic*) as an extra 'North Briton' on 1 Dec.; it was reprinted in the 'Middlesex Journal,' again in the 'Museum' and Almon, and was claimed by Francis in 1813.

A debate upon Mansfield followed on 5 Dec. A report was published at the time in several papers. On 10 Dec. Junius and Francis come into remarkable conjunction. On 21 Nov. Junius had written privately to Woodfall, hoping for information to be used against Mansfield, whom he is resolved to 'destroy.' On 1 Dec. Francis wrote a letter to Calcraft to be laid before Chatham, suggesting that Mansfield should be assailed by other methods, but not formally attacked in the house, where he was certain of a majority. Francis next got a hint of an argument against Mansfield from a friend at a tavern, reduced it to form, and sent it through Calcraft to Chatham. The paper, dated 9 Dec., is printed in the 'Chatham Correspondence' (iv. 48-9). Three days later Francis was flattered by hearing Chatham adopt his very words, and next day the speech 'flamed in the newspapers and ran through the kingdom.'

Chatham spoke on 10 Dec., and the 'London Evening Post' of the 11th reported that he had condemned Mansfield's conduct as 'irregular, extrajudicial and unprecedented,' the words used in Francis's private letter. Chatham's argument, however, was not given, and 'Nerva' in the 'Public Advertiser' of 14 Dec. showed that he had missed the point. On 17 Dec. 'Nerva' was answered by 'Phalaris,' who restates Francis's argument with such verbal closeness that there can be no doubt that he was Francis, or had read Francis's confidential communication to Chatham (see Herman Merivale in *Fortnightly Review*, March 1868). This letter, by omitting the three italicised words in 'I affirm *with Lord Chatham*,' became Chatham's speech in the report of the 'Museum' for January. In 1772 Junius cited this report in a note to the preface of the collected edition of his letters, and added 'it is exactly taken.' The 'Phalaris' letter, which was almost certainly by Francis, is included in the 'Miscellaneous Letters' of Junius; and the probability that Junius was the author is increased by his guarantee of its accuracy, and by the fact that he was keenly anxious to attack Mansfield; that he was writing the letter of 'Domitian' at least, and private letters to Woodfall, and that, if he was not 'Phalaris,' he made no direct attempt to support Chatham's assault upon the common enemy. A violent scene took place later in the debate of 10 Dec., at which Francis states that he was present, and it is described in the 'Museum,' obviously by an eye-witness. It ended in the expulsion of all strangers. Junius's private letter to Woodfall of 31 Jan. 1771 shows his extreme anxiety that the doors of the House of Lords might not be closed in the coming session. Francis, who attributes the closing to his publication of the 22 Nov. speech, declares that the closure was fatal to the opposition.

Francis and Junius were equally interested in the Falkland Islands quarrel. Francis thought that a war would necessarily place Chatham in power, and in that case he says 'I might have commanded anything.' He speculated in the funds, and by the peaceful settlement of the dispute in 1771 lost 500*l*. Calcraft told Chatham on 14 Jan. 1771 that war 'is more and more certain.' Junius told Woodfall, 16 Jan. 1771, that 'every man in the administration looks upon war as inevitable.' The 'Domitian' letter of 17 Jan. argues the same point, and on 30 Jan. Junius argues the case in a letter to which Johnson made a well-known reply. The remarks in this letter are curiously coincident with remarks from an unnamed correspondent, communicated to Chatham by Calcraft on 20 Jan.

The settlement of this question strengthened the ministry; and the opposition gradually declined and fell into discordant factions. Junius supported the city in the quarrel with the House of Commons. In the summer he again attacked Grafton, who in May 1771 accepted the privy seal; and was diverted by a sharp encounter with Horne, who was now quarrelling with Wilkes. He afterwards corresponded privately with Wilkes, suggesting means for pacifying the conflicting factions. The opposition grew daily weaker. At the end of 1771 Junius made his last assault upon Mansfield for bailing Eyre. The letter, composed with great labour, is said by Campbell and Charles Butler to prove that Junius was not a lawyer. Like the attack made by Francis, however, it turns upon a technical point, and Junius, like Francis, sent the proof-sheets of his letter to Chatham, asking him to co-operate in the House of Lords. The letter, which appeared 21 Jan. 1772, with another to Lord Camden, was a complete failure, and Junius, under that name, wrote no more.

On 21 Jan. 1772 D'Oyly, Francis's intimate friend, resigned his post at the war office. Barrington appointed Anthony Chamier [q. v.] in his place. Francis himself resigned in March. On 25 Jan. Junius told Woodfall of Chamier's appointment, and announced his intention of 'torturing' Barrington, requesting Woodfall at the same time to be careful to keep it secret that Junius was the torturer. The intention was fulfilled in the letters under various signatures, presumably intended to suggest different authors, which appeared on 28 Jan. and in the following months. They show Junius in his cruellest mood, and are in a vein of brutal pleasantry which, though it occurs in some of the other unacknowledged letters, is so unlike the more dignified style of Junius as to evade recognition. If Francis wrote them, they gave vent to the accumulated bile of an ambitious and arrogant subordinate against a dull and supercilious superior, whose politics he despised, who had turned out his dearest friend, and who had not yet had his fair share of abuse in Junius.

It is, however, remarkable that the facts, very partially known to us, do not fully explain Francis's wrath. The memoir in the 'Mirror' (1811), probably inspired by Francis, states that he resigned 'in consequence of a difference with Viscount Barrington, by whom he thought himself injured.' Yet in a private letter of 24 Jan. 1772 Francis says that Barrington had offered D'Oyly's place to him (PARKES and MERIVALE, i. 275), which he refused for 'solid reasons.' Barrington also wrote politely to Francis on 26 Feb. requesting him to make his own statement of the cause of his resignation, and desiring to use Francis's own words. The matter 'cannot remain a secret,' he says. In fact, however, the secret has been kept; no explanation is given by Francis himself or elsewhere. Francis's sixth child was born in this year; his father, who had long been hopelessly infirm, seems to have been partly dependent upon him. In losing his office, therefore, Francis would appear to have lost his chief means of support, while there were heavy claims upon him. He probably had some expectations through Calcraft's influence. He had been for some time thinking of an Indian appointment (*ib.* i. 260). He left England for a tour on the continent 7 July 1772, Calcraft promising to join him at Naples. Calcraft died 23 Aug. He had left 1,000*l.* to Francis by a codicil dated on the day of Francis's resignation, and an annuity of 200*l.* payable to Mrs. Francis if she should survive her husband and be left without due provision. Francis was also to be elected for his borough, Wareham. In his autobiography Francis leaves a spiteful character of Calcraft (*ib.* i. 359), curiously resembling a reference in Junius's letter of 5 Oct. 1771. Francis returned to England 14 Dec. 1772, anxious and only comforted by the friendship of D'Oyly. He was summoned to Bath, where his father was rapidly sinking, and returned to London on 12 or 13 Jan. The last letter from Junius to Woodfall had been dated 10 May 1772. A private note from Junius, taking a final leave of his publisher, is dated 19 Jan. 1773.

The evidence for the identity of Francis and Junius may be now briefly summarised. (1) Junius was especially acquainted with the affairs of the war office, and, in a less degree, of the state office. (2) Junius's fury at the dismissal of D'Oyly and Francis, coupled with his anxiety to conceal the fact that he was the author of these letters (private letter of 25 Jan. 1772), undoubtedly suggests some close personal interest. The publication of these letters in 1812, which first revealed the fact that they were written by Junius, suggested Francis to Taylor. (3) The facts above stated show that Junius throughout his career was acting, consciously or not, in the closest co-operation with Francis. Francis almost certainly wrote one of the 'Miscellaneous Letters' which fits into the Junius series. Junius guarantees the accuracy of a report by Francis of a speech in which Francis took a peculiar interest; and reports, probably due to Francis, make use of letters by Junius. Some presumptive proofs that Junius

had information known to Francis will be found in the 'Grenville Correspondence' (ii. cxiv seq.), where they are adduced to support the hypothesis that Junius was Lord Temple. (4) The papers of Francis show that his absences from London correspond with the silence of Junius. Horne on 16 Aug. 1771 taunts Junius for delaying till 13 Aug. to answer a previous letter of 31 July. Francis had left London at the end of July, and returned on 11, or possibly 12 Aug. Almost every letter assigned to Junius was delivered when Francis was probably in London. The chief exception is that Francis was at Margate when 'Q in the Corner' and 'A Labourer in the same Cause' were acknowledged in the 'Public Advertiser' of 6 July 1770. But the 'Labourer in the same Cause' is probably spurious, and the other may probably have been sent before Francis's departure (see *Notes and Queries*, 4th ser. xi. 130, 178, 202, 387, 425, for discussions of this point). (5) The evidence from handwriting is apparently very strong. In 1871 Mr. Twisleton published a careful examination by the expert Charles Chabot [q. v.], who gives in detail reasons which can be easily tested, and are apparently conclusive for identifying the handwriting of Junius and Francis. In the same book will be found a curious account of a poem sent in all probability by Francis about Christmas 1771 to a Miss Giles, in the handwriting of his cousin, Tilghman, and enclosed in an anonymous letter, which is identified by another expert, Mr. Netherclift, as in the handwriting of Junius. In one correction of the press, and probably in some corrections afterwards erased, Junius forgot to use his disguise, and writes a date in a hand indistinguishable from Francis's. This, however, has been disputed. (6) Some minor coincidences have been alleged. 'Bifrons' in the 'Miscellaneous Letters' says that he saw the books of the jesuits burnt in Paris. This probably refers to August 1761, when Englishmen were excluded by the war. But Francis wished to accompany, and possibly may have been sent with despatches to, Hans Stanley, who was then engaged in negotiations in Paris, and who described the scene in a despatch which Francis, if in England, must have seen. On the other hand, it is doubtful whether Junius wrote 'Bifrons' (see PARKES, i. 192, 196). The alleged kindness to Fox is of little or no importance, because the elder Francis and Calcraft had bitterly quarrelled with Fox, and Francis was as likely to have attacked as to have spared him. (7) Francis clearly belonged to the same political school as Junius, and was, like him, a whig doctrinaire.

There is a close general coincidence of opinion, with such slight divergences as are naturally explained by the changes of Francis's position in later life. Francis never wrote anything equal to Junius, though occasional passages suggest the same authorship. Upon this head, however, it is only safe to say that the identification presents no great difficulty, though the resemblance by itself affords scarcely any presumption. (8) Francis's conduct when challenged is on the whole confirmative. He seems (see afterwards) to have desired that the claim should be accepted, but to have been unwilling to make it himself. He appears to have denied the fact at times, though some alleged denials read like equivocations. To have claimed the authorship openly would have been to admit that he had been guilty of libelling his patron, Barrington, whose brother, the Bishop of Durham, was still alive, to say nothing of other admissions. Had he been conscious of innocence, an explicit denial would certainly have been called for. His actual course may be explained by such motives struggling with vanity, and confirmed by long habits of secretiveness and a probably exaggerated view of the importance of the facts. But other explanations are of course possible. (9) The moral resemblance is undoubtedly so close that it would be impossible to describe the character of Junius except in terms strikingly applicable to Francis. The chief arguments against Francis are that his authorship would imply an underhand malignity, which is not improbable in the author of Junius, whoever he may have been, and only too probable in Francis, whether he was or was not the author of Junius. It is also said that Woodfall, the printer of the letters, and Pitt stated that they knew Francis not to be the author. Both Pitt and Woodfall died, however, before the authorship had been publicly, if at all, attributed to Francis; and such second-hand reports are of little value (see, on the other side, Mr. Fraser Rae in the 'Athenæum,' 1888, ii. 192). On the whole, it may be said that Taylor established a *prima facie* presumption, which has been considerably strengthened by the publication of Francis's papers, and which is turned into something like proof, unless the coincidences of handwriting stated by Chabot and Netherclift can be upset. Nor is there any real difficulty in the assumption. The personal indications thrown out by Junius in his private letters to Woodfall and Wilkes are so indefinite and so probably mere blinds, that no inference can be drawn from them.

Francis made a short journey to the Hague two months after his father's death (5 March 1772). He there obtained permission from a M. de Pinto to translate his ' Essay on Circulation.' The translation was published under the name of his cousin, Stephen Baggs. Lord North had just passed his ' Regulating Act' for India, under which the governor of Bengal was to become governor-general of India, and to be controlled by a council of four. Francis had been thinking of retiring to Pennsylvania, where he had purchased a thousand acres through his brother-in-law, Alexander Macrabie. Hearing that one of the places in the council was not filled, Francis applied to Barrington, who recommended him to North in 'the handsomest and strongest letter imaginable,' and on North's advice was approved by the king and named in the bill, his colleagues being Warren Hastings, the new governor-general, Clavering, Monson, and Barwell. The appointment of a retired clerk to a place of 10,000*l.* a year has suggested the hypothesis that he was receiving hush-money as Junius. The post had already been refused by Burke and Cholwell at least, and was apparently going begging (PARKES and MERIVALE, i. 327). For obvious reasons the Junius hypothesis is improbable, though no further explanation can be given. The vague gossip reported by Lady Francis and the family, and given in Wade's ' Junius,' is inconsistent and incredible. After this Francis was on friendly terms with Barrington (*ib.* p. 329). He visited Clive, with whose son and widow he kept up an intimacy. After various difficulties with the court of directors, whose instructions to the new council were offensive to Francis, he finally sailed from Portsmouth 31 March 1774, leaving, it seems, a liberal allowance for his wife and her family.

Francis reached Calcutta 19 Oct. 1774. He came, according to Merivale (ii. 9, 239), strongly prejudiced against Hastings, although in 1787 he declared in the House of Commons that he and his colleagues had left England with the 'highest opinion' of Hastings. In any case Francis soon came to regard Hastings with sentiments resembling strongly the sentiments expressed towards Mansfield by Junius. In his earliest letters he denounced with great bitterness the corruption and rapacity which, as he declared, pervaded the whole Indian administration. Francis, Clavering, and Monson were the majority of the council, opposed by Hastings and Barwell. They reversed Hastings's policy and recalled his agents [see under HASTINGS, WARREN]. Francis was singularly energetic. He had four secretaries, his private secretary being his brother-in-law, Macrabie, and sometimes dictated to them all at once. He kept up a large correspondence, and preserved his papers in the most business-like method (MERIVALE, ii. 3, 24).

His quarrel with Hastings was soon embittered by the part which Francis took in the famous case of Nuncomar. On 11 March 1774 Francis received a visit from Nuncomar, who brought him a letter. Francis laid this before the council, declaring himself to be ignorant of its contents. It charged Hastings with corruption. In the interval between the committal and the execution of Nuncomar, Francis and his colleagues had some conflicts with the supreme court on questions arising out of the proceedings. On 31 July Nuncomar wrote a letter to Francis, entreating him to intercede for a respite. On 1 Aug. Nuncomar's counsel, Farrer, proposed to Francis that the council should send to the court a letter covering a petition from Nuncomar and supporting his prayer for a respite. Francis approved, but as Clavering and Monson declined, the matter dropped, and Nuncomar's last chance disappeared. He was hanged 5 Aug. On the 14th Clavering presented to the council a petition received from Nuncomar on the 4th. This petition suggested that he was judicially murdered on account of his attack upon Hastings. Hastings proposed that the letter should be sent to the judges, upon whose character it reflected. Francis, however, stated that he considered it as 'libellous' and 'wholly unsupported,' and carried a motion that it should be burnt by the common hangman and the copy of it expunged from the proceedings of the council. He tried upon the impeachment of Impey to explain his conduct in suppressing this document as libellous, although he and his colleagues made similar insinuations both before and after the event in the minutes of the council. He asserted that if he had acted weakly it was from a desire to save Clavering from the vengeance of Hastings; while it has been argued (STEPHEN, *Nuncomar and Impey*, ii. 108) that his real motive was to keep the charge against Hastings secret until it could be used to more effect. Francis's letters at the time seem to imply a very cautious reticence (MERIVALE, ii. 35). The question is discussed in two pamphlets published in 1788, 'Answer of Philip Francis to the charge brought . . . by Sir E. Impey' (by Francis), and 'A Refutation of . . . the Answer' (by Impey). Francis had before long quarrelled with Clavering. His position became uncomfortable, and upon the death of Monson (25 Sept. 1776) he was reduced to impotence, Hastings having the casting vote. He had meanwhile won 20,000*l.* at whist from Barwell, a sum reduced to 12,000*l.* by subsequent losses. He then gave up play and

invested his winnings. Although powerless in the council, he had hopes that Hastings would be superseded, and that he would be appointed to the vacant place. In June 1777 these hopes were dispelled upon Hastings's repudiation of his previous resignation and the decision of the supreme court in his favour. Clavering died 30 Aug. 1777. In the next month Francis wrote an elaborate letter to Lord North upon Indian affairs, separately printed in 1793. Wheler, sent out to succeed Hastings, arrived in Calcutta in November 1777, and generally acted with Francis as a member of council. They agreed in the following February to oppose 'the pernicious measures' of Hastings.

In 1778 Francis had an intrigue with the lovely wife, aged 16, of a Swiss officer in the East India Company's service, named Grand. In November Grand surprised Francis, who had entered Mme. Grand's room. An action was brought by Grand against Francis, who was sentenced to pay fifty thousand rupees damages by Impey (6 March 1779). Mme. Grand afterwards threw herself upon Francis's protection. She left India before him, and afterwards became the mistress, and in 1801 the wife, of Talleyrand.

In March 1779 Sir Eyre Coote succeeded Clavering as member of council and in command of the forces. Francis afterwards accused Hastings of buying Coote's support by large allowances, and says of Coote in November, in language suggesting Junius upon Barrington, 'I never heard of so abandoned a scoundrel.' The military difficulties now led to a truce with Hastings, in which Major Scott acted as negotiator. The political differences were compromised. Two of Francis's protégés were to be restored to the posts from which Hastings had removed them, and Francis undertook not to oppose Hastings in the management of the Mahratta war. Francis also joined with Hastings in opposing the pretensions of the supreme court under Impey. Francis and his new colleague Wheler were still on bad terms with Hastings. At last, in July 1780, Hastings accused Francis of breaking their agreement, and stated in an official minute that he had found Francis's private conduct to be 'void of truth and honour.' Francis's account was that his agreement referred only to the operations already begun and not to new movements intended by Hastings. A duel followed (17 Aug. 1780), in which Francis was severely wounded. He recovered in a few days, but took little active part in business afterwards, finding that Wheler was not hearty in supporting him. He left India at the end of 1780, and, after a long delay at St. Helena, reached

Dover on 19 Oct. 1781. Francis is said to have made judicious suggestions for the government of India, and to have proposed the permanent settlement of Bengal, afterwards carried out by Lord Cornwallis; but is remembered almost solely by his antagonism to Hastings.

Francis had realised a fortune amounting to over 3,000*l.* a year (MERIVALE, ii. 211). He had been accused of parsimony, and, as part of this fortune was due to his gambling, his salary of 10,000*l.* a year would enable him to make the rest without using the corruption imputed to many contemporary 'nabobs.' It has been suggested, but apparently without authority, that his appointment was clogged by the condition that he should pay part of his salary to a 'rider' (*Calcutta Review*). He was so unpopular on his arrival in England that no one, it is said (MERIVALE, ii. 204), except the king and Lord North, would speak to him when he first appeared at court. He seems (*ib.*) to have contributed many anonymous papers to the press. Attacks upon the Indian administration in the 'Intrepid Magazine' and 'A State of the British Authority in Bengal' (1781) are attributed to him. He was also supposed to have inspired a book called 'Travels in Europe, Asia, and America,' &c., published under the name of Macintosh. Francis solemnly denied the authorship; but he is shown to have paid Macintosh a sum of 1,000*l.* at this time, besides 'large advances' to his cousin, Major Baggs, although he equally denied that Baggs was his agent (*ib.* pp. 205, 206). An edition of Junius, without the name of printer or publisher, appeared in 1783, and has been attributed to Francis by Parkes (*Notes and Queries*, 17 Feb. 1855).

In April 1784 Francis was returned to parliament for Yarmouth, Isle of Wight. He failed as a speaker, although he prepared and reported his speeches with great care. Wyndham and Dr. Parr praised them highly; but he was pompous, didactic, and wanting in fluency (NICHOLL, *Recollections and Reflections*, 1822; WRAXALL, *Memoirs*, ii. 200), He was a keen whig, and became intimate with all the assailants of Hastings. He had made Burke's acquaintance before sailing for India, and during his stay here they had had some correspondence. Francis gave Burke information and advice in preparing the charges against Hastings, and in April 1787 he was proposed as one of the managers of the impeachment, but rejected after some sharp debates. The managers, however, asked him in very complimentary terms to assist them, and he was most eager and regular in his attendance at the trial. His own statement

of his share in preparing the impeachment and suggesting Burke's arguments is given by Merivale (ii. 287, 288).

In 1790 Francis was returned for Bletchingley. When Burke was alienated from the whigs by his views of the French revolution, Francis remonstrated with him, criticising his sentimental defence of Marie Antoinette with great severity, while Burke treated his dissent with special respect. Their correspondence, however, seems to have dropped, though Francis always spoke respectfully of his old friend.

Francis was an early reformer, and one of the founders of the 'Society of the Friends of the People,' of whose original programme (1793) he was in great part the author. He also was a strong opponent of the slave trade. In 1798 he was defeated in an election for Tewkesbury, but continued his intimacy with the whigs, and protested against Fox's secession. He became very intimate with Lord Thanet [see TUFTON, SACKVILLE], a radical reformer of the time, and was returned for Appleby in November 1802 by Thanet's influence. He had at this time many family losses, his daughter Harriet dying at Nice on 2 Jan. 1803, another daughter, Elizabeth, on 14 July 1804, and his wife on 5 April 1806.

One of his last performances was an elaborate speech upon India, 5 April 1805. He hoped for the governor-generalship upon the death of Cornwallis (5 Oct. 1805). In March 1806 he quarrelled with Fox for declining to promise him the appointment. The death of Pitt seemed to open the way, and at this period Francis was for some years on terms of close intimacy with the prince regent. Various accounts have been given of the negotiations which took place (see BROUGHAM, *Statesmen of the Time of George III*; and Lady Francis in MERIVALE, ii. 351–4). The governor-generalship was clearly out of the question, and Francis is said to have declined the government of the Cape. He had finally to content himself with the honour of adding K.C.B. to his name. Francis was re-elected for Appleby in December 1806, but on the election of 1807 he retired from parliamentary life.

The intimacy with the prince regent gradually declined as the prince dropped the whigs. Francis adhered to his rigid whiggism. At the end of 1814 he married his second wife, Miss Emma Watkins, daughter of a Yorkshire clergyman, born, as she states, ten years after the last Junius letter, or in 1782. He had corresponded with her from 1806, and seems to have been an affectionate husband. His amanuensis in later years was

Edward Dubois [q. v.], who published a life of Francis in the 'Monthly Mirror' for 1811. The publication of Taylor's 'Discovery of Junius' in 1813 (in which Junius is supposed to be the elder Francis, assisted by his son), and of 'Junius Identified' in 1816, put Francis in a difficult position. When the first was published, Francis wrote to the editor of the 'Monthly Magazine,' who wrote to him on the subject: 'Whether you will assist in giving currency to a silly, malignant falsehood is a question for your own consideration. To me it is a matter of perfect indifference.' After the appearance of the second, he behaved equivocally. His first present to his wife on their marriage was a copy of 'Junius's Letters,' and he left sealed up for her at his death a copy of 'Junius Identified.' She states that he never claimed to be Junius, but gives statements on his authority as to the circumstances of writing the letters, which could hardly have been made without expressly claiming the authorship. He withdrew from Brooks's Club in order, as she thought, to avoid awkward questions, and repelled direct inquiries with his usual severity. The anecdotes of Lady Francis (see MERIVALE, ii. 386–400) seem to establish this, although little reliance can be placed upon details.

Francis lived during his later years in St. James's Square, a place endeared to him, according to Lady Francis, because he had there acted as Chatham's amanuensis. He was known in society for his caustic humour, his intolerance of bores and long stories (which once led him to snub the prince regent), his real or affected penuriousness, and his old-fashioned gallantry to ladies. He suffered at the end from a painful disease, but retained his faculties to the last, and died quietly in his sleep 23 Dec. 1818.

A portrait of Francis by Hoppner is engraved in the first volume of Parkes and Merivale, and a caricature in the second. Francis had six children by his first wife: Sarah (b. 1763, died unmarried), Elizabeth (b. 1764, died unmarried 14 July 1804), Harriet (b. 1766, died unmarried 2 Jan. 1803), Philip (b. 1768, married Eliza Jane, daughter of Godshall Johnson of Putney, and left issue), Mary (b. 1770, married 1792 Godshall Johnson of Putney, who died 1800), and Catherine (b. 1772, married George James Cholmondeley).

Francis, whether Junius or not, was a man of great ability and unflagging industry; arrogant and vindictive in the extreme; unscrupulous in gratifying his enmities by covert insinuations and false assertions, yet courageous in attacking great men; rigid and even pedantic in his adherence to a set of princi-

ples which had their generous side; really scornful of meanness and corruption in others; and certainly doing much to vindicate the power of public opinion, although from motives which were not free from selfishness and the narrowest personal ambition. There may have been two such men, whose careers closely coincided during Francis's most vigorous period; but it seems more probable that there was only one.

Early collections of the letters of Junius were published by Newbery as the 'Political Convert,' 1769 (containing the Draper controversy); by Almon, 'Collection of Letters of Atticus, Lucius, Junius, and Others,' 1769; by A. Thomson, 'A Complete Collection of Junius's Letters' (reissued with additions). For a list of early editions see 'Notes and Queries,' 6th ser. v. 282, 342. Wheble printed collections 1770, 1771, 1772, 1775, the first without printer's name. The author's edition appeared in 1772. In 1783 appeared the new edition mentioned above. An edition by Robert Heron (for whom see *Notes and Queries*, 1st ser. vi. 445) appeared in 1802, another (with additions) in 1804, and Almon's edition appeared in 1806. The edition by George Woodfall, son of Henry Sampson Woodfall, 3 vols. 8vo, 1812, was edited with an anonymous introduction by J. Mason Good [q. v.] This edition included for the first time the private letters of Junius to H. S. Woodfall and to Wilkes. It also included a number of letters under different signatures not previously attributed to Junius. The publisher and editor had no private means of identifying Junius's letters; and some are almost certainly spurious. Others are identified by references in the private letters, or by the use of the letter 'C.' as a signature, or in notices to correspondents referring to letters. It is not certain that the same signature may not have been occasionally used by other correspondents. The identification is confirmed in a few cases by the letters to George Grenville (see above), which were not published till 1853. The original manuscripts of the letters to Woodfall and of a few of the later letters are now in the Woodfall MSS. in the British Museum, Addit. MSS. 27774–27788, where various other documents left by Woodfall are also preserved. Later editions of Junius are innumerable. The most convenient is Bohn's edition (1850 and later), edited by John Wade, which is a reprint of Woodfall's (1812) edition, with additional notes, taken in great part from Heron.

Francis printed separately many of his speeches in parliament, and the following pamphlets: 'Letter to Lord North,' 1793, and 'Letter to Lord Howick,' 1807, upon

India; 'Plan of Reform adopted by the Society of the Friends of the People in 1795,' reprinted in 1813; 'Proceedings in the House of Commons on the Slave Trade,' 1796; 'The Question as it stood in March 1798,' 1798; 'Reflections on the Abundance of Paper Money,' 1810; 'Letter to Lord Grey,' 1814 (upon the blockade of Norway), and 'Letter to Lord Holland,' 1816 (upon Irish policy); 'Historical Questions Exhibited,' in the 'Morning Chronicle' for January 1818 (upon the legitimacy of several royal families).

[The main authority for Francis's life is Memoirs of Sir Philip Francis, commenced by the late Joseph Parkes, completed and edited by Herman Merivale, 2 vols. 8vo, 1867 (founded on researches by Parkes, who had access to Francis's papers, but was very uncritical, and hastily put together by Merivale). See also the Memoirs by Dubois in the Mirror of 1811, reprinted in Taylor's Junius Identified; an article in the Gent. Mag. for January 1819, and one in the Annual Obituary for 1820, pp. 189–233. For the Indian career see Mr. Justice Stephen's Nuncomar and Impey, 1885; H. Beveridge's Trial of Maharaja Nanda Kumar, Calcutta, 1886; Calcutta Review, January 1845, pp. 561–608; Macaulay's Warren Hastings and the usual histories; H. E. Busteed's Echoes of Old Calcutta, 1882, pp. 72–165. Various anecdotes by Lady Francis are given in a letter printed in the notes to Campbell's Lord Loughborough in Lives of the Chancellors, 1847, vi. 344–7, in Wade's Junius, and in Parkes and Merivale; they are utterly untrustworthy. For remarks upon Francis's supposed authorship of Junius see Discovery of the Author of Junius (by John Taylor), 1813; the Identity of Junius with a Distinguished Living Character (by the same), 1816, and Supplement, 1817. For Taylor's statement that the book was exclusively by him, see Notes and Queries, 1st ser. iii. 258; Butler's Reminiscences, 1824, i. 73–107, ii. 120–6; E. H. Barker's Claims of Sir Philip Francis Disproved (privately printed 1827), 1828; Wraxall's Posthumous Memoirs, 1836, iii. 125–38; Dilke's Papers of a Critic, vol. ii.; A. Hayward's More about Junius, in Historical and Critical Essays; The Handwriting of Junius Investigated by Charles Chabot, with preface by Hon. E. Twisleton, 1871; Mahon's History, chap. xlvii.; Lecky's History, iii. 235–54; art. 'Chatham, Francis, and Junius,' by present writer, English Historical Review, April 1888; Mr. Fraser Rae, in Athenæum for 1888, ii. 192, 258, 319. A list of over fifty suggested authors is given in Halkett and Laing's Dictionary of Anonymous Literature and Cushing's Initials and Pseudonyms. Lists of books on the subject are in Lowndes's Manual, and Notes and Queries, 6th ser. v. 463. The following may be mentioned: In favour of BARRÉ, ISAAC: John Britton's Authorship of Junius Elucidated, 1841; of BOYD, HUGH [q.v.]: George Chalmers's Authorship of Junius Ascertained, with appendix to Supplemental

Apology, 1819; also Almon's Anecdotes, ii. 16, and Almon's Junius; of BURKE, WILLIAM: J. C. Symons's William Burke the Author of Junius, 1859; of CHATHAM: B. Waterhouse's Essay on Junius, 1841, John Swinden's Junius Lord Chatham, 1833, and William Dowe's Junius Lord Chatham, 1857; of CHESTERFIELD: W. Cramp's The Author of Junius Discovered in . . . Lord Chesterfield, 1821, and other books in 1823 and 1851; of DE LOLME: T. Busby's Arguments and Facts Demonstrating . . . 1816; of LAUGHLIN MACLEANE: Sir D. Brewster; of LORD LYTTELTON: Quarterly Review, vol. xc. (by David Trevena Coulton); of GOVERNOR POWNALL: Fred. Griffin's Junius Discovered, 1854; of LORD GEORGE SACKVILLE: G. Coventry's Critical Enquiry, 1825, and John Jaques's History of Junius, 1843; of LORD TEMPLE: Isaac Newhall's Letters on Junius, 1831, and W. J. Smith in Grenville Papers, iii. pp. xiii–ccxxviii; of JOHN HORNE TOOKE: John A. Graham's Memoirs of J. H. Tooke, 1829, and [J. Bellows] Posthumous Works of Junius, 1829; of D. WILMOT: Olivia Serres Wilmot's Junius: Sir Philip Francis denied; of DANIEL WRAY: James Falconer's The Secret Revealed, 1830. The Anecdotes of Junius, 1788, were reprinted from 'Anecdotes' prefixed to the so-called 'Piccadilly' edition of 1771, assuming E. Burke to be the author. The opinion was common at the time, from Burke's unique combination of literary and political fame, but was solemnly denied by him, and is intrinsically incredible. In 1841 Mr. N. W. Simons reprinted 'A Letter to an Honourable Brigadier-General' (1760), which he ascribed to Junius on (worthless) internal evidence.] L. S.

FRANCIS, THOMAS, M.D. (d. 1574), president of the College of Physicians, a native of Chester, was educated at Christ Church, Oxford, as a member of which he was admitted B.A. 19 June 1540, and M.A. 7 July 1544. 'After he had taken the degree of M. of A.,' says Wood, 'he applyed his studies to the theological faculty, but the encouragement thereof being in these days but little, he transfer'd himself to the school of physicians, and, with the consent and approbation of Dr. Wryght, the vice-chancellor, was entred on the physic line, 4 [7] Aug. 1550. In the year after, I find him supplying the place and office of the king's professor of physic, being, I presume, only deputy for Dr. John Warner' (Fasti Oxon. ed. Bliss, i. 143–4). He received the degree of M.B. and license to practise 9 March 1554–5, and commenced M.D. on the following 29 July (Reg. of Univ. of Oxford, Oxf. Hist. Soc. i. 198, 299). In the beginning of 1554–5 he succeeded Warner in the regius professorship, which he resigned in 1561 to become provost of Queen's College. The appointment was not a popular one, and 'serious disturbances' took place at his inauguration (Letter of Francis, Calfhill, and others to

Cecil, dated from Oxford, 11 May 1561 in *Cal. State Papers,* Dom. 1547–80, p. 175). He retired from the provostship in 1563. He was admitted a fellow of the College of Physicians, 21 Oct. 1560, at the comitia specially convened for that purpose. He was censor in 1561 and the three following years; was provisionally named elect 30 Sept. 1562 in place of Dr. John Clement, 'a second time gone abroad,' and was definitely appointed to that office 12 May 1564. He was president of the college in 1568, and consiliarius in 1571. Francis was physician in ordinary to Queen Elizabeth, and, according to Wood, much respected by her. While president he had some trouble with the quack Eliseus Bomelius [q. v.], whom he was obliged to prosecute for practising physic without a license from the college. Bomelius in his letters to Cecil offered to expose the ignorance of Francis in Latin and astronomy, but at the prospect of his enlargement apologised for having circulated such false statements (*ib.* pp. 292, 304). Francis lived in Silver Street, in the parish of St. Olave, London. He died in 1574. By his will, dated 8 April and proved 9 Nov. 1574, though he left his wife Anne comfortably provided for, he was more solicitous for the welfare of one 'Edwarde Marbecke alias ffraunces, a yonge childe, nowe or late withe me in house dwellinge.' He names as his executors Roger Marbeck and John Riche (will registered in P. C. C. 41, Martyn).

[Munk's Coll. of Phys, (1878), i. 61–2.] G. G.

FRANCISCUS À SANCTÂ CLARÂ. [See DAVENPORT, CHRISTOPHER (1598–1680), Franciscan and controversialist.]

FRANCK, RICHARD (1624?–1708), captain in the parliamentary service, was born and educated at Cambridge, but probably was not a member of the university, unless it be thought (with Sir W. Scott) that 'some degree of learning was necessary to have formed so very uncommon and pedantic a style' (*Memoir*, p. 1). When the civil war broke out he left Cambridge to 'seek umbrage in the city of London,' and became a Cromwellian trooper, when he probably obtained the rank of captain, for he is addressed in one of the recommendatory poems prefixed to his Scotch travels as 'my honoured friend, Captain Richard Franck.' He has indeed been thought to have served in the royalist army, but his panegyric on the Protector, his enumeration of the six great patriots of the English nation, Ireton, Vane, Nevill, Martin, Marvell, and Cromwell, together with his flouting of the cavalier angler, Izaak Walton, forbids the supposition. Nor

does his name appear among the army lists of the king. In the uncertainty and religious confusions which ensued upon the rise of Cromwell to power, Franck left England for a tour in Scotland. This must have been about 1656 or 1657, and his love of travel led him to the extreme north of the kingdom, 'when,' he says, 'to admiration I inspected that little artick world and every angle of it.' He returned to Nottingham, where he seems to have lived many years. About 1690 he went to America, where his second book was written, and in 1694 was in London at the Barbican. It may be gathered that he had a wife, whom in his 'Northern Memoirs' he calls Constantia. He wrote to her during his journey north. Of his death nothing can be learnt.

The book which has made Franck famous is an excellent specimen of euphuistic literature. Its title runs 'Northern Memoirs, calculated for the Meridian of Scotland. Wherein most or all of the Cities, Citadels, Sea-ports, Castles, Forts, Fortresses, Rivers, and Rivulets are compendiously described. Together with choice Collections of various Discoveries, Remarkable Observations, Theological Notions, Political Axioms, National Intrigues, Polemick Inferences, Contemplations, Speculations, and several curious and industrious Inspections, lineally drawn from Antiquaries and other noted and intelligible Persons of Honour and Eminency. To which is added the Contemplative and Practical Angler by way of Diversion,' with more of the same character. 'By Richard Franck, Philanthropus. Plures necat Gula quam Gladius, 1694.' The rest of the work is equally cumbrous. No less than four dedications must be confronted, a preface, an address in rhyme to his book, four recommendatory poems by as many writers, and then another poem 'to the poet' by the author, before the book itself is reached. It is in the form of a dialogue between Theophanes, Agrippa (a servant), Aquila (a friend), and himself, under the name Arnoldus, and the style is bombastic, stilted, and pedantic to a degree, 'drawn from the rough draught of a martial pen,' as Franck himself describes it. The author was evidently a mystic, deeply tinged with Böhme's tenets, and not improbably deranged on certain subjects. Sir W. Scott compares his style with that of Sir Thomas Urquhart's translation of 'Rabelais,' but in verbosity and affectation Franck exceeds Urquhart. 'Northern Memoirs' was written in 1658, put together in 1685, and not published till 1694. Its main interest centres in the places which Franck visited in Scotland, and the account of them which he gives.

His route was by Carlisle and Dumfries to Glasgow; thence to Stirling, Perth, Forfar, and Loch Ness; Sutherlandshire and Caithness, Cromarty, Aberdeen, Dundee, St. Andrews, Edinburgh, and Berwick, were next seen, and he made his way home by Morpeth. For anglers the book possesses great attraction. Franck is the first to describe salmon-fishing in Scotland, and both in that and trout-fishing with artificial fly he proves himself an excellent practical angler. His rules for fly-fishing, and especially for salmon-fishing, cannot be improved at present. Internal evidence shows that he had read the 'Compleat Angler;' indeed he tells us that he had argued with Walton at Stafford on the fact related by the latter of pickerel weed breeding pike, and that Walton laid it on Gesner and then 'huffed away.' Franck loses no opportunity of scoffing at him. He incidentally mentions Nottingham as being even in his time the nursery of many good anglers, describes their famous ' pith bait ' and the breeding of salmon, and commends the dressing of a fly which could not be improved upon at the present day. He is the first angler to name that curious fish of the Trent, the burbot, and highly commends the salmon of the Thames, especially those caught below bridge. The rudiments of angling he learnt in the Cam, but perfected himself in the Trent. His puritanism frequently breaks out while discoursing of angling. He says of religion after the Restoration, 'It is worn so threadbare that nothing save the name is left to cover it.' It is plain that he read Shirley's poems.

Franck's second book is entitled ' A Philosophical Treatise of the Original and Production of Things. Writ in America in a time of solitude,' London, 1687. The running head title of the work is 'Rabbi Moses.' It is written in the same high-flown language as ' Northern Memoirs,' but is devoid of interest. Franck also probably wrote ' The Admirable and Indefatigable Adventures of the Nine Pious Pilgrims . . . to the New Jerusalem. Written in America in a time of Solitude and Divine Contemplation. By a Zealous Lover of Truth . . .' London (Morphew), 1708. The introductory matter is signed ' Philanthropos ' as in Franck's other books. The style supports the ascription.

[Memoir by Sir W. Scott, prefixed to an edition of the Northern Memoirs, 1821, see Lockhart's Life, v. 134, ed. 1837; Westwood and Satchell's Bibliotheca Piscatoria, p. 100; Retrospective Review, viii. 170; Censura Literaria, vi. 11; Westwood's Chronicle of the Compleat Angler, 1864, p. 13; Notes and Queries, 5th ser. vi. 27.]

M. G. W.

FRANCKLIN, THOMAS (1721–1784), miscellaneous writer, son of Richard Francklin, bookseller near the Piazza in Covent Garden, London, who printed Pulteney's paper, ' The Craftsman,' was born in 1721, and admitted into Westminster School in 1735. In 1739 he was elected second from the school to Trinity College, Cambridge, where he was admitted on 21 June 1739, and took the degrees of B.A. in 1742, M.A. 1746, and D.D. in 1770. In 1745 he was elected to a minor fellowship, was promoted in the next year to be 'socius major,' and resided in college until the end of 1758. On the advice and encouragement of Pulteney he was educated for the church, but that statesman forgot his promises, and rendered Francklin no assistance in life. He was for some time an usher in his old school, and on 27 June 1750 was elected to the honourable, if not profitable, post of Greek professor at Cambridge. Later in the same year he was involved in a dispute with the heads of the university. Forty-six old boys of Westminster met between eight and nine o'clock on 17 Nov. at the Tuns Tavern to commemorate, as was their custom, the accession of Queen Elizabeth, and Francklin was in the chair. The party was just about to separate at eleven o'clock, when the senior proctor appeared and somewhat rudely called upon them to disperse. Many of the graduates present resented the summons, and hot words ensued. Several pamphlets were afterwards published, and among them was one from Francklin entitled ' An Authentic Narrative of the late Extraordinary Proceedings at Cambridge against the W . . . r Club,' 1751. Further particulars concerning the disturbance and the subsequent proceedings in the vice-chancellor's court will be found in Wordsworth's 'Social Life at the English Universities in the Eighteenth Century,' pp. 70–5. He resigned his professorship in 1759, and on 2 Jan. of that year was instituted, on presentation of his college, to the vicarage of Ware in Hertfordshire, which he held in conjunction with the lectureship of St. Paul's, Covent Garden, and a proprietary chapel in Queen Street, London. As a popular preacher his services were often in requisition. He was appointed king's chaplain in November 1767, and was selected to preach the commencement sermon at St. Mary's, Cambridge, on the installation of the Duke of Grafton as chancellor of the university in 1770. Through the favour of Archbishop Cornwallis he was appointed in 1777 to the rectory of Brasted in Kent, whereupon he vacated the living of Ware. For the greater part of his life Francklin was compelled, by want of lucrative preferment, to write for the press and for the stage. His plays were more numerous than original, but two of them met, through the excellence of the acting, with considerable success. He brought out in 1757 a periodical paper of his own composition entitled 'The Centinel,' and he was one of the contributors to Smollett's 'Critical Review.' Dr. Johnson and Sir Joshua Reynolds were among his friends, and through their influence he was exalted to the place of chaplain to the Royal Academy on its foundation, when he addressed the associates 'in good old lyric commonplaces,' and on Goldsmith's death in 1774 succeeded to the professorship of ancient history. It has been generally assumed that he was the 'Tho. Franklin' who signed the round-robin to Johnson on the Latin epitaph to Goldsmith; but Dr. Hill says, on account of the omission of the letter c in the name, and the difference in the handwriting from his acknowledged signature, 'he certainly was not,' but no other bearer of the name was sufficiently prominent among their friends to justify such a conspicuous honour. With the generality of literary men he was unpopular. One of his victims in the 'Critical Review' was Arthur Murphy, who solaced his feelings of indignation in 'A Poetical Epistle to Samuel Johnson, A.M.,' whereupon it is said that Francklin 'had recourse to the law for protection, and swore the peace' against Murphy (*Biog. Dramatica*, 1812 ed., i. 253-6). Churchill, in the 'Rosciad,' sneeringly says that 'he sicken'd at all triumphs but his own,' and in the poem of 'The Journey,' exclaims, with less reason, let

> Francklin, proud of some small Greek,
> Make Sophocles, disguis'd in English, speak.

After a laborious life Francklin died in Great Queen Street, London, 15 March 1784. He married, on 20 Jan. 1759, Miss Venables, the daughter of a wine merchant; she died in Great Queen Street, 24 May 1796.

Francklin's most profitable works consisted of translations and tragedies. His first venture was an anonymous rendering of Cicero's treatise, 'Of the Nature of the Gods,' which appeared in 1741, was reissued in 1775, and, after revision by C. D. Yonge, formed a part of one of the volumes in Bohn's 'Classical Library.' In 1749 he published 'The Epistles of Phalaris translated from the Greek; to which are added some select epistles of the most eminent Greek writers.' His translation of the tragedies of Sophocles was long considered the best in the English language. It came out in 1759, and was reprinted in 1809 and 1832, large selections from it were included in Sanford's 'British Poets,' vol. l.,

and it has recently been included in Professor Henry Morley's 'Universal Library' (vol. xliv.), while a separate impression of the 'Œdipus Tyrannus' was struck off in 1806. Equal popularity attended his version of 'The Works of Lucian from the Greek,' which was produced in 1780 in two volumes, and appeared in a second edition in 1781. The whole work was dedicated to Rigby, the politician, and parts were inscribed to other eminent men, the most famous of whom were Bishop Douglas, Dr. Johnson, 'the Demonax of the present age,' Sir Joshua Reynolds, and Edmund Burke. His translation of Lucian's 'Trips to the Moon' forms vol. lxxi. of Cassell's 'National Library,' edited by Professor Henry Morley. Francklin's plays are: 1. 'The Earl of Warwick,' which was produced at Drury Lane Theatre on 13 Dec. 1766, and was often represented. On its first appearance Mrs. Yates created a great impression in the part of Margaret of Anjou, and Mrs. Siddons in later years made that character equally successful. The whole play, which is said to have been taken without any acknowledgment from the French of La Harpe, was printed in 1766 and 1767, and was included in the collections of Bell, Mrs. Inchbald, Dibdin, and many others. 2. 'Matilda,' first presented at Drury Lane on 21 Jan. 1775, was also profitable to the author, as is shown in the balance-sheet in Garrick's 'Correspondence,' ii. 44. It appeared in print in 1775, and was also included in several theatrical collections. 3. 'The Contract,' brought out at the Haymarket on 12 June 1776, and printed in the same year, was a failure, although it deserved a better fate. The chief characters were two persons who had made a contract of marriage, parted, and on meeting again after many years, wished the engagement broken off. 4. 'Mary Queen of Scots,' which was several times announced but was never acted, and remained in manuscript until 1837, when it was edited by the author's eldest son, Lieutenant-colonel William Francklin [q. v.], once of the Hon. East India Company's service.

Francklin's other literary productions were very numerous. Their titles were: 1. 'Translation,' a poem, 1753, which condemned many previous attempts at translation, and appealed to abler men to undertake the task, ending with the preliminary puff of his proposal to print by subscription a version of Sophocles. 2. 'Enquiry into the Astronomy and Anatomy of the Ancients,' 1749, and said to have been reprinted in 1775. 3. 'Truth and Falsehood, a Tale,' 1755, issued anonymously, and panegyrising the then Duchess of Bedford. 4. 'The Centinel,' 1757 fol., 1758 12mo, a periodical paper, one of the numberless imitations of the 'Tatler and 'Spectator.' 5. 'A Dissertation on Ancient Tragedy,' 1760, given gratis to the subscribers to his translation of Sophocles. 6. 'A Letter to a Bishop concerning Lectureships,' ' a piece of humour ' on the manner of election to such posts, and the miserable pay attaching thereto. Between 1748 and 1779 Francklin printed nine single sermons preached on charitable and special occasions, the most important of which was that delivered at St. George's, Bloomsbury, in May 1756, on the death of the Rev. John Sturges, from which it appears that he had hoped to succeed him in that position. An entire volume of his sermons on 'The Relative Duties' was published in 1765, and passed into a fourth edition in 1788. He died without leaving adequate provision for his family, and in 1785 there appeared for his widow's relief two volumes of 'Sermons on Various Subjects,' followed by a third in 1787. Francklin lent his name, in conjunction with Smollett, to a translation of Voltaire's works and letters, but the 'Orestes' (produced at Covent Garden Theatre 13 March 1769 for the benefit of Mrs. Yates) and the 'Electra' (brought out at Drury Lane 15 Oct. 1774) are believed to have been his sole share in the publication. Some of his fugitive pieces were embodied in the 'Miscellaneous Pieces' brought together by Tom Davies, and there are many of his letters in the 'Garrick Correspondence.'

[Welch's Westm. School (1852 ed.), pp. 311, 321, 326; Forshall's Westminster, pp. 108–9, 229–30; Hill's Boswell, i. 355, iii. 83, iv. 34; Cussans's Hertfordshire, vol. i. pt. i. p. 154; Taylor's Sir Joshua Reynolds, i. 261–2, 310, 317, ii. 73, 162; Gent. Mag. 1759, p. 45, 1784, pt. i. pp. 238–9, 1796, pt. i. p. 446; Genest, v. 119–120, 242–6, 441–7, 528–9; Churchill's Works (1804), i. 7–8, 82, ii. 367; Nichols's Lit. Anecd. ii. 594, vi. 425; Hasted's Kent, i. 381; Records of Trin. Coll. Cambr.]　　W. P. C.

FRANCKLIN, WILLIAM (1763–1839), orientalist, born in 1763, was the eldest son of Thomas Francklin (1721–1784) [q. v.], by his wife Miss Venables. He was admitted on the foundation at Westminster in 1777, whence he was elected to Trinity College, Cambridge, in 1781. Preferring to engage in the profession of arms, he was admitted a cadet in the service of the East India Company in 1782, appointed ensign of the 19th regiment of Bengal native infantry 31 Jan. 1783, lieutenant 20 Oct. 1789, captain in the army 7 June 1796, captain in his regiment 30 Sept. 1803, major in the army 25 April 1808, major in his regiment 29 March 1810, lieutenant-colonel in the army 4 June 1814,

and in his regiment on 16 Dec. of the same year. On being invalided, 1 Oct. 1815, he was made regulating officer at Bhaugulpore. He retired in India in December 1825, and died 12 April 1839, aged 76. A distinguished officer, Francklin also enjoyed considerable reputation as an oriental scholar. In 1786 he made a tour in Persia, in the course of which he resided for eight months at Shiraz as an inmate of a Persian family, and was thus enabled to communicate a fuller account of the manners of the people than had before appeared. His journal was published as ' Observations made on a Tour from Bengal to Persia in . . . 1786–7; with a short account of the remains of the . . . Palace of Persepolis,' 4to, Calcutta, 1788 (reprinted in vol. ix. of J. Pinkerton's 'General Collection of Voyages,' 4to, 1808, &c.) A French version, 'Voyage du Bengal à Chyraz,' was published in vols. ii. and iii. of ' Collection portative de voyages traduits de différentes langues orientales,' 12mo, Paris [1797, &c.] His next work, 'The History of the Reign of Shah-Aulum, the present Emperor of Hindostan. . . . With an Appendix,' 4to, London, 1798, serves as an important continuation of the 'Seir ul Mutákherin, or History of Modern Times.' Francklin also published: 1. ' The Loves of Camarúpa and Cámalatà, an ancient Indian Tale . . . translated from the Persian' [version by Na'ámat Allah?], 12mo, London, 1793. 2. ' Remarks and Observations on the Plain of Troy, made during an Excursion in June 1799,' 4to, London, 1800. 3. 'Military Memoirs of Mr. George Thomas, who . . . rose . . . to the rank of a General in the service of the native powers in . . . India. . . . Compiled and arranged from Mr. Thomas's original documents (Appendix),' 4to, Calcutta, 1803; 8vo, London, 1805. 4. 'Tracts, Political, Geographical, and Commercial; on the dominions of Ava, and the North-Western parts of Hindostaun,' 8vo, London, 1811. 5. 'Miscellaneous Remarks, in two parts: 1st. On Vincent's Geography of Susiana. 2nd. Supplementary Note on the Site of the ancient City of Palibothra,' 4to, Calcutta, 1813. 6. 'Inquiry concerning the Site of ancient Palibothra,' &c. 4 pts. 4to, London, 1815–22. 7. ' Researches on the Tenets and Doctrines of the Jeynes and Boodhists; conjectured to be the Brachmanes of ancient India. In which is introduced a discussion on the worship of the serpent in various countries of the world,' 4to, London, 1827. To vol. iv. of 'Asiatick Researches' (1795), pp. 419–32, he contributed 'An Account of the present State of Delhi;' while to vol. ii. of 'Miscellaneous Translations from Oriental Languages,' published in 1834 by the Oriental

Translation Fund, he furnished an 'Account of the Grand Festival held by the Amír Timúr . . . A. H. 803. Translated . . . from the Mulfuzat Timuri, or Life of Timur, written by himself.' In 1837 he published his father's historical play, 'Mary Queen of Scots.' He maintained a learned correspondence with Dean Vincent, who was second master during the time he was at Westminster; and Francklin was one of the few persons to whom the dean acknowledged obligations in the preface to the 'Periplus,' 1800–5. Francklin was a member, and during the later years of his life librarian and member of the council, of the Royal Asiatic Society. He was also member of the Calcutta Asiatic Society.

[Preface to Thomas Francklin's Mary Queen of Scots; Welch's Alumni Westmon. (1852), pp. 407, 414–15; Dodwell and Miles's List of Officers of Indian Army, pp. 102–3; East India Registers; Journal of Royal Asiatic Society, vol. v. Annual Report, 11 May 1839, pp. ii–iii; Asiatic Journal, new ser. vol. xxix. pt. ii. p. 80.] G. G.

FRANK, MARK, D.D. (1613–1664), theologian, born at Brickhill, Buckinghamshire, in 1613, was admitted pensioner of Pembroke College, Cambridge, 4 July 1627. He was elected to a scholarship in 1630, and to a fellowship 8 Oct. 1634, having become M.A. the same year. In 1641 he became B.D., and was chosen junior treasurer of his college, and senior treasurer in 1642. Two years later he was ejected as a malignant by the parliamentary visitors, on his refusal to take the covenant, and ordered to leave Cambridge. We are told that he bore his long period of deprivation 'with patience and constancy.' Before his ejection he had attracted the favourable notice of Charles I by a sermon he preached at Paul's Cross before the lord mayor and aldermen in 1641 on Jeremiah xxxv. 18–19, which the king commanded to be printed. In this sermon he propounds the Rechabites as an example of obedience 'never more needful' than then, and gives a strongly drawn picture of the troubles of the time, describing the insults to the monarch, the bishops, and the clergy. 'It is a usual thing nowadays,' he says, 'to direct our governours what to do, what to read, what to command; then, forsooth, we will obey them.' At the Restoration Frank was re-established in his fellowship 10 Aug. 1660, and his learning and loyalty were rewarded by a long series of well-deserved ecclesiastical promotions. He was made D.D. by royal mandate in 1661, and was chosen master of his college 23 Aug. 1662, in succession to Dr. Laney, elevated to the see of Peterborough. Archbishop Juxon appointed him one of his chaplains, and he held the office of domestic chaplain and *ex-officio* licenser of theological works to Juxon's successor, Archbishop Sheldon, by whom he was presented to the archdeaconry of St. Albans, and to the treasurership of St. Paul's 19 Dec. 1660, and 22 April 1662 collated to the prebendal stall of Islington in the same cathedral. He was also presented to the rectory of Barley, Hertfordshire, 2 Feb. 1663–4, by Bishop Wren, a preferment he enjoyed but a short time, his death taking place the same year, at the age of fifty-one. He was buried in St. Paul's Cathedral, near the entrance of the north door. By his will he bequeathed 100*l*. and 360 volumes of books to St. Paul's Cathedral. Frank is chiefly known by a 'Course of Sermons for all the Sundays and Festivals throughout the Year,' originally published after his death, with a portrait, in 1672, and republished, in two volumes, in the 'Library of Anglo-Catholic Theology.' The series includes several sermons for the chief days of the christian year, there being nine for Christmas day, three for the Epiphany, five for Easter day, &c. The sermon on the Rechabites already mentioned, preached at Paul's Cross, is added, and one preached in St. Paul's Cathedral. These sermons deserve notice as the productions of a sound but not extreme churchman—plain, sensible, and evangelical discourses. In their scholarly character and shrewd incisiveness they recall the sermons of Bishop Andrewes, which they resemble also in their divisions and subdivisions, according to the fashion of the age. The divisions, however, are natural, not artificial, and are calculated to bring out and elucidate the real meaning of the text, and the lessons it was intended to convey.

[Attwood's Manuscript List of Masters of Pembroke; Kennet's Biographical Notices Lansd. MS. 986, No. 21, p. 54; Baker's MSS. vi. 297; biographical notice prefixed to sermons in Library A.-C. T.] E. V.

FRANKLAND, JOCOSA or JOYCE (1531–1587), philanthropist, the daughter of Robert Trappes, a citizen and goldsmith of London, by his wife Joan, was born in London in 1531. She married, first Henry Saxey, a 'merchant venturer,' and afterwards William (?) Frankland of Rye House, Hertfordshire, whom also she outlived. By her first husband she had an only son, William Saxey, a student of Gray's Inn, to whom she was greatly attached, and who died at Rye House 22 Aug. 1581, aged 23. Conjointly with him she had founded junior fellowships and scholarships at Caius and Emmanuel Colleges, Cambridge, and after his death and that of her second husband, who was perhaps unsympathetic, she determined to devote her wealth to educational endowments, as the most congenial tribute to the memory of her son. At Newport Ponds, Essex, she founded a free school. To Lincoln College, Oxford, she gave 3l. a year in augmentation of four scholarships founded by her mother, Joan Trappes, and to Brasenose College she left by her will, dated 20 Feb. 1586, both land and houses for the increase of the emoluments of the principal and fellows, and for the foundation of an additional fellowship, the holder of which was to be by preference a member of either the Trappes or Saxey families. She also provided maintenance for four scholars and a yearly stipend for an under-reader in logic and for a bible-clerk. In recognition of Jocosa Frankland's generosity her name was included in the grace after meat repeated daily in the college hall; and after her death, which occurred at Aldermanbury, London, 1587, the principals and fellows of Brasenose erected a monument to her memory in the church of St. Leonard's, Foster Lane, where she was buried. In the same church, which was destroyed in the fire of London, her father's tomb bore the too depreciatory epitaph :

When the bells be merely [merrily] rung
And the Masse devoutly sung
And the meate merely eaten,
Then shall Robert Trappis, his wyffe, and his
children be forgotten.

In the hall of Brasenose College is a portrait of Jocosa Frankland with some Latin verses inscribed, commencing :

Trapsi nata fui, Saxy sponsata marito,
  Gulielmo mater visa beata meo.
Mors matura patrem, sors abstulit atra maritum;
  Filius heu rapida morte peremptus obit.

The existence of the husband Frankland is throughout ignored. The portrait was engraved by Fittler. Another portrait is in the master's gallery in the Combination Room at Caius College, Cambridge.

[Wood's Hist. and Antiq. of Oxford, ed. Gutch, pp. 240, 358, 360, 369; Newcourt's Rep. Eccl. Lond., i. 393 ; Stow's Survey of London and Westm. ed. 1633, p. 325 ; Clutterbuck's Hist. of Hertfordshire, iii. 247 ; Cole MSS. v. 34, lvi. 350; Evans's Cat. of Portraits.]   A. V.

FRANKLAND, RICHARD (1630–1698), nonconformist tutor, son of John Frankland, was born on 1 Nov. 1630, at Rathmell, a hamlet in the parish of Giggleswick, Yorkshire. The Franklands of Thirkleby, Yorkshire (baronets from 1660), with whom John Frankland was connected, were originally from Giggleswick (Surtees Society,

vol. xxxviii.) Frankland was educated (1640–1648) at Giggleswick grammar school, and was admitted on 18 May 1648 as minor pensionary at Christ's College, Cambridge. The tone of his college, under the mastership of Samuel Bolton, D.D. [q. v.], was that of a cultured puritanism. Frankland, like Oliver Heywood [q. v.], received lasting impressions from the preaching of Samuel Hammond [q. v.], lecturer (till 1652) at St. Giles'. He was a hard student, and took his degrees with distinction (B.A. 1651, M.A. 1655).

After graduating, Frankland preached for short periods at Hexham, Northumberland ; Houghton-le-Spring, Durham; and Lanchester, Durham. At Lanchester he received presbyterian ordination on 14 Sept. 1653. 'Discouragements' led him to remove to a chaplaincy at Ellenthorp Hall, near Boroughbridge, West Riding, in the family of John Brook (d. 1693), twice lord mayor of York, and a strong presbyterian. Frankland left Ellenthorp to become curate to Lupthern, rector of Sedgefield, Durham. Sir Arthur Haslerig [q. v.] put him into the rich vicarage of Bishop Auckland, Durham, some time before August 1659. Some post was designed for him in the college at Durham, for which Cromwell had issued a patent on 15 May 1657. His patron, Haslerig, was interested in the success of this college, which died at the Restoration.

At Bishop Auckland, where two of his children were born, Frankland confined himself to his parochial duties. After the Restoration he was one of the first to be attacked for nonconformity. His living was in the bishop's gift, but Cosin (consecrated 2 Dec. 1660) did not interfere with a peaceable man. An attorney named Bowster demanded of him, 'publickly before the congregation,' whether he intended to conform. Frankland thought it would be time to answer this question when the terms of conformity had been settled; and meanwhile relied on the king's declaration (25 Oct. 1660) dispensing with conformity. Bowster, with a neighbouring clergyman, got possession of the keys and locked Frankland out of his church. He indicted them for riot, but the case was dismissed at the assizes for a technical flaw in the indictment. Cosin now offered to institute Frankland and give him higher preferment if he would receive episcopal ordination. He even proposed, but without result, to ordain him conditionally, and 'so privately that the people might not know of it.' By the act of 1661 Frankland was confirmed in the possession of his living; but the uniformity act of the following year ejected him.

In 1662 Frankland retired to his patrimony at Rathmell, where he lived some years in privacy. His children were baptised (1664 and 1668) at the parish church. At this period he did not join the ranks of the 'conventicle' preachers. Efforts were being made by the nonconformists of the north to secure the educational advantages offered for a short time by the Durham College. William Pell, who had been a fellow of Magdalene College, Cambridge, and a tutor at Durham, declined to start an academical institution, holding himself precluded by his graduation oath from resuming collegiate lectures outside the ancient universities. Application was then successfully made to Frankland, who was not hindered by the same scruple. Nonconformist tutors usually understood the oath as referring to prelections in order to a degree. Before opening his 'academy' Frankland was in London, where he felt 'a violent impulse upon his mind to go to the king.' By the help of ' the old Earl of Manchester, lord chamberleyne' (Edward Montagu, *d.* 5 May 1671), he gained an audience while Charles was on his way to the council. Frankland, in the divine name, enjoined Charles 'to reform your life, your family, your kingdom, and the church,' adding an impressive warning. '" I wil," saith the king, "do what I can."' After a few more words 'the king hasted away, saying, "I thank you, sir," and twice looking back before he went into the counsel-chamber, said, "I thank you, sir; I thank you"' (ASPLAND, from Sampson's *Day-book*, Addit. MS. 4460, p. 28).

Early in March 1670 Frankland began to receive students at Rathmell. His first student was George, youngest son of Sir Thomas Liddell, bart., of Ravensworth Castle, Durham, head of a family distinguished for its loyalty, though marked by puritan leanings. Some of his students were intended for the legal, others for the medical profession; his first divinity students belonged to the independent denomination. It was not till the indulgence of 1672 (15 March), from which Stillingfleet dates the presbyterian separation, that divinity students connected with that body were sent to Rathmell, and the earliest nonconformist 'academy' (as distinct from a mere school) became an important institution and the model of others. The course of studies in this 'northern academy' included 'logic, metaphysics, somatology, pneumatology, natural philosophy, divinity, and chronology.' The lectures were in Latin, and given by Frankland until he had trained up assistants, among whom were John Issot, Richard Frankland (the tutor's son) and John

Owen. The discipline of the house was strict, but Frankland always succeeded in gaining the confidence of his students, and maintained his authority with 'admirable temper.' Morning prayers were at seven, winter and summer; lectures were over by noon, but solitary study went on after dinner till six o'clock prayers, and supper was followed by discussion of the day's work, unhampered by the tutor's presence. Those who wished to graduate went on to Scotland, where they were promoted to a degree after one session's attendance. The total number of Frankland's students was 304; among the best known of his divinity students are William Tong (entered 2 March 1681), Joshua Bayes [q. v.], and John Evans, D.D. [q. v.] (entered 26 May 1697), leaders of the presbyterian interest in London. John Disney (1677–1730) [q. v.] entered as a law student on 5 July 1695. The ministry of dissent in the north of England was chiefly recruited from Frankland's academy, as the ejected of 1662 gradually died out.

The academy had six migrations from place to place. In consequence of the indulgence, Frankland had begun to preach at Rathmell, and though 'no very taking' preacher, his solid discourses gained him a call from a congregation in Westmoreland. At Natland, near Kendal, the dissenters of the neighbourhood held their worship, the parochial chapel being in ruins. Frankland moved hither with his academy in 1674 (between 20 Feb. and 26 May). The congregation increased under his care, and he extended his labours to Kendal and elsewhere. The first nonconformist ordination in Yorkshire was held (10 July 1678) at his instigation and with his assistance. He met with considerable opposition, but the first definite reference to proceedings against him occurs in a manuscript notebook of Oliver Heywood, under date 29 May 1681. Frankland had been excommunicated in the ecclesiastical court; his friends had obtained an absolution for him, upon which the official gave notice 'that Mr. Richard Frankland, the ringleader of the sectarys, hath voluntarily submitted himself to the orders of the church and is reconciled to it,' &c. (ASPLAND). The report ran that Frankland had conformed and got a good living. Early in 1683 the enforcement of the Five Miles Act compelled him to leave Natland as being too near to Kendal. He transferred his academy to Calton Hall, the seat of the Lamberts, in the parish of Kirkby Malham, West Riding, and in 1684 to Dawson Fold in Westmoreland, just outside the five-miles radius from Kendal. In 1685 (a year in which two of his former students were imprisoned at York, and the only year in which his academy received no accessions) he retired to Hart Barrow, near to Cartmell Fell, just inside the Lancashire border, and so convenient for escaping a writ for either county. Late in 1686 Frankland availed himself of James II's arbitrary exercise of the dispensing power, took out a fifty shilling dispensation, and removed to Attercliffe, a suburb of Sheffield, Yorkshire. He left Attercliffe at the end of July 1689, in consequence of the death of his favourite son, and returned to Rathmell. His pupil Timothy Jollie [q. v.], independent minister at Sheffield, began another academy at Attercliffe on a more restricted principle than Frankland's, excluding mathematics 'as tending to scepticism.'

Frankland carried his academy with him back to Rathmell, and during the remaining nine years of his life he admitted nearly as many students as in the whole previous period of over nineteen years. His congregation also throve, and he maintained harmony among its members at a time when many were beginning to relax their hold of the Calvinism to which he himself adhered. But while the Toleration Act protected him as a preacher, hardly a year passed without some fresh attempt on the part of the authorities to put down his academy. For not answering a citation to the archbishop's (Lamplugh) court he was again excommunicated; at the instance of Lord Wharton and Sir Thomas Rokeby, William III ordered his absolution, which was read in Giggleswick Church. Soon after the consecration of Sharp as archbishop of York (5 July 1691) new alarm was excited by the assembling of twenty-four nonconformist ministers at Wakefield (2 Sept.) to consider the 'heads of agreement' sent down from London as an irenicon between the presbyterian and independent sections. Frankland was the senior minister present, and earnestly promoted the union. Next year the clergy of Craven petitioned Sharp to suppress the academy. Sharp wrote to Tillotson for advice. Tillotson evidently did not like the business, and suggested to Sharp (14 June 1692), as 'the fairest and softest way of ridding' his 'hands of' it, that he should see Frankland and explain that the objection to licensing his academy was not based upon his nonconformity. His school was not required in the district, and it was contrary to the bishop's oath to license public instruction in 'university learning.' Sharp saw Frankland after a confirmation at Skipton and invited the nonconformist to Bishopthorpe. Here, with the help of a pipe of tobacco and a glass of good wine, a very friendly interview took place in the library,

Sharp courteously declining controversy and inviting confidential hints about the state of the diocese (Frankland to Thoresby, 6 Nov. 1694). The archbishop's goodwill did not stop further proceedings. From a letter of Richard Stretton, presbyterian minister at Haberdashers' Hall, London, to Ralph Thoresby, it appears that early in 1695 there was a prosecution against Frankland; on 10 Feb. the indictment was quashed. In 1697 he was brought before the spiritual court, but at Michaelmas the case was postponed, apparently by the archbishop's order. Calamy states that his troubles continued till the year of his death, but no further particulars are available. Oliver Heywood's diaries are full of references to the academy and its students, and to Frankland's labours at ordinations.

His health began to break in 1697, when he was troubled with gravel. But he persevered in his work to the last, and died in the midst of his scholars on 1 Oct. 1698. He was buried on 5 Oct. in Giggleswick Church, where his daughters placed an ornate mural tablet to his memory, being a facsimile of the monument to John Lambert, son of Major-general Lambert, in Kirkby Malham Church. His portrait, taken in early life, is in Dr. Williams's Library. His funeral sermon was preached some time after by John Chorlton [q. v.], who transferred the 'northern academy' to Manchester; the institution has continued with few interruptions to the present day. It is now the Manchester New College, removed in 1889 from London to Oxford. In the charge of the presbyterian congregation at Rathmell, Frankland was succeeded by James Towers.

He married Elizabeth Sanderson of Hedley Hope, in the parish of Brancepeth, Durham (buried 5 Jan. 1691), and had at least two sons (1. John, born 13 Aug. 1659, entered the academy 3 May 1678, and died in June 1679, 'the strongest man of his age in and about Natland;' 2. Richard, baptised 8 June 1668, entered the academy 13 April 1680, died of the small-pox, and was buried at Sheffield 4 May 1689) and three daughters (1. Barbary, born 16 April 1661, and buried 5 Aug. 1662; 2. Elizabeth, baptised 25 Aug. 1664 (this is the 'Mrs. Frankland' mentioned by Oliver Heywood as collecting materials for a memoir of her father); 3. Margaret, married 19 June 1701 to Samuel Smith (d. 1732) of York).

He published only 'Reflections on a Letter writ by a nameless Author to the Reverend Clergy of both Universities,' &c., London and Halifax, 1697, 4to (B.M. 4103, aaa. 9). The tract is excessively rare; from the state of one of the two known copies, Aspland conjectures that most of the impression was accidentally destroyed; it is more probable that it had a purely local circulation. It has a preface by Oliver Heywood (dated 11 March; not included in his works). The 'Letter' to which it is a reply was published in 1694 (dated 10 Dec.), and is a plea by a churchman for moderation towards unitarians; Heywood's preface suggests that it had got into the hands of Frankland's students. The 'Reflections,' written in failing health, are justly described by Heywood as 'able' and 'uncouth.'

[Oliver Heywood wrote (10 Oct. 1698) a life of Frankland which is lost; Hunter thinks it formed the basis of the notice in Calamy. The first real biography of Frankland was published in the Christian Reformer, 1862, pp. 1 sq., 80 sq., by the editor, Robert Brook Aspland [q. v.]; the copy used above has Aspland's manuscript emendations. Wesley's Reply to Palmer, 1707, p. 34; Calamy's Account, 1713, pp. 284 sq., 289; Continuation, 1727, i. xlii, 452; Clegge's Short Acct. of J. Ashe, 1736, p. 55 (account of the academy); Grey's Impartial Exam. of the Fourth Vol. of Neal, 1739, p. 112; Birch's Life of Tillotson, 1753, p. 270 sq.; Neal's Hist. of the Puritans, 1822, iv. 110; Thoresby's Diary, 1830; Thoresby's Letters, 1832; Hunter's Life of O. Heywood, 1842, p. 242, &c.; Christian Reformer, 1846, p. 290 sq. (James Yates on Durham College); Wallace's Antitrin. Biog. 1850, i. 286 sq.; Surtees Society, vol. xxxviii. 1860 (wills of Frankland family); Miall's Congregationalism in Yorkshire, 1868, pp. 259 sq., 337; Kenrick's Mem. of Presb. Chap. York, 1869, p. 43; Proceedings in Commem. of foundation of Manch. New Coll., 1886, p. 25 sq.; Hunter's MS., Addit. MS. 24485; extracts from admission book Christ's Coll. Cambr. per H. J. Ansell; extracts from parish registers at Bishop Auckland, per the Rev. J. Baker, and at Giggleswick, per the Rev. Cuthbert Routh; authorities cited above. For the list of Frankland's students, see Latham's Fun. Serm. for Daniel Madock, 1745, appendix; compare Monthly Repository, 1811, p. 9 sq., 1813, p. 181; Toulmin's Hist. Prot. Dissenters, 1818, p. 575 sq.; Hunter's MS., Addit. MS. 24442 (from the lists of Oliver Heywood and Eliezer Heywood).]   A. G.

FRANKLAND, THOMAS (1633–1690), impostor and annalist, was born in Lancashire in 1633. He was entered in May 1649 at Brasenose College, Oxford, and became a fellow in 1654. He proceeded to the M.A. degree on 28 June 1655, and in 1662 was proctor of the university. He took orders after his grace had been three times refused, but renounced them in order to practise medicine. He settled in London and passed as M.D., alleging when asked for particulars by members of either university that he had taken his degree at the other. He applied for admission to the Royal College of Physicians, producing a certificate to attest that the M.D. degree had been conferred on him at Oxford, 10 Oct. 1667. He was admitted a candidate of the college in December 1671, and on 29 July 1675 became a fellow. At a general election he was appointed junior censor of the college. His overbearing conduct in this office made him much disliked, especially by the juniors, some of whom caused a search to be made in the registers of Oxford University. The officers of the university certified by an instrument dated 15 Nov. 1677 that no record of his degree could be found. Frankland showed that he held the Cambridge M.D. degree, but it was proved that this had been obtained merely on the strength of his pretended Oxford degree, he having been admitted at Cambridge on 28 Feb. 1676 'to the same degree' as he held from Oxford. Other charges of receiving bribes for shielding empirics were brought against him. He was disqualified for membership of the College of Physicians, but his formal ejectment does not appear to have taken place before 26 June 1682, Wood says by the connivance of the senior members. Compelled to abandon medicine, Frankland had turned his undeniable talents to historical study, and in 1681 published anonymously 'The Annals of King James I and King Charles I,' a folio volume of 913 pages besides preface and index. This book is largely made up of speeches in parliament and documents of state. Frankland has also been credited with the authorship of 'The Honours of the Lords Spiritual asserted, and their privileges to Vote in Capital Cases in Parliament maintained by Reason and Precedent,' folio, 1679. According to Wood, Frankland forged a will as well as his doctor's certificate. His name occurs as the recipient of 800l. secret service money in 1689. His misdoings brought him to the Fleet prison, where he died in 1690, and was buried in the church of St. Vedast, Foster Lane.

[Wood's Athenæ Oxon., ed. Bliss, iv. 290, and Wood's Life prefixed, p. lxxviii; Munk's Coll. of Phys. i. 382; Rawlinson MSS. A. 306.]
A. V.

FRANKLAND, Sir THOMAS (1717?–1784), admiral, was the second son of Henry Frankland (died in Bengal 1738), a nephew of Sir Thomas Frankland, bart., for many years (1733–42) one of the lords of the admiralty, a younger brother of Sir Charles Henry Frankland, some time consul-general in Portugal, whose story forms the groundwork of Dr. O. W. Holmes's ballad of 'Agnes,' and is told in more accurate detail in 'Sir C. H. Frankland, or Boston in the Colonial Times,' by Elias Nason (8vo, 1865; see also *Appleton's Journal*, 1873, x. 273), and a direct descendant of Oliver Cromwell, being the great-grandson of his daughter Frances. He is described on his passing certificate, 3 Nov. 1737, as being upwards of twenty years of age, and as having been at sea for six years and eleven days. After serving as a lieutenant of the Chatham, with Captain Philip Vanbrugh, and of the Cumberland, with Captain James Steuart, both on the home station, he was promoted, in July 1740, to the command of the Rose frigate, and was sent out to the Bahamas, on which station, including the coast of Florida and Carolina, he remained till the summer of 1745. During this time he captured several of the enemy's vessels, privateers and guarda-costas, including one, in June 1742, commanded by Juan de Leon Fandino, the man who cut off Jenkins's ear in 1731, and who now, with a mixed crew of 'Indians, mulattoes, and negroes,' made a long and resolute defence against the very superior force; and another, in December 1744, 'whose principal loading consisted in pistoles, a few chests of dollars, and a great deal of wrought gold and silver; the quantity was so great that the shares were delivered by weight, to save the trouble of counting it' (BEATSON, i. 282). As the prize was not condemned by legal process, the value does not seem to have been clearly known, but after the treasure and the rest of the cargo were disposed of, two accidental finds of thirty thousand and twenty thousand pistoles were looked on as comparative trifles. In October 1746 Frankland was appointed to the Dragon of 60 guns, which he commanded on the Leeward Islands station till the peace. In 1755 he was again sent out to the West Indies, as commodore at Antigua, with his broad pennant in the Winchester. His arrival on his station was marked by a disagreement with his predecessor, Commodore Pye, who, being junior to Frankland, had committed the mistake of keeping his broad pennant flying in Frankland's presence, and was 'excessively angry' that Frankland would not allow it. He had also, in Frankland's opinion, been guilty, during the time of his command, of several gross irregularities, which Frankland officially reported, and which, on Pye's return to England, were inquired into by a court-martial [see PYE, SIR THOMAS]. It has been said that in this matter Frankland was moved by a personal dislike to Pye rather than by zeal for the service; but though his account may have been thus rendered more harsh, it is consonant with the general tenor of his service and character. His de-

termination to maintain his own rights and the prescribed regulations is best illustrated by his reply to an official letter indicating the wish of the first lord of the admiralty with respect to some patronage which Frankland, after his promotion to the rank of rear-admiral, conceived to belong to himself as commander-in-chief. 'You will please,' he wrote to the secretary of the admiralty on 12 May 1757, 'to acquaint Lord Temple that I have friends of my own to provide for; . . . it is a privilege I never have or can give up.' The admiralty took an early opportunity of recalling him; he returned to England in the following October, and had no further employment at sea, though rising in due course to the ranks of vice-admiral and admiral, In 1768, on the death of his elder brother. Sir Charles Henry, he succeeded to the baronetcy. In 1749 he had been elected as member of parliament for Thirsk, which he continued to represent, not taking any active part in politics, but speaking occasionally, and very much to the point, on naval matters; as, for instance, on the iniquities which pervaded the system of government contracts, 11 March 1779, and on the navy estimates, 17 June 1784. He died shortly after this last effort, on 21 Nov. He married, in May 1743, Sarah, daughter of Judge Rhett of South Carolina, by whom he had a large family.

[Official Letters and other Documents in the Public Record Office; Charnock's Biog. Nav. v. 18; Beatson's Nav. and Mil. Memoirs; Burke's Peerage and Baronetage.]   J. K. L.

FRANKLIN, ELEANOR ANNE (1797?–1825), poetess, first wife of John (afterwards Sir John) Franklin [q. v.], was daughter of William Porden, an architect of some eminence, and one of a line of architects. She early developed a taste for poetry and art, and while still a girl published 'The Veils, or the Triumph of Constancy, a poem in 6 Books' (8vo, 1815). A short poem on the Arctic expedition (8vo, 1818), and a visit to the Trent, then just come home, brought her the acquaintance of John Franklin. The acquaintance was renewed on Franklin's return from his first journey through Arctic America, and on 19 Aug. 1823 she became his wife. She had previously published another and more ambitious work, 'Cœur de Lion, an Epic poem in 16 cantos' (2 vols. 8vo, 1822). On her marriage there was, we are told, a distinct understanding that she would 'never, under any circumstances, seek to turn her husband aside from the duty he owed to his country and his profession' (*A Brave Man*, p. 18), a promise that she held even to the death. On 3 June 1824 she gave birth to a daughter; she seems never to have recovered her health, fell into a decline, and died on 22 Feb. 1825, six days after her husband had left England on his second journey through North America. Mrs. Franklin's poetry obtained in its day a certain social success, but it has none of the elements of vitality, and is now quite forgotten. Her versification is, however, smooth, and shows a delicate and cultivated mind. During her girlhood and short married life she gathered round her a pleasant society of men distinguished in art, literature, or science, and her correspondence not infrequently occurs in the memoirs of that time. She was always keen in the pursuit of knowledge and bright in conversation, but was qualified to retort one day at the Royal Institution, when she heard some one suggest that 'the young ladies had far better stay at home and make a pudding,' 'We did that before we came out.' A portrait is in the possession of the Gell family.

[A Brave Man and his Belongings (by one of Mrs. Franklin's nieces: printed for private circulation in 1874); Gent. Mag. 1825, i. 470–1.]

J. K. L.

FRANKLIN, JANE, LADY (1792–1875), second wife of Sir John Franklin [q. v.], whom she married on 5 Nov. 1828, was one of three daughters of John Griffin of Bedford Place. Before her marriage she was in the habit of accompanying her father in his frequent journeys both in England and on the continent. Shortly after her marriage Franklin was appointed to the command of a frigate in the Mediterranean, and during the time she travelled in Syria, Asia Minor, and other parts adjacent, joining her husband as opportunity offered. She afterwards accompanied him to Van Diemen's Land, and appears to have travelled not only over the whole of that island, but also in Australia and New Zealand. But she also devoted herself very earnestly to the improvement of the condition of the female convicts, on which, as well as on measures for the good of the honest labouring population, she is said to have expended very considerable sums. When apprehensions as to the safety of Sir John Franklin began to be felt, she was naturally one of the first to take alarm, and as early as 1848 stimulated the search both by personal influence and by the offer of a reward of 2,000*l.* Between 1850 and 1857 she fitted out, mainly if not entirely at her own expense, no less than five ships for the search (RICHARDSON, *Polar Regions,* p. 174); the last of these, the Fox, being the one that succeeded in bringing back the story of the lost expedition. To this work she devoted a very large part of her property. At this period, too, she seems to have sought relief from oppressing anxiety in constant travel. Her journeys embraced almost the whole of the civilised world, including Japan and Nevada. It was not, however, these that the Royal Geographical Society recognised in conferring on her their founder's medal in 1860, but rather the zeal and self-sacrifice with which she had maintained the search for the missing ships, and the success which, in 1859, had rewarded her efforts. She continued occasionally to attend the meetings of the society, where she was always an honoured guest. During the last months of her life she had been much occupied with the outfit of the Pandora yacht, which she had sent to try and make the north-west passage by the route on which her husband had failed. The Pandora failed also, but Lady Franklin did not live to hear the result. Her very last work was the completion of a monument to her husband's memory in Westminster Abbey. She wished to compose his epitaph, but thoughts and words would not flow in unison, and the task was completed by Lord Tennyson, Franklin's nephew by marriage. It was unveiled a fortnight after her death, and a note added by Dean Stanley tells that it was 'erected by his widow, who, after long waiting and sending many in search of him, herself departed to seek and to find him in the realms of light, 18 July 1875, aged 83 years.'

[Annual Register, 1875, cxvii. 143; McClintock's Narrative of the Discovery of the Fate of Sir John Franklin; Osborn's Career, Last Voyage, and Fate of Sir John Franklin; A Brave Man and his Belongings; Journal of the Royal Geographical Society, vol. xxv. p. lxxxvi.]

J. K. L.

FRANKLIN, SIR JOHN (1786–1847), Arctic explorer, the twelfth and youngest son of Willingham Franklin of Spilsby in Lincolnshire, was born on 16 April 1786. It had been intended to bring him up for the church, but a holiday visit to the seashore excited a strong desire to go to sea, which his father vainly endeavoured to overcome by sending him for a voyage in a merchant vessel as far as Lisbon. On his return he entered the royal navy on board the Polyphemus, then just sailing for the Baltic, where she played a leading part in the battle of Copenhagen. Two months later Franklin was appointed as a midshipman to the Investigator, under the command of his cousin, Matthew Flinders [q. v.], and on the point of sailing for Australia. While in the Investigator Franklin distinguished himself by his remarkable aptitude for nautical and astronomical observations; he was employed at Sydney as assistant in a little observatory which Flinders established, and won the notice of Captain King, the governor, who used to address him familiarly as Mr. Tycho Brahe. When the ship's company was broken up after the wreck of the Porpoise, Franklin accompanied Lieutenant Fowler to China in the Rolla, and, taking a passage home in the East India Company's ship Earl Camden, was with Commodore Dance in his extraordinary engagement with Linois (15 Feb. 1804), on which occasion Fowler commanded on the lower deck and Franklin took charge of the signals [see DANCE, SIR NATHANIEL]. On arriving in England Franklin was appointed to the Bellerophon [see COOKE, JOHN, 1763–1805], in which he was present in the battle of Trafalgar, again having charge of the signals, and being one of the few on the Bellerophon's poop who escaped unhurt. Two years later he joined the Bedford, and, continuing in her after his promotion to lieutenant's rank (11 Feb. 1808), was employed on the home station till the peace in 1814, when the ship was ordered to North America, to form part of the expedition against New Orleans. In a boat attack on some gunboats in Lac Borgne Franklin was slightly wounded; and he had besides a full share in the laborious duties of the campaign. Its failure may account for the fact that no attention was paid to the strong recommendation of Sir John Lambert, in command of the troops with which he had been serving, and that he remained a lieutenant, serving on board the Forth frigate, with Sir William Bolton, Nelson's nephew. With Franklin's appointment in January 1818 to command the hired brig Trent, fitting out to accompany Captain Buchan in the Dorothea, Franklin's career as an Arctic explorer commenced. Their instructions were to pass between Spitzbergen and Greenland, use their best endeavours to reach the pole, and thence, if possible, to shape a course direct for Behring's Straits. The two ships sailed on 25 April, sighted Spitzbergen on 26 May, and passed without difficulty along its western coast; they were then stopped by the ice, and, being driven into the pack on 30 July, the Dorothea received so much damage as to be in momentary danger of foundering. They got into Dane's Gat, where such repairs as were possible were executed, but it was still very doubtful whether she could live through the passage home, and further contact with the ice was clearly out of the question. Buchan's instructions fully authorised him in this contingency to move into the Trent and send the Dorothea home; but he was unwilling to appear to desert his shipmates in a time

of great danger. The Dorothea's state was such as to forbid her being sent home unattended, and Franklin's request that he might be allowed to go on rendered the task of superseding him the more disagreeable. So Buchan judged rightly that his proper course was to take the Dorothea home, with the Trent in close attendance on her. They arrived in England on 22 Oct.

Early in the following year Franklin was appointed to the command of an exploring expedition to be sent out with the general idea of amending the very defective geography of the northern part of America, and with more particular instructions 'to determine the latitudes and longitudes of the northern coast of North America, and the trendings of that coast from the mouth of the Coppermine River to the eastern extremity of that continent.' The details of the route from York Factory, named as a starting-point, were left to Franklin's judgment, guided by the advice he should receive from the agents of the Hudson's Bay Company, who would be instructed to co-operate with the expedition, and to provide it with guides, hunters, clothing, and ammunition. The small party, including Dr. (afterwards Sir John) Richardson [q. v.], Hood and Back, midshipmen [see BACK, SIR GEORGE], the last of whom had been with Franklin in the Trent, two seamen, and four Orkney boatmen, landed at York on 30 Aug. 1819, and started on 9 Sept. The scheme was, with portable boats or canoes, to follow the line of rivers and lakes, beginning with the Nelson and Saskatchewan, and ending with the Elk, Slave, and Coppermine. At Cumberland House, a long-established station on the Saskatchewan, it was found that further progress that season was impossible. One of the seamen and the Orkneymen were sent back, and, leaving Hood and Richardson to bring on the boats when the way should be open, Franklin and Back started on foot for Fort Chipewyan on the shore of Lake Athabasca, which they reached on 26 March 1820. It was Franklin's intention to make all arrangements for an onward march as soon as the boats should arrive. He now found that owing to the rivalry, amounting almost to war, between the two trading companies which disputed the territory, no supplies were available; and, when the boats came on, the expedition left Fort Chipewyan on 18 July with little more than one day's provisions and with a scanty supply of powder. On 2 Aug. they left Fort Providence on the northern shore of Great Slave Lake, the party consisting, what with Canadian voyageurs and interpreters, of twenty-eight men, besides three women and three children. The

due course was sent to Woodbridge school. Here, as he confessed, he was too fond of sports, violent in temper, and prone to lying. He was specially trained in writing and accounts with a view to his being apprenticed in London, but his ability led to his being sent to Cambridge, where he was admitted to Jesus College. His tutor was Bantoft, whom he succeeded in the office, but he gave up tuition on proving successful in a preaching competition against a Dr. Brooks for the college living of Kirton, Suffolk. Franklin found that he was unable to subsist in comfort on his living, which only produced 50l. a year, and set up a school, which proved to be educationally successful, but a commercial failure. Through a friend's influence he was appointed to the superior living of Bramfield, but here he received nothing at all, as the former incumbent declined to retire. He then obtained the living of Blythburgh, where he remained only a short time, being presented in 1659 to the vicarage of Westhall, where he again found an incumbent, speechless from palsy, who declined to move. Franklin was allowed, however, to perform the duties of the vicar on payment of ten shillings a week to his predecessor, who at length resigned and left him in possession. In 1662 he 'left his living rather than defile his conscience.' He became in 1663 private chaplain to Sir Samuel Barnardiston [q. v.], but after six months went to London and suffered for nonconformity. He was first seized for preaching at Colebrooke, and was lodged in Aylesbury gaol, his goods being confiscated. On his release he took a house in London, and held religious meetings there, but refusing the corporation oath he was again imprisoned. A sermon which he preached some time afterwards in Glovers' Hall was followed by his detention for six months in Newgate. Later he was seized in his own house at Bunhill Fields, and committed to the New prison; he was released shortly, but compelled to appear every sessions, and to give bail for his good behaviour. He died in 1684. He is described by Calamy as a man of great gravity and integrity, and a plain, serious preacher. Franklin subscribed his name, among those of fellow-ministers, to 'A Murderer Punished and Pardoned; or a True Relation of the Wicked Life and Shameful-happy Death of Thos. Savage, imprisoned, justly condemned, and twice executed at Radcliff, by us who were often with him in Newgate.' Otherwise he only published 'Death in Triumph over the most desirable ones,' a funeral sermon on Mrs. Mary Parry (1683), for, as he remarks in the preface to this publication, he had not the 'itching humour of the scribbling age, nor any desire to appear in print.' He left a manuscript entitled 'Memorable Occurrences of my Life,' which is the principal source for the facts of his career. Franklin was married.

[Calamy and Palmer's Nonconf. Mem. iii. 291; Davy's Athenæ Suffolc. i. 267.] A. V.

FRANKLYN, WILLIAM (1480?-1556), dean of Windsor, was born at Bledlow, Buckinghamshire, probably about 1480, and educated at Eton and King's College, Cambridge, where he graduated B.C.L. in 1504. He took orders, and in 1514 was appointed chancellor of the diocese of Durham and receiver of the bishop's revenues. In 1515 he became archdeacon of Durham and master of the hospital of St. Giles at Kepyer, Durham. In this and the following years Franklyn was active in directing measures in border warfare with the Scotch. His headquarters were at Norham, and it was probably about this period that a grant of arms was made him in consideration of the recovery of the castle at that place by his prowess and policy. In February 1518 he was installed prebendary of Heydour-cum-Walton in the diocese of Lincoln, and before 1522 he was rector of Houghton-le-Spring, Durham, and held the prebend of Eveston, in the collegiate church of Lanchester, in the same county. On Wolsey's accession to the see of Durham he confirmed Franklyn in the chancellorship, with power of appointing justices of the peace, coroners, stewards, bailiffs, and other officers, and the chancellor made himself very useful to the bishop in devising plans for increasing the revenues of the diocese. In one of many letters addressed by Franklyn to Wolsey in 1528 he points out the neglect of certain palatine rights which might be exercised with advantage, shows how collieries and lead mines might be more profitably worked, and suggests that some one else should be appointed chancellor and he himself Wolsey's surveyor of Yorkshire, for, though the chancellorship carried the best pay, 'I am young and can do more service thus.' He was still chancellor under Tunstall, Wolsey's successor at Durham, but he already enjoyed marked proofs of Wolsey's favour. He received a salaried appointment as counsellor resident with Henry Fitzroy [q. v.], duke of Richmond, natural son of Henry VIII; was presented to the prebend of Stillington, Yorkshire, in February 1526, and in the same year became president of Queen's College, Cambridge, which office he held only a year and nine months. His name appears in the commission formed, October 1528, to treat for peace with James V of Scotland, and he had a hand in the negotiations which led to the peace concluded 31 July 1534 at Holyrood. In May 1535 he was one of the council in the north executing the royal commission for assessing and taxing spiritual proceedings. On 17 Dec. 1536 Franklyn was by patent appointed dean of Windsor, and in 1540 he exchanged his Lincolnshire prebend for the rectory of Chalfont St. Giles, Buckinghamshire, the parsonage attaching to which he afterwards let on a lease of thirty-one years to John Storie, LL.D. [q. v.] As dean of Windsor he assisted at the christening of Edward VI and the funeral of Lady Jane Dudley, and his signature is affixed to the decree declaring the invalidity of the marriage of Henry VIII with Anne of Cleves. On 14 Jan. 1544–5 he surrendered to the crown his hospital of Kepyer and most of his benefices, and he also alienated the revenues of his deanery, some temporarily, others in perpetuity. The complaints against him on this score were so loud that after the accession of Edward VI he was compelled to resign. He retired to Chalfont St. Giles, where he died in January 1555–6, and was buried in the church. His will met with disapproval, for a grant was made to one J. Glynne of so much as he could recover of goods, chattels, and money, devised by Franklyn for superstitious purposes (*Cal. State Papers,* Dom. 1547–80, p. 233). A large number of letters addressed by Franklyn to Wolsey, Cromwell, and others are preserved in the Record Office and the British Museum. Franklyn is described by Foxe as 'a timorous man' (*Acts and Monuments,* ed. 1847, v. 469).

[Lipscombe's Hist. of Buckinghamshire, ii. 69, iii. 232; Le Neve's Fasti Eccl. Angl. ii. 156, iii. 213, 304, 373, 685; Hutchinson's Hist. of Durham, i. 404, 407, 443, ii. 540; Brewer's Letters and Papers of Henry VIII (Rolls Ser.), passim; Wood's Athenæ Oxon. ed. Bliss, i. 389; Strype's Eccl. Mem. ii. pt. i. pp. 9, 12; Rymer's Fœdera, xii. 282, 541; Camden Miscellany, vols. iii. xxiii.; Cooper's Athenæ Cantabr. i. 141; Cole's MS. Collection, vii. 129, xiii. 125, 126, xxxii. 112, 113, xlviii. 257. In the place first cited Cole doubts the identity of Franklyn, dean of Windsor, with Franklyn, archdeacon of Durham, seemingly only because he lacked proof of it.]   A. V.

FRANKS, Sir JOHN (1770–1852), Indian judge, second son of Thomas Franks (1729–1787), of Ballymagooly, Cork, by Catherine, daughter of Rev. John Day, born in 1770, graduated at Trinity College, Dublin, B.A. 1788, LL.B. 1791. He was called to the Irish bar 1792. He went the Munster circuit, and had a good practice as chamber counsel. He 'took silk' in 1823. In 1825 the board of control, on the recommendation

of his friend Plunket, then attorney-general, appointed him a judge of the supreme court at Calcutta. He received, as was customary, the honour of knighthood before his departure for India. He held this office till the effect of the climate on his health brought about his resignation in 1834. On his return he resided at Roebuck, near Dublin. He died 11 Jan. 1852. He was thrice married. By his first wife, Catherine, daughter of his cousin Thomas Franks of Carrig, Cork, he had two sons and three daughters. His heir was John Franks of Bally-scaddane, co. Limerick.

Franks was popular, both as advocate and judge. He was an intimate friend of Curran, and one of his executors, W. H. Curran, Curran's son, commemorates his 'peculiar aboriginal wit, quiet, keen, and natural to the occasion, and, best of all, never malignant' (*Gent. Mag.*)

[Gent. Mag. April 1852, p. 408; Graduates of Dublin, p. 208; Burke's Landed Gentry.]
F. W–t.

FRANKS, Sir THOMAS HARTE (1808–1862), general, was the second son of William Franks of Carrig Castle, near Mallow, co. Cork, by Catherine, daughter of William Hume, M.P. for the county of Wicklow, and aunt of Fitzwilliam Hume Dick, M.P. for Wicklow. He entered the army as an ensign in the 10th regiment on 7 July 1825, and had been promoted lieutenant on 26 Sept. 1826, captain on 1 March 1839, major on 29 Dec. 1843, and lieutenant-colonel on 28 March 1845, before he had ever seen service. During these twenty years he had been with his regiment in many parts of the world, and in 1842 he accompanied it for the first time to India. He was engaged in the first Sikh war, and the 10th regiment was one of those which were called up to help to fill the gap caused by the heavy losses at Mudki and Firozshah. At the battle of Sobraon the 10th regiment was on the extreme right of the line, and it did its duty nobly in carrying the Sikh position in front of it. Franks was wounded, and had a horse shot under him, and he was rewarded by the Sobraon medal and by being made a C.B. In the second Sikh war Franks's regiment was the first English one to come up to the siege of Múltán, and Franks, as one of the senior officers with the besieging force, held many independent commands, and rendered most valuable services. After the siege was over he joined Lord Gough on 10 Feb. 1849, and served with great distinction at Gujrát. He was promoted colonel on 20 June 1854, and was appointed to the command of the Jalandhar brigade on 11 May 1855. He had handed over his command, and was just going home on sick leave, when the mutiny of 1857 broke out. Thereupon he refused to go to England, and remained at Calcutta until his health was sufficiently restored to enable him to take the field. In January 1858 he was appointed to command the 4th infantry division in the field, with the rank of brigadier-general. This division, nearly six thousand strong, was intended to carry out a favourite scheme of Lord Canning. Franks was directed to march across the northeastern frontier of Oude, driving the mutineers before him, and then to meet Sir Jung Bahadur, the prime minister of Nepal, who had promised to bring a force of Goorkhas to the assistance of the English, after which the two corps together were to co-operate in Sir Colin Campbell's operations against Lucknow. This programme was successfully carried out; the junction with Jung Bahadur's Goorkhas was cleverly effected, and on 19 and 23 Feb. Franks inflicted two severe defeats on the rebel leader, Muhammad Hussein Nazim, at Chanda, and between Badshahganj and Sultánpur respectively. The effect of these victories, in which Franks only lost two men killed and sixteen wounded, was, however, minimised by the severe check which he received in an attempt to take Dohrighat. Sir Colin Campbell was much incensed at this defeat, and after the final capture of Lucknow he refused to give Franks another command in the field. This was a severe blow to Franks, who at once returned to England, where he was promoted major-general on 20 July 1858, made a K.C.B., and given the thanks of parliament. His health was entirely ruined by his exertions, and he died at Ibstone House, Tetsworth, Oxfordshire, on 5 Feb. 1862. Franks married (1) Matilda, daughter of Richard Kay, esq., and widow of the Rev. W. Fletcher; (2) Rebecca Constantia Elizabeth, widow of Samuel Brewis, esq., of Langley House, Prestwich, Lancashire.

[Hart's Army List; Gent. Mag. March 1862; Despatches of Lord Hardinge, Lord Gough, and Sir Harry Smith; Shadwell's Lord Clyde; Malleson's Indian Mutiny.] H. M. S.

FRANSHAM, JOHN (1730–1810), freethinker, son of Thomas and Isidora Fransham, was born early in 1730 (baptised 19 March) in the parish of St. George of Colegate, Norwich, where his father was sexton or parish clerk. He showed precocity at an elementary school. He wrote sermons, which the rector of St. George's thought good enough to submit to the dean. The aid of a relative, probably Isaac Fransham (1660–1743), an attorney, enabled him to study for the church. His relative dying, Fransham, at the age of fifteen,

was apprenticed for a few weeks to a cooper at Wymondham, Norfolk. By writing sermons for clergymen he made a little money, but could not support himself, though he went barefoot nearly three years. John Taylor, D.D., the presbyterian theologian, gave him gratuitous instruction. A legacy of 25l. determined him to buy a pony, not to ride, but to 'make a friend of,' as he told a physician consulted by his father, who thought him out of his wits. As long as the money lasted, Fransham took lessons from W. Hemingway, a land surveyor. He then wrote for Marshall, an attorney, but was never articled. One of Marshall's clerks, John Chambers, afterwards recorder of Norwich, took great pains with him. He made the acquaintance of Joseph Clover [q. v.], the veterinary surgeon, who employed him to take horses to be shod, and taught him mathematics in return for Fransham's help in classics.

In 1748 he joined a company of strolling players. He is said to have taken, among other parts, those of Iago and Shylock. The players got no pay and lived on turnips; Fransham left them on finding that the turnips were stolen. He sailed from Great Yarmouth for North Shields, intending to study at the Scottish universities and visit the highlands. But at Newcastle-on-Tyne he enlisted in the Old Buffs, was soon discharged as bandy-legged, and made his way back to Norwich with three halfpence and a plaid. After this he worked with Daniel Wright, a freethinking journeyman weaver. The two friends sat facing each other, so that they could carry on discussions amid the rattle of their looms.

After Wright's death, about 1750, Fransham devoted himself to teaching. For two or three years he was tutor in the family of Leman, a farmer at Hellesdon, Norfolk. He next took pupils at Norwich in Latin, Greek, French, and mathematics. He only taught for two hours a day, and had time to act as amanuensis to Samuel Bourn (1714–1796) [q. v.] He became a member of a society for philosophical experiment, founded by Peter Bilby. His reputation grew as a successful preliminary tutor for the universities; he reluctantly took as many as twenty pupils, being of opinion that no man could do justice to more than eight. His terms rose from a shilling a week to 15s. a quarter; out of this slender income he saved money, and collected two hundred books towards a projected library. If he got a bargain at a bookstall he insisted on paying the full value as soon as he knew it.

In 1767 he spent nine months in London, carrying John Leedes, a former pupil, through his Latin examination at the College of Surgeons. In London he formed a slight acquaintance with the queen's under-librarian, who introduced him to Foote. Foote, in 'The Devil upon Two Sticks' (1768), caricatured teacher and pupil as Johnny Macpherson and Dr. Emanuel Last. Fransham wore a plaid, which suggested the Mac, a green jacket with large horn buttons, a broad hat, drab shorts, coarse worsted stockings, and large shoes. The boys called him 'old horn-buttoned Jack.'

On his return to Norwich, the Chute family, who had a country house at South Pickenham, Norfolk, allowed him (about 1771) to sleep at their Norwich house (where his sister, Mrs. Bennett, was housekeeper) and to use the library. He taught (about 1772) in the family of Samuel Cooper, D.D. [see COOPER, SIR ASTLEY PASTON], at Brooke Hall, Norfolk, on the terms of board and lodging from Saturday till Monday. This engagement he gave up, as the walk of over six miles out and in was too much for him. When Cooper obtained preferment at Great Yarmouth, Fransham was advised by his friend Robinson to write and ask for a guinea. The difficulty was that Fransham had never written a letter in his life, and after he had copied Robinson's draft, did not know how to fold it. Cooper sent him 5*l.* The death of young Chute (of which Fransham thought he had warning in a dream) threw Fransham again on his own resources. He reduced his allowance to a farthing's worth of potatoes a day; the experiment of sleeping on Mousehold Heath in his plaid brought on a violent cold, and was not repeated. For nearly three years, from about 1780, he dined every Sunday with counsellor Cooper, a relative of the clergyman, who introduced him to Dr. Parr. From about 1784 to about 1794 he lodged with Thomas Robinson, schoolmaster at St. Peter's Hungate. He left Robinson to lodge with Jay, a baker in St. Clement's. Here he would never allow the floor of his room to be wetted or the walls whitewashed, for fear of damp, and to have his bed made more than once a week he considered 'the height of effeminacy.' In 1805 he was asked for assistance by a distant relative, Mrs. Smith; he took her as his housekeeper, hiring a room and a garret in St. George's Colegate. When she left him in 1806 he seems to have resided for about three years with his sister, who had become a widow; leaving her, he made his last move to a garret in Elm Hill. In 1807 or 1808 he made the acquaintance of Michael Stark (*d.* 1831), a Norwich dyer, and became tutor to his sons, of whom the youngest was James Stark, the artist.

Fransham has been called a pagan and a polytheist chiefly on the strength of his hymns to the ancient gods, his designation of chicken-broth as a sacrifice to Æsculapius, and his describing a change in the weather as Juno's response to supplication. His love for classical antiquity led him to prefer the Greek mathematicians to any of the moderns, to reject (with Berkeley) the doctrine of fluxions, and to despise algebra. Convinced of the legendary origin of all theology, he esteemed the legends of paganism as the most venerable, and put upon them a construction of his own. Taylor, the platonist, he observed, took them in a sense 'intended for the vulgar alone.' Hume was to him the 'prince of philosophers;' he read Plato with admiration, but among the speculations of antiquity the arguments of Cotta, in the 'De Natura Deorum,' were most to his mind. He annotated a copy of Chubb's posthumous works, apparently for republication as a vehicle of his own ideas. In a note to p. 168 of Chubb's 'Author's Farewell,' he puts forward the hypothesis of a multiplicity of 'artists' as explaining the 'infinitely various parts of nature.' In his manuscript 'Metaphysicorum Elementa' (begun 1748, and written with Spinoza as his model) he defines God as 'ens non dependens, quod etiam causa est omnium cæterorum existentium.' He thinks it obvious that space fulfils the terms of this definition, and hence concludes 'spatium solum esse Deum,' adding 'Deus, vel spatium, est solidum.' His chief quarrel with the preachers of his time was that they allowed vicious and cruel customs to go unreproved. Asked at an election time for whom he would be inclined to vote, he replied, 'I would vote for that man who had humanity enough to drive long-tailed horses.' He was fond of most animals, but disliked dogs, as 'noisy, mobbish, and vulgar,' and in his 'Aristopia, or ideal state,' he provided for their extermination.

Fransham brought under complete control a temper which in his early years was ungovernable. He rose at five in summer, at six in winter; a strict teetotaller, he ate little animal food, living chiefly on tea and bread-and-butter. To assure himself of the value of health, he would eat tarts till he got a headache, which he cured with strong tea. For his amusement he played a hautboy, but burned the instrument to make tea. Supplying its place with a 'bilbo-catch,' he persevered until he had caught the ball on the spike 666,666 times (not in succession; he could never exceed a sequence of two hundred). His dread of fire led him constantly to practise the experiment of letting himself down from an upper story by a ladder. In money matters he was extremely exact, but could bear losses with equanimity. He had saved up 100*l*., which he was induced to lodge with a merchant, who became bankrupt just after Fransham had withdrawn 75*l*. to buy books. To his friends' expressions of condolence he replied that he had been lucky enough to gain the 75*l*.

At the latter end of 1809 he was attacked by a cough; in January 1810 he took to his bed and was carefully nursed, but declined medical aid. When dying he said that had he to live his days again he would go more into female society. He had a fear of being buried alive, and gave some odd instructions as to what was to be done to prove him 'dead indeed.' On 1 Feb. 1810 he expired. He was buried on 4 Feb. in the churchyard of St. George of Colegate; his gravestone bears a Latin inscription. A caricature likeness of him has been published; his features have been thought to resemble those of Erasmus, while his double-tipped nose reminded his friends of the busts of Plato. He left ninety-six guineas to his sister; his books and manuscripts were left to Edward Rigby, M.D. (*d.* 1821); some of them passed into the possession of William Stark, and a portion of these is believed to have perished in a fire; William Saint, his pupil and biographer, seems to have obtained his mathematical books and most of his mathematical manuscripts.

He published: 1. 'An Essay on the Oestrum or Enthusiasm of Orpheus,' Norwich, 1760, 8vo (an anonymous tract on the happiness to be derived from a noble enthusiasm). 2. 'Two Anniversary Discourses: in the first of which the Old Man is exploded, in the second the New Man is recognised,' London, 1768, 8vo (anonymous satires; not seen; reviewed in 'Monthly Review,' 1769, xl. 83, and identified as Fransham's on the evidence of his manuscripts). 3. 'Robin Snap, British Patriotic Carrier,' 1769–70, fol. (a penny satirical print, published in Norwich; 26 numbers, the first on Saturday, 4 Nov. 1769, then regularly on Tuesdays from 14 Nov. 1769 to 30 Jan. 1770, and again 13 Feb.–24 April, also 15 May and 29 May 1770; the whole, with slight exceptions, written by Fransham; his own copy has a printed title-page, 'The Dispensation of Robin Snap,' &c.; 'snap' is the local term for the dragon carried about the streets of Norwich on the guild day.)

Of Fransham's manuscripts six quarto volumes remain. Five of these are described by Saint; they are prepared for the press and indexed, and contain a few allegorical drawings. They bear the general title 'Memorabilia Classica: or a Philosophical Harvest of Ancient and Modern Institutions.' In the first

volume is (No. 2) the original draft of his 'Oestrum,' and (No. 5) 'The Code of Aristopia, or Scheme of a perfect Government,' the most remarkable of his writings. He advocates (p. 175) a decimal system of coinage and measures. The second volume, 'A Synopsis of Classical Philosophy,' embodies his 'Essay on the Fear of Death,' expressing a hope of a future and more perfect state of being, a topic on which he had written in his nineteenth year. At the end of the third volume is his 'Antiqua Religio,' including his hymns to Jupiter, Minerva, Venus, Hercules, &c. The fourth volume includes the draft of his 'Anniversary Discourses,' and others in the same strain. The fifth volume contains thirty numbers of 'Robin Snap,' some of which were worked up in the published periodical. A sixth volume, 'Memorabilia Practica,' is perhaps that which is described by Saint as 'a mathematical manual;' it contains a very interesting compendium of all the subjects which he taught. Fransham's style is uncouth and emotional, but bears marks of genius; his prose becomes rhythmical when he is strongly moved.

There was an earlier JOHN FRANSHAM (*d.* July or August 1753), a Norwich linendraper, rent-agent to Horace Walpole, and correspondent of Defoe, 1704–7 (*Notes and Queries*, 5th ser. iii. 261 sq.), a contributor to periodicals (*ib.* ii. 37); author of: 1. 'The Criterion . . . of High and Low Church,' &c., 1710, 8vo; reprinted, Norwich, 1710, 8vo (by 'J.F.') 2. 'A Dialogue between Jack High and Will Low,' &c., 1710, 8vo (anon.; both of these are identified as Fransham's by a note in his handwriting); and in all probability the 'Mr. John Fransham of Norwich,' who published 3. 'The World in Miniature,' &c., 1740, 2 vols. 12mo. To him has also been ascribed a valuable tract by J. F., 'An Exact Account of the Charge for Supporting the Poor of . . . Norwich,' &c., 1720, 8vo (British Museum, 104, n. 44; catalogued under 'John Fransham'), but this is assigned, in a contemporary Norwich hand on Mr. Colman's copy, to James Fransham.

[Saint's Memoir, without date (preface dated Norwich, 3 Oct. 1811), is a perplexing jumble of contradictory accounts, and it is quite probable that the attempt made above to present the narrative in its true sequence has not been entirely successful. Saint's extracts from the manuscripts, made partly with the view of exhibiting Fransham's 'Christian character,' are well chosen. It would appear from a letter, dated 3 Aug. 1811, that 'the Rev. W. J. F.,' i.e. William Johnson Fox [q. v.], had something to do with the publication. An earlier memoir, in some respects better (dated Norwich, 20 March 1811), appeared in the Monthly Magazine, 1811,

Y

pt. i. pp. 342 sq., see also pt. ii. p. 463. Another is in Gent. Mag. vol. lxxxi. pt. ii. pp. 11, 127. A short biography is given in the Norfolk Tour, 1829, ii. 1232 sq. Fransham's manuscripts and other works are in the collection of J. J. Colman, esq., M.P.; information (respecting the Stark family) has been supplied by Mr. J. Mottram and (respecting the earlier John Fransham) by Mr. F. Norgate.]   A. G.

FRASER, Sir ALEXANDER (*d.* 1332), great chamberlain of Scotland, was the eldest son of Sir Andrew Fraser, who was sheriff of Stirling in 1293. His grandfather was Sir Richard Fraser of Touchfraser in Stirlingshire, and to him he succeeded in these and other lands. In 1296 his father was carried prisoner into England, and required to reside south of the river Trent. His family accompanied him thither, and as Edward I insisted on the Scottish barons sending their sons to his court, it is probable that Fraser spent some portion of his youth there. He, however, espoused the cause of Scottish independence, and, having left England, attached himself to Robert Bruce, with whom he fought at Methven in 1306. Bruce being defeated Fraser was led captive from the field, but he succeeded in escaping, and after Bruce had resumed the campaign he rejoined him with his friends and vassals at the Mounth in the Mearns, and aided him in inflicting the crushing defeat on his enemies, the Comyns, known as the 'harrying of Buchan.' He was also present at the battle of Bannockburn, on the eve of which he received the honour of knighthood. Shortly afterwards Fraser married a sister of King Robert Bruce, Lady Mary Bruce, who for four years was imprisoned by Edward I in a cage in the castle of Roxburgh. She was previously married to Sir Neil Campbell, who died in or about 1315. Fraser took a prominent place among the Scottish barons in the events of his time, and in 1319 was appointed lord chamberlain of Scotland. He was one of the barons who in 1320 sent the letter to the pope asserting the national independence of Scotland, as a reply to the efforts which were made by the English court to enlist the Roman see in their attempts to secure the subjection of the Scots. His seal is still appended to the document, which is preserved in the General Register House, Edinburgh. Fraser continued to hold the office of chamberlain until 1326. In recognition of his services he received large grants of lands from Bruce, including the lands of Panbride, Garvocks, Culpressach, Aboyne, Cluny, and the thanage of Cowie, all in the counties of Forfar, Kincardine, and Aberdeen. Besides these he possessed large estates in other parts of Scotland, and was sheriff of Stirling and also of the Mearns. After the death of Bruce he took an active part in the defence of the kingdom against the inroads of the English, and was slain at the battle of Dupplin on 12 Aug. 1332. His wife predeceased him in or before 1323, leaving two sons.

[Barbour's Bruce; Exchequer Rolls of Scotland, vol. i.; Robertson's Index; Fordun's Annalia, cap. cxlvi.; Wyntoun's Chronicle; Acts of the Parliaments of Scotland, i. 99–118; Lord Saltoun's Frasers of Philorth (1879).]   H. P.

FRASER, Sir ALEXANDER (1537?–1623), of Philorth, founder of Fraserburgh, was the eldest son of Alexander Fraser, son and heir of Alexander, seventh laird of Philorth. His mother was Lady Beatrix Keith, eldest daughter of Robert Keith, master of Marischal. He succeeded his grandfather in the family estates in 1569, his father having died in 1564, and he set himself to work out the ambitious schemes of his grandfather in aggrandising and improving the ancestral inheritance. Already the lands were erected into a barony, with Philorth as a baronial burgh, where a commodious harbour had been made. The castle also had been enlarged and improved. But the eighth laird outvied his predecessor. He enlarged and beautified the burgh, which was now created a burgh of regality, changed its name to Fraserburgh, and, notwithstanding strenuous opposition from the town of Aberdeen, obtained powers to build a grand university at Fraserburgh, with all the privileges enjoyed by the other universities in the kingdom. A college was actually built, of which, in 1597, the general assembly appointed Charles Ferm [q. v.], minister of Fraserburgh, to be principal; but the college was not a success. Fraser also erected a new family residence on Kinnaird Head, which he called Fraserburgh Castle. But the situation was too exposed, and the family were afterwards obliged to remove to a more sheltered position. What remains of the castle is now utilised as a lighthouse. He likewise built a new parish church not far from the castle. The town throve well, and has now become the most important fishing port on the Scottish coast. In connection with it Fraser is distinguished among the lairds of Philorth and Lords Saltoun as the 'founder of Fraserburgh.'

He was knighted by James VI, probably on the occasion of the baptism of Prince Henry in August 1594. Two years later he was chosen M.P. for the county of Aberdeen. In the latter part of his life he was obliged to place his affairs in the hands of trustees, and ultimately to sell several of his estates, in order to meet liabilities incurred in connection with his early projects.

His first wife died before 1606, and in that year he married Elizabeth Maxwell, eldest daughter of John, lord Herries, the staunch friend of Queen Mary, and widow of Sir John Gordon of Lochinvar. She also predeceased him. On 12 July 1623 he lay on his deathbed and made his will, dying shortly afterwards in the same month. He had five sons and three daughters. One of the sons, Thomas, is said to have written a history of the family. A portrait of the 'founder of Fraserburgh' was engraved by Pinkerton for his 'Scots Gallery of Portraits,' vol. ii., from the original in the possession of Mr. Urquhart at Craigston. His motto was, 'The glory of the honourable is to fear God.'

[Index Registri Magni Sigilli, in Signet Library, Edinburgh; Spalding's Miscellany, v. 358; Antiquities of Aberdeen, vol. iv.; Anderson's History of the Family of Fraser; Lord Saltoun's Frasers of Philorth (1879).] H. P.

FRASER, Sir ALEXANDER (1610?–1681), physician. [See FRAIZER.]

FRASER, ALEXANDER (1786–1865), painter and associate of the Royal Scottish Academy, was born at Edinburgh on 7 April 1786. He studied painting under John Graham at the academy of the Board of Trustees for the Improvement of Manufactures in Edinburgh, and had among his fellow-students William Allan, John Burnet, David Thomson, and David Wilkie. In 1809 he sent to the Exhibition of the Associated Artists in Edinburgh a painting of 'Playing at Draughts,' and at once became known as a painter of Scottish character and history, with a spirited and vigorous execution. In 1810 he sent from Edinburgh to the Royal Academy in London 'A Green Stall,' and in 1812 'The New Coat' and 'Preparing for the Fish Market.' From this date he was a frequent contributor to the leading exhibitions in London and Edinburgh. In 1813 he left Edinburgh to reside in London, and soon gained a good position. At this time his former fellow-pupil, Wilkie, was at the zenith of his popularity, and Fraser engaged with him to paint the details and still-life in Wilkie's pictures, which he continued to do for about twenty years. This did not, however, interfere with his own practice as a painter, though his connection with Wilkie and the similarity of their taste and subject not unnaturally led to his art being overshadowed by Wilkie's superior genius. In 1842 his 'Naaman cured of the Leprosy' obtained the premium at the British Institution for the best picture of the year. He was soon after elected an associate of the Royal Scottish Academy, in the foundation of which he had taken a share. Fraser last exhibited at the Royal Academy in 1848, and on approaching seventy years of age he was prevented by ill-health from practising his profession. He died at Wood Green, Hornsey, on 15 Feb. 1865. Fraser's pictures, which are very numerous, have always been popular. 'Cobbler and Bird,' dated 1826, a small panel picture, is at Woburn Abbey. 'The Interior of a Highland Cottage,' formerly in the Vernon Collection, is now in the National Gallery; it was engraved by C. Cousen for the Vernon Gallery. Others have been engraved, including 'Robinson Crusoe reading the Bible to his man Friday,' and 'Asking a Blessing,' both by C. G. Lewis; 'The First Day of Oysters,' by W. Greatbatch; 'The Noonday Meal,' by P. Lightfoot; 'War's Alarms,' by W. H. Simmons; 'The Cobbler at Lunch,' by William Howison; 'The Moment of Victory,' by C. Rolls, &c. His works should be carefully distinguished from those of Alexander Fraser, the present Scottish academician.

[Redgrave's Dict. of Artists; Gent. Mag. 3rd ser. (1865) xviii. 652; Cunningham's Life of Sir David Wilkie; Art Journal, 1865; Catalogues of the Royal Academy, British Institution, &c.; Graves's Dict. of Artists (1760–1880); information from Mr. J. M. Gray.] L. C.

FRASER, ALEXANDER GEORGE, sixteenth BARON SALTOUN (1785–1853), general, was the elder son of Alexander, fifteenth lord Saltoun of Abernethy in the peerage of Scotland, by Margery, daughter and heiress of Simon Fraser of Newcastle, a director of the East India Company. He was born in London on 12 April 1785, and on 13 Sept. 1793 succeeded his father in the Scotch peerage when still a minor. He entered the army as an ensign in the 35th regiment on 28 April 1802, and was promoted lieutenant on 2 Sept. following, and captain on 7 Sept. 1804. On 23 Nov. 1804 he exchanged into the 1st, afterwards the Grenadier guards, with which regiment he served continuously for many years. In September 1806 he accompanied the 3rd battalion of the 1st guards to Sicily, where it formed part of the guards brigade under Major-general Henry Wynyard, and in October 1807 he returned to England with it. In September 1808 he again left England, as lieutenant and captain of the light company of the 3rd battalion of the 1st guards, and his battalion formed one of the two comprising the guards brigade of Major-general Henry Warde which landed at Corunna with the army under Sir David Baird. From Corunna Baird marched to meet Sir John Moore at Mayorga, and in the terrible winter retreat which followed the guards distinguished themselves by their good order. Saltoun was present throughout the severe campaign, and at the battle of Corunna with his light company. In 1809 his battalion formed part of Major-general Disney's brigade of guards in the Walcheren expedition, and in 1811 it was sent to Cadiz, but too late to be present at Barrosa. At the close of 1812 he joined the 1st battalion of his regiment with the main army before Burgos, and from that time he went through the Peninsular campaigns with the 1st brigade of guards. He commanded the light infantry company of his battalion throughout the campaigns of 1813 and 1814, and was present at the battle of Vittoria, the battle of the Pyrenees, the forcing of the Bidassoa, the battles of the Nivelle and the Nive, and at the operations before Bayonne, especially in the repulse of the sortie. He was promoted captain and lieutenant-colonel on 25 Dec. 1813, and posted to the 3rd battalion of his regiment, but as it was in England he obtained leave to continue to serve with Lord Wellington's army in the Peninsula. He returned to England, and joined his old battalion on the conclusion of peace in 1814. On 6 March 1815 Saltoun married Catherine, a natural daughter of Lord-chancellor Thurlow, and in the following May he was again ordered on foreign service. At the battle of Quatre Bras he commanded the light companies of the 2nd brigade of guards, and at the battle of Waterloo he held the garden and orchard of Hougoumont against all the onslaughts of the French, while Sir James Macdonell of the Coldstream guards held the farmhouse itself. Saltoun had four horses killed under him during this day's fighting, and lost two-thirds of his men. When the guards made their famous charge on the Old Guard of France, the light companies were led on by Saltoun, who also received the sword of General Cambronne when that French officer surrendered. For his signal bravery in this great battle Saltoun was made a C.B., a knight of the orders of Maria Theresa of Austria and of St. George of Russia, and in 1818 he was made a K.C.B. He had been a representative peer of Scotland ever since 1807, and as a consistent tory he received the post of a lord of the bedchamber in 1821, in which year he was also made a G.C.H. On 27 May 1825 he was promoted colonel; in 1827 he became lieutenant-colonel commanding the 1st battalion of the Grenadier guards, and on 10 Jan. 1837 he was promoted major-general. In 1841 Saltoun received the command of a brigade

in the 'opium' war with China under Sir Hugh Gough, which he commanded at the battle of Chin-keang-foo and in the advance on Nankin. On Gough's departure from China Saltoun succeeded him in the command-in-chief of all the troops left in that country, a post which he held until 1843. For his services during this war he received the thanks of parliament, and in 1846 he was appointed colonel of the 2nd or Queen's regiment. He was promoted lieutenant-general in 1849, made a K.T. in 1852, and he died at his shooting-box near Rothes on 18 Aug. 1853, being succeeded as seventeenth Lord Saltoun by his nephew, Major Alexander Fraser. Saltoun held the very highest reputation as a gallant soldier; his bravery and coolness in action were proverbial in the army; his defence of the orchard of Hougoumont has made his name famous in English military history; and the Duke of Wellington once described him as a pattern to the army both as a man and a soldier. He was also an accomplished musician and a musical enthusiast, and was at the time of his death president of the Madrigal Society of London and chairman of the Musical Union.

[Foster's Peerage; Gent. Mag. October 1853; Royal Military Calendar; Hart's Army List; Hamilton's Hist. of the Grenadier Guards; Siborne's Waterloo.]   H. M. S.

FRASER, ALEXANDER MACKENZIE (1756–1809), major-general, was the third and posthumous son of Colin Mackenzie of Kilcoy, Ross-shire, by Martha, daughter of Charles Fraser of Inverallochy and of Castle Fraser in Aberdeenshire. He was educated at the university of Aberdeen, and at an early age he entered the banking-house of Sir William Forbes & Co. of Edinburgh, which he left in 1778 on being offered a commission by Lord Macleod in the 73rd, afterwards the 71st, highlanders. Mackenzie was speedily promoted lieutenant and made adjutant, and he served throughout General Eliott's famous defence of Gibraltar, during which he acted as aide-de-camp to Major-general Sir Charles Ross in his sortie, and was wounded by a splinter of rock. He was promoted captain on 13 Jan. 1781, and on the conclusion of the war he returned to England with Lord Macleod. The 71st regiment was next ordered to India, and when it departed Mackenzie was left behind on recruiting service. In 1784 he married Miss Helen Mackenzie, sister of the two highland generals, Thomas and Francis Humberstone Mackenzie, and great granddaughter of Kenneth, third earl of Seaforth, who was attainted for his complicity in the rebellion of 1713. Mackenzie threw up his commission in the army, and purchased the estate of Tore in Ross-shire, where he spent eight years in retirement until the outbreak of the great war with France in 1793. In that year his brother-in-law, Francis Humberstone Mackenzie, who was in 1797 created Lord Seaforth, raised the 78th highlanders, or Ross-shire buffs, and in May 1793 he appointed Mackenzie major in it. The new regiment was disciplined with unexampled rapidity, and in four months it was declared fit for service, and ordered to Guernsey. On 10 Feb. 1794 Mackenzie was promoted lieutenant-colonel, and in the following September he joined the army under the Duke of York at Flanders. During the terrible winter retreat before Pichegru he covered the division of Sir Ralph Abercromby, and had frequently to face round in order to check the rapid pursuit of the French army. His most distinguished services were in the sortie from Nimeguen on 4 Nov. 1794, when he succeeded in the chief command General de Burgh, disabled by wounds, and at Geldermalsen on 5 Jan. 1795, on which occasion Sir David Dundas rode up to him and said publicly, 'Colonel Alexander Mackenzie, you and your regiment have this day saved the British army.' In March 1795 he returned to England on the termination of the campaign, and received a commission to raise a second battalion of the 78th regiment, and in 1796 he was gazetted colonel-commandant. In that year he proceeded to the Cape of Good Hope with his second battalion, which he there amalgamated with the first battalion, forming a superb regiment of over thirteen hundred men. He acted for a short time as second in command to Major-general Sir J. H. Craig at the Cape, and then continued his way to India, where his battalion was quartered at Benares. It was his regiment which escorted Sir John Shore to Lucknow in 1797, when he went there to depose the nawab of Oude, and as one of the conditions of the treaty then made, Mackenzie took possession of Allahabad. In 1798 he joined Sir James Craig at Cawnpore, and commanded a wing of his army in the march against the Maráthás, and on 1 Jan. 1800 he left India for England. In 1802 he was promoted major-general, and in the same year was elected M.P. for Cromarty. In 1803 he inherited Inverallochy from his mother and Castle Fraser from his aunt, and he then took the additional name of Fraser. From 1803 to 1805 he commanded a brigade in England, and in 1805 in Hanover. In 1806 he was appointed to the staff of General Henry Edward Fox [q. v.] in Sicily, and in the same year he was elected M.P. for the county of Ross. While in Sicily he was selected for the command of an expedition to Egypt, for the British government had been induced by the urgent recommendations of the British consul-general, Major Missett, to direct General Fox to send a corps of five thousand men to Egypt. Mehemet Ali Pasha was then in power, and it was believed that owing to the disputes between the Mamelukes, the Porte, and the pasha it would be easy for a very small British army to obtain supremacy in Egypt. Fox was ordered to select one of his generals, fitted for both military and political affairs. 'It was probably on account of his conciliatory temper,' Bunbury writes, ' and his frank and engaging manners, that General Mackenzie Fraser was selected for the command of the expedition to Alexandria. He was a fine specimen of an open, generous, honourable highland chieftain. A man of very good plain sense, but one who had never studied the higher branches either of politics or of military science. Every one in the army loved Mackenzie Fraser, but no one deemed him qualified for a separate and difficult command ' (SIR HENRY BUNBURY, Narrative, p. 287). The force placed at his disposal consisted of seventy light dragoons, 180 artillerymen, and five thousand infantry, namely the 31st regiment, both battalions of the 35th, the second battalion of the 78th, the Regiment de Roll, the Chasseurs Britanniques, and the Sicilian volunteers. His transports were scattered on the way to Egypt, but on 18 March 1807 Captain Hallowell, better known as Admiral Sir Benjamin Hallowell Carew [q. v.], managed to get a thousand men ashore without any opposition. His other transports soon arrived with Sir John Duckworth's fleet from the Dardanelles, and on 21 March Fraser took possession of Alexandria. Then his greatest difficulties began; Major Missett, the consul-general, declared that it was impossible for him to get provisions for his army in Alexandria, a declaration proved to be false; he stated that the Albanian soldiers of Mehemet Ali were mere rabble, and recommended the general to send detachments to take possession of Rosetta and Rahmanieh. Fraser accordingly despatched a small force under Major-general Wauchope, his second in command, against Rosetta, and that general stupidly got involved in the narrow streets of the Egyptian city, where he was fired on by the Albanians from the windows and killed. His little force extricated itself with difficulty, with a loss of nearly half its numbers. Missett, however, insisted on the importance of taking Rosetta, and Fraser accordingly sent a brigade of 2,500 men to besiege that city. This expedition, though better conducted, was equally disastrous; Mehemet Ali sent all his best troops down the Nile; the British army was forced to retire with heavy loss, and one of the detacments at El Hamid, of thirty-six officers and 780 men, was entirely cut off by the Albanians. Fortunately, Major-general Sherbrooke at this time joined Fraser's army with a reinforcement of two thousand men, and the foolish and disastrous expedition came to an end after the treaty made by Sir Arthur Paget with the Grande Porte, and the restoration of the prisoners taken in the affair of Rosetta. On 23 April 1807 Fraser returned to Sicily, and when Sir John Moore left that country with his division for Sweden, Fraser commanded one of his brigades. Moore did not land in Sweden owing to the mad conduct of the king, and Moore's division went on to Portugal. Fraser there took command of an infantry division consisting of Fane's and Mackinnon's brigades, and he advanced with Sir John Moore into Spain. During the terrible retreat under that general through Galicia Fraser showed the highest military qualities, and his division, which was posted on the extreme left, greatly distinguished itself at the battle of Corunna. For his services at this battle he received a gold medal, and on 25 June 1808 he was promoted lieutenant-general. In the Walcheren expedition of 1809 he commanded the 3rd infantry division, with which he took the towns of Campveer on 30 July and Ramakens on 2 Aug. The pestilential climate of Walcheren greatly affected his health, and he returned to England only to die on 13 Sept. 1809 at the house of his brother-in-law, Sir Vicary Gibbs, the attorney-general, on Hayes Common. Fraser was one of the most popular, if not most able generals of his time; and an old comrade, writing to the 'Gentleman's Magazine' for October 1809, speaks of him as being 'mild as a lamb, and as a lion strong.'

[The authority for Mackenzie Fraser's life and career is a long article in the Military Panorama for May and June 1814; see also Gent. Mag. for September 1809, Sir Henry Bunbury's Narrative of some Passages in the Great War with France for the expedition to Egypt, and Napier's Peninsular War for Fraser's share in the campaign and battle of Corunna.] H. M. S.

FRASER, ANDREW (d. 1792), engineer. [See FRAZER.]

FRASER, ARCHIBALD CAMPBELL (1736–1815), of Lovat, thirty-eighth Macshimi, colonel 1st Inverness local militia, son of Simon Fraser, twelfth lord Lovat [q. v.], by his second wife, was born 16 Aug. 1736.

He was at school at Petty, and with some school companions was led by curiosity to the field of Culloden during the battle. Anderson (*Account of the Family of Fraser*) states that he afterwards acquired a sporting reputation under the name of FitzSimon. He was British consul at Tripoli at the time of the traveller Bruce's visit (BRUCE, *Travels*, I. xxxviii). He was appointed consul at Algiers in 1766 (*Cal. Home Office Papers*, 1766–9, par. 60) and held that post until 1774. Numerous references to his consular services in Barbary appear in the printed 'Calendars of Home Office Papers' for that period. He inherited the restored family estates in 1782, on the death of his elder half-brother Lieutenant-general Simon Fraser [see FRASER, SIMON, 1726–1782, Master of Lovat], whom he also succeeded as M.P. for Inverness-shire, which he represented in succeeding parliaments down to 1796. On the extension of the Local Militia Act to Scotland (48 Geo. III, c. 50) he was appointed colonel of the 1st Inverness-shire local militia, with headquarters at Inverness. Fraser, who is described as a typical gentleman of the old school, but very eccentric, some years before his death put up a monument to himself setting forth his public services—that, when on a mission to the Mahomedan states of Africa in 1764, he concluded a peace between these states, Denmark, and Venice; that during his ten years' consulate he ransomed imperialist, Spanish, and Portuguese subjects to the value of two millions sterling, and that not a single British subject during that time was sold into slavery; that he co-operated with the Duke of Montrose in procuring the restoration of the highland garb; that in 1785 he surveyed the fisheries of the western coast at his own cost, and petitioned for a repeal of the duties on coal and salt; that he encouraged the manufacture of wool, hemp, and flax; laboured to improve the soil; amended the breed of highland oxen; improved dairy practice; and, by providing employment for a hardy race of men returning from the wars, prevented emigration and preserved to the country their services, equally valuable in peace; that he put down insurrection on 10 Aug. 1792, and planned the system of placing arms in the hands of men of property, and, when invasion threatened, had the satisfaction of seeing its adoption and efficiency. These statements appear to require a good deal of qualification. Ninety years ago the old church at Kirkhill was pulled down and rebuilt on a site two hundred yards away; but the monument still survives on the wall of the Lovat mausoleum within the enclosure of the parish churchyard. The bombastic monument put up in his own glorification by Fraser's father, Lord Lovat (see HILL BURTON, *Life of Lord Lovat*), is fixed in the same wall. Fraser was author of 'Annals of . . . the Patriots of the Family of Fraser, Frizell, Simson, or FitzSimon' (published 1795, reprinted 1805, 8vo). Several brochures relating to the Lovat estates are entered under his name in the 'British Museum Catalogue of Printed Books.' He died on 8 Dec. 1815.

Fraser married, in 1763, Jane, daughter of William Fraser and sister of Sir William Fraser, bart., of Leadclune. By her he had six sons, all of whom died before their father.

SIMON FRASER (1765–1803), the eldest son, matriculated at Wadham College, Oxford, 4 July 1786; entered Lincoln's Inn 1789 and the Inner Temple 1793; was lieutenant-colonel of the Fraser Fencibles, a regiment raised in 1794 by James Fraser of Balladrum, a surviving officer of the old 78th Fraser highlanders, and disbanded in 1802; commanded the regiment in Ireland in 1798; sat in parliament for Inverness-shire from 1796 to 1802, and died, unmarried, at Lisbon on 6 April 1803.

[J. Anderson's Account of the Family of Frizell or Fraser (Edinburgh, 1825); J. Hill Burton's Life of Simon, Lord Lovat (London, 1845); Cal. of Home Office Papers, 1766–9, 1770–2; British Museum Cat. Printed Books; Official Lists of Members of Parliament; information from private sources. Fraser was one of the trustees of the Inverness bank according to a work entitled Observations on Objects interesting to the Highlands . . . By Invernessicus (Edinburgh, 1814, 8vo). A notice of the Fraser Fencibles will be found in General D. Stewart's Sketches of the Scottish Highlanders (Edinburgh, 1822), ii. 392–395, and a list of fencible and local militia regiments in Colburn's United Service Mag. December 1873.] H. M. C.

FRASER, JAMES (1639–1699), covenanting divine (commonly called from his patrimonial estate FRASER OF BRAE), was born in the parish of Kirkmichael, Ross-shire, on 29 July 1639. His father, Sir James Fraser, was the second son of Simon, seventh lord Lovat, by his second wife, Jane Stewart, daughter of James, lord Doun (son of the Earl of Moray). Sir James Fraser, a devout man, was elder for the presbytery of Inverness in the general assembly of 1638 which abolished episcopacy, and sat in several other general assemblies. The son was educated at a grammar school, and suffered much from his father's pecuniary difficulties. At a very early age he came under deep impressions of religion, abandoned the study of the law, and obtained license as a preacher of the gospel from a presbyterian minister in 1670. Coming under the notice of Archbishop Sharp as a preacher at conventicles, he was ordered to be apprehended in 1674; decreets and letters of intercommuning were passed against him 6 Aug. 1675. He was summoned before the council 29 Jan. 1676–7, and ordered to be imprisoned on the Bass Rock the next day. Here he remained two years and a half, being released on giving security for good behaviour in July 1679. He was depressed by the sudden death of his wife in October 1676, and by the many troubles of the time, as well as by his imprisonment. He yet found material for recording in his diary many matters that called for gratitude. While in prison he studied Hebrew and Greek, and gained some knowledge of oriental languages. He wrote also a treatise on justifying faith, of which many editions have been printed. Some of its views in favour of a universal reference in the work of Christ were strongly objected to by certain of his brethren who saw it in manuscript, and it was not till 1722 that the first part was published, the second appearing in 1749. In December 1681 he was again arrested and committed to Blackness Castle as a prisoner until he paid a fine of five thousand marks and gave security either to give up preaching or quit the kingdom. A brother-in-law caused the fine to be remitted, and Fraser was sent out of Scotland. On 21 July 1683 he was ordered to be imprisoned for six months in Newgate, London, for refusing the Oxford oath. Before 6 July 1687 he returned to Scotland, and was living in the bounds of Lothian and Tweeddale. In 1689 he was minister of Culross, Perthshire, where he exercised his ministry with diligence and earnestness. He was a member of the assemblies of 1690 and 1692, had a call from Inverness in September 1696, but died at Edinburgh 13 Sept. 1699. Fraser was a man of peculiar type, independent and sometimes singular in his views, an ultra-Calvinist, yet with a certain doctrine of universalism. He was twice married: first to a lady, Jean G——, 31 July 1672, who died in October 1676; and secondly to Christian Inglis, widow of Alexander Carmichael, minister of Pettinain, Lanarkshire.

Besides the book already mentioned, Fraser wrote memoirs of his life, published at Edinburgh in 1738. This book is to a large extent a record of his religious experience, with notices of his captivities and other events in his life up to his release from Newgate in 1684. Another work is entitled the 'Lawfulness and Duty of Separation from corrupt Ministers and Churches,' Edinb. 1744, being an argument against attending the ministrations of the ministers who accepted the conditions imposed on them by the king. A third, entitled 'Defence of the Convention of Estates, 1689,' vindicates that body for having declared that James VII had forfeited his right to the crown and that his throne was vacant. A sermon, ' Prelacy an Idol,' appeared in 1713.

[Douglas's Peerage, vol. ii.; Memoirs of the Rev. James Fraser of Brae (Wodrow Soc. Select Biog. vol. ii.); Anderson's Martyrs of the Bass (in the Bass Rock, 1848); Wodrow's History; Scott's Fasti, iv. 585; Walker's Theology and Theologians of Scotland.] W. G. B.

FRASER, JAMES (1700–1769), Scotch divine (sometimes called FRASER OF PITCAL-ZIAN), was born in 1700 at the manse of Alness in Ross-shire, where his father, the Rev. JOHN FRASER (d. 1711), was minister from 1696 till his death in 1711. The father, a native of the highlands, graduated at Aberdeen in 1678, attended dissenting meetings in London, was seized with Alexander Shiels in 1684, was sent to Leith, and thence, chained with Shiels, in the kitchen-yacht to Edinburgh, and was imprisoned in Dunottar Castle 18 May 1685. After three months of terrible suffering, he with his wife was among the hundred persons who were made a present of to the laird of Pitlochie and shipped for New Jersey, where they were to be disposed of for the laird's benefit. In New Jersey Fraser was set at liberty; went to New England, and preached as a licentiate at Waterbury, Connecticut. He returned to Scotland at the revolution, was ordained 23 Dec. 1691, and was settled first at Glencorse (1691–5), and afterwards at Alness (SCOTT, Fasti, pt. i. 281–2, pt. v. 291).

James Fraser, the son, was a man of considerable theological learning, and besides discharging his pastoral duties in a highly edifying way, showed no little ability as a biblical critic. He was licensed by the presbytery of Chanonry 6 Nov. 1723, and ordained 17 Feb. 1726, becoming minister of Alness. The treatise entitled ' The Scripture Doctrine of Sanctification' (Edinb. 1774) was suggested in consequence of the false view, as Fraser held, taken by Locke of the fifth and sixth chapters of the Epistle to the Romans, Locke applying them solely to the Gentiles. Starting from this point, the author was led into a very copious exposition of chapters vi. vii. viii. and an elaborate refutation of the Arminian views of Grotius, Hammond, Locke, Whitby, Taylor, Alexander, and others. His book has kept its ground in Scotland as an able and elaborate exposition of these important chapters, from the Calvinistic point of view. Fraser was a regular correspondent of Robert Wodrow, to whom he suggested the preparation of his work on witchcraft. He died

5 Oct. 1769. His widow, Jean Macleod, died 13 March 1778.

[A short account of the author prefixed to his work by the Rev. A. Fraser, Inverness, endorsed by Dr. John Erskine, Edinburgh, 1774; Scott's Fasti, pt. v. 291–2.] W. G. B.

FRASER, JAMES (d. 1841), publisher, was of an Inverness family. He carried on business at 215 Regent Street, and there published ' Fraser's Magazine,' so called from Hugh Fraser, a barrister, who, with Dr. Maginn, was the projector of the new tory review, afterwards familiarly known as ' Regina.' James Fraser never assumed the paternity of the magazine, which was always spoken of in his books and correspondence as ' The Town and Country.' The first number of ' Fraser's Magazine for Town and Country ' appeared in February 1830. The famous ' Gallery of Illustrious Literary Characters ' came out in it between 1830 and 1838; eighty-one portraits, chiefly by Daniel Maclise, with letterpress by Maginn. In 1833 a handsome quarto volume containing thirty-four of the portraits was issued, and in 1874 the complete gallery republished for the first time. The portraits were reduced in size and the literary matter much increased in ' The Maclise Portrait Gallery,' by William Bates, with eighty-five portraits, London, 1883, sm. 8vo. On 3 Aug. 1836 took place the cowardly attack by Grantley Berkeley [q. v.] upon the publisher in consequence of a severe criticism of his novel ' Berkeley Castle.' Cross actions were tried 3 Dec. on the part of Fraser for assault and Berkeley for libel. The one obtained 100l. damages for the assault and the other 40s. for the libel. Among the contributors to the magazine were Carlyle, Thackeray, F. S. Mahony (Father Prout), T. Love Peacock, Mr. J. A. Froude, Mr. W. Allingham, and many other well-known writers. After Fraser's death it fell to his successor, G. W. Nickisson, whose name first appeared on it in 1842. Five years later it was transferred to John W. Parker, of West Strand, by whom and by his successors it was continued under the same name to October 1882, when it was superseded by ' Longman's Magazine.'

Fraser published many books, among them Carlyle's ' Hero Worship.' The story of the dealings between the author and ' the infatuated Fraser, with his dog's-meat tart of a magazine,' is told in J. A. Froude's ' Thomas Carlyle ' (1882, vol. ii. and 1885, vol. i.) He was liberal and straightforward in business transactions and had much taste and judgment in literary matters. He died 2 Oct. 1841 at Argyll Street, London, after a lingering illness attributed by the newspapers of the day to the injuries inflicted upon him by Grantley Berkeley (see quotations in *Fraser's Magazine,* 1841, xxiv. 628–30).

[Literary Gazette, 9 Oct. 1841, p. 660 ; Gent. Mag. 1841, new ser. xvi. 553 ; Grantley Berkeley's Life and Recollections, 1865–6, 4 vols. ; Fraser's Mag. January 1837, pp. 100–43 ; W. Bates's Maclise Portrait Gallery, 1883 ; Notes and Queries 4th ser. vii. 31, 211, 5th ser. v. 249.] H. R. T.

FRASER, JAMES (1818–1885), bishop of Manchester, eldest son of James Fraser, of a branch of the family of Fraser of Durris, a retired India merchant, by his wife Helen, a daughter of John Willim, solicitor, of Bilston, Staffordshire, was born 18 Aug. 1818 at Prestbury, Gloucestershire. His father lost money in ironstone mines in the Forest of Dean, and dying in 1832 left his widow and seven children poorly provided for. Fraser's early years were chiefly spent at his maternal grandfather's at Bilston, but when his father removed to Heavitree, Exeter, he was put to school there. In 1832 he was placed under Dr. Rowley at Bridgnorth school, Staffordshire, and in 1834 removed to Shrewsbury school, where, first under Dr. Butler and then under Dr. Kennedy, he remained till 1836. Though entered at Balliol, and an unsuccessful competitor for scholarships at Corpus Christi College, Oxford, he was elected a scholar of Lincoln College and matriculated 16 March 1836, and went into residence in January 1837. He was a strong athlete, and had a passion for horses; but his poverty compelled him to deny himself the gratification of such tastes. As an undergraduate he lived a very recluse life, and no doubt acquired then his remarkable self-mastery. In 1837 he was an unsuccessful candidate for the Hertford scholarship, but in 1838 he all but won, and in 1839 did win, the Ireland scholarship. In November 1839 he took a first class in final honour schools, graduated B.A. 6 Feb. 1840, and was elected a fellow of Oriel. At this time he impressed his friends as shy and immature. At the end of his year of probation at Oriel he became reader of sermon notes, and tutor from 1842 to 1847 ; he graduated M.A. on 18 May 1842, and in January 1844 became subdean and librarian. Though in no respect a great tutor, his sympathies gave him unusual popularity among the undergraduates. On 18 Dec. 1846 he took deacon's orders, and, having indulged himself with a last fortnight's hard hunting in Leicestershire, forswore that pleasure for the rest of his life. He took some parochial work in Oxford, entered priest's orders Trinity Sunday 1847, and in July accepted the college living of Cholderton, Wiltshire, which

on this occasion was made tenable with a fellowship. Till 1856 he took pupils, and for twenty years occasionally was examiner at Oxford and elsewhere. In 1858 he examined for the Ireland, and in 1866 for the Craven scholarship at Oxford. On 12 Dec. 1851 he preached his first sermon as select preacher at Oxford, and was select preacher subsequently in 1861, 1871, 1877, and, though he did not preach any sermon, in 1885. In 1854 he became examining chaplain and subsequently in 1858 chancellor to Dr. Hamilton, bishop of Salisbury. Several of his sermons at Salisbury were published. On Bishop Hamilton's recommendation he was appointed assistant commissioner to the Royal Commission on Education in 1858 for a district of thirteen poor law unions in Dorsetshire, Devonshire, Somersetshire, Herefordshire, and Worcestershire. His report, made May 1859 and published in 1861, is, according to Mr. Thomas Hughes, 'a superb, I had almost said a unique, piece of work.' In 1860 he resigned his fellowship, on accepting the rectory of Ufton Nervet, Berkshire. In this parish, where he accomplished many parochial improvements, he developed his great capacity for business and for leadership. In March 1865 he was appointed a commissioner to report on education in the United States and America, and was in Canada and the United States from May till October. His report, made in 1866, stamped him as a man who was destined for ecclesiastical promotion, and in that year Lord Cranborne made him the offer of the bishopric of Calcutta, which he declined. In 1867 he prepared for the Commission on the Employment of Children in Agriculture, on the recommendation of the home secretary, a masterly report on the south-eastern district, comprising Norfolk, Suffolk, Essex, Sussex, and Gloucestershire. In June 1869 he preached before the queen, and on 18 Jan. 1870, expressly on the ground of his authority on educational questions, he received the offer of the bishopric of Manchester, and accepting it was consecrated on 25 March.

His new sphere was the most difficult of its kind in the kingdom. It was almost a new diocese. Its late bishop, Dr. Prince Lee, had lived a retired and a comparatively inactive life. It was a huge industrial community, with little interest in ecclesiastical affairs. Nonconformists of all denominations were numerous, and the district was in the crisis of the education question. To a new bishop the nonconformists' attitude was critical, and on the part of many hostile. The machinery of diocesan organisation was defective, and little was being done for church extension. Fifteen years afterwards Fraser died universally lamented. During his episcopate ninety-nine new churches, containing fifty-seven thousand sittings, nearly all free, and costing 685,000*l.*, were consecrated, twenty churches were rebuilt at a cost of 214,000*l.*, a hundred and nine new district parishes were created, and the whole fabric of diocesan machinery—conferences, board of education, and building society—had been created and was in perfect working order. The labour which his mere episcopal duties involved was prodigious; for the number of persons he confirmed was counted by scores of thousands. But in addition to this he threw himself into almost every social movement of the day. He was to be seen going about the streets on foot, his robe-bag in his hand; he addressed meetings several times a day; he spoke to workmen in mills, and to actors in theatres; he was diligent in attending his diocesan registry; he was a member of the governing bodies of Manchester and Shrewsbury grammar schools and of the Owens College, visitor of the high school for girls and of the commercial school, and president of the College for Women. 'Omnipresence,' said his foes, 'was his forte, and omniscience his foible.' Not being a born orator, or even a very good one, and speaking constantly on all topics without time for preparation, it is true that he said some rash things and many trite ones, and laid himself open to frequent attack; but his absolute frankness and fearlessness of speech won the heart of his people, and his strong good sense and honesty commanded their respect. He earned for himself the name of 'bishop of all denominations.' In 1874 he was chosen umpire between the masters and men in the Manchester and Salford painting trade, and his award, made 27 March, secured peace for the trade for two years. He was again umpire in March 1876, and in 1878, during the great north-east Lancashire cotton strike, the men offered to refer the dispute to him, but the masters refused. He always protested against the unwisdom of strikes and lockouts, and sought to make peace between the disputants. Outside the co-operative body he was the first to draw attention to that movement, having described the Assington Agricultural Association in his report on agriculture in 1867. When the co-operative congress was held in Manchester in 1878, he presided on the second day, and appeared in 1885 at that held at Derby.

He never was a professed theologian, but his views were on the whole of the old high church school. He had little sympathy with the tractarian high churchmen, and in all matters of practice he was extremely liberal, and more disposed to take a legal than an ecclesiastical view of such matters. His first appearance in convocation was to second Dean Howson's motion in favour of the disuse of the Athanasian Creed; his first speech in the House of Lords was on 8 May 1871, in support of the abolition of university tests; and he said characteristically to his diocesan conference, in 1875: 'If the law requires me to wear a cope, though I don't like the notion of making a guy of myself, I will wear one.' Yet he was fated to appear as a religious persecutor, to his own infinite distress. When first he went to Manchester the extreme protestant party looked to him for assistance in suppressing ritualism in the diocese. For some time he succeeded in pacifying them, and it was not until after the Public Worship Regulation Act was passed, of the policy of which he approved, that strife began. In 1878 complaint was made to him of the ritual practice of the Rev. S. F. Green, incumbent of Miles Platting. The first complaint the bishop was able to disregard, as wanting in *bona fides*; but in December the Church Association took up the case and made a formal presentation to him, and after some persuasion had been tried to induce Mr. Green to alter the matters complained of, the bishop felt obliged to allow the suit to proceed, upon a refusal to discontinue the use of the mixed chalice. The case was tried by Lord Penzance in June 1879, and was decided adversely to Mr. Green, who was eventually, in 1881, committed to Lancaster gaol for contempt of court. It was upon the motion of the bishop that he was at last released. The living meantime had become vacant, and the patron, Sir Percival Heywood, would present no one but Mr. Green's former curate, the Rev. Mr. Cowgill, whom the bishop had already refused to license. Mr. Cowgill declining to undertake not to continue Mr. Green's ritual, the bishop in December 1882 refused to institute him. The patron thereupon commenced an action against him for this refusal, which was eventually tried by Baron Pollock on 10 and 11 Dec. 1883, and judgment was given for the defendant. The bishop then presented to the living, and the contest closed.

On 24 April 1880 his mother, who had hitherto lived with him, died. Three months before he had married Agnes (to whom he had become engaged in 1878), daughter of John Shute Duncan of Bath, sometime fellow of New College, Oxford. In September 1885 he suffered from congestion of the veins of the neck, caused by a chill. He was obliged to curtail his work, and was thinking of resigning his bishopric when, on 22 Oct., he died rather suddenly. He was buried at Ufton Nervet on 27 Oct. Nonconformists of all denominations, with the Jewish and Greek congregations of Manchester, sent flowers to his funeral. On the same day a memorial service was held in Manchester, which was attended by prodigious crowds. Many places of business were closed; transactions on 'Change were for a time suspended; and a procession of magistrates, mayors, and members of parliament from all parts of Lancashire marched from the town hall to the cathedral. His charities were many. Though then a poor man, he expended on his parish of Cholderton 600*l.*, and on Ufton Nervet 2,000*l.*; while the strict accounts which he kept showed benefactions to his diocese to the extent of 30,000*l.* Yet, thanks to his habitual thrift and sound sense, he left over 70,000*l.* Except his reports to parliamentary commissions, and a few sermons and addresses, he published nothing. In 1888 his sermons (2 vols.) were edited by J. W. Diggle (afterwards bishop of Carlisle). His portrait was painted in 1880 by Sir J. E. Millais. There is a full-length figure of him in the Fraser chapel of Manchester Cathedral, with an inscription by Dr. Vaughan, and a statue in Albert Square, Manchester.

[Life (1887) by Thomas Hughes, Q.C. (to whom all Fraser's letters, &c., were committed by his family); The Lancashire Life of Bishop Fraser, 1889, by J. W. Diggle (bishop of Carlisle); Manchester Guardian, 23–9 Oct. 1885; London Guardian, 28 Oct. 1885.] J. A. H.

FRASER, JAMES BAILLIE (1783–1856), traveller and man of letters, eldest son of Edward Satchell Fraser of Reelick, Inverness-shire, was born at Reelick on 11 June 1783. In early life he went to the West Indies, and thence to India. In 1815, on the close of the war with Nepal, he made a tour of exploration in the Himalayas, accompanied by his brother, William Fraser [q. v.], then political agent to General Martindale's army, and an escort, the party being the first Europeans known to have traversed that part of the peninsula. The tour occupied two months, in the course of which the travellers penetrated as far as the sources of the rivers Jumna and Ganges. Fraser afterwards published an account of it, entitled 'Journal of a Tour through part of the Himálá Mountains, and to the Sources of the Rivers Jumna and Ganges,' London, 1820, 8vo. A folio volume of coloured plates illustrating the scenery accompanied the work. In 1821 he accompanied Dr. Jukes on his mission to Persia, reaching Teheran on 29 Nov., and afterwards, 27 Dec., set out in Persian costume with the intention of travelling through

Khorasan to Bokhara. He reached Meshed on 2 Feb. 1822, but there learning that the road to Bokhara was in a very disturbed state, turned westward by Kurdistan and the Caspian Sea, and terminated his travels at Tabriz. This expedition furnished him with materials for two new works, viz. 1. 'Narrative of a Journey into Khorasan in the years 1821 and 1822, including some Account of the Countries to the North-east of Persia. With remarks upon the National Character, Government, and Resources of that Kingdom,' London, 1825, 2 vols. 4to. 2. 'Travels and Adventures in the Persian Provinces on the Southern Banks of the Caspian Sea. With an Appendix containing short Notices on the Geology and Commerce of Persia,' London, 1826, 4to. Fraser next published 'The Kuzzilbash. A Tale of Khorasan,' London, 1828, 12mo. This romance purports to be founded on a manuscript discovered by the author while in India, and relates to the time of Nader-Shah. It was followed by a sequel, entitled 'The Persian Adventurer,' London, 1830, 3 vols. 12mo. Fraser's next effort was 'The Highland Smugglers,' London, 1832, 3 vols. 12mo, which was followed by 'Tales of the Caravanserai,' being vol. vii. of the 'Library of Romance,' edited by Leitch Ritchie, London, 1833, 12mo. He also contributed to the 'Edinburgh Cabinet Library,' vol. xv., 'An Historical and Descriptive Account of Persia from the earliest Ages to the present Time,' Edinburgh, 1834, 12mo (reprinted at New York in 1843). In the winter of 1833–4 he went on a diplomatic mission to Persia, riding from Semlin to Constantinople, and from Stamboul to Teheran, a distance of 2,600 miles, between Christmas 1833 and 8 March 1834. 'A Winter's Journey (Tâtar) from Constantinople to Teheran. With Travels through various parts of Persia,' &c., London, 1836, 2 vols. 8vo, gives a detailed account of this performance, while 'Travels in Kurdistan, Mesopotamia,' &c., London, 1840, 2 vols. 8vo, describes his return journey. On the visit of the Persian princes to England in 1835, he was chosen by the government to make all arrangements for their reception and entertainment during their stay in the country, which furnished him with matter for another work, viz. 'Narrative of the Residence of the Persian Princes in London in 1835 and 1836. With an Account of their Journey from Persia and subsequent Adventures,' London, 1838, 2 vols. 8vo. Returning to romance, he next published 'Allee Neemroo, the Buchtiaree Adventurer. A Tale of Louristan,' London, 1842, 3 vols. 8vo, and the same year 'Mesopotamia and Assyria from the earliest Ages to the present Time,'

Edinburgh, 12mo (being vol. xxxii. of the 'Edinburgh Cabinet Library,' reprinted at New York in 1845). Two more Eastern romances, viz. (1) 'The Dark Falcon. A Tale of the Attreck,' London, 1844, 4 vols. 8vo; and (2) 'The Khan's Tale,' London, 1850, 12mo, published in vol. xlvi. of the 'Parlour Library,' concluded his efforts in that species of composition. His last work was 'Military Memoir of Lieutenant-colonel James Skinner, C. B.,' London, 1851, 2 vols. 8vo. As a writer Fraser cannot claim any high rank. His works of travel had a certain value when first published on account of the extreme ignorance of the countries described which then prevailed; but owing to the author's lack of all but the most elementary knowledge of physical science they constituted no solid contribution to systematic geography. His tales are of no conspicuous merit. He was an amateur painter in water-colours. In later life he resided on and gave much attention to improving his estate at Reelick, of which county he was deputy-lieutenant. He died in January 1856. Fraser married in 1823 Jane, daughter of Alexander Fraser Tytler, Lord Woodhouselee [q. v.]

[Gent. Mag. 1856, new ser. xlv. 307; Imp. Dict. of Biog.; Edinb. Review, xliii. 87 et seq.; Brit. Mus. Cat.] J. M. R.

FRASER, JAMES STUART (1783–1869), of Ardachy, Inverness, general in the Indian army, was youngest son of Colonel Charles Fraser of that ilk, a scion of the house of Lovat, who fought as a marine officer under Admiral Hawke, and afterwards entered the Madras army, and died a colonel in command of a division at Masulipatam, 5 May 1795. Charles Fraser married Isabella Hook, and by her had six sons and three daughters; the eldest son, Hastings Fraser, who afterwards distinguished himself as a king's officer in India, died a general and colonel 86th Royal County Down regiment in 1854.

James 'Stewart' Fraser (as his baptismal register has it) was the youngest child, and was born at Edinburgh 1 July 1783. He was at school at Ham, Surrey, and afterwards at Glasgow University, where he showed a predilection for languages and astronomical studies. A Madras cadet of 1799, he was posted as lieutenant to the 18th Madras native infantry, 15 Dec. 1800. He served as assistant to Colonel Marriott on an escort conveying the Mysore princes to Bengal in 1807, and was aide-de-camp to Sir George Barlow [q. v.], governor of Madras, at the time of the mutiny of the Madras officers. He became a regimental captain 6 Nov. 1809, and private secretary to the government of

Madras 9 May 1810. He accompanied the Madras division in the expedition against the Isle of France (Mauritius) in the same year as deputy-commissary, and was on the personal staff of Colonel Keating, H.M. 56th regiment, in the landing at Mapou and advance on Port Louis. He was appointed barrack-master at Fort St. George, 29 March 1811; town-major of Fort St. George, and military secretary to the governor, 21 May 1813; and commandant at Pondicherry 28 Oct. 1816. He was employed as commissioner for the restitution of French and Dutch possessions on the Coromandel and Malabar coasts in 1816–17. This duty was facilitated by Fraser's literary and colloquial familiarity with the French language—a rather rare accomplishment among Anglo-Indians of that day—and he was specially thanked and commended by the government of India for 'the marked ability and conciliatory disposition' which had 'distinguished his conduct' throughout every stage of the long and tedious negotiations. He became major 10 Dec. 1819, and lieutenant-colonel 1 May 1824.

While commanding at Pondicherry Fraser married, at Cuddalore, 18 May 1826, Henrietta Jane, daughter of Captain Stevenson, admiralty agent for the eastern coast of India, and grand-niece of General Stevenson, who commanded the nizam's subsidiary forces at Assaye and Argaum. This lady, who was twenty years his junior, bore him a numerous family and died in 1860.

In 1828 Fraser was deputed to discuss the claims of the French at Mahé, and the same year was appointed special agent for foreign settlements. He became brevet-colonel 6 Nov. 1829. He was appointed secretary to the government in the military department 12 Feb. 1834. He was present in several actions during the conquest of Coorg, and carried out the negotiations that brought the war to a close. He was appointed resident at Mysore and commissioner of Coorg 6 June 1834, and assumed charge of the Mysore residency in October following. On 26 Sept. 1836 he was appointed regimental colonel 36th Madras native infantry, his previous regimental commissions having all been in his old corps, the 18th native infantry. He was appointed resident at Travancore and Cochin 5 Jan. 1836, and officiating resident at Hyderabad 1 Sept. 1838. Fraser 'repeatedly received the thanks of the government of Madras, the governor-general of India, and the court of directors of the East India Company for his eminent services. He appears, however, to have interfered in the disputes of the Syrian christians at Travancore and afterwards, and so to have incurred the displeasure of the Madras government' (information supplied by the India Office). On 28 June 1838 Fraser became a major-general, which was regarded as an exceptional case of rapid promotion by seniority. On 31 Dec. 1839 he was appointed resident at Hyderabad, and was vested with a general superintendence over the post-offices and post-roads of the nizam's dominions. While there in 1842 Fraser 'received the thanks of the government in council for his temper, decision, and energy on the occasion of the insubordination of certain native troops at Secunderabad' (general order, 12 April 1842). The court of directors in their despatch dated 3 Aug. 1842 referred to this affair, and stated that his 'conduct in the difficult and trying circumstances in which he was placed was such as they should have expected from the well-known judgment, temper, and energy of that distinguished officer and merits the highest approbation' (information supplied by the India Office).

At Hyderabad, which he regarded as being, for good or evil, the political centre of India, Fraser remained fourteen years, his residence ending before the enlightened administration of that state by Sir Salar Jung. For details of this period reference must be made to the bulky volume published by Fraser's son, Colonel Hastings Fraser, Madras staff corps, under the title, 'Memoirs and Correspondence of General J. S. Fraser' (London, 1885), 8vo, which is largely devoted to Hyderabad affairs. Fraser appears again and again, without much success, to have urged on the supreme government the need of taking a firmer tone with the nizam. 'Intrigue, corruption, and mismanagement are not to be corrected by whispers and unmeaning phrases,' he wrote in 1849, and in 1851 he drafted a letter of remonstrance, which was never sent from Calcutta, couched in the strongest terms (*Mem.* pp. 327–9). But latterly he dissented from the high-handed measures of Lord Dalhousie, then governor-general. His strained relations with Dalhousie led Fraser to resign his appointment at Hyderabad in 1852 and return to England. He revisited India more than once afterwards, but held no public appointment. He became lieutenant-general 11 Nov. 1851, and general 2 June 1862. Except the war-medal he received no mark of distinction for his long and distinguished services.

In person Fraser was tall, standing over six feet three inches, and spare-built. A photograph, taken late in life, forms the frontispiece to his son's memoir of him. He was a good rider, a keen sportsman, and a man of some general culture. A tried official, his acts appear to justify the character given of him by his son as 'a man of scrupulous integrity and unsullied honour, firm and faithful in all trials, and generous to a degree.' Fraser, who for some time had been totally blind, but otherwise retained all his faculties, died in his eighty-seventh year, at Twickenham Park, 22 Aug. 1869.

[Information furnished by the India Office; Burke's Landed Gentry; Hastings Fraser's Mem. and Corresp. of General J. S. Fraser (Lond. 1885); critical notices of the latter in the Times, 29 Aug. 1885, and in Athenæum, 1885 (i.), 244.]
H. M. C.

FRASER, JOHN (*d.* 1605), Scotch Recollect friar, was the fourth son of Alexander Fraser, and grandson of Sir William Fraser of Philorth, Aberdeenshire. He was educated for the church, took the degree of bachelor of divinity, and became abbot of Noyon or Compiègne in France. He died at Paris on 24 April 1605, and was buried in the Franciscan convent. He was the author of: 1. 'Offer maid to a Gentilman of Qualitie by John Fraser to subscribe and embrace the Ministers of Scotlands religion, if they can sufficientlie prove that they have the true kirk and laufull calling,' Paris, 1604, 8vo: another edition, 'newlie corrected,' printed abroad, s.l., 1605, 8vo. 2. 'A lerned epistle of M. Iohn Fraser: Bachler of Divinitie to the ministers of Great Britanie. Wherein he sheweth that no man ought to subscribe to their confession of faith. And that their presumed authorite to excommunicate anie man, especially Catholiques, is vaine and foolish' [Paris ?], 1605, 8vo. 3. 'In universam Aristotelis Philosophiam Commentarii.'

[Dempster's Hist. Ecclesiastica (1627), lib. vi. *n.* 549, p. 291; Anderson's Scottish Nation, ii. 260; Watt's Bibl. Brit.]
T. C.

FRASER, JOHN (1750–1811), botanist, was born at Tomnacloich, Inverness-shire, in 1750, and apparently came to London in 1770, when he married and settled as a hosier and draper at Paradise Row, Chelsea. Having acquired a taste for plants from visiting the Botanical Garden, Chelsea, then under the care of Forsyth, he sailed to Newfoundland in 1780 in search of new species, returning the same year. In 1784 he embarked for Charleston, whence he returned in 1785, only to start again the same year. His third, fourth, and fifth visits to North America were made in 1790, 1791, and 1795, he having in the latter year established a nursery at Sloane Square, Chelsea, to which his discoveries were consigned. Having introduced various American pines, oaks, azaleas, rhododendrons, and magnolias, in 1796 he visited St. Petersburg, where the Empress Catherine purchased a collection of plants from him. He then introduced into England the Tartarian cherries. Revisiting Russia in 1797 and 1798 he was appointed botanical collector to the czar Paul, and, commissioned by him, returned to America in 1799, taking with him the eldest of his two sons. In Cuba he met and was assisted by Humboldt and Bonpland. On his return the Czar Alexander declined to recognise his appointment by his predecessor, though he made two journeys to Russia to obtain remuneration. In conjunction with his sister he then introduced the weaving of hats from the leaves of a Cuban palm, an industry which was for a time successful. In 1806 he started on his seventh and last visit to America, again taking his son. While in Cuba he was thrown and broke several ribs ; but he returned, with many new plants, in 1810 to his nursery, which, however, was never very successful. He died at Sloane Square on 26 April 1811. His herbarium was presented in 1849 to the Linnean Society, of which he was a fellow, by his son. A lithograph portrait, from an original belonging to his family, was published in the 'Companion to the Botanical Magazine.'

[Life by R. Hogg, in Cottage Gardener, viii. 250; by Forsyth, in Loudon's Arboretum et Fruticetum Britannicum, p. 119; Faulkner's History of Chelsea ii. 41.]   G. S. B.

FRASER, Sir JOHN (1760–1843), general, colonel late royal York rangers, second son of William Fraser of Park, near Fraserburgh, factor to George Fraser, fourteenth lord Saltoun, by his wife, Katherine, daughter of John Gordon of Kinellar, was born in 1760. On 29 Sept. 1778 he was appointed to a lieutenancy in the 73rd highlanders, afterwards 71st highland light infantry, with a second battalion, afterwards disbanded, of which regiment he was on board Rodney's fleet in the actions with the Spanish Caraccas fleet under Don Juan de Langara and at the relief of Gibraltar. He served at the defence of Gibraltar in 1780–2, until the loss of his right leg, his second wound during the defence, compelled him to return home. He was captain of a garrison invalid company at Hull in 1785–1793, and at the outbreak of the French war raised men for an independent company. He became major 28 Aug. 1794, and lieutenant-colonel royal garrison battalion 1 Sept. 1795. He served at Gibraltar in 1796–8, part of the time as acting judge advocate and civil judge. On 1 Jan. 1800 he was appointed colonel of the royal African corps, composed of military offenders from various regiments pardoned on condition of life-service in Africa and the West Indies (see Notes and

Queries, 3rd ser. viii. 134). With this corps he served on the west coast of Africa in 1801–1804, and made a very gallant but unsuccessful defence of Goree against a superior French force from Cayenne. The place was compelled to surrender on 18 Jan. 1804, but not before the enemy's loss exceeded the total strength of the defenders at the outset (Ann. Reg. 1804, p. 135, and app. to Chron. pp. 526–8). After his exchange he was appointed to command an expedition against Senegal, which never started. In 1808 he became a major-general, served in Guernsey in 1808–9, and in the latter year was appointed to the staff at Gibraltar. He commanded that garrison until the arrival of General Campbell. He was then sent to negotiate for the admission of British troops into the Spanish fortress of Ceuta on the Barbary coast, and afterwards commanded the British garrison there until his return to England on promotion to the rank of lieutenant-general in 1813. In 1809, in recognition of its distinguished conduct in the West Indies, the royal African corps was reorganised as the royal York rangers, another royal African corps being formed in its place. Fraser retained the colonelcy of the royal York rangers until the regiment was disbanded after the peace. He was made lieutenant-governor of Chester Castle in 1828, and G.C.H. in 1832, and was a member of the consolidated board of general officers. He became general in 1838.

Fraser, who is described by his kinsman, Lord Saltoun, as a brave, chivalrous, upright old soldier, married, first, 15 April 1790, Evorilda, daughter of James Hamer of Hamer Hall, Lancashire, and by her had one son and two daughters, one of whom, Evorilda, married General Francis Rawdon Chesney [q. v.] Fraser married secondly, about three years before his death, Miss A'Court. He died at Campden Hill, Kensington, 14 Nov. 1843.

[Phillipart's Roy. Mil. Cal. (1820), ii. 253; Alex. Fraser, seventeenth Baron Saltoun's The Frasers of Philorth (Edinburgh, 1879, 3 vols. 4to), ii. 155–7 (an excellent engraved portrait of Fraser appears in i. 74 of the same work); Gent. Mag. new ser. xxi. 92.]   H. M. C.

FRASER or FRAZER, JOHN (d. 1849), poet, born at Birr, King's County, about 1809, was by occupation a cabinet-maker, but employed his leisure in literary studies. He wrote, under the nom de plume of J. de Dean, a considerable quantity of sentimental and patriotic verse of no great merit. He died at Dublin in 1849.

[Hayes's Ballads of Ireland (where some of his effusions are collected).]   J. M. R.

FRASER, LOUIS (*fl.* 1866), naturalist, was for some time curator to the Zoological Society of London, a post which he vacated to become naturalist to the Niger expedition of 1841-2. Returning home he entered the service of Lord Derby as temporary conservator of the menagerie at Knowsley. Here his time was fully occupied in making a scientific catalogue of the magnificent zoological collections. In November 1850 he received through Lord Derby the appointment of consul at Whydah, on the west coast of Africa (*Proceedings of Zoological Society*, pt. xviii. p. 245), from which he was recalled by Lord Palmerston. He then went to South America, where he collected many rare birds and other animals. He returned to England and became dealer in birds, opening shops successively at Knightsbridge and in Regent Street; but the speculation proved unsuccessful. He therefore left England, and obtained employment at Woodward's Gardens at San Francisco, which he is said to have quitted for some occupation in Vancouver's Island. He was certainly living in London in June 1866 (*ib.* pt. xxxiv. p. 367). His son, Oscar L. Fraser, F.L.S., is now (1888) second assistant to the superintendent of the zoological and general sections, Indian Museum, Calcutta. In addition to numerous papers in the publications of the Zoological Society, of which he was elected a corresponding member in 1857, Fraser was the author of 'Zoologia Typica; or Figures of New and Rare Mammals and Birds, described in the Proceedings, or exhibited in the Collections of the Zoological Society of London,' fol., London, 1849. The volume contains figures of twenty-eight mammals and forty-six birds, all of which were then of particular interest as representations of specimens originally described by the respective authors as the types of new genera or additional species of genera previously characterised; besides which the plates are enriched with drawings of many rare and beautiful plants. It was Fraser's intention that the work should appear at regular intervals, and be continued until it comprised figures of every new mammal and bird described in the Zoological Society's 'Proceedings,' of which figures had not appeared in any other publication, but circumstances compelled him to bring it to a premature close.

[Information from Mr. A. D. Bartlett; Preface to 'Zoologia Typica;' Thacker's Indian Directory (1888), p. 210.]   G. G.

FRASER, PATRICK, LORD FRASER (1819–1889), senator of the College of Justice, son of Patrick Fraser, a merchant of Perth, was born at Perth in 1819. He was educated at the Perth grammar school and at the university of St. Andrews. Going to Edinburgh he entered the office of William Fraser, clerk to the burgh of Canongate, and he afterwards served in the firm of Todd & Hill, writers to the signet. In 1843 he was called to the bar, and three years later he published 'The Law of Personal and Domestic Relations,' which attracted a great deal of attention among both professional and non-professional readers. He rapidly rose as a lawyer and acquired considerable reputation. He obtained the appointment of counsel for the crown in excise cases, and on Lord Ormidale's promotion to the bench in 1864 he was appointed sheriff of Renfrewshire. In his career at the bar he was engaged in some of the greatest causes of his day, including the Yelverton case and the two famous succession cases of Breadalbane and Udny. In 1871 the degree of LL.D. was conferred upon him by the university of Edinburgh, in recognition of the 'historical research, the vigour of thought, and boldness of criticism which characterise his work on personal and domestic relations.' In 1878 he was elected dean of the Faculty of Advocates, and in 1880 he was made a queen's counsel. On the resignation of Lord Gifford he was appointed a lord of session with the title of Lord Fraser, and on 15 Nov. in the same year he was appointed lord ordinary in exchequer cases. He steadily discharged his judicial duties, his bar and roll of causes generally being among the most crowded in the outer house. He died suddenly at Gattonside House, near Melrose, on 27 March 1889. He married Miss Sharp, daughter of a Birmingham merchant. She survived him, with a son—Mr. W. G. Fraser, a member of the Scottish bar—and four daughters.

Few men of his generation had read so extensively in all departments of Scottish legal literature, and he gave the fruits of his researches in a manner at once clear, concise, and popular.

His works are: 1. 'A Treatise on the Law of Scotland as applicable to the Personal and Domestic Relations; comprising Husband and Wife, Parent and Child, Guardian and Ward, Master and Servant, and Master and Apprentice,' 2 vols., Edinburgh, 1846, 8vo. 2. 'Tytler's History of Scotland examined; a review' (anon.), Edinburgh, 1848, 8vo. 3. 'Domestic Economy, Gymnastics, and Music; an omitted clause in the Education Bill. By a Bystander,' Edinburgh, 1855, 8vo. 4. 'The Conflict of Laws in Cases of Divorce,' Edinburgh, 1860, 8vo. 5. 'A Treatise on the Law of Scotland relative to Parent and Child, and Guardian and Ward,' 2nd edit. prepared by Hugh Cowan, Edinburgh, 1866, 8vo. 6. 'Sketch of the Career of Duncan Forbes of Culloden, 1737-47,' Aberdeen, 1875, 8vo. 7. 'Treatise on Husband and Wife, according to the Law of Scotland,' 2nd edit., 2 vols., Edinburgh, 1876, 8vo. 8. 'Treatise on the Law of Scotland relative to Master and Servant, and Master and Apprentice,' 3rd edit. prepared by W. Campbell, Edinburgh, 1881, 8vo.

[Catalogue of the Advocates' Library, Edinburgh; Times, Scotsman, Glasgow Herald, Dundee Advertiser, and North British Daily Mail of 29 March 1889; Dod's Peerage, 1888, p. 339; Debrett's House of Commons and Judicial Bench, 1888, p. 323.] T. C.

FRASER, ROBERT (1798–1839), Scottish poet, was born at Pathhead, Fifeshire, on 4 June 1798. In early life he served as an apprentice, first to a wine merchant and then to an ironmonger. In 1819 he entered into a partnership as an ironmonger in Kirkcaldy, and in 1833 began business on his own account. In 1836 he lost his fortune, through having become financial surety to a friend. He was almost entirely self-educated, and during intervals of leisure he acquired a knowledge of several foreign languages. He contributed original pieces and verse translations from German, Spanish, and other languages to the 'Edinburgh Literary Gazette,' the 'Edinburgh Literary Journal,' and various newspapers. His poetical work, which is wholly unpretentious, is distinguished by true feeling of its kind and nicety of touch. A selection was issued by David Vedder soon after his death. In 1838 he became editor of the 'Fife Herald.' He died on 22 May 1839. He married, in 1820, a Miss Ann Cumming, by whom he had eight children.

[Poetical Remains of the late Robert Fraser, with Memoir by David Vedder; Irving's Eminent Scotsmen; Conolly's Eminent Men of Fife.] W. B-E.

FRASER, ROBERT WILLIAM (1810–1876), Scotch divine and miscellaneous writer, son of Captain Robert Fraser, was born at Perth in 1810, and is said to have been educated at the Edinburgh University, though his name does not appear in the list of Edinburgh graduates published by the Bannatyne Club, 1858. He was, however, accustomed to append the letters A.M. to his name. He was licensed to preach by the Edinburgh presbytery in 1840, and in 1843 was presented to the parish of Burntisland, where he so greatly distinguished himself as a preacher that in 1844 he was chosen to succeed Dr. Thomas Guthrie as minister of

St. John's Church, Edinburgh. Here his eloquence in the pulpit and his devotion to his pastoral duties attracted a large congregation, which he retained until his death on 10 Sept. 1876. Fraser was the author of the following works: 1. 'Moriah, or Sketches of the Sacred Rites of Ancient Israel,' Edinburgh, 1849, 8vo. 2. 'Leaves from the Tree of Life. A Manual for the Intervals between the Hours of Divine Service in each Sabbath of the Year,' Edinburgh, 1851, 2nd edit. 1852, 16mo. 3. 'The Path of Life. A Discourse delivered on the Anniversary of the Birthday of George Heriot,' Edinburgh, 1851, 12mo. 4. 'Turkey, Ancient and Modern. A History of the Ottoman Empire. With Appendix,' Edinburgh, 1854, 8vo. 5. 'Elements of Physical Science, or Natural Philosophy in the form of a Narrative,' London, 1855, 12mo, 3rd edit. under the title of 'The Handbook of Physical Science,' London, 1866, 8vo. 6. 'The Kirk and the Manse. Sixty illustrative Views in tinted lithography of the interesting and romantic Parish Kirks and Manses in Scotland. With descriptive and historical Notices and an Introduction,' Edinburgh, 1857, 4to. 7. He edited 'Ebb and Flow, the Curiosities and Marvels of the Seashore. A Book for young People,' London, 1860, 8vo. 8. 'Head and Hand, or Thought and Action in relation to Success and Happiness,' Edinburgh, 1861, 8vo. 9. 'Seaside Divinity,' London, 1861, 8vo. 10. 'The Seaside Naturalist. Outdoor Studies in Marine Zoology and Botany, and Maritime Geology,' London, 1868, 8vo. 11. 'Gladdening Streams, or Waters of the Sanctuary. A Book for Fragments of Time in each Lord's Day in the Year,' Edinburgh, 1868, 24mo.

[Scotsman, 12 Sept. 1876; Brit. Mus. Cat.] J. M. R.

FRASER, SIMON, twelfth BARON LOVAT (1667 ?–1747), notorious Jacobite intriguer, was a descendant of Sir Simon Fraser, high sheriff of Tweeddale (now Peeblesshire). Another Simon Fraser, who fell at the battle of Halidon Hill in 1338, came into the possession of the tower and fort of Lovat, near the Beauly, Inverness-shire, anciently the seat of the Bissets; and in accordance with highland custom the clan Fraser were therefore called in Gaelic Macshimi, sons of Simon. In 1431 Hugh, grandson of Simon, was created a lord of parliament under the title Lord Lovat. Simon, twelfth lord, was the son of Thomas Fraser, styled afterwards 'of Beaufort' (Castle Downie, the chief seat of the family), third son of the eighth Lord Lovat, his mother being Sybilla, daughter of the Macleod of Macleod. According to his age at his death printed on his coffin, and to several statements made by himself, he was born about 1667. His birthplace was probably a small house in Tanich, Ross-shire, then occupied by his father, who suffered imprisonment for joining the expedition of Dundee in 1689; the next year served under General Buchan, and in 1696 joined with Lord Drummond and other noblemen in an attempt to surprise Edinburgh Castle (*Memoirs*, 1797, p. 211; letter to the Duke of Perth 9 Feb. 1704 in *Correspondence of Nathaniel Hooke*, i. 86). Simon was educated at King's College, Aberdeen, where, as would appear from his love of classical quotation and allusion, he acquired some proficiency in his studies. Indeed, he curiously united the peculiarities of a wild highland chief with those of a cultivated gentleman. When he had just taken the degree of M.A. in 1683, and was about to 'enter upon the science of civil law,' his studies were interrupted by the proposal that he should accept a commission in the regiment of Lord Murray, afterwards duke of Atholl. The proposal was, he states, extremely distasteful to him, and only assented to on the assurance that the design of Lord Murray in accepting the regiment was treacherously to aid King James with it 'in a descent he had promised to make during the ensuing summer.' In 1696 he accompanied Lord Murray (who in July was created Earl of Tullibardine) and his cousin, Lord Lovat, to London. He there so ingratiated himself with his cousin, whom he describes as of 'contracted understanding,' that Lord Lovat made a universal bequest to him of all his estates in case he should die without male issue, an opportune arrangement, for Lovat died very shortly after his return from London. By a deed made on 20 March it was found that the estates had been settled for life on Simon Fraser's father, Thomas Fraser of Beaufort, Simon having consoled himself for his filial piety in effecting this arrangement by securing for himself meanwhile a grant of five thousand merks Scots. The father thereupon assumed the title of Lord Lovat, and Simon styled himself Master of Lovat. Emilia, eldest daughter of the tenth lord, assumed, however, the title of Baroness of Lovat, and as she had the support of her mother's brother, the Earl of Tullibardine, lord high commissioner of Scotland, Simon prudently resolved to end the dispute by marrying the heiress. He attempted to get her into his hands, but the clansman who had been entrusted with conveying her, for whatever reason, failed to complete his commission, and brought her back to her mother. A treaty was then entered into for her marriage with the Master of Saltoun, whereupon Fraser raised a number of his followers, and,

falling in with Lords Saltoun and Tullibardine after they had left Castle Downie, captured them near Inverness, and conveyed them prisoners to the island of Aigas. He then invested Castle Downie, of which he soon obtained possession, and, finding the daughter had been removed beyond his reach, resolved, possibly rather from a sudden impulse of vengeance than from interested motives, to compel the mother to marry him instead. In the middle of the night he introduced into her chamber a clergyman, Robert Monroe of Abertarf, and the marriage was performed by force, the bagpipes being blown up to stifle the lady's cries (*State Trials*, xiv. 356). For some time afterwards the lady, whom he also removed to the island of Aigas, remained in a state of utter physical and mental prostration; but Fraser is said to have ultimately won her affection. At first he gave out that it was the lady herself who sent for the minister, and it has also been stated that she sent for a second minister; but in subsequent years, when he found it impossible to reap any benefit from the marriage, Lovat deemed it more convenient to treat the whole matter as a practical joke of his own, without legal validity. The Earl of Tullibardine at once took measures for punishing the outrage committed on his sister. Letters of 'intercommuning' and of fire and sword were issued against Fraser and his followers; proceedings were taken against him and his father and others in the court of justiciary, which ended on 6 Sept. 1698 in their being found guilty of high treason, and condemned to be executed as traitors (*ib.* xiv. 350-78). Simon removed his father to Skye, where he died in the castle of Dunvegan in 1699, when the son assumed the title of Lord Lovat. For some time he wandered with a band of trusty followers among the wilds of the northern highlands, eluding every effort to capture him, and occasionally inflicting severe losses on his pursuers. By cleverly working on the jealousy of the Duke of Argyll towards the rival house of Atholl he induced Argyll in the autumn of 1700 to intervene to procure him a pardon from King William. On Argyll's recommendation he took a journey to London, but King William was then on the continent, and Lovat utilised the opportunity to run over to France, where he paid two visits to the exiled court at St. Germain. His reason for doing so, he unblushingly states, was to dissipate the calumnies against the sincerity of his Jacobitism disseminated by the Marquis of Atholl, and he asserts that he was so successful that James promised when he came into power 'to exterminate that perfidious and traitorous family' (*Memoirs*, 103). He then met William at the Loo, having, according to his own account, agreed, at the special request of King James, to 'make his peace with the reigning government in order to save his clan.' He played before William the part of a devoted subject with such seeming sincerity that, if he is to be believed, William gave instructions that there should be drawn up for him 'an ample and complete pardon for every imaginable crime' (ib. 105). The limitation of the pardon, after it passed through the various forms, to offences against the state was, Lovat asserts, due to the 'unnatural treachery' of his cousin who had charge of the matter; but the records of the privy council, on the contrary, prove that William declined to interfere in regard to offences against private persons. For his outrage against the Dowager Lady Lovat he was consequently summoned before the high court of justiciary, and failing to appear was outlawed 17 Feb. 1701. On 19 Feb. of the following year the lady also presented a petition for letters of 'intercommuning' against him, which were a second time granted. After the death of King William, acting, he asserted, on the advice of Argyll, Lovat for greater security went to France, which he reached in July 1702. He can scarcely, however, have been following Argyll's advice when he pretended to have authority from some of the Scottish nobility and chiefs of the highlands to offer their services to the court of St. Germain (MACPHERSON, Original Papers, 629). King James was then dead, but Lovat succeeded in obtaining an audience, not only of Mary of Modena, but of Louis XIV. It was probably to secure this that he found it expedient to become a convert to the catholic faith, and as a matter of fact it was through Gualterio, the papal legate, that he opened communications with the French king. Louis bestowed on him a valuable sword and other tokens of regard. Lovat's proposal was that the Scottish Jacobites should raise as many as twelve thousand men, on condition that the French king should land five thousand men at Dundee and five hundred at Fort William. The unsatisfactory condition of Lovat's private affairs was his chief reason for coquetting with Jacobitism, and he doubtless did not intend to do more than coquet until he was more certain of success and rewards. Though his proposals were regarded with favour by Louis, the Scotch Jacobites at St. Germain were far from satisfied with his credentials. It was therefore resolved to send him to Scotland to make further inquiries, John Murray, a naturalised Frenchman, brother of the laird of Abercairny, accompanying him to act as a check on his pro-

cedure, and to afford some assurance of the genuineness of his information (instructions to Simon Fraser, lord Lovat, in MACPHERSON's Original Papers, i. 630–1). Murray confined his attention chiefly to the lowland nobles and gentry, while Lovat made a tour through the clans. Not improbably Lovat intended at first to do his utmost to promote a rising in the highlands, but the clans were distrustful. Lockhart of Carnwath asserts (as did also the tories at the time) that Lovat had all along been acting as the spy of Argyll and Queensberry, and that he went to the highlands with their knowledge; but it would rather appear that Fraser introduced himself to Queensberry because he had met with insufficient encouragement in the highlands. Lovat states that he was particularly on his guard with Queensberry in order to 'amuse him and throw him on the wrong scent;' and this he certainly did, in so far as he made Queensberry the instrument of gratifying his own personal revenge against the Duke of Atholl. He showed Queensberry a letter from Mary of Modena addressed to Atholl, in which she wrote: 'You may be sure that when my concerns require the help of my friends you are one of the first I have in my view.' The letter was probably intended for any nobleman whom Lovat might select, but Queensberry having also a special grudge against Atholl did not fail at once to accept the bait. He gave Lovat a pass to proceed to the continent to obtain further evidence against Atholl and others. Lovat was of course seriously desirous to ruin Atholl, and would have fabricated sufficient evidence for this purpose but for the interposition in the matter of Robert Ferguson, the plotter [q. v.] Lovat actually justifies his accusations by pleading that they were groundless; that Atholl was 'notoriously the incorrigible enemy of King James,' and that he was bound not to spare this 'incorrigible villain' (Memoirs, 175). He asserted that he never made any revelations to Queensberry except regarding those who were not Jacobites; but there can be little doubt that, besides revenging himself on Atholl, Lovat's aim was, as his enemies asserted, by 'treachery and villainy' to regain through Queensberry the 'complete possession of his province and estates.' His machinations were, however, completely upset by the revelations of Ferguson, for while Queensberry was by means of them driven from power and rendered unable to assist him, the double part Lovat had been acting became known to the Jacobites at St. Germain. With a pass from Queensberry, Lovat succeeded in reaching Holland, and after many hair-breadth escapes arrived in Paris, where he states he was on account of fatigue attacked by a serious illness, which lasted three weeks (*ib.* 243). Lovat had sent to the queen an account of his mission in Scotland ('Memorial to the Queen of all that my Lord Lovat did in his Voyage to England and Scotland by her Majesty's orders' in MACPHERSON's *Original Papers,* i. 641–50), but on account of information regarding his procedure brought by Murray he was arrested. His own account is that 'after spending thirty-two days in a dark and unwholesome dungeon' he was confined for three years in the castle of Angoulême, and for other seven years had his liberty restricted to the city of Saumur (*Memoirs,* written by himself, p. 270); but in the short 'Memoirs of the Life of Lord Lovat,' published in 1746, and the 'Life' erroneously attributed to a Rev. Archibald Arbuthnot, he is stated to have been a prisoner in the Bastille, to have become a curé at St. Omer, acquiring considerable fame as a preacher, and to have been admitted into the order of jesuits.

Meantime Emilia Fraser, the heiress of Lovat, whom Fraser had endeavoured to carry off, was married to Alexander Mackenzie, son of Roderick Mackenzie of Prestonhall, a judge in the court of session, and with the aid of the judge's legal knowledge Mackenzie, in the absence of Lovat, obtained on 2 Dec. 1702 a decree from the court of session for the estate, and his wife for the title, an execution of entail being further made in favour of the issue of the marriage. Mackenzie also got a deed executed 23 Feb. 1706, permitting the heirs, 'if they should think fit, in place of the surname of Fraser to bear the name of Mackenzie.' This procedure deeply offended the clan, and after several meetings of the gentlemen had been held they in 1713 despatched Major Fraser of Castle Leathers to France to discover the whereabouts of their chief and bring him home. After a vain attempt to induce the chevalier to sanction Lovat's release, Lovat and the major. with the aid of the jesuits and on the pretence that they were entrusted by the chevalier with a search commission, concerted an escape. Arriving in London, they were arrested in their lodgings in Soho Square, and kept for some time in a sponging-house, but obtained their liberty on Lord Sutherland, Forbes of Culloden, and others, becoming bail for them for 5,000*l.* Lovat did not, however, proceed northwards till the outbreak of the rebellion in 1715, when, perhaps less from revenge for his treatment by the Jacobites in France than from regard to his personal interests, he resolved to take the side of the government. His defection from the cause of the Pretender was a serious calamity, and if it

did not turn the balance against it rendered its defeat much easier than it would otherwise have been. Mar, writing in February 1716, says: 'Lovat is the life and soul of the party here; the whole country and his name dote on him; all the Frasers have left us since his appearing in the country.' He completely broke the back of the rebellion in the northern regions of Scotland by the capture of Inverness. His services were so valuable as to obliterate the memory of his former offences, but the rewards he obtained were by no means commensurate with his ambition. On account of a memorial signed by the Earl of Sutherland and others he received on 10 March 1716 a full pardon, and on 23 June was honoured by an audience of the king; but although Mackenzie had been outlawed and attainted for his connection with the rebellion, his lands could not be forfeited without a special act of parliament, and all that Lovat therefore received was a life-rent of the estates. In 1721, when his proxy was produced at an election of a representative Scottish peer, it was protested against on the ground that the peerage was vested in the person of Emilia, baroness of Lovat, by a decree of the court of session. For the same reason his vote was objected to in 1722 and 1727. In 1730 he commenced an action for 'reducing' the previous judgment of the court against him, as he had not been a party to the action in which it was decided, and on 30 July the dignity and honours of Lord Fraser of Lovat were declared to belong to him as eldest son of Thomas, lord Fraser of Lovat. The litigation was, however, continued, and it was not till 1733 that a compromise was agreed upon, whereby Hugh Mackenzie, son of the baroness, consented for a money consideration to renounce his claims to the honours and estates of Lovat.

Lovat's romantic adventures appealed to the clan sentiment. Burt also states that he made use of all arts to impress upon his followers 'how sacred a character that of chief or chieftain was;' and possibly in this instance he was himself thoroughly convinced of the truth of what he inculcated. At Castle Downie he kept a sort of rude court, and several public tables. 'His table,' says Sir Walter Scott, 'was filled with Frasers, all of whom he called his cousins, but took care that the fare with which they were regaled was adapted, not to the supposed quality, but to the actual importance of his guests' (*Tales of a Grandfather*). The manners and customs prevailing at Castle Downie were a reflection of the strange idiosyncrasy of the chief. A wild savagery in modes of punishment flourished along with an ardent sentiment of brotherhood; and ceremonious formality was associated with unsavoury pleasantries and indecorous orgies. The territory of Lovat had in 1704 been erected into a regality, and as in addition to this he was appointed sheriff of Inverness, he found considerable scope for the exercise of his remarkable talents in augmenting his influence in the north of Scotland. In 1724 he addressed to the king a 'Memorial concerning the State of the Highlands' (printed in App. to BURT's *Letters*, 5th ed. ii. 254) recommending the establishment of independent highland companies commanded by the chiefs, and when his recommendation was adopted he was appointed to the command of one of the companies. Lovat always professed a special friendship for the Argyll family, whose interests he pretended to represent in the northern regions; but even as early as 1719 this friendship did not prevent him from writing to Seaforth, promising to join him on behalf of the Pretender (*State Trials*, xviii. 586). The government having obtained information of his intentions, he went to London to make explanations, meantime giving instructions to his clan to take up arms on the side of the government. His mission to London so successfully dissipated the doubts regarding his fidelity, that King George agreed to be godfather to his child, Colonel William Grant of Ballindalloch being appointed to act as his proxy. This barren honour was perhaps less than Lovat had expected, for his communications with the Jacobite party were soon resumed. He was the first to join the association formed about 1737 to invite the chevalier to land in Scotland, a patent for a dukedom being the price by which his services were won. The government became suspicious, and deprived him both of his command of the highland regiment and of his office as sheriff. The humiliation stung him to the quick. He himself said that if Kouli Khan had landed in Britain he thought 'that would have justified him to have joined him with his clan, and he would have done it.' At the same time Lovat modified his desire for vengeance by a keen regard to other advantages, and when the Pretender actually arrived in Lochaber manifested no special enthusiasm for his cause. The friendly correspondence he continued to keep up with Duncan Forbes of Culloden (see *Culloden Papers*) was no doubt chiefly meant to delude the government, but it is evident that he also wished to avoid committing himself irrevocably to the Pretender till the success of the enterprise became more certain. It was not till after the battle of Prestonpans on 21 Sept. 1745 that he 'threw off the mask' so far as to send round the fiery cross to summon his followers, but even then his friendly communications did not cease with Duncan Forbes, to whom he explained that his son had joined the Pretender contrary to his wishes, and that 'nothing ever grieved his soul so much' as his son's resolution to join the prince. It was impossible to believe such protestations. Lord Loudoun therefore on 11 Dec. marched to Castle Downie, and seizing Lovat brought him to Inverness as a hostage for the clan's fidelity, but on 2 Jan. he made his escape. He now wrote to his son that nothing ever made him 'speak so much as a fair word' to President Forbes, except to save himself from prison (*State Trials*, xviii. 771), and that his chief desire now was that his son 'should make a figure in the prince's army;' but at the same time he asked him to take measures to secure the patent of the dukedom, stating that if it was refused he must keep to his oath that he would never draw sword till that was done. The northward retreat of the prince's forces had already begun. Desirous to back out of the enterprise even at the eleventh hour, Lovat now sent a message to his son desiring him to come home, professedly that he might raise more troops; but such a shallow pretext did not for a moment deceive the son, who advised his father 'not to lose on both sides' (*ib.* p. 764). After the disaster of 10 April 1746 at Culloden, the one half of the highland army retreated by Gortuleg, where Lovat was then staying at the house of one of the gentlemen of his clan. He was anxiously awaiting news of the result of the struggle, when the 'wild and desolate vale below him was suddenly filled with horsemen riding furiously towards the castle.' A lady who was there at the time as a child records that the sudden appearance of the confused multitude in the plain below her seemed to her a vision of the fairies, and that, in accordance with highland tradition, she strove to refrain from moving her eyelid lest the vision should disappear. Driven to bay, Lovat now vainly advised the prince to make one resolute stand, telling him that his great ancestor Robert Bruce after losing eleven battles won Scotland by the twelfth. The prince in the morning fled westwards, and Lovat sought a retreat he had prepared for himself on Loch Muilly. On the way thither he is said to have witnessed from a hill-top the blaze of Castle Downie, set fire to by the soldiers of Cumberland. He had boasted of his retreat that he 'would make a hundred good men defend it against all the forces that King George can have in Scotland' (Letter to his son in *State Trials*, xviii. 759), but he left this retreat for another seventy miles further off, in the lake of

Morar on the western coast. As he possessed the only boat on the lake, he felt pretty secure in his hiding-place, but the sailors from a man-of-war towed a boat over the peninsula separating the lake from the sea, and launched it on the lake. Lovat was discovered in the hollow of a tree, his legs muffled in flannel betraying his presence. He was carried in a litter to Fort William and thence by easy stages to London. At St. Albans he had an interview in the White Hart with Hogarth, with whom he had a previous acquaintance, and who then had the opportunity of sketching the famous portrait of him, impressions of which were immediately prepared for sale, and were in such demand that the rolling-press was kept at work day and night. On reaching London Lovat was lodged in the Tower. He was tried for high treason before the House of Lords, and, being found guilty on 18 March 1747, was beheaded at the Tower on the 9th of the following April. In accordance with the regulations as to cases of high treason, all help from counsel was denied him except in regard to strictly legal points. Old and infirm, he was thus placed at great disadvantage. Much evidence was admitted against him the legal validity of which was very questionable. He conducted himself with great tact, and the objections he made as well as his set speeches fully bore out his reputation for shrewdness. On the lord high steward putting the question whether he wished to offer anything further, 'Nothing,' said Lovat, ' except to thank your lordship for your goodness to me. God bless you all, and I wish you an eternal farewell. We shall not all meet again in the same place ; I am sure of that ' (*State Trials*, xviii. 840). The story of Lovat's life, and possibly also his great age, attracted an extraordinary crowd to witness his execution. A scaffold fell, causing the deaths of several people, on which Lovat grimly remarked, 'The more mischief the better sport.' When on ascending to the place of execution he saw the immense crowds beneath him, 'Why,' he said, 'should there be such a bustle about taking off an old grey head that cannot get up three steps without two men to support it ?' Before placing his head on the block he, with characteristic appropriation of the noblest sentiments, repeated the line from Horace :

Dulce et decorum est pro patriâ mori ;

and in a vein of becoming moralising, he also quoted Ovid :

Nam genus et proavos, et quæ non fecimus ipsi,
Vix ea nostra voco.

In the paper he delivered to the sheriff he declared that he died ' a true but unworthy member of the holy catholic apostolic church.' He had left a codicil to his will that all the pipers from John o' Groat's house to Edinburgh should be invited to play at his funeral ; but events having rendered this impossible, he had desired before his execution that he might nevertheless be buried in his tomb at Kirkhill, that 'some good old highland women might sing a coronach at his funeral.' He died in this expectation, but although the body was given to an undertaker for this purpose, 'leave not being given as was expected, it was again brought back to the Tower and interred near the bodies of the other lords' (*Gent. Mag.* xvii. 162).

During the lifetime of the Dowager Countess of Lovat, whom he had forcibly married, Lovat was twice married : first, in 1717, to Margaret, daughter of Ludovic Grant of Grant, by whom he had two sons and two daughters ; and secondly, to Primrose Campbell, daughter of John Campbell of Mamore, whom he is said to have induced to accept his addresses by inveigling her into a house in Edinburgh, which he asserted was notoriously one of ill-fame, and threatening to blast her character unless she complied with his wishes. By this lady he had one son. His eldest son by the previous marriage was Simon [see FRASER, SIMON, 1726–1782]. The second son, Alexander, rose to the rank of brigadier-general. Janet, the eldest daughter, married Macpherson of Clunie ; Sybilla, the younger, died unmarried. Archibald Campbell Fraser [q. v.], the son of the second marriage, succeeded to the estates on the death, without issue, of his half-brother Simon in 1782. Archibald survived his five sons, and on his death in 1815, the descendants not merely of Simon, twelfth Lord Lovat, but of Hugh, ninth Lord Lovat, became extinct, the estates and male representation of the family devolving on the Frasers of Strichen, Aberdeenshire. Besides the portrait taken at St. Albans, there is another of Lovat by Hogarth, done at an earlier period. The original St. Albans portrait came into the possession of the Faringtons of Worden, Lancashire (*Notes and Queries*, 4th ser. ii. 59, 191). There is an engraving of Lovat in the prime of life in Mrs. Thomson's 'Memoirs of the Jacobites.' The description of Lovat by a correspondent in the 'Gentleman's Magazine,' at the time of his trial, tallies closely with the Hogarth likeness : 'Lord Lovat makes an odd figure, being generally more loaded with clothes than a Dutchman with his ten pair of breeches ; he is tall, walks very upright considering his great age, and is tolerably well shaped ; he has a large mouth and short nose, with eyes very much contracted and down-looking, a very small forehead, almost all covered with a large periwig; this gives him a grim aspect, but upon addressing any one he puts on a smiling countenance' (xvi. 339). A gold-headed cane, said to be that handed by Lord Lovat to his cousin on the scaffold, was sold by auction in January 1870 for 24l. 10s., but the genuine cane was afterwards asserted never to have left the possession of the Frasers of Ford (*Notes and Queries*, 4th ser. v. 137, 213).

[John Anderson's Historical Account of the Family of Fraser, 1825; Genuine Memoirs of the Life of Lord Lovat, 1746; French translation published at Amsterdam, 1747, under the title Mémoires Autentiques de la vie du Lord Lovat, which is included in Mémoires de la vie du Lord Lovat, 1747 (containing in addition an account of Lord Kilmarnock, &c.); A Candid and Impartial Account of the Behaviour of Lord Lovat, 1747; The Life, Adventures, &c., of Lord Lovat, n.d., reprinted erroneously as by Rev. Archibald Arbuthnot, 1747; Memoirs of Lord Lovat, 1746, reprinted 1767; Memoirs of the Life of Simon Lord Lovat, written by himself in the French language, and now first translated from the original manuscript, 1797; Information for Simon Lord Lovat against Hugh Mackenzie, and various other legal documents on the Lovat Peerage Case, 1729; State Trials, xiv. 350-78, xviii. 530-858; Spalding Club Miscellany, ii. 1-25; Macpherson's Original Papers; Culloden Papers; Lockhart of Carnwath's Papers; Account of the Scotch Plot in Somers Tracts, xii. 433-7; Hooke's Correspondence; Correspondence of Lord Lovat, 1740-5, in University Library, Edinburgh (Laing collection); Ferguson's Robert Ferguson the Plotter, 1887; Gent. Mag. vols. xvi. and xvii.; Scots Mag. vol. ix.; Mrs. Thomson's Memoirs of the Jacobites, ii. 208-388; Hill Burton's Life of Simon Lord Lovat; Major Fraser's Manuscript, ed. Lieutenant-Colonel Fergusson.] T. F. H.

FRASER, SIMON (*d.* 1777), brigadier-general and lieutenant-colonel 24th foot, is described as the youngest son of Hugh Fraser of Balnain, Inverness-shire, by his wife, a daughter of Fraser of Forgie. Anderson likewise states that he entered the Dutch service and was wounded at the siege of Bergen-op-Zoom in 1748 (*Account of Frisel or Fraser*, pp. 195-6). The war department records at the Hague for this period are imperfect, but the name of Simon Fraser appears in the 'Staten van Oorlog' (or war budgets) of 1750-7 as a pensioned subaltern of the regiment of Drumlanrig, two battalions of the Earl of Drumlanrig's regiment of the Scots brigade in the service of Holland having been reduced to one in January 1749 (information supplied through the British Legation at the Hague). On 31 Jan. 1755 Fraser was ap-

pointed lieutenant in the 62nd royal Americans, which afterwards became the 60th royal rifles. This corps was then being raised by Lord Loudon, and Fraser's name appears in an order dated 23 March 1756, wherein he is described as a 'second lieutenant from the Dutch service,' and which directs the newly appointed officers to repair to their posts at New York and Philadelphia without delay (*London Gazette*, 9569). In January 1757 he became captain-lieutenant in the 2nd highland battalion, afterwards 78th or Fraser highlanders, commanded by the Hon. Simon Fraser, Master of Lovat [q. v.], in which regiment he was promoted captain 22 April 1759. He fought in the regiment at the siege of Louisburg, Cape Breton, and under Wolfe at Quebec, where a namesake, one of many in the regiment, Captain Simon Fraser, described by Stewart as of Inverallochy (*Scottish Highlanders*, vol. ii.), was killed. Fraser is said to have subsequently served on the staff in Germany. He was made brevet-major 15 March 1761, and on 8 Feb. 1762 was appointed to a majority in the 24th foot in Germany, with which regiment he afterwards served in Gibraltar and in Ireland, and of which he became lieutenant-colonel in 1768. When in Ireland Fraser served as first and principal aide-de-camp to the Marquis Townshend, then lord-lieutenant, and appears to have been repeatedly sent over to England to furnish the ministry with confidential information on Irish matters (*Cal. Home Office Papers*, 1766-9, under 'Fraser, Simon'). In one letter he is described as an 'intelligent and prudent man' (*ib.* p. 493). In 1770 he was appointed quartermaster-general in Ireland in succession to Colonel Gisborne. Several papers in the home office records testify to the active and intelligent interest he took in his profession (*ib.* 1770-2, p. 454). In 1776 Fraser accompanied his regiment to Canada, and was appointed to the command of a brigade, composed of the 24th foot and the grenadier and light companies of the army, which was posted on the south side of the St. Lawrence. As brigadier he accompanied General Burgoyne [see BURGOYNE, JOHN, 1722-1792] in the pursuit of the American troops retreating from Ticonderoga, and gained a victory over them at Hubbardton, 7 July 1777. He was present at the battle of Stillwater, near Saratoga, 19 Sept. 1777, and was mortally wounded by a rifle-ball in the action which took place on the same ground, sometimes called Behmus, or Behmise Heights, on 7 Oct. 1777. He died at eight o'clock the following morning. Madame Riedesel, wife of the Hessian brigadier with

Burgoyne's troops, has left a painful narrative of his last hours, to which the American historian, Bancroft, makes ungenerous allusion. Burgoyne refers in touching terms to his death, and afterwards inscribed an ode, 'To the Spirit of Fraser.' He was buried in one of the British redoubts, and much feeling was caused at the time by the Americans, in ignorance of what was going on, opening a heavy fire on the work (*Notes and Queries*, 1st ser. ix. 161, 431). A large painting of the event by J. Graham, afterwards engraved by Nutter, is preserved at Farraline House, Stratherrick (*ib.* 6th ser. xi. 134, 238). Landmann states that the grave could just be traced at the end of the last century (*Recollections*, i. 221).

Fraser married 14 Oct. 1769 Mrs. Grant, of Percy Street, London (*Scots Mag.* xxxi. 558), who appears to have been a relative of Colonel Van Phran, then Dutch commandant at the Cape (*Cal. Home Office Papers*, 1770–1772, p. 278), and by that lady left issue.

[Anderson's Account of the Family of Frisel or Fraser (Edinburgh, 1825, 4to); London Gazettes; Army Lists; Stewart's Sketches of the Scottish Highlanders (Edinburgh, 1822); Knox's Hist. Memoirs (London, 1769); Calendars Home Office Papers, 1766–9, 1770–2; Bancroft's Hist. United States, vol. vi.; Beatson's Nav. and Mil. Memoirs (London, 1794), vols. iv–vi.; Burgoyne's Orderly Book, ed. Dr. O'Callaghan (Albany, N.Y., 1870); Gent. Mag. xlvii. 398, 455, 549, 576 et seq.] H. M. C.

FRASER, SIMON (1726–1782), sometime Master of Lovat, thirty-seventh Macshimi, a lieutenant-general, colonel 71st or Fraser highlanders, was eldest son, by his first wife, Margaret Grant, of Simon, twelfth lord Lovat [q. v.], who was executed in 1747. He was born 19 Oct. and baptised 30 Oct. 1726 (baptismal register, Kiltarlity parish). When the rebellion broke out in 1745, he was studying at the university of St. Andrews, and was sent for by his father to head the clan against his inclinations. When the rebels advanced southwards the clan Fraser set up a sort of blockade of Fort Augustus. With six hundred of his father's vassals Fraser joined Prince Charles at Bannockburn, before the battle of Falkirk, 17 Jan. 1746, and was one of those who met in the house of Mr. Primrose of Dumphall, on the evening of the battle, uncertain of the issue. Thenceforward he was active in the prince's cause. He was not at Culloden, where the Frasers were led by Charles Fraser, jun., of Inverallochy, who, according to stories current at the time, was cruelly shot by the personal order of the Duke of Cumberland when lying grievously wounded on the field of battle.

The Frasers fought well and left the ground in some order, and when halfway between Culloden and Inverness met the master coming up with three hundred fresh men. He was one of forty-three persons included in the act of attainder of 4 June 1746. He surrendered to the government, and was kept a prisoner in Edinburgh Castle from November 1746 to 15 Aug. 1747, when he was allowed to proceed to Glasgow to reside there during the king's pleasure. A full and free pardon for him passed the seals in 1750. On 25 July 1752 Fraser entered as an advocate (AIKMAN, *List of Advocates*). He was one of the counsel for the pursuers in the trial of James Stewart of Aucharn, before a high court of justiciary, opened at Inverary 21 Sept. 1752, by Archibald Campbell, third duke of Argyll [q. v.], as lord justice-general, and Lords Elchies and Kilkerran as judges. The panel was arraigned as art and part in the murder, on 14 May previous, of Colin Campbell of Glenure, a factor appointed by the exchequer to the charge of a forfeited estate. A good deal of political significance attached to the trial, which is said to be the only one in which a lord justice-general and a lord advocate both took part (ARNOT, pp. 225–9). The evidence on which a conviction was obtained was entirely circumstantial, and it is admitted that the view of the law upheld by the crown side was utterly indefensible. Fraser and James Erskine were counsel for the widow of the murdered man, and the former's address to the jury is given in full in a printed report (*Trial of James Stewart*, p. 81). Fraser appears to have come to London with Alexander Wedderburn, afterwards Earl of Rosslyn and lord chancellor. Boswell refers to kindnesses shown by the father of Richard Brinsley Sheridan to Fraser and Wedderburn when they came to London as young men (*Life of Johnson*, 1877 ed. p. 394). Wedderburn entered the Middle Temple in 1753. Fraser, by his own account, was offered a regiment in the French service, but declined, preferring to serve the British crown (petition in *Gent. Mag.* xliv. 137). At the commencement of the seven years' war Fraser obtained leave to raise a corps of highlanders for the king's service. By his influence with his clan, without the aid of land or money, he raised eight hundred recruits in a few weeks, to which as many more were shortly added. The corps was at first known as the 2nd highland battalion, but immediately afterwards became the 78th or Fraser highlanders, the first of three British regiments which in succession have borne that numerical title. Fraser's commission as colonel was dated 5 Jan. 1757. Under his command the regiment went to America, and was much remarked for its brilliant conduct in the field during the ensuing campaigns, and the thrift and sobriety of the officers and men (KNOX, *Hist. Mems.*) Wolfe, in a letter to Lord George Sackville, speaks of the regiment as 'very useful, serviceable soldiers, and commanded by the most manly lot of officers I have ever seen' (*Hist. MSS. Comm.* 9th Rep. iii. 74). Fraser was with it at the siege of Louisburg, Cape Breton, in 1758, and in the expedition to Quebec under Wolfe, where he was wounded at Montmorenci. He was wounded again at Sillery, 28 April 1760, during the defence of Quebec, and commanded a brigade in the advance on Montreal. He appears to have been still serving in America in 1761. In 1762 he was a brigadier-general in the British force sent to Portugal, and was one of the officers appointed to commands in the Portuguese army, in which he held the temporary rank of major-general. At the peace of 1763 the 78th highlanders were disbanded, and Fraser was put on half-pay. In the 'Official Return of Lists of Members of Parliament' Fraser is shown in 1768 as a lieutenant-general in the Portuguese service, and in 1771 as a major-general in the British army. He petitioned the government for the restoration of his family estates (*Gent. Mag.* xliv. 137), and as it was held that his military services entitled him to 'some particular act of grace,' all the forfeited lands, lordships, &c., were restored to him on the payment of a sum of 20,983*l.* sterling, by a special act of parliament (24 George III, c. 37), ten years before the same grace was extended to any other family similarly circumstanced. The family title was not revived until 1837. At the outbreak of the American war of independence, Fraser, then a major-general, raised another regiment of two battalions, known as the 71st or Fraser highlanders, the third of five regiments which in succession have been so numbered. Many officers and men of the old 78th joined the colours, for Fraser appears to have been liked by his men, and possessed in a remarkable degree all the attributes of a highland military chieftain. Stewart relates a story of an aged highlander who, after intently watching Fraser haranguing his men in Gaelic, accosted him with the respectful familiarity then common,' Simon, you are a good soldier. So long as you live Simon of Lovat never dies' (*Scottish Highlanders*, vol. ii.) Mrs. Grant of Laggan, however, describes him as hard and rapacious under a polished exterior. Fraser did not accompany his regiment to America, where, after several years of arduous and distinguished service, the men were taken prisoners with

Lord Cornwallis at York Town, 19 Oct. 1781. The two battalions of the 71st or Fraser highlanders, and a corps known as the second 71st regiment, formed after the surrender at York Town, were disbanded at the peace of 1783, after Fraser's death. Fraser was returned to parliament for the county of Inverness, when away with his first regiment in Canada in 1761, and was thrice re-elected, representing the constituency until his death. A speech of his in the house, in which he accused the government of lukewarmness in prosecuting the war with the colonies, is given in 'Gent. Mag.' xlviii. 657. Fraser married a Miss Bristo, an English lady, by whom he left no issue, and who survived him and was alive in 1825 (see ANDERSON). He died in Downing Street, London, 8 Feb. 1782.

Fraser's only brother, the Hon. Alexander Fraser, born in 1729 (reg. Kiltarlity parish), became a brigadier-general in the Dutch service, and died unmarried in 1762. By a deed of entail dated 16 May 1774, and registered in Edinburgh 18 June and 28 July 1774, the recovered estates passed at Fraser's death to his younger half-brother, the Hon. Archibald Campbell Fraser [q. v.], M.P. for Inverness county and colonel of the Inverness local militia.

[Anderson's Account of the Family of Frisel or Fraser (Edinburgh, 1825, 4to); Foster's Peerage, under 'Lovat;' Aikman's List of Advocates, in Library of Faculty of Advocates, Edinburgh; Arnot's Scottish Criminal Trials (Edinburgh, 1785, 4to); Trial of James Stewart of Aucharn (Edinburgh, 1753); Army Lists, 1757–82; London Gazettes; Knox's Hist. Memoirs (London, 1769); Journal of Siege of Quebec, printed in Proc. Hist. Soc. of Quebec, 1870; Stewart's Sketches of the Scottish Highlanders (Edinburgh, 1822); Beatson's Nav. and Mil. Memoirs (London, 1794); Scots Mag. various vols. vi. to xliv.]   H. M. C.

FRASER, SIMON (1738–1813), lieutenant-general, is described by Stewart as the son of a tacksman (*Scottish Highlanders*, ii. App. xxxi.) He was senior of the Simon Frasers serving as subalterns (not captain-lieutenant as stated by Stewart) in the 78th or Fraser highlanders, commanded by Simon Fraser (1726–1782), Master of Lovat [q. v.], in the campaigns in Canada under Wolfe, Murray, and Amherst in 1759–61. He was wounded at the battle of Sillery 28 April 1760. When the regiment was disbanded in 1763 he was placed on half-pay as a lieutenant. In 1775 he raised a company for the 71st or Fraser highlanders, then forming under the command of his old colonel, Fraser of Lovat. He became senior captain and afterwards major in this regiment, with which he served in America in the campaigns of 1778–1781. When the regiment was disbanded in 1783, he was again placed on half-pay. In 1793 he raised a highland regiment, which was numbered as 133rd foot, or Fraser highlanders, and which after a brief existence was broken up and drafted into other corps. He became a major-general in 1795, commanded a force of British troops stationed in Portugal in 1797–1800, became lieutenant-general in 1802, and was for some years lieutenant-general and second in command of the forces in North Britain. He died in Scotland 21 March 1813.

[Stewart's Sketches of Scottish Highlanders (Edinburgh, 1822), vol. ii.; Army Lists; London Gazettes; Gent. Mag. vol. lxxxiii. pt. i. p. 591.]   H. M. C.

FRASER, WILLIAM (*d.* 1297), bishop of St. Andrews, chancellor of Scotland, was the son of Sir Gilbert Fraser, the ancestor of the Frasers of Touchfraser and Philorth, and also of the Frasers of Oliver Castle of Tweeddale. He took holy orders, and was rector of Cadzow (Hamilton) and dean of Glasgow. On the p.omotion of William Wishart in or before 1276 to the see of St. Andrews, Fraser was appointed chancellor of Scotland, and held the seals of office for several years. When Wishart died in 1279 Fraser was elected his successor, and proceeding to Rome, was there, on 18 June 1280, consecrated as bishop of St. Andrews by Pope Nicholas III.

At a meeting of the Scottish estates held shortly after the death of Alexander III, Fraser was chosen as one of six regents, three of whom were to govern north of the Firth of Forth and three south, pending the arrival of Margaret, the Maid of Norway, who was next heir to the throne. He supported the proposal for the marriage of the princess of Scotland to Edward, prince of Wales, and in connection with the negotiations therewith made a journey to the court of Edward I in Gascony. The Scots ratified the proposals in their parliament at Birgham on 17 March 1290, but these were frustrated by the death of the Maid of Norway at Orkney on her way to Scotland. In a Latin letter (the original of which is preserved in the Public Record Office, London) Fraser informed Edward I of the occurrence, and as there were a number of rival claimants for the vacant throne and a civil war seemed imminent, he requested the intervention of the English king for the preservation of the peace. After stating, among other things, that a number of the nobles had already taken arms, he concludes his letter thus: 'If Sir John de Baliol come to your presence, we advise that you be careful to treat with him so that whatever be the issue your honour and interest may be preserved. And if it prove true that our lady foresaid is dead (which God forbid), then, if it please your excellency, draw near the borders for the comfort of the Scottish people and preventing of bloodshed.' The consequence of the intervention of Edward I in this juncture was the enforcement of his claim as lord paramount of Scotland, and the Scots being divided among themselves were for the time obliged to yield. They tendered homage to the English king, and accepted his award as arbiter in the rival claims for the crown of Scotland in favour of John Baliol. On Baliol's accession to the throne Fraser resigned his office of regent and stood loyally by his sovereign during his short and unhappy reign. He was, however, a participator in some of the events which brought about the final rupture between Edward and Baliol. Appeals in certain judicial causes in which he was concerned were made from the court of Baliol to that of Edward. The Scottish king was summoned to appear before Edward in England to answer these appeals, but the Scots refused to allow him to do so, and Edward took steps to enforce his authority. To secure the friendship of France in the struggle, Fraser and several others were sent to negotiate a treaty with Philip IV. They were successful, but their aid was unavailing. Edward inflicted summary chastisement upon the Scots, and Baliol, forced by his countrymen to do so, abdicated the crown he had accepted at the English king's hands. Fraser retired to France, and during his absence, William Wallace having driven the English armies across the borders, the bishop's surrogates, William of Kinghorn and Patrick of Campania, deprived of their benefices every Englishman in the see of St. Andrews.

Fraser died in exile at Arteville in France, 19 Sept. 1297, having been bishop, as Wyntoun says, for seventeen winters. His body was buried in the church of the predicant friars at Paris, but his heart was enshrined in a rich casket and brought to Scotland and interred with much ceremony in the wall of the cathedral of St. Andrews.

Lord Hailes and other historians have described Fraser as a creature of Edward and a traitor to his country. With these accusations the late Lord Saltoun deals at length in his family history, 'The Frasers of Philorth' (ii. 96–115).

[Registrum Glasguense; Registrum Prioratus Sancti Andree; Fordun's Annalia, cap. lxviii., xci.; Wyntoun's Chronicle, bk. viii. chap. xiv.; Palgrave's Hist. Documents; Acts of the Parliaments of Scotland, vol. i.]   H. P.

FRASER, WILLIAM, eleventh Baron Saltoun (1654–1715), second son of Alexander Fraser, master of Saltoun, and Lady Ann Ker, was born on 21 Nov. 1654. He was educated at King's College, Aberdeen. His elder brother, Alexander, having died in 1672, he, on the death of his father in 1682, became Master of Saltoun, and in August 1693 he succeeded as Lord Saltoun on the death of his grandfather, Alexander, tenth lord. In the earlier period of his life the family fortunes were at a very low ebb, nearly all the estates being mortgaged heavily. To save them so far as possible, he was infeft in them in 1676 on a disposition by his father and grandfather, and having acquired a considerable dowry with his wife, Margaret Sharp, daughter of James Sharp, archbishop of St. Andrews, whom he married on 11 Oct. 1683, he succeeded, by judicious sales and otherwise, in redeeming the estates out of the hands of the creditors. He wrote a narrative of this part of the family history, so far as concerned the efforts of his father and himself, which is preserved at Philorth. Previous to his marriage he was in command of a regiment of infantry, under a commission from James, duke of York. In 1697 the marriage of his eldest son to Emilia Fraser, eldest daughter and heiress of Hugh, lord Lovat, was arranged, by which means the barony of Lovat would have been annexed to that of Saltoun. But Fraser of Beaufort and his son Simon (afterwards twelfth Lord Lovat [q. v.]), being next heirs of entail to Lovat, determined to frustrate the match, and took arms to enforce their plans. Lord Saltoun was forbidden to visit Beauly, where lay Castle Downie, the residence of Lovat, but disregarding their threats he did so, and was seized, imprisoned, and threatened with the gallows, which was erected in front of his prison, unless he bound himself to terminate the marriage negotiations. He was taken back to Castle Downie as a prisoner, and there is sufficient warrant for believing that Simon Fraser would have executed his threat. The marriage was broken off. As a lord of parliament Saltoun took his seat and the oath on 9 May 1695, and used his influence and vote in furtherance of the Darien scheme, and in opposition to the treaty of union with England. He died on 18 March 1715, his wife, by whom he left three sons and four daughters, surviving till 1734. The eldest son, Alexander (1684–1748), succeeded as twelfth lord, and his great-grandson, Alexander George Fraser [q. v.], sixteenth lord Saltoun, was the famous general.

[Lord Saltoun's The Frasers of Philorth; Acts of the Parliaments of Scotland, ix. 347, 350.] H. P.

FRASER, WILLIAM (1784?–1835), Indian civilian, youngest son of Edward Satchell Fraser of Reelick, Inverness-shire, arrived in India to take up a nomination to the Bengal civil service in 1799. After acting in subordinate capacities, he was appointed secretary to Sir David Ochterlony, then resident at Delhi, in 1805, and in 1811 he accompanied Mountstuart Elphinstone's expedition to Cabul as secretary. In 1813 he was promoted to be assistant to Mr. Seton, the resident at Delhi, and in 1815 was political agent to General Martindale's army, and subsequently travelled with his brother, James Baillie Fraser [q. v.], in the Himalayas. In 1819 he was sent to settle the hill state of Garhwal, which had just been freed from the Goorkhas. In 1826 he was appointed second member of the board of revenue of the north-western provinces, and in 1830 he was promoted resident and agent to the governor-general at Delhi, in succession to Sir T. F. Colebrooke. He held this appointment until the evening of 22 March 1835, when he happened to be riding along the junction of the roads leading from the Cashmere and Lahore gates of Delhi, attended only by a single sowar, and was suddenly shot dead by a Muhammadan, named Kureem Khan. The actual perpetrator of the deed was tried and hanged, and earnest efforts were made to find out who had suggested the murder. Suspicion fell upon a wealthy Muhammadan nobleman, Shams-ud-din, nawab of Firozpur, against whom Fraser had issued a decree, and after a long trial he too was found guilty and hanged. His trial greatly excited the Muhammadans of Delhi.

[East India Directory; Gent. Mag. February 1836.] H. M. S.

FRASER, WILLIAM, LL.D. (1817–1879), educationist, was born at Cullen in Banffshire about the end of 1817. At an early period he entered the Normal Seminary in Glasgow, where he soon became one of the head-masters and a zealous coadjutor of David Stow in carrying out his training system—a new feature in Scottish education. Soon after the disruption of the Scottish church, the Normal Seminary was claimed by the church of Scotland, and Stow, Fraser, and nearly all the other teachers, having become members of the free church, had to leave, but were soon provided with a new building. In 1849 Fraser, after completing his studies for the ministry, was ordained to the pastoral charge of the Free Middle congregation, Paisley. In this office he remained till his death, greatly distinguished both for his pulpit and pastoral labours, and especially his work among young men. In 1857, at the request of some gentle-men of influence, he undertook an inquiry into educational work throughout Great Britain and Ireland, the results of which were pub-lished in a large volume entitled 'The State of our Educational Enterprises,' embodying important suggestions for educational legis-lation, which were brought by an influential deputation before the lord advocate, and several of which were made use of in the Education Bill for Scotland. In 1872, as a recognition of his scientific work, the uni-versity of Glasgow conferred on him the de-gree of LL.D. For nearly thirty years he laboured unweariedly on behalf of a literary association and a natural science association in Paisley. In 1850 he instituted a special class for boys who had attended the Sunday-school, in order to give them higher instruc-tion; this class developed into the Paisley Young Men's Bible Institute, which he met with on Sunday evenings without intermis-sion for many years. Some of his prelections were published in a volume called 'Blending Lights, or the Relations of Natural Science, Archæology, and History to the Bible.' In 1857 he took on himself the resuscitation of the Paisley Philosophical Society, and be-sides rendering many other services made valuable collections which became the basis of a free museum in connection with a free library. Having proposed that a free library should be formed for Paisley, and this pro-ject being approved of, he was able to inti-mate on behalf of a wealthy citizen, Sir Peter Coats, a gift of site and buildings both for museum and library. Another of his under-takings was to compile a list of about three thousand volumes and raise a sum of 1,000l. in order to furnish a reference library as an addition to the free lending library. Fraser was twice a member of the Paisley school board. His services obtained more than one public recognition. In 1873, in acknowledg-ment of his long services as president of the Philosophical Society, he was presented with a microscope and a purse of sovereigns; in April 1879, on the part of the museum and library, with his portrait; and in August 1879, on the part of the community, with a cheque for two thousand guineas. He was highly respected in Paisley. He died 21 Sept. 1879.

[North British Daily Mail, Glasgow News, Paisley Daily Express, all of 22 Sept. 1879; Glasgow Herald, 29 Sept.; Renfrewshire Gazette, April 1879; Free Church of Scotland Monthly Record, January 1880.]   W. G. B.

FRAUNCE, ABRAHAM (fl. 1587–1633), poet, was a native of Shropshire, and was educated at Shrewsbury School, where his name is entered in the register in January

1571–2. Sir Philip Sidney, who entered the same school some eight years before, interested himself in his education, and sent him to St. John's College, Cambridge, where he became a pensioner 20 May 1575, a Lady Margaret scholar 8 Nov. 1578, and a fellow in 1580. He proceeded B.A. in 1579–80 and M.A. in 1583, and in 1580 acted in Dr. Legge's play, 'Richardus Tertius,' which was produced at the college. Having been called to the bar at Gray's Inn, he practised in the court of the marches of Wales. So long as Sidney lived he seems to have favoured Fraunce, and when Sidney died in 1586, Sidney's sister Mary, countess of Pembroke, took him under her patronage. To her he dedicated nearly all his works, one of which he called 'The Countess of Pembroke's Ivychurch,' from the name of one of his patroness's residences, and another 'The Countess of Pembroke's Emanuel.' Her husband Henry, earl of Pembroke, pre-sident of the council of Wales, recommended him to Lord Burghley in 1590 for the office of queen's solicitor in the court of the marches. He seems to have failed to obtain that ap-pointment, and to have soon after entered the service of John Egerton, first earl of Bridgewater [q. v.], who only became presi-dent of the council of Wales in 1631. Fraunce claims to have paid poetical honours to all the earl's daughters on their marriages. As late as 1633 he celebrated in verse the mar-riage of Lady Magdalen Egerton with Sir Gervase Cutler.

Fraunce proved himself one of the most obstinate champions of the school which sought to naturalise classical metres in Eng-lish verse. All his poems are in hexameters, and all are awkward and unreadable. Yet Fraunce gained the highest commendation from his contemporaries. As the protégé of Sir Philip Sidney, he was introduced at an early age into Sidney's circle of literary friends, which included Spenser, Sir Edward Dyer, and Gabriel Harvey. With Spenser he was very intimate, and he was able to quote, in his 'Arcadian Rhetorike,' 1588, the 'Faerie Queene' before its publication. Spenser refers to him in 'Colin Clout's come home again' (1595) as 'Corydon, . . . hablest wit of most I know this day,' a re-ference to Fraunce's translation from Virgil of Corydon's lamentation for Alexis. Thomas Watson was his closest literary associate. Both translated separately Tasso's 'Aminta,' and Fraunce translated Watson's Latin poem 'Amintas.' Nashe, in his epistle prefixed to Greene's 'Arcadia,' or 'Menaphon' (1589), writes of 'the excellent translation of Master Thomas Watson's sugared "Amintas"' by 'sweet Master France.' Fraunce is apparently mentioned in Clerke's 'Polimanteia' (1595) among the leaders of English contemporary poetry under the disguise of 'Watson's heire.' Lodge, in his 'Phillis' (1593), wrote of Fraunce and Watson as 'forebred brothers, who in their swan-like songs Amintas wept.' Similarly Spenser refers to them jointly when, in the 'Faerie Queene,' he speaks of 'Amyntas' wretched fate, to whom sweet poets' verse hath given endless date.' Gabriel Harvey, in his 'Foure Letters' (1592), commends Fraunce and others to 'the lovers of the muses . . . for their studious endeavours commendably employed in enriching and polishing their native tongue.' George Peele, in his 'Honour of the Garter' (1593), describes 'our English Fraunce' as 'a peerless sweet translator of our time.' Meres, in his 'Palladis Tamia' (1598), names Fraunce with Sidney, Spenser, and others as 'the best for pastoral.' Ben Jonson, with characteristic brusqueness, told Drummond of Hawthornden 'that Abram Francis in his English hexameters was a fool' (*Conversations*, p. 4).

Fraunce's earliest published work was the translation of Thomas Watson's 'Amyntas,' 1585, which he entitled 'The Lamentations of Amintas for the Death of Phillis ; paraphrastically translated out of Latine into English Hexameteres,' London, by John Wolfe for Thomas Newman and Thomas Gubbin, 1587 ; by Walter Charlewood, 1588. It was also republished in 1589, and an edition dated 1596 belongs to Sir Charles Isham. It is in the form of eleven eclogues, each called a ' day.' In 1591 appeared ' The Countesse of Pembrokes Yuychurch, conteining the affectionate life and unfortunate death of Phillis and Amyntas. That in a Pastorall : this in a Funerall : both in English Hexameters,' London, by Thomas Orwyn for William Ponsonby. In the dedication to the Countess of Pembroke, Fraunce writes : ' I haue somewhat altered S. Tassoes Italian and M. Watsons Latine " Amyntas " to make them both one English.' The pastoral which opens the volume is translated directly from Tasso's 'Aminta.' The second part, 'Phillis Funeral,' is a republication of Fraunce's older translation of Watson's 'Amyntas'—'The Lamentations of Amintas.' The eclogues here number twelve, the last one of the earlier edition being divided into two, and there are a few other alterations in the concluding lines. Robert Greene, in the dedicatory epistle to his 'Philomela: the Lady Fitzwaters Nightingale,' 1615, justifies his own title by Fraunce's example in giving to his 'Lamentations of Amintas' the title of 'The Countesse of Pembrokes Ivychurch.' There follow in the same volume, all in hexameters: 'The Lamentation

of Corydon for the loue of Alexis, verse for verse out of Latine,' from Virgil's Eclogue II (reprinted from Fraunce's 'Lawier's Logike,' 1588), and 'The Beginning of Heliodorus, his Aethiopical History.' In 1592 was published 'The Third Part of the Countesse of Pembrokes Iuychurch, entituled Amintas Dale, wherein are the most conceited tales of the Pagan Gods in English Hexameters, together with the ancient descriptions and philosophical explications,' London, for Thomas Woodcocke. This was dedicated to the Countess of Pembroke, is in both verse and prose, and resembles in plan Sidney's 'Arcadia.' A companion volume to this series was 'The Countess of Pembrokes Emanuel: conteining the Natiuity, Passion, Burial, and Resurrection of Christ, togeather with certaine Psalmes of Dauid. All in English Hexameters,' London, for William Ponsonby, 1591; also dedicated (in two hexameter lines) to the Countess Mary. Eight psalms are reduced to hexameters. Dr. Grosart reprinted this volume in his ' Fuller Worthies' Miscellanies,' vol. iii., 1872.

Fraunce's other works were: 1. 'Abrahami Fransi Insignium, Armorum, Emblematum, Hieroglyphicorum, et Symbolorum, quæ in Italia Imprese nominantur, explicatio: Quæ Symbolicæ Philosophicæ postrema pars est,' London, 1588. Dedicated to Robert Sidney, Sir Philip's brother. Two other unprinted portions of the same work are respectively in Bodleian MS. Rawl. Poet. 85, and at Penshurst. 2. 'The Arcadian Rhetorike, or the Precepts of Rhetorike made plaine by examples Greeke, Latin, English, Italian, French, Spanish, out of Homer's Ilias and Odissea, Virgil's Æglogs, Georgikes & Aeneis, Songs & Sonets, Torquato Tassoes Goffredo, Aminta, Torrismondo Salust his Iudith, and both his semaines Boscan & Garcilassoes sonets and Æglogs,' London, by Thomas Orwin, 1588 (entered in Stationers' Registers 11 June). A copy is in the Bodleian; none is in the British Museum. Fraunce here quotes the unpublished 'Faerie Queene.' 3. 'The Lawiers Logike, exemplifying the praecepts of Logike by the practice of the Common lawe,' London, 1588 (entered in Stationers' Registers 20 May 1588, when Fraunce's own name appears with the licensers, the bishop of London and the warden of the company. Dedicated to the Earl of Pembroke in rhymed hexameters. Quotations from Latin and English poets 'appear in the text, and Fraunce appends Virgil's second eclogue in the original and in his own hexametrical translation, afterwards reprinted at the end of the 'Ivychurch,' as well as analyses of the Earl of Northumberland's case and of Stanford's crown pleas. Manuscript drafts of this work are in the Bodleian (*Rawl. MSS.* D. 345, 1) and in the British Museum (*MS. Addit.* 34361). The latter, which belonged to Heber, has a dedication to Sir Edward Dyer, and an opening section entitled 'The Sheapheardes Logike.' 4. A Latin comedy called 'Victoria,' dedicated to Sir Philip Sidney (founded like Munday's 'Two Italian Gentlemen' on Pasqualigo's 'Il Fedele,' 1579), of which the MS. is at Penshurst (*Hist. MSS. Comm. Rep.* iii. 230), was first edited by Prof. G.C. Moore Smith and printed in Bang's 'Materialen zur Kunde des älteren englischen Dramas' (Band xiv. Louvain 1906).

Fraunce also contributed to Allot's 'English Parnassus' (1600), and five songs at the close of Sir Philip Sidney's 'Astrophel and Stella,' 1591, have been assigned to Fraunce on very doubtful grounds. His epithalamium on the marriage of Lady Magdalen Egerton and Sir Gervase Cutler (1633) was in 1852, according to Joseph Hunter, at Campsall, Yorkshire, among the papers of Dr. Nathaniel Johnston of Pontefract, but cannot now be found.

[Moore Smith's introd. to Fraunce's Victoria, 1906; Cooper's Athenæ Cantabr. ii. 119, 546; Warton's English Poetry; Corser's Collectanea; Collier's Bibl. Cat. i. 294–5; Langbaine's Dramatic Poets with Oldys's MS. notes in Brit. Mus. Cat. C. 28 g. 1; Hunter's MS. Chorus Vatum in Brit. Mus. MS. Addit. 24488, ff. 349–51; Gabriel Harvey's Works, ed. Grosart, i. 217; Notes and Queries, 4th ser. xi. 378, xii. 179, and 3rd ser. i. 44; Hazlitt's Bibl. Handbook and Miscellanies; Arber's Stationers' Reg. ii.; Grosart's Fuller Worthies' Miscellanies, iii.] S. L.

FRAXINETUS, SIMON (*fl.* 1200), poet. [See SIMON.]

FRAZER, ANDREW (*d.* 1792), lieutenant-colonel of engineers, son of George Frazer, a deputy surveyor of excise in Scotland, was probably employed on the works at Fort George after the Scottish rebellion of 1745–6. He was appointed practitioner engineer, with rank of ensign in the train, on 17 March 1759, and sub-engineer, with rank of lieutenant, in 1761. In 1763 he was ordered to Dunkirk, and served as assistant to Colonel Desmaretz, the British commissary appointed to watch the demolition of the works of that port in accordance with treaty obligations (*Cal. Home Office Papers,* 1760–6). On 18 Oct. 1767 he succeeded Desmaretz in that office (*ib.* 1766–9), and retained it until the rupture with France in 1778. In the British Museum MSS. are two reports from Frazer: 'A Description of Dunkirk,' 1769 (*Addit. MS.* 16593), and 'Report and Plans of Dunkirk,' 1772 (*ib.* 17779, f. 82). A letter from Frazer to Lord Stormont, British

ambassador at Paris in 1777 (*ib.* 24164, f. 172), indicates that he discharged consular functions at Dunkirk. He became engineer in ordinary and captain in 1772, brevet-major in 1782, and regimental lieutenant-colonel in 1788. He designed St. Andrew's parochial church, Edinburgh, built in 1785. Frazer, who had not long retired from the service, died on his way to Geneva in the summer of 1792. He married in 1773 Charlotte, daughter of Stillingfleet Durnford of the engineer department, and granddaughter of Colonel Desmaretz (*Scots Mag.* xxxv. 500); by her he was father of Sir Augustus Simon Frazer [q. v.] A portrait of Major Andrew Fraser (*sic*) is catalogued in Evans's 'Engraved Portraits' (London, 1836–53), vol. ii., with wrong date of death.

[Army Lists; Cal. State Papers (Home Office), 1760–6 et seq.; Brit. Mus. Addit. MSS. ut supra; Scots Mag. liv. 413. Some letters from Frazer at Dunkirk are indexed in Hist. MSS. Comm. 8th Rep. (i), 9th Rep. (iii.)] H. M. C.

FRAZER, SIR AUGUSTUS SIMON (1776–1835), colonel, the only son of Colonel Andrew Frazer [q. v.] of the royal engineers, by Charlotte, daughter of Stillingfleet Durnford, esq., of the ordnance office, was born at Dunkirk, where his father was then employed as a commissioner for superintending the destruction of the fortifications, on 5 Sept. 1776, and was sent for a short time to the Edinburgh High School. In August 1792 he joined the Royal Military Academy at Woolwich as a gentleman cadet, and on 18 Sept. 1793 he was gazetted a second lieutenant in the royal artillery. In December 1793, though only seventeen years old, he was ordered to join the army under the Duke of York in Flanders, and in January 1794, in which month he was promoted first-lieutenant, he was attached with two guns to the battalion of the 3rd guards, then in the field. With the guards he served throughout the retreat before Pichegru, and was present at the battles of Mouveaux, Cateau Cambrésis, Tournay, and Boxtel, and at all the other principal actions until the departure of the infantry from the continent. In May 1795 he was attached to the royal horse artillery, and in 1799, in which year he was promoted captain-lieutenant, he served in the expedition to the Helder and the battles of Bergen. On 12 Sept. 1803 he was promoted captain, and appointed to the command of a troop of royal horse artillery. In 1807 he commanded all the artillery employed in the expedition against Buenos Ayres, and was present in the disastrous assault on that city in July. Frazer next remained for some time on ordinary garrison duty in England, and he was promoted major by brevet on 4 June 1811. In November 1812 he exchanged troops of royal horse artillery with Major Bull, whose health had broken down in the Peninsula, and he joined the allied Anglo-Portuguese army in its winter quarters at Freneda. In April 1813, when he had been but a short time with the army, Lord Wellington determined to have an officer on his staff for the general command of all the horse artillery in the field, and offered the post to Frazer, as senior horse artillery officer with the army. In this capacity he served on the staff throughout the rest of the Peninsular campaigns, and was present at the affairs of Salamanca and Osma, the battle of Vittoria, the siege of San Sebastian, at which he commanded the right artillery attack, at the passage of the Bidassoa, the battles of the Nivelle and the Nive, the investment of Bayonne, and the battle of Toulouse. He soon became a great favourite with Wellington, and was largely rewarded for his services. He was promoted lieutenant-colonel by brevet on 21 June 1813, granted a gold cross and one clasp for the battles of Vittoria, San Sebastian, Nivelle, Nive, and Toulouse; made one of the first K.C.B.s on the extension of the order of the Bath; promoted lieutenant-colonel in the royal artillery on 20 Dec. 1814, and appointed to command the artillery in the eastern district. In 1815, when Napoleon escaped from Elba, Frazer at once took his old place as commanding the royal horse artillery upon the staff of the Duke of Wellington in Belgium. He was now allowed to bring nine-pounders into action instead of six-pounders, a change which certainly had a great deal to do with the effective fire of the English guns at Waterloo. When the war was over Frazer was appointed British artillery commissioner for taking over the French fortresses, and in the following year he was elected a F.R.S. For some time he commanded the royal horse artillery at Woolwich; in October 1827 he was appointed inspector of the ordnance carriage department there, and in July 1828 director of the Royal Laboratory. He was promoted a colonel in the royal artillery in January 1825, and died at Woolwich on 4 June 1835.

[Letters of Colonel Sir Augustus S. Frazer, K.C.B., commanding the Royal Horse Artillery in the army under the Duke of Wellington, written during the Peninsula and Waterloo Campaigns, edited by General Sir Edward Sabine, R.A.; Duncan's History of the Royal Artillery.]
H. M. S.

FRAZER, WILLIAM (d. 1297), bishop of St. Andrews. [See FRASER.]

FREAKE, EDMUND (1516?–1591), bishop successively of Rochester, Norwich, and Worcester, was born in Essex about 1516, and became a canon of the order of St. Augustine in the abbey of Waltham, in his native county. He appended his signature to the surrender of that house, dated 23 March 1539–40, and obtained an annual pension of 5l. He graduated in arts in the university of Cambridge, but the dates of his degrees are not known. He was ordained priest by Bishop Bonner on 18 June 1545. In 1564 he became archdeacon of Canterbury, and on 25 Sept. in that year he was installed a canon of Westminster. He was one of Elizabeth's chaplains, and was appointed to preach before the queen in Lent 1564–5. On 25 Oct. 1565 he was by patent constituted one of the canons of Windsor. He was instituted to the rectory of Purleigh, Essex, on 13 June 1567, on the queen's presentation; and on 29 March 1568 he was holding a canonry in the church of Canterbury. On 10 April 1570 he was installed dean of Rochester. On 10 June in that year a grace passed the senate of the university of Cambridge for conferring upon him the degree of D.D., he having studied in that faculty for twenty years after he had ruled in arts (COOPER, Athenæ Cantabr. ii. 96). In the following month he supplicated the university of Oxford for incorporation, but the result does not appear (WOOD, Fasti Oxon. ed. Bliss, i. 186). On 18 Sept. 1570 he was promoted to the deanery of Sarum. Shortly before 20 Nov. 1570 he resigned the rectory of Foulmire, Cambridgeshire, to which John Freake, M.A., was then instituted on the queen's presentation.

On 15 Feb. 1571–2 he was elected bishop of Rochester, the royal assent being given on the 28th of that month. He was consecrated at Lambeth 9 May 1572, being, as Archbishop Parker remarks, a serious, learned, and pious man (LE NEVE, Fasti, ed. Hardy, ii. 572). He was empowered to hold the archdeaconry of Canterbury and the rectory of Purleigh in commendam. On or about 29 May 1572 he became the queen's great almoner.

On 31 July 1575 he was elected bishop of Norwich, and on 12 Nov. following he had restitution of the temporalities (BLOMEFIELD, Norfolk, ed. 1806, iii. 558). He now resigned the archdeaconry of Canterbury. Serious complaints were made of his conduct as bishop. Writing to Secretary Walsingham on 28 Aug. 1578, Sir Thomas Heneage says the queen had been brought to believe well of divers zealous and loyal gentlemen of Suffolk and Norfolk, whom the foolish bishop had complained of to her as hinderers of her proceedings and favourers of presbyterians and puritans. On 9 Oct. following the privy council authorised commissioners to inquire into the matters in controversy between the bishop and Dr. John Becon [q. v.], his chancellor, the circumstances being so rare and strange as to seem incredible. On 12 Oct. the bishop wrote from Ludham to the council expressing his desire that Becon should not be readmitted to the office of chancellor of which he had deprived him. He adds that he had dissolved his court of audience, and that he intended to exercise the whole jurisdiction himself. The depositions taken by the commissioners contained grave charges against members of the bishop's household. It was alleged that Sir Thomas Cornwallis [q.v.] took care to place the chancellor with the bishop to serve his turn, that he intermeddled in high commissions and other matters, caused the default of the bishop's dealings against papists, shared in drunken banquettings of the bishop's servants, made scoffing excuses for coming to church, reproached the name of a minister, and vaunted his secretary's monkish profession at Brussels. Dr. Browne was charged with being the special means of acquainting Sir Thomas and the whole rabble of the papists with the bishop or Mrs. Freake, and linking them together. The bishop's wife was herself charged with purposing to remove the chancellor, directing her husband, speaking reproachfully of learned preachers, and wishing to turn every honest man out of the bishop's presence. The depositions sent by the commissioners to the council on 5 Nov. 1578 state that it was well known throughout all Norfolk that whatsoever Mrs. Freake would have done the bishop must and would accomplish, or she would make him weary of his life, as he complained with tears; and if any one came to the bishop without a present 'she will looke on him as the Divell lookes over Lincoln' (Cal. State Papers, Dom. Eliz., Addenda, 1566–79, p. 551). In December 1578 proposals were submitted for settling the controversy, and the bishop offered to compound with his chancellor, but it does not appear how the dispute terminated.

In 1579 there was a project to translate Freake to Ely, it being supposed that Dr. Richard Cox [q. v.] would resign that see. Freake, however, refused to accept the bishopric in the lifetime of Dr. Cox. When he found himself unable to correct the disorders occasioned by the puritans, he wrote from Ludham to the lord-treasurer, Burghley, on 29 Aug. 1583, requesting that he might either be removed to another diocese or else permitted to retire into private life (STRYPE, Annals, iii. 172, folio). Shortly after this he narrowly escaped getting into fresh trouble because two of the members of his household attended mass. On 26 Oct. 1584 the queen nominated him to the bishopric of Worcester. His election to that see took place on 2 Nov., and he was installed by proxy on 7 Feb. 1584–5. In the year of the Armada (1588) he and his clergy provided 150 'able foot men' who were ready to serve their country when and where they might be required. On 25 Jan. 1588–9 he wrote from Worcester to the queen, soliciting permission to be absent from parliament on account of ill-health. He is said to have died on 21 March 1590–1, but there is some doubt as to the accuracy of this date.

Cecily, his widow, died 'full of days' on 15 July 1599, and was buried at Purleigh. He had issue John, archdeacon of Norwich and rector of Purleigh; Edmund; and Martha, wife of Nathaniel Cole, sometime senior fellow of Trinity College, Cambridge, and ultimately vicar of Marsworth, Buckinghamshire.

His works are: 1. 'An Introduction to the loue of God. Accompted among the workes of S. Augustine, and set forth in his name, very profitable to moue all men to loue God for his benefits receaued,' London, 1574, 8vo. A translation, dedicated to Queen Elizabeth. Robert Fletcher [q. v.] turned it into English metre, London, 1581, 8vo. 2. 'A Sermon at S. Paul's cross, 18 Nov. 1565, on Matt. xviii. 21. Notes in Tanner MS., 50 f. 27 b.

[Abingdon's Cathedral of Worcester, pp. 65–7, 109; Addit. MS. 5869, f. 90; Ames's Typogr. Antiq. (Herbert), pp. 996, 998; Bedford's Blazon of Episcopacy, p. 81; Egerton MS. 1693, ff. 87, 100; Godwin, De Præsulibus (Richardson); Hackman's Cat. of Tanner MSS. 929, 930; Kennett MS. 48, f. 157; Newcourt's Repertorium, i. 927, ii. 476; Parker Correspondence, pp. 318, 319, 459, 475, 477; Rymer's Fœdera (1713), xv. 703, 705, 744, 749, 750; Calendars of State Papers, Dom. Eliz. (1547–80), pp. 382, 555, 562, 601, 602, 604, 607, 623, 642, (1581–90) pp. 32, 93, 190, 509, 575, 599, (Addenda, 1566–1579) p. 612, (Addenda, 1580–1625) p. 728; Strype's Works (general index); Stubbs's Registrum Sacrum Anglicanum, p. 85; Thomas's Survey of the Cathedral of Worcester, i. 116, ii. 210; Willis's Survey of Cathedrals, ii. 647; Wright's Elizabeth, ii. 145; Wright's Essex, ii. 668.] T. C.

FREAKE, JOHN (1688–1756), surgeon. [See FREKE.]

FREDERICA, CHARLOTTE ULRICA CATHERINA (1767–1820). [See under FREDERICK AUGUSTUS.]

FREDERICK, SAINT (d. 838). [See CRIDIODUNUS, FRIDERICUS.]

FREDERICK, COLONEL (1725?-1797), also known as FREDERICK DE NEUHOFF, author of 'Description of Corsica,' was, by his own account, the only son of Theodore Etienne, Baron de Neuhoff, king of Corsica, by his wife, an Irish lady named Sarsfield, daughter of Lord Kilmallock, and one of the suite of Queen Elizabeth Farnese of Spain. The date of his birth was supposed by his family to be about 1725 (*Ann. Necrology*, 1797-8). According to the 'Nouvelle Biog. Univ.' vol. xlv. (under ' Theodore '), on the authority of Theodore's private papers preserved in the archives of the French Foreign Office, Theodore absconded from Spain with his wife's jewels in 1720, spent the proceeds in speculations in Paris during the ' Mississippi' craze, which was at its height in the winter of 1719-1720, and, after visiting England and Holland, resided at Florence in the imperial service until he went to Corsica. His son Frederick appears to have been educated at Rome, and states (*Description of Corsica*, p. 34) that he 'served several campaigns under some of the most experienced generals of the age;' also that when the Corsicans were struggling for their liberties, he and two Corsican gentlemen, Buttafuoco and Colonna, who had served with distinction in the Corsican regiment in the pay of France, offered their services to Paoli, which were rejected. Frederick then came to England ' to share his father's misfortunes.'

Theodore in 1736 had been proclaimed king of Corsica, but having subsequently lost his throne, and failed to regain it by English aid, came to England an exile, and became a prisoner for debt in the Fleet. He obtained his discharge under the Insolvent Act by giving up all his effects to his creditors, his sole effects being his claim to the kingdom of Corsica, which was duly registered for their benefit. He died soon afterwards, on 11 Dec. 1756, and was buried in the churchyard of St. Anne's, Soho, where Horace Walpole, who had been very kind to him, erected a tablet to his memory. Frederick, his son, arrived in England about 1754, and appears to have assisted his father as far as he was able. He supported himself as a teacher of Italian, and had some fashionable pupils, including Macklin and Garrick. Another of his pupils was Alexander Wedderburn [q. v.], afterwards lord chancellor Loughborough, to whom Frederick appealed for help in his latter years. Frederick appears to have gone to Germany, and at some time or other held, it is said, some subordinate post in the cabinet of Frederick the Great. In 1768 he published in London his ' Mémoires pour servir a l'Histoire de la Corse,' and an English version

' Memoir of Corsica, containing the Natural and Political History of that important island . . . together with a variety of particulars hitherto unknown.' The work was alleged to have been compiled from the information of Edward Augustus, duke of York, brother of George III, who had died at Monaco the year before, and who was interested—or whom it was wished to interest—in Corsican affairs. After another brief visit to Germany, Frederick returned to England with a green uniform, a cross of military merit, and the title of colonel, and as ' Colonel Frederick' became the recognised although not accredited agent in London of the reigning grand duke of Würtemberg. He is said to have arranged for the duke the sale of a regiment of his subjects to the English East India Company, and he claimed to have made arrangements on behalf of the English government, during the latter part of the American war of independence, for the hire of three thousand Würtemburgers and one thousand Hohenlohe troops, and to have incurred heavy expenses in providing for their pay and subsistence, to prevent their entering the pay of Holland after their services were refused by the English government. Pitt refused to admit this claim, on the ground that it should have been settled by Lord Shelburne before leaving office. Frederick continued to press it again and again without success for many years afterwards, and alleged that he had forfeited the favour of the Duke of Würtemberg, through representations that the money had been paid to him and misapplied (see *Ann. Necrology*, 1797-8, pp. 351-61). As given by Frederick's biographer, the details suggest official shuffling. A man of many acquirements, intimately versed in the details of continental etiquette and diplomacy, a well-known frequenter of fashionable coffee-houses in London, where, despite many eccentricities, his gentlemanly bearing rendered him a general favourite, Frederick appears to have been employed on a variety of confidential services (*ib.*) One of these was the unsuccessful attempt of the Prince of Wales, afterwards George IV, and two of his royal brothers to raise a loan on the continent in 1791, when Frederick was employed as their agent. When Corsica was annexed in 1794, Frederick brought out a new edition of his book, under the title of ' Description of Corsica, with an Account of its Union to the Crown of Great Britain. Including a Life of General Paoli, and the Memorial presented to the National Assembly of France respecting the Forests in that Island' (London, 1795, 8vo). A duplicate copy of this book, now in the British Museum Library, contains numerous marginal notes in the author's handwriting, many of them relating to Paoli, made with a view to a fresh edition. Frederick had once been friendly with Paoli, but had quarrelled with him. Although most abstemious in his habits, Frederick appears to have often been in pecuniary straits, and as years rolled on, his liabilities became more pressing. At last, harassed by creditors, and neglected by his fashionable friends, he shot himself through the head, in the porch of Westminster Abbey, on the morning of 1 Feb. 1797. A coroner's jury brought in a verdict of 'lunacy,' and a week later he was laid beside his father in the graveyard of St. Anne's, Sono, where a tablet was put up by private subscription collected by Lady James.

In person Frederick was spare, of middle height, with an erect military gait, which he never lost, a pleasing countenance, and a dark olive complexion, bespeaking a southern origin, and contrasting in age with his silvery locks. During one of his residences on the continent Frederick married a German lady, who bore him two children, a son, Theodore Anthony 'Frederick,' a bright, promising lad, who was killed as an ensign in the British 15th foot at the battle of Germantown, Philadelphia, 4 Oct. 1777, and a daughter, married to a custom-house officer, named Clark, at Dartmouth. Mrs. Clark had several children, including a son, Frederick Anthony Clark, an ensign West Suffolk militia, and afterwards in the 5th foot, and a daughter Emily, an authoress and miniature painter. Miss Clark wrote 'Ianthe,' published by subscription in 1798, and a small book of poems, and some volumes of minor fiction published between 1798 and 1819. She was an exhibitor in miniature at the Royal Academy in 1799.

[The best biography of Theodore, king of Corsica, is in Nouv. Dict. Univer. vol. xlv., based on his private papers preserved in the French archives. The particulars agree with those given in Brit. Mus. Add. MS. 23798, f. 159. A sketch of his history, correct in the main, is given in Dr. J. Doran's 'Monarchs retired from Business,' i. 238–47. The best account of Colonel Frederick is given by a writer, who seems to have known him intimately, in a volume of neglected biography bearing the title 'Annual Necrology, 1797–8' (London, 1800, 8vo). The date of his death is, however, wrongly given as 1796, instead of 1797. For the latter see Gent. Mag. vol. lxvii. pt. i. p. 172, and Ann. Reg. 1797, p. 11. In Percy Fitzgerald's Life of George IV there is (i. 225–334) a succinct account of the attempt of the royal princes to raise a foreign loan; in the same work (ii. 1) it is asserted that the notorious Mrs. Mary Anne Clarke [q. v.], mistress of the Duke of York, was 'a daughter or goddaughter of Colonel Frederick'—an absurd misstatement for which there is not a shadow of foundation.]

H. M. C.

FREDERICK AUGUSTUS, DUKE OF YORK AND ALBANY (1763–1827), second son of George III and Queen Charlotte, was born at St. James's Palace on 16 Aug. 1763, and on 27 Feb. 1764 he was elected to the valuable bishopric of Osnaburg through the influence of his father as elector of Hanover. He was educated with the greatest care at Kew, and became the constant companion of his elder brother, afterwards George IV. In 1767 he was invested a knight of the Bath, and in 1771 a knight of the Garter. On 1 Nov. 1780 he was gazetted a colonel in the army, and in the following year was sent to Hanover to study French and German. He studied not only tactics but the minutiæ of regimental discipline, and varied his studies by visits to the Austrian and Prussian military manœuvres. He created a favourable impression in every court he visited, and in 1782 was presented to Frederick the Great. Meanwhile the Bishop of Osnaburg, as he was generally styled, was appointed colonel of the 2nd horse grenadier guards, now the 2nd life guards, on 23 March 1782; promoted major-general on 20 Nov. 1782, and lieutenant-general on 27 Oct. 1784, on which day he succeeded the Duke of Richmond as colonel of the 2nd or Coldstream guards. On 27 Nov. 1784 Prince Frederick was created Duke of York and Albany in the peerage of Great Britain, and Earl of Ulster in the peerage of Ireland. He retained the bishopric of Osnaburg till 1803.

In 1787 the Duke of York returned to England, where he was received with enthusiasm by all classes (see Gent. Mag. lvii. 734). He was the favourite of his father, and the Prince of Wales was devotedly attached to him. His kindly manners, generous disposition, and handsome face made him popular in society. He took his seat in the House of Lords on 27 Nov. 1787, and on 15 Dec. 1788 he made, on the question of the regency in opposition to Pitt's Regency Bill, a speech which attracted attention, as it was held to convey the sentiments of the Prince of Wales. On 26 May 1789 he fought a duel on Wimbledon Common with Colonel Lennox, afterwards Duke of Richmond, who was aggrieved by some of the duke's remarks. The duke coolly received the fire of Colonel Lennox, and then fired in the air. His coolness and his refusal to avail himself of his rank to decline the challenge were much applauded. In January 1791 a marriage was arranged for him with Princess Frederica Charlotte Ulrica Catherina (b. 7 May 1767), eldest daughter of Frederick William II, king of Prussia, whose acquaintance he made during his visits to Berlin. Parliament granted him an additional income of 18,000*l.* a year, and the king gave him 7,000*l.* a year on the Irish revenue, which sums, with the revenues of the bishopric of Osnaburgh, raised his income to 70,000*l.* a year. The marriage was celebrated at Berlin on 29 Sept. 1791, and at the queen's house, London, on 23 Nov. The princess was received with enthusiasm in London, where it is noted among other demonstrations of respect that a great sale was found even for imitations of the princess's slipper. The husband and wife soon separated, and the Duchess of York retired to Oatlands Park, Weybridge, Surrey, where she amused herself with her pet dogs, and died 6 Aug. 1820, being buried in Weybridge church.

On the outbreak of war in 1793 George III insisted that York should take command of the English contingent despatched to Flanders to co-operate with the Austrian army under the Prince of Coburg. The campaigns of 1793, 1794, and 1795 in Flanders served to prove that the English army was unable to cope with the enthusiastic French republicans, and that York was not a born military commander. His staff, and especially his adjutant and quartermaster-generals, Craig and Murray, were chiefly responsible; the duke showed himself brave but inexperienced, and there is much truth in Gillray's caricatures and Peter Pindar's squibs, which represented him as indulging too freely in the prevalent dissipation of his officers. In 1793 the allied army drove the French army out of Belgium, defeated it at Tournay and Famars, and took Valenciennes on 26 July. Then came a difference between the generals; the Prince of Coburg wished to march on Paris, while York was ordered to take Dunkirk. The armies separated, and Carnot at once concentrated all the best French troops and attacked the duke in his lines before Dunkirk. After severe fighting at Hondschoten on 6 and 8 Sept. the English had to fall back, and, after the defeat of the Austrians at Wattignies, finally joined them at Tournay, where both armies went into winter quarters. In February 1794 the duke joined the headquarters of the army in Flanders, and the new campaign opened with some slight successes at Cateau Cambrésis, Villiers-en-Cauche, and Troixville. But on 10, 14, and 18 May the French army under Pichegru attacked the English army at Tournay. In the last engagement the English were entirely defeated, and would have been destroyed but for the conduct of Generals Ralph Abercromby and Henry Edward Fox. York himself was nearly taken prisoner. After this defeat the English

army steadily fell back, in spite of the arrival in July of ten thousand fresh troops under the Earl of Moira. The duke was, in fact, driven out of Belgium after several severe engagements. There followed the terrible winter retreat of 1794–5, which concluded the unsuccessful campaign. York shared the perils of the retreat up to the beginning of December, in which month he returned to England.

The duke's reputation had not been raised. Nevertheless George III promoted him to be a field-marshal on 18 Feb. 1795, and made him commander-in-chief of the army 3 April 1798. Amherst, the retiring commander-in-chief, was an old man, who had allowed countless abuses in the discipline and administration of the army. The duke by his high rank could be considered as belonging to no party, and he was able from his position to put down much of the jobbery which had disgraced his predecessor's tenure of office. He was not a man of brilliant parts, but he determined to remove some of the abuses which he had seen in Flanders.

In 1799 he was appointed to command an army destined to invade Holland in conjunction with a Russian corps d'armée. The vanguard of this army, under Sir Ralph Abercromby and Admiral Sir Charles Mitchell, performed an important duty in capturing the Dutch ships in the Helder; but when the main force arrived under the duke on 13 Sept. nothing but disaster followed. Generals Brune and Daendaels collected an army, which, though defeated on 19 Sept., 2 Oct., and 9 Oct., managed to keep the English and Russians penned on the narrow strip of land seized by Abercromby, and on 17 Oct. the duke signed the disgraceful convention of Alkmaer, by which the victors were allowed to leave Holland on condition that eight thousand French prisoners of war should be surrendered to the republic. This failure confirmed the general opinion that the duke was unfit for the command of an army in the field.

The attention of the public was now turned to the state of the army; money was not spared by parliament, and while Abercromby was engaged in the Mediterranean in restoring the true spirit of discipline in the field, the duke devoted himself to the task of weeding out incapable officers, and encouraging those who did their duty. It was nothing short of a disaster that York was on 18 March 1809 forced to retire from his post of commander-in-chief. He had become entangled with a handsome adventuress, Mary Anne Clarke [q. v.], who made money out of her intimacy with the commander-in-chief, by promising promotion to officers, who paid her for her recommendations. This matter was raised in the House of Commons by Colonel Wardle on 27 Jan. 1809, and referred to a select committee, which took evidence on oath. The inquiries of this committee proved that York had shown most reprehensible carelessness in his dealings with Mrs. Clarke, but he could not be convicted of receiving money himself, and the House of Commons acquitted him of any corrupt practices by 278 votes to 196. Sir David Dundas, who succeeded the duke at the Horse Guards, continued his policy, and the action of the prince regent in replacing his brother at the head of the army in May 1811 was received with almost unanimous satisfaction. The House of Commons rejected Lord Milton's motion censuring the ministry for allowing the appointment by 296 votes to 47.

No other scandal marked the duke's career. He was twice thanked by the houses of parliament, in July 1814 and July 1815, after the battle of Waterloo, for the benefits he had bestowed on the army and his unremitting attention to his duties as commander-in-chief; and in 1818, on the death of Queen Charlotte, he was appointed guardian of the person of the king, with an allowance of 10,000l. a year. The death of George III made York heir to the throne, but he continued to hold his post at the Horse Guards. The real affection which George IV entertained for him made him an important personage, but he never interfered much with politics. He opposed catholic emancipation, and on 25 April 1825, in a speech in the House of Lords, declared his opinions in opposition to it in a speech which was held to embody the ideas of his royal brother. In July 1826 York was attacked with dropsy, and after a long illness, borne with exemplary fortitude, he died at the Duke of Rutland's house in Arlington Street on 5 Jan. 1827. His body lay in state in St. James's Palace, and on 19 Jan. 1827 he was buried in St. George's Chapel, Windsor, his brother, the Duke of Clarence, acting as chief mourner.

The conduct of York as commander-in-chief had the greatest influence on the history of the British army. He supported the efforts successfully to revive military spirit made by commanders in the field, and by his own subordinates, above all by his military secretary, Sir Henry Torrens. Without his strenuous support the regulations of Sir David Dundas [q. v.] could not have been successful, nor the quartermaster-general's department purified. He looked well after the soldiers and their comforts, but it was with the officers that he was most successful. He set apart every Tuesday as a levée day, in which any officer might have an audience.

He sternly put down the influence of personal favouritism. The purchase system was in force during his tenure of office, but a certain amount of military service in every rank was required before an officer could purchase a step, and it was impossible for boys at school to hold rank as colonels. The duke did much to eradicate political jobbery in military appointments, and set his face against systematic corruption. Though he had himself failed on the field, he generously recognised the superior merits of Wellington and his subordinates.

York was good-tempered and affable; he was a sportsman, and kept a racing stable, which was superintended by Greville, the diarist, and he possessed the open, if unintellectual, features common to his brothers. His name is better commemorated by his foundation of the Duke of York's School for the sons of soldiers, Chelsea, London, than by the column which bears his name at the end of Waterloo Place, St. James's Park, London.

[Annual Register for 1827, pp. 436–67, contains the best contemporary memoir of the Duke of York, and embodies all the pith of the obituary notices in the various newspapers and magazines, as well as the biography written by Sir Walter Scott for the Edinburgh Weekly Journal ; for his military career see Philippart's Royal Military Calendar and Sir F. W. Hamilton's Hist. of the Grenadier Guards ; for the campaigns of 1793–5 see Jones's Hist. of the late War in Flanders (London, 1796) ; for the expedition of 1799, Sir H. Bunbury's Narrative of some Passages in the late War ; and for his character see especially the Greville Memoirs, 1st series, and numerous allusions in Thomas Wright's Gillray the Caricaturist.]   H. M. S.

FREDERICK LOUIS, PRINCE OF WALES (1707–1751), eldest son of George II and Queen Caroline, and father of George III, was born 6 Jan. 1707 at Hanover, of which his father was electoral prince. Lady Mary Wortley Montagu, in 1716, speaks of the grace and charm of his behaviour (Works, ed. 1837, i. 316). In 1717 he was created Duke of Gloucester, the following year he was installed a knight of the Garter, and 11 June 1727 received the title of Duke of Edinburgh. In his infancy a marriage had been arranged by the mothers between him and his cousin, Sophia Dorothea Wilhelmina, princess royal of Prussia, afterwards margravine of Baireuth, it being also agreed that his sister, the Princess Amelia, should marry Prince Frederick of Prussia, afterwards Frederick the Great (see narrative of the 'Double Marriage Project' in CARLYLE's Frederick, bks. v. vi. and vii.) The arrangement was in 1723 virtually sanctioned by George I, but the final signature of the treaty was always delayed by the English king, and at his death in June 1727 was not completed. On the accession of George II Frederick still remained in Hanover, and being, in the words of Carlyle, 'eager to be wedded to Wilhelmina as one grand, and at present grandest, source of his existence,' entered into communications with her mother to have the marriage celebrated privately. The mother, who had set her heart on the match, eagerly consented, but having unsuspectingly informed Dubourgay, the English ambassador, of the project, he thought it his duty to prevent it. The antipathy existing between George II and Frederick William proved an insuperable barrier to the match, and after negotiations had been for some time in a state of suspense, they were definitely and finally broken off in 1730. In December 1728 the prince came to England; but, though welcomed by the nation, was received with marked coldness by his father. On 9 Jan. 1729 he was created Prince of Wales. The original cause of the estrangement between the prince and the king, the scandal of the reign, was probably the wreck of the marriage project, but though the breach was also widened by other circumstances, it can only be fully accounted for by the peculiarities of the prince's temper. His power of exasperating his relations, and especially his father, without committing against him any really great offence, indicated fatal incompatibilities of temper between them. His sister Amelia grudged him every hour he continued to live; the queen, his mother, wished a hundred times a day that he were dead, and is said to have remarked: 'My dear firstborn is the greatest ass, and the greatest liar, and the greatest *canaille*, and the greatest beast in the whole world, and I heartily wish he was out of it.' His father's stingy treatment of him in money matters, and his determination to keep him in a position of dependence, were peculiarly galling to the prince. His filial sentiments were, however, less replaced by indignation than contempt, which he loved on every opportunity to manifest, partly as a proof of his own superiority. He undoubtedly carried this feeling to an extreme when he wrote, or instigated the writing in 1735 of, 'Histoire du Prince Titi' (of which two English translations appeared in 1736), in which the king and queen were grossly caricatured. With George Bubb Dodington as his chief counsellor, he also formed an opposition court of his own, and used every influence to undermine the authority of Walpole, his father's favourite minister. Possessing easy manners and great good humour when his wishes were

not thwarted, he set himself deliberately to outshine his father in popularity, and the fact that he could pose before the public as one who was to some extent ill-used told greatly in his favour. Partly because of his money embarrassments, and partly possibly because he knew he would deeply pain his father, he entered into negotiations with the old Duchess of Marlborough for the hand of her favourite granddaughter, Lady Diana Spencer, afterwards Duchess of Bedford, stipulating that he should receive 100,000*l.* for her portion. A day is said to have been actually fixed for the secret marriage in the duchess's lodge in Windsor Great Park, but the project was discovered, just in time to prevent it, by Sir Robert Walpole. The marriage of the princess royal to the Prince of Orange in 1734 was regarded by Frederick as something in the nature of a personal grievance, from the fact that she had anticipated him not only in getting married, but in obtaining a permanent grant from parliament, and an establishment of her own. The rivalry between the two came prominently before the public in connection with the 'Tweedledum Tweedledee' controversy, as to the respective merits of the operas of Handel and his Italian rival Buononcini, the princess being a special friend and patron of Handel at the Haymarket, and the prince heading those of the nobility who supported Buononcini at Lincoln's Inn Fields. The marriage of the princess induced Frederick to go to the antechamber of St. James's and request an audience of the king, to whom he made three demands: permission to serve in the Rhine campaign, a fixed income suitable to his circumstances, and the arrangement for him of a suitable marriage. The first was peremptorily refused, but the king promised favourably to consider the second and third, provided Frederick in future acted with proper respect towards the queen. Some time afterwards, with the prince's consent, a negotiation was entered into for the hand of the Princess Augusta, daughter of Frederick, duke of Saxe-Gotha, and the marriage was solemnised at St. James's, 26 April 1736. Instead, however, of proving a means of reconciliation between the king and the prince, the marriage was the occasion of embittering their relations for the remainder of the prince's life. George II himself, when prince of Wales, had obtained an annuity of 100,000*l.* out of a civil list of 700,000*l.*, and the prince naturally thought himself entitled to at least an equal sum when the civil list had increased to 800,000*l.* The king proposed to give only 50,000*l.*, whereupon the prince resolved, on the advice of his friends the leaders of the opposition, to appeal to parliament against his father. The address on the subject was, however, rejected in both houses—by 30 in the commons, and by 103 to 40 in the lords. The mortification of the prince was permanent, and he felt his disappointment the more from the fact that he was deeply in debt. He showed his resentment by neglecting to acquaint the king and queen with his wife's condition before the birth of Augusta, his eldest child. When the pains of child-birth came on he hurried her from Hampton Court in the middle of the night to St. James's, where not only had no preparations been made, but the beds had not been properly aired, and the only lady in attendance was Lady Archibald Hamilton, the reputed mistress of the prince, who had accompanied them from Hampton Court. The prince excused himself on the ground that the princess had been seized with the pains of labour much sooner than he expected, but there is little doubt that the chief reason for his extraordinary conduct was to prevent the queen being present at the birth (see LORD HERVEY's *Memoirs*, ed. 1848, ii. 360–74). In any case the king rejected all his endeavours for conciliation, and on 10 Sept. 1737 sent him a message peremptorily ordering him to quit St. James's with all his family, as soon as the princess could bear removal. The order was immediately obeyed, the prince removing in the first instance to Kew, and subsequently to Norfolk House, St. James's Square. Copies of the correspondence which passed between father and son were sent by the king to each of the British ambassadors abroad and the foreign ambassadors in England, the latter being at the same time requested not to visit the prince's family, as 'a thing that would be disagreeable to his majesty' (*Marchmont Papers*, ii. 83; the letters between George II and the Prince of Wales were published in 1737). From this time the prince's home became a great centre of the opposition, Bolingbroke, Chesterfield, Carteret, Wyndham, and Cobham being numbered among the prince's special friends. Walpole, shortly before his overthrow, in the beginning of 1742, advised the king to make an effort to detach the prince from his party, on whom his patronage conferred undoubted influence in the country. Secker, bishop of Oxford, was therefore sent to the prince to intimate that if he would send to the king a letter couched in proper terms of regret for the past, and promising amendment for the future, an addition of 50,000*l.* would be made to his revenue, and in all probability his debts, which now reached an enormous sum, would be paid by the king; but the prince, who it may be supposed was well aware that Walpole's position was be-

coming desperate, replied that if the message had come directly from the king he might have been disposed to consider it favourably, but as it had evidently emanated from Walpole, he refused to entertain it so long as Walpole remained at the head of the government. After the resignation of Walpole a partial reconciliation with the king took place, but, possibly because the king took no steps towards increasing the prince's allowance, matters were soon again on their old footing. When the rebellion broke out in 1745, Frederick warmly solicited the command of the royal army. It is said to have been through the intercession of Frederick that Flora Macdonald received her liberty, after a short imprisonment for succouring the chevalier. Frederick died suddenly at Leicester House, 20 March 1751, from the bursting of an abscess which had been formed by a blow from a tennis ball. He had been ailing for a short time, and, when his death happened, Desnoyers, a dancing-master, had been amusing him by playing the violin at his bedside. Desnoyers supported him in his last moments. He was buried on 13 April, 'without either anthem or organ,' in Henry VII's chapel in Westminster Abbey. The princess survived to witness the coronation of her son, and, dying 8 Feb. 1772, was interred in Westminster Abbey. Frederick was the father, by his wife, of four sons besides George III, and of two daughters, viz. Edward Augustus, duke of York and Albany (1739–1767); William Henry, duke of Gloucester and Edinburgh (1743–1805); Henry Frederick, duke of Cumberland (1745–1790); Frederick William (1750–1765); Augusta (1737–1813), wife of Charles William Ferdinand, hereditary prince of Brunswick-Wolfenbüttel; and Caroline Matilda (1751–1775), wife of Christian VII, king of Denmark.

'The chief passion of the prince,' says Horace Walpole, 'was women; but, like the rest of his race, beauty was not a necessary ingredient.' A natural son, 'Cornwell Fitz-Frederick,' by Anne Vane ('Beautiful Vanella'), daughter of Gilbert, second lord Barnard, was buried in Westminster Abbey 26 Feb. 1735–6 (CHESTER, *Westm. Abbey Reg.* p. 345). He was also much addicted to gambling, but in all his money transactions his conduct was not regulated by any ordinary considerations of honour. Though he affected to patronise the arts and literature, his tastes were not otherwise refined, and in their pursuit he was not too regardful of his dignity. 'His best quality,' says Horace Walpole, 'was generosity, his worst insincerity and indifference to truth, which appeared so early that Earl Stanhope wrote to

Lord Sunderland what I shall conclude his character with: "He has his father's head and his mother's heart"' (WALPOLE, *George II*, i. 77). His popularity partly arose from the belief that he was hardly used by the king, and partly from the unpopularity of the king, and antipathy felt towards the prince's brother, the Duke of Cumberland, whose regency, should the king die before his successor was of age, was regarded with general dread. When Frederick's death became known, elegies were cried about the streets, to which the people responded with, 'Oh! that it was but his brother!' and 'Oh! that it was but the butcher!' Perhaps, however, the real sentiment of the nation was expressed in the lines beginning with

> Here lies Fred,
> Who was alive and is dead;

and ending with

> There's no more to be said.

Two songs of which Frederick was the author, one in French, the other in English, are printed in Walpole's 'George II,' i. 432–5.

[Lord Hervey's Court of George II; Walpole's Reminiscences, Memoirs, and George II; Wraxall's Memoirs; Coxe's Life of Walpole; Dodington's Diary; Opinions of Sarah, Duchess of Marlborough; Warburton's Horace Walpole and his Contemporaries, i. 225–69; Jesse's Court of England, ed. 1843, iii. 119–60; Carlyle's Frederick the Great; Stanhope's Hist.] T. F. H.

FREE, JOHN (*d.* 1465), scholar. [See PHREAS.]

FREEBAIRN, ALFRED ROBERT (1794–1846), engraver, was apparently the son of Robert Freebairn [q. v.], the landscape-painter, and is probably identical with the younger Freebairn who etched the 'Sketch-book' of Robert Freebairn, published in 1815. He was a student at the Royal Academy, and engraved some vignettes and illustrations after Arnold, Nixon, David Roberts, S. Prout, Pyne, and others for the 'Book of Gems' and other popular works. His later work seems to have been entirely confined to the production of engravings by the mechanical process, invented by Mr. John Bate, known as the 'Anaglyptograph.' This machine was specially adapted for reproducing in engraving objects with raised surfaces, such as coins, medals, reliefs, &c. Freebairn produced a large number of engravings by this process, some of which were published in the 'Art Union' (1846). His most important works in this style of engraving were 'A salver of the 16th century,' by Jean Goujon, and a series of engravings of Flaxman's 'Shield of Achilles;' the latter, a very remarkable work, was executed and published at Freebairn's own risk and expense. He only completed it shortly before his death, which occurred somewhat suddenly on 21 Aug. 1846, at the age of fifty-two, a few days after the decease of his mother. He was buried in Highgate cemetery.

[Redgrave's Dict. of Artists; Art Union, 1846, pp. 14, 161, 264.] L. C.

FREEBAIRN, ROBERT (1765–1808), landscape-painter, born in 1765, and apparently of Scottish descent, is usually stated to have been the last pupil of Richard Wilson, R.A. [q. v.] This does not seem certain, as Freebairn was articled to Philip Reinagle, R.A. [q. v.], and it was from Reinagle's house that he sent his first picture to the Royal Academy in 1782, the year of Wilson's death. He continued to exhibit landscapes up to 1786, when he appears to have gone to Italy. In 1789 and 1790 he was at Rome, and sent views of Roman scenery to the Academy. In 1791 he sent two views of the 'Via Mala' in the Grisons, probably taken on his return journey. His stay in Italy formed his style, and he brought back to England a storehouse of material, on which he drew plentifully during the remainder of his life, his productions being mainly representations of Italian scenery. When in Italy he was patronised by Lord Powis, and on his return to England by Lord Suffolk, Mr. Penn of Stoke Park, and others. His compositions were noted for their elegance rather than for grandeur, and were pleasing enough to enable him to secure sufficient patronage and commissions for his pictures, most of which he exhibited at the Royal Academy. He occasionally painted views of Welsh and Lancashire scenery, but his chief excellence lay in his Roman subjects. Some of his drawings were published in aquatint. Freebairn died in Buckingham Place, New Road, Marylebone, on 23 Jan. 1808, aged 42, leaving a widow and four children. After his death there was published in 1815 a volume called 'Outlines of Lancashire Scenery, from an unpublished Sketch-book of the late R. Freebairn, designed as studies for the use of schools and beginners, and etched by the younger Freebairn' [see FREEBAIRN, ALFRED ROBERT]. A Robert Freebairn, perhaps related to the above, edited several works of Scottish literature during the eighteenth century.

[Gent. Mag. (1808) lxxviii. 94; Redgrave's Dict. of Artists; Wright's Life of Richard Wilson, R.A.; Royal Academy Catalogues.] L. C.

FREEBURN, JAMES (1808–1876), inventor, was born in 1808 in the parish of St. Cuthbert's, Midlothian. At an early age he was apprenticed to a baker. At the age of seventeen he enlisted in the 7th battalion of the Royal Artillery, and for a time served as gunner and driver. In December 1827 he was made bombardier, in May 1831 corporal, in January 1835 sergeant, and in April 1844 sergeant-major. From May 1837 to September 1840 he served abroad in the West Indies. On his return home he began to devote his attention to the subject of explosives, and during 1846, in which year he was commissioned quartermaster of the 10th battalion Royal Artillery, he invented an elaborate series of metal and wood fuzes for exploding live shells, both on 'concussion' and by 'time.' In 1847 he effected improvements on his original idea, and his fuzes were approved by the master-general of ordnance, and adopted in her majesty's service. Freeburn continued in the Royal Artillery until 21 April 1856, when he retired with the honorary rank of captain, on retired half-pay of 10s. per diem. He died at Plumstead on 5 Aug. 1876.

[Royal Artillery Records, Woolwich; diagrams of Freeburn's inventions in the Royal Artillery Institution, Woolwich.]   J. B-y.

FREEKE, WILLIAM (1662–1744), mystical writer. [See FREKE.]

FREELING, SIR FRANCIS (1764–1836), postal reformer and book collector, was born in Redcliffe parish, Bristol, on 25 Aug. 1764. He began his official career in the Bristol post office. On the establishment of the new system of mail coaches, in 1785, he was appointed to aid the inventor, Palmer, in carrying his improvements into effect. Two years later he proceeded to London, and entered the service of the general post office, where he successively filled the offices of surveyor, principal and resident surveyor, joint secretary, and sole secretary, for nearly half a century. In a debate in the House of Lords in 1836 the Duke of Wellington stated that the English post office under Freeling's management had been better administered than any post office in Europe, or in any other part of the world. Freeling possessed 'a clear and vigorous understanding . . . and the power of expressing his thoughts and opinions, both verbally and in writing, with force and precision.' A baronetcy was conferred upon him for his public services on 11 March 1828. Freeling had been a warm admirer of Pitt, but he suffered no political partisanship to affect his administration of the post office. His leisure was devoted to the formation of a curious and valuable library. He was elected a fellow of the Society of Antiquaries in 1801, and was one of the original members of the Roxburghe Club, founded in 1812. Freeling died at his residence in Bryanston Square, London, on 10 July 1836. A marble monument was erected to him in the church of St. Mary Redcliffe, Bristol, with an inscription commemorative of his services. He was thrice married. By his first wife, Jane, daughter of John Christian Kurstadt, he had two sons. He was succeeded in the baronetcy by the elder, SIR GEORGE HENRY FREELING, born in 1789, who matriculated at New College, Oxford, 17 March 1807 (FOSTER, *Alumni Oxon.*); was for some time assistant secretary at the post office, and subsequently commissioner of customs (1836–1841); and died 29 Nov. 1841, leaving issue.

[Ann. Reg. 1836; Gent. Mag. 1836, 1838; Foster's Baronetage.]   G. B. S.

FREEMAN, JOHN (*fl.* 1611), divine, matriculated in the university of Cambridge as a sizar of Trinity College, 26 Nov. 1575. He graduated B.A. in 1580–1, was elected a fellow of his college in 1583, and commenced M.A. in 1584 (COOPER, *Athenæ Cantabr.* iii. 59). He was for some time preacher of Lewes in Sussex.

He published: 1. 'The Comforter, or a comfortable Treatise, wherein are contained many Reasons taken out of the Word, to assure the Forgiueness of Sinnes to the Conscience that is troubled with the feeling thereof,' London, 1591, 1600, 8vo. Dedicated to the whole congregation of Lewes. 2. 'A Sermon on Rom. viii. 2–28,' London, 1611, 8vo. 3. 'A Sermon on Rom. xi. 2–8,' London, 1611, 8vo.

[Ames's Typogr. Antiq. (Herbert), pp. 1179, 1185, 1200; Crowe's Cat. pp. 207, 210.] T. C.

FREEMAN, JOHN (*fl.* 1670–1720), painter, had some repute as a history painter in the reign of Charles II. In early life he went to the West Indies, and narrowly escaped death by poisoning. He returned to England, and was much employed, although 'his Genius was so impair'd by that Attempt on his Life, that his latter Works fail'd of their usual Perfection.' He was considered a rival of Isaac Fuller [q. v.] He drew in the Academy that then existed, and latterly was scene painter to the play-house in Covent Garden. Some plates in R. Blome's 'History of the Old and New Testament' are probably from his designs. It is not known when he died, but he can hardly have lived till 1747, and be identical with the I. Freeman who drew the large view of 'The Trial of Lord Lovat in Westminster Hall.'

[De Piles's Lives of the Painters; Redgrave's Dict. of Artists; Walpole's Anecdotes of Painting.]   L. C.

FREEMAN, PHILIP (1818–1875), archdeacon of Exeter, son of Edmund Freeman, of the Cedars, Combs, Suffolk, by Margaret, daughter of William Hughes of Wexford, Ireland, was born at the Cedars, Combs, 3 Feb. 1818, and educated at Dedham grammar school under Dr. George Taylor. At a comparatively early age, October 1835, he became a scholar of Trinity College, Cambridge, and in 1837 and 1838 was awarded Sir William Browne's medals for a Latin ode and epigrams. He was elected Craven University scholar in the latter year, graduated B.A. in 1839, and after being chosen fellow and tutor of St. Peter's College, in 1842 took his M.A. degree. He served as principal of the Theological College, Chichester, from 1846 to 1848, and was a canon and a reader in theology in Cumbrae College (the college built by the Earl of Glasgow in the island of Cumbrae, Buteshire) from 1853 to 1858, having at the same time charge of the episcopal church in that island. He was presented by the dean and chapter of Exeter to the vicarage of Thorverton, Devonshire, in 1858, was appointed a prebendary of Exeter Cathedral in November 1861, one of the four residentiary canons in 1864, and acted for some time as examining chaplain to the bishop of the diocese. Finally, he was appointed archdeacon of Exeter in April 1865. In connection with the works for the restoration of the cathedral and of his own parish church at Thorverton, in which he took great interest, he expended much time and money. In 1869, at the meeting of the British Association in Exeter, he protested in energetic language against some of the views propounded by Professor Huxley on Darwinism. He was an authority on liturgical and architectural questions, and wrote numerous works on those subjects, and was also a constant contributor to the 'Ecclesiologist,' the 'Christian Remembrancer,' and the 'Guardian.' In 1866 he engaged in a controversy with Archdeacon Denison as to the 'Real Presence.' While getting out of a train at Chalk Farm station, London, on 18 Feb. 1875, he met with an accident, from the effects of which he died at the residence of Thomas Gambier, surgeon, 1 Northumberland Terrace, Primrose Hill, London, 24 Feb. He was buried in Thorverton churchyard on 2 March. His will was proved on 3 April under 25,000l. He married, 18 Aug. 1846, Ann, youngest daughter of the Rev. Henry Hervey Baber [q. v.] She was born at the British Museum 11 Feb. 1821, and survived him. He was the author of and interested in the following works: 1. 'Carmen Latinum Comitiis Maximis recitatum, A.D. 1837. Newtonus,' Cambridge,

1838. 2. 'Church Principles as bearing upon certain Statutes of the University of Cambridge,' 1841. 3. 'Theses Ecclesiasticæ sive orationes in curia Cantabrigiensi habitæ,' 1844. 4. 'Thoughts on the Dissolution of the Camden Society,' 1845. 5. 'Proportion in the Gothic Architecture,' 1848. 6. 'An Appeal as to the Chichester Diocesan Training College and Bishop Otter's Memorial,' 1848. 7. 'Sunday,' a poem, 1851. 8. 'A Plea for the Education of the Clergy,' 1851. 9. 'Plain Directions for using Morning and Evening Prayer,' 1853. 10. 'A Short Account of the Collegiate Church of Cumbrae,' 1854. 11. 'The Principles of Divine Service. An inquiry concerning the manner of understanding the order of Morning and Evening Prayer and the administration of the Holy Communion,' 2 parts, 1855–62. 12. Four sermons for Advent, 1859. 13. 'Guessing Stories,' 1864; 3rd ed. 1876. 14. 'The Harmony of Scripture and Science,' 1864. 15. 'The Real Presence; the Worship Due. Correspondence between the Archdeacon of Taunton and the Archdeacon of Exeter,' 1866. 16. 'Rites and Ritual, a Plea for Apostolic Doctrine and Worship,' 1866; 4th ed., revised, 1866. 17. 'A Tract about Church Rates and Church Endowments,' 1866. 18. 'Church Rates, the Patrimony of the Poor; an attempt to set the subject in a new point of view,' 1867. 19. 'The History and Characteristics of Exeter Cathedral, with an Appendix on the Screens,' 1871. 20. 'The Admonitory Clauses in the Church's Homiletical Creed,' 1872. 21. 'The Architectural History of Exeter Cathedral,' 1873. 22. 'A Challenge to the Ritualists. Correspondence between the Archdeacon of Exeter and B. W. Savile on the attempt at Romanising the English Church,' 1874.

[Times, 26 Feb. 1875, p. 8, 1 March, p. 8; Illustrated London News, 6 March 1875, p. 223, 24 April, p. 403; Trewman's Exeter Flying Post, 3 March 1875, p. 5; Guardian, 3 March 1875, p. 259; information from G. Broke Freeman, esq., barrister, Lincoln's Inn.] G. C. B.

FREEMAN, SIR RALPH (*fl.* 1610–1655), civilian and dramatist, who was probably the son of Martin Freeman, first comes into notice as succeeding Naunton in the office of master of requests in 1618. He had married a relation of Buckingham, through whose influence he had also obtained a grant of pre-emption and transportation of tin for seven years in August 1613. In 1622 he had a grant in reversion of the auditorship of imprests, and also the auditorship of the mint. It was thought that through Buckingham Freeman would succeed Thomas

Murray as provost of Eton, but the appointment was given to Sir Henry Wotton. Freeman unsuccessfully applied to Buckingham to be allowed to succeed Wotton at Venice. In 1626 and 1627 he was on a commission for the arrest of French ships and goods in England. In 1629 he held the office of auditor of imprests, after a dispute as to its possession with Sir Giles Monpesson, and soon afterwards became master worker of the mint at a salary of 500*l.* per annum. He was one of the first appointed in February 1635 to the newly created office of 'searcher and sealer' of all foreign hops imported into England. On the death of Sir Dudley Digges, Freeman bid high for the mastership of the rolls, which was taken by Sir Charles Cæsar. He appears to have retired into private life shortly afterwards, and to have lived to an advanced age. In 1655 he published 'Imperiale,' a tragedy which he had written many years before, and had 'never designed to the open world;' he was induced to publish it by 'the importunity of his friends, and to prevent a surreptitious publication intended from an erroneous copy.' This unauthorised edition to which he refers had appeared so far back as 1639. The tragedy met with the approval of Langbaine. Freeman also published two verse translations from Seneca, both of which are above the average, the first being the 'Booke of Consolation to Marcia' (1635), and the other the 'Booke of the Shortnes of Life' (2nd ed. 1663). At the last-given date Freeman was still alive, and must have been an old man. He has been erroneously confounded with another Sir Ralph Freeman who was lord mayor of London, and died on 16 March 1633–4.

[Rolls Ser. (Dom.) 1603–10, p. 475, 1611–18, pp. 197, 511, 1619–23, pp. 53, 93, 335, 569, 1623–5, pp. 56, 70, 1627–8, pp. 32, 181, 1628–9, pp. 141, 590, 1634–5, p. 524, 1636–7, p. 445, 1638–9, p. 622; Baker's Biographia Dramatica.]
A. V.

FREEMAN, SAMUEL (1773–1857), engraver, worked chiefly in stipple, and is principally known as an engraver of portraits. Among these may be noted Samuel Johnson, after Bartolozzi, Garrick, and Henry Tresham, R.A., after Sir Joshua Reynolds, Sir R. K. Porter, and Miss L. E. Landon, after J. Wright (Freeman's original drawing from the portrait of Miss Landon is in the print room at the British Museum), Thomas Campbell, after Lawrence, Queen Victoria, after Miss Costello, and others. He engraved numerous portraits and other illustrations to the Rev. T. F. Dibdin's 'Northern Gallery,' &c. For Tresham's 'British Gallery' (1815) Freeman

engraved the Stafford Gallery replica of Raphael's 'Vierge au Diadème.' He also engraved some of the plates for Jones's 'National Gallery,' and numerous portraits for Fisher's 'National Portrait Gallery.' For Dallaway's edition of Walpole's 'Anecdotes of Painting' he engraved 'The Marriage of Henry VI and Margaret of Anjou' from an ancient painting. He died on 27 Feb. 1857, aged 84.

[Redgrave's Dict. of Artists; Catalogue of Dyce Collection, South Kens. Mus.] L. C.

FREEMAN, THOMAS (*fl.* 1614), epigrammatist, a Gloucestershire man, 'of the same family of those of Batsford and Todenham, near to Morton-in-Marsh' (WOOD, *Athenæ*), became a student of Magdalen College, Oxford, in 1607, and took his degree of B.A. 10 June 1611 (*Fasti*, ed. Bliss, i. 341). 'Retiring to the great city and setting up for a poet,' he published in 1614 a collection of epigrams in two parts, 4to, dedicated to Thomas, lord Windsor. 'Rvbbe and a Great Cast' is the title of the first part, and 'Rvnne and a Great Cast. The Second Bowle' of the second. It is a scarce and interesting volume. There are epigrams on Shakespeare, Daniel, Donne, Chapman, Thomas Heywood, and Owen, the epigrammatist; also an epitaph on Nashe. One piece, 'Encomion Cornubiæ,' is in Ellis's 'Specimens,' 1811, iii. 113.

[Wood's Athenæ, ed. Bliss, ii. 155–7.]
A. H. B.

FREEMAN, WILLIAM PEERE WILLIAMS (1742–1832), admiral. [See WILLIAMS.]

FREER, MARTHA WALKER (1822–1888), historical writer. [See ROBINSON.]

FREIND, SIR JOHN (*d.* 1696), conspirator. [See FRIEND.]

FREIND, JOHN, M.D. (1675–1728), physician and politician, a younger brother of Robert Freind [q. v.], was born at Croughton, near Brackley in Northamptonshire, where his father, William Freind, was rector. He was educated under Dr. Busby [q. v.] at Westminster, and in 1694 elected to Christ Church, Oxford. Here he attracted the notice of Dean Aldrich [q. v.], who had so high an opinion of his scholarship that he appointed him one of the editors of a Greek and Latin edition of the two antagonistic orations of Æschines and Demosthenes (8vo, Oxford, 1696), which has been several times republished; and also to superintend a reprint of the Delphin edition of Ovid's 'Metamorphoses.' While at Christ Church he became acquainted with Atterbury [q. v.], who was then one of the tutors, and with him he continued on intimate terms for the rest of his life. He also became involved in the famous controversy about the epistles of Phalaris, and naturally (with his fellow-collegians) made the mistake of supporting Boyle against Bentley. He took all his degrees at Oxford, and became B.A. in 1698, M.A. in 1701, M.B. in 1703, and M.D. by diploma in 1707. Having chosen medicine for his profession, he early began to write on medical topics, and invariably employed the Latin language. In 1704 he was appointed to deliver at the Ashmolean Museum in Oxford some lectures on chemistry, which were largely attended, and published some years later (1709). In the next year (1705) he accompanied the Earl of Peterborough in his brilliant campaign in Spain, as physician to the English forces, and remained there about two years. He then visited Italy, where he became personally acquainted with Baglivi and Lancisi and other celebrated physicians of the day, and returned to England in 1707. Here he at once plunged into politics, and published two books in defence of Lord Peterborough's conduct in Spain, which brought him into considerable public notice as a keen partisan. In 1709 he married Anne, the eldest daughter of Thomas Morice, esq., then paymaster of the forces in Portugal, who survived him, and died in 1737. He had by her an only son, John, who died unmarried in 1750. He was elected F.R.S. in 1712, and in the same year he accompanied the Duke of Ormonde in his campaign in Flanders as his physician. On his return to England he took his place among the chief London physicians, and maintained it until his death. He was admitted a candidate of the College of Physicians in 1713, and a fellow on 9 April 1716, the same day as his political antagonist and friendly rival, Dr. Richard Mead [q. v.] He delivered the Gulstonian lectures at the college in 1718, and the Harveian oration in 1720, and was censor in 1718, 1719. He was elected M.P. for Launceston in the tory interest in 1722, and was so deeply implicated in his old friend Bishop Atterbury's plot for the restoration of the Stuart family, that he was committed to the Tower on the charge of high treason in March 1722–3. Here he remained for about three months, with a mind sufficiently collected to allow him to employ his time in the composition of a Latin letter to Mead on smallpox, and also in the drawing out of the plan of his principal work, the 'History of Physic.' He is said to have owed his release from the Tower to the exertions of his friend Mead, who, when accidentally summoned to attend Sir Robert Walpole, refused to prescribe for

him till he had given his promise that Freind should be set free. Another well-known anecdote in connection with his imprisonment says that after his release Mead presented him with five thousand guineas which he had received from his patients while he had been in the Tower. In this there is evidently some mistake, though it is not certain whether it is in the amount handed over to Freind, or in the source from which it was said to have been derived. Not long after his release he was called to attend the children of the Princess of Wales, afterwards Queen Caroline, and this led to his being appointed her physician when she ascended the throne in 1727. That so strong a partisan as Freind, with his Jacobite propensities, should have had such a post offered to him, and still more that he should have accepted it, seems to have given rise to much ill-natured comment. Some said that his former friends and acquaintances began to shun and despise him; and his brother Robert (in the Latin dedication to the queen prefixed to the collected edition of his works) speaks of his having to bear 'non modo contumelias, sed etiam susurros.' We are not, however, obliged to suppose that there was on his part any unworthy sacrifice of his political opinions to his interest, and his old friend Atterbury after his death expressed this conviction. Both the king and the queen seem to have had a sincere regard for him, and to have treated him with much kindness; but he did not long enjoy his honourable appointment, as he died of a fever on 26 July 1728. He was buried at Hitcham, near Maidenhead in Buckinghamshire, where he was lord of the manor; and there is a monument to his memory in Westminster Abbey, with one of his brother Robert's lengthy epitaphs in elegant Latin, 'one half' of which (as Pope said) 'will never be believed, the other never read.' Personally he was much beloved by his friends, and the clause in his epitaph, 'societatis et convictuum amans' (strangely mistranslated in the 'Biog. Brit.,' as Aikin points out, 'towards his acquaintance affectionate'), testifies to his enjoyment of the convivial habits of his time. Professionally he was highly esteemed by his contemporaries both in this country and on the continent, though he cannot in any sense be reckoned among the really great physicians. He was not only an elegant scholar but a man of genuine learning, and his 'History of Physic' is still well worth consulting. His other works can hardly be considered to possess any permanent value, though they excited great attention and gave rise to some bitter controversies at the time of their publication, the details of which may be found in the works mentioned at the end of this article.

The following is a list of Freind's principal publications: 1. 'Emmenologia: in qua fluxus muliebris menstrui phænomena, periodi, vitia, cum medendi methodo, ad rationes mechanicas exiguntur,' Oxford, 8vo, 1703. As indicated by the title, Freind belonged to the mechanical school of physicians, supported by Baglivi, Borelli, Pitcairne, and others, and his works are defective in consequence of his adopting this theory as the basis both of his pathology and his treatment. There is an English translation by Dale, London, 1752, 8vo, and a French translation by Devaux, Paris, 1730, 12mo. 2. 'Prælectiones chymicæ: in quibus omnes fere operationes chymicæ ad vera principia et ipsius Naturæ leges rediguntur,' London, 1709, 8vo. There is an English translation, London, 1729, 8vo. These lectures (which had been delivered at Oxford five years before) are dedicated to Sir Isaac Newton, and in them Freind attempts to explain all chemical operations upon mechanical and physical principles. They were criticised in the 'Acta Eruditorum,' 1710, as being of a mystical or occult character, and this attack, together with his answer (which appeared in the 'Philosophical Transactions,' 1711), Freind reprinted in an appendix to the second edition of the lectures, 1717 (?). 3. 'Hippocratis de Morbis Popularibus liber primus et tertius. His accommodavit novem de Febribus commentarios Johannes Freind, M.D.,' London, 1717, 4to; reprinted Amsterdam, 1717, 8vo. This volume contains a Greek text and Latin translation, both based on those of Foes, with the nine essays mentioned in the title-page. Triller wrote a learned critique on the Hippocratic portion of the work, in a letter to Freind, Leipzig, 1718, 4to; and Dr. Woodward, in his 'State of Physick and of Diseases' (London, 1718, 8vo), laid the foundation of a dispute in which other physicians took part, and which was carried on with unbecoming acrimony on both sides. 4. 'De purgantibus, in secunda variolarum confluentium febre, adhibendis, epistola,' London, 1719, 8vo. This is a pamphlet written during the foregoing dispute, addressed to Dr. Mead. 5. 'De quibusdam variolarum generibus epistola,' London, 1723, 4to. This is the letter that was written from the Tower to Dr. Mead. 6. 'Oratio Anniversaria . . . habita ex Harvæi instituto,' London, 1720, 4to. 7. 'The History of Physick from the time of Galen to the beginning of the Sixteenth Century, chiefly with Regard to Practice,' London, 2 vols., 1725–6, 8vo, translated into French by Stephen Coulet, Leyden, 1727, 4to, and into Latin by

John Wigan, London, 1734, 2 vols. 12mo. This is Freind's principal work. It is addressed to Dr. Mead, and was intended as a sort of continuation of Daniel le Clerc's 'Histoire de la Médecine.' It is a book of classical and extensive learning, and is still the best work on the subject in the English language for the period of which it treats. At the commencement he praises Le Clerc's history itself, but points out various imperfections in his plan for a continuation. This offended John le Clerc, the brother of Daniel, who wrote a defence of his brother's 'History' in the 'Bibl. Anc. et Mod.' vol. xxiv., to which Freind did not reply. These seven are the works contained in Wigan's Latin edition of Freind's 'Opera Omnia Medica,' London, 1733, fol. ; Paris, 1735, 4to ; Venice, 1733, 4to. His two earliest professional essays appeared in the 'Philos. Trans.,' one on a case of hydrocephalus (September 1699), the other (March and April 1701), 'De spasmi rarioris historia,' giving an account of some extraordinary cases of convulsions in Oxfordshire, which appeared as a sort of epidemic, and occasioned great wonder and alarm at the time as being something almost supernatural. His 'Account of the Earl of Peterborough's Conduct in Spain,' 1706, with 'The Campaign of Valencia,' 1707, reached a third edition in 1708. There is a fine portrait of Freind by Michael Dahl belonging to the London College of Physicians, recently engraved for Dr. Richardson's 'Asclepiad,' vol. vi. ; and an account of a bronze medal struck in his honour is given in Francis Perry's 'Series of English Medals,' 1762, and in Dr. Munk's 'Roll of the College of Physicians,' 1878.

[John Wigan's preface to his edition of Freind's collected works; Biog. Brit.; Chaufepié, Nouveau Dict. Hist. et Crit. ; Haller's Biblioth. Medic. Pract. vol. iv.; Nichols's Lit. Anecd. ; Atterbury's Letters; Munk's Coll. of Phys. ; W. B. Richardson's Asclepiad, vol. vi.]   W. A. G.

FREIND, ROBERT (1667–1751), headmaster of Westminster School, eldest son of the Rev. William Freind (who spelt his surname Friend), rector of Croughton, Northamptonshire, was born at Croughton in 1667, and at an early age was sent to Westminster School, where he was admitted upon the foundation in 1680. He obtained his election to Christ Church, Oxford, in 1686, and graduated B.A. 1690, M.A. 1693, and B.D. and D.D. 1709. Freind served the office of proctor in 1698, and in the following year was appointed under-master of Westminster School in the place of Michael Maittaire, the well-known classical scholar. In 1711 he succeeded Thomas Knipe as the head-master, and in the same year was presented to the rectory of Witney in Oxfordshire. He was appointed a canon of Windsor by letters patent dated 29 April 1729, and was installed a prebendary of Westminster on 8 May 1731. On his retirement from the head-mastership in 1733 he was succeeded by John Nicoll, who had served nearly twenty years as the under-master of the school. On 26 March 1739 Freind resigned the living of Witney, which, through the influence of the queen and Lady Sundon, he had succeeded in making over to his son. The permission of Bishop Hoadly is said to have been obtained for this proceeding with the laconic answer, 'If Dr. Freind can ask it I can grant it.' In March 1737 he was appointed canon of Christ Church, but he resigned his stall at Westminster in favour of his son in 1744. Freind died on 7 Aug. 1751, aged 84, and was buried in the chancel of Witney Church. He married Jane, only daughter of Dr. Samuel De l'Angle, prebendary of Westminster, whose son, John Maximilian De l'Angle, became the husband of Freind's sister, Anne. Freind had four children, three of whom died under age. The other, William (1715–1766), succeeded his father in the living of Witney, and afterwards became dean of Canterbury [q. v.] There are two portraits of Freind at Christ Church, the one in the hall being painted by Michael Dahl. There is also in the library of the same college a bust of Freind, executed by Rysbrack in 1738. A portrait of Freind is also preserved along with the portraits of the other head-masters at Westminster School.

Freind was a man of many social gifts, a good scholar, and a successful schoolmaster. His house was the resort of the wits and other famous men of the time. Swift records in his 'Journal to Stella,' under date 1 Feb. 1711–12: 'To-night at six Dr. Atterbury and Prior, and I and Dr. Freind met at Dr. Robert Freind's house at Westminster, who is master of the school: there we sat till one, and were good enough company' (SWIFT, *Works*, 1814, iii. 30). Freind's own social position was not without its effect upon the school, which became for many years the favourite place of education for the aristocracy. Indeed the list of boys who recited the epigrams at the anniversary dinner in 1727–8 contains a far greater number of distinguished names than any other school at that period could have shown (*Comitia Westmonasteriensia*, 1728). In 1728 the numbers of the school reached 434, inclusive of the forty boys on the foundation. Duck, in an ode 'to the Rev. Dr. Freind on his quitting Westminster School,' alludes to several of his famous pupils (*Gent. Mag.* 1733, iii. 152).

With Atterbury and other old Westminster boys he helped in the production of Boyle's attack upon Bentley. Pope, it will be remembered, makes Bentley sneer at Freind's scholarship in the 'Dunciad' (iv. 223–4):—

> Let Freind affect to speak as Terence spoke,
> And Alsop never but like Horace joke.'

Freind's niece, however, married a son of Bentley, who is said after that event to have conceived a better opinion of Christ Church men, and to have declared that 'Freind had more good learning in him than ever he had imagined.' While a student Freind contributed some English verses to the 'Vota Oxoniensia (1689) 'On the Inauguration of King William and Queen Mary,' which were reprinted in Nichols's 'Select Collection of Poems' (vii. 122–4), where a Latin ode 'On the Death of Queen Caroline' in 1738 (*ib.* pp. 125–7), which has also been attributed to him, is by his son William. Two of his Latin poems, entitled 'Encænium Rusticum, anglice a Country Wake,' and 'Pugna Gallorum Gallinaceorum,' are printed in the 'Musarum Anglicanarum Delectus Alter,' 1698 (pp. 166–75, 189–93). 'Oratio publice habita in Schola Westmonasteriensi 7° die Maii, 1705, aucthore Roberto Friend, A.M.,' will be found among the Lansdowne MSS. in the British Museum (No. 845, pp. 47–51). A Latin ode to the Duke of Newcastle, written by Freind in 1737, appears in the 'Gentleman's Magazine' (vii. 631). Freind also wrote the dedication to the queen for the medical works of his brother John, which were published in 1733, and a number of epitaphs and other monumental inscriptions, the one on Lord Carteret's younger brother, Philip, whose monument is in the north aisle of Westminster Abbey, being perhaps the best known. With reference to the last-mentioned compositions of Freind, the following epigram, ascribed to Pope on somewhat doubtful authority (NICHOLS, *Select Collection of Poems*, v. 316), was written:—

> Friend, for your epitaphs I grieved
> Where still so much is said,
> One half will never be believ'd,
> The other never read.

Freind also published the two following works: 1. 'A Sermon preach'd before the Honble. House of Commons at S. Margaret's, Westminster, on Tuesday, Jany. 30, 1710–11, being the Anniversary Fast for the Martyrdom of King Charles I,' London, 1710, 4to and 8vo. 2. 'Cicero's Orator,' London, 1724.

died on 23 Aug. 1678. His remains were interred in the cathedral, where a splendid monument, with a Latin epitaph, describing his virtues, his learning, and his patriotism, was erected to his memory (DE BURGO, *Hibernia Domenicana*, p. 490 n.)

His works are: 1. 'A Course of Philosophy,' in Latin, 1630. Manuscript in Archbishop Marsh's library in Dublin. 2. 'Querees propounded by the Protestant partie, concerning the peace in generall, now treated of in Ireland . . .' Paris, 1644, 4to. 3. 'The Polititian's Catechisme for his Instruction in Divine Faith and Morall Honesty. Written by N. N.,' Antwerp, 1658, 12mo. This may be reckoned even more rare than the 'Unkinde Desertor' and 'Bleeding Iphigenia.' 4. 'Protesta y suplica de los Catolicos de Irlanda y de la Gran Bretaña. Al . . . Principe de la Iglesia, el Cardenal Julio Mazerino, y al . . . Señor D. Luys Mendez de Haro y Sotomayor, Conde-Duque de Olivares,' Seville, 1659, 4to, translated from the Latin. This protest is so rare that it appears to be unknown to the most diligent collectors of Irish tracts (*Bibl. Grenvilliana*, i. 257). 5. 'In nomine sanctissimæ Trinitatis vera descriptio moderni status Catholicorum in regno Hiberniæ, et preces eorum, ad Sanctissimum Dominum Clementem Papam nonum,' Cologne [1667], 8vo. The author's name, as designated by F. E. N. F. D. on p. 28, is 'Fernensis Episcopus, Nicolaus French, Doctor,' vide p. 26. 6. 'A Narrative of the Earl of Clarendon's Settlement and Sale of Ireland. Whereby the just English adventurer is much prejudiced, the ancient proprietor destroyed, and publick faith violated: to the great discredit of the English Church and government (if not recalled and made void), as being against the principles of Christianity and true Protestancy. Written in a Letter by a gentleman in the Country to a nobleman at court,' Louvain, 1668, 4to. This tract is extremely rare. It was reprinted, with some additions, under the title of 'Iniquity Display'd, or the Settlement of the Kingdom of Ireland, commonly call'd The Act of Settlement . . . laid open,' 1704, 4to. 7. 'The Dolefull Fall of Andrew Sall, a Jesuit of the Fourth Vow, from the Roman Catholick Apostolick Faith; Lamented by his Constant Frind . . .' 1674, 8vo, published under the initials N. N. There is an account of this work in 'Catholicon: or the Christian Philosopher,' 1818, v. 85–93. Sall replied to the attack in his 'True Catholic Apostolic Faith,' 1676. 8. 'The Bleeding Iphigenia, or an excellent preface of a work unfinished, published by the authors frind, with the reasons of publishing it,' no title-page, 1675, 8vo, published under the initials N. N. The Bleeding Iphigenia is Ireland. The author, lamenting Andrew Sall's abjuration of catholicism, inquires into the cause of persecution in Ireland and England. 9. 'The Vnkinde Desertor of Loyall Men and True Frinds,' 1676, 8vo. The 'unkinde desertor' is intended for a portrait of the Marquis of Ormonde. French's statements led to the Earl of Clarendon writing his 'History of the Rebellion and Civil Wars in Ireland,' in defence and justification of the marquis's conduct.

A collection of his 'Historical Works,' edited by Samuel H. Bindon, was published at Dublin in 2 vols., 1846, 12mo, forming part of Duffy's 'Library of Ireland.' Vol. i. contains the 'Bleeding Iphigenia,' the 'Settlement and Sale of Ireland,' letters, &c., and vol. ii. the 'Unkinde Desertor.'

[Bellings's Hist. of the Irish Confederacy, vol. i. pref. p. viii, ii. 215; Carte's Life of Ormonde; Clarendon's Hist. of the Rebellion and Civil Wars in Ireland; Clarendon State Papers, ii. 141; Cox's Hibernia Anglicana; De Burgo's Hibernia Domenicana, pp. 490, 657, 686–8, 692, 693, 695, 699, suppl. 861, 880, 881, 884, 895, 921; Gilbert's Contemporary Hist. of Affairs in Ireland (1641–52), i. 157–8, 168, 184–6, 288, 707, 716, 766, ii. 51, 106, 152–3, 196–8, 203, 290, 365, iii. 4, 5, 10, 178, 275, 301; Bibl. Grenvilliana; The Huth Library, ii. 553; Killen's Eccl. Hist. of Ireland, ii. 40, 81, 114; McGee's Irish Writers, p. 131; Moran's Spicilegium Ossoriense, pp. 390, 417, 438, 449, 454, 459, 475, 489, 499, 510; Notes and Queries, 2nd ser. vii. 45, 3rd ser. viii. 724; Rinuccini's Embassy in Ireland, translated by Hutton; Shirley's Library at Lough Fea, p. 116; Cat. of Library of Trin. Coll. Dublin, iii. 318; Walsh's Four Letters on Several Subjects to Persons of Quality; Walsh's Vindication of the Loyal Formulary on Irish Remonstrance.]

T. C.

FRENCH, PETER (*d.* 1693), missionary, a native of Galway, studied divinity in Ireland and in the south of Spain, and became a friar of the order of St. Dominic. Going to Spanish America, he laboured for thirty years as a missionary among the Indians of Mexico, great numbers of whom he converted from idolatry. He wrote in the Mexican language 'A Catechism or Exposition of the Christian Faith,' but whether it was printed does not appear. Returning to his native country, he was employed on the mission until his death, which took place in Galway in 1693.

[Quétif and Echard's Scriptores Ordinis Prædicatorum, ii. 735, quoting John O'Heyn's Epilogus Chronologicus exponens Conventus et Fundationes Ordinis Predicatorum in regno Hiberniæ, Louvain, 1706, p. 24; Ware's Writers of Ireland, p. 295; Hardiman's Galway, p. 254.] T. C.

FRENCH, WILLIAM, D.D. (1786–1849), master of Jesus College, Cambridge, was the son of a rich yeoman at Eye in Suffolk. He was sent to Ipswich grammar school, where the Rev. Mr. Howarth was head-master, and he afterwards entered Caius College, Cambridge. After a successful college career he came out in 1811 as second wrangler, the senior being Thomas Edward Dicey of Trinity, the two being bracketed equal as Smith's prizemen. Soon after French was elected fellow and tutor of Pembroke College, and in 1814 took his M.A. degree. He was only thirty-four years old in 1820 when he was appointed master of Jesus College by Dr. Sparke, bishop of Ely, in whose family he had been private tutor. In the following year he was made D.D. by royal mandate, and served the office of vice-chancellor, a position which he filled again in 1834, when he also acted as one of the syndics appointed to superintend the building of the Fitzwilliam Museum. He was presented by the lord chancellor to the living of Moor Monkton, Yorkshire, in 1827, and became a canon of Ely in 1832. He discharged his various functions with urbanity and integrity. His mathematical attainments were of the highest order, and to classical scholarship he added a considerable acquaintance with oriental languages. He took a distinguished part in the translations made by himself and Mr. George Skinner of the Psalms and Proverbs. He managed the affairs of his college so as greatly to improve its finances, and his name is connected with the remarkable restoration of Jesus College Chapel, begun under his direction by his gift of coloured glass for the eastern triplet. His published works are: 1. 'A new Translation of the Book of Psalms from the original Hebrew, with Explanatory Notes by W. French, D.D., and George Skinner, M.A.; a new edition, with corrections and additions, 8vo, London, 1842. 'A judicious and excellent work for review' (see British Critic, ix. 404). 2. 'A new Translation of the Proverbs of Solomon from the original Hebrew, with Explanatory Notes by W. French, D.D., and George Skinner, M.A.,' 8vo, London, 1831. He died at Jesus Lodge, Cambridge, on 12 Nov. 1849, in his sixty-third year, and was buried at Brockdish in Norfolk four days later.

[Gent. Mag. new ser. xxxii. 655; Luard, Graduati Cantabrigienses; Willis and Clark's Architectural Hist. of Cambr. ii. 151, iii. 199.] R. H.

FREND, WILLIAM (1757–1841), reformer and scientific writer, was born on 22 Nov. 1757 at Canterbury, being the second son of George Frend, one of its principal tradesmen. an alderman, and twice its mayor.

His mother was buried in the cloister yard, Canterbury, on 7 Feb. 1763, and his father married at the cathedral, on 25 Sept. 1764, Jane Kirby, who proved a kindly mother to her stepchildren (Canterbury Cath. Registers, Harl. Soc., pp. 95, 145). He was educated at the king's school in that city until 1771, and among his companions were his cousin Herbert Marsh, afterwards bishop of Peterborough, and Charles Abbott, afterwards Lord Tenterden. His father destined him for business, and he was sent to St. Omer to learn the French language, and then to a mercantile house in Quebec, where he remained for a few weeks, during which time he served as a volunteer at the beginning of the troubles with the American colonies. On his return home he expressed a wish to enter the church, and on the recommendation of Archbishop Moore he was entered as a minor pensioner at Christ's College, Cambridge, on 18 Dec. 1775, when Paley was one of the college tutors. After gaining various college prizes he took the degree of B.A. in 1780, being second wrangler and Smith's prizeman, and thus secured the favour of Dr. Caryl, master of Jesus College, by whose advice he migrated thither as a pensioner on 24 May 1780. Through the same interest Frend was elected foundation scholar on 6 June 1780 and fellow on 23 April 1781, from which year he also held the office of tutor. At the close of 1780 he was admitted deacon in the church of England, and advanced to the priesthood in 1783, when he was presented to the living of Madingley, near Cambridge, where he officiated zealously until June 1787. During this period of his life the post of tutor to the Archduke Alexander of Russia was offered to him, but the position was declined, although accompanied with a salary of 2,000l. per annum, a suitable establishment, and a retiring pension of 800l. a year for life. In 1787 he became a convert to unitarianism. He published his 'Address to the Inhabitants of Cambridge' in favour of his new creed, and he exerted himself very vigorously in support of the grace introduced into the senate house on 11 Dec. 1787 for doing away with subscription to the Thirty-nine Articles on taking the degree of M.A. For these offences he was removed by Dr. Beadon from the office of tutor by an order dated 27 Sept. 1788, and his appeal from this ejectment was dismissed by the visitor, the Bishop of Ely, by a decree dated 29 Dec. 1788. To relieve his mental anxiety and to deliberate calmly on the future, he took, in company with an old schoolfellow called Richard Tylden, a lengthy tour in France, the Low Countries, Germany, and Switzerland. When he returned home he resumed the study of Hebrew, which his travels had interrupted, and became so proficient as to be deemed 'in the opinion of learned Jews better versed in that language than any English christian of his day.' Priestley devised in 1789 a plan for a new translation of the scriptures, and through 1790 Frend was engaged on translating the historical books of the Old Testament. He also became very intimate with Robert Robinson, the learned dissenting minister of Cambridge, who died in 1790, and he corrected the press of Robinson's posthumous volume of 'Ecclesiastical Researches.' In 1793 he wrote a tract, printed at St. Ives but sold at Cambridge, entitled 'Peace and Union recommended to the Associated Bodies of Republicans and Anti-republicans,' in which he denounced many of the existing abuses and condemned much of the liturgy of the church of England. On 4 March certain members of the senate met on the invitation of the vice-chancellor, Dr. Isaac Milner, at his lodge in Queens' College, resolved that Frend should be prosecuted in the vice-chancellor's court, and deputed a committee of five to conduct the proceedings. On 23 April a summons was issued by that official requiring Frend's presence in the law schools on 3 May to answer the charge of having violated the laws and statutes of the university by publishing the pamphlet. After several sittings and a long and able defence, the vice-chancellor and heads gave their decision on 28 May that the authorship had been proved and that Frend had offended against the statute 'de concionibus.' Gunning, in his 'Reminiscences' (i. 280–309), reprints an account of the trial, and, while condemning the tone of the pamphlet, describes the proceedings as a party move and vindicates the tract from the accusation of sedition. He adds that the vice-chancellor was biased against the accused, and that the undergraduates, among whom S. T. Coleridge was conspicuous, were unanimous in his favour. Two letters from Dr. Farmer to Dr. Parr on this trial are in Parr's 'Works' (i. 447–8), and in the same set (viii. 30–2) is a long letter from Frend on the treatment which Palmer of Queens', another reformer, had just received. Frend was ordered to retract and confess his error, and as he declined was 'banished from the university' (30 May). An appeal against the sentence followed, but it was unanimously affirmed by the delegates on 29 June, and on 26 Nov. 1795 the court of king's bench discharged a rule which Frend had obtained for restoring him to the franchises of a resident M.A. The master and fellows of Jesus College decided, on 3 April 1793, that in consequence of this pamphlet he should not be allowed to reside in the college until he could produce satisfactory proofs of good behaviour. He thereupon appealed to the visitor, but on 13 July the appeal was dismissed, nor was he more successful in his application to the king's bench for a mandamus requiring the visitor to hear and determine the appeal. In spite of these proceedings he enjoyed the emoluments of his fellowship until his marriage, and remained, while he lived, a member of his college and of the senate of the university. Many years later, in 1837, Frend furnished Crabb Robinson with some anecdotes about his trial, and said that the promoters wished to expel him from the university, but that he demanded a sight of the university roll, when on reference to the original document it was discovered that an informality existed which made his expulsion invalid. On leaving Cambridge he came to London, and maintained himself by adding the profits of teaching and writing to his fellowship. In 1806 he exerted himself actively in the formation of the Rock Life Assurance Company, to which he was appointed actuary. A severe illness in 1826 compelled him to tender his resignation, which was accepted in the ensuing year, and an annuity of 800l. per annum was conferred upon him. His health subsequently recovered, and he resumed his active life until 1840, when he was attacked by paralysis, under which he lingered with almost total loss of speech and motion, though with the 'smallest possible decay of mind or memory.' He died at his house, Tavistock Square, London, on 21 Feb. 1841. As a unitarian and a whig he gloried in the spread of the opinions which he advocated. All reformers, such as Burdett and Horne Tooke, were numbered among his friends, and he maintained an active correspondence with the chief supporters of radicalism. He was frequently consulted by Palmer in support of his claim for a public grant for his services in improving the transmission of letters. Frend thought that the rate of postage should be reduced to a fixed charge of 2d. or 1d., and drew up a statement to that effect which reached a member of Peel's cabinet, but nothing came of it at that time. Disinterested benevolence and chivalrous assertion of his opinions were the leading traits in his character. He had been a pupil of Paley, and among his own pupils were E. D. Clarke, the traveller, Copley (afterwards Lord Lyndhurst), and Malthus; he was himself the last of 'the learned anti-Newtonians and a noted oppugner of all that distinguishes Algebra from Arithmetic.' In 1808 he married a daughter of the Rev. Francis Blackburne, vicar of Brignall in Yorkshire, and granddaughter of Archdeacon Blackburne. They had seven children, and their eldest daughter, Sophia Elizabeth, married in the autumn of 1837 Professor De Morgan.

Frend's works dealt with many subjects. His publications were: 1. 'An Address to the Inhabitants of Cambridge and its Neighbourhood . . . to turn from the false Worship of Three Persons to the Worship of the One True God,' St. Ives, 1788. The second edition was entitled 'An Address to the Members of the Church of England and to Protestant Trinitarians in General,' &c., and it was followed by 'A Second Address to the Members of the Church of England,' &c. These were reprinted in 'Six Tracts in Vindication of the Worship of One God,' and in other unitarian publications, and were answered by the Rev. H. W. Coulthurst, by George Townsend of Ramsgate in two tracts in 1789, and by Alexander Pirie in a volume issued at Perth in 1792. Frend responded in 'Thoughts on Subscription to religious tests . . . in a letter to the Rev. H. W. Coulthurst,' and in 'Mr. Coulthurst's blunders exposed, or a review of his several texts.' For these pamphlets Frend was expelled from the Society for Promoting Christian Knowledge (*An Account of some late Proceedings of the Society*, 1789). 2. 'Peace and Union recommended,' &c., 1793; 2nd ed. 1793, in which he described the evils of the then parliamentary system and of the game and poor laws, and explained the necessity for numerous reforms. The peccant passages are set out in the second edition in single inverted commas. His trial was described by himself in 'An Account of the Proceedings in the University of Cambridge against William Frend,' 1793, and in 'A Sequel to the Account,' &c., which dealt with the application to the court of king's bench in 1795. John Beverley [q. v.] also published accounts of the proceedings in 1793. 3. 'Scarcity of Bread: a plan for reducing its high price,' 1795, two editions. He urged subscriptions by the rich for the relief of the poor. 4. 'Principles of Algebra, 1796 (with a very long appendix by Baron Maseres); pt. ii. 1799. 5. 'A Letter to the Vice-chancellor of Cambridge, by Wm. Frend, candidate for the Lucasian Professorship,' 1798. 6. 'Principles of Taxation,' 1799, advocating a graduated system of income-tax. 7. 'Animadversions on Bishop Pretyman's Elements of Christian Theology,' 1800, to which Joshua Toulmin replied in a preface to his 'Four Discourses on Baptism.' 8. 'The Effect of Paper Money on the Price of Provisions,' 1801, which was provoked by the controversy between Sir Francis Baring and Walter Boyd. 9. 'The Gentleman's Monthly

Miscellany,' which lived for a few months of 1803, and was edited in whole or in part by Frend. 10. 'Evening Amusements, or the Beauty of the Heavens Displayed.' It lasted from 1804 to 1822, 'an astronomical elementary work of a new character, which had great success; the earlier numbers went through several editions.' 11. 'Patriotism: an Essay dedicated to the Volunteers,' 1804. 12. 'Tangible Arithmetic, or the Art of Numbering made Easy by means of an Arithmetical Toy,' 1805. 13. 'A Letter on the Slave Trade,' 1816. 14. 'The National Debt in its True Colours,' 1817. Reprinted in the 'Pamphleteer,' ix. 415–32. He advocated its extinction by an annual sinking fund. 15. 'Memoirs of a Goldfinch,' a poem, with notes and illustrations on natural history and natural philosophy (anon.), 1819. 16. 'Is it Impossible to Free the Atmosphere of London in a very considerable degree from Smoke?' 1819. A few copies only for friends, but it was reproduced in the 'Pamphleteer,' xv. 61–5. 17. 'A Plan of Universal Education,' 1832. A fragment of a volume, 'Letters on a hitherto Undescribed Country,' written some years before but never published. Frend, besides contributing two articles to 'Tracts on the Resolution of Affected Algebraick Equations,' edited by Baron Maseres in 1800, and one tract to the same editor's 'Scriptores Logarithmici,' vol. vi. 1807, suggested other matters to him in the same publications. Maseres in his 'Tracts on the Resolution of Cubick and Biquadratick Equations,' published voluminous supplements to his appendix to Frend's 'Principles of Algebra.'

[Gent. Mag. 1841, pt. i. pp. 541–3; Monthly Notices of Royal Astronomical Soc. v. 144–51, by De Morgan; Howell's State Trials, xxii. 523, 723; C. H. Cooper's Annals of Cambr. iv. 447–52; Baker's St. John's, Cambr. ed. Mayor, ii. 736; Dyer's Robinson, pp. 312–18; Crabb Robinson's Diary, i. 373, iii. 143, 192, 401; Rutt's Life and Corresp. of Priestley, ii. 24, 81–3, 94–5; Memoir of Augustus de Morgan, pp. 19–24, 39–40, 78–82, 109–10; [Mrs. Le Breton's] Memories of Seventy Years; Sidebotham's King's School, Canterbury, pp. 80–1.]   W. P. C.

FRENDRAUGHT, first VISCOUNT (1600–1650). See CRICHTON, JAMES.]

FRERE, BARTHOLOMEW (1778–1851), diplomatist, born in 1778, was the fifth son of John Frere [q. v.], F.R.S., M.P. for Norwich, and a younger brother of the Right Hon. John Hookham Frere [q. v.] He proceeded B.A. at Trinity College, Cambridge, in 1799, and M.A. in 1806. In 1801 he was appointed secretary of legation at Lisbon, whence he was transferred in the same capacity to Madrid in 1802 and Berlin 1805, and in 1807 became secretary of embassy at Constantinople, and witnessed the discomfiture of Mr. Arbuthnot and Admiral Duckworth. In 1808 he returned to Spain as secretary of embassy, and acted as minister plenipotentiary *ad interim* at Seville from November 1809 to January 1810, and at Cadiz from 29 Jan. to 2 March. Gazetted secretary of embassy at Constantinople in March 1811, he and his chief, Robert Liston, did not proceed to their post till the following year, when in June they relieved Stratford Canning [q. v.] from his responsibility as minister plenipotentiary. From 1815 to 1817, and again from 1820 to 1821, Frere took charge of the embassy at the Porte as minister plenipotentiary *ad interim*, but in August 1821 he finally retired on a pension, which he enjoyed for thirty years, till his death in Old Burlington Street, London, 29 May 1851, aged 74. He was a useful public servant of ordinary abilities.

[Foreign Office registers; Lane-Poole's Life of Lord Stratford de Redcliffe, i. 175, 179 ; Ann. Reg.]   S. L.-P.

FRERE, Sir HENRY BARTLE EDWARD, commonly called Sir Bartle Frere (1815–1884), statesman, belonged to a family associated for centuries with the eastern counties of England. His grandfather, John Frere [q. v.], was second wrangler in Paley's year (1763), was elected M.P. for Norwich, and at his death left seven sons, of whom John Hookham Frere [q. v.] was the eldest. Edward, the second son, was father of Henry Bartle Edward Frere. Edward Frere (1770–1844) married, 28 July 1800, Mary Anne, eldest daughter and coheiress of James Greene, esq., M.P. for Arundel in 1759, and had by her nine sons and five daughters. Henry Bartle was the sixth son. Born at Clydach, Brecknockshire, on 29 March 1815, he was sent at an early age to the grammar school at Bath. In the narrow range of subjects there taught Frere gained distinction, and he entered Haileybury in 1832. In this college he showed capacity for a wider scope of study. At the end of the first term he stood second on the list of scholars, and during the following term he gained the highest place, which he retained until the end of his course. In 1834 he received his appointment to a writership in the Bombay civil service. At this time the normal length of the voyage to India was from four to five months. But Lieutenant Waghorn's successful journey by Egypt having shown that the bowstring is shorter than the bow, Frere applied to the court of directors for permission to find his way to India by the same road. After some hesitation the direc-

tors granted the request, having learned that Lord William Bentinck proposed to send a steamer to Suez, which on its return voyage was to meet at Socotra a vessel carrying the mails to Bombay. In May 1834 the young civilian sailed from Falmouth, but on arriving at Malta found that the steamer was not expected at Suez until August. He was thus enabled to spend a month with his uncle Hookham Frere, then living in Malta on account of his wife's health. There he studied Arabic under the guidance of the well-known Dr. Wolfe, who on his departure vouched for him that he knew enough Arabic 'to scold his way through Egypt.'

Frere finally left Malta in a Greek brigantine for Alexandria, where he joined four other travellers who were taking the same route. He journeyed with them laboriously to Cairo, and thence to Thebes and Carnac, whence they struck across the desert on camels to Kosseir, on the Red Sea. Here, following the example of Waghorn, they embarked in open boats and reached Mocha, viâ Yambo and Jeddah. At Mocha they engaged passages for Bombay in an Arab dhow laden with pilgrims. After many dangers and a narrow escape from starvation they landed at Bombay on 23 Sept. The very unorthodox manner of arrival on Indian soil placed Frere under the necessity of proving his identity. He quickly settled down to the study of Hindustani, Marathi, and Gujarati, and, having in 1835 passed in all these languages, was appointed assistant to the collector at Poona. He devoted himself with characteristic zeal to his duties, and showed the same enthusiasm when subsequently detached to assist Henry Edward Goldsmid [q. v.] in investigating the system of land assessment of Indapore. Thoroughly to carry out the work it was necessary to investigate the extent and nature of each holding, and the result of this minute investigation was to prove that the assessments were much too high, and to convict the native collectors of extortion and oppression in collecting the land taxes.

In those days native officials were still frequently imbued with the traditions of oriental misgovernment. Many of their victims instead of complaining threw up their holdings and drifted elsewhere. Large tracts in the district were thus left uncultivated, and other farms were only imperfectly cropped. Frere and his companions proposed thoroughgoing remedies. They recommended that the rate of the land assessment should be reduced to sums easily payable by the cultivators, that security of tenure should be granted to every holder of land, and that more strenuous efforts should be made to check corruption on the part of the native officials. These recommendations were acted upon, and a most beneficial change produced. The people regained confidence. The spare land was eagerly taken up, and the district became one of the most prosperous in India. The obvious effects of this policy led to its wide extension throughout the Bombay presidency, as well as to Sind, Mysore, and Berár. Frere's zeal and ability thus gained for him promotion to the post of assistant revenue commissioner. This office he held until 1842, when he was appointed private secretary to Sir George Arthur [q. v.], the newly arrived governor of Bombay. Frere's new duties entailed considerable responsibility, more especially because Arthur had no experience of Indian administration. Upon Sir Charles Napier's annexation of Sind, the governor had to co-operate in the consolidation of the province. He was ably supported by Frere, who thus early gained an insight into the administration of the presidency. On 10 Oct. 1844 Frere married Miss Catherine Arthur, the second daughter of the governor, and shortly afterwards went home on sick certificate. On his return to India after an eighteen months' leave, he served for a time as assistant commissioner of customs, and was then appointed political resident at the court of the rajá of Sattara. The position of Sattara was defined by a treaty made on the conquest of the Marathá territory in 1818. Pertâb Sahib, the then rajá, a descendant of Sivaji, who established the Maratbá power in 1644, was the nominal ruler, but for several generations the imperial authority had been allowed to fall into the hands of the peshwas or mayors of the palace. By the treaty of 1818 the greater part of the southern Maratbá territory was annexed by the East India Company, Sattara being especially reserved for the rajá. Four years later the district was handed over to him, and a resident was appointed to his court. From being a mere puppet in the hands of the peshwa he had thus become a reigning sovereign. But he had grown disaffected to his benefactors, and had been at last sent as a state prisoner to Benares. Shahjí, his brother, was appointed to succeed him. Frere was nominated to Sattara during the reign of Shahjí, and for two years and a half he devoted his energies to improving the condition of the people. He directed especial attention to the improvement of the roads and the means of irrigation, and it was at his instigation that a tunnel, the first ever constructed in India, was made connecting a fertile valley with the town of Sattara. In 1847 Pertâb Sahib died, having adopted an heir who was inclined to put forward pretensions to the rajáship. Meanwhile

Shahjí was in bad health, and having no male issue was desirous of adopting a son and successor. In the beginning of April 1848 the rajá told Frere of his intention. He hoped that the government would sanction a handsome provision from the Sattara revenues for the support of the child whom he might take under his protection, and begged Frere to obtain the consent of the government to his adopting a member of the Bhonslay family as his son. Frere agreed to submit the rajá's request to the government, but warned him that the previous sanction of the court of directors might be necessary. This warning did not prevent the rajá from making the adoption a few hours before his death. Frere, who was absent at the time, having left at the rajá's earnest request to press his wishes on the government, hastened back to Sattara at the risk of his life, for the people were fanatically excited at the political position, and without the escort which the governor wished him to take. For nine months he administered the province, being careful in the meantime to avoid recognising in any way the adopted son. By the old treaty of 1818 the government of India had definitely ceded Sattara to the rajá, his heirs and successors, and Frere was of opinion, therefore, that they were in honour bound to recognise the title of the adopted son to the throne. This was strongly the opinion also of Mountstuart Elphinstone [q. v.] and Captain Grant Duff, the negotiators of the treaty, and of Sir George Clerk, the governor of Bombay, but the governor-general and the majority of his council took an opposite view. Lord Dalhousie recorded it as his strong and deliberate opinion that 'the British government is bound not to put aside or to neglect such rightful opportunities of acquiring territory or revenue as may from time to time present themselves,' and therefore should not give effect to the device of the Hindoo law for sustaining the succession by adoption. These views were supported by a majority in the court of directors, and Sattara was consequently annexed as British territory. Though Frere had not hesitated to urge officially an opposite opinion, he was selected as the officer most competent to discharge the duties of commissioner in the newly annexed province. In the exercise of his new powers he promoted cultivation by introducing cotton seed from New Orleans and sugar canes from Mauritius. He reformed the sanitary condition of the towns and villages, and provided them with abundant supplies of good water. He established suitable encampments for pilgrims, inaugurated municipal boards, introduced a system of popular education, and provided for the preservation of ancient monuments. He held that an essential condition of progress was the full power of the people to appeal to principles of justice. The judicial system of British India was, he considered, 'too refined and elaborate, and too difficult of access for general utility in ordinary cases.' 'A system of law,' he wrote, 'is to the social system of a country as the skin rather than the clothing to the animal frame; not only an appendage which may be made to fit, but one which must grow with the frame and accommodate itself naturally to the peculiarities and even the deformities of the body to which it belongs.'

In 1850 the chief commissionership of Sind, vacant by the resignation of Mr. Pringle, was in the appointment of the government of Bombay. The territory, nearly as large as England and Wales, was bordered on the west by some of the most turbulent tribes in existence; the inhabitants were idle and debauched, and in the case of the Sayyids violent and revengeful; and the country was still in the throes of annexation. An important party in the Bombay council desired the appointment of a military man accustomed to deal with turbulent populations; but Lord Dalhousie, the governor-general, deemed a civilian better fitted for the post. Lord Falkland, the governor of Bombay, decided to appoint Frere, and his colleagues threatened to resign if the appointment were not ratified. In a minute on the subject Lord Falkland wrote: 'The commissionership of Sind requires an union and balance of qualification which, in my opinion, are not possessed in a like degree by a member of the civil service senior to that gentleman [Frere], who is a civilian of sixteen years' standing, and whose firmness of purpose, mild disposition, and conciliatory manners cannot but insure for him in the exercise of his official functions the ready co-operation and respect of the military authorities.' Never was a forecast more happily fulfilled. Frere found his province distracted by factions and the people grossly ignorant. The dispossessed amirs claimed the sympathy of their former dependents as victims of foreign usurpation. Frere's first care was therefore to deprive the amirs of claims to commiseration by pensioning them off. Twenty-two families were thus treated, and by timely courtesy and consideration were converted into loyal supporters of the British government. He next turned his attention to the development of the province. He improved the harbour at Karàchi and gave municipal institutions to that and nineteen other towns. He established a library and museum at Karàchi, and, after the manner of Warren Hastings,

ordered every deputy-collector in the province to forward each season specimens of the raw products of their districts for exhibition in the museum. He improved and multiplied the roads and canals, built bungalows, baths, and places of shelter for travellers, and caused a topographical survey to be made of the province. He established village schools, a written language, and a judicial code. He built barracks for the troops and opened recreation grounds for the public. He thus gradually converted the people into an industrious and law-abiding peasantry. His attention was equally demanded by the political condition and social requirements of the tribes on the western frontier. He might either ignore them or endeavour to impress upon them a recognition both of the strength and amiable intentions of the British government. The first course would save immediate trouble, but in case of an outbreak in India would leave Sind exposed to a possibly hostile force on the frontier. It is needless to say that Frere adopted the second alternative. He opened relations with the khan of Khelat and established fairs at Sukkur and Karàchi, to which the frontier tribes were invited. The institution of these fairs is in accordance with the best traditions of oriental policy. The Chinese have long held similar gatherings on the Tibetan frontier, and with most beneficial consequences. The tribes mixed in the bazaars with the Sindis, and learned to respect the justice of English rule and the weight of English power. In Frere also they found a firm and just governor. With an even hand he punished the predatory hillman and the overbearing British subject. In cases of outrages committed by the tribesmen he demanded from the chiefs the rendition of the culprits alone and abstained from all retaliatory measures on the tribe generally. The consequence of this policy was that the culprits became outcasts among their own people, and in some instances surrendered to the British authorities, finding themselves cut off from the society of their fellow-men. At the end of five years, spent in teaching the native races industry and forethought, and in introducing into their midst the arts of civilised life, Frere came to England (1856) for the benefit of his health. After a well-earned rest of a year he returned to his post and was met on his landing at Karàchi in May 1857 with the news of the mutiny. Frere recognised the vitally serious nature of the outbreak, and at once called for a return of the British forces in Sind. It appeared that for the control of this vast territory there were only 1,350 sabres, four native infantry regiments, one Belooch battalion, three batteries of artillery, one European regiment, and a depôt of another. But Frere felt that when the Punjab was in danger this force was too large a one to be kept in Sind. His rule had been so successful that he could answer for the internal peace of the province, and he felt that, as he afterwards wrote, 'when the head and heart are threatened, the extremities must take care of themselves.' He therefore at once sent off his only European regiment to Mooltan, and by so doing secured this strong fortress during the worst days of the mutiny; at the same time he despatched a steamer to intercept the 64th and 78th regiments, which were on their way to Sind from the war in Persia, and to order them on to Calcutta. As the mutiny spread he directed a battery of artillery and a detachment of the 14th native infantry to march to the support of General Roberts at Guzerat. He further sent a portion of the remaining corps of Europeans into the south Marathá country, and the Belooch battalion to the further help of Sir John Lawrence in the Punjab. The removal of these several regiments left Frere only 178 European bayonets in Sind. And they were enough, though mutinies broke out at Shikarpur, Hyderabad, and Karàchi. Without exception these outbreaks were put down at once, and so slight a hold did the poison of disaffection get in Sind that at Karàchi the leaders in the revolt were tried by a court-martial composed of native officers, who dealt out exemplary punishments to the accused. But Frere was able to do more than give away the force he already had. He was able to create regiments, and when all natives were generally distrusted he raised troops who were as loyal as Europeans throughout the crisis. In the midst of all the work which was thus thrown upon him he found time to visit the khan of Khelat, and thus laid the foundation of an alliance which finally led up to the cession of Quetta and to the frontier treaty negotiated by Sir F. Goldsmid in 1872. Nor did he shrink from protesting with all the force of his influence and knowledge against the proposal of Sir John Lawrence to retire from Peshawur. While that fortress, Lahore, and Mooltan were in our possession, we were, he held, 'lords of the Punjab,' and he maintained that it would be better to stand at Peshawur a siege like that of Jellalabad than retire from it. He had time also to review in his own mind the acts of the Calcutta government, and a memorandum he then wrote on the constitution of the Indian army is as thoughtful and comprehensive as if written in the most peaceful leisure. Throughout the anxieties of the time he never for an instant relaxed his efforts

for the development of the province. In April 1858 he turned the first sod of the railway from Karàchi to Kotri; in the same year the Oriental Inland Steam Company commenced to run steamers between Karàchi and Mooltan, and in the following year the Eastern Narra canal was opened.

Frere's great services were recognised by men on the spot. 'From first to last,' wrote Sir John Lawrence, 'from the first commencement of the mutiny to the final triumph, that officer [Frere] has rendered assistance to the Punjab administration just as if he had been one of its own commissioners. . . . The chief commissioner believes that there is no civil officer in India who, for eminent exertions, deserves better of his government than Mr. H. B. E. Frere.' In England the value of his services was also cordially recognised. His name was especially mentioned in the vote of thanks passed by both houses of parliament.

In 1859 Frere received for the second time the thanks of both houses of parliament for his services during the mutiny, and at the same time he received the knight commandership of the Bath. He was in the same year appointed a member of the council of the governor-general. Up to that time the members of the council had always been chosen from the Bengal services, and the tradition was broken for the first time in Frere's favour. The news of his promotion came like an announcement of disaster to the people of Sind. From Shikarpur to Karàchi came expressions of deep regret from both native and foreign residents. From being a comparatively desolate and barren country it had become under his rule a fruitful and well-watered land. Trade had been developed and fostered, and the revenue had risen in eight years from twenty-three to forty-three lakhs of rupees. Six thousand miles of road were opened out and the Rohree supply channel was constructed, which irrigated many thousand square miles of territory. He gave proprietary rights and fixity of tenure to landowners who had previously held their possessions only at the will of their rulers. He secured to the people generally the enjoyment of their lives and property. He improved the postal service of the province and issued for use in Sind the first postage-stamps ever printed in India.

Frere, from being an almost independent ruler, now became a unit in a body whose deliberations were criticised on all sides, and whose decisions he could only affect to the extent of his influence and vote. Frere had always kept his mind open to the great problems of Indian policy, and was not unprepared to face the enormous difficulties of his new office. The finances were in terrible disorder. During 1859–60 the expenditure had exceeded the income by 9,000,000*l*., and the enormous addition to the military budget entailed by the mutiny appeared even likely to increase; the antagonism between the races was extreme, the whole military organisation unhinged. The disorder of the finances had induced the English government to appoint James Wilson [q. v.] to undertake the reform of the exchequer. From the first Frere worked cordially with Wilson, though not always agreeing with him in details. He heartily supported the steps he adopted for the reduction of expenditure, and especially turned his attention to the cost of the army, which threatened to become an uncontrollable burden. After all possible reductions the imposition of new taxes became necessary, and Frere supported Wilson in introducing the new income tax, which was strenuously opposed by large sections of the native community. The main credit for this and other financial measures of the time must of course belong to Wilson. Frere, however, did much of the work, and had charge of the exchequer in the interval between Wilson's death and the appointment of his successor, Laing. He again discharged the same duties for six months during the enforced absence of Laing from illness. A short experience of the governor-general's council convinced him that a radical change was necessary in both the supreme and local governments. The council, as it was then composed, was in his opinion manifestly insufficient for the work it had to do. The official section of the community was alone represented, to the exclusion of the mercantile classes and the natives. In the presidencies this anomaly was even more apparent. Bengal was governed by three hundred foreigners, all of whom were crown officials. The consequent bitterness of feeling was a continual irritant. Frere's strong sense of justice revolted against this inequality, and in season and out of season he urged on the authorities the necessity of reform. He held, with Lord Canning, that the existing executive councils should be supplemented by legislative bodies, in which the non-official classes of the presidencies should be represented. He urged strongly also the justice of employing native gentlemen in the administration of affairs. The equity and wisdom of these reforms were, when set forth, so apparent that they were successfully carried out, and the benefits resulting from them are now universally acknowledged even by those who at the time were opposed to them. The advocacy of these measures, which originated with Lord Canning, was

ably conducted by Frere, who was at this time Lord Canning's confidential and trusted adviser on all matters connected with India. It was due also to Frere that the unreasonable unpopularity of Lord Canning was greatly abated. He was able to enter into explanations on points of Lord Canning's administration impossible for Canning himself, and his genial hospitality to Europeans and natives served to break down prejudices and restore confidence in a way that no official acts or complacence could ever have done. In 1860 he accompanied Lord Canning on a visit to the north-west provinces, on which occasion the governor-general invested Scindia, Holkar, the nizam, and others with the Star of India as a reward for services rendered during the mutiny. Frere also introduced measures for the encouragement of the cultivation of cotton, tobacco, and indigo, and promoted in every way in his power the extension of roads and the construction of irrigation works.

In 1862 Frere was appointed governor of Bombay. Upon hearing this news Canning wrote: 'I do not know when I have read anything with such unmixed pleasure. God grant you health and strength to do your work in your own noble spirit and energy.' By the European community in Bombay it was recognised as a compliment that one of the foremost men in India should have been sent to rule over them, and by the natives his appointment was 'hailed with heartfelt satisfaction.' One of the first measures he carried out was to throw down the ramparts of Bombay, which stood as barriers against the sea breezes, and covered a space of ground daily becoming of more value. The sanitary advantages gained to the town by the demolition of these useless works became at once apparent, and as a financial measure it more than exceeded the expectations formed. The land fetched in the market 180 rupees a square yard, and on part of it were erected rows of public offices, designed by Gilbert Scott, which were then incomparably the finest modern buildings in the East. Municipal institutions, which always held a prominent part in Frere's administration, early gained his attention, and to him is due the municipality which now governs the city, and which in the first year of its existence was instrumental in reducing the death rate by two thousand. He established the Deccan College at Poona, as well as a college for instructing natives in civil engineering. He commenced the buildings of the Bombay University, and instituted English and vernacular schools in various parts of the presidency. He founded schools for the female children of soldiers and for the orphans of natives, and he developed the system of grants in aid, which insured the existence of many of these struggling institutions. He promoted the improvement of the harbour of Bombay, co-operated in establishing direct telegraphic communication with England, and lent support to the railway from Bombay to Rajputana, Delhi, and other parts. The development of these excellent works was chiefly due to Frere. But the circumstances of the time contributed largely to their success. The American war had suddenly raised the price of cotton and thrown an enormously increased business into the hands of the Bombay growers and merchants. The sudden inrush of wealth produced a feverish desire for speculation. Many new companies were started, and their shares rose to enormous premiums. One of the most rational undertakings was the 'Back Bay Company,' which undertook the reclamation of the land covered by the shallow water of the bay. The shares advanced to an absurd price. On the condition that a site should be provided on the reclaimed land for the terminus of the Baroda Railway, the Bombay government took four hundred shares. The government of India refused to sanction this transaction, and the shares on which 200,000*l.* had been paid up were sold in the market for 1,060,000*l.* When high mercantile authorities were carried away by this excitement, it is not surprising that Frere should have partially adopted their view, or that the directors of the Bank of Bombay, among whom were always two *ex-officio* members of the government, should have sanctioned advances to individuals whose business profits at the time were admitted to be enormous. At length the bubble burst. In June 1865 the restoration of peace in America caused the price of cotton to fall as suddenly as it had risen; a panic followed, and the speculative companies collapsed. The market was instantly flooded with paper, and the bank authorities, becoming alarmed, called in their advances. The history of the bank during this period was one series of disasters. In 1863, at the beginning of the speculating mania, a new charter was conferred upon the bank, and this charter unfortunately omitted several checks and safeguards which had been enforced under the older act of 1840. The choice of secretary was made unwisely, and under the weak administration of this gentleman, and the careless supervision of the directors, the conduct of the business of the bank was mainly conducted by a native broker named Premchund Roychund, who drew unlimited advances for himself and his

friends without either offering or being asked for the proper security. Rumours of the reckless conduct of the bank managers were current in London and Calcutta before they reached the ears of Frere on the spot. Twice Sir Charles Wood, the secretary of state for India, wrote warning Frere of the state of things, and the Indian government repeatedly addressed him on the same subject. On receipt of Sir Charles Wood's letters Frere gave the government directors stringent orders to see that the charter was on all points complied with, and, with a view to checking the superabundant speculation, he brought in a bill for the abolition of 'time bargains,' and forbade the members of the civil service to gamble in shares. But the inquiries of the Calcutta government as to the condition of the bank did not receive so ready a response, and it was not until a commission was appointed that the government of Bombay consented to allow the required information, which they regarded as unduly inquisitorial, to be given. Nothing, however, that was done was able to check the ruinous career of the bank. Having been of late managed on the Scottish system, it had been customary to make advances on personal security only. Finding, however, when the crash came, that it was impossible to recover at once the moneys lent out, the directors demanded securities for the amounts, and were compelled in many instances to receive as such the shares of wrecked companies. Though the failure of the bank was staved off for a time, it came at last. In January 1866 a petition was presented for winding up its affairs, when it was found that 1,889,933*l.* of the paid-up capital was lost. The ruin wrought by this failure was widely spread. Frere's conduct during the crisis has been adversely criticised; but the crash was inevitable. No individual action could have averted it.

Throughout this trying period Frere never relaxed from his philanthropic labours. With the able help of Lady Frere he inaugurated female education at Bombay. During the five years that Frere was at Bombay, Government House was freely thrown open to native gentlemen and their wives.

In 1867 Frere, having been appointed a member of the Indian council, returned to England. The crown conferred on him the order of G.C.S.I., and Oxford gave him the honorary degree of D.C.L. He became a member of the council of the Geographical Society, of which he was appointed president in 1873, and in 1872 he was elected president of the Asiatic Society. The university of Cambridge conferred on him the degree of LL.D. in 1874. But it was in matters directly affecting the government of India that his main interest was centred, and in various papers in periodicals and letters to the 'Times' he urged on the public the views which his deep insight into Indian character had enabled him to form. He took a statesmanlike view of our intercourse with Afghanistan, as appeared from a letter to Sir John Kaye which was much misrepresented in the party controversies of later times.

Stanley's visit to Dr. Livingstone had called public attention to the slave traffic in Africa, and Frere was sent by the foreign office in 1872 to Zanzibar to negotiate a treaty with the sultan, Sayd Burgash, for the suppression of the trade. The sultan undertook to do his utmost to put a stop to slavery in his dominions. On his return from this mission Frere was sworn in as a member of the privy council. The freedom of the city was conferred upon him (1874), and constituencies vied with each other to induce him to represent them in the House of Commons. His position on the Indian council, however, made it impossible for him to stand as a candidate. In 1875 he accompanied the Prince of Wales to Egypt and India, and by his knowledge of Indian society and Indian personages proved himself a most useful 'guide, philosopher, and friend.' A baronetcy and a G.C.B. awaited him on his landing in England (24 May 1876).

The successful confederation of the British colonies in North America with the Dominion of Canada had suggested to Lord Carnarvon, then colonial secretary, the idea of carrying out a similar system of confederation in South Africa. There was much to be said for the scheme in theory, and of all men Frere was best fitted by his successful dealing with similar difficulties in India to undertake such a work, had it been then practicable. It might reasonably be expected that he would be able to induce the inhabitants of South Africa to join a confederacy which would give to the inferior races all the protection and advantages of English rule, while preserving to them their national existences. Accordingly in 1877 Frere was appointed governor of the Cape and high commissioner for the settlement of native affairs in South Africa. But on landing at the Cape, Frere found that he had been set down at the very waters of strife. In the Cape parliament party feeling had reached a pitch which was well-nigh becoming dangerous to the state; the Transkei Kaffirs under Kreli were threatening the eastern colonies; the annexation of the Transvaal by Sir Theophilus Shepstone, which was publicly proclaimed twelve days after Frere's arrival at the Cape, was giving rise to agitation and unrest, and the Zulus were mustering armies which threatened the peace of Natal. As at the close of the first session of parliament the Kaffir affair presented itself as the most pressing question of the hour, Frere went to King William's Town and across the Kei at the risk of his life, with the intention of meeting Kreli to discuss the question in dispute, and explain the good will of the British government. Kreli made no response to this overture, and subsequently suddenly attacked the Fingoes, who were under British protection, in revenge for an outrage committed on some of his followers in a drunken brawl. The white settlers became alarmed with good reason. In their interest, as much as in that of the Fingoes, it became imperatively necessary that peace with the Kaffirs should be restored as speedily as possible, and Frere placed the matter in the hands of Sir Arthur Cunynghame, the general commanding. Meanwhile the conduct of some of the leading members of Frere's cabinet became openly and unconstitutionally obstructive. The position, complicated by the alarm of a savage war, was intolerable. Frere dismissed his cabinet, and Sir Gordon Sprigg, the leader of the opposition, accepted the seals of office as premier. From this time the war progressed favourably, first under Sir A. Cunynghame, and afterwards under General Thesiger, and a peace was finally brought about in 1878, after a trying succession of bush fights and rough skirmishes.

Tranquillity having been thus restored, Frere returned to Cape Town after an absence in Kaffraria of seven months. By the Sand River convention of 1852 the British government had guaranteed to the Boers the management of their own affairs, and engaged to respect their territory. The republic, however, had become greatly disorganised; the laws were not enforced, and the taxes had fallen into arrears. In 1876 the public debt amounted to 300,000l.; the confusion was chaotic, and neighbouring tribes were becoming dangerous. Sir Theophilus Shepstone was sent by the English government to report on the condition of affairs in the Transvaal. He came to the conclusion that the continued existence of the republic was dangerous to the welfare of 'her majesty's subjects and possessions in South Africa,' and in virtue of the power given to him formally annexed the state in April 1877. No resistance to this measure was made by the Boers. The president, Mr. Burgers, ordered the people to be loyal to their new ruler, and directed the state secretary to hand over the keys of the government offices to Sir Theophilus Shepstone. Little change was necessary in the personnel of the government, for nearly all the office-holders transferred their services to the new administration. A considerable section of the people dissented, and the president gave expression to the views of the malcontents by a protest against the annexation, while at a meeting of the late executive it was resolved to send Mr. Kruger and Dr. Jorrisen to London to lay the case of the non-annexationists before the colonial office. On their way through Cape Town the delegates had an interview with Frere, who gave them little encouragement, being convinced that they only represented a small and politically mischievous minority. Lord Carnarvon, acting on the opinions of Frere and Shepstone, returned an unfavourable answer to the memorial. In April 1878 the Boers despatched a second embassy to London, armed with a petition against annexation, signed by 6,591 qualified electors out of a total of 8,000. Considerable suspicion existed at the colonial office as to the way in which their signatures had been obtained, and Sir Michael Hicks Beach, the new colonial secretary, returned a similar answer to that given by Lord Carnarvon. A deputation to Frere in July 1878 met with no better success.

Meanwhile Cetewayo, who had been installed on the Zulu throne by Sir Theophilus Shepstone on the death of his father Panda in 1872, was beginning to threaten the Transvaal. An old controversy about a piece of disputed land lying between Zululand and the Transvaal furnished a ready excuse for gratifying his warlike instincts. The Boers asserted that this ground had been given them by Cetewayo in payment for the rendition of two of his half-brothers who had fled to the Transvaal for refuge, and that the gift had been confirmed by Panda, the king. Cetewayo replied that the grant had never been ratified by his father, and was therefore invalid. After the annexation, a commission decided, without going very thoroughly into the merits of the question, that as the gift made by Cetewayo was not shown to have been confirmed by the king, it must be held to be null and void. By the direction of the government, Frere went to Natal to revise the proceedings of the commission. He satisfied himself that, though the finding was technically correct, it was in equity too favourable to the Zulu. The position was one full of difficulty. Had he reversed the award, the Zulu would have regarded the act as one of hostility, while to confirm it absolutely was to leave the white settlers on the territory at the mercy of Cetewayo. Frere therefore confirmed the finding of the commission, with the proviso that the lives and

properties of the white settlers should be strictly respected and secured to them.

Cetewayo had already taken umbrage at the arrival of troops in Natal, caused by the threatening attitude of the Zulus. A reassuring answer was returned to a message sent by him; and this was accompanied by the award of the commission as modified by the high commissioner. Frere at the same time reiterated the demand for satisfaction for certain outrages committed on British subjects, and asked for assurances that Cetewayo would carry on his government in the spirit of the promises he had made when he was crowned by Sir Theophilus Shepstone. Frere specially demanded full satisfaction for the murder of two black women and for the detention of two English surveyors. He further required that the king should introduce a settled form of government into the country; should abolish the existing military system; should put a stop to the compulsory celibacy insisted on in certain regiments in the army; should receive a British resident at his capital; and should protect missionaries and their converts. Thirty days were given to Cetewayo to consider these terms, and, as at the end of that time no answer was received from him, Frere, considering that the use of that suasion which had been enjoined upon him by the English government was no longer possible and must yield to force, placed the matter in the hands of General Thesiger. It was this which constituted the disobedience to orders of which Frere was afterwards accused, and on this point Sir Henry Taylor, who was no mean authority on such matters, gives his verdict against him in a judicial letter addressed to Lord Blachford, and published in his 'Correspondence,' 1888. It must be admitted that the outrages complained of would not under other circumstances have been considered of an unpardonable nature. Cetewayo had already declared that he was unable to find the murderers, and had offered to make a money recompense to the relations of the murdered women. The surveyors thought so little of their detention that they made no complaint of the treatment they had received for a week after the event. Frere, in fact, had other reasons. 'The die for peace or for war,' he said, 'had been cast more than two years ago,' when the Zulus assumed their existing hostile attitude. It only remained, therefore, for General Thesiger to take such measures as he might deem advisable to protect Natal against the expected invasion of the Zulus. He had under his command about seven thousand men, many of whom were raw recruits, and more than half of whom were Kaffirs, while the Zulu hosts numbered forty-four thousand warriors. He had to decide between standing on the defensive behind the Tugela, or to cross the river and carry the war into the enemy's country. The Tugela, which was unusually high, was an obstacle to the Zulus; but Thesiger was unwilling to trust to the protection of so uncertain a barrier, and he determined, therefore, to advance into Zululand. The campaign began with the catastrophe at Isandlwana (22 Jan.) and ended triumphantly at Ulundi (4 July). Frere's responsibility ended when General Thesiger crossed the Tugela (11 Jan.) But he was not the man to throw off all participation in measures because his responsibility in them had ceased. When the news of Isandlwana reached Natal, he was still on the spot, and he exerted himself to the utmost to calm the panic which took possession of the settlers in anticipation of the momentarily expected invasion of the victorious Zulus. He directed measures for the defence of the colony, and appealed to England for reinforcements. So soon as he learned that fresh troops were on their way, he started for the Transvaal, whence disquieting rumours had reached him of the attitude of the Boers. Already the Boer forces were collected in camp, and every day it was expected that they would take the field. Accompanied by a small staff and an escort of twenty-five men, Frere rode 350 miles, a part of the way being through Zulu territory, to the Boer camp. He had left his escort at the frontier, and presented himself at the gate of the encampment, attended only by his staff (12 April). In spite of opposition and threats he rode into the camp, and invited the ringleaders to meet him in Pretoria to talk over their grievances. These he found to be genuine and great. The promises made by Sir T. Shepstone, 'upon the strength of which the inhabitants of the late republic were willing to give a peaceable trial to the new order of things,' had not been fulfilled, and the Boers found that they had given up their independence in exchange for delusive benefits. On condition that the Boers dispersed, Frere undertook to represent their complaints to the English government, and to urge the fulfilment of the promises which had been made to them.

Meanwhile in England the time for the general election was approaching. Many causes combined to make the Zulu war a favourable subject for attack. Frere was unsparingly assailed. The government met this by a despatch censuring Frere for his conduct in relation to the Zulu war, and announced what they had done in the House of Commons before informing the high commissioner of the fact. By this strange and

happily unusual course it happened that a Reuter's telegram first made Frere aware of the reflections which had been cast upon his character. Fortunately he had already come to terms with the Boers before the arrival of the telegram. In striking contrast with the estimate formed of his conduct of affairs by English politicians, the inhabitants of the districts through which he passed on his return to the Cape vied with each other in doing honour to one who was ready to sacrifice himself for the good of his country, and who was willing to risk his life to save his countrymen from the horrors of war. His journey southward was one continued ovation, and on arriving at Cape Town his horses were taken from his carriage and he was drawn by the populace to Government House. But bad news was awaiting him. On 1 June the Prince Imperial had met his death in Zululand, and almost at the same time the news arrived that Frere had been superseded in the office of high commissioner by Sir Garnet Wolseley, who was on his way to take command of the forces in South Africa. Frere, who remained governor of the Cape, was officially informed that this arrangement was intended to last for six months only, but when at the end of the Zulu war Wolseley was succeeded by Sir George Pomeroy Colley [q. v.], the same high office was continued to him to the exclusion of Frere. Many of Frere's friends were surprised that the slights thus put upon him did not cause him to resign his post. But Frere had not gone out to Africa for his own advantage, and so long as he believed he had work to do and power to do it, he felt bound to remain at his post. 'What,' asked a friend, 'will remain when you are superseded in the midst of your great work?' 'My integrity,' was the answer.

In the following spring Mr. Gladstone directed much of his oratory in Midlothian against Frere's conduct in South Africa, and charged him with having advocated an invasion of Afghanistan. In a remarkably temperate and able paper Frere urged on the colonial secretary the justice of contradicting this statement, for his position as an official rendered him unable publicly to justify himself. The contradiction, however, was not given, and it was left to Frere after his return to England to reply to the charges in a correspondence with Mr. Gladstone.

In July 1880 Frere was recalled, and he returned to England to find that the exigencies of party strife had estranged from him men who sat on both sides of the speaker's chair. Conscious of his integrity he was able to regard with comparative indifference the coldness with which he was received by politicians. With outwardly unruffled content he settled down quietly to the life of an English gentleman, and, as had always been his wont, used his best endeavours to do good to those about him. To raise the fallen, to instruct the ignorant, and to help the needy were objects which he had pursued throughout his career, and it came, therefore, as a familiar employment when he found himself advocating from platforms in England the claims of charitable institutions, educational establishments, and religious societies. During this period he was chosen for the third time president of the Royal Asiatic Society. The last letter he penned was one resigning this office. In his last year the university of Edinburgh conferred on him the degree of LL.D. On 29 May 1884 Frere died, after an illness of some weeks' duration. He was buried in St. Paul's Cathedral. His wife, a son, and four daughters survived him. The son, Bartle Compton Arthur, succeeded as second baronet. A statue of Frere was erected on the Thames Embankment by public subscription, and unveiled by the Prince of Wales in 1888.

To those who merely knew Frere as an acquaintance, his unvarying kindness and chivalrous courtesy will probably be considered as his leading characteristics; but those who had a deeper knowledge of his character will recognise that these outward graces were but the reflection of the brave, constant, unselfish, and religious nature of the man. Repeatedly he risked his life in the cause of duty, and it is not too much to say that in everything he did his last thought was of himself.

Frere was not an author in the sense of having written any large independent works. He, however, published separately a number of lectures delivered before societies, papers from scientific journals, speeches, and letters. Among the most important of these were: 'Report on the Nature and Effects of the "Thugg Duty,"' 1838?; 'The Scinde Railway,' 1854; 'Correspondence with the Revs. Gell and Matchett relative to certain Inscriptions on the Wall of a Shop in Hyderabad,' 1858; 'A Letter . . . on the reorganisation of the Indian Army,' 1858; 'Indian Missions,' 1870; 'Christianity suited to all Forms of Civilisation,' 1872; 'Eastern Africa as a Field for Missionary Labour,' 1874; 'On the impending Bengal Famine,' 1874; 'Correspondence relating to the Recall of Sir Bartle Frere,' 1880; 'The Union of the various portions of South Africa,' 1881; 'Afghanistan and South Africa: a Letter to the Right Hon. W. E. Gladstone . . . regarding portions of his Midlothian speeches,'

1881. He wrote also a memoir of his uncle, Hookham Frere, which is prefixed to the 'Works of J. H. Frere,' and an introduction to 'Old Deccan Days,' written by his daughter, Miss Mary Frere. He contributed several articles to 'Macmillan's Magazine' on Zanzibar, the Banians, and the Khojas, an article to the 'Quarterly Review' on Turkey and Salonica, and two articles to the 'Fortnightly Review' on the future of Zululand and the abolition of slavery in India and Egypt.

In religious opinions Frere was a strong churchman. But he was no bigot, and on several occasions he checked missionaries in their too zealous efforts to assert Christianity in defiance of the beliefs and prejudices of the natives of India.

[Journal of the Royal Asiatic Society, obituary notice, 1884; Celebrities of the Day—Life of Sir Bartle Frere, 1882; Sir Bartle Frere's Speeches and Addresses, 1870; Proceedings of the Legislative Council of India, vol. vi. 1860; Report of the Bombay Bank Commission, 1869; Parliamentary Papers, South Africa; Recreations of an Indian Official, 1872; Transactions of the Royal Historical Society, vol. iii.; Miss Colenso's History of the Zulu War, 1880; Greswell's Our South African Empire, 1885; Nixon's Complete Story of the Transvaal, 1885; Morley's Life of Gladstone, 1903. A life by John Martineau appeared in 1895 (2 vols.)] R. K. D.

FRERE, JAMES HATLEY (1779–1866), writer on prophecy, born in 1779, was the sixth son of John Frere, F.R.S. [q. v.], of Roydon, Norfolk, and Beddington, Surrey, by Jane, daughter and heiress of John Hookham of London (BURKE, Landed Gentry, 7th ed., i. 689). He married, 15 June 1809, Merian, second daughter of Matthew Martin, F.R.S., of Poets' Corner, Westminster (Gent. Mag. vol. lxxix. pt. i. p. 579), by whom he had five sons. He died at the residence of his third son, the Rev. John Alexander Frere, Shillington vicarage, Bedfordshire, on 8 Dec. 1866 (ib. 4th ser. iii. 124). His biblical studies were deemed worthy of notice by G. S. Faber, S. R. Maitland, and other well-known divines. He also took an interest in educational questions, and about 1838 introduced a phonetic system for teaching the blind to read. He had the advantage of having his plan carried out by a very clever blind man, who suggested several important changes. His characters consist of straight lines, half circles, hooked lines, and angles of forty-five degrees, together with a hollow and solid circle. He also invented the 'return' lines—that is to say, the lines in his book are read from left to right and from right to left alternately, the letters themselves being reversed in the return lines.

Although useful in enabling uneducated persons to read in a short space of time, Frere's system was found to vitiate pronunciation. In 1871 it was in use at only three home institutions. He devised a cheap method of setting up and stereotyping his books. 'The letters, formed of copper wire, are laid on a tin plate, previously washed over with a solution of zinc; when heat is applied to the under-surface, the letter becomes soldered on to the plate, and such plates produced extremely good printing' (CHAMBERS, Encyclopædia, new edit., ii. 226). Both T. M. Lucas of Bristol and William Moon of Brighton adopted this system of stereotyping. Aided by Miss Yates of Fairlawn, Frere was enabled to have 'The Book of the Prophet Isaiah' printed from embossed metallic plates according to his method, 4to, London, 1843-9. His other works are: 1. 'A Combined View of the Prophecies of Daniel, Esdras, and S. John, shewing that all the prophetic writings are formed upon one plan . . . Also a minute explanation of the prophecies of Daniel; together with critical remarks upon the interpretations of preceding commentators, and more particularly upon the systems of Mr. Faber and Mr. Cunninghame,' 8vo, London, 1815 (2nd edit., same year). 2. 'On the General Structure of the Apocalypse, being a brief introduction to its minute interpretation,' 8vo, London, 1826. 3. 'Eight Letters on the Prophecies relating to the last times; viz. The seventh vial, the civil and ecclesiastical prophetic periods, and the type of Jericho,' 8vo, London, 1831. 4. 'Three Letters on the Prophecies . . . in continuation of eight letters published in 1831,' 8vo, London, 1833; 2nd edit., with a prefatory address, 8vo, London [1859]. 5. 'The Art of Teaching to Read by Elementary Sounds,' 12mo, London, 1840. 6. 'A Letter to Lord Wharncliffe, in reply to the allegations made by the London Society for Teaching the Blind to Read, against the Phonetic Method of Instruction,' 8vo, London, 1843. 7. '"The Harvest of the Earth," prior to the vintage of wrath, considered as symbolical of the Evangelical Alliance . . . Also a letter to Dr. Wolff,' &c., 12mo, London, 1846. 8. 'The Great Continental Revolution, marking the Expiration of the Times of the Gentiles, A.D. 1847-8. In reply to a Letter from a Member of a Society of Prophetic Students. To which is added a Reprint of a Letter addressed to the Rev. Dr. Wolff on the expiration of the Times of the Gentiles A.D. 1847, and of other occasional papers, illustrative of the present period,' 8vo, London, 1848. 9. 'Preface to the Second Edition of the Great Continental Revolution, containing Remarks on the progress of Prophetic Events during the year 1848-9,' 8vo, London, 1849 (printed separately, for the convenience of purchasers of the first edition). 10. 'Notes, forming a brief Interpretation of the Apocalypse,' 8vo, London, 1850. 11. 'Directions for Teaching the Blind to Read on the Phonetic Principle,' 8vo [London, 1851]. 12. 'Grammar [embossed] for the Blind on the Principle of the Combination of Elementary Sounds,' 4to, London, 1851.

[Horace Frere's Pedigree of the Family of Frere, 4to, 1874; Brit. Mus. Cat.; Ripley and Dana's American Cyclopædia, ii. 719; Encyclopædia Britannica (9th edit.), iii. 826-8.] G. G.

FRERE, JOHN (1740-1807), antiquary, of Roydon Hall, Norfolk, and Finningham, Suffolk, born on 10 Aug. 1740, was the eldest son of Sheppard Frere of Roydon, by his wife Susanna, daughter of John Hatley of London and Kirby Hall, Essex. He belonged to an old family settled in Norfolk and Suffolk. His grandfather, Edward Frere, was a fellow of Trinity College, Cambridge, and a staunch adherent of Bentley the master. Frere was scholar and fellow of Caius College. He was second wrangler (Paley being senior), and graduated B.A. 1763, M.A. 1766. He became high sheriff of Suffolk in 1766, was a vice-president of the Marine Society in 1785, and was elected M.P. for Norwich in 1799. He was elected fellow of the Royal Society 20 June 1771, and was an active member. He published, in the 'Archæologia' for 1800 (xiii. 204), a paper 'On the Flint Weapons of Hoxne in Suffolk,' and showed discernment in assigning these stone implements (some of which, presented by him, are still in the collection of the Society of Antiquaries) 'to a very remote period indeed, even beyond that of the present world' (cp. JOHN EVANS, Ancient Stone Implements, p. 517). Frere also contributed to the 'Gentleman's Magazine' and other publications. His son, John Hookham Frere [q. v.], used to regret that more of his father's occasional papers had not been preserved. Frere was intimate with Richard Gough. His brother-in-law, Sir John Fenn, left him his library. Frere died at East Dereham, Norfolk, on 12 July 1807. A painted portrait of him is in the possession of Mr. J. T. Frere of Roydon Hall. He married, in 1768, Jane, only child of John Hookham of Beddington, a rich London merchant. This lady, besides a fortune and good looks, had 'rare gifts of intellect and disposition.' They had seven sons and two daughters. The eldest son was John Hookham Frere, the author and diplomatist [q. v.] The fourth, fifth, and sixth sons,

William, Bartholomew, and James Hatley, are also separately noticed. The seventh son, Temple (1781–1859), rector successively of Finningham, Roydon, and Burston, became canon of Westminster 3 Nov. 1838.

[J. Hookham Frere's Works (1872), memoir in vol. i.; Notes and Queries, 3rd ser. iii. 210, 257; Burke's Landed Gentry, editions of 1868 and 1886, s.v. 'Frere of Roydon;' Gent. Mag. 1807, vol. lxxvii. pt. ii. p. 691; Nichols's Lit. Anecd. viii. 58, 159, ix. 475; Nichols's Lit. Illustr. v. 175–7, 181, vi. 821; information from Mr. Frere of Roydon Hall.]　　　　　　　W. W.

FRERE, JOHN HOOKHAM (1769–1846), diplomatist and author, eldest son of John Frere [q. v.] of Roydon Hall, near Diss, Norfolk, by his wife Jane, only child of John Hookham of Beddington, Surrey, a rich London merchant, was born in London on 21 May 1769, and in 1785 went from a preparatory school at Putney to Eton, where he formed his lifelong friendship with Canning. In the following year the two friends joined with 'Bobus' Smith and some other schoolfellows in starting the 'Microcosm,' the first number of which appeared on 6 Nov. 1786, and the last on 30 July 1787. It ran through forty numbers, which were subsequently published in a collected form, with a dedication to Dr. Davies, the head-master. Frere contributed five papers to this periodical (Works, ii. 3–22). From Eton he went to Caius College, Cambridge, where he graduated B.A. in 1792 and M.A. in 1795. At college he gained several prizes for classical composition, but was prevented by illness from going in for honours. He was fellow of Caius from 1793 to 1816, and in 1792 obtained the members' prize for the Latin essay; the subject was 'Whether it be allowable to hope for the improvement of morals and for the cultivation of virtue in the rising state of Botany Bay'! On leaving the university Frere entered the foreign office and at a bye-election in November 1796 was returned for the pocket borough of West Looe in Cornwall, which he continued to represent until the dissolution in June 1802; but no speeches of his are reported in the volumes of 'Parliamentary History' for that period. In 1797 he joined with Canning in the publication of the 'Anti-Jacobin, or Weekly Examiner,' the first number of which appeared on 20 Nov. in that year. Gifford was the editor, and many of the pieces were written in concert by Canning, Ellis, and Frere. Jenkinson, afterwards the Earl of Liverpool, Lord Mornington, Chief-baron Macdonald, and Pitt were also among the contributors. Frere's contributions are collected in his 'Works' (ii. 57–161). Besides other pieces, he wrote the greater part of the 'Loves of the Triangles,' an amusing parody of Dr. Darwin's 'Loves of the Plants,' and shared with Canning the authorship of 'The Friend of Humanity and the Knifegrinder,' and with Canning and Ellis that of the 'Rovers, or the Double Arrangement.' After a brilliant career of eight months the 'Anti-Jacobin' was brought to a close on 9 July 1798. On 1 April 1799 Frere succeeded his friend Canning as under-secretary of state in the foreign office. In October 1800 he was appointed envoy extraordinary and plenipotentiary at Lisbon, and in September 1802 was transferred to Madrid, where he remained for nearly two years. In August 1804 Frere was recalled 'in consequence of circumstances having occurred that made it impossible for him any longer to communicate personally with the Prince of Peace' (Pitt's Speeches, 1806, iv. 383). The ministry, however, signified their approval of his conduct by granting him a pension of 1,700l. a year, and on 14 Jan. 1805 he was sworn a member of the privy council. In June 1807 the Duke of Portland appointed him envoy and minister plenipotentiary at Berlin, but owing to the treaty of Tilsit the mission had to be abandoned. On 4 Oct. 1808 Frere was sent out to Spain as minister plenipotentiary to the Central Junta. Affairs on the Peninsula were then in a very critical state, and his position as the British minister was one of heavy responsibility. In November Napoleon commenced his march upon Madrid. Sir John Moore, the commander of the British forces in the north of Spain, was inclined to retreat through Portugal. Frere, however, confident that Napoleon might be anticipated, urged Moore to advance upon Madrid, or, if retreat was inevitable, to retire through Gallicia. Moore yielded, and, after the disastrous retreat to Corunna, Frere was greatly blamed for the advice he had given. Though Ponsonby's motion in the House of Commons, on 24 Feb. 1809, for an inquiry 'into the causes, conduct, and events of the late campaign in Spain,' was defeated by 220 to 127 (Parl. Debates, xii. 1057–1119), the government determined to recall Frere, and on 29 April 1809 the Marquis of Wellesley was appointed ambassador to the court of Spain. Frere left in August, having been created 'Marquez de la Union' by the Central Junta, 'as a mark of their acknowledgment of the zeal with which he had laboured to promote the friendly union and common interest of the two countries.' With his second mission to Spain Frere's public career ceased. He afterwards declined the post of ambassador at St. Petersburg, and twice refused the offer of a peerage. On the death of his father in 1807

Frere succeeded to Roydon Hall and the other family estates in the eastern counties. On 12 Sept. 1816 he married Elizabeth Jemima, dowager countess of Erroll, the widow of George, fourteenth earl of Erroll, and a daughter of Joseph Blake of Ardfry, county Galway. In 1818 his wife became ill. After trying many changes of climate for the benefit of her health they went to Malta, where they took up their permanent residence. Here he amused himself with literary work, translating Aristophanes and Theognis, and learning Hebrew and Maltese. In August 1827 Canning died. Talking over the loss of his friend to his niece two years afterwards, Frere said: 'I think twenty years ago Canning's death would have caused mine ; as it is, the time seems so short, I do not feel it as I otherwise should' (*Works*, i. 209). His wife died in January 1831, and in November of that year Sir Walter Scott paid him a visit. Frere still continued to reside at Malta. He died at the Pietà Valetta on 7 Jan. 1846, in the seventy-seventh year of his age, and was buried beside his wife in the English burial-ground overlooking the Quarantine Harbour. A portrait of Frere by Hoppner was exhibited in the third Loan Collection of National Portraits in 1868 (*Cat.* No. 235). At Holland House, where he was a frequent visitor, there is a portrait of him by Arthur Shee, as well as a bust executed by Chantrey in 1817. As a diplomatist Frere is now almost forgotten, and it is only by the few that he is remembered as a brilliant wit and a sparkling writer of humorous poetry. His translations of Aristophanes cannot fail to be the most lasting memorials of his genius, and the manner in which he has successfully caught the spirit of the original comedies places him in an almost unique place as a translator. His metrical version of the 'Ode on Æthelstan's Victory' appeared in the second edition of Ellis's 'Specimens of Early English Poets' (1801, i. 32–4). It was written by Frere when at Eton, and is a remarkable example of the skilful adoption of the language and style of another period. Mackintosh, in his 'History of England,' says that it 'is a double imitation, unmatched, perhaps, in literary history, in which the writer gave an earnest of that faculty of catching the peculiar genius and preserving the characteristic manner of his original which, though the specimens of it be too few, places him alone among English translators' (i. 50). Scott, too, declares, in his 'Essay on Imitations of the Ancient Ballad,' that it was the only poem he had met with 'which, if it had been produced as ancient, could not have been detected on internal evidence' (*Poetical Works*,

1830, iii. 21). Three of Frere's translations from the 'Poem of the Cid ' were printed as an appendix to Southey's 'Chronicle of the Cid' (1808, pp. 437–68). In 1819 Frere formed one of Byron's 'cursed puritanical committee' which decided against the publication of the first canto of 'Don Juan.' Though one of the original projectors of the 'Quarterly Review,' Frere's only contribution to it was an article on 'Mitchell's Translations of Aristophanes,' which appeared in the number for July 1820 (pp. 474–505). It is signed 'W,' for Whistlecraft, and is a very early instance of a reviewer signing his contribution. Indolent, and unambitious for literary fame, Frere cared only for the appreciation of cultivated judges. Several of his productions were privately printed, and have become exceedingly rare.

He was the author of the following works : 1. 'Prospectus and Specimen of an intended National Work, by William and Robert Whistlecraft of Stowmarket in Suffolk, Harness and Collar Makers. Intended to comprise the most interesting particulars relating to King Arthur and his Round Table' (cantos i. and ii.), London, 1817, 8vo ; second edition, London, 1818, 8vo. This revival in English poetry of the octave stanza of Pulci, Berni, and Casti attracted great attention at the time. Byron, writing to Murray from Venice in October 1817, says: 'Mr. Whistlecraft has no greater admirer than myself. I have written a story in eighty-nine stanzas in imitation of him, called "Beppo"' (MOORE, *Life*, 1847, p. 369). 2. Cantos iii. and iv. (of the same work), London, 1818, 8vo. The four cantos were also published together in 1818 under the title of 'The Monks and the Giants Prospectus and Specimen,' &c.; fourth edition, London, 1821, 12mo ; another edition, Bath, 1842, 8vo. 3. 'Fables for Five-Years-Old,' Malta, 1830, 12mo. 4. 'The Frogs,' London, 1839. Frere says: 'The greater part of this play ['The Frogs'] had been printed upwards of twenty years ago, having been intended for private distribution ; an intention to which the writer adheres, being unwilling to cancel what had been already printed and in part distributed.' 5. 'Aristophanes. A Metrical Version of the Acharnians, the Knights, and the Birds, in the last of which a vein of peculiar humour and character is for the first time detected and developed' (anon.), London, 1840, 4to. These three plays, each of which are separately paged, were privately printed for Frere at the government press in Malta in 1839, and were afterwards published by Pickering in England in 1840 under the above title. Reprinted as No. 37 of Morley's 'Universal Library,' London, 1886, 8vo. In Coleridge's will, dated September 1829, the following interesting passage occurs : 'Further to Mr. Gillman, as the most expressive way in which I can only mark my relation to him, and in remembrance of a great and good man, revered by us both, I leave the manuscript volume lettered "Arist. Manuscript—Birds, Acharnians, Knights," presented to me by my dear friend and patron, the Right Hon. John Hookham Frere, who, of all men I have had the means of knowing during my life, appears to me eminently to deserve to be characterised as ὁ καλοκἀγαθός ὁ φιλόκαλος.' 6. 'Theognis Restitutus. The personal history of the poet Theognis, deduced from an analysis of his existing fragments. A hundred of these fragments, translated or paraphrased in English metre, are arranged in their proper biographical order with an accompanying commentary, with a preface in which the suggestion of Mr. Clinton, as to the true date of the poet's birth (viz. in Olymp. 59), is confirmed by internal evidence' (anon.), Malta, 1842, 4to. Reprinted (but without the introduction and the synopsis of historical dates) in the volume of Bohn's Classical Library containing 'The Works of Hesiod, Callimachus, and Theognis,' London, 1856, 8vo. 7. 'Psalms,' &c. (anon.), London [1848 ?], 4to.

[The Works of the Right Hon. John Hookham Frere in Verse and Prose, with memoir by Sir Bartle Frere, his nephew, 1874 ; Quarterly Review, cxxxii. 26–59 ; Edinburgh Review, cxxxv. 472–501 ; North American Review, cvii. 136–66 ; Fraser's Mag., new ser. v. 491–510 ; Contemporary Review, ix. 512–33 ; Macmillan's Mag., xxvi. 25–32 ; Professor Morley's Introduction to Frere's Aristophanes, 1886, p. 5–8 ; Princess Marie Liechtenstein's Holland House, 1874 ; Ann. Reg. 1846 ; Gent. Mag. 1846, new ser. xxv. 312–14, 338 ; Lowndes's Bibl. Manual (Bohn) ; Grenville Library Cat. ; Brit. Mus. Cat.] G. F. R. B.

FRERE, PHILIP HOWARD (1813–1868), agriculturist, the eldest son of William Frere [q. v.] by his wife Mary, daughter of Brampton Gurdon Dillingham, was born in 1813. He was educated at Eton and Trinity College, Cambridge, and in 1836 was placed among the senior optimes in the mathematical, and in the first class in the classical tripos. In the following year he was elected a fellow of Downing College, and in 1839 became tutor and bursar. The endowments of Downing consisted almost entirely of agricultural lands, the management of which devolved on the bursar, and Frere's previous residence on his father's estate at Balsham, Cambridgeshire, rendered him admirably suited to the post. He travelled much in Europe, and became a good linguist. His combination of a know-

ledge of agriculture and foreign languages led to his appointment as editor of the 'Journal of the Royal Agricultural Society' in 1862, when the council determined to raise the standard of their publication. He conducted the journal with success, contributing papers on agricultural subjects till his death at Cambridge in May 1868. Frere married in 1859 Emily, daughter of Henry Gipps, canon of Carlisle Cathedral, and vicar of Crosthwaite, Keswick, and left issue.

[Information from the Rev. W. H. Frere ; Journal of the Royal Agricultural Soc.] A. V.

FRERE, WILLIAM (1775–1836), lawserjeant and master of Downing College, Cambridge, the fourth son of John Frere [q. v.] of Roydon, Norfolk, and younger brother of John Hookham Frere [q. v.], was born 28 Nov. 1775. He was sent to Felstead and Eton, and in 1796 obtained a scholarship at Trinity College, Cambridge. In the same year he was elected to the Craven scholarship, and subsequently won several university honours, among them the senior chancellor's medal. He graduated fifth senior optime in 1798. In 1800 he became fellow of the newly founded Downing College. He was called to the bar, and joined the Norfolk circuit in 1802. He was serjeant-at-law in 1809, and three years later was elected master of Downing College, his appointment being unsuccessfully contested at law. He was made recorder of Bury St. Edmunds in 1814, and in 1819 became vice-chancellor of Cambridge University. He resided for a considerable part of each year on an estate which he bought at Balsham, Cambridgeshire. He proceeded LL.D. at Cambridge 1825, and D.C.L. at Oxford 1834. In 1826 he finally quitted the bar. He edited, with additions, Baron Glenbervie's 'Reports of Cases,' 1813, and the fifth volume of the 'Paston Letters' from the manuscript of Sir John Fenn [q. v.], his uncle. Some Latin and Greek verse by Frere was published with W. Herbert's 'Fasciculus Carminum stylo Lucretiano scriptorum,' 1797. He died 25 May 1836. He married in 1810 Mary, daughter of Brampton Gurdon Dillingham. His son, Philip Howard, is separately noticed. During Frere's time, chiefly through his wife, Downing College was a social centre at Cambridge.

[Information supplied by the Rev. W. H. Frere ; Gent. Mag. 1836, ii. 214.] A. V.

FRESNE, SIMON DU (*fl.* 1200), poet. [See SIMON.]

FRESTON, ANTHONY (1757–1819), divine, born in 1757, was the son of Robert Brettingham of Norwich, and nephew of Matthew Brettingham [q. v.], the architect.

While a child Anthony took the name of Freston, in pursuance of the will of his maternal uncle, William Freston of Mendham, who died in 1761, and devised to him his estates in Norfolk and Suffolk. He matriculated at Oxford as a commoner of Christ Church, 26 Dec. 1775, and proceeded B.A. in 1780 (FOSTER, *Alumni Oxon.* ii. 497). Having married a Cambridge lady, the widow of Thomas Hyde, he removed in 1783 to Clare Hall in that university, where he was incorporated B.A., and commenced M.A. the same year (*Graduati Cantabr.* edit. 1826, p. 119). In 1792 he was licensed to the perpetual cure of Needham, Norfolk, in his own patronage, and in 1801 he was presented by a college friend to the rectory of Edgworth, Gloucestershire. Dr. Huntingford, bishop of Gloucester, appointed him rural dean of the deanery of Stonehouse. He died on 25 Dec. 1819.

His works are: 1. 'Provisions for the more equal Maintenance of the Clergy,' 1784, 12mo (anon.) 2. 'An Elegy,' 1787, 4to. 3. 'Poems on Several Subjects,' 1787, 8vo. 4. 'A Discourse on Laws, intended to show that legal Institutions are necessary, not only to the Happiness, but to the very Existence of Man,' London, 1792, 4to. 5. 'Address to the People of England,' 1796, 8vo (anon.) 6. 'A Collection of Evidences for the Divinity of our Lord Jesus Christ,' London, 1807, 8vo. 7. 'Six Sermons on some of the more important Doctrines of Christianity; to which are added five Sermons on Occasional Subjects,' Cirencester, 1809, 8vo.

[Annual Biog. v. 444; Biog. Dict. of Living Authors, p. 122; Davy's Athenæ Suffolcenses, iii. 100; Gent. Mag. xc. pt. i. 279.] T. C.

FREVILLE, GEORGE (*d.* 1579), judge, of a family settled at Little Shelford, Cambridgeshire, from the reign of Edward II, was the second son of Robert Freville and Rose Peyton (see *MSS. Coll. Arms,* c. 41; *Inquis. p. m.* Cambr. 6 Edw. VI). He was educated at Cambridge, and studied common law at Barnard's Inn, and afterwards became a member of the Middle Temple, where he was reader in 1558, performing his duties by Edmund Plowden, his deputy, and again in Lent 1559. On the death of his elder brother John without issue in 1552, he succeeded to the family estates. On St. Matthias day 1552 he was elected recorder of Cambridge, and admitted to office 25 March 1553. He was in the special commission of oyer and terminer issued for Cambridgeshire 8 Aug. 1553, when indictments for high treason were found against the Duke of Northumberland and other adherents of Lady Jane Grey. By patent, 31 Jan. 1559, though not yet a ser-

jeant, he was created third baron of the exchequer. He obtained the royal permission to retain his office of recorder of Cambridge, but the town refused to submit to this. On 28 April 1564 he became second baron, and in May 1579 he died, and was succeeded by Robert Shute 1 June.

[Foss's Lives of the Judges; Cooper's Athenæ Cantabr. ii. 407; Annals of Cambr. vol. ii.; Dugdale's Orig. Jurid.; Baga de Secretis; Mem. Scacc. Mic. 405 P. and M. r. 56.] J. A. H.

FREWEN, ACCEPTED (1588–1664), archbishop of York, was the eldest son of the Rev. John Frewen [q. v.], rector of Northiam, Sussex. The family appears to have been originally of Worcestershire, as Richard Frewen, the father of John Frewen, was son of Roger Frewen, who was buried at Hanley Castle in 1543, and grandson of Richard Frewen, bailiff of Worcester in 1473. Accepted Frewen was born at Northiam, and baptised there 26 May 1588. A ruinous old house called 'Carriers,' opposite to Brickwall Park, is traditionally reported to have been the birthplace of the future archbishop. It is supposed that John Frewen, his father, rented it from John White of Brickwall from 1583, when he was presented to the living of Northiam, till he removed to the church-house about 1592. According to Anthony à Wood, Frewen was educated at the free school at Canterbury, and thence removed in 1604, when barely sixteen years of age, to Magdalen College, Oxford, where he became a demy, took his B.A. degree 25 Jan. 1608, and M.A. 23 May 1612. He was elected fellow in the latter year, and, according to the same authority, became divinity reader in the college. In 1617 in the college books we find leave given by the president and authorities for 'a year's absence to Mr. Frewen, acting as chaplain to Sir John Digby, ambassador in Spain.' Sir John was created Lord Digby in November 1618. Frewen appears to have accompanied him on a mission from King James to the Emperor Ferdinand in Germany in 1621. On 24 Dec. 1621 another year's absence was granted by the president and authorities to Frewen to act as chaplain to Lord Digby, who was accredited a second time as ambassador to the court of Spain. Lord Digby in 1622 was created Earl of Bristol. Frewen was at Madrid when Prince Charles arrived on his romantic visit, and, seeing the attempts to pervert him to the Romish faith, preached before him from the text 1 Kings xviii. 21, 'How long halt ye between two opinions? If the Lord be God, follow Him, but if Baal, then follow him,' urging him to be steadfast in the doctrines of the church of England.

The prince was much struck with the sermon, became attached to Frewen, and presented him with a miniature of himself, which is still in the possession of the family. On his accession to the throne the king appointed him one of his chaplains, putting him into the list with his own hand. In 1625 he was made canon of the tenth stall in Canterbury Cathedral, and vice-president of his college in the same year. In 1626 he was unanimously elected president of Magdalen on 24 Oct., and on 16 Dec. compounded for his D.D. degree, having taken that of B.D. 8 July 1619. In 1628 and 1629 he was vice-chancellor of Oxford, and on 13 Sept. 1631 installed dean of Gloucester. In 1635 he was made rector of Standlake in Oxfordshire, and also of Warnford in Hampshire, both livings being in the gift of his college. In 1638 and 1639, at the request of Archbishop Laud, the chancellor, he again discharged the office of vice-chancellor. In 1642 he was mainly instrumental in sending the university plate to the king at York, and lent 500l. to Magdalen College to present to the king towards the expenses of the war. On this the parliament ordered him to be arrested, but he withdrew, and did not return to Oxford till the king came there after the battle of Edgehill, at the end of that year.

Upon Frewen's appointment to the presidentship of Magdalen he made great alterations in the chapel. He paved the inner chapel with black and white marble, put up a new organ, stained windows, and new stalls, all which improvements were probably mainly at his own expense. ' In 1631,' says Calamy (*Nonconformists' Manual*, ii. 27), 'Dr. Frewen, president of Magdalen, changed the communion-table into an altar, the first that was set up in the university since the Reformation.' This created much sensation, and was inveighed against by several preachers at St. Mary's, when the matter was brought before the king and council, and the preachers banished the university. Dr. Williamson (formerly fellow of Magdalen), principal of Magdalen Hall, received a public and sharp rebuke for countenancing the factious parties. On 17 Aug. 1643 Frewen was nominated to the see of Lichfield and Coventry, and in April 1644 was consecrated in Magdalen College Chapel by John Williams, archbishop of York, assisted by four other prelates. On 11 May he resigned the presidentship. In 1652 his estate was declared forfeited for treason against the parliament, but by mistake he was designated Stephen Frewen. A similar error in his christian name enabled him to escape on a more perilous occasion, when Cromwell had offered 1,000l. to any one who

would bring him dead or alive. Being again described in the proclamation as Stephen Frewen, he got away to France, where he remained till the fury of the times was abated, when he returned and lived very privately. There is an apocryphal story in the ' Ballard MSS.,' xl. 110 (Bodleian Library), which probably refers to this period. The writer of the letter mentions an old house on Banstead Downs, which was occupied by a lady whose husband had fled to the continent on account of the civil troubles. The lady is said to have kept a kind of boarding-house, to which many ladies resorted. A clergyman, whose name was concealed, frequently preached to them. Notes were taken of his sermons by several of the ladies, and entered into a common note-book. The lady of the house made frequent journeys to London, taking with her bundles of manuscripts, which were supposed to be meant for the press. One of the ladies showed the notes to a gentleman, who made much use of them in his household. When the ' Whole Duty of Man' was published, this gentleman procured the book, and was surprised to find it exactly coincided with the notes in his possession. The mysterious clergyman at Banstead was discovered to have been Frewen, who was at that time supposed to be beyond sea. The story, however, has been ably confuted, and especially by Ballard himself in his memoir of Lady Pakington (*Memoirs of several Ladies of Great Britain*, p. 320), and the archbishop's noted aversion to female society would alone render the tale improbable.

After the Restoration he was nominated to the archbishopric of York, elected on 22 Sept. 1660, confirmed at Westminster in Henry VII's Chapel 4 Oct., and enthroned by proxy at York 11 Oct. In 1661 he was chairman of the Savoy conference. We have no official account of the conference from the bishops' side; but Richard Baxter describes Frewen as a mild and peaceable man, and one who took no active part in the proceedings.

Frewen died at Bishopthorpe 28 March 1664, and was buried under the east window of York Minster, where a sumptuous monument with a Latin inscription is erected to his memory. He was never married, and is said to have been ' so perfectly determined to preserve the chastity of his character as not to suffer a woman servant in his family.' The reason given for this, in a sixpenny pamphlet published in 1743 by Thomas Frewen of Brickwall, fourth in descent from the archbishop's brother Stephen, was 'fuit filius utero matris viventis excisus, which created in him so great an horror of that action that I believe it to have been his reason for living and dying a bachelor.' Frewen of Brickwall published this pamphlet to vindicate the archbishop's memory from the misrepresentations of Francis (whom, by the bye, he strangely calls Richard) Drake in his 'Eboracum, or History and Antiquities of York Cathedral and City.' Mr. Thomas Frewen also published a small volume of the archbishop's Latin speeches at Oxford when president of Magdalen and vice-chancellor. This is also dated 1743, and both pamphlets are dedicated to Edward Butler, LL.D., president of Magdalen and M.P. for the university. The archbishop died wealthy, and bequeathed the bulk of his fortune to his youngest brother Stephen, an eminent trader in London. Stephen Frewen (1600–1679) conveyed twenty-seven thousand guineas of the archbishop's money in specie in his carriage to London after the prelate's funeral ; but the money which he deposited with Sir Robert Vyner, the banker, was lent to Charles II, and lost by the closing of the exchequer. Stephen Frewen purchased Brickwall House, near Northiam, and other large estates in Sussex and other counties, and was ancestor of the present proprietor of Brickwall.

By his will the archbishop bequeathed to Magdalen College, 'my mother, that gave me my breeding, five hundred pounds, to be employed as my gift to the honour of the college, in some public way approved of by my worthy friend Gilbert [Sheldon], at the present time Lord Bishop of London ; as also I forgive unto it five hundred pounds lent it by me, *pecuniis numeratis*, in a time of necessity ;' to every bishop of the kingdom a ring with this inscription, 'Neque melior sum quàm patres mei,' no one to be under the value of 30*s.* ; to the Bishop of Rochester (Warner) a ring once Bishop Jewel's ; to every servant a year's wages, besides their due. Dr. Chamberlayne, in his 'State of England,' p. 190, assures us that Frewen's benefactions, besides abatements to tenants, amounted to 15,000*l.*

[Wood's Athenæ (Bliss), iv. 821–7 ; Bloxam's Registers of Magdalen College ; Le Neve's Lives of the Archbishops ; Burke's Landed Gentry ; a privately printed memoir in 'Hastings Past and Present', with notices of the most remarkable places in the neighbourhood,' by Mary Matilda Howard, 1855.] R. H–R.

FREWEN, JOHN (1558–1628), puritan divine, descended from an old Worcestershire family, was born in 1558. He is stated to have been baptised on 1 July 1560. His grandfather, Roger Frewen, and his father, Richard Frewen, were both possessed of property in Hill Croome and Earls Croome in Worcestershire. He was ordained priest by Bulling-

ham, bishop of Gloucester, 24 June 1582, and in November of the following year was presented by his father to the rectory of Northiam, Sussex. On his becoming resident at Northiam it is supposed that Frewen occupied a house known as 'Carriers,' situated about two hundred yards south of the present rectory-house, and then the property of his friend and neighbour, John White of Brickwall. His first publication is entitled 'Certaine Fruitfull Instructions and necessary doctrines meete to edify in the feare of God : faithfully gathered together by Iohn Frewen,' 18mo, London, 1587. Of this work, which is dedicated to 'M. Tho: Coventry,' father of the lord keeper, very few copies are known. Two years later Frewen published another manual with the title 'Certaine Fruitfull Instructions for the generall cause of Reformation against the slanders of the Pope and League,' 4to, London, 1589 (WOOD, *Athenæ Oxon.* ed. Bliss, iv. 823). In 1593 Frewen bought the Church House at Northiam, where he and his descendants continued to reside until the purchase of Brickwall, the present seat of the family. Church House still remains in the family. In 1598 he edited, and wrote the preface to, a pamphlet of eighty-eight pages, entitled 'A Courteous Conference with the English Catholickes Romane, about the six articles ministered unto the Seminarie Priests,' 4to, London. This loyal and excessively rare treatise had been left in manuscript by John Bishop, a recusant papist, a native of Battle, Sussex. Its design is to show the unlawfulness of revolting from the authority of the civil magistrate on account of religion. Frewen's uncompromising puritanism brought him at length into collision with some of his chief parishioners. At the Lewes summer assizes in 1611 they preferred a bill of indictment against him for nonconformity, but the grand jury ignored the bill, and Frewen vindicated himself in eight successive sermons, published as 'Certaine Sermons on the 2, 3, 4, 5, 6, 7, and 8 verses of the Eleventh Chapter of S. Paule his Epistle to the Romanes. Preached in the parish church of Northiam, in the county of Sussex,' 12mo, London, 1612. Copies are of comparatively rare occurrence. Exactly two hundred and fifty years later Octavius Lord, the then rector of Northiam, a descendant in the female line of Frewen, 're-preached' them by request on eight successive Sundays in the same pulpit. In 1621 Frewen published his 'Certaine choise grounds and principles of our Christian Religion, . . . wherein the people of the parish of Northiam, in the county of Sussex, have been catechized and instructed for the settling of their hearts and mindes in the mysteries of Salvation,' 12mo, London. Frewen's persecutors still continued to annoy him, and he was compelled to appeal to the ecclesiastical court at Lewes, 30 July 1622, when it was deposed that one Robert Cresswell of Northiam, 'gentleman,' had on 26 June 1621, on the open highway, insulted the rector, 'calling him old Fole, old Asse, old Coxscombe.' Cresswell was, after due citation, excommunicated. In 1627 Frewen sat for his portrait to Mark Gheeraerts [q. v.], and the picture is still preserved among the fine series of family portraits in the banqueting-room at Brickwall. 'It is a half-length, and represents the old puritan in full canonicals, except that he wears a very broad-brimmed hat. His right hand rests upon a Geneva bible, open at 2 Kings, chapter xxiii.—a favourite passage with the puritans, as it describes Josiah's zeal for religious reformation; his left hand grasps a skull.' The expression of the countenance is both benign and acute. It has been engraved by Scriven (EVANS, Cat. of Engraved Portraits, ii. 161). On 1 June of the same year, 'being aged and weake in bodie,' he made his will (registered in P.C.C. 38, Barrington). He died towards the end of April 1628, and was buried in the chancel of his own church on the following 2 May. He was married three times. By his first wife, Eleanor, who died in 1606, he had six sons: Accepted (1588–1664) [q. v.], Thankfull (1591–1656), purse-bearer and secretary of petitions to Lord-keeper Coventry, who suffered for his loyalty during the civil war and Commonwealth (cf. his will, P.C.C. 110, Ruthen; Cal. State Papers, Dom. 1660-1, p. 63, where he is described as 'clerk of appeals and clerk of the crown in chancery'); John (1595–1654), his father's successor in the rectory of Northiam; Stephen of Brickwall, citizen of London, master of the Skinners' Company, and fined for alderman of Vintry Ward; Joseph; and Mary, wife of John Bigg of Newcastle-upon-Tyne. In 1607 he married Helen Hunt, probably daughter of Richard Hunt of Brede, Sussex, and by her had Benjamin, citizen of London; Thomas, a captain in Cromwell's army for invading Ireland, and founder of the family at Castle Connel, near Limerick (Cal. State Papers, Dom. 1649-50, p. 573); and Samuel. The second Mrs. Frewen died in 1616, and Frewen married, on 29 July 1619 at St. Antholin's, Budge Row, London, a third wife, Susan Burdon, who survived him many years (Parish Register, Harl. Soc. p. 54).

In addition to his published writings he left a large unfinished work in manuscript, entitled 'Grounds and Principles of Christian Religion;' it consisted of seven books, of which two only (the fourth and fifth, of 95 and 98 folio pages respectively) have been preserved.

[Sussex Archæological Collections; Smyth's Obituary (Camd. Soc.), p. 43; Notes and Queries, 1st ser. viii. 222, 296-7, 2nd ser. x. 385; Cal. State Papers, Dom. 1650, p. 192, 1653-4, p. 114, 1655, p. 227; Wood's Athenæ Oxon. (Bliss), iv. 821, 823; Benjamin Brook's Lives of the Puritans, iii. 518; Lower's Sussex Worthies, pp. 45-9, 198, from the information of Thomas Frewen, esq. of Brickwall; Burke's Landed Gentry, 4th ed. p. 518, 7th ed. i. 689; Index of Leyden Students (Index Soc.); Commons' Journals, vi. 428; Le Neve's Pedigrees of the Knights (Harl. Soc.), p. 395; Will of John Frewen, M.D., of Northiam, dated 3 Jan. and proved 9 June 1659 (reg. in P. C. C.).]   G. G.

FREWEN, THOMAS, M.D. (1704-1791), physician, was born in 1704. He practised as a surgeon and apothecary at Rye in Sussex, and afterwards as a physician at Lewes, having obtained the M.D. degree previous to 1755. He became known as one of the first in this country to adopt the practice of inoculation with small-pox. In his essay on 'The Practice and Theory of Inoculation' (Lond. 1749) he narrates his experience in three hundred and fifty cases, only one having died by the small-pox so induced. The common sort of people, he says, were averse to inoculation, and 'disputed about the lawfulness of propagating diseases'—the very ground on which small-pox inoculation was made penal a century later (1842). The more refined studies of our speculative adepts in philosophy, he says, have let them into the secret that the small-pox and many other diseases are propagated by means of animalcula hatched from eggs lodged in the hairs, pores, &c. of human bodies. In 1759 he published another short essay on small-pox, 'Reasons against an opinion that a person infected with the Small-pox may be cured by Antidote without incurring the Distemper.' The opinion was that of Boerhaave, Cheyne, and others, that the development of small-pox after exposure to infection could be checked by a timely use of the æthiops mineral. Frewen's argument was that many persons ordinarily escape small-pox 'who had been supposed to be in the greatest danger of taking it,' and that the æthiops mineral was irrelevant. His other work, 'Physiologia' (Lond. 1780), is a considerable treatise applying the doctrines of Boerhaave to some diseases. One of his principles is: 'Wherever nature has fixed a pleasure, we may take it for granted she there enjoins a duty; and something is to be done either for the individual or for the species.' He died at Northiam in Sussex, on 14 June 1791, aged 86.

[Gent. Mag.; Giles Watts's Letter to Dr. Frewen on his behaviour in the case of Mr. Rootes, surgeon, Lond. 1755.] C. C.

FREWIN, RICHARD, M.D. (1681?–1761), physician and professor of history, son of Ralph Frewin of London, was admitted king's scholar at Westminster in 1693, and elected thence to a Westminster studentship at Christ Church, Oxford, in 1698. He took the degrees of B.A. in 1702, M.A. in 1704, M.B. in 1707, and M.D. in 1711. In 1708 he is described at the foot of a Latin poem which he contributed to 'Exequiæ Georgio principi Daniæ ab Oxoniensi academia solutæ' (Oxford, 1708) as professor of chemistry; he was also in 1711 rhetoric reader in Christ Church. As a physician he had an excellent reputation; he attended Dean Aldrich on his deathbed. John Freind's 'Hippocrates de Morbis Popularibus' is dedicated to him, and contains a letter from him (dated Christ Church, 20 July 1710), giving an account of a case of *variolæ cohærentes* which he had been attending. In 1727 he was unanimously elected to the Camden professorship of ancient history, no other candidate offering himself. Hearne relates that soon after his election he bought a hundred pounds' worth of books on history and chronology, ' on purpose to qualify him the better to discharge' the duties of the office. He died 29 May 1761, having survived his children, who died young, and three wives, Lady Tyrell, Elizabeth Woodward, and Mrs. Graves, daughter of Peter Cranke. He bequeathed 2,000l. in trust for the king's scholars of Westminster elected to Christ Church, and another 2,000l. in trust for the physicians of the Radcliffe Infirmary, and left his house in Oxford, now known as Frewin Hall, to the regius professor of medicine for the time being. His library of history and literature, consisting of 2,300 volumes, he left to the Radcliffe Library. There is in that library a volume containing a collection of dried specimens of plants made by him, with his notes in manuscript on their medicinal uses. Portraits are in the hall and common room at Christ Church, and a bust, presented by Dr. Hawley in 1757, in the library there.

[List of Queen's Scholars of Westminster; Cat. of Oxford Grad.; Oxford Honours Register; Bliss's Remains of Thomas Hearne, i. 212, 237; Hearne's MS. Diary, lxi. 123, cviii. 136, cxv. 158, cxvii. 75, cxxx. 138, cxxxv. 99, cxliv. 98–9; epitaph in St. Peter's in the East, Oxford, which, however, like the Gent. Mag. (xxxi. 284), erroneously gives his age as eighty-four; in the matriculation register he was entered 4 July 1698 as seventeen, from which it appears he must have been born in 1680 or 1681; Jackson's Oxford Journal, 6 June 1761; Ingram's Memorials of Oxford, iii. (St. Peter le Baily) 15; Notes and Queries, 3rd ser. vi. 150; London Mag. for 1761, p. 332; inscription on the back of his miniature in the Radcliffe Library; catalogue of his books in the Radcliffe Library.] E. C–N.

FRIDEGODE (*fl.* 950), hagiographer. [See FRITHEGODE.]

FRIDESWIDE, FRITHESWITH, or FREDESWITHA, SAINT (*d.* 735?), was, according to the earliest account, a king's daughter, who having chosen a life of virginity, refused marriage with a king. Being persecuted by her lover she fled from him, and at last took shelter in Oxford. Her lover pursued her thither; she invoked the help of God; the king was struck blind as he drew near the gates of the city with his company; he repented, and sent messengers to Frideswide, and his sight was restored. Hence the kings of England, it was believed, feared to enter Oxford in later days. The saint preserved her virginity, established a convent at Oxford, and died there (*Gesta Pontificum*, p. 315). William of Malmesbury, who was alive when Oxford University was in its first infancy, also speaks in his 'Gesta Regum' (i. 279) of a record in the archives of St. Frideswide's church dated 1002. This record is probably represented in an Oseney cartulary, Cotton MS. Vitell. E. xv. f. 5, late thirteenth century, quoted by Dugdale (*Monasticon*, ii. 143), which says that the saint was the daughter of Didanus, king of Oxford, who built for her a monastery there, that she obtained a place then called ' Thornbirie,' and afterwards ' Binseye,' where she had a holy spring, and that she worked miracles (PARKER, p. 91). There are also two twelfth-century manuscript lives, Cotton MS. Nero E. 1, and Bodl. MS. Laud. Misc. p. 114, which, taken together, though they differ from each other in several points (these differences are fully noted by PARKER), make the saint the daughter of Didanus and Sefrid; she was brought up by a matron named Algiva (Ælfgifu), was given a nunnery by her father, and was persecuted by Algar (Ælfgar), king of Leicester, whose messengers were struck blind, but restored to sight at her prayer. She fled by water to Benton (?), and abode there. Meanwhile Algar entered Oxford and was struck blind for the rest of his life. Frideswide went to Binsey or Thornbury, and founded a nunnery, and had a holy spring there. She worked miracles. The circumstances of her death are part of the common property of hagiology. She was buried in the church of St. Mary at Oxford, on the south side (*ib.*

pp. 95–101). There is a fourteenth-century life in Lansdowne MS. 436. It is not improbable that St. Frideswide, a member of the royal house of Mercia, should have founded a monastery at Oxford in the eighth century (BOASE, *Oxford*, p. 5). The belief that English kings feared to enter the city is curious, for Oxford was a favourite place for holding meetings of the witan in the eleventh century, and King Harold died there in 1040. It lingered late, for it is noted that Henry III 'defied the old superstition which was commonly repeated' by worshipping at the saint's shrine in 1264 (WYKES, iv. 143), and it was said that Edward I refrained from entering Oxford in 1275 from fear of the legend (*ib*. p. 264). The relics of St. Frideswide were translated on 12 Feb. 1180 (*ib*. p. 39). Wood says that Henry II was present at the ceremony (*Annals*, i. 166, comp. HARDY, *Descript. Cat.* i. 460); the church was within the walls. A second translation was performed on 10 Sept. 1289 to a new and splendid shrine erected near the old shrine (*Ann. Osen*. iv. 318). Probably at a later date the shrine was removed to the north aisle. The shrine was destroyed in 1538. Some bones, said to be those of St. Frideswide, were in the church in the reign of Mary, for in 1557 Pole considered that wrong had been done to the saint by burying Catherine Cathie, once a nun, the wife of Peter Martyr, near the virgin's sepulchre. Catherine's bones were accordingly cast out. In Elizabeth's reign Catherine's bones were reburied and were mixed with the relics of the saint, both being laid in the same receptacle, with the epitaph, 'Hic jacet religio cum superstitione' (*Monasticon*, ii. 141; FROUDE, vi. 36–8). St. Frideswide's monastery came into the hands of secular priests or canons probably during the Danish wars of the ninth century, and was held by them when the Domesday survey was made (*Domesday*, f. 157 *a*). The condition of the house was in bad repute, and in 1111 or 1121 Roger, bishop of Salisbury, established there a convent of regular canons of St. Augustine under Guimund as the first prior (*Gesta Pontificum*, p. 316). The convent was suppressed in virtue of a bull obtained by Wolsey from Clement VII, and bearing date 15 Sept. 1524, which was confirmed by the king 5 Jan. 1525. In July Henry granted the site and lands to Wolsey for the foundation of 'Cardinal's College.' The society was refounded by the king in 1532 under the name of 'King Henry VIII's College in Oxford.' Lastly, in 1545, the collegiate church was made cathedral, and called the church of 'Christ and the B. Virgin Mary,' and was again founded in the November of the next year as the 'Cathe-

dral church of Christ,' the old college becoming the house of Christ Church. St. Frideswide's day is 19 Oct., on which she is supposed to have died (LELAND, *Collectanea*, i. 342), and for which there is an office in the Sarum Breviary. Under the year 1268 Wood observes that after the translation of the saint it was the custom for the chancellor and scholars in the middle of Lent and on the festival of the Ascension to go in procession to the church of St. Frideswide as the mother-church of the university and town, and there worship (*Annals*, i. 272).

[Parker's Early Hist. of Oxford, pp. 86–104 (Oxf. Hist. Soc.); Acta SS. Oct. viii. 533 sq.; William of Malmesbury, Gesta Pontificum, p. 315 (Rolls Ser.), and Gesta Regum, i. 297 (Engl. Hist. Soc.); Ann. de Osen., Chron. T. Wykes, Ann. Monast. iv. 39, 143, 264, 318; Robert of Gloucester, ii. 545 (Hearne); Dugdale's Monasticon, ii. 134–75; Leland's Collectanea, i. 342 (Hearne); Wood's Annals, Hist. and Antiq. of Oxford, i. 166, 272 (Gutch); Hardy's Descript. Cat. i. 460 (Rolls Ser.); Leonard Hutten's Antiq. of Oxford, Elizabethan Oxford, pp. 51–61 (Oxf. Hist. Soc.); Boase's Oxford, pp. 4, 9, 38 (Historic Towns Ser.); Froude's Hist. of England, vi. 36–8 (ed. cr. 8vo); Dict. of Christian Biog. ii. 563.] W. H.

FRIEND, SIR JOHN (*d.* 1696), conspirator, was the eldest son of John Friend, a brewer, who resided in the precinct of St. Katharine's, near the Tower of London (LE NEVE, *Pedigrees of the Knights*, Harl. Soc. pp. 398–9; will of John Friend, the elder, P. C. C. 141, Mico). He followed his father's business. He built the 'stately brewhouse' called the Phœnix in the Minories, and amassed considerable wealth. For a while he maintained a fine country residence at Hackney. In 1683 he was appointed a commissioner of excise (HAYDN, *Book of Dignities*, p. 502). As colonel of the Artillery Company Friend, on occasion of their feast, 26 June 1684, had the honour of entertaining the Duke of York and Prince George of Denmark 'at a banquett in a fair large tent' in the Artillery Ground (LUTTRELL, *Relation of State Affairs*, 1857, i. 312). Though avowedly a protestant he remained a faithful adherent of James II, by whom he was knighted 3 Aug. 1685. After the revolution he was expelled from the artillery company at a meeting held in February 1689–90 (*ib.* ii. 13), and lost his seat at the board of excise. However, by a treasury order dated 18 Dec. 1690, he was relieved from the payment of excise duties (*Cal. State Papers*, Treas. 1556–1696, p. 148). James sent him a colonel's commission to raise a regiment of horse against the day when the French

Bristol, where he found the Gabriel already in port, and learned that the Michael had reached Great Yarmouth in safety. The report of Frobisher's two hundred tons of ore filled England with rejoicing. A large part of the treasure was deposited in Bristol Castle, the rest in the Tower of London, the queen commanding four locks to be placed upon the door of the treasury, the keys of which were to be handed over to Frobisher, Michael Lock, warden of the Tower, and the master of the mint. On 30 Nov. Lock had to inform Secretary Walsingham that a schism had grown up among the commissioners 'through unbelief, or I cannot tell what worse.' On 6 Dec. Sir W. Winter wrote to say that he could not get a furnace hot enough 'to bring the work to the desired perfection.' At length it was admitted that the ore was 'poor in respect of that brought last year, and that which we know may be brought next year' (Fox Bourne, i. 154). It was resolved to send out another and much larger expedition early next year, and it was resolved that it should not be stayed. After repairing to the court at Greenwich, where the queen, 'besides other good gifts and greater promises, bestowed upon the general a fair chain of gold,' Frobisher sailed from Harwich on 31 May with a fleet of fifteen vessels, in three divisions, headed by the Aid, Judith, and Thomas Allen, for the 'North-West parts,' and the fancied treasures of Meta Incognita. Taking a new route, he sailed down the Channel and along the southern coast of England and Ireland, and sighted Cape Clear on 6 June. Hence he sailed north-west until the 20th, when he reached the south of Greenland, where he landed, and named it West England, giving the name Charing Cross to the last cliff of which he had sight as he sailed past two days later. On 2 July the fleet sighted the islands off Meta Incognita, but could not proceed on account of the ice. After losing himself in the 'Mistaken Streight' (i.e. Hudson s), through no want of being warned by the more experienced Christopher Hall, master of the Aid. Frobisher anchored in the Countess of Warwick's Sound 31 July, where he found Fenton in the Judith, who arrived there ten days before him. Meanwhile Hall in the Thomas Allen was beating up in the open two or three of the other vessels which had lost their bearings in the storms and mist. After wasting nearly two months in finding the rendezvous and repairing damages there, the only results were the accidental discovery of a new strait by Frobisher, afterwards explored by Hudson, the further discovery of the upper part of Frobisher Bay by Best, and the loading the soundest vessels

with mineral that turned out to be worthless. The fleet sailed for England early in September, and arrived at various ports near the beginning of October. At first Frobisher was heartily welcomed, but popular feeling soon turned against him, on account of the mineral being declared to be inferior to that previously collected.

In an undated letter, written between 1576 and 1578, probably before the termination of his third voyage, his first wife, Isabel, whom he married 30 May 1559, wrote to Walsingham that whereas her former husband, Thomas Rickard of Snaith, left her with ample portions for herself and all her children, her present husband, 'whom God forgive,' had spent everything, and 'put them to the wide world to shift,' she and her children were starving at Hampstead, and begged Walsingham to help her in recovering a debt of 4l. due to her husband, and so to keep them from starving until Captain Frobisher's return (Fox Bourne, i. 177).

One curious fact of geographical interest in this voyage of 1578 remains to be noted. The *Emmanuel* Buss of Bridgwater, as she came homeward, to the south-east of Friesland (i.e. Greenland), discovered an island in lat. $57\frac{1}{2}°$ north, and sailed along the coast three days, 'the land seeming to be fruitful, full of woods, and a champaign country' (Best in Hakluyt, iii. 93). This island has been a source of perplexity to map-makers and navigators down to our day. It was doubtless an island, now submerged, a phenomenon by no means unknown in these regions, if we are to believe Ruysch, in his map of the 1507 Ptolemy. The following account of Buss (as the island was called) seems to have been entirely overlooked by recent writers on Frobisher. J. Seller, the hydrographer, in 1671, writes that Buss was twenty-five leagues long, and that it was 'also several times seen by Capt. Zach. Gillam, 1668,' &c. Again : 'This island (Buss) was further discovered by Capt. Thos. Shepherd in 1671, who brought home the map of the island that is here annexed' (*English Pilot*, 4th book, North Coast of America, Greenland to Newfoundland, London, 1671 ? fol. p. 5, Brit. Mus. 1804, b. 7).

In 1580 Frobisher had so far regained favour at court as to be employed as captain of one of the queen's ships, the Foresight, in preventing the Spaniards from giving assistance to the Irish insurgents in Munster. About this period he also received the reversionary title of clerk of her majesty's ships (Fox Bourne, i. 177).

In the autumn of 1581 a project for a fourth voyage to Cathay by the north-west was set forth by the Earl of Leicester and others, of which Frobisher was to have the command; but as the instructions issued to him in February 1582 were changed for the purposes of trade, and not discovery, as originally intended, Frobisher retired in favour of Fenton, who finally sailed in April 1582. In September 1585 Frobisher sailed from Plymouth in charge of the Primrose, in Drake's expedition to the West Indies as vice-admiral, where he distinguished himself in an assault upon Cartagena, and returned to England in July 1586 (HAKLUYT, iii. 534).

In 1588 Frobisher commanded the Triumph in the great Armada fight. On Sunday, 21 July (O. S.), in conjunction with Drake in the Revenge, and Hawkins in the Victory, he first beat the Spanish rear-admiral; later in the day he with Hawkins engaged Don Pedro de Valdez, leader of the Andalusian squadron, who, however, did not yield until Drake came to their assistance next morning, very much to Frobisher's annoyance. On Wednesday the 24th, when the English fleet was augmented from the Thames, Frobisher led one of the four newly formed squadrons. On Monday the 29th, Frobisher, with Drake and Hawkins, gave their final blows to the remains of the armada while in difficulties on the shoals off Gravelines. During the week previous Frobisher was knighted at sea by the lord high admiral, Charles, lord Howard of Effingham (ib. i. 600). Frobisher's services this year terminated with his appointment on 26 Nov. to the Tiger, in command of a squadron of six ships to sweep the Narrow Seas. On 7 May 1589 he was engaged off Ostend (JONES, p. 282). In May 1590 he proceeded to sea as vice-admiral to Sir John Hawkins [q. v.], with a fleet of twelve or fourteen ships, to intercept the Portuguese carracks coming from India, but without result, as means were found by Philip II to warn them to delay sailing (LEDIARD, p. 275). In the summer of 1591 Frobisher was residing at Whitwood in Yorkshire, when he married his second wife, Dorothy, widow of Sir W. Widmerpoole, daughter of Lord Wentworth. In the following May he was sent by Sir W. Raleigh in the Garland 'to annoy the Spanish fleet' off the coast of Spain, while Sir John Burroughs, his colleague, proceeded towards the Azores to intercept the Plate fleet from Panama. Frobisher soon afterwards capturing a large Biscayan ship with a valuable cargo of iron, &c., worth 7,000l., returned home, while Burroughs joined the Earl of Cumberland (MONSON, p. 23). In 1593 he paid his last visit to his Yorkshire home, where he became a justice of the peace for the West Riding.

In the autumn of 1594 Frobisher with the Dreadnought and ten sail co-operated with Sir John Norris in the relief of Brest and the adjoining port of Crozon, already in the hands of the Spaniards. In the last fight, when the garrison surrendered and the fort was reduced to ashes, Frobisher was wounded in the hip while leading his men on shore; this ultimately led to his death through unskilful surgery (LEDIARD, p. 308). He died soon after reaching Plymouth, where his entrails were buried in the church of St. Andrew, while his other remains were interred in St. Giles's, Cripplegate, 14 Jan. 1595 (JONES, p. 335). An impartial account of Frobisher is still a desideratum, as recent attempts to exalt his fame at the expense of Drake and Hawkins have only served to obscure it. Although a gentleman by birth, Frobisher was no scholar, as his letters prove (cf. ib. p. 284). Frobisher from his youth was trained in a rough school, whose highest ideal was courage, tempered by piracy, which was either patronised or reprobated according to its value or inconvenience to the state.

Frobisher's portrait, often reproduced, will be found in Holland's 'Herωologia.' Two cartographical relics remain to be noticed, 'a chart of the navigation of 1578,' and Frobisher's 'plot of Croyzon, 1594,' where he met with his death-wound (*Hatfield MSS., Hist. MSS. Comm.* 7th Rep. Appendix, pp. 192–3).

[Best's True Discourse, 1578, 4to (reprint in Hakluyt, 1599, vol. iii.); Collinson's Frobisher's Voyages (Hakluyt Soc.), 1867; Fox Bourne's English Seamen, 1862; Hakluyt's Navigations, 1589, fol. (for Ellis and Hall's Narratives); ib. Voyages, 1599–1600, 3 vols.; Holland's Herωologia, 1620; F. Jones's Life of Frobisher, 1878; J. J. Cartwright's Life of Frobisher in Chaps. of Yorkshire History, 1872; Lediard's Naval Hist. 1734, fol.; Sir W. Monson's 1st naval tract, War with Spain, 1682, fol.; Settle's True Report (2nd voyage), 1577, 8vo (reprint in Hakluyt, 1589); Frobisher MSS. in Brit. Mus. and State Papers.]   C. H. C.

FRODSHAM, BRIDGE (1734–1768), actor, was a native of Frodsham, Cheshire. He was admitted on the foundation of Westminster School in 1746, but forfeited his position by running away. In 1748, however, he was received back at the school, being apparently the only instance of a boy twice admitted on the foundation. He ran away a second time, and making his way to Leicester attached himself to a troop of players in that town. He was encouraged by J. G. Cooper of Thurgarton, Nottinghamshire, once also a Westminster boy, to make acting his profession, and joined the company at York. He quickly attained a very high degree of popularity, became the idol of the theatre-going public, and was known as the 'York Garrick.' Tate Wilkinson, with whom Frodsham acted more than once, considered his abilities unquestionable, and thought his Hamlet unequalled save by Garrick and Barry. Frodsham himself told Garrick, on whom he called as a brother genius, that he believed his own assumption of that character was almost equal to that of the better-known actors. With the exception of a fortnight, during which Frodsham paid a visit to London, because he thought he and Garrick ought to know one another, he rarely left York. He died 21 Oct. 1768 at Hull, his end being accelerated by drink. He had played at the theatre three nights before, and had announced that his next appearance would be in 'What we shall all come to.' Frodsham's too sympathetic friends put it about that his death was caused or hastened by ill-usage at the hands of Wilkinson, who was, however, exonerated by Frodsham's widow, Isabella.

[Wilson's Wonderful Characters, iii. 239; Wilkinson's Memoirs, iv. 33–48 ; Wilkinson's Wandering Patentee, i. 27–8, 58–9 ; Welch's Alumni Westmonasterienses ; Forshall's Westminster School Past and Present, p. 241.]

A. V.

FROST, CHARLES (1781?–1862), antiquary, born at Kingston-upon-Hull, Yorkshire, in 1781 or 1782, was the son of Thomas Frost, solicitor, of that town. He followed the same profession, and, as his father had been before him, was solicitor to the Hull Dock Company, which appointment he held for upwards of thirty-three years. From his father he acquired a love for genealogical and historical research. While still in his articles he diligently applied himself to mastering the writing of the thirteenth and fourteenth centuries, and it was not long before he had gained for himself a reputation as an expert black-letter lawyer. On 2 May 1822 he was elected F.S.A. In 1827 he published by subscription a work of permanent value entitled 'Notices relative to the Early History of the Town and Port of Hull ; compiled from original records and unpublished manuscripts, and illustrated with engravings, etchings, and vignettes,' 4to, London, 1827. He proves that Edward I was not the founder of the town as supposed by Leland and Camden, but that long previous to his visit to Cottingham in 1296 the ground on which Hull stands was the site of a populous and improving town called Wic or Wyke. The work was the subject of a long and flattering critique by Sir N. H. Nicolas in the 'Retrospective Review' for

December 1827 (p. 203). Another publication, also of local value, was his 'Address,' 8vo, 1831, delivered to the Hull Literary and Philosophical Society at the opening of the seventh session on 5 Nov. 1830, in which he alludes to the various literary societies which had been promoted in the town during the preceding half-century, and gives brief biographical notices of most of the Hull authors, whether natives or residents. A subsequent presidential address, delivered by him in 1852, was likewise published. Frost was president of the above society ten times between 1830 and 1855, and altogether he served the same office in connection with the subscription library for twelve years, between 1827 and 1854, one of the laws of that institution being suspended that he might occupy the position for five successive years, 1850–4, to enable him to carry into effect his scheme for the amalgamation of the two societies in the building in Albion Street which they now occupy. In the reading-room of the library is a full-length portrait of him by Schmidt. Frost was also one of the vice-presidents of the Hull meeting of the British Association for the Advancement of Science in 1853. Besides the works already named, he published two legal pamphlets. One was on the 'Propriety of making a remuneration to witnesses in civil actions for loss of time. . . . With some observations on the present system of taxing costs,' 8vo, London, 1815. The other consisted of a letter to Thomas Thompson on the subject of 'Equalising the poor rates of Hull by assessing the shipping belonging to the port to the relief of the poor,' published in 1820. Frost died at Hull, 5 Sept. 1862, aged 80 or 81.

[R. W. Corlass's Sketches of Hull Authors, ed. C. F. Corlass and William Andrews, 1879, pp. 33–4; Appendix to Frost's Address of 5 Nov. 1830, pp. 123–8 ; Gentleman's Magazine, vol. c. pt. ii. pp. 450–1, vol. ci. pt. i. pp. 523–4, 3rd ser. xiii. 508; Boyne's Yorkshire Library, pp. 162, 249; Law Magazine, January 1831, p. 13 n.]

G. G.

FROST, GEORGE (1754–1821), landscape painter, son of a builder at Ousden in Suffolk, was originally brought up to his father's business. He subsequently obtained a confidential situation in the office of the Blue Coach at Ipswich, which he continued to hold for the greater part of his life. He had a natural and early love of drawing, and without any instruction from others succeeded in producing some very excellent works. He studied nature very closely, and drew picturesque buildings and landscapes with a masterly hand, showing both originality and truth. He was a devoted admirer and imitator of

Gainsborough, and possessed some paintings and drawings by him, notably 'The Mall,' of which he executed a careful copy when in his seventy-seventh year. He was also an intimate friend of John Constable, R.A. His situation at Ipswich caused him to confine his subjects to that town and its neighbourhood, and he is little known elsewhere. He died on 28 June 1821, in his seventy-eighth year, after a painful illness.

[Gent. Mag. 1821, xci. 89; Redgrave's Dict. of Artists.]   L. C.

FROST, JOHN (1626?–1656), nonconformist divine, born at Langham, Suffolk, in or about 1626, was the eldest son of John Frost, rector of Fakenham in the same county. After attending schools at Thetford, Norfolk, and Bury St. Edmunds, Suffolk, he was admitted pensioner of St. John's College, Cambridge, 21 Feb. 1641–2, and fellow soon after taking his B.A. degree (MAYOR, *Admissions to St. John's Coll. Cambr.* pt. i. p. 62). He bore an active part in the educational work of the college as lecturer on logic and philosophy. In 1654 he began to preach regularly at St. Benedict's, Cambridge, and elsewhere in the town and county. He proceeded B.D. in the summer of 1656. A few months later he was invited to become 'pastor' of St. Olave's, Hart Street, London, but was cut off by small-pox, 2 Nov. 1656 (ZACHARY CROFTON, *Funeral Sermon*, 1657). To his 'Select Sermons,' fol., Cambridge, 1657 (with a new title-page, 1658), is prefixed his portrait at the age of thirty-one, by R. Vaughan.

[Brook's Puritans, iii. 291–3; Granger's Biog. Hist. of England, 2nd ed., iii. 46.]   G. G.

FROST, JOHN (1803–1840), founder of the Medico-Botanical Society of London, was born in 1803 near Charing Cross, London, where his parents were in business. Intending to enter the medical profession, he became the pupil of Dr. Wright, the apothecary of Bethlehem Hospital, but quarrelled with him, and gave up medicine for botany. Although only eighteen, he conceived a project which he carried into effect with remarkable success. In 1821 (16 Jan.) he founded the Medico-Botanical Society of London, having for its objects the investigation of the medicinal properties of plants, the study of the materia medica of all countries, with many other allied subjects, and the adjudging of rewards to original investigators. In this project he was first aided by Drs. Bree and Maton, and afterwards obtained an introduction to George IV, who not only appointed him botanical tutor to the two youthful Princes George (afterwards respectively king

of Hanover and Duke of Cambridge), but (in 1828) became patron of the new society. Sir James McGregor, director-general of the army medical board, was the first president, and it soon gained wide support. Frost was appointed director of the society and also lecturer on botany, both of which appointments are said to have been honorary. As the society grew, so did Frost's ambition, and he incessantly sought the support of royal personages and distinguished men all over Europe. He succeeded in obtaining the adhesion of eleven sovereigns, and by incredible perseverance procured their autographs, with those of many other celebrities, in a well-known book which he was always carrying about; each signature occupied a page, surrounded by a wreath of artistically painted flowers. The book disappeared when the society collapsed, and is not now known to exist (CLARKE, infra). It is recounted by Barham (*Life*, 1 vol. ed. pp. 119–21) that Frost, after many futile attempts, had an interview with the Duke of Wellington, dressed in a lieutenant-general's uniform, and succeeded in obtaining the duke's signature. The meetings of the society were not without interest. Frost directed everything and everybody, from the president downwards, and obtained some effective displays. Without any genuine qualification he made himself so generally known that within a few years he was elected a fellow of the Society of Antiquaries, of the Royal Society of Edinburgh, and of the Linnean Society, a member of the Royal Asiatic Society, lecturer on botany at the Royal Institution and at St. Thomas's Hospital; he also entered himself at Emmanuel College, Cambridge, intending to graduate in medicine, but his career of triumph was checked when the Royal Society blackballed him almost unanimously (BARHAM). Frost sent a hostile message to the secretary of the society (*Gent. Mag.* new ser. 1840, xiv. 664).

In 1824 Frost, at the age of twenty-one, was appointed paid secretary to the Royal Humane Society, with a residence in Bridge Street, Blackfriars. At the annual meetings of the Medico-Botanical Society he always delivered an oration, in which he related the progress of the society. His arrogance disgusted many of his friends. He presented himself at the annual meeting in 1829 to deliver his oration, decorated with a dazzling display of foreign orders and other distinctions, but was received with much hostility. A private meeting of the council under the presidency of Earl Stanhope subsequently declared the office of director abolished, and called a general meeting to confirm the decree. Frost replied to Earl Stanhope's accusations with spirit, but at an adjourned meeting on 8 Jan. 1830 he was not only deposed, but expelled from the society.

Not daunted by this rebuff, Frost sought success in new fields. He obtained about this time, according to an engraved card of his own, the appointment of surgeon to the Duke of Cumberland. He resigned the secretaryship of the Humane Society only to have his appointment as surgeon to the duke cancelled. Frost sought to regain his secretaryship to the Humane Society, but failed. Yet he succeeded in 1831 in establishing St. John's Hospital, Clerkenwell, and also did much to promote the Royal Sailing Society. In 1832 he obtained a grant from the admiralty of H.M.S. Chanticleer for a hospital ship off Millbank, for watermen above London Bridge, and enlisted a large body of distinguished patrons. Having, however, made himself responsible for a considerable sum of money on account of this scheme, and being disappointed of the pecuniary support on which he had relied, he fled to Paris to avoid the importunities of creditors, and lived there for some time under an assumed name. He finally settled in Berlin as a physician, taking the title of Sir John Frost, and is said to have gained considerable practice. He died after a long and painful illness on 17 March 1840. He married Harriet, only daughter of Mrs. Yosy, author of a work on Switzerland, but had no children.

Frost showed little scientific talent. His one object was self-aggrandisement. He wrote, besides his 'Orations,' nothing of note. A preface to Bingley's 'Introduction to Botany,' identical with an introductory lecture of his at the Royal Institution; a translation of the statutes of the Hanoverian Guelphic order, 1831; a paper 'On the Mustard Tree mentioned in the New Testament,' 1827; and some small papers on the oil of Croton Tiglium, published in pamphlet form in 1827, complete the list.

[Gent. Mag. new ser. 1840, xiv. 664–6; J. F. Clarke's Autobiographical Recollections of the Medical Profession, 1874, pp. 240–1, 267–72; Barham's Life (1 vol. ed. 1880), pp. 119–21.]
G. T. B.

FROST, JOHN (1750–1842), secretary of the Corresponding Society, born in October 1750, was educated at Winchester School, and brought up as an attorney. He early devoted himself to the study of politics. In 1782 he was a prominent member of a society which met at the Thatched House tavern for the purpose of advocating constitutional reforms, and among his associates were William Pitt, the Duke of Richmond, Lord Surrey, Lord Mahon, Major Cartwright, Horne Tooke, and John Wilkes. Pitt engaged in correspondence with Frost, and assured him that he regarded a thorough reform of the representation as 'essentially necessary to the independence of parliament and the liberty of the people.' At the breaking out of the French revolution Frost was one of the most enthusiastic of those who adopted republican principles. In 1792 Frost secretly sheltered in his house a number of political prisoners. The same year he took a leading part in founding the Corresponding Society, for which body he also acted as secretary. The society began an active propaganda for a reform of the parliamentary representation, and one of its manifestoes prepared by Frost and Hardy showed that 257 representatives of the people, making a majority of the existing House of Commons, were returned by a number of voters not exceeding the thousandth part of the nation.

Contemporaneously with the foundation of this society was formed the Society for Constitutional Information. Branches of both societies rapidly sprang up in the provinces. The Constitutional Society elected Frost a deputy to the convention of France in 1793, his colleague being Joel Barlow, whose expenses he paid. In this character he was present at the trial of the French king (1792–3), and he was denounced in one of Burke's speeches as the ambassador to the murderers.

On the information of the attorney-general Frost was arrested in February 1793 on a charge of sedition. He was brought to trial in the following May, the indictment describing him as 'late of Westminster, in the county of Middlesex, gentleman, a person of a depraved, impious, and disquiet mind, and of a seditious disposition.' The specific charge against the prisoner was that he had uttered these words in Percy's coffee-house, Marylebone: 'I am for equality; I see no reason why any man should not be upon a footing with another; it is every man's birthright;' that on being asked what he meant by equality, he replied, 'Why, no kings;' and being further asked whether he meant no king in England, rejoined: 'Yes, no king; the constitution of this country is a bad one.' Frost was defended by Erskine, but in spite of his advocate's eloquence he was found guilty. He was sentenced to six calendar months' imprisonment in Newgate, to stand once during that time in the pillory at Charing Cross for the space of one hour, between twelve and two o'clock; to find sureties for his good behaviour for the space of five years, himself in 500l. and two others in 100l. each; to be further imprisoned until the sureties were found; and lastly to be struck off the roll of attorneys. While one of the witnesses against Frost was waiting to hear sentence passed he was seized with a fit. It is said that Frost taunted him with his sufferings as a proof of divine vengeance. On the expiration of his sentence, 19 Dec. 1793, Frost was brought out of Newgate almost in a state of collapse. He was placed in a coach, and rolled in blankets. Kirby, the keeper, accompanied him to the house of Justice Grose, in Bloomsbury Square, where, with two sureties, he entered into his recognisances. As soon as he was at liberty the multitude took the horses out of the carriage and drew him along the streets, stopping at every marked place, and particularly before the Prince of Wales's house, to shout and express their joy. In this state he was conducted to his house in Spring Gardens, where Thelwall made a speech, entreating the crowd to separate peaceably.

The Corresponding Society continued its work of agitation, and during a debate in the House of Commons in May 1794 Pitt stated that it had laid in due form before the Society for Constitutional Information a deliberate plan for assembling a convention for all England, to overturn the established system of government. At length, on 28 July 1797, the members of the Corresponding Society assembled in a field near St. Pancras, when the proceedings were interrupted by the magistrates, who arrested the principal speakers, and kept them in custody until they procured bail. The society itself was then formally suppressed by the government.

Frost was a candidate for the representation of East Grinstead in 1802, and petitioned against his opponent's return, but a committee of the House of Commons found that the petition was frivolous and vexatious. In December 1813 Frost received from the prince regent, acting in the name and on behalf of the king, a free pardon, in consequence of which, on 8 Feb. 1815, the court of king's bench was moved to replace his name on the roll of attorneys. The court held that his want of practice and experience in the profession made him presumably unfit for the employment.

The effects of his imprisonment remained with him for many years, but he lived to the great age of ninety-one, dying at Holly Lodge, near Lymington, Hampshire, on 25 July 1842 (*Gent. Mag.* October 1842, pp. 442–3).

[Papers of the Corresponding and Constitutional Societies; Ann. Reg. 1842; Edinburgh Review, vol. xvi.; State Trials, vol. xxii.; Hampshire Independent, 30 July 1842.]   G. B. S.

FROST, JOHN (*d.* 1877), chartist, was the son of John and Sarah Frost, who kept the Royal Oak public-house in Mill Street, Newport, Monmouthshire, for nearly forty years. When about sixteen years of age he was apprenticed to a tailor in Cardiff. On his return to Newport in 1811 he commenced business as a tailor and draper, and shortly afterwards married the widow of a Mr. Geach, a timber dealer, by whom Frost had two sons and five daughters. In 1816 he began first to take an interest in politics, and from that time advocated the principles which were subsequently embodied in the People's Charter. In 1822 he suffered six months' imprisonment for libel. He took an active part in the struggle for reform, and when the Municipal Corporation Act came into operation Frost was elected a member of the town council of Newport. He was appointed a magistrate for the borough in 1835, and in the following year filled the office of mayor. In 1838 he was elected as the delegate to represent the chartists of Monmouthshire at the national convention of the working classes which met in London for the first time on 4 Feb. 1839. A few weeks afterwards he was removed from the commission of the peace by Lord John Russell, who was then home secretary, for using seditious language at local meetings (see the correspondence between Russell and Frost, given at length in the *Annual Register*, 1839, Chron. pp. 22–6). In consequence of this Frost's popularity among the chartists was greatly increased, and his name became well known throughout the country as one of the leaders of the chartist movement. During the course of the year a number of the more prominent chartists were convicted of sedition, and on 14 Sept. the convention, weakened in numbers by resignations and arrests, was dissolved on the casting vote of Frost, who acted as chairman on that occasion. Frost, however, was resolved to appeal to physical force, and on 4 Nov. led a large body of working men, chiefly miners, armed with guns and bludgeons, into Newport. Two other divisions, commanded respectively by Jones, a watchmaker of Pontypool, and Williams, a beershop keeper of Nantyglo, were to have joined forces with Frost in his attack upon the town, but the men of Nantyglo arrived late, and those from Pontypool never came. Frost with his division attacked the Westgate hotel, where, under the direction of Phillips, the mayor of the town, some thirty men of the 45th regiment and a number of special constables had been posted. The ill-armed and undisciplined mob were easily repulsed, twenty chartists being shot dead and many others being wounded. Frost was captured the same evening, and was tried before Lord-chief-justice Tindal, Baron Parke, and Justice Williams at a special assize which was opened at Monmouth on 10 Dec. 1839. He was defended by Sir Frederick Pollock and Fitzroy Kelly, and after a lengthy trial was found guilty of levying war against the queen. On 16 Jan. 1840 Frost, Williams, and Jones were sentenced to be hung, drawn, and quartered. On the 25th and the two following days a technical point which had been raised during the course of the trial was argued before all the fifteen judges in the court of exchequer chamber. The conviction was upheld, but owing to the considerable difference of opinion among the judges the capital sentence was on 1 Feb. commuted for one of transportation for life. Frost was sent to Van Diemen's Land, where he spent nearly fifteen years working in the gangs, serving as a police clerk, and in other capacities. Several efforts were from time to time made, especially by Thomas Slingsby Duncombe [q. v.] in the House of Commons, to procure the release of Frost and his associates. In 1854 he obtained a conditional pardon, the condition being that he should not return to the queen's dominions. He thereupon went to America, but receiving a free pardon in May 1856, he returned to England in July of that year. On 31 Aug. he delivered at Padiham two lectures on the 'Horrors of Convict Life,' which were afterwards printed, and in the following year he published 'A Letter to the People of Great Britain and Ireland on Transportation, showing the effects of irresponsible power on the Physical and Moral Conditions of Convicts.' Though it appears from internal evidence that it was his intention to write a series of letters on this subject, no more were published. Frost went to reside at Stapleton, near Bristol, where he lived for many years in comparative retirement, and died on 29 July 1877, being upwards of ninety years of age. Some account of the general convention and a list of the delegates will be found in the Place MSS. (*Brit. Mus. Addit. MS.* 27821).

[The Rise and Fall of Chartism in Monmouthshire (1840); the Dublin Review, viii. 271–85; Gurney's Trial of John Frost for High Treason (1840); Walpole's Hist. of England (1886), iv. 46–6C; Molesworth's Hist. of England (1874), ii. chap. v.; Gammage's Hist. of the Chartist Movement (1854); Life of Thomas Slingsby Duncombe (1868), i. 288–9, 294–5, 301, ii. 108–9, 194–5; Ann. Register, 1839; Haydn's Dict. of Dates (1881), p. 554; Daily News, 31 July 1877; Bristol Times and Mirror, 30 July and 4 Aug. 1877; Brit. Mus. Cat.]   G. F. R. B.

FROST, WILLIAM EDWARD (1810–1877), painter, was born at Wandsworth in September 1810. His artistic gifts were apparent from his earliest years. When about fifteen he was introduced to Etty, by whose advice he entered Sass's drawing school, and also studied at the British Museum. In 1829 he became a student of the Royal Academy, where he gained the first medals in each of the schools, except the antique, in which he was defeated by Maclise. During the next fourteen years he painted upwards of three hundred portraits. He began to exhibit at the Royal Academy in 1836, and in 1839 he was awarded the gold medal for his 'Prometheus bound by Force and Strength,' which was in the exhibition of the following year. In 1843 he sent to the competition in Westminster Hall a cartoon representing 'Una alarmed by the Fauns and Satyrs,' which obtained one of the third-class premiums of 100*l.*, and in the same year he exhibited at the Royal Academy 'Christ crowned with Thorns,' which was selected by an Art-Union prize-holder. These successes led him to relinquish portraiture, and to devote himself to subjects of a sylvan and bacchanalian character, drawn chiefly from the works of Spenser and Milton. His 'Sabrina' was exhibited at the Royal Academy in 1845, and engraved by Peter Lightfoot for the Art Union of London, and this was followed by 'Diana surprised by Actæon,' which secured his election as an associate in 1846, and was purchased by Lord Northwick. 'Una,' a subject from Spenser's 'Faerie Queene,' appeared in the exhibition of 1847, and was purchased by the Queen. In 1848 he sent to the Academy 'Euphrosyne,' one of his best works, painted for Mr. Bicknell, and now in the possession of Mr. J. L. Newall, by whom it was exhibited at Manchester in 1887. The group of 'L'Allegro' was afterwards painted from this picture as a gift from the Queen to the Prince Consort. In 1849 he exhibited at the Royal Academy 'The Syrens,' a picture remarkable for its beauty of colour, and in 1850 'The Disarming of Cupid,' painted for the Prince Consort, and 'Andromeda.' 'L'Allegro' and 'The Disarming of Cupid' were engraved respectively by T. Garner and P. Lightfoot for Hall's 'Royal Gallery of Art,' and are now at Osborne. In 1851 he exhibited 'Wood Nymphs' and 'Hylas;' in 1852 'May Morning,' and in 1854 'Chastity,' from Milton's 'Comus,' one of his most poetical conceptions, which was engraved by T. Garner for the 'Art Journal' of 1864. 'The Graces' and 'Bacchanalians' were exhibited in 1856, 'Narcissus' in 1857, and again at the International Exhibition of 1862, 'Zephyr with Aurora playing' in 1858, 'The Daughters of Hesperus' in 1860, 'Venus lamenting the absence of Adonis' and 'A Dance' in 1861, 'The Graces and Loves' in 1863, 'The Death of Adonis' in 1865, 'Come unto these yellow Sands,' from 'The Tempest,' in 1866, 'Hylas and the Nymphs' in 1867, 'By the Waters of Babylon' and 'Puck' in 1869, and 'Musidora' in 1871. Besides the works above mentioned he contributed many others—in all 110—to the exhibitions of the Royal Academy and the British Institution. It was not until 1870 that he became a Royal Academician, when he presented as his diploma work a 'Nymph and Cupid.' He retired in 1876, becoming an honorary R.A.

Frost died unmarried in Fitzroy Square, London, on 4 June 1877. He formed a large collection of engravings after the works of Thomas Stothard, R.A., and prepared, in conjunction with Mr. Henry Reeve, 'A complete Catalogue of the Paintings, Watercolour Drawings, Drawings, and Prints in the Collection of the late H. A. J. Munro, Esq., of Novar,' which was privately printed in 1865.

[Art Journal, 1849, p. 184, with portrait, from a sketch in oil by himself; Art Journal, 1857, pp. 5–7 (with woodcuts), 1877, pp. 234, 280; Illustrated London News, 21 Jan. 1871, with portrait; Athenæum, 1877, i. 744; Academy, 1877, i. 543; Times, 8 June 1877; Sandby's Hist. of the Royal Academy of Arts, 1862, ii. 219–221; Royal Academy Exhibition Catalogues, 1836–78; British Institution Exhibition Catalogues (Modern Artists), 1842–67.] R. E. G.

FROUCESTER, WALTER (*d.* 1412), abbot of St. Peter's, Gloucester, had previously officiated as chamberlain of the monastery. On the death of John Boyfield in January 1382 Froucester was elected his successor, being the twentieth abbot. Boyfield's rule had not been successful; he was weak and was in continual trouble with rival ecclesiastics, who, to the disadvantage of his monastery, generally got the better of him. Froucester, on assuming the direction, applied himself to the improvement of the brotherhood's position with marked success, taking and keeping the upper hand over all rivals, and yet without giving offence. By the prudence and economy of his domestic administration he succeeded in wiping off the greater part of the vast debt with which he found the monastery encumbered. From his private purse he supplied the church with ornaments of all kinds, books, vestments, and silver plate. He is best known for having brought to completion at great expense the beautiful cloisters, the building of which had been be-

gun in Horton's (abbot 1351–77) time, and left unfinished for several years. With the view of securing for his monastery full title to some of its possessions he despatched to Rome one of the brotherhood, William Bryt by name, who, after a stay of some years, succeeded in getting appropriated to the monastery the churches of Holy Trinity and St. Mary de Lode, Gloucester, and that of Chipping Norton, Oxfordshire. Froucester also obtained from Pope Urban, through the influence of the Duke of Gloucester, the privileges of wearing the pontifical mitre, ring, sandals, and dalmatic, which his predecessor had requested in vain. The occasion chosen by Froucester for his investment with these ornaments was 10 April 1390, the day on which the remains of St. Kyneburgh the Virgin were translated to St. Peter's, the ceremony being celebrated by the Bishop of Worcester and Froucester, and a number of ecclesiastics, in the presence of the Duke of Gloucester and many noblemen and ladies. He also obtained from the pope a dispensation allowing the brotherhood of St. Peter's to eat flesh from Septuagesima to Quinquagesima inclusive. By Froucester's orders the registers of the monastery were compiled afresh, and the history of St. Peter's was probably re-edited at the same time. It has sometimes been supposed, but unwarrantably, that this history, early copies of which exist in Queen's College Library, Oxford, and among the Cottonian MSS., was written by Froucester, because the chronicle closes during his abbacy; internal evidence shows that it was compiled from time to time. Froucester died in 1412, and was buried beneath an arch in the southwest portion of the choir of St. Peter's. Sir Robert Atkyns (*Ancient and Present State of Gloucestershire*, p. 66) calls him Trowcester.

[Historia et Cartularium Monasterii Sancti Petri Gloucestriæ (Rolls Ser. vol. xxxiii.), ed. W. H. Hart, i. x, xii, lxiii–lxviii, 6, 50, 54–8; Dugdale's Monast. Angl. i. 535; Rudder's New Hist. of Gloucestershire, p. 137.] A. V.

FROUDE, RICHARD HURRELL (1803–1836), divine, son of Robert Hurrell Froude, afterwards archdeacon of Totnes, was born 25 March 1803, at his father's rectory, **Dartington**, Devonshire. He was elder brother of William Froude [q. v.], and of the historian, James Anthony Froude. [see SUPPLEMENT.] He was educated at Ottery free school, where he lived in the house of George, elder brother of Samuel Taylor, Coleridge, and was sent to Eton in 1816. In 1821 he came into residence as a commoner of Oriel College, Oxford. He graduated as B.A. in 1824, when he was second class both in

'Literæ Humaniores' and mathematics. He was elected to a fellowship at Oriel at Easter 1826, took his M.A. degree in 1827, and in the same year became tutor in his college, retaining the office until 1830. He was ordained deacon at Christmas 1828 by the Bishop of Oxford, and priest in 1829. In 1826 (the present Cardinal) Newman became tutor of Oriel, and there made an acquaintance with Froude, which ripened into a close and affectionate friendship about 1829. Newman, in his 'Apologia,' speaks of Froude's bold and logical intellect. He already detested the reformers, admired the church of Rome, accepted tradition 'as a main instrument of religious teaching,' and was 'powerfully drawn to the mediæval church, but not to the primitive.' He was 'a high tory of the cavalier stamp,' a man of strong classical tastes, and fond of historical inquiry, but 'had no taste for theology as such.' He became an influential member of the party afterwards known as the Oxford school, and had a strong influence upon its founders. In 1831 he showed symptoms of consumption, and passed the winter of 1832 in the south of Europe for the sake of his health. He was accompanied by his father, and for part of the time by Newman. He was 'shocked by the degeneracy which he thought he saw in the catholics of Italy.' At Rome he began with Newman to write the 'Lyra Apostolica,' which appeared in the 'British Magazine.' His contributions signed β are exceptionally beautiful. After his return in the summer of 1833, he sailed in November 1834 to the West Indies, where he stayed until the spring of 1835. His health was not really improved, and he died at his father's house 28 Feb. 1836. He contributed three of the 'Tracts for the Times.' Two volumes of 'Remains' published at the end of 1837 were prefaced by Newman and edited by James B. Mozley [q. v.] The preface shows that although he hated 'protestantism,' he was still opposed to 'Romanism.' He was a 'catholic without the popery, and a church of England man without the protestantism' (*Remains*, i. 404). He was in fact at the stage reached by Newman at the same period. Two later volumes appeared in 1839. They show his strong prejudices more distinctly than the intellectual power which he undoubtedly possessed.

J. A. Froude wrote that he never saw any person 'in whom the excellencies of intellect and character were combined in fuller measure' (*Nineteenth Century* for April 1879).

[Life prefixed to Remains; Newman's Apologia, 1st ed. 75, 77, 84–7, 95, 109, 110, 125, 128, 129, 154; Mozley's Reminiscences (1882); Churton's Joshua Watson (1861), ii. 139–41; Coleridge's Keble, pp. xii. 111–13; Life of S. Wilberforce, i. 34, 95; J. B. Mozley's Letters, pp. 73, 102; Church's Oxford Movement, 1891; L. I. Guiney's Hurrell Froude, 1904.]

FROUDE, WILLIAM (1810–1879), engineer and naval architect, fourth son of the Venerable Robert Hurrell Froude, archdeacon of Totnes and rector of Dartington and Denbury in Devonshire, was born at Dartington parsonage, 28 Nov. 1810. He was educated at Westminster School, and then matriculated from Oriel College, Oxford, on 23 Oct. 1828, being for some time a pupil of his elder brother, Richard Hurrell Froude [q.v.] Here, although devoting much leisure to chemistry and mechanics, he took a first class in mathematical honours in 1832, his B.A. in the same year, and his M.A. in 1837. In the beginning of 1833 he became a pupil of Henry Robinson Palmer, vice-president of the Institution of Civil Engineers, and was by him employed on some of the surveys of the South-Eastern railway. In 1837 he joined the engineering staff of Isambard K. Brunel upon the Bristol and Exeter railway, where he had charge of the construction of the line between the Whiteball tunnel and Exeter. He evinced great attention to details, and in two elliptical skew-bridges introduced taper bricks so arranged as to make correct spiral courses, and it was while employed on this line that he propounded the 'curve of adjustment.' In the autumn of 1844 he was engaged on the survey of the Wilts, Somerset, and Weymouth railway, but shortly afterwards gave up the active pursuit of his profession in order to live at Dartington with his father, who was then in failing health. On the death of his father, in 1859, Froude left Dartington, and went to reside at Torbay, where in 1867 he built a house near Torquay, which he named Chelston Cross. As early as 1856 he had, at the request of Brunel, commenced an investigation into the laws of the motion of a ship among waves, which he continued at Torquay, and upon which he read a series of papers at the Institution of Naval Architects. He proved the mechanical possibility of that form of motion known as the trochoidal sea-wave. He also came to the conclusion that slow rolling ships are less likely to meet with waves which will cause them to roll, and that the rolling of a ship can be reduced by the means of a deep bilge-keel. The armour-clad and other ships of war of the British navy have been designed in accordance with this theory, so as to have steadiness at sea. In 1871 he demonstrated the effect of bilge-keels with a model of the Devastation, and in 1872 these keels were further tested by trials of the Greyhound and Perseus off Plymouth. At the suggestion of Edward James Reed, he proposed to the admiralty to conduct a series of experiments on the resistance of models. This offer was accepted in 1870, and from that time he devoted his energies to the conducting of experiments for the government on the resistance of ships, and on the cognate subject of their propulsion. The admiralty establishment at Torquay erected for carrying out these experiments contained a covered tank, 250 feet long, 33 feet wide, and 10 feet deep. Above the tank was suspended a railway, on which ran a truck drawn at any given speed, and beneath this truck the model was drawn through the water, and its resistance was measured by a self-acting dynamometer on the truck. His researches into the expenditure of power in screw-ships, the proportions of screw-propellers, and the information to be deduced from the speed-trials of ships, have been of immense importance to the royal navy and to the mercantile marine. His value as an adviser was recognised by his appointment as a member of the committee on design in 1870, and on the Inflexible committee in 1877, and by the confidence afforded to him by the successive heads of the admiralty. He became a member of the Institution of Civil Engineers 7 April 1846, and in 1877 was named a member of the council. On 2 June 1870 he was elected a fellow of the Royal Society, and on 27 April 1876 he received the degree of LL.D. from the university of Glasgow. In the same year he was given the royal medal of the Royal Society. He gave evidence before the royal commission on scientific research 29 May 1872, which contains details of the experiments which he undertook for the admiralty (Report of Royal Commission, 1874, ii. 147–52, in *Parliamentary Papers*, 1874, vol. xxiii.) His last work was the construction of a dynamometer capable of determining the power of large marine engines. This machine, which he did not live to see experimented on, was afterwards tried with complete success. In the winter of 1878 he went on a cruise to the Cape of Good Hope in H.M.S. Boadicea, and was about to return to England when he was seized with an attack of dysentery, and died at Admiralty House, Simon's Town, on 4 May 1879, and was buried in the Naval cemetery on 12 May. He was the author of papers in 'Minutes of Proceedings of Institution of Civil Engineers,' 'Journal of Bath and West of England Society,' 'Proceedings of Institution of Mechanical Engineers,' 'Transactions of the Institution of Naval Architects,' 'Reports of the British Association,' 'Naval Science,' 'Nature,' and other publications, most of them referring to his experiments in connection with ships.

[Minutes of Proceedings of Institution of Civil Engineers (1880), lx. 395–404; Proceedings of Royal Society of London (1879), xxix. pp. ii–vi; Nature (1879), xx. 148–50, 169–73; Times, 27 May 1879, p. 7, 3 June, p. 12, 7 June, p. 7; Mozley's Reminiscences (1882), ii. 14–17.]

G. C. B.

FROWDE, PHILIP (*d.* 1738), poet, was the son of Philip Frowde, deputy postmaster-general from 1678 to 1688 (HAYDN, *Book of Dignities*, p. 198). His grandfather, Colonel Philip Frowde, for his faithful adherence to Charles I and Charles II was knighted on 10 March 1664–5 (LE NEVE, *Knights*, Harl. Soc., p. 190), and appointed governor of the post office (*Cal. State Papers*, Dom. 1660–1667; *London Daily Post*, 28 Dec. 1738). From Eton, where young Philip was contemporary with Walpole (dedication to *The Fall of Saguntum*), Frowde passed to Magdalen College, Oxford, as a gentleman-commoner, and became one of Addison's pupils (A. B., *The History of Saguntum*, p. 51). He did not take a degree. To vol. ii. of 'Musarum Anglicanarum Analecta,' 8vo, Oxford, 1699, edited by Addison, Frowde contributed (pp. 145–7) 'Cursus Glacialis, Anglicè, Scating.' In May 1720 Curll published these justly admired verses as Addison's, together with an English version also supposed to be Addison's, and an impudent preface by one T. N., who states that although Addison was well known to be the author, he had always allowed Frowde to pass them as his own. An anonymous imitation in English appeared in 1774; there is also a translation in 'Miscellanea,' by J[ames] G[lassford], 4to, Edinburgh, 1818 (pp. 24–9). Frowde wrote likewise a frosty blank verse tragedy entitled 'The Fall of Saguntum,' 8vo, London, 1727, in which the influence of 'Cato' is clearly perceptible. It was acted at Lincoln's Inn Fields on 16 Jan. 1726–7 (GENEST, *Hist of the Stage*, iii. 191–192), Quin representing Eurydamas and delivering the prologue by Theobald. The tragedy obtained only about three representations, and is chiefly remarkable for an exquisitely absurd dedication to Sir Robert Walpole, who is described as 'bringing the learning and arts of Greece and Rome into the cabinet; either that to instruct in the depths of reasoning; or these in the rules of governing.' Previously to its performance an enthusiastic friend, A. B., possibly Frowde himself, undertook to explain for the benefit of 'a lady of quality' the numerous historical and classical allusions in the play in 'The History of Saguntum,' 8vo, London, 1727, in which he is also at pains to prove the dramatist's superiority over Silius Italicus, from whose 'Punica' the plot is partly derived. Another lugubrious tragedy in blank verse, 'Philotas,' 8vo, London, 1731 (another edition, 12mo, London, 1735), brought out at Lincoln's Inn Fields on 3 Feb. 1730–1, with Quin again in the cast, met with an even colder reception, though it was suffered to run for six nights (*ib.* iii. 310–11). Fielding has introduced an ironical encomium on ' Philotas' in 'Joseph Andrews.' Frowde died unmarried at his lodgings in Cecil Street, Strand, in December 1738, and was buried in the cemetery in Lamb's Conduit Fields (*London Daily Post*, 22 and 28 Dec. 1738 ; *Admon. Act Book*, P. C. C. 1739). His portrait, by T. Murray, painted in 1732, was engraved by Faber in 1738 (NOBLE, *Continuation of Granger*, iii. 307–8).

[Baker's Biog. Dram. 1812, i. 257–8, ii. 217, iii. 146 ; Hist. Reg. vol. xxiii. ; Chron. Diary, p. 49 ; Luttrell's Relation of State Affairs, 1857, i. 521, ii. 158, iv. 199 ; Will of Sir P. Frowde (P. C. C. 99 and 127, Bunce); Chester's London Marriage Licenses (Foster), col. 517.]   G. G.

FROWYK, SIR THOMAS (*d.* 1506), judge, a member of an important family of citizens of London, among whom king's goldsmiths, aldermen, and mayors are to be found (see PRICE, *Guildhall of the City of London*, 1886),was second son of Sir Thomas Frowyk of Gunnersbury, by his wife Joan, daughter and heiress of Richard and Joan Sturgeon. Born at Gunnersbury at least as early as November 1464, when he is mentioned by name in the will of his grandmother, Isabella Frowyk, he received his education at Cambridge. As Fuller (*Worthies*, ed. 1662, p. 183) says that he died before he was forty years old, which is confirmed by a statement in Croke's 'Keilwey's Reports' (ed. 1688, p. 85) that he died 'in florida juventute sua,' he must have joined the bar at a very early age, as his name occurs in the year-books of 1489. He was a member of the Inner Temple, and became serjeant in Trinity term 1494, according to the year-book. Dugdale, however, makes this event two years later. In May 1501 he was appointed a judge of assize in the western counties. In 1502, along with Mr. Justice Fisher and Conyngsbye, king's serjeant, he acted as arbitrator between the university and town of Cambridge, and by his award, 11 July, defined their respective jurisdictions. On 30 Sept. 1502 he succeeded Sir Thomas Wood as chief justice of the common pleas, and was knighted at Richmond the Christmas following. On

17 Oct. 1506 he died, and was buried at Finchley. According to Fuller, who says that he was ' one of the youngest men that ever enjoyed that office,' he was 'accounted the oracle of law in his age.' By his first wife, Joan Bardville, he had one son, Thomas (*d.s.p.*); his second wife, Elizabeth, married after his death Thomas Jakys ; Frideswide, Frowyk's daughter and heiress by her, married Sir Thomas Cheyney of Shirland.

[Foss's Judges of England ; Dugdale's Chron. Ser. ; Cass's South Mimms, p. 99, London and Middlesex Archæolog. Soc. 1877, which corrects Foss ; the Society's Transactions,iv. 260 ; Cooper's Athenæ Cantabr. i. 10 ; Weever's Monuments, p. 333 ; Plumpton Correspondence, Camd. Soc. pp. 152, 165 ; Bibl. Legum Angliæ, ii. 192 ; Rot. Parl. vi. 522 ; Notes and Queries, 1st ser. v. 332.]   J. A. H.

FRY, CAROLINE (1787–1846), author of ' The Listener.' [See WILSON.]

FRY, EDMUND, M.D. (1754–1835), typefounder, son of Joseph Fry (1728–1787) [q.v.], was born at Bristol in 1754. He studied medicine ; took the degree of M.D. at Edinburgh, and spent some time at St. George's Hospital, London. In 1782 his father admitted his two sons, Edmund and Henry, as partners in the type-foundry business in Queen Street, London. The father retired in 1787, when the new firm, Edmund Fry & Co., issued their first ' Specimen of Printing Types,' followed the next year by an enlarged edition. Several founts of the oriental type, which fill twelve pages, were cut by Fry. In 1788 the printing business was separated from the foundry, and remained at Worship Street as the 'Cicero Press,' under the management of Henry Fry. The foundry was removed to a place opposite Bunhill Fields in Chiswell Street, and new works erected in a street then called Type Street. Homer's series of the classics (1789–1794), printed by Millar Ritchie, were from the characters of the Type Street foundry. In 1793 ' Edmund Fry & Co., letter founders to the Prince of Wales,' produced a ' Specimen of Metal-cast Ornaments curiously adjusted to paper,' which gained vogue among printers. The next year Fry took Isaac Steele into partnership, and published a ' Specimen ' which ' shows a marked advance on its predecessors' (T. B. REED, *Old English Letter Foundries*, p. 306). In 1798 he circulated a ' Prospectus ' of the great work on which he had been occupied for sixteen years, published as ' Pantographia,' containing accurate Copies of all the known Alphabets of the World, together with an English explanation of the peculiar Force and Power of each Letter, to which are added Specimens of all well-authenticated

Oral Languages, forming a Comprehensive Digest of Phonology,' 1799, 8vo. The volume contains more than two hundred alphabets, including eighteen varieties of the Chaldee and thirty-two of the Greek. Many of the characters were expressly cut by Fry for his book. On the admission of George Knowles in 1799, the firm took the name of Fry, Steele, & Co. At the commencement of the present century the modern-faced type supplanted the old-faced. 'Specimens of modern cut printing types from the foundry of Messrs. Fry & Steele' are given in C. Stower's 'Printer's Grammar,' 1808, 8vo. About this time Fry reassumed sole management of the business. In 1816 a 'Specimen of Printing Types by Edmund Fry, Letter Founder to the King and Prince Regent,' was published. The firm soon after became Edmund Fry & Son, on the admission of his son, Windover. Fry cut several founts of oriental types for the university of Cambridge, the British and Foreign Bible Society, and other bodies. In a 'Specimen' printed in 1824 the name is changed back to 'Edmund Fry' at 'the Polyglot Foundry.' In 1828 he endeavoured to dispose of his business, and issued a descriptive circular (see REED, pp. 310–12). It was purchased by William Thorowgood of Fann Street, and the stock removed in 1829. It has since been in the hands of Thorowgood & Besley, then R. Besley & Co., and now Sir Charles Reed & Sons. In 1833 twenty designs for raised type for the blind were submitted to the Royal Scottish Society of Arts, who had offered a prize for the best example. Among them was one from Fry, to whom the gold medal was awarded a couple of years after his death (*Transactions*, 1837, i.), which took place at Dalby Terrace, City Road, London, at the age of eighty-one, on 22 Dec. 1835.

Fry was one of the most learned of the English typefounders, but retired with a very small competence. He was a member of the Company of Stationers. He was married twice: first to Jenny, daughter of Nicholas Windover, of Stockbridge, Hampshire, of whose issue one son only survived, Windover Fry (1797–1835); secondly to Ann Hancock, by whom he had a son, Arthur (1809–78). A portrait of Fry, painted by Frédérique Boileau, was shown at the Caxton Exhibition in 1877 (*Catalogue*, p. 336). A silhouette has been reproduced by Reed (*Letter Foundries*, p. 298) and Fry (*Memoir*, p. 16).

[Information from Mr. W. E. Fry; T. B. Reed's Old English Letter Foundries, 1887; T. Fry's Memoir of Francis Fry (not published), 1887; T. C. Hansard's Typographia, 1825; Joseph Smith's Descr. Cat. of Friends' Books, 1867, vol. i.; Gent. Mag. 1836, new ser. v. 557–8.]   H. R. T.

FRY, ELIZABETH (1780–1845), prison reformer, born at Earlham in Norfolk, 21 May 1780, was third daughter of John Gurney, banker in Norwich, and member of an old quaker family. Her younger brothers included Daniel Gurney [q. v.] and Joseph John Gurney [q. v.] Elizabeth in youth joined in social gaieties. Under the preaching and influence of an American named Savery she became deeply impressed by the gospel. Her earliest work was to visit the poor at Earlham and in Norwich, relieving the sick, and forming a class for the instruction of the children. At the age of twenty she married Joseph Fry, who appears to have been of a much colder and more commonplace nature than his wife. Their family was large. Amid all her public labours she never ceased to devote herself to their welfare; it was a great disappointment to her that some of them left the Society of Friends.

Soon after her marriage she was much exercised by the question whether or not she was called to the ministry among her people. Naturally she had an intense aversion to such a work, but on the death of her father, when she was twenty-nine, she was constrained to take part in the public service, and thereafter experienced such 'incomings of love, joy, peace,' that she no longer doubted, and was accordingly soon after recognised as a minister. She spoke with marvellous effect. The pathos of her voice was almost miraculous, and melted alike the hardest criminals and the most impervious men of the world. Cool observers who had witnessed the effects of her appeals in Newgate prison could hardly describe the scene without tears.

Her connection with prisons began practically in 1813. As a child of fifteen she had been deeply interested in the house of correction at Norwich, and had prevailed on her father to allow her to visit it. At the instigation of some of her friends who had come to know of the state of things at Newgate, and particularly of William Forster (1784–1854) [q. v.], she now turned her attention to the condition of the female prisoners. The state of things was appalling. Nearly three hundred women, with their children, were huddled together in two wards and two cells; some of them convicted, some not yet tried, innocent and guilty, misdemeanants and felons, all tumbled together; without employment, without nightclothes or bedclothes, sleeping on the bare floor, cooking and washing, eating and sleeping in the same apartment. A tap in the prison gave them the opportunity of supplying themselves with drink. Even the governor was afraid to trust himself in the place, and when the quakers were about to visit it he advised them to leave their watches behind. 'The begging,' as she afterwards described the scene to a committee of the House of Commons, 'swearing, gaming, fighting, singing, dancing, dressing-up in men's clothes were too bad to be described, so that we did not think it suitable to admit young persons with us.'

At first she tried no more than to supply the most destitute with clothes. Then she established a school, which was very successful. A matron was afterwards appointed. But the main cause of reformation was her personal influence and exertions. The reading of the scriptures was a leading part of her remedial measures, and her impressive tones and profound reverence made a deep impression. She was the heart and soul of an association formed in 1817 for the improvement of female prisoners in Newgate. The effects of her labours were thus described by the American minister of the day : 'Two days ago I saw the greatest curiosity in London, aye and in England too, compared to which Westminster Abbey, the Tower, Somerset House, the British Museum, nay parliament itself, sink into utter insignificance. I have seen Elizabeth Fry in Newgate, and I have witnessed there the miraculous effect of true christianity upon the most depraved of human beings. And yet the wretched outcasts have been tamed and subdued by the christian eloquence of Mrs. Fry. . . .'

Her success attracted the attention of all classes, including royalty. Transported criminals were sent in those days to New South Wales, and the voyage was performed without classification, employment, or superintendence. At New South Wales no arrangements were made for enabling them to earn an honest living. Mrs. Fry exerted herself greatly to induce the government to make proper regulations for the voyage, and to provide a suitable home and proper employments for them on arriving.

She took a lively interest in the condition of other prisons besides Newgate. Sometimes combining her work as a minister of the quaker communion with her prison labours, she would travel through the country, especially visiting places where there were prisons, ascertaining their condition, conferring with the local authorities, making suggestions to them, and forming ladies' associations for more effectually carrying out the object. Her visits, too, extended beyond the limits of the United Kingdom. In 1820 she corresponded with the Princess Sophie Mestchersky of Russia; the dowager-empress became deeply interested, and her son Nicholas allowed her

to convert a royal palace into a palace prison. Mrs. Fry, however, did not desire to encourage such sentimental philanthropy. In France, Louis-Philippe and his queen received her kindly; so did the king of Prussia and his family. At Kaiserswerth she had a most interesting time; Fliedner owned that her example had moved him greatly; while she was impressed, after visiting Kaiserswerth, with the importance of having trained nurses to attend the sick, and instituted an order of 'nursing sisters,' whose aid has been sought and valued by persons of all classes.

Although prison reform was her chief work, she attended to other questions. She was much impressed by the miseries of homeless wanderers in London during the rigorous winter of 1819-20, and especially by the death of a poor boy who was found frozen to death on a doorstep. A 'nightly shelter for the homeless' was the result, soup and bread, as well as a bed, being given to those who applied. The scheme prospered under a committee of ladies, of whom she was the head, and they did not limit their efforts merely to providing the night's lodging, but tried to find occupation for the unemployed. In like manner, finding Brighton to be greatly infested with beggars, she instituted a district visiting society designed to relieve real distress, to prevent mendicity and imposture, and encourage industry. Observing how the members of the blockade or preventive service were exposed to dreary idleness, she got them a supply of bibles and useful books, and by-and-by libraries were supplied to the preventive stations. A remark on the temptations of discharged prisoners led to the opening, by a lady who heard it, of the Royal Manor Hall Asylum.

In 1828 her husband became bankrupt, and he and his family sank from affluence to poverty. Much suffering was entailed on others, and Mrs. Fry could no longer help the needy as she had been accustomed to do. But she continued her duties as a minister, in addition to all her philanthropic work and her domestic duties. She was equally at home with all ranks; at one time we find her entertaining the king of Prussia at dinner, at another drinking tea with a poor shoemaker who had been able to procure but one luxury for her entertainment—a little fresh butter. She died at Ramsgate on 12 Oct. 1845, and was buried in the Friends' burial-ground at Barking. Mrs. Fry was the author of: 1. 'Observations on . . . Female Prisoners,' Lond., 1827. 2. 'Report by Mrs. Fry and J. J. Gurney on their late visit to Ireland,' Lond., 1827. 3. Preface to John Venn's 'Sermon on Gradual Progress of Evil,' Lond., 1830. 4. 'Texts for

Every Day in the Year,' Lond., 1831; translated into French, German, and Italian.

[Memories of [Mrs. Fry], by her daughter, R. E. C[resswell], 1845 ; Memoirs of the Life of Mrs. Fry, by two of her daughters, 1847 ; Abridged Memoir by Mrs. Cresswell, 1856 ; Memoirs of Mrs. Elizabeth Fry, by Thomas Timpson, 1847 ; The Life of Elizabeth Fry, compiled from her Journals, by Susanna Corder, 1853 ; Smith's Friends' Books, i. 811–13.]   W. G. B.

FRY, FRANCIS (1803–1886), bibliographer, born at Westbury-on-Trym, near Bristol, on 28 Oct. 1803, was the second son of Joseph Storrs Fry (1769–1835). He was educated at a large school at Fishponds, in the neighbourhood of Frenchay, kept by a quaker named Joel Lean, and commenced his business training at Croydon. From his twentieth year to middle age he devoted himself to the rapidly increasing business of the firm of J. S. Fry & Sons, cocoa and chocolate manufacturers, at Bristol, in which he was afterwards a partner. In 1833 he married Matilda, only daughter of Daniel and Anne Penrose, of Brittas, co. Wicklow. He took a part in the introduction of railways in the west of England, and was a member of the board of the Bristol and Gloucester railway, which held its first sitting 11 July 1839, retaining his position during the various amalgamations of the line until its union with the Midland. He was also a director of the Bristol and Exeter, the South Devon, and other railways. He took a principal share in managing the Bristol Waterworks (1846) until his death. In 1839 he removed to Cotham, between Bristol and Redland, and built a house close to the old Tower, represented in many of the books which he afterwards purchased. With William Forster, father of W. E. Forster [q. v.], and Robert Alsop he visited Northern Italy in 1850, as a deputation from the Society of Friends to various crowned heads, praying for their countenance in the abolition of slavery (B. SEEBOHM, *Memoirs of William Forster*, 1865, ii. 284). In 1852 he made proposals to the railway companies for a general parcel despatch throughout the United Kingdom. He catalogued the library of the Monthly Meeting at Bristol in 1860, and visited Germany. A discovery made by him at Munich about the books printed at Worms by Peter Schœffer the younger enabled him to decide that Tyndale's first English New Testament came from Schœffer's press. Two years later Fry produced his careful facsimile reprint, by means of tracing and lithography, of Tyndale's New Testament (1525 or 1526), the first complete edition printed in English, from the only perfect copy known, now in the Baptist

College, Bristol. In the same year he edited a facsimile reprint of the pamphlet known as the 'Souldier's Pocket Bible,' distributed to Cromwell's army, and discovered by G. Livermore of Boston, who had himself reprinted it the previous year. Several editions were circulated among the soldiers during the American civil war. It was somewhat altered and enlarged as the 'Christian Soldier's Penny Bible' (1693), also facsimiled and edited by Fry. In 1863 he issued a couple of small rare pieces illustrative of Tyndale's version, and in 1865 published his remarkable bibliographical treatise on the Great Bible of 1539, the six editions of Cranmer's Bible of 1540 and 1541, and the five editions of the authorised version. Fry visited many private and public libraries to collate different copies of these bibles, and was able to settle the peculiarities of the various issues. This work was followed by his account of Coverdale's translation of the Scriptures, and his description of forty editions of Tyndale's version, most of which vary among themselves. These three books are marked by laborious accuracy, great bibliographical acumen, and a profound acquaintance with the history of the English Bible.

He was a member of the committee of the Bristol Philosophical Society, as well as of the Bristol Museum and Library. Books and china formed his chief study. His collection of specimens produced at the Bristol factory between 1768 and 1781 was particularly complete. Many examples are described by Hugh Owen (*Two Centuries of Ceramic Art in Bristol*, 1873, pp. 78–9, 97, 243, &c.) His collection of bibles and testaments numbered nearly thirteen hundred, chiefly English, especially editions of the versions of Tyndale, Coverdale, and Cranmer, but with a number of first editions in other languages. He took an active interest in many associations for social improvement. He died 12 Nov. 1886, soon after the completion of his eighty-third year, and was buried in the Friends' graveyard at King's Weston, near Bristol.

His writings are: 1. 'A Catalogue of Books in the Library belonging to the Monthly Meeting in Bristol,' 3rd edit. Bristol, 1860, 8vo. 2. 'The First New Testament printed in the English Language (1525 or 1526), translated from the Greek by William Tyndale, reproduced in facsimile, with an Introduction,' Bristol, 1862, sm. 8vo. 3. 'The Souldiers Pocket Bible, printed at London by G. B. and R. W. for G. C. 1643, reproduced in facsimile, with an Introduction,' London, 1862, sm. 8vo (this consists of texts of Scripture, chiefly from the Geneva version, with special applications). 4. 'The Christian Soldiers Penny Bible, London, printed by R. Smith for Sam. Wade, 1693, reproduced in facsimile with an Introductory Note,' London, 1862, sm. 8vo (No. 3 altered, with the texts from the authorised version somewhat incorrectly quoted). 5. 'A proper Dyaloge betwene a gentillman and a husbandman eche complaynynge to other their miserable calamite through the ambicion of clergye with a compendious olde treatyse shewynge howe that we ought to have the Scripture in Englysshe, Hans Luft, 1530, reproduced in facsimile, with an Introduction,' London, 1863, 8vo. 6. 'The prophete Jonas, with an Introduction by Wm. Tyndale, reproduced in facsimile, to which is added Coverdale's version of Jonah, with an Introduction,' London, 1863, 8vo (Nos. 5 and 6 reproduced from the unique copies in the library of Lord Arthur Hervey). 7. 'The Standard Edition of the English New Testament of the Genevan Version,' London, 1864, 8vo (reprinted from the 'Journal of Sacred Literature,' July 1864). 8. 'A Description of the Great Bible, 1539, and the six editions of Cranmer's Bible, 1540 and 1541, printed by Grafton and Whitchurch; also of the editions in large folio of the Authorised Version printed in 1611, 1613, 1617, 1634, 1640; illustrated with titles and with passages from the editions, the genealogies and the maps, copied in facsimile, also with an identification of every leaf of the first seven and of many leaves of the other editions, on fifty-one plates, together with an original leaf of each of the editions described,' London, 1865, folio. 9. 'The Bible by Coverdale, 1535, remarks on the titles, the year of publication, &c., with facsimiles,' London, 1867, 8vo. 10. 'A List of most of the Words noticed exhibiting the peculiar orthography used in Tindale's New Testament,' Bristol, 1871, folio (single sheet, circulated to inquire as to the edition 'finished in 1535'). 11. 'A Bibliographical Description of the Editions of the New Testament, Tyndale's Version in English, with numerous readings, comparisons of texts, and historical notices, the notes in full from the edition of November 1534, an account of two octavo editions of the New Testament of the Bishop's version, without numbers to the verses, illustrated with 73 plates,' London, 1878, 4to. 12. 'Description of a Title-page of a New Testament dated anno 1532,' Bristol, 1885, 4to (with facsimile of title-page, two leaves).

[A Brief Memoir of Francis Fry of Bristol, by his son, Theodore Fry, privately printed, 1887, 8vo, with portraits of Fry and members of his family, and other illustrations; Joseph Smith's Descriptive Catalogue of Friends' Books, 1867, i. 814–15.]   H. R. T.

FRY, JOHN (1609–1657), theological writer, son of William Fry of Iwerne Minster, Dorsetshire, by Milicent, daughter of Robert Swaine of Tarrant Gunville, Dorsetshire, was born in 1609, being fourteen years of age at the herald's visitation of Dorset in 1623. Wood's account, to be received with caution, is that he 'had ran through most, if not all, religions, even to Rantisme.' In October 1640 he was elected a member for Shaftesbury in the Long parliament, but his election was declared void. Somewhat later (probably after the order of 6 Sept. 1643) he was placed on the county committee for Wiltshire, which acted in conjunction with the committee for plundered ministers. Dugdale calls him a colonel, but there is no evidence that he was in the parliamentary army. After Pride's purge (6 Dec. 1648) he was called to the parliament, put on the committee for plundered ministers, and on 6 Jan. 1649 was included in the commission for the trial of the king. He owed his appointment to his having severed himself from the 'rigid presbyterians,' though it does not appear that he joined any other religious body.

Fry is commonly called a regicide, but he attended only the early sittings of the high court. He was one of seven commissioners whose places had been filled by others, before 27 Jan., the date when sentence was passed; nor did he sign the warrant for the king's execution. It may be doubted whether his absence is to be explained by his having to meet a charge of blasphemy, or whether, as is more probable, that charge was brought against him in consequence of some reluctance on his part to proceed to extreme measures against the king.

For a number of years, according to his own account, Fry had been 'a searcher of the scriptures,' and his conversation had given the impression, a twelvemonth back, that he denied the deity of Christ, an impression which he declares to be groundless. But he was willing to extend toleration to antitrinitarians. On or about 15 Jan. 1649 he was in the committee-room of the House of Commons when Cornelius Holland [q. v.] asked him to give his aid in the committee for plundered ministers towards the liberation of a minister who had lain two or three years in prison for 'denying the personality of Christ.' This prisoner was almost certainly John Biddle [q. v.] Fry readily agreed to the request. Hereupon Colonel John Downes [q. v.], who was present, broke into passionate language on the subject of Fry's own opinions. Two or three days later Fry had a discussion with Downes in the painted chamber, where the high court was about to hold its sitting, and heard soon after that Downes had sought the Speaker's advice in framing a charge of blasphemy against him. The house suspended him till he should clear himself. He sent in a written paper declaring the sacred three to be 'equally God,' but objecting to the terms 'person' and 'subsistence.' This was accepted as satisfactory, and Fry was restored.

Next month he published a narrative of the case ('The Accuser Sham'd'), appending his exculpatory paper, with an offensive heading. This publication brought out several pamphlets in reply. One of them, in allusion to Fry's title-page, bore the title, 'M. Fry his Blasphemy and Error blown up and down the Kingdome with his owne Bellowes,' &c., 1649. Fry's most considerable opponent was Francis Cheynell [q. v.], who published his 'Divine Trinunity,' 1650, to meet the charge of tritheism preferred by Fry against some theological writers. Cheynell affirms that Fry was the first who had employed in English the expression 'Trinity of the Godhead.' His suspicion that Fry had been acquainted with 'the deified atheists of the Family of Love' is probably the foundation of Wood's accusation of 'rantisme.' Fry retorted in 'The Clergy in their Colours,' in which he disparaged the assembly's catechism, attacked the doctrine of free-will, argued against 'believing things above reason,' assumed the attitude of a critical free-lance ('my aym is not to write positive but negative things'), and satirised the 'wrye mouths, squint eyes, and screw'd faces' of popular divines.

Downes brought both of Fry's books under the notice of parliament. The house on 24 Feb. 1651 voted the publication of the narrative and paper a breach of privilege, condemned certain of Fry's statements as 'erroneous, prophane, and highly scandalous,' ordered the books to be burned in the New Palace Yard and the Old Exchange, and disabled Fry from sitting in parliament. Soon afterwards appeared an anonymous and undated pamphlet, 'A Discussion of Mr. Frye's Tenets lately condemned in Parliament,' &c., which Wood assigns to Cheynell without much ground. A more temperate reply was 'Θεῖος. Divine Beames of Glorious Light,' &c., 1651 (1 March). Wood says that Fry, after his expulsion, consorted with Biddle, but there is no evidence of his adoption of Biddle's views; his tendency was rather in a Sabellian direction.

He died at the end of 1656 or beginning of 1657. His will is dated 29 Dec. 1656, and was proved on 15 June 1657. He married Anna, probably daughter of Lindsay of Poole,

and had five sons and three daughters, one of his sons being Stephen Fry, M.D., of Trinity College, Oxford. At the Restoration Fry's property was forfeited for the part he had taken in the trial of the king.

He published: 1. 'The Accuser Sham'd; or, a Pair of Bellows to blow off that Dust cast ... by Col. Jo. Downs,' &c., February 1648 [i.e. 17 Feb. 1649], 8vo; prefixed is 'A Word to the Priests, Lawyers, Royalists, Self-Seekers, and Rigid-Presbyterians;' appended is 'A Brief Ventilation of that chaffie and absurd opinion of three Persons or Subsistences in the Godhead,' being his paper sent in to the house. 2. 'The Clergy in their Colours; or, a Brief Character of them,' &c., 1650, 8vo (published 28 or 29 Nov.)

[Wood's Athenæ Oxon. ed. Bliss, iii. 705 sq.; Rushworth's Hist. Coll. (abridged), 1798, vi. 563, 574, 594, 603; Noble's Lives of the English Regicides, 1798, i. 247; Wallace's Antitrin. Biog. 1850, iii. 206; works cited above; information from E. A. Fry.]   A. G.

FRY, JOHN (1792–1822), bookseller and author, was born in 1792. He was always in bad health, and devoted his leisure hours, when connected with the bookselling firm of Thomas Fry & Co., 46 High Street, Bristol, to the study of early English literature. Some of the prefaces of his pieces are dated from Kingsdown, Somersetshire. Besides his published works he left several in manuscript, among them one he styled 'Bibliophilia,' editions of the writings of the Rev. William Hamilton and William Browne, and biographical sketches of eminent Bristolians. After a lingering illness he died at Bristol, 28 June 1822, at the age of thirty. He published: 1. 'Metrical Trifles in Youth,' Bristol, 1810, 8vo. 2. 'The Legend of Mary Queen of Scots, and other ancient Poems, now first published from MSS. of the XVIth century, with an Introduction, Notes, &c.,' London, 1810, 8vo. 3. 'A Selection from the Poetical Works of Thomas Carew,' London, 1810, sm. 8vo (commended in 'British Critic,' February 1810). 4. 'Pieces of Ancient Poetry from Unpublished MSS. and Scarce Books,' Bristol, 1814, 4to (102 copies printed). 5. 'George Whetstone's Metrical Life of George Gascoigne, 1577,' Bristol, 1815, 4to (100 copies). 6. 'Bibliographical Memoranda in illustration of Old English Literature,' Bristol, 1816, 4to.

[Gent. Mag. December, vol. xcii. pt. ii. p. 566.]
H. R. T.

FRY, JOSEPH (1728–1787), typefounder, was born in 1728. He was the eldest son of John Fry (d. 1775) of Sutton Benger, Wiltshire, author of 'Select Poems,'

1774, 4th edition, 1793. He was educated in the north of England, and afterwards bound apprentice to Henry Portsmouth of Basingstoke, an eminent doctor (*Gent. Mag.* 1787, vol. lvii. pt. i. p. 385), whose eldest daughter, Anna, he afterwards married. He was the first member of his family to settle in Bristol, where he acquired a considerable medical practice, and 'was led to take a part in many new scientific undertakings' (HUGH OWEN, *Two Centuries of Ceramic Art in Bristol,* 1873, p. 218). After a time he abandoned medicine for business pursuits. He helped Richard Champion [q. v.] in his Bristol china works, and began to make chocolate, having purchased Churchman's patent right. The chocolate and cocoa manufactory thus started has been carried on by the family down to the present day. The success of John Baskerville caused Fry to turn his attention in 1764 to type-founding, and he entered into partnership with William Pine, the first printer of the 'Bristol Gazette,' who had a large business in Wine Street. Their new type may be traced in several works issued between 1764 and 1770. The manager of Messrs. Fry & Pine was Isaac Moore, formerly a whitesmith at Birmingham (E. ROWE MORES, *Dissertation upon English Typogr. Founders,* 1778, p. 83), after whose speedy admission to partnership the business was removed to London, and carried on as 'Isaac Moore & Co., in Queen Street, near Upper Moorfields.' Luckombe mentions Moore as one of three London founders (*History of Printing,* 1770, p. 244). In 1774 the London firm produced a fine folio bible, and in 1774–1776 a well-printed edition in 5 vols., 8vo. About this time they somewhat abandoned their earlier Baskerville style of letter, to follow the more popular Caslon character. In 1774 Pine printed at Bristol a bible in a pearl type, asserted to be 'the smallest a bible was ever printed with.' To all these editions notes were added to escape the penalty of infringing the patent. Two years later the firm became J. Fry & Co., and issued in 1777 reprints of the octavo and folio bibles. Pine subsequently withdrew entirely. Fry took his sons, Edmund (*d.* 1835) [q. v.] and Henry, into partnership in 1782, and bought largely at the sale of James's foundry in that year. The business was removed to Worship Street, where in 1785 was issued 'A Specimen of Printing Types made by Joseph Fry & Sons, Letter-founders and Marking Instrument Makers by the King's Royal Letters Patent.' In the advertisement the proprietors 'flatter themselves' that the types which are called new 'will mix with, and be totally unknown from, the most approved

founts made by the late ingenious artist, William Caslon.' The next year they published another 'Specimen,' with new founts, and including seven pages of oriental types. They now called themselves 'Letter-founders to the Prince of Wales.' Up to the time of his death Fry was a partner with Alderman William Fripp, as Fry, Fripp, & Co., soap-boilers. This business is now in the hands of Christopher Thomas Brothers. Fry also had some chemical works at Battersea, in which he was assisted by his son.

Fry died after a few days' illness on 29 March 1787, aged 59, having retired from business a short time before. Like his father and grandfather he was a member of the Society of Friends, and was buried in their burial-ground at the Friars, Bristol. After his death the chocolate and cocoa manufactory was carried on by his widow under the style of Anna Fry & Son. The previous title had been Fry, Vaughan, & Co. In 1795 the works were removed from Newgate Street to Union Street, where a Watt's steam engine was erected, the first in Bristol. The son was Joseph Storrs Fry (1766–1835), whose three sons, Joseph, Francis (1803–1886) [q. v.], and Richard, were subsequently joined with him as J. S. Fry & Sons, the name the firm has since borne. His widow was associated for a short time with her sons in the type-foundry. She died at Charterhouse Square, London, 22 Oct. 1803, aged 83.

[Hugh Owen's Two Centuries of Ceramic Art in Bristol, 1873, 8vo; T. B. Reed's Old English Letter Foundries, 1887, 4to; T. Fry's Memoir of Francis Fry (not published), 1887; a wood-cut of silhouette of Joseph Fry is given in each of these works. See also Printer's Grammar, 1787; T. C. Hansard's Typographia, 1825; J. Smith's Catalogue of Friends' Books, 1867, vol. i.]

H. R. T.

FRY, WILLIAM THOMAS (1789–1843), engraver, born in 1789, worked chiefly in stipple. He engraved four portraits for Fisher's 'National Portrait Gallery,' viz., Princess Charlotte, after Sir T. Lawrence, the Earl of Liverpool, after the same, Admiral Earl Howe, after Gainsborough Dupont, and the Rev. Samuel Lee, after R. Evans. He also engraved some fine portraits, after J. Jackson, R.A., including Robert Hills, the animal painter, John Scott, the engraver, and others. For Jones's 'National Gallery' he executed eleven engravings. He was extensively employed in his profession, and died in 1843. He occasionally exhibited his engravings at the Suffolk Street exhibition.

[Bryan's Dict. of Painters and Engravers; Graves's Dict. of Artists, 1760–1880; Redgrave's Dict. of Artists.]

L. C.

FRYE, THOMAS (1710–1762), painter, mezzotint engraver, and china manufacturer, was born near Dublin in 1710, and came to England early in life, in company with Stoppelaer, a brother artist. He at first practised as a portrait painter with some success, and in 1734 painted a full-length portrait of Frederick, prince of Wales, for the hall of the Saddlers' Company in Cheapside, engraved by himself in mezzotint, and published in 1741. A portrait by him of Leveridge, the actor, was engraved in mezzotint by Pether, who was Frye's pupil in the art. Through Mr. Ellis, whose portrait he painted, Frye obtained an introduction to Sir Joshua Reynolds, and became a familiar friend. In 1744 an American brought to London, and offered to the china manufactory, which seems to have been already in existence at Bow, some samples of an earth suitable for making china like that imported by the oriental merchants. It may have been through Frye, who was then residing at West Ham close by, that he obtained this introduction; at all events, on 6 Dec. 1744 a patent was taken out by 'Edward Heylin in the parish of Bow, in the county of Middlesex, merchant, and Thomas Frye of the parish of West Ham, in the county of Essex, painter,' for 'a new method of manufacturing a certain mineral whereby a ware might be made of the same nature or kind, and equal, if not exceeding in goodness and beauty, china or porcelain ware imported from abroad. The material is an earth, the produce of the Cherokee nation in America, called by the natives *unaker*.' A second patent was taken out on 17 Nov. 1749 by Frye alone, whose epitaph (published at length in *Gent. Mag.* 1764, xxxiii. 638) grandiloquently styles him 'the Inventor and first Manufacturer of Porcelain in England.' Frye became the manager of the china manufactory, which he constructed on the model of that at Canton in China, and called 'New Canton,' and brought Bow china into some repute. Pieces of this china are sometimes marked with his initials. After spending fifteen years in this profession, his health became seriously impaired by living among the furnaces, and he was forced to relinquish an active share in the business, which rapidly declined in later years. He retired into Wales to restore his health, and resumed his former profession as a portrait and miniature painter. After twelve months he returned to London, and settled in Hatton Garden. He now engraved and published the series of lifesize portrait heads in mezzotint, by which he is best known to the world at large. These are works of great power, and their artistic merit has been generally admitted.

It is stated that Frye used to frequent the theatre in order to make drawings of royalty and other people of quality, and that the king and queen, George III and Charlotte, used to pose themselves in order to give him special facilities for his object. It is also stated that the ladies whose portraits he thus drew declined to have their names affixed to the engravings, as they did not know in what company they might appear. Many of this series, eighteen in number, are unidentified, some being of his own family; among those identified, besides the king and queen and his own portrait, are Garrick, the Duchess of Northumberland, the Gunning sisters, Elizabeth countess of Berkeley, Miss Pond, the actress, and Miss Stothouse. Complete sets are scarce; one was formed by Mr. Charles and Lady Charlotte Schreiber at Langham House, Portland Place, and there are fine examples in the print room at the British Museum. Frye was very corpulent and subject to gout; adopting an over-spare diet, he fell into a consumption, and died on 2 April 1762, in his fifty-second year. He left a son, who turned out badly, and two daughters, who assisted him in painting the china at Bow; one, Catherine, married a painter of Worcester china of the name of Willcox, and with her husband was employed by Wedgwood in a similar capacity at his works at Etruria up to her death in 1776.

Frye's epitaph quoted above also states that 'no one was more happy in delineating the human countenance. He had the correctness of Vandyck, and the colouring of Rubens. In miniature painting he equalled, if not excelled, the famous Cooper.' A portrait by Frye of Jeremy Bentham, painted in 1761, is in the National Portrait Gallery.

[Redgrave's Dict. of Artists; Chaloner Smith's British Mezzotinto Portraits; Chaffers's Marks and Monograms on Pottery and Porcelain, 7th edit. 1886; Gent. Mag. cited above.] L. C.

FRYER, EDWARD, M.D. (1761–1826), physician, was born in 1761 at Frome, Somersetshire. He was sent to the grammar school there, and afterwards apprenticed to a general practitioner of medicine in Wiltshire. He studied medicine in London, Edinburgh, and Leyden, and graduated M.D. at Leyden 29 Jan. 1785. He travelled in Europe till 1790, when he came to London, and was admitted a licentiate of the College of Physicians. He became physician to the Duke of Sussex, and resided in Upper Charlotte Street, where he died 9 Jan. 1826. He attended Barry, the painter, in his last illness, and wrote his life, a work which was published in 1825. It shows little skill in biography, being full of indefinite statements, but has the merits of moderation in its praise of its subject, and of modesty in the concealment of the personality of its author.

[Munk's Coll. of Phys. ii. 412; Fryer's Life of Barry.]   N. M.

FRYER, JOHN, M.D. (*d.* 1563), physician, born at Balsham, Cambridgeshire, was educated at Eton and elected thence to King's College, Cambridge, in 1517. He graduated B.A. in 1521 and M.A. in 1525. On 5 Nov. 1525 he was incorporated at Oxford, being one of three masters of arts who had been preferred to Cardinal Wolsey's college in that university. Proving, however, 'violent Lutherans,' they were one and all obliged to leave. He was imprisoned for heresy in the Savoy, where he solaced himself with the lute, having good skill in music. On this account a friend commended him to the master of the Savoy, who replied 'Take heed, for he that playeth is a devil, because he has departed from the catholic faith' (WOOD, *Fasti Oxon.* ed. Bliss, i. 72). The date of his incarceration in the Savoy is nowhere recorded, but by 1528 he was again a prisoner, this time in the Fleet. On 16 Sept. 1528 he addressed from that prison an elegant Latin letter to Wolsey, wherein he extols the latter's generosity, 'which he had often experienced before.' 'To Wolsey,' he writes, 'he owed his restitution to life from that destruction into which he had precipitated himself by his own folly' (*Letters and Papers of Reign of Henry VIII,* ed. Brewer, vol. iv. pt. ii. No. 4741). Fryer's scholarship and personal qualities gained him the friendship of many eminent men, especially that of Edward Fox [q. v.], then provost of King's College. By Fox's assistance he was enabled to study medicine at Padua, where he took the degree of M.D. in 1535 (*ib.* ed. Gairdner, vol. ix. No. 648). It is probable that he was incorporated on this degree at Cambridge. In December 1535 he attended Fox to the diet at Smalcalde in Saxony (*ib.* vol. ix. Nos. 917, 1011). The following year he returned home (*ib.* vol. x. Nos. 321, 411, 418), and ultimately settled at London, residing in that part of Bishopsgate Street which is within the parish of St. Martin Outwich. He was admitted a fellow of the College of Physicians in 1536, was censor in 1541, 1553, 1554, 1555, and 1559, elect in 1547, consiliarius in 1548 and 1555 to 1560, and president in 1549 and 1550. To judge by a letter from him to Thomas, lord Cromwell, Fryer must have possessed no inconsiderable share of humour. He had attended the Bishop of Rochester in his last

illness. On the bishop's death his goods were seized to the king's use, so that for twelve days' labour and four nights' watching Fryer received nothing. Thereupon he besought Cromwell's mediation on his behalf, observing, 'Except your lordshype be good to me, I shal bothe lose my labour, my frende, and also my physycke; and truely if physycyens shuld take no monye for them that they kyll, as well as for them that they save, theyr lyvyngs shuldbe very thynne and bare.' As regards the amount of his recompense and reward for his pains he remarks: 'I beseche your lordshyppe it may be so motche the mor lyberall, becawse it shalbe the last payment; for of them that scape, we may take the lesse, becawse we hope they shale ons cum agayne in to our handys' (SIR H. ELLIS, *Original Letters,* 3rd ser. ii. 346-7). The bishop here alluded to has been erroneously supposed to have been Fisher; it was Hilsey who died in 1539. On 24 June 1560 Fryer was committed to the compter, but for what offence does not appear. He was liberated on the following day. In 1561 he was imprisoned in the Tower, on this occasion not for Lutheranism but for catholicism, 'wherein he was educated' (cf. *Cal. State Papers,* Dom. Ser. Addenda, 1547-65, p. 510). There is extant an examination of his servant, Thomas How, organ-maker, taken before Sir William Chester, lord mayor of London, 23 April 1561. It relates to the visit of his master to Dr. Martyn at Buntingford, Hertfordshire, and states that neither he nor his master to his knowledge had received the communion since the queen's accession (*ib.* 1547-80, p. 174). Fryer was liberated from prison in the beginning of August 1563, but died of the plague on the ensuing 21 Oct., and was buried at St. Martin Outwich. It is probable that he became outwardly reconciled to the English church before his death, as his will nuncupative (P. C. C. 2, Stevenson) is attested by the then curate of St. Martin's, one Albert Coopeman. His wife, Ursula, and several of his children also lost their lives by the pestilence. In her will, proved 28 Dec. 1563 (P. C. C. 39, Chayre), Mrs. Fryer, after desiring burial with her husband, names as her children three sons, Thomas, Jarmyn, and Reinolde, and two daughters, Mathe and Lucie.

[Cooper's Athenæ Cantabr. i. 225; Munk's Coll. of Phys. (1878), i. 31-2; Gillow's Bibliographical Dict. of the English Catholics, ii. 334.] G. G.

FRYER, JOHN, M.D. (*fl.* 1571), physician, who has been erroneously described as the son of John Fryer, M.D. (*d.* 1563) [q. v.], was born at Godmanchester, Huntingdon-shire, and educated at Cambridge, where he proceeded B.A. in 1544, M.A. in 1548, and commenced M.D. in 1555, when he subscribed the Roman catholic articles. His college is not known. He was one of the disputants in the physic act kept before Queen Elizabeth in the university 7 Aug. 1564. He subsequently settled at Padua for the sake of his religion. He is author of : 1. 'Hippocratis Aphorismi Versibus scripti . . . Per Iöannem Frerum Gormoncestrensem Anglum,' 8vo, London, 1567, 24 leaves, dedicated to Sir William Cecil. It was subsequently incorporated in Ἱπποκράτους οἱ ἀφορισμοί πεζικοί τε καὶ ἔμμετροι, edited by Ralph Winterton, 8vo, Cambridge, 1633. 2. Latin verses, viz. (*a*) on the death of Bucer ; (*b*) on the restoration of Bucer and Fagius ; (*c*) prefixed to Bishop Alley's 'The Poore Mans Librarie,' 1565 ; (*d*) prefixed to 'G. Haddoni Lucubrationes,' 1567 ; (*e*) prefixed to Nicholas Carr's 'Demosthenes,' 1571 ; (*f*) on the death of Nicholas Carr in 1568.

[Cooper's Athenæ Cantabr. i. 302 ; Gillow's Bibliographical Dict. of the English Catholics, ii. 334–5.]   G. G.

FRYER, JOHN, M.D. (*d.* 1672), physician, was a grandson of John Fryer, M.D. (*d.* 1563) [q. v.], and the eldest son of Thomas Fryer, M.D. (*d.* 1623, see MUNK, *Coll. of Phys.* ed. 1878, i. 72-4), both of whom were fellows of the College of Physicians. He studied his profession at Padua, where he graduated M.D. 6 April 1610, and was admitted a candidate of the College of Physicians 25 June 1612. He lived in Little Britain, London, in part of the house where his father 'did dwell.' By birth a strict member of the church of Rome, he was on 29 March 1626 returned to the parliamentary commissioners by the college as 'an avowed or suspected papist.' 'This,' observes Dr. Munk, 'was probably the reason he was not admitted a fellow, as it was without doubt the cause of his brother, Thomas Fryer, M.D. (*fl.* 1623), having been refused admission as a candidate.' After remaining a candidate for more than half a century, he was, in December 1664, when honorary fellows were first created, placed at the head of the list. On 5 Aug. 1628 he was admitted a member of Gray's Inn (*Harl. MS.* 1912, f. 106), but did not proceed to the bar. He died at his house in Little Britain, 12 Nov. 1672, at the advanced age of ninety-six, and was buried on 19 Nov. (SMYTH, *Obituary*, Camden Soc. p. 97), 'in the vault of St. Botolph's Church without Aldersgate, London, where his mother and

eldest sister, Elizabeth Peacocke, lye buried.' Fryer, for his unfilial and unbrotherly conduct, had been disinherited by his father, though the latter, by will dated 2 Dec. 1617, and proved 10 May 1623 (P. C. C. 40, Swan), left him 50*l.* in token of forgiveness. He denounced, however, his son's 'many great impieties to his parents, and especially towards his tender, carefull, and mercifull mother . . . too horrible and shamefull to repeate,' and desired the world to know that he had 'brought his parents, against all rites and against nature, and especially me, his father, before the greatest magistrates, to our discredites, as may appeare by letters sent from the highest, whᶜʰ at length they, having fully ripped upp all matters, although mutch against my will, turned utterly to his utter discredit.'

His father had purchased the manor of Harlton, Cambridgeshire, of the Barnes family, as appears from his monument in Harlton Church. His second brother, Henry, who died in Little Britain, 4 June 1631, by a fall from his horse (SMYTH, p. 6), had by his will dated 27 May of that year (P. C. C. 104, St. John) provided for some of his relatives, but directed his executors to settle Harlton and his other lands to such charitable uses as they thought fit. Fryer thereupon instituted proceedings in the court of wards. The executors consented to a reference to Mr. Justice Harvey, testator's cousin and an overseer of his will, and he certified that Fryer ought to have the whole estate. The matter was eventually submitted to the arbitration of Lord-Keeper Coventry, Bishop Laud, and Secretary Coke (*Cal. State Papers*, Dom. 1631–33, pp. 360–1, 470 ; 1633–34, pp. 376, 379). Fryer evidently gained the day, for by his will dated 1 Sept. and proved 21 Nov. 1672 (P. C. C. 129 and 150, Eure), he devised the property to his nephews and executors, John Peacock of Heath House, near Petersfield, county Southampton, and Andrew Matthew, carpenter, of the city of London. The version of the story as given by Lysons (*Magna Brit.* vol. ii. pt. i., 'Cambridgeshire') is erroneous.

[Munk's Coll. of Phys. (1878), i. 319–21.]
                                              G. G.

FRYER, JOHN, M.D. (*d.* 1733), traveller, eldest son of William Fryer of London, was a member of Trinity College, Cambridge, from which he transferred himself on 23 July 1671 to Pembroke College in the same university as a fellow-commoner (*Pembroke Coll. Register*). He took the two degrees in medicine, M.B. 'per literas regias' in 1671, and M.D. in 1683 (*Cantabr. Graduati*, ed. 1787,

p. 150), but he was not a member of the Royal College of Physicians as stated in the notice of his death in the 'Gentleman's Magazine.' On 9 Dec. 1672 he embarked at Gravesend for a lengthened tour in India and Persia, undertaken in the interests of the East India Company, and did not reach England again until 20 Aug. 1682. Nearly sixteen years elapsed before he could be persuaded to publish an account of his wanderings. At length, piqued at the frequent appearance of translations of foreign, especially French, books of travel in which English industry and enterprise were decried, and, as he adds, 'there being more than four hundred queries now by me to which I am pressed for answers,' he issued in handsome folio 'A New Account of East India and Persia, in eight Letters. Being nine years' travels, begun 1672, and finished 1681. . . . Illustrated with maps, figures, and useful tables,' London, 1698. This generally amusing book is also noteworthy as affording many curious particulars respecting the natural history and medicine of the countries visited. A Dutch version appeared, 4to, the Hague, 1700. Fryer married a niece of Rose Desborough, wife of Samuel Desborough [see under DESBOROUGH, JOHN], who mentions both in her will of 28 June 1698. He died 31 March 1733 (*Gent. Mag.* iii. 214). In the letters of administration P. C. C., granted 14 April 1733 to his daughter Anna Maria Sanderson, widow, he is described as late of the parish of Allhallows, Bread Street, London, a widower. In 1697 he was elected F.R.S. (THOMSON, *Hist. of Roy. Soc.*, appendix iv.), and continued a fellow until 1707 (*Lists of Roy. Soc.* in Brit. Mus.), but never contributed to the 'Philosophical Transactions' as asserted by Noble (*Continuation of Granger*, i. 234).

Fryer's portrait by R. White is prefixed to his 'Travels.' He himself wrote his name as 'Friar' or 'Fryar.'

[Authorities cited above.]   G. G.

FRYER, LEONARD (*d.* 1605?), sergeant-painter to Queen Elizabeth, received in 1598 the office of sergeant-painter for life. On 26 April 1605 another grant was made with survivorship to Leonard Fryer and John de Crites [see DE CRITZ] of the office of sergeant-painter, before granted to Leonard Fryer with reversion to John de Crites. As De Critz was shortly afterwards in sole possession of the office, it is probable that Fryer died about this time. In Painter-Stainers' Hall there is still preserved a richly chased cup presented by Fryer to the company in 1605.

[Cal. State Papers (Dom. Ser.), 1598 and 1605; An Account of the Worshipful Company of Painters.]   L. C.

FRYTH. [See FRITH.]

FRYTON, JOHN DE (*fl.* 1304), judge. [See BARTON, JOHN DE.]

FULBECK, WILLIAM (1560–1603?), legal writer, a younger son of Thomas Fulbeck, sometime mayor of Lincoln, was born in the parish of St. Benedict in that city in 1560. He studied at St. Alban Hall, Christ Church, and Gloucester Hall, Oxford, proceeding B.A. 1581, and M.A. 1584. In the last year he removed to London and entered Gray's Inn. He dates his 'Historicall Collection,' as Bacon did his 'Essays,' 'from my chamber in Graies Inne.' He applied himself with great devotion to legal studies, 'and, as 'tis said, had the degree of doctor of the civil law conferr'd on him elsewhere; but at what place, or by whom, I cannot yet find' (WOOD). He seems to have died about the end of Elizabeth's reign.

Fulbeck wrote: 1. 'A Book of Christian Ethicks, or Moral Philosophie,' 1587. 2. 'The Misfortunes of Arthur.' This is a masque written and prepared by eight members of Gray's Inn. Bacon helped to devise the dumb shows; Fulbeck wrote two speeches. It was produced before Queen Elizabeth at Greenwich 8 Feb. 1588. It was reprinted in Dodsley's 'Collection of Old English Plays,' 4th edit. 1874, vol. iv. 3. 'A Direction or Preparation to the Study of the Law.' This is the best known of Fulbeck's works. It was published in 1600, republished 1620; second edition, revised by T. H. Stirling, 1820. 4. 'An Historicall Collection of the Continual Factions, Tumults, and Massacres of the Romans and Italians during the space of one hundred and twentie yeares next before the Peaceable Empire of Augustus Cæsar, . . . beginning where the Historie of T. Livius doth end, and ending where Cornelius Tacitus doth begin,' 1601; republished in 1608, with a new title beginning 'An Abridgement, or rather a Bridge of Roman Histories, to passe the nearest way from Titus Livius to Cornelius Tacitus.' 5. 'A Parallele, or Conference of the Civil Law, the Canon Law, and the Common Law of England, . . . digested in sundry dialogues,' 1601, new edit. 1618. 6. 'The Pandectes of the Law of Nations, contayning severall discourses of the questions . . . of law, wherein the nations of the world doe consent and accord,' 1602. Fulbeck is a very curious writer, and often entertaining. His account of witches and the law of witchcraft (the third division of the fourteenth dialogue of the 'Parallele'), and his reasons why students should study in the morning and not after supper, in the 'Directions,' are examples. He enriches his works by quotations from many now forgotten writers. His classical allusions are often happy, and his remarks sound, notwithstanding his euphuistic style.

[Wood's Athenæ Oxon. (Bliss), i. 726 ; Notes and Queries, 29 July 1866, p. 69 ; Marvin's Legal Bibliography ; Brit. Mus. Cat.] F. W-T.

FULCHER, GEORGE WILLIAMS (1795–1855), poet and miscellaneous writer, born in 1795, carried on the business of a bookseller, stationer, and printer at Sudbury in Suffolk, where in 1825 he issued the first number of the 'Sudbury Pocket Book,' an annual which he continued to publish during his life, and to the pages of which, besides Fulcher himself, Bernard Barton, William and Mary Howitt, James Montgomery, and other less-known writers contributed. A selection from these contributions appeared under the title of 'Fulcher's Poetical Miscellany' in 1841, 12mo, reprinted in 1853. Fulcher also started in 1838 a monthly miscellany of prose and verse, entitled 'Fulcher's Sudbury Journal,' but this was not continued beyond the year. He made a courageous effort to treat pauperism poetically, publishing 'The Village Paupers, and other Poems,' London, 1845. 'The Village Paupers' is in the heroic couplet, and betrays in almost every line the influence of Crabbe and of Goldsmith's 'Deserted Village.' Of the miscellaneous poems 'The Dying Child' is the best. Fulcher also published 'The Ladies' Memorandum Book and Poetical Miscellany,' 1852 and following years; 'The Farmer's Daybook,' which reached a sixth edition in 1854, and he was engaged on a life of Gainsborough, a Sudbury man, at his death on 19 June 1855. This work, which represents much careful original research, and is written in a terse and scholarly style, was completed by his son, E. S. Fulcher, and published in London in 1856; a second edition appeared the same year. Fulcher was throughout life a diligent student, particularly of Crabbe and Cowper. Boswell's Johnson was also one of his favourite books. He was a practical botanist, and very sensitive to the beauties of nature. He took an active interest in local affairs, being one of the magistrates of the borough of Sudbury, president of the board of guardians, and several times mayor. He gave much to charities. He was buried in the churchyard of St. Gregory, Sudbury, the townspeople closing their shops, and the mayor, corpora-tion, and magistrates of the borough following the bier.

[Gent. Mag. 1855, xliv. 213 ; Allibone's Dict. of Brit. and Amer. Authors ; Brit. Mus. Cat.] J. M. R.

FULFORD, FRANCIS, D.D. (1803–1868), bishop of Montreal, second son of Baldwin Fulford of Fulford Magna, Devonshire, by Anna Maria, eldest daughter of William Adams, M.P. for Totnes, was born at Sidmouth 3 June 1803, and baptised at Dunsford, 14 Oct. 1804. He was educated at Tiverton grammar school, whence he matriculated at Oxford from Exeter College 1 Feb. 1821, and was elected a fellow of his college 30 June 1824, but vacated his fellowship 18 Oct. 1830 by marrying Mary, eldest daughter of Andrew Berkeley Drummond of Cadlands, Hampshire. Fulford proceeded B.A. in 1827, and M.A. 1838, and was created an honorary D.D. 6 July 1850. He was ordained a deacon in 1826, and became curate of Holne, Devonshire, afterwards removing to the curacy of Fawley. The Duke of Rutland instituted him to the rectory of Trowbridge, Wiltshire, in 1832, where he resided for ten years, and as a justice of the peace as well as a clergyman commanded respect and conciliated goodwill. In 1842 he accepted the rectory of Croydon, Cambridgeshire, which he held until 1845, when he was nominated by Earl Howe as minister of Curzon Chapel, Mayfair, London. On the projection of the 'Colonial Church Chronicle and Missionary Journal' in 1848 he was chosen editor, and in this way acquired a knowledge of the condition of the colonial church. On 19 July 1850 he was gazetted the first bishop of the new diocese of Montreal, Canada, and consecrated in Westminster Abbey on 25 July. He landed at St. John's on 12 Sept. and was enthroned in Christ Church Cathedral, Montreal, on 15 Sept. In the following month he was actively at work, and the church society of the diocese of Montreal was organised. On 20 Jan. 1852 the primary visitation was held, when he won great respect from all parties by his declaration that the church of England in Canada, politically considered, ' exists but as one of many religious bodies.' Montreal was next mapped out into ecclesiastical boundaries, and each district thus divided was set apart as the conventional parish of the neighbouring church. The bishop cheerfully co-operated with all the societies that were established for benevolent, scientific, and philanthropic purposes, and wrote papers for, and delivered lectures at, mechanics' institutes and working men's clubs. On 21 May 1857 he laid the foundation-stone of his new cathedral, where on Advent Sunday, 1859, he preached the opening sermon. Unfortunately the great cost of this building involved the diocese in a heavy debt, the thought of which so preyed on the bishop's mind that he practised the utmost economy throughout the remaining years of his life in an endeavour to pay off the amount. On 9 July 1860 the queen caused letters patent to be issued promoting Fulford to the office of metropolitan of Canada and elevating the see of Montreal to the dignity of a metropolitical see, with the city of Montreal as the seat of that see, and on 10 Sept. in the following year the first provincial synod of the united church of England and Ireland in Canada was held at Montreal. It was chiefly on the representation of the synod of Canada that the Archbishop of Canterbury held the pan-anglican synod at Lambeth 24-27 Sept. 1867, on which occasion the Bishop of Montreal visited England and took part in the proceedings. He, however, seems on this journey to have overtaxed his strength, and never afterwards had good health. He died in the see-house, Montreal, 9 Sept. 1868, and was buried on 12 Sept., when the universal respect which his moderation had won for him was shown by the bell of the Roman catholic church being tolled as the funeral procession passed.

Fulford was the writer of the following works : 1. 'A Sermon at the Visitation of Venerable L. Clarke, Archdeacon of Sarum,' 1833. 2. 'A Course of Plain Sermons on the Ministry, Doctrine, and Services of the Church of England,' 2 vols. 1837-40. 3. 'The Interpretation of Law and the Rule of Faith,' an assize sermon, 1838. 4. 'The Progress of the Reformation in England,' 1841. 5. 'A Pastoral Letter to the Clergy of the Diocese,' 1851. 6. 'An Address delivered in the Chapel of the General Theological Seminary of the Protestant Episcopal Church in the United States,' 1852. 7. 'A Charge delivered to the Clergy of the Diocese of Montreal,' 1852. 8. 'The Sermon at the Consecration of H. Potter to the Episcopate,' 1854. 9. 'Five Occasional Lectures delivered in Montreal,' 1859. 10. 'Sermons, Addresses, and Statistics of the Diocese of Montreal,' 1865. Fulford's latest publication was 'A Pan-Anglican Synod: a Sermon,' 1867.

[Fennings Taylor's Last Three Bishops appointed by the Crown (1870), pp. 21-130, with portrait ; Boase's Exeter College, pp. 125, 216 ; Illustrated London News, 3 Aug. 1850, p. 101, 24 Aug. p. 168, with portrait, 29 Nov. 1862, pp. 576, 587, with portrait, 26 Sept. 1868, p. 307 ; Morgan's Bibliotheca Canadensis, pp. 131-2.]

G. C. B.

FULKE, WILLIAM, D.D. (1538-1589), puritan divine, the son of Christopher Fulke, a wealthy citizen, was born in London in 1538, and is said to have been educated at St. Paul's School. As a London schoolboy he was a contemporary of Edmund Campion [q. v.], who defeated him in the competition for the silver pen offered as a prize to the city schools. He matriculated at St. John's College, Cambridge, in November 1555. He graduated B.A. in January 1557-8, and M.A. in 1563. By his father's desire he studied law at Clifford's Inn for six years, when, finding legal studies increasingly distasteful, he returned to Cambridge, and applied himself to mathematics, languages, and theology. He had already made one or two trifling essays upon astronomical subjects (see below). His father refused to help him after he relinquished the law, but his election to a foundation fellowship in 1564 placed him in comparative independence. He was thus enabled to study the text of holy scripture, having already taken up Hebrew and the other oriental languages then much neglected at Cambridge. In 1565 he was appointed principal lecturer of his college, in 1567 preacher and Hebrew lecturer, and in 1568 took his degree as B.D. Fulke on his return to Cambridge had attached himself to Thomas Cartwright (1535-1603) [q. v.], the puritan leader at Cambridge. He took a prominent part in the 'vestiarian' controversy, which was then distracting the university, and by his sermons and personal influence 'beat into the heads of younger sort such a persuasion of the superstition of the surplice,' that nearly three hundred at one time discarded it in the chapel of St. John's. The dispute led to scenes of violence, barely stopping short of bloodshed (STRYPE, Annals, II. i. 154). The contagion spread to other colleges. Discipline was relaxed, the whole university was in an uproar. Cecil found it necessary to interpose his authority as chancellor. He caused Fulke to be cited before him 'by special commandment' as the chief author of the dissension, intending, he said, 'to proceed with him himself' (ib. p. 156). Fulke was deprived of his fellowship, and expelled the college. He remained at Cambridge, took lodgings at the Falcon Inn in the Petty Cury, and continued to give lectures there and to hold public disputations. The puritans supported their champion successfully. The decree of expulsion was speedily removed, and he was readmitted to his fellowship 21 March 1566-1567, and on the 15th of the following April was elected a senior fellow. At this period of his life Fulke fell under grave suspicion of conniving at an incestuous marriage. Owing to relaxation of ancient ecclesiastical authority, connections within the prohibited degrees had become painfully common, and of these, says Strype, 'Cambridge was too guilty.' Fulke was so strongly suspected of being concerned in one of these illegal unions that he deemed it prudent to resign his fellowship. His case was heard before Bishop Cox of Ely, as visitor of the college, by whom he was acquitted, and in 1569 was a second time restored to his fellowship (STRYPE, *Parker*, i. 556). He so completely regained his reputation, that during the same year, on the vacancy of the headship, Dr. Longworth having left the college, then distracted by cabals, for fear of expulsion, Fulke, to the great disgust of Archbishop Parker, narrowly missed being elected master. Longworth, who offered himself for re-election, and Fulke, though of the same theological school, were the heads of the rival college factions. The feud became so hot that the Bishop of Ely expelled Longworth, a hot-headed and intemperate man, while Fulke, to escape a like fate, retired quietly (*ib.* i. 555–6). To console him for his disappointment, Leicester, the great favourer of the puritan party, who had supported his candidature, appointed him his chaplain, and obtained for him the livings of Warley in Essex and Dennington in Suffolk (RYMER, *Fœdera*, xv. 728), both of which he held till his death. By Leicester's influence also he obtained the degree of D.D. by royal mandate, 19 May 1572, being about to proceed to France with Edward Clinton, earl of Lincoln [q. v.] (STRYPE, *Annals*, II. i. 354–5). In the same year he was one of the friends who prevailed upon Cartwright to return from his banishment. He accompanied Cartwright in his visits to the puritans Field and Wilcox, then in prison for the publication of their 'Admonition to Parliament,' and urged them to persevere in the cause. On 10 May 1578 Leicester obtained for him the mastership of Pembroke Hall, Cambridge, vacant by the promotion of Dr. John Young to the see of Rochester, which he held till the end of his uneasy polemical life in 1589. He is said to have held frequent meetings with Chaderton, Whitaker, and other puritan divines at Cambridge for the study of holy scripture (CLARKE, *Lives*, p. 169). Fulke having no private means, and being burdened with a wife and family, found the stipend of the mastership insufficient, and got it augmented at the expense of the other members of the college. He is said by Bishop Wren to have been eager to increase the number of his college at the expense of its reputation. No fewer than twenty-six fellows were elected

in his mastership. He at once enlarged the buildings of the college by the erection of the University Hostel, to which he only contributed 20*l.*, leaving the main burden to be borne by the society. He also most inconsiderately bound his college by covenant with Queens' College to maintain six scholars, although the income was barely sufficient for three. On Chaderton's resignation in 1579 he was recommended to Lord Burghley by Dr. Still for the regius professorship of divinity, which was, however, more worthily conferred on Dr. Whitaker. In 1582 he unsuccessfully urged Cecil, then Lord Burghley, to set on foot a visitation of all the colleges in the university, by royal authority, with a view to the promotion of puritanism (*State Papers*, Dom. 10 Oct. 1582, p. 72). In 1580 he was appointed by the Bishop of Ely to hold a conference with Dr. Watson [q. v.], the deprived bishop of Lincoln, and Abbot Feckenham [q. v.], then imprisoned as papists in the bishop's castle of Wisbech, and in September 1581 was one of the divines deputed to hold a public disputation with his old schoolboy rival Campion in the Tower of London (STRYPE, *Annals*, II. ii. 361). In the same year he served the office of vice-chancellor of his university. In 1582 he was one of the body of twenty-five theologians appointed by the council to hold disputations with Romish priests and jesuits on the points of controversy between the two churches (STRYPE, *Whitgift*, i. 198). The last ten years of his life were the period of his greatest literary activity. No year passed without the appearance of one or more books in defence of protestantism, and in confutation of the doctrines of the church of Rome. His language was unmeasured, and, even in that age, he was conspicuous for the virulence of his invectives against his opponents. His learning was, however, extensive and sound, and he was an able master of controversy. His style is clear and incisive, though deformed by the coarseness of the time. He gained high reputation among protestants by his writings against Cardinal Allen [q. v.], and other leaders of the counter-reformation in England. His defence of the English translation of the Bible against the attacks of Gregory Martin, the seminarist of Rheims, bears a high reputation for learning and ability. It has been republished by the Parker Society, as well as his 'Discovery of the dangerous rock of the Papist Church, with the confutation of Stapleton and Martial.' His last work was a completion of Cartwright's unfinished confutation of the Rhemish translation of the New Testament, which was published in the year of his death, 1589, with a dedication

of Stebbing and minister of St. Martin's, Ironmonger Lane, London. He was educated at Queen's College, Cambridge, where he proceeded M.A. in 1660, and was incorporated at Oxford on 14 July 1663. He found himself, however, unable to conform, and was accordingly expelled from Warkworth, Northamptonshire, when acting as curate to Dr. Temple, the incumbent. Shortly afterwards he migrated to the west of England, preaching occasionally at Bath and Bristol. Finally he settled in London as assistant to Timothy Cruso [q. v.] at the English presbyterian meeting-house in Poor Jewry Lane. He continued with Cruso's successor, William Harris, until his death on 21 July 1701, at the age of sixty-four. His funeral sermon was preached by his friend, Jeremiah White, and published at London, 8vo, 1702. By his wife Bridget, who survived him, Fuller had two sons, born in Bristol, Francis [q. v.] and Samuel, who died about 1682. Calamy describes him as 'a facetious pleasant man,' while Samuel Palmer adds that he 'discovered great sagacity in judging of some future events.' Besides an address to the reader prefixed to Timothy Cruso's 'Three Last Sermons,' &c., 8vo, London, 1698, Fuller wrote: 1. 'Words to give to the Young-man Knowledg and Discretion. Or, the Law of Kindness in the Tongue of a Father to his Son,' 8vo, London, 1685. 2. 'A Treatise of Faith and Repentance. (A Discourse of self-denial; being an appendix to the treatise of Faith'), 8vo, London, 1685. 3. 'A Treatise of Grace and Duty,' 8vo, London, 1689. 4. 'Peace in War by Christ, the Prince of Peace. A Sermon [on Micah v. 5] preached . . . on the last Publick Fast, June the 26th, 1696,' 4to, London, 1696. 5. 'Some Rules how to use the World, so as not to abuse either That or our Selves,' 8vo, London [1695 ?] 6. 'Of the Shortness of Time' [a sermon on 1 Cor. vii. 9], 8vo, London, 1700. Job Orton found some of his works 'very excellent, entertaining, and useful.'

[Wood's Fasti Oxon, ed. Bliss, ii. 269; Calamy's Nonconf. Memorial, ed. Palmer, 1802–3, i. 159–160, iii. 46; Walter Wilson's Dissenting Churches, i. 56, 58, 64–6; Cantabr. Graduati, 1787, p. 150; Notes and Queries, 2nd ser. ix. 419, 5th ser. i. 209, 276.] G. G.

FULLER, FRANCIS, the younger (1670–1706), medical writer, second son of Francis Fuller, nonconformist divine [q. v.], and his wife Bridget, was born at Bristol, and entered at St. John's College, Cambridge, in 1687. He graduated B.A. at Cambridge in 1691, and M.A. in 1704. He had severe hypochondriasis following his too vigorous external treatment of an attack of itch. The hypochondriasis was accompanied by dyspepsia, and he cured himself by exercise on horseback and by emetics. This led him to write a book on the use of exercise in the treatment of disease, called 'Medicina Gymnastica, or a Treatise concerning the power of Exercise with respect to the Animal Œconomy, and the great necessity of it in the Cure of several Distempers,' 1704. A second edition was published in the same year, a third in 1707, a fifth in 1718, a sixth in 1728, and a ninth and last in 1777. Sydenham had been an advocate for fresh air and exercise as remedies in consumption and hypochondriasis, and Fuller enlarges upon his suggestions. He shows but little knowledge of disease; he thought highly of millipedes in the treatment of rheumatism, and of liquorice in that of consumption, but has the merit of recommending the regular use of chafing, or, as it is now called, massage, where exercise by locomotion is impossible. He died in June 1706.

[Rev. T. Fuller's Words to give to the Young Man Knowledge, London, 1685; Munk's Coll. of Phys. i. 401; Fuller's writings.] N. M.

FULLER, ISAAC (1606–1672), painter, born in 1606, is stated to have studied first in France under François Perrier, probably at the new academy in Paris, under whom he acquired some skill and robustness of style from copying the antique. Unluckily he was too fond of the tavern to become a great painter, and his talents were dissipated in ignoble indulgences. Still he produced some works which were not without merit. He resided for some time at Oxford, and painted an altarpiece for Magdalen College, and also one for Wadham College; the latter, which represented 'The Last Supper,' between 'Abraham and Melchizedek' and 'The Israelites gathering manna,' was executed in a singular method, the lights and shades being just brushed over, and the colours melted in with a hot iron. Fuller perhaps invented this method himself, and Addison wrote a poem in praise of it. While at Oxford he painted numerous portraits, and also copied Dobson's 'Decollation of St. John,' altering the heads to portraits of his own immediate friends. In London Fuller was much employed in decorative painting, especially in taverns, no doubt earning his entertainment thereby. The Mitre tavern in Fenchurch Street, and the Sun tavern near the Royal Exchange were among those adorned by him with suitable paintings. He painted the ceiling on the staircase of a house in Soho Square, and a ceiling at Painter-Stainers' Hall. As a portrait painter Fuller had some real power, and his own portrait, now in the Bodleian Library at Oxford, is skilfully, if capriciously, executed; it shows him in a curious head-dress of an eastern character, and gives a good idea of his character. James Elsum [q. v.] wrote an epigram on it. There is an original drawing for it in the Dyce Collection at the South Kensington Museum, and Fuller himself made a small etching of it. A portrait of Fuller, drawn by G. Vertue, is in the print room at the British Museum. Among other portraits painted by Fuller were Samuel Butler, the poet, Pierce, the carver, and Ogilby, the author (these two were in the Strawberry Hill Collection, and the latter has been engraved by W. C. Edwards), Norris, the king's framemaker (a picture much praised by Sir Peter Lely), Cleveland, the poet, Sir Kenelm Digby, and Latham, the statuary. Fuller painted five pictures on wood of some size, representing the adventures of Charles II after the battle of Worcester; these were presented to the parliament of Ireland, and subsequently were discovered in a state of neglect by Lord Clanbrassil, who had them repaired, and removed them to Tullamore Park, co. Down.

Isaac Fuller had also some skill as an etcher; he etched some plates of Tritons and mythological subjects in the style of Perrier. In 1654 he published a set of etchings entitled 'Un libro di designare,' which are very rare. He executed, with H. Cooke [q. v.] and others, the etchings in 'Iconologia, or Morall Emblems,' by Cæsar Ripa of Perugia, published by Pierce Tempest. In Dr. Thomas Fuller's [q. v.] 'Pisgah-sight of Palestine' (1650, bk. iv. chap. v.) there is a large folding plate of Jewish costumes, etched by Isaac Fuller. He perhaps also executed the plan of Jerusalem in the same book, on which the words 'Fuller's Field' occur in English. He was not connected by family with the author, and the costume of the portrait at Oxford suggests that he may have belonged to the Jewish race. Fuller died in Bloomsbury Square, London, on 17 July 1672. He left a son, who, according to Vertue, 'principally was imployed in torch-painting, a very ingenious man, but living irregularly dyd young.' Nothing further is known of his achievements.

[Walpole's Anecdotes of Painting (ed. Dallaway and Wornum); Vertue's MSS. (Addit. MSS. Brit. Mus. 23068, etc.); De Piles's Lives of the Painters; Dodd's manuscript History of English Engravers; Redgrave's Dict. of Artists; Bailey's Life of Thomas Fuller; Cunningham's Handbook to London; Catalogue of the Dyce Collection, South Kens. Mus.]   L. C.

FULLER, JOHN (*d.* 1558), master of Jesus College, Cambridge, was a native of Gloucester. He was educated at All Souls' College, Oxford, where he was admitted to the B.C.L. degree in July 1533, and became a fellow in 1536. He graduated D.C.L. in January 1546, and in the same year admitted himself a member of Doctors' Commons. In 1547 he was rector of Hanwell, Middlesex, but resigned the charge in 1551, having in 1550 been appointed vicar-general or chancellor to Thirlby, bishop of Norwich. At about the same time he became vicar of Swaffham, and rector of East Dereham and North Creake in Norfolk. On Thirlby's translation to the diocese of Ely, Fuller went with him as chancellor, and on 24 Sept. 1554 was installed his proxy in Ely Cathedral. In November following he was collated prebendary of the fifth stall. As chancellor he was also examiner of heretics, and condemned several, his judgment seldom inclining to leniency. He was proctor for the clergy of the diocese in two convocations, and held other preferments, being rector of Wilbraham, Fen Ditton, and Hildersham, Cambridgeshire. He resided in Queens' College, Cambridge, and when in London had rooms in Paternoster Row. He succeeded Pierpoint as master of Jesus College, Cambridge, in February 1557. In the following May he was elected to the prebend of Chamberlainwood in St. Paul's, London. He died 30 July 1558, and was buried, according to his directions, in the choir of Jesus College, to which institution he bequeathed one-third of his property, besides founding four fellowships. One-third he left to the poor of certain parishes, and the remainder to his cousins William and Margaret. His specific legacies included 13*l.* 6*s.* 8*d.* to All Souls' College, and two of his best geldings to the Bishop of Ely.

[Cole MSS. vii. 110, 203; Bentham's Hist. of Ely, p. 253; Shermanni Hist. Coll. Jes. Cant., ed. Halliwell, p. 37; Cooper's Athenæ Cantabr. i. 188; Le Neve's Fasti Eccl. Angl. i. 358, ii. 375, 496; Newcourt's Repert. Eccl. Lond. i. 136; Foxe's Acts and Monuments (ed. 1847), vii. 402, viii. 378; Blomefield's Norfolk, iii. 633, vi. 225, vii. 74, x. 210; Cooper's Annals of Cambr. ii. 83; Strype's Eccl. Mem. i. pt. i. p. 544; Lansdowne MS. 980, fol. 233 *b*; Coote's Civilians, p. 37; Boase's Reg. of Univ. of Oxford, i. 169.] A. V.

FULLER, JOHN, M.D. (*d.* 1825), historian of Berwick-on-Tweed, was some years in practice as a surgeon at Ayton, Berwickshire. During that time, in 1785, he published a pamphlet of 'New Hints relating to Persons Drowned and apparently Dead' (London, 8vo), in which he proposed transfusion from the carotid artery of a sheep as a means of resuscitation. It does not appear that the method was tried. On 21 Nov. 1789 Fuller, who appears to have had no previous connection with the university, received his M.D. degree at St. Andrews upon testimonials from Messrs. N. and T. Spens, physicians, Edinburgh, Alex. Wood, surgeon, and Andrew Wardrop, physician (*Minutes of the University*). Afterwards he practised at Berwick. While there in 1794, soon after the formation of the board of agriculture, he addressed to the board suggestions for the collecting of health statistics from counties periodically, and for the formation of a central medical institution and of a national veterinary college. At the request of Sir John Sinclair, president of the board, he prepared in a small compass the account of Berwick for the ' Statistical Account of Scotland ; ' but as he suggested that it required more extended treatment Sinclair agreed to its publication as a separate work, entitled ' History of Berwick ' (London, 1799), 4to, with plates. Fuller afterwards lived in Edinburgh. Sykes, the border historian, states that in 1824 Fuller issued prospectuses for a general view of the ' Border History of England and Scotland,' but that ' the work was not published during his [Fuller's] lifetime.' Fuller died at Edinburgh 14 Dec. 1825.

[Information supplied by the librarian, St. Andrews University ; also Monthly Rev. 1st ser. lxxii. 76; Fuller's Hist. of Berwick; Sykes's Local Recs. Durham and Northumberland, ii. 189 ; Scots Mag. 1825, p. 768.]   H. M. C.

FULLER, Sir JOSEPH (*d.* 1841), general, was appointed ensign Coldstream guards August 1792. He seems to have previously held the same rank in some foot regiment from 29 Sept. 1790, but his name does not appear in the army list. He became lieutenant and captain Coldstream guards 22 Jan. 1794. He was with his regiment at the sieges of Valenciennes and Dunkirk. Afterwards he served as aide-de-camp to Major-general Samuel Hulse in Ireland in 1798, in North Holland in 1799, and at home in the southern district until promoted to captain and lieutenant-colonel 18 June 1801. He accompanied the first battalion of his regiment to Portugal, with the expeditionary force under Major-general J. Coope Sherbrooke in December 1808 ; commanded a light battalion, formed of the light companies of the guards and some 60th rifles, in the operations on the Douro and advance to Oporto in 1809; and commanded the 1st battalion Coldstream guards at the battle of Talavera. He afterwards served with the regiment at home until promoted to major-general 4 June 1813.

He was appointed colonel of the 95th (Derbyshire) foot at its formation in January 1824; was made a knight bachelor 1826, G.C.H. in 1827, was transferred to the colonelcy of the 75th foot 1832, and became general 1838. Fuller was for many years president of the acting committee of the Consolidated Board of General Officers, formed to inspect army clothing, investigate claims for losses, and execute other duties previously performed by separate boards of general officers, a post he ultimately resigned through ill-health.

Fuller married, in 1815, Mary, eldest daughter of General Sir John Floyd, bart., by whom he had a family. He died at his residence in Bryanston Square 16 Oct. 1841, and was buried at Kensal Green.

[Philippart's Royal Mil. Calendar, 1820 ; Dod's Knightage, 1841 ; Gent. Mag. new ser. xvii. 98.]   H. M. C.

FULLER, NICHOLAS (1557 ?–1626), hebraist and philologist, the son of Robert Fuller by his wife Catharine Cresset, was a native of Hampshire, and was born about 1557. He was sent successively to two schools at Southampton, kept by John Horlock and Dr. Adrian Saravia respectively. He entered, in the capacity of secretary, the household of Horne, bishop of Winchester, who, by discussing points of theology at meal times, inspired him with an earnest desire for study. On Horne's death Fuller, through the influence of Dr. William Barlow, the late bishop's brother-in-law, was allowed to fill the same office to Bishop Watson. His work was now less to his taste, and, on Watson's death in 1584, he determined to have no more to do with civil affairs, of which, as he afterwards said, he was thoroughly wearied, and to live a scholar's life. His means were insufficient for his purpose, but he obtained an appointment as tutor to William and Oliver Wallop, and, accompanying them to Oxford, instructed them by day, while he pursued his own studies at night. He was a member of Hart Hall, and graduated B.A. 30 Jan. 1586, and M.A. 30 March 1590. He found a warm friend and adviser in Robert Abbot [q. v.], afterwards bishop of Salisbury. He took orders, and was presented to the living of Allington, Wiltshire, the income of which was very inadequate, ' ecclesiola ' rather than ' ecclesia ' he called it. The duties, however, were light, and Fuller applied himself to the study of languages, especially in their bearing on theology. He corresponded with foreign scholars, and in 1612 he published at Heidelberg, at Sir Henry Wallop's expense, ' Miscellaneorum Theologicorum, quibus non modo scripturæ divinæ sed et aliorum classicorum auctorum plurima monumenta explicantur atque illustrantur, libri tres.' Fuller was disgusted with the number of printer's errors which disfigured his work in this edition, and in 1616 printed another at Oxford under his own supervision. To this he added a fourth book and a preface, partly autobiographical. He had in the meantime, 14 Oct. 1612, become a prebendary of Salisbury Cathedral. Bishop Cotton, it was said, had heard of his learning, and visited Fuller with the object of testing it; he was so satisfied with the proofs he received that he at once offered him the prebend's stall. A third edition of the 'Miscellaneorum' was published at Leyden in 1622, with the addition of an 'Apologia,' a good-humoured reply to Drusius, the Belgian critic, who had virulently attacked him in his 'Notes on the Pentateuch.' Another edition issued in 1650, after Fuller's death, contained two more books. The work was also reprinted in Pearson's 'Critici Sacri.' Fuller left several manuscripts, some of which are preserved at Oxford; his 'Dissertatio de nomine יהוה' was published in Reland's 'Decas exercitationum philologicarum' (1707). He also compiled a lexicon, which may not have been completed, and was not published. He died in 1626. His learning was remarkable even among his fellow-students, and he is spoken of in high terms of admiration by Buxtorf (*Dissertatio de Nominibus Hebrais*) and by Pocock (*Nota Miscellanea in Portam Mosis*). The famous Thomas Fuller [q. v.] describes him as 'happy in pitching on (not difficult trifles, but) useful difficulties tending to the understanding of scripture,' and adds that 'he was most eminent for humility' (*Worthies*, Hants, p. 12, ed. 1662). Fuller was married, and had a son and daughter named Michael and Catharine.

[Preface to 2nd ed. of Miscellaneorum : Fuller's Worthies of England, loc. cit. ; Wood's Fasti Oxon. ed Bliss, i. 236, 257; Leigh's Treatise of Religion and Learning, pp. 201–2.] A. V.

FULLER or **FULWAR, SAMUEL,** D.D. (1635–1700), dean of Lincoln, second son of the Rev. John Fuller, vicar of Stebbing, Essex, who died minister of St. Martin's, Ironmonger Lane, in the city of London, and Dorcas, his wife, was born at Stebbing, and baptised 16 July 1635. He was educated at St. John's College, Cambridge, taking his degree of B.A. in 1654, M.A. 1658 (M.A. Oxon. 1663), B.D. 1665, D.D. 1679. He was elected fellow of St. John's 25 March 1656–7. Kennett tells us that he, together with his elder brother, Dr. Thomas Fuller, fellow of Christ's College and rector of Navenby, Lincolnshire, and

Willingale-Doe, Essex, received holy orders before the Restoration from their uncle, Dr. Thomas Fulwar (called Fuller by WOOD, *Fasti Oxon.* ii. 29), successively bishop of Ardfert 1641, and archbishop of Cashel 1660–1661 [q. v.]. The third brother, Francis, also ordained by his uncle, is described by Kennett as 'an uneasy man,' never staying long in one place, and died a presbyterian minister. Samuel Fuller became vicar of Elmdon, Essex, 8 Aug. 1663, and resigned the charge in 1668–1669 on receiving the rectory of Tinwell, Rutlandshire, from his patron the Earl of Exeter. William Fuller, bishop of Lincoln [q. v.], appointed him one of his chaplains, Kennett says, 'for his name's sake,' and on 25 March 1670 gave him the chancellorship of his cathedral. The next year, 26 June, he became rector of Knaptoft, Leicestershire, and on the death of Dean Brevint [q. v.] was elected dean of Lincoln 6 Dec. 1695. He had previously been appointed chaplain in ordinary to the king. Kennett informs us that Fuller obtained the deanery 'through the interest of the lay lords, who loved him for his hospitality and his wit.' The king, William III, refused for a time to appoint one whose qualifications were rather those of a boon companion than of an ecclesiastic, but at last yielded to importunity. The Exeter family were Fuller's powerful patrons, he having learnt 'how to accommodate himself to the genius of that house.' His portrait was hung up in 'the drinking-room' at Burley, and his rosy, jovial face was painted by Verrio on the great staircase of that mansion 'for Bacchus astride of a barrel.' Fuller had expected to be appointed to the mastership of his college (St. John's), and, says Kennett, 'seemed to please himself with a prospect of that station.' He was also disappointed of the rectory of St. Clement Danes, which he made no doubt his interest with the Exeter family would secure for him. According to Kennett Fuller's end was hastened by over-indulgence in the pleasures of the table: 'He was a plentiful feeder and at times a liberal drinker, though in small glasses, and his ill habit of body was imputed to Lincoln ale.' He died at the age of sixty-five, 4 March 1699–1700, and was buried in his cathedral, where a mural monument was erected to his memory, with a portrait bust in alto-relievo, and a very laudatory epitaph in latinity of remarkable excellence, the composition of the Rev. Anthony Reid, minor canon of the cathedral and master of the grammar school, to whom, writes Kennett, the dean had been 'a special familiar friend.' He is described as 'vir pius, beneficus, doctus, suavis, hospitalis,' possessing 'mores aureos, lepores, delicias,' and universally popular with men of the highest as well as of the lowest rank, the epitaph ending with 'exoriantur usque qui sic ornent hanc ecclesiam.' During his short tenure of office he made considerable alterations and improvements in the deanery house. Fuller printed a few separate sermons, among which was one preached before King William III at Whitehall, 25 June 1692, on Matt. xxii. 21–2, and published by royal command. He also published a defence of Anglican orders under the title 'Canonica Successio Ministerii Ecclesiæ Anglicanæ contra Pontificos et Schismaticos Vindicata,' Cambridge, 1690, 4to. Baxter holds Fuller up to obloquy as 'impudent beyond the degree of human pravity,' for publishing the doctrine that the bishop is the sole pastor of his diocese, and that 'the pastorate of parish priests was never heard of before the madness of that and the foregoing age' (*Baxter on National Churches*, c. xiv. § 20, p. 65).

[Kennett Collections; Lansdowne MS. 987, No. 94, p. 209; Brydges's Restituta, i. 162–4; Le Neve's Fasti.]   E. V.

FULLER, **THOMAS** (1608–1661), divine, born June 1608, was the son of Thomas Fuller, rector of Aldwincle St. Peters, Northamptonshire. Thomas Fuller the elder was a fellow of Trinity College, Cambridge, where he graduated B.A. 1587–8, and M.A. 1591. He became rector of St. Peter's in September 1602. About 1607 he married Judith, daughter of John Davenant, a London citizen, sister of John Davenant, afterwards bishop of Salisbury [q. v.], and widow of Stephen Payne, by whom he had Thomas and six younger children. He appears to have been a steady clergyman of moderate principles. Thomas Fuller the younger was for four years at a school kept by Arthur Smith, in his native village, where he learnt little. He was afterwards taught more successfully by his father. Aubrey (*Letters*, 1803, vol. ii. pt. ii. 355) says that he was a boy of 'pregnant wit,' and often joined in the talk of his father and his uncle Davenant. When just thirteen years old he was entered at Queens' College, Cambridge (29 June 1621). His uncle, who was at this time president of Queens' College and Lady Margaret professor of divinity, had also just been nominated to the bishopric of Salisbury. The tutors of the college were Edward Davenant, the bishop's nephew, and John Thorpe, whom Fuller calls his 'ever honoured tutor.' He graduated B.A. 1624–1625, M.A. 1628.

Bishop Davenant was a model uncle. He had appointed the elder Fuller to a prebendal stall at Salisbury in 1622, and had obtained the election of a nephew (Robert Townson) to a fellowship at Queens'. He wrote several letters in 1626 and 1627 to the master of Sidney Sussex (printed in BAILEY's *Life* from Tanner MSS. in the Bodleian) endeavouring to obtain a fellowship at that college for Fuller. Fuller, in spite of applications from the bishop, had been passed over at Queens'. According to his anonymous biographer, he had resigned his claim in favour of a more needy candidate from Northamptonshire, because two men from one county could not hold fellowships at the same time. He entered Sidney Sussex afterwards as a fellow-commoner, but he never obtained a fellowship. In 1630 he was appointed by Corpus Christi College to the perpetual curacy of St. Benet's, Cambridge, taking orders at the same time. Here he buried the carrier Hobson, who died of the plague in the winter of 1630–1. He contributed to a collection of Cambridge verses on the birth of the Princess Mary (4 Nov. 1631); and in the same year published his first book, 'David's Hainous Sinne, Heartie Repentance, Heavie Punishment,' in which his characteristic conceits supply the place of poetry. It was dedicated to the three sons of Edward, first Lord Montagu, of Boughton, in the neighbourhood of Aldwincle, with whose family he had many friendly relations. Edward, the eldest son, was at Sidney Sussex, of which his uncle, James Montagu, had been the first master. On 18 June 1631 Fuller was appointed by his uncle to the prebend of Netherbury in Ecclesia in Salisbury (*Appeal*, i. 286). He calls it 'one of the best prebends in England.' His father died intestate about this time, administration of his effects being granted to the son 10 April 1632. On 5 July 1633 Fuller resigned his Cambridge curacy, and in 1634 was presented by his uncle to the rectory of Broadwindsor, Dorsetshire, then in the diocese of Bristol. In 1635 he took the B.D. degree (11 June), when four of his chief parishioners showed their respect by accompanying him to Cambridge (*Life*, p. 10). His hospitality on the occasion cost him 140*l*. He twice speaks of having resided seventeen years in Cambridge, which would imply some stay there until 1638 (*Church History*, ed. Brewer, lxiv. § 43; *Appeal*, pt. i. 28). Before January 1638 he was married to a lady whose christian name was Ellen. Her surname is unknown. In the spring of 1639 he published the first of his historical writings, the 'History of the Holy Warre,' that is of the crusades. It shows much reading, and more wit, and was very popular until the Restoration.

In the spring of 1640 Fuller was elected

to the convocation as proctor for the diocese of Bristol. He gave an account of the proceedings in his 'Church History' and his 'Appeal.' Fuller's sympathies were always in favour of moderation. He objected to the severity of a proposed 'Canon for the restraint of Sectaries.' After the dissolution of parliament, the convocation was continued as a synod. Fuller says that it was only by an oversight that he and others did not formally protest against the prolongation of their sittings. The minority, however, submitted; a benevolence was voted, and canons were passed. Heylyn states that 'one of the clerks for the diocese of Bristol' (*Life of Laud*, pp. 405–6; see BAILEY, p. 191), probably meaning Fuller, proposed in committee a canon upon enforcing uniformity in ritual drawn up in 'such a commanding and imperious style' that every one disliked it except himself. The statement was made after Fuller's death. Fuller felt bound to subscribe the canons, in spite of his disapproval of some parts of them, and they received the royal assent.

Fuller was probably not in the convocation which met with the Long parliament (3 Nov. 1640). The House of Commons passed a bill, which fell through in the House of Lords, imposing fines upon those who had subscribed the canons. Fuller was set down for 200l. His uncle, the bishop, died 21 April 1641. A son, John, who survived him, was baptised at Broadwindsor 6 June 1641; and his wife died towards the end of the year. He abandoned both his living and his prebend about the same time. He says that he was 'never formally sequestered,' but he ceased to officiate or to receive the income. He settled in London, where he preached for a time at the Inns of Court, and soon afterwards became curate of the Savoy. He had finished the 'Holy and Profane State'—the most popular and characteristic of all his books—at the beginning of 1641. After being at press for a year it appeared in 1642. It was transcribed by the members of the community at Little Gidding [see FERRAR, NICHOLAS]. The discovery of one such copy led Dr. Peckard to attribute the authorship to Ferrar (see BAILEY, p. 229). Fuller was exceedingly popular as a preacher. His biographer says that he had two congregations, one in the church, the other listening through the windows. His hearers were chiefly royalists, and he fell under the suspicion of the parliamentary party. His position is indicated by the sermons published at the time. On 28 Dec. 1642, one of the fast-days appointed by the king to commemorate the Irish massacre, Fuller preached a sermon

strongly exhorting both sides to peace, and proposed petitions to the king and to parliament. He states (*Appeal*, pt. ii. p. 46) that he was one of six who tried to carry a petition from Westminster to the king at Oxford. It is not quite certain whether this is to be identified with a petition (printed in BAILEY, p. 267) presented to the king at Oxford by a 'Dr. Fuller' and others 18 Jan. 1643–4. Fuller was not then 'doctor,' and there were others of the name. On 27 March 1643, the anniversary of the king's accession, Fuller preached another sermon, expressing hopes of peace from the negotiations then just renewed. On 17 June, after the discovery of Waller's plot, parliament ordered that an oath should be generally tendered expressing abhorrence of the plot, and containing a promise not to join the royal forces. Fuller took the oath with certain reservations. On another fast-day, at the end of July, he preached a sermon upon 'Reformation,' condemning, among other things, Milton's tract of 1641 on the same topic in the 'Smectymnuus' controversy. He sufficiently showed his discontent with the zealots of the puritan side, and it was possibly at this time that he undertook the petition above mentioned. He incurred fresh suspicion, and was ordered to take the oath, without reservation, 'in the face of the church,' whereupon he withdrew to Oxford about August 1643.

Fuller settled at Lincoln College. He complains that 'seventeen weeks' at Oxford cost him more than seventeen years at Cambridge, even all that he had (*Church History*, bk. iv. § 43). This, though it has been differently understood, seems clearly to refer to the losses consequent upon his flight, not to the actual expense of living. He lost many of his books, and was deprived of his income. He was welcomed by the royalists, and preached before the king. But his position was not agreeable. His sermons on reformation produced a smart controversy with John Saltmarsh, who accused him of popish tendencies. Fuller replied in 'Truth Maintained,' published at Oxford, with supplementary letters to several persons, and to his 'dear parish, St. Mary Savoy.' Though Fuller was opposed to the puritans, he was regarded as lukewarm by the passionate loyalists of Oxford. Isolated and impoverished, he accepted (about December 1643) a chaplaincy to Sir Ralph Hopton, one of the most moderate and religious of the king's generals. Fuller followed the general's movements for a few months, amusing himself, it is said, even in the midst of campaigning, by antiquarian researches; but he was at Basing

House early in 1644, and his biographer states that he encouraged the garrison in their sallies on some occasions. The dates, however, are confused. He was preaching at Oxford 10 May 1644. Later in the year he followed Hopton to the west. By the autumn he was at Exeter, where the queen's fourth child, the Princess Henrietta, was born 16 June 1644. The king was at Exeter, after the surrender of Essex's army (1 Sept. 1644), and appointed Fuller chaplain to the new-born infant. He further pressed upon Fuller a presentation to a living in Dorchester. Fuller, however, declined an offer which could hardly have been carried into effect. He gave up his chaplaincy to Hopton and stayed quietly at Exeter as a member of the princess's household. He preached and worked at his 'Worthies,' and wrote his 'Good Thoughts in Bad Times,' published at Exeter in 1645. In the winter of 1645-6 the town was invested by Fairfax. On 21 March 1645-6, Fuller was appointed to a lectureship founded at Exeter by Laurence Bodley [q. v.] On 9 April following the town surrendered to Fairfax under honourable articles. Fuller went to London, and on 1 June sent in a petition (facsimile in BAILEY, p. 376), claiming the protection granted by the articles upon composition for his estate. He could not obtain terms which would permit of his being 'restored to the exercise of his profession.' He employed himself in writing his 'Andronicus,' published in the autumn. He had many influential friends who served him during the troubled times following so as to place him in a better position than most of the ejected clergy. Edward, lord Montagu (son of the first lord, who died 1644), had taken the parliamentary side. In the winter of 1646-7 he hospitably received his old college friend at Boughton House. Montagu was one of the commissioners who in February 1647 received the king at Holmby House. Fuller about the same period became intimate with Sir John Danvers [q. v.], in whose house at Chelsea he was a frequent guest. The intimacy continued until Danvers's death in 1655, although Danvers was one of those who signed the death-warrant of Charles. Fuller, it is said by his biographer, was so affected by the king's death as to throw aside the composition of the 'Worthies;' he preached a sermon on 'The Just Man's Funeral,' evidently referring to it; but he did not break with Danvers, one of the most regular judges at the trial. He was meanwhile leading an unsettled life, finding time to publish a few sermons and books of contemplation and occasionally preaching. In March 1647 he was lecturing in St. Clement's, Eastcheap, although from the preface to a sermon published in that year it appears that he was prohibited from preaching until further order. In 1648 or 1649 he was presented to the perpetual curacy of Waltham Abbey by the second Earl of Carlisle, who had come over to the parliament in March 1644 and compounded for his estate. Carlisle also made Fuller his chaplain. At Waltham, Fuller finished his 'Pisgah-sight of Palestine,' which appeared in 1650, after much delay due to the preparation of the plates. Book v. of Fuller's 'Church History' is dedicated to the third Earl of Middlesex, who lived at Copt Hall, near Waltham. The earl presented to Fuller 'what remained' of the library of his father, the first earl [see CRANFIELD, LIONEL]. Fuller was constantly at Copt Hall, and speaks of the 'numerous and choice library' (Appeal, iii. 617). He was also frequently in London during his curacy at Waltham. He had access to the library at Sion College, where he had a chamber for some time; and he made acquaintance with merchants, many of whom are mentioned among the numerous recipients of his dedications. He was again lecturer at St. Clement's, where he preached every Wednesday, and he was lecturer at St. Bride's in 1655-6, and, it is said, at St. Andrew's, Holborn (LLOYD, Memoirs, p. 524). He is mentioned as preaching in various London churches (BAILEY, pp. 527-8) during the following years. About the end of 1651 he married his second wife, Mary, daughter of Thomas Roper, viscount Baltinglasse, and descendant of James Pilkington, bishop of Durham. In March 1655 appeared his 'Church History,' which he had been preparing for many years. He had decided, after some hesitation, to bring the history down to his own time; and though necessarily written under constraint, the passages on which he speaks as a contemporary have a special value. His account of his authorities is given in the 'Appeal.' The book is divided into sections dedicated to a great number of patrons. This practice, adopted also in the 'Pisgah-sight,' was a rude form of the later method of publishing by subscription. It was ridiculed at the time by his opponent Heylyn, and by South, who pronounced the 'Terræ Filius' oration at Oxford in 1657 (printed in his 'Opera Posthuma Latina,' by Curll, 1717), where Fuller is described as running round London with his big book under one arm, and his little wife under the other, and recommending himself as a dinner guest by his facetious talk. This spiteful caricature had probably a grain of likeness. John Barnard (d. 1683) [q. v.], editor of Heylyn's 'Tracts' (1681), gives a similar account, which, though equally coloured by spite, gives some confirmation. The rising under Penruddock in 1655 caused a proclamation from Cromwell forbidding the exercise of their ministry to the ejected clergy. Fuller still preached under sufferance, and was helpful to less fortunate fellow-sufferers. Some time afterwards he was summoned before the 'triers,' when he succeeded in satisfying them, owing, as it seems, to the judicious management of John Howe (CALAMY, *Memoirs of Howe*, 1724, pp. 20, 21). In March 1658 he was presented to the rectory of Cranford, near Hounslow, by George Berkeley (1628–1698) [q. v.], first earl Berkeley, whose chaplain he also became. In 1659 Heylyn published his 'Examen Historicum,' the first part of which attacks Fuller's 'Church History.' He discovered 350 faults in Fuller's book; he condemned the 'scraps of trencher-jests interlaced in all parts' of the book; he ridiculed the multitude of dedications, and he was severe upon Fuller's tolerance of sectaries. Fuller replied with characteristic candour and good temper, though not without some smart retorts, in his 'Appeal for Injured Innocence.' An appended letter to Heylyn courteously proposes an amicable agreement to differ. Heylyn answered in the appendix to his 'Certamen Epistolare, or The Letter-combate.' They had afterwards a personal interview at Heylyn's house at Abingdon and parted on friendly terms.

In February 1660 Fuller published a pamphlet by 'a lover of his native country' in support of the demand for a free parliament, which went through three editions, the third with Fuller's name. Soon afterwards he published his 'Mixt Contemplations in Better Times,' dedicated to Lady Monck, from 'Zion College, 2 May 1660.' Fuller appears to have accompanied Lord Berkeley to meet Charles II at the Hague, and celebrated 29 May by a loyal 'Panegyrick' in verse (*Worthies*, Worcestershire, i. 84). He judiciously promises in the 'Worthies' to write no more poetry. Fuller, with some other divines, was created D.D. in August 1660 by letter from the king. He resumed his old lectureship at the Savoy, where his friend Pepys, who heard him, records on 12 May 1661 a 'poor dry sermon.' He also resumed his possession of the prebend at Salisbury, the income of which would, as he hoped, enable him to publish his 'Worthies.' At Broadwindsor he found one John Pinney in possession. Fuller, having heard him preach, allowed him to remain in the charge, apparently as curate. Pinney, however, was dismissed before January 1662. Fuller was also appointed 'chaplain in extraordinary' to the

king, and further preferment was anticipated. In the summer of 1661 he went to Salisbury, and, soon after his return, was attacked by a fever. It was probably typhus (BAILEY, p. 689); he was bled profusely ; and died at his lodgings in Covent Garden 16 Aug. 1661, crying out, as one account says, 'for his pen and ink to the last.' He was buried next day in the church at Cranford. His wife was buried in the same church 19 May 1679.

The 'Worthies' was published posthumously, with a dedication to Charles by John Fuller, the author's son, who had been admitted at Sidney Sussex College in 1657, and became a fellow in 1663.

The most authentic portrait of Fuller was engraved for Mr. Bailey's work, from the original in possession of Lord Fitzhardinge at Cranford House. An engraving prefixed to the 'Worthies,' and frequently reproduced, is apparently from another original. An engraving (showing a very different face) is in a few copies of the 'Abel Redivivus.' Another was prefixed to the anonymous 'Life.' Fuller is described as tall and bulky, though not corpulent, well made, almost 'majestical,' with light curly hair, rather slovenly in dress and often absent-minded, and careless 'to seeming inurbanity' in his manners. He was sparing in diet and in sleep. He seldom took any exercise except riding. His powers of memory were astonishing, and gave occasion for many anecdotes. He could, it was said, repeat five hundred strange names after two or three hearings, and recollect all the signs after walking from one end of London to the other. His anonymous biographer declares that he used to write the first words of every line in a sheet and then fill up all the spaces, which Mr. Bailey thinks 'not a bad method.'

Fuller's modern critics have generally confined themselves to simplifying Coleridge's phrase, 'God bless thee, dear old man!' He has been called 'dear Thomas,' and 'quaint old Tom Fuller,' with a rather irritating iteration. His power of fascinating posthumous as well as contemporary friends is easily explicable. His unfailing playfulness, the exuberant wit, often extravagant, rarely ineffective and always unforced, is combined with a kindliness and simplicity which never fails to charm. If not profound, he is invariably shrewd, sound-hearted, and sensible. He tells a story admirably, as Lamb observed, because with infectious enjoyment. His humour is childlike in its freedom from bitterness. His quick sense of the ridiculous, combined with a calm and cheerful temperament, made fanaticism impossible. It tempered his zeal instead of edging his animosities. Moderation was therefore his favourite virtue, or 'the silken chain running through the pearl-string of all the virtues' (*Holy State*, p. 201). He distinguishes it from 'lukewarmness,' of which he cannot be fairly accused. But it can hardly be said that he was quite free from the weakness of the moderate man. It is intelligible that Heylyn accused him of 'complying with the times,' and called him a 'trimmer.' Moderate men are 'commonly crushed,' he says himself, 'between extreme parties on both sides,' whereas he was patronised by both sides, and beloved both by Charles I and by a regicide. The truth seems to be that his perfectly genuine moderation enabled him to accommodate himself rather too easily to men of all parties. His many dedications seem to escape flattery by their witty ingenuity, and his popularity implies a certain share of the wisdom of the serpent. He steered rather too skilful a course, perhaps, through a revolutionary time; but he really succeeded in avoiding any really discreditable concessions, and never disavowed his genuine convictions. Coleridge's remarks upon Fuller are in his 'Literary Remains,' 1836, ii. 381–390; Lamb's 'Selections,' with comments, published in his 'Essays,' first appeared in Leigh Hunt's 'Reflector,' No. 4 (1811); the essay by James Crossley in the 'Retrospective Review,' iii. 50–71, and the essay by Henry Rogers (originally in the 'Edinburgh Review,' January 1842), prefixed to a volume of selections in Longman's 'Travellers' Library,' 1856, may also be noticed.

Fuller was apparently one of the first authors to make an income by their pens. He says in the beginning of his 'Worthies' that 'hitherto no stationer hath lost by me.' It does not appear how much he made by the stationers. His works are: 1. 'David's Hainous Sinne, Heartie Repentance, Heavie Punishment,' 1631 (reprinted in 1869, and by Dr. Grosart in Fuller's 'Poems and Translations in Verse,' 1868). 2. 'The History of the Holy Warre,' 1639, 2nd edit. 1640, 3rd 1647, 4th 1651 (besides other reprints), reprinted 1840. 3. 'Joseph's Party-coloured Coat,' 1640 (a collection of sermons), reprinted 1867 with 'David's Hainous Sinne,' &c. 4. 'The Holy State and the Profane State,' 1642, also 1648, 1652, 1663 (reprinted in 1840 and 1841). 5. 'Truth Maintained, or Positions delivered in a sermon at the Savoy, . . . asserted for safe and sound,' 1643. 6. 'Good Thoughts in Bad Times,' 1645 and 1646. 7. 'Andronicus, or the Unfortunate Politician,' 1646 (three editions) and 1649, also in second and later editions of 'Holy and Profane State.' In Dutch 1659.

8. 'The Cause and Cure of a Wounded Conscience,' 1647, reprinted in 1810, 1812, 1815. 9. 'Good Thoughts in Worse Times,' 1647, and with 'Good Thoughts in Bad Times' 1649, 1652, 1657, 1659, 1665, 1669, 1680; reprinted in 1810. 10. 'A Pisgah-sight of Palestine,' 1650, 1652, 1668; reprinted in 1869. 11. 'A Comment on the Eleven First Verses of the 4th Chapter of St. Matthew's Gospel,' 1652 (twelve sermons). 12. 'The Infant's Advocate,' 1652. 13. 'A Comment on Ruth,' 1654. 14. 'The Triple Recounter,' 1654. 15. 'The Church History of Britain,' also the 'History of the University of Cambridge since the Conquest' and the 'History of Waltham Abbey,' 1655; reprinted in 1837, edited by James Nichols, ru 3 vols., and again 1840, 1842, and 1868, and edited by J. S. Brewer for the Oxford University Press, 1845. The 'Histories' of Cambridge and Waltham were reprinted in 1840, edited by James Nichols, with the 'Appeal of Injured Innocence.' 16. 'A Collection of [four] Sermons, together with Notes upon Jonah,' 1656. 17. 'The Best Name on Earth, together with several other [three] sermons,' 1657 and 1659. 18. 'The Appeal of Injured Innocence,' 1659; reprinted in 1840 with the 'Histories' of Cambridge and Waltham Abbey. 19. 'An Alarum to the Counties of England and Wales' (three editions), 1660. 20. 'Mixt Contemplations in Better Times,' 1660; reprinted with former 'Contemplations' in 1830 and 1841. 21. 'A Panegyrick to His Majesty,' 1660. 22. 'The History of the Worthies of England,' 1662; reprinted in 1811 and 1840.

Fuller published several separate sermons, including 'A Fast Sermon on Innocents' Day,' 1642; 'A Sermon on the 27th March,' 1643; 'A Sermon of Reformation,' 1643; and 'A Sermon of Assurance,' 1647. He contributed poems to Cambridge collections of verses in 1631 and 1633; a preface to the 'Valley of Vision,' 1651 (a collection of sermons attributed to Dr. Holdsworth); an 'Epistle to the Reader,' and some lives to the 'Abel Redivivus,' 1651; a preface to the 'Ephemeris Parliamentaria,' 1654; and a life to Henry Smith's 'Sermons,' 1657. A minute and most careful account of the bibliography of all Fuller's writings is given by Mr. Bailey.

[The anonymous life of Fuller, first published in 1661 (reprinted with Brewer's edition of the 'Church History') is the original authority; Oldys's Life in the Biog. Brit. (1750) is founded on this, with a painstaking examination of Fuller's writings. Memorials of the Life and Works of Thomas Fuller, by Arthur J. Russell (1844), adds a little; but everything discoverable was first brought together in Mr. John Eglinton

Bailey's Life of Thomas Fuller, with Notices of his Books, his Kinsmen, and his Friends (1874). Life, Times, and Writings, by the Rev. Morris Fuller, 2 vols., 1884, is founded upon this. See also Lloyd's Memoirs (1677), pp. 523–4.]

L. S.

FULLER or **FULWAR, THOMAS,** D.D. (the two forms of surname seem to have been used indifferently) (1593–1667), archbishop of Cashel, one of the sons of the Rev. Thomas Fuller, vicar of Stebbing, Essex, a member of the same family with Fuller the church historian, was born in 1593. According to Kennett he was disinherited by his father 'for a prodigal.' This drove him to Ireland, 'with the happy necessity of being sober and industrious' (KENNETT, *Register,* p. 364). He may previously have graduated at Cambridge. His name does not appear in the registry of the university of Dublin, but he took orders in the Irish church. One of his name is found as prebendary of Cloyne, and in 1639 chancellor of Cork. In 1641 he was consecrated bishop of Ardfert, being the last prelate who held that see as an independent diocese before it was united to the see of Limerick. The Irish rebellion soon drove him with his family to take refuge in London, probably in the parish of St. Andrew's, Holborn. He dedicated a sermon on Luke ii. 48, preached at Gray's Inn 2 Oct. 1642, 'on the anniversary of the Irish rebellion,' to 'the worthy gentlemen and inhabitants of that parish who had been,' he says, 'the chief preservers of me and mine since our escape out of Ireland, where we had only our lives for a prey, and those lives your bounty hath cherished.' The ill-treatment he met with from the presbyterian party then dominant compelled him to retire to Oxford, where he was incorporated D.D. in 1645 (WOOD, *Fasti,* ii. 79). He seems to have remained in England till the Restoration, and in 1656 he ordained William Annand [q. v.], afterwards dean of Edinburgh (WOOD, *Athenæ,* iv. 258). After the Restoration he returned to Ireland, and was translated to the archiepiscopal see of Cashel (1 Feb. 1660–1). Kennett gives a somewhat highly coloured account of the archbishop's reception at Cashel, not only by churchmen but by others, who were converted by his 'indefatigable powers and exemplary piety' (KENNETT, *Register,* p. 312). He died 31 March 1667, in the seventy-fourth year of his age, and was buried in the chancel of his cathedral of St. John's, to which he bequeathed a silver chalice, paten, and flagon, still in use. As bishop of Ardfert he ordained his three nephews, who all rose to some eminence, the sons of his brother John, who succeeded his father as vicar of Stebbing:

Thomas, fellow of Christ's College, Cambridge, an acquaintance of Pepys, mentioned several times in his ' Diary,' subsequently, in 1658, chaplain to Colonel Lockhart, governor of Dunkirk, vicar of the college living of Navenby, near Lincoln, and rector of Willingale Doe, Essex, 1670, ' an inveterate preferment hunter,' who died at Navenby in March 1701 ; Samuel, afterwards dean of Lincoln [q.v.], and Francis the elder [q.v.] Archbishop Fuller is not mentioned by Ware among the Irish writers. He published a few sermons, of which the only one known to be extant is that upon the Irish rebellion.

[Kennett's Register; Cotton's Fasti Hibern.; Bailey's Life of Thomas Fuller.] E. V.

FULLER, THOMAS, M.D. (1654–1734), physician, was born at Rosehill, a country house in the parish of Brightling, Sussex, 24 June 1654. His family had for some time been seated there, and are believed by the parishioners to have grown rich during the period of iron-smelting in Sussex. A small inn which stands near the remains of the village stocks at the foot of the ascent on the top of which is Rosehill has for its sign the arms which are to be seen in some of the doctor's books (in the possession of C. J. Tatham of Clare College, Cambridge), argent, three bars with a canton in chief gules, and which are supposed to allude to the forging of bars and ploughshares by the ancestors of the family of Rosehill. Fuller was educated at Queens' College, Cambridge. He studied Descartes and Willis, and retained till old age a liking for their methods (*Exanthemologia,* p. xii). In 1676 he graduated M.B., and in 1681 M.D., and in February 1679 was admitted an extra-licentiate of the College of Physicians of London. He commenced practice at Sevenoaks, Kent, and there continued throughout life, attaining large practice and great popularity, which was increased in his old age by his undertaking at his own charge the proceedings in chancery necessary for a reform of the Senoke charity. He published three collections of prescriptions, 'Pharmacopœia Extemporanea,' 1702 (3rd edition, 1705 ; 4th, 1708 ; 6th, 1731), 'Pharmacopœia Bateana,' 1718 (based on the prescriptions of Dr. Bate [q. v.]), 'Pharmacopœia Domestica,' 1723. These were issued in Latin, but an advertisement of a pirated edition in English having appeared in the ' Postman,' 18 Sept. 1708, he published a translation of the first in 1710, of which a fifth edition appeared in 1740. In 1730 appeared his 'Exanthemologia, or an attempt to give a Rational Account of Eruptive Fevers, especially of the Measles and Small-pox,' the most interesting of his works. It contains many of his own notes of cases of small-pox, of measles, and of other fevers. He is the first English writer who points out clearly how to distinguish the spots produced by flea-bites (p. 145) from the spots seen in the eruptive fevers, and his is the first English book by a physician in which the qualifications necessary in a sick nurse are set forth in detail (p. 208). He narrates his cases with precision, and those illustrating the progress of small-pox after inoculation, of which he approved, are of permanent interest. He suffered from gout, and in 1727 he was threatened with blindness from cataract in both eyes to such a degree that he was unable to read the minute but clear handwriting of his youthful notes. He was, however, able to publish three collections of precepts:—' Introductio ad Prudentiam, or Directions, Counsels, and Cautions, tending to Prudent Management of Affairs in Common Life,' 2 vols. 1727 (2nd edition, 1740); ' Introductio ad Sapientiam, or the Art of Right Thinking,' 1731; ' Gnomologia: Adagies, Proverbs, Wise Sentiments, and Witty Sayings, Ancient and Modern, Foreign and British,' 1732. The first is most original, and includes 3,152 precepts for the guidance through life of his son John, of which some are copied with little alteration from the psalms, proverbs, and gospels, while none of the remainder rise above the level of the advice of Polonius, to which they have a general resemblance. He died 17 Sept. 1734, and is buried in Sevenoaks Church. He married Mary Plumer on 23 Sept. 1703. A portrait is prefixed to the ' Pharmacopœia Domestica,' 1739.

[Munk's Coll. of Phys. i. 400 ; Wadd's Nugæ Chirurgicæ, 1824 ; Works; Index Catalogue of Library of Surgeon-General's Office, Washington; Fuller's copy of Brown's Myographia, 1684.]
N. M.

FULLER, WILLIAM (1580 ?–1659), dean of Durham, born in or about 1580, was the son of Andrew Fuller of Hadleigh, Suffolk. He was a fellow of St. Catharine Hall, Cambridge, where he took the degree of D.D. in 1625, and is said to have been a good linguist and an excellent preacher. These gifts recommended him to James I, who made him one of his chaplains. By Sir Gervase Clifton he was presented to the rectory of Weston, Nottinghamshire. In the next reign he was continued in his chaplaincy, and on 3 July 1628 he received a dispensation to hold the vicarage of St. Giles-without-Cripplegate, London, in addition to the rectory of Weston (*Cal State Papers*, Dom. 1628–9, p. 190).

On the death of Henry Cæsar, 27 June 1636, he was promoted to the deanery of Ely (LE NEVE, *Fasti*, ed. Hardy, i. 348). In October 1641 some of the parishioners of St. Giles's petitioned parliament for his removal, complaining that, though the parish was very populous and the living worth 700*l.* a year, Fuller had 'pluralities of livings, and thereby was a non-resident,' and a ' popish innovator besides.' Altogether eight articles were exhibited against him. They alleged further that Fuller's curate, Timothy Hutton, ' repaired from his pulpit to the taverne on the Lords day, and there drinking uncivilly, danced and sung most profaine, & ungodly songs & dances, to the shame and disgrace of religion ' (*The Petition and Articles exhibited in Parliament against Dr. Fuller*, &c., 4to, London, 1641). The commons evidently thought it more dignified to summon him as a ' delinquent,' ' for divers dangerous and scandalous matters delivered by him in several sermons.' For refusing to attend he was ordered into the custody of the serjeant-at-arms, but upon giving substantial bail he was released on 11 Nov. 1641, and nothing apparently came of the matter (*Commons' Journals*, ii. 299, 307, 309, 311). In July 1642 Fuller and his curate, Hutton, were sent for as ' delinquents ' on a charge of having read the king's last declaration in church. Fuller denied having given orders for it to be read ; he had in fact enjoined Hutton not to read it ' till he had received farther direction.' He was thereupon forthwith discharged ' from any farther restraint without paying fees ; ' but the unfortunate curate, who confessed to having read it at the afternoon service, was committed a prisoner to the king's bench, where he remained for nearly a month (*ib.* ii. 650, 669, 703). Fuller's money was ordered to be confiscated ' for the service of the commonwealth,' 18 Feb. 1642–3 (*ib.* ii. 970). By warrant of the Earl of Essex, he asserts, 500*l.* was unjustly taken from him (*Will*). In 1645 he was in attendance upon the king at Oxford, and was incorporated in his doctor's degree on 12 Aug. of that year. Charles, who greatly admired his preaching, made him dean of Durham, in which he was installed on 6 March 1645–6 (LE NEVE, iii. 300). Ultimately he retired to London, and died in the parish of St. Giles, Cripplegate, on 13 May 1659, aged 79 (SMYTH, *Obituary*, Camden Soc. p. 50; *Probate Act Book*, P. C. C. 1659, f. 245 *b*). The authorities having refused his relatives' request that he might be buried in the church of St. Giles, he was interred at the upper end of the south aisle of St. Vedast, Foster Lane. By his wife Katherine, who survived him, Fuller left issue three sons.

William, Robert, and Gervase, and two daughters, Jane, married to Brian Walton, D.D., afterwards bishop of Chester, and Mary. Mrs. Walton, soon after the Restoration, erected a 'comely monument' over her father's grave. In his will, dated 14 Dec. 1658, and proved on 30 May 1659, Fuller requests that his 'written bookes and papers shall not be seene or disposed of without the privity and consent' of his son-in-law Brian Walton (registered in P. C. C. 273, Pell). He published: 1. 'A Sermon [on Ephes. iv. 7] preached before his Maiestie at Dover Castle,' 4to, London, 1625. 2. 'The Movrning of Mount Libanon . . . A Sermon [on Zech. xi. 2] preached . . . 1627. In commemoration of the Lady Frances Clifton,' &c., 4to, London, 1628. From the dedication to Sir Gervase Clifton we learn that Fuller had preached the funeral sermon of the first Lady Clifton, which, however, 'went out in written copies.'

[Wood's Fasti Oxon. ed. Bliss, ii. 79–80, 82; Newcourt's Repertorium, i. 357; Cal. State Papers, Dom. 1638–9, p. 298, 1640–1, pp. 213, 401, 1660–1, p. 232.]   G. G.

FULLER, WILLIAM, D.D. (1608–1675), bishop of Lincoln, was son of Thomas Fuller, merchant of London, by his wife, Lucy, daughter of Simon Cannon, citizen and merchant taylor. He was born in London, and was educated at Westminster School, from which he removed to Magdalen Hall, Oxford, as a commoner, about 1626, migrating to Edmund Hall, at which he took the degree of B.C.L. about 1632. After admission to holy orders he was appointed one of the chaplains or petty canons of Christ Church Cathedral. He was presented by the king to the rectory of St. Mary Woolchurch in the city of London on 30 June 1641, and resigned it on 16 Dec. of the same year, in which he was also appointed to the rectory of Ewhurst, Sussex. When Charles I shut himself up in Oxford in 1645, he became chaplain to Edward, lord Lyttelton, lord keeper of the great seal. As an ardent loyalist he suffered greatly in the civil wars, and in the parliamentary visitation of the university lost his position at Christ Church. During the protectorate he fell into 'a low condition.' Pepys tells us he supported himself by keeping a school at Twickenham, where he endeavoured to instil principles of loyalty and churchmanship into the minds of his scholars. While at Twickenham he had for his assistant William Wyatt, who had acted in the same capacity to Jeremy Taylor when he maintained himself by keeping school at Llanfihangel in Carmarthenshire, in conjunction with Nicholson, afterwards bishop of Gloucester. Wyatt was rewarded by his former

principal when bishop of Lincoln with the precentorship of that cathedral (WOOD, Fasti, ii. 254).

So consistent a loyalist naturally obtained speedy preferment at the Restoration. On 3 July 1660, little more than a month after the completion of the Restoration, Fuller was appointed to the deanery of St. Patrick's Dublin, and received the degree of D.C.L. at his own university on 2 Aug., by virtue of a letter of the chancellor, and also was admitted D.D. of Cambridge by the same authority. Other preferments in the Irish church followed: the treasurership of Christ Church, Dublin, on 11 July 1661, the chancellorship of Dromore in 1662, and finally the bishopric of Limerick, to which he was consecrated in Christ Church Cathedral on 20 March 1663–1664, with permission to hold his deanery in commendam for two years. Six months after he became dean of St. Patrick's, 27 Jan. 1660–1661, twelve bishops were consecrated at one time for as many vacant sees in St. Patrick's Cathedral by Archbishop Bramhall, the primate, Jeremy Taylor being then consecrated to the see of Down and Connor, and preaching the sermon. For this ceremonial an anthem was composed by Fuller, entitled 'Quum denuo exaltavit Dominus coronam.' It is evident that Fuller regarded his Irish dignities as little more than stepping-stones to some more acceptable English preferment. During the time he was dean of St. Patrick's we are told that he spent the greater portion of his time in England, leaving the sub-dean to preside at chapter meetings. But he manifested a warm interest in the repair of his cathedral, which during his tenure of office was restored from a ruinous condition to decency and stability (MASON, Hist. of St. Patrick's Cathedral, pp. 191–6). At last, after frequent disappointments, the long-looked-for translation to an English see took place. In 1667 Laney was translated from the bishopric of Lincoln to that of Ely. The see of St. Asaph, which had previously become vacant, had been promised by the king to Dr. Glemham, dean of Bristol, who was, however, anxious to exchange St. Asaph for Lincoln. Dr. Rainbow, the bishop of Carlisle, was not unwilling to accept Asaph. Dean Glemham's wishes were opposed in influential quarters, and Fuller, who was then laid up with the gout at Chester, on his way to Ireland, wrote to Williamson, Lord Arlington's secretary, on 25 May 1667, that, 'as when two contend for a post a third person is sometimes chosen, he hoped that Lord Arlington would propose, and the Archbishop of Canterbury approve of, his being translated from Limerick to Lincoln' (Calendar of State Papers, Dom.) His application proved successful, and in Wood's words he was removed to Lincoln 'after he had taken great pains to obtain it' (Wood, *Athenæ Oxon.* iv. 351). He was elected on 17 Sept. 1667. His episcopal palace at Lincoln having been hopelessly ruined during the civil wars, and Fuller feeling the importance of residing in his episcopal city instead of at the distant manor-house of Buckden, near Huntingdon, an arrangement was made with the dean and chapter by which the bishop had the occupancy of a mansion-house in the cathedral close during his visits to Lincoln (*Lincoln Chapter Acts*). Fuller enjoyed the friendship both of Evelyn and of Pepys. The former mentions having dined with him at Knightsbridge on 25 March 1674, together with the bishops of Salisbury (Seth Ward) and Chester (Pearson). Many references occur in Pepys's garrulous diaries to his 'dear friend' Dr. Fuller, with whom he dined on his appointment to St. Patrick's, and was 'much pleased with his company and goodness.' His elevation to the sees first of Limerick and then of Lincoln caused Pepys 'great joy,' and more especially as he found that his old friend 'was not spoiled by his elevation, but was the same good man as ever;' 'one of the comeliest and most becoming prelates he ever saw;' 'a very extraordinary, good-natured man.' He records the satisfaction with which he saw the bishop for the first time occupying his place in the House of Lords on 6 Nov. 1667, and a conversation he held with him on the probability of the Act of Toleration being carried, 23 Jan. 1668. In 1669 Fuller offered the archdeaconry of Huntingdon to Symon Patrick, afterwards bishop of Ely, which was declined by Patrick, 'thinking himself unfit for that government' (PATRICK, 'Autobiography,' *Works*, ix. 451). During his tenure of the see of Lincoln Fuller did much to repair the damages inflicted on his cathedral church by the puritans during the great rebellion. In a letter to Sancroft, Fuller expressed his intention of presenting the cathedral with 'a paire of faire brass candlesticks' to stand on the altar to take the place of 'a pitiful paire of ordinary brasse candlesticks which,' he writes, 'I am ashamed to see, and can indure no longer' (GRANVILLE, *Remains*, Surtees Soc. pt. i. p. 217 *n.*) He restored the monuments of Remigius, St. Hugh, and others, supplying appropriate epitaphs in excellent latinity, and, as his own epitaph records, he was intending further works of the same kind when he died at Kensington, near London, on 23 April 1675. His end, according to his epitaph, was as peaceful as his life had been: 'mortem obiit lenissima vita si fieri posset leniorem.' His

body was conveyed to Lincoln Cathedral, and interred there under an altar tomb in the retrochoir, by the side of the monument he had erected over the supposed grave of St. Hugh, which the inscription shows he had intended to be his own monument also: 'Hugonis Qui condit tumulum condit et ipse suum.' At the time of his death Fuller was engaged upon a life of Archbishop Bramhall, for which he had collected large materials, 'wherein,' writes Wood, 'as in many things he did, he would without doubt have quitted himself as much to the instruction of the living as to the honour of the dead' (Wood, *Athenæ Oxon.* iv. 351). Fuller was not married. One of his sisters, Catherine, married John Bligh, citizen and salter of London, afterwards of Rathmore, co. Meath, M.P. for Athboy, the founder of the noble family of Darnley. Another sister, Mary, married William Farmery of Thavies Inn. He bequeathed to the cathedral library of Lincoln the best of his books, and to Christ Church his pictures, chest of viols, and his organ. His will speaks of his having had to undertake lawsuits to protect his see 'from the encroachments of ungodly men.'

[Wood's Athenæ Oxon. iv. 351; Brydges's Restituta, i. 163; Mason's Hist. of St. Patrick's Cathedral, p. 192 sq.; Kennett's Biog. Notes Lansd. MS. 986, No. 85, p. 188; Collins's Fasti Eccl. Hibern. i. 385, &c.; Evelyn's Diary; Pepys's Diary; Cal. State Papers, Dom. sub ann. 1667; information from J. F. Fuller, esq.; Pegge's Anonymiana, pp. 5, 49.]   E. V.

FULLER, WILLIAM (1670–1717?), impostor, was born on 20 Sept. 1670 at Milton, Kent. By his own account he was son of Robert Fuller, son of Dr. Thomas Fuller, by the eldest daughter of the Hon. Charles Herbert of Montgomeryshire. His enemies declared that his mother was the dissolute daughter of a farmer named Sandys, and thought him very like his so-called guardian, Cornelius Harflet. In any case Fuller was apparently able to rely on the support of Charles Herbert, his alleged uncle, whose family had a seat at his birthplace. He was sent to school at Maidstone and Canterbury, and his putative father, Robert Fuller, having died when he was six months old, he was apprenticed in 1686 by Harflet to a rabbit furrier in London. From this position he was removed by William Herbert, first marquis of Powis, in May 1688, and shortly afterwards became page to the Countess of Melfort. James II's queen, Mary of Modena, noticed him, took him with her to France in December, and used him as emissary on several journeys to Ireland and England. He was at last recognised in London by a nephew of Harflet, and was placed in the charge of Tillotson, then dean of St. Paul's. In eight weeks Tillotson convinced him, as he alleged, of his political and religious errors. He thereupon disclosed all he knew to the Earl of Shrewsbury, and was formally thanked by William III, in whose presence Fuller cut open the buttons of his coat, and disclosed the letters he was carrying to various Jacobites. He continued to carry Jacobite letters, which he betrayed to the government, till exposed by his betrayal of another messenger, Matthew Crone. Crone's trial and conviction were delayed three weeks in consequence of an alleged attempt to poison Fuller, the principal witness, which kept him too ill to appear in court. Fuller followed William III to Ireland and to the Hague, living sumptuously on borrowed money and by the wages of his treachery. On returning to London he was arrested by angry creditors, and thrown into sponging-houses. Titus Oates assigned him lodgings in his house in Ax Yard, Westminster. Fuller neglected to pay the stipulated rent, or to repay loans from Oates, who at length put the law in motion. He was prevented from following the king to Holland in May 1691 by the marshal of the King's Bench, but shortly afterwards he escaped and crossed to Rotterdam. He stayed some weeks abroad, assumed various titles, and spent money lent by his dupes, or raised by forged bills, in luxurious living. When he returned to London he was at once arrested for debt, and wrote from prison to Tillotson and Lord Portland professing that he was able to disclose a plot against the throne. No notice being taken, Fuller addressed the House of Commons to the same effect, alleging that he could prove a Jacobite conspiracy against Halifax and other prominent noblemen. He stated at the bar of the house that he relied on the evidence of two witnesses named Delaval and Hayes. He received passports from the house and a blank safe-conduct from the king to bring these men from abroad; but on the day when he was to produce them he sent a message that he was too ill to attend. A committee was appointed to visit his bedside, when Fuller gave the London addresses of his witnesses. They could not be found, and on 24 Feb. 1692 the house resolved that Fuller was an impostor, cheat, and false accuser, and recommended that he should be put on his trial. His story had been so far believed that in December 1691 he had been granted an allowance of 30s. a day from the crown, and in January 20l. by the House of Commons. His trial took place on 21 Nov. 1692; he was convicted and sentenced to stand in the pillory at Westminster

and the Exchange, and to be imprisoned till he should pay two hundred marks to the king. Fuller remained in prison till June 1695, when he was released by the influence of Charles Herbert, who made him an allowance. Fuller formed a new intimacy with Oates, and published 'A Brief Discovery of the True Mother of the Prince of Wales,' 1696. Fuller repeated the old story, and declared that as a page in St. James's Palace he had witnessed on 10 June 1688 the transference of a warming pan from the chamber of a pregnant lady, Mary Grey, to that of the queen, and that this warming-pan contained the child of Mary Grey. The revived story met some belief, and Fuller quickly followed up his success with 'A Further Confirmation that Mary Grey was the true Mother,' &c., 1696, and 'Mr. William Fuller's Third Narrative containing new matters of Fact, proving the pretended Prince of Wales to be a grand Cheat upon the Nation, with an Answer to some Reflections cast upon him,' 1696. Fuller sent copies of his book to the king and leading statesmen. His petition to the House of Commons to be allowed to prove that the Prince of Wales was an impostor was received with contempt. After a fresh imprisonment for debt, he made an expedition into Hampshire, pretending to be on the track of fugitive Jacobites. In Southampton he again tried to raise loans by fraud, and remained there a year in prison. He made an unsuccessful journey to Flanders, and published 'A Trip to Hampshire and Flanders, discovering the vile Intrigues of the Priests and Jesuits, and the Practice of Englad's [*sic*] Bosom Enemies' (1701). Fuller had been disappointed at being cut off in Charles Herbert's will 'with mourning and a shilling' in favour of his own half-sister, who received the bulk of his fortune. This sister, who had been Fuller's partner in at least one of his earlier frauds, allowed him 3l. a week, which Luttrell says (*Diary*, iv. 261) he supplemented by marrying a widow with 1,500l. In 1701 he published 'The Life of William Fuller, gent., being a full and true Account of his Birth, Education, Employs and Intrigues, both of Publick and Private Concerns; his Reconciliation to the Church of England, and the occasion of his coming into service with the present Government.' In the same year he once more revived his story of Prince James's illegitimacy in 'Twenty-six Depositions of Persons of Quality and Worth, with letters of the late Queen . . . and others by Mrs. Mary Grey, proving the whole management of the supposititious Birth of the Prince of Wales, and that Mrs. Grey was barbarously murdered.' The book contained a

and Letters: as well by answer, as otherwise. Set forth in English by William Fulwood, Marchant.' The volume is dedicated in verse to the 'Master, Wardens, and Company of Marchant Tayllors,' and became very popular, running through several editions. It is divided into four books. The first, with much original matter, contains translations from Cicero and the ancients; in the second the translations are from Politian, Ficino, Merula, Pico della Mirandola, and other Italian scholars; the third contains practical and personal letters, mainly original; and in the fourth are six metrical love letters, besides prose specimens. In subsequent editions seven metrical letters are found and other augmentations. Fullwood's verse is spirited and vigorous.

[Corser's Collectanea Anglo-Poetica, vi. 397 (but Fullwood could scarcely have been a scholar of Richard Mulcaster: see J. C. Robinson's Register of Merchant Taylors' School); Nouvelle Biographie Universelle, art. 'Grataroli;' J. P. Collier's Extracts from Reg. of Stationers' Company, i. 50, 53, 62, 157; Sir S. E. Brydges's Censura Literaria, 2nd ed. x. 4.] R. B.

FULMAN, WILLIAM (1632–1688), antiquary, 'the son of a sufficient carpenter,' was born at Penshurst, Kent, in November 1632. His boyish promise is said to have attracted the notice of Henry Hammond [q. v.], then rector of Penshurst, who took him to Oxford, and procured him a place in Magdalen College choir, in order that he might be under the tuition of William White, master of the school. In 1647 he was elected to a scholarship at Corpus Christi College, and placed with an 'excellent tutor but zealous puritan' named Zachary Bogan [q. v.] On 22 July 1648 he was ejected by the parliamentary visitors. Along with another scholar of Corpus, one Timothy Parker, Fulman had deliberately 'blotted' and 'torn out' the name of Edmund Stanton, the parliament's president, which the visitors, on 11 July, had entered in the buttery book in place of Robert Newlin, the expelled president (Register of Visitors of Univ. of Oxford, Camd. Soc. pp. 90, 146, 494). Hammond, who was himself expelled, then employed him as his amanuensis. On this account he has been supposed, absurdly enough, to be the author of the 'Whole Duty of Man,' and the 'Gentleman's Calling.' When twenty-one years old he became, by Hammond's introduction, tutor to the heir of the Peto family of Chesterton, Warwickshire, in which capacity he continued until the Restoration. Then, resuming his scholarship at Corpus, he was created M.A. 23 Aug. 1660, and made fellow of that house. For several years he

stayed in college, 'a severe student in various sorts of learning.' In 1669 he accepted the college rectory of Meysey Hampton, Gloucestershire. There he was cut off by fever 28 June 1688, and was buried in the churchyard at the east end of the chancel, near his wife Hester, daughter of Thomas Manwaring, son of Roger Manwaring, bishop of St. David's. Wood, who knew him well, describes Fulman as 'a most zealous son of the church of England, and a grand enemy to popery and fanaticism. He was a most excellent theologist, admirably well vers'd in ecclesiastical and profane history and chronology, and had a great insight in English history and antiquities; but being totally averse from making himself known . . . his great learning did in a manner dye with him' (Athenæ Oxon. ed. Bliss, iv. 240). It seems that he was not sufficiently complacent or pushing to make his way in the world.

Fulman was the author of: 1. 'Academiæ Oxoniensis Notitia' [anon], 4to, Oxford, 1665, reissued at London in 1675, with additions and corrections from Wood's 'Historia et Antiquitates Universitatis Oxoniensis,' published the year before, the sheets of which Wood sent to Fulman as they came from the press. Fulman, according to Hearne (Collections, Oxf. Hist. Soc. i. 213), furnished the preface to Wood's 'Historia;' he also gave Wood his notes and corrections for the same work, which are now preserved in the Ashmolean Museum, No. 8540 (HUDDESFORD, Cat. of A. à Wood's MSS. 1761, p. 64), and a copy in the Bodleian Library, Rawlinson MS. C. 866. 2. 'Appendix to the Life of Edmund Stanton, D.D., wherein some Passages are further cleared which were not fully held forth by the former Authors,' s. sh. 8vo, London, 1673, a satirical attack on a very partial biography by the nonconformist Richard Mayow. He collected for publication the so-called 'Works' of Charles I, to which he intended prefixing a life of the king, but, being seized with the small-pox, the bookseller, R. Royston, engaged Richard Perrinchief for the task. It was printed in folio in 1662, when Perrinchief, though he used Fulman's work, assumed the whole credit to himself. He had carefully studied the history of the reformation in England, and at the suggestion of Bishop Fell sent to Burnet some corrections and additions for the first part of the latter's 'History.' He also read vol. ii. of the 'History' before it went to press, and 'with great judgment did correct such errors that he found in it,' assistance warmly acknowledged by Burnet (preface to pt. ii. of the History, ed. Pocock, ii. 2). Burnet, however, offended him by printing only an abstract of his notes in the 'Appendix,'

1681, though he asserts that he did so with Fulman's approval. Wood reiterated Fulman's complaints in his 'Athenæ.' Burnet alludes to the ill-bred pair at pages 10–12 of his 'Letter writ to the Lord Bishop of Cov. and Litchfield [Lloyd],' 1693, where he says 'that I might make as much advantage from Mr. Fulman as was possible, I bore with an odd strain of sourness that run through all his letters. Bishop Fell had prepared me for that; and I took everything well at his hands' (cf. his introduction to pt. iii. of the History, ed. Pocock, iii. 21–2). Fulman edited 'Rerum Anglicarum Scriptorum Veterum tom. i.,' fol. Oxford, 1684, with greater accuracy than Thomas Gale, who was responsible for two other volumes of British historians issued in 1687 and 1691. The same year saw completed his edition of 'The Works of Henry Hammond,' 4 vols. fol. London, 1684, the life having been written by Bishop Fell. He also collected large materials for the life of John Hales of Eton (cf. WALKER, Sufferings of the Clergy, 1714, pt. ii. p. 94), and for that of Richard Foxe [q. v.], bishop of Winchester, with an account of the distinguished members of Corpus Christi College. These and many other imperfect collections, contained in twenty quarto and two octavo volumes, he bequeathed to his college. Wood was refused access to them, at which he was very indignant; but his editor, Bliss, laid them under constant contribution in his edition of the 'Athenæ.' Bliss in appending a 'general catalogue' of these collections, praises Fulman for his accuracy and judgment; they are more fully described in H. O. Coxe's 'Catalogue of Oxford MSS.,' pt. ii. There are also a few of his manuscripts in the Rawlinson collection in the Bodleian Library (COXE, Catalogus Cod. MSS. Bibl. Bodl. pars v. fasc. ii.)

[Wood's Athenæ Oxon. (Bliss), vol. i. 'Life,' p. cxiii, 'Vindication,' p. clxix, iii. 499, 838, 932, iv. 239–44, and passim; Reliquiæ Hearnianæ (2nd edit.), ii. 196–7; Gough's British Topography, ii. 104; Chalmers's Biog Dict.; Nicolson's Historical Libraries, 1776, pt. ii. p. 127; Cambridge Univ. Lib. MSS. Catal. v. 443; Notes and Queries, 6th ser. x. 395.] G. G.

FULWAR. [See FULLER.]

FULWELL, ULPIAN (fl. 1586), poet, 'a Somersetshire man born, and a gentleman's son,' says of himself: 'When I was in the flower of my youth I was well regarded of many men, as well for my prompte wit in scoffing and taunting, as also for the comlynesse of my personage, beinge of very tall stature and active in many thinges, by meanes whereof I became a servitour' (Ars Adulandi, 8th Dialogue). His first known publication was a moral dramatic piece, written wholly in rhyme, 'An Enterlude Intituled Like wil to like, quod the Deuel to the Colier, very godly and ful of plesant mirth. . . . Made by Ulpian Fulwel. Imprinted at London . . . by John Allde,' 1568, 4to; another edition, 'London, printed by Edward Allde,' 1587, 4to. It has been reprinted in Dodsley's 'Select Collection of Old English Plays' (vol. iii. edit. 1874, &c.) In 1570 Fulwell was rector of Naunton, Gloucestershire (BIGLAND, Gloucestershire, ii. 236), to which he had presumably been presented by Queen Elizabeth. His next work was 'The Flower of Fame. Containing the bright Renowne & moste fortunate raigne of King Henry the VIII. Wherein is mentioned of matters, by the rest of our Cronographers ouerpassed. Compyled by Ulpian Fulwell. Hereunto is annexed (by the Aucthor) a short treatice of iii noble and vertuous Queenes. And a discourse of the worthie seruice that was done at Haddington in Scotlande, the seconde yere of the raigne of King Edward the Sixt. Imprinted at London by William Hoskins,' 1575, 4to. This curious and highly interesting medley was written somewhat on the model of the then popular 'Mirrour for Magistrates,' partly in verse and partly in prose; the events recorded being chiefly taken from Hall's 'Chronicles.' The author was assisted in his labours by 'Master Edmunde Harman,' formerly a groom of the privy chamber to Henry VIII, as he acknowledges in the dedication to 'sir William Cecill, baron of Burghleygh.' On fol. 39 there commences a sort of appendix containing commemorations in verse, and 'Epitaphs' on three of Henry's wives, Anne Boleyn, Jane Seymour, and Katherine Parr. In a 'Preamble to this parte of the Booke following,' he states that he will celebrate Henry's other wives if the present book should be well received. It has been included by Thomas Park in his edition of the 'Harleian Miscellany' (ix. 337–75). The following year Fulwell published a humorous work which attained considerable popularity, entitled 'Tee [sic] first part of the eight liberall science; Entituled, Ars adulandi, the art of Flattery, with the confutation thereof, both very pleasant and profitable, deuised and compiled by Vlpian Fulwell . . . Imprinted at London by William Hoskins,' 1576, 4to (the only copy known, that in the Capell collection, is fully described by SINKER, Cat. of English Books printed before MDCI. in Trin. Coll. Cambr., pp. 199–200). The copyright was sold by William Hoskins to Henry Bamford, 4 March 1576–7 (ARBER, Stationers' Registers, ii. 309), and by him to Richard Jones, 3 March 1577–8 (ib. ii. 325). Jones issued another edition, 'newly corrected and augmented,' 4to, London, 1579, and a third without a date, but probably in 1580. Collier is of opinion that a book called 'Flatteries Displaie,' licensed to Robert Waldegrave in December 1580, was the same work under a slightly different title. This book, which is inscribed to Lady Burghley, consists of several dialogues, chiefly in prose, with the exception of the sixth—between Diogenes and Ulpian—which is in verse, of the fourteen-syllable metre. In the first dialogue, between the author and the printer, whom he calls ' my olde fellow and friend, W[illiam] H[oskins],' Fulwell mentions his own poverty and thread-bare garments. Fulwell's attendance at court, as he sadly confesses to ' Diogenes' in the sixth dialogue, had brought him no hope of further preferment, though in answer to the latter's query he admits he had found one faithful friend in the world, and in some epigrammatic lines at the end he covertly expresses the name of his friend, Edmund Harman. In the ' eyghth Dialogue betweene Sir Symon the Parson of Poll Iobbam, and the Authour,' Fulwell endeavours to place the character of Sir Simon the Parson in the most odious light he can, and satirises the changes effected by the Reformation, though professing hopes that the queen will suppress the disorders. Although the author mentions a second part as intended, it does not appear to have been ever published. Fulwell became a commoner of St. Mary Hall, Oxford, in 1578, but probably did not take a degree. In 1572 he married at Naunton a lady whose baptismal name was Eleanor, and thenceforward for some years his signature occurs frequently in the register of that parish, chiefly in reference to the christening of his various children. In 1585 his name appears in connection with the burial of a son ; in the following year Joseph Hanxman became rector of Naunton.

[Wood's Athenæ Oxon. (Bliss), i. 540–2 ; Corser's Collectanea (Chetham Soc.), pt. vi. pp. 382–396 ; Payne Collier's Bibliographical Account of Early English Literature, i. 296–9 ; Cat. of the Huth Library, ii. 566 ; Notes and Queries, 3rd ser. xii. 183–4, 234 ; Carew Hazlitt's Handbook to the Popular Poetical and Dramatic Literature of Great Britain, p. 215 ; Carew Hazlitt's Collections and Notes, 1867–76, p. 175 ; Hartshorne's Book Rarities in Univ. of Cambr. p. 295 ; information from the rector of Naunton.] G. G.

FULWOOD, CHRISTOPHER (1590 ?–1643), royalist, probably born in London about 1590, was the eldest son of Sir George Fulwood, lord of the manor of Middleton by Youlgrave, Derbyshire. His father, who died in 1624, was admitted a member of Gray's

Inn in 1589 (*Harl. MS.* 1912, f 33), and appears to have passed the greater part of his life in the practice of the law in London, as in 1608 he is styled of Fulwood Street, Holborn (cf. his will registered in P. C. C. 55, Byrde). In 1605 Christopher was also entered at Gray's Inn, of which society he was admitted ancient 28 May 1622, appointed autumn reader in 1628, and treasurer 3 Nov. 1637 (*Harl. MS.* 1912, ff. 33, 183, 194, 248). When disengaged from his professional duties he resided at Middleton. His strict impartiality as a magistrate is commemorated by the ' apostle of the Peak,' William Bagshaw [q. v.] In 1640, at the Bakewell sessions, the curate of Taddington was charged with puritanism. Fulwood, who was chairman, ' though known to be a zealot in the cause of the then king and conformity, released him, and gave his accusers a sharp reprimand' (*De Spiritualibus Pecci*, 8vo, 1702, p. 17). Fulwood's influence in the district was of great value to the royalist cause. He was specially employed to raise the Derbyshire miners as a life-guard for his majesty in 1642, when the lord-lieutenant of the county, the Earl of Rutland, declined to appear in the service. He was soon at the head of a regiment of eleven hundred men, who were mustered on Tideswell Moor. His success appears to have alarmed the leaders of the parliamentarians in the neighbourhood, who, according to the local tradition, soon found an opportunity of seizing Fulwood while at his house at Middleton. The chief enemy of the king in the district was Sir John Gell of Hopton, and it was by Gell's emissaries that Fulwood was captured. It is said that while in his house he received notice of the near approach of the hostile detachment, and hid himself in a fissure separating an outlying mass of rock from its parent cliff, in the dale of the Bradford, a few hundred yards in the rear of the mansion. His pursuers saw him, and a shot from them inflicted a mortal wound. He was carried off towards Lichfield, a garrison town which had been taken by Gell on the preceding 5 March, but died on the way at Calton in Staffordshire, 16 Nov. 1643. The rock is still pointed out at Middleton. Before the close of 1644 the property had passed out of the hands of the family. Fulwood's two daughters, Elizabeth and Mary, sought refuge among their friends in London, where they died in obscurity. The mansion at Middleton began to be demolished about 1720.

[Dugdale's Origines Juridiciales (1666), pp. 297, 299 ; Jewitt's Reliquary, i. 89–93 ; Lysons's Magna Britannia, vol. v. ' Derbyshire,' pp. cxxix, 204 ; Cal. S. P., Dom. 1633–4, p. 516.] G. G.

FURLONG, THOMAS (1794–1827), poet, son of a farmer, was born in 1794 at Scarawalsh, situated between Ferns and Enniscorthy, co. Wexford. He obtained an appointment in the counting-house of an extensive distillery at Dublin, where he continued until his death. His first work was a poem, 'The Misanthrope' (Lond. 1819), composed, he stated, with the object of reclaiming a friend who, owing to early disappointments, had retired from society. It was withdrawn by the author on account of numerous typographical errors. He issued a second edition at Dublin in 1821, with other poems. A poem entitled 'The Plagues of Ireland: an Epistle,' appeared at Dublin in 1824, with a view to promoting catholic emancipation. He described his work as 'a little sketch and hasty picturing' of the more prominent evils and grievances which should be removed before that 'harassed land' of Ireland could calculate on the enjoyment of tranquillity. To 'The Plagues of Ireland' Furlong appended a few 'occasional poems.' He contributed largely to the 'New Monthly Magazine,' as well as to other periodicals, and projected a literary journal at Dublin. Thomas Moore, Charles Maturin, and Lady Morgan praised his work. At the instance of James Hardiman, author of the 'History of Galway,' Furlong undertook to produce metrical versions in English of the compositions of Carolan and other native Irish poets. While engaged on this work, and on a poem entitled 'The Doom of Derenzie,' Furlong died on 25 July 1827 at Dublin, and was interred in the churchyard of Drumcondra. Of the 'Doom of Derenzie' but one sheet had been revised by the author. It appeared posthumously (London, 1829). The poem treated the superstitions of the peasantry of Wexford. Several of Furlong's metrical translations, and a portrait of him, appeared in Hardiman's work on Irish minstrelsy (London, 1831). One of his compositions was, in 1845, included in Duffy's 'Ballad Poetry of Ireland.'

[Prefaces to Furlong's publications; Dublin Penny Journal, 1832; Hardiman's Irish Minstrelsy, 1831.]   J. T. G.

FURLY, BENJAMIN (1636–1714), quaker and friend of Locke, born at Colchester 13 April 1636, began life as a merchant there, and joined the early quakers. In 1659–60 he assisted John Stubbs in the compilation of the 'Battle-Door.' George Fox records that this work was finished in 1661, and that Furly took great pains with it. Some time previous to 1677 he went to reside at Rotterdam, where he set up as a merchant in the Scheepmaker's Haven. In 1677 George Fox stayed and held religious meetings at Furly's house in Rotterdam, and Furly then accompanied Fox, Keith, and others through a great part of Holland and Germany, acting as an interpreter. Later on in the same year he made a ministerial journey with William Penn. His house became the rendezvous of Leclerc, Limborch, and other learned men, and there he entertained Algernon Sydney, Locke (1686–8), and Locke's pupil, the third Lord Shaftesbury (1688–9). Sydney constantly wrote to him from 1677 to 1679. Edward Clarke of Chipley seems to have introduced Locke to him, and their correspondence lasted as long as Locke lived. Locke delighted in playing with Furly's children. Subsequently Furly renounced quakerism, again embraced it, but is supposed finally to have left it. He died at Rotterdam in 1714. Furly's chief works are: 1. 'A Battle-Door for Teachers and Professors to learn Singular and Plural,' &c. (in thirty-five languages), with Stubbs and Fox, 1660. 2. Preface to Ames's 'Die Sache Christi und seines Volks,' 1662. 3. 'The World's Honour detected, and, for the Unprofitableness thereof, rejected,' &c., 1663. He also wrote a number of prefaces to the works of other men, assisted Keith in writing 'The Universal Free Grace of the Gospel asserted,' and translated several works into English from the Dutch.

Furly's valuable library was sold by auction, and a catalogue, 'Bibliotheca Furleiana,' was published (1714). He was twice married. On the death of his first wife in 1691, Locke sent a letter of condolence. By her he had three sons, Benjohan (b. 1681), John, and Arent. The two eldest were merchants. The youngest was secretary to the Earl of Peterborough in Spain, and died there in 1705. Benjohan's daughter, Dorothy, married Thomas Forster, whose sons, Benjamin and Edward, are noticed above. Edward's grandson, Thomas Ignatius Maria Forster [q. v.], inherited much of Furly's correspondence, and printed part of his collection as 'Original Letters of Locke, Shaftesbury, and Sydney' in 1830, reissuing it in his privately printed 'Epistolarium' in 1830, 2nd edit. 1847. Much of Shaftesbury's correspondence with Furly is at the Record Office.

[Swarthmore MSS.; Fox's Journal, ed. 1763, pp. 328–518; Smith's Cat. of Friends' Books; Forster's Orig. Letters of Locke, 1830, cxviii–cxx; H. R. Fox Bourne's Life of Locke, ii.]
                A. C. B.

FURNEAUX, PHILIP (1726–1783), independent minister, was born in December 1726 at Totnes, Devonshire. At the grammar school of that town he formed a life-long friendship with Benjamin Kennicott (1718–1770) [q. v.] In 1742 or 1743 he came to London to study for the dissenting ministry under David Jennings, D.D., at the academy in Wellclose Square. He appears to have remained at the academy till 1749, probably assisting Jennings, whose 'Hebrew Antiquities' he afterwards ably edited (1766). After ordination he became (1749) assistant to Henry Read, minister of the presbyterian congregation at St. Thomas's, Southwark. On the resignation of Roger Pickering, about 1752, he became in addition one of the two preachers of the Sunday evening lecture at Salters' Hall (not the more famous 'mer-chants' lecture' at Salters' Hall on Tuesday mornings). Retaining this lectureship, in 1753 he succeeded Moses Lowman in the pastorate of the independent congregation at Clapham. His discourses were weighty and well composed, and in spite of an un-pleasing delivery and a habit of 'poring over his notes,' he drew a large congregation, and kept his popularity as long as he was able to preach. He received the degree of D.D. on 3 Aug. 1767, from the Marischal College, Aberdeen. From October 1769 to January 1775 he was relieved of the afternoon service on his lecture evenings by Samuel Morton Savage, D.D. As a leading member of the Coward Trust he had much to do with the revised plan of academical education adopted by the trustees on Doddridge's death. He was also from 1766 to 1778 a trustee of Dr. Williams's foundations.

Furneaux distinguished himself by his ex-ertions in behalf of the rights of noncon-formists. His name is closely associated with the progress of the 'sheriff's case,' which was before the courts for nearly thirteen years (1754–67). It arose out of an expedient adopted in 1748 by the corporation of Lon-don to raise money for building the Mansion House by fining nonconformists who declined to qualify for the office of sheriff in accordance with the Sacramental Test Act. Some 15,000l. had been thus obtained when, in 1754, three nonconformists resisted the imposition. The case reached the House of Lords in 1767, and in February of that year was decided in favour of the nonconformists. It was on this occa-sion that Lord Mansfield delivered the speech in which occurs the often-cited remark that the 'dissenters' way of worship' is not only lawful but 'established.' This speech was reported, without the help of a single note, by Furneaux, who possessed an extraordinary memory; he had, however, the assistance of another hearer of the speech, Samuel Wilton, D.D., independent minister of the Weigh-

house, Eastcheap. Mansfield, who revised the report, found in it only two or three trivial errors.

In 1769 appeared the fourth volume of Blackstone's 'Commentaries,' in which, under the head of 'Offences against God and Re-ligion,' nonconformity is treated as a 'crime.' Priestley was the first to animadvert on this opinion; Blackstone replied in a small pam-phlet (2 Sept. 1769). In the following year Furneaux published his 'Letters to Mr. Jus-tice Blackstone,' in which the moral argu-ment against enforcing religious truths by civil penalties is presented with remarkable power.

Furneaux was present on 6 Feb. 1772 in the gallery of the House of Commons with Ed-ward Pickard, presbyterian minister of Carter Lane, when the clerical petition for relief from subscription, known as the 'Feathers' peti-tion,' was under discussion. The speeches of Sir William Meredith and Sir George Savile in favour of the petition were reported by Furneaux from memory. In the course of the debate the remark was made by Lord North, who opposed the petition, that if similar relief were asked by the dissenting clergy there would be no reasonable objec-tion to it. Acting on this hint Furneaux and Pickard procured a meeting of noncon-formist ministers of the three denominations, who adopted an application to parliament (prepared by Furneaux) for relief from doc-trinal subscription. A relief bill passed the commons on 3 April 1772 without a division; on 18 May it was rejected in the lords. In support of a second bill to the same effect Furneaux published his 'Essay on Toleration' (1773). Relief was at length granted (1779), but not, as Furneaux desired, without a test. The new subscription, in which the Holy Scriptures were substituted for the Anglican articles, was devised by Lord North, and carried by the eloquence of Burke.

By this time Furneaux was incapable of taking any part in affairs. In 1777 he was seized with hereditary insanity, and remained under this affliction till his death on 27 Nov. 1783. He was unmarried, and no portrait of him is known. On the outbreak of his malady a considerable fund was raised for his support, Lord Mansfield being among the contributors. The fund accumulated after his death, and is still in existence. In ac-cordance with a scheme approved by the charity commissioners its income (the prin-cipal being over 10,000l.) is divided between two institutions maintained by unitarians, Manchester New College and the 'Ministers' Benevolent Society.'

He published: 1. 'Letters to the Honourable Mr. Justice Blackstone concerning his Exposition of the Act of Toleration,' &c., 1770, 8vo; 2nd edition, 1771, 8vo, has additions, and Mansfield's speech as appendix; reprinted, Philadelphia, 1773, 8vo. 2. 'An Essay on Toleration,' &c., 1773, 8vo. Also sermon on education (1755), a fast sermon (1758), funeral sermon for Henry Miles, D.D. (1763), sermon at ordination of Samuel Wilton (1766), ordination charge to George Waters and William Youat (1769), and sermon to the Society for Propagating Christian Knowledge in the Highlands (1775). In 1771 Furneaux was engaged in transcribing and editing the biblical annotations of Samuel Chandler, D.D. [q. v.], but the work was never published.

[Memoir by J. T. (Joshua Toulmin) in Protestant Dissenters' Magazine, 1798, p. 128 sq.; Wilson's Dissenting Churches, 1808, i. 199, 323, ii. 5, iv. 315; Belsham's Memoir of Lindsey, 1812, pp. 56, 57, 62 sq. (needs correction of dates); Chalmers's Gen. Biog. Dict., 1814, xv. 183 sq.; Rutt's Memoir of Priestley, 1831, i. 73, 137, 164, 169, 170, 318 sq.; Bogue and Bennett's Hist. of Dissenters, 1833, ii. 597 sq.; Jeremy's Presbyterian Fund, 1885, p. 157 sq.; information from the Registrar of Aberdeen University.] A. G.

FURNEAUX, TOBIAS (1735–1781), circumnavigator, was born at Swilly, near Plymouth, 21 Aug. 1735. Various letters show him to have been employed on the French coast, coast of Africa, and West India stations during war-time in 1760–1763, on board H.M.S. Edinburgh, Melampe, and Ferret. He was second lieutenant of H.M.S. Dolphin, Captain Samuel Wallis, in his voyage of discovery round the world (19 Aug. 1766–20 May 1768). He became commander in November 1771, and was soon afterwards appointed to command H.M.S. Adventure in company with Captain Cook's ship the Resolution in his second voyage. The Adventure was twice separated from the Resolution, and Furneaux's account of events during those periods is given in two chapters in Cook's narrative (vol. i. ch. vii., vol. ii. ch. viii.)

During the first separation (8 Feb.– 19 May 1773) he sailed fourteen hundred leagues alone, and explored in great part the south and east coast of Tasmania, or Van Diemen's Land, which had been wholly unvisited since its first discovery by Tasman in 1642. The chart sketched by him (page 115) appears to be the first of that coast on record, and the names given by him to localities, as Mewstone, Swilly, Storm Bay, Fluted Head, Adventure Bay, Bay of Fires, Eddystone Point, are retained in most cases in modern maps. Cook, who himself visited

the same coast on his third voyage, confirms in his narrative (i. 103–4) the substantial accuracy of Furneaux's survey except in one point, and named after him the islands discovered by him in what was then thought to be a deep bay, but is now known as Banks Strait, opening into Bass Strait.

Cook also gave the name of Furneaux to one of the groups of coral islets in what is now known as the Low Archipelago, visited by the two ships together, and named another group after the Adventure. The ships again became separated off the coast of New Zealand 22 Oct. 1773, and Furneaux, after cruising about some time in a vain endeavour to rejoin the Resolution, was ultimately obliged to return home alone, and reached Spithead 14 July 1774. The chief event occurring during this separation was the loss of a boat's crew commanded by Mr. Rowe, midshipman, with nine others, who were all killed and eaten by the natives in a cove of Queen Charlotte's Sound, New Zealand. During the whole voyage Furneaux made many attempts, some of which had permanent success, to introduce into the islands domestic animals and useful vegetables, especially potatoes. It is also noteworthy that he brought home in the Adventure, Omai, a native of Ulaietea, who remained in England for two years, and was taken back in Cook's third voyage. Omai was the first South Sea islander who had ever been seen in England.

Furneaux was made captain 10 Aug. 1775, and in that rank commanded the Syren (28) in Sir P. Parker's attack on New Orleans 28 June 1777. He died at Swilly 19 Sept. 1781, aged 46. Portraits of him by Northcote are preserved in the family.

[Hawkesworth's Narrative of Wallis's Voyage; Cook's Narrative of his Second Voyage; family papers.] H. F.

FURNESS, JOCELIN OF (*fl.* 1200), hagiographer. [See JOCELIN.]

FURNESS, RICHARD (1791–1857), poet, the son of Samuel Furness, a small farmer at Eyam, Derbyshire, was born on 2 Aug. 1791. Leaving school at the age of fourteen he was apprenticed to a currier at Chesterfield, and soon displayed a taste for versifying and an ardour for learning. From some French officers on parole he learned French and mathematics. He became proficient in music. When he was seventeen years old he joined the Wesleyan methodists, and undertook the duties of local preacher. Four years later he walked to London, and on his arrival enlisted as a volunteer soldier. He did not, however, give up preaching, and on one occasion, at the request of Dr. Adam

Clarke, he discoursed from the pulpit at the City Road Chapel. After a year he returned to his native county. He separated from the methodists about this time through resentment at his associates in calling him to account for writing a patriotic song which was sung at a meeting in a public-house. In 1813 he started business on his own account at Eyam as a currier, but trade was neglected for music, poetry, and mathematics, and his prospects were not improved when in 1816 he ran away with and married Frances Ibbotson of Hathersage. In 1821 he entered on the duties of schoolmaster in the free school of the small village of Dore, Derbyshire. He also acted as vestry and parish clerk, but showed his independence of mind and action by invariably closing his book and resuming his seat at the recitation of the Athanasian Creed. He likewise practised medicine and surgery, and when the ancient chapel of Dore was pulled down, his plans for a new one were adopted, and he not only superintended the erection of the building, but carved the ornamented figures which adorn the structure. On a change of incumbent at Dore he retired from his office of schoolmaster on a pension of 15*l.* The only duties he had now to perform were those of district registrar, which yielded him 12*l.* a year. In no year of his life did his income exceed 80*l.*

His first publication was a satirical poem entitled the 'Rag Bag,' 1832. His next was 'Medicus-Magus,' a poem, in three cantos,' Sheffield, 1836, 12mo, in which he depicted the manners, habits, and limited intelligence, in the more remote parts of Derbyshire, the local terms being elucidated by a glossary. The title was afterwards altered to 'The Astrologer.' Many of his miscellaneous poems were printed in the 'Sheffield Iris.' After his death a collected edition of his 'Poetical Works,' with a sketch of his life by Dr. G. Calvert Holland, was published (Sheffield, 1858, 8vo). His verse is antiquated but forcible. One of his short pieces, the 'Old Year's Funeral,' was thought by James Montgomery to be worthy of comparison with Coleridge's ode 'On the Departing Year.'

His wife died in 1844, and in 1850 he took as a second wife, Mary, widow of John Lunn of Staveley, Derbyshire. He died on 13 Dec. 1857, and was buried at Eyam church.

[Holland's Sketch; Hall's Biog. Sketches, 1873, p. 334; Holland and Everett's Memoir of James Montgomery, vi. 232.]   C. W. S.

FURSA, SAINT (*d.* 650), of Peronne in France, was an Irishman of noble birth. Two pedigrees of him are given in the 'Book of Leinster,' and also in the 'Lebor Brecc.'

One traces his descent from Rudraidhe Mac Sitri, ancestor of the Clanna Rudraidhe, of the race of Ir; the other from Lugaidh Laga, brother of Olioll Olum of the race of Heber; but they evidently refer to different persons, and Colgan has shown that there were two saints named Fursa, the first of whom flourished about 550. The 'Martyrology of Donegal,' as well as the 'Lebor Brecc' notes to the 'Calendar of Œngus,' clearly regards the first pedigree as that of Fursa of Peronne, but Colgan with Keating regards the Fursa of the second as the saint of Peronne, and this is clearly right, as Sigebert, king of East Anglia, received him in 637. His father was Fintan, son of Finlogh, a chieftain of South Munster; his mother, Gelges, was daughter of Aedh Finn of the Hui Briuin of Connaught. He was probably born somewhere among the Hui Briuin, and baptised by St. Brendan. His parents having returned to Munster, the child was brought up there, and from his boyhood he 'gave his attention to the reading of the Holy Scriptures and monastic discipline.' He retired to study in the island of Inisquin in Lough Corrib, under the abbot St. Meldan, called his 'soul-friend.' He afterwards built a monastery for himself at a place called Rathmat, which appears to be Killursa (Fursa's Church), in the north-west of the county of Clare.

After this he set out for Munster to visit his relatives. After his arrival he had the first of several remarkable cataleptic seizures, during which he had visions of bright angels, who raised him on their wings, and soothed him by hymns. In one trance famine and plagues were foretold. This evidently refers to the second visitation of the plague known as the Buidhe Connaill, 'the yellow or straw-coloured plague,' which visited Ireland about fourteen years after Fursa's death. The chief visions appear to have taken place in 627. Deeply impressed by them, Fursa travelled through Ireland, proclaiming what he had heard. At Cork he had a vision of a golden ladder set up at the tomb of St. Finn Barr [q. v.] and reaching to heaven, by which souls were ascending.

For ten years, in accordance with angelic directions, he continued 'to preach the word of God without respect of persons.' In the notes on the 'Calendar of Œngus' a strange story is told of his exchanging diseases with St. Maignen of Kilmainham. To avoid admiring crowds and jealousy, Fursa went away with a few brethren to a small island in the sea, and shortly after, with his brothers Foillan and Ultan, he passed through Britain (Wales), and arrived at East Anglia, where he was hospitably received by King Sigebert. After another vision—twelve years since his last seizure—he hastened to build the monastery Cnoberesburg or Burghcastle, in Suffolk, on land granted by the king. Then, committing it to the charge of Goban and Dichull, he went away to his brother Ultan, with whom he lived as a hermit for a year.

Owing to the disturbed state of the country he had to go to France and take refuge with Clovis, king of Neustria. The king being a child, the government was in the hands of Erchinoald, mayor of the palace, who gave him land at Latiniacum, now Lagny, on the Marne, six leagues from Paris. Here he erected a monastery in 644. According to the account in the 'Codex Salmanticensis,' it was when travelling with Clovis and Erchinoald that his last illness came on. He died on 16 Jan. probably in 650, at Macerias, now Mazeroeles. He was buried at Peronne, in the church built by Erchinoald, and with this place his name has since been associated. He was reputed to have performed miracles in his lifetime, and even his pastoral staff, if sent to a sick person, was supposed to have a healing power. The brethren whom he took with him formed the nucleus of an Irish monastery, and the succession appears to have been kept up by emissaries from Ireland, as we read in the 'Annals of the Four Masters' at 774, that 'Moenan, son of Cormac, abbot of Cathair Fursa (the city of Fursa, i.e. Peronne) in France, died.'

Fursa's visions were placed on record soon after his death in 'the little book' to which Bæda refers, and which Mabillon considers to be the life published by Surius at 16 Jan. Bæda describes the agitation of a monk who, when describing what he heard from Fursa's lips, though it was the severest season of the year, and he was thinly clad, broke out into a profuse perspiration from mere terror.

[Codex Salmanticensis, p. 77 (London, 1888); Bedæ Eccl. Hist. lib. iii. cap. 19; Lanigan's Eccl. Hist. ii. 448–64; Annals of the Four Masters, A.D. 774; Calendar of Œngus, p. xxxv; Dr. Todd's St. Patrick, p. 406.] T. O.

FURSDON, JOHN, in religion CUTH-BERT (d. 1638), Benedictine monk, the eldest son of Philip Fursdon of Fursdon in the parish of Cadbury, Devonshire, was born at Thorverton in that county. He became an enthusiastic disciple of Father Augustine Baker [see BAKER, DAVID], his father's chaplain, and proceeded to the Benedictine convent of St. Gregory at Douay, where, after completing the year of probation, he took the solemn vows as a professed father of the order, 25 Nov. 1620 (WELDON, Chronicle, Append. p. 8). Returning to the English mission, he

laboured chiefly in the southern counties, and he appears to have often resided in the families of Viscount Montagu and Lady Elizabeth Falkland. He was an instrument in the conversion of Lady Falkland's four daughters, and of Hugh Paulinus, or Serenus, Cressy [q. v.] Fursdon, who frequently passed under the assumed name of Breton, died in Lady Falkland's house in London on 2 Feb. 1637–8.

His works are: 1. 'The Life of the . . . Lady Magdalen, Viscountesse Montague, written in Latin . . . by Richard Smith [bishop of Chalcedon], and now translated into English by C. F.,' 1627, 4to, dedicated to Antony Maria, viscount Montague. 2. 'The Life and Miracles of St. Benedict,' 1638, 12mo, with plates. 3. 'The Rule of St. Bennet, by C. F.,' Douay, 1638, 4to, dedicated to 'Mrs. Anne Carie, daughter of the Lord Viscount Faulkland.' A new edition by 'one of the Benedictine Fathers of St. Michael's, near Hereford [i.e. Francis Cuthbert Doyle], was published at London, 1875, 8vo.

[Oliver's Catholic Religion in Cornwall, pp. 9 n., 310–11; Snow's Necrology, p. 44; Weldon's Chronicle, pp. 178, 210; Sweeney's Life of Augustine Baker, p. 40; Gillow's Bibl. Dict.; Fullerton's Life of Lady Falkland, p. 148 seq.] T. C.

FUSELI, HENRY (JOHANN HEINRICH FUESSLI) (1741–1825), painter and author, born at Zurich in Switzerland, 7 Feb. 1741, was the second son of Johann Caspar Fuessli, painter and lexicographer, and Elisabetha Waser, his wife. The family of Fuessli, still, as for many generations, resident in Zurich, has produced many members distinguished in art, literature, and science. Melchior Fuessli, an ancestor, had distinguished himself for original work. Johann Caspar Fuessli, a pupil of Kupetzky, the portrait-painter, was himself a well-known painter of portraits and landscapes, patronised by the petty royalty of the neighbouring states, and the author of the 'Lives of the Helvetic Painters.' His brothers, Heinrich and Johann Rudolf, were also artists, and the latter was the compiler of the 'Allgemeines Künstler-Lexicon;' each had a son named Heinrich, whose works should be carefully distinguished from those of John Henry Fuseli. Of Johann Caspar's numerous family five survived, including Heinrich; the eldest, Johann Rudolf, became an artist, entered the imperial service at Vienna, and possessed the family taste for lexicography; the youngest, Johann Caspar, was most noted for his achievements in entomology, another science to which the family was addicted; the daughters, Anna and Elisabetha, were noted for their skill in drawing birds and insects. This art-loving family was on intimate terms with the literary circle at Zurich, which claims to have started the romantic movement in general literature, represented by J. J. Bodmer, J. J. Breitinger, and the painter-poet, Salomon Gessner, who stood sponsor to the infant Heinrich. Fuessli was therefore nursed in an atmosphere of romanticism from his earliest days, and showed an early predilection for art. He received some instruction from his father and elder brother, but the father was discouraged by his own experience of an artist's career, and, distrustful of his son's mechanical powers, intended the boy for the clerical profession. Fuseli, however, secretly pursued his studies, and his habit of drawing with his left hand, while his father or tutor was reading aloud, caused him to be 'ambidexter,' a faculty which he retained through life. He studied eagerly his father's collection of prints after Michelangelo and other artists, and his childish productions all showed the love of weird fantasy characteristic of his later works. He made drawings to illustrate the old poem of 'Howleglas,' and subsequently etched them; and he studied with interest the works of Tobias Stimmer, Jost Amman, and other old Zurich artists. When about twelve his family removed into the country for his mother's health, and art for a time made way among the children for entomology. When he was about fifteen his father placed him at the Collegium Carolinum at Zurich, of which Bodmer and Breitinger were professors. Here he quickly attracted attention by his hot temper, his various extravagances in dress and behaviour, and his immense capacities for mental labour. He rapidly acquired a good knowledge of the English, French, and Italian languages, besides Greek and Latin, and was an ardent student of the works of Shakespeare, Richardson, Milton, Dante, and Rousseau, which, with the Bible, gave plenty of scope to his ever-active pencil. He made several essays in composition, both prose and verse, but never showed any aptitude for mathematics or other abstract sciences. He made many intimate friends, among them Johann Caspar Lavater, the physiognomist, the brothers Johann Jakob and Felix Hess, Leonard Usteri, and others who attained distinction in after life. In 1761 Lavater and Fuessli, whose kindred characters made them the closest of friends, entered into holy orders, and at once made their mark by their attempts to raise the style of pulpit oratory in Zurich. Before they could accomplish much they became involved in a cause which

soon agitated the whole town. One Felix Grebel, bailiff of Gruningen, one of the bailiwicks of Zurich, was accused of gross oppression and extortion. The young friends, in August 1762, sent an anonymous letter to Grebel threatening exposure. They next published a pamphlet, entitled 'The Under-Bailiff, or the Complaints of a Patriot,' and sent copies to the various members of the government. The authors were summoned to appear; Lavater and Fuessli came forward accordingly and proved their charges. Grebel was disgraced, but, as he was son-in-law of the burgomaster, and had powerful family connections, it was thought advisable for the young patriots to absent themselves for a time from Zurich. J. G. Sulzer, the author of a 'Theory of the Fine Arts,' who was about to return to Berlin, where he was professor, offered to take them with him, and in March 1763 Lavater, Fuessli, and the brothers Hess left Zurich. They visited Augsburg, where Fuessli was especially struck with Reichel's colossal statue of St. Michael at the arsenal, proceeded to Leipzig, where they met Ernesti, Gellert, and other celebrities, and reached Berlin to find that their fame had preceded them. Fuessli was at once employed to assist Rode on a set of illustrations to Bodmer's 'Noachide,' but after a short stay in Berlin visited Professor Spalding, the theologian, at Barth in Pomerania. At this time there was a desire to establish a channel of literary communication between Germany and England, and through Sulzer's kind agency Fuessli was summoned to Berlin and presented to the British minister, Sir Andrew Mitchell, at whose house, among others, he met Dr. John Armstrong [q. v.], afterwards his intimate friend. Mitchell was impressed by the young man's literary and artistic compositions, and offered to take him to England. Lavater and his other friends accompanied him as far as Göttingen, where he left them, and reached England towards the end of 1763. Thus introduced, he easily obtained access to several persons of importance, notably Mr. Coutts, the banker (who remained his steadfast friend and patron throughout), Millar, the bookseller, and Cadell, his successor, and Joseph Johnson, the well-known radical publisher in St. Paul's Churchyard. At Johnson's dinner-table he met some of the most remarkable persons in art and literature of the day. At first he appears to have thought only of a literary life, and supported life by translating books, although his pencil was never idle. In 1765 Fusseli, as he now called himself, published a translation of Winckelmann's 'Reflections on the Painting and Sculpture of the Greeks,' which provoked an animated reply from James Barry [q. v.] He also, at the suggestion of his friend, John Bonnycastle [q. v.], plunged into the controversy then raging between Voltaire and Rousseau, with a spirited pamphlet in defence of Rousseau; the greater part of this impression was accidentally destroyed by fire at Johnson's shop, and not much regretted by the author. In 1766 he became travelling tutor to Viscount Chewton, the eldest son of Earl Waldegrave, but his impetuous nature was not suitable to the office, and in 1767 he returned to London. Happening to obtain an introduction to Sir Joshua Reynolds, he produced a portfolio of his drawings; Reynolds was surprised to find that he had never been in Italy, and also that he was doubtful of his artistic abilities, and urged him most strongly to become a painter. Thus encouraged he devoted himself entirely to drawing, and tried his hand at oil-painting. His first picture, 'Joseph interpreting the dreams of the butler and baker of Pharaoh,' was purchased by his friend Johnson; it is now in the possession of Hon. Henry Dudley Ryder. In 1769 he started with Armstrong for a tour in Italy. They sailed for Leghorn, quarrelled during a tedious voyage, and parted upon their arrival. Fuseli (or Fuzely), as the artist now called himself to suit the Italian pronunciation, proceeded alone to Rome, where he arrived on 9 Feb. 1770. Here he remained eight years, studying most energetically the works of the great masters, and above all Michelangelo, by whose great genius he was influenced to an exaggerated degree, much as Spranger and Goltzius had been, though he was fully aware of their mistakes. His abilities gained him many friends and numerous commissions. In 1774 there appeared at the Royal Academy exhibition a drawing of 'The death of Cardinal Beaufort,' by — Fuseli at Rome; in 1775, at the exhibition of the Society of Artists at Exeter Change, 'Hubert yielding to the entreaties of Prince Arthur,' by Mr. Fuseli at Rome; and in 1777, at the Royal Academy, 'A Scene in Macbeth,' by — Fusole at Rome. A book of drawings made by him in Rome (preserved in the print room at the British Museum) contains numerous sketches, embodying many of the ideas from Milton, Dante, and Shakespeare, which he afterwards worked up into his more famous pictures. He visited Venice, Naples, and Pompeii, and on leaving Rome in 1778 returned through Lombardy to Switzerland; here he revisited his family and friends at Zurich, remained there six months, fell in love but was unsuccessful in his suit, and painted a picture of 'The Confederacy of the Founders of Hel-

vetian Liberty' for his native town. In 1779 he was back in London, and lodging at 100 St. Martin's Lane with John Cartwright [q. v.], a fellow student with him at Rome. Fuseli renewed his intimacy with his old friends (including Armstrong, who paid him a handsome compliment in his 'Art of Preserving Health,' ii. 236), and made several new ones, notably William Lock [q. v.] of Norbury and his son, and Dr. Moore [q. v.], author of 'Zeluco,' with whose family he became on terms of special intimacy. In 1780 he again exhibited at the Royal Academy, sending 'Ezzelin Bracciaferro musing over Meduna, slain by him for disloyalty during his absence in the Holy Land' (a subject of his own invention, formerly in the Angerstein Collection), 'Satan starting from the touch of Ithuriel's spear,' and 'Jason appearing before Pelias.' These pictures excited much attention, and obtained a prominent place by the direction of Sir Joshua Reynolds. In 1781 he painted, and in 1782 exhibited, his picture of 'The Nightmare,' which at once took the popular fancy, and insured his future success; he painted several versions of it (one is in the possession of the Earl of Harrowby), and numerous engravings were made from them. A large drawing of this subject is in the print room at the British Museum. In 1781 his father died at Zurich, and in the same year Fuseli painted an interview between himself and his aged tutor, Bodmer, which he sent to Zurich. In 1786 Alderman Boydell [q. v.] started his scheme of a Shakespeare gallery, and invited Fuseli to contribute; such a scheme had occupied Fuseli's mind at Rome when musing in the Sistine Chapel, as is shown by the sketch-book mentioned above. He contributed one small picture and eight large, including 'Titania and Bottom' (now in the National Gallery), 'Macbeth and the Witches,' and 'Hamlet and his Father's Ghost;' the last filled with awe the minds of the spectators, and, though extravagant in its execution, possessed real power. He also painted some pictures for Woodmason's 'Shakespeare.' On 30 June 1788 Fuseli married Sophia Rawlins of Bath Easton, near Bath, who is stated to have been one of his models, and often sat to him after marriage; she proved an affectionate and patient, if not very intelligent, wife, to whom he was sincerely attached. He now removed to 72 Queen Anne Street East (now Foley Street), and, in consequence of his marriage, overcame his reluctance to be connected with any associated body of artists, and became a candidate for the Royal Academy. He was elected associate 3 Nov. 1788, and academician 10 Feb. 1790, beating Bonomi [q. v.] on the latter occasion, to the great umbrage of Sir Joshua Reynolds. In 1790 Johnson, the publisher, issued proposals for an edition of Milton's poems, similar to Boydell's 'Shakespeare;' Cowper, the poet, was to edit the poems, and Fuseli to paint a series of pictures, to be engraved by Sharp, Bartolozzi, Blake, and other eminent engravers. Cowper's insanity and Boydell's hostility prevented the completion of the work, but Fuseli's mind was fired by the enterprise, and he conceived his 'Milton Gallery.' He devoted all his time to painting pictures for it, and on 20 May 1799 opened a gallery of forty pictures, taken from Milton's poems, at the rooms lately vacated by the Royal Academy in Pall Mall. It attracted considerable attention, but it was evident that the fantastic extravagance in which Fuseli's strength lay was unsuited to the stateliness of Milton's poems. The results grievously belied his expectations, and he closed the gallery after two months; in the following year he re-opened it with the addition of seven new pictures, but neither his own efforts nor those of his friends produced satisfactory results. Among the best known of these pictures were 'The Lazar House' (now in the possession of Lord North at Wroxton Abbey), 'Satan calling up his Legions,' 'The Bridging of Chaos,' 'Satan, Sin, and Death,' 'The Night Hag' (of which there is a large drawing in the print room at the British Museum), 'The Deluge,' 'Lycidas' (several versions of this exist), 'Milton dictating to his daughters,' &c. In 1799 Fuseli succeeded James Barry, R.A. [q. v.], as professor of painting at the Royal Academy, and in March 1801 delivered his first lectures. In December 1804 he succeeded Richard Wilson, R.A. [q. v.], as keeper, and moved from Berners Street, where he was then residing, to Somerset House. He thereby vacated his professorship, but in 1810, on Tresham's resignation, he volunteered to supply the vacancy until a suitable candidate could be found; the Academy then re-elected him to the post, and he continued to hold the joint offices during the remainder of his life. In 1802 he visited Paris in order to study the marvellous collection of works of art brought together by Napoleon, in which he found ample material for his future lectures. The rest of Fuseli's life was mainly occupied in his duties at the Royal Academy, in which he took an unfailing interest. In 1815, through the agency of Canova, a warm admirer, he received the diploma of the Academy of St. Luke at Rome. He remained in full possession of all his faculties up to the end; delivered his last course of lectures in 1825 in his eighty-fourth year; exhibited two

pictures that year at the Royal Academy, and left another unfinished on his easel. On Sunday, 10 April 1825, while on a visit at Putney Hill to his friend the Countess of Guilford (daughter of Mr. Coutts), with whom and her daughters he was on terms of great intimacy, Fuseli was taken ill, and died on Saturday, 16 April. His body was removed to Somerset House, and on 25 April was buried in the crypt of St. Paul's Cathedral, between the graves of Reynolds and Opie. His widow survived him for some years. He left no children.

Fuseli was below middle stature, but well proportioned. His forehead was high, his nose prominent and inclined to be aquiline, his eyes of a bright and penetrating blue; his hair was blanched at an early age by a fever in Italy, and his eyebrows were broad and bushy. He was always careful of his dress and person, and was an abstemious and frugal liver, as well as an early riser. He would often rise at dawn to go out into the country on some favourite entomological pursuit. Lavater, in his 'Physiognomy' (ed. 1789), inserts two portraits of Fuseli, one in early life and one from a drawing by Sir Thomas Lawrence; his reading of Fuseli's character from his features proved very accurate. Fuseli's countenance was remarkably expressive, and he showed in every feature and gesture the rapid and varying impressions of his mind, and the intensity of his emotions. Among other portraits of Fuseli are a profile done at Rome by J. Northcote, R.A. (in the possession of Mr. J. Carrick Moore); a portrait by Williamson done at Liverpool; a portrait by J. Opie, R.A. (who also painted Mrs. Fuseli), now in the National Portrait Gallery; a miniature by Moses Haughton, by some considered the best likeness of him; the well-known portrait by G. H. Harlowe, so familiar from engravings; a drawing by G. S. Newton, R.A.; a sketch by Sir George Hayter in January 1812, now in the print room at the British Museum; and a drawing by Sir Thomas Lawrence done shortly before his death. A bust was executed in Rome in 1778, another is at Wroxton Abbey, and two were done later by E. H. Baily, R.A., one taken after death.

As a painter Fuseli can only be judged by posterity from the wrecks of his great pictures. He suffered throughout from not having adopted the profession until late in life, and his industry and anatomical studies at Rome never compensated for his lack of early and methodical training. His natural impetuosity of temperament rendered him incapable of paying laborious attention to the ordinary technical details of painting. His method of colouring was faulty to an extreme, and his colour, though often fine, was strange, gloomy, and frequently unpleasing. In many of his pictures the lividness of his flesh-tints has been enhanced by the uniform blackness to which time has reduced the shadows. Were it not for the graver of Moses Haughton [q. v.], who lodged with Fuseli at Somerset House, and worked under his personal direction, John Raphael Smith, J. P. Simon, and others, he would be little known. His numerous sketches afford a better insight into his art than his completed pictures, in which the great power of his imagination is sometimes obscured. He sometimes indulged in considerable freedom of subject, but most of these sketches were destroyed. After his death a collection of eight hundred drawings by Fuseli were purchased from his widow by Sir Thomas Lawrence, and subsequently passed into the possession of the Countess of Guilford, but are now dispersed. While endeavouring to tread in the 'terribil via' of Michelangelo, he followed the precepts of Lavater in expressing by attitude, gesture, or other movements of the limbs or features, the passions or emotions which he wished to delineate in his characters. The artist most akin to him was William Blake, who engraved some of his drawings; Blake owed a great deal to the friendship of Fuseli, and both entertained a mutual esteem and affection for each other, with undoubted advantage on both sides. Among the pictures painted by Fuseli, in addition to his 'Milton' and 'Shakespeare' productions, were 'Perceval delivering Belisane from the enchantment of Urma,' 'Œdipus and his daughters' (now in the Walker Art Gallery at Liverpool), 'Paolo and Francesca de Rimini,' 'Ugolino in the Torre della Fame,' 'Dion seeing a Female Spectre overturn his Altars and sweep his Hall,' 'Psyche pursued by the Fates' (at Wroxton Abbey), 'Queen Mab' (in the possession of the Earl of Harrowby), 'Ariadne, Theseus, and the Minotaur,' 'William Tell leaping ashore' (notorious for its exaggerated limbs), 'Caractacus at Rome,' 'The Spirit of Plato appearing to a Student,' 'Cæsar's Ghost appearing to Brutus,' 'Hercules attacking Pluto,' 'Christ and his disciples at Emmaus' (now in the possession of Lord North at Kirtling Tower, Newmarket), scenes from the Nibelungenlied, &c. Most of these were exhibited at the Royal Academy, to which he contributed sixty-nine pictures in all; many have perished from natural decay or unmerited neglect. He published a few etchings, notably one of 'Fortune,' of which the original drawing is in the British Museum, and experimented in lithography.

He provided numerous illustrations to the small editions of the poets and classics, Bell's 'Theatre,' and other similar works then in vogue. The title of 'Principal Hobgoblin-Painter to the Devil,' humorously conferred on him, was neither undeserved nor resented by him.

As a teacher Fuseli was popular among his pupils, in spite of his eccentricities; he was also successful in his method, which seems to have consisted in inspiring his pupils with the desire to learn, rather than in giving them actual technical instruction, according to a favourite precept of his, that time and not the teacher makes an artist. Haydon, in whom Fuseli took great interest, Leslie, Etty, Mulready, and others have testified to his beneficial influence (see Builder, 1864, p. 4, for a similar tribute from a lady pupil). As an author Fuseli has hardly been esteemed as much as he deserves; he was a large contributor to the periodical literature of his day, especially to the 'Analytical Review;' he made numerous translations of works for Johnson and other publishers, and later in life few works on art of any importance were issued without a preliminary 'imprimatur' from Fuseli's pen, e.g. Blake's illustrations to Blair's 'Grave.' He revised Dr. Hunter's translation of Lavater's 'Physiognomy;' greatly assisted Cowper in his translation of Homer's 'Iliad;' and himself translated Lavater's 'Aphorisms on Man.' He also made a collection of 'Aphorisms on Art' of his own composition, which were published after his death, and are worth perusing. His lectures, especially the first three, which were published separately in 1801, show a wealth of learning and erudition unusual in an artist. His style, though often grandiose to absurdity, was in the fashion of the time. He indulged the family passion for lexicography by editing and re-editing Pilkington's 'Dictionary of Painters,' and by assisting his cousin in completing his uncle Rudolf's 'Allgemeines Künstler-Lexicon.' His devotion to the family science of entomology lasted through life, and is often evident in his pictures. Fuseli became one of the leading figures in London society, and was esteemed as much for his literary as for his artistic powers; he was an indispensable guest at Johnson the publisher's dinner-table, the resort of the leading radical celebrities of the day, and the circle was not complete without Fuseli's caustic wit and brilliant epigram. He was fearless in avowing his opinions, and when Johnson was imprisoned by the government for alleged sedition, he continued to visit him in prison as before. He made few enemies, and his freedom of speech and criticism, like other failings, became almost privileged.

With ladies Fuseli was a great favourite, and they thoroughly indulged his vanity and worshipped his genius. It may be doubted whether they ever stirred any feelings within him other than those of deep and sincere friendship. Of female beauty he had little appreciation, a fault conspicuous in his pictures. In early life he had a passing flirtation with Mary Moser, afterwards Mrs. Lloyd [q. v.], and with Angelica Kauffmann, R.A. [q. v.], for whom he always entertained feelings of respect and admiration. Later his domestic happiness was endangered by the apparent attempts of Mary Wollstonecraft, afterwards Mrs. Godwin [q. v.], to win his affections, in which affair Fuseli seems to have been not wholly free from blame, although he never showed or entertained any genuine affection for her. His numerous accomplishments and personal qualities fully entitled him to the influential position which he occupied. Anecdotes of his wit, eccentricities, and other peculiarities are innumerable. He was, as might be expected, devoted to the theatre, especially when Shakespeare was being played.

[Knowles's Life and Writings of Henry Fuseli; Allan Cunningham's Lives of British Painters; Redgraves' Century of Painters; Art Journal, 1860, 1861; Portfolio, iv. 50; J. T. Smith's Nollekens and his Times, vol. ii.; Gent. Mag. 1825, xcv. 568; Encyclopædia Britannica (9th ed.); Nouvelle Biographie Générale; Fuessli's Allgemeines Künstler-Lexicon; Nagler's Künstler-Lexicon; Seubert's Allgemeines Künstler-Lexicon; Builder, 1864, pp. 4, 22; manuscript additions by J. H. Anderdon to illustrated Royal Academy Catalogues in the print room, British Museum; private information.] L. C.

FUST, SIR HERBERT JENNER- (1778–1852), dean of the arches, second son of Robert Jenner of Doctors' Commons, proctor, and of Chislehurst, Kent, by his second wife, Ann, eldest daughter of Peter Birt of Wenvoe Castle, Glamorganshire, was born in the parish of St. Gregory, near St. Paul's, in the city of London, on 4 Feb. 1778. He was educated under Dr. Valpy at Reading and at Trinity Hall, Cambridge, where he graduated LL.B. in 1798, and LL.D. in 1803. Having chosen the law for his profession, he was called to the bar at Gray's Inn 27 Nov. 1800, admitted an advocate in the ecclesiastical and admiralty courts, and a fellow of the College of Doctors of Law 8 July 1803. On 28 Feb. 1828 he was appointed king's advocate-general, and knighted on the same day at St. James's Palace by George IV. He became vicar-general to the Archbishop of Canterbury in 1832, but resigned that place and the office of advocate-general 21 Oct. 1834, on his appointment as official principal of the arches and judge of prerogative court of Canterbury. On the 29th of the same month his name was added to the list of privy councillors. He assumed the additional surname of Fust 14 Jan. 1842 on succeeding to Hill Court, Gloucestershire, and Capenor Court, Somersetshire, which had belonged to his deceased cousin, Sir John Fust. The fellows of Trinity Hall elected him master in February 1843; but he never resided there, although he held this appointment, in conjunction with the deanery of the arches, to his decease. His name came very prominently before the public in the case of Gorham v. the Bishop of Exeter. In this case, which lasted three years, 1847–50, the bishop, charging Gorham with heresy, refused to institute him to the vicarage of Brampford Speke, Devonshire. In the end Gorham was instituted on 7 Aug. 1850, under an order made by the dean of the arches. Fust's decree of 2 Aug. 1849 in this matter was the subject of much discussion, and led to the publication of upwards of eighty pamphlets. In his latter days he became so infirm that he had to be carried in and out of his court by two footmen. He was a great authority on international law, on which subject he was frequently consulted by the chief politicians of his time.

Jenner-Fust died at 1 Chesterfield Street, Mayfair, London, 20 Feb. 1852, and was buried in the family vault at St. Nicholas, Chislehurst, Kent, on 26 Feb. He married 14 Sept. 1803 Elizabeth, daughter of Lieutenant-general Francis Lascelles. She was born 30 March 1784, and died at Chislehurst 29 July 1828. The names of Fust and of Jenner-Fust are found in print in connection with the following cases: 1. 'A Letter to the Archbishop of Canterbury in Refutation of Opinions delivered in the case of Breeks v. Woolfrey respecting Praying for the Dead,' 1839. 2. 'The Indeterminateness of Unauthorised Baptism occasioned by the Decision in the case of Mastin v. Escott,' 1841. 3. 'Report of the Trial of Doe on the demise of H. F. Bather, plaintiff, and Brayne and J. Edwards, defendants, with reference to the will of W. Brayne,' 1848. 4. 'Notices of the late Judgment in the case of Gorham v. the Bishop of Exeter; by J. King,' 1849. 5. 'The Sacrament of Baptism considered in reference to the Judgment of Sir H. Jenner-Fust; by H. Phillpotts, Bishop of Exeter,' 1849. 6. 'Gorham, clerk, against the Bishop of Exeter; the Judgment delivered in the Arches Court,' 1849. 7. 'Review of the Judgment in the case of Gorham v. the

Bishop of Exeter; by the Editor of the "Christian Observer," i.e. William Goode, jun.,' 1850. 8. 'A Medical Man, Dr. S. Ashwell, obtains a Will from a sick Lady during the absence of her Husband, whom he deprives of 25,000*l.* Judgment of Sir H. Jenner-Fust,' 1850. 9. 'Judgment in the Prerogative Court in the cause Cursham *v.* Williams and Chouler,' 1851. Jenner-Fust's portrait by F. Y. Hurlstone was engraved by William Walker in 1835.

[Gent. Mag. April 1852, p. 408; Law Times (1852), xviii. 216; Christian Observer, December, 1849, pp. 809–56, and October, 1850, pp. 698–713; Thornbury's Old and New London, i. 288, 292.] G. C. B.

FYCH or **FYCHE**, THOMAS (*d.* 1517), ecclesiastic. [See FICH.]

FYFE, ANDREW, the elder (1754–1824), anatomist, was born in 1754, probably at Corstorphine, near Edinburgh, where his father lived. He was appointed 'dissector' to Monro secundus, professor of anatomy in Edinburgh University, in 1777 (*Medical Commentaries*, iv. 242), having two years previously been awarded 'the annual prize medal given by the commissioners for improvements in Scotland, for the best drawing in the academy which they have established at Edinburgh.' For about forty years he superintended the dissections and gave demonstrations in the anatomical school under the second and third Monros. Sir Astley Cooper, who attended his demonstrations in 1787–8, says (*Life*, i. 172): 'I learned much from him. He was a horrid lecturer, but an industrious, worthy man, and good practical anatomist. His lecture was, "I say—eh, eh, eh, gentlemen; eh, eh, eh, gentlemen—I say, etc.;" whilst the tallow from a naked candle he held in his hand ran over the back of it and over his clothes: but his drawings and depictions were well made and very useful.' Mr. Bransby Cooper, who attended Fyfe in 1815–16, says: 'Mr. Fyfe was a tall thin man, and one of the most ungainly lecturers I ever knew. He had been assistant to Dr. Monro,' implying that he was now no longer assistant but lectured on his own account. It is doubtful when his assistancy ceased, but it is pretty certain that he lectured and taught anatomy somewhere in the Horse Wynd. He was entered as fellow of the Edinburgh College of Surgeons, 23 Oct. 1818, a few weeks before the entry of his son Andrew. He was a great writer of text-books, which are as dry as his lectures, but, being associated with and adapted to the university plan of teaching, they had a large sale. To the last his books were dated from the 'college,' that

is the university. The seventh edition of his 'Compendium,' 1819, bears on the title-page after his name 'teacher of anatomy, and many years assistant in the anatomical theatre, university of Edinburgh;' while the fourth edition of his 'System,' 1820, states that he was 'still conservator to the museum of the university.' It appears that his lectures at last failed to be remunerative, and that in his latter years he devoted himself to his text-books and engravings. He died on 31 March 1824. He had nine children, of whom three died in infancy. Four sons entered the medical profession. Fyfe's works are: 1. 'A System of Anatomy from Monro, Winslow, Innes,' &c. 2 vols. 1784, 2nd edit. 1787 (edited by A. F.), with the addition of Physiology based on Haller and others, and the 'Comparative Anatomy' of Monro primus. 2. 'A Compendium of the Anatomy of the Human Body,' 2 vols. 1800; 8th edit. 4 vols. 1823, entitled 'A Compendium of Anatomy, Human and Comparative,' the fourth volume dealing with comparative anatomy, based chiefly on Cuvier and Blumenbach; 9th edit. 1826; a 3rd American edit. in 2 vols. was published at Philadelphia in 1810. 3. 'A System of Anatomy' (first edition also called 'Compendium'), chiefly consisting of plates and explanatory references, Edinburgh, 1800, 3 vols. quarto, containing 160 plates and 700 figures; 4th edit. 1820. 4. 'Views of the Bones, Muscles, Viscera, and Organs of the Senses,' copied from the most celebrated authors, together with several additions from nature, 23 plates, folio, Edinburgh and London, 1800. 5. 'Outlines of Comparative Anatomy,' 1813; later edit. 1823, entitled 'A Compendium of Comparative Anatomy.' 6. 'On Crural Hernia,' 1818. In 1830 the plates to illustrate the 'Anatomy of the Human Body' (158 plates, 4to), and an octavo volume of 'Descriptions of the Plates,' were posthumously issued.

Fyfe's eldest son, ANDREW FYFE (1792–1861), was born 18 Jan. 1792, graduated M.D. at Edinburgh in 1814, and became fellow of the Edinburgh College of Surgeons in 1818, and president in 1842–3. He lectured privately on chemistry and pharmacy at Edinburgh for many years, having been assistant to Professor Hope. He published in 1827 'Elements of Chemistry,' 2 vols., a full and well-digested work; 3rd edit. 1833. He was an unsuccessful candidate in 1832 for the chair of materia medica at Edinburgh, but in 1844 became professor of chemistry in the university of Aberdeen, and retained his professorship till his death on 31 Dec. 1861 at Edinburgh, though for some years his lectures were given by a deputy. His knowledge of inflammable substances was great, and he often gave evidence in official inquiries on such subjects. He was much esteemed both by his students and in private life. He was twice married; his son, also named Andrew Fyfe, was a London physician.

[Struthers's Historical Sketch of Edinburgh Anatomical School, 1867, pp. 74–6; Life of Sir Astley Cooper, i. 166, 172; Life of Sir R. Christison, i. 68; Aberdeen Journal, 8 Jan. 1862; information from Dr. Andrew Fyfe, London.]

G. T. B.

FYFE, WILLIAM BAXTER COLLIER (1836?–1882), painter, was born at Dundee about 1836, and brought up in the neighbouring village of Carnoustie. Although the Scottish prejudices of his father's household were unpropitious to art, friends enabled him to become a student of the Royal Scottish Academy when only fifteen. Here his crayon portraits won prizes, and were highly praised. He afterwards studied at Paris during parts of 1857 and 1858. His first picture of importance, 'Queen Mary resigning her Crown at Loch Leven Castle,' appeared at the Royal Scottish Academy in 1861. In 1863, after having passed a year among the art treasures of France, Italy, and Belgium, he settled in London and devoted much of his time to portraiture, which he varied with landscapes and fancy subjects, but his summers were often spent in Scotland. His pictures of 'The Death of John Brown of Priesthill' and 'Jeanie Deans and the Laird o' Dumbiedykes' attracted much notice, and in 1866 he began to exhibit at the Royal Academy. In 1868 and 1869 he painted 'The Wood Merchant,' 'The "Scotsman," Sir?' 'The Flower Girl,' 'The Orange Girl,' 'Marketing,' and 'A Girl of the Period,' the last of which became very popular. These were followed during the next four years by 'The Young Cavalier,' 'The Page,' 'On Household Cares intent,' 'The Maid of Honour,' 'Bide a wee,' and 'What can a young Lassie dae wi' an auld Man?' several of which were engraved in the illustrated newspapers of Europe and America, and even of Asia. About 1874 Fyfe again visited Italy, and painted several Italian subjects. His best-known works of later date were 'A Good Catholic,' 'Wandering Minstrels,' 'The Love Letter,' 'A Quiet Christmas,' 'The Fisherman's Daughter,' 'A Chelsea Pensioner,' and 'The Raid of Ruthven,' his most important historical picture, which was exhibited at the Royal Academy in 1878, and afterwards at the Royal Scottish Academy. His last works were 'Hide and Seek,' 'A Fisher Girl,' and 'Nellie.' Among his portraits some of the most important were those of the Earl and Countess of Dufferin,

Lord Houghton, Sir David and Lady Baxter, Alderman Sir William M'Arthur, and Dr. Lorimer, first principal of the London Presbyterian College. His own portrait was one of his latest works.

Fyfe died suddenly at Abbey Road, St. John's Wood, London, on 15 Sept. 1882, in the forty-seventh year of his age, and was buried in Willesden cemetery.

[Times, 18 Sept. 1882; Architect, 23 Sept. 1882; Illustrated London News, 30 Sept. 1882, with portrait; Royal Academy Exhibition Catalogues, 1866–82.]

R. E. G.

FYNCH or FINCH, MARTIN (1628?–1698), ejected minister, was born about 1628, and entered the ministry about 1648. His maiden effort as an author was a criticism (1656) of the mystical theology of Sir Henry Vane. He was ejected from the vicarage of Tetney, Lincolnshire, by the uniformity act of 1662. In 1668 we find him in Norwich, where he acted as one of three 'heads and teachers' of a congregation of three hundred independents, who met for worship in the house of John Tofts, a grocer, in St. Clement's parish. On the issuing of the indulgence of 1672, Fynch took out a license to preach in the house of Nicholas Withers, in St. Clement's. He became pastor of the independent congregation in succession to John Cromwell (d. April 1685). Their meeting-place was the west granary in St. Andrew's parish. Fynch removed his flock to a brewhouse in St. Edmund's parish, which he fitted up as a meeting-house; and after the passing of the Toleration Act (1689) he secured a site in St. Clement's parish, being 'part of the Friars' great garden,' on which a handsome building was erected (finished 1693), originally known as the 'New Meeting,' but since 1756 called the 'Old Meeting.' John Stackhouse was Fynch's colleague from about 1691.

With the presbyterian minister at Norwich, John Collinges, D.D. [q. v.], who died 18 Jan. 1691, Fynch was in close relations, both personal and ecclesiastical. In accordance with the terms of the 'happy union' (mooted in 1690), these divines agreed to discard the dividing names 'presbyterian' and 'independent' and co-operate simply as dissenters. Fynch preached Collinges's funeral sermon, and defended his memory in reply to a pamphlet by Thomas Grantham (1634–1692) [q. v.]

Fynch suffered from failing eyesight, and was a victim to calculus, a malady prevalent in Norfolk. He died on 13 Feb. 1697 (i.e. 1698), and was buried in the graveyard on the north side of his meeting-house, immediately behind the pulpit. The epitaph on his flat tombstone is the main authority for the dates of his biography. After his death there was a rupture in his congregation, which lasted for twenty years.

He published: 1. 'Animadversions upon Sir Henry Vane's . . . The Retired Man's Meditations,' &c., 1656, 12mo. 2. 'A Manual of Practical Divinity,' &c., 1658, 8vo. 3. 'A Treatise of the Conversion of Sinners,' &c., 1680, 8vo. 4. 'An Answer to Mr. Thomas Grantham's . . . Dialogue between the Baptist and the Presbyterian,' &c., 1691, 8vo. 5. 'A Funeral Sermon for . . . John Collinges, D.D.,' &c., 1695, 4to.

[Calamy's Account, 1713, p. 448; Continuation, 1727, ii. 601; Palmer's Nonconf. Memorial, 1802, ii. 434 (a note by J. O., i.e. Job Orton, erroneously connects him with Peter, son of Henry Finch (1633–1704) [q.v.]); Browne's Hist. Congr. Norf. and Suff. 1877, pp. 260, 265 sq., 557 sq.; Fynch's Answer to Grantham.] A. G.

FYNES-CLINTON. [See CLINTON.]

FYNEUX or **FINEUX**, SIR JOHN (1441?–1527), judge, was the son of William Fyneux of Swingfield, Kent, his mother's name being Monyngs. The family of Fyneux or Fineux (sometimes also written Finiox or Fineaux) was of great antiquity in Kent. The judge is said by Fuller, on the authority of one of his descendants, a certain Thomas Fyneux, to have begun the study of law at the age of twenty-eight, to have practised at the bar for twenty-eight years, and to have sat on the bench for the same period. As he died not earlier than 1527, he must, if Fuller's statements are correct, have been born about 1441. He was a member of Gray's Inn and a reader there, though the dates of his admission, call, and reading are alike uncertain (DOUTHWAITE, Gray's Inn, p. 46). He was appointed in 1474 one of the commissioners for administering the marsh lands lying between Tenterden and Lydd, and in 1476 seneschal of the manors of the prior and chapter of Christ Church, Canterbury. This is probably the origin of David Lloyd's statement that he 'was steward of 129 manors at once' (Christ Church Letters, Camden Soc. p. 95). On 20 Nov. 1485 he was called to the degree of serjeant-at-law, his motto for the occasion being 'Quisque suæ fortunæ faber.' This is the earliest recorded instance of a motto being assumed by a serjeant on occasion of his call. In 1486 he was sworn of the council. On 18 May 1488 he was appointed steward of Dover Castle, on 10 May 1489 he received a commission of justice of assize for Norfolk, and on 14 Aug. following he was appointed king's serjeant (DUGDALE, Chron. Ser. p. 75;

POLYDORE VERGIL, xxvi. ad init.; Materials . . . Hen. VII, Rolls Ser. ii. 311, 448, 475). Lloyd says that he opposed the subsidy of a tithe of rents and goods demanded for the expenses of the war in Brittany. This must have been in 1488–9 (Rot. Parl. vi. 421; BACON, Literary Works, ed. Spedding, i. 88). On 11 Feb. 1493–4 he was raised to the bench as a puisne judge of the common pleas, whence on 24 Nov. 1495 he was transferred to the chief-justiceship of the king's bench. He was one of the triers of petitions in the parliament of 1496, and the same year was joined with the Archbishops of Canterbury and York and certain other peers as feoffee of certain manors in Staffordshire, Berkshire, Wiltshire, Kent, and Leicestershire to the use of the king. He was one of the executors of the will of Cardinal Morton, who died in 1500. In 1503 he was again a trier of petitions in parliament, and was enfeoffed of certain other manors to the uses of the king's will. In the act of parliament declaring the feoffment he is for the first time designated 'knight.' In 1509 he was appointed one of the executors of the king's will (DUGDALE, Chron. Ser. p. 74; Rot. Parl. vi. 509 b, 510, 521 a, 538 b; NICOLAS, Testamenta Vetusta, p. 35). He was also a trier of petitions in the parliament of 1515. In 1512 an act had been passed depriving all murderers and felons not in holy orders of benefit of clergy. This act, though its duration was limited to a single year, was vehemently denounced by Richard Kidderminster, abbot of Winchcombe, in a sermon preached at Paul's Cross in 1515, as altogether contrary to the law of God and the liberties of the church. The defence of the act was undertaken by Standish, warden of the Friars Minors. The general question of the amenability of the clergy to the temporal courts was thus raised and hotly debated, the controversy being further exasperated by a murder committed by the direction of the Bishop of London on one Hunne, who had rendered himself obnoxious to the clergy. The ferment of the public mind being general and extreme, the judges and the council were assembled by order of the king first at Blackfriars and subsequently at Baynard Castle, for a solemn conference upon the entire question. On the latter occasion a very dramatic incident occurred in which Fyneux played a principal part. Towards the close of the debate the Archbishop of Canterbury cited the authority of 'divers holy fathers' against the pretensions of the temporal courts to try clerical offenders; to which Fyneux replied that 'the arraignment of clerks had been maintained by divers holy kings, and sundry good holy fathers of the church had been obedient and content with the practice of the law on this point; which it was not to be presumed they would have been if they had believed or supposed that it was altogether contrary to the law of God; on the other hand they [the clergy] had no authority by their law to arraign any one of felony.' The archbishop having interposed that they had sufficient authority, but without saying when or whence they derived it, Fyneux continued that 'in the event of a clerk being arrested by the secular power and then committed to the spiritual court at the instance of the clergy, the spiritual court had no jurisdiction to decide the case, but had only power to do with him according to the intention and purpose for which he had been remitted to them.' To this, the archbishop making no reply, the king said: 'By the ordinance and sufferance of God ... we intend to maintain the right of our crown, and of our temporal jurisdiction, as well in this point as in all other points, in as ample a manner as any of our progenitors have done before our time; and as for your decrees, we are well assured that you of the spirituality yourselves act expressly against the tenor of them, as has been well shown to you by some of our spiritual council, wherefore we will not comply with your desires more than our progenitors in times past have done.' Shortly after this emphatic declaration, the assembly was dissolved. Fyneux's statement of the law on this occasion was referred to by Lordchancellor Ellesmere in the case of the postnati in 1608 as a precedent in favour of the authority of the extra-judicial opinions of judges then beginning to be seriously impugned (*Letters and Papers Henry VIII*, For. and Dom. vol. ii. pt. i. 42; BURNET, *Reformation*, i. 34; KEILWAY, *Reports* (Croke), 185; COBBETT, *State Trials*, ii. 666; BREWER, *Reign of Henry VIII*, i. 250). In 1522 Fyneux was elected into the fraternity of the Augustinian Eremites of Canterbury (*Christ Church Letters*, Camd. Soc. 95). There is evidence that he was living on 5 Feb. 1526-7; but he probably died or retired in that year (*Proceedings and Ordinances of the*

Privy Council, vii. 338; *Letters and Papers Henry VIII*, For. and Dom. vol. iv. pt. ii. 1670, pt. iii. App. 3096). He was buried in the nave of Canterbury Cathedral. By his will he was a donor to the priory of Christ Church, Canterbury, and to Faversham Abbey. He died possessed of various estates in Kent, his principal seat being at Herne. He is also said to have owned the house which was subsequently known as New Inn, and to have leased it to the lawyers at a rent of 6*l.* per annum (HASTED, *Kent*, iii. 617; DUGDALE, *Orig.* p. 230). The following maxims, preserved in Sloane MS. 1523, are ascribed to him: 'That no man thrived but he that lived as though he were the first man in the world, and his father were not before him. The prince's prerogative and the subject's privilege are solid felicities together, and but empty notions asunder. That people is beyond precedent free and beyond comparison happy who restraine not their sovereign's power to do them harm so far, as that he hath none left him to do them good.' Fyneux married twice: first, Elizabeth, daughter of William Apulderfield; secondly, Elizabeth, daughter of Sir John Paston, and granddaughter of William Paston [q.v.], justice of the common pleas in the reign of Henry VI. By his first wife he had issue two daughters, of whom the elder, Jane, married John Roper, prothonotary of the king's bench and father of William Roper, the son-in-law and biographer of Sir Thomas More, and of Sir John Roper, who was created Baron Teynham in 1616. This barony is still in existence. The only issue of Fyneux's second marriage was one son, William (*d.* 1557), whose granddaughter, Elizabeth, married Sir John Smythe of Ostenhanger or Westenhanger, Kent, father of Sir Thomas Smythe, who was created Viscount Strangford in the peerage of Ireland in 1628. A later descendant was created Baron Penshurst in the peerage of the United Kingdom in 1825. The title became extinct by the death of the eighth viscount on 9 Jan. 1869.

[Leland's Itinerary, vi. 6; Fuller's Worthies (Kent); Lloyd's State Worthies, i. 91-6; Foss's Lives of the Judges.]   J. M. R.

G

GABELL, HENRY DISON, D.D. (1764–1831), head-master of Winchester, was son of the Rev. Timothy Gabell of Winchester. Gabell was born at Winchester in 1764, and was elected a scholar of Winchester College in 1779, and subsequently of New College, Oxford, where he matriculated on 11 Oct. 1782; graduated B.A. on 8 July 1786; and held a fellowship from 1782 to 1790. Soon afterwards he was appointed master of Warminster school, where he had twenty boys to teach, with a salary of 30*l.*, and liberty to take private pupils. He was presented to the rectory of St. Lawrence, Winchester, in 1788, and was appointed second master of Winchester College in 1793. He graduated M.A. at Cambridge in 1807; succeeded Dr. Goddard as head-master of Winchester College in 1810; was presented to the rectory of Ashow, Warwickshire, in 1812, and that of Binfield, Berkshire, in 1820; resigned the head-mastership of Winchester College in December 1823, receiving a present of plate richly engraved from the scholars. He continued to hold the three livings of Binfield, Ashow, and St. Lawrence until his death, which took place at Binfield on 18 April 1831. Gabell married, on 11 Jan. 1790, Miss Gage, the daughter of a clergyman of Holton, Oxfordshire. Their third daughter, Maria, married, on 18 July 1818, Sir Joseph Scott, bart., of Great Barr Hall, Staffordshire. Gabell was a friend and correspondent of Dr. Parr, in the seventh volume of whose works some letters of his on points of classical scholarship will be found. He published: 1. A pamphlet entitled ' On the Expediency of Altering and Amending the Regulations recommended by Parliament for Reducing the High Price of Corn: and of Extending the Bounty on the Importation of Wheat and other Articles of Provision,' London, 1796, 8vo. 2. A discourse delivered on the fast-day in February 1799, London, 1799, 8vo.

[Gent. Mag. 1790 pt. i. p. 83, 1818 pt. ii. p. 178, 1823 pt. ii. p. 543, 1831 pt. i. p. 469; Kirby's Winchester Scholars, pp. 272, 296; Foster's Alumni Oxon. p. 503; Hoare's South Wiltshire, iii. ' Warm.' 40; Parr's Works, ed. Johnstone, vii. 470–501; Cat. Oxford Grad.; Grad. Cant.; Brit. Mus. Cat.]   J. M. R.

GABRIEL, afterwards MARCH, **MARY ANN VIRGINIA** (1825–1877), musical composer, the daughter of Major-general Gabriel, was born at Banstead, Surrey, 7 Feb. 1825. She was the pupil of Pixis, Döhler, and Thalberg, for the pianoforte, and of Molique and Mercadante for composition. Miss Gabriel married George E. March in November 1874, and died, from injuries received in a carriage accident, on 7 Aug. 1877. She had acquired great facility in composition, and published several hundred songs. Those entitled ' When Sparrows build,' ' Ruby,' ' Sacred Vows,' ' Only,' ' The Forsaken,' ' Under the Palms,' and ' The Skipper and his Boy,' became extremely popular. These drawing-room ballads may be said to stand midway between the bald jingle favoured by Miss Gabriel's early contemporaries and the attempted intensity of expression belonging to a later date; a music which, in spite of the composer's gifts of knowledge and imagination, does not attain to high artistic merit. Her operetta ' Widows Bewitched' was performed by the Bijou Operetta Company at St. George's Hall, 13 Nov. 1867, and held the stage for several weeks. Other similar works, ' Shepherd of Cournouailles,' ' Who's the Heir?' ' Lost and Found,' ' A Rainy Day,' about 1873 and 1875, were favourites in the drawing-room. The cantata ' Dreamland,' privately printed, was given in London about 1870; ' Evangeline,' produced at Kuhe's Brighton festival, 13 Feb. 1873, was very successful, and was heard at Rivière's Covent Garden Concerts of 24 Nov. and 1 Dec. Another cantata, ' Graziella,' closes the list of Miss Gabriel's longer compositions.

[Grove's Dictionary, i. 571; Musical World, vols. xlv. and lv.; Musical Times, vol. xviii.; The Choir, xv. 145, xvi. 344, xxii. 492; Music in Brit. Mus. Library.]   L. M. M.

GACE, WILLIAM (*fl.* 1580), translator, matriculated as a sizar of Clare Hall, Cambridge, in November 1568, and proceeded B.A. in 1572–3. He was author of the following translations: 1. ' A Learned and Fruitefull Commentarie upon the Epistle of James the Apostle. . . . Written in Latine by the learned Clerke, Nich. Hemminge . . . and newly translated into English by W. G.,' 4to, London, 1577. 2. ' Special and Chosen Sermons of D. Martin Luther collected out of his Writings. . . . Englished by W. G.,' 4to, London, 1578; another edition, 8vo, London, 1581. 3. ' A Guide unto godliness, moste worthy to bee followed of all true Christians. . . . Written in Latin by John Rivius; Englished by W. G.,' 8vo, London,

1579. 4. 'A right comfortable Treatise conteining sundrye pointes of consolation for them that labour & are laden. Written by D. Martin Luther to Prince Friderik, Duke of Saxonie; being sore sicke. . . . Englished by W. Gace,' 8vo, London, 1580.

[Cooper's Athenæ Cantabr. ii. 22–3; Brit. Mus. Cat.] G. G.

GADBURY, JOHN (1627–1704), astrologer, born at Wheatley in Oxfordshire on 31 Dec. 1627, was son of William Gadbury, farmer, by 'his stolen wife' (WOOD, Bliss, iv. 9), a Roman catholic, the daughter of Sir John Curson of Waterperry, knt. Curson seems to have disinherited his daughter, and the boy was apprenticed to Thomas Nicholls, an Oxford tailor, but left him in 1644. A partial reconciliation with his grandfather, Sir John Curson, enabled John Gadbury to be educated at Oxford. He joined a merchant adventurer named Thorn, living near Strand bridge, London, and married about 1648. He joined successively the presbyterians, the independents, and the 'family of love,' then under Abiezer Coppe [q. v.] Gadbury appears to have left him in 1651, by which time he was intimate with William Lilly [q. v.], Butler's 'Sidrophel.' In 1652 he returned to Oxfordshire to visit his grandfather, Sir John, and settled to study astrology under Dr. N. Fiske. He answered William Brommerton's 'Confidence Dismantled,' &c., 1652, in 'Philastrogus' Knavery Epitomized, with a Vindication of Mr. Culpepper, Mr. Lilly, and the rest of the Students in that noble Art,' &c., 'written by J. G[adbury], a lover of all ingenious arts and artists, Aprill the 5, 1651.' In 1654 he published 'Animal Cornutum, or the Horn'd Beast, wherein is contained a brief method of the grounds of Astrology.' In 1655 he presented to Sir John Curson the first of a long series of annual 'Ephemerides.' In 1656 he published his 'Emendation' of Hartgil's 'Astronomical Tables,' and also his own 'Cœlestis Legatus, or the Celestial Ambassadour, astronomically predicting the grand Catastrophe that is probable to befall the most of the kingdoms and countries of Europe,' two parts, 1656, 4to. In 1658 he published 'Genethlialogia, or the Doctrine of Nativities,' and 'The Doctrine of Horary Questions, Astrologically handled' (with his portrait engraved by T. Cross). In 'Nebulo Anglicanus' Partridge asserts that he meant to dedicate the 'Doctrine of Nativities' to Cromwell, and accuses him of becoming a royalist upon the Restoration. In August 1659 he published 'The Nativity of the late King Charls [sic], Astrologically and Faithfully performed, with

Reasons in Art of the various success and mis-fortune of His whole Life. Being (occasionally) a brief History of our late unhappy Wars,' still worth study. In 1659 he also published 'The King of Sweden's Nativity,' and probably 'Nuncius Astrologicus' and 'Britain's Royal Star.' In 1660 appeared his treatise on the 'Nature of Prodigies,' praising Fiske and mocking Lilly for having been indicted as a cheat before a Hicks's Hall jury in 1654. By 22 Nov. 1661 had appeared 'Britain's Royal Star, or An Astrological Demonstration of England's future Felicity,' founded on the position of the stars at the date of Charles II's proclamation as king.

In 1665 he published 'De Cometis, or A Discourse of the Natures and Effects of Comets, with an account of the three late Comets in 1664 and 1665,' 'London's Deliverance from the Plague of 1665,' and 'Vox Solis; or A Discourse of the Sun's Eclipse, 22 June 1666' (dedicated to Elias Ashmole). Previous to 1667 he published his 'Collection of Nativities' and 'Dies Novissimus; or Dooms-Day not so near as dreaded.' According to John Partridge [q. v.] Gadbury in 1666 had removed from Jewin Street to Westminster, where he attended the abbey each Sunday. Partridge maliciously accuses him of debauchery in 1667, and of complicity in the murder of one Godden, who had recently indicted him at the sessions. He published little except 'A brief Relation of the Life and Death of Mr. V. Wing,' 1669, 1670, his annual 'Ephemerides,' and his West India or 'Jamaica Almanack' for 1674, until 1675, when appeared his 'Obsequium Rationabile; or A Reasonable Service performed for the Cœlestial sign Scorpio, in 20 remarkable genitures of that glorious but stigmatized Horoscope, against the malitious and false attempts of that grand (but fortunate) IMPOSTOR, Mr. William Lilly.' In 1677 appeared 'The Just and Pious Scorpionist; or the Nativity of that thrice excellent man, Sir Matthew Hales, born under the Cœlestial Scorpion.' By 1678 he had possibly been received into the church of Rome, but this is extremely doubtful, and he was suspected of participation in some 'popish plots.' He was the accredited author of the clever narrative ballad, in four parts, 1679, 'A Ballad upon the Popish Plot' (Bagford Ballads). Thomas Dangerfield [q. v.] professed to have had eight meetings with Gadbury in September 1679, at the house of Mrs. Elizabeth Cellier [q. v.] Gadbury was summoned as a witness against Cellier at her trial in June 1680, and testified in her favour, having known her ten or twelve years (Case of Thomas Dangerfield, &c., together with John

Gadbury his testimony, with all his evasions, 1680, p. 27). Gadbury had been taken into custody on suspicion, 2 Nov. 1679. He denied connivance, before the king and council, and obtained release two months later. His enemies pretended that he had attempted ineffectually to bribe Sir Thomas Danby with a present of plate, and, on trebling the value of the present, he induced another person to gain for him a pardon. In compensation for 'wrongous imprisonment' he received 200*l.* in 1681. By this date he was a widower. In 1683 he published the works of his friend George Hawarth, *alias* Wharton. In 1684 appeared his 'Cardines Cœli, or An Appeal to the learned and experienced observers of Sublunars and their vicissitudes. In a Reply to the learned author of "Cometomantia."' He was falsely reported to have avowed himself a papist in 1685, but in 1686, in his 'Epistle to the Almanack,' indicated a prophecy for 'an eternal settlement in England of the Romanists.' In 1688–9 appeared 'Mene Tekel; being an Astrological judgment on the great and wonderful year 1688. London, printed by H. H. for the use of John Gadbury.' The misemployment of his name was satirical. Gadbury was falsely accused, on the strength of papers intercepted at the post office, of being implicated in a plot (June 1690) against William III. He was detained in custody eight or ten weeks, and had certainly refused as a nonjuror to take the oaths of allegiance. In 1693 he attended St. Margaret's Church, Westminster, as a protestant, and was then living in Brick Court, College Street, Westminster, when Partridge reproached him for ingratitude to Lilly, and accused him of being the author of the vindication, 'Merlini Liberati Errata.' He was reputed to have written 'The Scurrilous Scribbler dissected; a Word in William Lilly's ear concerning his Reputation,' printed on one side of a broadsheet, undated, of near this time (*Athenæ Oxon.* i. 36). Wood at first described Gadbury as a 'monster of ingratitude' to Lilly (Bliss, iv. 748), but, after a correspondence with Aubrey, accepted rectification of his statements, 20 Aug. and November 1692 (TANNER, *Coll.* Bodl. No. 451, and *MS. Ballard*, Bodl. xiv. 99). In 1693 appeared 'Nebulo Anglicanus; or The First Part of the Black Life of John Gadbury,' &c., by John Partridge. This contains a portrait of Gadbury as 'Merlinus Verax,' showing a round large-featured face, with long curling hair, fair-coloured, in the broad flapping hat of a pilgrim, with rosary and cross, but a label issuing from his mouth 'a special Protestant.' Partridge declared that Gadbury wrote 'Utrum Horum; Rome or

Geneva, Never a Barrel better herring,' and that it was 'designed against all religions, but most chiefly against the Reformed Protestant religion' (*Nebulo,* p. 24) ; also that Gadbury announced James II would return in 1694. Gadbury died near the end of March 1704, leaving a widow, and was buried in the vault of St. Margaret's Church, Westminster, 28 March 1704 (Bliss, iv. 9). It is extremely probable, judging from the racy vigour of his fourfold 'Ballad on the Popish Plot,' 1679, that many others of the fugitive broadsides were of his composition.

[Gadbury's works enumerated above; Wood's Athenæ Oxon. ed. Bliss, i. 36, ii. col. 680, 1051, iv. 9, 381, 748 ; John Gorton's General Biog. Dict., ed. H. G. Bohn, 1851, ii. sign. *B verso ; Granger's Biog. Hist. iii. 129, slight and inaccurate; Animadversion vpon Mr. John Gadbury's Almanack or Diary for the year of our Lord 1682, by Thomas Dangerfield, printed for the author, &c., 1682 ; Case of Thomas Dangerfield, 1680 ; Howell's State Trials ; Bagford and Luttrell Coll. Broadsides in British Museum ; Loyal Songs, 1685 ; Ballad Society's Bagford Ballads, wherein are given, on pp. 663–92, Gadbury's Ballad on the Popish Plot, assuming to have been written by a lady of quality, and on p. 1015 the libellous description of him, pseudo-autobiographical, from Partridge's Nebulo Anglicanus.]

J. W. E.

GADDERAR, JAMES (1655–1733), bishop of Aberdeen, was a younger son of William Gadderar of Cowford, Elginshire, and Margaret Marshall, the heiress of some lands in the same county. He graduated A.M. at Glasgow in 1675, having probably gone south with his eldest brother, Alexander, who from 1674 to 1688 was minister of Girvan, Ayrshire. Licensed in 1681 by the presbytery of Glasgow, he was presented the next year to the parish of Kilmalcolm, Renfrewshire (not Kilmaurs as often stated). In 1688, prior to the legal overthrow of prelacy, he and his brother were among the 'curates' 'rabbled' out of their parishes 'contra jura omnia divina humanaque' as he says in the epitaph he placed on his brother's tomb) 'tumultuantibus in apostolicum regimen ecclesiæ conjuratis.' In 1703 he published at London a translation from the Latin of Sir Thomas Craig's (unpublished) work on the 'Right of Succession to the Kingdom of England,' prefixing a 'Dedication' to the Faculty of Advocates at Edinburgh, and a 'Preface' in which, along with an account of Craig's work, he insinuates his own nonjuring politics and dislike of the presbyterians. In 1712 (24 Feb.), 'at the express desire' of Rose [q. v.], the deprived bishop of Edinburgh, he was consecrated in London a bishop for the Scottish episcopalians, by the non-juring bishop Hickes [q. v.] and the Scottish bishops Falconer and Archibald Campbell (d. 1744) [q. v.] He continued to reside with the last-mentioned in London, took part in the consecration of the nonjuring bishops Spinckes, Collier, and Brett, and entered enthusiastically into the negotiations made (1716–23), through Arsenius, metropolitan of Thebais, for intercommunion with the Eastern churches. These negotiations, abortive for their immediate purpose, served, says Bishop Keith, to bring about a more intimate acquaintance with Eastern tenets and usages than was then generally possessed in Britain. In 1721 Gadderar came to Scotland as the representative or vicar of Bishop Campbell, whose election as their ordinary by the episcopal clergy of Aberdeen had not been ratified by 'the college' of bishops. Both he and Campbell were known to be zealous supporters of 'the usages' at the Holy Communion: (1) the mixing water with the wine, (2) commemoration of the faithful departed, (3) invocation of the Holy Ghost in the consecration prayer, and (4) oblation before administration, which had already caused division among the English nonjurors. Lockhart of Carnwath [q. v.], the agent in Scotland of the exiled king, was afraid that if the controversy spread among the Scotch episcopalians the Jacobite cause would suffer; and at a meeting of the Scottish bishops at Edinburgh, which Gadderar attended on his way to Aberdeen, an effort was made to have 'the usages' condemned, but Gadderar, while professing his loyalty to James, was firm in his refusal to surrender the rights and interests of his church to any external authority. In Aberdeen he was cordially received, and was soon so strong that (July 1724) an agreement was made and signed between him on the one hand and the 'college' bishops on the other, by which three of 'the usages' were virtually sanctioned (in the 'permission' of the Scottish communion office), and the other, the mixed chalice, was allowed, provided the mixture was not done publicly; and Gadderar was confirmed as bishop of Aberdeen. In the same year he published at Edinburgh the first of the 'wee bookies,' a reprint with certain alterations of the communion office of Charles I's ill-fated Scottish liturgy of 1637. In 1725 Bishop Campbell formally yielded to him the see of Aberdeen, and the same year the episcopal clergy of Moray elected him to that see also. He administered both 'districts,' where the episcopalians were at that time both numerous and influential, with great vigour and acceptance till his

death. He had really been the restorer of the liturgy to the Scottish episcopal church; and it had been his influence which in 1727 secured at the synod of Edinburgh the restoration of diocesan, as distinguished from 'the college' episcopacy. He died at Aberdeen in 1733, and was buried in the grave of Bishop Scougall [q. v.] within the parish church of Old Machar. Until the revolution this church had been the cathedral of Aberdeen. On the Sunday following his death his flock made a collection from which his little debts were paid, and the charges of his funeral defrayed. Down to the beginning of the 19th century his name continued a household word among the episcopalian peasants of Aberdeenshire.

[Grub's Eccl. Hist. of Scotland, vols. iii. and iv.; Lockhart Papers; Scott's Fasti; Dowden's Annotated Scottish Communion Office; Blunt's Dict. of Sects; tombstone of Alex. Gadderar.]
J. C.

GADDESDEN, JOHN OF (1280?–1361), physician, was born about 1280, and wrote in the early part of the fourteenth century. He took his name from Gaddesden on the borders of Hertfordshire and Buckinghamshire, where an ancient house, opposite that gate of Ashridge Park which is nearest to the church of Little Gaddesden, is shown as his. He was a member of Merton College (WOOD), and a doctor of physic of Oxford. He began to study medicine about 1299, and soon attained large practice in London. He attended a son of Edward I, probably Thomas of Brotherton, in the small-pox, wrapped him in scarlet cloth in a bed and room with scarlet hangings, and says of the result: 'et est bona cura et curavi eum in sequenti sine vestigio variolarum' (Rosa, ed. Venice, 1502, p. 41 a). Between 1305 and 1307 he wrote a treatise on medicine, which soon became famous, and which he entitled 'Rosa Medicinæ.' He chose the name, he says, because as the rose has five sepals (additamenta), so his book has five parts, and adds that as the rose excels all flowers, so his book excels all treatises on the practice of medicine. The title was probably suggested by Bernard's 'Lilium Medicinæ,' which appeared at Montpellier in 1303, and is quoted in the 'Rosa.' Gaddesden's book is often spoken of as 'Rosa Anglica.' It is crammed with quotations from Galen, Dioscorides, Rufus of Ephesus, Haliabbas, Serapion, Al Rhazis, Avicenna, Averrhoes, John of Damascus, Isaac, Mesue, Gilbertus Anglicus, and from the 'Flos Medicinæ' of Salernum; but also contains a good many original remarks which illustrate the character of the author more than his medical knowledge. The book begins with an account of fevers based on Galen's arrangement, then goes through diseases and injuries beginning with the head, and ends with an antidotarium or treatise on remedies. It contains some remarks on cooking, and innumerable prescriptions, many of which are superstitious, while others prove to be common-sense remedies when carefully considered. Thus the sealskin girdle with whalebone buckle which he recommends for colic is no more than the modern and useful cholera belt of flannel. He cared for his gains, and boasts of getting a large price from the Barber Surgeons' guild for a prescription of which the chief ingredient is tree frogs (*Rosa*, ed. Pavia, p. 120). His disposition, his peculiarities, and his reading are so precisely those of the 'Doctour of Phisik' in Chaucer's prologue that it seems possible that Gaddesden is the contemporary from whom Chaucer drew this character. He is mentioned in line 434:

Bernard and Gatesden and Gilbertyn.

Many manuscripts of the 'Rosa Medicinæ' are extant. They usually begin with a calendar (as in *Breviar. Bartholomei* MS. Pembr. Coll., Oxford), which is absent in the printed editions. It was first printed at Pavia in 1492, again at Venice, 1502, and at Pavia, 1517, and for the last time at Augsburg in 1595 (two volumes). It was translated into Irish, and a manuscript written by Doctor Cormac Mac Duinntshleibhthe in 1450 contains part of this version (British Museum MS. Harleian 546).

Gaddesden was in priest's orders, and was appointed to the stall of Wildland in St. Paul's Cathedral, London, on 1 Aug. 1342. He died in 1361.

The best account of his writings is in Freind's 'History of Physick,' 1726, ii. 277. This account contains the error, repeated by Aikin's 'Biographical Memoirs of Medicine,' 1780, p. 11, that he held the stall of Ealdland. The John de Gatesdone who held this stall was another person, and died before 1262.

[Rosa Medicinæ, ed. 1502, Venice, ed. 1492, Pavia, Dr. Mead's copy in library of Medico-Chirurgical Society of London; Le Neve's Fasti Ecclesiæ Anglicanæ, ii. 382, 448; Hist. of the Royal Family, London, 1713; Harl. MS. 546, A.D. 1450; British Museum Addit. MS. 15582, A.D. 1563; Pembroke College, Oxford, MS. Breviarium Bartholomei, circa 1380.] N. M.

GADSBY, WILLIAM (1773–1844), particular baptist minister, the son of a labourer, was born at Attleborough in the parish of Nuneaton, Warwickshire, in January 1773. He went to Nuneaton Church school and to another school, and at thirteen was apprenticed to a ribbon weaver. As a lad he had the gift of public speaking, and often harangued his fellow workmen, ending with 'preaching to them hell and damnation.' In 1793 he met with a baptist minister named Aston from Coventry, and on 29 Dec. that year was formally baptised at the Cow Lane chapel, Coventry. Until he was twenty-two he worked as a ribbon weaver, and then went to Hinckley, Leicestershire, as a stocking weaver. In 1796 he married Elizabeth Marvin, and began business on his own account. Two years afterwards he commenced preaching regularly at Bedworth and Hinckley, but he continued his business, and used to carry his wares to market in a pack. At this time he was referred to as 'a very tried man, bearing very blessed marks and evidences of divine teaching within, though clownish and illiterate, almost to the extreme.' He settled at Manchester in 1805 as the pastor of the Back Lane baptist chapel, situate in George's, now Rochdale, Road, where he remained till his death. At first he met with considerable opposition, but gradually his sterling qualities were appreciated, and he attained great popularity. He had ready wit and quaint humour, and was an earnest and persuasive speaker, though he would often startle his hearers with some eccentric remark. 'He was called an antinomian, and probably he did not speak with sufficient discrimination or exactness on the nature of moral obligation, but no minister in Manchester lived a more moral life, or presented to his hearers a more beautiful example of christian discipline or self-control' (HALLEY). It is calculated that in the exercise of his ministry he travelled sixty thousand miles, and preached nearly twelve thousand sermons.

Between 1806 and 1843 he wrote frequently on religious subjects, and published a number of pamphlets, most of which were afterwards issued in a collective form in two vols. (1851) by his son, John Gadsby, who also in 1884 edited and published a volume of Gadsby's 'Sermons, Fragments of Sermons, and Letters.' Gadsby wrote many prosaic hymns and other verses, and published them in 'A Selection of Hymns,' 1814, in 'The Nazarene's Songs,' 1814, and elsewhere. He died at Manchester on 27 Jan. 1844, and was buried in the Rusholme Road cemetery. There is a tablet to his memory in his chapel, and a good portrait of him was engraved by W. Barnard after F. Turner.

[Memoir by his son, John Gadsby, 1844, new edit. 1870; Halley's Lancashire, its Puritanism and Nonconformity, 1872, p. 527; Procter's Bygone Manchester, p. 144; Manchester City News, 24 and 31 March 1888; Brit. Mus. Cat. of Printed Books; John Dixon's Autobiog. 1866, contains reminiscences of Gadsby.] C. W. S.

GAGE, FRANCIS, D.D. (1621–1682), president of Douay College, born 1 Feb. 1620–1, was son of John Gage of Haling, Surrey, by his second wife, Mrs. Barnes, a widow. He was half-brother of Sir Henry Gage [q. v.], governor of Oxford, of George [q. v.] and Thomas Gage [q. v.], missionary and traveller. He was a student in the English College at Douay from 1630 to 1641, when he went to Paris to pursue his theological studies under William Clifford [q. v.] at Tournay College, which had been granted by Cardinal Richelieu to the Bishop of Chalcedon for the education of the English clergy (Pref. to CLIFFORD, Little Manual, ed. 1705). In 1646 he was ordained priest, and in 1648 appointed tutor to Thomas Arundel, then residing in Paris. He graduated B.D. at the Sorbonne in 1649, and D.D. in 1654. He then came to the English mission, was appointed archdeacon of Essex, and resided with Lady Herbert, whom he afterwards accompanied to France, whence he proceeded to Rome in 1659 as agent to the English chapter (PANZANI, Memoirs, pp. 298, 301, 302). He remained in Rome until his recall in 1661, and then returned to the English mission. He was chaplain to Lady Strangford from 1663 to 1667, and afterwards tutor to Philip Draycot of Paynsley, Staffordshire, whom he accompanied on a continental tour. On 23 Jan. 1675–6 he was nominated president of Douay College, in succession to Dr. George Leyburn. The college flourished greatly under his management until 1678, when Oates's plot alarmed the English catholics, and made them very cautious in sending their children to the colleges abroad. But after the storm had subsided the number of students increased, being attracted to Douay by the fame of Gage's abilities. He died on 2 June 1682. Dodd, writing in 1742, says he was 'a person of extraordinary qualifications, both natural and acquired. His memory was of late years very fresh in the university of Paris, where upon several occasions he had distinguished himself, especially by his flowing eloquence. In regard of his brethren he behaved himself with remarkable discretion in several controversies which required management' (Church Hist. iii. 296).

He wrote 'Journal of the Chief Events of his Life, from his Birth in 1621 to 1627,' autograph manuscript, in the archives of the Old Chapter, Spanish Place, Manchester Square, London (Hist. MSS. Comm. 5th Rep. p. 463). It is believed he was the 'F. G.' who edited 'The Spiritual Exercises of . . . Gertrude More, of the . . . English Congregation of our Ladies of Comfort in Cambray,' Paris, 1658, 12mo.

[Gage's Hengrave, p. 235; Gillow's Bibl. Dict.; Hist. MSS. Comm. 5th Rep. pp. 465, 467–8, 472.]   T. C.

GAGE, GEORGE (fl. 1614–1640), catholic political agent, born after 1582, seems to have been son of John Gage of Haling, Surrey, and brother of Sir Henry Gage [q. v.], to whom he erected a monument (COLLINS, Peerage, ed. Brydges, viii. 256–7; Cal. Clarendon Papers, i. 166, 169). He was a great friend of Sir Toby Matthew, and seems to have received priest's orders with him from the hands of Cardinal Bellarmine at Rome on 20 May 1614 (OLIVER, Jesuit Collections, p. 140). James I despatched him to Rome towards the close of 1621, in quality of agent to the papal court, to solicit a dispensation for the marriage of the Prince of Wales with the Spanish infanta. The jesuits strove to retard the dispensation, and if possible to prevent the completion of the match. The negotiations lasted for nearly six years, and ultimately came to nothing. A detailed account of Gage's part in them is given in 'The Narrative of the Spanish Marriage Treaty' (Camd. Soc. 1869); Tierney's edition of Dodd's 'Church History,' v. 119–64; and in Mr. S. R. Gardiner's 'History of England, 1603–42.' Gage is described in 1627 as 'a prisoner in the Clink,' being the agent of the Bishop of Chalcedon and of the seminary of Douay (Discovery of the Jesuits' College at Clerkenwell, Camd. Soc. Miscellany, ii.) He is referred to in the list of priests and recusants apprehended and indicted by Wadsworth and his fellow-pursuivants between 1640 and 1651. It is there stated that he was found guilty 'and since is dead,' from which it may be inferred that he died in prison (LINGARD, Hist. of England, ed. 1849, viii. 646).

[Dodd's Church Hist. ii. 426; Gillow's Bibl. Dict. ii. 356, and additions and corrections, p. xiv; Gage's Hengrave; Cal. of State Papers, Dom. (1650), pp. 334, 370, 521, 559; Gardiner's Hist. of England, iv. 330, 350, 351, 372, 398, v. 69.]   T. C.

GAGE, SIR HENRY (1597–1645), royalist officer, son of John Gage of Haling, Surrey, and great-grandson of Sir John Gage [q. v.] (COLLINS, Peerage, ed. Brydges, viii. 256), was born about 1597, and, as his family were strong catholics, sent to Flanders at the age of ten to be educated. Thence, after a short residence in France, he went to Italy, 'where under that famous scholar Piccolomini he heard his philosophy, and with great applause did publicly defend it' (WALSINGHAM, Alter Britanniæ Heros, p. 2). At the age of twenty-two Gage entered the Spanish service, and for twelve months 'trailed a pike' in the garrison of Antwerp. He was then offered a company in the regiment raised by Archibald Campbell, seventh earl of Argyll, and distinguished himself in its command at the siege of Bergen-op-Zoom (1622) and Breda (1624). The reduction of the English regiments in Spanish service after the fall of Breda, and the outbreak of war between England and Spain, obliged him in the following year to return to England (*ib.* p. 3). Gage devoted his enforced leisure to the study of the theory of war, which was throughout his life his favourite pursuit (*ib.* p. 27). During this period he also translated Hermannus Hugo's account of the siege of Breda from Latin into English, and Vincent's 'Heraldry' from English into French (*ib.* p. 3). In 1630 Sir Edward Parham offered Gage the post of captain-commandant in an English regiment which was being raised for the service of Spain, and he spent the next twelve years in the war in the Netherlands. He obtained a commission to raise a regiment himself, levied nine hundred men, and, on the death of Sir William Tresham, 'had his regiment completed by the addition of the old unto it, which his highness the prince-cardinal bestowed upon him' (*ib.* p. 5). Gage's chief service during this period was the defence of Saint-Omer in 1638. In 1639 he suggested to the English government to offer the privilege of recruiting the English and Irish regiments in Spanish service to the number of ten thousand men, in return for 4,400 Spanish veterans to be used in Scotland. Secretary Windebanke authorised negotiations, but the Spanish government refused to hear of the proposed exchange (*Clarendon State Papers*, ii. 19–30, 50). Gage was also unsuccessfully employed in 1639 to negotiate a loan of 150,000*l.* from Spain as the price of protecting the Spanish fleet from the Dutch (*Cal. Clarendon Papers*, i. 185, 197). When the civil war broke out, Gage used his influence to intercept the parliament's supplies from Flanders, and is said to have 'deprived the rebels of thirty thousand arms, and afforded his majesty eight thousand of those that were intended to be borne against him' (WALSINGHAM, p. 9). He returned to England about the spring of 1644 to enter the king's service. When the king left Oxford he named Gage one of the military council appointed to assist the governor (3 June 1644; WALKER, *Historical Discourses*, p. 19). In spite of the opposition of the governor, he speedily infused a new spirit into the defence of Oxford (CLARENDON, *Rebellion*, ed. Macray, viii. 122). On 11 June he captured Borstall House, on 11 Sept. relieved Basing House, and on 25 Oct. helped to raise the siege of Banbury (WALKER,

pp. 26, 90, 109). The relief of Basing was one of the most remarkable exploits of the whole war; Gage's own account is given at length by Walker, and copied, with some additional particulars, by Clarendon (*ib.* pp. 90–5; CLARENDON, ed. Macray, viii. 123). On 19 Nov. Gage was again despatched to relieve Basing, but the besiegers retreated at his approach (WALKER, p. 119). As a reward for these services Gage was knighted on 1 Nov. 1644 (DUGDALE, *Diary*, p. 74), and on the dismissal of Sir Arthur Aston [q. v.] on 25 Dec. 1644 made governor of Oxford in his place (*ib.* p. 76; CLARENDON, *Rebellion*, viii. 165). 'It is incredible,' writes his biographer, 'what a general contentment all men took in his promotion and how few repined at his advancement' (WALSINGHAM, p. 19). On 10 Jan. 1645 an expedition was sent out from Oxford to break down Culham bridge, and in a skirmish with the garrison of Abingdon Gage was mortally wounded on 11 Jan. (Accounts of this fight from the parliamentary side are given in VICARS, *Burning Bush*, p. 93, and in a published letter by Colonel Richard Browne; for royalist accounts see WALSINGHAM, p. 21; and *Mercurius Aulicus*, p. 1332.)

Gage was buried in Christ Church Cathedral on 13 Jan. 1645. His epitaph is printed by Wood (*Colleges and Halls*, ed. Gutch, p. 479), and by Le Neve (*Monumenta Anglicana*, i. 217). Elegies on him are to be found in Walsingham's 'Life' (p. 23), and in 'Mercurius Belgicus,' 1685. Clarendon observes: 'The king sustained a wonderful loss in his death, he being a man of great wisdom and temper, and amongst the very few soldiers who made himself to be universally loved and esteemed' (*Rebellion*, viii. 166). Gage married, between 1625 and 1630, Mary Daniel, and left two sons and four daughters (WALSINGHAM, p. 4).

[Edward Walsingham's Alter Britanniæ Heros, or the Life and Death of the most honourable knight Sir Henry Gage, late governor of Oxford, epitomised, Oxford, 1645; Clarendon's Hist. of the Rebellion, ed. Macray, 1888; Clarendon State Papers; Sir Edward Walker's Historical Discourses, 1707; Manning and Bray's History of Surrey, ii. 542.]   C. H. F.

GAGE, Sir JOHN (1479–1556), statesman and military commander, was the only son of William Gage of Firle Place, Sussex, by Agnes, daughter of Benjamin Boleney of Bolney, Sussex, and a cousin of William of Wykeham, bishop of Winchester (*History of Hengrave*, pp. 227–31). Being under age at his father's death (1496) he was put under the guardianship of Stafford, duke of Buckingham, and 'educated for court and camp under his eye.' Gage accompanied Henry VIII on the French campaign of 1513 (30 June to 24 Nov.) His name frequently occurs between 1510 and 1522 as a commissioner of peace for Sussex (*State Papers*, Dom. Henry VIII, 1509–14, 1515–16, 1521–3). He was also appointed governor of Guisnes, and afterwards of Oye, in France. His name first occurs in connection with Guisnes in the State Papers for 1522, and in August of that year he received the additional post of comptroller of Calais (*ib.* 1521–3, pp. 945, 1029, &c.) He was recalled to England to take his seat on the privy council, and in 1528 created vice-chamberlain to the king, a post which he held till 1540, being also made captain of the royal guard. In 1529 he entered parliament as member for his own county, and on 22 May 1532 was installed K.G. (*Register of the Garter*, 1724, pp. 421, 423). Gage was constantly employed on commissions by the king. In 1532 he went over to survey some lands at Calais, and in the same year he was employed in the north of England from December till the spring. On his return to court he had a quarrel with Henry. 'Master vice-chamberlain departed from the king,' writes one of the courtiers to Cromwell, 10 April 1533, 'in such sort as I am sorry to hear; the king licensed him to depart hence, and so took leave of him, the water standing in his eyes.' For the sake of the long friendship between himself and Gage, Cromwell is requested to induce the vice-chamberlain to return to court 'within a fortnight,' and to be a means for obtaining the king's favour. The dispute was probably connected with Catherine of Arragon, for though Gage had signed the petition to the pope for the divorce (*ib.* 1530, p. 2929), he was in May examined 'about the Lady Catherine,' and, being a man 'more ready to serve God than the world,' he doubtless had spoken on her behalf to Henry (*ib.* 1533, pp. 418, 470). In the following January it was reported that the vice-chamberlain had 'renounced his office and gone to a charterhouse, intending, with the consent of his wife, to become a Carthusian' (*ib.* 1534, p. 8). This intention was not carried out, and Gage, though a zealous catholic, did not scruple to share in the spoils of the church (cf. grant of priory of Kelagh, 20 March 1540), and was also on the commission for the surrender of religious houses. The week before Easter 1540 he went with other commissioners to report on the state of affairs at Calais (*State Papers and Letters*, Henry VIII, viii. 299, 303). He was back at court before Cromwell's arrest, and profited greatly by his friend's disgrace,

receiving the posts of constable of the Tower, comptroller of the household, 9 Oct. 1540, and chancellor of the duchy of Lancaster. He had also been one of those employed to negotiate Henry's divorce from Anne of Cleves in July (*ib.* viii. 404).

Gage commanded the expedition against Scotland which ended in the defeat and death of James V at Solway Moss (1542), and brought his Scotch prisoners back with him to the Tower in the winter, riding before them in his office as constable when they were taken for trial to the Star-chamber (WRIOTHESLEY, *Chronicle*, Camden Soc. i. 139). He afterwards (1543) went again to Scotland to treat of the betrothal of Prince Edward to the infant queen of Scots. At the siege of Boulogne, where he shared the command with Charles Brandon, duke of Suffolk, being lieutenant of the camp and general captain of the cavalry, he was created a knight-banneret. Gage was present at the funeral of Henry VIII, and was appointed one of the executors of the king's will (BURNET, *Hist. of Reformation*, i. 369), receiving a bequest of 200*l*. Gage was a member of the privy council, but differences soon arose between him and Somerset, who when he became protector expelled him from the council and from his post of comptroller of the royal household, whereupon Gage joined Southampton, the leader of the catholic party, and was one of those who signed the declaration against the protector. Gage and Southampton only reassumed their seats on the council to resign them upon the accession to power of Dudley, earl of Warwick. Gage had, like Dudley, married into the Guilford family (Philippa, daughter of Sir Richard Guilford or Guldeford, first cousin to Dudley's wife, being Gage's wife), but had no sympathy with the plot for Lady Jane Grey, and was therefore suspended from his post as constable of the Tower a few days before she was there proclaimed queen. Gage, as a zealous catholic, was at once high in Mary's favour. He received her at the Tower gates on her arrival in London on 3 Aug. 1553 (WRIOTHESLEY, *Chronicle*, ii. 94), and was restored to his office of constable and created lord chamberlain of her household. He bore her train at the coronation (1 Oct. 1553), and helped to hold the pall over her (STRYPE, *Mem.* III. i. 28, 55, 56). As lord chamberlain Gage carried the news of Wyatt's rebellion to the lord mayor, 25 Jan. 1553 and shared the panic raised by the march of Knevett and Cobham into London. Gage was stationed at the outer gate of Whitehall (*Queen Mary and Queen Jane*, p. 131), and 'he and his guard, being only armed with brigandines, were so frightened, and fled in at the gate so fast, that he fell down in the dirt, and so the gate was shut' (STRYPE, *Mem.* III. i. 138). 'Old Gage fell down in the dirt, and was foul arrayed . . . and . . . came in to us so frightened that he could not speak' (NICHOLLS, *Narratives of the Reformation*, Camden Soc., pp. 165, 167). At Mary's marriage with Philip of Spain the lord chamberlain was again one of her train-bearers (25 July 1554). On Palm Sunday, 18 March 1555, he received Elizabeth under his charge as constable at the Tower gates (*Queen Mary and Queen Jane*, pp. 70, 168). He seems to have treated the princess severely, 'more for love of the pope than for hate of her person' (HEYLYN, *Hist. of Reformation*, ii. 259; BURNET, ii. 503), and on her release was, with Sir Thomas Pope [q. v.], placed as a guard over her at her own house. Gage died at his house, Firle, Sussex, on 18 April 1556, and was buried on 25 April, 'with II herolds, with a standard of arms, and four of images, and with a hearse, and two (white branches), two dozen of stuffs, and eight dozen of stockings' (MACHYN, *Diary*, p. 105), at West Firle Church, where he and his wife lie under a fine altar-tomb. By his wife Philippa he had four sons and four daughters. His portrait, painted by Holbein, is at Hengrave.

[Authorities cited above ; Hist. of Hengrave ; Sharp's Peerage, vol. ii. ; Gillow's Bibl. Dict. ; Foxe's Acts and Mon. v. 514.] E. T. B.

GAGE, JOHN (1786–1842), antiquary. [See ROKEWODE, JOHN GAGE.]

GAGE, JOSEPH or JOSEPH EDWARD, COUNT GAGE or DE GAGES (1678?–1753?), grandee of Spain, general in the Spanish army, was second son of Joseph Gage of Sherborne Castle, Dorsetshire, and grandson of Sir Thomas Gage, fourth baronet, of Firle, Sussex. Joseph Gage the elder (an English jesuit) entered the English College at Rome as a 'converter' 14 Oct. 1670. He married Elizabeth, daughter and heiress of George Penruddock of Southampton, who brought great estates to the Gage family, and by her, who died 5 Dec. 1693, had, besides daughters, two sons, whereof Thomas, the elder, conformed to the church of England, and became the first Viscount Gage and father of General Thomas Gage [q. v.], and Joseph or Joseph Edward, the younger, ultimately became Count Gage. The latter, who apparently married young, was in Paris in 1719, when he is said to have acquired Mississippi stock representing the value of 13,000,000*l.* Intoxicated with his success, Gage, whom French writers call Mons. Guiache, sent a gentleman to Augustus, king of Poland, to offer 3,000,000*l.* for the crown, which was declined. He next sent an agent to the king of Sardinia, to offer a vast sum for that island, which proposal was likewise rejected. Friends advised him to invest a quarter of a million in an English estate, to fall back upon in event of the failure of the Mississippi scheme. This was not done, and when the crash came he was ruined, and with his wife removed to Spain, where they were well received at Madrid. Gage at first tried gold-mining in Asturias, it is said without much result. A patent for fishing wrecks on the coasts of Spain and the Indies probably was more successful. At any rate, in 1741 Gage was presented by the king of Spain with a silver mine of great value, and was made a grandee of the third class. In August 1742 Gage was appointed to command the Spanish army in Italy, superseding the Duke de Montemar. The queen of Spain at this time, having put her son Don Carlos on the throne of Naples, was striving to place his brother Don Philip on the throne of Lombardy. In the remarkable campaigns which ensued in 1743–6 Gage proved himself an able, although an unsuccessful commander. Gage began by attempting to penetrate into Tuscany, but, foiled by the Austrians under Traun, retired to winter quarters in Bologna and the Romagna, the opposing imperialists wintering in the duchies of Parma and Modena. While in the Bolognese Gage received a peremptory order from the queen of Spain to fight within three days, under pain of dismissal like his predecessor. He displayed much address in obeying the mandate. Knowing that the Austrians were weakened in numbers and not expecting an attack, he resolved to surprise their position at Campo Santo, a short march distant. To divert the attention of the people of Bologna he gave a grand ball, whereat the Spanish officers were present, but withdrew during the night to join their men. The Austrians were, however, forewarned. A bloody engagement followed, begun by moonlight before dawn and continued till after dark, 4 Feb. 1743, with no decisive result. Eventually the Spaniards retired on the Neapolitan frontier. A 'Te Deum' was celebrated at Madrid for the victory, and Gage was made a grandee of the first class. The same year Gage was surprised by the Austrians under Count Brown at Villetri, but subdued the resulting panic, and by his masterly arrangements compelled Brown to retire. In his report of the affair to the king of Naples Gage generously admitted : 'I have been surprised in my camp, which has been forced. The enemy even reached the headquarters, but have been repulsed with loss. Your majesty's arms are victorious, and the kingdom of Naples is safe. Nevertheless, this has been entirely the action of your majesty's troops, and I cannot but admit that their valour has repaired my fault, which would be unpardonable if I sought to diminish it.' The operations of 1744 were of no special importance, but those of 1745 stand almost without parallel for boldness of conception and rapidity of execution. By astonishing marches the army under Don Philip, and a French force under De Maillebois, effected a junction with Gage near Genoa, 14 June 1745. By October all the territories of the house of Austria in Italy had been conquered. On 20 Dec. 1745 Don Philip was proclaimed king of Lombardy. The Austrians still held the citadel of Milan and Mantua. In the spring of 1746 Don Philip and Gage retired before the Austrians from the neighbourhood of Milan to Piacenza, Gage's policy being to compel the imperialists, strengthened by their recent peace with Prussia, to exhaust themselves by useless marches. The scheme was foiled by the meddlesomeness of the queen of Spain, who commanded Gage to fight at once at all risks. An attack followed on the Austrian camp at San Lazaro, twenty-two miles from Piacenza. The Austrians, again forewarned, continued the conflict during the night, and at daybreak, 4 June 1746, came out of their entrenchments and charged with such fury that the French and Spaniards were broken, and retired with a loss of six thousand killed and nine thousand wounded. Gage effected his retreat to Piacenza in good order. After this disaster Gage was superseded by the Marquis de las Minas. His name does not appear again as a military commander. He received the order of St. Januarius, and a pension of four thousand ducats from the king of Naples, in recognition of his services.

Concerning Gage personally much confusion of statement and some uncertainty prevail. Documents among the Caryll and Mackenzie Papers in British Museum Add. MSS. appear to show that he was married twice, first to Catherine, daughter of the fourth John Caryll of West Harting, secondly to the Lady Mary Herbert, daughter of the second Marquis (titular duke) Powis, who died in October 1745, granddaughter of the first Marquis Powis, who was created a duke by James II when in exile, and sister of the third marquis (titular duke), who died in March 1747. They also (*British Museum Add. MS.* 28238) throw doubt on the date of Gage's death, which is generally stated (as in *Gent. Mag.* xxiii. 144) to have occurred at Pampeluna, 31 Jan. 1753, in the seventy-fifth year of his age.

[W. Berry's Sussex Genealogies, in which the Gage pedigree ends with the fourth baronet; Collins's Peerage (1812 ed.), in which, as in other peerages, there are inaccuracies in respect of both the Gage and Powis family histories; Gillow's Bibliography of English Catholics, ii. 363–364, and references there given. Gillow, like most biographers, makes the erroneous statement that Gage married Lady Lucy Herbert, sister of the Lady Mary Herbert, wrongly describing her also as daughter of the first instead of the second Marquis Powis; J. P. Wood's Life of John Law (1824), p. 141; Allgemeine Deutsche Biog. iii. 369–73, under 'Brown, Ulysses Maximilian;' Gent. Mag. xiii. 162, xiv. 110, 230, 399, 455, xv. 54, 110, 223, 278, 335, 390, 446, 559, 671, xxiii. 144; Add. MSS., indexed under ' Caryll, Cath., daughter of fourth John Caryll,' and 'Herbert, Mary, second wife of Count Joseph Gage.']   H. M. C.

GAGE, THOMAS (*d.* 1656), traveller, was the second son of John Gage of Haling, Surrey, by Margaret, daughter of Sir Thomas Copley of Gatton in that county, and brother of Sir Henry Gage [q. v.] His father sent him to Spain in 1612 to study among the jesuits, hoping that he would enter that society, but the young man conceived a deadly aversion for them, and assumed the monastic habit in the order of St. Dominic at Valladolid, taking in religion the name of Thomas de Sancta Maria. In 1625 he was in the monastery at Xeres in Andalusia, when a commissary of his order inspired him with a desire to go to the Philippine Islands as a missionary. It is evident from his own narrative that wealth and pleasure supplied him with stronger motives than religious zeal. His father, who would rather have seen him a scullion in a jesuit college than general of the whole Dominican order, threatened to disinherit him, and to stir up the jesuits against him if he again set foot in England. The king had forbidden any Englishman to go to the Indies, and Gage was smuggled on board the fleet in an empty biscuit barrel. He left Cadiz on 2 July 1625 with twenty-seven of his brethren. In a skirmish at Guadaloupe the Indians killed several sailors, some jesuits, and a Dominican. The missionaries desired to return, but ultimately reached Mexico on 8 Oct. Gage remained till February 1625–6 in the monastery where missionaries were first received.

Gage was disgusted by what he learned of the Philippines, and determined to remain in Central America. The day before the missionaries were to start, he and three other Dominicans gave their companions the slip, and set out for Chiapa. Gage was kindly received by the provincial of his order, was appointed to teach Latin to the children of the town, and obtained the goodwill of the bishop and the governor. At the end of six months he proceeded to Guatemala, where he was made M.A. in 1627, applied himself to preaching, and was appointed professor of philosophy. After leaving Guatemala he lived for some years among the Indians, and learned the Cacchiquel and Poconchi languages. Trouble about ' some points of religion' made him 'desire the wings of a dove' to fly to England (*The English-American*, p. 180). Having amassed a sum of nearly nine thousand pieces-of-eight, he resolved to return to Europe, though his superior refused permission. Accordingly he left Amatitlan, where he was parish priest, on 7 Jan. 1636–7. He crossed the province of Nicaragua, following the coast of the Pacific. A Dutch corsair took a coaster in which he sailed, and robbed him of seven thousand crowns. He at last reached Panama, traversed the isthmus, and sailed from Portobello on board the Spanish fleet, which arrived at San Lucar 28 Nov. 1637.

Having attired himself in English secular costume, he returned to London after an absence of twenty-four years from his native country. Unable to satisfy his religious doubts, he resolved to visit Italy. At Loreto, according to his own statement, he finally renounced the catholic religion on convincing himself that the miracles attributed to the picture of our Lady at that shrine were fraudulent. He immediately returned to England, landing at Rye on 29 Sept. 1641. Without delay he made himself known to Dr. Brownrigg, bishop of Exeter, who took him to the Bishop of London, from whom he received an order to preach his recantation sermon at St. Paul's on 28 Aug. 1642. To give fuller proof of his sincerity, he resolved to marry (*ib.* p. 211). After a year's hesitation, during which he spent his means in London, he was determined, by the favour shown to papists at court, to join the parliamentary side (*ib.* p. 211). He was rewarded by his appointment, in 1642, to the rectory of Acrise, Kent (HASTED, *Kent*, iii. 348). About 1651 he was appointed rector or preacher of the word of God at Deal. To show his zeal he gave evidence against Father Arthur Bell, a near relation of Sir Henry Gage's wife, and against Father Peter Wright, his brother's chaplain, both of whom, on his testimony, were condemned to death as priests (cf. *Several Proceedings in Parliament*, 15–22 May 1651). He also attacked Archbishop Laud.

The appearance of his 'English-American; or New Survey of the West India's,' in 1648, caused a remarkable sensation. His account of the wealth and defenceless condition of the Spanish possessions in South America excited the cupidity of the English, and it is said that Gage himself laid before Cromwell the first regular plan for mastering the Spanish territories in the New World (BURNET, *Own Time*, ed. 1833, i. 137 ; LONG, *Hist. of Jamaica*, i. 221). He was appointed chaplain to General Venables's expedition, which sailed under Venables and Penn for Hispaniola. On 20 Dec. 1654 a frigate was ordered to carry him to Portsmouth (*Cal. of State Papers*, Dom. 1654, p. 586). The fleet failed at Hispaniola, but took Jamaica, where Gage died in 1656 ' in the States' service.' On 18 July in that year the council in London ordered that certain arrears of pay due to him should be given to his widow, Mary Gage, and they recommended the Jamaica committee at Ely House to settle upon her a pension of 6s. 8d. a week (*ib.* 1656–7, p. 28). His daughter Mary was buried at Deal 21 March 1652–3.

His works are : 1. ' The Tyranny of Satan, discovered by the teares of a converted sinner, in a sermon preached in Paules Church, on the 28 of August, 1642. By Thomas Gage, formerly a Romish Priest, for the space of 38 yeares, & now truly reconciled to the Church of England,' London, 1642, 4to. 2. ' The English-American his Travail by Sea and Land ; or a New Survey of the West India's, containing a Journall of three thousand and three hundred miles within the main Land of America,' London, 1648, fol., dedicated to Thomas, lord Fairfax ; 2nd edit. ' enlarged by the author and beautified with maps,' London, 1655, fol. This second edition is entitled ' A New Survey of the West India's.' The third edition appeared at London in 1677, and the fourth in 1711, 8vo. Southey, who has quoted this work in his notes on ' Madoc,' says that Gage's account of Mexico is copied verbatim from Nicholas's ' Conqueast of West-India,' which itself is a translation from Gomara. But though Gage might have borrowed some historical facts from previous writers, his book contained most interesting information derived from his personal observations and experiences. He was the first person to give to the world a description of vast regions from which all foreigners had been jealously excluded by the Spanish authorities. Gage's work was, at the command of Colbert, translated into French, with some retrenchments, 2 vols. Paris, 1676, 12mo, Amsterdam, 1680, 1699, 1721, 1722 ; it was translated also into Dutch, Utrecht, 1682, 4to, and into German, Leipzig, 1693, 4to. Selections from the French translation are inserted in Thevenot's ' Relations de divers Voyages curieux,' Paris, 1672 and 1696, fol. In 1712 there appeared at London 'Some Remarkable Passages relating to Archbishop Laud, particularly of his affection to the Church of Rome. Being the twenty-second chapter of Gage's Survey of the West Indies, as 'twas printed in the Folio Edition before the Restoration, but supprest in the Octavo since,' 8vo. 3. 'Rules for the better learning of the Indian tongue called Poconchi, or Pocoman, commonly used about Guatemala and some other parts of Honduras.' Printed at the end of 'The English-American.' 4. 'A Duell between a Iesuite and a Dominican, begun at Paris, gallantly fought at Madrid, and victoriously ended at London, upon fryday, 16 May 1651.' This tract relates to the evidence he gave against Peter Wright and Thomas Dade, a Dominican friar.

[Biog. Universelle; Brydges's Censura Literaria (1807), iv. 263, v. 225; Camus, Mémoire sur la Collection des Grands et Petits Voyages, pp. 116, 291, 292; Challoner's Missionary Priests (1843), ii. 259, 336; Chalmers's Biog. Dict.; Dodd's Church Hist. iii. 296; Foley's Records, ii. 520, vii. 284; Gage's Hengrave, p. 234; Lowndes's Bibl. Man. (Bohn), p. 853; Notes and Queries, 1st ser. vi. 291, vii. 609, viii. 144; Nouvelle Biog. Générale; Quétif and Echard's Scriptores Ordinis Prædicatorum, ii. 758.]

T. C.

GAGE, THOMAS (1721–1787), general, second son of Thomas Gage, first viscount Gage, in the peerage of Ireland, by his first wife Benedicta (or Beata Maria Theresa), only daughter and heiress of Benedict Hall of High Meadow, Gloucestershire, was born in 1721. On 30 Jan. 1741 he received his first commission as a lieutenant in Colonel Cholmondeley's newly raised regiment (afterwards 48th foot, and now the 1st Northampton). His name occurs in the Irish lists (*Quarters of the Army in Ireland*) in 1745 as a captain in Battereau's foot, the old 62nd, an Irish corps of two battalions, which fought at Culloden and was disbanded in 1748, and in 1748 as major in what then was the 55th foot. He appears to have been aide-de-camp to Lord Albemarle in Flanders in 1747–8 (MACLACHLAN, *Orders of William, Duke of Cumberland*). At the reductions of 1748, the 55th foot, of which Sir Peter Halket was colonel, was renumbered as the 44th foot (now the 1st Essex). Gage became lieutenant-colonel of the regiment 2 March 1751, and went with it to America under General Braddock [see BRADDOCK, EDWARD] in 1754. He commanded the advanced column in the march from the Monagahela to Fort Duquesne on 9 July 1755, where he was distinguished by his gallantry and was wounded. Subsequently he was employed with the 44th

at Oswego. In May 1758 he was appointed to raise a provincial regiment, which was brought into the line as the 80th or 'light-armed' foot. Later in the same year he commanded the light infantry in Abercromby's expedition against Ticonderoga. After the fall of Niagara in July 1759, Gage, as brigadier-general, was detached from Crown Point to supersede Sir William Johnson, a provincial officer by whom the command had been held after the death of Colonel Prideaux. He was directed to act against La Gallette, a French post on Lake Ontario, which he reported to be impracticable. He commanded the rear-guard of the force under Amherst [see AMHERST, JEFFREY], which united with Murray's forces from Quebec, before Montreal on 6 Sept. 1760, and completed the conquest of Canada. Gage was appointed governor of Montreal, where his mild rule contrasted with the severity of Murray at Quebec. He became a major-general in 1761, and in 1763 was appointed to act as commander-in-chief in North America, with his head-quarters at New York, during the absence of Amherst, who returned home (*Calendar Home Office Papers*, 1760–5, par. 967). He was confirmed in the appointment the year after (*ib.*) and retained it until 1772, when he returned to England (*ib.* 1770–2, par. 1573). His conduct received the approval of the home government (*ib.* 1766–9, par. 619). After his regiment, the 80th foot, was disbanded, Gage held the colonelcy of the 60th royal Americans for two months, and when Amherst was reinstated therein was transferred to the colonelcy of the 22nd foot. He became a lieutenant-general in 1770, before leaving America.

In 1774 Gage was appointed governor-in-chief and captain-general of the province of Massachusetts Bay, in succession to Hutchinson, and in May that year, pursuant to orders from home, took up his quarters in Boston, where he was well received, despite the unpopularity of the enactment closing the port against trading vessels, which had been put in force before his arrival. He had been employed there in 1768. Gage, a brave, though not a brilliant soldier, had six regiments with him in Boston, but his efforts to bring the colonists into a more submissive attitude towards the ministry at home proved as unavailing as thankless. He proclaimed the solemn league and covenant as a traitorous assemblage, and bade the magistrates arrest all persons aiding and abetting it. He likewise issued a proclamation for 'the encouragement of virtue and suppression of vice,' in which, according to an American historian, he gave great offence to many by ranking hypocrisy among the immoralities. He chose the new council for the province, and forbade the holding of town-meetings without special license. He also seized the provincial magazines at Cambridge and elsewhere, which resulted in some rioting. A once loyal province had been alienated to the verge of rebellion through ministerial blundering at home, and an accident sufficed to kindle the smouldering flame. On 18 April 1775 Gage, hearing that the colonists were collecting stores at Concord Town, twenty miles from Boston, sent a detachment of eight hundred men under Colonel Smith, 10th foot, to destroy them. The service was effected, but a collision with the militia occurred on the return march at Lexington, with which the war of independence may be said to have commenced. Gage's report of the affair is printed in facsimile in the 'Memorial History of Boston.' By a resolution of the provincial congress, the colonists refused longer to obey Gage as governor. Gage remained in Boston, where at the end of March he was reinforced by additional regiments from home. On 12 June Gage proclaimed martial law, and offered a free pardon to all who would avail themselves of it, except Samuel Adams and John Harvey. On the 16th the Americans took up a position on what was properly Breed's Hill, on Charleston Heights, opposite Boston, where on the morrow (17 June 1775) was fought the battle known as that of Bunker's Hill. Howe, with part of Gage's command, was sent to dislodge the American forces. Twice the position was assailed without success. The third time the slope was carried, and the Americans driven from their entrenchments. They merely retired from Breed's Hill to Bunker's Hill, whither the British did not follow them. Gage shut himself up in Boston, where great scarcity prevailed, and where he was blockaded on the land side by Washington. Gage was blamed at home and abroad. In an undated letter to Lord Suffolk about this time, Germain, the secretary of state for the colonies, laments that 'General Gage, with all his good qualitys, finds himself in a position of too great importance for his talents' (*Hist. MSS. Comm.* 9th Rep. iii. 83 *a*); and Burgoyne, in a letter from Boston dated 20 Aug. 1775, speaks of Gage as 'an officer totally unfitted for this command,' and enters into a detail of all he had left undone (*ib.* 81 *b*). Despite Germain's misgivings Gage was appointed commander-in-chief in North America in August 1775, but soon after resigned. He embarked at Boston for England on 10 Oct. 1775, leaving the command to Howe, was transferred from the colonelcy of the 22nd foot to that of the 17th dragoons, and afterwards of the 11th dragoons.

He became a full general in April 1782. He died 2 April 1787 (*Gent. Mag.* lvii. (i.) 366).

Gage married 8 Dec. 1758, at Mount Kembal, North America, Margaret, daughter of Peter Kembal, president of the council of New Jersey, by whom he had six sons and five daughters. His eldest surviving son, Major-general Henry Gage, succeeded his uncle, William Hall Gage, second viscount, as third viscount, and died, leaving issue, in 1808. The youngest son, Admiral Sir William Hall Gage, is separately noticed.

[For genealogical details see Archdall's Peerage of Ireland under 'Gage;' also Collins's Peerage (ed. 1812), viii. p. 267-8. The particulars of Gage's early military commissions in the War Office (Home Office) books are imperfect, owing to the regiments to which he belonged being on the Irish establishment. The services of the 44th foot during the period Gage belonged to it are given in T. Carter's Hist. Records 44th (East Essex) Regiment (London, 1865), in which Gage is wrongly described as a 'brevet lieutenant-colonel' in the affair of Fort Duquesne. The best account of the campaigns in America in which Gage was engaged, from the attempt on Fort Duquesne in 1755 to the fall of Montreal in 1760, will be found in F. Parkman's Montcalm and Wolfe (London, ed. 1884, 2 vols.) Some notices of Gage in America from 1760 to 1772 appear in Calendars of Home Office Papers, 1760-6, 1766-9, 1770-2. His account of the affair at Fort Duquesne and particulars of his later services in America, in his own words, with queries by Geo. Chalmers and Gage's answers, are given in vol. xxxiv. of the Collections of the Hist. Soc. of Massachusetts. For his doings at Boston reference may be made to Letters to the Ministry (1769, 12mo); Letters to the Earl of Hillsborough, &c. (1769, 8vo); Letters of Generals Gage and Washington (New York, 1775); Detail and Conduct of the American War under General Gage (London, 1780); also to Beatson's Nav. and Mil. Memoirs, vol. iv., Stedman's Hist. American War, Bancroft's Hist. United States, vol. iv., and similar works, which should be compared with Gage's order-books and letters. Gage's Regimental and General Orders, complete from 1759 to 1777, are in the British Museum, where they form Addit. MSS. 21656-7, 21680, 21683. His orders while in command at Niagara, and his correspondence with Colonel Bouquet, General Haldimand, and other officers of note, at various periods of his services in America, will also be found in Addit. MSS. In addition to materials in the Home and Colonial series in the Public Record Office, whereof those for the period 1760-72, as before stated, are noted in the published Calendars of Home Office Papers, a large number of letters to and from Gage in America are preserved among the Marquis of Lansdowne's papers, and are catalogued in Hist. MSS. Comm. 5th Rep. Some notices of him will also be found in the 6th Rep. and 9th

Rep. iii. See also Appleton's Enc. Amer. Biog. vol. iii., and Georgian Era, vol. ii.] H. M. C.

GAGE, Sir WILLIAM HALL (1777–1864), admiral of the fleet, sixth and youngest son of General the Hon. Thomas Gage [q. v.], was born on 2 Oct. 1777, and entered the navy on board the Bellona guard-ship at Plymouth, in 1789. After serving in several ships on the home, West Indian, and Mediterranean stations, including the Princess Royal flag-ship of Rear-admiral Goodall in the actions off Toulon on 13 March and 13 July 1795, and the Bedford, in the defence of the convoy against Richery off Cadiz, he was appointed to the Victory, carrying the flag of Sir John Jervis, and was promoted from her to be lieutenant of the Minerve frigate, in which he took part in the engagement with the Sabina on 20 Dec. 1796 [see NELSON, HORATIO, VISCOUNT], in the battle of Cape St. Vincent on 14 Feb., and in the cutting out of the Mutine brig on 29 May 1797. On 13 June 1797 he was made commander, and on 26 July was posted to the Terpsichore frigate, which for the next three years was actively employed in the Mediterranean, and especially in the blockade of Malta, and, having returned to England, was one of the frigates which detained the Danish ships under the convoy of the Freja, an affair which proved one of the main causes of the second armed neutrality and of the battle of Copenhagen (SCHOMBERG, Nav. Chron. iii. 373). In March 1801 Gage was appointed to the Uranie, and on 21 July took part in the cutting out of the French 20-gun corvette Chevrette from under the batteries in Camaret Bay (JAMES, Nav. Hist., ed. 1860, iii. 138). From 1805 to 1808 he commanded the Thetis frigate in the North Sea and Mediterranean, and in 1813–14 the Indus of 74 guns off Toulon under Sir Edward Pellew. In 1821 he became a rear-admiral. From 1825–30 he was commander-in-chief in the East Indies; and in the Downs, May to July 1833. He was nominated a G.C.H. on 19 April 1834, became a vice-admiral on 10 Jan. 1837, was commander-in-chief at Lisbon from April to December 1837, was a member of the board of admiralty 1842–6, and attained the rank of admiral on 9 Nov. 1846. From 1848 to 1851 he was commander-in-chief at Plymouth. This was the end of his long service, though in 1853 he was appointed rear-admiral of the United Kingdom, and vice-admiral in the following year. In 1860 he was nominated a G.C.B., and in 1862 was advanced to be admiral of the fleet. During his later years he lived at Thurston near Bury St. Edmunds, where he freely contributed both time and money to the restoration of the parish church and to the local charities, and where he died on 4 Jan. 1864.

[Marshall's Royal Nav. Biog. i. 836; O'Byrne's Naval Biog. Dict.; Gent. Mag. (1864, vol. i.), new ser. xvi. 388.]   J. K. L.

GAGER, WILLIAM (*fl.* 1580–1619), Latin dramatist, was a nephew of Sir William Cordell, master of the rolls [q. v.] He became a scholar of Westminster School, whence he was elected to Christ Church, Oxford, in 1574. He proceeded B.A. 4 Dec. 1577, M.A. 5 June 1580, and B.C.L. and D.C.L. 30 June 1589 (*Oxford Univ. Reg.*, Oxford Hist. Soc., ii. iii. 70). Gager soon proved a facile Latin verse writer, and wrote a series of Latin plays, which were performed in the university with great success. In 1581 a Latin tragedy, 'Meleager,' was produced in the presence of the Earl of Leicester, Sir Philip Sidney, and other distinguished persons. In June 1583, when Albert Alasco, prince palatine of Poland, was entertained by the university, two plays by Gager were acted at Christ Church, and the distinguished visitor expressed much satisfaction with them. The first was 'a pleasant comedie intituled "Rivales," ' the second 'a verie statelie tragedie named "Dido," wherein the Queenes banket (with Eneas narrative of the destruction of Troie) was livelie described in a marchpaine pattern,' and the scenic effects were 'all strange, marvellous, and abundant' (HOLINSHED, iii. 1355). The second and third acts of the 'Dido,' with prologue, argument, and epilogue, are extant in the Brit. Mus. MS. Addit. 22583, ff. 34–44. Early in February 1591–2 a fourth piece, 'Ulysses Redux,' was acted at Christ Church. In the manuscript volume already mentioned, which was formerly in Dr. Bliss's library, are extracts from a fifth play by Gager on the subject of 'Œdipus.' When Queen Elizabeth visited Oxford in September 1592, Gager wrote the prologue and epilogue for the comedy 'Bellum Grammaticale,' which was performed in the royal presence at Christ Church. Joseph Hunter suggested that Gager was identical with William Wager, the author of some moralityplays, but Wager's pieces were written before Gager left school: the theory is altogether untenable. Meres mentions 'Dr. Gager of Oxford' among 'the best poets for comedy'— not a very apt description, since Gager's chief works were tragedies—in his 'Palladis Tamia,' 1598.

Printed copies of only two of Gager's plays are now known—the 'Ulysses Redux' and 'Meleager'—both printed at Oxford by Joseph Barnes in 1592 The former, 'Ulysses Redux, tragœdia publice Academicis recitata octavo Idus Februarii 1591,' is dedicated to Lord Buckhurst. Copies are in the Douce collection at Oxford and at Bridgewater House. Commendatory verse by Alberico Gentili, Matthew Gwinne, Thomas Holland, and others is prefixed. The 'Meleager, tragœdia noua bis publice acta in Æde Christi Oxoniæ,' copies of which are in the British Museum and Bodleian libraries, is dedicated (1 Jan. 1592) to Robert, earl of Essex. Verses by Richard Edes [q. v.], Alberico Gentili [q. v.], and J. C. are prefixed. There is an epilogue addressed to the Earls of Pembroke and Leicester, and at the close of the volume is 'Panniculus Hippolyto Senecæ Tragœdiæ assutus, 1591;' an address to Elizabeth, dated 1592, with the prologue and epilogue to the 'Bellum Grammaticale.'

Gager sent a copy of the 'Meleager' to Dr. John Rainolds, then of Queen's College, afterwards president of Corpus Christi College, and with it he forwarded a letter defending the performance of plays at Oxford. Rainolds replied by denouncing the practice and by condemning the excess to which it had lately been carried at Christ Church. A letter of protest from Gager, dated 31 July 1592, is in Corpus Christi College Library (MS. ccclii. 6), and copies of other parts of Gager's share in the correspondence are in University College Library (MS. J. 18). Finally Rainolds wrote a detailed and spirited answer to Gager (preface, dated 30 May 1593), which was published in 1599 under the title of 'Th' overthrow of Stage-Plays by the way of controversie betwixt D. Gager and D. Rainolds, wherein all the reasons that can be made for them are notably refuted.' Rainolds attacked with especial vigour the appearance on the stage of youths in women's clothes. A Latin defence of Gager by Alberico Gentili, and a final reply by Rainolds, are appended to Rainolds's volume. A reprint of this volume and the manuscripts dealing with the controversy has long been promised by the New Shakspere Society.

Gager was a voluminous writer of Latin verse. He probably edited the 'Exequiæ D. Philippi Sidnæi,' Oxford, 1587, to which he largely contributed. He also wrote in the university collection issued on the deaths of Sir Henry Unton in 1596 and of the queen in 1603. The volume in the British Musuem (Addit. MS. 22583) which contains parts of Gager's tragedies of 'Dido' and 'Œdipus,' includes Latin-verse translations by him of Homer's 'Batrachomuomachia,' 'Susanna,' 'Præcepta quædam Isocratis ad Demonicum,' Musæus's 'Hero et Leander,' together with numerous verses and epigrams addressed

to friends, patrons, and relatives, like George Peele, Martin Heton, Richard Edes, Toby Matthew, the Earl of Leicester, Sir William Cordwell, Nicholas Breton, and Richard Hakluyt. Two long pieces, 'Musa Australis' and 'Ægloga,' are both addressed to Toby Matthew. Congratulatory odes on the queen's escape from the Babington plot, a few trifling English verses, and a prose 'Encomium Eloquentiæ,' conclude the volume. A Latin heroic poem, 'Piramus,' dated 5 Nov. 1605, is in MS. Royal, 12 A. lix. Latin verses by Gager appear before Breton's 'Pilgrimage to Paradise' (1592). In 1608 Gager seems to have publicly defended the thesis at Oxford 'that it was lawful for husbands to beat their wives.' William Heale of Exeter College replied in 'An Apologie for Women,' Oxford, 1609. On the death of Martin Heton, bishop of Ely, 14 July 1609, Gager wrote a Latin elegy, which was engraved on the bishop's tomb in Ely cathedral (BENTHAM, *Ely*, p. 197).

In 1590 Gager seems to have been disappointed of a fortune which he expected from an uncle, Edward Cordell, who died in that year. He attributed his disappointment to the action of his uncle's wife. In 1601 he became surrogate to Dr. Swale, vicar-general of Ely. On 29 May 1606, when his friend, Martin Heton, was bishop of Ely, Gager was appointed chancellor of the diocese of Ely. He was delegate and commissary for Archbishop Bancroft for the diocese of Ely in 1608, and custos of the spiritualities on the vacancy of the see in 1609. He was also vicar-general and official principal to Bishop Andrewes in 1613, 1616, and 1618.

[Wood's Athenæ Oxon., ed. Bliss, ii. 87–9; Halliwell's Dictionary of Plays; Stevenson's Supplement to Bentham's History of Ely (1817), 10, 20, 28, 33; Wood's Annals of Oxford, vol. ii. pt. i. pp. 216, 256; Hunter's MS. Chorus Vatum in Addit. MS. 24491, f. 90; Tanner's Bibl. Brit.]

S. L.

GAGNIER, JOHN (1670 ?–1740), orientalist, was born in Paris about 1670, and educated at the College of Navarre. His tutor, Le Bossu, having shown him a copy of Walton's 'Polyglott Bible,' he determined to master Hebrew and Arabic. After taking orders he was made a canon regular of the Abbey of St. Genevieve, but finding the life irksome he retired to England, and ultimately became an Anglican clergyman. In 1703 he was created M.A. at Cambridge by royal mandate (*Cantabr. Graduati*, 1787, p. 152). William Lloyd, bishop of Worcester, appointed him his domestic chaplain and introduced him at Oxford. Gagnier subsequently settled at Oxford, and taught

Hebrew. In 1706 he was enabled through Lloyd's liberality to publish in quarto an edition of the fictitious Joseph ben Gorion's 'History of the Jews,' in the original Hebrew, with a Latin translation and notes (HEARNE, *Remarks*, Oxf. Hist. Soc. i. 127). In 1707 he published at the Hague 'L'Église Romaine convaincue de dépravation, d'idolatrie, et d'antichristianisme,' 8vo. In 1710, at the instance of Sharp, archbishop of York, he assisted John Ernest Grabe [q. v.] in the perusal of the Arabic manuscripts in the Bodleian Library relating to the Clementine constitutions, on which Sharp had engaged Grabe to write a treatise against Whiston (*ib.* iii. 239). In 1717 he was appointed by the vice-chancellor to read the Arabic lecture at Oxford in the absence of the professor, John Wallis. In 1718 appeared his 'Vindiciæ Kircherianæ, sive Animadversiones in novas Abrahami Trommii Concordantias Græcas versionis vulgo dictæ LXX. Interpretum,' 8vo, Oxford, which, though vigorously written, was considered an unfair attack on Trommius, then an aged man. In 1723 he issued in folio Abū Al-Fidā's 'Life of Mahomet,' in Arabic, with a Latin translation and notes, dedicated to an early patron, Lord Macclesfield. The lord almoner's professorship of Arabic at Oxford was conferred on Gagnier in 1724. He had prepared an edition of Abū Al-Fidā's 'Geography,' and in 1726 or 1727 printed as a specimen seventy-two folio leaves, but was unable to proceed further from want of encouragement. The fragment was noticed in the 'Journal des Savants' for 1727. For the benefit of those who were unable to read his Latin translation of Abū Al-Fidā's 'Mahomet,' he compiled a 'Life' in French, which was published by Le Clerc at Amsterdam in 1732 (2 vols. 8vo). Of this work, which is quite unworthy of Gagnier's reputation, an edition in three volumes appeared at Amsterdam in 1748; and a German translation in two volumes at Köthen in 1802–4. He had previously furnished an anonymous continuation to Count H. de Boulainvilliers's 'La Vie de Mahomed,' 8vo, London, 1730. Gagnier died on 2 March 1740. He left a son, John, born in 1721, who died on 27 Jan. 1796, aged 75 (FOSTER, *Alumni Oxon.* 1715–1886, ii. 504; SURTEES, *Durham*, iii. 124,125). Gagnier's other publications are: 1. 'Lettre sur les Médailles Samaritaines,' printed in 'Nouvelles de la République des Lettres,' in the 'Journal de Trévoux,' 1705, and a Latin version in vol. xxviii. of Ugolinus's 'Thesaurus Antiquitatum' (p. 1283). 2. 'Tabula nova et accurata exhibens paradigmata omnium conjugationum Hebraicarum,' four

large leaves, Oxford, 1710, printed for the use of his pupils. 3. 'Carolina. Ecloga in diem natalem Willielminæ Carolinæ, serenissimæ Principis Walliæ,' 4to, London, 1719. 4. 'Liber Petra Scandali de principio et causa schismatis duarum ecclesiarum Orientalis et Occidentalis, ex Græco Arabice redditus,' 8vo, Oxford, 1721. 5. 'Animadversiones in novam Josephi Gorionidis editionem à Jo. Frid. Breithaupto publicatam,' printed in vol. v. of Le Clerc's 'Bibliothèque Choisie.' He also contributed to vol. ii. of J. A. Fabricius's edition of 'St. Hippolytus' (1716), 'Fragmenta ex catena in Pentateuchum,' &c., with a Latin translation. At the invitation of Dr. Mead he translated from the Arabic the treatise of Rhazes on the small-pox. 'Instructions sur les Nicodémites,' attributed to Gagnier, has been shown by Barbier to have been written by J. Graverol.

[Hearne's Remarks and Collections (Oxf. Hist. Soc.); Biographie Universelle (Michaud), xv. 360–2; Nouvelle Biographie Générale, xix. 166–7; Oxford Ten Year Book; Oxford Graduates.] G. G.

GAHAGAN, USHER (*d.* 1749), classical scholar, belonged to a good family of Westmeath, Ireland; was educated at Trinity College, Dublin, but took no degree, and then proceeded to study for the Irish bar. His parents had brought him up as a protestant, but he was converted in youth to Roman catholicism, and was thus prevented from being called to the bar. He soon married a rich heiress, whom he treated very cruelly, and a separation followed. His relatives were alienated by his conduct, and he came to London, where he tried to make a livelihood out of his classical scholarship. He edited in Brindley's beautiful edition of the classics the works of Horace, Cornelius Nepos, Sallust, Juvenal, Persius, Virgil, and Terence, all published in 1744; Quintus Curtius in 1746; Catullus, Propertius, and Tibullus, issued in 1749. He also translated into good Latin verse Pope's 'Essay on Criticism' ('Tentamen de re critica'), which appeared in 1747 with a Latin dedication to the Earl of Chesterfield, and a poem descriptive of the earl's recent reception in Dublin as lord-lieutenant. But Gahagan fell into very bad company in London. A compatriot, Hugh Coffey, suggested to him a plan for making money by filing coins or 'diminishing the current coin of the realm.' Another Irishman, of some education, Terence Connor, who is variously described as Gahagan's servant or lodger, was introduced into the conspiracy. For some months the scheme worked well. But the suspicions of the authorities were roused at the end of 1748. Coffey turned informer, and Gahagan and Connor were arrested in a public-house at Chalk Farm early in January 1748–9. The trial took place at the Old Bailey on Monday, 16 Jan. 1748–9, and both were convicted on Coffey's evidence. While awaiting execution in Newgate, Gahagan translated Pope's 'Messiah' and 'Temple of Fame' into Latin verse, and this was published immediately (1749), with a dedication to the Duke of Newcastle, prime minister, praying for pardon. Gahagan also addressed Prince George to the same effect in English verse, while Connor wrote a poetic appeal in English to the Duchess of Queensberry. These effusions are printed in the 'Newgate Calendar.' But all efforts failed, and the young men were hanged at Tyburn on Monday, 20 Feb. 1748–9. Some verses lamenting Gahagan's fate are quoted in the 'Newgate Calendar.' In the preface to the collected edition of Christopher Smart's poems, 'unfortunate Gahagan' is described as Smart's immediate predecessor in the successful writing of Latin verse.

[Knapp and Baldwin's Newgate Calendar, ii. 27–30; Gent. Mag. 1749, pp. 43, 90; London Mag. xviii. 62, 99, 102; Notes and Queries, 5th ser. i. 482; Southey's Commonplace Book, iii. 71; Brit. Mus. Cat.]   S. L.

GAHAN, WILLIAM (1730–1804), ecclesiastic and author, born in Dublin in June 1730, was of a Leinster sept, the original name of which was O'Gaoithin, anglicised Gahan. He was educated at Dublin, became a member of the Augustinian order there, and in 1747 entered the catholic university of Louvain, where he studied for eleven years and received the degree of doctor of divinity. Gahan returned to Ireland in September 1761, was appointed curate of the parish of St. Paul, Dublin, and subsequently retired to the convent of his order in that city, where he devoted much of his time to the composition of works for the use of Roman catholics on subjects connected with religion and morality. In 1786 he travelled through England, France, and Italy, and wrote an account of his experiences abroad, which has not been published. The most important public incident in the career of Gahan was in connection with John Butler (d. 1800) [q. v.], Roman catholic bishop of Cork, with whom he had intimate and confidential relations since 1783. Butler, in his seventieth year, on the death of his nephew, Pierce, became twelfth Lord Dunboyne in the peerage of Ireland, and possessor of the ancestral estates. Anxious to prevent the extinction of the direct line of his family, he resigned the bishopric of Cork, and sought

a papal dispensation to enable him to marry. The application having been rejected, Dunboyne publicly renounced the Roman catholic religion, and became a member of the established church. When suffering from illness in 1800, Dunboyne addressed a letter to the pope requesting readmission to the Roman catholic church. He also executed a will by which he bequeathed one of his estates to the Roman catholic college of Maynooth. The letter to the pope was transmitted through Troy, Roman catholic archbishop of Dublin, who expressed his disapprobation of any of the Dunboyne estates being alienated from the family. Under archiepiscopal sanction Gahan, in company with a friend of Dunboyne, attended on his lordship, received him into the catholic church, and urged, but in vain, the revocation of the will. After Dunboyne's death in 1800 the validity of the bequest to Maynooth was impugned by his sister in the court of chancery, and Gahan underwent several examinations there. The case came to trial at the assizes at Trim, in the county of Meath, in August 1802, before Viscount Kilwarden, the chief justice. Curran was one of the counsel for the college of Maynooth. In the course of the trial Gahan was required by the court, under penalty of imprisonment, to state certain details of his relations with Lord Dunboyne. These he conceived to have been confidential, in connection with his ministrations as a priest, and he firmly declined to disclose them. He was, for contempt of court, condemned by the judge to be imprisoned for a week. Gahan's confinement was of short duration, as, after the jury had returned their verdict, the court ordered his discharge, on the ground that the plaintiff had not suffered from his refusal to answer, and that he had acted on principle. A subsequent compromise between the litigants led to the endowment of a department of the college of Maynooth, designated the 'Dunboyne Establishment.' Gahan died at Dublin, in the convent of his order, on 6 Dec. 1804. His published works consist of 'Sermons and Moral Discourses' (6th ed. 1847), a history of the Christian church, translations from Bourdaloue, and several devotional books still extensively used.

[Case of C. Butler, 1802; Brenan's Ecclesiastical Hist. of Ireland, 1840; Case of Baron of Dunboyne, 1858–9; Episcopal Succession, Rome, 1876.]   J. T. G.

GAIMAR, GEOFFREY (fl. 1140?), wrote a history of England in French verse, extending from the time of King Arthur's successors to the death of William II. His errors in interpreting the 'Anglo-Saxon

Chronicle,' on which most of his history is based, render it probable that he was a Norman by birth, and he may have derived his name from a suburb of Caen, anciently known as Gaimara, and now Gémare. As he tells us in the concluding lines of his history, he wrote at the request of Custance, wife of Ralf Fitzgilbert, who was a friend of Walter Espec [q. v.] It is likely that this Ralf Fitzgilbert is the person to whom Gilbert of Ghent, second earl of Lincoln, granted the lordship of Scampton in Lincolnshire, and it is quite possible that he was an illegitimate member of the same family. Gaimar also speaks, as if from personal knowledge, of Henry I and his queen, Adelaide of Louvain, of Robert, earl of Gloucester, the king's illegitimate son, and of Nicholas de Trailli, a nephew of Walter Espec.

His history follows the 'Anglo-Saxon Chronicle' in the main, many of the differences being attributable either to gratuitous expansion or mistranslation. The insertion of the legendary story of Havelock, the founder of a Danish kingdom in East Anglia, is no doubt owing to the author's residence in Lincolnshire, and the same may be said of his version of the exploits of the more historic Hereward, which differs in some particulars from the well-known prose life. His account of the reign of William II, of which he must have had personal knowledge, is of more value, but is not chronologically accurate. He gives an amusing description of the court held in the New Hall at Westminster at Whitsuntide 1099, and, in narrating the death of the Red King, hints that Walter Tirel was moved to murder his master in consequence of a bragging assertion of his intention to invade France. He speaks also of the grief of the attendants and their careful removal of the corpse, which other writers say was left to a casual woodman, and he praises William for liberality and magnanimity as he does his successor, Henry I. There are four manuscripts of 'Lestorie des Engles,' as the work is called; MS. Bibl. Reg. 13. A. xxi. (Brit. Mus.); Lincoln Cathedral MS. A. 4–12; Durham Cathedral MS. C. iv. 27; and Arundel MS. No. 14, in the College of Arms. A previously written history of earlier times is more than once mentioned in the course of the poem, but it is not known to be extant.

[Monumenta Historica Britannica, pp. 91, 764; Michel's Chroniques Anglo-Normandes, vol. i.; Publications of the Caxton Society, vol. ii.; Church Historians of England, vol. ii. pt. ii. pp. xxi, 729; Lestorie des Engles solum la translacion Maistre Geffrei Gaimar, ed. Sir T. D. Hardy and C. T. Martin (Rolls Ser.), 1888;

Michel's Rapports sur les Anciens Monumens de la Littérature et de l'Histoire de la France, i. 44, 194, 244; Roquefort's De l'Etat de la Poésie Françoise, pp. 68, 82–4; Duval's Histoire Littéraire de la France, xiii. 63, xviii. 731, 738; De la Rue's Essais Historiques sur les Bardes, iii. 104, 120; Frere's Manuel de Bibliographie Normande; Pluquet's Mémoire sur les Trouvères Normands, in Mémoires de la Société des Antiquaires de Normandie, i. 375 n., 414–16; Jahrbücher der Literatur, Vienna, lxxvi. 266; Johann Vising's Étude sur le Dialecte Anglo-Normand du XII Siècle, Romania, ix. 480; Küpferschmidt's Die Havelok-Sage bei Gaimar und ihr Verhalten zum Lai d'Havelok; Gent. Mag. 1857, ii. 21; Archæologia, xii. 307–12; Freeman's Norman Conquest, iv. 485, 486, 806, v. 99, 581, 824; Freeman's William II, ii. 660; Lappenberg's England under the Anglo-Saxon Kings; Parker's Early History of Oxford (Oxford Historical Society), pp. 123, 126, 161, 180, 325; Woodward's History of Wales, pp. 200, 204; H. L. D. Ward's Catalogue of Romances in Manuscripts Department, British Museum, pp. 423, 496, 940; Sir Frederick Madden's Havelock the Dane (Roxburghe Club).]

C. T. M.

GAINSBOROUGH, THOMAS (1727–1788), painter, was born in 1727 at Sudbury, Suffolk, in a picturesque old house which had once been the Black Horse Inn. The day of his birth is unknown, but he was baptised at the independent meeting-house, 14 May 1727.

His father, John Gainsborough, was a dissenter, engaged in the wool manufactures of the town. He is said to have been a fine man, careful of his personal appearance, an adroit fencer, kind to his debtors, of good reputation, but not rigid in the matter of smuggling, enterprising and active in business, 'travelling' in France and Holland, and the introducer into Sudbury of the shroud trade from Coventry.

Mrs. John Gainsborough, whose maiden name was Burroughs, was the sister of the Rev. Humphrey Burroughs, curate of the church of St. Gregory, and master of the grammar school at Sudbury. They had nine children (five sons and four daughters), of whom Thomas was the youngest. The daughters were all married: Mary to a dissenting minister of Bath, named Gibbon; Susannah to Mr. Gardiner of the same city; Sarah married Mr. Dupont, and Elizabeth Mr. Bird, both of Sudbury. The sons' names were John, Humphry, Mathias, and Robert. Mathias died of an accident in his youth, and of Robert little is known, but both John and Humphry were remarkable for their mechanical ingenuity. John was well known in Sudbury as 'Scheming Jack.' He made a

D d

pair of copper wings and essayed in vain to fly, and among his other inventions were 'a cradle which rocked itself, a cuckoo which would sing all the year round, and a wheel that turned in a still bucket of water.' He also painted, and was about to sail to the East Indies to prove an invention for the discovery of longitude, when he died in London. The second brother, Humphry, was a dissenting minister at Henley-on-Thames, who declined to take orders though offered preferment in the church of England. His leisure hours were given to mechanics, and his experiments upon the steam engine are said to have been far in advance of his time. According to Fulcher his friends declared that Watt owed to him the plan of condensing the steam in a separate vessel. He invented a fireproof box, the utility of which was proved by a fire in a friend's house, and for a tide-mill of his invention he obtained a premium of 50l. from the Society for the Encouragement of Arts. A curious sundial of his contrivance is in the British Museum.

Thomas alone, of all the sons, cost his parents little. He supported himself after he was eighteen. From the first his bent towards art was decided. An intense love of nature and a facility for taking likenesses seem to have been born in him. His only known encouragement from without came from his mother, who was 'a woman of well-cultured mind, and, amongst other accomplishments, excelled in flower-painting.' He was sent to his uncle's grammar school, but spent all his holidays in sketching rambles. He told Thicknesse that 'there was not a picturesque clump of trees, nor even a single tree of any beauty, no, nor hedgerow, stem or post,' in or around his native town, which was not from his earliest years treasured in his memory. On one occasion he successfully forged his father's handwriting to a strip of paper bearing the words 'Give Tom a holiday.' When the fraud was discovered his father promptly prophesied that 'Tom will one day be hanged,' and, on seeing how the boy had employed the stolen time, declared that 'Tom will be a genius.' The lad one morning sketched the face of a man peeping over the fence of his father's (or a friend's) orchard. The man took to his heels when Gainsborough interrupted his assault upon a pear tree, but the sketch already taken was sufficient to identify the thief. From this sketch he afterwards painted a picture which was exhibited at the Grosvenor Gallery in 1885. It is on a board cut to the outline of the head, and when he went to Ipswich he set it up on the garden palings, to the deception of many, including Philip Thicknesse, who took it for a real man, and was so pleased that he called on the artist.

'At ten years old,' says Allan Cunningham, 'Gainsborough had made some progress in sketching, and at twelve was a confirmed painter,' and in his fifteenth year he was sent to London to the care of a silversmith 'of some taste,' to whom, according to a writer in the 'Gentleman's Magazine,' he always acknowledged great obligations. For some time he studied under Gravelot, the French engraver, at his house in James Street, Covent Garden, where he met Charles Grignon, who assisted him in his first attempts at etching. Here he acquired the skill which enabled him to etch the few plates (about eighteen) and the three aquatints which are mentioned in Bryan's 'Dictionary' (Graves). Fifteen of the etchings were published after his death by Boydell. He was employed by Gravelot in designing ornamental borders for Houbraken's portraits, and also by Alderman Boydell, but after entering the St. Martin's Lane Academy he left Gravelot's studio for that of Frank Hayman [q. v.] After three years under Hayman he hired rooms in Hatton Garden, where he painted landscapes for dealers at low prices, and portraits for three to five guineas. He also practised modelling of animals. After a year thus spent without very satisfactory results he returned to Sudbury in 1745.

He now continued his study of landscape and fell in love with Miss Margaret Burr, a beautiful girl with an annuity of 200l. a year, whom he soon married, being at that time nineteen years old, and one year older than his bride. According to the earlier biographers of the artist much mystery surrounded this young lady and the source of her annuity. It was said that she was the daughter of an exiled prince, or of the Duke of Bedford, and that the pair met accidentally 'in one of Gainsborough's pictorial excursions,' but even according to Fulcher her brother was a commercial traveller in the employ of Gainsborough's father, and her father, it is now asserted, was a partner in the business.

The newly married couple, after a brief residence in Friar Street, Sudbury, hired a small house in Brook Street, Ipswich, at a yearly rent of 6l. Here the artist made the acquaintance of Joshua Kirby [q. v.], who became his warm friend, and placed his son William with him when he went to London. He also appears to have had another pupil here, where he remained till 1760, gradually improving in skill and position. It was in 1754 that he met Philip Thicknesse, his earliest biographer, then lieutenant-governor of Landguard Fort, who describes his portraits at this time as ' truly drawn, perfectly like, but stiffly painted, and worse coloured.' Among his sitters was Admiral Vernon. For Thicknesse he painted a view of Landguard Fort with the royal yachts passing the garrison under the salute of guns, which was engraved by Major. To this Ipswich period belong his more carefully drawn and detailed landscapes in the Dutch manner, like the wood scene, with a view of the village of Cornard in Suffolk (No. 925 in the National Gallery), and known as 'Gainsborough's Forest,' under which name a print of it was published by the Boydells in 1790. Among his friends and patrons at Ipswich were Mr. Kilderbee, Mr. Edgar, a lawyer of Colchester, and the Rev. James Hingeston, vicar of Raydon, Suffolk (portraits of members of the Edgar and Hingeston families and other works of Gainsborough belonging to the Edgar family were exhibited at the Grosvenor Gallery in the winters of 1885 and 1888). Mr. Hingeston's son, in a letter quoted by Fulcher, gives a very pleasant picture of Gainsborough in these days. Gainsborough, he says, was generally beloved for his affability; received with honour by the country gentlemen, and winning the grateful recollections of the peasantry. The panels of several of the rooms in Hingeston's house were ' adorned with the productions of his genius. In one is a picture of Gainsborough's two daughters, when young; they are engaged in chasing a butterfly.' Music at this time, as afterwards, was the principal amusement of his leisure hours. Thicknesse lent him a violin, on which he soon learnt to play better than the lender; and he belonged to a musical club at Ipswich, and painted a picture of the members.

At the suggestion of Thicknesse, who passed his winters at Bath, Gainsborough removed to that city in 1760. Much to the alarm of his wife he took lodgings in the newly built Circus, at the rent of 50l. a year. But sitters flocked to him at once, and the portrait of Thicknesse, which was to have been painted as a kind of decoy-duck, was put aside and never finished. He soon raised his price for a head from five to eight guineas, and ultimately fixed it at forty guineas for a half, and a hundred for a whole length. The Society of Artists, founded in 1759, held their first exhibition in London in the following year, and he contributed to its exhibitions from 1761 to 1768, sending eighteen works in all. This society was incorporated by royal charter in 1765, and Gainsborough's name appears on the roll of members in 1766. In 1768 he was elected one of the original members of the Royal Academy, and contributed to its exhibitions from 1769 to 1772, when, in consequence of some misunderstanding with Sir Joshua Reynolds, he withdrew his contributions for four years, by the end of which time he was settled in London. After this quarrel, as after that of 1783, he sent a picture or so to the Free Society. During this period (1769–72) he exhibited several landscapes, large and small, with and without figures, but then, as afterwards, the majority of his contributions were portraits. As Gainsborough never signed and seldom dated his works, and as in the catalogues the landscapes are without titles and the portraits unnamed, except in the case of persons of importance, it is difficult to identify most of the pictures as exhibited in any particular year, but the following portraits are duly named: 1761, Mr. Nugent, afterwards Lord Clare; 1762, Mr. Poyntz; 1763, Quin the actor and Mr. Medlicott; 1765, General Honywood (on horseback) and Colonel Nugent; 1766, Garrick (for the corporation of Stratford-on-Avon, said by Mrs. Garrick to be the best portrait ever taken of ' her Davy '); 1767, Lady Grosvenor, John, duke of Argyll, and Mr. Vernon, son of Lord Vernon; 1768, Captain Needham and Captain Augustus Hervey (afterwards Earl of Bristol); 1769, Isabella, lady Molyneux, and George Pitt (eldest son of the first Lord Rivers); 1770, Garrick; 1774, Lady Sussex, Lord and Lady Ligonier (2), Mr. Nuthall and Captain Wade. All of these were whole lengths, except the Garrick of 1766, which was three-quarters. One at least of the unnamed portraits added greatly to his reputation. Writing to Fuseli at Rome, Mary Moser [q. v.] observes: ' I suppose there has been a million of letters sent to Italy with an account of our exhibition, so it will be only telling you what you know already to say that Gainsborough is beyond himself in a portrait of a gentleman in a Vandyke habit.' One of the pictures of this year is described in the catalogue as ' Portrait of a Young Gentleman,' and it has been suggested that the picture referred to by Miss Moser was none other than the famous ' Blue Boy.' Some of the pictures of the Bath period are identified by their having been in the possession of Mr. Wiltshire, the public carrier of Bath, who ' loved Gainsborough and admired his works,' and could not be persuaded to accept payment for taking his pictures to London. To him the artist, with his accustomed generosity, gave some of his finest pictures, including portraits of Quin and Foote the actors, Orpin, the parish clerk of Bradford-on-Avon (now in the National Gallery), and some landscapes, of which one, called by Fulcher 'The Return from Harvest,' but engraved by Finden as 'The Hay Cart,' contains portraits of Gainsborough's two daughters. It was sold in 1867 for 3,147l. 10s., and was exhibited by Lord Tweedmouth at the Grosvenor Gallery in 1885 under the title of 'The Harvest Waggon.' Besides those already named, Gainsborough painted while at Bath portraits of Lord Kilmorey, Mr. Moysey (there is a sketch of it in the National Gallery), Dr. Charlton, Mr. Thicknesse, the first Lord Camden, Cramer, the metallurgist, Richardson, the novelist, Sterne, Chatterton, and John Henderson, the actor. Of the last he became the firm friend and patron, and some lively letters which he wrote to him have been preserved, in which he praises Garrick as 'the greatest creature living in every respect,' and adds, 'he is worth studying in every action. . . . Look upon him, Henderson, with your imitative eyes, for when he drops you'll have nothing but poor old Nature's book to look in. You'll be left to grope about alone, scratching your pate in the dark, or by a farthing candle. Now is your time, my lively fellow. And do you hear, don't eat so devilishly. You'll get too fat when you rest from playing, or get a sudden jog by illness to bring you down again.' This is a fair sample of the style of Gainsborough's correspondence, spirited, careless, sometimes too free in expression, but always fresh and often witty. To his strong taste for music he added a passion for fine musical instruments, and William Jackson [q. v.] of Exeter, the composer, gives a humorous account in his 'Four Ages' of the manner in which Gainsborough acquired in rapid succession Giardini's violin, Abel's viol-di-gamba, Fischer's hautboy, the harp of a harper, and the theorbo of a German professor. Without accepting Jackson's theory that Gainsborough thought he could acquire the art of the musician by purchasing his instrument, we may well believe him when he says that 'though possessed of ear, taste, and genius, he never had application enough to learn his notes,' and that 'there were times when music seemed to be Gainsborough's employment and painting his diversion.' Both had something to do with his flight to London in the summer of 1774, the immediate cause being a quarrel with Thicknesse about that eccentric gentleman's unfinished portrait and his wife's viol-di-gamba.

On his return to London Gainsborough took up his residence in the west part of Schomberg House, Pall Mall (this part is still standing), for which he paid 300l. a year to John Astley the painter [q. v.], who occu-

pied the remainder. A few months after his arrival the king summoned him to the palace, and after this the full tide of prosperity flowed till his death. In 1777 he began again to exhibit at the Royal Academy, sending a large landscape and six portraits, among which were those of the Duke and Duchess of Cumberland, Lord Gage, and Abel. The large landscape was declared by Horace Walpole, in his notes on this year's catalogue, to be 'in the style of Rubens, and by far the finest landscape ever painted in England, and equal to the great masters.' Among the ten works he exhibited in 1778 were a portrait of Christie the auctioneer (a present from the artist) and the Duchess of Devonshire. He is said to have been dissatisfied with this portrait of the lovely duchess, and would not send it to Chatsworth. 'Her Grace is too hard for me,' he averred, and drew his pencil across the mouth. He exhibited another picture of the duchess in 1783, and a picture in the Wynn Ellis collection named 'The Duchess of Devonshire' was sold in 1876, and was bought by Messrs. Agnew for 10,605l., a price higher than any before given for a picture at Christie's [see CAVENDISH, ELIZABETH]. A few days afterwards it was stolen, and was not recovered till 1901, when it was acquired by Mr. J. Pierpont Morgan. Early in 1779 (says Fulcher) Gainsborough probably painted that full-length portrait of the son of Mr. Buttall, which is usually known as 'The Blue Boy,' and this portrait is said to have been painted to refute the opinion of Sir Joshua Reynolds in his eighth discourse 'that the masses of light in a picture should be always of a warm, mellow colour,' and the cold colours 'used only to support and set off these warm colours.' This discourse was delivered in December 1778, so that the picture of 1770 before referred to, if it really were a 'Blue Boy,' could not have been affected by it. Gainsborough probably painted more than one 'Blue Boy,' and there are many copies, but the picture belonging to the Duke of Westminster is the most famous of those to which the name has been given. There is no doubt that it is authentic and a masterpiece, and the questions as to when it was painted, whom it represents, whether it was meant to refute Sir Joshua's dictum, and whether it does refute it, or only evades it, cannot be discussed here. (The notes by Mr. F. G. Stephens to the Grosvenor Gallery Winter Catalogue of 1885 contain information and references bearing on these problems.)

At the exhibition of 1779 were portraits of the Duchesses of Gloucester and Cumberland, the Duke of Argyll, and Judge Perryn.

At that of 1780 (the first exhibition at Somerset House), among his sixteen contributions were six landscapes, and portraits of General Conway (governor of Jersey), Madame le Brun, the vocalist, Henderson, and Mr. Bate, afterwards Sir Bate Dudley, and others. The last is now in the National Gallery. In the exhibition of 1781 were portraits of the king and queen and Bishop Hurd, together with 'A Shepherd' and 'three landscapes,' which included two described by Walpole as 'pieces of land and sea so natural that one steps back for fear of being splashed.' The most celebrated works of 1782 were the portraits of the Prince of Wales and the dissipated Colonel St. Leger, which were painted to be exchanged as tokens of friendship between the prince and the colonel. The former is now in the possession of the St. Leger family, the latter at Hampton Court. This was also the year of the 'Girl with Pigs,' which was purchased by Sir Joshua Reynolds. In 1783 Gainsborough sent no less than twenty-six pictures to the Academy, fifteen of which were heads only, portraits of the royal family, a complete set with the exception of Prince Frederick. The other portraits were the Duchess of Devonshire, the Duke of Northumberland, Lord Cornwallis, and Lord Sandwich (for Greenwich Hospital), Sir Harbord Harbord, M.P., afterwards Lord Suffield (for St. Andrew's Hall, Norwich), Sir Charles Gould, Mrs. Sheridan, and Mr. Ramus. A landscape, a seapiece, and 'Two Shepherd Boys with dogs fighting,' conclude the list for 1783.

Next year, 1784, in consequence of a dispute about the hanging of a picture containing the portraits of the Princess Royal, Princess Augusta, and Princess Elizabeth, he withdrew all his pictures (eighteen) and never exhibited at the Academy again, and shortly afterwards opened an exhibition of his own works at his house in Pall Mall, which had no great success. Among the more celebrated pictures painted after this were the lovely portrait of Mrs. Siddons, now in the National Gallery, the 'View in the Mall of St. James's Park,' now belonging to Sir John Neeld, which is described by Hazlitt as 'all in a motion and flutter like a lady's fan—Watteau is not half so airy,' and the 'Woodman and the Storm,' since destroyed by fire, but well known from the engraving. Gainsborough had difficulties with the face of Mrs. Siddons, as with that of the Duchess of Devonshire. The tip of her nose baffled his draughtsmanship, and he is said to have thrown down his brush, exclaiming 'D—— the nose, there is no end to it.' In the early part of 1787, according to Allan Cunningham, while dining with Sir George Beaumont and Sheridan, he told Sheridan that he felt he should die soon, and made him promise to come to his funeral. In February of the next year, while attending the trial of Warren Hastings, 'he suddenly felt something inconceivably cold touch his neck,' and on his return home his wife and niece found on his neck 'a mark about the size of a shilling, which was harder to the touch than the surrounding skin, and which, he said, still felt cold.' This proved to be a cancer, of which he died 'about two o'clock in the morning of the 2nd of August 1788, in the sixty-second year of his age.'

Gainsborough's life in London seems to have differed little from his life elsewhere, except that he had more money to spend. In 1779 he writes to his sister Mrs. Gibbon that he lives at 'a full thousand a year expense.' He set up a coach, but only for a little while. He had lodgings at Richmond in the summer, and sometimes at Hampstead. There is a record of a short visit of his family to the Kilderbees of Ipswich in 1777, and after the close of the exhibition of 1783 he took a tour with Mr. Kilderbee to the Lake district, but as a rule he stayed in London, and was satisfied with his home circle and a few friends, among whom were Sir George Beaumont, Burke, and Sheridan. Though the favourite painter of the court, he was no courtier, and though the aristocracy and many eminent men, such as Pennant and Hurd, Blackstone and Clive, came and sat to him, he seems to have made no attempt to cultivate their society. But there is little known about his life in London, except what can be gathered from a few letters, a few anecdotes, and the names of his sitters. His home life seems to have been a happy one. Mrs. Gainsborough has been described as the kindest as well as the loveliest of wives, and he is said to have liked nothing so well of an evening as sitting by his wife making one rapid sketch after another. Though the quickness of his temper or other cause occasionally provoked a quarrel, it was of short duration. They exchanged pretty little notes of reconciliation in the names of their pet dogs, who carried them in their mouths. His two daughters were beautiful, but the marriage of Mary to Johann Christian Fischer [q. v.] the musician was not agreeable to her father, and both she and her sister Margaret were subject to mental aberration, from which Mrs. Gainsborough in her later years is said not to have been free. With his own family he seems to have been always on affectionate terms. He acted almost *in loco parentis* to Gainsborough Dupont [q.v.], his nephew, and made him an excellent artist. Dupont helped him with his pictures, engraved them, and finished those which he left uncompleted at his death. He helped his brother 'Scheming Jack' with many a five-pound note, only to be wasted in brass for mechanical experiments. He has left behind in a fine portrait a record of the affection which always subsisted between him and his brother Humphry. Indeed, in spite of his unevenness of temper and capriciousness, he appears to have been of so genial a disposition that he never had a downright quarrel with any of his relations or friends, if we except that with Philip Thicknesse, who quarrelled with everybody from his fellow-officers to his son.

Before he died there took place that meeting between him and his great rival Sir Joshua which is one of the most pathetic episodes in the history of art. The relations of Gainsborough and Sir Joshua, of Gainsborough and the Academy, had always been somewhat strained. Gainsborough's treatment of both was cavalier, to say the least of it, and he was unreasonable in the matter of the hanging of his pictures. He had taken his honours as an academician as a matter of course, but discharged none of the duties of his position, and never attended to his colleagues' invitations 'whether official or convivial.' They had, not unnaturally, resented this neglect, and once passed a resolution to scratch his name from the list of their members, which was generously rescinded, without any improvement in the behaviour of Gainsborough. Sir Joshua had called upon him, but he neglected to return his visit. Sir Joshua had sat to him at his request, but Gainsborough had neglected to finish his portrait. On the other hand Reynolds had behaved well and even handsomely towards him, had bought his 'Girl with Pigs,' and paid, or obtained for him from M. de Calonne, forty guineas more than he asked for it. He now declared him, at a meeting of the Artists' Club, to be 'the first landscape-painter in Europe,' thereby drawing upon him the famous retort of Richard Wilson, that 'Gainsborough was in his opinion the greatest portrait-painter at this time in Europe.' On the other hand, Gainsborough had simply ignored Sir Joshua, but a few days before his death Reynolds tells us that Gainsborough wrote to him ' to express his acknowledgments for the good opinion I entertained of his abilities, and the manner in which (he had been informed) I had always spoke of him; and desired he might see me once more before he died.' The impression left by the interview upon Reynolds was 'that his regret at leaving life was principally the regret of leaving his art ; and more especially as he now began, he said, to see what his deficiencies were, which he said he flattered himself in his last works were

in some measure supplied.' 'If any little jealousies had subsisted between us,' his old rival says, 'they were forgotten in those moments of sincerity, and the dying painter whispered to Reynolds, "We are all going to heaven, and Vandyck is of the party."'

According to his wishes he was buried near his friend Kirby in Kew churchyard. His pall-bearers were Sir Joshua Reynolds, Sir William Chambers, Paul Sandby, West (afterwards Sir Benjamin), Bartolozzi, and Samuel Cotes. Sheridan was there as he had promised, and his nephew, Gainsborough Dupont, was chief mourner.

In the December after Gainsborough's death Sir Joshua Reynolds delivered his fourteenth discourse to the students of the Royal Academy, which was chiefly devoted to the genius of Gainsborough. It is a noble and generous tribute to his rival's memory, and, if we make allowances for the then prevalent views, remains still the most full and weighty analysis of his work which has ever been written.

In March 1789 an exhibition of the works remaining in his possession at his death was opened at Schomberg House, which was full of those landscapes and rustic pictures which he could not sell during his life, although they (with a few notable exceptions) have fetched far higher prices than his portraits since his death. A list of these works is given by Fulcher, as well as of the large collection of Gainsborough's paintings exhibited at the British Institution in 1814. A still larger gathering was at the Grosvenor Gallery in the winter of 1885.

No artist was ever at once more new, more natural, and more English. Whether in landscape or pastoral or portrait, he drew his inspiration entirely from his subject, and tinged it with his own sentiment. Some touch of Watteau's grace may have come to him through Gravelot. He may have applied himself, as Reynolds says, to the Dutch and Flemish masters, but what he learned from Rubens and Vandyck 'he applied,' as Reynolds also says, 'to the originals of nature which he saw with his own eyes; and imitated not in the manner of those masters, but in his own.' So he became the father of modern landscape, and of modern pastoral also, breaking away from the 'classical' traditions of Claude on the one hand, and the affected pastorals of Boucher and his school on the other. In portraits he was scarcely less original, painting his ladies and gentlemen in a manner entirely pure and unaffected, yet with such spirit, grace, and dignity as nature had endowed them with. He chose to represent them in their most quiet and unconscious moments with the 'mind and music breathing from the face.' Principally because he painted his sitters so, he became the rival of Reynolds, weak where he was strong, and strong where he was weak, and yet often approaching him so nearly that the distance between them is scarcely measurable.

Gainsborough is well represented in the National Gallery and other public galleries in England. A list of these pictures will be found in Bryan's 'Dictionary.' A fine collection of his drawings is in the British Museum.

[Fulcher's Life, 1856; Thicknesse's Sketch of the Life and Paintings of Thomas Gainsborough, 1788; monographs by Sir Walter Armstrong (1894 and 1898), by N. D'Anvers (1897), and Gustav Pauli (1904); Gent. Mag. 1788; European Mag. 1788; Edwards's Anecdotes; Life and Time of Nollekens; Jackson's Four Ages; Cunningham's Lives (Heaton); Hazlitt's Conversations with Northcote; Northcote's Life of Reynolds; Leslie and Tom Taylor's Life of Reynolds; Reminiscences of Henry Angelo; Pilkington's Dict.; Redgrave's Dict.; Redgrave's Century of Painters; Bryan's Dict. (Graves); Graves's Dict.; Gainsborough, by Brock-Arnold (Great Artists Ser.); Peter Pindar's Works; Edgeworth's Memoirs; Sir W. Beechey's Memoirs; Correspondence of Garrick; Leisure Hour, xxxi. 620, 718; Sir Joshua Reynolds's Discourses; Waagen's Art Treasures; Walpole's Anecdotes (Dallaway); Leslie's Handbook; Ruskin's Modern Painters; Charles Blanc's École Anglaise; Chesneau's English School; Temple Bar (T. Gautier), v. 324; Works of Edward Dayes; Library of the Fine Arts, vol. iii.; Cat. of Grosvenor Gallery Winter Exhibition, 1885, by F. G. Stephens; Cook's Handbook to the National Gallery; Portfolio (Sidney Colvin), 1872, pp. 169, 178; Wedmore's Studies in English Art, 1st ser., 1876; Encycl. Brit.] C. M.

GAINSBOROUGH, WILLIAM (d. 1307), bishop of Worcester, was a Franciscan, who is first known as the divinity lecturer of the Franciscans at Oxford. His position seems to have suggested to Edward I that he should be employed as an ambassador to Philip IV of France, with whom the English king wished to be at peace. With Gainsborough was joined Hugh of Manchester, a leading Dominican, the Bishop of Winchester, and two laymen. After their negotiations in France they were empowered to proceed to Rome and enlist the good offices of Pope Boniface VIII (RYMER, Fœdera, ii. 866). At Rome Gainsborough commended himself to the pope, according to Bale, by his uncompromising adherence to the claims of spiritual suzerainty, which that pontiff was engaged in developing (BALE, Centuriæ, Cent. 4, No. 91). Gainsborough remained in Rome, where in 1300 he was made reader in theology in the papal palace (Chronicle of Lanercost, sub anno), and Boniface VIII found him a useful person for abetting his system of interference in the affairs of national churches. The see of Worcester became vacant by the death of Godfrey Giffard in 1301, and Edward I gave license to the chapter to elect his successor. They chose one of their own body, John of St. German, but on some trivial ground Archbishop Winchelsey refused to confirm his election. John took his case on appeal to Rome, where Boniface prevailed on him to resign his bishopric, and appointed Gainsborough by provision on 22 Oct. 1302 (WADDING, Annales Minorum, vi. 432). Gainsborough came to England early in 1303, and his appointment was accepted by Edward I, who, however, took care to guard the rights of the crown. The pope's provision conferred on him the temporalities and spiritualities of the see; Edward demanded that he should renounce this grant, and from this time forward an oath of renunciation was exacted from all bishops appointed by provision. Further a suit was brought against him, and he was condemned to pay one thousand marks, which was, however, remitted in 1306. Moreover, as the king had been guardian of the possession of the see during the vacancy, Gainsborough was required to pay five hundred marks for the seed which had been sown on his lands. As he was poor, and the monks of Worcester refused to help him by a loan, he was under great straits to provide for his enthronisation, which took place in May 1303 (an interesting description of the ceremony is given by THOMAS, Worcester Cathedral, Appendix No. 77). He walked barefoot through the city to the cathedral, probably with a view of overcoming by a display of humility the objection naturally felt by the monks to his appointment. Of Gainsborough's activity in his diocese we do not hear much. In October 1305 he was sent by Edward I to Rome as one of an embassy to Clement V, ostensibly for the purpose of arranging for a crusade, really to discuss the peace of Europe (RYMER, Fœdera, ii. 968). On his return he was present at the parliament held at Carlisle in 1306. In 1307 he was sent to France to arrange for the marriage of the king's son, Edward, with Isabella of France, and soon after his return received a further commission for an embassy to Rome. The commission was dated just before the death of Edward I, 5 July 1307 (ib. ii. 1058), but Gainsborough did not long survive his master. He died on his journey at Beauvais on 16 Sept., and was there buried.

Bale mentions that Gainsborough left behind him some volumes of scholastic theology, 'Quæstiones,' 'Disceptationes,' and 'Sermones.'

[Gainsborough's manuscript Register in the Worcester Diocesan Registry; Annales Wigornenses in Annales Monastici (Rolls Ser.), iv. 554-5; Wharton's Anglia Sacra, i. 531-2; Bale's Centuriæ, iv. 91; Thomas's Survey of the Cathedral Church of Worcester, pp. 154-8; Stubbs's Constitutional Hist. iii. 308.]   M. C.

GAINSFORD, THOMAS (*d.* 1624?), author, belonged to the Surrey family of Gainsford. He with Edward Stene apparently purchased of the crown Alne manor, Warwickshire, and a cottage in Stutton, Yorkshire, 27 Nov. 1599 (*Cal. State Papers*, Dom. 1598–1601, p. 347). He is known to have served in Ireland under Richard de Burgh, fourth earl of Clanricarde, as 'third officer' of the 'earl's regiment' when the Spaniards were dislodged from Kinsale on 24 Dec. 1601 (*Hist. . . . of . . . Tirone*, ded.) He was also engaged in the war against Tyrone in Ulster. As captain, Gainsford undertook to occupy land in Ulster at the plantation of 1610 (*Irish State Papers*, 1608–10, p. 367). On 4 Sept. 1624 Chamberlain wrote to Carleton that the deaths of the week in London included 'Captain Gainsford, the gazette maker' (*Cal. State Papers*, Dom. 1623–5, p. 334). This is doubtless a reference to our author. Gainsford published the following: 1. 'The Vision and Discourse of Henry the seventh concerning the unitie of Great Britaine, Lond., by G. Eld for Henry Fetherstone, 1610,' in verse of six-line stanzas; dedicated to 'the truly religious and resolute gentlemen of England.' An address from Henry VII to James I figures in the poem. Only two copies are now known, one at Bridgewater House, the other at the British Museum (COLLIER, *Bibliogr. Manual*, i. 300–1; CORSER, *Collectanea*, vol. vi.) 2. 'The Historie of Trebizond in foure books, by Thomas Gainsforde, esquier,' Lond., 1616, a collection of romantic stories. The books are separately dedicated to the Countess Dowager of Derby, the Countess of Huntingdon, Lady Frances Egerton, and Lady Chandos respectively. 3. 'The Secretaries Studie; or directions for the . . . judicious inditing of Letters,' Lond., 1616; no copy is in the British Museum. 4. 'The True and Wonderfull History of Perkin Warbeck,' Lond., 1618, dedicated to the Earl of Arundel; reprinted in 'Harleian Miscellany,' vol. iii. 5. 'The Glory of England, or a true Description of many excellent Prerogatives and remarkable Blessings whereby she triumpheth over all the Nations of the World,' Lond., 1618, dedicated to Buckingham. All 'the eminent kingdoms of the earth' are here compared with England to their disadvantage. A curious account of Ireland from the author's own experience concludes book i. Book ii. treats

of Russia, and compares London with Paris, Venice, and Constantinople. A revised edition appeared in 1619, and was reissued in 1620. 6. 'The True Exemplary and Remarkable History of the Earl of Tirone,' Lond., 1619, dedicated to the Earl of Clanricarde; of no great value, but interesting as a nearly contemporary record.

Mr. W. C. Hazlitt also conjecturally assigns to Gainsford 'The Rich Cabinet furnished with varietie of excellent discriptions, exquisite characters, witty discourses and delightfull histories, deuine and morrall,' Lond., for Roger Iackson, 1616. An appendix— 'an epitome of good manners extracted out of the treatise of M. Iohn della Casa called Galatea'—is signed T. G., together with a Latin motto. This signature resembles those in Gainsford's undoubted books, but the question of authorship is very doubtful. Some hostile remarks on players, ff. 116–18, are interesting. The book was popular; a fourth edition is dated 1668, and a sixth 1689. 'The Friers Chronicle, or the True Legend of Priests and Monkes Lives' (Lond., for Robert Mylbourne, 1623), has a dedication to the Countess of Devonshire, signed T. G., and has been attributed to Gainsford. But Thomas Goad (1576–1638) [q. v.] is more probably the author.

[Gainsford's Works; Manning and Bray's Surrey, iii. 174; Hazlitt's Bibliographical Handbook and Miscellanies; authorities cited above.]   S. L.

GAIRDNER, JOHN, M.D. (1790–1876), eldest son of Captain Robert Gairdner of the Bengal artillery, was born at Mount Charles, near Ayr, on 18 Sept. 1790. When he was only five years old his father was killed by the kick of a horse, and the care of five sons and a daughter fell upon his widowed mother, who lived to see them all grow up, and was regarded by them with deep and reverent affection. He received his school education at Ayr academy, but, he and his brother William [q. v.] having chosen a professional career, his mother removed with her family to Edinburgh in 1808, and there he took his degree of M.D. in 1811. He spent the winter of 1812 in London, studying anatomy under Mr. (afterwards the celebrated Sir Charles) Bell, and in 1813 commenced practice in Edinburgh in partnership with Dr. Farquharson, one of the leading physicians there. In the same year he became a fellow of the College of Surgeons, Edinburgh, and four years later began to act as examiner for that body, a duty which he continued to discharge till within a few years of his death. He always took a most lively interest in the affairs of the college, of which, besides being for many years treasurer, he was president from 1830 to 1832. This appointment, occurring at that particular date, brought him into connection with politics more than he would otherwise have been drawn, for it gave him a seat in the unreformed town council of Edinburgh as ' deacon of the chirurgeon barbers.' The election for the parliament of 1831 was entirely in the hands of the town council, and Gairdner, being a staunch reformer, seconded the nomination of the popular candidate, Francis Jeffrey [q. v.], then lord advocate under Earl Grey's government. The majority of the council, however, disregarding the popular fervour and a monster petition presented to them in Jeffrey's favour, elected Mr. Dundas, and had immediately to consult their own personal safety by escaping through back streets, while an infuriated mob attacked the lord provost and threatened to throw him over the North Bridge. It required all the personal influence of Jeffrey himself and his supporters to keep the popular excitement from proceeding to worse extremities.

The reforms, however, in which Gairdner took a most efficient part were those connected with his profession. With the zealous co-operation of Mr. William Wood, a lifelong friend, though of an opposite school of politics, he powerfully aided a movement for obtaining for medical students for the degree at Edinburgh University the right to receive some part of their professional training from extra-academical lectures, a change which, instead of weakening the university, as was apprehended by some, has very greatly strengthened it in the country at large, as well as in the colonies. He also gave evidence before parliamentary committees in London on behalf of the Edinburgh College of Surgeons in regard to the efforts made for many years to secure by act of parliament a legal status for duly licensed practitioners of medicine and surgery extending throughout the three kingdoms, an object finally attained by the Medical Act of 1859. He contributed largely to the literature of his profession by many valuable and some very elaborate memoirs in the 'Transactions of the Medico-Chirurgical Society of Edinburgh,' and in the medical journals, extending down to only a year or two before his death. He also published independently two interesting lectures, the first on the history of the Edinburgh College of Surgeons, the second on the early history of the medical profession in Edinburgh. Historical subjects had always a great attraction for him, and as an aid to chronological research he published in his later years a ' Calendar' printed on cardboard, with a card-board slide, for the verification of past or future dates as regards the correspondence of days of the week and month. He was also the author of some letters published anonymously at the time in the ' Scotsman' newspaper in answer to certain statements that had appeared elsewhere relative to the poet Burns and the society in which he moved. Gairdner's family ties and personal recollection of Ayrshire in his early days made him an important witness on this subject, and the letters were accordingly reprinted after his death and privately published, though still anonymously, in 1883, under the title ' Burns and the Ayrshire Moderates.'

Gairdner's independence of mind and deep religious convictions led him to join a small body of unitarians at a time when that sect was very unpopular, especially in Scotland. There is no doubt that, although he had a fair professional practice, this step was a considerable bar to his progress, yet personally he was universally respected. He took an active part in the setting up of a new unitarian chapel in Edinburgh; but after many years, failing to find in that sect what he considered to be pure christianity and freedom, he returned once more to the church of Scotland. His revolt against the established religion in his youth had been mainly owing to the prevalence of a narrow Calvinism; but in his later years he was more inclined to look for breadth and freedom to national churches than to sects. He married in 1817 his cousin Susanna Tennant, a grand-daughter of Dr. William Dalrymple of Ayr [q. v.], whom he survived sixteen years. He died on 12 Dec. 1876, at the age of eighty-six, survived by three sons and two daughters. One of the former writes this notice.

[Scotsman newspaper, 14 Dec. 1876; Edinburgh Courant of same date; Caledonian Mercury, May 1831; personal recollection.] J. G.

GAIRDNER, WILLIAM, M.D. (1793–1867), physician, son of Robert Gairdner of Mount Charles, Ayrshire, was born at Mount Charles on 11 Nov. 1793. After an education at the Ayr academy, he went in 1810 to the university of Edinburgh, where he graduated M.D. 13 Sept. 1813, taking dysentery as the subject of his inaugural dissertation. After further study in London he went abroad as physician to the Earl of Bristol. In 1822 he settled in London, where he had a house in Bolton Street, and in 1823 he was admitted a licentiate of the College of Physicians. In the following year he published an ' Essay on the Effects of Iodine on the Human Constitution.' Dr. Coindet of Geneva had in 1820 proposed to treat goitre and other glandular enlargements by the internal administration of iodine, and this essay is written in support of Coindet's views. While advocating the use of iodine it describes more minutely than any previous English book the ill effects of large doses. Gairdner's practice grew slowly, and he did not attain success till after long struggles. In 1849 he published 'On Gout, its History, its Causes, and its Cure,' a work which had four editions, of which the last appeared in 1860. It is a lucid exposition of the main clinical features of the disease, without pathological information, while as to treatment it advocates bleeding, moderate purgation, and the administration of colchicum. The older he grew, the author says, the more did his confidence in drugs abate. He married, 12 Jan. 1822, a Genevese lady who died before him. He continued his practice almost to the end of his life, and died at Avignon, after spending a winter in the south of France, on 28 April 1867. He left one daughter. He was a small man with a florid complexion, and his hair became white at an early age. He was a new whig in politics, and had an independent, inflexible spirit, which, if it sometimes increased the difficulties of his life, also enabled him to conquer them.

[Munk's Coll. of Phys. iii. 265; Works; Lancet, 1867; information from family.]   N. M.

GAISFORD, THOMAS (1779–1855), dean of Christ Church, Oxford, classical scholar, born 22 Dec. 1779 at Iford in Wiltshire, was the eldest son of John Gaisford, esq. He was educated at Hyde Abbey School, Winchester, under the Rev. Charles Richards, was entered as a commoner of Christ Church, Oxford, in October 1797, and elected student in December 1800 by the dean, Dr. Cyril Jackson. He took the degrees of B.A. in 1801, and M.A. in 1804. After acting for some time as tutor of his college and as public examiner in 1809–11, he was appointed on 29 Feb. 1812 to the regius professorship of Greek by the crown, when his predecessor, Dr. W. Jackson, was made bishop of Oxford. In 1815 he was presented by his college to the living of Westwell in Oxfordshire, which he held till 1847. His other preferments were, a prebend of Llandaff in 1823, of St. Paul's in 1823, and of Worcester in 1825. In 1829 he was offered the bishopric of Oxford on the death of Bishop Lloyd, but refused it. The same year he was collated to a stall at Durham by Bishop Van Mildert, which in 1831 he exchanged for the deanery of Christ Church, Oxford, with Dr. Samuel Smith, having the full consent of the two patrons, the Bishop of Durham and the crown. Here he spent the rest of his life. He took

the degrees of B.D. and D.D. by diploma in April 1831.

During the twenty-four years in which he presided over Christ Church, his attention was by no means only given to the superintendence of that great foundation, but he took a leading part in all university affairs. As Greek professor he was an official curator of the Bodleian Library, and always had its interest at heart; as delegate of the press for nearly fifty years he never wearied in his care. It is said that, when he was first appointed a delegate, the press did not pay its expenses, was in debt, and an annual loss to the university. Through his management a great change was effected; it was due to him that foreign scholars, like Bekker and Dindorf, were employed as editors. Nor was it only in his own department of classical literature that the press became eminent for its publications; it was owing to his recommendation that the series of works on English history, chiefly of the period of the great rebellion, were issued; and certainly the Oxford Press has been at no time more fruitful in the production of valuable works than in the years during which Gaisford exercised so marked an influence.

But it is as a scholar, and especially as a Greek scholar, second to scarcely any one of his time, that Gaisford will be remembered. In editing many of the chief Greek classical authors and several of the Greek ecclesiastical writers, his best years, indeed his whole life, were spent. When what he actually produced is compared with the work of others, whether English or foreign scholars, it seems almost marvellous that one man, even in the course of a long life and with ample leisure, could have done so much.

His first work was an edition of Cicero's 'Tusculan Disputations,' in 1805, from Davies's edition, with additional notes of Bentley [see DAVIES, JOHN, 1679–1732]. He superintended the reprint of Ernesti's edition of the 'De Oratore' in 1809, and probably of Davies's editions of the 'De Natura Deorum' in 1807, and the 'De Finibus' in 1809. In March 1806 he reviewed Walpole's 'Comicorum Fragmenta' in the 'Monthly Review,' his only contribution to periodical literature. He then turned his attention to the Greek drama, on which Porson had worked successfully at Cambridge, and to which Elmsley was devoting himself at Oxford, and edited several plays of Euripides. In 1810 appeared his edition of 'Hephæstion de Metris,' a work which at once made his name known as one of the foremost scholars of his day throughout Europe; even Reisig in his foolish attack on English scholarship spoke of this as 'bonum opus, ut fertur.' His 'Poetæ Græci Minores,' the first volume of which appeared in 1814, is described in the 'Museum Criticum' (i. 509) as a work on the acquisition of which every scholar is to be congratulated. In the course of the next few years appeared his editions of Stobæus, of Herodotus (which has formed the basis of all subsequent editions), of Sophocles, and above all of the Lexicon of Suidas (in which for the first time the manuscript in Corpus Christi College, Oxford, was collated), and lastly of the 'Etymologicon Magnum.' His first work on the ecclesiastical writers was an edition of the 'Græcarum affectionum curatio' of Theodoret, which appeared in 1839.

As a scholar he must be described as thoroughly judicious rather than brilliant. He was fonder of reprinting the notes of others, as in his variorum editions, than of producing notes of his own, and he has done little towards the emendation or interpretation of his authors as far as he was personally concerned. But his skill in collation and in bringing together all that he deemed valuable for the illustration of the authors he is editing is unrivalled, and perhaps no editions of classical works that this country has produced are so useful as Gaisford's.

Though all his published works are concerned with classical or patristic literature, his own studies were by no means confined to these. He was well read in history, theology, and civil law, and was a good Shakespearean scholar. A pleasing sketch of his conversation in 1815 is given in the 'Extracts from the Portfolio of a Man of the World' (Gent. Mag. October 1845, pp. 336–338). He married first, Helen Douglas, niece of the wife of Bishop Van Mildert; and, secondly, Miss Jenkyns, sister of Dr. Jenkyns of Balliol College. By his first wife he left three sons and two daughters. He died at Christ Church, 2 June 1855, and was buried in the nave of the cathedral on 9 June. In 1856 a prize was founded at Oxford to commemorate him, called the 'Gaisford Prize,' for composition in Greek verse and Greek prose.

The following is a list of his works: 1. 'Ciceronis Tusculanæ Disputationes,' from Davies's edition, with additional notes of Bentley from two Cambridge MSS., 1805. 2. 'Codices Manuscripti et impressi cum notis MSS. olim D'Orvilliani qui in Bibl. Bodleiana apud Oxonienses adservantur,' 1806. 3. 'Euripidis Alcestis' (for the use of Westminster School), 1806. 4. 'Euripidis Electra ex editione Musgravii' (for the use of Westminster School), 1806. 5. 'Euripidis Andromache' (for the use of Westminster School), 1807. 6. 'Euripidis Hecuba, Orestes, Phœnissæ,'

with Musgrave's notes, and various readings from a manuscript formerly in the possession of W. Hunter, 1809. 7. 'Cicero de Oratore ex editione Ernesti cum notis variorum,' 1809. 8. 'Hephæstionis Enchiridion de Metris, with Procli Chrestomathia,' 1810. This was reprinted in two vols. after his death in 1855, with the addition of the work of Terentianus Maurus de Syllabis et Metris. 9. 'Euripidis Supplices, Iph. in Aul., Iph. in Tauris,' from Markland's edition, with many notes of Porson, some tracts of Markland, and his correspondence with D'Orville, 1811. 10. 'Catalogus Manuscriptorum qui a cel. E.D. Clarke comparati in Bibl. Bodl. adservantur,' 1812. This is the first part, containing the account of the Greek MSS. Some inedited scholia on Plato and St. Gregory Nazianzen are inserted. 11. 'Poetæ Græci Minores,' 4 vols., 1814–20. Besides Hesiod and Theocritus and the minor poets, this contains the scholia on Hesiod and Theocritus. 12. 'Lectiones Platonicæ,' 1820. This is a collation of the Patmos MS. of Plato, brought to England by Dr. Clarke. Porson's notes on Pausanias are added. 13. 'Aristotelis Rhetorica, cum versione Latina et annott. variorum,' 2 vols., 1820. 14. 'Scapulæ Lexicon,' 1820. This was edited by Dr. H. Cotton, but Dr. Gaisford gave considerable assistance. 15. 'Stobæi Florilegium,' 4 vols., 1822. 16. 'Herodotus cum notis variorum,' 4 vols., 1824. The text has been reprinted separate from the notes. 17. 'Scholia in Sophoclem Elmsleii,' 1825. This was edited by Gaisford soon after Elmsley's death, who had transcribed the Laurentian MS. at Florence, but had printed only as far as p. 64. 18. 'Sophocles,' 2 vols., 1826. This is a variorum edition, giving the whole of the notes of Brunck and Schæfer. It is especially valuable for the extracts from Suidas, and the collation of the two Laurentian MSS. 19. Index to Wyttenbach's 'Plutarch,' which he had left unfinished, 1830. 20. 'Suidæ Lexicon,' 3 vols., 1834. 21. 'Parœmiographi Græci,' 1836. 22. 'Scriptores Latini rei metricæ,' 1837. 23. 'Theodoreti Græcarum affectionum curatio,' 1839. 24. 'Chærobosci Dictata in Theodosii canones necnon Epimerismi in Psalmos,' 1842. 25. 'Eusebii Eclogæ Propheticæ,' 1842. This is the first edition, printed from a Vienna manuscript. 26. 'Eusebii Præparatio Evangelica,' 2 vols., 1843. 27. 'Pearsoni Adversaria Hesychiana,' 2 vols., 1844, from the manuscript in Trinity College Library, Cambridge. 28. 'Etymologicon Magnum,' 1848. 29. 'Vetus Testamentum ex versione lxx. interpretum,' 3 vols., 1848. 30. 'Stobæi Eclogæ Physicæ et Ethicæ,' 2 vols., 1850. To the second volume is added the Commentary of Hierocles on the golden verses of Pythagoras. This contains the whole of Ashton's notes from the edition published by R. W[arren] in 1742. 31. 'Eusebii contra Hieroclem et Marcellum Libri,' 1852. 32. 'Eusebii Demonstratio Evangelica,' 2 vols., 1852. 33. 'Theodoreti Historia Ecclesiastica,' 1854.

Gaisford's portrait, by Pickersgill, has been engraved by Atkinson.

[Gent. Mag. July 1855, p. 98; Literary Churchman, Oxford, 16 June 1855, an article (by Dr. Barrow), reprinted in the Cambridge Journal of Classical and Sacred Philology, ii. 343; Classical Journal, xxiv. 121; The Crypt, ii. 169, iii. 201.] H. R. L.

GALBRAITH, ROBERT (d. 1543), judge, was a priest and treasurer of the Chapel Royal at Stirling, in which capacity he received a charter of the lands of Mydwyn Schelis, near Berwick, dated 5 July 1528. He was advocate to Queen Margaret Tudor, wife of James IV of Scotland, and as such made his protest on 1 Sept. 1528 in parliament against any prejudice to her claim for debt against the Earl of Angus being occasioned by his forfeiture. He was one of the advocates appointed when first the College of Senators was instituted, and was admitted an ordinary lord on 7 Nov. 1537. In 1543 he was murdered by John Carkettle, a burgess of Edinburgh, and others, on account of favour which he was alleged to have shown to Sir William Sinclair of Hermanston in a suit before him. The murderers were cited before parliament, but nothing is known of their fate. He left some reports of cases, which are cited as the 'Book of Galbraith' by the compiler of Balfour's 'Practicks.'

[Acts Scots Parl.; Acts of Sederunt, 1811, p. 5; Act Dom. Con. et Sess.; Diplomata Regia, pp. 5, 467; Tytler's Craig, p. 114; Arnot's Criminal Trials, p. 174; Brunton and Haig's Senators of the Royal College of Justice.] J. A. H.

GALDRIC, GUALDRIC, or WALDRIC (d. 1112), bishop of Laon and chancellor to Henry I, is probably the 'Waldricus cancellarius' who signs a charter to Andover Priory, Hampshire, towards the middle of William II's reign (DUGDALE, vi. 992). Galdric was also chancellor under Henry I, and in this capacity signs at Salisbury (3 Jan. 1103) about three months after his predecessor, Roger, had been made bishop of this see (ib. vi. 1083, cf. pp. 1083, 1106, 1273, and v. 149, where he seems to appear—February 1106?—as 'Walterus cancellarius'; SYM. OF DURHAM, p. 235; FLORENCE OF WORCESTER, ii. 51). By August 1107 he seems to have been supplanted by Rannulf (EYTON, Itin. of

Henry I), who was certainly chancellor in April 1109 (DUGDALE, vi. 1180; cf. SYM. OF DURHAM, ii. 239, 241; BOUQUET, xv. 66-7).

At the battle of Tenchebrai (28 Sept. 1106) a 'Gualdricus regis capellanus' took Duke Robert prisoner and was rewarded with the bishopric of Laon (ORD. VITALIS, iv. 230). This identifies the chancellor Waldric with the famous Galdric 'referendarius regis Anglorum' who bought this see in 1107 (GUIBERT OF NOGENT, iii. cc. 1–4). At this time, adds Guibert, Galdric was a simple clerk: but now, through Henry I's influence, 'although he had hitherto acted as a warrior,' he was hastily made a sub-deacon and canon of Rouen. Anselm of Laon, the greatest theological teacher in Western Europe, headed the opposition to the new appointment; and Galdric had to appear in person before Paschal II. Finally, Galdric, who had engaged Guibert of Nogent to defend his cause before the pope at Langres (c. 24 Feb. 1107), was confirmed by that prelate (ib.; for date cf. BOUQUET, xv. 36).

Nearly three years later Guibert accused Galdric of having planned the murder of Gerard of Kiersy, castellan of Laon, who was slain by Rorigo, the bishop's brother, at early dawn, 31 Dec. 1109, while praying at the cathedral altar. The royal provost drove the murderers from the city, with Galdric's archdeacons, Walter and Guy, at their head. Galdric, however, who had started for Rome before the murder, protested his innocence and bought the pope's pardon. On his return he summoned Guibert, who had excommunicated the murderers, into his presence at Conci; and there, openly surrounded by avowed accomplices in the crime, forced the abbot to promise to assist him in regaining Laon. When an attack upon the city failed he bribed Louis VI to effect his restoration, and immediately excommunicated all those who had helped to expel the murderers (GUIBERT, iii. cc. 5, 6).

Lack of money with which to pay the king's courtiers now drove him to 'his friend' King Henry. During his absence Archdeacon Walter and the nobles whom he had left as his deputies sold the people of Laon the right to establish a 'commune.' Galdric on his return was not allowed to enter the city till he had sworn to uphold the new constitution. But though King Louis had confirmed the new charter, the bishop and his nobles were bent on its abolition, 'striving,' says Guibert, 'in Norman or English fashion to drive out French liberty' (ib. iii. c. 7). Galdric now, in defiance of the canon law, caused his negro slave, John, to blind another slave— Gerard, a leader of the commune. For this the pope suspended him, till a second visit to Rome procured the restoration of his authority. From Rome Galdric returned, determined to destroy the commune. The French king slept in Galdric's palace on the night preceding Good Friday 1112 (18 April); and as the commune could only offer 400*l.* against the bishop's 700*l.*, he quashed the old charter. Next morning the city was in open revolt. Louis had to leave early (April 19), and Galdric at once began to levy for his own use the contribution each citizen had made to the 'commune.' In spite of warnings from Anselm, he continued to enforce the impost, till on the following Thursday the burgesses, raising the cry of 'Commune,' burst into the bishop's court. Galdric fled to the cellars beneath the cathedral. One of his own serfs, Tendegald, whom he had offended by nicknaming him 'Isingrinus,' after the fox in the popular fabliau 'Reynard the Fox,' pointed out the bolted coffer in which he was hidden. He was dragged out by the hair and massacred (25 April 1112). Tendegald cut his finger off to secure the episcopal ring. The naked corpse was then cast into a corner where it remained a mark for stones and insults from the passers-by till the next day, when Anselm had it buried in St. Vincent's Church, outside the city walls (GUIBERT, iii. cc. 7–9). D'Achery has printed the fragments of his epitaph (col. 1192).

Galdric was a typical secular bishop, 'unstable in word and bearing.' He loved to talk of war and of the dogs and horses which he had learned to prize in England (GUIBERT, iii. c. 4, &c.) He was recklessly extravagant. Anselm, who visited England in his company, heard a universal outcry against his ill-gotten gains. He retained for his own use the gift which the English queen sent for another church. He was a fierce hater and returned Guibert's 'History of the Crusade' unread because it was dedicated to his enemy, Bishop Lissard of Soissons. He scorned the 'commune,' declaring 'he could never perish by such hands;' and on the day before his death boasted that the 'commune' leader would not dare to 'grunt' 'if I sent my blackman John to tweak his nose.'

[Dugdale's Monasticon, ed. 1817, vols. i. vi. &c.; Orderic Vitalis, ed. Le Prevost, iv. 230 (bk. xi. c. 20); Guibert of Nogent ap. Migne, vol. clvi. cols. 911–12, &c.; Hermann of Laon ap. Migne, vol. clvi.; Sigebert's Chronicon Auct. Laud. ap. Pertz, vi. 445; Chron. Besuense ap. Pertz, ii. 250, and ap. D'Achery's Spicilegium, ed. 1665, i. 639; Jaffé's Regesta Paparum, p. 493. Bouquet, xii. 42, 174, 276, &c., xiii. 266, xiv; 66–7; Thierry's Lettres sur l'Histoire de France.] T. A. A.

GALE, DUNSTAN (*fl.* 1596), poet, was the author of a poem entitled 'Pyramus and Thisbe,' supposed to have been printed for the first time in 1597, as the dedication is addressed 'To the Worshipful his verie friend D. B. H. Nov. 25th, 1596.' It was published with Greene's 'History of Arbasto' in 1617, in the title of which it is spoken of as 'a lovely poem.' No earlier edition is known. Another edition was published in 1626. A poem called 'Perymus and Thesbye' was entered to William Griffith in 1562, and according to Warton printed in quarto for T. Hackett; but this was probably an earlier and quite different work.

[Collier's Bibl. and Critical Account, 1865; Ritson's Bibliographia Poetica.] R. M. B.

GALE, GEORGE (1797?–1850), aeronaut, was, according to the register of his burial, born about 1797. He was originally an actor in small parts in London minor theatres. He became a great favourite of Andrew Ducrow [q. v.] In 1831 he went to America, and played Mazeppa for two hundred nights at the Bowery Theatre in New York. He afterwards travelled in the west and joined a tribe of Indians. He brought six of them, with their chief, 'Ma Caust,' to London, and was scarcely distinguishable from his companions. They were exhibited at the Victoria Theatre till their popularity declined. Sir Augustus Frederick D'Este [q. v.] had become interested in them, and procured Gale an appointment as coast blockade inspector in the north of Ireland. On the strength of this appointment, which he held for seven years, he afterwards assumed the title of lieutenant. Tiring of this he made an unsuccessful attempt to return to the London stage, and then took to ballooning. He had a balloon manufactured at the old Montpelier Gardens in Walworth, and made his first ascent with success from the Rosemary Branch tavern at Peckham in 1848. He made many ascents, the 114th of which was from the hippodrome of Vincennes at Bordeaux, with the Royal Cremorne balloon, on 8 Sept. 1850. He was seated on the back of a pony suspended from the car. Gale descended at Auguilles. When the pony had been released from its slings, the peasants holding the balloon ropes, not understanding his directions, relaxed their hold, and Gale was carried up by the only partially exhausted machine. The car overturned, but he clung to the tackling for a time, and was borne out of sight. Next morning his body was found in a wood several miles away. He was buried at the protestant cemetery at Bordeaux on 11 Sept. Gale was a man of much courage and very sanguine. For some time after his death his widow, who had frequently made ascents in his company, continued to gain a livelihood by ballooning.

[Gent. Mag. 1850, pt. ii. 668; Annual Register, 1850; extract from burial register at Bordeaux kindly communicated by M. Paul Stapfer.] J. B-y.

GALE, JOHN (1680–1721), general baptist minister, was born in London on 26 May 1680. His father, Nathaniel Gale, is described as 'an eminent citizen' who had property in the West Indies. John was well educated. When sent to study at Leyden University, which he entered 7 Dec. 1697 (PEACOCK, Index, p. 39), he was already a proficient in classics and Hebrew. On 3 July 1699 he received the degrees of M.A. and Ph.D.; the latter, which had not been conferred within living memory, was specially revived in his favour. He printed his graduation thesis ' De Ente ejusque conceptu,' dedicated to his uncles Sir John and Sir Joseph Wolf. From Leyden he went to Amsterdam, where he made the acquaintance of Limborch and of Le Clerc, who became his correspondent. Returning home, he pursued his studies in private, especially in the departments of biblical and patristic learning. The university of Leyden offered him (1703) the degree of D.D., but this he declined, being unwilling to subscribe the articles of Dort. Before he was twenty-seven he had written (1706) his examination of Wall, a work (published 1711) which is said to have attracted, while yet in manuscript, the attention of Whiston, and to have first influenced him in the direction of baptist views. It was at Whiston's house in Cross Street, Hatton Garden, that William Wall (vicar of Shoreham, Kent) met Gale for a discussion.

Gale preached his first sermon in February 1706 at Paul's Alley, Barbican. His services were very acceptable, but owing to a 'heavy burden of domestick affairs' (BURROUGHS) he was not in a position to enter on a stated ministry. His residence was at Blackheath. In 1715 he took some part in assisting Joseph Burroughs [q. v.] at Paul's Alley, became alternate morning preacher in July 1718, constant morning preacher in November 1719, and again alternate morning preacher in April 1721. He was never in a pastoral charge, and hence was never ordained; but, in addition to his engagements at Paul's Alley, he undertook preaching duty at Virginia Street, Ratcliff Highway, and at Deptford.

Gale was a member of Whiston's little 'society for promoting primitive Christianity;' he acted as its chairman from 3 July 1715 (the first meeting) till 10 Feb. 1716. He did not, however, understand 'primitive Christianity' in Whiston's sense; he was a trinitarian by conviction, but a non-subscriber on principle. Accordingly, in the famous dispute at Salters' Hall in 1719 [see BRADBURY, THOMAS] he took the liberal side, as did all the general baptists. Barrington Shute's 'Account' of the proceedings was published (1719) in the form of an anonymous letter to Gale. To Shute, afterwards Viscount Barrington [q. v.], he probably owed his introduction to Lord-chancellor King and the whig bishops. Hoadly esteemed him; Bradford, bishop of Rochester, commends his 'learning, candour, and largeness of mind.'

In spite of a good constitution Gale died in his prime. In December 1721 he was attacked by a fever, which carried him off in three weeks; the exact date of his death is not stated. Funeral sermons were preached by Joseph Burroughs (24 Dec.) and John Kinch, LL.D. (31 Dec.) He left little to his family; a subscription enabled his widow to open a coffee-house in Finch Lane. Gale was tall in stature and had a striking countenance. Of two original portraits of him the best is by Joseph Highmore [q. v.], one of his hearers; this is engraved by Vertue.

He published: 1. 'Inquisitio Philosophica Inauguralis de Lapide Solis,' &c., Leyden, 1699, 4to. 2. 'Reflections on Mr. Wall's History of Infant Baptism,' &c., 1711, 8vo; new editions, 1820, 8vo, and 1836, 8vo (Wall wrote a 'Defence,' 1720, and other answers were published by Samuel Chandler [q. v.], 1719; Caleb Fleming [q. v.], 1745; and V. Perronet, 1749). Posthumous was 3. 'Sermons,' &c., 1726, 8vo, 4 vols. He had published separate sermons in 1713, 1717, and 1718. At the time of his death he was engaged on an answer to Wall's 'Defence,' an English translation of the Septuagint, and a 'history of the notion of original sin.'

[Funeral sermons by Burroughs and Kinch, 1722; Life, prefixed to Sermons, 1726; Crosby's Hist. English Baptists, 1740, iv. 371; Whiston's Memoirs of Clarke, 1748, p. 58; Nichols's Atterbury's Correspondence, 1784, iii. 538; Protestant Dissenter's Magazine, 1796, p. 41 sq. (sketch by J. T., i.e. Joshua Toulmin); Universal Theological Magazine, 1803, i. 6 sq. (account of Barbican congregation by John Evans); Wilson's Dissenting Churches in London, 1810, iii. 242 sq.; Monthly Repository, 1824, p. 712 sq.] A. G.

GALE, MILES (1647–1721), antiquary, eldest son of John Gale. His father, a descendant of the Gales of Scruton and Masham in Yorkshire, served under Count Mansfeld in the Low Countries (1622-5), returned to England, and lived in retirement on his estate at Farnley, near Leeds, refusing a commission from the parliament on the outbreak of the civil war. His mother was Joanna, daughter of Miles Dodson of Kirkby Overblow, Yorkshire. Miles was born at Farnley Hall on 19 June 1647. He was educated at Trinity College, Cambridge, where he graduated B.A. in 1666 and M.A. in 1670. Having taken holy orders he was presented to the rectory of Keighley (1680), which he continued to hold until his death in the night of 2–3 Jan. 1720–1. Gale was a friend of Gyles, the eminent glass-painter of York, and was much interested in antiquarian research. He compiled and presented to Thoresby's Museum, Leeds (1) 'Memoirs of the Family of Gale, particularly of the learned Dr. Thomas Gale, Dean of York, and Christopher Gale, Esq., Her Majesty's Attorney-general in North Carolina,' 1703; (2) 'A Description of the Parish of Keighley.' He married Margaret, daughter of Christopher Stones, D.D., chancellor of York (1660–87), by whom he had issue four sons and one daughter. Of his sons the eldest, Christopher, was attorney-general of North Carolina in 1703, judge of the admiralty of that province in 1712, and chief justice of Providence and the Bahama Islands in 1721. Several of his letters are printed in Nichols's 'Illustrations,' iv. 489–92. He married Sarah, relict of Harvey, governor of North Carolina.

[Thoresby's Diary, ii. 308, 312; Nichols's Lit. Anecd. iv. 5; Nichols's Lit. Illustr. iv. 490; Taylor's Biog. Leod. p. 575.]   J. M. R.

GALE, ROGER (1672–1744), antiquary, eldest son of Thomas Gale, dean of York [q. v.], by his wife Barbara, daughter of Thomas Pepys, esq., was born in 1672, and was educated at St. Paul's School, London, where his father was at the time high-master. He proceeded, with a Campden exhibition from the school, to Trinity College, Cambridge, in 1691, obtaining a scholarship there in 1693 and a fellowship in 1697. He graduated B.A. in 1694, and M.A. in 1698. The family estate of Scruton, Yorkshire, came into his possession on his father's death in 1702. Mrs. Alice Rogers bequeathed him the manor of Cottenham, Cambridgeshire, and Gale erected a monument in the church to the memory of his benefactress, but he soon sold the estate and chiefly divided his time between London and Scruton. He represented Northallerton in the parliaments of 1705, 1707, 1708, and 1710. He became a commissioner of stamp duties 20 Dec. 1714, and was reappointed 4 May 1715. From 24 Dec. 1715 he was a commissioner of excise, and was displaced in 1735 by Sir Robert Walpole, who wanted the post for one of his friends. Indignant letters on the subject

from Gale to his friend Dr. Stukeley appear in Stukeley's 'Memoirs,' i. 281, 321–4.

Gale was an enthusiastic antiquary. From his father he inherited a valuable collection of printed books and manuscripts, to which he made many additions. British archæology was his chief study, but he was also a skilled numismatist. He was liberal in assisting fellow-antiquaries. Browne Willis, a lifelong acquaintance, received from him a manuscript history of Northallerton, intended for, but never included in, Willis's 'Notitia Parliamentaria.' The manuscript passed to William Cole, and its substance was given by Gale in his work on Richmond. He helped Francis Drake in his 'History of York,' and prepared a discourse on the four Roman ways from his father's notes for Hearne's edition of Leland's 'Itinerary,' vol. vi. (HEARNE, Coll., Oxford Hist. Soc., iii. 220). Hearne, writing to Rawlinson on 8 Oct. 1712, describes Gale as 'my good and kind friend' (ib. p. 457). In August 1738 he presented some manuscripts to Trinity College, Cambridge. Dr. Stukeley was a friend as early as 1707 (STUKELEY, Memoirs, i. 33), and from 1717 onwards they were constantly in each other's society. In 1725 they made an antiquarian tour together. In 1739 Gale's sister Elizabeth became Dr. Stukeley's second wife. Sir John Clerk of Pennicuik [q. v.] was another intimate friend and fellow-student. Gale was the first vice-president of the Society of Antiquaries, and was treasurer of the Royal Society. He was a member of the Spalding and Brazennose Societies.

Gale published, with notes of his own, his father's edition of 'Antonini Iter Britanniarum,' London, 1709, and in the preface distinguishes between his own and his father's contributions. Gough had a copy of the book, with manuscript annotations by Gale and others. Hearne notes (30 May 1709) that the inscriptions 'are very faultily printed, and that the book is full of errors' (HEARNE, Coll., Oxf. Hist. Soc., ii. 203). In 1697 Gale translated for anonymous publication, from the French of F. Jobert, 'The Knowledge of Medals: or Instructions for those who apply themselves to the study of Medals both Antient and Modern.' A second edition appeared in 1715. In 1722 he issued by subscription, under the auspices of the Society of Antiquaries, 'Registrum Honoris de Richmond,' with valuable appendices. Gale contributed several papers to the 'Philosophical Transactions,' one, in 1744, being a letter to Peter Collinson [q. v.] on a fossil skeleton of a man found near Bakewell, Derbyshire. A paper on a Roman altar found at Castle

Steeds, Cumberland, is in the 'Gentleman's Magazine,' 1742, p. 135, and another on a Roman inscription at Chichester is in Horsley's 'Britannia Romania,' pp. 332 et seq. The 'Bibliotheca Topographica Britannica' for 1781 (ii.) contains, besides many letters to antiquarian friends and papers by his brother Samuel, Gale's accounts of Northallerton, of Scruton, of the Rollerich Stones, Warwickshire, of the Earls of Richmond, and a tour in Scotland. These papers, entitled 'Reliquiæ Galeanæ,' were edited by George Allan of Darlington, to whom they had been presented by Gale's grandson. Pennant, William Norris, and other fellows of the Society of Antiquaries took a keen interest in the publication, the expense of which was borne by Nichols (NICHOLS, *Lit. Anecd.* vi. 126, &c. viii. passim).

Gale married Henrietta, daughter of Henry Roper, esq., of Cowling, Kent. She died in 1720, and by her Gale had one son, Roger Henry. The antiquary died at Scruton on 25 June 1744, aged 72, and was buried there. He had some foreboding of his death, and a fortnight before selected oak planks to be employed in making his grave. He left directions that a flat stone should be placed above the vault containing the coffin, and should be so covered with earth 'that no one should know where the grave was' (STUKELEY, ii. 352, 356).

Gale gave many of his manuscripts to Trinity College, Cambridge, and his collection of coins to the Cambridge University Library, together with a catalogue prepared by himself. The chief papers remaining at Scruton appear in the 'Reliquiæ Galeanæ.' His library was purchased by Osborn the bookseller and dispersed in 1756 and 1758. A portrait by Vanderbanck, painted in 1722, was at Scruton.

[Nichols's Lit. Anecd. iv. 543–50 (for life), and passim for various references to his intercourse with antiquaries of the time; Hearne's Collections (Oxf. Hist. Soc.), vols. ii. and iii.; Dr. Stukeley's Memoirs (Surtees Soc.); Gough's British Topography; Reliquiæ Galeanæ in Bibl. Top. Brit. vol. ii.]   S. L.

GALE, SAMUEL (1682–1754), antiquary, youngest son of Thomas Gale, dean of York [q. v.], and brother of Roger Gale [q. v.], was born in the parish of St. Faith's, London, on 17 Dec. 1682. He was baptised on 20 Dec., Samuel Pepys being one of his godfathers. He was educated at St. Paul's School, where his father was master, but did not proceed to the university. About 1702 he obtained a post in the custom house, London. At the time of his death he was one of the land surveyors of the customs, and

searcher of the books and curiosities imported into England (*Gent. Mag.* xxiv. 47). Gale was one of the founders of the revived Society of Antiquaries, and was elected its first treasurer in January 1717–18 (*Archæologia*, vol. i. pp. xxviii, xxxiii). On resigning the treasurership in 1739–40, he was presented by the society with an inscribed silver cup. He was also a member of the Spalding Society, and of the Brazennose Literary Society at Stamford (founded 1745). Gale delighted in archæological excursions through England. For many years he and his friend Dr. Ducarel [q. v.] used in August to travel incognito, journeying about fifteen miles a day. They took up their quarters at an inn, 'penetrating into the country for three or four miles round.' They had with them Camden's 'Britannia' and a set of maps (NICHOLS, *Lit. Anecd.* vi. 402). In 1705 Gale visited Oxford, Bath, and Stonehenge, and wrote descriptive accounts. On 29 Aug. 1744 he made a pilgrimage with Dr. Stukeley to Croyland Abbey. On 16 May 1747 he visited Croyland Canons, the splendid mansion of the Duke of Chandos, and, lamenting its approaching demolition, went into the chapel, and preached an appropriate sermon, while his two companions sang an anthem and psalms (*Surtees Soc. Publ.* lxxiii. 389–90). Gale died of a fever on 10 Jan. 1754 at his lodgings, the Chicken-house, Hampstead. He was buried by Dr. Stukeley on 14 Jan. in the burial-ground of St. George's, Queen Square, London, near the Foundling Hospital. He was unmarried. A portrait of him was painted by his intimate friend, Isaac Whood, and is described by Nichols as being 'still at Scruton' (Roger Gale's estate). His collection of prints by Hollar, Callot, &c. was sold by auction in 1754 by Langford. Most of his books were sold to Osborn. The unpublished manuscripts of his own writings became the property of his only sister Elizabeth, and thus came into the hands of her husband, Dr. Stukeley, from whom they passed to Dr. Ducarel, and were then bought by Gough. Nichols printed many of them in the 'Reliquiæ Galeanæ' (1781, &c.), including the 'Tour through several parts of England' in 1705 (revised by Gale, 1730); 'A Dissertation on Celts;' 'Account of some Antiquities at Glastonbury,' 1711; 'Observations on Kingsbury, Middlesex,' 1751. (For others, see *Reliq. Gal.*) The only writings published by Gale himself were, 'A History of Winchester Cathedral,' London, 1715, 8vo (begun by Henry, earl of Clarendon), and two papers ('Ulphus' Horn at York,' 'Cæsar's passage over the Thames) in the 'Archæologia,' vol. i. Gale gave some valuable material to Drake for his 'Eboracum,' and probably furnished

Hearne with various readings of Leland's 'Itinerary.' Vertue's prints of the old chapel under London Bridge were designed under his patronage. Some of Gale's letters and a correspondence with Stukeley (who sometimes addresses him as 'Dear Mr. Samuel') are printed in Stukeley's 'Memoirs' (Surtees Soc.) Gale is described by Ducarel as a 'worthy and amiable' man, and by Nichols as being of 'uncommon abilities, and well versed in the antiquities of England.'

[Nichols's Lit. Anecd. iv. 550-5, and other references in Lit. Anecd. and Lit. Illustr.; Gent. Mag. 1754, xxiv. 47; Reliquiæ Galeanæ in vol. ii. of Nichols's Bibl. Topogr. Britannica; Family Memoirs of William Stukeley, &c. (Surtees Soc. 3 vols. 1882-7).]   W. W.

GALE, THEOPHILUS (1628-1678), nonconformist tutor, son of Theophilus Gale, D.D., vicar of Kingsteignton, Devonshire, and prebendary of Exeter, was born at King's-teignton in 1628. He was educated under a private tutor and at a neighbouring grammar school, and in 1647 was entered a commoner at Magdalen Hall, Oxford. At the visitation of 1648 he was made a demy of Magdalen College, and on 17 Dec. 1649 received the degree of B.A., a year earlier than usual, on the ground of his age and parts. In 1650 he was put into the place of one of the ejected fellows; he graduated M.A. on 18 June 1652. He was a successful tutor, among his pupils being Ezekiel Hopkins [q. v.], afterwards bishop of Derry. A hint in Grotius's 'De Veritate' (i. 16) gave him the idea of the derivation of all ancient learning and philosophy from the Hebrew scriptures, and to the elaboration of this theory he devoted the studies of his life. In ecclesiastical polity he was an independent, and a member of the church of this order formed by Thomas Goodwin, D.D. [q. v.], when president of Magdalen. He distinguished himself as a university preacher. At the end of 1657 he accepted an appointment as preacher in Winchester Cathedral, still retaining his fellowship. On the restoration of the monarchy (1660) his preferments went back to their former owners.

Unable to conform, Gale became tutor in the family of Philip, fourth baron Wharton. In September 1662 he accompanied his patron's two sons, Thomas (afterwards the first marquis) and Godwin, to the protestant college at Caen in Normandy. Here for two years he enjoyed the friendship of Bochart. Leaving his pupils at Caen, he seems to have spent a year in travel, returning in the autumn of 1665 to Wharton's seat at Quainton, Buckinghamshire.

Next year, his tutorial engagement being over, he proceeded to London, where, on his way to France, he had deposited his papers in the counting-house of a friend. He reached the city while the great fire was raging; by a mere chance his manuscripts had been saved. He settled at Newington Green and took pupils; acting also as assistant to John Rowe, minister of an independent congregation which met in St. Andrew's parish, Holborn, in defiance of the first conventicle act, not very operative in the dearth of ministrations caused by the great fire.

Gale now resumed the preparation of his great work. The first part of 'The Court of the Gentiles' was ready for the press in 1669; John Fell, D.D. [q. v.], then vice-chancellor, readily granted his license for printing it at Oxford. It was applauded as a marvel of erudition. Gale traces every European language to the Hebrew, and all the theologies, sciences, politics, and literature of pagan antiquity to a Hebrew tradition. A second part deals in a similar way with the origin of all philosophies. A third accounts for the errors of pagan philosophy and popish divinity on the theory of corruption by successive apostasies from a divine original. The fourth and largest part (in three books) is constructive, a reformed Platonism, ending with a powerful endeavour to rescue the Calvinistic doctrine of predetermination from moral difficulties. Excepting an essay on Jansenism, and a few learned sermons, Gale's other writings are mainly reproductions of his system in a Latin dress.

On the death of Rowe (12 Oct. 1677), Gale succeeded him as pastor, having Samuel Lee as a colleague. It would appear that he was now training students for the ministry; Wilson's manuscript list enumerates three, John Ashwood of Peckham, and the two sons of John Rowe, Thomas (who succeeded Gale) and Benoni. After the beginning of 1678 he printed proposals for publishing a 'Lexicon Græci Testamenti,' &c., which was ready for the press as far as the letter *iota*. His plans were cut short by his death, which occurred at the end of February or beginning of March 1678. He was buried at Bunhill Fields. All his real and personal estate he left for the education of poor nonconformist scholars. His library he bequeathed to Harvard College, New England, reserving the philosophical portion of it for the use of students at home.

He published: 1. 'The Court of the Gentiles, or a Discourse touching the Original of Humane Literature,' &c., pt. i. Oxford,

1669, 4to; 2nd edit. Oxford, 1672, 4to; pt. ii. Oxford, 1671, 4to; 2nd edit. London, 1676, 4to; pts. iii. and iv. London, 1677, 4to (bk. iii. of pt. iv. London, 1678, 4to); 2nd edit. London, 1682, 4to. 2. 'A True Idea of Jansenisme,' &c., 1669, 8vo (preface by John Owen, D.D.) 3. 'The Life and Death of Mr. Thomas Tregosse,' &c., 1671, 8vo (who was 'converted' by one of his own sermons). 4. 'Theophilie . . . the Saints Amitie with God,' &c., 1671, 8vo. 5. 'The Anatomie of Infidelitie,' &c., 1672, 8vo. 6. 'Idea Theologiæ,' &c., 1673, 8vo. 7. 'A Discourse of Christ's coming,' &c., 1673, 8vo. 8. 'Philosophia Generalis,' &c., 1676, 8vo. Also a sermon (1 John ii. 15), 1674, 8vo (reprinted in supplement to 'Morning Exercise at Cripplegate,' 1676, 4to); a preface to the 'Life of Rowe,' 1673, 12mo; and a summary prefixed to William Strong's 'Discourse of the Two Covenants,' 1678, fol. Wood (followed by Watt) assigns to him 'Ars Sciendi,' &c., 1681, 12mo; 1682, 8vo, by T. G., but this is the work of Thomas Gowan [q. v.]

[Wood's Athenæ Oxon., 1692, ii. 451, 750, 778; Reynolds's Funeral Sermon for Ashwood, 1706; Calamy's Account, 1713, p. 64 sq.; Continuation, 1727, i. 97 sq.; Palmer's Nonconformist's Memorial, 1802, i. 239; Wilson's Dissenting Churches in London, 1810, iii. 161 sq.; Wilson's manuscripts in Dr. Williams's Library (Dissenting Records, D*, p. 69); Gale's works.]
A. G.

GALE, THOMAS (1507–1587), surgeon, was born in London in 1507, and was apprenticed with John Field, also a well-known surgeon, to Richard Ferris, one of the chief barber-surgeons of the time. After practising for some time in London, he served in the army of Henry VIII at Muttrell in France in 1544 (*Treatise of Gunshot*, p. 74 *b*), and there had the good sense to refuse to imperil the lives of eleven soldiers by removing bullets the lodgments of which were uncertain. In 1557 he served under Philip II of Spain at the siege of St. Quentin, and two years later was established in practice in London (*Institution*, p. 8 *b*). He was master of the Barber-Surgeons' Company in 1561, and published a volume on surgery in 1563, dedicated to Lord Robert Dudley. It contains four separate treatises. 'The Institution of Chirurgerie,' the first, is a sort of catechism of surgery, in which Gale and his friend Field answer the questions of a surgical student named John Yates. The second is 'The Enchiridion of Surgery,' a compilation on general surgery, which contains the prescription for Gale's styptic powder often mentioned in contemporary works. Its chief ingredients were alum, turpentine, arsenic, and quick-

lime. The third is a treatise on gunshot wounds, in which he shows that gunpowder is not a poison, and the fourth is an antidotary or collection of prescriptions. A second volume appeared in 1566 containing some translations from Latin versions of Galen, 'A brief Declaration of the Worthy Art of Medicine,' and 'The Office of a Chirurgeon.' Gale knew but little Latin, and the translations are the work of his friend Dr. Cuningham. The writings of Gale are mainly compilations, and contain few cases from his own practice. They show him to have had less mother wit than his contemporary William Clowes the elder [q. v.], and less reading than John Banister (1540–1610) [q. v.] He died in 1587, and left a son, Thomas, also a surgeon, admitted to the guild 18 Jan. 1597.

[Works; MS. Transcript of Records at Barbers' Hall by Sidney Young.]   N. M.

GALE, THOMAS (1635?–1702), dean of York, born at Scruton in the North Riding of Yorkshire in 1635 or 1636, was the only surviving child of Christopher Gale of Scruton, by his wife Frances Conyers of Holtby in the same county (FOSTER, *Yorkshire Pedigrees*, vol. ii.) He was educated at Westminster School, under Busby, and being admitted king's scholar was elected in 1655 to Trinity College, Cambridge (B.A. 1659, M.A. 1662). He contributed verses to the 'Luctus et Gratulatio,' published by the university of Cambridge in 1658, on the death of Oliver Cromwell; to the 'Threni Cantabrigienses' on the deaths of the Duke of Gloucester and the Princess of Orange in 1661, and to the 'Epicedia Cantabrigiensis' in 1671. He became a fellow of his college, and was incorporated M.A. at Oxford the day after the opening of the Sheldonian Theatre, 13 July 1669 (WOOD, *Fasti Oxon.* ed. Bliss, ii. 312). He was appointed senior taxor in 1670. His eminence as a scholar obtained for him in 1666 the regius professorship of Greek at Cambridge, an office which he resigned in 1672 to become high master of St. Paul's School. On that occasion James Duport [q. v.] addressed to him a copy of verses which are printed at page 16 of the 'Musæ Subsecivæ,' 1676. He accumulated the degrees in divinity in 1675, and on 7 June 1676 was made prebendary of St. Paul's. On 6 Dec. 1677 he was elected into the Royal Society (THOMSON, *Hist. Roy. Soc.* App. iv. p. xxvii), of which he became a very active member. He frequently sat on the council, and presented many curiosities to the museum. In 1679 he wrote at the request of the society the inscription for the Bibliotheca Norfolciana. In January 1685–6 Gale and Sir

John Hoskyns were chosen honorary secretaries, and appointed for their clerk Edmund Halley [q. v.], one of Gale's pupils at St. Paul's (WELD, *Hist. Roy. Soc.* i. 266, 305). Gale's only contribution to the 'Philosophical Transactions' was some notes on Ralph Thoresby's 'Letter' to Martin Lister of 10 July 1697, concerning two Roman altars found at Collerton and Blenkinsop Castle in Northumberland (xix. 663). Gale continued at the head of St. Paul's School with increasing reputation until 1697, when he was preferred to the deanery of York, being admitted on 16 Sept. of that year. On leaving London he presented to his college a curious collection of Arabic manuscripts. At York Gale was noted for his hospitality, and for his admirable government, as well as for his care in restoring and embellishing the cathedral. He was further a benefactor to the deanery by obtaining in 1699 letters patent settling the dean's right to be a canon residentiary (DRAKE, *Eboracum*, pp. 480, 527, 565, 572). He died at York on 7 or 8 April 1702, in the sixty-seventh year of his age, and was buried on the 15th in the middle of the cathedral choir. He married Barbara, daughter of Thomas Pepys of Impington, Cambridgeshire, who was buried in St. Faith's Church, London, 5 June 1689. By her he left issue four sons: Roger (*d.* 1744) [q. v.]; Charles (*d.* 1738), rector of Scruton; Samuel (1682–1754) [q. v.]; and Thomas, and one daughter, Elizabeth (1687), who in 1739 became the second wife of William Stukeley, M.D. [q. v.] He had many eminent correspondents. Mabillon gave him the manuscript of Alcuin's 'De Pontificibus Eboracensibus,' published in his 'Historiæ Britannicæ Scriptores XV,' 1691, and Huet declared that Gale exceeded all men he ever knew both for modesty and versatility of learning (*Commentarius de Rebus ad eum pertinentibus,* 1718, bk. v. p. 315). To his eldest son Roger he left a noble library of books and manuscripts; the latter are catalogued in 'Catalogus Librorum Manuscriptorum Angliæ et Hiberniæ,' fol. Oxford, 1697 (iii. 185). By Roger Gale the manuscripts were given in 1738 to Trinity College, Cambridge, as was also a fine portrait of his father. There is another portrait of Gale (by Kneller) at Scruton. A drawing of him in the Pepysian collection at Magdalene College, Cambridge, was engraved by S. Harding. Gale edited: 1. 'Opuscula mythologica, ethica et physica,' Greek and Latin (anon.), 10 pts. 8vo, Cambridge, 1671 (see another edition 8vo, Amsterdam, 1688). 2. 'Historiæ poeticæ Scriptores antiqui. Accessêre breves notæ,' &c. (anon.) 8vo, Paris, 1675. His annotations on 'Antonini Liberalis Transformatio-

num Congeries were incorporated by G. A. Koch in his edition, 8vo, 1832. 3. 'Rhetores selecti. Demetrius Phalereus, Tiberius Rhetor, Anonymus Sophista, Severus Alexandrinus. Græce et Latine. (Demetrium emendavit, reliquos e MSS. edidit et Latine vertit T. Gale),' 8vo, Oxford, 1676 (another edition, by J. F. Fischer, 8vo, Leipzig, 1773). 4. 'Ἰαμβλίχου Χαλκιδέως περι Μυστηριων Λογος' (with Latin version and notes), fol. Oxford, 1678. 5. 'Ψαλτηριον. Psalterium. Juxta exemplar Alexandrinum editio nova, Græce et Latine' (anon.), 8vo, Oxford, 1678. 6. 'Herodoti . . . historiarum libri ix. Excerpta e Ctesiæ libris de rebus Persicis et Indicis,' &c. (anon.), Greek and Latin, fol. London, 1679 (another edition, fol. London, 1763). His 'Chronologia' was included in G. C. Becelli's Italian version of 'Herodotus,' 2 pts. 4to, Verona, 1733. 7. 'Historiæ Anglicanæ Scriptores Quinque ex vetustis Codicibus MSS. nunc primum in lucem editi. Vol. ii.' (anon.), fol. Oxford, 1687, including Walterus de Hemingford's 'Chronica' from 1066 to 1273. The first volume of this collection had appeared in 1684 under the anonymous editorship of William Fulman [q. v.] 8. 'Historiæ Britannicæ, Saxonicæ, Anglo-Danicæ Scriptores XV. ex vetustis Codd. MSS. editi opera Thomæ Gale,' &c. fol. Oxford, 1691. 9. 'Antonini Iter Britanniarum commentariis illustratum Thomæ Gale . . . Opus posthumum revisit, auxit, edidit R[ogerus] G[ale]. Accessit anonymi Ravennatis Britanniæ chorographia,' &c. 4to, London, 1709. Roger Gale also published his father's 'Sermons preached upon several Holydays observed in the Church of England,' 8vo, London, 1704. Gale translated anonymously Huet's 'Traité de la Situation du Paradis Terrestre,' 12mo, London, 1694. He communicated various readings from two manuscripts to the edition of 'Diogenes Laertius,' published at Amsterdam in two volumes, 4to, 1692; critical notes to Paulus Bauldri's edition of 'Lactantii de Mortibus Persecutorum,' 8vo, Utrecht, 1692; and notes to William Worth's edition of 'Tatiani Oratio ad Græcos,' 8vo, Oxford, 1700. J. C. Orelli included Gale's annotations in his edition of 'Sallust the Philosopher,' 8vo, 1821; and F. Oehler used his notes upon 'Maximus the Confessor' (*Anecdota Græca,* tom. i. 8vo, 1857). His manuscript notes on 'Herodotus' and 'Dion Cassius' are in the library of the university of Cambridge (*Catalogue,* vi. 73). He left too in manuscript editions of 'Origenis Philocalia' and of 'Iamblichus de Vita Pythagoræ.' From Ballard's Collection of MS. Letters in the Bodleian Library (xv. 32) it appears that Gale had an intention of continuing Archbishop Parker's 'Antiquitates Britannicæ.' Gale, by the king's command, composed the obnoxious inscription for the monument of London, for which he received from the city a present of plate.

[Nichols's Lit. Anecd. iv. 536–55; Welch's Alumni Westmon. (1852) pp. 143, 144; Biographia Britannica; Chalmers's Biog. Dict. xv. 221–5; Cole MSS. vol. xlv. ff. 242, 268, 462; Knight's Life of Colet, p. 282; Willis's Survey of Cathedrals, i. 70–2; Newcourt's Repertorium, i. 144; Evelyn's Diary; Noble's Continuation of Granger's Biog. Hist. i. 94–5; Evans's Cat. of Engraved Portraits, i. 132; Nicolson's Historical Libraries (1776), pts. i. and ii.; Stukeley's Diaries and Letters (Surtees Soc.); Hearne's Preface to Walterus de Hemingford, p. xxiii.; Le Neve's Fasti (Hardy) iii. 639.] G. G.

GALEON, WILLIAM (d. 1507), learned Augustinian, was born in Norfolk, and became a friar eremite in the Augustinian monastery of Lynn Regis. Bale says that he was already of 'mature years' when he went to Oxford, where he studied for several years among the brethren of his order in their college. He was chiefly renowned for his minute knowledge of theology, and took a D.D. degree probably before he left the university. He was much esteemed by his contemporaries, and 'having moved through several honourable stations,' was chosen provincial of his order in England. He died at Lynn in 1507 in the prime of life, and was buried in the church of his order there. Galeon was looked upon as a great ornament to his society, which he is said to have roused from slothfulness. Bale says that he gave many of his writings in his lifetime to his own religious house at Lynn. Bishop Pamphilus incorrectly states that Galeon died in 1500, aged 90. The works ascribed to him are: 'Lectiones in Theologia,' 'Disputationes Variæ,' 'Conciones per Annum.'

[Bale, viii. iii. 60; Pits, p. 687; Lansdowne MS. 978, f. 80; Wood's Athenæ Oxon. ed. Bliss, i. 11; Tanner's Bibl. Brit. p. 304; Stevens's Hist. of Abbeys and Monasteries, ii. 220; Dodd's Church History, i. 238.] E. T. B.

GALEYS, SIR HENRY DE (d. 1302?), mayor of London. [See WALEYS.]

GALFRIDUS. [See GEOFFREY.]

GALGACUS, or (according to the best readings) CALGACUS (fl. circa A.D. 84), Caledonian chieftain, held the command of the native tribes when Agricola, the Roman governor of Britain, invaded Caledonia in his last campaign. Agricola found him encamped near Mons Graupius (TACITUS, Agric. xxix.; so in the editions of Wex, Kritz, and Orelli, 2nd edit.; Church and Brodribb read

'Grampius;' SKENE, Celt. Scotl. i. 52, 'Granpius'), and a great battle ensued in which the Romans were victorious. The scene of this engagement has been variously identified with Dealgan Ross near Comrie, Ardoch, Fife, and Urie in Kincardineshire. Skene (Celt. Scotl. i. 54) supposes that previous to the battle the Romans occupied the peninsula formed by the junction of the Isla with the Tay, being protected by the rampart of the Cleaven Dyke, and that Galgacus was encamped at Buzzard Dykes. The date of the battle is usually given as A.D. 84. (SKENE, 'A.D. 86;' on the chronological difficulty, see Celt. Scotl. i. 51 note; MERIVALE, Hist. of the Romans, vii. 329). Before the fight Galgacus is represented by Tacitus (Agric. xxx–xxxii.) as delivering an harangue, denouncing the Roman plunderers of the world. ('Raptores orbis . . . ubi solitudinem faciunt, pacem appellant,' &c.) His personal fortunes in the battle are not stated, nor is his name subsequently mentioned. Tacitus speaks of him as 'inter plures duces virtute et genere præstans.'

[Tacitus, Agricola, xxix–xxxii. &c.; Skene's Celtic Scotland, i. 52–6.] W. W.

GALIGNANI, JOHN ANTHONY (1796–1873), and WILLIAM (1798–1882), publishers of Paris, were the sons of Giovanni Antonio Galignani (1757–1821), by Anne Parsons (1776–1822). The name is probably derived from the village of Gallignano, near Cremona, and Giovanni was a native of Brescia. There is a tradition that the father was originally a courier. In 1793 he taught Italian, German, and English at Paris. He thence removed to London, where in 1796 he published twenty-four lectures on a new method of learning Italian without grammar or dictionary. A second edition of this work was issued by Montucci in 1806. Galignani apparently married in London, and his two sons were born there, the elder on 13 Oct. 1796, the younger on 10 March 1798. Shortly after William's birth he returned to Paris, where he and his wife offered linguistic breakfasts and teas to persons desirous of mastering English or Italian, but for the latter language there appears to have been little demand, and 'Mrs. Parsons-Galignani' established an English bookshop and circulating library. In 1801 the Galignanis started a monthly (in 1817 it became a weekly) 'Repertory of English Literature.' A third son, Charles Alphonse, was born at Paris in 1811; he died at Geneva in 1829. On the fall of Napoleon in 1814 the father commenced issuing guide-books and founded 'Galignani's Messenger,' which was at first a tri-weekly but speedily became a daily paper, and circulated among English residents all over Europe, as the stamp duty and postage rendered London journals expensive. In 1815 he published a Paris guide in English and German, on opposite pages, for the use of officers of the allied troops. The elder son, while still under age, opened a bookshop at Cambrai, but returned to Paris at or before his father's death, when he became the chief partner. The two brothers issued reprints of many English books, sometimes paying authors for advance-sheets. Sir Walter Scott, for instance, on visiting what he calls the 'old pirate's den' in 1826, was, 'after some palaver,' offered a hundred guineas for sheets of his 'Life of Napoleon.' The 'den' was at the bottom of a court, 18 rue Vivienne, and though so central, a garden with large trees was attached to it. It served as a club for English residents and visitors, who paid six francs a month, the reading-room containing English and continental newspapers and eighteen thousand books. Both brothers obtained denizenship in December 1830, and in 1832 William was naturalised, Anthony (he had dropped his first name) remaining a British subject. In 1838 Thackeray, then in Paris, wrote for the 'Messenger.' In 1852 the copyright treaty put a stop to Galignani's reprints, and in 1855 the establishment was removed to the rue de Rivoli. A flourishing business and investments in house property brought the brothers a large fortune, of which they made a munificent use. Having a country house at Etiolles, of which parish William was for more than twenty years mayor, they presented the adjoining town of Corbeil with a hospital and extensive grounds. They were also liberal contributors to British charities in Paris, and erected at Neuilly a hospital for indigent English (now converted into an orphanage). In 1866 the British government presented them with a silver epergne in recognition of their benevolent efforts. Anthony, who was unmarried, died 29 Dec. 1873, and William, a widower since 1862, without issue, died 11 Dec. 1882. The elder was knight and the younger officer of the Legion of Honour. The latter bequeathed a site and funds for the erection at Neuilly of the 'Retraite Galignani frères' for a hundred inmates, fifty of them to pay five hundred francs yearly for their maintenance, the other fifty to be admitted gratuitously and to comprise ten booksellers or printers, twenty *savants*, and ten authors or artists, or parents, widows, or daughters of such. The aggregate benefactions of the brothers amount to between five and six million francs. A fine sculpture of them, by Chapu, has been erected at Corbeil.

[Information from M. Jeancourt-Galignani, nephew of Madame W. Galignani; tombstone at Père-Lachaise, Paris; advertisements in Petites Affiches, 1793–8, and in Paris Argus, 1802–4; Lockhart's Life of Scott; Journal des Débats, 4 Jan. 1874; Bulletin des Lois, 1830–2; will of William Galignani.]   J. G. A.

GALL, SAINT (550?–645?), originally named CELLACH or CAILLECH, abbot and the apostle of the Suevi and the Alemanni, appears to have been the son of Cethernach, an Irishman of noble lineage, of the sept of Hy-Cennsealach, his mother being, it is asserted, a queen of Hungary. He was uterine brother to St. Deicola [q. v.] He was brought up in St. Comgall's monastery of Bangor, at the mouth of Belfast Lough, by St. Columban [q. v.], was well instructed in grammar, learning both Latin and Greek, in poetry, and in the scriptures, was ordained priest on reaching the canonical age, and was distinguished by his holiness of life. When Columban went to Gaul, probably in 585, Gall accompanied him, and followed him when he was driven from Luxeuil. During his master's stay at Arbon and Bregenz Gall took an especially prominent part in the mission, and his ability to preach to the people in their own tongue seems to have made him the spokesman of the party. He burnt a place of idolatrous worship, and threw the offerings of the worshippers into the lake; and at Bregenz publicly destroyed their images, which were held in much veneration. The mission was chiefly supplied with food by his labour, for he made nets and caught much fish. One night while he was fishing he heard in the stillness the voice of the demon of the mountains crying from the heights to the demon of the lakes, and bidding him arise and help to turn out the strangers who were casting down their altars. The lake demon answered that one of them was even then troubling him, but he had no power to break his nets or do him harm, because he was for ever crying on a divine name. When Gall heard these voices he adjured the demons by the name of the Lord, and hastened to tell the abbot, who at once summoned the brethren to the church. Before they began to chant they heard the terrific sound of the voices of demons wailing on the mountain tops (WALAFRID STRABO, i. 7). When Columban left Bregenz in 612 Gall remained behind, for he was sick of a fever. The story that Columban believed his sickness to be feigned, and as a mark of displeasure ordered him not to celebrate mass until Columban's death, is not mentioned by Jonas, Columban's almost contemporary biographer. After Gall's recovery he went to stay with his friend the priest Willimar at Arbon, and there continued his preaching to the Suevi and Alemanni. Desiring probably to establish a separate centre for mission work, he retired to the forest and built a cell on the river Steinach. There he was soon joined by twelve others, and their little cluster of huts was the origin of the famous monastery of St. Gall. The story of his casting out an evil spirit from the only daughter of Gunzo, duke of the Suevi, who was betrothed to Sigebert, king of the Austrasians, must be rejected with all the incidents consequent on it, for it is impossible to find a Sigebert to whom it can refer (PAGIUS, an. 614, No. 30). When Columban was dying in 615 he sent Gall his pastoral staff, probably as a token of affection, not as a sign that any prohibition was removed. Gall was summoned to Constance in 616 to take part in the election of a bishop, and went thither with his two deacons, John and Magnoald. He was unanimously elected to the bishopric, but declined it, and persuaded the assembly to accept John. The sermon which he preached at John's consecration is still extant. On the death of Eustace, abbot of Luxeuil, in 625, Gall was elected to succeed him, but refused the office. In 645 he was persuaded by Willibald to visit Arbon, and while there fell sick of a fever, of which he died after fourteen days' illness on 16 Oct. He was buried at Arbon. The day of his death is usually the day of his commemoration, but 20 Feb. has also been appropriated to his memory. Although no materials exist for an exact estimate of the results of his work, it would not be too much to refer to him the evangelisation of the country between the Alps, the Aar, and the Lech. The new Bollandists propose as the chronology of his life that he was born in 554, ordained priest 584, followed Columban 590, built his cell 614, and died 627 (*Acta SS.* 7 Oct. ii. 881). The sermon preached at John's consecration is his only extant work. It is in Latin, and is printed by Canisius (*Lect. Antiq.* i. 785 sq., ed. Basnage). Dempster, who makes St. Gall a native of Albanic Scotland, attributes various works to him (*Hist. Eccl. Gent. Scot.* i. 299–301). The letter to Desiderius attributed to him by Tanner (*Bibl. Brit.* p. 307) appears to belong to Gallus, bishop of Clermont, consecrated 650 (LANIGAN, ii. 439).

[Vita S. Columbani, Jonas, Acta SS. O. S. B. sæc. ii. 2 sq.; Vita S. Deicoli, Acta SS. Bolland. Jan. 18, ii. 563; Vita S. Galli ap. Pertz, Mon. Germ. Hist. i. 1, and Acta SS. Bolland. with commentary. This life is supposed to be by Weten (*fl.* 771), master of Walafrid Strabo, who wrote his Vita S. Galli, Acta SS. O. S. B. sæc. ii. 215,

about 833, see Hist. Lit. de la France, iv. 479; Vita S. Magni, Canisius Lect. Antiq. i. 655, not valuable; Lanigan's Eccl. Hist. of Ireland, ii. 287, 432, 438; Ozanam's Etudes Germ. ii. 122; Montalembert's Monks of the West, ii. 429; art. in Dict. Christ. Biog., by the Rev. J. Gammack.]
W. H.

GALL, RICHARD (1776–1801), Scottish poet, the son of a notary, was born at Linkhouse, near Dunbar, in December 1776. Having attended the parish school of Haddington, he was apprenticed at the age of eleven to his maternal uncle, a carpenter and builder. He afterwards became a printer's apprentice in Edinburgh, and there he gave his leisure to study. He then became travelling clerk to a Mr. Ramsay, in whose employment he remained till his death, 10 May 1801. His powers attracted considerable attention during his lifetime, and he enjoyed the friendship of Burns and Thomas Campbell. Several of his songs were set to music, and became popular. Two of these, 'The Farewell to Ayrshire,' and 'Now bank and brae are clad in green,' were falsely assigned to Burns; the former was sent by Gall to Johnson's 'Scots Poetical Museum,' with Burns's name prefixed, and the latter appeared in Cromek's 'Reliques of Burns.' An edition of Gall's 'Poems and Songs' was published at Edinburgh in 1819.

[Roger's Scottish Minstrel; Allan Cunningham's Songs of Scotland.]
W. B-E.

GALLAGHER, JAMES (*d.* 1751), bishop, was a member of the Ulster sept of O'Galchobhair, anglicised Gallagher. He entered the priesthood of the Roman catholic church, and was, at Drogheda, in November 1725 consecrated bishop of Raphoe, Donegal. In 1735 he published at Dublin seventeen 'Irish Sermons, in an easy and familiar style, on useful and necessary subjects, in English characters, as being the more familiar to the generality of our Irish clergy.' In his preface the author mentioned that he had composed those discourses principally for the use of his fellow-labourers, to be preached to their respective flocks, as his repeated troubles debarred him 'of the comfort of delivering them in person.' He added: 'I have made them in an easy and familiar style, and of purpose omitted cramp expressions which be obscure to both the preacher and hearer. Nay, instead of such, I have sometimes made use of words borrowed from the English which practice and daily conversation have intermixed with our language.' By propaganda in May 1737 Gallagher was translated from the bishopric of Raphoe to that of Kildare, and in the same year he was appointed administrator of the diocese of Leighlin. In

April 1741 Gallagher, then at Paris, gave a certificate in commendation of a treatise, in Irish and English, on the Christian doctrine, composed by Andrew Donlevy, D.D., director of an Irish community in that city. This work, with Gallagher's certificate prefixed, was printed in the following year at Paris by James Guerin. Gallagher evaded the penal laws against Roman catholic ecclesiastics, and died in May 1751. Of several editions of his sermons, that issued at Dublin in 1877 has an English translation.

[Works of Sir J. Ware, 1746; Hibernia Dominicana, 1762; Transactions of Iberno-Celtic Society, 1820; Brady's Episcopal Succession, 1876; Comerford's Collections on Kildare and Leighlin, 1883.] J. T. G.

GALLAN, Saint (*fl.* 500). [See GRELLAN.]

GALLEN-RIDGEWAY, first BARON (1565?-1631). [See RIDGEWAY, SIR THOMAS.]

GALLENSIS, JOHN (*fl.* 1215), canon lawyer. [See WALLENSIS.]

GALLIARD, JOHN ERNEST (1687 ?-1749), musical composer, born about 1687, was son of a French hairdresser at Zell. His first music teacher was one Marschall; he afterwards learnt composition from Farinelli, director of concerts at Hanover (uncle to the celebrated sopranist), and Steffani. A printed catalogue of music formerly in Steffani's possession has the entry: 'Mr. Galliard's first lessons for composition under the tuition of Sig. Farinelli and Abbate Steffani, at the age of fifteen or sixteen, in 1702' (HAWKINS). He adopted the oboe as his instrument, and wrote in 1704 a sonata for oboe and two bassoons, on the manuscript of which is the following note in his own handwriting: 'Jaij fait cet air a Hannover, que Jaij Joué a la Serenade de Monsieur Farinelli ce 22me Juin, 1704' (*ib.*) He is said to have come to England in 1706, and to have been appointed chamber musician to Prince George of Denmark. Hawkins says that it was on the death of Draghi that Galliard received the sinecure appointment of organist at Somerset House, but it is probable that Draghi [q. v.] left the country long before Galliard's arrival. In the early part of his residence in England he composed various 'occasional' anthems, &c., for thanksgivings after victories; a Te Deum and Jubilate, and three anthems, 'I will magnify thee, O Lord,' 'O Lord God of Hosts,' and 'I am well pleased,' are mentioned. His connection with the stage, which lasted till 1736, began in 1712, with his setting of Hughes's opera 'Calypso and Telemachus,' performed at the Queen's Theatre in the Haymarket. This

work, sung by somewhat inferior singers, survived only five representations. Nicolini was on the point of leaving England at the time, and was not cast for a part in it; he encouraged and applauded it, and for this is praised in the 'Spectator' of 14 June 1712 (No. 405). Its failure was partly due to the serious character of its sentiments (BURNEY), and partly to the schemes of the friends of Italian opera (HAWKINS). It was afterwards revived with considerable success. In the following year he played in the orchestra of the Queen's Theatre, having an oboe solo in the accompaniment of the last air of the first act of Handel's 'Teseo.' From 1717 onwards he was constantly employed by Rich to provide music for the pantomimes, &c., that were given at Covent Garden and Lincoln's Inn Fields. His 'Pan and Syrinx,' to words by Lewis Theobald, was performed at the latter theatre in 1717. The list of works written for Rich is as follows: 'Jupiter and Europa,' and 'The Necromancer, or Harlequin Dr. Faustus,' pantomimes, 1723; 'Harlequin Sorcerer, with the Loves of Pluto and Proserpine,' pantomime, 1725; 'Apollo and Daphne; or the Burgomaster tricked,' pantomime, 1726; 'The Rape of Proserpine' (farce by Theobald), 1727; 'Circe' (also by Theobald); and 'The Royal Chace; or Merlin's Cave,' 1736. Music to Lee's 'Œdipus' was written, but not printed; the manuscript was in the library of the Academy of Ancient Music. 'The Royal Chace' contained the song 'With early Horn,' by the singing of which Beard won immense popularity. Galliard's other works comprise six English cantatas, set to words by J. Hughes, Congreve, and Prior; a sonata for flute, published at Amsterdam as op. 1; six sonatas for bassoon or violoncello, and six for flute or violin. In 1728 he wrote a two-part setting, in the style of his master Steffani, of the Morning Hymn of Adam and Eve, from 'Paradise Lost.' This was improved by Dr. Cooke, by the addition of orchestral parts and the rearrangement of certain numbers as choruses, and was published in this form in 1773. In his later years Galliard led a retired life. In 1742 he brought out a translation of Pier Francesco Tosi's 'Opinioni di Cantori Antichi e Moderni,' under the title of 'Observations on the Florid Song; or Sentiments on the Ancient and Modern Singers.' From the similarity of certain turns of expression, &c., with those employed by the anonymous translator (1709) of Abbé Raguenet's 'Parallèle,' Hawkins conjectured that translation to be by Galliard. The interest attaching to the discovery of the translator's identity is on account of a very outspoken 'Critical Discourse upon Operas in England,' &c., printed at the end of the translation. Burney points out that it would hardly be possible for Galliard to have obtained so thorough a command of English by this time. On the other hand the fearlessness of the criticism would seem to imply that the author was new to the ways of London musicians, and the question can hardly be considered as settled either way. In 1745 Galliard had a benefit performance at Lincoln's Inn Fields Theatre, at which was performed his music to the Duke of Buckingham's 'Julius Cæsar,' and a composition for twenty-four bassoons and four double basses. Hawkins says that music by Galliard to the same author's 'Brutus' was also performed at this concert; but in the Rev. J. Duncombe's 'Letters by Several Eminent Persons,' &c., 1773, ii. 63, it is stated that 'Brutus' was written not by Galliard, but by Buononcini. His last appearance as an oboist was probably, according to Burney, in 1722, on the occasion of his benefit, when he accompanied Mrs. Barbier in a song. He died early in 1749, and his collection of music was sold by auction soon afterwards. At the time of his death he was engaged upon an opera, 'Oreste e Pilade.' He was a prominent member of the Academy of Vocal Music (see *Add. MS.* 11732).

[Hawkins's Hist. ed. 1853, pp. 805, 828, &c.; Burney's Hist. iv. 639; Grove's Dict. i. 578; Fétis's Biographie Univ. des Musiciens; Companion to the Playhouse, 1764, vol. ii.; Walther's Musicalisches Lexikon; works in Brit. Mus. Cat., &c.] J. A. F. M.

GALLINI, GIOVANNI ANDREA BATTISTA, called SIR JOHN (1728–1805), dancing-master, born at Florence on 7 Jan. 1728, emigrated to England in an almost destitute condition about 1753, in which year he made his début at the Opera House, Haymarket, as a ballet-dancer, and achieved a remarkable and rapid success, so that the next season he was appointed principal dancer, and soon afterwards director of the dances, and finally stage-manager of that theatre. He also acquired great vogue as a dancing-master, and in that capacity was admitted into the house of the third Earl of Abingdon, where he won the heart of the earl's eldest daughter, Lady Elizabeth Peregrine Bertie, whom he married, though when or where remains uncertain. She had, however, assumed the name of Gallini in 1766, when (13 Oct.) she gave birth to two sons (*Gent. Mag.* 1766, p. 494). She lived for some years with Gallini on terms of affection, but they afterwards agreed to live separate. She died on 17 Aug. 1804. During a tour in Italy Gallini so delighted the pope by his dancing that he was honoured with

the knighthood of the Golden Spur, on the strength of which, though it conferred no right to the prefix, Gallini, on his return to England, assumed and was popularly conceded to have the title of Sir. By a fire which, on the night of 27 June 1789, destroyed the London Opera House, Gallini lost 400,000*l.* He is said to have advanced 300,000*l.* towards the rebuilding of it in the Italian style. Soon after the completion of the edifice he retired from the management, and the remainder of his life he spent in teaching dancing. He built the Hanover Square concert rooms, in part of which he resided until his death, which occurred suddenly in the morning of 5 Jan. 1805. Through his wife he acquired the manors of Hampstead Norris and Yattendon in Berkshire. There is a mural tablet in Yattendon church to his memory and that of his wife.

Gallini published: 1. 'A Treatise on the Art of Dancing,' London, 1762, 1765, 1772, 2 vols. 8vo (largely borrowed, with scant acknowledgment, from Louis de Cahusac's 'La Danse Ancienne et Moderne,' 3 tom., The Hague, 1754, 12mo). 2. 'Critical Observations on the Art of Dancing; to which is added a Collection of Cotillons, or French Dances,' London, 1770? 8vo.

[Collins's Peerage (Brydges), iii. 634; Gent. Mag. 1804 p. 795, 1805 p. 90; Notes and Queries, 2nd ser. ix. 147, 290; Doran's Knights and their Days. p. 472; Hist. of Newbury, 1839, p. 228; Watt's Bibl. Brit.] J. M. R.

GALLOWAY, SIR **ARCHIBALD** (1780?–1850), major-general and Indian writer, was the son of James Galloway of Perth. He obtained a cadetship in 1799, and on 29 Oct. 1800 was appointed ensign in the 14th Bengal native infantry. He afterwards served in the 29th, 10th, and 2nd Bengal native infantry regiments, and was gazetted colonel of the 58th Bengal native infantry on 22 Sept. 1836. Galloway took part in the defence of Delhi, and distinguished himself greatly by his gallantry at the siege of Bhurtpore. He was appointed by Lord William Bentinck a member of the military board, and was nominated a companion of the Bath on 20 July 1838 (*London Gazette,* 1838, ii. 1661). On 24 Sept. 1840 he was elected a director of the East India Company, and on 23 Nov. 1841 received the rank of major-general.

Galloway was decorated with the K.C.B. on 25 Aug. 1848 (*ib.* 1848, iii. 3157), and in the following year became chairman of the East India Company. He died in Upper Harley Street on 6 April 1850, aged 70. Galloway was thanked for his many and varied services to the Indian government by 'commanders-in-chief in India on nine different occasions, and by the supreme government of India, or the court of directors, and superior authorities in England on upwards of thirty occasions' (*Gent. Mag.* new ser. xxxiii. 660). By his wife, whose maiden name was Adelaide Campbell, and to whom he was married on 28 Nov. 1815, he left three sons and six daughters. An engraved portrait of Galloway was published by Dickinson of New Bond Street in August 1850. He was the author of the following works: 1. 'A Commentary on the Moohummuddan Law.' 2. 'Notes on the Siege of Delhi in 1804, with Observations on the position of the Indian Government under the Marquess of Wellesley,' 8vo. 3. 'On Sieges of India.' This work is said to have been reprinted, on the recommendation of General Mudge, by the court of directors, and used at their military college, and to have been distributed to the army for general instruction by the orders of the Marquis of Hastings (*ib.* p. 661). 4. 'Treatise on the Manufacture of Gunpowder.' 5. 'Observations on the Law and Constitution and present Government of India,' &c., second edition, with additions, London, 1832, 8vo.

[Chambers's Biog. Dict. of Eminent Scotsmen, 1869, ii. 75–6; Anderson's Scottish Nation, 1863, ii. 276; Gent. Mag. 1816 vol. lxxxvi. pt. i. p. 562, 1850 new ser. xxxiii. 660–2; Annual Register, 1850, App. to Chron. p. 218; Dod's Peerage, &c. 1850, p. 222; East India Registers and Army Lists; Dodwell and Miles's Indian Army List, 1838, pp. 116–17; Notes and Queries, 6th ser. xii. 288, 435.] G. F. R. B.

GALLOWAY, JOSEPH (1730–1803), lawyer, was born near West River, Anne Arundel, in Maryland, America, in 1730. Early in life he went to Philadelphia, where he speedily rose to eminence as a lawyer and politician, becoming speaker in the General Assembly of Pennsylvania. In the disputes between the proprietary interest and the assembly he took part with Franklin on the popular side. In May 1764 he supported a petition in favour of having the governors nominated by the king instead of the proprietors of the province, which was under discussion in the assembly. His speech, with a long preface by Franklin, was published in Philadelphia, and reprinted in London. John Dickinson, who had taken the other side, challenged him, and wrote a pamphlet against him. At the beginning of the rebellion Galloway was elected a member of the first congress in 1774, and submitted a plan for establishing a political union between Great Britain and the colonies. The scheme found little favour, but was published, with copious explanatory notes, in a pamphlet entitled 'A Candid Examination of the Mutual Claims of Great Britain and the Colonies,' New York and London, 1775.

In December 1776 the Howes issued a proclamation of indemnity, of which Galloway took advantage, and joined the British army under Sir William Howe. His accession was regarded as so important that he was allowed 200*l.* a year from the date when he joined the army till some other provision could be made. When Philadelphia was taken in 1777 he was appointed a magistrate of police for that city, with a salary made up to 300*l.* a year, and 6*s.* a day more for a clerk. He was likewise appointed superintendent of the port, with a salary of 20*s.* a day, making in all upwards of 770*l.* a year. When Philadelphia was evacuated in June 1778, he left for England. The insults to which he was subjected by the opposite party upon his departure are mentioned in a passage of John Trumbull's Hudibrastic poem 'MacFingal:'

> Did you not in as vile and shallow way
> Fright our poor Philadelphian Galloway?
> Your Congress, when the daring ribald
> Belied, berated, and bescribbled:
> What ropes and halters you did send,
> Terrific emblems of his end,
> Till, lest he'd hang in more than effigy,
> Fled in a fog the trembling refugee.

In 1779 he was examined before the House of Commons, when he said that he had left estates and property worth more than 40,000*l.* This evidence was published in one volume 8vo, London, 1779, and in 1855 was reprinted at Philadelphia by the council of the Seventy-six Society. He likewise published in 1779 'Letters to a Nobleman on the Conduct of the War in the Middle Colonies,' accusing General Howe of gambling and gross neglect of duty. A rejoinder by Sir William Howe was speedily followed by 'A Letter to Lord Howe on his Naval Conduct,' in which both brothers were charged with misconduct. He afterwards published 'Cool Thoughts on the Consequences of the American Rebellion,' and 'Historical and Political Reflections on the American Rebellion' (early in 1780).

Galloway's remaining years were devoted to a study of the prophecies. In 1802 and 1803 he published in two elaborate volumes: 1. 'Brief Commentaries upon such parts of the Revelations and other prophecies as immediately refer to the present times,' &c. 2. 'The Prophetic or Anticipated History of the Church of Rome, written and published six hundred years before the rise of that Church; in which the prophetic Figures and Allegories are literally explained, and her

Tricks, Frauds, Blasphemies, and dreadful Persecutions of the Church of Christ are foretold and described; prefaced by an Address, dedicatory, expostulatory, and critical, to the Rev. Mr. Whitaker, Dean of Canterbury;' to which is added 'A Pill for the Infidel and Atheist,' &c. He died at Watford, Hertfordshire, on 29 Aug. 1803. One daughter survived him.

[London Monthly Review, vols. xxxii. l. lii., &c.; Gent. Mag. 1780, 1803; Letter and Statement by General Howe, 1779; Trumbull's MacFingal, a satirical poem in four cantos, Hartford, 1782; Franklin's Life and Works, London, 1806; Duycknick's Cyclopædia of American Literature, vol. i.] J. T.

GALLOWAY, PATRICK (1551?–1626?), Scottish divine, was born about 1551. In 1576 he was appointed minister of the parishes of Foulis Easter and Longforgan, Perthshire. On 14 Nov. 1580 he was called to the Middle Church at Perth, and admitted on 24 April 1581. In June 1582 James VI came to Perth with his favourite, Esme Stuart, first duke of Lennox. Lennox had possessed himself of the revenues of the see of Glasgow, having prevailed on Robert Montgomery, minister of Stirling, to become a 'tulchan bishop,' with a pension of eight hundred marks. Galloway preached about this transaction; the privy council sustained his right to do so; yet Lennox obtained an order forbidding Galloway to preach so long as the king stayed in Perth. He went to Kinnoul and preached there, and again preached before the king at Stirling, after the raid of Ruthven, on 22 Aug. 1582. He was suspected of being privy to the plot of this famous raid, which issued in the banishment of Lennox. The king's other favourite, James Stewart, earl of Arran, kept his eye on Galloway, and at length, in April 1584, got an order for his apprehension. He kept out of the way, hiding for some time in the neighbourhood of Dundee. Hearing that his house in Perth had been searched, he fled to England in May. Here he preached in London, and afterwards in Newcastle-on-Tyne. In November 1585 he was permitted to return to his charge in Perth. The general assembly appointed him in 1586 visitor for Perthshire, and in 1588 visitor for Dunkeld and Perth.

Galloway, though no courtier, was a moderate man in church matters, and on this account found favour with the king, who employed him in editing some religious writings from his royal pen, sent for him to Edinburgh in 1590, and made him on 18 March minister in the royal household. On 4 Aug. of the same year he was elected moderator of the general assembly. He openly rebuked

the king on 3 Dec. 1592 for bringing back Arran to his counsels. He refused to subscribe the 'band,' or engagement, by which James sought on 20 Dec. 1596 to bind all ministers not to preach against the royal authority, objecting that their existing pledges of loyalty were sufficient. After the Gowrie conspiracy in August 1600, he twice preached before the king, at the cross of Edinburgh on 11 Aug., and at Glasgow on 31 Aug., maintaining the reality of the danger which the king had escaped. Calderwood says that his first 'harangue' did not persuade many, 'partly becaus he was a flattering preacher,' and partly because he named 'Andro Hendersoune' as the armed man in the study, and the king denied this. On 10 Nov. 1602 Galloway was again chosen moderator of the general assembly.

In January 1604 he was in attendance on James at Hampton Court, and acted as the medium of a communication from the Edinburgh presbytery to the king, in reference to the conference held in that month between the hierarchy and the representatives of the 'millenary' petitioners. Galloway was present during the actual conference. Of the preliminary proceedings on 14 Jan., when the king and privy council met the bishops and deans in private, he gives a hearsay account, which, brief as it is, throws more light on the attitude of the hierarchy than is shed by the official narrative of William Barlow (d. 1613) [q. v.] Galloway represents the bishops as arguing with great earnestness that to make any alterations in the prayer-book would be tantamount to admitting that popish recusants and deprived puritans had suffered for refusing submission to what 'now was confessed to be erroneous.' His statement of the 'great fervency' with which James urged instances of 'corruptions' in the Anglican church is confirmed by the remark, ascribed to Lancelot Andrewes [q. v.], that the king 'did wonderfully play the puritan for five hours,' though of this Barlow gives no hint.

Galloway was popular as a preacher, and his services were sought in 1606 as one of the ministers of St. Giles's, Edinburgh; first on 3 June by the town council, then on 12 Sept. by the sessions of the four congregations which met in different parts of the edifice. He was not, however, appointed till the end of June 1607. In 1610, and again in 1615 and 1619, he was a member of the high commission court. On 27 June 1617 he signed the protestation for the liberties of the kirk, directed against the legislative measures by which James sought to override the authority of the general assembly. The most obnoxious of these measures having been withdrawn, Galloway withdrew his protest. He gave a warm support to the five articles of Perth in August 1618, and did his best to carry out at St. Giles's in 1620 the article which enjoined kneeling at the communion. Of his last years little is known, and the exact date of his death is uncertain. It occurred before 10 Feb. 1626, and probably in January of that year, though it has been placed as early as 1624. He is described as 'a man of manie pensions,' some of which came from the abbey revenues of Scone, Perthshire. He was twice married: first in May 1583 to Matillo Guthrie (d. 1592); secondly, to Mary, daughter of James Lawson, minister at Edinburgh. He left two sons and two daughters. His eldest son, Sir James Galloway of Carnbee, Fifeshire, was created Baron Dunkeld in 1645. His grandson, the third baron, was outlawed in 1689 after Killiecrankie, and the title forfeited; he became a field officer in the French army, an example followed by his only son, with whom the line expired.

Galloway published: 1. 'Catechisme,' London, 1588, 8vo (WATT). 2. 'A Short Discourse of the . . . late attempts at his Majesty's person,' Edinburgh, 1600, 12mo. Posthumous were: 3. 'The Apology . . . when he fled to England' (1584); 4 and 5, the substance of his two sermons before James in 1600; and 6, his letter (10 Feb. 1604) to the Edinburgh presbytery, describing the Hampton Court conference; all first printed in Calderwood (1678). For James VI he edited 'A Fruitefull Meditation,' &c. (on Rev. xx.), 1588, 4to, and 'A Meditation,' &c. (on 1 Chron. xv.), 1589, 4to.

[Hew Scott's Fasti Eccles. Scotic.; Neal's Hist. Puritans, 1822, ii. 10 sq.; Bannatyne Miscell. 1827, i. 139 sq.; Cardwell's Hist. of Conferences, 1841, p. 212 sq.; Calderwood's Hist. Kirk of Scotland, 1842-9, iv. 110, v. 118, 521, vi. 50, 77, 241, vii. 436, &c.; Grub's Eccl. Hist. of Scotland, 1861, ii. 226 sq.; Anderson's Scottish Nation, 1870, ii. 105.] A. G.

GALLOWAY, THOMAS (1796-1851), mathematician, son of William Galloway and his wife, Janet Watson, was born in the parish of Symington, Lanarkshire, on 26 Feb. 1796. William Galloway occupied Symington mill. His father was a mechanical engineer, in high favour with John Carmichael, third earl of Hyndford [q. v.] After attending the parish schools of Symington and Biggar, and the New Academy, Lanark, Thomas Galloway became a student in the university of Edinburgh in November 1812. He was intended for the ministry. In 1811 some French prisoners came to live in his neighbourhood. Two of them were good mathe-

maticians, and from them he acquired a knowledge of the French mathematical methods. In 1815-16 he gained a prize for the solution of some mathematical problems, and was thenceforth Professor Wallace's favourite pupil. In 1820 he had completed the usual course and taken the degree of M.A., but did not apply for license, having now become satisfied that his vocation was the teaching of science. Professor Wallace assisted him in obtaining teaching and literary work, and thus two years were spent in Edinburgh. In 1823 he was elected a teacher of mathematics in the Royal Military College, Sandhurst, where 'his accuracy of knowledge and business-like habits rendered him both efficient and popular' (memoir in Transactions of the Royal Society). He married a daughter of Professor Wallace in 1831. On the death of Sir John Leslie in November 1832 he was one of three selected candidates for the chair of natural philosophy in the university of Edinburgh. Towards the close of 1833 he might have been appointed professor of astronomy in the same university, but meanwhile he had accepted the office of registrar or actuary to the Amicable Life Assurance Company of London, an office which he filled during the remainder of his life. He died from spasm of the heart, after some months of illness, at his residence, Torrington Square, London, on 1 Nov. 1851, and was buried at Kensal Green.

On 13 Feb. 1829 Galloway was elected a fellow of the Astronomical Society, and soon afterwards a fellow of the Royal Society. From 1843 he was on the council of the Royal Society. He contributed to the 'Transactions' (part i.) for 1847 a memoir on 'The Proper Movement of the Solar System,' for which the royal medal was presented to him on 30 Nov. 1848. His conclusion was that the data for a solution of the problem are as yet insufficient. He was a member of the council of the Royal Astronomical Society in 1834, one of the vice-presidents in 1837 and 1848, foreign secretary in 1842, one of the two secretaries in 1847, and a member of council in 1851. The 'Memoirs' of the society for 1846 contain a paper by him upon the 'Ordnance Survey of England,' and among the 'Monthly Notices,' in the fifth volume, a paper on 'The Present State of our Knowledge in relation to Shooting Stars.' An account of him was read at the annual meeting of the society on 13 Feb. 1852. He had on his deathbed enjoined the biographer 'that neither strength nor length of eulogy should be inserted in the report,' but his accuracy, mathematical ability, and knowledge of scientific history are adequately estimated. Galloway wrote the article 'Pendulum' for the

'Edinburgh Encyclopædia' (1830) and contributed to the seventh edition of the 'Encyclopædia Britannica' articles on 'Astronomy,' 'Balance,' 'Calendar,' 'Chronology,' 'Comet,' 'Figure of the Earth,' 'Precession of the Equinoxes,' and 'Probability.' The last paper was also issued in a separate volume. He wrote also in the 'Edinburgh Review,' his first contribution (No. 101, year 1830) being on 'The Recent History of Astronomical Science.' He also wrote for the 'Philosophical Magazine.' Among his later papers are some on 'Double Stars of the Southern Hemisphere,' 'The Dodo and its Kindred,' 'The Numeral Expression of the apparent Magnitude of the Stars,' and an article of eight pages on 'The Statistics of Coal.'

[Register of Births in Symington parish, 1796; Survey of Lanarkshire, 1796; Matriculation Roll of Edinburgh University, 1812; Transactions of the Royal Astronomical Society, 1829, &c.; obituary notice at annual meeting, 13 Feb. 1852; Transactions of the Royal Society, including obituary notice read on 1 Dec. 1851; Edinburgh Encyclopædia, vol. xvi.; Encyclopædia Britannica, 7th edit., and information from the publishers; Edinburgh Review, li. 81–114; Philosophical Magazine, xxxii. 318–26, xxxiii. 145–154, 407–77.]
J. T.

GALLY, HENRY, D.D. (1696–1769), divine and classical scholar, son of the Rev. Peter Gally, a French protestant refugee, was born at Beckenham, Kent, in August 1696. He was admitted a pensioner of Corpus Christi College, Cambridge, under the tuition of Mr. Fawcett, 8 May 1714, and became a scholar of that house in the following July. He graduated B.A. in 1717, M.A. in 1721, and was upon the king's list for the degree of D.D., to which he was admitted 25 April 1728, when George II visited Cambridge. In 1721 he was chosen lecturer of St. Paul's, Covent Garden, and on 23 Nov. in the same year was instituted to the rectory of Wavendon or Wandon, Buckinghamshire, on the presentation of his father (LIPSCOMBE, Buckinghamshire, iv. 396). Lord-chancellor King appointed him his domestic chaplain in 1725, and preferred him to a prebend in the church of Gloucester, 15 May 1728, and to another in the church of Norwich in 1731 (LE NEVE, Fasti, i. 450, ii. 498). He also presented him to the rectory of Ashney or Ashton, Northamptonshire, in 1730, and to that of St. Giles-in-the-Fields in 1732. Gally now resigned the rectory of Wavendon, in which he was succeeded by his father. The king made him one of his chaplains in ordinary in October 1735. Gally died on 7 Aug. 1769.

He was author of: 1. 'The Misery of Man,' 1723; being the substance of two sermons preached at St. Paul's, Covent Garden. 2. 'The Moral Characters of Theophrastus, translated from the Greek with notes. To which is prefixed a critical essay on Characteristic-Writings,' London, 1725, 8vo; dedicated to Lord Carteret, lord-lieutenant of Ireland. 3. 'The Reasonableness of Church and College Fines asserted, and the Rights which Churches and Colleges have in their Estates defended,' 1731, when a bill was introduced into the House of Commons to alter the tenure of their estates, and to ascertain the fines payable on the renewal of their leases. It was written in answer to a treatise by 'Everard Fleetwood,' i. e. S. Burroughs, to which replies were also written by Dr. Roger Long and Dr. William Derham [q.v.]. 4. 'A Sermon preached before the House of Commons on June 11, 1739, being the anniversary of his majesty's accession.' 5. 'Some Considerations upon Clandestine Marriages,' 1750, 8vo (two editions). This pamphlet was noticed in parliament in the debates on the Marriage Act (EARL OF ORFORD, Works, v. 37). 6. 'A Dissertation against pronouncing the Greek Language according to accents,' 1754, 8vo (anon.) 7. 'A second Dissertation against pronouncing the Greek Language according to accents, in answer to Mr. [John] Foster's Essay,' 1763, 8vo (anon.) These two essays were reprinted with Foster's 'Essay on the different nature of Accent and Quantity,' 1820.

He edited 'Some Thoughts concerning the proper method of Studying Divinity,' by W. Wotton, DD.

[Addit. MS. 5870, f. 128; Cantabrigienses Graduati (1787), p. 152; Gent. Mag. xxxix. 414; Lamb's Corpus Christi Coll. p. 469; Masters's Corpus Christi Coll. p. 291; Nichols's Lit. Anecd. ii. 274.]
T. C.

GALMOY, third VISCOUNT (1652–1740). [See BUTLER, PIERCE.]

GALPINE, JOHN (d. 1806), author of 'Synoptical Compend of the British Flora,' was elected an associate of the Linnean Society 20 Feb. 1798; the preface to his work above cited was dated Blandford, 1 Jan. 1806, and he died before 24 May of the same year. After his death three enlarged editions were printed by a London bookseller, dated respectively 1819, 1829, 1834.

[Archives, Linnean Society.]
B. D. J.

GALT, JOHN (1779–1839), novelist, was born 2 May 1779 at Irvine in Ayrshire. His father commanded a West-Indiaman. His mother was a woman of much character, shrewd, full of humour, and quaintly original in conversation. Galt as a child was delicate and sensitive, fond of ballads and story-books. At the age of ten his family removed to Greenock, and Galt completed at various schools the desultory education begun at home and at the grammar school of Irvine. He was then placed in the Greenock custom-house to acquire some clerkly experience, whence he was transferred to a desk in a mercantile house in Greenock. He read in the public library and joined a literary society. He wrote a tragedy on the story of Mary Queen of Scots, which was followed by a poem on the 'Battle of Largs.' He contributed verses to local newspapers and to an Edinburgh magazine, and wrote a memoir of John Wilson, author of 'The Clyde,' for Leyden's 'Scottish Descriptive Poems' (1803). In the period of revolutionary excitement Galt already displayed his toryism. He contributed to newspapers quasi-Tyrtean verse and helped in forming two companies of riflemen, which he avers (*Autobiography*, i. 41) were 'the first of the kind raised in the volunteer force of the kingdom.' Though happy enough at Greenock as a clerk, he felt restless. An insulting letter was addressed to his firm by a Glasgow merchant about 1803. Galt, apparently unauthorised, followed the writer to Edinburgh, where he forced him to write a formal apology. Instead of returning triumphant to Greenock, Galt threw up his situation and migrated to London. While looking about him there he published his poem in octosyllabics on the 'Battle of Largs.' He suppressed it immediately after publication (extracts from it are printed in the 'Scots Magazine' for 1803 and 1804), apparently because poetry might clash with business, and entered into a commercial partnership with a young Scotchman. In its third year the concern came to grief through the misconduct of one of its correspondents.

Galt now entered at Lincoln's Inn (but was never called to the bar), and began a life of Cardinal Wolsey, suggested during a visit to Oxford, where he found materials in the library of Jesus College. His composition was suspended on obtaining employment which took him to the continent in order to ascertain how far British goods could be exported in defiance of the Berlin and Milan decrees. From Gibraltar to Malta he was a fellow-traveller with Lord Byron, whom he also met at Athens. After visiting Greece and Constantinople and Asia Minor he took a house at Mycone in the Greek Archipelago suitable for the purpose of introducing English merchandise. He afterwards formed a connection with the Glasgow firm of Kirkman Finlay (*d.* 1828) [q. v.], who had formed a similar scheme. The plan collapsed after some

further travel, and ultimately Galt returned to London. There he was engaged by Kirkman Finlay to proceed to Gibraltar, apparently with a view to a scheme for smuggling English goods into Spain. The victories of the Duke of Wellington gave, Galt says, a death-blow to his hopes. He would have lingered on at Gibraltar, but a painful disease forced him to return to England for surgical advice. About this time he made a happy marriage with Elizabeth, only daughter of Alexander Tilloch [q. v.], editor of the 'Philosophical Magazine,' to which he was an occasional contributor. With the first restoration of Louis XVI in 1814, Galt paid a visit to France and Holland to promote 'an abortive scheme,' and then he returned once more to London.

Galt had already published in 1812 (1) 'Voyages and Travels in the Years 1809, 1810, and 1811, containing . . . Statistical, Commercial, and Miscellaneous Observations on Gibraltar, Sardinia, Sicily, Malta, Serigo [*sic*], and Turkey;' (2) 'The Life and Administration of Cardinal Wolsey;' (3) 'The Tragedies of Maddalon, Agamemnon, Lady Macbeth, Antonia and Clytemnestra.' The 'Voyages and Travels,' containing some interesting matter, are disfigured by grave faults of style and by rash judgments. He proposed that England should seize and hold for the benefit of her trade all islands anywhere accessible. He attacked continental aristocracies and priesthoods, and was contemptuously noticed in the 'Quarterly Review' for June 1812 ; while his ignorance and faults of judgment and style were pointed out in a bitter article on his 'Life of Wolsey' in the same review for September 1812. The latter work contained some curious and previously unpublished matter relating to Scotland. A second edition appeared in 1817 ; a third, 1846, 'with additional illustrations,' formed vol. i. of the 'European Library,' edited by William Hazlitt the younger. Galt's tragedies were praised with bitter irony in the 'Quarterly Review' for April 1814, and pronounced by Scott to be 'the worst ever seen.' In 1812 he also edited for a short time the 'Political Review,' and to Stevenson's edition of Campbell's 'Lives of the Admirals,' published in that year, he contributed the biographies of Hawke, Byron, and Rodney, that of Admiral Byron being revised by Lord Byron. In 1813 appeared his 'Letters from the Levant.' In 1814 he persuaded Colburn to commence a monthly publication, 'The Rejected Theatre,' containing dramas which had been refused by London managers, and other unacted dramas. It appeared in 1814–15 as the 'New British Theatre' (4 vols.), edited by Galt, who in the preface assailed the monopoly of the London patent theatres. It contained several dramas of his own, with his translation of two of Goldoni's pieces. One of Galt's plays, published in it, 'The Witness,' attracted the favourable notice of Walter Scott's friend, William Erskine, through whose influence it was some years afterwards performed at the Edinburgh Theatre as 'The Appeal,' with a prologue ostensibly written by Professor Wilson, but which Galt believed to be the joint product of Lockhart and Captain Hamilton, the author of 'Cyril Thornton;' Scott himself, he asserts, composed for it a comic epilogue, but did not acknowledge it. In 1816 appeared anonymously Galt's first known fiction, 'The Majolo,' founded on a Sicilian superstition. It had become imperative to write for money. He was introduced to Sir Richard Phillips, to whose magazine he contributed, and for whom he executed sundry compilations. In 1816 appeared part i. of Galt's 'Life and Studies of Benjamin West . . . prior to his Arrival in England, compiled from materials furnished by himself.' Part ii., continued to West's death in 1820, did not appear until 1820. He also published his poem, 'The Crusade,' another failure. In 1818 he removed from London to Finnart, near Greenock, to carry out a commercial scheme, on the failure of which he returned to London to aid the passing through parliament of a bill promoted by the Union Canal Company of Scotland. This effected, he issued, as 'collected by Samuel Prior' (1820), 'All the Voyages round the World;' 'A Tour of Asia, abridged from the most popular Voyages and Travels, by the Rev. T. Clark' (1820?), a pseudonym which, on account, he says, of his borrowings in it from his own 'Letters from the Levant,' he also used on the title-page of 'The Wandering Jew, or the Travels and Observations of Harreach the prolonged,' a conglomerate of history, biography, travel, and descriptive geography; 'The Earthquake,' founded on the Messina earthquake of 1783; and 'Pictures, Historical and Biographical,' drawn from English, Scottish, and Irish history (1821). In 1822 he edited, with a preface, Alexander Graydon's 'Memoirs of a Life chiefly passed in Pennsylvania,' published at Harrisburg, 1811 (see Quarterly Review, xxvi. 364).

In 1820 Blackwood accepted for his new magazine 'The Ayrshire Legatees,' Galt's first literary success. It follows the lines of 'Humphry Clinker.' A completely original work, 'The Annals of the Parish,' was published separately in 1821. It had been begun in 1813, and its completion and publication was prompted by the success of 'The Ayrshire

Legatees.' It is an admirable picture of rural Scotland, and the shrewdness, simplicity, and piety of the supposed narrator are masterly. Its value as a contribution to the social history of the west of Scotland is considerable. Scott pronounced it to be 'excellent,' and it was highly praised by the venerable Henry Mackenzie in 'Blackwood's Magazine' and by Jeffrey in the 'Edinburgh Review.' John Stuart Mill (Utilitarianism, edition of 1864, p. 9 n.) says that he adopted the word 'utilitarian' from Galt's 'Annals of the Parish' (ch. xxxvi.) The word had been used by Bentham himself long previously (Works, x. 390). In 1822 Galt published the 'Steamboat,' a collection of travellers' tales, and 'The Provost,' a picture of Scottish character, in 'Blackwood,' and 'Sir Andrew Wylie,' the most popular of his novels in England. It includes a portrait of his patron, Lord Blessington, to whom the second edition was inscribed. In 1823 appeared 'The Gathering of the West,' a jeu d'esprit on George IV's visit to Scotland, and, separately, 'The Entail,' which both Sir Walter Scott and Lord Byron are said to have read thrice. Galt was now so elated by success as to boast (GILLIES, iii. 59) that his literary resources were superior to those of Scott, with whom he resolved to compete in historical fiction. Three forgotten novels were the result: (1) 'Ringhan Gilhaize' (1823), (2) 'The Spaewife' (1823), and (3) 'Rothelan' (1824). In 1824 appeared his compilation 'The Bachelor's Wife.'

In 1823 Galt went to reside at Esk Grove, near Musselburgh, where he formed an intimacy with D. M. Moir [q. v.] He was appointed agent for the claims of some Canadians for losses incurred during the war of 1814. A scheme for the purchase of crown land in the colony by a company, the proceeds to be applied in satisfying the claims of his clients, was suggested by him. The home government would not consent to the plan, but the Canada Company, as it was ultimately called, resolved to go on with the purchase on its own account, and appointed Galt to the post of secretary. Galt devoted himself exclusively to the interests of his new employers, having done his best, though unsuccessfully, for his former clients. The home government appointed a commission, with Galt as one of its members, to investigate the matter in Upper Canada. On its return discussions took place, during which Galt wrote 'The Omen' (1825), praised by Scott in 'Blackwood's Magazine,' and the 'Last of the Lairds' (1826). Towards the close of 1826 he returned to Canada to organise a system of operations. At the end of eight months he became the company's Canadian superintendent, and directed the execution of his plans for the settlement of its lands. He threw himself into his task with great energy and success. One of his first labours was to found the town of Guelph in what is now the province of Ontario. In 1872 the township contained a population of fifty thousand. The company, however, did not obtain an immediate profit; its stock fell; Galt quarrelled with the lieutenant-governor, Sir Peregrine Maitland, and was at last superseded.

Bitterly disappointed, Galt returned in 1829 to England, and had to meet heavy claims. He was unable to pay 80*l.* due to Dr. Valpy, a 'friend' of long standing, for the education of his sons. According to Gillies (iii. 60–1), he was not only arrested, but suffered a long detention which contributed to the subsequent breakdown of his health. He was now entirely dependent on his pen for the support of himself and his family, and, still sanguine, he calculated that he could make 1,000*l.* a year by it. His first work after his return was 'Lawrie Todd, or the Settlers in the Woods' (1830, reissued in 1831 as No. 21 of 'Standard Novels'), which contains some graphic sketches of settler life in America. In the same year appeared 'Southennan' and a 'Life of Lord Byron' (issued as No. 1 of G. R. Gleig's 'National Library'), which, though valueless, went through four editions, and was translated into French and German. It involved Galt in a controversy with Hobhouse. For a few months in 1830, at the instance of Lockhart and John Murray, Galt edited the tory evening newspaper the 'Courier.' In 1831 Galt went to live at Barnes Cottage, Old Brompton, where he was visited by the Countess of Blessington (see THOMSON, ii. 110–11). In the same year appeared his readable compilation 'The Lives of the Players' (reprinted in 1886), and a novel, 'Bogle Corbet, or the Emigrants.' Among the periodicals to which he contributed was the recently founded 'Fraser's Magazine.' Carlyle, who met him at a dinner party given by its proprietor, says in his journal (21 Jan. 1832): 'Galt looks old, is deafish, has the air of a sedate Greenock burgher; mouth indicating sly humour and self-satisfaction; the eyes, old and without lashes, gave me a sort of wae interest for him. He wears spectacles, and is hard of hearing; a very large man, and eats and drinks with a certain west-country gusto and research. Said little, but that little peaceable, clear, and *gutmüthig.* Wish to see him again.' In a letter of the following February Carlyle speaks of him as 'a broad gawsie

Greenock man, old-growing, loveable with pity.' In 1832 appeared (1) 'The Member,' a satire on borough-mongering and political jobbery; (2) 'The Radical;' and (3) 'Stanley Buxton, or the Schoolfellows,' a novel. In this year he had the first of a long series of attacks 'analogous to paralysis.' It destroyed his hopes of an active connection with the British North American Land Company, of which a board of directors had been appointed with himself for its provisional secretary.

In 1833 Galt issued a volume of 'Poems,' 'Stories of the Study,' 2 vols., a novel, 'Eben Erskine,' and supplied the letterpress for the first and only instalment of 'Ouranologos, or the Celestial Volume,' in which the effects of line-engraving were to be combined with those of mezzotint, John Martin designing and engraving for it 'The Eve of the Deluge.' In the same year appeared his 'Autobiography,' remarkable for the absence of querulousness and for self-complacency. This was followed in 1834 by his 'Literary Life and Miscellanies,' 3 vols. The volumes were dedicated by permission to William IV, who sent him 200*l.* Mrs. Thomson (ii. 115) speaks of one donation to him of 50*l.* from the Literary Fund. His three sons had now received appointments in Canada, where one of them, the present Sir Alexander Galt, rose to be finance minister of the Dominion. Galt, poor and paralysed, found, towards the close of 1834, a home at Greenock with an affectionate sister. He bore his sufferings with great fortitude and cheerfulness. In 1836 he edited, with an introduction, 'Forty Years' Residence in America exemplified in the Life of Grant Thorburn [the original Lawrie Todd], Seedsman, New York, written by himself;' in 1839 appeared vols. iii. and iv. of 'Lady Charlotte Bury's Diary, illustrative of the Times of George IV,' with his preface and an appendix of personal reminiscences. He died at Greenock 11 April 1839, and was buried in the family grave. 'The Demon of Destiny, and Other Poems,' was edited posthumously by his friend Harriett Pigott, and privately printed in 1840. In Blackwood's 'Standard Novels' (vols. i. ii. iv. vi.) are reprints of his best fictions, 'The Annals of the Parish,' 'The Ayrshire Legatees,' 'Sir Andrew Wylie,' 'The Entail,' with some of his minor pieces. He printed at the end of the 'Autobiography' a list of his writings, not including his numerous contributions to periodicals. It is reproduced, with insignificant additions, at the end of the volume of 'Poems.' In not a single case has he given the date of publication. Galt left two sons, Sir Alexander Tilloch Galt, premier of Canada [see SUPPLEMENT], and Thomas Galt, who became a judge.

There is a portrait of Galt with a value-less notice of him in 'Fraser's Magazine' for December 1831, both of which are reproduced in Bates's reprint from that periodical of its 'Gallery of Illustrious Literary Characters' (1873). Moir describes him in his forty-fourth year, when in the full vigour of health, as of 'herculean frame.' He was more than six foot in height. 'His hair was thin, jet black; his eyes small, but piercing; his nose almost straight; long upper lip, and finely rounded chin.' In society 'his manner was somewhat measured and solemn, and cha-racterised by a peculiar benignity and sweet-ness.' Mrs. Thomson (ii. 103–4), referring to his conversation, dwells on his remarkable 'gift of narrative.' 'He spoke in a low mo-notonous voice, with much of the Greenock accent marring its sweetness, but adding to its effect,' what he said being 'simple, suc-cinct, unambitious in phrase.'

[The chief authorities for Galt's career are his Autobiography and Literary Life. But both works, though diffuse, are provokingly deficient in dates and definiteness of detail, imperfections which are to some extent rectified in D. M. Moir's excellent and sympathetic memoir prefixed to vol. i. of Blackwood's Standard Novels. There are interesting personal reminiscences of Galt in vol. ii. of Mrs. Thomson's Recollections of Lite-rary Characters (1854), 'John Galt,' and a few of less value in R. P. Gillies's Memoirs of a Lite-rary Veteran, 1851.]   F. E.

GALTON, Miss MARY ANN (1778–1856), author. [See SCHIMMELPENNINCK.]

GALWAY, EARL OF (1648–1720). [See MASSUE DE RUVIGNY, HENRI DE.]

GAM, DAVID (d. 1415), Welsh warrior, is more properly styled DAVYDD AB LLEWELYN. 'Gam' is a nickname meaning 'squinting,' which, like other Welsh nicknames, became equivalent to a surname. David's father was Llewelyn, the son of Hywel, the son of Eineon Sais. Llewelyn possessed fair estates in the parishes of Garthbrengy and Llanddew, which lay within the honour or lordship of Brecon, a dependency of the earldom of Hereford, and after 1399 lapsed to the crown by the acces-sion of Henry IV, who had long enjoyed that earldom. Peytyn was the name of Llewelyn's chief residence. David is described in a verse attributed to Owain Glyndwr as a short red-haired man with a squint. He was faithful to his lord, Henry IV, even during the revolt of Owain [see GLENDOWER, OWEN]. He was rewarded for his services by a large share in the South Welsh lands confiscated from rebels in 1401 (WYLIE, Hist. of Henry IV, p. 245). There is a story that David plotted against the life of Owain when attending the

Welsh parliament at Machynlleth. But it rests on no early authority, misdates the year of the Machynlleth parliament, and wrongly makes David a brother-in-law of Owain. There seems nothing to show that David ever wavered in his allegiance.

David was taken prisoner by Owain, pro-bably at a time when Owain's successes were very few. On 14 June 1412 David's father, Llewelyn ab Hywel, and the seneschal and receiver of Brecon were empowered to treat with Owain, and by ransom or by capturing rebel prisoners to extricate David from his rigorous imprisonment (Fœdera, viii. 753). It is said that David soon after got into trouble by killing a kinsman in an affray in Brecon town. In 1415 David, accompanied by three foot archers only, followed Henry V on his invasion of France (NICOLAS, Battle of Agincourt, p. 379). It is reported that when, on the eve of the battle of Agincourt, he was questioned by the king as to the num-ber of the enemy, he replied 'that there were enough to be slain, enough to be taken pri-soners, and enough to run away.' The story, however, first appears in Sir Walter Raleigh's 'History of the World' (p. 451). David was slain at the battle of Agincourt, which was fought on 25 Oct. 1415. The contemporary chroniclers who notice his death simply de-scribe him as an esquire (WALSINGHAM, ii. 313; cf. 'Chronicles of London,' quoted in NICOLAS, pp. 279–80). There is a tradition that he was knighted for his valour when dying on the field of battle, and the fact that one chronicler says that two recently dubbed knights were slain (Gesta Henrici Quinti, p. 58, Engl. Hist. Soc.) is thought to bear out the story. But one writer at least mentions both the two knights and David Gam (NICOLAS, p. 280). Lewis Glyn Cothi, a Welsh poet of the next generation, who celebrated the praises of David's children and grandchildren, regularly speaks of him, however, as 'Syr Davydd Gam' (Gwaith, pp. 1, 8). It has been suggested that David is the original of Shakespeare's Fluellen. This is not at all an improbable conjecture, as Fluellen is plainly a corruption of Llewelyn, and David was generally called David Llewelyn, or ab Llewelyn. The reference to him in Raleigh shows also that his name was familiar to the age of Elizabeth.

David is said to have married Gwenllian, daughter of Gwilym, son of Hywel Grach. He left a family. His son Morgan became the ancestor of the Games of Breconshire. His daughter Gwladus was by her second husband, Sir William ab Thomas of Raglan, the mother of William, the first Herbert earl of Pembroke.

[Besides authorities quoted in the text the biography of Gam in Theophilus Jones's Hist. of Breconshire, i. 160–1, ii. 156–69, with pedigrees; the pedigrees in Lewys Dwnn's Heraldic Visitation of Wales (Welsh MSS.Society); Gwaith Lewis Glyn Cothi; Sir Harris Nicolas's Battle of Agincourt; Tyler's Hist. of Henry V.]

T. F. T.

GAMBIER, SIR EDWARD JOHN (1794–1879), chief justice of Madras, third son of Samuel Gambier, first commissioner of the navy (1752–1813), by Jane, youngest daughter of Daniel Mathew of Felix Hall, Essex, and nephew of Admiral James, baron Gambier [q. v.], was born in 1794 and entered at Eton in 1808. He afterwards proceeded to Trinity College, Cambridge, where he took his bachelor's degree in 1817. He was ninth senior optime, and junior chancellor's medallist; he proceeded M.A. in 1820, and became a fellow of his college. He was called to the bar at Lincoln's Inn 7 Feb. 1822, and acted as one of the municipal corporation commissioners in 1833. The recordership of Prince of Wales Island was conferred on him in 1834, and he was knighted by William IV at St. James's Palace on 6 Aug. in that year. He was removed to Madras 28 Nov. 1836 as a puisne judge of the supreme court, and raised to the chief justiceship there 11 March 1842, being sworn in on 22 May. The duties of this high post he discharged with ability and efficiency until his retirement in 1849, when he received from the Hindu community of Madras a testimonial consisting of a silver centre-piece weighing 550 ounces, and Lady Gambier was at the same time presented with a handsome tripod centre-piece by the European ladies of Madras (*Illustrated London News*, 1 Feb. 1851, p. 77, with views of the testimonials). 'A Treatise on Parochial Settlement,' which he published in 1828, went to a second edition under the editorship of J. Greenwood in 1835. He died at 22 Hyde Park Gate, Kensington, London, 31 May 1879, in his eighty-sixth year. He married in 1828 Emilia Ora, daughter of C. Morgell, M.P.; she died on 25 Feb. 1877.

[Times, 4 June 1879, p. 11; Law Times, 7 June 1879, p. 105.]

G. C. B.

GAMBIER, **JAMES** (1723–1789), vice-admiral, was the grandson of a Norman Huguenot who left France on the revocation of the edict of Nantes, brother of John Gambier, lieutenant-governor of the Bahamas, and uncle of James, lord Gambier [q. v.] He was made a lieutenant by Admiral Mathews in the Mediterranean in 1743, and, after serving in the Buckingham and Marlborough, was in April 1746 promoted to the command of the Speedwell sloop, employed in the North Sea. In December 1747 he was posted to the Flamborough, and after commanding many different ships was in February 1758 appointed to the Burford, in which he assisted at the reduction of Louisbourg, and in the following year at the capture of Guadeloupe and the unsuccessful attack on Martinique, coming home in time to take part in the battle of Quiberon Bay. While at Halifax in 1758, acting under orders from Boscawen, he destroyed a number of pestilent liquor sheds, and pressed the sutlers—a piece of good service which afterwards caused him much annoyance, some of the sutlers prosecuting him at common law, against which he was still, two years later, claiming the protection of the admiralty. After the battle of Quiberon Bay, the Burford continued attached to the grand fleet till the peace. From 1766 to 1770 he commanded the Yarmouth guardship at Chatham, and from 1770 to 1773 was commander-in-chief on the North American station, with his broad pennant in the Salisbury. In July 1773 he was appointed comptroller of victualling, but was almost immediately afterwards advanced to be resident commissioner of the navy at Portsmouth, a post which he held till his promotion to be rear-admiral on 23 Jan. 1778. He was then sent out to New York as second in command under Lord Howe, and was left for short intervals as commander-in-chief, first, on Howe's departure from the station, and, secondly, on Byron's leaving for the West Indies. On 26 Sept. 1780 he was advanced to the rank of vice-admiral, and in 1783–4 was commander-in-chief at Jamaica, with his flag on board the Europa. His failing health compelled his early return to England, and he died at Bath on 8 Jan. 1789. He was twice married, and left issue by his first wife.

[Charnock's Biog. Nav. vi. 42; Gent. Mag. lix. pt. i. 182; Official Correspondence in the Public Record Office.]

J. K. L.

GAMBIER, **JAMES**, BARON GAMBIER (1756–1833), admiral of the fleet, son of John Gambier, lieutenant-governor of the Bahamas, and nephew of Vice-admiral James Gambier (1723–1789) [q. v.], was born at New Providence on 13 Oct. 1756, and at the age of eleven was entered on the books of the Yarmouth, guard-ship at Chatham, then commanded by his uncle. He was made lieutenant on 12 Feb. 1777, while serving on the North American station, and a year afterwards was promoted to the command of the Thunder bomb, which a few months later was picked up by the French fleet under D'Estaing. Gambier was soon exchanged, and on 9 Oct. 1778 was posted to the Raleigh frigate, in which, in May 1779, he took part in the relief of Jersey, and in May 1780 in the capture of Charlestown by Arbuthnot. He had no further employment afloat till April 1793, when he commissioned the Defence of 74 guns for service in the Channel. Gambier's notions of religion and morality were much stricter than those in vogue at that time; the Defence was spoken of as 'a praying ship,' and it was freely questioned whether it was possible for her to be 'a fighting ship' as well. The doubt, if it really existed, was set at rest on 1 June 1794, when the Defence was the first ship to break through the enemy's line. She was then closely engaged by two or three French ships, and sustained heavy loss. All her masts were shot away. The story is told that towards the close of the battle, as she was lying a helpless log on the water, Captain Pakenham of the Invincible, passing within hail, called to Gambier in friendly banter: 'I see you've been knocked about a good deal: never mind, Jimmy, whom the Lord loveth he chasteneth.' Gambier's conduct had, however, attracted Howe's notice, and he was one of those specially recommended for the gold medal. In the following winter he was appointed to the Prince George of 98 guns, but did not go to sea in her, being nominated as one of the lords of the admiralty; and though he was promoted to be rear-admiral on 1 June 1795, and again, on 14 Feb. 1799, to be vice-admiral, he remained at the admiralty till February 1801, when he hoisted his flag in the Neptune, as third in command of the Channel fleet. In the spring of 1802 he went out to Newfoundland as governor and commander-in-chief on that station, and on his return after two years was reappointed to the admiralty, where he continued till the change of ministry in February 1806, during which time he, in concert with Sir Roger Curtis [q. v.], was mainly responsible for the omission from the revised 'King's Regulations and Admiralty Instructions' (1 Jan. 1806) of the order to enforce the salute to the king's flag from all foreign ships within the king's seas, an order that had been maintained since the time of King John, if not from the time of William the Conqueror.

Gambier seems to have been as ignorant of naval history as careless of naval prestige, and must be considered as one of the chief of the perpetrators of the official blunder which, in the warrant of 9 Nov. 1805, appointing admirals of the red, spoke of the rank as restored to the navy, whereas, in point of fact, it had never previously existed. By the extensive

promotion accompanying this warrant Gambier became an admiral. He was recalled to the admiralty in April 1807, but hoisted his flag in July on board the Prince of Wales in command of the fleet which proceeded to the Baltic, and, in concert with the army under Lord Cathcart [see CATHCART, SIR WILLIAM SCHAW, first EARL CATHCART], bombarded Copenhagen on 2–5 Sept. On the 6th negotiations were concluded, and the surrender of the town and ships of war formally agreed to on the 7th. The ships, as many as were seaworthy, were hastily equipped, and on 21 Oct. the fleet, the transports, and the Danish navy sailed for England. The achievement was not one from which much glory accrued to either navy or army, for the British force was, both afloat and ashore, overpoweringly superior to the Danish. The strategical and political advantages were, however, very great, and the government bestowed rewards as though for a brilliant victory. Gambier was raised to the peerage as Lord Gambier; Cathcart was made a viscount; and the other flag or general officers were made baronets. Gambier resumed his seat at the admiralty, but vacated it in the following spring to take command of the Channel fleet. The period of his command, otherwise uneventful, was marked by the blockade of the French fleet in Basque Roads in the spring of 1809, and the attempt to destroy it by a flotilla of fireships and infernals, under the immediate orders of Lord Cochrane [see COCHRANE, THOMAS, tenth EARL OF DUNDONALD], who had been sent out by the admiralty for the special purpose. Gambier had already expressed his horror of that mode of warfare, and had pronounced the attempt to be hazardous, if not dangerous. It may well be that he was annoyed at this slight to his sentimental and professional opinions, and at being virtually superseded by a junior officer; it may well be also that Cochrane's manner was not calculated to remove Gambier's prejudice. There is no doubt that they disliked each other; that Cochrane considered Gambier as a canting and hypocritical methodist, while Gambier looked on Cochrane as a rash and insolent youngster, and though obliged, by the orders of the admiralty, to give him nominal support, steadily refused to make that support effective. The success was, therefore, very partial, and Gambier, on learning from the first lord of the admiralty that Cochrane would oppose the vote of thanks for the destruction of the French ships, at once applied for a court-martial. The admiralty was unwilling to grant it, but, finding that it could not be withheld, resolved that at any rate the board and Gambier, as the board's nominee, should be held blameless. Care was taken to assemble a friendly court; the president, Sir Roger Curtis, was a personal friend of Gambier's; as many inconvenient witnesses as possible were sent out of the way; and thus, after a grossly partial trial, Gambier was 'most honourably acquitted,' 9 Aug. 1809. He retained the command of the Channel fleet till 1811, after which he had no naval service, though in 1814 he was one of the commissioners for negotiating a treaty of peace with the United States. On 7 June 1815 he was nominated a G.C.B., and on 22 July 1830 was promoted to the rank of admiral of the fleet. He died on 19 April 1833. His portrait, by Sir William Beechey (Royal Academy, 1809), was exhibited at South Kensington in 1868, lent by the family. He married in 1788, but left no issue.

Gambier's long connection with the board of admiralty, his command at Copenhagen, and the scandal of Basque Roads have given his name a distinction not altogether glorious. His conduct on 1 June 1794 prevents any imputation of personal cowardice, but emphasises the miserable failure in April 1809, which certainly suggests that he was out of place in command of a fleet. He seems, indeed, to have had a very distinct preference for life on shore, and one of the most noticeable features in his career is the shortness of the time he spent at sea, which between his promotions to lieutenant and to rear-admiral amounted in all to five and a half years. His experience was thus extremely limited, nor have we any reason to suppose that his ability in any one point had a wider range. His kinship with the Pitts and Lord Barham stood him in good stead.

[The Memorials, Personal and Historical, of Admiral Lord Gambier, by Henrietta Georgina, Lady Chatterton [q. v.], a daughter of Gambier's sister, is, for the most part, a crude collection of correspondence which has no reference to Gambier; its general interest is slight, and it has no naval or biographical value whatever. See also Ralfe's Naval Biography, ii. 82; Marshall's Roy. Nav. Biog. i. 74; Lord Dundonald's Autobiography of a Seaman; Minutes of the Court-martial, 1809; James's Naval Hist. 1860, iv. 201, 395.] J. K. L.

GAMBLE, JOHN (d. 1687), musician and composer, was apprenticed (WOOD) to Beyland, one of Charles I's violinists, and afterwards played at a London theatre. In 1656 (according to the title-page) he published 'Ayres and Dialogues to be sung to the theorbo, lute, or base violl,' many of the verses for which were by Thomas Stanley. This music won Gamble renown at Oxford,

and Anthony à Wood in July 1658 was proud to entertain him and another eminent musician after their performance at Will Ellis's meeting-house. A second book of 'Ayres and Dialogues, for one, two, and three voyces,' was published in 1659 (GROVE); a manuscript commonplace book, formerly in the possession of Dr. Rimbault, but now in America, containing songs by Wilson for the 'Northern Lass,' and many compositions by H. and W. Lawes, as well as common songs and ballads, bears the same date (CHAPPELL). Gamble's admission to the king's household dated from the Restoration; his services as 'musitian on the cornet' were available at the Chapel Royal, where in 1660 the want of trained boys' voices was supplied by wind instruments and men's falsetto, and where at a later date cornets and sackbuts were employed on Sundays, holy days, and collar-days to heighten the effect of the music. Docquet-warrants of 1661 and 1663 record Gamble's claim to wages of twenty pence per diem and 16l. 2s. 6d. per annum for livery, from the midsummer of 1660; a petition in 1666 represents Gamble as having lost all his property in the fire of London; his name also appears in an exchequer document of 1674 (RIMBAULT, Roger North, 99) as one of the musicians in ordinary, with a salary of 46l. Gamble is said (WOOD, MS. Notes) to have played the violin in the king's band, and to have been composer of lessons for the king's playhouse. He signed a will in 1680, leaving his books of music and 20l. due to him out of the exchequer to his grandson, John Gamble, 'now servant to Mr. Strong,' cutting off other relatives with a shilling, and bequeathing the residue to his widow. Gamble died in 1687, advanced in years. His portrait, engraved by T. Cross, is prefixed to the volume of 'Ayres' of 1656.

[Wood's manuscript lives of English Musicians, Bodleian; Wood's Fasti, vol. i. col. 517; Wood's Life, p. 32; Locke's Practice of Music, 1673, p. 19; State Papers, Charles II, Dom., communicated by Mr. W. B. Squire; Rimbault's Memoirs of Roger North, p. 99; Chappell's Popular Music, i. 378; Chamberlayne's Angliæ Notitia, iii. 227; P. C. C. Registers of Wills; Grove's Dictionary, i. 580; Musical Times, xviii. 428.] L. M. M.

GAMBLE, JOHN (d. 1811), writer on telegraphy, was a member of Pembroke College, Cambridge, graduated B.A. 1784, M.A. 1787, became a fellow of his college, was chaplain to the Duke of York, and chaplain-general of the forces. He published (London, 1795) a quarto pamphlet of twenty pages entitled 'Observations on Telegraphic Experiments, or the different Modes which have been or may be adopted for the purpose of

Distant Communication.' This made some stir in the scientific world, and encouraged the writer to produce a more ambitious 'Essay on the different Modes of Communication by Signals' in 1797. This contained a number of elaborate and ingenious illustrative plates. The book gave a concise history of the progressive movements in the art of communication from the first beacon light to the telegraphy of the writer's day, with many valuable suggestions. Gamble, who was much esteemed in scientific circles, civil as well as military, died at Knightsbridge on 27 July 1811. He held the rectory of Alphamstone, and also that of Bradwell-juxta-mare, Essex. The latter was a most valuable living.

[Gent. Mag. 1811, ii. 193; Sabine's Hist. and Progress of the Electric Telegraph.] J. B-y.

GAMBOLD, JOHN (1711–1771), bishop of the Unitas Fratrum, was born on 10 April 1711 at Puncheston, Pembrokeshire. He received his early education from his father, William Gambold, a clergyman, and in 1726 entered as a servitor at Christ Church, Oxford. His taste was for poetry and the drama, but his father's death in 1728 preyed upon his spirits, and for a couple of years he abandoned himself to religious melancholy. In March 1730 he introduced himself to the acquaintance of Charles Wesley, his junior by two years, who had entered at Christ Church in the same year. Charles brought him under the influence of John Wesley, who admitted him to the society of the Oxford methodists, the 'Holy Club,' as it was called. Gambold's account (written in 1736) of the customs and pursuits of this society is of considerable historical value. He was much indebted to Wesley, but was 'slow in coming into his measures,' his turn being towards quietism rather than evangelistic activity. He shut himself up to the study of the earlier Greek fathers, and was captivated by their mysticism.

In September 1733 he was ordained by John Potter, bishop of Oxford, and in 1735 was instituted to the vicarage of Stanton-Harcourt, Oxfordshire. Here his sister kept house for him, and for about two years (1736–8) Keziah Wesley (youngest surviving sister of his friend) was a member of his household. Gambold attended to the duties of his small parish, but spent much time in retirement. He was working his way out of mysticism; John Wesley, on his return from Georgia (February 1738), found him 'convinced that St. Paul was a better writer than either Tauler or Jacob Behmen.' Wesley introduced him to the Moravian missionary, Peter Boehler, who gave addresses at Oxford

in Latin, Gambold acting as interpreter. Next year he met Count Zinzendorf, and was much impressed by him; at a later date he was the interpreter of Zinzendorf's German addresses. His religious musings found expression in a dramatic piece, the most important of his poems, written in 1740. In December of that year he had a visit from his younger brother, who gave him an account of the London Moravians; he was attracted by the homely warmth of their fellowship. Accompanying his brother to London (1741) he came under the influence of Philip Henry Molther. On 2 July 1741 he broke with Wesley. He preached before the university of Oxford on 27 Dec. 1741 a sermon of rather high church tinge. In October 1742 he resigned his living, having been for some little time with the Moravians in London. He was admitted a member of their society in November, while teacher in a boarding-school at Broadoaks, Essex. On 14 May 1743 he married Elizabeth, (b. 7 Dec. 1719, d. 13 Nov. 1803), daughter of Joseph Walker of Littletown, Yorkshire, and went to live in Wales, keeping a school at Haverfordwest, Pembrokeshire.

In November 1744 Gambold returned to London and became a stated preacher at Fetter Lane. In December 1745 Wesley found him unwilling to renew their former intercourse; they met again in 1763, but Gambold was still shy, yet Wesley spoke of him to the last (1770) as one of the most 'sensible men in England.' Gambold took part, in March 1747, in a synod of the brethren at Herrnhaag in the Rhine provinces. In 1749 he addressed a letter to Zinzendorf, proposing the formation of an 'Anglican tropus,' a plan for the admission, as Moravian brethren, of persons who should still remain members of the church of England. Gambold was willing to concede that an Anglican prelate should exercise some supervision in Moravian affairs, and assist at their ordinations; also that the common prayer-book should be adopted in their assemblies. The latter provision was not carried out; but, at a synod in London in September 1749, Wilson, the aged bishop of Sodor and Man, was chosen 'antistes' of the 'reformed tropus' (with liberty to employ his son as substitute), and accepted the office.

In 1753 the Moravian community was weakened by the secession of Benjamin Ingham [q. v.] and his following. Gambold exerted himself to repair the loss. At a synod held at Lindsey House, Chelsea, he was consecrated a 'chorepiscopus' in November 1754 by Bishops Johannes de Watteville, John Nitschmann, and David Nitschmann the younger. Till 1768 his home was in London, but his duties often took him on his travels. He had much to do with the reorganisation of Moravianism at the synod of Marienborn in July and August 1764, four years after Zinzendorf's death. In 1765 he founded the community at Cootehill, co. Cavan. His health failed in 1768, owing to a 'dropsical asthma,' and he retired in the autumn to Haverfordwest. There he continued his ministrations until three days before his death, which occurred on 13 Sept. 1771. He left a son and daughter. His portrait was painted by Abraham Louis Brandt, a Moravian minister; from this there is a fine mezzotint (1771) by Spilsbury, a reduced and inferior copy drawn by Hibbart (1789), and a small engraving by Topham (1816). His contemporaries were struck by his likeness 'in person and in mien' to Dr. Johnson (*Gentleman's Magazine*, 1784, p. 353).

Gambold never had an enemy, but he made few friends. The hesitations of his career are in part to be explained by the underlying scepticism of his intellectual temperament, from which he found refuge in an anxious and reclusive piety. This appears in his poems, e.g. 'The Mystery of Life,' his epitaph for himself, in which occurs the line, 'He suffered human life—and died,' and still more in his letters. His very remarkable 'Letter to a Studious Young Lady,' 1737, contains a curious argument to show that any absorbing pursuits will elevate the mind equally well. In an unpublished letter (15 April 1740) to Wesley he writes: 'I hang upon the Gospel by a mere thread, this small unaccountable inclination towards Christ.' He draws his own picture in the character of Claudius, the Roman soldier of his drama. His verse is often striking, and never conventional; many of his hymns have become widely known.

He published: 1. 'Christianity, Tidings of Joy,' &c., Oxford [1741], 8vo (university sermon). 2. 'Η καινὴ διαθήκη,' &c., Oxford, 1742, 12mo (Mill's text, Bengel's divisions; Gambold's name does not appear). 3. 'Maxims . . . of Count Zinzendorf,' &c., 1751, 8vo. 4. 'A Modest Plea,' &c., 1754, 8vo. 5. 'A Collection of Hymns,' &c., 1754, 8vo, 2 vols. (to this collection, edited by Gambold, he contributed eleven translations and twenty-eight original hymns; he had previously contributed to collections of Moravian hymns, printed in 1748, 1749, and 1752; a hymnbook for children is said to have been printed by his own hand at Lindsey House). 6. 'The Reasonableness and Extent of Religious Reverence,' &c., 1756, 8vo. 7. 'A Short Summary of Christian Doctrine,' &c., 1765, 12mo;

2nd edit. 1767, 12mo (catechism, in which the answers are entirely in the language of the Book of Common Prayer). Posthumous was 8. 'The Martyrdom of St. Ignatius,' &c., 1773, 8vo (written 1740; edited by Benjamin La Trobe). He assisted in editing the 'Acta Fratrum Unitatis in Anglia,' &c., 1749, 8vo; edited an edition of Lord Bacon's 'Works,' 1765, 4to, 5 vols.; revised the translation of Cranz's 'History of Greenland,' 1767, 8vo, 2 vols., and contributed prefaces, &c., to many Moravian publications from 1752 onward. He is said to have translated Rees Pritchard's 'Divine Poems' from Welsh into English. His works were first published at Bath in 1789, 8vo, with anonymous 'Life' by La Trobe. Thomas Erskine of Linlathen (1788–1870) [q. v.] re-edited them, Glasgow, 1822, 12mo; 2nd edit. 1823, 12mo. His 'Poetical Works' (not including the hymns) were published in 1816, 12mo (preface dated 'Darlington, 17 April').

[Life by La Trobe, 1789; Cranz's Hist. of the Brethren (trans. by La Trobe), 1780; Nichols's Anecdotes of W. Bowyer, 1782; Klinesmith's Hist. Records relative to the Moravian Church, 1831; Tyerman's Oxford Methodists, 1873; Gambold's Works; his manuscript letters among the large collection of unpublished documents formerly in the hands of Henry Moore, one of John Wesley's literary executors, now in the possession of J. J. Colman, esq., M.P.; information from Rev. S. Kershaw.] A. G.

GAMELINE (*d.* 1271), lord-chancellor of Scotland and bishop of St. Andrews, was one of the 'Clerici Regis Alexandri II' and archdeacon of St. Andrews. He was made lord-chancellor in 1250, and in 1254 was appointed one of the chaplains of Pope Innocent IV. In December 1255 he was elected to the see of St. Andrews by the prior and the convent of St. Andrews, the Culdees having been excluded from voting in the election. The appointment was confirmed by the king and council. He was consecrated the same year upon a warrant from the pope to Bishop Bondington of Glasgow. Pope Alexander IV commanded Gameline, December 1259, to prohibit King Alexander III from seizing the property of the church. This command was repeated by the same pope four years after, dated and sent to Gameline from Avignon. The bishop got into disfavour at court, and was banished from Scotland. He went to Rome to lay his case before the pope, who decided in his favour, excommunicated his adversaries, and ordered the sentence to be proclaimed throughout Scotland. A complaint was made by the pope to the king of England against the king of Scotland for encroaching upon the rights of the church and churchmen. Henry III of England ordered the baillies of the Cinque Ports to arrest Gameline should he enter England, saying : ' Whereas Master Gameline, Bishop of St. Andrews, has obtained, not without great scandal, certain requests at the court of Rome to the prejudice of our beloved and faithful son, Alexander, king of Scotland, who is married to our daughter, on which account we are unwilling to allow him to enter our dominions. . . . Given at Windsor January 1258.' Gameline baptised in 1263 the son of Alexander III, who died at the age of twenty. He himself died in 1271, and was buried at the north side of the high altar of his cathedral.

[Chronicle of Melrose, Keith, Fordun, Wynton, Rymer ; Gordon's Eccles. Chronicle, i. 162–9.]

J. G. F.

GAMGEE, JOSEPH SAMPSON (1828–1886), surgeon, eldest son of Joseph Gamgee, veterinary surgeon, now of Edinburgh, was born on 17 April 1828 at Leghorn, where his father was then residing. In 1829 the family removed to Florence, where young Gamgee was educated first at a private school, and afterwards at the public school. In 1847 he went to London, and entered as a student at the Royal Veterinary College, his father desiring him to follow his own profession. An introduction to Moncreiff Arnott, professor of surgery at University College, who gave him admission to his classes, followed by admission in 1848–9 to Professor Sharpey's and Dr. C. J. B. Williams's lectures, led the latter, who was pleased with his work, to suggest his joining the medical profession. This he did, first obtaining a veterinary diploma. In the University College medical school Gamgee was a most successful student, gaining several gold medals, and the Liston prize for surgery in 1853. In 1854 he became M.R.C.S. Engl., and early in 1855 was appointed surgeon to the British Italian Legion and had charge of the hospital at Malta during the Crimean war.

In 1857 Gamgee was appointed surgeon to the Queen's Hospital, Birmingham, and his services to the hospital and the medical school connected with it were of the highest value for many years. The structural arrangements of the hospital were largely improved and its funds benefited by his exertions. In 1873 he was mainly instrumental in starting the ' Hospital Saturday' collections in Birmingham, especially in factories and workshops, and his services were recognised by a presentation of four hundred guineas and an address by residents of Birmingham. This was but a sample of his services in matters of public health and medical reform. He was at various times president of the Birmingham and Midland branch of the British Medical Association and of the Birmingham Medical Institute. He was strongly opposed to indiscriminate hospital relief, and advocated thorough reorganisation of hospital out-patient departments. He vigorously supported the claims of the members of the Royal College of Surgeons to direct representation on its council, and of the members of the profession to direct representation on the general medical council. During the Franco-German war (1870–1) he was secretary of the Birmingham Society for Aid to the Wounded, and turned his surgery into an ambulance depôt. In 1881, after a severe attack of hæmaturia, he retired from active hospital work, and was appointed consulting surgeon ; but he continued to carry on a considerable practice. About the end of September 1886, while staying at Dartmouth, he slipped and fell, fracturing the neck of the femur. Later this injury was followed by uræmic poisoning, of which he died on 18 Sept., in his fifty-ninth year. He married in 1860 Miss Marion Parker, by whom he had seven children, of whom two sons and two daughters survived him. Mrs. Gamgee wrote all his works from his dictation, and materially aided in his literary work.

Gamgee was a surgeon of great practical skill and marked individuality. He was a strenuous advocate of the treatment of wounds by dry and infrequent dressing, and by rest and immobility, and he was an opponent of the extremes of Listerism. In 1853, at Florence, he had met the eminent Belgian surgeon, Baron Sentin, who had introduced the treatment of fractures by starched apparatus and bandages, and this treatment was the subject of his Liston prize essay and of his lifelong teaching. Several of his surgical appliances were largely adopted, especially by the army medical department, and his cotton wool absorbent pads, gauze tissue, and his millboard and paper splints are very widely used. The use of cotton wool was first suggested to him by reading Mathias Mayor's ' La Chirurgie Simplifiée,' Brussels, 1842 ; but its improved manufacture in an antiseptic condition was largely due to his suggestions. He was a brilliant operator, an excellent teacher, and a thoughtful and acute surgical attendant. His command of several continental languages gave him an extensive acquaintance with continental medical men and literature. For many years he was a frequent contributor to the ' Lancet.' A dramatic, fluent, and enthusiastic speaker, he had great influence on general and professional audiences. A conservative and church-man, he was tolerant and liberal-minded, and was much valued as a friend. He was most helpful to younger practitioners, and a great benefactor to the poor.

Gamgee wrote, besides several pamphlets: 1. 'On the Advantages of the Starched Apparatus in the Treatment of Fractures and Diseases of the Joints,' 1853. 2. 'Reflections on Petit's Operation, and on Purgatives after Herniotomy,' 1855. 3. 'Researches in Pathological Anatomy and Clinical Surgery,' 1856. 4. 'Medical Reform, a Social Question,' two letters to Viscount Palmerston, 1857. 5. 'History of a successful case of Amputation at the Hip Joint,' 1865. 6. 'Hospital Reform,' a speech, 1868. 7. 'Medical Reform,' 1870. 8. 'Lecture on Ovariotomy,' 1871. 9. 'On the Treatment of Fractures of the Limbs,' 1871. 10. 'On the Treatment of Wounds; Clinical Lectures,' 1878. A second edition of his works on fractures and wounds, consolidated and improved, appeared in 1883, entitled 'On the Treatment of Wounds and Fractures.' 11. 'On Absorbent and Antiseptic Surgical Dressings,' 1880. 12. 'The Influence of Vivisection on Human Surgery,' 1882.

[Birmingham Daily Gazette and Daily Post, 20 and 23 Sept. 1886; Lancet, 25 Sept. 1886, pp. 590, 607, 2 Oct. 1886, p. 658; Brit. Medical Journal, 25 Sept. 1886; information from Mr. Joseph Gamgee and Mrs. J. S. Gamgee.]
G. T. B.

GAMMAGE, ROBERT GEORGE (1815–1888), chartist leader and historian, born at Northampton in 1815, was apprenticed to a coachbuilder, and began his political career at the early age of seventeen, when he became a member of the Working Men's Association. He was a deputy to the national convention of 1838, convened to discuss the revolutionary programme, and in 1842 devoted himself to the work of lecturing on behalf of chartist principles in order to revive the spirit of the country. After two years of this work he settled at Northampton, and became chartist secretary for the district. In this capacity he was brought into frequent contact with Feargus O'Connor, whom he opposed. At this time he was by trade a shoemaker. In 1848, losing his employment at Northampton on account of his political propagandism, he removed to Birmingham. In 1852 he was the 'nominated' chartist parliamentary candidate at Cheltenham, but did not go to the poll. In 1853 he was elected into the paid executive of the National Charter Association, but next year failed to secure re-election. In 1854 he published his 'History of the Chartist Movement,' a work of no ability,

but moderate in tone and of considerable interest. After some years of study he qualified as a medical man, in which capacity he practised, first as assistant to Dr. Heath of Newcastle, and then alone at Sunderland. He died at Northampton 7 Jan. 1888.

[Gammage's Hist. of the Chartist Movement; Place MSS.; Newcastle Weekly Chronicle, 14 Jan. 1888; private information.]
E. C. K. G.

GAMMON, JAMES (*fl.* 1660–1670), engraver, is known by a few works, which, though they possess little merit as engravings, are valued for their rarity. They are for the most part poor copies of better known engravings. Gammon resided in London, and was employed by the booksellers. Among his engravings were portraits of James I, Charles I, Charles II, Catherine of Braganza, James, duke of York, Henry, duke of Gloucester, Mary, princess of Orange, Duke and Duchess of Monmouth, Richard Cromwell, George Monck, Duke of Albemarle (a copy from Loggan's print), Sir Tobias Mathew (prefixed to his 'Letters,' 1660), Edward Mascall the painter, and others. A portrait of Ann, duchess of Albemarle, was engraved by a Richard Gammon 'against Exeter House in ye Strand,' probably a relative of James.

[Strutt's Dict. of Engravers; Dodd's MS. History of Engravers (Brit. Mus. Addit. MS. 33401); Catalogue of the Sutherland Collection; Walpole's Anecdotes of Painting, ed. Dallaway and Wornum.]
L. C.

GAMON or GAMMON, HANNIBAL (*fl.* 1642), puritan divine, descended from a family originally resident at Padstow in Cornwall, was the eldest son of Hannibal Gamon, who married Frances Galis of Windsor, and settled as a goldsmith in London. He matriculated from Broadgates Hall, Oxford, on 12 Oct. 1599, at the age of seventeen, when he was described as the son of a gentleman, and he took the degrees of B.A. on 12 May 1603 and M.A. on 27 Feb. 1607. He was instituted to the rectory of Mawgan-in-Pyder, on the north coast of Cornwall, on 11 Feb. 1619, on presentation of Elizabeth Peter, the patroness for that turn on the assignment of Sir John Arundel, knight, the owner of the advowson. He was also nominated a chaplain to the first Lord Robartes, whom he aided in collecting the quaint library, mainly of divinity and philosophy, still preserved at Lanhydrock, near Bodmin. Many of the books have Gamon's autograph on the title. The collection includes several manuscript volumes in his handwriting, containing theological and medical notes and prescriptions. A letter at Lanhydrock from

J. Beauford of St. Columb Major, written in 1645, makes mention of his sons, Hannibal and Philip, and of his daughters. His ministry, says Wood, was 'much frequented by the puritanical party for his edifying and practical way of preaching.' On 20 April 1642 he was designated, with Gaspar Hickes of Landrake, as the representative of Cornwall in the Westminster Assembly of divines. Gamon does not seem to have taken his place in the assembly, possibly on account of the remoteness of his residence, and his absence from its proceedings appears to have given offence. Walker, in his 'Sufferings of the Clergy' (ii. 249), professes to have been informed that Gamon was 'so miserably harass'd that it broke his heart.' There is a gap in the parish registers from 1646 to 1660, and the date of his death is unknown. He signed the herald's visitation of Cornwall in 1620, and is stated therein to have married Eliza, daughter of the Rev. James Rilston of St. Breock. His son and heir, also called Hannibal, was then 'three quarters old,' and matriculated from Brasenose College, Oxford, on 9 March 1638.

Gamon was the author of a funeral sermon upon 'Ladie Frances Roberts' (London, 1627), and two assize sermons at Launceston in 1621 (London, 1622) and 1628 (London, 1629). A long letter from Degory Wheare to him, dated April 1626, is in Wheare's 'Epistolæ Eucharisticæ,' 1628 (pp. 85–93), and a short epistle is printed in Wheare's 'Charisteria' (p. 133), both of which works are included in Wheare's volume with the general title of 'Pietas, erga benefactores.'

[Wood's Athenæ Oxon. ed. Bliss, iii. 103–4; Fasti, pt. i. pp. 299, 306; Commons' Journals, ii. 535; Visit. of Cornwall (Harl. Soc.), ix. 74, 77; Boase and Courtney's Bibl. Cornub. vols. i. and iii.; Arber's Stationers' Registers, iv. 64, 170, 212; Edwards's Libraries, ii. 154; Hetherington's Westm. Assembly, ed. 1878, p. 104; Diocesan Registers at Exeter.]   W. P. C.

GANDELL, ROBERT (1818–1887), professor of Arabic at Oxford, youngest son o Thomas Gandell, was born in London in 1818, and educated at the Mill Hill school and King's College, London. He graduated in 1843 at Queen's College, Oxford, where he was Michel fellow from 1845 to 1850. In 1861 he was appointed Laudian professor of Arabic, in 1874 prebendary of Ashill in Wells Cathedral, and in 1880 canon of Wells Cathedral. He lectured on Hebrew for Dr. Pusey for many years. In 1859 he edited for the Oxford University Press a reprint of Lightfoot's 'Horæ Hebraicæ' with great care and accuracy. He further contributed a commentary (on conservative lines) upon the books of Amos, Nahum, and Zephaniah to the 'Speaker's Commentary.' He died in October 1887.

[Burgon's Lives of Twelve Good Men, vol. i. preface.]   D. S. M.

GANDOLPHY, PETER (1779–1821), jesuit, born in London on 26 July 1779, was son of John Vincent Gandolphi or Gandolphy of East Sheen, Surrey, by Anna Maria, daughter of Benedict Hinde of Worlaby, Lincolnshire. He was educated under the jesuits of the English province, partly at Liège academy and partly at Stonyhurst College, where on 4 Oct. 1801 he was appointed to teach humanities. He left Stonyhurst in 1804, and after receiving holy orders was appointed to the mission at Newport, Isle of Wight. Subsequently he was attached to the Spanish Chapel, Manchester Square, London, where he obtained great celebrity as a preacher. By the publication of his 'Liturgy' and his sermons 'in defence of the ancient faith' he incurred the displeasure of his ecclesiastical superior, Bishop Poynter, who suspended him and denounced his works. Gandolphy proceeded to Rome in order to appeal against the bishop's decision. There he obtained in 1816 official approbations of the two censured works from Stephen Peter Damiani, master of sacred theology and apostolic penitentiary at St. Peter's, and from Francis Joseph O'Finan, prior of the Dominican convent of St. Sixtus and St. Clement. The Sacred Congregation of Propaganda, wishing to terminate the controversy, by letters dated 1 March 1817, required that Gandolphy should be restored to the possession of his former missionary faculties on apologising to Bishop Poynter for whatever might have been disrespectfully stated by him in an address to the public hastily printed some months previously, and of which the bishop had complained to the holy see. Gandolphy accordingly drew up and subscribed an apology on 15 April (*Orthodox Journal*, v. 172). In a pastoral letter dated 24 April the bishop declared the apology to be insufficient. On 8 July Gandolphy made a full and unconditional apology in obedience to the bishop's demands.

From this humiliation he never recovered. In 1818 he resigned his chaplaincy at Spanish Place, and retiring to the residence of his relatives at East Sheen, died there on 9 July 1821.

Dr. Oliver says that Gandolphy 'wrote too rapidly not to err against theological precision,' but Bishop Milner remarks that there was 'no heterodox or dangerous principle in his mind.'

His works are: 1. 'A Defence of the Ancient Faith; or five sermons in Proof of the Christian Religion,' London, 1811, 8vo. 2. 'Congratulatory Letter to the Rev. Herbert Marsh, D.D. . . . on his judicious Inquiry into the consequences of neglecting to give the Prayer-Book with the Bible. Together with a Sermon on the inadequacy of the Bible to be an exclusive Rule of Faith, inscribed to the same,' London, 1812, 8vo, reprinted in 'The Pamphleteer' (1813), i. 413. This elicited a reply from Marsh, and several controversial pamphlets. 3. 'A Second Letter to the Rev. Herbert Marsh confirming the opinion that the vital principle of the Reformation has been conceded by him to the Church of Rome,' London, 1813, 8vo, reprinted in 'The Pamphleteer,' ii. 397. 4. 'Liturgy, or a Book of Common Prayer, and administration of Sacraments, with other Rites and Ceremonies of the Church. For the use of all Christians in the United Kingdom,' London, 1812, 12mo; Birmingham, 1815, 12mo. 5. A sermon on the text 'Render to Cæsar the things which are Cæsar's,' &c., London, 1813, 8vo. 6. 'A Defence of the Ancient Faith, or a full Exposition of the Christian Religion in a series of controversial sermons,' 4 vols., London, 1813–15, 8vo. 7. 'Letters addressed to the Archbishop of Canterbury, and the Protestant Clergy of England . . . or a Reply to the Calumnies and Slanders advanced against the Catholic Petitioners,' London, 1813 and 1817, 8vo. 8. 'Vetoism illustrated to future generations; or a letter to the editor of the "Ami de la Religion et du Roi," in answer to an article in the same journal,' London, 1819, 8vo. 9. 'Letter to a noble Lord on the conduct of Sir J. Cox Hippisley at Rome,' London, 1819, 8vo. 10. 'Lessons of Morality and Piety; extracted from the Sapiential Books of Holy Scripture,' London, 1822, 8vo.

[Baker's Hist. of St. John's (Mayor), ii. 834–841; Biog. Dict. of Living Authors, pp. 125, 431; Bodleian Cat.; De Backer's Bibl. des Écrivains de la Compagnie de Jésus (1869), i. 2029; Foley's Records, vii. 286; Gent. Mag. vol. lxxxiii. pt. ii. p. 362, vol. lxxxiv. pt. i. p. 470, vol. xci. pt. ii. pp. 185, 200; Gillow's Bibl. Dict.; London and Dublin Orthodox Journal (1842), xv. 103; Lowndes's Bibl. Man. (Bohn), p. 861; Oliver's Jesuit Collections, p. 98; Orthodox Journal, iv. 317, 350, 396, 405, v. 80, 163, 172, 176, 177, 203, 205, 232, 269, 378, vii. 428; Watt's Bibl. Brit.]   T. C.

GANDON, JAMES (1743–1823), architect, born in New Bond Street, London, on 29 Feb. 1742–3 at the house of his grandfather, a Huguenot refugee, was the only son of Peter Gandon, by his marriage with a Welsh lady named Wynne. He received a good classical and mathematical education and developed an early taste for drawing. His father having nearly ruined himself by a passion for alchemy, Gandon entered Shipley's drawing academy in St. Martin's Lane. In 1757 he was awarded a premium by the Society of Arts, and on the arrival of Sir William Chambers in London he became first a general assistant in his office, but afterwards his articled pupil. About 1765 he commenced business for himself, contributed to the Spring Gardens exhibitions in that and the succeeding years, and was chosen a member of the Free Society of Artists. In conjunction with John Woolfe, architect to the board of works, Gandon published a continuation of Colin Campbell's 'Vitruvius Britannicus,' 2 vols. fol. London, 1767–71, which contains (ii. 77–80) his design, obtained in competition, for the county hall and prison at Nottingham, erected in 1769–70, at a cost of 2,500l. In 1767 he exhibited at the Incorporated Society of Artists 'a mausoleum to the memory of Handel, erected in the demesne of Sir Samuel Hillier in Staffordshire.' On the foundation of the Royal Academy in 1768 he became a student, and won the first gold medal awarded in architecture (1769). In 1769 he obtained the third premium of thirty guineas for a design for the Royal Exchange, now the City Hall, Dublin (erected by T. Cooley); and in 1776 that of one hundred guineas for the New Bethlehem Hospital, London (erected by J. Lewis). Between 1774 and 1780 he exhibited drawings at the Royal Academy. After refusing a somewhat uncertain offer of court employment in Russia, he went to Dublin in 1781 to superintend the construction of the new docks, stores, and custom-house, the plans of which he had made in 1780 at the instance of Lord Carlow (afterwards Lord Portarlington). The building was completed in 1791. Gandon had to struggle against the nature of the ground and the armed opposition of the residents near the old custom-house. In 1784 he designed the united court-house and gaol for the city and county of Waterford, in 1785 the east portico and ornamented circular screen wall to the Parliament House in Dublin (since altered for the bank). Shortly afterwards the western screen and the Foster Place portico were added from his designs of 1786, under the superintendence of a Mr. Parke. On 3 March 1786 were laid the foundations of the Four Courts, Dublin, also from his designs. Part had been erected by T. Cooley in 1776–84. The courts were first used on 8 Nov. 1796; in 1798 the east wing of the offices was commenced; and in 1802 the screen, arcade, and wings of the offices were also completed by him. He was still harassed by an opposition which was carried into the Irish Parliament. He presented drawings for the Military Hospital in Phœnix Park (carried out under W. Gibson); in 1791–4 erected Carlisle Bridge; and on 1 Aug. 1795 laid the first stone of the King's Inns, Henrietta Street. In anticipation of the rebellion he removed to London in 1797, but returned in 1799 to finish the Inns of Court. About 1806 he defended himself in a vigorous letter against Lord-chancellor Redesdale, who had expressed dissatisfaction at the progress of the work. Resigning the control of the Inns of Court to his pupil, H. A. Baker, he retired in 1808 to Lucan, near Dublin, where he had bought, in 1805, an estate called Canon Brook. The improvements which he effected in planting are eulogised by contemporary writers (cf. CARLISLE, *Topographical Dict. of Ireland*, s.v. 'Canon Brook'). He prepared plans for private residences and further improvements in Dublin architecture. None of the latter were carried out. The small library at Charlemont House, Dublin, is perhaps a work of 1782; the excise office in London, pulled down in 1854, sometimes attributed to him, is a work of W. Robinson. After many years' torture from gout he died on 24 Dec. 1823, and three days later was buried by his own desire in the same vault with his friend Francis Grose [q. v.] in the private chapel of Drumcondra, near Dublin. He was elected in 1791 an original honorary member of the Architects' Club in London, and in 1797 a fellow of the Society of Antiquaries. He was also one of the original members of the Royal Irish Academy. He etched several plates after landscapes by Richard Wilson, R.A. His essays 'On the Progress of Architecture in Ireland,' and 'Hints for erecting Testimonials' are printed in Thomas J. Mulvany's 'Life of James Gandon,' 8vo, Dublin, 1846, which was arranged by his only son, James Gandon, and gives his portrait.

[Mulvany's Life; Dict. of Architecture (Arch. Publ. Soc.), iii. 10–11; Webb's Compendium of Irish Biography, pp. 217, 584; Redgrave's Dict. of Artists, 1878, pp. 165–6; Gent. Mag. xciv. pt. i. 464; Builder, 1847, v. 1.]   G. G.

GANDY, JAMES (1619–1689), portrait-painter, born in 1619, was probably a native of Exeter. He is stated to have been a pupil of Vandyck, and to have acquired to some degree the style of that master. He has even been supposed to have assisted Vandyck by painting the drapery in his pictures. In 1661 he was taken to Ireland by his patron, the Duke of Ormonde, and remained there

until his death in 1689. He executed a number of copies of portraits by Vandyck for the duke's collection at Kilkenny, some of which were sold at the dispersal of that collection as original works. His principal portraits were done in Ireland, and remain there. One of the Duke of Ormonde was in the possession of the Earl of Leicester. Gandy is worthy of notice as one of the earliest native English painters. He was father of William Gandy [q. v.]

[Pilkington's Dict. of Painters, ed. 1805; Walpole's Anecdotes of Painting, ed. Dallaway and Wornum; Cotton's Life of Reynolds; Northcote's Life of Reynolds (Appendix).]   L. C.

GANDY, JOHN PETER (1787–1850), architect. [See DEERING.]

GANDY, JOSEPH MICHAEL (1771–1843), architect, elder brother of John Peter Gandy-Deering [see DEERING], and also of Michael Gandy [q. v.], was a pupil of James Wyatt, and a student of the Royal Academy, where in 1790 he obtained the gold medal for his design for a triumphal arch. From 1793–9 he travelled, and in 1794 was at Rome, where in 1795 he received the pope's medal in the first class for architecture. He first exhibited at the Royal Academy in 1789 as Wyatt's pupil, sending a 'design for a casino,' and was from that time a frequent exhibitor up to 1838; he was elected an associate in 1803. In 1811 Gandy became connected with Sir John Soane [q. v.], and executed numerous drawings for him. His imagination and genius, which were of the first order, were now chiefly employed on works for which Soane got the chief credit. Certain drawings of great excellence exhibited at the Academy in Soane's name after he had become blind were no doubt the work of Gandy alone. Gandy, though an excellent draughtsman, seems to have been of too odd and impracticable a nature to insure prosperity, and it is said that his life was one of poverty and disappointment, ending, according to some accounts, in insanity. He died in December 1843, leaving a son, Thomas Gandy, who practised portrait-painting. Gandy was an excellent architect of the neo-classical school. Perhaps his best known work is shown in the Phœnix and Pelican Insurance offices at Charing Cross. He was largely employed on domestic architecture. Among his designs may be noted a 'Design for a National Institution appropriated to the Fine Arts, the Sciences, and Literature of our Kingdom;' this was embellished with busts and figures by Thomas Baxter, and engraved by John Le Keux. Gandy published in 1805 'Designs for Cottages, Cottage Farms, and other Rural Buildings, including entrance Gates and Lodges,' and 'The Rural Architect, consisting of various designs for Country Buildings, &c., with ground plans, estimates, and descriptions, &c.' A number of his drawings remain in the Soane Museum, Lincoln's Inn Fields. Some of the illustrations in Britton's 'Architectural Antiquities' are by him.

[Dict. of Architecture; Redgrave's Dict. of Artists; Leslie and Taylor's Life of Sir Joshua Reynolds, ii. 589; Sandby's Hist. of the Royal Academy, i. 400.]   L. C.

GANDY, MICHAEL (1778–1862), architect, younger brother of Joseph Michael Gandy [q. v.] and of John Peter Gandy-Deering [see DEERING], was a pupil of James Wyatt, whose office he left on receiving an appointment in the Indian naval service. He was thus employed for some years, and served in India and China. In 1812 he exhibited at the Royal Academy 'The Burning of Onrust and Kupers Island, Batavia, in 1800, drawn on the spot.' On his return he was employed for some time in the drawing-office of Mr. Holl, civil architect to the navy, afterwards by Francis Goodwin [q. v.], and eventually by Sir Jeffrey Wyatville [q.v.], with whom he remained for thirty-three years, until Wyatville's death in 1840. In 1842 he published with Benjamin Bond 'Architectural Illustrations of Windsor Castle (text by J. Britton).' He died in April 1862.

[Dict. of Architecture; Redgrave's Dict. of Artists.]   L. C.

GANDY, WILLIAM (d. 1729), portrait-painter, son of James Gandy [q. v.], was probably born in Ireland. He was for some years an itinerant painter in Devonshire and the west of England, went to Plymouth in 1714, and eventually settled in Exeter. According to Northcote, whose grandfather and father knew and befriended Gandy, the painter was a man of most intractable disposition, very resentful, of unbounded pride, and in the latter part of his life both idle and luxurious; he was at all times totally careless of his reputation as a painter, though he might have been the greatest painter of his time. He liked people to think that he was a natural son of his father's patron, the Duke of Ormonde, and that he was so much concerned in the duke's affairs that he was not able to make a public appearance in London. His portraits, though sometimes slight and sketchy, showed real genius, and have been frequently admired by great artists. The portrait of the Rev. Tobias Langdon in the college hall at Exeter excited the admiration of Sir Godfrey Kneller. Gandy may also be credited with having directed and stimulated the rising genius of Sir Joshua Reynolds. Reynolds saw Gandy's pictures early in life, and they made a great impression on his mind; he, like Northcote, often borrowed one of Gandy's portraits, probably the Langdon portrait, to study. His portraits are seldom found out of the west of England. He painted Northcote's grandmother, the Rev. Nathaniel Harding of Plymouth, the Rev. John Gilbert, vicar of St. Andrew's, Plymouth (engraved by Vertue as a frontispiece to Gilbert's 'Sermons'), John Patch, surgeon in the Exeter Hospital, the Rev. William Musgrave (engraved by Michael van der Gucht), Sir Edward Seaward in the chapel of the poorhouse at Exeter, Sir William Elwill, bart., and others. From his idleness and want of ambition Gandy frequently left his pictures to be finished by others. He died in Exeter, and was buried in St. Paul's Church on 14 July 1729.

[Northcote's notice of Gandy in Appendix to Life of Reynolds; Cotton's Life of Reynolds; Leslie and Taylor's Life and Times of Reynolds; Redgrave's Dict. of Artists.]   L. C.

GARBET, SAMUEL (d. 1751?), topographer, born at Norton, in the parish of Wroxeter, Shropshire, was educated at Donnington School and at Christ Church, Oxford, where he entered 12 June 1700, and graduated B.A. 23 May 1704, and M.A. 5 July 1707. He was ordained deacon 22 Sept. 1706, and became curate of Great Nesse. On 11 March 1712 he was elected second master of the free school at Wem, in Shropshire. In 1713 he also became curate of Edstaston. In 1724 he was offered, but declined, the headmastership of the Wem school. In 1742, 'having [as he says] kept up the credit of the school for thirty years, and being in easy circumstances, he thought fit to retire,' and devoted himself to the compilation of his 'History of Wem, and the following Villages and Townships,' which was published posthumously in 1818 (Wem, 8vo). In 1715 he had published a translation of Phædrus, bks. i. and ii. In 1751 he was still curate of Edstaston (Hist. of Wem, p. 280), and his death may have taken place in or after that year.

He married Anna, daughter of John Edwards of Great Nesse, by whom he had one son, Samuel, who graduated at Christ Church, Oxford, B.A. 1737, M.A. 1743, became curate of Wem and afterwards of Newtown, Shropshire, and died in 1768, being buried at Stoulton, near Worcester. According to Gough (Brit. Topogr. ii. 389) the younger Garbet had the principal hand in drawing up Valentine Green's 'Survey of the City of Worcester' (1764), and was 'a great historian, chronologist, and linguist,' though he published nothing in his own name.

[Garbet's History of Wem, especially pp. 208, 209; Cat. Oxford Grad.; Gough's Brit. Topogr.; Nash's Worcestershire, ii. 25.] W. W.

GARBETT, EDWARD (1817–1887), divine, was born at Hereford on 10 Dec. 1817, being the sixth son of the Rev. James Garbett (1775–1857), custos and prebendary of the cathedral. He was educated at Hereford Cathedral School, whence he proceeded to Brasenose College, Oxford (19 May 1837). He proceeded B.A. in 1841, coming out with second-class honours 'in litt. human.,' and M.A. in 1847. In early years he had wished to be a doctor, but afterwards showed a decided preference for the work of the ministry. Garbett was accordingly ordained deacon by the Bishop of Hereford in 1841 and licensed to the curacy of Upton Bishop, of which his father was then vicar. In the following year he removed to Birmingham as curate of St. George's, under his cousin, the Rev. John Garbett. At Birmingham he obtained his first preferment, the vicarage of St. Stephen's. An opportunity of removing to London was accepted, and in 1854 Garbett became perpetual curate of St. Bartholomew's, Gray's Inn Road. He had already shown some capacity for journalistic work, and was in the same year appointed to the editorship of the 'Record,' a position he filled with marked ability until his resignation in 1867. During this period there were few subjects of ecclesiastical importance upon which he did not write with force and discernment. He was for some time also editor of the 'Christian Advocate.' But journalism did not disqualify him for successful work either in the pulpit or the parish. In 1860 he accepted the Boyle lectureship on the nomination of Bishop Tait, and in 1861 was appointed a select preacher at Oxford. In 1863 came a removal to the living of Christ Church, Surbiton, and in 1867 his appointment as Bampton lecturer at Oxford. In the same year he resigned the editorship of the 'Record,' but continued for some time to write with more or less regularity in its columns. In 1875 Garbett was appointed an honorary canon of Winchester, and in 1877 he accepted from the lord chancellor the living of Barcombe, Lewes. He had previously declined invitations to succeed Dr. Miller at St. Martin's, Birmingham, and to fill the fashionable pulpit of St. Paul's, Onslow Square, London. During the earlier gatherings of the Church Congress Garbett's aid

was often asked. He read a paper at York in 1866, and again at the meetings of 1869, 1870, 1871, 1872, 1873, 1874, and 1879. Garbett's health was much broken by his work at Barcombe, and on 11 Oct. 1886 he was stricken with paralysis. He never recovered, but the end was deferred until 11 Oct. 1887. In his ecclesiastical views Garbett moved with the evangelical party, whose cause he championed with unfailing vigour. A clever but candid controversialist, widely esteemed in his own circle, he was one of the many men whose friends have anticipated for them honours they never attained.

His works were: 1. 'The Soul's Life,' 1852. 2. 'Sermons for Children,' 1854. 3. 'The Bible and its Critics' (Boyle Lectures), 1860. 4. 'The Divine Plan of Revelation' (Boyle Lectures), 1863. 5. 'The Family of God,' 1863. 6. 'God's Word Written,' 1864. 7. 'Religion in Daily Life,' 1865. 8. 'Dogmatic Truth' (Bampton Lectures), 1867. 9. 'Obligations of Truth,' 1874.

[Record, 14 and 21 Oct. 1887; Foster's Alumni Oxon. ii. 506; information supplied by Mrs. Garbett.] A. R. B.

GARBETT, JAMES (1802–1879), archdeacon of Chichester and professor of poetry at Oxford, born at Hereford in 1802, was eldest son of the Rev. James Garbett (1775–1857), prebendary of Hereford. He passed from the Hereford Cathedral School to Brasenose College, Oxford, where he was elected to a scholarship, 15 May 1819. He obtained a first class in classics in 1822, along with Lord Shaftesbury and Sotheron Estcourt, and bore through life a high reputation as a classical scholar. He proceeded B.A. 1822 and M.A. 1825; was fellow of Queen's College, 1824–5; fellow of Brasenose College, 1825–36; tutor, 1827; Hulmeian lecturer in divinity, 1828; junior dean, 1832; and Latin lecturer, 1834. The college living of Clayton-cum-Keymer, Sussex, was conferred on him in 1835, and he held it till his death. Garbett was a representative evangelical, and strongly opposed the tractarian movement at Oxford. In 1842 he was Bampton lecturer, and tried to show the needlessness of tractarian changes. In the same year he was elected professor of poetry, in opposition to Isaac Williams, the tractarian candidate. He was re-elected professor in 1847, and held the post till 1852. Some of his lectures, all delivered in Latin, were published, and illustrate his finished scholarship. He is said to have declined the Ireland professorship of exegesis in 1847. He certainly refused a seat on the university commission in 1853. He explained in a published letter to B. P. Symons, warden of Wadham (London, 1853), that he took the latter step, not because he was unfriendly to the commission, but because he objected to the mode of its appointment. He became a prebendary of Chichester in 1843, and archdeacon of the diocese, in succession to the present Cardinal Manning, in 1851. He died at Brighton on 26 March 1879.

Besides numerous sermons, archidiaconal charges, and controversial letters, issued separately, Garbett was author of the following: 1. 'An Essay on Warburton's "Divine Legation," a fellowship probationary exercise,' Hereford, 1828. 2. 'Christ as Prophet, Priest, and King, being a Vindication of the Church of England from Theological Novelties,' Garbett's Bampton lectures, 1842, 2 vols. 3. 'De Rei Poeticæ Idea,' 1843—lectures delivered as professor of poetry. 4. 'Parochial Sermons,' 1843–4, 2 vols. 5. 'Christ on Earth, in Heaven, and on the Judgment Seat,' London, 1847. 6. 'Beatitudes of the Mount in 17 Sermons,' London, 1854.

[Foster's Alumni Oxon. ii. 506; Guardian for 1879, i. 452, 456, 501, 564; Times, 27 and 28 March 1879; Brit. Mus. Cat.]

GARBRAND, or HERKS, JOHN (1542–1589), prebendary of Salisbury and friend of Bishop Jewel, was born at Oxford in 1542. Before that date his father, Garbrand Herks or HERKS GARBRAND, a Dutch protestant, fled from religious persecution in his native country, and settled as a bookseller at Bulkeley Hall, in St. Mary's parish, Oxford. In 1546 he was licensed to add wine to his commodities. At the beginning of Edward VI's reign he purchased many libraries from the suppressed monasteries, some of which subsequently entered the Bodleian Library. As early as 1551 he regularly supplied books to Magdalen College (BLOXAM, Reg. ii. 273). In 1556 his house was 'a receptacle for the chiefest protestants,' who worshipped in a cellar there (WOOD, Annals, ed. Gutch, ii. 107). The refugee had many sons, some of whom carried on the bookselling business in the later years of the century. Richard Garbrand was admitted a bookseller at Oxford 5 Dec. 1573, and was alive in 1590 (Oxf. Univ. Reg. II. i. 321). Thomas, born in 1539, was probationary fellow of Magdalen College from 1557 to 1570 (B.A. 1558, M.A. 1562), and was senior proctor 1565–6 (BLOXAM, iv. 145). William, born in 1549, was also fellow of Magdalen from 1570 to 1577 (B.A. 1570, M.A. 1574), when he seems to have been suspended for insubordination (ib. iv. 165). Four members of the third generation

of the same family are often met with. Ambrose, born at Oxford in 1584, received the privileges of an Oxford citizen in 1601 (Oxf. Univ. Reg. II. i. 398), and in 1616 was a chief officer of the London Stationers' Company (ARBER, Transcript, vol. iii.) John, born in 1585, was a scholar of Winchester in 1596, fellow of New College, Oxford, from 1606 to 1608 (B.A. in 1603–4, M.A. in 1608), and pursued the bookseller's trade at Oxford, dying about 1618, when his widow Martha remarried Christopher Rogers, principal of New Inn Hall (KIRBY, Winchester Scholars, p. 157; Oxf. Univ. Reg. II. i. 323, ii. 269, iii. 279). Tobias, born in 1579 [see under GARBRAND, JOHN, fl. 1695], and Nicholas, born in 1600, were both of Magdalen. The latter was demy 1614–19, fellow from 1619 to 1639 (B.A. 1618, M.A. 1621, B.D. 1631); vicar of Washington, Sussex, 2 Sept. 1638 to 1671, vicar of Patching, Sussex, 1660–71, prebendary of Chichester 1660–9 (BLOXAM, v. 43). As late as the end of the seventeenth century the family name was often written Garbrand, alias Herks.

John, one of the younger sons of Herks Garbrand, entered Winchester College in 1556, was admitted probationary fellow of New College, Oxford, 24 March 1560, and perpetual fellow in 1562, proceeding B.A. 22 April 1563, and M.A. 25 Feb. 1566–7. In 1565 Bishop Jewel, who was friendly with Garbrand's father, presented him to a prebendal stall in Salisbury Cathedral, where he subsequently held two other prebends. In 1567 he left Oxford to become rector of North Crawley, Buckinghamshire. In 1568 he was incorporated M.A. at Cambridge, and on 5 July 1582 proceeded B.D. and D.D. at Oxford. Until 1578 he was a prebendary of Wells, and for some time he was rector of Farthingstone, Northamptonshire, to the poor of which parish he gave 5l. (BRIDGES, Northamptonshire, i. 64) He died at North Crawley on 17 Nov. 1589, and was buried in the church. An inscription describes him as 'a benefactor to the poor.' Like his father and patron Jewel Garbrand was a puritan. When Jewel died in 1571 he bequeathed his papers to Garbrand, who by will devised them to Dr. Robert Chaloner and Dr. John Rainolds. Garbrand edited from Jewel's manuscripts three volumes of works by the bishop: 1. 'A View of a Seditious Bul' and 'A short Treatise of the Holie Scriptures,' London, 1582, with preface by Garbrand. 2. 'Certaine Sermons preached ... at Paules Crosse' and 'A Treatise of the Sacraments,' London, 1583, with dedication by the editor to Lords Burghley and Leicester, and Latin verses before the treatise. 3. 'Exposition upon Paul's two epistles to the Thessalonians,' London, 1583, with dedication by Garbrand to Sir Francis Walsingham. Garbrand wrote prefatory Latin verses for Wilson's 'Discourse upon Usurie,' 1572. Six letters in Dutch, dated in 1586, from J. Garbront to Herle, concerning naval affairs, are in Brit. Mus. Cat. Cotton. MS. Galba C. ix. ff. 253, 265, 283. Garbrand bequeathed some books to New College, Oxford.

[Cooper's Athenæ Cantabr. ii. 64, 544; Wood's Athenæ Oxon. ed. Bliss, i. 556 ; Jewel's Works, ed. Ayre (Parker Soc.); Oxford Univ. Reg. (Oxf. Hist. Soc.) I. ii. passim ; Wood's Fasti, ed. Bliss, vol. i. passim ; Le Neve's Fasti.] S. L.

GARBRAND, JOHN (*fl.* 1695), political writer, was born at Abingdon, Berkshire. His father, TOBIAS GARBRAND, M.D., of Oxford, was principal of Gloucester Hall (afterwards Worcester College), Oxford, under the parliamentary régime from 1648 to 1660, when he was expelled. He retired to Abingdon, practised medicine, and died 7 April 1689 (WOOD, *Fasti*, ed. Bliss, ii. 115). Another Tobias (1579–1638), probably the grandfather of the subject of this memoir, was demy of Magdalen (1591–1605), B.A. 1602, M.A. 1605, fellow 1605–19, vice-president 1618, vicar of Finden, Sussex, 5 March 1618–19, till his death in 1638 (BLOXAM, *Reg. Magdalen College*, iv. 232). This Tobias was grandson of Garbrand Herks, a Dutch bookseller of Oxford [see under GARBRAND, JOHN, 1542–1589]. John became a commoner of New Inn Hall, Oxford, in Midsummer term 1664, and proceeded B.A. on 28 Jan. 1667. He was afterwards called to the bar at the Inner Temple. He wrote: 1. 'The grand Inquest; or a full and perfect Answer to several Reasons by which it is pretended his Royal Highness the Duke of York may be proved to be a Roman Catholic,' 4to, London [1682?] 2. 'The Royal Favourite cleared,' &c., 4to, London, 1682. 3. 'Clarior è Tenebris ; or a Justification of two Books, the one printed under the Title of "The grand Inquest," &c. ; the other under the Title of "The Royal Favourite cleared,"' &c., 4to, London, 1683. 'By the writing of which books,' says Wood, 'and his endeavours in them to clear the Duke of York from being a papist, he lost his practice, and could get nothing by it.'

[Wood's Athenæ Oxon. (Bliss), iv. 786–7 ; Wood's Fasti Oxon. (Bliss), ii. 298 ; Will of Tobias Garbrand, April 1689 (P. C. C. 50, Ent).] G. G.

GARDELLE, THEODORE (1721–1761), limner and murderer, born in Geneva in 1721, was son of Giovino Gardelle of Ravenna, who was settled at Geneva. Gardelle was educated at Turretine's charity school, and ap-

prenticed to M. Bousquet, a limner and print-seller. He ran away to Paris, but eventually returned to Geneva, paying renewed visits to Paris. He left Geneva finally in 1756, taking with him a woman whom he passed off as his wife, and whom he seems to have deserted in Paris, and then went to Brussels, and eventually to England. A life of Gardelle (published in 1761) narrates that he became acquainted with Voltaire at Geneva, drew his portrait and enamelled it on a snuff-box, went to Paris with a recommendation from Voltaire to Surugue, the chief engraver to the king, and was advised by the Duc de Choiseul to try his fortune in London. The sordid circumstances of Gardelle's life render this account very doubtful. He arrived in London in 1760 and soon found employment as a miniature-painter. He lodged in Leicester Square in a house kept by a Mrs. Anne King, a woman of light character. On 19 Feb. 1761, when, according to his own account, they were alone in the house together they had an altercation over her portrait, which Gardelle had painted ; this ended in blows, Mrs. King eventually falling against a bed-stead and striking her head. To silence her screams he in terror cut her throat with a penknife. The more probable account is that Gardelle, having sent the servant out on some excuse, attempted violence, and that his victim's resistance frightened him to the murder. Having concealed the body he was unable to dispose of it for some days, but eventually cut it up and dispersed it under very revolting circumstances. Discovery soon ensued, and Gardelle was arrested on 27 Feb. He made an unsuccessful attempt at suicide with laudanum, but was convicted and executed at the corner of Panton Street, Haymarket, on 4 April 1761. His body was hung in chains on Hounslow Heath. Hogarth drew his portrait at his execution, which was engraved by Samuel Ireland in his 'Graphic Illustrations of Hogarth.'

[Life of Theodore Gardelle, London, 1761; Gent. Mag. 1761, xxxi. 171; Redgrave's Dict. of Artists.] L. C.

GARDEN, ALEXANDER (1730?–1791), botanist, was born at Charleston, South Carolina, about 1730. His father, Alexander Garden, was born in Scotland in 1685, and went out to Charleston in 1719 as a clergyman of the church of England, becoming rector of St. Philip's Church, and being chiefly remembered for a controversy in 1740 with the Rev. George Whitefield. He died in 1756. Garden was sent home to Scotland for his education, studied medicine at Edinburgh, where he graduated M.D., and was a pupil in botany of Alston. He returned to Charleston in 1752 (SMITH, *Correspondence of Linnæus*, i. 287), and went in 1754 for a time as professor to King's (afterwards Columbia) College, New York, but in 1755 married and established himself as a medical practitioner in his native town. Though having a large practice and a delicate constitution, he managed to devote considerable time to the study of botany and zoology. He corresponded with John Bartram, Peter Collinson, Gronovius, John Ellis, and, after 1755, with Linnæus. In his letters he expresses 'disgust and indignation' at the inaccuracy of Catesby's 'Natural History of Carolina,' and shows himself, as Sir J. E. Smith says, 'a thoroughgoing Linnean.' In the twelfth edition of Linnæus's 'Systema Naturæ' his name is subjoined to many new or little known species of fish and reptiles, and he also studied the more obscure classes of animals. He sent many new plants to Europe, including several magnolias and the *Gordonia*, which was, at his request, to have been named after him. Ellis having, however, already named it, chose the Cape Jessamine, introduced by Richard Warner [q. v.], to bear the name *Gardenia*. In 1761 he was chosen a member of the Royal Academy of Upsala, and in 1773 a fellow of the Royal Society, though not admitted until 1783. In 1764 he published an essay on the medicinal properties of the Virginia pink-root, and in the following year he described the genera *Stillingia* and *Fothergilla*, dedicated to Benjamin Stillingfleet and John Fothergill; and he also contributed to the 'Philosophical Transactions' in 1775. In the war of independence he sided with England, sending a congratulatory address to Cornwallis on his success at Camden in 1780, and in 1783 he came to England with his wife and two daughters.

On his arrival in England he settled in Cecil Street, Strand, became generally respected for his benevolence, cheerfulness, and pleasing manners, and was made vice-president of the Royal Society. He died in Cecil Street, 15 April 1791, in his sixty-second year.

His son ALEXANDER GARDEN (1757–1829), though educated at Westminster and Glasgow, joined the United States army, and received a grant of his father's estates, which had been confiscated. He afterwards published 'Anecdotes of the Revolutionary War,' 1822.

[Appleton's Cyclop. American Biog. p. 594; Ramsay's Hist. of South Carolina, vol. ii.; Rees's Cyclop.; Smith's Correspondence of Linnæus, i. 282–605; Loudon's Arboretum . . . Britann. p. 70.]
G. S. B.

GARDEN, FRANCIS, LORD GARDENSTONE (1721–1793), the second son of Alexander Garden of Troup, Banffshire, by Jean, eldest daughter of Sir Francis Grant [q. v.], lord Cullen, was born at Edinburgh on 24 June 1721. He was educated at Edinburgh University, and was admitted an advocate on 14 July 1744. In the following year, while serving as a volunteer under Sir John Cope, he narrowly escaped being hanged as a spy at Musselburgh Bridge. In 1748 he was appointed sheriff depute of Kincardineshire, and on 22 Aug. 1759 was elected one of the assessors to the magistrates of Edinburgh. On 30 April 1760 Garden was appointed with James Montgomery joint solicitor-general, but to neither of them was conceded the privilege of sitting within the bar (*Cat. of Home Office Papers*, 1760–5, pp. 54, 55–6). Garden was employed in the Douglas cause, and appeared before the chambre criminelle of the parliament of Paris, where he was opposed by Wedderburn, and greatly distinguished himself by his legal knowledge and the fluency of his French. He was appointed an ordinary lord of session in the place of George Sinclair, lord Woodhall, and took his seat on the bench on 3 July 1764 with the title of Lord Gardenstone. On the resignation of James Ferguson, lord Pitfour, in April 1776, Garden also became a lord of justiciary, a post from which he retired in 1787, with a pension of 200*l.* a year. Upon the death of his elder brother Alexander in 1785, Garden succeeded to the family estates in Banffshire and Aberdeenshire, as well as to a large fortune. In September 1786 he went abroad for the sake of his health, returning in the summer of 1788. He continued to hold the post of an ordinary lord of session until his death at Morningside, near Edinburgh, on 22 July 1793. He was buried in Greyfriars churchyard on 24 July, 'one and a half double paces north of the corner of Henderson's tomb,' but there is no stone to mark the exact spot. Garden was a man of many peculiarities, one of which was an extreme fondness for pigs. It is related that a visitor one morning called on Garden, but he was not yet out of bed. He was shown into his bedroom, and in the dark he stumbled over something which gave a terrible grunt. Upon which Lord Gardenstone said, 'It is just a bit sow, poor beast, and I laid my breeches on it to keep it warm all night' (*Original Portraits*, i. 24). His convivial habits during his early career at the bar have formed the subject of many characteristic anecdotes. Tytler says that Garden was 'an acute and able lawyer, of great natural eloquence, and with much wit and humour, had a considerable acquaintance with classical and elegant literature' (*Memoirs of Lord Kames*, iii. 293 note). In 1762 Garden purchased the estate of Johnson at Laurencekirk, Kincardineshire, and in 1765 began to build a new village, which so rapidly increased in the number of its inhabitants, that in 1779 it was erected into a burgh of barony. At the time of his death the village contained five hundred houses, with a population of twelve thousand. To encourage strangers to settle in it he offered land on very easy terms, and built an inn. He also founded a library and a museum for the use of the villagers, and did his best to establish in the district manufactures of various kinds. His 'Memorandums concerning the Village of Lawrence Kirk' will be found in the appendix to Knox's 'Tour through the Highlands of Scotland,' 1787, pp. 85–91. In May 1789 he erected at his own expense a Doric temple over St. Bernard's Well, near Edinburgh, having derived great benefit from the use of the waters. He never married. There are two portraits of him at Troup House, Banffshire, in the possession of Colonel Francis William Garden-Campbell, and a characteristic etching of him on horseback by Kay will be found in 'Original Portraits' (i. opp. p. 22, No. vii.)

Garden's works are: 1. 'Letter to the Inhabitants of Lawrence Kirk,' 1780, 8vo. 2. 'Travelling Memorandums, made in a Tour upon the Continent of Europe in the Years 1786, 1787, and 1788.' Vol. i., Edinburgh, 1791, 8vo and 12mo; vol. ii., Edinburgh, 1792, 8vo and 12mo. Vol. iii. was published after his death, and contains a short memoir of the author, Edinburgh, 1795, 8vo and 12mo. A second edition of vols. i. and ii. appeared at Edinburgh in 1792, 8vo. Garden also had a hand in 'Miscellanies in Prose and Verse,' Edinburgh, 1791, 12mo; second edit., corrected and enlarged, Edinburgh, 1792, 12mo.

[Travelling Memorandums, iii. (1795), 3–31; Gleig's Suppl. to the third edit. of the Encycl. Brit. (1801), i. 694–6; Brunton and Haig's Senators of the College of Justice (1832), pp. 526, 527–8; Kay's Original Portraits (1877), i. 22–5, 61, 350, 419, ii. 8, 71, 163; Tytler's Memoirs of Lord Kames (1814), iii. 293–304; Allardyce's Scotland and Scotsmen (1888), i. 126, 369–80; Chalmers's Biog. Dict. of Eminent Scotsmen (1869), ii. 80–2; Anderson's Scottish Nation (1863), ii. 281–2; Chalmers's Biog. Dict. (1814), xv. 270–2; Sir John Sinclair's Statistical Account of Scotland, i. 475–7, v. 176–8; Burke's Landed Gentry (1879), i. 618; Gent. Mag. (1793), lxiii. pt. ii. 769, 803; Scots Mag. (1748) x. 155, (1759) xxi. 446, (1789) li. 653–4, (1793) lv. 362; Edinburgh Mag. (1793), ii. 252; Notes and Queries, 3rd ser. v. 95; Brit. Mus. Cat.]

G. F. R. B.

GARDEN, FRANCIS (1810–1884), theologian, son of Alexander Garden, a Glasgow merchant, and Rebecca, daughter of Robert Menteith, esq., of Carstairs, N.B., was educated partly at home and partly at the college at Glasgow, whence he passed to Trinity College, Cambridge, where he took his degree of B.A. in 1833 and M.A. in 1836. In 1833 he obtained the Hulsean prize for an essay on the 'Advantages accruing from Christianity.' At Cambridge he belonged to the set of which R. Chenevix Trench, F. D. Maurice, and John Sterling were among the leaders, whose intimate friendship, together with that of Edmund Lushington and G. Stovin Venables, he enjoyed. His name occurs frequently in Trench's early letters (*Memorials*, i. 118, 182, 186, 236, &c.), and he was Trench's companion in Rome and its environs in January 1835. He was ordained deacon in 1836, as curate to Sir Herbert Oakeley at Bocking in Essex. In 1838–9 he was curate to Julius Charles Hare at Hurstmonceaux in Sussex, succeeding after an interval his friend Sterling. There was hardly sufficient sympathy between Garden and Hare for him to stay long as his curate, and he removed in 1839 to the curacy of St. James's, Piccadilly, from which he became successively the incumbent of Holy Trinity Church, Blackheath Hill (1840–4), junior incumbent of St. Paul's, Edinburgh (1845–9), curate of St. Stephen's, Westminster, assistant minister of the English chapel at Rome (1851–2), and finally, in 1859, he succeeded Dr. Wesley as sub-dean of the Chapel Royal, an appointment which he held till his death in 1884. In 1841 he undertook the editorship of the 'Christian Remembrancer,' which he retained for some years. In his earlier years Garden attached himself to the Oxford school, which was then exercising a powerful attraction over thoughtful minds. Trench describes a sermon he heard him preach in 1839 on 'the anger of God,' as 'Newmanite and in parts very unpleasant.' He subsequently became somewhat of a broad churchman, adopting the teaching of F. D. Maurice on the incarnation, the atonement, and other chief Christian doctrines, and contributing several thoughtful essays to the series of 'Tracts for Priests and People,' a literary organ of that school. The bent of his mind was essentially philosophical, disinclined to rest in any bare dogmatic statements without probing them to the bottom to discover the intellectual basis on which they rested. In 1848 he published 'Discourses on Heavenly Knowledge and Heavenly Love,' followed in 1853 by 'Lectures on the Beatitudes.' A pamphlet on the renunciation of holy orders, then beginning to be debated, appeared in 1870 under the title 'Can an Ordained Man become a Layman?' 'An Outline of Logic' was issued, which came to a second edition in 1871. He was also the author of 'A Dictionary of English Philosophical Terms,'1878; 'The Nature and Benefits of Holy Baptism;' 'The Atonement as a Fact and as a Theory.' He was a contributor to Smith's 'Dictionary of the Bible,' the 'Christian Remembrancer,' 'Contemporary Review,' and other periodicals. In 1837 he married Virginia, the daughter of Admiral Dobbie, who died early, leaving one daughter. The maiden name of his second wife was Boucher.

[Private information.]   E. V.

GARDEN, GEORGE (1649–1733), Scottish divine, a younger son of Alexander Garden, minister of Forgue in Aberdeenshire, and Isobell Middleton, was born at Forgue, and educated at King's College, Aberdeen, where in 1673, at the age of twenty-four, he was already a regent or professor. In 1677 he was ordained by Bishop Scougall, and appointed to succeed his father in the church of Forgue, the bishop's son, Henry Scougall [q. v.], preaching at his induction. Two years later Garden was promoted to Old Machar (the church of which was the cathedral of Aberdeen). In June 1678 he preached in the chapel of King's College the 'funeral sermon' on his friend, the admirable Henry Scougall. It is printed in many editions of Scougall's works, and throws light on the ideas of ministerial duty entertained among the clergy of the 'second episcopacy' (1662–1690). In 1683 Garden, already a D.D., became one of the ministers of St. Nicholas, the town parish of Aberdeen, where he continued till he was 'laid aside' by the privy council in 1692 for 'not praying for their majesties,' William and Mary. The commission of the general assembly of 1700 had him before them in connection with 'An Apology for M. Antonia Bourignon' (1699, 8vo), attributed to him. Garden, who issued translations of several of Madame Bourignon's works with prefaces of his own, refused to disavow the authorship, asserted that 'the said "Apology" as to the bulk of the book did represent the great end of Christianity, which is to bring us back to the love of God and charity, and further declared that the essentials of Christianity are set down in the said book, and that the accessories contained therein are not contrary thereto;' whereupon the commission suspended him from the office of the ministry, and cited him to the assembly of 1701. He did not appear, and the assembly deposed him and 'prohibited him from exercising the

ministry or any part thereof in all time coming.' Garden paid no regard to the sentence, and continued to officiate as before to the members of his former congregation who adhered to episcopacy. In 1703 he dedicated to Queen Anne, in terms of fervent loyalty to her, but with outspoken censure of the new presbyterian establishment, his magnificent edition of the works of Dr. John Forbes (1593–1648) [q. v.] ('Joannis Forbesii a Corse Opera Omnia'), which was published at Amsterdam. Though he had refused to take the oaths to William and Mary, Garden had never approved the arbitrary policy of James II; he accepted the conditions of the Toleration Act (1712); and when after the peace of Utrecht the episcopal clergy of Aberdeen drew up an address of congratulation to the queen, he and his brother James were chosen to present it. Introduced by the Earl of Mar, then secretary of state for Scotland, they were received with marked graciousness, and poured into her majesty's not unwilling ear (along with their thanks for the freedom they now enjoyed, 'not only in their exercise of the pastoral care over a willing people, but also in their use of the liturgy of the church of England'—then a new thing among the Scotch episcopalians) their complaints of the persecution they had lately suffered, and their entreaties for a further measure of relief. The queen's death made Garden and his brother Jacobites again; the insurrection of 1715 restored George for a brief period to the pulpit of St. Nicholas, and the brothers were among those who presented to the Pretender at Earl Marischal's house at Fetteresso, Kincardineshire, the address of the episcopal clergy of Aberdeen. On the suppression of the rising, Garden was thrown into prison; he managed shortly afterwards to escape to the continent, but returned to Aberdeen before 1720, when he was talked of for election as their bishop by the Aberdeen clergy. The support he had given to Bourignianism was held by the Scottish bishops, and by Lockhart [q. v.], the agent of the exiled prince, sufficient to disqualify him for such promotion. He died on 31 Jan. 1733 (SCOTT's Fasti has wrongly 1723). It illustrates the spread of 'high church' doctrine since the revolution among the Scottish episcopalians that he is called in his epitaph 'sacerdos.' He had fairly earned the praise awarded him of being 'literis et pietate insignis.' Besides his great edition of Forbes he was the author of the 'Queries and Protestation of the Scots Episcopal Clergy given in to the Committee of the General Assembly at Aberdeen June 1694,' 4to, London, 1694; 'The Case of the Episcopal Clergy,' pts. i. and ii. 4to, Edinburgh, 1703; and he is probably the

George Garden of Aberdeen who contributed to the 'Philosophical Transactions' of 1677 and 1693. His Bourignianism, says Grub doubtfully, was probably due to sheer weariness of the controversies wherewith his country had been so long distracted; moreover, his friend Henry Scougall had been in the habit of going to France as well as to Flanders for spiritual improvement. They may be called the Scottish Quietists. Garden's sermon preached at Scougall's funeral was printed first in 1726. His elder brother, JAMES (1647–1726), minister successively of Carnbee (1678–81), New Machar in Aberdeenshire, Maryculter in Kincardineshire, and of Balmerino in Fife, became professor of divinity at King's College, Aberdeen, and was deprived in 1696 for refusing to sign the Westminster Confession of Faith. 'He seems to have shared his brother's love of mystical theology, without falling into errors of doctrine' (GRUB); he shared also his brother's fortunes, and lies beside him in the churchyard of Old Machar. He is the author of a little treatise entitled 'Comparative Theology, or the True and Solid Grounds of a Pure and Peaceable Theology.'

[Records of the University and King's College, Aberdeen; Session Records; Acts of the General Assembly; tombstones; Lockhart Papers (where the name is spelled, as in Scotland it was often pronounced, Gairns); Scott's Fasti; Joseph Robertson's Book of Bon-Accord; Grub's Eccl. Hist.; Cunningham's Church Hist. of Scotland; Ray's Hist. of the Rebellion.] J. C.

GARDENSTONE, LORD. [See GARDEN, FRANCIS, 1721–1793, Scottish judge.]

GARDINER. [See also GARDNER.]

GARDINER, ALLEN FRANCIS (1794–1851), missionary to Patagonia, fifth son of Samuel Gardiner of Coombe Lodge, Oxfordshire, by Mary, daughter of Charles Boddam of Capel House, Bull's Cross, Enfield, Middlesex, was born on 28 Jan. 1794 in the parsonage house at Basildon, Berkshire, where his parents were temporarily residing. He was religiously educated, and in May 1808 entered the Royal Naval College, Portsmouth. On 20 June 1810 he went to sea as a volunteer on board H.M.S. Fortune, and after a time removing to the Phœbe, he served in that ship as midshipman until August 1814, when, having distinguished himself in the capture of the American frigate Essex, he was sent to England as acting lieutenant of that prize. Being confirmed as lieutenant 13 Dec. he afterwards served in the Ganymede, the Leander, and the Dauntless in various parts of the world, and returned invalided to Portsmouth 31 Oct. 1822. On 1 July in the following year he married Julia Susanna, second daughter of John Reade of Ipsden House, Oxfordshire; she died in the Isle of Wight on 23 May 1834. As second lieutenant of the Jupiter he was at Newfoundland in 1824, and in 1825 came back to England in charge of the Clinker, when he obtained his promotion as commander 13 Sept. 1826, after which period, although he often applied for employment, he never succeeded in obtaining any other appointment. Long before this his attention had been much directed to the unreclaimed state of the heathen nations, and he now resolved that he would devote his life to the work of a missionary pioneer. With this view he went to Africa in 1834, and, exploring the Zulu country, started the first missionary station at Port Natal. From 1834 to 1838 he was engaged in earnest endeavours to establish christian churches in Zululand, but political events and native wars combined to prevent any permanent success. From 1838 to 1843 he laboured among the Indians of Chili, and went from island to island in the Indian Archipelago, but his efforts were foiled by the opposition of the various governments.

His first visit to Tierra del Fuego took place 22 March 1842, when, coming from the Falkland Islands in the schooner Montgomery, he landed in Oazy harbour. The Church Missionary Society was now pressed to send out missionaries to Patagonia, but declined on the ground of want of funds. Similar proposals were unsuccessfully made to the Wesleyan and London Missionary Societies. At length in 1844 a special society was formed for South America, which took the name of the Patagonian Missionary Society, and Robert Hunt, a schoolmaster, was sent out as the first missionary, being accompanied by Gardiner. This attempt to establish a mission, however, failed, and they returned to England in June 1845. Gardiner, not discouraged, left England again 23 Sept. 1845, and, in company with Federico Gonzales, a Spanish protestant, from whom he learnt Spanish, went to Bolivia, where he distributed bibles to the Indian population, but not without much opposition from the Roman catholics. Having established Gonzales as a missionary at Potosi, he himself came back to England, landing at Southampton 8 Feb. 1847. He spent 1848 in making a survey of Tierra del Fuego with a view to a mission, and suffered great hardships. He then endeavoured to interest the Moravian Brethren and the Foreign Missions of the Church of Scotland in this enterprise, but neither of them was in a position to render any aid. At last, a lady at Cheltenham having given 700l., the mission was determined on. Accompanied by Richard Williams, surgeon, Joseph Erwin, ship-carpenter, John Maidment, catechist, and three Cornish fishermen, Pearce, Badcock, and Bryant, he sailed from Liverpool 7 Sept. 1850 in the Ocean Queen, and was landed at Picton Island 5 Dec. He had with him two launches, each twenty-six feet long, in which had been stowed provisions to last for six months. The Fuegians were hostile and great thieves; the climate was severe and the country barren. Six months elapsed without the arrival of further supplies, which were detained at the Falkland Islands for want of a vessel. The unfortunate men gradually died of starvation, Gardiner, himself the last survivor, expiring, as it is believed, 6 Sept. 1851. On 21 Oct. the John Davison, sent for their succour, arrived, and on 6 Jan. 1852 H.M.S. Dido visited the place, but all they could do was to bury the bodies and bring away Gardiner's journal. Two years later, in 1854, the Allen Gardiner was sent out to Patagonia as a missionary ship, and in 1856 Captain Gardiner's only son, Allen W. Gardiner, went to that country as a missionary. Gardiner married secondly, 7 Oct. 1836, Elizabeth Lydia, eldest daughter of the Rev. Edward Garrard Marsh, vicar of Aylesford, Kent. He wrote and published: 1. 'Outlines of a Plan for Exploring the Interior of Australia,' 1833. 2. 'Narrative of a Journey to the Zoolu Country in South Africa, undertaken in 1835, 1836.' 3. 'A Visit to the Indians on the Frontiers of Chili,' 1840. 4. 'A Voice from South America,' 1847.

[Gent. Mag. July 1852, pp. 92–4; Annual Register, 1852, pp. 473–8; The Martyrs of the South (1852); Marsh's Memoir of A. F. Gardiner (1857), with portrait; Marsh and Stirling's Story of Commander A. Gardiner (1867), with portrait; Marsh's First Fruits of South American Mission (1873); Garratt's Missionaries' Grave (1852); Bullock's Corn of Wheat dying (1870); W. J. B. Moore's They have done what they could (1866); O'Byrne's Naval Biog. Dict. p. 387; Illustrated London News, 1 May 1852, p. 331, and 8 May, pp. 380–1, with three views on Picton Island.] G. C. B.

GARDINER, ARTHUR (1716?–1758), captain in the navy, is described in his passing certificate, dated 3 Nov. 1737, as more than twenty-one years of age, and as having been at sea upwards of six years, chiefly in the Falmouth, with Captain John Byng [q.v.] On 4 July 1738 he was promoted to be lieutenant, and after serving in the Sutherland, and in the Captain with Captain Thomas

Griffin [q. v.], he was promoted on 6 June 1744 to the command of the Lightning bomb, from which on 27 May 1745 he was posted to the Neptune as flag-captain to Vice-admiral Rowley. On 1 Oct. he was moved into the Feversham, which he commanded for three years in the Mediterranean. From 1749 to 1754 he commanded the Amazon on the coast of Ireland, and, on paying her off, applied on 15 May 1754 for leave to go to France for eight or ten months. In May 1755 he was appointed to the Colchester, but left her in the following September to join the Ramillies as flag-captain to his old commander, now Admiral Byng. In this capacity he accompanied Byng to the Mediterranean; and when, after the action off Minorca, Byng was recalled, Gardiner too was superseded from his command. At Byng's trial several points in Gardiner's evidence bore heavily on the accused, especially as he was a personal friend and an unwilling witness. In February 1757 he was appointed to the Monmouth of 64 guns, and again sent to the Mediterranean. In February 1758 he was with the squadron under Admiral Osborn, shutting up M. de la Clue in Cartagena, when on the 28th the Marquis Duquesne, with three ships, attempted to raise the blockade. The ships were immediately chased, and took different courses. The Foudroyant, carrying Duquesne's broad pennant, was the ship in which M. de Gallissonnière had hoisted his flag in the battle of Minorca, and, notwithstanding her enormous size, Gardiner had been heard to say that if he fell in with her, in the Monmouth, he would take her or perish in the attempt. It is, perhaps, more probable that the story was invented afterwards; for it was by the mere accident of position that the Foudroyant was chased by the Monmouth, the Swiftsure and Hampton Court, each of 70 guns, following. As night closed in, however, the Monmouth ran the chase out of sight of the other two ships, and, having partially disabled her rigging, brought her to close action about seven o'clock. In the very beginning of the fight Gardiner was wounded in the arm by a musket bullet, though not so seriously as to compel him to leave the deck. About nine o'clock, however, he fell, shot through the head, and died a few hours afterwards. The fight was gallantly continued by the first lieutenant, Robert Carkett [q. v.], and on the Swiftsure coming up about one o'clock, the Foudroyant hauled down her colours. The great disproportion between the combatants, the Foudroyant being an unusually large and heavily armed ship of 80 guns, and the fact that the Monmouth alone had beaten her gigantic adversary almost to a standstill before the Swiftsure came up, as well as the circumstances of Gardiner's death, have all combined to render the action one of the most celebrated in our naval annals; and that this distinction should have been achieved by a pupil of Byng and Griffin is perhaps not its least remarkable feature.

[Charnock's Biog. Nav. v. 383; Beatson's Nav. and Mil. Mem. ii. 153; Minutes of the Court Martial on Admiral John Byng; Official letters and other documents in the Public Record Office.]

J. K. L.

GARDINER, BERNARD (1668–1726), warden of All Souls' College, Oxford, was younger son of Sir William Gardiner of Roche Court, first baronet and K.C.B., by his wife, Jane Brocas, heiress of Beaurepaire and Roche Court in Hampshire. He was born in 1668, became a demy of Magdalen College (whence he was temporarily ejected during the struggle with James II), and was elected fellow of All Souls in 1689, proceeding B.A. 26 Oct. 1688, B.C.L. 21 June 1693, and D.C.L. 9 June 1698. He was elected warden of All Souls in 1702, on the nomination of Archbishop Tenison; became custos archivorum in 1705–6, and was vice-chancellor from 1712 to 1715. Both as warden and vice-chancellor he was a prominent figure in his time, a conscientious, indomitable, stern, uncompromising man. In the former capacity he was engaged in a continuous struggle with his fellows in order to put an end to the abuses of non-residence, illusory dispensations from taking holy orders, and others of the same sort, the college during the process being subjected to two visitations from Archbishops Tenison and Wake respectively. The result was not, as he wished, to restore the college to the condition contemplated by the founder, but to establish it on the secular and non-resident basis which the lawyers and statesmen who were prominent among the fellows desired, and which, free from the undergraduate element, it has ever since retained. Gardiner's efforts to enlarge, rebuild, and beautify his college in the style of his age, as we now see it, were crowned with a success denied to his constitutional reforms. As vice-chancellor Gardiner was, along with Wake, the chief means of saving his university from the consequences of its pronounced and prevalent Jacobitism. He governed with a strong hand and made many enemies, especially Hearne the antiquary, to whom as a Hanoverian tory, manager of the university press, and keeper of the archives, the vice-chancellor was exceedingly obnoxious. Hearne described Gardiner as 'a person of very little learning and less honesty, standing for all places that he can make any interest to procure' (HEARNE, *Collections*, ed. Doble,

i. 85); but they had some amicable intercourse on antiquarian topics (cf. *ib.* iii. 397, 419, &c.) It was Gardiner's chief distinction that in the pursuit of the line of duty which he had prescribed for himself he put an end to the intolerable abuse of the 'terræ filius' or elected undergraduate, who by ancient custom had been permitted unlimited freedom of scurrilous speech at the annual act. At the critical periods of 1714 and 1715 these performances, which on such occasions always took a violent political direction, would probably have turned the scale against the permanent independence of the university, already temporarily menaced by the presence of the 'troop of horse' familiarly known to posterity by means of the famous epigram. He died on 22 April 1726 (*Hist. Reg.* 1726, p. 17). While warden of All Souls he married (29 Feb. 1711–12) Grace, daughter of Sir Sebastian Smythe of Tackley Park and Cuddesdon, Oxfordshire, and through their daughter Grace, wife of Dr. Whalley of Clerk Hill, Lancashire, part of the Brocas estates have been transmitted to the Gardiners of Roche Court.

[Montagu Burrows's Worthies of All Souls, 349 et seq.; Historical Family of Brocas of Beaurepaire and Roche Court, by the same author; Bloxam's Reg. Magdalen College, iii. 45.]

M. B.

GARDINER, GEORGE (1535?–1589), dean of Norwich, son of George Gardiner, was born at Berwick-on-Tweed about 1535. He was a scholar of Christ's College, Cambridge, where he proceeded B.A. in 1554. He took the M.A. degree in 1558, having in the meantime become a fellow of Queen's College, an appointment of which he was deprived on 6 Aug. 1561 by reason of his continued absence from Cambridge. In December 1560, at the instigation of Leicester, who was always a firm friend, he was presented by the queen to the living of Chatton, Northumberland. In or about 1562 he became a minor canon of Norwich Cathedral, and was appointed minister to the church of St. Andrew in the same city. He was promoted to be prebendary in 1565, and in 1570 was one of those who entered the choir of the cathedral and, among other outrages, broke down the organ. In the previous year, at a metropolitan visitation, articles had been lodged against him charging him with having been 'a man very unquiet, troublesome, and dissenting, setting debate between man and man.' It was also said that in Queen Mary's time he had persecuted persons supposed to favour the gospel at the universities. In 1571 Gardiner gave up his Norwich living on being instituted by the Merchant Taylors'

Company to the rectory of St. Martin Outwich, London, which he resigned in 1574, and in the same year he was collated to the living of Morley, Norfolk. In 1573 he became archdeacon of Norwich. He had represented to Leicester that the appointment had lapsed to the crown in consequence of a prolonged lawsuit between two candidates. The Bishop of Norwich (Parkhurst), whose own candidate was one of the disputants, refused to recognise Gardiner as archdeacon; but in October 1573 the bishop promised to support him for the deanery, then vacant, if he would give up the archdeaconry. But Gardiner had already had resort to Leicester and Burghley, and was nominated dean unconditionally, in spite of his bishop's opposition. Both Leicester and the queen ordered the bishop to desist, and ultimately Parkhurst and Gardiner became good friends. Gardiner erected a monument to Parkhurst's memory in the cathedral. In 1573 Gardiner was also appointed chaplain to the queen, and in the following year he was in attendance at court. In the same year he was on a commission of oyer and terminer for the county of Norfolk to examine into offences against the Act of Uniformity. In 1578 he was vicar-general of Norwich, apparently for only a short period. In 1575 he obtained the vicarage of Swaffham by gift of the queen, in 1579 the rectory of Haylesden, in 1580 that of Blofield, in 1583 that of Ashill, and in 1584 that of Forncett, all in Norfolk. He held as well the rectory of West Stow, Suffolk. He had also duties in London, and in February 1587 a formal complaint was made against him, among others, for neglecting to preach at St. Paul's Cross according to a monition. As dean of Norwich he greatly benefited the revenues of the cathedral. Part of the church lands had been annexed by Sir Thomas Shirley and others in a less degree on various pretexts. Gardiner, by dint of his influence at court and many lawsuits, finally, in 1588, obtained a royal warrant ordering the patentees to surrender the church lands, though not without some compensation. In the later years of his life Gardiner was much invalided by gout. He died about June 1589, and was buried in the south aisle of his cathedral, where his tomb, with its Latin inscription, still remains. He is described by Strype as 'a man of learning and merit and a hearty professor of the gospel.' Many of his letters are extant, and a number of them are printed in Strype's 'Annals.' Gardiner was married, and in 1573 was the father of four children.

[Cooper's Athenæ Cantabr. ii. 55; Strype's Annals of the Reformation, ii. 443–50, 485, 497, 533–7, iii. 57–62; Strype's Life of Parker, ii. 36, 87, 137, 154; Strype's Life of Aylmer, p. 201; Blomefield's Norfolk, ii. 350, iii. 620, 640, 668, iv. 301, v. 261, vi. 225, vii. 211, x. 432; Newcourt's Repert. Eccl. Lond. i. 420; Le Neve's Fasti, ii. 476, 481, 496, 500; Rymer's Fœdera, xv. 584, 725, 727; Lansdowne MS. 18, art. 15982, f. 116.]

A. V.

GARDINER, JAMES, D.D. (1637–1705), bishop of Lincoln, was the son, by his second wife, of Adrian Gardiner, apothecary, of Nottingham, 'who brought up many sons very well' (THOROTON, Nottinghamshire, p. 498, ed. 1677). He entered at Emmanuel College, Cambridge, in 1649, taking the degrees of B.A. 1652–3, M.A. 1656, and D.D. 1669. On the Restoration he obtained favour at court, became chaplain to the Duke of Monmouth, chaplain to the guards, and received the crown living of Epworth, Lincolnshire, and the stall of Stow-in-Lindsey in Lincoln Cathedral, 4 March 1660–1. He was also presented by Charles II (sede vacante) to the prebendal stall of Stratton in the cathedral of Salisbury, 3 Feb. 1665–6. In 1671 he received the sub-deanery of Lincoln from Bishop Thomas Fuller, in the room of Robert Mapletoft [q. v.] While holding this office he rebuilt his official residence, which had been reduced to ruins by the parliamentary forces on the storming of the castle and close in 1644. On the death of Dr. Honywood [q. v.] in 1681, he was recommended for the deanery of Lincoln by Archbishop Sancroft, but unsuccessfully, the dignity having been promised to Dr. Brevint [q. v.] On the serious illness of the latter in 1685, Gardiner applied to the archbishop for his interest for the anticipated vacancy, which, however, did not occur till 1695. Meanwhile, on the translation of Tenison from the see of Lincoln to that of Canterbury, Tenison successfully recommended his friend Gardiner as his successor, and Gardiner's was the first consecration performed by the new archbishop, 10 March 1694–5, being the first episcopal consecration since Tenison's own in 1691–2. Gardiner had permission to retain the stall of Stow-in-Lindsey in commendam for three years. Gardiner's ten years' episcopate was quiet and uneventful, and devoted to the conscientious discharge of his duty. He was a whig and a low churchman, and voted steadily with his party. He desired to be excused giving his opinion either way when, 22 Feb. 1699–1700, the case of Bishop Watson's deprivation came before the court of delegates. His colleagues were unanimous in confirming the sentence of the inferior court. Gardiner's conduct illustrates his irresolute character (LUTTRELL, Diary, iv. 616). When the bill against occasional conformity was thrown out by the House of

Lords, 7 Dec. 1703, he was one of the majority, ranging himself with Tenison, Burnet, Lloyd of Worcester, &c., against Compton of London, Mews of Winchester, and Sprat. Gardiner's charge at his primary visitation (2nd edit. 1697) shows an earnest desire for raising the tone of his clergy and promoting the spiritual good of his diocese in what he terms an 'atheistical and deluded age.' Many of his clergy he describes as unaccountably negligent, some grossly immoral; they indulged in the immoderate pursuit of pluralities, and were hard to reconcile to residence, cheapening their curates and calling 20*l.* or 30*l.* a year a competency. Catechising was disused, the fasts and festivals were unobserved; private baptism was too usual; for the sake of fees clandestine marriages were winked at; chancels were disused and left 'in a more nasty condition than the meanest cottage,' while the holy table was brought down into the mid-aisle, and the elements administered to persons in their seats. His faithfulness in the discharge of his duties and the gentleness of his character are set forth in a very admirable set of six sapphic stanzas on his monument in the retrochoir of Lincoln Cathedral. He died at his house in Dean's Yard, Westminster, 1 March 1704–5, his end being hastened by grief at the sudden death of his wife under peculiarly painful circumstances. He left three sons, James [q. v.], William, and Charles, and two daughters. He was an antiquary of some note, and assisted Simon Patrick [q. v.], afterwards bishop of Ely, when dean of Peterborough, in deciphering and transcribing the charters and muniments of the abbey. Besides his charge of 1697, his only published work is a sermon preached before the House of Lords on Psalm lxxix. 9, on the fast day, 11 Dec. 1695. He also published twenty sermons left in manuscript by the learned Dr. W. Outram, prebendary of Westminster, of which a second edition was printed in 1797. A portrait of him exists at Emmanuel, and it has been engraved.

[Willis's Cathedrals, i. 72; MSS. Tanner, No. 88, 170; Kennett, Lansdowne MS. 987, No. 126.] E. V.

GARDINER, JAMES, the younger (*d.* 1732), sub-dean of Lincoln, son of James Gardiner, bishop of Lincoln [q. v.], entered Emmanuel College, Cambridge, in 1695. He proceeded B.A. as sixteenth wrangler in 1699, and was elected fellow of Jesus College in 1700. He became M.A. in 1702. On 20 April 1704 he was presented by his father to the mastership of St. John's Hospital, Peterborough, and 29 April of the same year was installed

sub-dean of Lincoln Cathedral on the death of Dr. Knighton, and at the same time became prebendary of Asgarby. He is described by Browne Willis as 'an extraordinary benefactor to the church of Lincoln, having improved the house belonging to his dignity, rebuilt by his father, so very much that it may be esteemed the best house belonging to the minster' (WILLIS, *Cathedrals*, i. 99). He died at Lincoln, 24 March 1731–2, and was buried in the retrochoir of the cathedral, by the side of his father. His only daughter, Susanna, who had nursed him assiduously, followed him to the grave in little more than a month, 27 April, and was buried in the same grave in which his wife, Dinah, was also buried, 4 Sept. 1734. His monument bears a very lengthy epitaph, from which we may gather that he was a man of great suavity of disposition and beneficence, a cultured and popular preacher, and of some success as an author. He published: 1. 'The Duty of Peace amongst Members of the same State. A Sermon on Rom. xiv. 19,' London, 1713. 2. 'Practical Exposition of the Beatitudes,' 1713 (this, as well as the sermon, went to a second edition). He also translated 'Rapin of Gardens,' 1718, and contributed to the 'Oxford and Cambridge Miscellany Poems,' Lintot, 1709.

[Browne Willis's Cathedrals, i. 99; Le Neve's Fasti.] E. V.

GARDINER, JAMES (1688–1745), colonel of dragoons, eldest son of Captain Patrick Gardiner, of the family of Torwoodhead, by his wife, Mary Hodge of Gladsmuir, was born 11 Jan. 1687–8, at Carriden, Linlithgowshire. He was educated at the grammar school of Linlithgow, and having served very early as a cadet became ensign, at the age of fourteen, in a Scotch regiment in the service of Holland. In 1702 he exchanged into the service of Queen Anne, and he took part with distinction in the campaigns of Marlborough. At the battle of Ramillies, 23 May 1706, he was one of a forlorn hope sent to dispossess the French of the churchyard, and after planting the colours was disabled by a shot in the mouth. While lying helpless, after the battle, he saved himself from death by stating that he was a nephew of the governor of the neutral town of Huy. He was conveyed to a neighbouring convent, and on his recovery was exchanged. On 31 Jan. 1714–15 he was made lieutenant in Colonel Kerr's dragoons, now the 1st hussars; and on 22 July following captain in Colonel Stanhope's dragoons, disbanded in 1718. He was in this regiment at the battle of Preston, Lancashire, heading a small storming party, who in the midst of a hail of musketry, by which the majority of them were killed, advanced to the barricades and set them on fire. On 14 Jan. 1717–18 he was promoted major. His skill as a horseman attracted the attention of John Dalrymple, second earl of Stair [q.v.], to whom he became aide-de-camp. Stair's grand ceremonial entry into Paris as ambassador, in 1719, was arranged under the direction of Gardiner, who acted as master of the horse. On 20 July 1724 he was made major of the Earl of Stair's dragoons, now the 6th Inniskillings. Wodrow's statement, that he was made major of Stair's grey horse (*Analecta*, iii. 198), now called the Scots Greys, arose from the fact that Stair was colonel of the Greys both previously and subsequently (24 April 1706 to 20 April 1714, and 28 May 1745 to 27 May 1747); but from March 1715 to March 1734 he was colonel of the 6th dragoons, and it was only while he was colonel of this regiment that Gardiner served under him (information kindly supplied by Lieutenant-colonel Fergusson of Edinburgh from the war office). On 24 Jan. 1729–30 Gardiner was made lieutenant-colonel of the Inniskillings. According to his own statement, Gardiner in his early years was noted, even in Paris, for his dissolute life. While waiting for an assignation he happened to take up a book, according to Doddridge, Watson's 'The Christian Soldier,' or, according to Alexander Carlyle, Gurnall's 'Christian Armour.' Looking up during its perusal he saw what he ever afterwards regarded as a vision of Jesus Christ, and was immediately and permanently 'converted.' Alexander Carlyle, who states that he was 'very ostentatious' in his references to his conversion, describes him as 'a noted enthusiast, a very weak, honest, and brave man' (*Autobiography*, p. 16).

On 19 April 1743 Gardiner succeeded General Humphry Bland [q. v.] as colonel of the regiment of light dragoons now known as the 13th hussars, then quartered in East Lothian, in which district Gardiner had lately purchased a residence at Bankton, near Prestonpans. On the outbreak of the rebellion in 1745 Gardiner's and Hamilton's dragoons were retained in the low country, while Cope set out to oppose the Pretender in the highlands. On 14 Aug. four troops of Gardiner's dragoons marched to Perth by the ford of Dalreoch (KINGTON, *Lairds of Gask*, p. 104). He evacuated Perth on the approach of the Pretender's forces, and concentrated his dragoons in Stirling. He was confident that if they came to Stirling he would be able to 'give them a warm reception' ('Letters on the Suppression of the Rebellion,' in JESSE, *Pretenders and their Adherents*, ii. 345), but

asked in vain to be reinforced by Hamilton's dragoons from Edinburgh. The insurgents, learning that Stirling was held by Gardiner, resolved to cross the Forth by the fords of Frew, eight miles to the west. Gardiner set out to dispute the passage; but his numbers were much inferior to those of the enemy, and he could not depend on the temper of his men. He therefore, after making a reconnaissance, retreated on Edinburgh. Partly infected by the supineness and irresolution of Cope, and partly influenced by the tales of highland prowess at Killiecrankie in 1689, the dragoons both of Gardiner and Hamilton, when the Pretender's forces began to approach Edinburgh, left the city, and, notwithstanding the remonstrances of Gardiner and other officers, galloped eastwards in wild panic. They halted for the night in a field at Prestonpans, and Gardiner, 'quite worn out,' went to bed in his own house. Next morning they continued their march to Dunbar, where Cope was making his debarkation. Alexander Carlyle, then a young man, visited the camp and dined with Gardiner. On Carlyle referring to the retreat from Edinburgh—'A foul flight,' said he, 'Sandie, and they have not recovered from their panic; and I'll tell you, in confidence, that I have not above ten men in my regiment whom I am certain will follow me. But we must give them battle now, and God's will be done' (*Autobiog.* p. 132). On 20 Sept. the two armies came in sight of each other at Prestonpans, in the neighbourhood of Gardiner's own residence. When Cope took up his final position for the night, he had his rear to the high enclosing walls of Gardiner's residence and the Preston pleasure-grounds. Carlyle had another and his last interview with Gardiner in the evening. He found him 'grave, but serene and resigned; and he concluded by praying God to bless me, and that he could not wish for a better night to lie on the field.' He added that he expected they would be 'awaked early enough in the morning' (*ib.* p. 140). Gardiner's dragoons were posted on Cope's right wing, and after the discomfiture of Whitney's dragoons were ordered to charge the enemy, but after a faint fire only eleven, including Cornet Kerr (*ib.* p. 143), obeyed the word of command, the others wheeling round and galloping from the field. The battle was irretrievably lost, but Gardiner would not leave the infantry in the desperate plight in which they were now placed. At the beginning of the action he had received a bullet wound in his right breast, and soon afterwards a shot struck his right thigh. The officer in command of the foot was struck down, when 'the colonel immediately quitted his horse and snatched up the half-pike; and took upon him the command of the foot, at whose head he fought till he was brought down by three wounds, one in his shoulder by a ball, another in his forearm by a broad sword, and the third, which was the mortal stroke, in the hinder part of his head by a Lochaber axe. This wound was given him by a highlander, who came behind him while he was reaching a stroke at an officer with whom he was engaged' (*Gent. Mag.* xv. 530). He was carried, in a very weak condition, to the manse of Tranent, but lived till the forenoon of the following day. On the 24th he was buried in the north-west corner of Tranent Church, which he had been in the habit of attending. The mansion-house of Gardiner was destroyed by fire 27 Nov. 1852. By his wife, Lady Frances Erskine, daughter of the fourth Earl of Buchan, whom he married 11 July 1726, he had thirteen children, only five of whom, two sons and three daughters, survived him. Gardiner's daughter Richmond was the 'Fanny Fair' of the song "T was at the Hour of Dark Midnight,' written in commemoration of Gardiner by Sir Gilbert Elliot [q. v.], third baronet (1722–1777).

[Doddridge's Life of Colonel Gardiner, frequently printed; Doddridge's Sermon on the Death of Colonel Gardiner, 1745; Poem on the Death of Colonel Gardiner, 1746; Gent. Mag. xv. 530; Chambers's Biog. Dict. of Eminent Scotsmen; Cannon's Historical Records, 13th dragoons; Alexander Carlyle's Autobiography; Chambers's Hist. of the Rebellion; Burton's Hist. of Scotland; information kindly supplied by Lieutenant-colonel Fergusson of Edinburgh.]
T. F. H.

GARDINER, MARGUERITE, Countess of Blessington (1789–1849). [See Blessington.]

GARDINER, RICHARD, D.D. (1591–1670), divine, was born in 1591 at or near Hereford, and went to the grammar school of that town. In 1607 he entered Christ Church, Oxford, as a poor scholar, taking the degree of B.A. in 1611, M.A. in 1614, and D.D. in 1630. About this time he took holy orders, and, though he seems to have held no preferment, became known as a brilliant and quaint preacher. As deputy-orator to the university, some time previous to 1620, he delivered an 'eloquent oration' upon James I's gift of his own works to the library. James I, according to Wood, gave to Gardiner the reversion of the next vacant canonry at Christ Church in reward for a speech made before the king 'in the Scottish tone.' He was accordingly installed in 1629. In 1630 he was appointed one of the chaplains in or-

dinary to Charles I. He continued deputyorator, and in this capacity made the university oration to the king on his return from Edgehill. In 1647 he was examined several times before the parliamentary visitors, and deprived of his prebend. He lived obscurely at Oxford, befriending poor royalists, until the Restoration, when he was reinstated (July 1660). From this time he devoted all his means to charitable purposes and to the enrichment of the college. Among other benefactions in 1662–5 he gave 510*l.* towards rebuilding parts of Christ Church, and in 1663 he gave lands at Bourton-on-the-Water, Gloucestershire, to the support of two servitors on that foundation. He also erected a fountain in the quadrangle. He died at Oxford in 1670, aged 79, and was buried in the north choir aisle of Christ Church Cathedral, where a monument to his memory was erected, bearing a ludicrously laudatory inscription by South, who succeeded him in his prebend. Gardiner was a man of keen intellect, and his sermons are still worth reading.

His writings are: 1. 'Sermon at St. Paul's Ch. on his Majesty's day of Inauguration, 27 March 1642.' 2. 'Specimen Oratorium,' a collection of his official speeches, published in London in 1653, and again in 1657. In 1662 it was reprinted with additions, and republished in 1668 and 1675. 3. 'Sixteen Sermons preached in the University of Oxford and at Court,' 1659; besides several separate sermons.

[Wood's Athenæ Oxon. ed. Bliss, iii. 921; Wood's Hist. of Oxford; Le Neve's Fasti Eccl. Angl. ii. 521; Walker's Sufferings of the Clergy, ed. 1714, ii. 104; Watt's Bibl. Brit.] A. C. B.

GARDINER, RICHARD (1723–1781), called Dick Merryfellow, author, born at Saffron Walden, Essex, 4 Oct. 1723, was the son of the Rev. John Gardiner, LL.D., rector of Great Massingham, Norfolk, by a daughter of John Turner of Saffron Walden. After being educated at Eton and St. Catharine's Hall, Cambridge, where he took no degree, he went abroad for some years, and while returning to England was taken prisoner at sea by a French privateer and imprisoned at Dunkerque. On his release in 1748 he went to Norwich, and was persuaded by his relations to enter holy orders. He is said to have been a successful preacher, but in 1751, while still a deacon, he retired from the church. His unsuccessful suit to a young lady led him to publish in 1754 'The History of Pudica, a Lady of N-rf-lk, with an account of her five lovers, by William Honeycomb.' One of the lovers, named 'Dick Merryfellow,' was intended for himself. The satire is dull and acrimonious. Gardiner next took up the profession of arms, and in March 1757 he was promoted from being a lieutenant in the 12th regiment of foot to the command of a company of marines. In 1759 he commanded a detachment of marines in an engagement at St. Pierre, Martinique, and again at the siege of Guadeloupe on board the Rippon. On his return to England in the same year he published an unembellished diary of the experiences of the fleet, called 'An Account of the Expedition to the West Indies against Martinico, Guadeloupe, and other the Leeward Islands subject to the French King.' The work was originally dedicated to Lord Temple, who had procured Gardiner his commission. A third edition, which was published in 1762, together with a French translation, both beautifully printed by Baskerville, is dedicated to the queen. At the outbreak of the Spanish war in 1762 Gardiner raised a company of foot at his own expense, but was not permitted to sell his company of marines, which, after the siege of Paris, was reduced. Its commander being put upon half-pay, Gardiner retired to Swaffham, and amused himself by writing a large number of election squibs in verse and prose which, though poor even of their kind, were extensively circulated and well paid for. In 1773 Gardiner again obtained a commission, and was appointed captain in the 16th light dragoons with brevet rank of major; but he saw no more service, and shortly afterwards retired on half-pay. He then settled at Ingoldisthorpe, Norfolk, and finding his means insufficient for the support of his growing family he persuaded T. W. Coke [q. v.] to make him 'auditor-general' of his Holkham estates, with a salary of 600*l.* a year. The place was intended as a sinecure, but Gardiner recklessly altered existing arrangements, increased the rents, drove out tenants, and even endeavoured to choose guests and order dinner for his employer. In February 1777 he was dismissed with a gratuity of 200*l.* after a six months' tenure of his office. Early in 1778 he published an absurd 'Letter to Sir Harbord Harbord, with observations on Thomas William Coke,' assuming that Harbord had procured his dismissal. The insinuation was denied by Coke in the Norfolk newspapers, and similar publicity having been refused to Gardiner's rejoinder, he produced a 'Letter to T. W. Coke, Esq., of Holkham,' a long, tangled, and bitter tirade. He again took up the quarrel in the following year, when Harbord and Coke were candidates at parliamentary elections for Norwich and Norfolk county respectively; but each of his enemies was returned at the head of the poll. He died on 14 Sept. 1781, and

was buried in Ingoldisthorpe Church. At the time of his death he was preparing an elaborate 'Naval Register from 1739 to 1781,' which was never completed. A large number of his compositions were printed, chiefly consisting of prologues and epilogues to plays, elegies and epitaphs on friends and political skits; he was also mainly responsible for an ephemeral 'Lynn Magazine,' and prepared some articles for a projected county history of Norfolk. None of his work possesses any lasting merit. He married Ann, only daughter of Benjamin Bromhead of Thirlby, near Lincoln, and left a son, who became an officer in the army, and two daughters.

[Memoir of the Life and Writings (Prose and Verse) of R-ch-d G-rd-n-r, Esq.. *alias* Dick Merryfellow of Serious and Facetious Memory.] A. V.

GARDINER, SIR ROBERT WILLIAM (1781–1864), general, colonel-commandant royal horse artillery, second son of Captain John Gardiner, senior, 3rd buffs, by his wife Mary, daughter of J. Allison of Durham, was born 2 May 1781, entered the Royal Military Academy, Woolwich, as a cadet, 13 July 1795, and passed out as a second lieutenant royal artillery 7 April 1797. His subsequent military commissions were dated as follows: first lieutenant 16 July 1799, second captain 12 Oct. 1804, first captain 18 Nov. 1811, brevet-major 27 April 1812, brevet-lieutenant-colonel 8 March 1814, brevet-colonel 22 July 1831, regimental colonel 24 Nov. 1839, major-general 23 Nov. 1841, lieutenant-general 11 Oct. 1851, general 28 Nov. 1854, and colonel-commandant 23 March 1853. In October 1797 Gardiner embarked for Gibraltar, then partially blockaded by the French and Spanish fleets, and the year after was present at the capture of Minorca. He commanded a detachment of twelve guns with the force under General Don sent to Stade and Cuxhaven in November 1805, as the advance of the army proceeding to Hanover under command of Lord Cathcart. The troops having returned to England in January 1806, Gardiner effected an exchange to Sicily, which he reached just after the battle of Maida. He served in Sicily, part of the time as aide-de-camp to General Fox and afterwards to Sir John Moore, returning with Moore to England from Gibraltar in December 1807. As the regulations prevented him from serving on Moore's staff on the expedition to Sweden, he exchanged in order to accompany Sir Arthur Wellesley to Portugal. He was present at Roliça and Vimeiro. He was brigade-major of the artillery in the Corunna retreat. In the Walcheren expedition he was present at the siege of Middleburg and Flushing, and was invalided for fever. On his recovery he proceeded to Cadiz, and his battery took a prominent part in the battle of Barossa. He joined Lord Wellington's army in February 1812, and received a brevet majority for his services at the siege and capture of Badajoz (GURWOOD, *Wellington Despatches*, v. 580). He commanded a field battery at the battle of Salamanca, the capture of Madrid, the siege of Burgos (where he volunteered to serve in the siege batteries), and in the Burgos retreat. Early in 1813 Gardiner was appointed to the command of E (afterwards D) troop royal horse artillery, then attached to the 7th division, with which he fought at Vittoria in the Pyrenees, at Orthez, Tarbes, and Toulouse. He was made K.C.B. in 1814. In 1815 his troop was stationed in front of Carlton House during the corn riots, and subsequently proceeded to Belgium, where he commanded it through the Waterloo campaign and entered Paris. Gardiner was appointed principal equerry to Prince Leopold of Saxe-Coburg on the prince's marriage with the Princess Charlotte of Wales, and held the post until Prince Leopold became king of the Belgians, after which Gardiner continued to reside at Claremont. He was governor and commander-in-chief at Gibraltar from 1848 to 1855.

In 1844 Gardiner published a brief memoir of Admiral Sir Graham Moore, brother of Sir John Moore. Between 1848 and 1860 he published a number of pamphlets on military organisation, especially as regards artillery and national defence. In 1854 the committee of merchants at Gibraltar memorialised Lord Aberdeen's government against Gardiner's interference with the Gibraltar trade, which he described as contraband, and sought to render more reputable. The correspondence, together with a long report by Gardiner on 'Gibraltar as a Fortress and a Colony,' is printed in 'Parl. Papers,' 1854, vol. xliii. A scurrilous pamphlet, purporting to be a reply to the report, was distributed gratis, without any printer's name, by the committee of merchants in 1856. Gardiner was the author of many valuable reports on professional subjects, which are said to have contributed largely to the improvement in the artillery service which began after 1848 (DUNCAN, *Hist. Royal Artillery*, vol. ii.) Gardiner was a G.C.B. and K.C.H., and had the decoration of St. Anne of Russia for his services in Belgium and France. The Princess Charlotte of Wales appears to have written personally, but unsuccessfully, to the Duke of Wellington, asking him to recommend Gardiner for Portuguese and Spanish decorations (*Well. Suppl. Desp.* xi. 515)

When governor of Gibraltar, the queen of Spain sent him the Cross of Charles III, which the regulations of the service forbade his wearing.

Gardiner married, on 11 Oct. 1816, Caroline Mary, eldest daughter of Sir John Macleod, adjutant-general royal artillery, and granddaughter on the maternal side of the fourth Marquis of Lothian, by whom he had one son, General Henry Lynedoch Gardiner, C.B., of the Royal Artillery, for some years equerry in ordinary to Queen Victoria, and one daughter. Gardiner died at Melbourne Lodge, Claremont, 26 June 1864, aged eighty-three.

[Kane's List of Officers Royal Artillery (revised ed. 1869); Duncan's Hist. Royal Art.; Gent. Mag. 3rd ser. xvii. 383–5.] H. M. C.

GARDINER, SAMUEL (*fl.* 1606), was author of 'A Booke of Angling or Fishing. Wherein is shewed by conference with Scriptures the agreement betweene the Fishermen, Fishes, Fishing, of both natures, Temporall and Spirituall, Math. iv. 19. Printed by Thomas Purfoot,' 1606, 8vo. All that is known of him is that he was D.D. and chaplain to Archbishop Abbot. Only two copies of his book are known. One is in the Bodleian, the other in the Huth Library, whither it came from the library of Mr. Cotton, late ordinary of Newgate. It is dedicated to Sir H. Gaudie, Sir Miles Corbet, Sir Hammond Le-Strang, and Sir H. Spellman (*sic*). An analysis is given of the book in 'Bibliotheca Piscatoria' (p. 103), by Hone, and by the writer in 'The Angler's Note-Book' (2nd ser. No. 1, p. 5). Other instances of moralised angling are given in 'Bibl. Pisc.,' p. 41, and in Boyle's 'Reflections' (*Works*, 6 vols., London, 1772, passim, and especially ii. 399).

The following works were also written by Gardiner: 1. 'The Cognisance of a True Christian,' 1597. 2. 'A Pearle of Price,' 1600, dedicated to the Right Hon. Sir T. Egerton, lord keeper; Gardiner speaks of his having relieved 'my poore person and afflicted condition.' 3. 'Doomes Day Book or Alarum for Atheistes,' 1600. 4. 'A Dialogue between Irenæus and Antimachus about the Rites and Ceremonies of the Church of England,' 1605. 5. 'The Foundation of the Faythfull,' 1610. 6. 'The Scourge of Sacriledge,' 1611. Gardiner's favourite sport of angling furnishes him in both these latter sermons with curious opportunities to moralise; he tells in the latter how Satan plays an old sinner for a time, 'dallieth and giveth him length enough of line to scudde up and downe and to swallow up the baite, thereby to make him sure. So when he had goten a Pharisee by the gilles he made good sport with him,' &c. **7.** 'The Way to Heaven,' 1611.

[Gardiner's Works; Ames's Typogr. Antiq. (Herbert), pp. 1281, 1291, 1342; Hone's Year Book.] M. G. W.

GARDINER, STEPHEN (1483?–1555), bishop of Winchester, was the reputed son of John Gardiner, a clothworker of Bury St. Edmunds, where he was born between 1483 and 1490. In Betham's 'Genealogical Tables' (tab. DCX.) he appears as the son of one William Gardener and Helen, sister of Henry VII. The story that he was a natural son of Lionel Woodville, bishop of Salisbury, the younger son of Richard Woodville, earl Rivers, first appears in the pages of the 'Sceletos Cantab.' of Richard Parker, who wrote in the early part of the seventeenth century. The fact that no reference is made to the story by his personal enemies during his lifetime would seem sufficiently to discredit the assertion, which rests mainly on his being frequently called 'Mister Stevens' during the earlier part of his official career. This Parker supposed to be his mother's name, but it is really his christian name (from Stephanus), and secretaries in those days were frequently designated by their christian name only, as 'Master Peter' for Peter Vannes.

Gardiner was educated at Trinity Hall, Cambridge, and was subsequently elected a fellow of that society. He proceeded doctor of the civil law in 1520, and of the canon law in the following year. In both these branches of the legal profession he attained rapidly to eminence. In 1524 he was appointed one of Sir Robert Rede's lecturers in the university, and about the same year was made tutor to a son of the Duke of Norfolk, to whose family he remained firmly attached throughout his life. Through Norfolk's good offices he was introduced to Wolsey, to whom he became private secretary. In this capacity we find him as early as 1526 taking part in proceedings against heretics. In 1525 he was elected master of Trinity Hall, an office which he continued to hold until his ejectment in 1549. In the months of July and August 1527 he was with Wolsey in France, and the latter in a letter dated from Amiens proposes to King Henry to send Gardiner to him to receive his secret instructions, 'he being,' says the writer, 'the only instrument I have for the purpose.' Either in this year, or at some earlier time, he was in Paris, and there made the acquaintance of Erasmus, whom we find writing to him on 3 Sept. 1527, and recalling their pleasant meeting and also expressing his gratification at learning that Gardiner stands so high in the favour of their common patron, Wolsey. In the following year he was sent, together with Edward Fox, as ambassador to the pope, with instructions to visit France on their way. In a letter to Sir Gregory Casale, Wolsey says that the two ambassadors will show that the 'king's cause' (i.e. the proposed divorce) is founded both 'on human and divine law.' Wolsey himself suggested that in their official capacity Fox, as the royal councillor and first named in the king's letters, should have the precedence, and Gardiner 'the speech and utterance.' It was, however, agreed between the two that the latter should have the pre-eminence 'both of place, speech, and utterance ... without altercation or varyaunce, as our old amity and fast friendship doth require' (POCOCK, *Records of the Reformation*, i. 74). Their joint decision was justified by the sequel, for the tact and boldness of Gardiner working upon the fears and hesitating temperament of Clement VII ultimately wrung from the pontiff his consent to a second commission; on their return to England Henry expressed himself as highly pleased with the manner in which Gardiner had discharged his errand.

In July 1528 he appears as one of a commission appointed by Wolsey to revise the statutes which he had given for his colleges at Ipswich and Oxford, and in the following January on a royal commission designed to arrange, in conjunction with Francis I, a peace 'for the tranquillity of Italy and the defence of the pope's person.' On 1 March 1528–9 he was admitted archdeacon of Norfolk. In the following April Anne Boleyn writes to thank him for his 'willing and faithful mind.' Gardiner was at this time again in Italy, whither he had gone in January on the divorce business; but on 4 May he writes to Henry to say that though they have done their best to obtain from the pope the accomplishment of the royal desires they have not prevailed. A few days after he was recalled, and left Rome on 1 June, arriving in London with Sir Francis Bryan on the evening of the 22nd. On 28 July 1529, writing to Vannes, he says that he is going to court that day to enter upon his duties as secretary for the first time. From this date he is frequently referred to in the official correspondence as 'Mr. Stevens.' His influence with the king now began to increase rapidly. In the following year his former patron, Wolsey, was fain again and again to entreat his intercession with the king to procure some alleviation of his own lot. At a later period Gardiner professed to consider that Wolsey merited his fate (*Harleian MS.* 417), but he appears at this time really to have done his best in his behalf. He pleaded also warmly, though unsuccessfully, that the foundation at Ipswich might be spared, while Christ Church probably owes its existence to his efforts. In February 1530 he visited Cambridge, and took a leading part in the endeavours that were being made to win over the university to conclusions favourable to the divorce. His efforts, however, were strongly opposed by a large section of the academic body, and his servant Christopher was maltreated. The royal appreciation of his services was shown in the following July by a grant of the arable lands and rents of the honour of Hanworth. In 1531 he was collated to the archdeaconry of Leicester, and in October of the same year was incorporated LL.D. of Oxford. Although in relation to the divorce he still advocated 'a middle course,' he appears by this time to have altogether lost Catherine's confidence, and he was the compiler of the reply to the allegations made by her counsel in Rome. Henry now again evinced his sense of his desert by urging Clement to promote him to the see of Winchester. Gardiner was consecrated to the office on 27 Nov. 1531. Although, according to his own statement, he received 1,300l. less from the bishopric than his predecessor, Richard Fox, had done, he paid a fine of 366l. 13s. 4d. for his temporalities (*Letters and Papers Henry VIII*, v. 507). On 29 Dec. he again proceeded as ambassador to the court of France. He had now become so useful to his royal employer that Henry declared that in his secretary's absence he felt as though he had lost his right hand. Gardiner's conduct of the business entrusted to him gave entire satisfaction to Henry, and on 7 March 1531–2 he returned to England. Shortly after his return his skill as a canonist led to his services being again called into requisition in the preparation of the notable reply of the ordinaries to the address of the House of Commons to King Henry. Gardiner took up, as he generally did throughout his career, very high ground in defence of the privileges of his order, and maintained the right claimed by the bishops to make such laws as they might deem fit for 'the weal of men's souls.' Even Henry appears to have shown his displeasure at the tone of the document. Gardiner was present at Greenwich when, on 5 June, Henry transferred the great seal from Sir Thomas More to Sir Thomas Audley. There is some ground for supposing that he was at this time contemplating a less subservient line of action. He displayed remarkable assiduity in preaching in his diocese, and Volusenus, the Scottish scholar, who in 1532 dedicated to him his commentary

on Psalm l., takes occasion to praise in glowing terms the energy he thus exhibited and the example he was setting to the other bishops. In September of the same year Clement told the imperial ambassador in Rome that Gardiner had changed his mind on the whole question of the divorce, and had consequently left the English court (*ib.* v. 561). It is, however, in perfect keeping with that reputation for double dealing which he bore throughout his career, that in the same month he accompanied Henry to Calais with a personal following of twenty-four men; that in the following April Fisher on being placed under confinement was confided to his custody; that he was one of the assessors in the court which in the following month pronounced Catherine's marriage null and void; and that at the coronation of Anne Boleyn (8 June) he, along with the Bishop of London, 'bore up the laps of her robe' (*Harl. MS.* 41, fol. 2). He was one of those before whom Frith, the martyr, was summoned to appear at St. Paul's (20 June 1533); Frith had once been Gardiner's pupil at Cambridge, and the latter seems to have done his best to save him from his fate (*Grenville MS.* 11990; *Letters and Papers*, vi. 600).

On 3 Sept. he was again sent into France on the divorce business, proceeding first to Nice and then to Marseilles, and returning before the close of the year. In April 1534 he acted as one of the adjudicators to settle a dispute between the clergy and the parishioners of London respecting tithes. In the same month he resigned his post as secretary to King Henry, and was permitted to retire to his diocese. He was, however, shortly after again summoned to court, and the report was prevalent in London that his committal to the Tower was imminent. There seems to be no doubt that his position at this time was one of considerable difficulty. Henry regarded him with suspicion, imputing to him a 'colored doubleness' in his conduct with respect to the visitation of the monasteries, while he appears to have become obnoxious both to Cromwell and to Cranmer. At length, on 10 Feb. 1534–5, Gardiner took the decisive step and signed his renunciation of the jurisdiction of the see of Rome (WILKINS, *Concilia*, iii. 780); and shortly after (*not* in 1534, as Strype and others) published his famous oration, 'De vera Obedientia.' To the policy therein indicated he adhered with consistency almost to the close of his career. His arguments were devoted to establishing the following three main conclusions: (1) 'That human tradition ought to be regarded as inferior to divine precept. (2) That the Roman pontiff has no legitimate power or jurisdiction over other churches. (3) That kings, princes, and Christian magistrates are each entitled to supremacy in their respective churches, and are bound to make religion their first care.' Although Reginald Pole declared that the treatise contained nothing which a man of average intelligence would not be able to refute, it was generally accepted as a very able statement of the argument in the royal defence. Cromwell caused copies to be circulated on the continent, where it was hailed with delight by the protestant party, and in 1537 the Swiss reformers, Capito, Hedio, and Bucer, reprinted it at Strasburg, with a preface in which they strongly recommended the volume as an exposition of the true theory of the privileges and duties of the primitive bishop. Apprehensive, however, of the displeasure of the pope, Gardiner (or his friends) caused the report to be circulated among the Roman party that he had written the treatise under compulsion and in fear of death in case of refusal (*Calendar of State Papers*, x. No. 570).

It is certain that Gardiner's manifesto brought about no better understanding between himself and Cranmer, whom he continued to do his best to thwart and counteract. When the latter visited, as metropolitan, the diocese of Winchester, the bishop challenged his jurisdiction, maintaining that inasmuch as the archbishop had relinquished the title of legate of the holy see, he could no longer justly claim that of 'Primas totius Angliæ,' this being derogatory to the king's authority as 'head of the church' (Cleopatra, F. i. 260). In common with the majority of the bishops, however, Gardiner seems to have faithfully performed his share in the new translation of the New Testament which Cranmer had projected in 1533, for we find him writing (10 June 1535) to Cromwell, and stating that having finished the translation of SS. Luke and John, and being much exhausted by his severe labours, he intends to abstain altogether for a time from books and writing (*State Papers Henry VIII*, i. 430).

In the meantime the signal service which he had rendered to the royal cause had completely regained for him Henry's favour. In September 1535 the king's 'experience of his wisdom and moderation' induced him again to appoint him ambassador to the French court, with instructions 'to negotiate such articles in the treaty as shall be for the interest of the two crowns.' Gardiner arrived in Paris on 3 Nov., and his general conduct of the business gave Henry so much satisfaction that he directed Cromwell to intimate to him that, whatever might be the result of the negotiations he might be assured that the royal favour towards him would remain unaffected. In his answer to the petition of the rebels in 1536 Henry names Gardiner, along with Fox of Hereford and Bishop Sampson, as the three spiritual advisers whom he considers deserving of being called 'noble.' During Gardiner's stay in Paris he was consulted by Henry with respect to the proposals put forward by the protestants of Germany for the formation of a protestant league with England; and in February 1535-6 he forwarded a paper to Cromwell giving it as his opinion that Henry in his realm was 'emperor and head of the church of England,' but that, should he enter into the proposed league, he would become 'bound to the church of Germany, and would be able to do nothing without their consent' (STRYPE, *Mem.* I. i. 236). His policy continued, however, to be characterised by a certain disingenuousness; for while Campeggio, when contemplating his journey to England, mentions Gardiner as one of those on whose support he chiefly relies, the latter in the same year (1536) drew up a scheme whereby Henry might be enabled for the future altogether to ignore the bishop of Rome, suggesting that the substance of any bulls which the king might desire to retain in force should be reissued in the royal name without mention of the Roman pontiff.

But notwithstanding his compliant spirit and undoubted ability, Gardiner appears shortly after this again to have incurred Henry's suspicion. He was suspected of favouring the imperial interests, and Cromwell regarded him both with mistrust and dislike. In 1538 he was accordingly superseded as ambassador in Paris by Bonner. He retired to his diocese in a dejected and resentful frame of mind. In November of the same year he took part, however, in the trial of John Lambert for heresy at Westminster. His qualifications, both as a canonist and a diplomatist, were indeed too valuable to permit of his long remaining unemployed by the state. In 1539 he was again sent on an embassy to Germany. His intercourse with the protestant divines brought about no modification of his doctrinal views; and the six articles, which were promulgated soon after his return, were generally believed to have been mainly his work. Their reactionary character completed the breach between himself and Cromwell, and each felt that the overthrow of his adversary was now essential to his own safety. In the privy council Gardiner challenged the appointment by Cromwell of Barnes ('defamed for heresy') as commissioner to Germany. Cromwell's influence was still sufficiently powerful to procure Gardiner's dismissal from the council. But it was his last triumph, and in the following year his own fall and execution left his rival in almost undisputed possession of the royal favour and of supreme political influence. In the university of Cambridge Gardiner was also elected as his former opponent's successor in the chancellorship. Apart from his power to aid and protect the academic community, his election was recommended by his high attainments as a scholar and the discernment which he had already evinced as a judicious patron of rising merit among men of letters. He was, however, alarmed at the progress which the Reformation doctrines were making in the university, and his policy was chiefly retrograde. In May 1542 he issued an arbitrary edict forbidding the continuance of the new method of pronouncing Greek which had been introduced by Thomas Smith and Cheke. As regards the abstract merits of the question his view was probably the right one; but the measure had a disastrous effect in the manner in which it chilled the enthusiasm which those two eminent scholars had succeeded in arousing in connection with the revived study of the language.

In 1541 he was once more sent on an embassy to Germany. On his way he stayed at Louvain, and was hospitably entertained by the university, but these feelings of cordiality were soon changed when his hosts found leisure to make themselves acquainted with the drift of his treatise, 'De vera Obedientia' (copies of which he appears to have distributed among them), and he was not permitted to celebrate mass in the city.

In March 1542 the project of a new translation of the New Testament was again brought forward, at Cranmer's suggestion and with the royal sanction, in convocation, and the several books were once more portioned out to the different translators. Various writers, misled chiefly by Burnet, have represented the failure of the undertaking as arising partly from Gardiner's jealousy of Cranmer and partly from his real dislike to the project. 'His design,' says Burnet, 'was that if a translation must be made it should be so daubed all through with Latin words that the people should not understand it much the better for its being in English' (BURNET, ed. Pocock, i. 455, 498). But although it is true that Gardiner drew up a list of Latin words which he considered it would be safer to retain in their Latin form, it seems more just to interpret his anxiety in this respect as dictated by nothing more than those considerations which would naturally suggest themselves to the classical scholar and well-read theologian. He perceived the difficulty, not to say the danger, of attempting to supply exact English equivalents for words which learned divines had found it necessary to define with laborious and painful precision, and to whose definitions the decisions of the church had given the highest doctrinal importance. That Gardiner, by merely exhibiting the above list, should have alarmed Cranmer and brought the whole enterprise to an untimely end, would seem, to say the least, highly improbable. Mr. Dixon more reasonably represents Henry's interference, and the proposal to relegate the whole task to the two universities, as the result simply of the royal caprice (*Hist. of the Church of England*, ii. 285–9).

In September 1542 Gardiner, in conjunction with Tunstal, conducted the negotiations with the imperial ambassador in London. In the following year an event of a peculiarly painful character inspired his enemies with fresh hope. His private secretary was his own nephew, a young priest named Germayne Gardiner. He was now, along with three other clerics, brought to trial on the charge of denying the royal supremacy. The other three were acquitted, but Gardiner's nephew suffered the death of a traitor (BURNET, ed. Pocock, i. 567). That the event afforded an opportunity for aspersions on Gardiner's own loyalty is sufficiently probable. But the assertion of Strype that 'after this he never had favour or regard of the king more,' is altogether at variance with the evidence. Not less so is the story which exhibits Gardiner as the chief actor in a plot designed to bring about the disgrace of Catherine Parr, and falling himself under the royal displeasure in consequence. This rests on no contemporary authority, and is probably a protestant invention. It is discredited chiefly by the fact that at no subsequent period of his life, and especially in the proceedings at his deprivation, is any reference made to any such conduct on his part by his enemies (see MAITLAND, *Essays on the Reformation*, Nos. xv. and xvii.; FROUDE, *Hist. of England*, c. xxvii.) The evidence which convicts him of having been accessory to the plot of the prebendaries in 1543 for Cranmer's overthrow is better attested, but it is remarkable that, although somewhat under a cloud in 1546 for resisting an exchange of lands with the king, he appears to have retained the royal favour to the last. It is, however, undeniable that by the doctrinal reformers he was at this time looked upon as their chief enemy in England, although the complaint of Latimer that Gardiner had sought to deprive him of his bishopric was repudiated by the latter with considerable warmth, and apparently with truth.

In the funeral obsequies at Henry's interment Gardiner assumed the leading part, and was the chief celebrant at the mass. It appeared, however, that in the royal will—a document to which considerable suspicion attaches—he was unnamed. According to Fuller (*Church Hist.* bk. v. 254) Henry had made the omission purposely, and when his attention was drawn to it replied that ' he knew Gardiner's temper well enough, and though he could govern him, yet none of them would be able to do it.' On Edward's accession Gardiner was excluded from the council of state, and also removed from the chancellorship of the university of Cambridge.

To the innovations in matters of religious doctrine and practice which followed on the assumption of the supreme authority by the council, Gardiner offered a consistent and uncompromising resistance ; and on 25 Sept. 1547 was committed to the Fleet on the charge of having 'spoken to others impertinent things of the King's Majesty's Visitations, and refused to set forth and receive the Injunctions and Homilies' (*MS. Privy Council Book*, p. 229). After a fortnight Cranmer sent for him and endeavoured to prevail upon him to accept the homilies, hinting at the same time that if conformable in this respect he might hope again to become a privy councillor. Gardiner, however, continued contumacious. He was notwithstanding treated with considerable leniency, and after the proclamation of the general amnesty (24 Dec.) was permitted to return to his diocese. Amid the numerous changes which Somerset was now seeking to carry into effect he was especially anxious to have the formal concurrence of the episcopal order, and especially of Gardiner. The latter, although he alleged illhealth, was accordingly summoned to London (May 1548), and called upon to satisfy the council with respect to his views by the delivery of a public sermon. With this command he complied in a sermon preached at Paul's Cross (29 June), in which, however, while professing his readiness to yield a general obedience to the new legislation, he stoutly maintained the doctrine of the real presence, and omitted altogether to recognise the authority of the council. He was thereupon sent to the Tower, where he was detained in close confinement for a year.

On the fall of Somerset his hopes of regaining his freedom were destined to cruel disappointment. His repeated protests to the council against the illegality of his confinement were disregarded, and a petition to parliament which he drew up was not suffered to reach its destination. But at length the lords intimated a willingness to consider his case.

Commissioners were sent to interrogate him and to procure his signature to certain articles. As, however, these involved not only a recognition of the ecclesiastical supremacy of the council, but also a repudiation of the six articles, together with an admission of the justice of his own punishment, Gardiner refused to make so humiliating a submission. The council accordingly proceeded to sequestrate the fruits of his bishopric, while the conditions of his confinement were made still more rigorous. Burnet himself admits that Gardiner's treatment was now 'much censured, as being contrary to the liberties of Englishmen and the forms of all legal proceedings.' In December 1550 he was brought to Lambeth for formal trial by a court presided over by Cranmer. Among the charges brought against him was that of having armed his household when resident in his diocese, a measure which he fully justified by pointing out that it was a precaution warranted by the disordered state of the neighbourhood at that time. From the other charges he vindicated himself by a general oath of compurgation, and it is deserving of special note that he expressly attributed the omission of his name from the late king's will to the machinations of his enemies. On 15 Feb. 1550–1, however, he was deprived of his bishopric and sent back to the Tower, where he remained until the following reign. His successor in his see was Poynet, with Bale for his secretary. He had already (about February 1549) been deprived of the mastership of Trinity Hall.

On Mary's accession he was among the prisoners who knelt before her on her visit to the Tower, and was at once set at liberty. On 23 Aug. 1553 he was made lord high chancellor of the realm, and in this capacity placed the crown on her head at her coronation (1 Oct.), and presided at the opening of parliament (5 Oct.) In the same year he was re-elected to the chancellorship at Cambridge and to the mastership of Trinity Hall. For the severities put in force against the protestants in the earlier part of Mary's reign, Gardiner, in conjunction with Bonner, has generally been represented as mainly responsible. But it is certain that he sought (whatever may have been his motives) to save Cranmer's life, and also that of one with far less claims to mercy, Northumberland. Thomas Smith, who had been secretary to King Edward, was shielded by him from persecution, and even allowed 100*l.* per annum for his support ; while Roger Ascham was continued in office as secretary and his salary increased. Gardiner also honourably interposed to prevent the committal of Peter Martyr to prison, and furnished him with the funds necessary to enable him to return in safety to his own country. The attitude which he assumed in relation to the question of Mary's marriage, advocating the selection of a British subject, was also both statesmanlike and patriotic. On the other hand, he took a leading part in bringing back the country to that Roman allegiance against which he had written so forcibly and which he had so long repudiated; while his advocacy of the enactment of a declaration by parliament of the validity of Henry's first marriage and Elizabeth's consequent illegitimacy was an act of singular effrontery. His whole treatment of Elizabeth [see ELIZABETH] remains, indeed, one of the most sinister features in his later career, and it is asserted that after Wyatt's conspiracy he meditated her removal by foul means. His policy during the last two years of his life was partly determined by his jealousy of Reginald Pole, by whose accession to the archbishopric of Canterbury he foresaw that his own power in matters ecclesiastical would be rendered no longer paramount. He aimed at the restoration of the ecclesiastical courts and of episcopal jurisdiction with all their former, and even with augmented, powers; he procured in December 1554 the re-enactment of the statute 'De Hæretico Comburendo;' and he took a leading part in the proceedings which resulted in the burning of John Bradford and Rogers. He died of the gout at Whitehall on 12 Nov. 1555. On the account of the passion of our Lord being read to him in his last hours he exclaimed, when the reader reached the passage recording Peter's denial of his master, ' Negavi cum Petro, exivi cum Petro, sed nondum flevi cum Petro,' an ejaculation which can be interpreted only as an expression of his dying remorse for his repudiation of the Roman supremacy.

His bowels were buried before the high altar of St. Mary Overies in Southwark, where his exequies were celebrated on 21 Nov. His body was afterwards interred in his cathedral at Winchester, where his chantry chapel, a notable specimen of the Renaissance style, still exists.

There are portraits of him at Trinity Hall and in the picture gallery at Oxford. A picture alleged to be by Jan Matsys and to represent Gardiner was sold at the sale of the Secrétan collection in Paris (July 1889) for thirty thousand francs, and passed to the museum at Berlin. But there is no good evidence that it is a portrait of Gardiner.

The following is a list of Gardiner's printed works: 1. 'De vera Obedientia Oratio,' of which there are the following editions: (i) that of 1535, small quarto, 36 pp., Roman

type, with the colophon 'Londini in Ædibus Tho. Bertheleti Regii Impressoris excusa. An. M.D.XXXV. cum Privilegio' (this is probably the first edition); (ii) 'Stephani Wintoniensis Episcopi de vera Obedientia Oratio. Una cum Præfatione Edmundi Boneri Archidiaconi Leycestrensis sereniss. Regiæ ma. Angliæ in Dania legati, capita notabiliora dictæ orationis complectente. In qua etiam ostenditur caussam controversiæ quæ inter ipsam sereniss. Regiam Maiestatem & Episcopum Romanum existit, longe aliter ac diversius se habere, q; hactenus a vulgo putatum sit. Hamburgi ex officina Francisci Rhodi. Mense Ianuario 1536.' The treatise was reprinted in 1612 by Goldastus in his 'Monarchia S. Rom. Imp.,' i. 716, and by Brown (Edw.), 1690, in his 'Fasciculus Rerum expetend.' ii. 800, this latter with Bonner's preface. In 1553 there appeared the following: ' De vera Obediencia. An oration made in Latine by the ryghte Reuerend father in God Stephan, B. of Winchestre, nowe lord Chancellour of england, with the preface of Edmunde Boner, sometime Archedeacon of Leicestre, and the Kinges maiesties embassadour in Denmarke, & sithence B. of London, touchinge true Obedience. Printed at Hamburgh in Latine. In officina Francisci Rhodi. Mense Ia. M.D.xxxvi. And nowe translated into english and printed by Michal Wood: with the Preface and conclusion of the traunslator. From Roane, xxvi. of Octobre M.D.liii.' A second edition of this English version followed in the same year, purporting to be 'printed eftsones, in Rome, before the castle of S. Angel, at the signe of S. Peter. In novembre, Anno do. M.D.Liii.' Of this second (?) edition a scandalously inaccurate reprint was given in 1832 by Mr. William Stevens in an appendix to his 'Life of Bradford.' The original translation is characterised by Dr. Maitland as 'one of the most barbarous versions of Latin into a sort of English that was ever perpetrated.' 2. 'Conquestio ad M. Bucerum de impudenti ejusdem pseudologia. Lovanii, 1544.' 3. 'A Detection of the Devil's Sophistrie, wherewith he robbeth the unlearned people of the true byleef in the most blessed sacrament of the Aulter,' 12mo, London, 1546. 4. ' Epistola ad M. Bucerum, qua cessantem hactenus & cunctantem, ac frustratoria responsionis pollicitatione, orbis de se judicia callide sustinentem, urget ad respondendum de impudentissima ejusdem pseudologia justissimæ conquestioni ante annum æditæ. Louanii. Ex officina Seruatii Zasseni. Anno M.D.XLVI. Men. Martio. Cum Privilegio Cæsareo.' 5. ' A Declaration of those Articles G. Joy hath gone about to confute,' London, 4to, 1546. 6. ' An Explanation and

Assertion of the true Catholick Faith, touching the most blessed Sacrament of the Aulter; with a Confutation of a Book written against the same,' Rouen, 12mo, 1551; also, with Archbishop Cranmer's answer, fol. London, 1551. 7. 'Palinodia Libri de Vera Obedientia; Confutatio cavillationum quibus Eucharistiæ sacramentum ab impiis Capharnaitis impeti solet,' Paris, 4to, 1552; also Lovanii, 1554. 8. 'Contra Convitia Martini Buceri,' Lovanii, 1554. 9. 'Exetasis Testimoniorum quæ M. Bucerus minus genuine e S. patribus non sancte edidit de Cœlibatus dono,' 4to, Lovanii, 1554. 10. 'Epistolæ ad J. Checum de Pronuntiatione Linguæ Græcæ,' 8vo, Basel, 1555. 11. Sermon preached before Edward VI, 29 June 1548. In English in Foxe's 'Acts and Monuments.'

The library of Corpus Christi College in Cambridge also contains the following manuscripts (in the Parker collection), most of which are still unprinted: Vol. cxiii. No. 34, tractate against Bucer, maintaining the assertion 'Contemptum humanæ legis justa autoritate latæ gravius et severius vindicandum quam divinæ legis qualemcunque transgressionem.' Vol. cxxvii. (entitled 'Quæ concernunt Gardinerum') contains (No. 5) his sermon before King Edward (29 June 1548), giving his opinion on the state of religion in England, maintaining the doctrines of the real presence and clerical celibacy, but approving the renunciation of the papal power and the dissolution of the monasteries; (9) examination of witnesses in articles exhibited against him; (11) articles exhibited by him in his own defence before the judges delegate; (12) his 'Protestatio' against the authority of the same judges; (16, pp. 167–249) his 'Exercitationes,' or metrical Latin compositions, with which he is said to have beguiled the tedium of his confinement in the Tower. In Lambeth Library there is a manuscript in his hand, 'Annotationes in dialogum Johannis Œcolampadii cum suo Nathanaele de Mysterio Eucharistico disceptantis.'

[State Papers ; Calendars of Letters and Papers, Foreign and Domestic, of the Reign of Henry VIII, ed. Brewer and Gairdner, with prefaces to same; J. S. Brewer's Reign of Henry VIII to the Death of Wolsey, 2 vols., 1884 ; Dr. S. R. Maitland's Essays on the Reformation in England, 1849 ; N. Pocock's Records of the Reformation, 2 vols., 1870; Foxe's Acts and Monuments of the Christian Martyrs, ed. Cattley, 8 vols.; Cooper's Athenæ Cantabr. i. 139–40 ; J. B. Mullinger's Hist. of the University of Cambridge, ii. 58–63 ; R. W. Dixon's Hist. of the Church of England from the Abolition of the Roman Jurisdiction, 3 vols., 1878–84 ; Burnet, Lingard, Froude, &c.]   J. B. M.

GARDINER, THOMAS (fl. 1516), a monk of Westminster, probably died before the dissolution of the monastery, as his name is not among the signatures of the deed of renunciation (1540). He wrote a chronicle of English history from Brutus to the seventh year of Henry VIII, entitled 'The Flowers of England,' but the manuscript, which is among the Cotton MSS. (Otho C. vi.), has been so injured by fire as to be illegible.

[Holinshed, iii. 1590 ; Tanner's Bibl. Brit. p. 309.]   E. T. B.

GARDINER, Sir THOMAS (1591–1652), recorder of London and royalist, born in 1591, was third son of Michael Gardiner, rector of Littlebury, Essex, and Greenford, Middlesex, by Margaret, daughter of Thomas Brown, a merchant tailor of London (Visitation of London, 1633–5, Harl. Soc., i. 299). He was at one time ' of Clifford's Inn ;' was (15 May 1610) admitted a student of the Inner Temple ; was called to the bar in 1618, and on 18 Sept. 1621 was granted permission to read as a visitor in the Bodleian Library, Oxford (Oxf. Univ. Reg., Oxf. Hist. Soc., II. i. 282). He became a bencher of his inn in 1635, and was both autumn reader and treasurer in 1639. On 25 Jan. 1635-6 he was sworn recorder of the city of London. In 1638 he recommended the collection of ship-money, and showed himself henceforth a warm adherent of the court party. A certificate of his return to the Short parliament, dated 28 April 1640, as member for Callington, Cornwall, is extant among the House of Lords MSS. (Hist. MSS. Comm. 4th Rep. 25). He was a candidate for the representation of the city of London in the Long parliament, but was defeated at the poll. Had he been elected, the court party, according to Clarendon, had resolved to nominate him for the speakership. Clarendon (Hist. of Rebellion, iii. 1) describes him at the period as 'a man of gravity and quickness that had somewhat of authority and gracefulness in his person and presence, and in all respects equal to the service.' In spite of the growing divergence between Gardiner's political views and those of his city friends he was admitted to the freedom of the city (6 Oct. 1640). When Charles I visited the city on 25 Nov. 1641, Gardiner was knighted, and his speech specially commended by the king. In the following month, acting in alliance with the lord mayor, Sir Richard Gurney, he angrily denounced as illegal a petition circulated for signature in the court of common council against the right of the bishops and catholic lords to vote in the House of Lords. When the attorney-general, Sir Edward Herbert, was impeached (January 1641-

1642) Gardiner was appointed his leading counsel. On 9 March 1641–2 the lords directed him to open the defence, but he declined, and was committed to the Tower (*Lords' Journal*, iv. 639 *b*). On 12 March he petitioned for his release. A few days later the House of Commons resolved to impeach him on account of his support of the ship-money edict, and of his frequent avowals of sympathy with Charles I. The articles, seven in number, were sent up to the House of Lords 18 May, and were published five days later (cf. RUSHWORTH, *Hist. Coll.* iv. 780–2). Shortly afterwards Gardiner wrote to the king at York, reasserting his loyalty (cf. *Edward Littleton . . . His Flight to . . . York*, 1642). On 29 June 1643 his goods were ordered to be sold (*Commons' Journal*, iii. 149). Meanwhile he had joined the king at Oxford, and on 30 Oct. 1643 was nominated his solicitor-general. In 1644 he drew up a royal pardon for Laud (CLARENDON, viii. 213). In October 1644 he was apparently again a prisoner at the hands of the parliament (*Commons' Journal*, iii. 658), but in January 1644–5 he was one of the royalist commissioners at the futile Uxbridge negotiations, and on 3 Nov. 1645 was appointed by the king attorney-general. On 23 Sept. 1647 he paid to parliament a fine of 942*l.* 13*s.* 4*d.*, and his delinquency was pardoned (*ib.* v. 347). Thereupon he retired to Cuddesdon, near Oxford. On 12 Nov. 1650 the council of state issued an order permitting him to come to London for nine days on taking the engagement (*Cal. State Papers*, Dom. 1650). He died at Cuddesdon, where he was buried 15 Oct. 1652.

Gardiner married Rebecca Child, by whom he had many children. Two of his sons were slain in the civil wars within a few weeks of each other. The elder, Thomas, a captain of horse in the royalist army, was knighted by the king at Oxford as he sat at dinner on his reporting Prince Rupert's success at Newark, March 1643, and lost his life near Oxford at the end of July 1645. Henry, the younger son (*b.* 1625), also a royalist captain, was shot dead on 7 Sept. 1645 at Thame during a successful reconnaissance made by the royalists. Both were buried in Christ Church Cathedral in one grave amid 'universal sorrow and affection.' Wood praises the two young men very highly, and speaks of the younger's 'high incomparable courage, mixed with much modesty and sweetness' (WOOD, *Autobiog.*, ed. Bliss, x.) The fourth daughter, Mary (1627–1664), was second wife of Sir Henry Wood, and was mother of Mary Fitzroy, first duchess of Southampton (*d.* 1680).

[Information kindly supplied by Joseph Foster, esq.; Wood's Fasti, ed. Bliss, i. 404; Masters of the Bench of the Inner Temple, p. 31; Lloyd's Memoirs of Excellent Personages, 1668, p. 587; Gent. Mag. 1821, i. 577–9; Notes and Queries, 4th ser. iii. 531, 560, iv. 20; Overall's Remembrancia, p. 304; Lysons's Environs, ii. 440; Thurloe State Papers, i. 56; Commons' Journal, vols. ii. iii. v.; Verney's Notes on Long Parliament (Camd. Soc.), pp. 167–9; Clarendon's Rebellion; Chester's Westminster Abbey Registers, p. 161.] S. L.

GARDINER, WILLIAM or **WILLIAM NEVILLE** (1748–1806), minister plenipotentiary at Warsaw, second son of Charles Gardiner (*d.* 1765), and brother of Luke Gardiner, viscount Mountjoy was born on 23 April 1748, and on 31 Dec. 1767 was gazetted cornet in the old 18th light dragoons or Drogheda light horse. On 31 March 1770 he was promoted to a company in the 45th foot, then in Ireland. He went to America with his regiment, made the campaigns of 1775–6, part of the time as aide-de-camp to the commander-in-chief, Sir William Howe; and brought home the despatches after the battle of Long Island, for which he received a majority in the 10th foot. He served with the 10th in Philadelphia in 1777, and was wounded at Freehold during the operations in New Jersey, on 28 June 1778 (CANNON, *Hist. Rec. 10th Foot*). On 29 June 1778 he was appointed lieutenant-colonel 45th foot. Joining his old corps in England, he commanded it for three and a half years, during which time, in accordance with resolutions passed at a general county meeting of the Nottinghamshire gentry (August 1779), the 45th foot (now Sherwood Foresters) was ordered to assume the title of the 'Nottinghamshire Regiment,' so soon as three hundred men should have been recruited in the county. An extra bounty of six guineas per man was paid out of the county subscriptions. The title was given three years before county titles were bestowed on other line regiments (LAWSON LOWE, *Hist. Nottingham Regt. of Marksmen*). In January 1782 Gardiner was appointed lieutenant-colonel commandant of the 88th foot, and in February 1783 colonel of the 99th or Jamaica regiment of foot, a corps raised in England at the cost of the Jamaica planters, and the second of the six regiments which have successively borne that numerical rank. He appears never to have joined the corps, being employed in Ireland as aide-de-camp to the lord-lieutenant. The 99th was disbanded at the peace of 1783, and Gardiner, who was then put on half-pay, had no government employment until December 1789 (see memorial in *For. Office Recs.* in Public Record Office under

'Poland,' vol. cxxviii.), when the revolution occurred in the Austrian Netherlands (ALISON, *Hist. of Europe*, ii. 383–5; *Ann. Reg.* xxxiii. 1–35). He was then sent to report on the condition of the fortress of Luxemburg, which he describes as 'a most dangerous service' (*For. Off. Recs.* 'Flanders,' vol. ccxvi.) He was subsequently stationed at Brussels as a special envoy until 1792. His despatches from Ostend and Brussels during this period are among the Foreign Office Records in the Public Record Office, enrolled under 'Flanders,' 216, 217, 218, 219, 220 (1790–2), and his private letters during the same period addressed to the secretary of state are in Brit. Mus. Addit. MSS. 28064, 28065, and 28066. On 5 Jan. 1792 he was transferred as minister plenipotentiary to Warsaw, with an expression of approval for his 'zeal and assiduity.' Leaving his family as before in England, he reached Warsaw on 13 Oct. 1792. He was surprised to learn that there were already a hundred and twenty thousand Russian troops in the country. He had simply to watch and report the events, which followed in quick succession, and of which his weekly despatches (Public Rec. Off., *Foreign Off. Recs.*, 'Poland,' 128, 132, 133, 134, 135) supply many interesting details. The second partition of Poland in 1793 was followed by the insurrection, the success and speedy fall of Kosciusko, and the sack of Praga on 4 Nov. 1794 (*Ann. Reg.* xxxiv. 1–48; xxxv. 1–42). Gardiner speaks of the fine appearance and good order of the Russian troops which entered Warsaw at the invitation of King Stanislaus Augustus a few days later, but states that great atrocities were committed by the Cossacks at the storming of Praga. He was informed by the Russian authorities, without much courtesy, that his mission was at an end.

On 6 March 1795 Gardiner, who had attained the rank in 1793, was appointed major-general on the staff in Corsica, and on 21 March was appointed colonel of a new 99th foot, the third regiment bearing that number. The regiment was broken up in Demerara in 1796, and Corsica was abandoned the same year; but Gardiner was still detained in Warsaw by inability to pay his debts. His military emoluments were stopped, except 170*l.* for the governorship of Hurst Castle, during his employment under the foreign office. His salary was insufficient to keep his family at home, and during the sack of Praga he had to maintain three hundred persons at the embassy. It was not until April 1797 that, apparently through the urgent representations of Coutts, the banker, Gardiner was enabled to quit Warsaw. In

March 1799 he was in Dublin, where the commander-in-chief, Lord Cornwallis, strongly but unsuccessfully recommended him for military employment. 'He is like Lake in manner, but graver,' wrote Cornwallis (*Corresp.* iii. 77, 81). Gardiner sat in the last Irish parliament for Thomastown, King's County (*Off. List Members of Parl.* vol. ii.) In 1799 he attained the rank of lieutenant general, and was appointed colonel commandant of the newly raised 6th battalion 60th foot. He was subsequently transferred to the governorship of Kinsale from Hurst Castle. During the invasion alarms of 1803–5 Gardiner commanded the north inland district, one of the twelve military districts into which England was then divided. In 1805 he was appointed commander-in-chief in Nova Scotia and New Brunswick. He died 7 Feb. 1806.

Gardiner married in 1777 Harriet, youngest daughter of the Rev. Sir Richard Wrottesley, baronet of Wrottesley, and sister of the Duchess of Grafton, and by her left a son, Charles, major 60th foot, and four daughters.

[Debrett's Peerage, 1825, under 'Earl of Blessington;' Gent. Mag. lxxvi. pt. ii. 682, and correction at p. 771; Army Lists; Regimental Muster Rolls in Public Record Office and Foreign Office Recs. and Brit. Mus. Add. MSS. ut supra; information from Sir W. A. White, K.C.M.G., H.B.M. ambassador in Turkey.] H. M. C.

GARDINER, WILLIAM (1770–1853), musical composer, the son of a Leicester manufacturer, was born 15 March 1770. The elder Gardiner was an amateur of music, and composed at least one hymn tune, preserved in the first volume of 'Sacred Melodies,' yet he did little to encourage William's precocious talents, and judged that the smallest possible amount of general knowledge would suffice to fit him for the hosiery trade. The youth's inquiring mind found scope, however, in the meetings of the Adelphi Philosophical Society, formed in Leicester by Phillips (afterwards Sir Richard Phillips). For this society Gardiner wrote some striking papers —'Whether all the Celestial Bodies naturally attract each other?' 'What are those Bodies called Comets?' 'On Matter and its Properties,' &c. In 1790, the second year of the society's existence, this gathering of philosophical infants (fourteen out of the seventeen members were under age) was pronounced by the authorities dangerous in its tendency, and dissolved. Henceforward musical matters chiefly claimed Gardiner's attention during his leisure hours. Direction was given to his artistic taste by the arrival in Leicester of the Abbé Dobler with the last works of Haydn and Beethoven in his portmanteau. The consequent early performance (1794) there of Beethoven's E flat trio was referred to with gratitude by enthusiasts whom Gardiner met at the inauguration of the Bonn monument in 1848. Gardiner was shrewd enough to recognise without revering the genius of the great masters. He was responsible for such barbarous compilations as 'Sacred Melodies from Haydn, Mozart, Beethoven, and other composers, adapted to the best English poets and appropriated for the use of the British Church' (1812–15), and 'Judah, an Oratorio written, composed, and adapted to the Works of Haydn, Mozart, and Beethoven, by W. Gardiner' (1821). Garbled fragments out of masses, symphonies, quartets, and even operas, were here patched up with original matter by the compiler. Minuets and some less stately dances are disguised as heartrending slow movements; the first subject of the andante in Beethoven's seventh symphony does duty as a march of the Philistines, and confusion is increased by arbitrary changes of rhythm in well-known airs. Indulgence was sought for the experiment on the ground of the extreme dryness of the church music of the day. The popularity of the volumes, especially in the midland counties, for many years, may be supposed to have justified their production. Gardiner's independent compositions, such as the anthem 'One thing have I desired' (1843), the partsong 'At Evening when my work is done,' and a few songs are of greater merit. In the meantime he had edited, with notes, the 'Life of Haydn,' translated from the French of Bombet by the Rev. C. Berry, and the 'Life of Mozart,' from the German of Schlichtergroll, by R. Brewin (1817). The 'Music of Nature, an attempt to prove that what is passionate and pleasing in the art of singing, speaking, and performing upon musical instruments is derived from the sounds of the animated world, with illustrations' (1832), is a pleasant book of opinions, anecdotes, and historical scraps, but hardly successful in proving by illustration the conscious or unconscious reference by great composers to natural cries. As a precursor of modern attempts to combine the scientific with the artistic spirit, it has its place in musical history. After Gardiner's retirement from commercial life, he wrote and published (1838) 'Music and Friends, or Pleasant Recollections of a Dilettante,' furnishing a lively and good-natured account of his career, of life in his native town, and of its more or less eminent men. Gardiner's travels and correspondence, extending over a long period, had also brought him into contact with many celebrities, including Moore, Godwin, Peter Pindar, Bowring, Cobbett, Neukomm, Paganini, Weber,

Schroeder-Devrient, Malibran, Landseer, Mrs. Jordan, Kean, Elliston, Helen Maria Williams, Soult, &c. A last work, 'Sights in Italy, with some Account of the Present State of Music and the Sister Arts in that country' (1847), was the outcome of a tour made at the age of seventy-seven, yet written with a wonderful freshness of interest in pictures, persons, and performances. Gardiner was a foreign member of the Accademia di Santa Cecilia and attended one of its meetings in Rome; he was also corresponding member of the Institut historique de France. His popularity among all classes was due to his exuberant high spirits, kindness, and brilliant conversational powers. At the age of eighty-three he was still in vigorous bodily health, with bright, unclouded intellect. He died after a week's illness at Leicester, 16 Nov. 1853, and was buried in the new cemetery. His portrait by Miss M. A. Hull was published by Messrs. Allen of Leicester.

[Gardiner's works as above; Gent. Mag. new ser. xli. 92; Notes and Queries, 5th ser. x. 169, 6th ser. iv. 374; Musical World, xxxi. 765, 784; Russell's Memoirs of Moore, vols. i. ii. and vii.; Brown's Dict. of Musicians.]   L. M. M.

GARDINER, WILLIAM NELSON (1766–1814), engraver and bookseller, born at Dublin on 11 June 1766, was son of John Gardiner, 'crier and factotum' to Judge Scott, and Margaret Nelson, his wife, a pastrycook. He had an early taste for drawing. He was educated at Mr. Sisson Darling's academy, and later was, with his father, attached to the suite of Sir James Nugent of Donore, Westmeath. Showing some proficiency in various accomplishments, he was helped to pursue his artistic studies and to study for three years at the Dublin Academy, where he obtained a silver medal. He then came to London to try his fortune, and was at first employed by a Mr. Jones, a maker of profile shadow-portraits. Gardiner also supported himself by portrait-painting, but gave it up for the stage, both as scene-painter and actor. According to his own account, he attained some success in this line, but it did not last long, and he was eventually reduced to work for a Mrs. Beetham, who also made profile shadow-portraits. Being fortunate enough to make acquaintance with Captain Francis Grose [q. v.], the antiquary, he was placed by him with R. Godfrey, the engraver of the 'Antiquarian Repertory.' He acquired some considerable skill as an engraver in the chalk or stipple manner. Having taken an original engraving of his own to Messrs. Sylvester & Edward Harding, the publishers in Fleet

Street, he was employed by them in engraving plates for their publications in company with Bartolozzi and others. For them he worked on their 'Shakespeare Illustrated,' 'The Œconomy of Human Life,' 'The Biographical Mirror,' 'The Memoirs of Count de Grammont,' Lady Diana Beauclerk's illustrations of Dryden's 'Fables' and other works. His style was similar to that of Bartolozzi, and Gardiner claimed some of the plates bearing Bartolozzi's name as his own work. He subsequently worked for Bartolozzi. He occasionally painted, and in 1787, 1792, and 1793 exhibited pictures at the Royal Academy. He quitted his profession as an engraver, in which he might have succeeded, and returned to Dublin, where he did little more than spend all the money that he had earned. He returned to England with the intention of entering the church, and was entered at Emmanuel College, Cambridge. Finding that as an Irishman he had no chance there of a fellowship, he removed to Benet (i.e. Corpus Christi) College, and took his degree in 1797 as sixth senior optime. He remained at Cambridge for some time in the hopes of obtaining a fellowship, but, being unsuccessful, he relinquished all idea of taking holy orders and returned to London, where he obtained employment in copying portraits for his former patron, E. Harding. Subsequently he set up as a bookseller and publisher in Pall Mall. From his eccentricities of dress, behaviour, and conversation, he became a well-known figure at sales, and his shop was often visited by people out of curiosity. He avowed his political views as a whig with great freedom. The Rev. Thomas Frognall Dibdin [q. v.] introduced him in his 'Bibliomania' under the character of 'Mustapha,' and an engraved portrait of him exists in that character. Gardiner resented this keenly, and retaliated with stinging sarcasm in his published catalogues. Dibdin, in his 'Bibliographical Decameron,' refers again to this controversy. Gardiner did not meet with great success in his new profession, and became very dirty and slovenly in his habits, being a great snuff-taker. On 8 May 1814 he put an end to his own life, a deliberate act, in consequence, as he described it, of unbearable misery. He left a brief autobiography, printed in the 'Gentleman's Magazine' for June 1814. He married a Miss Seckerson.

[Gent. Mag. 1814, lxxxiv. pt. i. 622; Dodd's MS. Hist. of English Engravers (Brit. Mus. Addit. MSS. 33400); Dibdin's works cited above; Pasquin's Artists of Ireland; Redgrave's Dict. of Artists.]   L. C.

GARDNER.   [See also GARDINER.]

GARDNER, MRS. (*fl.* 1763–1782), dramatist and actress, appeared at Drury Lane Theatre as Miss Cheney 1 Oct. 1763, playing Miss Prue in Congreve's 'Love for Love.' On 13 Jan. 1764 she was Rose in the 'Recruiting Officer.' She played Miss Prue once more 20 Oct. 1764, and in June 1765 was the original Mrs. Mechlin in Foote's comedy of the 'Commissary,' with which the Haymarket reopened. On 19 Nov. 1765, at Covent Garden, as Mrs. Gardner, late Miss Cheney, she acted her favourite character of Miss Prue; 15 March 1766, at the same house, she was Belinda in the 'Man of the Mode,' and on 26 April was the original Fanny in 'All in the Right,' an unprinted farce from Destouches, attributed to Hull. When Foote [q. v.], after his recovery from his accident, reopened the Haymarket, Mrs. Gardner appeared there in many of the pieces. She was the original Margaret in the 'Devil upon Two Sticks,' 1768; Mrs. Circuit in the 'Lame Lover,' 1770; Mrs. Matchem in the 'Nabob,' 29 June 1772; and Mrs. Simony in the 'Cozeners,' 1774. At the Haymarket, under Foote, her reputation was made. She played, however, at the other houses characters chiefly belonging to broad comedy. In 1777, the year of Foote's death, she went to Jamaica. Returning thence she appeared in Dublin at the Capel Street Theatre, but quarrelled with the managers about a piece of hers which, in violation of their promise, they failed to bring out. On 13 Aug. 1782 she reappeared at the Haymarket, as Mrs. Cadwallader in the 'Author.' After this her name is not found in the bills. The 'Biographia Dramatica' says she played occasionally, and attempted (sola) an entertainment of her own composition.

Mrs. Gardner wrote 'Advertisement, or a Bold Stroke for a Husband,' a comedy acted at the Haymarket once, 9 Aug. 1777, for her benefit. Egerton (*Theatrical Remembrancer*) ascribes to her the 'Female Dramatist,' a musical farce acted at the Haymarket 16 Aug. 1782, the authorship of which has also been imputed to the younger Colman. Neither piece has been printed. She had an agreeable face and figure, and would have made a high reputation had she not fallen under the influence and copied the manner of Foote. She was the best actress in his company. Her husband, an insignificant member of the Covent Garden company, by whom she had a family, neglected her, and was treated by her with exemplary patience and constancy. He appears to have survived her.

[Genest's Account of the English Stage; Biographia Dramatica; Theatrical Biography, 1772.]
                                              J. K.

GARDNER, ALAN, first BARON GARD-NER (1742–1809), admiral, son of Lieutenant-colonel Gardner of the 11th dragoon guards, was born at Uttoxeter in Staffordshire, on 12 April 1742. In his passing certificate, dated 15 Feb. 1760, he is described as more than twenty years of age, and as having been upwards of six years at sea, 'part whereof in the merchants' service.' The two statements seem equally incorrect, but what appears certain is that he joined the Medway, under the command of Captain Denis [see DENIS, SIR PETER], in May 1755, and in January 1758 was moved into the Dorsetshire, also commanded by Denis, in which he was present in the battle of Quiberon Bay. On 7 March 1760 he was promoted to be lieutenant of the Bellona, again with Denis, but remained in the ship on Denis being superseded by Captain Faulknor, and took part in the capture of the Courageux on 14 Aug. 1761. On 12 April 1762 he was promoted to be commander of the Raven fireship, and on 17 May 1766 was advanced to post rank, and appointed to the command of the Preston, going out to Jamaica as flag-ship of Rear-admiral Parry. In 1768 he was removed into the Levant frigate, which he commanded on the same station till 1771. In 1775 he was appointed to the Maidstone of 28 guns, also sent out to the West Indies, from which in 1778 he was sent to join Lord Howe on the coast of North America, and was able to carry to Howe the first intelligence of the approach of the French fleet [see HOWE, RICHARD, EARL]. On 3 Nov. 1778 he captured a large and heavily armed French merchant ship, which he carried with him to Antigua, when he was appointed by Byron [see BYRON, HON. JOHN] to the Sultan of 74 guns. In her he had an important share in the battle of Grenada, 6 July 1779, as one of the seconds of the admiral; and in the following year was sent to England in charge of convoy. Towards the end of 1781 he commissioned the Duke of 98 guns, and accompanied Sir George Rodney to the West Indies, where he shared in the glories of 12 April 1782. He returned to England at the peace, and in 1786 was sent out to Jamaica as commander-in-chief, with a broad pennant in the Europa. After holding the command for three years he returned to England, and in January 1790 he was appointed to a seat at the board of admiralty, which he held till March 1795. He was also returned to parliament as member for Plymouth, which he continued to represent till 1796, when he was returned for Westminster. During the Spanish armament in 1790 he commanded the Courageux for a few months; and in February 1793, being advanced to flag-

rank, he went out to the West Indies, with his flag in the Queen, and in command of a considerable squadron; but for want of troops little was effected against the French colonies. On his return to England he was attached to the grand fleet under Lord Howe, and took part in the action of 1 June 1794, when the loss of the Queen was exceptionally severe. For his services on this occasion Gardner was created a baronet, and on 4 July was advanced to the rank of vice-admiral. He was again with the fleet under Lord Bridport off Lorient, on 23 June 1795, but had little share in the action. In April 1797, at the time of the mutiny at Spithead, he had his flag in the Royal Sovereign, and in a conference with the delegates on board the Queen Charlotte is described as having lost his temper and seized one of the delegates by the collar, threatening to have him and his fellows hanged. This led to a violent outburst, from which Gardner with difficulty escaped. On 14 Feb. 1799 he was promoted to be admiral of the blue; in August 1800 he was appointed commander-in-chief on the coast of Ireland, and in the following December was created a peer of Ireland, by the title of Baron Gardner. He continued, however, to represent Westminster in parliament till, in 1806, he was raised to the dignity of a peer of the United Kingdom, by the title of Baron Gardner of Uttoxeter. In 1807 he was appointed to the command of the Channel fleet, but the state of his health compelled him to resign it in the following year, and he died a few months afterwards, on 1 Jan. 1809. There is a pleasing portrait of him in the Painted Hall at Greenwich. He married at Jamaica, in 1769, Susanna Hyde, daughter and heiress of Mr. Francis Gale, and widow of Mr. Sabine Turner. By her he had several children, the eldest of whom, Allan Hyde, succeeded to his titles.

[Charnock's Biog. Nav. vi. 583 ; Ralfe's Nav. Biog. i. 407; Foster's Peerage; Jerdan's National Portrait Gallery.]   J. K. L.

GARDNER, DANIEL (1750 ?–1805), portrait painter, born at Kendal about 1750, came to London as a boy, and became a student of the Royal Academy. He attracted the notice of Sir Joshua Reynolds, and for a time became fashionable for his small portraits done in oil or crayons. They showed great elegance in composition, and a delicate perception of beauty; Hayley in his poems pays tribute to his taste and ease. Thomas Watson engraved several of his portraits in mezzotint, among them being 'Frances, Countess of Jersey,' 'Sir William Meredith, Bart.,' 'the children of Grey Cooper, Esq.,' 'Rebecca,

Lady Rushout, and her children;' also 'Abelard' and 'Heloise' (companion engravings), 'Circe,' 'Maria,' &c. Among other engravings from Gardner's pictures were 'Mrs. Gwyn and Mrs. Bunbury (the Horneck sisters) as the Merry Wives of Windsor' by W. Dickinson, 'Mrs. Swinburne' by W. Doughty, 'George Simon Harcourt, Visct. Nuneham,' by V. Green, 'Charles, Marquess Cornwallis,' by J. Jones, and others. Gardner only exhibited once at the Royal Academy, in 1771. Having realised some property by his art he retired from practice. He died in Warwick Street, Golden Square, 8 July 1805, aged 55. Two portraits and a family group were exhibited at the Grosvenor Gallery in 1888-9 by Mr. A. Anderdon Weston. Gardner also etched in 1778 a plate from a portrait by Hoppner of Philip Egerton, esq., of Oulton.

[Redgrave's Dict. of Artists; Grosvenor Gallery Catalogue, 1888-9; Chaloner Smith's British Mezzotinto Portraits.] L. C.

GARDNER, GEORGE (1812-1849), botanist, was born in Glasgow in May 1812. He studied medicine in the university of his native town; but when he had qualified as a surgeon he conceived a strong desire for botanical travel, and with the assistance of his teacher, Sir W. J. Hooker, obtained the support of the Duke of Bedford and others as subscribers for the plants that he might collect. In May 1836 he accordingly sailed for Brazil. Before starting he issued a pocket herbarium of 250 species of British mosses. In Brazil he first explored the Organ Mountains, and subsequently Pernambuco, the Rio, San Francisco, Aracaty, Ceara, and Piauhy, returning to Rio towards the end of 1840. He sent home sixty thousand specimens, representing three thousand species, and his entire collection comprised twice that number of species of flowering plants alone. He reached Liverpool, on his return, in July 1841, bringing with him six large Wardian cases of living plants. He described several new genera in a series of papers in Hooker's 'London Journal of Botany,' and in 1842 began in its pages an enumeration of Brazilian plants, and in those of the 'Journal of the Horticultural Society' 'Contributions to the History of the Connection of Climate and Vegetation.' In the same year he became a fellow of the Linnean Society, and in 1843 assisted H. B. Fielding in the preparation of an illustrated descriptive work entitled 'Sertum Plantarum,' London, 1844, 8vo. Being then appointed superintendent of the botanical garden of Ceylon, he devoted the voyage out to the preparation of the journal of his Brazilian travels, some accounts of which had already appeared, in letters to Sir W. J. Hooker, in the 'Companion to the Botanical Magazine,' and in the 'Annals of Natural History.' The detailed journal, the proof-sheets of which were revised by John Miers and Robert Heward, appeared in 1846 as 'Travels in the Interior of Brazil, principally through the Northern Provinces and the Gold and Diamond Districts, during the years 1836-1841.' In 1845 he visited Madras, and botanised in the Neilgherry Hills with Dr. Wight, with whom and Dr. M'Clelland he became associated as part editor of the 'Calcutta Journal of Natural History.' During 1846, 1847, and 1848 he published in that journal a monograph of the *Podostemaceæ* and 'Contributions towards a Flora of Ceylon;' and at the time of his death he had fully prepared for publication a manual of Indian botany, which, however, seems never to have been issued. He died of apoplexy at Neura Ellia, Ceylon, 10 March 1849. His herbarium, comprising fourteen thousand specimens, was mostly purchased for the British Museum.

[Proc. Linn. Soc. ii. 40; Hooker's Companion to the Bot. Mag. (1836), ii. 1, 344; London Journ. Bot. (1849), i. 154, (1851) iii. 188; Cottage Gardener, ii. 74; Gardener's Chronicle (1849), p. 263, (1851) p. 343.] G. S. B.

GARDNER, JOHN (1804-1880), medical writer and practitioner, was born in 1804 at Great Coggeshall in Essex. After completing his medical education (partly under the old system of apprenticeship) in 1829, he settled as licentiate of the Apothecaries' Society in London, where he continued to the end of his life. In 1843 he translated and edited Liebig's 'Familiar Letters on Chemistry in its relations to Physiology, Dietetics, Agriculture, and Political Economy,' which passed through several editions, and of which a second series was published a few years later. This led to his making Liebig's personal acquaintance at Giessen (of which university he was made M.D. in 1847), and to his being instrumental in establishing in 1844 the Royal College of Chemistry in Hanover Square, London, of which institution he was secretary till 1846. He also was the means of securing the services of Dr. A. W. Hofmann as the first professor there. He was an active-minded man, and took part in various useful projects. He was for a time professor of chemistry and materia medica to the General Apothecaries' Company, which he had assisted in founding for the preparation and sale of pure drugs under the supervision of scientific chemists and physicians. While connected with this company he was the means of introducing to the notice of the practitioners of this country many valuable drugs from America, among which may especially be mentioned podophyllin (see *Lancet*, 1862, i. 209, 286, 418). He wrote in various medical periodicals, belonged to the Chemical and Ethnological Societies of London, and in 1860 became, by examination, licentiate of the Royal College of Physicians, Edinburgh. He died in Lansdowne Crescent, Notting Hill, London, 14 Nov. 1880. He was a truly religious man, as appears from his principal work, entitled 'The Great Physician; the Connexion of Diseases and Remedies with the Truths of Revelation,' London, 8vo, 1843. With the exception of the last chapter, which contains a brief history of epidemic diseases or pestilences, the subject-matter of the volume is entirely theological, written from the standpoint of the well-known 'Bridgewater Treatises.' It was favourably noticed in some of the religious journals of the day, but the sale was not sufficient to encourage him to publish the second part of the work, which was to have consisted of medical matters. Among his other works may be mentioned: 1. 'Household Medicine,' 9th edition, 1878. 2. 'Longevity; the Means of Prolonging Life after Middle Age,' 5th edition, 1878. 3. 'Hymns for the Sick and Convalescent,' 2nd edition, 1879. In 1832 Gardner married Miss Julia Emily Moss, who survived him, and in 1881 wrote a little book on 'Marriage and Maternity.' By her he had a large family.

[Medical Directory, &c.; personal knowledge; information from his son, the Rev. Dr. D. M. Gardner.] W. A. G.

GARDNER, THOMAS (1690?–1769), historian of Dunwich, was 'salt officer' and deputy comptroller of the port of Southwold, Suffolk. He was an intelligent antiquary, made numerous local discoveries, and died possessed of large collections, of which the coins formed the most valuable portion. In 1745 he exhibited to the Society of Antiquaries 'A true and exact platt, containing the boundaries of the town of Dunwich, and the entries of certain records and evidences, and some things now in variance made the 14th of March 1589, by Ralph Agas' [q. v.] (GOUGH, *British Topography*, ii. 249). After much difficulty, occasioned by the loss of most of the town's records, Gardner published by subscription 'An Historical Account of Dunwich, antiently a city, now a borough; Blithburgh, formerly a town of note, now a village; Southwold, once a village, now a Town-corporate; with remarks on some places contiguous thereto. ... Illustrated with copper-

plates,' 4to, London, 1754. Prefixed to some copies is a modernised version of Agas's plan by Joshua Kirby. Agas's report of the state of the town and harbour referred to above is printed from the original manuscript then in Gardner's possession at pp. 20–2. Gardner died 30 March 1769, aged 79 (*Gent. Mag.* xxxix. 215), and was buried in Southwold churchyard near the south aisle, between his two wives Rachel and Mary, with the following inscription :—

> Betwixt honour and virtue here doth lie
> The remains of old antiquity.

(*Addit. MS.* 19082, f. 305). Mackenzie Walcott erroneously says 'his quaint epitaph records thus the names of his two wives' (*East Coast of England*, p. 47; cf. *Notes and Queries*, 3rd ser. iv. 265–6). It refers to the lines on their tombs.

[Authorities as above.] G. G.

GARDNER, WILLIAM (1844–1887), inventor of the Gardner gun, a native of Ohio, U.S.A., afterwards resided in England, where most of his inventions were developed. Possessing a strong mechanical bent he early abandoned the study of the law to carry out certain improvements in firearms. About 1870 he submitted to the British military authorities a magazine pistol, which was not approved. In 1876 he perfected the machine gun which bears his name, and which after long competitive trials was introduced into the British service five years later. Various improvements in firearms, &c., patented by him in the United Kingdom appear in the Patent Lists for 1882–4. Shortly before his death 'Captain' Gardner, as he was called, had perfected an improved quick-firing cannon. He died suddenly at Henley Lodge, St. Leonards-on-Sea, 20 Jan. 1887, aged 43.

[Information furnished by the general agent, Gardner Gun Co. (Lim.), London.] H. M. C.

GARDNER, WILLIAM LINNÆUS (1771–1835), Indian officer, was eldest son of Major Valentine Gardner, 16th foot. The father was elder brother of Alan, first lord Gardner [q. v.], and was with the 16th foot during its service in America from 1767 to 1782). Gardner's mother was his father's first wife, Alicia, third daughter of Colonel Livingstone of Livingstone Manor, New York. He was brought up in France, and when a boy was gazetted ensign in the old 89th foot, 7 March 1783, and placed on half-pay of the regiment on its disbandment some weeks later. He was brought on full-pay as ensign in the 74th highlanders in India, 6 March 1789, and promoted to a lieutenancy in the 52nd foot in India in October the same year. The regimental muster-rolls, which are incomplete, show him on the strength of the depôt-company at home in 1791–3. He became captain 30th foot in 1794, and at once exchanged to half-pay of a disbanded independent company. Of the circumstances under which he retired various stories were told. All that is known is that he appeared afterwards as a military adventurer in the chaotic field of central Indian discord. For some time he was in the service of Jeswunt Rao Holkar, the famous Mahratta ruler of Indore. Holkar sent him on a mission to the independent princes of Cambay, where he married his only wife, a native princess, on whose ancestors the emperors of Delhi, in days gone by, had conferred the highest hereditary honours. Holkar afterwards sent Gardner to treat with Lord Lake, and, suspecting treachery, grossly insulted him on his return. Gardner replied by attempting to cut down the maharajah. Failing, he escaped in the confusion, and went through a succession of the wildest adventures. At one time, when a prisoner of Emurt Rao, he was strapped to a gun under threat of death unless he promised to fight against the English. At another he jumped down a precipice fifty feet deep into a stream to escape his guards. Eventually he made his way into Lake's camp in the guise of a grass-cutter (1804). His wife and her attendants were allowed to depart unmolested from Holkar's camp through her family influence. Gardner served as a leader of irregular horse (captain) under Lake, and in the same capacity (lieutenant-colonel) performed important services under Sir David Ochterlony in Kamaun in 1814–15. In the latter connection Gardner (whose name, like that of his father, is spelt 'Gardiner' in many army lists) has been confounded by some writers with the first British resident in Nepaul, the Hon. Edward Gardiner, Bengal civil service (for whom see Debrett, Peerage, 1825, under 'Blessington,' and Dodwell and Miles, Lists of Bengal Civil Servants). He also rendered valuable service under Ochterlony in the settlement of Rajpootana in 1817–18. He was rewarded in 1822 with an unattached majority in the king's service antedated to 25 Sept. 1803.

The name of William Linnæus Gardner first appears in the East India Company army lists in January 1819, as a local lieutenant-colonel commanding a corps of irregular cavalry, afterwards described as Gardner's corps, as Gardner's local horse, and as the 2nd local horse, with which he was stationed at Khassgunge in 1819, at Saugor in 1821, at Bareilly in 1821–3, in Arracan in 1825, and at Khassgunge again in 1826–7. In January 1828, when the 2nd local horse was again at

Bareilly, Gardner is described as on leave, and his name does not again appear in either the British or Indian army list. No further record of him exists at the India Office. He resided at Khassgunge, now the chief town of the Etah district, North West Provinces, which was his private property (Hunter, Gazetteer of India, under 'Kásganj'), and there died on 29 July 1835, aged 65. His begum died a month after him (Parkes, vol. i.)

Gardner, a skilled rider and swordsman in his prime, is described in his latter years as a tall, soldierlike old man, of very courteous and dignified manners, and very kind to his ailing wife.

Gardner's or the 2nd local horse became the 2nd irregular cavalry, and since the Bengal mutiny, during which it was conspicuous by its loyalty, has become the 2nd Bengal cavalry.

[Foster's Peerage, under 'Gardner;' British and Indian army lists; information supplied by the India office; the incidental notices of Gardner in Mill's Hist. of India, vols. vii. and viii., and in Hunter's Gazetteer of India are inaccurate. Much information respecting Gardner will be found in Mrs. Fanny Parkes's Pilgrimage in Search of the Picturesque (London, 1850, 2 vols.) Mrs. Parkes, the wife of a Bengal civilian of rank, was personally acquainted with Gardner, and her book contains an account of him reprinted from the Asiatic Journal, Oct. 1834, and a letter from Gardner correcting misstatements therein.]

H. M. C.

GARDNOR, JOHN (1729–1808), painter, began life as a drawing-master, teaching drawing, painting, and calligraphy. As such he had an academy in Kensington Square. In 1763 he exhibited with the Free Society of Artists, sending two drawings with a specimen of penmanship. He exhibited with the same society in the following years up to 1767; in 1766 and 1767 contributions were also sent by 'Mr. Gardnor's pupils.' In 1767 he received a premium of twenty-five guineas from the Society of Arts. Gardnor seems now to have quitted the profession of drawing for the church, and took orders. In 1778 he was instituted to the vicarage of Battersea, which he continued to hold up to his death, which occurred on 6 Jan. 1808 at the age of 79; he was buried in Battersea Church. In 1782 Gardnor exhibited again, this time at the Royal Academy, sending two landscapes, and continued to be a frequent contributor of landscapes and views up to 1796. On 16 May 1787 Gardnor started with his nephew Richard on a tour to Paris, Geneva, Lausanne, Basle, Strasburg, and back down the Rhine. He made numerous drawings of the scenery on the Rhine, which he published in folio parts, the first of which appeared in 1788 entitled ' Views taken on and near the River Rhine, at Aix-la-Chapelle, and on the River Maese.' These views were engraved in aquatint by Gardnor himself, William and Elizabeth Ellis, Robert Dodd, Samuel Alken, and J. S. Robinson. A smaller edition was published in 1792, in which the aquatints were executed by Gardnor and his nephew. Gardnor also executed a series of views in Monmouthshire for D. Williams's 'History' of that county, published in 1796; they were engraved in aquatint by Gardnor himself and J. Hill. As vicar of Battersea Gardnor officiated on 18 Aug. 1782 at the wedding of William Blake [q. v.], the painter. In 1798 a sermon was printed which he preached before the armed association of Battersea.

GARDNOR, RICHARD (*fl.* 1766–1793), drawing-master, nephew of the above, was apparently his pupil. In 1766 he exhibited with the Free Society of Artists, and from 1786 to 1793 at the Royal Academy. His contributions were landscapes and views. He accompanied his uncle during his tour on the Rhine, and assisted him to engrave the plates in aquatint for the published work.

[Redgrave's Dict. of Artists; Graves's Dict. of Artists, 1760–1880; Manning and Bray's History of Surrey, iii. 341; Gardnor's Views on the River Rhine; Gilchrist's Life of Blake; Catalogues of the Free Society of Artists and Royal Academy.]   L. C.

GARDYNE, ALEXANDER (1585 ?–1634 ?), Scotch poet, an advocate in Aberdeen, was probably born about 1585, as he was master of arts before 1609, when he produced his ' Garden of Grave and Godlie Flowers.' This is a series of sonnets, elegies, and epitaphs, replete with fantastic conceits of thought and style, and including tributes to royalty and various friends, as well as reflective studies on such themes as fickle fortune, the wickedness of the world, and ' Scotland's Grief on His Majesties going into England.' Between 1612 and 1625 Gardyne wrote ' The Theatre of Scotish Kings,' based on Johnston's ' Reges Scoti,' and treating *seriatim* of the monarchs from Fergus to James VI. His next work, ' The Theatre of Scotish Worthies,' has not been preserved. In 1619 appeared a metrical version of Boece's Latin biography of Bishop Elphinstone. Gardyne's other writings consist mainly of commendatory verses prefixed to forgotten authors like Patrick Gordon and Abbakuk Bisset. In 1633 Gardyne and others were sworn before the sheriff principal of Aberdeen ' to continue as members and ordinar

advocats and procurators of this seat.' Another Alexander Gardyne (or Garden, as the names of both are sometimes given) was professor of philosophy at Aberdeen for some time after this, but he was probably the advocate's son. The death of Alexander Gardyne, the poet, is approximately assigned to 1634.

The ' Garden ' was printed in small quarto in 1609, by Thomas Finlason, Edinburgh. The ' Theatre ' was transcribed in 1625, and the copy, now in the Advocates' Library, Edinburgh, was printed in 1709 by James Watson, Edinburgh. The two works were edited in 1845 by W. Turnbull for the Abbotsford Club, and printed in a royal quarto volume, together with poems by John Lundie, an Aberdeen professor of Latin in Gardyne's time. The introduction includes a biographical disquisition by David Laing.

[Abbotsford Club volume as above; Kennedy's Annals of Aberdeen, ii. 166; Irving's Hist. of Scotish Poetry.]   T. B.

GARENCIÈRES, THEOPHILUS, M.D. (1610–1680), physician, was born in Paris in 1610. After mastering the primer he was made to read ' The Prophecies of Nostradamus,' and retained throughout life a love for them. He graduated M.D. at Caen in Normandy in 1636, came to England with the French ambassador, was incorporated M.D. at Oxford 10 March 1657 (WOOD, *Fasti Oxon.* ii. 791), and admitted a candidate at the College of Physicians of London 23 March in the same year. While in England he left the Roman church. In 1647 he published ' Angliæ Flagellum seu Tabes Anglica,' a work which is now very rare, and which owes its reputation to the error deduced from its title-page, that it is a treatise on rickets, three years earlier than that of Glisson. The ' Tabes Anglica ' of Garencières is pulmonary phthisis; the 187 pages of his duodecimo volume contain little of value, and not one word about rickets. In 1665 he published ' A Mite cast into the Treasury of the Famous City of London, being a Brief and Methodical Discourse of the Nature, Causes, Symptoms, Remedies, and Preservation from the Plague in this calamitous year 1665, digested into Aphorisms.' The book is dedicated to the lord mayor, contains thirty-five aphorisms, and recommends Venice treacle taken early as the best internal remedy for the plague, while poultices are to be applied externally to the glandular swellings. The preface is dated 14 Sept. 1665, from the author's house near the church in Clerkenwell Close. A second edition, enlarged to sixty aphorisms, appeared in the same year, and a third, containing sixty-one aphorisms, in 1666. In 1672 he published 'The True Prophecies or Prognostications of Michael Nostradamus, translated,' and in 1676 'The Admirable Virtues and Wonderful Effects of the True and Genuine Tincture of Coral in Physick.' Ten authors are quoted as praising coral, and it is stated to cure more than thirty separate diseases, but no cases or personal experience are given. Garencières lived for more than ten years (prefaces) in Clerkenwell, and was on friendly terms with Francis Bernard [q. v.], the learned apothecary, and afterwards physician to St. Bartholomew's Hospital. He died poor about 1680. His portrait as a medallion is engraved in his edition of 'Nostradamus.'

[Wood's Fasti Oxon. ii. 791; Munk's Coll. of Phys. i. 276; Works.] N. M.

GARGRAVE, GEORGE (1710–1785), mathematician, born at Leyburn, Yorkshire, in 1710, was educated by his uncle, John Crow, a schoolmaster in that place. Under him he acquired a considerable knowledge of the classics and mathematics. His natural bent was towards astronomy, and in after life he was reputed one of the best proficients in the less recondite branches of that science in the north of England. In 1745 he became associated with Joseph Randall in the management of the academy at Heath, near Wakefield. The academy, though of good repute, did not pay, and was given up in 1754. Gargrave then started at Wakefield a mathematical school, with such success that in 1768 he retired on a handsome competency. He died on 7 Dec. 1785, and was buried in the churchyard at Wensley. Gargrave was a musician of some skill, and his handwriting was remarkably clear and fine. He possessed a large and well-selected library, and a fine collection of astronomical and other scientific apparatus. He contributed to the 'Gentleman's Magazine' a translation of Dr. Halley's 'Dissertation on the Transit of Venus' (1760, p. 265); 'Observations on the Transit of Venus' (1761, p. 296); on the same subject (1769, pp. 278–9); 'Observations of an Eclipse of the Moon' (1776, p. 357); and 'Memoirs of Mr. Abraham Sharp, mathematician, mechanic, and astronomer' (1781, p. 461). He also left a manuscript treatise on the doctrine of the sphere.

[Gent. Mag. 1841, pt. ii. p. 36.] J. M. R.

GARGRAVE, SIR THOMAS (1495–1579), speaker of the House of Commons, and vice-president of the council of the North, son of Thomas Gargrave of Wakefield and Elizabeth, daughter of William Levett of Normanton, Yorkshire, was born in 1495 at a house in the Pear Tree Acres at Wakefield. In 1539 he was one of the learned members of the newly instituted council of the North. In 1547 he accompanied the Earl of Warwick into Scotland, acting as treasurer to the expedition. For these services he received there the honour of knighthood. After his return he purchased a considerable amount of land in Wakefield and its neighbourhood, including Kinsley Hall, where he resided for some years, and eventually the beautiful seat of Nostell Priory. In the first parliament of Edward VI in 1547 he was elected M.P. for the city of York, and again in 1553, and in 1555 was chosen to represent the county. During the reign of Queen Mary he was very active as a member of the council of the North, an arduous post owing to the constant inroads of the Scots and the unpopularity of the home government. On the accession of Elizabeth he was again elected to represent the county, and on 25 Jan. 1558–9 he was chosen speaker of the House of Commons. In this capacity he presented and read an address to the queen, praying her to take a husband. So far did he obtain the confidence of the queen that when the Duke of Norfolk was sent on an expedition to the north he was ordered to take no steps without previously consulting Gargrave. On 17 Jan. 1559–60 he was made vice-president of the council of the North, and from this time he was almost entirely occupied in the duties of this post. He was trusted implicitly by the queen and by Burghley. In January 1568–9, by command of the queen, he assisted Sir Francis Knollys to conduct Mary Queen of Scots from Bolton to Tutbury. Being again chosen vice-president during the presidency of the Earl of Essex, he took an active part in defeating the rebellion of the north under the Earls of Northumberland and Westmorland (1569). He held Pontefract Castle and the neighbouring bridges, and was thanked by the queen for his services. In 1570 he entertained Archbishop Grindal on his way to York. In 1574 he continued to act as vice-president under the Earl of Huntingdon. Gargrave's services in the north were very important. He was considered 'a great stay for the good order of those parts,' and in his own person was considered 'active, useful, benevolent, and religious.' He received from the queen at his request a grant of the Old Park of Wakefield. He died 28 March 1579, and was buried at Wragby. Gargrave was twice married, first to Anne, daughter of William Cotton, by whom he left an only surviving son, Sir Cotton Gargrave; and secondly to Jane, daughter of Roger Appleton, widow of John Wentworth of North

Elmsall. A portrait of him, formerly in the possession of Sir Levett Hanson [q. v.] of Normanton, is in the possession of G. Milner-Gibson-Cullum at Hardwicke, Bury St. Edmunds. A similar portrait was said to be in the possession of Viscount Galway at Serlby, Nottinghamshire.

[Cartwright's Chapters in the History of Yorkshire; Hunter's South Yorkshire, ii. 211; Banks's Wakefield and its Neighbourhood; Manning's Lives of the Speakers; Miscellanea Genealogica et Heraldica, i. 226; Calendar State Papers, Dom. Ser., 1539-1574, passim.]   L. C.

GARLAND, AUGUSTINE (*fl.* 1660), regicide, son of Augustine Garland, attorney, of Coleman Street, London, by his first wife, Ellen, daughter of Jasper Whitteridge of London, was baptised 13 Jan. 1602 (*Visitation of London*, 1633-5, i. 301; *Register of St. Antholin's, Budge Row, London*, p. 41; SMYTH, *Obituary*, p. 14). In 1618 Garland was admitted a pensioner of Emmanuel College, Cambridge (*Brit. Mus. Addit. MS.*, Cole, 5870, f. 168), and on leaving the university became a member of Lincoln's Inn. By the death of his father, in 1637, he succeeded to some property in Essex at Hornchurch and Waltham-holy-Cross, and at Queenborough in the island of Sheppey (will of Augustine Garland the Elder, P. C. C. 9, Lee). In his account of himself at his trial Garland says: 'I lived in Essex at the beginning of these troubles, and I was enforced to forsake my habitation. I came from thence to London, where I behaved myself fairly in my way' (*Trials of the Regicides*, ed. 1660, p. 264). On 26 May 1648 Garland was elected member for Queenborough in place of Sir E. Hales, expelled (*Return of Names of Members of Parliament*, p. 490). He signed the protest against the acceptance of the king's concessions (20 Dec. 1648), was appointed one of his judges, and acted as chairman of the committee selected to consider the method of the king's trial (WALKER, *Hist. of Independency*, ed. 1661, ii. 48; NALSON, *Trial of Charles I*, pp. 10, 14). 'I could not shrink for fear of my own destruction,' pleaded Garland on his own trial. 'I did not know which way to be safe in anything—without doors was misery, within doors was mischief' (*Trial of the Regicides*, p. 265). He attended twelve out of the sixteen meetings of the court, was present when sentence was given, and signed the death-warrant. Garland continued to sit in the Long parliament until its expulsion by Cromwell, took no part in public affairs under the protectorate, and was recalled to his place in parliament in May 1659 (*Old Parliamentary Hist.* xxi. 375). On 9 May 1660 he appeared before the lord mayor of London and claimed

the benefit of the king's declaration. Nevertheless he was put on his trial, and on 16 Oct. 1660 condemned to death. Besides his share in the trial he was accused of spitting in the king's face as Charles was led away from Westminster Hall after being sentenced. Garland strenuously denied the charge, saying, 'If I was guilty of this inhumanity I desire no favour from God Almighty' (*Trial*, p. 264). The death sentence was not put into execution, but Garland's property was confiscated, and he was kept prisoner in the Tower. A warrant for his conveyance to Tangier was issued on 31 March 1664, but whether he was actually transported is uncertain (*Cal. State Papers*, Dom. 1633-4, p. 536).

[Nalson's Trial of Charles I, 1684; Noble's Lives of the Regicides, 1798; Trials of the Regicides, ed. 1660.]   C. H. F.

GARLAND, JOHN (*fl.* 1230), grammarian and alchemist, was assigned by Bale and Pits to the eleventh century, and Dom Rivet, accepting this date, argued that he was also a native of France. They were not acquainted, however, with Garland's poem, 'De Triumphis Ecclesiæ.' Garland there describes himself as one whose mother was England and his nurse Gaul, and says that he had studied at Oxford under one John of London, a philosopher. From Oxford he went to Paris, and since he there studied under Alain de Lille [q. v.], who died in 1202, we may assume that he was born about 1180. When, at the close of the Albigensian crusade in 1229, Count Raymond VII had to consent to the establishment of a university at Toulouse, Garland was one of the professors selected by the legate to assist. In his 'Dictionarius Scolasticus' he says that he saw at Toulouse, 'nondum sedato tumultu belli,' the engine by which Simon de Montfort was killed. Wright infers that he had already been at Toulouse some time between 1218 and 1229, but the expression would not be inappropriate to the latter year. At Toulouse Garland remained teaching and writing for three years; but after the death of Bishop Fulk, in 1231, he says that the university began to decline, perhaps owing to the natural enmity of Fulk's Dominican successor Raymond for Parisian scholars. In any case Garland was among the first to leave, and after a variety of adventures made his way back to Paris in 1232 or 1233, and there he would appear to have spent the remainder of his life. The last event which he notices in the 'De Triumphis' is the preparation for the crusade by Ferdinand of Castile, which was prevented by his death in May 1252. Garland must have been now an old man, and as he does not mention Ferdinand's death we may conclude that he himself died in 1252 or shortly after.

Apparently Garland enjoyed a high reputation as a teacher. Roger Bacon says that he had heard him discourse on the orthography of 'orichalcum' (*Opus Minus*, c. vii., so Tanner; but the reference to Garland is not printed in Brewer's edition). His grammatical writings were much used in England, and were frequently printed at the end of the fifteenth century. Erasmus refers to him with some scorn as the chief source of instruction in an unenlightened age (*Op.*, ed. 1703, i. 514 F., 892 F.) He was in turn a theologian, a chronologist, and an alchemist— above all a grammarian; but though a persistent versifier, not a poet (M. LE CLERC). He has been the subject of much confusion, and some have supposed that there was more than one writer of the name. He has certainly been confused with Gerlandus, a French writer early in the twelfth century, whence probably the mistake as to his date. John the grammarian, who is assigned by Warton (*Hist. Engl. Poetry*, i. 216) to the eleventh, and by Bale and Pits to the thirteenth century, is probably only Garland without his surname, and confused with John Philoponus and John Walleys (Guallensis), the latter of whom was also an Englishman.

Garland's name is variously given as De Garlandia, Garlandius, Garlandus, or Gallandus. M. Le Clerc connects his name not with the noble French family, but with his teaching in the 'Clos de Garlande' or 'Gallande,' where was one of the most ancient schools of the university of Paris. Prince claims him in his 'Worthies of Devon' (ed. 1810, p. 400) for a family of the name resident at Garland by Chulmleigh in North Devon in the time of Henry III. The name Garland was also familiar in London; one John Garland was prebendary of St. Paul's in 1200 (LE NEVE, ii. 417). Another was sheriff of London in 1212.

Garland's works are—I. Poetry: 1. 'De Triumphis Ecclesiæ,' his most important poem, and the source of nearly all we know as to his life, consists of 4,614 elegiac lines, divided into eight books. It has for its main theme the celebration of the crusades. The first books begin from the passage of the Red Sea, and treat of early British legends, French Merovingian history, the third crusade, and the wars of John. Books iv. v. and vi. contain an account of the Albigensian crusade, valuable on account of the author's peculiar opportunities for obtaining information. There are some useful details as to mediæval siege operations. Book viii., called by the author the ninth, something having perhaps

been lost, treats of the crusade of Louis IX. The poem is ambitious, pedantic, and discursive. It is full of conceits, leonine verses, retrograde verses, and the like, but has the merit of frequently giving dates. There is only one known manuscript, viz. Cott. Claud. A. x. in British Museum. It has been edited by Thomas Wright for the Roxburghe Club. A full analysis will be found in 'Hist. Lit. de la France,' xxii. 2. 'Epithalamium Beatæ Mariæ Virginis.' In the 'De Triumphis' Garland says that at Toulouse he had written a poem upon this subject. In MS. Cott. Claud. A. x. there is a poem under the same title ascribed to Garland. The same poem is contained in Bodleian MS. Digby 65, where it has not previously been identified with Garland. The latter manuscript contains a prose prologue wanting in the Cotton. MS., which clearly connects the writer with the university of Paris, and thus corroborates Garland's claim to be the author. This poem contains about six thousand lines, divided into ten books. 3. 'De Miraculis Virginis' (Brit. Mus. MS. Bibl. Reg. 8 C. iv. 3). It contains nearly a thousand lines in a short rhyming metre, and is accompanied by a commentary. On f. 22 the author refers to himself as Johannes de Garlandia. 4. 'De Mysteriis Ecclesiæ,' or 'Libellus Mysteriorum,' a mystical explanation, in 659 hexameter lines, of the rites and vestments of the church. Written at the request of Fulk Basset, bishop of London [q. v.], in 1245, shortly after the death of Alexander of Hales, as is stated by the author. Printed in 'Comment. Crit. Codd. Biblioth. Gessensis,' pp. 86, 131-51, by F. Otto, who describes it as most useful for a knowledge of mediæval theology. Unfortunately, Otto used only two manuscripts, and those not of the best. There are many manuscripts, e.g. Cott. Claud. A. viii., Caius Coll. Cambr. 385, Bodl. Auct. F. 5, 6 f. 150 (incomplete, only lines 1-366 and 417-63). The last two contain commentaries in later and various hands. 5. 'Tractatus de Penitencia.' Frequently printed: Antoine Caillaut, Paris, n. d.; H. Quentell, Cologne, 1491, 1492, 1493, 1495. Other editions in sixteenth century. Bibliothèque MS. 8259, Bodl. MS. Digby 100, f. 171. 6. 'Facetus,' a poem on the duties of man to God, his neighbour, and himself. Ascribed to Garland in MS. Bibliothèque de S. Victor (MONTFAUCON, p. 1372), and accepted by Dom Rivet. But if, as he says (*Hist. Lit.* viii. p. xvi), it was used by Uguitio of Pisa, who wrote about 1194, it can scarcely be by Garland. 7. 'De Contemptu Mundi.' Usually, though wrongly, ascribed to St. Bernard, and printed in Mabillon's edition of his works (ii. 894-6) as 'Carmen Paræneticum.' The other printed copies are longer. Ascribed to Garland in Leyden MS. 360 (see *Hist. Lit.* viii. 89). 8. 'Floretus,' 1,166 leonine verses on the catholic faith and Christian morality. A scholiast, followed by Dom Rivet, ascribes it to the same author as the preceding. These last three poems are printed in the collection known as 'Auctores Octo,' Angoulême, 1491, Lyons, 1488, 1489, 1490. They were also frequently printed separately in the fifteenth and sixteenth centuries. 9. 'Satyricum Opus.' The first words are given by Pits, but nothing further is known. 10. 'Versus Proverbiales.' In Bodl. MS. Rawl. C. 496, along with 12, 15, 17, and 'Expositiones Vocabulorum,' which are perhaps by Garland. See also Bodl. MS. Laud. Misc. 707. 11. 'Aurea Gemma' (PITS). Perhaps identical with one of the former.

II. Grammatical: 12. 'Dictionarius Scolasticus.' A dictionary of phrases necessary for scholars. The author reviews the trades of Paris, and makes many allusions to that city. According to a note in MS. Bibliothèque Suppl. 294, it was printed at Caen in 1508 by L. Hastingue, but no copy is known to exist. Printed by Wright in 'Library of National Antiquities,' vol. i., and M. Geraud in 'Documents Inédits sur l'Histoire de France—Paris sous Philippe le Bel,' p. 580. 13. 'Dictionarius cum Commento.' Treats chiefly of sacred vestments and ornaments, MS. Caius College, Cambridge, 385. 14. 'Dictionarius ad res explicandas' (PITS). Probably identical with 'Commentarius Curialium,' which is contained in Caius College MS. 385, together with other works by John Garland, in whose style and manner it is written. At the end it is stated to have been written at Paris in 1240. 15. 'Cornutus' or 'Distigium' or 'Scolarium Morale.' Verses of advice to young students. Several of the numerous manuscripts give Garland as the author of the verses, not of the accompanying commentary. Printed Zwoll, 1481, Haguenau, 1489, and is the first part of the vocabulary printed by Wright in 'Library of National Antiquities,' i. 175. See Caius MS. 136. Dom Rivet suggests that the title of this work points to Garland as the scholiast on Juvenal and Persius who is called Cornutus; but this is only a conjecture. 16. 'Compendium Grammatice,' ascribed to Garland, Caius MS. 385. In verse, printed without date or place, and at Deventer, 1489. There is a key to this compendium in Caius Coll. MS. 136. 17. 'Accentarius sive de Accentibus,' ascribed to Garland, Caius MS. 385. Also in MS. Rawlinson, C. 496, as 'Ars lectoria Ecclesie.' In verse and with a commentary. 18. 'Synonyma' and

19. 'Equivoca,' both in hexameter verse. These two works were frequently printed with the commentary of Geoffrey the Grammarian [q. v.] by R. Pynson and W. de Worde, also by Hopyl, Paris, 1494, &c. The 'Synonyma' and a few lines of the 'Equivoca' were printed by Leyser and in Migne, cl. No doubt they were revised from time to time by teachers, and in their existing form may be by Matthew of Vendôme, to whom they are ascribed in some manuscripts. But see 'Hist. Lit.' xxii. 948–950. 20. 'Liber de Orthographia,' MS. Wolfenbüttel. Opening verses in Leyser and Migne, cl. 21. 'Liber Metricus de Verbis Deponentialibus,' printed Antwerp, 1486, Deventer, R. Paffroed, 1498, &c. 22. 'Merarius,' a short tract in Caius Coll. MSS. 136 and 385. Perhaps by Garland; used in 'Promptorium Parvulorum.' See Mr. Way's preface, p. xxxi. 23. 'Nomina et Verba Defectiva' printed. 24. 'Duodecim Decades,' printed as Garland's with 'Synonyma Britonis,' Paris, F. Baligault, 1496, (see HAIN, i. 554). 25. 'Libellus de Verborum Compositis,' Rouen, L. Hastingue, n. d. See Brunet. 26. 'Unum Omnium,' Pits. M. Gatien Arnault shows some reasons for supposing that this was a work on logic. Pits and others ascribe to John the Grammarian, along with the 'Compendium Grammatice,' (27) 'Super Ovidii Metamorphosin,' Bodl. MS. Digby 104—probably by John Walleys, under whose name it was printed, Paris, 1569—and (28) 'De Arte Metrica.' In Cambridge MS. More 121, as 'Poetria Magna Johannis Anglici.' Begins with panegyric on the university of Paris. In prose and verse.

III. Alchemical: 29. 'Compendium Alchymiæ cum Dictionario ejusdem Artis,' printed, Bâle 1560 and 1571, Strasburg 1566. According to Dom Rivet there are two distinct works—a compendium printed 1571, and an abridgment printed 1560; he also adds (30) 'A Key to the Abridgment and the Mysteries which it contains,' extant only in manuscript at abbey of Dunes. 31. 'Liber de Mineralibus,' printed, Bâle, 1560, after an edition of the 'Synonyma,' and along with (32) 'Libellus de Præparatione Elixir.' Fabricius suggests that the alchemist Joannes Garlandius should be distinguished from Joannes de Garlandia the grammarian and poet. Mansi, however, dissents. The commentary of Arnold de Villeneuve, which accompanies the 1560 edition, proves the celebrity of these writings. Pits ascribes to Garland a work entitled 'Hortulanus;' but this seems to be only a name used by him as an alchemist. In Ashmolean MS. 1478, iv. 1, which contains a translation of all these works and of Villeneuve's commentary, the author is called 'Jhone Garland or Hortulanus.' See also Bodl. MSS. Ashmolean 1416 and 1487, and Digby 119.

IV. Mathematical. In numerous manuscripts the two following chronological works are ascribed to John de Garlandia: (33) 'Computum' and (34) 'Tabula Principalis, contra Tabula de Festis Mobilibus et Tabula terminorum Paschalium.' But Gerlandus, canon of Besançon in the twelfth century, certainly wrote such works, and twelfth century manuscripts of them are extant (see *Analecta Juris Pontificii*, p. xii). There may also have been another Gerland in the eleventh century. See MSS. Digby, 40, and Ashmolean, 341. Garland may possibly have written such works. In the 'De Triumphis' he says that he gave the people of Toulouse rules how to find Easter, and there are also astronomical allusions in various works of his.

V. Musical: 35. 'De Musica Mensurabili Positio.' Jerome of Moravia, who wrote about 1265, used such a treatise, which he ascribes to Johannes de Garlandia, and this same treatise, though without any ascription, and with considerable variations, exists in a Vatican manuscript. Printed by Coussemaker, i. 175. 36. The author of the foregoing says that he had written 'Tractatus de Cantu Plano.' 37. 'Optima Introductio in Contrapunctum.' Assigned to Garland in manuscripts at Pisa and Einsiedeln, and in both he is described as a Parisian scholar. Printed by Coussemaker, iii. 12. 38. 'Introductio Musicæ Planæ et etiam Musicæ Mensurabilis.' Assigned to Garland in manuscript in Public Library at S. Die. Printed as before, i. 157. 39. Robert Handlo and John Hanboys, English writers on music in the fifteenth century, give some excerpts from a work of Garland. Here also there is possibly some confusion with Gerland the canon; M. Coussemaker, however, holds that some at least of these works belong to our writer, although he considers that Nos. 37 and 39 are of later date than Philip de Vitry (*ob.* 1361), who himself quotes John Garland.

This list is possibly incomplete. Some of the short tracts in such manuscripts as Caius Coll. 136 and 385, and Digby 100 may be by Garland; and he himself says that he wrote poems at Toulouse on Faith and Hope, on the Acts of the Apostles, &c. Whether or not he is the author of all that is extant under his name, the allusions in his undoubted works show that he might quite possibly have written on any of the subjects assigned to him.

[Bale, ii. 48; Pits, p. 184; Tanner, p. 309; Hist. Lit. de la France, viii. pp. xvi, 83–98, xxi. 369–72, xxii. 11–13, 77–103, 948–950 (the articles in vols. xxi. and xxii. are by M. Le Clerc); P. Leyser, Hist. Poetarum Medii Ævi; Mr. T. Wright's prefaces to De Triumphis and Library of National Antiquities; M. Geraud's preface to Dictionary; Mr. Way's Preface to Promptorium Parvulorum, vol. iii. (Camden Soc.) for grammatical works; Prof. Mayor's Latin-English and English-Latin Lexicography in Journal of Classical and Sacred Philology, vol. iv.; Coussemaker, Script. de Musica Medii Ævi, vols. i. and iii.; article by M. Gatien Arnault in Revue de Toulouse, xxiii. 117; Catalogues of Bodl. MSS.; Rev. J. J. Smith's Cat. of MSS. in Caius College Library. For fuller information as to the bibliography see the works of Fabricius (ed. 1858), Hain, Panzer, Graesse, Brunet's Manuel du Libraire (ed. 1860), Chevalier's Répertoire des Sources Historiques du Moyen Age, Bibliographie, and Dibdin's Typ. Ant.]   C. L. K.

GARNEAU, FRANÇOIS XAVIER (1809–1866), historian of Canada, was a member of an old French family from the diocese of Poitiers. His grandfather was a farmer at St. Augustin, and his father, by trade a saddler, took part in speculations which seriously hampered the education of his children. In 1808 he married Gertrude Amiot, and on 15 June 1809 his son François Xavier was born in Quebec. François' early education was obtained at a small town school kept by a Mr. Parent, but in a short time he came under the care of Mr. Perrault, who was an advocate of the system of Lancaster. Thence he passed at an early age into Mr. Perrault's office, having declined to take orders in the Roman church ('je ne me sens pas appelé au sacerdoce'). Leaving Mr. Perrault at the age of sixteen, he entered the office of Archibald Campbell, a notary, from whom he received great encouragement in the pursuit of his private studies. While he was in the office his patriotic ardour was often outraged by the view which the ordinary histories and his fellow-clerks took of the respective positions of the English and French settlers. He made up his mind to write a history which should give an impartial and accurate account (CASGRAIN, p. 26). A long time elapsed before his design was fulfilled. In 1828 he made a tour through the United States, in 1830 he was admitted a notary, and in 1831 (20 June) he started on a voyage to Europe, where he made a prolonged stay. After visiting London he went for a short time to Paris. On his return to London he was offered and accepted the position of secretary to Mr. Viger, then agent for Lower Canada, a connection which doubtless helped to bring him into contact with the radical party, with whom, indeed, he chiefly associated. On 10 May 1833 he started for home once more. In 1835 he became clerk at the bank of Quebec. Afterwards he was appointed translator to the Chamber of Assembly. From 1844 to 1864 he was greffier (town clerk) of Quebec. In 1841 he published with Mr. Roy a literary and scientific journal, 'L'Institut,' which ran only from 7 March to 22 May. Till 1845 his literary reputation was that of a patriotic poet in 'Le Répertoire National;' but he began his history as far back as 1840-1. Its merits were quickly recognised. In 1855 he was elected president of the Canadian Institute of Quebec, and he was appointed in 1857 on the council of public instruction. He died at Quebec 3 Feb. 1866, after a long illness. He married 25 Aug. 1835 Esther Bilodeau, by whom he had nine children, five dying young.

His principal writings were: 1. 'Histoire du Canada depuis sa découverte jusqu'à nos jours' 1845-6 (2nd edit. 1852; new edition, with introduction and fresh notes by Garneau's grandson, Hector Garneau). 2. 'Abrégé de l'histoire du Canada depuis sa découverte jusqu'à 1840.' 3. 'Voyage en Angleterre et en France, dans les années 1831, 1832, 1833;' originally published in the 'Journal de Québec,' 1854-5; then reprinted as a whole, 1855, but suppressed. Copious extracts appear in 'La Littérature Canadienne.'

[Casgrain's Un Contemporain; Chauveau's Memoir in Histoire, 4th edit.; Quebec Daily Mercury, Feb. 1866.]   E. C. K. G.

GARNER, THOMAS (1789–1868), engraver, born at Birmingham in 1789, received instruction in the art of engraving from Samuel Lines [q. v.] He resided in Birmingham nearly all his life, and was an active promoter of the study of art in that town. He was one of the founders of the Antique Academy there, subsequently known as the 'Royal Birmingham Society of Artists.' As an engraver he worked on subjects and portraits of local interest, and contributed to the annuals. By his plates for the 'Art Journal' he is best known. They included 'The Mountaineer' after P. F. Poole, R.A.; 'The Grecian Vintage' after T. Stothard, R.A.; 'L'Allegro' after W. E. Frost, R.A.; 'Il Penseroso' after J. C. Horsley, R.A.; 'Chastity' after W. E. Frost, R.A.; 'H.R.H. Princess Charlotte' after Sir Thomas Lawrence, P.R.A.; and the 'Village Diorama' after T. Webster, R.A. Garner died at Birmingham, 14 July 1868.

[Art Journal, 1868; Redgrave's Dict. of Artists.]   L. C.

GARNETT, ARTHUR WILLIAM (1829–1861), military and civil engineer, younger son of William Garnett [q. v.], born 1 June 1829, and educated at Addiscombe College, obtained his first commission in 1846, and proceeded to India in 1848 as lieutenant of the Bengal engineers. Assistant field engineer with the army before Mooltan, he was wounded in attendance on Sir John Cheape [q.v.] He joined the army under Lord Gough, held the fords of the Chenâb during the victory of Goojerât, and went forward with Sir Walter Raleigh Gilbert's flying column in pursuit of the Afghans. Having taken part in the first survey of the Peshawûr valley with Lieutenant James T. Walker (afterwards surveyor-general of India), he was next engaged on public works at Kohât, where in 1850 the sappers employed under his command in making a road to the Kothul were surprised in their camp by the Afreedees. Garnett and Lieutenant (afterwards Major-general Sir F. R.) Pollock, who was also stationed at Kohât, were surrounded, but held their position until Sir Colin Campbell (Lord Clyde), with General Charles J. Napier, arrived from Peshawûr and forced the Kohât pass.

Garnett reconstructed and strengthened the fort of Kohât, designed and built the fort at Bahadoor Kheyl for guarding the salt mines, as well as barracks, forts, and defensive works at other points on the frontier, including 'Fort Garnett,' named after him. He planted forest trees wherever practicable, constructed bridges, roads, and other works in circumstances of extreme difficulty. He was constantly interrupted by being called upon to take the field with the several expeditions in the Derajât, Meeranzaie valley, Eusofzaie country, Koorum valley, and Pei-war Kothul, &c., where there was frequently hard fighting. During the mutiny Garnett was kept at his post on the frontier, where his experience and influence with the hillmen were of the greatest value. He came to England on leave in 1860, studied dockyard works with a view to the needs of Bombay, and married Mary Charlotte Burnard of Crewkerne, by whom he had a posthumous daughter. Returning to India in 1861, he died of pleurisy, while temporarily assisting Colonel Yule, C.B., secretary to government in the department of public works. He was buried in St. Paul's Cathedral, Calcutta, where a monument was erected by his brother officers, other monuments being placed in the church at Kohât, which he had built, and in that of Holy Trinity at Brompton.

[Government Despatches in London Gazettes; Professional Papers Corps of Royal Engineers; Journal of Siege of Mooltan, 1848-9; series of general reports on the administration of the Punjâb territories from 1849 to 1859.]   F. B. G.

GARNETT, HENRY (1555–1606), jesuit, born in 1555 at Heanor, Derbyshire (not at Nottingham, as is commonly stated), was the son of Brian Garnett and his wife, Alice Jay. Father John Gerard states that his parents were well esteemed, and well able to maintain their family. He adds that his father was a man of learning who taught in the free school of Nottingham (*Narrative of the Gunpowder Plot*, ed. Morris, 1872, p. 297; *Tablet*, 25 May 1889, p. 817). Garnett was brought up as a protestant, and in 1567 was admitted a scholar of Winchester. He did not proceed in due course to New College, Oxford. According to his catholic biographers, he resolved to leave the school on embracing the catholic faith, although some of his teachers at Winchester who were inclined to catholicism tried to induce him to remain. Dr. Robert Abbot (1560–1617) [q. v.] asserts, on the contrary, that the warden admonished him not to remove to New College on account of his gross immoralities at school (*Antilogia Epist. ad Lectorem*). Jardine admits that the account of Garnett's early depravity has 'certainly more of the character of a tale of malignant scandal than of a calm narration of facts.' He quotes, however, some passages, including one from a statement attributed to Garnett in the Tower, to countenance a charge of drunkenness (*Narrative of the Gunpowder Plot*, pp. 172, 179 n.) Garnett removed from Winchester to London, where he began to study law, and became corrector of the press to Tottel, the celebrated law printer. While he was in this employment he formed an acquaintance with Chief-justice Popham, who recognised him on his first examination, and treated him throughout the inquiry with great respect. Coke, in his speech at Garnett's trial, represents him as a man having 'many excellent gifts and endowments of nature; by birth a gentleman, by education a scholar, by art learned, and a good linguist.' After remaining with Tottel about two years, during which his dislike to the protestant religion became confirmed, he determined to devote his life to the service of the Roman catholic church. He crossed to Spain, and thence proceeded to Italy in company with Giles Gallop, formerly a Winchester scholar and a fellow of New College, who afterwards became a jesuit. Having resolved to join the Society of Jesus, he entered the novitiate of St. Andrew 11 Sept. 1575, and made his noviceship under Father Fabius de Fabio. He pursued his higher studies in the Roman College under such masters as Christopher Clavius, Francis Suarez, Benedict Pereira, and Robert (afterwards Cardinal) Bellarmin, and became a great proficient in all kinds of learning. He was employed as penitentiary at St. Peter's, and for some time was professor of Hebrew at the Roman College; and during the sickness of Father Clavius he temporarily occupied his chair in the school of mathematics. Clavius found him so profoundly versed in mathematical sciences that he opposed his return to England as a missionary, and, by order of the Father-general Aquaviva, he was detained for two years in Clavius's school. When Clavius resumed his chair, Garnett obtained leave to go upon the English mission, and left Rome in company with Father Robert Southwell on 8 May 1586, landing safely in England on 7 July following. Writers of his own communion describe him as a man of such remarkable gentleness that Aquaviva, when urged by Father Parsons to send him upon the dangerous English mission, replied that he was greatly troubled, because by sending him there he was exposing the meekest lamb to a cruel butchery.

William Weston, *alias* Edmonds, at this time the only jesuit in England, gave his colleagues a hearty welcome on their arrival in London. On Weston's commitment to Wisbech Castle in 1587, Garnett was appointed to succeed him as superior of the English province. For eighteen years he governed the province with remarkable prudence, chiefly in London and its vicinity. His conduct, however, in supporting Weston and the jesuits in the Wisbech disputes (1695–6) gave much offence to some of his religion (TIERNEY, *Dodd*, iii. 41–5). In March 1596–7 he was living near Uxbridge, in a house called Morecroftes, and had at the same time a house in Spitalfields. He afterwards lived at White Webbs in Enfield Chase, called 'Dr. Hewick's house.' He sometimes penetrated in company with the gaolers into the London prisons to minister to members of his flock. More than once he narrowly escaped arrest at the hands of faithless catholics, who were seduced by the large rewards offered by the government for his capture. In a letter written on 1 Oct. 1593 to his sister Mary, whom he had sent to the Augustinian convent at Louvain, he announces that he had reconciled their aged mother to the Roman church, and expresses a hope that his other two unmarried sisters would embrace the religious state (OLIVER, *Jesuit Collections*, p. 100). On 8 May 1598 he was professed of the four vows. During his superiority there was a great increase of catholicism throughout the kingdom. He made great exertions to promote the prosperity of the seminaries abroad, secular and regular, and at his death he left behind him forty jesuits in the English mission.

When Guy Fawkes [q. v.] was arrested on

account of the gunpowder plot on 4 Nov. 1605, a letter was found upon him addressed to White Webbs, where Garnett had resided till within the last six months, and the suspicions of the government were consequently directed to him before three of the lay conspirators had been apprehended. Salisbury was most anxious to discover the priests who had been confessors to the conspirators. Thomas Bates, servant of Robert Catesby [q. v.], stated that his master and another conspirator had been at Lord Vaux's house at Harrowden, with Fathers Garnett, Greenway, and Gerard, and that he had been sent with a letter by his master, 'after they were up in arms,' to a house at Coughton, Warwickshire, the residence of the great catholic family of Throckmorton, where Garnett and Greenway then were. Upon this evidence the government, on 15 Jan. 1605–6, issued a proclamation declaring that the three jesuit fathers were proved guilty of the plot 'by divers confessions of many conspirators.' Gerard and Greenway escaped to the continent. Garnett had addressed to the privy council, on 30 Nov. 1605, from his retreat at Coughton, a protestation of his innocence (*Catholic Magazine*, 1823, pp. 198, 201). He remained at Coughton till 4 Dec., when he removed to Hindlip Hall, the seat of Thomas Habington [q. v.], near Worcester, by invitation of Father Thomas Oldcorne, *alias* Hall, who had acted as Habington's chaplain. This mansion contained several of the ingenious hiding-places common in the dwellings of the catholic gentry (see description and engraving of the house in NASH's *Worcestershire*, i. 584). Sir Henry Bromley, a neighbouring magistrate, was commissioned by the lords of the council to invest the house and conduct a rigorous search. Garnett and Oldcorne retired to one of the numerous secret receptacles, and their respective servants, Owen and Chambers, to another. The house was surrounded, all the approaches carefully watched and guarded, and several hiding-places were discovered, after a rigorous search, but nothing found in them excepting what Bromley described as 'a number of popish trash hid under boards.' In his letter to Salisbury (23 Jan.) he said: 'I did never hear so impudent liars as I find here—all recusants, and all resolved to confess nothing, what danger soever they incur.' On the fourth day of the search the two servants gave themselves up, being almost starved to death. The two jesuits, overcome by the confinement and foul air, also surrendered. Garnett afterwards said that 'if they could have had liberty for only half a day from the blockade,' they could have made the place tenable for a quarter of a

year. A contemporary manuscript states that 'marmalade and other sweetmeats were found there lying by them;' but that they had been chiefly supported by broths and warm drinks conveyed by a reed ' through a little hole in a chimney that backed another chimney in a gentlewoman's chamber.' According to Garnett's account, want of air and the narrowness of the space, blocked by books and furniture, made the confinement intolerable. They came out like 'two ghosts.'

On their way to London the prisoners were well treated at the king's charge, by express orders from the Earl of Salisbury. On their arrival they were lodged in the Gatehouse, and a few days afterwards were examined before the privy council. As Garnett was conducted to Whitehall the streets were crowded with multitudes eager to catch a sight of the head of the jesuits in England. He was sent to the Tower, and during the following days he was repeatedly examined. He made no confession, although threatened with torture, the application of which, however, had been strictly forbidden by the king. The lieutenant of the Tower then changed his tone, expressed pity and veneration for Garnett, and enabled him to correspond with several catholics. The letters were taken to the lieutenant, but contained no proof whatever against the prisoner. The warder then unlocked a door in Garnett's cell, and showed him a door through which he could converse with Oldcorne. Lockerson, the private secretary of Salisbury, and Forsett, a magistrate attached to the Tower, were concealed in a cavity from which they could overhear the conversations on five occasions. The reports of four of these conversations are still preserved.

Garnett was examined twenty-three times before the council. He at first denied the interviews with Oldcorne, but was drawn into admissions which led to charges of equivocation. A manuscript treatise upon this subject by an anonymous author, and annotated by him, was discovered, and has since been printed by Mr. Jardine (see GARDINER, *History*, 1885, i. 280, 281, and JARDINE, p. 204 *n.*) Writers of his own communion have regarded him as a martyr to the sacredness of the seal of the sacrament of confession. Garnett acknowledged that on 9 July 1605 Catesby asked him whether it was lawful to enter upon any undertaking for the good of the catholic cause if it should not be possible to avoid the destruction of some innocent persons together with the guilty. Garnett replied in the affirmative, but declared that he did not understand the application of the question. He admitted, however, that at the end of July he was fully informed of the plot by Greenway, though, as this information was obtained under the seal of sacramental confession, he was bound not to reveal it. Catesby had in confession disclosed the design to Greenway, who represented to him the wickedness of the project, but could not prevail upon him to desist. However, Catesby consented that Greenway should communicate the case, under the seal of confession, to Garnett; and if the matter should otherwise come to light, he gave leave that both or either of the priests might then make use of the knowledge which he thus imparted to them. Garnett declared that he was struck with horror at the proposal, and as he could not disclose the secret, he used every endeavour to prevail upon the conspirators to abandon their undertaking.

Garnett's trial took place at Guildhall on 28 March 1606. There was a crowd of spectators in the court, including several foreign ambassadors and many courtiers. The proceedings lasted from eight o'clock in the morning till seven at night, and the king was present privately during the whole time. Coke, the attorney-general, conducted the prosecution. The proof of complicity was the conversation with Catesby on 9 June. Mr. Gardiner points out that there was no evidence which would have satisfied a modern jury, and that the proceeding was rather political than judicial, the fear of the pope making it impossible that fair play should be given to Garnett's supporters. He holds, however, that there was 'strong corroborative evidence,' from Garnett's apparent 'approval of the plot' at a later period, as shown by his association with the conspirators (GARDINER, i. 277, 278). Nothing was said of the conversation with Greenway, about which no doubt whatever existed. Mr. Gardiner surmises that the government adopted this course because they knew they would be assailed with the most envenomed acrimony by the whole catholic world if they executed a priest for not revealing a secret confided to him in confession. Garnett's defence was that he had never heard of the plot except in confession. He was found guilty, and sentenced to be drawn, hanged, disembowelled, and quartered.

Several weeks elapsed before the sentence was executed, and Garnett was again brought several times before the council, and interrogated as to the teaching of the jesuits, and his own sentiments respecting the obligation of human laws and equivocation. At length, on 3 May 1606, he was drawn on a hurdle from the Tower to St. Paul's Churchyard, and there executed in front of the Bishop of London's palace. When he was on the scaffold the recorder vainly endeavoured to draw from him an admission of his guilt. He persisted in his denial that he had any positive information of the plot except in confession, though he allowed, as he had acknowledged before, that he had had a general and confused knowledge from Catesby. 'In all probability,' says Mr. Gardiner, 'this is the exact truth' (ib. i. 282).

Many catholics sought for relics of a man whom they regarded as a martyr, and within a year of his death wonderful accounts were circulated throughout the Christian world about a miraculous straw or 'ear void of corn' on which a drop of Garnett's blood had fallen. It was said that on one of the husks a portrait of him surrounded with rays of glory had been miraculously formed. Hundreds of persons, it was alleged, were converted to catholicism by the mere sight of 'Garnett's straw.' Archbishop Bancroft was commissioned by the privy council to call before him such persons as had been most active in propagating the story, and if possible to detect and punish the impostors. Many curious particulars on this subject will be found in Jardine's 'Gunpowder Plot' and Foley's 'Records.' Garnett's name occurs in the list of the 353 catholic martyrs which was sent to Rome by the English hierarchy in 1880, but is significantly omitted from Stanton's 'Menology of England and Wales, compiled by order of the Cardinal Archbishop and the Bishops of the Province of Westminster,' 1887, though in the second appendix to that work he is described as 'a martyr whose cause is deferred for further investigation.' There is a fine portrait of Garnett by John Wierix, engraved by R. Sadler.

His works are: 1. 'A Treatise on Schism.' 2. A manuscript treatise in confutation of 'A Pestilent Dialogue between a Gentleman and a Physician.' 3. A translation from Latin of the 'Summa Canisii,' with supplements on pilgrimages, invocation of saints, and indulgences, London, 1590, 8vo; St. Omer, 1622, 16mo. 4. 'Treatise on the Rosary of our Lady.' Several works on the subject were published about this period. Perhaps Garnett's was 'A Methode to meditate on the Psalter, or Great Rosarie of our Blessed Ladie,' Antwerp, 1598, 8vo (GILLOW, Bibl. Dict. ii. 393). 5. Letter on the martyrdom of Godfrey Maurice, alias John Jones. In Diego Yepes' 'Historia particular de la Persecucion de Inglaterra,' 1599. 6. 'A Treatise of Christian Renovation or Birth,' London, 1616, 8vo.

[Full accounts of Garnett's relations with the conspirators are given in David Jardine's Narrative of the Gunpowder Plot, 1857, and in Gardiner's Hist. of England, vol. i., and also, from a catholic point of view, in Lingard's Hist. of England, 1849, vol. vii., and Foley's Records, iv. 35–193. See also John Hungerford Pollen's Father H. Garnet and the Gunpowder Plot, 1888, John Gerard's What was the Gunpowder Plot, 1897, and Gardiner's What Gunpowder Plot was, 1897. A True and Perfect Relation of the whole Proceedings against . . . Garnet, a Jesuite, and his Confederats, was published by authority in 1606, but, as Jardine admits (p. 214), it is neither true nor perfect. On the vexed question of Garnett's moral guilt numerous works were published, and a bibliographical account of the protracted controversy is given by Jardine, p. 275 seq. In addition to the works already specified the principal authorities are : Addit. MSS. 21203, 22136 ; Dr. Robert Abbot's Antilogia adversus Apologiam Andreæ Eudæmon-Joannis ; Bartoli, Dell'istoria della Compagnia di Giesu ; l'Inghilterra, p. 514 seq.; Butler's Hist. Memoirs of the English Catholics, 1822, vol. ii. ; Challoner's Missionary Priests, vol. ii. App. ; De Backer's Bibl. des Écrivains de la Compagnie de Jésus, i. 2044, iii. 2205 ; Treatise of Equivocation, ed. by Jardine, 1851 ; Dodd's Church Hist. ii. 395, Tierney's edit., vols. iii. and iv. (with some of Garnett's letters from the originals); Specimens of Amendments to Dodd's Church Hist. by Clerophilus Alethes [John Constable], p. 195 ; R. P. A. Eudæmon-Joannis [i.e. the jesuit L'Heureux] . . . ad actionem proditoriam E. Coqui Apologia pro R. P. Hen. G——, 1610 ; A. Eudæmon-Joannis Cydonii . . . Responsio . . . ad Antilogiam R. Abbati, 1615 ; Gerard's Narrative of the Gunpowder Plot, printed in Morris's Condition of Catholics under James I ; Gillow's Bibl. Dict. ; Granger's Biog. Hist. of England, 5th edit. ii. 80 ; Kirby's Winchester Scholars, p. 141 ; Knight's Old England, ii. 145 ; The Month, xxxiv. 202 ; More's Hist. Missionis Anglic. Soc. Jesu, pp. 141, 310–30 ; Neut's Henri Garnet et la Conspiration de Poudres (Gand, 1876); Notes and Queries, 1st ser. x. 19, 73, 2nd ser. viii. 283, 6th ser. v. 403 ; Oliver's Jesuit Collections, p. 99 ; Panzani's Memoirs, p. 170 ; Southwell's Bibl. Scriptorum Soc. Jesu, p. 224 ; State Papers, Dom., 1605–6 ; Tanner's Societas Jesu usque ad sanguinis et vitæ profusionem militans.]   T. C.

GARNETT, JEREMIAH (1793–1870), journalist, younger brother of Richard Garnett [q. v.], was born at Otley in Yorkshire, 2 Oct. 1793. After being apprenticed to a printer at Barnsley, he entered the office of 'Wheeler's Manchester Chronicle' about 1814, and with a brief interruption continued there until 1821, when he joined John Edward Taylor [q. v.] in establishing the 'Manchester Guardian.' The first days of this now potent journal were days of struggle. Garnett was printer, business manager, and sole reporter. He took his notes in a rough shorthand extemporised by himself, and frequently composed them without the interven-

tion of any written copy. As the paper gained ground his share in the literary management increased, and in January 1844 he became sole editor upon the death of his partner, a position which he held until his retirement in 1861. During these forty years he exerted very great influence on the public opinion of Manchester and Lancashire generally, the admirable management of the 'Guardian' causing it to be largely read, both by tories and leaguers, who had little sympathy with its moderate liberal politics. He was active as a police commissioner, and in obtaining a charter of incorporation for the city. His pen and his advice were highly influential behind the scenes ; but his public appearances were infrequent. The most important was on the occasion of the expulsion of Thomas Milner Gibson and John Bright from the representation of Manchester in 1857, which was almost entirely due to his initiative. As a man he was upright and benevolent, but singularly averse to display as a writer for the press his principal characteristics were strong common-sense and extreme clearness of style. After his retirement he lived in Scotland and at Sale in Cheshire, where he died on 27 Sept. 1870.

[Manchester Guardian, 28 Sept. 1870 ; Manchester Free Lance, 1 Oct. 1870 ; Prentice's Historical Sketches and Personal Recollections of Manchester ; personal knowledge.]   R. G.

GARNETT, JOHN (1709–1782), bishop of Clogher, was born at Lambeth in 1709. His father, John Garnett, was rector of Sigglesthorne, in the East Riding of Yorkshire. His grandfather had been vicar of Kilham, and his great-grandfather a merchant in Newcastle. He graduated at Cambridge B.A. in 1728, and M.A. in 1732 ; was fellow of Sidney Sussex College, and Lady Margaret preacher to the university. In 1751 he went to Ireland as chaplain to the Duke of Dorset, lord-lieutenant, and in 1752 became bishop of Ferns, whence he was translated to Clogher in 1758. A very favourable account of his conduct in that see is given by Lynam, the biographer of Philip Skelton [q. v.], who calls him 'a prelate of great humility, and a friend to literature and religion. Though he had but one eye he could discover men of merit.' Garnett's patronage of Skelton no doubt propitiated Skelton's biographer ; but it is nevertheless evident that it would require an exceptional bishop to discern the claims of so exceptional a genius, a kind of Patrick Brontë plus great learning and first-rate abilities, who, says Lynam, 'would have continued in a wild part of the country all his days had not Providence placed Dr. Gar-the House of Commons from his offices of governor of the Turkey and other companies (*Journal*, iii. 37), and was expelled from the court of aldermen on 2 May 1643 (*Rep.* 56, f. 166 *b*). On Saturday 5 Nov. following the captains of the city trained bands arrested many of the wealthiest royalists in the city, including Garraway and his brother, for not contributing to the parliament's demand for money, and for 'other misdemeanours' (*A Catalogue of sundrie Knights, Aldermen, . . . who are in custody . . . by Authority from the Parliament*, 7 Nov. 1642; broadsheet in the Guildhall Library, *Choice Scraps, London*, v. 2, No. 16). Garraway's default was for 300*l.* (*House of Commons' Journal*, iii. 45). Lloyd says 'he was tossed as long as he lived from prison to prison, and his estate conveyed from one rebel to another' (*Memoires*, 1668, p. 633). He was still, however, governor of the Russia Company on 1 June 1644, when the House of Commons ordered his discharge from that office, and at the same time imprisoned him in Dover Castle during their pleasure (*Journal*, iii. 514). Garraway did not, however, die in prison, but in the parish of St. Mary Magdalen, Milk Street (*Burial Registers* of that parish), and was buried on 24 July 1646 in the church of St. Peter-le-Poer, Broad Street. His will, dated 8 March 1644, was proved in the P. C. C. 30 July 1646 (107, Twisse).

He lived in Broad Street, near Drapers' Hall, and in 1616 petitioned the company for a lease of his own house and another adjoining their hall, offering to rebuild the house in a substantial manner. This he did at a cost of over 1,000*l.*, erecting the front 'of bricke and stone done by daie woorke substantiall,' and in November 1628 the company granted him a lease of seventy years, at a yearly rent of 9*l.* (Drapers' Company's records). Garraway himself asserts that he was often a member of the House of Commons (*Speech*, 1642), but there is no record of the constituency which he represented.

He married Margaret, daughter of Henry Clitherow, a London merchant, who was buried on 25 June 1656 in St. Peter's Church, Broad Street. Garraway had ten children, William, John, Thomas, Elizabeth, Margaret, Ann, Katherine, Henry, Richard, and Mary, of whom the last three died in their childhood. From his daughter Elizabeth, who married Rowland Hale of King's Walden, Hertfordshire, Viscount Melbourne was descended (CLUTTERBUCK, *Hertfordshire*, iii. 133).

To his three sons he left large estates in Sussex, Kent, Devonshire, Northumberland, Westmoreland, and Yorkshire, which they seem to have obtained after his death without interference from the parliament, but difficulties were raised by the commissioners for sequestrations in Cornwall about some of his property in that county. The commissioners alleged that Garraway died a delinquent in prison for assisting the king against the parliament, and that all his family were known enemies of the parliament, a statement which John and Thomas Garraway in their reply assert to be scandalous and untrue (*Royalist Composition Papers*, 1st ser., xxviii. 843–870, passim). The following editions of the 'Speech' and its rejoinders are known: 1. 'The Loyal Citizen revived; a speech . . . at a Common Hall, January 17, upon occasion of a speech by Mr. Pym at the reading of His Majesties answer to the late petition,' 1642, folio sheet. Another edition, with a letter 'from a scholler in Oxfordshire,' &c., London, 1643, 4to. Reprinted in the 'Harleian Miscellany,' ed. 1744 and 1808, vol. v. 2. 'Oratie ghedaen door Alderman Garraway,' &c., Amsterdam, 1643, 4to. This is a Dutch translation of the 4to edition. 3. 'A briefe Answer to a scandalous pamphlet intituled "A Speech,"' &c. [anon.], London, 15 Feb. 1643, 4to.

[Gardiner's History of England, ix. 130, 153; information respecting the family kindly supplied by R. Garraway Rice, esq.]   C. W–H.

GARRETT, JEREMIAH LEARNOULT (*fl.* 1809), dissenting minister, was born at Horselydown, in the Borough, Southwark, near the Old Stairs, on 29 Feb. 1764. His parents were boat-builders, respectable people, but by no means 'evangelically' religious. The evangelical habit of mind, however, showed itself early in Jeremiah. While yet of the tender age of five he had, he tells us, 'views of the last day,' and before he was eight had 'strict views of the world being burnt up, and the wicked being turned into hell.' Soon after this date his father died. He was now sent to school, first at Christ's Hospital, Hertford, and afterwards at Jackson's academy, Hampton. After a year or two thus spent he was set to learn the tailoring trade, but disliking it was apprenticed to a builder of ship's boats at Wapping, who ill-used him. His master absconding for debt, he was apprenticed to another in the same way of business, from whom he met with better treatment. At the age of fourteen or fifteen he had 'a vision of an ancient form with more majesty than ever was or can be seen in mortality,' which laid its hand upon him, and which he took to be Christ. A dissenting minister at his earnest request was called in to see him, to whom he confessed his sins, the most flagrant of which was that seven years previously he had stolen a halfpenny. The minister thereupon 'pointed him to the blood of Christ,' which gave him great relief. Subsequently, however, he took to vicious courses, had a man-of-war's man who had assaulted him arrested, frequented theatres, fought with his fellow-apprentice, contracted debts, and a disease for which he was treated in the Lock Hospital. On emerging from the hospital he attended the ministrations of Wesley's preachers, as well as the services of the church, used 'to go out into the fields, and rave hell and damnation to sinners' to the detriment of his lungs, and came to be called a second Whitefield by the old women in Moorfields. A mysterious find of 80*l.* in his bed enabled him to pay his debts. At a somewhat later date he held forth at the old Rectifying House and the old Soap House, Islington, and in 1788 he laid the foundation-stone of the chapel since known as Islington Chapel in Church Street. Having thus established a certain reputation he was received into Lady Huntingdon's connexion and ordained. About this time he married; but was sorely tempted by love for a young woman of his congregation, whom he had saluted, according to the primitive Christian custom, with a 'holy kiss.' He removed to Basingstoke, and thence to Wallingford, and afterwards spent some three years in Guernsey. Returning to England, he ministered for a time at Ashby-de-la-Zouche, but developing lax views on baptism was ejected from Lady Huntingdon's connexion, and went into the business of a cotton dyer at Leicester. He soon, however, resumed preaching, and, after ministering for some time at Nottingham, established himself about the close of the last century at Lant Street Chapel, in the Borough, Southwark, having also a lecture at Monkwell Street Chapel, London. His views seem latterly to have inclined to antinomianism. The date of his death is uncertain.

He published: 1. 'The Power of an Endless Life contrasted with the Law of a Carnal Commandment. A Sermon preached at Monkwell Street on Thursday, 5 March 1801,' London, 1801, 12mo. 2. 'Rays of Everlasting Life,' not later than 1803. 3. 'Democracy detected, Visionary Enthusiasm corrected; or Sixpennyworth of Good Advice selected from the Scriptures of Truth,' London, 1804 (?) (an attack on Joanna Southcott, to which she replied in 'Answer to Garrett's Book, and an Explanation of the word Bride, the Lamb's Wife, in the Revelations,' London, 1805, 8vo). 4. 'The Songs of Sion. Principally designed for the use of Churches and Congregations distinguished by the name of the Children of Sion,' London, 1804? 12mo.

5. 'Huntington corrected, and Garrett's Doctrine protected from the Misconstruction of the Disaffected; or a Reply to a Book lately published called "The Doctrine of Garrett refuted by William Huntington,"' Southwark, 1808, 12mo. The controversy appears to have related to the doctrine of the eternal sonship of Christ, which Huntington accused Garrett of denying. A plate of Garrett's head may be seen by the curious in Joanna Southcott's 'Answer.'

[The principal authority for Garrett's life is his autobiography prefixed to the Songs of Sion. See also Nelson's Islington, p. 273.] J. M. R.

GARRETT, Sir ROBERT (1794–1869), lieutenant-general, colonel 43rd (light infantry) regiment, eldest son of John Garrett, of Ellingham, Isle of Thanet, by his wife Elizabeth, daughter of J. Gore, of St. Peter's, Isle of Thanet, was born in 1794, educated at Harrow School, and on 12 March 1811 became ensign by purchase in the 2nd queen's foot. With his regiment he was present at Fuentes d'Onoro, and in the attack on the forts of Salamanca, where he was the only surviving officer of his party, and received two wounds. He was promoted to a lieutenancy in the 2nd garrison battalion on 3 Sept. 1813, and on 2 Oct. following was transferred to the 7th royal fusiliers, with which he made the campaigns of 1813–14, and was again severely wounded in the Pyrenees. On 7 July 1814 he became captain by purchase in the old 97th (queen's own), and served with that corps in Ireland until it was disbanded, as the 96th foot, in 1818, when he was put on half-pay. He purchased an unattached majority in 1826, and in 1834, after nearly fifteen years on half-pay, was brought into the 46th foot, as major, and became regimental lieutenant-colonel in 1846. He served with the regiment, much of the time in command, at Gibraltar, in the West Indies and North America, and at home. He became brevet-colonel in January 1854.

When the 46th was doing duty, with Garrett in command, at Windsor in the summer of 1854, after the departure of the guards for the East, court-martials on two young officers of the regiment on charges arising out of a system of coarse practical joking at the expense of an unpopular subaltern, attracted much attention. The first case, which was virtually twice tried, gave much offence, as it was supposed to show that a poor officer had no security against the persecution of men of higher rank or wealth (*Nav. and Mil. Gazette*, 26 Aug. 1854). A clamour for further inquiry was met by the despatch of the regiment, a very fine body of men, under Garrett's command, to the Crimea, where it landed three friend Macklin and with Mrs. Woffington, with whom he maintained an intimacy productive of some scandal, and for whom he wrote his delightful song of 'Pretty Peggy.' He quarrelled with both. The rupture with Mrs. Woffington was made up after leading to a return of presents, with the exception of a pair of valuable diamond buckles, which Garrick, it is said, craved permission to keep. A more serious quarrel with Macklin initiated the charges of meanness Garrick had henceforward to endure. Fleetwood's extravagant management of Drury Lane had ended in bankruptcy. Garrick, as the heaviest sufferer, invited the actors of the company to meet him at his house in King Street, Covent Garden ('Mr. West's, Cabinet Maker'), and asked them to sign an agreement to stand by each other in refusing to act. He relied upon his popularity to obtain from the Duke of Grafton, the lord chamberlain, a license to open a new theatre. The duke, finding that Garrick drew 500l. a year, asked contemptuously if that 'was too little for a mere player,' and declined to give the license. A scheme of Garrick's to take the Lincoln's Inn Theatre fell through, and in the end the seceders made terms with their former manager, while Macklin, who is said to have opposed the original action, was made the scapegoat by Fleetwood and excluded. Garrick's endeavours to mediate between the manager and Macklin were vain, and a bitter and lasting quarrel between the two actors ensued. On 13 Sept. 1743 Drury Lane reopened, but the first appearance of Garrick was deferred until 6 Dec., when he appeared as Bayes. Two days previously he had written to the 'London Daily Post' a letter explanatory of his conduct. On the day of his appearance a pamphlet entitled 'The Case of Charles Macklin' was published, and a large party of Macklin's friends went to Drury Lane. Garrick had dispersed a 'handbill requesting the public to suspend their judgment.' His appearance provoked a storm of opposition, and he was not allowed to speak. On the 8th Garrick's explanation, said to be written by Dr. Guthrie the historian, and a letter from 'A Bystander,' appeared in the 'Daily Post.' Garrick was once more attacked. Fleetwood had, however, sent thirty prize-fighters into the pit; the dissentients were driven out of the house, and the riot ceased. Garrick's behaviour was scarcely chivalrous; but as others would have suffered by the fulfilment of his engagements to Macklin the general verdict was in his favour.

The great event of the season was Garrick's appearance, 7 Jan. 1744, as Macbeth, 'as written by Shakespeare.' D'Avenant's ver-

sion had till then held possession of the stage since the Restoration. Garrick's claim to have restored Shakespeare must be accepted with some allowance. At the subsequent revival, 19 March 1748, when Mrs. Pritchard played her great part of Lady Macbeth, he is known to have added a dying speech to his own part. Mrs. Giffard was Garrick's first Lady Macbeth. Samuel Foote [q. v.], destined to be a thorn in the side of Garrick, this season appeared at Drury Lane. The season of 1744–5 saw Garrick's first appearance as Sir John Brute in the 'Provoked Wife,' Scrub in the 'Beaux' Stratagem,' King John, Othello, and Tancred in the 'Tancred and Sigismunda' of Thomson. After 4 April Garrick, on account of illness, played no more. At the end of the season Fleetwood sold the patent to Lacy. Garrick renewed his intimacy with Mrs. Woffington, and even proposed marriage; but a total estrangement followed. During his illness Garrick declined advances from Mrs. Cibber to join her and Quin in taking Drury Lane, with which Lacy, it was supposed, could be induced to part. He accepted an invitation from Thomas Sheridan, the joint manager of the theatres in Aungier Street and Smock Alley, to appear in Dublin and share the profits with him. He appeared at Smock Alley as Hamlet 9 Dec. 1745. Lord Chesterfield, the lord-lieutenant, treated Garrick with studied coldness. The result was none the less a financial success. Orestes, a part he never essayed in England, Faulconbridge, and Iago were the new characters in which he appeared. Arriving in London 10 May 1746, Garrick arranged with Rich for six performances on sharing terms. On the 11th, accordingly, as King Lear he made his first appearance at Covent Garden. Hamlet, Richard, Othello, Archer, and Macbeth followed. He accepted also an engagement for Covent Garden for the following season. He associated himself, however, financially with Lacy, the manager of Drury Lane, whose resources had been crippled by the troubles of 1745, and became his partner in the new patent obtained from the lord chamberlain, the Duke of Grafton. Garrick appears to have paid 8,000l. for his share. The agreement, which bears the date 9 April 1747, is published in the 'Garrick Correspondence.' Hotspur was his only new Shakespearean character, but he was, 17 Jan. 1747, the original Fribble in his own farce of 'Miss in her Teens, or the Medley of Lovers,' and 12 Feb. 1747 the original Ranger in Dr. Hoadly's 'Suspicious Husband.' Quin had on other nights played in characters ordinarily taken by Garrick.

In spite of adverse circumstances, including a disabling illness of Garrick and the keen opposition of Barry and Mrs. Woffington at Drury Lane, the profits of the season, including the six nights in May, were estimated at 8,500*l*. The season of 1747–8 at Drury Lane began under the joint management of Garrick and Lacy. On 15 Sept. Garrick was ill, and unable to speak Johnson's famous prologue. Reformation in management began at once, the first step being the abolition of the practice of admitting by payment behind the scenes. He did not himself act until 15 Oct., when he reappeared as Archer. He spoke the prologue and presented the chorus in a revival of Henry V, and took for the first time Jaffier instead of Pierre in 'Venice Preserved.' From this time to his retirement, 10 June 1776, Garrick's connection with Drury Lane was unbroken. In the following season he played Benedick, produced on 29 Nov. 1748 his own version of ' Romeo and Juliet,' with an altered termination for Barry and Mrs. Cibber, and was the original Demetrius, 6 Feb. 1749, in 'Mahomet and Irene,' under which name was produced Johnson's tragedy of 'Irene.'

On 22 June 1749, first 'at the church in Russell Street, Bloomsbury, and afterwards at the chapel of the Portuguese embassy in Audley Street' (FITZGERALD, *Life of Garrick*, i. 240), Garrick married Eva Marie Violetti (1724–1822), the reputed daughter of a Viennese citizen named Veigel. She came to London in 1746, engaged as a dancer at the Haymarket, and became the guest of the Earl and Countess of Burlington, who on her marriage to Garrick are reputed to have settled on her 6,000*l*. Upon his marriage Garrick lived in Southampton Street, Strand, in the house now No. 27. He afterwards (1754) purchased the famous little house at Hampton. His marriage embroiled him further with the leading actresses, more than one of whom had regarded him as in some shape pledged to her. Mrs. Woffington had previously joined the rival house, and Mrs. Cibber quitted Garrick in anger. Barry also broke his engagement and went to Covent Garden. Garrick had thus to face the unconcealed hostility of Quin, Macklin, Barry, Mrs. Woffington, and Mrs. Cibber, and the more dangerous enmity of Foote. Johnson regarded him with temporary mistrust, if not with coldness, on account of the failure of 'Irene,' and an estrangement had arisen between himself and the aristocratic friends of his wife. Mrs. Ward had to assume the principal characters at Drury Lane, for which she was unfitted, until Miss Bellamy, whom Garrick was training, could be trusted with leading business. In addition to these, his

company comprised Yates, King, Shuter, Woodward, Mrs. Pritchard, and Mrs. Clive [q. v.] Weakened by the death of Mills, it was reinforced by the engagement of Palmer. Before the secession of Barry, Garrick played Comus for the benefit of Mrs. Forster, granddaughter of Milton. He had also played Iago to the Othello of Barry. An occasional prologue, written and spoken by Garrick 8 Sept. 1750, upon the reopening of Drury Lane with the 'Merchant of Venice,' alluded to the secession of Barry and Mrs. Cibber, and said that Drury Lane stage was sacred to Shakespeare, but that if ' " Lear " and " Hamlet " lose their force' he will give the public 'Harlequin,' and substitute the stage carpenter for the poet. In the epilogue he made Mrs. Clive speak of him as of a choleric disposition, but 'much tamer since he married.' So formidable was the opposition that his ruin was anticipated. Garrick, however, as his prologue stated, was ' arm'd cap-à-pie in self-sufficient merit.' ' Besides,' adds Tate Wilkinson (*The Mirror, or Actor's Tablet*, p. 156), ' he had industry, and his troops were under excellent discipline.' In the famous duel of this season, when ' Romeo and Juliet ' came out at both houses on 28 Sept. 1750, Garrick and Miss Bellamy were pitted against Spranger Barry and Mrs. Cibber. (For the epigram by Mr. Hewitt which appeared in the 'Daily Advertiser,' and for the comparisons instituted between the two Romeos, see BARRY, SPRANGER.) A second epigram, by the Rev. Richard Kendal of Peterhouse (*Poetical Register* for 1810–11, p. 369), institutes a comparison between the respective Lears of the same actors:—

> The town has found out different ways
> To praise its different Lears;
> To Barry it gives loud huzzas
> To Garrick only tears.
>
> A king! aye, every inch a king,
> Such Barry doth appear;
> But Garrick's quite another thing,
> He's every inch King Lear.

Garrick played in the season Osmyn in Congreve's ' Mourning Bride,' and Alfred in Mallet's masque of 'Alfred,' 23 Feb. 1751, and at Christmas 1750 carried the war into Rich's camp, producing 'Queen Mab,' a species of pantomimic entertainment in which Woodward played harlequin. Before Drury Lane reopened for the following season, 1751–2, Covent Garden lost Quin, who had practically retired, and Mrs. Woffington, who had gone to Dublin. Garrick meanwhile, together with other actors, had engaged Mossop. He played, 29 Nov. 1751, Kitely in his own alteration of Jonson's ' Every Man in his Humour,' was the original Mercour, 17 Feb. 1752, in 'Eugenia,' by Philip Francis, D.D. [q. v.], and produced Foote's comedy of 'Taste.' A visit in company with his wife to Paris had attracted little attention, though Garrick was introduced to Louis XV, and is said, on very dubious testimony, to have been the hero of a romantic adventure, in which by his skill in acting he detected the murderer of a Sir George Lewis (FITZGERALD, Life of Garrick, i. 270). Garrick once more produced a pantomime in 1752–3, and created a very powerful impression by his performance as the original Beverley in Moore's 'Gamester,' 7 Feb. 1753. In the following season Mrs. Cibber rejoined Garrick, whom she resembled so much that they might have passed for brother and sister. From this time forward until her death she did not leave him. Miss Macklin and Foote also joined the company, and Macklin took what was called a farewell benefit. Garrick took parts in the 'Boadicea' of Richard Glover [q. v.], the 'Virginia' of Samuel Crisp [q. v.], and Whitehead's 'Creusa.' To 18 March 1754 belongs the first production of 'Katharine and Petruchio,' Garrick's adaptation of the 'Taming of the Shrew,' which may be said to still hold possession of the stage. In this Garrick did not act; the Petruchio being Woodward and the Grumio Yates. The first important revival of the following season was the 'Chances,' altered by Garrick from Buckingham's previous alteration from Beaumont and Fletcher, and produced at the request of George II. In this, 7 Nov. 1754, he played Don John. Four days later for Mossop he produced 'Coriolanus.' 'Barbarossa,' by John Brown [q. v.], 17 Dec., was the first novelty. The 'Fairies,' an opera taken from the 'Midsummer Night's Dream,' 3 Feb. 1755, is generally attributed to Garrick, but is repudiated by him. He delivered as a drunken sailor a prologue to Mallet's masque of 'Britannia.' This was repeated many nights after the masque was withdrawn. On 8 Nov. 1755 Garrick produced the 'Chinese Festival,' a very dull divertissement by Noverre, a Swiss, which had been long in preparation. Meanwhile war with France having broken out, the French dancers provoked a strong opposition and much brawling. Garrick was accused of bringing over the enemies of his country to oppose his countrymen on the stage. On Tuesday the 18th the rioters overpowered the aristocratic patrons of the house, who drew their swords, did some 1,000l. worth of damage to the theatre, and attempted to sack the house of Garrick. The piece was then withdrawn. Three days later Garrick, dressed as Archer, came on the stage and heard cries which sounded like 'Pardon.' He then advanced, and firmly and respectfully 'explained how ill he had been treated by the wanton and malignant conduct of wicked individuals,' and declared that unless he was permitted to perform that night, 'he was above want, superior to insult, and would never, never appear on the stage again' (TATE WILKINSON, The Mirror, or Actor's Tablet, p. 215; not given in contemporary biographies). This was greeted with wild enthusiasm. 'Florizel and Perdita,' Garrick's alteration of the 'Winter's Tale,' was produced 21 Jan. 1756 with Garrick as Leontes, and the 'Tempest,' an opera taken from Shakespeare, with some additions by Dryden, on 11 Feb. and attributed to and repudiated by Garrick. In the next season, 28 Oct. 1756, Garrick produced 'King Lear,' with restorations from Shakespeare; also, 3 Dec., 'Lilliput,' a one-act piece, extracted from 'Gulliver' and acted by children whom he had trained; and, 24 March 1757, his own farce the 'Modern Fine Gentleman,' revived 3 Dec. as the 'Male Coquette.' He played for the first time, 6 Nov. 1756, his favourite character of Don Felix in the 'Wonder,' produced Foote's comedy the 'Author,' and strengthened his company by the addition of Miss Barton, subsequently Mrs. Abington [q. v.] Mrs. Woffington died before the next season commenced. On 2 Dec. 1757 he was Biron in his own alteration of Southern's 'Fatal Marriage,' and on 22 Dec. produced the 'Gamesters,' altered by himself from Shirley's 'Gamester,' and played in it the part of Wilding. When on 16 Sept. 1758 Drury Lane reopened, Garrick had lost Woodward. Foote, however, reappeared, and with him Tate Wilkinson. Garrick took Marplot in the 'Busybody,' Antony in 'Antony and Cleopatra,' abridged by Capel, and was the original Heartly in his own adaptation the 'Guardian,' 3 Feb. 1759. Moody was added to the company the following season, one of the early productions of which was 'High Life below Stairs.' Garrick produced on 31 Dec. 1759 his own unprinted pantomime 'Harlequin's Invasion.' In 1760–1 Garrick engaged Sheridan, who played leading business, Richard III, Cato, Hamlet, &c. Garrick was himself the Faulconbridge to Sheridan's King John. Some revival of jealousy and ill-feeling was the outcome of this experiment. He produced 'Polly Honeycombe,' by his friend George Colman the elder [q. v.], the authorship of which was attributed to and disowned by Garrick. He produced the 'Enchanter, or Love and Magic,' 13 Dec. 1760, a musical trifle, the authorship of which has been assigned to him. Foote during the season played in some of his own pieces. Garrick's alteration of 'Cymbeline,' 28 Nov. 1761, was, after the production of one or two pieces to commemorate the coronation, the first important event of 1761-2. On 10 Feb. 1762 Garrick was the original Dorilant in Whitehead's 'School for Lovers,' and on 20 March the Farmer in the 'Farmer's Return,' a trifle in verse of his own composition. For the following season the theatre was enlarged and further restrictions were imposed upon the presence of the public behind the scenes. Garrick was, 19 Jan. 1763, the original Don Alonzo in Mallet's 'Elvira,' and 3 Feb. the original Sir Anthony Branville in Mrs. Sheridan's comedy 'Discovery,' and played, 15 March, Sciolto in the 'Fair Penitent.' This is noticeable as the last new part he played. A production of the 'Two Gentlemen of Verona,' altered by Victor, was the cause of a serious riot. A certain Fitzpatrick put himself at the head of a set of young men known as 'The Town,' and demanded in their names, on 25 Jan. 1763, admission at half price at the end of the third act. A riot followed and was renewed next day, when Moody, for preventing a man from setting fire to the house, was ordered to go on his knees to apologise. He refused and was supported by Garrick, who, however, was compelled to promise that Moody should not appear while under the displeasure of the audience. Fitzpatrick, who had abused Garrick in newspapers and pamphlets, and spoken insultingly of him in a club at the Bedford (COOKE, *Life of Macklin*, 1804, p. 246), is the Fizgig of Garrick's 'Scribbleriad.' He was treated with much savagery by Churchill in the eighth edition (1763) of the 'Rosciad.' These things were largely responsible for Garrick's resolution at the close of the season 1762-3 to quit the stage, at least for a considerable time. A peaceful, and in the main long-suffering man, petted and rather spoilt by the distinguished men to whose society he was admitted, Garrick shrank from dependence upon the mob. The public interest was flagging. Receipts had fallen from hundreds to scores of pounds. Sir William Weller Pepys said, according to Rogers (*Table Talk*, ed. 1887, p. 7) that 'the pit was often almost empty.' Davies (*Life*, ii. 62) asserts that the opposition of Beard and Miss Brent at Covent Garden prevailed during the season against Garrick. It is difficult to believe, however, that Garrick and Mrs. Cibber jointly played on one occasion to an audience of five pounds. Change of air had been prescribed for Mrs. Garrick. It is a characteristic and an honourable trait in Garrick that Mrs. Garrick 'from the day of her marriage till the death of her husband had never been separated from him

for twenty-four hours' (*ib.* ii. 67). After a visit to the Duke of Devonshire, the Garricks went to Paris, where they arrived 19 Sept. 1763. Drury Lane, where Garrick left his brother George as his substitute, opened the following day, and gave, for one night only, 23 Nov., his alteration of the 'Midsummer Night's Dream.' A manuscript journal which Garrick rather spasmodically kept, together with his voluminous correspondence, enables us to trace the actor throughout his long and triumphant tour. Englishmen were well received in Paris after the peace. At the dinners of Baron d'Holbach he made the acquaintance of Diderot and the encyclopædists; he was made free of the Comédie-Française, and formed friendships with the members, especially Mlle. Clairon. At the house of a Mr. Neville he was induced by Mlle. Clairon to give various recitations in presence of Marmontel, D'Alembert, &c. After a stay of three weeks, and with a promise to return, he left Paris; proceeded by Lyons and Mont Cenis to Turin; received but did not accept an invitation from Voltaire to call on him at Ferney; visited the principal cities of Italy; stayed a fortnight at Rome; and reached Naples, where he was very popular with the aristocratic English colony of visitors and collected articles of virtu. By Parma, where the grand duke entertained him, he posted to Venice, which he quitted about the middle of June. Mrs. Garrick was restored to health by the mud baths of Albano, near Padua. The pair visited Munich, where Garrick had a bad attack, compelling him to go to Spa. He reached Paris once more near October 1764, and was welcomed more warmly than before. Beaumarchais, Marivaux, Grimm, and all the brilliant society received him with demonstrations more enthusiastic and more sincere than were often lavished upon English visitors. Mrs. Garrick was also received with the most respectful homage. French literature of this epoch furnishes many proofs of the influence he exercised. A dozen years later Gibbon found that Garrick was warmly remembered. Grimm or Diderot (July 1765) says that Garrick is the only actor who reaches ideal excellence, speaks enthusiastically of his freedom from grimace or exaggeration, and describes the effect which he produced by performing the dagger scene in 'Macbeth' in a room and in his ordinary dress (*Correspondance Littéraire de Grimm et Diderot*, vol. iv. pt. i. pp. 500-1, ed. 1813). The same authority declares Garrick to be of middle height, inclining to be little, of agreeable and *spirituel* features, and with a prodigious play of eye. He tells how Garrick simulated drunkenness with Préville in passing through Passy, and criticised his companion for not being drunk in his legs. He also gives a description of his method of narrating in a manner à faire frémir the incident of a father dropping his child from a window, losing his speech, and going mad (*ib.* pp. 502–3). Many other references, all eminently favourable to Garrick, are to be found in the correspondence. Garrick is said to have had an income of fifty to sixty thousand *livres de rente,* and it is added that 'he passes for a lover of money.'

Meanwhile Drury Lane was making money in a manner not altogether agreeable. Powell, a young actor whom Garrick had trained, and who made his début 8 Oct. 1763, had already become a public favourite, and was to prove, next to Barry, the most dangerous of all Garrick's rivals. Garrick was stimulated to return and resume acting. With characteristic and misplaced ingenuity he sent in advance a satirical pamphlet written by himself against himself, and called 'The Sick Monkey.' By publishing this 'fable' he hoped to escape the satire of others, and also to herald his reappearance. Much fuss was made about keeping the authorship secret, and Colman was urged to let no word of rumour escape. The thing, however, as it deserved, fell flat. On 27 April 1765 Garrick arrived in London. On the reopening of the theatre, 14 Sept. 1765, he introduced for the first time in England the system of lighting the stage by lights not visible to the audience. His first appearance 'by command' took place 14 Nov. as Benedick to the Beatrice of Miss Pope. His calculations had been just. Weary of the musical pieces, which during his absence had proved, at his suggestion, the staple of Drury Lane entertainments, the public received him with wild enthusiasm, and applauded everything, even to a facetious prologue of his own, which he spoke, and which is not in the best possible taste. An aftermath of success richer than the original harvest was in store for him. On 30 Jan. 1766 he lost by death his great ally, Mrs. Cibber, which wrung from him the remark that 'tragedy is dead on one side.' Quin, with whom he had of late been intimate, was also dead. On 20 Feb. he produced the 'Clandestine Marriage,' by himself and Colman. By refusing to take the part of Lord Ogleby, which was played by King, he gave rise to a coldness between himself and his collaborator extending over years. Early in 1766 Garrick ceased to act, and visited Bath. He played Kitely, 22 May, in aid of the fund for the benefit of retired actors. On 25 Oct. 1766 he produced his 'Country Girl,' an alteration of Wycherley's 'Country Wife,' and on 18 Nov. 'Neck or

Nothing,' a farce imitated from Lesage, the authorship of which, on no very satisfactory evidence, is assigned to Garrick. 'Cymon,' a dramatic romance founded on Dryden's 'Cymon and Iphigenia,' was played 2 Jan. 1767, and is more probably his. Garrick's 'Linco's Travels' saw the light 6 April 1767. Barry and Mrs. Dancer (subsequently Mrs. Barry) appeared in the season 1767-8. Garrick's 'Peep behind the Curtain, or the New Rehearsal,' was played 23 Oct. 1767. He wrote also a farewell address for Mrs. Pritchard on her quitting the stage, 24 April 1768. Palmer died at the close of the season and his wife retired. The following season saw the retirement of Kitty Clive, of all Garrick's feminine associates the one he most feared and in a sense esteemed. Havard was also dead. Meanwhile Colman had purchased the lease of Covent Garden, and been joined by Powell. A formidable rivalry was thus begotten, and the coolness between Garrick and Colman increased. Of the pieces by various authors produced by Garrick since his return from abroad Kelly's 'False Delicacy' and Bickerstaffe's 'Padlock' alone had a signal success. Before the beginning of the next season (1769-70) the memorable jubilee in honour of Shakespeare had been celebrated in Stratford. Garrick had the chief share in designing and carrying out this entertainment, to which the wits and the weather proved equally hostile. A full account of the spectacle (on 6, 7, and 8 Sept. 1769) is given in the third volume of Victor's 'History of the Theatres of London,' 8vo, 1771. Victor describes the entire pageant, including Garrick's 'Ode upon dedicating a Building and erecting a Statue to Shakespeare at Stratford-upon-Avon' (see also CRADOCK, *Memoirs,* i. 211). Garrick, who was much out of pocket by the fiasco, recouped himself by producing at Drury Lane, 14 Oct. 1769, the 'Jubilee,' a dramatic entertainment consisting of the pageantry designed for the Stratford celebration. This was repeated over ninety times. Garrick wrote the manuscript, which now appears to be lost. He had previously (30 Sept.) given the before-mentioned ode, which was republished with a whimsical parody upon it. Foote was persuaded to abandon an intended caricature of the whole proceedings, which gave Garrick many qualms. Kelly's 'Word to the Wise,' 3 March 1770, was the cause of a riot prolonged over some days by the friends of Wilkes, who saw in Kelly a government hireling. The piece was withdrawn after many scenes of disorder. 'King Arthur,' by Dryden, altered by Garrick, was produced 13 Dec. 1770. Cumberland's 'West

Indian' was given this season. The 'Institution of the Garter,' altered by Garrick from a dramatic poem by Gilbert West (*Biographia Dramatica*), was played 28 Oct. 1771. His 'Irish Widow,' taken in part from Molière's 'Le Mariage Forcé,' came out 23 Oct. 1772. On 18 Dec. he produced his mangled version of 'Hamlet,' which, in consequence of the opposition it aroused, was never printed. On 27 Dec. 1773 'A Christmas Tale,' assigned to Garrick, saw the light.

The season of 1774–5 opened 17 Sept. with the 'Drummer' and a prelude by Garrick never printed, called 'Meeting of the Company.' 'Bon Ton, or High Life above Stairs,' by Garrick, was played 18 March 1775. 'Theatrical Candidates,' a prelude attributed to Garrick, served in September 1775 for the opening of the season. 'May Day, or the Little Gipsy,' also attributed to him, followed, 28 Oct. During the spring of 1776 Garrick played for the last time a round of his favourite characters. His last appearance on the stage was made 10 June 1776 as Don Felix in the 'Wonder.' The profits of the night were appropriated to the Theatrical Fund, the customary address, one of the best and happiest in its line, being written and spoken by Garrick, who also took leave in a prose address. In the course of his farewell season his spirits and capacities were once more seen at their best. His successive representations had been patronised by all that was most brilliant in English society, and many of his distinguished French admirers were present. During one or two previous seasons the takings had diminished. Garrick's receipts had, however, been handsome, and the theatre had increased largely in value. Some important alterations in Drury Lane were made at the beginning of his last season. Consciousness of failing strength was a motive to retirement. The unrelenting animosity of contemptible scribblers, feuds with authors, and various managerial troubles had acted upon his singularly nervous temperament. Epigrams asserted that Garrick had been driven from the stage by three actresses, Miss Younge, Mrs. Yates, and Mrs. Abington. Garrick said that Mrs. Abington was 'the worst of bad women' (*Correspondence*, ii. 140). Miss Younge's letters are often querulous. The moiety of his patent and other possessions in Drury Lane Garrick sold to Richard Brinsley Sheridan, Lindley, and Dr. Ford for 35,000*l.*, a sum which must be considered moderate, since the other moiety, belonging to Willoughby Lacy, was purchased two years later for upwards of 45,000*l.* Of this latter sum 22,000*l.* was due to Garrick, who held a mortgage on

Lacy's share. Garrick maintained to the last his interest in Drury Lane, the fortunes of which, in spite of the success of the 'School for Scandal,' fell off under Sheridan's indolent management. His time, largely occupied with visits to country houses, allowed him to visit the theatre, and to offer suggestions, not always accepted in the best spirit, to actors who played characters previously his. A prologue by him was delivered on the opening of the season of 1776-7, and various prologues and epilogues were spoken during the following years at one or other of the patent houses. The best known of these are the prologues to 'All the World's a Stage' and to the 'School for Scandal,' both of them spoken by King. Both prologue and epilogue to the 'Fathers,' by Fielding, were also by Garrick, and constituted apparently his last contribution to the stage. 'Garrick's Jests, or the English Roscius in High Life. Containing all the Jokes of the Wits of the Present Age,' &c., 8vo, no date, is a catch-penny publication, for which Garrick is in no way responsible. Among his triumphs was the famous scene in the House of Commons, when 'Squire' Baldwin complained that Garrick had remained after an order for the withdrawal of strangers. Burke, who said that Garrick had 'taught them all,' supported by Fox and Townshend, successfully objected to the enforcement of the order in his case. Garrick foolishly retorted in some feeble and ill-natured verses against Baldwin (*Poetical Works*, ii. 538). While spending the Christmas of 1778 at Althorpe he was attacked by gout and stone, which had long beset him, and also by herpes. He was brought to No. 5 Adelphi Terrace, a house which he had taken in 1772, on 15 Jan. 1779. He rapidly sank, and died on 20 Jan. about 8 A.M. He was buried in Westminster Abbey on 1 Feb. with exceptional honours. The streets were crowded, and the string of carriages extended from the Strand to the abbey. The Bishop of Rochester received the cortège. The pall-bearers were the Duke of Devonshire, Lords Camden, Ossory, Spencer, and Palmerston, and Sir Watkin Wynne, and Burke, Johnson, Fox, and the 'Literary Club' generally were among the mourners. Sheridan wrote on his death the much-lauded monody, and Johnson uttered the famous phrase, 'I am disappointed by that stroke of death which has eclipsed the gaiety of nations, and impoverished the public stock of harmless pleasure.' These words Mrs. Garrick caused to be engraved on his monument in Lichfield. His tomb in Westminster Abbey is at the foot of Shakespeare's statue, where, 16 Oct. 1822, his wife, then ninety-eight years of age, was placed beside him. His monument, erected by his friend Wallis, is on the opposite wall, with an inscription by Pratt, substituted for one by Burke, rejected as too long. Of the monument and inscription Lamb said in the 'Essays of Elia:' 'I found inscribed under this harlequin figure a farrago of false thoughts and nonsense.' Burke's rejected epitaph said: 'He raised the character of his profession to the rank of a liberal art' (WINDHAM, *Diary*, p. 361). The only actor who has been buried in the Abbey since Garrick was Sir Henry Irving (on 20 October 1905). Garrick left behind him a sum that with no great exaggeration has been estimated at 100,000*l*. To his widow were left the houses at Hampton and in the Adelphi, with plate, wine, pictures, &c., 6,000*l*., and an annuity of 1,500*l*. No memorials were left to any of his friends, but his relations, including a German niece of Mrs. Garrick, had sums varying from 1,000*l*. to 10,000*l*., which last named amount was left to his brother George, who did not directly benefit by it. Of George, who had been his right-hand man, and who only survived him a few days, it was said with touching humour that he followed his brother so close because 'David wanted him,' a phrase which had been familiar in the theatre.

Garrick's correspondence is a mine of information, and from this and the recorded opinions of friends and observers, English and foreign, we have a livelier idea of his character than we possess of any actor, and of almost any contemporary. Of his weaknesses the best account is given in Goldsmith's masterly summary in 'Retaliation.' Garrick had the burning desire for admiration common to men of his craft. He was jubilant in success, petulant in defeat, timid in the face of menace, miserable in the absence of recognition. Naturally careful, he acquired a wholly unmerited reputation for meanness. Few actors indeed have been more reasonably and judiciously generous. His biographer, Davies, who is nowise given to over-praising Garrick, has collected many instances of his generosity. He was steadily beneficent in private as well as in public (*Life of Garrick*, ii. 395). His offer to Clairon in her fight against the ministry and the court of France elicited from Voltaire the question whether there was a marshal or a duke in France who would do the like. Davies also mentions that his death was deplored as a calamity in Hampton, and says that he heard Johnson express his knowledge that Garrick gave away more money than any man in London (*ib.* ii. 398). Garrick also 'dearly loved a lord,' a not unnatural

failing in one courted by lords. He was the object of special attention on the part of the Duc de Nivernois and other foreign ministers, and was probably more caressed than any man of his epoch. Impressionable in nature, and accustomed from his early days to a struggle for existence, belonging to 'a family whose study was to make fourpence do as much as others made fourpence halfpenny' (JOHNSON, *Life*, iii. 387), he was prudent and cautious even in the midst of his liberalities, and he was led to overestimate the value of social attention. Like most men of his epoch he was inclined to be a free, though, as Johnson said, 'a decent liver,' and he paid in ill-health the penalty of indulgence that does not seem to have been excessive. He confessed to fieriness of disposition, especially in disputes with Mrs. Clive or Mrs. Woffington. With the chief actresses of his company his relations during his married life were not always friendly, but he secured the esteem and the respect of the most petulant. Literature presents little that is pleasanter than his correspondence with his Pivy, a contraction of Clivey Pivey, as he called Mrs. Clive. One letter written by Mrs. Clive, 23 Jan. 1776, when she was sixty-five years of age, tells him that none of his surroundings could be sensible of half his perfections, and speaks in the highest terms of the manner in which he trained his company, endeavouring to beat his 'ideas into the heads of creatures who had none of their own' (*Garrick Correspondence*, ii. 128). Johnson, though he scolded Garrick and sneered at his profession, would, as Sir Joshua Reynolds said, let no one attack him but himself. 'It is wonderful,' he said, 'how little Garrick assumes.' Stockdale says (*Memoirs*, ii. 186) that Johnson said of Garrick: 'More pains have been taken to spoil that fellow than if he had been heir-apparent to the empire of India.' Most of the accusations levelled against Garrick are attributable to the reckless Foote and to petulant and unreasonable dramatists. His success made him from the outset many enemies, and each step of importance aroused a fierce polemic. In some cases, as in that of Kenrick, whose 'Love in the Suds; a Town Eclogue,' 1772, of which an imperfect copy is in the British Museum, charges Garrick with infamy, a public apology was made by Garrick's assailant. Other attacks, attributed to the Rev. David Williams, Leonard McNally, William Shirley, Fitzpatrick, Theophilus Cibber, Edward Purdon, and various nameless writers, were answered by friends of Garrick. 'An Essay on Acting, in which will be considered the mimical behaviour of a certain fashionable faulty actor, and the laudableness of such unmannerly, as well as inhumane proceedings,' &c., 1744, 8vo, is curious as a criticism by Garrick upon his own Macbeth, by publishing which he hoped to disarm the censure of others. Garrick also wrote an 'Answer to Mr. Macklin's Case,' London, 1743, of which a copy with no title-page is in the Forster collection at South Kensington. On a copy of a 'Letter of Abuse to D——d G——k.' London, 1757, 8vo, belonging to Joseph Reed, now no longer traceable, was the following note: 'This was probably written by Mr. Garrick himself.' The best known eulogy of Garrick is that of Churchill in the 'Rosciad,' 1761, in which, after dealing with minor actors, Shakespeare, on behalf of himself and Ben Jonson, bids

> Garrick take the chair,
> Nor quit it till thou place an equal there.

Garrick's easy acquiescence in this praise, which he professed to regard as a bid for the freedom of his theatre, led to the publication by Churchill of the 'Apology,' in which Garrick was made to wince. Henceforward Churchill was treated with consideration by Garrick, who more than once lent him money. For a list of the pamphlets and other works for and against Garrick that are accessible in the British Museum, the Forster collection, and some private libraries, reference may be made to Mr. Lowe's 'Bibliographical History of English Theatrical Literature,' 1888, in which work they occupy twelve pages. As a dramatist Garrick had vivacity and sweetness that almost do duty for art, a good knowledge of character, and complete familiarity with stage craft. In this respect he resembled Colley Cibber. His poetical works were collected in two volumes, small 8vo, 1785. Of the 540 consecutively numbered pages, almost three quarters are occupied with prologues and epilogues, in which Garrick was happy. These indeed constitute in themselves a minute chronicle of the stage. Songs, burlettas, epigrams, fables, and occasional verses, with 'Fizgig's Triumph, or the Power of Riot,' written against Fitzpatrick, and other satires make up the two volumes. His epigrams are good in their way. The only piece in which he reveals inspiration is in his song 'Peggy,' written to Mrs. Woffington. Garrick's plays have never been collected. His share in works, such as the 'Clandestine Marriage,' written in conjunction with George Colman cannot be settled, and the pieces generally which bear his name or are ascribed to him are almost invariably adaptations. Sometimes, as in the 'Country Girl,' his version of an unpresentable work of one of the older dramatists has retained possession of the stage. His

alterations of Shakespeare, however, of Ben Jonson, and other dramatists are not to be trusted as original productions, and are sometimes the reverse of creditable. His so-called dramatic works were published in three vols. 12mo, 1768, reprinted 1798. Lowndes justly speaks of this as 'a wretched and imperfect collection.' It contains sixteen plays. Most of the printed plays of Garrick are in the British Museum in 8vo. Many of them are included in the 'Modern British Drama' and the collections of Inchbald, Bell, &c. As a manager Garrick commands respect. His vanity did not prevent him from engaging the best obtainable talent. He pitted himself against men such as Spranger Barry, Macklin, and Quin, and he missed no opportunity of appearing with actresses such as Mrs. Clive, Mrs. Woffington, Mrs. Cibber, Mrs. Abington, and others of equal talent and reputation. To Mrs. Woffington he had, after essaying it, to resign the part of Sir Harry Wildair, and it was often said that he would not fairly match himself against Mrs. Clive, who was indeed a formidable opponent. In this respect, however, his conduct compares favourably with that of most of his profession. In his resentment against those who, he held, had gone out of their way to injure him, he declined to accept one or two pieces from their pens, and so played into the hands of Covent Garden. He had no enduring hostility, however, his temper generally being devoid of gall. He carried caution to an excess. Davies says that he acquired through this a hesitation in speech which did not originally characterise him. As a rule he was fairly accessible to authors, and if he produced few masterpieces, the fault was in the writers. In dramatists generally he displayed genuine interest, and after his retirement he took great pains to advance the fortunes of Hannah More. In his disputes the impression conveyed is generally that he was in the right. He generally treated the ebullitions of mortified vanity on the part of authors with tenderness. He kept the masculine portion of his company in fair order, though the feminine portion was generally mutinous. He made many important reforms, some of them learned during his journeys abroad, in discipline, in stage arrangement, and in matters of costume, in which he effected some improvement, pleading as a not very convincing reason for going no further that the public would not stand it. In many cases of difficulty he showed magnanimity, which his enemies sought vainly to stamp as prudence. Fortune fluctuated during his managerial career, but the result was that the property he conducted increased steadily in value under his management, that he retired with a larger fortune than any English actor except Alleyn had made in a similar enterprise, and with the respect and friendship of all the best men of his epoch. A list, founded principally upon information supplied by Genest, of the chief incidents at Drury Lane during Garrick's management appears in Mr. Fitzgerald's 'Life,' ii. 472–85.

Garrick's social gifts were among his strongest points. He was a bright and vivacious talker, except in the presence of Foote, when, says Davies (ii. 257), 'he was a *muta persona.*' Concerning his conversation, Johnson says it 'is gay and grotesque. It is a dish of all sorts, but of all good things. There is no solid meat in it; there is a want of sentiment in it. Not but that he has sentiment sometimes, and sentiment too very powerful and very pleasing, but it has not its full proportion in his conversation' (*Life* by BOSWELL, ii. 464). Garrick's position as an actor is in the front rank. That Horace Walpole and Gray disputed his supremacy, and Colley Cibber, Quin, and Macklin made grudging concessions of his merits, is little to the point. Every innovator in art encounters such opposition. George III said that 'he never could stand still, he was a great fidget,' and George Selwyn spoke depreciatingly of his Othello. Smollett attacked Garrick with much bitterness, but made amends by a high compliment in his continuation of Hume's 'History,' vi. 310, ed. 1818. George Colman the younger [q. v.] admits Garrick's unequalled power of imitating nature, though whenever he 'chose to show off as himself . . . he was almost sure to play that character worse than any other' (*Random Recollections*, i. 223, 227). Colman had been told that Garrick could make 'the twin stars which nature had stuck in his head look as dull as two coddled gooseberries,' and proceeds to describe at some length the manner in which he conveyed the expression in the eye of a deaf person. The most trustworthy, as the most unprejudiced, testimony to Garrick's method is that of Lichtenberg, the German critic, which is included in his 'Ausgewählte Schriften,' and has been more than once translated into English. Writing from England in October 1775, he furnishes to a friend elaborate criticisms of Garrick in various characters. Garrick is described by him as a model of strength and force as distinguished from the actors around him, by the intense life of his look, movement, and gesture, and compelling, as if by magnetic force, the sympathy of his audience with every assumed mood. Lichtenberg assigns Garrick an incontestable superiority over every English actor, and analysing various characters, notably Hamlet and Sir John Brute, conveys a lively idea of his powers of conception and execution. Samuel Derrick [q. v.], in his 'General View of the Stage' (pp. 231–2), after describing his appearance, says that he is the greatest if not the only actor in Lear and Abel Drugger, Macbeth and Benedick, Hamlet and Sir John Brute, Chamont and Archer, Tancred and Ranger, Jaffier and Bayes, Lusignan and Lord Chalkstone. This selection will be generally accepted. To this description may be added that in the 'Theatrical Review,' 1763, p. 74, quoted by Waldron in the Appendix to his edition of the 'Roscius Anglicanus,' p. 21: 'The voice of the performer is clear, impressive, and affecting, agreeable though not harmonious, sharp though not dissonant, strong though not extensive. In declamation it is uncommonly forcible, in variation unaffectedly simple. It is said to want power at the top, though the art of the actor all but conceals the defect. Dr. Burney says that Garrick, like other inhabitants of Lichfield, said 'shupreme,' 'shuperior.' Garrick's versatility, or, as Johnson called it, his 'universality,' was his distinguishing characteristic. The one character Johnson held he could not play was a fine gentleman (BOSWELL, v. 126). Hogarth, after seeing him in Abel Drugger, said: 'You are in your element when you are begrimed with dirt or up to your elbows in blood' (note to BOSWELL'S *Johnson*, iii. 35, taken from MURPHY'S *Garrick*, i. 31). Shireff, the miniature-painter, who was deaf and dumb, followed closely Garrick's performances, and said he understood him, 'his face was a language' (MURPHY, *Garrick*, ii. 185). Cooke's 'Memoirs of Macklin,' p. 110, tells of a Lichfield grocer who having seen Garrick in Abel Drugger apologised to Peter Garrick for saying that though the actor might be rich, he was 'one of the shabbiest, meanest, most pitiful hounds ever seen.' Standing in one of her tiffs at the wings in Drury Lane, Mrs. Clive turned away in anger at finding herself moved in her own despite, and said, 'D—— him, he could act a gridiron.' Stories of the kind from compilations French and English might be multiplied without end. The stories concerning his diminutive stature and his avarice sprang generally from rival actors. Burney and Hogarth, with Bannister and other actors of a later date, describe his facial play, the effect of the eye, which Burney says 'was surely equal to all Argus's hundred,' and the manner in which things inanimate seemed to share in the expression of emotion. Burney said of his coat that the very flaps and skirts seemed animated, while

Bannister asserted that in Lear his very stick acted. Home's 'Douglas' was first offered to Garrick, who returned it with an opinion that it was totally unfit for the stage (Dr. A. Carlyle, *Autobiography*, p. 325). Armstrong, on account of the rejection of his 'Forced Marriage,' maintained his anger for twenty years. Hawkins and Mickle for similar reasons remained hostile. Mickle inserted an angry note in his 'Lusiad.' Soon after he saw Garrick in 'Lear,' and after fetching a deep sigh said, 'I wish the note was out of my book' (Horne, *Essays*, p. 38, ed. 1808). 'Garrick in the Shades, or a Peep into Elysium,' 8vo, 1779, a farce published after his death, represents Garrick as hurt at the cold reception given him by Shakespeare.

Garrick collected books and bric-à-brac. His books, with additions by Mrs. Garrick, were dispersed in 1823 at a ten days' sale at Saunders's. From the Garrick collection of plays Lamb took for Hone's 'Table Book' many extracts, subsequently included in his 'Specimens of the English Dramatic Poets.' Garrick's will is printed in Murphy's 'Life.' Innumerable portraits and engravings of Garrick are to be found. One portrait by Hogarth represents him composing the prologue to 'Taste.' Sir Joshua Reynolds painted him several times. One of his most famous pictures is that presenting Garrick between Tragedy and Comedy. A portrait of Garrick as Kitely is, or quite recently was, in the Huth collection. A third portrait by Reynolds was presented to the Garrick Club in 1888 from his family collection by the Earl of Fife. The Garrick Club contains in addition among others a portrait assigned to Hogarth, pictures by Zoffany representing Garrick as Jaffier, as Macbeth, and as Lord Chalkstone, by Hayman as Ranger, by Morland (copied from Dance) as Richard III, by Loutherbourg as Don John in the 'Chances' and Richard III; by an unknown hand as Romeo and a steward of the Jubilee. In 1766 Gainsborough [q. v.] painted a portrait of Garrick for the corporation of Stratford-on-Avon, said by Mrs. Garrick to be the best portrait ever taken of 'her Davy.' Another by the same artist was painted in 1770.

[The chief authority for the Life of Garrick is contained in his Private Correspondence, published in 2 vols. folio, with a memoir by Boaden, in 1832. Much valuable matter not yet fully used is in the Forster collections at South Kensington Museum. Portions of this have been incorporated into Mr. Percy Fitzgerald's Life of Garrick, 2 vols. 1868. The Life of Garrick by Tom Davies, 2 vols. 1780 (first edit.), the opening sentence of which is attributed to Johnson, is the basis of much subsequent information.

Johnson professed his willingness to write a memoir, but the offer was declined by Mrs. Garrick. Murphy's Life of Garrick, 2 vols. 1801, contains matter not elsewhere found. More recent monographs are by Joseph Knight (the writer of this article), 1894, and by Sir Theodore Martin in Monographs, a collection of articles from Quart. Rev. 1906. Some previously unpublished correspondence by Prof. George Pierce Baker of Harvard Univ. appeared in 1907. See also memoirs of contemporary actors, Macklin, Cumberland, O'Keeffe, Colman and Foote; Boswell's Life of Johnson, by Dr. Birkbeck Hill; Dr. Hill's edition of Hume's Letters; Forster's Life of Goldsmith; Horace Walpole's Letters: Rogers's Table Talk; Victor's Works; Tate Wilkinson's Memoirs; The Dramatic Censor; Nichols's Anecdotes and Illustrations; Genest's Account of English Stage; Biographia Dramatica; Notes and Queries, 4th ser., passim; R. W. Lowe's Bibliographical Account of English Theatrical Literature (1888, pp. 136–147), which enumerates no less than 87 pamphlets dealing with Garrick's career.]   J. K.

GARROD, ALFRED HENRY (1846–1879), zoologist, eldest child of Dr. (afterwards Sir) Alfred Baring Garrod (1819–1907), an eminent physician, was born in Charterhouse Square, London, on 18 May 1846. He was educated at University College School, and entered University College in October 1862. He owed much of his scientific enthusiasm to Professor Sharpey's lectures on physiology, and also received a marked bias towards mathematical and mechanical studies from Professor De Morgan. In October 1864 he entered as a medical student at King's College, London, gaining a Warneford scholarship at entrance, and the medical scholarship in three successive years. In 1868 he became a licentiate of the Apothecaries' Society, and won an exhibition for natural science at St. John's College, Cambridge, where he commenced residence in October. During his university course he made several interesting researches on the causes of the varying temperature of the human body and on the circulation of the blood, and made some improvements in the sphygmograph. In 1870 he was elected to a foundation scholarship at St. John's, and in December 1871 he was placed senior in the natural sciences tripos. His election to a fellowship at St. John's in November 1873 was the first instance there of this distinction being given for natural science. In June 1871 Garrod was elected prosector to the Zoological Society, and he pursued his work in the dissecting room of the Zoological Gardens, Regent's Park, with devoted ardour till his death. The great quantity of material continually accumulating there for research drew him into almost exclusively zoological work. The anatomy of birds became his favourite study, and he was soon able to work out on a more extensive scale many of Nitzsch's observations on pterylography, and to add many new facts, especially in the myology of birds. In 1874 he was elected professor of comparative anatomy at King's College, London, which post he continued to hold till within a few weeks of his death. In 1875 he was appointed Fullerian professor of physiology at the Royal Institution, having previously lectured there on 'The Heart and the Sphygmograph' and on 'Animal Locomotion.' As Fullerian professor he gave twelve lectures in 1875 on 'The Classification of Vertebrate Animals,' in 1877 on 'The Human Form: Its Structure in relation to its Contour,' and in 1878 on 'The Protoplasmic Theory of Life, and its bearing on Physiology.' All these courses were illustrated by models and experiments, which he devised with great ingenuity, thus rendering the lectures very popular. In 1875 he delivered several of the Davis lectures at the Zoological Gardens, dealing with the various groups of ruminating animals. For several years he acted as one of the sub-editors of 'Nature,' writing many articles and reviews on biological subjects. In 1876 he was elected a fellow of the Royal Society, and undertook to write a comprehensive work, aided by a government grant, on the anatomy of birds, of which only a portion was completed at his death. In 1876–8 he was examiner in zoology in the Cambridge natural sciences tripos. In June 1878 he was seized with severe pulmonary hæmorrhage, but continued to work indefatigably. After conducting the tripos examination in December 1878, he wintered in the Riviera, but returned to London unrelieved. He continued to work as much as possible, occupying himself at last, when too ill to go to the gardens, with dissecting and comparing the trachea in different groups of birds. He died of phthisis on 17 Oct. 1879, aged 33.

Garrod was highly esteemed by a large circle of friends, and his rooms at the Zoological Society were a centre of work and inquiry, in which he was ever ready to afford assistance or to direct study. He was always cheerful and unselfish, with a strong and energetic character and a wide range of information and interest. In zoology Garrod's work is of permanent value. His most important paper on mammalian anatomy, 'On the Visceral Anatomy and Osteology of the Ruminants,' was read before the Zoological Society in 1877, developing important points in the classification of the group, and suggesting the adoption of a system of nomenclature which should indicate more precisely than

the binomial the true affinities of animals. His great energy enabled him to take full advantage of the exceptional opportunities of dissecting animals during his prosectorship. Thus he had dissected no fewer than five rhinoceroses belonging to three different species, and his papers on these are of great value. On the anatomy of birds he was in the front rank at the time of his death, and his papers 'On the Carotid Arteries of Birds,' 'On Certain Muscles in the Thigh of Birds, and on their value in Classification,' on columbæ, on parrots, and several on the anatomy of passerine birds, and on the trachea of gallinæ, are of permanent importance. Garrod's scientific papers were collected by a committee of zoologists, and published in one large volume in 1881, edited with a biographical notice by W. A. Forbes [q. v.], his successor in the prosectorship at the Zoological Gardens. A portrait of Garrod, etched by H. Herkomer, is prefixed to the volume. These papers will also be found in the Proceedings of the Royal Society, the Proceedings of the Zoological Society, Journal of Anatomy and Physiology, 'Ibis,' and 'Nature,' between 1869 and 1879. He contributed the important section 'Ruminantia' to Cassell's 'Natural History.' He also edited with valuable notes the translation of Johannes Müller's celebrated paper on the vocal organs of passerine birds (by Professor F. J. Bell), published by the Clarendon Press in 1879.

[Forbes's Biog. Notice prefixed to Garrod's Collected Scientific Papers, 1881; Ibis, 1881, p. 32.]   G. T. B.

GARROW, Sir WILLIAM (1760–1840), baron of the exchequer, was the third son of the Rev. David Garrow of Hadley, Middlesex, where he was born on 13 April 1760. He was educated by his father, who kept a school at Hadley, and at the age of fifteen was articled to Thomas Southouse, an attorney, whose offices were in Milk Street, Cheapside. Here he showed such ability that, on the recommendation of the attorney, he commenced studying for the bar. He was admitted a student of Lincoln's Inn on 27 Nov. 1778, and was for some time a pupil of Mr. Crompton, an eminent special pleader. He was called to the bar on 27 Nov. 1783. Garrow was already known as an orator in debating societies. In January 1784 his able prosecution of John Henry Aikles, who had been indicted for feloniously stealing a bill of exchange (*Sessions Papers*, 1783–4, No. ii. pt. vii.), quickly secured him plenty of business at the Old Bailey. At the general election in the spring of 1784 he acted as assessor to the sheriff of Hertfordshire, and afterwards was retained in the London scrutiny for Sawbridge, and in the Westminster scrutiny for Fox, on whose behalf he addressed the House of Commons in an able speech for nearly two hours (*Parl. Hist.* xxiv. 857–8). Garrow joined the home circuit, of which Erskine was then the leader, and in a remarkably short time established a great reputation at nisi prius as well as in criminal cases. He was appointed a king's counsel in Hilary term 1793, and at a by-election in April 1805 was returned to parliament for the borough of Gatton. In Hilary term 1806 he became attorney-general to the Prince of Wales, and at the general election in the autumn of that year was elected one of the members for the borough of Callington. Garrow was appointed solicitor-general in Lord Liverpool's administration in the place of Sir Thomas Plumer on 27 June 1812, and was knighted on 17 July following. At the general election in October 1812 he was returned for the borough of Eye, and upon the appointment of Plumer to the new office of vice-chancellor of England was made attorney-general on 4 May 1813. In Hilary vacation 1814 Garrow also received the appointment of chief justice of Chester in the place of Sir Richard Richards, made a baron of the exchequer. Sir Samuel Romilly protested in the House of Commons against the second appointment on the ground that the offices of attorney-general and judge were incompatible (*ib.* xxvii. 330–2). After being a law officer of the crown for nearly five years Garrow accepted the post of baron of the exchequer on 6 May 1817. He remained a puisne baron in that court for nearly fifteen years, retiring in the Hilary vacation 1832. He was admitted a member of the privy council on 22 Feb. 1832, and died at Pegwell Cottage, near Ramsgate, on 24 Sept. 1840, in the eighty-first year of his age.

Garrow was a consummate advocate. Remarkable alike for his acuteness and tact, he was unrivalled in the art of cross-examination. 'No man more clearly, more continuously presented his case to those he was addressing. His language was plain, but it was well strung together. He reasoned little, he jested less; he not rarely declaimed, and he had sufficient force to produce his effect. . . . His discretion, his perfect judgment, and entire self-command exceeded that of most men' (*Law Review*, i. 322). The rapidity with which he gained one of the foremost positions at the bar was remarkable, and it is doubtful 'whether Erskine or Gibbs ever had such a hold as Garrow of the common business of the court It is certain that he retained it far longer than either of them'

(*ib.* p. 325). As attorney-general he used his extraordinary powers with great leniency, and the single instance of a prosecution for libel during his tenure of that office contrasts most favourably with the number of ex officio informations in the time of Gibbs (*Parl. Debates*, xxxiv. 392). As a judge his powers were not conspicuous, but were shown to most advantage in the criminal court. His ignorance of the more abstruse branches of the law was remarkable, and Sir Samuel Romilly relates that in two cases before the House of Lords Garrow read a written argument, which somebody else had composed for him, 'without venturing to add a single observation or expression of his own' (*Memoir of Romilly*, 1840, iii. 128). Garrow made his maiden speech in the House of Commons during the debate on the charge against the Marquis of Wellesley, though he had 'not intended to speak that night, and had made a sort of league and covenant with himself to remain silent' (*Parl. Debates*, vi. 864–5). As a parliamentary speaker, however, he had little or no success. Garrow was elected a bencher of Lincoln's Inn, Easter term 1793, and acted as treasurer of the society in 1801.

By his wife, who died on 30 June 1808, he had two children, viz. the Rev. David Garrow, D.D., rector of East Barnet, who died on 11 April 1827, aged 45, and Eliza, who married on 6 April 1802 Samuel Fothergill Lettsom.

[Foss's Judges of England, 1864, ix. 86–90 ; Law Review, i. 318–28 ; Legal Observer, iii. 253–6 ; The Georgian Era, 1833, ii. 322 ; Ann. Reg. 1840, app. to chron. p. 177 ; Gent. Mag. vol. lxxii. pt. i. p. 373, vol. lxxv. pt. i. p. 386, pt. ii. p. 1238, vol. lxxviii. pt. ii. p. 658, vol. xcvii. pt. i. p. 474, new ser. xiv. 657–8 ; Whishaw's Synopsis of the Bar, 1835, p. 279 ; Haydn's Book of Dignities, 1851 ; Official Return of Lists of Members of Parliament, ii. 222, 230, 264 ; Notes and Queries, 5th ser. vii. 194 ; Lincoln's Inn Registers.]   G. F. R. B.

GARSIDE, CHARLES BRIERLEY (1818–1876), catholic divine, born 6 April 1818 at Manchester, was only son of Joseph Garside, surgeon and a distinguished ornithologist, by Mary Ann, daughter of Thomas Pearson. From the grammar school of his native city, where he obtained an exhibition in 1837, he was sent to Brasenose College, Oxford, in 1838. There he gained one of the Somerset scholarships, carried off the college prize for Latin and English essays in 1840, and became in the same year Hulme divinity exhibitioner. He graduated B.A. 28 May 1841, taking a third class *in literis humanioribus*, and commenced M.A.

27 June 1844. Having been ordained in 1842 by the Bishop of Gloucester, he became curate, first at Tetbury, Gloucestershire, next at Christ Church, Albany Street, Regent's Park, London, and afterwards, in 1847, at Margaret Street Chapel, Marylebone. At the time of the Gorham case he lost faith in the established church of England. He was received into the Roman catholic church, at St. Leonard's-on-Sea, 15 Aug. 1850, and was ordained priest at Rome by Cardinal Patrizi, 23 Dec. 1854, having in the previous month of May graduated as *Baccalaureus in Theologiâ* in the Collegio Romano. He was appointed domestic chaplain to Bertram, the last catholic Earl of Shrewsbury, in April 1855, assistant priest at St. Mary's, Chelsea, in 1857, and at St. Aloysius's, Somers Town, in May 1861. He died at Posilippo, near Naples, on 21 May 1876.

His works are: 1. 'The Impiety of Bartering Faith for Opinion,' London, 1850, 8vo. This pamphlet on the Gorham case was written before the author left the church of England. 2. 'Discourses on some Parables of the New Testament,' London [1869], 8vo. 3. 'The Preaching of the Cross. A brief discourse . . . introductory to the singing of sacred music illustrative of the Passion of Christ,' London, 1869, 8vo. 4. 'The Prophet of Carmel: a series of practical considerations on the History of Elias in the Old Testament, with a supplementary dissertation,' London [1873], 8vo, dedicated to Dr. (now Cardinal) Newman. 5. 'The Helpers of the Holy Souls, who and what they are; with some account of the Life of their Foundress, Mother Mary of Providence,' London, 1874, 8vo. 6. 'Blessed Margaret Mary Alacocque; a brief account of her Life. To which are added, a selection from her sayings, and the decree of her beatification,' London, 1874, 32mo. 7. 'The Sacrifice of the Eucharist, and other Doctrines of the Catholic Church, explained and vindicated,' London, 1875, 8vo.

[Axon's Annals of Manchester, p. 357; Browne's Annals of the Tractarian Movement (1861), p. 174; Gondon, Les récentes Conversions de l'Angleterre, p. 233; Men of the Time (1875); Cat. of Oxford Graduates, p. 252; Smith's Admission Register of the Manchester School, iii. 242; Sutton's Lancashire Authors, p. 41; Tablet, 27 May 1876, p. 686.]　　　　T. C.

GARTER, BERNARD (*fl.* 1570), poet, who describes himself on his title-pages as citizen of London, was, according to Hunter, second son of Sir William Garter of London, and father of a Bernard Garter of Brigstocke, Northamptonshire. But in the 'Visitation of London,' 1633–5 (Harl. Soc. i.), 'Barnerd Garter of Brikstocke,' Northamptonshire, is described as the son of Thomas Garter, the husband of Elizabeth Catelyne, and the father of George Garter, who was living in 1634. Garter wrote: 1. 'The tragicall and true historie which happened betweene two English lovers, 1563. Written by Ber. Gar., 1565. In ædibus Richardi Totelli,' an imitation in ballad metre of Arthur Broke's 'Romeus and Juliet,' 1561. A copy of this very rare book is in the library of Christie Miller at Britwell (cf. P. A. Daniel's reprint of BROOKE's *Romeus*, New Shakspere Soc. xxxiii.) 2. 'A New Yeares Gifte, dedicated to the Popes Holinesse and all Catholikes addicted to the Sea of Rome: prepared the first day of Januarie [1579] by B. G., Citizen of London,' London, by Henry Bynneman, 1579. This work, wrongly ascribed by Ritson to Barnabe Googe [q. v.], contains, besides verses against the catholics, a reprint of a letter sent in 1537 by Tunstall, bishop of Durham, and Stokesley, bishop of London, to Cardinal Pole, maintaining the royal supremacy; lives of Alexander II and Gregory VII; an account of the frauds of Elizabeth Barton, Maid of Kent [q. v.]; and 'invectives against the pope.' 'A new yeres geyfte made by barnarde Garter' was licensed for printing to Alexander Lacy in 1565, but no copy of so early a date has been met with.

A tract entitled 'The joyfull receavinge of the Quenes ma^tie into Norwiche' (licensed 30 Aug. 1578) includes a masque by Garter and Henry Goldingham, which is printed in Nichols's 'Progresses,' ii. 67. 'Pasquin in a Trance. A Christian and learned dialogue contayning wonderfull and most strange newes out of Heaven, Purgatorie, and Hell,' 4to, London, by Seres, n.d. (licensed 1565), has some prefatory verses to the reader signed 'Ber. Gar.;' it is a translation from the Italian of Celius Secundus Curio, and Mr. Collier is inclined to credit Garter with the whole. 'Among Coxeter's papers,' writes Warton, 'is mentioned the ballet of Helen's epistle to Paris from "Ovid," in 1570, by B. G.' This piece Warton also doubtfully claims for Garter. The 'B. G.' who wrote 'Ludus Scacchiæ: Chesse-playe, a game pleasant, wittie, and politicall,' London, 1597, is further identified with Garter by Hunter.

[Hunter's Chorus Vatum in Addit. MS. 24488, f. 318; Collier's Extracts from the Stationers' Reg. i. 101, 125, 139, ii. 66; Collier's Bibliographical Cat.; Hazlitt's Handbook and Collections; Ritson's Bibliographia Poetica; Warton's Hist. of English Poetry.]　　　　S. L.

GARTH, JOHN (*fl.* 1757), musical composer, of Durham, began his great work, the adaptation of the 'First Fifty Psalms of

Marcello' to the English version, in 1757. It was dedicated to the Bishop (Trevor) of Durham, and completed in eight volumes in the course of as many years. Garth's Op. 2, six sonatas for the harpsichord, pianoforte, or organ, with accompaniments for two violins and violoncello, became very popular. He also composed (Op. 3) six voluntaries for the organ, &c., six concertos for violoncello, six sonatas (Op. 7), thirty collects (1794), and instructions for the harpsichord.

[Calcott's MS. Dict.; Brown's Dict. of Musicians.]   L. M. M.

GARTH, Sir SAMUEL (1661–1719), physician and poet, eldest son of William Garth of Bowland Forest in the West Riding of Yorkshire, was born in 1661, and sent to school at Ingleton, at the foot of Ingleborough. In 1676 he entered at Peterhouse, Cambridge, and there graduated B.A. 1679, M.A. 1684, and M.D. 1691, after having in 1687 gone to Leyden to study medicine. He settled in London, where he was elected a fellow of the College of Physicians, 26 June 1693. In 1694 he delivered the Gulstonian lectures. His subject was respiration, but he never published the lectures, though requested to do so. He soon attained practice, was able to hold his own among the wits, and, without becoming an active politician, was known to be a whig. In 1697 he delivered the Harveian oration at the College of Physicians on 17 Sept., and it was ordered to be printed by the president and censors on the 27th of the same month. It is dedicated to Charles Montague, then first lord of the treasury and president of the Royal Society. Half of the oration is a panegyric of William III. On the last page Garth alludes to a scheme, which had been discussed in the college from 1687, for establishing a dispensary where poor people could obtain advice and prescriptions from the best physicians. While a large majority of the fellows of the college supported this scheme, a minority allied themselves with the apothecaries of the city, who tried to defeat the plan, chiefly by charging exorbitant prices for the drugs prescribed. In 1699 Garth published 'The Dispensary, a Poem,' which is a record of the first attempt to establish those out-patient rooms now universal in the large towns of England. 'The Dispensary' ridicules the apothecaries and their allies among the fellows. It was circulated in manuscript, and in a few weeks was printed and sold by John Nutt, near Stationers' Hall. A second and a third edition appeared in the same year, to which were added a dedication to Anthony Henley, an introduction explaining the controversy in the College of Phy-

sicians, and copies of commendatory verses. A fourth edition appeared in 1700, a sixth in 1706, a seventh in 1714, and a tenth in 1741. The poem continued to be generally read for fifty years, and some of its phrases are still quoted. It describes a mock Homeric battle between the physicians and the apothecaries, Harvey being finally summoned from the Elysian fields to prescribe a reform. 'Horoscope' represents Francis Bernard [q. v.], who had been apothecary to St. Bartholomew's Hospital, and whose courage during the plague led to his election to the medical staff. His note-books show that the insinuations about his practice were unfounded. His former position led him to take the apothecaries' side. Among his allies Dr. William Gibbons figures as Mirmillo, Dr. George Howe as Querpo, Dr. Edward Tyson as Carus, Dr. William Gould as Umbra, and Sir Richard Blackmore as the Bard. On the physicians' side Dr. Charles Goodall as Stentor is the most redoubtable combatant. Garth added and omitted or altered lines throughout the 'Dispensary' in later editions, but most readers will differ from Pope in the opinion that every change was an improvement. The copy of the third edition, which belonged to Garth's friend, Christopher Codrington, is in the library of the College of Physicians of London, and has the names added in his handwriting. Hallam (*Literature of Europe*, 4th ed. iii. 490) and other critics have suggested that the 'Dispensary' was a copy of Boileau's 'Lutrin,' but Garth owes more to Dryden's 'MacFlecknoe,' although, as the author admits in his preface, the lines in praise of King William's martial activity are copied from Boileau's verses in praise of Lewis ('Le Lutrin,' ii. 133 sq.)

In 1700 he obtained the permission of the censor's board (*Annals of the College of Physicians*, 3 May 1700) for the body of Dryden to lie in state at the college. He made a Latin oration in praise of the poet, and accompanied his remains to Westminster Abbey. In 1700 he translated the 'Life of Otho' in the fifth volume of Dryden's 'Plutarch,' and in 1702 the first philippic in 'Several Orations of Demosthenes,' published by Tonson. He became a member of the Kit-Cat Club, and wrote the verses inscribed on its toasting glasses to Lady Carlisle, Lady Essex, Lady Hyde, and Lady Wharton (printed at the end of the tenth edition of the 'Dispensary,' London, 1741). He wrote verses easily, and some, preserved in manuscript, were certainly intended to be read only by men far advanced in post-prandial potations (manuscript, in Garth's hand, belonging to Dr. Munk). His handwriting was always hurried and slovenly, but amidst the occupations of a large practice he found time to help the distressed. His notes to Sir Hans Sloane (*Sloane MS.* in Brit. Mus. 4045) always go straight to the point, as: 'Dear Sir Hans,—If you can recommend this miserable slut to be flux'd you'll do an act of charity for, dear sir, your obed' ser' S¹ Garth.' He married Martha, daughter of Sir Henry Beaufoy, and had one child, a daughter, who married Colonel William Boyle. Lady Garth died on 14 May 1717, and was buried in the parish church of Harrow. Garth continued to write throughout life; in 1711 he wrote a verse dedication of Lucretius, in 1715 'Claremont,' a poem on Lord Clare's villa; and in 1717 an edition of Ovid's 'Metamorphoses,' in English verse, of no great merit. He also wrote in verse a dedication of Ovid's 'Art of Love' to Richard, earl of Burlington, and one to Lady Louisa Lenox with Ovid's 'Epistles,' an epilogue to the tragedy of 'Cato,' a prologue to 'Tamerlane,' and a prologue to the 'Music Meeting in York Buildings.' He was knighted on the accession of George I, and became physician in ordinary to the king and physician-general to the army. The 'Chronological Diary,' 1714, states that he was knighted with the sword of Marlborough. He lived in Covent Garden, grew wealthy by practice, and died on 18 Jan. 1719, after a brief illness, and was buried beside his wife at Harrow. Pope wrote that Garth was 'the best natured of men,' and that 'his death was very heroical, and yet unaffected enough to have made a saint or philosopher famous.' His portrait, of kit-cat size, by Kneller, hangs to the left of the fireplace in the censor's room at the College of Physicians, and gives him a fresh complexion and cheerful expression, in a flowing wig. A drawing by Hogarth represents him at Button's coffee-house standing by a table at which Pope is sitting.

[Munk's Coll. of Phys. i. 498 ; Garth's Works; Johnson's Lives of the Poets, ed. 1781, ii. 313 ; An Historical Account of the Lives and Writings of our most considerable English Poets, London, 1720; Cibber's Lives of the Poets, London, 1753, iii. 263 ; Merrett's Short View of the Frauds and Abuses committed by Apothecaries, London, 1670 ; A Charter granted to the Apothecaries of London, London, 1695; Thomas Brown's Physick lies a-bleeding, or the Apothecary turned Doctor, London, 1697 ; The late Censors deservedly censured by Lysiponius Celer, M.D.L., London, 1698; The Necessity and Usefulness of the Dispensaries, London, 1702 ; The Present State of Physick and Surgery in London, 1701; Bellum Medicinale, 1701 ; Pitt's Craft and Frauds of Physic exposed, 1702 ; Spence's Anecdotes.]

N. M.

GARTHSHORE, MAXWELL (1732–1812), physician, son of the Rev. George Garthshore (*d.* 24 Jan. 1760, aged 72 ; see *Gent. Mag.* lxxxii. 387–8), fifty years minister in Kirkcudbright, was born at Kirkcudbright on 28 Oct. 1732. After being educated at the Kirkcudbright grammar school, he was apprenticed to a medical man in Edinburgh at the age of fourteen, and attended medical classes in the university. Before proceeding to his degree, Garthshore entered the army as surgeon's mate when in his twenty-second year. In 1756 he settled at Uppingham, succeeding (by the aid of his cousin, Robert Maitland, a prosperous London merchant) to the practice of Dr. John Fordyce [q. v.] After practising successfully at Uppingham for eight years, Garthshore was encouraged to remove to London, and to support his position there he graduated M.D. at Edinburgh 8 May 1764, and was admitted a licentiate of the London College of Physicians on 1 Oct. 1764. He obtained a large practice as an accoucheur, was appointed physician to the British Lying-in Hospital, and became a fellow of the Royal and Antiquarian Societies. He was a formal, fashionable physician of the old school, a sincere orthodox Christian, and extremely liberal to the poor, although parsimonious in his personal expenditure. It is stated that on one occasion he gave in a single gratuity more than his whole annual income (*Gent. Mag.* loc. cit.) The widow of the celebrated John Hunter was indebted to him for a comfortable provision when in very poor circumstances (OTTLEY, *Life of Hunter,* p. 139). His first wife, who brought him the small estate of Ruscoe in Kirkcudbrightshire, died in 1765, leaving him one son surviving. His second wife, Mrs. Murrel, whom he married in 1795, died some years before him. He died on 1 March 1812, and was buried in Bunhill Fields cemetery.

Garthshore bore a striking resemblance to the first Earl of Chatham, and was once pointed out in a debate in the House of Commons as the earl, whom every one believed to be present (*Gent. Mag.* loc. cit. p. 391). His portrait, by Slater, was engraved by Collyer. His only publications were his inaugural dissertation at Edinburgh, 'De papaveris usu . . . in parturientibus ac puerperis,' 1764 ; two papers read before the Society of Physicians in 1769, and published in the fourth and fifth volumes of 'Medical Observations;' some 'Observations on Extra-uterine Cases, and Ruptures of the Tubes and Uterus,' published in the 'London Medical Journal,' 1787 ; and 'A Remarkable Case of Numerous Births,' 'Phil. Trans.,' vol. lxxvii.

WILLIAM GARTHSHORE (1764–1806), son

of the above, was born in London on 28 Oct. 1764. He was educated at Westminster School and Christ Church, Oxford, where he graduated M.A. in 1789, and became a tutor. He afterwards was tutor to the Marquis of Dalkeith, and made an extensive tour in Europe with him. Returning in 1792, he was recommended to the government by the Duke of Buccleuch, and was appointed private secretary to Mr. Dundas (afterwards Lord Melville) when secretary for war in 1794. In the same year he married Miss Jane Chalié, daughter of a wealthy wine merchant. He was elected M.P. for Launceston in January 1795, and for Weymouth in September of the same year, and retained his seat till his death. In 1801 he was appointed a lord of the admiralty by Mr. Addington, which post he held till 1804; but the death of his father-in-law, his wife, and only child within a few days of one another (5 and 9 Aug. 1803) overthrew his reason, and he died on 5 April 1806. His property went to his father, who used to say, 'When William lived he made me poor; at his death he made me rich.'

[Gent. Mag. (1803), lxxiii. 793, 794, (1806) lxxvi. 389, (1812) lxxxii. pt. i. 300, 387–91, 673; Beatson's Parl. Reg. ii. 21, 94; Funeral Sermon by the Rev. George Greig, 1812; Georgian Era, ii. 399; Ottley's Life of John Hunter, pp. 28, 29, 114, 139; Welch's Alumni Westmon. (ed. 1852), p. 415; Foster's Alumni Oxon. vol. ii.]   G. T. B.

GARVEY, EDMUND (*d.* 1813), painter and royal academician, was probably of Irish parentage, as he first appears as an exhibitor at the Dublin exhibitions. He seems to have visited Italy, on his return from which he took up his residence at Bath. In 1767 he exhibited some views in Italy and Switzerland at the Free Society of Artists, and in 1768 a view of Piercefield in Monmouthshire. His works were nearly always either foreign scenery or views of gentlemen's seats, and were hard and dry in manner, though sometimes not unskilful in their imitation of nature, rather in the manner of R. Wilson, R.A. He first exhibited at the Royal Academy in 1769, and in 1770 was elected one of the first associates of that body. In 1771 he gained for a landscape a premium of ten guineas from the Society of Arts. He subsequently removed to London, and continued to exhibit at the Royal Academy up to 1808. In 1783 he was elected an academician, beating Joseph Wright of Derby [q. v.] He died in 1813. A collection of his pictures was sold by auction in 1816.

[Redgrave's Dict. of Artists; Graves's Dict. of Artists, 1760–1880; Sandby's Hist. of the Royal Academy; Bemrose's Life of Joseph Wright of Derby; Royal Academy Catalogues.]   L. C.

GARVEY, JOHN, D.D. (1527–1595), archbishop of Armagh, eldest son of John O'Garvey of Morisk, co. Mayo, was born in the county of Kilkenny in 1527. He was educated at Oxford, where he graduated in the reign of Edward VI; but through some negligence his name does not appear in the public register of the time (WOOD, *Athenæ Oxonienses*, ed. Bliss, ii. 838). His first ecclesiastical preferment was the deanery of Ferns, to which he was appointed by letters patent in 1558; in the following year, 13 July, he became archdeacon of Meath and rector of Kells, when he probably resigned the deanery, and in 1560 he was instituted to the prebend of Tipperkevin in St. Patrick's Cathedral, Dublin. On 27 Jan. 1561 he received 'letters of denization' from the crown (*Rot. Pat.*) He must have been in great favour with the higher powers, for, with liberty to retain at least two of his preferments, he was made dean of Christ Church Cathedral, Dublin, in 1565, and likewise a member of the Irish privy council. He was even designed for the archbishopric of Armagh in 1584, when it was conferred on John Long, D.D., as appears from a letter addressed by the lords justices of Ireland to Secretary Walsyngham, dated 14 May 1584 (*Calendar of State Papers*, Ireland, 1574–85, p. 512). In April of the following year he was promoted to the bishopric of Kilmore, on the recommendation of Sir John Perrot, lord deputy of the kingdom, and was allowed to hold *in commendam* his deanery and archdeaconry. From Kilmore he was translated in May 1589 to the archbishopric of Armagh, still retaining his minor preferments; and as a special mark of favour Queen Elizabeth, by mandate from Westminster, dated 12 July 1591, remitted the payment of his first fruits, amounting to 137*l.* 13*s.* 1*d.*, 'on account of his great hospitality, and also for his painful and true service to the queen of a long time continued, being her ancientest counsellor in that kingdom' (*Rot. Canc.*) In 1591, in answer to a circular appeal from Sir William Fitzwilliam, lord deputy, and council, he gave *in concordatum* 76*l.* towards building the college of Dublin. He had married Rose, widowed daughter of Thomas Ussher, and dying in Dublin 2 March 1595, he was buried in Christ Church, his successor in the archbishopric being his brother-in-law, Henry Ussher, D.D., archdeacon of Dublin.

Garvey is not included in Sir James Ware's 'History of the Writers of Ireland;' but on Wood's authority a small treatise is ascribed to him, entitled 'The Conversion of Philip Corwine, a Franciscan Friar, to the Reformation of the Protestant Religion, an. 1589,' which was published by Robert Ware in his 'Foxes and Firebrands,' Dublin, 1681, from the original found among Archbishop (James) Ussher's manuscripts. Philip 'Corwine' was nephew to Hugh Curwen, archbishop of Dublin [q. v.]

[Sir James Ware's Works, ed. Harris, i. 96, 231; Mant's Hist. of the Church of Ireland, i. 311, 315; Cotton's Fasti Ecclesiæ Hibernicæ, ii. 41, 180, 348, iii. 19, 116, 127, 157, 183, v. 89, 198; Stuart's Hist. of Armagh, p. 263; Dublin University Calendar, 1876, ii. 160.] B. H. B.

GARWAY, SIR HENRY (1575–1646), lord mayor of London. [See GARRAWAY.]

GASCAR, HENRI (1635–1701), portrait-painter, born at Paris in 1635, came to England about 1674 in the train or at the invitation of Louise de Keroualle, duchess of Portsmouth. Gascar (or Gascard, as he seems to have spelt his name at first) was already known as a skilful portrait-painter; among the portraits already painted by him was that of N. de Lafond, known as 'le gazetier Hollandais,' painted in 1667, and engraved by P. Lombart. The patronage of the Duchess of Portsmouth insured Gascar a rapid success in England. He exceeded Lely in the simpering affectation shown by his portraits of the ladies of Charles II's court, and in the lavishness with which he concealed his artistic deficiencies by sumptuous draperies and tawdry adornments. For a short time he became the fashion, and he is said to have amassed a fortune of over 10,000l. Some time before 1680 he was shrewd enough to see that his success was merely due to a fashionable craze, and he retired to Paris before this had entirely ceased. Among the portraits painted by him during this time in England were Charles II (engraved by Vanderbank), Louise, duchess of Portsmouth (twice; once engraved by Baudet), Barbara, duchess of Cleveland, and her daughter, Barbara Fitzroy, Charles Lennox, duke of Richmond, Frances Stuart, duchess of Richmond, George Fitzroy, duke of Northumberland, Nell Gwyn, Sophia Bulkeley (engraved by Dunkarton), Edmund Verney, and Philip Herbert, earl of Pembroke. It is stated that the last-named portrait was done by stealth for Louise, duchess of Portsmouth. A portrait by Gascar of James II as duke of York was in that king's collection (see Bathoe's catalogue). At Strawberry Hill there was a picture by Gascar apparently emblematic of the Restoration (see sale catalogue, twenty-second day, No. 95). On his return to Paris Gascar was elected a member of the academy there on 26 Oct. 1680. He subsequently went to Rome, where he enjoyed a high reputation, and died there 1 Jan. 1701, aged 66. About

1698 he painted a portrait of Joseph Ferdinand, the young son of Maximilian II, which was engraved at Munich by Zimmermann. A number of mezzotint engravings done from portraits by Gascar, but bearing no engraver's name, have been attributed to Gascar himself. There is no evidence that he really engraved them, but the inscriptions indicate the work of a foreigner. They are interesting as being among the earliest specimens of mezzotint engraving done in England.

[Dussieux's Artistes Français à l'Etranger; Mariette's Abecedario; Chaloner Smith's British Mezzotinto Portraits; De Piles' Lives of the Painters; Strutt's Dictionary of Engravers.]

L. C.

GASCOIGNE, SIR BERNARD (1614–1687), military adventurer and diplomatist, whose real name was BERNARDO or BERNARDINO GUASCONI, belonged to an ancient family settled at Florence, where he was born in 1614, being son of Giovanni Batista di Bernardo Guasconi and Clemenza di Lorenzo Altoviti. When he was four months old he lost his father, and he was brought up under the care of his maternal uncle, Alessandro Altoviti. He became one of the men-at-arms in the service of the Grand Duke of Tuscany, and distinguished himself in an action in Casentino, from which place he took his title on being made a nobleman of the province. Afterwards in his capacity as a *uomo d'arme* he served in Lombardy, Piedmont, and Germany. Then, coming over to England, he took up arms for Charles I. He obtained a commission in Colonel Nevil's regiment of horse, and on 4 Aug. 1644, when the king was at Liskeard, he surprised and captured a party of parliamentarian officers while they were carousing in Lord Mohun's house, which was within two miles of the Earl of Essex's headquarters. In 1647 he drew up for the instruction of Ferdinand II, grand duke of Tuscany, an account of the recent occurrences in England. He had the command of one of the regiments of horse which took possession of Colchester on 12 June 1648, bore a part in the ineffectual attempt made on 15 July to break through the beleaguering forces, and was taken prisoner when the town was surrendered to Fairfax on 28 Aug. He was condemned to be shot on the following day with Sir Charles Lucas and Sir Charles Lisle. His life was spared at the last moment, because the council of war feared that if they shot a distinguished foreigner their friends or children who visited Italy 'might pay dear for many generations' (CLARENDON, *Hist. of the Rebellion*, bk. xi.) On 3 Dec. 1649 Charles II renewed to him a grant of a pension of 1,000*l.* a year, originally made to Gascoigne by Charles I, which for the time could not be paid.

In 1650 Gascoigne was at Florence. He was in England again soon after the Restoration, and in or about September 1660 he petitioned the king that in lieu of his pension he might become the tenant of the Steel Yard in London, promising to dispose of the tenements to English merchants. A bill for Gascoigne's naturalisation was read a first time in the House of Lords on 26 June 1661, but was not further proceeded with (*Lords' Journals*, xi. 289; *Hist. MSS. Comm.* 7th Rep. 146). On 24 Sept. following the king leased to him the manor of Red Cross in Bristol for forty-four years at the rent of 20*l.* (*Sloane MS.* 856, f. 8). In Oct. he and Sir Charles Berkeley, jun., had a grant from the king of the extra-parochial tithes of the Earl of Bedford's level and other levels, reserving to the crown a fourth part thereof, as well as 600 acres already in lease. In that month also he obtained a patent of denization by the name of Sir Bernard Gascoigne of Florence. On 13 Oct. 1662 he had the royal warrant for a grant of the extra-parochial tithes in Long Sutton and other places in Lincolnshire and Norfolk, reserving a fourth part thereof to the king. This was to be in lieu of his pension of 1,000*l.* An order was made on 27 July 1663 for a warrant to pay him a pension of 600*l.* a year, he having received no benefit from the pension of 1,000*l.* granted to him by 'the late king' (i.e. Charles I), nor from a grant of extra-parochial tithes in Lincolnshire, on which he had expended 1,500*l.* The grant passed the great seal on 6 Aug., and on 2 Nov. a warrant was issued on his petition for the effectual payment of his pension, as he was then returning to his own country. He had a pass to Tuscany for himself, his servants, and nine horses, on 4 Jan. 1663-4.

In 1664 he wrote from Florence to Secretary Bennet, afterwards Earl of Arlington, informing him that he had agreed with an intelligencer at Venice for 100*l.* a year, and that he believed that Abbot Vittorio Siri, the historiographer, would, in consideration of 3,000*l.* a year, be willing to impart to the English government secret intelligence concerning affairs at the French court. John Kirton, writing from Florence, 1 March 1664-5, to Sir Ralph Verney, says : ' Sir Bernard Gascon hath got the palto of the tobacco, for which the Jews offer him 20,000 crowns' (*Hist. MSS. Comm.* 7th Rep. 460). In June 1665 he wrote to Bennet's secretary from Rome, requesting a pass for a ship of his from Holland. When Sir John Finch (1626-1682) [q. v.] went to Florence in 1665

as English minister, he was entertained in Gascoigne's house.

Gascoigne had a pass to return to England on 11 March 1666-7, and on 20 June 1667 he was admitted a fellow of the Royal Society of London. On the last-mentioned day a royal warrant was issued for the assignment of the yearly pension of 600*l.* granted to him in 1663, with 2,250*l.* arrears due thereon, to be paid from the impost of 5*s.* a tun on French wines, and on 8 Aug. 1667 there was a reference recommending to the treasury commissioners Gascoigne's petition for the lease of the imposition of 5*s.* per ton on all French vessels at the rent of 1,000*l.* a year. Gascoigne was in constant attendance on Cosmo, prince of Tuscany, during his visit to England in 1669. In the following year he took part in a frolic at Audley End, where the queen, the Duchess of Richmond, and the Duchess of Buckingham disguised themselves as country lasses and went to see the fair. Gascoigne 'on a cart-jade rode before the queen,' who was unluckily recognised, and 'thus by ill-conduct was a merry frolick turned into a pennance' (IVES, *Select Papers*, p. 40; *Hist. MSS. Comm.* 6th Rep. 367).

In 1672 Gascoigne was sent to Vienna as English envoy to conduct the negotiations for a marriage of the Duke of York with the daughter of the Archduke of Austria. Eventually the negotiations were broken off, and in May 1673 orders were sent to Gascoigne immediately to take his leave and retire from that court (*Letters addressed to Sir Joseph Williamson*, edited by W. D. Christie for the Camden Soc. i. 12). His name occurs on 3 Dec. 1678 in a list of papists found in the liberties of Westminster who were respited, upon certificates produced, for further consideration. In 1686 he received two several sums of 125*l.* of the royal bounty. He died in the Haymarket, in the parish of St. Martin-in-the-Fields, London, on 10 Jan. 1686-7.

He wrote : 1. ' Relazione della Storia d' Inghilterra del MDCXLVII, scritta dal Colonello e Residente in Londra Bernardino Guasconi ed inviata a Ferdinando II in Firenze,' Florence, 1886, 4to, with a brief notice of the author by G. Gargani. 2. ' A Description of Germany : its Government, Manner of Assembling Diets, Ceremony of Electing and Crowning the King of the Romans : as also an Account of their present Imperial Majesties Houshold.' This was sent to Charles II in 1672, when Gascoigne was envoy at Vienna. It is printed in T. Brown's ' Miscellanea Aulica, or a Collection of State Treaties,' London, 1702. His portrait, from a drawing in the king's copy of 'Clarendon,' was engraved by R. Cooper.

[Ackerman's Secret Service Payments (Camd. Soc.), 138, 141; Ayscough's Cat. of MSS. p. 226; Life of Mrs. Aphra Behn, prefixed to her novels (1718); Biog. Brit. iii. 2140 n.; Clarendon's Hist. of the Rebellion; Hist. of Colchester (1803), i. 241, 245; Cooper's Annals of Cambridge, iii. 533; Ellis Correspondence, i. 232; Ellis's Letters, 3rd ser. iv. 271; Evelyn's Diary (1850), ii. 48, 118; Fairfax Correspondence, iv. 47; Gargani's Memoir of Guasconi; Gent. Mag. ccxviii. 616; Granger's Biog. Hist. of England, 5th edit. iii. 51; Grey on 3 Neal, p. 326; Hist. MSS. Comm. vii. 514, xi. pt. ii. 69; Morant's Colchester, i. 58, 61, 66–8; Notes and Queries, 5th ser. vi. 447, vii. 15; Cal. State Papers, Dom. Charles II (1660–1), 249, 291, (1661–2) 113, 131, 132, 133, 515, (1663–4) 218, 232, 325, 430, 530, 607, (1664–5) 319, 436, 437, 543, (1665–6) 169, (1666–7) 51, 68, 556, (1667) 67, 72, 108, 116, 215, 370; Strickland's Queens of England (1865), iv. 442; Symonds's Diary, p. 48; Thomas's Hist. Notes, p. 581; Thomson's Hist. of the Royal Society, Append. p. xxv; Watt's Bibl. Brit.; Winstanley's Royall Martyrology, p. 89; Wood's Fasti Oxon. (Bliss), ii. 102.] T. C.

GASCOIGNE, SIR CRISP (1700–1761), lord mayor of London. [See GASCOYNE.]

GASCOIGNE, GEORGE (1525?–1577), poet, was eldest son of Sir John Gascoigne of Cardington, Bedfordshire, by his wife Margaret, daughter of Sir Robert Scargill of Scargill, Yorkshire. Through his mother's family he was kinsman to Sir Martin Frobisher [q. v.] His father's father, Sir William Gascoigne, was great-grandson of Sir William Gascoigne [q. v.], chief justice of the king's bench; was sheriff of Bedfordshire in 1507, 1514, and 1516; was knighted by Henry VIII, and was controller to the household of Cardinal Wolsey. The poet, when dedicating his 'Tale of Hemetes' to Queen Elizabeth in 1576, declares that he 'poured forth' in his writings 'such Englishe as I stole in Westmerland,' expressions that seem to imply that he was brought up in Westmoreland. He was educated at Trinity College, Cambridge, where Stephen Nevynson was his tutor. He left without a degree, and is said to have entered the Middle Temple before 1548. In that year he is often stated to have suffered imprisonment for dicing. This story is founded on an account of the arrest of 'Mr. Gastone the lawyare . . . a great dicer' in the 'Autobiographical Anecdotes of Edward Underhill,' 1551 (cf. Narratives of the Reformation, Camd. Soc.) But Gastone and Gascoigne are in all probability quite different persons. Gastone moreover is said in the same place to have 'an old wife,' whereas the poet seems at the time to have been a bachelor (cf. Notes and Queries, 2nd ser. ix.

15, 152). It is true that the poet's father disinherited him on account of his extravagance, and it was not till late in life that he checked his squandering propensities. In 1555 he became a student of Gray's Inn (Harl. MS. 1912, f. 33), and is probably the 'Gascoine' called as an 'ancient' of the inn on 24 May 1557. He paid a formal fine as an ancient in 1565. He sat in parliament as M.P. for Bedford in 1557–8 and 1558–9. In the spring of 1562, while riding between Chelmsford and London, he began a first poem entitled 'The Complaint of Philomene,' but soon flung it aside, and did not complete it till 1576. An early disappointment in love unfitted him for settled occupation. Travel in England and France occupied him about 1563–4. Returning to his home in Bedfordshire he visited his friends the Dyve family, and was introduced to Francis Russell, second earl of Bedford, and doubtless to Arthur, lord Grey de Wilton, who became his special patron. Lord Grey invited him to shoot deer in his company one winter, and presented him with a cross-bow. Gascoigne proved a poor shot, and excused himself in verse for his incapacity. In 1566 he produced at Gray's Inn 'The Supposes,' a prose adaptation of Ariosto's comedy 'Gli Suppositi.' Aided by Francis Kinwelmersh, who contributed acts i. and iv., he also wrote a blank-verse tragedy in five acts called 'Jocasta,' and adapted from Euripides's 'Phœnissæ.' Sir Christopher Yelverton supplied an epilogue. A folio manuscript of this play, dated 1568, was in the possession of Mr. Corser.

Gascoigne was now, he writes, 'determined to abandon all vain delights, and to return unto Gray's Inn, there to undertake again the study of common laws' (Poems, i. 63). Five fellow-students, Francis and Anthony Kenwelmersh, John Vaughan, Alexander Nevile, and Richard Courtop, challenged him to write five poems on as many Latin mottoes proposed by themselves; he consented, and in these verses, published some years later, freely reproached himself with past excesses. His first published verse was a sonnet prefixed to 'The French Littleton . . . by C. Holiband,' London, 1566. To retrieve his fortunes he married about this date Elizabeth, the well-to-do widow of William Breton, citizen of London. The lady's first husband, by whom she was mother of Nicholas Breton [q. v.], the poet, and of four other children, died on 12 Jan. 1559. Gascoigne must have married her some time before 27 Oct. 1568. On that day the lord mayor, in the interest of Gascoigne's step-children, directed an inquiry into the disposition of William Breton's property, which, it was suggested, was misused by their mother and Gascoigne. Whatever the result of the inquiry, Gascoigne seems to have secured a residence at Walthamstow out of Breton's estate, which he retained till his death.

His debts were still numerous, and he had to 'lurk at villages' and avoid the city. In 1572 he presented himself for election as M.P. for Midhurst, and was duly returned. But a petition was presented, apparently by his creditors, against his being permitted to take his seat. In this document he was not only charged with insolvency, but with man-slaughter and atheism, and with being 'a common rymer and a deviser of slanderous pas-quils against divers persones of great calling' (cf. *Gent. Mag.* 1851, pt. ii. 241–4). To avoid further complications, he resolved to go abroad. He took passage at Gravesend for Holland on 19 March 1572. A drunken Dutch pilot ran the vessel aground on the Dutch coast. Twenty of the crew were drowned, and Gascoigne, with two friends, Rowland Yorke and Herle, narrowly escaped with their lives. Gascoigne, who was nicknamed 'the Green Knight,' ob-tained a captain's commission under William, prince of Orange, and saw some severe service. But a quarrel with his colonel soon drove him to Delft, in order to resign his commis-sion to the prince. While the negotiation was in progress a letter addressed to Gas-coigne from a lady at the Hague, then in the possession of the Spaniards, fell into the hands of his personal enemies in the Dutch camp. A charge of treachery was raised, but the prince perceived the baselessness of the accusation, and gave Gascoigne passports enabling him to visit the Hague. Gascoigne afterwards joined an English reinforcement under Colonel Chester, and distinguished himself at the siege of Middleburg, when the prince rewarded him with a gift of three hundred guilders in addition to his ordinary pay. Soon afterwards he was surprised by three thousand Spaniards while commanding five hundred Englishmen with Captain Shef-field. The English retreated to Leyden, but their Dutch allies closed the gates against them. All surrendered to Loques, the Spanish general. Gascoigne and his fellow-officers were sent home after four months' imprison-ment. His knowledge of languages—Latin, French, Italian, and Dutch—enabled him to converse freely with his Spanish captors; and his friendliness with Loques exposed him to new charges of treachery. He wrote for his patron, Lord Grey of Wilton, two narratives of his adventures while they were in progress, the one entitled 'The fruites of warre, written uppon this Theame Dulce Bellum inexpertis,'

and the other 'Gascoignes voyage into Hol-lande, An. 1572.' His military adventures occupied less than three years.

In Gascoigne's absence a collected volume of his verse was published without his autho-rity by H[enry?] W[otton?], who had ob-tained the manuscript from another friend, G[eorge?] T[urberville?]. The volume bore the title 'A hundreth Sundrie Flowres bounde up in one small Poesie: Gathered partely by Translation in the fyne outlandish Gardins of Euripides, Ovid, Petrarke, Ariosto, and others, and partly by invention out of our owne fruite-full orchardes in England,' London, for R. Smith [1572]. The editor, in the course of the volume, says that Gascoigne, 'who hath never been dainty of his doings, and therefore I con-ceal not his name,' was author of the largest portion of the book. But in spite of the editor's assertion that more than one author is represented in the collection, there is little doubt that Gascoigne is responsible for the whole. The book opens with the 'Supposes' and 'Jocasta,' which are followed by 'A dis-course of the adventures passed by Master F[erdinando] I[eronimi],' a prose tale from the Italian, interspersed with a few lyrics; a number of short poems called 'The deuises of sundrie Gentlemen;' and finally a long unfinished series of semi-autobiographical re-flections in verse, entitled 'The delectable his-tory of Dan Bartholomew of Bath.' Many of the shorter pieces were suspected of attacking well-known persons under fictitious names. A loud outcry was raised, to which Gascoigne replied by reissuing, 'from my poore house at Walthamstow in the forest, 2 Feb. 1575,' the volume enlarged and altered, under his own name. The new title ran 'The Posies of George Gascoigne, Esquire. Corrected, perfected, and augmented by the authour,' London, for R. Smith. Some copies bear in the imprint the name of H. Bynneman as Smith's printer. An apologetic dedication is addressed to 'the reverend divines unto whom these posies shall happen to be presented.' The works are here divided into three parts, entitled respectively Flowers, Hearbes, and Weedes. The first part contains short poems and a completed version of 'Dan Bartholo-mew;' the second includes the 'Supposes,' the 'Jocasta,' and more short poems; the third part is chiefly occupied with a revised version of 'the pleasant fable of Ferdinando Ieronimi and Leonora de Valasco, translated out of the riding tales of Bartello,' i.e. Ban-dello. The volume concludes with a critical essay in prose entitled 'Certayne notes of In-struction concerning the making of verse or ryme in English, written at the request of Master Edouardo Donati.' Henceforth Gascoigne confined himself to literary work, but he still suffered much from poverty. In 1575 appeared his 'tragicall comedie,' called 'A Glasse of Government,' chiefly in prose, but with four choruses and an epilogue in verse, and two didactic poems introduced into the third act. A poem by him of fifty-eight lines, 'in the commendation of the Noble Art of Venerie,' was prefixed to George Turberville's 'Noble Art of Venerie or Hunting' (1575). Gascoigne accompanied Queen Elizabeth on her visit to the Earl of Leicester's castle of Kenilworth, 9–27 July 1575, and was commissioned by Leicester to write verses and masques for the entertainment of his sovereign. Many of these were issued in 1576, in a separate volume entitled 'The Princelye Pleasures at the Courte of Kenelwoorth,' to which George Ferrers, Henry Goldingham, and William Hunnis were also contributors. A reprint of this work is dated 1821, and it reappears in the appendix to Adlard's 'Amye Robsart,' 1870. Gascoigne's prose 'tale of Hemetes the heremyte, pronownced before the Q. Majesty att Woodstocke, [11 Sept.] 1575,' in the course of the progress from Kenilworth, was not included in 'The Princelie Pleasures,' nor was it printed in its author's lifetime. Gascoigne wrote it in four languages—English, French, Latin, and Italian. In 1579 Abraham Fleming [q. v.] had the boldness to annex this 'pleasant tale . . ., newly recognised both in Latin and English,' to his volume called 'The Paradoxe,' and allowed it to be supposed that he was the author. Gascoigne's original manuscript, with a dedication to the queen, and a drawing representing him in the act of offering it to her, is in the British Museum (Reg. MS. 18 A. 49, p. 27). It has been printed by Mr. W. C. Hazlitt in his collected edition of Gascoigne's works. It was also in 1576 that Gascoigne's well-known satire in blank verse appeared, dedicated to Lord Grey, and entitled 'The Steele Glas.' He completed this satire 12 April 1576, 'amongst my books in my house here at Walthamstow.' At the end of the volume was placed 'The Complainte of Phylomene,' Gascoigne's first poetic effort, begun thirteen years before. To the 'Steele Glas' a youthful friend, 'Walter Raleigh of the Middle Temple,' prefixed commendatory stanzas, the earliest by him to appear in print. In April 1576 a visit to Sir Humphry Gilbert at Limehouse suggested to Gascoigne the publication of Gilbert's account of the voyage to Cathay in 1566, which he duly prepared for the press. There followed two serious efforts in prose—'the fruites of repentaunce' Gascoigne called them—entitled respectively 'The Droomme of Doomesday,' a translation

from the Latin of Lothario Conti (May 1576; 1586), dedicated to Francis, second earl of Bedford, and 'A delicate Diet for daintiemouthde Droonkardes' (22 Aug. 1576), dedicated to Lewis Dyve. The first is described at length in Brydges's 'Restituta,' iv. 299–307; the second was reprinted by F. G. Waldron in 1789. Finally, in January 1576–7, Gascoigne dedicated to Queen Elizabeth, but did not print, a collection of moral elegies entitled 'The Griefe of Joye.' His manuscript is in the British Museum (Royal MS. 18 A. 61), and has been printed by Mr. W. C. Hazlitt. In May 1576 Gascoigne's health had begun to fail (*The Droomme of Doomesday*, ded.) The 'Delicate Diet' is dedicated (Aug. 1576) 'from my lodging in London.' But there seems good foundation for the categorical assertion of Richard Simpson that Gascoigne was present at the sack of Antwerp by the Spaniards in November 1576. On 10 Nov. 1576 Thomas Heton, governor of the English House at Antwerp, wrote to the privy council that he had sent accounts of the fall of Antwerp by 'this bearer, Mr. George Gascoigne [not Gaston, as printed in the Calendar], whose humanity in this time of trouble we for our parts have experimented.' There is little doubt that Gascoigne was the author of a prose tract, 'The Spoyle of Antwerpe. Faithfully reported by a true Englishman, who was present at the same. . . . London, by Richard Iones.' On this tract was founded 'A Larum for London, or the Siedge of Antwerp,' 1602, and Mr. Simpson prints both together in his 'School of Shakspere,' pt. i. (1872). The 'Spoyle' was reprinted in Mr. Arber's 'English Garner,' vol. viii. 1896.

In the autumn of 1577 Gascoigne went on a visit to his friend and biographer, George Whetstone, at Stamford, Lincolnshire, and he died at Whetstone's house on 7 Oct. 1577, being buried probably in the family vault of the Whetstones at Bernack, near Stamford. He seems to have left a son William.

Contemporaries praised Gascoigne. W. Webbe, in his 'Discourse of English Poetrie,' speaks of him as 'a witty gentleman and the very chief of our late rhymers,' who, though deficient in learning,' was sufficient in 'his gifts of wit and natural promptness.' Arthur Hall, in the preface to his translation of the 'Iliad' (1581), praises his 'pretie pythie conceits.' Puttenham, in his 'Arte of English Poesie,' writes of his 'good metre' and 'plentiful vein.' Francis Meres, in his 'Comparative Discourse of our English Poets' in his 'Palladis Tamia' (1598), numbers him among 'the best poets for 'comedies and elegies. Gabriel Harvey had a good word for his 'commendable parts of conceit and endeavour,' although he bemoaned his 'decayed and blasted estate' (*Foure Letters*, 1592). Likewise in his 'De Aulica' Harvey suggests that Gascoigne, with Chaucer and Surrey, should figure in the library of a maid of honour (*Gratulationes Valdinenses*, 1578, iv. 21). Edmund Bolton, classing him with the 'lesser late poets,' says that his 'works may be endured.' His 'Supposes' was revived at Trinity College, Oxford, in 1582, and he is represented in the many editions of the 'Paradise of Dainty Devices' (1st edit. 1576), and in 'England's Parnassus,' 1600. But he soon fell out of date. An epigram of Sir John Davies (1596) notes as an inconsistency in the character of 'a new-fangled youth,' that he should 'praise old George Gascoines rimes.'

Gascoigne's lyrics, such as 'the arraignment of a lover,' reissued as a broadsheet in 1581, 'a straunge passion of a lover,' 'a lullabie of a lover,' or 'Gascoignes good-morrow,' are his most attractive productions. But even here his hand is often heavy, and his command of language and metre defective. With rare exceptions his verse, 'in the measure of xij in the first line and xiiij in the second,' is now unreadable. As a literary pioneer, however, Gascoigne's position is important. 'Master Gascoigne,' writes Nash (pref. to GREENE, *Menaphon*, 1589), 'is not to be abridged of his deserved esteem, who first beat the path to that perfection which our best poets have aspired to since his departure.' His 'Supposes,' after Ariosto, is the earliest extant comedy in English prose; his 'Jocasta,' after Euripides, is the second earliest tragedy in blank verse; his 'Steele Glas' is probably the earliest 'regular verse satire;' his 'Certain Notes of Instruction concerning the making of verse,' in which he deprecates the sacrifice of reason to rhyme, or the use of obsolete words, is the earliest English critical essay; his 'Adventures of Ferdinando Ieronimi,' translated from Bandello, one of the earliest known Italian tales in English prose. Gascoigne's sole original comedy, the 'Glasse of Government,' which vaguely embodies some local knowledge acquired by the author in the Low Countries, seems to be 'an attempt to connect Terentian situations with a Christian moral.' It deals with the careers of four youths—two prodigals who reach bad ends, and two of exemplary virtue, who gain distinction and influence. Mr. Herford shows that it owes much to German school dramas like Gnapheus's 'Acolastus,' 1529, Macropedius's 'Rebelles,' 1535, and Stymmelius's 'Studentes,' 1549 (HERFORD, *Lit. Rel. of England and Germany*,

pp. 149–64). Shakespeare probably derived the name Petruchio and the underplot of Lucentio's suit to Bianca in the 'Taming of the Shrew' from Gascoigne's 'Supposes.' 'From this play also the ridiculous name and character of Dr. Dodipoll seems to have got into our old drama' (WARTON).

A collected edition of Gascoigne's works was published by Abel Jeffes in 1587. Copies are extant with two different title-pages, one running 'The pleasauntest workes of George Gascoigne, Esquyre: newly compyled into one volume,' the other beginning 'The whole workes of George Gascoige, Esquyre.' Besides the contents of the 1575 volume there appear here the 'Steele Glas,' the 'Complainte of Phylomene,' and the 'Pleasures at Kenelworth Castle.' Gascoigne is well represented in Chalmers's 'Poets.' In 1868–9 Mr. W. C. Hazlitt collected all his extant poems in two volumes (Roxburghe Library). Gascoigne's 'Complete Works' appeared in two volumes in 'Cambridge English Classics,' 1907–8, edited by Prof. J. W. Cunliffe. The critical essay was reprinted in Haslewood's 'Ancient Critical Essays,' 1815, and in Gregory Smith's 'Elizabethan Critical Essays,' 1904, and with his 'Steele Glas' and 'Complainte of Phylomene' by Professor Arber in 1868. Gascoigne has been wrongly credited with a virulent attack on the Roman Catholics, 'The wyll of the Deuyll and last Testament,' London, by Humphry Powell, n. d. (before 1550).

Gascoigne's portrait, subscribed with his favourite motto, 'Tam Marti quam Mercurio,' appears on the back of the title-page of the first edition of the 'Steele Glas.' Another portrait appears in the Reg. MS. containing 'The tale of Hemetes,' and has been reproduced by Mr. W. C. Hazlitt. There is an engraved portrait by Fry.

[Hunter's Chorus Vatum in Addit. MS. 24487, ff. 448–60, has been largely used by Mr. W. C. Hazlitt in the memoir prefixed to his edition of the poems. Whetstone's Remembraunce of the wel imployed life and godly end of George Gaskoigne, Esquire, London, for Edward Aggas [1577], has been reprinted by Professor Arber and others from the unique copy at the Bodleian Library. See also Cooper's Athenæ Cantabr. i. 374–8, 565–6; Collier's Hist. Dramatic Poetry; Collier's Bibl. Cat.; Wood's Athenæ, ed. Bliss, i. 434; Corser's Collectanea; Warton's Hist. of English Poetry; Simpson's School of Shakspere, a reprint of A Larum for London, pt. i. (1872); Nichols's Progresses, i. 485, 553.] S. L.

GASCOIGNE, JOHN (*fl.* 1381), doctor of canon law at Oxford, was possibly the 'Jo. Gascoigne, cler.' who is named in a seventeenth-century pedigree (THORESBY, *Duc. Leod.* p. 177) as brother to Sir William Gascoigne [q. v.], the chief justice, and to Richard

Gascoigne of Hunslet, who is said to have been father of Thomas [q. v.], afterwards chancellor of the university of Oxford. John Gascoigne was a member of that university and became a doctor of canon law, in which capacity he was called to give evidence before a commission of five bishops, appointed 20 June 1376 to examine into certain controversies between the masters of arts and the faculty of law at Oxford (RYMER, *Fœdera*, vii. 112; WOOD, *History and Antiquities of the University of Oxford*, i. 488, ed. Gutch). In 1381 he appears among the signatories of the judgment of William Berton, chancellor of the university, condemning the doctrine of Wycliffe touching the sacrament (*Fasc. Ziz.* 113, ed. Shirley). Possibly on the strength of this, for there is no further available evidence, Pits (*De Angliæ Scriptoribus*, p. 540), credits him with the authorship of a book ' Contra Wiclevum.' There has also been assigned to him a life of St. Jerome, which is really the work of Thomas Gascoigne [q. v.], and a 'Lectura de Officio et Potestate Delegati,' of which a copy was once to be found in the royal library (then at Westminster), but is no longer identifiable.

[Tanner's Bibl. Brit. p. 311.]   R. L. P.

GASCOIGNE, RICHARD (1579–1661?), antiquary, born, according to Oldys, at Sherfield, near Burntwood, Essex, was second son of George Gascoigne, at one time of Oldhurst, by Mary, daughter of John Stokesley. His elder brother, Sir Nicholas, died in 1617. The family descended from Nicholas, younger brother of Sir William Gascoigne [q. v.], the famous judge. A kinswoman, Margaret Gascoigne, married Thomas Wentworth, and was thus grandmother of the great Earl of Strafford, a relationship of which Gascoyne was always proud. He was admitted a scholar of Jesus College, Cambridge, 21 Oct. 1594, and graduated B.A. in Lent term 1599. He says in his will that failing health compelled him to leave Cambridge 11 Sept. 1599; otherwise he would have obtained a fellowship. Subsequently he seems to have lived at his house at Bramham Biggin, Yorkshire, but in later years he occupied lodgings in Little Turnstile, Lincoln's Inn Fields, suffering much from poverty. There he made a will, 23 Aug. 1661, which was proved by his landlady, executrix, and residuary legatee, Frances Dimmock, 24 March 1663–4.

Gascoigne spent his time and money in collecting antiquarian documents, and in compiling pedigrees of his Yorkshire kinsmen and neighbours. The Wentworth and Gascoigne pedigrees occupied him for a long period. As a pedigree-maker he charged high fees, which he often found a difficulty in obtaining after the work was done. He complains bitterly in his will of the failure of Sir Thomas Danby to pay him 100*l.* for a pedigree, but he kept Danby's evidences as security till he pawned them to his landlady for 30*l.* Dugdale met him in early life in London, and always writes in the highest terms of his learning and industry. In his ' Warwickshire,' ed. Thomas, p. 857, Dugdale describes him as his ' special friend . . . a gentleman well worthy of the best respects from all lovers of antiquities, to whose good affections and abilities in these studies his own family and several others of much eminency allied thereto are not a little obliged.'

Gascoigne bequeathed his printed books to Jesus College, Cambridge, with special injunctions for their preservation. He particularly mentions his copy of ' Vincent's correcting Raphes Brooke' as a book of great value. His ' evidences and seales' he left to his cousin, Thomas, son of Sir Thomas Gascoigne [q. v.] His picture of Lord Strafford he left to his executrix. But the chief part of Gascoigne's collections—' his paper books and transcripts of antiquities'—came, apparently in his lifetime, into the possession of William, second earl of Strafford (heir of Thomas Wentworth, first earl), who preserved them in his library at Wentworth Woodhouse, Yorkshire, until his death in 1695. They then passed with the earl's other property to Thomas Watson-Wentworth, son of the earl's sister Anne, by Edward Watson, second baron Rockingham. This Thomas Watson-Wentworth died in 1723, and his son of the same names, when about to be created Baron Malton (May 1728), deliberately burned the greater part of Gascoigne's manuscripts. Oldys witnessed this act of vandalism, and attributes it either to the owner's fear that the papers might contain something derogatory to the first Earl of Strafford, or to anxiety to demolish the old tower of Wentworth House, where the manuscripts were deposited, to make room for a more modern structure. Oldys prevailed with the reckless owner to preserve some few old rolls, public grants, and original letters of eminent persons, but there survived ' not the hundredth part of much better things that were destroyed' (*Memoir of Oldys*, first printed in *Notes and Queries*, 3rd ser. i. 3).

Some Whitby charters that belonged to Gascoigne are in the Rawlinson MSS. at the Bodleian; some collections about the Nevill family are in Brit. Mus. Addit. MS. 6118, p. 129. The Gascoigne pedigree in Thoresby's ' Ducatus' is by him, and he is said to have assisted Burton in his ' Account of Leicestershire.'

[Thoresby's Ducatus Leod. ed. Whitaker, pp. 179–81; Dugdale's Diary, ii. 278; transcript of Gascoigne's will, kindly supplied by Mr. Gordon Goodwin from Prerogative Court of Canterbury, 30 Bruce.]　S. L.

GASCOIGNE, RICHARD (d. 1716), Jacobite, was born in Ireland and descended from a good Roman catholic family. His grandfather was killed in fighting for Charles I, and his father fell in the service of James II at the siege of Limerick. On coming into an estate of the value of 200l. a year, he converted it into money and came up to London, where he speedily dissipated his fortune and was reduced to very low circumstances. He recovered his position, however, by his skill and luck at games of cards and dice, and was taken up by the leaders of the tory party, who entrusted him with the management of their affairs at Bath. He was there when the rebellion broke out in 1715, and hearing that his arrest had been ordered, he set out with such forces as he could gather together to join the army at Preston. He proclaimed the Pretender king at the principal towns he passed through on his northern march, and arrived at Preston only in time to be taken prisoner. He was brought up to Newgate with the other leaders, and was put on his trial for high treason. He pleaded 'not guilty,' but it was proved that some chests of arms which had been seized at Bath were purchased abroad by him, and he was sentenced to death. He was hanged at Tyburn, 25 May 1716, and 'died with the greatest unconcernedness of any of the unfortunate rebels' (PATTEN, Hist. of the Rebellion). In a paper which he handed to the sheriff on the scaffold, he declared that he was never in his life an agent nor employed by any person in any political design, and he denied all knowledge of the arms that were seized. He further said that he did not take up arms with any view of restoring the catholic religion, but solely on behalf of his lawful king James III. After his death a letter which he had written to a friend the night before his execution was printed.

[Patten's Hist. of the Rebellion of 1716, p. 117, 3rd edit.; New Newgate Calendar, i. 207 (ed. 1818); A True Copy of the Paper delivered to the Sheriffs of London, by Richard Gascoigne; Gillow's Bibliographical Dict. of English Catholics.]　A. V.

GASCOIGNE, THOMAS (1403–1458), theologian, son and heir of Richard Gascoigne and Beatrix his wife (Dict. Theol. i. 352 a), was born in 1403 (ib. ii. 516 a)—Bale says (Bodl. Libr. Selden MS. supra 64, f. 173 b) on the vigil of the Epiphany, i.e. 5 Jan.

1403–4—at Hunslet (Magd. Coll. Oxf. MS. 103 sub fin., ap. COXE, Catal. of Oxford MSS., Magd. Coll. 55), near Leeds, of which manor his father was the possessor (Dict. Theol. ii. 592 b; Munim. Acad. Oxon. ii. 671, ed. Anstey). Gascoigne's own mention of his parents' names disproves the correctness of the pedigree attested early in the seventeenth century and printed by Thoresby (Ducat. Leod. p. 177), according to which he was the son of Richard and Ann Gascoigne. This genealogy further makes Richard the brother of Sir William Gascoigne [q. v.], the chief justice; but had so near a relationship existed it is difficult to believe that Thomas, whose self-conceit was notorious, would have omitted to inform us of the fact. It is, however, most likely that he belonged to the same family.

Gascoigne seems to have lost his father in his youth (Dict. Theol. ii. 539 a), but he was left well provided for and able to live on his own means for the whole of his lifetime (ib.; cf. i. 352 a). He entered Oxford at a date which, computing backwards from his degree of doctor of divinity in 1434, and taking into account the periods required for that and his previous degrees, Mr. J. E. Thorold Rogers fixes as 'not later than 1416' (Loci, intr. xviii); but since we know that Gascoigne obtained a dispensation as to time with respect to his degree in 1434 (Magd. Coll. MS. 103, l. c.), it is probable that he matriculated some time after 1416, though hardly, as Tanner implies (Bibl. Brit. p. 311), so late as 1420. From his lifelong residence in Oriel College it may be inferred that he was a member of it from the first, though the circumstance that he was a benefactor of Balliol College has led to the unproved and improbable supposition that he once belonged to that society (WOOD, Hist. and Antiq. of Oxford, Colleges and Halls, ed. Gutch, p. 90). His private fortune made him ineligible to a fellowship at Oriel College, but he rented rooms there until 1449, when, in acknowledgment of his liberality in contributing towards the college buildings and giving books to the library, the provost and scholars granted him the use of his rooms rent free for the rest of his life (ROGERS, l. c.).

The respect in which Gascoigne was held at Oxford is shown by the frequency with which he was called upon to fill the offices of chancellor of the university, of commissary (or vice-chancellor), and of 'cancellarius natus.' Mr. Rogers's suggestion (intr. lxxxiii) that this last title, which designates simply the senior doctor of divinity acting as chancellor during a vacancy (cf. Munim. Acad. Oxon. ii. 533), was an 'exceptional title' conferred on Gascoigne, is put forth in ignorance of the university system of the time. Gascoigne was first chancellor in 1434 (*Dict. Theol.* i. 550 *a*), when Wood (*Fasti*, p. 45), though aware of Gascoigne's own statement, describes him as commissary, adding (p. 47) that he filled this post again in 1439. According to the same authority (p. 48) he was again chancellor in the summer of 1442, during the interval between the resignation of William Grey and the election, about Michaelmas, of Henry Sever, the first provost of Eton College and afterwards warden of Merton College. The presumption would be that Gascoigne was on this occasion 'cancellarius natus,' were not a doubt cast upon the record by the appearance of another person, John Kexby, as chancellor in July of this year (*Munim. Acad. Oxon.* ii. 526). Probably Wood has transferred to 1442 a notice which really belongs to the following year, when there is evidence that Gascoigne was 'cancellarius natus' on 13 March 1443-4 (*ib.* p. 533; WOOD, *Fasti*, p. 49). On the day following this notice, the university having sought in vain the acceptance of the post by Richard Praty, bishop of Chichester, Gascoigne was elected to the full dignity of chancellor. He resigned at the beginning of Easter term 1445 and was re-elected, but apparently was unwilling to continue in office. He remained, however, 'cancellarius natus' (*Munim. Acad. Oxon.* ii. 547 f.), and, Wood says (p. 50), ultimately consented to hold the chancellorship, but before the end of the year was succeeded by Robert Burton. Here again Wood is seemingly in error, since Gascoigne more than once says that he was only twice chancellor, though thrice elected (*Dict. Theol.* i. 311 *a*, ii. 567 *a*).

Of Gascoigne's activity as chancellor there are plentiful traces in the university registers. It is not indeed true, as stated by Mr. Rogers, that 'in 1443 he procured from the king a charter, or letters patent, to the effect that the chancellor of Oxford should always be *ex officio* a justice of the peace, and in the same year carried a statute by which compurgation should be disallowed in the university court, except at the chancellor's discretion' (intr. xix, xlv), since the document upon which this statement rests recites expressly that the former privilege was granted by kings Edward and Henry III, and refers generally to various enactments as to the latter, without a hint of their having been procured by Gascoigne, a further note showing them to date from the time of one of his predecessors (*Munim. Acad. Oxon.* ii. 535-8). These notices possess, however, the interest of having been written in the register Aaa. in Gascoigne's own hand for the guidance of future chancellors; and it was probably through his personal efforts (cf. *Dict. Theol.* i. 306 *a*, where he speaks of an interview with Henry VI) that the king in 1444 empowered the chancellor to expel all rebellious and contumacious persons from the precinct, extending twelve miles every way, of the university (*Munim. Acad. Oxon.* ii. 540). Some years later, in November 1452, Gascoigne was appointed with others to hear an appeal from the chancellor (*Register of the Univ. of Oxford*, i. 18, ed. C. W. Boase, 1885), and in the summer of the following year he once more acted as 'cancellarius natus' (WOOD, *Fasti*, p. 54).

He had been ordained priest in the prebendal church of Thame by Bishop Fleming in 1427 (*Dict. Theol.* ii. 397 *a*), and afterwards became rector of Dighton, probably Kirk Deighton in the West Riding of Yorkshire; but resigned this benefice some time— probably long—before 1446 (*ib.* ii. 304 *a*). In 1432, on the death of John Kexby (LE NEVE, *Fasti Eccl. Anglic.* iii. 164, ed. Hardy), Archbishop Kemp offered Gascoigne the chancellorship of the church of York; but he refused it, partly from a scruple to be enriched at the expense of two parish churches whose rents and tithes were appropriated to the office (*Dict. Theol.* ii. 517 *a*, cf. i. 432 *b*). Thirteen years later, in 1445, he was given the valuable living of St. Peter's-upon-Cornhill, in the city of London, but he resigned it within the year, 24 Feb. 1445-6, on the ground of feeble health (MS. ap. ROGERS, 232). Three years later, 7 Feb. 1448-9, he was installed at the presentation of Bishop Beckington in the prebend of Combe the Tenth in the church of Wells (*Dict. Theol.* ii. 517 *a*; WOOD ap. TANNER, l. c.)

Throughout his life Gascoigne was an active preacher, vehement in his hostility to the Wycliffite tradition, and as unsparing as Wycliffe himself of evils in the church wherever he found them. In 1436 he received the thanks of the university of Oxford for his sermons at Easter on the sacrament of the altar and in defence of the authority of holy scripture and of the king's prerogatives. It has been said (ROGERS, intr. xix) that on this occasion he was given the 'special title of "Doctor catholicus;"' but this statement is unsupported by the register, which is our only evidence on the point: this merely describes Gascoigne as 'doctorem hunc catholicum' because he argued 'egregie et catholice' (*Reg. F.* ep. iii., ap. TANNER, l. c.) In the last year of his life he headed the thanksgiving service for the deliverance of Belgrade (22 July 1456), and preached before the university at St. Frideswide's in commemoration of the event (*Dict. Theol.* i. 111 *b*). He had his own opinions as to the form according to which sermons ought to be composed, and set it forth once in a discourse preached at St. Martin's in Carfax, Oxford (*ib.* i. 409 *a*). Still he expresses in strong terms his repentance for not having preached more frequently than he did (*ib.* i. 352 *a*), a self-reproach doubtless influenced by the public discouragement of the practice of preaching on the part of his old Oriel contemporary, Bishop Peacock, of whom he always writes in terms of severe condemnation. Not less significant of the consistent honesty with which he combated the prevailing abuses of pluralities, non-residence, and general neglect of their duties by the clergy of his day (instances may be found in plenty in his 'Dictionary'), was his refusal of preferment or resignation of any benefice held by him, when he found its tenure incompatible with the due interests of the parishes concerned. The only benefice which he retained, his prebend at Wells, was of the small value of eight marks yearly (*ib.* ii. 517 *a*).

Gascoigne died 13 March 1457–8, according to the brass (now destroyed) upon his grave, having made his will on the previous day. The will, which was proved 27 March, is printed in the 'Munimenta Academica Oxon.' ii. 671 f. By it Gascoigne devised most of his books to the recently founded monastery of Sion in Middlesex. He had already presented many books to Balliol, Oriel, Lincoln, Durham, and All Souls' Colleges (see COXE, *Catal.* index; Rogers, intr. vii). He was buried in the antechapel of New College, possibly through the interest of Bishop Beckington, a former fellow; but the burial there of a member of another college may fairly be taken as evidence of the singular respect in which he was held. The inscription on his brass is given by Wood (*Colleges and Halls*, p. 207). The Gascoigne coat of arms is described by Thoresby (ubi supra), Thomas's 'difference' by Wood (l. c.)

Gascoigne's principal work is his 'Dictionarium Theologicum,' written at various times between 1434 and 1457 and preserved in two stout volumes in the library of Lincoln College, Oxford (MSS. 117, 118). Its alternative title is 'Veritates collectæ ex s. Scriptura et aliorum sanctorum scriptis in modum tabulæ alphabet.,' and its contents are mainly of a theological or moral interest. But it includes also much of an autobiographical character, and throws great light upon the history and condition of the university of Oxford and the English church in the writer's day. Some extracts from the book have been printed by Mr. J. E. T. Rogers under the title of

'Loci e Libro Veritatum' (Oxford, 1881); but the selection by no means exhausts the interest of the work, and the edition unfortunately abounds in errors of transcription. References to the work are here given from the manuscript itself. Extracts from the 'Dictionary' occur in several manuscripts, e.g. in the British Museum in the Cottonian MS. Vitellius C. ix., and the Harleian MS. 6949; and portions of it are sometimes cited as distinct works, e.g. 'Septem Flumina Babyloniæ,' 'Veritates ex Scripturis' (TANNER, l. c.)

Gascoigne also wrote a brief life of St. Jerome, of which Leland saw a copy in the library of Oseney Abbey (*Collect.* iii. 56, p. 57, ed. Hearne). This is perhaps the same with the compilation bearing Gascoigne's name, and occupying four leaves of the manuscript in Magdalen College, Oxford (93, f. 199; COXE, *Catal. Magd. Coll.* 51). He also translated into English a life of St. Bridget of Sweden for the edification of the sisters of Sion (*Loci*, p. 140). This is probably the life of St. Bridget which was printed without any author's name by Pynson in 1516, and has been re-edited by J. H. Blunt in his introduction to the 'Myroure of our Ladye,' pp. xlvii–lix (Early English Text Society, Extra Series, 1873). The 'Myroure' itself, a devotional treatise written for the use of the convent of Sion, is conjectured by the editor to be also the work of Gascoigne. It was printed by R. Fawkes in 1530, but of this edition only a few imperfect copies are known to exist. The lives of St. Bridget's daughter Katharine and of her confessor, which occur in the Digby MS. 172, ff. 25–53, have been assigned to Gascoigne (TANNER, l. c.) by an error, since the manuscript is expressly stated not to be his composition, though it contains some notes by him. Possibly these notes are identical with the 'Annotata quædam de s. Brigitta et miraculis eius,' of which a copy existed in the lost Cottonian manuscript Otho A. xiv. A volume in the Bodleian Library (Auct. D. 4. 5) contains a Latin psalter with notes by Gascoigne, and a Hebrew psalter (now bound separately and known as Bodl. Or. 621) has some glosses in his handwriting and his signature dated 1432. In the blank leaves at the end of the Latin psalter are several historical memoranda (ff. 99–107), one giving an account (unfortunately imperfect and not in his handwriting, but corrected with additions by him) of the condemnation and beheading of Archbishop Scrope, which is of the highest value, since it is probably the source from which the current narratives are derived. These memoranda are printed by Mr. Rogers (pp. 225–32). The following works are also attributed to Gascoigne: 'Epistola cuidam S. T. D. de rebus gestis in concilio Florentino' (Trin. Coll. Cambr., MS. 301, in *Catal. Codd. MSS. Angl.* ii. 96, 1697), 'Tractatus de indulgentiis ex compilatione doctoris Gascoyn' (unless this be the work of John Gascoigne [q. v.]), 'Ordinariæ Lectiones,' and 'Sermones Evangeliorum.'

[Gascoigne himself supplies most of the data for his biography in the Dictionarium Theologicum, and in notes written in manuscripts once belonging to him. One of these, at the end of the Bodleian manuscript 198, is printed by Mr. Rogers (p. 232); another at the end of the Magdalen College, Oxford, MS. 103, by Coxe, Catalogue of Oxford Manuscripts, Magd. Coll. 55. The remaining materials are chiefly found in the university registers (printed in the Munimenta Academica Oxon. ii.) and in Anthony à Wood and Tanner.] R. L. P.

GASCOIGNE, Sir THOMAS (1593?–1686), alleged conspirator, born about 1593, was eldest son of Sir John Gascoigne of Losingcroft, Parlington, and Barnbow, Yorkshire, by Anne, daughter of John Ingleby of Lawkland Hall, Yorkshire (cf. *Yorkshire Visitation*, 1666, Surtees Soc. 289). Sir John was made a Nova-Scotian baronet by Charles I in 1635, and died 3 May 1637. The family, which was strictly Roman catholic, descended from Nicholas, younger brother of Sir William Gascoigne the judge [q. v.] Sir Thomas's three brothers, John Placid (1599–1681), Francis, and Michael (*d.* 1657), all entered holy orders in the Roman catholic church; the first, a Benedictine, was abbot of Lambspring in Germany; the second was a secular priest, and the third was a missioner at Welton, Northumberland. Of his six sisters the third, Catherine, became abbess of Cambray, and the youngest, Justina, was prioress of the Benedictine convent at Paris when she died, 17 May 1690.

Gascoigne succeeded to the baronetcy and estates on his father's death in 1637, and was a popular and charitable country gentleman. He spent his time in supervising his large property, which included collieries. In March 1665–6 his name appeared on a list of Yorkshire recusants. His zeal for his religion led him in the spring of 1678 to endow with 90*l.* a year a convent of the institute of the Blessed Virgin which Mother Frances Bedingfield temporarily established at Dolebank, near Fountains Abbey. He corresponded on the subject with a jesuit, Father Pracid, *alias* Cornwallis. Next year Robert Bolron [q. v.], formerly manager of one of Gascoigne's collieries, who had been discharged in consequence of embezzlement, laid a deposition before the Earl of Shaftesbury in London to

the effect that he had been perverted to Roman catholicism while in Gascoigne's service, and had been lately offered 1,000*l.* by his master to engage with many members of the family and their neighbours in a plot to murder Charles II. Titus Oates, to whose following Bolron belonged, had recently disclosed his popish plot, and the excitement against Roman catholics was at its height. Gascoigne, aged 85, was consequently arrested at Barnbow on 7 July 1679, and carried to the Tower of London, while his eldest daughter, Lady Tempest, wife of Sir Stephen Tempest of Broughton Hall, Craven, also implicated by Bolron, was sent with two other friends to take her trial at York. Gascoigne was arraigned in the king's bench at Westminster on 24 Jan. 1679–80, and was brought to trial before a special jury drawn from his own county on 11 Feb. following. He pleaded not guilty. Besides Bolron the only witness for the prosecution was Lawrence Maybury, or Mowbray as he now called himself, lately footman in Gascoigne's service, who had been discharged for stealing money belonging to Lady Tempest. A letter to Gascoigne from Father Pracid, who was at the time in prison, about the founding of the convent at Dolebank in 1678, was put in. But witnesses called for the defence demolished the testimony of both the informers, and Gascoigne was acquitted. 'There was pretty positive evidence against him,' writes Luttrell, reflecting the unjust contemporary feeling, 'yet the jury (which was a very mean one), after nearly an hour's being out, gave in their verdict not guilty, to the wonder of many people.' Lady Tempest was tried and acquitted at York on 20 July following. Gascoigne soon retired to the English Benedictine monastery at Lambspring in Germany, of which his brother was abbot. He became a member of the confraternity, and died there in 1686, aged 93, being buried near his brother, who died five years earlier. William Carr, English consul at Amsterdam, visited him at Lambspring, and describes him as 'a very good, harmless gentleman . . . a person of more integrity and piety than to be guilty so much as in thought of what miscreants falsely swore against him in the licentious time of plotting' (*Remarks of the Government of several parts of Germany*, &c., Amsterdam, 1688, p. 145).

Gascoigne married Anne, daughter of John Symeon of Baldwins, Brightwell, Oxfordshire. Three sons and five daughters survived him. His successor and eldest surviving son, Thomas, died without issue in 1698; the title fell to the descendants of his second son, George, and became extinct on the death of the sixth baronet, Sir Thomas, 11 Feb. 1810. The second daughter, Catherine, became prioress of the Benedictine convent at Paris, and the youngest, Frances, was a nun at Cambray.

Dr. Oliver describes a portrait of Gascoigne in oils at the Chapel House, Cheltenham.

[Gillow's Bibl. Dict. of English Catholics; Thoresby's Ducatus Leodiensis, ed. Whitaker, pp. 179–81 (pedigree); Dodd's Church Hist. iii. 327; Howell's State Trials, vii. 959–1044; Oliver's Collections of English Benedictine Congregations, p. 494; Foley's Records of Soc. Jesus, iii. 103–4 n., v. 580; Luttrell's Brief Relation, i. 17, 22, 23, 35, 37, 51, 113; Depositions from the Castle of York (Surtees Soc.), 1881. The falsity of the charges against Gascoigne is exposed in An Abstract of the Accusations of Robert Bolron and Lawrence Maybury, servants, against their late master, Sir Thomas Gascoigne . . . with his trial and acquittal, Feb. 11, 1679–80, Lond., for C. R, 1680, fol. Bolron's fabricated story is told in the Narrative of R. B. of Shippen Hall, gent., London, 1680, fol.; in the Papists' Bloody Oath of Secrecy, London, 1680, fol. (reprinted in Harl. Miscellany, vii.), and in Animadversions on the Papists' . . . Oath of Secrecy given to R. B. by W. Rushton, a Jesuit, London, 1681, s. sh. fol. See art. BOLRON, ROBERT.]   S. L.

GASCOIGNE, SIR WILLIAM (1350 ?–1419), judge, eldest son of William Gascoigne, by Agnes, daughter of Nicholas Frank, was born at Gawthorpe, Yorkshire, about 1350. He is said to have studied at Cambridge and the Inner Temple, and he is included in Segar's list of readers at Gray's Inn, though the date of his reading is not given. From the year-books it appears that he argued a case in Hilary term 1374, and he figures not unfrequently as a pleader in Bellewe's 'Ans du Roy Richard le Second.' He became one of the king's serjeants in 1397, and was appointed by letters patent attorney to the Duke of Hereford on his banishment, for whom he also held an estate in Yorkshire in trust. His patent of king's serjeant was renewed on Hereford's accession to the throne in 1399, and he was created chief justice of the king's bench on 15 Nov. 1400 (DUGDALE, Chron. Ser. p. 55; DOUTHWAITE, Gray's Inn, p. 45; NICOLAS, Testamenta Vetusta, p. 144). He was a trier of petitions in parliament between 1400–1 and 1403–4. In July 1403 he was commissioned to raise forces against the insurgent Earl of Northumberland, and in April 1405 to receive the submission of the earl's adherents, with power to impose fines. The prime movers in the insurrection were put to death, among them being Thomas Mowbray, the earl marshal, and Richard Scrope, archbishop of York, both of whom were executed on 8 June 1405 at Bishops-

thorpe, near York. Walsingham, who records the fact of the execution, is silent as to the constitution of the court by which sentence was passed (Hist. Anglic. Rolls Ser. ii. 270). Capgrave, however (Chron. of England, Rolls Ser. p. 291), states that it consisted of the Earl of Arundel [see FITZALAN, THOMAS], Sir Thomas Beaufort [q. v.], and Gascoigne, and this statement is to some extent corroborated by a royal writ dated Bishopsthorpe 6 June 1405, by which Arundel and Beaufort are commissioned to execute the offices of constable and marshal of England (RYMER, Fœdera, ed. Holmes, viii. 399). The author of the 'Annales Henrici Quarti' (Trokelowe et Anon. Chron. Rolls Ser. p. 409) makes no mention of Gascoigne, but states that sentence was passed by Arundel and Beaufort. According to the 'English Chronicle,' 1377–1461, Camd. Soc. pp. 32–3, the Archbishop of Canterbury, Thomas Arundel, advised Henry to reserve Scrope for the judgment of the pope, or at least of the parliament; the names of the judges are not given. Clement Maidstone (WHARTON, Anglia Sacra, ii. 369–370) asserts that Gascoigne was to have tried the archbishop, but that he refused to do so on the ground that he had no jurisdiction over spiritual persons; that therefore the king commissioned Sir William Fulthorp, ' a knight and not a judge,' to try the case; and that he it was who passed sentence on the archbishop. With this account Sloane MS. 1776, f. 44, agrees, adding that Thomas Arundel, archbishop of Canterbury, concurred with Gascoigne, and that one Ralph Everis, also a knight, was joined with Fulthorp in the special commission. The life of Scrope, printed in 'Historians of the Church of York' (Rolls Ser.), ii. 428–33, is silent as to Gascoigne's refusal to sit, but states that the trial took place before Sir William Fulforde 'juris et literarum peritus.' This account appears to be of later date than any before cited, and is the one which was followed by Stow and most subsequent historians. That Sir William Fulthorp, though not a regular justice, nevertheless tried some of the insurgents, is clear from 'Parl. Roll,' iii.'633, but it is extremely unlikely that he should have tried a spiritual peer on a capital charge, and the evidence of clerical chroniclers must be received with caution on account of the strong temptation under which they lay to falsify facts in order to obtain the high authority of Gascoigne for the privileges of their order. Moreover, if Gascoigne had really made the signal display of independence attributed to him, he would probably have been punished either by removal or suspension from his office. That he was not removed is clear; for we find him in the following Michaelmas term trying cases as usual at Westminster, and it is very improbable that in the interval he had been suspended. It appears, indeed, from 'Parl. Roll,' iii. 578 *a*, that on 19 June he was still 'hors de courte,' and was not expected to return for some time, for his colleagues were authorised to proceed with certain legal business in his absence. But this seems merely to indicate that he was detained in the north longer than had been anticipated. On the whole the balance of probability seems to incline distinctly against the hitherto received account of his conduct in the case of Scrope, and in favour of Capgrave's explicit statement that he took part in the trial. With the story of his committing Prince Henry to prison, and of that prince's magnanimous behaviour towards him on his accession to the throne, it fares still worse. For the committal there is no evidence; the latter part of the story is demonstrably untrue. The committal to gaol for contempt of the heir-apparent to the crown would have been an event of such dramatic interest as could not fail, if it occurred, to have been recorded by some contemporary writer, and duly noted as a precedent by the lawyers. In fact, however, no contemporary authority, lay or legal, knows anything of such an occurrence, the earliest account of it being found in Sir Thomas Elyot's 'Governour' (1531), a work designed for the instruction and edification of princes, and in particular of Henry VIII, of no historical pretensions, but abounding in anecdotes drawn from various sources, introduced as illustrations of ethical or political maxims. (An exhaustive discussion of the question will be found in a paper by Mr. F. Solly Flood, Q.C., in the *Royal Historical Society's Transactions*, new ser. iii. pt. i.) From Elyot's 'Governour' the story passed into Hall's 'Chronicle' with the material additions, (1) that the contempt in question consisted in the prince's striking the chief justice a blow on the face with his fist, (2) that the king, so far from resenting Gascoigne's conduct, dismissed the prince from the privy council, and banished him the court (HALL, *Henry V*, ad init.) Both Elyot and Hall agree that the occasion of the prince's action was the arraignment of one of his servants before the chief justice, but Elyot represents the prince as at first merely protesting, and, when protest proved unavailing, endeavouring to rescue the prisoner. He says nothing of the assault, nor, though he states that the king approved of Gascoigne's conduct, does he hint that he endorsed it by adding any punishment of his own. Shakespeare, who drew on both accounts, identifies

the servant with Bardolph (*Henry IV*, pt. ii. act i. sc. 2. *Page*: 'Sir, here comes the nobleman that committed the prince for striking him about Bardolph'). The later scene (act v. sc. 2), where the new king calls upon the chief justice to show cause why he should not hate him, and after hearing his defence bids him 'still bear the balance and the sword,' is not only unfounded in, but is inconsistent with, historical fact. Gascoigne was indeed summoned as lord chief justice to the first parliament of Henry V, notwithstanding that his patent had determined by the death of the late king; but he had already either resigned or been removed from office when that parliament met on 15 May 1413, as the patent of his successor, Sir William Hankford, is dated the 29th of the preceding March (Foss, *Lives of the Judges*, iv. 169). His salary was paid down to 7 July, and by royal warrant dated 24 Nov. 1414 he received a grant of four bucks and does annually from the forest of Pontefract for the term of his life (DEVON, *Issues of the Exchequer*, p. 322; TYLER, *Life of Hen. V*, i. 379). It therefore seems probable that Henry's first intention was to continue him in his office, but that at his own request his patent was not renewed. His will, dated 'Friday after St. Lucy's day' (i.e. 15 Dec.) 1419, was proved in the prerogative court of Yorkshire on the 23rd of the same month. Fuller (*Worthies*) gives Sunday 17 Dec. 1412 as the date of his death. If we suppose that, though wrong about the year, he was right about the day of the week, then, as 17 Dec. 1419 happens to have been a Sunday, we may conclude that he died on that day. He was buried in the parish church of Harewood, Yorkshire, under a monument representing him in his robes and hood, his head resting on a double cushion supported by angels, a lion couchant at his feet. Foss remarks that he is the first English judge of whom we have any personal anecdotes. How little credit can be attached to these has already been shown; their character, however, evinces the profound respect in which Gascoigne was held by the people. He was clearly regarded as the ideal of a just judge, possessed with a high sense of the dignity of his office, and absolutely indifferent in the discharge of his duty to his personal interest and even safety.

Gascoigne married, first, Elizabeth, daughter of Alexander Mowbray of Kirklington, Yorkshire; secondly, Joan, daughter of Sir William Pickering, and relict of Sir Ralph Greystock, baron of the exchequer. By his first wife he had one son, William, who married Jane, daughter of Sir Henry Wyman. Their son, Sir William Gascoigne, served with distinction under Henry V in his French campaigns, and was high sheriff of Yorkshire in 1442, and his son William was created a knight of the Bath by Henry VII at the coronation of Queen Elizabeth in 1487. A descendant, Sir William Gascoigne, held the manor of Gawthorpe in the reign of Elizabeth ; but on his death without male issue, it devolved on his heiress, Margaret, who by her marriage with Thomas Wentworth, high sheriff of Yorkshire in 1582, became the grandmother of Thomas Wentworth, earl of Strafford. By his second wife Gascoigne had one son, James, who acquired by marriage an estate at Cardington, Bedfordshire, where his posterity were settled for some generations.

[Gough's Sepulchral Monuments, ii. pt. ii. 37 ; Thoresby's Leeds (Whittaker), ii. 179 ; Drake's Eboracum, pp. 353, 354 ; Hunter's South Yorkshire, p. 484 ; Dugdale's Warwickshire (Thomas), ii. 856 ; Walsingham's Hist. Angl. (Rolls Ser.), ii. 334 ; Gest. Abb. Mon. Sanct. Alb. (Rolls Ser.), iii. 509 ; Coll. Top. et Gen. i. 302, 311, v. 4, vi. 394 ; Lysons' Mag. Brit. i. 64 ; Addit. MS. 28206, f. 13 b ; Biog. Brit. ; Campbell's Lives of the Chief Justices ; Foss's Lives of the Judges.] J. M. R.

GASCOIGNE, WILLIAM (1612?-1644), inventor of the micrometer, son of Henry Gascoigne, esq., of Thorpe-on-the-Hill, in the parish of Rothwell, near Leeds, Yorkshire, by his first wife, Margaret Jane, daughter of William Cartwright, was born not later than 1612. He resided with his father at Middleton, near Leeds, and acquired a remarkable knowledge of astronomy. Charles Townley, writing to Ralph Thoresby 16 Jan. 1698-9, mentions that Gascoigne was a correspondent of Jeremiah Horrocks and William Crabtree, and adds : 'It is to the mutual correspondence of this triumvirate that we owe the letters my brother Townley has of theirs, de re Astronomica. They are many and intricate, and he thinks not to be made use of, without particular hints or instructions from himself' (Correspondence of Thoresby, i. 352). Gascoigne fell on the royalist side at the battle of Marston Moor on 2 July 1644. Aubrey's erroneous assertion (Lives of Eminent Men, p. 355), that at the time of his death he was ' about the age of 24 or 25 at most,' has been frequently repeated. Gascoigne left the manuscript of a treatise on optics ready for the press.

He invented methods of grinding glasses, and Sir Edward Sherburne states that he was the first who used two convex glasses in the telescope. When in 1666 Auzout announced his invention of the micrometer, Richard Townley, nephew of Christopher, presented Hook with a modification by himself of a similar instrument made by Gascoigne. A letter written by Crabtree to Horrocks in 1639 shows that Crabtree had seen Gascoigne use an instrument of the kind (SHERBURNE, Catalogue of Astronomers, pp. 92, 114). The instrument appears to have originally consisted either of two parallel wires or of two plates of metal placed in the focus of the eye-glass of a telescope, and capable of being moved so that the image of an object could be exactly comprehended between them. A scale served for the measurement of the angle subtended by the interval, and Gascoigne is said to have used this instrument for the purpose of measuring the diameters of the moon and planets, and also for determining the magnitudes or distances of terrestrial objects.

It is now generally admitted that Gascoigne was the original inventor of the wire micrometer, of its application to the telescope, and of the application of the telescope to the quadrant ; though the invention was never promulgated, even in England, until the undoubtedly independent inventions of Auzout and Picard suggested its publication.

[Annual Register, iv. 196 ; Gent. Mag. ccxv. (1863), 760 ; Knight's Cyclopædia of Biography ; Penny Cyclopædia ; Phil. Trans. ii. 457, xlviii. 190 ; Taylor's Biog. Leodiensis, p. 86 ; Thoresby Correspondence, i. 349, 357, 387, ii. 302.] T. C.

GASCOYNE, SIR CRISP (1700-1761), lord mayor of London, youngest son of Benjamin and Anne Gascoyne, was born at Chiswick, and baptised in the parish church on 26 Aug. 1700. He set up in business as a brewer in Gravel Lane, Houndsditch (OSBORN, Complete Guide, 1749, p. 137). His residence was at Barking in 1733, and the baptisms of his four youngest children are recorded there between 1733 and 1738. In 1755 he is described as of Mincing Lane, where he probably lived in the house of his father-in-law, Dr. Bamber, though still carrying on the brewhouse in Houndsditch in partnership with one Weston. Gascoyne was admitted a freeman of the Brewers' Company by redemption 17 Dec. 1741, he took the clothing of the livery 8 March 1744, fined for the offices of steward and the three grades of wardenship 19 Aug. 1746, and was elected an assistant 11 Oct. 1745, and master of the company for 1746-7.

He was elected alderman of Vintry ward 20 June 1745, and sworn into office on 2 July (Vintry Wardmote Book, Guildhall Library MS. 68). He served the office of sheriff of London and Middlesex in 1747-8. In December 1748 he took a prominent part, at the head of the committee of city lands, in passing through the common council an act for the relief of the orphans of the city of London, whose estates, vested in the guardianship of the corporation, had greatly suffered through the exactions of the civil war period and the illegal closing of the exchequer by Charles II (MAITLAND, *History of London*, 1756, i. 670). Gascoyne became lord mayor in 1752, and was the first chief magistrate who occupied the present Mansion House, the building of which had been commenced in 1739 on the site of Stocks Market. Owing to the change of style the date of the mayoralty procession was this year altered from 29 Oct. to 9 Nov. Gascoyne presided as lord mayor at the trial of the women Squires and Wells, convicted of kidnapping Elizabeth Canning [q. v.] His suspicions being aroused he started further inquiries, which resulted in proving that Canning's accusation was false. The mob took Canning's part, insulted the lord mayor, breaking his coach windows, and even threatening his life. Gascoyne justified himself in an address to the liverymen of London (London, 1754, folio; abstract in 'London Magazine,' xxiii. 317–20), and received a vote of thanks from the common council at the end of his year of office (MAITLAND, i. 708). Early in his mayoralty, 22 Nov. 1752, Gascoyne was knighted on the occasion of presenting an address to the king; he was also a verderer of Epping Forest, in which office he was succeeded by his eldest son (*London Magazine*, 1763). He purchased large estates in Essex, including the buildings and grounds of an ancient hospital and chapel at Ilford, and the right of presentation to the living.

Gascoyne died on 28 Dec. 1761, and was buried on 4 Jan. 1762 in Barking Church, in the north aisle of which is a large monument with an inscription, erected to his memory by his four children (OGBORNE, *History of Essex*, 1814, p. 39). His will, dated 20 Dec. 1761, was proved in the P.C.C. 4 Jan. 1762 (*St. Eloy*, 13). He married Margaret, daughter and coheiress of Dr. John Bamber, a wealthy physician of Mincing Lane, who purchased large estates in Essex and built the mansion of Bifrons at Barking (MUNK, *College of Physicians*, 2nd edit., ii. 107–8). A drawing of this house as it appeared in 1794 is preserved in the Guildhall Library copy of Lysons's 'Environs' (vol. iv. pt. i. p. 88). Gascoyne had four surviving children—Bamber, Joseph, Ann, and Margaret. His wife was buried in Barking Church 10 Oct. 1740.

Dr. Bamber died in November 1753, and his property descended in entail to BAMBER GASCOYNE (1725–1791), eldest son of Sir Crisp (*Gent. Mag.* 1753, p. 540). Bamber Gascoyne entered Queen's College, Oxford

(1743); was barrister of Lincoln's Inn (1750); was M.P. for Malden 1761–3, Midhurst 1765–70, Weobly 1770–4, Truro 1774–1784, and Bossiney 1784–6; and was also receiver-general of customs (FOSTER, *Alumni Oxon.*) and a lord of the admiralty (*Gent. Mag.* 1791, ii. 1066). On his death in 1791 the Bamber estates descended to his son Bamber (1758–1824), M.P. for Liverpool 1780–96, who cut off the entail, pulled down the house of Bifrons, and sold the site and park. His daughter and heiress married the second Marquis of Salisbury, who took the name of Gascoyne before that of Cecil, and became possessed of the Bamber property, worth, it is said, 12,000*l.* a year (MUNK). A mezzotint portrait of Sir Crisp by James McArdell, from a painting by William Keable, was published in the 'London Magazine' for July 1753. There is a smaller and anonymous print, probably of the same date.

[Information furnished by Mr. E. J. Sage; Brewers' Company's Records; Maitland's History of London, 1756, i. 694–701.] C. W.

GASCOYNE, ISAAC (1770–1841), general, third son of Bamber Gascoyne the elder, and grandson of Sir Crisp Gascoyne [q. v.], was born in 1770, and on 8 Feb. 1779 was appointed ensign in the 20th foot, from which he was transferred to the Coldstream guards in July 1780. His subsequent military commissions were lieutenant and captain 18 Aug. 1784, captain and lieutenant-colonel 5 Dec. 1792 (both in Coldstream guards), brevetcolonel 3 May 1796, lieutenant-colonel in 16th foot 7 June 1799, major-general 29 April 1802, colonel 7th West India regiment 10 Oct. 1805, lieutenant-general 25 April 1808, colonel 54th foot (now 1st Dorset) 1 June 1816, general 12 Aug. 1819. He was present with the guards in most of the engagements in Flanders in 1793–4, and was wounded in the brilliant affair at Lincelles in 1793, and again, in the head, a wound from which he suffered during the remainder of his life, when covering the retreat of Sir Ralph Abercromby's corps from Mouvaix to Roubaix, in the following year. He commanded the Coldstream battalion in the brigade of guards sent to Ireland about the close of the rebellion of 1798, and acted as a major-general on the staff there and elsewhere, a position he held in the Severn district before his promotion to lieutenant-general in 1808.

Gascoyne, who had a seat, Raby Hall, near Liverpool, was returned to parliament in 1796 for that borough, for which his eldest brother, Bamber Gascoyne, jun., had previously sat. For many years he was a familiar figure in the house, as well as on the turf at Newmarket. In politics he was a staunch conservative, and a consistent supporter of all measures for benefiting the army in days when such support was even more needed than at present. On 10 Aug. 1803 he seconded Mr. Sheridan's motion of thanks to the volunteers (*Parl. Debates*, under date). To his representations, it is said, was chiefly due the granting of the allowance of 25*l*. a company or troop to officers' messes, in lieu of the remission of wine duty, known as the 'prince regent's allowance;' also the increase of pay granted to captains and subalterns after the peace. He was an active and successful opponent of the paltry attempts repeatedly made to cut down the compassionate allowances to families of deceased officers.

Gascoyne, who had been returned for Liverpool after a very severe contest in 1802 and again in 1806, 1807, 1812, 1818, 1820, 1826, and 1830, was defeated at the election 4 May 1831, and retired from parliamentary life. He died at his residence, 71 South Audley Street, London, 26 Aug. 1841, of an inflammatory attack, in his seventy-second year.

[Army Lists; Parl. Debates, 1796-1831; Gent. Mag. new ser. **xvi.** 542.]　　　　H. M. C.

GASELEE, Sir STEPHEN (1762-1839), justice of the court of common pleas, was the son of Stephen Gaselee, an eminent surgeon at Portsmouth, where he was born in 1762. He was admitted a student at Gray's Inn on 29 Jan. 1781, but was not called to the bar until 20 Nov. 1793. He had the advantage of being a pupil of Sir Vicary Gibbs, under whose instruction he became a skilful special pleader. He joined the western circuit, and was so much respected as a careful and well-informed junior, that when, after twenty-six years' practice, he was made a king's counsel in Hilary term 1819, his professional income was probably diminished. Though he was not orator enough to commence practice as a leader, his deserved reputation for legal knowledge soon recommended him for a judge's place. On the resignation of Sir John Richardson, he was selected on 1 July 1824 to supply the vacant justiceship in the common pleas, became a serjeant-at-law 5 July 1824, and was knighted at Carlton House on 27 April in the following year. In that court he sat for nearly thirteen years, with the character of a painstaking and upright judge. He was a vice-president and an active member of the Royal Humane Society, and is said to have been the original of the irascible judge represented by Dickens in the trial of Bardell *v.* Pickwick, under the name of Justice Stareleigh. He resigned his judgeship at the end of Hilary term 1837, and after two years' retirement died at 13 Montague

Place, Russell Square, London, on 26 March 1839. His wife was Henrietta, daughter of James Harris of the East India Company's service.

[Foss's Judges, ix. 91; Foss's Biogr. Juridica, p. 292; Legal Observer, 6 April 1839, p. 450; Gent. Mag. September 1839, p. 315.]　　　G. C. B.

GASELEE, STEPHEN (1807-1883), serjeant-at-law, eldest son of Sir Stephen Gaselee [q. v.], was born at 77 Upper Guildford Street, Russell Square, London, on 1 Sept. 1807, and educated at Winchester School. He matriculated from Balliol College, Oxford, on 4 June 1824; graduated second class in classics 1828, when he took his B.A. degree; and proceeded M.A. in 1832. He was called to the bar at the Inner Temple 16 June 1832, and practised on the home circuit. On 2 Nov. 1840 he became a serjeant-at-law, and at the time of his decease was the oldest surviving serjeant. He unsuccessfully contested the borough of Portsmouth in the liberal interest 14 March 1855. Ten years later, 13 July 1865, he was elected M.P. for that borough, but lost his seat at the general election in 1868. For many years he was a director of the London and South-Western Railway, was a magistrate for the county of Middlesex, sometimes presided as assistant-judge at the Middlesex sessions, and was treasurer of Serjeants' Inn, in succession to Serjeant James Manning, in 1866. He died at 2 Cambridge Square, Hyde Park, London, 20 Oct. 1883. His wife, whom he married at Marylebone on 21 July 1841, was Alicia Mary, eldest daughter of Sir John Tremayne Rodd, K.C.B. She was born 7 Jan. 1814, and died at Bournemouth 11 Nov. 1886.

[Solicitors' Journal, 27 Oct. 1883, p. 802; Law Times, 27 Oct. 1883, p. 435; Times, 23 Oct. 1883, p. 10.]　　　G. C. B.

GASKELL, ELIZABETH CLEGHORN (1810-1865), novelist, born in Lindsey Row, now part of Cheyne Walk, Chelsea, 29 Sept. 1810, was the daughter, by his first marriage, of William Stevenson [q. v.] He was a native of Berwick-on-Tweed, who, after quitting the unitarian ministry, had taken to agricultural pursuits, had written upon commerce, and finally settled as keeper of the records to the treasury in London, where he continued to write. The death of his brother Joseph, a lieutenant in the royal navy, in a French prison must have suggested an incident in 'Cousin Phillis.' A strong love of the sea ran in the family. Mrs. Gaskell's mother was a daughter of Mr. Holland of Sandle Bridge in Cheshire (the 'Heathbridge' of 'Cousin Phillis'), a descendant of an ancient

Lancashire family. Within a month after her birth the child lost her mother, and after being entrusted for a week to the care of a shopkeeper's wife was by a family friend, a Mrs. Whittington, taken down to her own mother's sister, Mrs. Lumb, at Knutsford in Cheshire. This journey is represented by the travels of the 'babby' in 'Mary Barton' (chap. ix.) Her aunt, but recently married, was obliged, for painful reasons, to live alone with her daughter; and Elizabeth was to be a companion to this child, who had become a cripple. She found a second mother in her aunt, more especially after the death of her cousin. The aunt was poor, and lived in a modest house with an old-fashioned garden on the heath. She had, however, other relatives at Knutsford : her uncle, Peter Holland (the grandfather of the present Lord Knutsford), who resided there, furnished her with a type, the good country doctor, of which she was fond (see *Wives and Daughters* and *Mr. Harrison's Confessions*). As she grew into girlhood she paid some saddening visits to Chelsea, where her father had married again, but not happily. When about fifteen years of age she was sent to a school kept by Miss Byerley at Stratford-on-Avon, where she learnt Latin as well as French and Italian. Here she remained two years, including holiday times.

The quaint little country town of Knutsford, some fifteen miles from Manchester, supplied Mrs. Gaskell with the originals of her pictures of life at Cranford in her work of the name, and at Hollingford in 'Wives and Daughters' (see HENRY GREEN's *Knutsford*, 2nd edit. 1887, where is printed a letter on the antiquarian interest of the place from Jacob Grimm, who desires his kindest regards to Mrs. Gaskell). The disappearance of her only brother John Stevenson, on his third or fourth voyage as a lieutenant in the merchant navy about 1827, suggested an episode in 'Cranford' (see also the paper on 'Disappearances,' originally published in 'Household Words'). Her father died 22 April 1829. She occasionally visited London, staying with her uncle, Swinton Holland, in Park Lane ; and spent two winters at Newcastle-on-Tyne in the family of Mr. Turner, a public-spirited unitarian minister, and another at Edinburgh (the society of which afterwards suggested the introduction of · Round the Sofa'). At this time her youthful beauty was much admired, and at Edinburgh several painters and sculptors asked permission to take her portrait.

On 30 Aug. 1832 she married at Knutsford Church the Rev. William Gaskell [q. v.], minister of Cross Street Unitarian Chapel, Manchester. Her marriage proved extremely

happy, and her husband became the confidant of her literary life. Her 'Life of Charlotte Brontë' allows an incidental glimpse of her genial home, where in course of time she devoted much care to the education of her daughters. She occasionally co-operated in Mr. Gaskell's professional labours; she was ready at all times for works of charity, and gladly devoted some leisure to teaching, but otherwise, especially in later years, liked her time as well as her mind to be her own. Mr. and Mrs. Gaskell settled at Manchester, in Dover Street, whence in 1842 they moved to Rumford Street, finally in 1850 migrating to 84 Plymouth Grove. The first ten years of her married life passed uneventfully. When William Howitt announced in 1838 his intention of publishing 'Visits to Remarkable Places,' Mrs. Gaskell wrote offering an account of Clopton Hall, near Stratford-on-Avon. This was eagerly accepted, appeared in 1840, and is her first known publication. Family tradition recalls poems on a stillborn infant of her own and on a wounded stag, as well as the opening of a short story, probably begun even before her marriage. 'The Sexton's Hero' (first published in 1865) was also possibly composed before 'Mary Barton,' the work which made her famous. On a Rhine tour in 1841 Mrs. Gaskell first began her long intimacy with William and Mary Howitt.

In 1844 Mr. and Mrs. Gaskell visited Festiniog. Here their only boy (Willie) died of scarlet fever. To turn her thoughts she, by her husband's advice, attempted to write ; and there seems every reason to conclude that 'Mary Barton' was at once begun. She read Adam Smith, and perhaps others of the authorities at which, in 'North and South' (chap. xxviii.), she humorously represents a workman as 'tugging.' She sent the manuscript of the first volume to the Howitts, who ' were both delighted with it' (*Mary Howitt, an Autobiography*, 1889, ii. 28). The book was finished in 1847, and offered to more than one publisher. During the usual delay Mrs. Gaskell, as she afterwards declared, ' forgot all about it.' Early in 1848 Messrs. Chapman & Hall offered 100*l.* for the copyright, and on these terms 'Mary Barton' was published, anonymously, 14 Oct. 1848. Its success was electrical. Carlyle and Samuel Bamford [q. v.] sent congratulatory letters. Miss Edgeworth, just before her death, spoke enthusiastically of its interest, which she sometimes felt to be too harrowing (MME. BELLOC, p. 9). Landor addressed some enthusiastic verses to the 'Paraclete of the Bartons' (*Works*, 1876, viii. 255-6). Of all Mrs. Gaskell's books her earliest has enjoyed the most widespread reputation. It has been translated into French and German and many other languages, including Finnish; while at home the author became an established favourite. Some of the chief employers of labour in the Manchester district, however, complained that they were unjustly treated, and that she spoke rashly of some 'burning questions of social economy.' She was accused in the 'Manchester Guardian' (28 Feb. and 7 March 1849) of 'maligning' the manufacturers. Much the same position was taken in W. R. Greg's 'Essay on Mary Barton' (1849), which he thought worth reprinting many years afterwards (1876) in his volume entitled 'Mistaken Aims and Attainable Ideals of the Artisan Class.' Without discussing the point here, it may be observed, as Professor Minto has done, that John Barton must not be taken too hastily as a type of his whole class; that the book refers to the period of distress (1842) which suggested Disraeli's 'Sybil;' and that it has unquestionably contributed to the growth of sentiments which have helped to make the manufacturing world and Manchester very different from what they were forty years ago. The sincerity of its pathos and insight into the very hearts of the poor are of enduring value. Its humour is marked by the rather patriarchal flavour characteristic of Lancashire humour in general; nothing is more striking in Mrs. Gaskell's literary life than the ease and rapidity with which, in this respect, her genius contrived to emancipate itself.

The new writer was eagerly welcomed by Dickens. In May 1849 she dined with him and many well-known men, including Carlyle and Thackeray, to commemorate the publication of the first number of 'David Copperfield' (FORSTER, Life of Dickens, ed. 1876, ii. 100). When early in 1850 Dickens was projecting 'Household Words,' he invited Mrs. Gaskell's co-operation in the most flattering terms (Letters of Charles Dickens, 1880, i. 216–17). The first number of the new journal, published 30 March 1850, contained the beginning of 'Lizzie Leigh,' a story by Mrs. Gaskell, which was concluded 13 April. In the following years she contributed frequently to 'Household Words,' wrote an occasional paper for the 'Cornhill Magazine,' and perhaps for other journals. These contributions and Mrs. Gaskell's minor writings in general were afterwards published in a variety of combinations with the shorter of her novels, or under the titles of the longer of the tales themselves, viz. 'Lizzie Leigh,' 1855; 'The Grey Woman,' 1865; 'My Lady Ludlow,' 1859, the last named being republished under the title of 'Round the Sofa,' 1871. Mrs.

Gaskell could occasionally write with the single-minded intent of startling her readers (see 'A Dark Night's Work,' 1863, and 'The Grey Woman,' a story of the Chauffeurs, 1865), and again at times in the cheery workman's tract style, for which the benevolent purpose formed a quite sufficient excuse ('Hand and Heart,' in 'Household Words,' 1855 &c.) She was happiest in minor efforts like 'Morton Hall' or 'Mr. Harrison's Confessions,' both of which appeared in 'Household Words,' the first in 1853, the second in 1855. The very interesting tale of 'The Moorland Cottage,' written rather hurriedly, appeared as a Christmas book in 1850, with illustrations by Birket Foster. In it may be detected the first traces of the writer's more delicate vein of humour.

At the beginning of 1853, Miss Brontë having agreed to defer for a few weeks the publication of 'Villette,' in order to avoid comparisons (see her charming letter in the Life of Charlotte Brontë, ii. ch. xii.), Mrs. Gaskell published her second important novel, 'Ruth.' The story is in itself considerably more interesting than that of 'Mary Barton,' and the style, though still wanting in the more subtle charm of the authoress's later works, is unmistakably superior to that of her first book. No notice has hitherto been taken of the striking resemblance between certain characters in 'Ruth' and in Dickens's 'Hard Times,' published a year later.

Among Mrs. Gaskell's early contributions to 'Household Words' were those inimitable pictures of society in a little country town which were republished in June 1853 under the title of 'Cranford.' The original papers were printed at intervals from 13 Dec. 1851 to 21 May 1853, under headings which appear to have been in part devised by Dickens, who took a particular interest in the series (see his Letters, i. 270, 301). These delightful chapters of real life are both tinged with the most delicate sentiment, and constitute, in Lord Houghton's words, 'the purest piece of humoristic description that has been added to British literature since Charles Lamb.' The inhabitants of the little Cheshire town for which Mrs. Gaskell has secured literary immortality unhesitatingly acknowledged the fidelity of the portraiture. 'Cranford is all about Knutsford; my old mistress, Miss ——, is mentioned in it, and our poor cow, she did go to the field in a large flannel waistcoat, because she had burned herself in a lime pit' (H. GREEN, Knutsford, p. 114). A still more important work, 'North and South,' appeared in 'Household Words' from 2 Sept. 1854 to 27 Jan. 1855, in the course of which year it was republished with certain slight alterations. It is one of Mrs.

Gaskell's ablest and most interesting books. It exhibits, at least till near the close, a notable advance in constructive power; the characters are drawn with unprecedented firmness, and in some cases tinged with true humour, and though there is no loss of sympathy for the artisan the judgment of social problems shows greater impartiality and riper reflection. Her experience was widened and her interest in politics had grown deeper. She had made acquaintance with many able philanthropists, and in the company of Susanna Winkworth [q. v.] had moved about a good deal among the working classes, listened to discussions at workmen's clubs, and made herself the confidante of many a poor girl. Dickens was warm in his congratulations to Mrs. Gaskell ' on the vigorous and powerful accomplishment of an anxious labour' (*Letters*, i. 381). But for some defects of construction, due perhaps in part to the piecemeal method of weekly publication which the authoress heartily disliked, ' North and South' might safely be described as her most effective narrative fiction.

In August 1850 Mrs. Gaskell had, during a visit to Sir James Kay Shuttleworth in the Lakes, made the acquaintance of Charlotte Brontë (*Life of Charlotte Brontë*, ii. ch. vii.) The marked contrasts of temperament and literary idiosyncrasy between them had only strengthened a friendship as warm and as free from the faintest shade of jealousy as any that is recorded in literary biography. Miss Brontë visited Mrs. Gaskell at Manchester in 1851, and again in 1853 (*ib.* ii. chaps. ix. xii.), and Mrs. Gaskell became truly fond of, and 'very sorry for,' her guest. In the autumn of 1853 she returned Miss Brontë's visit at Haworth, and she was present with her husband at the wedding of Mr. and Mrs. Nicholls in June 1854. Some time after Miss Brontë's death (31 March 1855) Mrs. Gaskell consented, at Mr. Brontë's urgent request, to undertake his daughter's life. All through 1856 she was employed upon the biography, giving herself up to the work with the utmost assiduity, and sparing no pains to insure accuracy in her statements and descriptions. She spent a fortnight at Brussels in careful investigations. When in the spring of 1857 the book was at last ready for publication, Mrs. Gaskell made a journey with two of her daughters to Rome, where they were the guests of Mr. W. W. Story.

In a passage of the original edition of the 'Life' Mrs. Gaskell reproduced a supposed statement of facts, which had been explicitly made to her by Miss Brontë, and on the authenticity of which she of course placed absolute reliance. The truth of the statement was denied by the persons implicated, and the result was a retractation in the 'Times,' and the withdrawal from circulation of all the unsold copies of the first edition of the biography. Concerning certain other statements the authoress was much harassed by disclaimers and corrections, to which she sought to do justice in the later editions, and in the end she was obliged, as other biographers have been before her, to decline further personal correspondence concerning the book. The substantial accuracy of the picture drawn by Mrs. Gaskell of her heroine's life and character, and of the influences exercised upon them by her personal and local surroundings, has not been successfully impugned. As to her literary skill and power and absolute uprightness of intention as a biographer there cannot be two opinions. She expressly disclaimed having made any attempt at psychological analysis (*ib.* ii. ch. xiv.); but she was exceptionally successful in her endeavour to bring before her readers the picture of a very peculiar character and altogether original mind.

There seems no doubt that the strictures, just or unjust, passed upon her ' Life of Charlotte Brontë' gave rise in Mrs. Gaskell to a temporary distaste for writing. But her life nevertheless continued its usual course of active intellectual exertion, social kindliness, and domestic happiness. She had a great power of making friends, and of keeping them, and the extent of her circle took away the breath of a solitary like Charlotte Brontë (*ib.* ii. ch. xiii.) The Miss Winkworths and other intimates at Manchester, Lord Houghton—in whose judgment Mrs. Gaskell's house made that city a possible place of residence for people of literary tastes—and many other country and London friends, together with a never ebbing flow of American and continental admirers of her genius, diversified her home life and her excursions to London; and about the autumn of 1855 she began an intimacy with Mme. Mohl, in whose house she repeatedly stayed at Paris, and in whose historic salon, 'standing up before the mantelpiece, which she used as a desk,' she afterwards wrote part of her last story (M. E. SIMPSON, *Letters and Recollections of Julius and Mary Mohl*, 1887, p. 126, cf. *ib.* 163–7, 182–184, 201–2, 217–19, 232; see also K. O'MEARA, ' Mme. Mohl : her Salon and her Friends,' 4th paper, *Atlantic Monthly*, vol. lv. No. 330, April 1885 ; Mrs. Gaskell refers to Mr. and Mme. Mohl in *My French Master*, and pretty evidently to the lady and her power of ' sabléing' in the very sprightly paper, 'Company Manners,' contributed to *Household Words* in May 1854). But she never forgot old friends, and was always ready with useful advice to beginners in the art in which she had achieved fame. She possessed, too, a peculiar tact for training her servants. At one time she was much influenced by the example of the well-known prison philanthropist, Thomas Wright. During the cotton famine of 1862–3 she was a personal friend to many of the poor, and took a conspicuous part in organising and super-intending for six or seven hours a day a method of relief—sewing-rooms—which had occurred to her before it came to be largely adopted (MME. BELLOC, pp. 18–20).

After the stress of the cotton famine she set her hand to a new story. The plot of 'Sylvia's Lovers,' published early in 1863, turns on the doings of the press-gang towards the close of last century. She stayed at Whitby (here called Monkshaven) to study the character of the place, and personally con-sulted such authorities as Sir Charles Napier and General Perronet Thompson on the history of impressment. In its earlier portions the story maintains itself at the writer's highest level; the local colouring is true and vivid; the pathetic charm of the innocent Sylvia is admirably contrasted by the free humour of the figures of her father and his man Kester, although the effect is rather marred by the coincidences introduced to insure a symme-trical conclusion. In 1863–4 followed, in the first instance as a contribution to the 'Cornhill Magazine,' the prose idyll of 'Cousin Phillis.' The little book, which was not pub-lished as a complete story till November 1865, is beyond dispute in execution the most per-fect of Mrs. Gaskell's works, and has scarcely been surpassed for combination of the sun-niest humour with the tenderest pathos. Mrs. Gaskell's last story, 'Wives and Daughters,' also appeared in the 'Cornhill Magazine' from August 1864 to January 1866. It was reprinted as an unfinished work in the following February. It appeared at first in the magazine without her name. In it her later and more genial manner asserts itself with graceful ease. There is a certain weak-ness in the construction of the story; but its truthfulness of characterisation and its beau-tiful humanity of tone and feeling, ranging from the most charming playfulness to the most subduing pathos, stamp it as a master-piece in its branch of imaginative literature.

A collected edition of Mrs. Gaskell's works was first published in seven volumes in 1873. The 'Knutsford' collected edition, edited by the present writer, came out in eight volumes in 1906. Neither includes the 'Life of Char-lotte Brontë,' which was re-edited in 1900 by Mr. Clement K. Shorter. The collection of tales now included in 'Round the Sofa' was first brought out under the title of 'My Lady

Ludlow.' Of her chief writings French trans-lations have been published. 'Mary Barton' and 'Cranford' have also been translated into Hungarian. A Spanish version of 'Mary Barton' appeared in 1879.

Her strength began to fail when nearing the end of 'Wives and Daughters,' though her exertions never relaxed. On Sunday, 12 Nov. 1865, she was carried away by disease of the heart, 'without a moment's warning,' according to her epitaph. She was at the time conversing with (not reading to) her daughters, three of whom were around her, in the country house at Holybourne, near Alton in Hampshire, which she had purchased with the proceeds of her last book, and which she intended to present as a surprise to her husband. She was buried in the little sloping graveyard of the ancient unitarian chapel at Knutsford, where her husband was in 1884 laid by her side. A cross, with the dates of their births and deaths, marks their resting-place; but in the Cross Street Unitarian Chapel at Manchester they are commemorated by mural inscriptions, of which that to Mrs. Gaskell is from her husband's hand.

An interesting letter, dated 11 Nov. 1859, from 'George Eliot' to Mrs. Gaskell, grate-fully acknowledging her 'sweet encouraging words,' has been printed in the 'British Weekly.' George Sand, only a few months before Mrs. Gaskell's death, observed to Lord Houghton: 'Mrs. Gaskell has done what neither I nor other female writers in France can accomplish; she has written novels which excite the deepest interest in men of the world, and yet which every girl will be the better for reading.' None of our novelists has shown a more extraordinary power of self-development. She might have excelled in a different field. During the last months of her life, inspired perhaps by the example of Mme. Mohl's 'Essay on Mme. Récamier,' she had thoughts of writing a life of Mme. de Sévigné, and pursued some preliminary re-searches on the subject both at Paris and in Brittany. She had long taken a warm in-terest in French history and literature (cf. her papers *Traits and Stories of the Huguenots, An Accursed Race, Curious if True, My French Master*, &c.) Mrs. Gaskell had at one time been very beautiful; her head is a remarkably fine one in the portraits preserved of her, and her hand was always thought perfect. She had great conversational gifts, and the letters in her 'Life of Charlotte Brontë' show her to have been a charming correspondent. The singular refinement of her manners was noticed by all who became acquainted with her. Perhaps her natural vivacity caused her now and then to chafe a little at the rather tranquil conditions of her existence. In Manchester even nonconformity has few emotional aspects, and if Mrs. Gaskell's rectors and vicars usually lean in the direction of imbecility, she seems to show a half-ironical preference on secular grounds for church over dissent. It is noticeable that her imagination was much attracted by whatever partook of the supernatural, across the boundaries of which she ventured in more than one of her minor writings (e.g. 'My Lady Ludlow,' 'The Poor Clare,' 'The Old Nurse's Story'), and from which she does not seem to have shrunk in the confidential hours of home (see *Life of Charlotte Brontë*, ii. ch. xii.) But what was most characteristic as well as most fascinating in her must have been the sympathetic force of the generous spirit which animated her singularly clear and reasonable mind. In conversation with Charlotte Brontë, Mrs. Gaskell disputed her companion's sad view of human life: 'I thought that human lots were more equal than she imagined; that to some happiness and sorrow came in strong patches of light and shadow (so to speak), while in the lives of others they were pretty equally blended throughout.' To perceive this was to understand a lesson of the book of life which few modern imaginative writers have so powerfully and yet so unaffectedly impressed upon their readers.

[Family and private sources, except where otherwise indicated in the text. The only biographical sketch (previous to the present one) is a slight notice by Mme. Louise Sw. Belloc prefixed to E. D. Forgues's French translation of Cousin Phillis and other Tales (1879). This is partly founded on an obituary notice of Mrs. Gaskell signed 'M.' (Mrs. Charles Herford), which appeared in the Unitarian Herald, 17 Nov. 1865. Among other notices of her death was an admirable article by Lord Houghton in the Pall Mall Gazette, 14 Nov. 1865. The best critical paper on her writings is Professor W. Minto's in the Fortnightly Review, vol. xxiv. (July to December 1878).]   A. W. W.

GASKELL, WILLIAM (1805–1884), unitarian minister, eldest son of William Gaskell (*d.* 15 March 1819), sail-canvas manufacturer, was born at Latchford, near Warrington, on 24 July 1805. Of an old nonconformist family, he was early destined for the ministry. After studying at Glasgow, where he graduated M.A. in 1824, he was admitted in 1825 to Manchester College, York, being nominated by Thomas Belsham [q. v.] as a divinity student on the Hackney fund. Leaving York in 1828, he became colleague with John Gooch Robberds at Cross Street Chapel, Manchester, entering upon the ministry on 3 Aug. This was his lifelong

charge. Becoming senior minister in 1854, he had successively as colleagues James Panton Ham (1855–9), James Drummond, LL.D. (1860–9), and Samuel Alfred Steinthal. In his own denomination Gaskell held the highest positions. He was preacher to the 'British and Foreign' unitarian association in 1844, 1862, and 1875. At Manchester New College he was professor of English history and literature (1846–53) and chairman of committee from 1854, having previously been secretary (1840–6). Of the unitarian home missionary board he was one of the tutors from 1854 and principal from 1876, succeeding John Relly Beard [q.v.] From 1865 he was president of the provincial assembly of Lancashire and Cheshire. The jubilee of his Manchester ministry was commemorated in 1878 by the foundation of a scholarship bearing his name.

Gaskell exercised great influence in Manchester, especially in the promotion of education and learning. Though an effective and polished speaker, he rarely appeared on platforms. At Owens College he conducted the classes of logic and English literature during the illness of Principal Scott. On the formation of a working man's college in 1858 he was appointed lecturer on English literature, and retained that office on the amalgamation (1861) of this scheme with the evening classes of Owens College. His prelections were remarkable for their literary finish, and for the aptness and taste with which he drew upon an unusually wide compass of reading. The same qualities marked his discourses from the pulpit.

Gaskell died at his residence, Plymouth Grove, Manchester, on 11 June 1884; he was buried on 14 June at Knutsford. His portrait, painted in 1872 by W. Percy, is in the Memorial Hall, Manchester; another, painted in 1878 by Annie Robinson, is in the possession of his family; a marble bust, by J. W. Swinnerton, was placed in 1878 in the reading-room of the Portico Library, of which for thirty years he had been chairman. In 1832 he married Elizabeth Cleghorn Stevenson [see GASKELL, ELIZABETH CLEGHORN, the novelist], by whom he had a son (*d.* in infancy), a daughter, Florence (*d.* 1881), married to Charles Crompton, Q.C., and three daughters who survived him.

He published a considerable number of sermons and controversial tracts, including funeral sermons for the Rev. John Gooch Robberds (1854), David Siltzer (1854), J. O. Curtis (1857), Sir John Potter (1859), John Ashton Nicholls, with memoir (1859), and the Rev. William Turner (1859). Among his other publications may be noted: 1. 'Temperance Rhymes,' 1839. 2. 'Two Lectures on the Lancashire Dialect,' 1844; also appended to his wife's 'Mary Barton,' 5th edition, 1854. (For their samples of dialectical peculiarities these lectures are valuable. He wrote a number of hymns, most of which were contributed to a collection edited by J. R. Beard, D.D., 1837; some of the best will be found in 'Hymns of Praise and Prayer,' edited by James Martineau, D.D., 1874. His translation of Luther's 'Ein feste Burg' has found general favour. He was one of the editors of the 'Unitarian Herald' from its establishment in 1861 to the end of 1875.

[Manchester Guardian, 11 June 1884; Christian Life, 14 June 1884; Inquirer, 14 June and 21 June 1884; Monthly Repository, 1819, p. 194; Roll of Students, Manchester New College, 1868; Baker's Memorials of a Dissenting Chapel (Cross Street, Manchester), 1884; Thompson's Owens College, 1886, pp. 227, 232, &c.; private information.]   A. G.

GASKIN, GEORGE (1751–1829), prebendary of Ely, son of John Gaskin, a leatherseller (1710–1766), and of Mabel his wife (1707–1791), was born at Newington Green, London, in 1751. He was educated at a classical school in Woodford, Essex, and went to Trinity College, Oxford, in 1771. He proceeded B.A. in 1775, M.A. in 1778, and D.D. in 1788. He was ordained deacon in 1774, when he became curate of St. Vedast, Foster Lane. He was then appointed to fill the vacant office of lecturer in the parish of Islington, a post which he occupied for forty-six years. In 1778 he accepted the curacy of the parish of Stoke Newington. His first preferment was the rectory of Sutton and Mepal in the Isle of Ely. This, however, in 1791 he managed to exchange for the living of St. Bennet, Gracechurch Street, in order to be at hand for fulfilling his duties as secretary to the Society for Promoting Christian Knowledge. He was further employed on behalf of this society to visit and report upon the mission schools and churches of the Scilly Islands. He was a vigorous supporter of the Scotch episcopalians, and was selected as a member of the English committee for the obtaining of a bill known as 'An Act for granting Relief to Pastors and Ministers and Lay Persons of the Episcopal Communion in Scotland.' In 1797 he was further promoted to the rectory of Stoke Newington. On attaining his seventy-second year he was presented (25 May 1822) to a vacant stall in Ely Cathedral, through which preferment he was enabled to resign his secretaryship, and ultimately his post as lecturer of Islington. He then took a prominent position in assisting church institu-

tions in Western America, and in 1823 acted as trustee of the funds collected for the infant church of Ohio. He died on 29 June 1829, from a rapid succession of epileptic fits. Gaskin was married in early life to Elizabeth Broughton, daughter of the Rev. Thomas Broughton, rector of Allhallows, Lombard Street, and of Wotton, Surrey. His published works are few and unimportant, consisting of various sermons delivered on special occasions. He compiled and revised in 1798 the uncorrected writings of the Rev. Richard Southgate, curate of St. Giles-in-the-Fields, and rector of Warsop, Nottinghamshire, who bequeathed him all his manuscript papers. In 1821 he published an edition of sermons written by the American bishop, Theodore Dehon.

[Gent. Mag. xcix. 183, 282, 643, 1848 pt. ii. 35; funeral sermon by Aug. Clissold, 1829; Foster's Alumni Oxon.; Nichols's Lit. Illustr. and Lit. Anecd. &c.]   W. F. W. S.

GASPARS (JASPERS), JAN BAPTIST (1620?–1691), portrait-painter, was a native of Antwerp, and in 1641–2 was admitted a member of the guild of St. Luke in that city. He was a pupil of Thomas Willeboorts Bosschaert. He came to England towards the close of Charles I's reign, and was one of the purchasers at the dispersal by Cromwell of that king's art-collections. He worked a great deal for General John Lambert [q. v.], and after the Restoration became little more than an assistant to Sir Peter Lely. Lely employed Gaspars to paint for him the draperies and postures of his portraits to such an extent that Gaspars obtained the nickname of 'Lely's Baptist.' He acted in a similar capacity for Sir Godfrey Kneller, and it is also said for Riley. Gaspars was, however, a clever draughtsman, and drew good designs for tapestry. He painted some fair portraits himself, including portraits of Charles II at the Painter-Stainers' Hall and at St. Bartholomew's Hospital, and a portrait of Thomas Hobbes, the philosopher, presented by Aubrey the antiquary to Gresham College. That he made reduced copies of pictures for engravers is probable from the existence in the print room of the British Museum of a drawing from Vandyck's picture of Lord John and Lord Bernard Stuart, made apparently for R. Tompson's engraving. The print room also possesses two impressions of a large etching by Gaspars, humorously depicting 'The Banquet of the Gods.' Gaspars died in London in 1691, and was buried in St. James's Church, Piccadilly. There is a portrait of him in the early edition of Walpole's 'Anecdotes of Painting.'

[Pilkington's Dict. of Painters; Walpole's Anecdotes of Painting, ed. Dallaway and Wornum; Immerzeel's Levens en Werken der Hollandsche en Vlaamsche Kunstschilders; Rombouts and Van Lerius, Liggeren van de St. Lucas-Gilde te Antwerpen; Redgrave's Dict. of Artists.]

L. C.

GASPEY, THOMAS (1788–1871), novelist and journalist, son of William Gaspey, a lieutenant in the navy, was born at Hoxton on 31 March 1788. While a youth he wrote verses for yearly pocket-books, and when about twenty contributed to 'Literary Recreations,' a monthly publication, edited by Eugenius Roche of the 'Morning Post.' Soon afterwards he was engaged as parliamentary reporter on the 'Morning Post,' contributing also dramatic reviews, clever political parodies, and reports of trials for treason. In this paper he wrote an 'Elegy on the Marquis of Anglesey's Leg,' a jeu d'esprit which has been persistently attributed to Canning. On the 'Morning Post' he was employed sixteen years, then for three or four years on the 'Courier,' a government paper, as sub-editor. In 1828 he bought a share in the 'Sunday Times,' the tone of which paper he raised as a literary and dramatic organ, Horace Smith, the Rev. T. Dale, Alfred Crowquill, E. L. Blanchard, Gilbert à Beckett, and others contributing. His novels and other publications include the following: 1. 'The Mystery,' 1820. 2. 'Takings, or the Life of a Collegian, with 26 Etchings by Richard Dagley,' 1821, 8vo. 3. 'Calthorpe, or Fallen Fortunes,' a novel, 1821, 3 vols. 4. 'The Lollards, a Tale,' 1822, 3 vols. 5. 'Other Times, or the Monks of Leadenhall,' 1823. 6. 'The Witch-Finder,' 1824, 3 vols. 7. 'The History of George Godfrey,' 1828, 3 vols. 8. 'The Self-Condemned,' 1836, 3 vols. 9. 'Many-Coloured Life,' 1842. 10. 'The Pictorial History of France,' 1843, written in conjunction with G. M. Bussey. 11. 'The Life and Times of the Good Lord Cobham,' 1843, 2 vols. 12mo. 12. 'The Dream of Human Life,' 1849–52, 2 vols. unfinished. 13. 'The History of England from George III to 1859,' 1852–9, 4 vols. 14. 'The History of Smithfield,' 1852. 15. 'The Political Life of Wellington,' vol. iii. 1853, 4to.

He was for many years the senior member of the council of the Literary Fund. He was a very kindly man, genial, witty, and an excellent mimic. The last twenty years of his life were spent quietly on his property at Shooter's Hill, Kent, where he died on 8 Dec. 1871, aged 83, and was buried at Plumstead, Kent.

He married Anne Camp in 1810 or 1811,

and she died on 22 Jan. 1883. His son, Thomas W. Gaspey, Ph.D., of Heidelberg, who died on 22 Dec. 1871, was author of works on the Rhine and Heidelberg, and of several linguistic handbooks. Another son, William Gaspey (born at Westminster 20 June 1812, died at 17 St. Ann's Road, North Brixton, 19 July 1888), was a prolific writer in prose and verse.

[Information supplied by the late Mr. William Gaspey; British Museum, Advocates' Library, and other catalogues.]   C. W. S.

GASSIOT, JOHN PETER (1797–1877), scientific writer, was born in London 2 April 1797. He went to school at Lee, and afterwards was for a few years a midshipman in the royal navy. He married in 1818, and had nine sons and three daughters, six of whom survived him. Gassiot was a member of the firm of Martinez, Gassiot, & Co., wine merchants, of London and Oporto. He was a munificent friend to science. His house on Clapham Common was always open to his fellow-workers, and was provided with the best apparatus for scientific experiments. He was the chairman of the committee of Kew Observatory, which he helped to endow; he also endowed the Cowper Street Middle Class School, London, to which he bequeathed valuable apparatus; he founded the Royal Society Scientific Relief Fund; and was one of the founders of the Chemical Society in 1847. He was also a magistrate of Surrey. Gassiot wrote forty-four papers in various scientific periodicals; the first an 'Account of Experiments with Voltameters having Electrodes exposing different Surfaces,' appearing in the Electrical Society's 'Transactions,' 1837–40, pp. 107–10; and the last 'On the Metallic Deposit obtained from the Induction Discharge in Vacuum Tubes,' in the British Association Report for 1869, p. 46. His work was almost entirely concerned with the phenomena of electricity.

In the 'Philosophical Transactions' for 1840 and 1844, Gassiot, who was a fellow of the Royal Society, described experiments made with a view to obtaining an electric spark before the circuit of the voltaic battery was completed. For these experiments he constructed batteries of immense power, commencing with a water battery of five hundred cells, and ending with 3,500 Leclanché cells. In 1844 he published perhaps his most important research—his experiments with a battery of one hundred Grove's cells, specially made of glass, with long glass stems, so that each cell was effectually insulated from its neighbours. With this battery Gassiot was able to prove that the static effects of a battery increase with its chemical action, a fact which had been denied or doubted by other experimenters.

In 1844 Gassiot showed by experimenting with delicate micrometer apparatus (*Philosophical Magazine* for October) that Grove's arguments against the contact theory of electricity were correct. In conducting a series of experiments upon the decomposition of water by electricity, Gassiot showed that when the liquid was under a pressure of 447 atmospheres it offered no extra resistance to the passage of the electric current. In 1852 Grove discovered the dark bands, striæ, or stratification, of the electric discharge; and to the study of this phenomenon he devoted much time and money. He showed that these striæ accompany all electric discharges in vacuum tubes, and that they occur equally well when, as is the case when the discharge takes place in the Torricellian vacuum of a barometer, no contact-breaker is employed. His researches on this matter formed the subject of the Bakerian lecture before the Royal Society in 1858. Gassiot further proved that when vacuum tubes are exhausted of their gases beyond a certain limit, the electric discharge will not pass at all. Gassiot died in the Isle of Wight, 15 Aug. 1877.

[Journ. of Chemical Soc. for 1878, xxxiii. 227; Nature for September 1877, pp. 388, 399; Royal Soc. Cat. of Scientific Papers; information communicated by relatives.] W. J. H.

GAST, LUCE DE (*fl.* 1199?), knight and lord of the castle of Gast, near Salisbury, is mentioned in preambles to many manuscripts of the great prose romance of Tristan. It is stated that he wondered that no one had translated into French the Latin book containing the history of the Saint Graal, and at length decided to do so himself, although in language he belonged rather to England, where he was born (MSS. 6768 and 6771 in *Bibliothèque*, and *Add. MS.* 23929 in Brit. Mus.) Only the first part of Tristan is ascribed to Gast, the second being assigned to Hélie de Borron. It is at least questionable whether either writer ever existed. Gast professes, and in this Hélie de Borron supports him, to have been the first to make use of the records of the Round Table, and to have chosen Tristan for his hero, as being the most puissant knight that was ever in Britain before King Arthur, or afterwards, save only for Lancelot and Galahad. But whereas the Tristan is full of allusions to the Saint Graal and to Lancelot, these romances never mention Tristan as an Arthurian hero; the romance of Tristan was therefore probably the later composition. Nor is there any proof of the existence of a Latin original. In all probability the prose romance of Tristan was founded on the lost poem of Chrétien de Troyes, which must have been written about 1160. It is also noticeable that in the Quest of the Saint Graal, the Records (of the Quest, at all events) are said to be kept 'en l'aumoire de Salebères.' It looks as if the whole story of the knight, his castle, and the Latin book were an invention intended to give an appearance of authority to the romance. The Tristan was first printed at Rouen in 1489, and afterwards at Paris by Antoine Verard in two editions without date; again at Paris in 1514, 1520, 1533 (BRUNET, *Manuel du Libraire*, vol. v. col. 955). These printed copies follow the version as it was rearranged by writers of the fourteenth and fifteenth centuries, and differ greatly from the original work. One manuscript (Bibliothèque 6976) ascribes to Gast the 'Roman de Guyron le Courtois,' which is more commonly assigned to Hélie de Borron. The name is variously spelt Gast, Galt, Gant, or Gay. It has been endeavoured to identify it with one of two castles called Gât in Normandy, but all the manuscripts clearly describe Gast as 'voisin prochain de Salebères.'

[Paulin Paris' Manuscrits François de la Bibliothèque du Roi, vols. i. and iii.; Ward's Cat. of Romances in the Brit. Mus. vol. i.; Gaston Paris' Littérature Française au Moyen Age. The writer has also to thank Mr. Ward for some additional information.] C. L. K.

GASTINEAU, HENRY (1791–1876), painter in water-colours, was a student at the Royal Academy. He commenced his artistic career as an engraver, but soon relinquished that branch of art for painting, commencing in oil, but eventually settling down exclusively to water-colour. He joined the Society of Painters in Water-colours in 1818, and then exhibited for the first time. In 1821 he was elected an associate, and in 1823 a full member. He continued to exhibit for fifty-eight years continuously, during which he worked unweariedly at his profession, and with unflagging powers. He exhibited eleven pictures when eighty-five years of age. As a contemporary of David Cox, Copley Fielding, G. Cattermole, S. Prout, and others, he adhered throughout his life to the old style and manner of water-colour painting. Though he cannot be said to have attained the first rank in his profession, he showed great taste and discrimination in the treatment of his subjects, and, if these indicated little variation, he exhibited so refined a feeling for nature that they are highly valued by artists and others as examples of a thoroughly good workman in his art. Gastineau also devoted a great deal of his time to teaching, both privately and at various schools. Early in life he built for himself a house, Norfolk Lodge, in Cold Harbour Lane, Camberwell, and continued to reside there until his death on 17 Jan. 1876 in his eighty-sixth year. He was then the oldest living member of the Old Society of Painters in Water-colours. He left a family, one of whom, Maria Gastineau, was also a water-colour painter of some distinction. At the South Kensington Museum there are by him ' Penrhyn Castle ' and ' Netley Abbey.' Few comprehensive exhibitions of water-colour paintings have been without some example of his art. Some views in Scotland by him were published in lithography, which he seems to have occasionally practised himself. His favourite subject was scenery of a wild and romantic character.

[Art Journal, 1876, p. 106; Builder, 1876, p. 108 ; The Year's Art, 1885 ; Redgrave's Dict. of Artists; Graves's Dict. of Artists, 1760-1880.]

L. C.

GASTRELL, FRANCIS (1662-1725), bishop of Chester, born at Slapton, Northamptonshire, on 10 May 1662, and baptised the day of his birth, was the second of the two sons of Henry Gastrell of Slapton, a gentleman of property, descended from the Gastrells of Gloucestershire, by Elizabeth, daughter of Edward Bagshaw (*d.* 1662) [q. v.], of Morton Pinkney, Northamptonshire. The father died in early life, and left two sons and two daughters. Edward, the eldest son, inherited the family estate; Francis, the second, was in his fifteenth year admitted on the foundation at Westminster under Busby, and elected student of Christ Church, Oxford, 17 Dec. 1680. He graduated B.A. 13 June 1684, and M.A. 20 April 1687. He was ordained deacon 29 Dec. 1689, and priest 25 June 1690. On 23 June 1694 he proceeded B.D., probably because in that month he was elected preacher at Lincoln's Inn. In 1696 he published anonymously 'Some Considerations concerning the Trinity, and the ways of managing that Controversy.' He appears to combat Sherlock, dean of St. Paul's, more as a mediator than a partisan. The 'Considerations' were approved by John Scott [q. v.], author of the 'Christian Life,' and have been reprinted by Bishop Randolph in his 'Enchiridion Theologicum,' 1792. Sherlock replied in 1698, and Gastrell rejoined in a 'Defence of the Considerations' in the same year. In 1697 Archbishop Tenison appointed Gastrell Boyle lecturer, much to the mortification of Evelyn, who desired the reappointment of Bentley. Bentley, however, said himself that Gastrell was well fitted for

the task. The Boyle lectures were published as 'The Certainty and Necessity of Religion in general ; or the first Grounds and Principles of Human Duty Established,' 1697. In 1699 he published a continuation entitled 'The Christian Revelation and the Necessity of believing it established; in opposition to all the Cavils and Insinuations of such as pretend to allow Natural Religion and reject the Gospel' (2nd edition, 1703). Bishop Van Mildert quotes this book in his appendix to his own Boyle lectures, and styles Gastrell a forcible writer.

These works attracted the attention of Harley, afterwards Earl of Oxford. On 13 July 1700 Gastrell commenced D.D., and in the following year, when Harley was appointed speaker of the House of Commons, he nominated Gastrell chaplain, and in January 1702-3 he was installed canon of Christ Church. On 20 Aug. 1703 he married, at the church of St. Helen, Bishopsgate, his kinswoman, Elizabeth, only daughter of the Rev. John Mapletoft, professor of physic in Gresham College, rector of Braybrooke, Northamptonshire, and vicar of St. Lawrence, Jewry. On 19 Jan. 1704 he preached a sermon, afterwards printed, before the House of Commons upon the fast day 'for the present war and the late dreadful tempest.' In 1705 he contributed towards the rebuilding of Peckwater Quad at Christ Church. In 1707 he preached a sermon on religious education at the annual meeting of the charity children, the result of the movement for the education of the poor begun in 1697. In the same year (1707) his 'Christian Institutes, or the Sincere Word of God,' one of his most popular works, appeared. It was translated into Latin by A. Tooke, Gresham professor of geometry, 1718. Many abridgments have been published. In 1708 appeared anonymously 'Principles of Deism truly represented' (2nd edition, 1709), which has been attributed to Gastrell. In 1711 he was proctor in convocation for the chapter of Christ Church, and was nominated a queen's chaplain. In 1712 he published a sermon preached before the queen, and in 1714 another before the House of Lords. On 4 April 1714 he was consecrated bishop of Chester at Somerset House Chapel. He resigned the preachership of Lincoln's Inn, but was allowed to hold his canonry of Christ Church *in commendam.* In 1714 he published anonymously 'Remarks upon the Scripture Doctrine of the Trinity by Dr. Samuel Clarke.' Clarke, in his 'Reply to Mr. Nelson,' acknowledges the fairness and ability of his antagonist. Gastrell had in 1711 been appointed one of the commissioners for building fifty new churches in and about London, and in the same year became a member of the Society for the Propagation of the Gospel. After the death of Anne, Gastrell opposed the whig ministry in the House of Lords. On 6 Dec. 1716 his only son died of small-pox, and was buried in Christ Church Cathedral. In 1717 he warmly defended the university of Oxford when it was attacked in the House of Lords for a pretended riot on the birthday of the Prince of Wales. In 1719, out of zeal for the honour of the university, he was involved in a contest with the crown and the Archbishop of Canterbury as to the legal qualification for the wardenship of Manchester College. Samuel Peploe [q. v.] had been presented by George I, and obtained the necessary qualification of the B.D. degree from Archbishop Wake instead of going to Oxford. The court of king's bench declared in Peploe's favour. Gastrell vindicated himself in 'The Bishop of Chester's Case with relationship to the Wardenship of Manchester. In which is shown that no other degrees but such as are taken at the University can be deemed legal qualifications for any ecclesiastical preferment in England.' This was printed at both universities in folio, 1721. The university of Oxford decreed in full convocation a vote of thanks to the bishop. In 1723 Gastrell strongly opposed the bill for inflicting pains and penalties upon Atterbury, and censured the rest of the bishops, who, with the exception of Dawes, archbishop of York, concurred in the measure. In 1725 Gastrell published anonymously his 'Moral Proof of the Certainty of a Future State,' of which a few copies, printed a year before, had been given to friends. It was reissued in 1728.

On 24 Nov. 1725 he died of gout at Christ Church. Hearne asserts (manuscript *Diary*, cx. 56) that he refused to take a bottle of port wine which might have saved him, saying that he would rather die than drink. In his will he desires if he should die at Chester then to be buried there, but if at any other place as near his dear child as possible at Christ Church. He was accordingly buried at Christ Church. Upon the death of his wife in the parish of St. Margaret, Westminster, 31 Jan. 1761, a monument was erected at Christ Church. The bishop left an only daughter, Rebecca, who married Francis Bromley, D.D., rector of Wickham, Hampshire, second son of the Right Hon. William Bromley of Baginton (1664–1732) [q. v.], and was left a widow in 1753.

In one of Hearne's manuscript notebooks for 17 Jan. 1728 he says: 'Yesterday I called upon Dr. Stratford, Canon of Ch. Ch., who gave me a print of the late Bp. of Chester,

Dr. Gastrell, curiously done by Vertue at the charges of the present Earl of Oxford, from a paint by Dahl.' Gastrell is frequently mentioned by Swift in terms of admiration. He seems to have been the first prelate who truly conceived what the duties of a diocesan bishop ought to be. Consequently he compiled a thorough record of every parish, church, school, and ecclesiastical institution in his diocese. It is entitled 'Notitia Cestriensis, or the Historical Notices of the Diocese of Chester, by the Rt. Rev. Francis Gastrell, D.D., Lord Bishop of Chester.' This has been printed from the original manuscript for the Chetham Society, with illustrative notes and a memoir by the Rev. F. R. Raines, M.A., incumbent of Milnrow, in vols. viii. xix. xxi. and xxii. of the Chetham Society's Papers, Manchester, 1845–50, 4to. 'One of the most accomplished historians of the present day,' says Mr. Raines, ' declares this the noblest document extant on the subject of the ecclesiastical antiquities of the diocese.'

Peploe was appointed Gastrell's successor in the see of Chester. 'This is done,' says Tom Hearne, ' to insult the ashes of Bp. Gastrell.'

[Memoir by the Rev. F. Raines in Chetham Society's Transactions; Hearne's manuscript Diaries in the Bodleian Library. The notice of Gastrell in the Biog. Brit. is said to be by Browne Willis.]   R. H–R.

GATACRE, THOMAS (*d.* 1593), divine, was younger son of William Gatacre of Gatacre Hall, Shropshire, where the family had maintained an uninterrupted succession from the time of Edward the Confessor. His parents, zealous Roman catholics, intended him for the law, and he was admitted a student of the Middle Temple about 1553. John Popham, afterwards lord chief justice, was a fellow-student, and became his intimate friend. Some of Gatacre's kindred were 'high in place,' and while visiting them he was present at the examinations of protestant confessors, whose constancy impressed him in favour of their opinions. With a view to confirm him in the old faith, his parents removed him to the English college at Louvain, at the same time settling on him an estate which brought in 100*l.* a year. Finding him strengthened in his protestantism after six months at Louvain, his father recalled him to England, obtained his consent to the revocation of the settlement, and cast him off. Gatacre found friends, who provided him with the means of studying for eleven years at Oxford, and for four years at Magdalene College, Cambridge. There is no record of his graduation. In 1568 he was ordained deacon and priest by Grindal, bishop of London, and became domestic chaplain to Robert Dudley, earl of Leicester. On 21 June 1572 he was collated to the rectory of St. Edmund's, Lombard Street. In addition he was admitted to the vicarage of Christ Church, Newgate, on 25 Jan. 1577, but resigned this preferment in the following year. Fuller describes him as a 'profitable pastor.' His puritan principles are assumed by Brook, without much direct evidence. He died in 1593, his successor at St. Edmund's being instituted on 2 June in that year.

He married Margaret Pigott, of a Hertfordshire family, and left a son Thomas [see GATAKER, THOMAS].

[Ashe's Narrative, appended to Gray Hayres crowned with Grace, 1655; Fuller's Worthies, 1662, 'Shropshire,' p. 3; Clarke's Lives of Thirty-two English Divines, 1677, pp. 248 sq.; Biog. Brit. 1747, iv. 2155 sq.; Brook's Lives of the Puritans, 1813, ii. 68; Cooper's Athenæ Cantabr. 1861, ii. 164 sq.] A. G.

GATAKER, THOMAS (1574–1654), puritan divine and critic, was born on 4 Sept. 1574, in the rectory house of St. Edmund's, Lombard Street. His father was Thomas Gatacre [q. v.]; the son changed the spelling of his name 'to prevent miscalling' (ASHE). He was a bookish boy, and subject from childhood to excruciating headaches. In his sixteenth year (1590) he was entered at St. John's College, Cambridge, where he gained a scholarship and graduated M.A. His zest for Greek learning is shown by his attendance at the extra lecture given by John Bois [q. v.] at four o'clock in the morning 'in his bed.' With a fellow-student, Richard Stock, he contracted a close friendship, which riveted his attachment to the puritan principles inculcated by his tutors, Henry Alvey, B.D., and Abdias Ashton. In 1596 Gataker was nominated one of the first fellows of Sidney Sussex College. While the building was in progress he became tutor and chaplain in the household of William Ayloffe of Braxted, Essex, teaching Hebrew to Ayloffe, and preparing his eldest son for the university. From John Stern, suffragan bishop of Colchester, a near relative of Ayloffe's wife, he received ordination. Coming into residence at Sidney Sussex in 1599, the building being still unfinished, he gave accommodation in his rooms to another fellow, William Bradshaw (1571–1618) [q. v.], an act of courtesy which led to a long friendship. Gataker was successful in training students, but his career as a college tutor was short. A scheme was set on foot by Ashton and the famous William Bedell [q. v.] for providing preachers in neglected parishes round Cambridge. Gataker undertook Sunday duty at Everton, Bedford-

shire, where the vicar was reported to be 130 years of age. After half a year of this employment he left the university, on the advice of Ashton. The step seems to have followed the retirement of Bradshaw, who was in trouble through espousing the cause of John Darrel [q. v.], the exorcist (GATAKER, Life of Bradshaw, pp. 32 sq.)

Gataker removed to London about the end of 1600, and became tutor in the family of Sir William Cooke at Charing Cross, 'to whose lady he was near by blood.' He preached occasionally at St. Martin's-in-the-Fields. An old man-servant to the wife of James Ley (afterwards lord high treasurer) remarked that 'he was a prettie pert boy, but he made a reasonable good sermon' (Disc. Apol. p. 34). He obtained the lectureship at Lincoln's Inn through the good offices of James Montague, master of Sidney Sussex, who had come to London with the intention of bringing him back to fill a Hebrew chair. When he entered on his duties at Lincoln's Inn (1601) there was but one Sunday lecture at seven o'clock in the morning; he got this altered to the usual hour, and transferred the Wednesday lecture to the Sunday afternoon. His salary for the first five years was 40l., and never more than 60l. Till he married he continued to live with Cooke, spending his vacations at Cooke's country seat in Northamptonshire. In 1603 he commenced B.D., when he preached for the only time at St. Mary's, Cambridge, on 25 March, the day after the death of Elizabeth. The morning preacher had prayed for the queen; the news came down about noon; James had not yet been proclaimed; Gataker prayed 'for the present supream governor.' He refused in 1609, and subsequently, to proceed to D.D., giving two reasons, his not being well enough off to maintain the dignity, 'and also because, like Cato the censor, he would rather have people ask why he had no statue than why he had one.' He declined the lectureship at the Rolls, with double his existing emolument, besides preferment offered him in Shropshire by Sir Roger Owen, and in Kent by Sir William Sedley.

In 1611 he accepted the rectory of Rotherhithe, Surrey, mainly at the instance of his friend Stock, the alternative being the appointment of an unworthy person. While his health permitted he was assiduous in public and pastoral duty; his Friday catechetical lectures for children were crowded, and 'his parlour was one of the best schooles for a young student to learn divinity in.' In 1620 he spent a month (13 July–14 Aug.) in Holland, travelling with a nephew, in order to inform himself of the condition of Dutch protestantism, whose interests he thought imperilled by the foreign policy of England. He found time for close and continuous study, and for learned correspondence with such men as Ussher, but while in active ministerial employment he published little except controversial tracts against popery and on justification. He first appeared as an author (1619) in a pamphlet on the lawfulness of lots when not used for divination, which exposed him to attack as an advocate for games of hazard.

In 1643 Gataker was nominated a member of the Westminster assembly of divines. He was one of those who scrupled at the covenant in its original form, and procured the insertion of an explanatory clause relating to episcopacy. His views on church government tallied with those of Ussher, being in favour of 'a dulie bounded and wel regulated prelacie joined with presbyterie.' In 1644 he was put on the committee for examination of ministers. He had declined the mastership of Trinity College, Cambridge, offered him by the Earl of Manchester. On 4 March 1645 he was placed on a committee to select fit persons for translating the directory into Welsh. On 12 May he was elected one of the committee of seven charged with the preparation of the first draft of a confession of faith. In the discussions on this symbol he differed from the majority in the article of justification, and obtained a somewhat less rigid definition, which he accepted for the sake of unity. After 1645 the failure of his health precluded him from attendance either at the assembly or the local classis, as well as from preaching, though he still administered the sacraments, and did some little pastoral work. He signed the first address, 18 Jan. 1649, against the trial and execution of the king. He was reflected on for not resigning his benefice, but there was a difficulty in finding a man to suit patron and people. As for the emoluments, he goes minutely into his receipts and expenditure to prove that he was not 'gripple' (grasping). Practically he disbursed the whole net income of his preferment in improvements and the provision of a good curate. As an assembly man he did not receive half the charge of his boat hire.

Gataker in his enforced leisure published his critical labours on subjects both classical and biblical. His best known works are his edition of Marcus Antoninus and his commentaries on Isaiah, Jeremiah, and Lamentations in the assembly's 'Annotations' (1645 and 1651). His scholarship was minute and fastidious; a peculiarity of his Latin orthography is the invariable omission of u after q. He had a vast memory, enabling him to dispense with common-place books. From some conventional marks of the puritan he was free; the term 'Lord's day' he preferred to 'Sabbath,' and thought even 'Sunday' admissible, as sanctioned by Justin Martyr (Disc. Apol. p. 14). He criticised the style of the New Testament against the purists. He has been cited as favouring 'Jehovah' as the correct pronunciation of the tetragrammaton; in fact he leans to 'Jahveh,' but is content to retain the ordinary form, his main point being that any approach to the original is better than the substituted word 'Lord.' Shortly before his death he composed 'a pious epigram,' consisting of two quaint stanzas, of some power.

Gataker died of fever on 27 July 1654, and was buried in his church; no stone marks his grave. He would never allow his portrait to be taken; he is described as a spare man of medium stature, of fresh complexion, but early grey. He was four times married: first (shortly before 1611) to the widow (having two daughters) of William Cupp or Cupper; she died in childbed, leaving a son, Thomas, who went into trade, and died before his father; secondly, to a daughter of the Rev. Charles Pinner, and cousin of Sir Nicholas Crisp [q. v.]; she also died in childbed, leaving a son Charles [see below]; thirdly, to a sister of Sir George and Sir John Farwell; she died of consumption, having outlived a son and daughter, but leaving a daughter, who married one Draper, and survived her father; fourthly (in 1628), to a citizen's widow (d. 1652), by whom he had no issue.

He published: 1. 'Of the Nature and Use of Lots,' &c., 1619, 4to; 2nd edit., 1627, 4to. 2. 'A Just Defence,' &c. (of the preceding, against J. Balmford and E. Elton), 1623, 4to. 3. 'A Discourse of Transubstantiation,' &c., 1624, 4to. 4. 'Certaine Sermons,' &c., 1637, fol. (a collection, most having been separately printed). 5. 'Antithesis,' &c., 1638, 4to (in answer to 'Theses' on lots, by William Ames (1571 [not 1576]–1633) [q. v.] and Gisbert Voet). 6. 'Francisci Gomari Disputationis ... Elenchus,' &c., 1640, 8vo (on justification). 7. 'Animadversiones in J. Piscatoris et L. Lucii . . . de causa . . . justificationis,' &c., 1641, 12mo. 8. 'Master Anthony Wotton's Defence,' &c., 1641, 12mo (the 'defence' is by Samuel Wotton, son of Anthony; the preface and postscript are by Gataker). 9. 'A True Relation of Passages between Master Wotton and Master Walker,' &c., 1642, 4to. 10. 'An Answer to Master George Walker's Vindication,' &c., 1642, 4to. 11. 'De Nomine Tetragrammato,' &c., 1645, 8vo. 12. 'De Diphthongis,' &c., 1646, 12mo. 13. 'A Mistake . . . removed . . . answer to . . . a treatise of Mr. J. Saltmarsh,' &c., 1646, 4to;

with new title, 'Arminianism Discovered and Confuted,' &c., 1652, 4to. Saltmarsh replied in 'Reasons for Unitie,' &c., 1646, 4to, and Gataker rejoined in 14. 'Shadows without Substance,' &c., 1646, 4to. 15. 'De Novi Instrumenti Stylo Dissertatio,' &c., 1648, 4to. 16. 'Mysterious Clouds and Mists,' &c., 1648, 4to (answer to J. Simpson). 17. 'God's Holy Minde touching Matters Morall,' &c., 1648, 4to (on the decalogue; preface signed T. G.) 18. 'Cinnus, sive Adversaria Miscellanea,' &c., 1651, 4to. 19. 'Marci Antonini De Rebus Suis,' &c., 1652, 4to (Greek text, with Latin version and commentary). 20. 'De Baptismatis Infantilis Vi . . . disceptatio . . . inter . . . S. Wardium . . . et T. Gatakerum,' 1652 [i.e. 25 Jan. 1653], 8vo (against justification in baptism). 21. 'Vindication of the Annotations . . . against . . . W. Lillie, J. Swan, and another,' &c., 1653, 4to. 22. 'A Discours Apologetical, wherein Lilies lewd and lowd Lies . . . are cleerly laid open,' &c., 1654 [27 Feb.], 4to (postscript against John Gadbury [q. v.]; valuable for its autobiographical particulars). Posthumous were: 23. 'Adversaria Miscellanea,' &c., 1659, fol. (edited by C. Gataker; prefixed is Gataker's autobiography in Latin). 24. 'An Antidote against Errour concerning Justification,' &c., 1670, 4to (an unfinished exposition of Rom. iii. 28, begun 19 April 1640; not completed, out of respect to the Westminster assembly). 25. 'The Life and Death of Master William Bradshaw,' in Clarke's 'Lives of Thirty-two English Divines,' 1677, fol. Gataker's 'Opera Critica' were collected in two vols. folio, Utrecht, 1697–8. He edited S. Ward's 'Balme from Gilead,' 1617, 8vo, a selection of Galen's 'Opuscula,' annotated by Theodore Goulston, M.D. [q. v.], 1640, 4to, and other works.

CHARLES GATAKER (1614?–1680), son of the above, by his second wife, was born at Rotherhithe about 1614, and educated at St. Paul's School and Sidney Sussex College, Cambridge, where he graduated B.A. He afterwards entered as a commoner at Pembroke College, Oxford, and graduated M.A. on 30 June 1636. He was chaplain to Lucius Cary, second viscount Falkland [q. v.] Through the interest of Charles, earl of Carnarvon, he became about 1647 rector of Hoggeston, Buckinghamshire, where he died on 20 Nov. 1680, and was buried in the chancel. He edited some of his father's posthumous works, appending to No. 24 (above) his own first publication, viz., 1. 'The Harmony of Truth; or . . . St. Paul and St. James reconciled,' &c., 1670, 4to. On the same subject he had communicated anonymously in 1670 to Bishop Nicholson of Gloucester, and others, some 'Animadversions' upon Bull's

'Harmonia Apostolica,' 1669–70. Nicholson sent them to Bull, who replied in his 'Examen Censuræ,' 1675. He wrote also: 2. 'An Answer to five . . . questions . . . by a Factor for the Papacy,' &c., 1673, 4to (included is a letter, dated 1636, by Falkland). 3. 'The Papists' Bait,' &c., 1674, 4to (with another letter by Falkland). 4. 'Examination of the case of the Quakers concerning Oaths,' &c., 1675, 4to (answered by George Whitehead). 5. 'Ichnographia Doctrinæ de Justificatione,' &c., 1681, 4to.

[Discours Apologetical, 1654; Autobiog. of Gataker in Adversaria Miscellanea, 1659; Ashe's Gray Hayres crowned with Grace, a funeral sermon with memoir, 1655; Life in Clarke's Lives of Thirty-two English Divines, 1677, pp. 248 sq.; Wood's Athenæ Oxon. (Bliss), iii. 1257; Middleton's Biographia Evangelica, 1784, iii. 290 sq.; Brook's Lives of the Puritans, 1813, iii. 200 sq.; Chalmers's Gen. Biog. Dict. 1814, xv. 334 sq., 340 sq.; Neal's Hist. of the Puritans, 1822, iii. 451 sq.; Smith's Bibliotheca Anti-Quakeriana, 1873, p. 197; Mitchell and Struthers's Minutes of Westminster Assembly, 1874, pp. 67, 91, &c.; Mitchell's Westminster Assembly, 1883, pp. 156, 409, &c.]   A. G.

GATES, BERNARD (1685?–1773), musician, was the second son of Bernard Gates, gentleman, of St. Margaret's, Westminster, whose will was proved on 21 May 1718. His name appears in the list of children of the Chapel Royal in 1702. At the end of 1708 (after 1 Oct.) he was sworn a gentleman of the Chapel Royal in the place of J. Howell, who died on 15 July in that year. He held the sinecure office of tuner of the regals at court, and was a member of the choir of Westminster Abbey. He married before 1717, since on 6 June of that year his eldest child, a daughter named Atkinson, was buried in the north cloister of Westminster Abbey. This unusual christian name, which was borne by another daughter of Gates (buried 1736), was derived from a Mrs. Atkinson, who had been laundress to Queen Anne, and who had brought up Mrs. Gates, and made her her heiress. At some time before 1732 Gates was made master of the children of the Chapel Royal (the date given in Grove's 'Dict.' for this appointment is manifestly too late). On 23 Feb. 1732 Handel's 'Esther' was performed at Gates's house in James Street, Westminster, by the children of the chapel. The same singers sang the work at a subscription concert at the Crown and Anchor Tavern, and again at the room in Villiers Street, York Buildings. In 1734 Gates seceded from the Academy of Vocal Music, taking the children of the chapel with him. He had been a prominent member of the society from its inauguration. Gates sang one of the airs in the first performance of the 'Dettingen Te Deum' in 1743. In 1737 (10 March) Mrs. Gates died, and in 1758 Gates moved to North Aston, Oxfordshire. He died there on 15 Nov. 1773, and was buried in the north cloister of Westminster Abbey on the 23rd of the month. The inscription on his monument, which is the authority for many particulars as to his family, &c., gives his age as eighty-eight. His will, dated 5 Oct. 1772, was proved on 28 Nov. 1773. Failing the issue of a nephew, Bernard Downes, to whom the estate at North Aston was left, he bequeathed his property to Dr. Thomas Sanders Dupuis [q. v.], who had been his pupil, with a further remainder to Dr. Arnold. He directed that his chaise horse should be kept on his estate at Aston without working, that it should never be killed, and that when it died naturally it should be buried without mutilation of any kind. Hawkins says that in his singing there was such an exaggeration of the shake as to destroy the melody altogether, and that the boys of the chapel had adopted the same habit. He also says that Gates introduced into the chapel the system, then lately revived by Pepusch, of solmisation by the hexachords. A tablet to his memory was put up in the church of North Aston, at the expense of his pupil, Dr. Dupuis.

[Grove's Dict. i. 10, 587; Chester's Westminster Abbey Registers; Chapel Royal Cheque Book, ed. Rimbault; Add. MS. 11732; Notes and Queries, 3rd ser. iv. 204; Hawkins's Hist. ed. 1853, pp. 735, 832, 885; Burney's Hist. iv. 360, where the date of the first performance of Esther is given as 1731. It is pointed out in W. S. Rockstro's Life of Handel that the mistake arose from a confusion between the old and new styles.]   J. A. F. M.

GATES, SIR JOHN (1504?–1553), statesman, born about 1504, was the eldest son of Sir Geoffrey Gates (d. 1526) by Elizabeth, daughter of William Clopton (MORANT, Essex, ii. 146, 457). Henry VIII made him a gentleman of the privy chamber. In January 1535 he was placed on the committee for Essex and Colchester appointed to inquire into tenths of spiritualities (Letters and Papers of Reign of Henry VIII, ed. Gairdner, viii. 49). He became a justice of the peace for Essex in July 1536 (ib. xi. 85), and in the ensuing October was ordered to accompany the king on the expedition to quell the Lincolnshire rebellion (ib. xi. 233, 261). He was appointed one of three commissioners authorised to sign all documents by stamp in the name and on behalf of the king by patent dated 31 Aug. 1546 (State Papers of Henry VIII, i. 629). In December of the same year Gates, along

with Sir R. Southwell and Sir W. Carew, was despatched to Kenninghall, Norfolk, to bring back the Duchess of Richmond [see under FITZROY, MARY] and Elizabeth Holland, that they might give evidence against the Duke of Norfolk and the Earl of Surrey. He sent the king a graphic account of his proceedings (ib. i. 888–90). Henry rewarded him by a rich grant of lands and other property, including the college and rectory of Pleshey in Essex. He forthwith demolished the chancel of the church for the sake of making money of the materials, and obliged the parishioners to purchase what was left standing (MORANT, ii. 450, 454). He also obtained the under-stewardship and clerkship of Waltham Forest, and the clerkship of the court of Swanmote in the same (State Papers of Henry VIII, i. 896). At the coronation of Edward VI on 20 Feb. 1546–7 Gates was created a knight of the Bath, and took part in the jousts. On 23 June 1550, being then sheriff of Essex, he was ordered to enforce observance of the injunctions issued by Ridley, bishop of London, in regard to the 'plucking down of superaltaries, altars, and such like ceremonies and abuses.' In the following month he took measures to prevent the flight of the Princess Mary to Antwerp as contrived by the emperor Charles V. On 8 April 1551 the king made him his vice-chamberlain and captain of the guard, with a seat at the privy council, and gave him land to the value of 120l. In May 1552 he was chosen a commissioner to sell chantry lands and houses for payment of the king's debts; and on the following 4 July was made chancellor of the Duchy of Lancaster. Other favours were at this time conferred on Gates, who had become one of Northumberland's chief creatures, and supported him in promoting the celebrated 'devise' of succession in favour of Lady Jane Grey. He accompanied Northumberland in his expedition against Mary in July 1553. On 19 Aug. he was tried before a special commission, pleaded guilty, and was executed three days afterwards. Before he received the sacrament he expressed regret to Edward Courtenay, earl of Devonshire [q. v.], for his long imprisonment, of which he admitted himself in part the cause (Chronicle of Queen Jane, &c., Camd. Soc., p. 20). On the scaffold he warned the people against reading the Bible controversially as he had done. Three strokes of the axe severed his head. His possessions were forfeited to the crown.

[Morant's Essex, i. 323, and elsewhere; Gough's Pleshey; Harl. MS. 284; Chronicle of Queen Jane, &c. (Camd. Soc.); Bayley's Tower of London, App. p. xlix; Cal. State Papers,

Dom. 1547-80; Literary Remains of King Edward VI, ed. Nichols (Roxburghe Club); Froude's Hist. of England, ch. xxiii. xxx.]　　　G. G.

GATES, SIR THOMAS (*fl.* 1596–1621), governor of Virginia, was knighted in 1596 while serving in the expedition against Cadiz. He entered Gray's Inn 14 March 1597–8. In July 1604 he was in the Netherlands with Sir Henry Wotton, then proceeding to Vienna as ambassador. Sir Henry wrote in a letter of introduction to Winwood: 'I entreat you to love him [Gates], and to love me too, and to assure you that you cannot love two honester men.' Together with his fellow-captain Thomas Dale [see DALE, SIR THOMAS], Gates served subsequently in garrison in Oudewater, in South Holland. In April 1608 he obtained from the States-General leave of absence for one year. The special occasion for his absence was a commission from the king of England to proceed to Virginia. The first attempt to colonise Virginia having proved abortive, James I granted a new charter, dated 23 May 1609, with larger powers and privileges. Among the new adventurers were the Earl of Salisbury, Sir Francis Bacon, Captain John Smith, Sir Oliver Cromwell (uncle to the Protector), together with a number of public companies of London. The chief officers of the company were Sir Thomas Gates, lieutenant-general; Lord De la Warr, captain-general of Virginia; Sir George Somers, admiral; and Sir Thomas Dale, high marshal. The project excited great enthusiasm. Large sums of money were contributed, and so many persons desired to be transported that nine ships, with more than five hundred emigrants, were despatched in charge of Gates, Somers, and Captain Newport. They sailed from England at the close of May 1609, but only seven vessels arrived in Virginia. The ship of the three commissioners, the Sea Venture, was separated from the rest of the fleet by a furious hurricane, and stranded on the rocks of Bermuda. The passengers effected a landing, but six of the company died on the island. An account of the disaster written by one of the passengers, William Strachey, was published by Purchas in 1625, under the title of 'A True Reportory of the Wracke and Redemption of Sir Thomas Gates upon and from the Ilands of the Bermudas.' In 1610 appeared Silas Jourdan's 'Discovery of the Barmudas ... by Sir T. Gates ... with diuers others,' which was reprinted without acknowledgment with additional information in 1613. To both of these accounts Shakespeare is said to have been indebted for the groundwork of his play of 'The Tempest.' Gates and his fellow-voyagers remained nine months in Bermuda, where they con-

structed two vessels, partly from the wreck of the Sea Venture, and partly from cedars which they felled. Reaching Virginia on 24 May 1610, Gates found the colony in a desolate and miserable condition. After the departure of John Smith the colonists, uncontrolled by authority, had given way to excesses, and their numbers were further reduced by famine. They resolved to burn the town, but were prevented by Gates, who determined to sail for Newfoundland with the surviving colonists, in order to seek a passage for England. Lord De la Warr, however, arrived on 9 June 1610 with new colonists and supplies, and Gates returned with him to Jamestown.

Before the close of 1610 De la Warr despatched Gates to England for further supplies. The treasurer and council were inclined to abandon the enterprise altogether. Gates's report on oath, describing the territory, revived the hopes of the council. Nevertheless, many influential supporters withdrew from the undertaking, and their action seemed justified by the immediate return of De la Warr. But, as Gates still retained faith in the scheme, he succeeded in collecting new recruits. In March 1611 Sir Thomas Dale sailed from England with a year's supply in three ships for the colony; and about three months later Gates followed him with six ships carrying three hundred men, with ample supplies. Gates was accompanied by his wife and their two daughters. His wife died on the voyage, and his daughters had to be sent back. He arrived at Jamestown in August, and assumed the office of governor in succession to Sir Thomas Dale. Gates endeavoured to make religion the foundation of law and order. He effected a new settlement, and built a town called Henrico in honour of Prince Henry. His administration appears to have been discreet and provident. A third patent for Virginia, signed March 1612, granted to the shareholders in England the Bermudas and all islands within three hundred leagues of the Virginia shore, but this acquisition was subsequently transferred to a separate company. Gates returned to England in 1614, and endeavoured to revive and strengthen the fallen hopes of the London company of shareholders. He contemplated once more resuming his post in Virginia, but after De la Warr's death the treasurer and council appointed Captain Yeardley as captain-general and governor. Some time after his return to England in 1614 Gates repaired to the Netherlands, mainly for the purpose of obtaining the arrears of his pay, and was favoured by the States-General with immediate payment. Stith, in his 'History of Virginia,' cites a speech of Captain John Smith in 1621, wherein it is affirmed that Gates afterwards went to the East Indies and died there. From a list of shareholders in the English state paper office it appears that in 1623 fifty great shares, or five thousand acres of land in the colony of Virginia, stood in his name as owner. Nothing is known of his later career. His son, Captain Gates, served in the expedition of 1626 to Cadiz, and the next year at the Isle of Ré and Rochelle; at the latter place he was killed by a cannon-shot. Ten years afterwards his sisters petitioned the privy council for payment of the arrears due on his account, and the lord treasurer was authorised by the council to sign an order to that effect. The petitioners alleged that they were 'destitute of means to relieve their wants, or to convey themselves to Virginia, where their father, Sir Thomas Gates, Governor of that Isle [*sic*], died, and left his estate in the hands of persons who had ever since detained the same.'

[A Discovery of the Barmudas, otherwise called the Ile of Divels: by Sir Thomas Gates, Sir George Sommers, and Captayne Newport, with divers others. Set forth for the love of my country, and also for the good of the plantation in Virginia. By Sil. Jourdan, London, 1610; Purchas his Pilgrimage, or Relations of the World and the Religions observed in all Ages, London, 1625–6; Collections of the Massachusetts Historical Society, 4th ser. vol. ix., Boston, 1871; Justin Winsor's Narrative and Critical History of America, vol. iii.; Metcalfe's Knights; Bryant and Gay's Popular History of the United States; Appleton's Cyclopædia of American Biography.]
G. B. S.

GATFORD, LIONEL (*d.* 1665), royalist divine, a native of Sussex, was educated at Jesus College, Cambridge, of which he became a fellow. He proceeded B.A. in 1620–1, M.A. in 1625, and B.D. in 1633, was elected junior university proctor in 1631, and during the same year became vicar of St. Clement's, Cambridge. At Cambridge he was greatly shocked at the mild heresies of Dr. Eleazar Duncon [q. v.], and wrote a long letter on the subject to Lord Goring, 22 July 1633 (*Cal. State Papers*, Dom. 1633–4, pp. 150, 279). In 1637 he was presented by Sir John Rous to the rectory of Dennington, Suffolk. Soon after the outbreak of the civil war Gatford retired to Cambridge in order to write a pamphlet setting forth the doctrine of the church in regard to the obedience due to kings. On the night of 26 Jan. 1642–3 Cromwell seized his manuscript, then in the press at Cambridge, arrested Gatford in his bed at Jesus College, and sent both author and copy to London. On 30 Jan. the com-

mons ordered him to be imprisoned in Ely House, Holborn (*Commons' Journals*, ii. 953). Nothing daunted he contrived to publish in the following March a vigorous onslaught on anabaptists and other false teachers, called 'An Exhortation to Peace: with an Intimation of the prime Enemies thereof, lately delivered in a Sermon [on Psalm cxxii. 6], and newly published with some small Addition,' 4to, London, 1643. This was ordered by the commons on 3 July to be referred to the consideration of the committee for Cambridge (*ib.* iii. 153). After seventeen months' confinement Gatford was, upon an exchange of prisoners, set free, but was not allowed to return to Dennington, or to take duty elsewhere. He therefore went to Oxford, where he was kindly received by the mayor, Thomas Smith, in whose house he wrote, while the plague was raging, a whimsical tract, called 'Λόγος 'Αλεξιφάρμακος; or Hyperphysicall Directions in Time of Plague. Collected out of the sole authentick Dispensatory of the chief Physitian both of Soule and Body, and disposed more particularly . . . according to the method of those Physicall Directions printed by Command of the Lords of the Councell at Oxford, 1644,' &c. 4to, Oxford, 1644. Gatford soon after went to Cornwall as chaplain of Pendennis Castle (*Cal. State Papers*, Dom. 1661–2, p. 65). About July 1645 he drafted an address to Cornishmen (*Cal. Clarendon State Papers*, i. 271–2). In 1647 he was minister at Jersey, and there became a great favourite of Sir Edward Hyde, who made him his chaplain (*ib.* i. 316, 368, 416, ii. 19). His next publication was 'Englands Complaint: or a sharp Reproof for the Inhabitants thereof; against that now raigning Sin of Rebellion; but more especially to the Inhabitants of the County of Suffolk. With a Vindication of those Worthyes now in Colchester,' 4to, London, 1648. He fears that parliament will grant toleration to catholics, who will consequently return to power. He appears to have remained in exile about seven years. After his return he supported himself by taking boarders, and resided at different times at Kenninghall Place, Sanden House, Kilborough, and Swaffham in Norfolk. Thence he removed to Hackney, Middlesex, afterwards to Well Hall, Kent, and finally to Walham Green. He was much tormented by the county committees for persisting in keeping up the service of the church of England, and protested in 'A Petition for the Vindication of the Publique use of the Book of Common Prayer from some foul . . . aspersions lately cast upon it. . . . Occasioned by the late Ordinance for the ejecting of

scandalous . . . Ministers . . . ,' London, 1655.
Prefixed is a manly epistle to the parliament.
At the Restoration Gatford was created D.D.
by royal mandate. He found the chancel and
parsonage-house of Dennington in ruins, and,
as he could not afford to have them rebuilt,
petitioned the king for the vicarage of Plymouth, Devonshire, to which he was presented
on 20 Aug. 1661 (*Cal. State Papers*, Dom.
1661–2, pp. 65, 68). Gatford's last literary
labour was to defend his old patron, Sir John
Rous of Henham, Suffolk, from the attacks of
the puritan party in 'A true . . . Narrative of
the . . . death of Mr. William Tyrrell, and
the . . . preservation of Sr. John Rous . . .
and divers other gentlemen . . . ,' 4to, London, 1661. In August 1662 Dr. George, the
nonconformist vicar of Plymouth, was ejected,
but the corporation elected Roger Ashton as
his successor (ROWE, *Parish and Vicars of St.
Andrew, Plymouth*, p. 39). In 1663 the right
of appointing to the incumbency of Great
Yarmouth was disputed between the corporation of the town and the dean and chapter
of Norwich. Gatford, on the recommendation of Clarendon, then high steward of the
borough, was accepted by the corporation,
and allowed ' to officiate as curate during the
pleasure of the House.' Gatford died of the
plague in 1665, and the corporation allowed
his widow 100*l.* in consideration of the ' pains
he had taken in serving the cure for two
years' (PALMER, *Continuation of Manship*,
ii. 174–6; *Perlustration of Great Yarmouth*,
iii. 10). His son, Lionel Gatford, D.D., contributed a highly coloured account of his
parents' sufferings during the civil war to
Walker's ' Sufferings of the Clergy ' (pt. ii.
p. 255). Gatford has a Greek distich at
p. 20 of R. Winterton's ' Hippocratis Aphorismi,' 8vo, Cambridge, 1633.

[Addit. MSS. 5870 f. 172, 19091 ff. 259, 260 *b*;
Cal. of Clarendon State Papers, i. 305; Sober
Sadness, p. 35; Edward Simmons's Preface to
Woodnote's Hermes Theologus; Le Neve's Monu-
menta Anglicana, i. 304; Stow's Survey, ed.
Strype, bk. ii. p. 154; Le Neve's Fasti, ed. Hardy;
Cal. State Papers, Col. America and West Indies,
1661–8, p. 288; Cambr. Graduates.]   G. G.

GATLEY, ALFRED (1816–1863), sculptor, was born at Kerridge, about two miles
from Macclesfield in Cheshire, in 1816. While
still a child he learned the use of a stonemason's tools from his father, who owned and
worked two quarries in the Kerridge hills.
In 1837, by the aid of a few friends, he came
to London and obtained employment in the
studio of Edward Hodges Baily [q. v.] He
also studied in the British Museum, and two
years later became a student of the Royal
Academy, where he gained silver medals for

modelling from the antique, and in 1841 for the
first time exhibited a ' Bust of a Gentleman.'
In 1843 he left Baily and became an assistant to Musgrave L. Watson, and in the same
year he sent to the Royal Academy a marble
bust of ' Hebe,' which was purchased by the
Art Union of London and reproduced in
bronze. In 1844 he received the silver medal
for the best model from the life, and exhibited marble busts of ' Cupid ' and ' Psyche,'
and in 1846 he exhibited a bust of Marshal Espartero, and a model in bas-relief
of ' The Hours leading out the Horses of the
Sun,' now in the library of Britwell Court,
Buckinghamshire. In 1848 he sent to the
Royal Academy a bust of Dr. Sumner, archbishop of Canterbury, and in 1850 that of
Mr. Samuel Christie-Miller, who afterwards
became his steadfast friend. About 1851 he
executed a bust of Richard Hooker, now in
the Temple Church, but, although successful
in this and other works, he saw no prospect
of earning an adequate income in England,
and therefore towards the end of 1852 he
went to Rome, where he took a studio on
the Pincian Hill, and made the acquaintance
of John Gibson, whose enthusiasm for Greek
art he shared. Before long he completed a
bust of ' Alastor, or the Spirit of Solitude,'
and began statues of ' Echo ' and ' Night.'
A head in marble, ' The Angel of Mercy,' and
a design for a mural monument were his contributions to the Royal Academy in 1853.
Soon after his settlement in Rome, Mr.
Christie-Miller invited him to prepare designs
for the sculptural decorations of a mausoleum
to be erected to the memory of Mr. William
Henry Miller at Craigentinny, his estate near
Edinburgh. Gatley produced a model of a
large bas-relief representing ' The Overthrow
of Pharaoh in the Red Sea,' which was highly
praised by Gibson. Early in 1855 he was
entrusted with the companion bas-relief, ' The
Song of Moses and Miriam.' The Pharaoh
bas-relief was finished in time for the International Exhibition of 1862, but the ' Song
of Miriam ' was completed only just before
the sculptor's death. The two bas-reliefs
are in strong contrast to each other, the idea
of rejoicing being as powerfully given in the
one work as is that of fear and impending
destruction in the other. Gatley visited
England for the last time in 1862, but returned to Rome much depressed by his failure
to dispose of the works which he had sent to
the International Exhibition, where, besides
the noble bas-relief of ' Pharaoh,' he exhibited
his statues of ' Echo ' and ' Night,' as well as
four marble statuettes of recumbent animals—
lions, a lioness, and a tiger—which had gained
for him in Rome the name of the ' Landseer

of Sculpture.' He died from dysentery at Rome on 28 June 1863, and was buried in the English cemetery. His portrait, painted by a Portuguese artist named Da Costa, is in the sculptor's old home at Kerridge. His statue of 'Echo' is in the Peel Park Museum at Salford, and there also are a marble group of 'A Boy leading a Bull to Sacrifice,' and busts of Euripides and Paris copied in marble from antiques in the Vatican at Rome.

['Our Sculptor Friend,' by Miss M. A. Sumner, in Aunt Judy's Magazine, October 1885, pp. 722–736; Queen, 18 July 1863; Art Journal, 1863, p.181; Athenæum, 1863, ii. 117; Royal Academy Exhibition Catalogues, 1841–53.]   R. E. G.

GATLIFF, JAMES (1766–1831), clergyman, the son of James Gatliff of Manchester, 'chapman,' was baptised at St. Anne's Church, Manchester, 20 Sept. 1766, and educated at the Manchester grammar school. After serving in the militia he took holy orders, and in 1802, through the influence of his brother John, who was a fellow of the Manchester Collegiate Church, obtained the stipendiary curacy of Gorton Chapel near Manchester, and subsequently the incumbency of St. Thomas's Chapel, Heaton Norris. In 1808 he succeeded to the perpetual curacy of Gorton. He published a new edition of William Wogan's 'Essay on the Proper Lessons,' with a memoir of the author, 4 vols., 1818, which involved him in pecuniary difficulties with his publisher, and led to his imprisonment for debt and the sequestration of his living. After his liberation he published a statement of his case with the strange title of 'A Firm Attempt at Investigation; or the Twinkling Effects of a Falling Star to relieve the Cheshire Full-Moon' (i.e. the bishop of Chester), Manchester, 1820, 8vo. For some years he eked out a livelihood by preaching in Scotland, and in 1826 he returned to Gorton. In the following year he published 'Observations on the Life and Character of George Canning, delivered in a Discourse at Gorton Chapel.' He died in April 1831, and was buried in the chancel of his chapel.

[Booker's Didsbury (Chetham Soc.), p. 190; J. F. Smith's Reg. Manchester Grammar School (Chetham Soc.), i. 164, ii. 284, iii. 343; Higson's Gorton, 1852, pp. 130 seq.]   C. W. S.

GATTIE, HENRY (1774–1844), vocalist and actor, was born near Bath in 1774, and brought up to the trade of a wig-maker, but very early in life acquired a liking for the theatre. At the age of nineteen he had become well known at some musical associations. His first appearances on the stage were in vocal characters, such as Frederick in 'No Song No Supper,' Valentine in 'The Farmer,' and Captain Macheath. On 7 Nov. 1807 he came out at the Bath Theatre as Trot in Morton's comedy 'Town and Country,' and was next seen as Paul in 'Paul and Virginia,' but he soon settled down into playing as a general rule old men, Frenchmen, and Irishmen. Having been introduced by W. Lovegrove, the comedian, to Samuel James Arnold, the proprietor of the Lyceum Theatre, Gattie made his first appearance in London on 14 July 1813, in a new comic opera entitled 'M.P., or the Blue Stocking,' in which he took the character of La Fosse (Morning Post, 15 July 1813, p. 3), and afterwards played Sir Harry Sycamore and other old-men characters and footmen's parts. From this house he migrated to Drury Lane, where he was first seen, 6 Oct. 1813, as Vortex in 'A Cure for the Heartache.' He remained at Drury Lane until his retirement in 1833, filling up his summer vacations at the Haymarket, Lyceum, and other houses. At Drury Lane, where he was in the receipt of seven pounds a week, he was frequently the substitute for Munden, Dowton, Terry, and Charles Mathews, to none of whom, however, was he equal in talent. On 21 Aug. 1815 he took the part of the justice of the village in 'The Maid and the Magpie' at the Lyceum Theatre. His most celebrated and best-known impersonation was Monsieur Morbleu in Moncrieff's farce of 'Monsieur Tonson,' which was first played at Drury Lane on 20 Sept. 1821. His acting in this piece was much commended by George IV, who had commanded its performance on the occasion of a royal bespeak soon after its first production. Another of his characters was Dr. Caius in the 'Merry Wives of Windsor.' After a career of twenty-six years as an actor he retired from the stage in 1833, and opened a cigar-shop at Oxford, which became the resort of many of the collegians, by whom his dry humour was much appreciated. He was married, but had no family. His death took place at Reading 17 Nov. 1844, in the seventieth year of his age.

[Oxberry's Dramatic Biography (1826), iii. 37–46, with portrait; Genest, viii. 111, 399, ix. 96 et seq.; Era, 24 Nov. 1844, p. 6; Gent. Mag. December 1844, p. 654; Georgian Era, iv. 569.]   G. C. B.

GATTY, MARGARET (1809–1873), author of 'Aunt Judy's Tales,' youngest daughter and coheiress of the Rev. Alexander John Scott, D.D. [q. v.], Lord Nelson's chaplain in the Victory, was born at Burnham rectory, Essex, on 3 June 1809. Her mother died when she was two years old, and she was brought up at home by her father, a great lover and collector of books. At the age of ten she began to study in the print room of the British Museum, where she not only drew, but also made etchings on copper. The influence of German literature on some of her writings is very obvious, and probably had its beginning in her early admiration for Miss Elizabeth Smith. She was an excellent caligraphist, and long before illuminating was fashionable she illuminated on vellum, designing initials, reproducing the ancient strawberry borders with the gold raised and burnished as in the old models. On 8 July 1839 she married the Rev. Alfred Gatty, D.D., vicar of Ecclesfield, Yorkshire, where the remainder of her life was spent. In 1842 appeared 'Recollections of the Life of the Rev. A. J. Scott, D.D., Lord Nelson's Chaplain. By his Daughter and Son-in-law,' a very interesting book. She was forty-two years old when her first original work appeared. This was a series of stories brought out in 1851, under the title of 'The Fairy Godmothers, and other Tales,' which were most favourably received. This book was followed in 1855 by the first series of 'Parables from Nature,' with illustrations by herself. For some years she had made a study of seaweeds and zoophytes, and now formed the acquaintance of Dr. William Henry Harvey, the author of the 'Phycologia Britannica.' She was one of the first persons to show an interest in the use of chloroform on its introduction, and had it administered to herself to set a good example in Ecclesfield parish. In 1858 appeared her most popular child-book, 'Aunt Judy's Tales,' the title being taken from a family nickname of her daughter, Juliana Horatio Ewing [q. v.] During 1859 and 1860 she superintended the autobiography of Joseph Wolff, the Eastern traveller. By her advice he dictated his life, doing it in the third person, and ending the strange record with the formula, 'Wolff has done.' 'Aunt Judy's Letters' came out in 1862, but like many sequels was not equal in interest to the first work. In the same year she completed her book on 'British Seaweeds,' which was supervised by Dr. Harvey. It was written from fourteen years' experience, and was an attempt to combine scientific accuracy with the minimum of technicality. In May 1866 Mrs. Gatty established a monthly periodical for young people called 'Aunt Judy's Magazine.' This was a labour of love, and if the terms on which the editor lived with her contributors and child-correspondents were not very businesslike, they were at all events well adapted to so domestic a periodical. The juvenile subscribers to this magazine in

1868 and in 1876 raised two sums of 100*l.* each, with which two cots were endowed and maintained in the Hospital for Sick Children, Great Ormond Street, London. The magazine was edited after Mrs. Gatty's death by her daughter, H. K. F. Gatty, until October 1885, when it came to an end; but just before its conclusion another cot was founded in memory of Mrs. Gatty and of her daughter Mrs. Ewing. The fifth and last series of the 'Parables' was published in 1870. Besides being reprinted in America selections from the 'Parables' have been translated and published in the German, French, Italian, Russian, Danish, and Swedish languages. In 1872 her last books were brought out, 'A Book of Emblems' and the 'Book of Sun Dials.'

During the last ten years of her life Mrs. Gatty's health failed, and she gradually became disabled by paralysis. She bore her illness with the greatest resignation. Her writings are conspicuous for truthfulness, cheerfulness, humour, and the absence of false sentiment. She saw things from the point of view of the young people. She died at Ecclesfield vicarage on 4 Oct. 1873, and a memorial window, known as the Parable Window, was erected in Ecclesfield Church in 1874. Her second son, Sir Alfred Scott Scott-Gatty, became Garter King-of-Arms in 1904. Her husband, who was also a writer of repute, married again in 1889, and remained vicar of Ecclesfield till his death, 20 Jan. 1903, when nearly 90.

The following were Mrs. Gatty's works: 1. 'Recollections of the Rev. A. J. Scott,' 1842, with her husband. 2. 'The Fairy Godmothers, and other Tales,' 1851. 3. 'Parables from Nature,' 1855-71, 5 vols. 4. 'Worlds not Realised,' 1856. 5. 'Proverbs Illustrated,' 1857. 6. 'The Poor Incumbent,' 1858. 7. 'Legendary Tales,' with illustrations by Phiz, 1858. 8. 'Aunt Judy's Tales,' illustrated by Miss C. S. Lane, 1859. 9. 'The Human Face Divine, and other Tales,' 1860. 10. 'The Travels and Adventures of Dr. Wolff, the Missionary,' 1861, 2 vols., superintended by Mrs. Gatty. 11. 'The Old Folks from Home, or a Holiday in Ireland in 1861,' 1862. 12. 'Melchior's Dream,' by J. H. Gatty, ed. by Mrs. Gatty, 1862. 13. 'Aunt Judy's Letters,' 1862. 14. 'British Seaweeds, drawn from Professor Harvey's "Phycologia Britannica,"' 1863; another ed. 1872, 2 vols. 15. 'The History of a Bit of Bread,' by Professor J. Macé, translated from the French, 1864. 16. 'Aunt Sally's Life,' reprinted from 'Aunt Judy's Letters,' 1865. 17. 'Domestic Pictures and Tales,' 1866. 18. 'Aunt Judy's Magazine,' ed. by Mrs. Gatty, 1866-73, 6 vols. 19. 'Proverbs Illustrated, Worlds not Realised,' 1869. 20. 'The Children's Mission

Army,' reprinted from 'Mission Life,' 1869.
21. 'Mission Shillings,' reprinted from 'Mission Life,' 1869.   22. 'Waifs and Strays of
Natural History,' 1871.   23. 'Aunt Judy's
Song Book for Children.'   24. 'Select Parables from Nature, for Use in Schools,' 1872.
25. 'A Book of Emblems, with Interpretations thereof,' 1872.   26. 'The Mother's Book
of Poetry,' 1872.   27. 'The Book of Sun
Dials,' 1872.

[Parables from Nature, with a Memoir of the
Author (1885), pp. ix–xxi; A. Gatty's A Life at
One Living (1884), pp. 164–7; Illustrated London News, 18 Oct. 1873, pp. 369, 370, with portrait; Aunt Judy's Mag. Christmas volume (1874),
pp. 3–7; Athenæum, 11 Oct. 1873, pp. 464–5;
Sheffield Daily Telegraph, 6 Oct. 1873, p. 4, and
10 Oct. p. 3; Boase's Collectanea Cornubiensia,
p. 269.]   G. C. B.

GAUDEN, JOHN (1605–1662), bishop
of Worcester, was born in 1605 at Mayland
in Essex, of which parish his father was vicar.
He was educated at Bury St. Edmunds school,
and about 1618–19 entered St. John's College, Cambridge, where he took the degrees
of B.A. about 1622–3, and M.A. in 1625–6.
In 1630 he went to Oxford as tutor to two
sons of Sir William Russell, bart., of Chippenham in Cambridgeshire, whose daughter
Elizabeth, widow of Edward Lewknor, esq.,
of Denham in Suffolk, he had lately married.
Upon their departure he seems to have remained at Oxford as tutor to other pupils of
rank. He became a commoner of Wadham
College in September 1630, took his B.D. on
22 July 1635, and proceeded D.D. on 8 July
1641. In March 1640 he became vicar of
Chippenham, on the presentation of his pupil,
now Sir Francis Russell. He was also chaplain to Robert Rich, earl of Warwick. Wood's
statement that he was rector of Brightwell,
Berkshire, is disproved by an examination of
the registers. He shared Warwick's parliamentary sympathies, and was appointed to
preach before the House of Commons on
29 Nov. 1640. His sermon (printed in 1641)
brought him a large silver tankard, inscribed
'Donum honorarium populi Anglicani in
parliamento congregati, Johanni Gauden.'
In 1641 he was nominated by the parliament,
through Warwick's influence, to the deanery
of Bocking in Essex. He also procured a
collation from Archbishop Laud, the legitimate patron, then in the Tower. Baker says
he was admitted on 1 April 1642 as dean of
Bocking in Essex, 'atque rector ibidem, à
Gulielmo Archiepiscopo Cantuar. non nolente,
nec admodum volente, utpote non planè libero
et in arce Londinensi concluso.' Gauden was
chosen one of the assembly of divines in 1643,
according to his own account. From that

assembly he says he was shuffled out by a
secret committee and an unknown sleight of
hand, because he was for regulating, not rooting out episcopacy (see his *Ecclesiæ Anglicanæ
Suspiria*, p. 377, and his *Anti Baal-Berith*,
p. 89). We are also assured that he took the
'solemn league and covenant,' though he seems
to deny it, and published in 1643 'Certain
Scruples and Doubts of Conscience about
taking the Solemn League and Covenant.' He
ultimately gave up the use of the Common
Prayer, though it was continued in his church
longer than in any in the neighbourhood.

Gauden began to have misgivings as the
struggle developed. He published in 1648–9 a
'Religious and Loyal Protestation of John
Gauden, D.D., against the present Purposes
and Proceedings of the Army and others about
the trying and destroying our Sovereign Lord
the King; sent to a Colonell to bee presented
to the Lord Fairfax.' Shortly after the king's
death, if we may believe his own statement, he wrote 'Cromwell's Bloody Slaughter
House; or his damnable Designs in contriving the Murther of his Sacred Majesty
King Charles I discovered.' This, however,
was not printed till 1660. In 1662 it was
reprinted with additions as 'Στρατοστηλι-
τευτικόν. A Just Invective against those of
the Army and their Abettors, who murdered
King Charles I on the 30th Jan. 1648.
Written February 1648 by Dr. Gauden.'
While retaining his preferments, he published
in 1653 'Hieraspistes: a Defence by way of
Apology for the Ministry and Ministers of
the Church of England;' and again in the
same year, 'The Case of Ministers' Maintenance by Tithes (as in England) plainly
discussed in Conscience and Prudence.' On
the passing of the Civil Marriage Act he
published 'Ἱεροτελεστία γαμική. Christ at the
Wedding: the pristine sanctity and solemnity of Christian Marriages as they were
celebrated by the Church of England,' London, 4to, 1654. In 1658 he published 'Funerals made Cordials;' a funeral sermon upon
Robert Rich, heir-apparent to the earldom of
Warwick. In 1659 he printed 'A petitionary
Remonstrance presented to O. P. 4 Feb. 1655
by John Gauden, D.D., &c., in behalf of many
thousands his distressed brethren, ministers
of the Gospel, and other good scholars, deprived of all publique employment by his
Declaration, 1 Jan.' Gauden had thus maintained an ambiguous position, retaining his
preferments, and conforming to presbyterianism, though publishing books on behalf of the
church of England. In 1656 he was endeavouring to promote an agreement between
presbyterians and episcopalians on the basis
of Archbishop Ussher's model (THURLOE, v.

598). In 1659 he published a folio entitled 'Ἱερὰ Δάκρυα. Ecclesiæ Anglicanæ Suspiria, or the Tears, Sighs, Complaints, and Prayers of the Church of England.' Gauden preached the funeral sermon of Bishop Ralph Brownrig [q. v.], who died on 7 Dec. 1659, and published it with amplifications as a memorial. Gauden succeeded Brownrig in the preachership at the Temple. Upon the restoration of Charles II he was made chaplain to the king, and in November 1660 appointed to the bishopric of Exeter vacant by Brownrig's death. The revenues of the see were, according to Gauden, only about 500l. a year, but from the long intermission in renewing the leases of estates, the fines for renewal upon Gauden's appointment are said to have amounted to 20,000l. Before his promotion to Exeter he had published his 'Anti-sacrilegus; or a Defensative against the plausible pest or guilded poyson of that namelesse paper (supposed to be the plot of Dr. C. Burges and his partners) which tempts the King's Majestie by the offer of five hundred thousand pounds to make good to the purchasers of bishops' lands, &c., their illegal bargain for ninety-nine years,' 4to, 1660. Also 'Ἀνάλυσις. The loosing of St. Peter's bands; setting forth the true sense and solution of the Covenant in point of Conscience, so far as it relates to Episcopacy,' 4to, 1660. And again, 'Anti Baal-Berith, or the Binding of the Covenant and the Covenanters to their good behaviour by a Vindication of Dr. Gauden's Analysis,' 4to, 1661. In 1661 he published 'A pillar of gratitude humbly dedicated to the glory of God, the honour of his Majesty, the renown of this present Parliament, upon their restoring the Church of England to the primitive government of Episcopacy.' In 1662 he published a very faulty edition of Hooker's works, and prefixed a life of the author, which is unfavourably criticised by Isaac Walton. He now petitioned for advancement to the see of Winchester. On 25 July 1663 Pepys visited Dennis Gauden, the bishop's brother, who had nearly finished a fine house at Clapham. The house, as Dennis told Pepys, had been built for his brother 'when he should come to be bishop of Winchester, which he was promised,' as there was no house belonging to the see. Winchester, however, was given to Morley, bishop of Worcester, and Gauden was forced to be content with a translation to Worcester, to which he was elected on 23 May 1662, and confirmed on 10 June. It is said that vexation at having missed the aim of his ambition brought on a violent attack of the stone and strangury, of which he died on 20 Sept. following. He was buried in Worcester Cathedral, where there is a monument with his bust. His widow petitioned the king for the half-year's profits of Worcester, on the plea of the expenses of removal, but her petition was rejected on account of the large fines received at Exeter. Till his elevation Gauden presumably lived at Bocking, to which parish he gave 400l. for the schools.

Besides other writings of an ephemeral character, the 'Εἰκὼν βασιλική; the Pourtraicture of His Sacred Majestie in His Solitudes and Sufferings,' has been on very strong grounds attributed to Gauden. A copy of this book is said to have been bought the day after the king's execution (TOLAND, Life, 1722, p. 16), i.e. 31 Jan. 1649. It certainly appeared almost simultaneously with that event, and was put forth as the genuine work of Charles I. It soon went through forty-seven editions, was translated into Latin by John Earle (1601?-1665) [q. v.] in 1649, and was attacked in Milton's 'Iconoclastes' (1649). Some doubts as to whether the king was author are insinuated by Milton. They are noticed in the 'Princely Pelican,' a royalist pamphlet published six months later, and stated more explicitly in the Εἰκὼν ἀληθινή (probably August 1649), to which a reply was made in the Εἰκὼν ἡ πιστή. A sharp controversy upon the question broke out after the revolution of 1688.

Gauden, when appointed to Exeter, complained to Clarendon of the poverty of the see, and asked for a higher reward on the ground of some secret service. In a letter received 21 Jan. 1660-1 he explained that this was the sole 'invention' of the 'Eicon.' Clarendon said in his reply: 'The particular which you often renewed I do confesse was imparted to me under secrecy, and of which I did not take myself to be at liberty to take notice, and truly when it ceases to be a secret I know nobody will be glad of it except Mr. Milton. I have very often wished I had never been trusted with it' (Clarendon State Papers, iii. supplement, pp. xxvi, xxxii). When a vacancy was expected at Winchester, Gauden again pressed his claims upon Clarendon, upon the Duke of York, and Charles II, and afterwards upon Clarendon's enemy, George Digby, second earl of Bristol [q. v.] The claim was obviously admitted at the time by the persons concerned, although Clarendon in a conversation with his son in the last year of his life (1674) used language apparently denying Gauden's authorship (WAGSTAFFE, Vindication and Defence of Vindication). Burnet states that in 1674 the Duke of York told him that Gauden was the author. A memorandum written by Arthur Annesley, first earl of Anglesey [q. v.], in his copy of the book, to the effect that Charles II and the Duke of York made the same statement to him in 1675, came to light on the sale of Anglesey's library in 1686. Mrs. Gauden had made Gauden's authorship the ground of an application for the remission of claims upon his estate. A document written by her shortly before his death was found among papers referring to the 'Eicon' after her death in 1671. A list of these papers was given in 'Truth brought to Light' (1693), with an abstract of her narrative, which was fully printed in Toland's 'Amyntor' (1699). Anthony Walker, who had been Gauden's curate at Bocking, published in 1692 a 'True Account of the Author of a Book entituled,' &c. He professed to have been Gauden's confidant during the publication, and to have helped to send the book to press. The accounts of Gauden, his wife, and his curate are in some respects contradictory; but they agree in asserting that Gauden sent the book for approval to Charles I, through the Marquis of Hertford, during his imprisonment at Carisbrook, and that he afterwards published it from a copy which he had retained. A doubtful story that Mrs. Gauden expressed repentance (HOLLINGWORTH, *Character of Charles I*) is balanced by another that she swore upon the sacrament to its truth (*Ludlow no Liar*).

Royalist writers, on the other hand, state that Charles began the book at Theobalds in March 1641 (*Princely Pelican*). It was also said that the manuscript was lost at Naseby, and restored by a Major Huntington, of Cromwell's regiment. This story, mentioned by contemporary writers, was repeated by Huntington himself to Dugdale in 1679. Dugdale repeats the story with some variation in his 'Short View of the late Troubles' (1681). Huntington, however, says that the book was in the handwriting of Sir Edward Walker, with interlineations by Charles I. Now Walker wrote certain 'Memorials' which he gave to Charles I, which were lost at Naseby, recovered by means of an officer in the army, restored to the king, and afterwards published (WALKER, *Historical Discourses*, 1705, p. 228). It is therefore obvious that this, and not the 'Eicon,' was the book recovered by Huntington.

Much further evidence was produced in the later controversy. Dr. Hollingworth's 'Defence of Charles I,' 'Character of Charles I,' and 'Vindiciæ Carolinæ' in 1692, Thomas Long's examination of Anthony Walker's account in 1693, Thomas Wagstaffe's 'Vindication of King Charles the Martyr,' 1697 (3rd edit. 1711), and J. Young's 'Several Evidences concerning the Author,' &c., 1703, are the chief royalist pamphlets, the earliest of which were answered in Toland's 'Amyntor,'

1699, and by an author who, under the name of General Ludlow, wrote 'Ludlow no Lyar' in a 'Letter to Dr. Hollingworth,' Amsterdam, 1692. According to the royalists, Dr. William Dillingham [q. v.] is said on the authority of his son to have read part of the manuscript when Charles was at Holmby House, and afterwards recognised the passages in the 'Eicon;' Sir John Brattle stated in 1691 that he was employed with his father to arrange the papers at Hampton Court before Charles's flight; Colonel Hammond is reported to have said that he found manuscript sheets of the 'Eicon' in Charles's chamber at Carisbrook; Levet, a page, deposed in 1690 that he saw papers in Charles's handwriting during the Newport treaty, and was convinced of the identity; and Sir Thomas Herbert, writing in 1679, states that he found a copy among the king's papers in his own handwriting. Besides some similar evidence, one of the printers employed by Royston (printer of the book) stated that the manuscript, in the handwriting of Oudart, secretary to Sir Edward Nicholas, was brought by Symmons, rector of Raine, near Bocking, and understood to be sent from the king. Mrs. Gauden says that her husband sent the manuscript through Symmons, who was arrested on account of his share in the business, and died in prison. It is suggested that Gauden was allowed by Symmons to copy the book on its way to the press, and upon the Restoration determined to claim it for himself. An old servant of Gauden (WAGSTAFFE, p. 64) said that he had sat up with his master, who had to copy a manuscript and return it to Symmons in haste. The chief question of external evidence is whether more weight should be given to the statements of the persons who profess to have seen the manuscript in Charles's hands, especially before Gauden could have sent it (which evidence is mainly hearsay evidence, and was first produced forty years after the events referred to), or to the admission of Gauden's claim by the authorities at the Restoration. The internal evidence, from the resemblance of the 'Eicon' to Gauden's writings, and from the information apparently in possession of the author, has been much discussed, and most fully and recently by Mr. C. E. Doble in the 'Academy' for May and June 1883. He gives very strong reasons for accepting Gauden's claim.

[The history of the Εἰκὼν Βασιλικὴ, with all necessary references, is most fully given in 'Who Wrote ΕΙΚΩΝ ΒΑΣΙΛΙΚΗ?' two letters to the Archbishop of Canterbury by Christopher Wordsworth, master of Trinity College, Cambridge, 1824. A 'documentary Supplement,' 1825, contains the Gauden Letters, of which the originals are in the Clarendon MSS. at the Bodleian and the Lambeth Library. In 'King Charles I, Author of Icôn Basilike,' 1828, Wordsworth replied to Lingard, Hallam, and other critics, especially the Rev. H. J. Todd, who in 1825 published 'A Letter . . . concerning the Authorship,' &c., and in 1829 replied, chiefly upon the internal evidence, in 'Bishop Gauden the author of Εἰκὼν Βασιλικὴ.' An edition of the Eicon, with a preface by Miss C. M. Phillimore, appeared in 1879, and a reprint, edited by Mr. Edward Scott, with a facsimile of the original frontispiece, appeared in 1880. Both writers believe in the royal authorship. For Gauden's Life see Wood's Athenæ (Bliss), iii. 612–18; Baker's Hist. of St. John's College (Mayor), pp. 266, 678; Oliver's Lives of the Bishops of Exeter, pp. 150, 151; Biog. Brit. (1757), vol. iv.; and Calendars of State Papers.]   R. H–R.

GAUGAIN, THOMAS (1748–1810?), stipple-engraver, born at Abbeville in France in 1748, came when young with other members of his family to England. He studied engraving under R. Houston. He practised at first as a painter, and exhibited in 1778 at the Royal Academy, sending 'A Moravian Peasant,' 'The Shepherdess of the Alps,' and a portrait. He continued to exhibit there up to 1782. From 1780 he devoted himself principally to engraving, using the stipple method, and engraving some of his own designs. Four of these, printed in colours, viz. 'Annette,' 'Lubin,' 'May-day,' and 'The Chimney Sweeper's Garland,' he sent to the exhibition of the Free Society of Artists in 1783. Gaugain ranks among the best stipple-engravers of the period, and produced a large number of engravings. Among them may be noticed 'Diana and her Nymphs,' after W. Taverner, 'The Officers and Men saved from the Wreck of the Centaur,' after J. Northcote, 'Lady Caroline Manners,' after Sir Joshua Reynolds, 'The Death of Prince Leopold of Brunswick,' after J. Northcote, 'The Last Interview of Charles I with his Children,' after Benazech, 'Diligence and Dissipation,' a set of ten engravings after J. Northcote, 'Rural Contemplation,' after R. Westall, 'The Madonna,' after W. Miller, 'Warren Hastings,' from a bust by T. Banks, 'Charles James Fox,' from a bust by Nollekens, 'Lieut.-Col. Disbrowe,' after T. Barker, and numerous others after W. Hamilton, W. R. Bigg, G. Morland, J. Barney, J. Milbourne, Maria Cosway, and others. Gaugain lived for some years at 4 Little Compton Street, Soho. It is not certain when he died, but the engraving mentioned last was published in 1809, and he very probably died soon after that date.

[Redgrave's Dict. of Artists; Dodd's MS. Hist. of English Engravers; Graves's Dict. of Artists,

1760–1880; Leblanc's Manuel de l'Amateur d'Estampes.]   L. C.

GAULE, JOHN (fl. 1660), divine, studied at both Oxford and Cambridge, but did not graduate. He was an unlearned and wearisome ranter. For a time he appears to have been employed by Lord Lindsey, probably as chaplain. By 1629 he was chaplain to Lord Camden. He was then an ardent royalist, but afterwards paid assiduous court to the leading Commonwealth men, in the hope of obtaining preferment. Through the interest of Valentine Wauton he became vicar of Great Staughton, Huntingdonshire, by 1646. In the hope of being allowed to retain his living at the Restoration, he wrote a wretched tract, entitled 'An Admonition moving to Moderation, holding forth certain brief heads of wholesom advice to the late and yet immoderate Party,' 12mo, London, 1660, to which he prefixed a slavish dedication to Charles II. His other writings are: 1. 'The Practiqve Theorists Panegyrick. . . . A Sermon preached at Pauls-Crosse,' 12mo, London, 1628. 2. 'Distractions, or the Holy Madnesse. Feruently (not Furiously) inraged against Euill Men, or against their Euills,' 12mo, London, 1629. 3. 'Practiqve Theories, or Votiue Speculations, vpon Iesvs Christs Prediction, Incarnation, Passion, Resurrection,' 12mo, London, 1629. 4. 'Practiqve Theories, or Votiue Speculations vpon Abrahams Entertainment of the three Angels,' &c., 3 parts, 12mo, London, 1630. 5. 'A Defiance to Death. Being the Funebrious Commemoration of . . . Viscount Camden,' 12mo, London, 1630. 6. 'Select Cases of Conscience touching VVitches and VVitchcraft,' 12mo, London, 1646. 7. 'A Sermon of the Saints judging the World. Preached at the Assizes holden in Huntingdon,' 4to, London, 1649. 8. 'Πῦς-μαντία. The Mag-Astro-Mancer, or the Magicall-Astrologicall-Diviner posed and puzzled,' 4to, London, 1652. Another edition under the title of 'A Collection out of the best approved Authors, containing Histories of Visions,' &c., was published without Gaule's name in 1657.

[Prefaces to works cited above.]   G. G.

GAUNT, ELIZABETH (d. 1685), executed for treason, was the wife of William Gaunt, a yeoman of the parish of St. Mary's, Whitechapel. She was an anabaptist, and, according to Burnet, spent her life doing good, 'visiting gaols, and looking after the poor of every persuasion.' In the reign of Charles II she had taken pity on one Burton, outlawed for his part in the Rye House plot. Though she was a poor woman, keeping a tallow-chandler's shop, she gave him money to escape to Amsterdam. Burton returned with Monmouth, and after the defeat at Sedgemoor fled to London, where Mrs. Gaunt hid him in her house. Burton was base enough to earn a pardon by informing against his benefactress. Mrs. Gaunt was indicted for high treason, and tried at the Old Bailey on 19 Oct. Henry Cornish [q. v.] was tried at the same time. She was convicted and burnt at Tyburn (23 Oct. 1685). She suffered with great courage; Penn, the quaker, who was present at her execution, described how she laid the straw about her in order that she might burn quickly, and by her constancy and cheerfulness melted the bystanders into tears (BURNET, *Own Time*, ii. 270). She said that she rejoiced to be the first martyr that suffered by fire in this reign; but in a paper which she wrote in Newgate the day before her death laid her blood at the door of the 'furious judge and the unrighteous jury.' She was the last woman executed in England for a political offence. Her speech from the stake appeared in both English and Dutch at Amsterdam, 1685.

[Cobbett's State Trials, xi. 382–410; Ralph's Hist. i. 889–90; Macaulay's Hist. i. 664; Neal's Hist. of the Puritans, ii. 75.] E. T. B.

GAUNT, JOHN OF, DUKE OF LANCASTER (1340–1399). [See JOHN.]

GAUNT, or GANT, or PAYNELL, MAURICE DE (1184 ?–1230), baron of Leeds, Yorkshire, son of Robert Fitzharding by Alicia, daughter of Robert de Gaunt or Gant by Alicia Paganell or Paynell, was a minor at the death of his father in 1194–5, when his wardship was granted to William de S. Mariæ Ecclesia, afterwards bishop of London. He was of full age in 1205, when he instituted a suit to divest the prior of Holy Trinity of his rights over the church of Leeds, and the emoluments issuing therefrom. If, as is likely, he took these proceedings as soon as he was legally capable of so doing, the date of his birth would not be earlier than 1184. In 1207–8 he succeeded to the inheritance of his mother, and assumed her name. On 10 Nov. 1208 he granted a charter to the burgesses of Leeds, thus taking the first step towards the establishment of a municipal corporation there. The charter is preserved among the archives of the corporation of Leeds, and a translation may be read in Wardell's 'Municipal History of Leeds,' App. ii. On the levy of scutage for the Scotch war in 1212, he was assessed in respect of twelve and a half knights' fees in Yorkshire, which constituted the barony

of Paganell or Paynell, besides which he held the castle of Leeds and that of Beverstone in Gloucestershire, which had descended to him from his father, and the ruins of which still attest its ancient grandeur, though of the castle of Leeds not one stone remains upon another. He followed King John to the continent in 1214, but in the following year joined the assembly of the insurgent barons at Stamford. He was accordingly excommunicated pursuant to a brief of Innocent III early in 1216, and his estates were confiscated, the major portion of them being granted to Philip de Albini. He fought on the side of Lewis of France at the battle of Lincoln on 20 May 1217, and was taken prisoner by Ranulph, earl of Chester, but effected his release by the surrender of his manors of Leeds and Bingley, Yorkshire. By the following November he had returned to his allegiance, and his estates, except the manors of Leeds and Bingley, were restored to him. Henceforth he was steady in his loyalty, and grew in power and opulence. On the levy of scutage for the Welsh war in 1223, he was assessed in respect of estates in the counties of York, Berks, Lincoln, Somerset, Oxford, Surrey, Gloucester, and Leicester. In 1225 he was sent into Wales to assist William, earl of Pembroke, the earl marshal, in fortifying a castle there. Having without authority set about strengthening the fortifications of his own castle of Beverstone, he was called to account by the king in 1227, but obtained the royal license to continue the work (26 March). On 13 Aug. following he was appointed justice itinerant for the counties of Hereford, Stafford, Salop, Devon, Hants, and Berks. On 30 April 1230 he embarked with Henry for Brittany, but died in the following August. He married twice: first, by royal license (in return for which he pledged himself to serve the king with nineteen knights wherever he should require for the term of a year), Matilda, daughter of Henry de Oilli, who held the barony of Hook Norton, Oxfordshire; secondly, Margaret, widow of Ralph de Someri, who survived him. He left no issue. Before sailing for France he had surrendered to the king his manors of Weston Beverstone and Albricton in Gloucestershire. His nephew, Robert, son of his half-sister, Eva, wife of Thomas de Harpetre, succeeded to his manors in Somersetshire, doing homage for them on 6 Nov. following, and afterwards had a grant of the Gloucestershire and other estates from the king. The manor of Irneham with others in Lincolnshire, which had also belonged to Gaunt, were successfully claimed by Andrew Lutterell, a descendant of the Paganells, about the same time.

[Dugdale's Baronage, i. 402; Rot. de Obl. et Fin. (John), pp. 427, 469; Rot. Pat. p. 198; Rot. Claus. i. 232, 238, 246, 368, 376, ii. 59, 79, 180, 213; Excerpta e Rot. Fin. i. 201, 205, 207, 212; Matt. Paris (Rolls Ser.), ii. 585, 644; Collins's Peerage (Brydges), iii. 593-4; Taylor's Biog. Leodiensis, p. 61; Plot's Nat. Hist. of Oxfordshire; Foss's Lives of the Judges.] J. M. R.

GAUNT, SIMON DE (*d.* 1315), bishop of Salisbury. [See GHENT.]

GAUNTLETT, HENRY (1762-1833), divine, was born at Market Lavington, Wiltshire, on 15 March 1762, and educated at the grammar school of West Lavington, under the care of the Rev. Mr. Marks. After leaving school he was idle for some years, till, by the advice of the Rev. Sir James Stonehouse, he decided to enter the established church, and after three years' preparation was ordained in 1786, and became curate of Tilshead and Imber, villages about four miles distant from Lavington. He remained in this neighbourhood, adding to his income by taking pupils, till 1800, when he married Arabella, the daughter of Edward Davies, rector of Coychurch, Glamorganshire, and removed to the curacy of Botley, near Southampton. He left Botley in 1804 for the curacy of Wellington, Shropshire, which he occupied for a year, and then took charge of a chapel at Reading, Berkshire, not under episcopal jurisdiction. In two years' time he removed to the curacy of Nettlebed and Pishill, Oxfordshire, and thence in 1811 to Olney, Buckinghamshire. In 1815 the vicar of Olney died, and Gauntlett obtained the living, which he held till his death in 1833. Gauntlett was a close friend of Rowland Hill, and an important supporter of the evangelical revival in the English church, in company with his predecessors at Olney, John Newton and Thomas Scott. He published several sermons during his lifetime, and in 1821 'An Exposition of the Book of Revelation,' 8vo, which rapidly passed through three editions, and brought its author the sum of 700*l.* The second edition contained a letter in refutation of the opinion of 'Basilicus,' published in the 'Jewish Expositor,' that during the millennium Christ would personally reign. In 1836 the Rev. Thomas Jones published an abridgment of this entitled 'The Interpreter; a Summary View of the Revelation of St. John . . . founded on . . . H. Gauntlett's Exposition,' &c., 12mo. After Gauntlett's death a collection of his sermons, in two volumes 8vo, (1835), was published, to which a lengthy memoir by his daughter Catherine is prefixed. The appendix reprints portions of a rare work

upon the career of John Mason of Water Stratford, Buckinghamshire, and thirty-eight letters written by William Cowper to Teedon [see under COWPER, WILLIAM, 1731-1800]. Gauntlett published several collections of hymns for his parishioners. His son Henry John, the composer, is noticed below.

[The Memoir mentioned above; Brit. Mus. Cat. under 'Catherine T. Gauntlett' and 'H. Gauntlett.'] R. B.

GAUNTLETT, HENRY JOHN (1805-1876), composer, was born at Wellington, Shropshire, on 9 July 1805. His father, the Rev. Henry Gauntlett, who is noticed above, became in 1815 vicar of Olney, Buckinghamshire. The elder Gauntlett promised the congregation that if they would subscribe for an organ he would provide an organist from among his own children, intending to make two of his daughters play together. His son, then aged nine, undertook, by the time the organ was put up, to be able to play it. In a few weeks his promise was fulfilled, and he was regularly installed. He held the post for ten years. In order to celebrate the accession of George IV, he got up a performance of the 'Messiah,' first copying out all the parts, and training all the singers himself. He was at first educated with a view to taking orders. When he was about sixteen his father took him to London to see Crotch and Attwood, who were impressed by his musical powers. Attwood, then organist of St. Paul's, wished to take Gauntlett as his pupil and eventual successor. Unfortunately his father objected, and after a short sojourn in Ireland as tutor in a private family, he was in 1826 articled for five years to a solicitor in London. Soon after he was appointed organist of a church in or near Gray's Inn, at 60*l.* a year, and in 1827 became organist of St. Olave's, Southwark. In due time he became a solicitor, and practised successfully for fifteen years. He never lost an opportunity of gaining experience as an organist, and to that end applied to Samuel Wesley for instruction. From him he received many traditions of the older school, among others the original *tempi* of many of Handel's works. In 1836 he accepted the post of evening organist at Christ Church, Newgate, at a salary of two guineas a year! At this time he began that agitation in favour of enlarging the compass of the pedals of the organ which ended in the universal adoption of the 'CCC' organs throughout the country. On Mendelssohn's earlier visits to England no organ had been found on which the more elaborate works of Bach could be played. Gauntlett went to see the organ at Haarlem, and on his return was fortunate in obtaining the co-operation of Hill, the organ-builder. After strenuous opposition from many quarters the organ of Christ Church was transformed in time for Mendelssohn's arrival in the autumn of 1837, the bulk of the necessary funds being raised by private subscriptions. An interesting account of Mendelssohn's playing on the new instrument was written by Gauntlett in the 'Musical World' (15 Sept. 1837), a paper in which he took an active interest, and of which he was for some time editor and part proprietor. Many of the best articles in the earlier volumes are by him; one upon the 'Characteristics of Beethoven' attained a more than temporary celebrity. Among the other organs built and improved by Hill under Gauntlett's direction were those of St. Peter's, Cornhill; York Minster; the town hall, Birmingham, &c. In 1841 he married Henrietta Gipps, daughter of W. Mount, esq., J.P. and deputy-lieutenant, of Canterbury. In the following year Dr. Howley, archbishop of Canterbury, conferred upon him the degree of Mus. D. It was the first instance of such a degree being conferred since the Reformation, unless it be true that the degree conferred on Blow was given by Sancroft [see Blow, John]. About this time he superintended the erection of a new organ in St. Olave's, the old one having been destroyed by fire. The work was done by Lincoln, but subsequently voiced by Hill. The last of his schemes for the structural improvement of the organ was the application of electricity to the action. He took out a patent for this in 1852. In 1843 (3 Aug.) he gave a performance of works by John Bull at Christ Church, in the presence of the king of Hanover, who gave him permission to style himself his organist. The object of the performance was to ventilate the theories of Richard Clark (1780–1856) [q. v.] as to the origin of our national anthem. In 1846 he was chosen by Mendelssohn to play the organ part in the production of 'Elijah' at Birmingham on 26 Aug.; the task was not an easy one, for the organ part had been lost, and Gauntlett was compelled to supply one from the score, which he did to the composer's entire satisfaction. In the same year he resigned his post at St. Olave's. From this time he devoted himself to literary work and to composition, although he held various posts after this date. At Union Chapel, Islington (Rev. Dr. Allon's), he undertook to play the organ in 1853, the arrangement lasting until 1861, when he was appointed to All Saints, Notting Hill, remaining there for two years. His last appointment was to St. Bartholomew's, Smithfield, a post which he held for the

last four years of his life. He died at his residence, 15 St. Mary Abbotts Terrace, Kensington, on 21 Feb.1876, and was buried at Kensal Green on the 25th. His widow and six children survive him. Much of Gauntlett's literary work is hidden away in musical periodicals, in prefaces to unsuccessful hymn-books, and in similar places. The chants and hymn tunes written by him are many hundreds in number. Of the latter it is safe to say that tunes like 'St. Alphege,' 'St. Albinus,' and 'St. George' will be heard as long as public worship exists in England. His compositions in this class show correct taste, a pure style, free alike from archaisms and innovations, and a thorough knowledge of what is wanted for congregational use. Other compositions, such as ' The Song of the Soul,' a cycle of songs, and his excellent arrangements for the organ, are in all respects worthy of him. The following are the most important of the compilations, &c., on which he worked: 1. 'The Psalmist,' 1839–41. 2. 'Gregorian Canticles,' 1844. 3. 'Cantus Melodici,' 1845 (this was intended to be the title of a tune book, but it is prefixed only to an elaborate introductory essay on church music, the compilation for which it was designed being afterwards published, with another preface, as ' The Church Hymn and Tune Book,' see below). 4. 'Comprehensive Tune Book,' 1846. 5. 'Gregorian Psalter,' 1846. 6. 'Harmonies to Gregorian Tones,' 1847. 7. 'Comprehensive Choir Book,' 1848. 8. 'Quire and Cathedral Psalter,' 1848. 9. 'Christmas Carols,' 1848. 10. 'The Bible Psalms, . . . set forth to appropriate Tunes or Chants,' 1848. 11. '373 Chants, Ancient and Modern,' 1848. 12. 'The Hallelujah' (with Rev. J.J. Waite), 1848, &c. (A book with this title, a compilation made for Waite's educational classes, had been issued, in a meagre form, as early as 1842, by Waite and J. Burder; Gauntlett's connection with the former began in 1848, and lasted until Waite's death. See preface to the 'memorial edition' of the 'Hallelujah,' in which Gauntlett's work is fully acknowledged.) 13. 'The Stabat Mater, set to eight melodies,' 1849. 14. 'Order of Morning Prayer,' 1850. 15. 'Church Anthem Book,' 1852–4 (incomplete). 16. 'Church Hymn and Tune Book' (with Rev. W. J. Blew), 1851. 17. 'Hymns for Little Children,' 1853. 18. 'Congregational Psalmist' (with Dr. Allon), 1856. 19. 'Manual of Psalmody' (with Rev. B. F. Carlyle), 1860. 20. 'Christmas Minstrelsy' (with Rev. J. Williams), 1864. 21. 'Tunes New and Old' (with J. Dobson), 1866. 22. 'Church Psalter and Hymnal' (with Canon Harland), 1862. 23. 'The Service of Song,' 1870. 24. 'Parish

Church Tune Book,' 1871. 25. 'National Psalmody,' 1876. In 1856 he prepared and composed by far the greater part of a compilation entitled 'The Encyclopædia of the Chant,' for the Rev. J. J. Waite. This was only lately published (1885), with scanty acknowledgment of Gauntlett's important share in the work.

A set of 'Notes, Queries, and Exercises in the Science and Practice of Music,' 1859, intended for the use of those who have to choose organists, shows the extraordinary range of Gauntlett's musical culture. Mendelssohn said of him that ' his literary attainments, his knowledge of the history of music, his acquaintance with acoustical laws, his marvellous memory, his philosophical turn of mind, as well as practical experience, rendered him one of the most remarkable professors of the age' (quoted in *Athenæum*, No. 2522). His contributions to musical literature are to be found in the earlier volumes of the ' Musical World,' in the ' Church Musician,' 1850 and 1851, a periodical started and edited by himself, in the ' Sun,' ' Morning Post,' the 'Orchestra,' 'Notes and Queries,' &c. To the last he was a frequent contributor on general as well as on musical subjects. In an obituary notice in the ' Revue et Gazette Musicale,' he was stated to have been a contributor to the ' Athenæum;' this was denied in that periodical, and with truth, if the word ' contributor' is to be understood as a regular writer; it is scarcely a secret, however, that the learned and caustic review of a certain meretricious book on music was written by him for Grüneisen. Gauntlett was always fearless and outspoken in the expression of his artistic convictions; these were pure and his standard lofty. He was free from all trace of mercantile considerations. He was one of the most eager champions of Gregorian music, and his theories as to its performance and accompaniment were in advance of those held by most of his contemporaries. He was a devoted admirer of the works of Bach, and his playing of that master's organ fugues, &c., as well as his extempore playing, is said to have been exceedingly fine.

[Grove's Dict. i. 584, ii. 274 ; Athenæum, Nos. 2305, 2522, 2523; authorities quoted above; Brit. Mus. Cat.; Sermons by the Rev. Henry Gauntlett, with a Memoir by his daughter, 1835; the Town of Cowper, by Thomas Wright, 1886 ; information from Mrs. Gauntlett.]

J. A. F. M.

GAVESTON, PIERS, EARL OF CORNWALL (*d.* 1312), favourite of Edward II, was the son of a Gascon knight who had earned the favour of Edward I by his faithful service. He was brought up in the royal household as the foster-brother and playmate of the king's eldest son Edward, and thus early gained an ascendency over him. His character, as given by contemporary writers, is not altogether unfavourable. Baker of Swynebroke describes him as graceful and active in person, intelligent, nice in his manners, and skilled in arms. ' There is no authority for regarding Gaveston as an intentionally mischievous or exceptionally vicious man;' but by his strength of will he had gained over Edward a hold which he used exclusively for his own advancement. He was brave and accomplished, but foolishly greedy, ambitious, ostentatious, and imprudent. 'The indignation with which his promotion was received was not caused . . . by any dread that he would endanger the constitution, but simply by his extraordinary rise and his offensive personal behaviour' (STUBBS, *Const. Hist.* chap. xvi.) His master's inordinate affection for him entirely turned his head ; he scorned the great lords, and brought upon himself the envy and hatred of the very men whom he should have conciliated. His pride, says a contemporary, would have been intolerable even in a king's son. ' But I firmly believe,' continues the writer, ' that had he borne himself discreetly and with deference towards the great lords of the land, he would not have found one of them opposed to him' (*Chron. Edward I and II,* ii. 167).

Little is said of Gaveston in the reign of Edward I; but Hemingburgh (ii. 272) has handed down a curious story of his having instigated the prince to ask for him the county of Ponthieu, a demand which so enraged the king that he drove his son from his presence. Edward I determined to separate the friends, and on 26 Feb. 1307, at Lanercost, issued orders for the favourite's banishment, to take effect three weeks after 11 April, and bound both him and the prince never to meet again without command. But the king died on 7 July, and Edward II's first act after his accession was to recall his friend. The disgrace of Ralph Baldock, bishop of London, the chancellor, and of Walter Langton, bishop of Coventry, the treasurer, who was regarded as Gaveston's enemy, immediately followed. A large sum of money, amounting to 50,000*l.*, Langton's property, was seized at the New Temple, and, it is said, was given to the favourite, who also received from Edward a present of 100,000*l.*, taken from the late king's treasure, a portion of which sum had been set aside for a crusade to the Holy Land. All this wealth Gaveston is reported to have transmitted to his native country of Gascony.

On 6 Aug. 1307 Gaveston received a grant of the earldom of Cornwall and of all lands late belonging to Edmund, late earl of Cornwall, the son of the king of the Romans ; and on 29 Oct. following he was betrothed to Margaret de Clare, sister of the young Earl of Gloucester, and the king's own niece, and obtained with her large possessions in various parts of the kingdom. In his promotion to the earldom he had the support of the Earl of Lincoln, and by his marriage he became allied to a powerful house. But his pride could not be satisfied, and, as an instance of his personal vanity, one of the chroniclers notices that by royal command persons were forbidden to address him otherwise than by his title, an unusual practice at that period (*ib.* ii. 157). On 2 Dec. he held a tournament at Wallingford, in honour of the king's approaching marriage, but only increased his unpopularity with the barons, and particularly with the Earls of Warenne, Hereford, and Arundel, by defeating them in the lists.

On 30 Dec. Gaveston was appointed regent of the kingdom during Edward's absence in France on his marriage, although the king did not actually depart till 22 Jan. 1308, and was absent till 7 Feb. On 25 Feb. was celebrated the coronation, which had originally been appointed to take place a week earlier, and is even said to have been deferred on account of the growing discontent against the royal favourite. Here Gaveston's display eclipsed his rivals, and it is noticed as a special affront to the other nobles that he was appointed to carry in the procession the crown of St. Edward. His other services were the redemption of the 'curtana' sword, and the fixing of the spur on the king's left foot. His ostentation and the king's obtrusive partiality for him are also said to have disgusted the queen's relatives who were present, and who, on their return home, imparted their prejudice to the king of France. Seeing the storm rising, Edward postponed the meeting of the council, but at length, on 28 April, the barons assembled, and at once proceeded to call for Gaveston's banishment. Hugh Despenser (1262–1326) [q. v.] is said to have been the only man of importance who attempted to defend him. The king was forced to comply, and on 18 May issued his letters patent which proclaimed the sentence, the prelates undertaking to excommunicate Gaveston if he disobeyed; but, to soften the blow, Edward heaped fresh gifts upon him, and on 16 June appointed him lieutenant of Ireland, and at the same time prayed the pope to intervene for his protection. Gaveston sailed for his new command on 28 June from the port of Bristol, whither he was accompanied by the king in person, and remained in Ireland for a year. He established himself as Edward's representative at Dublin, and reduced the hostile septs in the neighbourhood, restored the fortresses, and carried out other works. But the king could not exist without his friend. Before many months had passed he was working for his recall ; in April 1309 he tried to move the king of France to intercede in his favour, and, although parliament refused to sanction the favourite's return, he at length prevailed upon the pope to absolve him. Early in July Gaveston was welcomed by the king at Chester.

At an assembly of the barons at Stamford on 27 July, the king accepted the articles of redress previously presented to him by the parliament, and, through the mediation of the Earl of Gloucester, the Earls of Lincoln and Warenne were drawn over to Gaveston's side, and a large number of the barons gave their formal assent to his return. But Gaveston's insolence only increased, and he appears to have chosen this inopportune moment for forcing upon the earls opprobrious nicknames in ridicule of their personal peculiarities or defects. The Earl of Lincoln was 'burstbelly' (boele crevée); Lancaster was 'the fiddler' (vielers), or 'play-actor' (histrio); Gloucester, his own brother-in-law, was 'horeson' (filz à puteyne); and Warwick was 'the black hound of Ardern.' 'Let him call me hound,' exclaimed the latter; 'one day the hound will bite him' (*Chron. Lanercost*, p. 216). He is specially accused at this period of appropriating the revenues of the kingdom to such an extent that the king was straitened for means to support the charges of his court, and the queen was subjected to unworthy reductions, of which she bitterly complained to her father.

Within three months of his return Gaveston had again estranged those to whom he had but just now been reconciled. A council was summoned at York in October, but Lancaster and others refused to appear. Fearful for his safety, Edward kept Gaveston close to his side, and they passed the Christmas of 1309 together at Langley. In February 1310 the bishops and barons were again summoned, and when they met in March the barons attended in arms. Edward was compelled to submit to the election of a commission of ordainers invested with power to frame ordinances for the reform of the government. In February Gaveston had withdrawn from court. In September the king marched against the Scots, and was joined by Gaveston at Berwick, where they remained until the end of July of the next year (1311). But then Edward was obliged to return to London to meet the parliament, which had been summoned for 8 Aug. Gaveston was therefore placed for safety in Bamborough Castle. In the parliament the new ordinances were presented to the king for confirmation, one of them specially requiring the perpetual banishment of the favourite. Edward resisted for some time, but on 30 Sept. was forced to assent. By the terms of his sentence Gaveston was called upon to leave the kingdom, sailing from the port of Dover before the feast of All Saints, and Scotland, Ireland, Wales, and Gascony, as well as England, were forbidden to him. He is said to have first attempted to pass into France, but, fearing to be made prisoner, he retired to Bruges in Flanders, where, however, through the hostile influence of the king of France, he was badly received. At Christmas he secretly returned to England, and for a while remained in hiding, moving from place to place. At the beginning of 1312 the king went to York, recalled Gaveston to his side, and restored his estates. On 18 Jan. he publicly announced his favourite's return and reinstatement. The hostile barons, with Lancaster at their head, at once took up arms, and demanded Gaveston's surrender, while Archbishop Winchelsey publicly excommunicated him and his abettors. The king and Gaveston now drew away further north, leaving York on 5 April, and remained at Newcastle till the beginning of May. But the barons were now approaching. Edward and his favourite, hastily retiring to Tynemouth, took ship and fled to Scarborough, a place of great strength, but not prepared to stand a siege. The king withdrew to York. Meanwhile the barons seized all Gaveston's goods in Newcastle, and advanced against Scarborough, which the Earls of Warenne and Pembroke were appointed to besiege. On 19 May Gaveston surrendered to Pembroke, who pledged himself for his prisoner's personal safety, and set out with him towards Wallingford, there to await the meeting of parliament in August. Arrived at Deddington in Oxfordshire, Pembroke left Gaveston under a guard, and departed on his own affairs. Scarcely had he gone, when Warwick, hearing that his hated enemy was so close at hand, surprised him before dawn on 10 June, and, making him his prisoner, carried him off to his castle of Warwick. There, on the arrival of Lancaster, Hereford, and Arundel, a consultation was hastily held, and it was determined to put their prisoner to death. The place chosen for the execution was Blacklow Hill, otherwise called—prophetically, as the chroniclers say—Gaversike, about a mile north of the town, in order that the Earl of Warwick

might be relieved of immediate responsibility. There his head was struck off on 19 June 1312, in the presence of Lancaster and his confederates; Warwick, however, apparently again with a view to future justification, remaining behind in his castle. The body was taken possession of by the Dominicans or preaching friars of Oxford, in which city it lay for more than two years. It was thence conveyed by Edward's orders to King's Langley in Hertfordshire, and buried there on 2 Jan. 1315, with great ceremony, in the house of the Dominicans, which had been lately built and endowed by the king. Gaveston left but one child, a daughter. His widow afterwards married Hugh de Audley the younger.

[Chronicles of Trokelowe, Lanercost, Walsingham, Baker of Swynebroke; Chron. of the Reigns of Edward I and Edward II (Rolls Ser.); Dugdale's Baronage; Stubbs's Const. Hist.; W. P. Dodge's Piers Gaveston, 1899; art. supra EDWARD II. In Marlowe's tragedy of Edward II, Gaveston plays a prominent part.] E. M. T.

GAVIN, ANTONIO (*fl.* 1726), author of 'A Master-Key to Popery,' a native of Saragossa, was educated at the university of that city and graduated M.A. Before he was twenty-three years of age he received ordination as a secular priest in the church of Rome. He subsequently embraced protestantism, escaped from Spain disguised as an officer in the army, reached London, where he was hospitably entertained by Earl Stanhope, whom he had met in Saragossa, and on 3 Jan. 1715–16 was licensed by Robinson, bishop of London, to officiate in a Spanish congregation. For two years and eight months he preached first in the chapel in Queen's Square, Westminster, and afterwards in Oxenden's chapel, near the Haymarket. His first sermon, which is dedicated to Lord Stanhope, was published as 'Conversion de las tres Potencias del alma, explicada en el Primer Sermon' [on Deut. xxx. 9, 10], 8vo, London, 1716. Stanhope, wishing to obtain for him some settled preferment in the church of England, advised Gavin to accept in June 1720 the chaplaincy of the Preston man-of-war, in which capacity he would have ample leisure to master English. On the ship being put out of commission he went to Ireland 'on the importunity of a friend,' and while there heard of the death of Stanhope at London on 5 Feb. 1721. Soon afterwards, by favour of Palliser, archbishop of Cashel, and Dean Percival, he obtained the curacy of Gowran, near Kilkenny, which he served nearly eleven months. He then removed to Cork, where he continued almost a year as curate of an adjacent parish, occasionally preaching at Cork, Shandon, and Gortroe. Gavin acquired considerable notoriety by compiling a farrago of lies and libels, interspersed with indecent tales, to which he gave the title of 'A Master-Key to Popery; containing . . . a Discovery of the most secret Practices of the secular and regular Romish Priests in their Auricular Confession,'&c., 8vo, Dublin, 1724, dedicated, curiously enough, to a child, the Hon. Grace Boyle. The British public swallowed Gavin's inventions with avidity. Thus encouraged, he published a second edition, 'carefully corrected from the errors of the first, with large additions,' 3 vols. 12mo, London, 1725-6, of which a French translation by François Michel Janiçon appeared, 3 vols. 12mo, London [Amsterdam], 1726-7. In the preface to the third volume Gavin writes: 'In less than two years 5,000 of my first and second volume are dispersed among the Protestants of Great Britain and Ireland; I shall assiduously apply myself to finish the fourth volume, which shall be a Master-Key both to Popery and to Hell,' undeterred, as he wishes his readers to infer, by the violent threats of the pope's emissaries. The concluding volume, which never appeared, was to have been entitled, according to the advertisement on the last page of vol. iii., 'Dr. Gavin's Dreams, or the Masterpiece of his Master-Key.'

[Prefaces to vols. i. and iii. of A Master-Key.]
G. G.

GAVIN, ROBERT (1827–1883), painter, was the second son of Peter Gavin, a merchant at Leith, where he was born in 1827. He was educated at the Leith High School, and when about twenty-one years of age he entered the School of Design in Edinburgh, and studied under Thomas Duncan. He painted a large number of familiar and rustic subjects, mainly landscape compositions with figures of children, which became very popular. Some of these, such as the 'Reaping Girl' and 'Phœbe Mayflower,' were reproduced in chromo-lithography. He was elected an associate of the Royal Scottish Academy in 1854. About three years later he appears to have become dissatisfied with his progress as an artist, and entered into partnership with a wine merchant; but after about a year he resumed the practice of his art. He was a regular contributor to the exhibitions of the Royal Scottish Academy, and between 1855 and 1871 exhibited a few pictures at the Royal Academy in London. In 1868 he made a tour in America, and painted several characteristic phases of negro life. Soon after his return home he went to Morocco, and resided for some years at Tangier, where he painted numerous Moorish pictures. In 1879 he became an academician, and presented as his diploma work 'The Moorish Maiden's First Love,' a damsel caressing a beautiful white horse; this picture is now in the National Gallery of Scotland. He returned to Scotland in 1880, and continued to paint subjects of Moorish life and manners until his death, which took place at his residence, Cherry Bank, Newhaven, near Edinburgh, on 5 Oct. 1883. He died unmarried, and was buried in Warriston cemetery.

[Annual Report of the Royal Scottish Acad. 1883; Scotsman, 8 Oct. 1883; Edinburgh Courant, 8 Oct. 1883; Royal Scottish Acad. Exhibition Catalogues, 1850–82; Royal Acad. Exhibition Catalogues, 1855–71.] R. E. G.

GAWDIE, SIR JOHN (1639–1699), painter. [See GAWDY.]

GAWDY, FRAMLINGHAM (1589–1654), parliamentary reporter, born on 8 Aug. 1589, was the eldest son of Sir Bassingbourne Gawdy, knight (d. 1606) of West Harling, Norfolk, by his first wife, Anne, daughter and heiress of Sir Charles Framlingham, knight, of Crow's Hall in Debenham, Suffolk. In 1627 he served the office of sheriff for Norfolk, and was afterwards appointed one of the deputy-lieutenants of the county. He sat for Thetford, Norfolk, in the parliaments of 1620–1, 1623–4, 1625–6, and 1640, and throughout the Long parliament. He has left 'Notes of what passed in Parliament 1641, 1642,' preserved in Addit. MSS. 14827, 14828. He was buried at West Harling on 25 Feb. 1654, leaving six sons and two daughters by his wife Lettice, daughter and coheiress of Sir Robert Knowles, knight, who had been buried at the same place on 3 Dec. 1630. Several of his and his wife's letters are in the British Museum (index to Cat. of Additions to the MSS. 1854–75, pp. 605–6). The manuscripts of the Gawdy family are calendered in part ii. of the appendix to the 10th Report of the Historical Manuscripts Commission.

[Blomefield's Norfolk, i. 306, and elsewhere; Official Return of Members of Parliament.]
G. G.

GAWDY, SIR FRANCIS (d. 1606), judge, was, according to the pedigrees in the Harleian MSS., the son of Thomas Gawdy of Harleston, Norfolk, by his third wife, Elizabeth, daughter of Thomas Shires, and therefore half-brother of Thomas Gawdy, serjeant-at-law, who died in 1556, and of Sir Thomas Gawdy [q. v.] Coke tells us that his 'name of baptism was Thomas, and his name of confirmation Francis, and that name of Francis, by the advice of all the judges, in anno

36 Hen. VIII, he did bear, and after used in all his purchases and grants' (*Comm. on Littleton*, 3 *a*). If, then, the pedigrees in the Harleian collection are correct, there were three sons of Thomas Gawdy of Harleston, by three different wives, each of whom received the baptismal name of Thomas. Francis Gawdy was admitted a student of the Inner Temple on 8 May 1549, being described in the register as ' de Harleston in com. Norfolk.' He was elected a bencher of that society in 1558, and was reader there in 1566 and 1571, in which latter year he was also elected treasurer (DUGDALE, *Orig.* pp. 165, 170). He was also, according to Browne Willis, returned to parliament for Morpeth the same year. In Michaelmas term 1577 he was called to the degree of serjeant-at-law, and on 17 May 1582 he was appointed queen's serjeant. In that capacity he opened the case against the Queen of Scots, on the occasion of the proceedings against her at Fotheringhay, 14 Oct. 1586, on the charge of complicity in Babington's conspiracy. He also took part in the proceedings against Secretary William Davison [q. v.], in whose indiscretion in parting with the Scottish queen's death-warrant without express authority Elizabeth sought the means of relieving herself of the odium attaching to the execution (STRYPE, *Annals* (fol.), iii. pt. i. 364 ; COBBETT, *State Trials*, i. 1173, 1233). On 25 Nov. 1589 he was appointed a justice of the queen's bench (DUGDALE, *Chron. Ser.* p. 95), somewhat against his will, according to his nephew, Philip Gawdy of Clifford's Inn (*Hist. MSS. Comm.* 7th Rep. App. 521 *a*). His daughter Elizabeth married in the following year Sir William Newport, *alias* Hatton, nephew of Sir Christopher Hatton. On the death of Sir Christopher Hatton in 1591, he was nominated one of the commissioners to hear causes in chancery during the vacancy of the office of chancellor (*Cal. State Papers*, Dom. 1591–4, p. 311). The first state trial in which he took part was that of Sir John Perrot in June 1592. He was a member of the special commission that sat at York House in June 1600 for the trial of Essex [see DEVEREUX, ROBERT, second EARL OF ESSEX], and was one of the advisers of the peers on Essex's trial for high treason in Feb. 1600–1 (*Coll. Top. et Gen.* iii. 291 ; SPEDDING, *Letters and Life of Bacon*, ii. 173, 283 ; COBBETT, *State Trials*, i. 1315, 1334). In 1602 he went the home circuit with Serjeant Heale, being instructed to substitute for capital punishment ' servitude in the galleys, rowed by many rowers, which her majesty has provided for the safety and defence of the maritime ports of her realm,' for a term of seven years in the case of all felonies except murder, rape, and burglary.

In a letter from his nephew, Philip Gawdy, to his brother, Bassingbourne Gawdy, written in 1603, Gawdy is said to have ' disdained to be made a knight.' Nevertheless his name appears in the list of knights made at Whitehall on 23 July 1603 (*Hist. MSS. Comm.* 7th Rep. App. 528 *a* ; NICHOLS, *Progr.* (James I), i. 206 ; METCALFE, *Book of Knights*). He was a member of the court that tried Sir Walter Raleigh for high treason in November 1603 (COBBETT, *State Trials*, ii. 18). There is a tradition that he stated on his deathbed that ' the justice of England was never so depraved and injured as in the condemnation of Sir Walter Raleigh' (SPEDDING, *Letters and Life of Bacon*, vi. 366). On 26 Aug. 1605 he was created chief justice of the common pleas (DUGDALE, *Chron. Ser.* p. 100). He died suddenly of apoplexy at Serjeants' Inn in the following year. The date cannot be exactly fixed, but the month was probably June, as the patent of his successor, Sir Edward Coke, was dated 30 June 1606. Spelman, who, however, writes with an evident bias against the judge, states, somewhat ungrammatically, that ' having made his appropriate parish church a hay-house or dog-kennel, his dead corpse, being brought from London to Wallington, could for many days find no place of burial, but in the meantime growing very offensive by the contagious and ill savours that issued through the chinks of lead, not well soldered, he was at last carried to a poor church of a little village thereby called Runcton, and buried there without any ceremony' (*Hist. of Sacrilege*, ed. 1853, p. 243). Gawdy married Elizabeth, daughter of Christopher Coningsby, son of William Coningsby [q. v.], judge in the time of Henry VIII (BLOMEFIELD, *Norfolk*, ed. Parkin, vii. 413). His wife being entitled in her own right to the manor of Eston Hall, Gawdy is said to have acknowledged a fine (apparently for the purpose of settling the estate), ' which done,' says Spelman, ' she became a distracted woman, and continued so to the day of her death, and was to him for many years a perpetual affliction' (*ib.* p. 242). Of this marriage the sole issue was the daughter already mentioned, who married Sir William Newport. She died in the lifetime of her father, leaving no male issue, but an only daughter, Frances, who was brought up by Gawdy, and in February 1605 married Robert Rich, who was created Earl of Warwick in 1618. Peck, in his ' Desiderata Curiosa' (fol.), bk. vi. 51, mentions as among the Fleming MSS. ' a large account of Babington's plot, as the same was delivered in a speech at Fotheringay, at the examination of Mary Queen of Scots, 14 Oct. 1586, by Judge

Gawdy.' This seems to be identical with the 'historical account of Babington's conspiracy,' which we learn from Cobbett's 'State Trials,' i. 1173, formed a principal part of Gawdy's speech as queen's serjeant on that occasion.

[Blomefield's Norfolk, ed. Parkin, vii. 412, 516, ix. 63; Inner Temple Books; Addit. MS. 12507, f. 79; Foss's Lives of the Judges.]   J. M. R.

GAWDY, SIR JOHN (1639–1699), painter, born on 4 Oct. 1639, was the second son of Sir William Gawdy, bart. (d. 1666), of West Harling, Norfolk, by his wife Elizabeth, daughter and heiress of John Duffield of East Wretham in the same county, and grandson of Framlingham Gawdy [q. v.] He was a deaf-mute, and became a pupil of Lely, intending to follow portraiture as a profession; but on the death of his elder brother, Bassingbourne, in 1660, he became heir to the family estates, and thenceforth painted only for amusement. Evelyn, who met him in September 1677, speaks of him as 'a very handsome person . . . and a very fine painter; he was so civil and well bred, as it was not possible to discern any imperfection by him' (Diary, 1850–2, ii. 111). He died, according to Blomefield, in 1699. By his wife Anne, daughter of Sir Robert de Grey, knight, of Martin, Lincolnshire, he left one son, Bassingbourne, and one daughter, Anne, married to Oliver Le Neve of Great Witchingham, Norfolk. His son dying unmarried on 10 Oct. 1723, the baronetcy became extinct. Three of Gawdy's letters are preserved in the British Museum (index to Cat. of Additions to the MSS. 1854–75, p. 606).

[Blomefield's Norfolk, i. 306–7; Redgrave's Dict. of Artists, 1878, p. 169; Burke's Extinct Baronetcy, p. 216.]   G. G.

GAWDY, SIR THOMAS (d. 1589), judge, is said by Blomefield (Norfolk, ed. Parkin, x. 115) to have been the son of John Gawdy of Harleston, Norfolk, by Rose, his second wife, daughter of Thomas Bennet, with which the pedigrees in the Harleian MSS. agree, except that they give Thomas as the christian name of the father. The minute in the Inner Temple register of the admission of the judge to that society also describes him as 'son of Thomas Gawdy, senior.' This Thomas Gawdy, senior, was identified by Foss with a certain barrister of that name, who was appointed reader at the Inner Temple in Lent 1548; was called to the degree of serjeant-at-law in 1552; was reappointed reader in Lent 1553, when he was fined for neglecting his duties; represented King's Lynn in parliament in 1547 (being then recorder of the town), and Norwich in 1553 (Hist. MSS. Comm. 11th Rep. App. pt. ii. 174); was appointed recorder of Norwich in 1563, and dying on the same day as his colleague, Serjeant Richard Catlin, in August 1566, shares with him a high-flown Latin epitaph in hexameter verse (author unknown) preserved in Plowden's 'Reports' (p. 180). If, however, any faith is to be placed in the pedigrees in the Harleian MSS., Thomas Gawdy the serjeant was not the Thomas Gawdy, senior, of the Inner Temple register, but his son by his first wife, Elizabeth. We learn from Strype (Mem., (fol.) iii. pt. i. 265) that Serjeant Thomas Gawdy was in the commission of the peace for Essex in 1555, and distinguished himself from his colleagues as the 'only favourer' of the protestants. From him descended the family of Bassingbourne Gawdy. Thomas Gawdy the younger received, according to 'Athenæ Cantabr.' p. 36, 'some education' in the university of Cambridge, 'probably at Gonville Hall.' He entered the Inner Temple on 12 Feb. 1549, and was elected a bencher of that society in 1551, being then one of the masters of requests. He was returned to parliament for Arundel, Sussex, in 1553, and was summoned to take the degree of serjeant-at-law in 1558, but the writ abating by Queen Mary's death he was not called on the accession of Elizabeth. He was elected reader at his inn in Lent 1560, and treasurer in 1561, and in Lent 1567 he was called to the degree of serjeant-at-law (Harl. MSS. 1177 f. 174 b, 1552 f. 161, 4755 ff. 87, 88, 5189 f. 26 b, 6093 f. 79; Addit. MSS. 27447 ff. 89, 91, 27959 f. 1; Lists of Members of Parliament (Official Return of); HORSFIELD, Sussex, App. 32; DUGDALE, Chron. Ser. pp. 91, 93, Orig. p. 165). There is preserved among the Gawdy MSS. a draft of a curious petition addressed by him to the queen in council, begging that he might be excused contributing a hundred marks to the exchequer on the three following grounds, viz.: (1) that he had never received payment of a loan of 10l. made by him to the late queen; (2) that he was in embarrassed circumstances from having built too much on his estates; and (3) that he was 'no great meddler in the law.' It bears no date, but that of April 1570 has been conjecturally assigned to it (Hist. MSS. Comm., Rep. on Gawdy MSS. 1885, p. 5). Gawdy was consulted by Dr. George Gardiner in 1573 with reference to a dispute concerning the title to an advowson (STRYPE, Ann., (fol.) ii. pt. i. 300). In November 1574 he was appointed justice of the queen's bench, and he was knighted by Elizabeth at Woodrising, on occasion of her Norfolk progress, on 26 Aug. 1578 (DUGDALE, Chron. Ser. p. 94; NICHOLS,

Progr. (Eliz.) ii. 225; METCALFE, *Book of Knights*). Disputes being chronic between Great Yarmouth and the Cinque ports as to fishing rights, which not unfrequently led to a kind of private warfare, a royal commission was appointed in 1575 to investigate and if possible adjust them, over which Gawdy presided (*Hist. MSS. Comm.* 9th Rep. App. 307 *a*, 316 *b*; MANSHIP, *Yarmouth*, ed. Palmer, i. 186–9). On 9 Oct. 1578 he was nominated one of a commission to inquire into certain matters in controversy between the Bishop of Norwich and his chancellor, Dr. Becon; in 1580 he gave an extra-judicial opinion in a case between the Earl of Rutland and Thomas Markham 'touching the forestership of two walks in Sherwood' (*Cal. State Papers,* Dom. 1547–80, p.601; *Addenda,* 1580–1625, p. 23). He was one of the commissioners who tried Dr. Parry for conspiracy to assassinate the queen in February 1584–5, and William Shelley for the same offence a year later. He also sat at Fotheringhay in October 1586 on the commission for the trial of the Queen of Scots on the charge of complicity in Babington's conspiracy. He assisted at the trial of the Earl of Arundel on 18 April 1589 for the offence of intriguing with foreign catholics to subvert the state (*Fourth Rep. Dep. Keep. Publ. Rec.,* App. ii. p. 273; COBBETT, *State Trials,* i. 1095, 1167, 1251). He amassed a large fortune, which he invested in the purchase of land, chiefly in his native county. In 1566 he bought the manors of Saxlingham and Claxton, and in 1582 that of Coldham, all in Norfolk. At his death, which took place on 4 Nov. 1589, he held besides Claxton, where he usually resided, and Gawdy Hall in Harleston, some twelve other estates in different parts of Norfolk, and also estates in Suffolk and Berkshire. He was buried in the north chapel of the parish church of Redenhall, near Harleston.

Coke describes Gawdy as 'a most reverend judge and sage of the law, of ready and profound judgment, and of venerable gravity, prudence, and integrity' (*Reports,* pt. iv. p. 54 *a*). He was succeeded on the bench by his half-brother Sir Francis Gawdy [q. v.] Gawdy married first, in 1548, Etheldreda or Awdrey, daughter of William Knightley of Norwich; secondly, Frances Richers of Kent (*Hist. MSS. Comm.,* Rep. on Gawdy MSS. 1885, p. 2). By his first wife he had issue one son, Henry, who survived him, was high sheriff of Norfolk in 1593, and was created a knight of the Bath by James I in 1603. Many letters of Sir Henry Gawdy to his cousin Sir Bassingbourne and others are calendared in the report on the Gawdy MSS. issued by the Historical Manuscripts Com-

mission. The judge also left three daughters, Frances, Isabell, and Julian, of whom the last named married Sir Thomas Berney of Park Hall, Reedham, Norfolk, and died in 1673.

[Foss's Lives of the Judges; Blomefield's Norfolk, ed. Parkin, iii. 269, 277, 358, v. 215, 364, 370, 499, x. 115, xi. 128.]　　　J. M. R.

GAWEN, THOMAS (1612–1684), catholic writer, son of Thomas Gawen, a minister of Bristol, was born at Marshfield, Gloucestershire, in 1612. He was admitted a scholar of Winchester School in 1625, and in 1632 was made perpetual fellow of New College, Oxford, where he graduated B.A. and M.A. After taking orders he travelled abroad, and at Rome made the acquaintance of Milton. On his return he became chaplain to Curle, bishop of Winchester, who in 1642 appointed him tutor to his son, then a commoner of Magdalen College, Oxford. That prelate also collated him to a benefice—probably Exton, Hampshire—and in 1645 to a prebend in the church of Winchester. Afterwards Gawen visited Italy a second time with the heir of the Pierpoints of Dorsetshire. At the Restoration he was presented to the rectories of Bishopstoke and Fawley, Hampshire, though he was never inducted into Fawley. He resigned all his preferments on being reconciled to the Roman catholic church, and to avoid persecution he withdrew to France, and through the interest of Dr. Stephen Goffe and Abbot Walter Montagu was admitted into the household of Queen Henrietta Maria. Subsequently he paid a third visit to Rome, married an Italian lady, and had a child by her. Wood says that because his wife had no fortune he deserted her and the child, and returned to England, 'his wealth being kept for the children of his brother.' Although living in retirement, he was in some trouble in 1679 over the popish plot. He died in Pall Mall on 8 March 1683–4, and was buried in the church of St. Martin-in-the-Fields.

Wood, who describes him as a learned and religious person, states that he was the author of: 1. 'A brief Explanation of the several Mysteries of the Holy Mass, . . .' London, 1686, 8vo. 2. 'Certain Reflections upon the Apostles' Creed touching the Sacrament,' London, 1686, 8vo. 3. 'Divers Meditations and Prayers, both before and after the Communion,' London, 1686, 8vo. These three treatises were issued and bound together. He was author of other works, apparently unprinted, including a Latin version of John Cleveland's poem, 'The Rebel Scot,' and a translation from the Spanish of the life of Vincent of Caraffa, general of the jesuits.

[Wood's Athenæ Oxon. (Bliss), iv. 130; Dodd's

Church Hist. iii. 275; Le Neve's Fasti; Kirby's Winchester Scholars, p. 171.] T. C.

GAWLER, GEORGE (1796–1869), governor of South Australia, son of Samuel Gawler, captain of the 73rd regiment, was born in 1796, educated at the military college, Great Marlow, and entered the army 4 Oct. 1810. He served with the 52nd light infantry through the Peninsular campaign from Nov. 1811 to the end, being wounded at Badajoz and San Munos. At Waterloo, he led the right company of his regiment, and attained the rank of colonel. In 1833 he contributed to 'The United Service Journal,' part ii., a paper ' The Crisis and Close of the Action at Waterloo, by an Eye-Witness,' which was re-issued as a pamphlet (Dublin, 1833), and caused great controversy. Gawler contended that his own regiment (the 52nd), supported by the rest of Adams's brigade, and not the guards, defeated Napoleon's final attack. Gawler defended his contention against Sir Hussey Vivian in 'The United Service Journal' for 1833, and was corroborated by W. Leeke in his ' Lord Seaton's Regiment at Waterloo,' 1866. On 12 Oct. 1838 he became governor of the newly founded colony of South Australia, then in considerable difficulties owing to dissensions between the late governor, Captain Hindmarsh, and the resident commissioner of the South Australian Colonisation Society. Gawler was himself made resident commissioner by the Colonisation Society. Embarrassments followed. The Wakefield system, upon which the colony was supposed to be founded, aimed at an equality between the labourers emigrating and the demand for their services. Gawler, by undertaking large public works, concentrated the labourers in Adelaide, and prevented the settlers from obtaining their aid. A consequent diminution in the sources of revenue accompanied an increase in expenditure. By the end of 1840 the financial position of the colony looked critical, and the home government dishonoured Gawler's drafts. He was recalled, and by a mishap his recall was first announced to him by his successor, George (afterwards Sir George) Grey (13 May 1841).

Gawler returned to England and devoted himself to religious and philanthropic pursuits. He died at Southsea 8 May 1869.

[South Australian Register, 1840–1; Rusden's Australia; Heaton's Australian Dict. of Dates; Stow's South Australia; South Australian, 1838–1841; Hampshire Telegraph and Sussex Chronicle, 15 May 1869.] E. C. K. G.

GAWLER, WILLIAM (1750–1809), organist, teacher, and composer, son of a schoolmaster, was born in 1750 in Lambeth. His Op. 2, a collection of varied pieces for harpsichord or pianoforte, with instructions, was published by Preston in the Strand in 1780. ' Harmonia Sacra,' containing psalm tunes, anthems, hymns, and a voluntary, appeared in 1781. In 1784 Gawler was appointed organist (with a salary of 63l.) to the Asylum for Female Orphans, Lambeth; he composed for their chapel music (Op. 16) to ' Twelve Divine Songs' by Dr. Watts, and collected the psalm tunes in use there in 1785; two sets of voluntaries for the organ (GROVE); and some patriotic songs. He was parish clerk at Lambeth for many years, and died 15 March 1809. His sister married Dr. Pearce, lecturer at St. Mary's, Lambeth, master of the Academy, Vauxhall, and afterwards subdean of the Chapel Royal.

[Allen's Lambeth, pp. 86, 336; Register of Wills, P. C. C., Legard, fol. 134; Gawler's works in Brit. Mus. Library; Gent. Mag. xl. 542; Nichols's Lambeth, p. 153; parish register of Lambeth; information kindly supplied by Mr. George Booth, secretary, Female Orphan Asylum, Beddington.] L. M. M.

GAY, JOHN (1685–1732), poet and dramatist, is generally stated to have been born in 1688. But the parish records of Barnstaple, produced at the ' Gay Bicentenary' held at that town in 1885, show that he was baptised at Barnstaple Old Church on 16 Sept. 1685. He came of an ancient but impoverished Devonshire family, being the youngest child of William Gay of Barnstaple, who lived in a house in Joy Street known as the Red Cross. William Gay died in 1695, his wife, whose maiden name was Hanmer, in 1694. John Gay, in all probability, fell to the care of an uncle, Thomas Gay, also resident at Barnstaple. He was educated at the free grammar school of that town, his masters, according to his nephew, the Rev. Joseph Baller (Gay's Chair, 1820, pp. 14–15), being Mr. Rayner and his successor, Mr. Robert Luck, the ' R. Luck, A.M.,' whose miscellaneous poems were published by Cave in April 1736, and dedicated to Gay's patron, the Duke of Queensberry.

O Queensberry! could happy Gay
This offering to thee bring,
'Tis his, my Lord (he'd smiling say),
Who taught your Gay to sing—

Luck writes, and it is asserted that Gay's dramatic turn was also derived from the plays which the pupils at Barnstaple were in the habit of performing under this rhyming pedagogue. It is also stated by Baller (ib. p. 16) that one of his schoolfellows and lifelong friends was William Fortescue [q. v.], afterwards master of the rolls. Little else survives respecting Gay's schooldays; but from the fact that there exists in the Forster

Library at South Kensington a large-paper copy of Maittaire's 'Horace,' copiously annotated in his beautiful handwriting, it must be assumed that subsequent to 1715, the date of the volume, he still preserved a love of the classics. His friends found no better career for him than that of apprentice to a mercer in London. With this vocation he was soon dissatisfied. Mr. Baller's account is that, 'not being able to bear the confinement of a shop,' he became depressed in spirits and health, and returned to his native town, where he was received at the house of another uncle, the Rev. John Hanmer, a nonconformist minister.

After a short stay at Barnstaple, his health, says Mr. Baller, became reinstated, and he returned to town, 'where he lived for some time as a private gentleman,' a statement scarcely reconcilable with the opening in life his friends had found for him. His literary inclinations were no doubt already developed, and it is probable that the swarming coffee-houses and taverns speedily supplied his 'fitting environment.' Rumour assigns to him, as his earliest employment, that of secretary to Aaron Hill [q. v.] His first poem, mentioned by Hill, was 'Wine,' which is said to have been published in 1708, and was certainly pirated by the notorious Henry Hills of Blackfriars (see *Epistle to Bernard Lintot*) in that year. Its motto is

Nulla placere diu, nec vivere carmina possunt,
Quæ scribuntur aquæ potoribus—

a contested theory, which seems to have exercised Gay nearly all his lifetime; for he is still debating it in his latest letters. He pretends in this production to draw 'Miltonic air,' but the atmosphere is more suggestive of the 'Splendid Shilling' of John Philips [q. v.] The concluding lines, which describe the breaking up of a 'midnight modern conversation' at the Devil Tavern, already disclose the minute touch of 'Trivia.'

'Wine' was not included in Gay's collected poems of 1720, perhaps because it was in blank verse. His next effort, which exhibits a considerable acquaintance with London letters, was the now rare 'twopenny pamphlet' entitled 'The Present State of Wit,' addressed 'to a Friend in the Country.' It is dated May 1711, and gives a curious account of periodical literature, especially of the recently completed 'Tatler' and the newly commenced 'Spectator.' 'The author,' says Swift (*Journal to Stella*, 14 May), 'seems to be a whig, yet he speaks very highly of a paper called "The Examiner," and says the supposed author of it is Dr. Swift. But above all things he praises the Tatlers and

Spectators, and I believe Steele and Addison were privy to the printing of it. Thus is one treated by these impudent dogs.' Swift, however, was wrong as to Gay's opinions. Such as they were—and he disclaims politics —he was a tory.

From a letter from Pope to Henry Cromwell, bearing date a few weeks later, it is plain he had already become slightly acquainted with Pope, whose 'Essay on Criticism' had been published just four days after the above-mentioned pamphlet. 'My humble service to Mr. Gay,' says Pope. They appeared together in Lintot's 'Miscellany' of May 1712 (the so-called 'Rape of the Lock' volume), to which Gay contributed a translation of one of Ovid's 'Metamorphoses.' But he must have been still practically unknown, as his name is not mentioned in the contemporary advertisements, although they duly announce even such *ignes minores* as Cromwell, Broome, and Fenton. A few weeks before had been advertised 'The Mohocks,' 'a tragi-comical farce, as it was acted near the Watch-house in Covent Garden,' notwithstanding which ambiguous statement it was never performed. 'This,' says the 'Biographia Dramatica,' iii. 55, 'has been attributed in general, and truly, to Mr. Gay.' It was dedicated to Mr. D***** (Dennis). In the same year (1712), and probably towards the close of it—since Pope's congratulations are dated December—he was appointed 'secretary or domestic steward' to the Duchess of Monmouth, whose husband had been beheaded in 1685. Early in 1713 (January) he published another poem, 'Rural Sports,' a georgic, which he dedicated to Pope. It is a performance of the 'toujours bien, jamais mieux' order, but nevertheless contains a good deal of unconventional knowledge of country life, especially of hunting and fishing. In September he contributed a clever paper on the art of dress to Steele's 'Guardian,' and it is possible that other pages of that periodical are also from his pen, while he is represented in the 'Poetical Miscellanies' of the same writer, which appeared in December, by two elegies ('Panthea' and 'Araminta') and a 'Contemplation on Night.'

At the beginning of 1714 Gay brought out the 'Fan,' one of his least successful efforts, and, though touched by Pope, now unreadable. This was succeeded by the 'Shepherd's Week,' a series of eclogues into which Pope had decoyed him in order to reinforce his own war with Ambrose Philips [q. v.], and sham pastoral. Gay was to depict rustic life with the gilt off, 'after the true ancient guise of Theocritus.' 'Thou wilt not find my Shepherdesses,' says the author's proem, 'idly piping upon oaten Reeds, but milking the Kine, tying up the Sheaves, or, if the Hogs are astray, driving them to their Styes . . . nor doth he [the shepherd] vigilantly defend his Flocks from Wolves [this was a palpable hit at Philips!], because there are none.' But the execution of the piece went far beyond its avowed object of ridicule, and Gay's eclogues abound with interesting folklore and closely studied rural pictures.

The 'Shepherd's Week' was dedicated to Bolingbroke, a circumstance which Swift hints (POPE, *Corr*. ii. 34) constituted that original sin against the court which subsequently so much interfered with Gay's prospects of preferment. But the allusions in this prologue (in rhyme) seem to show that the sometime mercer's apprentice had by this time made the acquaintance of Arbuthnot, and of some fairer critics whose favour was of greater importance to poetical advancement. 'No more,' he says, 'I'll sing Buxoma and Hobnelia,

> But Lansdown fresh as Flow'r of May,
> And Berkely Lady blithe and gay,
> And Anglesey whose Speech exceeds
> The Voice of Pipe or Oaten Reeds;
> And blooming Hide, with Eyes so Rare,
> And Montague beyond compare.'

'Blooming Hyde, with eyes so rare,' it may be remarked, was Lady Jane Hyde, daughter of the Earl of Rochester, and elder sister of the 'Kitty, beautiful and young,' afterwards Duchess of Queensberry.

Soon after the publication of the 'Shepherd's Week' Gay appears to have resigned his position in the household of the Duchess of Monmouth, and to have obtained the superior appointment of secretary to Lord Clarendon, who in June 1714 was despatched as envoy extraordinary to the court of Hanover. It was the influence of Swift or Swift's friends which procured Gay this post, and there exists a curious rhymed petition from the necessitous poet to Lord-treasurer Oxford for funds to enable him to enter upon his functions. For a brief space we must imagine him strutting 'in silver and blue' through the clipped avenues of Herrenhausen, yawning over the routine life of the little German court, and, as he told Swift, perfecting himself in the diplomatic arts of 'bowing profoundly, speaking deliberately, and wearing both sides of his long periwig before.' Then the death of the queen (1 Aug.) put an end to Clarendon's mission, and his secretary was once more without employment. He came back to England in September, and a letter from Pope, dated the 23rd of that month, winds up by recommending him to make use of his past

position by writing 'something on the king, or prince, or princess' (*ib*. ii. 417). Arbuthnot seems to have given him similar counsel. Gay's easily depressed spirits did not at first enable him to act on this advice, but he shortly afterwards recovered himself sufficiently to compose and publish in November an 'Epistle to a Lady, occasion'd by the Arrival of Her Royal Highness' (i. e. the Princess of Wales, who came to England on 13 Oct.), in which he makes direct reference to his hopeless waiting for patronage.

The only outcome of this seems to have been that their royal highnesses came to Drury Lane to see Gay's next effort, the tragicomi-pastoral farce of the 'What-d'ye-Call-it,' a play which belongs in part to the same class as Buckingham's 'Rehearsal,' inasmuch as it ridicules the popular tragedies of the day, and especially 'Venice Preserved.' The images of this piece were comic, and its action grave, a circumstance which must have been a little confusing to slow people, who, not having the advantage of the author's explanatory preface, could not readily see the joke. To Pope's deaf friend Henry Cromwell, who was unable to hear the words, and only distinguished the gravity of the gestures, it was, we are told, unintelligible. One of the results of this ambiguity was the publication by Lewis Theobald and Griffin the player of a 'Key to the What-d'ye-Call-it,' in which the travestied passages are quoted and the allusions traced. But there is originality and some wit in the little piece, which was published in March 1715, and it contains one of Gay's most musical songs, that beginning ''Twas when the seas were roaring.'

In the summer of 1715 (*ib*. ii. 458) Lord Burlington sent Gay to Devonshire, an expedition which he has pleasantly commemorated in the epistle entitled 'A Journey to Exeter.' In January of the following year he published his 'Trivia: or, the Art of Walking the Streets of London,' a poem, in the 'advertisement' of which he acknowledges the aid of Swift; and it is indeed not improbable that 'Trivia' was actually suggested by the 'Morning' and 'City Shower' which Swift had previously contributed to Steele's 'Tatler.' As a poem it has no permanent merit, but it is a mine of not-yet-overworked information respecting the details of outdoor life under Anne. Lintot paid Gay 43*l*. for the copyright, and from a passage in one of Pope's letters to Caryll (*ib*. ii. 460 *n*.) he must have made considerably more by the sale of large-paper copies. 'We have had the interest,' says Pope, 'to procure him [Gay] subscriptions of a guinea a book to a pretty tolerable number. I believe it may be worth

150*l.* to him in the whole.' This was scarcely bad pay for a poem which was sold to the public at 1*s.* 6*d.* But its popularity must have been confined to the first issues, for it was not until 1730 that it reached a third edition.

Gay's next production was the comedy entitled 'Three Hours after Marriage,' of which it is perhaps fairer to say that he bore the blame than that he is justly chargeable with its errors of taste. Although he signed the 'advertisement,' and was popularly credited with the authorship, he had Pope and Arbuthnot for active coadjutors. The piece was acted at Drury Lane, and published in January 1717. It ran feebly for seven nights. Dennis figured in it as Sir Tremendous, 'the greatest critic of our age,' while Woodward the geologist was burlesqued in Johnson's part of Fossile, to gain access to whose wife two suitors disguise themselves respectively as a mummy and a crocodile, expedients not at all to the taste of the stern censors of the pit. Another of the personages, Phœbe Clinket (played by Steele's friend, Mrs. Bicknell), was said to be intended for Anne Finch [q. v.], countess of Winchilsea, who was alleged to have spoken contemptuously of Gay (*Biog. Dram.* iii. 334). Like the 'What-d'ye-Call-it,' 'Three Hours after Marriage' was followed by 'A Complete Key,' which, however, was a criticism, and not a 'puff oblique.' It also prompted the farce of the 'Confederates' by Joseph Gay, the *nom de guerre* of John Durant Breval [q. v.]; and a pamphlet entitled 'A Letter to Mr. John Gay, concerning his late Farce, entituled a Comedy,' 1717.

In July 1717 William Pulteney, afterwards Earl of Bath, carried Gay with him to Aix, and (like Lord Burlington) was repaid by a rhymed epistle. The next year (1718) saw him in Oxfordshire at Lord Harcourt's seat of Cockthorpe, from which place he occasionally visited Pope, then working at the fifth volume of the 'Iliad' in another of Harcourt's country seats, an old gothic house and tower at Stanton Harcourt. Here occurred that romantic episode of the two lovers struck dead by lightning, of which Pope's 'Correspondence' contains so many versions, and which, from the fact that one of the earliest of these was printed in 1737 (POPE, *Prose Works*, i.), as written by Gay to his brother-in-law, Fortescue, has (by many people besides Sophia Primrose) been supposed to have been first chronicled by Gay. It is most probable, however, that the matrix (so to speak) of the story was a joint production sent by both writers to their friends, and colour is given to this conjecture by a passage in a letter from Lord Bathurst to Pope in August, in

which he thanks his correspondent and Gay for the melancholy novel they have sent him of the unhappy lovers (POPE, *Corr.* iii. 325, and iv. 399 *n.*)

Nothing further of interest in Gay's life is recorded until 1720, when Tonson and Lintot published his poems in two quarto volumes, with a frontispiece by William Kent, the architect. Its subscription list rivals that to Prior's folio of 1718, and bears glad witness to the munificence of the Georgian nobility to the more fortunate of their minstrels. Lord Burlington and Lord Chandos are down for fifty copies each, Lord Bathurst and Lord Warwick for ten, and so forth. The second volume included a number of epistles, eclogues, and miscellaneous pieces, the majority of which were apparently published for the first time, as well as a pastoral tragedy entitled 'Dione.' One of the ballads, the still popular 'Sweet William's Farewell to Black-ey'd Susan,' is justly ranked among the best efforts of the writer's muse. By these two volumes he is alleged to have cleared 1,000*l.*, no mean amount when it is remembered that one of them consisted wholly of pieces already in circulation. His friends clustered about him with kindly counsel in this unlooked-for good fortune. Swift and Pope recommended him to purchase an annuity with the money; Erasmus Lewis (Lord Bathurst's 'proseman,' as Prior was his 'verseman') wished him to put it in the funds and live upon the interest; Arbuthnot to entrust it to providence and live upon the principal. But the 'most refractory, honest, good-natured man,' as Swift called him, went his own refractory way. The younger Craggs had made him a present of some South Sea stock, and he seems to have sunk his poetical gains in the same disastrous speculation. He became speedily the master of a fabulous fortune of 20,000*l.* Again his advisers came to his aid, begging him to sell wholly or in part, at least as much, said Fenton, as will make you 'sure of a clean shirt and a shoulder of mutton every day.' But Gay was bitten by the South Sea madness. He declined to take either course, and forthwith lost both principal and profits (*Biog. Brit.* and JOHNSON, *Lives*, ed. Cunningham, ii. 288).

Among the other names chronicled in the subscription lists of the 'Poems' of 1720 were those of the Duke of Queensberry and his duchess, Catherine Hyde [see under DOUGLAS, CHARLES, third DUKE OF QUEENSBERRY], henceforward Gay's kindest friends. The portrait of the duchess by Jervas as a milkmaid of quality is in the National Portrait Gallery. After her marriage (March 1720) she seems to have taken the poet entirely under her protection. 'Any lady with a coach and six horses'—as Swift complained later, with a half-sorry recollection of his friend's 'rooted laziness' and 'utter impatience of fatigue' —'would carry him to Japan,' and he was certainly not the man to resent her grace's imperious patronage. 'He [Gay] is always with the Duchess of Queensberry,' writes Mrs. Bradshaw to Mrs. Howard from Bath in 1721; and five years later the poet himself tells Swift that he has been with his great friends at Oxford and Petersham 'and wheresoever they would carry me.' In the intervals he is with Lord Burlington at Chiswick or Piccadilly or Tunbridge Wells. Or he is helping Congreve to nurse his gout at 'the Bath,' or acting as Pope's secretary at Twickenham ('which you know is no idle charge'), or borrowing sheets from Jervas to put up Swift at the lodgings in Whitehall which were granted him by the Earl of Lincoln. But though his life sounds pleasant in the summary, it must often have involved many of the humiliations of dependency. According to Arbuthnot (POPE, *Corr.* ii. 32 n.), it would seem that the Burlingtons sometimes neglected the creature comforts of their protégé, and they and his other great friends either could not or would not procure his advancement. 'They wonder,' says Gay piteously to Swift in 1722, 'at each other for not providing for me, and I wonder at them all.' Still, from a reference in another letter to Pope (*ib.* ii. 426 and n.), it appears that he drew a salary of 150*l.* per annum as a lottery commissioner, a post which he held from 1722 to 1731; and, except that he lived in the Saturnian age of letters for those who had friends in power, there was no pressing reason why he should be singled out for special honours.

It is evident, too, that his circumstances— as far as they can be ascertained from chance references—were not improved by his own dilatory and temporising habits, nor was he of a fibre to endure the shocks of fortune. When his unsubstantial South Sea riches had vanished, he sank into a state of despondency which, 'being attended with the cholic,' says the 'Biographia Britannica,' 'brought his life in danger.' This illness, from a letter written to Swift in December 1722, must have preceded his appointment as a lottery commissioner. But he still continued to look discontentedly for further advancement, which was not forthcoming. 'I hear nothing of our friend Gay,' says Swift three years later, 'but I find the court keeps him at hard meat' (*ib.* ii. 55), and from other indications it would seem that Gay trusted much to the advocacy of Mrs. Howard (afterwards Coun-

tess of Suffolk), who probably had the will but not the power to help him.

After the 'Poems' of 1720 his next production was the tragedy of 'The Captives,' which was acted at Drury Lane in January 1724 with considerable success for seven nights, the third, or author's night, being by the express command of the Prince and Princess of Wales, to whom he had read his play in manuscript at Leicester House. Towards the close of the following year we get a hint of the work upon which his reputation as a writer mainly rests. 'Gay,' Pope tells Swift in December, 'is writing Tales for Prince William' (afterwards the Duke of Cumberland). The tales in question were the well-known 'Fables.' After considerable delay, caused to some extent by the slow progress of the plates, which were designed by Wootton, the animal painter, and Kent, the first series was published by Tonson & Watts in 1727, with an introductory fable to his highness. The work was well received; but, from a remark by Swift in No. 3 of 'The Intelligencer,' it must be inferred that some of the writer's sarcasms against courtiers were thought to be over bold. At all events, when the reward he had been led to anticipate came at last with the accession of George II, it was confined to a nomination as gentleman-usher to the little Princess Louisa. 'The queen's family,' he tells Swift in October 1727, 'is at last settled, and in the list I was appointed gentleman-usher to the Princess Louisa . . . which, upon account I am so far advanced in life, I have declined accepting, and have endeavoured, in the best manner I could, to make my excuses by a letter to her majesty. So now all my expectations are vanished; and I have no prospect, but in depending wholly upon myself, and my own conduct. As I am used to disappointments, I can bear them; but as I can have no more hopes, I can no more be disappointed, so that I am in a blessed condition' (*ib.* ii. 103).

In the same letter he refers to his next effort, the famous 'Beggar's Opera,' which he declares to be 'already finished.' The first idea was Swift's, and connects itself with the old warfare against Ambrose Philips. 'I believe,' says Swift in a letter to Pope of 30 Aug. 1716, 'that the pastoral ridicule is not exhausted, and that a porter, footman, or chairman's pastoral might do well. Or what think you of a Newgate pastoral?' Gay had essayed, upon another hint in this letter, a quaker eclogue, which is to be found in vol. ii. of the 'Poems' of 1720; but for the Newgate pastoral he had substituted a lyrical drama, which was now completed. Spence (*Anecdotes*, ed. Singer, p.120) says that

of 'Tidiver' (Tideford), Cornwall (VIVIAN, *Visitations of Cornwall*, ed. 1887, p. 172; *Visitation of London*, 1633–5, Harl. Soc. i. 306; will of the elder John Gayer, P. C. C. 86, Nevill). He settled in London, and was admitted to the freedom of the city as a member of the Fishmongers' Company. He was prime warden of that company in 1638. A prominent director of the East India Company, he was frequently chosen to serve on their committees, and probably visited India (*Cal. State Papers*, Col. East Indies, 1625–1629). In 1626 he gave land to the Orphan Boys' Asylum at Plymouth, founded by Thomas and Nicholas Sherwell. With Abraham Colmer and Edmund Fowell he founded in 1630 a charity called the Hospital of the Poor's Portion in Plymouth (LYSONS, *Magna Britannia*, vol. vi. pt. ii. pp. 404–5). Gayer was chosen sheriff of London 24 June 1635, and alderman of Aldgate ward 27 Oct. 1636 (OVERALL, *Remembrancia*, pp. 9–10). As sheriff he was active in enforcing the payment of ship-money. He also allowed many of the ships in which he had a share to be 'taken up' for the king's service, but in January 1636–7 requested the lords of the admiralty not to use this concession too frequently (*Cal. State Papers*, Dom. 1635–7). On 3 Dec. 1641 he was knighted at Hampton Court (METCALFE, *A Book of Knights*, p. 197). His name was removed from the committee for ordering the militia of the city of London, 21 Sept. 1642 (*Lords' Journals*, v. 366). He was one of the gentlemen called in by the commons, 24 Dec. 1642, and asked to lend 1,000*l.* upon the security of the public faith for the purpose of maintaining the army during negotiations for peace (*Commons' Journals*, ii. 901), but he refused. He was, however, elected lord mayor on 29 Sept. 1646. During his mayoralty the king was brought to Hampton Court. On 23 July 1647 parliament passed an ordinance for compulsory service in the militia, which caused such disturbances among the city apprentices that it was annulled on the 26th. The commons, however, acting on the report of the common council and committee of the militia, resolved on 24 Sept. to impeach Gayer and four aldermen of high treason for abetting the tumult (*Commons' Journals*, v. 315–16). They were committed next day to the Tower. Gayer protested in an ably written tract issued on 28 Sept., 'Vox Civitatis, or the Cry of the City of London against the tyranny ... of the ... Army, with the Vindication of those five worthy Patriots of this City,' &c. (anon.) On 29 Sept. he was ordered to deliver his ensigns of office to Alderman John Warner, who had been elected lord mayor in his place (*ib.* v.

318, 320). At the end of October the prisoners contrived to have printed and distributed a formal 'declaration' of their innocence, which appears to have been chiefly composed by Gayer. The articles of impeachment were not carried up to the lords until 13 March 1647–8 (*ib.* v. 494). On 15 April the lords ordered Gayer to be brought to the bar. In the interval he addressed a spirited protest to the lieutenant of the Tower, in which he demanded to be tried by a jury. He managed to have this letter published as 'A Salva Libertate sent to Colonell Tichburn, Lieutenant of the Tower, on Monday, April 17, 1648. . . . Being occasioned by the receipt of a Paper sent unto him by the said Lieutenant, wherein the said Lieu^t was seemingly authorised to carry him before the Lords on Wednesday next, being the 19th of April;' the printed sheet contained an eloquent appeal to the reader, urging that Gayer was defending the liberties of all Englishmen. A man distributing the sheet was sent to Newgate charged with being concerned in a plot to rescue Gayer. Gayer refused to kneel at the bar as a 'delinquent,' and for this contempt was fined 500*l.* He demanded a jury without success. Counsel were ordered to be assigned to him, and he was recommitted to the Tower (*Lords' Journals*, x. 196, 201, 208, 219, 221). On 23 May the lord mayor (Warner) petitioned the lords for the unconditional release of the imprisoned aldermen (*ib.* x. 276, 278), and on 3 June the commons resolved to proceed no further upon the impeachment (*Commons' Journals*, v. 583, 584). Three days afterwards the prisoners were discharged (*Lords' Journals*, x. 307, 308). Gayer was removed from his office of alderman by order of the parliament on 7 April 1649 (*Commons' Journals*, vi. 181). The year before, on being elected president, he presented Christ's Hospital with 500*l.* He died on 20 July 1649. In his funeral sermon by Nathaniel Hardy at his burial in St. Catherine Cree Church on 14 Aug. following he is stated (p. 25) to have been over sixty. By his wife, Katharine, daughter of Sampson (not Samuel) Hopkins of Coventry, Warwickshire, who died before him, he left issue John, Robert, Katharine ('now wife of Robert Abdy, marchant'), Mary, Sara, and Elizabeth. In his will, dated 19 Dec. 1648 (P. C. C. 133, Fairfax), he gave large bequests to numerous charities, including 500*l.* to Plymouth, and 200*l.* to the parish of St. Catherine Cree to provide for an annual sermon on 16 Oct. The story ran that he had once been lost in a desert, when a lion had passed without hurting him in consequence of his prayers and vows of charity. The sermon is therefore known as the 'Lion Sermon.' He gave 100l. to the Fishmongers' Company to provide for a yearly distribution to the poor of St. Peter's Hospital at Newington in Surrey, also 25l. in money to make 'a faire guilt standing cupp with a cover,' and his arms engraven thereon. What is said to be a good portrait of Gayer by Lely was in 1870 in the possession of Henry Godolphin Biggs of Stockton House, Wiltshire. A fine specimen of his autograph is preserved in the British Museum Addit. MS. 19399, vol. ii. 1646-1768, No. 171, f. 13.

[Smyth's Obituary (Camd. Soc.), p. 27, where Gayer's death is said to have occurred on 12 April 1649; Notes and Queries, 2nd ser. x. 128, 175, 238, 251; Stow's Survey (Strype), bk. v. pp. 59, 144; A. E. Gayer's Memoirs of Family of Gayer, 1870; Hatton's New View of London, i. 182; Report of Charity Commissioners, 1830, xii. 197.]

G. G.

GAYER, Sir JOHN (d. 1711?), governor of Bombay, was the son of Humfrey Gayer, merchant, of Plymouth, Devonshire (fourth son of John Gayer, who died in 1593), by his wife, Miss Sparke of the same town, and nephew of Sir John Gayer (d. 1649) [q. v.] (VIVIAN, Visitations of Cornwall, ed. 1887, p. 172; Visitation of London, 1633-5, Harl. Soc., i. 306; Cal. State Papers, Dom. 1629-31, p. 152). His uncle bequeathed to him 100l. At an early age he entered the service of the East India Company, and rose to be a sea-captain.

On being appointed by the owners commander of the ship Society, he was admitted into the freedom of the company on 7 April 1682. On 3 June 1692 he was chosen governor of the port and island of Bombay. In 1693, when Sir John Goldsborough [q. v.] was appointed 'General and Commander-in-Chief, &ca.,' Gayer (who had been knighted on 18 March) was appointed (10 April) 'our Lieutenant-Generall, Governour of Bombay, and Directore-in-Chief of all our Affaires and ffactoryes, . . . next and under Our Generall Sir John Goldsborough,' whom he was to succeed in case of death. He went out in December 1693 as governor of Bombay and general, reaching the Indian coast at Calicut on 5 March 1693-4, and there hearing of the death of Goldsborough. Gayer's prolonged tenure of office was much troubled by difficulties with the 'interlopers' and the growth of the New Company. In 1699 the forerunners of the New (or English) East India Company were followed by Sir Nicholas Waite (a dismissed agent of the old company) as president at Surat and king's consul. The servants of the Old (or London) Company refused to recognise the new men or even the

authority of Sir William Norris, who came out as King William's ambassador to the Great Mogul. Waite unscrupulously turned every engine against the Old Company, not even hesitating, it would appear, to stimulate the native excitement by charging his rivals with piracy. The native government was ready enough to take advantage of these rivalries. The ambassador arrived on 10 Dec. 1700, convoyed by four king's ships. A contest in bribery began between the agents of the two companies. Gayer, who had left his stronghold at Bombay and come to Swally, the roadstead of Surat, to arrange the disputes in which the governor of Surat was involved, was arrested there, in consequence apparently of Waite's charges. Along with his wife and some of his council, he was removed to Surat by a body of native troops, and confined to the factory. His confinement, with some temporary suspension, endured for years. He was still a prisoner in the beginning of 1709, when the companies had been amalgamated. Before going to Surat, Gayer had desired to retire on account of ill-health (see his letter to the company from 'Bombay Castle, Aug. the 18th, 1699'). In their letters to the court dated from Surat, 31 March and 25 April 1706, Gayer and his council give a frightful picture of the anarchy in Guzerat and the country between Surat and Ahmedabad. At length the Old Company, in a letter to Gayer, dated 20 April 1708, intimated that Waite had been removed, although his perverse violence had driven his council previously to confine him; and, as Gayer's captivity disqualified him from succeeding, William Aislabie, deputy-governor at Bombay, had been appointed general in his place. They also hinted that Gayer might have gained his liberty had he not stood so much on the punctilios of release. He was certainly released by 5 Oct. 1710. On that day he made his will in Bombay Castle, and died there, probably in the following year (Probate Act Book, P. C. C. 1712, f. 64). He was twice married, but left no issue. His first wife, a Miss Harper, had died in India, and he desired, should he himself die there, to be buried in her tomb. His will was proved at London by his second wife, Mary, on 17 April 1712 (registered in P. C. C. 70, Barnes). After making liberal bequests to his relatives and friends, he left 5,000l. for the benefit of young ministers and students for the ministry, especially desiring that the recipients should be of the same principles as Richard Baxter.

[Diary of William Hedges, Esq., ed. Colonel Sir Henry Yule (Hakluyt Soc.), ii. cxxxvii-clv; Luttrell's Brief Historical Relation of State Affairs, 1857, v. 97.]

G. G.

GAYNESBURGH, WILLIAM DE (*d.* 1307), bishop of Worcester. [See GAINS-BOROUGH, WILLIAM.]

GAYTON, CLARK (1720?–1787?), admiral, after serving as a midshipman in the Squirrel with Captain Peter Warren on the coast of North America, and subsequently as a lieutenant in the West Indies, was promoted by Commodore Knowles to command the Bien Aimé storeship on 12 Aug. 1744. In July 1745, being then at Boston, he was appointed by Commodore Warren to command the Mermaid, in which he came home in the following March in charge of convoy. He continued to command the Mermaid on the home station till September 1747. On 10 July 1754, applying for employment, he describes himself as a man with a large family and seven years on half-pay; and on 3 Feb. 1755 adds that before that almost his whole life had been spent at sea. In the following May he commissioned the Antelope, which he commanded on the home station till August 1756, when he was moved into the Royal Anne guardship at Spithead, and in April 1757 into the Prince, for service in the Mediterranean, as flag-captain to Admiral Henry Osborn [q. v.] On Osborn's return home, in the summer of 1758, Gayton was appointed to the St. George, in which he went out to the West Indies, and joined the squadron under Commodore Moore [see MOORE, SIR JOHN, *d.* 1779] at the unsuccessful attack on Martinique and the reduction of Guadeloupe, January 1759. A doubtful story is told that Gayton and other captains at the council of war pointed out that, from the commanding height of the citadel of Guadeloupe, ships were of little use against it: 'the commodore judged otherwise, and in arranging the attack sent Gayton a written order to engage the citadel, but afterwards, seeing the St. George suffering severely from the plunging fire, he sent a verbal order for her to haul off; to which Gayton replied that, as he had a written order to engage, he could not haul off without a corresponding written order; but before this could be sent the citadel ceased firing and was evacuated by the enemy' (CHARNOCK, v. 388). Captain Gardiner, the historian of the campaign (*An Account of the Expedition to the West Indies*, p. 23), who was present at the time, knows nothing of this; and as the order of attack, detailing the St. George, together with the Cambridge and Norfolk, to engage the citadel, was necessarily and according to custom in writing, the story has an air of extreme improbability. Towards the close of the year the St. George returned to England, and continued till the peace attached to the grand fleet in the Bay of Biscay. In 1769–70 Gayton commanded the San Antonio guardship at Portsmouth. In October 1770 he became a rear-admiral, and in May 1774 left England, with his flag in the Antelope, to take command of the Jamaica station, where, during 1776 and 1777, he had frequent and troublesome correspondence with the French commodore at Cape Français, or with the French governor, concerning right of search and alleged breaches of neutrality. In April 1778 Gayton returned to England, after which he had no further service. He had been advanced to the rank of vice-admiral in February 1776, and in April 1782 was raised to the rank of admiral. During his last years he was very infirm, and lived in retirement at Fareham in Hampshire, where he died about 1787.

[Charnock's Biog. Nav. v. 387; Official Correspondence in the Public Record Office.]

J. K. L.

GAYTON, EDMUND (1608–1666), author, son of George Gayton of Little Britain, London, was born there 30 Nov. 1608. In 1622–3 he entered Merchant Taylors' School, whence he was elected to St. John's College, Oxford, in 1625. He proceeded B.A. 30 April 1629, and M.A. 9 May 1633, and was elected fellow of his college. He developed some literary faculty, visited the wits in London, and became one of Ben Jonson's adopted sons. In 1636 he was appointed superior beadle in arts and physic in his university, and was in the same year one of the actors in 'Love's Hospital, or the Hospital for Lovers,' a dramatic entertainment provided by Laud when the king and queen were his guests at St. John's College (30 Aug. 1636). He studied medicine and received a dispensation from the parliamentary delegates for the degree of bachelor of physic 1 Feb. 1647–8. In 1648 the parliamentary delegates expelled him from his beadleship. He 'lived afterwards in London in a starving condition, and wrote trite things merely to get bread to sustain him and his wife' (WOOD). He composed verses for the pageant of Lord Mayor Dethicke, exhibited 29 Oct. 1655, the first pageant allowed since Cromwell was in power. Unfortunately when the performance took place Gayton was in a debtors' prison. On 22 Sept. 1655 he was taken to the Wood Street counter, and in 1659 was removed to the King's Bench. Later in the latter year he settled in Suffolk. At the Restoration he again became beadle at Oxford, and wrote many broadside verses. He died in his lodgings at Cat Street, Oxford, 12 Dec. 1666, and was buried in St. Mary's Church. Seven days before his death he had published his 'Glorious and Living

Cinque Ports.' When convocation proceeded three days after his death to elect a new beadle, Gayton was denounced by the vice-chancellor, Dr. John Fell, as 'an ill husband and so improvident that he had but one farthing in his pocket when he died.'

Wood calls Gayton a vain and impertinent author, Hearne calls him vain and trifling. But his chief publication, 'Pleasant Notes upon Don Quixot' (fol. London, 1654), a gossipy and anecdotal commentary in four books, in both prose and verse, is spiritedly written. It embodies many humorous anecdotes and quotations from the works of little-known contemporaries, besides references of high historical interest to contemporary society and 'our late stage.' Shakespeare is thrice mentioned, pp. 21, 95, 130, but Gayton regarded his 'father, Ben,' as the greater dramatist (cf. *Notes and Queries*, 5th ser. iii. 161, x. 301). There is prefatory verse by John Speed, Anthony Hodges, and others. In the headlines of the pages the work is called 'Festivous Notes.' An expurgated, corrected, and greatly abbreviated edition in 12mo appeared (with an index) in 1768 as 'Festivous Notes on the History and Adventures of the Renowned Don Quixote.' The editor, John Potter, writes of Gayton as 'a man of sense, a scholar, and a wit.' But Potter's introduction of original illustrations drawn from contemporary events, without any indication that they were not in Gayton's own work, drew down on him a sharp reprimand in the 'Critical Review,' September 1768, p. 203. Potter replied in a new edition in 1771. Gayton's other works are: 1. 'Chartæ Scriptæ, or a new Game at Cards call'd Play by the Booke,' printed in 1645; fantastic verse description of a pack of cards. An admiring versifier in a prefatory poem tells Gayton 'your Pen reviv'd Ben Iohnson from his grave agen.' 2. 'Charity Triumphant, or the Virgin Hero. Exhibited 29 Oct. 1655, being the Lord Mayor's Day,' London, 1655, dedicated to Alderman Dethicke. 3. 'Hymnus de Febribus,' 4to, London, 1655, dedicated to William, marquis of Hertford, with commendatory verse by Francis Aston: an account in Latin elegiacs of the symptoms, causes, &c., of fevers. 4. 'Will. Bagnall's Ghost, or the Merry Devil of Gadmunton in his Perambulation of the Prisons of London,' London, 1655, in prose and verse. 5. 'The Art of Longevity, or A Diæteticall Institution,' London; printed for the author 1659, dedicated to Elizabeth, wife of John Rous of Henham Hall, Suffolk. Sir Robert Stapylton, E. Aldrich, Captain Francis Aston, and others prefix verses. The book is a verse description of the wholesomeness or other-

wise of various foods. Chapter xv.—'Of the flesh of Swine, Deer, Hares, and Bears'—opens with a reference to the 'Every Man out of his Humour' of Gayton's 'father' Jonson. 6. 'Wit Revived, or a new excellent way of Divertisement digested into most ingenious Questions and Answers,' London, 1660, under the pseudonym 'Asdryasdust Tossoffacan.' 7. 'Poem upon Mr. Jacob Bobard's Yewmen of the Guards in the Physic Garden to the tune of the Counter Scuffle,' Oxford, 1662. 8. 'Diegerticon ad Britanniam,' Oxford, 1662. 9. 'The Religion of a Physician, or Divine Meditations on the Grand and Lesser Festivals,' London, 1663. 10. 'The Glorious and Living Cinque Ports of our fortunate Island twice happy in the Person of his Sacred Majestie' (Oxford, 1666), poems in heroic verse addressed to the Duke of York, Prince Rupert, Monk, Duke of Albemarle, and others engaged in the battle with the Dutch off the Downs, June 1666. 11. 'Poem written from Oxon. to Mr. Rob. Whitehall at the Wells at Astrop, Oxford, 1666.' An answer prepared by Whitehall was not printed.

Gayton also edited—'not,' writes Wood, 'without some enlargements of his own, which hath made many to suppose that they were . . . devised' by him—'Harry Martens Familiar Letters to his Lady of Delight,' Oxford, 1663, and is said by Wood to be the author of 'Walk, Knaves, Walk; a discourse intended to have been spoken at Court. . . . By Hodge Turberville, chaplain to the late lord Hewson,' London, 1659. Gayton likewise produced two Oxford broadsides, 'Epulæ Oxonienses, or a jocular relation of a banquet presented to the best of kings by the best of prelates, in the year 1636, in the Mathematic Library at St. Jo. Bapt. Coll. (song with music in two parts),' and 'A Ballad on the Gyants in the Physic Garden in Oxon.,' Oxford, 1662.

[Wood's Athenæ Oxon. ed. Bliss, iii. 756–8, iv. 275; Wood's Fasti; Robinson's Reg. Merchant Taylors' School; Notes and Queries, 7th ser. i. 317; Collier's Bibliographical Catalogue; Brit. Mus. Cat.] S. L.

GAYWOOD, RICHARD (*fl.* 1650-1680), engraver, was a pupil of Wenceslaus Hollar [q. v.], and worked in the style and method of that artist, though without attaining at any time to the same excellence. He was a friend of Francis Barlow [q. v.], and engraved many of his designs. From a letter written by Barlow to John Evelyn, the diarist, dated 22 Dec. 1656 (see EVELYN, *Diary and Correspondence*), it appears that the large etching from Titian's 'Reclining Venus,' Gaywood's most remarkable work, was commenced by Barlow, who made the drawing from the original picture; Barlow also commenced the work on the plate, but left the completion of the etching to Gaywood, and allowed him to put his name to it. The engraving was dedicated to Evelyn, who mentions Gaywood by name in his 'Sculptura.'

Gaywood was an industrious and prolific artist. His best work is shown in his etchings of birds and animals after Barlow. The bulk of his work consisted in portraits and frontispieces to books, for which he was largely employed by the publishers. Among the portraits, many of which are mere copies from engravings by Hollar or those in the 'Centum Icones' of Vandyck, were those of William Drummond of Hawthornden, and the early kings of Scotland in his 'History of Scotland,' 1655, Oliver Cromwell, James Shirley, Sir Peter and Lady Ellinor Temple, George Monk, duke of Albemarle (after Barlow), Madame Anne Kirk, General William Fairfax, Sir Bulstrode Whitelocke, John Browne, maker of mathematical instruments (Gaywood's original drawing of this is in the print room at the British Museum), and many others. Among the frontispieces and title-pages was that to J. Wecker's 'Secrets of Art and Nature,' 1660, signed ' Ric. Gaywood, sculp.' Among other plates were a set of social scenes, representing the 'Five Senses,' a view of 'Stonehenge,' 'The most magnificent Riding of Charles the II to the Parliament, 1661,' 'The Egg of Dutch Rebellion' (a satirical print), 1673, 'Capture of a Whale at Sea,' 'Democritus,' 'Heraclitus,' &c. Gaywood is stated to have lived to 1711, but this seems uncertain.

[Walpole's Anecdotes of Painting, ed. Dallaway and Wornum ; Redgrave's Dict. of Artists; Dodd's MS. Hist. of English Engravers, Brit. Mus. Add. MS. 33401 ; Cat. of the Sutherland Collection; prints in the print room at the British Museum.] L. C.

GEARE, ALLAN (1622–1662), nonconformist divine, was born at Stoke Fleming, near Dartmouth, Devonshire, in 1622. Sir Richard Carew of Anthony, Cornwall, whose clerk he was, taught him Latin. Soon after the outbreak of the civil war he was sent to Holland with a grandson of Carew, and money and plate. On 30 Sept. 1643 he entered Leyden University (*Leyden Students*, Index Soc. p. 39), and after residing there for eight years graduated M.A., being subsequently admitted *ad eundem* at Oxford. On his return home he was chosen minister of St. Peter, Paul's Wharf, London, a preferment which he held for six years. He then removed to Woburn in Bedfordshire as chaplain to the Earl of Bedford, and stayed there about two years. In 1656 he was elected minister of St. Saviour, Dartmouth, but was ejected for nonconformity in 1662. Some of the magistrates informed against him for preaching on a Sunday after the churches had closed. He was summoned before the commissioners at Exeter in very severe weather, and caught a fever, from which he died towards the end of December 1662. He was buried in St. Saviour's churchyard, amid considerable opposition. By his marriage with a daughter of John Canne [q. v.], minister of the English independent congregation at Amsterdam, he had five children. When at Leyden he is said to have written a treatise against the baptists, but he had no concern in the works mentioned by Calamy, whose account of him is in other respects very inaccurate.

[Palmer's Nonconf. Memorial, 1802–3, ii. 16–18.] G. G.

GEARY, SIR FRANCIS (1710 ?–1796), admiral, of a family long settled in Cardiganshire, entered the navy in 1727 on board the Revenge, one of the fleet sent into the Baltic under the command of Sir John Norris, and afterwards, under Sir Charles Wager, to the support of Gibraltar. He became a lieutenant in 1734, and on the outbreak of the war with Spain served in that rank on board the Victory, carrying Sir John Norris's flag, during 1740–1. On 30 June 1742 he was promoted to command the Squirrel of 20 guns, and, cruising in her off Madeira, captured a richly laden ship homeward bound from the Spanish main. In December 1743 he was appointed to the Dolphin, but in the following February was moved into the Chester of 50 guns, in which he cruised very successfully in the Channel, making or assisting in several rich captures, French and Spanish. In the early summer of 1745 he was ordered out to join Commodore Warren at the siege of Louisbourg, and on the surrender of that place was sent home express with the news, thus losing his share in the very rich prizes which were made there shortly after his departure [see WARREN, SIR PETER]. For a short time in the winter of 1746–7 he commanded the Prince Frederick in the Channel, and in September 1747 commissioned the Culloden of 74 guns, which formed part of the Channel fleet under Sir Edward Hawke, till the peace. In February 1755 he commissioned the Somerset, one of the fleet sent out to North America under Boscawen, and afterwards, through 1756 and the early months of 1757, cruising in the Channel under the orders of Vice-admiral Osborn, who hoisted his flag on board her, or of Sir Edward Hawke. In the summer of 1757, still in the Somerset, Geary was senior officer in command of a squadron sent out to Halifax as a reinforcement to Vice-admiral Holburne [see HOLBURNE, FRANCIS]; too late, however, to enable him to undertake any active operations. Early in 1758 Geary was appointed to the Lennox, one of the grand fleet under Lord Anson in the summer of that year. In the following February he was moved into the Resolution, one of the fleet off Brest under Sir Edward Hawke [q. v.] In June he was promoted to be rear-admiral of the white, receiving orders to hoist his flag on board the Resolution, from which in August he removed into the Sandwich. In the series of gales which, in the beginning of November, drove the fleet back into Torbay, the Sandwich sprung her mainmast, and, being also very sickly, was ordered into Plymouth to refit and send her invalids to hospital. She sailed again on the 19th, too late to share in the glories of the 20th. On her way to join the fleet she was met by orders to cruise off Ushant, which she did through almost continuously bad weather, till the end of December, when she returned to Plymouth, having been at sea for upwards of seven months without a break except the three or four days in November. In the following year, still in the Sandwich, Geary commanded a squadron detached from the main fleet to cruise off Rochfort, anchoring occasionally in Basque Roads. On this service he continued till the autumn, when he joined Hawke in Quiberon Bay and was sent home. He was shortly afterwards appointed port-admiral at Portsmouth, an office which he held for the next two years. In October 1762 he was promoted to the rank of vice-admiral, and in 1770 was again appointed commander-in-chief at Portsmouth. He had scarcely entered on this command before he was involved in a curious correspondence with Captain Elphinston, who, being there as a Russian rear-admiral and in command of a Russian squadron, took on himself to fire a morning and evening gun, a practice which Geary refused to allow [see ELPHINSTON, JOHN]. In 1775 he was advanced to be admiral of the blue, and in January 1778 became admiral of the white. In May 1780 he was appointed to command the Channel fleet, and hoisted his flag in the Victory; but, though Hawke in a private letter urged him to get to his old station off Brest, to 'watch those fellows as close as a cat watches a mouse,' and, if he had the good fortune to get up to them, to 'make much of them,' neither Geary's age nor health nor instruc-

tions permitted him to undertake so trying a service, and the season passed without any operation of importance. At the end of the summer cruise he was obliged by his weak health to resign the command. In August 1782 he was created a baronet, and, after some years spent in honourable retirement, he died on 7 Feb. 1796. He is spoken of as a man of a singularly calm and equable temper, and of a most kindly disposition, but without the restless energy or dogged determination of a great commander. He married in 1748 Mary, daughter and heiress of Mr. Philip Bartholomew of Oxon Heath in Kent, by whom he had issue.

[Charnock's Biog. Nav. v. 175; Foster's Baronetage; Official Letters in the Public Record Office.] J. K. L.

GED, WILLIAM (1690–1749), inventor of stereotyping, was born in Edinburgh in 1690, where he was subsequently a goldsmith and jeweller. Van der Mey of Leyden is credited with having in the sixteenth century produced a stereo block by simply soldering the bottoms of common types together. The expense connected with this method prevented its general adoption. The subject held the minds of printers until Ged took the matter actively in hand. In 1725 he took out a patent or privilege for a development of Van der Mey's method, which held the field until Carey of Paris supplied the idea of the matrix. At this period the best types were all imported from Holland at considerable cost, and only the coarser kinds were obtainable in London. In 1725 a printer asked Ged's opinion as to the feasibility of establishing a type-foundry in Edinburgh, and both agreed that if a cast could be taken from a made-up page of type, the inventors would realise a fortune. Ged made many experiments as to the best kind of metal, and at length decided on using a similar alloy to that employed in the manufacture of type. Clay and even copper were subsequently used by other experimenters. Ged succeeded in obtaining a fair cast of a page, thus producing a stereotype; but no Edinburgh printers would enter into the matter with him, and his endeavours to apply his invention were bitterly opposed by the compositors. Ged had to make his experiments in secret, assisted by subscriptions from friends and with the aid of his son James, who had been apprenticed to a printer. He tried his fortune in London, and made an arrangement with a stationer named William Fenner, and Thomas James, a typefounder, to start a partnership business. Ged accepted a challenge from a typefounder as to which of them should produce the best stereotype block in eight days from a page of bible type. Ged gained a signal victory, but he set all the typefounders, like the compositors, against him and his art. The Earl of Macclesfield procured for him a contract (dated 23 April 1731) for printing prayer-books and bibles for Cambridge University. Only two prayer-books were completed, and the lease was surrendered in 1738. Ged came to utter grief in London through the dishonesty of Fenner and the strength of trade jealousy. Driven back in 1733 to Scotland, he struggled further to establish his invention, but failed, and became broken-hearted. In 1739 he published at Edinburgh an edition of Sallust from stereotyped plates, prepared in 1736 (2nd edit. 1744). A page of these stereotypes belonged to Sir P. M. Threipland, bart., at Fingask Castle, Perthshire. But distrustful compositors, when setting up the type, introduced bad work purposely to bring Ged's plates into disrepute. Ged died in poverty 19 Oct. 1749, after his goods had been shipped at Leith for removal to London, where Ged desired to join his son James. James Ged was a Jacobite, was captain in the Duke of Perth's regiment in the '45 rebellion, and was taken at Carlisle, but was released in 1748. He afterwards tried anew to work his father's invention. But defeated at every point he emigrated to Jamaica, where his brother William (d. 1767) had set up as a printer. Subsequently, Andrew Wilson, the Earl of Stanhope's practical man, starting where Ged left off, worked out the plaster-of-Paris plan that preceded the papier-mâché system, which has established stereotyping in its present position. Ged's daughter, in a narrative of his career, said: 'He had offers from Holland repeatedly, either to go over there or sell to the Dutch his invention, but he would not listen, as he maintained that he meant to serve his own country and not to hurt it, as handing over his invention to Holland must have done, enabling the Dutch to undersell England.'

[Narrative of Ged, written by his daughter; Nichols's Biographical Memoir of W. Ged, 1781; Wilson and Grey's Modern Printing Machinery.]

J. B-y.

GEDDES, ALEXANDER, LL.D. (1737–1802), biblical critic, born in 1737, was son of Alexander Geddes, a small farmer at Arradowl, in the parish of Ruthven, Banffshire, Scotland, by his wife, Janet Mitchel. His parents were Roman catholics, and the principal book in their scanty library was the 'authorised' version of the English bible, which he read 'with reverence and attention,' after attending the village school. Before his eleventh year he knew all bible history

by heart. Afterwards he studied, together with his brother John [q. v.], subsequently a catholic bishop, under a tutor named Sheares. In 1751 he entered the catholic ecclesiastical seminary at Scalan in the highlands. There he acquired a knowledge of the Vulgate, but it was not till 1762 that he began to read the bible in the original languages. When twenty-one (1758) he was removed to the Scotch College at Paris, and attended lectures at the college of Navarre. He studied rhetoric with great success under Vicaire. In 1759 he attended the theological lectures of Buré and De Saurent in the college of Navarre, and those on Hebrew delivered at the Sorbonne by L'Avocat, professor of the newly founded Orleans chair. He devoted some attention to natural and experimental philosophy. Having reluctantly refused the proposal of Professor L'Avocat to settle in Paris and take work at the university, he returned to Scotland in 1764, and was ordered to Dundee to officiate as priest among the catholics of the county of Angus.

In May 1765 the Earl of Traquair invited him to reside in his house in Tweeddale. He was now able to devote all his time to biblical and philological studies, and to carry out the plan conceived at an early age of preparing a new version of the holy scriptures for Scottish catholics. After nearly two years in this peaceful retreat, he fell in love with a female relative of his patron, and in view of his sacerdotal vows deemed it his duty to beat a retreat, 'leaving behind him a little poem addressed to the lady, entitled "The Confessional"' (GOOD, Life of Dr. Geddes, p. 30).

After eight or nine months at Paris in a perturbed state of mind, he returned to Scotland in the spring of 1769 and accepted the charge of a catholic congregation at Auchinhalrig, Banffshire. For a time he gave much satisfaction, frequently discharging the double duty of the neighbouring mission at Preshome, and obtaining popularity as a preacher. His ultimate want of success was in great part attributable to money difficulties. He speculated in house property at considerable loss, and built a part of the present chapel at Tynet, on the eastern side of the park at Gordon Castle, leaving to his successor the task of completing it. In 1779 he published 'Select Satires of Horace, translated into English verse, and for the most part adapted to the present times and manners,' London, 4to. These happy imitations of Horace in Hudibrastic verse, praised by Dr. Robertson, Dr. Reid, and Dr. Beattie, of Aberdeen, established his literary reputation. Unfortunately he criticised some of Bishop Hay's recent acts which had been adopted by the administrators of the mission fund. Disputes followed; the bishop displayed undue severity. Geddes was irritable and unconciliatory. The result was an open rupture. At the close of 1779 it had been amicably arranged that Geddes should leave the mission. In February 1780 Bishop Hay expressed a desire to see him at Aberdeen on his way south, in the hope of making a satisfactory pecuniary settlement. On the very Sunday in Eastertide that the bishop was spending in the Enzie, Geddes was imprudent enough to accompany a small party of friends to hear a sermon preached by the presbyterian minister of Banff. The news spread to Aberdeen. Bishop Hay had an interview with Geddes. On 8 May 1780 he reprimanded him by letter for having attended the protestant service, and for having scandalised the catholics by hunting, contrary to the canons of the church; he finally threatened to suspend him *a divinis*. Eventually towards the end of the year the bishop gave Geddes 'dimissorials,' and he was thus enabled to seek more congenial employment. His literary ability had by this time become appreciated in the north, and in 1780 the university of Aberdeen conferred on him the degree of LL.D. He was also unanimously elected a corresponding member of the Society of Antiquaries of Scotland, which he had actively helped to establish. During his residence at Auchinhalrig he mitigated, by his liberality of sentiment, the rancour which had subsisted between his own congregation and their protestant neighbours, for 'he could ridicule the infallibility of the pope, and laugh at images and relics, at rosaries, scapulars, agnus Deis, blessed medals, indulgences, obits, and dirges, as much as the most inveterate protestant in his neighbourhood' (GOOD, p. 36).

On coming to London he officiated as priest in the imperial ambassador's chapel; formed an acquaintance with many eminent scholars, and was introduced to Lord Petre. The latter admitted him to close intimacy, allowed him an annual salary of 200*l*., and provided him with the books needed to carry out his scheme of translating the bible. The first imperfect sketch of his undertaking was published in 1780 under the title of an 'Idea of a New Version of the Holy Bible, for the use of the English Catholics.' It was then his intention to translate from the Vulgate, and to make the Douay version, with Bishop Challoner's amendments, in some respects the basis of his own; but he soon abandoned this plan. At the close of 1780 the imperial chapel at which he had officiated was suppressed by the emperor Joseph II. He preached, however,

occasionally at the chapel in Duke Street (now Sardinia Street), Lincoln's Inn Fields, till the Easter holidays of 1782, after which period he gave up all ministerial functions and seldom officiated. In 1783 he was introduced to Dr. Kennicott, who urged him to proceed with his biblical design, and also to Dr. Lowth, bishop of London, by whose advice he published a 'Prospectus of a New Translation of the Holy Bible, from corrected Texts of the Originals, compared with ancient versions; with various readings, explanatory notes, and critical observations,' London, 1786, 4to, with a dedication to Lord Petre. To this he added an appendix, entitled 'A Letter to the ... Bishop of London: containing Queries, Doubts, and Difficulties relative to a Vernacular Version of the Holy Scriptures,' London, 1787, 4to. After this he published several pamphlets on contemporary topics. In 1788 appeared his 'Proposals for printing by subscription a New Translation of the Bible, from corrected texts of the original; with various readings, explanatory notes, and critical observations,' London, 4to. In this he solicited the suggestions of scholars, and he received so many that in July 1790 he published 'Dr. Geddes' General Answer to the Queries, Counsels, and Criticisms that have been communicated to him since the publication of his Proposals for printing a New Translation of the Bible.' He adopted very few suggestions, but liberally expressed his obligations to their authors. His catholic brethren already doubted his orthodoxy, and regarded him with marked suspicion and distrust. Among the 343 subscribers to the projected work very few were members of the Roman church.

The first volume of the translation appeared under the title of 'The Holy Bible, or the Books accounted Sacred by Jews and Christians, otherwise called the Books of the Old and New Covenants, faithfully translated from the corrected Text of the Original; with various readings, explanatory notes, and critical remarks,' London, 1792, 4to; and a second volume appeared in 1797. These volumes include the historical books from Genesis to Chronicles, and the book of Ruth. In the notes, and in a subsequent volume of 'Critical Remarks,' Geddes absolutely denied the doctrine of the divine inspiration of the sacred writings, rejected contemptuously opinions universally received and respected by the catholic church, and generally adopted the German methods of rationalising the narrative of the Old Testament. Dr. Van Mildert, in his 'Boyle Lectures,' remarks that 'Geddes applied the whole weight of his learning and talents to an artful attack upon the divine authority of the scriptures,' and that he treated them as 'curious remains of antiquity.' In his 'Critical Remarks' he attacked the credit of Moses as an historian, a legislator, and a moralist. Even Dr. Priestley seemed to doubt whether 'such a man as Geddes, who believed so little, and who conceded so much, could be a Christian.'

Soon after the first volume of his translation appeared, an ecclesiastical interdict, signed by Drs. Walmesley, Gibson, and Douglass, as vicars apostolic of the western, northern, and London districts, was published, in which Geddes's work was prohibited to the faithful. Against this prohibition, which Bishop Thomas Talbot refused to subscribe, Geddes published a remonstrance, but he was suspended from all ecclesiastical functions. The only addition to his labours on the 'New Version' after the appearance of the 'Critical Remarks' was a translation of a portion of the book of Psalms. He died on 26 Feb. 1802, having on the previous day received absolution from Dr. St. Martin, a French priest, who, however, said afterwards that he could not with certainty affirm that he perceived the least disposition in Geddes to recant (GOOD, p. 525). Public mass for the deceased was prohibited by an express interdict of Bishop Douglass. Geddes was buried in Paddington churchyard, in the New Road, Marylebone, where a monument was erected to his memory in 1804 by Lord Petre, inscribed with the following sentences extracted by his own desire from his works:

Christian is my name, and Catholic my surname.
I grant, that you are a Christian, as well as I;
And embrace you, as my fellow disciple in Jesus:
And, if you are not a disciple of Jesus,
Still I would embrace you, as my fellow man.

Charles Butler, who, with other members of the catholic committee, remained throughout the doctor's friend, says of his translation of the bible: 'The frequent levity of his expressions was certainly very repugnant, not only to the rules of religion, but to good sense. This fault he carried, in a still greater degree, into his conversation. It gave general offence; but those who knew him, while they blamed his aberrations, did justice to his learning, to his friendly heart, and guileless simplicity. Most unjustly has he been termed an infidel. He professed himself a trinitarian, a believer in the resurrection, in the divine origin and divine mission of Christ, in support of which he published a small tract. He also professed to believe what he termed the leading and unadulterated tenets of the Roman catholic church. From her, however scanty his creed might be, he did not so far recede as was generally thought. The estrangement of his brethren from him was most painful to his feelings' (*Hist. Memoirs*, 3rd edit. iv. 481).

An engraved portrait of Geddes is prefixed to the eulogistic 'Memoirs' of his life and writings, by his friend, John Mason Good, London, 1803, 8vo.

In addition to the works already enumerated, he wrote: 1. 'Linton: a Tweeddale Pastoral,' Edinburgh, 8vo. 2. 'Cursory Remarks on a late fanatical publication, entitled "A Full Detection of Popery,"'London, 1783, 8vo. 3. 'Letter to the Rev. Dr. Priestley, in which the Author attempts to prove, by one prescriptive argument, that the Divinity of Jesus Christ was a primitive tenet of Christianity,' London, 1787, 8vo. 4. 'Letter to a Member of Parliament on the Case of the Protestant Dissenters; and the expediency of a general Repeal of all Penal Statutes that regard religious opinions,' London, 1787, 4to. 5. 'An Answer to the Bishop of Comana's Pastoral Letter, by a Protestant Catholic,' 1790, 8vo. This was elicited by the famous pastoral of Bishop Matthew Gibson (1734–1790) [q. v.] 6. 'A Letter to the Archbishop and Bishops of England, pointing out the only sure means of preserving the Church from the Evils which now threaten her. By an Upper-Graduate,' 1790, 8vo. 7. 'Epistola Macaronica ad fratrem, de iis quæ gesta sunt in nupero Dissentientium Conventu,' London, 1790, 4to. One of the happiest attempts extant in the macaronic style. An English version for the use of ladies and country gentlemen was published by the author in the same year. 8. 'Carmen seculare pro Gallica Gente tyrannidi aristocraticæ erepta. . . . A Secular Ode on the French Revolution,' London and Paris, 1790, 4to. 9. 'The First Book of the Iliad of Homer, verbally rendered into English verse; with critical annotations,' 1792, 8vo. 10. 'An Apology for Slavery,' 1792, 8vo. An ironical essay. 11. 'L'Avocat du Diable: the Devil's Advocate,' 1792, 4to, in verse. 12. 'Dr. Geddes' Address to the Public, on the publication of the first volume of his New Translation of the Bible,' London, 1793, 4to. 13. 'A Norfolk Tale, or a Journal from London to Norwich,' 1794, 4to. 14. 'Ode to the Hon. Thomas Pelham, occasioned by his Speech in the Irish House of Commons on the Catholic Bill,' 1795, 4to. 15. 'A Sermon preached before the University of Cambridge, by H. W. C[oulthurst], D.D., &c.; in doggrel rhymes,' 1796, 4to. Dr. Coulthurst had published 'The Evils of Disobedience and Luxury,' 1796. 16. 'The Battle of B[a]ng[o]r, or the Church Triumphant. A Comic-Heroic Poem,' 1797, 8vo.

17. 'A New Year's Gift to the Good People of England; being a Sermon, or something like a Sermon, in defence of the present War,' 1798, 8vo. 18. 'A Sermon preached on the day of the General Fast, 27 Feb. 1799, by Theomophilus Brown,' 1799, 8vo. 19. 'A Modest Apology for the Roman Catholics of Great Britain,' 1800, 8vo. 20. 'Critical Remarks on the Hebrew Scriptures, corresponding with a New Translation of the Bible; containing Remarks on the Pentateuch,' vol. i. London, 1800, 4to (no more published). 21. 'Bardomachia; Poema Macaronico-Latinum,' London, 1800, 4to, and also an English translation. The subject of this piece is a celebrated battle between two rival bards in a bookseller's shop. 22. 'A New Translation of the Book of Psalms, from the original Hebrew; with various readings and notes,' London, 1807, 8vo, edited by John Disney, D.D., and Charles Butler. Geddes's translation extends only to Psalm cviii., the remainder being taken from an interleaved copy of Bishop Wilson's Bible, corrected by Geddes.

[Memoirs by Good; Husenbeth's Life of Bishop Milnes, pp. 127, 397, 475; Buckley's Life of O'Leary, p. 363; Evans's Cat. of Engraved Portraits, No. 16218; Michel's Les Écossais en France, ii. 251; Notes and Queries, 3rd ser. i. 374, iii. 21, 67; British Critic, vols. iv. xiv. xix. xx.; Cotton's Rhemes and Doway, p. 405; Georgian Era, iii. 555; Gent. Mag. lxxii. 492, lxxiii. 511; Gillow's Bibl. Dict.; Cotton's Editions of the Bible in English, pp. 105, 107, 219, 222, 238; Stothert's Life of Bishop Hay, pp. 69, 185–91, 251, 287; Edinburgh Review, iii. 374; Horne's Introd. to the Holy Scriptures, 9th edit. v. 309, 324.]

T. C.

GEDDES, ANDREW (1783–1844), painter, son of David Geddes, deputy-auditor of excise, Edinburgh, was born on 5 April 1783 (see LAING, Etchings). He received a classical education at the high school and the university of Edinburgh, and in 1803 became a clerk in the excise office. His father was a connoisseur and collector of prints; the son was so strongly drawn to art that he spent his leisure in sketching and copying engravings, and, when he was free to choose his own way of life, he resolved—fortified by the advice of John Clerk, afterwards Lord Eldin—to proceed to London and study as a painter. In 1806 he began to attend the schools of the Royal Academy, and in the same year exhibited there his first picture, a 'St. John in the Wilderness.' In 1810 he opened a studio in York Place, Edinburgh, and was soon in good practice as a portrait-painter. Four years later he visited Paris in company with Burnet the engraver, and evi-

dent traces of the Venetian masters whom he studied in the Louvre appear in the 'Ascension,' an altar-piece executed after his return for St. James's, Garlick Hill. A 'Christ and the Woman of Samaria,' shown in the Academy of 1841, and a cartoon of 'Samson and Delilah' were later efforts in the direction of religious art. His next important picture was the 'Discovery of the Regalia of Scotland in 1818,' with full-length portraits of all the commissioners appointed for its search, a picture afterwards ruined by neglect, only the portrait heads which it included being preserved. It was exhibited in the Academy in 1821, and formed the chief feature in the collected exhibition of seventy of his works which he brought together in Waterloo Place, Edinburgh, in December of the same year, and which comprised portraits, sketches from the old masters made in Paris, and 'pasticcio compositions' in the manner of Rembrandt, Watteau, &c. Before 1823 he had finally established himself in London, for in that year he declined the suggestion of his artist friends in the north that he should return to Edinburgh with the view of filling the place of leading Scottish portrait-painter, vacant by Raeburn's death. In 1832 he was elected A.R.A. He married in 1827 Adela, youngest daughter of Nathaniel Plymer, miniature-painter; and in the following year started for the continent, where he resided, mainly in Italy, till the beginning of 1831, copying in the galleries, and at Rome painting portraits of Cardinal Weld, the Ladies M. and G. Talbot (afterwards Princesses of Doria and Borghese), J. Gibson, R.A., and James Morier. In 1839 he visited Holland for purposes of artistic study. He died of consumption in Berners Street, London, on 5 May 1844.

Geddes began the systematic practice of art comparatively late, and his works occasionally show defects of form; but he improved himself by a study of the great masters, and from the first his sense of colour and tone was unerring. He is represented in the National Gallery of Scotland by five works. The 'Portrait of the Artist's Mother' is entitled to rank as the painter's masterpiece. It forms the subject of one of his finest etchings. The portrait of George Sanders, miniature-painter, also in the Scottish national collection, is a good example of his cabinet-sized full-lengths, in which both the figures and the interiors in which they are placed are rendered with the most scrupulous finish of crisp detail. Among his works of this class 'David Wilkie, R.A.,' and 'Patrick Brydone, F.R.S.,' have been admirably mezzotinted by W. Ward, who also reproduced in the same method the life-sized portraits of the 'Very Rev. George H. Baird, D.D.,' the 'Rev. Thomas Chalmers, D.D.,' and 'William Anderson.' The list of Geddes's engraved works given by Laing may be supplemented by a few minor portrait book-plates and by the important mezzotint of 'Sir John Marjoribanks, bart., of Lees,' executed in 1835 by C. Turner. His copies from the old masters were highly valued, and have brought large prices. One of them, a full-sized transcript of Titian's 'Sacred and Profane Love,' hangs in the schools of the Royal Academy, London.

As an etcher Geddes ranks even higher than as a painter; his plates may be regarded as among the very earliest examples in modern English art of the brilliancy, concentration, and spirited selection of line proper to a 'painter's-etching.' His dry-points and etchings include portraits, landscapes, and a few copies from the old masters. Ten of them he himself published in 1826; forty-three are catalogued in Laing's volume, and there printed from the original coppers (much worn), or given in reproduction in cases when these no longer existed. Some six other uncatalogued subjects are to be found in the British Museum and in private collections.

There exist three oil-portraits of Geddes painted by himself: 1. Life-sized bust, in seventeenth-century costume, in the possession of Andrew Geddes Scott, Edinburgh. 2. Life-sized, to waist, unfinished (about 1826), in National Gallery of Scotland. 3. Cabinet-sized, to waist, in seventeenth-century costume (1812), in Scottish National Portrait Gallery (engraved, by J. Le Coute, in Laing's volume).

[David Laing's Etchings by Wilkie and Geddes, Edinburgh, 1875; Memoir by his Widow, London, 1844; Catalogue of his Exhibition in Edinburgh, 1821; Catalogues of National Gallery of Scotland and of Scottish National Portrait Gallery; P. G. Hamerton's Etchings and Etchers, 1880.]   J. M. G.

GEDDES, JAMES (d. 1748?), author, was born in the county of Tweeddale. He was educated at home and at the university of Edinburgh, where he distinguished himself in mathematics. He afterwards practised with success as an advocate, but died of consumption in or before 1748. In that year was published at Glasgow his 'Essay on the Composition and Manner of Writing of the Antients, particularly Plato.' A German translation appeared in vols. iii. and iv. of 'Sammlung vermischter Schriften zur Beförderung der schönen Wissenschaften,' 1759, &c.

[Preface to Essay.]   G. G.

GEDDES, JENNY (fl. 1637?), is popularly supposed to have been the name of the woman who inaugurated the riot in St. Giles's Church, Edinburgh, when an attempt was made to read Laud's service-book on Sunday, 23 July 1637, by flinging a stool at the head of David Lindsay, bishop of Edinburgh. In 'A New Litany' (c. 1640), a contemporary ballad on Scottish affairs, reference is made to 'Gutter Jennie' as a leader of the affray (cf. Scotish Pasquils, 1868, p. 57). A herb-woman, also of the same names, gave her stall to be burnt in a bonfire at the coronation rejoicings at Edinburgh, 23 July 1661 (Edinburgh's Joy for his Majesty's Coronation in England, p. 6). Nearly thirty years later a pamphleteer attributes the throwing of the first stool to an old 'herb-woman,' but does not give her name (Notes upon the Phoenix edition of the Pastoral Letter; Works of the Rev. Samuel Johnson, p. 320). Edward Phillipps, in his continuation of Sir Richard Baker's 'Chronicle' (1670), writes, 'Jane or Janot Gaddis (yet living at the writing of this relation) flung a little folding stool.' Kirkton, writing in 1679, says the woman's name was not known. Wodrow, on the authority of Robert Stewart, a son of the lord advocate of the revolution, asserts that it was 'Mrs. Mean, wife to John Mean, merchant in Edinburgh, who cast the first stool' (Analecta, Maitland Club, i. 64). Kincaid, in his 'History of Scotland,' 1787, says the woman's name was Hamilton, and she was 'grandmother to Robert Mein, late Dean of Guild Officer in Edinburgh.' The conflict among the early writers on the topic leaves the woman's name a very open question. The name 'Jenny Geddes' is said to have been applied indiscriminately at a later date to any woman who made herself conspicuous in times of public excitement at Edinburgh. A stool in the Edinburgh Antiquarian Museum, said to be the stool thrown in the cathedral, is of doubtful authenticity.

[Burton's Hist. of Scotland, 2nd edit., vi. 150-152; Notes and Queries, 4th ser. iv. 135, 207, v. 367, 7th ser. i. 467; Scottish Leader, November 1889.]   G. G.

GEDDES, JOHN (1735-1799), Scottish catholic prelate, elder brother of Alexander Geddes [q. v.], born at the Mains of Curridoun, in the Enzie of Banffshire, on 9 Sept. 1735, entered the Scots College at Rome in 1750, and after being ordained priest in 1759 returned to the mission in Scotland. He was superior of the seminary at Scalan from 1762 till 1767, when he was appointed to the mission of Preshome in succession to Bishop Hay. In 1770 he was sent to take charge of the college which Colonel Semple had founded in Madrid in 1627, and which had been under the jesuits until they were expelled from Spain. He procured the restitution of the effects of that college in favour of the secular clergy, and its removal to Valladolid, where he continued to superintend it for ten years. In 1779 he was appointed coadjutor to Bishop Hay, vicar-apostolic of the Lowland district of Scotland, and was consecrated bishop of Morocco *in partibus* on 30 Nov. 1780 at Madrid. He resided for the most part at Edinburgh, making occasional excursions through the country. He resigned the coadjutorship on account of paralytic attacks in 1797, and died at Aberdeen on 11 Feb. 1799.

He published: 1. 'A Treatise against Duelling.' 2. 'Life of St. Margaret, Queen of Scotland.' His collection of materials for a history of the catholic religion in Scotland, arranged as annals to A.D. 1795, is preserved among the manuscripts in the library of the catholic bishop of Edinburgh (*Hist. MSS. Comm.* 1st Rep. 121).

[Gordon's Catholic Mission in Scotland, p. 454 (with portrait); London and Dublin Orthodox Journal (1837), **iv.** 120; Notes and Queries, 4th ser. iii. 21.] T. C.

GEDDES, MICHAEL, LL.D. (1650?–1713), divine of the church of England, was born in Scotland about 1650, and educated in the university of Edinburgh, where he took the degree of M.A. in 1668 (LAING, *Cat. of Edinburgh Graduates,* p. 95). He was incorporated at Oxford on 11 July 1671, being one of the first four natives of Scotland who benefited by Bishop Warner's exhibitions intended for Balliol College. Some demur being made at Balliol, these scholars were first placed in Gloucester Hall (now Worcester College), but in 1672 they were removed to Balliol (WOOD, *Fasti Oxon.* ed. Bliss, ii. 330). Previously to their incorporation these four Scotchmen called on Anthony à Wood, and 'afterwards A. W. had them to the taverne against Alls. coll., and there liberally treated them with wine' (*Life of Wood,* ed. Bliss, p. lxviii). In 1678 Geddes went to Lisbon as chaplain to the English factory. In 1686 he was forbidden by the inquisition to continue his functions, although he pleaded a privilege which had never been called in question, founded on the treaty between England and Portugal. The English merchants wrote immediately to Compton, bishop of London, to protest against this invasion of their rights; but before their letter reached its destination Geddes was suspended by the ecclesiastical commissioners appointed by James II. They were therefore forbidden all exercise of their religion till the arrival of Mr. Scarborough, the English envoy, under whose

authority, as a public minister, they were obliged to shelter themselves. Finding matters in this situation, Geddes thought proper to return in May 1688 to England, and after the promotion to the see of Salisbury of Dr. Burnet, that prelate collated him to the chancellorship of that church on 12 June 1691. The Lambeth degree of LL.D. was conferred upon him, 16 April 1695, by Archbishop Tenison (*Gent. Mag.* cxvi. 636). He died in the early part of 1713. Bishop Burnet says: 'He was a learned and a wise man; he had a true notion of popery, as a political combination, managed by falsehood and cruelty, to establish a temporal empire in the person of the popes. All his thoughts and studies were chiefly employed in detecting this; of which he has given many useful and curious essays in the treatises he wrote, which are all highly valuable' (*History of the Reformation,* iii. 306).

His works are: 1. 'The History of the Church of Malabar, from the time of its being first discover'd by the Portuguezes in the year 1501. . . . Together with the synod of Diamper, celebrated in . . . 1599, done out of Portugueze into English. With some remarks upon the faith and doctrines of the Christians of St. Thomas in the Indies,' London, 1694, 8vo. 2. 'The Church-History of Ethiopia. Wherein the two great . . . Roman missions into that empire are placed in their true light. To which are added an epitome of the Dominican History of that Church, and an account of the practices and conviction of Maria of the Annunciation, the famous nun of Lisbon,' London, 1696, 8vo. 3. 'The Council of Trent no free Assembly: more fully discovered by a collection of letters and papers of the learned Dr. Vargas and other . . . Ministers who assisted at the said Synod. Published from the original manuscripts in Spanish . . . with an introductory discourse concerning Councils, showing how they were brought under bondage to the Pope,' London, 1697, 8vo. The manuscripts consisted of original letters addressed to Cardinal Granvelle, chief minister of the Emperor Charles. They came into the possession of Sir William Trumbull, who placed them in the hands of Bishop Stillingfleet, and that prelate requested Geddes to translate them (BURNET, *Hist. of the Reformation,* ed. Pocock, iii. 305). 4. 'Miscellaneous Tracts,' 3 vols. London, 1702–6, 8vo; 2nd edit. 1709; 3rd edit. 1715. 5. 'Several Tracts against Popery: together with the Life of Don Alvaro de Luna,' London, 1715, 8vo. 6. 'The most celebrated Popish Ecclesiastical Romance: being the Life of Veronica of Milan. Begun to be translated from the Portuguese by the late Dr. Geddes, and finish'd by Mr. Ozell,' London, 1716, 8vo.

[Cat. of Printed Books in the Advocates' Library, Edinburgh, iii. 348 ; Anderson's Scottish Nation, ii. 285 ; Birch's Tillotson, p. 333 ; Burnet's Hist. of the Reformation ; Chambers's Biog. Dict. of Eminent Scotsmen ; Hist. MSS. Comm. 5th Rep. 377 ; Le Neve's Fasti (Hardy), ii. 653 ; Lowndes's Bibl. Man. (Bohn) ; Cat. of Oxford Graduates (1851), p. 254 ; Preface to Geddes's Tracts on Popery ; Watt's Bibl. Brit.]   T. C.

GEDDES, WILLIAM (1600 ? – 1694), Scottish presbyterian divine and author, was a native of Moray, and graduated at the university and King's College, Aberdeen, in 1650. On 13 Nov. of the same year he became schoolmaster of Keith; was governor to Hugh Rose of Kilravock in 1652; and gave 20l. to the new buildings of King's College, Aberdeen, in 1658. He was admitted presbyterian minister of Wick about April 1664, was transferred to the parish of Urquhart, Elginshire, in 1677, resigned on refusal to take the test of 1682, returned to Wick, where he was readmitted minister in 1692, and died in 1694, aged about 94. Geddes published a volume of pious verse entitled 'The Saint's Recreation ; (third part) upon the Estate of Grace,' Edinburgh, 1683, 4to, dedicated to Anna, duchess of Hamilton, and Margaret Lesley, countess-dowager of Weems, i.e. Wemyss, with prefatory verse by many hands. The imprimatur at the beginning of the volume (18 March 1683) states that Geddes had received permission from the privy council to print ' Memoriale Historicum, or An Historical Memorial concerning the most remarkable occurrences and periods of Scripture; the Universal Histories of the Four Monarchs: the Scottish, English, French, and Turkish Histories;' as well as 'three other books which he intends for the press, viz. " Geographical and Arithmetical Memorials," " Memoriale Hebraicum for facilitating the Hebrew Language," " Vocabularium Latino-Hebraicum in Hexameter Verse," and " Familiæ Famigeratæ." ' In an 'Apology for the Author's delay,' which follows the imprimatur, Geddes acknowledges having received ' the price' of the books, and excuses himself for not having issued them. Hew Scott mentions the ' Memoriale Historicum,' which Geddes promises in his 'Apology' at an early date, as a published work. But no copy seems known. None of Geddes's other literary projects were carried out. George Park edited at Glasgow in 1753 a second edition of 'The Saint's Recreation,' adding ' fifteen select poems on divine subjects from other approven authors.'

[Hew Scott's Fasti Eccl. Scot. v. 174, 370; Geddes's Saint's Recreation.]   S. L.

GEDEN, JOHN DURY (1822–1886), Wesleyan minister, son of the Rev. John Geden, Wesleyan minister, was born at Hastings on 4 May 1822. In 1830 he was sent to Kingswood school. In 1836 he left school and devoted himself to study and teaching. In 1844 he became a candidate for the Wesleyan ministry, and was sent to Richmond College, Surrey. After the usual three years' course Geden was appointed assistant-tutor at the college. By the conference of 1851, which met at Newcastle-on-Tyne, Geden was stationed in that town, having Dr. Punshon as one of his colleagues. After a year each in this and the neighbouring circuit of Durham, he removed to Manchester, where he spent three years in the Oxford Road circuit. His ministry won the esteem of some of the most cultivated congregations of his church. On the death of Jonathan Crowther (1794–1856) [q. v.] in January 1856, Geden was requested to fill provisionally the vacant post of tutor in the sacred and classical languages at the theological college, Didsbury, Lancashire, and by the conference of the same year was formally appointed Crowther's successor. Geden's favourite field of study was oriental literature and philology, but he also studied various branches of philosophy and natural science. Soon after his appointment to Didsbury he became joint-editor of the ' London Quarterly Review,' established in 1853, and contributed to its pages many valuable papers, among them a review of Robertson's sermons (October 1861). Meanwhile Geden's services as an occasional preacher were in request over a wide surrounding district, and his reputation became established as one of the leading thinkers and writers of methodism, though he was not often a prominent figure in public ecclesiastical assemblies.

In the autumn of 1863 Geden made a journey to the East, and passed through parts of Egypt, the Sinaitic peninsula, and the Holy Land. A dangerous attack of dysentery at Jerusalem permanently injured his delicate constitution. Some memorials of this tour appeared subsequently in the ' City Road Magazine' during 1871–3. In 1868 Geden was elected into the legal hundred.

In 1870 Geden was invited to become a member of the Old Testament Revision Company, then first formed, and for many years he regularly attended the sessions of the company at Westminster. When no longer able to travel to London, and to face the discomforts of the Jerusalem Chamber, Geden still made many suggestions to his colleagues ; he was specially anxious to preserve the dignity and rhythm of the authorised version. In

1874, at the Camborne conference, in compliance with the request of the trustees of the Fernley lectureship, Geden delivered the fifth of the series on that foundation. He chose as his subject 'The Doctrine of a Future Life as contained in the Old Testament Scriptures,' vigorously opposing the view that the doctrine is not to be found in the Old Testament. The lecture was published by the Wesleyan Conference office. In 1878 Geden published (at the same office) 'Didsbury Sermons,' fifteen discourses, in which great energy of thought and brilliancy of style are combined with strict orthodoxy.

In 1883 failing health compelled him to retire. In January 1885 he received the honorary degree of D.D. from the university of St. Andrews. After prolonged suffering, patiently endured, he died on Tuesday, 9 March 1886.

Geden was twice married : first, to Elizabeth, daughter of the late Solomon Mease, esq., J.P., of North Shields ; and secondly, to Eliza Jane, daughter of the late Robert Hawson, esq., of Scarborough, whom he also survived. By his first wife he left two sons and a daughter. The elder son is an architect; the younger became a missionary in India, where he was in charge of Royapettah College, near Madras.

[Personal knowledge and information from the family.]   A. J. F.

GEDGE, SYDNEY (1802–1883), divine, the youngest son of Peter Gedge of Bury St. Edmunds in Suffolk, was born in 1802. He was educated at Bury St. Edmunds grammar school, whence he proceeded to St. Catharine's College, Cambridge. He graduated B.A. in 1824, coming out fourteenth wrangler, and in the first class in classics. In the following year he was elected a fellow of his college. For a short time he read in chambers at Lincoln's Inn, but threw up his intention of being called to the bar, and received holy orders. For some years he was curate of North Runcton in Norfolk. In 1835 he was appointed second master of King Edward's School, Birmingham, where he remained until 1859. He was an enthusiastic supporter of the Church Missionary Society, and held the post of honorary secretary in Birmingham during the whole time he was there. In 1859 he was presented by Lord Overstone to the vicarage of All Saints, Northampton, which he held, with the rural deanery, until his retirement from active parochial work in 1875. Thenceforward he chiefly occupied himself in advancing the cause of Christian missions, by speaking and preaching for the Church Missionary Society. His acute reason-

ing power and independence in action won him much influence in Birmingham and Northampton. His readiness, especially in later years, to believe in the purity of motive of those from whom he differed in opinion procured for him the warm regard of all with whom he came in contact. In politics he was a liberal. He died in August 1883 after a few days' illness, having enjoyed to the last full vigour of body and mind. Four of his sermons were published separately.

[Private information.]   S. F. G.

GEDY, JOHN (fl. 1370), abbot of Arbroath, 'the worthy abbot of Aberbrothock' of Southey's 'Inchcape Bell,' was in office in 1370 when he entered into an engagement regarding the judge or doomster of the regality. His seal is appended to the act of parliament which regulated the succession to the crown in 1371. The contract between him and the burgesses of Arbroath, dated 2 April 1394, sets forth that, on account of innumerable losses and vexations suffered for want of a port, the abbot and convent shall make and maintain at their expense, in the best situation, a safe harbour for the burgh. The burgesses engage, on the other hand, to clear away the stones and sand, to execute other parts of the work, and to provide a certain portion of the tools required. The burgesses agree to pay to the abbot yearly on the completion of the work three pennies sterling from each rood of land within the burgh in addition to three pennies then paid. The pope's bull conferring on the abbot the privilege of wearing the mitred crown and pontifical vestments was dated 6 July 1396. There is no evidence in the burgh records, or in those of the abbey or elsewhere, that makes any allusion to a bell being placed on the Bell Rock by Gedy or another abbot.

[Chartulary of the Abbey of Arbroath.]   J. G. F.

GEE, EDWARD, D.D. (1565–1618), divine, son of Ralph Gee of Manchester, was born in 1565. He entered as servitor of Merton College, Oxford, on 22 Feb. 1582-3, and was afterwards at Lincoln and Brasenose Colleges. He graduated B.A. in 1586, and two years after was elected fellow of Brasenose College. In 1590 he proceeded M.A., in 1598 was chosen proctor of the university, in 1600 took the degree of B.D., and in 1616 that of D.D. On 19 Sept. 1599 he was instituted rector of Tedburn St. Mary, Devonshire, on the presentation of Queen Elizabeth. He was also chaplain in ordinary to James I and a fellow of Chelsea College, appointed to the latter office by Dr. Matthew Sutcliffe, the founder. Lord-chancellor Egerton made him his chaplain, and presented him in 1616 to a prebend in Exeter Cathedral. He is characterised by Wood as 'a person well known for his sincerity in conversation, generality of learning, gravity of judgment, and soundness of doctrine.' In Prince's 'Worthies' and Polwhele's 'Devonshire' there is quoted a long epitaph on his wife Jane, who died at Tedburn in 1613. The brass containing the epitaph was removed from the church on rebuilding the chancel, and is now in the possession of the rector. He married again, for at his death, which took place at Tedburn in the winter of 1618, he left a widow named Mary.

Wood ascribes to him a manual of prayers entitled 'Steps of Ascension to God; or a Ladder to Heaven,' and states that this was printed in 24mo size, and that the twenty-seventh edition came out in 1677. It is, however, by his nephew, John Gee [q.v.], author of 'The Foot out of the Snare.' The first edition is dated 1625, and the initials of the author are on the title-page. After his death his brothers, John, vicar of Dunsford, Devonshire, and George, a minister in Lancashire, edited and published his 'Two Sermons: One, The Curse and Crime of Meroz. Preached at the Asises at Exon. The Other, a Sermon of Patience, at St. Maries in Oxford,' London, 1620, 4to. The second of these sermons was preached when he was fellow of Brasenose College.

[Wood's Athenæ Oxon. (Bliss), ii. 258; Wood's Fasti Oxon. i. 236, 251, 278, 285, 367; Prince's Worthies of Devon, 1701, p. 337; Le Neve's Fasti (Hardy), i. 422, ii. 491; Register of the University of Oxford (Oxford Hist. Soc.), vol. ii. pt. ii. p. 125; Notes and Queries, 6th ser. ii. 71; information supplied by the Rev. J. Ingle Dredge, the Rev. C. W. E. Tothill, and Mr. Winslow Jones.]   C. W. S.

GEE, EDWARD (1613–1660), presbyterian divine, was thought by Wood to be the son of Edward Gee, vicar of Tedburn [q. v.], and to have been born at Banbury, Oxfordshire, in 1613; but it has since been proved that he was the son of Edward's brother George, who was minister of Newton in the parish of Manchester (EARWAKER, *Manchester Court Leet Records*, iii. 302), and who probably lived at Banbury at the time of his son's birth. He was educated at Newton school and entered Brasenose College, Oxford, as a commoner on 26 Oct. 1626, taking the degree of B.A. in October 1630. He proceeded M.A. in June 1636, having in the meantime entered the ministry. He became chaplain to Dr. Richard Parr, at that time both bishop of Sodor and Man, and rector of Eccleston, near Chor-

ley, Lancashire. In June 1640 Gee was married at Eccleston to Elizabeth Raymond. Three years later he succeeded Dr. Parr as rector of Eccleston, which living was in the gift of Lord Saye as guardian of Richard Lathom; but he left the choice of minister to the people, and they nominated Gee. In March 1647–8 William Ashhurst wrote to the speaker Lenthall, asking that Gee, 'who had the approbation of all honest and good ministers,' might be continued in the living, and the request was complied with. In 1644 (13 Dec.) he was appointed a commissioner to ordain ministers in Lancashire, and in 1646 was elected a member of the sixth classis (Preston) of the Lancashire presbytery; and ultimately attained a leading position in that body. Adam Martindale (*Life*, p. 91) calls him a 'great knocker for disputation' and a 'solid and substantial man.' In 1648 he signed the 'Harmonious Consent of the Ministers of the Province of . . . Lancaster with their Reverend Brethren of . . . London.' In February of the same year his name is appended, as scribe to the provincial synod held at Preston, to 'A Solemn Exhortation made and published to the several Churches of Christ within the Province of Lancaster,' London, 1649, 4to. He was also one of the signers of the answer to the paper called 'The Agreement of the People,' 1649. He is credited (*Life of Martindale*, p. 98) with writing 'A Plea for Non (Sub) Scribers, or the Grounds and Reasons of many Ministers . . . for their Refusall of the late Engagement modestly Propounded,' 1650, 4to, pp. 136. About this time he wrote two other anonymous pamphlets: 1. 'An Exercitation concerning Usurped Power,' 4to, without date. 2. 'A Vindication of the Oath of Allegiance, in answer to a Paper disperst by Mr. Sam. Eaton,' 1650, 4to. Soon after this he was suspected, along with other Lancashire divines, of corresponding with the Scotch party and of encouraging dissatisfaction with the existing government (*Cal. State Papers*, Dom., 1651, p. 397). He was arrested pursuant to an order of the council of state of 2 Sept. 1651, but was released after a few weeks' confinement. In 1653 he published 'A Treatise of Prayer and of Divine Providence as relating to it,' 8vo, pp. 499, of which there was a second edition in 1666. He was joint author with Hollinworth of a preface to Brownsword's 'Rome's Conviction,' 1654, and in the same year became an assistant commissioner for ejecting 'ignorant and scandalous ministers and schoolmasters.' His last publication was 'The Divine Right and Originall of Civil Magistrates from God Illustrated and Vindicated,' 1658, 8vo, apparently written in favour of Charles II, then in exile. In November 1656 he preached a funeral sermon on Richard Hollinworth, and received the thanks of the Manchester classis. He died at Eccleston on 27 May 1660, and was buried in his church there.

[Wood's Athenæ Oxon. (Bliss), iii. 503; Wood's Fasti, i. 454, 489; Life of Martindale (Chetham Soc.); Newcome's Autob. (Chetham Soc.) i. 120; Life of Nath. Heywood, 1695, p. 5; Lancashire Church Surveys (Record Soc.); pp. 116, 117; Local Gleanings, i. 208, ii. 275, 300; Hibbert-Ware's Manchester Foundations, vol. i.; Raines's Notitia Cestriensis (Chetham Soc.), xxii. 372; Halley's Lancashire, its Puritanism, &c.; French's Chetham Church Libraries (Chetham Soc.), p. 178; Fishwick's Lanc. Library, p. 390; Fishwick's Kirkham (Chetham Soc.), p. 104; Brit. Mus. Cat.]   C. W. S.

GEE, EDWARD, D.D. (1657–1730), protestant writer, son of George Gee of Manchester, shoemaker, was born in 1657, being baptised at the Manchester collegiate church on 29 Aug. that year. After attending the Manchester grammar school he was admitted a sub-sizar at St. John's College, Cambridge, on 9 May 1676, graduated B.A. in 1679 and M.A. in 1683. He was incorporated in his master's degree at Oxford 4 March 1683–4. Subsequently, after December 1701, he is styled D.D., but the source of that degree is uncertain. He took a prominent part in the 'popish controversy' towards the end of James II's reign, in which contest he wrote the following quarto tracts: 1. 'Veteres Vindicati, in an expostulatory letter to Mr. Sclater of Putney,' &c., 1687. 2. 'An Answer to the Compiler of the Nubes Testium,' 1688. 3. 'A Vindication of the Principles of the Author of the Answer,' &c., 1688. 4. 'The Primitive Fathers no Papists,' 1688. 5. 'The Judgment of Archbishop Cranmer concerning the People's Right to, and discreet Use of, the Holy Scriptures,' 1689. 6. 'A Letter to Father Lewis Sabran' (on Invocation of Saints), 1688. 7. 'A Second Letter to Sabran,' &c., 1688. 8. 'A Third Letter to Sabran,' 1688. 9. 'A Letter to the Superiours who approve and license the Popish Books in England,' 1688. 10. 'The Texts Examined which Papists cite out of the Bible for the Proof of their Doctrine concerning the Worship of Images and Reliques,' 1688. 11. 'The Texts examined concerning the Seven Sacraments,' 1688. 12. Part II. of the same, 1688. 13. 'The Catalogue of all the Discourses published against Popery during the Reign of King James II,' 1689. Several of these are reprinted in Gibson's 'Preservative against Popery,' and Cardwell's 'Enchiridion.' He also published 'The Jesuit's

Memorial for the intended Reformation of England: with an Introduction and some Animadversions,' 1690, 8vo. This 'Memorial' was written by Robert Parsons [q. v.] In 1692 he printed 'Of the Improvement of Time, a Sermon,' 1692, 4to.

In May 1688 he was appointed rector of St. Benet's, Paul's Wharf, London, and soon after he was called chaplain in ordinary to William III and Queen Mary. On 6 Dec. 1701 he was installed prebendary of Westminster. Twenty years afterwards, on 9 Dec. 1721, he was instituted dean of Peterborough, but he resigned that office for the deanery of Lincoln, to which he was presented by the crown on 30 March 1722. A few days later he was installed prebendary of Lincoln. At the time of his death he was also incumbent of St. Margaret's, Westminster, and rector of Chevening, Kent. He died on 1 March 1729–30, and was buried in Westminster Abbey.

He married, on 25 Jan. 1702–3, Jane, daughter of Henry Limbrey of London and Hoddington in Upton-Gray, Hampshire, and by her had several children, whose names are recorded in the Westminster Abbey registers.

[Wood's Fasti Oxon. (Bliss), ii. 388, iv. 222; Chester's Westm. Abbey Reg. (Harleian Soc.), p. 327, &c.; Marriage Licences, Faculty Office (Harleian Soc.), p. 244; Jones's Popery Tracts (Chetham Soc.); Le Neve's Fasti (Hardy), ii. 36, 232, 540, iii. 363; Newcourt's Repertorium, i. 302; Notes and Queries, 5th ser. i. 16, 138, 237, 6th ser. i. 72.]   C. W. S.

GEE, JOHN (1596–1639), writer against Roman catholics, was grandson of Ralph Gee of Manchester, nephew of Edward Gee (1565–1618) [q. v.], and son of John Gee (d. 1631), incumbent of Dunsford, Devonshire, by his wife Sarah. He matriculated at Brasenose College, Oxford, 13 July 1612, aged 16, and migrated to Exeter College, where he graduated B.A. 28 Feb. 1616–7, and M.A. 17 Oct. 1621. After taking holy orders he obtained a benefice at Newton, near Winwick, Lancashire, in 1622. He would seem to have been temporarily converted to Roman catholicism, and settled in London, where he soon came to live on terms of intimacy with noted persons of the Roman catholic persuasion. He attended the 'Fatal Vespers' at Blackfriars (26 Oct. 1623), when the floor fell in and almost all the worshippers were killed [see DRURY, ROBERT (1587–1623)]. Gee escaped unhurt. He afterwards explained that the fame of the preacher Drury induced him to be present. A few days later the Archbishop of Canterbury summoned him to an interview. The archbishop's chaplains, Goad and Featley, conversed with him, and he readily consented to rejoin the church of England. The supplications of his aged father contributed to this decision. To prove the sincerity of his conversion he published in 1624 'The Foot out of the Snare; with a detection of sundry late practices and impostures of the Priests and Iesuites in England; whereunto is added a Catalogue of Popish Bookes lately dispersed in our Kingdome, the Printers, Binders, Sellers, and Dispersers of such Bookes, Romish Priests, and Iesuites resident about London, Popish Physicians practising about London,' London, 1624. The dedication is to the Archbishop of Canterbury and the members of both houses of parliament. The book is full of stories, many purporting to be drawn from the author's personal experience, of the deceptions and vices practised by popish priests. Its publication caused intense excitement, and it rapidly passed through four editions. Some Roman catholics, according to Gee, threatened to cut his throat. Many protestants deprecated its vindictive tone. To one Musket, a secular priest, who complained that Gee had falsely called him a jesuit, Gee replied with biting sarcasm in the fourth edition. The work is historically interesting from its wealth of contemporary allusions. It was reprinted in the 'Somers Tracts,' and the valuable catalogues appear in Foley's 'Records of the Society of Jesus' (i. 671–83). An appendix also appeared in 1624 entitled 'New Shreds of the Old Snare, containing The apparitions of two new female ghosts. The copies of diuers Letters of late intercourse concerning Romish affaires. Speciall Indulgences purchased at Rome, granted to diuers English gentle-beleeuing Catholiques for their ready money. A Catalogue of English Nunnes of the late transportations within these two or three yeares.' And in the same year Gee preached a sermon at St. Paul's Cross, which he published with a dedication to Sir Robert Naunton. A very popular book of prayers, entitled 'Steps of Ascension to God, or a Ladder of Heaven,' 12mo, London, 1625, is ascribed by Wood to' Gee's uncle Edward. But the preface shows that it was Gee's own work. The twenty-seventh edition bears date 1677. Gee was afterwards beneficed at Tenterden, Kent, where he died in 1639.

A brother, SIR ORLANDO GEE (1619–1705), twenty-three years John Gee's junior, was in the service of Algernon, earl of Northumberland, through whose influence he became in 1660 registrar of the court of admiralty, and was knighted 18 Aug. 1682. He married, first, Elizabeth, daughter of Sir William Maxey, and, secondly, Ann, daughter of Robert Chilcot of Isleworth, Middlesex. Sir Orlando was a benefactor to the parish church of Isleworth, where he was buried in 1705 (*Notes and Queries*, 4th ser. iv. 21–2). He married Elizabeth Barker by license dated 17 May 1662 (CHESTER. *Marriage Licences*, ed. Foster, p. 535).

[Boase's Register of Exeter College, pp. 211, 232; Foley's Records, i. 74; Wood's Athenæ Oxon., ed. Bliss, ii. 390–3; Hasted's Kent, iii. 102.]

S. L.

GEERAN or GUERIN, THOMAS (*d.* 1871), reputed centenarian, was, according to his two credulous biographers, son of Michael Geeran, a farmer, and was born at Scarriff, co. Clare, on 14 May 1766. The same authorities make the following doubtful statements respecting him. He remained at school until his twentieth year, during which time he learnt a little French and Latin, and became a master of arithmetic. On the death of his father he removed to Limerick, where he lived some years, until he enlisted in the army in March 1796. After a voyage of twelve months and two days he landed at Madras, joined the 71st highlanders, and was present in 1799 at the siege of Seringapatam. In 1801 his regiment was sent to Egypt. In 1809 he was present with his regiment at the battle of Corunna, and in 1815 at Waterloo. He returned to England in 1819, and was discharged from the army at Gosport, but without any pension. After this he worked at his trade of a sawyer in various parts of the country. Finally he settled at Brighton, where he made a living by relating his military experiences and dilating on his great age. He died in the infirmary of the Brighton union on 28 Oct. 1871, aged, according to his friends, 105 years and five months.

Mr. W. J. Thoms, F.S.A., investigated this case, and at the Public Record Office, London, obtained access to the original muster-rolls, pay-sheets, and description-rolls of the 71st regiment. From these he established the facts that Geeran had never served abroad with that regiment, and that the regiment had not been in many of the places as mentioned by him. Geeran's case was, on his own applications for a pension, investigated several times by the authorities of Chelsea Hospital, who failed to find any record of his services. However, from the pay-sheets of the regiment it appeared that a Michael Gearyn or Gayran enlisted on 3 March 1813, and deserted on 10 April following. If this were the same person as T. Geeran, as is most likely, he was in the army for about a month only, and at the time of his death was probably about eighty-three. Two lives of Geeran were written. The first, published by subscription for his benefit, was entitled 'Life of Thomas Geeran, a Centenarian, with photograph and autograph. [By H. R. Williams, M.A., Ph.D.] London; Brighton Circulating Library,' 1870. The second was called 'Longevity, with Life, Autograph, and Portrait of Thomas Geeran, a Centenarian, Brighton,' 1871. In these two works, published within two years, appear many notable contradictions.

[Thoms's Human Longevity, 1873, pp. 12, 131–54; Times, 20, 22, 24, 25, 27 Nov. 1871; Medical Times, 25 Nov. 1871, pp. 642–3.]

G. C. B.

GEFFREY, Sir ROBERT (1613–1703), London merchant and lord mayor, son of Robert Geffrey of Tredennack, was baptised at Landrake, Cornwall, on 24 May 1613. His parents were of humble means, and he appears to have left home at an early age for London, where he realised a large fortune. He is said by some to have been a Turkey merchant, and by others to have been in the East India trade; his house was in Lime Street, and there he carried on business for over fifty years. Geffrey was a large importer of tobacco, and suffered severe loss in the great fire of 1666; Chamberlayne, in his 'Present State of England,' states that he had 20,000*l*. worth of tobacco destroyed in 'the vast incendy' (*Notes and Queries*, 4th ser. xi. 310–11).

Geffrey was an influential member of the company of Ironmongers, and was one of the six persons appointed to represent them at Guildhall on 5 July 1660, when Charles II was entertained by the city. In 1664 he was warden, and in 1667 master, of the company, and when, in 1683, Charles II seized the company's charter under the *quo warranto*, Geffrey was deputed to deliver their petition of submission to the king. James II gave them a new charter, in which he reserved to the crown the right of displacing the master, wardens, and court of assistants, and appointed Geffrey the first master under the charter, in the place of William Hinton, who had been elected to the office in the regular course. By an order in council, dated 25 Sept. 1685, Geffrey and twenty-one others were dismissed from the office of assistant, and not replaced until 1688, when the king made a general restitution to the corporate bodies of their forfeited privileges (NICHOLL, *Hist. of the Ironmongers' Company*, 1866, pp. 275, 301, 322, 331).

On midsummer day 1673 Geffrey was elected sheriff of London and Middlesex, and at the mayoralty banquet in that year sixteen of the livery and twenty-two of the yeomanry of his company dined with him at Guildhall, the court of assistants contributing a hundred nobles, according to custom, 'towards the trimming of his house.' On this occasion Geffrey and his colleague, Henry Tulse, were knighted. Geffrey was elected on 22 June 1676 alderman of the ward of Cordwainer, and continued to represent this ward until his death, except for a brief period from 16 Aug. 1687, when all the aldermen were discharged by the king, to be reinstated in the following year (*City Records*, Repertory 81 f. 224, 92 f. 363). His mayoralty was in 1685, and the Ironmongers' Company prepared a splendid pageant for his inauguration, no member of the company having been mayor for fifty years before. The total expense incurred was 473*l*. 0*s*. 4*d*., which included 10*l*. given to Matthew Taubman, then city poet, for the speeches and songs composed for the occasion, entitled 'London's annual triumph . . . London, printed for Hen. Playford, near the Temple Church, 1685' (NICHOLL, p. 305). This pageant is now very scarce; a copy is preserved at the Bodleian Library, and another at the Guildhall Library; it is reprinted at length by Nicholl in his 'History' (pp. 306–21). The water procession was witnessed by the king from the leads of Whitehall (*London Gazette*, 2 Nov. 1685), and, this being the first mayoralty feast in the new reign, their majesties honoured the city with their presence at Grocers' Hall.

Geffrey was colonel of one of the regiments of the trained bands in 1681, and was elected president of Bridewell and Bethlehem Hospitals in March 1692–3. On William III's return to London, after the peace of Ryswick, in 1697, Geffrey was excused by the court of aldermen, on account of his age and infirmities, from riding before the king with the other aldermen (*City Records*, Rep. 102, f. 3). He died on 26 Feb. 1703–4, having been for many years father of the city, and was buried on 10 March in the church of St. Dionis Backchurch, where he had long been a parishioner (COLONEL CHESTER, *Registers of St. Dionis*, Harleian Soc., pp. 237, 272). He married Priscilla, daughter of Luke Cropley, a London merchant, but had no children. She died on 26 Oct. 1676, in her forty-third year (HATTON, *New View of London*, 1708, vi. 212). Geffrey had a colleague upon the court of aldermen named Jeffery Jeffreys, and one of the two, most probably Sir Robert, was very intimate with their famous namesake Sir George Jeffreys, the judge, and promoted his interests in the city. Woolrych, in his 'Life' of the judge (p. 25), says: 'Although it does not seem to be agreed whether they were in any way related to him, there being assertions on both sides, one of them, a great smoker, took a vast fancy to his namesake.'

Among the Tanner MSS. in the Bodleian Library (142, Art. 41) there is a letter from Geffrey to Archbishop Sancroft, dated 29 Sept. 1686; and many interesting letters written by him are said to be preserved in the collections of the Archer family at Trelaske (POLSUE, *Parochial Hist. of Cornwall*, ii. 397). By his will, dated 10 Feb. 1703, and proved in the P. C. C. 3 March 1703 (63 Ash), after many bequests to friends, relatives, hospitals, and clergymen's widows, he established certain trusts under the charge of the company of Ironmongers. A service was to be provided twice daily in the church of St. Dionis Backchurch, a school was to be maintained at Landrake, and the poor of St. Erney and Landrake to be relieved. The residue of his estate was to be devoted to the erection of almshouses in or near London. The company accordingly purchased a piece of ground in Kingsland Road, on which they built fourteen almshouses and a chapel, and appointed rules for their government on 17 Nov. 1715 (NICHOLL, pp. 569–73). There are now forty-two pensioners, each of whom receives 12*l.* per annum. In the foreground of the building is a statue of Geffrey, executed for the Ironmongers' Company in 1723 by John Nost, and, on the removal of the church of St. Dionis Backchurch in 1878, Geffrey's remains and those of his wife were re-interred in the burial-ground attached to the almshouses (*Notes and Queries*, 5th ser. xi. 57). A full-length portrait of Geffrey, by Sir Godfrey Kneller, is preserved at Bridewell Hospital, and has been engraved by Trotter (*London and Middlesex Archæol. Soc. Trans.* ii. 72). Another portrait in full length, at Ironmongers' Hall, was painted for the company by Richard Phillips for thirty guineas (NICHOLL, p. 344); a copy in water-colour is in the Guildhall Library (*MS.* 20).

[Luttrell, i. 76, 411, iii. 56; Boase and Courtney's Bibl. Cornub. i. 169–70, ii. 1192; Malcolm's Lond. Rediv. ii. 35, 38–9, 45–7, 571. The information given in Herbert's Twelve Great Companies, vol. ii. passim, is to be found in fuller detail in Nicholl's Hist. of the Ironmongers' Company.] C. W–H.

GEIKIE, WALTER (1795–1837), painter and draughtsman, son of Archibald Geikie, a perfumer, was born in Charles Street, George Square, Edinburgh, on 9 Nov. 1795. A nervous fever, which attacked him before he was two years old, left him deaf and dumb for life. His father gave him his earliest education, and afterwards placed him under Thomas Braidwood [q. v.], a successful teacher of the deaf and dumb, with whom he made rapid progress. His path in life was soon indicated by his passion for sketching. Accordingly at the age of fourteen he began to learn drawing from Patrick Gibson, and in 1812 was admitted a student of the Trustees' Academy, of which John Graham was then master. He took to painting in oil with great enthusiasm, but without much success. He began to exhibit in 1815, and contributed largely to the Royal Scottish Academy from its first exhibition in 1827. He was elected an associate of that body in 1831, and an academician in 1834. Most of his pictures are deficient in colour, but those in which he confined himself to groups of figures are less objectionable than his landscapes. There is one, a 'Cottage Scene, with figures,' in the National Gallery of Scotland; but his best paintings are a 'Scene in the Grassmarket,' 1828, 'All-Hallow Fair,' 1829, and 'Itinerant Fiddlers,' painted for the Earl of Hopetoun, and now at Hopetoun House, Linlithgowshire. His reputation rests chiefly on his clever sketches and etchings of everyday scenes in and around his native city, which he sought assiduously sketch-book in hand. These are executed with a spirit and dexterity which well convey the humour of the subjects. His first etching was that of 'John Barleycorn,' which was executed as a tailpiece to the ballad in David Laing's 'Fugitive Scottish Poetry,' 1825. He afterwards etched several other plates for the works of the Bannatyne Club. The first fourteen plates which he etched on his own account were published by himself, but others were sold to publishers, and the whole were eventually collected into a volume of 'Etchings illustrative of Scottish Character and Scenery,' with explanatory text, and a biographical introduction by Sir Thomas Dick Lauder, and published in 1833. They were republished with additional plates in 1885. Although deaf and dumb, Geikie possessed great social qualities, and his mirthful spirit and love of mimicry made him a great favourite among his brother artists. He died at Edinburgh, after a few days' illness, on 1 Aug. 1837, and was buried in the Greyfriars' churchyard. He left an immense collection of sketches in pencil and Indian ink, the greater number of which passed into the hands of Mr. James Gibson Craig and Mr. Bindon Blood.

[Sir Thomas Dick Lauder's Biographical Introduction to Geikie's Etchings illustrative of Scottish Character and Scenery, 1833; Chambers's Biog. Dict. of Eminent Scotsmen, 1875, ii. 95; Armstrong's Scottish Painters, 1888, p. 20; Exhibition Catalogues of the Royal Scottish Academy, 1827–37.] R. E. G.

GELASIUS or GILLA MAC LIAG (1087–1173), coarb of Armagh and primate of Ireland, is termed son or more correctly grandson of Rudhraidhe, and also, son of the poet, his father having been poet of the Hy Briuin of Connaught. In 1121 he was erenach, or hereditary warden, of Derry, and he is also termed coarb, or successor, of Colum Cille. During his tenure of these offices Armagh was the subject of frequent intrigues for the introduction of the organisation of the Roman church (see the learned Memoir introductory to the *Early History of the Primacy of Armagh*, by the Rev. Robert King). Malachy O'Morgair was forcibly installed as primate, but failed to get possession of Armagh, or of the credentials of the coarb, and retired to the bishopric of Down after nominating Gelasius as his successor. Gelasius had supported his views, and was acceptable to the advocates of the old order from his position at Derry, which had always been closely associated with Armagh. He was accordingly elected, and in 1137 became coarb of St. Patrick. The claim of Armagh to supremacy had long been acknowledged, but its jurisdiction in the modern sense was not yet established. To promote this object Gelasius in 1138 carried out a visitation of Munster, and obtained his 'full tribute.' Two years later he received 'a liberal tribute' in Connaught, and secured the adhesion of King Turlough to the new church regulations. In Tyrone he received a cow from each house belonging to a *biatach* or free-man, a horse from every chieftain, and twenty cows from the king himself.

The Irish churches had hitherto been generally of wood, but Gelasius, following the example of Malachy in building with stone, prepared for the work by erecting a large kiln, sixty feet in length on each side, 'opposite the Navan fort on the west side of Armagh.' The entry of this fact in the 'Annals of the Four Masters' shows the novelty of stone building in those days. In 1151 Cardinal Paparon arrived in Ireland, bringing with him four palls which had been formally applied for in the synod of Inispatrick in 1148. At the synod of Kells, held in the following year, Gelasius was present, but Cardinal Paparon and the legate Christian of Lismore took the precedence. Two additional archbishoprics (Tuam and Dublin) were constituted, and the palls were duly conferred on Gelasius and the others. The 'Four Masters' do not mention the palls, and there seems to have been a strong party opposed to these innovations, as well as to the establishment of the new archbishoprics.

Another synod was held at Drogheda in 1157, when Gelasius, with the papal legate,

seventeen bishops, and four kings, assembled to consecrate the church built at Mellifont, in the county of Louth, by the Cistercians, lately introduced by St. Bernard from Clairvaux. One king presented 140 cows and sixty ounces of gold, and two others gave the same quantity of gold, one of them adding a golden chalice.

Gelasius subsequently called a synod at Clane, co. Kildare, at which twenty-six bishops were present, when it was enacted that no one should hold the office of lector who had not been trained at Armagh; the object being to promote uniformity of doctrine and discipline throughout Ireland. The most important synod held in Ireland during his time was that of Cashel in 1172, presided over by the papal legate, and attended by the commissioners of Henry II, who subscribed its decrees. It was ordered that the Irish church should observe uniformity with the church of England ' according to the use, custom, rite, and ceremony of the church of Salisbury,' and the payment of tithes was for the first time made compulsory. Gelasius, now in his eighty-fifth year, was too infirm to attend, but, according to Cambrensis, gave his assent to all that was done. He died in 1173. His piety is praised by the 'Four Masters,' and the simplicity of his life appears from the story related by Cambrensis that ' it was his custom to take with him, whithersoever he went, a white cow, the milk of which formed his only sustenance.' He has been sometimes called the first archbishop of Armagh, as being the first who had the pall.

[Annals of the Four Masters, 1137–73; King's Memoir of the Primacy of Armagh; Petrie's Round Towers, p. 305; Lanigan's Eccles. Hist. iv. 102–3.]

T. O.

GELDART, EDMUND MARTIN (1844–1885), unitarian minister, second son of Thomas Geldart, sometime of Thorpe, near Norwich, and his wife, Hannah Ransome Geldart, author of a number of popular religious books for children (who died in 1861, aged 41), was born at Norwich on 20 Jan. 1844. He went for a short time to Merchant Taylors' School. When he was twelve years old his father, having undertaken the superintendence of the Manchester City Mission, removed from London to Bowdon, Cheshire, and Geldart was sent to a private school kept by a clergyman at Timperley. He now developed a taste for entomology, and projected and, along with his young friends Thomas and J. B. Blackburn, edited a periodical entitled 'The Weekly Entomologist,' published at twopence a number from August 1862 to

November 1863. After spending three months at Oxford, whither his schoolmaster had removed, he went to the Manchester grammar school, then under the mastership of Mr. F. W. Walker, afterwards of St. Paul's School. From this school he was elected to a scholarship at Balliol College, where he matriculated on 26 March 1863. He graduated B.A. in 1867, and was appointed assistant-master at the Manchester school. Ill-health compelled him to relinquish his post. He went abroad, and settled for a time at Athens, where he occupied himself as a teacher, and acquired a remarkable knowledge of the language and ideas of modern Greece. On his return to England he married Charlotte F. S. Andler, daughter of a Würtemberg government official. In 1869 he again accepted a mastership of classics and modern languages at the Manchester grammar school, and at the same date was ordained deacon by the Bishop of Manchester, and became curate of All Saints Church, Manchester. Two years later he took a curacy at St. George's Church, Everton, Liverpool, but did not retain it long, as his religious views underwent a change, and in 1872 he joined the unitarians. He graduated M.A. in 1873, and from the summer of that year until 1877 he acted as minister of the Hope Street Unitarian Chapel, Liverpool, and then removed to Croydon, where, after officiating as substitute for the Rev. R. R. Suffield [q. v.] at the Free Christian Church, he was appointed pastor of that church. He was esteemed an able and original preacher, and a man of pure motive, transparent character, and unselfish purpose. A year or two before his death he became imbued with socialistic opinions, and in his enthusiasm for 'humanity' went much further than his congregation thought prudent. Early in 1885 his connection with the Croydon Free Church terminated. He had been in ill-health, and on 10 April 1885 he left home for Paris for a holiday. He embarked at Newhaven, but was never heard of again, and it is supposed that he was lost on the night voyage to Dieppe. He was author of: 1. 'Modern Greek in relation to Ancient,' Clarendon Press, 1870. 2. 'The Living God,' 1872, one of the tracts issued by Thomas Scott of Ramsgate. 3. 'The Church at Peace with the World : a Sermon suggested by the Death of David Friedrich Strauss,' 1874. 4. Translation of the second volume of Keim's 'Jesus of Nazara,' 1876. 5. 'Faith and Freedom: fourteen Sermons,' 1881. 6. 'A Son of Belial: autobiographical Sketches by Nitram Tradleg,' 1882. This is a real autobiography, although the names are hidden under a slight disguise. Some of the characters are drawn with a very caustic pen.

'Nitram Tradleg' is his own name reversed. 7. 'A Guide to Modern Greek,' 1883; also a key to the same. 8. 'Simplified Grammar of Modern Greek,' 1883. 9. 'Sunday for our Little Ones: Unsectarian Addresses to the Young,' 1883. 10. 'The Gospel according to Paul: an Essay on the Germs of the Doctrine of the Atonement,' 1884. 11. 'Let there be Light: Sermon delivered at the opening of the New Free Christian Church, Croydon,' 1884. 12. Translation of Hahn's 'Folk-Lore of Modern Greece,' 1884. 13. Translation of Zacher's 'The Red International,' 1885. 14. 'Echoes of Truth: Sermons, &c., with Introductory Sketch by the Rev. C. B. Upton. Edited by Mrs. Geldart,' 1886, with portrait of Geldart.

[Biog. Sketch by John Morgan, reprinted from the Croydon Advertiser of 12 Dec. 1885; Inquirer, 2 May 1885; Unitarian Herald, 24 April 1885; Foster's Alumni Oxon. ii. 516; Crockford's Clerical Directory, 1872.] C. W. S.

GELDART, JAMES WILLIAM, LL.D. (1785–1876), professor of law at Cambridge, eldest son of the Rev. James Geldart, rector of Kirk Deighton, Yorkshire, who died 12 Nov. 1839, by Sarah, daughter of William Williamson of Linton Spring, Wetherby, Yorkshire, was born at Swinnow Hall, Wetherby, 15 Feb. 1785, and educated at Beverley grammar school. He was admitted at Trinity Hall, Cambridge, 5 May 1800, and became a scholar in December 1803. On 16 Feb. 1808 he was elected Skirne fellow of St. Catharine's Hall, but returned to Trinity Hall as a fellow and tutor on 4 Oct. 1809, and resided there as vice-master until 1820. He took the degree of LL.B. in 1806 and became LL.D. in 1814. On 28 Jan. 1814 he was admitted regius professor of civil law at Cambridge, on the nomination of the Earl of Liverpool, and continued to fulfil the duties of that post until 1847. After the death of his father, and on his own presentation, he became rector of Kirk Deighton in January 1840, and held that benefice until his death, which took place in the rectory house there on 16 Feb. 1876. He was buried in Kirk Deighton churchyard on 19 Feb. His literary work consists of 'An Analysis of the Civil Law. By Samuel Halifax, bishop of Gloucester. A new edition, with additions, being the heads of a course of Lectures read in the University of Cambridge by J. W. Geldart,' 1836.

Geldart married, 4 Aug. 1836, Mary Rachel, daughter of William Desborough of Kensingford Grey, Huntingdonshire, who survived him. He left two sons, the Rev. J. W. Geldart, rector of Kirk Deighton, and H. C. Geldart, who was sheriff of

Cambridgeshire and Huntingdonshire in 1887-8.

[Times, 19 Feb. 1876, p. 7; Illustrated London News, 6 May 1876, p. 450.] G. C. B.

GELDORP, GEORGE (*fl.* 1611–1660), portrait-painter, is usually stated to have been born in Antwerp, but it is possible that he was really born in Cologne, and that he was the son of the well-known painter, Geldorp Gortzius. He was at all events apprenticed in Antwerp, and in 1611 was admitted to the freedom of the guild of St. Luke in that city. He was a member of the 'Violieren' guild. On 5 Feb. 1613 he married Anna, daughter of Willem de Vos, the painter, and from 1615 to 1620 resided in a house called 'De Keyser' on 'De Meir,' subsequently moving to the 'Happartstraat' before leaving Antwerp for England. Geldorp seems to have come to England before 1623 if he painted the portrait of the Duke of Lenox, who died in that year. In December 1628 a return was ordered of the names, qualities, and conditions of all recusants resident in London; among the names was that of 'George Geldropp, a picture-drawer.' Geldorp numbered among his intimate friends the great painter Anthony Vandyck [q. v.], and it was perhaps owing to Geldorp that Vandyck came to England for the second time in 1632 and took up his residence in this country. The following incident throws some light upon this event. In December 1631 Sir Balthasar Gerbier [q. v.], then resident in behalf of Charles I at the court of Brussels, presented to the king a picture alleged to be by Vandyck, but discovered by Geldorp, who was in constant correspondence with Vandyck, to be only a copy. Gerbier angrily quoted Rubens to vouch for its authenticity. Vandyck came over in March or April 1632 to settle the matter, and lodged first in Geldorp's house. Geldorp had obtained the royal patronage, and had some share in the charge of the royal collections. He rented from the crown a large house and garden in Drury Lane. This house was much resorted to, for Mr. Rose, son-in-law of Richard Gibson the dwarf, told Vertue that Geldorp 'was mighty great with people of Quality in his Time, & much in their favor, he usd to entertain Ladies and Gentlemen with wine & hams & other curious eatables, & carryd on intreagues between them.' After the king's death Geldorp moved to a house in Archer Street, Westminster. As a painter Geldorp was much decried by his contemporaries. Sandrart says that he drew so badly that he used the drawings of others to make his portraits, pinning them over his own canvas and tracing through with

prepared chalk. Lely worked for Geldorp when he first came to England. The portraits that bear his name are by no means discreditable, and he made numerous copies of portraits by Vandyck, which are now no doubt often taken for originals. Geldorp was employed by William Cecil, second earl of Salisbury, to paint portraits of himself and other members of his family; the portrait of the earl (painted about 1626) is still at Hatfield House, where Geldorp's original receipt for the paintings, frames, and gilding (the latter being done by his wife) is also preserved. He also painted portraits of George Carew, earl of Totnes (now in the National Portrait Gallery), Lodovick Stuart, duke of Richmond and Lenox (exhibited at the Stuart Exhibition in January 1889, perhaps a copy, as the duke died in 1623), James Stuart, duke of Richmond and Lenox (engraved by Robert van Voerst), Robert Bertie, earl of Lindsey (also engraved by Van Voerst), George, marquis of Huntly, and others. In July 1637 Geldorp was employed by the great Cologne art-patron, M. Jabach, to negotiate with Rubens for his last completed work, the 'Martyrdom of St. Peter,' now in St. Peter's Church at Cologne. Geldorp was alive at the Restoration. According to Vertue numbers of works of art from the royal collection were stored for safety in his house. He is stated to have been buried at Westminster.

[Merlo's Kunst und Künstler von Köln; Vertue's MSS. (Brit. Mus. Addit. MSS. 23069, &c.); Van den Branden's Geschiedenis der Antwerpsche Schilderschool; Rombouts and Van Lerius's Liggeren der Antwerpsche Sint Lucasgilde; Carpenter's Pictorial Notices of Vandyck; Guiffrey's Vandyck; Cal. State Papers (Dom. Ser.), 1628; Redgrave's Dict. of Artists; information from G. Scharf, esq., C.B.] L. C.

GELL, Sir JOHN (1593–1671), parliamentarian, son of Thomas Gell of Hopton, Derbyshire, and Millicent, daughter of Ralph Sacheverell, was born 22 June 1593. He matriculated as a commoner of Magdalen College, Oxford, on 16 June 1610, but left the university without a degree. He married on 22 Jan. 1609, when only 16, Elizabeth, daughter of Sir Percival Willoughby of Wollaton, Nottinghamshire. In 1635 Gell became sheriff of Derbyshire, and was consequently charged with the levy of 3,500*l.* from that county for ship-money. This involved him in a quarrel with Sir John Stanhope of Elvaston, Derbyshire, who refused payment, and was summoned before the council for resisting the sheriff's men (*Strafford Correspondence,* i. 505). Stanhope died in 1638, but Gell is said to have gratified his animosity by plundering Stanhope's house and defacing his monument during the civil wars. The story is told in 'Mercurius Aulicus,' 15 Feb. 1642–3, and is repeated by Mrs. Hutchinson, but it is probably much exaggerated (*Memoirs of Colonel Hutchinson*, i. 180, 352, ed. 1885). Whether true or not, it did not prevent the subsequent marriage of Gell with Stanhope's widow, Mary, daughter of Sir Francis Radcliffe of Ordsal, Lancashire.

On 29 Jan. 1641–2 Gell was created a baronet, and the title remained in his family till 1719 (BURKE, *Extinct Baronetage*, p. 216). In October 1642 Gell raised a regiment of foot for the service of the parliament, and occupied Derby, of which town he was appointed governor by a commission from the Earl of Essex, dated 5 Jan. 1643 (*Hist. MSS. Comm.* 9th Rep. p. 343). Mrs. Hutchinson describes Gell's soldiers as ' good, stout-fighting men, but the most licentious, ungovernable wretches that belonged to the parliament. He himself nor no man knows for what reason he chose that side, for he had not understanding enough to judge the equity of the cause, nor piety nor holiness, being a foul adulterer all the time he served the parliament, and so unjust that without any remorse he suffered his men to plunder both honest men and cavaliers' (*Memoirs of Colonel Hutchinson*, i. 180). Gell's plunderings of the cavaliers are recorded in a pamphlet by Peter Heylyn, entitled 'Thieves, Thieves; or a Relation of Sir John Gell's Proceedings in Derbyshire in gathering up the rents of the Lords and Gentlemen of that country by pretended authority from the two Houses of Parliament,' 1643, 4to. Whatever Gell's moral defects may have been, he was one of the most active commanders in the service of the parliament; he captured many of the fortified homes of the royalists, held Derby throughout the war, and greatly contributed to the maintenance of Leicester and Nottingham. His military exploits are recounted in two narratives, drawn up either by Gell himself or under his immediate supervision, which are printed in Glover's 'History of Derbyshire' (vol. i. Appendix, pp. 62–75) and Shaw's 'History of Staffordshire.' The most notable of these services were his share in the capture of Lichfield and the battle of Hopton Heath (19 March 1643). The parliamentary newspapers and the pages of Whitelocke and Vicars mention him with great frequency. Mrs. Hutchinson accuses him of keeping ' the diurnal makers in pension, so that whatever was done in the neighbouring counties against the enemy was attributed to him ; and thus he hath indirectly purchased himself a name in story which he

never merited' (*Memoirs of Colonel Hutchinson*, i. 181). In July 1645 Gell was in command of fifteen hundred local horse, and might have intercepted the king's troops in their flight from Naseby to Leicester (CARTE, *Original Letters*, i. 129). His neglect to do so gave rise to grave suspicions, and other charges of misconduct as a military commander were brought against him in December (*Hist. MSS. Comm.* 9th Rep. p. 393).

Gell seems to have taken no part in the second civil war. In 1650 he was accused of taking part in plots against the Commonwealth, committed to the Tower on 27 March 1650, tried by the high court of justice in the following August, and on 27 Sept. found guilty of misprision of treason, and condemned to forfeit his personal estate and the rents of his lands for life (on Gell's trial, see WALKER, *History of Independency*, pt. iii. p. 24, and two tracts, *The True State of the Case of Sir John Gell*, and *A True Confutation of The True State of the Case of Sir John Gell*, by John Bernard, 1650, 4to). Gell was released from his imprisonment on 13 April 1652, and obtained a full pardon on 18 April 1653 (*Hist. MSS. Comm.* 9th Rep. p. 395). He next appears as one of the signatories of a Derbyshire petition to General Monck, urging him to summon a free parliament, and on 4 June 1660 made a declaration claiming the benefit of the king's act of indemnity (*ib.* p. 396). Gell died on 26 Oct. 1671 at his house in St. Martin's Lane, London, aged 79, and was buried at Wirksworth in Derbyshire, where his monument is still to be seen (COX, *Churches of Derbyshire*, ii. 559). His younger brother, Thomas (1594–1656), recorder and M.P. for Derby, served under John during the civil war in 1645 (cf. *Reliquary*, xi. 225).

[Glover's Hist. of Derbyshire, 1829 ; State Papers, Dom. ; Memoirs of Colonel Hutchinson, ed. C. H. Firth, 1885 ; Gell's Papers, now in the possession of H. C. Pole Gell, esq., of Hopton Hall, calendared in the 9th Rep. of the Historical Manuscripts Commission.]   C. H. F.

GELL, JOHN (*d.* 1806), admiral, of an old Derbyshire family, was promoted to be a lieutenant in the navy in 1760, and a commander in 1762. On 4 March 1766 he was posted to the Launceston of 44 guns going out to North America as flag-ship of vice-admiral Durell, who died within a few months of his taking command of the station. Gell, however, remained in the Launceston for the term of her commission, and after some years on half-pay was appointed in 1776 to the Thetis frigate, in which he was employed on the North American and afterwards on the home station. In 1780 he was appointed to the Monarca, a fine 70-gun ship captured from the Spaniards by Sir George Rodney on 16 Jan. immediately preceding. Towards the close of the year he was ordered to the West Indies, under the orders of Sir Samuel Hood; but the ship being dismasted in a violent gale, and compelled to return to England, he was afterwards sent out to the East Indies, where, as one of the squadron under Sir Edward Hughes [q. v.], the Monarca took part in each of the five indecisive engagements with the French under M. de Suffren. In 1784 she returned to England, and was paid off. During the Spanish armament in 1790 Gell commanded the Excellent for a few months; and on 1 Feb. 1793 was advanced to the rank of rear-admiral. He was then ordered out to the Mediterranean, with his flag in the St. George, in command of a squadron of four ships of the line and a frigate. On the way, off the coast of Portugal, they fell in with and captured a French privateer, the Général Dumourier, convoying a Spanish treasure-ship, the Santiago, which she had taken a few days before. The prizes were sent home, and, after some doubt in respect to the Santiago, were both condemned. The Spanish ship was of immense value, and her condemnation, under the circumstances, caused much dissatisfaction in Spain, and is said to have been one of the principal causes of the total change of Spanish policy and of the war with England (JAMES, *Naval History*, ed. 1860, i. 100).

Gell's squadron was but the advanced division of the fleet which, in several detachments, went out to the Mediterranean, and which, by the end of June, was collected at Gibraltar under the command of Lord Hood [see HOOD, SAMUEL, VISCOUNT]. As a junior flag-officer Gell was present with this fleet at the occupation of Toulon, and in October was sent with a small squadron to Genoa, where he took possession of the French frigate Modeste, the slight opposition offered being quelled by a volley of musketry, which killed one man and wounded eight (JAMES, i. 97; SCHOMBERG, *Naval Chronicle*, ii. 253). French writers have represented this as a wholesale massacre, which excused, if it did not warrant, as a measure of retaliation, the butchery in cold blood of the crew of the merchant brig Peggy nearly a year afterwards (BRUN, *Guerres Maritimes de la France, Port de Toulon*, ii. 261). In the following April Gell was compelled by ill-health to resign his command, and in doing so ended his active service. He became a vice-admiral on 4 July 1794, admiral on 14 Feb. 1799, and died of an apoplectic seizure on 24 Sept. 1806. There is a portrait by Sir Joshua Reynolds in the Painted Hall at Greenwich.

Charnock's Biog. Nav. vi.; 579; Gent. Mag. (1806) vol. lxxvi. pt. ii. p. 984.]   J. K. L.

GELL, ROBERT, D.D. (1595–1665), divine, born on 19 Feb. 1594–5 (*Sloane MS.* 1707, f. 13) at Frindsbury in Kent, of the family of Hopton, Derbyshire, was educated at Westminster School as a king's scholar, and matriculated at Christ's College, Cambridge, as sizar in 1615. He graduated B.A. 1617–18, M.A. 1621, B.D. 1628, and D.D. 1641, being fellow of Christ's from 1623 till after 1638. A chaplain to the Archbishop of Canterbury, he frequently preached before the university of Cambridge, in 1631 before Charles I, and in 1641 before the lord mayor and aldermen of London in the Mercers' Chapel. He was rector of St. Mary, Aldermanbury, London, at his death at Pampisford on 20 March 1665. About 1644 he married his wife Elizabeth, who owned property at Pampisford in Cambridgeshire; she died there on 12 Sept. 1668: a daughter Elizabeth erected an altar tomb to her parents in Pampisford churchyard in 1674. Gell left books or money to Christ's and Queens' colleges, and to the king's scholars of Westminster. He took much interest in astrology, and at least twice (1649 and 1650) preached before the Society of Astrologers. His works exhibit learning, wit, critical power, and a fund of allegorical illustrations. His published sermons include ' Ἀγγελοκρατία Θεοῦ, touching God's Government of the World by Angels,' 1650, and ' Noah's Flood returning,' preached before the lord mayor, 1655. ' An Essay towards the Amendment of the last English Translation of the Bible. The first Part, on the Pentateuch,' appeared in 1659, and ' Gell's Remaines: set in order by R. Bacon,' a collection of skeleton discourses, in 1676.

[Baker's Hist. London, art. ' St. Mary, Aldermanbury;' Wood's Athenæ Oxon. ed. Bliss, iii. 562; Notes and Queries, 2nd ser. iii. 19, 8th ser. xii. 401.]   A. C. B.

GELL, Sir WILLIAM (1777–1836), classical archæologist and traveller, born in 1777, was the younger son of Philip Gell of Hopton in Derbyshire, by his wife, Dorothy, daughter and coheiress of William Milnes of Aldercar Park, a lady who afterwards married Thomas Blore, the topographer [q. v.] William Gell's paternal grandfather, John Eyre, had assumed the name of Gell from his mother's family, the Gells of Hopton. Gell was educated at Jesus College, Cambridge, became a fellow of Emmanuel College, and graduated B.A. 1798, M.A. 1804. He at one time studied in the schools of the Royal Academy, but does not appear to have exhibited.

Most of his works are illustrated from sketches made by himself, which have been praised for their exactness and minuteness, though they do not show any exceptional artistic power. In 1801 he visited the Troad, where he made numerous sketches and fixed the site of Troy at Bounabashi (SCHLIEMANN, *Ilios*, p. 186). He published the 'Topography of Troy' in 1804, folio, a work to which Byron alludes in his 'English Bards' (first ed. 1809):

> Of Dardan tours let dilettanti tell,
> I leave topography to classic Gell.

While the 'English Bards' was printing Byron became acquainted with Gell, and altered the 'coxcomb Gell' of his manuscript to 'classic Gell.' In the fifth edition Byron, having then himself visited the Troad, altered 'classic' to 'rapid,' with the note: '" Rapid " indeed ! He topographised and typographised king Priam's dominions in three days' (BYRON, *Works*; MOORE, *Life of Byron*, 1 vol. ed. 1846, p. 76). On 14 May 1803 Gell was knighted on returning from a mission to the Ionian Islands. In 1804 he began a journey in the Morea, and left it in the spring of 1806 to visit Ithaca in company with Edward Dodwell, the traveller [q. v.] He afterwards published the 'Geography and Antiquities of Ithaca,' London, 1807, 4to; the 'Itinerary of Greece,' London, 1810, 4to (compiled 1801–1806), new edition, London, 1827, with a hundred routes in Attica, Bœotia, Phocis, Locris, and Thessaly; 'Itinerary of the Morea,' London, 1817, 8vo; and 'Narrative of a Journey in the Morea,' London, 1823, 8vo, in which he says (p. 306), 'I was once very enthusiastic in the cause of Greece ; [but] it is only by knowing well the nation that my opinion is changed.' Byron wrote an elaborate article (reprinted in MOORE, *Life of Byron*, Appendix) on the 'Ithaca' and 'Itinerary of Greece' in the 'Monthly Review' for August 1811. Gell does not appear to have been a collector of antiquities, and his writings on Greece have a topographical rather than an archæological interest.

In 1814 when Princess (afterwards Queen) Caroline left England for Italy, Gell accompanied her as one of her chamberlains. He gave evidence on 6 Oct. 1820 at her trial before the House of Lords, and stated that he had left her service merely on account of a fit of the gout, and had seen no impropriety between her and the courier Bergami (HANSARD, *Parl. Debates*). Gell, however, in his letters of 1815 and 1816, written under such signatures as 'Blue Beard,' 'Adonis,' 'Gellius (Aulus),' retails little bits of scandal about the queen. He had sixty or seventy letters of hers in his possession. 'What curious things they are !' he says. From 1820 till his death Gell resided in Italy. He had a small house with a pleasant garden at Rome, and painted (1828) his sitting-room 'in all the bright staring colours I could get, a sort of thing between Etruscan and Pompeii.' At Rome he went much into society. He had another house at Naples, where, 'surrounded by books, drawings, and maps, with a guitar, and two or three dogs,' he received a constant stream of distinguished visitors. At Naples he was especially intimate with Sir William Drummond, the Hon. Keppel Craven [see CRAVEN, KEPPEL RICHARD], and with Lady Blessington (from 1824), whom he visited at the Villa Belvidere, and to whom he addressed many lively letters (printed in MADDEN, *Countess of Blessington*, ii. 22–97 ; see also Gell's letters, *ib.* 488–500). When Sir Walter Scott visited Naples he saw more of Gell (between 5 Jan. and 10 May 1832) than of any English resident there. Gell, though greatly crippled, showed Scott the objects of interest near Naples, took him to Cumæ and (9 Feb. 1832) to Pompeii, where they dined 'at a large table spread in the Forum.' After Scott's death Gell drew up an account of their intercourse at Naples, part of which is printed in Lockhart's 'Life of Scott,' chap. lxxxii. It was to Gell that Scott made the well-known remark that Byron 'bet' (beat) him in poetry. From about 1815 till his death Gell suffered severely from gout and rheumatism, but he was always cheerful, and at this period did some of his best known archæological work. Between 1817 and 1819 he published, aided by J. P. Gandy [see DEERING, JOHN PETER], his 'Pompeiana : the Topography, Edifices, &c.,' London, 8vo. In 1832 he published (alone) 'Pompeiana : the Topography, Ornaments,' &c. 2 vols., London, 4to, giving the results of the Pompeian excavations since 1819. These books were well received in England and on the continent. Gell had obtained from the government special facilities for visiting the excavations, and made very numerous sketches (reproduced in the volumes) of objects which he declares would otherwise have perished unrecorded. In 1834 he published the 'Topography of Rome and its Vicinity,' 2 vols., London, 8vo (2nd edition by E. B. Bunbury, 1846 ; cf. A. NIBBY, *Le Mura di Roma*, 1820, 8vo, and his *Analisi*, &c., 1837, 8vo). To this work the Society of Dilettanti, of which Gell had become a member in 1807, contributed 200l. Gell was 'resident plenipotentiary' of the society in Italy, and regularly forwarded reports

(MICHAELIS, *Anc. Marbles*). He contributed to the letterpress of the 'Antiquities of Ionia,' issued by the society in 1797–1840. Gell was a fellow of the Society of Antiquaries and of the Royal Society, a member of the Royal Academy of Berlin (1827 ?), and of the Institute of France (elected about 1833). In 1834 Gell gave up his house at Rome. In the middle of 1835 he became seriously ill, but was tended kindly by his great friend Craven. He died at his Naples villa on 4 Feb. 1836, apparently worn out by his long sufferings from the gout. He was buried in the English burial-ground at Naples. Gell was unmarried. By his will (printed in MADDEN, ii. 500) he left his house and gardens at Naples to the English congregation there. His plate, carriage, &c., almost his only other property, he left to his servants. All his papers were bequeathed to Craven, his sole executor, who presented them to his (Craven's) Italian secretary Pasquini. The original drawings, nearly eight hundred in number, made by him during his travels through Spain, Italy, Syria, Dalmatia, the Ionian Islands, Greece, and European Turkey, were also left to Craven, and were bequeathed by him to the British Museum, where they were received in April 1852 (FAGAN, *Handbook to Departm. of Prints*, 1876, p. 185).

Gell was described by Lady Blessington (MADDEN, ii. 361) as 'gentle, kind-hearted, and good-tempered,' epithets which, judging from other testimonies, he seems to have deserved. He was extremely fond of society, and, according to Dr. Madden, delighted in 'lionizing' people, and was 'always hankering after patricians.' Bulwer Lytton (who visited him in 1833) found 'something artificial and cold about him *au fond*,' yet his urbane manners and companionableness made him very popular. Thomas Moore, who saw him in 1820, describes him (*Memoirs*, iii. 137) as 'full of jokes,' 'still a coxcomb, but rather amusing.' Others say that he had a real fund of wit, and when he died Lady Blessington said, 'J'ai perdu en lui mon meilleur causeur.' Gell had some acquaintance with Oriental languages, but is said not to have much cared for belles-lettres, nor was he a profound scholar. Written when Greece and even Italy were comparatively little known to English travellers and classical students, his works were for some time regarded as standard treatises, and much of the information they contain is still of value to the topographer and archæologist. Dr. Madden states (ii. 21) that 'there are several busts' of Gell, 'none of them a good likeness.' His portrait was painted (about

1831 ?) by Thomas Uwins, R.A., and came into the possession of Lady Blessington. A 'small waxen profile' of him was made at Rome about 1832 (MADDEN, ii. 65, 66).

[Madden's Literary Life of the Countess of Blessington, 1855, ii. 8–97, 488–500, &c.; Annual Register (1836), lxxviii. 190; Gent. Mag. 1836, new ser. v. 665–6; Athenæum, 19 March 1836, p. 209; Encyclop. Brit. 8th and 9th ed.; Michaelis, Anc. Marbles in Great Britain; Edinb. Rev. 1838, lxvii. 75–6; Gell's Works; Brit. Mus. Cat.; authorities cited in the article.]

W. W.

GELLIBRAND, HENRY (1597–1636), mathematician, born in the parish of St. Botolph, Aldersgate, London, 17 Nov. 1597, was the eldest son of Henry Gellibrand, M.A., fellow of All Souls' College, Oxford, and of St. Paul's Cray, Kent, who died 15 Aug. 1615. He became a commoner of Trinity College, Oxford, in 1615, and took the two degrees in arts, B.A. 25 Nov. 1619, M.A. 26 May 1623. He took holy orders, and served for a time a curacy at Chiddingstone, Kent, but was led to devote himself entirely to mathematics by one of Sir Henry Savile's lectures. He settled at Oxford, and became a friend of Henry Briggs [q. v.], on whose recommendation he was chosen professor of astronomy at Gresham College, 2 Jan. 1626-7. Briggs dying in 1630 he left his unfinished 'Trigonometria Britannica' to Gellibrand. Gellibrand held puritan meetings in his rooms, and encouraged his servant, William Beale, to publish an almanack for 1631, in which the popish saints were superseded by those in Foxe's 'Book of Martyrs.' Laud, then bishop of London, cited them both into the high commission court. They were acquitted on the ground that similar almanacks had been printed before, Laud alone dissenting, and this prosecution formed afterwards one of the articles exhibited against him at his own trial (PRYNNE, *Canterburies Doome*, 1646, p. 184). In 1632 Gellibrand completed Briggs's manuscript, and published it in 1633 as 'Trigonometria Britannica: sive de doctrina Triangulorum libri duo. Quorum prior ... ab ... H. Briggio ... posterior verò ... ab H. Gellibrand ... constructus, 2 pts. fol., Gouda, 1633. According to Ward, an English translation of Gellibrand's book was published in 1658 by John Newton as the second part of a folio with the same title. During 1633 he also contributed 'An Appendix concerning Longitude' to 'The strange and dangerous Voyage of Captaine Thomas James,' 4to, 1633, which has been frequently reprinted. Gellibrand died of fever 16 Feb. 1636, and was buried in the church of St. Peter the Poor, Broad Street, London. Works not mentioned above are : 1. ' A Discourse Mathematical of the Variation of the Magneticall Needle together with its admirable diminution lately discovered,' 4to, London, 1635. 2. 'An Institution Trigonometricall wherein . . . is exhibited the doctrine of the dimension of plain and spherical triangles . . . by tables . . . of sines, tangents, secants, and logarithms . . . Second edition . . . enlarged' (by William Leybourn), 8vo, London, 1652. The first edition had appeared in 1638. 3. ' An Epitome of Navigation . . . with tables . . .' An edition by E. Speidell appeared in 1698, and one by J. Atkinson, 1706. He wrote the preface to ' Sciographia, or the Art of Shadowes,' 8vo, London, 1635, composed by J[ohn] W[ells] of Brembridge in Hampshire. At the end of ' Trigonometria Britannica ' he stated that he had by him 'integram eclipsium doctrinam,' for the printer could not wait. Another manuscript, 'Astronomia lunaris,' written in 1635, was once in the possession of Sir Hans Sloane. A third manuscript, a ' Treatise of Building of Ships,' is mentioned by Wood as belonging to Edward, lord Conway. His Latin oration, ' in laudem Gassendi astronomiæ,' delivered in Christ Church Hall, Oxford, is in the British Museum, Addit. MS. 6193, f. 96. Gellibrand was a plodding industrious mathematician, without a spark of genius.

[Wood's Athenæ Oxon. (Bliss), ii. 622–3; Wood's Fasti Oxon. (Bliss), i. 386, 411 ; Ward's Lives of the Gresham Professors, pp. 81–5, 336; Chalmers's Biog. Dict. xvi. 390–2 ; Biographia Britannica ; Martin's Biographia Philosophica.]

G. G.

GEMINI, GEMINIE, or GEMINUS, THOMAS (*fl.* 1540–1560), engraver and printer, was the author of a compendium of anatomy, with copper-plate engravings by himself. The work, entitled ' Compendiosa totius Anatomie delineatio,' is an abridgment of Vesalius's great work on anatomy published at Basle in 1543. The illustrations in the text are copied from the woodcuts after Van Calcar's drawings in that work. The first edition was published in 1545, with a dedication to Henry VIII, which is signed ' tuæ Majestati semper mancipatissimus Thomas Geminus Lysiensis, Londini Quarto Calendas Octobres Anno 1545.' It has not yet been discovered whence Geminus came, the word ' Lysiensis ' having hitherto baffled the most learned investigations (see *Notes and Queries*, 4th ser. v. 360, 435, 516, ix. 6, 5th ser. xi. 37, 117, 139, 153). This first edition (published by John Herford) contains a very elaborate frontispiece, lightly but firmly engraved, with allegorical figures surrounding the royal arms in the centre. The engravings

are among the earliest copper-plate engravings known in England, having apparently been preceded only by the plates to Raynald's ' Byrthe of Mankynde ' in 1540, which have been sometimes also attributed to Gemini. In 1553 Gemini published a translation of his compendium, made by Nicholas Udall [q. v.] and others, with a dedication to Edward VI, in which he speaks of himself as ' not so perfeict and experte in the English tonge that I dare waraunt or trust myne owne dooynges,' and also as by the king's 'most gracious bountie' having his 'livyng and beyng here.' The same plates and title-page accompany this edition, which was printed by Nycholas Hyll. In 1559 Gemini published a third edition, this time dedicated to Elizabeth, who had just ascended the throne ; it was revised by Richard Eden. The same plates are here used again, with the addition of a large folding woodcut by another artist, which is sometimes met with separately, and was incorporated by Gemini into his own work. The same title-page also occurs, only the royal arms have been removed from the centre, and a portrait of Elizabeth (the earliest after her succession) inserted. This edition Gemini printed himself, having set up a press in Blackfriars. Gemini's anatomical plates passed into the possession of André Wechel, a publisher at Paris, who used them for a similar work published there in 1569. In 1553 Gemini published for Leonard Digges [q. v.] his 'Prognostication of right good effect,' and in 1556 his ' Tectonicon,' a work on mensuration. This work is stated to be ' Imprented at London in ye Blackfriers by Thomas Gemine, who is ther ready exactly to make all the Instruments apertaining to thes booke.' A later edition appeared in 1562. In 1559 he engraved a portrait of Mary (an impression was sold in Sir J. Winter Lake's collection, March 1808). Ortelius, in his 'Theatrum Orbis Terrarum,' published in 1570, refers to Gemini in London as the source from which he obtained the map of Spain in that work. Two notices of him occur in the register-books of the Stationers' Company, one in 1554 recording a fine inflicted on 'Thomas Gemyne, stranger,' for transgressing the rules. In the collection levied for Bridewell his name appears as a subscriber of twenty pence, a large sum in those days, showing him to have been a man of substantial position. Gemini is usually supposed to have been an Italian; the frontispiece to the 'Anatomy' mentioned above shows an unmistakably Italian character, that of the early woodcut engravings produced in Venice in the half-century before this book. Portions of the design, however, present some of the features of French engravings, executed in the manner and with the spirit of the Italian Renaissance (a facsimile will be found in Sir W. Stirling-Maxwell's 'Engraved Portraiture of the Sixteenth Century'). On the other hand the anatomical plates, though mere copies of the Basle woodcuts, show the hand of an engraver trained in Italy. It has been suggested that the frontispiece is by a different hand, and of the school of Fontainebleau (FISHER, *Catalogue of a Collection of Engravings*, &c., p. 309); it bears, however, a distinct statement that it was engraved by Gemini, and the portrait, inserted in 1559, is obviously the work of the same engraver. If Gemini designed the frontispiece himself, he was an artist of some merit. There does not seem any ground for supposing that he was a surgeon. Vesalius's book was so famous that the piracy of the text and plates was an easy and profitable undertaking.

[Ames and Herbert's Typographical Antiquities, ii. 872; Walpole's Anecdotes of Painters, ed. Dallaway and Wornum; Brit. Mus. Harl. MS. 5910 (Bagford), pt. iv. p. 165; Arber's Transcript of the Registers of the Stationers' Company; Brunet's Manuel du Libraire (sub voce 'Vesalius'); Gemini's own works and others referred to in the text.] L. C.

GENDALL, JOHN (1790–1865), painter, a native of Devonshire, showed an early taste for drawing, and was sent to London with an introduction to Sir John Soane [q. v.] Soane gave him his first commission, a drawing of one of the windows in Westminster, and introduced him to Rudolph Ackermann [q. v.], the print-seller and publisher in the Strand. Gendall was employed by Ackermann for some years in managing the business, in developing the new art of lithography, and in illustrating publications. He was sent by the firm on a sketching tour through Normandy; Gendall's sketches, with some by Augustus Pugin, were published in 1821 under the title of 'Picturesque Tour of the Seine from Paris to the Sea,' the text being by M. Sauvan. On 6 Nov. 1862 Gendall gave an illustrated description of this tour, with the sketches, at Exeter. He drew many views for Ackermann's topographical publications, such as 'Views of Country Seats;' and some of his views were engraved in aquatint by T. Sutherland, including three of Edinburgh, some of Richmond, Kew, and other places. On quitting Ackermann's house Gendall settled in the Cathedral Yard at Exeter, where he resided till his death. He now painted for his own recreation and profit, chiefly in oil, and his favourite subjects were the glens and rocky dells of his native county, or the scenery of the Teign, the Avon, and other Devonshire rivers. His paintings were highly appreciated. A friend once passed one off to some connoisseurs as a work of Turner. Turner himself thought highly of Gendall's work. Gendall never aimed at strength in colour, but rather sought to depict the calm repose of nature. He first exhibited at the Royal Academy in 1846, sending two scenes on the Avon. He continued to exhibit up to 1863, confining himself to views of Devonshire scenery. He was considered a very good judge of art; his advice was often sought and always readily given. Though afflicted with a long illness, he worked up to the close of his life. He died at Exeter, 1 March 1865, aged 75. A large collection of his paintings was sold by his executors soon after his death.

[Pycroft's Art in Devonshire (Devonshire Association, xiii. 233); Redgrave's Dict. of Artists; Graves's Dict. of Artists, 1760–1880; Royal Academy Catalogues (Anderdon's illustrated copy in print room, Brit. Mus.)] L. C.

GENEST, JOHN (1764–1839), writer, was the son of John Genest of Dunker's Hill, Devonshire. He was educated at Westminster School, entered 9 May 1780 a pensioner at Trinity College, Cambridge, and graduated B.A. 1784 and M.A. 1787. He took holy orders, and was for many years curate of a retired Lincolnshire village. Subsequently he became private chaplain to the Duke of Ancaster. Compelled by ill-health to retire, he went to Bath for the benefit of the waters. Here he appears to have remained until his death, which took place, after nine years of great suffering, at his residence in Henry Street, 15 Dec. 1839. His body is buried in St. James's Church. During his stay in Bath he wrote 'Some Account of the English Stage from the Restoration in 1660 to 1830,' Bath, 10 vols. 1832, 8vo, a work of great labour and research, which forms the basis of most exact knowledge concerning the stage. Few books of reference are equally trustworthy, the constant investigation to which it has been subjected having brought to light few errors and none of grave importance. Genest is not undeservedly hard on his predecessors who followed one another in error. The index to the book is ample, but its arrangement does not greatly facilitate research.

[Notes and Queries, 2nd ser. ix. 109, 231.] J. K.

GENINGES, EDMUND (1567–1591), catholic divine, was born in 1567 at Lichfield and brought up in the protestant religion. He became a page in the service of Richard Sherwood, a catholic gentleman, who afterwards went to Rheims and took holy orders. Geninges, at his own request, was also admitted into the college at Rheims, and after being ordained priest, while under the canonical age, at Soissons, 18 March 1589–90, by papal dispensation, he returned to England as a missioner. He was apprehended by Topcliffe while celebrating mass in the house of Swithen Wells in Gray's Inn Fields, London, 7 Nov. 1591, with two other priests and four laymen. On 4 Dec. they were brought to trial, Geninges being dressed in a fool's coat which had been found in Wells's house. The next day the jury found the three priests guilty of high treason for returning to the realm contrary to the statute of Elizabeth, and the laymen were convicted of felony for aiding and assisting the priests. They were all executed at Tyburn except Geninges and Wells, who were executed on 10 Dec. (O.S.) 1591 under peculiarly revolting circumstances before the door of the house in which they had been captured in Gray's Inn Fields.

'The Life and Death of Mr. Edmund Geninges, Priest, Crowned with Martyrdome at London, the 10 Day of Nouember in the year MDXCI,' appeared at St. Omer in 1614, 4to. There is a perfect copy of this extremely rare work in the Grenville Library, and another in the Huth collection. The titlepage, the portrait of Geninges, ' Ætatis suæ 24, A° 1591,' and eleven quaint prints illustrating his life from childhood, are all engraved by Martin Bas. The whole work is in prose except 'The Author to his Booke' and 'The Booke to his Reader,' three six-line stanzas, each on A 2. On A 3 is a letter signed 'J. W. P.' addressed to 'Maister J. G. P.' These initials probably represent John Wilson or Watson, the author of the 'Roman Martyrologie,' 1608, and John Geninges [q. v.], the brother of Edmund. It is not at all clear from the letter whether Wilson or John Geninges was the author of the biography. Challoner, however, ascribes the authorship to John Geninges. A reprint of the work 'without any substantial alteration' appeared at London in 1887, 4to, under the editorship of the Rev. William Forbes-Leith, S.J.

Another work relating to Edmund Geninges was printed under the title of 'Strange and Miraculous News from St. Omers, being an Account of the wonderful Life and Death of a Popish Saint and Martyr named Mr. Edmund Gennings, Priest, who was executed for treason some years since; with a relation of the miracles … at his death. Wherein may be observed what lying wonders the Papists are made to believe' [London, 1680?], fol.

[Challoner's Missionary Priests; Dodd's Church Hist. ii. 89; Douay Diaries, p. 423; Gillow's Bibl. Dict. ii. 415, 423; Granger's Biog. Hist.

of England, 5th edit. i. 275; Bibl. Grenvilliana, pt. i. p. 270; Harwood's Lichfield; Cat. of the Huth Library, ii. 589; Lowndes's Bibl. Man. (Bohn), p. 874; Stanton's Menology, p. 590; Stow's Annales (1615), p. 764.] T. C.

GENINGES, JOHN (1570?–1660), Franciscan friar, born at Lichfield in or about 1570, was brought up in the protestant religion, but became a catholic after the execution of his elder brother, Edmund Geninges [q. v.] He entered the English College at Douay, was ordained priest in 1607, and was sent on the mission in the following year. In 1614 or 1615 he was admitted into the order of St. Francis. In 1616, in his capacity of vicar and custos of England, he assembled at Gravelines about six of his brethren, including novices, and within three years he succeeded in establishing at Douay the monastery of St. Bonaventure, of which he was the first vicar and guardian. In 1621, with the assistance of Father Christopher Davenport [q. v.], he founded the convent of St. Elizabeth at Brussels for English nuns of the third order of St. Francis. On the restoration of the English province of his order he was appointed its first provincial, in a chapter held at Brussels on 1 Dec. 1630. He was re-elected provincial in the second chapter held at Greenwich on 15 Jan. 1633–4, for another triennium, and again in the fourth chapter at London on 19 April 1640. He died at Douay on 2 Nov. (O.S.) 1660. Dr. Oliver states that his portrait is preserved in the house of St. Peter's Chapel, Birmingham. To him is generally ascribed the authorship of the curious biography of his brother, published at St. Omer in 1614 [see GENINGES, EDMUND]. He also wrote 'Institutio Missionariorum,' Douay, 1651, 16mo.

[Dodd's Church Hist. ii. 416; Douay Diaries i. 19, 34; Gillow's Bibl. Dict.; Hist. MSS. Comm. 5 Rep. p. 468; Oliver's Catholic Religion in Cornwall, pp. 540, 541, 551; Parkinson's Collectanea Anglo-Minoritica, p. 261; Petre's Colleges and Convents, pp. 44, 90; Wadding's Scriptores Ord. Minorum.] T. C.

GENT, SIR THOMAS (d. 1593), judge, was the eldest or only son of William Gent, lord of the manor of Moyns, Steeple Bumpstead, Essex, of ancient family, by Agnes, daughter and coheiress of Thomas Carr of Great Thurlow, Suffolk. He was educated at Cambridge, probably at Christ's College, where one 'Gent' matriculated as a pensioner in 1548. He entered at the Middle Temple, and was called to the bar, and was Lent reader there in 1571 and 1574. He was appointed on 2 April 1571 to the lucrative office of steward of all the courts of Edward de Vere, earl of Oxford.

In the parliament which met on 2 April 1571 he sat for Malden, became a serjeant-at-law on 2 June 1584, and was appointed a baron of the exchequer on or before 1 Feb. 1586, on which day a commission of oyer and terminer for Suffolk in the 'Baga de Secretis' contains his name as a judge. Dugdale wrongly dates his elevation 28 June 1588. A special exemption was made in his favour from the act 33 Hen. VIII, c. 24, which forbade a judge from acting as a justice of assize in his own county. He was a member of the high commission in causes ecclesiastical, and appears to have been on circuit in Devonshire in February 1592 (GREEN, *Cal. of State Papers*, Dom. 1591–4). He died in January 1593, and was buried at Steeple Bumpstead. He married twice, first, Elizabeth, who was only daughter and heiress of Sir John Swallow of Bocking, and was buried at Steeple Bumpstead on 12 May 1585, by whom he had seven sons and five daughters; and second, in April 1586, Elizabeth, widow of Roger Hogeson of London, and sister of Morgan Robyns, by whom he had no issue. His arms are engraved in Dugdale's 'Orig. Jurid.' p. 227, from a window in the Middle Temple Hall. His character is highly praised by Newton in his 'Encomia.'

[Baga de Secretis; Burke's Landed Gentry, 1858; Cal. Chanc. Proc. temp. Eliz. i. 383, 384; Dugdale's Origines Juridiciales and Chron. Ser.; Foss's Judges of England; Harl. Misc. ed. Malham, ii. 18; Morant's Essex, ii. 336, 344, 354; Newcourt's Repert., ii. 62; Newton's Encomia, p. 121; Willis's Not. Parl. iii. 91; Wright's Essex, i. 632–4; Cooper's Athenæ Cantabr.] J. A. H.

GENT, THOMAS (1693–1778), printer, was born in Ireland on 4 May 1693, 'of meek and gentle parents . . . rich in grace, though not in shining ore' (*Life*, p. 23). His father was an Englishman, descended from a Staffordshire family. About the age of thirteen Gent was apprenticed to Powell, a Dublin printer, 'a Turk' and 'tyrant,' with whom he 'strove to live' three years (*ib.* p. 26). He absconded from his master, and arrived in London during August 1710, and got employment with Edward Midwinter of Pie Corner, Smithfield, a producer of ballads and broadsides for hawkers. Here he stayed three years, and then did 'smouting' or jobbing work for one or two other printers. Afterwards he went to John White of York, leaving London on foot on 20 April 1714, and performing the journey in six days. He remained at York a year, when the fact of his having run away from apprenticeship became known. His old master, Powell, drove him from Dublin when he visited his parents. In 1716 he was working for Midwinter in London again. Gent was made a member of the Company of

Stationers on 9 Oct. 1717, and admitted to the freedom of the city by virtue of his service with Midwinter (GENT, *Historia Compend. Anglicana*, Preface, p. 1). He worked with William Wilkins of Little Britain, a proprietor of newspapers, and subsequently with John Watts, printer, of Covent Garden, known as the partner of Jacob Tonson and the employer of Benjamin Franklin. Gent left Watts to enter the service of Francis Clifton, a Roman catholic, 'with whom he paid a mysterious visit to Dr. Atterbury at Westminster about some illicit printing (*Life*, pp. 87–90). Clifton issued for Gent a satirical jibe upon his fellow-workmen, entitled 'Teague's Ramble,' 1719 (reprinted by Owen, *Univ. Mag.* i. 194). He resumed employment with Midwinter, and set up an abridgment of 'Robinson Crusoe,' 1722, 12mo, with thirty woodcuts from his own rude designs. Together with Clifton and Midwinter he incurred suspicion for printing seditious libels. He opened an office in Fleet Street, and produced some books, besides Grub Street ballads and other compositions of his own, among them 'A Collection of Songs,' 'The Bishop of Rochester's Effigy,' &c. In 1724 he printed a Latin ode on the return of George I from Germany, and 'Divine Entertainments,' a book of emblems, with woodcuts, the last work he did in London of any consequence. The secret list of printers in London and Westminster presented to Lord Townshend in 1724 enumerates 'Gent, Pye-Corner,' among those 'said to be high-flyers' (NICHOLS, *Literary Anecdotes*, i. 303). Among his employers were Henry Woodfall and Samuel Richardson. On 10 Dec. 1724 he married Alice, widow of Charles Bourne, printer of York, whose business he had taken up. On 23 Nov. he issued the first number of the 'Original York Journal,' which he continued with an altered title to 1741 (*Life*, p. 193). He had now a fair prospect of commercial success, being the sole printer in the city and county of York. Newcastle was the only town in England north of the Trent which possessed a printing-press and local newspaper. Gent met with opposition from John White, a relative of his wife, who set up as printer in the city, but suffered more from the effects of his own quarrelsome temper. The first of his York printed books was a sermon by Thomas Clarke, 1724, 8vo. Two years later he issued several translations by John Clarke, schoolmaster in Hull. In 1730 appeared the 'History of York,' the first of his own works there printed and published. Proposals had been circulated the previous year, and a list of about 170 subscribers obtained. The 'History of Rippon,' on a similar plan, came out in 1734. About 16 June of the same year he set up the first printing-office at Scarborough. 'The Pattern of Piety,' with seven grotesque woodcuts, is the only known production of this press, which had no success.

Perhaps the earliest attempt to establish a serial in a country town was 'Miscellaneæ Curiosæ' (1734), a quarterly, devoted to 'enigmas and mathematical questions.' It only ran to six numbers. The projector was Edward Hauxley, a grammar school master. Gent printed and partly edited it. Next year his 'Annales Regioduni Hullini' came out, and six years later (1741) his quaint 'Historia Compendiosa Anglicana.' His temper did not improve with a failing business. At Martinmas 1742 he removed to a house in Petergate, where the first work produced was a poem of his own on St. Winifred. His curious shop-bill or advertisement of 1743 is reproduced by Charles Knight (*Shadows of the Old Book-sellers*, 1865, p. 99). About eight more books were printed when Gent brought out the prospectus of a 'History of the Ancient Militia in Yorkshire' (1760), which never came to anything. He was now in great poverty, and in 1761 was reduced to presenting a puppet-show of the tragedy of 'Jane Shore.' On Wednesday, 1 April 1761, his wife died, and in 1762 he published a 'History of the great Eastern Window in York Cathedral,' with many miserable woodcuts, the poorest of his topographical books. While passing it through the press he had to peddle lists of carriers, and to beg for alms. His last publication appears to have been 'Judas Iscariot' (1772), 'originally written in London at the age of eighteen, and late improved at eighty.' The last twenty years of Gent's life was one long struggle against want and disease; he died at Petergate, York, on 19 May 1778, in his eighty-sixth year, and was buried in the church of St. Michael-le-Belfry. He had only one child, who died at the age of six months (*Great Eastern Window*, p. 184).

His personal appearance, showing luxuriant hair, flowing beard, and irritable face, is believed to be admirably portrayed in the well-known mezzotint (1771) by V. Green, after a picture by N. Drake, which was painted and exhibited for his benefit. Mr. J. Chaloner Smith describes another print by Pether (*British Mezzotinto Portraits*, pp. 555-6, 983). There is an uncouth woodcut representing the printer sitting under a shelf full of his works, with a fiddle hanging on the wall. An engraving of his press in Coffee Yard, York, is given in many of his books; it is reproduced by Davies (*York Press*, p. 232).

His poetry is beneath criticism, but his topographical publications are still of value and in demand. They are not mere com-

pilations from earlier writers, but are full of minute examples of personal research, and contain many descriptions of objects now lost. He 'studied music on the harp, flute, and other instruments.' His 'Life' is very interesting, and deserves to be reprinted in its entirety. It is full of odd facts about printers and printing, quaint traits of character and curious gossip, throwing light on manners and habits in the early eighteenth century. Davies (*ib.* pp. 144–232) describes sixty-nine books printed by Gent, and the list is still incomplete. Besides the small pieces mentioned above Gent wrote: 1. 'Divine Entertainments, or Penitential Desires, Sighs and Groans of the Wounded Soul,' London, 1724, 12mo (verse; dedicated to the Princess of Wales). 2. 'The Ancient and Modern History of the famous City of York, and in a particular manner of York-minster,' York, 1730, small 8vo (a later edition with the same title has additions and alterations). 3. 'The Antient and Modern History of the loyal Town of Rippon, besides Travels into other parts of Yorkshire,' York, 1733, 8vo (contains a poem on Studley Park, with a Description of Fountains Abbey by Peter Aram, father of the murderer). 4. 'The Pattern of Piety, being the Spiritual Songs of the Life and Death of Job,' Scarborough, 1734, 12mo (verse). 5. 'Annales Regioduni Hullini, or the History of the royal and beautiful town of Kingston-upon-Hull,' York, 1735, 8vo (two editions; among the subscribers was Mr. Eugenius Aram; 'a facsimile of the original of 1735, with life by Rev. George Ohlson,' was printed at Hull, 1869, 8vo). 6. 'Pater Patriæ, being an elegiac Pastoral Dialogue, occasioned by the Death of Charles Howard, Earl of Carlisle' [York, 1738], 12mo (verse). 7. 'Historia Compendiosa Anglicana, or a Compendious History of England, as likewise a succinct History of Rome, annexed an Appendix relating to York,' York, 1741, 2 vols. sm. 8vo (the appendix contains life of St. Robert of Knaresborough, account of Pontefract, Pater Patriæ, Britain in Tears for Queen Caroline, review of the churches in York, and other pieces). 8. 'The Holy Life and Death of St. Winifred, and other religious Persons,' York, 1743, 12mo (in verse, five parts, and an epitome; some copies of this and others of Gent's pieces were collected together and issued with a title as 'The Pious and Poetical Works of Mr. Thomas Gent'). 9. 'The Contingencies, Vicissitudes, or Changes of this transitory Life, set forth in a Prologue spoken for the most part 18th and 20th February, 1761, at the Tragedy of Jane Shore, with a benedictive Epilogue of thanks' [York, 1761], 8vo (in verse; 'price 3*d.*, but left to the charity of the gentry'). 10. 'History of the famous great Eastern Window in St. Peter's Cathedral, York, previous thereto the History of Histories, likewise a Chronological Account of some Eminent Personages,' York, 1763, 8vo. 11. 'Divine Justice and Mercy displayed, set forth in the Birth, Life, and End of Judas Iscariot,' York, 1772, 12mo (reproduced as miniature 4to reprints, No. 1, S. & J. Palmer [1840], 12mo). 12. 'Historical Antiquities,' a translation into English, with some additions, of Dr. Heneage Dering's poem, 'Reliquiæ Eboracenses' [York, 1772?], 8vo (rudely printed on coarse paper, without title; it was never regularly published, see *Life*, p. 208, and DAVIES, *York Press*, pp. 220–1). 13. 'History of the Life and Miracles of Jesus Christ,' York [n. d.], 12mo (verse). 14. 'Piety displayed in the Holy Life and Death of St. Robert, Hermit of Knaresborough,' York [n. d.], 12mo (there is a second edition with additions). 15. 'The Life of Mr. Thomas Gent, Printer of York, written by himself' [edited by the Rev. Joseph Hunter], London, 1832, 8vo (written by Gent in 1746, in his fifty-third year; the manuscript was discovered by Thorpe the bookseller in a collection from Ireland; many interesting passages used by Davies are entirely omitted by the editor).

[Gent's own life is the chief source of information; the original manuscript is in the possession of Mr. Edward Hailstone, who also owns Gent's manuscript book of music, as well as the most extensive collection of his publications known. See also R. Davies's Memoir of the York Press, 1868; Life by the Rev. George Ohlson (see No. 5 above); Southey's The Doctor, 1837, iv. 92–131; Ch. Knight's Shadows of the Old Booksellers, 1865; The Bibliographer, ii. 154–7; Upcott's English Topogr. ii. 1356, 1376, 1411; Gough's British Topogr. ii. 428; Notes and Queries, 5th ser. ii. 217, 7th ser. i. 308, 356, 436, 471, ii. 149, 218, 329.]   H. R. T.

GENTILESCHI, ARTEMISIA (1590–1642?), painter, born at Rome in 1590, was daughter of Orazio Gentileschi [q. v.], from whom she received her first instructions in painting. She also worked under Guido Reni, and studied the style of Domenichino. She accompanied her father to England, and painted several pictures for Charles I, including 'David and Goliath,' 'Fame,' and a portrait of herself at an easel, which is now at Hampton Court. She quitted England, however, and returned to Italy before 1630, residing principally at Naples. She was renowned for her beauty and accomplishments as well as for her paintings. Scandal has been busy with her name; Lanière is said to have fallen a victim to her attractions in England, like the painter Romanelli of Viterbo

at Naples, who painted her portrait. She was especially famous for her portraits, but produced other remarkable works, including a 'Judith' and a 'Magdalen' in the Pitti Gallery at Florence; the former, by some considered her finest work, displays a temperament hardly feminine. She also painted a nude figure of 'Inclination' for Michelangelo Buonarroti the younger, which was considered so indecorous by his descendants that they employed a painter to fit it with suitable drapery. She married Piero Antonio Schiattesi, and is said to have died in Naples in 1642.

[Authorities under GENTILESCHI, ORAZIO, also Bottari e Ticozzi's Lettere Pittoriche, vol. i.; Bardi's Galleria Pitti.]   L. C.

GENTILESCHI, ORAZIO (1563–1647), painter, born at Pisa in 1563, was half-brother of the painter Aurelio Lomi, according to some accounts by a second marriage of their mother; but the account generally accepted is that he was the son of Giovanni Battista Lomi, Aurelio's father, and was placed at an early age under the charge of his maternal uncle, Gentileschi, at Rome, afterwards bearing his name. Gentileschi studied painting at Rome, and founded his style on the finest masterpieces there. He was employed by Pope Clement VIII on paintings in the library and other parts of the Vatican; he also painted for Cardinal Pietro Aldobrandini the tribune of St. Niccola in Carcere; for Cardinal Pinello a 'Circumcision' in Santa Maria Maggiore; for Cardinal Bentivoglio the portico of his palace; for Cardinal Scipione Borghese a summerhouse; also a large picture of 'The Conversion of St. Paul' in S. Paolo fuori le Mura, and other paintings in S. Giovanni Laterano, Santa Maria della Pace, and elsewhere. In the Palazzo Quirinale in 1616 and the Palazzo Rospigliosi he painted pictures in conjunction with his intimate friend, Agostino Tassi, the landscape-painter. In the Palazzo Borghese there is one of his finest paintings, 'Santa Cecilia and S. Valeriano.' In 1621, on the accession of Pope Gregory XV, he was induced by the Genoese envoy, Giovanni Antonio Sauli, to go to Genoa, where he painted fine works in the palaces of the nobility, especially that of Marc Antonio Doria at S. Piero d'Arena. Possibly he may have encountered Vandyck here. He was next invited to the court of Carlo Emmanuele I of Savoy at Turin, where he painted some excellent works. An 'Annunciation' by him was among the spoils removed by Napoleon to Paris, but was returned to the Turin Gallery (engraved in D'Azeglio's 'Galleria di Torino' and in the 'Musée Napoléon').

From Turin he proceeded to Paris, at the invitation of the queen-mother, where he found plenty of employment for about two years, and gained a new patron in George Villiers, duke of Buckingham. In 1626 he came to England, it is said at the invitation of Vandyck, though he may have come at the request of Buckingham, for whom he painted a 'Magdalen in a Grotto,' a 'Holy Family,' and a ceiling at York House in the Strand. Vandyck appears to have esteemed Gentileschi highly, and drew his portrait, which he had engraved by Vorsterman for his 'Centum Icones' (the original drawing is in the print room at the British Museum). Charles I treated Gentileschi with great honour, furnished a house for him at great cost, and gave him an annuity of 100l. Though over sixty years of age, he painted assiduously for his royal patron, especially at Greenwich Palace. Most of the pictures he painted for the king were dispersed after Charles's execution. Some are at Marlborough House, one of 'Lot and his daughters' was engraved by L. Vorsterman, another of 'The Repose in Egypt' is in the Louvre, and others are to be found at Madrid and Vienna. At Hampton Court there are two pictures by him, formerly in James II's collection, viz. 'A Sibyl' and 'Joseph and Potiphar's wife.' Gentileschi's patronage by the king and Buckingham excited the jealousy of Sir Balthasar Gerbier [q. v.], who seems to have claimed a monopoly of trading on their prodigal generosity to foreign artists. Like Gerbier, Gentileschi was employed on missions of secret diplomacy. Gerbier attacked Gentileschi in many ways, but does not appear to have shaken his position at court, as Gentileschi continued to reside in England up to his death in 1647, in his eighty-fourth year. He was buried in the chapel at Somerset House. He sometimes tried portrait-painting in England, but without much success. Gentileschi brought with him to England a large family, including three sons, Francesca, Giulio, and Marco, and a daughter Artemisia [q. v.] Francesco and Giulio were sent on picture-dealing errands to Italy, and after their father's death Francesco became a painter at Genoa, where he died about 1660; Marco was one of the suite of the Duchess of Buckingham at York House.

[Baldinucci's Notizie dei Professori del Disegno, iii. 710; Rosini's Storia della Pittura Italiana; Lanzi's Hist. of Painting in Italy; Walpole's Anecdotes of Painters, ed. Dallaway and Wornum; De Piles's Lives of the Painters; Cal. State Papers, Dom. Ser. 1629-31; Salvetti Correspondence (Hist. MSS. Comm. 11th Rep. app. x. pt. i. p. 97); Sainsbury's Original Papers relating to Rubens; Fine Arts Quarterly Review, iv. 413; Notes and Queries, 2nd ser. viii. 121; Law's Cat. of the Pictures at Hampton Court; Vertue's Cat. of King Charles I's Collection; Mariette's Abecedario.]   L. C.

GENTILI, ALBERICO (1552–1608), civilian, and one of the earliest systematic writers upon international law, the second son of Matteo Gentili, by his wife Lucrezia, daughter of Diodoro Petrelli, was born 14 Jan. 1552, at Sanginesio, an ancient walled town of the march of Ancona, where his father was a physician. The family had long been favourably known throughout the marches for attainments in law and medicine. Matteo had studied medicine at Pisa, and was also a man of wide general culture. Alberico was sent to the university of Perugia, where he attained the degree of doctor of civil law on 22 Sept. 1572. Two months later he was elected 'prætor,' or judge, of Ascoli, but shortly afterwards settled in his native town, where he filled various responsible offices, and in particular was entrusted with the revision of its statutes. Both father and son belonged to a confraternity suspected (no doubt justly) of meeting for the discussion of opinions hostile to the Roman church. The inquisition was upon the track of the heretics, and Matteo was obliged to fly from his country, taking with him Alberico and a younger son, Scipio, destined to become famous as a teacher of Roman law at Altdorf. At their first halting-place, Laibach, Matteo, doubtless through the influence of his brother-in-law, Nicolo Petrelli, a jurist high in favour with the court, was appointed chief physician for the duchy of Carniola. In the meantime the papal authorities had excommunicated the fugitives, and soon procured their expulsion from Austrian territory. Early in 1580 Alberico set out for England, preceded by a reputation which procured him offers of professorships at Heidelberg and at Tübingen, where Scipio was left to commence his university studies. Alberico reached London in August, with introductions to Battista Castiglioni. He soon became acquainted with Dr. Tobie Matthew, dean of Christ Church, and so with the Earl of Leicester, who, as chancellor of Oxford, furnished him with a letter which was publicly read in the convocation of the university on 14 Dec., recommending him as a learned exile for religion, and requesting his incorporation. On 14 Jan. 1581 Gentili was accordingly incorporated from Perugia as a D.C.L., so gaining the right of teaching law, which he first exercised in St. John's College. Contributions for his support were made also by Magdalen and Corpus Colleges, and from the university chest. He lodged at New Inn Hall, for many centuries a favourite haunt of the legal faculty. Matteo Gentili soon followed his eldest son to England, but after some years' practice of his profession in London became a confirmed invalid, and, dying in 1602, was buried at St. Helen's, Bishopsgate. Alberico in 1582 published a remarkable volume of dialogues in defence of the older school of jurists, as against the 'humanists' and their leader, Cujas. Henceforth he seldom passed a year without producing a new book, confining himself at first to the civil law, but before long dealing with the law of nations, the subject which he made peculiarly his own.

The Oxford civilians (lately, with those of Cambridge, congregated for London practice in the College of Advocates) were already recognised as experts in the rudimentary science of the law of nations. In 1584 Gentili was consulted by the government as to the proper course to be taken with the Spanish ambassador, who had been detected plotting against Elizabeth, and it was in accordance with his opinion that Mendoza was merely ordered to leave the country. Gentili chose the topic to which his attention had thus been directed as the subject of a disputation when Leicester and Sir Philip Sidney visited the schools at Oxford in the same year, and the disputation was, six months later, expanded into the 'De Legationibus,' dedicated to Sir Philip Sidney. In 1586 Gentili was appointed to accompany the embassy of Horatio Pallavicino to the elector of Saxony, and bade farewell to his English friends, apparently with no intention of returning. In the autumn he was at Wittenberg listening to a disputation by his brother Scipio, procuring a professorship there for Conrad Bruno, and dedicating a book to the Dukes of Brunswick and Lüneburg. But in June 1587 he was recalled to Oxford, through the influence of Walsingham, to become regius professor of civil law. In this capacity he delivered at the comitia of 1588 an oration on the 'Law of War,' which resulted in the publication in successive parts of his 'De Jure Belli Commentationes Tres' (1588-9), destined to develope nine years later into the work upon which his reputation mainly rests, the 'De Jure Belli Libri Tres.' The same subject was further illustrated in the 'De Injustitia Bellica Romanorum Actio' (1590); but, in the profusion of books which followed, Gentili touched upon an extraordinary variety of topics, dealing not only with questions of civil and international law, but also with witchcraft, casuistry, canon law, biblical exegesis, classical philology, the Vulgate, English politics, and the prerogative of the crown. He maintained the lawfulness of play-acting against Dr. J. Rainolds, afterwards president of Corpus, who had censured the performance of the 'Rivales' by William Gager [q. v.] before the queen on the occasion of her visit to the university in 1592. He was also involved in discussions as to the occasional permissibility of falsehood, and as to the remarriage of divorced persons. Strong language was freely used in these controversies, and Gentili had to complain of being described as 'Italus atheus.'

After 1590 Alberico seems to have finally taken up his residence in London with a view to forensic practice, leaving most of his work at Oxford to a deputy, and reappearing there only at the comitia or on the occasion of a royal visit. His name does not occur on the roll of the advocates of Doctors' Commons, but he certainly enjoyed a large business in the maritime and ecclesiastical courts. On 14 Aug. 1600 he was admitted a member of Gray's Inn, and in 1605 accepted, with the permission of King James, a permanent retainer as advocate for the king of Spain. Notes of many of the cases conducted by him in this capacity in the court of admiralty are preserved in his posthumously published work, the 'Advocatio Hispanica.' About 1589 he married a French lady, Hester de Peigni, by whom he had Robert [q. v.], Anna, a second Anna (all baptised at the French church in Threadneedle Street), Hester, and Matthew (baptised at St. Helen's, Bishopsgate Street).

Among the opinions of Alberico preserved in the British Museum is one with reference to a suit pending in June 1608 as to property in goods taken by a Tunisian pirate, and it seems he was to argue the case in court. He was probably unable to do so, for on the 14th of that month he made his will, died on the 19th, and on the 21st was buried, in accordance with his last wishes, by the side of his father in the churchyard of St. Helen's, Bishopsgate, two feet beyond the 'nun's grate.' Hester, the widow, died in 1648 at Rickmansworth, Hertfordshire, where her daughter Anna the younger became the wife of Sir John Colt of Woodoaks Manor, which passed by the marriage of their granddaughter, Gentilis Colt, into the Tichborne family. None of the other children are known to have had issue. The directions left by Alberico to his brother Scipio that all his manuscripts, except that of the 'Advocatio Hispanica,' should be burnt, were not carried out, since no less than fifteen volumes of them, for the most part commonplace books on topics of Roman law, were in 1805 purchased from the representatives of the great collector D'Orville of Amsterdam for the Bodleian Library.

The attractive character and varied accomplishments of Alberico procured him the friendship of such men as Walsingham, Sir Philip Sidney, Bodley, Saville, Henry Wotton, the Paulets, the Sherleys, the Earl of Leicester, and the Earl of Essex. In his exuberant literary activity we may distinguish four periods, viz. (1) of his polemic against the school of Cujas, (2) of his tractates and disputations upon questions of civil and international law, (3) of his controversies on theological and moral questions, and (4) of his disquisitions on politics. His enduring influence has been exercised through the writings of the second period, and by the teaching which accompanied it. There can be no doubt that, coming as he did from the original seat of civilian learning, and bringing with him traditions handed down from master to pupil in unbroken series since the days of Irnerius, he gave a new impulse to the study of Roman law, at a time when, as we are told, 'the books of the civil and canon law were set aside to be devoured with worms as savouring too much of popery.' He is described by a contemporary as one 'who by his great industrie hath quickened the dead bodie of the civill law.' The College of Advocates of that day was largely recruited from his pupils, many of whom became eminent in their profession. His teaching left its traces on John Selden, nor can it be an accident that in the generation which must have felt his influence Oxford produced two such Romanists as Sir Arthur Duck and Richard Zouch. Still more important were the services of Gentili to the law of nations, which he was the first to place upon a foundation independent of theological differences, and to develope systematically with a wealth of illustration, historical, legal, biblical, classical, and patristic, of which subsequent writers have availed themselves to a much greater extent than might be inferred from their somewhat scanty acknowledgments of indebtedness. His principal contributions to the science are contained in the 'De Legationibus,' the 'De Jure Belli,' and the 'Advocatio Hispanica.' The first of these was the best work upon embassy which had appeared up to the date of its publication. The last is a collection of arguments on questions of prize law, especially valuable as being much earlier in date than anything else of the kind which has been preserved to us. The 'De Jure Belli' is a vast improvement on the treatises even of Pierino Belli and Ayala on the same subject. In it Gentili combines for the first time the practical discussions of the catholic theologians with the theory of natural law which had been mainly worked out by protestants. Identifying the 'Jus Naturæ' with the consent of the majority of nations, and looking for its evidences to the writings of philosophers, to the Bible, and to the more generally applicable rules of the Roman law, he addresses himself to the novel and difficult task of collecting, criticising, and systematising the rules for the conduct of warfare. Nor does the author confine himself to the discussion of those rules in the abstract. It has been truly observed that the book may 'be regarded as a legal commentary on the events of the sixteenth century, dealing, from the point of view of public law, with all the great questions debated between Charles V and Francis I, between Flanders and Spain, between Italy and her oppressors.' The three books of the 'De Jure Belli' supply the framework and much of the materials of the first and third books of the 'De Jure Belli et Pacis' of Grotius; and it may well be questioned whether the additional matter which forms the second book of the latter work is not too important to be fitly introduced as a mere digression in a treatise on belligerent rights. The marvellous literary success of Grotius long obscured the fame of his predecessor, but in 1875 renewed attention began to be paid to the achievements of Gentili. Committees were formed, alike in his native and in his adopted country, to do him honour; inquiries were instituted which resulted in the ascertainment of many long-forgotten details of his career; a handsome monument was placed in St. Helen's Church as near as might be to his last resting-place; and his greatest work was re-edited at Oxford.

The following is probably a complete list of his writings: 1. 'De Juris Interpretibus Dialogi Sex,' London, 1582, 4to; reprinted London, 1584 and 1585, 8vo, and in Panciroli's 'De Claris Leg. interpr.' 2. 'Lectionum et Epistolarum quæ ad Jus Civile pertinent Libri I–IV,' London, 1583–7, 8vo. 3. 'De Legationibus Libri III,' London, 1585 (two editions), 4to; Hanau, 1594 and 1607, 8vo. 4. 'Legalium Comitiorum Oxoniensium Actio,' London, 1585, 8vo. 5. 'De Diversis Temporum Appellationibus,' Wittenberg, 1586, 8vo; Hanau, 1604, 4to, and 1607, 8vo; Wittenberg, 1646, 8vo. 6. 'De Nascendi Tempore Disputatio,' Wittenberg, 1586, 8vo. 7. 'Disputationum Decas Prima,' London, 1587, 8vo. 8. 'Conditionum Liber Singularis,' London, 1587, 8vo, and 1588, 4to. 9. 'De Jure Belli Commentatio Prima,' London, 1588, 4to; 'Commentatio Secunda,' 1588–9; 'Commentatio Tertia,' 1589; 'Commentationes I et II,' Leyden, 1589, 4to; 'Commentationes Tres,' London, 1589, 8vo; 'De Jure Belli Libri Tres,' Hanau, 1598, 1604, and 1612, 8vo; Oxford, ed. T. E. Holland, 1877, 4to; and in the 'Opera Omnia,' 1770, 4to. 10. 'De Injustitia Bellica Romanorum Actio,' Oxford, 1590, 4to. 11. 'Ad tit. de Malef. et Math. item ad tit. de Prof. et Med.,' Hanau, 1593, and 1604, 8vo. 12. 'De Armis Romanis et Injustitia Bellica Romanorum Libri II,' Hanau, 1599 and 1612, 8vo; printed also, merely as by A. G., in Polenus's 'Thesaur. Antiq., tom. i., ed. Venice, 1737. 13. 'De Actoribus et de Abusu Mendacii Disp. Duæ,' Hanau, 1599, 8vo (printed also in Gronovii 'Thesaur. Antiquit.,' vol. viii.) 14.' De Ludis Scenicis Epistolæ Duæ' (dated 1593), appended to 'The Overthrow of Stage Plays,' Middelburg, 1599, 4to, and Oxford, 1629. 15. 'Ad I Maccabæorum Disp.,' Frankfurt, 1600, 4to. 16. 'De Nuptiis Libri VII,' Hanau, 1601 and 1614, 8vo. 17. 'Lectiones Virgilianæ,' Hanau, 1603 and 1604, 8vo. 18. 'Ad I Maccabæorum Disp., et de Linguarum Mistura,' London, 1604. 19. 'De si quis Principi et ad Leg. Jul. Disp. Decem,' Hanau, 1604 and 1607, 8vo. 20. 'De Latinitate vet. Bibl. vers. male accusata,' Hanau, 1604, 8vo. 21. 'Laudes Academiæ Perusinæ et Oxon.,' Hanau, 1605, 8vo. 22. 'De Unione Angliæ et Scotiæ Discursus,' London, 1605, 8vo; Helmstedt, 1664, 4to. 23. 'Disputationes Tres (1) de libris Juris Can., (2) de libris Juris Civ., (3) Latinitate vet. Bibl.,' &c., Hanau, 1605, 8vo; Helmstedt, 1674, 4to. 24. 'Regales Disputationes, (1) de pot. Regis absol., (2) de Unione Regnorum, &c., (3) de vi Civium in Regem,' &c., London, 1605, fol. and 4to; Hanau, 1605, 8vo (' England's Monarch,' London, 1644, is a refutation of the 'false principles and insinuating flatteries' of this work). 25. 'De libro Pyano ad Jo. Howsonum Epistola' (dated 1603) in Howson's 'Theseos defensio,' Oxford, 1606. 26. 'Hispanicæ Advocationis Libri Duo,' Hanau and Frankfurt, 1613, 4to; Amsterdam, 1661 and 1664, 8vo. 27. 'In tit. de Verborum Significatione,' Hanau, 1614, 4to. 28. 'De Legatis in Testamento,' Amsterdam, 1661, 8vo. 29. 'A Discourse on Marriage by Proxy' is attributed to Alberico Gentili by Anthony à Wood. 'Alberici Gentilis J. C. Prof. Reg. Opera Omnia in plures tomos distributa,' Naples, 1770, was interrupted, after the appearance of vols. i. and ii., by the death of Gravier, the printer. It contains Nos. 9, 12, and 27. 'Mundus alter et idem, auct. Mercurio Britannico,' Hanau, 1607, though attributed by Bayle to Bishop Hall, is thought by Blaufus (*Vermischte Beyträge*, ii. 328) to be by Alberico Gentili. The following are Gentili's unpublished writings: 1. 'De Probationibus Libri IV.' 2. 'Consultationum Volumen.'

3. 'Quæstionum publice Disput. Liber.' 4. 'Commentarius ad Edict. de Annona' (Gentilis complains, in the dedication to 'De Diversis Temporum Appellationibus,' of the loss of all these, 'Quæ pessimo pontificiorum facinore mihi omnia perierunt,' possibly in his flight to Carniola). 5. 'Verborum et Historiarum Juris ex Accurs. et Bartol. Comm. duo' (mentioned in 'Dial. II'). 6. 'In Aldi Manutii Orthographiam Annotationes.' 7. 'De præmio Coronæ Muralis disputatio' (both mentioned in 'Ad. Maccab. I'). 8. 'De Poetis Disputatio.' 9. 'De potiore interpr. Decalogi in sec. tab.' (both mentioned in 'De Actoribus et Spectatoribus'). 10. A volume of 'Leggi ed ordini straordinarii da aggiungersi allo statuto composto e riformato dall' egregio ed eccellentissimo messer Alberigo Gentili' was, according to Benigni, presented by Alberico to San Ginesio. 11. The D'Orville MSS. in the Bodleian Library contain 'De papatu Romano Antichristo assertiones ex verbo Dei et SS. patribus, Alberico Gentili Italo auctore.' The manuscripts of the 'Condicionum Liber,' of the 'De Verborum Significatione,' and of the 'Advocatio Hispanica' are in the same collection. The library of Corpus Christi College possesses the manuscript of the correspondence between Dr. Rainolds and Alberico (ccciii, ccclii). All the works of Gentili were placed in the 'Index Librorum Prohibitorum' in 1603.

[Archives of San Ginesio, Perugia, and Oxford; D'Orville MSS. in Bodleian; Lansdowne MSS. vols. cxxxix. cxlv. in Brit. Mus.; State Papers, Dom. Eliz. vols. cxliv. cxlvii.; wills of Alberico and Hester Gentili at Somerset House; prefaces and dedications to the several works of Alberico Gentili; G. M. Konigius's Bibliotheca vetus et nova, Altdorfii, 1678; T. Benigni in Colucci Antichità Picene, vol. vii. Fermo, 1790; W. A. Reiger's Commentatio, Groningen, 1867; T. E. Holland's Inaugural Lecture, London, 1874, and his Preface to De Jure Belli, Oxford, 1877; G. Speranza's Studi, Rome, 1876; A. Fiorini, Di A. G. e del suo diritto di guerra, Leghorn, 1877; A. Saffi's Letture, Bologna, 1878.]   T. E. H.

GENTILI, ALOYSIUS, LL.D. (1801–1848), missionary-apostolic in England, born at Rome on 14 July 1801, was the son of a solicitor of Neapolitan descent. After completing his studies at the Sapienza, he took the degree of doctor of civil and canon law, and began to practise as an advocate. The death of his patron, Cardinal Gonsalvi, successively auditor of the rota and secretary of state, having destroyed his hopes of advancement, he studied the English, French, and Spanish languages, and became a professional teacher of Italian, in which vocation he had great success. He was made a knight by the duke Sforza Cesarini, who enjoyed the privilege of creating knights palatine and knights of the order of the Golden Spur. In 1830 he obtained an introduction to Rosmini, which led to his joining the Institute of Charity founded by that celebrated philosopher. Having been ordained priest in 1830, he was sent in 1831 to the first house of the institute, built on Monte Calvario, near Domo d'Ossola, and was appointed master of the novices. In 1835 the Institute of Charity was introduced into England, and Gentili and two other missionaries were sent by the Father-general Rosmini, and exercised their ministry first at Trelawney, Cornwall, and afterwards at Prior Park, near Bath, where Gentili was appointed superior of the college by Bishop Baines. Differences arose on educational and other subjects between the bishop and Gentili, who, after visiting Rome in 1839 to take his vows as presbyter of the institute, was sent back by his superior in 1840 to become chaplain to Ambrose Lisle Phillipps [see DE LISLE] of Grace Dieu Manor, Leicestershire. In 1842 he was removed to the mission at Loughborough, and after a time his talents and successes as a preacher led to his being appointed itinerant missionary. He commenced this new career in company with Father Furlong in 1845. After giving missions in all the large towns of England and Ireland, Gentili, while on a visit to the latter country, was seized with a feverish attack, and died at Dublin on 25 Sept. 1848. A detailed account of his missionary labours will be found in the 'Life of the Rev. Aloysius Gentili, LL.D., Father of Charity and Missionary Apostolic in England. Edited by the Very Rev. Father Pagani,' London, 1851, 8vo (with portrait).

[Pagani's Life of Gentili; Collins's Life of Gentili, 1861; Dublin Review, xxxi. 365; Lockhart's Life of Rosmini.]   T. C.

GENTILI, ROBERT (1590–1654?), infant prodigy, scapegrace, and translator, eldest son of Alberico Gentili [q. v.], was born in London 11 Sept. 1590, and was named after his godfather the Earl of Essex. He was educated in accordance with a theory that the youthful mind is better developed by conversation than by set study. Having always talked with his father in Latin, and with his mother in French, he could speak both languages, besides English, when seven years old. A few months afterwards he had been taken by the same method through the Eclogues of Virgil. In 1599, at the age of nine, he was matriculated at Christ Church, and in 1603 took the degree of B.A. as a member of Jesus College. In the following year

he was at St. John's, and on the nomination of Laud, then proctor, held the now obsolete university office of 'collector,' but was unfortunately dissuaded from publishing an account of his experiences in that capacity. One of the plans of Alberico for pushing the boy's fortunes was to allow him to dedicate in his own name several of his father's works to persons of influence. The illegal intrusion of Robert into a fellowship was less defensible. Alberico, finding that the boy was not making progress in his classical studies, set to work to procure his election to a law vacancy which had occurred at All Souls. For more than two years the college resisted alike letters from King James and representations from Archbishop Bancroft as to Robert's 'extraordinary forwardness,' on the ground that he had not reached the statutable age. Alberico wrote a learned argument to show that to enter upon one's seventeenth year was equivalent to completing it (Brit. Mus. *Addit. MS.* 12504), and, the appointment having lapsed to Bancroft as visitor, Robert was, on his nomination, admitted early in 1607 to be a probationer-fellow. His conduct was such as bitterly to disappoint the expectations of his parents, as appears from expressions in the wills of both, and in letters from his uncle Scipio, to whom he paid a visit at Altdorf in 1609. He was nicknamed at Oxford 'the king of the beggars,' and the archbishop was once obliged to summon him to Lambeth to answer for misbehaviour in college. In 1612 he took the degree of B.C.L., but in the same year resigned his fellowship, and disappears from view for a quarter of a century. He seems to have received some assistance from the king. A small annuity left to him by his mother, on condition that he should 'change no religion and come not to this country,' was revoked on his return to England in 1637, although he was then, according to some accounts, 'multum reformatus.' 'Alice, wife of Robert Gentilis,' had been buried in 1619 at St. Bride's, Fleet Street, but he married on 4 Jan. 1638, as a 'bachelor,' at St. Martin's-in-the-Fields, Mary, widow of Richard Simpson, and set to work to execute the following translations, all for Humphrey Mosely, of St. Paul's Churchyard, after the date of the last of which he is no more traceable : 1. 'The History of the Inquisition, composed by the Rev. Father Paul Servita,' London, 1639, 4to (reprinted in Sir Nathaniel Brent's 'Translation of the History of the Council of Trent,' folio, 1620, 1676). 2. 'The Antipathy between the French and the Spaniard,' otherwise entitled 'The Frenchman and the Spaniard, or the Two Great Lights of the World,' &c., London, 1641, 1642, 12mo (dedicated by

Robert Gentili to Sir Peter Pindar, with a promise, 'ere long, to present you with something which shall be mine own invention'). 3. 'The Success and Chief Events of the Monarchy of Spain, by Malvezzi,' London, 1647, 12mo. 4. 'Considerations on the Lives of Alcibiades and Coriolanus, by Malvezzi,' London, 1650, 12mo (dedicated to the daughter of Thomas, earl of Strafford, 'as a small token of the manifold obligements whereto I am everlastingly tied to you'). 5. 'The Natural and Experimental Historie of Winds,' &c., by the Right Hon. Francis, lord Verulam, &c., London, 1653, 12mo. 6. 'Le Chemin Abrégé, or a Compendious Method for attaining of Sciences,' London, 1654, 12mo, dedicated to John Selden. There is no positive clue to the authorship of this work, which contains 'the statutes of the academy in the city of Richelieu.'

[State Papers, Dom. James I; D'Orville MSS. in Bodl. Lib.; Archives of All Souls' College; A. Clark's Register of the Univ. of Oxford; dedications prefixed by Robert Gentili to his own and to several of his father's works; D. G. Morhof's Polyhistor, t. i. l. ii. c. 9, § 3.] T. E. H.

GENTLEMAN, FRANCIS (1728–1784), actor and dramatist, born in York Street, Dublin, 13 Oct. 1728, was son of a captain in the army. With Mossop and Dexter, both subsequently actors, he was educated at a grammar school in Digges Street under a clergyman named Butler. He obtained at the age of fifteen a commission in the regiment of his father, who died two years later. He exchanged into a newly raised company intended for active service, and had to leave the army on the peace of 1748. He then engaged with Sheridan at Smock Alley Theatre, where he appeared as Aboan in 'Oroonoko,' and remained for a season and a half. Notwithstanding what he calls 'an unconsequential figure and uncommon timidity,' he succeeded 'beyond his expectations.' Having inherited from an uncle in India a sum of 800l., he came to London, and states that he saved only 200l. from the lawyers. On his way from Dublin he met Macklin with a company at Chester, and produced 'Sejanus,' an alteration from Ben Jonson, printed 1752, 8vo. He afterwards joined Simpson's company at Bath, where he wrote 'The Sultan, or Love and Fame,' a tragedy (8vo, 1770), and next season produced 'Zaphna,' a tragedy, and an alteration of 'Richard II.' The manuscripts of the last two were stolen, and the pieces were unprinted. After going to Edinburgh, appearing as Othello and giving lessons in English, he visited Glasgow (where he met Boswell), Carlisle, Scarborough, Manchester, and Liverpool, returning to Chester, in which city he

played the 'Modish Wife,' his masterpiece, if such a term may be used, 8vo, 1774, and the 'Fairy Court,' never printed, which was acted by children, and ran for fifteen nights. He now retired to Malton in Yorkshire, stayed there five years, and married a wife, who died in 1773, leaving him two children. Here he wrote 'a thing in two volumes, entitled 'A Trip to the Moon.' To this period belongs 'A Set of Tables,' composed for the Prince of Wales. Expectations from the Marquis of Granby brought him to London; but Granby died in 1770, and Foote then gave him a summer engagement. His 'Sultan' had been revived in April 1769, apparently by a scratch company. The 'Tobacconist,' 8vo, 1771, a wretched comedy founded upon the 'Alchemist' of Ben Jonson, was given 22 July 1771. In this Gentleman played Sir Epicure Mammon. The 'Coxcomb,' a farce taken by him from 'Epicene,' was also played, once for a benefit, this season. His 'Cupid's Revenge,' taken from Hoadly's 'Love's Revenge,' a pastoral, 8vo, 1772, was played at the Haymarket July 1772. The 'Pantheonites,' a dramatic entertainment by Gentleman, 8vo, 1773, was acted for Jewell's benefit at the Haymarket, 3 Sept. 1773, Gentleman playing Skinflint. After the season was over, 18 Sept. 1773, his 'Modish Wife' was given. In 1770 Gentleman had published anonymously the 'Dramatic Censor,' 2 vols. 8vo, by which he is best known. It consists of a series of tolerable criticisms upon various plays of the time. The opinions expressed are fairly judicious. Vol. i. was dedicated to Garrick, and vol. ii. to Foote. A year previously he had printed the 'Stratford Jubilee,' a comedy, 8vo, 1769, and attacked Garrick in some sentences which the bookseller excised. Garrick had at this time assisted Gentleman, who had fallen upon evil times, and, though disliking him, helped him again. Among Garrick's papers is a quatrain upon this 'dirty dedicating knave,' who is 'Gentleman in name' only (PERCY FITZGERALD, *Life of Garrick*, ii. 379). In the 'Garrick Correspondence' are some pitiable appeals from Gentleman to which Garrick responded. One loan of five guineas is asked in August 1775 for the purpose of giving 'dramatic lectures of a nature different from any yet attempted' at 'Eaton' and Oxford (ii. 82). On 14 March of the same year, acknowledging a letter from Garrick with 'its solid contents,' Gentleman disavows the responsibility for his 'promulged (*sic*) theatrical sentiments,' and promises better behaviour for the future (*Private Correspondence*, ii. 48). Gentleman was now leading a shiftless life of expedients. He was indeed a poor creature, and writes despairingly: 'I heartily wish I had been fated to use an awl and end sooner than the pen, for nothing but a pensioned defender of government, a sycophant to managers, or a slave to booksellers can do anything more than crawl.' In addition to the pieces named, Gentleman wrote an alteration of 'Oroonoko,' Glasgow, 12mo, 1760, played at Edinburgh, and dedicated to Boswell, and the following unprinted pieces: 1. 'Osman,' a tragedy (every subscriber for a ticket for the performance at the Little Theatre in the Haymarket was to have a large or small paper copy according to his seat. It was subsequently acted at Bath). 2. 'Mentalist,' a dramatic satire acted at Manchester about 1759. 3. 'Orpheus and Eurydice' (a serious opera acted at the Smock Alley Theatre, Dublin, 1783. A piece similarly described was played for two or three nights at Covent Garden in February 1792). He published also: 1. 'Fortune,' a rhapsody (in verse), London, 1751, 4to (translated from an ode of Rousseau). 2. 'Characters,' London, 1766, 4to (in verse; a not very brilliant satire). 3. 'Royal Fables,' London, 1766, 16mo (rhymed fables in the manner of Gay). 'Narcissa and Eliza, a Dramatic Tale in Verse,' London, 1754, 4to, is assigned to him in the British Museum Catalogue. In 1774 was published in 12mo the 'Merry Wives of Windsor,' with an introduction and notes by the author of the 'Dramatic Censor.' He edited Bell's acting edition of Shakespeare. This edition, which only professes to present the dramas as they were then played, is harshly characterised by Reed in the 'Biographia Dramatica' as the worst that ever appeared of any English author. His 'Tobacconist' is included in the 'London Stage,' vol. ii., and in the collections of Dibdin and Oxberry. His late years were spent in Ireland. He died in George Lane, Dublin, on 21 Dec. 1784 (*Biographia Dramatica*, 18 Dec. 1784; REED, MS. *Notitia Dramatica*), having during the last seven years of his life undergone extreme sickness and want.

[The chief authorities for his life are found in a long preface to the Modish Wife. The particulars there given are copied, with more or less abridgment and alteration, in the Biographia Dramatica and other works of theatrical reference. The Garrick Correspondence, Genest's Account of the English Stage, Boswell's Life of Johnson (ed. Hill), Gent. Mag. (1784), and his own printed works supply further particulars. The authority on which some of the works cited are ascribed to Gentleman is not always evident.]

J. K.

GENTLEMAN, ROBERT (1746–1795), dissenting divine and tutor, was born at Shrewsbury in 1746. He was brought up under the ministry of Job Orton, who encouraged him in his studies. In 1763 he entered the Daventry academy under Caleb Ashworth [q. v.] On 15 Sept. 1765 Orton resigned the co-pastorate of the High Street congregation, Shrewsbury, and there was a division as to the appointment of his successor. The more conservative majority seceded, and Orton assisted them in building a new meeting-house. Gentleman was ultimately chosen as the first minister of this new society. He was a popular preacher, arianising in his theology, but of evangelical sentiment. He remained at Shrewsbury, where he kept a boarding-school, until 1779, when he accepted the position of divinity tutor at Carmarthen Academy (then at Rhydygorse, near Carmarthen), vacated by the removal of Jenkin Jenkins, D.D., to London. The experiment of housing the tutors and students in a residential college proved a failure, from the inability of Gentleman to maintain discipline. Bogue and Bennett say that the London 'congregational fund' withdrew its support from the academy owing to distrust of Gentleman's teaching; but this is an error; the support was withdrawn in 1755. He resigned his office in 1784, and the academy was removed to Swansea under Solomon Harris.

The dissenting congregation at Kidderminster had been divided after the death (1780) of Benjamin Fawcett [q. v.] Arian seceders erected a new meeting-house in 1782, but were without a pastor. Orton, who died at Kidderminster in 1783, made Gentleman his literary executor, and this circumstance probably recommended him to the Kidderminster seceders, who chose him as their first minister in 1784. His ministry was very successful. He died in his prime in July 1795, and was buried on 12 July in St. Mary's churchyard, Kidderminster.

He published: 1. 'The Young English Scholar's . . . Companion,' &c., Kidderminster, 1788, 12mo; another edit., 1797, 12mo. 2. 'Plain . . . Addresses to Youth,' &c., 1792, 8vo. From Orton's manuscripts he compiled 'A Short and Plain Exposition of the Old Testament,' &c., 1788–91, 6 vols. 8vo; 2nd edit., 1822, 8vo.

[Prot. Dissenter's Mag. 1795, pp. 180, 182, 312; Monthly Repository, 1822, p. 195; Bogue and Bennett's Hist. of Dissenters, 1833, ii. 535; Rees's Hist. Prot. Nonconf. in Wales, 1883, p. 496; Jeremy's Presbyterian Fund, 1885, pp. 20, 49, 66; extract from parish register, Kidderminster, per Rev. J. Hall.]

A. G.

GEOFFREY (d. 1093), bishop of Coutances, came of a noble Norman family settled at Montbrai, or, as pronounced in English, Mowbray, in the arrondissement of St. Lô; he was brother of Roger of Mowbray, and his sister Amicia married Roger of Albini. He was consecrated bishop of Coutances at Rouen on 10 April 1048, and is described as tall, handsome, and prudent. At the council of Rheims in October 1049 he was accused of simony; he confessed that his brother had bought the bishopric for him, but declared that it was without his knowledge, and that when he found it out he tried to avoid consecration. He was pronounced guiltless, and followed Pope Leo IX, who presided over the council in person, on his journey back to Rome. In the following May he was present at the council in Rome which condemned Berengar of Tours. Geoffrey had business of his own in Italy. His predecessor, Bishop Robert, had begun to rebuild the cathedral of Coutances. There were no funds sufficient to finish the building, no books, no ornaments, and only five canons. Geoffrey journeyed to Apulia, for the victorious Robert Guiscard and his brothers came from Hauteville in the diocese of Coutances, and he was well known to many of their followers. He told the adventurers of his needs, and they gave him liberal gifts from the spoils taken in their Italian wars. With these he returned to Coutances, and at once began to build. He completed the fabric of his church, which was consecrated on 8 Dec. 1056 in the presence of Duke William, built an episcopal residence with a fine hall and stabling, and added to the number of canons. This church appears to have been laid in ruins by Geoffrey Harcourt in 1356, and the present church was built chiefly by Bishop Sylvestre de la Cervelle in the later years of the same century. In 1063 Geoffrey attended a council at Rouen held by his metropolitan, Maurilius, and the next year incited Turstin and his wife and their son Eudo to found the abbey of the Holy Trinity at Lessay. He joined in the invasion of England, and the night before the battle of Hastings listened to confessions and pronounced absolution of sins; he and the bishop Odo are said to have come with a host of clerks and some monks in order to fight by their prayers (WILLIAM OF POITOU, p. 201; ORDERIC, p. 501); the bishop Odo certainly used a carnal weapon the next day; nothing is known of any part which Geoffrey may have taken in the fight. He is said to have been better skilled in war than in clerical matters, more apt at leading harnessed warriors in battle than at teaching surpliced clerks to sing psalms (ORDERIC, p. 703). At the coronation of the Conqueror on 25 Dec. 1066, the Archbishop of York having first put the question in English to the assembled multitude whether they would have William to reign over them, Geoffrey repeated it in French to the Normans (ib. p. 503). He received a vast number of grants of lands in England; Orderic says that he held as many as 280 manors (ib. p. 703); his estates lay in various parts of the kingdom (ELLIS, Introduction to Domesday, i. 400), but chiefly in the western shires; in 1086 he held seventy-seven manors in Somerset alone (EYTON). He is generally spoken of either by his christian name or by the title of his Norman see rather than by the name of his English residence, once at least in Domesday (Glouc. f. 165) as 'de Sancto Laudo' (Saint-Lô, the earlier seat of his bishopric), and he is described in the teste of a charter as 'de Seynt Loth' (Monasticon, i. 144).

Geoffrey appears to have accompanied William on his visit to Normandy in March 1067, for he was present at the dedication of the church of Jumièges on 1 July (Gallia Christiana, xi. 870). He took a prominent part in putting down the revolt in the west of England in 1069, leading a force raised from Winchester, London, and Salisbury to the relief of the castle of Montacute, which was besieged by the men of Somerset and Dorset. He slew some of the besiegers, put the rest to flight, and mutilated his captives (ORDERIC, p. 514). Worldly as he was, he lived on terms of friendship with the holy Bishop Wulfstan of Worcester, and tried to persuade him to dress more handsomely (Anglia Sacra, ii. 259). He presided at the trial of the suit between Archbishop Lanfranc and Bishop Odo on Pennenden Heath in Kent in 1071, representing the king and acting as his justiciar (ib. i. 335); the title was not as yet 'definitely attached to a particular post' (STUBBS, Const. Hist. i. 346). On 8 April 1072 he attended the king's council at Winchester, where the dispute between the archbishops of Canterbury and York was heard, was present at the adjourned hearing at Windsor, and attested the decree in favour of Canterbury, being described as 'bishop of Coutances and one of the nobles of England' (Vita Lanfranci, p. 304). In 1075 he was present at an ecclesiastical council which Lanfranc held in St. Paul's, for, as it is explained, though his bishopric lay over sea, he was assigned a place in the council because he had large estates in England (ib. p. 305). When Ralf of Wader, earl of Norfolk, and Roger, earl of Hereford, made an insurrection in this year, Geoffrey joined Odo of Bayeux in leading an army against Ralf; they advanced to Cambridge, and, in common with the other leaders on the king's side, cut off the right foot of each of their captives

(FLORENCE, ii. 11; ORDERIC, p. 535). Geoffrey laid siege to Norwich in company with Earl William of Warren, and received the capitulation of the town. In 1077 he was present at the dedication of St. Stephen's at Caen, and in 1080 attended a provincial council at Lillebonne. He wrote to Lanfranc apparently on behalf of some English ladies who had taken refuge in nunneries for fear of the Frenchmen, and was informed by the archbishop that in such cases ladies were not to be compelled to adopt a religious life (*Epp. Lanfranci*, No. 35). Either at this time (FREEMAN, *Norman Conquest*, iv. 676) or possibly in 1088, when his nephew, Robert of Mowbray, was earl, he for a while governed Northumberland (*Monasticon*, iii. 546; DUGDALE, *Baronage*, p. 56; HINDE, *Hist of Northumberland*, p. 92). He attended the funeral of the Conqueror in September 1087. When the Norman lords in England rebelled against Rufus in 1088, Geoffrey took part in the movement, and in company with his nephew Robert went to Bristol; they harried the neighbouring country, and brought their booty into the castle. William of Eu also acted in conjunction with them (*Peterborough Chronicle*; FLORENCE, ii. 24). Geoffrey was probably the constable of Bristol Castle, and received the king's dues from the town (*Domesday*, f. 163; FREEMAN, *William Rufus*, i. 40). He perhaps built the castle, which is said to have been exceedingly strong at this time, though it was afterwards strengthened by Robert, earl of Gloucester, and the outer wall of the town may also be set down as his work. He seems to have been included in the general pardon which the king granted to the greater Norman lords, and in the following November attended the king's court at Salisbury, where charges were preferred against William, bishop of Durham. There he urged that the prelates should withdraw and determine the question whether the bishop ought to be called upon to plead before he was restored to his bishopric. He spoke on behalf of the privileges of the clergy, but was overruled by Lanfranc (*Monasticon*, i. 247). At a later stage of the hearing one of Geoffrey's men made a claim against the Bishop of Durham, declaring that the garrison of his castle had taken two hundred cattle belonging to his lord (*ib.* p. 248). It is said that when Duke Robert sold the Cotentin to his brother Henry, Bishop Geoffrey refused to acknowledge the new count, declaring that his church should own no lord save him who was owned by the church of Rouen, and that frequent frays took place between the men of the bishopric and Henry's barons (*Gallia Christiana*, xi. 872; *Recueil des His-*

toriens, xii. 644 *n.*) He died at Coutances on 3 Feb. 1093, in the presence of Odo of Bayeux and other prelates who had come to visit him, and was buried in his cathedral church. He left his English estates to his nephew, Robert of Mowbray, earl of Northumberland.

[Freeman's Norman Conquest, vols. iii. and iv.; Gallia Christiana, xi. 870; Bessin's Concilia Rotom. Prov. i. 40, 49; Orderic and William of Poitou, ed. Duchesne; Anglo-Saxon Chron. (Rolls Ser.); Florence of Worcester (Engl. Hist. Soc.); Wace's Roman de Rou; William of Malmesbury, Gesta Pontiff.; B. Lanfranci Opera, ed. Giles; Anglia Sacra; Dugdale's Monasticon and Baronage, p. 56; Planché's Conqueror and his Companions, ii. 25; Gally Knight's Architectural Tour in Normandy, p. 100.] W. H.

GEOFFREY, GAIMER (*fl.* 1140?), historian. [See GAIMER.]

GEOFFREY, RUFUS (*d.* 1140), bishop of Durham and chancellor. [See RUFUS.]

GEOFFREY OF GORHAM (*d.* 1146), abbot of St. Albans, was descended from ancestors of noble rank both in Normandy and in Maine, of which county he was a native. He was a learned clerk, and, though a secular, was invited by Richard, abbot of St. Albans, to come to England and take charge of the abbey school. As he delayed to come, the post was given to another. The abbot, however, promised that he should have it at a future date, and he settled at Dunstable and kept a school there. While he was at Dunstable he composed a miracle-play of St. Katharine, either for the weavers of the town, for St. Katharine was the patron of their craft, or for his scholars (WARTON; WRIGHT). For the dress of his players Geoffrey persuaded the sacristan of St. Albans to lend him the choir copes of the abbey, for Dunstable Priory was not founded until some years later (*Monasticon*, vi. 238). On the night after the play, doubtless 24 Nov., the eve of the saint's feast day, Master Geoffrey's house was burnt, and with it his books and the St. Albans copes. To make up the loss to God and the saint, he determined to become a monk of St. Albans, and in after days as abbot took special care to provide the house with valuable choir copes. He became prior, and, on the death of Abbot Richard in 1119, was elected to succeed him. He made improvements in the internal economy of the abbey, built a fine guests' hall, and next to it a room called the queen's chamber, for the use of the queen, the only woman who was allowed to lodge within the abbey, and an infirmary with a chapel. Although he was anxious to complete a shrine which he was making for

Saint Alban, and on which he had spent 60*l.*, he nevertheless did not scruple in a year of famine to tear off from his work the silver plates which had not yet been gilded, and have them turned into money, which he spent in the relief of the poor. The next year he went on with the shrine, employing on it one of the brethren of the house named Anketil, a goldsmith, who had been moneyer to the king of Denmark. He finished it all except the crest, which he hoped to complete when gold and silver and jewels should become more plentiful, for the times were bad. On 2 Aug. 1129 he translated the saint's body in the presence of Alexander, bishop of Lincoln [q. v.], and others. He founded the hospital of St. Julian for lepers, on the London road, and founded, or more probably regulated, enlarged, and endowed, a nunnery at Sopwell, near St. Albans, as a cell of the abbey. At the same time he did some things which were detrimental to the wealth of his house, and appears to have shown undue favour to his sister's husband, Hugh, who held Westwick of the convent. He found it necessary to send some valuable plate to Pope Celestine II to content his claims, and also melted down other silver and gave it to Earl Warren, William of Ypres, and the Earl of Arundel, as a ransom for the town of St. Albans, which they threatened to burn during the wars of Stephen's reign, possibly when Geoffrey Mandeville was taken there in 1143. Both in worldly and spiritual matters he was in the habit of taking counsel with Christina, a recluse much famed for sanctity, for whom he built a nunnery at Markyate or Market street in Bedfordshire. He made many rich gifts to the abbey. He died on 26 Feb. 1146, after having ruled the house with much vigour for twenty-six years and some months. His epitaph is preserved by Weever.

[Gesta Abbatum S. Albani, i. 72–105 (Rolls Ser.); Vitæ Abbatum, pp. 1007–14, ed. Wats; Roger of Wendover, ii. 200 (Engl. Hist. Soc.); Matt. Paris, ii. 147, 178, vi. 39, 387 (Rolls Ser.); William of Newburgh, i. 35 (Engl. Hist. Soc.); Dugdale's Monasticon, ii. 184, iii. 362, 368; Warton's Hist. of English Poetry, i. cxii; Wright's Biog. Brit., Anglo-Norman, p. 109; Hone's Ancient Mysteries, pp. 199, 201.]   W. H.

GEOFFREY OF MONMOUTH (1100 ?– 1154), otherwise GALFRIDUS or GAUFRIDUS ARTURUS, GALFRIDUS MONEMUTENSIS, styled by Welsh writers GALFFRAI or GRUFFYD AB ARTHUR, bishop of St. Asaph and chronicler, was either born or bred at Monmouth about the commencement of the twelfth century, and may have been at one time a monk of the Benedictine abbey there. He was the son of Arthur, who, according to Welsh authorities, was family priest of William, earl of Gloucester, an apocryphal personage. Geoffrey was brought up as 'foster son' by his paternal uncle Uchtryd, archdeacon and subsequently bishop of Llandaff (*Archæologia Cambrensis*, 3rd ser. 1864, x. 124). He went to Oxford and made the acquaintance of Archdeacon Walter [see CALENIUS, WALTER] as early as 1129, when the two witnessed the Oseney charter subscribed by Geoffrey as Gaufridus Arturus (see *Journ. Arch. Instit.* 1858, p. 305). It was from Walter that Geoffrey professed to have obtained the foundation of his great work. He begins and ends his 'Historia Regum Britanniæ' with an acknowledgment that it was based upon a certain 'librum vetustissimum' ' Britannici sermonis, quem Gualterus Oxenfordensis archidiaconus ex Britannia advexit.' Before the book was half completed, however, Alexander, bishop of Lincoln [q. v.], desired Geoffrey to make a Latin version of the 'Prophecies of Merlin' from the Cymric. This was probably produced separately before the termination of his larger work (in which it was incorporated), as Ordericus Vitalis (*Historia Ecclesiastica*, bk. xii. cap. 47), writing about 1136–7, quotes from it. Alanus de Insulis wrote extensive commentaries upon the 'Prophecies' about 1170–80, and professed to have collated several manuscripts for the purpose. Towards 1140 Geoffrey went to Llandaff, 'and for his learning and excellencies an archdeaconry was conferred upon him in the church of Teilo' in that city, 'where he was the instructor of many scholars and chieftains' ('Gwentian Brut,' ut supra, p. 124). He probably accompanied his uncle Uchtryd, who had been made Bishop of Llandaff in that year. By this time the 'Historia Regum Britanniæ' had been issued in some form, as Henry of Huntingdon examined it at the abbey of Bec in Normandy, in January 1139, on his way to Rome with Theobald, archbishop of Canterbury. He made an abstract of its contents, which is extant in his works. Within a space of six months, in 1147–8, Geoffrey's two powerful friends, Robert, earl of Gloucester (to whom the 'Historia' is dedicated) and Bishop Alexander, as well as his uncle, died. He sought other patrons and addressed, at the beginning of 1149, his poem entitled 'Vita Merlini' to the new bishop of Lincoln, Robert de Chesney [q. v.], who had influence at the court of King Stephen.

Wright (*Biog. Lit.* 1846, p. 144) and Hardy (*Catalogue*, i. 350) agree in referring the final edition of the 'Historia Regum Britanniæ,' as we now possess it, to the autumn of 1147. Geoffrey was consecrated bishop of St. Asaph by Archbishop Theobald at Lambeth, 24 Feb. 1151-2, having been ordained priest at Westminster on the 16th of the same month ('Reg. Eccles. Christi Cantuar.' in WHARTON, *De Episc. Assav.* p. 305). On 16 Nov. 1153 he was a witness of the compact between Stephen and Henry II (see 'Brompton' in TWYSDEN, 1039, and 'Gervase,' *ib.* 1375). He does not seem to have visited his see, and died in 1154 'in his house at Llandaff, before he entered on his functions, and was buried in the church there' ('Gwentian Brut,' ut supra, p. 124). Another text of the Welsh Brut states that the death took place 'at mass' (ed. Williams ab Ithel, Rolls Series, 1860, p. 185).

Geoffrey of Monmouth was at least fifty years of age when he was ordained priest in 1152. His literary career was already over, and its record is a brilliant one notwithstanding the charges made on one side that his Cymric scholarship was faulty, and on the other that his Latinity is of vulgar order. The metrical 'Vita Merlini' has been considered too excellent a piece of composition for his pen, and therefore supposititious; but Mr. Ward gives good reason for believing it genuine. Indeed, the suggestion—however gratuitous—that Geoffrey was a Benedictine monk is almost a necessary one to account for the education evinced by his labours, not the most important part of them being the reduction of ancient British legends into respectable mediæval Latin history—a task accomplished with manifest literary skill and tact. His allusions to antecedent and contemporary writers are a proof that he was no mere monkish student eager to swallow wondrous stories, but a shrewd scholar equipped with all the learning of his age. 'He was a man whose like could not be found for learning and knowledge,' says the 'Gwentian Brut' (ut supra, p. 125), and had a charm of manner which made his society agreeable to men of high station.

The publication of the 'Historia Britonum' marks an epoch in the literary history of Europe. There followed in less than half a century after the completion of Geoffrey's Chronicle, the romances partly based upon it of the Grail, Perceval, Lancelot, Tristan, and the Round Table; and Geoffrey's stories of Merlin and King Arthur were naturalised in Germany and Italy, as well as in France and England. They are best known in English literature through Sir Thomas Malory's compilation (sec. xv.) of the Arthurian romances. Geoffrey's originality as an inventor of the tales related in his history has been much discussed. Of the larger portion of his text

and its principal elements, his own work is the oldest existing specimen; but there can be little doubt that he compiled it from the Latin 'Nennius,' still extant, and a book of Breton legends which has perished. The central idea of the latter book, described as *vetustissimus*, which undoubtedly came from Brittany, was the descent of the British princes from the fugitives of Troy—a notion to which a parallel is found in the traditions of the Franks in Gaul, and which seems to have arisen in both countries only after the invasion of the Teutonic tribes. The myth may be assumed to have sprung up in Britain about the end of the fifth century, or the beginning of the sixth; but it can hardly have had general credence or been set down in writing at the time when Beda was writing his 'History,' since he makes no allusion to it. Thus the *liber vetustissimus* could scarcely have been more ancient than the ninth century, and was probably less than two hundred years of age when Geoffrey inspected it. The name of Arthur outside the mythic story was an unfamiliar one in Britain, if not indeed quite unknown, when the so-called 'Nennius' was written (about A.D. 900). That the Breton contribution to Geoffrey's history was a considerable one must be admitted, notwithstanding Welsh denials of the fact, and the acceptance by many good authorities of a theory assuming definite Cymric characteristics in the narrative. History and philology tend equally to show that whatever differences exist at present between the Welsh and Breton languages have arisen gradually since the time of Henry I, and that before his time the two peoples were virtually identical.

The 'Historia Britonum' exercised a powerful influence in the unification of the people of England. The race-animosities of Breton, Teuton, and Frenchman would probably have endured much longer than they did, but for the legend of an origin common to them all, and to the Roman conquerors of Britain whose descendants were not yet extinct in the towns. Geoffrey's work was spread throughout the country and on the continent in an unlimited multiplication of copies. It was abridged by Alfred of Beverley as 'Historia de gestis Regum Britanniæ libris ix,' and translated into Anglo-Norman verse by Geoffrey Gaimar and by Wace about the middle of the twelfth century. Within a hundred years later Layamon and Robert of Gloucester gave the stories an English dress, and the chroniclers from Roger of Wendover to Holinshed followed Geoffrey as a sober historian. Shakespeare used his fictions through Holinshed. Milton, Dryden, Pope, Wordsworth, and Tennyson have all pressed Geoffrey's legends into their service.

The three Welsh chronicles known as the 'Brut Tysilio,' the 'Brut y Brenhinoedd,' and the 'Brut Gruffyd ab Arthur' have been clearly shown to be late translations or adaptations of Geoffrey's 'Historia,' made at a time when the word brut had, by frequent use as an appellative (both in Welsh and English) for the popular story with its continuations, become equivalent to chronicle. Editions of those various texts, or portions of them, have been given in the Myvyrian archæology and the Cambrian register. They must be distinguished from the 'Brut y Saeson' or 'Brut y Tywysogion' of Caradoc of Llancarvan, which is pure history, and has been printed in the Rolls Series and in the 'Archæologia Cambrensis.' Bale supplies the titles of several imaginary books supposed to have been written by Geoffrey. The treatise 'Compendium Gaufredi de Corpore Christi et Sacramento Eucharistiæ,' sometimes attributed to Geoffrey, of which two manuscripts are in the library of Corpus Christi College, Cambridge, is stated by Wright to be written by Geoffrey of Auxerre.

The following is a view of the printed editions. A list of the manuscripts (including compilations and extracts from his works) is given by Hardy (*Descriptive Cat.* 1862-71, 3 vols.); see also Ward (*Cat. of Romances,* 1883), and Potthast (*Wegweiser,* 1862-8, 2 vols.) 1. 'Britannie utriusque regum et principum origo et gesta insignia ab Galfrido Monemutensi ex antiquissimis Britannici sermonis monumentis in Latinum sermonem traducta et ab Ascensio cura et impendio magistri Junonis Cavelleti in lucem edita,' Paris, 1508, 4to, 1st edition (this, as well as the 2nd edition, were much altered by the editor); 'Britanniæ utriusque regum et principum origo et gesta . . . ab Ascensio rursus majore accuratione impressa,' Paris, 1517, 4to, 2nd edition; reprinted, after collation with a manuscript, in H. Commelini 'Rerum Britt. Script.,' Heidelb. 1587, folio, pp. 1-92. The first critical edition is 'Galfredi Monumetensis Historia Britonum, nunc primum in Anglia novem codd. MSS. collatis ed. J. A. Giles,' London, 1844, 8vo (also as a publication of the Caxton Soc.) The latest is 'Gottfried's von Monmouth Historia regum Britanniæ und Brut Tysilio, altwälsche Chronik in deutscher Uebersetzung, herausgegeben von San Marte [A. Schulz],' Halle, 1854, 8vo. 'The British History, translated into English from the Latin of Jeffrey of Monmouth, with a large preface concerning the authority of the history, by Aaron Thompson,' London, 1718, 8vo; a new edition, revised and corrected, by J. A. Giles, London, 1842, 8vo; again without the preface, in 'Six Old English Chronicles' (Bohn's Ser. 1848, small 8vo). 'Legendary Tales of the Ancient Britons, by L. J. Menzies,' London, 1864, small 8vo, is mainly drawn from Geoffrey. 2. 'Prophetia Anglicana Merlini Ambrosii Britanni, ex incubo olim (ut hominibus fama est) ante annos mille ducentos circiter in Anglia nati, Vaticinia et prædictiones, a Galfredo Monumet. Latine conversæ, una cum septem libris explanationum Alani de Insulis,' Francofurti, 1603, small 8vo; again as 'Prophetia Anglicana et Romana, hoc est Merlini Ambrosii Britanni,' Francof. 1608, 8vo, and also in 1649, 8vo. 3. 'Gaufridi Arthuri Monemuthensis Archidiaconi postea vero episcopi Asaphensis, de vita et vaticiniis Merlini Calidonii carmen heroicum,' Roxburghe Club, 1830, 4to, edited by W. H. Black; 'Galfridi de Monemuta Vita Merlini: vie de Merlin attribuée à Geoffrey de Monmouth, suivie des prophéties de ce barde, tirées du ive livre de l'Histoire des Bretons, publiées d'après les MSS. de Londres, par Francisque Michel et Thomas Wright,' Paris, 1837, 8vo. The 'Vita Merlini' and 'Vaticinia' are also in A. F. Gfroerer's 'Prophetæ veteres pseudepigraphi,' Stuttgart, 1840, 8vo, and in 'Die Sagen von Merlin von San Marte [A. Schulz],' Halle, 1853, 8vo.

[Much information has been collected by Mr. Ward in his valuable Catalogue of Romances in the MSS. Department of the British Museum, 1883; a biography is in Wright's Biographia Britannica Literaria Anglo-Norman period, 1846, pp. 143-50; the notices by Bale, Leland, Pits, and Tanner are full of fables. See also Haddan and Stubbs's Councils, 1859, i. 360-1; Wright's Essays on Archæological Subjects, 1861, i. 202-226; Legends of pre-Roman Britain, in Dublin Univ. Mag. April 1876, an excellent sketch of the literary influence of Geoffrey, by T. Gilray; Hardy's Catalogue of Materials relating to History, 1862-71, 3 vols.; T. Warton's Hist. of English Poetry (Hazlitt), 1871, 4 vols.; Encyclop. Brit. xx. s.v. 'Romance;' Skene's Four Ancient Books of Wales, i. 22-6; Romania, 1883, pp. 367-76; G. Heeger's Die Trojanersage der Britten, 1889, 8vo; N. Mitth. a. d. Gebiet Hist.-Antiq. Forsch., Halle, 1862, pp. 49-75; Dunlop's Hist. of Fiction (Wilson), 1888, 2 vols.; Der Münchener Brut, herausg. von Hoffmann u. Vollmöller, Halle, 1877, 8vo; Acta SS. Boll. 21 Oct. ix. 94-8; Archæological Journal, xv. 1858, pp. 299-312; a Letter from Bishop Lloyd in N. Owen's British Remains, 1777; L. A. Lemoyne de la Borderie, Études historiques bretonnes, 1883; Jahrb. für roman. u. englische Lit. bd. v. and ix.; P. Paris's Mémoire sur l'ancienne chronique dite de Nennius et sur l'histoire des Bretons de Monmouth, in Comptes Roy. Acad. des Inscr. 1865, vol. i.] H. R. T.

GEOFFREY (d. 1154), abbot of Dunfermline, monk, and afterwards prior of Christchurch, Canterbury, must have been elected prior about October 1126, for his predecessor, Conrad, died on 16 Feb. 1127, after having been abbot of Holme for eighteen weeks (J. DE OXENEDES, p. 294). Geoffrey witnesses as prior a charter granted to the monks of Rochester by Archbishop William (*Textus Roffensis*, Hearne's ed. p. 156, not Archbishop Ralph, as stated in *Anglia Sacra*). In 1128, at the request of David of Scotland, he became first abbot of Dunfermline in Fife, and was ordained by Robert, bishop of St. Andrews. Florence of Worcester, who is our authority for this, calls him a man of distinguished piety. The church of Dunfermline was dedicated during his tenure of the abbacy in 1150 (*Chron. Holyrood*). He is stated to have written 'Historia Apostolica,' a work which has apparently perished. He died in 1154 (*Chron. S. Crucis Edinb.*) His name is given as Gaufridus or Gosfridus; the former seems the more correct.

[Wharton's Anglia Sacra, i. 137, 161, 796; Dempster's Hist. Eccles. Scot. vii. 602.]

C. L. K.

GEOFFREY (d. 1178), abbot of Dunfermline, was nephew of Geoffrey (d. 1154) [q. v.], whom he succeeded as abbot in 1154 (*Chron. S. Crucis Edinb.*; *Anglia Sacra*, i. 161). He was the recipient of two bulls from Alexander III, the first undated, confirming the grant by Malcolm IV of the church of the Holy Trinity at Dunkeld to Dunfermline, the second dated June 1163, confirming all grants yet made or to be made to Dunfermline (*Reg. Dunf.* Bannatyne Club, p. 151). He appears as witness to several charters of Malcolm IV, of William the Lion, and of Bishops Arnold and Robert of St. Andrews. He was one of the ecclesiastics who at the convention of Falaise in 1175 conceded that 'the English church may have that right in the church of Scotland which it ought to have by right;' a cautious method of saying that the church of Scotland was and always had been independent of England. This would harmonise with Dempster's statement that he was a vigorous defender of the independence of the church of Scotland, and wrote 'pro exemptione ecclesiæ Scoticæ' (vii. 611). Geoffrey died in 1178 (*Chron. Melrose*).

[Hoveden, ii. 80; Gordon's Monasticon, p. 417.]

C. L. K.

GEOFFREY (1158–1186), count of Brittany, fourth son of Henry II, by his queen, Eleanor, was born on 23 Sept. 1158, and was probably called Geoffrey after his uncle, the Count of Nantes, then lately dead, his father, perhaps from his birth, hoping to provide for him by the acquisition of Brittany. As Henry had set up and supported Count Conan the Little, he had good reason to expect that he would not oppose his designs, but he had to reckon with the ill-will of Louis VII and the dislike of the Breton lords to Norman domination. During the war of 1166–7 which Henry undertook on Conan's behalf he proposed that Geoffrey should marry the count's daughter and heiress, Constance, who was then five, and should be recognised as the heir to Brittany. Conan agreed, and gave up Brittany to Henry, reserving for himself only the county of Guingamp and the honour of Richemont. In January 1169 Henry and Louis agreed at Montmirail that Geoffrey should do homage for Brittany to his eldest brother Henry, as duke of Normandy, and Henry did homage for it to Louis (ROBERT OF TORIGNI, ii. 12). Accordingly Geoffrey was sent over from England in May, was acknowledged on his arrival at Rennes by Stephen, the bishop, and other prelates, and received the homage of the Breton lords in the church of St. Peter. He joined his father at Nantes, and after Christmas accompanied him to different parts of Brittany, receiving homage from the lords who had failed to attend at Rennes (*Gesta Henrici*, i. 3). While Henry lay sick at Domfront in August 1170, he divided his dominions among his sons by will, and left Brittany to Geoffrey, with Constance as his wife. Conan died on 20 Feb. 1171, and Henry at once took measures to secure Brittany, and adjudged Guingamp and Richemont to Geoffrey. The following Christmas Geoffrey attended the court of his brother Henry at Bures. He and his brother Richard were living with their mother in England in 1173, and were sent by her to the French court to join the young prince Henry in a revolt against their father (*ib.* p. 40). The brothers took oath at a council at Paris that they would not make any peace with their father except by the advice of Louis and the French barons. Several Breton lords joined in the revolt. Geoffrey marched with his brothers in the French army to invade Normandy. At the conference held at Gisors on 25 Sept. Henry offered to give up to him all the hereditary estates of Constance as soon as he married her with the pope's consent. As, however, Louis was not willing that a reconciliation should as yet take place between Henry and his sons, the offer was not accepted. On 30 Sept. of the following year Henry made peace with his sons at a meeting held at Mont-Louis, near Amboise; he promised Geoffrey half the revenues of Brittany in money until his marriage with Constance, and accepted his homage. Geoffrey did his homage at Le Mans early in 1175, and before Easter was sent by his father into Brittany to destroy the fortifications which had been raised during the rebellion, Roland de Dinan being sent with him to act as his father's representative. By Roland's advice he acted obediently towards his father, and cultivated the goodwill of the Breton lords. He forfeited the possessions of Eudo of Porhoët, one of the most powerful of the rebel party (ROB. TORIGNI, ii. 53). In company with Richard he came over to England at Easter 1176, landed at Southampton, and spent the feast at Winchester with his father, who received his sons with great joy (*Gesta Henrici*, i. 115). After the festival was over, he received his father's permission to cross to Normandy (HOVEDEN, ii. 93); he returned to England and spent Christmas with the king at Nottingham. He seems to have stayed in England until the following August; he accompanied his father from Portsmouth to Normandy on the 17th, and was at once sent against the rebel lord Guyomar de Léon, whom he compelled to submit (ROB. TORIGNI, ii. 67). He spent Christmas with his father at Angers. On 6 Aug. 1178 Henry knighted him at Woodstock (R. DICETO, i. 426). He at once sailed to Normandy, and engaged in feats of arms on the border between Normandy and France and elsewhere, for he was anxious to share in the military renown of his brothers (*Gesta Henrici*, i. 207). He returned to England at Christmas, which he spent with the king at Winchester. After Easter 1179 he distinguished himself in another war against Guyomar, whom he utterly subdued, leaving him only two lordships until the following Christmas, when the defeated rebel promised that he would take his departure for the Holy Land, and giving his son only a small share of his father's estates (ROB. TORIGNI, ii. 81).

In the following November Geoffrey attended the coronation of Philip II, which took place before the death of Louis, and did homage to him for Brittany (CANON. LAUDUN., *Recueil des Historiens*, xiii. 683), and in 1181, in conjunction with his brothers Henry and Richard, upheld the new king against the lords who were in rebellion against him, humbling the Count of Sancerre, and giving Philip help against the Duke of Burgundy, the Countess of Champagne, and the Count of Flanders (DICETO, ii. 9). Towards the end of July he married Constance (ROB. TORIGNI, ii. 104 *n.*) He spent the festival of St. John 1182 with his father at Grandmont, and feasted with the monks there, and then went with Henry to help Richard, who was besieging the rebels in Périgueux (GEOFFREY OF VIGEOIS, *Recueil*, xviii. 212). He was at Caen with his father and brothers during the Christmas of 1182, and went with them to Le Mans, when Henry, in order to put a stop to the practices which his eldest son had been carrying on against his younger son Richard in Aquitaine, commanded both Richard and Geoffrey to do homage to their eldest brother. Geoffrey obeyed; Richard refused, and a fresh quarrel broke out between him and the younger Henry. The old king ordered Geoffrey and his eldest brother to make war upon Richard, and Geoffrey raised an army of Brabantine mercenaries, invaded Poitou, and wasted it with fire and sword. Henry saw that unless he interfered Richard would be crushed, and ordered his sons to come to a conference. Geoffrey paid no regard to this, went on with the war, and in February 1183 occupied the castle of Limoges, where he was joined by the younger Henry. On 1 March Henry II, who was reconciled to Richard, began the siege of the castle. During its progress he was twice shot at by the partisans of his sons, and in their presence (*Gesta Henrici*, i. 296). While the younger Henry drew off his father's attention by false promises, Geoffrey and his Brabantines wasted the country, robbing churches, burning towns and villages, and sparing neither age nor sex nor condition. He sent to his father in a time of truce, requesting him to order two of his lords, Jerome of Montreuil and Oliver FitzErnis, to come to him, as though he wished to offer terms through them. When they came, his men, in his presence and with his approval, wounded Jerome with the sword, and threw Oliver over the bridge into the river. Again, he pretended that he wished to confer with his father about bringing the war to an end, and by this means got admission into the town of Limoges, where he plundered the shrine of St. Martial, carried off gold and silver plate from other churches, and used his spoil to pay his mercenaries (*ib.* p. 299). The death of his eldest brother Henry on 11 June put Geoffrey in a different position. It was perhaps at this time (ROBERT OF TORIGNI puts it under 1182) that the war was carried into his own possessions, and that Henry's troops seized the castle of Rennes. Geoffrey besieged them, and destroyed the abbey of St. George and part of the town, and also destroyed the town and castle of Bécherel, belonging to Roland of Dinan. He made peace with his father at Angers. Henry declared his castles forfeited, and enforced a reconciliation with his brother Richard. In 1184, probably after Henry had returned to England in June (NORGATE, ii. 233),

Geoffrey joined his youngest brother John in making war on Richard, who retaliated by invading Brittany. Henry called his sons to England in November, and caused them to make peace with each other. He then sent Geoffrey to Normandy. Geoffrey held a parliament at Rennes in 1185, and promulgated a series of six articles called the 'Assize of Count Geoffrey,' to restrain the partition of baronies and knight's fees, to prevent the marriage of heiresses without permission, and generally to preserve the rights of the lord (MORICE, *Histoire de Bretagne*, i. 303). Before the spring was over, Geoffrey was worsted by Richard, who had renewed the war against him, and Henry was forced to go over to Normandy and bring Richard to order. Geoffrey was, however, wrathful with his father; he had set his heart on obtaining Anjou after the death of the young Henry, and his father would not give him the county, for he made Richard, now his eldest son, duke of Normandy and count of Anjou in the stead of Henry. Geoffrey's attempt to gain Anjou was no doubt at the bottom of Richard's quarrel with him, though it was nominally about boundaries. Philip of France urged Geoffrey's claim, and Geoffrey, when he found that his father would not be moved, went to Paris in 1186 and, it is said, engaged in a plot against him. Philip received him with joy, for Geoffrey is said to have proposed to transfer his homage for Brittany from his father and Richard and become the man of the king of France, receiving from him the office of grand seneschal. While he was in Paris he died on 19 Aug. at the age of twenty-eight, being killed, according to some accounts, in a tournament (*Gesta Henrici*, i. 350; HOVEDEN, ii. 309), according to others dying of disease (GERVASE, i. 336; RIGORD, *Recueil*, xvii. 20), of a fever (GIRALDUS CAMBRENSIS, *De Instructione Principis*, p. 34), or of a sudden complaint in the bowels which seized him on account of his threats against his father (*Gesta Henrici* u. s.) Philip lamented much for him, embalmed his body, and buried it in the church of Notre-Dame. Geoffrey was good-looking and fairly tall, a good soldier, and an eloquent speaker, but he was false and plausible, universally distrusted and known as a mischief-maker and a contriver of evil (*De Instructione Principis*, p. 35; *Topographia Hibernica*, p. 199; *Gesta Henrici*, i. 295, passim). He left a daughter named Eleanor (two daughters according to RALPH DE DICETO, i. 41), and his wife Constance with child. She bore on 29–30 April in the following year a son, Arthur [q. v.], the victim of his uncle King John's ambition.

[Gesta Henrici, vol. ii., R. Diceto, Gervase, Roger de Hoveden, all ed. Stubbs (Rolls Ser.); William of Newburgh (Engl. Hist. Soc.); Giraldus Cambrensis, De Instructione Principis, Anglia Christiana, and Topogr. Hibern., Opera, vol. v. (Rolls Ser.); Robert of Torigni, ed. Delisle; Canon. Laudunensis, Recueil des Historiens, vol. xiii., Rigord, tom. xvii., Geoffrey of Vigeois, tom. xviii.; Morice, Histoire de Bretagne, vol. i.; Norgate's Angevin Kings, vol. ii.]   W. H.

GEOFFREY DE **VINSAUF** (*fl.* 1200), poet. [See VINSAUF.]

GEOFFREY DE **MUSCHAMP** (*d.* 1208), bishop of Lichfield and Coventry, was probably a member of the family of Muschamp, barons by tenure of Wallovere in Northumberland (NICOLAS, p. 343). Geoffrey was appointed archdeacon of Cleveland in 1189, after the death of Henry II, and without the knowledge of King Richard. Geoffrey of York had made use of his position as chancellor to affix the late king's seals on his own authority, probably acting on directions given by Henry before his death. In spite of the manner of his appointment, Muschamp sided with the chapter in the subsequent quarrel between that body and the archbishop; he was one of the envoys sent on behalf of the chapter to Rome, whence in September 1194 they returned with letters of absolution. Soon after the archbishop, having made peace with Richard, got Muschamp disseised of his archdeaconry on the ground that the appointment was informal. At Southwell in 1195 Muschamp resisted John, bishop of Whithern, who was acting for the archbishop. In June of the same year he was present as archdeacon of Cleveland at the legatine visitation held by Hubert Walter at York. In 1198 he was elected bishop of Lichfield and Coventry, apparently by the monks of the latter place without reference to the canons of Lichfield (MATT. PARIS, ii. 444), but by the advice of Hubert and favour of King Richard. He was consecrated by Hubert at Canterbury on 21 June 1198 (his own autograph in the archives of Canterbury). He was present at John's coronation in May 1199 and at the council of Westminster in 1200. In 1204 he appears as a commissioner to decide the suit between the Bishop of Worcester and abbey of Evesham (*Chron. Evesh.* p. 130). According to Gervase (ii. 100) he was one of the bishops who fled from England in 1207. He died on 6 Oct. 1208, and is said to have been buried at Lichfield, which church he endowed with twenty marks annually for beer. Like other bishops of Lichfield and Coventry, he is also called bishop of Chester.

[Annales Monastici; Roger of Hoveden; Wharton's Anglia Sacra, i. 436, 446.]   C. L. K.

GEOFFREY (*d.* 1212), archbishop of York, has been generally described as a son of Henry II and 'Fair Rosamond' [see CLIFFORD, ROSAMOND]. This claim is quite untenable. The only contemporary writer who gives any account of Geoffrey's mother, Walter Map, says that she was a woman of the most degraded character, named Ykenai or Hikenai, and that she persuaded the young king to acknowledge Geoffrey as his son, despite a general assurance to the contrary (W. MAP, *De Nug. Curial.*, dist. v. c. 6). All the other writers of the time habitually describe Geoffrey as 'the king's son,' without hinting a doubt of his paternity. Gervase of Canterbury when seeking to discredit Geoffrey calls him 'regio natus ... sanguine, ut putabatur' (GERV. CANT. i. 520). Elsewhere he describes him as 'frater regis, sed nothus,' without further remark. It is clear that no doubt was felt by Henry or by Geoffrey himself, while both Richard and John always acknowledged Geoffrey as their brother, and Richard even suspected him of a design upon the crown, which could scarcely have entered the head of any one if his origin had been generally doubted. Map may have exaggerated the social degradation of Geoffrey's mother. From the fact that William Longsword, son of an elder William Longsword, who was an illegitimate son of Henry II, laid claim in the reign of Henry III to the estates of one Roger of Akeny, which suggests Ykenai, the late Mr. J. F. Dimock conjectured that these names might possibly be identical, and that Geoffrey's mother might be a knight's daughter or sister of Norman origin (GIR. CAMBR. *Opp.* vii. pref. xxxvii). The sole mention of this claim of William Longsword is in the Close Roll (12 Hen. III, m. 5, date 15 July). There is nothing to indicate the nature or origin of William's connection with the family of Akeny, and nothing but the slight verbal similarity to connect Akeny with Ykenai; while the great difference of age which almost certainly existed between Geoffrey and the elder William Longsword renders it very improbable that they were sons of the same mother. Some modern writers have referred to the 'Chronicle of Kirkstall' as authority for the statement that Geoffrey was born in 1159. But the 'Kirkstall Chronicle' in its present form dates only from the reign of Henry V; and the 'Galfridus filius regis [Henrici] secundi' whose birth it records is clearly Geoffrey's half-brother, Queen Eleanor's child of the same name, who certainly was born in September 1158. Gerald of Wales, in his 'Life of Geoffrey of York,' says that Geoffrey was scarcely twenty when appointed bishop of Lincoln, i.e. in April 1173, and elsewhere that he was about forty when consecrated to York, i.e. in August 1191. Neither of the dates thus indicated for his birth, 1151 or 1153, is in itself impossible. The later date seems the more probable. Map's language would seem to imply that he was regarded as an Englishman by birth. Map says that Ykenai presented him to the king 'at the beginning of his reign.' Now, Henry remained in England twelve months after his coronation in December 1154; he had also spent there nearly the whole of 1153; and his previous visit there had terminated in January 1150. Shortly after Henry's accession, in any case, Geoffrey was acknowledged as his son and taken into his household, where he was brought up on a footing of practical equality with Eleanor's children. While still a mere boy he was put into deacon's orders, made archdeacon of Lincoln, and endowed with a prebend at St. Paul's, till in April 1173 Henry caused the Lincoln chapter to elect him as their bishop. Shortly afterwards a revolt, in which Eleanor's three elder sons took part, broke out in Henry's continental dominions. Geoffrey at once levied contributions throughout his diocese for the royal treasury. Next spring he found it wiser to return the money which he had collected, and appeal to the men of Lincolnshire to follow him in person against the disaffected barons of northern England. After taking and razing Roger Mowbray's castle of Kinardferry in the Isle of Axholme, he joined his forces to those of Archbishop Roger of York; led the united host to a successful siege of Kirby Malzeard; threatened Mowbray's third fortress, Thirsk, by erecting a rival fort at Topcliffe; compelled the Bishop of Durham to give pledges for his loyalty, and frightened the king of Scots into withdrawing from his siege of Bowes Castle. One foreign writer attributes the crowning exploit of the war—the capture of the Scottish king at Alnwick in July (1174)—to 'the king's son, Mamzer,' a description which at this period can point to no one but Geoffrey (GEOFF. VIGEOIS, l. i. c. 67). It is, however, clear from the silence of the English historians that Geoffrey was not present on this occasion, although it is probable than some of his followers were, as the words of his biographer imply that he had an indirect share in it (GIR. CAMBR. *Vita Galfr. Archiep.* l. i. c. 3). He had at any rate well earned the greeting with which Henry met him at Huntingdon when the struggle was over: 'Baseborn indeed have my other children shown themselves; this alone is my true son!' On 8 Oct. Geoffrey, by his father's desire, followed him into Normandy, with the purpose of either proceeding in person to Rome or sending representatives to plead there for his confirmation in the see of Lincoln. The obstacles of his youth and his birth were overcome by a papal dispensation, and his election was confirmed by Archbishop Richard of Canterbury in the pope's name at Woodstock on 1 July 1175. Geoffrey himself returned to England on 18 July, and on 1 Aug. was received in procession at Lincoln. Henry sent him to study in the schools of Tours before he would allow him to be consecrated. Before Michaelmas 1178 he was home again, for the Pipe Roll of that year contains a charge of 7l. 10s. for the passage of ' Geoffrey, elect of Lincoln, and John, his brother,' from Southampton to Normandy; and at Christmas Henry, Geoffrey, and John were all in England together. For three more years Geoffrey continued to enjoy the revenues and administer the temporal affairs of his see without taking any further steps to become a real bishop, or even a priest. William of Newburgh declares he was 'more skilful to fleece the Lord's sheep than to feed them;' Walter Map, now precentor of Lincoln, who had succeeded Geoffrey in his canonry at St. Paul's, and had long been his rival at court, charges him with wringing exorbitant sums from his clergy (especially, it appears, from Map himself). To his cathedral church he seems to have been a benefactor; soon after his election he redeemed its ornaments, which his predecessor had pledged to a Jew—the famous Aaron of Lincoln—for 300l., and added to them by gifts of his own; he also gave two large and fine bells; he was active in reclaiming the alienated estates of the bishopric, and, according to his enthusiastic biographer, he began the process of filling his chapter with scholars and distinguished men, which in the next reign made Lincoln one of the chief centres of English learning (GIR. CAMBR. Vita S. Rem. c. xxiv.) For all spiritual purposes, however, the diocese had been without a chief pastor ever since 1166. In 1181 therefore Pope Alexander III bade Archbishop Richard either compel the elect of Lincoln to receive consecration at once or consecrate some other man to the see. It seems that Geoffrey hereupon appealed to the pope and managed to obtain from him a respite of three more years, but that Henry, having now planned another scheme for his son's advancement, determined to enforce the papal mandate (PET. BLOIS, Ep. lxxv. The editor of 'Fasti Eborac.' i. 253, and note n, refers to this letter as written to Roger, dean of Lincoln, and places it in 1174. But no Roger appears as dean of Lincoln till 1195; the letter is ad-

dressed simply ' Rogerio decano,' and the mention of the fifteen years' vacancy of the see shows that it cannot have been written earlier than the end of 1181, for Geoffrey's predecessor, Robert de Chesney [q. v.], died at the close of 1166). Accordingly Geoffrey, after consultation with his father, announced his resolve to give up the bishopric. His resignation was formally completed at Marlborough on the feast of Epiphany 1182. Geoffrey, it seems, was a very indistinct speaker, and when he recited the formula of resignation Archbishop Richard twice had to ask him what he was saying, whereupon Map answered for him, ' French of Marlborough,' alluding to a local tradition which said that whosoever drank of a certain well in that town spoke bad French for the rest of his life. The office for which Geoffrey had exchanged his bishopric was that of chancellor of England. To this, besides the archdeaconry of Lincoln which he still retained, Henry added the treasurership of York, the archdeaconry of Rouen, and a string of other benefices and honours, ecclesiastical and secular, among which are mentioned the honour of Wycombe in Berkshire, the 'county of Giffard in Normandy' (i.e. apparently the honour of Longueville-la-Giffart and its appurtenances in the Pays de Caux and the Roumois, escheated in 1164 by the death of Walter Giffard, earl of Buckingham; STAPLETON, Observ. on Norm. Exch. Rolls, p. civ), and the castles of Langeais and Baugé in Anjou, with a revenue amounting to five hundred marks a year in England and as many in Normandy.

In 1187 Geoffrey commanded one of the four divisions of Henry's troops against a threatened attack of Philip Augustus; in November 1188 he was entrusted with the duty of securing the Angevin castles against the united forces of Philip and Henry's son Richard; in June 1189, when the unnatural allies drove the king from his refuge at Le Mans, Geoffrey accompanied him in his flight, led the remnant of his body-guard safe into Alençon, hurried back with a fresh force to cover his retreat into Anjou, and never left him again, save on the day of Henry's submission at Colombières, when he begged permission to absent himself from the scene of his father's humiliation. Gerald has left a touching picture of the last scenes at Chinon, when Geoffrey's patient devotion won back the dying king from his ravings against his undutiful children, to die with a blessing on his one loyal son. The chancellor accompanied his father's corpse to its burial at Fontevraud; there he resigned his seal to his half-brother, the new king Richard; and ten days later (20 July 1189) Richard nominated him for the archbishopric of York. This nomination had been Henry's last earthly desire; and in later days Geoffrey seems to have confessed to Richard that while the seal remained in his possession after Henry's death, he had used it—possibly in accordance with Henry's intentions—for the purpose of sealing collations to three vacant stalls in York minster. On 10 Aug. Geoffrey was elected by a majority of the York chapter. The minority, headed by the dean, Hubert Walter, appealed against the election as invalidated by the absence of Hubert, and of the one existing suffragan of the province, Bishop Hugh of Durham; and this appeal, coupled with the inconsistent behaviour of Geoffrey himself, who desired the offered preferment, but still shrank from undertaking its responsibilities, caused Richard's formal confirmation of his appointment to be delayed till 16 Sept. On the 23rd Geoffrey was ordained priest at Southwell by a newly consecrated suffragan of his own, John, bishop of Whithern, in defiance of Archbishop Baldwin of Canterbury, who, by an unwarrantable stretch of his authority as metropolitan of all Britain, claimed for himself the exclusive right of ordaining and consecrating the elect of York. Shortly afterwards Richard commissioned his half-brother to escort the king of Scots on his journey to Canterbury, where he was to do homage to the new English king. Geoffrey on his way northward stopped at York; there his refusal, on grounds of ecclesiastical etiquette, to install some new members of the chapter who had been appointed by Richard during the vacancy of the see, revived the irritation both of the canons and of the king; his lay estates were confiscated, the messengers whom he had commissioned to fetch his pall from Rome were forbidden to cross the sea, and on his return to court he was confronted by all his opponents at once, all, on various grounds, renewing their appeal against his election. He succeeded, nevertheless, in getting it confirmed by the papal legate, John of Anagni, and in buying back Richard's favour by a promise of 3,000l. Owing, however, to the violence of party feeling in his chapter, and to the continued hostility of Hugh Pudsey, bishop of Durham, whom Richard left as justiciar in England during his own absence on crusade, there was no possibility of raising the money; and when Geoffrey appeared in Normandy in March 1190 with empty hands, Richard again seized his estates, sent envoys to Rome to hinder if possible his final confirmation by the pope, and made him take an oath not to set foot in England for three years. Geoffrey followed the king as far as Vézelay, and there managed to

purchase restitution by a payment of eight hundred marks down and a promise of twelve hundred more. He then withdrew to Tours, where he remained more than a year; for, although Clement III had issued a brief confirming his election as early as 7 March 1190, no mandate for his consecration followed till May 1191, when it seems to have been obtained by the diplomacy of Queen Eleanor. Richard, now at Messina, apparently began to think that in his own prolonged absence and that of the Archbishop of Canterbury—also bound on crusade—an archbishop of York might be useful as a check upon William of Longchamp, who, as chancellor of England and legate of the Roman see, was now virtually supreme alike in church and state. He therefore charged his mother to intercede with the pope in Geoffrey's behalf. The result was a mandate from Celestine III to Archbishop Bartholomew of Tours authorising him to consecrate Geoffrey. This was fulfilled on 18 Aug., and the new archbishop received his pall on the same day through the abbot of Marmoutier. Geoffrey now asserted that Richard, before they parted at Vézelay, had released him from his promise of absence from England; but William of Longchamp, doubting the truth of his story, had ordered his arrest as soon as he should touch the English shore. On 14 Sept. he landed at Dover in disguise, was recognised, and nearly captured, but made his escape to the neighbouring priory of St. Martin's; thence, after a five days' blockade, the chancellor's representatives dragged him by main force to prison in the castle. This outrage brought to a head the indignation which had long been rising on all sides against the chancellor; the pressure of the barons, with John as their leader, procured Geoffrey's release on parole; and in the struggle which followed Geoffrey and John made common cause against Longchamp. His fall in October left the Archbishop of York the highest ecclesiastical authority in England. On All Saints' day he was enthroned at York, and the strife with his chapter and his chief suffragan was at once renewed. On his last visit to York, at Epiphany 1190, he had excommunicated two of the chief dignitaries of the cathedral church for a gross violation of ecclesiastical decency (they had begun vespers without waiting for the archbishop-elect, and when he silenced them and recommenced the service himself, had put out the lights and left him to finish it alone in the dark). He also excommunicated Bishop Hugh of Durham, who refused him his profession of canonical obedience, and the prioress of St. Clement's (or Clementhorpe), who withstood his scheme for reducing her little nunnery to dependence on the abbey of Godstow. Bishop and prioress alike appealed to the pope; another feud broke out in the chapter; the queen-mother summoned Geoffrey and Hugh to London at mid-Lent 1192, and tried to bring them to reason; but the attempt only gave Geoffrey an opportunity for plunging into another quarrel, by causing his cross to be borne erect before him in the Temple Church, a ceremonial to which he had no right outside his own province. By threatening to seize all the estates of the see, the queen and the justiciars at last drove Geoffrey to patch up a reconciliation with all his opponents except his dean, Henry Marshall, and Bishop Hugh of Durham. In October three commissioners appointed by the pope to settle the dispute between Hugh and his metropolitan decided it in Geoffrey's favour, and brought Hugh to submission. Next spring (1193), upon Richard's imprisonment, Geoffrey and Hugh joined hands in resistance to John's attempted usurpation; Geoffrey first helped the sheriff of Yorkshire to fortify Doncaster, and then went to assist Hugh in besieging John's castle of Tickhill. About the same time the last obstacle to peace at York seemed to be removed by the advancement of the dean, Henry Marshall, to the see of Exeter. Geoffrey now wished to bestow the deanery on his brother Peter (probably a half-brother by the mother's side); Richard, however, wrote from Germany urging him to give it to John de Bethune; Peter was at Paris and could not be installed at once; and Geoffrey nominated one of his own chaplains, Simon of Apulia, telling him that he was only to keep the place for Peter. The canons refused to submit to this arrangement, and formally elected Simon as their dean; whereupon Geoffrey annulled his appointment altogether, and presented a favourite clerk of the king, Philip of Poitou, in his stead.

At this juncture came a demand from the justiciars for a fourth part of the revenue and movable goods of every man throughout the realm to furnish the king's ransom, backed by an urgent appeal from Richard himself. Geoffrey was zealous in the cause; but when he communicated the demand to his chapter the canons charged him with attempting to subvert the liberties of the church, and refused to have anything more to do with him. Both parties appealed to the pope on the question of the deanery; Richard, however, whom their envoys went to visit on the way to Rome, forbade the appeal, and summoned Geoffrey to his presence. Geoffrey was on the point of taking ship to obey this summons, when he was recalled by tidings that

his canons had risen in open mutiny, stopped the minster services and the ringing of the minster bells, stripped the altars, locked up the archbishop's stall, and blocked up the door which led from his palace into the church. Returning to York on 1 Jan. 1194, he excommunicated the canons and appointed other clerks to conduct the services in their stead. It appears that he at the same time took possession, for Richard's benefit, of the treasures of the minster, for it is certain that they were given for the king's ransom and afterwards bought back by the chapter (*Fabric Rolls of York Minster*, Surtees Soc. p. 152). Four of the chief rebels now again hurried to gain the ear of the king. Richard, angry at Geoffrey's failure to obey his summons, gave them leave to prosecute their appeal; they went on to Rome, and there persuaded Celestine III to confirm the appointment of Simon as dean, and to issue a sentence against Geoffrey which virtually condemned him unheard. On 31 May three commissioners were appointed to enforce the restoration of the expelled canons, with compensation for their losses. On 8 June three other commissioners were appointed to hold an inquiry at York into the various charges against Geoffrey. A third brief, issued a week later, granted to the chapter of York privileges which made them practically independent of the archbishop altogether. Geoffrey's old opponent, Hubert Walter, was now archbishop of Canterbury and justiciar of England. Shortly after Hubert's election, in June 1193, Geoffrey had again appeared at a council in London with his cross erect before him; and a Canterbury writer declares that when he set out to obey Richard's summons to Germany, he travelled along byways in order to have his cross carried before him unopposed through the southern province, and that a prohibition from Hubert was the real cause of his return to York (GERV. CANT. i. 523). When, in March 1194, the two primates came to meet Richard at Nottingham, which was in Geoffrey's province, Hubert in his turn appeared with his cross erect. An altercation followed. Richard at the moment could not afford to quarrel with either primate; he wanted the three thousand marks which Geoffrey offered him for the sheriffdom of Yorkshire, and therefore refused to listen to the complaints brought against him in the diocese; on the other hand, he begged him not to appear with his cross at the coronation in Winchester Cathedral on 17 April, whereupon Geoffrey stayed away from that ceremony altogether. On the 23rd, however, he presented himself with his cross erect before the king at Waltham. Richard answered Hubert's complaints by referring him to the pope for a settlement of the quarrel, and completed Geoffrey's momentary triumph by restoring his Angevin estates and forcing William of Longchamp to make compurgation for his share in the archbishop's arrest in 1191. On 12 May, however, Richard's departure over sea left Hubert supreme in the realm. The canons of York at once laid before him, as justiciar, a charge of spoliation and extortion against their primate. In August Hubert sent to York a committee of justices to investigate the case; they began by casting into prison certain servants of Geoffrey; they summoned Geoffrey himself to stand his trial before them, and, on his refusal, confiscated all his archiepiscopal estates except Ripon, replaced the canons whom he had expelled, and appointed two custodians to check him in the discharge of his functions as sheriff of Yorkshire. In September the appellants came back from Rome with their papal letters, one of which, ordering the restitution of the canons—now already accomplished by the secular arm—was published by Hugh of Durham in York minster on Michaelmas day. Geoffrey at once appealed against the papal sentences; then he went into Normandy to the king, and, by a present of a thousand marks and a promise of another thousand, obtained an order for the restitution of his rights and properties, as well as for the deprivation of the three prebendaries whom he himself had illegally collated under his dead father's seal in July 1189, and who had now turned against him. In January 1195 the papal commissioners opened their inquiry at York; there they were met by an announcement of Geoffrey's appeal, and they accordingly cited both parties to appear at Rome on 1 June. Geoffrey begged for a further respite, ostensibly on a plea of health, in reality, it seems, in consequence of the king's opposition to his journey. The pope granted him an adjournment to 18 Nov., but even then he did not appear. The papal commissioners in England, when urged to suspend him for this contumacy, refused, the chief of them, St. Hugh of Lincoln, declaring that he would rather be suspended himself (ROG. HOVEDEN, iii. 306). The sentence of suspension was, however, pronounced by the pope in person on 23 Dec. Meanwhile Geoffrey's long stay at the Norman court had ended in a fresh quarrel with his half-brother, and before the year closed Richard again deprived him not only of his archiepiscopal property, but also of the sheriffdom of Yorkshire. At length early in 1196 Geoffrey in despair betook himself to Rome. There the tables were suddenly turned. His ad-

versaries were compelled to own that they could not prove their case, and, in consequence, the pope was compelled to restore him to his archiepiscopal office. The king, however, determined that the sentence should be ignored, and Geoffrey, after a brief stay in France, again withdrew to Rome, where he apparently remained for about two years. A fresh charge made against him in 1196, of attempting to rid himself of his chief opponents at York by means of poison found on the person of one of his envoys in England, seems to have broken down completely; and at last, in 1198, Richard summoned both archbishop and canons to make peace in his presence in Normandy. Geoffrey arrived first; Richard granted him full restitution, and sent him back to Rome 'on the king's business and his own.' As soon as his back was turned, the canons presented themselves and got Richard to promise that the restoration should not take effect till Geoffrey's return. When Geoffrey came back another meeting took place at Les Andelys, but no agreement was reached. Once more Geoffrey went to Rome to lay his case before a new pope, Innocent III, and a remonstrance from Innocent moved Richard to make fresh overtures for reconciliation; but Geoffrey would not accept his conditions without first submitting them to the pope, and the pope insisted on the archbishop's restoration without any conditions at all, threatening, in default, to interdict first the province of York and then the whole kingdom of England. Before Innocent's letter was written Richard was dead. John, however, soon after his crowning ordered the archiepiscopal manors to be handed over to Geoffrey's representatives, and on Midsummer day (1199) he and Geoffrey met at Rouen as brothers and friends. The quarrel between the archbishop and his chapter lingered on for another year. An attempt of Cardinal Peter of Capua to mediate between them was frustrated by the interference of the Archbishop of Canterbury and the Justiciar Geoffrey FitzPeter, who persuaded the king to forbid Geoffrey's return to England save in his own company. It seems that Geoffrey accordingly came over with John in February 1200, and that shortly afterwards he and his chapter were at last formally reconciled at Westminster before two delegates of the pope.

Within a year another fray was well developed. John had summoned Geoffrey to return with him to France and he had not obeyed; he had refused to allow the king's officers to collect the carucage from his lands; he had never yet paid the three thousand marks promised to Richard for the sheriffdom of

Yorkshire. John ordered him to be disseised of all his estates, and transferred the sheriffdom to James de Poterne. James apparently took possession of his new office by main force. Geoffrey retaliated by excommunicating him and his followers, as well as the townsfolk of Beverley, who had broken into the archbishop's park, and all who ' without just cause had stirred up, or should stir up,' his royal brother against him. In October John returned to England, restored Geoffrey's temporalities, and appointed a day for him to answer for his proceedings before the king's court. When John visited York in March 1201, however, a temporary compromise was arranged. John took Geoffrey's barony in pledge for his debts, and appealed to the pope against him (*Rot. Chart.* p. 102). Two months after, Geoffrey managed to turn this truce into a peace by the usual means. John granted him a charter of forgiveness for the past, and confirmation in all his canonical and territorial rights for the future, in consideration of 1,000*l.* to be paid within twelve months, Geoffrey's barony remaining pledged to the crown meanwhile. Eight months later, however, it seems that Geoffrey had not yet received full compensation for the injuries done to him by John's servants during the quarrel (*Rot. Pat.* i. 5). Another dispute between the archbishop and his chapter about the appointment of an archdeacon had begun in the summer of 1200, and was not finally settled till June 1202, when the pope decided it against Geoffrey. In February or March 1204, John, being again at York, formally took the canons under his protection against Geoffrey and all men; and a year later, at the same place, Philip of Poitiers, bishop of Durham, the metropolitan chapter, and the heads of fourteen religious houses in the diocese appealed to Rome in the king's presence against a possible sentence of excommunication or suspension from their primate. One more reconciliation, patched up between the halfbrothers at Worcester in January 1207, lasted only a few weeks. On 9 Feb. John, after vainly endeavouring to win the consent of the bishops to a grant of a fixed proportion of revenue from every beneficed clerk for the needs of the royal treasury, laid a tax of a thirteenth of all chattels, movable and immovable, upon all lay fiefs throughout the realm, except those belonging to the Cistercian order, and on 26 May he called upon the archdeacons to procure a similar contribution from the clergy in general. The writ was issued from York, as if on purpose to goad the archbishop into a desperate act of defiance, for Geoffrey had headed the suc-

cessful opposition to John's first demand. He at once forbade his clergy to pay the tax, and denounced all who should do so as excommunicate. But no one dared to resist the king's demand, and Geoffrey, hurling a last anathema against the collectors and payers of the tax, and against all spoilers of the church in general, fled in despair over sea. His archiepiscopal property was of course seized by the king; he appealed to the pope, and Innocent interfered energetically, putting the church of York under interdict for his sake, but without effect.

Geoffrey was not heard of again till his death in 1212. In a note to Godwin, ' De Præsulibus Angliæ' (p. 677, ed. Richardson, 1743), he is said to have died on 18 Dec. at ' Grosmunt' in Normandy. Mr. Stapleton (*Observ. on Norm. Exch. Rolls*, p. clxx) gives the same date, and shows that Grosmunt stands for the religious house of Notre-Dame-du-Parc, commonly called Grandmont, near Rouen. No contemporary authority for either day or place is forthcoming; but Geoffrey was undoubtedly buried in the church of Notre-Dame-du-Parc, and there his grave and epitaph were still to be seen in the middle of the last century (DUCAREL, *Anglo-Norm. Antiq.*, pp. 37–8). The ' good men' of Grandmont were special favourites of King Henry II, brought by him from Aquitaine to undertake the care of a lazar-house into which he had converted his own hunting-lodge in the park outside Rouen. So it seems that the earliest and best affection of Geoffrey's life was also the most abiding. Unquestionably, secular office in his father's service, rather than the episcopal career into which he was urged against his own better judgment, was Geoffrey's true vocation. Yet even at York the worst charge that could ever be honestly brought against him was that of an impracticable self-will and an ungovernable temper. ' Vir quidem magnæ abstinentiæ et summæ puritatis' (T. STUBBS, p. 400) was the character that, when all struggles were over, he left behind him there.

[Giraldus Cambrensis, Vita Galfridi Archiepiscopi and Vita S. Remigii (Opera, ed. Brewer and Dimock, vols. iv. vii.); William of Newburgh, ed. Howlett; Annales de Waverley (Ann. Monast., ed. Luard, vol. ii.) Gervase of Canterbury, Ralph de Diceto, Gesta Henrici Regis and Roger of Hoveden, ed. Stubbs. The above are all in Rolls Series. See also T. Stubbs's Chronica Pontificum Ecclesiæ Eboracensis, pt. ii. (Hist. of Church of York, ed. Raine, vol. ii.); Walter Map, De Nugis (Camd. Soc.); Geoffrey of Coldingham (Hist. Dunelm. Scriptt. Tres, Surtees Soc.); Roger of Wendover, ed. Coxe (Engl. Hist. Soc.); Peter of Blois, Epistolæ, ed. Giles; Innocent. III Epistolæ, ed. Baluze; Chronicle of Kirkstall (MS. Cotton. Domit. xii.); Geoffrey of Vigeois (in Labbe, Nova Bibl. MSS. Librorum, vol. ii.); Close Roll xii. Hen. III; Rotuli Chartarum, Litterarum Patentium, and De Oblatis et Finibus (Record Comm.); Wilkins's Concilia; Le Neve's Fasti; Stapleton's Observations on Norman Exchequer Rolls (Mag. Rot. Scacc. Norm., vol. ii.); Eyton's Itinerary of King Henry II. Geoffrey's modern biographers are Godwin, De Præsulibus Angliæ; Dixon, Church Hist.; Dixon and Raine, Fasti Eboracenses; and, far above all, Dr. Stubbs's prefaces to Roger of Hoveden, vols. iii. and iv.] K. N.

GEOFFREY OF COLDINGHAM (*fl.* 1214), historian of Durham. [See COLDINGHAM.]

GEOFFREY (*d.*1235?), prior of Coventry, was a monk of Coventry elected prior in 1216. In Wharton's 'Anglia Sacra' (i. 464) the exact date is given as 17 July, but it must have been earlier, for the royal assent was granted to his election, and the sheriff of Leicester was ordered to give him seizin on 8 July (*Lit. Claus.* 18 Joh. p. 276). In 1223, on the death of William of Cornhill [q. v.], a quarrel arose between the monks of Coventry and canons of Lichfield about the election of a new bishop. Both parties petitioned the king for leave to elect, Geoffrey appearing as proctor for his own church. Leave was granted in ambiguous terms 'to those who were accustomed and ought to elect;' the monks thereupon chose Geoffrey, and presented him to Stephen Langton for confirmation. The archbishop refused, and after hearing the canons quashed the election; this sentence was on appeal confirmed by Pope Honorius III, who with the assent of all parties appointed Alexander de Stavenby bishop in 1224. In 1232 Geoffrey resisted the visitation of Bishop Alexander, on the ground that he was not bound to accept a visitor not of his own order; he was suspended, and went to Rome, where the case was decided against him. In 1234 he was engaged in a quarrel with the abbot of St. Augustine's, Bristol. He is the author of a chronicle quoted in Dugdale's 'Antiquities of Warwick' (pp. 100, 105) as by an approved writer. The royal assent to the election of his successor was given on 19 Sept. 1235 (*Pat.* 19 Hen. III, cited in *Monasticon*, iii. 183).

[Annales Monastici, 'Tewkesbury' and 'Dunstable;' Wharton's Anglia Sacra, i. 437–8; Dugdale's Antiq. Warwick.] C. L. K.

GEOFFREY THE GRAMMARIAN, *alias* STARKEY (*fl.* 1440), compiler of the 'Promptorium Parvulorum,' is said by himself in the preamble to the 'Promptorium' (Way's edition, pp. 1–3) to have been a friar-preacher at Lynn. He was bred, if not born, in Norfolk,

for he says that he had followed only the manner of speech of the county of Norfolk, which he had learnt from infancy and of which alone he had perfect knowledge. To this he adds that he was 'reclusus,' which word he probably uses in its strict sense of 'ankyr,' one who was shut up in a building specially appropriated to the purpose, and with a solemn service, by episcopal sanction; after which he could not leave his cell except in case of necessity or with the leave of the bishop; he himself explains 'ankyr' as 'recluse, Anachorita' (p. 12). The name of the author is given in Hearne's edition of Langtoft (ii. 624) as Richard Fraunces, on the strength of a manuscript note in a copy of Pynson's edition of 1499, but a similar note in another copy of the same edition gives the author as 'Galfredus Grammaticus dictus,' and with this Bale, himself an East-Anglian, and writing about a century after the author's time, agrees (p. 631). Bishop Tanner, finding as a note in the margin of the Lincoln MS. 'Galfredus Starkey,' conjectured this to be the full name of the author, but it is equally likely to be that of a former owner of the volume. Geoffrey speaks of himself as ignorant and unskilled, but, pitying the destitution of young clerks, he had drawn up for their use a slight compendium. This is the English-Latin dictionary known as the 'Promptorium Parvulorum,' also called 'Promptorius Parvulorum,' 'Promptorius Puerorum,' and 'Promptuarium Parvulorum Clericorum.' This last title is doubtless the most correct. The promptuarium of a monastery was a store-room, and the word is similarly used by other writers, e.g. 'Promptuarium Vocabulorum,' published at Antwerp in 1516. The author arranges the English words in alphabetical order, first placing under every letter the nouns and other parts of speech except the verbs, and then the verbs by themselves. Each English word is interpreted by one or more Latin words, whose gender, declension, &c., are noted, and in many cases English synonyms or paraphrases are added. The work is valuable as an authentic record of the English of the fifteenth century, as illustrative of the East-Anglian dialect, and explanatory of much debased Latin. Geoffrey himself gives his sources of information, chiefly consisting of the writings of previous grammarians, and especially of John Garland [q. v.] The 'Promptorium' was printed by Pynson 1499, by W. de Worde 1510, 1512, 1516, 1518, 1519 (?), 1522, and 1528, and by Julian Notary 1508. It has been edited for the Camden Society in 3 vols., by Albert Way, in whose third volume there is a very full account and discussion. The most important manuscript of the

'Promptorium' is Harl. MS. 221. Five others are known. Bale attributes to Geoffrey the following works: 'In Doctrinale Alexandri' (i.e. Neckam), lib. iii.; 'In Johannis Garlandi Synonyma,' lib. i.; 'In Equivoca ejusdem,' lib. i.; 'Expositiones Hymnorum,' lib. i.; 'Hortus Vocabulorum,' lib. i.; 'Medulla Grammatices,' lib. i.; 'Præceptiones Pueriles,' lib. i., all of which he says he had seen printed at Paris and London. The 'Synonyma' and 'Equivoca' were several times printed by Pynson and Wynkyn de Worde 'cum expositione Magistri Galfridi Anglici,' who may reasonably be identified with the author of the 'Promptorium.' From his quotation of the 'Incipit,' Bale's 'Medulla' seems to have been the same work as the 'Promptorium.' The colophon to Pynson's edition of 1499 says: 'Finit opus . . . quod nuncupatur Medulla grammatice.' There is, however, another 'Medulla Grammatice,' a Latin-English dictionary, of which seventeen manuscripts are extant; this has been with great probability ascribed to Geoffrey. The ascriptions in the manuscript are apparently by a later hand. The 'Hortus' or 'Ortus' is also a Latin-English dictionary (the first printed in England, W. de Worde, 1500); it seems to be a modified reproduction of the 'Medulla.' A 'Liber Hymnorum' is bound up with the Lincoln MS. (A. 3, 15) of the 'Medulla,' and is there stated to be by the same author. To Bale's list Pits erroneously adds 'In Poetria Nova,' a poem by Geoffrey Vinsauf. Bale and Pits give Geoffrey's date as 1490; 1440 is the date given by the author himself in his preamble.

[Way's edition of the Promptorium, vol. iii. (Camd. Soc.); article on Latin-English and English-Latin Lexicography by Professor J. E. B. Mayor in the Journal of Classical and Sacred Philology, vol. iv.; Dibdin's Typ. Ant. ii. 155–8, 406, 416; Bale, p. 631; Pits, p. 679; Tanner, p. 305.]   C. L. K.

GEORGE I (GEORGE LEWIS) (1660–1727), king of Great Britain and Ireland, and elector of Hanover, was born at Hanover 28 March 1660. His father, Ernest Augustus, married in 1658 to Sophia, youngest daughter of Elizabeth, queen of Bohemia, and granddaughter of James I of England, became bishop of Osnabrück in 1662, and in 1679 succeeded to the principality of Calenberg (Hanover). George William of Lüneburg-Celle had entered into an engagement to remain unmarried, and to transmit his dominions on his death to his younger brother, Ernest Augustus, or his descendants. The consequent prospect of uniting all the possessions of the younger branch of the

House of Brunswick suggested at an early date to Ernest Augustus the thought of obtaining from the emperor the creation of a ninth (Hanoverian) electorate. This purpose shaped the earlier career of his eldest son. The education of George Lewis must have been influenced by the clear and lively intellect of his mother, but, as was indignantly noted by her favourite niece, he was not in the habit of showing her affection (ELISABETH CHARLOTTE VON ORLÉANS, *An die Raugräfin Louise*, 22 April 1702; cf. KEMBLE, p. 20; HALLIDAY, *Hist. of the House of Guelph*, 1821, p. 162; see, however, his dutiful letters to her from the field, ap. KEMBLE, pp. 131–2; and cf. *ib.* p. 433 as to his grief at her illness). His campaigns in the wars of the empire began in 1675, when, as Ernest Augustus announced to his wife, 'her Benjamin bore himself bravely' in the battle of the Bridge at Conz (*Memoiren der Herzogin Sophie*, p. 104). In December 1680 he started, well furnished with money, on a journey to England, where he was well received at court, and believed to have a fair chance of the hand of the Princess Anne (HAVEMANN, iii. 426). But he was suddenly (see his statement to Lord Lansdowne ap. JESSE, ii. 283) recalled by his father, in conformity with whose schemes he on 21 Nov. 1682 married Sophia Dorothea, the only child of his uncle of Celle and his uncle's French wife, formerly his mistress. The arrangement as to the Celle succession still holding good, and primogeniture having been recently established by Ernest Augustus in the whole of his dominions, the future importance of the House of Hanover seemed better assured than ever, and in 1692 the father of George Lewis actually became elector. Meanwhile the prince continued his service under the imperial flag, taking an honourable part in Sobiesky's rescue of Vienna in 1683, in 1685 distinguishing himself at the capture of Neuhäusel in Hungary, and in the battle of Neerwinden, 29 July 1693, only escaping with his life through the devotion of General von Hammerstein (HAVEMANN, iii. 310, 311, and note, p. 357; cf. VEHSE, i. 70, as to his visit to Venice after his Hungarian campaign).

His wife had borne him two children, the future king, George II, and Sophia Dorothea, afterwards queen of Frederick William I of Prussia; but their conjugal relations, partly in consequence of the prince's amour with Madame von dem Bussche, sister of the Countess von Platen, had sunk from coldness into mutual repugnance. The faults were probably not all on one side, though George Lewis's dislike of his wife may have been intensified by his prejudice against her mother (see memoirs and correspondence of the Electress Sophia and her niece). Whether guilty or not (and no known evidence of her guilt exists, except in a correspondence of disputable authenticity), the Electoral Princess Sophia Dorothea was accused of a criminal intrigue with Count Philip von Königsmark, a Swedish adventurer of family, who had recently been in the Hanoverian military service. Whatever were the circumstances of the crime perpetrated in the palace at Hanover on the night of 1 July 1694, in which Königsmark vanished for ever from the sight of man, George Lewis at least, who had not yet returned from a journey to Berlin, had no hand in it. We may readily distrust the assertion of his relentless censor, the Duchess of Orleans (*Correspondance*, tr. par Brunet, 1869, i. 379), that he was wont to glory in its commission. Against the princess, who had previously attempted to quit Hanover and had manifestly meditated a second flight with Königsmark's help, sentence of divorce was pronounced on the ground of malicious desertion, and she was detained a prisoner at Ahlden, near Celle, till her death, 3 Nov. 1726. George henceforth knew her name no more; but she was not maltreated in her place of banishment, and on her death he, though reluctantly, allowed her to be buried with her parents at Celle (HAVEMANN, iii. 510). Horace Walpole's gossip about the king having been prophetically warned that he would not survive her a year (*Reminiscences*, p. ciii) is not worth repeating; but we may believe that George's hatred of his son was largely due to his knowledge of the son's regard for the mother.

In 1694 George Lewis began to take part in the government of the electorate, owing to the feeble health of his father, whom he succeeded on 23 Jan. 1698. The Celle dominions, which supported a military force about equal to the Hanoverian, did not fall in till seven years later; but already, 9 Jan. 1699, Leopold I had invested him with the electoral dignity. Finally, in 1708, his exertions on behalf of the grand alliance were rewarded by the long-delayed introduction of the elector of Hanover into the college of electors at the imperial diet, and in 1710 the hereditary arch-treasurership of the empire was conferred upon him. His influence, further strengthened by his *fœdus perpetuum* with Brandenburg (1700), by the reconciliation of the younger with the elder line of the House of Brunswick (1705), and by the Prussian marriage of his daughter (1706), increased with his honours (see HAVEMANN, iii. 400, as to his bold intervention on behalf of the protestant estates at Hildesheim, and as to the French offer of support in case

he should become a candidate on the next election to the imperial throne).

In 1699 he was first brought into personal contact with the question of the succession to the English throne. After the failure of William III in 1689 to include the Duchess Sophia and her descendants by name in the succession, no further step could for some time be taken in the matter by Sophia, her husband, or her son. A rather complicated series of negotiations, however, began with the visit of William III to George William of Celle at his hunting-seat of the Göhrde in 1698, at which George Lewis was present (KLOPP, viii. 245–8; cf. MALORTIE, iii. 147 seq.) In all these transactions the elector and his mother seem to have entirely identified their interests and conduct. The death of the young Duke of Gloucester (30 July 1700) brought the Hanover line to the front, and the act of 1701 definitely settled the succession, in default of issue from Anne and William, upon the Electress Sophia and her heirs, being protestant.

Meanwhile the elector of Hanover played an increasingly important part in the military affairs of Europe. In 1699 his troops helped to protect the Holstein Gottorp territory against Denmark, and thus to bring about the peace of Travendahl in the following year. In 1701 Hanover and Celle joined the grand alliance; and after the death of William III, its author, when there was some talk of George Lewis succeeding him in the stadholdership, they, in return for subsidies, placed more than ten thousand men under Marlborough's command, and furnished five regiments of horse to the States-General. Leibniz thought that the elector himself ought to have been appointed to the captain-generalship of the British forces (KEMBLE, p. 269). About this time (1702) Toland visited Hanover and Herrenhausen, and published his impressions three years afterwards. With the exception of certain palpable flatteries intended for the English market, his statements tally with other accounts. The elector is described as a popular prince, equitable in administration, frugal and punctual in his payments, a perfect man of business, but spending much time with his mistresses. Toland extols his military knowledge and personal courage, adding that he cares little for any diversion but hunting, and is very reserved in manner. He was not to be surpassed 'in his zeal against the intended universal monarchy of France, and was so most hearty for the common cause of Europe' (TOLAND, p. 70).

Marlborough visited Hanover in 1704 and 1705, and easily persuaded the elector to discountenance the tory scheme of bringing his mother over to England (suggestions to the same effect made to the elector by Peterborough and others in 1707 were rejected accordingly). George Lewis appears in return to have given good advice on the subject of the negotiations with Charles XII of Sweden. The elector formed intimate relations with Marlborough, and maintained them after the duke's loss of favour (for an earlier letter, 1702, see MACPHERSON, i. 621). In 1706 Halifax brought over the 'Regency Act,' by means of which the Hanoverian succession was to be actually accomplished, and the act which naturalised the Electress Sophia and her descendants, being protestants. The elector made polite acknowledgments (MACPHERSON, ii. 51 seqq.), but his policy was still governed by his dynastic interests at home and his devotion to the emperor. Rigidly abstaining from intervention in English affairs, and even more consistently than his mother avoiding any step which might give umbrage to Queen Anne or her ministers, he steadily seconded her in her policy of masterly inaction. Horace Walpole's assertion (*Reminiscences*, p. cvii) that during Anne's reign the elector was inclined to the tories and his mother to the whigs is a misrepresentation.

In 1707 George Lewis, after some well-warranted hesitation, accepted the supreme command of the army of the empire on the Upper Rhine. He found the troops in an unsatisfactory condition of discipline (September), and was much hampered by the slackness of the contributions and by the formalities surrounding his office. He showed much energy in combating these obstacles, but he was not initiated by Marlborough and Eugene into their plans for the campaign of 1708, or allowed to share its laurels. In 1709 his own offensive operations were thwarted, and on 20 May in the following year, indignant at the shortcomings of the emperor and the estates, he resigned his command (cf. his letters to Queen Anne, ap. MACPHERSON, ii. 178–81). But he was as loyal as ever to the war, and when sounded by Queen Anne deprecated further changes in her government. Hereupon the tory managers thought to gain his goodwill by bringing about his nomination to the command in the Low Countries. It was even said that Lord Rivers, who was sent to Hanover in 1710 to explain away the ministerial changes in England, was to insinuate the offer. But Marlborough had forewarned the elector, who managed to give replies of unimpeachable prudence to Rivers's explanations. George Lewis's chief interest in these years was probably the progress of the northern war, which led him to conclude defensive alliances with Poland (1709) and Denmark (1710), and to exert himself to

stave off hostilities in the German northeast. At first he demurred to the proposed partition of the Swedish territories, but insisted, in the event of its being taken in hand, that the duchies of Bremen and Verden should be allotted to Hanover. When in the autumn of 1712 the Danes occupied Bremen, he sent troops into Verden.

The polite overtures of both Harley and St. John in 1711 were very coldly met by the elector. He maintained a significant reserve concerning the peace negotiations, but found it necessary to send a plenipotentiary to Utrecht. He did not seem overcome when Thomas Harley arrived at Hanover (July 1712) with the act according precedence in England to his mother, himself, and his son, and though turning a deaf ear to Prince Eugene's suggestion that he should play over again the part of William the Deliverer, declined to second the policy of the British ministry at Utrecht or elsewhere. In his instructions to his envoy Grote he made no secret of his suspicions of Oxford, and his trust in the whig leaders; but he steadily maintained his attitude of non-intervention in English affairs, and notably declined to favour the suggestion (1713) that the electoral prince should be sent over to England. Even the news of Anne's serious illness at the end of the year failed to move him. Schulemburg's statement that George Lewis, could he have done so with honour, would have readily renounced his claim to the English succession (KLOPP, xiv. 590), remains a mere assertion. In any case, such a course became altogether impossible after the insulting letters written by Bolingbroke in Queen Anne's name, when, in consequence of the Hanoverian envoy Schütz's inquiry, the lord chancellor had sent to the prince his writ of attendance in the House of Lords [see GEORGE II]. Though one of the famous three letters was addressed to the elector (for it see MACPHERSON, ii. 621), it is certain that he had not joined with his mother and son in making the obnoxious inquiry (see the elector's own declaration to Clarendon, ap. COXE, i. 142–3, and Robethon's explicit statement, *Marchmont Papers*, ii. 399 seqq.; cf. KLOPP, xiv. 576 seqq.) In the memorial signed by the electress and himself on 7 May (1714), however, both the dotation of the former and the establishment of a member of the electoral family in England had been pointed out as expedient (see MACPHERSON, ii. 608 seqq.) The death of the Electress Sophia on 8 June seems to have induced the elector to manifest a livelier interest in the succession, in which he had now taken her place; nor was it an impulse of pure sentiment which on this occasion led to a reconciliation between him and his son (*March-mont Papers*, ii. 405). His conduct as heir-presumptive to the British throne was, how-ever, marked by his accustomed discretion and self-respect. He disavowed Schütz, and took no part in the publication of the queen's letters, replying to that addressed to himself calmly and courteously (see MACPHERSON, ii. 623–4). But he handed to Thomas Harley his outspoken memorial of 7 May, and en-trusted the announcement to the queen of his mother's death to Bothmar, by no means a *persona grata* to the existing *régime* (KLOPP, xiv. 601). At the same time he caused a fresh instrument of regency, containing his own nominations of lords justices, to be pre-pared, and at home took every precaution for the safety of his German dominions in the approaching crisis. Frederick William I of Prussia, who was on a visit to him at the end of July, and other allied princes offered him their help (RANKE, vii. 74).

Queen Anne died on 1 Aug. 1714, and on the same day the regency instruments were opened in the presence of George's represen-tatives, Bothmar and Kreyenberg. The ab-sence from the list of lords justices of Marl-borough's name was attributed to the remem-brance of the plan of campaign of 1708, but Lord Stanhope (i. 95) is probably right in sup-posing George to have been advised to omit the whig leaders in a body. Marlborough's nomination as captain-general, dated 6 Aug., was probably the first document signed by George I as king (KLOPP, xii. 654). On the day of Queen Anne's death the lords justices proclaimed the new sovereign in the usual localities in London, further proclamations following there and in Edinburgh on 5 Aug., and in Dublin with a proclamation for the disarming of papists on the 6th. The lords voted an address to King George on the 5th, and the commons on the 6th. The funds, which had risen three per cent. on 1 Aug., went up a further seven per cent. when the address of the commons became known.

On the evening of 1 Aug. Bothmar had despatched his secretary Goedeke to Hanover, where he arrived on the 6th, followed on the next day by the Earl of Dorset, sent by the lords justices on the morning of the 2nd to attend the king on his journey to England. According to a doubtful tradition, Lord Cla-rendon, who had arrived just before Queen Anne's death partly on a mission of condo-lence, partly to transmit Bolingbroke's reply to the memorial of 7 May, was the first Englishman to bend his knee before George I (so MALORTIE, who adds details; but see the doubts of Klopp, xiv. 646 n.) Craggs, who arrived at Hanover as early as the 5th,

was the bearer of a letter from the privy council dated the day before the queen's death (see *Political State*, viii. 206). Soon Hanover was full enough of princes, British and Ger-man diplomatists and others, to furnish reason or excuse for delay; but at last on 31 Aug. the king started without ceremony of any kind. Before leaving he had conferred some substantial favours upon the city of Hanover, and had committed the government of his electorate to a council presided over by his youngest brother, Ernest Augustus [q. v.] Bothmar became, and continued till 1727, minister for Hanoverian affairs in England (see KEMBLE, p. 331). The king was followed at some distance by his son. His prime minister (since 1709), Baron Bernstorff, and Privy-councillor Robethon, formerly private secre-tary to William III, and the draughtsman of the electoral court, had preceded him to the Hague. In his small suite were also his finance minister, Baron Görz, and his master of the horse, Baron Kielmannsegge. The ba-roness contrived (LADY M. W. MONTAGU, i. 127), in spite, it is said, of her creditors, to overtake the royal party in Holland; the king's other mistress *en titre*, Mlle. de Schulen-burg, followed without much delay. At the Hague, where the king was warmly received, he decreed the dismissal of Bolingbroke, naming Townshend secretary of state, a choice most acceptable to the United Provinces (cf. RANKE, vii. 75). On 16 Sept. the king em-barked at Oranie Polder in the yacht Pere-grine, accompanied by a squadron of twenty sail under Admiral Berkeley, anchored off Gravesend in a fog on the following night, and landed at Greenwich on the 18th at 6 P.M.

Here he held his first royal reception on the 19th, particularly distinguishing Marl-borough and the whig lords in attendance, but ignoring Ormonde and Harcourt, and barely noticing Oxford, introduced to him by Dorset as 'le comte Oxford dont V.M. aura entendu parler' (HOFFMAN'S *Report*, ap. KLOPP, xiv. 665; cf. STANHOPE and COXE). Among the addresses received was one signed by a number of leading highland names which figured in next year's rebellion (DORAN, i. 11). On the 20th George I held his royal entry into London, with the Prince of Wales by his side; but the honours of the day seem to have fallen to Marlborough (*Political State*, viii. 258). The king's court on the 21st was well attended; on the 22nd he presided over a meeting of the privy council held for formal purposes, but it was dissolved on the 29th, and a new one put in its place.

The new ministry was entirely whig, with the exception of Nottingham [see FINCH, DANIEL]. Lord Cowper, the new lord chancellor, had hastened to present his 'Impartial History of Parties' (see for this paper, which is not altogether historical and not at all impartial, the appendix to CAMPBELL'S 'Life of Lord Cowper' in his *Lives of the Lord Chancellors*, iv. 421–9), and Lady Cowper writes (*Diary*, p. 32): 'The King is, as we wish, upon the subject of Parties, and keeps my Lord's MS. by him, which he has read several times.' The notion of retaining the services of a few tories was soon relinquished (see as to Hanmer and Bromley *Political State*, viii. 350). A precedent of enduring importance was set by the selection of seven great officers of state, together with the veteran Somers without office, to form the cabinet council of the sovereign. George I seems to have shown considerable firmness in resisting solicitations, and the number of peerages (fourteen) and other honours bestowed by him at this time was not excessive. On 20 Oct. his coronation took place in Westminster Abbey with great pomp, both spiritual and lay peers of nearly every political complexion, including Bolingbroke, who had hitherto in vain sought to be admitted to the royal presence (LADY COWPER), appearing in their places (for details see *Political State*, viii. 347 seqq.; cf. LADY COWPER's lively description, *Diary*, p. 3 seqq.; Klopp cites an elaborate narrative in LÜNIG, *Theatrum Europæum*). In London the solemnity was unmarred by disturbances, but in Bristol and elsewhere it was celebrated by riots, with cries the reverse of loyal (cf. LADY COWPER, p. 19).

From 1714 to 1717 the conduct of affairs was in the hands of the administration in which Townshend exercised the chief influence, and in which his most intimate asssociate, Walpole, afterwards (October 1715) entered the cabinet as first lord of the treasury. The first thing necessary was the dissolution of Queen Anne's last parliament (4 Jan. 1715). It had readily voted the new sovereign a civil list of 700,000*l.*; indeed, some of the tories even proposed to increase this figure at which his predecessor's personal revenue had stood by a further 300,000*l.* (cf. *Wentworth Papers*, p. 411; according to WORTLEY MONTAGU, this proposal was made on behalf of the crown at the suggestion of Walpole). It had shown its loyalty to King George in other ways, but the majority was tory, with a variable infusion of Jacobitism. In the elections for the new parliament, which met on 17 March, no exertions on the part of the government were spared to secure a favourable verdict on the question of the succession challenged by the Pretender's manifesto of the previous 29 Aug. The tories, unwilling or unable to meet this issue directly, raised

the old cry of the church in danger, and the presbyterian principles of the house of Hanover were, with audacious ignorance or mendacity, held up to opprobrium (see the pamphlet, *English Advice to the Freeholders of England*, cited by WRIGHT). No doubt George I's mother was bred a Calvinist, but the line to which he belonged was Lutheran. Leibniz had been at pains to impress upon him the agreement between the Augsburg Confession and the Thirty-nine Articles; and George was not of a nature to make difficulties on such subjects (see *Correspondance de Leibniz avec l'Electrice Sophie*, iii. 342; cf. TOLAND, p. 56). He naturally brought his Lutheran travelling court chaplain with him to England (MALORTIE, i. 60); but he conformed unhesitatingly to the church of England (*Political State*, viii. 377, 464, and especially ix. 313; and see on the whole subject PAULI, *Aufsätze zur engl. Gesch. Neue Folge*, 1883, pp. 379 sq.)

In the new parliament, which was opened by the king in person, though his speech had to be read by the lord chancellor, the whigs commanded a very large majority. In its principal transactions the personal influence of George I had no determining share. His opinion as to the impeachment of the fallen tory leaders is unknown. The revival of the Riot Act (1715) was provoked by mobs which as a rule clamoured for the church rather than against the throne, though the cry of 'No George' was occasionally heard (cf. WRIGHT, i. 32–3), and though it was even rumoured that a plot had been laid in the city to assassinate the magistrates favourable to the king (*Treasury Papers*, 1716, p. 235). The Septennial Act (1716) in the first instance unmistakably added to the security of the reigning family. The king, however, was from the first profoundly unpopular with his subjects at large, and in London both with the world of fashion and with the public of the streets. This arose partly from his own want of royal graces, but still more from the rapacity attributed to his German mistresses and dependents. Outrageous corruption was imputed to the ladies, who reached the height of their honours as Duchess of Kendal (1719) and as Countess of Darlington (1722) respectively, and against the rest of the foreigners, down to the king's two favourite valets, Mustapha and Mahomet, captives of one of his Turkish campaigns, who, as pages of the backstairs, were said to carry on a brisk traffic in minor offices (JESSE, ii. 297; 'Honest Mah'met' is immortalised in POPE, *Moral Essays*, Ep. ii. 198).

The anticipation of the Jacobite insurrections of 1715–16 produced, however, a considerable display of loyalty outside as well as inside the houses. At this time George I, who had recently presented to the university of Cambridge the valuable library of Bishop Moore of Ely (he afterwards added a gift of 2,000*l.* for building purposes), refused to accept an address from the university of Oxford, which, among other ebullitions of disloyalty, had conferred an honorary degree upon Sir Constantine Phipps, just dismissed from the Irish lord chancellorship (as to the furious interchange of epigrams see DORAN, i. 348; cf. WORDSWORTH, *University Life in the Eighteenth Century*, p. 45). Five days before the proclamation of 'James III' at Braemar (6 Sept. 1715) Lewis XIV had died, who, after recognising George I and sending the Pretender out of France, was drifting into support of the invasion, for which he had allowed a small armament to fit out at Havre. His death, and the accession to power of the Duke of Orleans as regent, foredoomed the expedition to failure. George I appointed 7 June 1716 as a thanksgiving day. His government cannot be charged with unnecessary severity towards the prisoners taken in this rebellion. Of the six peers condemned to death, all but one (Wintoun) threw themselves on the king's mercy. The applications made on their behalf greatly troubled him, as he desired not to interfere. He pardoned Lord Nairn at the request of Stanhope, but the entreaties of the Countess of Derwentwater and those of the Countess of Nithsdale, who forced him to drag her on her knees to the door of the drawing-room, were in vain. When the house of peers, by a narrow majority, passed an address begging the king to reprieve such of the prisoners as deserved it for as long a time as he thought fit, he returned a dignified but evasive answer, which, according to Lady Cowper (*Diary*, p. 82), 'plainly showed the Lords concerned that they had played the Fool.' Nottingham, who had approved the address, and against whom the king was much incensed, was dismissed from office. Two of the condemned peers were, however, respited. The king naturally showed much annoyance at the escape of Lord Nithsdale, but was guilty of bad taste in attending the Duke of Montague's ball on the day of the execution of Lords Derwentwater and Kenmure (DORAN, i. 146–63; cf. STANHOPE, i. 194 seqq.)

The rebellion at an end and the Septennial Act passed, George I made known his wish to visit his electorate, in whose interests he had, July 1715, joined the coalition against Charles XII of Sweden. Townshend and his colleagues had warmly approved this step and the annexation of Bremen and Verden;

they had moreover sanctioned the despatch of a British fleet into the Baltic, ostensibly for the protection of our trade there. The two so-called treaties of Westminster show a lively desire on the part of ministers in the earlier half of 1716 to keep up the traditions of the Grand Alliance; but they were not privy to the whole of the designs of George I and Bernstorff, and there was reason enough to dread the shifting to Hanover of the centre of gravity of British foreign policy. The king, on the other hand, although warned of the unpopularity of the step, desired the repeal of the clause in the Act of Settlement debarring him from quitting the country without the consent of parliament. As the ministry shrank from the expedient of asking parliament to give this consent in each case, the repeal of the clause was carried without a dissentient voice. The tories hoped that he would incur unpopularity by this privilege, of which he made even freer use than they could have hoped. Besides his last journey he made six visits to Germany after his accession, which repeatedly covered nearly all the latter half of the year. Such remonstrances as were offered by his British advisers were ' often ineffectual, but always offensive' (COXE, i. 142).

In 1716 there existed a special obstacle to his journey in the difficulty of bringing about an understanding with the Prince of Wales, to effect which Bernstorff was set to work (LADY COWPER, p. 107). Already in the old days the son had been treated harshly, excluded from the council of state, denied a regiment and a sufficient income, and blamed for his confidences to ' the women,' i.e. his wife and the old electress (SCHULEMBURG, ap. KEMBLE, p. 512). The prince's eagerness about the succession had annoyed his more stolid father, and any reconciliation had been quite hollow. The prince was now anxious to have the title and office of regent during the king's absence; the king would have preferred a commission of regency, of which the prince would have been a member with carefully restricted authority. He also insisted on the dismissal of Argyll, the prince's favourite counsellor, and of other courtiers, and on this head the prince ultimately gave way (LADY COWPER, pp. 108, 111). But no precedent having been found by the privy council for a commission the sole direction of the government during his absence was assigned to the prince, under the obsolete title of ' guardian of the realm and lieutenant' (COXE, i. 142–4). Hereupon, 7 July 1716, the king sailed for the continent, a treasonable libel, ' King G——'s Farewell to England, or the Oxford

Scholars in Mourning,' being hawked about the streets on the occasion of his departure.

Hanover and Herrenhausen were ablaze with delight at the reappearance of their sovereign and the daily performance of French plays (HAVEMANN, iii. 496). George I, as Lord Peterborough phrased it, 'lived so happily here, that he seemed to have forgot the accident that happened to him and his family the 1st of August 1714' (LADY COWPER, pp. 194–5). He also paid a visit to his favourite watering-place of Pyrmont. But in truth political transactions of extreme importance were during this visit carried on by the king and Bernstorff, with the partial co-operation of Stanhope, who had accompanied the king as secretary of state. These negotiations ultimately led to the conclusion of the triple alliance between Great Britain, France, and the United Provinces (4 Jan. 1717). Before, however, this negotiation was finished, the czar Peter I had taken advantage of an internal quarrel in Mecklenburg to send troops into the duchy, and had thereby excited the resentment of George I and of other princes of the empire. George I proposed to crush the czar, and seize his person in pledge by means of the British squadron now in the Baltic; and though Stanhope, to whom Bernstorff communicated this plan, delayed his approval, he advised Townshend to assent to it. But Townshend, in the name of the Prince of Wales as well as of the ministry, demurred, and the crisis passed over without the proposed intervention. Meanwhile the king and Stanhope erroneously suspected Townshend of delaying the settlement of the treaty with France by insisting on the necessity of waiting for the Dutch signature; and the insinuations of the 'Hanoverian junto' against him were reinforced by the vehemence of Sunderland, who, dissatisfied with his position in the ministry, was allowed to attend the king abroad. The treasury at home was irritated by the attempts upon it by Bothmar and Robethon on their own behalf or on that of the mistress at the king's elbow; and George was in turn annoyed by Walpole's most respectful 'failure of memory' as to the promised refunding of a sum advanced by the king for the hire of Münster and Saxe-Gotha troops to help in suppressing the Scottish rebellion. But the most potent motive of the king's dissatisfaction with his English ministry was his revived jealousy of the Prince of Wales, who was making himself as popular as possible at home, and, besides showing renewed favour to Argyll, intimated through Townshend his desire, should the king remain abroad, to hold a parliament. Horace Walpole the elder, charged by Townshend,

November 1716, with his despatch of explanations to the king, found the latter strongly preoccupied against his chief minister, but succeeded, with Stanhope's praiseworthy aid, in producing a change of mood. In the middle of December, however, the king resolved on the removal of Townshend, though he was induced by Stanhope to offer him the lord-lieutenancy of Ireland to break his fall. This Townshend at first declined, but on the king's arrival in England (end of January 1717) he accepted the post, Walpole also remaining in office.

Parliament reopened 20 Feb. with loyal addresses inspired by the discovery of 'Görtz's plot' for an insurrection in England and the invasion of Scotland by Charles XII (29 Jan.); but this unanimity was only momentary. Walpole joined with other adherents of Townshend and the tories and Jacobites at large in seriously imperilling the vote of supply demanded against Sweden, and the result was the immediate dismissal of Townshend (5 April), whom Walpole and several of those who acted with him at once followed out of office. Stanhope became first lord of the treasury at the head of a reconstructed ministry, and the second period of the reign covered by his administration (1717–20) commenced. Beyond a doubt the important achievements of the 'German ministry,' as Stanhope's government was derisively called, were completely in accord with the wishes of the king, and the real director of our foreign policy in this period was Bernstorff, whose influence was now at its height (RANKE, vii. 104), though Stanhope's activity deserves a large share of the credit of the Quadruple Alliance. 'This king of England,' exclaimed the Duchess Dowager of Orleans (9 June 1718, ap. KEMBLE, p. 20), 'who is so dreadfully alarmed lest any one should imagine that he lets himself be ruled, how can he submit to be led in this way by that Bernstorff, and against his own children too?' Great Britain's gain from the foreign policy of this period was by no means confined to the indirect advantage of the definite acquisition by Hanover of Bremen and Verden (1719). The Utrecht settlement was maintained; the ambition of Alberoni was checkmated by the Quadruple Alliance (1718) and the war of 1719, which witnessed the collapse of another Spanish Armada; while the treaties of Passarowitz (1718) and Nystadt (1721) secured peace to the east and north of Europe. George I, as Ranke says (vii. 103), occupied a position in the European system resembling that of William III after Ryswick, with the advantage in his favour that France was his ally. But this was neither very obvious nor very interesting to the general public at home.

At home the government made no advance in popularity. George I had no love for high church, and the silencing of convocation, in which the ecclesiastical controversies of the times resulted (1717), must have had his approval, and Stanhope's liberal policy towards the nonconformists his goodwill. But he was prudent enough to perceive the impossibility of sweeping away by a repeal of the Test and Corporation Acts the disabilities of protestant dissenters and Roman catholics alike, and the Relief Act, carried December 1718, was a very modest measure (LECKY, i. 258). In the matter of Sunderland's Peerage Bill (finally rejected December 1719) the intervention of the king, who in his message to the lords requested that his prerogative should not stand in the way of the proposed limitation (COXE, i. 222), was thought to be influenced by fear of the creations which the Prince of Wales might make on his advent to the throne. Walpole, who with Townshend had entered into a bitter opposition to the government, was the chief adversary of the bill, but in July 1720 they rejoined the ministry. Stanhope's most serious embarrassment, however, was due to the action of Bernstorff, who finally ventured to conceive a scheme for the spoliation of Prussia with the aid of the emperor and Poland (see STANHOPE's letters, ap. COXE, i. Appendix, pp. 321–3). This Stanhope contrived (1719) to baffle by making a confidant of the Duchess of Kendal (ib. p. 239). All this time people in England refused to see in the king anything but a selfish and indolent voluptuary. Atterbury writes from his deanery, June 1718, that 'Hearne,' a nickname for George I, 'is soothed up with new pleasures and new mistresses . . . his indolence and ignorance of his affairs are more remarkable than ever' (DORAN, i. 311); and his unpopularity exposed him to perils culminating about the end of 1717 in an attempt at assassination by a coachmaker's apprentice, James Shepherd (JESSE, ii. 304), which he confronted with his habitual cool courage. It was remarked that he frequently visited the theatre in the solitude of a sedan-chair (DORAN, i. 320).

In 1719 and in 1720 George I visited Hanover, Herrenhausen, and Pyrmont, after on each occasion naming a council of regency composed of great officers of state, instead of naming the Prince of Wales regent. The dissensions between father and son had gone from bad to worse, and in 1718 a quarrel about the sponsorship of one of the prince's children led to the king's ordering him to quit St. James's Palace. The disgrace of the prince and princess was officially notified to foreign courts; Lord Cowper, who had opposed a bill by which the prince's income would have been made entirely dependent on the king's will, was obliged to give up the great seal (April 1718; cf. CAMPBELL, Lives, iv. 390); and the king planned obtaining an act of parliament by which the prince on coming to the British throne should be compelled to relinquish his German dominions (cf. LORD HERVEY, Memoirs, iii. 216–19, 291–3; and see CAMPBELL, u.s., as to the circumstances under which the scheme was dropped). At last, in April 1720, after much secret manœuvring, the king, through Walpole, made overtures for a reconciliation; an interview after some time followed, which, according to the prince's report to Lady Cowper, lasted five minutes, and in which the king's only audible words were 'votre conduite;' and the end was a reconciliation 'managed without Bernstorff or Bothmar, or any of the Germans knowing about it except the Duchess of Kendal' (see LADY COWPER's account, Diary, p. 141 sq.) Probably she was near the truth in her statement that Walpole undertook to make the prince do everything the king wanted. The management of the affair seems to have caused great consternation in the German clique (cf. as to the peacemakers Marchmont Papers, ii. 409–10).

The king's sojourn in Germany was in 1720 cut short by the news of the South Sea crash, and, taking an abrupt departure, he landed at Margate 9 Nov. But the ill-fated stock continued its precipitate fall; the country was in an uproar, and the king had to bear his share of the obloquy. The Duchess of Kendal was said to have received enormous sums from the company (WRIGHT, i. 79–80). It was rumoured that Sunderland, with the ulterior design of overturning the throne, was urging the king to marry the Duchess of Kendal. In view of the unpopularity of the king, some of his Hanoverian counsellors are said to have suggested a resignation of the crown to the Prince of Wales; while per contra he was recommended, with the help of a number of devoted officers of his army, to render the crown absolute by a coup d'état (COXE, ii. 21–2, referring to letters from the Hanoverian ministers among the Townshend Papers).

Wiser councils prevailed, and indeed already, shortly before the king's return, the man for the situation had been found. Walpole and Townshend—no longer Townshend and Walpole—resumed their former offices at the head of a government, the reconstruction of which had become indispensable through the death of Stanhope (4 Feb. 1721) and the removal by various causes of other whig leaders. With a speech written by Walpole, which promised well for the prosperity of the country, the king opened the last session of his first parliament (9 Oct. 1721), and the intrigues of Sutherland to oust him from the royal favour were thwarted by the king's avowed determination never again to part with his minister (COXE, ii. 71, 75). Walpole's long ministerial ascendency asserted itself at the very outset, when the king by his advice abandoned further interference in the affairs of the Swedish throne (*ib.* pp. 107–8). As the king spoke no English and Walpole neither German nor French, their conversation was carried on in such Latin as they could command (HORACE WALPOLE, *Reminiscences*, p. xcv). But the straightforwardness of George I harmonised with the *bonhomie* of Walpole, who in the next reign must have looked back with regret to the jovial hours the old king had spent with him over a bowl of punch after dinner in his small house at Richmond (*ib.* pp. xcvi–vii). George I bestowed a lucrative patent-place upon Walpole for life (HORACE WALPOLE), and created his son a peer. Townshend, too, was now in high favour (cf. COXE, ii. 125). A steady majority was secured to the ministry by the election for the parliament which met in October 1722, and which, by a year's suspension of the Habeas Corpus Act, promptly extinguished any ulterior danger from 'Atterbury's Plot.' This conspiracy, which proposed an invasion under Ormonde, the seizure of the king and royal family and of the chief civil and military authorities, had become known to the British government in May through the good offices of the regent Orleans. In it the last direct attempt against the throne of George I was nipped in the bud.

In 1723 George I's visit to Germany included an interchange of visits with Frederick William I of Prussia, to arrange a marriage between the Prussian Princess Wilhelmina and Frederick, eldest son of the Prince of Wales; but though ardently desired by Queen Sophia Dorothea, the marriage treaty, owing to subsequent difficulties between the two sovereigns, remained unsigned in this (as it did in the next) reign (CARLYLE, *Frederick II*, bk. v. c. i.; cf. c. iv. In the earlier chapter Carlyle cites from the *Memoirs of the Margravine of Baireuth* (see i. 77–80, ed. 1845) her amusing account of the 'Spanish manners' of her 'Grandpapa' in his visit to Charlottenburg). They, however, availed themselves of this opportunity to send a joint threat of re-

prisals to the elector of Mainz and the Bishop of Speier, who were continuing to oppress their protestant subjects (already in 1719 George I had made similar representations, without success, to the elector palatine. See MALORTIE, i. 131–2; cf. HAVEMANN, iii. 502). On this visit to Germany George I was, contrary to custom, accompanied by both secretaries of state, Lords Townshend and Carteret. The latter was on friendly terms with Bernstorff and Bothmar, and leant on the support of the Countess of Darlington and her sister Mme. de Platen, while the Duchess of Kendal adhered to Walpole and Townshend. A design for a marriage between a daughter of Mme. de Platen and the Count St. Florentin, son of La Vrillière, French secretary of state, to be accompanied by the bestowal of a dukedom upon the bridegroom's father, had found favour with King George. The lady's family reckoned upon the help of Sir Luke Schaub, a Swiss, formerly secretary to Stanhope, and 'a kind of Will Chiffinch to George I' (CUNNINGHAM, note to *Letters of Horace Walpole*, i. 83), now British minister at Paris. Townshend, however, with the aid of the Duchess of Kendal and her 'niece,' the Countess of Walsingham, obtained the dismissal of Bernstorff from the ministry of state at Hanover, and frustrated the efforts of Bothmar, who had come over to use his influence (COXE, ii. 104–5). The marriage took place at Paris, King George giving the bride a portion of 10,000*l.*; but the dukedom was withheld, and the king having angrily rejected a scheme of Lady Darlington and Schaub for a marriage between the youthful Lewis XV and the eldest daughter of the Prince of Wales, Schaub was superseded at Paris by his rival, Horace Walpole, and finally Carteret himself was deprived of the seals of secretary of state and sent as lord-lieutenant to Ireland (COXE; STANHOPE). In the troublesome affair of Wood's patent also the king followed the advice in which ultimately Carteret and Walpole concurred.

Baffled in the schemes proposed by them after the death of the regent Orleans (August 1723), the king and queen of Spain broke up the congress of Cambrai and brought about the first treaty of Vienna (April 1725). Spain was to call upon Great Britain to restore Gibraltar and Minorca; the demand was, if necessary, to be enforced by arms, and the Pretender to be seated on the British throne; while the emperor hoped to terrify or force the government of George I into guaranteeing the Pragmatic Sanction. George, who had better and earlier information at Hanover than his ministers had at Whitehall

(SIR ROBERT WALPOLE ap. STANHOPE, ii. 81), took the matter very coolly, expressing his hope to the Spanish ambassador that the reconciliation would last as long as the parties to it expected (COXE, ii. 210–13). It was not the king or his German advisers, but the British ministry acting through Townshend, who had accompanied the king on his journey to Hanover as soon as parliament was up (June 1725), that devised the counter-check of the treaty of Hanover (3 Sept.) between Great Britain, France, and Prussia. George I shrank from a course which might bring invasion upon Hanover, and the ban of the empire upon himself, and all this for the sake of purely English questions, such as Gibraltar and Minorca, the Ostend Company and the Pretender. It is all the more to his credit that he assented to the treaty, bearing with his usual indifference the opposition clamour against a compact which showed 'Hanover riding triumphant on the shoulders of England' (CHESTERFIELD ap. STANHOPE, ii. 82). Such comments were quite as loud as the welcome which greeted George I on his landing at Rye (3 Jan. 1726) after being exposed to imminent peril during the violent storm which had detained him three days on his voyage.

The king's speech from the throne (20 Jan.) prefaced vigorous preparations in Scotland against the threatened invasion. But Fleury's accession to power in France (June) strengthened the Hanover alliance, which was joined by the United Provinces, Sweden, and Denmark. To bring about pacific relations between the two Scandinavian powers, and thereby to assure to Hanover an undisturbed tenure of Bremen and Verden, was one of the chief objects of George I during his sojourn at Herrenhausen in the summer of 1726. Though before long Prussia fell away from the alliance of Hanover (October), warlike demonstrations, partly intended to keep off the intervention of Russia, commenced on the part of Great Britain. When at the opening of parliament in January 1727 the royal speech had referred to the designs of the allies of Vienna, Palm, the imperial minister in London, presented a memorial to the king denying the existence of secret articles in the treaty and demanding reparation for the expressions in the speech. Palm had easily secured the support of Bothmar and the Hanoverians; he had found means, it is said, to impress the Duchess of Kendal, notwithstanding the price annually paid by the administration for her goodwill, and was in communication with the opposition, now controlled by Bolingbroke. All parties, however, agreed in resenting or professing to

resent the memorial as insulting to both king and country; an indignant address was voted by the commons, and Palm received his passports (COXE; STANHOPE). Both the British and the Hanoverian forces were very considerably increased; a subsidy voted for twelve thousand Hessians at a cost of 240,000l. a year, however, excited much discontent (LORD HERVEY, Memoirs, ch. i.) Soon afterwards the emperor agreed to preliminaries of peace with Great Britain and her allies (31 May), and Spain only delayed following his example in order to save appearances. Bolingbroke, who had now completely gained over the Duchess of Kendal, revenged himself for the failure of his schemes by thrusting upon the king through her hands a memorial inveighing against Walpole, and demanding an audience. The king transmitted the paper to his minister, and by his advice the audience was granted. Immediately afterwards the king received Walpole himself in high good humour, but would give him no other account of what had passed but 'bagatelles, bagatelles!' As, however, George continued his confidential visits to Walpole, and on his last departure for Hanover ordered him to have the royal lodge and Richmond Park ready for his return, Walpole can hardly have erred in concluding that Bolingbroke's intrigue had failed. The Duchess of Kendal seems to have thought the same, though Bolingbroke and his friends roundly asserted that on the king's return he was to have been made prime minister in Walpole's place. Walpole was probably by no means free from apprehensions; but the strong sense of George I could hardly have allowed him to lose sight so completely of the interests of the country, and of his own (COXE, ii. 252–5, and Preface i. xi–xii; cf. HORACE WALPOLE, Reminiscences, pp. xcvii, and LORD HERVEY, Memoirs, i. 18).

The last journey of George I to Germany was begun 3 June 1727. On the 9th he slept at Count de Twillet's house near the little Dutch town of Delden, after supping heartily and in the best of humours. Next day he continued his journey at 7 A.M., leaving the Duchess of Kendal behind him, and attended by two Hanoverian high court officials, Hardenberg and his favourite Fabrice. An hour afterwards he fainted. The courtiers thought it an apoplectic stroke; but he retained consciousness, and after being bled ordered by signs that the journey should be continued to Osnabrück, where he arrived at the house of his brother the bishop (Duke of York) some time after 10 P.M., unconscious and wholly paralysed. He lived through the next day, and died calmly on Wednesday morning, 12 June, in the presence of a few attendants, including his faithful valet Mustapha. His remains were deposited in the palace vaults, whence they were after a time taken to those at Hanover, and interred there on the night of 30 Aug. (MALORTIE, i. 137–51; cf. COXE's account, ii. 255–7, derived from the personal inquiries of Wraxall). George I's will, which was rumoured to contain a legacy of 40,000l. to the Duchess of Kendal, and a large legacy to his daughter, the queen of Prussia, was destroyed by George II, and its duplicate likewise. According to Horace Walpole (*Reminiscences*, pp. cxxi–ii, where see Wright's note), Lady Suffolk told him, by way of plausible excuse for George II, that George I had burnt two wills made in favour of his son. 'They were probably the wills of the Duke and Duchess of Zell (i.e. Celle), or one of them might have been that of his mother, the Princess Sophia.' According to the same authority (*ib.* p. cx) George I's daughter-in-law, Queen Caroline, found in his cabinet at his death a proposal from the Earl of Berkeley, first lord of the admiralty, to seize the Prince of Wales and convey him to America, 'whence he should never be heard of more.'

The sudden death of George I, who had started on his journey in his usual vigorous health (he had had a threatening of apoplexy at Charlottenburg in 1723), and was only in his sixty-eighth year, took the world by surprise. Some unkindly legends were invented in connection with his decease; but probably few unselfish tears were shed, and none in his own family. Between his son and him all was hatred; his genial daughter-in-law he called 'cette diablesse' (*ib.* p. ciii); the only one of his own blood for whom he had much tenderness seems to have been his sister Queen Sophia Charlotte (LADY COWPER, *Diary*, p. 149). To his English subjects he had always remained a stranger. He never troubled himself to learn their language, though already as a boy he had acquired a certain facility in speaking Latin, French, and Italian. English literature found in him no patron, and occupied itself but little with his name. The expression of elation attributed to him that Newton was his subject in one country and Leibniz in the other is not much in his style, especially as he was rather illiberal to the latter at Hanover, and denied him his heart's desire, a summons to London (*Correspondance de l'Electrice Sophie*, iii. 325–328; cf. VEHSE, i. 234–5; KEMBLE, p. 533). Early in the last year of his life he received Voltaire 'very graciously' (DORAN, ii. 22). He was fond of music; but the diversions especially affected by him were stag-hunting at the Göhrde, a hunting seat rebuilt in 1706 and frequently visited by him (MALORTIE, ii.

148–52, 187, 188), and shooting (in Richmond Park), late suppers (JESSE, ii. 315–16) and masquerades, which Bishop Gibson offended him by denouncing (LADY COWPER, p. 81 *n.*) Like his mother he was fond of walking exercise, and indulged in it both in the gardens of his favourite Herrenhausen, and in those of Kensington Palace, which he offended the London world by enlarging at the expense of Hyde Park (DORAN, ii. 14–15; cf. as to his walks, SCHULEMBURG's complaint ap. VEHSE, i. 28).

From his father George I had inherited, with other 'noble passions,' a double portion of the paternal gallantry. His new subjects were much shocked by his mistresses, but chiefly because they were German and therefore written down ugly. In the last year or two of his reign 'he paid the nation the compliment of taking openly an English mistress' in the person of Anne Brett, daughter of Henry Brett [q. v.] (HORACE WALPOLE, *Reminiscences*, pp. cv–vi). But the ascendency of the Duchess of Kendal (Mlle. de Schulemburg), though Horace Walpole thought her 'no genius,' only came to an end with the life of the king; it was periodically disputed by the Countess of Darlington (Mme. de Kielmannsegge). By the former George I was supposed to be father of the Countess of Walsingham; by the latter of the subsequent Viscountess Howe. His stolid infatuation for these women, whom he loaded with Irish and then English peerages, estates, and the profits of vacant offices, and his cynical laxity towards the processes by which some of his German officials, courtiers, and servants sought to improve their opportunities, excited much aristocratic jealousy and popular ill-will; yet Bernstorff and Bothmar, as well as Robethon and perhaps some others, rendered services of real value. Many of George I's shortcomings might have been forgiven had it not been for his want of personal attractiveness. 'He had no notion of what is princely,' wrote the Duchess of Orleans—a censure justified by much more than his undisguised hatred of the parade of royalty and his dislike, noted by the same critic, of intercourse with people of quality. His whole person was commonplace, his countenance inexpressive though handsome, his address awkward, and his general manner dry and cold (for a description of his person and dress towards the close of his reign, see *ib.* p. xciv; cf. COXE, i. 102). Not much religious feeling had been implanted in him by education, and in one of the 'philosophical conversations in his mother's circle he professed to be a materialist' (*Correspondance de l'Electrice Sophie*, ii. 163); but he gave explicit instructions for the religious education of his grandson (HAVEMANN, iii. 568); in German ecclesiastical affairs he was a staunch and active member of the Corpus Evangelicorum, and in England he showed respect to the institutions of the national religion, and interested himself intelligently in projects for 'church extension' in London (*Political State*, x. 59, 63–4). He was at the same time quite free from superstition (an instance of quasi 'touching,' DORAN, *London in Jacobite Times*, i. 345, notwithstanding) and from bigotry of any kind. He was never passionate or in extremes; and in his electorate had doubtless been rightly esteemed a just and therefore beneficent prince. In the case of those who had taken part in the rebellion of 1715 and on other lesser occasions he showed a complete absence of vindictiveness. Towards the exiled family of the Stuarts he repeatedly displayed generosity of feeling (see HORACE WALPOLE, *Reminiscences*, p. cxv; cf. JESSE, *Memoirs of the Court of England*, ii. 309; DORAN, i. 48–9); and both at Hanover and in England he showed compassion to persons imprisoned for debt (*Political State*, viii. 210; JESSE, ii. 310). On the other hand he was, unlike the Stuarts, rarely unmindful of services rendered to him; and in some degree justified the boast, fathered by flattery both on him and on his son, that it was 'the maxim of his family to reward their friends, do justice to their enemies, and fear none but God' (*Political State*, viii. 327). No doubt could exist as to his courage, which he had shown on many a battle-field, and of which he gave constant proof in London, often dispensing with guards, and appearing almost unattended in places of public resort (DORAN, i. 25). In Lord Cowper's opinion (see *ib.* i. 140), had the insurrection of 1715 been successful, King George I would have speedily passed from the throne to the grave; for neither he nor his family would have condescended to save themselves by flight.

A considerable share in the permanent establishment of the new order of things in this kingdom belongs to George I. Though his own tendencies were entirely in the direction of absolute government, he mastered rebellion and kept down disaffection without giving the aspect of tyranny to a constitutional rule. He was possibly, as Shippen sneered, no better acquainted with our constitution than he was with our language; but he learnt to accustom himself to a system of government under which William III had constantly chafed. Before his accession to the British throne he kept out of the conflict of parties; afterwards there was but one that he could trust. Among the whigs he preferred the more to the less

pliant leaders, but even on this head he ultimately gave way.

The whigs and the country needed him as he needed them. The foreign policy of Great Britain, unsettled since the advent of the tories to power, and the conclusion of the peace of Utrecht, required to be directed by one who commanded the situation, and who enjoyed the confidence of Great Britain's old allies. The triple and quadruple alliances made that peace a reality, and the ambition of Spain, even when linked with the dynastic interests of Austria, broke helplessly on the rock of a firm alliance between Great Britain and France. The interests of Hanover were, it is true, paramount in the eyes of George I, but with the exception of the ill-judged designs against the czar in 1716, the interests of Hanover were in substance those of England, and when they seemed to conflict in 1725, the king was found ready to postpone the less to the greater. Unlovable in himself and in his chosen surroundings, George I was worthy of his destiny, and shrank from no duty imposed upon him by the order of things.

Portraits by Kneller are at Windsor and in the National Portrait Gallery.

[The best connected account of the public and private life of George I as a German prince is to be found in Havemann's Geschichte der Lande Braunschweig und Lüneburg, vol. iii. (Göttingen, 1857). See also Schaumann's art. 'George I' in Allgemeine deutsche Biographie, vol. viii. (1878). Toland's Account of the Courts of Prussia and Hanover (published 1705; the characters of George I and his son and daughter-in-law were reprinted in an enlarged form 1714) describes him and his surroundings in 1702. Scattered notices occur in the Memoiren der Herzogin Sophie, &c., ed. Köcher (Leipzig, 1879) and the Correspondance de Leibniz avec l'Electrice Sophie, ed. Klopp (3 vols. Hanover, 1874); and in the Letters of Elizabeth Cnarlotte, Duchess of Orleans (Stuttgart, 1843 and 1867, Paris, 1869, &c.) The official events and ceremonials at the court of Hanover before and after his accession to the British throne are detailed in C. E. von Malortie's Beiträge zur Geschichte des Br.-Lüneb. Hauses und Hofes (Hanover, 1860–2). More varied, and less decorous, information is supplied in vol. i. of E. Vehse's Geschichte der Höfe des Hauses Braunschweig in Deutschland und England (Hamburg, 1853), on which Thackeray founded his lecture. A sufficient survey of the literature concerning Sophia Dorothea and her catastrophe is given in the Quarterly Review for July 1885, art. 'The Electress Sophia.' For the official correspondence of the Elector George Lewis concerned with the question of the Hanoverian succession, see Macpherson's Original Papers, 2 vols. 1775, and J. M. Kemble's selected State Papers and Correspondence, &c. (1857); the entire history of these transactions and of the events connected with them has been elaborated at great length by Klopp in Der Fall des Hauses Stuart, of which vols. ix–xiv. (1881–8) contain plentiful materials for the history of George I ; for a review of recent literature on the subject see the English Historical Review for July 1886, art. 'The Electress Sophia and the Hanoverian Succession.' For the reign of George I the standard modern authorities are the Histories of Lord Stanhope and Lecky (the former of which is here cited as 'Stanhope' in the 5th edit. 1858), with Coxe's Life of Walpole (here cited as 'Coxe' in the edition of 1816). Ranke's Englische Geschichte, vol. vii., summarises the foreign policy of the period. Detailed annalistic information will be found in (Boyer's) Political State of Great Britain, of which vols. viii–x. treat the opening period of the reign. Many facts of interest in the earlier half of the reign are narrated in the Diary of Lady Cowper (1714–20) (1864), and in that of her husband the lord chancellor (1833). Two amusing papers on the court and state of affairs after the accession, with details concerning the king's ministers and mistresses, are printed in vol. i. of the Letters and Works of Lady Mary Wortley Montagu (1861). Horace Walpole's (Lord Orford) Reminiscences, written in 1788, here cited from vol. i. of Cunningham's edition of the Letters (1856), furnish further touches. See also Lord Campbell's Lives of the Lord Chancellors of England, vol. iv. (1846); the Marchmont Papers, vol. ii. (1831) ; and for anecdotal history Thomas Wright's England under the House of Hanover, illustrated from the caricatures and satires of the day, 2 vols. 1848, republished 1867 ; Jesse's Memoirs of the Court of England from the Revolution of 1688, vol. ii. (2nd edit. 1846), and Dr. Doran's London in the Jacobite Times (2 vols. 1877).] A. W. W.

GEORGE II (1683–1760), king of Great Britain and Ireland, only son of George I by Sophia Dorothea, daughter of George William, duke of Lüneburg-Celle, born at Herrenhausen on 10 Nov. (N.S.) 1683 and christened George Augustus, remained under the care of his mother until her divorce on 28 Dec. (N.S.) 1694. Thenceforward he lived with his grandparents, Ernest Augustus, elector of Hanover, and his consort, the Electress Sophia, granddaughter of James I, and was instructed in history and the Latin, French, and English languages. He is said to have cherished the memory and believed in the innocence of his mother, and on one occasion to have made an attempt, frustrated by the vigilance of her guards, to penetrate into her prison (Lebensbeschreibung, 4–7; Walpole, Memoirs, iii. 314 ; Walpoliana, i. 59; Memoirs of Sophia Dorothea, 1845, i. 290; Coxe, Walpole, i. 269, 270). When the Electress Sophia and her issue were placed in the order of succession to the English throne (1701), the whigs proposed to in-

vite the electress and her grandson to England. The project was defeated by the tories, but the Electress Sophia and her issue were naturalised by act of parliament (1705), and the prince was invested with the order of the Garter and created Baron of Tewkesbury in Gloucestershire, Viscount Northallerton in Yorkshire, Earl of Milford Haven in Wales. and Marquis and Duke of Cambridge (9 Nov. 1706). Meanwhile he had married at Herrenhausen on 2 Sept. (N.S.) 1705 Wilhelmina Charlotte Caroline, daughter of John Frederic, markgraf of Brandenburg-Anspach [see CAROLINE, 1683–1737]. In June 1708 he joined the army of the allies, under Marlborough, at Terbanck, and on 11 July (N.S.) distinguished himself at the battle of Oudenarde, heading a cavalry charge, being unhorsed, and more than once in imminent peril of death (Lebensbeschreibung, 7–11 ; Parl. Hist. v. 1237, 1294; KLOPP, ix. 144, 260, xi. 36, 297 ; Lords' Journ. xvii. 132; NICOLAS, Hist. of British Knighthood, vol. ii., Chron. List, lxix ; RIMINI, Memoirs of the House of Brunswick, 413, 421 ; COXE, Marlborough, ed. Wade, ii. 237; LUTTRELL, Relation of State Affairs, v. 626, vi. 33, 338, 359, 434; PÖLLNITZ, Neue Nachrichten, 1739, Erst. Th. 116; PÖLLNITZ, Maison de Brandebourg, 1791, i. 306 ; Marlborough Despatches, ed. Murray, iv. 71, 104, 272). On 22 Dec. 1710 he was installed knight of the Garter, Lord Halifax acting as his proxy. In 1711 an act of parliament was passed giving him precedence as Duke of Cambridge before all the nobility of Great Britain. Prince Eugene now strongly urged him to visit England, but the elector forbade the journey. The Electress Sophia, however, applied through Schütz, the Hanoverian minister at London, for the writ necessary to enable the prince to take his seat in the house of peers. This was done with the concurrence of the principal whig and opposition tory lords. Schütz was informed by the lord-chancellor (Harcourt) that Queen Anne, though surprised, would not refuse the application. The news was well received by the nation, and the prince was eagerly expected. Anne, however, wrote to the elector, the Electress Sophia, and the prince in terms which left no doubt of her dislike to the proposal, which was dropped after a reply of cold politeness from the prince. After the death of Anne (1 Aug. 1714) the prince accompanied his father to England, was declared Prince of Wales at the first council held by the new king (22 Sept.), and so created by letters patent on 27 Sept. The princess followed with her two daughters, Anne and Amelia, in October. On 29 Oct. the king, accompanied by the prince and princess, dined with the lord mayor, and on the 30th the prince's birthday was celebrated by a ball, the princess, according to Lady Cowper, dancing 'very well,' and the prince 'better than anybody' (*Lebensbeschreibung*, 12–26; KLOPP, xiv. 359, 583–93; MACPHERSON, *Orig. Papers*, ii. 563, 573, 590–2, 625; LEIBNIZ, *Corresp. avec l'Electrice Sophie*, ed. Klopp, iii. 454, 487; *Three Letters sent from Her Most Gracious Majesty, viz., one to the Princess Sophia*, &c., London, 1714; BOYER, 1714, pt. ii. 267, 327, 340, 375; *Hist. Reg. Chron. Diary*, 1714–16; LADY COWPER, 11). On 12 Feb. 1715 the prince took the oaths as Duke of Rothesay, and on 17 March his seat in the House of Lords. 'I have not,' he had said before leaving Herrenhausen, 'a drop of blood in my veins which is not English.' He had won popular favour by his gallantry at Oudenarde, celebrated by Congreve in a ballad in which the prince figured as 'young Hanover brave.' On 1 Feb. he was chosen governor of the South Sea Company; on 8 April appointed president of the Society of Ancient Britons, recently established in honour of the princess; and on 5 May captain-general of the Honourable Artillery Company. In the debate on the civil list (13 May) the tories proposed that one-seventh of the 700,000*l.* to be voted should be specially appropriated to his use; and, though the motion was lost, it was understood that it was the desire of parliament that the allowance should be made. On 16 Feb. 1716 the prince was elected chancellor of Trinity College, Dublin. The prince vexed the Hanoverian courtiers by calling the English people 'the handsomest, the best-shaped, the best-natured and lovingest people in the world.' He paid court to one of the princess's maids of honour, the beautiful Mary Bellenden, daughter of John, lord Bellenden. She was already attached to her future husband, Colonel John Campbell, afterwards fourth duke of Argyll, and repulsed the prince decisively. He once, according to Horace Walpole (*Reminiscences*), appealed to her by counting over his money in her presence, till she exclaimed: 'Sir, I cannot bear it. If you count your money any more, I will go out of the room.' The prince avenged himself by inflicting petty annoyances upon her, and transferred his passion to another of the princess's maids of honour, Henrietta Howard [q. v.], afterwards Countess of Suffolk. She became his recognised favourite, and after his accession was provided with rooms in St. James's Palace, her husband being quieted by an annuity of 1,200*l.* In 1734 she was replaced by Madame Walmoden. The prince had been on bad terms with his father while both were still in Hanover, and a reconcilia-

tion after the death of the Electress Sophia was only temporary. The Hanoverians were offended by the prince's display of affection for his new country, while an intimacy which he soon formed with his groom of the stole, John Campbell, second duke of Argyll [q. v.], brought upon him the hatred of Argyll's enemies, Marlborough, Cadogan, and Sunderland. Argyll was deprived of all his offices after his suppression of the rebellion of 1715, owing, it is said, to the machinations of these combined factions. The king also required the prince to sever himself from Argyll, and the prince was only appointed guardian of the realm when the king went to Hanover (July 1716) on condition of yielding to this demand. Argyll, however, was received with distinction at the receptions which the prince now held at Hampton Court. The prince's popularity grew apace. Towards the end of September 1716 he made a progress from Hampton Court to Portsmouth, distributing largess copiously all the way, held a review of the troops and inspected the ships at Portsmouth, and was everywhere received with the utmost enthusiasm. He increased his popularity by his energy in superintending the suppression of a fire at Spring Gardens on 3 Dec., to which he walked from St. James's Palace in the early morning. He displayed great coolness a few days later at Drury Lane Theatre, when an assassin attempted to enter his box with a loaded pistol, and was only secured after taking the life of the guard in attendance (BOYER, 1714 pt. ii. 251, 1715 pt. i. 4, 141, 152, 302, 316, 423, 1716 pt. i. 407, 735, pt. ii. 118, 140, 284, 468, 644; PÖLLNITZ, *Memoirs*, iv. 328; LADY COWPER, 51, 58, 107–17; KEMBLE, *State Papers*, 512; HORACE WALPOLE, *Reminiscences*, cxxiii et seq.; *Walpoliana*, i. 85; HERVEY, i. 56; *Chesterfield Letters*, ed. Mahon, ii. 440; CAMPBELL, *Life of John, Duke of Argyll*, 1745, 267–75; *Hist. Reg.* 1716, 355; *Lebensbeschreibung*, 37–40).

At this time Sunderland, who had followed the king to Hanover, was intriguing to compass the downfall of Townshend, then secretary of state. He persuaded the king that Townshend and Argyll were in league with the prince to make him an independent power in the state. This brought about the dismissal of Townshend (December 1716). He accepted the lord-lieutenancy of Ireland, but was dismissed from that post also on 9 March 1717. On 2 Nov. the princess was delivered of a son. The king was to be one of the infant's godfathers, and the prince desired that his uncle, Ernest Augustus, duke of York (1674–1728) [q. v.], should be the other. The king insisted that the Duke of Newcastle, with whom the prince was on bad terms, should take the Duke of York's place. Directly after the baptism in the princess's bedroom, the prince shook his fist in Newcastle's face, exclaiming in his broken English, 'You are a rascal, but I shall find you.' The king hereupon confined the prince to his room, as though to prevent a duel. Two submissive letters from the prince induced the king to restore him his liberty, but he was still excluded from St. James's Palace, the princess having the option of remaining there with her children or accompanying the prince and leaving them behind her. She joined the prince at the Earl of Grantham's house in Arlington Street. Thence on 23 Jan. 1718 they removed to Leicester House, Leicester Fields, where they resided, attended only by their own servants, and without any of the insignia of state. A bill was now drafted in the cabinet to give the king absolute control of the prince's income, but was dropped mainly in consequence of the determined opposition of Lord-chancellor Cowper [q. v.] At Leicester House and at Richmond Lodge, their summer residence, the prince and princess now gathered round them a brilliant court, which was immediately thrown into opposition by an official announcement that all who should attend the prince's receptions must forbear his majesty's presence [see CAROLINE, QUEEN, 1683-1737]. On 3 Feb. the prince was removed from the governorship of the South Sea Company, the king being elected in his place (COXE, *Walpole*, i. 93-107; WALPOLE, *Reminiscences*, cxi; *Marchmont Papers*, ii. 84; SALMON, *Chron. Hist.*, ed. Toone, i. 462-3; *Lebensbeschreibung*, 41-50). In order further to humiliate the prince, the king determined if possible to deprive him permanently of the custody of his children. The 'care and approbation' of his grandchildren's marriages was undoubtedly vested in the sovereign, but there was no precedent to decide whether he had also the custody and education of them. The king had a case submitted to the common law judges, and the prince on his part took the opinion of several eminent counsel. The judges met to try the case at Serjeants' Inn on 22 Jan. 1717-18. The majority of the judges, Eyre and Price alone dissenting, decided for the king on the ground that the right of disposing of his grandchildren in marriage carried with it all the other rights of a father, to the exclusion of the true father (HOWELL, *State Trials*, xv. 1200 et seq.) The famous proposal for limiting the number of peers was calculated to humiliate the prince, and was ultimately defeated by his friends in the opposition. The king also sought to obtain an act of parlia-

ment to sever the connection between England and Hanover on the prince's accession to the throne, but abandoned the idea in deference to an adverse opinion of Lord-chancellor Parker, afterwards Earl of Macclesfield. A scheme for kidnapping the prince and transporting him to America, projected by the Earl of Berkeley, first lord of the admiralty, and reduced to writing by Charles Stanhope, elder brother of the Earl of Harrington, was apparently regarded by the king as a measure which might be resorted to in case of extremity. The draft was carefully preserved by him, and was found among his papers at his death. Walpole may have exaggerated the story, for which, however, there is some ground (see WALPOLE, *Reminiscences*, p. cx; COXE, *Walpole*, i. 300, ii. 630). The discredit brought by this unnatural feud upon the Hanoverian dynasty at length determined the whigs to attempt to bring about a reconciliation. An opportunity presented itself in the spring of 1720. The Hanoverians were clamouring for the repeal of the clause in the Act of Settlement (12 and 13 Will. III, c. 2 sec. 3) which excluded them from the English and Scottish peerage and all offices under government in Great Britain. Sunderland, not being able to secure the repeal of this clause, was compelled to make overtures to Townshend and Walpole in order to strengthen his position. Walpole refused to enter the ministry as long as the feud between the king and the prince continued. Overtures for a reconciliation were made in April 1720. A fragmentary account of the negotiations given in Lady Cowper's 'Diary' does not reveal the precise terms of the agreement. It is clear, however, that the prince was induced to write a submissive letter to the king, and to express penitence in a short private audience with the king. He was then permitted to visit the young princesses, and returned, amid the acclamations of the populace, to Leicester House under an escort of beefeaters, who mounted guard there for the first time since the rupture. On the 25th the foreign ambassadors had an audience of the prince. The king still treated the prince with marked coldness, left the regency in the hands of lords justices when he went to Hanover (14 June), and had not restored to the prince the custody of his children when Lady Cowper's 'Diary' terminates (5 July). On this footing matters stood during the remaining years of George I's life, the prince living a somewhat retired life, and being uniformly deprived of the regency during the king's visits to Hanover. His most intimate friends were the Earl of Scarborough, his master of the horse, and Sir Spencer Compton [q.v.], speaker of the House of Commons (COXE, *Walpole*, i. 116–33, 271; *Parl. Hist.* vii. 594–624; LADY COWPER, 129 et seq.; BOYER, 1720, pt. i. 450, 660; HERVEY, ii. 475–9; *Suffolk Corresp.* i. 53; WALPOLE, *Reminiscences*, cvi et seq.; *Lebensbeschreibung*, 51–5). On the death of George I, the news was carried to the prince at Richmond by Sir Robert Walpole (14 June). The new king received the intelligence without any display of emotion, and curtly told Walpole to go to Chiswick and take his instructions from Sir Spencer Compton, whom he thus designated prime minister. The king forthwith proceeded to Leicester House, where he held his first council the same day. At the meeting the archbishop of Canterbury produced the late king's will, in the expectation that it would be read. The king, however, put it in his pocket, and it was seen no more. A duplicate had been deposited with the Duke of Brunswick, and rumours of its contents got abroad. It contained a legacy to the queen of Prussia, no part of which was ever paid, though Frederick the Great, soon after his accession, endeavoured to recover it by diplomatic action (GLOVER, p. 55; HERVEY, i. 30 et seq.; *Marchmont Papers*, ii. 412; WALPOLE, *Reminiscences*, cxvi et seq.; FREDERICK THE GREAT, *Polit. Corresp.* i. 38).

Compton declined to form an administration. The king, by the advice of the queen, continued Walpole in office, who in return arranged that the civil list should be settled on a scale of unprecedented liberality, 830,000*l.* in lieu of a previous 700,000*l.*, that 50,000*l.* should be allowed for the queen's establishment, with Somerset House and Richmond Lodge for her residences, and that her jointure should be fixed at 100,000*l.* The king replaced Lord Berkeley by Sir George Byng, Viscount Torrington, at the admiralty, but made no other material change in the administration. The coronation ceremony was performed on 11 Oct. with great magnificence, the queen being ablaze from head to foot with jewels, most of them hired. On his birthday (30 Oct.) the king went in state with the queen and royal family to dine with the lord mayor at Guildhall. In April 1728 he visited Cambridge, and received from the university the degree of D.D.; on 29 Sept. he assumed his stall as sovereign of the order of the Garter at Windsor. The continuance of Walpole in office disappointed many hopes both at home and abroad. The party which had gathered round the prince during his disgrace tried vainly to regain favour by paying court first to Mrs. Howard, and then to Mrs. Clayton, afterwards Lady Sundon. Lord Scarborough remained master of the

horse, Sir Spencer Compton was created Lord Wilmington (1728), Lord Hervey became the favourite of the queen, Argyll and Chesterfield gradually drifted into opposition. Abroad it had been generally anticipated that the king's accession would be followed by a change of policy. Articles had been signed preliminary to a congress of the great powers to arrange a general pacification, but pretexts were found by the Spanish court to defer the ratification. Meanwhile the emperor menaced Hanover, the siege of Gibraltar was not raised, Spanish men-of-war and privateers continued to harass English commerce. The continuity of Walpole's policy, however, remained unbroken. By retaining in British pay the twelve thousand Hessians hired by the late king, and subsidising the Duke of Brunswick, he defeated the emperor's designs on Hanover, and Spain at length ratified the articles. The congress met at Soissons on 14 June (N.S.) 1728, and broke up without any material result except the detachment of the emperor from Spain. Spain, thus isolated, was reduced to conclude a separate peace with Great Britain by the treaty of Seville, 9 Nov. (N.S.) 1729 (HERVEY, i. 59, 89, 94, 100, 103, 107, 131, 164; COXE, *Walpole*, i. 301–3; *Hist. Reg.* 1728, p. 312; NICHOLS, *Lit. Anecd.* ii. 454 *n.*; *Walpoliana*, i. 86; *Parl. Hist.* viii. 642, 680; DE GARDEN, iii. 145; JENKINSON, ii. 306). On 17 May 1729 the king, having previously appointed the queen regent of the realm, left England for Hanover, where he had many affairs to settle. The king's divorced mother, Sophia Dorothea, had died 22 Nov. 1726, leaving a will by which she bequeathed her allodial estate to her friend the Count von Bar. This being by German law invalid, the property devolved upon George and his sister, the queen of Prussia. The Count von Bar had deposited the will in the imperial court at Vienna, and George took proceedings in concert with the king of Prussia to recover it, and there was much tedious litigation before the estate was realised and partitioned, nor was the king of Prussia altogether satisfied with the share which he obtained in right of his wife. He was also annoyed when his wife's uncle, Ernest Augustus, bishop of Osnabrück, who died 14 Aug. 1728, left George his entire estate, except his jewels, which he bequeathed to the queen of Prussia. The two sovereigns had never been on good terms. They had met as boys at Hanover and fought; they had been rivals in love, Frederick William having been passionately attached to Queen Caroline before her marriage; their characters were antipathetic, Frederick William scornfully nicknaming George 'the comedian,' and George returning the compliment by calling Frederick William 'the archbeadle of the Holy Roman Empire.' Both were engaged under the emperor's orders in the desperate attempt to settle the affairs of Mecklenburg, which had long been in a state of anarchy, and were far from unanimous as to the means to be employed. George had also a standing grievance in the king of Prussia's practice of impressing Hanoverian subjects for his army on Hanoverian soil. George conceived himself slighted because on his journey to Hanover he was permitted to traverse Prussian territory at his own expense. Accordingly he omitted to inform Frederick William of his arrival at Herrenhausen in May 1729, and the omission being brought to the notice of Lord Townshend by the Prussian minister, he coldly (and untruly) replied that it was in accordance with usage. Some Hanoverian soldiers carried off hay from Prussian territory, and some Prussian soldiers, travelling with passports in Hanover, were detained by the king's express orders. Frederick William at first demanded satisfaction by duel, seconds were named, and a meeting arranged. Diplomacy, however, averted the duel and suggested an arbitration. Of this, however, George would not hear. Thereupon Frederick William mobilised forty-four thousand troops, and began massing them on the Hanoverian frontier. George also made a show of warlike preparations, but eventually accepted the arbitration. The arbitrators met at Brunswick towards the end of September, and after some delay arranged (April 1730) for an exchange of the Prussians arrested by George against some of the Hanoverians impressed by Frederick William, and the cessation of military preparations. The affair of the hay was allowed to drop. Meanwhile George had returned to England in September 1729 (HERVEY, ii. 467; *Hist. Reg.* 1729, pp. 221–57; BOYER, 1729, pt. i. 516, pt. ii. 178, 282–8; HOPPE, *Gesch. der Stadt Hannover*, 182; VEHSE, i. 244; BUCHOLTZ, *Versuch in der Geschichte des Herzogthums Mecklenburg*, 638; BÜSCHING, *Beyträge zu der Lebensgeschichte*, &c., i. 305 et seq., 318 et seq.; *Lebensbeschreibung*, 162–72; *A Letter from an English Traveller to his Friend in London relating to the Differences betwixt the Courts of Prussia and Hanover*, London, 1730; FREDERICK THE GREAT, *Memoirs of the House of Brandenburg*, iii. 69, 72–3, London, 1768; a detailed account of this curious quarrel will be found in CARLYLE, *Frederick the Great*, ii. 266–99). The petty squabble thus at length composed left behind it so much bitterness as effectually to put an end to a negotiation which had long been pending for a cross match between the houses of England and

Prussia, by the marriage of Frederic Louis, Prince of Wales, to the Princess Sophia Dorothea Wilhelmina of Prussia, and of the crown prince of Prussia to George's second daughter, Princess Amelia. The Prince of Wales, who was, or fancied himself, ardently in love with Wilhelmina, had been brought to England for the first time, in deference to the urgent representations of the ministry in December 1728, and was soon openly on bad terms with his father. The king pretended in 1729 that the civil list was deficient to the extent of 115,000*l.* No such deficit could be proved, but the House of Commons was induced by Walpole to vote the amount under the name of an arrear (*Hist. Reg.* 1728, p. 319; COXE, *Walpole*, i. 299; *Parl. Hist.* viii. 605, 702; CARLYLE, *Frederick the Great*, ii. 312 et seq.) The prince was sarcastic on his father's conduct in this matter, and provoked because the regency had not been left in his hands during the king's absence in Hanover. The prince soon had a 'minister' of his own, viz. Bubb Dodington, afterwards Lord Melcombe [q. v.] When Walpole introduced his celebrated Excise Bill the king favoured it because it would tend to swell the civil list. The prince accordingly countenanced the opposition which defeated it (HERVEY, i. 120–126, 182, 212). The king kept the prince very short of money, allowing him only 36,000*l.* out of the 100,000*l.* which, when the civil list was settled, was understood to be for his use. The king patronised Handel, and the prince with many of the nobility deserted the Haymarket for the rival opera house in Lincoln's Inn Fields. The prince found further cause of offence in the marriage of the princess royal to the Prince of Orange in 1734, alleging that he was entitled to a settlement before his sister. The king became extremely unpopular, and the prince fancied himself the idol of the people [see FREDERICK LOUIS, PRINCE OF WALES, 1707–1751]. The attention of the king was diverted from the prince by the course of events on the continent. On the death of Augustus the Strong, elector of Saxony and king of Poland (1 Feb. 1732–3), the succession of his heir Frederic Augustus to the throne of Poland was disputed by Stanislaus Leczinsky. Louis XV supported Stanislaus in order to have a pretext for attacking the emperor, who favoured Frederic Augustus. On 14 Oct. 1733, after the election of Frederic Augustus in place of Stanislaus, Louis declared war and invaded the emperor's dominions. The emperor appealed to England for help. The king and queen were eager for war on his behalf, and were with the utmost difficulty restrained by Walpole. The king then entered into a negotiation with the view of effecting an alliance between Spain and the emperor. The terms arranged were that the emperor should marry the second archduchess to a Spanish prince, who should succeed to the kingdom of Naples and Sicily on the emperor's death, and that Spain should meanwhile guarantee the integrity of the empire. The negotiation went forward in London under the personal superintendence of the king, who earnestly pressed the imperial ambassador to close the bargain. He, however, hesitated, urging the need of express instructions, and before these came Spain had concluded an alliance with France. The emperor was beaten in the Rhine, in northern Italy, and in Naples, where the Spaniards crowned Don Carlos (May 1734). The Young Pretender served in their army as a volunteer, and was received by Don Carlos with distinction. The king, excited by these events, would hear and talk of nothing but war, and the queen was in much the same temper. Walpole at last prevailed. He warned the queen that if England took any part in the foreign imbroglio 'her crown would at last as surely come to be fought for as the crown of Poland.' The queen yielded and the king followed suit, and thus, to quote Lord Hervey, 'the shadow of the Pretender beat the whole Germanic body' (CARLYLE, *Frederick the Great*, iii. 195 et seq.; *Nouv. Biog. Gén.* 'Stanislas;' HERVEY, i. chap. xii. and xv.) Before parliament rose, however, George obtained power to augment his land forces during the recess, and on 19 Sept. he concluded a treaty with Denmark for the hire of six thousand horse and foot. The treaty, which was to last for three years, was laid before and approved by parliament early in the following year (*Parl. Hist.* ix. 651, 851). In May 1735 the king went to Hanover, where he met and soon became attached to Amelia Sophia, the young and beautiful wife of Adam Gottlob, count von Walmoden. With engaging frankness he confessed his love to the queen, adding, 'You must love the Walmoden, for she loves me' (HERVEY, i. 424–8, 497–500; BIELFELD, *Lettres*, 1763, i. 187; VEHSE, i. 272). He had not been long in Hanover before the emperor made him the tempting offer of the command of the army of the Rhine as the price of the English alliance. He had, however, been so well schooled by Walpole before he left England that he was able to say 'No.' Having met the Princess Augusta of Saxe-Gotha, he fixed on her as an eligible match for the Prince of Wales. Before leaving Hanover he promised the Estates that he would take the burden of the contingent of troops which the electorate was bound to furnish for the imperial army

upon his own exchequer, instead of asking them for a subsidy. He returned to England in October in ill-health and worse humour, loudly expressing his regret for Hanover and disgust with England. He had left Madame Walmoden behind, and the queen suffered much in consequence from his ill-temper (HERVEY, ii. 6, 17, 28, 33, 43; BOYER, 1735, pt. i. 561, ii. 459, 492). The marriage of the prince with the Princess Augusta took place on 27 April 1736, being hurried on by the king, who ardently desired to escape to Hanover and Madame Walmoden again. The king raised the prince's allowance to 50,000*l.*, which, according to Lord Hervey, was regarded by the prince and 'most people' as equivalent to robbing him of 50,000*l.*, the other half of the income due to him (HERVEY, ii. 117–20). The king set out for Hanover on 22 May, and reached Herrenhausen on the 28th. He had not long been there when an officer was found under suspicious circumstances under the windows of Madame Walmoden, who declared it to be a plot of her enemies. George laid the whole affair before the queen, advising her to consult Walpole, who had more experience than she, and more impartiality than himself (*ib.* 128; BOYER, 1736, ii. 1). The king's birthday drew near, but the king showed no sign of returning, a mark of indifference which he had hitherto spared the queen. She was at first inclined to try what resentment could do to re-establish her ascendency, but at the instance of Walpole and Hervey abandoned this idea, and wrote the king a submissive and tender letter, begging that he would return and bring Madame Walmoden with him. This elicited a very frank and friendly letter from the king, in which he gave a minute description of Madame Walmoden's personal charms, and desired the queen to have the rooms which Lady Suffolk had occupied prepared for her reception, which was accordingly done. The king's protracted stay in Hanover was keenly resented by all classes, while his neglect of the queen and devotion to his foreign mistress excited further disgust. The national discontent found expression in a multitude of pasquinades and lampoons, most of which, according to Lord Hervey, only flattered the king's vanity by their testimony to his eminence as a lover (HERVEY, ii. 174–92). It was not until December that the king left Hanover. His return was delayed for some days by a violent storm which caused great excitement in England, most people confidently expecting to hear that the royal yacht had foundered. The king at last insisted, against the advice of Sir Charles Wager, on putting to sea. 'Let it be what weather it will,' he exclaimed, 'I am not afraid,' to which Wager replied laconically, 'If you are not, I am.' Wager at last gave way, but after a short experience the king was glad enough to be put on shore again at Helvoetsluys, and admitted that he was so satisfied with the storm that he did not desire ever to see another. The king's unpopularity was not in the least diminished by his danger. It was a common occurrence to hear people in the streets wish him at the bottom of the sea, and even the soldiers drank damnation to him. The queen sincerely rejoiced at his safety, wrote to congratulate him on his escape, and was answered in a lengthy epistle of thirty pages full of rapturous expressions of love and devotion. He landed on 15 Jan. 1736–7 at Lowestoft, and arrived on the 17th at St. James's in good humour and bad health. He had caught a severe cold on the passage, and this soon developed into a regular fever, which, though apparently never really dangerous, caused some apprehension. Meanwhile it was determined by the junto that now governed the prince that the question of his revenue should be formally raised in parliament. The rumour of this only roused the king. He resumed his levees, behaved with unusual graciousness to everybody, successfully dissembled his anxiety, and began visibly to improve in health. The general impression was that the prince's friends were likely to secure a majority in parliament, and Walpole induced the king to send a message to the prince notifying his intention to settle upon him the 50,000*l.* a year allowed him since his marriage, which had so far remained in the discretion of the king, and also a suitable jointure upon the princess. The prince professed gratitude for a concession more apparent than real; but on 22 Feb. Pulteney in the House of Commons, and on the following day Lord Carteret in the House of Lords, moved that an address might be presented to the king, praying that an annuity of 100,000*l.* might be settled on the prince. It was urged that it was a tacit condition of the grant of the civil list that such an allowance, being the same as the king had when he was prince, should be made. The motion, however, was lost in both houses, the victory being mainly due to the dexterous use made by Walpole of the king's attempt at a compromise (*ib.* pp. 236–81; *Parl. Hist.* ix. 1352 et seq.) Both king and queen keenly resented the action of the prince, and were hardly restrained by Walpole from turning him out of St. James's; nor, though he was permitted to remain in the palace, would the queen speak to him or the king even recog-

nise his existence, and Walpole had much ado to induce them so far to keep faith with the prince and the public as to settle a jointure of 50,000*l.* a year upon the princess, at the same time exempting the prince's allowance from taxation, and enabling him to make leases of the lands within the Duchy of Cornwall (HERVEY, ii. 283, 341; Stat. 10 Geo. II, c. 29). The king at this time paid much attention to one of his daughters' governesses, Anne Howard, widow of Henry Scott, first earl of Deloraine, and wife of William Wyndham, sub-governor to the Duke of Cumberland. Lady Deloraine was, says Lord Hervey, 'one of the vainest as well as one of the simplest women that ever lived; but she had one of the prettiest faces ever formed, and though now five-and-thirty had a bloom that not one woman in ten thousand has at fifteen' (HERVEY, ii. 351). She is supposed to have been the original of Pope's Delia (*Satires*, i. l. 81). For a time Madame Walmoden seemed to be forgotten.

The prince's disobedient conduct in hurrying his wife by night, while in the very pangs of labour, from Hampton Court to St. James's to lie in there, caused a complete rupture between him and the king and queen (31 July 1737). Through the influence of Walpole the prince was indeed permitted to remain at St. James's, but angry letters were exchanged, and the king refused to see the prince. The king and queen condescended, however, to become godparents to the young princess (Augusta), who was baptised on 29 Aug., but, offended by the manner in which this attention was received by the prince, gave him on 10 Sept. notice to quit St. James's Palace. The foreign ministers were requested to forbear his society, and the court was informed that all who were received by him would be excluded from the king's presence. The king even pushed his spite so far as to forbid the prince to remove his furniture from the palace (HERVEY, ii. 348, 362–409, 421–34, 439–40; *Marchmont Papers*, ii. 83; HARRIS, *Life of Lord Chanc. Hardwicke*, i. 363 et seq.) During the last illness of Queen Caroline the prince begged to be allowed to see her (11 Nov.), but the king sent Lord Hervey to him with a curt refusal, and the queen died without seeing him, or expressing any desire to do so. As her death drew near, the king showed much clumsy tenderness, teased her with various suggestions about her food and drink, fairly sobbed when she urged him to marry again after her death, and with much difficulty got out the words, 'Non, j'aurai des maîtresses,' to which the queen replied, 'Ah! mon Dieu! cela n'empêche pas' (HERVEY, ii. 499–504, 513–14). He was loud in his praise of the queen's understanding and various virtues, descanting by the way on his own merit, and particularly on the courage which he had exhibited during the storm, and his own recent illness. The queen died on 20 Nov. 1737 at 10 P.M. The king after kissing the face and hands of the corpse several times went to bed, but for several nights had attendants to sit up with him. His grief for the queen was heartfelt, and did much to redeem his character with the nation, to which it came as a surprise (*ib.* pp. 534–43; COXE, *Walpole*, i. 553). True to his promise he lost little time in bringing Madame Walmoden from Hanover, a step much favoured by Walpole, who hoped to manage him through her influence. She landed in England in June 1738, and was accommodated in St. James's Palace. She was permitted to exercise a certain amount of patronage, and was created Countess of Yarmouth in 1739, but she never acquired any ascendency over the king in affairs of state. A dispute about the title to the castle of Steinhorst in Holstein, which George claimed to have acquired by purchase, nearly led to a war with Denmark, but was compromised in March 1739 by the king of Denmark selling his rights for seventy thousand thalers. About the same time George concluded a treaty with Denmark similar to that of 1734. It was approved by parliament on 10 May (WALPOLE, *Reminiscences*, cli; SALMON, *Chron. Hist.* ed. Toone, i. 557; *Parl. Hist.* x. 1366; *Lebensbeschreibung*, 236–46). Walpole soon found that the king was secretly thwarting his foreign policy, and talked of resigning. Of this, however, George would not hear. He had become weary of peace, but hoped that Walpole might be induced to adopt a warlike policy. His bellicose temper was now the temper of the nation, which clamoured for war with Spain. The Assiento treaty, by which English trade with Spanish America had been limited to the supply of a fixed number of negroes by the South Sea Company, had led to bitter disputes through the restrictions imposed by the Spanish government in order to prevent evasions. It was to expire in 1743. Walpole, anxious for peace, endeavoured to provide for the future arrangements by negotiation. Plenipotentiaries were named, met, and separated without coming to any agreement, and on 23 Oct. 1739 the king had his way and declared war. In May 1740 he went to Hanover, and made some ineffectual attempts to secure the alliance of Frederick the Great. He returned to England in October. The capture of Porto Bello by Admiral Vernon in December was followed by an attempt on Carthagena which failed (April 1741); after

which the war was allowed to languish, the attention of the king and people being diverted to the gigantic struggle in which the death of Charles VI (20 Oct. N.S. 1740) and the ambition of Frederick the Great had involved the continent of Europe. On the outbreak of the first Silesian war, fear for the safety of Hanover, and indignation at what he regarded as a flagrant breach of international law, combined with his natural gallantry to enlist George II on the side of the queen of Hungary. The nation was with the king, the cabinet was divided. Walpole succeeded in staving off hostilities for a time, but in April 1741 a subsidy of 300,000*l.* was voted to the queen of Hungary. George, in spite of a strong remonstrance from Walpole, hurried to Hanover in the following month, accompanied by Lord Harrington, secretary of state for the northern province, and there concluded (24 June N.S.) a treaty with Maria Theresa providing for prompt quarterly payment of the subsidy, and also for the immediate despatch of a force of twelve thousand Hessian and Danish troops pursuant to a treaty of 1732. For the defence of Hanover he collected an army of twenty-eight thousand men, and twelve thousand more were assembled at Lexden Heath, near Colchester, ready for emergencies. A force of thirty thousand Prussians under Leopold of Anhalt Dessau was encamped on the borders of Brandenburg and Brunswick, and in the middle of August the French under Belleisle and Maillebois crossed the Rhine eighty thousand strong, and marched straight on Osnabrück. George felt himself caught in a trap, and hastily concluded a treaty with France pledging Hanover to neutrality (28 Oct. N.S.), and returned to England. No term being fixed for the duration of the treaty, the king broke it as soon as it was convenient to do so (COXE, *Walpole*, i. 536–62, 573–604, 615–26, 635–40, 674–9, 685; COXE, *Pelham*, i. 17; FREDERICK THE GREAT, *Polit. Corresp.* i. 7–45, 311–65; FREDERICK THE GREAT, *Hist. de mon Temps* (1788), i. 208; JENKINSON, i. 379; DE GARDEN, iii. 258–60; MARTENS, *Supplément*, i. 262). On 9 Feb. 1741–2 Walpole, having lost command of the House of Commons, accepted a peerage, and three days later resigned. The king was moved to tears when he took his leave. By Walpole's advice he offered the first lordship of the treasury to Pulteney, who declined, stipulating, however, for a peerage and a seat in the cabinet without office. He was accordingly created Earl of Bath. The first lordship of the treasury was given to Spencer Compton, now Lord Wilmington. Carteret succeeded Harrington as secretary of state for the northern province. The Duke of Newcastle and Lord Hardwicke retained their places, and Henry Pelham, brother of the Duke of Newcastle, became paymaster of the forces. The Prince of Wales was reconciled to the king. Of the new ministers Carteret was the only one who knew German, and he soon monopolised the confidence of the king, with whose ambition to play a prominent part in European politics he sympathised (COXE, *Walpole*, i. 698-700; GLOVER, i. 8; *Gent. Mag.* 1742, pp. 107-8, 163, 387). How far the policy which for the next three years was pursued was due to Carteret's, how far to the king's initiative, cannot be precisely determined [see CARTERET, JOHN]. Its general scope was to engage the Dutch in alliance for the defence of the Austrian Netherlands against France and Prussia, to afford Maria Theresa all possible aid short of an actual declaration of war in her favour, and to endeavour to mediate a peace between her and Frederick with the ulterior object of detaching Frederick from France, and uniting him in a defensive alliance with Great Britain. In response to a royal message, the House of Commons placed half a million at the disposal of the king to employ as he might see fit on behalf of the queen of Hungary (*Parl. Hist.* xii. 591). His mediatorial efforts, coinciding as they did with the brilliant successes of the Prussian arms, resulted in the treaty of Breslau, by which Maria Theresa ceded Silesia to Frederick (11 June, N.S. 1742). By a separate 'act of guarantee' George pledged himself to do his utmost to secure the faithful observance of the treaty by both parties (24 June, N.S.). It was confirmed by a definitive treaty of peace signed at Berlin on 28 July, N.S. On 18 Nov., N.S., George concluded a defensive alliance with Frederick. The king next offered his good offices as mediator between the new emperor, Charles VII, and the queen of Hungary, providing in the meantime for the defence of the Austrian Netherlands against France, and a possible diversion in favour of the queen in Flanders, in the event of the negotiations falling through. No effort was spared to induce the Dutch to co-operate. Carteret himself was sent to the Hague to extort from the States-General a decisive answer, and obtained a promise of a contingent of twenty thousand men. The king's Hanoverian forces were taken into British pay, and, strengthened by reinforcements from England, were gradually pushed into the Netherlands during the autumn and winter. A defensive alliance was concluded with Russia on 11 Dec. N.S. (FREDERICK THE GREAT, *Polit. Corresp.* ii. passim; FREDERICK THE GREAT, *Hist. de mon Temps* (1788)

i. 242; COXE, *Pelham*, i. §§ iv, v; WENCK, i. 640, 649, 734-9, 781). In May 1743 the Dutch contingent was actually mobilised, and cantoned about Maestricht and Namur. The British, Hanoverian, and Austrian forces meanwhile concentrated in the neighbourhood of Mainz, where they remained for a time to secure the election of the Austrian candidate, the Graf von Ostein, as chairman of the imperial diet (22 April, N.S.) (ADELUNG, *Pragmatische Staatsgeschichte Europens*, iii. pt. ii. 113, 121). On 27 April George left England, and after staying a few weeks at Hanover joined the army about the middle of June, taking with him Carteret and Cumberland. The French meanwhile, under Marshal Noailles, had crossed the Rhine, and lay seventy thousand strong about Seligenstadt on the south bank of the Main. The allied or Pragmatic army, numbering about forty thousand men, had its base at Hanau on the north bank, but on 26 June (N.S.) was encamped at Aschaffenburg. During the night the French crossed the river at Seligenstadt, and took up a strong position at Dettingen, where the allies encountered them while retreating on Hanau in the morning. While hesitating whether to force their way through or retire on Aschaffenburg, they were imprudently attacked by Noailles, who thus forfeited the advantage of his position, was repulsed with great loss, and finally driven across the river. The king, whose horse bolted early in the action, placed himself on foot at the head of his troops, brandished his sword, and exclaimed, 'Now, boys, now for the honour of England; fire and behave bravely, and the French will soon run.' He remained in the field throughout the day, exposing his person with the utmost gallantry (*Gent. Mag.* 1743, pp. 217, 278, 328-30, 381). Though the king was nominally in command of the British and Hanoverian forces, the responsibility for such strategy as was exhibited on this occasion does not rest with him, but with the generals who formed his council of war, and particularly with Lord Stair. Nothing was done to improve the victory in a military sense, but its effect on England was enormous. The king suddenly became a popular hero, and Handel composed a Te Deum in honour of the occasion. The moment seemed favourable for diplomatic action, and accordingly George, with the help of Carteret, who had accompanied him to the field, attempted to arrange a treaty by which the emperor should renounce his claims on the Austrian succession, permit the Grand Duke of Tuscany to be crowned king of the Romans, and withdraw from the French alliance, in consideration of being guaranteed peaceful possession of Bavaria, his imperial title, and an annual subsidy from England. The treaty was actually drafted at Hanau, and provisionally signed, but lapsed in consequence of the lords justices, in whom the regency had been vested during the king's absence, refusing to ratify it, and thus the fruits of the victory were entirely thrown away. From Hanau the king and Carteret went to Worms, and there concluded (13 Sept. N.S.) a treaty of alliance with the queen of Hungary and the king of Sardinia, by which the contracting parties mutually guaranteed all dominions which they did or ought to possess, and Great Britain granted the king of Sardinia a subsidy of 200,000*l.*, and engaged to maintain a strong fleet in the Mediterranean. This treaty, which was intended principally as a security against Spanish designs on Italy, was ratified in due course. In November the king returned to England (*ib.* 1743, pp. 391, 447, 610; COXE, *Pelham,* i. 75–7, 164; *Marchmont Papers,* i. 25; WENCK, i. 682; DE GARDEN, iii. 294; *Parl. Hist.* xiii. 101).

Early in 1744 the Young Pretender was received at the French court with marks of distinction, and in March France formally declared war on England. George's diplomacy was now mainly directed towards inducing the Dutch to come to an open rupture with France, and obtaining succours from Frederick the Great, pursuant to the defensive alliance of 18 Nov. (N.S.) 1742. The Dutch, however, could be prevailed upon no further than to furnish a contingent of six thousand men, and Frederick readily found pretexts for refusing to render any assistance. A further treaty for a subsidy of 150,000*l.* to the queen of Hungary was signed on 1 Aug. On 10 Aug. (N.S.) Frederick declared war upon her, and forthwith marched into Bohemia. This step produced a ministerial crisis in England. The majority of the cabinet were disgusted with the unexpected length of the war. They took Lord Chesterfield and his faction into their counsels, and submitted to the king a joint note in effect demanding Carteret's dismissal. The king was very reluctant to comply. 'Lord Carteret has served *me* very well,' he said to the Duke of Newcastle. But as the junto at length threatened to resign *en masse,* the king yielded, and dismissed Carteret (24 Nov. 1744). A ministry of all the factions was then formed under Henry Pelham. The new ministry was bent on making peace as soon as possible. In the meantime they desired to carry on the war upon a concerted plan, and with a clear understanding as to the distribution of expense. Lord Chesterfield was sent to the Hague to treat on this point with the Dutch. The negotiation issued, however,

in the union or quadruple alliance of Warsaw (8 Jan. N.S. 1745), by which the country was burdened with the payment to the elector of Saxony for the defence of Bohemia of two-thirds of an annual subsidy of 150,000*l.* 'so long as necessity should require,' Holland becoming responsible for the residue (*Gent. Mag.* 1743 pp. 389, 444, 668, 1744 pp. 154, 167, 226, 285, 1745 p. 55; FREDERICK THE GREAT, *Polit. Corresp.* iii. 104, 142, iv. 5–15, 81, 83, 203, 211, 241, 246; *Marchmont Papers,* i. 3, 15, 65, 73–88; COXE, *Lord Walpole,* p. 275; COXE, *Pelham,* i. 189, 198, 209; WENCK, ii. 163, 171; DE GARDEN, iii. 319; LORD CHESTERFIELD, 'Apology for a late Resignation,' *Works,* ed. Mahon, v. 58 et seq.)

The course of events during the summer was, except for the unexpected conquest of Cape Breton by Sir Peter Warren, disastrous to the allies. The attempt to rouse the Dutch to energetic action signally failed, and the loss of the battle of Fontenoy (11 May, N.S.) placed the Netherlands at the mercy of the French. Frederick the Great gained a brilliant victory over the Austrians at Hohenfriedberg (3 June N.S.); the Young Pretender landed in Scotland in July. George, who had gone to Hanover in May, hereupon returned to England (31 Aug.) The ministry seized the opportunity to present him with a strongly worded memorial on the expediency of bringing the queen of Hungary to make peace on the terms of the treaty of Breslau. George, after indignant protests, at length consented to make an offer of mediation between Frederick and the queen. A negotiation carried on at Hanover in the autumn led to the treaty concluded at Dresden (25 Dec. N.S.), confirming the cession of Silesia, Great Britain giving Prussia a separate guarantee of quiet possession. Meanwhile the brilliant successes of the French under Marshal Saxe in the Netherlands, from which the British troops had been withdrawn on the outbreak of the Jacobite rebellion, alarmed the Dutch, who sent urgent appeals to England for help. The king would fain have afforded it, but the ministry refused. They also demanded that Pitt, whose anti-Hanoverian speeches had made him peculiarly obnoxious to the king, should be appointed secretary at war. The king would not hear of it. Harrington and Newcastle thereupon (10 Feb. 1744–5) resigned, and the king sent for Pulteney, earl of Bath, and Carteret, now lord Granville. This was met by the resignation of the rest of the ministers. Bath and Granville failed to form an administration, and the old ministers returned to power on the 14th, more resolute to terminate the war than before. The king was most dejected, called himself a prisoner

he had begun to recover (*Life of Hardwicke*, iii. 283; WALPOLE, *Letters*, iv. 1). In the hope of dividing the whigs, he persuaded Henry Fox to desert his party, and take the management of the commons, acting in this as in all else on Bute's suggestion (*Bedford Correspondence*, iii. 134). Persons about the court said that the 'king would now be king indeed,' and that the 'prerogative was to shine out.' The whigs were now to feel the royal displeasure. The Duke of Devonshire [see CAVENDISH, WILLIAM, fourth duke], whom the princess-dowager bitterly called the 'prince of the whigs,' and who had refused to take part in the discussions about the peace, was lord chamberlain. He called at St. James's in October, but the king sent him out a message by a page, 'Tell the duke I will not see him.' The duke resigned his office; his brother, Lord George Cavendish, a member of the household, also resigned, and the king accepted his resignation in person, and with marked discourtesy. Lord Rockingham remonstrated with the king, resigned his office in the bedchamber on 4 Nov., and was treated in the same manner. The same day the king with his own hand erased Devonshire's name from the list of privy councillors. Newcastle, Grafton, and Rockingham were deprived of their lieutenancies, and with the king's approval a general proscription of the whigs was carried out, which extended to inferior officials, such as clerks, and even to pensioners (*Rockingham Memoirs*, i. 135–60). When the king went to open parliament on the 25th, he was not cheered in the streets. The royal influence, however, was strong in parliament, and the preliminaries of peace were approved. This was a signal triumph. 'Now,' the princess said, 'my son is king of England.' George was delighted, and when the peace of Paris was concluded in February 1763, declared that 'England never signed such a peace before' (*Bedford Corr.* iii. 199).

Meanwhile a storm of indignation rose against Bute, and the king himself did not wholly escape it; for the minister was held to be a 'favourite.' Favouritism in its special sense was not one of George's weaknesses; while he had of course personal preferences, he showed favour to Bute, and in later times to other ministers not for personal, but for political, reasons. The influence which Bute exercised over him was jeered at in many ways, and among them by a caricature entitled 'The Royal Dupe' (WRIGHT, p. 285). Although the ministerial majority was strong in parliament—for, in addition to the practice of intimidation, 52,000*l.* a year was spent in maintaining it—Bute felt himself unable to brave the popular indignation, and resigned

on 8 April. George received his resignation with unexpected alacrity; he considered him 'deficient in political firmness,' and seems to have been rather glad to get rid of him as a minister (MALMESBURY, *Diaries*, iii. 163; ROSE, *Diaries*, ii. 192; WALPOLE, *George III*, iv. 133). By Bute's advice he appointed George Grenville to the treasury, laying down as a basis of the administration which he was to form, that none of the Newcastle and Pitt ministry were ever to return to office during his reign, but that favour might be shown to those whigs who would support his government (*Bedford Corr.* iii. 224). The speech with which the king closed parliament on 19 April was scurrilously commented on by Wilkes in No. 45 of the 'North Briton,' where it was treated not as the king's, but as the minister's speech. George ordered that Wilkes should be prosecuted, urged forward the violent measures taken against him, treated the matter as a personal quarrel, and dismissed Temple from his lord-lieutenancy for sympathy with Wilkes (*Grenville Papers*, ii. 162, 192; WALPOLE, *George III*, iii. 296; LECKY, iii. 71). Grenville took office with the intention of shielding the king from dictation, but George found him masterful. The administration was bad, and the king was anxious to make some change in it. In August he offered cabinet office to Hardwicke, and even spoke of giving a court office to Newcastle, but Hardwicke would not come in alone, and George would not submit to take in a party in gross.

On the 21st George was much disturbed by the death of Lord Egremont, which weakened the tory side of the cabinet. By the advice of Bute he sent for Pitt, and on 27 Aug. requested him to state his opinions. Pitt dilated on the defects of the peace and the dismissal of the whigs, whom, he said, he should restore. George listened graciously, but said that his 'honour must be consulted.' He was in a difficult position; he wanted to get rid of his present ministers, and hoped that Pitt would have consented to be his minister without bringing with him any of the party which he hated. A decision was to be made on the 29th. The day before, Sunday, the 28th, Grenville saw the king, who was confused and flustered. The result of their conversation was that when Pitt the next day stated his terms, which were the treasury for Temple, and the restoration of the great whig families, the king refused them. 'My honour is concerned,' he said, 'and I must support it.' He asked Grenville to continue in office. The minister lectured him, and received the king's promise that Bute should not interfere. A few days later Bute made an attempt to win Pitt over. Grenville was indignant, and reproached the king, and when George promised that nothing of the sort should happen again, dryly answered that he hoped not. He insisted on Bute's retirement from London, and refused to allow the king to give the office of keeper of the privy purse, which Bute vacated, to one of Bute's friends. 'Good God! Mr. Grenville,' exclaimed the humiliated king, 'am I to be suspected after all I have done?' Bedford joined the administration; Bute left London, and for a time the king and his ministers were on better terms (*Grenville Papers*, ii. 197, 205, 210; *Life of Hardwicke*, iii. 278). George approved of their depriving military officers of their commands for voting against the government on the question of general warrants. 'Firmness and resolution,' he said, 'must be shown, and no one saved who dared to fly off.' He was much annoyed by the hereditary Prince of Brunswick, who came over in January 1764 to marry his sister Augusta, and who openly sympathised with the opposition. The king's unpopularity was shown by the enthusiasm with which the prince was received, and king and prince behaved rudely to each other. George disliked his ministers more and more; the administration was thoroughly bad, and was marked by want of concert, slackness, and haste. Grenville did his duty, but made himself personally hateful to the king by lecturing and thwarting him. Still George agreed with the chief measures taken by the ministers, and fully concurred in the Stamp Act, which became law on 22 March 1765. Meanwhile on 12 Jan. he was attacked by a serious illness, which lasted more or less until early in April, and during which symptoms of derangement appeared (MRS. PAPENDIEK, i. 33; *Quarterly Review*, cxxxi. 240).

On the king's recovery he wished that parliament should make provision for a regency in case of his death or incapacity, and proposed that he should be empowered to name from time to time the person he desired, keeping the nomination secret to 'prevent faction' (*Grenville Papers*, iii. 126). The ministers brought in a bill limiting his choice to the queen or any other person of the royal family. Bedford, out of dislike to Bute, was anxious to shut the king's mother out of any chance of power, and Halifax and Sandwich told George that unless this was done the bill would not pass the commons. He yielded to the representations of his ministers, apparently without grasping the full import of their proposal, and the princess was pointedly excluded. He soon became conscious of what he had done, had an interview with Grenville, in which he was much agitated, and even

shed tears, and besought the minister to replace her name. Grenville would only promise to yield if pressed in the commons, and the king's mortification was increased when, after a ludicrous exhibition of his ministers' weakness, the house insisted on replacing his mother's name. On 6 May, the day after his interview with Grenville, he asked his uncle, the Duke of Cumberland, who had considerable influence with the opposition, and whom he had from his boyhood treated with neglect and suspicion, to negotiate with Pitt, Temple, and the great whig families as to the formation of a 'strong and lasting administration' (Duke of Cumberland's Statement, *Rockingham Memoirs*, i. 189). On the 18th he cavalierly announced to Grenville his intention of dismissing his ministers (*ib.* p. 203). Bedford, who believed that Bute was at the bottom of the intended change, scolded the king (*Bedford Corr.* iii. 280). Meanwhile Pitt refused the offer of the court, and the king sent Cumberland to Lord Lyttelton, who also refused to attempt to form an administration. During these negotiations the Spitalfields weavers were raising riots, on account of the rejection of a bill intended to benefit their industry. They marched to the king's lodge, and not finding him there followed him to Wimbledon, where he listened to their complaints, and persuaded them to return to their homes. But disorders broke out afresh, and were perhaps only checked by the vigorous action of the king, who personally gave orders that troops should be in readiness to prevent disturbance. He was anxious not to appear to avoid the rioters, and declared his willingness to 'put himself at the head of the army, or do anything else to save his country' (*Grenville Papers*, iii. 177). When Lyttelton refused the king's offer, Cumberland advised George to recall his ministers. He had a humiliating interview with Grenville on the 21st. The ministers compelled the king to promise that he would neither see Bute nor retain Bute's brother, Stuart Mackenzie, as privy seal in Scotland, though George had promised that he should keep the office (*ib.* p. 187). Although the king was in after days constantly suspected of acting by Bute's advice, it seems perfectly certain that he kept his word, and that he never willingly saw Bute again, or had any direct or indirect consultation with him after this. Grenville used his power mercilessly. 'When he has wearied me for two hours,' George once said, ' he looks at his watch to see if he may not tire me for one hour more.' The king allowed his dislike of his ministers to be seen, and on 12 June Bedford scolded him for not allowing his authority and his favour to go together, and accused him of listening to the misrepresentations of Bute. George heard him in silence, though he certainly was shamefully treated (*Bedford Corr.* iii. 288, 289). He again sent Cumberland to Pitt, who had two interviews with the king, and undertook to form an administration; but his arrangements were brought to an end on 25 June 1765 by Temple's refusal to accept the treasury. In his distress the king again turned to his uncle, who, with Newcastle's help, formed an administration under the Marquis of Rockingham, and on 10 July George at last got rid of Grenville. The humiliation of turning to the Rockingham whigs was a less evil than the retention of the old ministry. 'I would rather,' he said, 'see the devil in my closet than George Grenville' (*Rockingham Memoirs*, ii. 50).

George, though outwardly civil, thwarted his new ministers, and would not create peers on their recommendation. Indeed he probably from the first intended to get rid of them as soon as he could find others more subservient to himself. George saw with concern the abuses of the government in Ireland, and when Lord Hertford accepted the viceroyalty in October 1765, wrote him a paper of instructions, which was probably his own composition. It shows remarkable knowledge of the secret sources of mischief, and contains straightforward directions for destroying them by an honourable and decided policy (FROUDE, *English in Ireland*, ii. 39–43). Rockingham pressed to be allowed to treat with Pitt in January 1766. The king did not like the idea, probably because he did not wish to see the administration strengthened, and also because he did not want Pitt unless as, in a special sense, his own minister. He yielded, but Pitt was impracticable. George did not approve the repeal of the Stamp Act, though he was willing to modify it; but he asserted that he had all along preferred repeal to force, if one or the other was necessary. As Rockingham found that he was opposed by the king's friends, he obtained the king's sanction to the repeal in writing (*Rockingham Memoirs*, i. 301). George acted a double part, pretending to be pleased when his ministers were in a majority, but allowing the court party to see that his sympathies were really on the other side. Rockingham seems to have taxed him with this conduct (*ib.* pp. 299, 321; *Bedford Corr.* iii. 327). The repeal of the Stamp Act received the royal assent on 18 March. The retirement in May of the Duke of Grafton, one of the secretaries of state, was due to underhand negotiations carried on by Lord-chancellor Northington, who was one of the king's party. In July Northington openly quarrelled with his colleagues, and by his advice

the king sent for Pitt. George received Pitt with pleasure, put all arrangements under his control, and dismissed his ministers ungraciously. Pitt was created Earl of Chatham, and formed an administration of which he was the real, and Grafton the ostensible, head. George thus won a decided success. He got rid of the administration of the great whig families, and was delighted at securing Pitt, who, he had good reason to believe, would 'destroy all party distinctions,' and 'root out the present method of parties banding together' (*Chatham Corr.* iii. 21, 127). Chiefly through the king's policy the whigs were now divided into hostile sections. He was personally gratified by the restoration of Stuart Mackenzie to his former office.

The new administration fell at once into a state of weakness and division. Against his own will the king allowed Chatham to treat with Bedford, and when the negotiation failed told his minister that 'due firmness would show the Bedfords of what little consequence they were' (*ib.* p. 137). The administration became more tory in character, and derived what little strength it had from the support of the king's friends. Chatham's illness reduced it to incapacity. The king was almost in despair, for he was afraid of being forced to receive Grenville. On 2 March 1767 he entreated Chatham to see his messenger if only for a quarter of an hour, in order that the 'world might know' that he was still advising him; on 30 May that Chatham would see Grafton, if only for five minutes; and on 2 June, when the administration seemed about to break up, that he would lay a plan before him (*ib.* pp. 137, 227, 267). He earnestly begged him to retain office. 'Your name,' he wrote, 'has been sufficient to enable my administration to proceed;' he hoped that his minister would recover, and help him 'in resisting the torrent of factions.' Chatham resigned on 14 Oct. 1768 (*ib.* pp. 318, 338–44). On 28 March, when Wilkes was elected for Middlesex, it was thought that the mob would attack the queen's house. George declared that he wished that they 'would make the attempt, that he might disperse them at the head of his guards' (*Grenville Papers*, iv. 268). He took an active part in the arrangements for preserving order, urged the expulsion of Wilkes from the house, insisted that 'due firmness' should be used in resisting riots, approved the firing on the mob in St. George's Fields, and required the Westminster justices to show firmness in using the military. In 1769 he followed a similar course as regards Wilkes. On 22 March, after Wilkes had been declared incapable of sitting in the 'present parliament,' while the king was talking with his ministers in St. James's Palace, a mob beset the gates, and a hearse was driven into the courtyard decorated with insulting emblems, and having on the roof a man dressed as an executioner, masked, and with an axe in his hand. A sharp though short struggle took place before the rioters were dispersed. During the whole time the king remained perfectly unruffled, and talked as calmly as usual (*ib.* p. 416; WRAXALL, *Memoirs*, i. 333). In July the lord mayor presented a petition to the king from the livery against the ministers, complaining specially of the employment of soldiers in repressing disturbances, and of the late affair in St. George's Fields; other petitions, one from ten thousand freeholders of Yorkshire, were also presented against the violation of the right of electors in the Wilkes case, and on 19 Dec. was published Junius's 'Address to the King,' which was made the subject of legal proceedings (*Ann. Register*, 1769, pp. 200–5; *Letters of Junius*, i. 225; MAY, *Const. Hist.* ii. 252). The speech with which George opened parliament on 9 Jan. 1770 began with a reference to a distemper then prevailing 'among horned cattle;' it was bitterly and unjustly ridiculed by Junius as containing 'nothing but the misery of a ruined grazier, and the whining piety of a methodist' (*Letters*, i. 272; STANHOPE, *History*, v. 246). Chatham's return to parliament had been welcomed by the king the previous July, but the earl attacked the administration with such vigour that its fall became imminent. When it was necessary to dismiss Lord-chancellor Camden, George urged Charles Yorke to accept the great seal. Yorke refused, for he shrank from deserting his party, the 'Rockinghams.' On the next day, 17 Jan. 1770, the king at the levee called him into his closet, charged him on his loyalty to accept the office, and declared that if he did not do so it should never be offered to him again. Thus pressed Yorke yielded, and his acceptance caused his death on the 20th (*Life of Hardwicke*, iii. 465–79). Grafton resigned on the 28th, and the king gave the treasury to Lord North, at that time chancellor of the exchequer. Chatham renewed his attacks, and reflected on the king by inveighing against the 'invisible counsels of a favourite,' meaning that George allowed Bute to direct his policy, which was certainly not the case. Grafton defended the king, but Chatham renewed his accusation. On 14 March George received a petition from the lord mayor (Beckford) and the livery, declaring that the House of Commons did not represent the people, praying for a dissolution, and referring to a 'secret and malign influence which under each administration had defeated every good, and

suggested every bad intention' (*Ann. Register*, 1770, p. 200). He made a short and not undignified reply, which seems to throw great doubt on the story that when the lord mayor was leaving the presence, he 'turned round to his courtiers and burst out a laughing' (JUNIUS, i. 284). He was determined not to dissolve, for he knew that a new house would force him to part with his ministers, and perhaps to receive the whig families back into power. 'I will have recourse to this,' he said, laying his hand upon his sword, 'sooner than yield to a dissolution.' On 23 May he received another petition from the common council of much the same kind. After he had made a short answer the lord mayor addressed him in a magniloquent and impertinent speech, to which he returned no answer. The increase of the ministerial majority in parliament gratified him. Beckford's death (21 June 1770) brought the active hostility of the city to an end, and the distrust which existed between the followers of Chatham and of Rockingham strengthened the position of the administration. George had gained a signal success, for he had found in North a minister of considerable sagacity, courage, and parliamentary tact. His scheme of government was fully realised; parties were broken up; the 'power of the crown, almost dead and rotten as prerogative, [had] grown up anew, with more strength and far less odium under the name of influence' (BURKE). George had succeeded in setting up a system of personal rule through a minister who commanded a large majority in parliament, and consented to shape his policy in accordance with commands given him in the closet. During the next twelve years he carried out his own system of government, and the affairs of the country were directed by an irresponsible king acting through responsible ministers.

George continued to indulge his love for a retired and simple life. He still lived much at Kew, and while there enjoyed domestic pleasures and homely pursuits (for a courtly account of his life at Kew during the summer see *Annual Register*, 1775, ii. 1); he took much interest in farming, a taste which increased as time went on, and in later days wrote some letters to Young on agriculture (YOUNG, *Annals of Agriculture*, vii. 65, 332); was said to have farmed for profit, and to have looked sharply after it, and was made fun of in satires and caricatures as 'Farmer George.' He liked trifling mechanical occupations, and was at this time constantly ridiculed as the 'royal button-maker' (WRIGHT). While not illiberal in his charities, he and his queen were extremely economical. His health was at this time good; he was afraid of becoming fat, and was therefore very abstemious and took much exercise without regard to weather, sometimes riding from Windsor to London in the rain, and after he had dressed holding a levee, and, when that was over, giving audience to his ministers and setting off for Windsor in his carriage about 6 P.M., without having taken anything but a little tea and bread and butter, which he would often eat as he walked up and down (WRAXALL, *Memoirs*, i. 282). He never missed a drawing-room or a levee. The graciousness of his manners to men whom he respected is recorded by Dr. Johnson, whose well-known interview with him took place in February 1767. Johnson afterwards said: 'They may talk of the king as they will, but he is the finest gentleman I have ever seen' (BOSWELL, *Life*, ii. 37–43, ed. 1807). He worked hard, and was inspired by a genuine desire to do good to his people, and a belief that what he thought right necessarily was so. His letters to North, for whom at this time he felt a strong affection, show the deep interest which he took in the progress of affairs. The distribution of the crown patronage was now entirely in his hands, and he gave orders about every appointment, whether it was to the place of housekeeper at one of his palaces, or to a colonelcy of the guards, or to an episcopal see. Patronage was one of the chief means by which he maintained and managed his party in parliament. Another of these means was the manifestation of his feelings by word or manner when people who had either satisfied or displeased him presented themselves at court; and a third was the disposal of the civil list revenues. The income settled on the crown, swelled as it was by the profits of the duchies of Cornwall and Lancaster and revenues from Scotland, Ireland, and other sources, was sufficient for all ordinary needs, and far more than sufficient for a king who lived so simply, yet in 1769 the ministers were forced to ask parliament for 513,511*l.* for payment of debts; inquiry was demanded, but in the end the money was granted without investigation. Much waste went on, as was abundantly proved in 1777, but large sums were no doubt spent in corruption of various kinds (MAY, *Const. Hist.* i. 237, 341). George was now thoroughly acquainted with political business. He identified himself with North's administration, and wrote his minister constant letters, sometimes two or three in a day, with his own hand. These letters he used to date according to the minute of writing, a custom which illustrates the importance which he attached to trifles, and possibly also his feeling that everything connected with himself

was of special moment. He was at all times ready to listen to suggestions from men who were not his constitutional advisers, and from 1770 to 1782 Charles Jenkinson, afterwards Lord Hawkesbury and Earl of Liverpool, is said to have exercised an influence which was 'sometimes paramount to, or subversive of, the measures proposed by his first minister' (WRAXALL, *Memoirs*, i. 416). When the new parliament met in 1771, the result of the elections and the disorganisation of the whigs secured the success of the king's policy.

George saw with some alarm the rise of the quarrel between the House of Commons and the printers, and, while writing of the printers as 'miscreants,' hoped that matters would not be allowed to grow serious. On 17 March, however, he considered it necessary for the commons to commit the Lord-mayor Crosby and Alderman Oliver, but was glad that the ministers were content to leave alone so dangerous an antagonist as Wilkes (*Letters to North*, i. 64, 67). He also took an active interest in the opposition to Savile's 'Nullum Tempus' Bill, which was designed to protect the subject against the dormant claims of the crown, such as that revived to the prejudice of the popular whig magnate the Duke of Portland. Family troubles crowded on the king. In November 1770 he was forced to find, not without difficulty, 13,000*l.* to pay damages and expenses incurred by his brother, the Duke of Cumberland, in a divorce case, and early in 1772 was much troubled at the news of the disgrace of his sister, the queen of Denmark [see under CAROLINE MATILDA]. On 8 Feb. he lost his mother; she had probably long ceased to influence his political conduct, but this was not generally believed, and the mob followed her body to the grave with insults (WALPOLE, *Last Journals*, i. 17). Shortly before this event he heard with indignation of the marriage of the Duke of Cumberland to Mrs. Horton, and soon afterwards of the marriage of his favourite brother, William Henry, duke of Gloucester, to the widow of Earl Waldegrave. The two dukes were forbidden the court, and it was announced that the king would not receive those who called on them. It was some years before he forgave the Duke and Duchess of Gloucester. These marriages and the scandals connected with them called forth a message from the king to parliament recommending the Royal Marriage Bill, which prohibited descendants of George II, except the issue of foreign princesses, from marrying before the age of twenty-five without the king's consent. After that age they might marry provided that no objection was raised by parliament to the proposed match, of which a year's notice had to be given to the privy council. All marriages contracted contrary to the act were to be null, and the parties to incur the penalties of præmunire. This bill was the king's own work, and he made it a personal matter. 'I expect every nerve to be strained,' he wrote, 'to carry the bill with becoming firmness, for it is not a question that immediately relates to administration, but personally to myself;' adding that he should 'remember defaulters.' Nevertheless the bill was violently opposed. Chatham pronounced it 'newfangled and impudent,' and the king heard with anxiety that there was a strong feeling against it in the commons. He asked North for a list of 'those that went away and those that deserted to the minority; that,' he added, 'would be a rule for my conduct in the drawing-room to-morrow' (*Letters to North*, i. 97; *Chatham Corr.* iv. 199, 203; LECKY, *Hist.* iii. 463; STANHOPE, *Hist.* v. 311; see art. FOX, CHARLES JAMES). The bill was carried by considerable majorities. He expressed strong dislike to the motion for abolishing compulsory subscription to the articles of religion by clergymen, physicians, and others, observing that 'presbyterians often resembled Socinians rather than Christians.' Affairs in the north of Europe directly and indirectly conduced to set Great Britain in opposition to France. During the war between Russia and the Porte a French fleet would have entered the Baltic had not England interfered. George was anxious to prevent a war, and recommended his ministers to 'speak out' as to their determination not to allow France to take part against Russia. The policy he recommended was successful; France was forced to leave the Turk to his fate, and Russia obtained substantial gains by the treaty of Kainardji. He was hostile to Lord Clive [q.v.], who was supported generally by the opposition, and on 22 May 1773 expressed his amazement 'that private interest could make so many individuals . . . approve of Lord Clive's rapine' (*Letters to North*, p. 135).

On 16 Dec. 1773 the irritation of the American colonists at the retention of the tea duty broke out in a riot at Boston. George shared the opinion of most of his people that the colonists might safely be despised, and that if firmness was used they would soon submit. Accordingly in 1774 he felt much satisfaction at the Boston Port Bill, and the bill for regulating the government of Massachusetts Bay. He had no wish to see fresh taxes laid on the colonists, but considered it necessary to maintain the duty in order to keep up the right of taxation. The meeting of congress in September convinced him that the colo-

nists must 'either triumph or submit,' and he declared in November that blows must decide whether they were to be his subjects or independent (*ib.* pp. 202, 215). Meanwhile in the spring he was annoyed at the awkward predicament in which North was placed in the debate on the matter of the printer Woodfall, and insisted on the dismissal of Fox for his conduct in the affair. Although he was mortified at the return of Wilkes for Middlesex, the general result of the elections to the new parliament delighted him. In spite of the eloquence of the opposition, the ministers had a majority of 190 to 200 in the commons in favour of their American policy. War actually broke out on 19 April 1775, and in August the king as elector of Hanover arranged for the employment of Hanoverian troops to garrison Gibraltar and Minorca. He received no subsidy for lending these troops, but asked to be reimbursed for expenses and levy-money. He also busied himself about the hire of other German forces and recruiting matters at home. A proposal for the hire of Russian troops made in a letter written with his own hand called forth a rebuff from the empress Catherine which greatly annoyed him. (For the part taken by George in the negotiations for the hire of foreign troops see a chapter by E. J. Lowell in 'History of America,' ed. Winsor, vii. 16–23, 74–7.) He was indignant at the attacks which Chatham made in the course of the session on the policy of the ministers with respect to the colonists. Chatham was, he said, the 'trumpet of sedition;' his political conduct was 'abandoned.' For himself, he was 'fighting the battle of the legislature' (*Letters to North*, p. 267); and not only the legislature but the nation at large upheld his determination. At the same time he was not so embittered against the colonists as to refuse proposals of accommodation, for his influence was certainly exercised in February 1775 on behalf of North's Conciliation Bill. He did not believe that the war would be of long duration, and rejected Howe's advice that it should be carried on by sea only. As the war continued, his feelings became more bitter, and though the opposition in parliament and outside it gathered strength, the nation widely shared in them. The city of London disapproved of the ministerial policy; the royal proclamation for the suppression of rebellion was received with hisses on the Exchange, and the city tried to provoke a quarrel with the king by refusing to present an address, except to him on the throne. 'I am ever ready,' the king said, 'to receive addresses and petitions, but I am the judge where.' He was pleased at the capture of New York in September 1776, and believed it to have been 'well planned and executed with alacrity,' which was perhaps rather too high praise (*ib.* ii. 39). He was now thoroughly embittered against the rebels; he warmly approved of the bill passed in February 1777 for securing and detaining persons suspected of high treason in America, and of the employment of Indians in the war; 'every means of distressing America must,' he wrote, 'meet with my concurrence,' and he hoped that 'Howe would turn his thoughts to the mode of war best calculated to end the contest' (*ib.* i. 274, ii. 84). At no time probably in the course of the war was the country at large more fully in sympathy with his policy than during this year. The news of Burgoyne's surrender on 17 Oct. deeply affected him; the disaster was, he wrote on 4 Dec., 'very serious, but not without remedy;' the cause could not be given up.

On 9 April of this year (1777) the king through North made the commons acquainted with his debts, which on 5 Jan. preceding amounted to 600,000*l.* Although part of this deficit was no doubt due to relief given to the loyalist refugees, by far the larger part arose from corrupt practices, and from the waste which prevailed in every department of the household; highly paid sinecure offices abounded, the king's turnspit was a member of the house, there had been scandalous mismanagement, and while the 'lustre of the crown was tarnished' by the king's economical and almost sordid mode of life, the wages of his menial servants were six quarters in arrear, and his tradesmen were almost ruined. The accounts laid before the house were unsatisfactory, and there were neither vouchers nor audit-books. Enormous sums had been spent in pensions and in various other ways which extended and maintained the influence of the crown. The excess in pensions and annuities during the last eight years, as compared with the last eight years of the reign of George II, amounted to 194,144*l.*, while, although the last years of the last reign included the great period of the seven years' war, the excess in secret service money during the same number of years just past was 63,559*l.* Indeed it is not unlikely that something like a million had already been spent during the reign on purposes which could not conveniently be avowed. All these matters were freely discussed in parliament (*Parl. Hist.* xix. 103, 160, 187; *Annual Register,* 1777, pp. 71–88; MASSEY, *Hist.* ii. 230–2). Nevertheless the house granted 618,340*l.* for discharge of arrears, and an addition of 100,000*l.* to the annual 800,000*l.* of the civil list. When at the close of the session the speaker, Sir Fletcher Norton, brought up the

bill, he dilated on the magnificence of the gift, 'great beyond example, great beyond your majesty's highest expense.' The court party were grievously offended, and an attempt was made to censure the speaker, but Fox brought forward a resolution approving his conduct, which was carried nem. con.

As the king was going to the Haymarket Theatre on 25 July 1777, a mad woman attacked and did some damage to his chair. In September he pressed North to accept from him the payment of his debts, offering, if needful, as much as 20,000*l.*, and expressing his love for him as a man and his esteem for him as minister, adding, 'I shall never forget your conduct at a critical minute'—on the retirement of Grafton (*Letters to North,* ii. 83). North had begun to disapprove of the colonial policy forced upon him by the king. War with France, declared in May 1778, was imminent. He felt that he could not conciliate the colonies and that conciliation was necessary, and on 31 Jan. he begged the king to accept his resignation and send for Chatham. He repeated his request in March. Men of every rank and political section looked on Chatham as the only hope of the country, and this was made known to George from various sides. He was immovable—not, as it would seem, so much from motives of public policy as from private feelings. He appealed to North's personal affection and sense of honour not to desert him. With Chatham he would hold no direct communication; but if he liked to serve under North 'he would receive him with open arms.' North might address him on this basis, with the distinct understanding that Chatham was not to bring in any member of the opposition. The administration must remain with North at its head, and include Thurlow, Sandwich, Gower, and others of its present members. He 'would rather lose his crown' than submit to the opposition, who, he declared, would 'make me a slave for the remainder of my days.' His conduct was chiefly governed by this and similar personal considerations; for he did not refuse to allow North to bring in conciliatory measures, and Chatham was as fully convinced as he was of the necessity of preventing American independence. North's negotiations were fruitless. That the king's conduct was culpable admits of no question (*ib.* ii. 149–56; *Memorials of Fox,* i. 180–7; LECKY, *Hist.* iv. 82). George declared on 18 March 1778 that he was 'fairly worn down,' but would not change his administration or receive 'that perfidious man.' Chatham's fatal illness made him hope that North would be more inclined to retain office. He was 'rather surprised' at the vote about the earl's funeral and monument; if it expressed admiration of his general conduct, 'it is,' he said, 'an offensive measure to me personally.' North renewed his entreaties to be allowed to resign, but was overpersuaded, and continued to carry out the king's policy. George showed his gratitude by giving him the lucrative post of warden of the Cinque ports. During the spring he made visits of inspection to Chatham and Portsmouth; on 28 Sept. he made a tour for the purpose of holding reviews at Winchester, Salisbury, and Warley in Essex, and on 22 Nov. reviewed the troops encamped on Coxheath, near Maidstone (*Annual Register*, 1778, p. 232 sq.) During 1779 he gave several proofs of his determination to uphold the administration. Referring to the debates on the manifesto of the king of Spain, who declared war in June, he wrote that he must know how members voted, and spoke of what might happen ' if the prerogative is not soon brought into effect' (Letter to Weymouth, 17 June, JESSE, ii. 243). A protest of the opposition lords against the conduct of the war seemed to him ' very wicked' (*Letters to North*, ii. 259). He was strongly opposed to Keppel, whose cause was maintained by the opposition. The feeling of the nation seems to have begun to change about this time, and the opposition, though numerically weak in parliament, grew more popular. North urged his former entreaties again and again without success, until in November 1779 George allowed him to negotiate with Camden and Shelburne for a coalition under a new first minister. In February 1780 the king, who was watching the debates on Burke's economic reform bills with painful intensity, was annoyed at the smallness of the ministerial majority on the proposal to regulate the pension list, and, as usual, recommended ' firmness' to North (*ib.* p. 305). Dunning [q. v.] carried his famous resolution concerning the influence of the crown in April 1780; George attributed the rising discontent of the commons to 'factious leaders and ruined men, who wish to overturn the constitution' (*ib.* p. 314). He allowed North to make some overtures to the Rockingham party in June, but objected to receive Fox [see under FOX, CHARLES JAMES] or the Duke of Richmond on account of some personal displeasure. The overtures were abortive. It seems that the king felt keenly the humiliation which was gradually coming upon him; for it is said that he seriously contemplated retiring to Hanover, and that liveries were ordered and other preparations made for his departure (*Memorials of Fox*, i. 287 *n.*)

George, however, had other causes for uneasiness. On 6 June 1780 the 'no popery' riots

reached a serious height, in consequence of the feebleness of the attempts to check them at an earlier stage. All responsible authority seemed paralysed, and the king himself came forward to supply its place. He wrote to North blaming the supineness of the magistrates, and called a special privy council for the next day. At the council it was alleged that the reading of the riot act and other formalities were necessary before the military could be called upon to act. George declared that if there was further hesitation he would lead the guards in person to disperse the rioters. It was 'black Wednesday,' and London was almost at the mercy of an infuriate mob. 'I lament,' George said, 'the conduct of the magistrates; but I can answer for one who will do his duty.' Attorney-general Wedderburn upheld, and had indeed suggested, the king's opinion that soldiers might in cases of necessity act against rioters without the civil power. The council at last agreed, and George promptly sent to the adjutant-general bidding him issue a proclamation that officers were at once to order their men to act (TWISS, *Life of Eldon*, i. 293; *Annual Register*, 1780, p. 266). His intrepidity, firmness, and good sense saved London from further havoc. On the 19th his action was declared by Lord Mansfield to have been in strict conformity with the common law. The feeling of the country was now against the administration. This change, though partly due to the failure of the war, must mainly be attributed to the exposure which the opposition made of the enormous and corrupt expenditure of the crown. The majority in the commons which had so long supported the royal policy was broken up, and the fruitless attempt at negotiation with the Rockinghams was followed by an unexpected dissolution. George used every means to influence the result of the general election. He was startled when the bill came in. It amounted to about 50,000*l.*, besides some pensions. 'The sum,' he wrote, 'is at least double of what was expended on any other general election since I came to the throne' (*Letters to North*, ii. 423). He was anxious to get Keppel unseated at Windsor, and to secure the election of the court candidate, and is said to have canvassed in person against the admiral, going into the shop of a silk mercer, one of Keppel's supporters, and saying in his usual hurried way, ' The queen wants a gown, wants a gown. No Keppel; no Keppel' (*Rockingham Memoirs*, ii. 425). The elections improved the prospects of the administration. They were ruined by the capitulation of Cornwallis on 19 Oct. 1781. George bore the blow with fortitude, though the fact that his reply to Lord George

Germain's announcement of the news was not, as usual, dated according to the hour and minute of writing shows that he was much moved. In his speech in opening parliament on 25 Nov. 1781 he spoke of the necessity of 'most active exertions.' During the early part of 1782 he was much distressed by the constant decrease of the majority. The separation of the colonies would, he was convinced, 'annihalate (*sic*) the European position of the kingdom.' On 11 March he commissioned Lord-chancellor Thurlow to treat with Rockingham for an administration 'on a broad bottom;' but though he was willing to concede the demands for peace and economy, the negotiation failed on the 18th, because he would not pledge himself to accept Rockingham's selection of ministers. He wished to put Rockingham at the head of an administration partly formed by himself (*ib*. pp. 451–9). On the 20th North persuaded him to acknowledge that his administration could not stand any longer, and Thurlow renewed the negotiation with Rockingham. But the king would not consent to a reform of the household, and sent for Shelburne on the 21st, after North's resignation had been announced. Shelburne was bound to Rockingham, and on the 22nd George sent for Lord Gower, who refused his offer. He was then advised by Shelburne to accept Rockingham, and was forced to again bow his head to the yoke (LECKY). Nevertheless, he refused to see Rockingham personally until after the administration was formed, and by employing Shelburne as an intermediary sowed the seeds of discord among his new ministers. He delivered the seals to Rockingham on 27 March 1782. When North's resignation was imminent, and during the crisis which followed, he again entertained the idea of retiring to Hanover. His humiliation was notorious, and the triumph of the whigs was caricatured in the 'Captive Prince.'

The new administration included the Chatham section of the whigs under Shelburne as well as the Rockinghams, and the king, with the help of Thurlow, whom Rockingham had consented to retain as chancellor, set himself to weaken it by division. While he withheld his confidence from Rockingham, he gave it freely to Shelburne, and by bringing Dunning into the cabinet, without consulting his first minister, secured the Shelburne party an equal number of votes with the followers of Rockingham. George was annoyed at being forced by Rockingham to recommend the reform of the civil establishment, and would not speak to him on the subject, though he wrote his objections to Shelburne, telling him not to show his letter to any one except Thurlow (*Life of Shelburne*,

iii. 157–9). Burke's efforts to reduce the expenditure of the crown were followed by some petty and apparently unworthy measures of economy in the king's household arrangements (PAPENDIEK, i. 161–3). Rockingham died on 1 July 1782, and his death was followed by a disruption of the whigs, brought about, in part at least, by the king's management. This disruption made so great a change in the balance of power that Fox said that on Rockingham's death 'the crown devolved on the king.' Fox recommended the king to send for the Duke of Portland, and on finding that Shelburne was appointed to the treasury, gave up office with other members of the Rockingham party. On 5 Dec. the king, in his speech on opening parliament, announced that he had offered to declare the American colonies free and independent. 'Did I,' he afterwards asked, 'lower my voice when I came to that part of my speech?' (WALPOLE, *Journals*, ii. 577). George seems, like most other people, to have disliked Shelburne, and the minister thought that the king plotted against him. This was probably untrue, but George had by this time given people occasion to suspect him; 'by familiarity of intercourse he obtained your confidence and availed himself of his knowledge to sow dissension' (NICHOLLS, i. 342). He was certainly wholly on Shelburne's side when on 18 Feb. 1783 the combined parties led by Fox and North were in a majority in the commons (*Court and Cabinets*, i. 156). Shelburne's resignation on the 24th caused him much annoyance (*ib*. p. 303), for he could not endure the idea of falling into the hands of the coalition. The next day he pressed Pitt to take Shelburne's place, but he refused on the 27th. He made proposals in vain to Gower, and then tried to persuade North to leave the coalition, offering him the treasury if he would desert Fox, whom he regarded with vehement personal hatred. His distress of mind was great, and he again thought of retiring to Hanover. At length he yielded to Fox's demand, and sent for the Duke of Portland, but finding that Fox insisted on the dismissal of Thurlow, and that Portland treated him cavalierly, and refused to show him the list of proposed appointments to inferior offices, he broke off the negotiation (*ib*. p. 206). William Grenville, who was at this time admitted to his confidence, was impressed by his mental agitation; he spoke with 'inconceivable quickness.' On 23 March 1783 he again applied to Pitt. He was indignant at North's desertion; 'after the manner I have been personally treated by both the Duke of Portland and Lord North,' he wrote on the 24th, 'it is impossible that I can ever admit either of them into my service' (*Life of Pitt*, i. App. ii.) But Pitt again refused, and on 2 April the long interministerium ended in George's acceptance of the coalition administration. During this period George constantly resided at Kew from May to November, though he was sometimes at Windsor. He lived in great retirement, going into London on Wednesdays and Fridays to hold levees and talk with his ministers. His chief amusements were hunting and walking; and he occasionally had artists to play or recite before him. His life was quiet and respectable, and his court intensely dull (for particulars see authorities stated below).

The king hated his new ministers, and told Temple that he meant to take the first opportunity of getting rid of them, expressing his 'personal abhorrence' of North, who had, he considered, betrayed him (*Court and Cabinets*, i. 303). He thwarted them as much as he could, and used to wish that he 'was eighty, or ninety, or dead.' The proposal of the ministers to grant the Prince of Wales 100,000*l.* a year greatly angered him, and he would probably have openly quarrelled with them had not Temple advised him not to do so on a private matter. The ill conduct of the prince caused him much uneasiness [see under GEORGE IV]. Bad as the prince was, his father was not blameless in his treatment of him. George's temper was sullen and unforgiving, and it is probable that his eldest son was not lying when he said that he knew that his father hated him (MALMESBURY, ii. 129). Fox's India bill gave the king the opportunity he wanted. Thurlow roused his jealousy by presenting him on 1 Dec. with a paper pointing out the effect which the bill would have on the royal authority (*Court and Cabinets*, i. 288). On 11 Dec., after the bill had passed the commons, he gave Temple a paper stating that 'whoever voted for the bill was not only not his friend, but would be considered by him as his enemy' (*ib.* p. 285). The bill was thrown out by the lords on 17 Dec.; on the same day the king's action was commented on in the commons, and a resolution was passed declaring that to 'report any opinion or pretended opinion of his majesty upon any bill' depending in parliament to influence votes was a 'high crime and misdemeanor.' The next day the king dismissed the ministers, and at once sent for Pitt. He took the deepest interest in Pitt's struggle against the hostile majority in the commons, and steadily refused to dismiss his new ministers, or to dissolve parliament before the opposition had lost its majority in the house and its popularity in the country [see under Fox, CHARLES JAMES, and PITT, WILLIAM]. He

prorogued parliament in person on 24 March 1784, with a view to its dissolution the next day.

In one sense Pitt's success, which was completed by the result of the general election, was a victory for the king. George got rid of the ministers whom he hated, he gained a minister who as long as he lived proved himself able to preserve him from again falling into the hands of the whigs, and he found himself more popular than he had been since his accession. But he had, on the other hand, to give up the system of personal government for which he had hitherto struggled. The result of the crisis was a diminution of the direct influence of the crown, and an immense increase in the power of the first minister. For many years George could not have afforded to quarrel with Pitt, for he was his one hope of salvation from Fox whom he hated (LECKY). The 'king's friends' consequently disappeared as a party, most of them becoming supporters of the minister whom he wished to keep in office. George never expressed the same personal affection for Pitt that he had for North, and he did not always like his measures. He disapproved of the Westminster scrutiny [see under Fox] and of Pitt's plan for parliamentary reform (*Life of Pitt*, i. App. xv.), but refrained from opposing it, and appears to have disliked the proceedings against Warren Hastings, from whom he allowed the queen to accept an ivory bed (*ib.* p. 296); the court took its tone on this question from him and the queen, but he did not interfere in the matter. Although on 7 Aug. 1783 he had virtually refused to receive a minister from the United States (*Memorials of Fox*, ii. 140), he consented to receive John Adams on 1 June 1785. He behaved with dignity during the interview, though he showed that he was affected by it, and assured the minister that as he 'had been the last to consent to the separation,' so he 'would be the first to meet the friendship of the United States as an independent power' (Adams to Jay, ADAMS, *Works*, viii. 257, ed. 1853). On 2 Aug. 1786 an attempt was made to stab him at the gate of St. James's by a mad woman named Margaret Nicholson; he behaved with perfect composure (*Annual Register*, 1786, p. 233; PAPENDIEK, i. 260).

In the spring of 1788 the king suffered much from bilious attacks, supposed to have been brought on by the worry and fatigue of business, combined with exhaustion produced by the violent exercise which he was in the habit of taking to prevent corpulence (*ib.* pp. 297, 298, 303). On 12 June he went to Cheltenham to drink the waters, and while there resided at Lord Fauconberg's house, Bays Hill Lodge (D'ARBLAY, *Diary*, iv. 214). He returned to Windsor on 16 Aug., and on 16 Oct. got wet while walking. The next day he was taken ill, and on the 22nd signs of derangement appeared. However, he got better, and on the 24th held a levee, in order, he said, 'to stop further lies and any fall of the stocks' (*Life of Pitt*, i. 385). His mind dwelt on the loss of the American colonies (MALMESBURY, iv. 20). While at Windsor on 5 Nov. he became delirious, and for a while it was thought that his life was in imminent danger. He suffered from intense cerebral irritation, which showed itself in sleeplessness and increasing garrulity. On the 29th he was removed by his physicians to Kew, the removal being effected by deception (D'ARBLAY, *Diary*, iv. 341). On 5 Dec. his physicians stated to the privy council that his disease was not incurable, but that it was impossible to say how long it might last. He was then put under the charge of Dr. Willis. It is said that before this date he was treated with brutality (MASSEY, *Hist.* iii. 199, 207). The stories are probably greatly exaggerated, for they all seem to refer to a period of only five days, during which he was at Kew before Dr. Willis came there. (Mrs. Papendiek's account of the king's illness in 'Court and Private Life,' ii. 7–31, goes far to disprove, with one exception, p. 20, the stories of harsh usage; her narrative differs in some respects from that given by Madame d'Arblay.) He was, however, subjected to unnecessary restraints which tended to increase his mental irritation. Willis, who declared that his recovery at an early date was certain, changed this system, and soon gained complete control over him (*Court and Cabinets*, ii. 35). During his illness violent debates took place on the regency question [see under GEORGE IV, BURKE, Fox, PITT]. On 19 Feb. 1789 the chancellor announced that he was convalescent, and on 10 March he resumed his authority. His recovery was hailed with delight, and London was illuminated. He attended a public thanksgiving at St. Paul's on 23 April (*Annual Register*, 1789, p. 249; PAPENDIEK, ii. 83–90), but was still suffering from dejection and lassitude on 5 May. The undutiful conduct of the Prince of Wales and Frederick Augustus [q. v.], duke of York, caused much unhappiness in the royal family. On 25 June George, by his physicians' advice, left Windsor for Weymouth, where he resided at Gloucester Lodge. He was greeted with acclamations everywhere. In after years he constantly spent either the whole or some weeks of the summer at Weymouth. His life there was very simple. He

bathed, yachted, rode, and made excursions, going this year to Lord Morley's at Saltram, 15–27 Aug., and visiting the ships at Plymouth. On 18 Sept. he returned to Windsor in complete health. On 21 Jan. 1790 an insane man threw a stone at him as he was going in state to open parliament (*Annual Register*, 1790, pp. 194, 205). During the summer, when there was some unusually hot weather (*ib.* p. 209), the state of the king's health caused some anxiety to his physicians, who endeavoured to keep him from dozing during the day and brooding over French affairs, and told the queen that she must devote herself entirely to him (PAPENDIEK, ii. 214–16). A signal proof of his determination to uphold Pitt was given in 1792, when he reluctantly agreed to dismiss Thurlow from the chancellorship, because Pitt found it impossible to work with him (*Life of Pitt*, ii. 149, 150).

The proceedings of the 'Friends of the People' and other revolutionary societies strengthened the king's feelings against Fox and the parliamentary section which sympathised with the French revolution (*ib.* App. xiv.) The general feeling of the country was with him, and was signified and excited by caricatures, one of which, by Gillray, published in July 1791, and entitled 'The Hopes of the Party,' represented the king as brought to the block by Fox and Sheridan, with Priestley assisting at his execution. He was gratified by the declaration of war against France in 1793 (*ib.* xvii.; NICHOLLS, i. 136, 400), and received with 'infinite pleasure' the reports of the defeats of motions for peace. On 30 Jan. 1794 he held a review of Lord Howe's fleet at Spithead. He struggled hard to keep his son the Duke of York in command in the Low Countries, but Pitt insisted so strongly on the evils attending a division of command that, though 'very much hurt,' he at last agreed to his recall (*Life of Pitt*, iii. App. xxi.) Lord Fitzwilliam's Irish policy highly displeased him; it was overturning the 'fabric that the wisdom of our forefathers esteemed necessary;' the admission of Roman catholics to vote and office would be 'to adopt measures to prevent which my family was invited to mount the throne in preference to the House of Savoy,' and the proposal must have been instigated by a 'desire to humiliate the old friends of the English government,' or to pay 'implicit obedience to the heated imagination of Mr. Burke' (*ib.* xxx.) He thought that Fitzwilliam should be recalled. He consulted Lord Kenyon and Sir John Scott as to whether it would be consistent with his coronation oath to assent to an Irish Roman catholic relief bill; they answered that his oath did not prevent his doing so, but Lord Loughborough, whom he also consulted, was on the other side, and gave his reasons in writing (CAMPBELL, *Lives of the Chancellors*, vi. 296–8). The year (1794) was one of scarcity and of much discontent among the lower classes, and as the king proceeded to open parliament on 29 Oct. his carriage was surrounded by a mob shouting 'Bread!' 'Peace!' and 'Down with George!' A missile was shot through the window of his coach, and as he returned stones were thrown; he behaved with great coolness, and the next evening was much cheered on appearing in Covent Garden Theatre (*Annual Register*, 1795, ii. 39). This attack led to the enactment of the Treasonable Attempts Bill. On 1 Feb. 1796 a stone was thrown at his carriage and hit the queen, as they were returning from Drury Lane Theatre. He was strongly opposed to negotiations with France in 1797, and wrote his opinion to Pitt on 9 April; Pitt answered in a decided tone. The next day George sorrowfully acquiesced, and negotiations were opened at Lille (*Life of Pitt*, iii. 52, App. ii–vi.) On 19 Dec. he went in state to St. Paul's to give thanks for the victories of Cape St. Vincent and Camperdown. As he was entering his box in Drury Lane Theatre on 15 May 1800, he was shot at by a madman named James Hadfield. He showed great unconcern, and slept as quietly as usual during the interval between the play and the afterpiece (KELLY, *Reminiscences*, ii. 156; WRAXALL, *Memoirs*, ii. 29).

The homeliness of the king's manners, his lack of dignity in private life, and the minute economy of his domestic arrangements became more conspicuous as he grew older. They were ridiculed in caricatures chiefly by Gillray, and in verse by Dr. Wolcot (Peter Pindar) and others. In 1791 the king is represented in a print as toasting muffins, and in 1792 as applauding the happy thought of the queen, who is instructing her daughters to drink tea without sugar to save 'poor papa' expense. He is said while at Weymouth to have had household necessaries sent from Windsor to avoid the high prices of the watering-place, and Peter Pindar describes 'Great Cæsar' as handling the soap and candles which came by the mail. In a caricature of 1795 Gillray ridicules his 'affability,' or love of gossiping and asking questions, in a print representing him as chattering to a cottager who is carrying food to his pigs. The most famous story of George's eccentric and undignified habits is preserved by Peter Pindar in verse, and by Gillray in a caricature of November 1797, and records how he stopped while hunting at an old woman's cottage and learnt from her how the apple got inside the

dumpling (see GILLRAY, *Caricatures*; WOLCOT, *Works of Peter Pindar*, i. 337; WRIGHT, *Caricature History*, pp. 458–65). He was, however, decidedly popular, especially with the middle class; the court was not fashionable, and a certain number of the working class were discontented, though the nation was as a whole strongly loyal. The king's virtues and failings alike were such as won the sympathy of average Englishmen of the middle class, and the affliction from which he had lately suffered greatly increased his subjects' affection for him.

George was fully persuaded of the necessity for a legislative union with Ireland, and took much interest in the progress of the scheme. At the same time he did not forget the proposals for Roman catholic relief which had caused him uneasiness in 1795, and saw that it was possible that the Irish union might cause their renewal in one shape or other. 'I only hope,' he said to Dundas in the autumn of 1799, 'that the government is not pledged to anything in favour of the Roman catholics,' and on Dundas replying that it would be a matter for future consideration, and pointing out that the coronation oath only applied to the sovereign in his 'executive capacity, and not as part of the legislature,' he angrily broke in with 'None of your Scotch metaphysics, Mr. Dundas—none of your Scotch metaphysics' (MACKINTOSH, *Life of Sir James Mackintosh*, i. 170). While he was at Weymouth on 27 Sept. 1800, the chancellor, Loughborough, who happened to be staying with him, showed him a private letter which he had received from Pitt summoning him to a cabinet council on the subject of catholic emancipation, and thus betrayed to him the minister's design before Pitt had thought fit to say anything to him about it. The news caused him great anxiety (CAMPBELL, *Lives of the Chancellors*, vi. 306, 322). He further received letters from Dr. Moore, archbishop of Canterbury, and Dr. Stuart, archbishop of Armagh, condemning the design. On 13 Dec. he also received a paper from Loughborough, stating the objections to emancipation (*Life of Sidmouth*, i. 500–12). Meanwhile no communication took place between the king and his ministers on the subject. At the levee on 28 Jan. 1801, one of the days on which the speaker was swearing-in the members of the new parliament, George asked Dundas what the ministers were 'going to throw at his head,' and declared that it was the 'most Jacobinical thing he ever heard of,' adding, 'I shall reckon any man my personal enemy who proposes any such measure' (WILBERFORCE, *Life of Wilberforce*, iii. 7). The next day he wrote to the speaker, Addington, desiring him to 'open Mr. Pitt's eyes' as to the danger of the proposal, though he speaks of Pitt's approval of it as not absolutely certain (*Life of Sidmouth*, i. 285). On 1 Feb. 1801 he received a letter from Pitt, written the night before, which contained the first intimation from his minister as to the course he intended to adopt. In this letter Pitt stated that he should be forced to resign unless the measure could be brought forward with the king's 'full concurrence, and with the whole weight of government.' In reply George offered that if Pitt would abstain from bringing forward the measure, he, for his part, would be silent on the subject, adding, 'further I cannot go, for I cannot sacrifice my duty to any consideration.' On 5 Feb. 1801 the king sorrowfully accepted his minister's resignation (*Life of Pitt*, iii. App. xxiii–xxxii.) During the progress of the correspondence he received a letter from Loughborough written with the object of ingratiating himself. George showed Pitt, in a letter written on 18 Feb., that his esteem for him was unabated. He sent for Addington, who succeeded in forming an administration, but before the new ministers received their seals the worry and excitement of the crisis caused the king another attack of insanity. For some days he dwelt with much agitation on the sacredness of his coronation oath (*Life of Sidmouth*, i. 286; MALMESBURY, iv. 22). On the 15th he took a severe cold; on the 22nd his mental alienation was unmistakable, and on the 23rd he was unconscious until evening, when he said, 'I am better now, but I will remain true to the church' (*Life of Pitt*, iii. 294). On 2 March his disease reached a crisis (ROSE, *Diaries*, i. 325), and from that day he continued to get better. He ordered his physician Willis to write to Pitt on the 6th. 'Tell him,' he said, 'I am now quite well—quite recovered from my illness, but what has he not to answer for who is the cause of my having been ill at all?' Pitt sent the king an assurance 'that during his reign he would never agitate the catholic question,' on which George said, 'Now my mind will be at ease' (*ib.* p. 360; *Life of Pitt*, iii. 304). On 14 March he received Pitt's resignation with many expressions of kindness, and handed the seals to Addington, whom he styled the next day 'his own chancellor of the exchequer.' He also gave the great seal to Eldon, from, as he said, 'my heart' (*Life of Sidmouth*, i. 353; *Life of Eldon*, i. 368). The excitement of these interviews occasioned a relapse, and he was forced to live for some time in complete seclusion at Kew, under the care of the Willises; he was not sufficiently recovered to

be out of their hands until 28 June, when he left for Weymouth. This illness aged him considerably, and it was observed that he stooped more and was less firm on his legs (MALMESBURY, iv. 62). In the course of the summer he offered to pay 30,000*l.* from the privy purse for the settlement of Pitt's debts; this offer was gratefully declined (ROSE, *Diaries*, ii. 214). A wild plot to overturn the government and assassinate the king was discovered in October 1802 [see DESPARD, EDWARD MARCUS].

George did not expect much from the negotiations with France, and spoke of the peace as 'experimental' (MALMESBURY, iv. 63, 69; *Life of Eldon*, i. 398). It is doubtful whether he cordially approved of the tone adopted by his ministers towards France, but the rumour that he regretted Pitt in October was an exaggeration; he was personally fond of Addington, whose character and opinions were in many points like his own; though two years later, after Addington had left office, he came to believe that he had parted with him feeling that he 'was not equal to the government of the country' (ROSE, ii. 156). Nothing was told him about the negotiations between Pitt and Addington in 1803 until they were ended; then on 20 April Addington informed the king of them, evidently making his own story good, for George was indignant at Pitt's conduct, talked of his 'putting the crown in commission,' and said that Pitt 'carried his plan of removals so extremely far, and so high, that it might reach him' (MALMESBURY, iv. 185). He attributed the attacks made upon the administration to 'faction.' On 13 June he heard of the surrender of Hanover to the French, and received the news 'with great magnanimity and a real kingliness of mind' (*ib.* p. 270). During the alarm of invasion on 26 Oct. he held a review of twenty-seven thousand volunteers in Hyde Park; he declared that if the French landed he would meet them at the head of his troops, and drew up a scheme of arrangements to be adopted in case of invasion (*Auckland Correspondence*, iv. 184). About the middle of January 1804 he caught a severe cold; he had been much annoyed by the conduct of the Prince of Wales in publishing the correspondence of 1803 on the subject of his offer to serve in the army, and this may have made his attack more serious; at all events his mind became again deranged, and for a while his life was in danger. The disease fluctuated a good deal; on 27 Feb. he was sensible, but perfect quiet was necessary for some time longer. His condition prolonged the existence of the administration; the opposition could not let matters continue as they were, and yet a change seemed impossible while he remained incompetent. On 26 April Addington came to him in company with Eldon, the chancellor, and announced that he must resign. The next day Eldon gave him a letter which Pitt had written a few days before, stating his political views; it appears to have been received graciously. On 2 May, Addington having resigned, Eldon, in whom the king placed perfect confidence, gave him another letter from Pitt offering to form an administration on a broad basis. To this the king returned an irritable reply, which he evidently hoped would put an end to Pitt's offer (*Life of Pitt*, iv. 296, App. viii.; *Life of Eldon*, i. 440–3; MALMESBURY, iv. 296–8; ROSE, ii. 113). Eldon, however, arranged matters, and on 7 May the king saw Pitt; he assented to the inclusion of the Grenvilles in the new administration, but refused to allow him to invite Fox to join it. George is said to have considered the proposal of Fox's name as merely 'ostensible' (COLCHESTER, *Diary*, i. 539), but he expressed his determination in strong terms to Addington, and later declared that he would not admit Fox 'even at the hazard of a civil war' (ROSE, ii. 156). During the change of ministers he was occasionally excitable, and showed an excessive love of talking (*Life of Eldon*, i. 445). In May, though collected when talking of business, he was flighty in private life, was harsh and irritable, made sudden changes in the household, and caused the queen much distress (MALMESBURY, iv. 310, 319). The slowness of his recovery is said to have been due to the employment of another physician in place of the Willises, against whom he had strong feelings. Discussions about the Prince of Wales seem to have added to the discomfort at the palace, for the queen was anxious on her son's behalf, while the king declared that he 'could never forgive him' for publishing his letters (ROSE, ii. 168). Somewhat ungraciously he consented to give his son an interview, but the prince failed to keep his appointment. Meanwhile the king had determined to support Pitt and was displeased when Addington opposed a government measure (*Life of Pitt*, iv., App. xvi.) He set out for Weymouth on 24 Aug. 1804, and while there regained his health. On his return he stayed at Mr. Rose's house, Cuffnells, in Hampshire, 29 Oct. to 2 Nov. (see the account of his conversation with ROSE, *Diary*, ii. 155–196). He told his host that he had nearly lost the sight of his right eye, and could scarcely read a newspaper by candle-light with any spectacles. Family disputes troubled him, and he and the queen, who feared an

outbreak of madness, lived entirely apart (MALMESBURY, iv. 336; *Auckland Correspondence*, iv. 213, 220). During the autumn he took much interest in arrangements for the education of his granddaughter, Princess Charlotte, but was annoyed by the manner in which the prince treated him with reference to the matter. The reconciliation between Pitt and Addington delighted him. Addington's approaching return to office enabled George to renew his intercourse with him, and on 29 Dec. he was invited to share the king's dinner, which consisted of mutton chops and pudding (*Life of Sidmouth*, ii. 342).

The king's health improved during the early part of 1805, though for a time he still showed some signs of flightiness, insisting on 'wearing a flowing brigadier wig on state occasions' (HORNER, *Memoirs*, i. 283). His speech at the opening of the session was the last which he delivered in parliament, and was printed before it was delivered to enable him to read it with more ease (*Court and Cabinets*, iii. 411). By July he had become almost entirely blind; he had a cataract in his right eye, and could see but little with his left. Although he got on well with Pitt, he still liked to have his own way, especially with regard to church appointments. He had laid great stress on his 'personal nomination' of Dr. Stuart to the archbishopric of Armagh in 1800. He knew that Pitt intended to recommend Bishop Tomline for the archbishopric of Canterbury, which was likely to become vacant during the year (1805). As soon, therefore, as the king heard of the archbishop's death, he walked from the castle to the deanery at Windsor, called the dean, Manners Sutton, out from dinner, and congratulated him as archbishop. When Pitt came with his recommendation, George insisted on his acquiescing in his nomination; the interview was stormy, but he carried his point (*Life of Pitt*, iv. 252, App. xxi.; ROSE, ii. 67). In July, after the secession of Sidmouth (Addington), Pitt tried to induce the king to consent to an invitation to Fox to join the ministry, but he refused. Pitt followed him to Weymouth in September and again pressed his request in a long interview, and only desisted through fear of disturbing his mind (*Life of Pitt*, iv. 334; ROSE, ii. 199; LEWIS, *Administrations*, p. 260). He was much affected by Pitt's death on 23 Jan. 1806, and could not see his ministers for two days. He then sent for Lord Hawkesbury (Jenkinson), who declined attempting to form an administration. By the advice of his ministers he sent for Lord Grenville on the 26th, and when Grenville said that he must consult Fox, answered, 'I thought so and meant it so;' he would have no 'exclusions' (HORNER, *Memoirs*, i. 331; COLCHESTER, *Diary*, ii. 32). The only difficulty arose from his wish that the army should be under the direct control of the crown, while the incoming ministers contended that the control should belong to a ministerial department. It was settled by their promise that they would introduce no changes in the army without his approval (*Life of Sidmouth*, ii. 415). He received Fox graciously, expressing a wish to forget 'old grievances,' and when Fox died on 13 Sept., said that the country could ill afford to lose him, and that he little thought that he should ever live to regret his death (LEWIS, *Administrations*, p. 292; *Life of Sidmouth*, ii. 435). Grenville's proposals as to the changes of office consequent on Fox's death were accepted by the king with satisfaction (*Court and Cabinets*, iv. 77). His sight grew worse, and at the beginning of 1807 it was remarked that he was becoming apathetic, and only wished to 'pass the remainder of his days in rest and quiet' (MALMESBURY, iv. 358). He was roused on 9 Feb. 1807 by the proposal of his ministers to introduce a clause in the Mutiny Bill removing a restriction on Roman catholics, and at once expressed his strong dissent. A further communication from the cabinet led him to imagine that the proposal did not go beyond the Irish act of 1793; he therefore, on 12 Feb., promised his assent, declaring that he could not go one step further. On finding on 3 March that he was mistaken as to the scope of the act, which would have admitted English Roman catholics to hold commissions in the army and navy, without the restrictions of the Irish act, he was much disturbed, and on 11 March declared that he was surprised at the extent of the proposal which Lord Howick then laid before him, informing Lords Grey and Howick that he would not go beyond the act of 1793. On the 15th he received a note from the cabinet agreeing to drop the bill, but adding that, in view of the present state of Ireland, they should feel at liberty to propose 'from time to time' such measures respecting that country 'as the nature of the circumstances shall appear to require.' In answer he wrote requiring a 'positive assurance from them that they would never again propose to him any concessions to catholics.' He was informed on 18 March that his ministers considered that it would be inconsistent with their duty as his 'sworn counsellors' to give him such an assurance. The king then said that it was impossible for him to keep his ministers; that between dismissing them and 'forfeiting his crown he saw no medium,'

and he accepted their resignation. He had on 13 March received a letter from the Duke of Portland advising him to refuse his assent to the bill, and offering to form an administration (*ib*. iv. 358–72; ROSE, ii. 318–33; *Colchester Diary*, ii. 96, 99; *Memoirs of the Whig Party*, ii. 173–205). On 19 March 1807 he commissioned Eldon and Hawkesbury to request the duke to do so, remarking that he had no restrictions, no engagements or promises to require of him. During this interview he was calm and cheerful. A resolution condemning the acceptance by ministers of pledges which should bind them as regards offering advice to the crown was moved in both houses; it conveyed a distinct censure on the king's conduct; in the lords it was supported by 90 against 171, and in the commons by 226 against 258 (LEWIS, *Administrations*, p. 296).

During 1808 the king, who was now quite incapacitated from reading or writing, led a quiet and cheerful life. He was much distressed by the scandal about the Duke of York in 1809. The conduct of the Prince of Wales with reference to this affair added much to his trouble (*Court and Cabinets*, iv. 291, 325). He supported his ministers, who were quarrelling among themselves, and his influence is said to have enabled them to retain office (*ib*. pp. 234, 288). Early in June (1808) he sanctioned Canning's proposal that Lord Wellesley should be substituted for Lord Castlereagh as war minister, but in September, when Portland's resignation was imminent, he by no means approved of Canning's pretensions to the position of first minister, and was in a perfect agony of mind lest he should be forced to admit Grenville and Grey to office (*Memoirs of Castlereagh*, i. 18; *Life of Eldon*, ii. 80–94). He wrote a dignified paper to the cabinet on the impropriety of the duel between Canning and Castlereagh. Having offered Perceval the headship of the administration, which was now disorganised by the retirement of the two secretaries as well as of Portland, he with much reluctance allowed Perceval on 22 June to make overtures to Grenville and Grey for the purpose of forming an extended administration (*Life of Eldon*, ii. 98; ROSE, ii. 390, 394). He was much relieved by their refusal. At Perceval's request he exacted no pledge on the catholic question from his new ministers, though he assured them that he 'would rather abandon his throne' than 'consent to emancipation.' On 25 Oct. the jubilee of the reign was kept with great rejoicings (*Jubilee Year of George III*, 1809, reprinted 1887). For some months after this George, who was then blind, lived in seclusion; he still rode out, and walked on the terrace of Windsor Castle accompanied by his daughters. His temper was gentle and his manner quiet; he attended daily morning service at chapel. In the autumn of 1810 he was much distressed by the illness of his favourite daughter Amelia [q.v.] On 24 Oct. he showed signs of approaching derangement of mind (ROSE, ii. 447), and on the 29th Perceval found him incapable of transacting business. His malady continuing, the Regency Bill was passed in January 1811, but on 5 Feb. Eldon, who went to see him in order to ascertain that it was necessary to put the great seal in commission for the purpose of giving the royal assent to the bill, found him so much better that he was embarrassed (ib. p. 481). The king spoke of the regency with resignation, and almost with cheerfulness. The bill gave the care of the king's person to the queen. On 21 May 1811 he was able to ride through the Little Park at Windsor, a groom leading his horse. Soon after this, however, he became worse (Auckland Correspondence, iv. 66), and the remainder of his life was spent in mental and visual darkness, with very few momentary returns of reason. His bodily health was good. On the death of the queen in 1818 the guardianship of his person was entrusted by parliament to the Duke of York. Early in January 1820 his bodily powers decayed, and on the 29th he died very quietly in his eighty-second year, six days after the death of his fourth son, Edward, duke of Kent. After lying in state on 15 Feb. he was buried on the night of the 16th in St. George's Chapel, Windsor. He had fifteen children by his queen, Charlotte—nine sons (the first christian name only is given in each case): George, who succeeded him (1762–1830); Frederick, duke of York (1763–1827); William, duke of Clarence, afterwards William IV (1765–1837); Edward, duke of Kent (1767–1820); Ernest, duke of Cumberland and king of Hanover (1771–1851); Augustus, duke of Sussex (1773–1843); Adolphus, duke of Cambridge (1774–1850); Octavius (1779–1783); and Alfred (1780–1782); and six daughters: Charlotte, queen of Würtemberg (1766–1828); Augusta (1768–1840); Elizabeth, princess of Hesse-Homburg (1770–1840); Mary, duchess of Gloucester (1776–1857); Sophia (1777–1848); and Amelia (1783–1810).

At Windsor Castle are portraits of George by Dupont, Gainsborough, and Beechey. At Hampton Court is a family picture by Knapton, including George as a boy, besides portraits by West and Beechey. Portraits by Richard Wilson (as a boy) and by Allan Ramsay are in the National Portrait Gallery.

A colossal equestrian statue by Westmacott terminates the long walk in Windsor Park.

[Jesse's Memoirs of the Life and Reign of George III, 3 vols. 2nd edit. 1867, contains many personal details, but is greater in gossip than in weightier matters; Adolphus's History of England during reign, 7 vols. 1840, has the merits and defects of a nearly contemporary work; Massey's History, 4 vols. 2nd edit. 1865, ends at 1802, dispassionate, though judging George rather severely; Mahon's (Stanhope's) Hist. vols. iii–vii. 3rd edit. 1853, ends at 1783, clear and trustworthy, though dull; May's Const. Hist. 3 vols. 5th edit. 1875; Lecky's Hist. of England during the Eighteenth Century, vols. iii–vi. 1882–7. For early years Earl Waldegrave's Memoirs, 1821, 4to, ends 1758; Bubb Dodington's Diary, 1785, ends 1761; Lady Hervey's Letters, 1821; Harris's Life of Lord-chancellor Hardwicke, 3 vols. 1847, especially useful for 1760; Walpole's Memoirs of Reign of George II, 2 vols. 4to, 1822; Earl of Chesterfield's Letters, 5 vols. ed. Mahon, 1845. Monthly Magazine, vols. li. lii., Notes and Queries, 1st ser. vol. x., Authentic Records, 1832, and Thoms's Hannah Lightfoot, &c., 1867, contain the 'Fair Quaker' scandal. Walpole's Memoirs of reign, 4 vols. 1845, Last Journals, 2 vols. 1859, and Letters, ed. Cunningham, 9 vols. 1880, must be taken with allowance for the writer's love of gossip and personal hostility to the king. Political correspondence and memoirs, representing party views, chiefly valuable down to 1783, are: Russell's Bedford Correspondence, vols. ii. and iii. 1842, ends 1770; Grenville Papers, vols. ii. iii. and iv., ed. W. J. Smith, 1852, valuable to 1770; Albemarle's Memoirs of the Marquis of Rockingham, 2 vols. 1852; Chatham Correspondence, 4 vols. 1838; Albert von Ruville's Life of Pitt, Earl of Chatham, 3 vols. Stuttgart, 1905, English translation, 1907; Corresp. of George III with Lord North, 1768–83 (from originals at Windsor), ed. Donne, 2 vols. 1867, with good introd. and notes; Fitzmaurice's Earl of Shelburne, 3 vols. 1875; Russell's Memorials and Correspondence of C. J. Fox, 4 vols. 1862, down to Fox's death in 1806; Nicholls's Recollections, 2 vols. 1820; Justin Winsor's Narrative and Critical Hist. of America, 1888, vol. vii. chaps. i. and ii. Letters of Junius, 2 vols. ed. Bohn. Authorities chiefly valuable after 1783 are: Lewis's Administrations of Great Britain, 1864; for personal details, court, &c.: Autobiography and Correspondence of Mrs. Delany, ed. Lady Llanover, 6 vols. 1861–2, vols. ii. and iii. 2nd ser.; Diary and Letters of Madame d'Arblay, 7 vols. 1842–6; Mrs. Papendiek's Journals, or Court and Private Life in the Time of Queen Charlotte, ed. Mrs. Broughton, 2 vols. 1887; Jubilee Year of George III, an Account of the Celebration of 25 Oct., reprinted 1887; Quarterly Review, vols. xxxvi. cxxxi. Memoirs and correspondence, chiefly political: Wraxall's Historical and Posthumous Memoirs, 5 vols. 1884, of no great value for the king's life; Duke of Buckingham's Court and Cabinets, 4 vols. 1853, begins 1782, contains the correspondence of the Grenville family; Earl of Malmesbury's Diaries and Correspondence, 4 vols. 1844, for domestic affairs vol. iv. is chiefly valuable; Malmesbury seceded from Fox in 1793, and was fully in the confidence of Pitt and Portland; Earl Stanhope's Life of Pitt, 4 vols. 1862, has many letters written by the king in the appendixes; Campbell's Life of Loughborough, Lives of the Chancellors, vol. vi. 1847, for Loughborough's intrigue on catholic question; Lord Auckland's Journal and Correspondence, 4 vols. 1861; Rose's Diaries, 2 vols. 1860, of the highest value, for Rose was an intimate friend of Pitt, held office in both his administrations, and in 1804 had some interesting conversations with the king; Twiss's Life of Eldon, 3 vols. 1844 (from 1801 (i. 364) on to the time of his final derangement (ii. 165) the king treated Eldon with implicit confidence); Pellew's Life of Sidmouth, 3 vols. 1847, a strong ex parte statement (see Lewis's Administrations), and should be read along with Rose, Malmesbury, and Stanhope's Pitt; Lord Castlereagh's Memoirs and Correspondence, vols. i–v. 1849; Lord Holland's Memoirs of the Whig Party, 2 vols. 1854; Lord Colchester's Diary, 3 vols. 1861; Memoirs of F. Horner, 2 vols. 1853. Thackeray's Four Georges is of no historical value. For caricatures see Gillray in British Museum; Wright's Caricature Hist. of the Georges, 2nd edit. 1867; and satires, Wolcot's Works of Peter Pindar, 4 vols. 12mo, 1809.]   W. H.

GEORGE IV (1762–1830), king of England, eldest son of George III and of Queen Charlotte of Mecklenburg-Strelitz, was born at St. James's Palace about half-past seven on the morning of 12 Aug. 1762. On the 17th he was created by patent Prince of Wales and Earl of Chester, and on 8 Sept. was baptised by Archbishop Secker under the names of George Augustus Frederick, his sponsors being the Dukes of Cumberland and Mecklenburg-Strelitz and the Princess Dowager of Wales. He was inoculated and handed over to the care of a retinue of nurses, under the control of Lady Charlotte Finch. On 26 Dec. 1765 he was created a knight of the Garter, and was presented to the public in October 1769 at a drawing-room formally held in his name. In the main, however, he was brought up along with his brother, Frederick Augustus [q. v.] duke of York, with strict and almost excessive plainness and seclusion, at the Bower Lodge at Kew. In 1771 his regular education began under Markham, bishop of Chester, Dr. Cyril Jackson, a Swiss gentleman, M. de Sulzas, and Lord Holdernesse. In 1776 these tutors were replaced by Hurd, bishop of Lichfield, Mr. Arnold, and Lord Bruce, and the latter was soon succeeded by the Duke of Montague. The prince's education was extensive, and included classics, modern languages, elocution, drawing, and husbandry.

He learnt readily, and showed some taste for Tacitus, but he soon displayed a troublesome disposition. He was headstrong with his tutors and disrespectful to the king. He was addicted to lying, tippling, and low company.

As he approached his nineteenth birthday he pressed his father for a commission in the army and greater personal liberty, but the king refused the request. In 1780, however, he was provided with a small separate establishment in a portion of Buckingham House; the arrangement took effect on 1 Jan. 1781, and he was forthwith launched upon the town. He immediately became closely attached to Fox and the whigs, and though Fox advised him not to identify himself with any political party (Diary of Lord Malmesbury, ii. 75), his partisanship was undisguised, and at times indecent (WALPOLE, Last Journals, ii. 599, 600). He was at this time stout, of a florid complexion, with gracious and engaging manners, considerable social facility, and some accomplishments. He sang agreeably, played on the violoncello, dressed extravagantly, quoted poetry, and conversed in French and Italian. He fell under the influence of the Duke of Cumberland and the Duc de Chartres; he gamed and drank, and was so extravagant that he spent 10,000l. on his clothes in a year. In 1780 he became involved in an intrigue with Mary Robinson, a beautiful actress, by whose performance of Perdita at Drury Lane he was captivated. He provided for her a splendid establishment, and when after two years the connection terminated, she obtained from him his bond for 20,000l., which she afterwards surrendered. He left her to want in her latter days (see MARY ROBINSON, Memoirs of Perdita). When the Rockingham ministry came in, he shared the triumph of Fox and the enmity of the king. In June 1783 it became necessary to consider his future allowance. The ministry proposed 100,000l. a year, charged on the civil list. The king thought this an extravagant sum, and offered to provide 50,000l. a year himself. After a ministerial crisis upon the question, it was ultimately decided that the prince, now harassed with debts, should receive from parliament a vote of 30,000l. to liquidate them, and 50,000l. a year from the king. To this the duchy of Cornwall added 13,000l. per annum. He came of age in August, established himself at Carlton House, and took his seat in the House of Lords on 11 Nov. 1783.

The prince's first vote in parliament was given for Fox in one of the India Bill divisions on 15 Dec., and he assisted Fox in his Westminster election. Fox had fallen (18 Dec.), and the prince shared his unpopularity. For some time he lived in the closest alliance with the whig leaders, and sought amusement in an endless round of routs and masquerades, boxing matches, horse races, and drinking bouts. He lavished vast sums on alterations and decorations at Carlton House. He spent 30,000*l.* a year on his stud. By the end of 1784 he was 160,000*l.* in debt. He appealed to the king for aid, and talked of living incognito on the continent in order to retrench. The king refused either to help him or to allow him to travel. With every month he became more and more embarrassed. In 1786 he opened negotiations with the ministry for a parliamentary vote of 250,000*l.* He endeavoured to put pressure on the king by proposing to devote 40,000*l.* a year, two-thirds of his income, to paying his debts; broke up his establishment, shut up part of Carlton House, and sold his horses and carriages at auction. He lived in borrowed houses, travelled in borrowed chaises, and squandered borrowed guineas. At length a meeting of his friends was held at Pelham's house, and early in 1787 it was decided to appeal to parliament, and accordingly Alderman Newenham, member for the city of London, gave notice of a motion on the subject for 4 May.

The prince's friends were embarrassed by the allegation that, in breach of the Royal Marriage Act of 1772, he was secretly married without the king's consent, and to a Roman catholic. In 1784 he had become acquainted at Richmond with the widow of Mr. Fitzherbert of Swinnerton, Staffordshire [see FITZHERBERT, MARIA ANNE], then a beautiful and accomplished woman of eight-and-twenty. He fell violently in love with her. She resisted his importunities. To work upon her feelings he stabbed himself so as to draw abundance of blood without risking his life, and sent complaisant friends to bring her to see him in this state of despair. She withdrew to Holland, where he persecuted her with endless couriers and correspondence. His ardour passed all bounds. He would go to Fox's mistress, Mrs. Armstead, to tell her of his love, cry by the hour, beat his brow, tear his hair, roll on the floor, and fall into fits of hysterics (see for his use of phlebotomy on these occasions, HOLLAND's *Memoirs of the Whig Party*, ii. 68). At length in December 1785 Mrs. Fitzherbert was prevailed upon to return, on condition that a formal ceremony of marriage should be gone through. Fox, suspecting what was intended, wrote to the prince advising him to have nothing to do with a marriage. The prince replied that he was not going to marry, but on 21 Dec. he secretly went through the ceremony of marriage, by a clergyman of the church of England, with Mrs. Fitzherbert in her draw-

ing-room in Park Lane, in the presence of her brother, John Smythe, and her uncle, Henry Errington. They thenceforth lived together openly, and in the society of his friends, male and female, she was treated with the respect due to his wife. The rumour of this union seriously endangered his chance of obtaining parliamentary assistance in 1787. The leading whigs, headed by the Duke of Portland, had declined to injure their party by espousing his cause. At the meeting at Pelham's the prince denied that he was married to Mrs. Fitzherbert, but Fox alone was eager to support him. Newenham's notice of motion was at once followed by dark hints from Rolle, M.P. for Devonshire, of an inquiry into the supposed marriage. On 30 April Fox, authorised and instructed by the prince, rose to deny that any marriage had been entered into, or form of marriage gone through. To the prince the announcement was of inestimable value; it encouraged his friends, and disarmed his enemies; but having obtained his end by throwing over Mrs. Fitzherbert, he found it necessary to pacify Mrs. Fitzherbert by throwing over Fox. Next day he owned to Grey that a ceremony had been gone through, and asked him to say something in the House of Commons to modify what Fox had said, but Grey haughtily declined (HOLLAND, *Memoirs of the Whig Party*, ii. 139; RUSSELL, *Memorials of Fox*, ii. 289). He told Mrs. Fitzherbert that Fox had 'exceeded his instructions.' Fox found his mouth closed. To vindicate himself was to charge the prince with lying, and for a whole year he refused to speak to him. Mrs. Fitzherbert had to console herself for her husband's slight with the increased respect which she received from the Duchesses of Portland and Devonshire, and all the leaders of whig society. Pitt now saw that no ground remained for refusing assistance which could creditably be brought forward. On 21 May a royal message was brought down, recommending an increase in the prince's income, and promising 10,000*l.* a year from the civil list; 161,000*l.* was voted to pay the debts, which amounted to that sum, and 20,000*l.* for the completion of Carlton House. The prince promised to be more careful in future.

The reconciliation which followed with the king was short-lived. In August the Duke of York returned from abroad, and the prince, in his company and that of Fox, Sheridan, Brummell, and Lord Rawdon, soon fell into new extravagance. Resenting the exclusion from Brooks's of his henchmen, Payne and Tarleton, he founded a new club under the management of his German cook, Weltjie, where boundless drinking and gaming went on. Here, when he was sober enough to play at all, he lost thousands of pounds a night. His I O U's became a speculative security among usurers. To add to these follies, he began in 1784 to build his costly absurdity, the Brighton Pavilion, decorated in the oriental, especially the Chinese, style. He had taken a fancy to Brighton since his first visit in 1782, and soon made it equally fashionable and dissolute. It was from Brighton that he was summoned post haste to Windsor in November 1788 by the news of the king's insanity.

The king's madness was in part brought on by distress at the prince's irregularities. On catching sight of his son, the unhappy father flew at him, clutched him by the collar, and threw him against the wall. The prince was overcome, and could only shed tears. Next day, however, he recovered himself, and assumed the direction of affairs in the castle. It was thought the king would die, and already Thurlow, the chancellor, began to ingratiate himself with the prince. The prince accepted his overtures, but also made overtures of his own through Payne to Lord Loughborough. Soon, however, it became plain that a regency would have to be provided for, and a warfare of intrigue between the prince and the queen, the whigs and the Pittites, began, first for the regency, and then for the custody of the king's person. Finding that the ministry proposed to fetter the regent with many restrictions to be imposed by parliament, the whigs put forward on behalf of the prince a claim to an indefeasible title in right of his birth to a regency without any restrictions at all. On Lord Loughborough's advice a plan was prepared by which the prince was to assume power and summon parliament by a sort of *coup d'état*. When parliament met on 20 Nov. 1788, the day to which it had been prorogued, an adjournment took place for a fortnight. The arrival of Fox from the continent gave greater consistency to the policy of the whigs, and on his advice the prince became reconciled to the Duke of Portland. By 29 Nov. matters had so far progressed that Loughborough was prevailed upon to waive his claims to the great seal in favour of Thurlow, and the prince was in a fair way to have his new ministry settled. Parliament met on 4 Dec., and a series of debates followed, in which Pitt easily exposed the inconsistency and unconstitutionality of the whig theory of the prince's right to the regency. The prince wrote to the chancellor complaining of Pitt for want of respect to him in general, and in particular for settling his proposals for the regency without any communication to himself. On 16 Dec. Pitt introduced his three resolutions as a preliminary to bills to provide for the exercise of the powers of the crown. Though the prince had openly canvassed for votes against them, the second was carried by 268 to 204, and the others were passed also. They were carried in the House of Lords by 99 to 66, and a bill was prepared. Meantime the dissensions between the queen and the prince had grown very grave. He was charged with exhibiting his mad father to visitors in the most unfeeling manner, and with insulting the queen by sealing up the king's papers and jewels which had been left at Windsor on his removal to Kew. The prince retaliated with bitter complaints of the queen, and permitted his henchmen to speak of her in his presence in a ribald manner. On 30 Dec. Pitt communicated to him the heads of the bill: the queen was to have the custody of the king and the control of his household, and although the prince, as regent, was to exercise the royal powers generally, he was not to create peerages, except in the case of his brothers as they came of age, or to convey away the king's real or personal property, or to grant pensions or offices, except during pleasure. The prince, having consulted Burke and Fox, replied on 2 Jan. 1789 in a letter, which was also revised by Loughborough and Sheridan, complaining of the restrictions as a plan for dividing the royal family, and for dislocating all the royal powers. On 16 Jan. Pitt's proposals were brought forward in the form of resolutions, and these having been passed by both houses the bill was introduced. It passed the commons on 12 Feb., and reached the lords, but in the beginning of February the king's health had begun to improve, and the progress of the bill was now suspended. Meantime the Irish parliament, on Grattan's motion on 11 Feb., had agreed to an address to the prince praying him to assume the royal powers unrestricted, and despatched a deputation of six members to London to offer him the regency in Ireland entirely unfettered. It arrived on 25 Feb., only to find the king all but restored to health. By the end of the month the king was tolerably sane again. The prince, suspecting that his recovery was exaggerated, desired to see him; but the queen, in spite of long written remonstrances, excluded him from the king's presence, so that the meeting did not take place till 23 Feb. The conversation at this interview was guarded and general, and the king suffered no relapse; but the queen contrived to prevent further interviews, and on 7 March the king was induced practically to decline to see his son. On 23 April, when the king returned thanks at St. Paul's for his recovery, the prince attended the service, but his indecorous levity on the occasion was much remarked. He also addressed to the king in writing long remonstrances against the animosity shown by the queen in the affair of Colonel Lenox's duel with the Duke of York, and a memorial explanatory of his conduct during the king's insanity, but the father and son continued to be estranged.

By 1789 the prince was again almost as deeply in debt as ever. More than double the amount granted by parliament had been spent upon Carlton House. His creditors were clamorous and dunned him in the streets. During the king's illness he and his brother, the Duke of York, with the assistance of Weltjie, the cook, had begun raising money abroad upon their joint post-obits, conditioned for payment when either should ascend the throne. Some 30,000l. was obtained in this way upon most usurious terms, but with the king's recovery these bonds lost their attraction to speculators. The prince had also, in 1788, endeavoured to raise 350,000l. in Holland upon the security of the bishopric of Osnaburg. It was brought out as a formal loan; Thomas Hammersley, a banker of Pall Mall, was to receive subscriptions and pay dividends. The loan was taken up abroad, and large sums were obtained in this way through persons named Boas, De Beaume, and Vaucher. Interest at six per cent. was paid till 1792, but when the bonds at maturity were presented for payment the prince's agents repudiated their liability. Importunate claimants were expelled the kingdom under the Alien Act. The affair began to wear the aspect of a deliberate fraud. Mrs. Fitzherbert, too, had brought her jointure into the common stock of her own and the prince's funds, and was soon almost penniless. To pay the bailiffs out of her house, the prince pawned his diamonds. Yet mere want of money was not allowed to interfere with his numerous amusements. Faro at Mrs. Hobart's, cricket at Brighton, private theatricals at Richmond House, and masked balls at Wargrave engrossed his attention. He became an ardent patron of the turf till an imputation of swindling fell at least upon his jockey, and drove him from it in dudgeon. In 1788 he won the Derby, and in the four years following took 185 prizes. His jockey, Sam Chifney [q. v.], was suspected of spoiling the prince's horse, Escape, for his first race at Newmarket on 20 Oct. 1791, in order to affect the betting upon the next day's race, which the horse was allowed to win. The Jockey Club censured Chifney, and sent Sir Charles Bunbury to warn the prince that if he suffered Chifney to ride for him no gentleman's horse would start against him. The prince took deep offence. He never revisited New-

market, but he continued racing for at least twenty years longer. He bought seven horses one after another in hopes of winning the Ascot Cup, and even so late as 1829 attended the Ascot meeting (see *Greville Memoirs*, 1st ser.) After 1792 he retired into the country, and for some time lived principally at Bagshot Park, at Kempshott Park, near Basingstoke, and at Critchill House in Dorsetshire.

At last he became so involved that for the sake of an increase of income he consented to a marriage as the only condition upon which the king could be induced to assist him. In June 1793 he employed Lord Malmesbury to arrange his affairs for him. He owed 370,000l., and had executions in his house. He talked of going abroad; he sold five hundred horses and shut up Carlton House; he proposed to live in the country and devote three-fourths of his income to the payment of his debts. By August 1794 matters had proceeded so far that he had promised the king to give up Mrs. Fitzherbert and to marry the Princess of Brunswick. A reconciliation was all the more easy because, since the disunion among the leading whigs in 1792, the prince had nearly severed himself from his old friends. In November Lord Malmesbury was despatched to the court of Brunswick with a formal proposal for the princess's hand, and the prince, though he had then only seen her portrait, displayed in his correspondence with the emissary the impatience and ardour of a lover. None the less he was at the same time wholly under the influence of Lady Jersey, whose husband he appointed his master of the horse, and this person after the wedding was thrust upon the princess as her principal lady in waiting. When the Princess Caroline [q. v.] arrived at St. James's on 5 April 1795, she and the prince met for the first time, and he found the shock of his emotions upon that occasion so severe that, having kissed her in silence, he was obliged to drink a dram of brandy in a corner of the room. The ceremony of marriage took place on the evening of 8 April at the Chapel Royal, St. James's, and the prince was only brought through it with decorum by the prompting of his father, who was more familiar than he was with the prayer-book. Long afterwards the princess accused him of having been dead drunk most of the wedding night (*Diary of the Times of George IV*). The honeymoon was spent partly at Windsor, partly at Kempshott, but very shortly a quasi-separation took place between the prince and his wife. The marriage had been entirely without affection on either side, and he treated her without respect or even decorum. On

the assistance of the Hertford influence they would retain their places, that Eldon did not trouble himself to pronounce judgment in a single one of the many cases pending before him. The prince sent for Lord Wellesley, who, though he had thought himself betrayed in January, now proposed to form an administration upon the basis of catholic emancipation and the vigorous prosecution of the Peninsular war. After some negotiations with the whigs, on 23 May, which were met by Grenville's well-founded doubt of the prince's sincerity, the prince, on 25 May, gave Wellesley full liberty in forming an administration. Although he had vacillated upon Grattan's motion in favour of emancipation earlier in the year, at one time desiring his friends to oppose it, at another to support it, he now promised the marquis his full support on the catholic question, but bitterly opposed the inclusion of any of the opposition in the ministry. As a body he said he would rather abdicate the regency than come in contact with them, and, when Wellesley pointed out to him that no ministry founded on a principle of exclusion could be honourable or permanent, the conflict between his antipathy to Grey and the necessity in which his situation placed him was so acute that for the time being he became almost deranged with irritation (see BUCKINGHAM, *Courts and Cabinets of the Regency*). Wellesley's efforts failing, the prince had recourse on 27 May to Moira, who endeavoured to reconcile the regent to Grey by sending the Duke of York on 31 May to remonstrate with his brother. The result merely was that the prince quarrelled with the duke. What rankled in his mind was Grey's phrase used in the House of Lords on 19 May, that there was 'an unseen and pestilent secret influence behind the throne, which it would be the duty of parliament to brand with some signal mark of condemnation.' On 1 June he again had recourse to Wellesley, who came to Grey authorised to form an administration in conjunction with him. But Grey found that it was already settled with the prince that Moira, Erskine, and Canning were to be in the cabinet, and that only four places were to be open to the nominees of himself and Grenville. He refused to negotiate on the principle of disunion and jealousy and the supposed balance of contending interests, and on 3 June Wellesley announced to the House of Lords that, owing to the 'dreadful animosities' with which he met, he had failed to form any administration.

Though not very openly talked of, the last remaining point upon which the prince would not give way was the household, where Lady Hertford's son, Lord Yarmouth, held high office. Grey and Grenville required that the household should go out with the other ministers. The regent now began to be frightened. He invested Moira with authority to form a government. Moira asked if this included the filling up of the household, and although the prince consented, Moira, for some inexplicable reason, undertook that the existing household should not be dismissed. Accordingly he found, on again applying to Grey and Grenville, that he had effectually prevented the success of his attempts, and after three weeks of negotiations the crisis came to an end by Lord Liverpool becoming first lord of the treasury on 9 June 1812.

The prince next came into conflict with his wife and with the Princess Charlotte, who showed herself warmly attached to her mother's cause. At the beginning of 1813 she intimated to her father that she would no longer submit to be under governesses; but under the pressure which, with the assistance of Eldon, he put upon her, she gave way. The prince, always jealous of his wife, conceived that she had incited the Princess Charlotte to this resistance, and brought the intercourse of mother and child before the privy council, which decided that the restrictions upon it ought to continue as before. Upon the pretext that the Princess of Wales had caused the publication in the 'Morning Chronicle' on 10 Feb. of the letter she had addressed to George on 14 Jan.—a letter of strong remonstrance composed by Brougham—the prince refused to allow her to see her daughter. Later on he made a pretext of himself requiring Kensington Palace, in order to deprive his wife of her residence there. To relieve himself of the embarrassment of managing the Princess Charlotte, he decided to procure her marriage, and selected the Prince of Orange as her husband, but after a few months the princess's resistance baffled his design. When the exiled king of France came up to London before the restoration in 1814, the prince carefully excluded his wife and daughter from any share in the festivities, and when the allied sovereigns visited England he sent Sir Thomas Tyrwhitt to the czar requesting him not to carry out his intention of visiting the Princess of Wales. The ceremonies attending their reception were entirely after the regent's own heart, and he played his part in the pageants with a satisfaction alloyed only by the marked disfavour with which the public, even at that juncture, received him. When he endeavoured to induce the committee of White's Club to exclude the Princess of Wales from their ball, they took such offence that they abandoned their ball altogether

At length his difficulties cleared away. The Princess Charlotte was allowed to become betrothed to Prince Leopold in January 1816. In the previous August the Princess of Wales had finally left England. The regent, whose excesses had impaired even his constitution, and brought him to the verge of death in September 1816, obtained an opportunity of recruiting his health and his reputation by living a quiet life, and attracting as little public attention as possible.

Unfortunately, he continued to come before the public in the most unpopular way. Tierney brought to light the enormous extravagance of his expenditure since he had become regent. The 100,000*l.* then provided by Perceval as his outfit had been diverted to the payment of pressing debts. 160,000*l.* had since been lavished on furniture for Carlton House. His silversmith's bill was 130,000*l.*, and, in spite of the scheme for liquidating his debts which had now been many years in operation, they still amounted to 339,000*l.* It is hardly surprising that after these revelations a populace, impoverished and almost starving after so long a war, wrote ominously upon his walls, 'Bread, or the Regent's head.' He had retired to the less conspicuous publicity of Brighton; but his very unpopularity made residence in London important, and Lord Liverpool strongly insisted upon the inconvenience and even danger of his absence. He appeared in public surrounded by troops, and in vain attempted to elude the hatred of the crowd by stealing across the park to the Chapel Royal in a private carriage. The mob hung hissing upon his carriage-wheels. As he returned from opening parliament in January 1817 they stoned his coach, and were said to have fired on him with air-guns. For his protection the act of 1795, for the security of the king's person, was extended to cover the person of the regent. His unpopularity increased, and his hold on the people diminished, after the death of the Princess Charlotte on 6 Nov. 1817, an event by which he was himself as a father so deeply affected that he sought relief for his feelings by being cupped and bled. He diverted himself by yachting and attending regattas; and as soon as, by his mother's death on 17 Nov. 1818, Buckingham House, the old 'Queen's House,' fell into his hands, he threw himself with ardour into the congenial extravagance of reconstructing it. Nash, the architect, was taken under his patronage, and the quarter of London about the Regent's Park, together with Regent Street, the Quadrant, and Waterloo Place, was erected during the regency with his sanction and encouragement.

George III died on 29 Jan. 1820. The new king nearly died in the hour of his accession to the throne. He had been too ill to attend his father's deathbed, and the inflammation, due to a chill, from which he suffered was, on the night of 1 Feb., so acute that he was in danger of suffocation, and was saved only by a bleeding so severe that it alone almost killed him. No less than 130 oz. of blood was taken from him (COLCHESTER, *Diary*, iii. 111). On recovering his first step was, on 6 Feb., to consider how to deal with the prayer in the Book of Common Prayer which prays for 'our most Gracious Queen' (*Croker Papers*). His next was to employ the servant whom he most relied upon, Sir William Knighton, to compromise, buy up, or pay off his outstanding and long-overdue debts, bonds, and notes of hand, and during the next ten years Knighton was constantly and successfully engaged in delicate and secret negotiations with this object. He then pressed his ministry to attack the queen, against whom he had since 1818 been collecting evidence; and now, upon her determination to return to England and assert her claims, he resolved to take steps for a divorce. His ministers were at first loth to assist him, and in a cabinet minute of 10 Feb. 1820 recorded their opinion that the evidence was inadequate. 'The cabinet,' writes Croker, 'offer all but divorce. The king will have divorce or nothing.' As the queen drew nearer to England, George urged Lord Liverpool to endeavour to come to some compromise with Brougham, by which she would be induced to remain on the continent; but the queen reached England in the first days of June. On the 6th the king sent to the House of Lords a message recommending to their attention the evidence which had been collected against her, and the divorce proceedings began. During the remainder of the year, though the king remained inexorably resolved that they should go on to the end, his hand did not openly appear in the matter. The Divorce Bill was a ministerial bill, and the proceedings went on in the House of Lords without the king's intervention. Even after it had been withdrawn he bore himself with outward indifference to its failure.

In the spring of 1821 he was engrossed with the preparations for his coronation, the outlay on which was on the most profuse and elaborate scale. Sheltered by his ministers he was able to refuse the queen's request to be present at the ceremony, and even carried this affectation of indifference so far as to return her letters unopened to Lord Liverpool (1 May 1821), 'in conformity to a resolution adopted more than twenty years ago, and since invariably adhered to by the king, that the king would never again receive or open any letter or paper addressed to him personally by the queen' [see CAROLINE, AMELIA ELIZABETH]. The ceremony took place with great pomp, but the expense was so enormous and the exclusion of the public so complete that it produced only unpopularity. The royal robes alone cost 24,000*l.*, the crown 54,000*l.* The king next made preparations for visiting Ireland, and landed at Howth, from the Lightning packet, on 12 Aug., undeterred by the news of his wife's death (7 Aug.), which he had just received. 'The king was uncommonly well during his passage and gayer than it might be proper to tell,' but in deference to his bereavement he postponed his entry into Dublin until the 17th. He quitted Ireland on 3 Sept., after a series of festivities, to which all parties contributed with enthusiastic loyalty; but the weather was so unfavourable that it was not till the 13th, after considerable peril, that he landed at Milford. He next arranged to visit Hanover. He left England 24 Sept., and, travelling viâ Calais and Brussels, in about a week reached Osnaburg and Hanover, where he remained till the end of October. It was on this journey that he encountered his old friend Brummell, almost destitute, at Calais, and passed him by without recognition or relief. To complete the tour of his dominions he next visited Scotland, and landed at Leith on 14 Aug. 1822, remaining in Edinburgh till the 29th. Lord Londonderry's death occurred during his absence, and on his return to town he was engaged in the arrangements for a reconstitution of the ministry. He resisted as long as he could the introduction of Canning into the cabinet, but at length he yielded on 8 Sept. When Canning had retired in 1820 the king had parted from him with expressions of goodwill, but subsequently he took offence because Canning's friends in the House of Lords opposed the Divorce Bill, as he supposed at Canning's instigation. Greville also reports that Canning had insisted that the expense of the Milan commission should be defrayed by the king and not by the state (see this exclusion of Canning from office 1820–2, discussed in STAPLETON, *Correspondence of Canning,* vol. i.) For some time after Canning became foreign secretary he found himself thwarted by the king, who derived from some of the other ministers, especially Lord Westmorland, private information and advice, and even communicated directly with the foreign ambassadors. Now, however, and for the remainder of his life, he withdrew himself almost completely from the public view. Except to open and pro-

rogue parliament, he made no public appearance in London after his visit to the two theatres in 1823. He spent his time, attended, without any concealment, by his mistress, Lady Conyngham, at Brighton, and latterly almost entirely at Windsor, where he built a pagoda at Virginia Water and established a menagerie. Signs of dropsy had begun to appear, and, apprehensive of being ridiculed for his unwieldy bulk, he took extraordinary precautions to prevent himself from being seen even while driving in Windsor Park. As the catholic question grew more pressing his opposition to emancipation became more decided, and it was also with great reluctance that he was brought to consent to the recognition of the Spanish-American republics (see STAPLETON, *Correspondence of Canning*). In 1825 it was known that he supported the Duke of York in his almost passionate denunciation of the measures for the relief of the catholics. At the end of the year he came to an understanding with Canning, that his objections to catholic relief were to be respected, and thenceforward their relations became more amicable. Upon the retirement of Lord Liverpool (February 1827) he was at first desirous of keeping Canning out of the first place, making some peer, to be selected by the cabinet, Liverpool's successor, and retaining the existing ministry; but this proving impracticable, and the delay in the formation of a ministry being now serious, he commissioned Canning on 10 April to form a ministry. During this crisis his health was bad, and excitement and indecision rendered it worse. In a long interview with the Duke of Buckingham he explained that his chief anxiety had been to keep together a cabinet which would let the catholic question rest. Next the Duke of Wellington resigned his position of commander-in-chief, and the king was with difficulty convinced that it would be unconstitutional for him to assume the direct command of the army himself. After Canning's death (8 Aug. 1827) all the troubles of the spring began again. Contrary to expectation the king, instead of selecting a 'protestant' premier, commissioned Lord Goderich to form an administration. He was very anxious to have Herries included as chancellor of the exchequer, and after considerable pressure induced him to accept the seals. It was thought that he desired this because Herries was intimate with Knighton, his confidential servant, and was consequently, though wrongly, supposed to be likely to yield to the king's wishes on money matters. During the existence of Lord Goderich's weak ministry in 1827–8 the king assumed considerable freedom in disposing of patronage and appointments without consulting his ministers. By the end of the year 1828 dissensions had broken out in the cabinet, and Lord Goderich resigned. The Duke of Wellington was sent for and formed a strong protestant administration. The only person whom the king had refused to accept as a minister was Grey, but the duke had no difficulty in forming a tory ministry. For twelve months the king enjoyed comparative peace, though it was with reluctance that he accepted the Test and Corporation Acts; but when the ministry was compelled in 1829 to face the necessity for catholic emancipation, he offered a resistance which not even his habitual awe of the firm management of the Duke of Wellington could overcome, and he was all the less fitted for a contest by the fact that he suffered from chronic inflammation of the bladder, and his dropsical and gouty swellings were increasing, both preventing him from taking any wholesome exercise and necessitating the use of large quantities of laudanum. All through the autumn of 1828, in proportion as Peel and Wellington became favourable to emancipation, the king became more suspicious of them and more determined against it. Lord Anglesey's encouragement of the catholic association in December threw him into a fury, and early in January 1829 his agitation was so great that it was thought that the family tendency to insanity might break out in him. He talked freely of laying his head on the block rather than yield. On 26 Jan. the duke went to Windsor with a cabinet minute, stating the intentions of the ministry to introduce a Catholic Relief Bill, and the grounds on which they were acting. This he carefully got signed by his majesty. Thus pinned down, the king assented to the speech with which the session was opened, announcing that the ministry would propose a measure of catholic relief. Soon, however, influenced by the Duke of Cumberland, he began to waver. The Duke of Wellington was obliged to see him again on 26 and 27 Feb., and after an interview of five hours he was again brought to acquiesce in the policy of his ministers. But the defeat of Peel at Oxford revived his hopes. On 1 March he obstinately refused to direct his household to vote for the Relief Bill, and protested he would rather abdicate. A cabinet was then held, and he was reminded that he had signed a memorandum of his adhesion to this policy. On 4 March he sent for the duke, the chancellor, and Peel, and said he must have a clearer explanation of their policy. He was told the oaths of supremacy were to be repealed. He protested he had never understood that, and could never consent to it, and after five hours of discussion the resig-

nation of his ministers was tendered and accepted. Next day, however, he repented, and wrote to the duke that he would yield, and the ministry was allowed to proceed with its bill. For some time he continued to complain to his visitors of the violence done to his feelings, and the injudicious provision which compelled O'Connell to undergo a second election in Clare was inserted to gratify his resentment ; but his resistance to his ministers, except in a few matters of patronage, and indeed his political activity of any kind, was now at an end. His health began clearly to fail. No one but Knighton could induce him even to sign the necessary documents of state. He lay all day in bed and passed his nights in restless wakefulness. He kept his room at a high temperature and drank excessive quantities of cherry brandy. By February of 1830 he had become partially blind, and his singular delusions, such as that he had commanded a division at Waterloo and ridden a winning race at Goodwood, were in high force. On 12 April he drove out for the last time. Those about him knew, though he did not, that he was sinking. In May the Duke of Wellington caused the Bishop of Winchester to attend on him to prepare him for his end. Though Knighton thought he might rally, Halford and Tierney had given him over. On the 23rd he signed a request to parliament that a stamp might be substituted for the sign-manual. On 8 June he learned with fortitude that his end was near. In the night of the 25th he suddenly died. He was buried in St. George's Chapel, Windsor.

When his affairs came to be looked into, a curious condition of things was revealed. He seemed to have had a mania for misplaced hoarding. All the coats, boots, and pantaloons of fifty years were in his wardrobe, and to the end he carried the catalogue of them all in his head, and could call for any one of them at any moment. He had five hundred pocket-books, and all contained small sums of money laid by and forgotten ; 10,000l. in all was thus collected. There were countless bundles of women's love letters, of women's gloves, of locks of women's hair. These were destroyed. In 1823 Lord Eldon had made the king's will, and the executors were Lord Gifford and Sir W. Knighton, but his private effects were of comparatively small value.

The character of George IV was a singular mixture of good talents and mean failings. Undoubtedly he was clever and versatile, and, lazy though he was, he acquired a fair dilettante knowledge of many things. When he chose he could prove himself a capable man of business, nor could a person who associated with all the distinguished men of two generations, and won the regard of not a few of them, have been either without natural merit of his own, or incapable of profiting by their society. He had considerable mimetic talent (see *Macvey Napier's Correspondence*, p. 276; CAMPBELL, *Chief Justices*, iii. 245), and could assume a most gracious and winning manner at will, which accounted for, if it did not justify, his title of the 'first gentleman in Europe.' Undoubtedly he was master of that art which is called 'deportment.' 'Louis XIV himself,' says Wraxall, 'could scarcely have surpassed the son of George III in a ballroom, or when doing the honours of his palace, surrounded by the pomp and attributes of luxury and royal state.' But he often chose to be coarse, gross, and rude in his own demeanour, and the tone of manners of which he set the fashion was unrefined and vulgar. His flatterers called him a good musician, but Croker, who knew him well, says in 1822: 'His voice, a bass, is not good, and he does not sing so much from notes as from recollection. He is therefore as a musician very far from good.' In conversation he was very amusing and talkative, and passionately fond of gossip, and what he most sought for in his companions was deference without awe, and a capacity for keeping him amused. But his memory was very inaccurate, and his word wholly untrustworthy. The long statement which he dictated to Croker in 1825 for publication, which is given in the 'Croker Papers,' purported to correct the errors in the account given in Moore's 'Life of Sheridan' of the negotiations for a change of ministry in 1811 and 1812; but as an authority for the events of those years it is not to be relied upon. It is rather a political apology and a statement of the view which he would have desired the world should take of his conduct down to 1812, than a statement of fact. He was extraordinarily dissolute. In addition to his five more or less historic connections with Mrs. Robinson and Mrs. Fitzherbert, and Ladies Jersey, Hertford, and Conyngham, Lloyd and Huish, who devote much curious industry to this topic, enumerate eleven other persons by name and two others unnamed who were at one time or other his mistresses, and intimates the existence of very many other more temporary intrigues. Greville, who knew him well, and had no reason to judge him unfairly, says of him: 'This confirms the opinion I have long had, that a more contemptible, cowardly, unfeeling, selfish dog does not exist than this king.' In substance this is likely to be the judgment of posterity. There have been more wicked

kings in English history, but none so unredeemed by any signal greatness or virtue. That he was a dissolute and drunken fop, a spendthrift and a gamester, 'a bad son, a bad husband, a bad father, a bad subject, a bad monarch, and a bad friend,' that his word was worthless and his courage doubtful, are facts which cannot be denied, and though there may be exaggerations in the scandals which were current about him, and palliation for his vices in an ill-judged education and overpowering temptations, there was not in his character any of that staple of worth which tempts historians to revise and correct a somewhat too emphatic contemporary condemnation. All that can be said in his favour is this. The fact that his character was one which not even his own partisans could respect or defend caused the personal power of the monarch, which was almost at its highest when he became regent, to dwindle almost to a shadow years before he died.

Three portraits by Sir Thomas Lawrence and a marble statue by Chantrey are at Windsor. Portraits by West as a boy (with the Duke of York), and by Owen after Hoppner, are at Hampton Court. An unfinished portrait by Lawrence is in the National Portrait Gallery.

[Duke of Buckingham's Courts and Cabinets of George III, the Regency, and George IV, 1853; Lord John Russell's Memorials of Fox, 1862; Lord Holland's Memoirs of the Whig Party, 1854; Moore's Sheridan; Moore's Diary; Memoirs of Lord Malmesbury; Memoirs and Correspondence of Lord Auckland, 1861; Cornwallis Correspondence; Stanhope's Pitt; Life and Letters of Sir Gilbert Elliot, first lord Minto, 1874; Lord Colchester's Diary, 1861; Croker Papers, ed. Jennings; Greville Memoirs, 1st ser.; Twiss's Life of Eldon, 1844; Life of Sir J. Romilly; Lady Bury's Diary of Times of George IV; Cobbett's History of the Regency; Lives of George IV, by G. Croly, P. Fitzgerald, R. Huish, H. L. Lloyd, and Wallace; Langdale's Memoirs of Mrs. Fitzherbert; Jesse's George III; Horace Walpole's Journals and Correspondence; Gronow's Reminiscences; Massey's History of England, 1865, ending in 1802; Thackeray's Four Georges; Mrs. Delany's Autobiography, ed. Lady Llanover, 1861–2; Wraxall's Memoirs, 1884.] J. A. H.

GEORGE, PRINCE OF DENMARK (1653–1708), husband of Queen Anne, second son of Frederick III of Denmark and Sophia Amalia, daughter of George, duke of Brunswick-Lüneburg, the grandfather of George I, was born on 23 April 1653 (so HÜBNER; DOYLE dates his birth 21 April). His governor from 1661 to 1665 was Otto Grote, a man of great ability, to whom the house of Hanover afterwards largely owed its new electoral dignity (VEHSE, *Höfe d. H. Braun-*

schweig, i. 39 ; cf. *Allgemeine deutsche Biographie*, ix. 178). In his youth the prince travelled through France, Italy, and Germany, and gained some experience of naval training as well as of active service under arms (BURNET, v. 391–2). In 1674 efforts were made to place him on the Polish throne, but his aversion to catholicism caused the scheme to break down, and Sobiesky was elected (see a notice of ' C. H. Brasch, det polske Kongevalg,' 1674, Copenhagen, 1882, in *Revue Historique*, xxv. pt. ii. 397). After a preliminary visit to England in 1681 he was, on 28 July 1683, married to the Princess Anne, the second daughter of the Duke of York. Charles II presented his niece on her marriage with Wandsworth manor-house, where she lived with her husband for eighteen years. In the year after his marriage Prince George was created a K.G. (LUTTRELL, i. 294). He made a good personal impression at the English court, but as his brother, Christian V, was now at peace with France, the match was attributed to French influence, and the conversion of the prince to the church of Rome was thought likely to follow. But he had been brought up a strict Lutheran, and even after his wife's accession to the throne 'kept his chapel in the Lutheran way,' though ready to 'conform occasionally' to the church of England (BURNET, v. 53). A French intrigue, carried on in England by an agent named Bonrepos (March 1686), for converting the Princess Anne to catholicism, was thought by the agent to be favoured by Prince George (KLOPP, iv. 205–6), but it failed completely ; in the summer of the following year he paid a visit to Denmark (LUTTRELL, i. 407, 411). Prince George, from whom, ' whether drunk or sober,' Charles II had failed to extract anything at all, seems in the next reign to have made no difficulty in acquiescing with his wife in the schemes for the overthrow of her father's throne ; and after William's landing, though he accompanied the royal army on its march, and on its retreat as far as Andover, where he supped with James II, on the same evening (25 Nov. 1688) rode away with the Duke of Ormonde, the Earl of Drumlanrig, and Mr. H. Boyle to join the Prince of Orange at Sherborne, where they came in on 30 Nov. King James is said, in allusion to the phrase repeated by the prince as each fresh case of desertion became known, to have exclaimed, ' So Est-il possible is gone too,' and to have kindly ordered his servants and equipage to follow their master (CLARKE, *Life of James II*, ii. 227, and note ; cf. *Diary of Henry, Earl of Clarendon*, ii. 208, and 213 and notes; for the prince's letter to the king see Kennet, p. 531).

The prince, who took his wife's subsequent departure from London very coolly (CLARENDON, ii. 216), soon joined her in her progress at Oxford, and returned with her to Whitehall. His adhesion was rewarded by the king's assent to the act for his naturalisation (April 1689; see LUTTRELL, i. 517), and by his admission a few days afterwards into the English peerage as Baron of Ockingham, Earl of Kendal, and Duke of Cumberland ; a year later he was made chief commissioner of appeal for prizes (DOYLE). These honours may have had some connection with the successful efforts of William III to hold Denmark to his alliance, and to obtain Danish troops for Scotland and Flanders (LUTTRELL, i. 587, 603, ii. 117, 148; cf. as to the alliance of 1696, *ib.* iv. 142). But the extreme personal coldness which King William soon began to show towards Prince George proved one of the causes of the estrangement between the princess and her sister the queen (see art. ANNE ; cf. *Marchmont Papers*, ii. 418). In August 1691, when applying in vain with the princess for a Garter for Marlborough, Prince George reminded the king that this was the only request he had ever addressed to him (KLOPP, vi. 26). After the death of Queen Mary (December 1694), the relations between them assumed a more friendly aspect. But the death of the prince's only surviving son, the young Duke of Gloucester (1700), made it indispensable to introduce the house of Hanover by name into the succession, and the proposal made by Lord Normanby during the debates on the Act of Settlement, that in the event of Anne's accession to the throne the title of king should be conferred on her husband, was rejected (May 1701 ; *ib.* ix. 266).

When Anne became queen (March 1702) her first thoughts were for her husband, and one of the first orders issued in the new reign was designed as a mark of attention to the Danish court (cf. LUTTRELL, v. 152). She had to relinquish the intention of associating him with herself in the royal dignity (a motion to this effect in the commons was made and lost as late as November 1702), and her plan for inducing the States-General to name him their captain-general in William III's place came to nothing (KLOPP, x. 18, 32, 72). When Marlborough was appointed captain-general of the army, George received the sounding title of generalissimo of all her forces (17 April 1702), Marlborough declaring himself ' ravished' to serve under the prince (*Marlborough Despatches*, i. 44). Of a far more questionable nature was his appointment (21 May) to the office of lord high admiral, with a council to conduct the administration of the navy in his name. To these honours were added the lord wardenship of the Cinque ports and the captain-generalship of the London Artillery Company (June). A bill exempting the prince from the operation of the clause in the Act of Settlement excluding foreigners from offices passed the lords with great difficulty, but no opposition was offered to the annuity of 100,000*l.* proposed for the prince, 'though it was double of what any queen of England ever had in jointure' (BURNET, v. 55–6; cf. STANHOPE, pp. 77–8). To hold his office of lord high admiral it was necessary for the prince to 'conform occasionally' to the church of England by receiving the sacrament according to its rites; but he deferred to the queen in voting for the Occasional Conformity Bill in 1702, though assuring an opponent of the bill, 'My heart is vid you.' When it came up again in 1703, and the queen, to oblige the Duke of Marlborough, slackened her opposition, the prince was allowed to absent himself from the division (STANHOPE, vol. iii.) At the end of the year he took an active part in the reception of the Archduke Charles, titular king of Spain, on his visit to Windsor (BURNET, v. 83). But in general he played no part in public affairs. In 1706 he carried a message of encouragement from the queen to Godolphin (ELLIOT, *Life of Godolphin*, 1888, pp. 288–9), but in 1707 the tory intriguers endeavoured to gain his support by representing to him that the influence of Marlborough and the lord treasurer shut him out from his proper share in the control of affairs (BURNET, v. 336). According to an unkind story the queen's secret interviews with Harley first became publicly known through the indiscreet remark of her husband that she had hurt her eyes by sitting up late at night (SOMERVILLE, p. 267). In June 1708 Godolphin complained of his, as well as the queen's, ill-will (KLOPP, xiii. 166), and at the beginning of the year the whigs had begun to threaten that if the queen did not retract her promise to appoint certain tory bishops they would, among other things, 'show up' the admiralty in such a way that the prince should be obliged to give up his post as high admiral (Lord Raby to Leibniz, 17 Jan., ap. KEMBLE, p. 464). The inefficient system of naval administration of which the prince was the figure-head had almost from the first given rise to loud complaints (BURNET, v. 90), and an address on the subject had been voted by the House of Lords in 1704, and very sharply answered by the queen (KLOPP, xi. 33–4; it seems to have been a factious motion). Parliament was to meet on 16 Nov. with the whigs in the majority, and already their demand for the ad-

mission of Somers into the cabinet was coupled with renewed menaces against Prince George, who had for some time been suffering very severely from asthma. His obnoxious favourite, Admiral George Churchill, to whom the conduct of the naval administration had been chiefly entrusted, was persuaded by his brother, the Duke of Marlborough, to offer his resignation. But the whigs were determined to transfer the management of the admiralty from the prince to Lord Pembroke, in order that his offices might be given to Somers and Wharton; and in order to screen her suffering husband from a personal attack the queen (22 Oct. 1708) signified to Godolphin her assent to the admission of Somers. Whether the resignation of the prince would have been still insisted on remains uncertain, for on 28 Oct. he died; 'nature was quite worn out in him, and no art could support him long' (Godolphin to Marlborough, ap. COXE, chap. lxxv.) The queen, who during his illness had shown the most unremitting care to her husband, was inconsolable for his loss, and gave touching proofs of her remembrance of him by her generosity to his servants and dependants (cf. *Wentworth Papers*, pp. 63–4; *Treasury Papers*, 1714–19, pp. 270, 373). During his lifetime she had regretted his excessive good-nature to them (CLARENDON, *Diary*, ii. 315). Steele was gentleman usher to the prince (see A. DOBSON, *Richard Steele*, 1886, pp. 55–6).

Prince George was said, probably with truth, to have neither many friends nor many enemies in England. He was too old for active service after Anne's accession. His incapacity at the head of the admiralty was due to the system which placed him there, at least as much as to himself (see note to BURNET, v. 392). He was a fellow of the Royal Society, and seems to have taken an intelligent interest in navigation and in the sciences connected with it. He liberally promoted the publication of Flamsteed's important astronomical work (see *Treasury Papers*, 1714–19, p. 197). In 1702 he resigned his share of prizes taken during the war to such merchants as should fit out privateers (LUTTRELL, v. 179), and it was his intention (and the queen's after his death) to settle the royal house and park at Greenwich upon the Naval Hospital (*Treasury Papers*, 1714–19, p. 157). Although the Copenhagen professor who devoted a funeral oration to him (*ib.* 1708, pp. 14, 115) may not have found his achievements a fertile theme, he seems to have been too freely caricatured. In Macky's 'Characters' it is said of him that 'he is very fat, loves news, his bottle, and the queen,' but he is there further described as 'a prince of a familiar, easy disposition, with a good understanding, but modest in showing it.' Burnet (v. 391), who asserts that Prince George 'knew much more than he could well express,' adds that 'his temper was mild and gentle,' and that 'he was free from all vice.' The evident sincerity of these simple tributes and his long, happy wedded life should help to temper the ridicule which his name has suffered.

Kneller, Riley, and Dahl painted the prince's portrait. That in the National Portrait Gallery is by Wissing. Others are at Althorp and Middleton.

[Most of the authorities cited above are given in full under QUEEN ANNE; several particulars mentioned there concerning Prince George of Denmark have not been repeated here. Doyle's Official Baronage, i. 498, s. v. 'Cumberland,' contains a collection of passages descriptive of the prince's person, with a woodcut after Kneller.]   A. W. W.

GEORGE, JOHN (1804–1871), Irish judge, eldest son of John George of Dublin, merchant, by Emily Jane, daughter of Richard Fox, was born in the city of Dublin on 18 Nov. 1804, and received his education at Trinity College, Dublin. The university of Dublin conferred on him the degrees of B.A. 1823, and M.A. 1826, and in the latter year he was called to the bar at King's Inns. On 16 May 1827 he was also called to the bar at Gray's Inn, London. Having returned to Ireland, he was created a queen's counsel 2 Nov. 1844. He represented Wexford county in parliament as a conservative from 1852 to 1857, and again from May 1859 to 1866. He acted as solicitor-general for Ireland under Lord Derby from February to July 1859. He became a bencher of King's Inns in 1849, and a member of the Irish privy council in 1866, and was appointed a judge of the court of queen's bench, Ireland, in the November of the latter year, a post which he held until his death. He was highly esteemed as patient and painstaking in the discharge of his duties, strictly impartial and independent in his judgments, and courteous and dignified in his demeanour on the bench. He died at 45 Fitzwilliam Square, Dublin, 15 Dec. 1871, having married, first, in 1832, Susan Rosanna, daughter of Isaac Matthew D'Olier of Collegues, co. Dublin—she died in 1847; and secondly, 10 Aug. 1848, Mary, eldest daughter of Christopher L'Estrange Carleton.

[Times, 16 Dec. 1871, p. 5, and 18 Dec. p. 5; Illustrated London News, 23 Dec. 1871, p. 618.]
                                                    G. C. B.

GEORGE, WILLIAM, D.D. (d. 1756), dean of Lincoln, born in London, was educated at Eton and admitted to King's College, Cam-
bridge, in 1715. He proceeded to his degree of B.A. 1719, M.A. 1723, and D.D. 1728. On leaving the university he became assistant-master, and eventually principal, of Eton School, a position he maintained during several years with unusual distinction. It was during his residence at Eton that George was married to Miss Bland, daughter of Dr. Bland, his predecessor, and in 1731 he is further mentioned as canon of Windsor and chaplain in ordinary to his majesty. He quitted his scholastic career in 1743, when he was appointed to the vacant provostship of King's College, Cambridge. At his election to this office he engaged in a keen competition with Dr. Chapman, who was also a candidate, but he eventually succeeded in defeating his opponent by a small majority of votes. Within the same year he was also elected vice-chancellor of Cambridge. In 1747, the deanery of Winchester falling vacant, he was nominated for that office; but in order to oblige his friend, Dr. Samuel Pegge, he consented to exchange it for the deanery of Lincoln, where he was installed in 1748. He also resigned in favour of Dr. Pegge his rectory of Whittington, near Chesterfield in Derbyshire. He died on 2 Aug. 1756. George was a popular and eloquent preacher, and several of his sermons have been printed, among which may be mentioned a sermon preached before the Society for the Propagation of the Gospel, 1732, and a second delivered before the House of Commons in 1752. He is also described as an accurate Greek scholar and good Latin poet. Some fine specimens of his poetry have been preserved in the 'Musæ Etonenses' (1755), edited by J. Prinsep, including among others a series of poems entitled 'Ecclesiastes' and some exquisite lines on the death of Prince Frederick. The latter became unusually famous, from the high commendation pronounced upon them by Pope Lambertini, Benedict IV, who gave them the title of 'cardinal,' and is said to have observed that if the author had been a catholic he would have made him a cardinal; but since that could not be, he would bestow the honour upon the verses themselves.

[Nichols's Lit. Illustr. and Lit. Anecd.; Le Neve's Fasti; Alumni Etonenses, pp. 49, 295; Cooper's Mem. Cambr.; Oratio habita in funere reverendi et doctissimi viri Guil. George, S.T.P., by W. Barford, M.A.]   W. F. W. S.

GERALD, SAINT and BISHOP (d. 731), of Magh Eo, now Mayo, was, according to the life published by the Bollandists, and attributed by Colgan to Augustin Magraidin (1405), a monk from the neighbourhood of Winchester, who, with some companions, migrated to Ireland, in order to lead a solitary life. Another account connects his leaving England with the defeat of St. Colman, bishop of Lindisfarne, at the conference at Whitby on the Easter question. The party landed in Connaught and made their way northward to Sligo. Gerald built a church in Mayo which he called Cill n-ailither, or the Church of the Pilgrims. Parties of West- and East-Saxons having from time to time joined him there, the district acquired the name of Tech Saxan, which is still preserved in the prebend of Tagh Saxan in the cathedral of Tuam. He is also said to have built an oratory for his adherents in the plain of Mayo, on land given by Raghallach, king of Connaught (640-5), but it must have been a later king, as the best authority places his own death in 731. Here he was buried and his memory was venerated. This has been confounded with the monastery built in the same neighbourhood by St. Colman of Lindisfarne for his Saxon followers. It has been suggested that St. Colman placed his followers under the charge of Gerald as their countryman, but Bede distinctly states that St. Colman's monastery was a new one, and Dr. Petrie holds that St. Colman's abbey church was founded in the seventh century, and this of St. Gerald, also known as 'Tempull Garailt,' in the beginning of the eighth. Another story connects him with St. Fechin of Fobhar, who belonged to the second order of Irish saints (542–99). Fechin approved a proposal of the rich to pray for a pestilence to diminish the numbers of the lower orders on occasion of a famine, that there might be enough for the survivors. Gerald opposed the wicked proposal, which is said to have been punished by a plague. These anachronisms show that little value can be attributed to the details of the life. His fame was probably due to the later prosperity of his monastery. Ussher quotes from the 'Book of Ballymote' a statement that there were a hundred Saxon saints at Mayo in the time of Adamnan, St. Gerald's successor, and the Litany of Oengus in the 'Book of Leinster' has an invocation of '3,300 saints with Gerald the bishop, and with the fifty saints of Leyney in Connaught, who are [buried] at Mayo of the Saxons.' Local names and traditions also attest the reality of this English mission. Gerald is termed in the 'Annals' the 'Pontifex of Mayo of the Saxons,' and more distinctly 'episcopus' in the extract from the Litany of Oengus. The date of his death is given by Ussher as 697, and by the 'Four Masters' as 726, but the 'Annals of Ulster,' which appear to be the best authority, place it at 731. His day is 13 March.

[Bollandists' Acta Sanct., 13 March, ii. 290, &c.; Calendar of Oengus, p. clxxxi; Petrie's Round Towers, pp. 143, 144; Book of Leinster, p. 373, b. 59; Lanigan's Eccl. Hist. iii. 166–8; Ussher (Works), vi. 607–10.]   T. O.

GERALD, JOSEPH (1763–1796), political reformer. [See GERRALD.]

GERARD or **GIRARD** (*d.* 1108), archbishop of York, was the nephew of Walkelin, bishop of Winchester, and his brother Simeon, abbot of Ely, and therefore, possibly, a distant kinsman of the Conqueror. He was precentor of the cathedral of Rouen (ROB. DE MONTE, ed. Stevenson, p. 680), and afterwards a clerk of William Rufus's chapel and chancery. William despatched him in 1095, in company with William of Warelwast, afterwards bishop of Exeter, to the papal court on a secret and delicate mission in connection with the dispute between the king and Anselm. The alleged object of their embassage was to investigate the claims of the two rival popes. Its real purpose was to acknowledge Urban, if in return he would consent to send William a pallium for him to bestow on the Archbishop of Canterbury, neither Anselm nor any other person being named, and would also confer on the king some kind of legatine authority. Gerard and Warelwast met Urban probably at Cremona. The result of their negotiation was the mission to the king of a papal legate, Cardinal William of Albano, with whom they returned by the middle of May, the pallium being secretly in the legate's custody (EADMER, *Hist. Novorum*, p. 68). A year later (1096) Gerard, though not yet even in deacon's orders, was rewarded with the bishopric of Hereford for his successful intrigue. Anselm, then staying with his friend Gundulf at his manor of Lambeth, ordained Gerard deacon and priest the same day, and consecrated him the following day, 8 June 1096 (*ib.* p. 74). He was present at the consecration of Gloucester Abbey, 15 July 1100 (SYM. DUNELM. p. 225). The story told by Walter Map (*De Nugis Curial.* p. 224), that Gerard crowned Henry I (5 Aug. 1100) and received from him the promise of the first vacant archbishopric, that Henry repented, and that Gerard held him to his word, may safely be rejected. Anselm being absent from England, and Thomas, archbishop of York, lying on his deathbed, Maurice, bishop of London, was the prelate who crowned Henry. Gerard was present, for his name appears as one of the witnesses to Henry's famous charter of issued liberties, on the day of his coronation; but though the Oseney 'Chronicle' supports Map's story (*Annal. Monast.* iv. 14), the part he took in the ceremony must have been merely secondary (MATT. PARIS, *Chron. Maj.* ii. 117, 554; WENDOVER, *Chron.* ii.164). Orderic states that Edith, better known as Matilda, Henry's queen, was crowned by Gerard (ORD. VIT. 784 A), but other authorities, with greater probability, assign both the marriage and the 'hallowing to queen' to Anselm. A week later the death of Archbishop Thomas, 18 Nov., placed the northern primacy at Henry's disposal, and he without delay conferred it on Gerard. A conflict between the two primatial authorities once more broke out. Anselm, as primate of all England, demanded Gerard's profession. Gerard claimed exemption as a brother primate. It was essential, however, that Gerard should obtain the pallium from Rome, and for this purpose letters from Anselm substantiating his claim were necessary. On applying for them, he was told that he must either make his profession at once or promise to make it on his return. Gerard evasively replied that ' when he came back he would do all that could be justly demanded of him.' Anselm professed himself satisfied, and furnished Gerard with the necessary letters to Pope Paschal (ANSELMI *Epist.* lib. iii. ep. 48). Gerard also carried one from Henry himself.

The dispute about investiture was then running high. The decision was to be submitted to the pope. Each party was to be represented. Anselm sent two monks, Henry three prelates, of whom the new archbishop was the chief, the other two being Robert of Chester (i.e. Lichfield) and Herbert de Losinga of Norwich, both men of very questionable respectability (CHURCH, *Essays*, p. 205). Gerard, clever and unscrupulous, with much reputation for learning, pleaded his royal master's cause with so much ability, that he was openly complimented by Paschal and the whole curia. The pallium was conferred on him, and he and his companions returned bearing sealed letters to Anselm and the king. Both missives refused the king's demands and peremptorily required him to submit to the papal see. But Gerard and his companions asserted that the pope had secretly assured them that so long as Henry acted as a good king, the decrees about investitures would not be enforced. Anselm's deputies denied any such assurance. The solemn word of Gerard and his episcopal companions, however, was held to outweigh the testimony of two 'paltry monks.' Paschal when appealed to repudiated in the most solemn terms the alleged understanding, and placed Gerard and the other bishops under sentence of excommunication until they had confessed their crime and made satisfaction (EADMER, pp. 132, 140, 145, 151; cf. ANSELMI *Epist.* lib. iii. ep. 131).

Eventually the required profession of canonical obedience to Anselm was made by Gerard, though so tardily that more than one letter was despatched by Paschal before it was rendered. The last of these, dated 12 Dec. 1102, arrived after the profession had been made, and remained unopened and unread (ANSELMI *Epist.* iii. 131; EADMER, p. 173; *Anglia Sacra*, ii. 170). Although Thomas Stubbs, eager for the privileges of the see of York, vehemently repudiates the story (TWYSDEN, p. 1710 B), we may safely accept the well-authenticated statement that Gerard laid his hand upon that of Anselm, with the promise that he would exhibit the same obedience he had paid him when bishop of Hereford (EADMER, p. 187; FLOR. WIG. ii. 56; GERVAS. CANTUAR. ii. 375; SYM. DUNELM. ii. 239; HOVEDEN, i. 164). Gerard, however, continued to assert the co-ordinate dignity of the two primatial sees, and at the important council held at Westminster, September 1102 (if we may credit the tale told by Thomas Stubbs), indignantly kicked over the lower seat which had been prepared for him with a curse, 'in the vulgar tongue, on the head of the author of such an indignity,' and refused to take his place except on a level with his brother primate (TWYSDEN, *ib.*)

The next year Gerard again came into open collision with Anselm. Three bishops were awaiting consecration, William Giffard [q. v.] to Winchester, the famous Roger [q. v.] to Salisbury, and Reinhelm [q. v.] to Hereford. On Anselm's refusal to consecrate the latter two as having received investiture from the king, Henry commanded Gerard to perform the rite. Gerard consented. Reinhelm, shrinking from so gross an infringement of the rights of Canterbury, refused to accept consecration at Gerard's hands. Giffard, who had already received investiture from Anselm, appeared on the day of consecration in St. Paul's Cathedral, but when the ceremony had begun he interrupted the service, and openly repudiated Gerard's pretensions. The assistant bishops thought it prudent to proceed no further, and the assembly broke up in confusion. Roger, who stood awaiting consecration, left the cathedral as he entered it, a simple priest (EADMER, p. 69; FLOR. WIG. p. 1103; MATT. PARIS, *Chron. Maj.* ii. 122; *Hist. Angl.* i. 191). During Anselm's three years of exile Gerard devoted himself to re-establishing discipline in his vast diocese, not yet recovered from the Conqueror's devastations. Gerard's conduct displeased Paschal, who in an objurgatory letter took him severely to task for the support he had given to the king against the primate. The indulgence of the holy see had been heavily taxed and would not be extended much longer (ANSELMI *Epist.* lib. iv. ep. 38). Although any confidential intercourse between Anselm and Gerard would seem to have been rendered impossible by the decided line each took in the dispute regarding investiture, their correspondence is not wanting in dignified courtesy. Before it was recognised that Anselm's return was indispensable to the English church, letters had passed between them practically effecting a reconciliation. Gerard, with the bishops of Lichfield, Norwich, and others, addressed a moving letter to Anselm entreating him to return at once as the only means of remedying the miseries under which the church was labouring (*ib.* lib. iii. ep. 121). On Anselm's return and the great settlement of the investiture dispute, the reconciliation seems to have been completed, and Gerard was the first of the six assistant prelates at the long-deferred episcopal consecration at Canterbury, 11 Aug. 1107, when no fewer than five bishops received the archiepiscopal blessing (GERVASE, ii. 376; EADMER, iv. 77; WILL. OF MALMESBURY, *Gesta Pont.* p. 117; SYM. DUNELM. ii. 239). Gerard died 21 May 1108, at his palace at Southwell, when on his way to a council held in London to enforce clerical celibacy. He had been suffering from a slight indisposition. After dinner he went to walk in the garden attached to the palace, and after a little time lay down to sleep on a sunny bank, requesting his chaplains to leave him alone for a while. On their return he was dead. Under the cushion which had been his pillow was found a book by Julius Firmicus, a writer on judicial astrology, a science to which the archbishop was much devoted. His enemies interpreted his death, without the rites of the church, as a divine judgment for his addiction to magical and forbidden arts. Gerard had failed to secure the affections of the clergy or the people of his diocese. The funeral cortège was very scantily attended on its route, and on its entry into York it was not, as was customary, received in pomp by the citizens and the clergy, but by noisy boys who pelted the bier with stones. As the archbishop had departed without the last sacraments, the canons refused him interment within the walls of his cathedral, barely allowing him a turfed grave outside its doors. From this ignominious resting-place his body was transferred to the cathedral by his successor, Archbishop Thomas II. That Gerard was a learned man, an eloquent orator, and an able politician, there is no question. Thomas Stubbs says that he had few superiors in knowledge and eloquence, and William of Newburgh styles him clever and learned, epithets which are confirmed by

William of Malmesbury. But he is charged by these authorities with covetousness and a licentious life, to which popular rumour added the practice of magical arts. Canon Raine says: 'Gerard was a reformer and a successful politician, and in both these characters he would be sure to create enemies.' Our chief knowledge of him is from ecclesiastical historians, from whom an unprejudiced verdict on one who so vigorously supported the regal against the pontifical power is hardly to be looked for. Two of Gerard's letters appear among those of Anselm (lib. iii. ep. 121, iv. ep. 39). Some Latin verses of no high poetical merit are preserved in a manuscript of the Cottonian collection (Titus D. xxiv. 3). He enriched the cathedral of York with five churches which were granted him by Henry I, one of which, Laughton, was constituted a prebend.

[Raine's Fasti Eboracenses, containing references to all original authorities; Eadmer, Hist. Nov. (Rolls Ser.); Gervase of Canterbury, Chron. ed. Stubbs (Rolls Ser.); William of Malmesbury, De Gestis Pont. (Rolls Ser.); Hoveden, Chron. ed. Stubbs (Rolls Ser.); Florence of Worcester, Chron. (Engl. Hist. Soc.); Symeon of Durham (Rolls Ser.)] E. V.

GERARD, ALEXANDER, D.D. (1728–1795), theological and philosophical writer, born at the manse of Chapel of Garioch, Aberdeenshire, 22 Feb. 1728, studied at Marischal College, Aberdeen, and was licensed as a preacher of the church of Scotland in 1748. Two years later he became a professor of philosophy in Marischal College, following the old arrangement, by which each professor had to conduct the students over several branches of study. This arrangement was founded on the notion that logic ought to be the first study, and that its principles ought to be applied in the study of all other branches; but Gerard in 1755 published an acute pamphlet, in which he advocated a modification of the arrangement of studies, and prepared the way for the abolition of the old system.

In 1756 he gained a prize offered by the Philosophical Society of Edinburgh for the best essay on taste, and in 1759 this work was published. Its fundamental definition is that taste consists chiefly 'in the improvement of those principles which are commonly called the powers of imagination,' including the sense of novelty, sublimity, beauty, imitation, harmony, ridicule, and virtue. The work has thus a much wider scope than that which, according to modern ideas, belongs to the subject of taste. Under the sense of beauty Gerard gave a prominent place to the principle of association, in which he has been followed by Alison [see ALISON, ARCHIBALD].

In 1760 Gerard was appointed professor of divinity in Marischal College, and likewise minister of the Greyfriars Church in Aberdeen. In 1771 he resigned both these offices, on his appointment to the chair of divinity in King's College. He was a member of a well-known literary and philosophical society in Aberdeen with which Drs. George Campbell, Thomas Reid, James Beattie, Blackwell, Gregory, and other distinguished men were connected, and where not a few papers were first produced which proved the germs of important contributions to literature. He was one of the chaplains of the king, supported the 'moderate' party in the church, and filled the chair of moderator of the general assembly in 1764. Gerard died 22 Feb. 1795. Other works published by him were: 1. 'The Influence of the Pastoral Office on the Character examined; with a View especially to Mr. Hume's Representation of the Spirit of that Office,' Aberdeen, 1760. 2. 'Dissertations on Subjects relating to the Genius and the Evidences of Christianity,' Edinburgh, 1766, a defence of the manner in which the evidence of Christianity was presented by its great author, and a contention that Christianity is confirmed by the objections of infidels. 3. 'An Essay on Genius,' London, 1774. 4. 'Liberty a Cloak of Maliciousness, both in the American Rebellion and in the Manners of the Times,' Aberdeen, 1778. 5. Sermons, 2 vols. 2nd edit. London, 1782. 6. 'The Corruption of Christianity,' Edinburgh, 1792. 7. 'The Pastoral Care' (posthumous), London, 1799. His son, Gilbert Gerard, D.D. [q. v.], assisted him in the last-named book.

[Scott's Fasti, iii. 475; Darling's Cyclopædia Bibl.; Kennedy's Annals of Aberdeen; Smith's Hist. of Aberdeen; Chambers's Eminent Scotsmen.]   W. G. B.

GERARD, ALEXANDER (1792–1839), Himalayan explorer, was son of Gilbert Gerard, D.D. [q. v.], grandson of Alexander Gerard, D.D. [q. v.], and brother of James Gilbert [q. v.] and Patrick [q. v.] He was born in Aberdeen 17 Feb. 1792, and probably was the student of that name who appears in the album of the King's or Marischal College in 1804. He received a Bengal cadetship in 1808. He was appointed ensign 13th Bengal native infantry 9 Sept. 1808 and lieutenant in that corps 28 Nov. 1814. He was employed in the survey of the route to Lahore in 1812, and as surveyor to the board of commissioners in the ceded provinces in October 1814, and was adjutant of the second battalion of his regiment in 1815. He was surveyor of Seharunpore in 1817; was posted to the Sirmoor battalion 12 June 1820; was assistant to the resident in Malwa and Rajpootana 29 June 1822; was surveyor of the Nerbudda valley 19 Nov. 1825, and surveyor in Malwa and Rajpootana from 11 Sept. 1826 to 18 Aug. 1827 (information supplied by the India Office). In the course of his service Gerard carried out many arduous and important survey duties, especially in the Himalayas, where he ascended heights previously believed to be inaccessible, and penetrated into Thibet as far as the frontier picquets of Chinese would allow. To him we are indebted for our earliest notions of the geological structure and remains of the Himalayan ranges. The first notice of him appears in 'Asiatic Researches,' xv. 339, as the companion of Major Herbert in the survey of the Sutlej. The same volume contains Gerard's 'Observations on the Climate of Subathoo and Kotguhr' (ib. pp. 469–88). His labours in completing the geographical survey of the Sutlej valley were subsequently described by Henry Thomas Colebrooke [q. v.] in 'Transactions Asiatic Soc. London,' i. 543. (See also 'Edinburgh Journal of Science,' v. 270–278, vi. 28–50.) In 1817–18 Gerard was exploring the Himalayas with Dr. Govan, and in 1819 with his brother, Dr. James Gilbert Gerard [q. v.], 1st Nusseerabad battalion. In 1821 he performed the most important of his Himalayan journeys. Leaving Subathoo he ascended the Himalayan upper ranges, carefully noting the places inhabited by the way, determining with the aid of the barometer, checked by trigonometrical admeasurements wherever practicable, their ranges of elevation above the level of the sea, the temperatures, natural productions, and character of the tribes dotted about on ledges previously supposed to be uninhabited and uninhabitable. Gerard and his company reached the Borendo pass, 15,121 feet above the sea-level, on 15 June. Here the native guides refused to proceed further, and Gerard had to shape his course to the source of the Pabur by another route. The Charang pass, at an altitude of 17,348 feet, was ascended on 9 July, half a mile of the slope being so slippery with gravel and half-melted snow that Gerard had to crawl upwards on all fours, burying his arms deep in the snow to secure his hold. Another ascent was that of the Keeobrung pass, 18,312 feet above the sea. Yet another was that of Mount Tahigung, where part of the ascent was at an angle of forty-two, an incline declared by Humboldt to be impracticable. The height ascended was 19,411 feet, and the total computed altitude of the mountain 22,000 feet. A small collection of geological specimens, made by Gerard in Chinese Tartary during this journey between lat. 31° 30' and 32° 30' N.

and long. 77°–79° E., at an elevation of 19,000 feet above the sea, and resembling the fossils of the oolite in Europe, was exhibited before the Geological Society of London after his death. A narrative of Gerard's 'Journey from Subathoo to Shipké in Chinese Tartary' appeared posthumously in 'Journ. Asiat. Soc. of Bengal' (1842), xi. 363–91, and his 'Journal of a Journey from Shipké to the frontier of Chinese Thibet' was published in the 'Edinburgh Journal of Science' (1824), i. 41–52, 215–225. Bishop Heber, who met Gerard at Ummeerpore after his return from this journey, describes him as a man of very modest exterior and of great science and information, and enlarges eloquently in his journal on Gerard's achievements and enterprising spirit (HEBER, *Journal of a Journey in the Upper Provinces*, ii. 59). Sir H. T. Colebrooke made selections from Gerard's geological notes on the Himalayas, whereof duplicates were sent to the Geological Society, London, from which and from Gerard's letters was compiled the 'Geological Sketch of the Himalayas,' which appeared in 'Geological Trans.' (London), i. (2nd ser.) 124. Gerard was a good Persian scholar and versed in other oriental tongues. He was a most accurate topographer and a very entertaining and observant traveller. Unfortunately, except in the fragmentary shapes just indicated, no accounts of his travels were published during his lifetime. Broken health, the result of the amazing hardships endured in the course of his survey duties and travels, led to his retirement from the service on 22 Feb. 1836, and brought him to a premature grave. He died at Aberdeen on 15 Dec. 1839, in the forty-eighth year of his age, after three days' illness, from a fever, to the attacks of which he was periodically subject.

In 1840 Sir William Lloyd, knight, of Brynestyn, near Wrexham, a Welsh country gentleman, who had been a major in the Hon. East India Company's Bengal infantry and an Indian surveyor, brought out a book, under the editorship of his son, George Lloyd, entitled 'Narrative of a Journey from Caunpoor [Cawnpore] to the Borendo Pass in the Himalayas, *viâ* Gwalior, Agra, Delhi, and Sirhind, by Major Sir William Lloyd, knight. . . . Also Captain Alexander Gerard's Account of an attempt to penetrate by Bekhur to Garoo and Lake Manasarowara. Also a Letter from the late James Gilbert Gerard, esq., M.D., detailing a Visit to the Shatool and the Borendo Passes with the purpose of determining the Line of Perpetual Snow on the Southern Face of the Himaleyas,' 2 vols. 8vo, London, 1840. The second volume of this work consisted of the narratives of Alexander and James Gilbert

Gerard, which were prepared for the purpose by Alexander, who died while the sheets were in the printer's hands. Afterwards, Alexander Gerard's papers, or some of them, appear to have been entrusted to Mr. George Lloyd, who published therefrom 'An Account of Koonawar in the Himalayas,' London, 1841, 8vo. To this account are appended narratives of Alexander Gerard's Himalayan journeys in 1817–18 and 1819.

The paper on 'Pendulum Experiments' (1851), entered under the name in 'Cat. Scientific Papers,' vol. ii., was by another Alexander Gerard (LL.D. Aberdeen, 1875, teacher of mathematics in Robert Gordon's Hospital, now Gordon College, Aberdeen). He belonged to a different family.

[Chambers's Biog. Dict. of Eminent Scotsmen (in part inaccurate); Gent. Mag. new ser. xiii. 324; authorities under GERARD, PATRICK.]

H. M. C.

GERARD, CHARLES, first BARON GERARD OF BRANDON in Suffolk, VISCOUNT BRANDON, and EARL OF MACCLESFIELD (*d.* 1694), was the eldest son of Sir Charles Gerard, by Penelope, sister and heiress of Sir Edward Fitton of Gawsworth, Cheshire, and grandson of Ratcliffe, second son of Sir Gilbert Gerard [q. v.], master of the rolls in the reign of Elizabeth. An Englishman, 'Anglus Lancastrensis,' of his name entered Leyden University 23 March 1633. He was also educated in France under John Goffe of Magdalen College, Oxford, brother of Stephen Goffe [q. v.] PEACOCK, *Leyden Students*, p. 40; *Athenæ Oxon.*, ed. Bliss, iii. 525; *Cal. State Papers*, Dom. 1633–4, p. 280). Dugdale states that he was 'trained in the discipline of war from his youth in the United Provinces,' and that on the outbreak of the civil war in England he joined the king at Shrewsbury, and raised a troop of horse at his own charges (*Baronage*, ii. 41). At Edgehill, however, he commanded a brigade of infantry, the steadiness of which largely contributed to avert absolute defeat. In this battle, as also in the operations before Lichfield in April 1643, he was wounded. He was present at the siege of Bristol (July 1643), and arranged the very rigorous terms of the capitulation. He fought with distinction in the first battle of Newbury (20 Sept. 1643), and took part in the relief of Newark (March 1644), when he was again wounded, thrown from his horse, and taken prisoner, but released on parole shortly before the besiegers capitulated (CLARKE, *Life of James II*, i. 17; CLARENDON, *Rebellion*, iii. 292, iv. 35, 145, 614; WARBURTON, *Memoirs of Prince Rupert*, ii. 237, 259; BAKER, *Chron.* pp. 551–3; *Mercur. Aulic.* 20 Sept. 1643,

23 March 1643-4). Shortly afterwards he was appointed to succeed the Earl of Carbery in the general command in South Wales, then strongly held by the parliament, and by 19 May 1644 had succeeded in collecting a force of two thousand five hundred horse and foot with which to begin operations. He marched by Chepstow to Cardiff, which surrendered to him, and took Kidwelly. By 12 June he had already penetrated into Carmarthenshire, and before the 18th he was in possession of Carmarthen. He rapidly reduced Cardigan, Newcastle Emlyn, Laugharne, and Roch Castles, and seems to have experienced no check until he was already threatening Pembroke about the middle of July, when the garrison of that place by a sortie routed a portion of his force and obtained supplies. On 22 Aug. he took Haverfordwest, and before the end of the month had invested Pembroke and was threatening Tenby. His forces are said to have been largely composed of Irish levies, of whose barbarous atrocities loud complaint is made in the 'Kingdom's Intelligencer,' 15-23 Oct. 1644. In September he received orders to join Rupert at Bristol, and in October he began his retreat, marching by Usk and Abergavenny, and thus evading General Massey he reached Bristol towards the end of the month. November he spent in Oxford or the neighbourhood, whence in December he transferred his headquarters to Worcester, where he remained until 11 March 1644-5. Hence he marched to Cheshire to co-operate with Rupert, Maurice, and Langdale against General Brereton. Their united forces succeeded in relieving Beeston Castle on 17 March (*Mercur. Aulic.* 19 May and 31 Aug. 1644; *Perfect Occurr.* 21 July 1644; *Diary or Exact Journal,* 7 Nov. 1644; *Manchester's Quarrel with Cromwell,* Camd. Soc. p. 17; *Weekly Account,* 31 Oct. and 3 Dec. 1644; *Addit. MS.* 18981, f. 326; WARBURTON, *Memoirs of Prince Rupert,* i. 500; ORMEROD, *Cheshire,* ed. Helsby, ii. 275). Gerard was then ordered back to South Wales, where the parliamentary general, Laugharne, had gained some successes. He marched through Wales from Chester in a south-westerly direction, carrying all before him and ravaging the country as he went. After a brush with Sir John Price at Llanidloes, he fell in with Laugharne before Newcastle Emlyn on 16 May, and completely defeated him. Haverfordwest and Cardigan Castle, which had been recovered by the roundheads, were evacuated on his approach. Picton Castle offered a stout resistance, but was carried by assault. Carew Castle also fell into his hands. Pembroke and Tenby, closely invested, alone held

out. The ascendency of the royalists being thus re-established in South Wales, Gerard received orders to move eastward again, and was marching on Hereford at the head of five thousand horse and foot when the battle of Naseby was fought (14 June 1645). After the battle the king and Rupert, with the fragments of their army, fell back upon Hereford in the hope of effecting a junction with Gerard, who, however, seems to have been unexpectedly delayed; and Rupert, pushing on to Bristol, sent orders that part of Gerard's forces should join him there, while the king required a portion of the cavalry to attend his person. From Hereford Charles retreated to Abergavenny and thence to Cardiff, with the hope of raising a fresh army in Wales, but found the Welsh much disaffected, owing (according to Clarendon) to the irritation engendered by the extraordinary rigour with which Gerard had treated them; so that when news came that Hereford had been invested by the Scottish army and must fall unless relieved within a month, Charles could only induce the Welsh to move by superseding Gerard, promising at the same time to make him a baron. Gerard chose the title of Baron Brandon, for no better reason, says Clarendon, than 'that there was once an eminent person called Charles Brandon who was afterwards made a duke' (WARBURTON, *Memoirs of Prince Rupert,* iii. 120; CLARENDON, *Rebellion,* v. 186, 221-2, 227-9; see art. BRANDON, CHARLES, DUKE OF SUFFOLK, *d.* 1545). Two dates have been assigned to the patent creating him Baron Gerard of Brandon, viz. 8 Oct. and 28 Nov. 1645 (DUGDALE, *Baronage,* ii. 41; NICOLAS, *Historic Peerage,* ed. Courthope; DOYLE gives 8 Nov.)

Gerard had become lieutenant-general of all the king's horse, and assumed the command of his body-guard. On the night of 4 Aug. 1645 he escorted Charles from Cardiff to Brecknock, and thence to Ludlow, and throughout his progress to Oxford (28 Aug.) Thence they returned to Hereford (4 Sept.), the Scots raising the siege on their approach. At Hereford on 14 Sept. Charles heard of the fall of Bristol, and determined if possible to join Montrose in the north. Escorted by Gerard he made for Chester, and succeeded in entering the city, having first detached Gerard to the assistance of Sir Marmaduke Langdale, who was endeavouring to muster the royalists in force outside the city, with the view of raising the siege. After much apparently purposeless marching and counter-marching the royalists risked an engagement with the besiegers on Rowton Heath (23 Sept. 1645), but were totally defeated by General Pointz. Gerard was carried off the field desperately wounded. The king then evacuated Chester and retired to Newark, where he arrived with Gerard on 4 Oct., and fixed his headquarters for the winter. Gerard was dismissed the king's service before the end of the month for taking part with Rupert and some other cavaliers in a disorderly protest against the supersession of Sir Richard Willis, the governor of the place ('Iter Carolinum,' in *Somers Tracts*; SYMONDS, *Diary*, Camd. Soc.; *Parliament's Post*, 23–30 Sept. 1645; *Perfect Diurnal*, 29 Sept.–6 Oct. 1645; *King's Pamphlets*, small 4to, vol. ccxxvii. Nos. 18, 21, 24–6; *Hist. MSS. Comm.* 7th Rep. App. 454 *a*, 9th Rep. App. 435–6; CARTE, *Ormonde Papers*, i. 338; BAKER, *Chron.* 364; WARBURTON, *Memoirs of Prince Rupert*, iii. 206–7). Gerard now attached himself closely to Rupert's party, which consisted of about four hundred officers. They established themselves at Worton House, some fourteen miles from Newark, and made overtures to the parliament with the view of obtaining passes out of the country. Parliament, however, required that they should take an oath never again to bear arms against it. The cavaliers therefore temporised, being really anxious for a reconciliation with the king on honourable terms. They were ordered to the neighbourhood of Worcester by parliament, and there remained during the winter, but early in the following year returned to their allegiance and the king at Oxford. There Gerard raised another troop of horse, with which he scoured the adjoining country, penetrating on one occasion as far as the neighbourhood of Derby, where he was routed in a skirmish. At one time he seems to have been in command of Wallingford, but when the lines of investment began to be drawn more closely round Oxford he withdrew within the city walls, where he seems to have remained until the surrender of the place (24 June 1646). He probably left England with Rupert, as we find him at the Hague on 27 Dec. 1646 (*True Informer*, 31 Oct. 1645; *Mercur. Britann.* 27 Oct.–3 Nov. 1645; *Perfect Passages*, 28 Oct. 1645, 21 Feb. 1645–6; *Contin. of Special Passages*, 31 Oct. 1645; *Perfect Diurnal*, 19 Nov. 1645, 10 Feb. 1645–6; *Mod. Intell.* 21 Nov. and 13 Dec. 1645, 24 Jan. 1645–6, 27 Dec. 1646; WOOD, *Annals of Oxford*, ed. Gutch, ii. 477; *Perfect Occurr.* 2 May 1646). From this time until the Restoration his movements are very hard to trace. He was at St. Germain-en-Laye in September 1647 with Rupert, Digby, and other cavaliers. He was appointed vice-admiral of the fleet in November 1648, and on 8 Dec. passed through Rotterdam on his way to Helvoetsluys to enter on his new duties.

In April 1649 he was at the Hague as gentleman of the bedchamber to the king. He apparently belonged to the 'queen's faction,' which was understood to favour the policy of coming to an understanding with the commissioners from the Scottish parliament, who were then at the Hague, but were denied an audience by Charles. In October of the same year he was with Charles in Jersey when the celebrated declaration addressed to the English people was published, and he was a member, and probably an influential member, of the council which advised the king to treat with the Scottish parliament as a 'committee of estates.' He returned with the king to the Hague, where this policy was put in execution. On 18 March 1649–50 Hyde writes from Madrid to Secretary Nicholas praising Gerard somewhat faintly as a 'gallant young man' who 'always wants a friend by him;' to which Nicholas replies on 4 May that Gerard is 'the gallantest, honestest person now about the king, and the most constant to honourable principles.' In the following November (1650) Nicholas writes to Gerard that he has the commission appointing him general of Kent, but that the fact must be kept secret 'because the king in his late declaration promised the Scots to grant none.' In March 1650–1 Gerard left the Hague for Breda in attendance on the Duke of York, who was anxious to avoid certain 'things called ambassadors,' as Nicholas scornfully terms the Scottish envoys. In the following November he was in Paris, where he seems to have remained for at least a year (*Hist. MSS. Comm.* 4th Rep. App. 275, 547, 5th Rep. App. 173; CARTE, *Ormonde Papers*, i. 93, 155, 338, 426; WHITELOCKE, *Mem.* 349; BAILLIE, *Letters*, Bannatyne Club, iii. 8; HARRIS, *Life of Charles II*, p. 74; *Clarendon State Papers*, iii. 13; *Nicholas Papers*, Camden Soc., 171, 199, 279; *Cal. State Papers*, Dom. 1651–2, p. 3; *Egerton MSS.* 2534 ff. 117, 127, 2535 f. 483). On 13 May 1652 he was appointed to the command of the corps of life guards then being raised. In 1653 he went to Utrecht, where Dr. Robert Creighton [q. v.] 'wrought a miracle' upon him. He remained there through part of 1654, was present at the siege of Arras, serving under Turenne as a volunteer in August of that year (GUALDO PRIORATO, *Hist. del Ministerio del Cardinale Mazarino*, ed. 1669, iii. 319), and then returned to Paris, where he divided his energies between quarrelling with Hyde, intriguing on behalf of Henrietta Maria, and instigating his cousin, John Gerard, to assassinate the Protector. The plot, to which the king appears to have been privy, was discovered, and John Gerard was beheaded in the

Tower. Gerard had presented his cousin to the king early in 1654 [see under GERARD, JOHN, 1632–1654]. A letter from one F. Coniers to the king, dated London, 11 Jan. 1655, preserved in 'Thurloe State Papers' (i. 696), accuses Gerard of having treated with Thurloe for the poisoning of Cromwell. This the writer professes to have discovered by glancing over some papers incautiously exposed in Thurloe's chambers. The story is obviously a mere invention. In July 1655 Gerard was at Cologne, closely watched by Thurloe's spies. As Hyde wrote to Nicholas from Paris, 24 April 1654, Gerard was never without projects (Cal. Clarendon Papers, ii. 341). From Cologne he went to Antwerp 'to attempt the new modelling of the plot,' returning to Paris in September. There he appears to have resided until May 1656; busily employed in collecting intelligence. In this work he seems to have been much aided by the postal authorities, who, according to one of Thurloe's correspondents, allowed him to intercept whatever letters he pleased. In July he was at Cologne awaiting instructions. In February 1657 he was at the Hague, corresponding under the name of Thomas Enwood with one Dermot, a merchant at the sign of the Drum, Drury Lane. The only fragment of this correspondence which remains (Thurloe State Papers, vi. 26) is unintelligible, being couched in mercantile phraseology, which gives no clue to its real meaning. Thence he went to Brussels, where in April he received instructions to raise a troop of horse guards at once and a promise of an allowance of four hundred guilders a day for his family. From Brussels he returned to Paris in March 1657–8. He was almost immediately despatched to Amsterdam, apparently for the purpose of chartering ships, and he spent the rest of that year and the first six months of the next partly in the Low Countries and partly at Boulogne, returning to Paris between August and September 1659. There he appears to have spent the autumn and part of the winter, joining Secretary Nicholas at Brussels in the following January. Thence in the spring he went to Breda, and in May 1660 returned with the king to England. He rode at the head of the life guards in the king's progress to Whitehall on the 29th (Cal. State Papers, Dom. 1651–2 pp. 3, 240, 1655 p. 341, 1655–6 p. 327, 1656–7 pp. 92, 340, 1657–8 pp. 201, 306, 313, 314, 346, 1659–60 pp. 81, 82, 136, 217, 308; Hist. MSS. Comm. 5th Rep. App. 184, 7th Rep. App. 459 b; COBBETT, State Trials, v. 518–519; Thurloe State Papers, i. 696, ii. 57, 512, 579, iii. 659, iv. 81, 100, 194, v. 160, vi. 26).

On 29 July Gerard received a grant in re-version of the office of remembrancer of the tenths and first-fruits. On 13 Sept. his estates, which had been forfeited by the parliament, were restored to him. On 15 May 1661 he petitioned for the post of ranger of Enfield Chase, which he obtained. His title, however, was disputed by the late ranger, the Earl of Salisbury, and he was soon involved in litigation with Captains Thomas and Henry Batt, keepers of Potter's Walk and bailiffs of the Chase, whose patents he refused to recognise. Both matters were referred to the lord chancellor for decision. As against the Batts, Gerard succeeded on the technical ground that their patent was under the great seal, whereas by statute it should have been under that of the duchy of Lancaster. It does not appear how the question with the Earl of Salisbury was settled. In 1662 Gerard was granted a pension charged on the customs. Towards the end of the year he was sent as envoy extraordinary to the French court, where he was very splendidly received. About this time he became a member of the Royal African Company, which obtained in January 1663 a grant by letters patent of the region between Port Sallee and the Cape of Good Hope for the term of one thousand years. Litigation in which he was this year engaged with his kinsman, Alexander Fitton [q. v.], afterwards lord chancellor of Ireland, was watched with much interest by his enemies. The dispute was about the title to the Gawsworth estate in Cheshire, of which Fitton was in possession, but which Gerard claimed. The title depended on the authenticity of a certain deed which Gerard alleged to be a forgery, producing one Granger, who swore that he himself had forged it. Gerard obtained a verdict at the Chester assizes and ejected Fitton. Fitton, however, published a pamphlet in which he charged Gerard with having procured Granger's evidence by intimidation. Gerard moved the House of Lords on the subject, and the pamphlet was suppressed (Hist. MSS. Comm. 5th Rep. App. 184, 7th Rep. App. 125 a, 459 b; Lords' Journ. xi. 171 b, 541 a–561 a; Cal. State Papers, Dom. 1651–2–65; Cal. Amer. and West Indies, 1661–8; Thurloe State Papers, i. 696, ii. 57, iii. 659, iv. 81, 100, 194, v. 160, vi. 26, 756, 870, vii. 107, 247; KENNETT, Register, 846; PEPYS, Diary, 21 Feb. 1667–8; ORMEROD, Cheshire, ed. Helsby, iii. 551; NORTH, Examen, 558; B. M. Cat., 'Gerard, Charles,' 'Fitton, Alexander'). In March 1665 Gerard was granted a pension of 1,000l. per annum to retire from the post of captain of the guard, which Charles desired to confer on the Duke of Monmouth. His retirement, however, did not take place until 1668, when Pepys says that he received 12,000l. for it. Pepys also states that it was his practice to conceal the deaths of the troopers that he might draw their pay; and one of his clerks named Carr drew up a petition to the House of Lords charging him with peculation to the extent of 2,000l. per annum. The petition found its way into print before presentation, and was treated by the house as a breach of privilege, voted a 'scandalous paper,' and ordered to be burned by the common hangman. Carr was sentenced to pay a fine of 1,000l., to stand in the pillory for three hours on each of three different days, and to be imprisoned in the Fleet during the king's pleasure. Gerard subsequently indicted him as a deserter from the army.

On 5 Jan. 1666–7 Gerard had been appointed to the general command of the Hampshire and Isle of Wight militia, with special instructions to provide for the security of the Isle of Wight and Portsmouth in view of the threatening attitude of the Dutch. In this capacity he was busily engaged during the spring and summer of 1667 in strengthening the fortifications of Portsmouth. He continued to hold the post of gentleman of the bedchamber, with a pension of 1,000l. attached to it, during the reign of Charles II. On 23 July 1679 he was created Earl of Macclesfield. On the occasion of the Duke of Monmouth's unauthorised return from abroad in November 1679, Gerard was sent by Charles to him 'to tell him out of his great tenderness he gave him till night to be gone.' The messenger was ill-chosen, Gerard being himself one of the band of conspirators of which Monmouth was the tool. His name appears in the 'Journal of the House of Lords,' with that of Shaftesbury, as one of the protesters against the rejection of the Exclusion Bill on 15 Nov. 1680. Lord Grey de Werke in his 'Confession' (p. 61) asserts that Gerard suggested to Monmouth the expediency of murdering the Duke of York by way of terrorising Charles. In August 1681 he was dismissed from the post of gentleman of the bedchamber. On 5 Sept. 1682 he entertained the Duke of Monmouth at his seat in Cheshire. In 1684 the question of the Gawsworth title was revived (partly no doubt as a political move) by an application on the part of Fitton to the lord keeper, Guilford, to review the case. Roger North tells us that as Fitton was then in favour at court, while Gerard was 'stiff of the anti-court party,' it was generally anticipated that the lord keeper would, independently of the merits of the case, decide in favour of Fitton. In fact, however, he refused the application on the ground that the claim was stale, a 'pitch of heroical justice' which North cannot adequately extol, and which so impressed Gerard that he expended a shilling in the purchase of the lord keeper's portrait (*Cal. State Papers, Dom.* 1663–7; *Hist. MSS. Comm.* 7th Rep. App. 486 *a*, 495 *a*, 8th Rep. App. 115 *a*; Pepys, *Diary*, 13 Oct. 1663, 14 Sept. and 16 Dec. 1667, 16 Sept. 1668; *Lords' Journ.* xii. 173–5, xiii. 666; *Hatton Corresp.* Camd. Soc. i. 206, ii. 7; Earwaker, *East Cheshire*, ii. 556; Burnet, *Own Time*, 8vo, iii. 56 *n.*; Luttrell, *Relation of State Affairs*, i. 120, 216; North, *Life of Lord-Keeper Guilford*, 206; *Examen*, 558). The grand jury of Cheshire having presented him on 17 Sept. as disaffected to the government and recommended that he should be bound over to keep the peace, Gerard retaliated by an action of scandalum magnatum against a juryman named Starkey, laying the damages at 10,000l. The case was tried in the exchequer chamber on 25 Nov. 1684, and resulted in judgment for the defendant. On 7 Sept. 1685 a royal proclamation was issued for Gerard's apprehension. He fled to the continent, and sentence of outlawry was passed against him. The next three years he spent partly in Germany and partly in Holland, returning to England at the revolution of 1688. During the progress of the Prince of Orange from Torbay to London, Gerard commanded his body-guard, a troop of some two hundred cavaliers, mostly English, mounted on Flemish chargers, whose splendid appearance excited much admiration. In February 1688–9 he was sworn of the privy council, and appointed lord president of the council of the Welsh marches, and lord-lieutenant of Gloucester, Hereford, Monmouth, and North and South Wales. His outlawry was formally reversed in the following April. His political attitude is curiously illustrated by his speech in the debate on the Abjuration Bill. Lord Wharton, after owning that he had taken more oaths than he could remember, said that he should be 'very unwilling to charge himself with more at the end of his days,' whereupon Gerard rose and said that 'he was in much the same case with Lord Wharton, though they had not always taken the same oaths; but he never knew them of any use but to make people declare against government that would have submitted quietly to it if they had been let alone.' He also disclaimed having had much hand in bringing about the revolution. In July 1690 he was one of a commission appointed to inquire into the conduct of the fleet during a recent engagement with the French off Beachy Head, which had not terminated so successfully as had been anticipated. He died on 7 Jan. 1693–4 suddenly in a fit of vomiting, and was buried on the 18th in Exeter vault in Westminster Abbey (COBBETT, *State Trials*, x. 1330; LUTTRELL, *Relation of State Affairs*, i. 305, 357, 399, 502, 505, 513, 522, ii. 74, iii. 250; BURNET, *Own Time*, fol. i. 780, 8vo iv. 79 n.; ORMEROD, *Cheshire*, iii. 553, 556; *Coll. Top. et Gen.* viii. 9). Gerard married Jane, daughter of Pierre de Civelle, a Frenchman resident in England. Little is known of her except that in 1663 she was dismissed by Charles from attendance on the queen for tattling to her about Lady Castlemaine, and that on one occasion while being carried in her chair through the city she was mistaken for the Duchess of Portsmouth, saluted as the French whore, and mobbed by the populace (*Hatton Corresp.* Camd. Soc. i. 175). By this lady Gerard had issue two sons (Charles [q. v.], who succeeded to the title, and Fitton) and three daughters, Elizabeth, who married Digby, fifth lord Gerard of Bromley (*Coll. Top. et Gen.* viii. 12), and was buried in Westminster Abbey, Charlotte and Anne.

[Granger's Biogr. Hist. (4th ed.), iii. 219; Doyle's Baronage; Banks's Extinct Peerage, iii. 304; Burke's Extinct Peerage; Phillips's Civil War in Wales; Duke of Manchester's Court and Society from Elizabeth to Anne, i. 335, i. 123.] J. M. R.

GERARD, CHARLES, second BARON OF BRANDON in Suffolk, VISCOUNT BRANDON, and EARL OF MACCLESFIELD (1659?–1701), the eldest son of Charles Gerard, first Earl of Macclesfield [q. v.], by Jane, daughter of Pierre de Civelle, was born at Paris about 1659, and naturalised by act of parliament in 1676–7 (*Coll. Top. et Gen.* viii. 12; *Hist. MSS. Comm.* 9th Rep. 80, 83; *Lords' Journ.* xiii. 47 b, 71 a). His earliest recorded achievement was the killing in his cups of a footboy belonging to a certain Captain With by a box on the ear in St. James's Park on the night of 17 May 1676. He absconded for a time, but was not brought to justice (*Hatton Corresp.* Camd. Soc. i. 127; RERESBY, *Memoirs*, ed. 1813, pp. 318–19). He was returned to parliament for the county of Lancaster on 9 Sept. 1679, and again on 22 Feb. 1680–1. As one of the grand jury that presented James, duke of York, as a popish recusant at Westminster in 1680, he fell under suspicion of entertaining treasonable designs against the government, was committed to the Tower on 8 July 1683, and only released on 28 Nov., on entering into his own recognisances for 10,000l., with four sureties for 5,000l. each. The trial took place in the following February, and resulted in an acquittal. Having, however, taken part with his father in entertaining the

Duke of Monmouth, he was presented jointly with him by the grand jury of Cheshire on 17 Sept. 1684 as disaffected to the government, was committed to the Tower on 31 July 1685, indicted at the king's bench of high treason on 14 Nov., convicted, mainly on the evidence of Lord Grey de Werk, of complicity in the Rye House plot on the 25th, and sentenced to death three days later. The king, however, granted a reprieve, and in January 1686–7 released him on bail. He received the royal pardon on 31 Aug., and obtained a reversal of the attainder which had followed his conviction on 26 Nov. in the same year (CLARKE, *Life of the Duke of York*, i. 590; RAPIN, ii. 713; 'Proceedings upon the Bailing of Lord Brandon Gerard,' *Brit. Mus. Cat.*; LUTTRELL, *Relation of State Affairs*, i. 265, 292, 301, 355, 363, 392, 407, 421; *Hist. MSS. Comm.* 3rd Rep. App. 270, 7th Rep. App. 501 b; BRAMSTON, *Autobiogr.* Camd. Soc. 215; *Somers Tracts*, viii. 406). On 17 Jan. 1688–1689 he was returned to parliament for the county of Lancaster, which he continued to represent until his elevation to the peerage. In January 1689–90 he was appointed custos rotulorum for Cheshire, and on 23 May following lord-lieutenant of Lancashire. He was an intimate friend and a connection by marriage of Lord Mohun [q. v.], for whom he became bail in 1692, on that nobleman's being committed to stand his trial for the murder of Mountfort. On 24 Jan. 1693–4 (his father having died on the 7th) he took his seat in the House of Lords. In the following February he was appointed to the command of a regiment of horse, and a few weeks later advanced to the rank of major-general. He took part in the unsuccessful attack on the outworks of Brest (8 June), in which General Talmash received a mortal wound, and on the fleet returning to Plymouth he was appointed Talmash's successor. In this capacity he accompanied Lord John Berkeley throughout his cruise along the northern coast of France, in the course of which Dieppe and Havre were bombarded (July). In March 1695–6 he was appointed lord-lieutenant of North Wales. He was accredited in June 1701 envoy extraordinary to the court of Hanover to present the electress-dowager Sophia with a copy of the Act of Succession. Toland, the freethinker, who with Lord Mohun accompanied him to Hanover, and who wrote an account of the mission, says that he was appointed solely from his father having been known in the court of Bohemia. The envoys left England early in July, and returned in the autumn. Toland describes their reception as extremely cordial. Gerard was presented by the electress with her own picture and an electoral crown, both set in diamonds, and by the elector with a huge basin and ewer of solid gold. He returned about the end of October, and had hardly communicated the results of the mission to the lords justices when he caught a fever, of which on 5 Nov. he died. He was buried in Westminster Abbey on the 14th. He left no lawful issue, and was succeeded by his brother, Fitton Gerard, who died a bachelor on 26 Dec. 1702, when the title became extinct (LUTTRELL, *Relation of State Affairs*, ii. 3, 274, 638, iii. 250, 267, 269, 280–2, 327–8, 331–2, 346, 352, iv. 26, 674, v. 58, 67, 105–6, 250; *Lords' Journ.* xv. 350 *a*; BURNET, *Own Time*, fol. ii. 271; TOLAND, *Account of the Courts of Prussia and Hanover*, 2nd ed., pp. 58, 65; *Coll. Top. et Gen.* viii. 13). Gerard married, in June 1683, Anne, daughter of Sir Richard Mason of Whitehall and Sutton in Surrey. The marriage proved unhappy, and on 2 March 1684–5 Gerard wrote his wife, then on a visit to her mother, a lengthy letter, in which he forbade her to return. While the countess was still living apart from her husband, she was delivered of two children, a girl in 1695, and a boy on 16 Jan. 1696–7, whose births she attempted to conceal. The girl was christened Ann Savage, and was put out to nurse, first at Walthamstow, and then at Chelsea, where she died. The boy was born at Fox Court, Gray's Inn Lane, entered on the register of St. Andrew's, Holborn, as 'Richard, son of John Smith and Mary,' and nursed first at Hampstead by a certain Mary Peglear, and then at Maiden Lane, Covent Garden, by a woman named Ann Portlock. Notwithstanding these precautions the facts came to the knowledge of the earl, who accordingly, in the summer of 1697, applied to the court of arches for a divorce *a mensa et thoro*. The application was strenuously resisted by the countess, and while the suit was still pending the earl in December 1697 instituted proceedings in the House of Lords for a divorce. In opposition, the countess alleged that she had been turned out of her husband's house during his absence by the late earl; that the earl owed his life to her intercession with the king when he lay under sentence of death in 1685; that nevertheless he had secluded her from his bed and board; and she urged that if the bill passed, her marriage settlement ought to be rescinded, and her fortune restored to her. The lords considering that a *prima facie* case was made out, a bill to dissolve the marriage and illegitimate the children was introduced by the Duke of Bolton on 15 Jan. 1697–8. It occasioned much animated debate, there being no precedent for a dissolution of marriage by act of

parliament in the absence of a decree of a spiritual court. On 3 March 1697–8, however, the bill was read a third time, Halifax and Rochester alone protesting, and on 2 April it received the royal assent. It contained clauses settling an annuity on the countess, indemnifying the earl against her debts, and declaring her children illegitimate. That the father of both of them was Earl Rivers had been sworn in the ecclesiastical court; the House of Lords did not pronounce on the question; but while the bill was in progress it was matter of common talk that the boy went by the name of Savage, and that Rivers was the putative father. With this boy, whose history after 1698 is wrapped in obscurity, the poet Richard Savage [q. v.] sought in after years to establish his identity. Savage claimed to have discovered the fact from certain letters of Lady Mason, the mother of the countess, which he had found among the papers of his nurse on her death. The countess married soon after the divorce Colonel Henry Brett [q. v.], with whom she lived, apparently happily and virtuously, until his death. She survived him many years, dying on 11 Oct. 1753, upwards of eighty years of age.

[London Marriage Licenses, ed. Foster; Luttrell's Relation of State Affairs, iv. 323, 332, 336, 362; Lords' Journ. xvi. 224; Parl. Hist. v. 1173–1174; Duke of Manchester's Court and Society from Elizabeth to Anne, ii. 98–9; Gent. Mag. 1753, p. 491; Johnson's Lives of the Poets (Savage). Savage's story is examined ably and in detail in four articles by Mr. W. Moy Thomas in Notes and Queries, 2nd ser. vi, 361–5, 386–9, 425–8, 445–8.] J. M. R.

GERARD, SIR GILBERT (*d.* 1593), judge, was the eldest son of James Gerard of Ince, Lancashire, by Margaret, daughter of John Holcroft of Holcroft in the same county. After residing for some time at Cambridge he was admitted a member of Gray's Inn in 1537, where he was called to the bar in 1539. He became an 'ancient' of the inn in 1547, was elected reader in the autumn of 1554, and treasurer, jointly with Nicholas Bacon, on 16 May 1556. He was returned to parliament for Wigan in 1553, for Steyning, Sussex, in the following year, and again for Wigan in 1555. He was summoned to take the degree of serjeant-at-law by writ issued 27 Oct. 1558, and returnable in the Easter term following, which therefore abated by Queen Mary's death. Elizabeth preferred to make Gerard her attorney-general, which she did on 22 Jan. 1558–9. He thus never took the degree of serjeant-at-law. Dugdale states, on the authority of 'credible tradition,' that in the time of Queen Mary, 'upon the Lady Elizabeth being questioned at the council table,' Gerard 'was permitted to plead on her behalf, and performed his part so well that he suffered imprisonment for the same in the Tower during the remaining term' of the reign. What truth there may be in this statement is not clear. That Gerard had rendered some important service to Elizabeth is made probable by the fact that she appointed him attorney-general immediately on her accession, but it is also clear that he was not then in prison (ORMEROD, *Cheshire*, ed. Helsby, iii. 893; WOTTON, *Baronetage*; GREGSON, *Portfolio of Fragments, Lancashire* (Harland), p. 237; *Athenæ Cantabr.* ii. 141; DOUTHWAITE, *Gray's Inn*, p. 53; DUGDALE, *Orig.* pp. 91, 295, 298; *Lists of Members of Parliament, Official Return of*). He was employed in Ireland in 1560 to reform the procedure of the court of exchequer, and to this end drew up certain 'orders and articles for the better collecting the queen's rents, revenues, and debts,' to which the lord-lieutenant (the Earl of Suffolk) affixed the seal on 2 Sept. (*Sloane MS.* 4767, f. 22). In 1561 he was made counsel to the university of Cambridge, and in May 1563 commissioner for the sale of crown lands. In 1565 he went the home circuit, and on 23 July was entertained with Sir John Southcote and other judges at a magnificent banquet given by Archbishop Parker at the palace, Canterbury. On 12 June 1566 he was appointed one of the special commission for hearing causes 'infra virgam hospitii,' i.e. within the bounds of the palace or other place where the sovereign might for the time be residing. He seems to have been a member of the ecclesiastical commission in 1567, when he materially assisted Archbishop Parker in introducing certain reforms into Merton College, Oxford. During a great part of 1570 he was actively engaged in trying participators in the northern rebellion, as one of a special commission constituted for that purpose, with the Earl of Sussex at its head, and which sat principally at York and Durham. In January 1571 he received a letter of thanks from the senate of the university of Cambridge for his services in connection with the passing of the statute 13 Eliz. c. 29, confirming the charters and privileges of the university and for services rendered in connection with other statutes. He appears in a deed (printed in 'Trevelyan Papers,' Camden Soc., ii. 74–83) of 23 Oct. 1571 as trustee for the queen of certain manors in Chelsea and elsewhere mortgaged to her by the Earl of Wiltshire to secure 35,000*l.* He probably drew the interrogatories administered to the Duke of Norfolk concerning his intrigues with the Bishop of Ross and Ri-

dolfi on 13, 18, and 31 Oct. 1571, on each of which occasions he was present at the examination and signed the depositions (MURDIN, *State Papers,* pp. 158–63; *Hist. MSS. Comm. Cal. Cecil MSS.*, 1883, pp. 535, 544), and he ably seconded the queen's serjeant, Nicholas Barham [q. v.], in the prosecution of the duke on the charge of conspiring to depose the queen, which followed on 16 Jan. 1571–2. His argument is reported at considerable length in Cobbett's 'State Trials,' i. 1000–11. He also in the following February took part in the prosecution of Robert Higford or Hickford, the duke's secretary, for the offence of adhering to and comforting the queen's enemies (*ib.* p. 1042), and on 5 May he was occupied at the Tower with Sir Ralph Sadler and other commissioners in taking the examination of Thomas Bishop, another of the duke's dependents. The same day he sent to Burghley the depositions of the Bishop of Ross, taken on interrogatories prepared by himself two days before with remarks on the obstinacy of the bishop. He also drew the interrogatories for the examination of the Earl of Northumberland in the following June. A curious case submitted to him the same year by Fleetwood, recorder of London, is preserved in Strype's 'Annals' (fol.) ii. pt. i. 240, pt. ii. App. bk. i. No. xxv. One Blosse (*alias* Mantel) had asserted that Edward VI was still alive, and that Elizabeth had about 1564 married the Earl of Leicester and had four children by him. Blosse was accordingly charged with treason before Fleetwood, who reserved the case in order that Gerard might advise whether it fell within the statutes of treason. Gerard held that it did not, and the man was released. In 1573 Gerard was a member of three commissions : (1) a commission of gaol delivery for the Marshalsea, (2) a commission of inquiry as to the ownership of certain ships and Spanish goods on which an embargo had been laid (both in the month of April), and (3) in October a commission of oyer and terminer for Middlesex (*Cal. State Papers,* Dom. 1547–80, pp. 225, 433, 443; Addenda, 1566–79, pp. 251, 261, 267, 270, 305–6, 400; Scotland, 1509–1603, p. 911; STRYPE, *Parker* (fol.), i. 190, 253; RYMER, *Fœdera*, ed. Sanderson, xv. 660, 718, 720, 725). In 1576 the Irish lord deputy, Sydney, requested the privy council to send Gerard to Ireland to advise him on various legal questions. It does not appear whether he was sent or not. He was a member of the ecclesiastical commission of this year. On 23 Feb. 1579 he took the examination of the Irish rebel, Richard Oge Burke, second earl of Clanricarde, at Durham House, Strand. On 5 July following he received the honour of knighthood at Greenwich. On 30 May 1581 he was appointed master of the rolls, when he received a letter of congratulation from the senate of the university of Cambridge. He was a member of the commission which tried on 16 Dec. 1583 John Somervyle, on 25 Feb. 1584–5 John Parry, and on 7 Feb. 1585–6 William Shelley, for the offence of conspiring the queen's death, and on 23 June 1585 he was one of the judges who assembled in the Star-chamber to take the inquest on the death of the Earl of Northumberland, who had committed suicide in the Tower three days before. At this time he represented Lancaster in parliament, having been returned on 16 Nov. 1584. He was a member of the tribunal that on 28 March 1587 tried Secretary William Davison for misprision and contempt in laying the death-warrant of the Queen of Scots before the council, and of that which on 18 April 1589 tried the Earl of Arundel, who was charged with having for some years carried on treasonable intrigues with Roman catholics on the continent. A letter from Gerard to Mr. Auditor Thompson, dated 2 July 1589, begging one of his fee bucks to give to his friend, Mr. John Lancaster of Gray's Inn, on occasion of his reading, is preserved in Harl. MS. 6994, f. 184. On 26 July 1591, at the Sessions House, Newgate, Gerard tried three fanatics, Hackett, Copinger, and Arthington, for the crime of libelling the queen and defacing the royal arms. Their defence was that they were moved to this conduct by the Holy Spirit. It did not, however, save them from conviction. On the death of Sir Christopher Hatton, 20 Nov. 1591, Gerard was appointed chief commissioner of the great seal, in which capacity he acted until 28 May 1592, when Sir John Puckering became lord keeper. The last state trial in which he appears to have taken part was that of Sir John Perrot, who was arraigned on 27 April 1592 on the charge of having, when lord deputy of Ireland in 1587, imagined the death of the queen (*Cal. State Papers*, Ireland, 1574–85, pp. 92, 161; STRYPE, *Grindal* (fol.), 208; *Ann.* (fol.), iv. 71; METCALFE, *Book of Knights*; DUGDALE, *Chron. Ser.* 97; *Fourth Rep. Dep.-Keeper Public Records*, App. ii. 272, 275; COBBETT, *State Trials*, i. 1095, 1114, 1229, 1251, 1315; *Lists of Members of Parliament, Official Return of*; HARDY, *Catalogue of Lord Chancellors*, &c., 67). Gerard died on 4 Feb. 1592–3, and was buried in the parish church of Ashley, Staffordshire. His principal seat was at Bromley in the same county, which he purchased from his kinsman, Sir Thomas Gerard of Etwall, Derbyshire, and where he built a house, described by Dugdale

as a 'stately quadrangular fabric of stone.' The house is no longer standing, but an engraving of it is preserved in Plot's 'Staffordshire,' p. 102. Gerard married Anne, daughter of William Ratcliffe of Wilmersley, Lancashire, by whom he had two sons and four daughters. His eldest son, Thomas, was created Baron Gerard of Gerard's Bromley on 21 July 1603. From Gerard's second son, Ratcliffe, descended Charles Gerard [q. v.], created on 8 Nov. 1645 Baron Gerard of Brandon, and on 23 July 1679 Earl of Macclesfield.

[Dugdale's Baronage, ii. 417–18; Courthope's Historic Peerage; Foss's Lives of the Judges; Erdeswick's Staffordshire, ed. Harwood, p. 99.]

           J. M. R.

GERARD, GILBERT, D.D. (1760–1815), theological writer, son of Alexander Gerard, D.D. [q. v.], was born at Aberdeen 12 Aug. 1760, and studied at Aberdeen and Edinburgh. On being licensed he became minister of the Scotch church at Amsterdam, and during his residence there acquired a considerable knowledge of modern languages and literature, which he turned to account in contributions to the 'Analytical Review.' In 1791 he returned to Aberdeen to occupy the chair of Greek in King's College, which he filled admirably. On his father's death, in 1795, he succeeded him in the chair of divinity, and in 1811 he added to his professorship the second charge in the collegiate church of Old Aberdeen. He prepared for publication 'A Compendious View of the Evidences of Natural and Revealed Religion' (Lond. 1828), the joint production of himself and his father, being the substance of the lectures delivered by them from the chair of divinity. The only contribution to literature exclusively his own was 'Institutes of Biblical Criticism' (Edinburgh, 1808), in which he discussed elementary questions in connection with the interpretation of the sacred scriptures. The language of scripture, the text, the versions, the ordinary rules of interpretation, were considered, but the book does not even hint at the much more vital questions raised by modern critics. He was a king's chaplain, and filled the chair of the general assembly in 1803. He became minister of Old Machar 19 Sept. 1811, and died 28 Sept. 1815.

Gerard married, 3 Oct. 1787, Helen, daughter of John Duncan, provost of Aberdeen, by whom he had six sons and five daughters. Three sons, all Indian explorers and writers on geographical science, Alexander, James Gilbert, and Patrick, are separately noticed.

[Scott's Fasti, iii. 488; Darling's Cyclopædia Bibl.; Kennedy's Annals of Aberdeen; Smith's Hist. of Aberdeen; Chambers's Eminent Scotsmen.]

           W. G. B.

GERARD, JAMES GILBERT, M.D. (1795–1835), surgeon on the Bengal establishment, son of Gilbert Gerard, D.D. [q. v.], brother of Alexander [q. v.] and of Patrick Gerard [q. v.], was born in 1795. Probably he is the 'Gerard, Jacobus, Aberdoniensis,' who entered the King's or Marischal College as in 1807, but there is some doubt. On 27 Nov. 1814 he was appointed assistant-surgeon on the Bengal establishment and became surgeon 5 May 1826. He accompanied his brother Alexander in several of his Himalayan journeys, and was author of ' Observations on the Spité Valley and the circumjacent Country within the Himalayas' in 'Asiat. Researches' (1833), xviii. 238–79, and of the ' Account of a Visit to the Shotool and Borendo Passes' in Sir William Lloyd's book. His regimental service was chiefly in the hills with the 1st Nusseerabad battalion. In 1831 he volunteered to accompany Sir Alexander Burnes [q. v.] in his expedition across the Hindu Khoosh to Bokhara. Sufficient credit has not been given to Gerard for the scientific accuracy which his assistance lent to the geographical information collected by Burnes (Journ. Roy. Geog. Soc. Lond. xii. 133). From his notebooks his brother Alexander prepared a map of the return route from Herat to Peshawur. His brother writes : 'His trip to Bokhara with Colonel Sir Alexander Burnes was a mad-like expedition for him, as he had long been unwell and was obliged to leave his bed to go, and could only travel in a palkee [palanquin]. It was . . . at his own particular request that Burnes applied for him. The trip killed him, for he had several attacks of fever on his way to Bokhara, and Burnes again and again urged him either to return or stop at Cabool until he recovered, but he would do neither. . . . On his return he was detained three months at Meshed, and no less than eight at Herat, by fever, so that on his arrival at Subathoo his constitution was completely worn out. He . . . gradually declined. Patrick and I were with him the whole time he survived, which was just a year, for I got leave of absence to prepare a map of the route from his notes ; for he observed the bearings, estimated the distances, and noted the villages all the way from Herat to the Indus. . . . It was a splendid map, 10 ft. long by 3 ft. wide, on a scale of 5 in. to the mile. At my brother's dying request I presented it to Sir Charles Metcalfe, then governor-general, from whom I received a thousand thanks. The map is now [1840] with the army on the Indus, and . . . they have found the position of the roads wonderfully correct, considering the distances were estimated by time and the bearings taken with a small pocket-compass.' Gerard died at Subathoo 31 March 1835.

The German geographer, Ritter, has noticed the valuable services rendered by the three brothers Gerard to the cause of geographical science (RITTER, Der Erdkunde von Asien (1829), Band ii. S. 546).

[See under GERARD, PATRICK.]　H. M. C.

GERARD, JOHN (1545–1612), herbalist, was born in 1545 at Nantwich, Cheshire, and was connected with the Gerards of Ince, as evidenced by his coat of arms on the title of his 'Herball.' He went to school at Willaston, two miles from his native place, and having studied medicine, he travelled in Scandinavia and Russia, possibly also in the Mediterranean.

In 1562 Gerard was apprenticed to Alexander Mason, a surgeon in large practice, who was twice warden of the Barber-Surgeons' Company. Gerard was admitted to the freedom of the same company 9 Dec. 1569, but there is no record of his admission to the livery. On 21 Feb. 1577–8 he was summoned by the master to answer a charge of defaming the wife of a brother freeman. He was elected a member of the court of assistants of the body, 19 June 1595. Gerard was then well known as a skilled herbalist. He was superintendent of the gardens of Lord Burghley in the Strand, and at Theobalds in Hertfordshire. He was living in Holborn, where he had a garden, to which he devoted great attention, and published a list of the plants therein in 1596. The only copy of that edition (in duodecimo) known to exist is in the Sloane collection in the British Museum. It is of peculiar interest as being the first catalogue of any one garden, public or private. A second edition, this time in folio, with English names as well as Latin in opposite columns, was brought out in 1599. Between these dates Gerard had suffered from ague. In August 1597 he was appointed junior warden of his company. In the previous year he had suggested that the company should keep a garden for the cultivation and study of medicinal plants. A piece of land at East Smithfield was selected, but was found unsuitable. Money was subscribed for the purchase of a garden elsewhere ; but although the scheme was under discussion on 2 Nov. 1602, when 'the committee for Mr. Gerrard's garden' held a meeting, no active steps were taken.

In December 1597 appeared the folio volume which has made Gerard's name a household word, his 'Herball' (London, by J. Norton), dedicated to Lord Burghley. This is in the main a translation begun by Dr. Priest of Dodoens's 'Pemptades,' arranged in the order of Lobel's 'Adversaria;' it contained more than eighteen hundred wood-cuts, only sixteen of which were original, the majority being the identical cuts used by Bergzabern (better known as Tabernæmontanus) in his 'Eicones,' 1590, which were procured from Frankfort by the king's printer, John Norton. The volume has many of Gerard's own remarks inserted, such as localities in various parts of England for scarce plants, and many allusions to persons and places now of high antiquarian interest. He lays claim to a purely scientific object, but accepts much contemporary folk-lore, which does not detract from the interest of his volume. In the opening pages figure some quaint verses by 'Thomas Thorney, master in chirurgerie,' and an epistle by George Baker (1540–1600) [q. v.] On 15 Jan. 1598, and again 20 July 1607, he was appointed an examiner of candidates for admission to the freedom of the Barber-Surgeons' Company, then exercising as complete control of the surgeons practising in London as the various medical boards do at the present time. In 1604 he was granted a lease of a garden adjoining Somerset House by the queen-consort of James I, but in 1605 he parted with his interest in it to Robert, earl of Salisbury, second son of Lord-treasurer Burghley. In the legal documents connected with this lease Gerard is described as 'herbarist' to James I. Upon payment of a fine of 10l. Gerard was released from the office of 'second warden and upper governor' of his company 26 Sept. 1605. He was chosen master of the Barber-Surgeons' Company 17 Aug. 1607. He died in February 1611–12, and was buried in St. Andrew's Church, Holborn (18 Feb.), but there is no monument to mark the spot.

In 1633 Thomas Johnson edited a new edition of the 'Herball,' which was so well received that a reprint of it, word for word, was brought out in 1636. The genus *Gerardia* was founded by Linnæus in commemoration of John Gerard, and it now includes about thirty species, chiefly North American. In 1639 the Barber-Surgeons' Company paid 25s. 6d. for a copy of Gerard's 'Herball' for their library. Gerard's works were: 1. 'Catalogus arborum, fruticum, ac plantarum tam indigenarum quam exoticarum in horto Ioannis Gerardi civis et chirurgi Londinensis nascentium,' London, 1596, 12mo, pp. iv, 18, 2nd edit., 1599, fol.; the same, reprinted by B. D. Jackson, 1876, 4to, with modern names and memoir of the author. 2. 'Herball,' London, 1597, fol.; the same edited by T. Johnson, London, 1633, and again in 1636.

A fine portrait of Gerard is prefixed to the 'Herball.'

[Life of Gerard in reprint of Catalogus, 1876; Arber's Reprint of Stationers' Registers, iii. 21; information from the Archives of the Barber-Surgeons' Company, kindly supplied by Mr. Sidney Young.]   B. D. J.

GERARD, JOHN (1564–1637), jesuit, second son of Sir Thomas Gerard, knight, of Bryn, Lancashire, by Elizabeth, eldest daughter and coheiress of Sir John Port, knight, of Etwall, Derbyshire, was born on 4 Oct. 1564, probably at New Bryn. He received part of his education in the English College at Douay, where he arrived 29 Aug. 1577, and apparently accompanied the students in their migration to Rheims in the following March. It seems that he subsequently returned to England, and was matriculated in the university of Oxford as a member of Exeter College about October 1579 (BOASE, *Register of Exeter Coll.*, pp. 186, 218). Being unable conscientiously to comply with the religious observances of the college, he left it within twelve months and went home. In 1581 he proceeded to Paris, and studied for some time in Clermont College, which belonged to the jesuits, but ill-health compelled him again to return to England. An unsuccessful attempt which he afterwards made to leave this country without a government license resulted in his apprehension and imprisonment in the Marshalsea prison, from which he obtained his release in October 1585. In the following year he was admitted into the English College at Rome, where he was ordained priest. He joined the Society of Jesus in Rome on 15 Aug. 1588, and was at once sent on the English mission. His activity soon attracted the attention of the government, but for a long time he baffled all the attempts of spies and pursuivants to apprehend him. Eventually, while on a visit to London, he was betrayed by a servant, and was imprisoned successively in the Compter, the Clink, and the Tower, where, by order of the privy council, he underwent the horrible torture of being suspended by the wrists for hours at a time, and was nearly crippled for life. A graphic account of his extraordinary escape from the Tower in October 1597, by swinging himself along a rope suspended over the Tower ditch, is given in his autobiography. With characteristic courage he continued his missionary labours, and the government never captured him again. In 1603 Gerard, in the belief that submission to James I might bring about a removal of catholic disabilities, discountenanced Watson's plot, and gave information about it to the government. Though Gerard's trust in James was soon dissipated, 'there is strong reason to believe,' writes Mr. Gardiner, 'that he was not made acquainted with the particulars' of the Gunpowder plot. The government, however, thought they could inculpate him along with Greenway and Garnett. After the discovery of the plot the search for him was therefore renewed with redoubled vigour, and it became absolutely necessary that he should leave England. Dressed in livery he embarked with the suites of the ambassadors of Spain and Flanders, and crossed the Channel on 3 May 1606, the day on which Father Henry Garnett [q. v.] was executed.

Proceeding to Rome, he was appointed English penitentiary at St. Peter's. In 1609 he was professed of the four vows, and was nominated 'socius' of Father Thomas Talbot, rector and novice-master in the English jesuit novitiate at Louvain. He took a leading part in the establishment of the college of his order at Liège, and became its first rector and master of novices (1614–22). After acting for some time as instructor of the tertians at Ghent, he was recalled in 1627 to Rome, and became spiritual director of the students of the English College, where he died on 27 July 1637.

His works are: 1. 'The Exhortation of Jesus Christ to the Faithful Soul,' London, 1598, 8vo; St. Omer, 1610, 8vo. A translation from the Latin of Landsberger. 2. 'The Spiritual Combat; translated from the Italian,' London, 12mo; Rouen, 1613, 12mo. 3. 'A Narrative of the Gunpowder Plot,' 1606,' manuscript fol. preserved at Stonyhurst College, ff. 170. Printed under the editorship of Father John Morris in 'The Condition of Catholics under James I,' London, 1871, 8vo; 2nd edition, 1872. Portions of Gerard's valuable narrative were printed in the 'Month' in 1867–8, and these, rendered into French by Father J. Forbes, appeared in the 'Études Théologiques,' Paris, 1868, and were reprinted separately in 1872. A German translation of Father Morris's first edition was published at Cologne in 1875. 4. 'Narratio P. Johannis Gerardi de Rebus a se in Anglia gestis,' manuscript at Stonyhurst, compiled in 1609 for the information of his superiors. Considerable use was made of this autobiography by Father Morris in writing the 'Life' of Gerard, which is contained in 'The Condition of Catholics under James I.' A third edition of the 'Life,' rewritten and much enlarged, was printed at London, 1881, 8vo. The translation of the autobiography is from the pen of the Rev. G. R. Kingdon, S.J. It has been printed separately as the forty-sixth volume of the 'Quarterly Series,' under the title of 'During the Persecution,' London, 1886, 8vo, and is of very high interest.

[Life by the Rev. John Morris; Catholic Spectator, 1824, i. 257, 325, 360, 389; De Backer's Bibl. des Ecrivains de la Compagnie de Jésus, 1869, i. 2089; Dodd's Church Hist. ii. 419; Douay Diaries; Gardiner's Hist. of England, 1603–42, i. 114, 243; Gillow's Bibl. Dict.; Lives of Philip Howard, Earl of Arundel, and his Wife, p. 233; Husenbeth's Colleges and Convents on the Continent, p. 49; London and Dublin Orthodox Journal, ii. 67; More's Hist. Missionis Anglicanæ Soc. Jesu, pp. 249, 253, 256, 261, 263, 337, 339, 414; Oliver's Jesuit Collections, p. 101; Southwell's Bibl. Scriptorum Soc. Jesu, p. 452.]
T. C.

GERARD, JOHN (1632–1654), royalist colonel, was second son of Lieutenant-colonel Ratcliffe Gerard and first cousin to Charles Gerard, lord Brandon, d. 1694 [q.v.] (DUGDALE, Baronage, p. 418). He entered the king's army as an ensign, and speedily rose to the rank of colonel, commanding both in England and France. There were seven colonels besides himself of the name of Gerard in the army. In November 1653 he appeared as a witness at the trial of Don Pantaleone, a brother of the Portuguese ambassador, for the murder of an Englishman. The night before the murder Gerard had overheard Pantaleone and his friends talking of English affairs in the street and had given them the lie, whereupon they had attacked him, and, though a little man, yet 'he threw him off that was upon him, and so was hustling with him a good while,' but was rescued by a passer-by, after he had received a stab in the shoulder (COBBETT, State Trials, v. 462). Early in 1654 Gerard went over to France, where he was presented to Charles II by his cousin, Lord Gerard. Soon after his return to England (May) he was arrested, with two others, on a charge of conspiring against the government. In company with a royalist major, one Henshaw, whom he had met in France, Gerard and others were to attack the Protector with a band of thirty horse as he rode to Hampton Court, and, after killing him, to besiege Whitehall (State Papers, Dom. 1654, pp. 219, 233–40, 274–436), seize the Tower, and proclaim Charles king. The trial began on 3 June before the high court of justice. Gerard declared that he had been to Paris on private business, and that Charles had desired his friends not to engage in plots. The reluctant evidence of his younger brother Charles, to whom he sent his forgiveness from the scaffold, pointed to treasonable conversations with Henshaw and the rest in taverns. Gerard and Vowell, a schoolmaster, were sentenced to death. Gerard successfully petitioned to be beheaded instead of hanged. The royalist writers published his dying speech, and affirmed that he fell into a trap set by Cromwell. This view has been elaborately restated by Mr. Reginald Palgrave in the 'English Historical Review' for October 1888, in the course of a controversy between that writer and Prof. C. H. Firth. But no certain proof has been adduced of Cromwell's complicity. Gerard died with undaunted courage on 10 July 1654, the same day as Don Pantaleone.

[Dr. Lloyd's Memoirs, 1668, p. 557; Cobbett's State Trials, v. 518–38; Carte's Hist. of England, iv. 662–3; Clarendon's Rebellion, vii. 28, 29, 30; Winstanley's England's Worthies, London, 1659; Mercurius Politicus, November 1653 and June 1654; Letters of Dorothy Osborne, pp. 287–8.]

E. T. B.

GERARD, MARCUS. [See GHEERAERTS.]

GERARD, PATRICK (1794–1848), writer on geographical science, son of Gilbert Gerard, D.D. [q. v.], and brother of Alexander [q. v.] and of James Gilbert Gerard [q. v.], was born 11 June 1794. He probably entered the King's or Marischal College, Aberdeen, in 1808, and received a Bengal cadetship in 1812. He was appointed ensign in the 8th Bengal native infantry on 19 Aug. 1812; became lieutenant therein on 16 Dec. 1814, and brevet captain on 19 Aug. 1827. He became captain in the 9th native infantry on 11 April 1828, and was placed on the invalid establishment in India on 8 Aug. 1832. Most of his service was regimental, part of it attached to the hill corps, of which his brother James Gilbert [q. v.] was surgeon, the 1st Nusseerabad battalion. He died at Simla on 4 Oct. 1848.

Gerard was author of 'Observations on the Climate of Subathoo and Kotguhr' in 'Asiat. Res.' xv. 469–88, meteorological observations made hourly for the space of nearly two years; of 'Account of the Climate and Agriculture of Subathoo and Kotguhr' in 'Edinburgh Journal of Science' (1828), ix. 233–41, cf. Froriep's 'Notizen' (1829), xxiii. cols. 65–71; and of 'Remarks on some Mineral Products of the Himalayas' in 'Delhi Medical Journal' (1844), i. 62–71. A joint paper by Alexander and Patrick Gerard, entitled 'Account of a Journey through the Himalaya Mountains,' appeared in 'Edinburgh Philos. Journal' (1824), x. 295–305. 'A Journal of Meteorological Observations made in India from 1817 to 1829,' by Patrick Gerard, forms British Museum Addit. MSS. 24017–22.

[India Office Records; Royal Society's Cat. of Scientific Papers, vol. ii.; President's Address in Proceedings of the Geological Soc. of London, 1840; Lloyd's Narrative of a Journey, and Account of Koonawar. Brit. Mus. Cat.; information relating to Aberdeen courteously supplied by the registrar of Aberdeen University.] H. M. C.

GERARD, RICHARD (1613–1686), cavalier, second son of Sir Thomas Gerard of Bryn, Lancashire, by Frances, daughter of Sir Richard Molineux of Sefton, in the same county, was born in 1613, went to Maryland, soon after the charter had been granted to Lord Baltimore in 1634, but returned to England the following year, raised a troop of foot for the king of Spain, and served in the Netherlands between 1638 and 1642, when he quitted the Spanish service and entered that of Henrietta Maria, then at the Hague. He raised and commanded the bodyguard which escorted her from the Hague to Bridlington Bay, Yorkshire, where he obtained from the Earl of Newcastle a lieutenant-colonel's commission (16 March 1642–3). Thence he went to Oxford, and on the way thither was wounded in an attack on Burton-on-Trent. He took part in the second battle of Newbury (27 Oct. 1644), after which he retired to Oxford, and there remained until the surrender of the place. He attended the king at Hurst Castle, and carried letters between him and the queen in France. On the Restoration he was appointed (1 Jan. 1660–1) cupbearer in ordinary and waiter to the queen-mother. He died on 5 Sept. 1686 at Ince, Lancashire, the manor of which he had bought from his cousin, Thomas Gerard, and was buried in the parish church of Wigan. Gerard married, first, Frances, daughter of Sir Ralph Hansby of Tickhill Castle, Yorkshire, by whom he had issue one son only, who died in infancy; secondly, Judith, daughter of Sir Nicholas Steward of Pattishall, Northamptonshire, by whom he had issue six sons and three daughters.

[Gregson's Portfolio of Fragments (Lancashire), p. 239; Wotton's Baronetage, i. 56; Dodd's Church Hist. (fol.) iii. 62.] J. M. R.

GERARD, GARRET, or GARRARD, THOMAS (1500?–1540), divine, matriculated at Corpus Christi College, Oxford, on 9 Aug. 1517, graduating B.A. in June 1518, and M.A. in March 1524. Some time during his residence at Oxford he removed to Christ Church, then Cardinal College, and also went to Cambridge, where he took his B.D. and D.D. (CLARK, Register of Matriculation and Degrees, Oxford, p. 104; COOPER, Athenæ Cantabrigienses, i. 75). Gerard was one of the first English protestants, and showed his zeal by distributing Lutheran books. In December 1525 Erasmus begs his commendations to him among other 'booksellers.' In 1526 he became curate to his friend Forman, rector of All Hallows, Honey Lane, but Foxe says that he was at Oxford at Easter 1527, and had been there since Christmas 1526, selling Latin books and Tyndall's translation of the New Testament to the scholars. He had also distributed books at Cambridge. Foxe says that he had intended to take a curacy in Dorsetshire under a feigned name, but gave up the design, and was at Reading some time this year (1527) 'corrupting the prior,' to whom he sold more than sixty of his books. By Christmas, however, he was again hiding at Oxford, 'privily doing much hurt,' until in the middle of February 1528 he was seized by the commissary. He escaped by the help of a friend, but was again captured at Bedminster, near Bristol, on 29 Feb., and taken to the Somerset county gaol at Ilchester. After an examination on 9 March he was sent to London, examined before the Bishop of Lincoln and the lord privy seal, and afterwards forced to recant before them and the bishops of London (Tunstall) and Bath and Wells. Lincoln complains (1 April) to Wolsey that Gerard is 'a very subtyll, crafty, soleyn, and untrue man,' as his answers differ from the scholars. Foxe gives a detailed but inaccurate account of this capture under a wrong date (1527), in which he states that one of the proctors gave secret information as to his whereabouts, and after an attempted escape he was taken at Hinksey, and condemned to carry a fagot on his back from St. Mary's to Christ Church, of which college he was then called a student, 'with his red hood on his shoulders like an M.A.,' and was afterwards imprisoned at Osney till further orders. Gerard finally obtained his pardon from Wolsey, and was employed by him the same year in copying documents (see Foxe, *Acts and Monuments*, v. 414, 421-9, Appendix, p. vi; *State Papers*, Henry VIII, Brewer, iv. pt. i. 1524-6, pt. ii. 1526-8, index). By 1535 he had obtained the king's license to preach. On 11 July he preached at Jervaulx Abbey, Yorkshire; a monk who interrupted him was taken into custody, and he was sent with letters from Sir Francis Bigod to Cromwell as a mark of favour (*State Papers*, 1535, viii. 405, 420). Cranmer recommended him unsuccessfully to Cromwell for the living of St. Peter's, Calais, as a 'forward and busy Lutheran.' In June 1536 he was chaplain to the Bishop of Worcester, though in May his old enemy the Bishop of Lincoln had complained of his want of learning and discretion to Cromwell (*ib.* 1536, x. 371, 463). Through Cranmer's influence with Cromwell Gerard was inducted on 14 June 1537 to All Hallows, Honey Lane. He also became chaplain to Cranmer, who sent him in August to preach at Calais. To please Cromwell, who

had taken him into favour, Bonner appointed him to preach after Stephen Gardiner [q. v.] and Robert Barnes [q. v.] at St. Paul's Cross in Lent 1540. Gerard, like Barnes, argued against Gardiner's sermon on passive obedience, and both of them, together with another Lent preacher, Jerome [q. v.], vicar of Stepney, were ordered to publicly recant from the pulpit of St. Mary Spital in Easter week. A contemporary (see *Chronicle of Henry VIII*, 1889, pp. 193-6) calls Jerome 'a great heretic,' and Gerard 'a good Christian,' and says that Gerard in his sermon declared that his two predecessors deserved to be burnt for their heresies, while himself 'warmed so much to his sermon that he preached in favour of the pope.' The recantation was held to be ambiguous, and they were all three sent to the Tower and attainted as detestable heretics. Their names and Cromwell's were specially excepted from the king's general pardon of all offences committed before 1 July, and ten days after Cromwell's execution they were drawn on a sledge through the middle of the city to Smithfield, and burnt at one stake (30 July 1540), the two heretics, says the Spanish chronicler, in one sack, and the good Christian in another. Three Romanists were hanged on the same day. Gerard suffered with great courage, renouncing all heresy and begging forgiveness for faults of rashness and vehemence.

[Besides the State Papers, Henry VIII, and Foxe's Acts and Monuments, vol. v., see Burnet's Reformation, i. 590; Wood's Athenæ, ed. Bliss, ii. 760; Wood's Fasti, i. 45; Cranmer's Works, ed. Jenkyns, i. 445; Original Letters (Parker Soc.), 1537-8, i. 207, 209-10; Tunstall Register, f. 137; Todd's Cranmer, i. 138; Soames's Hist. of the Reformation, ii. 437-42; Collier's Ecclesiastical History, v. 76-9, &c.] E. T. B.

GERARD, Sir WILLIAM (*d.* 1581), lord chancellor of Ireland, son of Gilbert Gerard of Ince, Lancashire, by Eleanor, daughter of William Davison, alderman, of Chester, and cousin of Sir Gilbert Gerard [q.v.], master of the rolls, was admitted in 1543 a member of Gray's Inn, where he was called to the bar in 1546. He became an 'ancient' of that inn in 1555, and was elected reader there in the autumn of 1560, but owing to illness did not read. He entered parliament as member for Preston in 1553, and sat for Chester, of which place he was recorder, from 1555 to 1572. He was also from an early date a member of the council of Wales, of which he became vice-president in 1562, retaining, however, the recordership of Chester as late as 1567. He is probably identical with the 'Mr. Gerrard' mentioned by Strype (*Ann.* fol. i. pt. ii. 547) as active in urging Bishop Downham of

Chester to put down the papists in the neighbourhood of Wigan in 1568. He was also for some years a justice of assize for the counties of Brecknock, Glamorgan, and Radnor (*Harl. MS.* 2094, f. 62; WOTTON, *Baronetage*, i. 53; GREGSON, *Portfolio of Fragments, Lancashire* (Harland), 237; ORMEROD, *Cheshire* (Helsby), i. 195; DOUTHWAITE, *Gray's Inn*, 55; DUGDALE, *Orig.* 294; *Cal. State Papers*, Dom. 1547-80 p. 152, 1581-90 p. 326). On 23 April 1576 he was appointed lord chancellor of Ireland, with a grant of the deanery of St. Patrick's in reversion, expectant on the death of the then incumbent, Dr. Weston. The appointment was extremely satisfactory to the viceroy, Sir Henry Sidney, who, as president of the council of Wales, had had ample opportunity of judging of Gerard's capacity. 'I have had long experience of him,' he wrote to the council, 'having had his assistance in Wales now sixteen years, and know him to be very honest and diligent, and of great dexterity and readiness in a court of that nature' (*Sydney Papers*, pp. 95-6). The despatches which Gerard sent to Walsingham soon after his arrival in Ireland give a very lively picture of the state of affairs there. A great part of the country, he reports, 'is depopulated, and the most of the inhabitants in the other parts so wretched, poor creatures, in person and substance as not to be able to defend themselves.' The 'poor churls' are wasted and impoverished by a 'multitude of idle thieves.' His 'plot' is to get these hanged, which can only 'be put in execution by circuiting the Pale' twice a year. 'English justices must be the executioners.' Subsequently he describes the Irish courts as 'shadows,' and the justices as 'rather overleapt as scarecrows than reverenced as magistrates' (*Lib. Hibern.* i. pt. ii. 15; *Cal. State Papers*, Ireland, 1574-85, pp. 91, 101; *ib. Carew*, 1575-1588, p. 55). On 8 Feb. 1577 he writes to Walsingham, that 'the whole Irishry must be subjected to the sword;' remarks strongly on the cruelty of the landlords, whose tenants are 'only starved beggarly misers,' and describes the cess as 'a burden laid on the poor which breaketh all their backs.' On 22 March he writes that 'he will soon die if he have not the help of two English lawyers.' The cess, which constituted the chief grievance in the Pale at this time, was a prerogative in the nature of a purveyance exercised by the deputy, by levying contributions in kind for the use of the garrison at a fixed price, known as the 'queen's price.' In December 1575 a petition had been presented to Sir Henry Sidney, in which a money composition was offered in lieu of the cess, and Sidney had referred the question to the privy council.

The matter advancing no further, a memorial was presented and sent to the privy council in January 1577. Elizabeth treated the petitioners as 'presumptuous and undutiful' subjects, had them rigorously examined, and, on their maintaining the illegality of the impost, gave orders for their punishment, at the same time sharply censuring Sidney for having been too lenient with them in the first instance. This led Sidney and Gerard to investigate with much care the history of the cess, a work involving considerable research among the public records. Their labours resulted in establishing that the cess had existed from the time of Edward III. This proof of its antiquity did not, however, blind Gerard to the fact that some modification of the impost was required by justice and humanity, and in the autumn of 1577 he was deputed by the council of the viceroy to represent the state of the country to the privy council, and urge upon them, among other reforms, the adoption of some more equitable method of raising money. In the letter of the Irish council which formed his credentials, he is described as one who in the course of 'long journeys' 'has seen the exactions, extortions, and Irish impositions which decay the poor and hinder justice,' and who, 'by his search into the parliament rolls and rolls of account,' 'has seen the government of this estate in times past.' He arrived at court on 6 Oct. 1577, and remained until the end of the following May, when he returned to Ireland with despatches from Walsingham. So far as concerned the cess, his mission was a complete failure. The honour of knighthood was conferred on him, on 11 Oct. 1579, by Sir William Pelham, then lord justice. He returned to England the same month. On 23 Nov. he was appointed a master of requests. He returned to Ireland in the summer of 1580, but was compelled by illness to come home in the following January. He never went back again, but seems to have resided at Chester until his death on 1 May 1581. He was a zealous protestant, and one of the most active members of the Irish ecclesiastical commission. Towards the close of his life his tenure of the deanery of St. Patrick's is said to have weighed on his conscience. He was buried in the church of St. Oswald, Chester (*Cal. State Papers, Carew*, 1575-88, pp. 55, 78, 111, 157, 193, 354, Ireland, 1574-85, pp. 101, 104, 111, 113-15, 169, 191, 241, 277, 280, 291, 302, Dom. 1547-80, pp. 635, 637, Dom. Add. 1580-1625, p. 171; WALSINGHAM, *Journal*, Camd. Soc. vi. 33, 37; HOLINSHED, *Chron.* ed. 1808, vi. 421; ORMEROD, *Cheshire* (Helsby), i. 194, 297). Gerard married Dorothy, daughter of Andrew Barton of Smythils, Lancashire, by whom he had two sons and four daughters. His eldest son married Jane, daughter of William Almer of Pentyokin, Denbighshire (*Harl. MSS.* 1441 f. 15 *b*, 2094 f. 62). A certain bent towards historical research is indicated by his labours in connection with the cess, and also by a 'Discourse on the Estate of the Country and People of Wales in the Time of King Edward I, and from that Time until the Establishment of the Council in the Marches of Wales, with orders devised to avoid and remove evil Practices and Abuses at this day used,' which he forwarded to Walsingham as the fruit of his experience in the Principality in 1576 (*Cal. State Papers*, Dom. 1547–80, p. 515). A 'Short Treatise on Ireland,' preserved among Lord Calthorpe's MSS., is also attributed to him (*Hist. MSS. Comm.* 2nd Rep. App. 40 *a*).

[O'Flanagan's Lives of the Lord Chancellors of Ireland; Mason's Hist. of the Collegiate and Cathedral Church of St. Patrick, p. 172.]

J. M. R.

GERARDS, MARCUS. [See GHEE-RAERTS.]

GERBIER, SIR BALTHAZAR (1591?–1667), painter, architect, and courtier, born about 1591 (*State Papers*, Dom. xl. 133) at Middelburg, in Zeeland, was the son of Anthony Gerbier, by his wife, Radigonde Blavet, protestant refugees from France. 'My Great Grand-father,' he gave out, 'was Anthony Gerbier, the Baron Doully,' and he at one time assumed in England the title of Baron Douvilly, though his claims are doubtful (*ib.* xxv. 68). His father dying, he accompanied one of his brothers into Gascony, where he picked up a knowledge of drawing, architecture, fortifications, and 'the Framing of Warlike Engines,' which brought him the favour of Prince Maurice of Orange. The prince recommended him to Noel de Caron, the Dutch ambassador in London, with whom he passed over to England in 1616. He entered the service of George Villiers, afterwards duke of Buckingham, and was employed 'in the contriving of some of the Duke of Buckingham's Houses,' particularly York House, of which he was appointed keeper, and in painting miniatures. The Jones collection in the South Kensington Museum contains a miniature portrait of Charles I, done in grisaille by Gerbier, dated 1616. He was also employed in collecting for the duke (cf. GOODMAN, *James I*, ii. 260, 326, 369). In 1623 he followed Prince Charles and Buckingham to Spain, where he made a portrait of the Infanta, which was sent over to King James; and in 1625 he went with Buckingham to Paris. He was equally ready at devising machines for a mask or the mines 'which were

to have blown up the Dycke at Rochell,' and at conducting a state intrigue at some foreign court. He now kept the ciphers of the duke's foreign correspondence; and his pamphlets contain numerous allusions to his frequent missions abroad. His first public employment, he tells us, was in Holland, probably in connection with the negotiation carried on by Weston at Brussels in 1622. In 1625 Gerbier met Rubens in Paris, who had then spoken to Buckingham of the advantages of a peace with Spain. In January 1627 Rubens repeated these proposals to Gerbier, who was again in Paris. Gerbier was sent to Brussels to carry out negotiations founded on these proposals, while ostensibly buying pictures. The negotiations, however, failed. Gerbier shared Buckingham's unpopularity, and a bill for his naturalisation was in danger of being thrown out by the commons in the summer of 1628 (*ib.* cviii. 52). On 3 Dec. 1628 he took the oath on entering the service of the king after Buckingham's assassination, and was knighted in the same year. In 1629 and 1630 his name is mentioned in connection with contracts for pictures and statues (*ib.* cxxxiii. 29, cxli. 82, clviii. 48, 54). It must have been about this time that Vandyck painted the family piece of Gerbier, his wife, and his nine children, now at Windsor.

In 1631 Gerbier was appointed 'his Mat[ies] Agent at Brussels,' and on 17 June he sailed with his wife and family. Charles put special trust in him, and sent him direct orders, occasionally in contradiction to those sent through the secretary of state (cf. HARDWICKE, *State Papers*, ii. 54). But in November 1633 Gerbier betrayed to the Infanta Isabella, for the sum of twenty thousand crowns, the secret negotiations of Charles with the revolutionary nobles of the Spanish Netherlands.

During 1636–7 the court at Brussels, instigated, as he thought, by the 'Cottingtonian faction,' asked for his removal; but Rubens supported him, and Charles's confidence remained unbroken. While in London towards the end of June 1641, having, without the king's leave, let himself be drawn into a lawsuit before the House of Lords, he accused Lord Cottington of betraying state secrets, and, though his commission was signed for his departure to Brussels, he was detained and examined by the lords. The charge broke down, and Gerbier was superseded at Brussels. Upon the death of Sir John Finet [q. v.] he succeeded to the place of the master of the ceremonies, which had been granted to him by patent, 10 May 1641. He was impoverished by debts incurred abroad, and could only with difficulty bring over his family from Brussels (*ib.* cccclxxxii. 3, 4, 5,

8, 104, cccclxxxiii. 10, &c.) He was accused of giving shelter to papist priests; and in September 1642 his house at Bethnal Green was attacked by a mob. He immediately published a pamphlet entitled 'A Wicked and Inhumane Plot ... Against Sir Balthazar Gerbier, Knight,' &c., in which he declares himself a protestant. After repeated petitions for the money due to him (*ib*. ccccxlxxxix. 67, ccccxci. 101, cccxcvii. 88, &c.) he obtained from the king, at the suit of the elector palatine, permission to retire beyond the seas, together with letters to Louis XIII, who died (14 May 1643) before Gerbier landed at Calais.

In May 1641 Gerbier had made proposals to Charles for the erection of ' mounts ' or banks, combining pawnbroking with banking business (*ib*. ccccxlxxviii. 96). He made similar proposals at Paris in three pamphlets, 'Remonstrance tres humble ... touchant le mont-de-piété, et quelques mauvais bruits que nombre d'usuriers sèment contre ce pieux, utile et nécessaire establissement,' 1643 : 'Justification particulière des intendants de monts-de-piété,' &c., 1643. 'Exposition ... sur l'establissement des monts-de-piété,' 1644. Gerbier states that he was favoured by the Duke of Orleans. The duke and the old Prince of Condé were to be protector-generals of the establishment. He received a patent under the great seal of France. The queen regent was thereupon accused of protecting a protestant. One 'Will Crafts [Crofts] immediately whipt in,' alleging that Gerbier was not the father of the children in his family, and had made them protestants by force. Gerbier's project was stopped; three of his daughters were carried to an English nunnery called Sion, and he himself constrained to quit France. His papers and money were seized between Rouen and Dieppe by seven cavaliers. Crofts, with whom Gerbier associates Davenant, spread their calumnies even to England. Gerbier forthwith printed at Paris, in May 1646, a rambling defence of himself in English, entitled 'Baltazar Gerbier Knight to all men that Love Truth;' and 'A Letter from Sr Balthazar Gerbier, Knight. To his Three Daughters inclosed in a Nunnery att Paris.' Both were distributed in England, and copies, it would seem, were sent to the speaker of the House of Commons. To the Countess of Clare he sent, in manuscript, 'his last Admonitions to his Daughters,' dated Paris, 24 Nov. 1646 (*Harl. MS.* 3384). Eventually his daughters appear to have returned to him.

In 1649, while he was in France, his house at Bethnal Green was broken into by order of the parliamentarians, and his papers relating to his foreign negotiations carried to the paper room at Whitehall (*State Papers, Dom.* xl. 132), and on 12 Nov. of the same year it was agreed by the council that those of Gerbier's papers ' taken to be used at the trial of the late king,' which do not concern the public, be re-delivered to him. He appears to have returned to England shortly after the execution of the king. He now proposed a scheme for an ' Academy' on the model of Charles I's ' Museum Minervæ,' which had ceased with the civil war. He issued a prospectus in some four or five different forms (1648, 4to). It was to give instruction in all manner of subjects, from philosophy, languages, and mathematics, to riding the 'great horse,' dancing and fencing. It was opened on 19 July 1649 at Gerbier's house at Bethnal Green. Many of the lectures were printed: 'The First Lecture, of an Introduction to Cosmographie . . .' 1649 ; 'The Second Lecture being an introduction to Cosmographie . . .' 1649 ; 'The First Lecture, of Geographie . . .' 1649 ; 'The Interpreter of the Academie for forrain Langvages, and all noble sciences, and exercises . . .' 1649 ; 'The First Lecture touching Navigation . . .' 1649 ; ' The Interpreter of the Academie . . . concerning military architecture . . .' 1649 ; 'A Publique Lecture on all the Languages, Arts, Sciences, and noble Exercises ...' 1650 ; 'The Art of Well Speaking . . .' 1650 ; 'The Academies Lecture concerning Justice . . .' 1650. Walpole says of one of these tracts that 'it is a most trifling superficial rhapsody,' which is equally true of all Gerbier's writings. Gerbier was the object of many unfavourable reports, absurd and undeniable. He protested that he was an honest patriot, in a little book entitled ' A Manifestation by Sr Balthazar Gerbier, Kt,' 1651, containing some autobiography; but the ' Academy' broke down. He now published several political pamphlets : ' Some Considerations on the Two grand Staple-Commodities of England . . .' 1651 ; 'A new-year's result in favour of the Poore . . .' 1652; 'A Discovery of Certain Notorious Stumbling-Blocks . . .' 1652. There is also attributed to him an attack on the late king, entitled ' The nonesuch Charles, his Character, extracted out of original Transactions, Dispatches, and the Notes of several public Ministers . . .' 1652. In 1652 an order was passed by the committee for trade and foreign affairs to request the council to give Gerbier a pass to go beyond the seas, and to bestow 50*l*. on him, because he had waited on them for a long time, 'to acquaint them with some particulars relating to the service.' The following year he published at the Hague a small book entitled ' Les Effects pernicieux de Meschants Favoris et Grands Ministres d'Estat . . .' 1653. A few years afterwards he was at the Hague, engaged in a project concerning a gold and silver mine in America, described in 'Waerachtige Verklaringe nopende de Goude en Silvere Mijne,' &c., and 'Tweede Deel van de Waerachtige Verclaringe nopende de Goude en Silvere Mijne,' &c. These were followed by 'Derde Verclaringe aengaende de Goude ende Silvere Mijne aenghewesen door den Ridder Balthazar Gerbier, Baron Douvily, dienende tot wederlegginghe van een Fameux Libel uytgespogen tegens de Waerheyd van de saecke ende zyn Persoon.' These three tracts are dated 'In 's Gravenhage, 1656,' a fourth appearing at the Hague in November 1657: 'Waarachtige Verklaringe van den Ridder Balthazar Gerbier, B. Douvilij; noopende sijn saeke van Goude en Silvere Mijnen,' &c. He had made some proposals to the English committee for trade and foreign affairs (*Proceedings*, 28 May 1652), but they would grant him no monopolies. In 1658 he offered his assistance to the English government during the war with Spain, promising to get up a revolt in the towns of the Spanish Netherlands (THURLOE, vii. 275). He now obtained a patent from the States-General, and styled himself 'Patroon ende Commandeur van de Geoctroyeerde Guiaense Colonie' in his 'Gebedt,' or prayer for the success of the undertaking, published in 1659 at Amsterdam. He sailed from Texel to carry out his mining schemes in Guiana with his wife and family and a number of colonists. He touched at Cayenne, where a mutiny took place, 7 May 1660, among his followers. They killed his daughter Katherine and wounded another. He was saved by the arrival of the governor. On 9 Sept. 1660 he had returned to Amsterdam, and was making his depositions of the murder before the magistrates there, publishing two tracts: 'Informatie voor de Rechtsgeleerde die van wegen d'Edele Heeren Bewinthebbers van de Gheoctroyeerde West-Indische Compagnye gherequireert syn hare advisen te geven op den Moorde in Cajany begaen, en waervan gemelt is in het Sommier Verhael door den Baron Douvily in druck contbaer gemaeckt,' and 'Sommier Verhael van sekere Amerikaensche Voyagie, gedaen door den Ridder Balthasar Gerbier,' &c. Upon the restoration he resolved to return to England, sending before him a pamphlet he printed at Rotterdam, entitled 'A Sommary Description, Manifesting that greater Profits are to bee done in the hott then in the could parts off the Coast off America,' &c., with a second, headed, 'Advertissement for men inclyned to Plantasions in America.' He also addressed to Charles II, on 5 Dec. 1660, 'An Humble Remonstrance

concerning expedients whereby his sacred Matie may increase his revenue, with greate advantage to his Loyall subjects.' On 10 Dec. 1660 a warrant was issued to suspend him from the office of the master of the ceremonies. In 1661 he came to England and petitioned the king for the restitution of his appointment, and the payment of moneys owing to him by Charles I; at the same time presenting various schemes for increasing the revenue and beautifying London.

Being unable to regain his position at court, he once more turned to architecture, and in 1662 supplied the designs for Lord Craven's house at Hampstead Marshall, in Berkshire, since destroyed by fire. In the same year he published 'A Brief Discourse concerning the Three chief Principles of Magnificent Building,' &c., and in the following year, 1663, 'Counsel and Advise to all Builders,' &c.; the most interesting of his pamphlets from incidental references to English architecture in the seventeenth century. There are forty dedicatory epistles, addressed to various eminent persons, from the queen-mother and the Duke of York to Sir Kenelm Digby. His last piece was called 'Subsidium Peregrinantibus. Or an Assistance to a Traveller,' &c., Oxford, 1665. He died at Hampstead Marshall in 1667 while superintending the building of Lord Craven's house, and was buried in the chancel of the church there.

Besides the family piece at Windsor, Vandyck painted a half-length of Gerbier himself; two engraved portraits are prefixed to some of his pamphlets. Some of his drawings are in the Pepysian Library, Magdalene College, Cambridge. He had three sons, George, James, and Charles, and five daughters, Elizabeth, Susan, Mary, Katherine, and Deborah. George Gerbier wrote a play and other literary pieces, and seems to be identical with George Gerbier D'Ouvilly [q. v.] Three of Gerbier's daughters in great distress petitioned the king for the payment of 4,000*l.*, owing to their father by Charles I (*State Papers*, Dom. lxxix. 68).

[Works cited; Walpole's Anecdotes of the Painters, ed. Wornum, 1849; Sainsbury's Papers illustrative of the Life of Sir Peter Paul Rubens, 1859; Gardiner's Hist. of England; Brit. Mus. Cat.]

GEREDIGION, DANIEL DU O, Welsh poet. [See EVANS, DANIEL, 1792–1846.]

GEREE, JOHN (1601?–1649), puritan divine, was born in Yorkshire. In 1615, being then in his fifteenth year, he became either batler or servitor of Magdalen Hall, Oxford. He graduated B.A. on 27 Jan. 1619, M.A. on 12 June 1621. Having taken orders he obtained the living of Tewkesbury, Gloucestershire. For not conforming to the ceremonies he was silenced (after 1624) by Godfrey Goodman [q. v.], bishop of Gloucester, and reduced to live 'by the helps of the brethren.' In 1641 he was restored to his cure by the committee for plundered ministers, and remained there till, on 14 March 1646, he was appointed to the rectory of St. Albans, Hertfordshire. Here he engaged in friendly controversy with John Tombes, the baptist, who had been his fellow-student at Oxford. He left St. Albans in 1647, having been appointed preacher at St. Faith's, under St. Paul's, London. His residence in February 1648 was in Ivy Lane, Paternoster Row. In London, as elsewhere, his sermons were largely attended by puritans. He was strongly averse to episcopacy, and published his 'Case of Conscience,' 1646, to prove that the king might consent to its abolition without breaking his coronation oath. He was attached to the monarchy, and his veneration for the person of the king was such that he 'died at the news of the king's death' (BAXTER). The exact date of his death is not given, but it was in February 1649. Wood supposes him to have been buried at St. Faith's.

He published: 1. 'The Down-Fall of Antichrist,' &c., 1641, 4to. 2. 'Judah's Joy at the Oath,' &c., 1641, 4to, 2 parts (includes answer to Henry Burton [q. v.]) 3. 'Vindiciæ Ecclesiæ Anglicanæ,' &c., 1644, 4to (for a further reformation, but against separatists). 4. 'Vindiciæ Pædobaptismi . . . answer to Mr. Tombs,' &c., 1646, 4to. 5. 'Astrologo-Mastix . . . Iniquity of Judiciall Astrology,' &c., 1646, 4to. 6. 'The Character of an old English Puritane, or Non-Conformist,' &c., 1646, 4to. 7. 'A Case of Conscience Resolved,' &c., 1646, 4to (see above; E. Boughen 'sifted' it in a reply, 1648, 4to). 8. 'Vindiciæ Vindiciarum,' &c., 1647, 4to (defence of No. 4, against Tombes and Harrison). 9. 'Σινιορραγία. The Sifter's Sieve Broken,' &c., 1648, 4to (defence of No. 7). 10. 'Ἵππος Πυρρός, the Red Horse. Or the Bloodines of War,' &c., 1648, 4to. 11. 'Θειοφάρμακον. A Divine Potion . . . the cure of unnaturall health-drinking,' &c., 1648, 4to. 12. 'Καταδυνάστης: Might overcoming Right . . . Answer to M. J. Goodwin's "Might and Right well met,"' &c., 1649, 4to (against the arbitrary removal of members of parliament; answered by Goodwin and Samuel Richardson). He prefixed epistles to W. Pemble's 'Vindiciæ Fidei,' 1625, 4to; T. Shephard's 'Certain Select Cases Resolved,' 1648, 12mo; and W. Fenner's 'The Spirituall Mans Directory,' 1651, 4to. Urwick mentions his 'Catechism,' 1647.

STEPHEN GEREE (1594–1656?), elder brother of the above, was born in Yorkshire, and in 1611 became a student in Magdalen Hall, Oxford, where he graduated B.A. on 5 May 1615. He took orders, was vicar of Wonersh, Surrey, and about 1641 became rector of Abinger, Surrey. He was a strong puritan. He probably died in 1656 or soon after. Besides some sermons, including a funeral sermon for Elizabeth Machel (1639), he published: 1. 'The Doctrine of the Antinomians . . . confuted,' &c., 1644, 4to (answer to Tobias Crisp [q. v.]) 2. 'The Golden Meane . . . Considerations . . . for the more frequent administration of the Lord's Supper,' &c., 1656, 4to.

[Wood's Athenæ Oxon. 1691 i. 820, 830, 839, 1692 ii. 64, 132; Brook's Lives of the Puritans, 1813, iii. 102, 265; Urwick's Nonconformity in Herts, 1884, p. 131 sq.] A. G.

GERMAIN, LADY ELIZABETH or BETTY (1680–1769), was second daughter of Charles, second earl of Berkeley. The Duchess of Marlborough wrote of her in 1738 that 'notwithstanding the great pride of the Berkeley family she married an innkeeper's son,' and maliciously adds in explanation that 'she was very ugly, without a portion, and in her youth had an unlucky accident with one of her father's servants.' The innkeeper's son was Sir John Germain [q. v.], and she was his second wife. They met at the Hot Wells, Bristol, and were married in October 1706. She was many years younger than her husband, but her good sense made their union happy. They had three children, two boys and a girl, who all died young, and in acknowledgment of her devotion in nursing them Germain left her the estate of Drayton in Northamptonshire, and the vast property which he had inherited from his first wife. He expressed the wish on his deathbed that she would marry a young man and have children to succeed to her wealth, but hoped that otherwise her fortune might pass to a younger son of Lionel, duke of Dorset, who had married Elizabeth, daughter of Lieutenant-general Walter Philip Colyear, his friend and colleague in the Dutch service. Though almost persuaded in her old age to marry Lord Sidney Beauclerk, a handsome and worthless fortune-hunter, she remained a widow for more than fifty years, and fulfilled her husband's wishes by leaving the estate of Drayton, with 20,000l. in money, to Lord George Sackville, the duke's second son, who then assumed the name of Germain [see GERMAIN, GEORGE SACKVILLE]. She died at her house in St. James's Square, London, on 16 Dec. 1769. Her elder sister married Thomas Chamber of Hanworth, Middlesex, and had two daughters, who, as their parents died young, were brought up entirely under her guardianship. The elder niece married Lord Vere, the younger became the wife of the well-known Lord Temple. The disposition of Lady Betty's money is set out in a letter from Vere to Temple (*Grenville Papers*, iv. 490–2). She left 120,000*l.* in the funds. Horace Walpole paid a visit to Drayton in 1763, and found the house 'covered with portraits, crammed with old china.' Many of her curiosities were sold after her death by auction. The cameos and intaglios collected by Thomas Howard, earl of Arundel, were bequeathed to Germain by his first wife, the divorced Duchess of Norfolk. Lady Betty offered the collection to the British Museum for 10,000*l.*, and, as the offer was declined, gave them in 1762 to her great-niece, Lady Mary Beauclerk, who married Lord Charles Spencer, brother of the third Duke of Marlborough. These gems were described in two folio volumes entitled 'Gemmarum antiquarum delectus quæ in dactyliothecis Ducis Marlburiensis conservantur,' 1781–90; the engravings were chiefly by Bartolozzi, and the Latin text by Jacob Bryant [q. v.] and William Cole (1753–1806) [q. v.] The gems were part of the Marlborough collection sold in 1875 for 36,750*l.*

She is acknowledged to have 'outlived the irregularities of her youth, and she was esteemed for her kindness and liberality.' She gave 500*l.* to the Foundling Hospital in 1746. Her politics were indicated by a present of 100*l.* to Wilkes during his imprisonment in the Tower. Swift was chaplain to her father, then a lord justice in Ireland. Her name is often mentioned in the 'Journal to Stella,' and Lady Betty often disputed with the dean on political topics. Many letters to and from her are included in Swift's 'Works' and in the 'Suffolk Correspondence.' Her spirited letter in defence of Lady Suffolk against the censure of Swift is especially singled out as doing her 'great honour.' She added a stanza to the dean's ballad on the game of traffic, written at Dublin Castle in 1699, which produced from him in August 1702 a second ballad 'to the tune of the Cutpurse.' Young dedicated to Lady Betty his sixth satire on women, and according to a correspondent in Nichols's 'Literary Anecdotes,' ii. 11, she was credited with having written a satire on Pope. The manuscripts at Drayton, now the property of Mrs. Stopford-Sackville, are described in the Hist. MSS. Comm. 9th Rep. pt. iii., and among them are communications to and from Lady Betty. There are at Knole, near Sevenoaks, two rooms still known as her bedroom and dressing-room.

[Suffolk Corresp. i. 71–3, ii. 18–20, 43, 54–7, 159, 171–3, 213–15; Swift's Works (1884 ed.), xiv. 55–8, xvii. and xviii. passim, xix. 531; Pope's Letters, iii. (Works, viii.) 352–3; Lipscomb's Buckinghamshire, ii. 40; Grenville Papers, i. 135–136, iii. lxviii–ix; Walpole's Corresp. (Cunningham), i. cliv, 187, iv. 99–101, 505, v. 290, viii. 142; Wraxall's Memoirs (1884 ed.), iii. 131–3; Nichols's Lit. Anecd. ii. 4; Gent. Mag. 1746 p. 439, 1769 p. 609; Bridgman's Sketch of Knole (1817), pp. 36–7; Brady's Knole (1839), pp. 118–121; Life of the Countess of Huntingdon (1844 ed.), ii. 48–9; Redford's Art Sales, i. 4, ii. 195–198.]
        W. P. C.

GERMAIN, GEORGE SACKVILLE, first VISCOUNT SACKVILLE (1716–1785), known from 1720 to 1770 as LORD GEORGE SACKVILLE, and from 1770 to 1782 as LORD GEORGE GERMAIN, was third and youngest son of Lionel Cranfield Sackville, seventh earl and first duke of Dorset, the friend of George II, who was lord-lieutenant of Ireland, 1731–7 and 1751–6, and died in 1765, by his wife Elizabeth, daughter of Lieutenant-general Colyear, and niece of the Earl of Portmore. He was born 26 Jan. 1716, and was educated at Westminster School. After residing for some time in Paris with his father, he accompanied him to Ireland, and entered Trinity College, Dublin, where he took his degree as B.A. in 1733, and was created M.A. in 1734. On 23 April 1737 he was appointed clerk of the council in Dublin, with Edward Dering as his deputy, and in July 1737 captain in the present 6th dragoon guards (carabineers), then on the Irish establishment as the 7th or Lord Cathcart's horse. This appears to have been Sackville's first military commission. His next was in 1740, when he was promoted to lieutenant-colonel of the 28th foot (now 1st Gloucester), of which Major-general Bragg [q. v.] was at the time colonel. In 1741 he was returned to parliament as one of the members for Dover, and sat for that borough in each succeeding parliament up to 1761 (his father being at the time lord warden of the Cinque ports). On 20 April 1743 Bragg's regiment was reviewed by the king at Kew, and at once embarked for Flanders. It does not appear to have been at Dettingen, but Sackville was one of the officers appointed king's aides-de-camp, with the brevet of colonel, a few days after the battle, by an order dated 27 June 1743 (*Home Office Mil. Entry Book,* xvii. 246). Sackville took part in the succeeding campaigns, and at Fontenoy, 11 May 1745, was shot in the breast at the head of his regiment, which penetrated so far into the enemy's camp that Sackville was laid in the French king's tent to have his wound dressed.

The regiment had seventeen killed, seventy-four wounded, and forty-eight missing that day, though its presence in the battle is not mentioned in the published history of the 28th foot. Bragg's was one of the regiments ordered home on the receipt of news of the rising in Scotland, and the Duke of Cumberland wrote on 20 Sept. 1745 that he was 'exceedingly sorry to lose Lord George [Sackville], as he has not only shown his courage, but a disposition to his trade which I do not always find in those of higher rank' (De la Warre MSS. in *Hist. MSS. Comm.* 4th Rep. p. 282). Bragg's regiment was sent to Ireland, and on 9 April 1746 Sackville was appointed colonel of the 20th foot (now 1st Lancashire fusileers), which he joined at Inverness just after the battle of Culloden. He was stationed at Inverness, Dundee, and elsewhere in Scotland until the summer of 1747, when he returned to Flanders, apparently in advance of his regiment (*ib.*) In 1748 he was sent by the Duke of Cumberland on a mission to Marshal Saxe (*ib.* 9th Rep. (iii.)). After the peace the 20th foot was at home, and the major commanding, James Wolfe, in a letter dated 2 Aug. 1749, deplores the expected transfer of Sackville to a colonelcy of dragoons. 'Unless Mr. Conway fall to our lot,' he says, 'no possible successor can in any measure make amends for his loss' (WRIGHT, *Life of Wolfe*, pp. 133–4). In November that year Sackville was transferred to the colonelcy of the 12th dragoons (now lancers), and in 1750 to that of his old corps, the present 6th carabineers, by that time the 3rd Irish horse or carabineers. Sackville was first and principal secretary to the lord-lieutenant, and secretary of war for Ireland during his father's viceroyalty in 1751–6, and during part of the time sat for the borough of Portarlington, Queen's County, in the Irish House of Commons, retaining his English seat the while. Abstracts of Sackville's papers relating to Irish affairs during 1750–6 are given in 'Hist. MSS. Comm.' 9th Rep. (iii.), pp. 40–58. They furnish little of political importance. A letter is quoted in which Sackville is described as 'the gayest man in Ireland except his father.' Sackville became a major-general in 1755, and, after vacating the Irish secretaryship, was appointed to command a brigade of line encamped on Chatham upper lines. In 1757, Lieutenant-general Charles Spencer, duke of Marlborough, and Major-generals Lord George Sackville and Waldegrave were appointed by warrant under the royal sign manual, to inquire into the conduct of General Sir John Mordaunt in the Rochfort expedition, a precedent existing in the case of Sir John

Cope at Prestonpans (CLODE, *Administration of Justice under Military Law*, p. 172). The court reported unfavourably of Mordaunt's conduct; but the court-martial which followed took a different view. The same year Sackville was appointed lieutenant-general of the ordnance, and was transferred to the colonelcy of the 2nd dragoon guards (queen's bays). Another descent on the French coast having been decided on, the command was given to the Duke of Marlborough, with Sackville and Lord Ancram as his lieutenants. A force of thirteen thousand guards and line and six thousand marines sailed from Spithead in June 1758. Having reconnoitred St. Malo, they landed in the bay of Cancale a few miles distant, and marched across country to the port, in two columns, the first commanded by Sackville. After burning some shipping, they returned to Cancale, and, hearing of the approach of a powerful French force, re-embarked somewhat precipitately. On 29 June the expedition appeared off Cherbourg, but the weather proving tempestuous, the admiral (Howe) forbore to attack, and returned to the Isle of Wight, where the troops were put on shore for refreshment, and their leaders returned to London, vowing they would 'go buccaneering' no more. Sackville's account of the expedition will be found in 'Hist. MSS. Comm.' 9th Rep. (iii.) 71–4. Contemptible as a military operation, it appears to have had the effect of diverting French reinforcements from Germany, whither part of Marlborough's troops were sent as a British reinforcement to the allied army under Prince Ferdinand of Brunswick. The troops under Marlborough, with Sackville as his second in command, arrived in Hanover in September 1758. Marlborough died at Münster soon after, of an epidemic which had broken out among the British soldiers, and was succeeded by Sackville as 'commander-in-chief of all his majesty's forces, horse and foot, serving on the Lower Rhine or to be there assembled with the allied army under the command of Prince Ferdinand of Brunswick, commander-in-chief of the said army' (see *Proceedings of Sackville's Court Martial*). Sackville was sworn of the privy council the same year. Haughty in official intercourse and of an exacting temper, Sackville, according to the popular story, was speedily on bad terms both with Prince Ferdinand and with his own second in command, Lord Granby. Nothing of special importance, however, occurred until the battle of Minden or Thornhausen, 1 Aug. 1759. The French attack on the allied army in position commenced soon after dawn, and before 10 A.M. six regiments of British foot and two of Hanoverians on the allied left, aided by the British guns, had repulsed four attacks by the flower of the French horse, and had driven back an infantry brigade sent up in support. The moment appeared opportune for pursuit, and repeated orders were sent to Sackville to advance with the British cavalry, which was away behind a wood on the right. The orders were regarded as not sufficiently precise by Sackville, who, after some expostulation with Colonel Fitzroy, the bearer of the last order, peremptorily halted Granby, who had already got the blues in motion, and went off to confer with Prince Ferdinand. In the end the movement was made, but, to the vexation of the whole army, the moment for decisive action had gone by, and the British cavalry lost their share in the honours of the day. Prince Ferdinand pointedly omitted Sackville's name, while mentioning Granby, in his general order to the army after the battle, and in his despatch to England. Sackville having remonstrated, the prince replied: ' Je vous dirés doré tout simplement que je n'ai pu voir avec indifference ce qui s'est fait avec la cavallerie de la droite. Vous commandés tout le Corps Brittanniques ; ainsi votre poste fixé ne devait pas etre tout la cavallerie, mais vous deviés egalement conduire les uns et les autres suivant que vous en trouviés l'occasion pour cooperer a la reussite d'une journée si glorieuse pour l'armée. Je vous ai fourni la plus belle occasion pour profiter et pour faire decider le sort de cette journée, si mes ordres avaient etés remplis au pied de la lettre. . . . Le temoinage que j'ai rendu à mylord Granby je lui dois parce qu'il le merite à tous egards et qu'il ne ma manquée dans tous d'occasions. Ce n'est pas une règle que puisque je loue l'un que je blame l'autre. Mais il ne me peut pas être indifferent si mes ordres ne s'executent point et qu'on ne veut ajouter foi aux porteurs de cet ordre' (*Hist. MSS. Comm.* 9th Rep. (iii.) 80). Sackville obtained leave to return home, and arrived in London three weeks after the date of the battle. On 10 Sept. he was dismissed the service by a war-office letter from Lord Barrington, informing him that ' his majesty has no further need of your services as lieutenant-general and colonel of dragoon guards.' He was succeeded in his command in Germany and at the ordnance by his rival Granby. Horace Walpole writes of Sackville: ' He immediately applied for a court-martial, but was told it was impossible, as the officers were all away in Germany. This was in writing from Lord Holdernesse, but my lord Ligonier in words was more squab. "If he wanted a court-martial he must go seek it in Germany." All that could be taken from him is his regiment, about

2,000*l.* a year, his command in Germany 10*l.* a day, 3,000*l.* to 4,000*l.*, lieutenant-general of the ordnance 1,500*l.* a year, a fort 300*l.* He retains his patent place in Ireland, about 1,200*l.* a year, and 2,000*l.* of his wife and himself. With his parts and ambition it cannot end here ; he calls himself ruined, but when parliament meets he will probably attempt some sort of revenge' (WALPOLE, *Letters*, iii. 249). Sackville was one of the very few men of acknowledged ability in parliament who were not connected with the party in power (MACAULAY, *Essay on Chatham*). He pressed for a court-martial, which the government appeared in no hurry to grant. He published an ' Address to the English Public,' and an ' Answer to Colonel Fitzroy.' When at last it was decided to refer to the law officers of the crown the question of the legality of trying an officer no longer in the service by court-martial for offences committed while serving, he was officiously warned that if the finding of the court were adverse, he would certainly be shot, like Byng. Sackville persevered with a dogged resolution that gave the lie to the common suggestion of cowardice (see the pamphlets under 'Sackville' in WATTS, *Cat. Printed Books* ; also *Brit. Mus. Cat. Prints and Drawings*, Div. i. iii. (ii.), 1197–1202. In some of the satires it is suggested that Sackville was bribed by France). The law officers having pronounced in favour of the trial—an opinion on which it would not now be safe to rely (CLODE, *Admin. Mil. Law*, p. 92)—a general court-martial, composed of eleven lieutenant-generals and four major-generals, under the presidency of General Sir Charles Howard, K.B., assembled at the Horse Guards, 3 Feb. 1760. Before this tribunal Sackville was arraigned on the charge of disobedience of orders. The disobedience (the judge-advocate, Charles Gould, was careful to explain) was confined to orders relating to the battle of Minden. Sackville objected to General Belford, of the artillery, as being under the influence of Granby. The objection was allowed.

After repeated adjournments caused by the illness of the president and the expiry in the meantime of the Mutiny Act, it was considered necessary to summon a new court. The court, with the same president, was accordingly convened afresh at the Horse Guards on 25 March 1760. Sackville, who took a high-handed tone with the court, made an able and spirited defence. On 5 April the court agreed to its finding and sentence, which was that Sackville was ' guilty of having disobeyed the orders of Prince Ferdinand of Brunswick, whom he was by his commission bound to obey as commander-in-chief, according to the rules of war,' and that 'the court is further of opinion that he is, and he is hereby adjudged to be, unfit to serve his majesty in any military capacity whatever.' George II confirmed the sentence, and directed that it be recorded in the order-book of every regiment with the following remarks : 'It is his majesty's pleasure that the above sentence be given out in public orders, not only in Britain, but in America, and every quarter of the globe where British troops happen to be, that officers, being convinced that neither high birth nor great employments can shelter offences of such a nature, and that, seeing they are subject to censures worse than death to a man who has any sense of honour, they may avoid the fatal consequences arising from disobedience of orders.' To complete Sackville's disgrace, the king called for the privy council books and erased his name therefrom. These last two acts were announced in the 'London Gazette,' 26 April 1760.

Sackville, who had retained his seat for Dover, was returned at the general election of 1761 for East Grinstead, Sussex, and Hythe, Kent, and elected to sit for the latter. The harshness with which the court-martial sentence had been carried out had not escaped public notice, and in the new reign there came the inevitable reaction. In 1762 Sackville spoke in the house for the first time since his disgrace (*Parl. Hist.* xv. 1222), and in April 1763, not eighteen months after the coronation of George III, we find Lord Bute writing to Sir Harry Erskine that the king admits and condemns the harsh usage of Sackville, 'but is prevented by state reasons from affording him the redress intended' (*Hist. MSS. Comm.* 9th Rep. (iii.) 11 *b*). Sackville's name was soon after restored to the list of privy councillors, and he was received at court. In 1765, in which year he succeeded to the Knole Park estates on the death of his father, he was appointed joint vice-treasurer of Ireland, a post from which he was dismissed the year after. At the general election of 1768 he was returned for East Grinstead, which borough he represented in succeeding parliaments until his elevation to the peerage. Sackville was now a recognised follower of Lord North. From July to October 1769 were published the famous 'Letters of Junius,' with the authorship of which Sackville was early and very generally accredited. Sir William Draper was confident that the authorship lay between Sackville and Burke. The evidence in favour of Sackville's authorship, collected by J. Jaques, will be found among the Woodfall letters in the British Museum (*Addit. MS.* 27783), but the opinion

has never been accepted by writers of authority. In 1770 Sackville was empowered by act of parliament to assume the name of Germain, in accordance with the provisions of the will of Lady Betty Germain [q. v.] In December of the same year Germain (Sackville) was greatly rehabilitated in public estimation by his duel with Captain George Johnstone, late governor of Pensacola, and then M.P. for Cockermouth. 'Governor' Johnstone, as he was called, a noisy politician, had expressed his surprise that Germain, on some particular occasion, should be so concerned about his country's honour when he cared so little for his own. Germain demanded an apology, which was refused. A meeting took place in Hyde Park. At the second exchange of shots Johnstone's bullet struck the barrel of Germain's pistol. 'Mr. Johnstone, your ball struck the barrel of my pistol,' said Germain. 'I am glad, my lord, it was not yourself,' rejoined Johnstone, who afterwards declared that in all the affairs in which he had any hand, he never knew a man behave better than Germain (*Scots Mag.* xxxii. 724). 'Lord George Germain is a hero, whatever Lord George Sackville may have been,' was Horace Walpole's characteristic comment (*Letters*, v. 269–70). In 1775 Germain, who continued to take an active part in politics, was appointed by Lord North a lord commissioner of trade and plantations, a post he held until 1779, and likewise secretary of state for the colonies, which he held until the resignation of the North cabinet in 1782. Germain zealously supported all the rigorous measures directed against the colonists, and acquired much influence with the king. He was the object of some virulent party attacks (see RUSSELL, *Life of Fox*, note at p. 157 ; also *Parl. Hist.* 1776–81 ; and WALPOLE, *Letters*, vii. 11, 72). On the resignation of the North ministry, the king desired to confer some mark of favour on Germain, who asked for a peerage. He is said also to have asked to be made a viscount, as otherwise he would be junior to his own secretary, Lord Walsingham, to Loughborough, who was his lawyer, and to Amherst, who had been his father's page. On 11 Feb. 1782 he was created Viscount Sackville of Drayton Manor, Northamptonshire, and Baron Bolebroke of Sussex, in the peerage of the United Kingdom (copy of patent, *Addit. MS.* 19818, f. 271). A motion in the House of Lords by the Marquis of Carmarthen that Germain, being still under sentence of court-martial, was an unfit person for a peerage, was rejected, as was a similar motion on the day he took his seat. Sackville's last years were spent chiefly in retirement on his estates. His health was latterly enfeebled by suffering of long standing from stone, and his death is said to have been hastened by his efforts to be in his place in the House of Lords at the discussion of certain 'propositions' sent up by the Irish parliament. He died at his residence, Stoneland Lodge, Sussex (now included in Buckhurst Park), on 26 Aug. 1785, in the seventieth year of his age (*Gent. Mag.* lv. pt. ii. 667, 746).

Sackville married, in September 1754, Diana, second daughter and coheiress of John Sambroke, only brother of Sir Jeffreys Sambroke, bart., of Gubbins, Hertfordshire. She died on 15 June 1778, leaving two sons and three daughters.

In person Sackville was tall, robust, and active. Although haughty and distant in manner in public, he was agreeable in private intercourse. His abilities appear to have been much above the average; his experience of public life and affairs was exceptionally wide and varied; he was quick in the despatch of business, and Walpole describes him as one of the best speakers in the House of Commons (*Letters*, iv. 194). He had no pretensions to scholarship, and those who knew him best declare that, although possessing a fine library, he rarely opened a book. There is no evidence of the 'transcendent abilities' as a statesman which have been sometimes claimed for him. Richard Cumberland, the dramatist [q. v.], his neighbour at Stoneland, describes him in his declining years, riding about his estate, followed by an aged groom, who had grown grey in his service, taking an intelligent interest in the welfare of his cottagers and retainers, or in the village church, in quaint Sir Roger de Coverley style, nodding approval of the sermon or rating the rustic choir for singing out of tune. A portrait by Sir Joshua Reynolds has been engraved.

[Collins's Peerage (1812 ed.), vi. 308–17; Doyle's Official Baronage, iii. 205; Rich. Cumberland's Character of the late Viscount Sackville (1785, 8vo), a pamphlet of which there are several copies in the British Museum. A biography of Sackville is given in Georgian Era, ii. 53. The Memoirs of the Rev. Percival Stockdale (London, 1809), i. 428–40, contains an account of Sackville at Brompton Camp and elsewhere. The statement at p. 433 should be compared with the rather apocryphal story in Colburn's United Serv. Mag. 1830, ii. 475. In the British Museum, among the printed books catalogued under 'Sackville, afterwards Germain,' will be found copies of Sackville's Address to the Public (London, 1759, fol.), and his vindication of himself in a letter to Colonel Fitzroy (1759, 8vo); also copies of the court-martial proceedings, printed 'by authority.' Among the maps is (30520[1]) an ingenious one

of the battle of Minden, showing the successive movements of the troops from 27 July to 2 Aug. 1759, which was prepared by Captain (afterwards General) Roy, and laid before the court-martial. Reference may also be made to J. Jaques's Hist. of Junius (London, 1843); Walpole's Letters, under 'Sackville' and 'Germain;' Wraxall's Memoirs, passim; Rich. Cumberland's Memoirs (ed. 1807), pp. 484–96. This, the quarto edition, contains a well-engraved portrait. Sackville's more important speeches will be found in Parliamentary History, vols. xvi–xxvi. His papers are now at Drayton House, Northamptonshire, and are the subject of a very full report forming Hist. MSS. Comm. 9th Rep. pt. iii. They include three series of Irish papers, papers relating to Cherbourg and St. Malo, Minden papers, and Sackville's correspondence when secretary of state for the colonies, 1775–82. This collection also includes a large bundle of letters from Sackville to his friend General Sir John Irwin, by whose widow they were sold to the Duke of Dorset. They cover the period 1761–84. Other letters and papers in various private collections are indexed under 'Sackville' or 'Germain' in other Hist. MSS. Comm. Reports; but the Sackville Family MSS., reported on in Hist. MSS. Comm. 7th Rep., contain no papers of so late a date. Besides numerous papers in the Public Record Office, Dublin, and in the Home and Colonial Series in the Public Record Office, London, the following papers exist in the British Museum: Sackville's Correspondence with Amherst and others, Addit. MS. 21697; with General Haldimand, Addit. MSS. 21702–4; Letters to General Grant, 1778–1779, Eg. MS. 2135, ff. 45, 52; to Lord Lisburne, 1779, Eg, MS. 2136, ff. 142, 145; to Governor Burt, Eg. MS. 2135, f. 79; Correspondence with Sir Henry Clinton, Addit. MS. 24322, ff. 47, 71; and with General Vaughan, Eg. MS. 2135 ff. 83–179.]   H. M. C.

GERMAIN, SIR JOHN (1650–1718), soldier of fortune, passed as the son of a private soldier in the life guards of William II, prince of Orange. His mother, who was very handsome, is stated to have been that prince's mistress, and Germain is said to have assumed ' as his seal and armorial bearing' a red cross, implying pretensions to exalted parentage. His military qualities, independently of this supposititious relationship, endeared him to William III, whom he accompanied to England in 1688, and with whom he served in later years in Ireland and Flanders. His personal appearance and courage won favour with women, and his relations with Lady Mary Mordaunt, only surviving child of Henry, earl of Peterborough, and wife of Henry, seventh duke of Norfolk, made his name notorious. They were charged with having committed adultery in 1685, 1690, and 1691, and the duke introduced into the House of Lords a bill for a divorce in 1691 and 1692, but it was rejected on each occasion. In November 1692 the duke brought an action in the court of king's bench against Germain, and claimed 50,000*l.* damages, when 'lascivious conversation' between him and the duchess was proved, but to the astonishment of the court the jury awarded only a hundred marks in damages and costs. A third bill for a divorce passed the House of Lords in 1700. At the death of her father, 19 June 1697, the duchess inherited great estates, including that of Drayton in Northamptonshire, which Charles, the next Earl of Peterborough, tried in vain to secure for himself. A license for the marriage of 'Sir John Germain, of St. James's, Westminster . . . and Lady Mary Mordaunt, of same, spinster,' was granted at the faculty office of the Archbishop of Canterbury at London on 15 Sept. 1701, and shortly afterwards they were married. She died on 17 Nov. 1705, aged 46, and a tomb of grey marble, with her figure above it, was placed under the east window of the north chancel aisle of Lowick Church. By her will Drayton and other property, valued at 70,000*l.*, passed to Germain, who had been knighted at Kensington on 26 Feb. 1698, and exalted to a baronetcy on 25 March in the same year. Immediately on the death of Germain's wife it was rumoured that her brother, the Earl of Peterborough, intended to enter upon legal proceedings for obtaining her property, and in November 1707 a great trial took place, when the tithes were assigned to the peer, but the remainder was left to the husband. A second trial, with the same result, occurred in 1710, and for the rest of Germain's life he was involved in constant trouble over the estate. Upon his marriage to Lady Elizabeth Berkeley [see GERMAIN, LADY ELIZABETH], it was given out by Peterborough that if Drayton was left to her she should remain in undisturbed possession, and the peer kept his word. Germain died on 11 Dec. 1718, aged 68 years. A tomb of grey marble, with his effigies, and with representations of their three small children before him, was erected to his memory by his second wife near the monument of her predecessor. His 'defective morals were accompanied by a total want of education. A modern colonnade, the pillars of which were at first set up with their capitals downwards,' was constructed by him at Drayton, and he is said to have believed that St. Matthew's Gospel was written by his compatriot, Sir Matthew Decker [q.v.] In his last moments he is said to have been in great distress and desired the sacrament, but Dr. Clarke of St. James's, Westminster, refused to give it to him (NICHOLS, *Lit. Anecd.* iv. 720).

[Walpole's Corresp. (Cunningham), viii. 58, 297; Prior's Malone, pp. 442–3; Wraxall's Memoirs (1884 ed.), iii. 131–3; Harl. Soc. xxiv. 240 (1886); Le Neve's Knights (Harl. Soc.), p. 461; Burke's Extinct Baronetcies; Luttrell's Relation of State Affairs, vol. ii. passim; Bridges's Northamptonshire (1791 ed.), ii. 247–52.]

W. P. C.

GERMANUS (378 ?–448), bishop of Auxerre, and missionary to Britain, son of noble parents whose names are given as Rusticus and Germanilla, was born at Auxerre about 378, and after attending schools in Gaul went to study at Rome. There he practised as an advocate, and on his return to Gaul married a lady named Eustachia, and became one of the six dukes of Gaul (for the office of dux see *Recueil des Historiens*, i. 750; there were five duces in Gaul about this time, *ib.* p. 125; GIBBON, ii. 320). Auxerre appears to have been in his province. He was fond of hunting, and used to hang the heads of the beasts which he slew on a large pear-tree in the middle of the city. Amator, the bishop, vainly remonstrated with him on this practice, which gave some countenance to pagan superstition, and one day, when Germanus was absent, cut down the tree and threw away the heads. Germanus thought of slaying Amator, but the bishop, who felt unworthy of the honour of martyrdom, circumvented him by going to the prefect Julius, and requesting that, as he knew that his end was near, he might secure Germanus as his successor. When he returned to Auxerre he gathered the people in the church, and Germanus came with the rest. The bishop caused all present to lay aside their arms, ordered the doors to be barred, and then seized the duke, cut his hair, made him a cleric, and bade him live as one who was to be a bishop. Soon after this Amator died, and Germanus was unanimously chosen to succeed him, and was consecrated 7 July 418. He at once adopted a new manner of life, his wife became to him as a sister, he distributed his goods among the poor, and practised many austerities, such as abstaining from salt, oil, and other things, and sleeping on ashes laid upon boards. He founded a monastery on the other bank of the Yonne, and often went across to visit the abbot and monks there. He had power over demons, laid a ghost which haunted a ruined house, and when on one of his journeys he found that the people who received him were in trouble because their cocks could not crow, he blessed the fowls' grain, and ever after the birds crowed so much that they became a nuisance (ad molestiam fatigabant) to the neighbours (*Vita*, i. c. 5). In 429 a message came from Britain to the bishops of Gaul, begging them to give some help to the catholic cause in Britain against the spread of Pelagianism. A council was held. Germanus had perhaps already been commissioned by Pope Celestine to undertake the work as his representative, and he and St. Lupus, bishop of Troyes, were chosen by the council to go on a mission to Britain (Prosper of Aquitaine gives the date, and records the commission from Celestine; he was himself in Rome on a mission to Celestine in 432; Constantius, who was a contemporary of Germanus, and wrote his life less than fifty years after his death, only speaks of the Gallic council; the two accounts are not inconsistent. *Councils and Eccl. Docs.* i. 17 *n.* a; TILLEMONT, *Mémoires*, xiv. 154; but Lingard's explanation seems forced, *Anglo-Saxon Church*, i. 8). As the two bishops journeyed they came to Nanterre, near Paris. From the crowd which assembled to see them Germanus singled out a young girl named Genovefa, and bade her dedicate herself to God; she became famous as Ste. Geneviève of Paris. It was winter when the bishops crossed, and Germanus calmed the sea by pouring oil upon it. The connection between the British and Gallic churches was very close at this period, and among the disciples of Amator, who tarried with Germanus, was St. Patrick, a native probably of Strathclwyd.

The bishops held a disputation with the heretic teachers evidently near Verulamium (St. Albans). Their opponents appeared richly dressed, and followed by a crowd of admiring disciples, but were vanquished by the 'torrent of eloquence mixed with the thunders of the apostles and evangelists' which the bishops launched against them. The victory was declared by the shouts of the multitude. The bishops then visited the tomb of St. Alban, in which Germanus deposited some precious relics, taking away a piece of earth red with the martyr's blood. To this visit belongs the famous story of the Alleluia victory, which is told by Constantius. The Britons besought the bishops' help against the incursions of the Picts and Saxons. Germanus bade them take courage. A large number of them who were, it is said, unbaptised received the rite. Immediately after Easter, 430, Germanus drew the Britons up in battle array in a valley closely shut in by mountains. When the enemy came, the British host thrice repeated after their leader the shout of Alleluia, and the hostile army fled in confusion, leaving abundance of spoil. On his return to Auxerre, Germanus found the people oppressed with taxation, and ob-

tained a remission of the tax from the prefect. He built a church at Auxerre in honour of St. Alban and placed in it what he had brought from the martyr's tomb ('Mir. S. Germani,' *Acta SS.* July vii. 258). In 447 a message came to him from Britain requesting that he would again help the church there against the Pelagians. He went over in company with Severus, bishop of Treves, worked a miraculous cure which strengthened the catholic cause, and by his preaching entirely overthrew the Pelagian heresy. On his return to Gaul he found the Armoricans suffering under an invasion of Alans. They had been goaded to revolt, and the patrician Aetius instigated the Alans to invade them in order to reduce them to submission. Germanus seems at one time to have ruled the Armoricans as duke; he went to meet the Alans and begged their king Eochar to withdraw his forces. As Eochar would not listen, he seized the king's bridle; his courage and bearing overawed the king, who granted the Armoricans a respite to allow time for Germanus to plead their cause with the imperial government. Germanus at once set out for Italy, reached Milan on 19 June 448, and proceeded to Ravenna. At Ravenna he was received with much honour, and the empress-mother, Galla Placidia, sent him food on a silver dish. He gave the food to his attendants, sold the dish, and distributed the price among the poor, sending back to the empress in return some bread on a wooden platter. The empress had the platter encircled with gold, and kept the bread as a cure for sickness. While at Ravenna he dreamt that the Lord appeared to him and gave him provision for a journey; he asked on what pilgrimage he was to be sent, and received answer that he was to be sent on no pilgrimage but was to go home. He knew that this meant that he was soon to be taken to his home in heaven. He fell sick and died on 31 July 448. His body was sent back to Gaul with great magnificence; bridges and roads were mended all along the route by which the funeral car was to travel. He was buried in a chapel close by Auxerre on 1 Oct. When Auxerre fell into the hands of the Huguenots on 27 Sept. 1567, his bones, it has been asserted, were scattered; on the other hand it is claimed that they were concealed by the catholics; the subject is fully discussed by the Bollandists. There are many Welsh legends about the doings of Germanus in Britain. Maes-y-Garmon, near Mold in Flintshire, has been fixed upon as the site of the Alleluia victory (USSHER, *Antiqq.* p. 179). The book called by the name of 'Nennius,' probably of the ninth century, represents him as working many miracles, as anathematising Vortigern for incest, and taking part in other matters which are clearly unhistorical. Another legend attributes to him the foundation of the colleges of Llancarvan and Llanilltyd, while a Cornish missal claims 'his preaching and relics for Cornwall, and attributes his mission to Pope Gregory.' Gildas does not mention him, and Constantius says nothing of these legends. The utmost that can be said of them is that it is possible that they signify that Germanus 'did more for British Christianity than Constantius knew of, or felt an interest in recording' (BRIGHT). Germanus is brought into the mythical stories of the antiquity of Oxford (inserted passage in ASSER).

[Vita S. Germani by Constantius, a priest of Lyons, who was highly esteemed by Sidonius Apollinaris (Ep. i. 1, iii. 2), and who wrote between twenty-five and fifty years after the death of the bishop, Acta SS. Bolland. July vii. 211, with earlier commentary; Vita S. Germani by Heric, who wrote about 877, dedicating his work to Charles the Bald (Heric also wrote two books of miracles; he says that he derived some of his information from an aged British bishop named Mark, ib. 232 seq.); Vita S. Lupi, ib. p. 74; Vita S. Genovefæ, Acta SS. Bolland. Jan. i. 138 seq.; Prosper Aquit. Chron.; Migne's Patrol. li. 594; Bædæ Hist. Eccl. cxvii-xxi., borrowed from Constantius; Nennius, Hist. Brit. passim (Engl. Hist. Soc.), see Stevenson's preface; Welsh legends of Nennius used in Higden, Polychron. v. 274 (Rolls Ser.); Ussher's Antiquitates (1687), pp. 172 seq.; Rees's Welsh Saints, pp. 122-4; Haddan and Stubbs's Councils and Eccles. Docs. i. 16-21, 139; art. 'Germanus' (8), St., in Dict. Christ. Biog., by Canon Bright, D.D.]   W. H.

GERRALD, JOSEPH (1763-1796), political reformer, was born on 9 Feb. 1763, at St. Christopher, West Indies, where his father, the descendant of an old Irish family, had settled as a planter. When a child he was brought to England by his parents and passed from a boarding-school at Hammersmith to the care of Samuel Parr at Stanmore. Parr conceived the highest opinion of his abilities, but was nevertheless obliged to expel him for 'extreme indiscretion.' At twelve years of age he was left an orphan, and on his majority he succeeded to a fortune embarrassed by his father's extravagance, and to be still further wasted by his own improvidence. Having returned to the West Indies he married —according to one account 'rashly'—a lady of St. Christopher, who soon afterwards died leaving him with two children. Reduced to comparative poverty, he went to America, where for four years he practised at the bar in Pennsylvania. In 1788 he came to England to prosecute a lawsuit in connection with his property. From this time he engaged in politics, taking a prominent part in the agitation for parliamentary reform. He renewed his acquaintance with Dr. Parr in a grateful letter.

In 1793 he was sent along with Maurice Margarot as a delegate from the London Corresponding Society to the 'British Convention of the Delegates of the People' assembled at Edinburgh. The avowed object of the convention was to obtain universal suffrage and annual parliaments. It had 'secret committees' and 'conventions of emergency,' its members addressed each other as 'citizens,' and generally adopted the language of the French revolutionists. Gerrald was received at Edinburgh with enthusiasm; he was an eloquent speaker, his morning levée at the Black Bull inn was crowded with admiring worshippers, and every night he was attended by a numerous train when he visited and harangued the different 'sections.' On 5 Dec. 1793 he and Margarot were arrested for sedition, but admitted to bail. He returned to London, and prepared to wait his trial. Meantime Margarot and the secretary of the convention, William Skirving [q. v.], with other political reformers, had received sentences of transportation; Gerrald's friends, especially Parr, entreated him to insure his safety by flight.

Gerrald considered that he was in honour pledged to surrender himself, but he was under no illusion as to the consequences. In a letter to the home secretary, Henry Dundas [q. v.], he said that he was starting not to take his trial, 'for trial implies candid examination,' but to receive his sentence of transportation for fourteen years, to which Margarot had already been condemned. The trial took place on 3, 10, 13, and 14 March 1794, the presiding judge being Lord Braxfield [see MACQUEEN, ROBERT], to whose presence on the bench Gerrald made the formal objection, which was overruled, that he had already prejudged the case. While assisted by counsel appointed by the court, Gerrald defended himself in a forcible address to the jury. He was convicted and sentenced to fourteen years' transportation (HOWELL, State Trials, xxiii. 947-98).

The prosecutions of Gerrald and his fellow agitators excited great indignation, and formed the subject of several debates in parliament. Gerrald remained in prison in London for upwards of twelve months, having for companion his young daughter; during this time he was visited by many friends. In May 1795 he was suddenly shipped to Botany Bay, without being allowed time to make any preparations for the voyage. Parr addressed an indignant letter on the subject to Windham, then secretary at war, and, assisted by others, sent after Gerrald money, books, and personal necessaries; he also took under his protection Gerrald's son. Touching letters written at this period bear witness to the affection which existed between Parr and his former pupil (PARR, *Works*, i. 453–5).

Gerrald reached Sydney, New South Wales, on 5 Nov. 1795, in very weak health, and was received by friends who had suffered in the same cause. Among these was Margarot, against whom accusations had been made by his companions, and from whom Gerrald soon separated. He was permitted by the governor of the settlement to purchase a small house and garden. Five months after his arrival (16 March 1796) he died of consumption, aged 33. Gerrald's name appears on the obelisk ('The Martyrs' Monument') erected on Calton Hill, Edinburgh, in 1844, to commemorate the struggle for parliamentary reform.

[Howell's State Trials, xxiii. 803–1011, 1411–1414; Parl. Hist. xxx. 1298, 1449, 1486, xxxi. 54, 263, xxxiii. 617; Adolphus's History, v. 532–41; Lives and Trials of the Reformers, 1836, pt. i.; Memoirs and Trials of the Political Martyrs of Scotland persecuted during 1793 and 1794, Edinburgh, 1837; An Examination of the Trials for sedition which have hitherto occurred in Scotland, by the late Lord Cockburn (posthumously published 1888); Johnstone's Memoir of Dr. Parr prefixed to his Works, i. 448–57; Rogers's Monuments and Monumental Inscriptions, i. 92.] J. M. S.

GERVASE OF CANTERBURY (GERVASIUS DOROBORNENSIS) (*fl.* 1188), chronicler, was born, apparently of a Kentish family, about 1141. As he had a brother Thomas in his monastery, who is conjectured to be identical with one Thomas of Maidstone, we have a possible clue to his birthplace; but the information is too imperfect to warrant more than an hypothesis. Gervase became a monk of Christ Church, Canterbury, on the first Saturday in Lent, 16 Feb. 1163 (*Hist. Works*, i. 173). The new archbishop, Thomas Becket, received his profession, and it was he who conferred holy orders upon him (p. 231). Dom Brial's statement (*Recueil des Historiens de France*, xvii. præf. pp. xi, xii, 1818) that Gervase was prior of St. Ceneri before he went to Canterbury is impossible on chronological grounds. Of his earlier years in the monastery nothing is recorded beyond an incidental notice (ii. 396) of his presence at the archbishop's burial on the morrow of his murder, 30 Dec. 1170. Thenceforward his works contain more and more information as to the

events connected with his church and monastery, which he seems never to have quitted for any length of time. He gives, for instance, a minute account of the burning of the cathedral, 5 Sept. 1174 (i. 1–6), though this record is apparently not quite contemporary, since it is probable that he did not begin writing until 1185; and he takes an active interest in the disputes of his monastery, which continued in an acute form until long after the election of Archbishop Baldwin in December 1184. His writings are of great interest for the history of the important religious body to which he belonged. 'He writes throughout as the champion of the cathedral convent against the whole world, and especially against the archbishop, wherever the interests of the archbishop and convent are opposed. Where there is no such opposition he is willing to act and write as the archbishop's champion, and his interest is never more vivid or his argument stronger than where the rights of the archbishop and convent are identical' (STUBBS, i. pref. p. xvi).

The earliest controversy in which Gervase appears to have been personally concerned was one between the archbishop and the abbot of St. Augustine's, Canterbury, which lasted from 1179 to 1183, and on which he wrote two 'imaginations' or statements of the case (i. 68–83). These have the look, however, rather of exercises than of statements drawn up for use in the contest. The same criticism applies also, though with not so high a degree of probability, to a set of tracts or statements prefixed to Gervase's 'Chronicle' (i. 32–68), which relate to the disputes between Archbishop Baldwin and the monastery of Christ Church (1185–91). There are several traces of his personal action in the affair, and on one occasion, in December 1186, he was sent with other monks to announce to the archbishop the appeal of the monastery to Rome (i. 343 f.) It is further possible that he was in part the author of some of the letters drawn up on behalf of his monastery, and printed by Bishop Stubbs in his collection of 'Epistolæ Cantuarienses' (*Chronicles and Memorials of the Reign of Richard I*, vol. ii. Rolls Series, 1865). The relation of the smaller tracts to the Chronicle which follows them, as well as of the Chronicle to the life of St. Thomas by Herbert of Bosham, furnishes a satisfactory argument for fixing 1188 as the date at which Gervase began the composition of the larger work. That opens at the accession of Henry I (1100), and was continued apparently year by year until 1199. The materials for its earlier portions are chiefly derived from Henry of Huntingdon and Florence of Worcester—of the latter

Gervase seems to have used a continuation no longer extant—together with perhaps the chronicle of St. Augustine's, Canterbury, and the 'Historia Pontificalis' of John of Salisbury. Afterwards his authorities are the lives of St. Thomas and the 'Gesta regis Henrici,' attributed to Benedict of Peterborough; and by degrees the work acquires the character of an independent chronicle, though its interest is to a great extent limited to the affairs of the author's monastery. Gervase contemplated the production of a second book of this history (i. 594); but no such work is now known to be in existence, and there is no proof that it was ever written.

In November 1189 he went with a deputation to Westminster, and accepted Richard I's proposal to arbitrate between the monastery and the archbishop (*Epp. Cantuar.* 315 ff.; cf. GERVASE, i. 462–72). In 1193, as sacrist of the convent, he met the new archbishop, Hubert Walter, 3 Nov., at Lewisham, and delivered to him his cross, the speech which Gervase made on the occasion being duly recorded by him (i. 520–2). Before 1197 he had ceased to hold the office of sacrist (p. 544), and we possess no further notice of his life or doings. It is only from the internal evidence afforded by his 'Gesta Regum' that we can infer with probability that he ceased to write in 1210, in or soon after which year his death may be presumed to have taken place. The day of his death is equally uncertain, since three Gervases appear in the Canterbury necrologies under 1 Jan., 14 March, and 30 April.

Besides the 'Chronica' with the preliminary 'Tractatus de Combustione et Reparatione Cantuariensis Ecclesiæ,' and other short pieces already mentioned, Gervase was the author of a smaller chronicle known as the 'Gesta Regum' (ii. 1–106). This work is in its earlier portions a compilation from Geoffrey of Monmouth, William of Malmesbury, and other known sources, and in part an abridgment of the larger Chronicle. From the point where the latter ends, the death of Richard I (1199), it assumes an independent character, and is of considerable value for the first half of John's reign. The fact that the notices of the year 1210 are immediately followed by a narrative beginning with 1207 combines with other evidence to support the view that Gervase's own work ends here; the continuation runs on to 1309, with some additions down to 1328.

Further, Gervase wrote a history of the archbishops of Canterbury, 'Actus Archiepiscoporum Cantuariensium,' from St. Augustine to the death of Archbishop Hubert; and a topographical work, the 'Mappa Mundi,' containing a list of the counties of England, Wales, and part of Scotland, with the ecclesiastical foundations in each, their dedications, &c., hospitals, castles, and waters and springs; together with a list of bishoprics in the British Isles and on the continent of Europe.

Gervase is not one of the great historians of his age, but he illustrates with fidelity the tone and temper of his monastic world. Much of what he writes has the value of contemporary knowledge and observation, or at least of personal recollection; and much bears the impress of recording the local tradition of the writer's religious house. Even that which is not original has at least the value of a contemporary or nearly contemporary corroboration of the statements which it repeats.

The 'Chronicle' and 'Actus Archiepiscoporum' were first printed by Twysden in his 'Historiæ Anglicanæ Scriptores decem,' col. 1290–1683; the whole of the works were edited with prefaces by Bishop Stubbs ('The Historical Works of Gervase of Canterbury,' in two volumes, Rolls Series, 1879, 1880).

[The older bibliographers, Leland, Bale, Pits, Cave, and Tanner, add nothing to the information afforded by Gervase's works, now that they are all printed. What other scanty materials exist are collected and made use of in Bishop Stubbs's preface to his edition.]   R. L. P.

GERVASE OF CHICHESTER (*fl.* 1170), commentator, was one of the band of learned young men who gathered round Thomas, archbishop of Canterbury. Although one of his party, he did not follow him into exile (BOSHAM). Leland and Bale say that he was brought up at Paris and was a fine preacher, statements which, though highly probable, have not perhaps any authoritative basis. He is said to have written a commentary on the Psalms, and a life of Archbishop Thomas. For this life there is some authority. One of his works, a commentary on Malachi, is extant, MS. Reg. 3 B. x. It is followed by two homilies, and is prefaced by some hexameters in which the author speaks of Thomas as affording a model of sacerdotal life, and says that he is preparing to write a life of him. On the strength of this he has been credited with the life ascribed by Giles to Roger of Pontigny, and printed by Canon Robertson in the 'Materials for the Life of Becket,' iv., as by an anonymous author. It is certainly not by Gervase, for the author was one of those who accompanied the archbishop. Leland says that Gervase's work is cited in a life by Helias of Evesham, but if it ever existed it is now lost.

[Herbert of Bosham, vii. c. 1., Materials for Life of Becket, iii. 527, ed. Robertson; Stubbs's

Gervase of Canterbury, introd. xxxiii. (Rolls Ser.); Leland's Scriptt. p. 216; Bale's Scriptt. p. 206, ed. 1559; Pits, De Angliæ Scriptt. p. 224; Wright's Biog. Lit. ii. 217; Hardy's Catalogue, ii. 351, 394.]

W. H.

GERVASE OF TILBURY (*fl.* 1211), author of the 'Otia Imperialia,' was no doubt a native of Tilbury in Essex, though he appears to have been brought up in Rome, and to have spent some years of his early life in Italy. He took orders, and studied and taught law at Bologna, having among his pupils John Pignatelli, afterwards archdeacon of Naples, with whom he kept up a friendship in later years (*Otia*, ed. Leibnitz, i. 964). In 1177 he was present at the meeting of the Emperor Frederick I and Pope Alexander III at Venice. It is possible that he may have supplied an account of the interview to Roger of Hoveden, Gervase of Canterbury, and the chronicler known as the Abbot Benedict, for they seem to have had some common source of information (STUBBS). Soon after this he appears to have been in England for some time; he had interest at court, for he was connected with Earl Patrick of Salisbury, and the earl's son Philip was his close friend (*Otia*, p. 964). He attached himself to the young king Henry, son of Henry II, wrote for his amusement a volume, now lost, called 'Liber Facetiarum' (*ib.* p. 914), and evidently was much distressed at his death, which took place on 11 June 1183 (*ib.* p. 947). Possibly this event led to his leaving England. While still a young man he was a clerk in the household of William, archbishop of Rheims (cons. 1176, *d.* 1202), brother of the third wife of Louis VII, the father-in-law of the young king Henry. This was during the time when the archbishop was especially active in persecuting the 'publicani' or 'paterins,' and probably not earlier than 1183 (ROBERT OF AUXERRE, *Chronicle of St. Martin's, Chronicle of Anchin; Recueil*, xviii. 251, 291, 536). In later life he told Ralph of Coggeshall how at this time he one day tried to seduce a young woman, and gathered from the answer with which she repelled his advances that she was a 'paterin.' The archbishop came up while they were talking; Gervase told him of his suspicions, and the girl and her old instructress were condemned and burnt as heretics (COGGESHALL, pp. 122–4). Like many other Englishmen at this period, he visited Sicily, and there entered the service of William II, the son-in-law of Henry II of England, and stood high in his favour. William gave him a house at Nola in order that he might have a place to which to retire from the heat and bustle of Palermo (*Otia*, p. 964). He was at Salerno at the time of the siege of Acre by

the Christians, 1190–1. As Earl Patrick of Salisbury was uncle of the Countess Ela, wife of William Longsword, uncle of the Emperor Otto IV, he had interest with the emperor, who was the grandson of Henry II. Otto took him into his service, and made him marshal of the kingdom of Arles. He seems to have married at Arles, for he had a palace there in right of his wife (*ib.* p. 991), and was related to Humbert, the archbishop, by marriage (*ib.* p. 988). To Otto he dedicated his book entitled 'Otia Imperialia,' on which he was engaged in 1211, the year in which Otto, having been excommunicated by Innocent III, was disowned by the German princes. Although he wrote for the emperor, Gervase does not use violent language about this quarrel; he recommends peace, and says that Otto ought to gratify the pope, to whose help he owed his crown, and who was the vicar of God (*ib.* p. 941). In one passage he advances the theory that Charles (Charlemagne) owed the imperial title to papal beneficence (*ib.* p. 944). The 'Otia' is full of queer scraps about natural history, geography, politics, and folklore. The style is lucid and natural, such as would be used by an educated man of the world who was constantly in the habit of writing Latin. It is evident that Gervase had little if any acquaintance with ancient literature, or indeed with patristic writings. He divides his work into three parts (decisiones). In the first he treats of the events recorded in the early chapters of Genesis. While discussing the temptation of Eve he illustrates the probability of the theory that the serpent had a woman's face by the existence of werewolves in England. He further treats of fairies and sylvan spirits, of the sons of Adam, the origin of music, and other matters. His second part is mainly devoted to geography, politics, and history; it contains a topographical description of Rome (*ib.* ii. 767), and an account of the history of Britain and of the kings of England down to his own day, together with a good deal of political geography. A special value attaches to his view of the theory of the empire and his remarks on the history of the imperial election (*ib.* i. 941, 943). The third part is a record of marvels, and presents a most curious picture of the beliefs of the time. Gervase probably ended his days in England; he was a canon when he told Ralph of Coggeshall the story of the 'paterin' girl, his wife was then perhaps dead, and the changes in the empire must have caused his resignation or loss of place. The 'Otia Imperialia' is the only work of his which is now known to exist. Besides this book and the 'Facetiarum Liber' he also wrote a book entitled 'De

transitu B. Virginis et gestis discipulorum'
(*Otia*, i. 928, 968, 976). For a long time
he was believed to be the author of the
'Dialogus de Scaccario' and the lost 'Tricolumnus.' Madox first showed this was
impossible. Two books attributed to him by
Bale, 'De Mundi descriptione' and 'De Mira-
bilibus Orbis,' are parts of the 'Otia,' and a
third, the 'Galfridi Munmuthensis Illustra-
tiones,' was probably a compendium from
Geoffrey's work. There is a manuscript of
the 'Otia Imperialia' in Cotton MS. Vespasian, E. iv., and others in the National
Library in Paris (STEVENSON). Portions of
it were printed in Duchesne's 'Historiæ Francorum Scriptores,' iii. 363–379, Paris, 1641,
fol., and separately by J. J. Mader, Helm-
stadt, 1673, 4to. Large portions, though,
according to Mr. Stevenson, not the whole,
were published by G. G. Leibnitz in his
'Scriptores Rerum Brunsvicensium,' i. 884–
1004; with emendations and additions, ii.
751–84; Hanover, 1707–10. The third part
was edited with notes by F. Leibrecht, Hanover, 1856, 8vo, and extracts are given by
Stevenson in his edition of Ralph of Coggeshall, Rolls Series.

[Otia Imperialia, Scriptt. Rerum Brunsvic. ed.
Leibnitz, vol. i. Introd. sec. 63, pp. 811–1004, ii.
751–84; Stubbs's Gervase of Canterbury, Pref.
p. xxviii sq. (Rolls Ser.), Lectures, pp. 140, 166;
Stevenson's Ralph of Coggeshall, Pref., pp. xxiii,
xxix, 122–4, 419 sq. (Rolls Ser.), Bale's Scriptt.
i. 250; Pits, De Angliæ Scriptt. p. 274; Hardy's
Catalogue, i. 298, iii. 25, 26 (Rolls Ser.); Wright's
Bibl. Brit. ii. 283–9; Madox's History of the
Exchequer, ii. 410.] W. H.

GERVAYS, JOHN (*d.* 1268), bishop of
Winchester. [See JOHN.]

GETHIN, GRACE, LADY (1676–1697),
learned lady, daughter of Sir George Norton
of Abbot's Leigh, Somersetshire, was born in
1676, married Sir Richard Gethin, baronet,
of Gethin Grott, Ireland, and died on 11 Oct.
1697. She was buried at Hollingbourn, Kent,
and a monument was erected to her in Westminster Abbey. A sermon was founded to
be preached in the abbey upon Ash Wednesday in memory of her. A collection of
papers found after her death was published
in 1699 as 'Reliquiæ Gethinianæ;' a second
edition appeared in 1700, and a third, to
which a portrait was prefixed, in 1703. The
last includes a copy of verses by Congreve,
and to it is appended a funeral sermon by
Peter Birch [q. v.], published separately in
1700. The book is more creditable to the
taste than to the knowledge of her executors. Many passages are from Bacon's 'Essays,' copied in her commonplace book and

mistaken for her original composition by
several of her biographers.

[Reliquiæ Gethinianæ, 1703; Ballard's Learned
Ladies, 1775, pp. 252–3; Noble's Granger, i. 280;
Stanley's Memorials of Westminster Abbey; Col-
linson's Somersetshire, iii. 153.] L. S.

GETHING, RICHARD (1585?–1652?),
calligrapher, a native of Herefordshire, and
a scholar of John Davies [q. v.], the famous
writing-master of Hereford, was thought to
surpass his master in every branch of his art.
Coming to London, he started in business at
the 'Hand and Pen' in Fetter Lane. In 1616
he published a copy-book of various hands in
twenty-six plates, oblong 4to, which are very
well executed. In 1645 he brought out
his 'Chirographia,' consisting of thirty-seven
plates engraved by Goddart. In it Gething
says 'he has exactly traced and followed
certain pieces, both in character and language, of the ablest calligraphotechnists and
Italian masters that ever wrote, with certain
pieces of cursory hands, not heretofore extant, newly come in use.' Another edition of
the 'Chirographia,' probably published after
his death, is entitled 'Gething Redivivus, or
the Pen's Master-Piece. Being the last work
of that eminent and accomplished master in
this art, containing exemplars of all curious
hands written,' London, 1664, oblong 8vo.
Prefixed is his portrait engraved by J. Chantry.
In 1652 he published 'Calligraphotechnia, or
the art of faire writing set forth and newly
enlarged.' It contains thirty-six folio plates,
and his portrait inscribed 'Richardus Ge-
thinge, Herefordiensis, æt. 32.' This work
is probably an enlargement of his first book,
as some of the plates are dated 1615 and 1616.
Moreover there is a dedication to his 'very
good master, Sir Francis Bacon, knight,' afterwards the lord chancellor.

Massey considers that 'on account of his
early productions from the rolling press, he
may stand in comparison with Bales, Davies,
and Billingsley, those heads and fathers, as I
may call them, of our English calligraphic
tribe;' and Fuller, speaking of Davies and
Gething, quaintly remarks: 'Sure I am, when
two such Transcendant Pen-Masters shall
again come to be born in the same shire, they
may even serve fairly to engross the Will
and Testament of the expiring Universe.'

[Wood's Athenæ Oxon. (Bliss), ii. 261;
Granger's Biog. Hist. of England, 5th edit. iii. 194,
Massey's Origin and Progress of Letters, p. 80;
Works of John Davies, ed. Grosart, i. xiii.]
T. C.

GETSIUS, JOHN DANIEL (1592–1672),
divine and tutor, born at Odernheim in the
Palatinate in 1592, was a descendant of the
ancient family of the barons of Goetz, origi-

nally driven from France during the persecution of the Albigenses. His father took refuge in Hesse when the emperor invaded the
Palatinate, but died in his son's infancy. His
wife placed the son under the care of Daniel
Tossanus, a learned protestant divine, and
sent him afterwards to the university of Mar-
burg, where he took the degree of doctor of
philosophy in 1618. Religious difficulties
forced him to fly from Hesse to his mother's
brother, Justus Baronius; but his uncle, himself a convert from protestantism, quarrelled
with the nephew for refusing to follow him.
Getsius, after a short stay in Holland, proceeded to London, and finally, at the end of
1619, to Cambridge. Here he remained for
more than two years under the protection
of Dr. John Preston, and took the degree of
B.A. In 1623 he went to the Hague to
solicit the help of the king of Bohemia. At
the king's desire the university of Oxford
granted to him and four more of his countrymen a pension of 18*l.* per annum. This was
paid to him for four years, and enabled him
to study for seven years at Exeter College,
where he gave lessons in Hebrew and was
permitted to take pupils. On 15 July 1628
he was incorporated B.A. of Oxford. In
1629, by the advice of Dr. Prideaux, he went
with Robert Jago, an M.A. of Exeter College,
to Dartmouth in Devonshire, where he 'taught
school and preached at Townstall, the mother
church, for about seven years.' In 1636 he
was presented to the vicarage of Stoke Gabriel, about five miles from Dartmouth, where
he continued his school, preparing gentlemen's sons for the university. One of his
pupils, Valentine Greatrakes, out of gratitude
for his care, gave him a small life annuity
from certain rents in Cornworthy, near Stoke
Gabriel. In October 1643 he preached by
command before Prince Maurice, who had
been sent by the king to reduce Dartmouth.
He was afterwards arrested by the parliamentarians, and threatened with banishment.
Finally, by the aid of Arthur Upton of Lupton, who had made his acquaintance at Exeter
College, he was released with a severe reprimand for the obnoxious sermon.

He died on 24 Dec. 1672, and was buried
in his church at Stoke Gabriel, leaving two
sons, the youngest of whom, Walter, vicar of
Brixham, Devonshire, supplied Wood with
the facts of his father's life. Getsius wrote:
1. 'Tears shed in the Behalf of his dear
Mother the Church of England, and her sad
Distractions,' Oxford, 1658, 8vo. 2. 'The
Ship in Danger,' sermon on Acts xxvii. 21,
22' (the discourse preached before Prince
Maurice). 3. 'Syllabus omnium Vocum
Græcarum Nov. Test. una cum Etymologia

Verborum et Nomenclatura omnium Tropo-
rum, Nominum propriorum et Vocabulorum
Hebræorum, Syriacorum, Græcorum, Latino-
rum, aliorumque, quæ in N. T. occurrunt.'
4. An abstract of the Bible in Latin heroic
verse. 5. 'Treatise about the Quinquarticu-
lar Controversy that was canvassed in the
Council of Dort.' Of these only the first
seems to have been published; 3 and 4 were
for the use of youths in schools.

[Wood's Athenæ Oxon. iii. 973; Fasti, i. 443.]
R. B.

GHEERAERTS, GEERAERTS, or
GARRARD, MARCUS, the elder (1510 ?–
1590 ?), painter and engraver, was son and
pupil of Egbert Gheeraerts, a painter, who
was admitted as master painter in the guild
of St. Luke at Bruges in 1516. According
to the chronology compiled by Delbecq from
the lost manuscript of Lucas de Heere [q. v.],
Gheeraerts was born at Bruges in 1510,
though a later date, about 1530, seems more
probable. In 1558 he was admitted to the
freedom of the painters' guild, and was second
'vinder' to the guild. His biographers extol
his excellence in drawing, painting (especially landscape), miniature-painting, engraving, architecture, designs for glass-painters,
and tapestry, &c. In 1558 he prepared the
designs for the tomb of Charles the Bold,
duke of Burgundy, copying the famous tomb
of Mary of Burgundy in the church of Notre-
Dame at Bruges, where both tombs now
remain. In 1561 he was commissioned to
complete the triptych of the 'Passion' left
unfinished by Bernard van Orley at his
death, which hangs still in the same church.
In 1562 he engraved for the town the fine
bird's-eye view of the town of Bruges,
the original copper-plates of which are still
preserved among the town archives at
Bruges. In 1563 he painted a triptych of 'The
Descent from the Cross' for the church of
the Recollets at Bruges. Payments to Gheeraerts for his services occur in the town archives from 1557 to 1565. Gheeraerts was
especially noted for his drawings of animals.
In 1559 he drew a series of bears, which were
afterwards etched and published by Marc de
Bye. In 1566 he published at his own cost
an edition of 'Æsop's Fables,' entitled 'De
warachtighe Fabulen der Dieren,' with etchings by himself, poetry by Eduwaert de Dene,
a dedication to Hubert Goltzius, and an introductory poem by Lucas de Heere. There
are several editions of this work, and the
plates were frequently copied. Gheeraerts's
original drawings are in existence, and were
sold in the Van der Helle sale at Paris in
February 1868. He made designs for several

other series of engravings representing animals, ornaments, allegory, mythology, &c., among which may be noted a remarkable series of initial letters with designs from the 'Passion' published by Joannes Sadeler.

Gheeraerts embraced the reformed religion, and, like many of his confederates, sought refuge in England at the outbreak of the Alvan persecution in 1568. He was probably accompanied by his son, Marcus Gheeraerts the younger [q.v.] On 9 Sept. 1571 he married at the Dutch Church, Austin Friars, London, a second wife, Susanna de Crets of Antwerp, no doubt a relative of the queen's sergeant-painter, John de Critz [q.v.] By her he had three children: Rachel, born 1573; Sara, born 1575; and Tobias, born 1576, all baptised at the Dutch Church. In 1577 he seems to have gone to Antwerp, as in 1577 he was admitted a member of the guild of St. Luke there. He was a member of the chamber of rhetoric called 'The Violet,' and remained in Antwerp till 1586. He is said to have died in 1590 in England, but this seems uncertain. He was certainly dead before 1604, when Carel van Mander published his 'Lives of the Flemish Painters,' as Van Mander complains of the want of courtesy of the son, Marcus Gheeraerts the younger, in declining to supply information concerning his father's end.

[Van Mander's Vie des Peintres, ed. Hymans; Michiel's Histoire de la Peinture Flamande; Moens's Registers of the Dutch Church, Austin Friars; Rathgeber's Annalen der Niederländischen Malerei; Baldinucci's Notizie dei Professori di disegno, ii. 604; Biographie Nationale de Belgique; Rombouts and Van Lerius's Liggeren der Antwerpsche Sint Lucasgilde; Nagler's Monogrammisten, iv. 1571; Guilmard's Les Maîtres Ornemanistes; Weale's Bruges et ses Environs; information from Mr. W. H. James Weale.]   L. C.

GHEERAERTS, GHEERAEDTS, GEERAERTS, GERARDS, or GARRARD, MARCUS, the younger (1561–1635), painter, born at Bruges in 1561, was son of Marcus Gheeraerts the elder [q.v.] by his first wife. He is stated to have been a pupil of Lucas De Heere [q.v.], and as such to have been entered in the guild of St. Luke at Antwerp in 1577. But the actual entry in the guild-book is to a different effect, and refers to his father. De Heere's painting-school at Ghent was broken up in 1568, when he, the elder Gheeraerts, and others who embraced the reformed religion took refuge in England. The younger Gheeraerts may possibly have been taught by De Heere during the latter's residence in England, though he more probably was his father's pupil. In 1577 or 1578 either the father or the son drew the procession of the

knights of the Garter, which was subsequently engraved by Hollar for Ashmole's 'Institution, Laws, and Ceremonies of the Most Noble Order of the Garter.' This may very well be an early work of the younger Gheeraerts, though it is usually attributed to his father. Subsequently Gheeraerts acquired a great reputation for his portraits, and became the fashionable court-painter of the age. His portraits were remarkable for their truth to nature, and are always well painted, though their manner seems somewhat hard and cold. The rich costumes and accessories are always carefully executed. He painted Elizabeth several times, the most noticeable examples being the small full-length portrait at Welbeck, belonging to the Duke of Portland, the portrait with a fan of white feathers, belonging to Lord Tollemache, and those at Burghley House and Hampton Court, painted in her old age. Many other court notabilities were painted by him. The portrait of William Camden in the Bodleian Library at Oxford was executed by him in 1609, and signed 'Marcus Gheeraedts.' On 19 May 1590 Gheeraerts was married at the Dutch church, Austin Friars, to Magdalena de Crits of Antwerp, a relative no doubt of his father's second wife, and of John De Critz [q.v.], the queen's sergeant-painter. By her he had six children, baptised at the Dutch church, including two sons of the name Marcus, the younger being born in 1602. After the death of Elizabeth, Gheeraerts continued in his position as court-painter to James I and Anne of Denmark, and painted portraits of their two sons, Princes Henry and Charles. He died in London on 19 Jan. 1635, in his seventy-fourth year. His own portrait, painted by himself in 1627, was etched by W. Hollar in 1644. Gheeraerts is mentioned by Francis Meres, in his 'Wit's Commonwealth' (1598), among the notable painters in England. His name occurs in various returns of foreigners resident in London; in 1593 he is returned as 'Marks Garratt, housekeeper; borne in Bruges in Flanders; Maudlyn his wife, born in Andwarpe in Brabonde; a Paynter; one daughter;' in 1611, among the goldsmiths, 'Marcus Garrard of Bruges: 2 children; living here 49 years;' and again in 1618 as 'Marcus Garret; born at Bridges in Flaunders; noe free denizen; picture drawer to his majesty; professing the Apostolick faith taught and held by the church in England; sovereign King James.' Among the most important pictures attributed to Gheeraerts are: 'The Procession of Queen Elizabeth to Blackfriars on 16 June 1600, of which two examples exist, one at Sherborne Castle, belonging to Lord Digby, and a similar picture at Melbury, belonging to Lord Ilchester (Vertue engraved this picture for the Society of Antiquaries, but it was then wrongly described as a ' Visit of Elizabeth to Hunsdon House in 1571 ') ; and 'The Conference of English and Spanish Plenipotentiaries in 1604,' purchased for the National Portrait Gallery at the Hamilton Palace sale in July 1882. Portraits by Gheeraerts are at Woburn Abbey, Penshurst, Barrow Green, Ditchley, Hatfield, Burghley, and other noble residences. He published a ' Handbook to the Art of Drawing,' a translation of which into English was published in 1674. Care should be taken to distinguish from his works the pictures by Geraert Pietersz van Zyl, in imitation of Vandyck, who signed his works ' Geraers.'

[Walpole's Anecdotes of Painters, ed. Dallaway and Wornum ; Hamper's Life of Dugdale, Appendix ; Cooper's Foreigners resident in London, 1618–88 (Camden Soc.) ; Catalogues of Pictures at Woburn Abbey, the National Portrait Gallery, Manchester Exhibition, National Portrait Exhibition, 1866, &c. ; Waagen's Art-Treasures of Great Britain ; information from George Scharf, C.B., F.S.A., and W. J. C. Moens, F.S.A. ; authorities in preceding article.] L. C.

GHENT or GAUNT, JOHN OF, DUKE OF LANCASTER (1340–1399). [See JOHN.]

GHENT, SIMON DE (d. 1315), bishop of Salisbury, was born at Westminster (MATT. OF WESTM. p. 431). In 1284 he was archdeacon of Oxford, and was present in this year when Devorguila assigned lands to her newly founded college of Balliol (TANNER, p. 307 ; WOOD, v. 72). Archbishop Winchelsey gave him a prebend in Salisbury Cathedral on 27 April 1284, when he was already archdeacon of Oxford. He was elected chancellor of the latter university in December 1290 or 1291, and continued to hold the office till 1293 (TANNER, p. 307). He was also a canon of Salisbury and York before his election to the bishopric of Salisbury on 2 June 1297, on the death of Nicholas Longespée (LE NEVE, ed. Hardy, iii. 599). At this time he was ' magister . . . vir in arte Theologica peritus' (MATT. OF WESTM. p. 431). Archbishop Winchelsey consecrated him at Canterbury on 20 Oct. 1297 (STUBBS, p. 49, from Cant. Profession Rolls). In June 1299 Edward I employed him as his envoy, when the Bishop of Vicenza, at the instance of Boniface VIII, was arranging a peace between France and England (RYMER, ii. 841). Owing to Winchelsey's illness he was one of the three prelates who crowned Edward II on 25 Feb. 1308 (Annales Paulini, p. 260 ; cf. RYMER, iii. 52). Next year he was summoned to

Newcastle for military service against the Scots at Michaelmas 1309 (RYMER, iii. 149). By this time he was one of the leading English politicians. His name is third on the list of the ordainers in March 1310, and on 17 March he was one of the thirty-two nobles who pledged themselves that the king's concessions on this occasion should not be turned into a precedent (Ann. Lond. pp. 170, 172). He died on 31 March 1315 in his London house, near St. Bridget's Church, and was buried at Salisbury, in the north part of the choir, where his tomb was already an object of pilgrimage in the days of his successor, Robert de Mortivaux (Annales Paulini, pp. 277–8 ; Salisbury Register, quoted in JONES, Fasti, p. 92).

Simon's episcopate is remarkable for his refusal to admit the pope's nominee, Cardinal Reymund, to the deanery of Salisbury (JONES, p. 92 ; Diocesan Hist. p. 117). He was an ardent reformer, and is found instituting inquiries as to pluralists and lay vicars, suspending prebendaries for neglect of duty, and admonishing his chancellor for neglecting the cathedral fabric, and his treasurer for not reading the divinity lectures he was bound to give (ib. pp. 117–18). Early in his episcopate he addressed letters of remonstrance to Boniface VIII, because of the intrusion of foreigners into cathedral stalls. These letters (dated 29 March 1302) are preserved in Balliol College Library, No. 169 (JONES, p. 92 ; COXE, Catalogue, i. 46). In 1305 Simon was at variance with the burgesses of Salisbury, from whom, according to his rights, he claimed a tallage whenever the king had one from his towns. The citizens resisted, and rather than make the payment renounced their privileges (April 1305). Ultimately, however, they prayed for the restoration of the old dues. A charter (8 May 1306) restored the bishop's right of tallage, a gild-hall was established under Simon's patronage, and the city was strengthened by a wall and a moat running through the episcopal demesne. A curious document shows the bishop's anxiety for the townsmen's spiritual welfare, and another recounts the steps he took to preserve the privileges of his close from infringement at the great tournament of 1305 (HATCH, pp. 70–80, 737–43 ; GODWIN, p. 347).

Simon's writings are: 1. ' Regula Anchoritarum, sive de Vita Solitaria,' in seven or eight books (manuscripts at Magdalen College, Oxford, No. 67, and in the British Museum, Vitell. E. vii. 6, Nero A. xiv., is an old English translation, addressed to the nuns at Tarent in Dorsetshire). 2. A ' Meditatio de Statu Prælati' (TANNER, p. 307). 3. ' Statuta ecclesiastica,' by which at the beginning of the seventeenth century the church of Salisbury was still in a great measure ruled (GODWIN, i. 347). 4. The letters to the pope mentioned above.

[Annales Paulini, Bridlingtonienses, Londonienses, ap. Chron. of Edward I and II (Rolls Ser.), ed. Stubbs; Matt. of Westminster, Frankfort, 1601; Le Neve's Fasti, ed. Hardy; Fasti Ecclesiæ Sarisberiensis, ed. the Rev. W. H. Jones; Diocesan Histories, Salisbury, by the Rev. W. H. Jones; Stubbs's Registrum Sacrum Anglicanum; Rymer's Fœdera, ed. 1705-6; Hatch's Hist. of Salisbury, 1843; Dodsworth's Cathedral Church of Salisbury, 1814, pp. 42, 141-2; Godwin, De Præsulibus, ed. Richardson, vol. i. 1743; Planta's Cat. of Cotton. MSS. p. 205.]   T. A. A.

GIB, ADAM (1714-1788), Scotch antiburgher divine, ninth son of John Gib, was born at Castletown, his father's property, in the parish of Muckhart, Perthshire, 7 April 1714. He was educated at the university of Edinburgh. His first serious impressions were caused by his unexpectedly witnessing the execution of a criminal in the Grassmarket. While he was attending the undergraduate classes the controversy was going on in the general assembly which led to the formation of the secession church under Ebenezer Erskine [q. v.] and others, and Gib was so impressed with the harsh treatment of the seceders, that he threw in his lot with them. His father was at first extremely displeased with him, but was afterwards reconciled; and as his eldest son was a prodigal he settled on Adam the succession to the estate. When the will was read Adam asked his brother if he would reform, and on his promising to do so put the will into the fire. Gib joined the 'Associate Presbytery' founded by Erskine and others in 1735, and was licensed to the West Kirk of Stirling 5 March 1740. In 1741 he was ordained to the charge of the important secession congregation in Bristo Street, Edinburgh. In 1745, when Edinburgh fell into the hands of the Pretender, Gib displayed characteristic courage. Most of the presbyterian ministers had fled from the city. Gib, however, withdrew with his flock only to the suburbs, and for five Sundays at Dreghorn, near Colinton, three miles from Edinburgh, where the insurgents had a guard, he fearlessly lifted up his voice against the 'popish pretender' and his cause. He prayed with great earnestness for George II, for the preservation of the protestant succession, and for the suppression of the unnatural and antichristian rebellion. The services were conducted in the open air, and among the audience were sometimes some of the Pretender's soldiers, who did not molest the preacher. Gib actually took prisoner a rebel spy a few hours before the battle of Falkirk (17 Jan. 1745-6), and would no doubt after the battle have suffered from the vengeance of the victors, but when searched for he could not be found. About 1747 Gib entered into another species of warfare. Among the seceders a dispute had arisen about the lawfulness of an oath to be taken by burgesses or burghers. Gib took the side of those who deemed the oath unlawful, and ultimately became the leader of the antiburgher section of the secession. The antiburgher synod was constituted in his house at Edinburgh 10 April 1747. This involved him and his flock in litigation as to the property of the church in Bristo Street. With characteristic intrepidity he stuck to the building for years, after decisions had been given against him, renewing the litigation on some other point, till at last retreat became inevitable. His people built a large meeting-place for him in Nicolson Street, where, till near his death, which took place at Edinburgh on 18 June 1788, he ministered to an immense congregation, and where he was succeeded as minister by Dr. John Jamieson [q. v.], the well-known author of the 'Scottish Dictionary.'

All his life Gib was an active controversialist, chiefly on points involved in the position of the seceders. His one object was to maintain and defend what he considered to be the truth. Rude, scornful, and despotic as he was, and earning for himself the sobriquet of 'Pope Gib,' he commanded the homage due to disinterested courage. He published the following: 1. 'A Warning against Countenancing the Ministrations of George Whitefield,' Edinburgh, 1742. This he afterwards regretted that he had written. 2. 'The Proceedings of the Associate Synod at Edinburgh, concerning some Ministers who have Separated from them,' Edinburgh, 1748. 3. 'A Solemn Warning by the Associate Synod,' Edinburgh, 1758. 4. 'Address to the Associate Synod met at Edinburgh,' Edinburgh, 1763. 5. 'An Exposure of a False and Abusive Libel entitled "The Procedure of the Associate Synod in Mr. Pirie's Case Represented,"' Edinburgh, 1764. 6. 'A Refuge of Lies scooped away, in Answer to a most False and Abusive Libel,' Edinburgh, 1768. 7. 'Tables for the Four Evangelists' [anon., 1770]; 2nd edit., with author's name, 1800. 8. 'The Present Truth, a Display of the Secession Testimony,' 2 vols., Edinburgh, 1774. 9. 'An Antidote against a New Heresy concerning the True Sonship of Jesus Christ,' a sermon against William Dalgliesh of Peebles [q. v.], Edinburgh, 1777. 10. 'Vindiciæ Dominicæ, a Defence of the Reformation-standards of the Church of Scotland concerning the Administration of the Lord's Supper and the One Sonship of Jesus

Christ' [anon.], Edinburgh, 1780. 11. 'A Display of the Fraudulent and Gross Abuses committed upon the Secession-testimony' [anon.], Edinburgh, 1780. 12. 'Καινὰ καὶ Παλαιά: Sacred Contemplation in three parts: I. A View of the Covenant of Works; II. A View of the Covenant of Grace; III. A View of the Absolute and Immediate Dependence of all things on God,' Edinburgh, 1786.

[M'Kerrow's Hist. Secession Church; M'Kelvie's Annals and Statistics of the United Presbyterian Church; Chambers's Eminent Scotsmen; Anderson's Scottish Nation; Scots Mag. vol. xxvii.; Walker's Theology and Theologians of Scotland; Notes and Queries, 7th ser. ix. 183.] W. G. B.

GIBB, FREDERICK (d. 1681), miscellaneous writer, son of Bernard Gibb, advocate, was born at Dunfermline, studied medicine, and took, 9 Sept. 1651, the degree of doctor at the university of Valence. He spent his life abroad. He died 27 March 1681.

Gibb, who adopted occasionally the name of Philalethes, wrote some unimportant works, among which some verses, contributed to a volume of de Thou, published by Daniel Elzevier in 1678, and an harangue made in 1679 in praise of the hog, and dedicated to François Gaverol, a famous lawyer of Nismes, seem most worthy of note. Gibb's grandson, Jean Frederic Guib (as the name came to be spelt), is mentioned as having written some remarkable criticisms of parts of Bayle's Dictionary.

[Michel's Les Écossais en France, ii. 422.] F. W-T.

GIBB, JOHN (1776–1850), civil engineer and contractor, was born at Kirkcows, near Falkirk, a small property belonging to his father, a contractor, in 1776. The elder Gibb having died when John was only twelve, the son served an apprenticeship to a mechanical trade. After this he was employed as contractor's assistant, and later as subordinate engineer by his brother, then serving under John Rennie on the construction of the Lancaster and Preston canal. He afterwards went to Leith, being engaged by his father-in-law, Mr. Easton, in the making of the docks there. Commencing practice on his own account as a contractor, he gradually established a reputation for professional skill. He was employed in the construction of Greenock harbour under Rennie, where Telford's attention was drawn to his exceptional ability and great managerial tact. Telford engaged him as resident engineer at the Aberdeen harbour works. Gibb removed thither in 1809, and superintended the erection of extensive piers and other details. He executed many commissions with credit under Telford, Ren-

nie, Robert Stephenson (of Edinburgh), and Sir William Cubitt; chief among his labours being the repair of the Crinan canal in 1817, various harbours on the east coast of Scotland, the great Glasgow and Carlisle turnpike road (which involved stone bridges of extensive span, such as that of Cartland Craigs, near Lanark, over the glen of the Mouse), various lighthouses, the Dean road bridge, near Edinburgh, several railway viaducts, and the famous Glasgow bridge, the lowest over the Clyde, and a model of its class, which was designed by Telford and completed by Gibb and his son. Gibb's special eminence lay in operations connected with harbour construction and river engineering. He died at Aberdeen on 3 Dec. 1850, being at the time one of the oldest members of the Institute of Civil Engineers.

[Thomson's Eminent Scotsmen; Anderson's Scottish Nation.] J. B-Y.

GIBB, ROBERT (d. 1837), landscape-painter, a native of Dundee, was an associate of the Royal Institution, Edinburgh, and contributed to the exhibitions of that body from 1822 to 1830. He was an original associate of the Scottish Academy, became a full member in July 1829, and contributed to its exhibitions from 1830 to 1834. His works, which are chiefly landscapes, though he occasionally produced figure-pictures, are carefully handled and show considerable feeling for nature. He is represented in the National Gallery of Scotland by views of 'Borthwick Castle' and 'Craigmillar Castle.' He died, at an early age, in 1837. (He is to be distinguished from Robert Gibb, portrait and figure painter, who was elected A.R.S.A. in 1878 and R.S.A. in 1882.)

[Harvey's Notes on the Early History of the Royal Scottish Academy; Catalogues of the Royal Institution, Edinburgh, Royal Scottish Academy, and National Gallery of Scotland.] J. M. G.

GIBBES, CHARLES, D.D. (1604–1681), divine, sixth son of Sir Ralph Gibbes, who was knighted at Whitehall in 1603, was born at Honington, Warwickshire, in 1604, matriculated from Magdalen Hall, Oxford, 26 June 1621, graduated B.A. 20 Feb. 1622–3. He was elected in 1624 probationer-fellow of Merton College, where, Wood tells us, he became 'a noted disputant, orator, and quaint preacher.' He proceeded M.A. on 25 June 1628, and in April 1638 was presented to the rectory of Gamlingay, Cambridgeshire, which he held until 1647, when he resigned it in anticipation of sequestration, being a zealous royalist. He appears also to have held about the same time the prebend of Combe Octava in the church of Wells. During the interregnum he taught at a school at Canterbury. On 30 April 1661 he was presented to the rectory of Stanford Rivers, Essex, and on 21 May 1662 was installed prebendary of Westminster; the same year he received the degree of D.D. from the university of Oxford. He died at Stanford Rivers on 16 Sept. 1681, and was buried in the parish church of that place. He published 'XXXI Sermons preached to his parishioners upon several subjects and occasions. Never before made publick,' London, 1677, 4to. At his death he was engaged in editing a volume of 'sermons and discourses' by his brother-in-law, Dr. Walter Raleigh.

[Dugdale's Warwickshire, p. 458; Oxf. Univ. Reg. (Oxf. Hist. Soc.), ii. ii. 392, iii. 417; Wood's Athenæ Oxon. (Bliss), iv. 12; Wood's Fasti Oxon. i. 405, 439; Le Neve's Fasti Eccl. Angl. iii. 362; Walker's Sufferings of the Clergy, pt. ii. p. 75; Colville's Warwickshire Worthies.]   J. M. R.

GIBBES, Sir GEORGE SMITH, M.D. (1771–1851), physician, was the son of the Rev. George Gibbes, D.D., rector of Woodborough, Wiltshire. From Dr. Mant's school at Southampton he proceeded to Exeter College, Oxford, graduated B.A. in 1792, was elected a fellow of Magdalen, graduated M.B. in 1796 and M.D. in 1799. He joined the College of Physicians in 1803, and was made a fellow the year after. In 1817 he delivered the Harveian oration before the college. He practised at Bath, where he was a prominent figure. In 1800 he published his 'Treatise on the Bath Waters,' followed by a second treatise on the same in 1803. In 1804 he was elected physician to the Bath Hospital. Later he became physician extraordinary to Queen Charlotte, and in 1820 was knighted by George IV. He took an active part in municipal business at Bath, and was a member of the corporation until 1834. In 1835 he gave up practice and went to live at Cheltenham. He died at Sidmouth on 23 June 1851, aged 80. He was twice married, first to a daughter of Edward Sealey of Bridgwater, who died in 1822; and secondly, in 1826, to Marianne, daughter of Captain T. Chapman, 23rd regiment.

His first essay was in the 'Philosophical Transactions,' 1794, on the conversion of muscle into a substance resembling spermaceti (pamphlet on same theme, Bath, 1796). In 1799 he issued a syllabus of a course of chemical lectures given at Bath. Then came his two editions on the Bath waters. In 1809 he published 'A Phlogistic Theory ingrafted upon M. Fourcroy's "Philosophy of Chemistry,"' pt. i. pp. 32, Bath. His most considerable medical work was 'Pathological Inquiries, or an Attempt to Explain the

Phenomena of Disease,' &c., Bath, 1818, a semi-popular but philosophical exposition of the principles of medicine, published for private circulation, of which this is a specimen: 'The gout does the work which is left unfinished by the reactive energies of the digestive organs; and, as far as its curative powers go, produces a salutary outlet for the accumulated evils' (p. 47). His address at the opening of the Bath Literary and Philosophical Institution was published, 1825, pp. 15. He was a fellow of the Royal Society and of the Linnean Society, having communicated to the latter an account of the contents of a bone-cave on the north-west side of the Mendip Hills, one of the earliest explored bone-caves in England (Trans. v. 143). To Nicholson's 'Journal of Natural Philosophy' he contributed a number of papers on the Bath waters and other chemical subjects (vols. ii. iii. xiv. xix.), and to Tilloch's 'Philosophical Magazine' a 'Description of the Diacatoptron' (xxxix. 1812).

[Gent. Mag. July 1851; Munk's Coll. of Phys. 1878, iii. 13.]   C. C.

GIBBES or GHIBBES, JAMES ALBAN, M.D. (1611–1677), Latin poet, was born (not, as stated by Wood, at Rouen, but) at Valognes, for in his will, still preserved at Rome, he speaks of himself as 'nativo di Vallone, appresso Cadomo, diocesi di Constanza.' Although Valognes is sixty miles from Caen, it is the only place in the diocese of Coutances answering to this description. His father, William Gibbes, a native of Bristol, where his family had considerable property, was educated at Brasenose College, Oxford, but marrying Mary Stonor, who belonged to an Oxfordshire catholic family, he embraced catholicism. They settled at London, but being disquieted on account of their religion went to France in 1609, where, two years afterwards, James Alban was born. He did not set foot in England till his ninth year, when he rejoined his parents, who had shortly before returned thither, the father ultimately becoming physician to Queen Henrietta Maria. Gibbes was sent to the English college at St. Omer, and afterwards travelled in the Low Countries, Spain, Germany, and Italy. At Padua he was the pupil of the eminent anatomist, Vesling or Wesseling. In 1644 he settled at Rome, where Evelyn visited him in that year and was shown by him over a hospital and orphanage of which he was physician. Evelyn spells his name Gibbs, but the latter had inserted h in it, apparently for the sake of pronunciation, and italianised it into Ghibbesio. He passed the remainder of his life at Rome, with the exception of two years at Modena as tutor to Almerico, second son to Duke Francis I, a post which ill-health obliged him to relinquish. His handsome face, wonderful power of mimicry, entertaining conversation, and mastery of six living languages, coupled with his medical skill, gained him a succession of patrons, viz. Cardinal Caponi, Cardinal Spada, in whose house he resided till Spada's death, and Prince Giustiniani, with whom Gibbes thenceforth resided. He composed several Latin eulogies on Pope Leo X, and enjoyed the favour of his three successors. Alexander VII in 1647 gave him a vacant professorship of rhetoric at Sapienza College worth 60*l.* a year, as well as a canonry at San Celso; to Clement IX he dedicated two odes, and Clement X seems to have given him a retiring pension. In 1667 the Emperor Leopold I sent him the diploma of poet laureate. In 1668 appeared at Rome in four books dedicated to Clement IX his 'Carminum Pars Lyrica ad exemplum Q. Horatii Flacci,' with the author's portrait prefixed. The rich gold chain and medal accompanying the emperor's diploma, Gibbes, after much deliberation and by the advice of Oxford scholars at Rome, presented to Oxford University. In a letter of 5 April 1670 to the vice-chancellor announcing the gift, he speaks of his father's connection with the university, and mentions his own thirty years' absence from England. In the following February, 1670–1, Oxford, at the suggestion of the Duke of Ormonde, chancellor, conferred the degree of M.D. on Gibbes, 'the Horace of his age,' as Wood styles him, but the diploma was not signed till August 1673. Gibbes, who valued the honour as one never before awarded to an English catholic, wrote twice meanwhile to inquire the cause of the delay. In 1673 appeared a second volume of his Latin verses, and in 1676 was published again at Rome 'Carmina Marmoribus Arundelianis fortasse perenniora,' in honour of Cardinal Philip Thomas Howard [q. v.] Wood, on the evidence of those who remembered Gibbes, describes him as 'a very conceited man, a most compact body of vanity.' His recently published will shows inordinate anxiety for the preservation of his four portraits, for the erection of a monument and bust over his tomb in the Pantheon, for the custody of his books as a separate collection at the English college at Rome, and for the publication of his manuscripts. His monument and portraits have disappeared; his manuscripts were apparently never published. The poet laureate medal is still at Oxford. He was a collector of art curiosities, and bequeathed to Prince Giustiniani a linnet with two cages of his own make. He left legacies to William Byam and to an English

convent at Rome, where his sister had been educated. His residuary legatee was Benedetto Hercolani, whom he had trained as a physician and whom he directed to take the name of Ghibbesio. He died 26 June 1677. His heir slightly altered the epitaph appended by Gibbes to his will, and omitted the sixteen Latin verses with which it ended. His manuscripts, bequeathed to Sapienza College, consisted of Greek and Latin poems dedicated to the Emperor Leopold, epigrams dedicated to the Earl of Castlemaine, Latin letters 'ad principes viros,' and thirty-three orations dedicated to Oxford and Cambridge universities. The Alessandrina, Casanatense, and Vittorio Emanuele libraries at Rome possess fourteen of his published works. Besides the three volumes of Latin poems mentioned above, he issued 'Epistolarum Selectarum Tres Centuriæ' and 'Pinacotheca Spadia sive Pontificorum Romanorum Series.' No copy of his 'De Medico,' written, according to Wood, on the model of Cicero's 'De Oratore,' seems now known.

[Art. by Domenico Bertolotti, in Il Buonarroti, a Roman periodical, 16 Aug. 1886, reprinted as Un Professore alla Sapienza di Roma nel Secolo XVII poco conosciuto, Rome, 1886, 8vo; preface to his poems, by Carolus Cartharius, who mistakes Gibbes's age; Wood's Fasti Oxon. ed. Bliss, ii. 326, 338–42; Evelyn's Diary; Pryce's Hist. of Bristol.] J. G. A.

GIBBON, BENJAMIN PHELPS (1802–1851), line-engraver, son of the Rev. Benjamin Gibbon, vicar of Penally, Pembrokeshire, was born in 1802. He was educated at the Clergy Orphan School, and afterwards articled to Edward Scriven, the chalk-engraver. He inclined in early life to the stage, but on the expiration of his articles he placed himself under the line-engraver John Henry Robinson, and soon attained great proficiency. His plates, some of which are engraved in line and others in a mixed style, are distinguished by delicacy of touch. They are mostly from the works of Sir Edwin Landseer, after whom he engraved 'The Twa Dogs,' 1827; 'The Travelled Monkey,' 1828, a small plate engraved for the 'Anniversary;' 'The Fireside Party,' 1831; 'Jack in Office,' 1834; 'Suspense,' 1837; 'The Shepherd's Grave,' 1838; 'The Shepherd's Chief Mourner,' 1838; 'Be it ever so humble, there's no place like Home,' 1843; 'The Highland Shepherd's Home,' 1846; and 'Roebuck and Rough Hounds,' 1849. He engraved also 'Wolves attacking Deer,' 1834, after Friedrich Gauermann, in which the landscape was engraved by E. Webb; and 'The Wolf and the Lamb,' after Mulready. He, however, took more interest in portraits than in subject pictures, although he did not engrave many. They include a half-length portrait of Queen Victoria, after William Fowler, engraved in 1840, and a head of his master, Edward Scriven, after Andrew Morton, engraved for Pye's 'Patronage of British Art,' 1845. His death, occasioned by an attack of English cholera, took place at his residence in Albany Street, Regent's Park, London, on 28 July 1851, in his forty-ninth year. He died unmarried, and left scarcely half finished a plate from Webster's picture of 'The Boy with many Friends,' which was completed by P. Lightfoot.

[Art Journal, 1851, p. 238; Athenæum, 6 Sept. 1851, p. 956; Redgrave's Dict. of Artists of the English School, 1878; Algernon Graves's Catalogue of the Works of Sir Edwin Landseer, 1875.]

R. E. G.

GIBBON, CHARLES (_fl._ 1589–1604), miscellaneous writer, was a member of Cambridge University, but there is no record of his having graduated. He was probably in holy orders, and appears to have resided at Bury St. Edmunds, London, and King's Lynn. He was the author of: 1. 'The Remedie of Reason: not so comfortable for matter as compendious for memorie,' 1589, 4to. 2. 'A compendious Forme for domesticall Duties; also our Trust against Trouble,' 1589, 4to. 3. 'Not so newe as true, being a caueat for all Christians to consider of. Wherein is truelie described the iniquities of this present time, by occasion of our confused living, And justly approved the world to be never worse by reason of our contagious lewdness,' 1590, 4to. 4. 'A Work worth the Reading, wherein is contained fiue profitable and pithy questions, very expedient as well for parents to perceive howe to bestowe their children in mariage, & to dispose their goods at their death, as for all other Persons to receive great Profit by the rest of the matters herein expressed,' 1591, 4to. 5. 'The Praise of a Good Name; the Reproach of an Ill Name,... with certain pithy Apothegues very profitable for this age,' 1594, 4to. This book, which is dedicated to 'some of the best and most ciuill sort of the inhabitants of St. Edmond's Bury,' appears to have been written in answer to some calumny under which the author was smarting. 6. 'The Order of Equalitie, contriued and divulged as a generall Directorie for common Sessements; serving for the indifferent defraying, taxing, & rating of common Impositions and Charges, lyable to Citties, Townes, or Villages,' &c., Cambridge, 1604, 4to. The last-named work, which is perhaps the most important, is an appeal for proportional equalisation of the incidence of taxation.

[Ames's Typogr. Antiq. (Herbert), pp. 1101, 1231, 1244–6; Brit. Mus. Cat.; Bodl. Libr. Cat.; Huth Libr. Cat.; Lowndes's Bibl. Man. ii. 884; Cooper's Athenæ Cantabr. ii. 396.]   A. V.

GIBBON, EDWARD (1737–1794), historian, was the descendant of a family settled at Rolvenden in Kent since the fourteenth century (an article in the _Gent. Mag._ 1788, p. 698, by Sir Egerton Brydges, gives an account of the ancestry differing from that in Gibbon's autobiography). A Matthew Gibbon (baptised 23 Feb. 1642) became a linendraper in Leadenhall Street. Matthew had two sons, Thomas, who became dean of Carlisle, and Edward (_b._ 1666), who became an army contractor, made a fortune, and was a commissioner of the customs during the last four years of Queen Anne. Bolingbroke declared his knowledge of English commerce and finance to be unsurpassed. In 1716 he was elected a director of the South Sea Company. On the breaking of the bubble his property was confiscated by the act of pains and penalties, but he was allowed to retain 10,000_l._ out of an estate valued at 106,543_l._ 5_s._ 6_d._ He succeeded in making a second fortune almost equal to the first, and at his death in December 1736 was owner of a large landed property and of a 'spacious house with gardens and lands' at Putney. By his wife, daughter of Richard Acton, goldsmith in Leadenhall Street, a member of the Shropshire family, he was father of a son, Edward, and two daughters, Catherine, wife of Edward Elliston, whose daughter married Lord Eliot [see ELIOT, EDWARD], and Hester, who died unmarried in 1790. Hester was a disciple of William Law (1686–1761) [q. v.], in whose 'Serious Call' she is said to be represented by 'Miranda,' while 'Flavia' represents her sister. Her religious views produced some difficulties with her family, though she remained upon civil terms with her nephew, the historian, and left him her money (see GIBBON, _Misc. Works_, ii. 126, 345, 432; CANON OVERTON'S _William Law_; and [WALTON'S] _Notes and Materials_ for Law's life: in the last is a letter from Gibbon in 1786). Law came into the family as tutor of Edward Gibbon, said to be the 'Flatus' of the 'Serious Call.' Edward was sent to Westminster and to Emmanuel College, Cambridge, whither Law accompanied him. After making the grand tour he was elected for Petersfield in 1734. He was a tory, if not a Jacobite, and took part in the final attack upon Sir Robert Walpole. He married Judith, daughter of James Porten, by whom he was the father of Edward Gibbon, born at Putney 27 April 1737. Five other sons and a daughter died in infancy, the daughter alone living long enough to be remembered by her brother. The father ceased to sit in parliament after the dissolution of 1747. The son's health was very precarious in childhood, and his life often in doubt. His mother being also delicate, he owed his preservation chiefly to the tender care of his aunt, Catherine Porten. He was precocious, especially in arithmetic. He was taught at a day-school in Putney, and when seven years old learnt a little Latin from John Kirby, a poor curate, and author of a philosophical romance called 'Automathes' (1745) and an English and Latin Grammar (1746). In January 1746 he was sent to the school of a Dr. Wooddeson at Kingston-on-Thames, where the delicate boy was bullied as a Jacobite by his fellows, and birched into Latin grammar by his master. His mother died in December 1747, and his father, in deep affliction, retired to Buriton, a house near Petersfield, Hampshire, where he had an estate. The son was left in the house of his maternal grandfather, James Porten, near Putney Bridge, under the care of his aunt, Catherine. The boy became deep in Pope's 'Homer,' the 'Arabian Nights,' Dryden's 'Virgil,' and many romances and histories. Porten became bankrupt in the spring of 1748, and at the end of the year Catherine Porten set up a boarding-house for Westminster School, chiefly, it is said, for the benefit of her nephew. He accompanied her, and entered the school in January 1749 [Dr. Vincent, dean of Westminster, told Gibbon that 1748 was the correct date (*Misc. Works*, ii. 489)]. Miss (called Mrs.) Porten died in the summer of 1786, when Gibbon wrote of her to Lord Sheffield in the most affectionate terms. To her he owed 'a taste for books which is still the pleasure and a glory of my life' (*ib.* ii. 389). In two years he 'painfully climbed into the third form.' A 'strange nervous affection,' which 'alternately contracted his legs' and produced excruciating pain, enforced frequent absences. At the end of 1750 he was sent to Bath for his health. He read a little Latin with a clergyman there, but his infirmity prevented any regular teaching, and it seemed probable that he would remain for life an 'illiterate cripple.' About 1751 his health improved rapidly, and he was sent in January 1752 to be a pupil of Philip Francis the elder [q. v.] at Esher. Francis, it was found, preferred London excursions to the drudgery of teaching. The elder Gibbon in despair took his son to Oxford, and entered him as a gentleman commoner of Magdalen College 3 April 1752. His taste for miscellaneous reading was by this time directed into a fixed channel. An accidental glance at Echard's 'Roman History' had in 1751 excited his curiosity,

and led him through a wide course of study curiously coincident with the direction of his later researches. He came to Oxford with a 'stock of erudition which might have puzzled a doctor, and a degree of ignorance of which a schoolboy might have been ashamed.' His tastes were confirmed by an 'assiduous perusal' of the 'Universal History,' of which sixty-five volumes were published from 1747 to 1766. At Oxford, however, Gibbon spent the fourteen 'most idle and unprofitable' months of his whole life. The university was plunged in port and prejudice. He incurred debts and paid visits to London of which no notice was taken. He retained an interest in theological controversy, in which his aunt had encouraged him. A perusal of Middleton's 'Free Inquiry' (1749), then the subject of a lively controversy, led him to the church of Rome. Middleton insinuated that the continuity of the claim to miraculous powers implied that the claim had been groundless from the first. Gibbon inferred that it was still valid. Bossuet completed the conversion, with the help, it seems, of the jesuit Parsons. [A story mentioned by Johnson (BOSWELL, ed. Hill, ii. 448), that Gibbon had once been a Mahommedan, is ingeniously conjectured by Macaulay to have arisen from a passing wish to study Arabic at Oxford. See Milman's note in *Memoirs* (1839), p. 68.] Gibbon applied to a Roman catholic bookseller in London named Lewis, and was by him recommended to a jesuit named Baker, chaplain to the Sardinian ambassador, by whom he was received into the church, 8 June 1753. He communicated the news to his father, who at once took him to the house of David Mallet [q. v.] at Putney, by whose free thinking the boy was scandalised. It was then decided to place him under the care of Pavillard, a Calvinist minister at Lausanne. Gibbon reached Lausanne 30 June 1753, having left London on 19 June. Ignorant of the language, and being upon a moderate allowance among foreigners, Gibbon soon adapted himself to his situation. French then became a second native language. He soon made friendships, especially with a youth named Deyverdun, and Pavillard gently and judiciously led him into various intellectual occupations. He studied the logic of Crousaz, then dominant at Lausanne. He discovered an argument against transubstantiation; 'the articles of the Romish creed disappeared like a dream;' and on Christmas day 1754 he received the sacrament in the church of Lausanne. A letter announcing the news to Miss Porten shows that he was already writing English like a Frenchman. He now took to the study of Latin literature with extraordinary energy, cheered by the companionship of Deyverdun. He soon abandoned mathematics, but read Grotius, Puffendorf, Locke, Bayle, and Pascal's 'Provincial Letters.' He travelled through Switzerland in 1755, and studied the constitutions of the cantons. He opened a correspondence with some learned men, and had a glimpse of Voltaire. In 1757 he met Susanne Curchod, afterwards Mme. Necker and mother of Mme. de Staël. Her father was minister of Crassy, where Gibbon was permitted to visit her more than once in the latter part of 1757. They became mutually attached. There were difficulties in the way of a marriage ; Gibbon was dependent upon his father, without whose consent the match was agreed on both sides to be impossible, and Mlle. Curchod was unwilling to leave her own country. They hoped, however, that time might remove these obstacles. In August 1758 he returned to England, passing through France disguised in the regimentals of some Swiss officers in the Dutch service. He was welcomed by his aunt, but approached his father with some awe. During his absence the father had married a second wife, Dorothea Patton. Gibbon, at first prejudiced against his stepmother, soon became attached to her as to a second mother. She had no children of her own. His father disapproved of the relation to Mlle. Curchod, and Gibbon, being entirely dependent upon him, 'sighed as a lover,' but 'obeyed as a son.' He dropped all communication with her, although she continued to cherish hopes and refused good matches for his sake.

Gibbon was now introduced to London society, but made few friends except the Mallets. He spent nine months in London during the next two years, and the remainder at Buriton, where he lived as much as he could in the library, but was occasionally compelled to visit horse races, entertain country squires, or canvass at elections. He began to form a library of his own and to make abstracts of books. He had begun his French 'Essai sur l'Étude de la Littérature' at Lausanne in 1758. He finished it in February 1759, and published it, at his father's desire, in 1761. A letter from Dr. Maty [q. v.], who had encouraged the young author, is prefixed. It succeeded better abroad than at home, and was reprinted at Geneva in 1762. An English translation appeared in 1764. After the publication of his history it was much sought for and pirated in Dublin, but he refused to republish it himself. Sainte-Beuve says (Causeries du Lundi, viii. 446) that the French is 'correct but artificial.' Gibbon and his father had meanwhile become captain and major in the

Hampshire militia, their commissions being dated 12 June 1759. The regiment was embodied in May 1760. They were quartered at various towns in the southern counties until they were disembodied at Southampton 23 Dec. 1762. Though his companions were often boorish, Gibbon was forced to become 'an Englishman and a soldier.' He studied military literature, and 'the captain of Hampshire grenadiers' was 'not useless to the historian of the Roman empire.' He made the acquaintance of Wilkes, then colonel of the Buckinghamshire militia.

After this 'long fast' from literature he returned with fresh appetite to his studies, and 'never relapsed into indolence.' He had already begun to choose a subject for a prolonged effort. During brief absences from the militia he had resolved, after considering various projects, upon a life of Sir Walter Raleigh. He found the subject too narrow, too much exhausted, and too likely to lead to party controversy. He afterwards thought of a history of the Swiss, or of Florence under the Medici. He used his first liberty in a visit to the continent, staying from 28 Jan. to 9 May 1763 in Paris, where he saw some of the eminent authors of the time. He returned to Lausanne, and stayed till April 1764. He met Mlle. Curchod—a fact which he does not mention in his autobiography—but treated her with marked coldness. She at last demanded an explanation, receiving a cold reply, and she consented to exchange love for friendship. She suggested, however, that he should visit Rousseau. Her friend Moultou, a pastor, had prepared Rousseau to administer some good advice to the backward lover. Gibbon did not pay the visit, and soon afterwards, meeting Mlle. Curchod at a gathering at Ferney, behaved in such a way as to bring about a final rupture. Gibbon's behaviour, which was first made known in the letters published by M. d'Haussonville, seems to have deserved Rousseau's condemnation of which he complains in his autobiography. It was only a misfortune that the lady's passion was stronger than his own ; but he need not have behaved to her with a coldness bordering on brutality. They were, however, reconciled. She married Necker in 1764. Gibbon met her in Paris in 1765, when he saw her daily, and each took a certain pride in proving to the other that the wound was healed. They afterwards saw each other frequently, and their correspondence in later years was not only polite but affectionate, though not perhaps quite unaffected. At Lausanne Gibbon met Holroyd, afterwards Lord Sheffield. Their intimacy grew and flourished until Gibbon's death. He went through an elaborate course of antiquarian reading to prepare for a journey to Italy, which occupied a year (April 1764 to May 1765). He spent the first summer at Florence and studied Italian. He reached Rome in October. On 15 Oct. 1764, he says, while 'musing amidst the ruins of the Capitol, where the barefooted friars were singing vespers in the temple of Jupiter . . . the idea of writing the decline and fall of the city first started into my mind.' He visited Naples, Venice, and Verona, crossed Mont Cenis to Lyons, and reached his father's house 25 June 1765.

Gibbon retained his commission in the militia, becoming major and colonel commandant, until 1770. This involved a month of drilling each year. He lived quietly at Buriton, where he had become warmly attached to his stepmother, and where his friend Deyverdun, who was now seeking literary and educational employment, spent many months with him. In the winter he went to London, and formed a 'Roman Club' to preserve the friendships formed abroad. He still contemplated his great work 'at an awful distance,' and with Deyverdun's help composed in French an introduction to a history of Switzerland. It was read (1767) before a literary society of foreigners in London, and their disapproval caused its abandonment. Hume, however, saw and approved it. Gibbon co-operated with Deyverdun in publishing 'Mémoires Littéraires de la Grande-Bretagne,' in imitation of the 'Journal Britannique' (1750-5) of Dr. Maty. Two volumes were published in 1767 and 1768, to which Gibbon contributed a review of Lyttelton's 'Henry II,' and other articles. It made him known to Lord Chesterfield, to whom it was dedicated, and to David Hume (for contents of vol. i. see *Miscellaneous Works*, ii. 69). A third volume was interrupted by Deyverdun's appointment through Gibbon to be travelling tutor to Sir Richard Worsley. He was to receive after four years an annuity of 100*l.* for life. In 1770 Gibbon published his 'Critical Observations on the Sixth Book of the Æneid,' a sharp attack upon the hypothesis suggested by Warburton in his 'Divine Legation.' Gibbon was not unnaturally provoked by Warburton's arrogance, but he admits that he was too contemptuous, and that he should not have concealed his name. From 1768 he had been settling down to his chief task. His father died 10 Nov. 1770. He had mortgaged his estates and sold Putney with his son's consent; he was troubled by lawsuits, had lost money by farming, and his strength and spirits had decayed. Gibbon, who had been a thoroughly good son, now became independent. Two years passed before he could get rid of Buriton; but in 1772 he settled at 7 Bentinck Street, Cavendish Square, London, which he only quitted occasionally to visit his friend Holroyd at Sheffield Place, Sussex. He became member of the fashionable clubs and well known in London society. In 1774 he joined Johnson's famous club (founded in 1764). He was elected 'professor in ancient history' at the Royal Academy in succession to Goldsmith (*d.* 1774). Boswell (*Letters to Temple*, pp. 233, 242) calls him an 'ugly, affected, disgusting fellow,' who 'poisons the literary club to me,' and classes him among 'infidel wasps and venomous insects.' He signed the famous 'round-robin' requesting Johnson to use English for Goldsmith's epitaph. Boswell's dislike may have prevented Gibbon's name from appearing more frequently in reports of conversation, but he does not appear to have been intimate with Johnson. On 11 Oct. 1774 he was returned by the Eliot influence for Liskeard, Cornwall. He soon resigned himself to be 'a mute,' and voted in support of the ministry throughout the American war.

The first volume of his history, which he had begun to compose in London, appeared in the beginning of 1776. Three editions were speedily sold. His fame was as rapid as it has been lasting. Some warm praise from Hume 'overpaid the labour of ten years.' Robertson, third of a 'triumvirate' in which he scarcely ventured to claim a place, was equally warm, and welcomed his later volumes. Adam Ferguson, Joseph Warton, Lord Camden, and Horace Walpole were among his admirers. Strahan & Cadell, his publishers, allowed him two-thirds of the profits, which on the first edition amounted to 490*l.* He composed the first and two last chapters three times, and the second and third twice, and at starting was often tempted to throw away the labours of seven years. The famous chapters upon the growth of Christianity produced, as Hume foretold—though Gibbon himself seems to have been unprepared for it —a series of attacks. He replied to Henry Edward Davies [q. v.], James Chelsum [q. v.], and some others, in a 'Vindication' (January 1779), printed in octavo in order that it might not be bound up with the history. 'Victory over such antagonists was a sufficient humiliation.' Antagonists of higher reputation were Joseph Milner, David Dalrymple (Lord Hailes), Joseph Priestley, and Richard Watson, afterwards bishop of Llandaff (see a list in LOWNDES, *Manual*). No one, however, was a match for Gibbon in learning; and his accuracy in statement of facts is now admitted, though his philosophical explanation is no longer accepted. A six months' visit to the

Neckers in Paris, where he saw Buffon, and had a smart dispute with the Abbé de Mably, delayed his second volume. The fastidious Mme. du Deffand was pleased with him and said that he deserved to be a Frenchman. He also spent some time in studying anatomy under Hunter, and attending lectures upon chemistry. He was employed by the ministry to draw up a ' Mémoire Justificatif ' in answer to a French manifesto. This service and the friendship of the attorney-general, Wedderburne, led to his appointment in the summer of 1779 as one of the lords commissioners of trade and plantations, with a salary of 750*l.* Gibbon was not a keen politician, and his agreement in some of the criticisms made by the opposition gave rise to the charge that he had been bought off by the government (*Walpole's Letters*, viii. 24, 57 ; Russell, *Fox*, i. 265; *Notes and Queries*, 1st ser. viii. 312). He confesses rather cynically his regard for his personal interest, and his indifference to the great questions raised by the American contest. The duties of his office were too slight to interrupt his literary labours. On 13 March 1780 a clause in Burke's ' Establishment Bill ' for abolishing the board of trade was passed by 207 to 199; but the bill was ultimately lost. Parliament was dissolved 1 Sept., and Gibbon lost his seat for Liskeard, Eliot having joined the opposition. Some letters to his cousin upon this occasion are preserved at Port Eliot (*Hist. MSS. Comm.* 1st Rep. pp. 41-2). He now (at the beginning of 1781) published the second and third volumes of his history. Though at first more coldly received, they soon rose to a level with the previous volume in general esteem. The Duke of Gloucester on accepting a volume said affably, ' Another damned thick book ! Always scribble, scribble, scribble ! Eh, Mr. Gibbon ? ' (Best, *Memorials*, p. 68).

Gibbon was returned to parliament for Lymington on a bye-election (25 June 1781), through the influence of North. The board of trade was abolished in 1782. Gibbon, who adhered to the North and Fox coalition ' from a principle of gratitude,' had a promise of some other place, and applied for the post of secretary of embassy at Paris. Fortunately he did not obtain an appointment which would have involved the interruption of his great work. He had some thoughts of concluding it with the third volume. He desired independence, however, was weary of parliament, and had become absorbed in his fourth volume. His friend Deyverdun, after travelling with several pupils, was now settled at Lausanne with a moderate competence in a house given by an aunt. Gibbon proposed to join him in a retreat, where his fortune would go

further and where he would have leisure and access to books. Deyverdun gladly accepted the proposal, and Gibbon sent his library to Lausanne and settled there himself in September 1783. His last hope of the secretaryship only vanished at the beginning of that month (*Misc. Works*, ii. 321). He occupied a convenient house with a beautiful garden of four acres. He rapidly finished his fifth and sixth volumes ; he was now ' straining for the goal,' and between eleven and twelve on the night of 27 June 1787 wrote the last words in a summer-house in his garden. The three last volumes (written from March 1782 to June 1784, July 1784 to May 1786, and May 1786 to June 1787) were sent to press and published in 1788. He notes that the first rough copy was sent to the press, and that no one saw it except the printer and the author. Adam Smith, acknowledging the gift of these volumes from ' his dear friend,' pronounces that they place the author at the ' very head of the literary tribe ' in Europe. He returned to England to visit Holroyd, now Lord Sheffield, and superintended the publication. This was delayed till his fifty-first birthday, 27 April 1788, and celebrated by a dinner at the house of his publisher (Cadell). He was present at the impeachment of Warren Hastings in June, and was complimented in Sheridan's speech. He then returned to Lausanne, where he was deeply affected by the loss of his friend Deyverdun, 4 July 1789. Deyverdun had made arrangements in his will by which Gibbon was enabled to secure the possession of the house for his life.

He lived quietly and regularly at Lausanne, where he was treated with the highest respect by the natives. He shared the enjoyments of the little society of the place ; played shilling whist, gave an occasional ball, and was rather vexed than pleased when the ' fashion of viewing the glaciers ' led to the ' incursions of foreigners.' The outbreak of the French revolution brought many refugees to Lausanne, including the Neckers. Gibbon, who shared the common abhorrence of the later events, was alarmed by the approach of the French. In 1791 Sheffield with his family spent some months with Gibbon. He promised to return the visit, and was preparing to start when, on 26 April 1793, he heard of Lady Sheffield's death. He resolved immediately to join his friend, and arrived in England at the end of May. After staying at Sheffield Place till October, he visited his stepmother at Bath and Lord Spencer at Althorp, returning to London in November. Since his early youth his health had been good, in spite of occasional attacks of gout. A complaint, for which he had consulted a surgeon in 1761, had been strangely neglected by him ever since, and now assumed alarming proportions. Some operations became necessary, and on a visit to Sheffield Place at Christmas he was evidently very weak. He returned to London, and on 15 Jan. said that he thought himself a 'good life for ten, twelve, or perhaps twenty years.' He was taken ill that night and died at a quarter to one on the following afternoon, 16 Jan. 1794. He was buried in Sheffield's family burial-place at Fletching, Sussex, where a Latin epitaph by Dr. Parr was placed upon his monument. He left his fortune to the two children of his uncle, Sir Stanier Porten, the Eliots, his other relations being too prosperous to need it. His papers were left to Lord Sheffield, whose grandson, the third earl, sold the whole collection to the British Museum in 1895 (*MSS. Addit.* 34874–87). In the same year the British Museum also acquired documents concerning Gibbon from M. William de Charrière de Sévery, of Lausanne (*MSS. Addit.* 34715–6).

Gibbon composed his 'Memoirs' in his last stay at Lausanne. He had contemplated a series of lives of great Englishmen from the Reformation, and the direction of a scheme, abandoned on his death, for the publication of the original documents for English history, to be edited by Pinkerton with introductions to the volumes by himself.

A portrait of Gibbon by Warton in 1774 was engraved for the 'Miscellaneous Works.' He was ugly, and his features were so overlaid by fat, even at this time, as to be almost grotesque. His portrait by Reynolds, painted in 1779 (*Misc. Works,* ii. 232), was at Sheffield Place, and engraved by Wall for his 'Decline and Fall.' A silhouette in the 'Miscellaneous Works' (1796 and 1837) gives a comic representation of his figure. Absurd stories were told of his clumsiness. Mme. de Genlis speaks of his falling on his knees before Madame de Montolieu, who had to summon a servant to enable him to rise. His corpulence increased his aversion to exercise, and after his military service he appears to have led a most sedentary life, though never working at night except when finishing his history. His manners appear to have struck most people as rather affected, and his dress was a little too fine. Sheffield describes his charm in congenial society. Though a very unromantic lover, a lukewarm patriot, and rather cynical in his philosophy, Gibbon was a most amiable friend. In his relations to his father, his aunt, his stepmother, to Sheffield and Deyverdun, he was not only amiable but faithful and affectionate to a remarkable

degree. No personal quarrel is recorded; his servants were attached to him; and his career as a man of letters, labouring without haste and without pause at one great task, is a proof of his moral as well as his intellectual qualities. He must have possessed in the highest degree patience, calmness, unswerving industry, and a just estimate of his own abilities. The criticisms upon his book, the last and ablest of which is in J. C. Morison's 'Gibbon' (Mr. Morley's 'English Men of Letters'), are nearly unanimous. In accuracy, thoroughness, lucidity, and comprehensive grasp of a vast subject, the 'History' is unsurpassable. It is the one English history which may be regarded as definitive. The philosophy is of course that of the age of Voltaire and implies a deficient insight into the great social forces. The style, though variously judged, has at least the cardinal merit of admirable clearness, and if pompous is always animated. Whatever its shortcomings the book is artistically imposing as well as historically unimpeachable as a vast panorama of a great period. Gibbon's fortunate choice of a subject enabled him to write the one book in which the clearness of his own age is combined with a thoroughness of research which has made it a standard for his successors.

Gibbon's library was bought by W. Beckford (1759–1844) [q. v.], who left it in Lausanne, and ultimately gave it to a physician named Scholl. Scholl sold half of it in 1830 to a bookseller, by whom it was dispersed, and the other half for 500*l.* to an Englishman, who ultimately gave it back to him. This half is apparently still preserved (*Notes and Queries,* 5th ser. v. 425, vii. 414). The Hôtel Gibbon at Lausanne stands on part of Gibbon's garden. His house was still standing in 1868.

In 1796 Sheffield published 2 vols. 4to of Gibbon's 'Miscellaneous Works.' In 1814 he published a second edition in 5 vols. 8vo, containing much additional matter, which was also published in 4to. The original 4to was republished in one vol. 8vo without the additional matter in 1837. The 'Works' include letters, notes, and diaries of his early studies, a fragment called 'Antiquities of the House of Brunswick,' dated 1790, published separately in 1814, his previously published works, and a number of youthful essays. The 'Memoirs of my Life and Writings,' first printed in the 'Works' (1796), were compiled from six different sketches. Gibbon says that his name may 'hereafter appear among the thousand articles of a Biographia Britannica;' and his memoir is a model for that purpose as for others. Milman edited Sheffield's text of the 'Memoirs' in 1839.

Sheffield in his will forbade the publication of further papers, and Dean Milman was only allowed to inspect them on condition of not publishing anything. All the six original drafts (now in the British Museum) were first printed in 1896. Another edition of the 'Memoirs,' annotated by George Birkbeck Hill, came out in 1900. Some additional 'Private Letters of Gibbon 1753–1794' were edited by R. E. Prothero in 1896 (2 vols.)

The centenary of Gibbon's death was celebrated by the Royal Historical Society in London in November 1894 (*Proceedings of the Gibbon Commemoration, 1794–1894*, 1895).

Of editions of the 'Decline and Fall' may be mentioned the Oxford edition in 8 vols. 8vo (revised and compared with original manuscripts), 1828; that by H. H. Milman, 12 vols. 8vo, 1838, 1839; that by Dr. W. Smith (including notes of Milman and Guizot), 8 vols. 8vo, 1854, 1855; and that by Prof. J. B. Bury, 7 vols. 1896–1900. French, German, and Italian translations appeared during Gibbon's life and subsequently; there are also translations into Polish, modern Greek, and Magyar. The French translation, revised and annotated by M. and Mme. Guizot, appeared in 1812.

[Gibbon's Miscellaneous Works as above; Autobiographies, ed. Murray (1896), and Private Letters, ed. Prothero (1896); Egerton Brydges's Autobiography, i. 227, ii. 17; Gent. Mag. for 1794, i. 5, 94, 178, 199, 382; M. d'Haussonville's Salon de Mme. Necker (1882), i. 34–84; Boswell's Johnson; Walpole's Letters; Colman's Eccentricities for Edinburgh (for some absurd anecdotes); Mme. du Deffand's Letters to Horace Walpole (1810), iii. (on his visit to Paris in 1777); Letters of Gibbon in Campbell's Loughborough (Lives of the Chancellors) and Notes and Queries, 2nd ser. ii. 145, 385; Sainte-Beuve's Causeries du Lundi, viii. 431–72; J. C. Morison's Gibbon in Men of Letters Series.] L. S.

GIBBON, JOHN (1629–1718), writer on heraldry, eldest son of Robert Gibbon, draper, of London, fourth son of Robert Gibbon of Rolvenden, Kent, by his wife Mary, daughter of Lionel Edgar of Framsden, Suffolk (*Visitation of London*, 1633–5 (Harl. Soc.) i. 310), was born on 3 Nov. 1629. He was brother of Edward Gibbon's great-grandfather, Matthew Gibbon. On 11 Dec. 1639 he was admitted a pupil of Merchant Taylors' School (ROBINSON. *Register*, i. 145), whence he proceeded to Jesus College, Cambridge, but did not take a degree. On his father's death in 1643 he inherited a marshy and valueless estate in Kent, but lived at Allesborough in Worcestershire, in the house of Thomas, lord Coventry, as domestic tutor.

Gibbon visited Europe as a soldier and a traveller, acquired good knowledge of French and Spanish, passed some time 'very happily' in Jersey, crossed the Atlantic, and resided 'a great part of anno 1659 till February the year following . . . in Virginia, being most hospitably entertained by the Honourable Colonel Rich. Lee, sometimes secretary of state there' (*ib.* pp. 155, 156). In Virginia his passion for heraldry found gratification at a war-dance of the native Indians. Their little shields of bark and their naked bodies were painted with the colours and symbols of his favourite science, showing 'that heraldry was ingrafted naturally into the sense of humane race' (*ib.* pp. 156–7). Gibbon returned home after the Restoration, and on 9 Feb. 1664–5 took up his abode in the house belonging to the senior brother in St. Katharine's Hospital, near the Tower, where he resided till 11 May 1701 (STOWE, *Survey*, ed. Strype, 1720, bk. i. p. 204). He received a patent for the office of Blue Mantle pursuivant at arms on 10 Feb. 1668, through the influence of Sir William Dugdale, then Norroy, but was not actually created such until 25 May 1671 (NOBLE, *Hist. of College of Arms*, p. 293), when, as he relates, 'it was my hard hap to become a member of the Heralds Office when the ceremony of funerals (as accompanied with officers of arms) began to be in the wane. . . . In eleven years time I have had but five turns,' which out of gratitude he commemorates at length (*Introductio, &c.*, p. 161). He never received further promotion, as he injured himself by his arrogance towards his less learned superiors in the college, whose shortcomings he had an unpleasant habit of registering in the margins of the library books, which he also filled with calculations of his own nativity. He firmly believed his destiny so fixed by the stars which presided at his birth that good or ill behaviour could never alter it (NOBLE, ut supra, p. 363). Among his friends, however, he could number Dugdale, Ashmole, Dr. John Betts, and Dr. Nehemiah Grew, 'and in the society of such men,' remarks Edward Gibbon, 'he may be recorded without disgrace as the member of an astrological club' (*Autobiography*). In religion and politics he was a high tory. In the latter end of the reign of Charles II he wrote in the support of the Duke of York. Upon James's return from Flanders in 1679 he published a little essay entitled 'Dux bonis omnibus appellens, or The Swans Welcome.' Another whimsical piece was 'Day Fatality; or, some Observations of Days lucky and unlucky; concluding with some Remarks upon the fourteenth of October, the auspicious Birthday of his Royal Highness James, Duke of York,' fol. [London], 1678, and again in 1679. It was reprinted by Aubrey in his 'Miscellanies,' with additions at the end by himself, and in vol. viii. of the quarto editions of the 'Harleian Miscellany.' In 1686 appeared a 'second impression, with . . . additions. To which is added, Prince-Protecting Providences and the Swans Welcome. All by an Officer at Arms, author of a book, Introductio ad Latinam Blasoniam,' 2 pts. fol. Gibbon's other political writings are: 1. 'A Touch of the Times; or, two letters casually intercepted' [London, 1679], against Henry Care [q. v.], author of the 'Weekly Packet of Advice from Rome.' 2. 'Unio Dissidentium. Heir apparent and presumptive made one. By J. G., B.M.,' fol. [London? 1680?]. 3. 'Edovardus Confessor redivivus . . . in the sacred Majesty of King James the II.; being a Relation of the admirable and unexpected finding of a sacred relique of that pious prince, . . . since worn sometimes by his present majesty' [anon.], 4to, London, 1688. At page 157 of his 'Introductio' Gibbon makes humorous reference to his antagonist, 'little Mr. Harry Care,' whose arguments he had ridiculed in a pamphlet called 'Flagellum Mercurii Antiducalis.' The triumph of the whigs proved a lasting check to Gibbon's preferment, and he was suspended from his office until he could bring himself to take the oath of allegiance.

Among his contemporaries Gibbon's reputation as a writer on heraldry and genealogy ranked deservedly high. In 1682 he published at London his 'Introductio ad Latinam Blasoniam. An Essay towards a more correct Blason in Latine than formerly hath been used,' 8vo, 'an original attempt, which Camden had desiderated, to define, in a Roman idiom, the terms and attributes of a Gothic institution. His manner is quaint and affected; his order is confused; but he displays some wit, more reading, and still more enthusiasm. An English text is perpetually interspersed with Latin sentences in prose and verse; but in his own poetry he claims an exemption from the laws of prosody' (EDWARD GIBBON, Autobiography). He also compiled from British and foreign authorities an elaborate account of the important services rendered by heralds in former times, which compilation, named by him 'Heraldo-Memoriale,' he communicated to Strype for insertion in an abridged form in the latter's edition of Stow's 'Survey,' 1720 (bk. i. pp. 143-5). He was able to render Strype other aid (ib. bk. i. p. 204, bk. ii. pp. 7, 8). Three of his letters occur in the 'Strype Correspondence' in the University Library, Cambridge (Cat. of MSS. v. 148).

Gibbon died in the parish of St. Faith, London, on 2 Aug. 1718 (affidavit appended to will registered in P. C. C. 160, Tenison), and was buried on the 6th in the church of St. Mary Aldermary (Registers of St. Mary Aldermary, Harl. Soc. p. 215). His wife, Susannah, had been buried in the same church on 24 Aug. 1704 (ib. p. 208).

[Addit. MS. 5870, f. 78 ; Brit. Mus. Cat.]
G. G.

GIBBON or **GIBBONS, NICHOLAS,** the elder (fl. 1600), theological writer, matriculated as pensioner at Clare Hall, Cambridge, in June 1585. He proceeded B.A. in 1588-9, M.A. in 1592, and was incorporated at Oxford July 1592. He has been identified with the Nicholas Gibbon of Heckford, Dorsetshire, whose son of the same name, born at Poole in 1605, became rector of Corfe Castle [see GIBBON, NICHOLAS, the younger, 1605-1697]. He published 'Questions and Disputations concerning the Holy Scripture, wherein are contained . . . expositions of the most difficult places,' London, 1601, 4to. This work of nearly six hundred pages deals with the first fourteen chapters of Genesis, and is described on the title-page as 'the first part of the first Tome. By Nicholas Gibbens, Minister and Preacher of the Word of God.'

[Cooper's Athenæ Cantabr. ii. 430; Wood's Athenæ Oxon. ed. Bliss, iv. 787; Wood's Fasti, i. 259; Hutchins's Dorset, i. 297; Brit. Mus. Cat.]
R. B.

GIBBON, NICHOLAS, the younger (1605-1697), divine, son of Nicholas Gibbon of Heckford, Dorsetshire [see preceding art.], was born at Poole in 1605. He was admitted into Queen's College, Oxford, in 1622, but soon afterwards migrated to St. Edmund Hall. He took the degrees of B.A. in 1626, M.A. in 1629, B.D. and D.D. in 1639. In 1632 he became rector of Sevenoaks. Charles I, when at Carisbrooke Castle in 1647, sent for him in order to consult him on questions of church government. He was ejected from Sevenoaks in 1650 or earlier, and had to work as a farm labourer in order to support himself and his eleven children. While thus engaged he was brought before the committee in Kent, and asked how he spent his time. He answered that he studied during part of the night, and performed manual labour by day, and showed his hardened hands, remarking to some who scoffed, 'Mallem callum in manu quam in conscientiâ.' He was then offered possession of his living if he would take the covenant, and he refused to do so. At the Restoration he regained the rectory of Sevenoaks, and was also put in possession of the rectory of Corfe Castle, to which he had been presented more than ten years before. He died at Corfe Castle on 12 Feb. 1697.

His writings were: 1. 'The Tender of Dr. Gibbon unto the Christian Church for the Reconciliation of Differences,' s. sh. fol. 1640 (?). 2. 'The Reconciler, earnestly endeavouring to unite in sincere affection the Presbyters and their dissenting brethren of all sorts,' 1646. 3. 'A Paper delivered to the Commissioners of the Parliament (as they call themselves) at the personal Treaty with his Majesty King Charles I in the Isle of Wight, anno 1648.' 4. 'A Summe or Body of Divinity Real,' 1653. This is a large diagram in which the attempt is made to illustrate the connection between the various truths of religion by means of lines, semicircles, and similar devices. 5. 'Theology Real and truly Scientificall; in overture for the conciliation of all Christians, and (after them) the Theist, Atheist, and all Mankind into the Unity of the Spirit and the Bond of Peace,' 1663. 6. 'The Scheme or Diagramme adjusted for future use in a larger Prodromus ere long to be published, and whereof this is then to be a part: at present printed for private hands.' This is a key to the 'Summe or Body.' Baxter, to whom he showed one of his schemes of divinity, denounces it as 'the contrivance of a very strong headpiece, secretly and cunningly fitted to usher in a Socinian Popery,' and describes its author as an impostor (*Reliquiæ Baxterianæ*, pt. i. p. 78, pt. ii. p. 205, pt. iii p. 69).

[Wood's Athenæ Oxonienses, iv. 787-9; Fasti, i. 422, 451, 508, 510; Walker's Sufferings of the Clergy, pt. ii. pp. 251, 252; Hutchins's Dorset (3rd ed.), i. 539, 542, 543; Hasted's Kent, i. 358; Bodleian Library and Brit. Mus. Catalogues of Printed Books.] E. C–N.

GIBBONS. [See also GIBBON.]

GIBBONS, CHRISTOPHER (1615-1676), musical composer, elder of the two surviving sons of Orlando Gibbons [q. v.], was born in 1615, and baptised in St. Margaret's, Westminster, 22 Aug. of that year. He was probably called after his father's patron, Sir Christopher Hatton. He received his musical education in the choir of Exeter Cathedral under his uncle, Edward Gibbons [q. v.] (the double mistake of stating him to have learnt music under Ellis Gibbons [q. v.] and at Bristol originated in a clerical error of Wood). In 1638 he succeeded Thomas Holmes as organist of Winchester Cathedral, a post which he held, in name at all events,

until 23 June 1661. He joined a royalist garrison, along with other cathedral officials, in the civil war. In July 1654 Evelyn heard 'Mr. Gibbon,' probably Christopher, play the organ in Magdalen Chapel, Oxford. At the Restoration he was appointed one of the organists of the Chapel Royal, to which he had belonged in Charles I's time (WOOD, *Fasti*, ii. 277). He was also made organist of Westminster Abbey, and private organist to Charles II. On 23 Sept. 1646 he married, at St. Bartholomew's the Less, Mary, daughter of Dr. Robert Kercher, a late prebendary of Winchester, and in February 1661 he petitioned the king that he might obtain his tenant right by virtue of this marriage to a tenement in Whitchurch manor belonging to the cathedral (*Cal. State Papers*, Dom., Charles II, vol. xxxi. No. 65). His wife died in April 1662, and was buried on the 15th of the month in the north cloister of Westminster Abbey. In that year the famous German organist Froberger, who had been robbed on his way to England, and was almost destitute, appealed to him for the post of organblower. On the occasion of the king's marriage, Gibbons was playing before the court, when Froberger overblew the bellows, and drew down upon him the rage of his employer. Shortly afterwards Froberger, having filled the bellows, struck a crashing discord on the keys, and resolved it in so masterly a manner that he was recognised by a lady who had been his pupil. By the king's command a harpsichord was brought in, and he played to the admiration of all present, and even drew an apology from Gibbons for his rudeness (MATTHESON, *Grundlage einer Ehrenpforte*, p. 88). In July 1663 the king requested the university of Oxford to confer upon Gibbons the degree of Mus.D. (*Cal. State Papers*, Dom. Charles II, vol. lxxvi. No. 12), and accordingly the honour was conferred on him, *per literas regias*, on the 7th of the month. His 'Act Song,' performed in the church of St. Mary on the 11th (WOOD, *Fasti*, ii. 158), is preserved in the library of the Music School, Oxford. He received 5*l.* on the occasion from the dean and chapter of Westminster (GROVE). In 1653 he composed, in conjunction with Matthew Lock, who like himself had been a choir-boy at Exeter under Edward Gibbons, the music to Shirley's masque, 'Cupid and Death,' which was performed before the Portuguese ambassador on 26 March (the manuscript is in the British Museum, Add. MS. 17799). Gibbons died 20 Oct., and was buried in the cloisters of Westminster Abbey 24 Oct. 1676. His nuncupative will, dated three days before his death, was proved 6 Nov. following by his second wife, Elizabeth, whose own will, dated 19 March 1677-8, was proved 22 Jan. 1682-3. She is assumed to be the person whose burial in the cloisters on 27 Dec. 1682 is entered as that of Elizabeth Bull (see CHESTER, *Registers of Westminster Abbey*, pp. 190, 206, where the name of Gibbons's second wife, whether her maiden name or that of a former husband, is stated to have been Ball).

Gibbons excelled less as a composer than as an organ-player, and it was no doubt in the latter capacity that he acted as Blow's instructor. The only printed works by him are contained in 'Cantica Sacra' (the second set, published by Playford, 1674; see DERING, RICHARD). His contributions to the book are 'Celebrate Dominum,' 'Sing unto the Lord,' 'Teach me, O Lord,' and 'How long wilt thou forget me,' all for two voices. The second and fourth of these, as well as 'O give thanks' and 'The Lord said unto my lord,' are in manuscript in the British Museum (Add. MSS. 17799, 17820, 17840); the volume of anthems in Blow's writing in the Fitzwilliam Museum at Cambridge contains, besides the three English anthems in 'Cantica Sacra,' 'Let Thy merciful ears' and 'Teach me, O Lord,' both by Gibbons; and Hawkins mentions 'God be merciful,' 'Help me, O Lord,' and 'Lord, I am not high-minded,' among 'those of most note.' A three-part song, 'Ah, my soul, why so dismay'd,' is in Add. MS. 22100. A portrait of Gibbons is in the Music School, Oxford.

[Authorities quoted above; Grove's Dict. i. 565, 595, ii. 157, iv. 647; Hawkins's Hist. ed. 1853, p. 713; Winchester Chapter Books, communicated by Mr. W. Barclay Squire; Notes and Queries, 3rd ser. x. 182, 4th ser. v. 288; Companion to the Playhouse, 1764, vol. i.; Evelyn's Diary, 12 July 1654.]   J. A. F. M.

GIBBONS, EDWARD (1570 ?–1653 ?), musical composer, supposed to have been son of William Gibbons, one of the 'waits' at Cambridge, was brother of Orlando [q. v.] and uncle of Christopher Gibbons [q. v.] He received the degree of Mus.B. at Cambridge, and on 7 July 1592 was incorporated in the same degree at Oxford. At midsummer in that year he became organist and master of the choristers at King's College, Cambridge, succeeding Thomas Hammond, who returned to the duties in 1599. Between those two dates the 'Mundum Books' of the college contain entries showing that Gibbons, or 'Gibbins' as he is more usually called, received 20s. a quarter as his own salary, and 11s. 8d. for the tuition of the choristers. He had to provide for the making, mending, &c., of the choristers' clothes. About the beginning of the century he went to Bristol,

being appointed cathedral organist, priest-vicar, sub-chanter, and master of the choristers. In 1611 he was given the post of organist and custos of the college of priest-vicars at Exeter Cathedral, and he remained there until 1644. In 1634 a complaint was made that he was in the habit of neglecting his duties, and he, with two other of the vicars-choral, replied to the charge (*Hist. MSS. Comm.* 4th Rep. Appendix, pp. 137, 139). Hawkins states, but only as a matter of hearsay, that on the outbreak of the civil war he advanced a sum of 1,000*l.* to the king, and that in consequence of this he was deprived of a very considerable estate by those afterwards in power, and was, with his three grandchildren, driven from his house, though he was then over eighty years of age.

In the Music School at Oxford a few manuscript compositions by him are preserved, and in the Tudway collection (Brit. Mus. Harl. MS. 7340) his 'How doth the city sit solitary' is included.

[Wood's Fasti Oxon. vol. ii. col. 258; Mundum Books of King's College, Cambridge, vol. xx.; Lib. Communarum, ib. vols. xxi–xxiii.; Grove's Dict. i. 594 (the dates of his appointment at Exeter are given in Grove, without reference to authoritative documents of any kind); Hawkins's Hist. ed. 1853, p. 573. The Cathedral Registers at Bristol date back only to 1660, so that the exact date of his appointment there cannot be discovered.]   J. A. F. M.

GIBBONS, ELLIS (*fl.* 1600), musical composer, brother of Edward and Orlando Gibbons [q. v.], is said to have been organist of Salisbury Cathedral at the end of the sixteenth century. The only compositions extant by him are two madrigals, 'Long live fair Oriana' and 'Round about her Chariot,' contained in 'The Triumphs of Oriana,' published 1603.

[Grove's Dict. i. 594; Hawkins's Hist. ed. 1853, p. 573. The Chapter Act Books at Salisbury contain no mention of Gibbons's name; the volume for 1599–1603 is missing, however, and may have contained the entries both of his appointment and of that of his successor.]   J. A. F. M.

GIBBONS, GRINLING (1648–1720), wood-carver and statuary, was born at Rotterdam on 4 April 1648 of Dutch origin. This is proved by a letter preserved in the Ashmolean MSS. (20243) in the Bodleian Library at Oxford, dated 12 Oct. 1682, wherein Gibbons invokes Ashmole's skill in prognostication with reference to a 'consarne of great consiquens,' and encloses a letter from his sister, giving an account of his birth, to enable Ashmole to calculate his astrological figure. The mixture of Dutch and English in the letter reveals his nationality. Thoresby, in his 'Diary' (ed. Hunter, 2 vols., London, 1830), describes Gibbons as his countryman, i.e. a native of Yorkshire, and also states that Gibbons worked at York under Etty, the architect. It has also been suggested that he was son of Simon Gibbons, a skilful carpenter, who worked under Inigo Jones in the reign of Charles I. He lived for some time in Belle Sauvage Court, Ludgate Hill, where he is stated to have carved a pot of flowers over a doorway, which shook with the motion of the carriages which passed by; this seems unlikely, as all Gibbons's wood-carving, though marvellously light in appearance, is really perfectly rigid and strong. He carved capitals and other ornaments for the theatre in Dorset Garden. Wishing to apply himself to his profession of wood-carving without interruption, he moved to a small lonely house at Deptford, and set to work on a copy of Tintoretto's great picture of the 'Crucifixion' at Venice, which contained more than a hundred figures, and was encased in an elaborate frame of flowers and fruit. While working on this he was discovered on 18 Jan. 1671 by John Evelyn, the diarist [q. v.], who lived at Sayes Court, close by. Evelyn was astonished and delighted at the wonderful talents of young Gibbons, obtained the king's permission to show him Gibbons's work, and invited his friends, including Sir Christopher Wren and Samuel Pepys, to inspect it. On 1 March Gibbons brought his carving to Whitehall, where it was inspected by the king, who had it carried to the queen's bedchamber to be shown to her. Owing to a want of appreciation on her part, the work, contrary to expectation, was not purchased by the king. Gibbons eventually sold it to Sir George Viner for 80l. Evelyn spared no trouble to advance his young protégé, whose novel genius soon became well known, and his fortune secured. The specialty of his wood-carving lay in carving pendent groups and festoons of flowers, fruit, game, and other ornaments, as large as life, and carefully copied from nature. These were executed with a taste and delicacy which, though often imitated, has always remained unequalled. They were usually carved in lime-wood. For church panels and mouldings he used oak, for medallions boxwood or pearwood, but cedar rarely, except for the architraves in large mansions. The king purchased from him a carving, on the same scale as the 'Crucifixion,' representing the 'Stoning of St. Stephen,' containing seventy figures, and carved out of three blocks of wood. This the king gave to the Duke of

Chandos, who placed it at Cannons, and when that mansion was demolished the carving was bought by Mr. John Gore, M.P., from whom it descended to Mr. J. Gurdon Rebow of Wyvenhoe Park, Essex. Another large carving is in the ducal palace at Modena, probably sent as a present from the king. Wren promised Evelyn to employ Gibbons, and the new St. Paul's Cathedral afforded him an opportunity. The choir stalls in that cathedral are the work of Gibbons, and the festoons on the exterior were executed in his style, and perhaps under his superintendence. Several of Wren's city churches contain work by Gibbons, who also executed the busts, coats of arms, and ornaments to complete the interior of Wren's new library at Trinity College, Cambridge. Gibbons was employed by the king at Windsor, Whitehall, and Kensington. Nearly all the mansions of the nobility built at this time were decorated to some extent with carvings executed under Gibbons. At Chatsworth, where there is an extensive series of carvings executed by Gibbons or under his direction, there is a wonderful carving of a point-lace cravat and other still-life, presented by Gibbons to the Duke of Devonshire after the completion of the works. A similar but less elaborate piece of work was in possession of Baroness Burdett-Coutts. Belton House (near Grantham), Blenheim, Wimpole, Cassiobury, Burghley, Petworth, Somerleyton, Houghton, Melbury, Gatton, and many others rank his carvings among their chief treasures. Those at Belton House may be noted, not only as particularly fine specimens, but as examples of a successful process of restoration invented by W. G. Rogers [q. v.]; this process has been since successfully applied to numbers of the carvings elsewhere. The wooden throne at Canterbury Cathedral, given by Archbishop Tenison, was carved by Gibbons. It would be impossible to enumerate all Gibbons's carvings, but his portrait medallions are worthy of special notice. His talents were not devoted to wood-carving alone, for his works in marble give him claim to distinction as a statuary. Good examples of his work in this line are the tomb of Baptist Noel, viscount Campden, at Exton; the font in St. Margaret's, Lothbury; the bust of Sir Peter Lely on his tomb in St. Paul's, Covent Garden (destroyed by fire in 1795); the pedestal of Charles II's statue in the courtyard at Windsor; the statues of Charles II at the Royal Exchange and at Chelsea Hospital; and of James II (in bronze) at Whitehall. Gibbons himself could not have executed all the commissions given him with his own hands, and he employed numerous carvers to carry out his designs. Among them were Selden, who lost his life in saving the carved room at Petworth from a destructive fire; Watson, who executed most of the famous carvings at Chatsworth; Henry Phillips, who worked with Gibbons at Whitehall; and others. In statuary he was assisted by Dyvoet of Mechlin and Laurens of Brussels, who executed the statue of James II at Whitehall; and by Arnout Quellin of Antwerp in various works. The pedestal of Charles I's statue at Charing Cross, so often attributed to Gibbons, was executed by Joshua Marshall, master-mason to the king, possibly from Gibbons's designs. Gibbons was master-carver in wood to the crown from the time of Charles II to that of George I, and also held an office in the board of works. He resided from 1678 in Bow Street, Covent Garden; in January 1701 his house fell down, but fortunately none of the family were injured (*Postman*, 24 Jan. 1701). He died in the house rebuilt there on 3 Aug. 1720, and was buried on 10 Aug. in St. Paul's, Covent Garden; his wife had been buried there on 30 Nov. 1719. They had nine or ten children, all baptised at St. Paul's, including five daughters, one of whom, Catherine, married Joseph Biscoe, and was buried at Chelsea, 23 Jan. 1731–2, leaving two sons. Another daughter, Elizabeth, had administration of her father's effects granted to her on 7 Sept. 1721; she was then unmarried. Gibbons's portrait was painted by Sir Godfrey Kneller (formerly at Houghton, now at St. Petersburg), and, with his wife, by Closterman; both were engraved in mezzotint by John Smith. Evelyn describes Gibbons, when he first met him, as 'likewise musical, and very civil, sober, and discreete in his discourse.'

[Walpole's Anecdotes of Painting, ed. Dallaway and Wornum; Evelyn's Diary; Builder, 1862; Notes and Queries, 4th ser. iii. 504, 573, 606, iv. 43, 63, 106, 259; Audit Office Declared Accounts in Publ. Rec. Off. (giving prices of various works); Cunningham's Lives of British Painters, Sculptors, and Architects; information from Mr. A.W. Gibbons and Mr. G. A. Rogers; authorities quoted in the text.]   L. C.

GIBBONS, JOHN, D.D. (1544–1589), jesuit, born at or near Wells, Somersetshire, in 1544, was sent to Oxford in 1561, and became a member, as Wood surmises, of Lincoln College, but left the university without taking a degree, and proceeding to Rome spent seven years in the German College there, and in 1576 was created doctor of philosophy and divinity. Afterwards Gregory XIII collated him to a canonry in the collegiate church of Bonn in Germany. In 1578 he entered

the Society of Jesus at Trèves, eventually became rector of the jesuit college there, and was 'much admired by all for his great humility, gravity of manners, zeal, and charity, and, above all, for his admirable regimen of that house' (WOOD, *Athenæ Oxon.* ed. Bliss, i. 555). He died on 3 Dec. 1589, while on a visit to the monastery of Himmelrode, near Trèves.

He was the author of 'Concertatio Ecclesiæ Catholicæ in Anglia, adversus Calvino-Papistas et Puritanos, a paucis annis singulari studio quorundam hominum doctrina et sanctitate illustrium renovata,' Trèves, 1583, 8vo. Some of the lives of the martyrs in this valuable historical and biographical work were written by John Fenn [q. v.] The work was afterwards greatly enlarged by John Bridgewater [q. v.], the latinised form of whose name is Aquepontanus. An account of its multifarious contents will be found in the Chetham Society's 'Remains,' xlviii. 47–50.

Southwell asserts that Gibbons was the real author of 'Confutatio virulentæ Disputationis Theologicæ, in qua Georgius Sohn, Professor Academiæ Heidelbergensis, conatus est docere Pontificem Romanum esse Antichristum a Prophetis et Apostolis prædictum,' Trèves, 1589, 8vo; but it is distinctly stated on the title-page that John Aquepontanus. or Bridgewater, was the author.

[De Backer's Bibl. des Écrivains de la Compagnie de Jésus (1869), col. 2116; Dodd's Church Hist. ii. 146; Foley's Records, iv. 480, vi. 526, vii. 298; Gillow's Bibl. Dict. i. 295, ii. 245, 437; Lansd. MS. 96, art. 25, 26; More's Hist. Missionis Soc. Jesu, p. 19; Morris's Troubles of our Catholic Forefathers, ii. 19 seq.; Oliver's Catholic Religion in Cornwall, p. 312; Oliver's Jesuit Collections, p. 103; Pits, De Angliæ Scriptoribus, p. 788; Southwell's Bibl. Script. Soc. Jesu, p. 453; Tanner's Bibl. Brit. p. 315.]   T. C.

GIBBONS, ORLANDO (1583–1625), musical composer, was the son of William Gibbons, who was admitted one of the 'waits' of Cambridge on 3 Nov. 1567. Orlando was born at Cambridge in 1583, and in February 1596 entered the choir of King's College. His elder brother, Edward [q. v.], was organist and master of the choristers during the whole time the boy was in the choir. The first entry of the name (spelt 'Gibbins') in the list of choristers is in the account for commons for the eighth week after Christmas 1595, from which time the name appears regularly in the weekly lists until the second week after Christmas 1597, when it is placed at the top of the list as that of the senior chorister. The name is again found, only in a single entry, in the list for the third week after Michaelmas 1598, but, as it is not at the top, it probably refers to a younger brother. At Michaelmas 1601, 1602, and 1603 he received from the college sums varying from 2s. to 2s. 6d. for music composed ' in festo Dominæ Reginæ,' and at Christmas 1602 and 1603 similar payments were made to him for music for the Feast of the Purification. Although the christian name is not given, these entries in all probability refer to him. Gibbons was appointed organist of the Chapel Royal in London on 21 March 1604, in the place of Arthur Cock, deceased. In 1606 he took the degree of Mus.B. at Cambridge (BAKER, *Reg. Acad. Cant.* quoted by WOOD; *Fasti*, i. 406), and at that time it was stated that he had studied music for seven years. If this is to be relied upon, his attention must have been turned to composition about the time of his leaving the choir of King's. The Orlando Gibbons who was a M.A. of Cambridge, and was incorporated in the same degree at Oxford in 1607, cannot have been the composer, but may possibly have been that bearer of the name who was baptised at Oxford 25 Dec. 1583, which was, strangely enough, the year of the composer's birth. In 1611 the composer first came before the world as the associate of Byrd and Bull, in the collection of virginal pieces called 'Parthenia.' His pieces are placed at the end of the volume, and consist of two galliards, a fantasia of four parts, 'The Lord of Salisbury his Pavin,' the 'Queen's Command,' and a preludium. The fantasia is perhaps the most remarkable piece of instrumental music of the period; it is a sustained work in fugal form written with consummate contrapuntal skill, and developed with the hand of a master. A state paper of the same year contains Gibbons's petition to the Earl of Salisbury for a lease in reversion of forty marks per annum of duchy lands, without fine, as promised him by the queen (*Cal. State Papers*, Dom. Ser. James I, vol. lxvii. No. 140). In 1612 there appeared ' The First Set of Madrigals and Mottets of 5 Parts: apt for Viols and Voyces. Newly Composed by Orlando Gibbons, Batcheler of Musicke, and Organist of his Maiesties Honourable Chappell in Ordinarie. London· Printed by Thomas Snodham, the Assigne of W. Barley, 1612.' The dedication to Sir Christopher Hatton, knight of the Bath, implies that the composer was on terms of intimacy with his patron. 'They were most of them composed in your owne house and doe therefore properly belong vnto you, as Lord of the Soile; the language they speak you prouided them, I onely furnished them with Tongues to vtter the same.' From the last sentence it has been inferred that Sir Christopher wrote the words, some of which are remarkably good. There are no motets, as the title would lead us to expect, but the thirteen complete madrigals, some of which are divided into two, three, or even four sections, each as long as an ordinary madrigal, are among the masterpieces of their class. The 'Silver Swan' is generally considered as the most perfect work of the kind of the English school, and its wonderful conciseness, the exceeding beauty of each part, and the charm of its melodic treatment, fully explain its lasting popularity. In contrast to this, the sustained power of the set of four, beginning ' I weigh not fortune's frown,' is very remarkable.

The composer's connection with the family of his patron is shown in the title given to one of the twenty-seven pieces preserved in what is known as ' Benjamin Cosyn's virginal book,' in Buckingham Palace. The galliard on p. 170 of that volume is called in the index the 'La. Hatten's Galliard.' The virginal book at Cambridge known as 'Queen Elizabeth's' contains a pavane, and another composition in the same form is in Addit. MS. 29996; Addit. MS. 31403 contains, besides the 'preludium' with which 'Parthenia' concludes, six pieces by Gibbons, called variously 'voluntary' or 'fantazie.' The 'Wood soe wilde' is an air with variations.

His work for stringed instruments, though far less extensive than either his sacred or secular vocal music, is exceedingly interesting, since his compositions are among the first designed distinctively for instruments. In earlier times, and in his own set of madrigals, the viols were only permitted to take the vocal parts, and in the set of pieces for three stringed instruments in Addit. MSS. 30826–8, three of which are by Gibbons, and more particularly in his own ' fantasies,' the first signs of transition may be seen from the exceedingly dry 'In nomines' of the older generation to the chamber music of the period of the Restoration. The title presents considerable difficulties to the biographer. It runs: 'Fantasies of Three Parts composed by Orlando Gibbons, Batchelour of Musick and Late Organist of his Majesties Chappell Royall in Ordinary. Cut in Copper, the like not heretofore extant. London: At the Bell in St. Paul's Churchyard.' There is no date to the part-books and the word 'Late' is inexplicable, since there is no evidence that Gibbons gave up his post or was dismissed from it during his life. The date must have been earlier than 1622, as it is dedicated to Edward Wray, as one of the grooms of the king's bedchamber, and in that year Wray lost his place (*Cal. State Papers*, Dom. Ser. James I, vol. cxxviii. No. 96).

Besides his published madrigals no secular or vocal compositions exist in manuscript except a kind of burlesque madrigal entitled 'The Cries of London,' for six voices, preserved in Addit. MSS. 29372–7, in the library of the Royal College of Music and elsewhere. Other compositions of the kind, as the 'Country Cry,' &c., are found, but without composer's names, in Addit. MSS. 17792–17796 and 29427. These may or may not be by Gibbons. The more important manuscript collections are rich in copies of his church compositions, which consist of two sets of 'preces,' two full services in F and D minor respectively, and some twenty-one anthems preserved entire. Another, 'I am the Resurrection and the Life,' is in the incomplete set of part-books (Add. MSS. 29366–8). The complete sacred compositions were edited with great care and skill by the late Sir F. A. Gore Ouseley (London, 1873). In a copy of some of the anthems (Addit. MS. 31821) sundry pieces of information, apparently given on the authority of Dr. Philip Hayes, are noted in pencil, concerning the circumstances under which the anthems were written. Thus 'Blessed are all they' is 'a wedding anthem made for my Lord of Somerset;' 'Great King of Gods' was 'made for the King's being in Scotland, 1617;' and 'This is the record of John' was 'made for Laud, the president of John's, Oxford, for John Baptist's Day.' The second of these entries may explain one of the titles given in Grove's 'Dictionary,' 'Fancies and Songs made at K. James I's being in Scotland,' of which no trace is to be found. Another title there given, 'A Song for Prince Charles for 5 voices with wind instruments,' is also not forthcoming. As Laud was president of St. John's College from 1611 to 1621, we have a limit of time for the composition of one of the most interesting of Gibbons's works, which shows to what an extent the new methods of music which came into vogue at the beginning of the century had been assimilated by one who excelled most of his contemporaries in the older polyphonic style. One other anthem is dated by a manuscript copy in the library of St. George's Chapel, Windsor. It is there recorded that the anthem 'Behold, Thou hast made my days,' was composed at the request of Anthony Maxey, dean of Windsor, and was performed at his funeral. In an autograph copy of the same work in the library of Christ Church, Oxford, it is stated to have been 'Composed at the entreaty of Dr. Maxey, Dean of Windsor, the same day se'nnight before his death.' Dean Maxey was succeeded on 11 May 1618 by De Dominis [q. v.], archbishop of Spalatro. Besides the anthems the sacred works comprise two hymns for four and five voices respectively, contributed to Sir William Leighton's 'Teares and Lamentacions,' published 1614. Only four of the sixteen hymn tunes contained in George Wither's 'Hymns and Songs of the Church' (1623, reprinted by J. Russell Smith in 1856) are contained in Ouseley's edition. The tunes are in two parts, and are studiedly simple in style ; in his dedication to the king Wither says of Gibbons, 'He hath chosen to make his music agreeable to the matter, and what the common apprehension can best admit, rather than to the curious fancies of the time ; which path both of us could more easily have trodden.' Two slight references to Gibbons before this date may be mentioned, On 17 July 1615 two bonds of the value of 150*l.*, forfeited by one Lawrence Brewster of Gloucester and his sureties for his non-appearance before the high commission court at Lambeth, were granted to Gibbons (*State Papers*; *Coll. Sign-Manuals*, James I, vol. v. No. 38). On St. Peter's day 1620 he had a dispute with one Eveseed, a gentleman of the Chapel Royal, when the latter 'did violently and sodenly without cause runne uppon Mr. Gibbons, took him up and threw him doune upon a standard wherby he receaved such hurt that he is not yett recovered of the same, and withall he tare the band from his neck to his prejudice and disgrace' (*Old Cheque Book*, ed. Rimbault, p. 102). It is proved beyond any doubt that Gibbons accumulated the degrees of bachelor and doctor of music at Oxford, on 17 or 18 May 1622, on the occasion of the foundation of the history professorship by Camden, who requested the university to confer the musical degrees upon his friend Heather, the first professor, and Gibbons. Wood failed to find the official record of the degree in Gibbons's case, but a letter from Dr. Piers to Camden, quoted in Hawkins's 'History' (ed. 1853, p. 572 *n.*), establishes the matter. It is also certain that Gibbons's anthem 'O clap your hands' served as Heather's exercise for the degree. A copy bearing the unequivocal inscription 'Dr. Heather's Commencement song, compos'd by Dr. Orlando Gibbons,' was sold at Gostling's sale, and is now in the possession of Mr. W. H. Cummings. In 1623 the composer was rated as residing in the Woolstaple, Westminster (where Bridge Street now stands) (*Books of St. Margaret's, Westminster*, quoted in *Notes and Queries*, 3rd ser. x. 182). In 1625, on the occasion of the reception of Henrietta Maria by Charles I, Gibbons was commissioned to compose the music for the ceremony, and was commanded to be present at Canterbury. Here, on 5 June, Whitsunday, he died of a kind of apoplectic seizure, and was buried in the cathedral. His widow erected a monument over his tomb with a Latin inscription, under a bust of the composer, surmounted by his arms. He is said in it to have died 'accito ictuque heu Sanguinis Crudo.' There was at the time some suspicion that Gibbons had died of the plague, and the tradition that small-pox was the cause seems to have been early circulated. It is actually inserted in all the translations of the inscription, and has been accepted by all musical historians as a satisfactory equivalent of the Latin words; but fortunately in November 1885 Mr. W. Barclay Squire communicated to the 'Athenæum' (No. 3029) a letter discovered by him among the State Papers from Sir Albertus Morton to his fellow secretary of state, Lord Edward Conway, and it is endorsed 'June 6, 1625. Mr. Secretarie Morton Touchinge the musitian that dyed at Canterburie and suggested to have the plague.' The writer encloses a medical certificate of death signed by Drs. Poe and Domingo, stating that his sickness was at first 'lethargicall,' that subsequently convulsions came on, and he 'then grew apoplecticall and so died.' His widow, Elizabeth, was the daughter of John Patten of Westminster, yeoman of the vestry of the Royal Chapel. Between 1607 and 1623 she bore him seven children, of whom one only, Christopher [q. v.], attained distinction in music. She outlived him only by a year, her will being proved 30 July 1626. A portrait of the composer by an unknown artist is in the Music School at Oxford. It is a copy from a lost original once in the possession of a Mrs. Fussell.

[Authorities and documents quoted above; Grove's Dict. i. 594, iv. 310, 312, 313, 647; Hawkins's Hist. pp. 572-3; Chester's Westminster Abbey Registers, p. 190; Cooper's Annals of the University and Town of Cambridge, iii. 176; Ouseley's Preface to complete Sacred Works of Gibbons, 1873; Old Cheque Book of the Chapel Royal; Catalogues of Christ Church and Music School Libraries, Oxford, and Fitzwilliam Museum, Cambridge; Wood's Fasti, i. 406 n.; Brit. Mus. Addit. MSS. 17840, 17841, 17792-6, 29289, 29366-8, 29372-7, 29430, 30933, 31281, 31403-5, 31415, 31443, 31460, 31462, &c.; Wither's Hymns and Songs of the Church, reprint of 1856 (the British Museum copy of the 1623 edition wants the dedication, in which Gibbons's name appears); Athenæum, No. 3029; Mus. Ant. Soc. reprint of Gibbons's Madrigals and Fantasies, pref. &c. Musical Society, No. 1, 1886; Dart's Hist. of Canterbury, pp. 51, 52.]
J. A. F. M.

GIBBONS, RICHARD (1550?–1632), jesuit, younger brother of Father John Gibbons [q. v.], was born at Winchester about 1550, and, after making his lower studies in England, went through a two years' course of philosophy at Louvain and in the German College at Rome. He entered the Society of Jesus on 1 Sept. 1572. He again studied philosophy for three years, and was professor of mathematics and philosophy for thirteen years, partly in Rome and partly in France. He was also a professor of canon law and Hebrew for some time in Italy, Spain, and Portugal, besides holding a like office at Tournay, Toulouse, Douay, and Louvain, where he was also prefect of studies. For a while he was preacher in the jesuit college at St. Omer. He was professed of the four vows in the college of Coimbra in Portugal in 1591. His latter years were spent at Douay, where he was occupied in printiing ancient manuscripts, and in translating, editing, and annotating various learned works. He died at Douay on 11 June (O.S.) 1632.

He published: 1. 'A Spiritual Doctrine, conteining a Rule to Live Wel, with divers Praiers and Meditations,' from the Spanish of Luis de Granada, Louvain, 1599, 12mo, dedicated to Sir William Stanley, 'coronel' of the English regiment. 2. 'Francisci Toleti . . . Cardinalis de Instructione Sacerdotum et peccatis mortalibus libri VIII. Quibus accessit . . . Martini Fornarii de Ordine Tractatus,' edited by Gibbons, Douay, 1608, 8vo. 3. 'Meditations uppon the Mysteries of our Holy Faith, with the Practise of Mental Praier touching the same,' from the Spanish of Luis de la Puente, 2 parts [Douay?], 1610. John Heigham is credited with a similar translation, St. Omer, 1619, reprinted 1852 (GILLOW, Dict. of the English Catholics, iii. 258). 4. 'Joannis Nider . . . Præceptorium: sive orthodoxa et accurata Decalogi explicatio,' edited by Gibbons, Douay, 1611, 8vo. 5. An edition of the 'Sermones funebres' of Joannes de Sancto Germiniano, 8vo; Douay, 1611, 12mo; Antwerp, 1611 and 1630, 8vo. 6. 'Francisci Riberæ . . . in librum duodecim Prophetarum commentarii . . . ab infinitis mendis typographicis expurgati, et ubique dictionibus Hebraicis et Chaldaicis in Latinam prolationem permutatis lucidati,' Douay, 1612, fol. 7. 'Ludovici de Ponte Meditationum de Vita et Passione Christi libri II. ex Hispanico in Latinum versi,' Cologne, 1612, 12mo. 8. 'Divi Amedei . . . Episcopi Lausaniæ de Maria Virginea Matre Homiliæ,' St. Omer, 1613, 12mo. 9. 'The First Part of the Meditations of the Passion and Resurrection of Christ our Saviour' [1614?], 12mo, from the Latin of Father Vincent Bruno. 10. 'Historia admiranda de Jesu Christi stigmatibus ab Alphonso Paleato Archiepisc. Bononiensi explicata,'

&c., 2 vols. Douay, 1616, 4to. 11. 'Opera Divi Ælredi Rhievallensis . . . ex vetustis MSS. nunc primum in lucem producta,' Douay, 1616 and 1631, 4to; Douay and Paris, 1654, 4to. 12. 'Beati Gosvini Vita celeberrimi Aquicinctensis Monasterii Abbatis septimi, a duobus diversis ejusdem Cœnobii Monachis separatim exarata, e veteribus MSS. nunc primum edita,' Douay, 1620, 12mo. 13. 'Historia Anglicana Ecclesiastica a primis gentis susceptæ fidei incunabulis ad nostra fere tempora deducta . . . auctore Nicholao Harpsfeldio Archidiacono Cantuariensi . . . nunc primum in lucem producta,' Douay, 1622, fol. 14. 'Christian Doctrine,' from the Italian of Cardinal Bellarmine. 15. 'Opuscula F. Androtii, S.J.'

[De Backer's Bibl. des Écrivains de la Compagnie de Jésus (1869), col. 2116; Dodd's Church Hist. iii. 113; Duthilloeul's Bibl. Douaisienne (1842), Nos. 265, 596, 600, 620, 1583; Foley's Records, iv. 484, vi. 528, vii. 299; Gillow's Bibl. Dict. ii. 439; More's Hist. Missionis Anglic. Soc. Jesu, p. 20; Oliver's Catholic Religion in Cornwall, p. 312; Oliver's Jesuit Collections, p. 104; Southwell's Bibl. Scriptorum Soc. Jesu, p. 718.]
T. C.

GIBBONS, THOMAS (1720–1785), dissenting minister and miscellaneous writer, was the son of Thomas Gibbons, who was at one time minister of a dissenting congregation at Olney in Buckinghamshire, and afterwards of a congregation at Royston in Hertfordshire. He was born at Reak, Swaffham Prior, near Cambridge, on 31 May 1720, and received the early part of his education at various schools in Cambridgeshire. When about fifteen years of age he was sent to Dr. Taylor's academy in Deptford, and afterwards to that of John Eames [q. v.] in Moorfields. In 1742 he was appointed assistant to the Rev. Thomas Bures, minister of the Silver Street presbyterian congregation, and in the next year he was chosen minister of the independent congregation of Haberdashers' Hall. In 1754 he was elected one of the three tutors of the Mile End academy, where he gave instruction in logic, metaphysics, ethics, and rhetoric, till the end of his life. He was chosen Sunday evening lecturer in the Monkwell Street meeting-house in 1759. He received the degree of M.A. from New Jersey in 1760, and that of D.D. from Aberdeen in 1764. He died in the Hoxton Square coffee-house, 22 Feb. 1785.

A list of between forty and fifty works by him may be found in the 'Protestant Dissenters' Magazine,' ii. 492, 493, and in Wilson's 'Dissenting Churches,' iii. 181, 182. The following appear to have been the chief of them: 1. 'Juvenilia; poems on various subjects of devotion and virtue,' 8vo, 1750. 2. 'Rhetoric,' 8vo, 1767. 3. 'Hymns adapted to Divine Worship,' 12mo, 1769. 4. 'The Christian Minister, in three Poetic Epistles,' 8vo, 1772. 5. 'Female Worthies,' 2 vols. 8vo, 1777. 6. 'Memoirs of the Rev. Isaac Watts, D.D.,' 8vo, 1780. 7. 'Sermons on evangelical and practical subjects,' 3 vols. 8vo, 1787. His favourite form of composition seems to have consisted in elegies on the death of his friends and others. For this, and for the want of poetical power which he showed in all his efforts, he was ridiculed in 'An Epistle to the Rev. Mr. Tho. G-bb-ns on his Juvenilia,' 1750. He was also satirised by Robert Sanders in 'Gaffer Greybeard' as 'Dr. Hymnmaker' (NICHOLS, Lit. Anecd. ii. 730). Dr. Johnson enjoyed his society (BOSWELL, Johnson, 3 June 1781, 17 May 1784).

[Benj. Davies's Israel's Testament (funeral sermon on Gibbons), 1785, pp. 19–20 note; Protestant Dissenters' Magazine, ii. 489–93; Wilson's Dissenting Churches, iii. 178–83; Gent. Mag. xxxix. 261, lv. pt. ii. p. 159.] E. C-N.

GIBBONS, WILLIAM, M.D. (1649–1728), physician, born at Wolverhampton 25 Sept. 1649, was the son of John Gibbons of that town. From Merchant Taylors' School he went to St. John's College, Oxford, graduating B.A. in 1672, M.B. in 1675, and M.D. in 1683. He practised as a physician in London, joined the College of Physicians in 1691, became fellow in 1692, and censor in 1716. He is not remembered by any writings, but chiefly as the Mirmillo of the 'Dispensary' of Sir Samuel Garth [q. v.] He was one of the few college fellows who opposed the project of dispensaries for the poor, and so incurred the satire of Garth, who makes him say:

While others meanly asked whole months to slay, I oft despatched the patient in a day.

He is described by a contemporary (NICHOLS, Lit. Illustr. ii. 801) as 'pretty old Dr. Gibbons,' and as taking his fees with alacrity. The Harveian oration of the year following his death (1729) ascribes to him erudition, honesty, candour, love of letters, piety, benevolence, and other Christian virtues. According to Wadd (Mems., Maxims, and Memoirs, p. 148), the credit of making mahogany fashionable belongs to Gibbons. His brother, a West Indian shipmaster, brought home some of that wood as ballast, and gave it to the doctor, who was building a house. The carpenters finding it too hard for their tools, it was thrown aside; but some of it was afterwards used to make a candle-box, which looked so well that a bureau of the same wood was taken in hand. When finished and polished, the bureau was so pleasing that it became an object of admiration to visitors, among others the Duchess of Buckingham, who had one made like it and so brought the wood into fashion. Gibbons left no writings. He died on 25 March 1728. He was a liberal benefactor to Wolverhampton, his native place. There is a portrait of him in St. John's College, Oxford.

[Munk's Coll. of Phys.; Wadd's Mems. p. 148; Robinson's Merchant Taylors' School Reg. i. 268.]

C. C.

GIBBS, MRS. (*fl.* 1783–1844), actress, born about 1770, was the daughter of Logan, an Irishman, somehow 'connected with' some of the country theatres. John Palmer, her godfather, brought her on the stage at the Haymarket, where, 18 June 1783, she made her first appearance as Sally in 'Man and Wife,' by George Colman the elder. Next day, Oxberry, in his notice of Mrs. Gibbs, remarks, George Colman, subsequently her 'chere ami' (*sic*), produced his first piece, 'Two to One.' But 'Two to One' was produced 19 June 1784. After one season at the Haymarket, Miss Logan accompanied Palmer in his unfortunate expedition to the Royalty Theatre in Wellclose Square. At the opening of the house on 20 June 1787, as Mrs. Gibbs, she played Biddy in Garrick's 'Miss in her Teens.' Nothing is known of her husband, Gibbs. She played at the Royalty the principal characters in the serious pantomimes, given to evade the privileges of the patent houses. While at this house Mrs. Gibbs came on the stage as the Comic Muse through a trap, and gave an imitation of Delpini. Her support of Palmer offended the managers, by whom she was practically boycotted. On 15 June 1793 she played, at the Haymarket, Bridget in the 'Chapter of Accidents,' by Miss Lee. This was announced as her first appearance at the theatre. Oxberry says she had previously played at both Drury Lane and Covent Garden. A close intimacy sprang up between George Colman the younger [q. v.] and Mrs. Gibbs, which ultimately resulted in marriage. For her Colman is said to have written expressly the parts of Cicely in the 'Heir-at-Law,' Haymarket, 15 July 1797; Annette in 'Blue Devils,' Covent Garden, 24 April 1798; Grace Gaylove in the 'Review,' Haymarket, 2 Sept. 1800; and Mary in 'John Bull,' Covent Garden, 5 March 1803. In these characters, and in others such as Katherine in 'Katherine and Petruchio,' and Miss Hardcastle in 'She stoops to conquer,' she obtained reputation as a second Mrs. Jordan. She made occasional appearances at Drury Lane and Covent

Garden, but the Haymarket remained her home. Here in late years she played parts such as Mrs. Candour and Miss Sterling ('Clandestine Marriage'). Oxberry speaks of her as possessing genius, talent, and industry, and adds that her Curiosa in the 'Cabinet' is one of the richest specimens of comic acting extant. In such parts as Nell in the 'Devil to Pay' she rivalled Mrs. Davison [q. v.] or Fanny Kelly, though surpassing both in vivacity and in the 'fullness and jollity' of her voice. She was an admirable laugher, and, though not much of a singer, had a peculiarly pleasing voice. She had a plump figure, a light complexion, and blue eyes, on the beauty of which Gilliland and Oxberry dwell. The 'Monthly Mirror' says (August 1800) 'that after the secession of Mrs. Stephen Kemble she had deservedly occupied all characters of tender simplicity and unaffected elegance.' She won the high esteem of her contemporaries, and the stories told concerning her are mostly to her credit. She appears to have been generous in disposition, and to have befriended her fellow-actresses. After Colman's death in 1836 she lived in retirement in Brighton, and her death seems to have passed unchronicled. She is included among actresses still living in Mrs. Cornwell Baron Wilson's 'Our Actresses,' 1844.

[Genest's Account of the English Stage; Oxberry's Dramatic Biography, vol. iv.; Monthly Mirror, various years; Peake's Memoirs of the Colman Family; Biography of the British Stage, 1824; New Monthly Magazine, various years; The Drama, or Theatrical Pocket Magazine; Gilliland's Dramatic Mirror.]

J. K.

GIBBS, JAMES, M.D. (*d.* 1724), physician and poet, son of James Gibbs, vicar of Gorran in Cornwall, was a student of Exeter College, Oxford. In a letter to Archbishop Tenison, preserved among the manuscripts in Lambeth Library, he solicits Tenison's 'favour and assistance' in promoting 'a new metrical version of the Psalms.' The letter is undated, but in 1701 the first fifteen of the psalms were published in London, and a second edition followed in 1712. A copy of the latter was discovered in Swift's library, containing some severe marginal criticism by the dean. Gibbs died at Tregony, Cornwall, in 1724.

He published: 1. 'A Consolatory Poem, humbly addressed to Her Royal Highness, Upon the much lamented death of His Most Illustrious Highness, William Duke of Gloucester,' London, 1700, fol. 2. The First Fifteen Psalms of David, translated into Lyric Verse, propos'd as an essay, supplying the Perspicuity and Coherence according to the

Modern Art of Poetry . . . With a Preface containing some observations of the great and general Defectiveness of former Versions in Greek, Latin, and English,' London, 1701, 4to. The title-page of the second edition (1712) states that 'some of the lords spiritual freely proposed to recommend' it to 'parliament and convocation.' 3. 'Observations of various eminent cures of scrophulous distempers, commonly called the King's Evil, such as tumours, ulcers, cariosity of bones, blindness, and consumptions . . . to which is added An Essay concerning the animal spirits and the cure of convulsions. . . .' Exeter, 1712, sm. 4to. It contains an essay written in vindication of a trial at Launceston in 1710 concerning the cure of a lad from Plymouth. Some of the cases relate to persons living at Tregony, Gorran, and other places in Cornwall. In manuscript are: 'Carmen in honorem principis Poetarum, doct. Gibbesii, cum diploma a Cæsarea Majestate in Musarum templo concessum est,' Worcester Coll. MS. No. 58, pp. 99–101; 'Proposal of J. Gibbs to the Archbishop of Canterbury for a New Translation of the Psalms, with a printed translation of the first and second Psalm into English verse,' Lambeth MS. 937, art. 24, 25.

[Boase and Courtney's Bibl. Cornub. i. 171–2, iii. 1193; Nichols's Lit. Anecd. i. 286; works of Swift, 1843, ii. 369–72.]   W. F. W. S.

GIBBS, JAMES (1682–1754), architect, son of Peter Gibbs, a Roman catholic merchant, and Isabel Farquhar, his second wife, was born 23 Dec. 1682, at his father's house of Footdeesmire, in the Links of Aberdeen. A son by the first wife was the only other surviving child. Gibbs was educated at the grammar school and the Marischal College of Aberdeen, where he took the degree of M.A. His father and mother both dying, he studied for some time in Aberdeen, living with his aunt, Elspeth Farquhar, and her husband, Peter Morison. He afterwards resolved to seek his fortune abroad, and in Holland made the acquaintance of John Erskine, eleventh earl of Mar [q. v.] Mar supplied him with letters and money, enabling him to travel to Rome and study architecture under Carolo Fontana, surveyor-general to Pope Clement XI, and architect to St. Peter's. The illness of his only brother induced him to return in 1709. His brother was already dead, and, after settling his affairs in Scotland, he went to London, where he was patronised by Mar and by John, second duke of Argyll. The first public building upon which he was employed after his arrival from Italy was St. Mary-le-Strand, one of fifty new churches. The foundation-stone was laid

15 Feb. 1714, and the building consecrated 1 Jan. 1723. The steeple was substituted for a campanile, when a column with a statue of Queen Anne was abandoned in consequence of her death. The base of the campanile having been already built, he was obliged to make the plan of the steeple oblong instead of square. The consequent shallowness of the steeple, as seen from the north or south side, is the only serious defect in the design of this building. Although one of Gibbs's very finest works, it can scarcely be called truly distinctive of him, as its delicate beauty suggests the influence of Wren. In 1719 Gibbs added the steeple and the two upper stages to the tower of Wren's church of St. Clement Danes in the Strand. His next church was 'Marybone Chapel,' better known as St. Peter's, Vere Street, begun in 1721 by Harley, earl of Oxford. He designed about this time the monument in Westminster Abbey to Matthew Prior, who died 18 Sept. 1721. In the following year was commenced the most famous of his buildings, St. Martin-in-the-Fields. Gibbs prepared several plans, and among them 'two Designs made for a Round Church, which were approved by the Commissioners, but were laid aside on account of the expensiveness of executing them, though they were more capacious and convenient than what they pitch'd upon.' The first stone was laid on 19 March 1722, and the church consecrated in 1726. The east end of the interior of this church shows very markedly the influence of his Roman studies. In June 1722 he began the Senate House at Cambridge. This was but one wing in a large scheme never completed. A wing to the south was to have contained 'the consistory and Register office,' and one on the west 'the Royal Library.' Sir James Burrough [q. v.] had some share in the original design. The large church of Allhallows in Derby, his next undertaking, was commenced in 1723, and finished in 1725. The fifteenth-century tower remains, joined to Gibbs's work. In 1723 was erected the monument to John Holles, duke of Newcastle, in Westminster Abbey, executed, from Gibbs's designs, by Francis Bird [q. v.], and the most sumptuous of all the many monuments designed by him. The other monuments in the abbey by Gibbs are those to Mrs. Katherina Bovey, 1727; John Smith, 1718; John Freind, M.D., 1728; the monument erected in 1723 by James, marquis of Annandale, to his mother and younger brother; and the monument to Ben Jonson in Poets' Corner. King's College, Cambridge, was another of his designs commenced about this time. The west side of the great quadrangle was begun in 1724, and

was still unfinished in 1731 owing to the poverty of the college. It was completed in 1749. Gibbs intended to erect a similar block on the site now occupied by the screen, and a hall and provost's lodge on the south side.

In 1728 he published 'A Book of Architecture, containing Designs of Buildings and Ornament.' It contains drawings for all the buildings hitherto erected by him, with some alternative designs. His next important work was the quadrangle of St. Bartholomew's Hospital, begun in 1730, for which Gibbs gave all his drawings, time, and attendance 'out of Charity to ye poor.' He published in 1732 his 'Rules for Drawing the several Parts of Architecture in a More exact and easy manner than has been hitherto practised, by which all Fractions, in dividing the principal Numbers and their Parts, are avoided.' On 11 June 1737 were laid the foundations of his greatest work, the Radcliffe Library at Oxford. Nicholas Hawkesmore had made several designs for this library in 1713, and Gibbs himself made more than one design. In 1747, the year of its completion, he published the full drawings for this library in a thin folio, entitled 'Bibliotheca Radcliviana: or, a short description of the Radcliffe Library at Oxford.' Towards the end of his life Gibbs was afflicted with the stone, and went to Spa in 1749. It was probably to soothe his tedium that he now made his well-written translation of the 'De rebus Emanuelis' of Osorio da Fonseca, published in 1752, and entitled 'The History of the Portuguese during the Reign of Emmanuel. Written originally in Latin by Jerome Osorio, Bishop of Sylvis.' His last architectural work seems to have been the church of St. Nicholas, Aberdeen. Some years before his death he sent to the magistrates of Aberdeen, as a testimony of his regard for his native place, a plan for the new fabric, which was begun in 1752. This church was still unfinished when he died, 5 Aug. 1754, aged 71. He was buried, by his own wish, within the old church, now the parish chapel, of Marylebone, where, on the north wall below the gallery, is yet remaining a simple marble tablet to his memory. He died a bachelor, and with few relations; and by his will, dated 9 May 1754, left the bulk of his fortune, valued at 14,000l. or 15,000l., to the son of his old patron, the Earl of Mar, with bequests to some other friends, to St. Bartholomew's and the Foundling Hospitals, and his printed books, drawings, &c., to the Radcliffe Library. These books and drawings are now preserved in the museum at Oxford. The books include some fine editions of the classics and many early Italian works on architecture. There are also many of his designs. Gibbs was a Roman catholic, like his father, but 'justly esteemed by men of all persuasions.' His portraits and busts indicate thoughtfulness, penetration, and self-control, but scarcely great power. His architecture shows fine discernment rather than fine invention. His reverence for classic architecture led him to an excessive respect for tradition, but his work is lifted far above the level of mere imitation, and has a distinctive style of its own. He never fell into the vagaries of some of his contemporaries, and made no attempt at Gothic. His good taste may be attributed to his Italian training, which also narrowed his art to the mere consideration of fine composition and proportion. Although, as Walpole says, his designs want the harmonious simplicity of the greatest masters of classic architecture, he deserves higher praise than Walpole gave, and is now regarded as perhaps the most considerable master of English architecture since Wren.

There are several engraved portraits of him; the most important are by M'Ardell after Hogarth, M'Ardell after S. Williams, and P. Pelham after H. Hysing. There are also busts of him at the Radcliffe Library, Oxford, and in the church of St. Martin-in-the-Fields, London.

['A short Accompt of Mr. James Gibbs, Architect,' contained in a manuscript volume in the Soane Museum, entitled 'A few short Cursory Remarks on some of the finest Antient and Modern Buildings in Rome, and other parts of Italy, by Mr. Gibbs,' &c.; The Scots Magazine, September 1760; A Book of Architecture, by James Gibbs, 1728; Wornum's edition of Walpole's Anecdotes of Painting in England, 1849; Willis and Clark's Architectural History of Cambridge, i. 560, iii. 445, 535-6.]

GIBBS, JOSEPH (1700?-1788), organist, published about 1740 'Eight Solos for a Violin, with a Thorough Bass for the Harpsichord or Bass Violin. London. Composed by Joseph Gibbs of Dedham in Essex, dedicated to Sir Joseph Hankey,' &c., and subscribed for largely by organists and others. Gibbs became organist at the church of St. Mary-at-Tower, Ipswich, about 1748, and displayed so much zeal and talent in that capacity, and in his compositions, that on his death, after forty years' service, in December 1788, he was honoured by his fellow-townsmen with a public funeral, and buried in front of the organ. The church has since undergone a thorough restoration, which has obliterated Gibbs's grave.

[Gent. Mag. lviii. pt. ii. 1130.] L. M. M.

GIBBS, PHILIP (fl. 1740), dissenting minister and stenographer, was appointed in 1715 assistant to the Rev. Robert Bragge, at the independent chapel in Paved Alley, Lime Street, London. He was chosen one of the first of Coward's Friday evening lecturers at the meeting-house in Little St. Helen's, Bishopsgate. In 1729 he removed from Lime Street to Hackney, where he was joint pastor with the Rev. John Barker. He had avowed himself a Calvinist, but he eventually adopted unitarian opinions, and was in consequence dismissed from his ministry in 1737.

His works are: 1. 'Christ the Christian's Propitiation and Advocate.' In 'Twelve Sermons preach'd at Mr. Coward's Lecture,' London, 1729, p. 438. 2. 'An Historical Account of Compendious and Swift Writing,' London, 1736, 8vo; dedicated to John Jacob. This is the earliest history of shorthand. It gives an account of all the English systems from Timothy Bright [q.v.] to James Weston, and contains information not to be found elsewhere. 3. 'An Essay towards a farther Improvement of Short-Hand,' London, 1736, 8vo, pp. 56, engraved throughout. Gibbs's system of stenography is clumsy and complicated, and greatly inferior to that of William Mason, published in 1707. 4. 'A Letter to the Congregation of Protestant Dissenters at Hackney, amongst whom the Author now stately ministers. With a postscript to all others to whom he has formerly preach'd,' London, 1737, 8vo (three editions). 5. 'Explications and Defences of P. Gibbs's Letter to the Congregation of Protestant Dissenters meeting in Mare Street, Hackney,' London, 1740, 8vo. This and the preceding work relate to the author's conversion to unitarianism. 6. A pamphlet on the controversy between the rival shorthand inventors, Byrom, Weston, and Macaulay. About 1740.

[Byrom's Journal, ii. 3; Wilson's Dissenting Churches, i. 174, 249, ii. 42; Lewis's Hist. of Shorthand, pp. 109; Levy's Hist. of Short-hand Writing, p. 80; Shorthand (a magazine), i. 80; Westby-Gibson's Bibl. of Shorthand, p. 72; Cat. of Dr. Williams's Library, ii. 158, iii. 104.]
T. C.

GIBBS, SIR SAMUEL (d. 1815), major-general, was appointed an ensign in the 102nd foot in October 1783. He removed in 1788 to the 60th, with which he served in Upper Canada, until he was promoted in 1792 to a lieutenancy in the 11th. He joined this regiment at Gibraltar, and returned with it to England in February 1793, when he was appointed aide-de-camp to Lieutenant-general James Grant. He served with the 11th in Corsica, and on board Lord Hood's fleet in the Mediterranean from the spring of 1794 till the end of 1795, when he obtained a company. After acting for some months as captain and adjutant in the garrison at Gi-

braltar, he returned to England in April 1796, and was reappointed to his former position of aide-de-camp. In May 1798 he accompanied the expedition which was sent under the command of Sir Eyre Coote (1762–1824?) [q. v.] to cut the sluices at Ostend, and was taken prisoner, but included in the exchange of prisoners which took place the following Christmas. In 1799 he succeeded to the rank of major, and accompanied the 11th to the West Indies, where he commanded it in an attack on St. Martin's in the expedition against the Danish and Swedish islands, and in the island of Martinique. In 1802 he was promoted lieutenant-colonel of the 10th West India regiment, and returned to England on the declaration of peace in the same year. He was subsequently appointed to the 59th foot, which he commanded in the expedition to the Cape of Good Hope in 1805 and 1806. From the Cape he proceeded to India, and commanded his regiment in the Travancore war of 1808–9. On 25 July 1810 he received the brevet rank of colonel, and in March 1811 accompanied the expedition under Sir Samuel Auchmuty, which was sent by Lord Minto to conquer Java from the Dutch. He greatly distinguished himself in this expedition, and is repeatedly mentioned in the despatches of Sir Samuel Auchmuty to Lord Minto. On 26 Aug. he supported, with the 59th and the 4th battalion of Bengal volunteers, the attack made by Colonel Gillespie on Fort Corselis, and took one of the redoubts of this stronghold by storm; and on 16 Sept. he led the final attack against the Dutch general Janssens, which resulted in the surrender of the island. Shortly afterwards Gibbs left India, and in 1812 was appointed to the command of the two British regiments stationed with the allied forces at Stralsund. In the following year he served in Holland, and on 4 June was appointed major-general. In the autumn of 1814 he was appointed second in command under Sir E. Pakenham of the expedition sent out to succour the British forces in the United States. This expedition landed on Christmas day, and on 26 Dec. began the operations which preceded the attack on New Orleans on 8 Jan. 1815. In this attack Gibbs, who commanded one of the main columns, was severely wounded, and died on the following day. By a proclamation of the prince regent on 2 Jan. 1815 he was made a knight commander of the Bath.

[Roy. Mil. Cal.; British Campaign at Washington and New Orleans, by an Officer, London, 1821; Gent. Mag.; Thornton's Hist. of India.]
E. J. R.

GIBBS, Sir VICARY (1751–1820), judge, was the second son of George Abraham Gibbs, chief surgeon to the hospital at Exeter, by his wife, Anne, daughter of Anthony Vicary of the same city. He was born in the Cathedral Close at Exeter on 27 Oct. 1751, and was sent to Eton, where he gained much distinction by his compositions in Latin verse, a specimen of which will be found in the 'Musæ Etonenses,' 1795, i. 295–6. In 1770 he was elected a scholar of King's College, Cambridge, of which he afterwards became a fellow, and where he greatly distinguished himself as a Greek scholar. He was elected Craven university scholar in 1772, and graduated B.A. in 1775, and M.A. in 1778. Gibbs was admitted a member of Lincoln's Inn on 24 Aug. 1769. For some years he practised as a special pleader, and thus acquired by degrees a large connection. 'When the attornies,' he remarked, 'have no one else to go to, they come to me! other pleaders have the luck of getting some easy cases. I never remember having had a single one. They were all difficult, and had nothing short about them but the fees.' He was called to the bar in February 1783, and joined the western circuit. Ten years later he defended William Winterbotham, a baptist minister indicted for preaching two seditious sermons at Plymouth (HOWELL, State Trials, xxii. 823–908). He was appointed recorder of Bristol in February 1794, a post which he held until November 1817. In the autumn of 1794 Gibbs assisted Erskine in the defence of Thomas Hardy and Horne Tooke (ib. xxiv. 199–1408, xxv. 1–745), and it was owing to his forcible exposition of the law and his clear application of the facts, as well as to the marvellous eloquence of Erskine, that the prisoners were both acquitted. At the end of the trial Sir John Scott (afterwards Lord Eldon), then the attorney-general, sent the following note to Gibbs across the table: 'I say from my heart that you did yourself great credit as a good man, and great credit as an excellent citizen, not sacrificing any valuable public principle; I say from my judgment that no lawyer ever did himself more credit, or his client more service; so help me God!' Gibbs had now raised himself by his own sheer legal ability to the front rank of the profession, and at the end of the year received a silk gown. In the following year he was appointed solicitor-general to the Prince of Wales, and in 1799 was promoted to the post of attorney-general to his royal highness. In 1804 he became chief justice of Chester, and in December of that year was returned to parliament for the borough of Totnes. In February 1805 he accepted the office of solicitor-general in Pitt's

last administration, and was knighted on the 20th of the same month. Gibbs resigned office on Pitt's death in the following year. But on 7 April 1807 he was appointed attorney-general in the Duke of Portland's administration, and a few days after was returned to parliament for Great Bedwin. At the general election in May 1807 he was elected, after a very close contest, one of the members for the university of Cambridge. After holding the post of attorney-general for five years, he was made a serjeant-at-law on 29 May 1812, and appointed a puisne judge in the court of common pleas. On 8 Nov. 1813 Gibbs became lord chief baron in the place of Sir Archibald Macdonald, and was sworn a member of the privy council on the last day of the same month. Upon the resignation of Sir James Mansfield, Gibbs was finally promoted, on 24 Feb. 1814, to be the chief justice of the common pleas. After presiding over this court for more than four years he resigned, owing to ill-health, on 5 Nov. 1818. He died on 8 Feb. 1820 at his house in Russell Square, in his sixty-ninth year, and was buried in the family vault at Hayes, Kent, where a monument was erected to his memory, the inscription being written by his friend, Lord Stowell.

Gibbs was a small man, not more than five feet four inches in height, and of a meagre frame. His merits as a skilful special pleader and an acute and learned lawyer have been universally acknowledged. He was wholly destitute of humour, and possessed of so caustic and bitter a manner that he acquired the name of 'Vinegar Gibbs.' Confident of his own legal strength, he was equally uncivil and outspoken to his own clients, and once gave his opinion of a proposed defence in these words: 'The defence is good in law, but the person who suggested it ought to be hanged.' Though somewhat narrow-minded and impatient on the bench, Gibbs was a thoroughly conscientious judge, and Taunton's 'Reports' bear record to the accuracy and extent of his legal knowledge. In politics Gibbs was a strong and decided tory. As a parliamentary speaker he met with little success, and confined himself entirely to legal topics. His first reported speech in the House of Commons was made on 11 March 1805 (Parliamentary Debates, iii. 850–3), and the most important was that delivered by him in the defence of the Duke of York on 9 March 1809 (ib. xiii. 240–65). As attorney-general he waged incessant war against the press, and between 1808 and 1810 no less than forty-two ex officio informations were filed. Cobbett was convicted for an article in the 'Register,' while in 1811 the Hunts and Perry and Lambert were acquitted of the charges brought against them, arising out of articles which had appeared in the 'Examiner' and the 'Morning Chronicle' respectively. In 1811 Lord Holland in the House of Lords and Lord Folkestone in the House of Commons drew attention to the extraordinary increase in the numbers of these prosecutions, and Gibbs made a long speech in his own defence, declaring that 'it would be found that every prosecution of that nature had been conducted with the greatest lenity' (*ib.* xix. 129–74, 548–612). The statute passed at his instigation authorising the arrest of any person who should be prosecuted by indictment or information in the king's bench (48 Geo. III, c. 58), was of so oppressive a nature that it was never put into force. Gibbs was elected a bencher of Lincoln's Inn in Easter term 1795, and acted as treasurer of that society in 1805. He married, in June 1784, Frances Cerjat Kenneth, daughter of Major William Mackenzie, a sister of Francis, lord Seaforth, by whom he had an only child, Maria Elizabeth, who married General Sir Andrew Pilkington, K.C.B. Lady Gibbs survived her husband many years, and died at Hayes on 1 May 1843, aged 88. His portrait by William Owen, R.A., is in the possession of his granddaughter, Mrs. Burrell Hayley of Catsfield, Sussex. It has been engraved by S. W. Reynolds and T. Lupton, and a replica of the picture is preserved at Eton College. Mrs. Hayley has another portrait of Gibbs by Mrs. Hoare of Bath, and a third by her brother, Mr. Prince Hoare, is in the possession of Mr. H. Hucks Gibbs of Aldenham House, near Elstree. Gibbs's speeches in the defence of Hardy and Tooke were published separately in 1795. A collection of his opinions, transcribed and selected from the numerous volumes of manuscripts which Gibbs left behind him, was many years ago presented to the Truro Law Library.

[Townsend's Lives of Twelve Eminent Judges (1846), i. 239–98; Foss's Judges of England (1864), viii. 287–94; Brougham's Statesmen of the Time of George III (1839), 1st ser. pp. 124–134; The Georgian Era (1833), ii. 318; Annual Register, 1820, chron. p. 163*; Gent. Mag. (1794) lxiv. pt. ii. 1061, (1820) xc. pt. i. 190, 275, 640, (1843) new ser. xix. 667, (1853) xxxix. 436; Burke's Landed Gentry (1879), i. 365; Grad. Cantabr. (1856), pp. 150, 445; Notes and Queries, 5th ser. v. 220, 275; Haydn's Book of Dignities (1851); Official Return of Lists of Members of Parliament, pt. ii. pp. 217, 236, 242; Lincoln's Inn Registers.]   G. F. R. B.

GIBSON, SIR ALEXANDER, LORD DURIE (*d.* 1644), Scottish judge, was son of George Gibson of Goldingstones, a clerk of session (*d.* 1590?), by his wife Mary Airth,

of the ancient family of Airth of that ilk in Stirlingshire. Thomas Gibson (1488–1513), member of an old family in Fife, had two sons, George and William [see GIBSON, WILLIAM, *fl.* 1540, lord of session]. George, the elder son of Thomas, was grandfather of George, father of Sir Alexander and of Archibald, who was bred to the church.

Alexander graduated M.A. at the university of Edinburgh, August 1588. On 14 Dec. 1594 he was admitted third clerk of session. James VI was present at his admission, and promised to reward the first and second clerks for their consent. On 10 July 1621 he was appointed a lord of session, when he took the title of Lord Durie, his clerkship being conferred on his son Alexander, to be held conjointly with himself. He is described in many charters as 'Alexander Gibson de Durie, Miles' before December 1628. In that year, according to Douglas, he was created a baronet of Nova Scotia, but does not appear to have actually assumed the dignity. In 1633 he was named a commissioner for reviewing the laws and collecting the local customs of the country. In 1640 he was elected a member of the committee of estates, and on 13 Nov. 1641 his appointment as judge was continued under a new commission to the court. While the office of president of the College of Justice continued elective, Durie was twice chosen head of the court, namely for the summer session on 1 June 1642, and for the winter session of 1643 (BRUNTON AND HAIG, *Senators of the College of Justice*, p. 264). He died at his house of Durie 10 June 1644, having from 11 July 1621, the day after his elevation to the bench, to 16 July 1642 preserved notes of the more important decisions. They are the earliest digested collection of decisions in the Scottish law, and are often referred to as 'Lord Durie's Practicks.' They were published (with his portrait prefixed) by his grandson, Sir Alexander Gibson (*d.* 1693) [q. v.], folio, Edinburgh, 1690. Durie married, 14 Jan. 1596, Margaret, the eldest daughter of Sir Thomas Craig [q. v.] of Riccarton, by whom he had three sons, Sir Alexander of Durie (*d.* 1656) [q. v.], Sir John of Pentland, and George of Balhousie. William Forbes, in the preface to his 'Journal of the Session' (1714), says that Durie 'was a man of a penetrating wit and clear judgment, polished and improved by much study and exercise.' He was constantly studying the civil law, as appears from the preface to Sir Thomas Craig's 'Jus Feudale,' and his abilities are further proved, according to Forbes, by his own book, by his frequent election to the vice-presidency of the court of session, to which no one else was appointed in his time, and by a story of his being kidnapped by a suitor, the Earl of Traquair, who thought him unfavourable in a cause before the court, and kept him for three months in a dark room in the country, when, the cause being decided, he was returned to the place where he had been seized. This story forms the subject of Scott's ballad of 'Christie's Will' [see ARMSTRONG, WILLIAM, 1602 ?–1658 ?] in the 'Minstrelsy of the Scottish Border.' Patrick Fraser Tytler, in the appendix to his 'Life of Sir Thomas Craig,' mentions another version of the kidnapping of Durie in 1604, when he was only a clerk of session. Mr. Tytler thinks this was another and different incident.

[Douglas's Baronage of Scotland, 1798; manuscript Scottish Charters; Tytler's Life of Sir Thomas Craig, Edinburgh, 1823; Anderson's Scottish Nation; family memoranda.]

R. H–R.

GIBSON, SIR ALEXANDER, LORD DURIE (d. 1656), Scottish judge, was eldest son of Sir Alexander Gibson (d. 1644) [q. v.], by Margaret, eldest daughter of Sir Thomas Craig of Riccarton. He was made a clerk of session conjointly with his father upon the latter's promotion to the bench in 1621. He opposed Charles I's policy respecting the service-book, protested against the royal proclamations of 1638, and petitioned the presbytery of Edinburgh against the bishops, November 1638. He was commissary-general of the forces raised to resist Charles I in 1640, but was afterwards knighted 15 March 1641, and made lord clerk register 13 Nov. 1641. He was made a commissioner of the exchequer 1 Feb. 1645, and sat on the committee of estates (1645–8). He became lord of session in 1646, when he took the title of Lord Durie. He was deprived of his offices in 1649 by the act of classes, after joining 'the engagement.' He was one of the Scottish commissioners chosen to attend the English parliament in 1652 and 1654. Lamont writes in 1650, 'Both Durie and his lady was debarred from the table because of their malignancie.' He died in June 1656. He was twice married; first to Marjory Hamilton, by whom he had one daughter; secondly to Cecilia, daughter of Thomas Fotheringham of Powrie, by whom he left Sir Alexander Gibson of Durie, knt., commissioner to parliament in England for Fife and Kinross 1656–9, and for Fife 1659, who died at Durie 6 Aug. 1661.

[Brunton and Haig's College of Justice, pp. 317–18; Lamont's Diary (Maitland Club, 1830); family memoranda.]

R. H–R.

GIBSON, SIR ALEXANDER (d. 1693), clerk of session, was eldest son of Sir John Gibson of Pentland and Addiston, co. Edinburgh (knighted circa 1647), by Jean, daughter and heiress of Alexander Hay of Kennet, Clackmannanshire. Sir John was second son of Sir Alexander Gibson, the first lord Durie (d. 1644) [q. v.] Douglas states that Sir John was a distinguished royalist, and was created a knight-banneret at the battle of Worcester, but there seems no other evidence than his assertion. Alexander was principal clerk of session and clerk to the privy council in Scotland. He was knighted in 1682, and died in 1693. He edited his grandfather's (Sir Alexander, first lord Durie) 'Decisions of the Lords of Council and Session,' also called 'Lord Durie's Practicks,' on the recommendation and permission of the court of session and the privy council. The volume was printed in folio, Edinburgh, 1690. Sir Alexander married Helen, daughter of Sir James Fleming of Rathobyers, Mid-Lothian, by whom he had (with five daughters) two sons, Sir John of Pentland, knighted in or before 1690, and died in 1704, and whose line ceased with his son; and Alexander, who purchased the estate of Durie from his brother John, and married Elizabeth, daughter of Sir John Foulis, and left an eldest son and heir, John, who married Helen, daughter of the Hon. William Carmichael of Skirling, second son of the first Earl of Hyndford, by Helen Craig of Riccarton, and sister and heiress of the fourth earl. The descendants of this marriage (the elder line having failed) are now the lineal male representatives of Sir Alexander Gibson, first lord Durie; and the present head of the family is the Rev. Sir William Gibson-Carmichael, bart., of Castle Craig, Dolphinton, N.B.

[Family memoranda.] R. H–R.

GIBSON, ALEXANDER (1800–1867), botanist, was born at Laurencekirk, Kincardineshire, on 24 Oct. 1800. After taking his degree of doctor of medicine at Edinburgh, he obtained an appointment as assistant-surgeon in the East India Company's service in January 1825, in which year he went out to India, and served some years in the Indian navy. While thus engaged he studied the native languages, and passed examinations in Hindustani, Mahrati, and Gujerati. In 1836 he was appointed vaccinator for the Deccan and Kandesh, and while in this migratory office his knowledge of botany and agriculture procured him in 1838 the post of superintendent of the botanical garden at Dapuri. Here Dr. Gibson paid special attention to the introduction and cultivation of exotic trees and plants, and his successful efforts to procure several drugs for the use of the medical department received special commendation from the court of directors. In 1847 he was promoted to the more important post of conservator of forests in the Bombay presidency, and for fourteen years he rendered invaluable service to the government in this capacity. Among other qualifications he possessed an iron constitution, which enabled him, in the discharge of his duties, to penetrate and to live in jungles which would have been fatal to most Europeans. His reports were collected and published by the government, and on his retirement in 1860 he received from the governor in council a public acknowledgment of his unremitting zeal, and of the beneficial results which the measures conducted under his direction had secured to the state. He was elected a fellow of the Linnean Society on 19 April 1853, and died on 16 Jan. 1867. His works were: 1. 'Forest Reports, Bombay Presidency,' Bombay, 1849–1855, 8vo. 2. 'Handbook to the Forests of the Bombay Presidency,' Bombay, 1863, 8vo. 3. 'Bombay Flora,' ed. by N. A. Dalzell, Bombay, 1861, 8vo. He also edited Hove's 'Tours for Scientific Research' from a manuscript in the Banksian Library, Bombay, 1855, 8vo.

[Proc. Linn. Soc. 1866–7, p. 33.] B. D. J.

GIBSON, ALEXANDER CRAIG (1813–1874), antiquary, born at Harrington, Cumberland, on 17 March 1813, was the eldest son of Joseph Gibson, a native of that place, by his wife Mary Stuart Craig, who was of a Moffat family. He served his time to the practice of medicine in Whitehaven, and after studying at Edinburgh began his professional duties at Branthwaite and Ullock in his native county, where he remained about two years, removing to Coniston in 1843. Here he married in May 1844 Sarah, daughter of John Bowman of Hoadyood in Lamplugh. In 1849 he removed to Hawkshead, but in 1857, finding the work too heavy, settled at Bebington in Cheshire, where he remained in practice until his failing health compelled him to retire in 1872. Gibson was from his youth a contributor to newspapers. His first separate book, 'The Old Man, or Ravings and Ramblings round Coniston' (Kendal, 1849, 12mo), had already been printed in chapters in the 'Kendal Mercury.' It was an attempt to carry out a suggestion of Professor Wilson (Christopher North) that each locality in the Lake district should be carefully described by one well acquainted with it. The book went through several editions. About the same time he contributed to 'Tait's Magazine' a ballad in the Annandale dialect, 'The Lockerbie Lycke.'

This he reprinted in his volume entitled 'The Folk-speech of Cumberland and some Districts adjacent, being Short Stories and Rhymes in the Dialect of the West Border Counties' (Carlisle, 1869, 12mo, 2nd ed. 1873). This work has much interest from Gibson's intimate acquaintance with the dialect of the district, and from his keen sense of the humour of the dales-folk. He contributed largely to the 'Transactions of the Historic Society of Lancashire and Cheshire' and other antiquarian associations. He was also author of 'The Geology of the Lake Country' in Miss Martineau's 'Guide;' and of numerous articles in medical and other periodicals. He was F.S.A., M.R.C.S. Engl. 1846, L.S.A. 1855, and L.M. Edinb. (Univ. Edinb.) He died at Bebington on 12 June 1874.

[Whitehaven News, 18 June 1874; Medical Directory, 1871; private information.] A. N.

GIBSON, DAVID COOKE (1827–1856), artist and poet, born at Edinburgh 4 March 1827, was the son of a portrait-painter who died early of consumption, leaving a widow, David, and a daughter. After four years at the Edinburgh High School, he was admitted to the Board of Trustees' Academy. He passed through the ornamental class under Charles Heath Wilson, studied the collection of casts from the antique under Sir William Allan, and afterwards the colour class and life class under Thomas Duncan. Before he was seventeen years of age he was the chief support of his mother and sister, resigning all chance of a college career to devote himself to portrait-painting. His mother, Ann Gibson, died soon after September 1844, and his sister on 2 Dec. 1845 of consumption. Gibson had inherited the same disease, and the insinuation that his constitution was broken by vice is absolutely false. It is supported by a perversion of his dying words; his life was perfectly pure, though he was a social favourite, fond of dancing, an excellent mimic, eminently handsome and graceful, though diminutive in figure. In January 1846 he obtained three prizes at the Trustees' Academy. A month later two of his small pictures were badly hung at the Royal Scottish Academy, and he imprudently asked to withdraw one of these. He made a tour to London, Belgium, and Paris, studying in the great galleries. His copy of Vandyck's 'Charles I' was bought by Sir Edwin Landseer after Gibson's death. Returning to Edinburgh he worked hard at portraits. He removed to London in April 1852. At this time he wrote an immense quantity of easy and sometimes humorous verse. He had disappointments, was discontented, and listened to socialists and sceptics. He was attracted by the pre-Raphaelites, and his picture, 'The Little Stranger,' exhibited at the Royal Academy in 1855, was sold for 100l. After revisiting Scotland he was advised to go abroad for his health, and passed the winter of 1855–6 at Malaga. Some of his Spanish pictures were exhibited in the Royal Academy in 1856, and some of them were bought by John Phillips, R.A. After despatching his painting Gibson visited the Alhambra in March 1856, and made many sketches. Creswick had bought one of Gibson's pictures before the opening of the Academy for 150l. Gibson returned to England in June, but unfortunately lingered there too long. He broke a blood-vessel in September, and died 5 Oct. 1856. In the following May his 'Gipsies of Seville' was exhibited in the Academy. He had bequeathed to Dr. Tweedie his picture of the Alhambra Towers with the Sierra Nevada in the distance, 'A Pleasing Prospect,' and it was chromolithographed and published.

[Personal remembrance; Royal Academy Exhibition Catalogues, 1855–7; Art Journal, 1855, p. 172, 1856–68; Struggles of a Young Artist, being a Memoir of David C. Gibson (anon., by William Macduff), 1858, valuable only for portrait, extracts from his journals of travel, and his poems, among which are 'Angelo and Zelica,' written at Malaga, in imitation of J. G. Lockhart; Dumfries Herald, Greenock Advertiser, and Macphail's Ecclesiastical Journal.] J. W. E.

GIBSON, EDMUND (1669–1748), bishop of London, son of Edmund Gibson of Knipe by his wife Jane Langharne, and nephew and heir of Thomas Gibson, M.D. [q. v.], was baptised at Bampton, Westmoreland, 19 Dec. 1669, and educated at the free grammar school there. In 1686 he was admitted as a 'poor serving child' at Queen's College, Oxford, and proceeded B.A. 25 June 1691. As early as 1691 he appeared in print, as the editor of a macaronic poem by William Drummond (1585–1649 [q. v.]), entitled 'Polemo-Middinia,' with 'Christ's Kirk on the Green' by James I of Scotland, and an original dissertation on macaronic poetry. Gibson's energies were now attracted towards Anglo-Saxon studies, then somewhat the rage at Oxford, through the reputation and teaching of Dr. Hickes [q. v.] In 1692 he published an edition of the 'Saxon Chronicle,' with a Latin translation and notes, a preface, and a chronological index. In the same year Gibson published an account of the manuscripts in the library made by Tenison when rector of St. Martin-in-the-Fields, and in the collection of Sir W. Dugdale bequeathed to the Ashmolean Museum at Oxford (cf. HEARNE,

VOL. VII.

Coll. ed. Doble, ii. 45–6). This served to bring him to the notice of Tenison, lately (1691) made bishop of Lincoln, and led to his future promotion. An edition of Quinctilian was published in 1693 by Gibson, who, according to Hearne, 'took little pains in it,' and in the same year he supplied notes to an edition by James Brome [q. v.] of Somner's 'Roman Ports and Forts in Kent,' and in 1694 issued his own Latin translation of Somner's 'Julii Cæsaris Portus Iccius.' Gibson proceeded M.A. 21 Feb. 1694, was admitted a fellow of his college, and took holy orders. In 1695 he published an English translation of Camden's 'Britannia,' with the aid of William Lloyd, of Jesus College, who revised the whole work. Dr. John Smith furnished the additions on the bishopric of Durham in the second edition; the observations on Oxfordshire were by Bishop Kennett; large collections made from Dodsworth's papers were communicated by Dr. Nat. Johnston (2nd edition, 2 vols. fol. 1722; 3rd edition, 1753, and again 1772). Gibson's edition of Sir Henry Spelman's English works, published in the author's lifetime, together with his posthumous works, both in Latin and English, appeared, with a life of the author, under the title of 'Reliquiæ Spelmannianæ,' 1698. Gibson had now been made domestic chaplain to Archbishop Tenison and librarian at Lambeth. Through the same patronage he became lecturer of St. Martin-in-the-Fields, rector of Stisted (1700), and rector of Lambeth (1703). Being thus closely connected with the archbishop, Gibson was necessarily involved in the acrimonious controversy as to the rights and powers of convocation which raged at that period and produced a vast crop of pamphlets. On the meeting of the convocation of Canterbury, at the beginning of 1701, Atterbury endeavoured to substantiate his views that the relations between the upper and lower houses of convocation were similar to those existing between the houses of lords and commons; that the lower house had a right to prorogue itself and arrange for its own sittings, and was not subject to the archbishop. This view was strongly combated by Gibson and others. Gibson's first pamphlet, published 1700, was entitled 'A short state of some present questions in Convocation.' Soon afterwards (1701) he published 'The right of the Archbishop of Canterbury to prorogue the whole Convocation,' and the next year two other pamphlets on the same subject. These led to a more important work, which forms now the text-book for all proceedings in convocation. It is entitled 'Synodus Anglicana; or the Constitution and Proceedings of an English Convocation,

London, 1702, a work showing great research and clear judgment (ed. Cardwell, Oxford, 1854). In the following years other pamphlets in defence of his views on convocation were published by Gibson anonymously. Many of his single sermons were also published. In 1710 Gibson was promoted to the archdeaconry of Surrey. In 1713 he brought out his great work, a magnificent monument of research, entitled 'Codex Juris Ecclesiæ Anglicanæ; or the Statutes, Constitutions, Canons, Rubrics, and Articles of the Church of England digested under their proper heads, with a Commentary Historical and Juridical,' 2 vols., fol. London, 1713. This was reprinted at Oxford in 1761, and is still the highest authority on church law. An abstract, 'A System of English Ecclesiastical Law,' by R. Grey (1730), reached a fourth edition. In 1715 Gibson's patron, Archbishop Tenison, died, and the vacancy at Canterbury was filled by the translation of Dr. Wake from Lincoln. The new primate, who was of a kindred mind with Gibson in his opinions and studies, recommended him strongly as his successor at Lincoln, and in 1716 he was consecrated Bishop of Lincoln. During the four years of his occupancy of this diocese the only works attributed to Gibson are several separate sermons. In 1720, on the death of Bishop Robinson, Gibson was translated to London. Here his literary activity quickly revived, and both by writing and action he resolutely resisted prevailing evils. Masquerades were much patronised by the court, and caused great scandal. Gibson remonstrated privately with the king, and procured a petition signed by several bishops for the abandonment of these entertainments. The establishment of Whitehall sermons by members of the universities appointed by the Bishop of London was due to him. It may have been to make way in London for a bishop of less strict views that Gibson was offered translation to the rich see of Winchester. But this he declined, and by pastoral letters, charges, sermons, and tracts continued to oppose the prevailing laxity. His 'Family Devotions,' 1705, 8vo, reached an eighteenth edition in 1750. Some of his pastorals were directed against the deists and freethinkers (1728–9). Of these the second was answered by John Jackson in 'Four Tracts on Human Reason.' Another pastoral was directed against the methodists, especially George Whitefield. Gibson collected and edited, in three volumes folio, with prefaces, 'A Collection of the principal Treatises against Popery in the Papal Controversy, digested under proper heads and tables,' London, 1738. His 'Earnest Dissuasive from Intemperance' appeared in 1743 (15th edition, 1771), and his

'Pastoral Letter for Reformation of Life' in 1745. His 'Serious Advice to Persons who have been Sick,' his 'Sacrament of the Lord's Supper explained,' and his 'Sinfulness of profaning the Lord's Day' all reached numerous editions. Gibson long lived on intimate terms with Sir Robert Walpole; and after Archbishop Wake was incapacitated by illness, he was Walpole's chief adviser in ecclesiastical matters. 'His [Walpole's] esteem for the Bishop of London had been so great that when he was reproached with giving him the authority of a pope he replied: "And a very good pope he is"' (COXE). Gibson's influence was sufficient to prevent the consecration of Rundle to the see of Gloucester (1734), as he was believed to hold deistical opinions. In 1736, however, Gibson alienated Walpole by his strenuous opposition to the Quakers' Relief Bill. The rejection of this measure in the House of Lords was partly caused by this opposition, which appears to have been ill-judged. The bill provided for the recovery of tithes and church rates from quakers by distraint. Gibson procured votes against it, and Walpole never forgave him. Horace Walpole remarks (Letters, ii. 130) that, in spite of the quarrel, Gibson always spoke of the statesman in the highest terms. At the death of Wake in 1737 Gibson, who had always been regarded as the 'heir-apparent of Canterbury,' was passed over, and the primacy was conferred on Potter, bishop of Oxford. At the death of Potter, ten years afterwards, it was offered to Gibson, but declined by him on account of age and infirmities. Contemporary notices represent Gibson as a patron of learned men. When librarian of Lambeth he commenced the catalogue of the library, finished by Dr. Ducarel, and arranged a collection of manuscripts left by Archbishop Tenison. Gibson died at Bath on 6 Sept. 1748. A portrait was engraved by Vertue in 1727. He is said to have married a sister of John Bettesworth, dean of the arches. He was survived by seven of twelve children. The bishop's brother John was provost of Queen's College, Oxford, from 1717 to 1730.

[Some Account of the Right Rev. Dr. E. Gibson, Lond. 1749, attributed to Richard Smalbroke, bishop of Coventry; Coxe's Walpole, ii. (1798); Nichols's Lit. Anecd. of the Eighteenth Century; Wood's Athenæ Oxon. ed. Bliss, iv. 540; Lathbury's Hist. of Convocation, 1853; Biog. Brit. 1766, suppl.; Hearne's Collections (Oxford Hist. Soc.), i. ii. iii.]   G. G. P.

GIBSON, EDWARD (1668–1701), portrait-painter, was nephew of William Gibson (1644–1702) [q. v.], from whom he received instruction in painting. He commenced painting portraits in oil, but subsequently found more employment in crayons. In this line he showed some genius, and was making great progress when he died in January 1701 in his thirty-third year. He resided in Catherine Street, Strand, and was buried at Richmond, Surrey. He drew his own portrait in crayons twice, in one dressed as a Chinese, in the other as a quaker. One portrait of himself, dated 1690, was at Tart Hall, and another, dated 1696, was formerly in Sir Thomas Lawrence's collection, and was sold at Christie's on 27 March 1866.

[De Piles's Lives of Painters; Vertue's MSS. Addit. MS. Brit. Mus. 23068; Walpole's Anecd. of Painting, ed. Dallaway and Wornum; Manning and Bray's Hist. of Surrey, i. 433.]   L. C.

GIBSON, FRANCIS (1753–1805), miscellaneous writer, son of Joseph and Mary Gibson of Whitby, Yorkshire, was baptised at Whitby 16 Jan. 1753. He became a seaman, voyaged to North America, and afterwards, as master mariner in a ship of his father's, to the Baltic. In 1787 he was, on the recommendation of Lord Mulgrave, appointed to the collectorship of customs at Whitby, which office he held till his death, 24 July 1805. He was twice married, and had issue.

Gibson wrote: 1. 'Sailing Directions for the Baltic,' 1791. These are said to have been employed with advantage by the Copenhagen expedition of 1801 under Sir Hyde Parker and Nelson. 2. 'Streanshall Abbey, or the Danish Invasion,' Whitby, 1800. This is a play in five acts, dedicated to Lady Mulgrave. It was first performed at the Whitby Theatre 2 Dec. 1799. It went through two (probably limited) editions in the year of its publication. 3. 'Memoirs of the Bastile,' a translation of an account published under the sanction of the National Assembly of France, Whitby, 1802. 4. 'Poetical Remains,' Whitby, 1807.

[Life by W. Watkins, prefixed to Poetical Remains.]   F. W–T.

GIBSON, GEORGE STACEY (1818–1883), botanist and philanthropist, was born 20 July 1818 at Saffron Walden, Essex, being the only son of Wyatt George Gibson, a lineal descendant of Sir Henry Wyatt. His mother's maiden name was Deborah Stacey. Born to ample private means, though occupied by a large banking business and many charitable institutions, especially those connected with the Society of Friends, of which he was for many years 'clerk of the yearly meeting,' he at an early age imbibed a taste for botany. His keen observing powers added six species to the known British flora, and furnished the material for a series of interesting communications to the 'Phytologist' between 1842 and

1851. He also communicated to Hewett Watson records of plants from various counties of England, Wales, and Scotland. In 1845 he married Elizabeth, daughter of Samuel Tuke of York, and in 1847 became a fellow of the Linnean Society. In 1862 he published 'The Flora of Essex,' the result of nearly twenty years' work, which was in several respects an advance on preceding county floras. After this date other duties took him away from active scientific work; but he retained to the last a keen interest in science, especially photography, electric lighting, and the rearrangement of the excellent local museum at Walden. He was senior partner of the firm of Gibson, Tuke, & Gibson, and in 1877 and 1878 held the office of mayor of his native town, the charities of which he endowed munificently both during his life and at his death. He died of kidney disease, in Bishopsgate Street, London, on 5 April 1883. Exactitude and conscientiousness were his characteristics alike in science and in business, and he modestly submitted all his botanical discoveries to the judgment of his friends William Borrer, Edward Forster, and Professor C. C. Babington. His herbarium is in the Saffron Walden Museum.

[Memoirs, illustrated by two different portraits, in Journ. of Bot. 1883, and in Trans. Essex Field Club, vol. iv., by G. S. Boulger.]   G. S. B.

GIBSON, JAMES, D.D. (1799–1871), Free church polemic, was born at Crieff, Perthshire, on 31 Jan. 1799, went to school in his native place, and entered the university of Glasgow in his twelfth year. Towards the close of his preparatory course he became tutor in a Lanarkshire family, and in 1820 was licensed to preach by the presbytery of Hamilton. He afterwards accepted a situation as tutor in a Roxburghshire family, where he remained more than three years. In 1825 he became travelling companion to Captain Elliot, a cousin to the Earl of Minto. They went to Portugal and resided a considerable time in Lisbon. Returning to Glasgow Gibson was appointed assistant to the Rev. Mr. Steel, of the West Church, Greenock. After two years of work he made another continental tour with a pupil, receiving a testimonial from the Greenock congregation on his departure. In these tours he specially studied the moral and religious condition of the countries visited. Gibson was afterwards appointed assistant to Dr. Lockhart in the college parish, Glasgow, and received ordination as a minister. He was distinguished for accurate scholarship, a well cultivated mind, and sincere piety, but was not an attractive or effective preacher. He was drawn into the voluntary controversy as a de–

fender of church establishments. He argued that the errors supposed to be due to the action of the Emperor Constantine had existed at an earlier date. He became editor of the 'Church of Scotland Magazine' in 1834, an office which he held for three years. Some influential members of the church placed at his disposal about 2,000l., which might either be accepted as a gift or devoted to the purpose of building a church for him. A church was accordingly built in the suburb of Kingston, into which he was inducted in 1839. The disruption came in 1843, when Gibson joined the Free church, and on the Sunday following he was interdicted from entering his own church. A place of worship in connection with the Free church was built for him in the same locality. For some years he acted as clerk to the Glasgow free presbytery. In 1855, having a promise of 30,000l. from Dr. Clark of Wester Moffat, with whom Gibson was on friendly terms, the general assembly of the Free church resolved to erect a theological college in Glasgow, and next year Gibson was elected professor of systematic theology and church history. He was conspicuous as a debater in the courts of the Free church, and strenuously opposed anything like innovation. Gibson died on 2 Nov. 1871. Besides contributing to volumes of lectures against infidelity, popery, and voluntaryism, he edited the 'Scottish Protestant,' vols. i. and ii., Glasgow, 1852, and wrote treatises on 'The Marriage Affinity Question,' 8vo, Edinburgh, 1854 ; 'Principles of Bible Temperance,' 8vo, Glasgow, 1855 ; 'Present Truths in Theology,' 8vo, Glasgow, 1863 ; 'The Connection between the Decalogue and New Testament Morality,' 8vo, Glasgow, 1865 ; and 'The Public Worship of God : its Authority and Modes,' 8vo, Glasgow, 1869.

[Free Church Monthly, January 1872; Disruption Worthies, 1876; newspaper reports; published works.]   J. T.

GIBSON, Sir JAMES BROWN, M.D. (1805-1868), physician, studied medicine and graduated M.D. at Edinburgh. He entered the military service in 1826 as hospital assistant, and was duly promoted to be assistant-surgeon and surgeon. He served in the Crimean war, and was body surgeon to the Duke of Cambridge. In 1860 he was made director-general of the army medical department, and a K.C.B. in 1865. He retired in 1867, and died at Rome on 25 Feb. 1868.

[Lancet, 1868, i. 331.]   C. C.

GIBSON, JAMES YOUNG (1826-1886), translator from the Spanish, born at Edinburgh 19 Feb. 1826, was the fourth son of William Gibson, a merchant of that city.

In his sixteenth year he entered the Edinburgh University, in which he completed his full course of study, though he took no degree, and proceeded in 1847 to the divinity hall of the united presbyterian church, where he remained till 1852. During the vacations of 1851-2 he studied at the university of Halle in Germany. On the completion of his theological course in 1853 he was licensed by the Edinburgh presbytery, and about that time became tutor in the family of Henry Birkbeck of Keswick Hall, Norfolk. Having placed his name for some months on the probationers' roll, he received three nearly simultaneous offers of ministerial work. He finally accepted an appointment at Melrose, and accordingly in July was ordained to the ministry. His health broke down, and in 1859 he resigned his appointment. The next few years he devoted to study and foreign travel, and to recruiting his strength. In 1865 he travelled to Cairo and visited the Holy Land. In 1871 he accompanied Mr. Alexander J. Duffield, the translator of 'Don Quixote,' on a tour of inspection among the iron mines in Spain. They spent 1872 in travelling over the country. Gibson became interested in Spanish poetry, and after Mr. Duffield's return home proceeded to Madrid, where he began the first of his translations. He settled in London in 1872. In 1878 he was again invalided. While recovering he corrected the proof-sheets of Mr. Duffield's translation of 'Don Quixote,' in the first two volumes of which his poetical renderings were inserted. The translation was published in 1881. The unexpected success of this first essay led to Gibson's translation of the 'Viage al Parnaso,' which appeared in 1883. In 1883 he married, at Wildbad in Germany, after a three years' engagement, Margaret Dunlop, daughter of John Smith, solicitor, of Irvine in Ayrshire. In 1884 he settled with his wife at Long Ditton, near Surbiton. Here he completed the translation of 'Numantia,' published in 1885. Gibson died suddenly at Ramsgate, 2 Oct. 1886. He was buried in the Dean cemetery, Edinburgh. A number of his unpublished translations were printed after his death, with a memoir by his sister-in-law, Agnes Smith.

His published works are : 1. 'Journey to Parnassus, composed by Miguel de Cervantes Saavedra, translated into English tercets with preface and illustrative notes . . . to which are subjoined the antique text and translation of the letter of Cervantes to Mateo Vazquez,' London, 1883, 8vo. 2. 'Numantia. A Tragedy by Miguel de Cervantes Saavedra. Translated from the Spanish, with introduction and notes by James Y. Gibson,' 1885, 8vo. 3. 'The Cid. Ballads and other poems and translations from Spanish and German, by the late James Young Gibson. Edited by M. D. Gibson. With Memoir by Agnes Smith,' 2 vols. London, 1887, 8vo.

[Memoir by Agnes Smith; Times, 15 Oct. 1887; Athenæum, 16 Oct. 1887; Academy, 16 Oct. 1887; Sonnets of Europe, Canterbury Poets Series; Mr. Duffield's translation of Don Quixote.] W. F. W. S.

GIBSON, Sir JOHN (1637–1717), colonel, son of Sir John Gibson, knt., of Alderstone, in Ratho parish, near Edinburgh, entered the Dutch army, and obtained a captain's commission dated 9 March 1675; as major, in 1688, he accompanied William of Orange to England. He obtained from the English war office his commission as lieutenant-colonel on 28 Feb. 1688–9; became colonel of a newly raised regiment on 16 Feb. 1693–4; and colonel of a regiment to be raised (afterwards the 28th foot, now 1st battalion Gloucestershire) on 12 Feb. 1701–2, holding the command until 1 Feb. 1704–5. He was lieutenant-governor of Portsmouth from 28 May 1689, until his death on 24 Oct. 1717. He was commander-in-chief in 1697 of the land-forces sent to capture Newfoundland. He left England in March and returned in October, having secured the fishing rights of the English settlers. After unsuccessfully contesting the representation of Portsmouth in January 1695–6, he was elected for the borough in 1701–2, and was knighted by Queen Anne 6 Sept. 1705.

He left two sons, Francis and James, and two daughters; Anne Mary, the eldest, married General Robert Dalzell (1662–1758) [q. v.]

[Archives in the Hague War Office and Record Office; London Gazette; English private letters, Brit. Mus.; Luttrell's Brief Relation of State Affairs, containing very many references to Gibson's career at Portsmouth.] F. N. R.

GIBSON, JOHN (d. 1852), portrait-painter, was a native of Glasgow, where he was largely employed. He contributed to the exhibition of the West of Scotland Academy. In October 1852 he took an active part on the committee engaged in hanging the pictures; he was subsequently present at the private view on 7 Oct., and attended the dinner afterwards. After returning home he revisited the exhibition gallery for some purpose, and was found lying dreadfully injured at the bottom of the stairs. He lingered till the following night, 8 Oct., when he died at an advanced age.

[Gent. Mag. new ser. 1852, xxxviii. 551; Glasgow Chronicle, 13 Oct. 1852.] L. C.

GIBSON, JOHN (1794–1854), glass-stainer and sheriff of Newcastle, was a native of Newcastle, where he practised as an ornamental and house painter, and especially devoted himself to the art of enamelling in glass. Many of the churches at Newcastle and in the neighbourhood possess windows painted by him. Among them may be mentioned a figure of 'Jesus Christ with the Cup of the Last Supper' in the east window of St. John's Church at Newcastle, and a figure of 'Jesus Christ bearing the Cross' in the east window of St. Nicholas Church in the same town. Gibson devoted himself ardently to the study and promotion of the fine arts, and formed an extensive and valuable gallery. His taste and judgment were highly appreciated in Newcastle. He was elected a town councillor for North St. Andrews ward, and in 1854 served the office of sheriff of Newcastle. Shortly after vacating this office he died at his residence, the Leazes Terrace, on 25 Nov. 1854, aged 60.

[Gent. Mag. new ser. 1855, xliii. 108; Newcastle Guardian, 2 Dec. 1854; Newcastle Journal, 2 Dec. 1854; Mackenzie's Hist. of Newcastle, pp. 345, 761.] L. C.

GIBSON, JOHN (1790–1866), sculptor, son of a market gardener, was born at Gyffin, near Conway, in 1790. At the age of seven he drew geese and other animals on a slate from memory. When he was nine years old his parents removed to Liverpool, where a stationer named Tourmeau lent him drawings and casts to copy. At fourteen he was bound apprentice to Messrs. Southwell & Wilson, to learn cabinet-making, but after a year he preferred to learn wood-carving, and his indentures were altered accordingly. The next year he wished to be apprenticed to Messrs. Francis, at whose works he had seen carvings in marble. They employed Luge, afterwards Chantrey's head workman, and Gibson soon copied a head of Bacchus by him, and made his first attempt in marble by carving a small head of Mercury in his leisure hours. Messrs. Francis offered to pay his employers 70l. to cancel Gibson's indentures. On their refusal Gibson neglected his wood-carving, and vowed he would be sent to prison rather than continue it. In the end his stubbornness triumphed, and he was apprenticed to Messrs. Francis, where his work attracted the attention of William Roscoe, for whom he carved a bas-relief for a chimneypiece, and executed a cartoon of Satan and his Angels, both of which are now in the Roscoe Institution at Liverpool, together with a bust of Roscoe by Gibson. A bas-relief in Sefton Church to the memory of Mr. Blundell, and other of his early works, bear the name of Francis. At Liverpool he attended Dr. Vose's lectures on anatomy, and had access to Allerton and the collections of Roscoe, whose advice that 'the Greek statue is nature in the abstract' appears to have permanently influenced his art. Solomon D'Aguilar, his wife and his daughters, Mrs. Lawrence, and Mrs. Robinson were also very kind to him. Mrs. Robinson devoted herself to improving his mind, and was a constant friend and correspondent till her death in 1829. Through the D'Aguilars Gibson was introduced to John Kemble, who sat to him for a small bust, the only one ever taken of the actor. In 1816 he commenced to exhibit at the Royal Academy, sending two busts (one of H. Park, esq.), and 'Psyche borne by Zephyrs' (this is called a drawing in Redgrave's 'Dictionary,' but it is catalogued among the sculpture, and it is recorded in his life that Flaxman, who did not know Gibson, placed it in a good light). His last work in Liverpool was a mantelpiece for Sir John Gladstone, the father of Mr. W. E. Gladstone.

Gibson came to London in 1817, with introductions to Christie, the auctioneer, and to Brougham. Christie introduced him to Watson Taylor, who commissioned the bust of Roscoe, now in the Liverpool Institution, and busts of all his family, from himself and his wife down to the baby, 'a little thing with no shape at all.' Busts of two Master Watson Taylors were exhibited in 1817, the artist's address being still given as Liverpool in the Royal Academy Catalogue. A bust of Watson Taylor was exhibited in 1819.

Gibson had dreamed that he was carried by an eagle to Rome, and to Rome he determined to go, 'if he went there on foot.' He went thither, taking his unfinished bust of Roscoe with him, but not before he had been introduced to Fuseli, West, Flaxman, Blake, and Chantrey. He arrived on 20 Oct. 1817 in Rome, where he was received by Canova in the most generous manner. 'I am rich,' said the famous sculptor, 'I am anxious to be of use to you in your art as long as you stay in Rome.' From Canova he received his first instruction in the art of sculpture, working in the Italian's studio, and afterwards under him in the academy of St. Luke's. He also received instruction from Thorwaldsen, then living at Rome. He was at once admitted to the intimate society of these eminent sculptors, and naturally formed a high estimate of the advantage to a sculptor of a residence in Rome as the artistic capital of the world. His first original work in Rome was a 'Sleeping Shepherd,' life size, and his first

commission was for the group of 'Mars and Cupid' now at Chatsworth. So inexperienced was he at this time (1819) that he asked the Duke of Devonshire only 500l. for it, though it cost the artist 520l. before it was finished in marble. To the years 1821–2 belong the 'Psyche and Zephyrs,' executed for Sir George Beaumont (for which he more wisely asked 900l.), and a bas-relief of 'Hero and Leander' for the Duke of Devonshire. In 1824 he executed his figure of 'Paris' for Watson Taylor, and the 'Sleeping Shepherd Boy' for Lord George Cavendish. 'Hylas and the Nymphs' was ordered by Mr. Hyland in 1826, and transferred to Mr. Vernon, who left it to the nation. In the winter of the same year Sir Watkin Williams Wynn ordered the figure of 'Cupid drawing his Bow,' and in the following year the 'Psyche and Zephyrs' was at the Royal Academy, but Sir George Beaumont, who had ordered it, was dead. As Flaxman was also dead, and Chantrey rich and lazy, Gibson was again urged to go to London and 'make his fortune,' but he resolved to stay where he could do the best work without regard to fortune. He did not even visit England till 1844.

From 1827 to 1844 Gibson executed among other works a 'Nymph untying her Sandal,' for Lord Yarborough (exhibited 1831); a seated statue of Dudley North, his first portrait statue; 'Cupid disguised as a Shepherd' (exhibited 1837), for Sir John Johnstone, a very pretty figure, which was repeated eight times; 'Cupid tormenting the Soul' (exhibited 1839), for Lord Selsey, which he looked upon as one of his best works. He was persuaded that the god appeared to him and directed him to colour the statue. It was repeated for Mr. Yates and Mr. Holford, and the latter repetition was tinted. In 1833 he was elected an associate of the Royal Academy, and in 1838 a full member. In 1838 Mr. Henry Sandbach, with his wife, the granddaughter of William Roscoe, went to Rome. Mrs. Sandbach formed with him an elevating friendship, which lasted till her death in 1854. For her husband he executed his 'Hunter and Dog,' his most vigorous work 'in the round,' and 'Aurora' (exhibited 1847). For the 'Hunter' he had a very fine model 'in the prime of youth,' but in addition 'went often to study the casts from the Elgin marbles.'

When Gibson came to London in 1844, he disapproved of the place inside the custom house at Liverpool, where it was proposed to place his colossal statue of Huskisson which was exhibited at the Royal Academy in that year. A previous statue of Huskisson in marble had been erected in the cemetery, and

Mrs. Huskisson, another devoted friend, gave him a commission for a third, to be erected in the open area surrounding the building. The second marble statue is now at Lloyd's, Royal Exchange. While he was in England he was publicly entertained at Glasgow on the occasion of the erection of his statue of Kirkman Finlay [q.v.] in the Merchants' Hall, and he received the command of the queen to execute a statue of herself, and her permission to present a bust of her to Liverpool, to be placed in St. George's Hall, where is also his statue of George Stephenson. In the statue executed for the queen he for the first time ventured to introduce a little colour, tinting the diadem, sandals, and borders of drapery with blue, red, and yellow. For this departure from modern practice, the subject of much dispute then and since, he claimed the example of the Greeks, and at this time (1846) he wrote : ' My eyes have now become so depraved that I cannot bear to see a statue without colour,' and ' Whatever the Greeks did was right.'

Gibson remained in Rome during the political agitations of 1847–9, not without personal danger. On the approach of the French army he retired with his brother Benjamin to Lucca, returning in time to see the pope re-enter the city. In 1850 he came to England to model the statue of the queen for the houses of parliament (prince's chamber), which with its noble figures of Justice and Clemency was in hand for five years. He also took five years to complete for Mr. Preston the celebrated statue of Venus, known as 'The Tinted Venus.' This was a replica of a statue (uncoloured) which he had executed for Mr. John Neeld, shortly after his return from Lucca to Rome. He describes it as ' the most carefully laboured work I ever executed, for I wrought the forms up to the highest standard of the ideal. The expression I endeavoured to give my Venus was that spiritual elevation of character which results from purity and sweetness, combined with an air of unaffected dignity and grace. I took the liberty to decorate it in a fashion unprecedented in modern times. I tinted the flesh like warm ivory, scarcely red, the eyes blue, the hair blond, and the net which contains the hair, golden.' He became almost as enamoured of this statue as Pygmalion of Galatea. ' At moments,' he wrote, ' I forgot that I was gazing at my own production; there I sat before her, long and often. How was I ever to part with her ?' He was at last compelled to give her up, by the remonstrances of Mrs. Preston, four years after the statue was completed. This ' Venus,' with Lady Marian Alford's 'Pandora,' and Mr. Holford's 'Cupid,' all coloured, were exhibited at the International Exhibition of 1862.

On 13 Aug. 1851 Gibson lost his youngest brother Benjamin, who died at Lucca, aged 40. The two brothers had long lived together, and Benjamin, from his superior education, had served as ' classical dictionary.' Benjamin Gibson wrote several monographs on classical subjects for English antiquarian publications (see *Gent. Mag.* 1851, ii. 552). In 1853 Gibson won a new friend in the American sculptress, Miss Hosmer, whom he instructed gratuitously. He was amply repaid by her ' bright and helpful companionship.' He spent many summers at Innsbruck, and of later years in England and Switzerland, or the Tyrol. In his journeys he was absolutely dependent on some devoted companion. Living in the heaven of his art, he had no time to devote to sublunary matters, and was as guileless, and in many things as helpless, as a child. He forgot invitations, posted letters without addresses, got out at wrong stations, lost his luggage. Once when asked why he took with him three packages, one of which was never opened, he replied, ' The Greeks had a great respect for the number three—yes, the Greeks, for the number three.' Miss Hosmer said, ' He is a god in his studio, but God help him out of it !'

Gibson was consulted about the Albert Memorial, which of course he wished to be entirely ' classical,' and declined to execute the ' Group of Europe,' as he could not winter in England. His subsequent offer to execute it in Rome came too late. In 1862 he modelled a bas-relief of ' Christ blessing little Children ' for Mr. Sandbach, his first and only subject from the scriptures. He persevered in spite of misgivings as to his power of expressing the divine through the human, and succeeded better than might have been expected. For some years before his death his health had failed, and his pure and happy life came to an end at Rome on 27 Jan. 1866. This life cannot be better described than in his own words: ' I worked on all my days happily, and with ever new pleasure, avoiding evil, and with a calm soul—making images, not for worship, but for the love of the beautiful.'

Gibson may be said to have been the last and one of the best of the ' old school' of European sculpture, based on the teaching of Winckelmann, and carrying out strictly the ' purist' view of sculpture as the embodiment of abstract ideas in beautiful form. He was not, and did not wish to be, original. ' It is the desire of novelty that destroys pure taste,' he said. He studied from nature incessantly, but ever strove to treat her in the manner of the Greeks. He once expressed an opinion that Pheidias would have said of Michael Angelo, 'Here is a most clever and wonderful sculptor, but a barbarian.' He refused to execute the statues of Huskisson and Sir Robert Peel (Westminster Abbey) unless he was allowed to drape them classically. He said: 'The human figure concealed under a frock coat and trousers is not a fit subject for sculpture. I would rather avoid contemplating such objects.' It was not to be expected that sculpture executed with strict regard for such strict principles should be 'popular' in England in Gibson's time, but there was little excuse for the abuse which the press poured on many of his finest works. They were always pure in sentiment, refined in form, and executed with perfect skill. His brother artists felt and recognised his merit, and he had always a cultivated circle of admirers who smoothed the way of life for him by affectionate companionship and plentiful employment. He died worth 32,000*l.*, which (with the exception of a few small legacies) he left, with the contents of his studio, to the Royal Academy. There, in a room specially devoted to them, may be seen the original sketches and casts of all his principal works, besides a few works in marble. Not the least beautiful, and certainly, except the 'Hunter,' the most spirited of his works, are some of his bas-reliefs, as 'The Hours leading the Horses of the Sun,' and 'Phaeton driving the Chariot of the Sun,' executed for Lord Fitzwilliam.

[Life of John Gibson, R.A., containing his Autobiography, and edited by Lady Eastlake; Redgrave's Dict.] C. M.

GIBSON, KENNET (1730–1772), antiquary, born at Paston, Northamptonshire, in 173C, was the son of Thomas Gibson, M.A., rector of Paston. He was educated at Eton, and admitted a minor pensioner of Christ's College, Cambridge, 7 May 1748 (*College Register*). He graduated B.A. in 1752 as fourteenth junior optime, and was ordained. He was afterwards rector of Marholm, or Marham, Northamptonshire, and curate of Castor in the same county. On 3 July 1769 he issued proposals for printing by a guinea subscription a commentary upon part of the fifth journey of Antoninus through Britain, but his death in 1772 interrupted the design. In 1795 the manuscript was offered to John Nichols by the possessor, Daniel Bayley, fellow of St. John's College, Cambridge. Nichols published it with considerable additions in 'Miscellaneous Antiquities in continuation of the Bibliotheca Topographica Britannica' as 'A Comment upon part of the Fifth Journey of Antoninus through Britain, in which the situation of Durocobrivæ [Durobrivæ?],

the seventh station there mentioned, is discussed; and Castor in Northamptonshire is shown, from the various Remains of Roman Antiquity, to have an undoubted Claim to that Situation. To which is added a Dissertation on an Image of Jupiter found there. By the Rev. Kennet Gibson. . . . Printed from the original MS. and enlarged with the Parochial History of Castor . . . to the present time. To which is subjoined an Account of Marham,' &c. (by Richard Gough), 4to, London, 1800; 2nd edition, enlarged, 4to, London, 1819.

[Nichols's Lit. Anecd. vi. 636, ix. 237.] G. G.

GIBSON, MATHEW (*d.* 1741?), antiquary, was educated at Queen's College, Oxford, where he graduated B.A. 9 Dec. 1700 and M.A. 26 June 1703. At an early date he made the acquaintance of Thomas Hearne, and corresponded with him. An entertaining letter from him to Hearne appears in 'Letters from the Bodleian Library,' 1813, i. 197. It is dated from 'Lord Scudamore's, near Hereford,' 19 Nov. 1709. Hearne wrote in his diary in April 1734: 'Mr. Mathew Gibson, rector of Abbey Dore, called on me. He said that he knew Mr. Kyrle (the "Man of Ross") well, and that he was his wife's near relation—I think her uncle. He said that Kyrle did a great deal of good, but 'twas all out of vanity and ostentation. I know not what credit to give to Mr. Gibson on this account, especially since he hath more than once spoken against that good worthy man, Dr. Ottley, late bishop of St. David's. Besides, this Gibson is a crazed man, and withal stingy, though he is rich, and hath no child by his wife' (*Reliq. Hearnianæ*, iii. 132). He was instituted to the living of Abbey Dore 27 Nov. 1722. His successor, the Rev. Digby Coates, was instituted 21 July, 1741, ' on vacancy caused by death of the last incumbent' (*Diocesan Register*). He wrote 'A View of the Ancient and Present State of the Churches of Door, Home-Lacy, and Hempsted, endowed by John, lord viscount Scudamore, with some memoirs of that Ancient Family, and an appendix of records and letters,' London, 1727, a handsome quarto, of which there are two copies in the British Museum Library.

[Oxford Graduates; Nichols's Lit. Anecd. viii; Reliquiæ Hearnianæ, ed. Bliss, 1869, iii. 131-2; Hearne's Collections (Oxford Hist. Soc.), i. 279, ii. 171, 311; Cooke's Continuation of Duncumb's Hereford, iii. 112; information from the Diocesan Registry, Hereford.] H. M. C.

GIBSON, MATTHEW, D.D. (1734–1790), catholic prelate, fourth son of Jasper Gibson of Stonecrofts, near Hexham, Northumberland, was, according to his own statement, born on 25 March (O.S.) 1734, but, according to the Hexham register, he was baptised on 23 March, a difference possibly due to the change in style. He was educated in the English College at Douay, where he was ordained priest, and appointed professor, first of philosophy, and afterwards of divinity. In 1768 he returned to England. He was chosen archdeacon of Kent and Surrey in 1770, and appointed vicar-general in the northern district to Bishop Walton in 1776, and special vicar in 1777. On Walton's death he was chosen to succeed him as vicar-apostolic of the northern district of England, and was consecrated in London to the see of Comana, *in partibus*, on 3 Sept. 1780. Finding that the catholic catechisms then in use were very inaccurate, he corrected the mistakes and published 'The London, or Little Catechism,' London, 1784, 12mo. Thomas Eyre [q. v.], president of Ushaw College, helped him, and described it as 'by far the most perfect in the English tongue, in every sense and in every respect.' All the English bishops gave their approbation to this catechism. On 21 Oct. 1789 Gibson and the three other vicars-apostolic issued the well-known encyclical letter on the subject of the 'Protestation Oath,' in which the term 'protesting catholic dissenters' was assumed by the catholic committee [see BUTLER, CHARLES, 1750–1832]. He died at Stella Hall, Ryton, Durham, on 19 May 1790, and was buried at Newbrough Church, near Stonecrofts. He was succeeded in the northern vicariate by his younger brother, Dr. William Gibson [q. v.]

[Kirk's MS. Biographical Collections, quoted in Gillow's Bibl. Dict. ; Brady's Episcopal Succession, iii. 223, 265, 266 ; Amherst's Hist. of Catholic Emancipation, i. 164, 168.]   T. C.

GIBSON, PATRICK (1782?–1829), landscape-painter and writer on art, was a native of Edinburgh. The date of his birth is usually given as December 1782, but the parochial register of Dollar states that he died in 1829, 'aged fifty-four years.' He received a classical education in the high school, Edinburgh, and in a private academy, and studied art under Alexander Nasmyth and in the Trustees' Academy, then taught by John Graham. From 1805 he resided in Lambeth, exhibiting in the Royal Academy in 1805, 1806, and 1807, and in the British Institution in 1811. In 1808 he was in Edinburgh, where he joined the Society of Associated Artists, to whose exhibitions he contributed from that date till 1816, and he was represented in the modern exhibitions of the Institution for the

Encouragement of the Fine Arts in Scotland in 1821 and 1822. In the earlier exhibition catalogues his name occasionally appears as 'Peter' Gibson. In June 1818 he married Isabella, daughter of William Scott, a well-known teacher of elocution ; and his wife is stated to have been an accomplished musician and the composer of the tune entitled 'Comfort' (information from Mr. James Christie). In 1826 he became a foundation member of the Scottish Academy, to whose exhibitions he contributed (1827–9) landscape and architectural subjects, both Scottish and foreign. In 1824 he had been appointed professor of painting in Dollar Academy, and he died there on 23 Aug. 1829 (see *Parochial Register of Dollar*). In his works in oil, of which there is an example—'Landscape Composition'—in the National Gallery of Scotland, Gibson founded his style upon Claude and Poussin. His water-colours are delicate and careful, executed with washes of rather subdued and low-toned pigments. An interesting volume of them is in the library of the Board of Manufactures, Edinburgh, and a portrait of himself by his own hand in this medium is in the Scottish National Portrait Gallery. He was an accomplished etcher, and published in 1818 a quarto series of six 'Etchings of Select Views in Edinburgh, with Letterpress Descriptions.' He was excellently qualified as a writer on art by his general culture, and his acquaintance, both practical and theoretical, with the subject. He contributed a comprehensive article on 'Design' to the 'Encyclopædia Edinensis;' and articles on 'Drawing,' 'Engraving,' and 'Miniature-painting' to Dr. Brewster's 'Edinburgh Encyclopædia.' His 'View of the Progress and Present State of the Arts of Design in Britain,' in the 'Edinburgh Annual Register' for 1816, is especially valuable for its notices of minor Scottish painters. In Anderson's 'Scottish Nation' he is stated to have contributed an article on the 'Progress of the Fine Arts in Scotland' to the 'New Edinburgh Review ;' but an examination of the five volumes of this publication has failed to disclose the paper. He was author of a curious anonymous *jeu d'esprit* on the exhibition of the Royal Institution, Edinburgh, 1822 ; and, under the pseudonym of 'Roger Roundrobin, Esq.,' of a 'Letter to the Managers and Directors' of the same institution, 1826. A treatise on 'Perspective,' written shortly before his death, was printed but not published. He also contributed to the daily press ; and Laing (*Etchings of Wilkie and Geddes*) is inclined to attribute to his pen a notice of Geddes's exhibition in the 'Edinburgh Evening Courant,' 15 Dec. 1821.

[Authorities quoted above; Catalogues of National Gallery of Scotland, Scottish National Portrait Gallery, Royal Academy, British Institution, Associated Artists, Edinburgh, Royal Institution, Edinburgh, and Royal Scottish Academy; A. Graves's Catalogue of Artists; and information from Mr. Graves.] J. M. G.

GIBSON, RICHARD (1615–1690), dwarf and miniature-painter, is stated to have been a native of Cumberland. He became page to a lady at Mortlake, who discovered his talent for drawing, and placed him under the instruction of Francis Clein [q. v.], the manager of the tapestry works there. Subsequently he became page to Charles I and Henrietta Maria. He obtained considerable success as an artist, especially as a miniature-painter. Evelyn, the diarist, extols his powers (*Numismata*, p. 268). He also copied the style and many of the pictures by Sir Peter Lely. Cromwell patronised him, and Gibson drew his portrait several times. Under Charles II he continued to be a favourite at court, and was appointed instructor in drawing and painting to the princesses Mary and Anne at Richmond Palace. When Mary was married to the Prince of Orange (4 Nov. 1677), he accompanied her to Holland, and remained in her suite for some time. Among his other patrons was Philip Herbert, earl of Pembroke, who showed him many favours. Gibson's miniatures are numerous; among them may be noted the large head of Henrietta Maria (painted on chicken-skin after Vandyck) at Windsor Castle. It was the loss of a miniature painting by Gibson representing 'The Good Shepherd,' and highly valued by Charles I, who owned it, which is said to have caused Abraham Van der Doort [q. v.], the keeper of the royal collections, to commit suicide. Gibson was three feet ten inches in height, and was fortunate enough to find a consort, Anne Shepherd, of the same height. The diminutive pair were married in the presence of Charles I and Henrietta Maria, and the king gave the bride away. Waller, the poet, wrote some verses to commemorate this curious event. They both lived to a great age, and left nine children, five of whom lived to maturity and attained the natural size. Gibson died on 23 July 1690 in his seventy-fifth year, and his wife in 1709, aged 89; they were buried at St. Paul's, Covent Garden. So remarkable a couple offered good subjects for the artist's pencil, and numerous portraits exist. Vertue says that Mr. Rose, the jeweller, Gibson's son-in-law, possessed pictures of Gibson and his master, Clein, in green costume as archers, together with Gibson's bow (archery being a sport of which he was very fond), a portrait of Gibson leaning on a bust, painted by Lely in 1658, a head of Gibson by Dobson, and one of Mrs. Gibson by Lely. Lely also painted a picture of the two dwarfs hand in hand, which was originally the property of the Earl of Pembroke, and subsequently that of Earl Poulett at Hinton St. George, Somersetshire. The figures were engraved by A. Walker for Walpole's ' Anecdotes of Painting' (4th ed.) A head of Gibson, drawn by himself, is in the print room at the British Museum. Mrs. Gibson is represented in the portrait of Mary Villiers, duchess of Richmond and Lenox (formerly Lady Herbert), at Wilton House, of which various replicas exist elsewhere. SUSAN PENELOPE GIBSON (1652–1700), daughter of the above, painted some miniatures, a portrait of Bishop Burnet being best known. She married Rose, a jeweller, from whom Vertue obtained most of his information.

[Walpole's Anecdotes of Painting, ed. Dallaway and Wornum; Vertue's MSS., Brit. Mus. Addit. MSS. 23068, &c.; Davy's MSS., Brit. Mus. Addit. MS. 19131; Redgrave's Dict. of Artists; De Piles's Lives of British Artists; Pilkington's Dict. of Painters; Strickland's Lives of the Queens of England, vol. vii.] L. C.

GIBSON, SOLOMON (*d.* 1866), sculptor, younger brother of John Gibson, R.A. [q. v.], passed his life in Liverpool, where he practised as a sculptor. At the age of sixteen he modelled a small figure of Mercury, which is his best-known work. A copy of this he presented to Sir Thomas Lawrence, who sent him ' as an encouragement ' a ten-pound note. John Kemble greatly admired this work, which he saw Gibson modelling. Lord Colborn bought a bronze cast of the figure from a curiosity dealer in Holland, and showed it to John Gibson as the work of an unknown genius, when to his great surprise Gibson informed him it was by his brother. Gibson was a man of eccentric character. Though well versed in the Greek and Latin classics, and with a good knowledge of ancient Welsh literature—on which subject he wrote many papers—' there was an absence of purpose in the direction of his studies, and he passed through life a strange and useless though not a commonplace man.' For many years he was dependent on the bounty of his brother. In January 1866, hearing of his brother's illness in Rome, he determined to go to see him, and set out, but only reached Paris, where he was taken ill and died three days afterwards, on 29 Jan.

[Eastlake's Life of John Gibson, R.A.; Memoir of Solomon Gibson by Joseph Mayer, F.S.A., manuscript in writer's possession; private information.] A. N

GIBSON, THOMAS (d. 1562), printer, medical practitioner, and theological writer, was a native of Morpeth, Northumberland, and Wood conjectures that he received his education at Oxford, ' because that several of both his names and time were conversant with the muses in that university ' (*Athenæ Oxon.* ed. Bliss, i. 331). It is certain, however, that a Thomas Gibson took the degree of M.B. in the university of Cambridge in 1511 (COOPER, *Athenæ Cantabrigienses,* i. 217). He was noted for his extraordinary success in curing diseases, and also for his strong antipathy to the Roman catholics. He wrote much, and from 1535 to 1539, or afterwards, carried on the business of a printer in London (AMES, *Typogr. Antiquities,* ed. Herbert, pp. 490, 676). With one exception all the known productions of his press were compiled by himself. Bishop Latimer on 21 July 1537 recommended him to Cromwell for employment in printing a book, and says : ' He ys an honeste poore man, who will set ytt forth in a good letter, and sell ytt good chepe, wher as others doo sell too dere, wych doth lett many to by' (*State Papers, Henry VIII,* ii. 564). In the reign of Mary he fled to the continent with his wife and daughter. They became members of the English protestant congregation at Geneva on 20 Nov. 1557 (BURN, *Livre des Anglois à Genève,* p. 11). On the accession of Elizabeth he returned, and in 1559 had a license from the university of Cambridge to practise physic. He died in London in 1562.

The following works are attributed to him : 1. ' The concordance of the new testament, most necessary to be had in the handes of all soche, as desire the communicacion of any place contayned in the new testament,' London, 1535, 8vo. This is the earliest printed concordance in the English language. The epistle to the reader, written by Gibson, intimates that he was the compiler. 2. ' A treatise behouefull, as well to preserue the people from the pestilence, as to helpe and recouer them, that be infected with the same; made by a bishop and doctour of phisick in Denmark; which medicines haue been proued in many places in London,' London, 1536, 4to. 3. 'The great Herball newly corrected,' London, 1539, fol. 4. ' A breue Cronycle of the Byshope of Romes Blessynge, and of his Prelates beneficiall and charitable rewardes, from the time of Kynge Heralde vnto this day,' London, printed by John Day, n.d., 12mo. In English verse. 5. ' The sum of the actes and decrees made by diverse bishops of rome,' translated from the Latin, London [1540?], 8vo. 6. ' Treatise against unskilful Alchimists.' 7. ' Treatise of curing common

diseases.' 8. ' De utroque homine.' 9. ' Of the ceremonies used by Popes.' 10. ' The various states that Britany hath been in.' In five books or parts, left unfinished.

[Bale, De Angliæ Scriptoribus, i. 719 ; Cat. of Early English Books in Brit. Mus. iii. 1320 ; Dibdin's Typogr. Antiquities, iii. 400, 401, iv. 171 ; Hodgson's Northumberland, vol. ii. pt. ii. p. 438 ; Hutchinson's Biog. Medica, i. 354 ; Latimer's Works (Corrie), ii. 380; Maitland's List of Early Printed Books, pp. 198, 242; Tanner's Bibl. Brit. p. 316.]   T. C.

GIBSON, THOMAS, M.D. (1647–1722), physician, was born at High Knipe, in the parish of Bampton, Westmoreland, in 1647. After attending Bampton school he was sent to Leyden University, where he graduated M.D. on 20 Aug. 1675. He was admitted a licentiate of the Royal College of Physicians on 26 June 1676, and an honorary fellow on 30 Sept. 1680. He was a presbyterian, and a visit which he and his second wife paid to his nephew John, provost of Queen's College, Oxford, is sourly described by Hearne (*Hearn. Reliq.* ii. 105). On 21 Jan. 1718–19 he was appointed physician-general to the army. He died on 16 July 1722, aged 75, and was buried in the ground adjoining the Foundling Hospital belonging to St. George the Martyr, Queen Square. He married, first, Elizabeth (1646–92), widow of Zephaniah Cresset of Stanstead St. Margaret's, Hertfordshire, and third daughter of George Smith of that place (CLUTTERBUCK, *Hertfordshire,* ii. 214) ; and secondly, Anne (1659–1727), sixth daughter of Richard Cromwell, the lord protector (*ib.* ii. 97), but left no issue. Edmund Gibson [q. v.] was his nephew and heir. Gibson published ' The Anatomy of Humane Bodies epitomized,' 8vo, London, 1682 (6th edition, 1703), compiled for the most part from Alexander Read's work, but long popular.

[Munk's Coll. of Phys. 1878, i. 413 ; Atkinson's Worthies of Westmoreland, ii. 185–8; will in P. C. C. 138, Marlborough.]   G. G.

GIBSON, THOMAS (1680?–1751), portrait-painter, drew portraits well, and the accessories as well as the expression were attractive. According to the painter Highmore, Sir James Thornhill [q. v.] sometimes applied to Gibson to sketch for him in his large pictures figures in difficult action. Vertue, who was on terms of great friendship with Gibson, says that other artists were offended with Gibson because he refused to raise his prices. He further says he was a man of most amiable character, but suffered from ill-health, and for this reason about 1730 disposed of his pictures privately among his friends, and retired from practice to Oxford. He subsequently returned to London, and is said to have resumed his practice. He died in London on 28 April 1751, aged about 71. At the Society of Antiquaries there is a portrait of Vertue by Gibson, painted in 1723 (engraved by Vertue himself); at the Royal Society a portrait of Flamsteed the astronomer; at the Bodleian Library, Oxford, portraits of Flamsteed and John Locke; and at the National Portrait Gallery a portrait of Archbishop Wake. Many of his portraits were engraved by J. Faber, J. Simon, G. White, G. Vertue, and others, including Sir Robert Walpole, Admiral Sir Charles Wager, Dr. Sacheverell, Robert, lord Molesworth, and the Rev. Samuel Clarke.

[Walpole's Anecdotes of Painting, ed. Dallaway and Wornum ; Redgrave's Dict. of Artists; Chaloner Smith's British Mezzotinto Portraits.]
L. C.

GIBSON, THOMAS MILNER- (1806–1884), statesman, was born at Port of Spain, Trinidad, West Indies, 3 Sept. 1806, and baptised on 8 Nov. His father, Thomas Milner Gibson, son of the Rev. Thomas Gibson, of a family settled at Dovercourt-cum-Harwich and Ipswich, was a major of the 37th foot, who after serving in Trinidad returned to England, where he died in May 1807. His mother, Isabella, daughter of Henry Glover of Chester, after the death of her husband, remarried, in July 1810, Thomas Whiting Wootton, who died in 1844. The only child, Thomas, coming to England with his parents in 1807, was after some time sent to a unitarian school at Higham Hill, Walthamstow, kept by Dr. Eliezer Cogan [q. v.], where he had Benjamin Disraeli for one of his companions. He was next at a school at Blackheath, then was entered at the Charterhouse in 1819, and five years afterwards was at a private tutor's in Nottinghamshire. At Trinity College, Cambridge, he came out thirty-sixth wrangler in 1830, when he proceeded B.A. He was returned as member for Ipswich in the conservative interest on 27 July 1837, but two years later resigned, after becoming a convert to the liberal doctrines of the period. He appealed to the electors to receive him in his new capacity, but was defeated at the poll, 15 July 1839, by Sir T. J. Cochrane. He then contested Cambridge, but it was some time before he was again seen in the House of Commons. Like many other able young men, he found in free trade and its development the cardinal point of his political creed. In the intervals of his exclusion from parliamentary life, while the agitation was being organised for the abolition of the corn laws,

he entered heart and soul into the movement, and became one of Cobden's most influential allies, and one of the prominent orators of the league. This gave him a seat for Manchester, which he won, 1 July 1841, after a severe struggle with Sir George Murray. On the formation of Lord John Russell's ministry in July 1846, with the object of carrying out a free trade policy, he was appointed vice-president of the board of trade, and became a privy councillor on 8 July. The object of Lord John Russell was to strengthen the government by an alliance with the chiefs of the league. Gibson, although he only held office until April 1848, will always be remembered as one of the first official exponents of free trade. Like Lord Palmerston and Charles Buller, he combined great powers of argument with a happy use of ironical humour. His speeches on the sugar duties in 1848 were marked by a thorough mastery of the whole question, and were some of the best delivered on that topic, and his addresses throughout the anti-cornlaw agitation, both in and out of parliament, convinced his audiences. In March 1857 he seconded Cobden's vote of censure of Lord Palmerston's Chinese policy, but together with his friend and colleague John Bright lost his seat for Manchester, his objection to the Crimean war having proved distasteful to his constituents ; however, on 14 Dec. he found refuge at Ashton-under-Lyne, which he continued to represent until 1868, when, being defeated on 17 Nov. by Thomas Walton Mellor, he retired from public life. In March 1869 he was offered but declined the governorship of the Mauritius; he also refused to accept the honour of K.C.B. On the motion for the second reading of Lord Palmerston's bill to amend the law of conspiracy, Gibson moved a vote of censure on the government, which was carried by 234 against 215, and Palmerston resigned 19 Feb. 1858. During Lord Palmerston's ministry, 1859–65, and in the short-lived government of Lord John Russell which followed, 1865–6, Gibson was president of the poor law board, 25 June to 10 July 1859, and president of the board of trade, with cabinet rank, from July 1859 to July 1866, having held the latter place longer than any of his predecessors. He took an active part in the promotion of the commercial treaty with France. The abolition of the newspaper stamp, the advertisement duty, and the excise on paper was, to a very great extent, due to his exertions. In 1850 he became the president of the Association for the Repeal of the Taxes on Knowledge, and took every opportunity of urging on the government the necessity of doing away with the three restrictive duties. This subject was at the same time most ably advocated throughout the country by John Francis [q. v.] The last of these taxes was repealed 1 Oct. 1861, and Gibson's great services were recognised by a public testimonial consisting of a centrepiece and two candelabra, which were presented to him 4 Feb. 1862 (*Illustrated London News*, 15 Feb. 1862, pp. 162, 176, with woodcuts of the plate). Sampson's 'History of Advertising,' 1875, is dedicated to him 'in recognition of the service he rendered to advertising and journalism.' Gibson retired from office with a pension of 2,000*l.* a year, and thenceforth spent his time either at his country residence, Theberton House, Suffolk, or in yachting in the Mediterranean. He was one of the best known amateur yachtsmen of his day, able to navigate his own ship, and at the time of his death was the senior member of the Royal Yacht Squadron. It is curious that he was the last person who cruised in the Mediterranean with a free pass from the dey of Algiers, 1830, and this fact is commemorated on a tablet in the English church there. His knowledge of nautical affairs made him a useful elder brother of the Trinity House, while after his retirement until his death he was one of the most diligent of the public works loan commissioners. He was a J.P. and D.L. for Suffolk, and on 7 Feb. 1839 had by royal license assumed the additional surname of Milner before that of Gibson, in order to testify his respect for the memory of Robert Milner of Ipswich. He died on board his yacht, the Resolute, at Algiers on 25 Feb. 1884, and was buried in Theberton churchyard 13 March (*Bury Free Press*, March 1884). On the day of his funeral a graceful tribute to his memory was published in the 'Times' by Sir T. H. Farrer, permanent secretary of the board of trade, in the name of those who served under him. 'Many an opposition was disarmed,' he wrote, 'and many a struggle in the house or on the platform anticipated and avoided, by the patient good temper with which, in the smoking-room or the lobby, he would discuss while appearing to gossip and lead while appearing to listen. . . . To us it seemed that the public business of our department never received greater attention than when it was in his hands.' His portrait in oils by James Holmes, engraved by W. Holl, and dedicated to the members of the Reform Club, is in the possession of Jasper Milner-Gibson, esq., and his portrait in water-colours by C. A. Du Val, engraved by S. W. Reynolds, belongs to Gery Milner-Gibson-Cullum, esq.

There is no record of Gibson having been an author, but the following works refer to his public career: 1. 'Malt Tax: a Letter to the Members of the House of Commons by J. Fielden, exposing the misstatements of Mr. Milner Gibson,' 1865. 2. 'Railways, in a Letter to the President of the Board of Trade: a Plan for the Reform of the Railways of the United Kingdom,' 1865.

He married, 23 Feb. 1832, Susanna Arethusa, only child of the Rev. Sir Thomas Gery Cullum, bart., of Hardwick House, Suffolk, and granddaughter of Sir T. G. Cullum [q. v.] She was born at Southgate Green, Bury St. Edmunds, 11 Jan. 1814, and was for many years a leader in society, and an advocate of mesmerism and spiritualism when those sciences were in their infancy. Her political and literary salon was opened to many distinguished exiles, Napoleon, Mazzini, Victor Hugo, Louis Blanc, and others, as well as to the leading English literary celebrities, especially Dickens, to one of whose sons she stood sponsor. An account of her salon is to be found in Edmund Yates's 'Recollections,' i. 252–3 (1884), and again in Mrs. Lynn Linton's curious 'Autobiography of Christopher Kirkland' (1885), ii. 15 et seq. Latterly she became a Roman catholic, and died at 11 Avenue du Bois de Boulogne, Paris, 23 Feb. 1885, aged 71, and was buried in the cemetery, Bury St. Edmunds, 3 March (*Bury and Norwich Post*, 3 March 1885). By her husband she had a large family, of whom only two survived, Jasper Milner-Gibson of Theberton House, and Gery Milner-Gibson-Cullum of Hardwick House, both in Suffolk.

[Francis's Orators of the Age, 1847, pp. 294–300; Evans's Lancashire Authors and Orators, 1850, pp. 101–5; Illustrated News of the World, 6 March 1858, p. 76, with portrait; Grant's Newspaper Press, 1871, ii. 299, 311–19; Nicoll's Great Movements, 1881, pp. 268–331, with portrait; Illustrated London News, 27 Feb. 1858, p. 207, 31 Dec. 1842, p. 541, with portrait, and 8 March 1884, pp. 217, 227, with portrait; Graphic, 15 March 1884, pp. 249–50, with portrait; Times, 26 Feb. 1884, p. 10, and 13 March, p. 4; information from Gery Milner-Gibson-Cullum, esq., Hardwick House, Bury St. Edmunds; Morley's Life of Cobden; J. G. Francis's John Francis, 1888; Men of the Time, 11th ed. pp. 168, 457; Anecdotal Photographs in Truth, 12 May 1881.] G. C. B.

GIBSON, WILLIAM (*fl.* 1540), lord of session, was the second son of Thomas Gibson of Durie in Fifeshire, who lived in the reign of James IV of Scotland. He was educated for the church at the university of Glasgow, where he was incorporated in 1503 and graduated in December 1507. He afterwards became vicar of Garvock, Kincardineshire, and in 1518, when present at a meeting of the Glasgow University council, was designated rector of Inverarity Forfarshire.

On 17 April 1526, when witnessing a document, he is styled 'that venerable and circumspect man Master William Gibson, dean of Restalrig.' His predecessor was Patrick Covyntre, who had presided at his graduation, one of thirteen ambassadors for negotiating a peace with England in 1516, who died about 1524. Gibson must, therefore, have become dean about 1525. On 27 Aug. 1527, after Gibson had become dean, James V added the rectory of Ellem to Restalrig.

In 1532 Gibson was appointed a lord of session. To remedy defects in the administration of justice in civil causes, which had rested with the nobility, James V had resolved to institute the College of Justice, of which the first idea is said to have been suggested by the parliament of Paris. This court was to consist of fourteen judges and a president. Ten thousand 'golden ducats of the chamber' were to be levied from the Scottish bishoprics and monastic institutions, and in return for this it was stipulated that one half of the judges should be ecclesiastics, and that the president should always be a churchman.

According to Sir Robert Douglas, followed by Brunton and Haig, Gibson was, on account of his extensive abilities, frequently employed in embassies to the pope. Contemporary history does not record many such embassies at that period, but there was one connected with the dispute between James V and the prelates about the expenses of the College of Justice, and probably Gibson had some credit for the amicable settlement of that matter. For some reason he was in favour with the pope, who bestowed on him an armorial bearing of three keys, with the motto 'Cœlestes pandite portas.' This has been retained by representatives of the family ever since, but they do not now possess the estate of Durie.

In 1539 James Beaton, archbishop of St. Andrews, died, and the charge of all ecclesiastical affairs was committed to his nephew the cardinal, David Beaton [q. v.], who in 1540 desired to associate Gibson with himself as suffragan. He was to hold his other preferments and to receive a pension of 200l. a year from the cardinal and his successors. To this arrangement the pope's sanction was needful, and in letters dated 4 May 1540 James V and Cardinal Beaton answer for Gibson's knowledge of law and theology, and for his high moral character. It was probably in connection with this appointment that the king gave him the title of 'Custos Ecclesiæ Scoticæ.' The precise date of his death is uncertain, but it appears to have been before 1545. On 27 April 1540 Dr. John Sinclair

was appointed a lord of session, while abbot of Snaw, which designation he still held in 1542. From that date there is a blank in the register till 1545, when the name of Gibson has disappeared, and Sinclair is on the list of judges as dean of Restalrig.

[Douglas's Baronage of Scotland, p. 568; Brunton and Haig's Senators of the College of Justice, p.13; Reg. Univ. Glasguensis, ii. 18,124, 138, 285; Charters of the Collegiate Churches of Midlothian (Bannatyne Club), pp. 273, 280, 290, and preface thereto, pp. xliii–v; Epist. Reg. Scot., printed 1724, pp. 63–6; Tytler's Hist. of Scotland, v. 198; Spotiswood's Church Hist. pp. 67–8, fol. London, 1666.] J. T.

GIBSON, WILLIAM (1629–1684), quaker, was born at Caton in Lancashire in 1629. During his early life he was a puritan, and a soldier in the parliamentary forces. While forming part of the garrison at Carlisle he joined a party to insult a quaker meeting, but was so attracted by the preacher's words that he attended other meetings, and finally left the army. In 1654 he was committed to Lancaster gaol for 'public testimony.' In 1655 and 1656 he was several times imprisoned for short periods for the same offence, and is believed to have been recognised as a quaker minister about this time. In 1660 he was again imprisoned at Lancaster for some months on account of his refusal to take the oaths of allegiance and supremacy, and in 1661 at Shrewsbury for some unknown cause. During the same year he was seized on the road to a meeting in Denbighshire by a party of soldiers, and sent to gaol with a number of other quakers. They were all liberated at the assizes except Gibson, who was kept in prison and cruelly treated by the gaolers. They once threw him down a flight of stone stairs, and caused a six months' illness. On his discharge he married in 1662, and settled at Warrington in Lancashire, where he is believed to have engaged in trade. Subsequently he seems to have removed to London, and in 1672 his name appears in a list of quakers discharged from the king's bench under the general proclamation of Charles II. During 1676 and 1677, while living in Fenchurch Street, his goods were several times distrained on account of his not paying tithes. From a letter protesting against the eviction of the Friends from Danzig, dated 8 Aug. 1679, Gibson appears to have been engaged in ministerial work in Holland during that year. He died in London, aged 55, on 23 Nov. 1684, and was buried from a meeting in White Hart Court at the Friends' burial-ground, near Bunhill Fields, his funeral being attended by upwards of a thousand quakers. His published writings are: 1. 'A Salutation of the Father's Love unto the Young Men and Virgins, who are in the Openings of the Prophesies in Visions and in Revelations,' &c., 1663, written in 1661 in Shrewsbury gaol. 2. 'The Everlasting Rule born witness unto . . . in words,' 1667. 3. 'Universal Love, being an Epistle given forth by the Spirit of God through His Suffering Servant, William Gibson,' 1671; republished 1672; written in Maidstone gaol. 4. 'Tythes ended by Christ with the Levitical Priesthood,' &c., 1673. Part by T. Rudyard and George Watt. 5. 'A False Witness examin'd and rebuk'd,' &c., 1674. 6. 'The Life of God which is the Light and Salvation of Men Exalted: or an Answer to six Books or particular Treatises given forth by John Cheyney . . .' 1677. 7. 'Election and Reprobation Scripturally and Experimentally Witnessed unto, &c.,' 1678. 8. 'A Christian Testimony born by the People of God, in scorn call'd Quakers, in London . . .' 1679. Part by Thomas Rudyard. 9. 'A General Epistle given forth in obedience to the God of Peace . . .' &c., 1682.

[Neal's Hist. of the Puritans, ed. 1822, v. 267; Gough's Hist. of the Quakers, iv. 3; Besse's Sufferings, i. 255, &c.; Smith's Catalogue of Friends' Books.]   A. C. B.

GIBSON, WILLIAM (1664–1702), miniature-painter, was nephew of Richard Gibson, the dwarf [q. v.], from whom he received instruction. He was also a pupil of Sir Peter Lely, and was very successful in his copies of Lely's works. He attained great eminence as a miniature-painter, and was largely employed by the nobility. At the sale of Lely's collection of prints and drawings by the old masters, Gibson bought a great number, and added considerably to them by subsequent purchases. He resided in the parish of St. Giles-in-the-Fields, and died of a 'lethargy' in 1702, aged 58. He was buried at Richmond in Surrey.

[Walpole's Anecd. of Painting, ed. Dallaway and Wornum; De Piles's Lives of the Painters; Brit. Mus. Addit. MS. 19131 (Davy MSS.) fol. 257; Manning and Bray's Hist. of Surrey, i. 433.]   L. C.

GIBSON, WILLIAM (1720–1791), self-taught mathematician, born at Boulton, near Appleby, Westmoreland, in 1720, worked on a farm from childhood, and afterwards obtained a farm of his own at Hollins, near Cartmel Fell, Lancashire. He received no education whatever in youth, but in early manhood taught himself to read a book on arithmetic, and developed an extraordinary power of working out sums of all kinds in his head.

He afterwards taught himself writing, and studied geometry, trigonometry, algebra, and astronomy, in all of which he proved himself an expert. He finally acquired a knowledge of the higher mathematics in all their branches, and answered correctly for many years the problems propounded in the 'Gentleman's Diary,' the 'Ladies' Diary,' the 'Palladium,' and similar publications. His fame spread, and he was consulted by mathematicians in various parts of England. About 1750 he opened a school at Cartmel for eight or ten pupils, who boarded at his farmhouse. He also obtained a good practice as a land-surveyor. He died from a fall at his house at Blawith, near Cartmel, on 4 Sept. 1791, leaving a widow and ten children. A son of the same name, employed at the Bank of England, died at Pentonville on 13 Feb. 1817, aged 64.

[Gent. Mag. 1791 pt. ii. 1062–4, 1817. pt. i. 188; Chalmers's Biog. Dict.]

GIBSON, WILLIAM, D.D. (1738–1821), catholic prelate, fifth son of Jasper Gibson of Stonecrofts, near Hexham, Northumberland, was born on 2 Feb. 1738, and educated in the English College at Douay, where he was ordained priest. He came back on the mission in 1765, and for many years he resided in the family of the Silvertops of Minster-Acres. He was president of Douay College from 1781 till 1790, when he was appointed vicar-apostolic of the northern district of England in succession to his elder brother, Matthew Gibson [q. v.]. His consecration as bishop of Acanthos, in partibus, took place at Lulworth Castle, 5 Dec. 1790. He entered actively into the disputes between the bishops and the 'catholic committee' on the question of catholic relief [see BUTLER, CHARLES, 1750–1832], and was mainly instrumental in establishing a new college for the refugees from Douay, by which the famous English College has been perpetuated at Ushaw [see ALLEN, WILLIAM, cardinal, and EYRE, THOMAS]. He died at Durham, which had always been his episcopal residence, on 2 June 1821, and was buried at Ushaw College.

He compiled a French grammar for the use of Douay College, and translated from the French of M. de Mahis 'The Truth of the Catholic Religion proved from the Holy Scriptures,' Newcastle-on-Tyne, 1799, 8vo. 'A Conversation between the Right Hon. Edmund Burke and the R.R. Dr. Gibson,' in reference to the proposed government veto on the appointment of catholic bishops, appeared at London, 1807, 8vo.

His portrait, drawn by W. M. Craig, and roughly lithographed by Vowkes, is inserted in the 'Catholic Miscellany' for September 1825. There is a fine full-length portrait of him in the refectory at Ushaw.

[Gillow's Chapels at Ushaw, with an historical introduction (Durham, 1885); Gillow's Bibl. Dict.; Brady's Episcopal Succession, iii. 268; Douay Diaries, p. 71; Oliver's Catholic Religion in Cornwall, p. 40; Petre's Colleges on the Continent, p. 4; Amherst's Hist. of Catholic Emancipation, i. 169, ii. 40, 54, 81, 127, 132.] T. C.

GIBSON, WILLIAM, D.D. (1808–1867), Irish presbyterian divine, son of James Gibson, a merchant in Ballymena, co. Antrim, was born there 8 May 1808. He attended school in his native town and in the Belfast Academical Institution, where he took the medal for classics in 1829. His collegiate training was obtained partly in Belfast and partly in Edinburgh. In 1833 he was licensed, and in 1834 ordained minister of First Ballybay, co. Monaghan. In 1835 a pamphlet which he wrote on 'The Position of the Church of Ireland and the Duty of Presbyterians in reference to it' had a wide circulation. In 1840 he became colleague to the Rev. Samuel Hanna, D.D., in Rosemary Street Church, Belfast. In 1842 he was the chief means of establishing the 'Banner of Ulster,' a newspaper devoted principally to the interests of Irish presbyterianism. In 1847 he was appointed professor of Christian ethics in the assembly's college, Belfast. In 1859 he became moderator of the general assembly. He died suddenly in June 1867. His chief work was 'The Year of Grace, a History of the Ulster Revival of 1859,' Edinburgh, 1850.

[Personal knowledge; obituary notices.]
T. H.

GIBSON, WILLIAM SIDNEY (1814–1871), miscellaneous writer, born at Parson's Green, Fulham, in 1814, was for some years on the staff of a Carlisle newspaper. He entered Lincoln's Inn, and was called to the bar by that society in 1843. The same year he was appointed registrar of the Newcastle-upon-Tyne district court of bankruptcy. When the Bankruptcy Act of 1869 (32 & 33 Vict. c. 71) abolished this among other like courts, Gibson retired on a pension, and devoted himself entirely to antiquarian and literary studies. He died at the Grosvenor Hotel, London, 3 Jan. 1871, and was interred in the disused burial-ground of the Old Priory, Tynemouth, 'for which a special permission had been obtained from the home office during the lifetime of the deceased.' He was an honorary M.A. of Durham, and a fellow of the London Society of Antiquaries and many other learned societies.

Gibson wrote: 1. 'The Certainties of Geology,' 1840. 2. 'Prize Essay on the History and Antiquities of Highgate,' 1842 (written for a Highgate society). 3. 'The History of the Monastery founded at Tynemouth in the Diocese of Durham,' 2 vols., 1846–7 (a review of this, which originally appeared in the 'Newcastle Guardian,' was republished, Newcastle-on-Tyne, 1846). 4. 'An Essay on the Filial Duties,' 1848. 5. 'A Letter to the Lord Chancellor on the Amendment of the Law of Bankruptcy,' 1848. 6. 'Descriptive and Historical Notices of some remarkable Northumbrian Castles, Churches, and Antiquities, in a Series of Visits to the ruined Priory of Finchale, the Abbey Church of Hexham, &c., with Biographical Notices of Eminent Persons' (three series, 1848–54; the second series entitled 'Dilston Hall,' &c.) 7. 'Remarks on the Mediæval Writers on English History, intended as a popular Sketch of the Advantages and Pleasures derivable from Monastic Literature,' 1848. 8. 'Marvels of the Globe,' two lectures, 1856. 9. 'Lectures and Essays,' two series, 1858–63. 10. 'A Memoir of Northumberland, descriptive of its Scenery, Monuments, and History,' 1860, and, in a different form, 1862. 11. 'Descriptive and Historical Guide to Tynemouth, with Notices of North Shields, &c.,' Tynemouth and North Shields, 1861. 12. 'A Memoir of Lord Lyndhurst,' 1866; new edition, 1869. Gibson also wrote 'A Memoir of the Life of Richard de Bury, Bishop of Durham,' articles for Colburn's 'New Monthly Magazine' and other periodicals, and was an early contributor to 'Notes and Queries.'

[Colburn's New Monthly Magazine, April 1871; Solicitors' Journal and Reporter, 14 Jan. 1871, p. 260; Notes and Queries, 4th ser. vii. 48, xi. 28.] F. W–т.

GIDDY, DAVIES (1767–1839), president of the Royal Society. [See Gilbert.]

GIDEON, SAMPSON (1699–1762), capitalist and financier, was of Jewish race. His father, Rowland Gideon (d. 1720), a West India merchant, who was a freeman of the city of London and on the court of the Painter Stainers' Company (admitted 17 Feb. 1697), had changed his name from the Portuguese name of Abudiente on settling in England. Sampson Gideon was born in London in 1699, and began business when only twenty years old with a capital of 1,500l., which in less than two years had increased to 7,900l. He was admitted a sworn broker in 1729, with a capital of 25,000l. His fortune mounted up rapidly, and was invested mainly in landed estates, which at his death in 1762 were valued at 580,000l.

Gideon became, writes a contemporary, 'the great oracle and leader of Jonathan's Coffee House in Exchange Alley,' afterwards the Stock Exchange in Threadneedle Street (NICHOLS, *Anecdotes*, ix. 642). He began to be consulted by the government in 1742, when Walpole desired his advice in raising a loan for the Spanish war. His aid became still more important to Pelham in 1743 and 1744, when the French fleet held the Channel and the funds were falling. In 1745, when the advance of Charles Edward to Derby threw the city into a panic, he freely lent his property and his credit to the government, and raised a loan of 1,700,000*l.* In 1749 he advised and carried through the consolidation of the national debt and the reduction of its interest, and in 1750 is said to have raised a million, three per cent., at par. He also, in 1753, raised a loan for the citizens at Danzig. At the beginning of the seven years' war in 1756, he paid a bounty from his estates for the recruiting of the army; and in the great years of the war, 1758–9 (as is shown by letters from the Dukes of Newcastle and Devonshire), he was almost wholly relied on by the government for the raising of loans. He added little to his fortune from this time till his death, and even sold parts of his estates, owing to his preoccupation with government finance.

He built a fine house at Belvedere, near Erith (which is now used for a merchant sailors' asylum), and collected a remarkable gallery of pictures by the old masters, which is now at Bedwell Park, Hertfordshire, the seat of his descendant, Mrs. Culling Hanbury. According to Horace Walpole, Gideon purchased, in 1751, many paintings that had belonged to Sir Robert Walpole. Though so closely connected with the government, he took no part in support of the measure introduced by the Pelhams in 1750 for the naturalisation of the Jews. It was his ambition to be made a baronet; but, this being considered impossible on account of his religion, a baronetcy was conferred in 1759 on his son Sampson, then a boy of fifteen under education as a Christian at Eton. He possessed, besides his mansion at Belvedere, large estates at Salden in Buckinghamshire, at Spalding and Caistor in Lincolnshire, and at Borough Fen, near Peterborough. As lord of the manor of Spalding he was elected in 1750 member of the well-known antiquarian 'Gentlemen's Society at Spalding' (NICHOLS, *Anecdotes*, vi. 85).

Gideon married Elizabeth Erwell, a member of the church of England. He ceased all open connection with the Portuguese synagogue at Bevis Marks in 1753, yet he never himself joined the Christian church. 'He breeds his children Christians,' Horace Walpole wrote correctly in 1753. Gideon's youngest daughter, Elizabeth, married (1757) William Hall Gage, second viscount Gage. All his estates descended to his only son, Sampson (1744–1824), who married (6 Dec. 1766) the daughter of Chief-justice Sir John Eardley Wilmot, assumed the surname of Eardley in July 1789, and was in October 1789 created Lord Eardley in the Irish peerage. The peerage became extinct at his death in 1824, his two sons, Sampson Eardley, a *détenu* after the peace of Amiens, and Colonel Eardley of the guards, having died before him. Lord Eardley's three daughters married respectively Lord Saye and Sele, Sir Culling Smith (father of Sir Culling Eardley Eardley [q. v.]), and J. W. Childers, esq., of Cantley, near Doncaster, among whom his estates were divided.

Gideon was a man of remarkable amiability and generosity, ' of strong natural understanding, and of some fun and humour.' At his death, which took place at Belvedere on 17 Oct. 1762, it was found that he had continued to pay his contribution to the synagogue under the name of Peloni Almoni, and he was buried with much ceremony in the Jewish cemetery at Mile End. He left legacies by will, dated 17 April 1760, to many charities, both Jewish and Christian, including the Portuguese synagogue and the Corporation of the Sons of the Clergy, to which he had been an annual subscriber of 100*l.* during his lifetime. To the Duke of Devonshire, one of his executors, he left the reversion of his estates if his children died without issue. Much of Gideon's correspondence with the Duke of Newcastle (1756–1762) and others is among the Addit. MSS. at the British Museum.

[Private information; J. Picciotto's Sketches of Anglo-Jewish History, 1875, pp. 60 sq.; Nichols's Illustrations, vi. 277–84 (by J. Eardley Wilmot); Horace Walpole's Letters, ed. Cunningham, ii. 260, 395; Nichols's Anecdotes, ix. 642–3.]

W. H. F.

GIFFARD. [See also GIFFORD.]

GIFFARD, SIR AMBROSE HARDINGE (1771–1827), chief justice of Ceylon, eldest son of John Giffard (1745–1819), high sheriff of Dublin in 1794, accountant-general of customs in Dublin, and a prominent loyalist, was born at Dublin in 1771. His mother was Sarah, daughter of William Morton, esq., of Ballynaclash, co. Wexford. The Giffards were an ancient Devonshire family; but the grandfather of the chief justice, who was the disinherited grandson of John Giffard of Brightleigh, settled in Ireland. Giffard received his christian names from his father's intimate friend, Ambrose Hardinge. After studying for the law he was called to the bar of the Inner Temple, and was appointed chief justice of Ceylon in April 1819. Giffard's leisure was devoted to literature, and a selection of poems was published at Ceylon about 1822. Specimens are reproduced in the 'Traditions and Recollections' of the Rev. J. Polwhele. Owing to the eastern climate Giffard's health failed, and he was granted leave of absence, but he died on 30 April 1827, while on the homeward voyage, in the Lady Kennaway, East Indiaman. Before his death a knighthood was conferred upon Giffard, but the title was never gazetted. He married in 1808 Harriet, daughter of Lovell Pennell, esq., of Lyme Regis, and left five sons and five daughters. Admiral Sir George Giffard (1815–1888) was his third son.

[Gent. Mag. 1827; Burke's Peerage, s. v. 'Halsbury.']   G. B. S.

GIFFARD, BONAVENTURE, D.D. (1642–1734), Roman catholic bishop, and president of Magdalen College, Oxford, second son of Andrew Giffard of Chillington, in the parish of Brewood, Staffordshire, by Catherine, daughter of Sir Walter Leveson, was born at Wolverhampton in 1642. His father was slain in a skirmish near Wolverhampton early in the civil war (SMITH, *Brewood*, p. 38). The family still exists, and traces a pedigree without failure of heirs male from before the Conquest. Bonaventure was educated in the English College at Douay, and thence proceeded on 23 Oct. 1667 to complete his ecclesiastical studies in Paris. He received the degree of D.D. in 1677 from the Sorbonne, having previously been ordained as a secular priest for the English mission. James II soon after his accession made Giffard one of his chaplains and preachers. On 30 Nov. 1686 he and Dr. Thomas Godden [q. v.] disputed with Dr. Jane and Dr. Simon Patrick before the king and the Earl of Rochester concerning the real presence (MACAULAY, *Hist. of England*, ed. 1858, ii. 149–53). In 1687 Innocent XI divided England into four ecclesiastical districts, and allowed James to nominate persons to govern them. Accordingly Giffard was appointed the first vicar-apostolic of the midland district by propaganda election on 12 Jan. (N.S.) 1687–8. His briefs for the vicariate and the see of Madaura, *in partibus*, were dated 30 Jan. 1687–8, and he was consecrated in the banqueting hall at Whitehall on Low Sunday, 22 April (O.S.) 1688, by Ferdinand d'Adda, archbishop of Amasia, *in partibus*, and nuncio apostolic in

England. Some writers say, however, that Bishop John Leyburn was the consecrator. Giffard's name is attached to the pastoral letter from the four catholic bishops which was addressed to the lay catholics of England in 1688.

On the death of Samuel Parker, bishop of Oxford, who had been appointed president of Magdalen College by the king in spite of the election of John Hough by the fellows, Bishop Giffard, by royal letters mandatory, was appointed president. He was installed by proxy on 31 March 1688, and on 15 June 'took possession of his seat in the chapel, and lodgings belonging to him as president' (WOOD, *Athenæ Oxon.* ed. Bliss, iv. 235, 898). His brother, Andrew Giffard, a secular priest, and eleven other members of the church of Rome were then elected fellows. The college was practically converted into a Roman catholic establishment, and mass was celebrated in the chapel (BURNET, *Hist. of James II*, ed. Routh, 1852, p. 262). By virtue of special authority from the king, Giffard on 7 Aug. expelled several fellows who had refused to acknowledge him as their lawful president. On 3 Oct. Sancroft, archbishop of Canterbury, with other bishops then in London, advised the king to restore the president (Hough) and fellows. James, according to Macaulay, did not yield till the vicar-apostolic Leyburn declared that in his judgment the ejected president and fellows had been wronged. Giffard and the other intruders were in their turn ejected by Mew, bishop of Winchester, visitor of the college, on 25 Oct. 1688. Luttrell (*Relation of State Affairs*, i. 469) relates that the catholic fellows and scholars embezzled much of the college plate; but Bloxam remarks that it is only due to them to say that a diligent inspection completely disproved the charge (*Magdalen College Register*, ii. p. clviii).

At the revolution Giffard and Bishop Leyburn were seized at Faversham, on their way to Dover, and were actually under arrest when James II was brought into that town. Both prelates were committed to prison, Leyburn being sent to the Tower, and Giffard to Newgate. They were both liberated on bail by the court of king's bench on 9 July 1690, on condition that they would transport themselves beyond sea before the end of the following month (LUTTRELL, *Hist. Relation of State Affairs*, ii. 73).

In 1703 Giffard was transferred from the midland to the London district, on the death of Leyburn. He also took charge of the western district from 1708 to 1713 in the absence of Bishop Ellis [see ELLIS, PHILIP]. Dodd says he lived privately in London, under the connivance of the government, who gave him very little disturbance, being fully satisfied with the inoffensiveness of his behaviour (*Church Hist.* iii. 469). It is certain, however, that he was exposed to constant danger. He tells Cardinal Sacripanti in 1706 that for sixteen years he had scarcely found anywhere a place to rest in with safety. For above a year he found a refuge in the house of the Venetian ambassador. Afterwards he again lived in continual fear and alarm. In 1714 he wrote that between 4 May and 7 Oct. he had had to change his lodgings fourteen times, and had but once slept in his own lodging. He added: 'I may say with the apostle, *in carceribus abundantius.* In one I lay on the floor a considerable time, in Newgate almost two years, afterwards in Hertford gaol, and now daily expect a fourth prison to end my life in' (*Catholic Miscellany,* 1827, vii. 170).

In 1720 he applied to the holy see for a coadjutor. Henry Howard, brother to the Duke of Norfolk, was accordingly created bishop of Utica, *in partibus,* and nominated to the coadjutorship, *cum jure successionis,* on 2 Oct. 1720, but he died before the end of the year, and in March 1720-1 the propaganda appointed Benjamin Petre coadjutor in his stead. Giffard died at Hammersmith on 12 March 1733-4, in his ninety-second year, and was buried in the old churchyard of St. Pancras. The tomb has disappeared, but the inscription upon it is printed in 'Notes and Queries,' 3rd ser. xii. 191 (cf. *Addit. MS.* 27488, f. 130). Giffard bequeathed his heart to Douay College, and it was buried in the chapel, where a monument with an epitaph in Latin was erected to his memory (BRADY, *Episcopal Succession,* iii. 161).

Dodd highly commends Giffard for his charity to the poor, and Granger says he was much esteemed by men of different religions. He procured many large benefactions for the advancement of the catholic religion and the benefit of the clergy, and at his death left about 3,000*l.* for the same ends (GILLOW, *Dict. of the English Catholics,* ii. 456).

Two of his sermons preached at court were published separately in 1687, and are reprinted in 'Catholic Sermons,' 2 vols. Lond. 1741 and 1772. Many interesting letters written by him are printed in the 'Catholic Miscellany' for 1826 and 1827. There is a fine picture of him at Chillington, a life size, half length. His portrait has been engraved by Claude du Bosc, from a painting by H. Hysing.

[Bloxam's Magdalen Coll. and King James II, pp. 214, 242, 243, 244, 245, 250, 253 *n.,* 265, 270, 271; Bloxam's Magdalen Coll. Reg. i. 121 *n.,*
ii. pp. clii, cliii, clv, iii. 184, 196; Brady's Episcopal Succession, iii. 147, 149-61, 203, 206, 245, 283, 289; Cansick's Epitaphs at St. Pancras, i. 29; Catholic Mag. (1833), iii. 103; Catholic Miscell. (1826) v. 131, 310, vi. 12, 83, 158, 227, 320, 378, (1827) vii. 30, 169, 322; Dodd's Church Hist. iii. 425, 469, 486; Gillow's Bibl. Dict. ii. 451, 454; Granger's Biog. Hist. of England, 5th edit. vi. 107; Laity's Direct. for 1805 (portrait); Lingard's Hist. of England (1849), x. 296; Luttrell's Hist. Relation of State Affairs, i. 68, 430, 435, 445, ii. 65, 73, v. 469; Noble's Contin. of Granger, iii. 171; Notes and Queries, 1st ser. vii. 242, 3rd ser. i. 263, xi. 455, 509, xii. 76, 189, 190, 512, 4th ser. i. 64; Palmer's Life of Cardinal Howard, p. 203; Panzani's Memoirs, pp. 338, 361, 365, 373, 378, 387; Smith's Brewood; Wood's Athenæ Oxon. (Bliss), iv. 598; Wood's Fasti, ii. 402.]   T. C.

GIFFARD, Sir GEORGE MARKHAM (1813–1870), lord justice of appeal, fourth son of Admiral John Giffard, and Susannah, daughter of Sir John Carter, was born at his father's official residence, Portsmouth dockyard, 4 Nov. 1813. He was educated at Winchester College and at New College, Oxford, where he was elected to a fellowship in 1832 and took the degree of B.C.L. on 4 March 1841, entered at the Inner Temple, of which he eventually became a bencher, and was called to the bar in November 1840. He rapidly obtained an excellent equity practice, and was for many years a leading chancery junior counsel. In 1859 he became a queen's counsel, and attached himself to the court of Vice-chancellor Sir William Page Wood, and, in spite of a severe illness which kept him from his work for many months after he received silk, he soon obtained a leading position in that court. When Vice-chancellor Wood in March 1868 became a lord justice of appeal, Giffard succeeded him, and was again his successor on his promotion from the court of appeal to the woolsack in December, when he also became a member of the privy council. After an illness of some length he died at his house, 4 Prince's Gardens, Hyde Park, London, on 13 July 1870. He was both quick and learned, indifferent to rhetorical display, terse in argument, and a refined and cultivated scholar. He was a decided liberal in politics, but never contested any constituency. In 1853 he married Maria, second daughter of Charles Pilgrim of Kingsfield, Southampton.

[Solicitors' Journal, 16 July 1870; Law Times 16 July 1870. For descriptions of him by the Lord-chancellor and Lord-justice James, see Times, 16 and 20 July 1870; Cat. Oxf. Graduates; Kirby's Winchester Scholars.]

J. A. H.

GIFFARD, GODFREY (1235?–1302), chancellor of England and bishop of Worcester, was the son of Hugh Giffard of Boyton in Wiltshire, a royal justice, and of his wife Sibyl, daughter and coheiress of Walter de Cormeilles. He was born about 1235 (*Calendarium Genealogicum*, p. 281). He was the younger brother of Walter Giffard [q. v.], ultimately archbishop of York, whose successful career insured the preferment of Godfrey. When his brother was bishop of Bath and Wells, he became canon of Wells (NEWCOURT, *Repert. Eccl. Lond.* i. 59) and rector of Mells. He was also rector of the greater mediety of Attleburgh in Norfolk (BLOMEFIELD, *Norfolk*, i. 523), archdeacon of Barnstaple from 1265 to 1267, and, after Walter became archbishop of York, archdeacon of York and rector of Adlingfleet in 1267 (RAINE, *Fasti Eboracenses*, p. 315 from Reg. W. Giffard). Complaints were afterwards made at Rome of the way in which the archbishop gave this and many other benefices to his brother, though Godfrey was only in minor orders and deficient in learning. After Walter became chancellor of England in 1265, Godfrey in 1266 was made chancellor of the exchequer (MADOX, *Hist. of Exchequer*, i. 476), and next year was allowed to appoint a fit person to act for him when his own affairs gave him occasion to withdraw from the exchequer (*ib.* ii. 52). When in 1266 Walter was translated to York, he resigned the chancellorship, and Godfrey was appointed his successor. He was still chancellor when the monks of Worcester elected him as their bishop on the translation of Bishop Nicholas of Ely [q. v.] to the see of Winchester. Henry III accepted his appointment, and he received the temporalities on 13 June 1268. After some little resistance, Archbishop Boniface confirmed his election, but it was not until 23 Sept. that he was consecrated by the archbishop at Canterbury ('Ann. London.' in STUBBS, *Chronicles of Edward I and II*, i. 79). He was enthroned in his cathedral on Christmas day (WYKES in *Annales Monastici*, iv. 220). He still retained the chancellorship, and in 1268 received a grant of five hundred marks a year for the support of himself and the clerks of the chancery (MADOX, i. 76), but before 1270 he had resigned the office.

In 1272 he acted with the Bishop of Lichfield in treating with Llewelyn of Wales (SHIRLEY, *Royal Letters*, ii. 343). In May 1273 he was sent abroad with Nicholas of Ely, bishop of Winchester, and Walter Bronescomb, bishop of Exeter, to meet Edward I on his return from the Holy Land. He was made a commissioner along with Roger Mortimer to investigate certain grievances of the Oxford scholars, and in 1278 acted as an itinerant justice in Herefordshire, Hertfordshire, and Kent (Foss, *Judges of England*, ii. 94). In 1279 he succeeded to the very extensive property, inherited and acquired, of his brother the archbishop. He was one of the four negotiators selected in 1289 by Edward I to treat at Salisbury with the Scottish and Norwegian envoys about sending Margaret of Norway to Scotland (*Fœdera*, i. 720).

Giffard ruled over the see of Worcester for more than thirty-three years, and his activity was almost confined to his own diocese. He was engaged in constant disputes with his monastic chapter, long accounts of which, written from the monks' point of view, have come down to us in the 'Annals of Worcester' (*Annales Monastici*, vol. iv.) The great subject of contention was whether the bishop should be allowed to annex some of the more valuable livings in his gift to the prebends of the college at Westbury, which led to tedious litigation, ultimately decided in favour of the monks. But the claim of the bishop to receive the monks' 'profession' produced other suits. In 1288, at an ordination at Westbury, an unseemly dispute between the precentor of Worcester and John of Evreux, archdeacon of Gloucester, a favourite nephew of the bishop, as to who had the right to call over the names of the candidates, led to the expulsion of the former from the chancel with the connivance of the bishop (*Ann. Wigorn.* p. 496). A little later a truce was patched up, but at Bromsgrove the bishop 'would not permit the prior to exercise his office, regardless of the peace that had been made, which we believe to have been as vain as a peace with the Welsh.' The monks also complained of his taking away the chapel at Grafton from them, and of the constant efforts of the bishop to visit and to exercise jurisdiction over them. In 1290 he held a visitation, and required the convent to support his 140 horses, and went away in anger. Though in 1290 he, at Bishop Burnell's mediation, revoked the statutes of the priory and agreed to postpone the lawsuits, he soon after procured from Rome a 'very bad bull' against them.

Giffard was involved in another great dispute with the Abbot of Westminster. He had deposed William of Ledbury, prior of Malvern, for gross crimes. The monks of Westminster took up William's cause, as Malvern was a cell of their abbey, and obtained the king's support. In the end Giffard was glad to compromise the case, and received a grant of land at Knightwick not to visit Malvern as his predecessors had done (1283), and Ledbury was restored. This settlement Archbishop Peckham denounced as simoniacal. Giffard had already been involved, like the other suffragans to Canterbury, in the struggle against Peckham's excessive claims of metropolitical jurisdiction. He afterwards, however, became friendly with him, and sent the archbishop many costly presents (*Reg. Peckham*, No. dli.) Giffard's many favours to the Franciscans, whose general in 1277, and again in 1282, admitted him as a brother of the order, must have procured him the friendship of the Franciscan primate. His remissness in allowing the monks of the cathedral to steal the body of one Henry Poche from the Franciscans and bury it in their churchyard was in 1290 a new source of difference.

In 1300 Giffard had become sick and infirm. He was in March visited by Archbishop Winchelsey at Wyke. Next year William of Gloucester produced thirty-six articles against him before the archbishop, when visiting the diocese. They were mostly small, technical and legal, and included, besides the old complaints of the chapter, a charge of manumitting serfs without its consent, and unduly favouring his nephews. They were, however, elaborately investigated, and the bishop's answers, which seem fairly satisfactory, are recorded with the charges in his register. Giffard died on Friday, 26 Jan. 1302, and was buried on 4 Feb. by John, bishop of Llandaff, in Worcester Cathedral, on the south side of the altar of the lady chapel, where his tomb is still to be seen. (There is an engraving of it in Thomas's 'Survey of Worcester Cathedral,' p. 44.)

Giffard's will, dated 13 Sept. 1300, left a large number of legacies to kinsfolk, including his sister Mabel, abbess of Shaftesbury, and to various churches. His heir was John, son of his younger brother, William Giffard (*Calendarium Genealogicum*, p. 625) who, fighting on the baronial side at Boroughbridge, was hanged at Gloucester, and forfeited his estates to the crown. They were soon, however, restored, and in later times the Giffards of Weston-sub-Edge assumed the arms of the see of Worcester in memory of an ancestor who had done so much for the family (HOARE, *Wiltshire*, i. 204).

Despite his quarrels with the chapter, Giffard was a benefactor of his cathedral, and beautified the pillars of the choir and lady chapel by interlacing them with little pillars. In 1280 he laid the first stone of the pavement of the cathedral (*Ann. Wigorn.* p. 479). One of his first acts was to obtain leave to fortify and finish Hartlebury Castle which Bishop Cantelupe [q. v.] had begun He extorted from Bishop Cantelupe's executors a legacy left to the see, for supplying a stock of cattle on the lands of the bishopric. He obtained a grant of fairs to Stratford-on-Avon and Blockley. He also secured permission to fortify his palace at Worcester and Wydindon like that at Hartlebury.

[The fullest account of Giffard is in Thomas's Survey of Worcester Cathedral, pp. 135–54, largely derived from his still surviving Register, large extracts of which, including his will and the 'Articuli contra Godfridum episcopum Wygornensem et responsiones ejusdem,' are printed in the 'Appendix chartarum originalium.' His relations with Malvern Priory are fully told in Thomas's Antiquitates pricratus majoris Melverniæ, which prints from the Register all his acts relating to that convent; Martin's Registrum Epistolarum Johannis Peckham (Rolls Ser.) gives several of his letters and a large number of Peckham's to him, and in the introduction to vol. ii. Mr. Martin summarises the Malvern question; Raine's Fasti Eboracenses, in the notice of Walter Giffard, gives what is known of his early history; Dugdale's Baronage, i. 424, or still better, Hoare's Wiltshire, i. 196–204, for an account of his family; Annals of Winchester, Wykes, and more particularly the Annals of Worcester in Annales Monastici, vols. ii. and iv.; Foss's Judges of England, iii. 93–4; Roberts's Calendarium Genealogicum.]   T. F. T.

GIFFARD, HENRY WELLS (1810–1854), captain in the navy, son of Admiral John Giffard (*d.* 1851), entered the navy in 1824; was a midshipman of the Asia at the battle of Navarino, 20 Oct. 1827; was promoted to the rank of lieutenant on 4 March 1831; and after serving in the Mediterranean and on the East Indian station was made commander on 22 Feb. 1838. In 1839 he commissioned the Cruiser of 16 guns, in which he went out to China and took part in the capture of Chusan and Canton. He was advanced to post-rank on 8 June 1841; but continuing in command of the Cruiser, was present at the reduction of Amoy and Chinghae. He returned to England in 1842, and in 1846-7 was captain of the Penelope, bearing the broad pennant of Sir Charles Hotham, on the coast of Africa. In June 1852 he was appointed to the Tiger, paddle-wheel frigate, for service in the Mediterranean, and in 1854 attached to the fleet in the Black Sea. On 11 May the Tiger, in company with two other steamers, was detached from the fleet off Sebastopol, and early on the following morning in a dense fog took the ground close under a cliff a little to the south of Odessa. As soon as she was discovered from the shore, the Russians brought up a battery of field-pieces, and from the edge of the cliff opened a plunging fire of shot, shell, and carcasses, to which the Tiger's guns were unable to reply. The ship was soon set on fire, shell and shrapnel were sweeping her decks, resistance was impossible, and Giffard, severely wounded in the leg, was carried down to the surgeon. Under these circumstances he ordered the ship to be surrendered, and the officers and men, becoming prisoners of war, were hastily sent ashore; Giffard, whose leg had just been amputated, being passed into a boat through a maindeck port. Every care and attention seems to have been shown to the wounded, but the shock to Giffard's system, added to the anxiety and depression of spirits, proved fatal, and he died on 1 June. 'He died as he lived, a religious man, much regretted by all,' is the comment of one of the Tiger's officers. He was buried at Odessa with military honours.

Giffard married, in 1846, Ella Emilia, daughter of Major-general Sir Benjamin C. Stevenson, G.C.H., and left issue, among others, Vice-admiral George Augustus Giffard, C.M.G. (b. 1849), who, as a lieutenant of the Alert, served in the Arctic expedition of 1875–6.

[O'Byrne's Nav. Biog. Dict.; United Service Journal, 1854, pt. iii. p. 337.]   J. K. L.

GIFFARD, JOHN, BARON GIFFARD OF BROMSFIELD (1232–1299), was a soldier and baron in the reigns of Henry III and Edward I, descended from Osbern Giffard, a Norman noble, who under William I acquired various estates, of which Bromsfield (now Brimpsfield) in Gloucestershire and Sherrington in Wiltshire were the chief. From Osbern was descended Richard, one of the justices appointed at Northampton in 1176 (HOVEDEN, ii. 87), whose grandson, Elias, was one of the barons who fought against King John. The son of this Elias was John Giffard, who succeeded his father in 1248 at the age of sixteen (Inq. p.m. in Calendarium Genealogicum, p. 25). During his minority the queen had the guardianship of his lands, which probably prejudiced him against the court. His first experience of war was against the Welsh between 1257 and 1262. He seems to have been attached to the household of Simon de Montfort, and when the civil war broke out early in 1263 he ravaged the lands of Roger Mortimer; later in the same year he was one of the barons who captured the alien bishop of Hereford, attacked Sir Matthew de Besil at Gloucester, and afterwards besieged Prince Edward there in March 1264. Next year he was excommunicated by the Archbishop of Canterbury, and in April, while governor of Kenilworth, attacked Warwick Castle and captured its earl and countess. He was present at Lewes, where he

was captured early in the day, imprisoned in the castle, and rescued at its close. He had himself captured Alan de la Zouch, a dispute as to whose ransom, or, according to Wykes (iv. 60, perhaps supported by document in Cal. Gen. p. 172), an order to surrender some lands which he had occupied, alienated him from Montfort. Giffard now attached himself to Gilbert de Clare, whom he appears to have influenced in taking up the royalist cause (Ann. Lond. Rolls Series, ii. 67). He took an active part in the events which preceded Evesham, was present at that battle, 4 Aug. 1265, and in recognition of his services received pardon for his past conduct (Pat. Roll, 49 Hen. III). During the following years of peace we hear of him only as receiving licenses to hunt in the royal forests, except that in 1271, for forcibly marrying Matilda, widow of William Longespée and heiress of W. de Clifford, he had to pay a fine of three hundred marks to the king (ib. 55 Hen. III; Cal. Gen. p. 151). He was employed in all the wars of Edward I's reign; in Wales, where he was one of the knights commanding the English when Llewellyn was killed, in Gascony, and in Scotland. He was at the council of Berwick in 1292; was summoned to parliament by writ in 1295; and in 1297, during Edward's absence in Flanders, he was one of the council of regency, and as such must have had a share in the 'Confirmatio Cartarum.' He died on 30 May 1299. Giffard is constantly described as a valiant and skilful soldier and a prudent and discreet man (cf. 'The Song of the Barons,' WRIGHT, Political Songs, p. 59). In 1283 he had founded Gloucester Hall (now Worcester College) outside the walls at Oxford, and made provision for the sustenance there of thirteen Benedictine students. His son John, by a third wife, took part with Thomas of Lancaster in the next reign, and was attainted and executed in 1322, when his castle of Bromsfield was destroyed.

[Annales Monastici, Rishanger's Chronicle, Hist. S. Petri Gloucestriæ, Robert of Gloucester, all in the Rolls Series; Rishanger, De Bellis (Camden Soc.); W. Hemingburgh (Engl. Hist. Soc.); History of Broughton Giffard, by the Rev. J. Wilkinson, in Wiltshire Natural History and Archæological Magazine, vol. v.; Blaauw's Barons' War; Burke's Dormant and Extinct Peerages; Banks's Dormant and Extinct Baronage, i. 324. Some further slight information may also be found in the Patent Rolls and Calendarium Genealogicum.]   C. L. K.

GIFFARD, ROGER, M.D. (d. 1597), president of the College of Physicians, was the son of Ralph Giffard of Steeple Claydon, Buckinghamshire, by his wife Mary, daughter of Sir Edward Chamberlain of Woodstock,

Oxfordshire. He was educated at Merton College, Oxford, of which house he became a fellow, and took the degree of B.A. on 14 Aug. 1556, proceeding M.A. on 15 Feb. 1559–60 (*Reg. of Univ. of Oxford*, Oxford Hist. Soc. i. 232, 238, 321). On 8 April 1562 he was elected junior university proctor, and was re-elected on 21 April 1563 (WOOD, *Fasti Oxon.* ed. Bliss. i. 160, 162). As a bachelor of medicine of 23 June 1563, 'sometime fellow of Merton College, now or lately fellow of All Souls' College,' he was, on 30 Aug. 1566, created M.D. by Drs. Walter and Henry Baylie by virtue of a commission directed to them by the convocation, which had selected him to dispute before Elizabeth on her intended visit to the university in the ensuing September (*ib.* i. 176). Giffard was afterwards appointed physician to the queen. He was censor of the College of Physicians from 1570 to 1572, consiliarius from 1585 to 1587, and again in 1591, and president from 1581 to 1584. He died on 27 Jan. 1596–7, and was buried in the parish of St. Bride, Fleet Street. His will, made on the day of his death, was not proved until 1 Aug. 1597 (registered in P. C. C. 77, Cobham). Therein he bequeathed to Lord-keeper Sir Thomas Egerton 'the Jewell wherein the Quenes ma^ties picture is which he vsed to weare aboutes his necke.' He possessed lands in the county of Durham and a lease of the farm of Tollesbury in Essex. By his wife Frances, who survived him, he had a son Thomas, a daughter Mary, another daughter married to Thomas Harries, and probably other children. Giffard was a man of wide culture, well read in French, Italian, and Flemish literature. He requested his executors to deliver to Merton College 'suche of his bookes as Mr. Henry Savill should choose to be placed in the Librarye of the same Colledge for the vse of the ffellowes and Schollers of the same howse.'

[Munk's Coll. of Phys. 1878, i. 68–9.] G. G.

GIFFARD, STANLEY LEES (1788–1858), editor of the 'Standard' newspaper, youngest son of John Giffard of Dromartin, co. Dublin, and brother of Sir Ambrose Hardinge Giffard [q.v.], was born in Dublin 4 Aug. 1788. He was first educated by Thomas White, the schoolmaster of Sheridan the politician and Moore the poet. He then studied at Trinity College, Dublin, where he proceeded B.A. 1807, M.A. 1811. He afterwards took the degree of LL.D., entered at the Middle Temple, and was called to the bar by that society in 1811. Making no way as a barrister, he soon turned his attention to literature. After some anonymous hack-work in classics and Hebrew he began his journalistic

career by an engagement on the 'St. James's Chronicle,' of which paper he was editor for some years. He was chosen editor of the 'Standard' when that paper was founded in 1827, and this post he filled for more than a quarter of a century. During this period he opposed catholic emancipation, championed the cause of the Irish state church, and defended the corn and navigation laws (being attacked by name in Mr. Bright's speech at the famous repeal meeting in Covent Garden Theatre in 1845). Giffard died at Folkestone, Kent, 6 Nov. 1858. His first wife was Susannah Meares Moran, and his third son by her, Hardinge Stanley, was raised to the peerage as Lord Halsbury in 1885 on first becoming lord chancellor, and was promoted to an earldom in 1898, during his third tenure of the chancellorship, which he retained till 1905. His second wife was Mary Anne, daughter of Henry Giffard, R.N.

Giffard's life is almost entirely bound up with that of the paper he edited. He was once candidate for the representation in parliament of Trinity College, Dublin, but withdrew before the poll. He contributed articles to the 'Quarterly' and 'Blackwood,' and began a 'Life of the Great Duke of Ormonde,' and 'Vindiciæ Anglicanæ,' being an account of the 'English in Ireland.' No part of this was published. Giffard was thus described in the 'Standard' obituary notice: 'In the obduracy of his sympathies and antipathies in politics he was a man after Dr. Johnson's own heart; and with him departed perhaps the last of the school of Georgian political writers, who brought so great a fund of learning to the pursuit of the press.' The story told in Grant's 'History of the Press' and elsewhere, that in the early days of the 'Standard' the Duke of Newcastle sent the editor 1,200*l.* as a mark of admiration of the article against catholic emancipation which had appeared on the previous day, is an entire fiction.

[Standard, 9 Nov. 1858, p. 5; Catalogue of Dublin Graduates, p. 221; Grant's Hist. of the Newspaper Press, ii. chap. iv.; Gent. Mag. December 1858, p. 652; Burke's Peerage, s. v. 'Halsbury.'] F. W–T.

GIFFARD, WALTER (*d.* 1279), archbishop of York, son of Hugh Giffard, of Boyton in Wiltshire, by Sibyl, daughter and coheiress of Walter de Cormeilles, was probably his parents' eldest son, and was brother of Godfrey, bishop of Worcester (1235?–1302) [q.v.] In 1256 he and his mother received the king's license to dwell in the castle, and Adam de Marisco [q. v.], the Franciscan, wrote a letter to the chancellor of the university, recommending Giffard in terms which perhaps imply that he was a scholar of some repute (*Monumenta Franciscana*, p. 257). He became a canon and archdeacon of Wells, and one of the pope's chaplains. On 22 May 1264 he was elected to the see of Bath and Wells, and received the temporalities on 1 Sept. As the primate Boniface was in France, he went over to Paris for consecration, which he received at Notre-Dame on 4 Jan. following from Peter d'Acquablanca, bishop of Hereford, having first sworn that he would not take part against Henry III. The barons, in anger at his having gone abroad against their will, ravaged nearly all his manors. By the primate's order he excommunicated the Earl of Leicester and his party on his return to England (WYKES, p. 164). Giffard was a handsome, gay, and genial man. He was fond of luxury, and in later life grew fat, which injured his health and temper. At the same time he was a man of high character, and was able and industrious (*Chronicle of Lanercost*, pp. 71, 103; WYKES, p. 194; RAINE, p. 303). On 10 Aug. 1265, immediately after the battle of Evesham, the king made him chancellor, with a stipend of five hundred marks a year (FOSS, *Judges*, ii. 353). In the August of the following year he was appointed one of the arbitrators for drawing up the award of Kenilworth, the agreement by which the disinherited lords were allowed to recover their estates. On 15 Oct. he was appointed by Clement IV to the archbishopric of York by provision, resigned the chancellorship, was enthroned on 1 Nov., and received the temporalities on 26 Dec. He at once entered on a dispute with Archbishop Boniface of Canterbury about the right to carry his cross erect in the southern province, and made an appeal to Rome. Although he was rich both by inheritance and in virtue of his office, he could not keep clear of debt, incurred partly on account of the expenses of his translation, partly also by this suit in the papal court, and also probably by his liberality and his magnificent manner of living. He maintained a kinsman named William Greenfield while studying at Oxford. This was probably the William of Greenfield [q.v.] who afterwards became archbishop of York (RAINE). The year after his translation Giffard paid sixteen hundred marks to Italian money-lenders, and five hundred and fifty marks to certain merchants of Paris, and in 1270 sent two hundred marks to his agents at Rome to expedite his affairs, hoping 'for the present to keep out of the whirlpool of usury' (*ib.* from Register). He appears to have been kind to his relatives, and gave his brother Godfrey the archdeaconry of York. This was made a cause of complaint against

him at Rome, for it was alleged that Godfrey was only in minor orders, and was not learned (*ib.*) Giffard was active in discharging the duties of his office, and was a 'strict and fearless reformer of abuses' (*ib.*) He made a visitation of his province, and came to Durham during a vacancy in the see; the prior of St. Cuthbert's endeavoured to distract him by a rich entertainment. The archbishop, however, insisted on making a visitation, was shut out from the cathedral church, and excommunicated the prior and his monks (*Scriptores Tres*, p. 56; *Chronicle of Lanercost*, p. 103). On 13 Oct. 1269 he officiated at the translation of St. Edward the Confessor. When leaving England, Edward, the heir to the throne, appointed him by will in 1270 one of the tutors of his sons, and he assisted him in bringing Earl Warenne to justice for the murder of Alan la Zouche at Westminster (WYKES, p. 234). On the death of Henry III on 20 Nov. 1272 the great seal was delivered to the archbishop as first lord of the council, in virtue of an arrangement made in the preceding year, the see of Canterbury being vacant, and he, in conjunction with Roger Mortimer and Robert Burnell, was appointed to govern the kingdom until the new king's return, and to acquaint him with the death of his father. The regents were confirmed by a great council which met at Westminster after St. Hilary's day the following year, received the oaths of the baronage and certain representatives of the commons, swore fealty themselves, and governed the kingdom discreetly until the king came back on 2 Aug. 1274 (STUBBS, *Constitutional History*, i. 104, where references are given). It is said that the king would not allow Giffard to be present at his coronation on 19 Aug., on account of the quarrel between him and Archbishop Kilwarby of Canterbury with respect to the right of carrying the cross (WYKES, p. 260); he seems to have come to the ceremony, but not to have been allowed to take part in it (*Annals of Dunstable*, p. 263). He was one of the guardians of the kingdom during Edward's absence in 1275. He died at York on 22 April, or a few days later, in 1279, and was buried in his cathedral church, probably in the choir. His body was afterwards removed by Archbishop Thoresby to a tomb which he had erected in the presbytery (RAINE).

[Life by Canon Raine in Fasti Eboracenses, pp. 302–17, with extracts from Giffard's Register; Wykes, and the Waverley, Dunstable, and other annals in Annales Monastici (Rolls Ser.); Chron. of Lanercost (Bannatyne Club), pp. 7, 103; Historiæ Dunelm. Scriptt. Tres, p. 56 (Surtees Soc.); Foss's Judges, ii. 353; Rymer's Fœdera, i. 497.]

W. H.

GIFFARD, WILLIAM (*d.* 1129), bishop of Winchester, probably of the same family as Walter Giffard, earl of Buckingham, was canon and subsequently dean of the cathedral of Rouen, and chancellor of William Rufus. Giffard was appointed by Henry I to the see of Winchester, which had been vacant since the death of Bishop Walkelin more than two years before, immediately on his accession to the throne and before his coronation, and was put in possession by him of the temporalities of the bishopric (HENRY OF HUNTINGDON, p. 232). Malmesbury tells us that the episcopal office was violently forced upon Giffard by Henry, and that he accepted it with the greatest reluctance, assailing his electors, the monks of Winchester, with threats and reproaches (WILL. OF MALMESBURY, *Gesta Pont.* p. 110). But if the charge that he purchased the see of Henry for a large sum of money, implied in Matthew Paris's word 'remuneratus,' is to be accepted as historical, this reluctance was entirely feigned, and merely assumed to hide the real nature of the transaction (MATT. PARIS, *Hist. Angl.* ii. 181). After Henry's coronation, Giffard was one of the bishops who witnessed the king's letter to Anselm excusing himself for being crowned in the archbishop's absence, and begging him to return without delay (ANSELM, *Epist.* iii. 41). On Anselm's return to England he recognised Giffard's election, inducted him to his office, and invested him with the ring and pastoral staff. The dispute which immediately arose between Anselm and Henry respecting homage caused a long delay in his consecration. However, as a bishop-elect who had received induction and the insignia of office, his episcopal position was fully acknowledged. In common with other prelates he witnessed Henry's charter of liberties, issued immediately after his coronation, and took part in the council of Westminster, 20 Sept. 1102. On the persistent refusal of Anselm to consecrate bishops as long as the king maintained his demand that they should do homage to him for their benefices and become his 'men,' Henry ordered Gerard [q. v.], the newly appointed archbishop of York, to act as consecrator. Giffard at first manifested no reluctance to be consecrated by him, but at the last moment, when the ceremony had already commenced in St. Paul's, Giffard interrupted the service by a refusal to accept consecration at Gerard's hands. A scene of violent confusion arose. The populace loudly applauded Giffard's courage. The king, however, viewed his conduct with great indignation, and sentenced him to banishment and confiscation. Anselm's intercession was, as might be expected, fruitless (EADMER, *Hist. Nov.* lib. iii. p. 64).

Anselm did all in his power to mitigate the severity of Giffard's exile. He wrote numerous letters on his behalf to the leading personages in Normandy, Duke Robert, the Archbishop of Rouen, and others, entreating them to protect his friend (ANSELM, *Epist.* iii. 70, iv. 24, 25, 26). But Anselm's appeal to Robert proved of little use. The injuries Giffard received at Duke Robert's hands led him to consult Anselm whether he could lawfully transfer a castle he held of the duke to the duke's brother, Henry I. Anselm's reply was a firm negative. He was not yet consecrated, and if he were to make over what he held of Robert to the king of England, his enemy, he would be liable to the charge of having done it to buy his consecration (*ib.* iii. 98). Anselm subsequently wrote to Giffard exhorting him not to recede from his good resolution (*ib.* iii. 105). The relations between Giffard and Anselm grew closer, and on Anselm's leaving England in 1103, Giffard accompanied him across Europe to Rome (MATT. PARIS, *Hist. Angl.* ii. 192; HOVEDEN, i. 161). Henry's anger must have sufficiently abated to allow of Giffard's early return to England, for we find him signing the letter of the bishops to Anselm in 1105 entreating him to come back to his distressed church (ANSELM, *Epist.* iii. 121). On Anselm's return and the final settlement of the dispute concerning investitures, 1 Aug. 1107, the way was opened for Giffard's long-deferred consecration. Giffard was still only in deacon's orders. Anselm suggested that he should come to him in the approaching Ember season for priest's orders, with the view of being consecrated the next day (*ib.* iv. 7). On Sunday, 11 Aug., the solemn ceremony took place at Canterbury, and seven years after his election Giffard with four others, Roger of Salisbury, Reinhelm of Hereford, William of Warelwast of Exeter, and Urban of Llandaff, was consecrated by Anselm, Gerard, and six assistant bishops.

Giffard settled down in his diocese, and devoted himself to his episcopal duties. In July 1108 he assisted Anselm in the consecration of Richard de Beames, bishop of London, and in August of the same year of Ralph d'Escures, bishop of Rochester, afterwards archbishop of Canterbury. In the following year, 27 June 1109, two months after Anselm's death, he was one of the assistants of the Bishop of London at St. Paul's Cathedral in the consecration of Thomas as successor to Gerard in the archbishopric of York, and in 1123 he assisted the same bishop of London in consecrating William de Corbeil to the archbishopric of Canterbury. In 1111, according to the 'Annals of Winchester,' he deposed Geoffrey the Prior, and in the same year gave the enormous sum of eight hundred marks to Henry I (*Annal. Monast.* ii. 43, 44), probably to purchase the royal consent for the removal of the so-called 'new minster' at Winchester, which stood in very inconvenient proximity to the cathedral on the north, to a new site outside the city under the name of Hyde Abbey. Feuds between the two monastic bodies had been of constant occurrence (*Annal. Waverl. ib.* p. 214; Hoveden, i. 168). In 1121 Giffard was deputed by the palsied Archbishop Ralph to celebrate the espousals of Henry I and Adela of Louvain (Will. of Malmesbury, ii. 132). In 1122 a very fierce quarrel broke out between Giffard and the monks of Winchester, who complained that he had alienated their revenues, and appropriated to himself nine of their manorial churches. At the end of two years their feud was healed by the intervention of the king, who had supported the convent in the quarrel. The monks threw themselves at the feet of the bishop, confessing their fault and promising satisfaction; and the bishop prostrated himself at their feet in turn, promising to give back all they asked for, and confirming the grant by a charter (*Annal. Winton.* p. 47). So complete was the reconciliation that Giffard himself assumed the habit of a monk, as being one of their body, loving to take his midday sleep with the brethren in the dormitory, and to sup with them in the refectory, and then always taking the lowest place with the novices. When stricken for death he was carried in the conventual habit to the infirmary, where he breathed his last (*ib.* p. 49). Giffard first introduced the Cistercian reform into England, being the founder, 24 Nov. 1128, of the earliest house of that order at Waverley, near Farnham in Surrey. This took place only a few weeks before his death, 25 Jan. 1128-9. He was also the founder of a house of Austin canons on the episcopal manor of Taunton, and was a considerable benefactor to St. Mary Overies in Southwark, in the immediate proximity of which he erected a palace as the London residence of the bishops of Winchester. He was buried in the nave of his cathedral church, close to his predecessor Walkelin. Contemporary historians give Giffard a high character, which he appears to have well deserved. Henry of Huntingdon calls him 'vir nobilissimus,' while the Winchester annalist describes his patience, piety, and gentleness. He was not calculated to be a leader of men, but he could follow faithfully and courageously such a leader as Anselm.

[Will. of Malmesbury's Gesta Pont. pp. 109, 110, 117, 132; Matt. Paris's Chron. Maj. ii. 118, 123, 124, 134, 136, 151, 156; Annal. Monast. ii. 42, 44, 46, 47, 214, 221; Henry of Huntingdon, pp. 233, 315; Sym. Dunelm. ii. 235, 236, 239, 240, 245, 283; Eadmer's Hist. Nov. pp. 64, 69; Hoveden, i. 161, 164, 168, all in Rolls Ser.; Flor. Wig. (Engl. Hist. Soc.), p. 1103; Anselm's Epist. ll. cc.; Freeman's Norman Conquest, v. 225; Freeman's William Rufus, ii. 349; Cassan's Bishops of Winchester.]   E. V.

GIFFORD. [See also GIFFARD.]

GIFFORD, ADAM, Lord Gifford (1820–1887), lord of session and founder of the Gifford lectureships, eldest son of James Gifford and his wife, Catherine Ann West, was born at Edinburgh on 29 Feb. 1820. His father, who had risen from a comparatively humble position, became treasurer and master of the Merchant Company, an elder in the Secession church, and a zealous Sunday-school teacher. His mother was vigorous in body and mind, and a very independent thinker. She was the only teacher of her sons Adam and John, till Adam was eight years old, when the boys were sent to learn Latin and Greek at a small school kept by John Lawrie in West Nicolson Street. Adam Gifford was afterwards a pupil at the Edinburgh Institution, founded in 1832. In early life he became a Sunday-school teacher in the Cowgate, besides sometimes taking a service on a Sunday forenoon with the poor children of Dr. Guthrie's ragged school.

In 1835 Gifford was apprenticed to his uncle, a solicitor in Edinburgh; at the same time he attended classes in the university, and became a member of the Scots Law Debating Society. He soon became managing clerk in the office, but decided to become an advocate, and in 1849 was called to the bar. He was clear-headed, persevering, and had good connections, but, from unwillingness to push himself, advanced slowly. He acquired by degrees an extensive practice. As an advanced politician he expected nothing from the government, but in 1861 he was appointed an advocate-depute. In that capacity he conducted on behalf of the crown, in 1863, the prosecution against Jessie M'Lauchlan in the Sandyford murder case. In 1865 he was appointed to succeed W. E. Aytoun [q. v.] as sheriff of Orkney and Zetland; but continued his practice as an advocate, having appointed a resident sheriff-substitute.

On 28 Jan. 1870 Gifford was nominated a judge, and on 1 Feb. took his seat in the court of session as Lord Gifford. Symptoms of paralysis appeared in 1872, and gradually developed themselves, but he worked on till 1881. On 25 Jan. of that year he resigned, and retired with a pension. He died on 20 Jan. 1887. On the 27th he was buried in the old Calton cemetery. He was survived by one son, Herbert James Gifford; his wife, Maggie, only daughter of James Pott, W.S., to whom he was married on 7 April 1863, having died on 7 Feb. 1868.

Gifford was an able judge, with strong common sense and little respect for technicalities. He often lectured to literary and philosophical societies. By his will, recorded on 3 March 1887, a sum, estimated at 80,000*l.*, was bequeathed to found lectureships on natural theology, 25,000*l.* being assigned to Edinburgh, 20,000*l.* to Glasgow and Aberdeen, and 15,000*l.* to St. Andrews. The object was to found 'a lectureship or popular chair for promoting, advancing, teaching, and diffusing the study of natural theology, in the widest sense of that term, in other words, the knowledge of God,' and 'of the foundation of ethics.' All details and arrangements were left to be settled by the accepting trustees in each town, subject only to certain leading principles and directions stated in the will. The first appointments were made and lectures delivered in 1888.

[Private information obtained from relatives; Lord Gifford's will, in General Register House; *Scotsman* newspaper, 1870, and 21 Jan. 1887.] J. T.

GIFFORD, ANDREW (1700–1784), baptist minister and numismatist, was the son of Emanuel Gifford, and grandson of Andrew Gifford, both baptist ministers at Bristol. He was born on 17 Aug. 1700, and was sent to the academy of Samuel Jones at Tewkesbury. After leaving that academy he studied for a time under Dr. John Ward. He seems to have performed ministerial work in Nottingham in 1725, and to have been assistant to his father at Bristol in 1726, in which year he was invited to become pastor of the congregation in Devonshire Square, London. He declined this position, but in the beginning of 1730 he accepted a call from the baptist meeting in Eagle Street, London. He was chaplain to Sir Richard Ellys [q. v.], and after Sir Richard's death to Lady Ellys, from 1731 to 1745. In 1754 he received the degree of D.D. from Aberdeen.

He collected coins, of which he had a great knowledge, and was a fellow of the Society of Antiquaries. Owing to this, and to the influence of powerful friends with whom he had become acquainted during his chaplaincy to Ellys, and also probably owing to the fact that his old tutor, Dr. John Ward, was one of the trustees, he was appointed assistant librarian in the British Museum in 1757. He held this office till his death on

19 June 1784. He edited for the Society of Antiquaries 'Folkes' Tables of English Silver and Gold Coins,' which was published, in 2 vols. 4to, in 1763. His own collection of coins was purchased by George II for his private cabinet, but he left a valuable collection of books, manuscripts, pictures, and curiosities to the baptist academy at Bristol. His second wife, Grace Paynter, whom he married in 1737, died in 1762. She brought him a fortune of 6,000*l.* (*Gent. Mag.* vii. 637, xxxii. 600). He had no children. Pastor of the Eagle Street meeting till his death, he bequeathed 400*l.* to it, making the six deacons his executors.

Two of his sermons were published, one on 'the Great Storm in 1703,' 1734, and the other, preached ten days before his death, 'To the Friendly Society,' 1784.

[John Rippon's Funeral Sermon on Andrew Gifford, p. 34 ff.; Wilson's Dissenting Churches, i. 439; Nichols's Lit. Anecd. v. 461, vi. 367; Gent. Mag. liv. 478, 485, 595.] E. C–N.

GIFFORD, GEORGE (*d.* 1620), divine, was a student at Hart Hall, Oxford, 'several years before 1568' (Wood, *Athenæ*, Bliss, ii. 201). He took no degree at Oxford, and seems to have graduated B.A. (1569–70) and M.A. (1573) from Christ's College, Cambridge. It is probable that he is the George Gifford who, aged 30, was ordained by the bishop of London both deacon and priest in Dec. 1578. In 1573 he published a translation from the Latin of Fulke's 'Prelections upon the Sacred and Holy Revelations.' His next work, 'Country Divinity, containing a Discourse of Certain Points of Religion which are among the common sort of Christians, with a Plain Confutation thereof,' London, 1581, 8vo, was probably the cause of his presentation in August 1582, by Richard Franks, to the living of All Saints' with St. Peter's at Maldon, Essex (Newcourt, *Repert.* ii. 398). In 1582 he published a 'Dialogue between a Papist and a Protestant applied to the capacity of the unlearned,' and in 1584 a tract 'Against the Priesthood and Sacrifice of the Church of Rome . . . ,' London, 1584, 8vo. He also published 'A Cathechism containing the sum of Religion . . . ,' London, 1583, 8vo, and 1586. He won a reputation as 'a great and diligent preacher' (Brook, *Lives of the Puritans,* ii. 273), and was much valued at Maldon for the reformation effected by his preaching (Strype, *Annals,* III. ii. 470). In January and February 1584 he joined a synod of nonconformist Essex ministers in London (Bancroft, *Dangerous Positions,* 2nd edit. reprint, p. 75), and publicly refused to subscribe the articles of the established church. For this he was suspended. A further charge that he had preached limited obedience to civil magistrates and used conventicles and secret teachings was disproved, and he is said to have been released and again arrested on a charge of nonconformity. He was tried before the high commissioners in May or June 1584. Fifty-two of Gifford's parishioners sent in a petition praying for his restoration to his living; in it they testified to his usefulness in Maldon and to his innocence of the charges against him. Burghley interceded, seconded by Sir Francis Knowles, with Whitgift (May 1584) on his behalf (NEAL, *Puritans*, i. 291). Both the archbishop and Aylmer, bishop of London, were immovable, as they considered Gifford to be 'a ringleader of the nonconformists,' and he was therefore deprived of his living, to which on 18 June another vicar, Wyersdale, was instituted (DAVID, *Annals of Nonconformity in Essex*, p. 126). He was, however, allowed to hold the office of lecturer and continued preaching at Maldon, a fact which makes Neal's statement that he remained 'several years' in prison impossible. The Essex nonconformists complained that all their best ministers were suspended and replaced by ignorant ones, while twenty-seven of the suspended Essex clergy, headed by Gifford, petitioned the privy council for the redress of their grievances (BROOK, *Puritans*, p. 275). In 1586 Wyersdale desired to resign the living in Gifford's favour. Aylmer would not, however, permit this, and on his next visitation (1587) suspended Gifford for a time from his lectureship (HANBURY, *Memorials*, i. 69; STRYPE, *Annals*, III. ii. 479; DAVID, *Annals*, pp. 107, 126). Gifford went as one of the representatives of the Essex nonconformist ministers to a puritan synod held privately either at Cambridge or at Warwick, 8 Sept. 1587 (STRYPE, *Annals*, III. i. 691, ii. 477–8). He had also subscribed to the 'Book of Discipline,' and in 1589 he attended a synod held at St. John's College, Cambridge, to discuss corrections of the book (BANCROFT, p. 89). Gifford next attacked the Brownists, the heads of which, Henry Barrow [q. v.] and John Greenwood (*d.* 1593) [q. v.], had been since 1586 in prison, in 'A Short Treatise against the Donatists of England, whom we call Brownists . . . ,' London, 1590, 4to. Greenwood replied to this from the Fleet, whereupon Gifford answered with 'A Plain Declaration that our Brownists be full Donatists . . . Also a reply to Master Greenwood touching read prayer, wherein his gross ignorance is detected, which, labouring to purge himself from former absurdities, doth plunge himself deeper into his mire.' Dedicated to Sir

William Cecil, London, 1590. Gifford then published 'A Short Reply unto the last printed books of H. Barrow and J. Greenwood . . . wherein is laid open the gross ignorance and foul errors . . . ,' London, 1591, 4to, with a preface disavowing personal motives. Barrow replied in his 'Plain Refutation.' Gifford took no further part in theological controversy. He preached in 1591 at St. Paul's Cross. In 1597 he was made one of a presbytery elected in Essex. He died in 1620 at a good old age at Maldon, continuing to preach to the last. Besides the above he published: 1. 'Four Sermons preached at Maldon, 1584, "penned from his mouth, and corrected and given to the Countess of Sussex as a New Year's Gift,"' London. 2. 'A Discourse of the Subtle Practises of Devils by Witches and Sorcerors,' London, 1587, 4to. 3. 'Eight Sermons preached at Maldon, 1589.' 4. A 'Dialogue concerning Witches and Witchcrafts,' London, 1593 and 1603, 4to (reprinted by the Percy Society). 5. A 'Treatise of True Fortitude,' London, 1594, 8vo. 6. 'Commentary or Sermons upon the whole Book of Revelations,' London, 1596, 4to. 7. 'Four Sermons upon several parts of Scripture,' London, 1598, 8vo. 8. 'Exposition on the Canticles,' London, 1612, 8vo. 9. 'Fifteen Sermons on the Song of Solomon,' London, 1620, 8vo.

Probably JOHN GIFFORD, D.D., who proceeded B.A. from Christ Church, Oxford, 1613, and M.A. 1616, and afterwards D.D., was George Gifford's son. He was rector of St. Michael Bassishaw from 1636 till 1642, when the parliament expelled him on account of his royalist tendencies (WALKER, *Sufferings*, p. 170). A John Gifford, D.D. of Cambridge, wrote 'Dissertatio de ratione alendi Ministros evangelicos in statu Ecclesiæ stabilito,' Hamburg, 1619, 8vo).

[Strype's Life of Aylmer, ed. 1831, p. 73; Strype's Whitgift, ii. 190; Hanbury's Memorials, i. 49–69.] E. T. B.

GIFFORD, GEORGE (*fl.* 1635), engraver, one of the earliest English engravers, is principally known from the interesting portrait of Bishop Hugh Latimer, engraved as frontispiece to the edition of Latimer's sermons published in 1635. It is well engraved, in a manner superior to that of some of the contemporary engravers. Gifford engraved a portrait of John Bate as frontispiece to the second edition of his 'Mysteries of Art and Nature,' published in the same year. He also engraved a portrait of Sir Edmund Marmion. An engraving of St. Peter, evidently one of a set, in the print room at the British Museum, bears his name in full. All his engravings are scarce.

[Walpole's Anecdotes of Painting, ed. Dalla-way and Wornum; Dodd's MS. Hist. of English Engr. (Brit. Mus. Addit. MS. 33401).]   L. C.

GIFFORD or GIFFARD, GILBERT (1561 ?–1590), Roman catholic spy, belonged to the well-known Roman catholic family seated at Chillington, Staffordshire. His father, John Gifford (d. 1612), suffered imprisonment for recusancy. Gilbert is said as a schoolboy to have challenged a schoolfellow to a duel. After spending some months at Anchine he entered Douay College, then at Rheims under the direction of William Allen (1532–1594) [q. v.], on 31 Jan. 1576–7. In the register he was described as 'clarus adolescens.' In 1579 he removed to the English College at Rome, and in October publicly defended theses embracing all philosophy before a large assembly of prelates and noblemen (FOLEY, Records, vi. 68). He and a friend and fellow-student, Edward Gratley, made the acquaintance at Rome of Solomon Aldred, a Roman catholic spy of Sir Francis Walsingham, who lived there with his wife, and had English secret service money to dispose of. Gifford readily entertained proposals to enter the English secret service at some future date. His superiors at the English College admired his intellectual capacity and did not suspect his intentions, but they complained of his dissimulation and deceitful character, and before 1582 expelled him on grounds that are not exactly defined. He returned to Rheims to teach theology on 23 June 1582, after having apologised to Cardinal Allen for past misconduct. On 29 March 1583 Allen wrote, objecting to his remaining at either seminary, Douay or Rome. In 1583 he paid a second visit to Rome. On 16 March 1584–5 he was ordained sub-deacon, and on 6 April 1585 deacon by Cardinal de Guise, in the church of St. Remigius at Rheims. He left Douay College on 8 Oct. 1585, and went to Paris.

Gifford definitely entered Walsingham's secret service in 1583 (JEBB, De Vita et Rebus Gestis Mariæ, 1725, ii. 281). While at Rheims he seems to have become acquainted with John Savage, afterwards an associate of Babington, a Roman catholic, who had thought of killing Elizabeth. At Paris he placed himself in communication with Thomas Morgan, a representative of Mary Queen of Scots. Morgan gave him a letter (15 Oct. 1583) recommending him to Queen Mary, then confined at Chartley. He was represented to be an enthusiastic adherent who could be trusted to convey her private correspondence from and to Chateauneuf, the French ambassador and her chief agent in London. He arrived in London about December, and was received unsuspectingly at the French embassy. Some catholic noblemen, as well as the Countess of Arundel and many catholic youths of good family, entertained him, but neither they nor members of his own family suspected his treacherous occupation. He soon presented himself to Phelippes, the chief of Walsingham's spies, and lived in his house for a short time, receiving instructions, and 'practising secretly among the catholics.' In January he went to Chartley and ingratiated himself with Queen Mary, who readily accepted his offer to direct the conveyance of her secret correspondence to London. Her gaoler, Sir Amias Paulet, knew that Gifford was an accredited government spy, and at first doubted his intentions, but quickly placed implicit trust in him.

Gifford had arranged with Phelippes and Walsingham to place all Mary's letters at their disposal. He had to adopt means to avoid rousing the slightest suspicion on the part of Mary or her London agent. Much importance attaches to his methods. He told Mary, the French ambassador, and others of Mary's friends that he secured the services of a catholic brewer of the village to take her letters in his barrels to a neighbouring catholic gentleman, who conveyed them to another catholic gentleman, and that the latter forwarded them by a servant to the French embassy in London. Letters were, he pretended, also sent from London in the same way when he himself or one of his trusted servants did not carry them direct. Mr. Froude accepted this story and, exaggerating its details, assumed that Gifford kept the letters he received from Mary only just time enough to copy them, and then at once sent them to London by means of his secret and circuitous device. As a matter of fact Gifford's account of his device was a lying tale, concocted to lull the suspicions of Mary and her friends. He himself, on receiving Mary's letters from her, usually copied them in conjunction with Paulet, but he also invariably sent the originals to Phelippes's house in London, and Phelippes at his leisure employed some agent who could be trusted to deliver them to the French ambassador. A letter written by Queen Mary on 31 Jan. was thus not delivered at the French embassy till 1 March. It lay in the interval in Phelippes's rooms. The French ambassador was nevertheless thoroughly deceived, and gave Gifford in March letters received for Queen Mary in the previous two years, which he had had no opportunity of sending her. All these Gifford took in batches to Phelippes, who deciphered them for Walsingham before forwarding them to Mary. In April Gifford was again at Chartley, and still retained the full confidence not only of Queen Mary but of her keeper Paulet. In the next few months he paid many visits to London and Paris. He was well acquainted with Anthony Babington [q. v.], John Ballard, and their fellow-conspirators, and encouraged them to pursue their plot, at the same time keeping Walsingham well informed of its development. At Paris he saw Mendoza, the Spanish ambassador who had been expelled from London, and is reported to have given him the first intelligence of the Babington conspiracy. Mendoza freely promised Spanish aid. Roman catholic writers assert that it was Gifford who suggested and arranged the whole conspiracy. At present the better supported view is that the priest Ballard was its originator. Gifford continued to satisfy both his masters. He carried the fatal letters from Queen Mary to Babington, which contained her approval of the conspiracy, and duly showed them to Walsingham and his agents before they reached their destination. On 8 July 1586 he was in London, and gave Walsingham a book denouncing Parsons and the jesuits which he and Gratley had written some time before. Walsingham highly prized the manuscript, and is said to have distributed printed copies. By the end of July Gifford's work was done. All the details of Babington's plot were settled by the conspirators, and had been brought by Gifford to Walsingham's knowledge. He seems to have felt the danger of his position and hurried to Paris (29 July). After the conspirators' arrest he wrote to Phelippes and Walsingham, hoping that his departure would not be judged 'sinistrously.' On 3 Sept. he offered to do further work for Walsingham, but the offer was not accepted. That he was capable of almost any villany is clear, but that he was the concoctor of the Babington plot, and that he interpolated those passages in Queen Mary's letters which convicted her of complicity in the conspiracy and brought her to the scaffold, are charges that have some *prima facie* justification, but have not yet been proved.

Both sides soon suspected Gifford to be a traitor, although neither knew the exact extent of his treachery. His catholic associates were certainly cognisant of some portion of his action in England. Fitzherbert, writing from Paris (February 1586-7), hoped that he would 'prove honest.' In the spring of 1587 he travelled to Rheims and Rouen under the name of Jaques Colerdin. At Rheims he was ordained priest (14 March 1586-7), and expressed an intention of seeking a professorship at Rome. In 1588 he was again at Paris, dressed as disguised priests dressed in Eng-

land. He quarrelled with Sir Charles Arundel, one of the chief English catholic exiles, who accused him of writing against the jesuits. In December 1588 he was found in a brothel and brought before the bishop of Paris. The bishop committed him to prison; Sir Edward Stafford, the English ambassador, made some endeavours to procure his release, but Gifford thought to serve his own ends better by bringing serious charges against Stafford. His catholic enemies proved more powerful than he anticipated, and he died in prison in November 1590. He announced to Walsingham in 1588 the arrival in Paris of Father John Gerard [q.v.], and is said to have written to Cardinal Allen while in prison an account of the injuries he had done the catholic cause.

[Father Morris's Letter-book of Sir Amias Paulet, passim; Father Morris's Troubles of our Catholic Forefathers, 2nd ser. pp. 86, 361, 379, 388, 453, 492; Foley's Records of the Society of Jesus, vi. 8 et seq. (account of Gifford by Cardinal Sega written in 1596), pp. 15, 68, 135; Records of English Catholics, (1) Douay Diaries, (2) Letters, &c., of Cardinal Allen; Teulet's Papiers d'État (Bannatyne Club); Cal. State Papers (Dom.), 1581-90. Mr. Froude's account of Gifford in History of England, vol. xii., is full of errors, as Father Morris has shown in the Letter-book of Paulet.] S. L.

GIFFORD, COUNTESS OF (1807-1867). [See SHERIDAN, HELEN SELINA.]

GIFFORD, HUMPHREY (*fl.* 1580), poet, was probably the second son of Anthony Gifford of Halsbury, Devonshire. He published in 1580 'A Posie of Gilloflowers, eche differing from other in colour and odour, yet all sweete,' 4to, of which a copy (supposed to be unique) is preserved in the King's Library, British Museum. One section is in prose, the other in verse. The prose is prefaced by a dedicatory epistle 'To the worshipfull his very good Maister, Edward Cope of Edon, Esquier,' whom Gifford describes as 'the onely maister that euer I serued;' and the poetry is dedicated 'To the Worshipfull John Stafford of Bletherwicke, Esquier.' Little interest attaches to the prose, which chiefly consists of translations from the Italian; but some of the poems (in particular a spirited war song) have merit. The poems, with selections from the prose, have been reprinted by Dr. Grosart in 'Occasional Issues,' and again in 'Miscellanies of the "Fuller Worthies' Library."'

[Grosart's Introduction to A Posie of Gilloflowers; Ellis's Specimens.] A. H. B.

GIFFORD, JAMES, the elder (1740 ?–1813), unitarian writer, son of James Gifford, mayor of Cambridge in 1757, was born at

peer of France. It is said that Gifford was preferred to the see on the understanding that he should retain it during the minority of the Duke of Guise's son, who was then but a child, and it was generally believed that he annually paid a considerable portion of the archiepiscopal revenues to the Guise family. Weldon says it was intended at the time of Gifford's advancement that the abbey of St. Remigius at Rheims should be annexed to the archbishop's *mensa* in order to help to defray the cost of his maintenance and table. The Duke of Guise wanted the abbey for his infant son, then called the Abbé of St. Denis, but the king refused to give it to him without Gifford's consent. As, however, Gifford was under great obligations to the Guise family, he gave his consent, and thereby deprived himself of 40,000 livres a year (*Chronicle*, p. 160). His promotion to the archbishopric gave general satisfaction, and he passed the remainder of his life in preaching, enforcing discipline among the clergy, and providing for the wants of the poor. He died on 11 April 1629 (N. S.), and was buried beneath the high altar in the church of the Blessed Virgin at Rheims, but his heart, by his own direction, was delivered to the Benedictine nuns of St. Peter's monastery in that city, and deposited in the chapel of their house with great solemnity on 11 May. He was eulogised in funeral sermons by Henri de Maupas, abbot of St. Denis at Rheims, afterwards bishop successively of Le Puy and Evreux, and by Guillaume Marlot, the historian of Rheims. Both discourses were printed, and are excessively scarce. The title of the second, which contains many interesting biographical details, is ' Discours funèbre sur la mort de feu Monseigneur le Reverendissime Gabriel de Ste Marie, Archevesque, Duc de Reims . . . seconde édition,' Rheims, 1630, 12mo, pp. 130.

Portraits of him were formerly preserved in the English Benedictine monastery of St. Edmund in Paris and at the monastery of Rheims (WELDON, p. 163).

Dodd says : ' He was remarkably mild, yet not without a reserve of life and spirit, when errors or neglect of discipline gave provocation ; upon which occasion he thought a little passion was not ill employed. As to his political disposition he was more of the French than Spanish faction ; and what some may think a blemish in his character, a favourer of the league. There are no proofs of his countenancing any attempts against the person or government of Queen Elizabeth ; though a certain miserable wretch thought to lessen his own guilt by casting out words to that purpose ' (*Church Hist.* ii. 361).

His works are: 1. 'Oratio Funebris in exequiis venerabilis viri domini Maxæmiliani Manare Præpositi ecclesiæ D. Petri oppidi Insulensis,' Douay, 1598, 8vo. 2. ' Orationes Diversæ,' Douay, 4to. 3. ' Calvino-Turcismus. Id est Calvinisticæ perfidiæ cum Mahumetana Collatio . . . Quatuor libris explicata. Authore G. Reginaldo,' Antwerp, 1597 and 1603, 8vo. A work begun by Dr. William Reynolds, and completed and edited by Gifford. Matthew Sutcliffe replied to it in 'De Turco-Papismo, hoc est De Turcorum et Papistarum adversus Christi ecclesiam et fidem Conjuratione, eorumque in religione et moribus consensione et similitudine,' London, 1599 and 1604. 4. 'The Inventory of Errors, Contradictions, and false Citations of Philip Mornay, Lord of Plessis and Mornay,' translated from the French of Fronto-Ducæus, S.J., at the instance of the Duke of Guise. 5. A treatise in favour of the League, written at the request of the Duke of Guise. 6. ' Sermones Adventuales,' Rheims, 1625, 8vo. Preached originally in French, and translated by himself into Latin. 7. Several manuscript works which perished in the fire that destroyed the monastery at Dieulewart, 13 Oct. 1717.

He also assisted Dr. Anthony Champney in his 'Treatise on the Protestant Ordinations,' 1616.

[Collect. Topogr. et Geneal. vii. 223; Dodd's Church Hist. ii. 358 ; Douay Diaries ; Downside Review, i. 433 ; Duthilloeul's Bibl. Douaisienne, 2nd edit. p. 47 ; Gillow's Bibl. Dict. ii. 457 ; Herald and Genealogist, vii. 69 ; Maihew's Congr. Anglic. Ord. S. Benedicti, 1625 ; Marlot's Hist. de Reims, 1846, iv. 450, 535 ; Oliver's Catholic Religion in Cornwall, pp. 484, 485, 516, 535 ; Pits, De Angliæ Scriptoribus, p. 809 ; Reyner's Apostolatus Benedictinorum in Anglia, ii. 198 ; Smith's Brewood, 1874, p. 38 ; Snow's Benedictine Chronology, p. 37 ; Wood's Athenæ Oxon. ed. Bliss, ii. 453, 879.] T. C.

GIFFORD, WILLIAM (1756–1826), editor of the 'Quarterly Review,' born in April 1756, was the son of Edward Gifford, whose great-grandfather had ' possessed considerable property at Halsbury,' near Ashburton, Devonshire. Gifford's grandfather was extravagant, and was disinherited or spent what fortune he received. The father was a wild lad who twice ran away from school, first going to sea, and afterwards consorting with Bamfylde Moore Carew [q. v.], the king of the gipsies. He was then articled to a plumber and glazier, became possessed of two small estates (probably by his father's death), and married Elizabeth Cain, daughter of a carpenter at Ashburton. He set up in business at South Molton, got into scrapes, and after four or five years escaped from prosecution for a riot in a methodist chapel by going to sea, where he obtained a position on an armed transport. His wife returned to Ashburton, where William Gifford was soon afterwards born. He was taught reading by a schoolmistress, and learnt old ballads from his mother. In 1764 the father returned with 100*l.* prize-money won at the Havannah. He sold his little property, and set up in business as a glazier. The son was sent to the Ashburton free school, under Hugh Smerdon. Three years later the father died of drink, leaving his widow, with an infant son. She tried to carry on the business, was plundered by her assistants, and died in a year. Her goods were seized by a creditor, 'C.,' who was also William's godfather. The infant was sent to the almshouse, and 'bound to a husbandman.' William Gifford, when his own prospects improved, did his best to help his brother. The boy was sent to sea, but died soon afterwards. Meanwhile the godfather, C., under the pressure of Ashburton sentiment, which held that he had sufficiently paid himself, sent William Gifford to school, where he began to show taste for arithmetic. C. soon tired of the expense, and sent Gifford to work on a farm. The boy had suffered a permanent injury from an accidental blow on the chest, and was incapable of the labour of ploughing. The godfather then tried to export him to Newfoundland, but he was rejected by an employer on account of his puny frame. He was therefore when about thirteen placed in a small Brixham coaster. He stayed in it for a year, acquired a love of the sea, and had a narrow escape from drowning. At Christmas 1770 his godfather took him back to Ashburton, the Brixham fishermen having spread reports of the child's neglected condition, and again roused Ashburton opinion. He was once more sent to school, and now began to make rapid progress. He helped the master in teaching other pupils, and aspired to succeed to the mastership, Smerdon being now infirm. The godfather, however, insisted upon binding him apprentice to a shoemaker, his indentures being dated 1 Jan. 1772. Gifford's new master was an ignorant dissenter, whose whole reading was confined to the 'Exeter Controversy.' Gifford procured a black-letter romance, a few loose magazines, and a Thomas à Kempis. He had also a 'Treatise on Algebra,' and managed by stealth to read 'Fenning's Introduction,' belonging to his master's son, from which he got the necessary preparation. He beat out pieces of leather, and worked his problems on them with a blunted awl. He

also composed a few rhymes of a satirical kind, and sometimes made sixpence in an evening by reciting them. His master unluckily discovered his occupations and his little store of books, which had been increased by his earnings. He was deprived of his treasures, and ordered to desist from writing. His ambition was crushed by the death of his schoolmaster and the election of another person. He fell into gloom, from which he was roused by the kind attentions of a 'young woman of his own class.' William Cookesley, a surgeon in the town, had heard of Gifford's doggerel. He talked to the author, gave him good advice, and got up a subscription to buy the remainder of his term of apprenticeship, and enable him to educate himself. His last eighteen months were thus remitted, his master receiving 6*l.*, and he was enabled to study at the school to considerable purpose. The subscribers paid for another year's schooling, and in 1779 the master (Thomas Smerdon) thought him fit for the university. Cookesley, through a friend, Thomas Taylor of Denbury, procured him a bible clerkship at Exeter College, Oxford. This, with occasional help from friends, would, it was thought, enable him to get a degree. He matriculated 16 Feb. 1779, and graduated B.A. 10 Oct. 1782. He had begun to translate Juvenal. With the help of Cookesley he sent out proposals (1 Jan. 1781) for publishing the whole by subscription. Cookesley died on 15 Jan. following. Gifford was greatly depressed by the loss of his patron, and found himself unable to continue his translation. He sought relief in the study of other languages, and the college authorities enabled him to take a few pupils. As his spirits revived he again took up the Juvenal, but found it so bad that he resolved to abandon the attempt, and returned as far as he could subscriptions already received. He was corresponding with a Devonshire clergyman, William Peters, to whom he sent letters under cover to Lord Grosvenor. He accidentally omitted Peters's name upon a letter, which was thereupon read by Grosvenor. Grosvenor became interested, and sent for Gifford, who candidly stated that he had 'no prospects.' Grosvenor hereupon said that he would be responsible for Gifford's 'present support and future establishment,' and until other prospects offered invited the young man to reside with him. Gifford accepted the invitation, became the permanent friend of Grosvenor, and member of his family, acting also as travelling tutor to his son. Two tours upon the continent occupied 'many years.'

At Grosvenor's house Gifford proceeded with his 'Juvenal,' which, however, did not appear until 1802, when the autobiography from which the preceding facts are taken was given in the preface. Gifford first became known by the two satires, the 'Baviad' (1794) and the 'Mæviad' (1795), published together in 1797. Gifford attacks the so-called Della Cruscans, a small clique of English at Florence, including Mrs. Piozzi, Mr. Merry, and other scribblers, who published poems in a paper called 'The World' under such signatures as 'Anna Matilda.' They were so silly as to be too small game for satire. The 'Mæviad' also assails some of the small dramatists of the time.

John Williams, author of some discreditable books by 'Anthony Pasquin,' prosecuted Gifford in the Michaelmas term of 1797 for a libel contained in a note to the 'Baviad.' Gifford's counsel, Garrow, read some passages from Pasquin to the jury, who immediately nonsuited the plaintiff. The trial is reported in the eighth edition of the 'Baviad' and 'Mæviad'(1811). In 1800 Gifford had a quarrel with a better-known antagonist, John Wolcot, 'Peter Pindar.' Wolcot attributed to William Gifford a criticism in the 'Anti-Jacobin Review' really written by John Gifford [q. v.] He assaulted the wrong Gifford, who was entering the shop of his bookseller, Wright (now Hatchard's), but after a brief scuffle was bundled out into the street and rolled in the mud. The affray was celebrated in a mock-heroic 'Battle of the Bards,' by 'Mauritius Moonshine' (1800). Taylor (*Records of my Life*, ii. 279) asserts that he explained the mistake, and that thereupon the combatants exchanged friendly messages. An 'explanation' must have been difficult and its results transitory. Gifford published an 'Epistle to Peter Pindar' (1800), in the preface to which he endorsed his namesake's attack upon Wolcot (whom he had never previously mentioned), and in which he calls Wolcot an unhappy 'dotard,' a 'brutal sot,' a 'miscreant,' a 'reptile,' and an 'atheist,' besides giving anecdotes of his cruelty, blasphemy, and debauchery. Wolcot would be afraid of seeking legal redress after the fate of John Williams. He retaliated in various passages in his works, to which it seems rather strange that Gifford should have submitted. Gifford is accused of supplanting his friend Peters with Lord Grosvenor, and of keeping his patron's favour by the basest services (PETER PINDAR, *Works*, 1812, iii. 493–6, iv. 331–3). Taylor tells us that Peters quarrelled with Gifford for the reason assigned; but the other imputation is sufficiently discredited by its author's character.

Gifford was becoming known in the political world. In 1797 Canning and his friends were projecting the 'Anti-Jacobin, or Weekly Examiner.' The illness of Grant, who had been engaged as editor, caused the substitution of Gifford. The paper appeared from 20 Nov. 1797 to 9 July 1798. Gifford wrote in it himself, and became connected with Canning and his distinguished co-operators. After this paper had dropped a monthly magazine called 'The Anti-Jacobin Review' was started by John Gifford [q. v.], but had no connection with its predecessor.

When the 'Quarterly Review' was started, with the concurrence of Canning, Scott, and other eminent tories, Gifford became the editor. The first number appeared in February 1809. Its success is a presumption that he must have had some good qualities as an editor, though he was so well supported that a good start was insured. An imperfect list of the authors of articles in the early numbers is in the 'Gentleman's Magazine' for 1844 (i. 137, 577), 1845 (i. 599), and 1847 (ii. 34). Among his most regular contributors were Scott, Southey, Croker, and Barrow. His own contributions seem to have been mainly literary. According to Southey, he looked upon authors as Izaak Walton looked upon worms—something beyond the pale of human sympathy. His rigorous adherence to the old school in literature and his hatred of radicals gave especial bitterness to his judgments of the rising authors. He was probably the author of the famous assault upon Keats's 'Endymion' (number dated April 1818, which appeared in September following). His antipathy was repaid in full by the radicals. Hazlitt replied to some attacks in a bitter 'Letter to W. Gifford' (1819), part of which was reprinted as an appendix to Leigh Hunt's 'Ultra-Crepidarius,' a satire in verse (1823). Byron, however, speaks with exaggerated deference of Gifford, to whom 'Childe Harold' was shown (against the author's wishes) in manuscript, and to whom nearly all the later poems were submitted. Byron always professed to agree in theory, though not in practice, with Gifford's admiration for the old or 'classical' school. Southey's frequent references show that Gifford exerted to the utmost the editor's right of altering and interpolating. Southey was frequently so stung by this and by some differences of opinion that he would, he says, have broken off the connection if he could have afforded to do so. Gifford doubtless knew that Southey had good reasons for submission. The first article left unspoilt by Gifford, one phrase excepted, was in November 1821 (SOUTHEY, *Selected Letters*, 1856, iii. 283). Gifford was a little man, almost deformed, and had long been full of ailments, which may partly explain his sourness. His health began to break in 1822, but, at Murray's request, he continued to edit the review until the publication of the sixtieth number. He announces his resignation to Canning on 8 Sept. 1824. His illness had caused the review to be two numbers in arrear. John Taylor Coleridge [q. v.] took his place until Lockhart succeeded in 1825. Gifford died 31 Dec. 1826, in his house at 6 St. James's Street, and was buried in Westminster Abbey 18 Jan. 1827. He had received at first 200*l.* a year, afterwards raised to 900*l.*, for editing the 'Quarterly Review.' He also held a commissionership of the lottery at 100*l.* a year, and was paymaster of the gentlemen-pensioners at 1,000*l.* a year. On 5 March 1826 he acknowledged 'a splendid and costly proof of affection,' apparently of a pecuniary nature, presented to him by Canning, in which Lord Liverpool and John Hookham Frere had taken part. Gifford seems to have been of penurious habits. He left the bulk of his savings, amounting to 25,000*l.*, to the Rev. Mr. Cookesley, son of his first patron, the lease of his house to the widow of his friend Hoppner, the painter to whom the 'Baviad' was dedicated, other sums to the poor of Ashburton, and 2,000*l.* to found two exhibitions at Exeter College. He also left 3,000*l.* to the relatives of his beloved servant-maid, Ann Davies, who died 6 Feb. 1815, and upon whom he wrote an elegy of which the second line runs, 'I would I were where Anna lies.' He was amiable in private life, kind to children, and fond of dogs.

His portrait by Hoppner prefixed to his 'Juvenal' is said to be very like him. It is now in the possession of Mr. John Murray. Gifford's works include valuable editions of the old dramatists: Massinger, 1805, 1813; Ben Jonson, 1816; Ford, 1827; his notes upon Shirley were used in Dyce's edition, 1833; and some manuscript notes on Shakespeare are in a copy in the British Museum. The editions have always had a very high reputation for thoroughness and accuracy, and although as a literary critic Gifford was crabbed and strangely wanting in taste, the fault was redeemed by strong common sense.

A second edition of his 'Juvenal' appeared in 1817, and a translation of 'Persius' in 1821. A reply to strictures of the 'Critical Review' upon the 'Juvenal' appeared in 1803, and a collection of 'beauties' from Gifford's prose and verse, edited by A. Howard, in 1834.

[Nichols's Illustrations, vi. 1–39, containing his autobiography (often reprinted) and anecdotes first published in the Literary Gazette; Annual Obituary (1828), pp. 159–200; Gent. Mag. (1827), i. 105–12 (with portrait); Canning's Official Correspondence, by E. J. Stapleton (1887), i. 129, 224, ii. 183, 227, 233; Jerdan's Autobiography, ii. 270, iv. 108–19; John Taylor's Records of my Life, ii. 279, 372–8; Southey's Life and Correspondence (1849) and Selections from Letters (1856); Boase's Register of Exeter College, pp. 126, 146; Moore's Life of Byron; Lockhart's Life of Scott; Hazlitt's Spirit of the Age, pp. 277–303 (a bitter attack); Moore's Diary (1856), ii. 230, 248, viii. 70, 215.] L. S.

GIGLI, GIOVANNI (*d.* 1498), bishop of Worcester, was a native of Lucca. He was a skilled ecclesiastical lawyer, entered the papal service, and was sent to England as papal collector by Pope Sixtus IV. He seems to have made himself useful to Edward IV, and was appointed a canon of Wells in 1478. Still he did not cease to serve the pope, and in the synod of London, 1480, he set forth that the pope had sold his jewels and melted his plate to provide money for the defence of Rhodes; but despite his eloquence the English clergy refused to tax themselves (WILKINS, *Concilia*, iii. 613, where Gigli appears as Joannes de Sighs). Gigli was a humanist of considerable attainments, and in 1486 wrote an epithalamium in Latin hexameters on the marriage of Henry VII with Elizabeth of York. In 1489 Gigli was employed by Pope Innocent VIII as his commissioner for the sale of indulgences in England. Soon afterwards Henry VII, who had reasons of his own for establishing intimate relations with the papacy, sent Gigli to Rome as his diplomatic agent. In 1492 Burchard (*Diarium*, ed. Thuasne, i. 490) calls him 'orator antiquus regis Angliæ.' Gigli's services were rewarded in 1497 by the bishopric of Worcester, to which he was appointed by a provision of Pope Alexander VI, dated 30 Aug. He was consecrated in Rome, appointed Thomas Wodyngton as his vicar-general, and was enthroned by proxy. He had no time to visit his see, for he died in Rome on 25 Aug. 1498, and was buried in the English College there, where a tomb was erected to him by his nephew, Silvestro. The inscription is given by Thomas, 'Survey of Worcester Cathedral,' p. 202.

Gigli's 'Epithalamium,' which is a good example of the complimentary verses of the period, is in the British Museum, Harleian MS. 336.

[To the sources quoted in the text may be added Wharton's Anglia Sacra, i. 538, and the manuscript Register of Bishop Gigli in the Worcester Diocesan Registry.] M. C.

GIGLI, SILVESTRO (1463–1521), bishop of Worcester, was a native of Lucca, and succeeded his uncle Giovanni [q. v.] in the see of Worcester. It would seem that he had been trained by his uncle, and helped him in his diplomatic duties at the Roman court; for in the grant of the temporalities of his see by Henry VII he is called 'archi-presbyter Luccensis, causarum nostrarum in curia Romana solicitator' (THOMAS, *Survey of Worcester Cathedral*, Appendix, p. 130). He was appointed to the see by provision of Alexander VI, dated 24 Dec. 1498, and was enthroned by proxy in April 1499. He remained in Rome as resident ambassador of Henry VII, and as such took part in the ceremonies of the papal court (BURCHARD, *Diarium*, ed. Thuasne, iii. 354). At the end of 1504 he was sent by Pope Julius II as the bearer of some tokens of the pope's favour to Henry VII, and he distinguished himself by his eloquence before the king at Richmond (BERNARD ANDRÉ, *Annales Henrici VII*, ed. Gairdner, p. 86). After that he seems to have stayed a few years in England, more engaged as a master of ceremonies about the court than in the work of his diocese (*ib.* pp. 122–3). When Henry VIII became more intimately connected with European politics, he sent to Rome as his ambassador Christopher Bainbridge [q. v.], archbishop of York, in 1509, but found it necessary to employ Gigli as well, and appointed him in 1512 one of his ambassadors to the Lateran council. Pope Leo X found Gigli a more congenial person than Bainbridge, who was not popular at the papal court. The two English ambassadors were not on good terms, and there were frequent disputes between them. So patent were their quarrels that when Bainbridge died in 1514, poisoned by a servant, Gigli was suspected of being the author of the murder (ELLIS, *Original Letters*, i. Nos. 35–7). Pope Leo X inquired into the matter, and Gigli was acquitted. Wolsey supported him, and could afterwards count upon his gratitude. It is only fair to say that there was no evidence against Gigli; that Bainbridge's temper seems to have stung his servant to a desire for revenge and plunder; that the man was lightheaded, and committed suicide in prison. The accusation did not affect Gigli's credit, and he was Wolsey's confidential agent in securing the cardinalate and the grant of legatine powers. From this time Gigli was the chief diplomatic agent of Wolsey in Rome, and was in constant correspondence with him and Henry VIII. He was also a man of letters and a correspondent of Erasmus. He died in Rome on 18 April 1521.

[Thomas's Survey of Worcester Cathedral, pp. 202–3; Burchard's Diarium; Paris de Grassis, Diarium, Brit. Mus. Addit. MSS. 8440–4; Cal. of State Papers of Hen. VIII, vols. i -iii.; Brewer's Reign of Hen. VIII; Memorie per servire all' Is-toria del Ducato di Lucca, ix. 140; manuscript Reg. in Worcester Diocesan Registry.] M. C.

GILBART, JAMES WILLIAM (1794–1863), writer on banking, descended from a Cornish family, was born in London 21 March 1794. In 1813 he entered as clerk a London bank, which stopped payment on account of the panic of December 1825. He was for some time after this engaged as cashier in the employment of a Birmingham firm, but soon returned to London, where in 1827 he published 'A Practical Treatise on Banking, containing an account of the London and Country Banks, a view of the Joint-Stock Banks of Scotland and Ireland, with a summary of the Evidence delivered before the Parliamentary Committees relative to the suppression of Notes under five pounds in those countries' (6th ed. 1856. Revised ed. 1871, republished in America at Rio de Janeiro and in Spain). Gilbart had already written a number of articles for popular periodicals. He was also connected with the Union Club, a debating society founded by J. S. Mill, of which Macaulay was a member.

In 1829 Gilbart went to Ireland, and managed in succession the branches at Kilkenny and Waterford of the Provincial Bank of Ireland.

Gilbart continued his literary activity, and became so well known that when joint-stock banks were established in London, there was a competition for his services. He agreed to become manager of the London and Westminster Bank, 10 Oct. 1833. The bank opened its doors 10 March 1834, and both before and after Gilbart had hard and delicate work to pilot the new institution through early difficulties. In 1836 the Bank of England obtained an injunction against his bank 'prohibiting their accepting any bills drawn at less than six months after date.' This seemed likely to kill the bank's country connection, but Gilbart skilfully evaded the danger by getting the country banks to draw upon his bank bills 'without acceptance.' He took this plan from the method adopted by his adversary in dealing with the Bank of Ireland. Not content with this, Gilbart wrote on the subject, gave evidence before various parliamentary committees, and saw his labours completely successful, when in 1844 Peel's Bank Charter Act enacted (*inter alia*) that joint-stock banks could sue and be sued by their public officers, and could accept bills at six months after date.

Gilbart's interest in his profession was shown in 1851 by his giving a prize of 100*l.* for the best essay 'On the Adaptation of Recent Inventions, collected at the Great

Exhibition of 1851, to the purposes of Practical Banking.' In 1859 he retired on a pension of 1,600l. per annum from the bank. He died at Brompton Crescent, London, 8 Aug. 1863.

Besides being a fellow of the Royal Society, Gilbart was a member of the Statistical Society (to whose 'Transactions' he contributed various papers) and various other learned bodies. He took part in the International Statistical Congress held in July 1860. His writings on banking are valuable as the work of a man of good education and strong practical sense, who has a thorough mastery of the subject. 'They contain,' remarks McCulloch, 'much useful information, presented in a clear compendious form.' Besides the works noticed Gilbart wrote: 1. 'The History and Principles of Banking,' 1834, republished, revised, and incorporated with the 'Practical Treatise on Banking,' as 'The History, Principles, and Practice of Banking,' by A. S. Michie, in Bohn's Series, 1882. 2. 'The History of Banking in Ireland,' 1836. 3. 'The History of Banking in America, with an inquiry how far the Banking Institutes of America are adapted to this country, and a Review of the causes of the recent Pressure on the Money Market,' 1837. 4. 'An Inquiry into the Causes of the Pressure on the Money Market during the year 1839,' 1840. 5. 'The London Bankers, an Analysis of the Returns made to the Commissioners of the Stamps and Taxes by the Private and Joint-Stock Bankers of London, January 1845,' 1845. 6. 'Lectures on the History and Principles of Ancient Commerce,' 1847. 7. 'A Record of the Proceedings of the London and Westminster Bank during the first thirteen years of its existence; with portraits of its principal officers,' 1847 (privately printed). 8. 'Logic for the Million,' 1851 (6th ed. 1860, also 'Logic for the Young,' adapted from Watts's 'Logic,' 1855). 9. 'Elements of Banking,' 1852. 10. 'The Laws of the Currency, as employed in the Circulation of Country Bank Notes in England since the passing of the Act of 1844,' 1855 (reprinted, with a portrait, from the journal of the Statistical Society). 11. 'The Moral and Religious Duties of Public Companies' (in 1856, with portrait). 12. 'The Philosophy of History,' 1857 (not published). 13. 'The Logic of Banking, a familiar exposition of the principles of reasoning, and their application to the Art and Science of Banking,' 1859. 14. 'The Social Effects of the Reformation,' 1860 (a reply to Cobbett's 'History of the Reformation'). All Gilbart's chief works went through several editions. They

were republished in a collected form in six volumes in 1865.

[Memoir prefixed to Works; Bankers' Mag. September 1863, p. 652; Gent. Mag. September 1863, p. 385; McCulloch's Literature of Political Economy; Brit. Mus. Cat.]   F. W–T.

GILBERT THE UNIVERSAL (d. 1134?), bishop of London, is described as 'natione Britannus' by Richard of Poitiers, who probably means a Breton rather than a Welshman (ap. BOUQUET, p. 415). Le Neve makes him a relative of 'Henry, bishop of Ely' (? Hervey, bishop of Ely, 1109–33), at whose 'suggestion he left his school at Nevers' for England (ed. Hardy, ii. 188; cf. STUBBS, p. 162). Le Beuf prints a charter which shows that in 1120 he was a 'magister' at Auxerre, probably directing the episcopal schools there (LE BEUF, iv. App. No. 19), and the Nevers necrology proves him to have been treasurer in this city also (ib. ii. 468), where, according to Henry of Huntingdon, he was teaching at the time of his appointment to London (ed. Arnold, p. 307; cf. HARPSFELD, p. 350). Other contemporary authority makes him at that epoch a canon of Lyons (Cont. of FLORENCE OF WORCESTER, ii. 89). He was already 'grandævus' when, thanks to Henry I and Archbishop William de Corbeil of Canterbury, he was consecrated on 22 Jan. 1127 bishop of London, in succession to Richard de Belmeis [q.v.] (ib.; HENRY OF HUNTINGDON, p. 247; MATTHEW PARIS, ii. 153). Florence seems to date his consecration 27 Henry I (i.e. 1127); but as his predecessor did not die till January 1127–8 (STUBBS, p. 25), it should perhaps be 1128 (FLORENCE OF WORCESTER, p. 89; cf. RALPH DE DICETO, i. 245; HENRY OF HUNTINGDON, p. 247). About 1 Aug. 1129 Gilbert took part in the great council of London which condemned the marriage of priests (HENRY OF HUNTINGDON, pp. 250–1); on 4 May 1130 he was present at the Canterbury consecration, and a little later at that of St. Andrew's in Rochester (Anglo-Saxon Chron. ii. 227). It was perhaps about this time that he sent his blessing to St. Bernard, who praised the poverty of his life (Epp. Bernardi, No. 24). His name appears twice in the pipe roll of Henry I, which is ascribed to 1130–1 (Rot. Mag. Pip. pp. 55, 61). He seems to have died on 12 Aug. 1134, while accompanying the bishop of Llandaff (Urban) to Rome (Auxerre Martyrology, p. 716; RALPH DE DICETO, i. 247; MATTHEW PARIS, ii. 159). Orderic Vitalis, however, appears to put his death in 1136 (v. 78); Mabillon assigns it to 1133 (Note ap. MIGNE, clxxxii. coll. 127–8), and the 'Margam Annals,' by implication, to 1134 (Ann. Margam, p. 13).

Henry of Huntingdon accuses Gilbert of excessive avarice. To the surprise of his contemporaries he died without making a will, and Henry I confiscated his 'infinite' wealth (HENRY OF HUNTINGDON, *De Cont. Mundi*, pp. 307–8). When appointed to London, Gilbert's reputation was almost unequalled, and he had no peer from England to Rome (*ib.*) Harpsfeld suggests that he owed his cognomen 'Universal' to his encyclopædic attainments (HARPSFELD, p. 350). His nephew tells us that he was a great benefactor to his diocese (*De Mirac. Sancti Erkenwaldi*, by his nephew, quoted in WHARTON, pp. 51–2; cf. HARDY, i. 294); St. Bernard commends his humility, and the church of Auxerre celebrated the anniversary of his death in recognition of wealth it had received from him (*Auxerre Martyrology*, p. 716).

The 'Auxerre Martyrology' styles Gilbert 'veteris et novi testamenti glossator;' his nephew assigns him a treatise on the Old Testament, written before his elevation to London (WHARTON, p. 51); and St. Bernard speaks of his eagerness 'divinam . . . revocare et renovare scripturam' (*Ep.* 24). These phrases seem to point to an exposition of the whole Bible, which, however, appears to be now lost, except a treatise on Lamentations. This compilation, of which in the last century there were two copies at St. Aubin's, Angers, winds up with the words 'Hæc . . . hausi Gislebertus Autissodoriensis ecclesiæ diaconus' (*Hist. Lit.* p. 240). Gilbert may also be the author of treatises on other parts of scripture (Isaiah, Jeremiah, the Psalms, &c.), which in some manuscripts are joined to this exposition. But his writings appear to have been partly confused with those of his namesake, Gilbert of Auxerre, who is said to have died in 1223 (*ib.* pp. 240–2), and even with those of Gilbert Foliot [q.v.], bishop of London (*ib.*) The whole question as to his works is discussed in the 'Histoire Littéraire,' Fabricius, Tanner, and the other writers cited below. His great renown may be inferred from the ascription of so many works to his pen; from his nephew's boast 'ut supra vires [esset] illius actus describere, quæ universa Latinitas laudat;' from Henry of Huntingdon's words, 'artibus eruditissimus . . . singularis, unicus;' and from Richard of Poitiers' testimony, which couples him with Alberic of Rheims, as two of the greatest teachers of the time (WHARTON, p. 52; HENRY OF HUNTINGDON, p. 307; RICHARD OF POITIERS, p. 414). He is styled 'the Universal' by Florence's continuator, Henry of Huntingdon, Orderic, the Anglo-Saxon Chronicle, and nearly all the contemporary writers who mention him.

[Histoire Littéraire de France, vol. xi.; Stubbs's Registrum; Le Beuf's Histoire d'Auxerre, ed. 1855; Hardy's MS. Materials for English Hist. (Rolls Ser.); Henry of Huntingdon (Rolls Ser.), ed. Arnold; Ralph de Diceto (Rolls Ser.), ed. Stubbs; Anglo-Saxon Chron. (Rolls Ser.), ed. Thorpe; Matt. Paris (Rolls Ser.), ed. Luard; Margam Annals in Ann. Mon. (Rolls Ser.), ed. Luard; Orderic Vitalis, ed. Le Prevost (Soc. de l'Hist. de France); Epistolæ Sancti Bernardi ap. Migne, vol. cxxxii.; Martyrology of Auxerre ap. Martène's Ampliss. Collectio, vol. vi.; Richard of Poitiers ap. Bouquet, vol. xii.; Pipe Roll of Henry I, ed. Hunter; Florence of Worcester, ed. Thorpe (Engl. Hist. Soc.); Wharton's Historia de Episcopis Londiniensibus.] T. A. A.

GILBERT OF LOUTH (*d.* 1153?), abbot of Basingwerk, was sent by Gervase, founder and first abbot of Louth in Lincolnshire, about 1140 to an Irish king (M. Paris says to King Stephen, but it is clear from Henry of Saltrey that the king was an Irish one) in order to obtain a grant to build a monastery in Ireland. The grant was made, and on Gilbert complaining that he did not understand the language, the king gave him as an interpreter the knight Owen, who, according to the legend, had descended into purgatory. From Owen, Gilbert received an account of his vision, which he in his turn imparted to Henry of Saltrey, who wrote it down in the 'Purgatorium S. Patricii' (printed in Colgan and in Migne, vol. clxxx. col. 989). One manuscript (Vatican Barberini 270, ff. 1–25) has the title 'Purgatorium Sancti Patricii curante Gilberto Monacho Ludensi post Abbate de Basingwerek in Anglia.' There seems to be no other authority for making Gilbert the author of the 'Purgatorium.' Gilbert after spending some years in Ireland returned to England, became abbot of Basingwerk in Flintshire, and died about 1153 (SALTREY ap. COLGAN, *Acta Sanctorum*, ii. 279).

[Hardy's Catalogue of British History, i. 72–7, ii. 247; Wright's Purgatorium Sancti Patricii; Matthew Paris, ii. 193–203 (Rolls Series).] C. L. K.

GILBERT THE GREAT or THE THEOLOGIAN (*d.* 1167?), abbot of Cîteaux, is described as an Englishman in an epistle prefixed to the commentary 'In Oraculum Cyrilli,' of which he is said to be the author (cf. TANNER). Going to France he entered the Cistercian order, and in 1143 became abbot of Ourcamp. In 1163 he succeeded Fastradus as eighth abbot of Cîteaux and general of the order (*Recueil des Historiens*, xiii. 278). In this capacity he drew up statutes for the knights of Calatrava in 1164, and in 1165 obtained from Alexander III a charter exempting his order from all episcopal jurisdiction. He supported

Geoffrey of Clairvaux against the pope and the king of France; and under his rule Becket found a refuge at Pontigny, although regard for the interests of his order compelled Gilbert to convey to the archbishop the threats of Henry II against the Cistercians (*Materials for Hist. of Becket* (Rolls Ser.), iii. 397). In May 1167 he made an agreement with the chapter of Autun, and probably died 17 Oct. of that year, although some fix his death in 1168. All writers celebrate the learning and piety to which he owed his cognomen, but seem to confuse him with other Gilberts. Bale and Pits ascribe to him various works, of which, with one or two exceptions, nothing seems known. Among them there are ' Commentaries on the Psalms,' the opening words of which correspond with Bodl. MS. Auct. D. 4. 6; a treatise styled 'Distinctiones Theologicæ' is also assigned to Gilbert in Bodl. MSS. 29 and 45. Mabillon prints a sermon which he ascribes to Gilbert in his edition of S. Bernard's works, ii. 745. There are also three letters from Gilbert to Louis VII in Duchesne's 'Historiæ Francorum Scriptores,' iv. 670, 679, 744; these, however, are all short, and contain nothing to justify the high praise bestowed on their author for his literary ability. Henrique includes Gilbert among the saints of the Cistercian order. Bale and Pits wrongly give his date as 1280, and say that he had studied at Paris and Toulouse.

[Bale, p. 337; Pits, p. 361; Tanner, p. 317, under ' Gilbert the Cistercian;' Hist. Lit. de la France, xiii. 381–5; Gallia Christiana, iv. 987; Menologium Cisterciense Oct. 17.] C. L. K.

GILBERT OF HOYLAND (*d.* 1172), theological writer, has been the subject of much confusion with other Gilberts, and especially with his contemporary Gilbert the Great or the Theologian (*d.* 1167 ?) [q. v.], who was likewise an Englishman and a Cistercian. Gilbert of Hoyland was a disciple and friend of St. Bernard of Clairvaux, by whom he was admitted to the Cistercian order; in 1163 he became abbot of Swineshead in Holland in Lincolnshire, of which district he was probably a native. The supposition of some writers that he was a Scotsman, and of Mabillon that he was Irish, seems to have no further foundation than an idea that Hoyland meant Holy Island. According to the chronicle of Clairvaux, Gilbert died at the monastery of Rivour in the diocese of Troyes in 1172 (MIGNE, clxxxv. 1248). His name day is given as 25 May (*Menologium Cisterciense*, p. 172). We know nothing further as to his life, but in his thirteenth sermon he condemns the rival popes Victor and

Alexander, though without mentioning any names; and in the forty-first he refers to Ælred, abbot of Rievaulx [see ETHELRED, 1109 ?–1166], as lately dead, which fixes the date of this discourse at 1166. His forty-eight sermons on the Cantica Canticorum, chapters 4–5, are in continuation and imitation of those of St. Bernard, than whom, says Mabillon, he has scarcely less elevation. These sermons are printed in Mabillon's edition of St. Bernard's ' Works,' vol. ii., and in Migne's ' Patrologia,' clxxxiv., together with seven ' Tractatus Ascetici ' in the form of epistles, four epistles and a sermon ' De Semine verbi Dei.' The sermons were printed separately at Florence 1485, Strasburg 1487, and Antwerp 1576. Bale and Pits also assign to Gilbert of Hoyland commentaries on the Epistles of St. Paul, the Psalms, St. Matthew (Gilbertus Abbas in *Bodl. MS.* 87), and the Apocalypse; ' Sententiæ Theologicæ; De Statu Animæ; ' ' De Casu Diaboli.' These are, however, of doubtful authority. According to Oudin (ii. 1484) the commentaries should be assigned to Gilbert of Poitiers. The ascription to Gilbert of Hoyland of a share in the life of St. Bernard is also incorrect.

[Histoire Littéraire de la France, xiii. 461–9; Hardy's Catalogue of British History, ii. 551; Mabillon's Prefaces to vols. iv. and v. of St. Bernard's Works; Bale, p. 246; Pits, p. 269; Tanner, p. 317; Fabricius, p. 55.] C. L. K.

GILBERT OF SEMPRINGHAM (1083 ?–1189), founder of the order that bears his name, was born about 1083 (*Vita* ap. *Acta Sanct.* p. 573, where, however, ' sex ' may be a corruption of ' senex;' cf. CAPGRAVE, fol. 157b2 and *Digby MS.* 36, fol. 48a2, 46b1). His father, Jocelin, was a wealthy Norman knight, his mother an Englishwoman of lower rank (*Digby MS.* 7 *a*; but cf. DUGDALE, p. v). The family estates were in or near Lincolnshire (*Digby MS.*). Of an ungainly figure, and showing no promise of military vigour, Gilbert, as he himself told his followers, was treated with contempt at home. Then he was set to literature, at which after a time he worked vigorously, and went to France. Here he ultimately became a teacher (*ib.* fol. 8), and acquired a great reputation for learning. While still a young man he returned home, and began to instruct the boys and girls of his own neighbourhood (*ib.*) His father gave him the churches of Sempringham and ' Tirington;' and though there was some opposition to Jocelin's right of appointment, Gilbert retained both livings (*ib.*)

His labours now attracted the notice of Robert Bloet, bishop of Lincoln (*d.* 10 June 1123), in whose house he ministered as a clerk. Later he lived in the court of Robert's successor, Alexander (*d.* 25 Feb. 1148). The economy thus effected enabled him to give his Tirington income to the poor; but he refused the archdeaconry which one of these prelates pressed him to accept. It was probably some time before he took deacon's orders, and strongly against his own will, that he became priest (*ib.* fol. 12ar, 2, 13b1; for dates see HENRY OF HUNTINGDON, pp. 244, 280).

Gilbert founded his order, which he primarily intended for women only, before the death of Henry I (1135); but the difficulty of finding fitting inmates led him to admit men, several of whom he chose from his early scholars. Bishop Alexander helped when establishing his first house near St. Andrew's Church at Sempringham; and as the fame of Gilbert's piety spread this example was followed by the wealthy nobles, and finally by Henry II (*Digby MS.* 14a2, 1662, 17a2; cf. *Instit.* p. 30). By the advice of William, abbot of Rievaulx (*d.* 1145 or 1146), Gilbert crossed the channel to obtain the papal sanction for the orders he had drawn up to govern his followers; but at first without effect (*Instit. St. Gilb.*, ap Dugdale, p. 29, &c.; for date see JOHN OF HEXHAM, p. 317). When advancing years made him anxious to lay aside his responsibility, he visited France, leaving his flock under the care of his 'chief friends' the Cistercians. At the great Cistercian assembly at Cîteaux (September 1147 or 1148) he met Eugenius III, who grieved that it was now too late to make him archbishop of York. On this occasion or another Gilbert acquired the friendship of St. Bernard and St. Malachy (*d.* 2 Nov. 1148), the famous archbishop of Armagh, from each of whom he received an abbot's staff (*ib.* fol. 19; DUGDALE, pp. xi, xii; cf. CAPGRAVE, fol. 157a2; for the dates, cf. O'CONOR, iii. 762; ST. BERNARD, *Vita Malachiæ*, col. 1114, and JAFFÉ, p. 629; WILL. OF NEWBURGH, i. 54–5).

On returning home Gilbert completed arrangements for the ordination of some of his canons, and revised the rules of his order. Later he found a successor in an old pupil, Roger of Sempringham, provost of Malton Church. To Roger, Gilbert vowed obedience, and received a canon's habit at his hands at Bullington near Wragby (*Digby MS.* 28 a; DUGDALE, p. 17; CAPGRAVE, 157a2).

Gilbert supported Becket against Henry II, and sent him money openly in his exile. For this he was called before the king's curia in London. Things might have fared ill with him had not messengers arrived from the king, who was abroad, with orders to reserve Gilbert for the royal judgment (*Digby MS.*, 29b–31a1; DUGDALE, pp. 17, 18; CAPGRAVE, 157b1). Gilbert was held in such regard that when he came to court the king used to visit him; Queen Eleanor and her sons esteemed him highly, and when Henry heard of his death during the war against his rebellious children he broke out, 'I knew he must be dead because of the ills that have increased upon me' (*Digby MS.*, 37b1, 2; DUGDALE, p. 21; cf. *Digby MS.*, 101b1, 2, 105b2, 106). Gilbert's later years were troubled by the evil conduct of two of his most trusted servants, Gerard and Ogger Carpenter. This Ogger, with his poverty-stricken parents and three brothers, Gilbert had brought up from his boyhood. His rapacity and ingratitude brought on his patron a reprimand from Pope Alexander III, and the old man had to write to Rome in his own defence. Nearly all the English bishops wrote in the same strain, as did also Henry II, who refused the bribes of Gilbert's enemies, though admitting the lax discipline into which the new order had fallen (DUGDALE, pp. 18–19; *Digby MS.*, 31a1–34a2; HARPSFELD, p. 386; cf. *Digby MS.*, fol. 97b–109). Gilbert grew feeble from old age; but when he was over a hundred years his eyesight alone failed him. He received extreme unction on the night of Christmas 1188 in 'Kaadeneia' Abbey; then, fearing lest his body should be detained for burial elsewhere, had himself carried by by-paths to Sempringham, 'the head of his monasteries.' Here the rulers of all his churches came to receive his last blessing. Then, with his successor only by his couch, he remained in a kind of stupor, from which he woke repeating the words 'He has dispersed, he has given to the poor,' Psalm 112, v. 9. 'This is your duty for the future,' he added to the watcher at his side. Next morning he died about matins, Saturday, 4 Feb. 1189 (DUGDALE, pp. 22–3; *Digby MS.*, fol. 46–8; cf. CAPGRAVE, fol. 187b2). He was buried, wrapped in his priest's robes, between the great altars of St. Mary and St. Andrew at Sempringham. King John and many other nobles visited his tomb (9 Jan. 1201), and after due inquiries he was canonised by Innocent III (11 Jan. 1202), largely owing to the efforts of Archbishop Hubert Walter, to whom the principal account of his life is dedicated (DUGDALE, pp. 23, 38; *Digby MS.*, fol. 46–8; cf. CAPGRAVE, 187b2). His body was translated, 13 Oct. 1202, in the presence of Archbishop Hubert and many other prelates and nobles (*ib.* pp. 27–9; DUGDALE, p. 27). During his lifetime Gilbert had founded thirteen 'conventual churches,' and at his death his order numbered seven hundred men and fifteen hundred 'sisters.' Each house was ruled by two 'probate' senes and two 'maturæ sorores.' The moral dangers inherent in his system, of which in later years Walter Map speaks so apprehensively, had made their appearance before 1166, as may be seen from the disgusting story of the 'Wotton nun' told by Ailred of Rievaulx (*Digby MS.*, 147b2; CAPGRAVE, fol. 157a2; cf. DUGDALE, fol. 97. Ailred's narrative may be read in Bale, p. 225–7, and in Migne, vol. cxcv. col. 789–96).

Gilbert's writings include a treatise, 'De Constructione (or de Fundatione) monasteriorum' (*Digby MS.*, fol. 14a2, 31a1; cf. DUGDALE, pp. 9, 18, 19), rules and regulations for his own order, which were confirmed by Eugenius III, Hadrian IV, and Alexander III (*Digby MS.*, 21ab; DUGDALE, p. 13), and are printed in Dugdale, pp. 29, &c.; and a letter to his order (*Digby MS.*, 45a–46a2). De Visch adds a volume of letters and certain discourses, 'conciones' or 'exhortationes' (p. 113; cf. BALE, p. 661).

Gilbert's life, written by one of his own order, and dedicated to Archbishop Hubert, is preserved, along with many other documents relating to the saint, in a fifteenth-century manuscript (*Digby MS.*, 36) (see fol. 4a1, 6a1). The author had known Gilbert personally, and wrote at the request of Abbot Roger (*ib.* fol. 7b1, 6a1). Cotton. MS. Cleopatra, B. 1, fol. 31–173, as printed in the 'Monasticon' (pp. i–xcix), following p. 795, seems to be an abbreviated, or perhaps an earlier, form of this biography (cf. *Digby MS.*, 6a1, 2). Two shorter lives are printed in the Bollandists' 'Acta Sanct.' for 4 Feb., pp. 570–573, one of which is a reprint of Capgrave. Both the Cottonian and Digby MSS. give an account of Gilbert's canonisation. The latter is prefaced by a dedicatory letter to Archbishop Hubert (fol. 4–6). It also includes two treatises on St. Gilbert's miracles (fol. 38–46a2, with which cf. DUGDALE, p. 22, and fol. 63b–77a). It concludes with the correspondence relating to Gilbert's translation and canonisation, and a number of interesting letters written to him or on his behalf by Henry II, Alexander III, Henry, bishop of Winchester (*d.* 6 Aug. 1171), William, bishop of Norwich (*d.* 16 Jan. 1174), Archbishop Roger of York (*d.* 20 Nov. 1181), Cardinal Hugo, and other prelates, which seem to throw the Ogger dispute between 1170 and 1175 (for dates see ROGER HOVEDEN, ii. 70; FLOR. WIG. ii. 153; RALPH DE DICETO, ii. 10, i. 347).

[Digby MS. 36 in Bodleian Library, Oxford; Dugdale's Monasticon, ed. 1817, &c., vol. vi. pt. ii. pp. i–xcix inserted between pp. 945 and 947; Walter Map's De Nug. Cur. ed. Wright (Camd. Soc.), 1850; William of Newburgh, ed. Howlett (Rolls Ser.); Ralph de Diceto and Roger of Hoveden (Rolls Ser.), ed. Stubbs; William of Newburgh, ed. Howlett; John of Hexham (Rolls Ser.); Bollandists' Acta Sanctorum, February, vol. i.; Capgrave's Legenda Angliæ, 1516; St. Bernard's Works, ap. Migne, vol. clxxxii.; Epistolæ Eugenii, vol. iii. ap. Migne, vol. clxxx.; Ailredi Opera, ap Migne, cxcv. 789–96; Harpsfeld's Hist. Eccles. Anglic. pp. 265–7; Planta's Cat. of Cotton. MSS.; De Visch's Bibliotheca Script. Ord. S. Cisterc. Douai, 1649; Henriquez's Menologium Cisterciense, 1630; Butler's Lives of the Saints, ed. 1847, ii. 48–50; Baring-Gould's Lives of the Saints, ii. 99–105, ed. 1872, Bale ed. 1559, pp. 214–17; Pits, pp. 252–3.] T. A. A.

GILBERT OF MORAY (*d.* 1245), bishop of Caithness, and the last Scotsman enrolled in the Kalendar of Saints, was a member of the noble family of Moray, and son of William, lord of Duffus and Strabrook, who had vast estates in the north. Fordun (bk. viii. ch. xxvi.), in his account of the council of Northampton in 1176, gives at length the speech of a young canon named Gilbert, who defended with great eloquence the rights of the church of Scotland. It has been sought by Bower, Spotiswood, and others to identify this Gilbert with the bishop of Caithness; but it is absurd to suppose that if, as they say, he thus made a brilliant reputation, he would have waited nearly half a century for a bishopric. After a good religious and secular education, Gilbert became archdeacon of Moray, in which capacity his name occurs in several charters dated between 1203 and 1221 (given with facsimiles in *Registrum de Moravia*). He was elected bishop of Caithness by the assent of all the clergy and people in 1223. It does not appear that he was ever, as has been asserted, chamberlain of Scotland, for he is never mentioned with that title in the charters which he granted or witnessed, nor does any chamberlain named Gilbert appear in any authentic document till long after St. Gilbert's death. Probably, however, he administered the property of the crown in the north, and was employed in the guardianship and repair of castles. Through the position which he thus held and through the influence of his family he was able to play a great part in civilising his province, winning popularity where his two predecessors had both been murdered. He built the cathedral of Dornoch at his own cost, and drew up for its chapter a constitution, preserved in the records of his bishopric. According to Dempster (vii. 663) he wrote 'Exhortationes ad ecclesiam suam,' and 'De libertate Scotiæ.' He died on 1 April 1245; he was soon afterwards canonised, and was held in great reverence till the Reformation.

[Kalendar of Scottish Saints, p. 355; Breviary of Aberdeen; Registrum de Moravia, p. xliii, all published by the Bannatyne Club; Records of the Bishopric of Caithness in Bannatyne Miscellany, vol. iii.] C. L. K.

GILBERT THE ENGLISHMAN (*fl.* 1250) is said to be the first practical English writer on medicine, but the Master Richard quoted by Gilbert in his 'Compendium' was perhaps an earlier English writer on the subject. According to Bale and Pits, Gilbert, after studying in England, went abroad to extend his knowledge; and on returning to England he became physician to Hubert Walter. For these statements no authority is given, and it is improbable that Gilbert was physician to Hubert, since he must have survived the archbishop for half a century or more. For Gilbert's true date we have the internal evidence of his 'Compendium,' wherein he quotes Richard, who lived in the early half of the thirteenth century, and also Averroes, whose works were not translated till towards the middle of that century. Again he says that he had met Bertrand, son of Hugh, lord of Jubilet, in Palestine; a Hugh of Jubilet was engaged in an ambuscade in 1227, and had a son named Bertrand, who is probably the person referred to. On these data we may fix Gilbert's time of writing about 1250; Dr. Freind puts it as late as 1270. His work must have been written within the century, for Gilbert is himself quoted in the 'Rosa Medicinæ' of John of Gaddesden (1280?–1361). Gilbert was undoubtedly an Englishman, and studied and practised abroad. In one manuscript he is called chancellor of Montpelier, and he mentions among his patients a Count of Forez; he also uses medical terms which seem to be derived from the Romance languages rather than from English, such as 'bocium gulæ,' 'bosse de la gorge,' a swelling in the throat.

Dr. Freind praises Gilbert for having exposed the superstitious customs of the monks, and adopted a rational method of medicine. Gilbert does not, however, appear to have been much in advance of other writers of the time, nor to have had much originality; M. Littré says that his writings abound in ridiculous and superstitious formulæ, although they contain something of more value, and ought not to be neglected in the medical history of the thirteenth century.

Gilbert's chief work was a 'Compendium Medicinæ,' also called 'Lilium or Laurea Medicinæ.' This work is divided into seven books which treat (1) of fevers, (2) of diseases of the head and nerves, (3) of the eyes and face, (4) of diseases of the external members, (5 and 6) of internal diseases, (7) of diseases of the generative system, gout, cancer, diseases of the skin, poisons, &c. Like his contemporaries, Gilbert is generally content to borrow from the writings of the Greeks and Arabs, citing among others Aristotle, Avicenna, Rases, and Averroes. The most characteristic feature of the work is that it contains a small number of observations drawn from his own experience. It was printed in 1510 at Lyons as 'Compendium Medicinæ Gilberti Anglici tam morborum universalium quam particularium, non tantum medicis, sed et cyrurgicis utilissimum. Correctum et emendatum per dominum Michaelem de Capella.' It was also printed at Geneva in 1608 as 'Laurea Anglicana seu compendium totius medicinæ.' Numerous manuscripts have survived. Other works by Gilbert are: 2. 'Commentarii in Versus Ægidii de Urinis.' It is certain that Gilbert composed such a commentary, and it is quoted by John of Gaddesden; these quotations, however, show that it is not the commentary still extant and ascribed to Gilbert (MSS. Sorbonne, 6988 and 992; there is also a manuscript in Merton College Library under the name of Gilbertus Anglicus). 3. Pits ascribes to Gilbert a 'Practica Medicinæ.' In the catalogue of the Bibliothèque, a work in MS. 7061 is assigned under this title to Gilbert. But in the manuscript it is entitled simply 'Tractatus magistri G. de Montepessulano' (Montpélier), and the same work in MS. 996 Sorbonne is called 'Summa magistri Geraudi.' 4. 'Experimenta magistri Gilberti Cancellarii Montepessulani' (Bibliothèque MS. 7056). This is a collection of receipts, many of which bear Gilbert's name and are certainly his, for they agree closely with passages in his 'Compendium' without being identical. 5. 'Compendium super Librum Aphorismorum Hippocratis.' 6. 'Eorundem Expositio.' These two works exist in Bodleian MS. 720. 7. 'Antidotarium,' MS. Caius College. Bale and Pits also add 8. 'De Viribus Aquarum et Specierum.' 9. 'De Proportione Fistularum.' 10. 'De Judicio Patientis.' 11. 'De re Herbaria.' 12. 'De Tuenda Valetudine.' 13. 'De Particularibus Morbis.' 14. 'Thesaurus Pauperum.' Nothing further is known about them. Tanner following Leland calls Gilbert Leglæus; this is due to confusion with Gilbert de Aquila or L'Aigle, who lived at least a century later.

[Bale, p. 256; Pits, p. 277; Tanner, p. 474; Freind's History of Physick, 4th edit. 1750, ii. 250, 267–276; Wright's Biographia Britannica Literaria; Histoire Littéraire de la France, xxi. 393–403, article by E. Littré.] C. L. K.

GILBERT OF ST. LIFARD (*d.* 1305), bishop of Chichester, probably derived his surname from the collegiate church of Saint Lifard or

Leofard, close by Meung-sur-Loire, in the diocese of Orleans, formerly a monastery of that saint (STEPHENS, *Memorials of Chichester*, p. 102; ST. MARTHE, *Gallia Christiana*, viii. 1513), and was therefore a foreigner; but nothing seems certainly known of his early history. He was a lawyer practising in the ecclesiastical courts, and particularly in the court of arches. In 1269 he received a grant for his expenses from Archbishop Walter Giffard [q. v.] of York, whose official he now became (RAINE, *Fasti Eboracenses*, p. 310). In 1274 the same archbishop authorised him to borrow sixty marks. In 1276 he and other agents of the archbishop's court got into difficulties for unlawfully extending their jurisdiction in the wapentake of Pickering to matters not relating to wills (*Rotuli Hundredorum*, i. 108). While in the north he became the friend of William of Greenfield [q. v.], afterwards archbishop.

Gilbert's patron, Archbishop Giffard, died in 1279, and then, or earlier, he seems to have gone back to the south. In 1282 he was already treasurer of Chichester Cathedral (MARTIN, *Reg. Epistolarum J. Peckham*, i. 300). In the same year he was appointed by Archbishop Peckham as one of a small commission of men 'learned by long experience in the customs and rights of the church of Canterbury,' to inquire into the complaints of the bishops of the province as to the recent extension of the metropolitical jurisdiction by way of appeals (*ib.* i. 335). They drew up five articles of reformation, limiting and defining the functions of the archbishop's official (*ib.* i. 337-9), and on 24 July 1282 Gilbert was acting as Peckham's official himself, and as one of the three agents engaged in settling the dispute of the archbishop with the monks of his cathedral (*ib.* i. 389). Mr. Stephens describes him as 'official for the peculiars of the see of Canterbury, which were numerous in Sussex,' but it is plain that he acted generally. In 1283 Peckham interfered in a dispute Gilbert had with the prior of Lewes, as he was so much occupied with the archbishop's business that it was impossible for him to rebut in person the attacks the prior was constantly making against him before the royal justices (*ib.* ii. 593). In 1286 he was still official, and assisted Peckham in condemning heretics in the church of St. Mary-le-Bow (*ib.* iii. 921). He also held the livings of Hollingbourn and Boughton-under-Blean with the chapel of Hernehill (*ib.* iii. 1008), both in the diocese of Canterbury. He held all these offices until 1288.

On 30 Jan. 1288 Gilbert was elected bishop of Chichester by his brother canons.

The royal assent was given on 24 June, and his temporalities were restored the same day. On 5 Sept. he was consecrated bishop by his old patron, Peckham, at Canterbury (LE NEVE, *Fasti Eccl. Angl.* i. 241, ed. Hardy). One of his first acts as bishop was to convoke a diocesan council at Chichester, where on St. Faith's day (6 Oct. 1289) a large body of constitutions was drawn up. The strictness and zeal shown in them were quite those of a follower of the Franciscan archbishop. They provided that the clergy should be moral and respectable, should not go to tournaments, or keep concubines or consort with such as did, should be careful and diligent in divine worship and in visiting the sick; that rectors should choose respectable and duly ordained priests to act for them, and be on their guard against counterfeit friars (WILKINS, *Concilia*, ii. 169-172, prints them in full). These rules became sufficiently well known to be re-enacted in substance by Archbishop Greenfield [q.v.] in 1306.

In 1292 Gilbert had a quarrel with Richard Fitzalan (1267-1302) [q. v.], earl of Arundel, who had hunted over the bishop's woods in Houghton Chase (TIERNEY, *Arundel*, pp. 204-207). The earl only submitted after he had been excommunicated and his lands placed under interdict. In 1294 Edward I in his distress laid violent hands on 2,000*l.* in money which Gilbert had deposited for safety in St. Paul's ('Ann. Dunst.' in *Ann. Monastici*, iii. 390). Yet Edward and Gilbert were generally on good terms, and the bishop made the king costly presents on the latter's frequent visits to Chichester 'in honour of St. Richard' (*Sussex Archæological Collections*, ii. 140-1). On 12 Dec. 1299 Chichester was visited by Archbishop Winchelsey.

Gilbert was a good and holy bishop. He is described as 'the father of orphans, the consoler of widows, the pious and humble visitor at rough bedsides and hovels, the bountiful helper of the needy, the sanctity of whose life was attested by the large number of miracles worked at his tomb' (*Flores Historiarum*, p. 456, ed. 1570). He was also a liberal benefactor of his cathedral. He bequeathed 1,250 marks for purposes of the fabric, a hundred shillings for two boys 'to cense the body of Christ at the daily high mass,' and endowed the precentorship for a mass on his anniversary. But his great work at Chichester was the rebuilding, in a singularly beautiful form of 'decorated' architecture, the eastern bays and the east end of the lady chapel of the cathedral. He died at Amberley on 12 Feb. 1305 ('Annales Londonienses' in STUBBS, *Chronicles of the Reigns of Edward I and Edward II*, i. 134, published in the Rolls Series), and was buried in his own lady chapel, in a tomb against the south wall.

[Stephens's Memorials of the See of Chichester, pp. 102–9; Raine's Fasti Eboracenses; Martin's Registrum Epistolarum Johannis Peckham (Rolls Ser.); Annales Monastici (Rolls Ser.); Flores Historiarum, ed. 1570; Le Neve's Fasti Ecclesiæ Anglicanæ, ed. Hardy, i. 241–2, 267; Sussex Archæological Collections; Wilkins's Concilia, vol. ii.; Stubbs's Chronicles of Edward I and Edward II (Rolls Ser.)]   T. F. T.

GILBERT, Mrs. ANN (1782–1866), writer of poetry for children, is better known by her maiden name, ANN TAYLOR, her most popular works having been written before her marriage in conjunction with her younger sister Jane, the author of the 'Contributions of Q. Q.' She was the eldest child of Isaac Taylor ' of Ongar,' and was born at a house opposite Islington Church on 30 Jan. 1782. One of her brothers was Isaac Taylor [q. v.], author of the 'Natural History of Enthusiasm.' From 1786 to 1795 her home was at the village of Lavenham in Suffolk, whither her father, who depended for his livelihood upon engraving, had removed for the sake of economy. Early in 1796, at a time when the trade in engravings was at a very low ebb, he was fortunately chosen minister of a congregation of nonconformists at Colchester. Here he educated his family himself. Ann and Jane worked long hours at engraving under his superintendence. The first literary venture of the family was a poetical solution of the enigma, charade, and rebus in the ' Minor's Pocket Book' for 1798, which Ann sent to the 'Pocket Book' for 1799. Her solution won the first prize, and in consequence she became a regular contributor to the annual, and established a connection with its publishers, Darton and Harvey. They employed the sisters on various books for children, the chief of which were ' Original Poems for Infant Minds,' in two volumes, published in 1804 and 1805, and ' Rhymes for the Nursery' in 1806. Their 'Hymns for Infant Minds' followed in 1810. In 1811 Isaac Taylor was called to the pastorate of a congregation at Ongar in Essex. He remained there for the rest of his life, and as his own and his wife's works and most of those of his children were published after this date the family became known as the 'Taylors of Ongar.' In 1812, while staying with Jane Taylor and her brother Isaac at Ilfracombe, Ann received a letter from the Rev. Joseph Gilbert [q. v.] asking if he might be allowed to visit her with a view to marriage. He had never seen her, knowing her only from the report of her friends, and from her writings. After he had been to Ongar and favourably impressed her parents, she consented to his visit. He was successful in his suit, and they were married on 24 Dec. 1813.

For many years the care of a somewhat numerous family impeded her writing. Soon after the birth of her eldest son she said ' the dear little child is worth volumes of fame.' She lived with her husband at Rotherham from 1814 to 1817, at Hull from 1817 to 1825, and at Nottingham from 1825 till his death in 1852. During her married life she published in 1839 'The Convalescent, Twelve Letters on Recovery from Sickness,' and in 1844 ' Seven Blessings for Little Children,' and she also contributed about a quarter of the whole number of hymns in Dr. Leifchild's collection of 'Original Hymns' published in 1842. On her husband's death she wrote a ' Memoir of the Rev. Joseph Gilbert,' which was published along with ' Recollections of some of his Discourses by one of his sons' in 1853.

As a widow she continued to live in Nottingham. Though she was now above seventy, she made regular summer tours with an old friend, Mrs. Forbes, through England, Scotland, and Wales. She revisited in this way all the scenes of her youth, and saw many new places. When she was eighty she said 'the feeling of being a grown woman, to say nothing of an old woman, does not come naturally to me.' Her journeys continued till 1866. She died at Nottingham on 20 Dec. of that year.

In 1874 was published the 'Autobiography and other Memorials of Mrs. Gilbert, edited by Josiah Gilbert ' (2 vols. 8vo, 3rd ed. 1 vol. 1878). In this work the history of her life, suggested by the frontispieces, which show Ann Taylor first as a sweet-tempered child, and again as a sweet-tempered old lady, is told in a charming manner by herself till the date of her marriage, and after that by her son with help from her letters. The fact that the 'Original Poems for Infant Minds,' the 'Rhymes for the Nursery,' and the ' Hymns for Infant Minds ' are still republished is a strong testimony to their suitability for their purpose. The authorship of Ann and Jane Taylor's joint works is often attributed exclusively to Jane, but this is a mistake. Ann wrote at least as much of them as Jane, and her contributions, though they perhaps contain less of poetic merit than Jane's, are better adapted for children. Many of the best of the 'Poems' and 'Rhymes,' as, for instance, 'My Mother' and the 'Notorious Glutton,' were written by Ann. So, too, were some of the best known of the 'Hymns,' such as the one which begins 'I thank the Goodness and the Grace.'

Besides the works already mentioned Ann Taylor wrote, in conjunction with her sister: 'Limed Twigs to catch Young Birds,' 1815; 'Rural Scenes;' 'City Scenes;' 'Hymns for Infant Schools;' 'Original Anniversary Hymns for Sunday Schools;' 'Incidents of Childhood,' 1821; 'The Linnet's Life,' 1822; and (alone) 'The Wedding among the Flowers,' 1808.

[The Autobiography mentioned in the text; Isaac Taylor's Family Pen; Brit. Mus. Cat. of Printed Books.] E. C–N.

GILBERT, ASHURST TURNER (1786–1870), bishop of Chichester, son of Thomas Gilbert of Ratcliffe, Buckinghamshire, a captain in the royal marines, by Elizabeth, daughter of William Long Nathaniel Hutton, rector of Maids Moreton, Buckinghamshire, was born near Burnham Beeches, Buckinghamshire, 14 May 1786, and educated at the Manchester grammar school from 1800 to 1805, when he was nominated to a school exhibition, and matriculated from Brasenose College, Oxford, on 30 May. At the Michaelmas examination of 1808 he was placed in the first class *in literis humanioribus*, one of his four companions being Sir Robert Peel, bart. He graduated B.A. 16 Jan. 1809, and succeeded to one of Hulme's exhibitions on 8 March following. Having been elected to a fellowship, he proceeded M.A. 1811, and B.D. 1819. He was actively engaged for many years as a college tutor, and in 1816–18 was a public examiner. On the premature death of Dr. Frodsham Hodson in 1822 he was elected principal of Brasenose on 2 Feb., and took his D.D. degree on 30 May. For twenty years he filled that post, and discharged the duties of his office with dignity and kindness. From 1836 to 1840 he was vice-chancellor of the university. On the death of Dr. P. N. Shuttleworth he was nominated by the Duke of Wellington to the bishopric of Chichester, 24 Jan. 1842, and consecrated at Lambeth Palace on 27 Feb. On retiring from Brasenose he received from the fellows and graduate members a costly service of table plate. To the oversight of his diocese Dr. Gilbert brought the same zeal, energy, and kindness which had previously marked his university career. He took much interest in Lancing College and other educational institutions. Though his personal leanings were in favour of high church opinions, he was averse to any approach to Romanism and romanising ceremonials, and on 14 Oct. 1868 he interdicted the Rev. John Purchas from using ultra-ritualistic services at St. James's Chapel,

Brighton. This case led to much litigation, and eighteen works were printed in connection with the matter.

Gilbert died of paralysis of the lower bowels at the palace, Chichester, on 21 Feb. 1870, and was buried in Westhampnett Church, Sussex, on 25 Feb. He married on 31 Dec. 1822 Mary Anne, only child of the Rev. Robert Wintle, vicar of Culham, Oxfordshire, who died in the palace, Chichester, 10 Dec. 1863. His blind daughter, Elizabeth Margaretta Maria, is separately noticed.

Gilbert was the author of: 1. 'A Pastoral Letter to the Clergy and Laity of the Diocese of Chichester,' 1843. 2. 'Church Questions: a Letter to Colonel Wyndham, M.P.,' 1845. 3. Sermons, 1847, 1854, 1856, 1859, and 1862, being six pamphlets. 4. 'A Course of Sermons preached in St. Paul's Church, Brighton. By the Bishop of Winchester and others. Edited by the Rev. H. M. Wagner,' 1849. 5. 'Memorial of the Parishioners of the Parish of Westbourne to the Bishop of Chichester, with his reply, also a Letter from H. Newland, rector,' 1851. 6. 'Pictorial Crucifixes: a Letter to the Rev. A. D. Wagner,' 1852, to which there was a reply entitled 'Pictorial Crucifixes: a Letter to the Bishop of Chichester. By a Priest,' 1852. 7. Charges, 1853, 1856, 1859, three pamphlets. 8. 'A Statement of the Proceedings of the Bishop of Chichester against John Mason Neale, the Warden of Sackville College, East Grinstead,' 1853. 9. 'Teaching and Practice in the Parish of Lavington: a Correspondence between the rector, R. W. Randall, and the Bishop of Chichester,' 1859.

[Times, 22 Feb. 1870, p. 10, and 26 Feb. p. 5; Illustrated London News, 5 March 1870, p. 259, and 28 May, p. 563; Manchester School Register, ii. 221–4; Guardian, 23 Feb. 1870, p. 215; Our Rulers in the Lord, a Sermon on the Sunday after the Funeral of the Bishop of Chichester, by the Rev. H. B. W. Churton, 1870.] G. C. B.

GILBERT, CHARLES SANDOE (1760–1831), historian of Cornwall, son of Thomas Gilbert, was born in the parish of Kenwyn, near the city of Truro, in 1760. In conjunction with a Mr. Powell he became an itinerant vendor of medicines in Cornwall and Devonshire, where Gilbert & Powell's pills, plaisters, tinctures, and drops were considered the universal remedies, and brought in much wealth to their proprietors. On Powell's retirement 'Doctor Gilbert' continued the business alone, but afterwards took in a Mr. Parrot. Later on he had establishments at 29 Market Street, Plymouth, and at Fore Street, Devonport, being assisted by a staff of six travellers, who continually visited the towns and villages of the two counties. His medicines were also extensively advertised in the local newspapers. About 1810 Gilbert acquired information which led him to believe that he might claim descent from the Gilberts of Compton Castle, Devonshire, and under that persuasion he applied himself to the study of antiquities, genealogy, heraldry, and the collateral sciences, which ultimately led him to undertake a general history of Cornwall. Henceforth in his journeys through Cornwall he took notes of all he saw and heard, and also made his travellers collect information respecting local occurrences. After 1812 he was accompanied in several of his annual excursions in Cornwall by Henry Perlee Parker, since well known as an historical painter, who aided him by his pencil. After years of assiduous labour the first volume appeared in 1817, bearing the title of 'An Historical Survey of the County of Cornwall, to which is added a Complete Heraldry of the same, with numerous Woodcuts,' 592 pages. The second volume came out in 1820, 962 pages, and is generally found bound in two parts, the latter commencing after the conclusion of the heraldry at p. 373, where a half-title is found embellished with a view of St. German's Church, and the words 'Historical and Topographical Survey of the County of Cornwall.' As a parochial history, taken as a whole, it is an admirable work, and is still one of the best and most useful of the numerous books on Cornwall. Copies are seldom met with, and when found command high prices. In the majority of instances the twenty-five engraved plates of coats of arms are wanting. During the progress of the 'Historical Survey' Gilbert appears to have neglected his business, and, although he was patronised by successive dukes of Northumberland, and obtained a number of subscribers, the work cost double the estimate, and on 29 Oct. 1825 he was gazetted a bankrupt. In the following year he removed to London, where, taking Gilbert Morrish into partnership, he opened a chemist's shop at 27 Newcastle Street, Strand. Here he was interviewed by the Rev. John Wallis (WALLIS, *Cornwall Register*, 1847, p. 312); and died at the same address 30 May 1831, being buried in the churchyard of the Savoy, where a head-stone was erected to his memory.

[Notes and Queries, 4th ser. ix. 141 ; Journ. Royal Inst. of Cornwall, 1879, pp. 343-9, by Sir J. Maclean ; Boase and Courtney's Bibl. Cornub. pp. 173, 1194 ; Davies Gilbert's Hist. of Cornwall, 1838, i. xiii-xiv.]   G. C. B.

GILBERT, CLAUDIUS, the elder (*d.* 1696 ?), ecclesiastic, was nephew of Henry Markham, a colonel employed in Ireland under the Commonwealth. Gilbert officiated as a nonconformist or independent clergyman in Ireland. Under the civil establishment of the Commonwealth in 1655 he received an annual allowance of 200*l.* as minister for the precinct of Limerick. In that town he actively opposed the quakers, who in 1656 endeavoured to propagate their doctrines there, with a zeal which led to their expulsion by the governmental authorities. In 1657 Gilbert published at London, 'The Libertine School'd, or a Vindication of the Magistrates' Power in Religious Matters ; in answer to some fallacious quæries scattered about the City of Limerick, by a nameless author, about the 15th of December, 1656 ; and for detection of those mysterious designs so vigorously fomented, if not begun, among us by Romish engineers, and Jesuitick emissaries, under notionall disguises.' This publication, dated from Gilbert's study in Limerick, 22 Dec. 1656, was dedicated to Henry Cromwell, commander-in-chief of the forces, and his council for the affairs of Ireland. The signature of Gilbert stands first among those clergymen who, as 'servants in the ministry of the gospel,' presented an address to Henry Cromwell, lord deputy, in Dublin in May 1658. In that year Gilbert published at London, 'A Soveraign Antidote against Sinful Errors, the Epidemical Plague of these latter dayes; extracted out of divine records, the dispensatory of Christianity for the prevention and cure of our spiritual distempers.' This was dedicated to Colonel Henry Ingoldsby, governor of the precinct of Limerick and Clare, under date of 23 Jan. 1656. In 1658 Gilbert also published at London 'The Blessed Peace-maker and Christian Reconciler; intended for the healing of all unnatural and unchristian divisions in all relations; according to the purport of that divine oracle announced by the Prince of Peace himself.' This treatise, dated at Limerick 23 March 1656, was dedicated to Major-general Sir Hardress Waller and his wife Elizabeth. A fourth treatise by Gilbert was issued at London in the same year, entitled 'A pleasant Walk to Heaven through the New and Living Way which the Lord Jesus consecrated for us and His sacred Word reveals unto us.' The date, Limerick, 19 May 1657, is appended to the 'epistle dedicatory' to the author's uncle, Colonel Henry Markham, and his wife Esther. On the title-pages of his above-mentioned works Gilbert is designated 'bachelor of divinity and minister of the gospel at Limerick in Ireland.' In 1659 the commissioners of the revenue in Ireland were directed by government to provide a house for Gilbert while preaching in Dublin. After the Restoration Gilbert appears to have become connected with the established church in Ireland, and to have settled in Belfast as a friend of Arthur Chichester, first earl of Donegal, who in his will made him a bequest. In 1666 Gilbert became prebendary of Ballymore in the church of Armagh (COTTON, *Fasti*, iii. 51). Under the designation of 'minister of Belfast' Gilbert in 1683 published in London a translation of Pierre Jurieu's reply to Bossuet, under the title 'A Preservative against the Change of Religion; or a just and true idea of the Roman catholic religion opposed to the flattering portraictures made thereof, and particularly to that of my lord of Condom; translated out of the French original.' Gilbert prefixed a dedication, dated 3 July 1682, to the sovereign, burgesses, and inhabitants of Belfast. Gilbert's publications indicate proficiency in Hebrew, Arabic, Latin, Greek, Italian, French, and Spanish.

[Records of Government in Ireland, 1650–60; Brit. Mus. Lansdowne MS. 1228; Fuller and Holms's View of Sufferings of Quakers, 1731; Reid's Hist. of Presbyterian Church in Ireland, 1853; Benn's Hist. of Belfast, 1877.] J. T. G.

GILBERT, CLAUDIUS, the younger (1670–1743), ecclesiastic, only son and heir of Claudius Gilbert the elder [q. v.], minister at Limerick and Belfast, was born in the latter town in 1670. He received his early education in Belfast, entered Trinity College, Dublin, on 23 March 1685, became a fellow of that institution in 1693, and received the degrees of doctor of laws and doctor of divinity in 1706. Gilbert was for some time professor of divinity in his college, of which he was appointed vice-provost in 1716. He obtained the rectorship of Ardstraw in the county of Tyrone in 1735, and died in October 1743. He bequeathed considerable sums to various charities, and gave about thirteen thousand volumes of printed books to Trinity College. A catalogue of his books, compiled by himself, is in the possession of that institution, but it does not contain any matter of special literary interest. Gilbert's donation is commemorated by an inscription over his collection in the library of the college, and a bust of him in white marble, executed in 1758, is preserved there.

[Archives of Trinity College, Dublin; Boulter's Monument, London, 1745; Dublin Journal, 1758.] J. T. G.

GILBERT (formerly GIDDY), DAVIES (1767–1839), president of the Royal Society, was born in the parish of St. Erth, Cornwall, on 6 March 1767. His father, the Rev. Edward Giddy, sometime curate of St. Erth, died 6 March 1814 having married in 1765 Catherine, daughter and heiress of John Davies of Tredrea, St. Erth; she died in 1803. Davies Giddy, the only child, was educated at the Penzance grammar school and at a boarding-school at Bristol. He matriculated from Pembroke College, Oxford, as a gentleman-commoner, 12 April 1785, and was created M.A. in 1789 and D.C.L. in 1832. His tastes were literary, and at an early age he cultivated the company of men of letters. He joined the Linnean Society, and was one of the promoters of the Geological Society of Cornwall, founded in 1814. He was president of the latter society, and never omitted to pay an annual visit to Cornwall to preside at its anniversary meetings. While at Oxford he contracted an intimacy with Thomas Beddoes, M.D. [q. v.], who in 1793 dedicated to him his 'Observations on the Nature of Demonstrative Evidence.' During 1792–3 Giddy served the office of high sheriff for his native county. One of the most noted events in his life is the part he performed in encouraging the early talents of Sir Humphry Davy [q. v.] Among others whom he helped to advance in life were the Rev. Malachi Hitchins [q. v.] and the Rev. John Hellins [q. v.] He made calculations to assist Richard Trevithick and the two Hornblowers in their endeavours to improve the steam-engine, and calculated for Thomas Telford the length of the chains required for the Menai Bridge. On 26 May 1804 he was elected to parliament for the borough of Helston in Cornwall, and at the next election, 1 Nov. 1806, was returned for Bodmin, which town he represented until 3 Dec. 1832. He was one of the most assiduous members who ever sat in the House of Commons, and perhaps unequalled for his service on committees. He helped to pass the act repealing the duty on salt, with a view to assisting the pilchard fishery of Cornwall. He devoted to public business nearly the whole of his time, and was remarkable for the short period which he spent in sleep. He took a prominent part in parliamentary investigations connected with the arts and sciences. On 18 April 1808 he married Mary Ann, only daughter and heiress of Thomas Gilbert of Eastbourne. By this marriage he acquired very extensive estates in the neighbourhood of that town, which, added to the landed property in Cornwall he afterwards inherited from his father, placed him in very affluent circumstances. On the levels of Pevensey, a portion of his Sussex estates, he planned and accomplished extensive improvements. He took the name and arms of Gilbert in lieu of those of Giddy, pursuant to royal sign-manual 10 Dec. 1817, and the family names of his children were also changed by another sign-manual on 7 Jan. following. In 1811, when the high price of gold produced an effect on the currency, he printed an argumentative tract entitled 'A Plain Statement of the Bullion Question,' to which replies were written by Samuel Banfill and A. W. Rutherford. During the Corn Bill riots, March 1815, his residence, 6 Holles Street, London, was attacked by the mob (*European Mag.* March 1815, p. 273). In 1819 he suggested with success the establishment of the observatory at the Cape of Good Hope. On the death of Sir Joseph Banks in 1820, when Sir Humphry Davy was elected president of the Royal Society, his friend Gilbert accepted the office of treasurer. Ill-health obliging Davy to quit England in 1827, the treasurer took the chair at the meetings of that session, and when a continuance of illness obliged the president to resign, Gilbert was elected president 30 Nov. 1827. The want of a hospitable town residence and of a commanding decision of deportment, the cabals of some discontented members, and the understood desire of the Duke of Sussex to obtain the chair, induced Gilbert to resign the presidency 30 Nov. 1830. During his tenure of office, under the provisions of the Earl of Bridgewater's will he nominated the eight writers of the 'Bridgewater Treatises' [see EGERTON, FRANCIS HENRY]. All his appointments did not give satisfaction, and it was a question whether the earl's money had been distributed in strict accordance with his desires (*Correspondence regarding the Appointment of the Writers of the Bridgewater Treatises between D. Gilbert and others*, Penryn, 1877, 8vo. Privately printed by his nephew, John D. Enys). Gilbert selected Brunel's design for the Clifton suspension bridge (1830). Gilbert was elected a fellow of the Society of Antiquaries in 1820, and he promoted antiquarian and historical research with much liberality. On his recommendation Thomas Bond's 'History of East and West Looe' was printed in 1823 [see BOND, THOMAS]. In 1827 he edited 'A Collection of Christmas Carols,' and in 1826 and 1827 'Mount Calvary' and 'The Creation of the World,' two mystery plays in the ancient Cornish language. His most extensive work, however, was 'The Parochial History of Cornwall, founded on the manuscript histories of Mr. Hals and Mr. Tonkin,' 1838, 4 vols. To this work, which is arranged in the alphabetical order of the parishes, the author added much topographical and biographical matter, while Dr. Henry Samuel Boase [q. v.] contributed the geology of each parish. The author was in failing health when these volumes were brought out, and a

great deal of the work had to be done by persons who were ignorant of Cornish names. The book has consequently never had much repute as a county history. He also contributed to the 'Archæologia,' the 'Philosophical Transactions,' the 'Journal of the Royal Institution,' and other scientific periodicals. A detailed account of these papers, as well as of his other writings, will be found in the 'Bibliotheca Cornubiensis.' In 1825 he established a private press in his house at Eastbourne, where his eldest daughter, Catherine, afterwards the wife of John Samuel Enys of Enys, Cornwall, acted as the compositor. Nothing of much length was printed, but upwards of two hundred short pieces on slips, fly-sheets, &c., were struck off. For an account of many of these see Boase's 'Collectanea Cornubiensia,' pp. 276–7. He died at Eastbourne 24 Dec. 1839, and was buried on 29 Dec. in the chapel appropriated to the interments of the Gilridges and Gilberts north of the chancel of Eastbourne Church. A tablet bearing a long biographical inscription is in the church of his birth-place, St. Erth, Cornwall. His portrait in oils, by Thomas Phillips, R.A., is preserved in the rooms of the Royal Society, London. His wife, who died at Eastbourne 26 April 1845, took an interest in agriculture, and wrote 'On the Construction of Tanks' in the 'Journal of the Royal Agricultural Society' (1840), i. 499, and 'On Self-supporting Agricultural Schools' in the 'Journal of the Statistical Society' (1842), v. 289. His only son, John Davies Gilbert, F.R.S., born at Eastbourne 5 Dec. 1811, died at Prideaux Place, near Padstow, Cornwall, 16 April 1854. Three daughters also survived Gilbert.

[Drew's Imperial Mag. (1828), x. 585–93, with portrait; Jerdan's National Portrait Gallery (1831), ii. 1–8, with portrait; Weld's Hist. of the Royal Society (1848), ii. 419–28, 456–60, Walker's Memoirs of Distinguished Men (1864), pp. 53–5; Lower's Worthies of Sussex (1865), pp. 212–15; Gent. Mag. (February 1840), pp. 208–11; Boase and Courtney's Bibliotheca Cornubiensis (1874), pp. 173–5, 1194–5; Meteyard's Group of Englishmen (1871), pp. 82–4, 92, 225, 230, 316; information from the family.] G. C. B.

GILBERT, ELIZABETH MARGARETTA MARIA (1826–1885), philanthropist, born at Oxford on 7 Aug. 1826, was the second daughter and third of the eleven children of Ashurst Turner Gilbert [q. v.], principal of Brasenose College, Oxford, and afterwards bishop of Chichester, by his wife Mary Ann, only surviving child of Robert Wintle, vicar of Culham, Oxfordshire. She was at an early age a fine child, with flashing black eyes, but when only three years old a bad attack of scarlet fever deprived her of sight. Her parents wisely determined that she should be brought up with her sisters, although she was once severely burnt by falling against the fire. At the age of twenty she could understand French, German, and Italian, and had been thoroughly educated. She began to be keenly interested in the state of the blind poor. The invention, in 1851, of the Foucault frame enabled her to write freely, and she began to correspond with William Hanks Levy, a young blind teacher employed at the St. John's Wood school. In May 1854 she hired a cellar in New Turnstile, Holborn, at the cost of 1s. 6d. a week, for the sale of the work of seven blind men who worked at their own homes, and were paid the full selling price, less the cost of material. Levy was engaged as manager. Ultimately the institution developed into 'The Association for Promoting the General Welfare of the Blind,' at 21 South Row, New (Euston) Road, now 127 Euston Road. In accordance with Levy's wish, none but blind persons were employed, although Miss Gilbert rather disapproved of their isolation. She proposed in a thoughtful paper the establishment of a normal school for training teachers for the blind. Finding that much time might be saved by the use of blocks upon which baskets could be modelled, she sent Levy to France to obtain the necessary tools. In 1865 the association, now much advanced, removed to 210 Oxford Street, and afterwards to 28 Berners Street. Miss Gilbert materially assisted Levy in writing a book on 'Blindness and the Blind,' 8vo, 1872. She also took much interest in the foundation of the Normal College for the Blind. In November 1874 she sent a paper to a special committee appointed by the Charity Organisation Society to consider means of helping the blind, but was too ill to attend the meeting. Her delicate health caused her much suffering. She died on 7 Feb. 1885, at 5 Stanhope Place, Hyde Park, London.

[Frances Martin's Elizabeth Gilbert and her Work for the Blind; Athenæum, 17 Dec. 1887.]

G. G.

GILBERT, Sir GEOFFREY or JEFFRAY (1674–1726), judge, was the son of William Gilbert and Elizabeth, sister of a certain Mistress Gibbons, who was housekeeper of Whitehall in the time of Cromwell (*Hist. MSS. Comm.* 7th Rep. App. 244 *b*). Attempts have been made, but without success, to connect him with Sir Humphrey Gilbert the navigator [q. v.] Nichols (*Literary Anecdotes*, i. 408) says that he was a relation and an intimate friend of the nonjuring divine,

Thomas Brett, D.D. [q. v.], though himself a whig. He was admitted a member of the Inner Temple on 20 Dec. 1692, and was called to the bar in June 1698. His rise in the profession was rapid. On 4 Feb. 1714–15 he was appointed a puisne judge of the king's bench in Ireland, and by patent dated 5 July following he was created chief baron of the court of exchequer in that country. His name is connected with the celebrated constitutional case of Annesley *v.* Sherlock, in which a conflict occurred between the English and the Irish House of Lords. The Irish house had, in 1703, solemnly and unanimously resolved (1) 'that by the ancient known laws and statutes of this kingdom her majesty hath an undoubted jurisdiction and prerogative of judging in this her high court of parliament in all appeals and cases within her majesty's realm of Ireland; (2) that the determinations and judgments of this high court of parliament are final and conclusive, and cannot be reversed or set aside by any other court whatsoever.' These pretensions were so far from being admitted by the English House of Lords that in 1717–18, having reversed on appeal the decision of the Irish house in Annesley *v.* Sherlock—a case relating to real property in Ireland—they ordered the court of exchequer in that country to give effect to their decree. The court accordingly (Gilbert presiding) issued, on 22 Feb. 1717–18, an injunction commanding the sheriff of Kildare to reinstate the plaintiff Annesley in the possession of certain lands which the Irish house had adjudged to belong to Sherlock, and, on the sheriff neglecting so to do, and alleging in justification the prior order of the Irish house, imposed on him sundry fines, and ultimately issued an attachment against him; whereupon he absconded, and afterwards (28 July 1719) petitioned the Irish house on the subject. The Irish house resolved that Gilbert and his colleagues in the court of exchequer were 'betrayers of his majesty's prerogative,' and committed them to the custody of the usher of the black rod. Thereupon the English house resolved that the barons had 'acted with courage according to law in support of his majesty's prerogative, and with fidelity to the crown of Great Britain,' and ordered that an address should be presented to his majesty recommending them for special distinction. An act of parliament followed, declaring the pretensions of the Irish house to independent jurisdiction to be null and void, which act remained in force until the concession of Grattan's parliament in 1782. Gilbert resigned the office of lord chief baron on 18 May 1722, and was appointed on the 24th to a seat on the English exchequer bench. On

7 June he took the degree of serjeant-at-law, and on the 9th his seat in the English court. On the resignation of Thomas Parker, lord Macclesfield, he was appointed a commissioner for the custody of the great seal, and was knighted (7 Jan. 1724–5). The commissioners delivered the seal to Lord King on 1 June. On 3 June Gilbert was appointed lord chief baron of the court of exchequer. On 12 May 1726 he was elected a fellow of the Royal Society. He was prevented from presiding in the court of exchequer by a severe illness, of which he died at Bath on 14 Oct. 1726. He was buried in the church of St. Peter and St. Paul, commonly known as the Abbey Church, Bath. A monument to his memory was placed in the Temple Church, with an elaborate inscription said to have been written by one of his executors, Phillips Gibbon. He left no children, and probably did not marry.

Gilbert is said to have beguiled his leisure with mathematical studies. As a legal author he achieved permanent though only posthumous distinction. Among his papers were found the following works, which were published at various dates during the last century: 1. 'Law of Uses and Trusts,' London, 1734, 1741, 1811, 8vo. The last edition was by E. B. Sugden, afterwards Lord St. Leonards. 2. 'Law and Practice of Ejectments,' London, 1734, 1741, 1781, 8vo (the last edition being by Runnington). 3. 'Reports of Cases argued and decreed in the Courts of Chancery and Exchequer from 4 Queen Anne to 12 Geo. I,' London, 1734, 1742, fol. 4. 'History and Practice of Civil Actions in the Common Pleas,' London, 1737, 1761, 1779, 8vo. A brief treatise on the constitution of England is prefixed to this work. 5. 'Historical View of the Court of Exchequer,' London, 1738, 8vo, a first instalment of a work published in its entirety in 1758 under the title of 'A Treatise on the Court of Exchequer,' London, 8vo. 6. 'Treatise of Tenures,' Dublin, 1754; another edition in 1757; the 5th edition, in 1824, by Charles Watkins and R. S. Vidal, 8vo. 7. 'Law of Devises, Revocations, and Last Wills,' London, 1756, 1773. 8. 'Treatise on Rents,' London, 1758, 8vo. 9. 'History and Practices of the High Court of Chancery,' London, 1758, 8vo; an edition also appeared in Ireland in the same year. 10. 'Cases in Law and Equity, argued, debated, and adjudged in the King's Bench and Chancery in the 12th and 13th years of Queen Anne, during the time of Lord-chief-justice Parker. With two treatises, the one on the Action of Debt, the other on the Constitution of England,' London, 1760, 8vo. 11. 'The Law of Evidence,' London, 1761, 8vo. An edition, known as the 4th, enlarged, appeared in 1777, others in 1791, 1792, 1796, the last in four volumes, royal octavo, by Capel Lofft, with a life of the author prefixed, also, by way of introduction, an abstract of Locke's 'Essay concerning Human Understanding.' The first volume was reprinted in 1801, with notes and references to contemporary and later cases by J. Sedgwick, 8vo. 12. 'The Law of Executions, with the History and Practice of the Court of King's Bench, and some cases touching Wills of Lands and Goods,' London, 1763, 8vo. 13. 'Law and Practice of Distress and Replevin,' London, 1780, 1794 (ed. Hunt), 1823 (4th edit. by Impey). Gilbert also wrote 'A History of the Feud,' which came into the possession of Hargrave, but has remained in manuscript. A manuscript treatise on 'Remainders' has also been ascribed to him.

Gilbert's published works are marked by precision and lucidity of style, and very considerable mastery of his subject, and evince a real desire to exhibit it in a logical shape. The treatise on evidence, which is referred to by Blackstone as a classic, 'which it is impossible to abstract or abridge without losing some beauty and destroying the chain of the whole' (*Comm.* 12th edit. bk. iii. c. 23, p. 367), remained the standard authority on the subject throughout the eighteenth century. Blackstone also praises the 'History and Practice of Civil Actions in the Court of Common Pleas' as a work which 'has traced out the reason of many parts of our modern practice from the feudal institutions and the primitive construction of our courts in a most clear and ingenious manner' (*ib.* c. 18, p. 272). There is evidence in the 'History and Practice of the High Court of Chancery' (1758) of some acquaintance with Roman law, and of a very clear perception of the analogy between the prætorian code and English equity. Gilbert may thus fairly claim to have used, with eminent success, both the historical and the analytic methods, and even to have discerned the importance of the study of the Roman law, then generally neglected in England.

[Howell's State Trials, xv. 1302–23; Lords' Journ. (Ireland), ii. 625–7; Hist. Reg. Chron. Diary (1720), pp. 85–108, (1722) pp. 28–9, (1725) p. 28, (1726) p. 39; Bunbury's Rep. p. 113; Lord Raymond's Rep. 1380–1, 1420; Life by Capel Lofft, prefixed to Law of Evidence, ed. 1796; Foss's Lives of the Judges.] J. M. R.

GILBERT, GEORGE (1555–1583), founder of the Catholic Association in the reign of Queen Elizabeth, was born in Suffolk in 1555, and was grandson of William Gilbert of Clare, Suffolk (cf. VINCENT'S *Grants of Arms*, ii. 380, in library of College of Arms). At an early age he succeeded, on his father's death, to extensive landed estates. While travelling with the royal license on the continent he was reconciled to the catholic church by Father Robert Parsons at Rome in 1579. On his return to London he, in conjunction with Thomas Pound of Belmont, formed a 'Catholic Association,' consisting of young men of birth and property without the incumbrance of wives or offices. They promised ' to content themselves with food and clothing and the bare necessities of their state, and to bestow all the rest for the good of the catholic cause.' The association was solemnly blessed by Pope Gregory XIII on 14 April 1580. Its members lodged together in the house of Norris, the chief pursuivant, in Fetter or Chancery Lane. Norris had great credit with Aylmer, bishop of London, and was liberally paid by Gilbert. At Fulham the bishop's son-in-law, Dr. Adam Squire, was in Gilbert's pay. Through the connivance of these men the members of the association were able to receive priests and to have masses celebrated daily in their house until, after the arrival of the jesuits Parsons and Campion in England, the persecution grew more severe. In 1581 Gilbert deemed it prudent to withdraw to the English College at Rheims, where he was cordially welcomed by Dr. William Allen, who described him as 'summus patrum presbyterorum patronus.' Proceeding afterwards to Rome, he entered the English College as a pensioner, and devoted himself to promoting the catholic cause in England. Gregory XIII ordered him to France on diplomatic business. Gilbert was so eager about his preparations that he died of a fever on 6 Oct. 1583. While on his deathbed he was admitted into the Society of Jesus. The pope declared his death a serious blow to catholicism in England.

Gilbert incurred great expense by covering the walls of the English College at Rome with frescoes of the English martyrs. He left the superintendence of this work to Father William Good [q. v.], who had the pictures engraved and published, under the title of ' Ecclesiæ Anglicanæ Trophæa,' Rome, 1584, fol.

Gilbert's portrait has been engraved by W. P. Kiliam, from a drawing by J. G. Hemsch.

[Foley's Records, iii. 658-704; More's Hist. Missionis Anglicanæ Soc. Jesu, p. 83; Oliver's Jesuit Collections, p. 104; Simpson's Life of Campion, p. 123; Tanner's Societas Jesu Apostolorum Imitatrix, p. 180.]   T. C.

GILBERT, SIR HUMPHREY (1539?–1583), navigator, was the second son of Otho Gilbert of Compton, near Dartmouth. Sir Walter Raleigh was his step-brother by the second marriage of his mother, Catharine, daughter of Sir Philip Champernowne. He was educated at Eton and Oxford, and devoted himself to the study of navigation and the art of war. His first public service appears to have been under Ambrose Dudley [q. v.], earl of Warwick, at Havre in Normandy, where he was wounded in fighting against the French catholics, 26 Sept. 1563 (STOW, p. 654; *Cotton. MS.* Aug. I. ii. 78 *a*). In July 1566 he served as captain under Sir Henry Sidney in Ireland, and in the ensuing autumn took part in the operations against Shane O'Neil. In November, being sent home with despatches by the lord deputy Sidney, he took the opportunity of presenting to the queen a petition for privileges 'concerning the discoueringe of a passage by the North [west] to go to Cataia,' as an alternative to an earlier one presented by Anthony Jenkinson and himself in the previous April for discovery by the North-east (MORGAN and COOTE, ii. 177–9). The queen found other employment for both petitioners. Early in 1567 Gilbert was sent back to Ireland in order to assist Sidney in establishing an imported colony of West of England men near Lough Foyle in Ulster, with Gilbert for president. The undertaking failed, however, and Gilbert returned once more to soldiering.

Sent back to England in the summer of 1568, Gilbert there fell dangerously ill. The queen told Sidney that he was to have his full pay during his absence, and promotion on his return to Ireland. In October 1569, after defeating the celebrated McCarthy More, Gilbert was placed in entire charge of the province of Munster, where he had to keep the Irish chieftain and his followers in subjection. In December he wrote to the lord deputy saying that he was determined to have neither parley nor peace with any rebel, as he was convinced that no conquered nation could be ruled with gentleness. Thereupon Sidney knighted him at Drogheda, 1 Jan. 1570. Shortly afterwards Gilbert returned to England and married Anne, daughter of Sir Anthony Ager of Kent, by whom he had five sons and one daughter. In 1571 he was returned as M.P. for Plymouth. While in parliament he was sharply rebuked by Peter Wentworth for ' untruly informing her majesty of a motion made in the house on the queen's prerogatiue,' and was called ' a flatterer, a lyer, and a naughtie man,' and when he would have spoken in self-defence, ' had the denial of the house three times' (*Dev. Assoc. Trans.* xi. 466, 479).

In the autumn of 1572 Gilbert was sent to the Netherlands with a band of fifteen hundred English volunteers to assist the Zeelanders against their Spanish tyrants. After making an incursion nearly up to the gates of Bruges he crossed the Wester Schelde to Flushing. He was repulsed in an assault upon Goes, and his raw levies were not allowed to take refuge in Flushing until they had withstood a night attack by the Spaniards from Middelburg. At the end of August Gilbert again assaulted Goes unsuccessfully, as he was obliged to raise the siege by Mondragon's famous march of eight miles across the 'drowned lands' of the Ooster Schelde from Bergen-op-Zoom. The English fled before the more disciplined troops of Spain, and Gilbert returned to England in disgust (Fox Bourne, *English Seamen*, i. 114; Markham, *Fighting Veres*, pp. 43–8). For the next five years (1573–8) Gilbert lived in retirement at Limehouse, where he had resided for a year before he went to the Netherlands. During the winter of 1574, being visited here by George Gascoigne [q. v.], the poet, and asked by him 'how he spent his time in this loitering vacation from martial stratagems,' Gilbert took his friend into his study and there showed him 'sundry profitable and very commendable exercises which he had perfected plainly with his own pen' (Gascoigne's Pref. to Gilbert's *Discourse*). One of these 'exercises' was Gilbert's 'Discourse of a Discouery for a New Passage to Cataia.' It was written partly in support of his still unanswered petition of November 1566, and partly to quiet the fears of his elder brother, Sir John, who, having no issue, was adverse to Sir Humphrey embarking personally in such an enterprise. It led to the bestowal of a license (5 Feb. 1575) upon Sir Martin Frobisher [q. v.] for his discovery towards Cathay. It was afterwards edited by George Gascoigne in 1576, with additions, and probably without Gilbert's authority. On 6 Nov. 1577 Gilbert set forth another 'discourse:' 'How Her Majesty might annoy the King of Spain by fitting out a fleet of war-ships under pretence of a voyage of discovery, and so fall upon the enemy's shipping, destroy his trade in Newfoundland and the West Indies, and possess both Regions' (*State Papers*, Dom. cxviii. 12). There was no response to this discourse, but on 11 June 1578 Gilbert obtained from the queen his long-coveted charter for discovery, to plant a colony, and to be governor (Hakluyt, iii. 135–7). The first expedition in connection with it, in which he was assisted by his step-brother, Sir Walter

Raleigh, left Dartmouth on 23 Sept. 1578. Owing to divided councils it was a failure from the outset, and after putting back into Plymouth the fleet left once more on 18 Nov., only to court disaster at sea at the hands of the Spaniards off Cape Verde. Gilbert, finding it impossible with the residue to carry out his project, returned to Plymouth in May 1579 (Holinshed, iii. 1369). Although Sir Humphrey had sunk all his money and his influence at court in this unfortunate venture, the project was not abandoned, but in the meantime he turned to his old employment in Ireland. The summer of 1579 saw him serving under Sir John Perrot, admiral of the queen's ships sent to encounter the insurrection raised by James Fitzmaurice, aided by Spanish ships off Munster [see Fitzgerald, James Fitzmaurice, *d.* 1579]. In July 1581 he writes to Walsingham from Minster in Sheppey that he might be paid a little sum of money for his work in Ireland in 1579, whereby he had lost so much that he was reduced to utter want. It was a miserable thing, he added, that after seven-and-twenty years' service he should now be subjected to daily arrests, executions, and outlawries, and have even to sell his wife's clothes from off her back (*State Papers*, Dom. cxlix. 66). The next four years appear to have been employed by Gilbert chiefly in raising money for his colonising scheme, and in collecting information. His charter would expire in 1584, and to facilitate his operations he resolved to assign some of the privileges contained in it to other speculators, on condition that their enterprises should be carried on under his jurisdiction. Thus we meet with 'Articles of agreement between Sir H. Gilbert and such of Southampton as adventure with him' (*ib.* clv. 86). The result was that in the summer of 1583 he was enabled to set out once more on his long-cherished project for the settlement of Newfoundland.

On Tuesday, 11 June 1583, Gilbert sailed out of Plymouth Sound with a fleet of five ships, viz. the Delight as admiral, the barque Raleigh (furnished by his step-brother, and the largest vessel), the Golden Hind (commanded by Edward Hayes, the narrator of the voyage), the Swallow, and the Squirrel. Two days later the barque returned to Plymouth, probably by the connivance of Raleigh, on the plea of sickness aboard. After parting company with the Swallow and Squirrel in a fog on 20 July, Gilbert proceeded with his two remaining vessels until 30 July, when he sighted the northern shores of Newfoundland, near the Straits of Bellisle. Following the coast to the south, and after crossing Conception Bay, where he met with the Swallow, he held on his course to the harbour of St. John. There on 3 Aug. he found the Squirrel at anchor. The next day being Sunday he went ashore, and was so delighted with his surroundings that he at once decided to make this harbour the centre of his colony.

On Monday, 5 Aug., Gilbert took possession, in the name of the queen, of the harbour of St. John and two hundred leagues every way for himself, his heirs, and assigns for ever. After his commission had been read and interpreted to all concerned, he proclaimed 'that if any person should utter words sounding to the dishonour of her majesty, he should lose his ears and have his ship and goods confiscate.' Thus was planted the first English colony in North America. Within a fortnight he found himself the governor of a mixed colony of raw adventurers, many of whom were lazy landsmen and sailors useless except at sea. Not a few had been taken out of English prisons and intended for servants to the colonists. The best of these begged that they might be taken back to England or anywhere from the lawlessness with which Gilbert was unable to cope. Leaving the Swallow to carry home the sick and those who wished to return direct to England, Gilbert left the harbour of St. John with his other three ships on 20 Aug. with a view of searching the coast towards the south on board the little Squirrel. In their attempts to make for Sable Island eight days later the ships fell in with the flats and shoals between Cape Breton Island and the edge of the bank of Newfoundland. On 29 Aug. the largest ship, the Delight, struck aground and was lost. Among the drowned was the learned Hungarian, Stephen Parmenius, whose elegant Latin verses upon Gilbert are preserved to us by Hakluyt (iii. 138–43). Two days later Gilbert, with his two remaining ships, changed his course for England, intending a speedy return in the following spring. At the moment of tacking about there was seen a great sea monster, which Hayes describes as 'a lion in the ocean sea, or a fish in the shape of a lion.' Gilbert 'took it for bonum omen, rejoicing that he was to war against such an enemy, if it were the devil.' The imaginations of the eye-witnesses were most probably assisted by their vivid recollections of the monsters so graphically depicted upon the famous Olaus Magnus map of 1539. On 2 Sept., after sighting Cape Race, Gilbert paid his farewell visit on board the Golden Hind, where he was entreated by his friends and followers to stay for his own safety, and to abandon his own smaller vessel, the Squirrel. This was a craft of ten tons, whose decks were already overloaded with small

ordnance and nettings. With his characteristic waywardness he returned to the ill-fated Squirrel. On 9 Sept. in the afternoon, after emerging from a storm encountered to the south of the Azores, Gilbert was seen sitting abaft the Squirrel with a book in his hand; as often as he came within hearing distance of the Hind, he was heard to utter the well-known words, 'We are as near to heaven by sea as by land.' At midnight the watch on board the Golden Hind, observing the lights of the Squirrel to disappear suddenly, cried out 'the general was cast away,' which was too true; for in that moment the frigate was devoured and swallowed up of the sea' (HAKLUYT, iii. 159).

An unbiassed review of Gilbert's career serves to show that his fame deserves something better than the undiscriminating eulogies so lavishly bestowed upon his memory by his biographer in the 'Biographia Britannica.' Although usually described as a navigator, Gilbert was more of a soldier than a seaman; he seems to have been strangely wanting in the power of winning the unquestioning obedience of his followers. Of the genuineness of his patriotism, piety, and learning there can be no question. Another of his 'exercises' was written probably at Limehouse after his return from the Netherlands in 1572. From a literary point of view it adds more to Gilbert's fame as a gentleman and a scholar than anything he ever undertook either as a soldier or a colonist. It is entitled 'The Erection of (Queen Elizabethes) Achademy in London for Education of her Maiesties Wardes and others the youths of nobility and gentlemen.' It is a curious anticipation of recent efforts to obtain a charter for the establishment of a teaching and examining university in London. Three clauses relating to library economy may be a specimen: 'There shalbe one keeper of the Liberarie of the Achademy, whose charge shall be to see bookes there saffely kepte, to cawse them to be bound in good sorte, made fast orderly set, and shall keepe a Register of all bookes in the said Librarie, that he may give accompte of them when the Master of the Wardes or the Rector of the Achademy shall appointe; and shalbe yearely allowed 26 li. Note.—This keeper, after every marte, shall cawse the bringers of bookes into England to exhibit to him their Registers before they vtter any to any other person, that he may peruse the same, and take choyse of such as the Achademie shall wante, and shall make the Master of the Wardes or Rector of the Achademy, privy to his choyse, upon whose warrante the bookes so provided shalbe payed for. And there shalbe yearly allowed for the buying of bookes for the said

Liberary and other necessary instruments ... 40 li.' The next clause anticipates the provisions of the Copyright Act, and directs all printers 'to deliuer into the Liberary of the Achademy, at their own charges, one copy, well bounde, of euery proclamacion, or pamflette, that they shall printe' (Brit. Mus. *Lansdowne MS.* 98 I.) Dr. Furnivall printed Gilbert's scheme in a volume entitled 'Queen Elizabethes Achademy' (Early English Text Soc. 1869). A portrait of Gilbert will be found in Holland's 'Herωologia,' p. 64.

[Biog. Brit. vol. iv. 1750; Sir H. Ellis in Archæologia, xxi. 506; Fox Bourne's English Seamen under the Tudors; Furnivall's Queen Elizabethes Achademy (Early English Text Soc.), extra series, No. viii.; Sir H. Gilbert's Discourse, ed. G. Gascoigne, 1576; Hakluyt's Voyages, 1599; Holinshed's Chronicles, 1587, fol.; C. R. Markham's Fighting Veres, 1888; Morgan and Coote's Early Voyages to Russia, &c. (Hakluyt Soc.), 1886, 2 vols.; Sir G. P[eckham's] True Report, 1583; Stow's Annales, 1615; State Papers, Dom. Series (Lemon), 1577–83; Hist. MSS. Comm. 2nd Rep. App. pp. 40 *a*, 45 *b*, 97 *aa*; cf. Froude's Short Studies, ii. 136 sq.]   C. H. C.

GILBERT, JOHN (*fl.* 1680), son of John Gilbert of Salisbury, was born in 1659, entered Hart Hall, Oxford, as a commoner early in 1674, where he graduated B.A. on 16 Oct. 1677, and M.A. 25 June 1680 (WOOD, *Fasti*, Bliss, ii. 360, 372), afterwards took holy orders, and was vicar of St. John Baptist's Church, Peterborough. He published: 1. 'Answer to the Bishop of Condom (now of Meaux), his Exposition of the Catholic Faith, &c., wherein the Doctrine of the Church of Rome is detected, and that of the Church of England expressed,' &c. London, 1686, 4to; with which was printed 2. 'Reflections on his Pastoral Letter.' He has been confounded with an older John Gilbert who was appointed a prebendary of Exeter on 18 March 1674–5.

[Wood's Athenæ Oxon. (Bliss), iv. 794; Noble's Continuation of Granger's Biographical Hist. ii. 118.]   J. M. R.

GILBERT, JOHN (1693–1761), archbishop of York, was the son of John Gilbert, fellow of Wadham College, Oxford, vicar of St. Andrew's, Plymouth, and prebendary of Exeter, who died in 1722. He was educated at Trinity College, Oxford, where he graduated B.A. on 5 May 1713. He proceeded M.A. from Merton College 1 Feb. 1717–18. Owing to his connection with the cathedral of Exeter and his aristocratic connections, he began early to climb the ladder of preferment. On 1 Aug. 1721 he was appointed to the chapter living of Ashburton; on 4 Jan. 1722–3 he succeeded to the prebendal stall

vacated by his father's death; on 4 June 1724 he was appointed subdean of Exeter, which he vacated on his installation to the deanery, on 27 Dec. 1726; on 8 Jan. 1724 he was granted the degree of LL.D. at Lambeth (*Gent. Mag.* 1864, i. 637). In January 1726 he received from the crown a canonry at Christ Church, which he held *in commendam* with the bishopric of Llandaff, to which he was consecrated on 28 Dec. 1740. In 1749 he was translated to Salisbury. In 1750 he succeeded Bishop Butler as clerk of the closet, and in 1757 the archiepiscopate of York, to which the office of lord high almoner was added, crowned his long series of ecclesiastical preferments. He did little honour to the primacy. His health had already begun to break, and he rather languished than lived 'through a pontificate of four years, when he sank under a complication of infirmities' (RASTALL, *Hist. of Southwell*, p. 328). He died at Twickenham on 9 Aug. 1761, aged 68, and was buried in a vault in Grosvenor Chapel, South Audley Street. Gilbert seems to have possessed few qualifications to justify his high promotion in the church. He was neither a scholar nor a theologian. Nor were these deficiencies compensated by graces of character. A friendly witness, Bishop Newton, speaks of his being regarded as 'somewhat haughty' (NEWTON, *Autobiography*, p. 82); while Horace Walpole, whose pen when writing of the clergy is always dipped in gall, describes him as 'composed of that common mixture of ignorance, meanness, and arrogance' (WALPOLE, *Last Ten Years of George II*). John Newton, Cowper's friend, when seeking to obtain ordination from him, found him 'inflexible in supporting the rules and canons of the church' (*Letters*, ii. 57). His imperious character is illustrated by his refusal to allow the civic mace to be carried before the mayor of Salisbury in processions within the cathedral precincts, for which he claimed a separate jurisdiction, disobedience to which, it is said, caused an unseemly personal scuffle between him and the mace-bearer (CASSAN, *Bishops of Salisbury*, p. 274). We learn from Bishop Newton that he was the first prelate to introduce at confirmations the practice, now passing away, of the bishop laying his hands on each candidate at the altar rails, and then retiring and solemnly pronouncing the prayer once for the whole number. This mode was first observed at St. Mary's, Nottingham; it 'commanded attention, and raised devotion,' and before long became the regular manner of administering the rite (NEWTON, *Autobiography*, pp. 59, 60). Gilbert married Margaret Sherard, sister of Philip, second earl of Harborough, and daughter of Bennet Sherard, esq., of Whissendine, by Dorothy, daughter of Henry, lord Fairfax, who predeceased him. His only child Emma was married on 6 Aug. 1761 to George, third baron Mount-Edgcumbe, at her father's house at Twickenham, three days before his death. Gilbert's only publications were occasional sermons: (1) on the consecration of Bishop Stephen Weston of Exeter, on 2 Tim. i. 7, 1724; (2) before the House of Lords on 30 Jan., Eph. iv. 26, 1742; (3) for the education of the poor of the city of London, Gal. vi. 10, 1743; (4) for the Society for Promoting the Gospel, Rom. i. 16, 1744; (5) for the London Infirmary, Matt. vii. 12, 1745; (6) on the general fast, Lev. viii. 24, 17 Feb. 1758–9. There are portraits of Bishop Gilbert, in the robes of the chancellor of the order of the Garter, in the great dining-room of the palace of Salisbury, in the hall of Christ Church, Oxford, and at Mount-Edgcumbe.

[Abbey's English Church and her Bishops, ii. 47; Cassan's Lives of the Bishops of Salisbury, ii. 268 seq.; Bishop Newton's Autobiog.; Horace Walpole's Last Ten Years of George II; Gent. Mag. 1740 (index), 1773 p. 438.]   E. V.

GILBERT, JOHN GRAHAM- (1794–1866), painter. [See GRAHAM-GILBERT.]

GILBERT, JOSEPH (1779–1852), congregational divine, born in the parish of Wrangle, Lincolnshire, on 20 March 1779, was son of a farmer who had come under the influence of Wesley. After receiving some education at a free school on the confines of the parishes of Wrangle and Leake, he was apprenticed to a general shopkeeper at Burgh. On the expiration of his term he became assistant in a shop at East Retford, Nottinghamshire, of which he by-and-by became proprietor. Here he began to associate with a small body of congregationalists, for whom he sometimes preached. In 1806 he gave up business and entered Rotherham College. In 1808, at the request of Dr. Edward Williams [q. v.], its principal, he published his first book, a reply to a work by the Rev. William Bennet, entitled 'Remarks on a recent Hypothesis respecting the Origin of Moral Evil, in a Series of Letters to the Rev. Dr. Williams, the author of that Hypothesis.' His college course finished, he became minister at Southend, Essex. After a residence of eighteen months there he was appointed classical tutor in Rotherham College. On 8 Dec. 1818 he was ordained pastor of the Nether Chapel, Sheffield, still retaining the tutorship, spending the Sundays and Mondays in Sheffield and the rest of the week at Rotherham. In July 1817 he became minister of Fish Street Chapel, Hull, during his pasto-

rate of which he published, in 1825, a 'Life of Dr. Williams,' his old friend and preceptor. In November 1825 he removed to James Street Chapel, Nottingham. A new meeting-house was built for him in April 1828 in Friar Lane, Nottingham, and in this he ministered thenceforth. In 1835 he delivered in London the course of congregational lectures by which he is now best known, entitled 'The Christian Atonement, its Basis, Nature, and Bearings, or the Principle of Substitution illustrated as applied in the Redemption of Man' (London, 1836). His health giving way, he resigned his charge in November 1851, and he died on Sunday, 12 Dec. 1852.

He was twice married, in May 1800 to Miss Sarah Chapman, daughter of a surgeon at Burgh, and in December 1813 to Ann, eldest daughter of the Rev. Isaac Taylor of Ongar [see GILBERT, MRS. ANN].

In addition to the works already mentioned he published during his Rotherham tutorship a sermon on 'The Power of God in the Soul of Man.' After his death one of his sons issued 'Recollections of Discourses' which he preached in the years of 1848–50, with 'A Biographical Sketch' by his widow prefixed (small 8vo, London, 1853).

[Biographical sketch, as above.]   T. H.

GILBERT, JOSEPH FRANCIS (1792–1855), painter, born in 1792, took up art amidst great family difficulties. In 1813 he was residing at High Street, Portsmouth, and exhibited at the Royal Academy a 'Landscape and Figures.' In 1814 he sent 'The Rustic Traveller crossing the Style,' and occasionally exhibited in the following years. Subsequently he removed to Sussex, and resided for many years at Chichester. He continued to exhibit at the British Institution, Suffolk Street, Royal Manchester Institution, and other exhibitions, principally views in Sussex. Some of his works have been engraved, including 'A View of the Ruins of Cowdray' (by T. Clark), 'Priam winning the Gold Cup,' 'The Goodwood Race-course,' &c. In 1847 he was a competitor at Westminster Hall with an oil-painting of 'Edwin and Emma' from Mallet's poem. He died 25 Sept. 1855, in his sixty-fourth year.

[Redgrave's Dict. of Artists; Graves's Dict. of Artists, 1760–1880; catalogues of exhibitions.]   L. C.

GILBERT, MARIE DOLORES ELIZA ROSANNA (1818–1861), dancer and adventuress, known by her stage name of LOLA MONTEZ, was born at Limerick in 1818. Her father, Edward Gilbert, was gazetted an ensign in the 44th foot on 10 Oct. 1822, and proceeding to India joined his regiment and died of cholera at Dinapore in 1825. He had married a Miss Oliver, a lady who had Spanish blood in her veins, and she very soon after her husband's death married a Captain Craigie. In 1826 Marie Gilbert was sent from India to Scotland to be educated under the care of some of Captain Craigie's relatives at Montrose. Her further education took place in Paris, and on its completion she went to Bath, where her mother was then residing. To avoid a marriage with an old man, Sir Abraham Lumley, she ran away to Ireland with Captain Thomas James, and on 23 July 1837 married him at Meath under the name of 'Rosa Anna Gilbert, spinster.' Her husband held a commission in the 21st regiment of Bengal native foot, and on his returning to his duties she accompanied him to India. She returned to England early in 1842, and on 15 Dec. in that year her husband obtained in the consistory court, London, an order for a divorce, by reason of her having committed adultery with a Mr. Lennox while on the voyage home. The case is entitled James v. James (*Times*, 16 Dec. 1842, p. 6; *Morning Herald*, 16 Dec. 1842, p. 6). She then studied the dramatic art under Miss Fanny Kelly, but showing more promise as a dancer, she was instructed for four months by a Spanish teacher, and after a short visit to Spain made her début at Her Majesty's Theatre, London, under Benjamin Lumley's management, on 3 June 1843, as 'Lola Montez, Spanish dancer,' but being badly received did not again make her appearance (*You have heard of them*, by Q., 1854, pp. 98–106; *Era*, 11 June, 1843, p. 5). In the 'Era' of 18 June 1843, pp. 5–6, there is a letter from her denying that she was an Englishwoman, and stating that she was born in Seville, but it is to be observed, in contradiction of this assertion, that when she came on the stage the occupants of the omnibus-box immediately cried out, 'Why, there is Betty James.' An opening was made for her at the Royal Theatre, Dresden, where, and at Berlin, her success in the rôle of a Spanish dancer was considerable. From Berlin she proceeded to Warsaw, where she associated herself with the Polish party, and was in consequence ordered to quit the country; but she was notwithstanding well received at St. Petersburg by the emperor Nicholas, and became the recipient of many costly presents. She was afterwards in Paris, where she was very intimate with Dujarier, editor of 'La Presse,' who was killed in a duel with Beauvallon on 11 March 1845. This duel made a great sensation, and led to a celebrated trial at Rouen, when Alexandre Dumas, herself, and other celebrities appeared as witnesses (LAROUSSE, *Grand Dictionnaire*, vi.1365–6; *American Law Journal*, Philadelphia, July 1848, pp. 1–9). In 1847 she appeared as a dancer at Munich, and completely captivated the old king of Bavaria, Ludwig Carl Augustus. Five days after her appearance she was officially introduced at court, when the king said : ' Gentlemen, I present to you my best friend.' On 7 March 1847 she was naturalised by a royal ordinance, and then letters patent named her successively Baronne de Rosenthal and Comtesse de Lansfeld. The king also accorded her a pension of twenty thousand florins, and built for her a splendid mansion. Her abilities were considerable, she had a strong will and a grasp of circumstances, her disposition was generous, and her sympathies large. She exercised marvellous fascination over sovereigns and ministers. She now ruled the kingdom of Bavaria, and, singular to say, ruled it with wisdom and ability. Her audacity confounded alike the policy of the jesuits and of Metternich. Through her influence the ultramontane D'Abel ministry, which had held office for ten years, was dismissed, and another cabinet, under Prince Wallenstein, a man of liberal tendencies, was brought into power (*Times*, 2, 8, 9, 12, 18 March 1847). In the 'Times' of the last-mentioned date is a letter from her from 'Munich, 11 March,' giving her own version of the state of affairs in Bavaria, and in the same paper of 9 April is another letter stating that she was born in Spain, was called Lola Montez, and had never been known by any other name. The influences of Austria and of the jesuits were, however, at work against the favourite, and a free distribution of money aided in turning public opinion against her. She accorded her patronage to an association of students called the Alemannen, who held liberal principles. On 9 Feb. 1848 a fight took place between the Alemannen and the conservative students, and in an émeute which followed Lola's life was in danger. On 18 March, owing to the continued hostility of the students, she caused the university to be closed by a royal decree; but an insurrection took place, she was banished from the kingdom, and the king was forced to abdicate on 21 March. She at first had expectations of being recalled, and, dressed as a boy, ventured to return to the neighbourhood of Munich in hopes of meeting the king, but finding no security in the country she fled to Berne (*Mola Lontes oder Tanz und Weltgeschichte*, Leipzig, 1847; *Lola Montez und die Jesuiten*, von Dr. Paul Erdmann, Hamburg, 1847; *Anfang und Ende der Lola Montez in Bayern*, München, 1848, and another edition, München, 1848; *Illustrated London*

News, 20 March 1847, p. 180, with portrait, and 3 April, pp. 215–16; *Times*, 24 March 1848, p. 7; *Fraser's Mag.* January 1848, pp. 89–104, and March, pp. 366–8). Early in 1849 she came to England, where she was advertised to appear at Covent Garden Theatre, London, in a drama entitled 'Lola Montez ou La Comtesse pour une heure;' but, it being very doubtful whether the lord chamberlain would have licensed the piece, the advertisements were withdrawn. On 19 July 1849 she married, at St. George's, Hanover Square, George Trafford Heald. He was only just of age, a son of George Heald of the chancery bar, and had been gazetted a cornet in the 2nd life guards on 29 June 1848. On 6 Aug. 1849 she was summoned to the Marlborough Street police-court on a charge of bigamy. The case was not promoted by the husband, but by Miss Susanna Heald of Horncastle, Lincolnshire, who had been her nephew's guardian (*Times*, 7 Aug. 1849, pp. 6–7). To avoid possible punishment, as it appeared that the final order for her divorce in the consistory court had never been made, she fled with Heald to Spain, where she is said to have borne him two sons. He sold out of the army soon after his marriage, and is reported to have been accidentally drowned at Lisbon in 1853. She was afterwards in America, arriving at New York in the same vessel with Kossuth on 5 Dec. 1851, and making her appearance at the Broadway Theatre on 29 Dec. in the ballet of 'Betley the Tyrolean.' She remained there until 19 Jan. 1852. As a danseuse she disappointed public expectation, although for some time she attracted crowded houses. On 18 May she reappeared at the same theatre in Ware's drama entitled 'Lola Montez in Bavaria,' in which she represented herself as the danseuse, the politician, the countess, the revolutionist, and the fugitive, and played for five nights (IRELAND, *New York Stage*, ii. 593–5). On 19 Jan. 1852 she was at the Walnut Street Theatre, Philadelphia. In 1853 she went to California, where on 2 Aug. she married P. P. Hull, the proprietor of the 'San Francisco Whig,' but did not live long with him. At this period it was stated that her first and second husbands were dead, but this was not correct, as Captain James, who had retired from the Indian army on 28 Feb. 1856, did not die until 17 May 1871. After a visit to Europe she went to Australia, and on 23 Aug. 1855 played at the Victoria Theatre, Sydney. In the following year, while playing at Melbourne, she horsewhipped Mr. Seekamp, the editor of the 'Ballarat Times,' on account of an article he had inserted in his journal reflecting on her

character. Shortly after this she had a disagreement with Mr. Crosby, the lessee of a theatre where she was engaged, which led to a personal encounter between herself and Mrs. Crosby. In August 1856 she went to France, whence in 1857 she sailed for America, and made her appearance at the Green Street Theatre, New York, in 'The Eton Boy,' 'The Follies of a Night,' and 'Lola in Bavaria.' She next appeared as a public lecturer, speaking of beautiful women, gallantry, heroines of history, and similar subjects. These lectures were printed in America and England in 1858, and there is also a German edition of some of them entitled 'Blaues Blut. Handbuch der Noblesse. Von E. M. Vacano, Berlin,' 1864. She also published at New York in 1858 a work on 'The Art of Beauty,' of which there is a French edition called 'L'Art de la Beauté ou secrets de la toilette des Dames,' Paris, 1862, with a portrait of the author. The lectures, which were written for her by the Rev. C. Chauncey Burr, proved pecuniarily successful, but she soon wasted the greater part of the proceeds. Shattered in health and deserted by her associates, she met in New York in 1859 Mrs. Buchanan, wife of the well-known florist, a schoolfellow whom she had known long ago at Montrose. This meeting was the turning-point of her career; she devoted the remainder of her life to visiting the outcasts of her own sex at the Magdalen Asylum, near New York. While thus labouring she was stricken with paralysis, and after great suffering died, sincerely penitent, in a sanitary asylum at Asteria, New York, 17 Jan. 1861, and was buried in the Greenwood cemetery 19 Jan., where a tablet was erected to her memory.

[Autobiography and Lectures of Lola Montez, London, 1858, with portrait; Lectures of Lola Montez, including her Autobiography, London, 1858; Les Contemporains, 'Lola Montès, par Eugène de Mirecourt,' Paris, 1870, with portrait; H. H. Phelps's Players of a Century, 1880, pp. 265–7, 297; Larousse's Grand Dictionnaire, x. 645; Temple Bar, July 1880, pp. 362–7; F. L. Hawks's Story of a Penitent, Lola Montez, New York, 1867; Mortemar's Folly's Queens (1882), pp. 10–14, with portrait; New York Herald, 20 Jan. 1861, p. 4; Era, 10 Feb. 1861, p. 10.]

G. C. B.

GILBERT, NICOLAS ALAIN (1762–1821), catholic divine, born at St. Malo in Britanny in 1762, became parish priest of Saint-Pern. During the French revolution he was several times imprisoned, and narrowly escaped with his life. On coming to England he was stationed at Whitby, Yorkshire, where he established a mission. After the restoration of Louis XVIII in 1815 he returned to France, and became noted for his zeal in preaching missions in that country. He attacked with much force the doctrines of the revolution. He died in Touraine on 25 Sept. 1821. His works are : 1. 'A Vindication of the Doctrine of the Catholic Church on the Eucharist,' London, 1800, 12mo. 2. 'An Enquiry if the Marks of the True Church are applicable to the Presbyterian Churches,' Berwick, 1801, 12mo. 3. 'The Catholic Doctrine of Baptism proved by Scripture and Tradition,' Berwick, 1802, 12mo. 4. 'A Reply to the False Interpretations that John Wesley has put on Catholic Doctrines,' Whitby, 1811, 12mo. 5. 'The Method of Sanctifying the Sabbath Days at Whitby, Scarborough, &c. With a Paraphrase on some Psalms,' 2nd edition, prepared by the Rev. George Leo Haydock [q. v.], York, 1824, 12mo. 6. Many poems and hymns which have not appeared in a collected form.

[Biog. Universelle, Supplément, 1838, lxv. 332; Gillow's Haydock Papers, 223, 225, 228; Nouvelle Biog. Générale, xx. 503; Gillow's Bibl. Dict. ii. 465, and Additions, p. xv.] T. C.

GILBERT, RICHARD (1794–1852), printer and compiler, was born in St. John's Square, Clerkenwell, London, in 1794. His father, Robert Gilbert, who died 10 Jan. 1815, aged 51, was a printer, and a partner in the firm of Law & Gilbert of St. John's Square, the successors to a very old-established house. The son, Richard, commenced life as an accountant of the Society for Promoting Christian Knowledge in Bartlett's Buildings, but on the death of his father joined his brother Robert, who died in 1818, as a printer at St. John's Square. His business became much enlarged after his marriage, 11 Sept. 1823, with Anne, only daughter of the Rev. George Whittaker of Northfleet, and sister of George Byrom Whittaker, bookseller and publisher, and sheriff of London in 1823. On the death of his brother-in-law, 13 Dec. 1847, Gilbert and his family acquired a very considerable fortune, and his only son, Robert Gilbert, succeeded to his uncle's share in the business as a wholesale bookseller and publisher. In 1830 Richard Gilbert, who had since his brother's death carried on the printing business alone, took into partnership William Rivington, youngest son of Charles Rivington, bookseller, Waterloo Place, and under the style of Gilbert & Rivington continued the establishment until his death. He wrote and published in 1829 the 'Liber Scholasticus: an Account of Fellowships, Scholarships, and Exhibitions at Oxford and Cambridge, and of Colleges and Schools having

University advantages attached to them or in their patronage.' A second edition of this book appeared, which was entitled 'The Parent's School and College Guide,' 1843. He compiled and edited 'The Clerical Guide or Ecclesiastical Directory,' 1817 ; second edition, 1822 ; third edition, 1829 ; fourth and last edition, 1836. The compiler's name appears on the title-page of the third edition. This work gives a complete account of the prelates and beneficed clergy in England and Wales, and was the predecessor of the annual 'Clergy List,' which made its appearance in 1841. He also projected and edited 'The Clergyman's Almanack,' 1818, and 'Gilbert's Clergyman's Almanack and Churchman's Miscellany,' 1835, both published by the Company of Stationers. He was attached to the church of England, and was mainly instrumental in the erection of St. Philip's and St. Mark's churches in the neighbourhood of Clerkenwell. In 1841 he was elected one of the stockkeepers of the Company of Stationers. He was for many years one of the general committee, and finally one of the auditors, of the Royal Literary Fund for the Relief of Authors, and was an active governor of Christ's and St. Bartholomew's Hospitals. He died at 70 Euston Square, London, 26 Feb. 1852, aged 58, and was buried in the vaults of St. John's Church, Clerkenwell, on 4 March.

[Gent. Mag. May 1852, pp. 525–6; Pink's Clerkenwell (1881), pp. 330, 691, 693.] G. C. B.

GILBERT, SAMUEL (d. 1692?), floriculturist, was chaplain to Jane, wife of Charles, fourth baron Gerard of Gerard's Bromley, and rector of Quatt, Shropshire. In 1676 he published a pamphlet entitled 'Fons Sanitatis, or the Healing Spring at Willowbridge in Staffordshire, found out by . . . Lady Jane Gerard,' London, 12mo, pp. 40, some of the cures recorded in which work are attested by himself. It has therefore been suggested that he also practised as a physician (Journal of Horticulture, 1876, p. 172). He married Minerva, daughter of John Rea [q. v.], of whom he speaks as the greatest of florists ; and, as his own writings contain many verses, it has been suggested that he also composed those in Rea's 'Flora, Ceres, and Pomona,' 1676. Gilbert seems to have lived with his father-in-law at Kinlet, near Bewdley, and after the death of the latter, in 1681, published the 'Florist's Vademecum and Gardener's Almanack,' 1683, subsequent editions of which appeared in 1690, 1693, 1702, and 1713. This little work is arranged according to the months, and to the second edition are added various appendices and a portrait of the author, engraved by R.

White, which was reproduced in the 'Journal of Horticulture' (loc. cit.) Gilbert had one son, Arden, and four or five daughters. The date of his death is uncertain.

[Works mentioned above.]   G. S. B.

GILBERT, THOMAS (1610–1673), ejected minister, is described by Calamy as 'a Scottish divine.' He is probably the Thomas Gilbert who graduated M.A. at Edinburgh on 25 July 1629, and became 'minister verbi.' His name does not occur in Scott's 'Fasti.' According to his epitaph his first preferment was to the rectory of Cheadle, Cheshire. In 1654 he was presented by Francis Allein to the vicarage of Ealing, Middlesex. He appears to have been a zealous puritan. His epitaph describes him as 'the proto-martyr, the first of the ministers that suffered deprivation in the cause of non-conformity.' Hence it may be inferred that he lost his living at the Restoration, owing to some informality in the appointment. His name is not in Newcourt's list of vicars of Ealing. He emigrated to New England, and became pastor at Topsfield, Massachusetts. He died in 1673, aged 63 years, and was buried on 28 Oct. at Charlestown, Massachusetts.

[Mather's Magnalia Christi Americana, 1702, iii. 221; Calamy's Account, 1713, p. 467; Continuation, 1727, ii. 611; Palmer's Nonconf. Memorial, 1802, ii. 446; Cat. Edinb. Graduates, 1858, p. 43.]   A. G.

GILBERT, THOMAS (1613–1694), ejected minister, son of William Gilbert of Prees, Shropshire, was born in 1613. In 1629 he became a student in Edmund Hall, Oxford, his tutor being Ralph Morhall. After graduating B.A. on 28 May 1633, he obtained some employment in Ireland, but returned to Oxford and graduated M.A. on 7 Nov. 1638. Through the favour of Philip, fourth baron Wharton, he obtained the vicarage of Upper Winchendon, Buckinghamshire, and (about 1644) the vicarage of St. Lawrence, Reading, Berkshire, when he took the covenant. He sided with the independents, according to Tanner (a statement which seems questionable), and was created B.D. on 19 May 1648 at the parliamentary visitation of Oxford. About the same time he exchanged his cure at Reading for the rectory of Edgmond, Shropshire. Tanner says he was appointed in the room of an ejected royalist, but of this there is no record in Walker. He gained great influence, and was nicknamed the 'bishop of Shropshire.' In 1654 he was made assistant to the commissioners for ejecting insufficient ministers in Shropshire, Middlesex, and Westminster Peck prints a letter (28 Aug. 1658) from Gil-

bert to Henry Scobell. At the Restoration he lost the rectory of Edgmond, and he was ejected from Winchendon by the Uniformity Act of 1662. Hereupon he retired to Oxford, where he and his wife lived quietly in St. Ebbe's parish. He is said by Calamy to have been the means of keeping South from becoming an Arminian. He still preached frequently in the family of Lord Wharton and in other private houses. On the issue of Charles II's indulgence (15 March 1672) Gilbert joined with three ejected presbyterians in gathering a congregation at a house 'in Thames Street, without the north gate.' This did not last long, as the indulgence was quashed in the following year.

Gilbert did not again take charge of a congregation. He was badly off in his later years, 'his children having drained him,' and was assisted by private friends, including several heads of colleges. He was deeply versed in school divinity, and a better Latin than English poet. Wood calls him 'the common epitaph-maker for dissenters;' Calamy says he wrote but three, for Thomas Goodwin, D.D. [q. v.], John Owen, D.D., and Ichabod Chauncey [q. v.] When Calamy was at Oxford (1691–2), he found Gilbert regularly attending the ministry of John Hall (1633–1710) [q. v.], bishop of Bristol and master of Pembroke, for one of the Sunday services, and for the other that of Joshua Oldfield at the presbyterian meeting, an example followed by other Oxford dissenters. He was on intimate terms with Hall, Bathurst, master of Trinity, Aldrich, Wallis, and Jane. Calamy describes him as 'very purblind,' as 'the completest schoolman' he ever knew, in his element among 'crabbed writers,' yet sometimes 'very facetious and pleasant in conversation.' Calamy has preserved some of his stories, told after a supper of 'buttered onions.' Gilbert died at Oxford on 15 July 1694, and was buried in the chancel of St. Aldate's.

He published: 1. 'Vindiciæ supremi Dei Dominii . . . oppositæ nuper Doct. Audoeni Diatribæ de Justitia,' &c., 1655, 8vo (disputes the necessity of satisfaction, against Owen). 2. 'An Assize Sermon at Bridgnorth,' &c. (James ii. 12), 1657, 4to. 3. 'Julius Secundus,' &c., Oxford, 1669, 12mo (preface, assigning this dialogue to Erasmus); 2nd edit., Oxford, 1680, 8vo (with addition of 'Jani Alex. Ferrarii Euclides Catholicus'). 4. 'England's Passing-Bell, a Poem,' &c., 1675, 4to (commemorates the plague, the great fire, and the Dutch war). 5. 'Super auspicatissimo regis Gulielmi in Hiberniam descensu . . . carmen,' &c., 1690, 4to. Probably posthumous was 6. 'A Learned and

Accurate Discourse concerning the Guilt of Sin,' &c., 1695, 8vo, though Calamy speaks as if it had been first printed in Gilbert's lifetime. It was written before 1678 and reprinted, 1708, 8vo, from Gilbert's manuscript; again reprinted, Edinburgh, 1720, 8vo. It teaches that pardon covers future as well as existing sin. He had a hand in the 'Annus Mirabilis' for 1661 and following years, and wrote the largest part of a Latin version (Amsterdam, 1677, 8vo) of Francis Potter's 'Interpretation of the Number 666,' Oxford, 1642, 4to.

By a misprint Chalmers calls him 'William' Gilbert, a blunder which has misled other writers. Thus Watt assigns to him 'Architectonice Consolationis,' &c., 1640, 4to, a funeral sermon on 1 Thess. iv. 18, for Jane Gilbert, by William Gilbert, D.D., rector of Orsett, Essex. There was also a William Gilbert, ejected from a lectureship at Witney, Oxfordshire, in 1662.

[Wood's Athenæ Oxon. 1691 i. 874, 893, 1692 ii. 511, 747, 783; additions in the editions of Tanner, 1721, ii. 916, and Bliss, 1820, iv. 406 sq.; Calamy's Account, 1713, pp. 109, 542, 573; Calamy's Continuation, 1727, i. 146, ii. 718; Calamy's Own Life, 1830, i. 268 sq.; Peck's Desiderata Curiosa, 1779, ii. 509; Palmer's Nonconf. Memorial, 1802 i. 309, 1803 iii. 145; Chalmers's Gen. Biog. Dict. 1814, xv. 495.] A. G.

GILBERT, THOMAS (1720–1798), poor-law reformer, born in 1720, son and heir of Thomas Gilbert of Cotton in Staffordshire, was admitted at the Inner Temple in 1740, and called in 1744. In 1745 he accepted a commission in the regiment formed by Lord Gower, brother-in-law of the Duke of Bridgewater. He was for many years land-agent to Gower, and his brother, John Gilbert, acted for the duke in the same capacity. Through their interest he sat in parliament for Newcastle-under-Lyme from November 1763 to the dissolution in 1768, and for Lichfield from that year till 1795, when he retired to make room for Lord Granville Leveson Gower. In 1765 the sinecure place of comptroller of the great wardrobe was given to him, and he retained it until its abolition through Burke's bill reforming the civil list. He also held from the date of its foundation until his death the office of paymaster of the fund for securing pensions to the widows of officers in the navy. But his most important office was the chairmanship of committees of ways and means, to which he was appointed shortly after Pitt's accession to power on 31 May 1784. Gilbert was zealous in amending the poor-laws. He succeeded in 1765 in passing through the commons a bill for grouping parishes for poor-law purposes in large districts, such as

hundreds, but it was rejected in the upper house by 66 votes to 59. In 1776 a committee of the House of Commons reported on the condition of the workhouses and alms-houses, and Gilbert, after having worked at the subject energetically for many years, introduced into the commons three bills in 1782. The first two, on the amendment of the laws relating to houses of correction, and for enabling two or more parishes to unite together, passed into law; but the third, for reforming the enactments relating to vagrants, miscarried. Gilbert proposed in 1778 that during the war with the American colonies a tax of twenty-five per cent. should be levied upon all government places and pensions. James Harris, the author of 'Hermes,' ridiculed the tax, and called its author 'a kind of demi-courtier, demi-patriot.' George III told Lord North that it was utterly impracticable. Nevertheless it was carried in committee against Lord North, and in spite of the opposition of Burke and Fox, by a majority of eighteen votes, but on the report it was rejected by a majority of six. Horace Walpole mentions the current belief that this proposal was aimed at Rigby, who had refused to give a vacant place at Chelsea Hospital to the brother of its author's second wife. Gilbert endeavoured, unsuccessfully, to carry a general act for the improvement of highways, and succeeded in passing many local acts for roads in the midland counties. Through his advice the Duke of Bridgewater engaged the services of James Brindley [q. v.], and Gilbert joined with Brindley in purchasing an estate near Golden Hill in Staffordshire. He supported many of the canals then projected for the central districts of England, and he was one of the promoters of the Grand Trunk. In 1787 he introduced another poor-law bill, grouping many parishes together, taxing dogs, and imposing an additional charge for the use of turnpikes on Sundays. He also advocated the abolition of ale-houses in the country districts, except for the use of travellers, and the stricter supervision of such establishments in towns. His views for doing away with imprisonment for small debts were not adopted until many years later, but his propositions for encouraging the formation of friendly societies by grants from the parochial funds were largely provided for in an act passed in 1793. To promote the residence of the clergy he procured the passage of the act still known as 'Gilbert's Act,' enabling the governors of Queen Anne's Bounty to lend capital sums for the erection of such houses on easy terms. His first wife was a Miss Phillips, to whom he had presented a lottery ticket which drew one of the largest prizes of the year; she bore him two sons, one of whom became a clerk-extraordinary to the privy council, and the other served in the navy. He married, secondly, Mary, daughter of Lieut.-Colonel George Craufurd, and with her he retired into Staffordshire, devoting his time and his money to the improvement of his estate. Gilbert died at Cotton on 18 Dec. 1798, and his friend John Holliday printed anonymously a monody on his death, praising his generosity for building and endowing in 1795 the chapel of ease of St. John the Baptist at Lower Cotton. He was bencher of the Inner Temple in 1782, reader 1788, and treasurer 1789.

Gilbert's publications on his schemes of reform were very numerous. He published in 1775 'Observations upon the Orders and Resolutions of the House of Commons with respect to the Poor;' and 'A Bill intended to be offered to Parliament for the better Relief and Employment of the Poor in England.' These were followed in 1781 by a 'Plan for the better Relief and Employment of the Poor,' together with bills for those objects; followed by a 'Supplement.' At the same time he brought out as a separate tract 'A Plan of Police,' which passed into a second edition, 'with objections stated and answered,' in 1786. In 1782 he brought out a volume of 'Observations on the Bills for amending the Laws relative to Houses of Correction,' &c. The Poor-law Bill of 1787 was preceded by three tracts: (1) 'Plan to amend and enforce the Act 23 George III;' (2) 'Heads of a Bill for the better Relief and Employment of the Poor and for the Improvement of the Police;' (3) 'Considerations on the Bills for the better Relief of the Poor,' &c. His opinions found many supporters and opponents. He was supported by John Brand (d. 1808) [q. v.] in 1776, and was attacked in 'Observations on the Scheme before Parliament for the Maintenance of the Poor,' 1776 (anonymous, by Edward Jones of Wepré Hall, and printed at Chester). A candid friend published in 1777 some critical 'Remarks on Mr. Gilbert's Bill for Promoting the Residence of the Parochial Clergy;' and Sir Henry Bate Dudley criticised his Poor-law Bill in 1788 in 'Remarks on Gilbert's Last Bill.' Gilbert edited in 1787 'A Collection of Pamphlets concerning the Poor,' written by Thomas Firmin [q. v.] in 1678, and others. His report on the king's household in 1782, and some letters from him on its management, are among the manuscripts of the Marquis of Lansdowne (*Hist. MSS. Comm.* 3rd Rep. p. 145). Other letters are referred to in the 7th Rep. p. 238. Stebbing Shaw, in the preface to his 'History of Staf-

fordshire,' records his obligations to Gilbert and praises his plantation at Cotton.

[Eden's State of the Poor, i. 362–6, 389–95, 600–1; Nichols's Lit. Anecd. ix. 203–4; Smiles's Engineers, i. 347–51; Gent. Mag. 1784 pt. i. p. 460, 1798 pt. ii. pp. 1090, 1146; Horace Walpole's Reign of George III, ii. 89; Walpole's Last Journals, ii. 221, 595; Correspondence (Cunningham's ed.), iv. 340, viii. 396; Corresp. of George III and North, ii. 146; Letters of first Earl of Malmesbury, i. 380–1; G. Robertson's Ayrshire Families, p. 177; John Holliday's British Oak, p. 56.] W. P. C.

GILBERT, Sir WALTER RALEIGH (1785–1853), lieutenant-general, son of the Rev. Edmund Gilbert, vicar of Constantine and rector of Helland, Cornwall, by his wife, the daughter of Henry Garnett of Bristol, was born in Bodmin in 1785. He belonged to the Devonshire family of Gilbert of Compton to which Sir Humphrey Gilbert [q. v.] also belonged. Sir Humphrey's mother was by a second marriage mother of Sir Walter Raleigh. In 1800 Gilbert obtained a Bengal infantry cadetship. In 1801 he was posted as ensign to the late 15th Bengal native infantry, in which he became lieutenant 12 Sept. 1803, and captain 16 April 1810. In that corps, under command of Colonel (afterwards Sir) John Macdonald, he was present at the defeat of Perron's brigades at Coel, at Ally Ghur, the battle of Delhi, the storming of Agra, the battle of Laswarrie, and the four desperate but unsuccessful attacks on Bhurtpore, where he attracted the favourable notice of Lord Lake. Afterwards he was in succession barrack-master and cantonment magistrate at Cawnpore, commandant of the Calcutta native militia, and commandant of the Rhamgur local battalion. He was promoted major 12 Nov. 1820, lieutenant-colonel of the late 39th Bengal native infantry, then just formed in 1824, and colonel of the late 35th native infantry in 1832. He became a major-general in 1841, and lieutenant-general in 1851. He commanded a division of the army under Sir Hugh Gough [q. v.] in the first Sikh war, at the battles of Moodkee and Ferozeshah in December 1845, and at Sobraon 10 Feb. 1846. Gough in his despatch spoke highly of Gilbert's services. Gilbert commanded a division of Gough's army in the second Sikh war, at the battles of Chillianwallah, 13 Jan. 1849, and Goojerat, 21 Feb. 1849. After Goojerat, Gilbert with his division crossed the Jhelum in pursuit of the remains of the Sikh host, part of which surrendered to him at Hoormuck on 3 March, while the rest, sixteen thousand fine troops with forty-one guns, laid down their arms to him at Rawal Pindi three days later. He pursued their

Afghan allies to the entrance of the Khyber Pass. Gilbert, who had been made K.C.B. in 1846, was appointed G.C.B. and a provisional member of the council of India in 1850, and created a baronet in 1851. He was colonel of the 1st Bengal European fusiliers.

Gilbert was well known as a sportsman in India, and a supporter of the turf. He married in 1814 a daughter of Major Ross, royal artillery, by whom he had issue. He died in London 12 May 1853, aged 68. A memorial obelisk was erected on the Beacon at Bodmin. On the death of his son, Sir Francis Hastings Gilbert, second baronet, British consul, Scutari, Albania, at Cheltenham 17 Nov. 1863, the baronetcy became extinct.

[Prince's Worthies of Devon and Tuckett's Devonshire Genealogies for notices of the family; Sir John Maclean's History of Trigg Minor, i. 112, 310–3; East India Registers and Army Lists; Innes's Bengal European Regiment; Shadwell's Clyde, 1881; Thackwell's Second Sikh War; Gent. Mag. new ser. xxxix. 652, 3rd ser. xv. 810.] H. M. C.

GILBERT, WILLIAM, M.D. (1540–1603), physician (who sometimes spelt his name Gilberd), was son of Hierom Gylberd, a Suffolk gentleman, who was recorder of Colchester, and great-grandson of Thomas Gilberd, who was made a burgess of Colchester in 1428. He was born at Colchester in 1540, and when twenty years of age graduated B.A. at St. John's College, Cambridge, and was elected a fellow on 21 March 1561. He graduated M.A. in 1564, and M.D. in 1569, becoming a senior fellow of his college on 21 Dec. 1569. In 1573 he settled in practice in London, and soon after became a fellow of the College of Physicians. He lived on St. Peter's Hill in London, was appointed physician to Queen Elizabeth, and attained considerable practice. He became censor of the College of Physicians in 1581, and was appointed to that office in seven subsequent years. He was treasurer of the college for nine years, and in 1600 was elected president. In that year he published in London 'De Magnete, Magneticisque corporibus, et de Magno Magnete Tellure, Physiologia Nova.' It was the first great physical book published in England, and has fulfilled for its author Dryden's prophecy: 'Gilbert shall live till loadstones cease to draw.' His merit was immediately recognised both in England and on the continent, where he won eulogy from Galileo. Bacon mentions Gilbert with respect in the 'Novum Organum' (ed. Leyden, 1650, pp. 263–5 and elsewhere). The author had worked at his subject for many years, revising and experimenting. He begins by a summary of existing knowledge about the magnet, exactly resembling the commencement of a modern scientific essay. The next part is characteristic of his own time, and is an account of the names of the loadstone and their etymology. The remainder is an investigation of the properties of the magnet, illustrated by diagrams and relating numerous experiments. The attraction of the magnet, its direction in relation to the poles of the earth, its variation and declination are treated in separate divisions. He does not neglect to point out the practical bearing of these points in navigation, and how the declination may be used in discovering the latitude at sea. His general conclusion is that the phenomena of magnetism are explained by regarding the earth as one vast spherical magnet. Edited by Wolfgang Lochmans, Gilbert's treatise on the magnet reappeared in Latin at Sedan in 1628 and 1633. English translations were published in 1893 and 1900. Some of his other scientific papers on meteorology which belonged to Sir William Boswell [q. v.] were printed at Amsterdam in 1651, after his death, edited by his brother, 'De Mundo Nostri sublunari Philosophia Nova.' He was appointed physician to James I on his accession, but died on 30 Nov. 1603. Two novel instruments for navigation, of Gilbert's invention, are described in Thomas Blundevile's 'Theoriques of the Seuen Planets' (1602). He was unmarried, and bequeathed all his books, globes, instruments, and a cabinet of minerals to the College of Physicians. They perished in the great fire of London in 1666. He was buried at Colchester, in the Holy Trinity Church, where his monument and epitaph, erected by his brothers Ambrose and William (of the same name as himself), still remains. It is a panel surrounded by a frame of Jacobean pattern, surmounted by pinnacles bearing globes and fourteen shields of armorial achievements. His portrait, by Harding, once in the schools at Oxford, was engraved by Clamp. A Gilbert Club was founded in 1889, with Lord Kelvin as president, to celebrate the tercentenary of Gilbert's work and to publish translations of the 'De Magnete' and like works.

[Gilbert of Colchester: An Elizabethan Magnetizer, by Dr. Silvanus P. Thompson, 1891; Munk's Coll. of Phys. i. 77; Works; Morant's History of Colchester, 1748.] N. M.

GILBURNE or GILBORNE, SAMUEL (fl. 1605), actor, mentioned in the 1623 folio of Shakespeare, was apprentice to Augustine Phillips, a member of the same company. Phillips left by will (4 May 1605) 'to Samuell Gilborne, my late apprentice,' 40s., much wearing apparel, 'my purple cloke, sword, and dagger, and my base viall' (see

Chalmers's 'Further Account of the Early English Stage,' p. 483, and Payne Collier's 'English Dramatic Poetry,' iii. 410). No other reference to Gilburne has been traced. Malone's 'Historical Account of the English Stage,' Basle, 1800, simply writes opposite the name, 'unknown,' p. 268.

[Works cited.]   J. K.

GILBY, ANTHONY (d. 1585), puritan divine, was born in Lincolnshire (FULLER, Worthies, ii. 67), and educated at Christ's College, Cambridge, where he graduated B.A. 1531-2, M.A. 1535 (COOPER, Athenæ Cantabr. i. 516). He entered the ministry, and early joined the ranks of the reformers, afterwards becoming one of their most acrimonious and illiberal writers, and a 'dear disciple' of Calvin. Fuller calls him 'a fast and furious stickler against church discipline' (Church Hist. bk. ix. p. 76). He was a learned man, a good classical scholar, and a student of Hebrew. Besides translating commentaries of Calvin and Theodore Beza, he wrote two original commentaries on Micah (London, 1551, containing a prayer for the king, 1547) and Malachi (no date, London). His first controversial work was a reply to Gardiner's work on the sacrament of the altar, entitled 'An Answer to the Devilish Detection of Stephen Gardiner, Bishop of Winchester . . . Compiled by A. G. anno 1547, the 24th of January,' London, 1547-8, 8vo. That he had held a living in Leicestershire is shown by his 'Epistle of a Banished Man out of Leicestershire, sometime one of the Preachers of God's Word there,' prefixed to Knox's 'Faithful Admonition,' which was published abroad in 1554. On Mary's accession Gilby fled from England with his wife and children, and was one of the first of the exiles who took refuge at Frankfort (1554).

At Frankfort Gilby entertained Foxe the martyrologist. He took a prominent part in the quarrel with Dr. Cox over the communion service, and retired with Whittingham, Knox, and other leading reformers to Geneva in 1555. In September Christopher Goodman [q. v.] and Knox were made pastors of the new congregation, and, Knox being absent in France, Gilby was chosen to fill his place (Troubles at Frankfort, Phenix, ii. 44). He took part in the Geneva translation of the Bible, which appeared in quarto in 1560, and also helped to compile the 'Form of Common Order,' used by the English congregation at Geneva. While in exile Gilby published two original works of bitter invective, and Bancroft reproaches him, with the rest of the Geneva divines, for justifying civil rebellion (Dangerous Positions, p. 50). After Mary's death

he was one of the eighteen reformers who signed (15 Dec. 1558) the circular letter from Geneva to all the other exiled churches praying them to be reconciled to one another (Troubles at Frankfort; STRYPE, Annals, I. i. 152). He soon returned to England, where he acquired many influential friends. His chief patron, Henry, earl of Huntingdon, presented him some time before 1564 to the living of Ashby-de-la-Zouch in Leicestershire. He continued to 'roar' against the English church (FOULIS, Wicked Plots, p. 59), and published (1570, STRYPE, Annals, II. i. 8; or 1566 (?), AMES (Herbert), p. 1616) 'a very hot and bitter letter to divers ministers against the habits,' exciting them against the bishops. This address was entitled 'To my loving Brethren that is troubled about the Popish Apparel, two short and comfortable Epistles.' In 1571 Archbishop Parker commanded Grindal, archbishop of York, to prosecute Gilby for nonconformity. Grindal refused, on the ostensible ground that Ashby was not in his diocese, but more probably from fear of the Earl of Huntingdon. Nicholls, who abused Gilby, insinuates that he was once summoned to Lambeth and silenced, but there is no evidence for this statement (Defence of the Church of England, ed. 1740, p. 21). Gilby replied to the charges of his superiors in a tract, written during the lifetime of Parker (who died in 1575), and published in 1578: 'A View of Anti-Christ, his Laws and Ceremonies in our English Church, unreformed,' &c., London, 1578. In 1572 Gilby is said to have met Wilcox, Simpson, and others privately in London, and agreed to help in the compilation of 'An Admonition to Parliament.' The conference resulted in two very bitter pamphlets, bound up with a letter from Beza to Leicester, which appeared after the prorogation of parliament, by 'poor men whom the ecclesiastical authorities have made poor.' 'Father Gilby' was respected for his godly life and learning at Ashby, where he lived 'as great as a bishop' until his death in 1585, having in December 1582 resigned his living to his son-in-law, Thomas Widdowes (NICHOLS, Leicestershire, iii. 619). He corresponded with some of the most celebrated divines of the day, and was on terms of great intimacy with Thomas Bentham [q. v.], bishop of Lichfield and Coventry. He had two sons and two daughters. GODDRED GILBY, the elder son, who was with his father at Geneva, translated Cicero's 'Epistle to Quintus,' London, 1561, 12mo, and Calvin's 'Admonition against Judicial Astrology,' n.d. The younger, Nathaniel, of Christ's College and fellow of Emmanuel, Cambridge, was tutor to Joseph Hall [q. v.], bishop of Norwich, whose mother was one of Gilby's congregation (HALL, *Works*, ed. Pratt, i. 2).

Besides the works already enumerated, Gilby published: 1. 'A brief Treatise of Election and Reprobation,' London, 1547 (?); reissued, along with a treatise on the same subject by Foxe, as an appendix to Beza's 'Treasure of Trueth,' translated by Stockwood (London, 1576). 2. 'An Admonition to England and Scotland to call them to repentance,' printed with Knox's 'Appellation,' Geneva, 1558. 3. 'A Pleasant Dialogue between a Soldier of Berwick and an English Chaplain . . .,' London, 8vo, 1581. 4. 'The Testamentes of the Twelve Patriarches,' from the Latin of Robert Grosseteste, London, 1581, often wrongly attributed to Arthur Golding. A letter to protestant writers, dated 10 March 1566, is prefixed, and reappears in 'Part of a Register' (1593), which reprints Gilby's 'View of Anti-Christ.' Gilby also translated Calvin's 'Commentaries upon the Book of Daniel' (1570: the address signed by the translator, A. G., has been erroneously attributed to Arthur Golding [q. v.]); Beza's 'Paraphrase of the Psalms,' 1580, and Beza's 'Paraphrase of fourteen Holy Psalms,' 1590.

[Authorities cited above; Strype's Life of Grindal, p. 252; Strype's Annals, i. i. 343; Life of Whitgift, i. 55; Brit. Mus. Cat. of Books before 1640.] E. T. B.

GILBY, WILLIAM HALL (*d.* 1821 ?), geologist, was the son of William Gilby, M.D., an English physician, and studied under Professor Jameson at Edinburgh, where he graduated M.D. in 1815, his thesis being 'Disceptatio . . . de mutationibus quas ea, quæ e terra gignuntur, aëri inferent,' Edinb. 1815, 8vo, pp. 26, at which time he was annual president of the Royal Society of Medicine in that city. He wrote several papers, chiefly on geological subjects, his last being on the respiration of plants in the 'Edinburgh Philosophical Journal' for 1821. The date of his death has not been ascertained, but, as he was a frequent essayist until that year, he probably died either then or very shortly after. He was a member of the Geological Society before its incorporation.

[Disceptatio, title-page, &c.] B. D. J.

GILCHRIST, ALEXANDER (1828–1861), biographer, son of James Gilchrist (author of 'The Intellectual Patrimony,' 1817), was born at Newington Green, London, 25 April 1828. In 1829 his father moved to an old water-mill on the Thames at Mapledurham, near Reading. Alexander was an affectionate and sympathetic child, and 'almost as soon as he could walk' his father's

constant companion. At the age of twelve he was sent to University College School, and at sixteen left it to study law. He entered the Middle Temple in 1846, and was called to the bar in 1849. Legal studies, however, proved uncongenial, and he preferred the 'most modest literary achievement' to 'brilliant legal success.' Though he met with some disappointments from editors, his talents were recognised in 1848 by Dr. Price, editor of the 'Eclectic Review.' All his writings for three or four years appeared in the 'Eclectic,' and one upon Etty, published in 1849 and reissued separately, brought him a commission from David Bogue to write Etty's life. On 4 Feb. 1851 he married Anne Burrows [see GILCHRIST, ANNE] at Earl's Colne, Essex. He wrote an article on decorative art as illustrated by the Great Exhibition, and then collected materials for the 'Life of Etty,' which appeared in 1855. He afterwards wrote lives of artists for an edition of 'Men of the Time.'

In 1853 he settled at Guildford. In a visit to London a sight of some of Blake's illustrations of the Book of Job decided him to undertake a life of the artist. He had previously only known the illustrations to Blair's 'Grave' and Allan Cunningham's life of the artist. He now resolved to write a full life of Blake. In 1856 he settled in Chelsea, at the express wish of Carlyle, who was his next-door neighbour, and with whom he and his wife had some pleasant intercourse. He was for two years afterwards chiefly occupied in winding up the business affairs of a brother who had died suddenly. He then devoted himself to Blake, contributing also to the 'Literary Gazette' and the 'Critic.' In the spring of 1861 he made the acquaintance of D. G. Rossetti. He had not finished Blake when he died of scarlet fever on 30 Nov. 1861. He had made preparations for lives of Wordsworth, the Countess d'Aulnoy, Lord Herbert of Cherbury, and Sir Kenelm Digby. His loss called forth strong expressions of sympathy from Mr. Madox Brown and D. G. Rossetti—the latter calling him 'a far-sighted and nobly honest writer on subjects of which few indeed are able to treat worthily.'

The 'Life of Blake' was completed by his widow, and published in 1863. She also edited a second edition in 1880, and prefixed to it a 'Memoir of Alexander Gilchrist.'

[Memoir as above.] H. H. G.

GILCHRIST, ANNE (1828–1885), miscellaneous writer, daughter of John Parker Burrows, solicitor, by his wife Henrietta (Carwardine), was born at 7 Gower Street, London, 25 Feb. 1828. Her father died in 1839.

At the age of five she was sent to a school in Highgate kept by the Misses Cahusac. When ten years old she fell into an uncovered well, and was saved by her brother, John T. Burrows (d. 1849), who held her by the hair until help came. She describes her sensations in 'Lost in the Wood' in 'Magnet Stories' (1861). Her thoughts were early turned to religious questions, her tendency to liberal opinions being combined with a tenderness for the prejudices of others. A thoughtful letter, written in 1849, upon this subject is given in her 'Life' (p. 25). On 4 Feb. 1851 she married Alexander Gilchrist [q. v.], living with him at Guildford and Chelsea. The marriage was a very happy one, and she shared her husband's tastes, criticised his writings, and wrote to his dictation. Her first article, 'Our Poor Relation,' appeared in 'Household Words' in 1857, and was favourably noticed by Dickens.

In 1861 she nursed her family (two boys, two girls, and her husband) through an attack of scarlet fever, of which her husband died. In 1862 she settled at Shottermill, near Haslemere, Surrey, and completed her husband's 'Life of Blake.' Her study of Blake won for her the friendship of the Rossetti family, and she had a lifelong correspondence with Mr. W. M. Rossetti. The reading of Rossetti's 'Selections of Walt Whitman' led her to a study of Whitman's poetry. The result appeared in 'A Woman's Estimate of Walt Whitman,' published in the American 'Radical' in 1869. Another essay upon the same subject, called 'A Confession of Faith,' was written in 1883. A letter to D. G. Rossetti upon his poems, especially his 'Jenny,' written in 1870 (Life, p. 197), gives an interesting statement of her views upon poetry.

In August 1876 she went to the United States, returning in June 1879. In Philadelphia she translated Victor Hugo's 'Légende des Siècles,' and while at Northampton, Mass., wrote 'Three Glimpses of a New England Village,' published in 'Blackwood's Magazine' in 1884. After returning to England she edited a second edition of the 'Life of Blake,' and in 1882 began her 'Life of Mary Lamb' (published in 1883), clearing up some errors and bringing out with true sympathy the lovable characters of Lamb and his sister. She contributed notices of Mary M. Betham and William Blake to this dictionary in 1884. She lived after her return from America at Hampstead, and was at work upon a study of Carlyle when she died 29 Nov. 1885. Her children were Percy C., Beatrice, Herbert H., and Grace.

The 'Life and Writings' published by her son in 1887 contains several essays in which she gives expression to her religious beliefs. Mr. William Rossetti in a prefatory notice says that she had an 'eminently speaking face, of which the eyes, full, dark, liquid, and extremely vivacious,' were the marked feature. She had, he remarks, strong sense, great cordiality without false sentiment, and a high self-respect which excluded any undue deference to conventional distinctions. She was a good talker and listener, and discharged her domestic duties thoroughly, while finding time for intellectual activity.

[Life and Writings of Anne Gilchrist, by H. H. Gilchrist (1887); personal knowledge.]

H. H. G.

GILCHRIST, EBENEZER, M.D. (1707–1774), physician, was born at Dumfries in 1707, studied medicine at Edinburgh, London, and Paris, and graduated at Rheims. In 1732 he returned to Dumfries, where he practised with a reputation which extended beyond the locality, until his death, on 12 June 1774. He became known by reviving certain modes of treatment which he found in the ancient writers. In his first papers on nervous fevers (typhus), published in the 'Edinburgh Medical Essays and Observations,' vols. iv. and v. (1746–8), he recommended the use of wine and warm baths. His best known work, 'The Use of Sea Voyages in Medicine' (1756; 2nd edit., with a supplement, 1757; 3rd edit. 1771; French transl. 1770), contains a very full analysis of the benefits of sea-exercise and sea-air, especially in consumption, together with cases. The analytical or theoretical handling of the subject is judicious and has hardly been surpassed, but the experience is meagre, and limited too much to short voyages. In the 'Essays Physical and Literary' (vol. iii. 1770, and reprint 1770), he published an account of the symptoms and circumstances of the sibbens, the endemic form of syphilis among the poor in the west of Scotland, said to date from the Cromwellian occupation. His other papers are a defence of inoculation for small-pox, an account of the epidemic catarrh (influenza) of 1762, and on cases of vesical hypertrophy, all in 'Essays, Physical and Literary,' vols. ii. and iii.

[Encycl. Brit., 3rd ed.; Watt's Bibl. Brit.; Gilchrist's writings as above.]

C. C.

GILCHRIST, JAMES (d. 1777), captain in the navy, was promoted to be a lieutenant in the navy on 28 Aug. 1741, and in 1749 was serving in the Namur when, on 12 April, she was lost with all hands on board [see BOSCAWEN, Hon. EDWARD]. As only those who were on shore with the admiral, or sick in hospital, escaped, it would seem probable that Gilchrist was Boscawen's flag-lieutenant. When the news of the peace was confirmed, he was sent home in command of the Basilisk bomb, bringing the few survivors. He arrived at Plymouth on 17 April 1750, putting in there on account of the inclemency of the weather, which the men were unable to stand, being, he wrote, entirely naked. On 18 July 1755 he was advanced to post-rank and appointed to the Experiment frigate, which he joined on 8 August. In September he was sent over to the coast of France, where in eleven days he captured no fewer than sixteen, mostly small, vessels. In the beginning of 1756 he was sent into the Mediterranean, where he joined Admiral Byng, and was present at the action off Minorca on 20 May. He was afterwards appointed by Sir Edward Hawke, in rapid succession to the Chesterfield, the Deptford, and the Trident; was then sent home as a witness at the trial of Admiral Byng, and in April 1757 was appointed to the Southampton, a 32-gun frigate, in which, off Portland, on 25 July, he fought a severe action with two French frigates of superior force (LAUGHTON, Studies in Naval History, p. 333), and succeeded in beating them off. With better fortune he met, on 12 Sept, the French frigate Émeraude, which he captured after a sharp action of thirty-five minutes' duration, and brought into Falmouth. During the following year he was still employed in Channel service, in the course of which he captured two large privateers; and on 28 March 1759, being in company with Captain Hotham in the Melampe [see HOTHAM, WILLIAM, LORD], on a cruise in the North sea, met and engaged the 40-gun French frigate Danae, which, after a hard-fought action, lasting all through the night, struck her flag in the morning. Gilchrist was shot through the shoulder by a one-pound ball, a wound that for the time endangered his life, and rendered his arm permanently useless. He never served again, but lived in retirement at his family seat of Hunsfield in Lanarkshire, where he died in 1777. One of his daughters married the ninth earl of Dundonald, and was the mother of Thomas Cochrane, tenth earl of Dundonald [q. v.]

[Charnock's Biog. Nav. vi. 122; Official Correspondence in the Public Record Office.]

J. K. L.

GILCHRIST, JOHN BORTHWICK (1759–1841), orientalist, born at Edinburgh in 1759, was educated at George Heriot's Hospital in that city, an institution to which he bequeathed a liberal donation. Having studied for the medical profession and obtained the appointment of assistant-surgeon in the East India Company's service on 3 April 1783, he went out to Calcutta. He was promoted to a surgeoncy on 21 Oct. 1794 (DODWELL and MILES, Medical Officers of Indian Army, pp. 22–3). At that time the company were satisfied if their servants possessed a tolerable knowledge of Persian, the language of the courts and the government; but Gilchrist saw that to hold effective intercourse with the natives Hindustani should be substituted. Clad in native garb he travelled through those provinces where Hindustani was spoken in its greatest purity, and also acquired good knowledge of Sanskrit, Persian, and other Eastern tongues. His success inspired a new spirit in the company's servants, and the study of Hindustani became more popular. To further facilitate its study, Gilchrist published 'A Dictionary, English and Hindoostanee,' 2 parts, 4to, Calcutta, 1787–90; 'A Grammar of the Hindoostanee Language,' with a supplement, 4to, Calcutta, 1796; and 'The Oriental Linguist, an . . . Introduction to the Language of Hindoostan,' 4to, Calcutta, 1798 (another edition, 4to, Calcutta, 1802). The governor-general, Lord Wellesley, liberally aided his exertions, and upon the foundation of the Fort William College at Calcutta in 1800 appointed him its head. With the object of collecting a body of literature suitable as text-books for the study of the Urdū language by the European officials, he gathered together at Calcutta the best vernacular scholars of the time, and their works, due to his initiative, 'are still unsurpassed as specimens of elegant and serviceable prose composition, not only in Urdū but also in Hindī' (Encyclop. Britannica, 9th ed., xi. 849). To Gilchrist is thus due the elaboration of the vernacular as an official speech. His own writings at this period include 'The Anti-jargonist . . . being partly an abridgment of the Oriental Linguist,' 8vo, Calcutta, 1800; 'The Stranger's East Indian Guide to the Hindoostanee, with an Appendix by A. H. Kelso,' 8vo, Calcutta, 1802 (2nd edition, 8vo, London, 1808, 3rd edition, 1820); 'The Hindee Story Teller, or entertaining expositor of the Roman, Persian, and Nagree Characters,' 8vo, Calcutta, 1802; and 'A Collection of Dialogues, English and Hindoostanee, on the most familiar and useful subjects,' 8vo, Calcutta, 1804 (2nd edition, 8vo, Edinburgh, 1809; 3rd edition, 8vo, London, 1820). He also edited 'The Hindee Moral Preceptor, and Persian Scholar's shortest road to the Hindoostanee Language, or vice versa [consisting of Saedi's Pand

Namah in Persian, with a Hindustani translation, paradigms of Persian grammar, with their equivalents in Hindustani on opposite pages, &c.] Translated . . . and arranged by . . . natives' (with a preface in English, and a literal prose version as well as a paraphrase in English verse by Gilchrist), 8vo, Calcutta, 1803; and 'The Oriental Fabulist, or polyglot translations of Esop's and other Ancient Fables from the English Language into Hindoostanee, Persian, Arabic, &c., in the Roman character, by various hands,' 8vo, Calcutta, 1803. In 1804 ill-health compelled him to return home. On his departure he received from the governor-general in council a letter to the court of directors in London, commending him to their favour as one who had done much to promote the study of oriental languages. Lord Wellesley also gave him a letter of introduction to Mr. Addington, afterwards Lord Sidmouth. Gilchrist fixed his residence for a while at Edinburgh, the university of which created him LL.D. on 30 Oct. 1804 (*Cat. of Edinb. Graduates*, 1858, p. 260). He retired from the company's service on a pension of 300*l*. on 6 Jan. 1809. His fiery temperament, violent politics, which savoured strongly of republicanism, and no less violent language, appear to have considerably astonished his fellow-citizens, especially at civic meetings. These peculiarities, together with his readiness to take offence, involved him often in serious quarrels. Among other eccentricities he set up an aviary of Eastern birds at his house on the north side of Nicolson Square, the building being fully exposed to the public gaze. In conjunction with James Inglis he started a bank in Edinburgh, under the style of Inglis, Borthwick Gilchrist, & Co.; but the enterprise came to grief owing to the suspicion with which other banks regarded it.

Gilbert compressed his ' Anti-jargonist,' 'Stranger's Guide,' ' Oriental Linguist,' and various other works on the Hindustani language, into two portable volumes, with the general title of ' The British Indian Monitor,' 8vo, Edinburgh, 1806–8, and also penned a fierce political tirade entitled ' Parliamentary Reform on Constitutional Principles ; or British Loyalty against Continental Royalty,' &c., 8vo, Glasgow, 1815. In 1816 Gilchrist removed to London to find more congenial occupation in giving private lessons in oriental languages to candidates for the Indian service. Two years later, the East India Company having resolved that their servants, and more especially medical officers, should, previously to their leaving England, be instructed in the rudiments of Hindustani, created a professorship, and

conferred it on Gilchrist. His classes were accordingly removed to the Oriental Institution, Leicester Square. He was allowed a salary of 200*l*. a year, besides 150*l*. more for a lecture room on condition that he should teach the students without charging them more than three guineas each. Gilchrist declined to accept the three guineas, but of his own authority made a regulation that students should be admitted to attend his class only on producing a receipt from his publishers proving the purchase of what he or the latter considered an adequate quantity of his oriental text-books. These cost from 10*l*. to 15*l*. Thus, by professing to teach them gratuitously, Gilchrist got from his pupils nearly four or five times the sum prescribed by his employers. His irregular method of teaching was also unfavourably criticised. In 1825 the company withdrew their support. Gilchrist had previously complained bitterly of what he considered their cruelty, parsimony, and ingratitude. His great object appears to have been to induce the company to compel all their juvenile officers to attend his lectures (instead of their assistant-surgeons only), by which his receipts would be enormously swelled. Failing in this, his official reports grew from year to year more lengthy and bitter. Having at last collected the whole together under the title of ' The Orienti-Occidental Tuitionary Pioneer to Literary Pursuits by the King's and Company's Officers of all ranks . . . and departments . . . Fourteen Reports, &c. . . . A Panglossal Diorama for a Universal Language and Character . . . and a . . . new Theory of Latin Verbs,' he formed a folio volume of abuse against his employers and almost every one connected with them in the diffusion of oriental learning. He carried on the class till the end of 1826, when he handed it over to Sandford Arnot and Duncan Forbes [q. v.] He engaged at the same time to give gratuitously a weekly lecture, but finding that the sale of his text-books decreased he tried to recover his old position. In the beginning of 1828 he ill-naturedly endeavoured to form a Hindustani class in the immediate neighbourhood of the institution. Arnot and Forbes, whose patience had been sorely tried by his vagaries, attacked him severely in the appendix to their first annual report of the London Oriental Institution, issued on 1 April of that year. During the remainder of his life Gilchrist lived in retirement. He died at Paris on 9 Jan. 1841. By his wife, Miss Mary Ann Coventry, he had no children. In August 1850 she married at Paris General Guglielmo Pepe of the kingdom of Naples.

Gilchrist's other publications are : 1. 'The

Hindee-Roman Orthoepigraphical Ultimatum; or, a systematic . . . view of Oriental and Occidental visible Sounds on fixed . . . principles for acquiring the . . . pronunciation of many Oriental Languages; exemplified in one hundred popular anecdotes . . . and proverbs of the Hindoostanee story-teller. Second edition. (A . . . prospectus and . . . synopsis of the Persian Naghree and Roman characters),' 8vo, London, 1820. 2. 'Dialogues English and Hindoostanee : for illustrating the Grammatical Principles of The Stranger's East Indian Guide,' 8vo, London, 1820. 3. 'The Hindee Moral Preceptor; or Rudimental Principles of Persian Grammar . . . rendered . . . plain . . . through the medium of sixty exercises in prose and verse, including [selections from the Hikáyát-i Latif and others] the . . . Pundnamu or Ethics of Shuekh Sundee ; with a Hindoostanee literal version, and an English metrical paraphrase of each poem. . . . Second edition,' 2 pts., 8vo, London, 1821. A different book altogether from that bearing a similar title, as even the Hindustani version of the Pand Námah is entirely new. 4. 'The General East India Guide and Vade-Mecum : being a Digest of the work of the late Capt. Williamson, with many improvements and additions,' 8vo, London, 1825. 5. 'A New Theory and Prospectus of the Persian Verbs, with their Hindoostanee synonimes in Persian and English,' 4to, Calcutta, 1831. 6. 'A Practical Appeal to the Public, through a Series of Letters, in Defence of the New System of Physic by the illustrious Hahnemann. . . . Letter the first,' 8vo, London, 1833.

[W. Anderson's Scottish Nation, ii. 298–300 ; Memoir in Chambers's Eminent Scotsmen, ii. 106–7, written from personal knowledge ; Annual Reg. 1841, lxxxiii. 181 ; East India Reg. 1803 pt. i. p. 83, 1805 p. 91 ; Brit. Mus. Cat. No record of the eighteenth-century alumni of Heriot's Hospital has been preserved.] G. G.

GILCHRIST, OCTAVIUS GRAHAM (1779–1823), antiquary, was born at Twickenham in 1779. His father, Stirling Gilchrist, lieutenant and surgeon in the 3rd dragoon guards, on the return of his regiment to England quitted the service and retired to Twickenham. Octavius was one of a family of sixteen. He was educated at Magdalen College, Oxford, but left the university early without a degree, in order to assist a relative (Alderman Joseph Robinson, grocer) in business at Stamford. In 1803 he was elected F.S.A.; and in the following year he married Elizabeth, daughter of James Nowlan, merchant, of the Hermitage, Wapping. He printed in 1805, for private circulation, a little volume

of 'Rhymes,' 8vo ; and in 1807 he published a full and valuable edition of the 'Poems,' 8vo, of Richard Corbet [q. v.], sometime bishop of Oxford and Norwich. To his friend William Gifford he addressed in 1808 'An Examination of the Charges maintained by Messrs. Malone, Chalmers, and others of Ben Jonson's enmity towards Shakespeare,' 8vo, pp. 62 ; and in 1811 'A Letter on the late edition [by H. Weber] of Ford's Plays, 8vo,' pp. 45. Gifford, in his editions of Jonson and Ford, acknowledged the help that he received from Gilchrist's investigations. The 'Quarterly Review' for June 1812 contains a severe article by Gilchrist on Stephen Jones's edition of Baker's 'Biographia Dramatica.' Jones published a reply entitled 'Hypercriticism Exposed,' 1812. Early in 1814 Gilchrist printed, but never circulated, proposals for publishing 'A Select Collection of Old English Plays in 15 vols. 8vo, with Biographical Notices and Notes Critical and Explanatory : ' the scheme was abandoned owing to the appearance of Dilke's 'Old English Plays.' Notes of Gilchrist are incorporated in the third edition (by J. P. Collier) of Dodsley's 'Old Plays,' 1825–7. The 'Quarterly Review' for October 1820 had some uncomplimentary remarks on William Lisle Bowles [q. v.], in a review of 'Spence's Anecdotes.' Bowles hastened to reply in 'The Pamphleteer,' vol. xvii., ascribing the 'Quarterly' article to Gilchrist, who (while disclaiming the authorship) published a vigorous 'Letter to the Rev. William Lisle Bowles,' Stamford, 1820, 8vo. An acrimonious controversy ensued. Gifford (introduction to Ford's *Works*) declared that 'in the extent and accuracy of his critical knowledge' Gilchrist was 'as much superior to the Rev. Mr. Bowles as in good manners.' On 30 June 1823 Gilchrist died at his house in the High Street, Stamford ; he had long been suffering from a consumptive complaint. His library, which contained some choice Elizabethan and early printed books, was sold by auction 5–11 January 1824. Gilchrist probably supplied much of the material for Drakard's 'History of Stamford,' 1822.

[Gent. Mag. lxxix. 53, xci. 291, 533, vol. xciii. pt. ii. p. 278 ; information kindly supplied by Justin Simpson, esq., Stamford.] A. H. B.

GILDAS (516?–570?), British historian, tells us that he was born in the year of the battle of Mount Badon (Mons Badonicus), but gives no indication of the date of the battle. The tenth-century Latin chronicle, which is our next best authority after him for early Welsh history, puts this battle seventy-two years after the point at which its own record begins (*Harl. MS.* 3859, generally quoted as 'Annales Cambriæ MS. A'). The editors of the 'Monumenta Historica Britannica' make the chronicle begin in 444, which would give 516 for the date of both the battle and Gildas's birth. Apparently following or inspiring 'Nennius,' the chronicle treats the battle of Mons Badonicus as the special victory of Arthur, while Gildas makes no mention whatever of Arthur; but he is so vague that it is unsafe to argue too much from his omissions. M. Arthur de la Borderie has recently maintained that the true date of Gildas's birth is fixed by a passage in Bæda (*Hist. Ecclesiastica*, bk. i. ch. xvi.), which dates the battle in the forty-fourth year after the arrival of the English in Britain, that is in 493. Advocates of the later date have supposed that Bæda, who is copying Gildas at this point, has misunderstood his author; but M. de la Borderie maintains that this and many other difficulties are avoided by adopting the earlier date. That date is also consistent with the statement of the monk of Ruys and the ninth-century author of the life of St. Paul Aurelian, that Gildas was a disciple of St. Illtyd, and a friend of St. Brigitta. But the materials hardly permit of a satisfactory solution (see *Revue Celtique*, vi. 1–13, 'La date de la naissance de Gildas,' par ARTHUR DE LA BORDERIE). If we follow Ussher and Mr. Stevenson (Preface to *Gildas*, p. ix), we put the date of Gildas's birth in 520. We can also gather from Gildas that he was an ecclesiastic, doubtless a monk. The whole tone of his work shows him a man of gloomy temper, irritated and saddened by the triumphs of the Saxons, and profoundly conscious of the vices and weaknesses of his countrymen. He enumerates the chief British kings who were his contemporaries, and expatiates in turgid and vague rhetoric upon their wicked characters. They are Constantinus, 'the tyrant of Damnonia,' Aurelius Conanus (Cynan), Vortiporius, 'tyrant of the Demetians' (South Welsh), Cuneglasus (Cyneglas), and the 'island dragon' Maglocunus (Maelgwn). The tenth-century chronicle places the death of Maelgwn in 547, and the 'conversion of Constantine to the Lord' in 589.

Gildas also tells us that he crossed the sea; that though strongly pressed by his friends to write his book, he refrained from doing so from want of information, and when after ten years' hesitation he undertook the task, he had still to trust to foreign accounts, 'broken by repeated chasms and not sufficiently clear.' He also says that at the time of his writing forty-three years and one month had elapsed from the siege of Mons Badonicus and the year of his own birth. It may be inferred from the above statements, and the known connections between Britain and Armorica, that Gildas wrote his work in Brittany, and that he crossed over thither not later than 550. This agrees with the positive statement of Gildas's eleventh-century Breton biographer, who says that he went to Gaul when in his thirtieth year. He is reputed to have founded there the monastery of St. Gildas at Ruys, on the peninsula that protects Vannes from the sea. This is very likely to be the case. His biographer was a monk of Ruys, who wrote to exalt the fame of his founder. The abbey itself became very famous as the place of the retirement of Abelard. The tenth-century annals of Wales seem to place Gildas's death in 570. He was regarded as a saint, and his day was kept on 29 Jan. Writing at the end of the ninth century, Alcuin in his epistles twice refers to Gildas's book, and calls him the wisest of the Britons (JAFFÉ, 'Monumenta Alcuiniana,' in *Bibl. Rer. Germ.* vi. 206, 371). Alcuin spells his name 'Gildus.' The twelfth-century manuscript of Gildas's history styles him in its rubrics 'Saint Gildas the Wise.' Gildas's statements gained wide currency from the use of his book by Bæda in the introductory chapters of his 'Ecclesiastical History.' Bæda speaks of him in one place as 'Gildus, the historian of the Britons' (*Hist. Eccl.* lib. i. chap. xxii.) Gildas remained a popular saint in Brittany, where in 1026 another monastery, that of St. Gildas du Bois (about midway between Vannes and Nantes), was founded in his honour (SAINTE-MARTHE, *Gallia Christiana*, xiv. 847). About 1830 a popular metrical hymn on his merits was published at Vannes in Breton (*Cannen Spirituel. Buhé Sant Gueltas*).

A much more detailed account of Gildas's life is to be found in the pages of the monk of Ruys. But apart from its late date and plainly legendary character, its statements harmonise so little with chronology that they can be safely disregarded. A second life of Gildas is also extant, which seems to have been the result of the renewed intercourse between Brittany and Wales in the twelfth century. It is ascribed to Caradog of Llancarvan [q. v.], the friend and fellow-worker of Geoffrey of Monmouth and William of Malmesbury. Though Caradog's authorship is denied by the editor of the life, it does not seem to be altogether unlikely. It is equally untrustworthy with the Breton life, from which, however, it differs in some important points. For instance, Caradog makes Gildas be buried at Glastonbury, while the monk of Ruys of course buries him at Ruys. Those who have given any credence to either have been compelled to start the hypothesis that there were two persons of the name of Gildas, one of whom, flourishing in the fifth century, they call 'Gildas Albanius,' while the author of the British history they call 'Gildas Badonicus.' But this is mere guesswork, and leaves so many difficulties that other writers have assumed the existence of three, if not four, historical Gildases.

Gildas's historical work is called in the rubric of the oldest extant manuscript, 'Liber querulus de excidio Britanniæ.' It is divided in the editions into a first part called 'Historia Gildæ,' and a second part 'Epistola Gildæ;' but it is plainly a continuous work, and the division seems due to early transcribers. The literary merit of the work is very small, and its historical value depends mainly upon the absence of better authorities. The style is extraordinarily verbose, rhetorical, involved, and obscure, while very few definite facts can be extracted. Bæda describes it as a 'sermo flebilis.' It was believed by William of Malmesbury, Henry of Huntingdon, Geoffrey of Monmouth, and Giraldus Cambrensis, that the curious compilation now generally assigned to Nennius [q. v.] was the work of Gildas, but that is plainly impossible. Pits and Bale attribute a long list of works to Gildas, but they have no good authority for doing so.

Gildas's history was first printed at London by Polydore Vergil in 1525, and has been many times reprinted. In 1568 John Joscelyn, Archbishop Parker's secretary, published a new edition. In 1691 it was again printed by Gale in the third volume of his 'Rerum Anglicarum Scriptores.' The best editions are that of Mr. Stevenson (English Historical Society, 1838), reprinted in 1844 by Sainte-Marthe (Schulz) at Berlin, and that in the 'Monumenta Historica Britannica' (1848). 'The Epistle of Gildas, faithfully translated out of the Original Latine, with introduction by J. Habington' (London, 1638, 12mo), was the first version in English. Another English translation can be found in Bohn's 'Six Old English Chronicles,' pp. 295–380. There are only two manuscripts of Gildas extant, both in the Cambridge University Library.

[Hardy's Preface to Monumenta Historica Britannica, pp. 59–62; Stevenson's Prefaces and Notes to the English Historical Society's edition of the Historia; Wright's Biographia Britannica Literaria, Anglo-Saxon period, pp. 115–35; Schöll, De Ecclesiasticæ Britonum Scotorumque Historiæ fontibus, cap. i.; Skene's Four Ancient Books of Wales, vol. i. cap. iii.; A. de la Borderie in Revue Celtique, vol. vi.; Brit. Mus. Cat.

of Printed Books; Dictionary of Christian Biography; Bædæ Historia Ecclesiastica Gentis Anglorum; Annales Cambriæ MS. A., confused in Mon. Hist. Brit. and in Rolls Ser. edition with less authoritative sources, but recently carefully printed by itself from the tenth-century Harleian MS., by Mr. Phillimore in the Transactions of the Cymmrodorion Society, ix. 141–83. Walter, Das alte Wales, pp. 41–2, gives a list of several other sources, many of very little critical value. The Life of Gildas by the monk of St. Gildas de Ruys has been published completely by Mabillon in the Acta Sanctorum Ordinis S. Benedicti, i. 138–89, and less fully in the Bollandist Acta Sanctorum, January, tom. iii. 573 sq. The Life ascribed to Caradog was first published from the manuscript in Corpus Christi Coll. Cambridge, by Stevenson in the Engl. Hist. Soc. edition of Gildas; for other lives see Hardy's Descriptive Cat. of Materials, i. pt. i. 132–7, 151–6, pt. ii. 799.] T. F. T.

GILDAS minor or **NENNIUS** (*fl.* 796), historian. [See NENNIUS.]

GILDERDALE, JOHN (*d.* 1864), divine, was educated at Howden grammar school in Yorkshire. His tastes were early disposed towards a seafaring life, but he eventually adopted a literary and scholastic profession. On the completion of his school career he matriculated from St. Catharine's Hall, Cambridge, where he graduated B.A. in 1826, proceeded to his degree of M.A. in 1830, and to that of B.D. in 1853. He proceeded 'ad eundem' in the university of Oxford 25 June 1847. After leaving Cambridge he was appointed lecturer of the parish church of Halifax, Yorkshire, through the influence of Dr. Musgrave, archdeacon of Craven. This office, however, he resigned on being presented to the living of Walthamstow, where he was also principal and trustee of the Forest School in that parish. He died at Candle Stourton, Dorsetshire, on 25 Sept. 1864, in the sixty-second year of his age.

Gilderdale published: 1. 'An Essay on Natural Religion and Revelation, considered with regard to the legitimate use and proper limitation of Reason,' London, 1837, 8vo. This work is dedicated to the Rev. William Dealtry, D.D. [q. v.], rector of Clapham and chancellor of the diocese of Winchester. 2. 'A Course of Family Prayers for one month, with Short Forms for several occasions, dedicated to the Ven. Charles Musgrave, Prebendary of York and Vicar of Halifax.' London, 1838, 12mo. 3. 'A Letter to Lord Brougham on National Education,' London, 1838, 8vo.

[Gent. Mag. 1864, pt. ii. p. 661; Foster's Alumni Oxon.; Guardian, October 1864.]
W. F. W. S.

GILDON, CHARLES (1665–1724), miscellaneous writer, was born in 1665 at Gillingham, near Shaftesbury in Dorsetshire. His father was a member of Gray's Inn, and had suffered on the royalist side in the civil war. The family was Roman catholic. Gildon was sent to Douay when twelve years old, to be educated for the priesthood. He returned when about the age of nineteen, and on coming of age inherited his father's property. He ran through it in a short time, and increased his difficulties by marrying at the age of twenty-three. He afterwards led the life of a hack-author. Seven years' close application to study led him to abandon catholicism for deism. In 1695 he published the 'Miscellaneous Works of the Deist, Charles Blount' (1654–1693) [q. v.], and in a preface signed 'Lindamour' defended the practice of suicide. Gildon afterwards announced his conversion from deism by Charles Leslie's 'Short and Easy Method,' 1697. In 1705 he published the 'Deist's Manual,' defending the orthodox creed, with a letter from Leslie appended. He afterwards came into conflict with Pope. The first offence seems to have been given by Gildon's 'New Rehearsal, or Bays the younger, containing an examen of Mr. Rowe's plays, and a word or two on Mr. Pope's " Rape of the Lock," ' 1714. He there attacks Pope as 'Sawney Dapper,' and accuses him of having himself written the panegyric prefixed to his 'Pastorals' in the name of Wycherley. Pope afterwards asserted that Gildon had abused him in a life of Wycherley, and had been rewarded by a present of 10l. 10s. from Addison. No such life of Wycherley is forthcoming; the story is in several ways inconsistent, and is part of Pope's elaborate concoction of falsehoods against Addison (ELWIN, Pope, iii. 234, 537; CARRUTHERS, Life of Pope, 1857, 130, 236). In the 'Epistle to Arbuthnot' (1735) Pope speaks of Gildon's 'venal quill,' words substituted for the 'meaner quill' of an earlier version (1724), to countenance this accusation. Pope also attacked Gildon (1728) in the 'Dunciad' (bk. iii. l. 173). The story about Addison is worthless; but Gildon was one of the unfortunate scribblers of the time, and appears from Dunton's account to have been a dependent of the whigs. He died 12 Jan. 1723–4, and was described by Boyer (Political State of Great Britain, xxvii. 182) as a person of 'great literature but mean genius.' The last epithet is sufficiently justified by his works. Besides those above mentioned, the following are attributed to him : 1. 'History of the Athenian Society,' 1691 [see DUNTON, JOHN, for this society]. 2. 'Postboy robbed of his Mail . . . containing some 500 letters to several persons of quality.' 3. 'Miscellany Poems upon various occasions,' 1692. 4. 'Examen Miscellaneum,' 1701. 5. 'A Comparison of the two Stages,' 1702. 6. 'Life and Adventures of Defoe.' 7. 'Canons, or the Vision, addressed to James, Earl of Carnarvon' (afterwards Duke of Chandos) [see BRYDGES, JAMES], 1717. 8. 'The Laws of Poetry laid down by . . . Buckingham . . . Roscommon, and . . . Lansdown, illustrated and explained,' 1721. He was author of the following plays : 1. 'The Roman Bride's Revenge,' 1697. 2. 'Phaethon, or the Fatal Divorce,' 1698 (plot from the 'Medea' of Euripides). 3. 'Measure for Measure' (adapted from Shakespeare), 1700. 4. 'Love's Victim,' 1701. 5. 'The Patriot, or the Italian Conspiracy,' 1703 (from Lee's 'L. J. Brutus'). In 1699 he edited Langbaine's 'Dramatic Poets,' with a continuation. He also wrote an essay prefixed to a volume published by Curll, and intended to pass as a seventh volume to Rowe's 'Shakespeare' (6 vols., 1710) (Notes and Queries, 2nd ser. xii. 349).

[Cibber's Lives of the Poets (1753), iii. 326–329; Nichols's Lit. Anecd. i. 24, 25, viii. 297; Dunton's Life and Errors (1818), pp. 181, 191, 734; Biog. Dram.; Genest's Hist. of the Stage, ii. 112, 137, 221, 247, 276.]   L. S.

GILES, FRANCIS (1787–1847), civil engineer, born in 1787, was brought up as a surveyor, and executed in the early part of his career, under John Rennie, an important portion of numerous surveys which subsequently became models of later practice. Among these were surveys of the Thames, the Mersey, the Wear, and the Tyne, and of the harbours of Dover, Rye, Holyhead, Dundee, and Kingstown. He afterwards engaged in business as an engineer, and executed many important harbour and canal works and river improvements. He also had a hand in the construction of some of the largest works on the Newcastle and Carlisle railway, and in part of the South-Western railway. The Warwick bridge in Cumberland is considered, as regards elegance of design, his masterpiece, though a cutting of 102 feet deep which he made through the Cowran Hills is a most remarkable work. Giles was in great request as an arbitrator, adviser, and consulting engineer, and enjoyed a lucrative practice. He was most prominent for his long opposition to George Stephenson's railway enterprises. When the Liverpool and Manchester railway project was under consideration, Giles gave evidence, which had much weight from his long experience and engineering reputation. 'No engineer in his senses,' he maintained, 'would go through

Chat Moss if he wanted to make a railway from Liverpool to Manchester.' 'His estimate for the whole cutting and embankment over Chat Moss was 270,000*l.* nearly. . . . It would be necessary to take the Moss completely out at the bottom, in order to make a solid road.' Giles afterwards became a railway locomotive engineer. He was an active member of the council of the Institution of Civil Engineers, and took a prominent part in the discussions of that body, besides contributing some valuable plans and charts to its collections. Giles died on 4 March 1847, in his sixtieth year.

[Minutes of Proceedings of Inst. of Civil Engineers, 1848; Smiles's Lives of the Engineers.]
J. B–Y.

GILES, JAMES (1801–1870), landscape-painter, was born at Glasgow, 4 Jan. 1801. His father, a native of Aberdeenshire, was an artist of some local repute, but his death threw his son at an early age upon his own resources. At thirteen he maintained himself, his mother and sister by painting, and before he was twenty taught private classes in Aberdeen. Shortly afterwards he made a tour through Scotland and visited the continent, and on his return home he was introduced to the Earl of Aberdeen, with whom he became very intimate. His earliest successes were in portrait-painting, but his visit to Italy gave him a taste for classic landscape, which he never entirely lost, for the mist seldom hangs about his mountains, even when the scene is laid near 'dark Lochnagar.' He was a keen angler, and fond of painting the result of a successful day's fishing. These pictures were his best works. He first exhibited at the Royal Institution for the Encouragement of the Fine Arts in Scotland, but in 1829 he became an academician of the Royal Scottish Academy, and contributed numerous works to its exhibitions from that time until near the close of his career. He also exhibited frequently at the British Institution in London, and occasionally at the Royal Academy and the Society of British Artists. His picture of 'The Weird Wife' is in the National Gallery of Scotland. His last work was a painting of himself, his wife, and youngest son, which he left unfinished. He died at his residence in Bon Accord Street, Aberdeen, after a lingering illness, 6 Oct. 1870. He was twice married, and by his first wife had a son, who gave great promise as an artist, but died of consumption at the early age of twenty-one.

[Scotsman, 8 Oct. 1870; Redgrave's Dict. of Artists of the English School, 1878; Exhibition Catalogues of the Royal Institution for the En-couragement of the Fine Arts in Scotland, the Royal Scottish Academy, the Royal Academy, the British Institution, and the Society of British Artists.]
R. E. G.

GILES, JOHN ALLEN, D.C.L. (1808–1884), editor and translator, son of William Giles and his wife Sophia, whose maiden name was Allen, was born on 26 Oct. 1808 at South-wick House, in the parish of Mark, Somerset, the residence of his father and grand-father, and at the age of sixteen entered Charterhouse as a Somerset scholar. From Charterhouse he was elected to a Bath and Wells scholarship at Corpus Christi College, Oxford, on 26 Nov. 1824. In Easter term 1828 he obtained a double first class, and shortly afterwards graduated B.A., proceeding M.A. in 1831, in which year he gained the Vinerian scholarship, and took his D.C.L. degree in 1838. His election to a fellowship at Corpus on 15 Nov. 1832 followed his college scholarship as a matter of course. He wished to become a barrister, but was persuaded by his mother to take orders, and was ordained to the curacy of Cossington, Somerset. The following year he vacated his fellowship, and was married to Miss A. S. Dickinson. His 'Scriptores Græci minores' had been published in 1831, and his 'Latin Grammar' reached a third edition in 1833. In 1834 he was appointed to the head-mastership of Camberwell College School, and on 24 Nov. 1836 was elected head-master of the City of London School. He failed to preserve discipline; the school did not do well under him, and he resigned on 23 Jan. 1840; his resignation, however, has been attributed to some misfortune connected with building speculations (*Times*, 7 March 1855, p. 12). He retired to a house which he built near Bagshot, and there took pupils, and engaged in literary work. After a few years he became curate of Bampton, Oxfordshire, where he continued taking pupils, and edited and wrote a great number of books. Among them was one entitled 'Christian Records,' published in 1854, which related to the age and authenticity of the books of the New Testament. The bishop of Oxford, Samuel Wilberforce, required him, on pain of losing his curacy, to suppress this work, and break off his connection with another literary undertaking on which he was engaged. After some letters, which were published, had passed on the subject, he complied with the bishop's demand.

On 6 March 1855 Giles was tried at the Oxford spring assizes before Lord Campbell, on the charges of having entered in the marriage register book of Bampton parish church a marriage under date 3 Oct. 1854, which took place on the 5th, he having himself performed the ceremony out of canonical hours, soon after 6 A.M.; of having falsely entered that it was performed by license; and of having forged the mark of a witness who was not present. He pleaded not guilty, but it was evident that he had committed the offence out of foolish good nature, in order to cover the frailty of one of his servants, whom he married to her lover, Richard Pratt, a shoemaker's apprentice. Pratt's master, one of Giles's parishioners, instituted the proceedings. Giles spoke on his own behalf, and declared that he had published 120 volumes. His bishop also spoke for him. He was found guilty, but strongly recommended to mercy. Lord Campbell sentenced him to a year's imprisonment in Oxford Castle. His fate excited much commiseration in the university, and after three months' imprisonment he was released by royal warrant on 4 June (*Times*, 7 March and 7 June 1855). After the lapse of two or three years he took the curacy, with sole charge, of Perrivale in Middlesex, and after remaining there five years became curate of Harmondsworth, near Slough. At the end of a year he resigned this curacy, and went to live at Cranford, in the immediate neighbourhood, where he took pupils, and after a while removed to Ealing. He did not resume clerical work until he was presented in 1867 to the living of Sutton in Surrey, which he held for seventeen years, until his death on 24 Sept. 1884. His literary tastes and some peculiarities of manner and disposition are said to have injured his popularity, but he was kind and courteous. His wife survived him, and he left two sons, one in the Bengal police, the other, Herbert Allen Giles, Professor of Chinese at the University of Cambridge. He also left two daughters, the elder married to Dundas W. Cloeté of Churchill Court, Somerset, the younger unmarried.

Much of Giles's literary work was hasty, and done as task work for booksellers. Still, historical scholars, especially those who began to study before the publication of the Rolls Series of editions, have reason to remember him with gratitude, although his editions of historical works are frequently disfigured by carelessness, and lack of arrangement, indexes, and every kind of critical apparatus. Many of his works require no notice. Besides those already noticed he published a 'Greek Lexicon,' 1839. Between 1837 and 1843 he published the 'Patres Ecclesiæ Anglicanæ,' a series of thirty-four volumes, containing the works of Aldhelm, Bæda, Boniface, Lanfranc, Archbishop Thomas, John of Salisbury, Peter of Blois, Gilbert Foliot, and other authors. Several volumes of the Caxton Society's publications were edited by him, chiefly between 1845 and 1854. Among these were 'Anecdota Bædæ et aliorum,' 'Benedictus Abbas, de Vita S. Thomæ,' 'Chron. Angliæ Petroburgense,' 'La révolte du Conte de Warwick,' and 'Vitæ quorundam Anglo-Saxonum.' His 'Scriptores rerum gestarum Willelmi Conquestoris' was published in 1845. He contributed to Bohn's Antiquarian Library translations of 'Matthew Paris,' 1847, 'Bede's Ecclesiastical History,' and the 'Anglo-Saxon Chronicle,' 1849, and other works. In 1845 he published 'Life and Times of Thomas Becket,' 2 vols., translated into French, 1858; in 1847, 'History of the Ancient Britons,' 2 vols., and in 1848, 'Life and Times of Alfred the Great.' In 1847–8 appeared his 'History of Bampton,' 2 vols., and in 1852 his 'History of Witney and some neighbouring Parishes.' While at Bampton, in 1850 he published 'Hebrew Records' on the age and authenticity of the books of the Old Testament, and in 1854 'Christian Records on the Age, Authorship, and Authenticity of the Books of the New Testament,' in which he contends, in a preface dated 26 Oct. 1853, that the 'Gospels and Acts were not in existence before the year 150,' and remarks that 'the objections of ancient philosophers, Celsus, Porphyry, and others, were drowned in the tide of orthodox resentment' (with reference to this book see *Letters of the Bishop of Oxford and Dr. J. A. G.*, published in a separate volume). In 1853 he began to work on a series called 'Dr. Giles's Juvenile Library,' which went on appearing from time to time until 1860, and comprises a large number of school-books, 'First Lessons' on English, Scottish, Irish, French, and Indian history, on geography, astronomy, arithmetic, &c. He contributed 'Poetic Treasures' to Moxon's 'Popular Poets' in 1881.

[Information from the president of Corpus Christi College, Oxford, and private sources; Times, 7 March, p. 112, and 7 June, 1855, p. 10; Ann. Register, 1855, pp. 50, 51; Crockford's Clerical Directory, 1860; Oxford Univ. Cal. 1889; Brit. Mus. Cat.] W. H.

GILES, NATHANIEL (1559?–1634), composer, was born in or near Worcester about 1559 (cf. *Harl. MS.* 1532 f. 144), and was a chorister at Magdalen College, Oxford, from 1567 to 1571. In 1577 he was clerk in the same chapel, but remained there only one year. He took the degree of Mus.B. at Oxford on 26 June 1585, and on 1 Oct. 1595 became organist and master of the choristers at St. George's Chapel, Windsor. In June 1597 he succeeded William Hunnis as a gentleman of the Chapel Royal and master of the children. Hawkins's statement that on the accession of Charles I he received the appointment of one of the organists of the Chapel Royal appears to be without foundation, as the Cheque Book contains no mention of such an appointment. He applied in 1607 for the degree of Mus.D., but, 'for some unknown reason' (HAWKINS), declined to perform his exercise, and the degree was not conferred upon him until 5 July 1622, when it was proposed that he should dispute with William Heyther on three questions concerning music. The fact that the dispute did not take place may be perhaps explained by Heyther's insufficient knowledge of music, for it is beyond question that his exercise had to be written for him by his friend Orlando Gibbons [q. v.] It was certainly due to no lack of learning on Giles's part, for his 'Lesson of Descant of thirtie-eighte Proportions of sundrie kindes' on the plain-song 'Miserere' (quoted by Hawkins) is a monument of erudition, and is no doubt the cause of Burney's attack on him as a pedant and nothing else. Two inscriptions at Windsor show that he died on 24 Jan. and was buried 2 Feb. 1633–4. The longer of these gives various erroneous statements concerning the tenure of his offices; it also states that his wife was Anne, eldest daughter of John Stayner of Worcestershire.

Though few in number Giles's compositions seem to have enjoyed a wide popularity. His service in C and his five-part anthem 'O give thanks unto the Lord' were printed in Barnard's collection, and are found in many of the manuscript collections of church music. Blow's manuscript in the Fitzwilliam Museum at Cambridge gives a 'new service' (evening only) in 'A re,' and a verse anthem 'I will magnify,' besides the two more familiar works, and in the Brit. Mus. Addit. MS. 29372 there is a five-part madrigal, 'Cease now vain thoughts.' Giles was noted for his religious life and conversation. A son of his, of the same name, was canon of Windsor and prebendary of Worcester.

[Grove's Dict. i. 595; Bloxam's Registers of Magdalen College, i. 15, &c.; Hawkins's History, ed. 1853, pp. 573, 574, 961; Burney's History, iii. 324; Wood's Fasti, vol. ii. col. 405; Catal. Fitzwilliam Museum; Old Cheque Book, Chapel Royal.] J. A. F. M.

GILFILLAN, GEORGE (1813–1878), miscellaneous writer, was born on 30 Jan. 1813, in the village of Comrie, Perthshire, where his father, the Rev. Samuel Gilfillan (1762–1826) [q. v.], was minister of the secession congregation. His mother, Rachel Barlas, 'the star of the north,' was daughter of the Crieff secession minister. Of twelve children George was the eleventh. When

thirteen years old his father died, and he entered Glasgow College, where he became a class-fellow of Archibald Campbell Tait, afterwards archbishop of Canterbury, Dr. John Eadie, and Dr. Hanna. He profited by the teaching of Sir Daniel Sandford, Robert Buchanan, and James Milne. He went to Edinburgh, and received warm encouragement from the professor of moral philosophy, John Wilson, better known as 'Christopher North.' Among his intimate friends, for life, were Thomas Aird [q. v.], Thomas de Quincey, and Thomas Carlyle, each of whom powerfully influenced him, but the last least. When twenty-two years of age, in 1835, he was licensed by the united presbytery of Edinburgh. He declined an invitation from his father's congregation at Comrie, and settled in March 1836 at Dundee in the School-Wynd Church, where he remained till his death.

In 1844 Gilfillan contributed gratuitously to the 'Dumfries Herald,' of which his friend Aird was editor, a brilliant series of literary estimates of living writers. These papers he republished under the title 'A Gallery of Literary Portraits,' Edinburgh, 1845, with eleven poor lithographic portraits by Friedrich Schenck. The book was instantly popular. Thenceforward literature claimed a large part of Gilfillan's time. During the following thirty years he published a hundred volumes or pamphlets, besides innumerable contributions to newspapers and magazines. But he never neglected his ministerial duties. His congregation increased. He worked hard for the cause of voluntaryism, although maintaining private friendship with episcopalians and state presbyterians; and was always zealous in the cause of liberal and progressive thought. In 1843 he published a sermon entitled ' Hades; or the Unseen,' which reached three editions. It was attacked by Dr. Eadie in the 'United Secession Magazine,' May 1843, by the Rev. Alexander Balfour, and others. The Dundee presbytery examined it on 25 July 1843, and decided the matter in Gilfillan's favour. In September 1869 he wrote a letter to the Edinburgh 'Scotsman,' declaring that 'the standards of the church contained much dubious matter and a good deal that is false and mischievous.' In February 1870 this declaration was brought by the Edinburgh presbytery before the Dundee presbytery, who again found there was no cause for further procedure. In 1847 he opposed the ultra-sabbatarianism of those who strove to stop all Sunday travelling or 'Sunday walks.' Gilfillan persistently opposed the project of union between the united presbyterians, to which body he belonged, and the free kirk that had seceded.

Gilfillan actively promoted mechanics' institutes, popular lectures, and free libraries. He brought distinguished men, such as Professor John Nicol, the astronomer, R. W. Emerson, and Dr. Samuel Brown, to lecture at Dundee and at mechanics' institutes elsewhere. In May 1841 he himself lectured against the corn laws; in January 1844, at the Watt Institution, on the reconciliation of geology and scripture; in 1846 on 'literature and books' and against American slavery. He actively sympathised with Kossuth and Garibaldi, and supported the Burns centenary and the Shakespeare tercentenary. In 1865 he lectured on Ireland, but 'without hope that it would ever come abreast of Great Britain;' he had visited it and examined its evils for himself. Lectures on America followed.

Gilfillan generously assisted his fellow-authors, among those he helped being Sydney Dobell, Alexander Smith, and John Stanyan Bigg. As an editor of the old poets, a labour that occupied much of his time, Gilfillan was not very successful. He wrongly disdained the minute rectification of texts by a careful collation of the earliest editions or manuscripts, and his introductory essays and memoirs are not remarkable for accuracy. He died suddenly on Tuesday morning, 13 Aug. 1878, at Arnhalt, Brechin. His funeral, 17 Aug., at Balgay cemetery, was attended by a procession two miles long. Gilfillan's many friends acknowledged that success never spoilt him, and all recognised his generosity and sincerity. Though living so busy a life, he found time in vacations for much foreign travel. In November 1836 he married Margaret Valentine of Mearns, who survived him. It was a happy marriage, although they had no children.

The following are his more important works: 1. 'Hades,' already mentioned, 1843. 2. 'Gallery of Literary Portraits,' first series, 1845 (Jeffrey, Godwin, Hazlitt, Robert Hall, Shelley, Chalmers, Carlyle, De Quincey, Wilson, Irving, Landor, Coleridge, Emerson, Wordsworth, Lamb, Keats, Macaulay, Aird, Southey, Lockhart, and others); second series, 1850; third, 1854; reissued 1856-7. 3. 'Alpha and Omega' (one of his best books), 2 vols. of scripture studies, 1850. 4. 'Book of British Poesy,' 1851. 5. 'Bards of the Bible,' 1851; 6th edition 1874. 6. 'Martyrs and Heroes of the Scottish Covenant,' 1852. 7. 'The Fatherhood of God,' 1854. 8. 'Life of Robert Burns,' 1856 and 1879. 9. 'History of a Man ; a semi-autobiographical Romance,' 1856. 10. 'Christianity and our Era,' 1857. 11. 'Remoter Stars in the Church Sky' (short memoirs of preachers, among whom is his father, Samuel Gilfillan), 1867. 12. 'Modern Christian Heroes, including Milton, Cromwell, and the Puritans,' 1869. 13. 'Life of Sir Walter Scott,' 1870 and 1871. 14. 'Comrie and its Neighbourhood,' 1872. 15. 'Life of the Rev. William Anderson of Glasgow,' 1873. 16. 'Edinburgh, Past and Present.' His only poem of importance was the volume entitled 'Night ; a Poem,' 1867, which found favour among his friends. His editions with lives of the poets in James Nicol's series appeared at Edinburgh between 1853 and 1860. Among his published lectures were the 'Christian Bearings of Astronomy,' 1848; the 'Connection between Science, Literature, and Religion,' 1849 ; 'The Influence of Burns on Scottish Poetry and Song,'1855; an introduction (and probably much more) to 'The Age of Lead, a Satire by A. Pasquin,' 1858 ; 'The Apocalypse of Jesus Christ,' 1851; 'Christian Missions,' 1857; and 'The Life and Works of David Vedder,' 1878. He had completed the literary portion of a new 'Life of Burns' shortly before his death. At that time he was engaged on a 'History of British Poetry,' and on a memoir, intended to be his *magnum opus*, 'Reconciliation, a Life History,' a sequel to his 'History of a Man.' Selections from the critical and reflective, but not from the narrative, portions of this unpublished manuscript, were posthumously issued at Edinburgh, 1881, inadequately edited by Frank Henderson, M.P., under the title 'Sketches, Literary and Theological.'

On 25 March 1878 there was signed the deed of investment of the 1,000*l*. 'Gilfillan Testimonial Trust,' the proceeds of a public subscription raised in Gilfillan's honour in 1877. After the death of his wife Margaret the money was to be devoted to founding Gilfillan scholarships for the deserving youth of either sex.

[Personal knowledge of many years; obituary notices in the Scotsman and Dundee newspapers, and his own works as enumerated above.]

J. W. E.

GILFILLAN, JAMES, D.D. (1797–1874), Scotch divine, son of the Rev. Samuel Gilfillan [q.v.], a rather notable minister of the secession body, and brother of the Rev. George Gilfillan [q. v.], was born at Comrie, Perthshire, on 11 May 1797, and, having received his early education at a school in his native village, entered Glasgow College in 1808, when only eleven and a half years old. After spending six sessions there he entered the divinity hall of the antiburgher synod in Edinburgh, and in 1821 was licensed by the Edinburgh presbytery of the united secession church. He was ordained on 24 Dec. 1822 in Stirling secession congregation. He was an excellent preacher of the old type, but is best known as author of 'The Sabbath, viewed in the light of Reason, Revelation, and History,' which was published in 1861, and rapidly gained favour. He had it in hand for twenty years, and expended on it an enormous amount of labour. In 1866 the university of Glasgow conferred on him the degree of D.D. In 1869 he demitted the charge of his congregation, and went to reside at Portobello, near Edinburgh, where he died on 28 Jan. 1874.

[Obituary notices; United Presbyterian Magazine, September 1874.]   T. H.

GILFILLAN, ROBERT (1798–1850), Scotch poet, was born 7 July 1798 at Dunfermline, and was the son of a master weaver. In 1811, on the removal of the family to Leith, Gilfillan was there apprenticed to a cooper, whom he served, with a somewhat languid interest, for seven years. For three years after 1818 he was a grocer's shopman in Dunfermline, mingling freely with contemporaries interested like himself in literature, and receiving generous appreciation of his growing poetical gift. This time he considered the happiest part of his life. Returning to Leith he was successively clerk to a firm of oil and colour merchants, confidential clerk to a wine merchant, and collector of police rates. This last post he held from 1837 till his death, 4 Dec. 1850. During the same period he was grand bard to the grand lodge of freemasons in Scotland, being in this respect a successor of Burns. Gilfillan never married, and a niece reared under his care kept house for him in his latter years.

Beginning his poetical career in local newspapers while still an apprentice, Gilfillan speedily came to be recognised as a genuine Scottish singer. Favourable references to him in the 'Noctes Ambrosianæ,' and especially to his 'Peter M'Craw,' a clever humorous satire of 1828, induced him to publish, and he issued a small volume of 'Original Songs' in 1831. Two other enlarged editions appeared in his lifetime, and several of his best songs were aptly set to music by Peter M'Leod. Gilfillan contributed in his later years to the 'Dublin University Magazine' and the 'Scotsman,' and also to the Scottish anthology, 'Whistle-Binkie.' After his death a collective edition of his works (1851), with a prefatory biography, was prepared by William Anderson (1805–1866) [q. v.] Besides 'Peter M'Craw,' Gilfillan's best songs are his touching 'Fare thee well' and his plaintive and melodious emigrant's song, 'Why left I my Hame?' which instantly won and retained a wide popularity.

[Anderson's Scottish Nation, and edition of Gilfillan's Poems; Whistle-Binkie; Wilson's Poets and Poetry of Scotland.]   T. B.

GILFILLAN, SAMUEL (1762–1826), secession minister, son of a merchant in the village of Bucklyvie, Stirlingshire, was born there on 24 Nov. 1762. He was the youngest of a family of fifteen children. In his early years he displayed great fondness for reading, and the habit was encouraged by his mother, with a view to his entering upon the work of the ministry. In November 1782 he went to the university of Glasgow, passed through the arts course, and afterwards studied theology under Professors William Moncrieff of Alloa and Archibald Bruce of Whitburn, of the antiburgher secession church. During his period of study Gilfillan maintained himself principally by teaching. He was licensed to preach by the associate presbytery of Perth in June 1789, and shortly afterwards received calls from the congregations at Barry in Forfarshire, and Auchtergaven and Comrie in Perthshire. The synod sent him to Comrie, a small village in the upper part of Strathearn, and he was ordained on 12 April 1791.

In July 1793 he married Rachel, eldest daughter of the Rev. James Barlas of the adjacent parish of Crieff, known for her beauty and other charms as 'the star of the north.' Gilfillan himself was a handsome man of stately bearing. His income was at first 50l. a year, and his congregation numbered only sixty-five members. Within a few years his popularity doubled that number, but his stipend never reached 100l. The Gilfillans managed on this to bring up a large family and educate three sons for the ministry. Gilfillan preached with much success both in Gaelic and English. His son says that he had 'little logical faculty,' but a powerful memory, a lively fancy, and a power of moving the hearts of his hearers. He was a strict Calvinist.

His published writings, most of which had been used as sermons, include numerous articles contributed to the 'Christian Magazine,' a periodical conducted by ministers of his church, which, says Hugh Miller, 'was not one of the brightest of periodicals, but a sound and solid one' (*My Schools and Schoolmasters*, p. 543). His articles were signed 'Leumas' (Samuel reversed). A number of these were included in 1822 in a volume of 'Short Discourses on various important subjects for the use of families.' His 'Essay on the Sanctification of the Lord's Day,' published in 1804, passed through ten English editions, and was translated into various foreign languages. Another small treatise on 'Domestic Piety' was published in 1819, and an enlarged edition in 1825. Two essays on 'Hypocrisy' and 'Meditation,' and a small 'Manual of Baptism,' were also published in 1825. In 1826 was issued what has been considered his best work, 'Discourses on the dignity, grace, and operations of the Holy Spirit;' and he was occupied preparing his 'Treatise on Relative Duties' for the press when he died. He also contributed some articles to the columns of 'The Student,' a Glasgow University periodical, in 1817. A posthumous work giving a collection of his letters, chiefly to afflicted persons, to which a memoir was prefixed, was published in 1828 by his eldest son, the Rev. Dr. James Gilfillan [q. v.] of Stirling, himself the author of a work on 'The Sanctification of the Sabbath.'

Along with several other ministers of the same church Gilfillan in 1819 planned and put in execution a scheme for the erection of lending libraries in the highlands, to consist principally of religious books. Of such libraries fourteen were actually set in operation with good results. Gilfillan died on 15 Oct. 1826, from an inflammation produced by eating sloes. He was buried close beside the river Earn four days later. He was survived by his widow and eight out of twelve children. Two sons, James and George, are separately noticed.

[Memoir by the Rev. Dr. James Gilfillan (see above); the Rev. George Gilfillan's Remoter Stars in the Church Sky, 1867, p. 26; Christian Magazine, 1797–1820.] H. P.

GILL, ALEXANDER, the elder (1565–1635), high-master of St. Paul's School, born in Lincolnshire 7 Feb. 1564–5, was admitted scholar of Corpus Christi College, Oxford, in September 1583, and proceeded B.A. 1586 and M.A. 1589. Wood believed that he was a schoolmaster at Norwich, where he was living in 1597. On 10 March 1607–8 he was appointed high-master of St. Paul's School in succession to Richard Mulcaster [q. v.] Milton was among his pupils from 1620 to 1625. 'He had,' says Wood, 'such an excellent way of training up youth that none in his time went beyond him; whence 'twas that many noted persons in church and state did esteem it the greatest of their happiness that they had been educated under him.' The escapade of his son [see GILL, ALEXANDER, the younger] in 1628 caused him much disquietude, and he successfully exerted himself—supplicating 'on his knees,' says Aubrey —to obtain at the hands of Laud, with whom he was on friendly terms, a remission of the punishment inflicted by the Star-chamber. He died at his house in St. Paul's Church-

yard 17 Nov. 1635, and was buried 20 Nov. in Mercers' Chapel. A transcript of his will, dated 30 July 1634, is among Wood's MSS. (D 11) at the Bodleian Library. His widow Elizabeth received a pension from the Mercers' Company till 1648. He had two sons, Alexander [q. v.] and George, who was in holy orders (cf. MASSON, i. 211). A daughter, Annah Banister, received grants from the Mercers' Company in 1666 and (as a widow) in 1673.

Gill was not only famous as a schoolmaster, but 'was esteemed by most persons to be a learned man, a noted Latinist, critic, and divine.' He published: 1. 'A Treatise concerning the Trinitie of Persons in Unitie of the Deitie' (written at Norwich in 1597), London, 1601, 8vo; reprinted with 3 (see below), 1635. This was a remonstrance addressed to Thomas Mannering, an anabaptist, who 'denied that Jesus is very God of very God,' and said that 'he was but man only, yet endued with the infinite power of God.' 2. 'Logonomia Anglica, qua gentis sermo facilius addiscitur,' London, by John Beale, 1619, 2nd edit. 1621; dedicated to James I. Gill's book, written in Latin, opens with suggestions for a phonetic system of English spelling by reviving the Anglo-Saxon signs for the two sounds of *th* and similar means. In his section on grammatical and rhetorical figures Gill quotes freely from Spenser, Wither, Daniel, and other English poets, with whose works he shows an intimate acquaintance. For Spenser he had a special affection, preferring him to Homer (pp. 124–5); nearly all his examples were taken from the 'Faerie Queen.' 3. 'Sacred Philosophie of the Holy Scripture,' London, 1635, 8vo, a commentary on the Apostles' Creed, with a reprint of 1—an attempted demonstration of the truth of the Apostles' Creed in opposition to the beliefs of Turks, Jews, and other heretics.

[Wood's Athenæ Oxon. ed. Bliss, ii. 597–600; Gardiner's Reg. St. Paul's School, p. 32; Masson's Life of Milton, i. 78–82; Aubrey's Lives, ii. 286.] S. L.

GILL, ALEXANDER, the younger (1597–1642), high-master of St. Paul's School, son of Alexander Gill the elder [q. v.], was born, probably at Norwich, in 1597. He obtained a scholarship at St. Paul's School, London, of which his father became high-master in 1608; matriculated from Trinity College, Oxford, 26 June 1612; became an exhibitioner of Wadham College in 1612, and bible-clerk there 20 April 1613; proceeded B.A. 1616, and M.A. 1619. He afterwards returned to Trinity, where he took the degrees of B.D. (27 June 1627) and D.D.

(9 March 1636-7) (*Oxf. Univ. Reg.*, Oxford Hist. Soc. II. ii. 326, iii. 344). Gill was of very unruly disposition, and was, according to the pamphleteers of the day, on bad terms with the university authorities; but he displayed much skill as a writer of Latin and Greek verse. As early as 1612 he published a Latin threnody on the death of Prince Henry. At Michaelmas 1621 he was appointed under-usher of St. Paul's School. Milton was among his pupils; a close intimacy sprang up between them, and many of Milton's Latin letters to Gill are preserved. On 20 May 1628 the poet writes in extravagant terms of Gill's Latin verses. On 2 July following he sent Gill some of his own Latin verses for him to criticise and correct. On 4 Dec. 1634 Milton again thanks Gill for a gift of Latin verses. Meanwhile Gill had fallen into serious trouble, and lost his post at St. Paul's School. He was visiting his friends at Trinity College, Oxford, about Michaelmas 1628, when he drank a health to Felton, Buckingham's assassin, and made some disrespectful remarks about the king. William Chillingworth [q. v.], with whom, according to Aubrey, Gill was in the habit of corresponding, was of this party, and deemed it fitting to inform Laud of what had passed. Gill was committed to the Gatehouse at Westminster (4 Sept.) by Laud's orders, and was examined in the Star-chamber by Laud and Attorney-general Heath on 6 Sept. Laud's report of the proceedings sent to the king appears in his correspondence (*Anglo-Cath. Libr.* vii. 16-18). A search at Oxford in the rooms of William Pickering of Trinity College, an intimate friend of Gill, disclosed letters and verses by him (some dated in 1626), abusing Buckingham and Charles I. Gill admitted his guilt, and was sentenced (1 Nov.) to degradation from the ministry, to a fine of 2,000*l.*, and to the loss of both ears (one to be removed at Oxford, and the other in London). Gill's father immediately petitioned for a remission of the sentence, and Edward, earl of Dorset, supported the appeal (AUBREY). Laud, a friend of the elder Gill, consented to mitigate the fine, and to forego the corporal punishment. On 30 Nov. 1630 a free pardon was signed by Charles I. Gill, now dismissed from his ushership, received small gratuities from the governors of St. Paul's School in 1631, 1633, and 1634. He tried to retrieve his reputation by publishing in 1632 a little volume of collected Latin verse, entitled 'Πάρεργα sive Poetici Conatus,' containing a fulsome dedication to the king and a profoundly respectful poem to Laud, dated 1 Jan. 1631-2, besides much verse to other royal or noble personages, and odes on the successes of Gustavus Adolphus in Germany.

According to Wood, Gill obtained temporary employment at the school of Thomas Farnaby [q. v.] in Cripplegate. On 18 Nov. 1635, the day following his father's death, he was elected his father's successor in the highmastership of St. Paul's School. In 1639 complaints were made of his excessive severity towards a boy named Bennett, and at the end of the year he was dismissed. In the school accounts there is an entry of 13*l.* 7*s.* 11*d.* as 'charges for displacing Dr. Gill,' which implies some resistance on his part. On 28 Jan. 1639 Gill appealed to the king to reverse the decision on the ground that it was based on 'the unjust complaint of a lying, thieving boy' (*Cal. State Papers,* Dom. 1639-40, p. 389). The king referred the petition to Archbishop Laud and 'some other lords.' The Mercers' Company, the governing body of the school, insisted on their right to deal with Gill as they pleased. Laud argued that Gill could not be removed, according to canon law, without his ordinary's knowledge (LAUD, *Works*, iv. 80-1). But the company gained the day, and Laud's remarks about the canon law formed the subject of the tenth charge brought against him at his trial. Two coarse doggerel poems, headed respectively 'On Doctor Gill, master of St. Paul's School,' and 'Gill upon Gill . . . uncas'd, unstript, and unbound,' dwelt on Gill's whipping propensities and savage temper. They were first issued with the 'Loves of Hero and Leander,' London, 1651, and reappear in 'The Rump,' 1660. Aubrey writes that Dr. Gill had 'his moods and humours as particularly his whipping fits.' During his last year at the school Gill was refused the usual extra payments and gratuities allowed by the Mercers' Company to the high-master of St. Paul's. On 22 Feb. 1639-1640 a pension of 25*l.* was granted him, and 50*l.* was given him later in discharge of his claims. He died at the close of 1642, having 'taught certain youths privately in Aldergate Street, London, to the time of his death' (WOOD). He was buried in the church of St. Botolph without Aldersgate.

Besides the works noted above, Gill printed 'Arithmeticorum 'Ανάμνησις' at the end of N. Simpson's 'Arithmeticæ Compendium,' 1623; 'Panthea. In honorem illustriss. spectatiss. omnibus Animi Corporisque Dotibus instructiss. Heroinæ, qua mihi in Terris,' &c., 4to (WOOD); 'A Song of Victory upon the Proceedings and Success of the Wars undertaken by the most puissant King of Sweden,' in English verse, London, 1632, 4to (WOOD). Gill's ''Επίνικιον,' a poem on

Gustavus Adolphus's victories, dated 1631, of which a manuscript copy is among the Tanner MSS. (306) at the Bodleian Library, was reprinted separately from the 'Πάρεργα,' according to Wood, and also at the close of 'A New Starr of the North,' London, 1632. A Latin congratulatory poem on Charles I'sreturn from Scotland, by Gill, was printed by John Waterson in 1641 (four leaves). A copy is at Lambeth (44, E. 1). Wood further credits Gill with an elegy on Strafford in 1641, and describes a manuscript book, which 'I have also seen,' containing other Latin verses (fifteen poems in all), some addressed to friends, and some descriptive of Gustavus Adolphus's victories. This book does not now seem extant, but its contents are partly represented in manuscript pieces in Corpus Christi College, Oxford, in the Bodleian Library (Tanner MS. 306), and in the British Museum (Burney MS. 368, f. 16). Nine of the pieces mentioned by Wood are also extant with twelve others by Gill ('Epithalamia,' an interchange of complimentary verse with Isaac Oliver, verses to Bacon, &c., besides five letters to Laud) in a manuscript volume belonging to Thomas Frewen, esq., of Brickwall Hall, Northiam, Sussex. The volume belonged to Charles Blake, D.D. [q. v.], and was intended for the press (cf. *Gent. Mag.* 1851, i. 345–7).

Gill and Ben Jonson had a long-standing feud, which began as early as 1623, in consequence of the elder Gill's patronage of Wither's satires. In the Ashmolean MSS. at the Bodleian Library are some abusive but interesting English verses by Gill on Ben Jonson's 'Magnetick Lady,' which Dr. Bliss printed in his edition of Wood's 'Athenæ' (ii. 598–599) under the error (afterwards corrected) that they were by the elder Gill. Zouch Townley defended Jonson from Gill's illiberal attack in a short poem (*ib.*)

[Masson's Life of Milton, i. 83, 190, 193, 207–213, 510, 528, 623; Coxe's Cat. MSS. at Oxford; Wood's Athenæ Oxon. ed. Bliss, iii. 42–4; Gardiner's Reg. St. Paul's School, pp. 32, 38, 400; Aubrey's Lives, ii. 286–7.]   S. L.

GILL, JOHN, D.D. (1697–1771), baptist minister, was born of poor parents at Kettering, Northamptonshire, on 23 Nov. 1697. He spent a very short time at Kettering grammar school. In November 1716 he was baptised, and shortly after began preaching. In 1718 he was ordained at Higham Ferrers, Northamptonshire. In 1719 he removed to the baptist congregation at Horselydown, Southwark, which in 1757 was removed to a chapel near London Bridge. A Wednesday evening lectureship was founded for him in Great Eastcheap by his admirers in 1729,

and this he held till 1756. In 1748 he was created D.D. at Aberdeen. He died at Camberwell, 14 Oct. 1771.

Gill's principal works were: 1. 'Exposition of the Song of Solomon, 1728. 2. 'The Prophecies of the Old Testament respecting the Messiah considered,' 1728, written in answer to Collins. 3. 'Treatise on the Doctrine of the Trinity,' designed to check the spread of Sabellianism among the baptists, 1731. 4. 'The Cause of God and Truth,' in answer to Whitby's discourse on the five points, 4 vols. 1735–8. 5. 'Exposition of the Holy Scriptures,' his *magnum opus*, in which he utilises his extensive rabbinical learning. The New Testament portion appeared in 3 vols. folio in 1746–8; the Old Testament, in 6 vols. folio, was completed in 1766. 6. 'Dissertation on the Antiquity of the Hebrew Language, Letters, Vowel Points, and Accents,' 1767. 7. 'A Body of Doctrinal Divinity,' 1767. 8. 'A Body of Practical Divinity,' 1770. 9. A collection of sermons and tracts, with memoir, 1773, 3 vols. 4to.

[Memoir by Dr. Rippon, 1816.]   T. H.

GILL, WILLIAM JOHN (1843–1882), captain royal engineers, son of Major Robert Gill, Madras army, was born at Bangalore in 1843. He was educated at Brighton College, where one of his contemporaries was Augustus Margary, his precursor in travel from China to the Irawadi. From Brighton he went to the Royal Military Academy at Woolwich, and obtained a commission in the royal engineers in 1864. In September 1869 he went to India and served there till March 1871. Just before his return to England a distant relation left Gill a handsome fortune, which enabled him to gratify his desire for exploration. On his return from India he was stationed until 1876 at Aldershot, Chatham, and Woolwich.

He first became known as a traveller when he joined Colonel Valentine Baker in the journey to Persia, of which an account was published by Baker early in 1876, under the title of 'Clouds in the East.' The journey occupied from April 1873 to the end of that year. The party travelled to Tiflis and Baku, and thence across the Caspian to Ashurada and Astrabad, intending to explore the Atrek valley. Disappointed in this, they proceeded to Teheran and wandered among the Elburz mountains north of that city, crossing the range by a pass 12,000 feet in height, in search of ibex and mouflon. Then skirting the great mountain Demavend they descended into the dense forests of Mazanderan, and, recrossing the mountains to Damghan, followed the northern border of the desert of Khorasan, and after visiting Meshhed struck north to Kila't, the famous stronghold of Nadir Shah. From this they passed on to the Darah-gaz district, and recrossing the great frontier range (Kurendagh) explored the upper course of the Atrek, and thence went south-west by Jahgirm to Shahrúd, and rejoined the high road from Meshhed to Teheran. The survey made by Gill under great difficulties in this expedition embraced valuable additions to geographical knowledge, and formed the subject of a paper read by him at the Belfast meeting of the British Association in 1874, and published in the 'Geographical Magazine.'

In 1874 Gill stood for Hackney in the conservative interest against Messrs. Reed and Holms, in which, although defeated, he polled 8,994 votes. Six years later he stood for Nottingham, but was again unsuccessful.

In 1876 Gill was ordered to Hongkong, and, while quartered there, he obtained leave to travel in China. He reached Pekin in September. After a trip in the north of Pechili to the borders of Liaotung and the sea terminus of the great wall, he ascended the Yang-tse as far as Chung-Ching in Szechuen, with Mr. Evelyn Colborne Baber for a companion. From Chung-Ching he travelled to Cheng-tu-fu, the famous capital of Szechuen. Here he was delayed, and utilised his time in an excursion to the alps in the north of Szechuen, the 'Min mountains' of the ancient Yü-Kung, from which the great Kiang of the Chinese flows down into Szechuen. No traveller had preceded Gill in that part of China. The journey, which formed a loop of some four hundred miles and occupied a month or more, brought the traveller for the first time into partial contact with those highland races whom the Chinese call Mantzu and Sifan. On his return to Cheng-tu, Gill started with Mr. Mesny, who had joined him there, for Eastern Tibet and the Irawadi. His first place of halt was Tachienlu (8,340 ft.), whence he mounted at once to the summit level of the great Tibetan tableland, continuing his journey by Lit'ang (13,280 ft.) to Bat'ang (8,546 ft.) in a tributary valley of the great Kinsha, and then crossing that river he turned south, travelling parallel to the river for twenty-four marches on his way to Talifu, the western capital of Yunnan. Here the most laborious part of his task was done, as the route thence to the Irawadi had been already surveyed by Mr. Baker after the murder of Margary. Having descended the Irawadi, Gill went to Calcutta and back to England, after twenty months of travel. The story of this journey was eventually (1880)

published in two volumes under the title of 'The River of Golden Sand,' but the scientific results were embodied in an elaborate memoir contributed to the 'Journal of the Royal Geographical Society,' and in a map of forty-two sheets on a scale of two miles to one inch. The merits of his enterprise and record of his travel secured in 1879 the gold medal of the Royal Geographical Society, and in the following year that of the Paris Geographical Society.

On his return home he was appointed to the intelligence branch of the war office. When the negotiations at St. Stefano were going on, Gill started with a friend, rather suddenly, for the Danube, to visit the scenes of recent war, but they were prevented from getting beyond Giurgevo by Russian officials, whom they ridiculed in 'Vanity Fair' (see 'Arrested by the Russians,' June 8, 12, 15, 1878). In the spring of 1879 Gill was sent to Constantinople on duty, in association with Major Clarke, R.A., as assistant boundary commissioner for the new Asiatic boundary between Turkey and Russia, consequent on the Berlin treaty. In the summer of 1880, when the news of the defeat of Maiwand reached England, Captain Gill obtained leave and hurried to the scene, but he did not reach Quetta until Roberts had relieved Kandahar. He was allowed to join Sir C. Macgregor, as a survey officer, in his expedition against the Maris, and was mentioned in despatches. On the termination of the expedition Gill embarked at Karachi for Bandar Abbás, and travelled by Sirgán, Kermán, Yezd, and Teheran, to Meshhed. He hoped to get to Merv, but complaints from M. de Giers of English officers haunting the frontier brought about a recall, and he returned to England by Russia, reaching London 1 April 1881.

In October of the same year the transactions of the French at Tunis had drawn Gill's attention to North Africa, and he obtained leave of absence with the view of obtaining detailed knowledge of the provinces between Tunis and Egypt. At Malta he engaged a dragoman, a Syrian from Beyrout, by name Khalil-Atik, who won his master's regard, rejoined him on the last fatal expedition, and perished with him. Gill went to Tripoli, where he was detained for some months, waiting for a permit to travel from Constantinople, which never came. But Gill dispensed with it, and several interesting journeys were accomplished and a large mass of information collected. His first journey was parallel to the coast westward to Zuara and Farwa, a second to Nalut in the hill country W.S.W. of Tripoli and thence eastward to Yifrin, and then N. by F. to Tripoli; lastly from Tripoli

S. into the hill country by Wádi Mijinin, then E. to Homs upon the coast, and back along the coast by Lebda to the capital. From Tripoli he went to Benghazi, and hoped to travel through the Cyrenaica to Egypt, but, stopped by the Turkish authorities, he returned to England viâ Constantinople, arriving in London on 16 June 1882.

On the 21st of the following month he started on his last expedition. He went to Egypt on special service with the rank of deputy-assistant adjutant-general. During the short time he was at home he had been employed in collecting information for the admiralty regarding the Bedouin tribes adjoining the Suez Canal, and in arranging with Professor Palmer for the despatch of the latter to the desert. On the outbreak of hostilities Gill was directed to join Admiral Hoskins at Port Said, as an officer of the intelligence department. The task of cutting the telegraph wire from Cairo, which crossed the desert to El Arish and Syria and so to Constantinople, by which Arabi obtained information and support from Constantinople, devolved upon Gill. He went to Suez (6 Aug.), where he met Professor Palmer and Lieutenant Charrington (the flag-lieutenant of the admiral commanding), and they went together into the desert, Palmer and Charrington to proceed to Nakhl to meet a sheikh from whom they were to purchase camels, and Gill accompanying them with the view of cutting the telegraph. Professor Palmer, who had with him 3,000l. in English sovereigns, had engaged the services of Meter Abu Sofieh, who had falsely represented himself as a head sheikh, to conduct them. The fact that the party had money was known not only to Meter but to others, and there can be no doubt that Meter deliberately plotted to rob if not to murder them. On their arrival in Wady Sudr they were attacked by Bedouins, made prisoners, and murdered in cold blood the next day, 11 Aug. The knowledge of what took place after they entered the desert, the punishment of the murderers, and the recovery of the fragmentary remains of the murdered men were due to Colonel Sir Charles Warren, R.E., who, accompanied by Lieutenants A. E. Haynes and E. M. Burton, R.E., were sent out by the government on a special mission for this purpose. The remains were sent to England and solemnly laid to rest in the crypt of St. Paul's Cathedral at a special funeral service on 6 April 1883. A stained glass window has been placed in Rochester Cathedral to the memory of Captain Gill by his brother officers of the corps of royal engineers.

[Corps Records; R. Eng. Journ. vol. xii.; Parl. Blue-book C. 3494, 1883.] R. H. V.

GILLAN, ROBERT (1800–1879), Scotch divine, was born at Hawick, Roxburghshire, in 1800. His father, the Rev. Robert Gillan, son of another minister of the same name, was appointed minister of Ettrick, 11 May 1787, and transferred to Hawick 30 Dec. 1789. He retired from the ministry of his church 7 May 1800, and died at Edinburgh 7 May 1824, aged 63, having married, 4 April 1798, Marion, daughter of the Rev. William Campbell. He was the author of 'An Account of the Parish of Hawick' in Sir John Sinclair's 'Statistical Account of Scotland,' 1791, vol. viii.; 'Abridgments of the Acts of the General Assemblies of the Church of Scotland,' 1803, other editions in 1811 and 1821; 'View of Modern Astronomy, Geography, &c.;' 'A Compendium of Ancient and Modern Geography,' 1823; and he edited 'The Scottish Pulpit, a Collection of Sermons,' 1823. Robert Gillan, the third of that name, studied at the high school and university of Edinburgh, where he was early noted for his extensive scholarship and impressive oratory. On 7 July 1829 he was licensed to preach the gospel by the presbytery of Selkirk, and ordained minister to the congregation at Stamfordham, Northumberland, in October 1830. He removed to the church at South Shields in October 1833, succeeding to Holytown, Lanarkshire, in 1837, where he continued to 1842. After being at Wishaw in the same county for six months, he accepted the parish of Abbotshall, Fifeshire, on the secession of the non-intrusion ministers in May 1843, and from that place was brought to St. John's, Glasgow, on 25 Feb. 1847. Here he remained during a long period, became very popular, and preached to large congregations. He took an active interest in all religious or social movements, and was an early opponent of the law of patronage. The university of Glasgow conferred on him the degree of D.D. in 1853. The incessant activity of the Glasgow charge at length told on his health, and on 10 Jan. 1861 he accepted charge of the small church of Inchinnan, Renfrewshire. He was, however, still able to work, and being appointed one of the first two lecturers on pastoral theology, he prepared an admirable course of lectures, which were on two separate occasions delivered at the four Scottish universities. On 11 Oct. 1870 he was publicly entertained in Glasgow, and presented with his portrait. He was devotedly attached to the established church of Scotland, and as moderator presided over the general assembly of 1873. He died at the manse, Inchinnan, 1 Nov. 1879. His wife died 23 Jan. 1847. By her he had a son, the Rev. George Green Gillan, a chaplain in the

H.E.I. Co.'s service. Gillan was the author of: 1. 'A General Fast Sermon,' 1832. 2. 'The Intellectual and Spiritual Progress of the Christian in the Church of Scotland Pulpit,' 1845, ii. 13–31. 3. 'Sermons at Glasgow,' 1855. 4. 'The Decalogue, a Series of Discourses on the Ten Commandments,' 1856.

[Hew Scott's Fasti Ecclesiæ Scoticanæ (1867), i. pt. ii. 489, 548, ii. pt. ii. 269; John Smith's Our Scottish Clergy (1848), pp. 182–8; Church of Scotland Home and Foreign Missionary Record, 1 Dec. 1879, pp. 549–50; Irving's Book of Scotsmen (1881), p. 162.] G. C. B.

GILLE or GILLEBERT (*fl.* 1105–1145), bishop of Limerick, termed by Keating GIOLLA EASBOG, was consecrated in Ireland, but it is uncertain whether he was an Irishman or a Dane, Limerick being then a Danish city. If he were abbot of Bangor, as Lanigan thought, he would probably have been an Irishman, but Keating, to whom Lanigan refers, does not say so. He had travelled abroad, and became acquainted with Anselm at Rouen. Their friendship continued, and on his appointment to Limerick he appears to have written of it to Anselm. A correspondence followed, which may be seen in Ussher's 'Sylloge.' In his letters Anselm urged Gille to use all his influence to abolish certain ecclesiastical usages which prevailed in Ireland, referring among other things to the appointment of bishops 'contrary to the order of ecclesiastical religion,' and to consecration by a single bishop, and in places where bishops ought not to be. For these he wished, as Lanigan observes, to substitute the Roman usages. In compliance with Anselm's advice, Gillebert first attempted to introduce the Roman liturgy instead of the various liturgies in use from time immemorial in Ireland, and which he calls 'schismatical,' an expression which, as Lanigan says, only showed his ignorance. In pursuance of this design he wrote a tract entitled 'Of the Ecclesiastical Use' (or order of divine service). This, which appears to have been merely a copy of the Roman liturgy and office, has not come down to us, though the treatise on 'Church Organisation' which he prefixed is extant, and has been published by Ussher. In the latter he describes the hierarchy of the Roman church, and illustrates the gradations of dignity by a comparison with the corresponding secular ranks. The ascending series terminates with the pope, whose correlative is the emperor of Rome; but as the Irish had nothing to do with the empire the foreign character of the system was apparent. This treatise appears to have been written before he became legate, but the date of his appointment to that office is not known.

A further step towards the introduction of the Roman system was the holding of the council of Rathbreasail, in which it was proposed to divide Ireland into twenty-six dioceses, the boundaries of which were set out in full detail. There has been much discussion as to the identity of this synod, which is not mentioned in the 'Annals,' and is only found in Keating, who took it from the lost 'Book of Clonenagh.' Mr. King thought it was the same as the synod of Fiadh mic Aenghusa, but they are expressly distinguished by Keating, though he allows that they were held about the same time, i.e. about 1111; and Mr. King was in error as to the situation of Fiadh mic Aenghusa, which, according to the 'Annals of Lough Cé,' was near Uisnech in West Meath. Another synod in this latter place was also supposed by Colgan to have been identical with that of Fiadh mic Aenghusa, and thus there would have been only a single synod. There is no doubt, however, that there were really three, held about the same time. That of Uisnech was a mere assembly of the local clergy to rearrange the parishes of West Meath. The synod of Fiadh mic Aenghusa was an important one, at which King Muircheartach was present and a large number of bishops, clergy, and laity. But the synod of Rathbreasail (at Mountrath in Queen's County) was an ecclesiastical assembly at which no layman of importance was present, and the president of which was Gillebert, the other names mentioned being Ceallach or Celsus, the primate, and Maelisa mac Ainmire, termed by Keating 'noble bishop of Cashel,' but in the 'Annals of the Four Masters' bishop of Waterford. There were therefore present the bishops of two Danish cities with Celsus, a favourer of the new ideas, who thus combined to revolutionise the constitution of the Irish church. But no immediate result followed. It was merely an arrangement on paper, and Gillebert was as unsuccessful in this as in his attempt to supersede the Irish liturgies. In both cases the current of national feeling was against him. This synod is remarkable as the first over which a papal legate presided, Gillebert having been the first holder of the office, and also as the first Irish synod which closed its proceedings in Roman fashion with an anathema.

Gillebert died, according to the 'Chronicon Scotorum,' in 1145.

[Lanigan's Eccl. Hist. iv. 37–43; King's Primacy of Armagh, pp. 30, 81–5; Ussher's Sylloge (Works, iv. 500–14); Keating's Forus Feasa, Reign of Muircheartach; Reeves's Eccl. Antiq. pp. 139–41, 162; Annals of Four Masters, A.D. 1111; Chron. Scot. A.D. 1107–45.] T. O.

GILLESPIE, GEORGE (1613–1648), Scottish divine, second son of John Gillespie (d. 12 Aug. 1627), minister of Kirkcaldy, Fifeshire, and Lilias, daughter of Patrick Simson, minister of Stirling, was born at Kirkcaldy on 21 Jan. 1613. His father was a 'thundering preacher;' the eldest son was Captain John Gillespie; a younger son was Patrick Gillespie, principal of Glasgow University [q. v.] George went to St. Andrews University at a very early age, if it be true that he graduated A.M. in 1629 (SCOTT). More probably he entered in that year. In November 1629 the session records of Kirkcaldy state that he held a bursary of twenty merks from the presbytery. Leaving the university he became chaplain to John Gordon, first viscount Kenmure [q. v.], on whose death (September 1634) he became chaplain to John Kennedy, earl of Cassilis, and tutor to his son, Lord Kennedy. In 1637, in the midst of the excitement which attended the 'Jenny Geddes' episode (23 July), the young tutor published his 'Dispute against the English Popish Ceremonies obtruded upon the Church of Scotland.' It was anonymous, and is supposed to have been printed in Holland. The Scottish privy council on 16 Oct. ordered all copies of it to be collected and burned, a measure which simply served to call attention to it.

On a supplication from the parish of Wemyss, Fifeshire, Gillespie was presented to this charge by the town council of Edinburgh on 5 Jan. 1638. The preliminaries to his ordination were taken on the motion of the archbishop (Spotiswood); but meantime all the members of the presbytery of Kirkcaldy, except three, subscribed the 'national covenant' of 28 Feb. They ordained Gillespie on 26 April, Robert Douglas [q. v.] presiding, this being the second instance of a non-episcopal ordination since the revival of the hierarchy. On the presentation of Lord Elcho he was instituted (8 Nov.) to the parsonage of Methill, Fifeshire, a quoad sacra parish (now in the parish of Wemyss). He preached before the general assembly which opened at Glasgow on 21 Nov., and was memorable for its deposition of the bishops. His discourse from Proverbs xxi. 1 was criticised by the Earl of Argyll as inimical to the king's prerogative. By this time his authorship of the 'Dispute' had become well known, and his remarkable powers in debate were making his influence felt.

On 21 Aug. 1640 the covenanting army of Scotland invaded the English border. Gillespie was one of the army presbytery, and made his first visit to London with the Scottish commissioners for the treaty of peace, after the armistice agreed upon at Ripon on 26 Oct. Next year he was called to Aberdeen, but the assembly, on 2 Aug. 1641, at his earnest request forbade his removal. Overtures were also made for his settlement at St. Andrews. After the re-establishment of presbyterianism (26 Aug.), Gillespie preached before Charles at Holyrood (12 Sept.), and was one of the covenanting leaders on whom the king bestowed a pension (16 Nov.) The town council of Edinburgh had already (12 Oct.) presented him to the Greyfriars Church, Edinburgh; he was translated thither on 23 Sept. 1642.

In 1643 Gillespie was nominated one of the Scottish commissioners to the Westminster Assembly. He took his place in the assembly on 16 Sept., and on 25 Sept. joined in subscribing the new covenant ('solemn league and covenant' of 17 Aug.) He was the youngest member of the assembly, being now in his thirty-first year, but his prestige as a disputant has closely associated his name with the details of its systematising work. Robert Baillie, D.D. [q. v.], who calls him 'that brave youth,' writes in unreserved admiration of his logical powers and his pointed speech. Legend has not dealt very accurately with Gillespie's actual contributions to the labours of the assembly. His encounter with Selden, in the debate on church government, was not a 'single combat,' as has been represented. Selden spoke on 20 Feb. 1644, maintaining that Matthew xviii. 15–17 has no reference to ecclesiastical jurisdiction. Herle immediately followed with an able reply. Gillespie's speech, from carefully prepared notes, was not delivered till next day, and it was Thomas Young who then met Selden on grounds of scholarship. Gillespie's 'seven arguments' were well chosen, but it is incredible that Selden should have said, 'That young man, by this single speech, has swept away the learning and labour of ten years of my life.'

Gillespie's attendance at the assembly was first interrupted by the order which sent him to Edinburgh with Baillie, in January 1645, to introduce the directory to the general assembly, which opened on 22 Jan. He is said to have drawn the act of assembly sanctioning this form of worship. His return to London (9 April) was delayed a month, the ship in which he sailed being carried away to Holland. He assisted on the committee (appointed 12 May) for preparing the draft of a confession of faith. Professor Candlish successfully traces his hand in that section of chapter i. which deals with the internal evidence of the divine origin of holy scripture. On the final reading of the confession (4 Dec. 1646) he carried a technical alteration in the chapter on the civil magistrate. He took his last leave of the assembly on 16 July 1647. This disposes of the legend which connects him with the shorter catechism (not begun till 5 Aug.) Scott mentions the fable that Gillespie drew it up 'in the course of a single night.' More persistent is the story about the answer in that catechism to the question 'What is God?' which, according to one account, was taken from the opening words of a prayer by Gillespie. Pictorial shape was given to this version of the story, by Dean Stanley's order, in the decorations of the Jerusalem Chamber, Westminster Abbey. The larger catechism has a kindred answer, brought to its present shape by successive revisions, which were not concluded when Gillespie left London. He presented the confession of faith to the general assembly which opened at Edinburgh on 4 Aug. 1647, and obtained its ratification.

Gillespie was elected to the High Church of Edinburgh by the town council on 22 Sept. He was chosen moderator of the general assembly which met on 12 July 1648, and was appointed on the commission to conduct the treaty of uniformity in religion with England. His intellectual powers were at their height, for it was then that William, earl of Glencairn, declared 'there is no standing before this great and mighty man.' But his end was near. He fell into a rapid consumption. With a dying hand he wrote his tract against confederacies with 'malignants;' similar testimonies were embodied in his will, and dictated to an amanuensis when he could no longer hold a pen. In hope of recruiting his health he went with his wife to Kirkcaldy, and died there on 16 Dec. 1648. A Latin epitaph was placed on his tombstone at Kirkcaldy. By order of the committee of estates the stone was broken by the hangman at the cross of Kirkcaldy in January 1661. In 1746 the inscription was replaced by his grandson, George Gillespie, minister of Strathmiglo, Fifeshire. To his widow, Margaret Murray, a grant of 1,000*l.* sterling was voted by the committee of estates on 20 Dec. 1648; the grant was ratified by parliament on 8 June 1650, but owing to the invasion by Cromwell in that year it was never paid. He left three sons: (1) Robert, a covenanting minister, who suffered imprisonment on the Bass Rock, lived for some time in England, and was at Auchtermuchty, Fifeshire, in 1682; his widow and children were recommended by parliament to the royal bounty on 17 July 1695; (2) George; (3) Archibald, died 1659; and a daughter, Elizabeth, who married James Oswald, an Edinburgh merchant.

Excepting a posthumous treatise, all Gillespie's writings are of a controversial character. Such interest as they now possess is less due to the skill of his dialectic than to his elevation of tone and the genuineness of his religious nature. His early maturity and untimely death have invested his memory with much of its peculiar charm. His mind was not illiberal. While opposed to toleration, as tending to perpetuate division as well as error, he saw nothing impracticable in 'a mutual endeavour for a happy accommodation' (*Minutes*, p. 28). Speaking in favour of a catechism, he declares, 'it never entered into the thoughts of any to tie to the words and syllables' (*ib.* p. 93). The fame of his 'rugged name' is preserved in Milton's sonnet under the form 'Galasp.'

He published: 1. 'Dispute against the English Popish Ceremonies,' &c., 1637, 4to (anon.) 2. 'An Assertion of the Government of the Church of Scotland,' &c., 1641, 4to. 3. 'A Sermon . . . before the . . . House of Commons . . . March 27,' &c., 1644, 4to (Ezek. xliii. 11). 4. 'A Dialogue between a Civilian and a Divine, concerning . . . the Church of England,' &c., 1644, 4to (anon.) 5. 'A Recrimination . . . upon Mr. Goodwin, in Defence of Presbyterianism,' &c., 1644, 4to (anon.) 6. 'Wholesome Severity reconciled with Christian Liberty. Or, The true Resolution of a present Controversie concerning Liberty of Conscience,' &c., 1645, 4to (anon., often erroneously catalogued as two distinct works). 7. 'A Sermon . . . before the . . . House of Lords . . . August 27 [Mal. iii. 2] . . . added, A Brotherly Examination of . . . Mr. Coleman's Sermon,' &c., 1645, 4to. 8. 'Nihil Respondens,' &c., 1645, 4to (answer to 'A Brotherly Examination Reexamined' by Thomas Coleman [q. v.]) 9. 'Male Audis; or, An Answer to Mr. Coleman on his Male Dicis . . . with some Animadversions upon Master Hussey,' &c., 1646, 4to. 10. 'Aaron's Rod Blossoming: or, The Divine Ordinance of Church Government,' &c., 1646, 4to (dedicated to the Westminster Assembly). 11. 'One Hundred and Eleven Propositions concerning the Ministry and Government of the Church,' &c., Edinburgh, 1647, 4to. Posthumous were: 12. 'An usefull Case of Conscience . . . associations and confederacies with Idolaters, Infidels, Hereticks,' &c., 1649, 4to. 13. 'A Treatise of Miscellany Questions,' &c., 1649, 4to (published by his brother, Patrick Gillespie, deals *inter alia* with questions which came before the Westminster Assembly). 14. 'The Ark of the New Testament opened . . . by a Minister of the New Testament,' &c., 1661, 4to, 2nd pt. 1677, 4to (published by, and sometimes ascribed to, his brother Patrick).

15. 'Notes of Debates and Proceedings of the Assembly of Divines and other Commissioners at Westminster, from Feb. 1644 to Jan. 1645 . . . from unpublished manuscripts: edited by David Meek,' &c., Edinburgh, 1846, 8vo (Wodrow intimates, in 1707, that Gillespie wrote six volumes of notes; in 1722 he specifies twelve or fourteen volumes; only two are extant). The 'Works,' edited by Hetherington, were collected in two vols., Edinburgh, 1843–6, 8vo.

[Memoir by Hetherington prefixed to Works; Hew Scott's Fasti Eccles. Scotic.; Livingstone's Divine Providence exemplified, 1754; Wodrow's Analecta (1842) and History (1828); Howie's Biographia Scoticana (1781), edition of 1862 (Scots Worthies), p. 353 sq.; Grub's Eccl. Hist. of Scotland, 1861, vols. ii. and iii.; Anderson's Scottish Nation, 1870, ii. 301; Mitchell and Struthers's Minutes of Westm. Assembly, 1874; Mitchell's Westm. Assembly, 1883.] A. G.

GILLESPIE, JAMES (1726–1797), founder of a hospital at Edinburgh, was probably born at Roslin in 1726. He had one sister and a younger brother John, who was afterwards his partner in business. His parents belonged to the denomination of reformed presbyterians, or Cameronians, who maintained the perpetual obligation of the solemn league and covenant. At an early age James, with his brother John, was in business as a tobacconist in Edinburgh. They were steady young men, and in 1759 purchased a snuff mill, with land attached, in the parish of Colinton, three miles west from Edinburgh. By additional instalments in 1766 and 1768 he acquired the whole estate of Spylaw, and in 1773 added the adjoining lands of Bonaly and Fernielaw. No more land was purchased, but money accumulated. He lent 500*l.* in 1776 on security of house property at Leith, and in 1782, under the designation 'James Gillespie of Spylaw,' advanced 1,000*l.* on a bond over the estate of Woodhall in his own neighbourhood.

The business in Edinburgh was managed by his younger brother in a shop now (1889) marked 231 High Street, a little way east from the cross. It is still designated 'The Gillespie Tobacco Shop.' James, 'the laird,' as he was called, resided at Spylaw, superintending the manufacture of snuff. A kind of snuff known as 'Gillespie' is still generally sold by tobacconists. He was an exceptionally unassuming man, living in a patriarchal style among his small tenants, to whom he was always forbearing. A carriage was bought, but of the plainest description, and was scarcely ever used except during the last year of his life.

James Gillespie survived his brother two years, and carried on the business till his death at Spylaw on 8 April 1797, in his seventy-first year. He was buried in the churchyard at Colinton, in the same vault with his brother John. Neither of them was married.

Lord Cockburn, in his 'Memorials,' calls Gillespie 'a snuff-seller who brought up an excellent young man as his heir, and then left death to disclose that, for the vanity of being remembered by a thing called after himself, he had all the while had a deed executed by which this, his nearest, relative was disinherited.' Gillespie's will, however, was executed in 1796, only a year before his death, and after he had been offended by the youth whom he had conditionally promised to 'make a man.' By his will Gillespie bequeathed his estates, together with 12,000*l.* sterling (exclusive of 2,700*l.* to found a school), to build a hospital for the maintenance of old men and women. On 19 April 1801 the governors were incorporated by royal charter. They consist of the master, treasurer, and twelve assistants of the Merchant Company of Edinburgh, five members elected by the town council of Edinburgh, and two of the city ministers. By a provisional order obtained in virtue of the Endowed Institutions (Scotland) Act, 1869, which came into operation 24 July 1870, the governors were empowered to make certain alterations. They have dispensed with the hospital, and now give the pensioners a fixed yearly allowance, while the benefits of the school have been greatly extended. In July 1887 there were 167 female and 42 male pensioners, who received either 10*l.* or 25*l.* each yearly, and in November of the same year there were 1,450 children enrolled in the school.

In the hall of the Merchant Company is a bust of James Gillespie, and a portrait of him painted by Sir James Foulis of Woodhall; and in Kaye's 'Edinburgh Portraits' are heads of both brothers, in which the faces are exhibited with some exaggeration, especially of one prominent feature. In the same publication is a genial biographical sketch.

[Information obtained from the secretary of the Edinburgh Merchant Company; Register of Sasines in General Register House, Edinburgh; Old Statistical Account of Colinton Parish, published in 1796; New Statistical Account, 1839; Kaye's Edinburgh Portraits, vol. ii.; Somerville's Life and Times, p. 335; Cockburn's Memorials of his own Time, p. 173.] J. T.

GILLESPIE, PATRICK (1617–1675), principal of Glasgow University, was third son of John Gillespie, minister of Kirkcaldy, by his wife Lilias, daughter of Patrick Simson, minister of Stirling [see GILLESPIE, GEORGE]. He was baptised 2 March 1617, was educated at St. Andrews, where he graduated in 1635, became minister of the second charge of Kirkcaldy in 1642, and of the High Church of Glasgow in 1648. From that time he took a very prominent part in public affairs, first as an extreme covenanter, and next as a friend and supporter of Cromwell. He strenuously opposed the 'engagement' for the rescue of Charles I, helped to overthrow the government that sanctioned it, and advocated the severest measures against all 'malignants.' He considered the terms made with Charles II unsatisfactory, and after the battle of Dunbar (3 Sept. 1650) he assembled a meeting of gentlemen and ministers in the west, and persuaded them to raise a separate armed force, which was placed under the command of officers recommended by him. He was the author of the 'Remonstrance' (December 1650) addressed to parliament by the 'gentlemen, commanders, and ministers attending the Westland Force,' in which they made the gravest charges against the public authorities, condemned the treaty with the king, and declared that they 'could not own him and his interest in the state of the quarrel' with Cromwell. This seditious paper was condemned by church and state. Soon after the commission of assembly passed resolutions in favour of allowing 'malignants,' on profession of their repentance, to take part in the defence of the country. Against this Gillespie and his friends protested, and as the general assembly, which met in July 1651, was likely to approve of the resolutions of the commission, they protested against its legality. For this he and two others were deposed from the ministry. They and their sympathisers disregarded the sentence, and made the first schism in the church since the Reformation. Many of the protesters, as the dissenters were called, preferred Cromwell to the king, and some of them became favourable to independency. Gillespie was the leader of this section, and there was no one in Scotland who was in greater favour with the Protector or who had more influence with him. Hence his appointment to the principalship of the university of Glasgow in 1652, notwithstanding protests on the grounds that the election belonged to the professors, that he was insufficient in learning, and had been deposed from the ministry. In 1653 Cromwell turned the general assembly out of doors, and in the following year he called up Gillespie and two other protesters to London to consult with them as to a new settlement of Scottish ecclesiastical affairs. The result was the appointment of a large commission of protesters, who were empowered to 'purge' the church of ministers

whom they thought 'scandalous,' and to withhold the stipend from any one appointed to a parish who had not a testimonial from four men of their party. This was known as 'Gillespie's Charter,' and was particularly odious to the resolutioners, who formed the great majority of the church. In September 1655, having gone to Edinburgh to preach, Gillespie was interrupted by a part of the congregation, who asked how he dared to appear there, being a deposed minister and 'an enemy and a traitor both to kirk and kingdom,' and then rose and left the church. Not 'much dashed' he gave out for his text 'I would to God that not only thou, but also all that hear me this day, were both almost and altogether such as I am.' A few weeks later, when preaching in the High Church of Edinburgh (14 Oct. 1655), he prayed for 'his highness the Lord Protector, and for a blessing on all his proceedings,' being the first to do so publicly in Scotland. About this time he got the synod of Glasgow, in which he had great influence among the young ministers and 'yeoman elders,' to annul the sentence of deposition passed by the general assembly, and he was sent as a correspondent to the synod of Lothian, in order to get their act acknowledged, but, much to his indignation, he was not admitted. Soon after Gillespie and other protesters went to London to seek an increase of power, but Sharp, who had been sent up by the resolutioners, was there to oppose them. Sharp was backed by the English presbyterians. Gillespie and his friends 'plyed hardly the sectaries,' and 'did pray oft with them both privately and publicly,' but though they were 'affectionately for them,' and 'with all their power befriended them,' they were not successful. Gillespie spent about a year in London, and during this visit was seriously ill. He lived in state, preaching before the Protector in 'his rich velvet rarely cut cassock,' and was the intimate friend of Owen and Lockyer, Lambert and Fleetwood. He obtained from the Protector a large addition of revenue to the university out of church property. After his return home he quarrelled with the town council, and was libelled for neglect of duty and maladministration of funds, but the accusation was not pushed to extremities. In May 1659 he again visited London, and obtained from Richard Cromwell an addition of 100l. a year to his income out of the college revenues. On 28 Oct. 1659 'he was desired' for the Outer-High Church, Edinburgh. At the Restoration he sent his wife to court to intercede for him. It was said that he offered to promote episcopacy, but this he denied. He was deprived of his office, and imprisoned in Stirling Castle. In March 1661 he was brought to trial, when he professed penitence, and threw himself upon the mercy of the court. He had powerful friends, and even Sharp used his influence on his behalf, so that he escaped with a sentence of confinement to Ormiston for a time. The king thought him more guilty than James Guthrie, and said that he would have spared Guthrie's life if he had known that Gillespie was to be treated so leniently. Lord Sinclair wished to have him appointed to Dysart, but Sharp said that one metropolitan was enough for Scotland, and that two for the province of Fife would be too many. He could obtain no further employment in the ministry, and died at Leith in February 1675. His superior abilities, fluent delivery, and popular manners made him at one time a man of great personal influence. He was, however, ambitious, domineering, and extravagant, so that it was said no bishop in Scotland had ever lived at so high a rate. He deserves to be considered a benefactor to the university of Glasgow, as he renewed and enlarged the buildings, and added to its permanent revenues, if he left it deeply in debt. His works were: 1. 'Rulers' Sins the Cause of National Judgments,' a sermon, 1650. 2. A posthumous work, 'The Ark of the Testament opened,' published in 1677, with a preface by Dr. John Owen, who highly commends it, and expresses his great esteem for the author, and his 'respect for his labours in the church of God.'

[Scott's Fasti, iv. 518; Baillie's Letters, vol. iii.; Records of the Kirk; Lamont and Nicoll's Diaries; Cook's Hist. of the Church of Scotland; Life of Archbishop Sharp; Beattie's Hist. of the Church of Scotland during the Commonwealth.]

G. W. S.

GILLESPIE, SIR ROBERT ROLLO (1766–1814), major-general, of an old Scottish family which acquired property in Downshire early in the eighteenth century, was only child of Robert Gillespie of Comber, co. Down, where he was born on 21 Jan. 1766. The father was married thrice, twice without issue. Robert was child of the third marriage with a sister of James Bailie of Innisharrie, co. Down, member for Hillsborough in the Irish House of Commons.

Robert went to a private school at Kensington, known as Norland House, and afterwards to the Rev. Mr. Tookey of Exning, near Newmarket, to prepare for Cambridge. He strongly preferred a military career, and on 28 April 1783 was appointed to a cornetcy in the 3rd Irish horse, now the 6th dragoon guards (carabineers). Three years afterwards,

on 24 Nov. 1786, he contracted a clandestine marriage in Dublin with Annabell, fourth daughter of Thomas Taylor of Taylors Grange, co. Dublin, whom he met at the deanery, Clogher, a few weeks before. Soon after Gillespie was second to an officer named Mackenzie, in a duel with a brother of Sir Jonah Barrington. It was proposed that the matter should end after two fruitless discharges, but a quarrel then arose between Barrington and Gillespie. Gillespie drew a handkerchief from his pocket, and challenged Barrington to fight across it. Shots were fired, and Barrington fell dead. Gillespie fled, and took refuge with some of his wife's relations. Afterwards he and his wife escaped to Scotland, whence he returned, and surrendered to take his trial. He was tried on a charge of wilful murder at Maryborough, Queen's County, at the summer assize of 1788, when, despite the adverse summing-up of Judge Bradstreet, the jury, which included several half-pay officers, brought in a verdict of 'justifiable homicide,' and Gillespie was discharged upon his own recognisances to come up and plead the king's pardon in the court of king's bench, Dublin, during the ensuing term. Gillespie refused the persuasions of friends to sell out and settle down on his estate, his father having died in 1791; he resolved to see active service, and accepted promotion in 1792 to a lieutenancy in the newly raised 20th Jamaica light dragoons. At Madeira, on the voyage out, the ship was driven out of the roads by a violent storm, and Gillespie and some others escaped to shore in an open boat across a mountainous sea. At Jamaica he had yellow fever, from which he recovered, and when the French planters in St. Domingo applied to Jamaica for aid, he offered his services as a volunteer, his regiment, in which he got his troop in January 1794, remaining in the colony. He was present at the capture of Tiburon in February 1794, and afterwards at Port-au-Prince, where he was fired at while swimming ashore with a flag of truce to demand the surrender of the town. He displayed much gallantry at the capture of Fort Bizotten, and received several wounds in the attack on Fort de l'Hôpital. After the fall of Port-au-Prince Gillespie took advantage of a temporary cessation of hostilities to return home. He rejoined his wife, and travelled about at home for a time. Appointed major of brigade to General Wilford he re-embarked for the West Indies in 1796. He became regimental major the same year. He accompanied General Wilford to St. Domingo, where he was appointed adjutant-general, and was much feared by the republicans. A gang of eight desperadoes broke into his quarters, murdered his slave-boy, and

committee to perform the act of induction. The general assembly cancelled this appointment, and required the presbytery of Dunfermline itself to ordain. Six of the ministers, including Gillespie, justified their continued refusal in a written statement to the general assembly (22 May 1752). The assembly resolved, by a majority of 93 to 65, that one of the six should be deposed. Gillespie, who had presented an additional paper, was selected, and a sentence of deposition was thereupon pronounced against him from the moderator's chair. He received the sentence with dignified meekness, and replied in these words: 'Moderator, I desire to receive this sentence of the general assembly passed against me with real concern and awful impressions of the divine conduct in it; but I rejoice that to me it is given, in the behalf of Christ, not only to believe on him, but also to suffer for his sake.' The bearing of Gillespie under the hurried proceedings excited a strong reaction in his favour. During the summer he preached in the open air to congregations of vast numbers, but was obliged at last to take up his position on the highway, and in the winter he removed to the neighbouring town of Dunfermline, where a church was provided, most of his former congregation adhering to his ministry. In the next assembly an effort was made to have him reponed, but Gillespie held that no good would be done unless the policy of the church were reversed.

Gillespie joined none of the existing branches of the secession, because he was opposed to the ecclesiastical limitations of church communion which they had imposed. For six and a half years he stood alone. At the end of that time he was joined by Thomas Boston the younger [q. v.], minister of a large congregation in Jedburgh. Three years afterwards, in 1761, the people of Colinsburgh in Fife, having been driven out of the church by an unpopular appointment, applied to Gillespie and Boston for help. They ordained a minister for the discontented worshippers of Colinsburgh, and the three congregations of Dunfermline, Jedburgh, and Colinsburgh formed themselves into a presbytery, for the 'relief' of Christians oppressed in their church privileges (22 Oct. 1761). For twelve years afterwards Gillespie continued to labour with much earnestness and zeal. He died 19 Jan. 1774. He married, 19 Nov. 1744, Margaret Riddell, who died 27 April 1787. It is said, on the authority of Dr. Erskine, that Gillespie cooled in his attachment to the relief church, and even advised his people to go back to the establishment. This, however, is strenuously denied, and there is no direct evidence for the charge. He was a laborious and conscientious minister. His secession was not due to any personal ambition.

In 1774 was published, probably posthumously, Gillespie's 'Practical Treatise on Temptation,' which appeared with a preface and strong recommendation by Dr. Erskine. It is remarkable for the prominent place which it assigns to the devil as the author of temptation. In another work, published at Edinburgh in 1771, 8vo, Gillespie handled the subject of supposed immediate revelations from God, contending that such revelations were not now granted to the church.

The relief church went on increasing for nearly a century. In 1847 the relief united with the secession, which had been founded in 1733. The united presbyterian church, which was formed by the union, numbered 518 ministers, of whom 400 had been of the secession church and 118 of the relief.

[Scott's Fasti, iv. 580; Gavin Struthers's History of the Relief Church, 1839; Gavin Struthers's History of the Rise of the Relief Church, 1848; William Lindsay's Life and Times of the Rev. Thomas Gillespie; M'Kelvie's Annals and Statistics of the United Presbyterian Church; Life of Dr. John Erskine, by the Rev. Sir Henry Moncreiff Wellwood, bart., D.D.; Carlyle's Autobiography; Buchanan's Ten Years' Conflict.] W. G. B.

GILLESPIE, THOMAS (1777–1844), professor at St. Andrews, born at Closeburn, Dumfriesshire, in 1777, was educated at Wallace Hall School and Dumfries Academy, and at Edinburgh University. At the university he distinguished himself as a classical scholar and as a debater; at the conclusion of his college course he was licensed as a preacher, 4 Jan. 1810. On leaving college he acted as tutor in the family of Sir James Hay of Dunragit. In 1813 he was presented to the living of Cults, Fifeshire, where he devoted his leisure to literature. In 1824 he received the degree of LL.D. from Glasgow. In 1828 he was appointed assistant and successor to the professor of humanity at St. Andrews, and in 1836 he was elected to the professorship. He died at Dunino, near St. Andrews, on 11 Sept. 1844. He contributed numerous articles both in prose and verse to the leading periodicals, including essays in 'Blackwood' and in 'Constable's Miscellany,' and sketches in Wilson's 'Tales of the Borders.' In 1822 he published a volume of sermons, entitled 'The Seasons contemplated in the Spirit of the Gospel.' An 'Analecta' for the use of his class appeared in 1839. He was twice married; his second wife was daughter of the Rev. Dr. Campbell, parish minister of Cupar, and sister to Lord-chancellor Campbell.

[Roger's Hist. of St. Andrews; Conolly's Eminent Men of Fife; Scott's Fasti, iv.485.] W. B-E.

GILLESPIE, WILLIAM (1776–1825), poet, was the eldest son of the Rev. John Gillespie (1730–1806), minister of Kells in Galloway. He was baptised 18 Feb. 1776. He attended the parish school, and also received private instruction from the schoolmaster, who lived in the manse. In 1792 he entered Edinburgh University, where he studied theology and also, as a secondary subject, medicine. From early years he had been devoted to painting, poetry, and music. A common print of a view of Kenmure Castle was executed from a drawing made by him when about fourteen years of age. While at Edinburgh he wrote a poem entitled ' The Progress of Refinement,' which was not, however, published till some years later. He found subjects for some of the poems (which were published along with it) in a tour through the western highlands, which he took with Alexander Don, to whom he was tutor. At the end of his university course he was licensed as preacher by the presbytery of Kirkcudbright (1 Aug. 1798), and on 7 Aug. 1800 was ordained assistant and successor to his father. On 29 April 1806 his father died, after having been minister of Kells for forty-two years, and he became sole minister. In 1820 he was chaplain to the stewartry of Kircudbright yeomanry cavalry, and the commandant wrote to him, asking whether in his service before the force he would pray for the queen. He returned an evasive answer, but in the prayer for the royal family he inserted the words, ' Bless also the queen.' On this the commandant ordered him to consider himself under arrest, that is to say, as was subsequently explained, not at liberty to go out of the county (30 July). Gillespie then published the sermon which he had preached before the yeomanry, with a preface and appendices explaining the circumstances, and proving the illegality of his arrest.

On 26 July 1825 he married Charlotte Hoggan; but while on his wedding tour he was attacked by erysipelas, and died on 15 Oct. in the fiftieth year of his age. He was long remembered in his parish for the refinement of his tastes, his hospitality, and his kindness to students.

Besides contributions to the ' Scots Magazine ' and other periodicals, his works were : a life of John Lowe, author of ' Mary's Dream,' in Cromek's ' Remains of Nithsdale and Galloway Song,' pp. 342–60 ; ' The Progress of Refinement, an allegorical poem, with other poems,' Edinburgh, 1805, 8vo ; ' Consolation, with other poems,' Edinburgh, 1815, 8vo ; ' The Rebellion of Absalom : a discourse preached at Kirkcudbright on the 30th July last,' Dumfries, 1820, 8vo.

[Thomas Murray's Literary Hist. of Galloway, 2nd ed. pp. 275–82 ; private information ; Brit. Mus. and Bodleian Library Catalogues ; Hew Scott's Fasti, ii. 716.]   E. C—N.

GILLIES, ADAM, Lord Gillies (1760–1842), Scottish judge, born in 1760, youngest son of Robert Gillies of Little Keithock, Forfarshire, and brother of Dr. John Gillies [q. v.], historian, was admitted an advocate on 14 July 1787. On 20 March 1806 he became sheriff-depute of Kincardineshire, on 30 Nov. 1811 succeeded Lord Newton as an ordinary judge of the Royal College of Justice, and in March 1812 succeeded Lord Craig as a lord of justiciary. On Lord Meadowbank's death he was appointed, 10 July 1816, a lord commissioner of the jury court. In 1837 he resigned his seat as a lord of justiciary, and was appointed a judge of the court of exchequer in Scotland. He died at Leamington on 24 Dec. 1842. He took little part in politics ; in early life his views were whig, but subsequently they became tory. As a judge he was strong, learned, and impartial.

[Ann. Reg. ; Brunton and Haig's Senators of the Royal Coll. of Justice ; Anderson's Scottish Nation.]   J. A. H.

GILLIES, JOHN, D.D. (1712–1796), theological writer, was born in 1712, at the manse of Careston, near Brechin, where his father, John Gillies, was minister, and after prosecuting his literary and divinity courses and being employed as tutor in several families of note, became minister of the college church, Glasgow, 29 July 1742. In this charge he remained till his death fifty-four years after (29 March 1796). It is said of him that besides preaching three times every Sunday, he delivered discourses in his large church three times a week to crowded audiences, published for some time a weekly paper, and regularly visited and catechised his parish. His first wife was Elizabeth (d. 1754), daughter of the Rev. John McLaurin, a distinguished preacher [q. v.], and his second, Joanna (d. 1792), sister of Sir Michael Stewart. Gillies is best known for a work entitled ' Historical Collections relating to the Success of the Gospel,' 2 vols. Glasgow, 1754. To this an appendix was added in 1761, and a supplement in 1786. Another work of considerable magnitude was entitled ' Devotional Exercises on the New Testament,' 2 vols. London, 1769, 8vo. He published, likewise, ' Exhortations to the Inhabitants of the South Parish of Glasgow,' 2 vols. Glasgow, 1750, 12mo ; ' Life of the Rev. Mr. George Whitefield,' London, 1772, 8vo ; ' Essays on the Prophecies relating to the Messiah,' Edinburgh, 1773, 8vo ; ' Hebrew Manual for the use of Students ; ' ' Psalms of

David,' with notes, Glasgow, 1786; and Milton's 'Paradise Lost,' illustrated by texts of scripture, London, 1778, 12mo. He wrote a life of John MacLaurin for MacLaurin's 'Sermons and Essays,' Glasgow, 1755. Dr. John Erskine prefixed an appreciative notice of his life to the supplement to his 'Historical Collections.'

[Scott's Fasti, iii. 19; Memoir by Dr. Nicol, prefixed to New Testament Meditations; Erskine's Sketch ut supra; Chambers's Eminent Scotsmen; Anderson's Scottish Nation.]   W. G. B.

GILLIES, JOHN, LL.D. (1747–1836), historian and classical scholar, born at Brechin in Forfarshire, on 18 Jan. 1747, was the eldest son in the large family of Robert Gillies, a merchant in Brechin, and proprietor of Little Keithock, by his wife Margaret, the daughter of a Brechin merchant named Smith. Adam Gillies (1787–1842) [q. v.], the Scotch judge, was a younger son. John Gillies was educated at Brechin, and at Glasgow University under Leechman and Moore. When at home he passed the day 'studying in his father's garret.' Before he was twenty he was selected to teach the Greek class in the university during the illness of Moore, the professor of Greek. While at the university he wrote a 'Defence of the Study of Classical Literature,' which was printed, apparently in a periodical. Soon afterwards he came to London to follow literature, but gave up his engagements on going abroad as tutor to the Hon. Henry Hope, second son of John, second earl of Hopetoun. He lived some years in Germany and visited other parts of Europe. In 1777 the earl settled an annuity on him. Gillies was afterwards travelling tutor to the earl's two younger sons John (Sir John Hope, afterwards Baron Niddry, and fourth earl) and Alexander (Sir A. Hope, G.C.B., lieutenant-governor of Chelsea Hospital). About 1784 he returned to England and carried on his literary work. In 1784 he took the degree of LL.D. He was also a corresponding member of the French Institute, a fellow of the Royal Society, and of the Society of Antiquaries. In 1793 he was appointed royal historiographer for Scotland on the death of Dr. Robertson. In 1794 he married, and at that time had a house in Portman Square, London. From 1830 he lived in retirement at Clapham, where he died on 15 Feb. 1836 in his ninetieth year. 'He had no disease of any kind, and departed without a pang ... or the change of a single muscle' (Gent. Mag.) Mathias (Pursuits of Lit. 7th ed., dial. ii. pp. 118, 120) says that Gillies was 'a man of good intentions, a passable scholar, an indefatig-

able reader, and of most respectable character,' but there was no touch of genius in his writings. Miss Burney found him in conversation 'very communicative and informing' (Diary, &c. of Mme. d'Arblay, v. 225). He is described (Public Characters, p. 235) as a man of about middle height, with a handsome figure, and an open and ingenuous countenance.

Gillies is remembered as the author of a once popular 'History of Greece.' This book, written in a readable but somewhat pompous style, was published in 1786, London, 2 vols. 4to, and in 4 vols. 8vo, and other editions (including French and German translations) followed: Basle, 1790, 8vo; London, 1792–3, 8vo; London, 1825, 8vo; Vienna, 1825. The first volume of Mitford's 'Greece' had been published in 1784, but the work was not completed till 1810. Gillies also wrote a 'History of the World' (from Alexander the Great to Augustus), 2 vols., London, 1807, 4to; noticed, not unfavourably, in the 'Edinburgh Review' (xi. 40–61), and 'A View of the Reign of Frederick II of Prussia' (London, 1789, 8vo), whose court he had visited. Professor Smyth (Lect. on Mod. Hist.) says the book is little more than a panegyric. Gillies also translated: 1. 'The Orations of Lysias and Isocrates,' 1778, 4to. 2. 'Aristotle's Ethics and Politics,' with introductions and notes, 1797, 4to; 1804, 8vo; 1813, 8vo (cf. Thomas Taylor's 'Answer to Dr. G.'s Supplement to his new Analysis of Aristotle's Works, in which the unfaithfulness of his Translation of Aristotle's Ethics is unfolded,' 1804, 8vo; cf. also the strictures in Publ. Char. p. 234). 3. 'Aristotle's Rhetoric,' 1823, 8vo.

[Gent. Mag. 1836, new ser. v. 436–7; Jervoise's Land of the Lindsays, pp. 182, 221, 222; Public Characters, 1800–1, pp. 223–5; Irving's Book of Scotsmen; Chambers's Biog. Dict. of Eminent Scotsmen (Thomson); Allibone's Dict. of Engl. Lit.; Mathias's Pursuits of Lit.; Brit. Mus. Cat.]   W. W.

GILLIES, MARGARET (1803–1887), miniature and water-colour painter, was the second daughter of William Gillies, a Scotch merchant settled in Throgmorton Street, London, where she was born on 7 Aug. 1803. Having lost her mother when eight years old, and her father having met with reverses, she and her younger sister, Mary, were placed under the care of their uncle, Adam Gillies, lord Gillies [q.v.], one of the judges of the court of session in Scotland, by whom they were educated, and subsequently introduced to the best society in Edinburgh. There she met Sir Walter Scott, Lord Erskine, Lord Jeffrey, and other famous men; but before she was twenty she determined to earn for herself an honourable livelihood, and returned with her sister to her father's home in London. Mary Gillies became an authoress, and died in 1870, while Margaret took the somewhat bold step of becoming a professional artist. She received some lessons in miniature-painting from Frederick Cruickshank, and quickly gained a reputation in that branch of art, although she had had no regular artistic training. Before she was twenty-four she was commissioned to paint a miniature of the poet Wordsworth, at whose residence, Rydal Mount, she spent several weeks. She painted also a portrait of Charles Dickens, and one of Mrs. Marsh, the novelist, and for many successive years contributed portraits to the exhibitions of the Royal Academy. She then went for a while to Paris, where she worked in the studios of Hendrik and Ary Scheffer, and on her return to England she exhibited from time to time portraits in oil. It was, however, not long before she devoted herself to water-colour-painting, usually choosing domestic, romantic, or sentimental subjects, and it is on these that her chief distinction rests. In 1852 she was elected an associate of the Old (now the Royal) Society of Painters in Water-colours, and was a constant contributor to its exhibitions down to the year of her death. Some of the best of her exhibited works were 'Past and Future,' 1855, and 'The Heavens are telling,' 1856, both of which have been engraved; 'Rosalind and Celia,' 1857; 'Una and the Red Cross Knight in the Cavern of Despair,' 'An Eastern Mother,' and 'Vivia Perpetua in Prison,' 1858; 'A Father and Daughter,' 1859; 'Imogen after the Departure of Posthumus,' 1860; 'Beyond,' 1861; 'The Wanderer,' 1868; 'Prospero and Miranda,' 1874; 'Cercando Pace,' a beautiful drawing in three compartments, 1875; and 'The Pilgrimage,' which was exhibited at the Royal Jubilee Exhibition at Manchester in 1887. Her last work was 'Christiana by the River of Life,' exhibited in 1887. She lived for many years in Church Row, Hampstead, but died at The Warren, Crockham Hill, Kent, on 20 July 1887, of pleurisy, after a few days' illness.

[Times, 26 July 1887; Academy, 30 July 1887; Miss Clayton's English Female Artists, 1876, ii. 87–94; Exhibition Catalogues of the Royal Academy, 1832–61; Exhibition Catalogues of the Royal Society of Painters in Water-colours, 1852–87; Mary Howitt: An Autobiography, 1889, ii.]   R. E. G.

GILLIES, ROBERT PEARSE (1788–1858), autobiographer, a member of the Forfarshire family of Gillies, was born at or near Arbroath in 1788. His father, Dr. Thomas Gillies, was possessed of a landed estate, which on his death in 1808 his son inherited. Gillies had already collected a library of books, written poetry, and studied under Dugald Stewart and Playfair at the university of Edinburgh. He was admitted advocate in 1813, and, losing most of his fortune in consequence of a rash speculation, settled in Edinburgh in 1815, where he devoted himself to literary pursuits. He was one of the early contributors to 'Blackwood's Magazine,' and figures as 'Kemperhausen' in Christopher North's 'Noctes Ambrosianæ.' He was a well-known figure among the literary men who frequented the Ballantynes, and was a special friend of Scott. Reminiscences of his intercourse with Scott were published by Gillies in 1837. Like Scott, Gillies was attracted for some time by the literature of Germany, from which he made many translations, published for the most part in 'Blackwood's Magazine.' He resided in Germany for a year, and met Goethe and Tieck. Gillies also corresponded with Wordsworth, who encouraged him in his early pecuniary difficulties in a sonnet (*Miscellaneous Sonnets*, pt. ii. no. 4), commencing—

> From the dark chambers of dejection freed,
> Spurning the unprofitable yoke of care,
> Rise, Gillies, rise: the gates of youth shall bear
> Thy genius forward like a wingèd steed.

Gillies likewise attracted the attention of Byron, who in his 'Diary' (23 Nov. 1813) remarks on his work: 'The young man can know nothing of life; and if he cherishes the disposition which runs through his papers will become useless and perhaps not even a poet, which he seems determined to be. God help him! No one should be a rhymer who could be anything else.'

Most of Gillies's remaining means disappeared in the commercial panic of 1825, and he became involved in a series of lawsuits. Scott assisted him in various ways, and finally suggested to him the idea of a journal of foreign literature. Gillies succeeded in inducing the London firm of Treuttel & Würtz, Treuttel, junr., & Richter to take up the project, and the result was the foundation of the 'Foreign Quarterly Review' in July 1827. Gillies as editor was to receive 600l. per annum, but he was to pay the contributors out of this. To the first number articles were contributed by Sir W. Scott (who declined to receive remuneration for his work), Robert Southey, the Rev. G. R. Gleig, W. Maginn, and others.

Gillies now removed to London, where he led a somewhat chequered life. His affairs remained hopelessly involved, and when about 1833 he passed a whole year without being arrested for debt, the fact seemed to him remarkable. In 1840 he removed to Boulogne, where he remained till 1847, when incautiously returning to England, he was at once thrown into prison, and was not liberated till 1849.

Gillies died at Kensington, 28 Nov. 1858. He was married and had a family. He turned to account his acquaintance with famous men in his 'Memoirs of a Literary Veteran' (3 vols., 1851), where he gives personal reminiscences of many. Among the most notable besides Scott were James Hogg, Lord Jeffrey, Thomas de Quincey, John Kemble, Mrs. Siddons, and John Galt. Selections from this work with a biography were edited by Richard Henry Stoddard, as the tenth volume of the 'Bric à Brac Series,' New York, 1876.

Gillies's other works consisted, besides fugitive contributions, of the following: 1. 'Wallace, a fragment,' 1813. 2. 'Childe Alarique, a poet's reverie, with other poems,' 1814. 3. An edition of James the First's 'Essays of a Prentise in the Divine Art of Poesie,' 1814. 4. 'Confessions of Sir H. Longueville,' a novel, 1814. 5. 'Rinaldo, the Visionary, a Desultory Poem,' 1816. 6. 'Illustrations of a Poetical Character, in six tales, with other poems' (2nd edit. 1816). 7. 'Oswald, a metrical tale,' 1817. 8. 'Guilt, or the Anniversary,' a tragedy from the German of A. G. A. Muellner, 1819. 9. Extempore, to Walter Scott, Esq., on the publication of the new edition of the 'Bridal of Triermain' (1819, by 'S. K. C.,' probably by Gillies. When the 'Bridal' was first published, Scott encouraged the idea [LOCKHART, p. 236] that Gillies was the author). 10. 'German Stories, selected from the works of Hoffmann, De la Motte-Fouqué, Pichler, Kruse, and others,' 3 vols. 1826. 11. 'A Winter Night's Dream.' 12. 'The Seventh Day,' 1826. 13. 'Tales of a Voyager to the Arctic Ocean,' 6 vols., two series, 1826 and 1829. 14. 'Ranulph de Rohais: a Romance of the Twelfth Century,' 3 vols. 1830, 8vo. 15. 'Thurlston Tales,' 3 vols. 1835. 16. 'Palmario,' 1839.

[Memoirs above referred to; Lockhart's Life of Scott; Wordsworth's Poems; Dictionary of Living Authors, 1816.] F. W-T.

GILLILAND, THOMAS (*fl.* 1804–1816), writer, is the subject of severe attack in the 'Satirist.' According to it, he attracted attention as a frequenter of the green-room of Drury Lane Theatre. Upon inquiry it appeared that he was 'no other than the famed Mr. Thomas Gilliland, ci-devant scout to Anthony Pasquin.' A remonstrance against his presence was made by Charles Mathews

the elder, and signed by actors who objected to the appearance among them of 'this spy upon the private conduct of public men.' He met this by a voluntary withdrawal (*Satirist*, i. 420). He is said to have written for a living, and to have been 'countenanced' by 'Monk' Lewis and 'Anacreon' Moore (*ib*. iii. 534). Gilliland is responsible for various compilations of which the 'Dramatic Mirror' alone can be said in any sense to survive: 1. 'A Dramatic Synopsis, containing an Essay on the Political and Moral Use of a Theatre, involving Remarks on the Dramatic Writers of the Present Day and Strictures on the Performers of the two Theatres,' London, 1804, 8vo. This production, which contains some sensible opinions, was subsequently expanded into: 2. 'The Dramatic Mirror, containing the History of the Stage from the Earliest Period to the Present Time,' &c., London, 1808, 2 vols. 12mo, a work of little merit, giving some information concerning the country theatres. It supplies biographies of the principal actors from the time of Shakespeare and of dramatic writers subsequent to 1660, is illustrated with portraits and other engravings, and is dedicated to the Prince of Wales. 3. 'Elbow Room, a Pamphlet containing Remarks on the shameful Increase of the Private Boxes of Covent Garden,' &c., London, 1804, 8vo. 4. 'Jack in Office, containing Remarks on Mr. Braham's Address to the Public, with a full and impartial consideration of Mr. Kemble's conduct with regard to the above gentleman,' London, n.d. (1804, 8vo, *Brit. Mus. Cat.*) The two works last named are satires upon Kemble's management. 5. 'The Trap, a Moral, Philosophical, and Satirical Work, delineating the Snares in which Kings, Princes, and their Subjects have been caught since the days of Adam; including Reflections on the Present Causes of Conjugal Infidelity. Dedicated to the Ladies,' London, 1808, 2 vols. 12mo, a satire dull and indecorous. 6. 'Diamond cut Diamond: Observations on a Pamphlet entitled "A Review of the Conduct of His Royal Highness the Prince of Wales," comprising a free and impartial View of Mr. Jefferys as a Tradesman, Politician, and Courtier. By Philo Veritas,' 5th edition, enlarged, London, 1801, 8vo. These works are in the British Museum. On the title-page to the 'Trap' is mentioned: 7. 'Diamond new Pointed.' A portrait prefixed to the 'Dramatic Mirror' presents the not unpleasing features of a man aged somewhere near thirty. Gilliland was alive in 1816, in which year his name appears in 'A Biographical Dictionary of Living Authors.'

[Books cited; Lowndes's Bibl. Man.] J. K.

s s

GILLING, ISAAC (1662?–1725), presbyterian minister, elder son of Richard Gilling, baker, was born at Stogumber, Somersetshire. He was educated at a nonconformist academy in Taunton, maintained (1678–85) by George Hammond, an ejected minister. John Fox (1693–1763) [q. v.], his relative and biographer, says that when Gilling began to preach ' he preached often in the churches, though he was never a regular conformist.' He received presbyterian ordination at Lyme Regis, Dorsetshire, 25 Aug. 1687, being at that time ' curate of Barrington and Seavington St. Mary in Somerset' (WILSON). His next employment was at Axminster, Devonshire, as usher in a Latin school; while here he preached to a congregation of independents. He then became pastor of the presbyterian congregation at Silverton, Devonshire. Here he married a lady (from Brampford-Speke) 'somewhat deformed,' but of good estate. From Silverton he was called to the charge of the presbyterian congregation at Newton Abbot, Devonshire, in succession to William Yeo, an ejected minister (d. 1699).

Gilling, who was a scholarly and genial divine, kept a flourishing boarding-school at Newton Abbot, and got into trouble during the reign of Anne for doing so without the bishop's license. He was more than once obliged to abscond to prevent arrest, the last occasion being in 1712, when (in a disguise) he accompanied Fox to London. In ecclesiastical politics he was for a consolidation of the dissenting interest, and was an active member of the Exeter assembly, formed in 1691 as a union of presbyterians and independents on the London model. Of this body he was for many years the scribe; his quarto volume of manuscript minutes (to 1718) is preserved in Dr. Williams's library. In the disputes of 1719 he sided with the minority against subscription, and hence was excluded from the assembly and deserted by more than half his hearers, who formed a new congregation under Samuel Westcot. Other disappointments followed; Gilling lost heart, fell into a lingering sickness, and died on 20 or 21 Aug. 1725. His age is not given, but the date of his ordination shows that he could not have been born later than 1662. He was buried in his meeting-house. He had wished to be interred in the church or churchyard at Newton Abbot; but the parish being a peculiar, the ordinary, Sir William Courtenay, refused to permit the interment, saying ' they might bury him in one of the marshes.'

By his first wife Gilling had a son Isaac, educated as a physician at Paris and entered at Leyden 4 Oct. 1723, who did not turn out well, and a daughter, married to John Fox. His second wife, née Atkins, of Exeter, led him into extravagances.

He published: 1. 'The Qualifications and Duties of Ministers,' &c., Exeter, 1708, 8vo. 2. 'The Life of the Reverend Mr. George Trosse,' &c., 1715, 8vo (an abridgment and continuation of Trosse's very singular autobiography, originally published at Exeter, 1714, 8vo, by J. H. [Joseph Hallett], but superseded by Gilling's more decorous narrative, 'one of the best pieces of evangelical biography'). 3. 'The Mischief of . . . Uncharitable Judging,' &c., Exeter, 1719, 8vo. Also funeral sermons for the Rev. S. Atkins, 1702, Samuel Atkins, jun., 1703, Susanna Reynell, 1704, and the Rev. S. Mullins, 1711. He prepared for the press the papers of Walter Moyle [q. v.]

[Biographical sketch, by J. Fox, in Monthly Repository, 1821, pp. 327 sq., see also pp. 132 sq.; Wilson's Dissenting Churches, 1814, iv. 393; Evans's manuscript List of Diss. Congr. (1715 sq.), partly printed in James's Hist. Litig. Presb. Chapels, 1867, p. 657; manuscript list of ministers in records of Exeter Assembly; Northcote's transcript of Fox's manuscripts in Plymouth Public Library.] A. G.

GILLINGWATER, EDMUND (1735?–1813), topographer, born at Lowestoft, Suffolk, about 1735, was the son of Edmund and Alice Gillingwater of Lowestoft. He was apprenticed to a barber. When about twenty-two years of age he removed to Norwich, which he left on 5 Dec. 1761 for Harleston, Norfolk. There he carried on a small business as stationer and bookseller in the Old Market Place, and was appointed an overseer of the poor. While holding the latter office he published 'An Essay on Parish Work-Houses; containing Observations on the present State of English Work-houses; with some Regulations proposed for their improvement,' 8vo, Bury St. Edmunds, 1786. Gillingwater retired from business about 1788. Two years later he brought out by subscription 'An Historical Account of the ancient Town of Lowestoft in the County of Suffolk. To which is added some cursory remarks on the adjoining parishes and a general account of the Island of Lothingland,' 4to, London [1790]. Another useful compilation was his 'Historical and descriptive Account of St. Edmund's Bury . . . the Abbey,' &c. [with an appendix], 12mo, Saint Edmund's Bury, 1804. He also made considerable, though not very valuable, collections for a history of Suffolk, consisting chiefly of extracts from printed books. These after his death came into the possession of H. Jermyn, and were sold at his auction. Samuel Burder in the preface (p. xiii) of his ' Oriental Customs,' 1802, acknowledges his 'obligations to Mr. Gillingwater, of Harleston in Norfolk, for the very liberal manner in which he favoured him with his manuscript papers,' which consisted of additions to, and corrections of, Harmer's ' Observations on divers Passages of Scripture.' Gillingwater died 13 March 1813, aged 77, and was buried in the churchyard of Redenhall-with-Harleston, beside his wife, Mary Bond, who had died 18 May 1802, aged 65. He left no children.

[Tymms's East Anglian, iv. 253–5, 276 ; manuscript note by David Elisha Davy, in a copy of ' An Essay on Parish Work-Houses,' in the British Museum ; Nichols's Lit. Anecd. iii. 200 ; Nichols's Illustr. vi. 545–9.] G. G.

GILLIS, JAMES, D.D. (1802–1864), catholic prelate, born at Montreal, Canada, on 7 April 1802, was the son of James Gillis, a native of the parish of Bellie, Banffshire, Scotland, who had emigrated in early life and acquired a considerable fortune. He was educated at the Sulpician College in Montreal, and in 1816 went to Scotland with his parents. In 1817 he entered the seminary of Aquhorties as an ecclesiastical student, and thence was transferred to the seminary of St. Nicholas at Paris, where he was a fellow-student with Dupanloup, afterwards bishop of Orleans. He left St. Nicholas in October 1823 and entered the seminary of Issy, a house belonging to the Sulpicians, to study philosophy and theology, but his health gave way and he was obliged to return to Scotland in April 1826. He was ordained priest at Aquhorties in 1827. In the following year he was deputed by Bishop Paterson to collect money in France for the repairs of St. Mary's Chapel, Broughton Street, Edinburgh, and during his stay in France he conceived the idea of reviving the conventual life and restoring the religious orders in Scotland. On the outbreak of the revolution in 1830 he with difficulty effected his escape and returned to Scotland. In 1831 he became secretary to Bishop Paterson, and having subsequently collected funds for the purpose in France, he founded St. Margaret's convent in Edinburgh for nuns of the Ursuline order. It was opened on 16 June 1835, being the first religious house established in Scotland since the reformation. On 22 July 1838 he was consecrated bishop of Limyra, *in partibus*, having in the previous year been appointed coadjutor to Bishop Andrew Carruthers [q. v.], on whose death, 24 May 1852, he succeeded to the vicariate-apostolic of the eastern district of Scotland. In the course of a tour which he made in France in 1857 he, at the request of Dupanloup, pronounced

the panegyric of Joan of Arc in the cathedral of Orleans. On this occasion the heart of Henry II, king of England, who died at the castle of Chinon on the Loire in 1189, was presented to him by the mayor of Orleans as a tribute of thanks for the eloquent panegyric. In 1859 Gillis introduced the jesuits into his 'district.' He died at Edinburgh on 24 Feb. 1864.

He published : 1. ' A Letter to the Moderator of the General Assembly of the Church of Scotland, containing a refutation of certain statements made by the Revd. Frederick Mound . . .,' Edinburgh, 1846, 8vo. 2. ' Letter to the Duke of Argyll on the subject of his speeches as chairman of the late annual meeting of the Edinburgh Bible Society,' Edinburgh, 1849, 8vo. 3. ' A Discourse on the Mission and Influence of the Popes, delivered on the day of thanksgiving for the return to Rome of Pius IX,' London, 1850, 8vo. 4. ' Facts and Correspondence relating to the admission to the Catholic Church of Viscount and Viscountess Feilding,' Edinburgh, 1850, 8vo. 5. ' The new Penal Law considered in its bearing upon Scotland ; or two Letters addressed to the Earl of Arundel and Surrey' (on Lord John Russell's Ecclesiastical Titles Assumption Bill), Edinburgh, 1851, 8vo. 6. ' Letter to Duncan Maclaren, Lord Provost of Edinburgh, on the proposed " Voluntary" Amendment of the Lord Advocate's Educational Bill for Scotland,' Edinburgh, 1854, 8vo. 7. ' A Lecture on Education,' Edinburgh, 1856, 8vo. 8. 'Panégyrique de Jeanne d'Arc, prononcé dans la Cathédrale d'Orléans à la fête du 8 mai 1857,' 3rd edit. London, 1857, 8vo. 9. ' A paper on the subject of Burns's pistols,' Edinburgh, 1859, 8vo, read before the Society of Antiquaries of Scotland, to which the bishop presented a brace of pistols that had belonged to the poet Burns.

[Gordon's Catholic Mission in Scotland, p. 480 (with portrait) ; Hist. of St. Margaret's Convent, Edinb., 1886 (with portrait) ; Times, 26 Feb. 1864 ; Catholic Directory (1867), p. 11 ; Weekly Register, January–June 1864, pp. 131, 147, 163 ; Cat. of the Advocates' Libr. Edinb.] T. C.

GILLOTT, JOSEPH (1799–1873), steel pen maker and art patron, the son of a workman in the cutlery trade, was born at Sheffield 11 Oct. 1799, and commenced life as a working cutler, soon becoming a 'noted hand' at forging and grinding knife blades. In 1821, no longer finding any work in his native place, he removed to Birmingham, where his employment was in the ' light steel toy trade,' the technical name for the manufacture of steel buckles, chains, and other works and ornaments of that kind. About 1830 his attention was called to the manufacture of steel pens. Such pens were then laboriously cut with shears out of the steel, and trimmed and fashioned with a file. He adapted the 'press' to the making of pens. With much ingenuity and unflagging perseverance he experimented on different qualities of steel and the various ways of preparing it for use. One of his chief troubles was the extreme hardness of the pens. This he obviated by cutting side slits in addition to the centre slit, which had been solely in use up to that period. To this was afterwards added the cross grinding of the points; and these two processes imparted an elasticity to the pen, making it in this respect nearly equal to a quill. For some years he kept his method of working secret, fashioning his pens with his own hand, assisted by a woman, his first pens being 'blued' in a frying-pan over a garret fire. At first he worked for others, selling his pens for a shilling each to a firm of stationers called Beilby & Knott. His business rapidly increased. It was at first established in Bread Street, Birmingham, then removed to Church Street, then to 59 Newhall Street, and finally to his great works in Graham Street, Newhall Hill, in 1859. The simplicity, accuracy, and readiness of the machinery employed enabled him to produce steel pens in large quantities, and as he sold them at high prices he rapidly made a fortune. He ultimately employed 450 persons, who produced upwards of five tons per week, and the price of the pens was reduced from 1s. each to 4d. the gross. From his earliest years as an employer he spared no cost or pains to benefit his workpeople to the utmost of his power. His works afforded all convenience and comfort to the persons employed. He established a benevolent society among the workpeople, to which he subscribed liberally. He seldom changed his managers, and never had a dispute with his 'hands.' As soon as he had money to spare he began to buy pictures. The collection constantly grew both in quality and in size, until at last his house in the Westbourne Road, Edgbaston, and his residence at Stanmore, near London, were crowded with gems of English art. The great strength of the collection lay in Turners and Ettys, the last-named artist being a special friend of the collector. He appreciated Turner's talents before they had been generally recognised, and purchased his paintings when others doubted. The collection was also very rich in examples of Linnell, Maclise, Mulready, David Roberts, Prout, and other English artists. After the owner's death the paintings were sold for 170,000l. Webster's 'Roast Pig,' a picture painted on commission,

for which Gillott gave 700 guineas, realised 3,550 guineas. His collection of violins, on which he much prided himself, was also disposed of, producing 4,000l. For many years Gillott's face was familiar at the Birmingham Theatre, where he attended nearly every evening, and then adjourned to the Hen and Chickens Hotel to smoke his 'churchwarden' and converse with his friends. Until about ten days before his death failing eyesight was the only sign he gave of old age. On the day after Christmas day 1872 he entertained as usual some of his children and their friends; the next morning he was attacked by a complication of pleurisy and bronchitis, and died at Westbourne Road, Edgbaston, Birmingham, 5 Jan. 1873. He married Miss Mitchell, a sister of John and William Mitchell, the steel pen makers. On 16 March 1873 his personalty was sworn under 250,000l.

[Practical Magazine (1873), i. 322–5, with portrait; Timmins's Birmingham and Midland Hardware District (1866), pp. 634–7; Mayhew's Shops and Companies of London (1865), pp. 98–100; Edwards's Personal Recollections of Birmingham (1877), pp. 89–100; Annual Register, 1872, p. 38.]   G. C. B.

GILLOW, JOHN, D.D. (1753–1828), president of Ushaw College, son of Robert Gillow of Westby, Lancashire, and his wife, Agnes Fell, was born on 25 March 1753. He was sent in 1766 to the English College at Douay, where he was ordained priest, and occupied for eleven years the chairs of philosophy and divinity. In 1791 he returned to England to take charge of the mission at York, where he laboured for twenty years. Some curious mission stories concerning him are related in 'Footsteps of Spirits,' written anonymously by the Rev. James Augustine Stothert. On 11 June 1811 he was installed president of Ushaw College, near Durham, in succession to Thomas Eyre (1748–1810) [q. v.] The college flourished greatly under his management. He was highly esteemed, not only by catholics, but by members of all denominations; and his opinion was often solicited by the vicars-apostolic during the agitation which preceded the passing of the Catholic Relief Act. He died at Ushaw on 6 Feb. 1828.

A fine portrait of him, engraved by C. Turner from a painting by James Ramsay, was published in 1814, and reproduced in the 'Orthodox Journal' of 19 Oct. 1833. The original hangs in the refectory at Ushaw.

[Catholic Miscellany, ix. 31; Kirk's Manuscript Collections, cited in Joseph Gillow's Bibl. Dict.; Henry Gillow's Chapels at Ushaw, hist. introd. pp. 37–9.]   T. C.

GILLOW, THOMAS (1769–1857), catholic divine, fourth son of Richard Gillow of Singleton, Lancashire, by Isabel, sister and heiress of Henry Brewer of Moor House, Newton-cum-Scales, received his education in the English College at Douay. When the professors and students were imprisoned by the French revolutionists, he succeeded in making his escape to England, and continued his studies in the college at Crook Hall, Durham. After being ordained priest in 1797 he was appointed chaplain to the Clavering family at Callaly Castle, Northumberland. In 1817 he was selected by the propaganda to preside as bishop over the vicariate of the West Indies, but he declined the episcopate. In 1821 he left Callaly Castle, to take charge of a new mission at North Shields, where he laboured till his death, on 19 March 1857. He was the author of: 1. 'Catholic Principles of Allegiance illustrated,' Newcastle-on-Tyne, 1807, 8vo. 2. 'A Letter to the Rev. William Hendry Stowell on the Rule of Faith,' North Shields, 1830, 8vo.

[Information from Joseph Gillow, esq.; Catholic Miscellany (1830), new ser. iii. 193; funeral oration by J. W. Bewick; Gillow's Bibliographical Dictionary; Brady's Episcopal Succession, vol. iii.]　　　　　　T. C.

GILLRAY, JAMES (1757–1815), caricaturist, was born in 1757. His father, who is said to have been a Lanark man with the same christian name, had served as a trooper under the Duke of Cumberland in Flanders, and fought at Fontenoy. About 1746, having lost an arm, he became an out-pensioner of Chelsea Hospital, and afterwards filled for forty years the post of sexton to the Moravian burying-ground at Chelsea, where he was himself interred in 1799. His son James is the only one of his descendants of whom any record has been preserved. Nothing is known of his early training beyond the fact that at a fitting age he was (like Hogarth) apprenticed to a letter-engraver. Whether this was because he had shown a talent for drawing is not stated, but he seems to have begun to design during his apprenticeship. Becoming tired of a monotonous employment, he ran away and joined a troop of strollers. Quitting these again, after a brief experience, to enter himself as a student of the Royal Academy, he began speedily to acquire that grasp and knowledge of figure drawing which is one of his characteristics. Concurrently with his labours at the Academy, he is thought to have studied engraving with W. W. Ryland [q. v.], whose dot-manner he practised, and with Bartolozzi. He must have begun in good time to exercise his satiric talent, for an early etching which is ascribed to him, a caricature of Lord North, with an owl on his head, entitled 'A Committee of Grievances and Apprehensions,' is dated 12 June 1769, or when he was a boy of twelve. Other anonymous efforts succeeded, for some of which he is believed to have used the initials of Pitt's caricaturist, James Sayer, but he was first revealed in his own name by a design called 'Paddy on Horseback' (the horse being a bull), which bears date 4 March 1779. After 1780 his works, which had hitherto been chiefly devoted to social subjects, became almost exclusively political, and his long career as a political caricaturist may be said to have begun in 1782 with the series of designs in which he signalised the popular victory of Rodney over De Grasse off Guadeloupe.

From this time until 1811, when he engraved his last plate, he continued to pour out the characteristic pictorial satires which for nearly thirty years delighted Londoners, and induced an astonished German visitor to declare that England was 'altogeder von libel.' The royal family, the court, the nobility, the ministry, 'all sorts and conditions of men,' were freely ridiculed by this daring censor, who, after publishing with Holland of Oxford Street, Fores of Piccadilly, and others, finally took up his residence with, and practically confined his efforts to, the establishment of Miss (by courtesy Mrs.) H. Humphrey, which, originally located in the Strand, passed afterwards to New Bond Street, then to Old Bond Street, and ultimately to No. 29 St. James's Street. Here, while the artist was working above in his eager, feverish way, often wounding his fingers by the 'burr' thrown up in the rapid progress of his needle over the copper, his brightly coloured works were dispensed in the shop beneath by Miss Humphrey or her giggling assistant, Betty Marshall. One of his prints, 'Very Slippy-Weather' (10 Feb. 1808), represents the famous old shop, with its accustomed crowd outside (a crowd often so great that the passer-by had to quit the footway in order to get by), and decorated by many well-known designs. Another, 'Twopenny Whist' (11 Jan. 1796), shows Miss Humphrey herself in a white satin trimmed cap, Mortimer the picture dealer, a German friend, Schotter, and the radiant Betty, who is exhibiting the trump card. Mortimer, who was Miss Humphrey's neighbour in St. James's Street, also appears in 'Connoisseurs examining a collection of George Morlands' (16 Nov. 1807). Gillray continued to be an inmate of Miss Humphrey's house until he died. She made a handsome income by his labours, and in return supplied her retiring and somewhat morose lodger with every requirement. His health at length yielded to growing habits of intemperance, fostered, it is only charitable to suppose, by the constant strain upon his inventive powers, and about the end of 1811 he sank into comparative imbecility, passing a great part of the latter years of his life confined in an upper chamber of Miss Humphrey's house. Once, as witnessed by Stanley the picture-dealer, and the artist, Kenny Meadows, he was with difficulty restrained from throwing himself out of window. His last appearance, unclad, unshorn, and haggard, was in the shop which his creations had made so popular. He had escaped for a moment from the vigilance of his guardians, but was speedily reconducted to his room, and on the same day, 1 June 1815, he died, aged 58 years. He was buried near the rectory house in the churchyard of St. James's, Piccadilly, where there is a flat stone to his memory.

The miniature of Gillray in the National Portrait Gallery, painted by himself on ivory, represents an elderly man in a blue-grey coat and high collar, with shaven face, dull grey eyes, and grey hair. It has been engraved in mezzotint by Charles Turner (19 April 1819) and in stipple by J. Brown. In character he is described as a 'silent, shy, and inexplicable' personage, who took his pleasures in his own solitary fashion, a course which, coupled with his vocation as a caricaturist, favoured exaggerated rumours as to his peculiarities. But those who knew him intimately found him no more than reserved and undemonstrative, and never detected in him those evidences of grosser tastes with which he has been charged. His relations with Miss Humphrey were, perhaps inevitably, a fertile subject of scandalous speculation, but in justice to the poor lady, who when his mind gave way treated her demented lodger with the greatest kindness, an emphatic contradiction has been given to report. That, as might perhaps be expected, marriage was more than once mooted is not improbable, and there is a pleasant legend that the pair once actually set out for St. James's Church upon this errand. But the artist turned back before they reached their destination, having decided on the way that things were better as they were, a sentiment in which the lady apparently acquiesced.

Gillray's work extended to some fifteen hundred pieces. Many of his most popular efforts were levelled at 'Farmer George' and his wife, whose frugal habits he ridiculed in 'Frying Sprats' and 'Toasting Muffins' (23 Nov. 1791), and also in 'Anti-Saccharites' (27 March 1792), where the royal pair are subjecting the unwilling princesses to a régime of sugarless tea. He contrasts them again in 'Temperance enjoying a Frugal Meal' (28 July 1792) with their luxurious son and heir, who is depicted (2 July) as 'A Voluptuary under the Horrors of Digestion,' a design which George Cruikshank afterwards recalled in his famous 'First Gentleman in Europe' recovering from a debauch. In 'Monstrous Craws at a Coalition Feast' (29 May 1787) and 'A New Way to Pay the National Debt' (21 April 1786) he satirised their avarice and the penniless condition of the Prince of Wales, whose marriage in 1788 prompted 'Wife or no Wife' (27 March) with its admirable sketch of Lord North as a sleeping coachman, and 'A Scene on the Continent' (5 April). 'Ancient Music' (10 May 1787) deals with one of the most defined royal tastes by showing their majesties enraptured at a discordant concert of ministers. Another exceedingly caustic design, prompted by some depreciatory utterance of royalty, is 'A Connoisseur examining a Cooper' (18 June 1792), in which, by the light of a candle on a save-all, King George blinks at a miniature of his special abhorrence, Oliver Cromwell. In 'The King of Brobdingnag and Gulliver' (26 June 1803) and the sequel plate, which exhibits a diminutive Napoleon manœuvring a tiny boat in a cistern for the amusement of the royal family, the laugh is more against the terrible Corsican. The circle at the palace, where Gillray's latest efforts were always regularly supplied wet from the press, are said to have been delighted with this production. They were even pleased with 'Anti-Saccharites,' which is by no means complimentary to Queen Charlotte, but it is scarcely to be wondered at that they were highly offended by 'Sin, Death, and the Devil' (9 June 1792), in which the queen, as a loathsome hag, is shown interposing between Pitt and the black-browed Chancellor Thurlow. It may be doubted whether a more outrageous political attack has ever been made upon royalty. Certainly for daring and power (and it may be added for aptitude of allusion) it would be difficult to match this savage performance.

In several of Gillray's remaining designs the young premier, William Pitt, plays a prominent part. In 'The Vulture of the Constitution' (3 Jan. 1789), 'An Excrescence' (20 Dec. 1791), 'God Save the King' (27 May 1795), 'Presages of the Millennium' (4 June 1795), 'The Death of the Great Wolf,' a travesty of West (17 Dec. 1795), 'The Plumb Pudding in Danger' (26 Feb. 1805), 'Uncorking Old Sherry' (10 March 1805), and 'Disciples Catching the Mantle' (25 June

1808), he is either the sole or the conspicuous figure. The dusky muzzle of Charles James Fox is nearly as often under Gillray's needle, e.g. in 'Spouting' (14 May 1792), 'The Slough of Despond' (2 Jan. 1793), 'Blue and Buff Charity' (12 June 1793), and 'The Worn-out Patriot' (13 Oct. 1800). Sheridan's mottled and once handsome face is also often reproduced, and Burke's (to cite but one example) in the famous 'Dagger Scene' (30 Dec. 1792), which includes all the other notabilities above named. 'A Smoking Club' (13 Feb. 1793) also contains portraits of Pitt, Fox, and Sheridan. The last two appear again in a remarkable work entitled 'Doublures of Characters, or Striking Resemblances in Physiognomy,' executed in November 1798 for the 'Anti-Jacobin Magazine,' and comprising portraits of Sir Francis Burdett, Horne Tooke, and the Dukes of Norfolk and Bedford. The exploits of Nelson and Napoleon, the Broad Bottom administration, and the French revolution naturally prompt many plates. But the catalogue of the strictly political caricatures would be endless. The more important are 'Market Day' (2 May 1788); 'Fatigues of the [Duke of York's] Campaign in Flanders' (20 May 1793); 'The Loyal Toast,' i.e. the Duke of Norfolk's 'Majesty of the People' (3 Feb. 1798); 'The Apotheosis of Hoche' (11 Dec. 1798); 'The Union Club' (21 Jan. 1801); 'Confederated Coalition' (1 May 1804); 'L'Assemblée Nationale' (18 June 1804); 'More Pigs than Teats' (5 March 1806); its supplement, 'The Pigs Possessed' (18 April 1807); and 'The Great Balloon' (8 Aug. 1810), a satire upon the installation of Lord Grenville as lord chancellor of Oxford, which is also the last political engraving bearing the artist's name.

Many of Gillray's social, or rather non-political, subjects are still popular. 'The March to the Bank' (22 Aug. 1787), 'The Bengal Levee' (9 Nov. 1792), 'Heroes Recruiting at Kelseys,' the fruiterer in St. James's Street (9 June 1797), the burlesque on inoculation, called 'The Cow Pock' (12 June 1802), 'A Broad Hint of not meaning to Dance,' and 'Company shocked at a Lady getting up to Ring the Bell' (20 Nov. 1804), 'Harmony before Matrimony' and 'Matrimonial Harmonics' (25 Oct. 1805), are all favourite examples in this kind. Of satires aimed more directly at individuals, may be cited the prints called 'Sandwich Carrots' (3 Dec. 1796), with its attractive barrow-woman; 'Push Pin' (17 April 1797) as played by 'Old Q.' and Miss Vanneck; 'A Peep at Christie's' (24 Sept. 1796); 'The Marriage of Cupid and Psyche' (3 May 1797), showing the dumpy Lord Derby with his second wife,

the tall Miss Farren; and 'The Bulstrode Siren' (14 April 1803), Mrs. Billington and the Duke of Portland. To this class of non-political caricature belongs also Gillray's last work, 'Interior of a Barber's Shop in Assize Time,' engraved from a design by H. W. Bunbury [q. v.] It is dated 9 Jan. 1811, but during the eclipse of the artist's powers had long been painfully 'in hand.' It was published 15 May 1818.

Among Gillray's miscellaneous works is a series of stippled plates in red, entitled 'Hollandia Regenerata,' which was published in Holland with Dutch inscriptions, and was intended 'to ridicule the republican costumes and appointments.' Occasionally he made excursions into serious art. In June 1784 he designed and engraved two oval subjects from Goldsmith's 'Deserted Village,' which in style are said to resemble Stothard. He also executed three or four marine subjects, a likeness of Dr. Arne in profile after Bartolozzi (1782), 'Colonel Gardiner's last Interview with his Wife and Daughters before the Battle of Preston Pans' (1786), and two portraits of Pitt. Besides these he is known to have etched several plates bearing fictitious names. In a design called 'A Domestic Musical Party' (1804) he essayed lithography, and he cut or drew a few subjects on wood, now so rare that of one of them, 'A Beggar at a Door,' only a solitary impression is known to exist. Another was a medallion portrait of Pitt which appears as the title-page vignette in Bohn's collection of Gillray's works.

Gillray's most enduring work, however, was done as a caricaturist, and as a caricaturist pure and simple he holds a foremost place in that division of English graphic art. Much of the intensity, the almost ferocious energy, of his satire is scarcely conceivable in these milder days, but, that admission made, it is impossible not to admire his inexhaustible fertility of fancy, the frequent grandeur of his conception, the reckless audacity of his attack, and his skill in selecting the vulnerable side of his victims. His executive facility was unexampled. Often, equipped only with a few slight outlines of his characters on tiny cards (some of which are still preserved by collectors), he would, without further preliminary study, rapidly cover a copper plate with intricate groups of figures, composed and contrasted with consummate skill. George Cruikshank, who knew him towards the close of his career, describes his enthusiasm over his work as extraordinary and even as painful to witness, since it seemed in its hurrying excitement like a premonition of insanity. There are, indeed, discernible traces of coming trouble in his last works.

[Gillray's 'original coppers' were purchased at Miss Humphrey's death by H. G. Bohn. A selection of them had been published in 1818, and again with illustrative description by M'Clean in 1830, 2 vols. In 1851 Bohn issued 582 of them in one atlas folio volume, with a separate octavo key by Thomas Wright and R. H. Evans. The chief authority for Gillray, however, is the Works of James Gillray, the Caricaturist, with the History of his Life and Times, described on the title-page as edited by Thomas Wright, but now understood to have been the work of Joseph Grego, the author of Rowlandson, the Caricaturist, and published (n.d.) by Chatto & Windus. It has 'over four hundred illustrations,' many of which were drawn on wood by Grego. Besides this, George Stanley's sketch in Bryan, ed. 1858, pp. 283–3*, Buss's English Graphic Satire, 1874, pp. 113–29, and Everitt's English Caricaturists, 1886, may be profitably consulted.]   A. D.

GILLY, WILLIAM STEPHEN (1789–1855), divine, born on 28 Jan. 1789, was the son of William Gilly (d. 1837), rector of Hawkedon, Suffolk, and of Wanstead, Essex. In November 1797 he was admitted at Christ's Hospital, London, whence he proceeded in 1808 to Caius College, Cambridge, but graduated B.A. as a member of St. Catharine Hall in 1812 (List of Exhibitioners of Christ's Hospital, ed. 1885, p. 39). He proceeded M.A. in 1817, and accumulated his degrees in divinity in 1833. In 1817 he was presented by Lord-chancellor Eldon to the rectory of North Fambridge in Essex. He paid the first of many visits to the Vaudois in 1823, and during the following year published a 'Narrative of an Excursion to the Mountains of Piemont, and Researches among the Vaudois, or Waldenses,' 4to, London, 1824; 3rd edition, 8vo, 1826. Much sympathy for the Vaudois was evoked in England by Gilly's book. A subscription, headed by the king and Barrington, bishop of Durham, was started for their relief, and was devoted in part to the endowment of a college and library at La Tour in Piedmont. On 13 May 1826 Gilly was collated to a prebendal stall in Durham Cathedral (LE NEVE, Fasti, ed. Hardy, iii. 317). The following year he became perpetual curate of St. Margaret, Durham, and in 1831 vicar of Norham, near Berwick-on-Tweed. In 1853 he was appointed canon residentiary of Durham. With a view to bettering the condition of the agricultural labourers in north Northumberland, he wrote 'The Peasantry of the Border; an Appeal in their behalf,' 8vo, Berwick-upon-Tweed, 1841 (2nd edition, London, 1842), in which he called the attention of landowners

to the miserable condition of the cottages. Gilly died at Norham on 10 Sept. 1855. He married, in December 1825, Jane Charlotte Mary, only daughter of Major Colberg, who survived him (Gent. Mag. vol. xcv. pt. ii. p. 640). His other works include: 1. 'The Spirit of the Gospel, or the Four Evangelists, elucidated by explanatory observations,' 8vo, London, 1818. 2. 'Horæ Catecheticæ, or an exposition of the duty and advantages of Public Catechising in Church,' 8vo, London, 1828. 3. 'Waldensian Researches during a second Visit to the Vaudois of Piemont,' 8vo, London, 1831. 4. 'A Memoir of Felix Neff, pastor of the High Alps,' 8vo, London, 1832 (many editions). Lord Monson published in 1840 some folio 'Views' in illustration of this memoir. 5. 'Our Protestant Forefathers,' 12mo, London, 1835 (many editions). 6. 'Valdenses, Valdo, and Vigilantius; being the articles under these heads in the seventh edition of the Encyclopædia Britannica,' 8vo, Edinburgh, 1841 (the third article was reprinted separately in 1844). 7. 'The Romaunt Version of the Gospel according to St. John. With an introductory history,' 8vo, London, 1848. 8. 'A Comparative View of the progress of Popular Instruction. Two Lectures,' 12mo, Durham, 1848. He contributed a preface to 'Narratives of Shipwrecks of the Royal Navy, between 1793 and 1849,' compiled principally from official documents at the admiralty by his son William O. S. Gilly, and another to J. L. Williams's 'Short History of the Waldensian Church,' 1855. His three letters on the 'Noble Lesson' and Waldensian MSS., communicated to the 'British Magazine' for 1841, are reprinted in the appendix to J. H. Todd's 'Books of the Vaudois,' 1865.

[Gent. Mag. new ser. xliv. 437–9, 626.]
G. G.

GILMOUR, SIR JOHN (d. 1671), Scottish judge, son of John Gilmour, writer to the signet, was bred to his father's profession, but on 12 Dec. 1628 he was admitted an advocate. His professional connection lay among the royalist party, and he was appointed by the committee of estates counsel for the Earl of Montrose in 1641. When the court of session was re-established at the Restoration, he was appointed lord president on 13 Feb. 1661, his appointment was approved by parliament on 5 April, and the sittings of the court were resumed on 1 June. He received a pension of 500l. per annum as lord president. He also was sworn of the privy council, and was made a lord of the exchequer. He was elected commissioner for the shire of Edinburgh in the parliament of 1661, which he continued to represent till his death, and at the same time he was appointed a lord of articles. He obtained the insertion of a clause in the Militia Act that the kingdom should not be obliged to maintain any force levied by the king otherwise than as it should be agreed by parliament or a convention of estates. He spoke in parliament in defence of the Marquis of Argyll, but without avail, and, joining the Lauderdale party, helped, especially by personal audiences with the king in London, to overthrow Middleton in 1663. In 1664 he became a member of the court of high commission, and exerted his influence without success to mitigate the severity of the bishops who were members of it. In the privy council he refused to vote for the execution of the insurgents taken at Pentland, to whom quarter had been promised; but he signed the opinion of the court of session to the effect that forfeiture could be pronounced against accused persons in their absence if they had been duly cited to appear. On 22 Dec. 1670 he resigned his judgeship in consequence of ill-health, and died next year. Reports of his decisions from 1661 to 1666 are preserved. He is described by Sir George Mackenzie in his 'Idea Eloquentiæ Forensis' as a man of rough eloquence and powerful common sense, but little learning. There is a portrait of him by Scougal at Inch, near Edinburgh.

[Books of Sederunt; Acts Scots Parl.; Wodrow's Analecta; Fountainhall's Decisions, i. 500; Fountainhall's Chronological Notes, p. 224; Omond's Lord Advocates; Anderson's Scottish Nation; Douglas's Peerage, ed. Wood, i. 99; Brunton and Haig's Senators of the Royal Coll. of Justice.] J. A. H.

GILPIN, BERNARD (1517–1583), the 'Apostle of the North,' was born at Kentmere, Westmoreland, in 1517. He came, both by father and mother, of 'ancient and honourable' families. His mother was daughter of William Laton of Delamain, Cumberland. Having received the rudiments of education at a grammar school in the north, Gilpin was sent to Queen's College, Oxford, at the age of sixteen. At Oxford he was much attracted to the works of Erasmus, and received help in acquiring Greek and Hebrew from Mr. Neale, a fellow of New College, and afterwards the author of the famous Nag's-head fable. Gilpin proceeded B.A. in 1539–40, and M.A. in 1541–2, and was about the same time elected fellow of his college and admitted into holy orders by the Bishop of Oxford. He took his B.D. degree in 1549. His scrupulous conscience was much troubled by an oath required of him at his ordination (thought necessary on account of the recent

breach with Rome), that he held all such ordinations, past or future, to be valid. Cardinal Wolsey's foundation of Christ Church had now been completed by the king, and the most promising scholars were sought for to be admitted as students. Among these Gilpin was one of the first elected. As yet he had no inclination towards the reformed opinions in religion, and in fact undertook to hold a public disputation with John Hooper in defence of the old doctrinal views. In this he obtained considerable reputation, insomuch that in the next reign, when Peter Martyr was established as divinity professor at Oxford, Gilpin was put forward to dispute with him. It was now that, searching diligently into the records of the primitive church, Gilpin began to have doubts as to the truth of the modern Roman doctrines. He applied for help to Tunstall, bishop of Durham, who was his mother's uncle, and learnt from him the comparatively modern origin of the doctrine of transubstantiation and the equivocal character of some of the papal ordinances. Afterwards he conferred with Dr. Redman, another relative, who defended the Book of Common Prayer, then newly issued. Although influenced by these arguments and a diligent search of the scriptures and fathers, Gilpin still had difficulties. At this juncture he was induced to accept the vicarage of Norton, in the diocese of Durham; but before taking possession of it he was called upon to preach before Edward VI at Greenwich (1552). In this sermon Gilpin inveighs against the abuses of the time in the scandalous robbery of church property and incomes. 'A thousand pulpits in England are covered with dust,' he says. He does not treat much of doctrine. Bishop Tunstall, who no doubt saw in which direction Gilpin's mind was moving, now advised him to travel abroad. But first Gilpin insisted, much against the bishop's will, on resigning his benefice. He then proceeded abroad, where he remained some years, first at Louvain and afterwards at Paris. At Paris he lived in the house of Vascosanus, the printer, and occupied himself with carrying through the press a work of Tunstall on the Eucharist. Returning into England in the latter years of Queen Mary, Gilpin was in 1556 promoted by Tunstall to the rectory of Easington and the archdeaconry of Durham. The persecution prevalent in England under Mary, though the mild temper of Tunstall would not allow it to be felt in the diocese of Durham, seems to have decided Gilpin to set forth reforming views with greater distinctness and earnestness. He also reproved vigorously the faults of the clergy. Consequently he was soon denounced to the bishop as a heretic, but Tunstall replied to his accusers: 'Father's soul! let him alone; he hath more learning than you all.' The bishop even conferred on Gilpin the important rectory of Houghton-le-Spring, ' being a very large parish, containing fourteen villages, with very large possessions' (CARLETON). His house was like a bishop's palace, and far superior to many palaces, and his position that of a clerical magnate. Gilpin now entered upon that extended sphere of work and influence which gained for him the title of the 'Apostle of the North.' Taking compassion on the miserably neglected state of parts of Northumberland and Yorkshire, he used every winter to make a progress through Riddesdale and Tyndale and some other districts, where scarcely any preachers were to be found, preaching and distributing alms. The people almost worshipped him, and numerous anecdotes are preserved by his biographers of the extraordinary influence which he had over them. At Houghton Gilpin's charities were on the most extensive scale. He would sometimes strip his cloak off and give it to an ill-clad beggar. Riding with his servants in the country on one occasion, he saw a poor husbandman's horse fall down dead in the plough. Immediately Gilpin told one of his servants to unsaddle his horse and give it to the poor man. His habit was on Sundays to feast all his parishioners, in three divisions, according to their ranks, at his table. But his most valuable work was the foundation, on a scale of great munificence, of a grammar school. From this school many scholars were sent to the universities. Some were supported there at Gilpin's cost. A large number of the boys attending the school were boarded and lodged in Gilpin's house free of all charge. Gilpin's zeal and munificence soon made for him a great and dangerous reputation. His enemies, unable to persuade Tunstall to proceed against him, laid thirty-two articles of accusation before Bonner, bishop of London. The bishop, acting probably under the queen's commission, sent a pursuivant to bring him to London. On the way Gilpin accidentally broke his leg, which probably saved his life, as before he was able to travel Queen Mary died. At the death of Oglethorpe, bishop of Carlisle (1559), Gilpin was much pressed to accept the bishopric. But he steadily refused, his reason being that, having so many friends and kindred in the diocese who were not in accord with him in opinions, he would be much hampered in his work. In the following year the provostship of Queen's College, Oxford, was offered to him. This he also declined.

When, after the passing of Queen Elizabeth's Injunctions, commissioners went through the country to enforce conformity, Gilpin had considerable difficulty in signing the required declaration. Sandys, bishop of Worcester, Gilpin's cousin, was one of the commissioners, and he insisted on Gilpin preaching before them at Auckland against the supremacy of the pope. This he consented to do; but a sermon preached the day before by Dr. Sandys on the Eucharist so shocked him that he had the greatest difficulty to bring himself to perform his task. On the next day, when the subscription was to be made, Gilpin endeavoured to avoid it, but was told that if he refused all the clergy in the north would follow his example. This induced him at last to consent, though he does not appear to have been fully satisfied with the settlement of the church of England. In June 1560 Gilpin entertained at Houghton Sir William Cecil and Dr. Wotton, sent as ambassadors to Scotland. During the northern rebellion (1569) his house and barns were plundered by the rebels; but upon its repression Gilpin was very active in endeavouring to save the lives of the misguided people implicated. Great attempts were now made by the puritan party to obtain the countenance and support of Gilpin for their 'discipline.' He was intimate with Bishop Pilkington, the successor of Tunstall at Durham, who was much inclined to favour the puritans, and with Thomas Lever, another puritan leader. But his great reverence for the fathers and for primitive antiquity preserved him from accepting these modern views. His laborious ministrations, his boundless charities, and, above all, his unsparing and outspoken denunciation of the abuses then prevalent, made Gilpin many enemies. Among these was Richard Barnes [q. v.], who succeeded Pilkington as bishop of Durham. Barnes was not congenial to Gilpin, and his brother, who acted as chancellor, was notorious for gross abuses. The bishop insisted, at a visitation at Chester-le-Street, that Gilpin should preach. Gilpin was not prepared with a sermon, but, being urged by the bishop, delivered in the plainest and most forcible language a strong censure of the proceedings of the bishop and chancellor. The bishop accompanied Gilpin to his house, and on entering it seized his hand, exclaiming: 'Father Gilpin, I acknowledge you are fitter to be bishop of Durham than myself parson of this church of yours. I ask forgiveness for errors past; forgive me, father. I know you have hatched up some chickens that now seek to pick out your eyes; but so long as I shall live bishop of Durham be secure, no man shall injure you' (CARLETON). Gilpin's health had begun to fail, when he was knocked down by an ox in the market-place at Durham, and received injuries from which he never quite recovered. He died 4 March 1583, in the sixty-sixth year of his age. An affectionate memoir of this good man has been written by George Carleton [q. v.], bishop of Chichester, who was one of the scholars at Gilpin's school at Houghton, and also by William Gilpin [q. v.], a descendant of the family. The only printed work of his which remains is the sermon preached before Edward VI in 1552. This sermon was on the text Luke ii. 41–9, printed with Carleton's memoir at London in the edition of 1636, also printed in Gilpin's 'Life.'

[Life of Bernard Gilpin, by George Carleton, Bishop of Chichester, in Latin, London, 1628, in English, London, 1629; Life of Bernard Gilpin, by W. Gilpin, 1753, reissued in Gilpin's Lives of Reformers, vol. ii. London, 1809; Strype's Life and Acts of Edm. Grindal, London, 1710, fol.; Wood's Fasti (Bliss), i. 129.] G. G. P.

GILPIN, GEORGE (1514?–1602), diplomatist and translator, usually called THE ELDER to distinguish him from the eldest son of his elder brother, was the second son of Edwin Gilpin of Kentmere, Westmoreland, by Margaret, daughter of Thomas Layton of Dalemain, Cumberland, and elder brother of Bernard Gilpin [q. v.] In W. Gilpin's 'Life of Bernard' (London, 1753, sect. 3) some particulars are given respecting George. When Bernard in 1553 left England, he visited George at Mechlin, where he was studying the civil law. The visit was 'probably upon a religious account,' but lasted only a few weeks. In 1554, on Mary's accession, George received a letter from Bishop Tunstall, just released from the Tower, offering Bernard a valuable benefice if he would return to England. George was anxious that his brother should accept the offer, and would seem at this time to have been still a papist. He must, however, have become a protestant soon after, and in Elizabeth's reign become absorbed in politics. He was till his death one of the queen's most trusted agents in her negotiations with the states of the Low Countries. The Earl of Bedford is said to have first brought him to court. Frequent references to him occur in the Domestic and Foreign Series of the 'Calendar of State Papers,' from 1561 till his death in 1602. In 1561 the queen in a letter to Sir Thomas Gresham promises to befriend his secretary Gilpin in any reasonable suit, and he would seem to have shortly afterwards become a salaried servant of the English government. In 1577 he petitioned Burghley to ask the

queen 'for arrearages of certain concealed lands.' He became before his death councillor to the council of estate in the Low Countries. J. L. Motley is of opinion that an unfortunate despatch written by him prevented the relief of Antwerp in 1585, but speaks of him as 'the highly intelligent agent of the English government in Zeeland' (United Netherlands, 1867, i. 287–8, 298–9, 403). An instance of his diplomatic ability in the conduct of disputes with the Hanse Towns is given by C. Molloy (De Jure Maritimo et Navali, 1769, ii. 144). His death is announced in a letter to Dudley Carleton, dated 2 Oct. 1602, which mentions the difficulty of finding a successor. Many of Gilpin's letters are to Dudley Carleton. Calisthenes Brook, writing to Carleton in Paris, calls him 'your cousin Gilpin' (Cal. State Papers, Dom. Ser. Addenda, 1580–1625, pp. 153, 410). Gilpin published a (now rare) translation of the 'Apiarium Romanum' (1571) by Philip von Marnix, seigneur de St. Aldegonde. The first edition is entitled 'The Beehive of the Romishe Churche. Wherein the author, a zealous Protestant, under the person of a superstitious Papist, doth so driely refell the grose opinions of Popery, and so divinely defend the articles of Christianitie, that (the Sacred Scriptures excepted) there is not a booke to be founde either more necessarie for thy profite, or sweeter for thy comforte. Translated out of Dutch into Englishe by George Gilpin the Elder,' 1579, 8vo. The volume is dedicated to Master Philip Sidney, esq. The second edition is entitled 'The Beehive of the Romishe Churche. A Worke of all good Catholikes to be read, and most necessary to be understood. Wherein the Catholike Religion is substantially confirmed, and the Heretikes finely fetched over the coales. Translated out of Dutch into English by Geo. Gilpin the Elder. 1 Thess. v. 21. Newly imprinted, with a table thereunto annexed,' 1580, 8vo. Abraham Fleming [q. v.] compiled the table. Other editions followed in 1598, 1623, and 1636.

[Cal. of State Papers, Dom. Ser. and For. Ser. from 1560 to 1602; Ames's Typogr. Antiq. (Herbert), ii. 1119; Brit. Mus. Cat.; Biographie Universelle, vol. xxvii. under 'Marnix.'] R. B.

GILPIN, RANDOLPH (d. 1661), divine, came of that branch of the Gilpin family of Kentmere and Scaleby, which was seated at Bungay in Suffolk. His exact descent cannot be determined from the pedigree appended to William Gilpin's 'Memoirs of Dr. Richard Gilpin,' published by the Cumberland and Westmoreland Antiquarian Society in 1879. He was educated at Eton, from which he was elected in 1611 to King's College, Cambridge, and proceeded M.A. in 1618. He was poser in 1627 (HARWOOD, *Alumni Eton.* p. 213). He acted as chaplain to the fleet which sailed to the relief of Rochelle in 1628. During the same year he was presented by Francis Gilpin to the rectory of Barningham, Suffolk (*Addit. MS.* 19079, f. 81). He did not live very harmoniously with his parishioners. Disputes about certain alleged customs in tithing led to a multiplicity of suits in various courts of law. Gilpin thereupon petitioned the king, 17 Oct. 1637, praying that the whole matter might be referred to the Archbishop of Canterbury and the Bishop of Norwich (*Cal. State Papers,* Dom. 1637, pp. 478-9). The cause came on for hearing in the inner Star-chamber, 24 Jan. 1636, when an order was made in adjustment of the tithes, but Gilpin did not escape a lecture from Laud on the duty of living in peace with his flock (*ib.* Dom. 1637-8, p. 183). During the Commonwealth he occupied himself in the composition of a little work which he dedicated to Eton School ; it is entitled 'Liturgica Sacra ; Curru Thesbitico, i.e. Zeli inculpabilis vehiculo deportata, & viâ devotionis Regiâ deducta a Rand. Gilpin, Sacerd. Vel, Opsonia spiritualia omnibus verè Christianis, etiam pueris degustanda,' 8vo [London ?], 1657. At the Restoration he was created D.D. by royal mandate (*Graduati Cantabr.*) He also obtained from the king the rectory of Worlingham, Suffolk, 10 May 1661 (*Addit. MS.* 19112, f. 246 b). He died a bachelor in 1661. His will, dated 9 Nov. 1661, requests that he may be buried in St. Mary's Church, Bungay.

[Authorities as above.]   G. G.

GILPIN, RICHARD, M.D. (1625-1700), nonconformist divine and physician, second son of Isaac Gilpin of Strickland-Kettle, in the parish of Kendal, Westmoreland, and Ann, daughter of Ralph Tonstall of Coatham-Mundeville, Durham, was born at Strickland, and baptised at Kendal on 23 Oct. 1625. He was educated at Edinburgh University, graduating M.A. on 30 July 1646, and studying first medicine, then divinity. Neither the date nor the manner of his ordination is known. He began his ministry at Lambeth, continued it at the Savoy as assistant to John Wilkins, afterwards bishop of Chester (CALAMY), and then returning to the north preached at Durham. In 1650 William Morland had been sequestered from the rectory of Greystoke, Cumberland, worth 300*l.* a year. For about two years the living had been held by one West, a popular preacher, who died of consumption. Gilpin succeeded him in 1652 or early in 1653. No fifths were paid to Mor-

land. In the large parish of Greystoke there were four chapels, which Gilpin supplied with preachers. His parish was organised on the congregational model, having an inner circle of communicants and a staff of deacons. The presbyterian system, which it seems that Gilpin would have preferred, had not been adopted in Cumberland. In August 1653 Gilpin set on foot a voluntary association of the churches of Cumberland and Westmoreland, on the lines of Baxter's Worcestershire 'agreement' of that year, but giving to the associated clergy somewhat larger powers than Baxter approved. The organisation worked smoothly and gained in adherents ; the terms of agreement were printed in 1656 ; in 1658 Gilpin preached (19 May) before the associated ministers at Keswick. He used his opportunities of influence with great judgment and disinterestedness, always acting as a peacemaker. His chief trouble was with the quakers, who abounded in his district ; one of his relatives at Kendal, bearing his own surname, had been for a short time a quaker. Gilpin was in the habit of giving medical advice as well as spiritual counsel to his flock. By his purchase of the manor of Scaleby Castle, some twenty miles north of Greystoke, beyond Carlisle, he acquired a position in the county which gave him a lead in public affairs. His reputation for learning, scientific as well as scholastic, was recognised in his appointment as visitor to the college at Durham, for which Cromwell issued a patent on 15 May 1657.

At the Restoration Gilpin was one of the most prominent religious leaders in the north of England. In the redistribution of ecclesiastical preferment he was not overlooked. He was offered the see of Carlisle, for which his capacity for organisation admirably fitted him. Calamy ascribes his refusal to his modesty, reinforced by the recollection that his kinsman, Bernard Gilpin [q. v.], had declined the same dignity at the hands of Elizabeth. The explanation is probably correct, as he had no inflexible ideas on the subject of church government. He preached at Carlisle at the opening of the assize on 10 Sept. 1660. When Richard Sterne became bishop (2 Dec.), Gilpin was not called upon to vacate his living. He resigned it on 2 Feb. 1661 in favour of the sequestered Morland, retired to Scaleby, and preached there in his large hall. He is also said to have preached occasionally at Penruddock, a village in Greystoke parish, where John Noble, one of his deacons, gathered in his own house a nonconformist congregation, afterwards ministered to by Anthony Sleigh (*d.* 1702).

Shortly after the passing of the Uniformity Act (1662) Gilpin removed to Newcastle-upon-Tyne, to minister to the hearers of the ejected lecturer, Samuel Hammond [q. v.] As early as 1663 Bishop Cosin complained of him. He did not wait for the indulgence of 1672, but openly disregarded the Conventicle Acts (1664, 1670) and the Five Mile Act (1665). Consequently he was several times presented for holding a conventicle, but escaped with fines, and does not seem to have been interfered with after 4 Aug. 1669. At Newcastle he acquired considerable repute as a physician 'among persons of rank and quality;' to legalise his practice he graduated M.D. at Leyden on 6 July 1676. Calamy describes his preaching in enthusiastic terms. He was a born orator, and though he never used notes his discourses were remarkable for method, as well as rich in pathos. His 'skill in government' was taxed by 'a numerous congregation of very different opinions and tempers.' Calamy says (Abridgment, 1702, p. 415) 'he left them in peace; tho' fearful of what hath since happ'ned among them' [see BRADBURY, THOMAS; Madame Partis, mentioned in that article, was Gilpin's daughter]. From 1694 to 1698 Gilpin had as assistant William Pell [q. v.], ejected from Great Stainton, Durham. Pell was followed by Timothy Manlove (d. 3 Aug. 1699), and Manlove by Bradbury.

Early in February 1700 Gilpin was seized with a feverish cold; his last sermon 'he rather groan'd than spake,' the text (2 Cor. v. 2) being strangely appropriate. He died on 13 Feb., and was buried on 16 (BARNES) or 21 (HEYWOOD) Feb. in All Saints' Church, Newcastle. He was of short stature, with a mobile countenance; his likeness is given in Grosart's edition of the 'Dæmonologia,' from a painting in the possession of a descendant, Dr. Gilpin of Halifax, Nova Scotia. He was twice married; his second wife, who survived him, was Susanna, daughter of William Brisco of Crofton, Yorkshire. She removed to Scaleby Castle, and died on 18 Jan. 1715. His children were : (1) William, born 5 Sept. 1657, remained a churchman, became recorder of Carlisle (1718), was noted for artistic and antiquarian tastes, married Mary, daughter of Henry Fletcher of Tallantire, Cumberland, and was buried 14 Dec. 1724; (2) Isaac, born 12 July 1658, died 21 Feb. 1719; (3) Susanna, born 17 Oct. 1659, married Matthias Partis; (4) Anne, born 5 Dec. 1660, married Jeremiah Sawrey of Broughton Tower, Lancashire; buried 11 April 1745; (5) Elizabeth, born 3 Aug. 1662; (6) Richard, born 4 May 1664, died young; (7) Mary, born 28 Dec. 1666; (8) Dorothy, born 13 Aug. 1668, married, first, Jabez Cay, M.D., of Newcastle-upon-Tyne; secondly, on 29 Dec. 1704, Eli Fenton; died April 1708; (9) John, born 13 Feb. 1670, merchant at Whitehaven, made a fortune in the Virginia trade; married Hannah, daughter of Robert Cay of Newcastle-upon-Tyne; buried 26 Nov. 1732; (10) Frances, born 27 July 1671, died young; (11) Bernard, born 6 Oct. 1672, died young in Jamaica; (12) Frances, born 27 Jan. 1675, died young; (13) Thomas, born 27 July 1677, died 20 June 1700.

He published : 1. 'The Agreement of the Associated Ministers and Churches of Cumberland and Westmerland' (sic), &c., 1646, 4to (anon.) 2. 'The Temple Rebuilt,' &c., 1658, 4to (sermon, Zach. vi. 13, to associated ministers). 3. 'Disputatio Medica Inauguralis de Hysterica Passione,' &c., 1676, 4to. 4. 'Dæmonologia Sacra; or, a Treatise of Satan's Temptations,' &c., 3 pts., 1677, 4to; 2nd edit. Edinburgh, 1735, 8vo; new edition, by A. B. Grosart, Edinburgh, 1867, 8vo (a work of religious experience, the first title somewhat misleading). 5. 'The Comforts of Divine Love,' &c., 1700, 8vo (funeral sermon for Manlove). Posthumous was 6. 'An Assize Sermon . . . at Carlisle,' &c., London and Newcastle, 1700, 4to (preached in 1660, see above). Among Gilpin's manuscripts was a treatise on the 'Pleasantness of the Ways of Religion,' which Calamy desired to see in print; it has since perished. The communion cups of the church of the Divine Unity, Newcastle-upon-Tyne, which bore the inscription, 'Church Plate, Dr. Richard Gilpin, Pastor, 1693,' were sold some years back 'to provide a set of more modern pattern.'

[Memoir, by Grosart, prefixed to Dæmonologia Sacra, 1867; Memoirs by W. Gilpin, 1879; Calamy's Account, 1713, pp. 154 sq.; Continuation, 1727, i. 226; Walker's Sufferings, 1714, ii. 306; Monthly Repository, 1811, pp. 514 sq.; Cat. Edinb. Graduates, 1858, p. 65; George Fox's Journal, 1694, p. 123; Thomas Story's Journal, 1747 (interview with Gilpin in 1691); Memoir of Ambrose Barnes, ed. Longstaffe (Surtees Soc.), l. 153; Turner's Northowram Register (Heywood's and Dickenson's), 1881, pp. 99, 197, 244; List of Chapels claimed by Presbyterians (Tooting Case), 1887, p. 48; Mearns's English Ulster, 1888, p. 34; information from the Rev. F. Walters, Newcastle.]
A. G.

GILPIN, SAWREY (1733–1807), animal painter, born at Carlisle 30 Oct. 1733, was seventh child of Captain John Bernard Gilpin and Matilda Langstaffe, his wife, and younger brother of the Rev. William Gilpin [q. v.] He learnt drawing as a child from his father, and as he showed an early predilection for the profession of an artist his father sent him to London at the age of fourteen, and placed him with Samuel Scott [q. v.], the marine painter, who then resided in Covent Garden. Gilpin, however, found greater diversion in sketching the market carts and horses than in his master's line of art, and it soon became evident that animals, and especially horses, were the most appropriate subject for his abilities. He left Scott in 1758, and devoted himself to animal painting from that time. Some of Gilpin's sketches were shown to the Duke of Cumberland, who was very much struck with them, and employed Gilpin to draw from his stud at Newmarket and at Windsor, where the duke was ranger of the Great Park. He afforded Gilpin considerable material assistance in his profession. Subsequently Gilpin resided at Knightsbridge for some years. He became one of the best painters of horses that the country has produced, and was nearly as successful in other delineations of animal life. He sometimes attempted historical pictures on a larger scale in which horses were prominent, but with rather less success. He was an animal painter only, and required the assistance of others to paint the landscapes and figures in his pictures; for the former he had frequently the assistance of George Barret the elder, R.A. [q. v.], to whom he gave similar service in return, and for the latter he had recourse sometimes to John Zoffany, R.A.[q.v.], and Philip Reinagle [q. v.] Gilpin first appears as an exhibitor with the Incorporated Society of Artists in 1762, and exhibited there, chiefly pictures of horses, up to 1783. In 1768, 1770, 1771, he exhibited a series of pictures illustrating 'Gulliver's visit to the Houyhnhnms,' one of which was engraved in mezzotint by V. Green; in 1770 a drawing of 'Darius gaining the Persian Empire by the neighing of his horse;' in 1771 'The Duke of Cumberland visiting his stud (with a view of Windsor Castle from the Great Park, by W. Marlow).' In 1773 he became a director of the society, and in 1774 president. In 1786 he exhibited at the Royal Academy, and continued an exhibitor till his death. In November 1789 he missed being elected an associate by the casting vote of the president, Sir Joshua Reynolds, in favour of J. Bonomi. He was, however, elected an associate in 1795, and royal academician in 1797. Many of his pictures of horses, dogs, and sporting scenes have been engraved, notably 'The Death of the Fox' (Royal Academy, 1788), finely engraved by John Scott, and 'Heron-Hawking' (Soc. of Artists, 1780), engraved by T. Morris. After losing his wife Gilpin resided for some time with his friend Samuel Whitbread in Bedfordshire. He subsequently returned to London, and spent his declining years with his

daughters at Brompton, where he died 8 March 1807, in his seventy-fourth year. Gilpin also executed some etchings of horses and cattle, and contributed numerous drawings for the illustration of his brother's (the Rev. W. Gilpin) published and unpublished works. His portrait is in the series of drawings by G. Dance, engraved by W. Daniell. His son, William Sawrey Gilpin, is separately noticed.

[Redgrave's Dict. of Artists; Graves's Dict. of Artists, 1760–1880; Bryan's Dict. of Painters and Engravers, ed. R. E. Graves; Redgraves' Century of Painters, i. 350; Sandby's Hist. of the Royal Academy, i. 310; Seguier's Dict. of Painters; Gilpin's Memoirs of Dr. R. Gilpin; Catalogues of the Royal Academy and Society of Artists.]   L. C.

GILPIN, WILLIAM (1724–1804), miscellaneous writer, was born on 4 June 1724 at Scaleby Castle, near Carlisle. He was the son of Captain John Bernard Gilpin and Matilda, daughter of George Langstaffe, and a collateral descendant of Bernard Gilpin [q. v.] Sawrey Gilpin [q. v.], the artist, was his younger brother. Gilpin went to school at Carlisle, and subsequently at St. Bees, and in 1740 matriculated at Queen's College, Oxford, where, as he says, he spent six or seven years under a system of teaching 'no better than solemn trifling.' He graduated B.A. in 1744, and was ordained in 1746 by Sir George Fleming, bishop of Carlisle, to the curacy of Irthington, of which parish his uncle, the Rev. James Farish, was vicar. He shortly afterwards returned to Oxford, and proceeded M.A. in 1748, but left the university owing 70l.; to meet the debt he wrote his 'Life of Bernard Gilpin' (London, 1753, 8vo), which has been several times reissued. The work is a useful biography. Gilpin then held a curacy for a short time in London, but soon afterwards took a school at Cheam, Surrey, from a James Sanxay, where he remained nearly thirty years. About this time he married his first cousin, Margaret, daughter of William Gilpin, such unions having been frequent in his family.

At Cheam Gilpin showed himself an educational reformer considerably in advance of his time. For corporal punishment he substituted a system of fines and imprisonment, with due provision for exercise, imposed by a jury of boys. The fines were spent on the school library, on fives-courts, and other improvements, and on a dole of bread to the poor. He encouraged a love of gardening and habits of business among his pupils, and 'thought it of much more use to' them 'to study their own language with accuracy than a dead one.' Among his pupils, who averaged eighty in number, were Addington (Lord

Sidmouth), the first Lord Redesdale, and his brother, Colonel William Mitford, the historian. During his long summer vacations Gilpin undertook those sketching tours by the publication of which he afterwards became so well known. Thus in 1769 and 1773 he visited Cambridge, Norfolk, Suffolk, and Essex; in 1770 and 1782 the Wye and South Wales; in 1774 the coasts of Hampshire, Sussex, and Kent; and in 1776 Cumberland, Westmoreland, and the Scotch highlands. In 1755 the 'Life of Bernard Gilpin' was followed by that of Latimer, and in 1765 by those of Wycliffe, Cobham, Huss, Jerome of Prague, and Zisca, all of which have passed through several editions. In 1768 Gilpin published 'An Essay on Prints,' the fifth edition of which appeared in 1802. In 1777 he was presented by William Mitford to the vicarage of Boldre in the New Forest, his home for the remainder of his life. He refused another living owing to his dislike to pluralities, and all his work was henceforward devoted to the good of his parish. He lived upon his income of 600l. a year, and, so as not to deprive his children of his savings, devoted the 'profits of his amusements,' i.e. of his literary and artistic work, to parochial improvements. He promoted the establishment of a new poor-house, of which he wrote an account printed by his friend, Edward Forster of Walthamstow, for the Society for Bettering the Condition of the Poor; and he built and endowed a parish school with a house for the master. In 1779 he published 'Lectures on the Church Catechism,' originally prepared for his school-pupils. This work was repeatedly reprinted; and Bishop Barrington gave him the prebend of Beaminster Secunda in Salisbury Cathedral in recognition of its merits. In 1782 he published his 'Observations on the River Wye and several parts of South Wales . . . relative chiefly to picturesque beauty, made in the summer of the years 1770 and 1782,' the first of a series of five works with similar titles, and illustrated by aquatint drawings, which created, as has been truly said (*Gent. Mag.* vol. lxxiv. (1804) pt. i. pp. 388–9), 'a new class of travels,' though they also exposed the author to the satire of William Combe's 'Dr. Syntax.' The style of the writings has been characterised (loc. cit.) as 'too poetic . . . but full of ingenious reflections, and free from exaggeration . . . truthful and warm, but free from false vague enthusiasm.' His drawings are described by Michael Tyson (Nichols, *Lit. Anecd.* viii. 643) as 'rather studies for landscape-painters than portraits of particular places.' Some skill in drawing seems to have been here-

ditary in his family, his father being a skilful draughtsman, and Benjamin West being one of his cousins. The work on the Wye and South Wales went into five editions before 1800, in which year it was issued in French at Breslau. In 1789 it was followed by two volumes on his tour 'in the mountains and lakes of Cumberland and Westmoreland,' which was reissued in 1792, and of which both French and German editions were issued, with better aquatints than those of the original, at Breslau in 1800. In the same year appeared two volumes on the highlands of Scotland, which were equally successful. In 1790 he published another religious educational work, an 'Exposition of the New Testament,' which became as popular as his 'Lectures on the Catechism;' and in the same year appeared one of his best-known works, 'Remarks on Forest Scenery and other Woodland Views (relating chiefly to picturesque beauty), illustrated in the scenes of the New Forest.' For this work his brother Sawrey etched a set of drawings. About this time he printed a 'Funeral Sermon and Life of William Baker,' a parish impostor who entirely deceived the simple-minded vicar; and imaginary 'Lives of John Trueman and Richard Atkins, for the use of servants'-halls, farmhouses, and cottages.' In 1784 he had followed up his series of biographies of reformers by one of Cranmer. When about seventy-one he was attacked by dropsy, and, though mainly cured by the use of digitalis, was no longer able to serve his extensive parish without help, and therefore secured the assistance of the Rev. Richard Warner [q. v.] as curate. From Warner's 'Literary Recollections' we gather much of our information about Gilpin's later years. Unable to preach, he issued in 1799 and 1800 two volumes of 'Sermons to a Country Congregation; and Hints for Sermons,' a third volume of which appeared in 1803, and a fourth, posthumously, in 1805. In continuation of his works on landscape he published in 1792 three essays, on picturesque beauty, on picturesque travel, and on sketching landscapes, with a poem on landscape painting; and, in 1798, 'Picturesque Remarks on the Western Parts of England and the Isle of Wight.' He then collected together all his original drawings and had them sold by auction, by which means he was enabled to endow with 1,200l. the school he had built at Boldre, while a further sale after his death realised nearly 1,600l. Among minor works issued during his lifetime were 'Three Dialogues on the amusements of Clergymen' (1796); 'Moral Contrasts; or the Power of Religion . . .' (1798); and an edition of C. D'Oyley's 'Life of Our

Blessed Saviour' (1801). He vested all his unpublished works in trustees for the benefit of the school, in accordance with which bequest there appeared 'A Clergyman's Legacy to his Parishioners,' 1804; 'Observations on the Coasts of Hampshire, Sussex, and Kent, with two Essays on the... Mode in which the Author executed his own Drawings,' 1804; the fourth volume, and a new edition, of his sermons, 1805; 'Dialogues on Various Subjects,' 1807; and 'Observations on ... Cambridge, Norfolk, Suffolk, and Essex,' 1809.

Gilpin died on 5 April 1804 at his house at Vicar's Hill, Boldre, and is buried in the churchyard of his parish. His wife survived him for three years. Of his four children two daughters, both named Margaret, died in infancy; John Bernard married and settled in Massachusetts, and William graduated at Oxford in 1778, succeeded his father in the Cheam school about the same time, and died rector of Pulverbatch, Shropshire, in 1848 at the age of ninety-one. In 1791 Gilpin had written for his grandchildren 'Memoirs of Dr. Richard Gilpin of Scaleby Castle in Cumberland and of his Posterity in the two succeeding Generations,' which remained in manuscript until 1879, when it was issued by the Cumberland and Westmoreland Antiquarian Society, with an account of the author by himself, written in 1801, and a full pedigree of the family. This has been the source of much of our information. Some 'Original Letters from William Gilpin' were published by R. Warner in 1817. There is an engraved portrait of Gilpin by G. Clinch, from a painting by H. Walton.

[Gent. Mag. vol. lxxiv. (1804) pt. i. pp. 388-9; Nichols's Lit. Anecd. i. 639, ii. 253, viii. 643, 657; Nichols's Lit. Illustr. i. 778; Biog. Univers. xvii. 388; and the works above mentioned.]

G. S. B.

GILPIN, WILLIAM SAWREY (1762-1843), water-colour painter and landscape gardener, born in 1762, was son of Sawrey Gilpin, R.A. [q. v.] He practised as a water-colour painter and drawing-master, and his father's reputation enabled him to obtain considerable practice. He exhibited a view of the 'Village of Rydal, Westmoreland' at the Royal Academy in 1797, and in 1800 sent 'A Park Scene.' So high did Gilpin stand in his profession, that at the original meeting of water-colour painters on 30 Nov. 1804, at which the Old Water-colour Society was founded, he was voted to the chair, and elected the first president of the society. The inferior quality of his work as a painter was, however, very evident at the first exhibition in 1805, and he resigned the post of president in 1806, after filling it with great ability. Gilpin was appointed drawing-master to the branch of the Royal Military College at Great Marlow, and subsequently at Sandhurst. He continued a member of the Water-colour Society, and was one of the members who seceded in 1813, but he continued to exhibit up to 1814. Later on in life he seems to have devoted himself entirely to landscape gardening, and obtained almost a monopoly of the chief practice in it. His principal works were in Ireland at Crum Castle, Enniskillen Castle, and the seats of Lord Cawdor and Lord Blayney; in England he laid out the gardens at Danesfield, near Henley-on-Thames, and at Sir E. Kerrison's seat near Hoxne, Suffolk. In 1832 he published, with plates, 'Practical Hints for Landscape Gardening, with some remarks on Domestic Architecture as connected with Scenery' (2nd ed. 1835). Gilpin died at Sedbergh Park, Yorkshire, aged 81. He left two sons by his wife, Elizabeth Paddock.

[Redgraves' Century of Painters, i. 469; Redgrave's Dict. of Artists; Gent. Mag. 1843, new ser. xx. 209; Gilpin's Memoirs of Dr. R. Gilpin.]

L. C.

GINKEL, GODERT DE, first EARL OF ATHLONE (1630-1703), eldest son of Godard Adriaan van Reede, baron Ginkel, was born at Utrecht in 1630. He was educated for a military career, and took part in the battle of Senef in 1674. Though a member of the equestrian order of Utrecht, he never took his seat in that assembly, and in 1688 he accompanied the Prince of Orange to England (A. J. VAN DER AA, Biographisch Woordenboek der Nederlanden; BOSSCHA, Neêrlands Heldendaden te Land, ii. 172; LODGE, Peerage, ed. Archdall, ii. 153). His first service in England was the suppression of the mutiny of a Scotch regiment at Harwich on occasion of the proclamation of William and Mary. He overtook the mutineers not far from Sleaford in Lincolnshire, and immediately attacked them, though strongly ensconced among the fens of the district. His energy struck terror into them, and they surrendered at discretion (MACAULAY, Hist. of England, ch. xi.) Accompanying William to Ireland in 1690, he distinguished himself at the battle of the Boyne, and was afterwards present at the first siege of Limerick in the autumn of the same year (TINDAL, Hist. of England, iii. 137, 147; STORY, Impartial History, p. 96). On the departure of William he was appointed general-in-chief of the Irish forces. He retired into winter quarters at Kilkenny, endeavouring, however, as far as possible to check the predatory excursions of the Irish guerilla bands, or 'rapparees.' The rapparees were an active race and difficult to come at, while his own soldiers were ill-supplied, their pay was in arrear, they were growing mutinous and were pillaging the neighbourhood (BURNET, *Hist. of his own Time*, ii. 66). In the spring of 1691 large supplies of money and provisions arrived, and Ginkel prepared to open the campaign with vigour. Collecting his troops in the vicinity of Mullingar, he marched straight on Athlone, the strongest fortress in the hands of the enemy and the key to the west of Ireland. The Duke of Würtemberg at the same time marched northward from Clonmel to join him, although in the opinion of General Mackay the plan gave a dangerous opportunity to St. Ruth, commanding the enemy, to attack before the juncture had been effected (*Life of Mackay*, p. 110). Ginkel, after capturing and regarrisoning Ballymore, a fort erected by Sarsfield to cover Athlone and Lanesborough, successfully accomplished his object, and with his combined force marched westward, appearing before the walls of Athlone on 19 June 1691. So strongly fortified was that town both by nature and by art that St. Ruth exclaimed: 'His master ought to hang him for trying to take Athlone, and mine ought to hang me if I lose it.' Nevertheless, after a series of gallant assaults, Ginkel succeeded on 30 June, by a brilliantly conceived though extremely hazardous plan, in capturing the place (see MACAULAY's graphic description in *Hist. of England*, ch. xvii.) He used his victory with moderation, leaving nothing 'unattempted which might contribute to bringing the enemy over by fair means.' A proclamation by the lords justices promising pardon and a restoration to their estates to all who submitted within a certain specified time, made, according to Story, 'a great noise' all over the kingdom, and was the precedent for the articles of Galway and Limerick. But though many sued for pardon, the proclamation came too late to have any general effect; St. Ruth especially exerted himself to prevent his soldiers taking advantage of it. On 11 July Ginkel, having repaired the fortifications of Athlone and left a garrison there, fixed his headquarters at Ballinasloe, on the borders of Roscommon and Galway, about four miles from Aughrim, where St. Ruth had taken up his position. At five in the afternoon of 12 July the battle began, and after two hours of equal fighting was decided by the death at a critical moment of St. Ruth. Fighting obstinately and only yielding inch by inch, the Irish at length broke and fled. A horrible carnage ensued, and one who was present tells us that from the top of a neighbouring

hill he saw the country to the distance of near four miles white with the naked bodies of the slain. After a few days' rest Ginkel moved towards Galway. According to the 'Memoirs of King James,' he might have finished the war at one blow had he marched straight on Limerick; as it was, he gave the Irish time to rally their scattered forces and complete their fortifications. Passing through Loughrea and Athenry, and cutting off all chance of assistance from Baldearg O'Donnell, he sat down before Galway on 19 July. Two days after, D'Usson, the governor, consented to a capitulation on favourable terms, pleading as an excuse the bad state of the fortifications, the ill-will of the citizens, many of whom were protestants, but above all the discouragement of the soldiers (RANKE, *Hist. of England*, v. 29). On the 26th Ginkel entered the city and was received with profound respect by the mayor and aldermen; D'Usson departed the same day with about 2,300 men for Limerick, 'the last asylum of the vanquished race.' Ginkel followed without loss of time, for the season was well advanced and the lords justices were anxious for a settlement before the arrival of fresh supplies from France. Disappointed in the expectation that the dissensions of the besieged would lead to a surrender, Ginkel carefully invested Limerick on all sides. Then, having completed his arrangements, he crossed the Shannon on 22 Sept., directing his main attack against the fort commanding the Thomond Bridge. A few hours afterwards the fort was stormed, and the besieged, deeming further resistance futile, beat a parley. An English squadron had meanwhile appeared in the estuary of the Shannon. On 3 Oct. the town, with the exception of the castle and cathedral, which were for a time left in the keeping of the Irish, was delivered up to Ginkel on conditions which have since excited considerable controversy, but which, so far as Ginkel was concerned, were faithfully kept (MACAULAY, *Hist. of England*, ch. xvii.; T. D. INGRAM, *Two Chapters of Irish History*, pp. 91–154; *Hist. MSS. Comm.* 7th Rep. App. pp. 203, 207, 210). The capture of Limerick having practically put an end to the war, Ginkel, after a short delay, proceeded to Dublin, where he was greeted with public demonstrations of respect and gratitude. On 5 Dec. he sailed for England on board the Monmouth yacht, and two days afterwards arrived at Chester (STORY, *Continuation*, p. 282). His journey to London resembled a triumphal progress, and on his arrival there he was publicly thanked by the speaker of the House of Commons for his services, to which he judiciously replied by ascribing his success to the bravery of his English soldiers.

Shortly afterwards he was created Baron of Aughrim and Earl of Athlone (4 March 1692). He obtained a large grant of forfeited lands in Ireland, afterwards confirmed to him by the Irish parliament, but was subsequently deprived thereof by the Act of Resumption (HARRIS, *Life of King William*, pp. 353, 478). On 6 March 1692 he accompanied William to the continent, and after witnessing the capture of Namur by Lewis, and taking part in the battle of Steinkirk, he presided over the court-martial which tried and condemned Grandval for his plot to assassinate William. In the following year he served at the battle of Landen (19 July 1693), and narrowly escaped being drowned in his efforts to restore order during the retreat of the allies. In the campaign of 1695 he commanded the Dutch horse in the army of the elector of Bavaria, and played a prominent part at the recapture of Namur (TINDAL, *Hist. of England*, iii. 288, 295). Early in the following spring he assisted Cohorn in surprising Givet and destroying the immense military stores collected there by Lewis for the ensuing campaign (MACAULAY, *Hist. of England*, ch. xxii.) On the renewal of the war in 1702 he consented to waive his claim to the supreme command of the Dutch troops, and to serve under Marlborough, being chiefly instrumental in the capture of Kaiserswerth (TINDAL, *Hist. of England*, iii. 562; STANHOPE, *Reign of Queen Anne*, pp. 47, 49). He frankly admitted the superiority of Marlborough, by whom he was supplanted. 'The success of this campaign,' he generously said, ' is solely due to this incomparable chief, since I confess that I, serving as second in command, opposed in all circumstances his opinion and proposals' (COXE, *Life of Marlborough*, i. 147). He died on 11 Feb. in the following year (1703) at Utrecht, after two days' illness (*Europ. Merc.* 1703, p. 160). He married Ursula Philippina van Raasfeld, by whom he had several children.

FREDERICK CHRISTIAN GINKEL, second EARL OF ATHLONE (1668–1719), the eldest son, succeeded him. He early acquired considerable reputation as a soldier in the wars of William's and Anne's reigns, and rose to the position of lieutenant-general of the Dutch cavalry and governor of Sluys. During the siege of Aire, on the river Lys (1710), he was entrusted with the command of a convoy, but being intercepted by the enemy was defeated, and notwithstanding great personal bravery taken prisoner (DE QUINCY, *Hist. Militaire*, ii. 300). He married Henrietta van Nassau Zuilenstein, youngest daughter of William van Nassau, earl of Rochefort, by whom he had two sons. He died on 15 Aug. 1719

(VAN DER AA, *Biog. Woordenboek*). On the death of William Gustaaf Frederick, ninth earl of Athlone, on 21 May 1844, the peerage became extinct (BURKE, *Extinct Peerage*).

[A. J. Van der Aa's Biographisch Woordenboek der Nederlanden; Lodge's Peerage (Archdall); Burke's Extinct Peerage; Bosscha's Neêrlands Heldendaden te Land; Compleat Hist. of the Life and Military Actions of Richard, earl of Tyrconnel, 1689; Story's Impartial History of the Wars in Ireland and Continuation; O'Kelly's Macariæ Excidium (Irish Archæol. Soc.); Clarke's Life of James II; Mémoires de Berwick; Tenac, Hist. de la Marine, t. iii.; Rawdon Papers; Diary of the Siege of Athlone, by an Engineer of the Army, a witness of the action, licensed 11 July 1691; Mackay's Life of General Mackay; Captain R. Parker's Memoirs; An exact Journal of the Victorious Progress of their Majesties' forces under the command of General Ginckle this Summer in Ireland, 1691; Diary of the Siege of Lymerick, 1692; Burnet, Hist. of his own Time; Tyndal's Hist. of England; M. O'Conor's Military History; London Gazette; Walter Harris's Life of William III; Europische Mercurius; De Quincy, Histoire Militaire de Louis le Grand; Letters of the Duke of Marlborough, ed. Sir George Murray; Rousset's continuation of Dumont's Batailles gagnées; Coxe's Life of Marlborough; Narcissus Luttrell's Diary, 1678–1714; Macaulay's Hist. of England, with references to documents preserved in the Public Record Office and in the archives of the French war office; Stanhope's Reign of Queen Anne; Ranke's Hist. of England; Hist. MSS. Comm. 4th Rep. App. 317–25, where are a number of letters from Ginkel, chiefly addressed to Coningsby in 1690 and following years. Among the manuscripts of the Earl of Fingall is one entitled 'A Light to the Blind, whereby they may see the . . . Dethronement of J[ames] the Second, king of England,' &c. 1711. The manuscript, strongly Jacobite in tone, appears to have been lent to Sir James Mackintosh, who made copious extracts from it, which were in turn placed at the disposal of Lord Macaulay, and frequently referred to by him. A full account of the manuscript is given by Mr. J. T. Gilbert in Hist. MSS. Comm. 10th Rep. App. t. v. p. 107 sqq.] R. D.

GIPPS, SIR GEORGE (1791–1847), colonial governor, born at Ringwould in Kent in 1791, was the son of the Rev. George Gipps, rector of the parish. He was educated at the King's School, Canterbury, and at the Military Academy at Woolwich. In 1809 he joined the royal engineers, receiving his commission as second lieutenant 11 Jan., and that of first lieutenant 21 Dec. in the same year. In May 1811 he embarked for Portugal, and in 1812 was present at the siege of Badajoz, where he was wounded while leading one of the columns of assault on Fort Picurina (25 March). In 1813 and

1814 he was with Sir John Murray's army in Catalonia, taking part in the fight at the pass at Biar, the battle of Castalla, the capture of Fort Balaguer, the siege of Taragona, and the blockade of Barcelona. In November 1814, holding then commission as captain, he was ordered to Flanders, but was not present at the battle of Waterloo, having been detached for the purpose of putting Ostend in a condition of defence. On the withdrawal of the army of occupation from French territory, he was permitted to remain for some time out of military service, and occupied himself in European travel. Returning home, he was employed at Chatham, but in November 1824 was sent to the West Indies, where he remained five years, arriving home 18 Dec. 1829. He drew up elaborate reports on those colonies, with especial reference to the question of slavery (some are still extant in manuscript), and thus impressed the government with some idea of his capacity. He was subsequently a member of two government commissions appointed to define the boundaries of constituencies under the first Reform Bill. In 1834 he became private secretary to Lord Auckland, first lord of the admiralty. The next year he was sent as commissioner, together with Lord Gosford and Sir Charles Grey, to Canada, to endeavour to allay the discontent then fast rising in the country. The commission, though not wholly successful, did much by its attempts to extend the principle of local self-administration. He returned home in April 1837, and was appointed to the governorship of New South Wales. He sailed in October, and on 24 Feb. 1838 assumed the government of the colony, which was just entering the stage of self-government. Gipps devoted himself to the maintenance of order and to the development of the colonial resources. In the first direction he declared (1839) his intention of protecting the aborigines, an intention emphasised by the new Border Police Act, and by the punishment of those concerned in the Myall Creek murders. But the most strenuous of his efforts were devoted to the attempt to open up the country by means of exploration, an equable land system, and immigration. Unfortunately, some friction was excited in 1840 between himself and the popular party owing to a quarrel with W. C. Wentworth, mainly caused by the frankness with which Gipps commented on Wentworth's claim to purchase enormous tracts of land from the New Zealand chiefs at an almost nominal value.

The work of exploration was vigorously promoted by Gipps and by private adven-

turers. In 1838 the Clarence River was discovered; in 1840 there were the expeditions headed by M'Millan and Count Strzelecki, in 1844 those of Leichardt and Mitchell. With regard to the land system and immigration Gipps was 'determined to apply the whole of the money derived ' from the land to the encouragement of immigration (September 1842; as to immigration, cf. resolution of the legislative council, 22 Sept. 1840). The land revenue he looked upon not as the property of the colonies only, but in great part as the property of the empire. He offered bounties on immigration to such an extent as to provoke a sharp reprimand from Lord John Russell (cf., however, despatches, Parl. Papers, 1844, xxxv. 10). He determined to prevent a too sudden dispersion of the population over the land by instituting sales by auction with high upset prices, and by only placing small lots of land in the market at a time (LANG, i. 287). Thus he was led to consider the scheme of Gibbon Wakefield, which he criticised with much vigour. In 1840, acting with the approval of the legislative council, he suspended the operation of the instructions to sell at a fixed price transmitted from home 'in the most authoritative way,' and in consequence of his opposition these royal instructions were, in part, revoked. Thus far he had acted in general harmony with his legislative council, though conflict had threatened; he was obliged (1840) to withdraw the Local Government Bill which he had promoted. His proposal to enforce payment of the arrears of quit rents also occasioned complaints.

The remainder of his career was one of unceasing strife. In the first place the popular party, supreme through the alteration of the constitution in 1842, attacked the settlement of judicial salaries, the appropriation of the civil list, and the liability of the colony to bear the gaol expenses. In the second place, the governor in April 1844 issued new squatting regulations, whereby, without obtaining the consent or asking the advice of the legislative council, he placed new imposts upon the squatting runs according to the number of sheep they could depasture. He had further demanded the payment of all arrears of quit rents. These measures, conducted as they were in a somewhat arbitrary manner, united all classes against him. He was denounced for asserting the absolute right of the crown to the territorial revenue, and for claiming authority on the part of the crown and the governor to impose taxes arbitrarily and without consent of the council (cf. Parl. Papers, 1846, vol. xxix.) The Pastoral Association of New South Wales was formed, and for the first time the squatters claimed rights of pre-emption over the runs. Gipps was upheld by Lord Stanley, whom he counselled, how-ever, to permit a purchase of homesteads with 320 acres on terms assuring a temporary security in the tenure of the run. Early in 1846 Gipps sought relief from his post, the usual term of office being already exceeded. When accepting his resignation Lord Stan-ley complimented him both publicly and privately on his official conduct.

He arrived in England 20 Nov. 1846. He died at Canterbury 28 Feb. 1847, leaving a widow and one child, afterwards General Sir Reginald Gipps, G.C.B. There is a monument to his memory in Canterbury Cathedral.

[G. W. Rusden's Hist. of Australia; Lang's New South Wales; Parl. Papers, 1843–6; colo-nial newspapers, and private information.]

E. C. K. G.

GIPPS, SIR RICHARD (1659–1708), master of the revels at Gray's Inn, son of John Gipps of Great Whelnetham, Suffolk, and Mary, daughter of David Davidson, alder-man of London, was baptised at Great Whel-netham 15 Sept. 1659 (*Reg.*) He was admitted a student of Gray's Inn 5 Feb. 1675–6; the only other record of his membership of that society previous to 1682 is a decree of censure on him for a breach of authority. On 3 Nov. 1682 Gipps assumed the office of master of the revels to the society. These continued every Saturday for two terms, and were patronised by royalty. On 27 Nov. of that year Gipps was knighted by Charles II at Whitehall. On 23 Jan. 1682–3 he went in great state to Whitehall to invite the king, queen, and court to a masque held on the following Candlemas day (2 Feb.) at Gray's Inn, which was performed with great splendour (LUT-TRELL, *Relation*). Subsequently Gipps ap-pears to have retired to his seat in Suffolk, and devoted himself to antiquarian pursuits and the history of his native county. His manu-script collections for this purpose are in the British Museum (Harl. MS. 4626) and the Bodleian Library, Oxford (Tanner MSS.) Sir John Cullum, bart. [q. v.], transcribed Gipps's collections for the history of Suffolk gentry, and made considerable additions. This manuscript is in the possession of G. Milner-Gibson-Cullum, F.S.A., at Hardwick, Bury St. Edmunds, who also owns the original copperplate of the admission ticket to the aforesaid masque. Besides Great Whelnet-ham Gipps inherited property at Brockley and Rede Hall in Suffolk, which he sold. He married an heiress, Mary, daughter of Edward Giles of Bowden, Devonshire, with

whom he obtained a large estate, and by whom he had four children. He died 21 Dec. 1708, and was buried at Great Whelnetham. His portrait, painted by J. Closterman, was finely engraved in mezzotint by J. Smith. Care should be taken to distinguish him from Sir Richard Gipps of Horningsheth, a con-temporary, neighbour, and distant relative, who was knighted by Charles II at Saxham, Suffolk, on 20 Oct. 1676.

[Davy's Suffolk Collections, Brit. Mus. Addit. MS. 19132; Gage's Hist. of Thingoe Hundred; Page's Supplement to the Suffolk Traveller; Le Neve's Pedigrees of Knights (Harleian Soc. Publ.); Douthwaite's Hist. and Assoc. of Gray's Inn; Nichols's Lit. Illustr. iii. 435, vii. 408.] L. C.

GIPPS, THOMAS (*d.* 1709), rector of Bury, Lancashire, was educated at St. Paul's School, London, which he left as Campden ex-hibitioner in 1654. He subsequently went to Trinity College, Cambridge, where he gained a fellowship. He proceeded B.A. in 1658 and M.A. in 1662, and became rector of Bury, Lancashire, in 1674, on the presentation of the Earl of Derby, whose chaplain he was. In 1683 he published 'Three Sermons preached in Lent and Summer Assizes last, at Lancas-ter, and on one of the Lord's Days in the late Guild of Preston,' and in 1697 'A Sermon against Corrupting the Word of God, preacht at Christ Church in Manchester.' He charged the presbyterians during the civil wars with altering Acts vi. 3, 'whom *we* might appoint' into 'whom *ye* might appoint,' to favour the notion of the people's right to elect their own ministers. This led to a sharp controversy with James Owen of Oswestry, in which Gipps was shown to be in error. Four or five curious pamphlets were published on each side. Gipps died at Bury 11 March 1709. He gave some books to the library of St. Paul's School in 1673.

[Raines's Vicars of Rochdale (Chetham Soc.), i. 129; Fishwick's Lancashire Library; Baines's Lancashire (Harland), i. 517; Graduati Cantabr. 1823; Oliver Heywood's Diaries (Turner), 1881, ii. 223 (as to his countenancing the persecution of dissenters); Gardiner's Register of St. Paul's School, pp. 46, 408; Account of the Life of James Owen, 1709, p. 106; Knight's Life of Colet, p. 327; information from the late Canon Hornby.] C. W. S.

GIRALDUS DE BARRI, called CAMBREN-SIS (1146?–1220?), called also Sylvester by his enemies, was born at the castle of Maenor Pyr or Manorbeer in Pembrokeshire, of which he gives an elaborate description (*Itin. Cambriæ*, p. 92, DIMOCK), in 1146 or 1147 (WHARTON, *Anglia Sacra*, ii. xx). He was the youngest son of William de Barri, by his second wife Nesta, granddaughter of Rhys ap Theodor, prince of South Wales. As a child he showed early aptitude for learning, and was remarked for his veneration for the church and church matters, influenced by his uncle, David Fitzgerald, then bishop of St. David's [see DAVID, d. 1176]. Though he was at first slow at learning, he must have made up for this by diligence, as his early Latin poems (Opp. i. 341–84), written probably in 1166, indicate a careful study of many of the Latin poets. While still young he made three journeys to Paris, studying, and lecturing on the Trivium, and obtaining especial praise for his knowledge of rhetoric. He was probably ordained soon after his return to England in 1172, when he was appointed by the archbishop to secure payment of tithes from the Welsh. He soon made a mark by his vigour in such cases as that of the sheriff of Pembrokeshire, who was excommunicated for seizing the cattle belonging to the priory of Pembroke, and that of the archdeacon of Brecknock, who was suspended for concubinage. The result of this was that the archbishop took the archdeaconry into his own hands and gave it to Giraldus. He relates in his 'De Rebus a se gestis' various instances of his energy in his new office: continuing to insist on the payment of tithes, risking the resentment of the Flemings, a colony settled on the borders by the English kings, disregarding all comfort when he had to perform severe duties in rough weather, resisting and even excommunicating the Bishop of St. Asaph when he attempted to trespass on the rights of St. David's, and giving the king a pretty strong opinion on the character of the people, the bishops being thieves of the churches, as the laymen were of the property of others. On the death of his uncle, the bishop of St. David's, in 1176, the Welsh hoped to see the restoration of a metropolitan of their own, and to make the see independent of Canterbury. The canons nominated Giraldus, with three other archdeacons, for presentation to the king, intending to secure him for their bishop. But the king, who had always followed the Norman policy of appointing Norman bishops to Welsh sees, would not listen to them. The people who heard the Te Deum sung expected that Giraldus had been elected. But he saw that it would not do, and repudiated the nomination. The king's anger, however, fell upon him; he consulted with the archbishop (Richard), refused to follow his advice to nominate Giraldus, and spoke of his fear of the archdeacon from his connection with the royal blood of Wales. The canons gave way at once, and in spite of Giraldus's exhortations to the papal legate

and the archbishop for the appointment of a man of good character, who had acquaintance with the habits and language of the people, Peter de Leia was elected. Giraldus left the country and went to Paris to study canon law and theology. He tells us of his large audiences, gives an account of his first lecture (De Rebus a se gestis, i. 46), and was even supposed by some who heard him to have studied many years at Bologna. Want of money prevented his return to England for some time; but in 1180 he returned by Arras, where he saw Philip, count of Flanders, playing at the quintain, and reached Canterbury, where he was entertained by the archbishop. He proceeded at once to Wales, and was appointed commissary to the bishop of St. David's, who had ceased to reside in his diocese; but finding that the bishop suspended and excommunicated the canons and archdeacons, while he left plunderers of monasteries and robbers of churchyards unpunished, Giraldus gave up the charge and obtained from the archbishop the reversal of the sentence on the canons. In 1184 he was made one of Henry II's chaplains, and was sent by the king to accompany his son John in his expedition to Ireland. While there he preached at the council of Dublin, giving a very severe review of the character of the clergy and the low state of the people (ib. p. 67). He was offered while in Ireland the bishoprics of Wexford and Leighlin, and apparently at a little later time the bishopric of Ossory and the archbishopric of Cashel (ib. p. 65; De jure Menevensis ecclesiæ, p. 338), but declined them all. It is to this journey that we owe the treatise 'Topographia Hibernica,' dedicated to Henry II, which appeared in 1188. It gives an account of the general features of the country, its productions, climate, &c., mixed up with many marvellous stories. The 'Expugnatio Hibernica,' which probably appeared the same year, dedicated to Richard, though containing much that is interesting and valuable, can scarcely be considered as 'sober, truthful history' (DIMOCK, preface, p. lxix). He remained in Ireland till 1186, and on his return read his work publicly at Oxford, entertaining all his hearers on three successive days (De gestis, p. 72). In 1188, after the king had taken the cross, Archbishop Baldwin preached the crusade; the king sent him especially into Wales for this purpose. He took with him Giraldus and the justiciary, Ranulph de Glanville [q. v.] Giraldus tells us that the archbishop produced little effect till he bade Giraldus take up the preaching; then, although he spoke in French and Latin, which the people did not understand, such crowds came to take the cross that the archbishop could scarcely defend himself from the pressure, and compelled the archdeacon to pause for a time. He compares the tears which his exhortations produced with those which followed St. Bernard's preaching in French to the Germans, and adds that John afterwards attacked him for emptying Wales of its defenders by his preaching. He gives a full account of his journey in the 'Itinerarium Cambriæ,' which appeared in 1191 (DIMOCK, pref. p. xxxiii). Soon after this he crossed to France in company with the archbishop (who intended him to write a history of the Crusade) and Ranulph de Glanville. But on the death of Henry II he was, by the archbishop's advice, sent to keep the peace in Wales, lest it should be disturbed at that critical time. He arrived there, after having had a narrow escape from the loss of all his property at Dieppe, was joined as justiciary with the chief justice (Longchamp), and managed to keep the country at peace. He now obtained absolution from his crusading vow. He was offered the bishopric of Bangor, vacant by Bishop Guy's death in 1190, and of Llandaff by John in 1191. These offers, though in addition to what had been offered in Ireland they greatly pleased him, 'secura quidem et alta mente calcavit.'

In 1192 he turned his back on the court, took advice from an anchoret, and as the war between Richard and Philip prevented his going to Paris, where he had hoped to go with his books and devote himself to study, he went to Lincoln and remained there till the death of Peter de Leia, bishop of St. David's, in 1198, probably then writing his 'Gemma Ecclesiastica' and his lives of the Lincoln bishops. The chapter of St. David's again nominated him with three others, Giraldus the first and foremost, for their bishop. The archbishop (Hubert) refused to listen to the election; he was determined no Welshman should have the bishopric. Six, or at least four, of the canons were ordered to cross the sea and present themselves before Richard in Normandy; they followed him from place to place; before they reached him he was dead. They met John, were well received by him, and were given letters to the justiciary, bidding him not to molest them in their election. They returned and saw Giraldus at Lincoln; he went back to St. David's, and was unanimously elected to the bishopric on 29 June, the canons requesting him to go to Rome and receive consecration from the Pope, so as to obtain the dignity of a metropolitan. In spite of the archbishop's opposition, Giraldus accepted the suggestion, started

for Rome in August, and arrived there with some difficulty in November. He saw the pope (Innocent III), presented him with six of his works, 'quos ipse studio magno compegerat,' and had the satisfaction of learning that the pope read them carefully, and showed them to the cardinals, giving the preference to the 'Gemma Ecclesiastica.' But his suit was a failure; the archbishop had sent letters beforehand to the pope and cardinals, stating that Giraldus had been elected by three only of the canons, the rest of the chapter refusing their consent, and that he did not think him fit for the post (*De gestis*, p. 122). Giraldus has preserved his lengthy answer to this in the first book of his treatise 'De Invectionibus' (Opp. iii. 16). The pope required evidence of the fact that St. David's was independent of Canterbury. Giraldus's arguments on his side will be found in his treatise 'De jure Menevensis ecclesiæ,' which exhibits (to use Mr. Brewer's words) a 'strange mixture of antiquarian research with a total absence of all historical criticism.'

To give full details of the process of the suit would be impossible within the present limits; they may be studied in his treatise just mentioned. Some few of the leading facts may be told. He went to the Welsh laity for support, and the princes of North and South Wales threatened the clergy who would not support him with the loss of their friendship. Then in 1202 the king took the lands belonging to the bishopric into his own hands, and the revenues of Giraldus in his archdeaconry were seized. He was accused of stirring up the Welsh to rebellion. The justiciary proceeded against him; he was summoned to appear before a commission at Worcester; on his appearing there the trial came to nothing in consequence of the absence of the principal judges. He went to Canterbury, asserted that the archbishop, not he, was the king's enemy; returned to Wales, excommunicated two of his chief opponents, was cited to appear before the papal commissioners, and appealed to the pope. The sheriff of Pembroke was ordered to attach the goods and chattels of all his clerical adherents; Giraldus endeavoured to summon a general council of the clergy of the diocese, and with some difficulty obtained this at Brecknock; but it came to nothing (his account of this in his book *De Gestis Giraldi* is lost). At length a commission was held at Brackley; the canons of St. David's disowned his election. He had now to conceal himself; no one in Wales was allowed to harbour him, and the ports were watched to prevent his crossing. After a variety of adventures (*De jure Menevensis ecclesiæ*, pp.

224–38), he crossed from Dover to Gravelines, and, going by St. Omer and Cambray, reached Spoleto, and finally Rome. Here the pope received him kindly; he presented the letters of the princes of Wales in his favour, impeached the witnesses against him, defended the priority of his own election to the subsequent one, and detailed all his sufferings and oppressions. The pope at length gave sentence, annulling both the elections that had taken place. Thus after the suit had continued for four years, during which Giraldus had twice visited England, three times going to Rome, it was no nearer a settlement. He had now no course but to return; he did not get home without difficulty, being taken prisoner in France and carried to Châtillon on the Saone as an English subject. When he regained his liberty he went to Rouen, where he found the Bishop of Ely, sent to settle the matter of the election to St. David's, to which the chapter had nominated again. Giraldus impeached their nominees on various grounds; he repeated his charge before the archbishop's officials at Canterbury. He went to Brecknock, then to St. David's, then to London; at Lambeth he again protested against the election made in his absence; at the meeting of the canons in St. Catharine's chapel at Westminster he proposed Walter Map, archdeacon of Oxford, and Roger, dean of Lincoln. At length Geoffrey Henlaw, prior of Llanthony, was elected, and Giraldus gave way. He was at once reconciled with the king and the archbishop, the expenses of the suit were repaid him, and he was promised an ecclesiastical income of sixty marks a year (ib. p. 324). He then resigned his archdeaconry, which was given at the request of the archbishop to Giraldus's nephew. He lived to see yet another election to St. David's, on the death of Geoffrey Henlaw in 1214. He begins his treatise 'De jure Menevensis ecclesiæ' by discussing the question why he was then passed over. He states that Welshmen were never promoted to Welsh sees, that he was unpopular with the Welsh clergy because he was known to be opposed to their evil habits; but yet that the better portion of the chapter asked him to allow himself to be nominated. Had they been unanimous, and the king and archbishop agreed, he would have accepted the bishopric, in spite of its poverty (p. 134); but he foresaw the troubles in which he would have been involved, and refused his consent.

We have, of course, only Giraldus's own account of his career, which it is likely enough his excessive vanity and self-confidence may have coloured. His pen in writing of his enemies, as of Bishop Longchamp of Ely for

instance, is very bitter. Still, on the whole, there is no reason to doubt the truth of his statements. His contemporaries did not take the same view of the chief object of his life. Gervase of Canterbury puts it down as Archbishop Hubert's greatest merit that he had retained seven bishops in subjection to Canterbury and put down the rebel cleverness ('rebellem astutiam') of Giraldus (Actus Archiepiscoporum, Rolls Ser. ii. 412).

On the death of St. Hugh of Lincoln, some of the canons of Lincoln thought of electing Giraldus to that see, if they had free election (De jure Menevensis ecclesiæ, p. 340); he mentions also that there was talk in the Roman curia of his being made a cardinal. The closing years of his life seem to have been spent in peace and retirement. He would take no part in the troublous time following the election of Stephen Langton. He lived certainly till 1216. He had begun a treatise, 'De instructione Principum,' at an earlier date, but since he speaks in it of John in such a way as leaves no doubt that John was dead, Giraldus could not have completed it before 1216. He was buried in the cathedral of St. David's.

His works have been edited in the Rolls Series (7 vols.) by J. S. Brewer and J. F. Dimock, 1861–77. All are included, except the 'De Instructione Principum,' which is to appear in an eighth and concluding volume, edited by Mr. G. F. Warner. Full accounts of probable dates of composition and publication will be found in the prefaces to the volumes. Giraldus's separate works were: 1. 'Topographia Hibernica' (in Camden's 'Anglica, Hibernica, Normannica, Cambrica, a veteribus scripta,' Frankfort, 1602, and in Opp. v. by Dimock). 2. 'Expugnatio Hibernica' (in Camden's collection and Opp. v. Dimock). 3. 'Itinerarium Cambriæ' (by Powel, London, 1585; by Camden; by Sir R. C. Hoare, with a translation, London, 1806; and Opp. vi. Dimock. A portion is in Wharton's 'Anglia Sacra,' ii. 447). 4. 'Descriptio Cambriæ' (published as the last). 5. 'Vita Galfridi Arch. Eboracensis' (Wharton, ii. 375, and Opp. iv. Brewer). 6. 'Symbolum Electorum' (Opp. i. Brewer). 7. 'Invectionum Libellus' (Books 1–4, in Opp. iii., Books 5, 6, in Opp. i. Brewer). 8. 'Speculum Ecclesiæ' (Opp. iv. Brewer). 9. 'Vita S. Remigii,' with lives of bishops of Lincoln and others (Wharton, ii. 408; Opp. vii. Dimock). 10. 'Vita S. Hugonis' (Opp. vii. Dimock). 11. 'Gemma Ecclesiastica' (Opp. ii. Brewer). 12. 'Vita S. Davidis archiepiscopi Menevensis' (Wharton, ii. 628; Opp. iii. Brewer). 13. 'Vita S. Davidis II episcopi Menevensis' (Wharton, ii. 652; Opp. iii. Brewer). Brewer, though a little doubtful, is inclined to think that this is by Giraldus.

Wharton gives a different opinion. 14. 'Vita S. Ethelberti' (Opp. iii. Brewer). 15. 'De rebus a se gestis' (Wharton, ii. 457; Opp. i. Brewer). The third book of this is but a fragment of the whole, containing only nineteen out of 236 chapters, of which the titles are preserved. 16. 'Epistola ad Stephanum Langton' (Wharton, ii. 435; Opp. i. Brewer). 17. 'De Giraldo Archidiacono Menevensi' (Opp. i. Brewer). 18. 'De libris a se scriptis' (Wharton, ii. 439; Opp. i. Brewer). 19. 'Catalogus brevior librorum' (Wharton, ii. 445; Opp. i. Brewer). 20. 'Retractationes' (Wharton, ii. 455; Opp. i. Brewer). 21. 'De jure et statu Menevensis ecclesiæ' (Wharton, ii. 514; Opp. iii. Brewer). 22. 'De instructione principum,' in three parts (the last two edited by Brewer for the Anglia Christiana Society, 1846).

[Giraldus, De rebus a se gestis and De jure Menevensis ecclesiæ; Chronology of his life in Wharton's Anglia Sacra, ii. 374; Wharton's preface, ii. xx; Life of Giraldus Cambrensis prefixed by Sir R. C. Hoare to his translation of the Itinerarium Cambriæ, London, 1806; Brewer's preface to vol. i. of his edition of the works, to which the present writer is greatly indebted.] H. R. L.

GIRARDUS CORNUBIENSIS (*fl.* 1350?) was author of two works: 1. 'De gestis Britonum,' and 2. 'De gestis Regum West-Saxonum,' our knowledge of which is chiefly due to citations in the 'Liber de Hyda,' and in Rudborne's 'Chronicle' (in WHARTON, *Anglia Sacra*, i.) The former chronicle gives the 'De gestis Regum West-Saxonum,' chaps. x. xi. and xiv. as a source for the history of Alfred and his daughter Æthelflaed, and bk. v. c. x. of the same work as the authority for ascribing to Edward the elder the restoration of the public schools at Cambridge. Rudborne quotes bk. iii. chap. vi. of the same work for the history of Cynegils of Wessex, and also twice refers to the 'De gestis Britonum' for details in the early history of the church of Winchester. Besides these the 'Liber de Hyda' gives an extract on the war between Guy of Warwick and Colbrand, which is said to be chap. xi. of the 'De gestis Regum West-Saxonum;' the same extract with the same reference exists at the end of a manuscript of Higden's 'Polychronicon' (Magdalen College, Oxford, 147), and was printed by Hearne as an appendix to the 'Annals of Dunstable,' ii. 825–30. Lydgate, in his unprinted poem on Guy of Warwick, says that he had translated it 'out of the Latyn . . . of Girard Cornubyence' (Bodl. MS. Laud Misc. 683, f. 77 *b*). Girard, as his name shows, was probably a native of Cornwall, but since he is thus quoted only

in chronicles written in Hampshire, we may perhaps conclude that he was resident at some monastery in the latter county; and also as the 'Liber de Hyda,' Rudborne, and Lydgate all date from the earlier half of the fifteenth century, we may possibly argue that Girard lived not long before. We do not, however, know anything for certain, and Girard has often been confused with Giraldus Cambrensis [q. v.] Sir T. D. Hardy gives his supposed date as the time of King John; but the reference to Cambridge makes it unlikely that Girard lived at that period.

[Courtney and Boase's Bibliotheca Cornub. vol. i.; Hardy's Cat. of Brit. Hist. iii. 50; Liber de Hyda, pp. 62, 111, 118–23 in Rolls Ser.; Wharton's Anglia Sacra, i. 180, 186, 189.] C. L. K.

GIRAUD, HERBERT JOHN (1817–1888), physician, chemist, and botanist, second son and youngest child of John Thomas Giraud (1764–1836), a surgeon at Faversham, Kent (mayor in 1814), by Mary, daughter of William Chapman of Badlesmere Court, Kent, was born at Faversham on 14 April 1817. His grandfather, Francis Frederick Giraud (1726–1811), was born of Waldensian protestant refugee parents at Pinache in Würtemberg in 1726, and was brought to England by his uncle, the Rev. William Henry Giraud, vicar of Graveney, Kent, in 1736, entered at All Souls, Oxford, in 1744, was ordained in 1749, and was from 1762 to 1808 head-master of the Faversham grammar school. Herbert John Giraud was educated at the university of Edinburgh, where he graduated M.D. with honours in 1840. Entering the medical service of the East India Company in 1842, he became successively professor of chemistry and botany (in 1845) and principal of the Grant Medical College, Bombay; he was also chief medical officer of Sir Jamsetjee Jeejeebhoy's Hospital, chemical analyst to the Bombay government, surgeon-major and deputy-inspector-general of the Bombay army medical service, and dean of the faculty of medicine in Bombay University (1863). He died 12 Jan. 1888 at Shanklin, Isle of Wight, where he had lived since his retirement in 1867. He married in 1842 Christina, daughter of Dr. David Shaw of the Bombay medical service, by whom he had two daughters, the elder of whom married Major-general Harpur of the Bombay staff corps. A list of ten botanical and chemical papers by Giraud is given in the Royal Society's 'Catalogue of Scientific Papers,' vol. ii. The most valuable of the botanical papers is on the embryo of Tropæolum, 'Linnean Transactions,' xix. 161. Several of the chemical papers relate to toxicology in India. Giraud was often consulted as an expert in medico-legal cases in the Bombay presidency.

[Men of the Time, 1875, 1884 ; Times, 13 Jan. 1888; information from Mr. F. F. Giraud, Faversham, nephew of H. J. Giraud.] G. T. B.

GIRDLESTONE, CHARLES (1797–1881), biblical commentator, the second son of Samuel Rainbow Girdlestone, a chancery barrister, was born in London in March 1797. His younger brother was Edward [q. v.], canon of Bristol. He was educated partly at Tunbridge School, under Dr. Vicesimus Knox [q. v.], and in 1815 was entered as a commoner at Wadham College, Oxford, where he held two exhibitions, one for Hebrew, the other for botany. In 1818 he graduated B.A., with a first class in classics and a second in mathematics, at the same time as Edward Greswell [q. v.], Josiah Forshall [q. v.], and Richard Bethell (afterwards Lord Westbury), also of Wadham. In the same year he was elected to an open fellowship at Balliol, which had then begun (under Dr. John Parsons, afterwards bishop of Peterborough) to rank with the foremost colleges at Oxford. He was appointed catechetical, logical, and mathematical lecturer in the college. He was ordained deacon in 1820 and priest in 1821, taking his M.A. degree in the same year. About this time he became tutor to the twin sons of Sir John Stanley of Alderley Park; it was this connection which led to his being appointed rector of Alderley some years later. In 1822 he was curate at Hastings (then a small fishing town), and in 1824 at Ferry Hincksey, near Oxford. He was classical examiner for degrees at Oxford in 1825–6, and select preacher to the university in 1825 and 1830. Shortly after his marriage (1826) he was presented by Lord Dudley and Ward, on the recommendation of Dr. Copleston (then provost of Oriel) [q. v.], to the vicarage of Sedgley, a district of about 20,500 inhabitants, forming one parish, in the south of Stafford mining district. Here, with the assistance of his patron, he built several district churches, schools, and parsonages. The place suffered severely from the first invasion of cholera into this country. There were 1,350 cases of cholera and 290 deaths in six weeks in August and September 1832. Immediately after the epidemic was over, Girdlestone published 'Seven Sermons preached during the prevalence of Cholera,' with a map of the district, and a preface giving an account of the visitation and of the religious impressions produced by it at the time upon the people. Girdlestone henceforth took a lively interest in all sanitary matters. In 1843–4 he was one of the earliest

supporters of the Metropolitan Association for Improving the Dwellings of the Industrial Classes, and in 1845 he published twelve very useful 'Letters on the Unhealthy Condition of the Lower Class of Dwellings,' founded on the official reports recently issued by the poor law commissioners and the health of towns commission. In 1837, when Edward Stanley [q. v.] was appointed bishop of Norwich, Girdlestone accepted the living of Alderley, Cheshire, which the bishop vacated. The offer was made to him through the influence of his former pupil, Edward John Stanley, then under-secretary for foreign affairs. But the advantages of comparative rest at Alderley after his severe work at Sedgley were marred by protracted litigation with the first Lord Stanley (patron of the living) and other landowners of the parish, caused by the Tithes Commutation Act of 1836. The arrangements made under the act were destined to affect not only himself, but also his successors, and Girdlestone felt bound to defend their pecuniary rights. The matter was practically decided in his favour, but the result of the dispute was the complete alienation of the Stanleys at the Park. He passed part of 1845 and 1846 in Italy and elsewhere on the continent in the hope of improving his delicate health. On his return to England he accepted the important rectory of Kingswinford in the Staffordshire mining district, offered him by Lord Ward, afterwards Earl of Dudley, cousin of his former patron. Here Girdlestone had to face the second great cholera epidemic of 1849, when Kingswinford suffered severely. He resigned in 1877 ; at the time one of his sons was his *locum tenens.* He had himself for many years resided at Weston-super-Mare in Somersetshire on account of his health, where he died in April 1881, at the age of eighty-four. In 1826 he married Anne Elizabeth, only daughter of Baker Morrell, esq., solicitor to the university of Oxford, who survived him about a year. By her he had one daughter, who died in infancy, and eight sons, of whom seven survived him, the sixth, Robert Baker, being principal of Wycliffe Hall, Oxford, from 1877 to 1889.

Girdlestone was a man of sincere piety, and an energetic and enlivening preacher. Both as a politician and as a churchman he chose in early life the *via media,* but after middle age he sided with the evangelicals and conservatives, though always an advocate of church reform and reform of convocation, of revision of the prayer-book and also of the authorised version of the Bible. At Oxford, as select preacher, he advocated in a sermon, afterwards published, 'Affection between Churchmen and Dissenters,' and in later life he spoke of 'those noxious errors, Tractarian and Neological.' His principal work was his commentary on the Bible, which occupied him for several years. The New Testament was first published in 2 vols. 8vo, 1832–5, which was sufficiently well received to induce him to publish the Old Testament in 4 vols., 1842. It is intended for family reading, and is an excellent specimen of an explanatory and practical commentary written in the early period of modern biblical criticism and addressed especially to the moderate evangelical school. In later life he employed himself in thoroughly revising it on more distinctly protestant principles, and a new edition, in 6 vols. large 8vo, was published in 1873. He published also eleven small volumes of sermons and several single ones; these were once very popular. On one occasion Girdlestone heard one of them read from the pulpit by a preacher who was quite unconscious of the author's presence. Among numerous other works may be mentioned: 1. Two volumes of 'Devotions for Family Use and for Private Use,' 1835. 2. Two volumes of 'Select Hymns for Public Use and for Private Use,' 1835. 3. Twenty-eight numbers of 'Sedgley Church Tracts,' 1831–6. 4. 'Concordance to the Prayer Book Version of the Psalms,' 1834. 5. The Bible version and the prayer-book version of the Psalms, in parallel columns, 1836. 6. 'Questions of the Day, by the Creature of an Hour,' 1857 (anonymous). 7. 'Christendom, sketched from History in the Light of Holy Scripture,' 1870. 8. 'Number, a Link between Divine Intelligence and Human,' 1875. 9. 'Thoughts on Dying Daily,' 1878. 10. An expurgated edition of 'Horace with English notes of a Christian tendency, for the Use of Schools,' in conjunction with the Rev. W. A. Osborne, 1848.

[Personal knowledge and recollections; information from the family; a short memoir, with a photographic portrait, in the Church of England Photographic Portrait Gallery, London.]

W. A. G.

GIRDLESTONE, EDWARD (1805–1884), canon of Bristol, youngest son of Samuel Rainbow Girdlestone, a chancery barrister, was born in London 6 Sept. 1805. An elder brother, Charles, is noticed above. He matriculated from Balliol College, Oxford, 10 June 1822, and in 1823 was admitted a scholar of his college, became B.A. in 1826, M.A. in 1829, and was ordained to the curacy of Deane, Lancashire, in 1828. Having taken priest's orders he became vicar of Deane in 1830. Lord-chancellor Cranworth, to whom he was personally unknown, conferred on him in 1854 the place of canon residentiary of Bristol Cathedral, in right of which he succeeded to the vicarage of St. Nicholas with St. Leonard, Bristol, in 1855, which he resigned in 1858 for the vicarage of Wapley with Codrington, Gloucestershire. In 1862 he became vicar of Halberton, Devonshire, and ultimately in March 1872 vicar of Olveston, near Almondsbury, Bristol. He was well known under the title of 'The Agricultural Labourers' Friend,' an appellation of which he was very proud. It was in 1867 that his first public efforts on behalf of the labourers were made, and at a meeting of the British Association at Norwich in the following year he suggested an agricultural labourers' union. He wrote, spoke, travelled, and organised in behalf of this object, and his name became associated with the meetings of various learned and philanthropic bodies. He was the means of removing upwards of six hundred families from the districts of the west of England, where work was scarce and poorly paid, to the more active and prosperous north. He caught cold while on a journey to visit King Edward VII, then Prince of Wales, at Sandringham, and died at Bristol, 4 Dec. 1884. He was buried in the graveyard of Bristol Cathedral, 9 Dec. He married in 1832 Mary, eldest daughter of Thomas Ridgway of Wallsuches, in Deane parish. He was the author of: 1. 'Sermons,' 1843, &c., eight pamphlets. 2. 'The Committee of Council on Education, an imaginary Enemy, a real Friend,' 1850. 3. 'G. Marsh, the Martyr of Deane,' 1851. 4. 'Sermons on Romanism and Tractarianism,' 1851. 5. 'The Education Question,' 1852. 6. 'Apostolical Succession neither proved matter of fact nor revealed in the Bible nor the Doctrine of the Church of England,' 1857. 7. 'Reflected Truth, or the Image of God lost in Adam restored in Jesus Christ,' 1859. 8. 'Remarks on "Essays and Reviews,"' 1861. 9. 'Revelation and Reason,' a lecture, 1883.

[Church of England Photographic Portrait Gallery, 1859, pt. vi., with portrait; Church Portrait Journal, August 1884, pp. 57–60, with portrait; Times, 5 Dec. 1884, p. 10, and 10 Dec. p. 6.]

G. C. B.

GIRDLESTONE, JOHN LANG (1763–1825), classical translator, born in 1763, was fellow of Caius College, Cambridge, where he proceeded B.A. 1785, M.A. 1789. He took orders, was rector of Swainsthorpe (1788), vicar of Sheringham, Norfolk (1803), and master of the classical school at Beccles. He died in 1825. Girdlestone wrote 'All the Odes of Pindar translated from the original Greek' (Norwich, 1810).

[Gent. Mag. May 1825, p. 473 (where a work on the authorship of Junius is incorrectly attributed to Girdlestone; it is really by Thomas Girdlestone [q.v.]); Romilly's Cantabr. Graduati, 1760–1856, p. 152.] F. W–T.

GIRDLESTONE, THOMAS, M.D. (1758–1822), translator of Anacreon, born in 1758 at Holt, Norfolk, was entered on the physic line at Leyden 8 May 1787 (*Index of Leyden Students,* Index Soc. p. 40). Entering the army as a doctor, he served for some time under the command of Colonel Sir Charles Stuart, governor of Minorca, to whose friendship he attributed his success in life. After passing some years with the army in India, he settled in Great Yarmouth, Norfolk, where he succeeded Dr. John Aikin [q.v.], and practised with great success for thirty-seven years. Tall, slender, and upright, scrupulously dressed in black, with silk stockings and half-gaiters, a white cravat, an ample shirt frill, powdered head and pigtail, he might be seen daily perambulating the town with his gold-headed cane. In 1803 he was one of the promoters of the public library at Great Yarmouth. He died suddenly on 25 June 1822. By his marriage with the widow of the Rev. John Close, and daughter of Robert Lawton of Ipswich, Suffolk, he had an only son, Charles Stuart Girdlestone, an ardent ornithologist, who formed a large collection of birds, principally shot by his own gun in the neighbourhood of Yarmouth. He died unmarried in 1831, aged 33. Girdlestone possessed a good medical library, which was sold by auction soon after his death. He contributed largely under various signatures to the medical journals of the day, and published with his name (1) 'Essays on the Hepatitis and Spasmodic Affections in India,' &c., 8vo, London, 1787; (2) 'A Case of Diabetes, with an Historical Sketch of that Disease,' 8vo, Yarmouth, 1799. He had some correspondence with R. Langslow upon apoplexy, which was published by the latter in 1802. In 1805 Girdlestone published an address to the inhabitants of Great Yarmouth strongly urging vaccination. During his residence in Yarmouth he compared the translation of the 'Odes of Anacreon,' by D. H. Urquhart, then residing at Hobland Hall, with the original Greek, and in 1803 he published his own translation, after having 'kept it from the press nearly eleven years.' Other editions followed in 1804 and 1809. He also wrote a paradoxical essay maintaining that Arthur Lee was the author of 'Junius,' entitled 'Facts tending to prove that General Lee was never absent from this country for any length of time during the years 1767, 1768, 1769, 1770, 1771, 1772, and that he was the author of Junius,' 8vo, London, 1813. The copy in the British Museum contains copious manuscript notes by the author, together with copies of four letters from General Lee to Sir Charles Davers. The 'Reasons' had previously appeared without Girdlestone's name, 8vo, London, 1807. He likewise published several views of ancient buildings, including the church of St. Peter in Wolverhampton, Dudley Castle, and the abbeys of Lilleshall, Haughmond, and Buildwas in Shropshire, with short descriptions appended to each.

[Gent. Mag. vol. xcii. pt. i. p. 643; Palmer's Perlustration of Great Yarmouth, i. 179–81, ii. 142, 221, 380; Brit. Mus. Cat.] G. G.

GIRLING, MARY ANNE (1827–1886), founder of the sect called 'The People of God,' daughter of Mr. Clouting, a small farmer, was born in the parish of Little Glemham, Suffolk, on 27 April 1827. She received little instruction when young, but afterwards managed to acquire a fair amount of knowledge. At first she was in communion with a methodist connexion, but left it when the congregation refused to listen to her inspirations. In the meantime she had become the wife of George Stanton Girling, first a seaman, then a fitter in an iron foundry, and afterwards a general dealer at Ipswich. About Christmas 1864 she began to believe that she was a new incarnation of the Deity. One sign of this was the stigmata which appeared on her hands, feet, and side. She was wont to describe with minute details the extraordinary emotion which overwhelmed her at the moment when she experienced the divine call. From that period she went about proclaiming the new revelation and speaking as with absolute knowledge of hidden mysteries. She gathered around her a small company of men and women, belonging for the most part to the labouring classes. Their first meeting-place for public worship was at 107 Bridge Road, Battersea, London, where in August 1870 they attracted much attention. They were generally called shakers, but they themselves never accepted that name, but always spoke of their community as the children of God. On 2 Jan. 1872 they removed from London and settled in the New Forest, Hampshire, where Miss Wood, a wealthy lady, had purchased for them a residence and a farm, known as New Forest Lodge. She gave 2,250l. for the property, on which there remained a mortgage of 1,000l. Here the community increased to 160 persons, who learnt to regard Mrs. Girling, 'their mother,' with tenderness, love, and reverence. She owed her authority over her people to her belief in herself and to her great force of will. Their faith in her endured through cold, hunger, and suffering, and many and repeated misfortunes. It was believed that they would all live for ever, and that sooner or later everybody would acknowledge the divinity of Mrs. Girling, who would then rule over a peaceful world. She was a tall, lean woman, with an upright carriage, a strong, intelligent countenance, bright eyes, a very good expression, and a rather winning voice. She had scruples against going to law, which afterwards made her an easy prey to her enemies. Although the community was industrious and lived in a state of celibacy, it got into debt and was ejected in a somewhat arbitrary manner from New Forest Lodge in December 1873. This ejection took place in very severe weather, and the pitiable condition of the people excited much commiseration. They encamped on the roadside for two days, when they had notice to leave, and part of the community returned to their homes in various parts of the country. A Mr. Beasley then offered them the use of a shed, where they remained for three weeks, but the place was not large enough for them all to sit down at one time. They next found a friend in the Hon. Auberon E. M. Herbert, who gave them the use of a barn on the Ashley Arnewood farm, Lymington. After staying in this barn five weeks, they removed to a field which they formerly had on lease with New Forest Lodge; when this lease expired they were again turned into the roadway, and there they lived night and day for five weeks. In 1879 Mrs. Girling rented a small farm of two acres called Tiptoe Farm, near Hordle, Lymington. Here they erected a number of wooden huts with canvas roofs, with a larger and superior hut as a place of public worship. The only publication issued by Mrs. Girling is a small four-page tract entitled 'The Close of the Dispensation: the Last Message to the Church and the World.' It is signed 'Jesus First and Last (Mary Ann Girling), Tiptoe, Hordle, near Lymington, Hants, 1883.' In it she says: 'I now close this letter with the true and loving declaration that I am the second appearing of Jesus, the Christ of God, the Bride, the Lamb's Wife, the God-mother and Saviour, life from heaven, and that there will not be another.' Latterly the children of God escaped public notice, except from excursionists visiting the place. The cold and exposure at last told on Mrs. Girling, and she fell ill. During her illness she did not lose faith in what she had preached, and believed that she would never die, but would live until the second coming of Christ. She died of cancer at Tiptoe, Hordle, on 18 Sept. 1886, aged 59, and was buried in Hordle churchyard 22 Sept. After the funeral those of the community who had friends returned to them, and only six persons were left to occupy the camp at Tiptoe. Mrs. Girling left children, among them a younger son, William Girling.

[Irish Monthly, October 1878, pp. 555–64; Times, 20 Sept. 1886, p. 9; Standard, 20 Sept. 1886, p. 3; Pall Mall Gaz. 18 Sept. 1886, p. 8, and 27 Sept. p. 3; Lymington Chronicle, 23 Sept. 1886, p. 3, and 30 Sept. p. 3; Vanity Fair, 25 Sept. 1886, p. 181; information from Brother H. Osborne of Tiptoe, Hordle.]   G. C. B.

GIRTIN, THOMAS (1775–1802), watercolour painter, was born on 18 Feb. 1775. Though 1773 is given by several authorities as the year of his birth, his tombstone records that he died in 1802, aged 27 years, and his descendants now living believe this to be correct. His father was an extensive rope and cordage maker in Southwark, and died when Thomas was about eight years old. His mother afterwards married a Mr. Vaughan, a pattern-draughtsman, and Girtin lived with them at No. 2 St. Martin's-le-Grand till 1796. He received some instruction from a drawing-master named Fisher in Aldersgate Street, and was afterwards apprenticed to Edward Dayes [q. v.], who imprisoned him for refusing to serve out his indentures. He soon made the acquaintance of J. M. W. Turner, then a boy of his own age, employed like him in washing in skies for architects, and colouring prints for John Raphael Smith [q. v.], the engraver, painter, and printseller. They also frequently met in Adelphi Terrace, at the houses of Dr. Thomas Monro and Mr. Henderson, the well-known patrons of young artists, and went out sketching together on the shores of the Thames and in the neighbourhood of London, and in 1793 on a more extended tour. From drawings left by Mr. Henderson's son to the British Museum we learn that Girtin copied drawings by Thomas Malton and Mr. Henderson himself, that he made studies after pictures by Canaletti, and copied in pen and ink the prints of Piranesi. These drawings, and one after Morland's picture of 'Dogs hesitating about the Pluck,' show his early freedom and skill in the use of water-colour and pen and ink. One of his earliest employers was James Moore, F.S.A., an amateur artist, with whom he travelled to Scotland and other places. Some of Moore's sketches, after being worked upon by Girtin, are said to have been engraved and published with Moore's name only attached as artist. In 1794 he began to exhibit at the Royal Academy, when he sent a drawing of

Ely Cathedral, and this was followed in 1795 by views of Warwick Castle and the cathedrals at Lichfield and Peterborough. About 1796 his genius was greatly developed by a visit to the north of England, the fruits of which were shown in the Royal Academy exhibition of 1797, to which he sent ten drawings, including one of Jedburgh Abbey, two of St. Cuthbert's, Holy Island, four views of York, and one of Ouse Bridge in that city. Though mainly occupied with architectural subjects, which he treated with striking originality and poetical feeling, he also made many sketches of pure landscape, recording the grand effects of light and shade upon the swelling moors and rolling downs with a breadth and power never equalled (at least in water-colour) before. About this time he was employed in making topographical sketches for J. Walker's 'Itinerant.' Of his fifteen drawings engraved in this magazine the 'Bamburgh Castle' is notable for the grandeur of its design. He early achieved a high reputation, and might have found lucrative employment as a drawing-master but for his disinclination to teach those who had no artistic gift. His dislike of fashionable society is also said to have stood in the way of his worldly success. 'When travelling to the north he would take his passage in a collier; and his delight was to live in intercourse with the crew, eating salt beef, smoking, and exchanging jokes,' and on shore found amusement and subjects among the 'motley groups' in inn kitchens.

The graver charges which have been brought against Girtin's character are based principally, if not entirely, on the unsupported statements of Dayes and Edwards. Dayes, with whom he had quarrelled, and whom he had surpassed in art, was probably the author of Edwards's statements. Girtin doubtless had an early taste for social pleasures of a somewhat Bohemian kind, but there is no sufficient proof that he was vicious, or that his early death was the result of culpable self-indulgence. The only evidence, except vague statement, is on the other side. He was a welcome guest at houses where dissipated habits would not have been tolerated— at those, for instance, of Lord Hardwicke, the Earl of Essex, the Hon. Spencer Cowper, and Lord Mulgrave. The Earl of Elgin wished him to accompany him to Constantinople as a sort of artistic adviser to his wife.

He married the daughter of Phineas Borrett, a respectable goldsmith with a house of business in Staining Lane and a residence at Islington. Throughout his short career he worked with unfailing industry and unimpaired faculty. But perhaps there is no

stronger testimony to his character than the composition of the little coterie which he chose to form his sketching society, the first of its kind established in London. The members met in turn at each other's houses, and the host provided tea, coffee, and cold supper, and kept the sketches, which were made from a subject from English poetry specially set for the evening. The names of the members were Robert Ker Porter, Augustus Callcott (both afterwards knighted), T. R. Underwood, G. Samuel, P. S. Murray, John Sell Cotman, L. Francia, W. H. Worthington, J. C. Denham, and T. Girtin. And finally, there is abundant testimony as to the loving regard in which he was held by his friends. Hands more friendly and more trustworthy than those of either Dayes or Edwards wrote of his 'noble, generous, unselfish nature,' and testified that 'he was beloved by all that knew him,' that 'his house, like his heart, was open to all,' and that 'he was warm-hearted, liberal, and generous as the sun.'

In 1797 Girtin had removed from his mother's house to 35 Drury Lane. In 1798 he was at 25 Henrietta Street, Covent Garden, in 1799 at 6 Long Acre, and in 1800 his address in the Royal Academy Catalogue is at the house of his father-in-law, Phineas Borrett, at 11 Scott's Place, Islington. In these years he exhibited drawings of different places in England and Wales and Scotland, all in water-colour; but in 1801, the year in which his old friend and rival, Turner, was elected an associate of the Royal Academy— urged probably by the desire to obtain the same honour—he sent an oil picture for the first time to the exhibition. This picture was 'Bolton Bridge,' and the last he ever exhibited.

His health had broken down, symptoms of pulmonary disease appeared, and he was recommended to try change of air. The peace of Amiens allowed him to go to Paris in the spring of 1802. Here, notwithstanding the state of his health, he appears to have worked with unabated industry. Besides a number of architectural sketches in outline, taken of Paris and other towns through which he passed, he executed a beautiful series of twenty drawings of Paris for the Earl of Essex (now in the possession of the Duke of Bedford), which were etched by himself, and, after aquatint had been added by other hands, were published by his brother, John Girtin, a writing engraver in Castle Street, Leicester Square. He became homesick, and returned to England in May, and from two of his views of Paris painted scenes for Covent Garden Theatre. To this time must probably be ascribed also the completion, if not the entire execution, of a panorama of London (one of the first of its kind), which was taken from the top of the Albion Mills, on the south side of Blackfriars Bridge. It was on exhibition in Castle Street, Leicester Square, at the time of his death, and afterwards at the exhibition-room in Spring Gardens. It was then bought and sent to St. Petersburg. Girtin did not cease working till within eight days of his death, which took place at his lodgings in the Strand on 9 Nov. 1802. He left a widow and an infant son, and was buried in the churchyard of St. Paul's, Covent Garden. His funeral was attended by his brother artists, Sir William Beechey, Edridge, Hearne, and Turner, and a flat stone was laid over his grave.

Girtin was the true founder of the modern practice of 'painting' as distinguished from 'tinting' in water-colours. The difference is described by a contemporary, W. H. Pyne [q. v.], as follows: 'This artist prepared his drawing on the same principle which had hitherto been confined to painting in oil, namely, laying in the object upon his paper with the local colour, and shadowing the same with the individual tint of its own shadow. Previous to the practice of Turner and Girtin drawings were shadowed first entirely through, whatever their component parts—houses, cattle, trees, mountains, foregrounds, middle-grounds, and distances—all with black or grey, and these objects were afterwards stained or tinted, enriched and finished, as is now [1824] the custom to colour prints. It was this new practice, introduced by these distinguished artists, that acquired for designs in water-colours upon paper the title of paintings.' This change of practice was accompanied by many changes in manipulation. He used a large and full brush, and a paper rougher, more absorbent, and of a warmer tone than had been previously employed. It was a cartridge paper, bought of a stationer at Charing Cross, with slight wire marks and folded. It can be recognised now by the line of the fold, which often greatly mars the beauty of his drawings by a row of unseemly spots down the very centre of them.

Girtin was distinguished by the breadth and simplicity of his style, by the depth and harmony of his colour, by the bold distribution of his masses, whether of form or light, by the solemnity and serenity of his sentiment, seen equally in the treatment of pure landscape and of architecture. He seized at once the general character of a scene, and by a truthful and happy generalisation conveyed his impression of it without hesitation or loss of freshness. In execution he was rapid and masterly. 'It was a great treat to see Girtin at his studies,' says one writer, who proceeds to describe his extraordinary facility; another speaks of 'the swordplay of his pencil;' and his drawings, from their mere technical dexterity, are still the admiration of artists. By increasing the range of atmospheric effect in painted landscape, by the purity and force of his artistic gift, by his feeling of natural poetry, and in many other ways, he has exercised a vast and noble influence on modern landscape-painting. This influence has been indirect, through the works of his great contemporary Turner, and those of such followers as Cotman, Francia, Bonington, and De Wint, but it has not been less true on that account. 'Had Tom Girtin lived, I should have starved,' said Turner, and Mr. Ruskin has written of his work: 'He is often as impressive to me as Nature herself; nor do I doubt that Turner owed more to his teaching and companionship than to his own genius in the first years of his life.' Most of Girtin's finest drawings are in private hands, but by the bequests of Mr. Chambers Hall in 1855, and of Mr. Henderson in 1878, the British Museum possesses many interesting examples of his work, and one large and magnificent drawing of Bridgenorth. There are also some good drawings of his at South Kensington.

Several portraits of Girtin's handsome face are in existence, one in oils by Opie, now in the possession of his grandson, which has been engraved in mezzotint. His friend Edridge drew him several times; one of the sketches and a finished drawing are in the British Museum. George Dance the younger [q. v.] executed a lithograph portrait of him, and also included him in his book of portraits engraved by William Daniell, A.R.A.

[Redgrave's Dict. of Artists, 1878; Bryan's Dict. of Artists (Graves); Dayes's Works; Edwards's Anecdotes; Library of the Fine Arts, vol. iii.; Somerset House Gazette; Gent. Mag. 1802, 1803; Chalmers's Dict.; Miller's Turner and Girtin's Picturesque Views; Thornbury's Life of Turner; Monkhouse's Turner; Portfolio, April and May 1888; Cat. of National Gallery at South Kensington; Wedmore's Studies in English Art; Liber Fluviorum; Rivers of England; Catalogues of Burlington Fine Arts Club, 1871, 1875, 1884; Leslie's Handbook for Young Painters; Dance's Portraits.] C. M.

GISA or GISO, sometimes called GILA (d. 1088), bishop of Wells, a native of Saint Trudo in Hasbain, in the diocese of Liège, was one of the chaplains or clerks of the chancery of Eadward the Confessor (on these

cellor's medallist. A political career was open to him, but he preferred the quiet life of a country squire and clergyman. He took orders, and in 1783 he was presented to the perpetual curacy of Barton-under-Needwood, settling in the same year at Yoxall Lodge, inherited by him on his father's death in 1779, within three miles of his church. He married Mary, daughter of Thomas Babington of Rothley Temple, Leicestershire, in 1784, and passed the rest of his life at Yoxall. His son James succeeded him as perpetual curate of Barton in 1820. In April 1823 he was appointed to the fifth prebend, and in 1826 to the first prebend in Durham. He died 24 March 1846, leaving six sons: Thomas (1794–1852) [q. v.], John, William, James, Matthew, and Walter; and two daughters, Mary, wife of William Evans of Allestree, Derby, and Lydia, wife of the Rev. E. Robinson.

Gisborne was an intimate friend of Wilberforce, whom he had known at college, and who spent many summers at Yoxall and Rothley Temple. Among his other friends were Bishop Barrington of Durham, Hannah More, and most of the eminent evangelicals. His ethical writings are directed against Paley's expediency, and endeavour to provide a basis of absolute right; but his criterion is mainly utilitarian. His sermons were held to rank with the best contemporary performances; but he shows more refinement and good feeling than intellectual force. The then unenclosed Needwood Forest was to him what Selborne was to Gilbert White, and his enjoyment of natural scenery is impressed in poems modelled chiefly upon Cowper. Many of his books went through several editions.

His works are: 1. 'Principles of Moral Philosophy,' 1789; 4th ed. 1798. To later editions were added 'Remarks on Decision of the House of Commons on 2 April 1792, respecting the Abolition of the Slave Trade,' first published in 1792. 2. 'An Inquiry into the Duties of Men in the Higher Ranks and Middle Classes,' 1794; 6th ed. 1811. 3. 'Walks in a Forest,' 1794; 8th ed. 1803. 4. 'Inquiry into the Duties of the Female Sex,' 1797; 8th ed. 1810, German translation 1803. 5. 'Poems Sacred and Moral,' 1798; later editions included an ode to the memory of William Cowper, published separately in 1800. 6. 'Familiar Survey of the Christian Religion,' 1799; 8th ed. 1836, Welsh translation 1801. 7. 'Sermons,' 1 vol. 1802. 8. 'Sermons on Christian Morality,' 1809; 2 vols. 1804–6. A collective edition of the above was published in 1813 in 9 vols. 8vo. 9. 'Sermons on Epistle to the Colossians,' 1816. 10. 'Testimony of Natural Theology to Christianity,' 1818. 11. 'Essays on Recollection

of Friends in a Future State,' 1822. 12. 'Inquiry concerning Love as one of the Divine Attributes,' 1838; besides pamphlets on Church Establishment, 1829 and 1835; Maynooth, 1844, &c.

[Gent. Mag. 1846, i. 643, 661; Burke's Landed Gentry; Le Neve's Fasti; Life of William Wilberforce; Sir J. Stephen's Essays on Ecclesiastical Biography (Clapham Sect).]   L. S.

GISBORNE, THOMAS, the younger (1794–1852), politician, born 1794, was the eldest son of Thomas Gisborne [q. v.], prebendary of Durham, by Mary, daughter of Thomas Babington, of Rothley Temple, Leicestershire. He was a country gentleman of a good estate and interested in business at Manchester. He was elected for Stafford in 1830, and again in 1831, as a supporter of the Reform Bill. In the first reformed parliament he represented the northern division of Derbyshire, and was re-elected in 1835. In 1837 he lost his seat; but in 1839 he stood for Carlow, and, though beaten at the poll, was seated on petition. In 1841 he stood unsuccessfully for South Leicestershire, but in 1843 was elected for the town of Nottingham. He was a staunch whig or radical; supported the ballot, the abolition of church rates, and the extension of the suffrage; but was most conspicuous as a supporter of the free trade agitation. He was a vigorous speaker, with much humour. He died 20 July 1852 at Yoxall Lodge, Staffordshire. He published some speeches and pamphlets; and in 1854 appeared four 'Essays on Agriculture,' of which three had already appeared in the 'Quarterly Review' (Nos. 168, 171, 173). By his first wife, Elizabeth Fysche, daughter of John Palmer, who died 20 June 1823, he had four children, Thomas Guy, Henry Fysche, Thomas Bowdler, and Elizabeth Maria. In 1826 he married Susan, widow of Francis Dukinfield Astley, by whom he had no children.

[Gent. Mag. 1852, ii. 315.]

GISBURNE, WALTER OF (fl. 1300), chronicler. [See HEMINGFORD.]

GLADSTANES, GEORGE (d. 1615), archbishop of St. Andrews, was the son of Herbert Gladstanes, clerk of Dundee, and one of the bailies of that town. He was born there between 1560 and 1565, and after spending some time at its grammar school went in 1576 to the university of St. Andrews, where he graduated as master of arts in 1580. He probably afterwards studied theology under Andrew Melville. He was for some time a teacher of languages in Montrose, and was appointed reader in that town in 1585.

Before 23 July 1587 he was ordained minister of St. Cyrus or Ecclesgreig in Kincardineshire, and had at the same time the church of Aberluthnott, or Marykirk, also under his care. During his residence at St. Cyrus he was on several occasions in danger of his life from armed attacks on his house by William Douglas the younger of Glenbervie and others, but was relieved by the exertions of his neighbours.

Gladstanes was a member of the general assembly of 1590 (SCOT, *Apologetical Narration*, Wodrow Soc., p. 57). In May 1592 he was presented by the king to the vicarage of Arbirlot in Forfarshire, and was again a member of assembly in that year, and also in 1595, when he was nominated with several others as assessors with the king in the choice of two royal chaplains. About this time he served on several commissions appointed by the general assembly, one of which was for advising with the king on church affairs. The ministers in St. Andrews, Messrs. Black and Wallace, having offended by their preaching, the king ordered them to be summarily removed from their charge, and brought Gladstanes from Arbirlot to fill their place. He was inducted at St. Andrews on 11 July 1597, James Melville very reluctantly preaching on the occasion.

When the king in the following year introduced the proposal that the church should be represented in parliament, he was warmly supported in the assembly by Gladstanes, who was appointed one of three commissioners chosen to sit and vote in parliament in name of the ministry. He became vice-chancellor of the university of St. Andrews in July 1599, and on 14 Oct. 1600 was made bishop of Caithness by the king. He sat in parliament as bishop, and was challenged by the synod of Fife, meeting at St. Andrews 3 Feb. 1601, for doing so, when he declared he was obliged to answer 'with the name of *Bishop* put against his will, because they would not name him otherwise' (CALDERWOOD).

Gladstanes continued to be minister of St. Andrews. He was employed by the assembly on various commissions for dealing with the papists, for the plantation of kirks, and for visiting presbyteries. On 24 Nov. 1602 he was admitted a member of the privy council of Scotland, being the second clerical member of that body, and after the accession of James VI to the crown of England was appointed in 1604 one of the commissioners for the union of the two kingdoms. He went to London in the latter part of that year, but before starting he, along with his brethren of the presbytery of St. Andrews, renewed the national covenant, or Scots confession of faith,

and subscribed it. When at London, on 12 Oct. 1604, he was appointed by James VI archbishop of St. Andrews; but on his return, fearing the displeasure of his co-presbyters, he did not disclose what had taken place. At a meeting of the presbytery on 10 Jan. 1605 he openly declared that he claimed no superiority over his brethren. Some of his friends asked him, according to Calderwood, how he could bear with the presbytery. 'Hold your tongue,' he replied; 'we shall steal them off their feet.'

Gladstanes long refrained from assuming the title of archbishop of St. Andrews. The king required him to resign the old archiepiscopal residence of the castle of St. Andrews, in order that it might be conferred on the Earl of Dunbar, and Gladstanes resigned it formally both at Whitehall and in the Scottish parliament. He received in exchange the provostry of Kirkhill, &c.,with an annual pension of three hundred merks (13*l*. 6*s*. 8*d*. sterling). James also compelled him to yield another of the old primatial residences, Monimail, Fifeshire, in order that he might confer it on Sir Robert Melville of Murdocairnie. Gladstanes then obtained a few vicarages in Forfarshire. But at a later date the king purchased back the castle of St. Andrews as a residence for the archbishops of St. Andrews, and Gladstanes dwelt in it for a time.

Gladstanes had a great aversion to Andrew Melville. Martine states that the king brought Gladstanes to St. Andrews, where Melville was principal of the university, for the very purpose of balancing and putting a check on Melville, and of preventing the students from imbibing Melville's principles. 'And,' he adds, 'many a hote bickering there was between them thereupon' (*Reliquiæ Divæ Andreæ*). In a letter to the king on 19 June 1606 Gladstanes says: 'Mr. Andrew Melvil hath begun to raise new storms with his eolick blasts. Sir, you are my Jupiter, and I under your Highness, Neptune, I must say, *Non illi imperium pelagi . . . sed mihi sorte datur.* Your Majesty will relegat him to some Æolia, *ut illic vacua se jactet in aula.* James commanded Melville with certain others to appear before him in London, and he was never permitted to return to St. Andrews. The ostensible occasion of the summons was the king's desire for the conference at Hampton Court, which Gladstanes also attended as one of the representatives of the bishops (22 Sept. 1606). Before going he promised the presbytery of St. Andrews that he would do nothing 'to prejudice the established discipline of the church.' The presbytery, however, supplied to Andrew Melville documents to show that Gladstanes had signed the covenant, and forwarded the explanations which he had given to the presbytery after his former visit to London in 1604, to be made use of at court as occasion should require.

In this year, 1606, the assembly, at the bidding of James, enacted that there should be permanent moderators for presbyteries and synods, and Gladstanes was appointed president of the presbytery of St. Andrews, and also of the synod of Fife. The presbytery proved recalcitrant. The privy council issued a special charge (17 Jan. 1607) to the members to obey the act of assembly within twenty-four hours under pain of being put to the horn or denounced rebels. To secure full submission four commissioners from the king attended the synod meeting at Dysart on 18 Aug. to induct Gladstanes as permanent moderator, but resistance continued. The brethren answered severally they 'would rather abide the horning and all that follows thereupon than lose the liberty of the kirk' (CALDERWOOD). The leaders of the opposition were imprisoned, and one was put to the horn.

About the same time Gladstanes was empowered to constitute a chapter consisting of any seven of the ministers of his diocese he might choose. He was a zealous member of the Scottish legislature, giving much attention to his duties, both in the privy council and in parliament. In 1609 Gladstanes and James were at variance on a question of the perquisites of the archbishopric, Gladstanes claiming that as of old the estates of bastards, the customs of St. Andrews, and confiscated goods pertained to the episcopal see. James wished them for the crown, and Gladstanes humbly tendered his submission, but asked to be heard on the subject (Acts of the Parliaments of Scotland, vi. 453). In the same year he projected another journey to court, and wrote to the king in May asking the requisite permission. In September he was far on his way, and from Standford on the 11th of that month intimated his approach in a letter of remarkable sycophancy, calling James his 'earthly creator' (Original Letters relating to Ecclesiastical Affairs of Scotland, Bannatyne Club, i. 205).

The court of high commission was established shortly after the return of Gladstanes from his visit to London, and was the combined result of the efforts of Gladstanes and his archiepiscopal colleague in the west of Scotland. Spotiswood, Gladstanes' successor in the primacy, had already to a large extent supplanted him in the king's estimation. In 1610 Gladstanes begged hard of James to nominate him for the moderatorship of the general assembly, but the king declined.

Gladstanes at this time was a good deal resident in Edinburgh, where, as James Melville states, he kept a 'splendid establishment,' and was surrounded by 'crowds of poor ministers' (Melvini Epistolæ, p. 125). Gladstanes in a later letter to James speaks of his influence with complacency. 'All men,' he says, 'do follow us and hunt for our favour upon the report of your majesty's good acceptance of me and the bishop of Caithnes.' James placed the regulation of the stipends of the clergy in the power of the bishops, and also distributed money among them. In 1610, just before the meeting of the assembly in June, he placed ten thousand merks at the disposal of Archbishops Gladstanes and Spotiswood for the members of that meeting (Register of the Privy Council of Scotland, viii. 844).

Although created a bishop in 1600, Gladstanes had never received consecration at the hands of a prelate. The bishops of Glasgow, Brechin, and Galloway were therefore consecrated at London by Abbot, bishop of London, in November 1610. On their return they consecrated Bishop Gladstanes at St. Andrews, on 13 Jan. 1611, along with several others. After this date he is mentioned as residing in the castle of St. Andrews. He held the bishopric until his death, which took place at St. Andrews on 2 May 1615. It was said to be caused by a loathsome disease. His body had to be buried immediately in the parish church; but a public funeral was accorded to him in the following month at the expense of the king (7 June).

Gladstanes, in his connection with the university of St. Andrews, revived the professorship of canon law, to which he nominated his own son-in-law (Ecclesiastical Correspondence, tempore James VI, i. 433*), and he also made great efforts for the restoration of degrees in divinity. On this subject he wrote in 1607, requesting his majesty in his 'incomparable wisdom' to send him 'the form and order of making bachelors and doctors of divinity,' that he might 'create one or two doctors to incite others to the same honour, and to encourage our ignorant clergy to learning' (ib. p. 109). But the royal permission was not granted until the year following Gladstanes' death. Spotiswood, his successor, eulogises him as a man of good learning, ready utterance, and great invention, but of too easy a nature (Hist. Spottiswoode Soc. iii. 227).

Gladstanes married Christian, daughter of John Durie, minister of Montrose, who survived till 1617, and by whom he had one son and three daughters. The son, Alexander, was appointed archdeacon of St. Andrews, and was deposed in 1638. One of the daughters married Sir John Wemyss of Craigton, another John Lyon of Auldbar, and the third, named Elizabeth, married, about 1632, Dr. George Haliburton, whose son George, born in 1635, became bishop of Brechin and Aberdeen.

A large number of the letters of Archbishop Gladstanes to James VI and others are printed, with many more joint productions of him and his brother bishops, in 'Ecclesiastical Letters relating to the Affairs of Scotland' (Bannatyne Club), 2 vols., and also in the memoir of him in 'Wodrow's Lives' (Maitland Club), vol. i.

[Gordon's Ecclesiastical Chronicle for Scotland (1867), i. 339–59; Acts of the Parliaments of Scotland, vol. vi. passim; Register of the Privy Council of Scotland, vols. v. vi. vii. and viii.; Scott's Fasti Ecclesiæ Scoticanæ, iv. 833, v. 456, vi. 789, 863; Calderwood's History, iv. 660, v. vi. vii. passim; Scot's Narration; Row's History; Spotiswood's History; Diary of Mr. James Melville, and Dr. McCrie's Life of Andrew Melville.]   H. P.

GLADSTANES, JOHN, LL.D (d. 1574), advocate, is first mentioned on 21 Feb. 1533, at which date he was designated 'M. Johannes Gladstanes, licentiatus utroque jure.' In 1534 there was a James Gladstanes of Coklaw, an estate with a defensible tower in Roxburghshire, which had been possessed by the family for many previous generations. It is averred that John Gladstanes was a member of the Coklaw family, and his mother was a Fraser; but circumstances rather indicate the upper ward of Lanarkshire as the locality of his birth. Among the students incorporated in the university of St. Andrews in 1506 appears the name of 'Johannes Gledstains,' among determinants in 1507 'Johannes Gledstanys,' and among licentiates in 1509 'Johannes Gledstains.' There is little doubt that the future lord of session is indicated in these references. In 1533 he was a young man, and with his cousin, Robert Fraser, applied to the council for a passport to spend some time in France and elsewhere. It was declared under the great seal that both young men were well born, and belonged to ancient and honourable families.

Gladstanes was in practice as an advocate early in 1534. At a sitting of the lords of session on 2 March that year, it was decided, in compliance with a royal letter, to appoint a new official, to be called 'Advocatus Pauperum.' He was to swear that he would act for the king's lieges who should prove that they were too poor to afford a lawsuit. This advocate was to have 10l. yearly from the king's treasurer. The court thereupon chose

Master Thomas Marjoribanks and Master John Gladstanes conjunctly and severally to be advocates for all the poor. On 27 April 1535, in consequence of another royal letter, it was arranged that Friday in each week should be set apart for the poor, as they could not afford to be kept long in waiting. On 23 March 1536 Gladstanes appears as witness to a document at Dundee.

In the sederunt on 30 Sept. 1546 Gladstanes appears for the first time as a lord of session. On that day he was appointed their procurator, to receive certain dues from the prelates. On 1 and 4 Feb. 1549 the accounts were audited; a sum of 40l. was available for each of the judges, and a surplus of 17l. 7s. 10d. was divided equally between the king's advocate and Gladstanes. As a gift from the court Gladstanes likewise obtained the arrears of the contribution due by the minister of Failford, Ayrshire, superior of the Trinity or Red Friars. He died without issue in April 1574, leaving to a nephew some oxgates of land in Quothquam, Lanarkshire.

[Register of the Great Seal of Scotland; original manuscript in General Register House, Edinburgh; Retours in Register House; Munimenta de Melros, p. 486; Regist. Episc. Brechinensis, ii. 319; Regist. Univ. Glasguensis, ii. 75–469; Acta Dom. Con. et Sess. 1811, pp. 24, 45; Lord Hailes's Catalogue of the College of Justice; Brunton and Haig's Senators of the College of Justice; Records of University of St. Andrews.]   J. T.

GLADSTONE, Sir JOHN (1764–1851), merchant, of Liverpool, was born at Leith 11 Dec. 1764, where his father, Thomas Gladstones (1732–1809), was a shopkeeper and corn merchant. His mother was Helen, daughter of Walter Neilson, esq., of Springfield. John, at the age of twenty-two, entered the service of Corrie & Co., corn merchants, in Liverpool. His shrewdness was great, his energy indomitable, and he was soon taken into partnership. The first vessel which went from Liverpool to Calcutta after the trade of the East had been thrown open was despatched by him. While still young he was sent out to buy corn in America on account of a European scarcity. He was unable to procure it, as the American crops had suffered, and meanwhile twenty-four vessels had been engaged to convey to Europe the grain he was despatched to purchase. The prospect of sending them back in ballast was ruinous, but by a singular display of energy he managed to stock the holds of every one of the vessels with commodities which were sold in Britain subsequently at a very trifling loss. In 1813 he published two letters addressed to the Earl of Clancarty, president of the Board of Trade, insisting 'on the inexpediency of permitting the importation of cotton wool from the United States' during the existing war. Gladstone was a partner in the firm of Corrie, Gladstone, & Bradshaw for sixteen years, and greatly increased its business. Upon a dissolution of partnership he became sole proprietor, and the firm was known as Gladstone & Co. With characteristic care for others, he drafted over from Leith his six brothers, one by one, in order to provide them with careers. His business, in which he amassed a large fortune, was mainly with the East Indies, but some ten years before he retired he also developed a West-Indian trade. The firm acquired large plantations in Demerara and elsewhere, whence they brought over sugar and other produce in their own ships. Like all West-Indian merchants Gladstone was a slaveowner, and he championed the interests of the planters in the controversy respecting the abolition of the slave trade. An elaborate discussion of the subject took place between himself and James Cropper [q. v.], the well-known abolitionist, in the columns of the 'Liverpool Mercury' and 'Courier,' in the autumn of 1823, and the articles were republished in pamphlet form in 1824. In 1830, when the great Emancipation Bill was in view, Gladstone issued, in the form of a letter to Sir Robert Peel, 'A Statement of Facts connected with the Present State of Slavery,' in which, while acknowledging the heavy social responsibilities of slaveowners, he deprecated the total abolition of slavery in the interests of the negro as well as of the planter. This pamphlet reached a second edition. Mr. W. E. Gladstone in his famous first speech (3 June 1833) in the House of Commons defended his father from a charge brought by Viscount Howick, afterwards third Earl Grey, against the management of an estate of his in Demerara called Vreedens Hop, and expressed approval of the principle of compensation to the planters (HANSARD, *Parl. Debates*, 3rd ser. xviii. 330-7; *Mirror of Parliament* for 1833, pp. 2079-83).

Gladstone sat in parliament for many years. In early life he had been a liberal, and a supporter of William Roscoe, M.P. for Liverpool, but admiration for Canning led to a change in his political allegiance, and he voted in parliament as a staunch tory on all imperial questions. In 1812 he invited Canning to contest Liverpool, and was at first sole guarantor of the statesman's election expenses. He himself first entered parliament as member for Lancaster in 1818, when his friends in Liverpool subscribed 6,000*l.* towards his election expenses, which amounted to 6,000*l.* more. He was elected for Wood-

stock in 1820, and for Berwick in 1826, but he was unseated at Berwick on petition in 1827. He spoke rarely in the debates, and chiefly on commercial questions. He disapproved the repeal of the corn laws, and described the disastrous results which he anticipated from the measure in a pamphlet, which reached a second edition in 1839. In 1846, when the bill for the repeal was passing through the House of Lords, he published in the same sense ' Plain Facts intimately connected with the intended Repeal of the Corn Laws : its Probable Effects on the Public Revenue and the Prosperity of the Country.' But before his death he expressed a conviction that Sir Robert Peel was right.

Gladstone took at all times a prominent part in the support of charitable and religious institutions at Liverpool and his native town of Leith. He built St. Thomas's Church, Seaforth, in 1814-15, and St. Andrew's Church, Liverpool, about 1816, besides a church at Leith. In 1840 he established, also at Leith, an asylum for women labouring under incurable diseases.

He dropped the final *s* of his name by royal letters patent dated 10 Feb. 1835; was created a baronet by Sir Robert Peel on 18 July 1846, and died 5 Dec. 1851, at his estate of Fasque, Kincardineshire, which he had purchased twenty years previously, and where he built and endowed an episcopal chapel about 1847. His fourth son, the Right Hon. W. E. Gladstone, wrote of him : ' No one, except those who have known him with the close intimacy of family connection, could properly appreciate the greatness of that truly remarkable man.'

Sir John married (1) in 1792 Jane, daughter of Joseph Hall of Liverpool, who died without issue in 1798 ; and (2), on 29 April 1800, Anne, daughter of Andrew Robertson, esq., provost of Dingwall, Ross-shire, and sheriff-substitute of that county. Sir John's second wife died 23 Sept. 1835 ; by her he was father of four sons and two daughters. The eldest son, Sir Thomas Gladstone of Fasque (1804–1889), the second baronet, was conservative M.P. for Queenborough 1830, for Portarlington 1832–5, and Leicester 1835–7. The third son, John Neilson (1807–1863), a captain in the navy, was elected M.P. for Devizes in 1852 and 1859. The fourth son was the eminent statesman, William Ewart Gladstone, M.P. (1809–1898), who was four times prime minister [see SUPPLEMENT].

[Notes supplied by the Right Hon. W. E. Gladstone, M.P.; Gent. Mag. 1852, pt. i.187–8 (chiefly from the Liverpool Courier); Foster's Baronetage; John Morley's Life of W. E. Gladstone,

1903; Picton's Memorials of Liverpool. A Life of Sir John Gladstone, by Dr. Samuel Smiles, was at one time in contemplation.]

GLADWIN, FRANCIS (d. 1813?), orientalist, served in the Bengal army. His devotion to oriental literature drew upon him the attention of Warren Hastings, who warmly encouraged the opening of the intellectual world of Asia to European research. In 1783–6 Gladwin, under this influence, published his translation of a portion of the encyclopædic work of Abul Fazl Allámi, under the title of 'Ayeen Akbery; or the Institutes of the Emperor Akber.' The work, warmly recommended to the patronage of the court of directors by the governor-general, was brought out in Calcutta in three volumes 4to. In 1785 Hastings established the still existing Asiatic Society of Bengal, of which Gladwin was a member. In 1788 he published a 'History of Hindostan' (Calcutta, 1 vol. 4to), and in the same year a translation of the 'Narrative of Transactions in Bengal' during the viceroyships of Azim-us-Shán and Ala Vardi Khán. From this time Gladwin continued to bring out numerous translations from Persian writers, and several grammatical works and vocabularies, the last being a Persian-Hindustani-English dictionary which appeared in 1809. In 1801 he was appointed a professor in the college of Fort William, established by the Marquis Wellesley, for the better instruction of young gentlemen appointed to the Indian civil service. Next year he presented the college press with new founts of oriental types; but in May of that year (1802) he was transferred to Patna as collector of customs. Here he appears to have passed the remainder of his days. In 1808 he was promoted to be commissary resident at Patna, an office of which the precise nature cannot now be ascertained. There is no publication of Gladwin's later in date than 1809; his estate was administered to in 1813.

Gladwin was not a great scholar, but displayed singular ardour and devotion. In the preface to his 'Gulistán,' 1806, he speaks of his desire to furnish the college of Fort William with a collection of the best 'Persian Classicks,' which he intended to print in eight quarto volumes. There were to be careful editions of the texts, with biographies, criticisms, notes, and indices. A part only of this task was fulfilled. Some of the letters addressed by Gladwin to Warren Hastings are in Brit. Mus. MS. Addit. 29168–70, 29170, 29179.

[Gladwin's prefaces; Biog. Dict. of Living Authors (1816), p. 432; Nichols's Lit. Anecd. vi. 637; Gent. Mag. (1830) ii. 627.]   H. G. K.

GLAMMIS, BARONS. [See LYON, PATRICK, seventh BARON, 1510?–1558; LYON, PATRICK, eighth BARON, d. 1578.]

GLAMMIS, LADY (d. 1537). [See DOUGLAS, JANET.]

GLAMMIS, MASTER OF (d. 1608). [See LYON, SIR THOMAS.]

GLAMORGAN, titular EARL OF (1601–1667). [See SOMERSET, EDWARD, second MARQUIS OF WORCESTER.]

GLANVILL, JOHN (1664?–1735), poet and translator, born at Broad Hinton, Wiltshire, about 1664, was the son of Julius Glanvil of Lincoln's Inn, by his wife, Anne Bagnall of St. Dunstan-in-the-West, London (CHESTER, London Marriage Licences, ed. Foster, col. 551). His grandfather was Sir John Glanville (1590–1661) [q. v.] He became a commoner of Trinity College, Oxford, in 1678, was elected scholar 10 June 1680, and took the two degrees in arts, B.A. 24 Oct. 1682, M.A. 24 Nov. 1685. In 1683 he stood for a fellowship at All Souls, but on the election falling to Thomas Creech [q. v.] Glanvill was highly affronted, 'so conceited he was of his own parts.' He lost all chance of a fellowship at his own college 'because he would be drunk and swear,' and was ultimately expelled (HEARNE, Remarks and Collections, Oxf. Hist. Soc. i. 265). He therefore entered himself at Lincoln's Inn, and was called to the bar. He died a bachelor and very wealthy 12 June 1735, aged 71, at Catchfrench, in St. Germans, Cornwall, an estate which he had purchased in 1726 (monumental inscription in Parochial History of Cornwall, ii. 42). His will, dated 23 Dec. 1724, was proved with two codicils 16 June 1735 by his nephew and heir, John Glanvill, citizen and apothecary of London (registered in P. C. C. 122, Ducie). He was the author of: 1. 'Some Odes of Horace imitated with Relation to His Majesty and the Times,' 4to, London, 1690. 2. 'Poem ... lamenting the Death of her late Sacred Majesty of the Small-pox,' 4to, London, 1695. 3. 'A Panegyrick to the King' [in verse], 4to, London, 1967 [1697]. 4. 'The Happy Pair,' a new song [anon.], fol. London [1706?]; other editions 1710? 1750?. 5. Poems, consisting of originals and translations,' 8vo, London, 1725. 6. 'Two Letters to Francis Gregor,' dated Catchfrench, August 1730 and October 1730, printed in Gregor's preface to Sir John Fortescue's 'De Laudibus legum Angliæ,' fol. 1737, pp. xxvii–xxxii. He also translated from the Latin Seneca's 'Agamemnon,' act i., which, together with 'A Song,' is in 'Miscellany Poems and Translations by

Oxford Hands,' 8vo, London, 1685 (pp. 196–199). In the 'Annual Miscellany' for 1694, being pt. iv. of 'Miscellany Poems,' &c., 8vo, London, 1694, he has translations from Seneca and Horace. He also translated Fontenelle's 'A Plurality of Worlds,' 12mo, London, 1688; other editions, 12mo, London, 1695; 16mo, London, 1702. The best of his poems have been reprinted in vol. iv. of Nichols's 'Collection.'

[Wood's Athenæ Oxon. (Bliss), iv. 689–90; Wood's Fasti Oxon. (Bliss), ii. 383, 396; Boase and Courtney's Bibl. Cornub. i. 176, 111, 1196; Chalmers's Biog. Dict.; Brit. Mus. Cat.; Will of Julius Glanvill, February 1710 (P. C. C. 33, Smith).]

G. G.

GLANVILL, JOSEPH (1636–1680), divine, third son of Nicholas Glanvill of Halwell, Whitchurch, Devonshire, was born at Plymouth in 1636, and entered Exeter College, Oxford, 2 April 1652. He took his B.A. degree 11 Oct. 1655; moved to Lincoln College in 1656, and graduated thence as M.A. in 1658. He became chaplain to Francis Rous [q. v.], one of Cromwell's lords and provost of Eton. On Rous's death in 1659 Glanvill returned to Oxford. He travelled from Oxford to Kidderminster to hear Baxter preach, but was not able to obtain a personal interview. He mentions this in an enthusiastic letter, dated 3 Sept. 1661, sent with his first treatise to Baxter. This was the 'Vanity of Dogmatizing,' in which he attacks the scholastic philosophy dominant at Oxford. He used, according to Wood, to lament that he had not been at Cambridge, where the new philosophy was in more esteem. He became an admirer of the Cambridge platonists, especially Henry More, and a friend of the founders of the Royal Society, of which (14 Dec. 1664) he was elected a fellow. He conformed upon the Restoration, and in 1660 received the rectory of Wimbish, Essex, from his brother Benjamin, a London merchant. In November 1662 he was presented to the vicarage of Frome Selwood, Somersetshire, by Sir James Thynne in place of John Humphrey, expelled for nonconformity. He exchanged this in 1672 for the rectory of Streat and Walton in the same county. On 23 June 1666 he was inducted rector of the Abbey Church at Bath. He became chaplain in ordinary to Charles II in 1672, and in 1678 received a prebend at Worcester through the influence of his wife's relation, the Marquis of Worcester. Some letters cited by Mr. Glanville Richards show that he was much troubled by the fanatics of Bath, who seemed to have gone back in spirit to 1643. During the excitement of the Popish plot he wrote a tract called 'The Zealous and Impartial Protestant,' in which he attacks the various nonconformist sects with great vivacity, and argues that the best preservative against popery is the maintenance of the privileges and discipline of the church of England. Baxter, for whom he makes a complimentary exception, protested against this intolerance in his 'Second Defence of the Nonconformists,' 1681. He says that Glanvill's principles were opposed to persecution, and prints the admiring letter already cited. Glanvill, he says, was a man 'of more than ordinary ingeny' whose death he regrets. Baxter says elsewhere (*Reliquiæ Baxterianæ*, 1696, i. 378) that Glanvill admired him 'far above my desert,' and offered to defend him when he was silenced. Glanvill died at Bath 4 Nov. 1680. He was buried in the Abbey Church, in the north aisle of which is an inscription to his memory. By his first wife, Mary Stocker, he had two children, of whom Maurice became rector of Wimbish in 1681. By his second, Margaret Selwyn, he had three children, Sophia, Henry, and Mary.

Glanvill was a voluminous author. His style is often admirable, not unfrequently recalling that of Sir Thomas Browne. His intellect was versatile, active, and sympathetic, but he is rather rhetorical than logical. In his dislike to the scholastic philosophy he followed Bacon and the founders of the Royal Society. Though he was in this direction a thorough-going sceptic, he was opposed to the materialism of Hobbes. His defence of witchcraft was the natural result of an attempt to find an empirical ground for a belief in the supernatural, and he formed with Henry More a virtual association for 'psychical research.' Glanvill himself visited the house of Mr. Mompesson at Tedworth, Wiltshire, and heard drummings and saw strange phenomena, caused by a vagabond drummer who had been turned out of the house, and revenged himself by witchcraft. The story oddly resembles that told by Wesley and by modern 'spirit-rappers.' It suggested Addison's 'Drummer.' Although Glanvill accepted More's theory of a preexistence of souls, and he admired the 'Platonists,' he does not appear to have gone deeply into their philosophical system. His works are: 1. 'The Vanity of Dogmatizing,' 1661. It contains (p. 196) the story of the 'Scholar Gipsy,' which suggested one of Matthew Arnold's finest poems, and (pp. 182, 203) some very curious anticipations of the electric telegraph ('to confer at the distance of the Indies by sympathetick contrivances may be as natural to future times as to us is a litterary correspondence') and other inventions. A passage at p. 189 is quoted by G. H. Lewes to show that Glanvill anticipated Hume's theory of causation. 2. 'Lux Orientalis' (a defence of More's doctrine of 'Præexistence of Souls;' it was reprinted in 1682 with George Rust's [q.v.] 'Discourse of Truth,' in 'two short and useful treatises,' with annotations [by Henry More]), 1682. 3. 'Scepsis Scientifica,' 1665 (the 'Vanity of Dogmatizing' recast, the gipsy and other passages omitted, reprinted in 1885 with preface by the Rev. John Owen). With the 'Scepsis' appeared 4. 'Reply to the exceptions of Thomas Albius; or scir$_i^e$ tuum nihil est' (Albius or Thomas White [q. v.] had replied to the 'Vanity of Dogmatizing' in a treatise called 'Sciri, sive sceptices et scepticorum à jure disputationis exclusio,' 1663), defending the scholastic philosophy, 1665, and 5. 'Letter to a friend concerning Aristotle' (this and the last with the 'Scepsis'). 6. 'Philosophical considerations touching Witches and Witchcraft,' 1666; most of the impressions having been destroyed in the fire, this was reissued in 1667. The fourth edition (1668) is entitled 'A Blow at modern Sadducism, in some philosophical considerations about Witchcraft,' &c. With it appeared 7. 'An Account of the famed disturbance by the drummer at the house of Mr. Mompesson,' and 8. 'A Whip for the Droll; Fidler for the Atheist,' a letter to H. More occasioned by the drummer of Tedworth. The 'Sadducismus Triumphatus,' 1681, is a reprint of the 'Blow,' with a translation from More's 'Enchiridion Metaphysicum' and a 'Collection of Relations.' The third edition (of 1689) includes also the 'Whip for the Droll.' 9. 'Plus Ultra, or the Progress and Advancement of Knowledge since the days of Aristotle,' 1668 (presented to the Royal Society 18 June 1668). This book was partly the result of an interview with Robert Crosse [q. v.], who had got the best of an argument about Aristotle, Glanvill being unprepared. Crosse retorted in privately circulated ballads and letters. 10. Sermons in 1667, 1669, 1670. 11. 'The Way of Happiness, or its Difficulties and Encouragements,' 1670 (also, as a 'Discourse concerning Difficulties,' &c.) 12. 'ΛΟΓΟΥ ΘΡΗΣΚΕΙΑ, or a Seasonable Recommendation and Defence of Reason in affairs of Religion against Infidelity,' &c., 1670 (a 'statement of fundamentals' resembling that of Herbert of Cherbury). 13. 'Philosophia Pia; a Discourse of the Religious Temper of the Experimental Philosophy professed by the Royal Society,' 1671. 14. 'A Prefatory Answer to Mr. Henry Stubbe ... in his animadversions on "Plus Ultra"' (Henry

Stubbe [q. v.] had attacked Glanvill in 'Legends no Histories, or Specimens of Animadversions on the History of the Royal Society'); the second part, also separately, being called the 'Plus Ultra reduced to a non plus,' 1670. He replied to the 'Prefatory Answer' in two prefaces to Ecebolius Glanvil, in a tract upon 'Lord Bacon's relation of the Sweating Sickness,' and a 'reply to a letter of Dr. Henry More,' both in 1671. 15. 'A further discovery of Mr. Henry Stubbe,' 1671 (at the end is 'Ad clerum Somersetensem προσφώνησις'). 16. 'An Earnest Invitation to the Lord's Supper,' 1673, 1674; 10th edit. 1720. 17. 'Seasonable Reflections' (four sermons). 18. 'Essays on several Important Subjects,' 1676 (seven essays, of which the first six are restatements of his previous arguments. The best and most remarkable is an essay on 'Anti-fanatical Religion and Free Philosophy,' in continuation of Bacon's 'New Atlantis.' James Crossley [q. v.] had a manuscript entitled 'Bensalem,' from which he says that this is an extract, WORTHINGTON, *Diaries*, i. 300). 19. 'An Essay concerning Preaching' (with 'A Seasonable Defence of Preaching'), 1678. 20. 'Some Discourses, Sermons and Remains,' with portrait and preface by A. Horneck, 1681. 21. 'The Zealous and Impartial Protestant,' 1681. Glanvill contributed some notices of Bath to the 'Transactions of the Royal Society' (Nos. 28, 39, 49), and has a poem in the 'Letters and Poems in honour of . . . the Duchess of Newcastle,' 1676.

[Wood's Athenæ (Bliss), iii. 1244; Life prefixed to fourth edition of Sadducismus Triumphatus, 1726; Prince's Worthies of Devon, 1810, p. 431; Glanville Richards's Records of the Anglo-Norman House of Glanville, pp. 76–80, 162; Birch's Royal Society, ii. 297; Biographia Brit.; Worthington's Diaries (Chetham Soc.), i. 214, 299, 300; Boase's Register of Exeter Coll., xxxi, lxxii; Boyle's Works, 1744, v. 627–9 (five letters from Glanvill). For criticisms of Glanvill's Works, see Hallam's Literature of Europe, iii. 358–62; Retrospective Review, 1853, i. 105–18; Pyrrhonism of Joseph Glanvill (article by W. Barnes, the Dorsetshire poet); Lecky's Rationalism in Europe, i. 120–8; Tulloch's Rational Theology, ii. 443–55; Preface to John Owen's edition of the Scepsis Scientifica, 1885; G. C. Robertson's Hobbes, p. 217; Rémusat's Philos. Angl. 1875, ii. 184–201.] L. S.

GLANVILLE, BARTHOLOMEW DE (*fl.* 1230–1250), is the name erroneously given to BARTHOLOMEW ANGLICUS or the Englishman. Leland, without citing any authority, called him De Glanville. Bale copied Leland in 1557, and added a list of writings wrongly attributed to Bartholomew. J. A. Fabricius

(*Bibl. Latina*, 1734) pointed out that there was some confusion; while Quétif and Echard had previously given detailed reasons for refusing the name De Glanville to the Minorite friar, Bartholomeus Anglicus. The majority of later writers also erroneously assign Bartholomeus Anglicus to the fourteenth century, a mistake perhaps due to Trittenheim, who placed Bartholomew undated between articles dated 1350 and 1360. Wadding, to whom our first precise notices are due, was unconscious that he placed the same man both in the thirteenth and in the fourteenth centuries (viii. 202). Bartholomew the Englishman, a Minorite (*c.* 1230–50), is first met with in 1230, when a letter was recorded from the general of the friar minors in the new province of Saxony, asking the provincial of France to send Bartholomew and another Englishman to help in the work of that province. In the following year a manuscript Saxon chronicle states that two were sent, Johannes Anglicus, 'and Bartholomew, also an Englishman, as teacher of holy theology to the brethren in that province.' The Parmese chronicler, Salimbene, writing in 1283 (SBARALEA, p. 115 ; DOVE, p. 3) of an elephant belonging to the Emperor Frederick II in 1237, refers to Bartholomew's chapter on elephants in the 'De Prop. Rerum,' and, naming him 'Anglicus,' calls him a 'great clerk who read through the whole Bible in lectures at Paris.' Bartholomew of Pisa (second half of fourteenth century) calls him 'de provincia Francia,' while John de Trittenheim, abbot of Spanheim (end of fifteenth century), still speaks of him simply as 'Bartholomeus natione Anglicus,' and relates his success as a teacher at Paris. From all which it appears that Bartholomew was an Englishman born, that he studied in the Paris schools, entered the French province of the Minorite order, and became a famous professor of theology in Paris; finally, that the newly organised branch of the order in Saxony desired his services, and that he was sent thither from France in 1231. M. Leopold Delisle, to whose recent paper this notice is much indebted, would claim Bartholomew as a Frenchman, but we venture to think the evidence lies wholly the other way; he was living in France and Germany, and therefore was carefully distinguished from the first as 'Anglicus.' That he was a Minorite 'de provincia Francia' does not prove that he was a Frenchman. The date of his great work 'De Proprietatibus Rerum' can only be approximately fixed by internal evidence and that of the manuscripts. Jourdain noted before 1819 that there are some of Aristotle's treatises always quoted by Bartholomew according to a translation from an Arab version, which fell out or use about 1260; and that while citing Albert the Great, who was teaching in Paris till 1248, he does not refer to Vincent de Beauvais, Thomas d'Aquinas, Roger Bacon, or Gilles de Rome, all workers of the thirteenth century. Salimbene shows that the book was known in Italy in 1283; two manuscripts (in the Paris Library) also show it was known and prized there in 1297 and 1329. That it was current in England in 1296 is proved by a manuscript at Oxford (*Ashm.* 1512), which was copied in November of that year. Manuscripts of the book are frequent in English and French libraries; many are of the end of the thirteenth or early part of the fourteenth century.

The work is a compilation in nineteen books from various departments of human knowledge. It was the encyclopædia of the middle ages. The facts are arranged with a religious and moral object. To its author was given the title of 'magister de proprietatibus rerum.' The Latin text long remained a classic in universities; it was one of the books hired at a regulated price by the scholars of Paris. It was first printed at Basle about 1470, and went through fourteen or more editions before 1500; it was translated into French for Charles V by Jean Corbichon in 1372, into English by John of Trevisa (from the Latin) in 1398, and into Spanish and Dutch a century later. Trevisa's English version was printed by Wynkyn de Worde about 1495, and by Berthelet in 1535. 'Batman uppon Bartholome his booke De Proprietatibus [with Trevisa's translation], newly corrected and amended, with additions,' London, 1582, fol., was by Stephen Batman [q. v.], and Douce believed that Shakespeare was well acquainted with the volume. The book was certainly the source of common information on natural history throughout the middle ages.

Trittenheim also attributes to Bartholomew a book of sermons, and cautiously mentions that 'he is said to have written other things,' but according to Sbaralea this statement is doubtful.

[M. L. Delisle in Hist. Littéraire, xxx. 334; Wadding's Annales Minorum, ed. 1733, ii. 248, 274; Salimbene, ed. Parma, 1857; A. Dove's Doppelchronik von Reggio, &c., Leipzig, 1873; J. H. Sbaralea, Supplementum ad Scriptores trium ordinum S. Francisci, p. 115; Quétif and Echard's Scriptores Ordinum Prædicatorum, 1719, i. 486; Joh. Trithemius, De Ecclesiasticis Scriptoribus, in Fabricius's Bibl. Eccles. p. 150; Amable Jourdain, Recherches sur les traductions latines d'Aristote, 1819, pp. 35, 398. Biographical compilers, who have copied or added one unauthorised detail after another, are Leland (Script. Brit.), Bale, Pits, Wadding (viii. 202), Tanner,

Cave's Wharton (Script. Eccles. ii. ii. 66), Oudin (Comm. de Script. Eccles. iii. 969), and Jöcher. Chevalier, in his Répertoire, gives Bartholomew the wrong name and date, therein following several of the authorities named by him. See also Hist. Littéraire, vol. xxiv.]　L. T. S.

GLANVILLE, GILBERT DE (d. 1214), bishop of Rochester, was a kinsman of Ranulf de Glanville [q. v.], and a native of Northumberland. Herbert de Bosham in his life of Becket mentions him among the scholars attached to the archbishop, and describes him as learned both in the canon and civil law, adding that although the last to join them he was one of the most faithful. Becket just before his death sent Glanville on a mission to the pope. He may be the Canon Gilbert who was sent as a messenger to the court in 1164, and who was present at the meeting at Gisors on 18 Nov. 1167, and the Master Gilbert twice mentioned by John of Salisbury in his letters. Glanville became archdeacon of Lisieux in 1184 (Gallia Christiana, xi. 780). He was, however, a clerk of Archbishop Baldwin, by whose influence he was elected bishop of Rochester at Oxford on 17 July 1185. He was consecrated at Canterbury on 29 Sept., after a protest by the monks of Canterbury as to the disregard of their rights in the election (see GERVASE, i. 324). As a scholar and lawyer Glanville entered into the antimonastic movement of the day. In Baldwin's dispute with the monks of Canterbury he acted on several occasions for the archbishop, and was also engaged in a long quarrel with his own monks. This quarrel appears to have been due to his assertion of his rights as bishop, and his interference in the management of the cathedral property. Hadenham, the Rochester chronicler, says that he deprived the monks of many of the possessions which Bishop Gundulph had bestowed on them. The dispute, after lasting several years, was at length decided against the monks. Glanville claimed, as chaplain of the province, to act for the archbishop in his absence; this right was disputed by the Bishop of London, especially in the case of the consecration of the Bishop of Worcester in 1190, when the matter was compromised by Longchamp performing the ceremony as legate, and again in 1203, when Glanville protested against the consecration of the Bishop of Ely by the Bishop of London (WENDOVER, iii. 174). Meantime in October 1186 Glanville had been one of the embassy sent to Philip of France. In February 1188 he and the archbishop preached the crusade at Geddington. He was in Normandy at the time of Henry II's death, came over to England in August 1189, was present at Richard's coronation and at

the council of Pipewell, and was one of the witnesses to the treaty of December 1189 by which William the Lion repurchased the rights conceded at Falaise in 1174. During Richard's absence on the crusade he supported Longchamp against John, endeavoured to mediate between the two parties, and when the chancellor took flight was one of those who escorted him to Dover in 1191. He took part in the election of his friend Hubert Walter, whom he supported against his monks in 1198. He was summoned to Germany by Richard in 1193, and on his return excommunicated John in February 1194. He was present at Richard's second coronation, at John's coronation, and at Lincoln when the king of Scots did homage. In 1207, after suffering much injury at John's hands, he fled to Scotland, but is also mentioned among the bishops who went to Rome next year. In 1212 he was commissioned by Pandulph to absolve the Scots from their homage to John. He died on 24 June 1214, and was buried on the north side of the altar in Rochester Cathedral, where is his tomb with a recumbent effigy. Glanville frequently acted in a judicial capacity; in 1190 he was appointed to adjudicate respecting Hugh Nonant of Coventry, who had improperly taken the office of sheriff; in the same year he was one of the justices appointed to hold the pleas (Pipe Roll, 1 Richard I); in 1192 he was one of the judges appointed by the pope to annul the excommunication of Hugh of Durham by Geoffrey of York; and in 1206 he was a commissioner to investigate the dispute between the abbey of Evesham and the Bishop of Worcester (Chron. Evesham, pp. 191, 222). He was a benefactor of his diocese, and, despite his quarrel with his monks, built them a new cloister, and gave them an organ and other presents. He likewise founded a hospital for the poor at Strood. Tanner ascribes to him some sermons, which he says are extant, without mentioning where.

[Annales Monastici, Hoveden, Gervase of Canterbury, Diceto, Materials for the Hist. of Thomas Becket, all in the Rolls Ser.; Wharton's Anglia Sacra, i. 346, 390; Dugdale's Monasticon, i. 156; Tanner, p. 326.]　C. L. K.

GLANVILLE, SIR JOHN, the elder (1542–1600), judge, born in 1542, second son of John Glanville of Tavistock, was bred an attorney. He is the first attorney who is recorded to have reached the bench. He entered at Lincoln's Inn on 11 May 1567, and was called to the bar on 24 June 1574. He was reader there in Lent 1589, and again in the autumn, having been made a serjeant in the meantime. He was member of parliament for Launceston in 1585, for Tavistock in 1586, and for St. Germans in 1592. He was in 1594 interested in St. Margaret's tin works in Cornwall (GREEN, *Cal. State Papers*, Dom. 25 Feb. 1594). On 30 June 1598 he was made a judge of the common pleas, and died on 27 July 1600. He was buried in Tavistock Church, where there is an elaborate tomb, with a recumbent statue of him in his robes, engraved in Polwhele's 'Devon.' He married Alice, daughter of John Skerret of Tavistock, who survived him, and had by her seven children, of whom the second son was John [q. v.], speaker of the House of Commons in 1640. He died rich, and built the mansion of Kilworthy, near Tavistock.

[Wood's Fasti, ed. 1820–2, p. 64 ; Polwhele's Hist. of Devonshire, and Hist. of Cornwall, v. 137, 138; Black Book, v. 64, 183 ; Prince's Worthies of Devon ; Dugdale's Origines, p. 251 ; W. U. S. Glanville-Richards's Records of the House of Glanville; Foss's Lives of the Judges.]

J. A. H.

GLANVILLE, SIR JOHN, the younger (1586–1661), serjeant, second son of Sir John Glanville [q. v.], judge of the common pleas, and Alice Skerret his wife, was born at Kilworthy, near Tavistock, in 1586. He was brought up to be an attorney, but entered at Lincoln's Inn, was called to the bar about 1610, and became reader there in Hilary term 1630. In 1614 he was elected member for Plymouth, and was successively re-elected in 1620, 1623, 1625, 1626, and 1628, and played a conspicuous part as one of the opponents of the crown in parliament. In 1624 he prepared a collection of cases, nine in number, relating to the elections of burgesses to parliament, decided by election committees of the House of Commons, which were published in 1775 by John Topham of Lincoln's Inn, and his opinion carried great weight in the discussion upon Sir Thomas Wentworth's election for Yorkshire, which was ended by the decision on 5 July 1625 that the election was void. He prepared the protest against the dissolution of parliament, which the house hastily adopted on 12 Aug. 1625, while black rod was waiting at the door, and had applied himself so pertinaciously to criticising 'the expense of the kingdom,' that by way of punishment, and to keep him out of parliament, he was sent with the fleet to Cadiz in September 1625 as secretary to the council of war. He took part in the impeachment of Buckingham in 1626, having the management of articles 6, 7, and 8 in the conference between the two houses on 17 and 18 April 1628; carried, by 191 votes to 150, the addition of a 13th article ; and was one of those charged with laying the Petition of Right

before the House of Lords, and his speech delivered in a general committee of both houses on 22 May 1628, giving the reasons why the house should not agree to the form of the petition of right proposed by the House of Lords, was printed and published in the same year. He became eminent in his profession ; appeared before the Star-chamber for Lord Poulett against the Rev. Richard Gore on 13 Nov. 1635 ; was counsel for Lord Dacre in a suit about the manor of Dacre in Cumberland in 1637, and in the same year advised the Bishop of Bath and Wells in his dispute with Sir Francis Popham about the right of presentation to the living of Buckland St. Mary in Somerset. In the year following he was appointed by the lord keeper referee in a chancery suit about the rights of copartners in gavelkind. He was also proctor for the dean and chapter of Windsor. He was appointed recorder of Plymouth as early as 1614, and became a serjeant on 20 May 1637. Shortly afterwards he became recorder of Bristol, and seems to have been in good relations with the court, for on 21 Aug. 1639 he tried one Davis for nonconformity, having been already in conference with Laud, Coke, and the attorney-general about the conduct of the case, and, as the Bishop of Bristol wrote to Laud, 'did his part copiously, gravely, and with semblance of great severity.' He was elected for Bristol, and having been pointed out by rumour as likely to be speaker in the Short parliament, was elected on 15 April 1640. He was then reported to have made his submission to the king. His address to the king on his appointment is entered in the 'Lords' Journals,' iv. 50–4. He spoke so strongly against ship-money (see *Harl. MS.* 4931, fol. 49), that the court party believed he would put to the house any protestations that might be made against it, and accordingly prevented him from coming down to the house on the day the Short parliament was dissolved. He adhered, however, to the king subsequently, was made a king's serjeant on 5 July 1640, with leave to continue to hold the recordership of Bristol, was knighted in 1641, and went with the king to Oxford in 1643, where he received the degree of D.C.L. He also acted as a judge with others in 1643 at Salisbury to try the Earls of Northumberland, Pembroke, and Salisbury for assisting the parliament, whereupon the commons ordered a committee to draw up an impeachment of treason against Glanville and his colleagues. Next year, when he had fallen into the hands of the parliament, he was ordered to be impeached for condemning Captain Turpine to death, and on 25 Sept. 1644 was disabled to be a member of the house for his delinquency. He was imprisoned in the Tower in 1645; but partly by Whitelocke's intercession, and by giving up one-fifth of his rents yearly as composition for the fine of 2,320*l.* imposed upon him, he was released on 27 July 1648, and retired to Hampshire (see EVELYN, *Diary*, ed. 1850, i. 293). He was, however, elected member of parliament by the university of Oxford during the Commonwealth. In March 1654 he was anxious to resume his practice at the bar, and accordingly petitioned the council, by whom his petition was referred to a committee. At the Restoration he was again appointed a king's serjeant. He died on 2 Oct. 1661, and was buried at Broad Hinton Church, Wiltshire. About 1615 he married Winifred, daughter of William Bouchier of Barnsley, Gloucestershire, by whom he had seven children, four sons: William, who succeeded to his estates; John, a barrister; Francis, who fell at Bridgewater during the civil war on the king's side; and Julius. He had extensive estates, having bought Laverstoke in Hampshire in 1637, and Highway in 1640, which cost 4,700*l.*, and was patron of the livings of Broad Hinton, Wiltshire, and Lamerton in Devonshire. Fuller calls him one of 'the biggest stars' of the law.

[W. U. Glanville-Richards's Records of the House of Glanville; Grosart's Voyage to Cadiz (Camden Soc.), 1883; Woolrych's Eminent Serjeants; Bruce and Hamilton's Domestic State Papers; Whitelocke's Memorials; Lloyd's Loyal Sufferers; Wood's Athenæ Oxon. (ed. Bliss), ii. 720; Waylen's Hist. of Marlborough; Prince's Worthies of Devon; Fuller's Worthies, p. 257; Burnet's Life of Hale; Burton's Parliamentary Diary, iii. 236; S. R. Gardiner's Hist. of England, v. vi. vii. ix.; Forster's Sir John Eliot; Wood's Journals, iii. 814; Fuller's Ephemeris; Rushworth, i. 572.]   J. A. H.

GLANVILLE, RANULF DE (*d.* 1190), chief justiciar of England. His family, which probably derived its name from Glanville, near Lisieux, seems to have settled in Suffolk at or soon after the Norman conquest, and to have become moderately wealthy. Ranulf, it is said, was born at Stratford, that is at Stratford St. Andrew, near Saxmundham. Throughout his life he seems to have been connected with this part of the country, and to have had considerable possessions thereabout. He married Bertha, daughter of Theobald de Valoines, lord of the neighbouring township of Parham, and he left three daughters, among whom his estates were divided. He founded the priory of Butley, the abbey of Leiston, and a hospital at Somerton. We first hear of him as sheriff of Yorkshire. This office he held from 1163 until the spring of 1170, when Henry II removed all the sheriffs and instituted a rigorous inquiry into their doings. The great rebellion of 1173 gave him a chance of showing what was in him. In the course of that year he was made sheriff of Lancashire, seemingly at a moment when an incursion of Scots was imminent, and he was also custodian of the honour of Richmond, which was in the king's hand. Early in 1174 the Scots under William the Lion crossed the border; Henry was busy with his enemies in Poitou; Richard Lucy, his justiciar, was detained in the midlands; the greatest of the English feudatories were in revolt; an invasion of England from the Flemish shore was threatened. In this strait, on 13 July 1174, a decisive victory was won over the Scots at Alnwick; they were taken by surprise and routed; their king and many of their leaders were captured. The chief commanders of the English host were Robert Stuteville, the sheriff of Yorkshire, and Glanville, who probably led the men of Lancashire and Richmondshire; a messenger from him carried the good news to Henry, and it was to him that the king of Scots yielded himself a prisoner (JORD. FANT. pp. 355, 363; BEN. i. 65; HOV. ii. 62; NEWB. pp. 183, 189; GIR. CAMBR. v. 300; COGG. p. 18; STUBBS, *Const. Hist.* § 144). After this exploit Glanville becomes prominent. Almost at once he was reappointed to the shrievalty of Yorkshire, which he held thenceforth until the end of the reign, and for some years he was sheriff of Westmoreland also. In 1176 he was a justice in eyre, in 1177 ambassador to the Count of Flanders, in 1179 a justice in eyre and one of the six members of the permanent royal court that was then formed (BEN. i. 108, 136, 239); in 1180 he succeeded Richard Lucy as chief justiciar of England (HOV. ii. 215). Thenceforward he was the king's right-hand man—'the king's eye' a chronicler calls him (RICH. DEV. p. 385). In 1182 he was appointed an executor of Henry's will (GERV. i. 298), and in the same year he led an army against the Welsh (BEN. i. 289); in 1186 we find him negotiating, now a peace in the Welsh marches, and now a truce with the French king (BEN. i. 353–5; DIC. ii. 43). During the last year of the reign he passed rapidly to and fro between England and France, collecting forces and aiding his master in the final struggle with his rebellious sons (BEN. ii. 40; GERV. i. 447). Henry apparently had found just the servant he wanted, and was well served to the last. Naturally, therefore, Richard may not have known how to deal with Glanville. Perhaps for a moment he gave way to resentment. Glanville had to pay a large sum—15,000*l.* it is said (RICH.

DEV. p. 385)—but Richard was raising money for the crusade upon every excuse, and he seems to have seen the value of the old states-man. Glanville was present at the corona-tion (3 Sept. 1189), and was employed to suppress the riots which arose out of the en-suing Jew-bait (NEWB. i. 297). According to one story, he resigned the justiciarship, misdoubting Richard's policy (*ib*. i. 302); an old man, worn out by work, he wished to ful-fil the crusader's vow which he had taken some years before (BEN. ii. 87). According to another, Richard deposed him and forced him to go on the crusade (RICH. DEV. p. 386). Very possibly the king hoped to make him useful, but did not dare to leave him behind in England. Anyway, he, with Archbishop Baldwin and Hubert Walter, accompanied Richard to Marseilles (July 1190); and thence he sailed for the siege of Acre (BEN. ii. 115). At Acre he died. His death seems to have happened before 21 Oct. 1190 (*Ep. Cant.* p. 329), and to have been caused, not by the sword of the infidel, but by the eastern cli-mate (COGG. p. 29).

The picture that we get of him is that of an active, versatile man, ready at short notice to lead an army, negotiate a peace, hold a council, decide a cause; above all things faith-ful to his master. We read of his sagacity and of his eloquence; of the pride that he took in the expeditious justice of the royal court (MAP, *Nug. Cur*. p. 241). There is against him one very bad story of how he sought to pervert the law in order that he might compass the death of a certain Gilbert Plumpton, against whom he had a private grudge; and this story comes from a good source (BEN. i. 314). He must have had a hand in carrying through the great legal changes which mark the reign of Henry II. In after days tradition made him the inventor of the assize of novel disseisin and the action of replevin (*Mirror of Justices*, c. 2, §§ 25, 26), but that he was a trained lawyer we are not told by any writer of his time. We are told, however, that when in power he was much influenced by his secretary and nephew, Hu-bert Walter. This is the Hubert Walter who became dean of York, bishop of Salisbury, archbishop of Canterbury, chief justiciar and chancellor, and who bore a high reputation for legal learning ('omnia regni novit jura,' GERV. ii. 406). Perhaps later ages have as-cribed to Glanville juristic attainments which in truth were those of his more clerkly kins-man and successor.

But he has long been best known as the reputed author of a 'Treatise on the Laws and Customs of England,' the oldest of our legal classics. His right to this fame depends mainly on the words of the contemporary chronicler Roger of Hoveden, who under the year 1180 says that the king appointed as justiciar Ranulf Glanville, 'cujus sapientia conditæ sunt leges subscriptæ.' On this statement there follow : (1) a set of laws pro-fessedly made by the Conqueror; (2) the col-lection of laws generally known as 'Leges Ed-wardi Confessoris;' (3) the treatise in ques-tion; (4) certain ordinances of Henry II. Probably Hoveden only means that Glanville, as justiciar, sanctioned these various docu-ments, or that they contained the rules which he administered; it can hardly be intended that he composed what announce themselves as laws of the Confessor and the Conqueror, and it seems very plain that the hand that wrote the treatise was not the hand that com-piled the 'Leges Edwardi.' Thus as to the authorship of the treatise Hoveden's evidence falls short, and it is not certain that we have any first-hand evidence. An examina-tion of all the many manuscripts which give the treatise might perhaps settle this point; but it is believed that as a general rule they simply state that the book was written during Glanville's justiciarship ('justiciæ guberna-cula tenente . . . Ranulpho de Glanvilla'). There is good internal evidence that it was written during the last years of Henry's reign, and apparently it was not finished until after October 1187 (lib. viii. cap. ii. iii.) Its object is to describe the procedure of the king's court; more than once the author says that he is ignorant of what goes on in other courts. He does not speak in a tone of authority; in Eng-land there is a confused multitude of laws which it were hopeless to define; but he will try to set down some matters of daily im-portance. He writes as a lawyer keenly inte-rested in legal problems, and not ashamed to confess that he does not know the answer to all the questions that he raises. The book looks more like the work of one of the clerks of the royal court than like that of the chief justiciar, who, during the last years of Henry's reign, can have had little time for writing a legal treatise. The conjecture seems permis-sible that it was written by Hubert Walter. When in the middle of the thirteenth century Bracton [q. v.] was going over the same ground with this treatise before him, and wanted ex-amples of proper names in order to show how fatal it was for a pleader to make mistakes in them, the two names which occurred to him were his own and that of Hubert Walter (f. 188*b*). If he had coupled Glanville's name with his own, we should have thought it very natural that he should thus associate himself with the writer in whose steps he was follow-ing. However, ever since the book was printed it has been known among lawyers as 'Glanville.' It is a brief but clear and orderly book, and must have done much towards settling the procedure of the royal court and defining the common law. The impulse to write a treatise of this kind was probably due to the reviving study of Roman law, and of that law the author knew a little; but he shows no desire to adopt it wholesale, and does not even take the arrangement of the 'Institutes' as his model. His book, one of the very first treatises on law produced on this side of the Alps, became a venerated authority among English lawyers; Coke acknowledges that he owed it a heavy debt. Upon it some Scottish lawyer founded the text-book known, from its first words, as 'Regiam Majestatem.' How far this fairly represents Scottish law is a debated question. 'Glanville' is of great value to students of legal and social history, continental as well as English, and is well known in France and Germany.

[Occasional notices of Glanville in Gesta Henrici ('Benedict'), R. Hoveden, Gervase of Canterbury, William of Newburgh, R. de Diceto, R. Coggeshall, Giraldus Cambrensis, Jordan Fantosme, Rich. of Devizes, Epistolæ Cantuarienses (all in Rolls Ser.); Jocelin of Brakelond, and Mapes, De Nugis Curialium (Camd. Soc.); Madox's Hist. Exchequer; Stubbs's Const. Hist. and prefaces to Hoveden; Monasticon (under 'Butley' and 'Leystone'); List of Sheriffs in 31st Rep. of Dep.-keeper of Publ. Records. There is some genealogical information in Glanville-Richards's Records of the House of Glanville; but much of this is incorrect or very questionable. For Hoveden's testimony as to Glanville's authorship of the treatise see Stubbs's Preface to vol. ii. of Hoveden (Rolls Ser.) The treatise was printed by Tottel without date, about 1554; later editions in 1604, 1673, 1780; English translation by Beames, 1812; published in France by Houard in Traités sur les coutumes Anglo-normandes; in Germany by Phillips, Englisch. Rechtsgesch.; also printed in Acts of Parliament of Scotland, vol. i., and collated with the Regiam Majestatem. A new edition by Sir T. Twiss (Rolls Ser.) is advertised.]   F. W. M.

GLAPTHORNE, HENRY (*fl.* 1639), dramatist, of whom no biographical particulars have come down, published: 1. A tragedy, 'Argalus and Parthenia. As it hath been Acted at the Court before their Maiesties: And at the Private-House in Drury-Lane, By thier Maiesties Servants,' 1639, 4to. 2. 'The tragedy of Albertvs Wallenstein. . . . Acted with good allowance at the Globe on the Banke-side, by his Majesties Servants,' 1639, 1640, 4to; dedicated 'To the great Example of Vertue and Trve Mecenas of Liberall Arts, Mr. William Murrey of his Majesties Bed-chamber,' with a prefatory copy

of Latin iambics by Alexander Gill (1597–1642) [q. v.] 3. 'The Hollander. A Comedy written 1635,' 1640, 4to, dedicated to Sir Thomas Fisher, knight. 4. 'Wit in a Constable. A Comedy written in 1639,' 1640, 4to, dedicated to Thomas, lord Wentworth 5. 'The Ladies Priviledge,' 1640, 4to, a comedy dedicated to Sir Frederick Cornwallis. The last three plays were acted at the Cockpit in Drury Lane and at court. Two tragedies of Glapthorne, 'The Duchess of Fernandina' and 'The Vestal,' were entered in the Stationers' Register, 9 Sept. 1653, but were not printed. Another tragedy, 'The Paraside, or Revenge for Honor,' was entered 29 Nov. 1653 as the work of Glapthorne. This is probably the play published in 1654 under the title of 'Revenge for Honour,' with Chapman's name on the title-page. Chapman had certainly no hand in it, but it may have been revised by Glapthorne. 'The Noble Trial,' entered 29 June 1660, is to be identified with 'The Lady Mother,' a comedy preserved in Egerton MS. 1994, and printed in vol. ii. of Bullen's 'Collection of Old English Plays.' A note at the end of the manuscript copy, in the handwriting of William Blagrave (assistant to Sir Henry Herbert, master of the revels), shows that 'The Lady Mother' was licensed in October 1635; and from a passage in ii. 1 it would seem that the play was produced at Salisbury Court Theatre in Whitefriars. Glapthorne's plays are not of high merit; he had little dramatic power, but occasionally writes with grace. In 1639 he published a thin volume of indifferent 'Poëms,' which he dedicated to Jerome [Weston], earl of Portland. Several pieces are addressed to a lady whom he designates as Lucinda; one is headed 'To Lucinda, he being in prison.' In 1641 he edited 'Poems Divine and Humane,' of his friend Thomas Beedome [q. v.], prefixing an address to the reader, and commendatory verses in Latin and English. His last publication was 'Whitehall. A Poem. Written 1642. With Elegies,' &c., 1643, dedicated 'To my noble Friend and Gossip, Captaine Richard Lovelace.' The elegies are of small account, but 'Whitehall' is not without interest. Glapthorne's works (with the exception of 'The Lady Mother') were collected in 1874, 2 vols.

[Memoir prefixed to vol. i. of Glapthorne's Plays and Poems, 1874; Retrospective Review, x. 122–59; Bullen's Collection of Old English Plays, ii. 101–2.]   A. H. B.

GLAS, GEORGE (1725–1765), mariner, son of the Scottish sectary, John Glas [q. v.], was born at Dundee in 1725. He is said to have been brought up as a surgeon, in which capacity he made several voyages to the West Indies. According to another account he was once a midshipman in the royal navy. He afterwards obtained command of a vessel in the Brazil trade, in which he made several voyages to the west coast of Africa and the Canary Isles. On one of his trips he discovered a river between Cape Verde and Senegal, navigable some way inland, and came to the conclusion that it would be a suitable site for a new trading settlement. He returned home and laid his scheme before government, but his conditions, an exclusive grant of the country for all trading purposes for thirty years, were thought too high. After some negotiations Glas came to an agreement with the commissioners of trade and plantations, by which he was guaranteed the sum of 15,000l. on condition of his obtaining a free cession of the country by the natives to the British crown. On the faith of this arrangement Glas entered into an agreement with a company or firm of merchants, who provided him with a ship and cargo. Accompanied by his wife and daughter, Glas sailed from Gravesend in August 1764, and arrived safely at his destination, which he named Port Hillsborough. He had little difficulty in persuading the natives to cede their territory, and a treaty was drawn up and signed by all the headmen of the district. A famine at this time prevailed on the coast, and Glas resolved to proceed to Teneriffe, to obtain grain and other provisions for his settlement. He was obliged to leave the ship with his companions, as they had no place on shore to stay in, and set out in the long-boat, with five men, in November 1764. He arrived safely at Lanzarate, one of the Canary group, where an English vessel was on the point of sailing home, by which Glas forwarded his treaty to the authorities in London. But the jealousy of the Spaniards was by this time aroused, and shortly after his arrival Glas was arrested, by orders from Teneriffe, on a charge of contraband trading at Lanzarate, and was sent prisoner to Teneriffe, where he was treated with great harshness. Among the home office records is a letter from 'Mr. George Glass,' dated Teneriffe, 15 Dec. 1764, in which he reports his seizure and close confinement in the castle. He suggests that the Spaniards dreaded interference with the important fishery carried on by natives of the Canary Isles on the African coast between Capes Bojador and Blanco, and asked for his release (Calendar Home Office Papers, 1760-5, par. 1631). A letter to the secretary of the admiralty from Captain Thomas Graves, H.M.S. Edgar, off Senegal, dated 22 March 1765, states that opportunity was taken 'to

enquire into the seizure and detention of Captain Glass by the governor of Santa Cruz, Teneriffe. The governor was not very satisfactory in his reasons for imprisoning that unfortunate poor man. It was then demanded to see him, for he is shut up from ye sight of every one but his own keepers, said to be kept in irons, and denied the use of pens, ink, and paper; but this ye governor refused, and would assign no reason why the poor man was kept under such rigid confinement, even to barbarity, though pressed to it in the strongest and most lively terms' (Admiralty Records, Captains' Letters, G. 15). Papers representing the case accompanied the letter, and with it is another from Captain Boteler, H.M.S. Shannon, which states that the explanation (ultimately?) given by the Spanish authorities was that Glas came to Allegranza Lanzarate from the coast of Africa without a pass, and was selling contraband (ib.; Calendar Home Office Papers, 1760-5, p. 550). About the same time, March 1765, the settlers at Port Hillsborough were attacked by the blacks, who killed the chief officer and six men. Dreading a renewal of the attack, the survivors made their escape in the boats to Teneriffe, where Mrs. Glas first learned of her husband's detention. Steps appear to have been taken by the British government to obtain his release (ib. par. 2033, no details given), and in October 1765 he was set at liberty. The English barque Sandwich touching at Teneriffe, Glas with his wife and daughter embarked in her for England. Among the crew were a number of Spaniards or Portuguese, who had somehow become aware of the fact that there was treasure on board. Rising one night, when the vessel was off the south coast of Ireland, these men murdered the captain and those of the crew who were not in the plot, and stabbed Glas as he rushed upon deck on hearing the noise. He was killed on the spot. Mrs. Glas and her daughter, locked in each other's arms, were thrown overboard. The murderers then scuttled the ship and escaped with their booty to the shore. But, contrary to their expectations, the ship, instead of sinking, drifted on shore not far off, with the evidence of the tragedy still fresh and reeking. A search was made for the murderers, who were discovered carousing in a roadside public-house, were arrested, tried in Dublin, and executed after confessing their guilt and giving particulars of the crime.

Glas appears to have been a man of some ability. He translated from a manuscript of J. Abreu de Galinda, a Franciscan monk of Andalusia, then recently found at Palma, 'An Account of the Discovery and History of the

Canary Islands,' which was published by Doddridge in 1764, the year Glas left England, and went through several subsequent editions; and he appears to have had in preparation at the time of his death a descriptive account of north-western Africa.

[Chalmers's Biog. Dict. ; Anderson's Scottish Nation, ii. 308; Calendar Home Office Papers, 1760–5, under 'Glas.' A full account of the murder is given in Gent. Mag. xxxv. 545.]

H. M. C.

GLAS, JOHN (1695–1773), Scottish sectary, only son of Alexander Glas (d. 1724), minister of Auchtermuchty, Fifeshire, afterwards of Kinclaven, Perthshire, and Christian, daughter of John Duncan, minister of Rerwick, Kirkcudbrightshire, was born at Auchtermuchty on 21 Sept. 1695. From the parish school of Kinclaven he went to the Perth grammar school, and thence to St. Leonard's College, St. Andrews, where he graduated A.M. on 6 May 1713. He finished his studies in Edinburgh. On 20 May 1718 he was licensed by Dunkeld presbytery, was called to Tealing, Forfarshire, on 19 Feb., and ordained there on 6 May 1719. He soon became very popular as a preacher. On 13 July 1725 he formed a society of nearly a hundred persons within his parish for a monthly celebration of the Lord's supper and closer religious fellowship. His father first warned him that his principles were those of an independent. At the end of the year he addressed a letter to Francis Archibald, minister of Guthrie, Forfarshire, denying the binding obligation of the national covenants. His views in opposition to state churches and the right of the civil authority to interfere in religious matters were embodied in his 'Testimony of the King of Martyrs,' 1727, a publication which brought him before the church courts, when he withdrew his signature from the formula, and renounced some passages in the confession of faith. The synod of Angus and Mearns suspended him on 18 April 1728, a sentence confirmed by the general assembly in May. As he disregarded the suspension, the synod deposed him from the ministry on 15 Oct. On appeal to the assembly, great efforts were made in his favour by influential elders, including Duncan Forbes (1685–1747) [q. v.], then lord advocate, who pleaded for indulgence to the speculative opinions of a man of high character and usefulness. At length, on 12 March 1730, the commission of assembly affirmed the deposition.

Glas removed to Dundee, where he formed a church to his mind, the members of which were popularly termed Glassites. His principles have been described as akin to Brownism,

but they approached more nearly to the type of independent presbyterianism set forth by early English puritans, e.g. by William Bradshaw (1571–1618) [q. v.] But Glas did not, with Bradshaw, recognise the prerogative of the sovereign in religious matters, a congregation with its presbytery being 'subject to no jurisdiction under heaven.' He introduced sundry practices on the ground of apostolic direction, such as the 'osculum pacis,' and later the agape, in the shape of a common meal, whence his followers received the nickname of 'kailites.' With the formation of other congregations came the question of providing a ministry. Only two clergymen joined him, and this at a later date, namely, George Byres of St. Boswells, Roxburghshire, in 1738, and Robert Ferrier of Largo, Fifeshire, in 1768. Glas, though himself a good scholar, set aside the strong presbyterian feeling in favour of an academical training for the clergy. He was at one with the quakers also on the point of ministerial emolument, though he went beyond them in his estimate of the common duty of the church to be responsible for the maintenance of all its members. The first 'elder' appointed to carry on the new organisation was James Cargill, a glover and an able preacher, who had charge of the congregation at Dunkeld.

In 1733 Glas left Dundee for Perth, where he built the first meeting-house of the new sect amid considerable opposition. At Perth the cause received an important accession in the person of Robert Sandeman [q. v.], who, in his twentieth year, joined Glas and two others in an application to the 'associate presbytery,' recently organised by Ebenezer Erskine [q. v.] Two years later (22 May 1739) the general assembly of its own motion restored Glas to 'the status of a minister of Jesus Christ, but not to that of a minister of the kirk of Scotland,' leaving him incapable of holding a charge in the church until he should have renounced such tenets as were inconsistent with its constitution.

Unlike that of the Erskines, Glas's popularity deserted him upon his secession. Though he deviated but slightly from Calvinistic orthodoxy, there was a dry literalism about some of his views unfavourable to fervour. Faith he defined as a bare intellectual acceptance of certain facts. With the Wesleyans he discarded the doctrine of 'final perseverance,' but the methodist 'conversion' was as unreal to him as the Calvinistic 'assurance.' He showed his good sense by rejecting (1759) the Hutchinsonian discovery of a complete system of physical science in holy scripture, maintaining that 'the Bible was never designed to teach mankind philosophy.' His notes on scripture texts (1747) exhibit a good deal of theological acumen; his monograph on the heresy of Aerius (1745) is a scholarly piece of work; and still better is his reconstruction, from Origen's citations, of the 'True Discourse' of Celsus, of which he prepared (1753) a translation with notes. His sacred 'songs' have no poetical merit.

Glas was of even and cheerful disposition, in company free from professional stiffness, and not without a sense of humour. 'I too can be grave at times,' he replied to an austere critic, 'when I want money, or want righteousness.' His strength of character in trying circumstances was remarkable. After the execution of the murderers of his son, his first thought was of the 'glorious instance of the divine mercy, if George Glas and his murderers should meet in heaven.' Glas died at Perth on 2 Nov. 1773. He married Katharine (d. December 1749), eldest daughter of Thomas Black, minister at Perth, and had fifteen children, all of whom he survived. Of his sons, Alexander was the writer of some of the best of the 'Christian Songs' published by the sect; George [q. v.] was the ablest of the family; Thomas became a bookseller at Dundee. His daughter Katharine married Robert Sandeman. In Scotland the sect is still known as Glassites; in England and America, to which it spread through the influence of Sandeman's labours, the name Sandemanian is given to it. In addition to the parent body there are several smaller sects which owe their origin to the writings of Glas, e.g. the Johnsonian baptists and the 'separatists' who follow the teaching of John Walker of Dublin.

Glas's 'Works' were collected in his lifetime and published, Edinb. 1761–2, 4 vols. 8vo; a second and more complete edition was issued at Dundee, 1782–3, 5 vols. 8vo. The most characteristic are: 1. 'The Testimony of the King of Martyrs concerning his Kingdom,' &c., Edinb. 1727, 8vo; also 1728, 8vo; 1729, 8vo; 1747, 8vo (preface by Robert Ferrier); 1776, 12mo; 1777, 12mo; 1813, 12mo. 2. 'An Explication,' &c., 1728. 3. 'The Speech before the Commission,' &c., 1730. 4. 'A Letter to Mr. John Willison . . . concerning Illiterate Ministers,' 1734. 5. 'The Scheme of Justification by Faith agreeable to Common Sense,' &c., 1753. Others are noticed above. Not included in the 'Works' is 6. 'Christian Songs,' 6th edit. Perth, 1784, 12mo; 9th edit. Edinb. 1805, 12mo (has unauthorised alterations); 13th edit. Perth, 1847, 12mo (the printer was R. Morison, who had printed the 6th edition sixty-four years previously; in this edition are sixteen compositions by Glas, besides two doubtful ones).

[Hew Scott's Fasti Eccles. Scotic.; Wilson's Dissenting Churches in London, 1810, iii. 261 sq.; Hurd's Religious Rites, 1811, pp. 644 sq.; Grub's Eccl. Hist. of Scotland, 1861, iv. 55; Anderson's Scottish Nation, 1870, ii. 307; Hunt's Religious Thought in England, 1873, iii. 222 sq.; Russell's Congregationalism, in Religions of the World, 1877, pp. 224 sq.; Glas's Works.]   A. G.

GLASCOCK, WILLIAM NUGENT (1787?–1847), captain in the navy, entered the navy in January 1800 on board the Glenmore frigate with Captain George Duff, whom he followed in 1801 to the Vengeance, in which he served in the Baltic, on the coast of Ireland, and in the West Indies. In 1803 he was appointed to the Colossus and afterwards to the Barfleur, in which he was present in the action off Cape Finisterre on 22 July 1805, and later on at the blockade of Brest under Admiral Cornwallis. In November 1808 he was promoted to be lieutenant of the Dannemark, and served in her at the reduction of Flushing in August 1809; in 1812 he was a lieutenant of the Clarence in the Bay of Biscay. He afterwards served in the Tiber, Madagascar, and Meander frigates on the home station, and in the Sir Francis Drake, flagship of Sir Charles Hamilton [q. v.], on the Newfoundland station, and was promoted from her to the command of the Carnation sloop in November 1818. In 1819 he commanded the Drake brig, from which he was obliged to invalid. In 1830 Glascock was appointed to the Orestes sloop, which he commanded on the home station during 1831; but in 1832 he was sent out to the coast of Portugal, and during the latter months of the year was stationed in the Douro, for the protection of British interests in the then disturbed state of the country [see SARTORIUS, SIR GEORGE ROSE; NAPIER, SIR CHARLES (1786–1860)]. He continued in the Douro, as senior officer, for nearly a year, during which time his conduct under troublesome and often difficult circumstances won for him the approval of the admiralty and his promotion to post-rank, 3 June 1833, accompanied by a special and complimentary letter from Sir James Graham, the first lord. He did not, however, leave the Douro till the following September, and on 1 Oct. he paid off the Orestes. From April 1843 to January 1847 he commanded the Tyne frigate on the Mediterranean station, and during the following months was employed in Ireland as an inspector under the Poor Relief Act. He died suddenly on 8 Oct. 1847 at Baltinglass. He was married and left issue. Glascock devoted the long intervals of half-pay, both as commander and captain, to literary labours, and produced several volumes of naval novels, anecdotes, reminiscences, and reflections, which, as novels, are stupid enough, and in their historical parts have little value, but are occasionally interesting as social sketches of naval life in the early part of the century. The titles of these are: 1. 'The Naval Sketch Book, or The Service Afloat and Ashore,' 2 vols. 12mo, 1826. 2. 'Sailors and Saints, or Matrimonial Manœuvres,' 3 vols. 12mo, 1829. 3. 'Tales of a Tar, with characteristic Anecdotes,' 12mo, 1836. 4. 'Land Sharks and Sea Gulls,' 3 vols. 12mo, 1838. His 'Naval Service, or Officers' Manual,' 2 vols. post 8vo, 1836, comes under a different category, and proved, as it was meant to be, a useful manual for young officers; it passed through four editions in England; the last, published in 1859, has a short advertisement by Glascock's daughter, in which she says that 'the work has been translated into French, Russian, Swedish, and Turkish, and adopted by the navies of those powers, as well as by that of the United States.' It is now, of course, quite obsolete, though still interesting to the student of naval history and customs.

[O'Byrne's Nav. Biog. Dict.; Marshall's Roy. Nav. Biog. xii. (vol. iv. pt. ii.) 490 (a very detailed memoir, evidently supplied by Glascock himself); United Service Magazine, 1847, pt. iii. p. 465.]   J. K. L.

GLASS, JOSEPH (1791?–1867), philanthropist, born in 1791 or 1792, was the inventor of the chimney-sweeping machine now in use. A less successful machine was invented in 1805 by Smart, but until the production of Glass's invention the friends of the sweep were unable to carry the bill for the suppression of climbing-boys. Glass, having perfected his machine and proved its practicability, was examined before a committee of the House of Lords; the result being the act of parliament for the suppression of the old system of sweeping chimneys (1 July 1842). Glass received the silver medal and the prize of 200l., but he never patented his invention. He was actively engaged for many years, first in advocating the claims of the sweeps, and afterwards in prosecuting the masters who attempted to evade the provisions of the act. The law was made more stringent in 1864. Glass died at Brixton, Surrey, 29 Dec. 1867, in his seventy-sixth year.

[Athenæum, 11 Jan. 1868, p. 60; Times, 1 Jan. 1868, p. 1, col. 1; Gent. Mag. 4th ser. v. 259.]   G. G.

GLASS, SIR RICHARD ATWOOD (1820–1873), manufacturer of telegraph cables, was born at Bradford, Wiltshire, in 1820, and educated at King's College, London. He began life in a London accountant's office, where in the course of his business duties he became acquainted with Mr. Elliot, who was associated with the wire-rope manufactory of Kuper & Co. In 1852 Glass, who had a mechanical as well as a financial turn of mind, first adapted the wire-rope covering to submarine cables. It was first applied to the Dover and Calais cable, then partially completed. Afterwards the plan was adopted for many other cable services with great success. In the early days of submarine telegraphy Glass gave most valuable patronage and support to the enterprise by the manufacture of various descriptions of cable. The Atlantic cables of 1865 and 1866 were made under his direct superintendence. After being knighted for these services in 1866, Glass quitted the Telegraph Construction and Maintenance Company, and subsequently became chairman of the Anglo-American Telegraph Company. He was returned member for Bewdley, Worcestershire, in 1868, and sat for that constituency from December of that year until the March following, when he was unseated on petition. He married in 1854 Anne, daughter of Thomas Tanner, and died on 22 Dec. 1873 at Moorlands, Bitterne, Southampton.

[Ann. Reg. 1873; Sabine's Hist. of the Electric Telegraph; Times, 23 Dec. 1873.]   J. B–y.

GLASS, THOMAS, M.D. (1709–1786), physician, son of Michael Glass, dyer, of Tiverton, where he was born 14 May 1709, was entered as a medical student at Leyden on 29 Oct. 1728, and graduated M.D. in July 1731 ('Dissertatio Medica Inauguralis, De Atrophia in genere,' 4to, Leyden, 1731). He practised first at Tiverton and from 1741 at Exeter, where he became a physician of the Devon and Exeter Hospital on its foundation. To his brother Samuel Glass, a surgeon at Oxford, he imparted a process of preparing magnesia alba. Samuel perfected the preparation, published in 1764 an 'Essay' on its use, and greatly benefited thereby. He ultimately sold the secret to a firm of chemists. Meanwhile, in the summer of 1771, Thomas Henry [q. v.], a Manchester apothecary, communicated to the College of Physicians what he maintained to be an 'improved' method of preparing magnesia alba, and his paper was printed in vol. ii. of the college 'Transactions.' After Samuel Glass's death on 25 Feb. 1773 (*Gent. Mag.* xliii. 155), Henry published in the following May 'Strictures' on the magnesia sold 'under the name of the late Mr. Glass,' proving by a searching analysis that it was not properly made, and advertising his own preparation as 'genuine.' Thomas Glass replied in 'An Examination of Mr. Henry's "Strictures" on Glass's Magnesia,' 8vo, London, 1774, but was effectively answered by Henry during the same year. To 'Medical Observations and Inquiries' (vi. 364) Glass contributed an 'Account of the Influenza, as it appeared at Exeter in 1775.' He wrote also: 1. 'Commentarii duodecim de febribus ad Hippocratis disciplinam accommodati,' 8vo, London, 1742 ('Editio nova, curante Ern. Godofr. Baldinger,' 8vo, Jena and Leipzig, 1771). 2. 'An Account of the antient baths, and their use in physic,' 8vo, London, 1752. 3. 'A letter . . . to Dr. Baker on the means of procuring a distinct and favourable kind of small-pox,' &c., 8vo, London, 1767. 4. 'A second letter . . . to Dr. Baker on certain methods of treating the small-pox during the eruptive state,' 8vo, London, 1767. 5. 'An Essay on Revealed Religion,' 1772. Glass was considered the greatest English authority after Sir William Watson on inoculation for the small-pox. A German translation of their papers was published at Halle in 1769.

Glass died at Exeter on 5 Feb. 1786 and was buried in St. David's churchyard. His will, dated 8 Nov. 1783, was proved at London on 27 Feb. 1786 (registered in P. C. C. 90, Norfolk). He bequeathed to the dean and chapter of Exeter all his 'medical printed books,' to be placed in their library for the use of any physician of the city. By a codicil dated 15 Dec. 1784 he made provision for the education of poor children in Exeter. By his wife Mary, daughter of Sir Nathaniel Hodges, who died before him, he had four daughters, Mary (Mrs. Parminter), who predeceased her father, Elizabeth, Ann (Mrs. Lowder), and Melina or Melony (Mrs. Daniell). His portrait, by Opie, in the board-room of the Devon and Exeter Hospital, was engraved by Ezekiel.

[Notes and Queries, 8th ser. viii. 462; will of Samuel Glass, proved 31 March 1773 (P. C. C. 110, Stevens).] G. G.

GLASSE, GEORGE HENRY (1761–1809), classical scholar and divine, the son of Dr. Samuel Glasse [q. v.], was born in 1761. He was sent to Christ Church, Oxford, in 1775, aged 14, and graduated B.A. 28 April 1779, and M.A. 14 Jan. 1782. He took holy orders, and in 1785 his father resigned to him his living of Hanwell, Middlesex. He also filled the office of domestic chaplain to the Earl of Radnor, the Duke of Cambridge, and the Earl of Sefton successively. His intellectual attainments greatly impressed his friends. In 1781 he published a translation of Mason's

'Caractacus,' 'Καράκτακος ἐπὶ Μώνῃ : sive cl. Gul. Masoni Caractacus Græco carmine redditus cum versione Latina,' which was very favourably reviewed. In 1788 appeared Glasse's rendering in Greek verse of Milton's 'Samson Agonistes.' The ease with which Glasse handled the classical languages is illustrated by his Latin version of Colman's 'Miss Bayley's Ghost,' which was sung by Tom Moore at a masquerade given by Lady Manvers, and afterwards published in the 'Gentleman's Magazine' (lxxv. 750). He published a large number of sermons. including 'Contemplations on the Sacred History, altered from the works of Bishop Hall,' 4 vols., 12mo, 1792, and 'Sixteen Discourses abridged from the works of Bishop William Beveridge [q.v.], with Supplement of Ten Sermons by G. H. Glasse,' London, 1805, 8vo. The most popular of his works was 'Louisa: a narrative of fact supposed to throw light on the mysterious history of the Lady of the Haystack' (1801), translated from 'L'Inconnue, Histoire Véritable.' This work, which quickly reached a third edition, was an attempt to prove that a mysterious refugee at Bristol was identical with Félix-Julienne de Schonau, otherwise Freulen, who declared herself to be the natural daughter of the emperor Francis I, and who was the unnamed heroine of the anonymous French work 'L'Inconnue.' Glasse frequently contributed to the 'Gentleman's Magazine,' and wrote a paper in 'Archæologia' in 1787. He ran through a large fortune in sixteen years, and then found himself in such difficulties that on 30 Oct. 1809 he hanged himself in the Bull and Mouth Inn, St. Martin's-le-Grand, London. At the inquest his solicitor testified that his embarrassments were so great as to fully account for mental derangement. Glasse is described as 'short and fat, his face full and rather handsome, with an expression of benevolence and intelligence.' He married, first, Anne Fletcher of Ealing, who died in June 1802, within a few days of their eldest daughter, and afterwards in May 1805 Harriet, the daughter of Thomas Wheeler.

[Gent. Mag. lxxix. 1082–3; Nichols's Lit. Anecd. ix. 131–3; St. James's Chronicle, 31 Oct. 1809; Notes and Queries, 1st ser. x. 496, 2nd ser. iii. 249; Cat. of Oxford Graduates; Brit. Mus. Cat.] A. V.

GLASSE, HANNAH (*fl.* 1747), was author of a popular treatise on cookery. The first edition is a thin folio, entitled 'The Art of Cookery Made Plain and Easy, which far exceeds any Thing of the kind ever yet Published. . . . By A Lady. London. Printed for the Author; and sold at Mrs. Ashburn's a China-Shop, the Corner of Fleet-Ditch, 1747.' A list of nearly two hundred subscribers includes 'Mrs. Glasse, Cary-Street,' and 'Mr. Glasse, Attorney at Law.' In an address 'To the reader' the author declares, 'I have attempted a Branch of Cookery which Nobody has yet thought worth their while to write upon,' and continues: 'If I have not wrote in the high polite Stile I hope I shall be forgiven; for my Intention is to instruct the lower Sort.' The extravagance of French cooks is severely condemned. The volume has at the end 'A certain Cure for the Bite of a Mad Dog, attributed to Dr. Mead.' It became deservedly popular. In 1751 the fourth edition was issued in octavo. It contains a few pages of appendix, and has the autograph of H. Glasse engraved in facsimile across the title at the top of the beginning of the text. This autograph was printed in facsimile in the same place in subsequent editions. The ninth edition appeared in 1765, and many other editions succeeded. Mrs. Glasse was author also of 'The Compleat Confectioner: or the Whole Art of Confectionary Made Plain and Easy, &c. &c. By H. Glasse, Author of the "Art of Cookery."' This is not dated, but is to be sold, like the 'Art of Cookery,' at 'Mrs. Ashburner's China Shop.' The introductory address, 'To the Housekeepers of Great Britain and Ireland,' has the facsimile autograph 'H. Glasse,' which is repeated at the beginning of the text as in the 'Art of Cookery.' The British Museum Catalogue suggests 1770 as its date of publication. Mrs. Glasse also published 'The Servant's Directory, or Housekeeper's Companion,' &c., London, 1770, 8vo. In the fourth edition of 'The Art of Cookery,' on the flyleaf opposite the title-page, is an elaborate advertisement in copperplate, announcing that Hannah Glasse is 'Habit Maker to Her Royal Highness the Princess of Wales, in Tavistock Street, Covent Garden,' &c. She may be identical with the 'Hannah Glass of St. Paul's, Co. Garden, Warehouse-keeper,' placed in the list of bankrupts for May 1754 in the 'Gentleman's Magazine' (xxiv. 244). A report is mentioned in Boswell's 'Life of Johnson' (1848, p. 592) that Mrs. Glasse's 'Cookery' was by Dr. John Hill, but the style of the book and the existence of the other works noted above are irreconcilable with this view. The attribution to Mrs. Glasse of the proverb 'First catch your hare' has occasioned some discussion. The proverb is not found in her 'Art of Cookery,' but her words 'Take your hare when it is cased' may have suggested it.

[Notes and Queries, 2nd ser. vi. 322, 444, viii. 206, xi. 264, 6th ser. xi. 90, 196; Brit. Mus. Cat. The Brit. Mus. copy of the Servant's Di-

rectory is unfortunately missing; Brewer's Dict. of Phrase and Fable.]   R. B.

GLASSE, SAMUEL, D.D. (1735–1812), theologian, son of the Rev. Richard Glasse of Purton, Wiltshire, born in 1735, was a scholar of Westminster School from 1749 to 1752, when he was elected a junior student of Christ Church, Oxford (4 June). He proceeded B.A. in 1756, M.A. in 1759, and accumulated the degrees of B.D. and D.D. on 7 Dec. 1769. In 1764 he became a fellow of the Royal Society, and in 1772 chaplain in ordinary to his majesty. His first preferment was the rectory of St. Mary's, Hanwell, Middlesex, which he afterwards resigned in favour of his son, George Henry Glasse [q. v.], in 1785. The church was rebuilt during his residency, and he contributed largely towards the new edifice. In 1782 he became vicar of Epsom, and four years later rector of Wanstead, Essex. He was appointed to the prebend of Shalford in the cathedral of Wells in 1791, which he retained until 1798, when he was installed as prebendary of Oxgate in St. Paul's Cathedral. He died in Sackville Street, Piccadilly, on 27 April 1812, in his seventy-ninth year. Glasse was the intimate friend of George Horne, bishop of Norwich.

Glasse was a popular and eloquent preacher, and an active country magistrate. The sermons he delivered before public bodies and on behalf of special charities were often printed between 1773 and 1803. In 1777 he translated and edited a French work, entitled 'Address from a Lady of Quality to her Children in the Last Stage of a Lingering Illness,' Gloucester, 1778, 2 vols. 8vo. He felt a keen sympathy with Raikes in his organisation of Sunday schools, and was the author of 'The Piety, Wisdom, and Policy of promoting Sunday Schools,' London, 1786, 4to, and of an article in the 'Gentleman's Magazine,' lvii. 11, January 1788, entitled 'A Short Sketch and Character of Mr. Raikes.' He published in 1787 'A Narrative of Proceedings tending towards a National Reforming previous to, and consequent upon, his Majesty's Royal Proclamation for the Suppression of Vice and Immorality. In a Letter to a Friend, &c. by a Country Magistrate,' London, 1787, 8vo. He likewise assisted Man Godscall in his pamphlet, 'A General Plan of Parochial and Provincial Police,' London, 1787, 8vo.

[Welch's Alumni Westmon. pp. 349, 358, 359, 534; Foster's Alumni Oxon.; Lysons's Environs, ii. 553; Manning's Surrey, ii. 623; Malcolm's Lond. Red. iii. 20; Nichols's Lit. Hist. ix. 131; Gent. Mag. lii. 552, lvi. 719, lxi. 686; Watt's Bibl. Brit.; Life of Bishop Horne, by C. Jones, i. 41.]   W. F. W. S.

GLASSFORD, JAMES (*d.* 1845), legal writer and traveller, was son of John Glassford of Dougalston [q. v.], by his third wife, Lady Margaret Mackenzie, sixth daughter of the third Earl of Cromarty. Glassford was admitted a member of the Faculty of Advocates in 1793, and became sheriff-depute of Dumbartonshire. He succeeded to Dougalston on the death of his elder brother Henry in 1819. He was one of the commissioners of inquiry into the state of education in Ireland, and in that capacity visited Ulster, Leinster, and Munster in 1824, and Connaught in 1826. He also acted as one of the commissioners for inquiring into the duties and emoluments of the clerks and other officers of the courts of justice in Scotland. He died at Edinburgh on 28 July 1845. His published works are as follows: 1. 'Remarks on the Constitution and Procedure of the Scottish Courts of Law,' Edinburgh, 1812, 8vo. 2. 'An Essay on the Principles of Evidence, and their application to subjects of Judicial Enquiry,' Edinburgh, 1812, 8vo. 3. 'Exemplum Tractatus de fontibus Juris, and other Latin Pieces of Lord Bacon. Translated by James Glassford, Esq., Advocate,' Edinburgh, 1823, 8vo. 4. 'Frondes Caducæ,' Chiswick, 1824, 16mo. 5. 'Letter to the Right Hon. Sir John Newport, Bart., M.P., on the subject of the Fees payable in the Courts of Justice and the Stamp Duties on Law Proceedings,' London, 1824, 8vo. 6. 'Letter to the Right Hon. the Earl of Roden on the present state of Popular Education in Ireland,' London, 1829, 8vo. 7. 'Lyrical Compositions selected from the Italian Poets,' with translations, Edinburgh, 1834, 8vo (favourably noticed in the 'Edinburgh Review,' January 1835). A second edition was published in 1846 after the author's death, greatly enlarged. Several of these translations were republished in London in 1886 in a volume of the 'Canterbury Poets,' entitled 'Sonnets of Europe,' edited by Mr. Samuel Waddington. 8. 'Notes of Three Tours in Ireland in 1824 and 1826,' Bristol, 1838, 8vo. This work was printed for private distribution in 1831. It was republished, however, during the following year, and is identical with the former edition, except for the insertion of a new title-page. 9. 'Letter by the Chancellor D'Aguesseau to a Friend on the subject of the Christian Mysteries, by James Glassford, Esq., and extracted by permission from the Scottish "Christian Herald."' This letter is published among a number of treatises entitled 'Unitarianism tried by Scripture and Experience, . . . with a General Introduction by a Layman,' London, 1840, 8vo. 10. 'Miscellanea,' Edinburgh, 4to, pp. 83. This volume, printed at Edinburgh for private circulation, contains translations of Addison's 'Machinæ Gesticulantes,' Froude's 'Cursus Glaciales,' &c. Glassford also published 'Elegiæ,' without place or date, pp. 31; another edition, pp. 39.

[Martin's Privately Printed Books, pp. 244, 426; Edinb. Review, lx. 1835; Sonnets of Europe (Canterbury Poets Series).] W. F. W. S.

GLASSFORD, JOHN (1715–1783), merchant of Glasgow, born in 1715, was a tobacco merchant on a large scale. He was one of the original members of the Glasgow chamber of commerce, and took a prominent part with Larnshaw, Ritchie of Busbie, and Spiers of Elderslie, in developing the trade of Glasgow. The firm of Spiers & Glassford, of which he was a member, imported in 1774 more than one-fourth of the entire 40,500 hogsheads of tobacco received by the forty-six firms then existing in Glasgow. Glassford was also the most extensive shipowner of his time in Scotland. He possessed twenty-four fine vessels regularly trading between the Clyde and America, and the West Indies. Glassford, who was made bailie of Glasgow in 1751, resided in the old Shawfield Mansion, on the north side of Trongate, facing Stockwell Street, which was built in 1712 by David Campbell, M.P. for Glasgow, and was subsequently razed to make way for the present Glassford Street. Glassford purchased the extensive lands of Dougalston, Dumbartonshire, in 1767, and greatly improved the estate by planting and building. He was three times married. By his second wife, Anne, daughter of Sir John Nisbet of Dean, he was father of Henry Glassford, M.P. for Dumbartonshire from 1806 to 1810, who died 14 May 1819; his third wife, whom he married 21 March 1769, was Lady Margaret Mackenzie, daughter of the third Earl of Cromarty, and by her he was father of James Glassford [q. v.] She died at Glasgow 29 March 1773. Glassford died at Dougalston on 27 Aug. 1783.

[Irving's Book of Scotsmen; Pagan's Sketches of Glasgow; Glasgow Past and Present; articles in the Glasgow Herald; Douglas and Wood's Peerage of Scotland, i. 400; Foster's M.P.'s of Scotland.] J. B-y.

GLASTONBURY, JOHN OF (*fl.* 1400), historian. [See JOHN.]

GLAZEBROOK, JAMES (1744–1803), divine, son of William Glazebrook, was born at Madeley, Shropshire, on 11 Oct. 1744. When he was a young man of twenty-three, working as a collier and getter of ironstone, he was brought under the influence of the Rev. John Fletcher of Madeley [q. v.], and he determined to become a clergyman. With this view he was educated at Lady Huntingdon's college at Trevecca in South Wales. He was ordained deacon by the Bishop of Lichfield and Coventry in December 1771, and six years later he received priest's orders. In 1779 he married Dorothy, daughter of Dr. Thomas Kirkland, and removed to Warrington, where he became incumbent of a new church, St. James's, Latchford, consecrated in 1781. In that year he joined in a sharp controversy with Gilbert Wakefield on infant baptism. Wakefield afterwards acknowledged that his opponent was 'a man of talents, very superior in his education and advantages, and deserves the warmest commendations for the pains which he must have taken with the cultivation of his understanding in very untoward circumstances.' On being appointed vicar of Belton, Leicestershire, in 1796, being then broken in health, he left Warrington, though he retained St. James's incumbency. He died at Belton on 1 July 1803. His son, Thomas Kirkland, is noticed below.

He wrote : 1. 'A Defence of Infant Baptism,' &c., 1781. 2. 'The Sacrifice of Thanksgiving, a Sermon,' 1789. 3. 'The Practice of what is called Extempore Preaching recommended,' 1794. 4. 'The Minister's Enquiry into the State of his People, a Sermon,' 1798. 5. 'Sermons on various Important Subjects (with Life by T. W. Whitaker),' 1805.

[Rylands's Genealogies of Bate and Kirkland; Ormerod's Cheshire, 2nd edit. i. 603; New's Memorials of Selina, Countess of Huntingdon, 1858, pp. 214, 228.] C. W. S.

GLAZEBROOK, THOMAS KIRKLAND (1780–1855), author, son of the Rev. James Glazebrook [q.v.], was born at Ashbyde-la-Zouch, Leicestershire, on 4 June 1780. He lived for many years at Warrington, where he carried on the business of a glass manufacturer, and where he engaged in the promotion of many useful institutions and societies. He was the captain of a local volunteer corps in 1803, and was always an ardent politician of the tory party. He wrote : 1. 'The First Eclogue of Virgil, translated into English Verse,' 1807. 2. 'A Guide to Southport, North Meoles, in the County of Lancaster,' 1809; 2nd edit. 1826. 3. 'Lissa' (a poetical fragment). 4. 'A Letter addressed to the Members of the Warrington Institution,' 1814. 5. 'Alphabetical and Chronological List of Companies, Trades, &c.,' 1831. He also printed many occasional songs and poetical effusions.

He married in 1801 Elizabeth Twanbrook of Appleton, Cheshire, by whom he had a large family. He died at Southport on 17 Jan. 1855, after residing there for twenty years.

[Kendrick's Warrington Worthies; Fishwick's Lancashire Library, p. 176; Rylands's Bate and Kirkland Genealogies, 1877; information from Mr. J. P. Rylands.] C. W. S.

GLEIG, GEORGE (1753–1840), bishop of Brechin, came of a family of Scotch episcopalians, which had adhered to the house of Stuart and suffered for it. He was born on his father's farm at Boghall, in the parish of Arbuthnot, Kincardineshire, on 12 May 1753. After some instruction at the school of Arbuthnot he entered, at about thirteen years of age, King's College, Aberdeen, where he carried off the first prizes in mathematics and the moral and physical sciences. In 1773 he took orders in the Scottish episcopal church, and was appointed almost immediately to the charge of Crail and Pittenweem, Fifeshire. In 1786 he went to London, chiefly to negotiate for the repeal of the penal laws, and appears to have obtained from Moore, archbishop of Canterbury, a draft of a bill to which the government might assent. The Scotch bishops, however, desired a measure of relief not involving the requirement to pray for the king by name. This 'foolish attempt,' as Gleig described it, was fatal to the scheme. Bishop Skinner was then allpowerful in the church, was suspicious of his efforts, and had resented Gleig's criticism of his consecration sermon in the 'Gentleman's Magazine' for 1785 (pt. i. p. 438). Though he was elected by the clergy bishop of Dunkeld in November 1786, in September 1792, and for the third time in the summer of 1808, the hostility of Skinner rendered the election on all three occasions ineffectual.

Gleig removed from Pittenweem to Stirling in 1787. He became a frequent contributor to the 'Monthly Review,' the 'Gentleman's Magazine,' the 'Anti-Jacobin Review,' and the 'British Critic.' He also wrote several articles for the third edition of the 'Encyclopædia Britannica,' and on the death of the editor, Colin Macfarquhar, in 1793, was engaged to edit the remaining six volumes (xiii–xviii.) Three of his principal contributions to this work were the articles on 'Instinct,' 'Metaphysics,' and 'Theology.' The two supplementary volumes, which appeared in 1801, he wrote almost unaided. King's College, Aberdeen, conferred on him the degree of LL.D.; he was elected fellow of the Royal Society of Edinburgh, contributed to their 'Transactions,' and became also fellow of the Society of Antiquaries of Scotland.

On 28 Sept. 1808 Gleig was unanimously chosen successor to Bishop Strahan in the episcopate of Brechin, and having bound himself to maintain the Scotch office—a test imposed upon him by Skinner, now primus—

he was consecrated in St. Andrew's Church, Aberdeen, on 30 Oct. He at once attacked the old abuses. He immediately addressed to his clergy a long circular pastoral letter, dated 18 Nov. 1808, recommending strict adherence to the English liturgy in every office of the church, except that of the Holy Communion. In 1810 he suggested a plan for enabling the clergy to improve their education. On 20 Aug. 1816 he was appointed primus, but failed to fulfil the promise of his ordinary episcopate. The chief cause of his comparative failure in administration was his persistent and abortive interference in diocesan elections. During 1820–3 Gleig contributed some able articles to the 'Scottish Episcopal Magazine,' the organ of his friend, Dr. Russell. In June 1823 he made another journey to London, and did what he could to forward a measure for securing the *regium donum* for the church. Increasing infirmities obliged him to send in his resignation of the primacy on 15 Feb. 1837. He died 9 March 1840, and was buried in a chapel attached to the Greyfriars Church, Stirling, which belongs to the Graham Moirs of Leckie. In 1789 he married Janet, widow of Dr. Fullton, and youngest daughter of Robert Hamilton of Kilbrackmont. By this lady, who died 15 June 1824 (*Scots Mag.* new ser. xv. 255), he had three sons and one daughter. He survived all his children except the youngest son, George Robert Gleig [q. v.] Besides various sermons and charges Gleig was the author of: 1. 'Some Account of the Life and Writings of William Robertson . . . late Principal of the College of Edinburgh,' 8vo (1812), prefixed or intended to be prefixed to an edition of Robertson's works. 2. 'Directions for the Study of Theology in a Series of Letters from a Bishop to his Son on his admission into Holy Orders,' 8vo, 1837 (in great part a reprint from periodicals). He likewise edited Jerome Lobo's 'Voyage to Abyssinia,' 8vo, 1789, and Thomas Stackhouse's 'History of the Holy Bible,' 4to, 1817. He was attacked for lax views upon original sin expressed in his edition of Stackhouse. His letters to Alexander Henderson of Edinburgh, from 1810 to 1818, are in the British Museum (Additional MS. 28960), as is also a single letter addressed in 1792 to John Douglas, bishop of Salisbury (Egerton MS. 2186, f. 62).

[Life by William Walker, incumbent of Monymusk (1878); Life by G. R. Gleig in Encycl. Brit. (8th edit.) x. 676–7, which is full of extraordinary inaccuracies; Life in Encycl. Brit. (9th edit.) x. 677.]   G. G.

GLEIG, GEORGE ROBERT (1796–1888), chaplain-general of the forces, son of George Gleig [q. v.], bishop of Brechin, was born at Stirling 20 April 1796. His childhood was spent at his father's country house at the foot of the Ochill Hills. So delicate was he in his early years that his life was at one time despaired of. Gleig received his early education from his father, and was then sent to the Stirling grammar school. His lessons were mastered with unusual ease, and then he kept the class idle by telling stories. From the grammar school he was removed at the age of ten and placed under Dr. Russell at Leith. He finished his school course at thirteen, and was sent to Glasgow University. Gaining a Snell exhibition to Balliol College, he proceeded to Oxford in 1811, but soon resigned his exhibition to enter the army.

Gleig obtained an ensigncy in the 85th regiment, joined his company at the Cove of Cork, and served with it there until February 1813. The 85th was then remodelled, Gleig was promoted in the course of a few months, and went out to Spain as lieutenant. He served in the Peninsular campaigns of 1813 and 1814, being present at the siege of San Sebastian, the passage of the Bidassoa, the battle of the Nivelle, where he was twice wounded, the battle of the Nive, where he was again wounded, and the investment of Bayonne. When not on active duty he would amuse his comrades by the production of squibs and songs. For his services in the war he received the medal with three clasps. He afterwards served in the American war, and took part in the engagements at Bladensburg, Baltimore, New Orleans, the capture of Washington, and Fort Bowyer. He was thrice wounded in America.

After the battle of Waterloo Gleig went upon half-pay, and returned to Oxford to keep his terms in 1816. He proceeded B.A. from Magdalen Hall in 1818, and M.A. in 1821. In 1819 he married a ward of his father, and daughter of Captain Cameron the younger of Kinlochleven. He lived for twelve months at Rockliffe Hall, Cumberland, and prepared himself for taking orders. He was ordained by the Archbishop of Canterbury (Dr. Manners Sutton) in 1820, and appointed to the curacy of Westwell in Kent, worth only 70l. per annum. In 1821 the archbishop presented him to the perpetual curacy of Ash, valued at 130l. per annum, and in 1822 added the rectory of Ivy Church, worth 250l. He tried to increase his income by taking pupils, but finding the interruption of domestic quiet intolerable, he gave up the scheme.

While curate of Westwell, Gleig wrote his 'Campaigns of the British Army at Washington and New Orleans.' In 1826 he sold his half-pay, and wrote 'The Subaltern,' which first appeared in 'Blackwood's Magazine.' It professes merely to relate the adventures of the hero during his service with the Duke of Wellington's army, and is distinguished by literary skill, vivacity, and accuracy. In 1829 Gleig published 'The Chelsea Pensioners,' a large portion of which consisted of actual historical narrative; and he was an early contributor to 'Fraser's Magazine,' started in 1830.

From 1830 Gleig's life was one of strenuous labour. He had a growing family, and a large and populous parish to superintend; but he shortly gave to the world 'The Country Curate' (1830), 'Allan Breck,' and in 1834 'The Chronicles of Waltham.' He then took to history, and wrote a 'Life of Sir Thomas Munro,' in three volumes, 1830; a 'History of India,' in four volumes, 1830-5 (in 'Family Library'); the 'Story of the Battle of Waterloo,' 1847; 'The Leipsic Campaign;' 'Lives of Military Commanders,' three volumes, 1831 (in Lardner's 'Cabinet Cyclopædia'); a 'Sketch of the Military History of Great Britain,' 1845; and 'Sale's Brigade in Afghanistan,' 1847. He also wrote biographies of Lord Clive (1848) and Warren Hastings (3 vols. 1841), the last of which was the text of Macaulay's essay. Macaulay says that the work consisted of 'three big, bad volumes, full of undigested correspondence and undiscerning panegyric.'

Gleig was a strong conservative in politics, but took little part in public affairs, except in attacking the Reform Bill of 1832. In 1834 he was appointed to the chaplaincy of Chelsea Hospital by Lord John Russell, who refused to revoke the appointment when assured of Gleig's tory sentiments. Gleig was highly esteemed at Chelsea for his philanthropy and zeal. The flag, in capturing which he was wounded at Bladensburg, was always suspended from his pulpit in the hospital chapel. In 1838 he published in three volumes 'Chelsea Hospital and its Traditions.' Gleig was made chaplain-general of the forces in 1844. He proposed a plan for promoting the education of soldiers and their children, and was appointed in 1846 inspector-general of military schools.

In 1857 Gleig issued 'India and its Army,' and in the following year he republished, chiefly from the 'Edinburgh' and 'Quarterly' reviews, his 'Essays, Biographical, Historical, and Miscellaneous.' Gleig edited from 1850 for Longmans a cheap and useful educational library called 'Gleig's School Series,' to which he contributed a history of England, &c. In 1862 he produced a 'Life of Arthur, first Duke of Wellington,' founded upon Brialmont's biography, with the addition of some original matter. He had known

the duke personally, besides having served under him. Gleig was also the author of a number of theological works, including 'The Soldier's Manual of Devotion,' 1862, a 'History of the Bible,' 2 vols. 1830-1, 'The Great Problem: can it be Solved?' London, 1876, and two volumes of sermons, 1829 and 1844.

Gleig resigned the post of inspector-general of military schools in 1857, and that of chaplain-general of the forces in 1875. He continued, however, to hold till his death the appointment of prebendary of Willesden in St. Paul's Cathedral, to which he had been preferred in 1848. Gleig outlived all the original contributors to 'Fraser's Magazine.' His is one of the figures in Maclise's 'Portrait Gallery.' He was likewise for some years before his death the only surviving early contributor to 'Blackwood,' and the last surviving officer who served under the Duke of Wellington in the 85th.

Early in 1888 Gleig's health began to fail. He died on 9 July 1888 at Stratfield Turgis, near Winchfield, having retained his faculties almost to the last. Gleig was a staunch churchman, and a decided enemy to cant in every form.

[Fraser's Mag. vol. x.; Bates's Maclise Portrait Gallery, 1883; Waller's Imperial Dict.; New Monthly Mag. 1837; Times, 11 July 1888; Athenæum, 14 July 1888; Gleig's works.]

G. B. S.

GLEMHAM, EDWARD (*fl.* 1590-1594), voyager, of Benhall in Suffolk, esquire, in 1590 fitted out, as owner and sole adventurer, the ship Edward and Constance, of 240 tons, in which he sailed from Gravesend in August. He proceeded in the first instance to the Azores, where he landed on St. George's Island with a party of eighty-six men; but finding himself unable to hold the island, as he appears to have intended, he concluded a truce with the governor, and withdrew. He then met with six Spanish ships, two of which he succeeded in destroying; afterwards he had a fierce engagement with four galleys bound for Marseilles, which he beat off; and having refitted at Algiers, entered the Mediterranean, where he captured a large vessel laden with sugar and other valuable merchandise, which was afterwards claimed as Venetian property. The case, as tried in the admiralty court, seemed doubtful, and the judgment was that Glemham was to have the goods 'on a bond in double of their value, to pay their just value within two months after proof has been made, or for so much as is proved to belong to Venetians or others not subjects of the King of Spain' (*Calendar of State Papers,*

Domestic, 17 May 1592). An account of the early part of the voyage was published anonymously in 1591 [sm. 4to, 8 leaves, black letter; reprinted 1820, 8vo], under the title of 'The Honorable Actions of that most famous and valiant Englishman, Edward Glemham, esquire, latelie obtained against the Spaniards and the Holy Leauge in foure sundrie fightes. . . .' Some commendatory verses at the end of the narration express a wish that he may safely return, 'freighted with gold and pearl of India'— a wish which seems to have been fulfilled only in respect of the safety. A second voyage, undertaken very shortly after the first, was described by the same writer in a small pamphlet published in 1594 (sm. 4to, pp. 24, black letter; reprinted 1866 in Collier's *Illustrations of Old English Literature*, vol. i.), under the title of 'Newes from the Levane Seas. Describing the many perilous events of the most woorthy deserving Gentleman Edward Glenham, Esquire. . . .' Glemham's ventures seem to have been unfortunate, if we may judge from the fact that, starting with a good property, 'feasting his friends and relieving the poor plentifully,' and having a wife 'sole heir of a right worshipful knight, famous in his life and of great possessions,' he sold Benhall away from the family to Edward Duke, who died in 1598 (PAGE, *Supplement to the Suffolk Traveller*, p. 169). In the 'Newes from the Levane Seas,' the name is frequently spelt Glenham, but this appears to be wrong, as the family was called after Glemham in Suffolk, their ancient seat (COLLINS, *Peerage*, edit. 1768, vi. 427).

[Authorities as above.] J. K. L.

GLEMHAM, SIR THOMAS (d. 1649?), royalist, was the son of Sir Henry Glemham of Little Glemham, Suffolk, and Anne, daughter of Thomas Sackville, earl of Dorset (*Visitations of Suffolk*, p. 140). He was entered at Trinity College, Oxford, as a commoner in 1610 (*Trin. Coll. Reg.*; WOOD, *Fasti*, ed. Bliss, ii. 88). Glemham was knighted by James I on 10 Sept. 1617, and represented Aldeburgh in the first two parliaments of Charles I (METCALFE, *Book of Knights*; *Official Return of Names of Members of Parliament*, i. 466, 471). He is said to have served in the German wars, and took part in the siege of Bois-le-Duc in 1629 under Lord Wimbledon (DALTON, *Life of Wimbledon*, ii. 293). In the first Scotch war Glemham was lieutenant-colonel of the Earl of Warwick's regiment, in the second colonel of the 9th regiment of foot in the Earl of Northumberland's army (PEACOCK, *Army Lists*, p. 80). When Charles left York,

in August 1642, he appointed Glemham to command in York, and to assist with his advice the Earl of Cumberland, the lord-lieutenant of that county [see CLIFFORD, HENRY, fifth EARL OF CUMBERLAND]. Clarendon on this occasion describes Glemham as a gentleman of a noble extraction and a fair but impaired fortune. He had a good reputation for courage and integrity, but was wanting in energy (*Rebellion*, v. 445). Glemham's attempts against the parliamentary posts near York proved failures, and he was practically blockaded in that city when relieved by the Earl of Newcastle in December 1642 (SLINGSBY, *Diary*, ed. Parsons, pp. 78, 83). Newcastle removed Glemham from the government of York, but appointed him colonel-general of his field army (*Life of the Duke of Newcastle*, ed. 1886, p. 165). In January 1644, when the Scotch army invaded England, Glemham was sent to oppose them in command of the forces of Northumberland. A correspondence then took place between him and the members of the committee of both kingdoms present with the Scots (RUSHWORTH, v. 606–10). Glemham was again appointed governor of York after the battle of Marston Moor, and on the departure of the Marquis of Newcastle to the continent, but was obliged to capitulate a fortnight later (15 July 1644; RUSHWORTH, v. 637–40). He then made his way to Carlisle, which he held against the Scots until 25 June 1645, when want of provisions forced him to surrender (JEFFERSON, *History of Carlisle*, pp. 51–5). 'He was the first man that taught soldiers to eat cats and dogs,' says Lloyd, speaking of this siege (*Memoirs of Excellent Personages*, ed. 1668, p. 552). With the remains of the garrison, about two hundred foot, Glemham joined the king at Cardiff. Sir Edward Walker remarks that within three days of Glemham's arrival General Gerard was made Lord Gerard of Brandon in Suffolk, although Glemham had an interest in the place, and was an heir of the family of Brandon (*Historical Discourses*, p. 134). Charles, however, appreciated Glemham's services if he did not reward them, and he was sent to take the command of Oxford, which he did on 8 Oct. 1645 (DUGDALE, *Diary*, p. 82). In his new post Glemham greatly improved the fortifications, and made preparations for a stubborn defence. But he was obliged to surrender, after a strong protest, by the orders of the members of the privy council present in Oxford, and by that of the king himself (24 June 1645; DUGDALE, *Diary*, p. 88; *Clarendon MS.* 2240; *Old Parliamentary Hist.* xiv. 449). In contravention of the articles on which he surrendered, Glemham was for about a month imprisoned in the Fleet, but on applying to Fairfax was released by the House of Commons on 21 Aug. 1645 (CARY, *Memorials of the Civil War*, i. 143). Sir Thomas and his son Sackville compounded for their estates for the sum of 951*l*. 15*s*. (DRING, *Catalogue*, ed. 1733, p. 44). Nevertheless, he was ready to take up arms in the second civil war, and appeared in Scotland with that object in the spring of 1648. The commissioners of the English parliament demanded his surrender from the parliament of Scotland (31 March 1648), but could not obtain it (*Old Parliamentary Hist.* xvii. 91, 105, 115). Glemham assisted Sir Philip Musgrave to seize Carlisle, but seems to have taken no further part in the war (RUSHWORTH, vii. 1105). The exact date of his death is uncertain. His will was proved by his brother, Henry Glemham, 13 March 1649–50 (WOOD, *Fasti*, ii. 88).

[Wood's Fasti Oxon. ed. Bliss, ii. 88 ; Lloyd's Memoirs of Excellent Personages, 1668 ; Rushworth's Historical Collections; Clarendon's Hist. of the Rebellion.]   C. H. F.

GLEN, ANDREW (1665–1732), botanist, graduated B.A. from Jesus College, Cambridge, in 1683, and M.A. in 1687. According to Pulteney he was fellow of St. John's College, but Baker does not give his name in his list of fellows. According to the 'Graduati Cantabr.' he was fellow of Jesus College. In 1685 he formed an herbarium of seven hundred native and two hundred foreign plants, the latter collected on the continent. He afterwards travelled in Sweden and resided some time in Turin, where in 1692 he collected two hundred more specimens. In 1694 he became rector of Hathern, Leicestershire. His wife, Elizabeth, died in 1705, leaving three daughters, Elizabeth, Mary, and Margaret. Glen himself died at Hathern, where he is buried, on 1 Sept. 1732. His only published work was an assize sermon, dated 1707, but he is commemorated by Pulteney as a friend of Ray.

[Pulteney's Sketches of the Progress of Botany, ii. 63–4; Nichols's Lit. Anecd. viii. 196; Nichols's Hist. Leicestershire, iii. 84–6.]   G. S. B.

GLEN, WILLIAM (1789–1826), Scotch poet, was born in Queen Street, Glasgow, 14 Nov. 1789. He belonged to an old Renfrewshire family, and his father was a Russian merchant. After leaving school Glen, about the age of seventeen, entered a house trading with the West Indies. When he had become familiar with the business he went for some years to one of the islands as representative of the firm. Returning to Glasgow he started business for himself, but retired, owing to reverses, in 1814. An uncle in Russia now supported him, and his mode of life became rather unsettled. For some time he would appear to have given the rein to his social instincts and his poetic gifts as the laureate of his boon companions. In 1818 he married Catherine Macfarlane, daughter of a Glasgow merchant, and jointtenant with her brother of a farm at Port Monteith, Perthshire. During most of his remaining years Glen lived here, dependent on his wife's resources and his uncle's generosity, and a general favourite in the district. His old weakness for social amusement and late hours unfortunately still haunted him, and it may have hastened the consumption that ultimately proved fatal. Feeling his end approaching, Glen induced his wife to accompany him to Glasgow, on the conclusive plea that it was ' easier to take a living man there than a dead one,' and they were not long settled when he died, December 1826. His wife and only daughter afterwards managed the orphanage at Aberfoyle.

As a boy Glen eagerly learned of the fallen house of Stuart, and his pathetic song ' Wae's me for Prince Charlie,' which is charged with the true Jacobite spirit, constitutes the recognised dirge of the lost cause. Several other songs of Glen's are on occasional themes—such as ' The Battle of Vittoria,' ' The Battle Song,' and three on Napoleon—and there are love songs and narrative pieces, all more or less meritorious. The Jacobite lament, however, which has made the tune of ' Johnnie Faa ' its own, stands out so clearly above all the others that Glen is generally known only as the singer of this one song. He published in 1815 a 12mo volume of ' Poems, chiefly Lyrical,' and in 1874 Dr. Charles Rogers edited his ' Poetical Remains,' with a memoir.

[Poetical Remains of William Glen, as above ; Whitelaw's Book of Scottish Song; Wilson's Poets and Poetry of Scotland.]   T. B.

GLENBERVIE, BARON. [See DOUGLAS, SYLVESTER, 1743–1823.]

GLENCAIRN, EARLS OF. [See CUNNINGHAM, ALEXANDER, first EARL, *d.* 1488; ALEXANDER, fifth EARL, *d.* 1574; WILLIAM, fourth EARL, *d.* 1547; and WILLIAM, ninth EARL, 1610?–1664.]

GLENCORSE, LORD (1810–1891), lord justice general of Scotland. [See INGLIS, JOHN.]

GLENDOWER, OWEN (1359?–1416?), Welsh rebel, more accurately OWAIN AB GRUFFYDD, lord of Glyndyvrdwy or Glyndwr

(*Rawlinson MS.* B. 464, f. 42; OWEN and BLAKEWAY, *Shrewsbury*, i. 181), was probably born in 1359; on 3 Sept. 1386 he was between twenty-seven and twenty-eight years old (*Scrope and Grosvenor Roll*, i. 254, ed. Nicolas). On his father's side he traced back his descent through the princes of Powys Vadog to Bleddyn ab Cynvyn. His father's name was Gruffydd Vychan, i.e. the Little, modernised into Vaughan (Gruffydd Llwyd in PENNANT, *Tour in Wales*, i. 311, ed. 1778). This surname was doubtless to distinguish him from his father, Owain's grandfather, whose name was also Gruffydd, and who was the son of Madog, son of Gruffydd Vychan, son of Gruffydd of Bromfield [see GRUFFYDD AB MADOG, *d.* 1269] (BRIDGEMAN, *Princes of South Wales*, pp. 250–2). The lands of Glyndyvrdwy had long been in the family. Early in Edward II's time Gruffydd ab Madog (*b.* 1298) was married to Elizabeth, daughter of Sir John L'Estrange of Knockin, near Oswestry (*Rot. Parl.* i. 306), and the lordships and manors of Glyndyvrdwy and Sycharth were entailed on this couple and their heirs (*ib.* iv. 440). Glyndyvrdwy was in Edeyrnion and a part of the old shire of Merioneth. It included the valley of the Dee between Corwen and Llangollen. Sycharth, then within the Welsh marches, is now part of the parish of Llansilin, on the borders of Shropshire and the modern county of Denbigh. Owain claimed to be descended from the old line of north Welsh princes, and thence from Cadwaladr Vendigaid and the fabulous Brutus (see Owain's letter in ADAM OF USK, pp. 69–71). He also claimed descent from the old houses of Deheubarth, and, through his mother Helen, from Llewelyn ab Gruffydd (LELAND, *Itinerary*, v. 44; PENNANT, i. 302; *Harl. MS.* 807, f. 94). It is pretty clear, however, that Llewelyn's legitimate stock died out in his daughters. Owain also possessed in South Wales the manors of Yscoed and Gwynyoneth, but his main influence was in the north. He derived a revenue of three hundred marks a year from his lands, and was thus among the few Welsh gentlemen of large estate. He had in the north two great houses, of which the chief was at Sycharth, which, by his hospitality, became known as a 'sanctuary of bards.' The poet Iolo Goch [q. v.] has left a glowing description of the splendour of this house (text and translation in *Y Cymmrodor*, v. 264–73; and another translation in PENNANT, i. 305). It was called Saghern by the English (ELLIS, *Original Letters*, 2nd ser. i. 11). Owain had another house of only less importance at Glyndyvrdwy itself (*ib.* i. 12). Owain had a younger brother named Tudor. It was afterwards believed that great pro-

digies attended Owain's birth, and contemporaries thought that he had magic help in his struggle against the English. The story, often told, that at the time of his birth the horses in his father's stables were found standing in blood, is really told of Edmund Mortimer in all the original authorities ('Annales Hen. IV' in TROKELOWE, p. 349; WALSINGHAM, *Hist. Angl.* ii. 254; *Cont. Eulogium Historiarum*, iii. 398; MONK OF EVESHAM, p. 179; HOLINSHED).

Owain became a student of English law at Westminster, and was perhaps called to the bar ('juris apprenticius' *Ann. Hen. IV*, p. 333). He remained a student of ancient deeds. He subsequently became squire to the Earl of Arundel, who had large estates in North Wales and was lord of Dinas Bran, the great fortress overlooking Llangollen, not far from Owain's estates (*Cont. Eul. Hist.* iii. 388; CAPGRAVE, *De illustribus Henricis*, p. 110). In 1385 he served in the Scottish campaign of Richard II (*Scrope and Grosvenor Roll*, i. 254). He was summoned as a witness in the famous suit of Scrope and Grosvenor, and on 3 Sept. 1386 gave evidence at Chester in favour of Robert Grosvenor's right to wear the arms azure a bend or (*ib.* i. 254).

Arundel was a strong partisan of the popular party, and Owain subsequently took service with Henry of Lancaster himself, afterwards Henry IV ('scutifer regi moderno,' and therefore not of Richard II, as is generally said; *Ann. Hen. IV*, p. 333; WALSINGHAM, ii. 246). His connections were therefore thoroughly Lancastrian and constitutional. Yet Wales in general was strongly attached to King Richard, and when Henry IV on his accession made his son Henry prince of Wales, the French metrical chronicler prophesied that the new prince would not gain the lordship without force (*Archæologia*, xx. 204). Tumults became common from the time of Richard's deposition. Prince Henry's council, under Henry Percy, the famous 'Hotspur,' had little success in restoring order.

One of Owain's strongest neighbours was Reginald, lord Grey of Ruthin [q. v.], with whose house the king's tenants in Glyndyvrdwy had long been in conflict. A dispute was now caused by Owain's claim to some land in Grey's possession. It is said by the continuator of the 'Eulogium Historiarum' (whose dates are often wrong) that Owain journeyed to Westminster to complain before the Hilarytide parliament in 1401 of Grey's usurpation (*Cont. Eul. Hist.* iii. 388). But Owain was already in arms in 1400. If the story be true, it must refer to the parliament of October 1399, but there is no record of the transaction in the 'Rolls of Parliament.' The continuator tells us how the Bishop of St. Asaph, John Trevor, warned the parliament not to despise Owain. The lords replied that they did not care for the barefooted rogues, and Owain went home in a rage with his grievances unredressed.

Owain soon had another complaint. Grey had neglected to deliver a writ summoning Owain to the Scottish expedition, until it was so late that obedience was impossible. Grey then denounced him before the king as a traitor for not appearing (MONK OF EVESHAM, p. 171). Owain now plundered and burnt Grey's estates, and cruelly murdered some of Grey's household (*Ann. Hen. IV*, p. 333). Grey was much occupied at the time with a quarrel with Gruffydd ab Davydd ab Gruffydd, 'the strongest thief in Wales.' The revolt spread. The rumours that King Richard was still alive kindled Welsh feeling for their deposed favourite (cf. ADAM OF USK, p. 54). Owain, despite his Lancastrian connections, put himself at the head of the movement, which soon developed into a Welsh national rising against Saxon tyranny.

The rebels were from the first brilliantly successful. The clashing jurisdictions of the Prince of Wales and the marcher lords made united action among the English impossible. The castles were ill-equipped and undermanned, and, when not in Welsh hands, were in charge of Welsh deputies. The civil administration was almost entirely in native hands, and a large Welsh element had crept in even among the 'English towns.' Before long all North Wales was in revolt. Owain soon assumed the title of Prince of Wales, and gave himself the airs of a sovereign (EVESHAM, p. 171; ADAM OF USK, p. 46). The Welsh scholars at Oxford and Cambridge left their books and joined in the rebellion. The Welsh labourers from England hurried off to Owain with whatever weapons they could seize (*Rot. Parl.* iii. 457). In Wales the farmers sold their cattle to buy arms (ELLIS, 2nd ser. i. 8). Secret meetings were held everywhere, and the bards wandered about as messengers of sedition. Many castles and 'English boroughs' fell into Owain's hands. The great border stronghold of Shrewsbury, with its negligent town-guard and large Welsh population, was hardly beyond the range of danger (*Fœdera*, viii. 160).

Henry IV heard of the Welsh rising at Leicester on his way back from his expedition to Scotland. On 19 Sept. he issued from Northampton summonses to the levies of ten shires of the midlands and borders. He entered Wales a few days later, and wandered for a month throughout the north. He penetrated as far as Anglesey, where he drove out the Franciscan friars of Llanfaes, who, like their brethren in England, were keen partisans of King Richard, and therefore of Owain (*Cont. Eul. Hist.* iii. 388, but cf. WYLIE, p. 147) ; but as the army began to suffer from want of provisions, and Owain kept obstinately in hiding, Henry had to return to England with a few captives. On 9 Nov. he was at Westminster, where he granted all Owain's forfeited estates to his brother, John Beaufort [q. v.], earl of Somerset.

Owain for some time hid himself with only seven companions (ADAM OF USK, p. 46). His bard, Iolo Goch, lamented his disappearance in impassioned strains (the Welsh in LLOYD, *Hist. of Powys Fadog*, i. 220 ; English translation in *Y Cymmrodor*, iv. pt. ii. 230–2). But the rebels were soon as active as ever. In January parliament pressed hard for coercive laws. The king to a great extent accepted their proposals, but still aimed at conciliation, and on 10 March, at the petition of the Prince of Wales, issued a general pardon, from which Owain, himself, and the brothers Gwilym and Rhys, sons of Tudor, were the only exceptions. The commons of Carnarvon and Merioneth humbly tendered their thanks, and offered to pay the usual taxes. Yet with the return of spring the rebels were again active. Gwilym and Rhys seized Conway Castle on Good Friday, though on 28 May they had to give it up. On 30 May Percy won a battle near Cader Idris. He believed he had now subdued the three shires of Gwynedd, but, angry at being left to bear the expense, threw up his command. Before leaving Wales he entered into suspicious dealings with Owain.

Owain's movements during this time are very obscure. He was plainly keeping himself in the background until his agents had got all things ready. A curious letter addressed to his partisan, Henry Don, explains clearly enough his general plan of operations (it is printed in OWEN and BLAKEWAY'S *Shrewsbury*, i. 181–2). In the spring of 1401 Owain suddenly appeared in South Wales, in the 'marches of Carmarthen,' driven there perhaps by Percy's activity in Gwynedd, or perhaps by the desire of extending the rising to the south. On 26 May the king received the news that Owain had held a great assembly of rebels in that district, 'with the purpose of invading England, and of destroying our English tongue' (*Ordinances of the Privy Council*, ii. 55). Henry at once hurried to Worcester to prepare for a second expedition into Wales, but, finding the accounts of it exaggerated, he abandoned the invasion to attend to pressing business in London. Owain at once hurried to Powys, where on one of the

defence of the mathematical fellows, which is printed at pages 67–76 of 'An Authentic Narrative of Dissensions in the Royal Society.'

[Anderson's Scottish Nation, ii. 314–16; Chambers's Eminent Scotsmen, ii. 116–17; Gent. Mag. lxxxvii. pt. ii. 571–2; Army Lists; Cat. of Lib. of Faculty of Advocates, iii. 414.] G. G.

GLENLEE, LORDS. [See MILLER, SIR THOMAS, 1717–1789; MILLER, SIR WILLIAM, 1745–1846.]

GLENNY, GEORGE (1793–1874), horticultural writer, was born 1 Nov. 1793. He was apprenticed to the watchmaking, but early showed a taste for flowers, which was wisely encouraged by his father. In 'a few words about myself,' addressed to the editor of 'Lloyd's Newspaper' a day or two before his death, Glenny wrote: 'Sixty-seven years ago I had a very fine collection of auriculas and twenty rows of tulips, and visited several good amateur growers, from whom I received great encouragement and occasionally presents of plants and flowers. I cultivated my stock at Hackney. . . . From observation of the doings of the most successful amateurs I had become a very successful grower of the auricula, the tulip, ranunculus, polyanthus, and other florists' flowers. I had learned something from everybody and took many prizes.' It is related of him that in after years he once entertained fifty-seven guests at his table, and was able to set before each individual a silver prize-cup won in showing auriculas, dahlias, tulips, and roses as an amateur. His first literary attempts appeared in the 'Antigallican Monitor' and other forgotten prints. In 1820 he contributed a series of letters to a publication called 'The British Luminary,' of which he became editor. Soon after he became associated with a paper called 'The British Press,' and then editor of the 'Royal Lady's Magazine and St. James's Archives,' to which the Ettrick Shepherd, Miss Pardoe, Miss Mitford, the sisters Strickland, and others contributed. As a writer of authority on horticultural subjects his efforts date from 1832, when he started the 'Horticultural Journal,' and commenced the papers on the 'Properties of Flowers,' which may be regarded as the most important of his works. The object was to formulate 'rules for judging flowers by a perfect model, instead of by comparison with popular favourites.' Other writers, like Maddocks, had attempted to draw up rules for the purpose, but Glenny maintained, with reason, that these 'criterions,' of which the best collection is given in 'Loudon's Encyclopædia,' were incomplete and ill-defined. From this time Glenny acted as editor of various new ventures, the 'Gar-

dener's Gazette,' the 'Garden Journal,' the 'Practical Florist,' 'Glenny's Journal,' &c. As an editor he is described as exacting and quarrelsome. One of his literary ventures deserves mention. A reduction in the price of the newspaper stamp in 1836 caused the old 'unstamped' journals of advanced tendencies, issued by Hetherington of Holywell Street and others, to be replaced by little stamped sheets, equally anarchical in tone. Glenny proposed to buy up these mischievous publications, and reissue them as cheap journals of healthier tone, in which he was supported by several noblemen and gentlemen of position. The project ended in a loss of 2,000l., and caused Glenny to abandon politics. In 1832 Glenny started the Metropolitan Society of Florists and Amateurs, which has done much good service to floriculture. In 1839 he was one of the founders of the Royal Gardeners' Benevolent Institution, to which he subscribed the first twenty guineas. 'One of his most important public services consisted in obtaining the removal of the absurd restraints to the enjoyment of Kew Gardens which were thought necessary in his earlier days. Here his slashing style told well. . . . For many years previous to his death his sole occupation was to contribute the garden column to "Lloyd's Weekly Newspaper," and the work was most admirably performed' (*Gard. Mag.* 23 May 1874, p. 269).

Glenny, who retained his faculties to the last, passed quietly away at his residence, Gipsy Hill, Norwood, 17 May 1874, aged 80. No complete list of Glenny's writings exists. That in the 'British Museum Catalogue of Printed Books' is imperfect and overladen with cross-references. Among them may be mentioned, in order of appearance, 'Glenny's Almanac,' started in 1837; 'Gardening for the Million,' 1838; 'Cottage Gardening,' 1847; 'Every Man his own Gardener,' 1848, based on the earlier work of Abercrombie, and adapted in Welsh by R. M. Williamson (Bardd y Môn) under the title 'Y Garddwr Cymreig' (Carnarvon, 1860?); 'Properties of Flowers,' originally published in 'Horticultural Journal,' 1832–5, but republished in a second edition in 1864; 'Properties of Fruits and Vegetables,' 1865. Some of Glenny's works have been edited, and the issue of the 'Almanac' continued, by his son, George M. F. Glenny, Paxton House Nurseries, Fulham, S.W.

[Glenny's Almanac, 1875; Cassell's Working Man, No. 25; Gardener's Chronicle, 23 May 1874, p. 676; Gardener's Magazine, ed. S. Hibberd, 23 May 1874, p. 269, with portrait; Lloyd's Weekly London Newspaper, 24 May 1874.] H. M. C.

GLENORCHY, Viscountess (1741–1786). [See CAMPBELL, WILLIELMA.]

GLISSON, FRANCIS, M.D. (1597–1677), physician, second son of William Glisson of Rampisham in Dorsetshire, was born there in 1597. He entered at Caius College, Cambridge, in 1617, graduated B.A. 1621, and M.A. 1624. He was incorporated M.A. at Oxford 25 Oct. 1627, and in 1634 took the degree of M.D. at Cambridge. In 1635 he was elected a fellow of the College of Physicians of London, and in 1636 was appointed regius professor of physic at Cambridge, an office which he held till his death. He lectured on anatomy, a term which then included pathological and comparative as well as normal human anatomy, at the College of Physicians, and in 1640 he delivered the Gulstonian lectures. Up to this date he resided chiefly at Cambridge, but a little later took a house in the parish of St. Mary at the Walls in Colchester, and soon obtained much practice there. He was in the town during the siege of 1648, and his house escaped, though fifty-three in that parish were destroyed. On 21 Aug. he was sent out by the royalists to Lord Fairfax to ask for better terms (MORANT, Colchester, i. 63), but, after two interviews, failed to obtain any concession. After the siege Colchester was much impoverished, and Glisson went to London. On previous visits to London he had lodged above a cutler's shop next to the Three Kings in Fleet Street (Sloane MS. 2251, in Brit. Mus.), and he ultimately took a lease of a house in New Street, near Shoe Lane, in the parish of St. Bride, Fleet Street. This was renewed 22 May 1666, and he resided in the parish till his death. Before he came to London he had petitioned for the payment of the arrears of his salary as professor, having received no part of it for five years, and at last, on 7 April 1654, an order in council was issued at Whitehall ordering his payment (original in Sloane MS. 2251, in Brit. Mus.) He attended the meetings which led to the formation of the Royal Society, and he was one of its first fellows. In 1650 he published 'De Rachitide sive morbo puerili qui vulgo The Rickets dicitur, Tractatus.' This work was printed by William Dugard, and published by Laurence Sadler and Robert Beaumont in Little Britain, and, with the exception of 'Caius on the Sweating Sickness,' a much less thorough treatise, was the first monograph on a disease published in England. Rickets is mentioned as a cause of death in the bills of mortality for 1634 (GRANT, Bills of Mortality), and has no doubt existed ever since children were given solid food during the period of suckling, but Glisson seems to have shared the belief of his time, that the disease had but lately developed and first appeared in England. The origin of the book was Glisson's own observation of the chief symptoms of rickets, enlarged joints and bent bones, in the children of his native county of Dorset. He communicated his notes to other fellows of the College of Physicians, of whom seven added some remarks of their own. Dr. George Bate [q. v.] and Dr. A. Regemorter [q. v.] were appointed to aid Glisson in preparing a treatise on the subject. As the work went on it became clear that he had made nearly all the observations and conclusions, and the other physicians desired him to take as his due the whole honour of the work. After more than five years of this open scientific discussion the book appeared. In 1645 Dr. Whistler [q. v.], to whom, as a student in London, the knowledge of the investigation at the College of Physicians of this new disease was easily accessible, published at Leyden 'Disputatio Medica inauguralis de morbo puerili Anglorum quem patrio idiomate indigenæ vocant The Rickets.' An examination of the dissertation shows that Whistler's knowledge was second-hand, obtained from Glisson himself in England (Vir Consummatissimus, pt. v.), and indeed he only lays personal claim to one thing, the proposal of the name Pædosplanchnosteocaces for the disease. Whistler was a young man trying to utilise an imperfect knowledge of the well-known but not yet printed discovery of a great scientific investigator. What little information there is in his thesis is due to Glisson, while Glisson owes nothing to him. The 'Tractatus de Rachitide' will always remain one of the glories of English medicine. To his description of the morbid anatomy as observable to the naked eye, subsequent writers, and even so laborious a pathologist as Sir William Jenner, have added little. All writers on the diseases of children agree in their admiration of the book. Its 416 pages are full of original observation. The propositions arrived at are stated in a scholastic manner, and some of the accompanying hypotheses are associated with physiological doctrines now forgotten, but these are not mixed up with the observations of patients during life and after death, which make the book a work of permanent value. It has had many editions, and has been translated into English (PHILIP, Armin. 1681). In 1654 his next work appeared, 'Anatomia hepatis,' a full account of the anatomy, normal and morbid, of the liver. From the clear description given of it in this book the fibrous sheath of the liver is always spoken of at the present day as Glisson's capsule, and thus he is one of those physicians whose name is known to every student of medicine in England. He became a censor of the College of Physicians in 1656, and was elected president in 1667, 1668, and 1669. He gave 100*l.* towards the rebuilding of the college in 1669. In 1672 he published 'Tractatus de Natura Substantiæ energetica, seu de vita naturæ ejusque tribus primis facultatibus,' dedicated to Lord-chancellor Shaftesbury. In the preface he mentions that he had for many years been Shaftesbury's physician. The love of scholastic forms visible in all his writings is prominent in this philosophical dissertation. In 1675 he was obliged to appoint Dr. Brady, master of Caius, his deputy as physic professor at Cambridge (*Sloane MS.* 2251, in Brit. Mus.), and in 1677 he published in London, in the summer, his last work, 'Tractatus de Ventriculo et Intestinis,' a long anatomical treatise based on some of his past lectures. It is dedicated in touching language to the university of Cambridge and the College of Physicians of London, the two societies in which he had spent his life. He died in London 16 Oct. 1677, and was buried in his parish church of St. Bride, Fleet Street. His portrait at the age of seventy-five hangs in the College of Physicians, and is engraved with his arms beneath it, sable on a bend argent three mullets, pierced, gules, with a crescent for difference, in the 'Tractatus de Natura Substantiæ.' His will was proved by his executor, Paul Glisson, 27 Nov. 1677. It contains bequests to numerous nephews and nieces, brothers and sisters, to Caius College and to Trinity Hall.

Dr. Robert Taylor, in his eloquent Harveian oration of 1755, eulogised Glisson along with Harvey and Haller.

[Works; Munk's Coll. of Phys. i. 218; Philip Morant's History and Antiquities of Colchester, London, 1748; Norman Moore's Cause and Treatment of Rickets, London, 1876, and The History of the First Treatise on Rickets; St. Bartholomew's Hospital Reports, vol. xx.; copy of will from P. C. C., Hale, f. 116; Sloane MSS. 1106, 2251, in British Museum. These contain some rough drafts in Glisson's hand, letters to him, notes of lectures, and some entire series of lectures. C. de Rémusat's Histoire de la Philosophie en Angleterre (Paris, 1875, ii. 163–8) gives an account of his philosophical views.]   N. M.

GLOUCESTER, DUKES OF. [See THOMAS OF WOODSTOCK, 1355–1397; HUMPHREY, 1391–1447; RICHARD III, 1452–1485; HENRY, 1639–1660; WILLIAM HENRY, 1743–1805; WILLIAM FREDERICK, 1776–1834.]

GLOUCESTER, EARLS OF. [See CLARE, GILBERT DE, sixth EARL, *d.* 1230; CLARE, RICHARD DE, seventh EARL, 1222–1262; CLARE, GILBERT DE, eighth EARL, 1243–1295; CLARE, GILBERT DE, ninth EARL, 1291–1314; MONTHERMER, RALPH DE, *d.* 1325?; DESPENSER, THOMAS LE, 1373–1400.]

GLOUCESTER, MILES DE, EARL OF HEREFORD (*d.* 1143), was the son and heir of Walter de Gloucester, hereditary castellan of Gloucester and sheriff of the shire, by Berta, his wife.

Walter's father and Miles's grandfather, Roger 'de Pistres,' had been sheriff before him, but was dead in 1086 (*Domesday Book*).

Miles's father Walter was in favour with Henry I, three of whose charters to him are extant (*Duchy of Lancaster: Royal Charters*). He held the post of a royal constable. Early in 1121 his son Miles was given the hand of Sibyl, daughter of Bernard de Neufmarché, the conqueror of Brecknock, with the reversion of her father's possessions (*ib.*) In the Pipe Roll of 1130 Walter is found to have been succeeded by his son, having died (or retired to Llanthony Abbey, according to its chronicle) in or before 1129 (*Rot. Pip.* 31 Hen. I).

The son Miles was now (i.e. from 1128 at least) sheriff of Gloucestershire and Staffordshire, a justice itinerant, and a justice of the forest. He had also (though the fact has been doubted) been granted his father's office of constable by a special charter (*Dugdale MSS.*) In conjunction with Pain Fitzjohn [see FITZJOHN, PAIN], sheriff of Herefordshire and Shropshire, he ruled the whole Welsh border 'from the Severn to the sea' (*Gesta Stephani*, p. 17).

On the accession of Stephen he set himself to secure the allegiance of these two lords-marchers, who at length, on receiving a safe-conduct and obtaining all they asked for, did him homage (*ib.*) It was at Reading that they met the king early in 1136. This we learn from two charters there tested, one of which was printed by Madox (*History of the Exchequer*, p. 135), by which Stephen confirms to Miles, 'sicut baroni et justiciario meo,' the shrievalty of Gloucestershire, the constableship of Gloucester Castle, and the 'honour' of Brecknock.

Miles is next found attending the Easter court at Westminster as one of the royal constables (RYMER, *Fœdera*, new ed. i. 16), and, shortly after, the Oxford council in the same capacity (RICHARD OF HEXHAM, ed. Raine, p. 149). He was then despatched to the aid of the widow of Richard Fitz-Gilbert [see CLARE, RICHARD DE, *d.* 1136?], who was beleaguered in her castle by the Welsh and whom he gallantly rescued (*Gesta*, p. 13). Meanwhile he had married his son and heir, Roger, to Cecily, daughter of Pain Fitzjohn, who inherited the bulk of her father's possessions (*Duchy Charters*). Two years later (1138) he received, in his official capacity, King Stephen at Gloucester in May (*Cont.* FLOR. WIG. ii. 105). He has been said to have renounced his allegiance a few weeks later (*Angevin Kings*, i. 295), but careful investigation will show that he was with Stephen in August (1138) at the siege of Shrewsbury, and that his defection did not take place till 1139. In February (1139) Stephen gave Gloucester Abbey to Miles's kinsman Gilbert Foliot [q. v.], at his request (*ib.* ii. 114). In the summer (1139), however, he joined his lord, the Earl of Gloucester, in inviting the empress to England (*ib.* ii. 110, 117). On her arrival he met her at Bristol, welcomed her to Gloucester, recognised her as his rightful sovereign, and became thenceforth her ardent supporter. She at once gave him St. Briavels Castle and the Forest of Dean. His first achievement on her behalf was to relieve Brian Fitz-Count [q. v.], who was blockaded at Wallingford (*Gesta*, p. 59). In November (1139) he again advanced from Gloucester and attacked and burnt Worcester (*Cont.* FLOR. WIG. p. 119). He also captured the castles of Winchcombe, Cerne, and Hereford (*Gesta*, p. 60). Meanwhile he was deprived by Stephen of his office of constable (*Cont.* FLOR. WIG. p. 121). He took part (*Gesta*, p. 69) in the victory at Lincoln (2 Feb. 1141), and on the consequent triumph of the empress he accompanied her in her progress, and was one of her three chief followers on her entry (2 March) into Winchester (*Cont.* FLOR. WIG. p. 130; WILL. MALM. p. 743). We find him with her at Reading when advancing on London (*Add. Cart.* pp. 19, 576), and on reaching St. Albans she bestowed on him a house at Westminster (*Duchy Charters*, No. 16). He was among those who fled with her from London shortly after, and it was on his advice, when they reached Gloucester, that she ventured back to Oxford (*Cont.* FLOR. WIG. p. 132). There, on 25 July (1141), she bestowed on him the town and castle of Hereford and made him earl of that shire (*Fœdera*, i. 14), in avowed consideration of his faithful service. With singular unanimity hostile chroniclers testify to his devotion to her cause (*Gesta*, p. 60). He even boasted that she had lived at his expense throughout her stay in England (*Cont.* FLOR. WIG. p. 133). As 'Earl Miles' he now accompanied her to Winchester (*Gesta*, p. 79), and on the rout of her forces (14 Sept.) he escaped thence, with

the greatest difficulty, to Gloucester, where he arrived 'exhausted, alone, and with scarcely a rag to his back' (*Cont.* FLOR. WIG. p. 135). Towards the end of the year (1141) we find him at Bristol making a grant to Llanthony Priory in the presence of the empress and the Earl of Gloucester (*Mon. Angl.* vi. 137). In 1142 he is proved by charters to have been with the empress at Oxford and to have received her permission to hold Abergavenny Castle of Brian Fitz-Count (*Duchy Charters*, No. 17). It is probably to the summer of this year that we must assign a formal deed of alliance between the Earl of Gloucester and himself, as a hostage for the performance of which he gave the earl his son Mahel. In 1143 his pressing want of money wherewith to pay his troops led him to demand large sums from the church lands. The Bishop of Hereford withstood his demands, and, on the earl invading his lands, excommunicated him and his followers, and laid the diocese under interdict (*Gesta*, p. 102; *Mon. Angl.* vi. (1), 133). The earl's kinsman, the Abbot of Gloucester, appealed to the legate on his behalf against the bishop's severity (FOLIOT, *Letters*, No. 3). On Christmas-eve of this year (1143) the earl was slain while hunting by an arrow shot at a deer (SYM. DURH. ii. 315; GERVASE, i. 126; *Gesta*, pp. 16, 95, 103). A dispute at once arose for possession of his body between the canons of Llanthony and the monks of Gloucester. The case was heard before the bishops of Worcester, Hereford, and St. David's, and was terminated by a compromise on 28 Dec. (1143). The earl was then buried at Llanthony (*Gloucester Cartulary*, i. lxxv; FOLIOT, *Letters*, No. 65) in the chapter-house.

He had transferred the original house of Austin canons at Llanthony in Monmouthshire to a site on the south side of Gloucester in 1136. This house was thenceforth known as 'Llanthonia Secunda' (*Mon. Angl.* vi. (1), 127, 132).

The earl was succeeded by his son and heir, Roger, who bore hatred to the church for his father's excommunication, and compelled the prior of Llanthony, as a friend of the Bishop of Hereford, to resign (*ib.* p. 133). He even troubled his kinsman, Gilbert Foliot, on his becoming bishop of Hereford (FOLIOT, *Letters*, No. 6), and was by him, after three warnings, formally excommunicated (*ib.* No. 78). Subsequently, however (*temp.* Stephen), he founded Flaxley Abbey, a Cistercian house, within the Forest of Dean (*Flaxley Cartulary*), possibly on the spot of his father's death. The Gloucester 'Cartulary' also shows him as confirming the gifts of his predecessor. In the early part of 1144 we find him at Devizes with the empress (*Duchy Charters*, No. 19), and he is again found there with her son in 1149 (*Brit. Arch. Assoc.* xl. 146 [for 'Bedford' read 'Hereford']), with whom he marched northwards to Carlisle (GERVASE). Another duchy deed (Box A) records his formal alliance with Earl William of Gloucester. On the accession of Henry (1154) he resisted his authority, but was persuaded (*circa* March 1155) by the Bishop of Hereford to surrender his castles (GERVASE), and thereupon received a charter confirming him in almost all his father's possessions (*Cart.* 1 John m. 6). He was with the king at Bridgnorth in July (*Mon. Angl.* v. 483) and at Salisbury soon after (*Journ. Arch. Inst.* No. 61, p. 312). Dying without issue in the same year (1155) his earldom became extinct, but the shrievalty of Hereford and Gloucester passed to his brother Walter. On the death of the latter and two other brothers without issue the family possessions passed to their sisters, Bertha bringing Abergavenny to Braose, but Margaret, the eldest sister, taking the bulk (*Liber Niger*) to the Bohuns afterwards (1199), in recognition of their descent from Miles, earls of Hereford, and constables of England.

[Domesday Book (Record Commission); Rymer's Fœdera (ib.); Pipe Roll, 31 Hen. I (ib.); Rotuli Chartarum (ib.); Cartulary of St. Peter's, Gloucester (Rolls Ser.); Symeon of Durham (ib.); Gesta Stephani in vol. ii. of Chronicles of the Reigns of Stephen, &c. (ib.); Gervase of Canterbury (ib.); Florence of Worcester (Engl. Hist. Soc.); William of Malmesbury (ib.); Round's Ancient Charters (Pipe Roll Soc.); Dugdale's MSS. (Bodl. Library); Additional Charters (Brit. Mus.); Duchy of Lancaster Charters (Public Record Office); Dugdale's Monasticon Anglicanum; Madox's History of the Exchequer; Hearne's Liber Niger; Gilbert Foliot's Letters (Giles's Patres Ecclesiæ Anglicanæ); Crawley-Boevey's Cartulary of Flaxley Abbey; Norgate's England under the Angevin Kings; Ellis's Landholders of Gloucestershire (Bristol and Glouc. Arch. Soc. vol. iv.); Archæological Journal; Journal of British Arch. Assoc.]

J. H. R.

GLOUCESTER, ROBERT OF (*fl.* 1260–1300), historian. [See ROBERT.]

INDEX

TO

THE SEVENTH VOLUME.

Lives in Supplement, Vol. XXII

Lives in Supplement, Vol. XXII

Lives in Supplement, Vol. XXII

Lives in Supplement, Vol. XXII

Lives in Supplement, Vol. XXII

Lives in Supplement, Vol. XXII

Gleichen, Count, p. 1260.

END OF THE SEVENTH VOLUME

PRINTED IN
GREAT BRITAIN
AT THE
UNIVERSITY PRESS
OXFORD
BY
CHARLES BATEY
PRINTER
TO THE
UNIVERSITY